THE HISTORY OF PARLIAMENT

THE HOUSE OF COMMONS 1820–1832

Already published:

The House of Commons, 1386–1421, ed. J. S. Roskell,
Linda Clark and Carole Rawcliffe (4 vols., 1992)

The House of Commons, 1509–1558, ed. S. T. Bindoff
(3 vols., 1982)

The House of Commons, 1559–1603, ed. P. W. Hasler
(3 vols., 1981)

The House of Commons, 1660–1690, ed. B. D. Henning
(3 vols., 1983)

The House of Commons, 1690–1715, ed. E. Cruickshanks,
S. Handley and D.W. Hayton
(5 vols., 2002)

The House of Commons, 1715–1754, ed. Romney Sedgwick
(2 vols., 1970)

The House of Commons, 1754–1790, ed. Sir Lewis Namier
and John Brooke (3 vols., 1964)

The House of Commons, 1790–1820, ed. R. G. Thorne
(5 vols., 1986)

In preparation:

The House of Commons, 1422–1504
The House of Commons, 1604–1629
The House of Commons, 1640–1660
The House of Commons, 1832–1868
The House of Lords, 1660–1832

'Matchless eloqu[e]nce thrown away' (Henry Hunt: see p. 788)
February 1831 (© History of Parliament Trust)

THE HISTORY OF PARLIAMENT

THE
HOUSE OF COMMONS
1820–1832

D. R. Fisher

V

MEMBERS

E–K

PUBLISHED FOR THE HISTORY OF PARLIAMENT TRUST
BY CAMBRIDGE UNIVERSITY PRESS
2009

CAMBRIDGE UNIVERSITY PRESS

Cambridge, New York, Melbourne, Madrid, Cape Town, Singapore, São Paulo, Delhi

Cambridge University Press
The Edinburgh Building, Cambridge CB2 8RU, UK

Published in the United States of America by Cambridge University Press, New York

www.cambridge.org
Information on this title: www.cambridge.org/9780521193146

First published 2009

Printed in the United Kingdom at the University Press, Cambridge

A catalogue record for this publication is available from the British Library

ISBN 978-0-521-19317-7 Volume 1 hardback
ISBN 978-0-521-19320-7 Volume 2 hardback
ISBN 978-0-521-19322-1 Volume 3 hardback
ISBN 978-0-521-19325-2 Volume 4 hardback
ISBN 978-0-521-19328-3 Volume 5 hardback
ISBN 978-0-521-19331-3 Volume 6 hardback
ISBN 978-0-521-19334-4 Volume 7 hardback
ISBN 978-0-521-19314-6 7-volume set hardback

Contents

Contributors

S.R.B.   Stephen Bairstow

M.P.J.C.   Martin Casey

R.B.C.   Richard Cockett

M.M.E.   Margaret Escott

S.M.F.   Stephen Farrell

D.R.F.   David Fisher

S.R.H.   Simon Harratt

R.M.H.   Robin Healey

T.A.J.   Terry Jenkins

S.K.   Sharman Kadish

P.J.S.   Philip Salmon

H.J.S.   Howard Spencer

Editorial note

A raised asterisk (*) following a name denotes a Member of the House of Commons during the period covered by these volumes, where such inference is not apparent from the surrounding text. A raised dagger (†) against a name indicates a Member sitting outside the period and for whom an entry is to be found in earlier or later volumes. Where two (or more) Members bear exactly the same name and style they have been differentiated by the addition of roman numerals according to when they first entered Parliament, for instance John Fane I, John Fane II. This numbering is specific to this section of the *History* only, and does not reflect a Member's seniority by age or within his family. For other conventions concerning the arrangement and content of biographies, the reader should refer to the section on 'Method' in Volume I (pp. xxi–xxvi).

Abbreviations

In addition to standard and self-explanatory abbreviations, the following abbreviations are used in this volume.

In the preliminary paragraphs:

abp.	archbishop
adn.	archdeacon
adv.	advocate
att.-gen.	attorney-general
Bar.	Baron
bp.	bishop
called	called to the bar
c.bar. exch.	chief baron of the exchequer
cdr.	commander
ch.	child, children
chan.	chancellor
c.j.	chief justice
coh.	coheir(ess)
commn.	commission
commr.	comissioner
c.p.	common pleas
cr.	created
ct.	court
cttee.	committee
dep.	deputy
d.s.p.	died *sine prole* (without issue)
d.v.p.	died *vita patris* (in the lifetime of his father)
e.	elder, eldest
E.I.	East Indies, East India
exch.	exchequer
f.m.	field marshall
Ft.	Foot regiment
g.s.	grammar school
[GB]	Great Britain

h.	heir(ess)
h.s.	high school
[I]	Ireland, Irish
jt.	joint
k.b.	king's bench
l.c.b.	lord chief baron of exchequer
l.c.j.c.p.	lord chief justice of common pleas
mq.	marquess
o.	only
posth.	posthumous
preb.	prebend, prebendary
q.m.g.	quartermaster general
q. sess.	quarter sessions
rect.	rector
recvr.	receiver
res.	resigned
ret.	retired
[S]	Scotland, Scottish
SCJ	Senator of the College of Justice
s.p.	*sine prole* (without issue)
s.p.m.	(without male issue)
suc.	succeeded
treas.	treasurer
[UK]	United Kingdom
vic.	vicar
vol.	volunteer
w.	wife
W.I.	West Indies, West Indian
wid.	widow
yr.	younger

In the endnotes:

Add.	Additional manuscripts, British Library
AHR	*American Historical Review*
Al. Cant.	*Alumni Cantabrigienses* ed. Venn
Al. Ox.	*Alumni Oxonienses* ed. Foster
Althorp Letters	*Letters of Lord Althorp* (private, 1929)
Ann. Reg.	*Annual Register*
AO	Archive(s) Office
Arbuthnot Corresp.	*The Correspondence of Charles Arbuthnot* ed. A. Aspinall (Camden ser. 3, lxv, 1941)
Arbuthnot Jnl.	*The Journal of Mrs. Arbuthnot, 1820–1832* ed. F. Bamford and the Duke of Wellington, 2vv (1950)

Argyll Mems.	8th Duke of Argyll, *Autobiography and Memoirs* ed. Dowager Duchess of Argyll, 2vv (1906)
Arniston Mems.	*The Arniston Memoirs. Three Centuries of a Scottish House* ed. G.W.T. Omond (1887)
Arnould, *Denman*	Sir J. Arnould, *Memoirs of Thomas, Lord Denman,* 2vv (1873)
AS	Archive Service
Ashley, *Palmerston*	Evelyn Ashley, *The Life of Henry John Temple, Viscount Palmerston,* 2vv (3rd edn. 1877)
Bagot, *Canning and Friends*	*George Canning and his Friends* ed. J. Bagot, 2vv (1909)
Balfour, *Aberdeen*	Lady Frances Balfour, *The Life of George, 4th Earl of Aberdeen,* 2vv (1922)
Baring Jnls.	*Journals and Correspondence of Francis Thornhill Baring, Baron Northbrook, 1808–1852* ed. Earl of Northbrook, 2vv (private, Winchester, 1905)
Bentham Corresp.	*The Correspondence of Jeremy Bentham* ed. T.L.S. Sprigge et *al,* 5vv (1968–81)
Berry Jnls.	*Extracts from the Journals and Correspondence of Miss [Mary] Berry, 1783–1852* ed. Lady Theresa Lewis, 3vv (1866)
BIHR/HR	*Bulletin of the Institute of Historical Research/ Historical Research*
Bk.	*Book*
BL	British Library
Blakiston, *Lord William Russell*	Georgiana Blakiston, *Lord William Russell and his Wife, 1815–1846* (1972)
Bodl.	Bodleian Library, Oxford
Borthwick	Borthwick Institute of Historical Research, York
Brougham, *Life and Times*	*The Life and Times of Henry, Lord Brougham, written by Himself,* 3vv (1871)
Broughton, *Recollections*	Lord Broughton, *Recollections of a Long Life* ed. Lady Dorchester, 6vv (1909–11)
Buckingham, *Mems. Geo. IV*	Duke of Buckingham and Chandos, *Memoirs of the Court of George IV, 1820–1830,* 2vv (1859)
Bulwer, *Palmerston*	Sir Henry Lytton Bulwer, *The Life of Henry John Temple, Viscount Palmerston,* 3vv (1870–4)
Bunbury Mem.	*Memoir and Literary Remains of Sir Henry Edward Bunbury* ed. Sir C.J.F. Bunbury (private, 1868)
Burke Corresp.	*The Correspondence of Edmund Burke* ed. various, 10vv (Cambridge, 1958–78)
Burke LG	*Burke's Landed Gentry*
Burke PB	*Burke's Peerage and Baronetage*
Buxton Mems.	*Memoirs of Sir Thomas Fowell Buxton* ed. C. Buxton (1848)

Cam. Soc.	Camden Society
Canning's Ministry	*The Formation of Canning's Ministry, February to August 1827* ed. A. Aspinall (Camden ser. 3, lix, 1937)
Canning Official Corresp.	*Some Official Correspondence of George Canning* ed. E.J. Stapleton, 2vv (1887)
Castlereagh Corresp.	*Correspondence, Despatches, and Other Papers of Viscount Castlereagh* (ser. 3) ed. Marquess of Londonderry, 4vv (1853)
CB	*Complete Baronetage*
CITR	*Calendar of Inner Temple Records*
CJ	*Journals of the House of Commons*
Cockburn Jnl.	*Journal of Henry Cockburn, 1831–1854*, 2vv (Edinburgh, 1874)
Cockburn, *Jeffrey*	Lord Cockburn, *Life of Lord Jeffrey*, 2vv (Edinburgh, 1850)
Cockburn Letters	*Letters Chiefly Connected with the Affairs of Scotland, from Henry Cockburn to Thomas Francis Kennedy, 1818–1852* (1874)
Cockburn Mems.	Henry Cockburn, *Memorials of His Time* ed. K.F.C. Miller (Chicago, 1974)
Colchester Diary	*The Diary and Correspondence of Charles Abbot, Lord Colchester* ed. Lord Colchester, 3vv (1861)
Countess Granville Letters	*Letters of Harriet, Countess Granville, 1818–1845* ed. F. Leveson Gower, 2vv (1894)
Cowley Diary	*The Diary and Correspondence of Henry Wellesley, First Lord Cowley, 1790–1846* ed. F.A. Wellesley (1930)
CP	*Complete Peerage*
Crabb Robinson Diary	*Diary, Reminiscences and Correspondence of Henry Crabb Robinson* ed. T. Sadler, 2vv (3rd edn. 1872)
Creevey Pprs.	*The Creevey Papers* ed. Sir Herbert Maxwell, 2vv (2nd edn. 1904)
Creevey's Life and Times	*Creevey's Life and Times* ed. J. Gore (1937 edn.)
Croker Pprs.	*The Correspondence and Diaries of John Wilson Croker* ed. L.J. Jennings, 3vv (1884)
CUL	Cambridge University Library
D. Am. B.	*Dictionary of American Biography*
Disraeli Letters	*Benjamin Disraeli Letters* ed. various, 7vv (Toronto, 1982–2004)
DNB	*Dictionary of National Biography*
DWB	*Dictionary of Welsh Biography*
Dyott's Diary	*Dyott's Diary, 1781–1845* ed. R.W. Jeffery, 2vv (1907)

EcHR	*Economic History Review*
Edgeworth Letters	*Maria Edgeworth. Letters from England, 1813–1844* ed. C. Colvin (Oxford, 1971)
Eg.	Egerton mss, British Library
EHR	*English Historical Review*
Ellenborough Diary	Lord Ellenborough, *A Political Diary, 1828–1830* ed. Lord Colchester, 2vv (1881)
Farington Diary	*The Diary of Joseph Farington* ed. various, 16vv (Yale, 1978–84)
Fox Jnl.	*The Journal of Henry Edward Fox, 1818–1830* ed. Lord Ilchester (1923)
Gen. Mag.	*Genealogist's Magazine*
Gent. Mag.	*Gentleman's Magazine*
Geo. IV Letters	*The Letters of King George IV* ed. A. Aspinall, 3vv (Cambridge, 1938)
GL	Guildhall Library
Gladstone Diaries	*The Gladstone Diaries* ed. M.R.D. Foot and H.G.C. Matthew, 14vv (Oxford, 1994)
Glenbervie Diaries	*The Diaries of Sylvester Douglas (Lord Glenbervie)* ed. F. Bickley, 2vv (1928)
Glenbervie Jnls.	*The Glenberve Journals* ed. W. Sichel (1910)
Greville Mems.	*The Greville Memoirs* ed. L. Strachey and R. Fulford, 8vv (1938)
Gronow Reminiscences	*The Reminiscences and Recollections of Captain Gronow*, 2vv (1900 edn.)
Heber Letters	R.H. Cholmondeley, *The Heber Letters, 1783–1832* (1950)
HEHL	Henry E. Huntington Library, San Marino, California
Heron, *Notes*	Sir Robert Heron, *Notes* (2nd edn. 1851)
Highland Lady	*Memoirs of a Highland Lady* ed. Lady Strachey (1911)
HJ	*Historical Journal*
HLB/HLQ	*Huntington Library Bulletin*, later *Huntington Library Quarterly*
HLRO	House of Lords Record Office (Parliamentary Archives)
HMC	*Historical Manuscripts Commission*
Hobhouse Diary	*The Diary of Henry Hobhouse (1820–1827)* ed. A. Aspinall (1947)
Holland, *Further Mems.*	Lord Holland, *Further Memoirs of the Whig Party, 1807–1821* ed. Lord Stavordale (1905)
Holland, *Mems. Whig Party*	Lord Holland, *Memoirs of the Whig Party during My Time* ed. Lord Holland, 2vv (1852)

Holland House Diaries	*The Holland House Diaries* ed. A.D. Kriegel (1977)
Horner Pprs.	*The Horner Papers* ed. K. Bourne and W.B. Taylor (Edinburgh, 1994)
Howard Sisters	*Three Howard Sisters* ed. Lady Leconfield and J. Gore (1955)
HP	*History of Parliament*
Huskisson Pprs.	*The Huskisson Papers* ed. L. Melville (1931)
IGI	International Genealogical Index
IHR	Institute of Historical Research
IR	Death duty registers
JBS	*Journal of British Studies*
JEH	*Journal of Ecclesiastical History*
JMH	*Journal of Modern History*
JRL	John Rylands University Library, Manchester
Lady Holland Jnl.	*The Journal of Elizabeth, Lady Holland (1791–1811)* ed. Lord Ilchester, 2vv (1908)
Lady Holland to Son	*Elizabeth, Lady Holland to her Son, 1821–1845* ed. Lord Ilchester (1946)
Lady-in-Waiting	Lady Charlotte Bury, *The Diary of a Lady-in-Waiting* ed. A.F. Steuart (1908)
Lady Lyttelton Corresp.	*Correspondence of Sarah Spencer, Lady Lyttelton, 1787–1870* ed. Mrs. Hugh Wyndham (1912)
Lady Palmerston Letters	*Letters of Lady Palmerston* ed. T. Lever (1957)
Later Corresp. Geo. III	*The Later Correspondence of George III* ed. A. Aspinall, 5vv (Cambridge, 1962–70)
Le Marchant, *Althorp*	Sir Denis Le Marchant, *Memoir of John Charles, Viscount Althorp, Third Earl Spencer* (1876)
Leveson Gower Corresp.	*Lord Granville Leveson Gower. Private Correspondence, 1781 to 1821* ed. Countess Granville, 2vv (1916)
Lieven Letters	*Letters of Dorothea, Princess Lieven, during her residence in London, 1812–1834* ed. L.G. Robinson (1902)
Lieven-Palmerston Corresp.	*The Lieven-Palmerston Correspondence, 1828–1856* ed. Lord Sudeley (1943)
Lieven-Grey Corresp.	*Correspondence of Princess Lieven and Earl Grey* ed. G. Le Strange, 2vv (1890)
Life of Campbell	*Life of John, Lord Campbell* ed. Mrs. Hardcastle, 2vv (1881)
Life of Wilberforce	R.I. and S. Wilberforce, *Life of William Wilberforce* (1838)
LJ	*Journals of the House of Lords*
LMA	London Metropolitan Archives

Macaulay Letters	*The Letters of Thomas Babington Macaulay* ed. T. Pinney, 6vv (Cambridge, 1974–81)
Malmesbury Letters	*A Series of Letters of the First Earl of Malmesbury, his Family and Friends, from 1745 to 1820* ed. Lord Malmesbury, 2vv (1870)
Malmesbury Mems.	Earl of Malmesbury, *Memoirs of an Ex-Minister*, 2vv (1884)
Martin, *Lyndhurst*	Sir Theodore Martin, *A Life of Lord Lyndhurst* (1883)
Martineau Letters	*Harriet Martineau. Selected Letters* ed. V. Sanders (Oxford, 1990)
Maxwell, *Clarendon*	Sir Henry Maxwell, *The Life and Letters of George William Frederick, Fourth Earl of Clarendon*, 2vv (1913)
Melbourne's Pprs.	*Lord Melbourne's Papers* ed. L.C. Sanders (1889)
Melville, *Cobbett*	L. Melville, *The Life and Letters of William Cobbett*, 2vv (1913)
MI	Monumental Inscription(s)
Mill Works	*Collected Works of John Stuart Mill* ed. various, 33vv (Toronto,1963–91)
Misc. Gen. et Her.	*Miscellanea Genealogica et Heraldica*
Monypenny and Buckle, *Disraeli*	W.F. Monypenny and G.E. Buckle, *The Life of Benjamin Disraeli, Earl of Beaconsfield*, 6vv (1910–20)
Moore Jnl.	*The Journal of Thomas Moore* ed. Wilfrid S. Dowden, 6vv (Newark, Delaware, 1983–91)
Moore Mems.	*Memoirs, Journal and Correspondence of Thomas Moore* ed. Lord John Russell, 8vv (1853–6)
Morley, *Gladstone*	J. Morley, *The Life of William Ewart Gladstone*, 3vv (1903)
Mus.	Museum
NAI	National Archives of Ireland
N and Q	*Notes and Queries*
NAS	National Archives of Scotland
n.d.	no date
NLI	National Library of Ireland
NLS	National Library of Scotland
NLW	National Library of Wales
NLWJ	*National Library of Wales Journal*
NMM	National Maritime Museum
n.s.	new series
O'Connell Corresp.	*The Correspondence of Daniel O'Connell* ed. M.R. O'Connell, 8vv (Dublin, 1972–80)
OIOC	Oriental and India Office Collections, British Library

Oldfield, *Rep. Hist.*	T.H.B. Oldfield, *Representative History of Great Britain and Ireland*, 6vv (1816)
Oldfield, *Key* (1820)	T.H.B. Oldfield, *Key to the House of Commons* (1820)
OR	*Official Return of Members of Parliament* (1878–91)
Overstone Corresp.	*The Correspondence of Lord Overstone* ed. D.P. O'Brien, 3vv (Cambridge, 1971)
Oxford DNB	*Oxford Dictionary of National Biography*
Palmerston-Sulivan Letters	*The Letters of the Third Viscount Palmerston to Laurence and Elizabeth Sulivan, 1804–1863* ed. K. Bourne (Camden ser. 4, xxiii, 1979)
P and P	*Past and Present*
par.	parish
Parker, *Graham*	C.S. Parker, *Life and Letters of Sir James Graham*, 2vv (1907)
Parker, *Peel*	C.S. Parker, *Sir Robert Peel from his Private Papers*, 3vv (1891)
Parl. Deb.	*Hansard's Parliamentary Debates*
Peel Letters	*The Private Letters of Sir Robert Peel* ed. G. Peel (1920)
Peel Mems.	*Memoirs of Sir Robert Peel* ed. Lord Stanhope and E. Cardwell, 2vv (1856)
Pellew, *Sidmouth*	G. Pellew, *The Life and Correspondence of Henry Addington, First Viscount Sidmouth*, 3vv (1847)
PH	*Parliamentary History*
Phipps, *Plumer Ward Mems.*	E. Phipps, *Memoirs of the Political and Literary Life of Robert Plumer Ward*, 2vv (1850)
PP	*Parliamentary Papers*
Prince of Wales Corresp.	*The Correspondence of George, Prince of Wales, 1770–1812* ed. A. Aspinall, 8vv (1963–71)
PROB	Probate Records: wills, administrations and valuations
PRO NI	Public Record Office of Northern Ireland
Raikes Jnl.	*A Portion of the Journal kept by Thomas Raikes from 1831 to 1847*, 4vv (1856–7)
Reid, *Lord Durham*	S.J. Reid, *Life and Letters of the First Earl of Durham*, 2vv (1900)
Reid, *Monckton Milnes*	T.W. Reid, *The Life, Letters and Friendships of Richard Monckton Milnes, First Lord Houghton*, 2vv (1890)
RO	Record Office
Romilly Mems.	*Memoirs of the Life of Sir Samuel Romilly, written by himself; with a Selection from his Correspondence*, 3vv (1840)

Russell Early Corresp.	*Early Correspondence of Lord John Russell, 1805–40* ed. R. Russell, 2vv (1913)
Russell Later Corresp.	*The Later Correspondence of Lord John* Russell ed. G.P. Gooch, 2vv (1925)
Russell Letters	*Letters to Lord G. William Russell*, 3vv (private, 1915–20)
Russell, *Recollections*	Earl Russell, *Recollections and Suggestions* (1875)
Scott Jnl.	*The Journal of Sir Walter Scott* (Edinburgh, 1950 edn.)
Scott Letters	*The Letters of Sir Walter Scott: 1878-1828* ed. H.J.C. Grierson, 10vv (1932-6)
Scottish Electoral Politics	*Papers on Scottish Electoral Politics, 1832–1854* ed. J.I. Brash (Scottish Hist. Soc. ser. 4, xi, Edinburgh, 1974)
ser.	series
Shelley Diary	*The Diary of Frances, Lady Shelley* ed. R. Edgcumbe, 2vv (1912)
SHR	*Scottish Historical Review*
Smith Letters	*The Letters of Sydney Smith* ed. N.C. Smith, 2vv (Oxford, 1953)
Somerset Letters	*Letters, Remains, and Memoirs of Edward Adolphus Seymour, Twelth Duke of Somerset* ed. W. Mallock and Lady G. Ramsden (1893)
Spencer-Stanhope Letter-Bag	A.M.W. Stirling, *The Letter-Bag of Lady Elizabeth Spencer Stanhope, 1806–1873* (1913)
Stirling, *Coke of Norf.*	A.M.W. Stirling, *Coke of Norfolk and his Friends* (1912 edn.)
Taylor Autobiog.	*Autobiography of Henry Taylor, 1800–1875*, 2vv (1885)
Taylor Pprs.	*The Taylor Papers: being a Record of Certain Reminiscences, Letters and Journals in the Life of Sir Herbert Taylor* ed. E. Taylor (1913)
TCD	Trinity College, Dublin
Three Diaries	*Three Early Nineteenth Century Diaries* ed. A. Aspinall (1952)
TNA	The National Archives
Torrens, *Melbourne*	W.M. Torrens, M*emoirs of William, 2nd Viscount Melbourne*, 2vv (1878)
Trans.	*Transactions*
TRHS	*Transactions of the Royal Historical Society*
Twiss, *Eldon*	H. Twiss, *The Public and Private Life of Lord Chancellor Eldon*, 3vv (1844)
Two Brothers	*Correspondence of Two Brothers: Edward Adolphus, Eleventh Duke of Somerset, and his brother, Lord*

	Webb Seymour, 1800–1819 and after ed. Lady G. Ramsden (1906)
Two Duchesses	*The Two Duchesses: Georgiana, Duchess of Devonshire, Elizabeth, Duchess of Devonshire. Family Correspondence, 1777–1859* ed. V. Foster (1898)
UCL	University College, London
UCNW	University College of North Wales (now Bangor University)
VCH	*Victoria County History*
Victoria Letters (ser. 1)	*The Letters of Queen Victoria: a selection from Her Majesty's Correspondence between the years 1837 and 1861* ed. A.C. Benson and Lord Esher, 3vv (1907–11)
Victoria Letters (ser. 2)	*The Letters of Queen Victoria, 1862–1885* ed. G.E. Buckle, 3vv (1926–8)
Victoria Letters (ser. 3)	*The Letters of Queen Victoria, 1886–1901* ed. G.E. Buckle, 3vv (1930–2)
Vis.	*Visitation*
Von Neumann Diary	*The Diary of Philipp Von Neumann, 1819–1850* trans. and ed. E. Beresford Chancellor, 2vv (1928)
Walpole, *Russell*	S. Walpole, *Life of Lord John Russell*, 2vv (1889)
Ward, *Llandaff Letters*	*Letters to the Bishop of Llandaff by the Earl of Dudley* ed. E. Copleston (1840)
Ward, *Letters to 'Ivy'*	*Letters to 'Ivy' from the First Earl of Dudley* ed. S.H. Romilly (1905)
WCA	Westminster City Archives
Wellesley Mems.	R.R. Pearce, *Memoirs and Correspondence of Richard, Marquess Wellesley*, 3vv (1846)
Wellesley Pprs.	*The Wellesley Papers: Life and Correspondence of Marquess Wellesley*, 2vv (1914)
Wellington and Friends	*Wellington and his Friends* ed. 7th Duke of Wellington (1965)
Wellington Despatches	*Despatches, Correspondence and Memoranda of the Duke of Wellington* ed. 2nd Duke of Wellington, 8vv (1867–80)
Wellington Pol. Corresp.	*The Prime Ministers' Papers: Wellington Political Correspondence I: 1833–November 1834* ed. J. Brooke and J. Gandy (1975); *II: November 1834–April 1835* ed. R.J. Olney and J. Melvin (1986)
WHR	*Welsh History Review*
Wilberforce Corresp.	*The Correspondence of William Wilberforce* ed. R.I. and S. Wilberforce, 2vv (1840)
Wilberforce Priv. Pprs.	*Private Papers of William Wilberforce* ed. A.M. Wilberforce (1897)

William IV-Grey Corresp.	*Correspondence of Earl Grey with King William IV* ed. Lord Grey, 2vv (1867)
Williams Wynn Corresp.	*Correspondence of Charlotte Grenville, Lady Williams Wynn, and her Three Sons, Sir Watkin Williams Wynn, Charles Williams Wynn, and Sir Henry Williams Wynn* ed. R. Leighton (1920)

MEMBERS
E–K

EAST, Sir Edward Hyde (1764–1847), of 12 Stratford Place, Mdx.

GREAT BEDWYN   11 Feb. 1792–1796
WINCHESTER   18 Feb. 1823–1831

b. 9 Sept. 1764, in Jamaica, s. of Edward East of Whitehall, Jamaica and Amy, da. of James Hall of Jamaica. *educ.* Harrow 1776; Magdalen, Oxf. 1782; I. Temple 1781, called 1786. *m.* 23 Dec. 1786, Jane Isabella, da. of Joseph Chaplin Hankey of East Bergholt, Suff., 1s. 1da. kntd. 26 Feb. 1813; *cr.* bt. 25 Apr. 1823. *d.* 8 Jan. 1847.
C.j. Bengal 1813-23; bencher, I. Temple 1823, reader 1830, treas. 1831; PC 29 June 1831; member, judicial cttee. of PC 1833.
Vol. London and Westminster light horse 1794-6.

East, whose family's fortune derived from Jamaican plantations, had been active in the defence of West India interests during his first spell in Parliament, and gained another colonial perspective by his appointment as an Indian judge in 1813. According to his son James Buller East*, who accompanied him to Bengal, he found there a primitive and inefficient judicial system and encountered resistance from settlers to his attempt to introduce trial by jury.[1] One of the cases to come before the Calcutta supreme court during his stewardship was that of his own son-in-law, James William Croft, who was found guilty in March 1819 of the seduction (and impregnation) of the daughter of a family friend. Croft, who was moderately fined and banished, had apparently induced her to fake insanity and suicide to cover her flight. East's reference to a 'factious cabal' of enemies in a letter to Charles Philip Yorke*, 27 Aug. 1820, suggests that there may have been calls for his removal as a result of this episode, though he had already determined on a return to England.[2] He blamed the ensuing delay in the acceptance of his resignation on the aspirations of George Canning*, the president of the board of control, to the governor-generalship of India, and his wish to delay any new judicial appointments until he could make his own nominations. He also appeared to hold Canning responsible for the difficulties which later emerged over his pension. (In his anxiety to leave, he accepted the comparatively low settlement of £1,300 per annum, with a promise of an increase to £2,000 when funds permitted.) Still in post in November 1821, he complained that he had been 'unwell for nearly the last two months, my stomach having been long aching, accompanied with debility and occasionally with headache', and he had yet to receive confirmation of his resignation when he left for Britain in February 1822 aboard the *Thomas Greville*, which docked at the end of May.[3] He was chiefly remembered in India for his efforts in promoting native education, notably the foundation of the Hindu college, and on his departure was commended by the inhabitants of Calcutta for his even-handed dispensation of justice 'to people of different countries, languages and habits'. A statue of him was commissioned to stand in the grand jury room over which he had presided.[4]

Whilst in India East had tried to keep abreast of political developments at home. An opponent of parliamentary reform, in August 1820 he opined:

> The system of radical reform ... has only corrupted or is capable of corrupting some of the lower classes of people. Those above them who affect to talk this nonsense, have in reality a revolution in government in prospect, and use the other merely as a popular stalking horse of the day. The government and gentlemen of England have, I am sure, sufficient strength to combat and overthrow this hydra.

He identified public finance as the crucial issue of the hour and reckoned it 'not improbable that ... reducing some of the taxes, now highly raised, would tend to increase rather than diminish the revenue, by increasing ... consumption'.[5] On belatedly learning the outcome of the 1820 general election the following month, he felt himself vindicated in not falling prey to alarmism, but admitted fearing that the minds of the lower classes will in time be perverted by the incessant insidious attacks upon the very frame of government and society through the daily and systematic abuse of the press, urging every abstract ...right to such an excess as to make it a wrong and a public mischief.[6]

East's knighthood was upgraded to a baronetcy within a year of his return, upon which he resumed regular attendance of the West India planters' committee.[7]

In February 1823 he came forward for a vacancy at Winchester caused by the retirement of his son's father-in-law James Henry Leigh, whose second residence at Adlestrop House, Gloucestershire, was to become one of his bolt holes.[8] On the hustings he derided the 'absurd' notion that agricultural distress demonstrated the need for parliamentary reform, sought to justify the French wars and the return to a 'wholesome currency', and promised to support such 'moderate reduction of taxation as would not endanger our national freedom, credit and security'.[9] He was returned unopposed on the interest of the 1st duke of Buckingham, who, by way of a denial that Winchester was really controlled by his wife, informed William Fremantle* that East had 'no partialities or predilections except for my opinion and votes for the Catholic question'. He 'has sworn allegiance to me exclusively', he later insisted.[10] Fremantle thought Buckingham protested too much, but East duly supported Catholic relief (to which the duchess of Buckingham was strongly opposed), and as the duke's private auditor from 1827 made valiant but futile attempts to save him from financial ruin.[11] A regular attender, described as 'an agreeable but not very effective speaker' by a radical commentary of 1825, he invariably supported the Liverpool ministry.[12] He was in their majorities against repeal of the assessed taxes on houses valued under £5, 10 Mar., and limiting the sinking fund, 13 Mar. 1823. That day Buckingham's son Lord Chandos* requested his attendance to vote against a select committee on the game laws, though in the event there was no division.[13] He divided against repeal of the Foreign Enlistment Act, 16 Apr., and inquiry into the prosecution of the Dublin Orange theatre rioters, 22 Apr. He was a majority teller against a motion for parliamentary reform, 24 Apr., when he observed that the architects of the 1688 Revolution had not seen fit to alter the electoral system and denied that the representative base had narrowed, citing the transfer of Grampound's seats to Yorkshire and warning against a more general measure, 'the benefit of which must be precarious and questionable, while the hazard is great and certain'. Ricardo, who spoke next, dismissed

his arguments as 'too often repeated, and too often refuted, to have any weight'. He voted against reform of the representation of Scotland, 2 June 1823, and Edinburgh, 26 Feb. 1824, 13 Apr. 1826. On 11 July 1823 he spoke in support of a clause to the East India mutiny bill empowering the governor of Bombay to summons courts martial.[14] That month Buckingham attempted to intercede with government to obtain a improved pension for East; he tried again two months later, without success.[15]

East presented constituency petitions against the licensing duties, 20 Feb., and the assessed taxes, 22 Mar. 1824.[16] The latter was possibly the spur for his minority vote for their repeal, 3 Mar. 1825, and he later boasted of having twice opposed government at the request of his constituents, though the second instance apparently went unrecorded.[17] He was appointed to the select committee on the criminal law, 16 Mar., and voted against inquiry into the prosecution of the Methodist missionary John Smith, accused of inciting slave riots in Demerara, 11 June 1824. That November Buckingham mentioned him as a candidate for the governorship of Madras to Charles Williams Wynn*, president of the board of control, who dismissed the suggestion as ludicrous.[18] He divided for suppression of the Catholic Association, 25 Feb., and Catholic relief, 1 Mar., 21 Apr., 10 May 1825. He was in the majorities for the duke of Cumberland's annuity bill, 20 May, 6, 10 June. On 6 June 1825 he warned that the interference of Parliament would only strengthen the attachment of Indian Hindus to the custom of burning widows, but applauded the efforts of local authorities to discourage the practice. He presented a petition from Winchester silk throwers for protection from imports, 21 Feb. 1826.[19] Confirming Hume's assertion that slave owners in India had no legal redress against runaways, 1 Mar., he added that on his West Indian property he had 'always thought it his duty to have it managed in the way most advantageous to the slaves' and cited his record of support for ameliorative measures, but urged a consensual approach to abolition and the compensation of owners. Next day he voted against a motion condemning the Jamaican slave trials. He divided with ministers for the report on the salary of the president of the board of trade, 10 Apr. He was added to the select committee to consider a petition of grievance against the East India Company, 11 May 1826.

At the 1826 general election he stood again for Winchester, promising to continue to support ministers 'for so long as they promote the general good' and Catholic relief. He was returned unopposed.[20] In

February 1827 he was the conduit for Buckingham's communications of admiration for Frederick Robinson, the chancellor of the exchequer, and the latter's less than effusive response. Privately, he considered that the 'melancholy and sudden' event of Liverpool's stroke 'must throw the government into great difficulty for a time at least, if it do not even produce interior conflict', and doubted the general assumption that Canning would soon be in sufficient health to resume his place, 20 Feb.[21] He voted for Catholic relief, 6 Mar. 1827, 12 May 1828 (as a pair). He divided for the duke of Clarence's annuity bill, 16 Mar., but against the corn bill, 2 Apr. With the apparent encouragement of East, Buckingham had taken against the Canning administration after being passed over for the governor-generalship of India, and in April instructed his Members to oppose them, before decreeing a course of abstention the following month. East does not appear to have broken either injunction, though Fremantle reported that his true allegiance was 'to the duchess and Chandos', who had gone into outright opposition, 19 Apr. 1827.[22] In January 1828 the duke of Wellington was advised by Sir Henry Hardinge* that although East counted himself a supporter of the Goderich ministry, he was convinced that 'things cannot and ought not to last' and was anxious for 'a reconciliation or change by which your grace and Mr. Peel may be at the head of affairs'.[23] Like Chandos, East voted against repeal of the Test Acts, 26 Feb. He assumed responsibility for a bill to amend the law governing the liability of British citizens in India to have their property seized for debt, 25 Mar., but the initiative for the measure was later taken by Robert Cutlar Fergusson. He divided with the Wellington ministry against a motion on chancery delays, 24 Apr. He welcomed the second reading of the settlement by hiring bill, but suggested that entitlement to poor relief from a particular parish should be dependent on residence and 'industrious labour' for a set number of years, 29 Apr. He approved legislation to extend recent English legal reforms to India, 4 June. He voted against ordnance reductions, 4 July. He presented a petition from West India proprietors for an impartial inquiry into colonial slavery, 22 July 1828. It appears that he joined Chandos in unsuccessfully urging the appointment of Buckingham as Irish viceroy in December 1828, but without the knowledge of his patron, who was in Italy.[24] He was, of course, expected by Planta, the patronage secretary, to divide for the ministry's concession of Catholic emancipation, though he only did so on the bill's third reading, 30 Mar. 1829, which was his sole recorded vote of the session. On 20 May 1829 he attended a special meeting of the West India plant-

ers, at which Chandos was elected as permanent chairman.[25] His profile remained low during 1830, when he was in the majorities against the transfer of East Retford's seats to Birmingham, 11 Feb., parliamentary reform, 18 Feb., the enfranchisement of Birmingham, Leeds and Manchester, 23 Feb., and Jewish emancipation, 17 May. On 2 June 1830 he attended a meeting of Members with West India interests, where he seconded a motion of support for the ministerial proposals on the rum duty.[26]

At the 1830 general election he offered again for Winchester, promising to maintain his general support for government and contrasting the state of the nation with the revolutionary conditions prevailing in France. He was returned unopposed.[27] On 26 Oct. he proposed the re-election of Charles Manners Sutton as Speaker with an appropriate eulogy. He had naturally been listed by ministers as one of their 'friends' and he was in their minority in the crucial division on the civil list, 15 Nov. 1830. He was censured for his absence from a Winchester meeting for parliamentary reform in mid-February 1831, and although he presented and endorsed the resulting petition, 28 Feb., it was with the qualification that he would oppose any measure 'which goes to the forfeiture or confiscation of privileges now held by any persons, without ... proof of abuse'.[28] He presumably felt that the Grey ministry's reform bill fell into this category, for he voted against its second reading, 22 Mar., and for Gascoyne's wrecking amendment, 19 Apr. On 18 Mar. 1831 he spoke against an increase in the duty on imports to the West Indies.

At the subsequent dissolution East retired from Winchester in favour of his only son James Buller East, rather than face a contest against two reformers, noting his 'advancing years' and support for 'ancient and honourable franchises, which to the last I have defended in Parliament'.[29] On 11 Aug. 1831 he asked Brougham, the lord chancellor, to use his influence in favour of his reappointment as chief justice of Bengal, citing the weight of his experience as a counter to any objection on account of his age. 'All my property lies unfortunately in the West Indies and is involved in the ruin of Mr. [William] Manning's* bank', he explained, adding that 'several near and dear relatives, besides my own immediate household, are thrown nearly helpless upon me, and all I have to rely on is my pension'.[30] (As early as August 1810, he had predicted that his Jamaican estates were 'more likely to break my heart than benefit me'.)[31] Brougham evidently suggested that a domestic post might be more suitable, but 'under the pressure ... to which I before alluded', East vainly renewed his application in November 1831. Brougham had already satisfied his wish, first expressed in 1822, for a seat on the privy council, and in August 1833 named him to its judicial committee. As a mark of gratitude East, who was plainly glad of the work, sent Brougham an engraving of his Calcutta statue.[32] Thereafter he acted as a 'constant assessor' of Indian appeals, on which subject he had earlier wearied another former colonial judge, Sir James Mackintosh*.[33] Amidst his financial difficulties he retained an interest in politics, and was almost certainly the 'Sir East' whom Benjamin Disraeli[†] encountered at a 'regular Bucks party' in 1839 in the company of 'a widow daughter', and reported to be 'enthusiastically blue, and boring Chandos about my genius'.[34] From 1831 he chaired meetings of the West India planters, of whom he led a delegation to Peel, the prime minister, in August 1842.[35]

East moved to Minchenden House, Southgate, Middlesex, in July and thence to Sherwood House, Battersea, Surrey, presumably for reasons of economy.[36] He was discovered in his locked bedroom by his butler, 'lying on his left side, apparently dead', at the latter address in January 1847, in circumstances sufficient to merit an inquest, though the jury agreed with the doctor that the cause of death was 'sanguineous apoplexy, induced solely from natural causes'.[37] The only legacies realized from his will, dated 11 July 1844, were those of his library, which passed to his son and executor, and the £1,093 in government stock placed in trust for his daughter Anna Eliza. After the settlement of debts his personal estate was insufficient to meet his other bequests to family and servants, and at his own request he received a 'plain and simple' burial in the family vault at Kensal Green.[38]

[1] BL OIOC Mss Eur. A. 145, f. 1. [2] Add. 45038, f. 35; The Times, 15 Nov. 1819. [3] Add. 45038, ff. 43, 49, 53, 57. [4] Gent. Mag. (1847), i. 422-3; H.D. Sandeman, Selections from Calcutta Gazettes, v. 429, 439-42; Bengal Obituary (1848), 269. [5] Add. 45038, f. 35. [6] Ibid. f. 41. [7] Inst. of Commonwealth Stud. M915/3/4; 4/1-2. [8] N. Kingsley, Country Houses of Glos. 48. [9] Hants Chron. 24 Feb. 1823. [10] J.J. Sack, The Grenvillites, 29-30; Bucks. RO, Fremantle mss D/FR/46/11/71; 12/76. [11] Sack, 201, 211-12, 215-16. [12] Session of Parl. 1825, p. 462. [13] Fremantle mss 46/11/78. [14] The Times, 12 July 1823. [15] Fremantle mss 51/5/19; Buckingham, Mems. Geo. IV, ii. 269-70. [16] The Times, 21 Feb., 23 Mar. 1824. [17] Hants Chron. 19 June 1826. [18] Buckingham, ii. 165. [19] The Times, 22 Feb. 1826. [20] Hants Chron. 19 June 1826. [21] Add. 45038, ff. 59, 61, 64. [22] Fremantle mss 46/12/100; Sack, 210-11. [23] Wellington mss WP1/913/8. [24] Sack, 215; Wellington mss WP1/998/13. [25] Inst. of Commonwealth Stud. M915/4/1, 2. [26] Ibid. M915/11/7. [27] Hants Telegraph, 2 Aug. 1830. [28] The Times, 23 Feb. 1831. [29] Hants Chron. 2 May 1831. [30] Brougham mss. [31] Add. 45038, f. 9. [32] Brougham mss, East to Brougham, 11 Aug., 19 Nov. 1831, 7 June, 18 Sept. 1831; Buckingham, i. 338-9. [33] Gent. Mag. (1847), i. 423; Add. 51655, Mackintosh to Holland [26 Apr. 1832]. [34] Disraeli Letters, iii.

936. [35] Inst. of Commonwealth Stud. M915/4/2; Add. 40513, f. 320. [36] Brougham mss, East to Brougham, 12 July 1832. [37] The Times, 13 Jan. 1847. [38] PROB 11/2055/400; IR26/1770/266.

H.J.S./P.J.S.

EAST, James Buller (1789–1878).

| WINCHESTER | 1831–1832 |
| WINCHESTER | 1835–Feb. 1864 |

b. 1 Feb. 1789, o.s. of Sir Edward Hyde East*, 1st bt., and Jane Isabella, da. of Joseph Chaplin Hankey of East Bergholt, Suff. educ. Harrow 1802; Christ Church, Oxf. 1806; I. Temple 1807, called 1813. m. 27 June 1822, Caroline Eliza, da. of James Henry Leigh*, s.p. suc. fa. as 2nd bt. 8 Jan. 1847. d. 19 Nov. 1878.
Bencher, I. Temple 1856, reader 1869.

East, who was head boy at Harrow, took a second class degree at Oxford and was among the group of Christ Church alumni who founded Grillion's Club in 1813.[1] That year he went to India on his father's appointment as chief justice of Bengal, where he practiced at the Calcutta bar and served as a local magistrate, a combination he found exhausting, as he told his Christ Church contemporary Frederick Douglas[†], though effective in banishing 'the contemplation of ennui'.[2] On arrival, he was inspired to reforming zeal by the state of the judicial system, which he found to be riddled with doubtful practices and incompetence. Yet while he remained a staunch critic of the administration of the East India Company and iniquities such as its salt monopoly, by June 1815 he had begun to weary of the country, 'a worn out nation' which he found topographically uninspiring, whose 'ignorant and debased' natives lacked a literary tradition and a proper antiquarian devotion to their architectural heritage.[3] In August 1816 East, who closely followed the parliamentary careers of Douglas and another college friend John Nicholas Fazakerley*, belatedly warned Douglas against the 'captivating solicitations' of George Canning* and Lord Wellesley, whose political conduct he compared unfavourably with

> the direct opposition of the honest and manly opponents of government, notwithstanding the accession of Jacobinism, vulgarity and presumption which has been made to that party by Mr. [Henry] Brougham. From this you will presume that I am still attached to the party whom I consider as the representatives of Pitt's administration, strict anti-Jacobins and anti-citizens of the world and anti-philosophers, and I believe as sincerely rational and patriotic and moral as those who pretend to higher merits.

He added that he had been 'just as ministerialist in this quarter of the globe', citing his support for the war against Nepal waged by Lord Moira, the Indian governor-general, the previous year.[4] In September 1821 he made a recuperative tour of the upper provinces of Bengal, having been 'unwell for several months', according to his father, with whom he set sail for England in February 1822.[5] On his return he apparently did not resume legal practice. His family's wealth derived from a Jamaican estate and in February 1824 he was elected to the standing committee of the West India planters and merchants, of which his father was a stalwart, but he attended only a handful of meetings over the next decade.[6]

East may have considered entering Parliament in 1826 as a protégé of the 1st duke of Buckingham, his father's patron.[7] He certainly proclaimed his 'attachment and esteem' to Buckingham when he came forward for Winchester as his father's replacement at the 1831 general election. On the issue of parliamentary reform, to which his father was opposed, his election address was evasive, but on the hustings he was forced into admitting that he was not a 'strenuous advocate' of the Grey ministry's proposals and only supported the enfranchisement of large towns. After a controversial three-hour poll he was narrowly returned in second place.[8] A silent attender in this period, he voted against the second reading of the reintroduced reform bill, 6 July, for use of the 1831 census to determine the disfranchisement schedules, 19 July, for postponing consideration of Chippenham's status, 27 July, and against the bill's passage, 21 Sept. He divided against the second reading of the revised bill, 17 Dec. 1831, going into committee on it, 20 Jan., the enfranchisement of Tower Hamlets, 28 Feb., and the bill's third reading, 22 Mar. 1832. That month he was listed as a founder member of the Carlton Club. He voted against the second reading of the Irish reform bill, 25 May. He divided against ministers on the Russian-Dutch loan, 26 Jan., 12 July, and was appointed to the select committee on the affairs of the East India Company, 27 Jan. 1832.

At the 1832 general election East offered again for Winchester, where the freemen were now swamped by the newly enfranchised householders. Though he was unrepentant over his stance against reform, having 'felt it his duty to oppose so extensive and sudden a change', he promised to 'uphold and promote' the new system. He was defeated by his opponent of the previous year, but persevered and topped the poll as a Conservative in 1835.[9] He sat until his retirement in 1864, and served as secretary of Grillion's from 1854 to 1870.[10] He inherited his father's baronetcy in 1847, but derived no benefit from his debt-encumbered estate, beyond the contents of his library, despite being named as his residual legatee.[11] In 1850 he purchased Bourton House, near Moreton-in-the-Marsh, Gloucestershire, where he died a widower and s.p. in November 1878, when the baronetcy became extinct.[12] By his will, dated 27 Nov. 1877, he provided annuities for his cousins Charlotte Mary Elizabeth Brace East and Frances Hyde Hinton East, and left Bourton House, diamond heirlooms and about £70,000 to his cousin Gertrude Charlotte Mary D'Este Maclaverty.

[1] List of Members of Grillion's Club (1864). [2] BL OIOC O/6/6; Mss Eur. A145, f. 8; Bengal Almanac (1818), app. vii. [3] OIOC Mss Eur. A145, ff. 1, 8, 26. [4] Ibid. f. 14. [5] Add. 45038, ff. 47, 53, 57. [6] Inst. of Commonwealth Stud. M915/4/1, 2. [7] J.J. Sack, The Grenvillites, 31. [8] Hants Chron. 2, 9 May; The Times, 4 May; Portsmouth Herald, 8 May 1831. [9] Hants Chron. 10, 17 Dec. 1832. [10] Grillion's Club, (1914), 18, 21. [11] PROB 11/2055/400; IR26/1770/266. [12] VCH Glos. vi. 200; The Times, 25 Nov. 1878.

H.J.S./P.J.S.

EASTHOPE, John (1784–1865), of 39 Lothbury, London.

ST. ALBANS	1826–1830
BANBURY	1831–1832
LEICESTER	1837–1847

b. 29 Oct. 1784, 2nd surv. s. of Thomas Easthope, barge master, of Tewkesbury, Glos. and Elizabeth, da. of John Leaver of Overbury, Worcs. m. (1) 4 Aug 1807, Ann (d. 11 Feb. 1840)[1], da. of Jacob Stokes of Leopard House, Worcester, 1s. d.v.p. 3da; (2) 19 Sept. 1843, Elizabeth, da. of Col. George Skyring, wid. of Maj. John Longley, s.p. cr. bt. 24 Aug. 1841. d. 11 Dec. 1865.
  Director, Canada Co. 1826-60.

Easthope's paternal grandfather Thomas Easthope was a native of Bridgnorth, Shropshire, where the family had long been settled. He married Frances Asbury there in 1738 and with her had three sons, Thomas (bap. 1748), the father of this Member, Edward (bap. 1751) and Francis Asbury (bap. 1758). He later moved to Tewkesbury, Gloucestershire, where his son Thomas became a barge master, and he evidently married for a second time. By his will, dated 14 Sept. 1781, he devised property in the parish of St. Leonard, Bridgnorth to his son Francis, who was then abroad, and his leasehold inn, the Hole in the Wall, in the parish of St. Mary Magdalene, to Thomas. He was dead by early 1782.[2] John Easthope, the third son of Thomas, was born at Tewkesbury in 1784, but not baptized until 11 Sept. 1788, along with his brother Edward and sister Ann. One of his two elder brothers,

Francis Asbury and Thomas, apparently died comparatively young.[3] His father's economic circumstances and date of death are unknown; but Easthope was later described as a man of 'vulgar origin' who had been 'the architect of his own fortune'.[4] He worked as a clerk in the banking house of Thomas and Timothy Cobb at Banbury, Oxfordshire, but subsequently went to London to try his fortune. Although he was listed among Bridgnorth freemen resident in London in 1812, he first appeared in the directories as a stockbroker at 2 Hercules Court, Threadneedle Street in 1818.[5] (John Bentall, who shared the same address, had been there since at least 1811.) By 1820, Easthope was in partnership with one Allen at 9 and 10 Exchange Buildings, Threadneedle Street, and by 1827 their firm had moved to 39 Lothbury. He engaged in a series of successful speculations and built up a useful though not spectacular fortune; he was said to have done particularly well during the financial crisis of 1825-6, which proved disastrous to many other commercial speculators. He was reckoned to be worth about £150,000 by 1841.[6]

As soon as the death of the Whig sitting Member created a vacancy for the open and venal borough of St. Albans, 9 Dec. 1820, Easthope, writing from Finchley, offered himself as 'a sincere and steady' supporter of 'constitutional freedom'. According to Lord Duncannon*, the opposition whip, he started 'at our instigation', though he was unknown to Tierney, the Whig leader in the Commons and uncle of the deceased Member. (Easthope never joined Brooks's.) He attacked 'the present degraded and tottering administration' and deplored their 'unmanly and persecuting proceedings against the queen', in which they had 'become the dupes of a wicked conspiracy'. He promised to scrutinize public expenditure with 'the utmost jealousy' and to campaign for 'the most rigid economy', and asserted that 'a temperate and constitutional reform of the Commons ... is indispensable'.[7] The Whig Lord Spencer and his son Lord Althorp*, who had the remnants of an interest at St. Albans, and would in normal circumstances have given Easthope their blessing, remained neutral, out of deference to their long personal friendship with the father of Charles Ross*, one of his two ministerialist rivals.[8] Easthope finished third, but he polled respectably enough to suggest that he might succeed on a future occasion, and he indicated that he would try again.[9] Immediately afterwards he sought the support of Althorp in the event of his having the election declared void on account of the bribery of the winner, Sir Henry Wright Wilson, which he claimed he would have no difficulty in proving. Although Althorp was

committed not to oppose Ross, he made a very half-hearted attempt to persuade Ross's father to give Easthope a clear run at any by-election in return for his support for Ross at the election after that. When the Rosses refused to make way for him Easthope abandoned his intention of petitioning.[10] He continued to cultivate the borough, and in October 1825, when he dated his address from Friern Barnet, he offered himself for the next general election, Ross, now seated elsewhere, having withdrawn his pretensions. Shortly before he conducted his canvass in December, he strenuously repudiated 'vague insinuations' in the local press of impropriety in his financial dealings.[11] A contest was expected, but shortly before the election in June 1826 one of the contenders pulled out, leaving Easthope to come in unopposed with the ministerialist sitting Member. On the hustings, he adopted a far less strident tone than in 1821. He expressed satisfaction at the 'present aspect of public affairs', particularly applauding Canning's liberal foreign policy and Peel's first attempts to lessen the severity of the penal code. He reiterated his desire for tax reductions, but suggested that in present circumstances it was 'impossible' to achieve substantial cuts without damaging 'national credit or public honour'. In general terms he observed:

> If the ministry act as they have hitherto done, I will come forward in their support; but I shall watch over the interests and privileges of my country, and place myself in the ranks of their bitterest opponents when they offer a stab to the liberties of England.

In his written address of thanks he declared his devotion to the Protestant religion, but admitted his support for 'extending to those who conscientiously differ from us, every manifestation of kindness and conciliation that is compatible with national security'. The editor of the local Tory newspaper approved the 'moderate and manly' line taken by Easthope, but cast doubt on the sincerity of his professions of friendliness to the Liverpool ministry.[12]

Easthope's conduct in the House justified this cynicism. He voted with opposition against the duke of Clarence's grant, 16 Feb., 2 Mar., and was in the small minority on the army estimates, 20 Feb. 1827. He voted for Catholic relief, 6 Mar. He divided for inquiry into Leicester corporation's electoral activities, 15 Mar., and for the production of information on the mutiny at Barrackpoor, 22 Mar., and the Lisburn magistrates' conduct over the Orange procession, 29 Mar. He was in the opposition minority for the postponement of the committee of supply the following day. He voted for inquiries into the Irish miscellaneous estimates and chancery delays, 5 Apr. He voted for the disfranchisement of Penryn, 28 May. He was in the majority for Althorp's election expenses bill later that day, and, as a director of the recently established Canada Company, voted for the grant to improve water communications in that country, 12 June. He was not reported as speaking in debate in his first session, but in May and June 1827 he presented a number of petitions, some from Dissenting congregations in London, for repeal of the Test Acts.[13]

Easthope presented more of the same, 15, 18, 19, 25 Feb. 1828, and voted for repeal the following day. He voted against the extension of the East Retford franchise to the neighbouring hundred, 21 Mar., and for inquiry into chancery delays, 24 Apr. On behalf of the Canada Company, 27 Mar., he responded to Waithman's motion for inquiry into its dealings with government by saying that its directors had nothing to hide and were 'governed by a laudable spirit of liberality'; and he deplored Poulett Thomson's 'wanton' attack on the directors of the Hibernian Joint Stock Company, 24 Apr. He was in the minorities of 58 and 27 for further relaxation of the restrictions on the import of foreign corn, 22, 29 Apr. On the 29th he supported the unsuccessful bid by the Members for Hertfordshire and his colleague Alderman Smith to allow the legislation for the erection of a new court house at St. Albans to be proceeded with despite an inadvertent failure to comply with standing orders. Easthope, who voted for Catholic relief, 12 May, was in the small minorities for more effective control over crown proceedings for the recovery of excise penalties, 1 May, a revision of civil list pensions, 10 June, and the Irish assessment of lessors bill, 12 June. He argued that allowing any 'evasions' of the Scottish and Irish bank notes bill would render that irksome but essential measure nugatory, 16 June. Later that day he opposed Hume's bid to force country bankers to supply quarterly returns of notes circulated. He divided for the usury laws amendment bill, 19 June, and voted against government on the cost of building works at Buckingham House, 23 June, the ordnance estimates, 4 July, and the silk duties, 14 July 1828.

Easthope presented and endorsed a petition from the Catholics of Heythrop, Oxfordshire, for redress of grievances, 6 Feb., voted for emancipation, 6, 30 Mar., and presented favourable petitions from Protestant Dissenters, 13, 16 Mar. 1829. On 12 and 19 June 1829 he pressed ministers to intervene with the Spanish government to obtain satisfaction for British bondholders who had suffered financial losses. He was one of the 28 oppositionists who voted with the

Wellington ministry against the amendment to the address, 4 Feb. 1830; but he divided for the transfer of East Retford's seats to Birmingham, 11 Feb., Lord Blandford's parliamentary reform scheme, 18 Feb., the enfranchisement of Birmingham, Leeds and Manchester, 23 Feb., and investigation of the Newark petition accusing the duke of Newcastle of improper electoral interference, 1 Mar. He voted to get rid of the Bathurst and Dundas pensions, 26 Mar., and for Jewish emancipation, 5 Apr., 17 May. On 7 Apr. he presented the Hertfordshire petition complaining of distress and called for reductions in expenditure and the removal of all restrictions on commerce and trade: he subsequently voted for economies, 3, 21 May, 7, 14 June. He was one of O'Connell's minority for reform of the Irish vestry laws, 27 Apr., and voted against government on the Terciera incident the next day. He presented petitions from the Dissenters of Nether Chapel, Sheffield for abolition of the death penalty for forgery and action against suttee, 11 May; he voted for the former, 24 May, 7 June. He voted for inquiry into the civil government of Canada, 25 May, and parliamentary reform, 28 May. He was shut out of the division on the sale of beer bill, 1 July. He was in the minorities of 11 for a reduction in judges' salaries, 7 July, and 27 for Brougham's condemnation of colonial slavery, 13 July 1830. He offered again for St. Albans on the death of the king, but his initial canvass convinced him that he could not win the anticipated contest; it was reported that he had lost support on account of his failure to 'attend to the local interests of the borough' with sufficient zeal. He decided to cut his losses, but before making public his retirement notified Althorp, who would have supported him personally, to give him the chance to alert another opposition candidate to the opportunity. Althorp thought he had behaved 'very well by us'.[14] At the general election of 1831 Easthope stood for Banbury, where the local reformers were up in arms against the patron Lord Bute, whose nominee was assaulted and driven out of town. He was returned after a token contest.[15]

He voted for the second reading of the reintroduced reform bill, 6 July 1831, and was a steady supporter of its details, though he was briefly made *hors de combat* by a broken collar bone sustained in a fall from his horse in August,[16] and was in the minority for the total disfranchisement of Aldborough, 14 Sept. He voted for the passage of the bill, 21 Sept., and the motion of confidence in the Grey ministry, 10 Oct. He divided with them on the Dublin election controversy, 23 Aug. At about this time Greville noted Easthope's connections with the French government as a broker in the London market.[17] He voted for the second reading of the revised reform bill, 17 Dec. 1831, and again was a reliable supporter of its detailed provisions. He voted for the third reading, 22 Mar., and the address calling on the king to appoint only ministers who would carry it unimpaired, 10 May, and against an amendment to the Scottish reform bill, 15 June. He sided with ministers on the Russian-Dutch loan, 26 Jan.,12, 16, 20 July, and relations with Portugal, 9 Feb.; but he voted in the minority against their temporizing amendment to Buxton's call for the abolition of slavery, 24 May. On 22 May he agreed to postpone his motion for a disclosure of information on the circulation of Bank of England notes, to which ministers were opposed, to accommodate their proceedings on the proposed renewal of the Bank's charter. They duly resisted and defeated it, 26 July 1832, when Easthope explained that his object was to expose the incompetence of the Bank's directors, its culpability for the panic of 1825 and its unfitness for a continuation of its 'exclusive privileges'. By then it was known in Banbury that he did not intend to stand again at the next general election.[18]

He unsuccessfully contested Southampton at the 1835 general election and Lewes at a by-election in April 1837; but he was successful at Leicester at the general election later that year and sat there for ten years. He was defeated at Tewkesbury in 1841 and Bridgnorth in 1847. James Grant wrote in 1841 that while Easthope was an infrequent speaker in the House, 'not only is he listened to with attention, but he speaks with great ease, and usually with much effect', by virtue of 'the strong good sense' which he purveyed and 'the lucidness with which he arranges his ideas and facts'. His unpolished diction was a source of amusement to some.[19] In the summer of 1834 he was persuaded by government party managers to purchase the ailing *Morning Chronicle*. (One of them rather churlishly described him as 'a liberal, honest and most active man, but not well backed in opinion or instruction; and like all men of vulgar origin accessible to the praise of great men'.) He paid about £16,500 for the paper and placed its columns at the disposal of ministers, though their relationship was not always harmonious. He was rewarded with a baronetcy by Lord Melbourne in 1841. He disposed of his interest in the *Chronicle* in 1847.[20]

By 1838 Easthope's firm was styled Easthope and Son; the latter died in France in January 1849, about two years after the business had moved to 38 Throgmorton Street. It had disappeared from the directories by 1857. With his second wife, Easthope, for all his supposed vulgarity, was a generous and

accomplished dinner host to the great and the good, both in London and Paris.[21] In the mid-1840s he acquired a residence at Fir Grove, Weybridge, Surrey; and it was there that he died in December 1865.[22] By his will, dated 18 Nov. 1863, he left his wife 300 shares in the Cordova and Seville Railway, the Weybridge house and four labourers' cottages there. He devised a freehold estate at Weybridge and Chertsey and the remaining 950 shares in the Spanish Railway Company to his grandson John Andrew Doyle, his residuary legatee. He directed that his London house in Great Cumberland Place be sold and the proceeds combined with his personal estate to honour a bond of £10,000 due to his wife and daughter Louisa Doyle, and to furnish legacies amounting to £3,000.

[1]*Gent. Mag.* (1840), i. 332. [2]IGI (Glos. and Salop); PROB 11/1087/74. [3]IGI (Glos.). [4]*Hist. of 'The Times'*, i. 463; [J. Grant], *Portraits of Public Characters* (1841), i. 76. [5]*VCH Oxon.* iii. 333; x. 91. [6]*Oxford DNB*; Grant, i. 77-78. [7]*The Times*, 11, 15 Dec., 1, 4 Jan. 1821; Add. 76124, Duncannon to Spencer [11 Dec.]; Grey mss, Tierney to Grey, 13 Dec. 1820. [8]Add. 76124, Duncannon to Spencer [11, 13 Dec.], Howarth to same, 11 Dec., reply, 12 Dec., Spencer to A. Ross, 12 Dec., reply, 13 Dec. 1820. [9]*The Times*, 10-13, 15, 16, 18 Jan.; *Cambridge Chron.* 12 Jan. 1821. [10]Add. 76378, Althorp to A. Ross, 24 Jan. 1821. [11]*Herts Mercury*, 29 Oct., 19, 26 Nov. 3, 17, 24 Dec. 1825. [12]Ibid. 3, 10, 17 June 1826. [13]*The Times*, 22, 26, 31 May, 9, 16, 30 June 1827. [14]*Herts Mercury*, 3, 10 July; *Althorp Letters*, 150-1. [15]*VCH Oxon.* x. 91; *Jackson's Oxford Jnl.* 30 Apr., 7, 14 May; *The Times*, 4 May 1831. [16]*The Times*, 15 Aug. 1831. [17]*Greville Mems.* ii. 186. [18]*VCH Oxon.* x. 91. [19]Grant, i. 79-81; *Disraeli Letters*, ii. 604. [20]*Oxford DNB*; A. Aspinall, *Politics and the Press*, 101, 240-1, 257, 260; *Greville Mems.* iv. 139; *Hist. of 'The Times'*, i. 305-6, 462-3. [21]Broughton, *Recollections*, vi. 110; *Disraeli Letters*, ii. 604; iv. 1456. [22]*Gent. Mag.* (1866), i. 128.

D.R.F.

EBRINGTON, Visct. *see* **FORTESCUE, Hugh**

EDEN, Hon. Robert Henley (1789–1841), of 19 Whitehall Place, Mdx.

FOWEY   1826–5 Feb. 1830

b. 3 Sept. 1789, at Dresden, 3rd but 1st surv. s. of Morton Eden, 1st Bar. Henley [I], and Lady Elizabeth Henley, da. of Robert Henley†, 1st earl of Northington. *educ.* Eton 1802-7; Christ Church, Oxf. 1807; L. Inn 1811, called 1814. *m.* 11 Mar. 1824, Harriet Eleanora, da. of Sir Robert Peel†, 1st bt., of Drayton Manor, Staffs., 4s. (3 *d.v.p.*). *suc.* fa. as 2nd Bar. Henley [I] 6 Dec. 1830; took name of Henley by royal lic. 4 Apr. 1831. *d.* 3 Feb. 1841.

Commr. of bankrupts 1817-26; KC, duchy of Lancaster 1819-25, sjt.-at-law 1825-6; master in chancery 1826-40; commr. on cts. of co. palatine of Lancaster 1829.

Eden's father, the brother of William Eden, 1st Baron Auckland, served with distinction in a succession of diplomatic postings before retiring as ambassador to Austria in 1799, with an Irish peerage and a pension of £2,000 per annum.[1] After being called to the bar in 1814 Eden practised as an equity draftsman and attended the Oxford and Brecon sessions. He was ambitious and, with the support of his Christ Church contemporary Robert Peel*, a rising member of Lord Liverpool's ministry, he soon accumulated a commissionership of bankrupts and a duchy of Lancaster counsellorship.[2] In 1818 he published *Reports in Cases in Chancery, 1755-66* (which were largely the principal judgments of his maternal grandfather Lord Northington as lord chancellor); the following year he produced an updated edition of *Brown's Reports* and in 1821 he delivered himself of a monumental *Treatise on the Law of Injunctions*. His main professional interest was in reform of the bankruptcy laws, and in 1823 and 1824 he published explanatory comments on the bills introduced by William Courtenay to amend and consolidate them. His *magnum opus* appeared in 1825, in the form of *A Practical Treatise on the Bankrupt Law*, which he dedicated to lord chancellor Eldon; a revised and expanded edition was published the next year. On his brother Frederick's death in November 1823 Henry Brougham* commented that it was 'a very great loss to … Henley, who had as fair prospects as any young chancery lawyer could have, of *very early promotion*, and now of course he must look to a barren title in Irish peerage without fortune'.[3] He did himself no harm soon afterwards by marrying Peel's sister. When he sought a vacant mastership in chancery his brother-in-law, as home secretary, strongly supported his application, which was crowned with success in March 1826.[4] The previous month he had revealed his parliamentary ambitions by canvassing Oxford on the prospect of a vacancy, which did not materialize.[5] It was thought that he might come in there at the general election that summer, but in the event he stood for Fowey on the Austen interest and was returned, as he told Peel, 'after three days very arduous contest'; he survived a subsequent petition.[6]

One leading Tory found Eden to be 'an agreeable man', but Peel's professed 'conviction that a new avenue of distinction' had been opened to him proved unfounded, as he made little mark in the House.[7] He divided against Catholic relief, 6 Mar., and the spring guns bill, 23 Mar. 1827. In the disputes arising from the collapse of Liverpool's ministry and Canning's accession to power he naturally sided with his brother-in-law, concluding, on a review of the evidence, that Canning had been guilty of blatant 'duplicity'.[8] He moved for an account of recent sittings of the bankruptcy commissioners, 15 May.[9] He introduced a Bankruptcy Acts amendment bill, 30 May, but it did not progress beyond the second reading. He voted in the minority against the Coventry magistracy bill, 18 June 1827. In late August he relayed to Peel news of the turmoil in cabinet, observing that the new premier Lord Goderich's 'whole conduct … appears to have been as pusillanimous in *manner* as it is in *substance*'.[10] He divided against repeal of the Test Acts, 26 Feb., and Catholic relief, 12 May 1828. He introduced another Bankruptcy Acts amendment bill, 1 May, but it foundered in the Lords. He presented a Fowey petition for removal of the restrictions on small banknotes, 5 June. Next day he spoke in defence of the officers of Millbank prison, particularly the chaplain. He voted with the duke of Wellington's ministry on the ordnance estimates, 4 July 1828. In February 1829 Planta, the patronage secretary, who had earlier included Eden on his list of possible movers and seconders of the address, predicted that he would side 'with government' for Catholic emancipation. In the House, 18 Feb., he declared that he 'viewed with the greatest dismay the efforts that were making to grant further concessions of political power to the Roman Catholics', and warned that 'the measure now contemplated would bring great misery on the country'. However, this was mere bluster, and he voted for emancipation, 6, 30 Mar. 1829. That autumn the Ultra Tory leader, Sir Richard Vyvyan*, listed him among those 'present government connections who will be hostile to a new one'. He vacated his seat, for reasons which have not been ascertained, at the start of the 1830 session.

In December 1830 Eden succeeded his father to the Irish peerage and the main family property at Watford, near Daventry, Northamptonshire.[11] He was determined to retain his mastership in chancery, notwithstanding a widespread feeling that by doing so he would degrade the nobility, since one of his duties was to act as a messenger from the Lords to the Commons. He assured Brougham, now lord chancellor, that the other masters were willing to relieve him of the necessity of such attendance, and he invoked the views of Lords Eldon and Tenterden in his support.[12] In 1831 Henley (as he was now styled in both name and title) published a *Memoir* of Lord Northington, partly, it seems, to enhance his claim, as Northington's heir at law, to a United Kingdom peerage. Applying directly (but unsuccessfully) for this object to the prime minister Lord Grey, he acknowledged that

> my fortune and pretensions are not such as to justify a claim to the full extent of the honours of my grandfather and uncle. But the inheritance which I have received from them through my mother, with my private fortune

derived from other sources, are such as to entitle me to affirm that they are sufficient to support both in my own person and in that of my descendants the rank of a baron.[13]

In 1832 he made a considerable impact with his *Plan of Church Reform*, which called for 'a timely and judicious correction of abuses' and went quickly to eight editions. He wished to eradicate pluralism, non-residence and sinecures, redistribute church revenues and create new sees. Most controversially, he suggested the establishment of a commission, partly salaried, to manage episcopal property. The scheme infuriated many churchmen and provoked a lively response. Henley, for his part, repeatedly pressed Brougham to persuade ministers of the need for action, and in September 1832 he formed the Church Reformation Society, of whose provisional committee he became chairman. His ideas were in close accord with those of Peel, whose ecclesiastical commission of 1835 proceeded on broadly similar lines.[14] Church reform was part of the platform on which Henley, professing to be 'connected with no party', canvassed Middlesex at the general election of 1832. He denounced the agitation by the political unions, advocated the speediest end to colonial slavery as was consistent with safety and fairness, but declined to commit himself on free trade in corn and silk. However, his vulnerability on a number of issues exposed him to incessant popular abuse: he was accused, unfairly, of belonging to a family of pensioners, while his hostility to parliamentary reform and repeal of the Test Acts (which he now publicly repented), and his insistence on the inalienability of church property, were seized on by his opponents. At length his nerve broke and he withdrew shortly before the poll. Brougham's private secretary noted that

> Henley had by no means a bad chance of success ... [but his] want of spirit saved his adversary. He is not qualified for a popular election. He is very gentlemanly and by no means without talent, and he has a fine person – tall and well-proportioned – but he is entirely without the art of public speaking, and he is singularly indecisive ... He is best adapted to private life. An excellent husband and father, and a kind friend, he has effaced the recollections of a very irregular youth by years of active benevolence and virtue.[15]

During 1840 it became apparent that Henley was insane, and he was relieved of his duties as a master in chancery. He died in February 1841 and was succeeded by his elder son Anthony Henley (1825-98), Liberal Member for Northampton, 1859-74, who received a United Kingdom peerage as Baron Northington in 1885; his personalty was sworn under £30,000.[16]

[1] *Oxford DNB.* [2] Add. 40269, f. 313; 40277, f. 86. [3] Add. 51564, Brougham to Lady Holland [6 Nov. 1823]. [4] Add. 40385, ff. 155, 280; 40386, f. 48. [5] Add. 40342, f. 311; 40385, ff. 114, 168. [6] Add. 40387, f. 174; *West Briton*, 9 June 1826. [7] Surr. Hist. Cent. Goulburn mss 304/66A, Goulburn to wife, 25 Feb. 1827; Add. 40387, f. 175. [8] Add. 40393, f. 248. [9] *The Times*, 16 May 1827. [10] Add. 40394, f. 192. [11] The personalty was sworn under £45,000 (PROB 8/224; 11/1780/24). [12] Brougham mss, Henley to Brougham, 18 Dec. 1830. [13] Ibid. Henley to Brougham and Grey, 8 Apr. 1831. [14] Ibid. Henley to Brougham, 24 Aug., 1 Sept. [Sept.], [Oct.] 1832; Add. 40403, f. 69; G.F.A. Best, *Temporal Pillars*, 252-3, 280-91, 311, 319. [15] Brougham mss, Henley to Brougham, [?20 Oct.]; *The Times*, 9, 16, 22, 24 Nov., 15 Dec. 1832; *Three Diaries*, 286-7. [16] *The Times*, 5 Feb. 1841; *Gent. Mag.* (1841), i. 425, which erroneously gives 1 Feb.; PROB 8/234; 11/1942/187.

D.R.F.

EDGCUMBE, Ernest Augustus, Visct. Valletort (1797–1861).

FOWEY	11 May 1819–1826
LOSTWITHIEL	1826–1830
PLYMPTON ERLE	1830–14 Dec. 1830
LOSTWITHIEL	20 Dec. 1830–1832

b. 23 Mar. 1797, 2nd but 1st surv. s. of Richard Edgcumbe[†], 2nd earl of Mount Edgcumbe, and Lady Sophia Hobart, da. of John Hobart[†], 2nd earl of Buckinghamshire; bro. of Hon. George Edgcumbe*. *educ.* Harrow until 1811; Sandhurst. *m.* 6 Dec. 1831, Caroline Augusta, da. and coh. of R.-Adm. Charles Feilding, 2s. 1da. *styled* Visct. Valletort 1818-39. *suc.* fa. as 3rd earl of Mount Edgcumbe 26 Sept. 1839. *d.* 3 Sept. 1861.
Ensign and lt. 1 Ft. Gds. 1814-19; col. Cornw. militia 1821; col. and militia a.d.c. to William IV 1830-7, to Queen Victoria 1837-57.
Mayor, Lostwithiel 1823, 1830.

Valletort, whom the duke of Bedford described as 'amiable, good-hearted, affectionate and very far from deficient in understanding',[1] had been seated on petition for Fowey, where his father had some influence, in May 1819, and was returned unopposed in 1820. He gave silent support to Lord Liverpool's ministry, but his attendance was intermittent. He divided against economies in revenue collection, 4 July 1820. Early in 1821 it was reported that he had 'returned from Paris, having lost his money at the salon and his heart to Miss Fitzgerald, but, like his kind, perfectly happy without either'.[2] He voted in defence of ministers' conduct towards Queen Caroline, 6 Feb. He divided against Catholic relief, 28 Feb. He voted against repeal of the additional malt duty, 3 Apr., and Hume's economy and retrenchment motion, 27 June 1821. He divided against parliamentary reform, 20 Feb., and reform in Scotland, 2 June 1823. He voted against reduction of the sinking fund, 3 Mar., repeal of the Foreign Enlistment Act, 16 Apr., and inquiries into the prosecution of the Dublin Orange rioters, 22 Apr., and delays in chancery, 5 June 1823. In January 1824 he was said to be 'still a great cripple', presumably after an accident, and 'thinks he is lame for life';[3] his only recorded vote that session was against inquiry into the trial of the Methodist missionary John Smith in Demerara, 11 June. He voted for the Irish unlawful societies bill, 25 Feb. 1825. He was named as a defaulter, 28 Feb., but attended next day to divide for Catholic relief, one of several conversions that Edward Littleton* attributed to the influence of Plunket's speech.[4] He 'felt proud of the triumph which his reason had enabled him to achieve over the strong and early prejudices which he had unjustly entertained' on the subject, 21 Apr., and expressed confidence that emancipation would 'ultimately succeed'; he voted for relief that day, and again, 10 May. He presented, without comment, an East Stonehouse petition for revision of the corn laws, 26 Apr. 1825.[5] He divided against reform of Edinburgh's representation, 13 Apr. 1826. At the general election that summer he abandoned Fowey, which he had allegedly neglected, and was returned unopposed for Lostwithiel on his father's interest.[6]

He divided for Catholic relief, 6 Mar. 1827, 12 May 1828. He presented a Lostwithiel anti-slavery petition, 16 June, and voted with the duke of Wellington's ministry against reducing the salary of the lieutenant-general of the ordnance, 4 July 1828. In February 1829 Planta, the patronage secretary, listed him as being 'with government' on Catholic emancipation; he voted accordingly, 30 Mar. 1829. He wrote to Gilbert John Heathcote, 9 Feb. 1830, that if he 'really wish[ed] the government well' he should attend the House on the forthcoming 'general field day on a motion of Hume's for retrenchment', as 'a vote now is worth a dozen later'. He regretted that 'Huskisson and his party are as bitter and jesuistical in and *out* of the House as possible'.[7] He divided against the transfer of East Retford's seats to Birmingham, 11 Feb., Lord Blandford's reform plan, 18 Feb., and the enfranchisement of Birmingham, Leeds and Manchester, 23 Feb. Amidst continued heckling, he condemned this last proposal as the 'first approach of the advanced guard of those reformers' who were bent on making a 'violent and ill-directed assault ... against all the political institutions of this country'. He was convinced that 'reform will produce no practical good' and dismissed attempts to blame the lack of parliamentary representation for the economic ills of large industrial towns such as Birmingham, whose interests were 'sufficiently

represented by the general mass' of Members. He considered it his duty to support Wellington's 'energetic and efficient administration' and hoped to see a strong and consistent opposition in the House, rather than 'a number of parties, all taking a different course'. In opposing O'Connell's 'injurious' reform motion, 28 May, he claimed to be equally 'attached to rational liberty'. He agreed that all men had equal rights to the protection of property and person, but 'other constitutional rights' were 'defined by the law'. He rejected radical complaints about corruption, asserting that the House contained 'as much honour ... talent and ability as ever has been congregated in any assembly', and he trusted that the country would never fall into the hands of 'factious demagogues'. He divided against Jewish emancipation, 17 May, and paired against abolishing the death penalty for forgery, 7 June 1830. The following month he declined the post of vice chamberlain of the household, explaining to Wellington that 'under present circumstances' he would 'feel greater pleasure in being permitted to give His Majesty's government my support in the House ... as an independent man', which he believed would be 'in some degree more efficient'. However, he was persuaded to accept an appointment as aide-de-camp to William IV.[8] At the general election that summer he was returned for Plympton Erle on his father's interest.

The ministry regarded Valletort as one of their 'friends', but he privately informed Wellington, 11 Nov. 1830, that he must oppose them on Sir James Graham's motion against the appointment of the high Tory controversialist Henry Phillpotts as bishop of Exeter. He regretted the need for such action at a time when he would have preferred to help strengthen the government, but he warned that many other Members, who were well disposed to ministers and the Church of England, but who also had to serve the public, felt the same way; the duke invited him to Downing Street to hear an explanation.[9] He voted with ministers in the crucial civil list division, 15 Nov. Next month he transferred to the vacant seat for Lostwithiel. He trusted that his 'locality may not be taken as an indication of my sentiments' and said he would support Lord Grey's ministry whenever possible, 9 Dec. 1830, but he hoped that they would 'not inflict permanent injury upon the country' by taking their planned reduction of salaries too far. He insisted that their reform bill would be 'productive of no benefit whatever', 21 Mar. 1831, as it would not satisfy the majority of the people who remained excluded from the franchise. He urged that 'this is not a time to try experiments' and that 'you cannot make the slightest change without producing consequences of a most lamentable description', and he advised Members to 'give the benefit of their doubt to that state of representation which exists'. He regretted the want of sympathy between Parliament and the people, but claimed that this was 'mainly' due to the language used by ministers, who 'instead of attempting to allay excitement, do everything in their power to increase it'. He voted against the bill's second reading next day. He feared that the redistribution of seats to large towns would 'destroy [the] balance of interests ... in the country' by giving 'a more than due influence to the commercial', 13 Apr. He divided for Gascoyne's wrecking amendment, 19 Apr., and condemned the resulting dissolution as 'the height of criminality' by ministers whose 'reckless boldness' had induced them to appeal to the country before it 'returned to a state of calmness and quiet', 21 Apr. 1831. He stood for Cornwall at the general election and promised to approach the reform question with 'a mind unbiased by party ... feelings', declaring that he would 'no longer ... oppose all attempts to amend the representative system, provided ... they do not ... endanger the existence of those institutions upon which depend the property, the rights and the liberties of all'. However, he came bottom of the poll and was returned again for Lostwithiel.[10]

He sought Wellington's approval before attending the Pitt dinner in May 1831, as he believed that 'nothing can ... be effected but by a union of action upon all occasions and ... we must always look upon you as our guide and our leader'.[11] He divided against the second reading of the reintroduced reform bill, 6 July, when he repeated his criticism of ministers who had 'fixed the eyes of the people on the blots of the constitution and closed them against its excellences'. He also blamed the revolution in France for inciting popular opinion in Britain. He declared himself to be 'a reformer', but he could 'never give my consent to so faulty and anomalous a plan'. One Whig minister observed that 'the roaring of Valletort' had provided some light relief in a dull debate.[12] He demanded that the House should know 'exactly and clearly' the principles on which the disfranchisement of boroughs was based before it considered particular cases, 15 July, and voted to use the 1831 census for scheduling purposes, 19 July. He described the disfranchisement of boroughs as 'arbitrary and unjust', 22 July, and used the example of Plympton Erle to show 'the utter absurdity of the bill'. He accused ministers of being willing to 'break through the rules laid down by themselves, if ... they can disfranchise a place', but not if it would 'save a borough'. He also denied that Lostwithiel, which was due to be disfranchised, was an 'old and impotent' borough. He denounced the resolutions by the

City of London reform meeting as 'a most presumptuous attempt to deter Members from the conscientious discharge of their duty', 3 Aug. He voted against the bill's passage, 21 Sept., when he admitted that the pro-reform feeling 'appears to be firmly and permanently fixed in the public mind' but doubted whether the majority favoured this 'wild, extravagant and arbitrary' measure. He looked to a 'fearless' Upper House to save 'our ancient constitution' and said ministers would be responsible for any 'mischief' arising from the bill's rejection. On 13 Oct., following the bill's defeat in the Lords, he accused ministers of 'a dereliction of ... duty' by 'holding up the institutions of the country to disrespect', and declared that it was 'a libel on the English peerage' to say that they had acted from self-interest. He urged the government to 'diminish the violent character of the measure', so that he and others could vote for it, rather than 'risk ... the consequences which would probably follow' from a second rejection by the Lords. He attended the Cornwall reform meeting, 26 Oct., but his speech was constantly interrupted. He condemned recent attempts to 'influence the lower orders against the higher' and declared that there 'never was such a collection of deliberate and direct lies ever penned' as those in the *Black Book*. He thought the 'demand for the *whole* bill was most ridiculous' and recommended a gradual approach, repeating his willingness to support a 'more moderate measure'. He warned that the people were 'deceived' if they believed they could intimidate the Lords, as were those 'whose wish it was to drive the rich from their estates'. He predicted that once the bill was passed and 'the preponderance of power ... thrown into the hands of the manufacturer', the 'immediate' result would be the repeal of the corn laws.[13] In the House, 16 Aug. 1831, he sought an explanation for the government's failure to prevent the French seizure of the Portuguese fleet on the Tagus, which had 'compromised' Britain's 'honour', and expressed suspicion that ministers were prepared to use the British fleet on behalf of 'the revolutionists of Belgium'.

Valletort was absent from the division on the second reading of the revised reform bill, 17 Dec. 1831, presumably owing to his recent marriage, but he privately stated that he would 'not like to put my name to anything so comprehensive and specific' as the proposed Cornish declaration for moderate reform.[14] He voted against going into committee on the bill, 20 Jan. 1832. He thought it was a 'strange way to reward the services' of the Helston yeoman cavalry by depriving the borough of one seat because of their exemption from assessed taxes, 23 Feb. On 20 Mar. he maintained that the supporters of reform were a motley alliance of 'the mob ... who are influenced more by impulse than reason', those with a 'senseless desire of change, for the sake of change' and those who 'openly avow that they look upon this measure merely as a stepping stone to ulterior measures ... incompatible with monarchy'. He remained convinced that a majority in the country, some of whom were subject to intimidation or were 'too timid ... to stem the current', would have been 'better pleased with a more moderate experiment upon the constitution', and he regretted that ministerial intransigence had made it impossible for him to withdraw his opposition. His 'deepest dread' was that the Commons would consequently become 'the mere organ of the excited feelings, the tool of the passing will of the democracy ... ready at its bidding to act as the instrument for annihilating the independence' of the Lords. He divided against the bill's third reading, 22 Mar. He voted against ministers on the Russian-Dutch loan, 22 Jan., and paired against them, 12 July. He presented a Liskeard petition in favour of the factory bill, 27 Feb. 1832.

That summer he offered for East Cornwall and called on 'all who are real friends of the constitution' to unite in defence of 'those institutions on which our greatness as a nation ... depends'. He warned that repeal of the corn laws would be 'deeply injurious to the agricultural classes, especially the small proprietor and labourer', but said he was willing to support certain reforms 'as may be adapted to the spirit of the age' and advocated changes in the method of collecting tithes. However, he retired before the poll.[15] He succeeded to his father's title and estates in Devon and Cornwall in 1839. He died in September 1861 and was succeeded by his eldest son, William Henry Edgcumbe (1832-1917), Conservative Member for Plymouth, 1859-61.

[1] Add. 51668, Bedford to Lady Holland, 11 Jan. 1824. [2] *Countess Granville Letters*, i. 209. [3] Add. 51668, Bedford to Lady Holland, 11 Jan. 1824. [4] TNA 30/29/6/3/93. [5] *The Times*, 27 Apr. 1825. [6] Treffry mss (Aspinall transcripts), Lucy to Austen, 23 July 1824, 20 Nov. 1825; Carew Pole mss CC/N/59, Mount Edgcumbe to Pole Carew, 21 June 1826. [7] Lincs. AO, Ancaster mss 3/ANC 9/10/30. [8] Wellington mss WP1/1124/8. [9] Ibid. 1150/20; 1154/20. [10] *West Briton*, 29 Apr., 6, 13, 20 May 1831. [11] Wellington mss WP1/1185/10. [12] Add. 51573, Spring Rice to Lady Holland, 6 July 1831. [13] *R. Cornw. Gazette*, 29 Oct. 1831. [14] Carew Pole mss CC/N/64, Valletort to Pole Carew, 21 Dec. 1831. [15] Ibid. CO/CC/14, election address, 3 Sept.; *R. Cornw. Gazette*, 26 June, 18 Aug., 3 Nov. 1832.

T.A.J.

EDGCUMBE, Hon. George (1800–1882), of Mount Edgcumbe, Cornw.

PLYMPTON ERLE	1826–2 Dec. 1826

b. 23 June 1800, 3rd but 2nd surv. s. of Richard Edgcumbe[†], 2nd earl of Mount Edgcumbe (*d.* 1839), and Lady Sophia Hobart, da. of John Hobart[†], 2nd earl of Buckinghamshire; bro. of Ernest Augustus Edgcumbe, Visct. Valletort.* *educ.* Harrow 1812; Balliol, Oxf. 1818. *m.* 19 May 1834, Fanny Lucy, da. of Sir John Shelley, 6th bt.,* 2s. 4da. (1 *d.v.p.*). *d.* 18 Feb. 1882.
  Sec. of legation, Switzerland 1828-30, 1837-8, Tuscany 1831-7, Hanover 1838-58.
  Maj. Cornw. militia 1826-55.

Edgcumbe was returned for Plympton Erle in 1826 on his father's interest, presumably in the absence of a paying guest. His father observed that 'George is extremely surprised and flattered with the honour, but I fear his *diplomatic* duties (to say nothing of his *military*) will interfere greatly with his *parliamentary*'.[1] He took no recorded part in the House's proceedings before vacating on 2 Dec. 1826, and he subsequently pursued his diplomatic career. Lady Granville described him as 'very inoffensive ... not handsome ... not clever ... not useful, but there is nothing below mediocre, and he is very obliging and good-natured'; even his mother-in-law considered him to be an 'excellent creature'.[2] On his father's death in 1839 he received £1,000 in addition to the £10,000 already settled on him at the time of his marriage.[3] He died in February 1882; his eldest son, Richard Edgcumbe (1843-1937), was serjeant-at-arms, 1880-1921.

[1] Carew Pole mss, Mount Edgcumbe to Pole Carew, 21 June 1826. [2] *Countess Granville Letters*, i. 301; *Shelley Diary*, ii. 254. [3] The personalty was sworn under £30,000 (PROB 8/233; 11/1935/713).

T.A.J.

EDMONSTONE, Sir Charles, 2nd bt. (1764–1821), of Duntreath, Stirling.

DUNBARTONSHIRE	1806–1807
STIRLINGSHIRE	1812–1 Apr. 1821

b. 10 Oct. 1764, 3rd but 1st surv. s. of Sir Archibald Edmonstone, 1st bt.[†], of Duntreath and 1st w. Susanna Mary, da. of Roger Harenc, merchant, of London and Foot's Cray Place, Kent. *educ.* Westminster 1772; Eton 1775-80; Christ Church, Oxf. 1780; L. Inn 1779, called 1788. *m.* (1) 1 June 1794, Emma (*d.* 30 Nov. 1797), da. of Richard Wilbraham Bootle[†] of Rode Hall, Cheshire, 1s. 1da.; (2) 5 Dec. 1804, Hon. Louisa Hotham, da. of Beaumont Hotham[†], 2nd Bar. Hotham [I], 4s. 2da. *suc.* fa. as 2nd bt. 20 July 1807. *d.* 1 Apr. 1821.
  Clerk in chancery 1797-1807.

Edmonstone was returned unopposed for Stirlingshire in 1820 with the support of the 3rd duke of Montrose and Lord Liverpool's ministry. Soon afterwards a serious illness effectively ended his parliamentary career: no trace of activity has been found, and he was granted periods of leave, 21 June 1820, 9 Mar. 1821. In November 1820 Montrose reported to Lord Melville, the government's Scottish manager, that Edmonstone intended to 'vacate at the meeting of Parliament instead of at the latter end of the session', and that his eldest son Archibald was already canvassing Stirlingshire. However, by early January 1821 he was said to be 'wholly *non compos*' and 'unable to sign his name', and the by-election therefore had to be delayed.[1] He lingered until April 1821, dying at Brighton.[2] He was succeeded by Archibald (1795-1871), and then by the eldest son from his second marriage, William Edmonstone (1810-88); his personalty was finally sworn under £16,000.[3] Archibald Edmonstone's subsequent candidature for Stirlingshire was unsuccessful.

[1] NAS GD51/1/198/26/47; 5/522. [2] *Gent. Mag.* (1821), i. 381; Sir A. Edmonstone, *Fam. of Edmonstone of Duntreath*, 57. [3] PROB 11/1643/268; IR26/861/488.

D.R.F.

EDWARDES, Hon. Edward Henry (1798–1829), of 16 Great Ryder Street, Mdx.

BLETCHINGLEY 1820–1826

b. 5 Nov. 1798, 1st s. of William Edwardes[†], 2nd Bar. Kensington [I], and Dorothy Patricia, da. of Richard Thomas. *educ.* Eton c. 1810-15; Christ Church, Oxf. 1817; St. John's, Camb. 1825. *unm. d.v.p.* 16 Aug. 1829.

Edwardes's father, Lord Kensington, looking forward in 1819 to the commencement of his eldest son's political career, remarked that 'whatever his views are I shall support them, but at present I think he is very much of my opinion'.[1] Kensington had latterly inclined towards the Canningite wing of Lord Liverpool's ministry, and it was this connection which secured Edwardes's unopposed return for Bletchingley in 1820 on the Russell interest. He apparently joined Brooks's Club, 21 May 1820. However, his parliamentary career was a singularly uneventful one: nearly three years elapsed without a trace of any activity, prompting a radical publication to denounce him as 'a truant'.[2] The likely reason for this absenteeism was illustrated by the reaction to his first recorded vote, 22 Apr. 1823, for Burdett's motion for inquiry into the prosecution of the Dublin Orange rioters,

which resulted in a government defeat. His father's profession of political tolerance was tested and found wanting, as Thomas Creevey* recounted:

> [Kensington] has been down to Canning at Gloucester Lodge ... to tender his son's resignation of his seat ... the said son having voted with Burdett on Tuesday, although his seat was given him by Canning. The latter said he had observed Edwardes go out in the division, but behaved very handsomely indeed about it; said he was a young one and might think differently in the future, and, in short, desired that he might have his head and do as he liked for some time longer. But ... [Kensington] observed there was no chance of his mending, for ... his mother was in his confidence and he had entrusted to her his decided opinion against the government.[3]

Thereafter Edwardes confined his activities to the issue of Catholic relief, on which he was in agreement with his father: he voted for it, 1 Mar., 21 Apr., and paired for it, 10 May 1825. He relinquished his seat at the dissolution in 1826.

He had been admitted to St. John's College, Cambridge as a fellow commoner in December 1825, though as at Oxford earlier, he did not take a degree. He died unmarried and *v.p.* at Brighton in August 1829, 'of a rapid decline'. His address was then given as Llandawke, Carmarthenshire, and administration of his effects, valued at £200, was granted to his father.[4]

[1] Bodl. Clarendon dep. C.431, bdle. 5, Kensington to Joseph Foster Barham, 19 Jan. 1819. [2] *Black Bk.* (1823), 153. [3] *Creevey Pprs.* ii. 72. [4] *The Times*, 20 Aug. 1829; PROB 6/205/169.

H.J.S.

EDWARDS VAUGHAN (formerly **EDWARDS**), **John** (1772–1833), of Rheola, Neath, Glam. and 14-16 Regent Street, Mdx.

GLAMORGAN 1818–1820

WELLS 1830–1832

bap. 29 Mar. 1772, s. of John Edwards of Belvedere House, Lambeth, Surr. and w. Catherine. *m.* (1) 17 Dec. 1799, Ann (*d.* 16 Apr. 1807), da. and h. of Thomas Williams of Court Herbert, Glam., 1s.; (2) 26 Nov. 1807, Sarah, da. and h. of Thomas Barwix of the Stock Exchange, London, wid. of John Dalton of Russell Square, Mdx., 1s. 1da. *suc.* fa. 1818; William Vaughan of Glanelai, Glam. and took additional name of Vaughan 29 July 1829. *d.* 16 Aug. 1833.
Sheriff, Glam. 1823-4.

Edwards, whose brief tenure as Member for Glamorgan was ended in 1820 by the concerted opposition of the local gentry, left behind a reputation as an opportunist, an unscrupulous demagogue and 'a low lived blackguard', whose canvassing methods consisted of 'a large distribution of ale and money'.[1] He accumulated substantial wealth through two advantageous marriages and inheritances from his father and his chief political supporter in Glamorgan, William Vaughan, whose name he added to his own in 1829.[2] His work as a parliamentary solicitor had originally drawn him into a business association with the architect John Nash, who may have been a relative, and he subsequently invested money in Nash's projects, including the ill-fated Regent's Canal Company. Nash enlarged and remodelled the house at Rheola which Edwards had inherited from his father, and they shared the premises in Regent Street which Nash completed in 1824. Edwards's connection with Nash confirmed the widespread prejudice against him as a speculator and adventurer. George IV's proposal in 1829 that Nash should be awarded a baronetcy, with remainder to his 'nephew' Edwards, 'a gentleman of excellent character ... and a most *loyal man*, besides being well known to *me personally*', was blocked by the duke of Wellington, the premier, on the ground that Nash's business affairs were under investigation by the Commons. The fact that Edwards had been a solicitor and that his son still worked in the profession was apparently regarded as another obstacle to the conferment of an hereditary title.[3]

Prior to 1825 fears had persisted in Glamorgan landed circles that he planned to make another attempt on the county at the next general election.[4] However, in May that year he was requisitioned to stand for Wells on the 'independent' interest against the sitting Members. He canvassed the city that summer with his friend Richard Williams, a London banker, and professed 'a strict adherence to the constitution ... in church and state', denounced the Catholic religion as 'subversive of liberty' and promised to support 'popular rights'. He and Williams were defeated at the general election of 1826 and their petition against the result was rejected, but the party with which they were associated later captured control of the corporation.[5] Early in 1830 it was reported that Edwards Vaughan (as he was now known) had suffered 'a fit of apoplexy ... accompanied with ... loss of sight'.[6] He was sufficiently recovered by the general election that summer to offer for Wells with John Lee Lee, the son of his key ally in the corporation; they were returned ahead of a candidate backed by the old corporation interest.[7]

The Wellington ministry regarded him as one of their 'friends', but continued ill health prevented him

from taking much part in parliamentary proceedings. He was absent from the crucial civil list division, 15 Nov. 1830. He attended to vote against the second reading of the Grey ministry's reform bill, 22 Mar., and paired for Gascoyne's wrecking amendment, 19 Apr. 1831. Defying expectations, he offered for Wells at the ensuing general election and defended his opposition to a measure that would have deprived the freemen of their privileges and increased the representation of 'Catholic Ireland'. However his later statement, expressing the hope that the next bill would be framed in such a way as he could support, helped to avert a potentially dangerous contest and allowed him and Lee to come in unopposed.[8] In June 1831, after the riots at Merthyr Tydfil, the Tory Herries reported to Peel that Edwards Vaughan, 'who was rather a doubtful supporter of ours, told me ... that he attributed all this mischief to the spirit which ... ministers have elicited and that there is no length to which he is not prepared to go in opposition to them'.[9] Yet no trace of his activity has been found for the first session of the 1831 Parliament. He was granted one month's leave on account of ill health, 17 Sept. He divided against the second reading of the revised reform bill, 17 Dec. 1831, the enfranchisement of Tower Hamlets, 28 Feb., and the third reading, 22 Mar. 1832. He voted against ministers on the Russian-Dutch loan, 26 Jan., and paired against them on this issue, 12 July 1832. He is not known to have spoken in debate, but he presented petitions against the Shaftesbury road bill, 30 Mar., and the Exeter improvement bill, 16 Apr. 1832. That summer, despite having been dangerously ill, he was suspected of planning to offer for Glamorgan as a Conservative at the forthcoming general election, but nothing came of this.[10] He stood again at Wells, where he explained that his main objection to the Reform Act lay in the uniform £10 householder franchise for all boroughs, because 'in some it presented a very respectable constituency, whilst in others it was quite the reverse'. Trailing well behind the other candidates after the first day's polling, and 'suffering from extreme bodily affliction', he retired from the contest.[11]

Edwards Vaughan died in August 1833 and left all his real estate to his son by his second marriage, Nash Vaughan Edwards Vaughan (1811-68), who later inherited Nash's property. His wife and son were named as guardians of 'the property and estate of my son (by my first wife) John Williams Edwards', who was still living. His personalty was sworn under £14,000.[12]

[1] R. Grant, *Parl. Hist. Glam.* 39-40, 144-53; *Glam. Co. Hist.* vi. 10.
[2] R.D. Rees, 'Parl. Rep. S. Wales, 1790-1830' (Reading Univ. Ph.D.

thesis, 1962), ii. 361-5. [3] T. Davis, *John Nash*, 76-78, 97-98; *Geo. IV Letters*, iii. 1563. [4] Mid-Glam. RO, Bute mss D/DA11/47, Bute to Knight, 9 July; Merthyr Mawr mss, Nicholl to son, 14 Sept. 1824. [5] *Bristol Mirror*, 28 May, 23, 30 July 1825, 1 July 1826. [6] NLW, Bute mss L73/21. [7] *Keene's Bath Jnl.* 9 Aug. 1830. [8] *Bristol Mirror*, 30 Apr., 7 May 1831. [9] Add. 40402, f. 89. [10] Bute mss L75/90, 93; NLW, Penrice and Margam mss 9239. [11] *Bristol Mirror*, 15 Dec. 1832. [12] PROB 11/1828/793; IR26/1342/659.

T.A.J.

EGERTON, Sir Philip de Malpas Grey, 10th bt. (1806–1881), of Oulton Park, Cheshire and 18 Jermyn Street, Mdx.

CHESTER	1830–1831
CHESHIRE SOUTH	1835–1868
CHESHIRE WEST	1868–5 Apr. 1881

b. 13 Nov. 1806, 1st s. of Rev. Philip Grey Egerton, rect. of Malpas and Tarporley, Cheshire, and Rebecca, da. of Josias Du Pré of Wilton Park, Bucks. *educ.* Eton 1820-4; Christ Church, Oxf. 1825. *m.* 8 Mar. 1832, Anna Elizabeth, da. of George John Legh of High Legh, Cheshire, 2s. 2da. *suc.* fa. as 10th bt. 13 Dec. 1829. *d.* 5 Apr. 1881.
Capt. Cheshire yeoman cav. 1825, lt.-col. 1847.

Egerton, one of the most eminent antiquaries and palaeontologists of his time, was the eldest of the seven sons and a daughter born to the Rev. Philip Egerton, a leading freemason, who in 1825 succeeded his brother Sir John Grey Egerton[†] to the Egerton baronetcy and 9,000-acre Oulton Park estate, which had been denuded of timber to meet electioneering costs in Chester.[1] His mother was the daughter of a nabob and sister of James du Pré[†]. He was educated at Eton and Oxford, where he studied geology under William Buckland and William Conybeare and became a close friend of William Willoughby, Viscount Cole (afterwards 3rd earl of Enniskillen), with whom he travelled in Germany, Switzerland and Italy in search of fossil fishes, the subject of his work and reputation as a palaeontologist.[2] His coming of age was celebrated at Oulton and at Chester's *Albion* hotel, the venue of his late uncle's Egerton or 'Independent' party, for whom his kinsman General Charles Egerton had almost recaptured one of the borough seats from the Grosvenors in 1826 and seemed set to do so at the next opportunity.[3] Egerton graduated in 1828, was elected a fellow of the Royal Geological Society the following year and in December 1829 succeeded his father, who died worth less than £8,000 and having willed everything to his widow, to the baronetcy and entailed estates.[4] At the 1830 general election Egerton canvassed early and came in unopposed for Chester with

the 2nd earl Grosvenor's son Robert. His notices and speeches made frequent references to the Egertons' achievements, and he promised to support 'every measure for economizing the resources of the country, reducing the burdens of the people', and abolishing sinecures and useless places. He declined to attend the nomination for Cheshire, where Lord Grosvenor's heir Lord Belgrave, who had stood down at Chester, was a successful candidate.[5] As his late uncle Sir John had wished, Egerton was a major beneficiary of the will (proved under £25,000) of the dowager Lady Egerton (*d.* 11 Aug. 1830).[6]

The Wellington ministry interpreted Egerton's election as a gain and classified him as one of their 'friends', and he divided with them when they were brought down on the civil list, 15 Nov. 1830. Afterwards, he joined Grosvenor in issuing an equivocal declaration of support for moderate reform; but, unlike him, he refused to endorse the Chester reform meeting's petition in favour of the Grey ministry's bill, and caused a great stir by stating in an explanatory letter to the mayor, 14 Mar. 1831:

> Upon subjects of local interest I should at all times pay the utmost deference to your opinions; but on one of great national importance, like the present ... I shall consider it my bounden duty to throw every obstacle in the way of so crude and dangerous a measure.

He added that in the likely event of a dissolution the freemen could judge his conduct.[7] He divided against the bill at its second reading, 22 Mar., and for Gascoyne's wrecking amendment, 19 Apr. 1831. He is not known to have spoken in debate in this period, but he presented petitions from Chester against slavery, 23 Nov. 1830, the first and second Chester-Liverpool railway bills, 23 Mar., and the reform bill, 19 Apr. 1831. Certain of defeat, he stood down at the dissolution that month.[8] There was talk of proposing him for the county, where at the ensuing general election he signed the anti-reformers' declaration of support for the abortive candidature of Lord Henry Cholmondeley*. According to the reformers, he had hoped to be returned for Castle Rising in his place.[9]

Egerton married a daughter of the leading Cheshire Tory George John Legh in March 1832 and, backed by the Cheshire Conservatives and his Carlton Club colleagues, he stood for the new Cheshire South constituency in December 1832, but was narrowly defeated by two Liberals.[10] He was returned without a contest in 1835 and remained a Member for life, coming in for West Cheshire in 1868 after boundary changes.[11] When he died of a heart attack brought on by bronchitis at his London home in Albemarle Street in April

1881, he was the antiquary to the Royal Academy, a trustee of the British Museum and of the Royal College of Surgeons, a member of the senate of the University of London, and had seats on the councils of the Royal Society and the Geological Society, which awarded him the Woollaston medal in 1873 for his services to palaeontology. He was the first recipient in 1879 of the Kingsley Medal, awarded by the Chester Society of Natural Sciences, of which he was vice-president.[12] His scientific works included catalogues of his collections and over 80 articles in the Royal Geological Society's transactions. He also published an edited commentary on *William, Lord Grey de Wilton* (1847); *Papers relating to the Elections of the Knights of the Shire for the County Palatine of Chester* (1852); *A Short Account of the Possessors of Oulton* (1869), and *Annals of Grillion's Club, 1812-62* (1880), of which he was president in 1837.[13] He was succeeded in the baronetcy and entailed estates by his eldest son Philip le Belward Grey Egerton (1833-91), and provided for his widow (*d.* 1882), two daughters and younger son Rowland, to whom he left his unentailed estates and fossils at his museum in Oulton.[14] As he had wished, the British Museum purchased his fossil fish collection for the Natural History Museum, and his original drawings of them were donated to the Geological Society 'to be added to the Agassiz collection'.

[1] P.M.G. Egerton, *Short Account of Possessors of Oulton*, 35-36; Cheshire and Chester Archives, Egerton of Oulton mss DEO/14-15; *HP Commons, 1790-1820*, iii. 676. [2] *Oxford DNB*. [3] *Chester Chron.* 16, 23 Nov. 1827. [4] PROB 8/223; 11/1768/163. [5] *Chester Courant*, 6 July; *Chester Chron.* 9, 16, 23 July, 6 Aug.; *Macclesfield Courier and Herald*, 10 July 1830; Grosvenor mss 12/5. [6] PROB 11/1775/546; IR26/1043/915; 1226/555. [7] *Chester Courant*, 15, 22 Mar.; *Chester Chron.* 18 Mar. 1831. [8] *The Times*, 5 Apr.; *Chester Chron.* 29 Apr.; *Chester Courant*, 3 May 1831. [9] *The Times*, 29 Apr., 5, 14 May; *Chester Courant*, 10, 17 May 1831. [10] *The Times*, 26 Sept., 9, 18 Oct., 4, 18, 21, 23, 26 Dec. 1832; *VCH Cheshire*, ii. 145, 158. [11] *The Times*, 3, 6, 14, 21 Jan. 1835. [12] *Chester Chron.* 9 Apr. 1881. [13] *Oxford DNB*; *Ann. Reg.* (1881), Chron. p. 115. [14] Egerton of Oulton mss DEO/220/2.

M.M.E.

EGERTON, Wilbraham (1781-1856), of Tatton Park, Cheshire.

CHESHIRE   1812-1831

b. 1 Sept. 1781, 2nd but 1st surv. s. of William Egerton[†] of Wythenshawe, Lancs. and 2nd w. Mary, da. of Richard Wilbraham Bootle[†] of Rode Hall, Cheshire. *educ.* Eton 1796; ?Brasenose, Oxf. 1800. *m.* 11 Jan. 1806, his cos. Elizabeth, da. of Sir Christopher Sykes[†], 2nd. bt., of Sledmere, Yorks., 7s. (4 *d.v.p.*) 3da. *d.v.p. suc.* fa. in Egerton estates 1806. *d.* 25 Apr. 1856.

Sheriff, Cheshire 1808-9
Capt. R. Cheshire militia 1803; lt.-col. Macclesfield regt. 1809, lt.-col. commdt. 1812; capt. king's Cheshire yeomanry 1819, lt.-col. 1831, lt.-col. commdt. 1835.

In 1812, Egerton, an anti-Catholic Tory whose estates made him one of the richest commoners in England, had come in unopposed for his native Cheshire, which his father had represented, 1802-6. He had proved to be a staunch advocate of protection for corn, salt and silk and a ready presenter of petitions, whose support for the Liverpool government was tempered by his readiness to represent local interests.[1] In 1820 he sought to distance himself from the controversy surrounding the retirement and subsequent nomination of his colleague Davenport, which thwarted the ambitions of the Tories George John Legh of High Legh and Thomas Legh*.[2]

Despite occasional complaints about his indolence and reluctance to speak in debate, Egerton retained his seat unchallenged until the reform era. He presented a petition for relief from distress from the manufacturers of Stockport, 24 June, and divided with government on the revenue, 4 July 1820.[3] He voted against censuring their handling of Queen Caroline's case, 6 Feb. 1821. Having been present, 11 Jan., he intervened on behalf of the sheriff of Cheshire, James France France, when a petition criticizing his conduct at the contrived county meeting on the subject was presented, 9 Feb., and was a majority teller against the ensuing motion of complaint, 20 Feb.[4] He divided as hitherto against Catholic relief, 28 Feb. 1821, 30 Apr. 1822, 1 Mar., 21 Apr., 10 May, and the attendant Irish franchise bill, 26 Apr. 1825, and presented anti-Catholic petitions from the dean and chapter of Chester, 16 Apr. 1823, 25 Mar., 18, 28 Apr. 1825.[5] He voted against parliamentary reform, 9 May 1821, 2 June 1823. He had spoken in defence of the Peterloo magistrates in 1819 and did so again when Burdett revived the issue, 16 May 1821, justifying their decision to issue a warrant for Henry Hunt's* arrest and explaining the impossibility of executing it without the aid of the military. He voted against abolishing capital punishment for forgery, 23 May 1821. He divided with government against more extensive tax cuts, 11, 21 Feb., admiralty reductions, 1 Mar., and abolition of one of the joint-postmasterships, 13 Mar., but against them on the salt tax, which he said was 'so unequal in its operations and so oppressive to the lower orders', 28 Feb., 28 June 1822. He presented and endorsed his constituents' petitions against the navigation bill, 30 May, 4 June, the poor removal bill, 30 May, and the licensing bill, 3, 5, 7 June.[6] He voted against inquiry into the lord advocate's handling of the Scottish press, 25 June 1822. In July he ensured that the home secretary Peel consulted opinion in Cheshire before appointing a new prothonotary to the palatine court.[7] George Canning*, an unexpected guest at Tatton in September 1822, when his coach broke down, described it as

a magnificent house in the midst of a most beautiful park and gardens, in short, one of the finest country seats that I ever saw – and the interior of the house, the whole style, and particularly ... the goodness of the dinner all corresponding with the external appearance. There was nobody but the family, consisting of Mr. and Mrs. E. and a female relation and three Eton boys and two lesser ones.[8]

Egerton divided against tax concessions, 10 Mar., and inquiries into chancery delays, 5 June, and the currency, 12 June 1823. He presented Cheshire petitions against the proposed alterations in the duties on silk, 8, 17 Mar., beer and excise licenses, 31 Mar., 6, 7, 11, 17 May, and hides, 17 May, and voted in the minority against ending the prohibition on long wool exports, 21 May 1824. He strongly endorsed a petition entrusted to him against repealing the duty on imported salt, 9 June 1824.[9] He voted against condemning the indictment in Demerara of the Methodist missionary John Smith, 11 June, having presented a Macclesfield petition advocating it, 26 May 1824.[10] He brought up Stockport's petition for repeal of the Beer Act, 25 Feb. 1825,[11] and voted for the bill outlawing the Catholic Association that day. He presented distress petitions from the silk towns of Macclesfield, 6 Feb., and Congleton, 15 Feb. 1826.[12] Supporting inquiry into the silk trade on their behalf, 24 Feb., he said that if a select committee 'did not make out such a case as would justify government in abandoning their measures', he would cease to support the petitioners' claims. He voted against Russell's electoral bribery resolutions, 26 May 1826. Nothing came of a reported challenge by an un-named third man at the general election in June, when attention focused on the close contest for Chester, in which he took no part.[13]

Egerton voted against Catholic relief, 6 Mar. 1827, 12 May 1828, having presented a petition in its favour, 28 Apr. 1828. He voted against the Liverpool ministry's corn importation bill, 2 Apr. and presented petitions against the alehouse licensing bill, 4 May, and for repeal of the Test Acts, 11 May 1827.[14] The pro-Catholic Canning's appointment as premier dismayed him, and he was quick to congratulate Peel on his appointment as home secretary by the duke of Wellington in January 1828 and to declare his confidence in their administration.[15] He divided against repealing the Test Acts, 26 Feb., voted in the minority against providing a pension for Canning's family, 13 May, and with government against ordnance reductions, 4 July. He presented his constituents' petitions against the General Turnpike Act, 6 Mar., the 1827 Malt Act, 6 Mar., the friendly societies bill, 21, 24 Apr., and further reduction of the silk duties, 30 May 1828. As the patronage secretary Planta noted in February 1829, Egerton remained 'opposed to the principle' of Catholic emancipation. He presented and endorsed hostile petitions from the 'loyal inhabitants of Lymm', 16 Feb., and the controversial Knutsford meeting, 24 Feb., but he would 'not say' whether the latter expressed 'the feelings of the county of Chester'.[16] He presented others, 26 Feb., 9, 11, 16, 30 Mar., and voted against the relief bill, 6, 18, 27, 30 Mar. Testifying to the unparalleled distress and the 'ruinous state' of the trade, he supported the silk workers' petitions for protection, 26 Feb., 31 Mar., 14, 28 Apr., and advocated inquiry, 1 May. He carried the second reading of controversial Cheshire constabulary bill, 13 Apr. 1829.

At the county meeting, 25 Jan. 1830, Egerton spoke briefly in favour of petitioning 'for relief from the present dreadful distress', but his views on the petition promoted by Davenport's son Edward Davies Davenport* were not reported. Presenting it, 15 Feb., he strongly endorsed its requests for the appointment of an investigative committee and the 'most rigid economy', but distanced himself from its claim that distress emanated from currency change.[17] He voted against Lord Blandford's reform proposals, 18 Feb., and the proposed enfranchisement of Birmingham, Leeds and Manchester, 23 Feb. He presented petitions against renewing the East India Company's charter from Congleton, 19 Feb., and the white salt manufacturers of Cheshire and Lancashire 15 Mar., and against the truck system from Congleton, 26 Feb., and Stockport, 28 Apr. He presented a favourable petition, 17 Mar., but divided against abolishing the death penalty for forgery, 7 June. He cast a wayward vote against the Bathurst and Dundas pensions, 26 Mar., and divided against Jewish emancipation, 17 May. He presented petitions, 30 Apr., 3 May, and voted to restrict on-consumption under the sale of beer bill, 21 June, 1 July. He was a member of the lobbying committee appointed by the magistrates to oppose the abolition of Cheshire's palatine jurisdiction under the administration of justice bill, and he presented petitions hostile to it, 6, 18, 19 May, and vainly moved to have the clause abolishing Chester's equity court 'struck off', 5 July.[18] Conscious that his support had waned and of manoeuvring by potential challengers, he canvassed Cheshire thoroughly before the general election in August 1830, when the 2nd Earl Grosvenor's heir Lord Belgrave replaced Davenport as his colleague.[19] He faced strong criticism on the hustings for his self-serving stance on local bills, his ministerialist votes and his opposition to the abolition of slavery and parliamentary reform. Responding, he tried to explain that he would vote only for those reductions in public expenditure that he considered prudent and in the best interests of the state, and advocated a 'gradual abolition of slavery, without injury to private interests'. He refused to commit himself to supporting 'any particular' measure of reform and said he had 'not made up his mind' on the 'propriety of transferring the franchise to the great towns', but asserted that he had 'supported the transfer of the franchise from Penryn to the extensive and populous county of York'. He added that he was prepared to back any measure calculated to limit the cost of county elections.[20]

The Wellington ministry naturally counted Egerton among their 'friends' and he divided with them when they were brought down on the civil list, 15 Nov. 1830. He presented an anti-slavery petition from Stockport, 12 Nov. On the 23rd he silenced opposition to an application for leave for his son Tatton Egerton, who was shortly to be married. He presented petitions against the East India Company's monopoly, 8 Dec., the truck system, 8 Dec., the calico duties, 18 Dec. 1830, 10 Feb. 1831, and the register of deeds bill, 7 Feb.; and in favour of the liability of landlords bill, 25 Feb., and reform, 28 Feb., 15 Mar., on which he was said to be 'wavering till he hears the result of the Cheshire meeting'.[21] He divided against the Grey ministry's reform bill at its second reading, 22 Mar. Presenting favourable petitions next day from the county, Macclesfield, Nantwich and Stockport, he expressed support for 'a moderate reform' and declared that the bill went too far:

Taking it as a whole, I conceive it to be a dangerous measure, and cannot give it my support. I heartily regret that I am thus compelled to differ with those who have so long sent me to represent their wishes in this House. Nevertheless, I am, in some degree, consoled by the reflection that I am discharging my duty, which I owe to the House, the country and my own conscience.

With opposition certain in the event of a dissolution, by 26 Mar. he had resolved not to stand for Cheshire again. His political ally Lord Kenyon wrote: 'I am sorry Wilbraham Egerton has been frightened out of the representation of Cheshire. He has always been an honest and upright Member ... and we are but too sure to have a worse in his room'.[22] He presented petitions against the Thornset-Stockport road bill, 18, 25 Mar.,

and the first and second Liverpool-Chester railway bills, 16, 18 Mar., 12, 15 Apr. He also presented petitions on 15 Apr. from cotton manufacturers opposed to the factory apprentices bill and from the grand jury and magistrates of Cheshire for repeal of the 1830 Beer Act. He voted for Gascoyne's wrecking amendment to the reform bill, 19 Apr. 1831, and retired at the dissolution that month. He signed the Cheshire anti-reformers' declaration of support for Lord Henry Cholomondeley* at the ensuing general election.[23]

Egerton backed Tatton when he contested the new Cheshire North constituency successfully in 1832 and remained steady in his support for the Cheshire Conservatives.[24] He commanded the yeomanry during the 1839-40 Chartist riots and applied in vain to Peel as premier for a peerage in 1841.[25] In 1848 the dowager countess of Bridgwater appointed him a trustee under the will of his late kinsman the 7th duke (d. 1823), but his claim to the Bridgwater fortune was ignored when the Lords ruled on the case, 19 Aug. 1853.[26] He died at Tatton, to which his eldest son succeeded him, in April 1856, having been predeceased in 1853 by his wife. He made generous bequests to his younger sons Edward Christopher Egerton (1816-69), Conservative Member for Macclesfield, 1852-68, and Charles Randle Egerton, and provided £15,000 and a £22,500 trust fund for the widow of his son Thomas Egerton (d. 1847), rector of Myddle.[27]

[1] HP Commons, 1790-1820, iii. 677-8. [2] Chester Courant, 29 Feb., 7 Mar.; Chester Chron. 10, 17, 24 Mar.; Macclesfield Courier, 18, 25 Mar. 1820. [3] The Times, 15 June 1820. [4] Chester Chron. 30 Jan.; The Times, 10, 21 Feb. 1821. [5] The Times, 17 Apr. 1823, 26 Feb., 26 Mar., 19 Apr. 1825. [6] Ibid. 31 May, 4-6, 8 June 1822. [7] Add. 40348, ff. 95, 117, 138, 140; 40349, ff. 15, 36. [8] Harewood mss WYL 250/8/26, Canning to wife, 6 Sept. 1822. [9] The Times, 9, 18 Mar., 1 Apr., 7, 8, 12, 18 May, 10 June 1824. [10] Ibid. 27 May 1824. [11] Ibid. 26 Feb. 1825. [12] Ibid. 7, 16 Feb. 1826. [13] Chester Chron. 26 May, 9, 30 June; Macclesfield Courier, 17, 24 June 1826. [14] The Times, 5, 12 May 1827. [15] Add. 40395, f. 82. [16] The Times, 18 Dec. 1828; Chester Courant, 6 Jan. 1829. [17] Chester Courant, 26 Jan.; The Times, 28 Jan.; Chester Chron. 29 Jan. 1830. [18] Cheshire and Chester Archives QCX/1/2. [19] Macclesfield Courier, 3, 10, 31 July; Chester Courant, 6 July; Stockport Advertiser, 9 July 1830; Grosvenor mss 12/1,4. [20] Macclesfield Courier, 7 Aug.; Chester Chron. 13 Aug. 1830. [21] Kenyon mss, Lloyd Kenyon to Lord Kenyon, 19 Mar. 1831. [22] Ibid., Egerton to Kenyon, 27 Mar., Kenyon to wife, 31 Mar.; Chester Courant, 2, 29 Mar.; The Times, 5 Apr. 1831. [23] Macclesfield Courier, 30 Apr., 7, 14, 21 May; Chester Courant, 3, 10, 17 May 1831. [24] The Times, 23 July, 26 Sept. 1832; VCH Cheshire, ii. 158. [25] JRL, Egerton of Tatton mss EG/T3; Add. 40489, ff. 53-55. [26] B. Falk, Bridgewater Millions, 181, 222. [27] Gent. Mag. (1856), i. 455-6; PROB 11/2232/380; IR26/2063/381.

M.M.E.

EGERTON, William Tatton (1806–1883), of Tatton Park, Cheshire.

LYMINGTON   1830–1831

CHESHIRE NORTH   1832–Aug. 1858

b. 30 Dec. 1806, 1st. s. of Wilbraham Egerton* of Tatton Park and Elizabeth, da. of Sir Christopher Sykes[†], 2nd bt., of Sledmere, Yorks. *educ.* Eton 1820; Christ Church, Oxf. 1825. *m.* 18 Dec. 1830, Lady Charlotte Elizabeth Loftus, da. of John Loftus[†], 2nd mq. of Ely, 4s. (2 *d.v.p.*) 4da. (1 *d.v.p.*). *suc.* fa. 1856; *cr.* Bar. Egerton 15 Apr. 1859. *d.* 21 Feb. 1883.

Ld. lt. Cheshire 1868-*d.*

Capt. King's Cheshire yeomanry 1827, maj. 1863, ret. 1866.

Egerton's family were extremely wealthy Cheshire landowners, whose association with the Tatton estate went back to 1598. His grandfather and namesake William Tatton Egerton (1749-1806) had sat for the county, 1802-6, and his father Wilbraham Egerton, 1806-31; but before Egerton assumed the same role he was returned for Lymington at the 1830 general election, as the nominee of its Tory patron Sir Harry Neale*. He was listed by the Wellington ministry as one of their 'friends' and voted in their minority in the crucial division on the civil list, 15 Nov. 1830. His application for a month's leave, made through his father, 23 Nov., was challenged by Hume, who withdrew his opposition on being informed that Egerton was to be married. His wife, recalled her kinswoman Lady St. Helier, was an 'extraordinary woman', who 'said out loud everything she thought', but 'was not a person who had many friends, because people were afraid of her and what she might say'.[1] Egerton, who is not known to have spoken in debate in this period, voted against the second reading of the Grey ministry's reform bill, 22 Mar., and for Gascoyne's wrecking amendment, 19 Apr. 1831. He was left without a seat at the ensuing general election, when Neale apparently thought it necessary to return a nominee of greater political weight.[2]

At the 1832 general election he successfully stood as 'a thorough going Tory' for Cheshire North, where he sat for the next 26 years. Raised to the peerage by the second Derby ministry, he continued to act with the Conservatives in the Lords.[3] 'An enormously rich man', whose fortune might have been even larger as a reversionary heir to the Bridgwater millions of his distant cousin the 7th earl of Bridgwater, he and his wife apparently 'lived carefully and without any ostentation' at their London home and at Tatton Hall, where he died from a 'severe attack of bronchitis' in

February 1883. He was evidently a model landlord and a local meeting paid tribute to his 'interest in everything connected with agriculture'.[4] By his will, dated 28 Sept. 1878, the bulk of his landed estate and his house in St. James's Square, Westminster passed to his eldest son and heir in the barony Wilbraham Egerton (1832-1909), Conservative Member for Cheshire North, 1858-68, and Mid-Cheshire, 1868-1883. His four other surviving children received legacies of between £30,000 and £40,000 each. His youngest son Alan de Tatton Egerton (1845-1920), to whom he also devised estates in Durham, sat as a Conservative for Mid Cheshire, 1883-85, and Knutsford, 1885-1906, when he succeeded his brother in the barony.

[1] N. Pevsner and E. Hubbard, *Buildings of England: Cheshire*, 354; S.E.M. Jeune, *Mems. of Fifty Years*, 79. [2] Hants RO 27M74/F102, Neale to Peel [Apr. 1831]. [3] *The Times*, 18 Oct. 1832, 23 Feb. 1883. [4] Jeune, 79-80; B. Falk, *Bridgewater Millions*, 181, 222-4; *Chester Chron.* 24 Feb. 1883.

H.J.S./P.J.S.

ELFORD, Jonathan (1776–1823), of Uplands, Tamerton Folliott, Devon.

WESTBURY   1820–23 Nov. 1820

b. 5 Nov. 1776, o.s. of Sir William Elford[†], 1st bt. (*d.* 1837), banker, of Bickham and 1st w. Mary, da. and h. of Rev. John Davies of Plympton. *educ.* ?Plympton g.s.;[1] Oriel, Oxf. 1795. *m.* 10 May 1810, Charlotte, da. of John Wynne of Abercynlleth, Denb., *s.p.*[2] *d.v.p.* 11 Mar. 1823.

Capt. E. Devon militia 1803.

Elford's father, a partner in the Plymouth Bank and a controversial Member for Plymouth, 1796-1806, was solicitous for his only son. His attachment to the prime minister, William Pitt, earned him a baronetcy in 1800, but his attempts to secure the receivership of Devon for Jonathan were in vain. In 1805 he sought a commissionership of public accounts, but nothing had been done by the time Pitt died, though Elford later claimed to have been given a firm promise of early provision for his son. The Grenville ministry, trying to deflect Sir William from standing for Plymouth in 1806, offered a post in the revenue department at the Cape of Good Hope, worth £1,000 a year, for himself or Jonathan, but Elford refused to be bought off, stood and was beaten. In 1807 he asked the Portland ministry for a promise of the collectorship of customs at Plymouth for his son in the event of his own success there at the approaching general election: it was 'a valuable situation, and one which would be extremely agreeable to Jonathan and also to us, as it would keep him near us'. Elford had to withdraw from the field at Plymouth, and although he was returned for a treasury borough, he held the seat for only a year and left the House with Jonathan still unprovided for.[3] He became a freeman of Plymouth in 1810.[4]

Elford was returned at the general election of 1820 for Westbury, presumably as a paying guest of the proprietor, Sir Manasseh Masseh Lopes*, who had recently been imprisoned for electoral corruption. He was named to the select committee on turnpikes, 16 May, but is not known to have voted or spoken in the House before he and his colleague vacated their seats in November 1820 to allow Masseh Lopes, whose sentence had been remitted, to return himself with a wealthy Bristol merchant. Elford died in March 1823, leaving his estate, including personalty sworn under £7,000, to his widow.[5] He was spared the ignominy of the family's ruin by the collapse of his father's bank in 1825, to which his own debts had contributed.[6]

[1] L. Elford, *The Elford's* [*sic*] (BL typescript), pt. ii. p. 2b. [2] *Gent. Mag.* (1810), i. 484. [3] *HP Commons, 1790-1820*, iii. 679-81; TNA, Dacres Adams mss 10/6. [4] Elford, pt. ii. p. 2b. [5] PROB 11/1670/277; IR26/954/348. [6] *Oxford DNB sub* Sir William Elford.

D.R.F./S.M.F.

ELIOT, Edward Granville, Lord Eliot (1798–1877), of 47 Dover Street, Mdx.

LISKEARD	16 Jan. 1824–1832
CORNWALL EAST	1837–19 Jan. 1845

b. 29 Aug. 1798, o.s. of William Eliot*, 2nd earl of St. Germans, and 1st w. Lady Georgiana Augusta Leveson Gower, da. of Granville Leveson Gower[†], 1st mq. of Stafford. *educ.* Westminster 1809-11, Christ Church, Oxf. 1815. *m.* 2 Sept. 1824, Lady Jemima Cornwallis, da. and coh. of Charles, 2nd Mq. Cornwallis, 6s. (3 *d.v.p.*) 2da. (1 *d.v.p.*). *suc.* fa. as 3rd earl of St. Germans 19 Jan. 1845; GCB 24 Jan. 1857. *d.* 7 Oct. 1877.
   Ld. of treasury Apr. 1827-Nov. 1830; envoy extraordinary to Spain 1834-7; chief sec. to ld. lt. [I] Sept. 1841-Jan. 1845; PC [GB] 3 Sept. 1841; PC [I] 12 Oct. 1841; postmaster-gen. Jan.-June 1846; ld. lt. [I] Jan. 1853-Mar. 1855; ld. steward of household Nov. 1857-Feb. 1858, June 1859-Jan. 1866.

Eliot, like his father, initially pursued a diplomatic career, serving as an attaché at The Hague and accompanying Sir William A'Court[†] on his mission to Spain in 1822.[1] In January 1824 he was returned unopposed for Liskeard on his father's interest, following the latter's succession as 2nd earl of St. Germans, and he sat undisturbed until 1832. He attended fairly regularly

and gave silent support to Lord Liverpool's ministry. He voted against the motion condemning the trial of the Methodist missionary John Smith in Demerara, 11 June 1824. He divided for the Irish unlawful societies bill, 25 Feb., against Catholic relief, 1 Mar., 21 Apr., 10 May, and against the Irish franchise bill, 26 Apr., 9 May 1825. He voted for the financial provision for the duke of Cumberland, 30 May, 10 June 1825. He presented a Liskeard anti-slavery petition, 24 Feb.,[2] but divided against the motion condemning the Jamaican slave trials, 2 Mar. 1826. He voted against reducing the salary of the president of the board of trade, 10 Apr. 1826. He divided for Catholic claims, 6 Mar. 1827, when he explained that he had changed his mind on the subject after giving it his 'fullest consideration'. He was 'convinced that the tranquility of Ireland depended on the passing the measure', which would help in 'appeasing the animosity and rancour which almost desolated the country', and argued that the government would then be better placed to protect the 'just and lawful rights' of the Irish church. He voted for the duke of Clarence's annuity bill, 16 Mar. Next month he was appointed a lord of the treasury in Canning's coalition ministry, and on securing re-election at Liskeard he pledged to 'exert himself in his new office to promote ... those measures which he conceived calculated to secure the peace and prosperity of the empire'.[3] He remained in place when Lord Goderich became prime minister in August 1827, but was apparently advised by his father to resign 'if another Whig appointment was made'; by the end of the year he had 'signified [his] intention of taking flight' if Lord Holland joined the cabinet.[4] In January 1828, with his father abroad, he sought advice from Lord Harrowby, the former lord president of the council, as to whether he should retain his position under the duke of Wellington. He observed that had the new government been 'wholly composed of Ultra Tories', he would have 'felt no hesitation in at once resigning', but as Huskisson and 'some others of Mr. Canning's friends' were to be included, he was inclined to remain. However, he knew that many other Canningites considered Huskisson's adhesion 'dishonourable', and feared that 'even in the subaltern position which I occupy my conduct and motives might be misrepresented', which mattered because 'one's character ought to be above the possibility of suspicion'. If he resigned, he foresaw difficulty in finding 'a body of men in the ... Commons whose moderation would keep them as clear of the Whigs ... as of the Ultras', although 'if such men there be I should be much disposed to enroll myself in their number'. He finally accepted Harrowby's advice to participate in a 'reunion of the scattered parts of Lord Liverpool's administration', which afforded the only defence against an Ultra government. At this time, Edward Littelton* identified Eliot as one of an 'important party' of 'young men' in the Commons, including Lord Francis Leveson Gower, Lord Sandon and John Stuart Wortley, who 'hang much together ... united ... against High Tory principles'.[5] He divided for Catholic claims, 12 May 1828. In January 1829 he informed Wellington that his father, who was still abroad, had resolved to withdraw his support from the government unless it acted immediately to settle the Catholic question. Eliot thought it 'more fair' to the premier to notify him at once of 'the position in which I stand rather than leave you to learn my defection at a moment when my adherence would be counted on'; the irritated duke reportedly 'had a great mind to turn him out now'.[6] He voted for emancipation, 6, 30 Mar., and presented a favourable petition, 12 Mar. 1829. Early in February 1830 he reportedly left London briefly, owing to the death of his mother-in-law.[7]

In the autumn of 1830 Eliot was of course listed among the 'friends' of Wellington's ministry, and he voted with them in the crucial civil list division, 15 Nov. 1830. He presented a Liskeard anti-slavery petition, 13 Dec. 1830. The Grey ministry's reform bill proposed to open Liskeard to the £10 householders but to reduce its representation to one seat. Eliot divided against the second reading, 22 Mar., and for Gascoyne's wrecking amendment, 19 Apr. 1831. He voted against the second reading of the reintroduced bill, 6 July, for use of the 1831 census in scheduling boroughs, 19 July, and to postpone consideration of Chippenham's inclusion in schedule B, 27 July. However, he divided against the adjournment motion, 12 July, and for the proposed division of counties, 12 Aug. He accepted that no case could be made for removing Liskeard from schedule B, 29 July, but expressed concern at the bill's effect on boroughs in remote parts of England where property values were low. He was 'conscious of having done nothing to forfeit the confidence of the inhabitants' and trusted that he would again be returned for the borough. He argued that Rochester and Chatham should be separated and given one Member each, 9 Aug. He voted against the bill's passage, 21 Sept. He emerged at this time as a prominent opposition spokesman on foreign policy, drawing on his previous diplomatic experience. He thought there was insufficient justification for dismantling the Belgian frontier fortresses, which could only benefit France, 27 July, and urged the government to show the 'utmost possible caution'. On 3 Aug. he warned that there was a strong feeling in the

Netherlands against 'not merely the hostile spirit, but what they consider the duplicity of this country', in failing to compel Belgium to adhere to the original agreement for the separation of the countries. He asked the foreign secretary, Lord Palmerston, questions about the nature of the great powers' guarantee of Belgian integrity, 6 Aug., and maintained six days later that the Dutch king had a 'clear right' to resume hostilities, given the Belgian monarch's determination to retain Luxemburg and Limburg in defiance of the original protocols. He seconded Vyvyan's motion for papers regarding the international conferences on Belgium, 18 Aug. 1831, observing that the Dutch king had behaved 'as a just and benevolent monarch' to the Belgian people; Charles Arbuthnot* considered that Eliot's speech was 'much the best of the two'.[8]

In November 1831 he privately advised against the proposed Cornish declaration for moderate reform, as he was unwilling to pledge support for 'any specific measure ... in all its details' and believed it would 'divide and weaken the Conservative party' in the county. He was not prepared to admit the necessity for 'devising a new constitution', which, however moderately framed, must 'form an irresistible precedent for future innovations'.[9] He divided against the second reading of the revised bill, 17 Dec. 1831, the enfranchisement of Tower Hamlets, 28 Feb., and the third reading, 22 Mar. 1832. He supported the motion for papers regarding the enlistment of men for an expedition against Portugal, 9 Feb., arguing that France had no cause for complaint about the treatment of its citizens and that it was a matter of 'gross impolicy' for Britain to refuse to recognize Dom Miguel's regime, which meant 'closing the door of such a market' at a time of distress in the manufacturing sector; he was a minority teller. In a survey of Palmerston's foreign policy, 26 Mar., he predicted that war in Europe was inevitable, whether it broke out first in Italy, Portugal or the Netherlands, and he feared that 'instead of being looked upon ... as the protectors of the weak' Britain was 'beginning to be regarded in the light of oppressors'. He warned of France's aggressive intentions and pointed to evidence of a 'deep hatred for the English'. He made no motion, having intended only to stimulate a general debate. He questioned Palmerston about the naval blockade of Madeira, 7 May. He divided against ministers on the Russian-Dutch loan, 12 July, and four days later supported the motion for papers regarding the convention of 1815, as the Commons could not 'sanction such a profligate expenditure of ... public money without sufficient reason'. He voted against the malt drawback bill, 2 Apr., and favoured bringing colonial expenditure 'under one head' so that the

Commons could be kept fully informed of what was required, 13 Apr. 1832.

At the dissolution of 1832 Eliot retired from Liskeard after an unsuccessful canvass. In his address he defended his family's 'honourable connection' with the borough and expressed disappointment that the services of one who was 'independent in circumstances and unfettered by any professional avocations' were not required at 'what I cannot but consider an awful crisis'.[10] Following his diplomatic mission to Spain, which resulted in the 'Eliot Convention' of 1835 on the treatment of prisoners of war, he was returned for East Cornwall in 1837 as a 'moderate Conservative'.[11] He held office in Peel's second ministry and later served in various Liberal governments. He succeeded to his father's earldom and Cornish estates in 1845. Richard Monckton Milnes[†] knew no man 'of more noble and moderate spirit ... more free from selfishness and almost from party ambition'.[12] He died in October 1877 and was succeeded in turn by his eldest surviving son, William Eliot (1829-81), Liberal Member for Devonport, 1866-8, and his second surviving son, Henry Eliot (1835-1911).

[1] Cornw. RO, St. Germans mss, 3 June 1822; Add. 41544, ff. 90-93, 115-17. [2] *The Times*, 25 Feb. 1826. [3] *West Briton*, 11 May 1827. [4] Wellington mss WP1/895/15; 903/20; Hatherton diary, 10 Feb. 1828. [5] Harrowby mss, Eliot to Harrowby, 21, 29 Jan., reply, 22 Jan.; Hatherton diary, 29 Jan. 1828; P. Jupp, *British Politics on Eve of Reform*, 264-5. [6] Wellington mss WP1/988/14; *Ellenborough Diary*, i. 339. [7] Lincs. AO, Ancaster mss 3 ANC 9/10/20. [8] Aberdeen Univ. Lib., Arbuthnot mss, Arbuthnot to Hardinge, 19 Aug. 1831. [9] Carew Pole mss CC/N/64, Eliot to Pole Carew, 16, 21 Nov. 1831. [10] Ibid. CC/CO/14, Eliot's address, 7 Dec. 1832. [11] *Dod's Parl. Companion* (1838), 105. [12] Reid, *Monckton Milnes*, i. 271.

T.A.J.

ELIOT, **Hon. William** (1767–1845), of 58 Grosvenor Street, Mdx.

St. Germans	7 Jan. 1791–1802
Liskeard	1802–17 Nov. 1823

b. 1 Apr. 1767, 4th but 2nd surv. s. of Edward Eliot[†], 1st Bar. Eliot (*d.* 1804), and Catherine, da. and h. of Edward Elliston of Gestingthorpe, Essex; bro. of Hon. Edward James Eliot[†] and Hon. John Eliot[†]. *educ.* Liskeard sch.; Pembroke, Camb. 1784. *m.* (1) 30 Nov. 1797, Lady Georgiana Augusta Leveson Gower (*d.* 24 Mar. 1806), da. of Granville Leveson Gower[†], 1st mq. of Stafford, 1s. 3da. (2 *d.v.p.*); (2) 13 Feb. 1809, Letitia (*d.* 20 Jan. 1810), da. of Sir William Pierce Ashe A'Court[†], 1st bt., of Heytesbury, Wilts., *s.p.s.*; (3) 7 Mar. 1812, Charlotte (*d.* 3 July 1813), da. of Lt.-Gen. John Robinson[†] of Denston Hall, Suff., *s.p.*; (4) 30 Aug. 1814, Susan, da. of Sir John Mordaunt[†], 7th bt., of Walton, Warws., *s.p. suc.* bro. John

Eliot[†] as 2nd earl of St. Germans 17 Nov. 1823. *d.* 19 Jan. 1845.

Sec. of legation, Berlin 1791-3, chargé d'affaires 1793; sec. of embassy, The Hague 1793-5 and minister plenip. *ad. int.* 1793-4; plenip. on spec. mission to Brunswick 1794; minister to Elector Palatine and Diet of Ratisbon 1796-8.

Ld. of admiralty July 1800-Jan. 1804; under-sec. of state for foreign affairs June 1804-Jan. 1805; ld. of treasury Mar. 1807-Jan. 1812.

Eliot, whose active days as a diplomat and junior minister were behind him, was again returned for the family borough of Liskeard in 1820. He was an occasional attender who continued to give silent support to Lord Liverpool's ministry. He voted in defence of their conduct towards Queen Caroline, 6 Feb. 1821. He divided against Catholic relief, 28 Feb. He voted against repeal of the additional malt duty, 3 Apr., was in the minority for inquiry into the currency, 9 Apr., but voted for the duke of Clarence's grant, 18 June. He divided against the disfranchisement of ordnance officials, 12 Apr., parliamentary reform, 9 May, and the forgery punishment mitigation bill, 21 May 1821. His last known vote was against more extensive tax reductions, 21 Feb. 1822. He was granted ten days' leave to attend to private business, 18 Apr. 1822, and soon afterwards went to 'reside a year or two on the continent', leaving his affairs in the hands of his elder brother,[1] whom he succeeded to the peerage by special remainder in November 1823.[2] In the Lords, he supported the Wellington ministry's Catholic emancipation bill in 1829. The death of his wife in 1830 made him a widower for the fourth time. He died in January 1845 and was succeeded by his only son, Edward Granville Eliot*, who achieved the political eminence which had eluded him.[3]

[1] *Castlereagh Corresp.* xii. 474-5. [2] He inherited the Port Eliot estate in Cornwall, but the bulk of the personalty, which was sworn under £45,000, went to the 1st earl's widow, the residuary legatee (PROB 11/1683/180; IR26/1017/230). [3] *Gent. Mag.* (1845), i. 429, 667.

D.R.F.

ELIOTT LOCKHART, **William** (1764–1832), of Borthwickbrae, Roxburgh.

Selkirkshire	1806–1830

b. 30 Nov. 1764, 1st s. of John Eliott of Borthwickbrae and 2nd w. Margaret, da. and h. of Walter Laing. adv. 1786. *m.* 5 Mar. 1792, Marianne, da. and h. of Allan Lockhart of Cleghorn, Lanark, 5s. (2 *d.v.p.*) 2da. Took additional name of Lockhart on *d.* of fa.-in-law 1805. *d.* 6 Aug. 1832.

Lt. and capt. Roxburgh and Selkirk fencibles 1794, lt.-col. 1795-1801; maj. R. Lanark militia 1801; maj. commdt. Roxburgh yeoman cav. 1802, lt.-col. 1821-8.

Eliott Lockhart, whose eldest son John, a cornet in the 12th Dragoons, was killed at Waterloo, lost his youngest son Gilbert, at the age of 15, in 1825. By then he was in his fifth consecutive Parliament as the thoroughly undistinguished Member for Selkirkshire, where he sat on the interest of the 5th duke of Buccleuch.[1] At the general election of 1820 he was 'most busy in stirring rebellion in the camp of the enemy' in Haddington Burghs, where his influence in Jedburgh was reported to have helped to get the other burghs to 'throw off the fetters of Lord Lauderdale'; in the event his favoured candidate was beaten.[2] He continued, when present, to give general though not slavish support to Lord Liverpool's administration.[3] On 4 May 1820 he notified Lord Melville, their Scottish manager, that he would be unable to attend the House 'for a fortnight' as he was going to Orleans with two of his surviving sons, who were 'to remain there for some months'.[4] He divided in defence of ministers' conduct towards Queen Caroline, 6 Feb., and with them on the state of the revenue, 6 Mar., and the ordnance estimates, 11, 12 Apr.; but on 31 May 1821 he was in Hume's minority for a reduction of ordnance salaries. He did not vote on the Catholic question, 28 Feb. 1821, but he divided for relief, 21 Apr., 10 May 1825. He was given periods of leave to attend to urgent private business, 21 May 1821, on account of ill health, 16 Apr. 1822, and because of illness in his family, 15 Feb. 1825. He voted for inquiry into the Scottish royal burghs, 20 Feb., and with Hume for returns of naval pay, 22 Feb. 1822. He sided with ministers against abolition of one of the joint-postmasterships, 13 Mar., but voted in the hostile majority on this, 2 May. He was in Lord Althorp's minority of 24 for a permanent 18s. bounty on wheat exports, 9 May 1822. He voted with government against repeal of the assessed taxes, 10, 18 Mar., the production of information on the Dublin Orange theatre riot, 24 Mar. 1823, in defence of the prosecution of the Methodist missionary John Smith in Demerara, 11 June, for the Irish insurrection bill, 14 June 1824, for the president of the board of trade's salary, 10 Apr., and against reform of Edinburgh's representation, 13 Apr. 1826. He is not known to have spoken in debate, but he presented constituency petitions for repeal of the duty on notaries' licences, 31 Mar. 1824, and against interference with the Scottish banking system, 16 Mar. 1826.[5] At the April 1826 by-election for Roxburghshire he supported Buccleuch's successful candidate Henry Hepburne Scott, but

his 'reckless piece of activity' in moving the writ put paid to hopes of postponing the business until the approaching general election in order to avoid Hepburne Scott's 'paying his fees twice over' in a short space of time.[6] He appears to have been largely absent from the 1826 Parliament, though he was named to the committees on the Scottish entails bill, 11 Mar., and the Scottish alehouses bill, 12 May 1828, and was added to the select committee on Scottish entails, 10 Mar. 1829. He divided for Catholic relief, 6 Mar. 1827, but not in 1828 or 1829 when, having been listed as likely to vote with the Wellington ministry for emancipation, he defaulted on a call of the House, 5 Mar. It is not clear whether it was he or John Ingram Lockhart who voted for the duke of Clarence's annuity, 16 Mar. 1827; but it was almost certainly the latter who divided against inquiry into chancery delays, 24 Apr. 1828. Eliott Lockhart presented a Selkirkshire agriculturists' petition for enhanced protection against foreign wool imports, 5 June 1828. He had planned to postpone his retirement from Parliament, which his declining health made desirable, until Buccleuch's brother Lord John Scott† came of age in July 1830. In the event, Scott had no intention to enter Parliament at that juncture, and with Buccleuch's blessing Eliott Lockhart stood down at the 1830 dissolution.[7] In March 1831 he helped to draft the Selkirkshire freeholders' petition protesting against the merger of the county with Selkirkshire proposed in the Grey ministry's first reform scheme.[8] He died in August 1832 and was succeeded by his eldest surviving son, Allan Eliott Lockhart (1803-78), Peelite Conservative Member for Selkirkshire, 1846-61.

[1] *Caledonian Mercury*, 25 Mar. 1820, 10, 15 June 1826. [2] NLS mss 11, f. 28. [3] *Black Bk.* (1823), 171; *Session of Parl. 1825*, p. 473. [4] NAS GD51/1/190. [5] *The Times*, 1 Apr. 1824, 17 Mar. 1826. [6] NAS GD157/2294/6; 2968/5. [7] NAS GD224/581/4, Eliott Lockhart to Buccleuch, 11 Mar., Buccleuch to J. Johnstone, 4 June, Lord Montagu to Eliott Lockhart, 4 June; Pringle mss box 16, Eliott Lockhart to J. Pringle, 13 June 1830. [8] *Scott Jnl.* 637.

D.R.F.

ELLICE, Edward (1783–1863), of Wyke House, nr. Brentford, Mdx.

COVENTRY	1818–1826
COVENTRY	1830–17 Sept. 1863

b. 12 Sept. 1783,[1] 2nd surv. s. of Alexander Ellice (*d.* 1805), merchant, of Montreal, Canada and London and w. Anne Russell. *educ.* Winchester; Marischal Coll. Aberdeen 1797. *m.* (1) 30 Oct. 1809, Lady Hannah Althea Grey (*d.* 28 July 1832), da. of Charles, 1st Earl

Grey, wid. of Capt. George Edmund Byron Bettesworth, RN, 1s.; (2) 25 Oct. 1843, Lady Anne Amelia Keppel, da. of William Charles, 4th earl of Albemarle, wid. of Thomas William Coke I*, 1st earl of Leicester, *s.p. d.* 17 Sept. 1863.

Sec. to treasury Nov. 1830-Aug. 1832; PC 3 Apr. 1833; sec. at war Apr. 1833-Dec. 1834.

Ellice, who was born in London, was his father's business heir and a successful trader to the North Americas, Canada and the West Indies, where his failure to sell out in time eventually cost him £70,000.[2] Drawn into politics in Middlesex as a friend of Henry Brougham*, Robert Byron, Sir Francis Burdett*, John Cam Hobhouse* and his brother-in-law Samuel Whitbread[†], he aligned with the 'Mountain' before gravitating to the main Whig opposition, led in the Lords by his wife's brother Lord Grey. Nevertheless, he continued to adopt a radical profile for the Foxites and liberals of Coventry, which had first returned him in 1818. A regular attender, he had spoken frequently on Canada and fiscal policy, criticized the timetable, but not the principle of the resumption of cash payments, and opposed the Liverpool ministry's repressive measures after Peterloo. As a spokesman for the Coventry silk and ribbon weavers, he had sponsored the 1819 ribbon and silk weavers regulation bill which extended the Spitalfields regulations to Coventry and urged inquiry into manufacturing distress.[3] At the dissolution in 1820, he was thought of for London, but persisted at Coventry, where, with Peter Moore, he overcame an 'awkward' and highly publicized challenge at the general election by William Cobbett[†], who capitalized on his absence from the Coventry Peterloo meeting and caused him to spend £6,000.[4] To Cobbett in 1820, Ellice was

> a *City* organ ... By marriage ... related to Lord Grey ... a very tall man, more than six feet high, as big as ... Hume about the shoulders and breast, but with a frame *tapering downwards* ... a forehead *falling back on the sides* ... the eye, set in a shallow socket ... large, round dull and of downward cast ... The voice of Ellice is ... soft and fat. He has nothing of the *keenness* of 'Change Alley about him. He would seem to have taken lessons to acquire the Bond Street *Croak*. In short, imagine a great *schoolboy of forty*, and you have the man fully about your eyes.[5]

Nicknamed 'Bear' Ellice on account of his size and stake in the North American fur trade, or, as Carlyle put it, 'rather for his oiliness than for any trace of ferocity ever seen in him', Brougham considered him a 'clever, sensible and most kindly disposed person, but not always very wise. He had that most pernicious kind of good nature that made him at all times wish

to play the part of *Mr. Harmony*'.[6] Preferring business and society to reading, he kept abreast of events through his City contacts, Brooks's, dinner parties, newspapers and a voluminous correspondence. As with Brougham, most of his letters are undated and 'difficult to decipher'.[7] For Ellice, who also organized financial support for his nephew Samuel Charles Whitbread* in Middlesex, the 1820 election was ill-timed.[8] He had tacitly withdrawn from Ellice, Inglis and Company the previous October and his negotiations with Lord Selkirk's executors, which in 1821 enabled him to effect the merger he had sought since 1803 between the North West Company and the Hudson Bay Company, were at a delicate stage.[9] He wrote in June 1821 that he had recovered '£4-5,000 a year to myself by it'.[10] Caricatured in May 1822 as a 'Royal Exchange consul general', he was an early supporter of the Greek Patriots and, as a member of their London committee, instrumental in floating the loans. He bore the brunt of the ferocious newspaper campaign prompted by the second loan's failure to deliver a Greek navy in 1825 and endured the opprobrium of the London press throughout 1826. He was similarly taunted in the House and in Coventry.[11]

As a spokesman and occasional teller for the Whig opposition on trade and commerce in the 1820 Parliament, Ellice divided against administration in almost all major divisions, and occasionally in the 'Mountain's' small minorities for lower taxes and retrenchment. He attended the House unstintingly until 1823, when disillusionment briefly set in, but soon rallied on behalf of the silk trade and the Greek Patriots. He was especially active in the select committees on foreign trade (1821-24) and a major contributor to the debates on agriculture, 1821-2, and corn and the currency, 1825-6. He approved and voted for a scot and lot franchise for Leeds under the Grampound disfranchisement bill, 2 Mar. 1821,[12] and divided for reform, 18 Apr., 9 May 1821, 20 Feb., 25 Apr. 1822, 20 Feb., 24 Apr., 2 June 1823, 13, 27 Apr. 1826, and to curb electoral bribery, 26 May 1826. He capitalized on the Hull freeholders' petition, 15 Mar., and Sykes's 'badly timed' county franchise bill, 26 Apr. 1826, to draw attention to the unrepresented Coventry freeholders. He divided for Catholic relief, 28 Feb. 1821, 1 Mar., 21 Apr., 10 May, and against the attendant Irish franchise bill, 26 Apr. 1825.[13] He echoed the plea of the London merchants' petition for easing commercial restrictions to relieve distress, 8 May 1820, but, deliberately differing from the political economist David Ricardo, he pointed to the 30-50 per cent fall in the price of manufactured goods since the return to cash payments and advised the board of trade to consider placing less reliance on the bonded warehouse system and stamp duties to service public debt. He presented a Hawick petition for easing trade restrictions, 16 May, and spoke and was a minority teller that day for inquiry into military expenditure. He was a minority teller against referring the agricultural distress petitions to a select committee, 30 May, and criticized the tactics by which it was conceded; but he withdrew a tabled motion, calculated to prevent its appointment, as he did 'not want to be linked with anything that made distress worse, or put agriculture before manufacturing'.[14]

He supported the 1820 parliamentary campaign on behalf of Queen Caroline, but the 'radical fever' and uncertainty it generated and the prospect of subjecting the bill of pains and penalties to 'the labyrinth of Mr. Hume's cross-examinations, motions of adjournment, committal of *non mi ricordo* to Newgate, etc.' in the Commons perturbed him. He observed to Grey's son-in-law John Lambton*, 14 Sept.:

> If all parties, as the saying is, had their deserts, the ministers should be taken to Tower Hill, or rather, as they have been merciful to the radicals at York ... transported to Botany Bay, and His Majesty carried to a horse-pond. But guilt or punishment is now out of the question, and the cry is, show us the way out of it, how are we to escape?[15]

He voted against the prorogation proposed by the queen's radical partisans, 18 Sept., but stated his future commitment to opposing the bill. Following its abandonment, he watched the queen's procession to St. Paul's with Burdett, 29 Nov., and attended the Covent Garden meeting, 7 Dec. 1820, but left early to disassociate himself from its radical address.[16] He was consulted that month over Grey's terms, should he be called to office, and sought London accommodation for him for the 1821 session.[17] He supported the 1821 parliamentary campaign on the queen's behalf and assisted Sir Robert Wilson* following his dismissal from the army for forcing a way through the City for the crowd at her funeral in September. Wilson had been his companion in Paris the preceding day, and in debate, 13 Feb. 1822, Ellice testified to this and to their prior suspicions of a plot implicating Wilson.[18]

He stressed the high commercial cost of government indecision on the timber duties, but refrained from accusing the vice-president of the board of trade Thomas Wallace I and the select committee of neglect for failing to announce the duties promptly, 14, 15 Feb. 1821.[19] A long-term opponent of the 1815 corn laws, he disputed Curwen's 'inflated' claims, 22 Feb., and objected to proceeding with the corn aver-

ages bill before the agriculture committee reported, 2 Apr. Opposing the additional malt duty when opposition carried the division, 21 Mar., he explained, in what the radical Whig Henry Grey Bennet* termed a 'tolerable speech with many good points in it', that his motives for supporting the motion differed from those of its proposer Western, and he 'admonished the gentry' that, having rejected currency 'depreciation', they might 'bid adieu' to high remunerating prices and should 'bend their attention entirely to the reduction of expenses'.[20] On the Bank cash payments bill, he resolutely defended Robert Peel* and the 1819 committee's decision to restore the gold standard, 19, 20, 29 March, 5, 9, 13 Apr., but he conceded that they had been misled by the 'apparent price' of gold in 1818, 19 Mar. He tried to remedy their failure to direct the Bank to issue small notes on demand by securing a rider to the measure, 13 Apr.[21] On the budget, 1 June, and again, 22 June, he criticized the 'farce of borrowing to reduce the national debt' and the 'grossly immoral' state lottery. Dissenting from Hume, he explained that he was against seeking piecemeal reductions in the duke of Clarence's grant: it would be better 'openly to take away from the crown the power of granting pensions, than by a side-wind to force claimants upon it', 18 June. He made representations on behalf of the redundant London customs officers, 22 June, and pressed the case of the Canadian claimants who had not been compensated for wartime damage, 25 June 1821.[22] He succeeded in killing the cruelty to horses bill at his second attempt, 20 June.[23] Despite his private criticism of Henry Hunt* and the radicals,[24] he divided with them for receipt of the Lancaster convict Broadhurst's petition, 7 Mar., on Peterloo, 16 May, conditions in Ilchester gaol, 21 June 1821, 22 Mar 1822, and for remission of Hunt's gaol sentence, 24 Apr. 1822.

From Wyke, Ellice corresponded almost daily with Grey during the Dowager Lady Grey's final illness in the winter of 1821-2.[25] He thought the Grenvillite accession to government might help enable them to carry Catholic relief in 1822;[26] and when they failed, he wrote of the House: 'Hume speaks and Castlereagh, it amounts to this ... The debates are almost disgusting. Everyone relying upon some partial effect against a great chimera which they dare not examine, and preaching'.[27] He contended, when Edward Curteis brought up the Sussex distress petition, 13 Feb. 1822, that the 'notion of protecting and prohibitive duties ... still maintained by ... Webb Hall and other visionaries, in their reveries, had long been given up and exploded, both in Parliament and the country', and suggested that tax reductions were the only remedy. Still publicly defending the 1819 currency change, although privately he conceded that an adjustment was imperative, he pronounced the £4,000,000 exchequer bills loan (which he had known about since January) 'helpful', 18 Feb.[28] He shared Grey's belief that ministers would 'give up [the] sinking fund debt and all to keep their places' and pressed them to concede a public accounts committee, 22 Feb., 18 Apr.[29] He opposed the navy five per cents bill, 4, 8, 11 Mar., and attacked the estimates, 14, 15, 18, 25 Mar. To the annoyance of Brougham, who was 'on the circuit', he also called for government assistance for the depressed Canadian timber trade, 13 Mar., and clashed openly with Hume over Canada, 15 Mar.[30] Directing Lord Duncannon* to reprimand him and notify the gossips Thomas Creevey* and Michael Angelo Taylor*, Brougham wrote, 20 Mar. 1822:

> I am sick beyond all description at reading the newspapers of yesterday, giving accounts of the debate on Monday. Ellice must be plainly told that if he from mere vulgar vanity and flattery will get up and attack Hume, he must expect the most severe punishment. I assure you if I had been in the House I should have made an example of him, which neither he nor the House would have forgotten for a twelvemonth.[31]

As a principal speaker and minority teller for ordnance reductions, 25 Mar., Ellice observed that the distressed petitioners' pleas had been 'useless', and he delivered a harsh verdict on the 1822 agriculture committee report, based entirely on the 1821 evidence, 3 Apr. 1822. Replying, Lord Londonderry accused him of changing his views since 1819, which of course he denied. He resumed his criticism of the report and the 'agricultural bank', 2, 6, 13 May. Objecting to the report being brought up that day, he expressed support for Huskisson and Ricardo's 'suggestions, but not their conclusions', and attacked the sinking fund as a complicated, ineffectual and outmoded device for taking money from men's pockets, encouraging loans and foreign investment, that pandered to the City and operated a 'perpetual transfer of capital'.[32] Peel made him concede, during the debate, that he had never been an advocate of an unrestrained paper currency, but he refused to admit that he had failed to grasp the full consequences of the 1819 Act. Changing tactics, he drew on the testimony of Thomas Attwood and Hume and accepted (to cheers) that the current 'distress … arose, in a great measure, and indeed chiefly, from paying the interest of the debt in a currency of higher value' than that in which it was contracted. He and Western lost the division by 153-22.[33] Ellice participated in the discussions on the independent South American colonies, 30 Apr., and the navigation laws, 6, 7, 18 May, and voiced qualified support for the colonial trade bill, 17, 18 May.[34] Responding to the budget, he made the usual complaints about high expenditure and pleaded for retrenchment and changes in the usury laws, 1 July. He voiced the Coventry silk manufacturers' concerns over the warehousing bill, 20 May, 21 June, and condemned the barilla duties as a means of assisting the soap manufacturers at Scotland's expense, 29 July. His late session attendance was motivated by concern for the Canadian government and trade bill (introduced by Wilmot Horton, 30 Mar.), which he had urged on the government. He secured its committal (by 48-14), 18 July, but he was bested that day by the bill's opponent Sir James Mackintosh, and his speech was misreported to convey the impression that the proposed union of Upper and Lower Canada was a prelude to their annexation by the United States. His remarks on bringing up a favourable petition from the Canada merchants on the 23rd again disappointed, and the bill was timed out.[35] Following Londonderry's suicide in August, Ellice remained in close contact with John Evelyn Denison*, Duncannon and Wilson and briefed Grey on Canning's succession to the foreign office and as leader of the House. In October 1822 he rented a house in Brighton for the winter.[36]

To thwart Cobbett and his distress petition, he prepared resolutions for Lord Althorp's* friend Edmund Lechmere Charlton† to propose at the Herefordshire reform meeting of January 1823.[37] Preparing for the session, and depressed by a recent illness and family bereavements, he wrote to Grey (who agreed) of his concern lest opposition treat the Catholic question and Dublin theatre 'outrage' concurrently, and decided not to encourage Burdett to attempt a Catholic relief bill that session. He added:

> There was at one time a large party of my way of thinking with Burdett at our head. Lord Lansdowne and Mackintosh have now attached many of our supporters, and the only doubt I have on the subject is whether we can make our objection effectual to them, and carry the bill on its presentation or second reading.[38]

Opposing the national debt reduction bill as a principal speaker and minority teller with Hume, 17 Mar., he acknowledged that they could not object to its provisions for abolishing the old sinking fund machinery, but ridiculed the allusion to a £2,000,000 surplus. He found fault with and was a minority teller against the silk manufacture bill which ended the prohibition on imports, 9 May, 11 June, but maintained that the combination laws and restrictions on artisan emigration were more damaging, 22 May, 9, 11 June. He welcomed the two-year adjustment period secured.[39] He expressed support for the reciprocity duties proposed by the president of the board of trade Huskisson and urged their extension to ship building, 6 June. After consulting Canning, 8 July 1823, he agreed to defer a motion he had prepared on French interference in the West Indies.[40]

Ellice spent November in Durham with Lambton and was unable to avoid that autumn's endless intrigues over the 'mad' Northumberland Member Beaumont, whose seat Grey coveted for his heir Lord Howick*.[41] He had difficulty motivating himself to attend the House for long periods in February 1824 and, feeling bored, he complained that 'the same system is going on'. Nevertheless, he divided fairly steadily with his friends (and in Curwen's majority criticizing the duke of Atholl's jurisdiction in the Isle of Man, 18 Feb).[42] By March, he had rallied as expected on the silk duties, and he accompanied delegations to Downing Street from the silk towns and succeeded in securing a qualified endorsement of free trade from certain Coventry manufacturers (but not the weavers).[43] Ellice was always inclined to be a repetitive speaker, prone to convoluted sentences. Between 1824 and 1826 he frequently tried to represent his personal support for Huskisson's liberal trade policies and his constituents' demands for protection in the same breath – generally to little effect. He protested at precipitate tariff changes and inadequate concessions, 23 Feb. 1824. He confirmed his support for free trade on presenting petitions for protection for silk, 5, 8, 9, 10, 18 Mar., and, seeking a middle way, he cautioned Huskisson against singling out silk, which was 'not native', for experimental deregulation, 18, 19, 22 Mar. He secured some concessions on stock-in-hand and a two-year 'trial period' acceptable to the Coventry manufacturers.[44] He tried to discourage Hume from legislating on the sugar duties 8 Mar., and the hide regulation bill, 18 Mar.[45] He quibbled over the Windsor Castle grant, 5 Apr., and raised minor points on taxation and a wide range of commercial issues, including the West India Company bill, 10 May, marine insurance, 27 May, and the East India trade bill, which he backed, 11 June. He endorsed the London petition for recognition of the South American republics and moved to receive Captain McNeal's report, 15 June. On 12 Apr. 1824 he promoted the London Oil Gas Company bill, which Moore, a shareholder in the rival Imperial Gas Light Company, opposed, 12 Apr., 3 May 1824; and their appearance as rival tellers, 12 Apr. 1824, 22 Feb. 1825, created a furore and prompted Hume to demand the annulment of the votes of interested Members.[46] He announced a motion to exempt Canadian corn stocks

in bond from duty under the warehoused corn bill, 18 May 1824.[47]

When in March 1825 he received a £200 demand from Harriette Wilson to keep his name out of her *Memoirs*, Ellice forwarded it to the press.[48] In the House, where the political gap between him and his erstwhile allies was now evident, he preferred to quibble over differential duties with the chancellor Robinson than to engage in the discussions on the sinking fund, suggested by Hume, 28 Feb. Nor, although sympathetic, did he share Moore's commitment to securing the immediate repeal of the Bubble Act, 22, 29 Mar. His speech on the Peruvian Mining Company bill, 16 Mar., was wary and reflected his private unease over the 'new schemes and companies and committees' which took up so much of the House's 'time that one scarcely knows which way to turn or how to find time to attend to anything'.[49] He welcomed the partial restoration of the combination laws, 3 May, 14, 23, 27 June. On corn, as with silk, his expressed opinions were confused. He declined to endorse the City's petition for a 20s. duty and release of corn from bond, duty free, 28 Mar., silently presented a protectionist petition from Aberdeenshire, 5 May, and pressed for concessions for Canadian corn, 9 June. He declined to 'join the Whigs' in opposing the Mauritius trade bill, 6, 29 June.[50] He was vice-president of the Shipowners' Association, 1825-6, and a director of the newly incorporated Van Diemen's Land Company, which memorialized Huskisson stating their concern at the short-term commercial damage to shipping caused by the recent relaxation of the navigation laws and colonial policy.[51] He agreed with the banker Hudson Gurney's assessment that bullion was 'too susceptible to panic and fluctuations' and maintained that the 'small notes bill, like the corn laws, was devised to protect certain great interests from the losses which Peel's bill had inflicted on all other debtors' and to 'conciliate them to that measure', 27 June 1825.

That summer Ellice took a Norfolk mansion, Snettisham, near King's Lynn, which provided refuge for his family and Hobhouse while the furore generated by the Greek loan was at its height. Creevey, an early guest, predicted that the scandal would bankrupt Ellice.[52] He had anticipated and suffered little personally by the December 1825 banking crisis, which he attributed to 'poor regulation' and 'overuse of paper'. Drawing parallels with 1814 and 1819, he noted the 'calm before the storm' when he returned to the City in January 1826. He also speculated about a silver standard.[53] On the address, 2 Feb., he reiterated his views on distress, South America and the currency and cautioned against precipitately adopting the Scottish banking system in England. He approved the decision to end the circulation of small notes and criticized the 'continued madness of ministers' experiments with the manufacturing industry', corn and silk.[54] He endorsed the principle of the Bank charter and promissory notes bills, which Alexander Baring and the Whig country bankers opposed, divided for it, 10, 13 Feb., and made further supportive interventions, 7, 13, 17, 21 Mar. He also seconded John Maberly's amendment for a select committee on banking and a metallic currency, 20 Feb., causing Peel to accuse him of inconsistency. He replied that the small notes bill was a 'virtual repeal' of the 1819 Bank Act: 'It gave power to the Bank, a temptation to increase its issues, which with the best intentions, that body would not always be able to withstand'. Additionally, he declared against free trade in corn as long as the national debt remained high. He presented distress petitions, 9, 14 Feb., preparatory to seeking inquiry into the silk trade, 23 Feb., when, with John Williams seconding, he described the grievances of different branches of the trade and criticized the proposed 30 per cent duty. He said he had hoped to secure an 'internal prohibition of foreign silk' and welcomed similar concessions announced on dyes and soap.[55] Mrs. Arbuthnot attributed his heavy defeat (222-40) to Huskisson's superior reply.[56] Laying the ground for Tierney's speech on the exchequer loan, 28 Feb., he accused ministers of 'making half-baked proposals they cannot substantiate with returns or accounts'. He voted to increase the president of the board of trade's salary, 6, 10 Apr., after seeking prior guarantees that equivalent savings were possible, and for corn law revision, 18 Apr., and harried ministers over the sudden economic downturn in manufacturing, 1, 19 May. Speaking on 4, 9, 12, 13, 26 May, he made the late banking crisis the scapegoat for all recent commercial failures. Grey, who had consulted him over the Northumberland elections, when Howick was twice defeated, ignored his advice to seek a cheaper alternative seat.[57] Ellice was suggested for Middlesex at the dissolution in May 1826, but he refused to spend more than £2,500 and contested Coventry, where he and Moore were defeated by the corporation candidates.[58] His 'bad press' from the Greek loan fiasco persisted.[59]

Out of Parliament, Ellice communicated regularly with Denison, Grey, Hobhouse and Wilson, started to put his own and Lambton's finances in order and advised Grey on land sales following Howick's defeat in Northumberland.[60] He tendered for Appleby, but considered the asking price too high, and vainly took soundings elsewhere through Burdett and Taylor.[61] He attributed his failure to unseat the Coventry Members on petition to political in-fighting in the wake of Liverpool's stroke, the narrow anti-Catholic majority in the Commons, 6 Mar., and the composition of the committee:

> Two good 'No Popery' men cannot be spared out of a majority of four, and more especially where two Catholics will help repeal them, and these are the principles of justice on which one has to rely in such a tribunal.[62]

The political turmoil of the next twelve months convinced him that any seat would have been a bad investment, although he again toyed with the idea when considering an alignment with Althorp in July 1827 and with the liberal Tories when Huskisson was leader of the House in Lord Goderich's short-lived ministry.[63] Differing from Grey, he continued to write flatteringly to Lord Durham (Lambton) of Huskisson.[64] He lobbied, but failed to persuade the Lords to carry the Coventry magistracy bill, introduced in the wake of the election committee report, and testified (on Coventry elections) before the committee on borough polls, 10 May 1827.[65] Between January 1828 and the dissolution in 1830 Ellice lived mainly in Dawlish. He travelled on the continent with his son Edward, watched the political situation and monitored the progress of Howick and others of the 1826 intake. He twice failed to secure the election of his brother Russell as an East India Company director: a 'useless battle of "independence" against the chairs, and all the agency money, and with troops who do not understand successive defeats' (7 Apr. 1830).[66] In January 1830, when the duke of Wellington was expected to 'send for Grey', Ellice observed:

> There appear to be four distinct parties preparing for Parliament. First government. Second, a direct and entire opposition led by Lord Palmerston in the Commons and Lord Melbourne in the ... Lords, with Charles Grant and the ex-liberals, etc. ... [and] a large support from our friends, who have only made the condition that Huskisson is not to lead, or as others will have it, to have anything to do with the party and on this point they willingly give up their leader Lord Lansdowne. The third party are what they call the *Watchers*, under ... Althorp in the ... Commons, and to this I fear Brougham proposes to attach himself. The fourth, the discontented and still more bitter old Tories, who will make no peace with Peel, and are probably the most formidable, backed as they will be by the distress and loud complaints from every part of the country.[67]

Largely through Howick, he also monitored attendance that session at Brooks's and at meetings of the revived opposition in Althorp's rooms.[68] Despite

Lord Hertford's hostility, he came in for Coventry at the 1830 general election with the Ultra Fyler after a token poll.[69] Afterwards, he reported regularly to Grey on reactions to the political situation in the City and at Brooks's, where he noticed that there was 'great jealousy of Brougham's assumption of the office of leader'.[70]

Ellice was of course listed among the ministry's 'foes' and voted to bring them down on the civil list, 15 Nov. 1830. Offering to assist Grey in office, 19 Nov., he advised:

> What you have most to avoid is the appearance before the public, of rather providing places for *worn out*, useless people than providing proper and efficient persons, even for the lowest office. For God's sake, have none of the followers and retainers of the last 20 years' governments, where it is possible to do without them. They will always be jealous of newcomers; and their diminished hope of advancement [means that they will be] incessantly endeavouring in concert with their old allies and the press, to undermine all your arrangements.[71]

Grey made him his patronage (treasury) secretary at £2,500 a year, and he was immediately lampooned as 'Mr. Jobbery' and as one of Grey's family cabinet.[72] He repeatedly cautioned Grey against making further 'family' appointments.[73] It was reported in the City that Ellice and Poulett Thomson, the vice-president of the board of trade, would make half a million pounds if they remained in office for two years.[74] Ellice was also appointed with Auckland, Brougham and Durham to Grey's new committee 'to regulate the public press, as far as regards government'.[75] As patronage secretary he had the management of elections, oversaw the trade in seats and attended the House frequently but rarely engaged in debate. He covered for or assisted ministers as necessary, and ordered or brought up returns and bills. His votes indicated the government's line, and with Duncannon and occasionally Sheil and even O'Connell for the Irish and Thomas Kennedy and others for the Scottish Members, he drew up lists and acted as a whipper-in. Liaising with Brougham, who as lord chancellor was Speaker of the Lords, he briefed the leader of the Commons Althorp and Grey on morale and warned of possible difficulties and defections. He discussed the House's business schedules and occasionally compared lists with the Tory whip Holmes, and entertained colleagues and likely defectors at his house, then 3 Richmond Terrace. Early doubts about his suitability were assuaged and he was seen as 'no mean' judge of the Commons.[76] He recommended an immediate dissolution and, when this was vetoed, tried to allow for losses at by-elections gen-erated by the change in ministry by leasing William Russell's* Saltash seats, which he found difficult to manage effectively. He engineered a vacancy at New Windsor for the Irish Secretary Smith Stanley following his defeat at Preston in December 1830.[77] He deputized for Althorp during his father's illness, 10 Dec., and opposed, to Tory taunts, a motion for printing the evidence on the Evesham election petition, 14 Dec. He presented returns and ordered accounts on imports and exports, 15 Dec., and carried the third reading of the patents bill, 17 Dec. 1830.

He was named to the public accounts committee, 17 Feb., assisted with the contentious seaborne coal bill, 16, 21 Feb., brought his knowledge of Canada to the debate on emigration, 22 Feb. 1831, and was directed to bring in the assisted emigration bill with the colonial under-secretary Howick. He had John Stuart Wortley added to the East India Committee that day and dealt with irregularities in the Liverpool-Leeds railway bill, 23 Feb. When he presented petitions for parliamentary reform, 26 Feb., *The Times* maliciously commented: 'There is one person, in particular, unfavourably known in the City for his connection with the celebrated Greek loan. This person should have shrunk from public life altogether, but particularly he should not have been placed in a situation connected with the revenue of the country!' He decided against treating it as a libel. He brought up two Coventry petitions favourable to the government's reform bill, 15 Mar., and thereby succeeded in marginalizing local concern over the voting rights of serving apprentices and a third Coventry petition, for the ballot, entrusted to Hunt. He presented further reform petitions, tabled several reports and accounts and had the sugar duties bill deferred, 19 Mar. He had had it circulated privately that the timber duties would probably not be carried.[78] Before the details of the reform bill were announced, he had predicted a majority for it of 67, but the second reading was carried by only a single vote, 22 Mar.[79] According to Brougham's private secretary Denis Le Marchant†, Ellice heard beforehand that John Calcraft would 'switch' to them. By April he counted his brothers-in-law Sir Charles and Walter Burrell among the likely Tory defectors, and was monitoring the Lowthers. (He later became the government's agent in distributing honours to those whose nomination boroughs the Reform Act abolished.)[80] He correctly predicted the bill's defeat on Gascoyne's wrecking amendment, 19 Apr., and prepared for a dissolution.[81] He has been variously credited with raising £15,000 in subscriptions by the 23rd (£25,000 overall), purchasing 'Tory' boroughs with £10,000 of secret service money to assist candidates and binding a party together by the cry of 'The Bill! The whole bill, and nothing but the bill!'[82] His correspondence reflects the problems he faced in finding candidates and making them pay their own way.[83] After first ensuring the co-operation of the Coventry Political Union, he came in at a personal cost of £2,500, with a new colleague, Henry Lytton Bulwer, after defeating Fyler in a five-day poll.[84] During it he wrote:

> Everything is put upon me, and I am blamed for anything that goes wrong, or rather that does not accord with the particular wishes or feelings of any person connected with the government ... I cannot find candidates, and what is still more difficult, the persons exactly suited to the particular places requiring them, and above all, men that know their own minds with money to fight any borough and almost any county in the kingdom ... All is going right where we have people of nerve and determination to deal with, something wrong where we have undecided and weak candidates on our hands ... I must go back in the mail to Coventry tonight to prevent mischief.[85]

Forwarding the returns to Brougham before leaving London, 17 May 1831, 'partly for a holiday, but more especially to avoid dunning for money', he reckoned on a 'majority of 150 at least. Tolerably good accounts from Scotland – 13 of 15 burgh returns, 9 gains altogether'.[86] Lord Dudley, who met him in Paris shortly afterwards, informed William Ord*, 'I know very well what fault may be found with him [my friend the *Bear*] "*minus aptus acutis naribus horum hominum*"(Horace), but he has an active vigorous understanding, a cheerful temper and more than all he is a generous kindhearted man'.[87]

Deputizing for Althorp, Ellice ordered papers for the public accounts committee and announced the Irish tobacco bill, 23 June 1831. He naturally divided steadily with his colleagues for the reintroduced and revised reform bills and was dismayed by their defeats on Saltash, 26 July,[88] and Lord Chandos's amendment enfranchising £50 tenants-at-will, 18 Aug. He also faced a rebellion over Saturday sittings. The antireformers Henry Goulburn, Frederick Hodgson and Sir Charles Wetherell tried to embarrass him by taking up the cause of the unfranchised apprentices and freeholders of Coventry, 13 July, and the radicals deployed the same tactic when he presented Coventry's petition for corn law revision; he endorsed it as the 'next important subject after reform', 12 Sept.[89] That month, the Irish lord lieutenant Lord Anglesey, having heard Ellice praised by the Irish Members, suggested him as a possible replacement as Irish secretary for Smith Stanley.[90] He was not tempted. He advised Grey on appointments to the royal household and coronation honours and kept a close watch on the intrigues of Lord Wharncliffe and the reform bill's prospects in the Lords.[91] Assisted by the Preston Member John Wood, he carried the Waterloo Bridge bill, 16 Sept., and he was a majority teller for authorizing public spending on improving Windsor Castle and Buckingham House, 28 Sept. He had anticipated the reform bill's Lords defeat, and mustered support for Lord Ebrington's confidence motion, 10 Oct.[92] He also sought Ebrington's assistance to keep 'Althorp up to the mark', 26 Oct.[93] He came to the assistance of Poulett Thomson when papers on smuggling were ordered, 15 Dec. 1831. Le Marchant recalled that when Peel's brother-in-law George Dawson* told Ellice that the revised final reform bill was 'a damned deal worse than the last', he 'justly answered that a greater compliment could not be paid it'.[94] Keen to avoid another dissolution, he refused to delay the bill's committee stage beyond 20 Jan. 1832 and hoped that Grey's visit to the king in Brighton that month and the threat of peerage creations would be enough to ease its passage through the Lords.[95] He and Duncannon had to act precipitately to avoid defeat on the Russian-Dutch loan, 26 Jan., and he complained to Grey that they had received too little support from Althorp.[96] The premier's speech affirming the government's determination to enforce the payment of Irish tithes, 7 Feb., 'set all the Papists and radicals furious with Lord Grey and the Bear', who was now reported to be looking 'gloomy'.[97] Discussions with Lord Powis's son Robert Clive* had reassured him that the reform bill's passage in the Commons, 22 Mar., was not in doubt.[98] In April he suggested making 'about five or six' new peers to carry it. (The diarist Greville inflated the figure to 56.)[99] He doubted whether he could secure a respectable majority on their confidence motion following its Lords' defeat, 10 May, and repeatedly warned that attendance would fall off following its passage, leaving the ministry vulnerable.[100] He was a teller against a Conservative amendment opposing the dismemberment of Perthshire by the Scottish reform bill, 15 June 1832. To the annoyance of Smith Stanley, who contemplated resignation, he advised Grey against attempting an Irish tithe bill.[101]

By June, preliminary arrangements for the 1832 general election were in place for England and Wales, but the lord advocate Francis Jeffrey* complained that he had been 'warning Ellice of trouble in Scotland in vain for the last couple of months and that government may suffer'.[102] Grey, partly on Althorp's advice, and to avoid trouble, had paid little heed to Ellice's pleas, first voiced in March, that he be permitted to resign on account of his own deteriorating health and his wife's terminal illness.[103] Between March and June, he sent

Grey several letters of resignation, and, justifying his *'fixed determination* to get out of office the moment I can', he wrote, 30 June:

> It may have its attractions for younger people, or other men having higher views than I aspire to. It has none for me and I would not have the last 12 months over again, if you will give me the choice of all the offices under the government. But possibly any change will have a bad appearance during the remainder of the Parliament. Whether I go or stay, I will manage the next election for you, it being also understood that George Ponsonby is to assist in the management of the present House during the remainder of the session. In the state of Hannah's health, I must be considered a free agent to go and come, as I am able. My retirement will eliminate all objections to [Charles] Wood's* appointment to either situation ... You must have an infusion of younger, more active, and intelligent men, who will take an interest in what is going on in the House, make themselves acquainted with the new-comers and lay themselves out to conciliate and satisfy them. There is not a single soul except Duncannon who ever speaks to or takes the least notice of any of our most zealous and steady supporters.[104]

He retired when his wife died, 27 July, and after her funeral he 'set off for a wandering expedition anywhere, to the North in the first instance ... and with the intention of not returning to town, if I can avoid it, for the next six months'.[105] For six weeks in August and September 1832, before setting out for the continent, he canvassed and sent reports on the Scottish constituencies to Grey and the first lord of the admiralty Sir James Graham.*[106]

Ellice contested Coventry successfully in December 1832 and retained the seat for the Liberals for life. He was severely challenged at the by-election following his appointment to the cabinet as secretary at war in April 1833, and became a veteran of six further polls. He resigned with Lord Melbourne in December 1834 and did not hold office again, but he remained a confidential adviser to successive Liberal ministries and was instrumental in founding the Reform Club. Noting Ellice's high political connections, Creevey portrayed him unflatteringly in 1836 as 'very vain (who is not?), he is a sieve, and so much the more agreeable for those who squeeze him'. His second marriage in 1843 to Thomas William Coke I's widow ended tragically with her death in late pregnancy the following year. Ellice died in his sleep (of angina) at Ardochy, Invernessshire, in September 1863, a week after presiding at a dinner to mark the completion of the Northern Railways. Obituarists recalled him as a gentleman of the 'Old School', as ready to advise on affairs of love as affairs of state.[107] To Le Marchant, he was

a general favourite in the House, his readiness to oblige being as remarkable as the extent of his influence and connections. Never, perhaps, had there been a more efficient and popular (political) secretary of the treasury. He was always a firm and consistent Liberal of the radical school ... His knowledge was not derived from books, for he was too fond of society to be a deep reader, but he had picked up much useful information on the questions of the day that most engaged public attention, and he could speak readily, fluently, and plausibly on them. Courage and dexterity supplied his deficiencies. A pleasant address, and an exemption from the social prejudices of the Whigs, told also in his favour. Altogether he was a most valuable member of the party. Careless of his own personal interests, his sagacity and independence gave him deserved weight, especially when out of office, with men in power. He suggested most of Lord Melbourne's appointments, and was concerned in many of Lord John Russell's.[108]

His will was sworn and administered by his only son and heir Edward Ellice (1810-80), Liberal Member for Huddersfield, 1837, and St. Andrews Burghs, 1837-80.

[1] *Oxford DNB.* [2] J.C. Clarke, 'The fortunes of the Ellice family: from business to politics, 1760-1860' (Oxf. Univ. D. Phil. thesis, 1974), 168-76. [3] *HP Commons, 1790-1820*, iii. 685-6. [4] NLI, Vesey Fitzgerald mss 7858, p. 169; Grey mss, Ellice to Grey, 4, 16 Mar.; NLS, Ellice mss, Grey to Ellice, 20 Mar. 1820; Broughton, *Recollections*, ii. 121; M.D. George, *Cat. of Personal and Pol. Satires*, x. 14039-43. [5] *Pol. Reg.* 25 Mar. 1820. [6] T. Carlyle, *Reminiscences* ed. C.E. Norton, 136; Brougham mss, autobiog. fragment. [7] *Scotsman*, 19 Sept. 1863; A. Aspinall, *Brougham and the Whig Party*, 263. [8] Grey mss, Ellice to Grey, 16, 31 Mar., 7 Apr. 1820. [9] Clarke, 96, 100-9, 177. [10] Grey mss, Ellice to Grey, 4 [June] 1821. [11] *Westminster Rev.* vi (June 1826), 123-31; Add. 36460, ff. 289-93; Broughton, iii. 74-75; George, x. 15146. See also R.E. Zegger, *Hobhouse*, 114-42. [12] *The Times*, 3 Mar. 1821. [13] Ibid. 27 Apr. 1825. [14] Brougham mss, Brougham to Grey, 1 June 1820. [15] Lambton mss. [16] Grey mss, Ellice to Grey, 29 Nov., 7 Dec. 1820. [17] Ibid. same to same, 4, 13, 14 Dec. 1820, 4, 6, 8, 11, 15 Jan. 1821; Broughton, ii. 139. [18] Grey mss, Ellice to Grey, 25 Sept., 13 Oct. 1821, 1, 14 Feb. 1822. [19] *The Times*, 15, 16 Feb. 1821 [20] HLRO, Hist. Coll. 379, Grey Bennet diary, 42; B. Hilton, *Corn, Cash, Commerce*, 136. [21] *The Times*, 20, 29 Mar., 6 Apr. 1821; Hilton, 133, 136. [22] *The Times*, 23, 26 June 1821. [23] Ibid. 21 June 1821. [24] Grey mss, Ellice to Grey, 4 Oct., 7, Dec. 1819, Apr. 1820. [25] Ibid. same to same, 13 Oct., 6 Nov., 13, 16, 22 Nov., 25, 26 Dec. 1821, 1, 4, 6, 10, 26 Jan., 1, 4, 14 Feb. 1822. [26] Ibid. same to same, 4, 23 Jan. [late Jan.] 1822. [27] Ibid. same to same [Feb. 1822]. [28] Ibid. same to same [Jan.]; *The Times*, 23 Feb. 1822. [29] Grey mss, Ellice to Grey [14 Feb. and n.d. 1822]; *The Times*, 23 Feb. 1822. [30] Ibid. 9, 12 Mar. 1822. [31] Bessborough mss F53. [32] Hilton, 162. [33] *The Times*, 14 May 1822. [34] Ibid. 7, 8 May 1822. [35] Ibid. 21, 25 June, 24 July; Grey mss, Ellice to Grey, 24 July 1822. [36] Grey mss, Ellice to Grey [Aug.], 24 Sept., 5 Oct. 1822. [37] Ibid. same to same, 7, 14, 21 Jan. 1823. See HEREFORDSHIRE. [38] Grey mss, Ellice to Grey, 15, 20, 26 Feb.; Ellice mss, Grey to Ellice, 23 Feb. 1823. [39] Coventry Local Stud. Lib. *Coventry Pamphlets*, v. [40] Grey mss, Ellice to Grey [8 July 1823]. [41] Ibid. same to same, 14, 15 Nov. 1823, 3 Feb., 6, 8, 11, 15 Mar., Ridley to Grey, 13 Mar. 1824. [42] Ibid. Ellice to Grey, 4-6 Feb. 1824. [43] Ibid. same to same, 27 Feb., 1 Mar. 1824. [44] Ibid. same to same, 11 Mar.; *The Times*, 9, 13 Mar. 1824. [45] *The Times*, 19 Mar. 1824. [46] Ibid. 13 Apr., 4 May 1824. [47] Ibid. 19 May 1824. [48] George, x. 14833; *The Times*, 14 Mar. 1825.

[49] Grey mss, Ellice to Grey, 9 Feb. 1825. [50] *The Times*, 7, 30 June 1825. [51] Add. 37863, f. 99. [52] Add. 36461, f. 203; Broughton, iii. 119-20; *Creevey Pprs.* ii. 93-94. [53] Grey mss, Ellice to Grey, 5, 18 Dec. 1825, 8, 20 Jan. 1826; Add. 36461, f. 326, 402. [54] Northants. RO, Agar Ellis diary, 2 Feb.; Add. 51580, Carlisle to Lady Holland, 5 Feb. 1826. [55] *Greville Mems.* i. 159-60; Wellington mss WP1/851/4; *The Times*, 15, 24 Feb. 1826. [56] *Arbuthnot Jnl.* ii, 17. [57] Grey mss, Ellice to Grey, 29 May, 5 June, reply, 29 May 1826. [58] *Coventry Herald*, 9, 23 June; *Coventry Mercury*, 26 June 1826. [59] *Ann. Reg.* (1826), Hist. pp. 371-6; Grey mss, Ellice to Grey, 1 Jan. 1827. [60] Grey mss, Ellice to Grey, 13 Aug., 29 Sept., 8 Oct., 1826, 15 Jan.; Ellice mss, replies, 7 Feb., 22 Oct. 1827. [61] Grey mss, Ellice to Grey, 23, 27 Sept. 1826, 11 June; Brougham mss, J. Brougham to Ellice, 9 Sept. 1827. [62] Grey mss, Ellice to Grey, 14 Nov. 1826, 8 Mar. 1827. [63] Ibid. same to same, 29 Sept. 1827, 12 Jan. 1828; Lambton mss, Ellice to Lambton, 3 Dec. 1827; *Canning's Ministry*, 344. [64] Lambton mss, Ellice to Lambton [13 Feb. 1828]; Ellice mss, Grey to Ellice, 24 Jan. 1830. [65] *PP* (1826-7), iv. 1117-19. [66] Grey mss, Ellice to Grey, Jan. 1828-June 1830, *passim.*; *Ellenborough Diary*, ii. 34. [67] Grey mss, Ellice to Grey, 18 Jan. 1830. [68] Ellice mss, Grey to Ellice, 6, 11, 17 Feb.; Grey mss, Howick jnl. 6, 21 Mar. 1830; A. Mitchell, *Whigs in Opposition*, 226-7. [69] Grey mss, Grey to Ellice, 14, 18 July; *Coventry Mercury*, 25 July, 1 Aug. 1830. [70] Grey mss, Ellice to Grey [Aug], 28 Oct; Ellice mss, replies, 5, 29 Oct. 1830; Aspinall, 184. [71] Grey mss. [72] *Three Diaries*, 25. [73] Grey mss, Ellice to Grey [Jan.] 1832. [74] *Greville Mems.* i. 159-60; ii. 75. [75] Agar Ellis diary, 9 Dec. 1830. [76] *Life of Campbell*, i. 500; *Three Diaries*, 299. [77] Broughton, iii. 78; Ellice mss, Ellice to Russell, 25 Dec., reply, 27 Dec. 1830; Vivian to Ellice, 9 Jan.; Brougham mss, Ellice to Brougham [4 Apr.] 1831. [78] *Three Diaries*, 66. [79] PRO NI, Anglesey mss D619/31D/27; *Cockburn Letters*, 299. [80] Le Marchant, *Althorp*, 303; Grey mss, Ellice to Grey [Apr. 1831]; *Oxford DNB*. [81] *Three Diaries*, 80. [82] Broughton, iii. 109; Le Marchant, 319; N. Gash, *Politics in Age of Peel*, 325-7. [83] Brougham mss, Ellice to Brougham, Monday [2 May 1831]. [84] N. LoPatin, 'Popular Politics in Midlands', *Midlands Hist.* xx (1995), 103-18. [85] Brougham mss, Ellice to Brougham [2 May 1831]. [86] Brougham mss. [87] Northumb. RO, Blackett-Ord mss 324/A/33. [88] Hatherton diary, 26 July 1831. [89] *Three Diaries*, 113. [90] Anglesey mss D619/27B, p. 52; NLW, Coedymaen mss 218. [91] Grey mss, Ellice to Grey, 31 May, Wed., various [autumn 1831]. [92] Agar Ellis diary, 29 Sept. 1831; *Three Diaries*, 146. [93] Devon RO, Earl Fortescue mss 1262M/FC 87. [94] NLS mss 24762, f. 49. [95] Add. 40402, ff. 2, 181. [96] *Three Diaries*, 184, 196-7; Grey mss, Ellice to Grey, 6 Feb. 1832. [97] *Croker Pprs.* ii. 150; *Baring Jnls.* i. 92. [98] Grey mss, Ellice to Grey, 10 Feb. 1832. [99] *Baring Jnls.* i. 93; *Greville Mems.* ii. 282. [100] Grey mss, Ellice to Grey, 10 Feb., 17 Apr. 1832. [101] Ibid. same to same, 1 July 1832; Le Marchant, 425; E.A. Smith, *Lord Grey*, 294-5. [102] Add. 51593, Hamilton Dalrymple to Holland, 24 May 1832. [103] Grey mss, Ellice to Grey, 17, 27 Mar., 17, 24 Apr., 27 July 1832. [104] Ibid. Ellice to Grey, 17, 27 Mar., 17, 24 Apr., 27 July 1832. [105] Add. 51588, Ellice to Lady Holland [3 Aug. 1832]. [106] Grey mss, Ellice to Grey, 10, 18, 31 Aug., 10, 17 Sept.; Cumb. RO, Sir James Graham mss D/GN3, Graham to Ellice, 21 Aug. 1832. [107] *Creevey Pprs.* ii. 309; *The Times*, 19 Sept.; *Revue des Deux Mondes*, 15 Oct. 1863. [108] Le Marchant, 489-90.

M.M.E.

ELLIS, Augustus Frederick (1800–1841).

SEAFORD	1826–Apr. 1827
SEAFORD	5 Sept. 1827–7 Mar. 1831

b. 17 Sept. 1800, 2nd s. of Charles Rose Ellis* (*d.* 1845) and 1st w. Elizabeth Catherine Caroline, da. of John Augustus Hervey, Lord Hervey. *educ.* Eton 1811-14. *m.* 25 June 1828, Mary Frances Thurlow, da. of Sir David Cunynghame, 5th bt., of Milncraig and Livingstone, Ayr, 2s. 3da. *d.v.p.* 16 Aug. 1841.

Cornet 9 Drag. 1817, lt. 1818; capt. (half-pay) 76 Ft. 1821; capt. 16 Drag. 1822; maj. (half-pay) 1825; maj. 60 Ft. 1826, lt.-col. 1828-d.

'Gussy' Ellis and his elder brother Charles Augustus, 6th Baron Howard de Walden, whose right to that title (claimed on the status of his maternal great-grandfather, the 4th earl of Bristol, as sole heir to it) had been confirmed in 1807, were with their father in Paris in 1817. Lady Granville thought them 'very handsome men, the second like his mother', dead for 14 years.[1] They both entered the army that year. Howard gave up his commission in the Grenadier Guards in October 1822, when he became a précis writer in the foreign office under their father's close friend and political mentor Canning. He was promoted to under-secretary in May 1824, resigned four years later and subsequently turned to diplomacy, holding senior posts in Sweden, Portugal and Belgium from 1832 until his death in 1868. Ellis was described in 1820 by George Agar Ellis, just returned with his father for Seaford, as 'a good looking, gentlemanlike youth of an amorous complexion'; but two years later Henry Fox* dismissed him as 'a bore'.[2] His father seems to have enlisted the aid of his fellow Canningite Huskisson, a member of the government, to pave the way for his promotion to a regimental captaincy in May 1822. He was in London in March 1824.[3]

At the general election of 1826 Ellis stood for Seaford on the interest of his father, who was about to be created Lord Seaford. He was returned with their coadjutor John Fitzgerald after a contest forced by two Whigs.[4] There is no trace of parliamentary activity before he vacated his seat in April 1827 to accommodate Canning on his appointment as prime minister. He resumed it on Canning's death only four months later, when he was 'with the British troops in Portugal'.[5] In November 1827 Lord Seaford, on the eve of going to Paris, wrote to Huskisson, the leader of the Canningite group:

> Let me refer you ... to Howard on the subject of Augustus's return to attend his duty in Parliament. Whenever you wish him to attend, he shall come over. But Howard will explain to you for what reasons it might be desirable for him to remain till his regiment returns, subject always, however, to your decision, on which side the balance preponderates.[6]

He was evidently summoned (as was his father) when Huskisson found himself under attack for taking office under the duke of Wellington, and was sworn in, 31 Jan. 1828. He voted with Huskisson against repeal of the Test Acts, 26 Feb. A month later Seaford asked him to urge Fitzgerald to pester ministers to secure a modification of a pending bill to amend the regulations governing assessment for the poor rates, which might adversely affect their borough interest.[7] He voted for Catholic relief, 12 May 1828, and after Huskisson's resignation from the ministry later that month, which prompted his brother's departure from the foreign office, was duly listed as one of the Canningite remnant. He was, however, a reluctant and ineffectual parliamentarian, whose attendance seems to have lapsed even more after his promotion to lieutenant-colonel of the 60th Royal Rifles in December 1828. He voted for Catholic emancipation, 6, 30 Mar., and the transfer of East Retford's seats to Birmingham, 5 May 1829, and against government on the question of British interference in Portugal, 10 Mar. 1830.

At the general election that summer he stood again with Fitzgerald for Seaford, where they were attacked by two strangers whose intrusion, though ostensibly aimed at Lord Seaford's electoral domination, was regarded as part of the Wellington ministry's vendetta against the Huskissonites. Criticized for failing to support the sale of beer bill, he was defended during the campaign by Fitzgerald, who said that Ellis had 'warmly approved of its principle'. He came second in the poll, but only four votes clear of one of the interlopers. In returning thanks, he brushed aside the charges of 'tyranny' levelled against his father and deplored 'the baseness of some old friends' who had encouraged the opposition. He confirmed that he would have supported the beer bill had he not been 'detained in Seaford by indisposition'. He also

> spoke with much warmth of feeling on the desire which existed in a certain quarter of sacrificing the remnants of a party, obnoxious because they were the friends of a deceased statesman; a dead set ... had been made at four or five Members, known to be favourable to his political views.[8]

Ministers listed him as one of 'the Huskisson party', and he was absent from the division on the civil list which brought them down, 15 Nov. 1830. Four months later, just after the Grey ministry's reform bill, which proposed the disfranchisement of Seaford, was made public, he was unseated on his opponents' petition. According to his father, Ellis, who 'dislikes Parliament as interfering with his military duties', immediately 'announced to his friends that he should not offer himself again as a candidate'. Lord Seaford commented that the election committee's decision

> though in one sense a disappointment, had its compensation, and, under all circumstances, one that was fully equivalent. It not only gave him a reason for withdrawing, but it relieved him from a very disagreeable dilemma,

of either voting for the disfranchisement of his constituents who had many of them supported him zealously and disinterestedly, or of opposing the government on a measure on which they staked their existence.

Accordingly he did not stand at the 1831 general election even though, so his father believed, he 'might ... have come in'.[9]

Had he survived his father, Ellis would have inherited 'the greatest portion' of his 'money in the funds'.[10] As it was, he died v.p. in August 1841 in Jamaica, where he was commanding the second battalion of his regiment: 'his death was accelerated by his indefatigable attention and anxiety to arrest the mortality which had already destroyed so many of his regiment'.[11] Administration of his estate, which was sworn under £4,000, was granted to his widow, 3 June 1842.[12] By his will of 1843 Seaford, in compliance with Ellis's dying request, bequeathed her a bust of her late husband by Chantray. Seaford, who had been paying her £300 a year to make up her jointure to £800 in accordance with her marriage settlement, released Ellis's estate from all claims in respect thereof.[13]

[1] *Countess Granville Letters*, i. 95. [2] Keele Univ. Lib. Sneyd mss SC8/43; *Fox Jnl.* 110. [3] Add. 38743, f. 26; TNA 30/29/9/5/22. [4] *Brighton Herald*, 3, 7 June 1826. [5] *The Times*, 10 Sept. 1827. [6] Add. 38752, f. 42. [7] Add. 38754, f. 234; 38755, f. 207. [8] *Brighton Herald*, 10, 17 July; *Brighton Guardian*, 14, 21 July, 4 Aug. 1830. [9] TNA 30/29/9/5/78, 81. [10] W. Suff. RO, Acc 941/56/30. [11] *Gent. Mag.* (1841), ii. 558. [12] PROB 6/218/42. [13] PROB 11/2023/670.

D.R.F.

ELLIS, **Charles Rose** (1771–1845), of 2 Audley Square, Mdx. and Seaford House, Suss.

HEYTESBURY	22 Mar. 1793–1796
SEAFORD	1796–1806
EAST GRINSTEAD	1807–1812
SEAFORD	1812–1826

b. 19 Dec. 1771, 2nd s. of John Ellis of Jamaica and Elizabeth, da. of John Pallmer, c.j. of Jamaica. *educ.* Christ Church, Oxf. 1789. *m.* (1) 2 Aug. 1798, Elizabeth Catherine Caroline (*d.* 21 Jan. 1803), da. and h. of John Augustus Hervey, Lord Hervey, 2s. (1 *d.v.p.*) 1da. *d.v.p.*; (2) 2 Oct. 1840, Anne Louisa Emily, da. of Hon. George Cranfield Berkeley[†], wid. of V.-Adm. Sir Thomas Masterman Hardy, 1st bt., *s.p. cr.* Bar. Seaford 15 July 1826. *d.* 1 July 1845.

Capt. St. James's vols. 1798.

Ellis was Canning's closest friend and most trusted political confidant. The owner of two Jamaican plantations, and chairman since 1810 of the committee of West India planters and merchants, he was 'the leader of the West India party' in the Commons.[1] Since 1815 he had lived mostly on the continent, accompanied by his two sons, whom he started in the army in 1817, and his sickly daughter, Eliza.[2] In November 1819 he was staying with his fellow-Canningite Huskisson at Eartham, Sussex. Four months later, from a base in Brighton, where Eliza was 'very, very ill', he presided over his unopposed re-election on his own interest for Seaford.[3] He did not immediately resume his parliamentary career, probably because of his daughter's illness, which terminated in her death, 18 Aug. 1820. In November Lady Granville, who thought him 'an angel of a man', was delighted to find him 'in such good spirits again'. 'If esteem is the measure of one's affection', she went on, 'there can be no bound to that he inspires. I think more highly of him than of anybody I know'.[4]

In October 1820 Ellis was advised by Canning, who consulted him on his personal embarrassment over the proceedings against Queen Caroline, that 'non-attendance would be the safest and most desirable course' when the bill of pains and penalties reached the Commons. He went with Canning to Walmer Castle in early December to air the problem with Lord Liverpool, his late wife's uncle; and although the premier initially persuaded Canning to delay his intended resignation, Ellis brought him to accept it as inevitable.[5] He found the queen's affair 'so disgusting a subject that one hates to enter upon it' and had 'some thoughts' of going to Paris with Canning in the first week of 1821.[6] After reconsideration, as he told Lord Granville, he 'determined to wait over the liturgy question'; and on 26 Jan. he replied to Hamilton's comments on Canning's resignation, vindicating it and vouching for his concurrence in the decision to omit the queen's name from the liturgy. The Whig George Howard* thought it 'a lame defence', and George Macpherson Grant* deemed it 'very unsatisfactory'.[7] Ellis voted against the opposition censure motion, 6 Feb. A fortnight later he was confident that even they, having 'worn the queen nearly threadbare', knew her 'game to be up'. At the same time he was worried, as he observed to Sir Charles Bagot, ambassador to Russia, that the issue of parliamentary reform was

> now assuming a formidable shape. Many of the country gentlemen, supporters of government, formerly anti-reformers, are now for a moderate reform 'for the sake of satisfying the country' (as if the reformers would be the dupes of a tinkering job of reformation!) But the real motive is funk, and that is a feeling so likely to spread and

to spread so wildly that I begin to think the reform question far more serious than I used.[8]

Ellis, who voted for Catholic relief, 28 Feb. 1821, had resumed the active chairmanship of the West India committee in January. He was one of the West Indian Members who presented a Jamaican petition for relief from distress to the king, 23 Feb., and he led the deputation which impressed on Liverpool and the chancellor Vansittart the need for adequate protection against East Indian sugar, 28 Mar.[9] He voted with government against repeal of the additional malt duty, 3 Apr., and the disfranchisement of ordnance officials, 12 Apr. At about this time he reintroduced Canning to Holland House (Ellis had been brought up in Jamaica with Lady Holland), where he had not been for 15 years.[10] He was given a month's leave to attend to 'urgent private business', 30 Apr. 1821. 'Astounded' to learn from Canning in November that the only question under discussion with Liverpool was whether or not he should take the governor-generalship of India, he had 'scarcely a doubt' that he would turn it down. Unlike Canning, he thought Liverpool would then be obliged to make him 'another offer' more calculated to 'answer the purpose of remedying the inconvenience of his out of office position in the House of Commons'.[11]

Ellis voted against more extensive tax reductions, 21 Feb., and abolition of one of the joint-postmasterships, 12 Mar. 1822. He spoke of 'the severe distress under which the colonies now laboured', 20 Mar., and seconded a motion for a return of senior West Indian appointments, 22 Mar. That day he chaired the meeting of the West India committee which adopted a petition complaining of distress, and he duly presented it and had it referred to the foreign trade committee (of which he was a regular member), 28 Mar.[12] On Hume's motion for inquiry into the government of the Ionian Islands, 14 May, he, Canning and Huskisson were reported to have 'walked out of the House shortly before the division, in a manner which seemed to indicate a wish rather to challenge observation than avoid it'.[13] He argued that a lessening of West Indian protection against East Indian sugar would be 'the ruin of those who had virtually abolished the slave trade', 17 May, and he presented petitions against equalization of the duties, 31 May, 3 June.[14] Later that month and in July he was centrally involved in unsuccessful negotiations with ministers for measures to relieve distress.[15] He was in the minority of 21 in favour of the export of flour ground from bonded corn, 10 June, but he voted with ministers against repeal of the salt duties, 28 June, and for the Canada bill, 18 July 1822.

Ellis considered that the rumoured offer of the exchequer to Canning after Lord Londonderry's* suicide would be 'little short of an insult'. On his acceptance of the foreign office, where Ellis's elder son Charles Augustus, Lord Howard de Walden, was taken on as a précis writer in October 1822, Ellis and Granville were said to have persuaded him to tone down his 'violent and indignant' letter of acceptance to the king.[16] During the autumn and early winter he was tormented by 'intolerable aching pain' in his leg, which not only crippled him and confined him to London, but made it impossible for him to sleep in a horizontal position. He was on the mend by late December 1822, when he helped Canning, with whose schemes to remodel the government he was au fait, to make the disgruntled Huskisson swallow his exclusion from the cabinet. He also lent himself to Canning's abortive bid to take from Robinson, the new chancellor of the exchequer, the Downing Street house which went with the job.[17]

Ellis, who was asked by Canning to disseminate his view that further 'interference' after the unanimity shown on the address, 4 Feb., would precipitate war between France and Spain, voted with government against parliamentary reform, 20 Feb., and on the sinking fund, 3 Mar. 1823. It was said that his frequenting of Holland House fuelled suspicions of Canning among some of his ministerial colleagues.[18] He was much exercised early in 1823 with the problem of East Indian sugar and its threat to the West Indian economy and the campaign for the abolition of slavery. He had interviews with Liverpool, 20, 28 Feb., and chaired a general public meeting of the West India interest, 12 Mar., when a petition was adopted.[19] In the House, 3 Mar., he denied the free traders' allegation that ministers were pledged to equalize the duties; and on 19 Mar. he presented petitions against it from Antigua, Barbados and Montserrat. He was largely satisfied with the government's agreement to maintain the level of protection on the 1814 basis for the term of the East India Company's charter; but he warned Huskisson, now president of the board of trade, of

the growing discontent among the proprietors in the colonies ... [which] has already arrived at the point that there exists an almost unanimous feeling, that no colonies are so much oppressed as the British. And when to this feeling, with reference to the unproductiveness of their property, shall be added the apprehensions of its insecurity in consequence of the announced systematic attack of the emancipators, I fear little would be wanting but the opportunity to induce all the resident proprietors, with the concurrence too of many of the absentees, to connect themselves with any country strong enough to protect them.

Personally, he 'could never reconcile myself to being, or making Howard, a Yankee'; and, to counteract the 'mischief' of the abolitionists' campaign, he wished ministers to take 'the inquiry into and the improvement of the condition of the negroes into their own hands'.[20] He was made chairman of the West India subcommittee on the amelioration of slavery, 25 Apr. 1823.[21] He voted against repeal of the Foreign Enlistment Act, 16 Apr., and inquiry into the prosecution of the Dublin Orange rioters, 22 Apr. In a substantial speech on Buxton's motion for the abolition of slavery, 15 May, he put the case for the planters, who had merely inherited a system sanctioned in law by successive governments and Parliaments. Warning of the perils of hasty emancipation by 'compulsory enactments', he advocated careful preparation of the slaves by education and religious instruction. He denied that colonial legislatures had been 'culpably slow' in implementing amelioration, though he admitted that 'the sanguine expectations' which had informed his own motion of 1797 on this subject had not been realized. He said that the owners would concur in 'every fair and reasonable proposal' for amelioration, blamed the lax morals and irreligion of Caribbean society on the corruption of the colonial church establishment and supported Canning's counter-resolutions for amelioration and cautious progress to emancipation. After presenting petitions from London West India merchants against equalization, 22 May, he led the opposition to Wolryche Whitmore's call for inquiry into the sugar duties, arguing his case as a question of simple justice to the West Indies which went to the core of colonial policy. He voted against Scottish parliamentary reform, 2 June, and inquiry into chancery delays, 5 June 1823.

Ellis showed his characteristic generosity of spirit in asking Liverpool to provide one George Ricketts, for whom he had secured an offer of the command of a boat in the Irish preventative service, with an alternative post which would not expose his war wound to 'severe weather'; but Liverpool, less inclined to 'charity', gave him short shrift.[22] Though still handicapped by his leg he was able to go with Canning to Lord Morley's at Saltram in October 1823. Increasingly concerned at the state of the West Indian colonies, he corresponded with Lord Holland on how to encourage the implementation of measures of amelioration in Jamaica.[23] He chaired a meeting of the West India committee, 21 Nov., held to adopt resolutions, which he transmitted to ministers, drawing attention to the 'awful warning' of the slave insurrection in Demerara and pressing them to repudiate the calumnies of the abolitionists, reform the colonial church establishment and guarantee adequate compensation in the event of emancipation.[24] As he subsequently told Lady Holland, he had 'a very difficult job' in 'preventing the calling of a general meeting, for discussing and ordering the publication of a very indiscreet set of resolutions professing to be an exposition of our case'. Although he had done 'tolerably well' from that year's sugar crop, he was made uneasy by

> a very bad spirit among the whole people, which was not wanting to render the disposition of the negroes sufficiently alarming, and which will increase the danger in that quarter, while it will embarrass us in fighting our battle in Parliament and will have the effect of rendering our countrymen in England less temperate and discreet than they were last year.[25]

Ellis led deputations to government on the 'agitated state' of the West Indies and the economic difficulties of the planters early in 1824. He chaired a public meeting at the *London Tavern*, 10 Feb., when he moved the adoption of an address to the king asserting the proprietors' property rights and entitlement to compensation if they were violated.[26] He voted against reform of Edinburgh's representation, 26 Feb., but, he told Granville, 'my amusement has been chiefly in the line of sugars and rums'. He welcomed the government's concession on the latter, at which some West Indians were inclined to look askance, 8 Mar., 9 Apr.[27] He had privately expressed willingness to 'change situations with a negro slave' for the day of the debate on Canning's proposals for amelioration, 16 Mar.; but he answered Buxton with a forceful restatement of the planters' case. While he emphasized their readiness to co-operate, already formally signified to ministers, he attacked the abolitionists for creating the current climate of unrest which made safe progress difficult. The 'only sure foundation', he contended, was the government's scheme for improvement by religious instruction, founded on reform of the church establishment. He raised minor objections to the proposal to admit slaves as witnesses and more serious ones to that to confer compulsory powers for the purchase of freedoms. To Granville he commented that Canning's opening speech had been 'a masterpiece of dexterity and discretion', though he regretted his characteristic indulgence in his 'talent of ridicule' by 'quizzing our colonial assemblies', which was 'calculated to produce bad blood'. On the whole, however, he thought that 'all the principles and doctrines which he laid down were so sound and discreet, that it has given the greatest satisfaction to moderate and disinterested people, and my countrymen forgive the manner for the sake of the matter'.[28] He welcomed the bill to incorporate the West India Company, 10 May, as 'an admirable means for the employment of barren capital' which would 'diffuse more widely a sense of the importance of the West India islands'. He deemed the case of the prosecution of the missionary John Smith for inciting rebellion among slaves in Demerara to be an issue 'between the Methodists and the government, in which we [the West Indians] are not implicated': and he gave a silent vote against Brougham's censure motion, 11 June.[29] He voted for the Irish insurrection bill, 14 June 1824, and, pleased with Howard's recent promotion to under-secretary, contemplated the end of 'the shortest and most successful session that I remember since I have been in Parliament'.[30]

Ellis visited Granville at The Hague in July and August 1824. In mid-October he was at Seaford, whence he sent to Huskisson a letter from George Hibbert[†], the agent for Jamaica, asking him to urge government to authorize the temporary use of molasses in the distilleries. Huskisson had no personal objections but pointed out the practical difficulties, which Ellis, who had little enthusiasm for the idea, thought would strengthen his hand when it was discussed by the West India committee. He chaired its meetings of 22 Oct. and 3 Dec. 1824, and led a deputation which made an unsuccessful approach to ministers on the subject in February 1825.[31] He protested against any violation of the 'solemn compact' on the East Indian sugar duties, 18 Mar. 1825, and expressed anxieties about the government's plans for those on rum and brown sugar. Despite his 'surprise' at the projected reduction of duty on Mauritian sugar, he generally welcomed Huskisson's plans to remove restrictions on West Indian trade, 21 Mar., as likely to stimulate the colonial economies and create the prosperity and tranquillity essential to emancipation. He supported the West India Company bill, 16 May, but on 3 June deplored the Mauritius trade bill which, by placing on the same footing as West Indian sugar the produce of a country where the slave trade had been notoriously carried on, would have an 'injurious' moral effect. He voted for the Irish unlawful societies bill, 25 Feb., Catholic relief, 1 Mar., 21 Apr., 10 May, and for the duke of Cumberland's grant, 10 June 1825.

Ellis was host to Canning at Seaford in November 1825, when he again discussed with Holland the problems of implementing amelioration in Jamaica, before going to Paris for Christmas.[32] He was not surprised that the threatened opposition of 'the commercial and banking supporters of government' to the emergency bank restriction bill in February 1826 turned out to be 'only a bubble'; but he acknowledged that 'the distress *is really* very great'. Much of his own time was taken up with West Indian matters, though 'not to ... good purpose'. He conferred with ministers on the planters' worries over the intensive anti-slavery agitation, 21 Feb.[33] He voted silently with government on the Jamaican slave trials, 2 Mar.; but, as he wrote to Granville, he felt that

> our slavery debates have been far from satisfactory. The Jamaica trials were a terrible case, and, what rendered it provoking, as well as mischievous in its effect, if the colonial office had expressed a single word of disapprobation of what, when brought before Parliament, they could not defend, or had taken a single spontaneous step towards reforming the state of the laws which they now agree cannot be tolerated, no parliamentary attack could have been made. The Saints feel they have gained so much ground that they have announced their intention of renewing their attacks after Easter.[34]

Ellis, who voted against reform of Edinburgh's representation, 13 Apr., said that proprietors generally 'treated slaves with kindness and humanity' in the debate on alleged maltreatment in Berbice and Demerara, 20 Apr. He argued that when they did not they were 'subject to the control and animadversion of Parliament', insisted on their right to 'adequate compensation' and pointed out that for all the 'disgust and horror' rightly excited by the Berbice evidence, further investigation had revealed that there had been only 67 genuine cases of abuse in 14 years. Fearing that 'the remainder of the session seems to be intended to be employed very much in attacks on us devoted West Indians', he privately applauded Canning's conciliatory declaration of 20 Apr. that the proceedings of the Anti-Slavery Society were a hindrance to government and that there was no hidden agenda behind the amelioration proposals contained in the order in council of 1824. This, he observed to John Allen

> ought to induce the West Indians to adopt those measures, for the sake of afterwards gaining the support of the government in opposition to the Saints. But whether my countrymen will have the sense and temper to feel the expediency of this compromise is more than I can venture to expect, though I am not quite without a hope.[35]

In his last known speech in the Commons, which he had separately published, Ellis answered Brougham's attack on the slow progress of amelioration, 19 May 1826. He did so not as 'the indiscriminating champion of the colonial legislatures', for he had been personally criticized for interfering by the Jamaican assembly; but he defended their record, appealed to them to meet Canning half way and ended by quoting Fox's pronouncement that unilaterally imposed emanci-

pation would be 'mischievous'. A week later he was genuinely surprised to be informed by Canning that he was to be offered a peerage, which Canning had requested in response to the king's expressed wish to mark his appreciation of his services. As Canning wanted nothing for himself, he had nominated Ellis as the 'person who after my own family is the nearest to me in the world'. After 24 hours' consideration Ellis accepted, opting for the title of Seaford.[36] He did so with a pleasure which gives the lie to Lady Carlisle's speculation that he and his sons did not 'much like' it, which 'some people say Canning merely does ... to show his power'. Greville wrote sourly that 'everybody cries out against it': as Ellis 'has no property, and is of no family, and his son is already a peer', it 'is thought very ridiculous and that he would have done much better to have declined it'.[37] In anticipation, Ellis retired from the Commons at the dissolution and returned his younger son for Seaford.

He remained active for several years in the Lords and on the West India committee, despite telling Bagot in October 1827 that 'the dreadful catastrophe' of Canning's death had robbed him of 'all interest in politics for the future', beyond a wish to ensure that 'those who created the difficulties and the worries which wore him out might not have the triumph of gratifying their spite, or succeeding in their speculations'.[38] In February 1828 he left Paris in response to a summons from Huskisson, who was under fire from some Canningites for taking office with Wellington. He defended the decision in the Lords, 25 Feb., and in London society, having at least one 'pretty violent altercation' over the dinner table with Lord George Cavendish Bentinck*, Canning's nephew.[39] Later that year Howard married Cavendish Bentinck's sister Lucy, whom Seaford provided with a jointure of £2,000, secured partly on her own fortune and partly on one of his Jamaican estates.[40] He was a pragmatic supporter of the Grey ministry's reform bills and reconciled himself without too much difficulty to the disfranchisement of his borough, where his son was in any case ousted on petition in March 1831: the first bill, though flawed, was not

> revolutionary in the sense of a tendency to convulsion or anarchy, for it takes property and a higher rate of qualification than formerly as the basis of representation, and gives nothing [to] and takes away prospectively much direct influence from the rabble.[41]

He was 'a great sufferer' by the slave insurrection in Jamaica in late December 1831; but, according to Holland, he bore the 'cruel misfortunes' of this and his elder brother John's death in February 1832 with 'unaffected calmness and philosophy'.[42] He visited Jamaica in 1833-4 to survey the damage and adopted his agent's scheme to repair the sugar works on the New Montpelier estate and convert the Old into a breeding ground for working cattle. He expected an immediate loss of £10,000 and that the single plantation would yield at best two thirds of the crops of the two; but he hoped that this streamlining and other economies would ensure that 'the future ultimate loss' would 'not be considerable to those who come after me, if indeed property of any sort should be allowed to last so long in this country'.[43] He was reported to have declined the government of Canada in 1835.[44]

Since at least 1826 Seaford, a widower for 23 years, had been paying court at Dieppe, Brighton and other resorts to Lady Hardy, 17 years his junior, the estranged wife of Nelson's comrade in arms. Hardy died in 1839 and the following year Seaford married his 'droll' widow, who brought him three stepdaughters.[45] He subsequently rented from Lady Georgiana Bathurst a house at Woodend, near Chichester, where he took 'quiet enjoyment' in 'solitude'.[46] He died there in July 1845. By his will, dated 7 Sept. 1843 and proved under £20,000, he left his wife, who lived until 1877, an immediate legacy of £500, confirmed her jointure and gave her the option of continuing to reside rent free at Woodend. He released the Old Montpelier estate from all claims other than those of his wife, provided for the widow of his younger son, who had died in 1841, and devised his plantations, Seaford property and town house in Audley Square to Howard, now a diplomat, in whose title the barony of Seaford merged.[47]

[1] Session of Parl. 1825, p. 462. [2] Countess Granville Letters, i. 95. [3] Add. 51818, Ellis to Holland, 12 Nov. 1819; Harewood mss HAR/GC/26, Canning to wife, 9, 18 Feb.; Keele Univ. Lib. Sneyd mss SC8/43; Northants. RO, Agar Ellis diary, 3-6 Mar. [1820]. [4] Bagot, Canning and Friends, ii. 101; Countess Granville Letters, i. 190; ii. 14. [5] W. Yorks AS (Leeds), Stapleton mss, Canning to Ellis, 14 Oct. 1820; Add. 38742, f. 85; TNA 30/29/9/5/12, 13; Arbuthnot Corresp. 18; J. E. Cookson, Lord Liverpool's Administration, 288-9. [6] Bagot, ii. 106-7; Harewood mss 26, Canning to wife, 13, 19 Dec. 1820. [7] TNA 30/29/9/5/14; Geo. IV Letters, ii. 895; Castle Howard mss, Howard to Lady Morpeth, 28 [Jan.]; Macpherson Grant mss 361, Macpherson Grant to Lady Stafford, 27 Jan. 1821. [8] Cumbria RO, Bagot mss, Ellis to Bagot, 23 Feb. 1821. [9] Inst. of Commonwealth Stud. M915/3/4/457, 479, 481-2; J.L. Ragatz, British Caribbean Hist. 145; Add. 38744, ff. 153, 155. [10] Lord Ilchester, Home of Hollands, 251; Fox Jnl. 66. [11] Add. 38743, f. 26. [12] The Times, 23, 29 Mar. 1822; Inst. of Commonwealth Stud. M915/4/1/1-2, 4. [13] The Times, 23 May 1822. [14] Ibid. 1 June 1822. [15] Inst. of Commonwealth Stud. M915/4/1/30, 33-34, 38-39, 41-42, 46-48. [16] TNA 30/29/9/5/15; Greville Mems. i. 133. [17] TNA 30/29/9/3/9; 29/9/5/15-20; Add. 38296, f. 395; 38743, f. 279; Hobhouse Diary, 101-2. [18] Add. 38568, f. 118; Grey mss, Lambton to Grey, 13 Feb. 1823. [19] Inst. of Commonwealth Stud. M915/4/1/73, 76, 80, 96-97, 114; The Times, 4 Mar. 1823. [20] Add. 38744, ff. 151, 194-203. [21] Inst. of Commonwealth Stud. M915/4/1/114. [22] Add. 38296, ff. 395-400; 38297, ff. 9, 39, 146. [23] Add. 51818, Ellis to Holland, 10, 13, 18 Oct. 1823. [24] Inst. of Commonwealth Stud. M915/4/1/138; Add. 40359, ff. 58-63. [25] Add. 51818, Ellis to Lady Holland, 4 Dec. 1823. [26] Inst. of Commonwealth Stud. M915/4/1/150-3, 158, 159, 162, 164, 172; The Times, 11 Feb. 1824; TNA 30/29/9/5/21. [27] The Times, 10 Apr. 1824; Inst. of Commonwealth Stud. M915/4/1/177-80. [28] TNA 30/29/9/5/21, 22, 24. [29] Ibid. 29/9/5/32. [30] Ibid. 29/9/5/33, 34. [31] Add. 38746, ff. 15, 36, 38, 40, 44; TNA 30/29/9/5/34, 35; Inst. of Commonwealth Stud. M915/4/1/241, 268, 272. [32] Bagot, ii. 296; Add. 51818, Ellis to Holland, 24 Nov. 1825; Lady Holland to Son, 42; TNA 30/29/9/5/37. [33] TNA 30/29/9/5/38; Inst. of Commonwealth Stud. M915/4/1/317. [34] TNA 30/29/9/5/39. [35] Add. 52195, Ellis to Allen, 25 Apr. 1826. [36] Geo. IV Letters, iii. 1235, 1243; Bagot, ii. 350-2; Add. 38301, ff. 213, 231. [37] Castle Howard mss, Lady Carlisle to Morpeth, 1 June [1826]; Greville Mems. i. 160-1. [38] Add. 38749, f. 312; 38752, f. 42; TNA 30/29/9/5/48; Bagot, ii. 425-7. [39] Add. 38754, ff. 234, 279; Countess Granville Letters, ii. 5, 10; Colchester Diary, iii. 549-50; Greville Mems. i. 205-6. [40] Suff. RO (Bury St. Edmunds), Hervey mss Acc. 941/56/30, Seaford to Bristol [12 Oct.1828]. [41] TNA 30/29/9/5/78, 81. [42] Holland House Diaries, 60, 137; Add. 51818, Seaford to Holland, 10, 13 Dec. 1831. [43] Add. 51818, Seaford to Holland, 2 Aug. 1833-14 Oct. 1834; Hervey mss 56/30, to Bristol, 16 Aug. 1833. [44] Holland House Diaries, 298. [45] Add. 52017, J. R. Townshend to H. E. Fox, 9 Nov. 1826; TNA 30/29/9/5/47, 49, 50, 58, 131; Lady Holland to Son, 89; Countess Granville Letters, ii. 293, 312; Ilchester, Chrons. Holland House, 271-2; Lieven-Palmerston Corresp. 190. [46] Add. 51818, Seaford to Lady Holland, 18 Oct. 1843. [47] Gent. Mag. (1845), ii. 419-20; PROB 11/2023/670; IR26/1722/642.

D.R.F.

ELLIS, Henry (1788–1855).

BOSTON   1820–16 Feb. 1821

b. 1 Sept. 1788,[1] illegit. s. of Robert Hobart†, 4th earl of Buckinghamshire (d. 1816).[2] educ. Harrow 1799-1803;[3] by William Nicholson of Soho Square, Mdx. 1804-5;[4] Fort William Coll. Calcutta 1805.[5] m. 10 June 1820, at Cape Town, Louisa Amelia Wilson of Leominster, Herefs., 3s.[6] KCB 27 Apr. 1848. d. 28 Sept. 1855.

Writer E.I. Co. (Bengal) 1805; asst. to sec. of secret, political and foreign depts. 1807, to Lt.-Col. John Malcolm* on Persian expedition 1808; head asst. to dep.-sec. of secret, political and foreign depts. 1809; first asst. to resident at Poonah 1810; res. 1811.

Private sec. to pres. Bengal bd. of control 1812-14; plenip. to Persia 1814; sec. during Anglo-American negotiations 1815; third commr. in Lord Amherst's embassy to China 1816-17; dep. colonial sec. and commr. of stamps, Cape Colony 1819-21; commr. of customs 1824-5; clerk of the pells 1825-34; commr. bd. of control Dec. 1830-Dec. 1834; PC 11 July 1832; ambassador to Persia 1835-6; spec. mission to Brazil 1842-3; attended Brussels conference on affairs of Italy 1848.

Ellis was born in Dublin, the illegitimate son of Robert Hobart, chief secretary to the Irish viceroy, 1789-93. Hobart had already fathered one natural son, Charles, and it seems likely that both boys were the product of his liaison with Margaretta, the wife of Thomas Adderley. After Adderley's death they married in 1792, prompting Lady Holland to remark that Hobart had 'exhibited his high sense of a *point d'honnour*'.[7] Charles and Henry could trace their patronym to Sir Richard Ellys[†] who, on dying without issue in 1742, had bequeathed his Nocton estates near Lincoln to his distant relations the Hobarts. They entered Harrow in September 1799, but Charles left after only four terms to prepare himself for entry to the East India Company's service and joined the Fort St. George establishment as a writer late in 1801. (He was dismissed from the service in disgrace in 1822.) Henry left Harrow at the end of the summer term of 1803 and was coached in 'mathematical and other studies' for a year before successfully petitioning to join the Bengal establishment. On arrival at Calcutta he enrolled at Fort William College, where he was grounded in Hindustani, Persian, Arabic and Sanskrit. He left in 1807 to take on the first of a number of junior civil service posts. He resigned from the Company's service in 1811 but stayed in India and the following year, when his father, now earl of Buckinghamshire, became president of the board of control, he was appointed secretary to the president of the board at Calcutta. His linguistic and diplomatic skills secured him the post of plenipotentiary to Persia in 1814, and the following year he helped to negotiate the Anglo-American peace treaty. When Lord Amherst was asked to head an embassy to China Ellis was appointed public secretary with the official rank of third commissioner.[8] Their ship, the *Alceste*, left England in February 1816 and a year later, returning home after a largely unsuccessful mission, was wrecked off Borneo. As one of the survivors, Ellis accompanied Amherst and a skeleton crew in an open boat to Java, whence they returned in the East Indiaman *Ternate* to rescue the remaining crew.[9] On the voyage home a visit was paid to St. Helena, where Ellis conversed with Buonaparte on a variety of topics. According to one biographer, Buonaparte was later incensed by a passage in Ellis's account of the embassy to China, published in 1817, in which he accused Buonaparte of revelling in the annoyance caused by his complaints about accommodation. He even went so far as to suggest that 'some commis to Lord Bathurst', the colonial secretary, had invented the offending passage and 'imposed the insertion of it' on Ellis.[10]

Four days before Ellis had embarked for China his father had died, leaving all the unentailed Hobart properties to his legitimate daughter Sarah, who had married Frederick John Robinson* in 1814. Ellis and his brother each received a mere £25 annuity from Nocton rents.[11] In an attempt to mend his fortunes, and with the backing of Robinson, who had just been appointed president of the board of trade, Ellis canvassed Boston as the Pink candidate early in 1818. Robinson wrote to Lord Liverpool, the premier, on the eve of the general election anticipating success and requesting that Ellis, as a 'steady friend' of government, be considered for a post 'compatible with a seat in Parliament'. Liverpool, however, dismissed Ellis as a 'political adventurer' and suggested that he apply directly to government departments.[12] His opponents at Boston also regarded him with suspicion. After accusing him of being a placeman willing to pay £3,000 for a seat they published a report of an address in which he had attacked his enemies for wishing 'to make Boston the theatre of those scenes of blood and murder which were excited in the streets of Paris by Jacobin tunes'. When cornered Ellis admitted his ministerial allegiance, prompting the Blues to dub this 'China lemon' a 'treasury tool'. He finished bottom of the poll, blaming 'turn-coats' for his failure, but vowed to return.[13] Early in 1819 he secured the post, worth £1,500 a year, of deputy colonial secretary at the Cape, where he arrived in July. For the next 18 months, under the governor Lord Charles Somerset[†], whose son he had accompanied in China, he worked among the settlers, particularly those at Algoa Bay.[14]

At the 1820 general election he was solicited by the Pinks to stand again for Boston, despite objections from some of their supporters to his absence on unspecified 'engagements abroad'. His agent John Macleod, ship's surgeon on the China mission, repeatedly denied allegations that as a placeman with a 'snug situation' at the Cape he was unlikely to appear, and after a two-day poll he was returned in second place.[15] His defeated opponent, William Johnson*, petitioned against his return, claiming that it was invalid because at the time he held an office of profit under the crown. In debate on 25 and 26 May 1820 the minister Thomas Courtenay argued that Ellis should be given more time to appear and defend himself, but William Williams replied that the country could not wait and Sir Robert Heron contended that the dey of Algiers was as eligible to sit for Old Sarum as Ellis was to represent Boston. The Whigs George Tierney and Henry Brougham agreed with the foreign secretary Lord Castlereagh that it was impossible to prove that Ellis had held a crown office on the day of his return. The matter rested there until 31 Jan. 1821, when Johnson reintroduced his petition. An election committee was appointed and Ellis was deemed ineligible and unseated, 16 Feb. 1821.[16]

He left the Cape, 3 Mar. 1821, and seems not to have returned there, although by the following December he had negotiated the purchase of a government farm in the colony yielding annual rents of 640 rix dollars.[17] During Robinson's tenure of the exchequer from 1823 he was appointed first a commissioner of customs and then clerk of the pells at £3,000 a year. He gave evidence before select committees on the East India Company in the summer of 1830 and published his observations, which included a recommendation that its exclusive privileges be abandoned, in *A Series of Letters on the East India Question* (1830). When Robinson, now Lord Goderich, became colonial secretary in the Grey ministry, Ellis was appointed a commissioner of the board of control. In June 1831 Goderich included him in the emigration committee and in November recommended him to Grey for the new life appointment of comptroller general of the exchequer, following the proposed reorganization of that department. Goderich argued that not only was Ellis the fittest candidate in terms of experience, but that he had shown 'an indefatigable zeal and activity in support of the present government'. Moreover

> he lives amongst a great variety of society: he is much connected with the literary people of the day, amongst whom (and they are by no means an unimportant class) *I know* that he has fought *our battle*, not only upon reform, but upon the *general policy and conduct* with no common earnestness and success.[18]

Grey evidently consented, but when the exchequer was revamped in 1834 he went back on his word and installed Sir John Newport* as comptroller. Goderich, now earl of Ripon, remonstrated in vain, but Grey did concede that Ellis should be compensated for the loss of his office, which was abolished in the reorganization.[19] According to Ripon, Ellis's departure from the board of control followed his own resignation from the ministry in May 1834, but Ellis seems to have remained nominally in office until the incoming Conservative ministry ejected him in December. In July 1835 he was appointed ambassador to Persia, but he was recalled in November 1836, and Ripon later complained bitterly to Lord Aberdeen of the Melbourne ministry's 'unjust treatment' of Ellis 'in respect to the Persian mission'.[20] At the 1837 general election Ellis, with Ripon's backing, stood as a Conservative for Lincoln, where he was described as 'a half-and-half Liberal of the Stanley school'.[21] He was unsuccessful, and a disappointed Ripon recommended him to Sir Robert Peel as a 'very useful assistant' in the event of some 'accidental vacancy' occurring.[22] When Ripon returned to office with the Conservatives in 1841, he persuaded

Lord Aberdeen, the foreign secretary, to allow Ellis to head a trade delegation to the Brazils, maintaining that no other diplomat knew more of 'the true principles of commercial policy'. He concluded his testimony by acknowledging a friendship with Ellis of 40 years, adding, 'as I owe so much of my actual position in the world to the generosity of his father, I have always felt myself bound to do what I could, to help him in his course through life'.[23] Ellis received a knighthood and a pension of £1,400 on his retirement from the diplomatic service, to go with the pension awarded in compensation for his abolished office. He died at his home in Brighton in September 1855.[24]

[1] BL OIOC J/1/19, f. 224. [2] Add. 43547, f. 185. [3] Harrow School Archives. [4] OIOC J/1/19, f. 225. [5] *Bengal Past and Present*, xxiv (1922), 114, 124. [6] P. Philip, *British Residents at the Cape*, 115; PROB 11/2220/834. [7] *Holland Jnl.* i. 236. [8] OIOC J/1/18, ff. 294-8. [9] *Ann. Reg.* (1817), Chron. pp. 432-49 contains a full account of the shipwreck extracted from John McLeod's *Voyage of the Alceste* (1817). [10] B. O'Meara, *Napoleon in Exile*, ii. 404-6. [11] PROB 11/1578/121. [12] Add. 38270, ff. 306, 321. [13] *Hist. Boston Election* (Boston, 1818), *passim*. [14] Ellis, *Jnl. of Embassy to China*, 18. [15] *Late Election for Boston* (Boston, 1820), 9, 25, 27, 32. [16] *CJ*, lxxv. 155, 213, 238, 245, 389; lxxvi. 18, 73-77. [17] *Recs. Cape Colony* ed. G. Theal, xiv. 187-8. [18] Grey mss, Goderich to Grey, 20 Nov. 1831. [19] Add. 40863, ff. 78, 112. [20] Add. 43072, f. 195. [21] *The Times*, 15 May 1837. [22] Add. 40424, f. 8. [23] Add. 43072, f. 195. [24] *The Times*, 5 Oct. 1855.

R.M.H./P.J.S.

ELLIS, Thomas (1774–1832), of Abbeyfeale, co. Limerick and 9 Merrion Square, Dublin.

DUBLIN   30 June 1820–1826

b. 10 June 1774,[1] 1st s. of Capt. Richard Ellis of Abbeyfeale and Youghal, co. Cork and Mary, da. of Robert Hilliard of co. Kerry. *educ.* Trinity, Dublin 1790; I. Temple 1793, called [I] 1796. *m.* 3 Dec. 1804, Dymphna, da. of Col. William Thomas Monsell of Tervoe, co. Limerick, 4s. *suc.* fa. 1814. *d.* 26 Jan. 1832.
Master in chancery [I] 1806-*d.*

Ellis was descended from Thomas Ellis of county Monaghan, who was attainted in the reign of James II, married twice and died in 1714. The third son of his first marriage, Richard Ellis of Monaghan and Drumnalee, county Cavan, died in 1774, leaving two sons, Thomas, who died without issue in 1790, and Richard, born in 1738, the father of this Member. He became an ensign in the 66th Regiment in 1758, was promoted to lieutenant in 1760, to captain in 1771 and to major in the army in 1782. He appears to have retired about two years later. He married in November 1770 Mary Hilliard of Kerry, acquired an estate in county Limerick and died in 1814. His third son

Conyngham (1783-1815) entered the army and died of wounds received at Waterloo; and the youngest, Henry (1784-1857), joined the navy. Thomas Ellis, the eldest son, was bred to the Irish bar, to which he was called in 1796. Ten years later, with the blessing of the Grenville ministry, he bought from the incumbent Thomas Walker one of the four Irish masterships in chancery for £9,850, a price, he told the Irish judicial commissioners in 1815, based on an estimated annual income of about £3,000 in fees. In 1821 a hostile radical publication put his earnings at £4,410 a year.[2] Ellis drew attention to himself politically in Dublin on 11 Feb. 1819 when, at the *Rotunda* meeting of Protestants to petition for Catholic relief, he seconded Lord Frankfort's unsuccessful wrecking amendment and provoked outrage with his allegation that signatures had been obtained for the requisition 'by interest ... fear ... private friendship ... [and] threats'.[3] He subsequently served at least once on the committee of the Grand Orange Lodge of Ireland.[4]

On the death of Henry Grattan, the revered champion of Catholic claims, 4 June 1820, Ellis, backed by Dublin corporation and the Orange interest, challenged Grattan's son and namesake for the vacant city seat, as the avowed opponent of emancipation. He led throughout a bitter and violent contest.[5] Enraged Irish Whigs were determined to thwart him, and in the Commons, 30 June (the day on which he was formally returned), Sir John Newport, Member for Waterford, proposed the addition to the Irish court of chancery bill (brought in on 1 June) of a clause to prevent Irish masters in chancery from sitting in Parliament. He supported his case with Ellis's own admission to the judicial commissioners that his duties as master required 'regular [daily] attendance for ten months in the year'. Lord Castlereagh, the foreign secretary and leader of the Commons, concurred in the principle that a man could not satisfactorily fulfil the roles of master and Member, but argued that as Ellis was currently a candidate it would be invidious to exclude him *ex post facto*. After a heated debate, in which Newport and his backers insisted that if Ellis was returned he could simply resign his mastership in order to take his seat, and a number of Orange Members argued for his exemption, the clause was added.[6] On 3 July John Maxwell Barry, Orange Member for Cavan, moved the addition to the bill of a clause removing its retrospective operation, but it was defeated by 65-42. Ellis's Dublin supporters campaigned and petitioned both Houses against his exclusion. In the Lords, 20 July, Lord Redesdale proposed and Lord Liverpool, the prime minister, and lord chancellor Eldon supported, an amendment to the bill to exempt Ellis, which they

carried by 22-10. The amended measure passed the Lords on 24 July 1820, but made no further progress that session. Grattan's petition against Ellis's return was not pursued.[7]

He was therefore technically free to take his seat, but it was a certainty that his eligibility would again be challenged next session. In late July 1820, when he was in London, he sought from Liverpool 'a candid explanation of the wishes of government' as to what he should do. Liverpool, who had only belatedly realized who Ellis was, promised to consult his cabinet colleagues when they reassembled.[8] Ellis showed his face in the Commons to present a petition for relief from Dublin paper stainers, 31 Jan. 1821.[9] Lushington, Whig Member for Ilchester, had given notice of a motion to declare him ineligible for Parliament as a master. Ellis professed to be satisfied with Liverpool's assurance that while ministers had not yet decided whether to oppose it or to remain neutral, he would 'in any event ... be allowed to make my election of either vacating my seat or my office (as my mind is made up to retain my office)', and he left the matter in their hands:

> There never was a period when the best interests of the country so much required not only that the government should be strong, but that they should appear to be strong. I came into Parliament for the purpose of supporting them, and should exceedingly lament exposing them to embarrassment or annoyance by an indiscreet advocacy of my cause. At the same time I am quite sure that the principle of my case, if once established, may subject them to so many inconveniences, that it would be more prudent to resist in the outset, than when a decision of the House had afforded a precedent that could not be easily overlooked or explained.[10]

He voted in defence of ministers' conduct towards Queen Caroline, 6 Feb., and on the 22nd opposed inquiry into the conduct of the sheriff of Dublin at the December 1820 county meeting in her support, arguing that in calling in troops he had 'taken the wrong side of a difficult discretion', rather than acted unconstitutionally. On 27 Feb. he introduced a bill to regulate the fees of Irish attorneys (amending an Act of 1734), which received royal assent on 6 Apr.[11] He divided silently against Catholic relief, 28 Feb. When Lushington proposed his motion, 5 Mar., Ellis was allowed to speak in his own defence before the question was put: he claimed that the 'charges ... against him' were 'exaggerated in their nature and exasperated in the detail', but he did not disavow his 1815 statement and said that if he found that the combined duties of master and Member trenched more on his time 'than the interests of his family justified him in appropriating', he would vacate his seat. Having said what, as Henry Bankes* put it, was 'rather prejudicial than advantageous to him', he left the chamber and in his absence Castlereagh, for government, opposed the motion, but indicated that they would back any 'prospective measure' to exclude Irish masters thereafter.[12] The motion was defeated by 112-52. In 1823 the government carried an Irish chancery regulation bill which replaced the masters' fees with a fixed annual salary of £3,000 (plus £200 a year compensation) and thereby debarred them from Parliament in future.[13]

Ellis voted with government on the state of the revenue, 6 Mar., and against repeal of the additional malt duty, 21 Mar., 3 Apr., and army reductions, 11 Apr. 1821. His adverse comments on the pro-relief petition from Catholics of Staffordshire and Warwickshire, 16 Mar., were 'almost inaudible' in the gallery; but his forthright attack on the relief bill as 'a solemn humbug', 2 Apr., when he made a sneering reference to Daniel O'Connell's* family as one of 'mushroom celebrity', was sufficiently clear:

> He had himself been nourished in all the bosom of Popery; he had at one time cherished the warmest desire to give liberty and equality to creeds of every class; and nothing else than a firm conviction of the dangers to be apprehended from the unrestrained freedom of the Catholic faith, had compelled him at length to adopt a different opinion.[14]

He denied the allegation that the Bank of Ireland had refused to accept sovereigns as deposits, 28 Mar.[15] He presented petitions from officials of the Irish common law courts for compensation for losses under the current regulation bill, 11 Apr., and from Dublin for repeal of the window tax, 4 May 1821.[16] He voted with government against reduction of the salt duties, 28 Feb., and abolition of one of the joint-postmaster-ships, 13 Mar. 1822. He complained that Irish ships trading to England were liable to the same duties as foreign ones, 15 Mar.[17] On the 20th he secured the appointment of a select committee on Dublin local taxation, which he argued pressed unfairly on the poor and which he wished to make more equitable. The inquiry was reappointed in 1823 and 1824, when Ellis carried a bill to deal with the problem.[18] He was a member of another select committee on the subject, 23 Feb. 1825.

Ellis presented and endorsed Dublin parish petitions for repeal of the 'objectionable' window tax, 22, 24 Apr. 1822.[19] Opposing on the former day Newport's motion for inquiry into the state of Ireland, he delivered, according to Bankes, a 'very intemperate and injudicious speech'.[20] It was a 'furious tirade' against rebellious working class Catholics and their turbulent priests and recommended giving ministers 'almost absolute power' to crush insurrection, after which the 40s. freeholders should be disfranchised, illicit distillation stopped and 'religious and moral education' fostered. Charles Williams Wynn* reported that William Plunket, the Irish attorney-general, who followed Ellis, gave him 'a severe drubbing', though he suspected that Ellis was 'but too correct' in describing the current 'conspiracy' as 'exclusively Catholic'.[21] Sir James Mackintosh* noted:

> Ellis ... a furious Orangeman ... suspected of being prompted by Peel to throw out those topics among the vulgar which the [home] secretary's own caution would not risk, gave an entirely new turn to the debate ... Plunket sprang upon his prey. I have never seen such a chastisement. He fixed his eye on Ellis and treated him with a degree of scorn, disgust and contempt which I scarcely thought possible from one man to another.[22]

The Whig George Agar Ellis* recorded that Ellis's 'absurd, abusive, intolerant anti-Catholic speech ... was answered most admirably'.[23] Ellis divided against Canning's Catholic peers bill, 30 Apr. He presented a petition from the Dublin chamber of commerce for the retention of protecting duties, 5 June 1822.[24]

In January 1823 O'Connell reported from Dublin that Ellis was 'very busy' in Orange attempts to 'overawe' Lord Wellesley's Irish administration.[25] Ellis assured the House that the sheriff of Dublin desired full inquiry into his part in the prosecution of the Orange theatre rioters, 15, 22 Apr., when he voted in the majority against government on the issue. He divided against parliamentary reform, 20 Feb., 2 June, repeal of the Foreign Enlistment Act, 16 Apr., and inquiries into British chancery delays, 5 June, and the currency, 12 June. He presented petitions from Dublin tanners for repeal of the leather tax, 14 Apr., and from Irish linen manufacturers for protection against the importation of foreign flaxen yarn, 29 Apr.[26] He brought up anti-Catholic petitions from Dublin and Westmeath, 16 Apr.[27] On 27 May he supported the Irish joint-tenancy bill, alluding to the case of a farm worth £15 which had been divided to produce 40 free-hold votes. He encouraged Phillimore to go ahead with his Catholic marriages bill, 12 June 1823, professing to favour removal of all their 'disabilities' short of giving them political power.[28] He presented another Dublin tanners' petition for repeal of the leather tax, 17 Mar., and pleaded their case, 25 Mar. 1824.[29] He carried a measure to light Dublin with oil gas, but his bills to regulate its tolls and coal trade foundered; he explained and was a minority teller for the latter,

13 Apr.[30] He defended the grant for the Royal Dublin Society and the activities of Dublin aldermen as police magistrates, 19 Mar. He presented a petition from the Dublin chamber of commerce for repeal of the usury laws, 31 Mar., and voted in that sense, 8 Apr. 1824, 8, 17 Feb. 1825. He brought up a Dublin tradesmen's petition against the combination laws, 31 Mar. 1824, and was added to the select committee on the subject, 19 Apr. 1825.[31]

He thought that landed rather than personal security should be required for Irish assessments, 13 May 1824.[32] He was a teller for the ministerial majority against interference with Irish first fruits revenues, 25 May 1824. Ellis, who shook hands with O'Connell when he visited the Commons in February 1825,[33] voted for the Irish unlawful societies bill that month. He presented a Dublin petition against Catholic relief, 1 Mar., when he voted to that effect, as he did again, 21 Apr., 10 May.[34] Under instructions from Dublin merchants, he approved the St. Katharine's Docks bill, 22 Feb. 1825. Next day he presented a Dublin curriers' petition against assimilation of the English and Irish duties.[35] He divided with ministers on the Jamaican slave trials, 2 Mar. 1826. On 19 Apr. he introduced a bill to prevent the wilful destruction by tenants of houses in Ireland, which received royal assent on 26 May.[36] He denied Hume's allegation that he and his fellow masters showed partiality in their choice of Irish newspapers to carry official proclamations and was a teller for the majority for the relevant grant, 21 Apr.; he stood his ground when Hume raised the issue again, 5 May.[37] He presented two anti-Catholic petitions from Dublin, 26 Apr., and was in the majority against the spring guns bill, 27 Apr. 1826.[38] He duly retired from Parliament at the dissolution the following month, when he threw his weight behind the anti-Catholic Tory George Moore* for Dublin.[39] A stalwart anti-reform member of the corporation of Dublin, he seconded Moore at the general election of 1831 and proposed the recorder Frederick Shaw* at the by-election later that year.[40] He died in harness, in January 1832.[41] His Limerick estate passed to his eldest son Richard (1805-79), while his younger sons Conyngham (?1816-91), Francis (1819-81) and Frederick (b. 1826) entered the church, the law and the army respectively.

[1] King's Inns Admissions Pprs. ed. E. Keane, P.B. Phair and T.U. Sadleir, 152. [2] PP (1817), x. 162, 165; Extraordinary Red Bk. (1821), 121. [3] The Times, 16 Feb. 1819. [4] PRO NI, Leslie mss MIC606/3/J/7/21/4. [5] Dublin Evening Post, 8, 10, 13, 20, 22, 24, 27 June; The Times, 26, 28, 30 June, 1, 4, 5 July 1820. [6] Christ Church, Oxf. Phillimore mss, Plunket to Phillimore [6 July 1820]; PP (1817), x. 172; Add. 52444, f. 187; CJ, lxxv. 155, 267-8, 296, 378-9. [7] Dublin Evening Post, 4, 8, 13 July 1820; CJ, lxxv. 444, 460-2, 478; LJ, liii.

267, 293, 298, 305, 334, 342, 351. [8] Add. 38286, f. 323. [9] The Times, 1 Feb. 1821. [10] Add. 38289, f. 62. [11] The Times, 28 Feb. 1821; CJ, lxvi. 115, 117, 124, 137, 147, 160, 181, 221, 237. [12] Dorset RO, Bankes mss D/BKL, Bankes jnl. [13] CJ, lxxviii. 365, 375, 385, 390, 402, 408, 418-19, 470, 471; LJ, lv. 812, 839, 846, 852, 857; The Times, 13 Aug. 1824. [14] The Times, 17 Mar. 1821; O'Connell Corresp. ii. 895. [15] The Times, 29 Mar. 1821. [16] Ibid. 12 Apr., 5 May 1821. [17] The Times, 16 Mar. 1822. [18] Ibid. 21 Mar. 1822; CJ, lxxix. 59, 173, 189, 289, 391, 426, 492, 501, 502. [19] The Times, 23, 25 Apr. 1822. [20] Bankes jnl. [21] Buckingham, Mems. Geo. IV, i. 318-19. [22] Add. 52445, ff. 78-79. [23] Agar Ellis diary, 22 Apr. [1822]. [24] The Times, 6 June 1822. [25] O'Connell Corresp. ii. 990, 992. [26] The Times, 15, 30 Apr. 1823. [27] Ibid. 17 Apr. 1823. [28] Ibid. 13 June 1823. [29] Ibid. 18, 26 Mar. 1824. [30] CJ, lxxxix. 88, 167, 184, 189, 251, 262, 288, 300. [31] The Times, 1 Apr. 1824. [32] Ibid. 14 May 1824. [33] O'Connell Corresp. iii. 1169. [34] The Times, 2 Mar. 1825. [35] Ibid. 24 Feb. 1825. [36] Ibid. 20 Apr. 1826; CJ, lxxxi. 261, 292, 299, 305, 310, 363, 373. [37] The Times, 6 May 1826. [38] Ibid. 27 Apr. 1826. [39] Dublin Evening Post, 10 June 1826. [40] Dublin Evening Mail, 4, 6, 9 May, 19 Aug. 1831. [41] Gent. Mag. (1832), i. 189.

D.R.F./S.M.F.

ELLIS, Wynn (1790-1875), of 30 Cadogan Place, Mdx.[1]

LEICESTER	1831-1834
LEICESTER	22 Mar. 1839-1847

b. July 1790, s. of Thomas Ellis of Oundle, Northants. and w. Elizabeth Ordway of Barkway, Herts. m. 1814, Mary Maria, da. of John Smith of Lincoln, s.p. d. 20 Nov. 1875. Sheriff, Herts. 1852-3.

Ellis came from a 'respectable' Oundle family who claimed descent from the Flintshire Ellises. After receiving a 'good' education he went to London where his natural business acumen brought him quick success. He began trading as a retail haberdasher, hosier and silk mercer at 16 Ludgate Street in about 1812 and, as he prospered, he took over other firms to create the largest silk business in the City and from about 1830 diversified into the wholesale trade as head of Everington, Ellis and Company.[2] He intended to offer himself for election as an alderman for Castle Baynard ward in April 1831, but relinquished this ambition when he was invited to stand on the 'liberal interest' for Leicester at the general election, having declined a request from the independent party at Shaftesbury to stand there at the next opportunity.[3] He was returned unopposed with his fellow supporter of the Grey ministry's reform scheme William Evans after a moderate reformer pulled out late in the day.[4] For the vacancy in Castle Baynard he subsequently nominated Samuel Wilson, who was unanimously elected as the popular candidate.[5]

Ellis voted for the second reading of the reintroduced reform bill, 6 July 1831, and divided steadily for its details in committee. His only reported speech on the bill was against Mackinnon's proposal to restrict the franchise in large towns, which he said would 'give us anything but a popular constituency', 26 Aug. He spoke in support of the Leicester petition presented by Evans for repeal of the corn laws, 18 July, and was one of the minority of six who voted for Hunt's motion to that effect, 15 Sept. He divided for printing the Waterford petition calling for the disarming of the Irish yeomanry following the massacre at Newtownbarry, 11 Aug., but voted with government against charges of improper interference in the Dublin election, 23 Aug., and the issue of a new writ for Liverpool, 5 Sept. He voted for the passage of the reform bill, 21 Sept., and Lord Ebrington's motion of confidence in the ministry, 10 Oct. 1831. He voted for the second reading of the revised reform bill, 17 Dec. 1831, and was again a generally steady supporter of its details, though he was one of the minority of 32 who refused to ratify the enfranchisement of £50-tenants-at-will, 1 Feb. 1832. He voted for the third reading, 22 Mar. He divided with government on the Russian-Dutch loan, 26 Jan., 12, 20 July, and relations with Portugal, 9 Feb. He voted for inquiry into the state of the glove trade, 31 Jan. 1832, having endorsed the Worcester glovers' petition for protection against foreign imports, 15 Dec. 1831, when he warned that free trade would 'ruin all our fancy manufactures'. On a petition from the silk industry, 21 Feb. 1832, he disputed the assertion that 'increased consumption of material' created more employment, since the 'fancy branches' of this trade had long been in decline. He was added to the select committee on the trade, 15 Mar., when he spoke of the inadequacy of customs records as a means of estimating the number of importers. The same day he voted in the minority of 31 for inquiry into the Peterloo massacre. He presented a petition from the Leicestershire Political Union for repeal of the newspaper stamp duty, 8 May. He divided for the address asking the king to appoint only ministers who would carry undiluted reform, 10 May, and next day, bearing 'testimony to the earnest feelings' in favour of the reform bill entertained by the people of the 'great northern towns', urged the House to refuse to grant supplies until the measure had passed, 11 May. He voted for a committee to consider the abolition of slavery, 24 May. He divided for the second reading of the Irish reform bill, 25 May, but was in the minorities in favour of an extension of the franchise to £5 freeholders, 18 June, and preservation of the rights of freemen, 2 July. He was forced to withdraw a petition from the Leicester Political Union for a more radical measure for Ireland, 28 June, because the Speaker deemed it to be from 'an unrecognized body', but he

presented it in an acceptable form, 6 July. He voted for a proposal to make permanent provision for the Irish poor by imposing a tax on absentees, 19 June, in the minorities for amendments to the boundaries bill designed to prevent aristocratic domination of Stamford and Whitehaven, 22 June, and for a reduction in the barracks grant, 2 July. He spoke in support of the Leicester petition for rationalization of the laws governing the recovery of debts, since debtors were 'too frequently tempted to avail themselves of the law's delay', 5 July. On 7 Aug. 1832 he endorsed the London silk manufacturers' relief petition. As an active member of the select committee, he regretted that it had not accompanied its evidence with a report, as this would have vindicated his own opinion that the 'fancy trade' had been lost to foreign incursion. He argued that much greater protection was due to the industry and that it was government's duty to protect silk manufacturers against the French monopoly in raw silk. He also drew attention to the 'great distress' in the silk manufacturing districts and touched on the 'wretched depraved habits' of women reduced to prostitution:

> Bad, however, as is their present state, it is yet much better than it will be, if these duties on foreign thrown silk be repealed, an event which I can only look upon as entailing wretchedness on the whole population of women and children so employed, and which … will be an act of great injustice to, and destructive of the property of, the mill-owners.

Ellis complained publicly of badly 'impaired' health in August 1832, but he represented Leicester in three further Parliaments.[6] His business continued to flourish and in 1871 it was merged to form the 'large establishment' of James Howell and Company.[7] He bought Ponsbourne Park in Hertfordshire in 1836, but sold it shortly before his death.[8] He extended Tankerton Tower, a small castellated mansion near Whitstable in north Kent, which his wife's maternal uncle had purchased in the 1790s.[9] Ellis became well known as an admirer and patron of the fine arts and amassed a valuable if somewhat idiosyncratic picture collection, which he bequeathed to the National Gallery. It was said that he believed more in 'work and wages than in eleemosynary acts', but he left charitable bequests in excess of £180,000, the principal beneficiary being Charles Simeon's patronage trust with a legacy of £50,000. He died in November 1875 and his personal estate was proved in London under £600,000, 31 Dec. 1875.[10]

[1] Ellis's first name is incorrectly spelt 'Wynne' by *Oxford DNB*. [2] Ibid.; *Warehousemen and Drapers Trade Jnl.* (27 Nov. 1875), 618. [3] *The Times*, 29 Apr.; Dorset RO, Rutter mss D50/3, Rutter to

Tinney, 26 Mar., Ellis to same, 31 Mar., Tinney to Rutter, 4 Apr. 1831. ⁴ *Leicester Jnl.* 29 Apr., 6 May 1831. ⁵ *The Times*, 1, 3 Oct. 1831. ⁶ *Leicester Chron.* 25 Aug. 1832. ⁷ *Warehousemen Jnl.* 618, 641, 660. ⁸ J. Cussans, *Herts.* ii. 270-1. ⁹ *North East and North Kent* ed. J. Newman, 491. ¹⁰ *Oxford DNB.*

S.R.H.

ELLISON, Cuthbert (1783–1860), of Hebburn Hall, co. Dur.

NEWCASTLE-UPON-TYNE   1812–1830

b. 12 July 1783, 2nd s. of Henry Ellison (*d.* 1795) of Hebburn and Gateshead and Henrietta, da. of John Isaacson of Newcastle-upon-Tyne, Northumb. *educ.* Bradenham 1791-6; Harrow 1796-1801; Christ's, Camb. 1801. *m.* 21 July 1804, Isabella Grace, da. and coh. of Henry Ibbetson of St. Anthony's, Northumb., 7da. (5 *d.v.p.*). *suc.* bro. Henry 1798. *d.* 13 June 1860.

Sheriff, Northumb. 1808-9, co. Dur. 1827-8; mayor, Hartlepool 1809.

Lt.-col. commdt. Gateshead vols. 1803-14.

Ellison, a Tyneside grandee and patron of the mining engineers Sir Humphry Davy and John Budde, was noted for his shrewdness, largesse and 'most frugal manner of conducting extensive coal concerns'.[1] A pro-Catholic Tory committed to cutting public expenditure, he had been thwarted in his ambition to sit for county Durham in 1807, but came in for Newcastle-upon-Tyne in 1812 as the candidate of the incorporated companies and the shipping interest. He spoke only on issues of local importance. The renegade Whig Sir Charles Monck† of Belsay Hall, who had, as Member for Northumberland, liaised with him on constituency business, considered him 'quite unsafe to be reckoned upon in the case of a job'.[2] Prolonged absences abroad on account of his own and his family's ill health, coupled with his inability to prevent the establishment of a rival customs house in Tynemouth, encouraged opposition to him in Newcastle at the general election of 1820, but with his brother Robert (*d.* 1843), a soldier, deputizing, he saw off a challenge from lord chancellor Eldon's nephew William Scott* and was returned *in absentia* with the sitting Whig Sir Matthew White Ridley after a one-day poll.[3]

Ellison's conduct in the 1820 Parliament restored his reputation. He presented the Tyne ship owners' petition against altering the timber duties, 26 Feb. 1821. He divided with the Liverpool ministry on the Queen Caroline affair, 6 Feb., the additional malt duty repeal bill, 3 Apr., and retrenchment, 27 June, but he cast a wayward vote for restoring the queen's name to the liturgy, 13 Feb. 1821. He divided for Catholic relief, 28 Feb. 1821, 1 Mar., 21 Apr., 10 May 1825, and

was described in a radical publication of that session as a Member who 'attended occasionally and voted with ministers'.[4] He voted against parliamentary reform, 9 May 1821, 26 Feb. 1824, 13 Apr. 1826. According to his 1826 election speech, he also voted in the minority for transferring Grampound's seats to Yorkshire, 12 Feb. 1821.[5] He divided with ministers on taxation, 21 Feb., but for reductions in the 'comparatively useless' junior admiralty lordships, 1 Mar., and to abolish one of the joint-postmasterships, 2 May. He officiated at the proceedings in Newcastle to mark the duke of Sussex's visit in September 1822, hosted the Recorder's Club dinner there in October and became a founder-trustee that month of the Literary and Philosophic Society.[6] He divided with government against repealing the Foreign Enlistment Act (which he had opposed in 1819), 16 Apr., and on chancery arrears, 5 June, and the Scottish juries bill, 20 June 1823. However, brandishing the ship owners' hostile petition, he voted against their reciprocity bill, 4 July 1823.[7] Both families 'delighted' in the connection brought about by his daughter Henrietta's marriage in 1824 to the Whig John Lambton's* brother William.[8] Reporting on 2 Mar. 1824 from the select committee on the Newcastle coal trade, Ellison defended the northern coal owners against allegations of price fixing, and he criticized ministers' decision to cut the duty on coal transported over land, but not coastwise, 1 Apr., 4 May.[9] He called again for a reduction in the duty on coal exports, 17 June 1825. He voted, 8 Apr., and presented petitions, 9 Apr., for the usury laws repeal bill, and against colonial slavery, 7 May. He opposed inquiry into the indictment in Demerara of the Methodist missionary John Smith, 11 June 1824, believing, he later explained, that Smith's treatment and trial so clearly contravened Canning's 1823 resolutions as to make further investigation unnecessary.[10] He voted for the Irish insurrection bill, 14 June 1824, and, true to his 1815 votes, he divided against the award to the duke of Cumberland, 6 June 1825. Uncharacteristically, he breached a pairing arrangement to vote personally for the anti-Catholic Tory Matthew Belb at the Northumberland by-election of February 1826.[11] He presented anti-slavery petitions, 28 Feb., 17 Mar., and endorsed protectionist ones from the ship owners of North Shields, 27 Apr., and Newcastle, 5 May 1826.[12] He chose not to vote in Northumberland at the general election in June. On the hustings at Newcastle, where his fourth return was never in doubt, he condemned tariff reform and precipitate relaxation of the navigation laws, defended his voting record, and called for greater protection for shipping and manufacturing.[13]

Ellison presented and endorsed the Newcastle ship owners' petition for protection, 3 May 1827. However, before Gascoyne withdrew his inquiry motion on the 7th, he informed the ship owners that although he was prepared to vote for it 'in deference to their wish', he had become convinced by the president of the board of trade Huskisson's counter-arguments that it was unnecessary and would serve no purpose. He presented petitions for repeal of the Test Acts, 30 May, 20 June 1827.[14] He brought up and strongly endorsed the Newcastle coal owners' petition against removing one pound country bank notes from circulation (under the Small Notes Act), 6 June 1828, and one from North Shields for the abolition of colonial slavery, 24 June. His votes to reduce government spending on the Royal Cork Institution, 20 June, and Buckingham House, 23 June, were wayward ones, but he divided with the Wellington administration against ordnance reductions, 4 July 1828. Ellison had divided for Catholic relief, 6 Mar. 1827, 12 May 1828, and he voted for emancipation, 6, 30 Mar. 1829, as the patronage secretary Planta had predicted, having presented and endorsed favourable petitions from Newcastle, 13 Feb., 17, 26, and Gateshead, 26 Mar. However, he also testified to the 'respectability' of the signatories to the hostile Northumberland petitions presented by Bell, 17 Mar.[15] He brought up his constituents' protectionist petitions against French shoe imports, 26 Mar., one in favour of anatomical dissection, 13 Apr., and several against the labourers' wages bill, 12 May 1829. As a Tyneside Member, Ellison was appointed to the East India select committee, 9 Feb., and that on the coal trade, 11 Mar. He voted against enfranchising Birmingham, Leeds and Manchester, 23 Feb., but to transfer East Retford's seats to Birmingham, 5 Mar. 1830. He aligned with the revived Whig opposition in the divisions on the Bathurst and Dundas pensions, 26 Mar., the public buildings grant, 3 May, the Irish lord lieutenancy, 11 May, and privy councillors' emoluments, 14 May, but voted against Jewish emancipation, 5 Apr., 17 May. He divided as previously (4 June 1821) for the abolition of capital punishment for forgery, 7 June. Ellison was alerted on 29 May by his Newcastle agents to the prevailing local hostility to Ridley, and John Hodgson* of Elswick's willingness to poll as a third man, and he immediately authorized spending on a canvass and freeman admissions there. Accordingly, his decision on 8 June 1830 to stand down on health grounds, despite assurance of success, surprised all but his closest friends.[16] Returning to Newcastle for the election, he conceded on the hustings that he was the 'victim' of the anti-Ridley campaign; but he denied that his retirement had been procured through a pact between them.[17]

From Florence in March 1831 and again in March and August 1832 Ellison declined invitations to stand for the new Gateshead constituency at the first post-reform election, and preferred to hold aloof from Durham and Northumberland politics.[18] Deterred from living in his 85-room mansion at Hebburn by encroaching industrialization and especially the construction in 1853 of Andrew Leslie's shipbuilding yards, he spent his later years at Juniper Hill, near Dorking, Surrey, and his London house in Whitehall Gardens, where, predeceased by his wife and four of their daughters, he died in June 1860. He was recalled for his philanthropy towards Gateshead Dispensary, the Literary and Philosophical Society and Infirmary in Newcastle and the Victoria and Albert Museum, South Kensington, to whom his wife had bequeathed their watercolour collection. His youngest daughter Sarah and many grandchildren were the principal beneficiaries of his will, which was proved in London, 27 Aug. 1860, and administered by Sarah's husband Sir Walter Charles James† of Betteshanger, afterwards 1st Baron Northborne. Having no sons, his entailed estates passed to Robert's son, Cuthbert George Ellison, who died without issue in 1867, and then to his sister Hannah's son Ralph Carr (d. 1884), who assumed the name of Ellison.[19]

[1] Diaries and Corresp. of James. Losh ed. E. Hughes (Surtees Soc. clxxiv) [hereafter Losh Diaries, ii], 68; F.W.D. Manders, Hist. Gateshead, 325-6. [2] HP Commons, 1790-1820, ii. 148-51, 312; iii. 702-3; Grey mss, Monck to Grey, 3 Oct. 1812. [3] Newcastle Courant, 12, 26 Feb., 11, 18 Mar.; Tyne Mercury, 14 Mar. 1820; Northumb. election pprs. [BL J/8133.i.13.], ii. 805-13 [4] Session of Parl. 1825, p. 462. [5] Newcastle Chron. 17 June 1826. [6] Ibid. 4 Sept.; The Times, 6 Sept. 1822; R.S. Watson, Hist. Lit. and Phil. Soc. of Newcastle, 68-72, 83; Diaries and Corresp. of James Losh ed. E. Hughes (Surtees Soc. clxxi) [Losh Diaries, i], 173. [7] The Times, 5 July 1823. [8] Grey mss, Lambton to Grey, 4 Jan. 1824. [9] The Times, 5 May 1824. [10] Newcastle Chron. 17 June 1826. [11] Creevey mss, Creevey to Miss Ord, 7 Mar. 1826. [12] The Times, 1, 17 Mar., 6 May 1826. [13] Northumb. election pprs. ii. 573, 579, 585, 591; The Times, 26 May, 2, 12 June; Newcastle Chron. 27 May, 10, 17 June 1826. [14] The Times, 4, 31 May, 21 June 1827. [15] Losh Diaries, ii. 166. [16] Tyne and Wear Archives, Ellison of Hebburn mss DF/ELL/A66, passim; Newcastle Chron. 12 June 1830; P.D. Brett, 'Newcastle Election of 1830', Northern Hist. xxiv (1988), 101-23. [17] Newcastle Chron. 7 Aug. 1830. [18] Manders, 268-9. [19] Gent. Mag. (1860) ii. 205-6; R.E. and E.E. Carr, Fam. of Carr, i. 114, 121-2.

M.M.E.

ELPHINSTONE *see* **BULLER ELPHINSTONE, James Drummond**

ENCOMBE, Visct. *see* **SCOTT**, **John**

ENNISMORE, Visct. *see* **HARE**, **Richard** *and* **HARE**, **William**

ERLE DRAX GROSVENOR, Richard Edward
(1797–1828), of Charborough Park, nr. Blandford
Forum, Dorset.

NEW ROMNEY   22 Feb. 1819–1826

bap. 10 Mar. 1797,[1] o.s. of Richard Erle Drax Grosvenor†
of Charborough and Swell Court, Som. and Sarah
Frances, da. and h. of Edward Drax† of Charborough.
educ. Westminster 1809-10; Christ Church, Oxf. 1815;
European tour 1818-19. *unm. suc.* fa. 1819. *d.* 18 Aug.
1828.[2]

Erle Drax Grosvenor, whose father had vainly pestered successive administrations for a peerage, was
again returned unopposed for New Romney on the
Dering interest in 1820.[3] He was nominally a supporter of the Liverpool ministry, but was a complete
cipher in the House.[4] He probably voted in defence
of ministers' conduct towards Queen Caroline, 6
Feb., and certainly divided against Catholic relief, 28
Feb. 1821, but no other trace of parliamentary activity has been discovered. He retired from Parliament
at the dissolution of 1826. He died, a bachelor, in
August 1828. No will or administration has been
found. His estates passed to his sister Jane, the wife
of John Samuel Wanley Sawbridge. In 1905 they were
inherited by her grand-daughter, the widow of the
17th Lord Dunsany, who then rejoiced in the names
of Ernle Elizabeth Louisa Mary Grosvenor Plunkett
Ernle Erle Drax. She was succeeded in 1916 by her
younger son Reginald Aylmer Ranfurly Plunkett
Ernle Erle Drax.

[1] IGI. [2] M.I. printed in J. Hutchins, *Dorset*, iii. 507. *Gent. Mag.*
(1828), ii. 283 and *Burke LG* give 13 Aug. [3] *HP Commons, 1790-1820*,
iii. 706-7. [4] *Black Bk.* (1823), p. 160; *Session of Parl. 1825*, p. 466.

                                                        D.R.F.

ESTCOURT (afterwards **BUCKNALL** and
BUCKNALL ESTCOURT), **Thomas Grimston**
(1775–1853), of New Park, nr. Devizes, Wilts. and
Estcourt House, nr. Tetbury, Glos.

DEVIZES   23 Jan. 1805–18 Feb. 1826
OXFORD UNIVERSITY   22 Feb. 1826–1847

b. 3 Aug. 1775, 1st. s. of Thomas Estcourt† of Estcourt
House and Hon. Jane Grimston, da. of James Grimston†,
2nd Visct. Grimston. *educ.* Harrow 1788-92; Corpus,
Oxf. 1793; L. Inn 1795, called 1820. *m.* 12 May 1800,
Eleanor, da. and coh. of James Sutton† of New Park,
6s. (1 *d.v.p.*) 3da. (1 *d.v.p.*). *suc.* fa. 1818; took name of
Bucknall by royal lic. 1 May and additional name of
Estcourt by royal lic. 3 July 1823. *d.* 26 July 1853.

Cornet Wilts. yeomanry 1794, lt. 1799; capt. Herts.
militia 1798; maj. Wilts. yeomanry 1802-3; maj. Devizes
vols. 1803, lt.-col. commdt. 1803-36, (militia) 1808; capt.
Tetbury troop of Glos. yeoman cav. 1831.

Chairman, q. sess. Wilts. (Devizes) 1802-36; high
steward, Malmesbury 1808-12; recorder, Devizes
1828-33.

A leading gentry family, the Estcourts had been
established at Tetbury, on the Gloucestershire and
Wiltshire border, since the fourteenth century.
Thomas Grimston Estcourt, whose father was
Member for Cricklade, 1790-1806, inherited New
Park from his father-in-law in 1801, and began to
cultivate an interest in Devizes. He became a capital
burgess councillor and justice of the borough in 1802,
and three years later he was elected there, in succession
to his wife's uncle, Henry Addington†, on his creation
as Viscount Sidmouth. He was generally a supporter
of the administration of Lord Liverpool, following
the lead of Sidmouth, the home secretary. A man of
obvious integrity and assiduity, though no great distinction, many Members apparently wished him to
be proposed for the Speakership on Charles Abbot's
resignation in May 1817.[1] Estcourt survived his first
contest for Devizes at the general election of 1818,
receiving votes from 25 of the 27 members of the corporation who polled, though he himself voted for his
friend and colleague, John Pearse, and the leading corporator, William Salmon.[2] Disappointed in his aspirations to a county seat, he observed a studied neutrality
in the Wiltshire contest in 1818, but voted for John
Dugdale Astley* against John Benett* in the by-election in 1819. Acknowledging to Charles Arbuthnot*, 7
Feb. 1820, that this had created in his constituents 'an
unfortunate sensation towards me', he refused to exert
the very little influence he claimed to have over Devizes
freeholders on behalf of the ministerialist William
Long Wellesley* at the subsequent general election.[3]
Although at that time he wished to resign as the magistrate for Devizes, he continued to fulfil the duties,
which were 'not trifling', and to attend the meetings
of the corporation and Bear Club.[4] Disregarding his
mother's advice to retire, 26 Feb., he stood another
contest there with Pearse, against Wadham Locke,
the popular candidate they had defeated in 1818. He
offered on the basis of his known principles and diligence, and was again elected with a large proportion
of the votes, 10 Mar. 1820.[5] According to an entry in
his pocket diary, he was present at the Gloucestershire
election, 13 Mar.[6] He attended the Wiltshire county
meeting to congratulate George IV on his accession,
22 Mar., and, chairing the Wiltshire Society meeting,
12 May, he spoke in favour of charitable education as

the 'most effectual means of stemming the torrent of wretchedness and infatuation'.[7] He was thanked by the corporation of Devizes, 7 Oct. 1820, for his assistance in quashing a legal claim against the validity of the recent election of a new mayor.[8]

He presented a Devizes petition in favour of restoring Queen Caroline's name to the liturgy, 24 Jan. 1821, when he said that he had been returned by 36 not 12 electors, but he voted with ministers against the censure motion on the affair, 6 Feb. He was appointed to select committees on agricultural distress, 7 Mar., and poor returns, 28 Mar. (as he was in every session until 1826). He paired against Catholic claims, 28 Feb. He voted against the additional malt duty repeal bill, 3 Apr., and Hume's attempt to disqualify civil officers of the ordnance from voting in parliamentary elections, 12 Apr. In late April 1821 he accepted Sidmouth's invitation to chair the commission of inquiry into Ilchester gaol, and his report was presented to the House, 8 Feb. 1822.[9] He was again named to the select committee on agricultural distress, 18 Feb., and he voted against more extensive tax reductions for its relief, 21 Feb., and abolition of one of the joint-postmasterships, 13 Mar. He divided against the Catholic peers relief bill, 30 Apr. He testified that Henry Hunt's* conduct had been 'perfectly correct', 24 Apr., but spoke against the production of the magistrates' journal relating to Ilchester gaol, 13 May, 5 June.[10] He voted against repeal of the Foreign Enlistment Act, 16 Apr. 1823. He spoke in favour of punishment by whipping, 30 Apr., when he was a teller for the majority against granting leave for a bill to abolish it. He divided against inquiry into chancery administration, 5 June, and the usury laws amendment bill, 17, 27 June 1823.

Following the death of his uncle, Harbottle Bucknall, rector of Pebmarsh, Essex, in early 1823, Estcourt inherited the estate of Oxhey, Hertfordshire, under the will of John Askell Bucknall, who had died in 1796. Obliged by its terms to take the name of Bucknall, he quickly obtained permission to add his former surname to it, and was thenceforth known as Bucknall Estcourt.[11] He voted against reform of the representation of Edinburgh, 26 Feb. 1824. He presented Devizes petitions against the importation of manufactured silks and the tobacco duties, 8 Mar., and for the abolition of slavery, 11 Mar.[12] He brought in his vagrants bill, 9 Apr., chaired a committee on the subject, whose report he presented to the House, 6 May, advocated some of its clauses, 3, 5 June, and led the managers in a conference with the Lords, 18 June, after which they dropped their amendments;

it received royal assent, 21 June.[13] He was appointed to committees on the county gaols bill, 12 Apr., and county rates, 19 May (to which he was again named in the following two sessions), subjects with which he was well acquainted since he was in the middle of chairing a two-year inquiry into the Wiltshire accounts.[14] He presented a Devizes petition for inquiry into the trial of the Methodist missionary John Smith in Demerara, 1 June, but voted against condemning ministers over it, 11 June.[15] He presided at the Bear Club dinner, 27 Aug. 1824.[16] Bucknall Estcourt, who oversaw the passage of the Devizes improvement bill during the session, contributing £1,000 towards its expenses, moved the first and second readings of the county rates mortgage bill, 21 Mar., 29 Apr. 1825.[17] Named as a defaulter, 28 Feb., he was present to be excused, 1 Mar., when he voted against Catholic claims. He asked Sir Francis Burdett, 22, 23 Mar., to delay the second reading of his relief bill, 'to which he intended to give his strenuous opposition', until after the quarter sessions week, so that it would receive proper attention from the House. He voted steadily against it, and presented anti-Catholic petitions from the inhabitants of Devizes, 19 Apr., and the clergy of Berkshire, 3 May.[18] He voted for the duke of Cumberland's annuity bill, 10 June 1825.

When a vacancy occurred at Oxford University in early 1826, Bucknall Estcourt, to the surprise of some, was promoted as an uncontroversial candidate. Peel, who sat for the other seat and had succeeded Sidmouth as home secretary, thought him 'a most respectable man, and an excellent Member of Parliament', and that he would be 'at least a creditable Member'; and Edward Bouverie Pusey described him as a 'thoroughly respectable country gentleman, of respectable talents also'.[19] Much speculation centred on whether Canning, the foreign secretary, would stand, and it was understood that Bucknall Estcourt, despite differing with him on the Catholic question, would then withdraw. Nothing came of that, however, though he did have to see off a strong challenge from Sir Charles Wetherell, Member for Oxford and solicitor-general. In the end, having resigned from Devizes, he was elected unopposed.[20] One newspaper correspondent, complaining that he had been referred to as 'a Mr. Estcourt', claimed that he had been 'frequently looked to as the most proper person to be invited to start as the True Blue or Tory Member for one of the counties in which his property lies'. He attended the by-election in Devizes, 1 Mar. 1826, and it was clearly with his approval that George Watson Taylor was elected to replace him.[21]

He asked Peel, 27 Feb. 1826, to introduce him to the House on taking his seat that night.[22] He commented that crime had increased because of the impoverishment of the lower classes, 9 Mar., and presented a petition for lights to be displayed on carriages at night in order to prevent accidents, 14 Mar. He explained the reasons behind moving for leave to bring in a bill to amend the Alehouses Licensing Act, 17 Mar., and argued that some measure of regulation was necessary to preserve the public peace, 21 Apr., when, however, he acknowledged that the changes could not be implemented that session and moved to postpone the second reading. He introduced a new measure designed to extend the Act for one year, 26 Apr., spoke in its favour, 27 Apr., 8 May, and was a teller for the majority against an amendment to allow magistrates to hold adjourned meetings for the purpose of granting licenses, 12 May.[23] He voted against resolutions to curb electoral bribery, 26 May. He attended the Devizes election, 9 June 1826, when he nominated Watson Taylor.[24] He was elected for Downton, one of Lord Radnor's bor-' oughs, 10 June, but chose to sit for Oxford University, where he was also returned unopposed four days later. He proposed his friend Lord Robert Edward Henry Somerset* at the Gloucestershire election, 16 June, and spoke at the Pitt Club dinner in Gloucester, 27 July 1826.[25] In his 'Account of measures adopted to better the condition of the poor at Long Newnton', he described how arable land ought to be allotted to cottagers in order to remove them from the system of parochial relief.[26] That autumn he and Peel arranged a post-election visit to Oxford, where he was made a doctor of civil law, 27 June 1827.[27]

Bucknall Estcourt voted against Catholic relief, 6 Mar., and presented a hostile petition, 7 Mar. 1827.[28] On 13 Apr. he wrote to Sidmouth, from Boodle's, that

the duke of Wellington is said to have declared at Lady Jersey's last night that the resignations did not arise from the Catholic question, but on account of 'the man'. Sir George Warrender* has been sitting by my side and loudly pressing upon those around that the resignation of the ministry was solely occasioned by the king having determined to exercise his prerogative in the appointment of Canning to be his minister, in opposition to the will of the seven ministers who insisted that the commander-in-chief should be premier. This is clearly erroneous.[29]

In the House, 21 Mar., he informed Sir James Graham that he would be proposing another alehouses' licensing bill, which he duly introduced, 9 Apr. Thomas and Francis Phippen's *Letter to Estcourt*, dated 27 Apr., argued against it. He said that he wanted the bill referred to a select committee and to Peel, 4 May, but

again ran out of time, and, having introduced another bill to extend the Act for one year, 31 May, put off the substantive measure, 18 June.[30] He advocated revision of the game laws, 28 Mar., and presented petitions from the magistrates of Wiltshire for this, 29 Mar., 4 May. He disagreed with Hume's amendment to the writ of right bill, 9 Apr., expressed his intention of opposing the Dissenters' marriages bill, 30 May, but approved the changes made to it, 19 June, and urged that no precipitate action be taken on the issue of the Canadian clergy reserves, 15 June.[31] Surprisingly, he was listed as voting in the majority in favour of the third reading of Lord Althorp's election expenses bill, 28 May. He voted for the grant to improve water communications in Canada, 12 June 1827.

At the Wiltshire Agricultural Society dinner, 18 July 1827, he argued that the fortunes of agriculture stood higher than in the previous year and that Parliament would not sanction measures hostile to its interests.[32] In his published *Substance of the Charge Delivered to the Grand Jury at the Quarter Sessions* (1827) he blamed the increase in crime squarely on 'a negligence of character in those occupying the lower walks of life', and condemned the practice of paying wages out of the poor rates. His sentence of two years' hard labour on Catherine Cook for stealing eight cups was criticized in an address from William Lisle Bowles, vicar of Bremhill, and during the subsequent furore he offered to resign.[33] He commented on the political world in a letter to Sidmouth, 30 Nov. 1827:

Surely we are in a glorious state of confusion, and daily sinking deeper into the mire! If some improvement does not take place before the meeting of Parliament what will be the course for steady, orthodox, loyal and constitutional men to pursue? Can we support, or rather must we not oppose, a government constituted of such a variety of adverse principles, as to retain no semblance of a principle on which they move, and the consequence seems to be anything but a firm, uncompromising line of policy?[34]

In another letter, 4 Jan. 1828, he added that

I cannot help feeling strongly disposed against a government in which nought but the signs of weakness, discordance, innovation and hostility to church and king are found to console us in our embarrassments. I hate faction as much as I do Whiggery, and am therefore anxious to ascertain when and where I am to find the real friends of the sovereign and the supporters of the constitution.

He welcomed Peel's reappointment to office under Wellington, and was glad to have attended the first day, because, as he reported to his mentor, 31 Jan., 'I found a pretty full muster of those with whom I generally act', and the 'impression made on my mind on

Tuesday [29 Jan.] was favourable to the existence of the government, notwithstanding the omission of some, and ... in particular ... of ... Lord Eldon'.[35] He was listed among the 'supporters' of the Wellington ministry in John Herries's* 'scheme of a finance committee', 10 Feb. 1828, but was not appointed to it.[36] He objected to the Scottish parochial settlements bill, 19 Feb., 14 Mar., 6 May. He voted against repeal of the Test Acts, 26 Feb., and asked for a delay on this, 28 Feb., when he said he would vote for suspension rather than repeal. An active committeeman, he chaired one on the metropolitan police, which was appointed, 28 Feb., and reported its findings to the House, 11 July.[37] He again promised to reintroduce his alehouses' licenses bill, 29 Feb., and asked for leave to do so, 14 Mar., when he stated that its purpose was to do away with all unnecessary difficulties in the way of obtaining licenses. He moved its first reading, 21 Mar., commented on it, 24 Mar., 2 Apr., and, on moving the second reading, 21 May, agreed that criticisms of it could usefully be raised in committee. There he strongly defended the concurrent jurisdiction clause, 19 June, which allowed county justices to sit on committees for granting licenses in small jurisdictions so that decisions would not be left in the hands of a few, possibly interested, local magistrates, but it was defeated by 46-53. He agreed to further amendments, 25 June, and his bill received royal assent, 15 July.[38] Although the bishop of Oxford opined that it was 'a great pity that Mr. Estcourt has not head and tongue enough to be put forward', he defended the opinion of Peel and their constituency that commutations of tithes should not be made permanent, 17 Mar., and acted as a teller for the majority in favour of instructing the select committee on the subject to consider limiting their duration.[39] He supported the Oxford University petition against Catholic claims, 29 Apr., which he voted against, 12 May. He raised points about payment of the Canadian Protestant clergy, 12 June, cider excise licenses, 26 June, and the game bill, 4 July. He proposed, but withdrew, amendments to limit the hours during which breweries could open for the sale of beer, 8, 10 July. He resigned as justice of Devizes, 31 July, and was elected as its recorder, 11 Aug. 1828.[40]

Bucknall Estcourt was kept away from the early part of the following session by the death of his mother, 3 Feb. 1829, and the convocation of Oxford therefore forwarded its anti-Catholic petition to Peel.[41] He, however, had decided to follow the cabinet's new policy in favour of introducing a bill to emancipate the Catholics. Bucknall Estcourt regretted this, and wrote to him, 6 Feb., to 'express my apprehension that I shall not be able to view the state of public affairs in

relation to the Roman Catholic question in the light in which they seem to have been presented to you'.[42] Listed by Planta, the patronage secretary, among those 'opposed to the principle of the bill', he supported the efforts of his son, Thomas Henry Sutton Bucknall Estcourt*, to organize Wiltshire opinion against it, but asked for his name to be removed from the putative anti-Catholic declaration in order to save his colleague further embarrassment.[43] In the House, 23 Feb., he denied that it had often sanctioned Catholic relief, as 'in private, this has been the *dictum* of many gentlemen: "we vote for the committee, but it by no means follows that, for that reason, we shall vote for acceding to the claims when we are on the committee".' He presented anti-Catholic petitions, 26 Feb., when he reiterated his opposition, and later that day he reported to his son that he had had the 'extreme satisfaction of being abused by Lord Milton for intolerance'.[44] He moved the writ for Oxford University, 20 Feb., on Peel's offering himself for re-election, but apparently played little or no part, and did not vote, in the by-election in which he was defeated.[45] He denied that the majority of the junior members of the University were pro-Catholic, 2 Mar. On the 6th he explained that he had formerly stayed silent on the subject because he had trusted Peel to defend the established church, argued that the Parliament elected in the less divisive atmosphere of 1826 was not qualified to decide the question, pleaded for the integrity of the Revolution settlement as a defence against Popery and criticized the government's failure to put down the agitation in Ireland. He duly voted against the claims, 6 Mar., and the second reading of the emancipation bill, 18 Mar., bringing up more hostile petitions, 9, 18, 30 Mar. He moved an amendment to alter the words of the oath, 23 Mar., but Peel opposed it and it was lost by 99-261; he divided against allowing Catholics to sit in Parliament that day. He voted against the second reading of the related Irish franchise bill, 19 Mar., and made his protest against it, 26 Mar. He called for greater securities, 27 Mar. 1829, when he voted against receiving the report, and he divided against the third reading three days later.

It may have been through his influence that Lord Ailesbury, who was looking to fill vacancies at Marlborough with anti-Catholics and whom he met on 20 Feb. 1829, brought in his son there.[46] He took his seat, 17 Mar., but was overshadowed by the activities of his father, who no doubt should most often be identified as the 'Mr. Estcourt' named in the reports of debates. He was reappointed to the select committee on the metropolitan police, 15 Apr. 1829, and probably chaired it again, but it never reported.[47] He defended the findings of the previous year's committee, 19,

25 May, when supporting Peel's successful bill. He voted in the minority against the committal of the silk trade bill, 1 May. He said that there was insufficient time left in the session for the House to consider the disfranchisement of East Retford, 5 May. He spoke and acted as a teller for the majority against the third reading of the St. James's, Westminster, vestry bill, 21 May. He rejected the argument of a petition against his Alehouses Licensing Act, 22 May. The same day, ministers having failed to indicate that the Maynooth grant would be discontinued after the current year, he carried out his threat to force a division against it, on which he was in the minority of 14. Either he or his son voted for a reduction in the grant for a sculpture of the marble arch, 25 May. The death of his wife, 23 June 1829, caused him to miss the Devizes Bear Club annual dinner for the first time in 25 years.[48]

Bucknall Estcourt voted against parliamentary reform, 18 Feb., and the enfranchisement of Birmingham, Leeds and Manchester, 23 Feb. 1830. He spoke in favour of committing the Avon and Gloucestershire Railway bill and declared that he would vote for this, 12 Mar. He supported one Dursley petition against distress and presented another, 16 Mar. He asked for a postponement of the debate on Jewish emancipation, 23 Mar., and voted against the proposal, 5 Apr., 17 May. He opposed the poor law amendment bill, 26 Apr., when he suggested possible improvements. He was a teller for the majority against postponing the third reading of the watching of parishes bill, 17 May, and spoke in its favour, 15 June. Although hostile to the principle of the sale of beer bill, he offered it his support, as a friend to free trade, 21 May, 3 June. However, he moved an amendment, 1 July, to limit its provisions to parishes of more than 300 houses, which he was persuaded to withdraw. Since he referred to having voted for previous amendments, it may have been he, not his son, who did so, 21 June, 1 July. He made comments on the Scottish and Irish paupers bill, 26 May, 4 June, the metropolitan police, 15 June, and the church commissioners, 17 June. His only other known vote that session was against abolition of the death penalty for forgery, 7 June 1830.

Having again been returned for Oxford University at the general election of 1830, he attended the proceedings at Devizes, 2 Aug., and the county meeting to congratulate William IV on his accession, 17 Aug., and he received praise for his work as recorder at the dinner for the new mayor, 29 Sept.[49] As a landlord, magistrate and militia officer, he was very active in the forcible suppression of the agricultural riots in both Wiltshire and Gloucestershire in the autumn, taking

leave from the House for this reason, 30 Nov., and he served on the special commission set up to try offenders in Wiltshire.[50] Though listed by ministers among their 'friends', he voted against them in the division on the civil list, 15 Nov., which precipitated their downfall. In a letter to Sidmouth, 12 Dec. 1830, in which he condemned the weak response of central government during the agrarian crisis, he wrote about the new Grey administration that

> of them, I suppose it is too early to offer any opinion, and the calamitous state to which we were reduced under their predecessors' reign too grievous not to inspire an earnest hope that whether Whig, Tory or Radical, an amelioration of our condition may be their work; all that Lord Grey is reported to have said seems very sensible, and in reference to Scotch banking full of hope.[51]

He was granted three weeks' leave to carry out his legal duties, 8 Feb. 1831. On 2 Mar. the House allowed him to give evidence to the Lords committee on the poor laws, where he blamed the rural atrocities on the low level of wages and advocated the distribution of land to cottagers and the abandonment of the Speenhamland system, 18 Mar. He was appointed to the select committee on secondary punishments, 17 Mar., and in his evidence to it, 20 Apr., he spoke of the efficacy of imprisonment, hard labour and transportation.[52] Lord Ellenborough recorded, 18 Mar. 1831, that 'Estcourt told me the speeches of Peel and others against the [reform] bill had produced a great effect and the opponents were honoured, but the ministers supported, and the tide ran strongly in favour of reform'.[53] He divided against the second reading of the bill, 22 Mar., justified the petition of the corporation of Devizes against it and denied allegations about Sidmouth's influence there, 18 Apr., and voted for Gascoyne's wrecking amendment, 19 Apr. At the subsequent general election he was again returned unopposed for Oxford University. He attended the elections at Devizes, 4 May, Cricklade, 6 May, when he voted for the successful candidates Robert Gordon and Thomas Calley, and Gloucestershire, 10 May, having previously signed a declaration in favour of Somerset's return and been a member of the committee which had persuaded him to withdraw the day before.[54] He supported the complaint of his colleague, Sir Robert Inglis, that the usual references to the providence of God's blessings had been omitted from the address, 22 June, and brought up the University's anti-reform petition, 24 June. He pressed ministers, 4 July, over whether they or a draftsman were responsible for the clause in the reintroduced reform bill which would apparently disfranchise many by allowing the payment of rent at shorter than quarterly intervals. He voted against the second reading, 6 July, for using the census of 1831 to determine the disfranchisement schedules, 19 July, and to postpone consideration of the partial disfranchisement of Chippenham, 27 July. That month he privately threatened to 'ask questions across the House soon' if ministers did nothing to provide relief for the poor before the onset of winter.[55] He signed the Wiltshire declaration against reform.[56] He objected to the enfranchising clauses, 6 Aug., on the grounds that the manufacturing interests of the west country would be left underrepresented, and he suggested that one seat be given to both Trowbridge and Bradford in Wiltshire. Urging continued progress on the settlement by hiring bill, 12 Aug. 1831, he classed it as 'of greater importance to the peasantry of this country, than the measure which at present occupies so much of the time of this House'.

He asked Lord Althorp, the leader of the House, to adjourn the reform bill over the planned Saturday sitting, 12 Aug., as he thought that the 'disorderly state of the House' was due 'mainly to the uneasiness arising from constant attendance on the subject', and he raised minor queries about it, 19, 20 Aug. 1831. He spoke against the Deacles, 22 Aug., 27 Sept., asked when the Irish education supply would be taken, 22 Aug., and (unless it was his son) voted for the censure motion against the Irish government over the Dublin election, 23 Aug. He defended the powers of magistrates under the Sale of Beer Act, 24 Aug., 5 Sept., but stated his disapproval of the measure. He presented and endorsed a petition from the non-resident freemen of Worcester against their disfranchisement, 27 Aug., when he moved an amendment to preserve the existing rights of voting. He argued that this would not conflict with ministers' intentions to reduce nomination influence and electoral expenses, but would preserve ancient privileges and chartered rights, and he acted as a teller in the division, which was lost by 89-17. Three days later it was probably he, not his son, who voted to preserve the right of voting to non-resident freemen for their lives. He commented on the definition of the distance from a town within which £10 householders would be eligible to vote, 30 Aug., 13 Sept. He raised fears that the costs of registration would fall upon county rates, 3, 5 Sept., and his amendment that commissioners not magistrates should decide the location of polling places in counties was negatived, 13 Sept. He voted in favour of issuing the Liverpool writ, 5 Sept., and against the third reading of the reform bill, 19 Sept., and its passage, 21 Sept. He defended the Church of Ireland, 12, 14 Sept., and voted to end the Maynooth grant after the current year, 26 Sept. He

was a teller for the majority in favour of amending the vestries bill, 29 Sept., and regretted that changes to it were not pressed, 30 Sept. He justified the conduct of magistrates in Ireland, 5 Oct., and repeated his ideas on how to better the condition of the labouring poor, 11 Oct. 1831.

Writing in despondent mood to Sidmouth, 14 Nov. 1831, Bucknall Estcourt foresaw

> much of misery in store for us before this notable ministry will bring us back even to the point from which they started, not that there is much of which to boast in the state to which R. C. emancipation, want of credit and confidence and inattention to agricultural distress had reduced us under the administration of our friends.

He reported that there had been little local reaction against reform, and that he had done militia duty in Bristol in the aftermath of the riots there.[57] He was appointed to the select committee on Irish tithes, 15 Dec., and on 27 Dec. Lord Brougham asked for his suggestions on amending the poor laws.[58] He voted against the second reading of the revised reform bill, 17 Dec. 1831. He divided against the vestries bill, 23 Jan. 1832, and (unless it was his son) against the production of information on military punishments, 16 Feb. On the reform bill, he asked whether joint-tenants in a single house valued at more than £10 a year would be entitled to vote, 7 Feb., and moved an amendment to relieve magistrates of the additional duties and costs under it, which Lord John Russell promised to consider, 11 Feb. He voted against the enfranchisement of Tower Hamlets, 28 Feb., and the third reading of the bill, 22 Mar. He presented an Oxford petition against the Purton Pill Railway bill, 17 Feb., and was instrumental in having it thrown out, 22 Mar.[59] He spoke in favour of allowing vestries to employ labourers in order to relieve agricultural distress, 17 Feb., 9 July. It may have been his son, rather than he, who voted in the minority against the malt drawback bill, 2 Apr., and for making permanent provision for the Irish poor by a tax on absentees, 19 June, and the bill to exclude insolvent debtors from Parliament, 27 June. He defended the vote of supply for the professors of Oxford and Cambridge, 13 Apr., and moved the committal of the beer bill, 18 July. His only other recorded votes were with opposition against the Russian-Dutch loan, 26 Jan., 12 July. At the Devizes Bear Club dinner, 24 Aug., he declared that 'at his time of life, and under existing circumstances, it must be manifest, that his humble services to his country, were drawing near to a close'.[60] However, at the general election in December 1832 he was again returned for Oxford University, where he sat until his retirement in 1847. Having moved his principal residence to Estcourt House in 1831, he resigned as a capital burgess councillor and recorder of Devizes in 1833 and as chairman of the Wiltshire quarter sessions in 1836.[61] He died in July 1853, being succeeded by his eldest son, then Member for Wiltshire North, who afterwards resumed the name of Estcourt (in addition to that of Sotheron).

[1] *HP Commons, 1790-1820*, iii. 715; Glos. RO, Sotheron Estcourt mss D1571 F438. [2] *Devizes Gazette*, 14 June 1900. [3] *HP Commons, 1790-1820*, ii. 411; *Wilts. Pollbook* (1819), 86; Sotheron Estcourt mss F209. [4] Sotheron Estcourt mss F209, Estcourt to Pembroke, 7 Feb. 1820; *Devizes Gazette*, 30 Sept. 1824; Wilts. RO, Devizes borough recs. G20/1/21, 22. [5] Sotheron Estcourt mss F220; *Devizes Gazette*, 16 Mar. 1820. [6] Sotheron Estcourt mss F279. [7] *Devizes Gazette*, 23 Mar., 18 May 1820. [8] Devizes borough recs. G20/1/21. [9] Devon RO, Sidmouth mss 152M/OA, Ilchester gaol commission; Sotheron Estcourt mss X25; *PP* (1822), xi. 277. [10] *The Times*, 6 June 1822. [11] PROB 11/1279/440; 1668/186; *London Gazette*, 6 May, 19 July 1823. [12] *The Times*, 9, 12 Mar. 1824. [13] Ibid. 4, 7 June 1824; Sotheron Estcourt mss X26. [14] Sotheron Estcourt mss X42-49. [15] *The Times*, 2 June 1824. [16] *Devizes Gazette*, 2 Sept. 1824. [17] Ibid. 24 Mar., 6 Oct.; *The Times*, 19 Feb., 30 Apr. 1825. [18] *Devizes Gazette*, 21 Apr.; *The Times*, 4 May 1825. [19] Add. 40342, f. 307; 40385, f. 153; 43231, f. 171; Hatherton mss, Littleton to ?Leigh, Feb. 1826; H.P. Liddon, *Life of Pusey*, i. 90-91. [20] Add. 40342, ff. 309-18; 40385, ff. 151, 162, 168, 170, 173; *Jackson's Oxford Jnl.* 4, 18, 25 Feb.; *Devizes Gazette*, 9 Feb. 1826; Sotheron Estcourt mss F285; X27. [21] *Devizes Gazette*, 16 Feb., 2 Mar. 1826. [22] Add. 40385, f. 288. [23] *The Times*, 15, 18 Mar., 22, 27, 28 Apr., 9, 13 May 1826. [24] *Devizes Gazette*, 15 June 1826. [25] *Gloucester Jnl.* 19 June, 29 July 1826. [26] *Devizes Gazette*, 21 Dec. 1826. [27] Add. 40387, f. 209; 40389, ff. 207, 210. [28] *The Times*, 8 Mar. 1827. [29] *Canning's Ministry*, 108. [30] *The Times*, 22 Mar., 10 Apr., 5 May, 1, 19 June 1827. [31] Ibid. 30 Mar., 10 Apr., 5, 31 May, 16 June 1827; NLS mss 3436, f. 159. [32] *Devizes Gazette*, 19 July 1827. [33] Sotheron Estcourt mss X51-59. [34] Ibid. F665. [35] Sidmouth mss. [36] Add. 40395, f. 221. [37] Sotheron Estcourt mss X30. [38] Ibid. X29. [39] Add. 40343, f. 193. [40] Devizes borough recs. G20/1/22. [41] N. Gash, *Pillars of Government*, 70. [42] Add. 40398, f. 114. [43] Sotheron Estcourt mss X114, T.G. to T.H.S. Bucknall Estcourt, 1, 6, 8, Mon. [?9] Feb. 1829. [44] Ibid. [45] *Oxf. Univ. Pollbook* (1829), 22-23. [46] Sotheron Estcourt mss F288; X114, T.G. to T.H.S. Bucknall Estcourt, 2-4 Mar. 1829. [47] Ibid. X30. [48] *Devizes Gazette*, 3 Sept. 1829. [49] Ibid. 5 Aug., 30 Sept; *Salisbury Jnl.* 23 Aug. 1830. [50] H. Bull and J. Waylen, *Hist. Devizes*, 557; *Devizes Gazette*, 25 Nov., 2, 9 Dec.; Sotheron Estcourt mss X60-63; Lansdowne mss, Bucknall Estcourt to Lansdowne, 21, 26-28, 30 Nov., 1, 2 Dec. 1830. [51] Sotheron Estcourt mss F665. [52] *PP* (1831), vii. 558; viii. 609. [53] *Three Diaries*, 69. [54] Sotheron Estcourt mss F290; *Cricklade Pollbook* (1831), 24; *Gloucester Jnl.* 23 Apr., 14 May 1831. [55] W. Suss. RO, Goodwood mss 635, ff. 19, 37. [56] *Devizes Gazette*, 11 Aug. 1831. [57] Sotheron Estcourt mss F665. [58] Ibid. F209. [59] Ibid. F244, Bragge Bathurst to Bucknall Estcourt, 25 Mar. 1832. [60] *Devizes Gazette*, 30 Aug. 1832. [61] Sotheron Estcourt mss F438; Add. 34571, f. 126; Devizes borough recs. G20/1/22.

S.M.F.

ESTCOURT *see also* **BUCKNALL ESTCOURT**

ETWALL, **Ralph** (1804–1882), of Andover, Hants.

ANDOVER   1831–1847

b. 30 May 1804, 1st s. of Ralph Etwall, attorney, of Andover and Elizabeth, da. of Richard Bird of Snoddington. *educ.* Trinity, Oxf. 1821; L. Inn 1824. *m.* 17 Oct. 1837, Mary Anne, da. of John Evans, wid. of one Hannam.[1] *s.p.* suc. fa. 1832. *d.* 15 Dec. 1882.

Lt. Andover yeoman cav. 1830.

Etwall, 'the gambler', was memorably portrayed by William Day, the son of his racehorse trainer, as

the most ungainly person, and for a gentleman the most uncouth, that I ever saw ... He was peculiar ... and one of his peculiarities was that he would never allow you to give any of his servants the smallest gratuity. He used to say that he paid them, and that was enough.

Likewise, he refused to tip other people's servants, 'no matter what they might have done for him'. His parsimony in this respect contrasted with his expenditure on racing and coursing, which always ran to 'more than his faint means would grant continuance', according to Day, who added that Etwall's lack of polish and 'want of education' could not be blamed on his upbringing and background, given that his parents possessed 'two or three freehold estates' in the neighbourhood of Andover.[2] The family had long been resident in the district. Etwall's grandfather Ralph Etwall (*d.* 1798), an attorney, had at various times held the corporate posts of bailiff, town chamberlain and town clerk. His first appointment in 1752 had galvanized the moribund corporation, which embarked upon a number of important public works. His son Ralph Etwall held the same municipal offices in broken spells, 1797-1828, was appointed a commissioner of lotteries with a salary of £350 in 1817, and after staging a successful revolt against the corporation's nominal patron the following year was thenceforth regarded as its 'co-patron'.[3] His marriage brought estates in north Hampshire at Snoddington and Longstock, where the inhabitants were regaled with 'good strong beer and other refreshments' at a coming of age celebration for Etwall in 1825.[4] He had been admitted to Lincoln's Inn the previous year, but was never called to the bar. At the 1831 general election he offered as a reformer for Andover, following a successful appeal by the inhabitants for the corporation to drop the anti-reform sitting Members Thomas Assheton Smith and Sir John Walter Pollen, both of whose families had employed his father as steward. In private his father had complained that the Grey ministry's bill would exclude many 'respectable inhabitants' from the franchise, but on the hustings

Etwall pledged to give it his unqualified support, commenting that 'on the triumph of the great measure ... depended the happiness and prosperity of the nation'. He was returned unopposed.[5]

Etwall, who is not known to have spoken in debate in this period, voted for the second reading of the reintroduced reform bill, 6 July, at least twice against the adjournment, 12 July, and gave steady support to its details, though he divided for the disfranchisement of Saltash, over which ministers provided no clear lead, 26 July, Lord Chandos's amendment to enfranchise £50 tenants-at-will, 18 Aug., and the total disfranchisement of Aldborough, 14 Sept. 1831. On 10 July he joined Brooks's, sponsored by 'Mr. Coke' and Sir Ronald Ferguson*. He voted for the passage of the bill, 21 Sept., the second reading of the Scottish measure, 23 Sept., and Lord Ebrington's confidence motion, 10 Oct. He divided with ministers on the Dublin election controversy, 23 Aug. He voted for the second reading of the revised reform bill, 17 Dec. 1831, again supported its details, and divided for the third reading, 22 Mar. 1832. He voted with government on relations with Portugal, 9 Feb. He divided for the address calling on the king to appoint only ministers who would carry the reform bill unimpaired, 10 May, and the second reading of the Irish bill, 25 May. He was in the minority for a select committee on colonial slavery, 24 May, but voted with ministers on the issue, 20 July 1832.

Etwall's father died 11 Nov. 1832, leaving him the Longstock estate and his house at Andover, along with the £6,500 residue of his personalty, which was proved in total under £40,000.[6] The duke of Wellington, who described Etwall to Lady Salisbury, 23 Nov., as 'a radical gentleman who has an enormous fortune', doubted if any Conservative could dislodge him from Andover in 1832, and he successfully defended his seat until 1847, when he retired.[7] He subsequently advocated shorter parliaments and repeal of the corn laws, and at the 1837 general election came out in favour of the secret ballot.[8] His wedding that year was celebrated at St. Sepulchre, Holborn, London, and both he and his bride were described as residents of Smithfield. The marriage was apparently childless, and his wife died 20 Oct. 1850 at Nursling, Hampshire.[9] According to Day, Etwall had ceased to race the previous year, having been ruined by the costs of maintaining his establishment and the expenses of contested elections. Afterwards he 'lived many years in seclusion' in France, evading his creditors, and paying occasional visits to friends in England *incognito*. At some unspecified point he returned and earned a living as an anonymous contributor to newspapers on racing matters.[10] In 1872 he wrote to the premier Gladstone, who brushed aside his claim for preferment.[11] He had apparently made over the Longstock estate to his brother William, while his mother and his sisters, Elizabeth and Ann, occupied the house at Andover, which he was reputed have visited under cover of darkness to beg for money.[12] Neither his mother (*d.* 1866) nor Ann (*d.* 1890) made any reference to him in the wills which they drew up in 1861. Etwall died intestate, still 'in straitened circumstances', in December 1882, 'at his residence in Connaught Street, Hyde Park'.[13] (An assertion that he died in exile in France is incorrect.)[14] No grant of administration has been found. A local newspaper commented blandly that 'the Etwall family, representatives of whom have always resided in the town ... have always retained general esteem, and done a large amount of good in a quiet unostentatious way'.[15]

[1] Marriage certificate (Bishopsgate district registry). [2] H.W. Earney, *Men of Andover* (Andover Local Archives Cttee. no. 6), 2-4; W. Day, *Reminiscences of the Turf* (1886), 241. [3] *Reg. of Unreformed Corporation of Andover* (Andover Local Archives Cttee. no. 7), unpaginated; J. Spaul, *Andover*, 60-61; *Black Bk.* (1820), 38; Oldfield, *Key* (1820), 174. [4] *VCH Hants*, iv. 450, 513; *Salisbury Jnl.* 6 June 1825. [5] *Salisbury Jnl.* 2, 9 May 1831; Hants RO, Andover borough recs. 37M85 11/PE/43; Hants RO 15M84 5/5/26. [6] PROB 11/1809/754; IR26/1290/811. [7] Hatfield House mss. [8] *Dod's Parl. Companion* (1838), 106-7; (1841), 149; (1847), 177-8; *Salisbury and Wilts. Herald*, 29 July 1837. [9] *Gent. Mag.* (1850), ii. 674. [10] Day, 242, 246-7; Earney, 4. [11] Add. 44541, f. 176. [12] *VCH Hants*, iv. 450; Andover borough recs. 37M85 18/AP/9: notes by S. Longstaff. [13] Day, 247; *The Times*, 16 Dec. 1882. [14] Earney, 2. [15] *Andover Standard*, 22 Dec. 1832.

H.J.S./P.J.S.

EUSTON, earl of *see* **FITZROY**, **Henry**

EVANS, **George De Lacy** (1787–1870), of 12 Regent Street and 6 Waterloo Place, Mdx.[1]

RYE	17 May 1830–1830
RYE	1831–1832
WESTMINSTER	11 May 1833–1841
WESTMINSTER	19 Feb. 1846–1865

b. 7 Oct. 1787, 3rd s. of John Evans of Lisready and Milltown, co. Limerick and Mary Ann, da. of Patrick Lacy of Milltown. *educ.* RMA, Woolwich. *m.* 21 June 1834, Josette, da. of Lt.-Col. Robert Arbuthnott, wid. of Philip Hughes, cdr. E.I. Co. marine service, *s.p.*[2] KCB 13 Feb. 1838; GCB 5 July 1855. *d.* 9 Jan. 1870.

Ensign 22 Ft. 1807, lt. 1808; lt. 3 Drag. 1812; capt. 5 W.I. Regt. 1815, half-pay 1817; brevet maj. 1815; dep. q.m.g. with Wellington's army 1815; brevet lt.-col. 1815;

brevet col. 1837; maj.-gen. 1846; col. 21 Ft. 1853-d.; lt.-gen. 1854; gen. 1861.

Evans, the youngest son of a small landowner and farmer, was born at Moig, county Limerick. His mother's family had a strong military tradition and, like his elder brother Richard Lacy Evans (?1782-1847), who became a cadet in the East India Company's forces in 1800, he followed this line. He entered the army in India as a volunteer in 1806, obtained a commission the following year and was promoted in 1808. He declined an invitation to join Sir John Malcolm's* mission to Persia, preferring active service in the Deccan. In March 1812 he secured a transfer to the 3rd Dragoons in the Peninsula, where he served for two years in a staff capacity, playing a conspicuous and daring role in all the major engagements. In March 1814 he was attached as deputy quartermaster to the corps sent under General Ross to act with Cochrane's fleet on the American eastern seaboard. He showed bravery at Bladensberg, 24 Aug. 1814, and later that day led the successful attack on Washington. He fought at Baltimore, 12 Sept., and in the New Orleans operations in December 1814, when he was twice wounded. Promoted to captain in January 1815 and major in May, he joined the staff of the duke of Wellington's army and served with distinction at Quatre Bras and Waterloo. His merits were recognized by promotion to lieutenant-colonel, his third step in three months. He remained some time with the army of occupation, was placed on captain's half-pay in 1817 and on his return to Britain served briefly with the troops sent to Glasgow during the disturbances of 1819. He later claimed to have made numerous unsuccessful offers to serve abroad in the following years, and to the end of his life he resented this stagnation of his career, which he attributed to personal malice on the part of the military hierarchy. He wrote an untitled and undated pamphlet on Waterloo, in refutation of a French account, and *Facts Relating to the Capture of Washington* (1829), a defence of Ross against the criticisms of Admiral Cockburn.[3]

By 1824 Evans was on very friendly terms with Robert Otway Cave* of Stanford Hall, Leicestershire, who later left him £20,000 in a codicil to his will. (A chancery suit was required to obtain the money in 1847.)[4] He was involved in Otway Cave's successful campaign for a seat for Leicester in 1826, when he advised him to compromise his pro-Catholic views in order to secure influential support: 'hereafter when you are more independent in point of fortune you may be disposed to change your mind and it will be time enough then to do it'.[5] He made a name for himself in the late 1820s as a Russophobe. In August 1828 he published *On the Designs of Russia*, in which he argued fancifully that success in the conflict with Turkey would put world domination easily within Russia's grasp and called for armed intervention by Britain and France. The book, which sold 500 copies, received considerable attention in the press, though few reviewers concurred in Evans's views. Late in 1829, after the peace of Adrianople, he produced a more temperate work, *On the Practicability of an Invasion of British India*. This consisted largely of quotations from a number of authorities designed to illustrate the Russian threat to India and to establish that Britain possessed the economic resources to meet it. He welcomed the passage of Catholic emancipation and argued that, despite appearances, the aggregate of national wealth was greater than ever:

> Still pauperism spreads, and demoralization with it. The evil, however is not the diminution, but the inequality of wealth; and, unfortunately, the nature and repartition of the taxes, instead of tending to remedy, are calculated to promote ... this inequality. If means, however, are to be found, in one order of society, for alleviating any excessive pressure on another, we may be well assured that the present government will fearlessly advance to effect that end.

Evans succeeded in stimulating an official investigation of the possible Russian threat to India. Lord Ellenborough, president of the board of control, discussed his book with the premier Wellington and sent copies for evaluation to the experts Sir James Macdonald* and Malcolm. Both complimented Evans for drawing timely attention to an important problem, but concluded that although Russian activity required careful monitoring, there was no immediate danger to British India.[6]

In March 1830 Evans, a thin, swarthy scruffy individual,[7] was invited to contest a by-election for Rye by the leaders of the independent interest there, who for five years had been trying to wrest control of the borough from the Lamb family. He was beaten at the poll but petitioned and secured a decision on the right of election which gave him the seat.[8] He was sworn in on 19 May. On 27 May he presented the petition of the inhabitants of Rye complaining of an abuse of magisterial power by Herbert Barrett Curteis*, who earlier that month had sent in coast guards to curb disorders resulting from the townsmen's destruction of a sluice which was impeding the free navigation of Rye harbour and the river Rother. Evans outlined the recent history of the dispute on this issue between the townsmen and the neighbouring landowners, who included Curteis and his father, Member for Sussex. He argued that his constituents had been 'morally justifiable' in wrecking the sluice: not only had the landowners defied a chancery decree of 1826 by failing to modify it, but they had in 1830 introduced a bill intended to annul that decree. On the advice of Joseph Hume*, Evans let the matter drop, lest he prejudice the question, on which there was considerable sympathy for the inhabitants of Rye in official circles. The admiralty subsequently intervened to impose a compromise which temporarily satisfied the bill's opponents. Evans voted for parliamentary reform, 28 May, abolition of the death penalty for forgery, 7 June, modification of the sale of beer bill, 1 July, against increased recognizances in libel cases, 9 July, and to abolish colonial slavery, 13 July 1830.

His electoral success at Rye was celebrated with a triumphal procession and dinner, 16 June 1830, when he joined in calls for the example set there to be followed throughout the country. He stood for the borough with his fellow-reformer Benjamin Smith at the general election, when he was probably instrumental in encouraging the contests which occurred in the other 'oppressed' Cinque Ports of Hastings (where Otway Cave stood), Hythe, New Romney and Winchelsea. The patron of Rye, the Rev. George Augustus Lamb, defied the May ruling on the right of election, against which he had appealed to Parliament, and Evans and Smith were beaten at the poll. They petitioned, but when an election appeal committee reversed the decision of May they gave up the legal struggle.[9] Evans, 'the complete idol of the Cinque Ports', attended several meetings at Rye in the interim. On 19 Oct. 1830 he welcomed the revolution in France, but thanked the admiralty for their intervention in the harbour dispute and spoke warmly of Wellington as lord warden of the Cinque Ports, trusting to his good offices to ensure fair play in the impending trial of the right of election. These conciliatory utterances may have provided the basis of the charge of 'political dishonesty', excused only by his 'poverty', which was made against him two years later by an enemy: 'he came into the House as a radical, then went over [to] the duke, and being refused the post of king's aide-de-camp he joined the Whigs, and would have been with them now if they had paid him'.[10] After the unfavourable decision of the appeal committee he urged the Hastings and Rye independents to join forces with their fellows throughout the country in agitating for parliamentary reform and the destruction of corrupt oligarchies. On 3 Mar. 1831, two days after the unveiling of the Grey ministry's reform scheme, he addressed meetings at Hastings and Rye in its support,

though he stated his personal wish that it had included the ballot and triennial parliaments.[11] The following day he spoke at the Westminster reform meeting, and was reported as having said that 'ten thousand persons were ready to march up to London' from Sussex if the bill was defeated. He subsequently denied any intention to incite armed insurrection, claiming that he had merely expressed his fear that obstructive opposition to the measure could provoke serious disorder; but Francis Place, the Westminster radical activist, later claimed that Evans was one of several army officers who had been 'ready to lead' a show of force to ensure the success of the bill.[12]

At the general election of 1831 Evans was encouraged by John Cam Hobhouse* to go to Preston to oppose Henry Hunt, who was felt in respectable reforming circles to have betrayed the cause by denouncing the bill as inadequate. He had been 'left bare' of money by his activities at Rye, which had cost him £4,000; but Place secured an apparent promise of payment of his expenses from Hobhouse's fellow-Member for Westminster Sir Francis Burdett and the managers of the Loyal and Patriotic Fund. Furnished with letters of introduction from Place, Evans arrived at Preston on 27 Apr., when he declared his hostility to all trade monopolies, especially the corn laws, advocated reform of the established church and defended the reform bill despite its shortcomings.[13] He was too late to stand any chance of success, the more so as Hunt's colleague Wood refused to join forces with him, and he was in any case summoned back to Rye during the night by a deputation from his supporters there. The squabbles which had arisen since the 1830 election among the Rye independents were temporarily laid aside and Evans again stood with Smith. They made no attempt to poll the votes which had been deemed ineligible by the appeal committee, but serious disorder occurred when their supporters, provoked by Lamb's parade of physical and military force, barricaded the streets and intimidated those who wished to vote for his nominees. Lamb was forced to concede one seat in return for a promise to keep the peace and Evans was returned.[14] Place subsequently tried to extract £100 from the Loyal and Patriotic Fund to cover Evans's travelling expenses but, to the disgust of both men, payment was refused.[15] Evans intruded himself on the freeholders of Leicestershire, 6 May 1831, when he defended Otway Cave's role in the intrigues which had preceded the return of two reformers and attacked the conduct of one of them, Thomas Paget, whom Burdett considered to be 'a pendant of Hunt'.[16] He attended the annual Westminster purity of election dinner, 23 May 1831, when, responding to a toast to himself and the electors of Rye, he gave one to 'the heroic Poles'.[17]

Evans proved to be a voluble and dogged but largely ineffective parliamentarian in this period. He was a self consciously poor speaker, and his ignorance of parliamentary protocol frequently led him astray.[18] He responded to the anti-reformer Wetherell's condemnation of the 'barricades at Rye', 21 June 1831, blaming the trouble on Lamb's provocative tactics and the inhabitants' resentment of his corrupt domination of the borough. He denied Hunt's allegation that he had been sent to Preston by the Parliamentary Candidate Society and boasted that but for the lateness of his arrival he would have 'performed a great public service' by turning him out, 23 June. He could not agree to O'Connell's proposal for disbandment of the Irish yeomanry, 27 June, preferring their gradual reduction and a proportionate augmentation of regular troops. In the same debate he called for improved treatment of half-pay officers, though he doubted the practicability of Hume's suggestions. He voted for the second reading of the reintroduced reform bill, 6 July, and two days later, after another clash with Hunt, repeated his view that its defeat would entail 'lamentable and melancholy circumstances'. He also vowed to propose abolition of the law of primogeniture. He voted for most of the details of the reform bill, though he was in the minorities against the division of counties, 11 Aug., and for the disfranchisement of Aldborough, 14 Sept. He criticized ministers over the slow progress of the bill, 26 July, when he applauded the disfranchisement of New Romney. On the proposal to deprive Rye of one Member, 30 July, he put the case for uniting it with Winchelsea to return two. He appealed for support to the opponents of reform, but had an uncomfortable time in trying to gloss over the violence which had attended his election and withdrew his motion when ministers resisted it. He welcomed the enfranchisement of Brighton, 5 Aug. On 24 Aug. he presented petitions from Bury for an extension of its boundaries to prevent the exercise of undue influence and from Rye complaining of 'useless delays' in the progress of the bill. The Speaker deemed the latter unacceptable and he withdrew it, as he did one from Manchester against the enfranchisement of tenants-at-will which was also ruled out of order, 5 Sept. He voted for the third reading and passage of the bill, 19, 21 Sept., when he addressed the Westminster meeting to petition the Lords in its favour as a Member

of that estate miscalled the House of Commons ... [He] was heartily wearied of listening to debates upon reform for the last three months, nor did he participate in the zeal which seemed to animate both parties within the walls of Parliament, for he conceived that they assumed to themselves more power and influence over the decision of the question than in his opinion they really possessed. The bill had been submitted to the empire at large before it was proposed to the acceptance of the legislature, and the public had sealed its fate from the beginning by their unanimous acquiescence.[19]

He voted for the second reading of the Scottish reform bill, 23 Sept. 1831.

Evans carped at the size of the grants for convict settlements and additional churches, 18 July, and for the Society for the Propagation of the Gospels and the defence of Canada, 25 July 1831. He approved government's agreement with France on the dismantling of some of the Belgian frontier fortresses, 25, 27 July. On 21 July he moved for information on the case of Thomas and Caroline Deacle of Marwell, who had been arrested for conspiracy during agricultural disturbances in Hampshire in November 1830. The charges were subsequently dropped and Deacle sued six magistrates for unlawful arrest. All were acquitted except William Bingham Baring*, who was found guilty of assault, but Deacle was awarded a derisory £50 in damages. Evans, who admitted that he knew no more of the business than what he had read in the press, found little support and, with ministers coming to Baring's defence, he did not persevere. His unauthorized initiative only angered the Deacles and on 22 Aug., conceding that he had unintentionally done them 'great injury', he presented their petition to be heard at the bar of the House to clear their names. They expected him to press for a full inquiry, but he unhappily prevaricated until it became clear that no further litigation would take place. When he moved for a select committee, 27 Sept., he found ministers firmly against him and was beaten by 78-31. He later claimed that after raising the case, a 'heinous' offence in the eyes of 'party men of all kinds', he was subjected to 'a considerable indication of odium and hostility, on the part of the lower official people'.[20] He voted in the minorities for swearing in the Dublin election committee, 29 July, against the issue of a new writ, 8 Aug., and for disarming the Irish yeomanry, 11 Aug., but rallied to government in the divisions on alleged interference in the Dublin election, 23 Aug. The Polish revolution of 1830 had reinforced his Russophobia and on 16 Aug. he drew attention to the plight of the Poles and moved for information on their conflict with Russia. Ministers, seeing no scope for British interference, resisted and Evans was reprimanded by the Speaker for accusing the House of neglecting its moral duty. He presented petitions on the subject, 7, 16 Sept. He repeated his criticisms of the Irish yeomanry, 3 Oct. Next day, on the pretext of paving the way for 'some specific measure for the maintenance of the public peace' in 'the present awful crisis', he moved for disclosure of the military preparations alleged to have been made in case of insurrection in November 1830. Lord Porchester* thought it a 'queer' motion, and it found no seconder.[21] At the Westminster meeting to protest against the Lords' rejection of the reform bill, 10 Oct., Evans stressed 'the necessity of a peaceable, though firm demeanour in the present trial';[22] but when supporting Lord Ebrington's confidence motion later the same day he caused a stir in the House with his declaration that

> no government can exist in this country opposed to reform, except one prepared to maintain its power by force and the sword ... If any government should attempt to govern on such principles ... I would be one of the first to draw my sword in resistance against it.

He again failed to secure a declaration of support for Poland, 13 Oct., but promised a comprehensive motion on the subject next session. He endorsed the prayer of a petition presented by Hunt for the exclusion of bishops from the Lords, 18 Oct., and gave notice of a motion for the following day for a delay of no more than a month in the reintroduction of the reform bill. In the event he withdrew it, having been assured in the interim that the prorogation would be brief. He presented a petition for the creation of peers and disfranchisement of bishops to secure the bill, 20 Oct. 1831.

Evans, who became alarmed by the violence of the reform riots, was present at a meeting of the committee formed to organize a public meeting to launch the National Political Union, 27 Oct. 1831. According to Place, he subsequently acted 'a rather disgraceful part' by colluding with Burdett, to whom 'he had been toadeating', in his belated attempt to postpone the meeting, at which it was planned to create an alliance between middle and working class reformers. Evans attended the meeting, 31 Oct., but evidently played no conspicuous role in the subsequent proceedings of the Union and presumably resigned from it with Burdett some weeks later.[23] He addressed reform meetings at Lewes, 4 Nov., when he denounced the bishops and voiced his confidence that ministers would introduce an improved reform bill, and at Rye, 7 Nov.[24] A week later he chaired a meeting of the inhabitants of St. James's, Westminster to form a Loyal Association to back government in carrying reform, and expressed his support for 'armed associations for the citizens of the metropolis, to protect themselves equally from the borough monger and the

pickpocket'.[25] Later that month he applied to the lord lieutenant of Sussex and to Wellington for authority to raise a corps of volunteers to protect property in and around Rye, but was refused.[26]

Evans voted for the second reading of the revised reform bill, 17 Dec. 1831, but was not a particularly assiduous attender during its progress through committee. He blamed 'an accidental indisposition' for his absence from the division on the enfranchisement of Tower Hamlets, 28 Feb. 1832.[27] He voted for the third reading, 22 Mar. He was in the government majorities on the Russian-Dutch loan, 26 Jan., and relations with Portugal, 9 Feb. On 14 Feb. he advanced the view that cholera was 'not a dangerously contagious disorder', and the next day argued that the prevention bill would 'produce more injury than good, by retarding the commerce of the country'. His suggestion of a commission of inquiry into the origin and spread of the disease was ignored, and he had no more success on 23 Feb., when he was accused of risking catastrophe by seeking to play down the seriousness of the outbreak. He deplored the 'spirit of party' in opposition attacks on his friend Admiral George Sartorius, who had enlisted under Dom Pedro in the Portuguese civil war, and clashed with Hobhouse, now war secretary, over the cost of the foreign half-pay establishment, 17 Feb. He complained – mistakenly, so the Speaker thought – of the exorbitance of solicitors' fees for conducting cases against bills before committees, 22 Feb. It was at about this time that he told Otway Cave:

> I have been ... till the last day or two far from right inside, finding myself more alarmed a day or two back at hearing my own voice that I have come to the conclusion of inflicting a sentence or two almost each day so as to habituate myself to the matter if possible, however humiliating it maybe to make such small attempts so often and perhaps indifferent. I think I have got some propositions for economy in the military department which may be of use ... You will be delighted to hear that the tithe system is to be done away, but it remains to be proved that the remedy is a good one.[28]

He welcomed the French invasion of Italy, 13, 26 Mar., when he also denied that the Foreign Enlistment Act had been violated by Dom Pedro's expedition. He was in correspondence with Sartorius and his former regimental colleague George Lloyd Hodges, who was commanding Dom Pedro's British Legion, and seems to have considered joining them in Portugal, but nothing came of the notion. On 16 Apr. he challenged Peel to say whether he wished the government to intervene against Dom Pedro. He attacked the purchase system of promotion in the army, 28 Mar., and supported Hume's criticism of military pensions, 2 Apr. He voted with government for the navy civil departments bill, 6 Apr., but later that day was in the minority against the arrears of tithes bill. He told Otway Cave that Robert Ferguson* had 'not behaved courteously' in shouldering him aside on the Polish issue; but, he went on, 'I do not mind that much. I do not like to annoy [the foreign secretary] Lord Palmerston if I could help it, and I am thus relieved from bringing forward this question and yet can speak on it'.[29] He did so briefly on 18 Apr. 1832, having earlier welcomed the government's plans for Irish education.

Evans voted for the address asking the king to appoint only ministers who would carry undiluted reform, 10 May 1832. At the Westminster meeting called to protest at their resignation the following day he condemned proceedings in the Lords as 'a desperate experiment on the presumed baseness of the House of Commons, and the cowardice and pusillanimity of the people of England', and advocated the withholding of taxes to secure reform.[30] Later, in the House, he deplored the prospect of Wellington's accession to power, which he thought could only be maintained by military force. Place later implied, albeit vaguely, that during the days of crisis which followed, Evans was one of a number of army officers who were 'ready to serve the people against the Tories'.[31] On 23 May he defended the right of soldiers to 'entertain political opinions', but attacked Wellington for 'bartering his purely-earned glories of victory for the doubtful honours of a political career'. He presented a Rye petition for supplies to be withheld until the reform bill had been carried, 1 June. Evans voted for the Liverpool disfranchisement bill, 23 May, the abolition of colonial slavery, 24 May, and the second reading of the Irish reform bill, 25 May. On 7 June he advocated reduced factory hours for children and unsuccessfully sought information on municipal recorderships, which he believed were abused by peers for electoral purposes. He supported repeal of the taxes on knowledge, 14 June, and voted for an absentee tax to relieve Irish poverty, 19 June, when he also supported the suspension of flogging in the army, though he was not prepared to risk such an experiment in time of war. He was in minorities for amendments to the coroners bill, 20 June, and to the boundaries bill, 22 June. Supporting Ferguson's motion on Poland, 28 June, he welcomed Palmerston's admission that Britain had a right to remonstrate with Russia, but demanded armed intervention in alliance with France. He was in the government majorities on the Russian-Dutch loan, 12, 16, 20 July. He spoke and voted for inquiry into the inns of court, 17 July, backed Hume's attempts to exclude the recorder of Dublin from the

House, 18, 24 July, and promised to propose the exclusion of full-pay army officers at a future date. On 25 July he questioned ministers about arrangements for the burial of London cholera victims and argued that the only 'just' way to prevent smuggling was to lower customs duties. Next day he proposed wholesale reductions, amounting to £2,000,000, in the military establishment, an area in which he felt that ministers had been badly remiss. Hobhouse, moving the previous question, observed that 'looking at the deserted benches, it does not seem as if the House was disposed to join' Evans 'in his gallop through the establishments of the army'. The resolutions were negatived. Evans spoke and voted for reception of a petition for the abolition of tithes and supported a call for resistance to the repressive policies of the German Diet, 2 Aug. He moved but did not press a resolution for intervention in support of Poland, 7 Aug., and the following day supported the Greek Convention bill, welcoming the establishment of an independent Greek state, though on 10 Aug. he insisted that the Greek government should pay its due debts. He was reproved by Hume for being too ready to accept the salary proposed for lord chancellor Brougham, 9 Aug. 1832.

In February 1832 Place had supplied Evans with statistics on rates and taxes. In July, wishing to draw attention to his belief that the Reform Act, by requiring borough voters to have paid their current year's poor rates and assessed taxes by the end of that month in order to qualify, would drastically reduce the size of the electorate at the impending general election, he persuaded Evans to move for returns on the subject, 27, 30 July. On 7 Aug. Evans, having been coached by Place, alleged that two-thirds of potential borough voters might be disfranchised and proposed that the regulations should be relaxed. Only Hume supported him and he was beaten by 66-2. According to Place, he was 'so alarmed' by the fear of making a fool of himself that he wanted to 'drop the matter', but Place provided him with evidence to support motions for more returns and for an address for the convening of a short session to tackle the problem, 9 Aug., when he painted an alarming picture of the anticipated extent of disfranchisement in the Lancashire industrial towns. For the government Lord Althorp, insisting that the problem had been greatly exaggerated, would have none of it. Evans raised the subject again when supporting a Westminster petition for redress, 11 Aug., but on 15 Aug. 1832 was forced to concede that information lately received showed his 'suppositions' about Lancashire to have been wildly erroneous, though he still thought that 'great disfranchisement' would occur in London.[32]

O'Connell had a notion of Evans's standing for Limerick as a Repealer at the 1832 general election, but nothing came of it.[33] He was beaten at Rye by a member of the Curteis family, who had been given a decisive advantage by the extension of the constituency's boundaries. He was additionally handicapped by his estrangement from some of his former supporters in the borough, where divisions among the independents had reappeared after the 1831 victory. He also stood for Westminster in response to the invitation of elements hostile to Hobhouse. As at Rye, he espoused a radical programme of the ballot, shorter parliaments, repeal of the assessed taxes and the taxes on knowledge, church reform, abolition of tithes, free trade and factory reform. 'It furnishes serious ground for apprehension and regret', he declared, 'that the ministers do not intend to proceed in the work of reform, in that manner which the country has been led to expect'. Hobhouse's supporter Le Marchant dismissed Evans as a 'demagogue' and described him on the hustings:

He looked anything but the representative of an English constituency – in short, anything but English. Those who could recollect the jolly good-humored convivial countenance of Mr. Fox, or the comely elegance of Burdett, could have drawn comparisons rather odious ... Tall and thin, with very sallow complexion, and jet black hair and whiskers, one might almost have mistaken him for an Italian assassin. His speech was dull and but ill adapted to his audience.

Evans came a poor third on that occasion, but had his revenge six months later when Hobhouse resigned both his office and his seat to put his popularity to the test.[34] He lost the seat in 1841, but regained it in 1846 and held it for 19 years. He achieved further notoriety by taking command of the controversial British Auxiliary Legion on the side of the queen regent of Spain against Don Carlos, 1835-7. Some observers ridiculed him as 'a vain coxcomb' who 'fancies himself a great general', and as 'the *Brummagem* Wellington', but his services set him on the road to belated promotion.[35] In 1854, at the age of 66, he commanded the second division of the army in the Crimea with striking bravery. He returned home a hero, but with his health damaged.[36] He died of bronchitis in January 1870. In codicils to his will, which was sworn under £80,000, he left legacies totalling £57,000.[37]

---

[1] See E.M. Spiers, *Radical General: Sir George De Lacy Evans, 1787-1870* (1983). [2] *Gent. Mag.* (1832), i. 376; (1834), ii. 208; (1861), i. 354. His wife brought him a son, Philip Alexander Hughes, by her first husband and a considerable fortune (Spiers, 65; *The Times*, 18 July 1870). [3] Spiers, 1-18; Add. 43252, ff. 333-9. [4] Leics. RO, Braye

mss 130-44; PROB 11/2010/19; 2020/547; *The Times*, 4 Mar. 1845, 6 Mar. 1847. [5] Braye mss 3453, 3457, 3536. [6] J. Gleason, *Genesis of Russophobia*, 85, 101-4; Spiers, 19-29; *Quarterly Rev.* xxxix (1829), 1-41; *Ellenborough Diary*, ii. 92, 122-3, 149-50; Add. 21178, ff. 34-77. [7] [J. Grant], *Random Recollections of Commons* (1837), 257. [8] Spiers, 40-44; *Brighton Guardian*, 10 Mar. 1830. [9] *Brighton Guardian*, 23 June, 28 July, 4, 11 Aug. 1830. [10] *Hastings Iris*, 23 Oct., 13 Nov. 1830; *Three Diaries*, 285. [11] *Hastings Iris*, 1, 29 Jan., 5 Feb., 5 Mar. 1831. [12] *Morning Chron.* 5, 9 Mar. 1831; *Ann. Reg.* (1831), Hist. p. 80; Add. 27789, ff. 276, 280. [13] Spiers, 44-45; *Preston Chron.* 30 Apr. 1831; Add. 36466, ff. 317, 333. [14] *Hastings Iris*, 30 Apr., 7, 21 May 1831. [15] Add. 27789, ff. 375-8, 36466, ff. 332, 335, 345, 354. [16] *Leicester Jnl.* 13 May 1831. [17] Add. 56555, f. 140; *The Times*, 24 May 1831. [18] Grant, 255-6. [19] *The Times*, 22 Sept. 1831. [20] Spiers, 46-48; Evans, *Letter to Electors of Westminster* (1833), 32. [21] Hants RO, Carnarvon mss 75M91/L12/9. [22] *Morning Herald*, 11 Oct. 1831. [23] Add. 27791, ff. 38, 44; 27822, f. 31; *Morning Advertiser*, 1 Nov.; *The Times*, 5 Nov. 1831. [24] *Brighton Guardian*, 9, 16 Nov. 1831. [25] *The Times*, 16 Nov.; *Brighton Guardian*, 23 Nov. 1831. [26] Spiers, 49. [27] *The Times*, 1 Mar. 1832. [28] Braye mss 3541. [29] Ibid. 3540. [30] *The Times*, 12 May 1832. [31] Add. 27789, f. 280; 27790, ff. 243-4; 27793, f. 104. [32] Add. 27796, ff. 80-90; 35149, ff. 135, 172-9; Spiers, 50. [33] *O'Connell Corresp.* iv. 471. [34] Spiers, 50-52; *Croker Pprs.* ii. 195, 210; D. Miles, *Francis Place*, 208-10; *Westminster Election* (1832), 15-28; *Three Diaries*, 284. [35] Spiers, 66-100; *Greville Mems.* iii. 209; *Raikes Jnl.* iii. 155. [36] *Oxford DNB*; Spiers, 146-72. [37] *The Times*, 11, 18 Jan., 18 July 1870.

D.R.F.

EVANS, Henry (*d.*1842), of Old Town, co. Cork.

WEXFORD	1 Mar. 1819–1820
WEXFORD	1826–13 May 1829

4th s. of Nicholas Green Evans of Carker House and Hannah, da. of Randall Roberts of Britfieldstown. *m.* (1) 1 May 1801, Elizabeth, da. and coh. of Andrew Nash of Rossnalee, 1s. 1da.; (2) 1812, Mary Anne, da. of Peter Holmes of Peterfield, co. Tipperary, *s.p. d.* 13 Dec. 1842.

Lt. RN 1782, cdr. 1794, capt. 1797, r.-adm. (ret.) 1821, v.-adm. 1841.

Evans retired from Wexford at the 1820 dissolution as the nominee of its former Member Richard Nevill, who in alternate turn with Lord Ely had controlled the representation since the Union. On Nevill's death in 1822 he assigned his interest in the borough to Evans, whose brother Nathaniel had married Nevill's first cousin, until his grandson Sir Edward Cholmeley Dering* came of age, it having been long established that the 'cordial union' between the patrons would be 'continued to their issue male, and in failure thereof to their nominees'.[1] To the annoyance of Dering's mother Lady Henrietta Geary, however, Evans, 'without consulting any of the Nevill family', signed a document, which was circulated to the freemen, saying that by keeping the 'cordial union' with Nevill's 'nominee', Ely had 'fulfilled the compact' and was therefore 'not to be considered as pledged to any future support of the Nevill interest', 29 June 1822.[2]

At the 1826 general election Evans returned himself as the locum of his patron's interest, with the support of Ely.[3] He signed the petition of Irish landed proprietors against Catholic claims, 15 Feb.,[4] and voted thus, 6 Mar. 1827, 12 May 1828, when he declared that he had 'lived eleven years in Ireland' and could not believe in the 'good effects which are to be produced by these amalgamations and dovetailings' of Protestants and Catholics, and that the same sentiments were shared by his constituents. He denied a charge that he was merely the nominee of 'the mayor and a few burgesses of Wexford'. He defended the right of naval officers on the post list to be made admirals and strongly objected to being called a 'yellow admiral' by Sir George Cockburn, who apologized, insisting that the term had not been intended as a slight, 16 May. He complained that it was easy for those 'who lived during the war in comfort and composure, while the navy were defending them from invasion, to talk now only of the dead weight' of military pensions, but warned that 'mistaken reductions' would impair the future efficiency of the service, 19 May 1828. He clashed repeatedly with Hume on the navy estimates the following year, arguing that officers who 'had been fighting battles in a foreign country and enduring every possible hardship, while the Honourable Member was at home in bed', had legitimate claims, and on 27 Feb. citing the 'verse of an old song': 'When sailors we are wanting, we give them bread and beer, but now the French are beaten, there's nothing left to fear'. On 9 Feb. he presented and endorsed the first of some 25 Irish petitions against Catholic emancipation, which on the 16th he declared was 'inconsistent with the Protestant constitution of this country' and 'in conformity with the oath I took on entering this House, I must in conscience always oppose'. He announced that he had 'joined the Brunswick institution' because the 'Roman Catholic combinations growing around me' rendered 'the life of every Protestant in Ireland in danger', 12 Feb., but dismissed comparisons with the Catholic Association, saying their 'religion is impious and idolatrous' whereas the Brunswickers were 'satisfied with their king, their constitution, and their laws', 19 Feb. He was, of course, listed by the patronage secretary Planta as 'opposed to the principle' of emancipation and he voted accordingly, 6, 18 Mar.; but he was absent from the division on the third reading, 30 Mar. He warned that the Catholics 'we are about to introduce into Parliament are, as we have all sworn, idolators', 17 Mar., and paired for a bid to prevent their sitting, 23 Mar. He doubted that raising the Irish freehold qualification to £10 would be 'sufficient to protect the Protestant interests' and proposed

£15 instead, 26 Mar., arguing that a £20 qualification 'would throw the influence too much into the hands of the aristocracy' while that of £10 gave 'too much influence to the democracy'. In his last known speech next day, he complained that

> the old ship, the constitution, which last year we thought safely at anchor, with ... [Peel] as her commander ... [had broken] from her anchors, and is, I think, fairly at sea. Protestant ascendancy and the 40s. freeholders have both been thrown overboard, and a great number of their supporters will, I suppose, also fall into the sea.

His comments evidently hit their mark, for on 30 Mar. Peel, 'borrowing the metaphor of the gallant admiral', replied that 'it does not always follow that the pilot is bound to steer the same course to guard the ship from danger'. On 30 Apr. 1829 Dering, who was 'just of age', announced that Evans had advised him that 'indisposition will oblige him to retire' and declared his candidature for the vacancy.[5] Four days later Evans informed Ely that 'finding my interference in Wexford has given no satisfaction to either party, and been attended with considerable trouble and expense to myself', he had taken steps to vacate and would 'decline all further interference in the borough'.[6] On 13 May 1829 he took the Chiltern Hundreds, leaving Ely and Dering to engage in a 'furious family contest for the borough', in which the controversial agreement he had made with Ely in 1822 featured prominently. A few days before the poll 'an attempt was made between the parties to reconcile their differences', in support of which Evans made 'a long disclosure of the circumstances of the case', but to no avail.[7] His own vote for Dering was later struck off by an election committee 'on the grounds of his not having been sworn in as a freeman'.[8] Evans was one of the three Protestant landlords whom the Doneraile conspirators were hanged for plotting to murder in October 1829.[9]

Evans died at Old Town in December 1842 and was succeeded by his only son Nicholas.[10]

[1] *PP* (1835), xxviii. 179. [2] Ibid. (1820), iv. 357; *The Times*, 9 Mar. 1830. [3] *Dublin Evening Post*, 22 June; *Wexford Evening Post*, 23 June 1826. [4] Add. 40392, f. 3. [5] *Wexford Herald*, 9 May 1829. [6] *PP* (1830), iv. 357. [7] *Wexford Herald*, 3 June; *The Times*, 23 May, 9 June 1829. [8] *The Times*, 15 Mar. 1830. [9] *O'Connell Corresp.* iv. 1616. [10] *Gent. Mag.* (1843), i. 322.

P.J.S.

EVANS, William (1788–1856), of Allestree Hall,
Derbys.

b. 17 Jan. 1788, 1st surv. s. of William Evans, banker
and industrialist, of Darley Abbey and Elizabeth, da. of
Jedediah Strutt of Belper. *m.* 31 July 1820, Mary, da. of
Rev. Thomas Gisborne of Yoxall Lodge, Staffs., 1s. *suc.*
fa. 1796.; grandfa. Thomas Evans of Derby 1814. *d.* 8
Apr. 1856.

Cornet, Derbys. yeoman cav. 1812, capt. 1816; sheriff,
Derbys. 1829-30.

Evans inherited a share in the Derby bank, Darley
cotton and paper mills, Derby waterworks and Bonsall
lead smelting business founded by his grandfather
Thomas Evans and his father William Evans, who died
when he was eight-years-old.[1] It was his stepfather
(and uncle) Walter Evans (his father's younger half-
brother, who married William's widow Elizabeth *née*
Strutt) who ran the cotton mills and created at Darley
a model community for his employees, with a school
and church.[2] Evans's younger brother Samuel was in
charge of the paper mill. Evans was again returned
unopposed for East Retford (where he had spent
heavily in 1818) at the general election of 1820, evidently with the continued private acquiescence of the
anti-Catholic Tory 4th duke of Newcastle. In his first
Parliament he had taken an independent line, but in
his second he confirmed his liberal inclinations by
acting with the Whig opposition to the Liverpool ministry, though he was not a 'thick and thin' attender.[3]
His only known vote in support of Queen Caroline
was for restoration of her name to the liturgy, 13 Feb.
1821. He divided for Catholic relief, 28 Feb. 1821, 1
Mar., 21 Apr., 10 May 1825. He voted with fair regularity for economy, retrenchment and reduced taxation, but was in the ministerial majorities against
repeal of the additional malt duty, 3 Apr. 1821, and of
some assessed taxes, 10 Mar. 1823. On the army estimates, 14 Mar. 1821, he said that he saw no prospect
of relieving distress by the simple remission of taxes,
deprecated military expenditure in the colonies and
advocated the enlistment of a colonial yeomanry. He
was granted ten days' leave to attend to urgent private
business, 18 May 1821. Before voting for inquiry into
Sir Thomas Maitland's[†] government of the Ionian
Islands, 7 June 1821, he condemned Maitland's
arbitrary use of a power 'too great for any man to be
entrusted with'. He presented and endorsed a petition
for mitigation of the criminal code and of the punish-

ment for forgery, 20 June 1821.[4] His first recorded vote
for parliamentary reform was on 25 Apr. 1822, and he
supported it in the divisions of 24 Apr., 2 June 1823,
26 Feb. 1824, 27 Apr. 1826. He was in the minority
of 25 for a fixed duty of 20s. on wheat imports, 9 May
1822, and voted to relax the corn laws, 26 Feb. 1823, 18
Apr. 1826. In the silk trade debates, 5, 19 Mar. 1824,
he argued that free trade would be more beneficial to
industry and commerce than the remission of direct
taxes. He presented an East Retford petition for repeal
of the Insolvent Debtors Act, 25 Feb. 1823.[5] He supported Phillimore's proposal to moderate the Profane
Swearing Act, 18 Mar. 1823. He was named to the
committee on the county gaols bill, 13 Apr. 1824, and
on 14 May proposed to add a clause empowering magistrates to commit to such prisons.[6] He approved the
principle of the game bill, 25 Mar., and spoke in favour
of the grant for new churches, 12 Apr. 1824.[7] He presented petitions in favour of the cruelty to animals bill,
11 Mar. 1825.[8] As a mill owner, he recognized the need
to improve working conditions and supported the
cotton factories regulation bill, 17 May 1825, but he
repudiated any comparison between the experiences
of factory workers and colonial slaves: shorter working
hours would not be injurious 'even to the interests of
the manufacturers', because children would be able
to perform with 'greater vigour'. On 3 Mar. 1826 he
questioned the need to maintain volunteer corps to
preserve public order and criticized magistrates for
neglect of their duties in this regard.

In 1820 Evans, who was incensed at the determination of foreign governments to continue the slave
trade, had become a regular patron of the African
Institution. He was appointed a director the following
year. He addressed the institution in May 1823, and
presented a number of anti-slavery petitions in that
and the following year.[9] He was closely associated with
Zachary Macaulay and the extra-parliamentary abolitionist movement. This association brought him into
contact with Thomas Babington Macaulay*, whom
he entertained at Allestree in the summer of 1824.
Macaulay delighted in his company, though he found
Mrs. Evans

> the very freezing point of the moral thermometer. Cold
> water seems warm after raspberry ice. And Mr. Evans
> gains in the same manner: though indeed he is too honest
> and amiable to need a foil.[10]

After privately encouraging Thomas Fowell Buxton*
to expose the government's vacillation on slavery
abolition,[11] on 16 Mar. 1824 he said in the House that
Canning's proposals to ameliorate the condition of
colonial slaves were inadequate and that it was illusory

to imagine that slaves could obtain legal redress in cases of oppression. He voted in condemnation of the conviction of the Methodist missionary John Smith for inciting rebellion among slaves in Demerara, 11 June. He served as secretary to the African Institution in 1824 and wrote to lobby Peel, the home secretary, 5 May, against the bill to incorporate the East India Company, since this would hamper the progress of emancipation. He unsuccessfully opposed the West India Company bill on the same grounds, 10, 16 May 1825, and defended missionary societies against imputations of promoting insurrection, 15 June 1824.[12] He obtained statistics on the slave trade, 7 Mar., 5 May 1825, 14 Apr. 1826.[13] He protested against the principle of giving preference to slave labour in the colonies, 21 Mar., but approved the recently relaxed tariffs as an 'enormous advantage to the country', 25 Mar. 1825. He seconded the resolution of the Derbyshire meeting called to petition for the abolition of slavery, 12 Jan. 1826.[14] He voted in condemnation of the Jamaican slave trials, 2 Mar., and against colonial military expenditure, 10 Mar. 1826: 'they heard much of the loss and waste of human life in Sierra Leone in preventing slavery; but there was no mention at all of the excessive waste of life' in supporting it. He presented more anti-slavery petitions in the ensuing weeks.

Evans's decision not to seek re-election for East Retford, whose venality he found increasingly distasteful and where his parliamentary conduct was thought to be 'too independent' for Newcastle's liking, was public knowledge by October 1824.[15] At the general election of 1826 he came forward for Leicester. According to William Gardiner he was anxious to expose the corporation over the issue of honorary freemen, the nomination of which he condemned on the hustings. He declared himself an opponent of the corn laws and advocated free trade and Catholic emancipation. As an abolitionist he was assiduously supported by his kinsman Thomas Babington† and Zachary Macaulay, but was anxious to secure the assistance of the retiring Whig Member Thomas Pares.[16] Anticipating a hard contest, he received the professional services of Thomas Macaulay, who drafted satirical squibs in his favour.[17] After a fierce contest, which cost him about £17,000, he was defeated by the corporation candidates, who had coalesced against him.[18] Later in the year Evans commended Zachary Macaulay's decision to prosecute *John Bull* for printing 'malicious libels' in support of the West India interest and offered to share the cost of doing so. At about this time he was hoodwinked by Zachary Macaulay's nephew into making a large loan in support of their trading house in Sierra Leone under the misguided assumption that Macaulay

was cognisant of the application.[19] He spoke at a Derby meeting called to petition for relaxation of the corn laws, 9 Nov. 1826.[20] In November 1828 Evans was a guest of the Friends of Civil and Religious Liberty at Leicester and agreed to their proposal to nominate him as a prospective candidate for the borough.[21] In 1829 he became a shareholder in the new university of London.[22] He duly offered for Leicester at the general election of 1830 and received the tacit support of the retiring Member Robert Otway Cave, who did not wish to divide the popular vote and tried elsewhere. Evans, who was supported by Matthew Babington and Pares, alluded to the causes of the July revolution in France, but believed it imprudent for Britain to interfere. He asserted his desire for economies and parliamentary reform, but declined to support 'every ill-digested visionary proposition to that end' or to commit himself to the ballot, though he pledged himself to combat municipal corruption at Leicester. He said he had come round to favouring the total repeal of the corn laws. He was returned unopposed.[23]

The Wellington ministry listed him among the 'bad doubtfuls' with the endorsement 'opposition'; and he voted against them in the division on the civil list which brought them down, 15 Nov. 1830. He presented numerous anti-slavery petitions to the 1830 Parliament, though he supported the proposal not to print repetitious ones, 11 Nov., while reserving the right to move the printing of those 'more argumentative than the great mass'. Next day he voted to relax West Indian import duties on wheat. He warned the House against the empty promises of West Indian slave owners and protested against the postponement of emancipation in order to consider the question of compensation for their vested interests, 23 Nov. He secured a return of information on the foreign slave trade, 7 Dec., and on the 20th refuted the arguments of Members who exaggerated the obstacles to the immediate abolition of slavery and pressed the Grey ministry to settle the question without delay: otherwise, 'they will lose my poor support'. Before he presented an Anstey reform petition calling for the ballot, 2 Dec., he corresponded with Pares in order to verify its authenticity and told him:

> I hope much from the new ministry, but the state of a large portion of the country is deplorable and alarming, and the mighty question with which ministers have now to deal must render their situation most difficult and serious.[24]

On 15 Dec. he presented and endorsed the prayer of a Shepshed reform petition and urged Members to reassure the country of their intentions in the forthcoming debate:

I agree with the petitioners in thinking that the operation of the corn laws is injurious to the lower classes, and that several of the taxes, especially those on the necessaries of life, fall with peculiar weight upon their comforts. I, therefore, wish to have many of the existing taxes repealed, and a well regulated property tax imposed in their stead.

He conveyed his apologies to the Leicester reform meeting chaired by Thomas Paget* in January 1831.[25] He presented and endorsed a Loughborough petition for reform and relief from distress, 3 Feb., but said he believed that repeal of the corn laws 'should not be sudden and immediate'. He brought up a Leicester petition for abolition of the truck system, 11 Feb., and declared his support for Littleton's bill for that purpose, though he doubted whether it would 'produce any effectual relief to the working classes'. The same day he largely approved of the government's budget, but condemned the proposed transfer tax and again advocated the imposition of a property tax as a 'fairer' alternative. On 17 Feb. he was given leave to bring in a bill to restrain corporations from the abuse of municipal funds for electoral purposes. On the 19th he dined with Jeremy Bentham.[26] He presented a Leicester petition in support of the corporate funds bill, 25 Feb., and defended its principle on the second reading, 11 Mar., and in committee, 14 Apr. The measure passed the Commons on 18 Apr., but was overtaken by the dissolution. Evans's refusal to pledge himself to support the ballot had disappointed some of his constituents, but he indicated in a public letter, 3 Jan., that he was now 'disposed ... to think more favourably' of it.[27] However, on 26 Feb. he said in the House that he still could not commit himself to support the proposal, advocated in a Leicester petition, as he 'did not know anything which would throw greater discredit on the country, or be more objectionable to the respectable portion of the community'. Excusing himself from attending the forthcoming Leicester reform meeting, he told Paget in a public letter, 8 Mar., that he considered that with their reform scheme ministers had 'nobly redeemed their pledge' and deserved 'all the support the people can give them'.[28] He presented and endorsed reform petitions from Leicester and other towns in the county, 17 Mar., and spoke of his constituents' disinterested enthusiasm for the reform bill as proof of the 'rational view which the people take of the proposed measure'. He was named to the select committee on cotton mills, 18 Mar. Next day he presented an individual's petition complaining of the partisan conduct of Leicester corporation in 1826, but could not find a seconder for his motion to have it printed. He also brought up

a Leicester beer sellers' petition complaining of corporation harassment. He voted for the second reading of the reform bill, 22 Mar., and against Gascoyne's wrecking amendment, 19 Apr. 1831. He was reported to be 'jubilant' at the government's decision to dissolve Parliament and appeal to the country.[29]

Evans stood again for Leicester as a reformer at the general election, even though he admitted that 'his anxiety to be in Parliament was not now so great', and was returned unopposed after a third man gave up at the last minute.[30] He obtained leave to reintroduce his corporate funds bill, 23 June 1831. It passed its third reading, 23 July, but foundered in the Lords, 25 July. He voted for the second reading of the reintroduced reform bill, 6 July, and divided steadily for its details. On 25 Aug. he argued that urban tenants who rented on a weekly basis were no less independent than those on annual leases. He presented and endorsed a Leicester manufacturers' petition for repeal of the corn laws, 18 July. He voted for printing the Waterford petition calling for the disarming of the Irish yeomanry following the massacre at Newtownbarry, 11 Aug., but divided with government against charges of their improper interference in the Dublin election, 23 Aug. At a Leicester dinner to celebrate the coronation, he explained that he had recently taken a week's rest from Parliament, as constant attendance had damaged his health, but he congratulated his audience on the 'successful progress' of the reform bill.[31] He was present to vote for its passage, 21 Sept., and the second reading of the Scottish bill, 23 Sept. Writing to Pares, 4 Oct., he expressed misgivings about the English bill's prospects in the Lords, but took some consolation from the enthusiasm shown at the Derbyshire reform meeting.[32] He voted for the motion of confidence in the ministry, 10 Oct. On 19 Oct. 1831 he presented and backed the prayer of a Northampton shoemakers' petition for repeal of the newspaper stamp duties. He obtained leave to reintroduce his corporate funds bill, 12 Dec. 1831. It passed the Commons, 28 Jan., and received royal assent, 1 Aug. 1832. He voted for the second reading of the revised reform bill, 17 Dec. 1831, was again a steady supporter of its details, though he was one of the minority of 32 who refused to accept the enfranchisement of £50-tenants at will, 1 Feb., and voted for the third reading, 22 Mar. He belatedly joined Brooks's Club, 15 Feb. Next day he voted in the minority of 28 for information on military punishments. He presented a Leicester petition supporting the proposed Leicester to Birmingham railway, 6 Apr. He divided in favour of the Irish registry of deeds bill, 9 Apr. He voted for the address asking the king to appoint only ministers who would carry undiluted reform, 10 May, and on the 18th presented a Leicester petition for supplies to be withheld until it had been secured. He was in Buxton's minority for the immediate abolition of colonial slavery, 24 May, having been 'almost the only person' among his close friends who had urged him to persevere with it in the face of ministerial hostility, and was a member of the select committee appointed to consider it, 30 May.[33] He voted for the second reading of the Irish reform bill, 25 May, and against a Conservative amendment to the Scottish measure, 1 June. He divided against Baring's bill to exclude insolvent debtors from Parliament, 6 June, and for an amendment to the boundaries bill designed to prevent aristocratic domination of Stamford and Whitehaven, 22 June. He voted to open inquests to the public, 20 June, and presented and endorsed a Leicester petition calling for the establishment of local courts to facilitate the recovery of debts, 5 July. He sided with government on the Russian-Dutch loan, 12, 16, 20 July 1832.

Evans was returned at the head of the poll for Leicester at the general election of 1832, but was defeated by two Conservatives in 1835. He declined to contest the borough in 1837, when he came in for North Derbyshire as a supporter of the ballot.[34] He vacated his seat in 1853 and died in April 1856. After providing for his wife, sisters and a host of relatives and godchildren, he left all his residual property to his only son Thomas William Evans (1821-92), Liberal Member for South Derbyshire, 1857-68, 1874-85, who was created a baronet in 1887. Evans's personalty was sworn under £250,000.[35]

[1] PROB 11/1276/302; 1553/127. [2] See *Dyott's Diary*, ii. 56. [3] *Session of Parl. 1825*, p. 462. [4] *The Times*, 21 June 1821. [5] Ibid. 26 Feb. 1823. [6] Ibid. 15 May 1824. [7] Ibid. 13 Apr. 1824. [8] Ibid. 12 Mar. 1825. [9] Ibid. 9, 15 May, 28 June 1823, 9, 10, 30 Mar. 1824. [10] *Macaulay Letters*, i. 197-8. [11] *Buxton Mems.* 145. [12] Add. 40364, ff. 262, 264. [13] *The Times*, 8 Mar., 6 May 1825, 15 Apr. 1826. [14] *Derby Mercury*, 18 Jan. 1826. [15] *LJ*, lxii. 312, 320, 349; Fitzwilliam mss 118/3, 4, 7, 9. [16] W. Gardiner, *Music and Friends*, ii. 627; *Leicester Jnl.* 5 May, 9 June; J. Clive, *Macaulay*, 96-98; Derby Local Stud. Lib. Pares mss, Evans to Pares, 15 May 1826. [17] *Macaulay Letters*, i. 211-12. [18] *LJ*, lxii. 352; Leics. RO, Braye mss 3455; Gurney diary, 23 Sept. 1826. [19] E. A. Knutsford, *Zachary Macaulay*, 403, 417, 436. [20] *Derby Mercury*, 15 Nov. 1826. [21] Braye mss 3502. [22] UCL, College mss, Evans to Coates, 24 Apr. 1829. [23] *Leicester Jnl.* 2, 9, 16 July, 6 Aug. 1830. [24] Pares mss, Evans to Pares, 2 Dec. 1830. [25] *Leicester Chron.* 1 Jan. 1831. [26] Derby Local Stud. Lib. Strutt mss, E. to F. Strutt, 11 Feb. 1831. [27] *Leicester Herald*, 9 Feb. 1831. [28] *Lincoln and Newark Times*, 16 Mar. 1831. [29] Strutt mss, E. to F. Strutt, 21 Apr. 1831. [30] *Leicester Jnl.* 29 Apr., 6 May 1831. [31] *Leicester Chron.* 17 Sept. 1831. [32] Pares mss. [33] *Buxton Mems.* 291. [34] A. Temple Patterson, *Radical Leicester*, 232. [35] PROB 11/2232/383; IR26/2063/371

S.R.H.

EVANS, William Bartrum (1801–1850), of 32 Hertford Street, Mdx.[1]

LEOMINSTER 1831–1832

b. 23 Nov. 1801, 1st. s. of John Evans (*d.* 1853), attorney, of London and Sarah, da. of Charles Bartrum of Rye Lane, Peckham, Surr. *educ.* Harrow 1814-16; Trinity Coll. Camb. 1819; L. Inn 1819, called 1825. *m.* 18 Jan. 1833, Jane, da. of John Boyd of Broadmeadows, Selkirk, 2s. 2da. *d.v.p.* 22 Nov. 1850.

Evans, whose father initially practised with Thomas Bartrum in St. Mildred's Court, Poultry, was baptized at St. Andrew Undershaft on Christmas Day 1801, and named after his grandfathers Bartrum and William Evans of Teddington. He spent his childhood in London, where his father became clerk to the Commercial Dock Company and established a practice in Hertford Street, and also in Dublin, where John Evans, a landowner in Tipperary, had business interests.[2] He was sent to Harrow and Cambridge and qualified as a barrister in May 1825, but he does not appear to have practised. That August his sister Eleanor married James Lennigan of Castle Ffogarty, Tipperary, and the family afterwards spent more time in Ireland. His mother died at Sea Point, Black Rock, near Dublin, 22 Mar. 1828.[3] Evans meanwhile had absconded with the Dublin upholsterer James Jordan's wife Catherine (*née* Hinton), who, generally under the assumed name of Estcourt, lived with him at various addresses in Walworth, Paris, Dublin, Southwark and Cheltenham. She bore him three children before the relationship ended in 1832.[4] Little is known of the background to Evans's candidature for Leominster, where, standing on the reform and corporation interests, he topped the poll at the general election of 1831.[5] The Ledbury banker John Biddulph, who first met him at the Herefordshire Association dinner, 28 May, described him as 'a stranger to the country'; but his paternal grandparents had owned land in nearby Eaton and Elton, which after his grandfather's death in 1813 had been sold to John Chambre, 10th earl of Meath, the defeated Whig candidate in 1812, for whom the Chaworth and Eaton Barony was revived at the coronation in 1831.[6]

Evans voted for the second reading of the Grey ministry's reintroduced reform bill, 6 July, and steadily for its details, including the total disfranchisement of Saltash, which ministers no longer pressed, 26 July 1831. He divided for the bill's passage, 21 Sept., attended the reform dinner at Stationers' Hall in honour of the leader of the House Lord Althorp and the bill's architect Lord John Russell, 24 Sept.,[7] and voted for Lord Ebrington's motion of confidence in the ministry, 10 Oct. He had sponsored the Leominster races, 17 Aug., and was thanked publicly for supporting the bill when the borough celebrated Meath's elevation to the British peerage, 8 Sept., and at the Herefordshire reform meeting, 5 Nov.[8] Summoned by circular, 6 Dec.,[9] he divided for the second reading of the revised reform bill, 17 Dec. 1831, frequently for its details, and for the third reading, 22 Mar. 1832; but, as the disappointed editor of the *Hereford Journal* pointed out, he cast a wayward vote against enfranchising £50 tenants-at-will, 1 Feb., which had been conceded.[10] He voted for the address calling on the king to appoint only ministers who would carry the bill unimpaired, 10 May, for the second reading of the Irish measure, 25 May, and against a Conservative amendment to the Scottish bill, 1 June 1832. He divided with government in both divisions on the Dublin election controversy, 23 Aug. 1831, on the Russian-Dutch loan, 26 Jan., 12, 16 July, on Portugal, 9 Feb., and the navy civil departments bill, 6 Apr.; but against them for immediate inquiry into colonial slavery, 24 May 1832. He voted to make coroners' inquests public, 20 June 1832. On 15 Dec. 1831, as a spokesman against the newspaper duties, the 'tax on knowledge', Evans requested detailed returns of the stamps issued and the conveyance of newspapers and pamphlets in all parts of Britain and the colonies, in a maiden speech that drew heavily on an article on the subject in the July *Westminster Review*. The motion was carried, but subject to a government amendment adding the words 'so far as the same can be made out'.[11] He or William Evans, Member for Leicester, presented a petition 'for the appointment of a day for national humiliation and prayer' from Holy Trinity, Sloane Street, Chelsea, 17 Jan., and one of them was appointed to the select committee on colonial slavery, 30 May 1832. Evans had been expected to act as a steward at the Herefordshire Association anniversary dinner at the *Freemasons' Tavern* that day, but he failed to attend and he did not stand for Parliament again.[12]

At Selkirk on 18 Jan. 1833 he married Jane Boyd, who knew of his previous liaison, and whose kinsman, the lawyer Archibald Boyd, acted for Evans and his father when Jordan and Catherine, who already received £100 a year, attempted extortion in 1833-4 and 1848.[13] Evans died *v.p.* at his home in Hertford Street in November 1850, leaving a widow and three children; a fourth, his second son, Harry Saville Ward Evans (1851-89), the sportsman and captain of the Cambridge University volunteer corps, was born posthumously. Evans left everything to his wife (*d.* 1894), who, with their children, inherited most of

John Evans's English property and £120-160,000 in investments in 1853, when the Irish holdings passed to the Lennigans.[14] In 1863 Jane Evans purchased the 15,000-acre Forde Abbey estate at Thorncombe, Dorset, once rented by Jeremy Bentham. Evans's four legitimate children died without issue and it passed through the Boyds to the Freman Roper family in 1906.[15]

[1] Evans's second name was also spelt Bertram. [2] GL ms 4108; PROB 11/2180/793; IR26/576/228. [3] *Gent. Mag.* (1828), i. 381-2; *Dublin Evening Post*, 25 Mar. 1828. [4] Evans mss (NRA 29106); Herefs. RO, Evans mss E42/46. [5] *Hereford Jnl.* 4 May; *Worcester Jnl.* 5 May; *Worcester Herald*, 7 May 1831. [6] Herefs. RO, diaries of John Biddulph of Ledbury [Biddulph diary] G2/4/J/59, 28 May 1831; *Burke LG* (1886): Evans of Forde Abbey; PROB 11/1544/242; Meath mss A/1/304-10; J/3/26; *Hereford Jnl.* 29 Sept. 1813. [7] Evans mss E42/1-2. [8] *Hereford Jnl.* 3, 10, 17, 24 Aug., 14 Sept., 9 Nov. 1831. [9] Evans mss E42/3. [10] *Hereford Jnl.* 8 Feb. 1832. [11] *Westminster Rev.* xxix (1831), 238-66. [12] Biddulph diary, 28 May 1831; *Hereford Jnl.* 2 May, 13, 20 June, 12 Dec. 1832. [13] IGI (Selkirk); Dorset Hist. Cent. Forde Abbey Estate mss D/FAE/F/18; Evans mss E42/5-46. [14] *Hereford Times*, 7 Dec. 1850; *Gent. Mag.*(1853), ii. 430; PROB 8/244; 11/2130/284; 11/2180/793; IR26/1965/686. [15] J. Hutchins, *Dorset*, iv. 528; will of Jane Evans, proved at Principal Registry, 28 July 1894.

M.M.E.

EVELYN, Lyndon (?1759–1839), of 28 York Place, Portman Square, Mdx. and Kinsham Court, Herefs.

WIGTOWN BURGHS	27 Feb. 1809–1812
DUNDALK	2 Jan. 1813–1818
ST. IVES	1820–1826

b. ?1759, 1st s. of Francis Evelyn of Dublin. *educ.* Trinity, Dublin 1 Nov. 1773, aged 14; King's Inns 1778, called [I] 1781. *m.* (1) 31 Dec. 1789, Elizabeth (*d.* 6 Sept. 1826), da. of John Pimlot of Marple Hall, Chester and Bromley, Kent, 2s. *d.v.p.* 1da.; (2) c. 1829, Sarah Allen, 1s. 2da. *d.* 30 Apr. 1839.

Chief examiner, ct. of chancery [I] 1795-c.1804; commr. Grand Surr. Canal Dock Co. from 1815.

Evelyn, an Irish barrister, was returned in second place for St. Ives in 1820 on the 'independent' interest.[1] He attended more infrequently than in the past and, despite having joined Brooks's Club, 3 June 1816, he gave silent general support to Lord Liverpool's ministry. He voted in defence of their conduct towards Queen Caroline, 6 Feb. 1821. He paired for Catholic relief, 28 Feb., and against repeal of the additional malt duty, 3 Apr., and was granted one month's leave for urgent private business, 15 May 1821. He divided against more extensive tax reductions, 11, 21 Feb., and abolition of one of the joint-postmasterships, 14 Mar. 1822. He voted against Hume's amendment to limit the sinking fund, 13 Mar., and presented a St. Ives petition for repeal of the coastwise coal duty, 24 Mar. 1823.[2] He divided against ministers that day for papers regarding the Orange conspiracy to murder the Irish viceroy, but with them against inquiry into the prosecution of the miscreants, 22 Apr. He voted against repeal of the Foreign Enlistment Act, 16 Apr. 1823. He divided for Catholic relief, 1 Mar., 21 Apr., 10 May 1825. He voted for the separate salary of the president of the board of trade, 10 Apr. 1826. In June 1822 a rumour had circulated at St. Ives that he had vacated his seat. Although this was unfounded, there seems to have been no expectation that he would stand again, and he retired at the dissolution in 1826.[3]

In 1824 Evelyn purchased the Kinsham estate from the earl of Oxford, and he later added other properties in Herefordshire and Radnorshire. Shortly before his death in April 1839 he provided a dowry of £16,000 for his daughter from his first marriage, on her marriage to Randall Plunkett, son of the 14th Baron Dunsany. He left an annuity of £250 to his second wife, £5,000 each to their two daughters and the residue, including his estates, to their son Francis (b. 1828); all three children had been born out of wedlock and were described as 'adopted'. Plunkett, who had spent time in a debtors' prison, challenged the will, and the protracted litigation that followed meant that Francis's inheritance was heavily encumbered when his rights were confirmed in 1861.[4]

[1] West Briton, 17 Mar. 1820. [2] The Times, 25 Mar. 1823. [3] Cornw. RO, Johnstone mss DD/J2/109, Edwards to Hawkins, 22 June 1822; AD 207/1, Hawkins to Roberts, 5 Mar. 1825. [4] PROB 11/1910/287; IR26/1513/162; TNA J90/170, 729.

S.K./T.A.J.

EWART, William (1798–1869), of Mossley Hill, Liverpool, Lancs. and 16 Eaton Place, Mdx.[1]

BLETCHINGLEY	23 July 1828–1830
LIVERPOOL	30 Nov. 1830–28 Mar. 1831
LIVERPOOL	1831–1837
WIGAN	9 Mar. 1839–1841
DUMFRIES BURGHS	1841–1868

b. 1 May 1798, 2nd. s. of William Ewart (d. 1823), merchant, of Liverpool and Margaret, da. and coh. of Christopher Jaques of Bedale, Northallerton, Yorks; bro. of Joseph Christopher Ewart[†]. educ. Eton 1811-17; Christ Church, Oxf. 1817; M. Temple 1820, called 1827; continental tour 1821-3. m. 15 Dec. 1829, his cos. Mary Anne, da. and coh. of George Augustus Lee, cotton merchant, of Singleton, Lancs., 1s. 4 da. (2 d.v.p.) d. 23 Jan. 1869.

Commr. on capital punishment 1864-6.

Ewart's father, a general commission merchant, was described by George Canning, at whose elections he assisted, as 'unquestionably the most powerful commercial man in Liverpool'. He was a son of the Scottish minister and landowner, the Rev. John Ewart of Troqueer, Dumfries, godfather of the future prime minister William Ewart Gladstone[†], and senior partner in the firm of Ewart, Rutson and Company.[2] He died worth £330,000, 8 Oct. 1823, having purchased the church living of Kirklington in Yorkshire for his youngest son Peter (d. 1852) and partnerships in Ewart, Myers and Company of Liverpool, and Ewart, Taylor and Company of London for his sons John (1796-1839), a common councillor and sometime chairman of the Liverpool East India Association, and Joseph Christopher (1799-1868), an early promoter of the Liverpool-Manchester railway. Together, they financed Ewart's early parliamentary career.[3] Tutored privately with his brothers by a 'Mr. Bold', and at Eton by the Rev. William Heath, he excelled in Latin verse at Oxford, where Edward Pusey, Lord Morpeth* and Edward George Geoffrey Smith Stanley* were his closest friends, taking the Christ Church prize in 1819 and the Newdigate the following year. Eschewing the ecclesiastical career his father had intended for him for politics, he toured the continent, 1821-3, studied trade and political economy, qualified as a barrister and practised briefly on the Northern circuit.[4] Returning from it to London in May 1828, he replied to a query from Thomas Gladstone* about London Clubs:

The Crown Club, as far as I have been able to ascertain, does not bear a good character. I can learn nothing of the infant University. Both these Clubs, and several others, are in such a state of immaturity that you will be able to make your own election when you arrive in town, and where the choice is within your reach, I should not be justified in choosing for you. The junior University will perhaps be destroyed in its birth by the extension of the senior establishment. We are to decide in a few days whether our club is to be increased from 1,000 to 1,500 and lodged in a new edifice of magnificent construction near St. James's Park. I inserted your name among the candidates about a year ago.[5]

He owed his return for Bletchingley in July that year as the paying guest of William Russell* of Brancepeth to Canning's friend William Huskisson, whose politics he espoused and whose Liverpool elections were partly bankrolled by his brothers.[6] Russell's kinsman Charles Tennyson*, who met Ewart that October, complimented Huskisson on his choice.[7]

A slight, slender, studious and rather sallow young man with longish hair,[8] he took a seat near Huskisson, 5 Feb., and divided with him for Catholic emancipation, 6, 30 Mar. 1829. His maiden speech on 27 Mar., an endorsement of the measure in which he expressed reservations over the attendant franchise bill (which Huskisson opposed), was 'flat' but well received, and 'read well'. He soon established himself as a regular speaker on commercial and humanitarian issues and Huskisson, although perturbed by his 'diffidence', praised his 'talents and considerable acquirements'.[9] He voted with Tennyson to transfer East Retford's seats to Birmingham, 5 May, declared that the case for disfranchisement was proven and spoke against issuing a new writ, 29 May. At Prestwich in December 1829 he married Mary Anne Lee (d. 1837), seven years his junior, the daughter of his father's youngest sister and heiress to a Lancashire cotton fortune. She had a £20,000 marriage settlement. Stating that he was sorry to differ from Huskisson, Ewart chose not to vote for Knatchbull's amendment regretting the omission of distress from the king's speech and cited cotton trade statistics to substantiate his claim that reports of a slump in trade in the Liverpool and Manchester district were exaggerated, 4 Feb. 1830. He voted as previously on East Retford, 11 Feb., and to enfranchise Birmingham, Leeds and Manchester, 23 Feb., and divided steadily from March until the dissolution in July with the Huskissonites who supported the revived Whig opposition, including for Jewish emancipation, 5 Apr., 17 May, to make forgery a non-capital offence, 24 May, 7 June, and to consider the abolition of colonial slavery, 13 July. When the Hull ship owners' distress petition was presented, 2 Apr., he countered criticism of Huskisson's economic policies by demonstrating that the tonnage carried by British vessels was increasing faster than that conveyed by American ones. He introduced petitions for and urged inquiry into 'inadequate' law court accommodation, 18 Feb., 10 May, and welcomed the changes to king's bench proposed by Henry Brougham, 29 Apr., 7 July. Preparing for the next Parliament, he proposed legislating to end capital punishment for non-violent crimes, 13 July, and ordered returns on the northern turnpikes in which his relatives had vested interests, 20 July 1830.

Left without a seat at the general election of 1830, Ewart swiftly staked his claim to that vacated by Huskisson's death, 15 Sept., so precipitating a realignment in Liverpool politics and a 20-year breach (signalled by the return of portraits) with the Gladstone family, who denied him their support.[10] Willing only to make way for Charles Grant*, who declined, and amid mercantile rivalry and mounting concern that he lacked political weight, he defeated his schoolfellow and political ally John Evelyn Denison*, Lady

Canning's nephew, in a protracted contest remarkable for its closeness, cost (about £100,000) and corruption. During it Lord Grey replaced the duke of Wellington as premier and appointed Denison secretary to the India board, and Ewart's first child Mary Anne (a pioneer and benefactor of university education for women) was born.[11] His addresses and speeches stressed his Liverpool origins and Huskissonite connections, opposition to the East India Company and Bank monopolies and support for civil and religious freedom, free trade and reform of the corn and game laws.[12] Justifying his recent anti-slavery vote, he explained:

> I voted in favour of the motion, not in favour of the expressions which may have fallen from some of the speakers ... It is not likely that I should unguardedly acquiesce in any measure by which the interests of my native town and ... near relations should be *unjustly* compromised. I know also that some of the West Indian proprietors themselves voted on that occasion with Mr. Brougham. I may refer particularly to our respected fellow townsman Mr. [Joseph] Birch.[13]

He wanted the West India planters compensated but expected the colonies, 'not Britain', to pay.[14]

In later life Ewart described his commitments as Member for Liverpool as onerous, thankless and permitting no free time. He advocated inquiry and early emancipation with compensation when Lord Chandos brought up the West India planters' distress petition, 13 Dec., and spoke similarly on presenting Liverpool's petition, 15 Dec. 1830, when, to the general satisfaction of the merchants, he praised their support for Canning's 1823 resolutions and maintained that to be effective abolition should be gradual.[15] He brought up petitions against colonial slavery, 15 Dec., and for Jewish emancipation, 16 Dec. 1830; and one against the Liverpool poor bill, 2 Mar., whose third reading he carried, 14 Mar. 1831. Referring to recent innovations in Lancashire textile production, he made light of foreign competition and congratulated the chancellor Lord Althorp on his budget, 15 Feb., reserving censure for the locally unpopular taxes on steamboat passengers, 17 Feb., soap, 10 Mar., and timber, which, echoing the trading associations' petitions, he deemed too steep, 15, 17 Mar. 1831.[16] Criticism of his performance persisted, especially his failure to secure concessions on the sugar duties, transport bills and Chinese trade.[17] His return had been petitioned against, alleging bribery, 13, 20 Dec., and with steps to reform the Liverpool franchise also in train, he scotched reports that he would vacate to impede investigation of corruption there, advocated an extended franchise 'to represent wealth' and spoke proudly of his middle class origins, 20 Dec. 1830.[18] Ignoring its references to the recent by-election and demand for a householder franchise, he voiced general support for the Liverpool reform petition presented by Smith Stanley, 26 Feb., and presented another that day from the ratepayers. In hostile exchanges with his colleague Isaac Gascoyne, 14 Mar., he fully endorsed a heavily signed petition in favour of the ministerial reform bill, which his brothers had helped to procure, and claimed that Canning would no longer have 'ruled out' reform.[19] He divided for the bill's second reading, 22 Mar. Unseated on petition, 28 Mar. 1831, and 'half dead with anxiety', he left for Liverpool to seek re-election, unaware of the writ's suspension and that a botched report by the election committee chairman John Benett had 'unintentionally' disqualified him as a by-election candidate.[20] Three weeks later, after Gascoyne had wrecked the reform bill, precipitating a general election, he was rapturously received by the merchants at Liverpool Exchange. Backed by the newly constituted reform committee, he topped the poll.[21]

On 5 July 1831 he wrote to the leader of his local party, the Liverpool Unitarian minister William Shepherd, that

> there appears to be a determination on the part of every Member of the present Parliament, liberal and otherwise, to express his sentiments about reform. I therefore infer that a reformed Parliament will be a very long winded one; as they are, I believe in America. I intend to explain myself to the Speaker and my constituents as soon as I can get an opportunity. Last night I rose several times in vain. The Speaker's eye is not very easily caught.[22]

He voted for the reintroduced reform bill at its second reading, 6 July, and steadily supported it in committee, where he endorsed its provisions for Downton, 21 July, Manchester and Salford, 2 Aug., the Liverpool suburb of Toxteth Park, 6 Aug., the £10 borough vote, terms of qualification, 25, 26 Aug., and two-day polls, 5 Sept. His votes on Saltash, 26 July, and Aldborough, 14 Sept., were wayward ones. He divided for the bill's third reading, 19 Sept., and passage, 21 Sept., the second reading of the Scottish reform bill, 23 Sept., and Lord Ebrington's confidence motion, 10 Oct. Praising ministers, he refuted suggestions by his new colleague Lord Sandon and others that Liverpool was dissatisfied with the revised reform bill, 7, 12 Dec. He divided for its second reading, 17 Dec. 1831, generally for its details, and the third reading, 22 Mar. 1832. He dismissed Daniel O'Connell's assertion that the bill would increase the electoral power of landowner combinations, 27 Jan., but divided against enfranchis-

ing £50 tenants-at-will, 1 Feb. His opposition to a proposal for a £15 qualification in large towns, 3 Feb., annoyed Liverpool corporation.[23] Pleading a lack of time for letter writing, he informed Shepherd, 22 Feb., that

> the brief moments of leisure interposed between the mechanical movements of a Member of the Lower House – oscillating as we do from the committee rooms to the green benches and back again – have not been sufficient even for a few short lines. We are now looking out for a constitutional reinforcement of peers ... I wish the ministers were more popular both in the House and in the country. I am afraid that many neutrals will become adversaries when the reform bill is passed.[24]

To taunts of 'Toxteth Park' he was mocked by the anti-reformers for defending the bill's 'meagre' provision for Liverpool, 28 Feb., 5 Mar. According to Edward Littleton's* diary

> a disgraceful and most ungentlemanly scene took place ... [that day] between Croker and Ewart ... in which Croker's manner was more violent and worse than his language. The chairman put it to him whether it was 'worth while' to continue such language to Ewart, on which Croker rejoined, 'Sir, I agree with you', and then with a most courteous motion of the hand towards Ewart, said, 'It is not worth while'. The whole House felt indignant, and [Smith] Stanley insisted on explanations before the parties left the House. Bernal, the chairman, then called not on Croker! but on Ewart! to explain. He must have been asleep. However the affair was made up.[25]

Ewart suggested to Shepherd that he should rely only on the *Mirror of Parliament*'s account of the debate and explained:

> Croker was in a fury; but he assailed me first. [Smith] Stanley did not extricate me well, though kindly, from the skirmish. Toxteth Park has been made a rallying point by Peel and Croker. I suspect that ... Peel has an eye to Toxteth, as he has always had to Liverpool.[26]

He voted for the address calling on the king to appoint only ministers who would carry the reform bill unimpaired, 10 May, and, as directed by the meeting, he endorsed the Liverpool petition requesting the withholding of supplies pending its passage, 15 May.[27] He voted for the second reading of the Irish reform bill, 25 May, and against a Conservative amendment to the Scottish measure, 1 June. Alluding to his 1829 vote, he endorsed his constituents' critical petition requesting extension of the English bill's provisions to Ireland, 21 June 1832.

Dogged by bribery allegations and the controversy surrounding the Liverpool by-election writ (necessitated by Denison choosing to sit for Nottinghamshire), he deemed delay to the latter insupportable, 6 July, and was a minority teller for issuing it, 8 July 1831. He had informed Shepherd, 5 July, that 'the proceedings of Benett have been, and are, in my opinion, absurd' and signalled his intention of avoiding a quarrel with him, 'as much as I should his acquaintance'.[28] He denied any involvement in corruption and, in several brief interventions, he praised the innovative multi-booth facilities erected by Liverpool corporation 14 July, 29 Aug., 2, 5 Sept. He was a teller for the minority, 5 Sept., and the majority for issuing the writ, 12 Oct. 1831. He generally contrived to be absent when the Liverpool disfranchisement bill was heard but, 'hoodwinked' by its promoter Benett, who brought it up unexpectedly, 24 May 1832, he failed to evade close questioning by Croker and the anti-reformers and condemned the measure as an act of vengeance and injustice. He was glad to see it lapse, 13 July 1832. He voted in the minority for appointing 11 of its original members to the reconstituted Dublin election committee, 29 July, but divided with government on the election controversy, 23 Aug. 1831, the Russian-Dutch loan, 26 Jan., 12, 16, 20 July, Portugal, 9 Feb., and the navy civil departments bill, 6 Apr. 1832. However, he voted with the radicals against them for printing the Waterford petition for disarming the Irish yeomanry, 11 Aug., and inquiry into the Deacles' case, 27 Sept. 1831, military punishments, 16 Feb., and Peterloo, 15 Mar. 1832. Noting the last, which, by explanation, Ewart had equated to impeachment, Thomas Gladstone commented: 'He is indeed far gone'.[29]

After suffering several postponements and disparaging comments from Peel, on 27 Mar. 1832 Ewart obtained leave to introduce his bill to end capital punishment for the non-violent theft of animals, money and effects from domestic premises. He backed it with petitions (7, 17 May, 22, 28 June) and a plethora of statistics and arguments demonstrating that in these instances the death penalty inhibited sentencing, rarely followed conviction and was no deterrent, 2 Apr., 30 June, 3, 4, 5, 6, 21 July. It received royal assent on 11 July (2 & 3 Gul. IV, c. 62), and served as a basis for his subsequent achievements as an abolitionist. He naturally supported the forgery punishment mitigation bill, 22 June, 21, 25 July, 11 Aug. 1832. He was appointed to the East India select committees, 28 June 1831, 27 Jan. 1832. In debate, 28 June 1831, he described the difficulties faced by British merchants at Canton and pressed for consular representation there and measures to promote the China trade. He presented the East India Association's petition against renewing the Sugar Refinery Act, 16 Aug.,

but apparently refrained from voting when the bill's second reading was made a party issue, 12 Sept. 1831. On 7 Oct., he said that he hoped to see the problems arising from it referred to the West India select committee, to which he was named, 6 Oct., 15 Dec. 1831. He criticized the opposition raised by the planters' spokesman Burge to the crown colonies relief bill and expressed confidence in it and in the November 1831 orders in council, 8 Aug. 1832. Drawing on information supplied by Liverpool traders, he urged ministers to lodge formal protests over the Brazilian government's tardiness in compensating British merchants, 16 Apr., and also against Russia for invading Poland, 18 Apr., 7 Aug. However, echoing Huskisson's former pleas, he warned that war inhibited the extension of liberal principles, 7 Aug. 1832. As a spokesman for the Liverpool merchants and tradesmen, who submitted bills and petitions, he reiterated his criticism of the duties on soap and timber, 1 July 1831, adding those on marine insurance, hemp and railway carriages to the list, 8 July 1831, 2 Apr., 9 Aug. 1832. He justified government expenditure on the Liverpool Revenue Buildings, 1 July 1831, 8 Feb. 1832, detailed the hardship the quarantine laws imposed on shipping, 8 Aug. 1831, and, using his experience as a member of the select committee on Irish communications, opposed the proposed curtailment of the Liverpool-Dublin packets, 4 Apr. 1832. Although personally in favour of registration in principle, he joined in criticism of the general register bill, 11 Oct. 1831, 14 Feb. 1832. With the general election and the Irish vote in mind, he supported Liverpool's bid to host the Lancashire assizes, 19, 22 June, and petitions in favour of the Maynooth grant, 22 June, 23 July, and against the bill for the removal of Irish vagrants, 28 June, 16 July 1832.

Ewart contested Liverpool successfully in 1832 and 1835 as a Liberal free trader, inclined to radicalism. Following defeats there and at Kilkenny in 1837, when the general election coincided with a slump in trade, he published a pamphlet questioning the achievements of the Reform Act.[30] He lost the 1838 Marylebone by-election before being accommodated in 1839 at Wigan. At the general election of 1841 he returned to his family's Scottish roots, becoming Member for Dumfries Burghs, which he represented until his retirement at the dissolution in 1868. He devoted much of his long widowhood and parliamentary career to humanitarian issues and improving the management of business in the Commons. His contribution to improving public services, especially in the fields of education and free library provision, was a pioneering one. (The Ewart Library in Dumfries is named in his honour.) He died of pneumonia in January 1869 at the Wiltshire estate of Broadleas, near Devizes, which he had purchased in 1854 with his brother Joseph, and he was interred with him at nearby Bishop's Cannings. He left the bulk of his estate to his only son, William Lee Ewart (1836-92), and provided for other family members.[31]

[1] Draws on W.A. Munford, *William Ewart, M.P., 1798-1869: portrait of a radical* (1960). [2] Add. 38743, f. 2; *Oxford DNB*. [3] PROB 11/1690/510; IR26/1001/815. [4] Liverpool RO, Ewart Letters 920/MD293, fa. to Ewart, 8 July 1817, Canning to Ewart sen. 21 May 1820. [5] St. Deiniol's Lib. Glynne-Gladstone mss 519, Ewart to T. Gladstone, 3 May [1828]. [6] Ibid. 227, Huskisson to J. Gladstone, 18 July 1828. [7] Add. 38757, f. 147. [8] [J. Grant], *Random Recollections of Commons* (1835 edn.), 278. [9] Ibid. 277-9; Glynne-Gladstone mss 278, Huskisson to J. Gladstone, 10 Apr. 1829. [10] Glynne-Gladstone mss 196, T. to J. Gladstone, 17, 18, 27 Sept., 2 Oct.; 453, J. Ewart to T. Gladstone, 2 Oct. 1830; 329, W. Ewart to J. Gladstone, 15 Dec., Joseph Ewart to same, 27 Dec. 1850. [11] Brougham mss, William Shepherd to Brougham [postmark 30 Sept.]; Hatfield House mss, bdle. 3, Leigh to Salisbury, 30 Nov.; Glynne-Gladstone mss 243, G. Grant to J. Gladstone, 30 Nov. 1830; *Greville Mems.* ii. 76-77; *Oxford DNB sub* Ewart, Mary Anne. [12] *Albion*, 27 Sept., 18 Oct., 6 Dec.; *Gore's Advertiser*, 24 Oct., 2 Dec. 1830; J. Picton, *Memorials of Liverpool*, i. 421-5. [13] Glynne-Gladstone mss 2871. [14] Ibid. 243, G. Grant to J. Gladstone, 19 Nov. 1830. [15] Ibid. 196, T. to J. Gladstone, 13 Dec. 1830 and undated. [16] Ibid. 197, T. to J. Gladstone, 23 Feb. 1831. [17] *Liverpool Chron.* 15, 22 Jan.; Glynne-Gladstone mss 197, T. to J. Gladstone, 5, 7, 23 Feb., 26 Mar. 1831. [18] 4 Dec. 1830. [19] *Liverpool Chron.* 5, 12 Mar.; Glynne-Gladstone mss 196, T. to J. Gladstone, 14 Mar. 1831. [20] Glynne-Gladstone mss 103, J. Gladstone to Denison, 3 Apr.; 197, T. to J. Gladstone, 7, 8 Feb., 19, 21, 25, 28 Mar.; 244, G. Grant to same, 22, 27 Mar. 1831; Manchester New Coll. Oxf. Archives, William Shepherd mss vii, f. 53; *PP* (1830), iii. 1-418. [21] Glynne-Gladstone mss 197, T. to J. Gladstone, 28 Apr.; 244, G. Grant to same, 23 Apr., 2-4 May; *Gore's Advertiser*, 28 Apr., 5 May; *Liverpool Chron.* 30 Apr., 7 May 1831. [22] William Shepherd mss vii. [23] Glynne-Gladstone mss 199, T. to J. Gladstone, 6, 9, 11 Feb. 1832. [24] William Shepherd mss vii, f. 87. [25] Hatherton diary, 5 Mar. 1832. [26] William Shepherd mss vii, f. 87. [27] *Albion*, 14 May; *Gore's General Advertiser*, 17 May 1832. [28] William Shepherd mss vii, f. 53. [29] Glynne-Gladstone mss 199, T. to G. Gladstone, 16 Mar. 1832. [30] *The Reform of the Reform Bill and its anticipated results*. [31] *Dumfries and Galloway Standard and Advertiser*, 27 Jan; *Devizes and Wilts. Gazette*, 28 Jan.; *The Times*, 28 Jan. 1869; *Oxford DNB*.

M.M.E.

EWING, James (1784-1852), of 18 Park Crescent, Regent's Park, Mdx.[1]

WAREHAM   1830-1831

b. 11 Jan. 1784, s. of ?James Ewing and w. Margaret.[2] *educ.* Westminster 1801. *m.* (1) 18 Nov. 1812, Mary Ann Carige (*d.* 27 Oct. 1813), 1da.;[3] (2) 13 Feb. 1816, Jane Morton (*d.* 28 Aug. 1842),[4] at least 3da. (1 *d.v.p.*);[5] (3) 23 Oct. 1843, Louisa, da. of Mungo Dick of Richmond Hill, Surr.,[6] 1da. *d.* 18 Dec. 1852.

Writer, E.I. Co. (Bengal) 1802; asst. to magistrate at zillah ct., Chittagong 1807; register to ct. of appeal, Dacca 1807, officiating register of city ct. 1810; register and asst. to magistrate, Bhaugulpore 1810, officiating magistrate 1812, officiating judge and magistrate

1813-14; judge and magistrate of zillah ct., Sylhet 1814; deputed to visit interior parts of Sylhet on public duty 1820; officiating judge of provincial ct., Dacca 1821; at home 1823-8; judge of diwani adalat and magistrate, Dacca 1828; officiating judge, Patna 1828; at home 1828-34, out of service 1834.

Ewing was an obscure Irishman, whose family it has not been possible to trace. He may have been the son of James Ewing of Prussia Street, Dublin, whose will was proved in 1790, or James Ewing of Templemoyle, county Londonderry, whose will was proved in 1791.[7] When Ewing applied for a writership in the East India Company in April 1803, he was unable to provide proof of his date of birth, other than in a statement from his mother, then resident at Great Neston, Cheshire, but he noted that he believed himself to have been born in St. Paul's parish, Dublin.[8] Following his appointment, which was backdated to July 1802, he arrived in India in February 1804, and there held a series of minor legal offices, was twice married and evidently made a considerable fortune.[9] On the death of his uncle Robert Ewing, formerly of Londonderry and York Place, Portman Square, London in December 1827, he inherited two thirds of his estate, which included personal wealth sworn under £60,000. The other third went to his sister Margaret, wife of the Rev. William Curwen, rector of Harrington, Cumberland, a younger son of John Christian Curwen, Member for Carlisle and Cumberland. His other sister, Martha, was disinherited for having contracted a clandestine marriage with one Francis Wheatley, 'a man of the most depraved and worthless character'.[10] Following a five-year spell on furlough in the mid-1820s, he returned again to England in 1828 and left the Company's employment six years later.

At the general election of 1830 he was returned unopposed for the seat he had purchased at Wareham from its patron, John Calcraft, paymaster of the forces in the duke of Wellington's administration.[11] As 'John Ewing', he was listed by ministers among their 'friends'; 'do not know' was written beside his name. He was absent from the division on the civil list which led to their downfall, 15 Nov. 1830, but voted against the second reading of the Grey ministry's reform bill, 22 Mar., and for Gascoyne's wrecking amendment, 19 Apr. 1831. He made no reported speeches in the Commons, which he left at the dissolution in 1831, when Calcraft, who had rejoined his Whig friends, made the seat available to government for a reformer. He died at Richmond, Surrey, in December 1852, dividing his real and personal property between his wife and daughters.[12] The sole surviving executor was his second daughter (the first with his second wife) Anna Caroline Morton, who married in 1843 Caledon Du Pré Alexander of Auberies, Essex, son of Josias Du Pré Alexander*, former Member for Old Sarum. The eldest daughter, Mary Ann, had married in 1836 her first cousin Robert Ewing Curwen, and the youngest daughter, Louisa, married in 1863 her first cousin Winthrop Mackworth Praed of Mickleham Downs, nephew and namesake of the former Member for St. Germans, Great Yarmouth and Aylesbury.

[1] Not to be confused with the Glasgow merchant and lord provost James Ewing (1775-1853), Member for Glasgow, 1832-4. [2] BL OIOC J/1/19, f. 74; the 'Robert' mentioned as Ewing's father in *Rec. of Old Westminsters*, i. 317 (using this information) was in fact his uncle. His father's Christian name certainly began with 'J' (*Gent. Mag.* (1831), i. 365) and is presumed to have been James. [3] OIOC N/1/9, ff. 34, 119. [4] Ibid. N/1/10, f. 15; *Gent. Mag.* (1842), ii. 441. [5] Margaret Eliza Ewing (OIOC N/1/10, f. 311). [6] *Gent. Mag.* (1843), ii. 648. [7] *Index to Prerogative Wills of Ireland* ed. Sir A. Vicars, 159; *Indexes to Irish Wills* ed. G. Thrift, v. 41. [8] OIOC J/1/19, f. 74. [9] Ibid. f. 70; H.T. Prinsep, *Bengal Civil Servants*, 115-16. [10] *Gent. Mag.* (1827), ii. 646; PROB 11/1735/17; IR26/1160/30. [11] *Dorset Co. Chron.* 5 Aug. 1830; [W. Carpenter], *People's Bk.* (1831), 249. [12] *Gent. Mag.* (1852), i. 218; PROB 11/2165/21; Cent. Kent. Stud. Scott mss U1471 T92 (NRA 20728).

S.M.F.

FAIRLIE *see* **CUNNINGHAM FAIRLIE**

FANE, **Sir Henry** (1778–1840), of Fulbeck, nr. Grantham, Lincs. and Avon Tyrell, Hants.

LYME REGIS	1802–1818
SANDWICH	30 Mar. 1829–1830
HASTINGS	1830–1831

b. 26 Nov. 1778, 1st s. of Hon. Henry Fane† of Fulbeck and Anne, da. and h. of Edward Buckley Batson, London banker, of Avon Tyrrell and Upwood, Dorset; bro. of Vere Fane*. *educ.* Eton 1791. *unm.* 3s. (1 *d.v.p.*) 1da. illegit. *suc.* fa. to Fulbeck 1802; KCB 5 June 1815; GCB 24 Jan. 1826; *suc.* mother to mat. grandfa.'s estates 1838. *d.* 25 Mar. 1840.

Cornet 6 Drag. Gds. 1792; lt. 55 Ft. 1792, capt. 1793; a.d.c. to ld. lt. [I] 1793-4; capt. 4 Drag. Gds. 1793, maj. 1795, lt.-col. 1797; lt.-col. 1 Drag. Gds. 1804; brevet col. 1805; a.d.c. to the king 1805; brig.-gen. 1808; maj.-gen. 1810; col. 23 Drag. Gds. 1814; col. 4 Drag. Gds. 1814; inspector of cav. 1814-15; lt.-gen. [on continent] 1817; lt.-gen. 1819; col. 1 Drag. Gds. 1827-d.; c.-in-c. India 1835-9; gen. [in E. Indies] 1835; gen. 1837.

Surveyor-gen. of ordnance Mar. 1829-Jan. 1831.

Fane had a murky private life, which he concealed for many years from all his immediate family except his younger brother and confidant Vere. During his service in Ireland in 1793 he formed 'a strong attachment' to Isabella, daughter of Hamilton Gorges, Member for county Meath, 1801-2, and the wife since 1791 of Edward Cooke, the powerful under-secretary at Dublin Castle and later under-secretary at the colonial and foreign offices. As Fane explained to Vere in 1814, Gorges had 'sold' her to Cooke for £1,500, thereby condemning her to 'the sort of miserable life that was to be expected' in the circumstances:

> As she considered it nothing less than prostitution living with a man she hated, and loving another, she told her husband so, and insisted upon separating from him. He detained her in his house above a twelvemonth, combating this resolution: but finding he could not prevail, at last a regular separation took place, and she went to England to live with some relations there. I believe the world invented a story of my having run away with her; for which there was no more foundation than what I have told you. For *several years* after this, although we were in the constant habit of meeting and spending weeks together, such was her strength of mind, that our intercourse continued, as it had been, perfectly innocent. At last, however, in 1801, in an unlucky hour, passion got the better of prudence; and the consequence was, in nine months a child … Since then we have lived together as man and wife, and have had six children, four of whom are alive: three boys and a girl.

One of the boys died young. The surviving children were Henry Fane (1802-85), who became a cornet in his father's regiment in 1822 and retired as a half-pay lieutenant-colonel in 1838; Arthur Fane (1809-72), who took holy orders, and Isabella Fane (1804-86), who died a spinster. Fane kept 'utter silence' about these 'domestic affairs' to avoid causing 'vexation' to his mother until 'the interest of my children' made it necessary to enlighten her. He was also influenced by a sense of delicacy towards Mrs. Cooke's family (her sister was married to the son of the archbishop of Tuam and she was 'in several ways related to all the Beresfords') and by sympathy for 'the unfortunate dropsical secretary' Cooke, 'to whom I should be sorry to add one pang more than I have already occasioned'. Although Fane praised Mrs. Cooke as 'the best of mothers', to whom their children were 'more attached than I should have thought it possible', she later became alienated from them as a result of what Arthur termed 'incompatibility of disposition', which 'renders reciprocal love out of the question'. When Fane was knighted Mrs. Cooke, who since 1794 had held the patent office of housekeeper and wardrobe keeper of Dublin Castle, worth £600 a year, styled herself 'Lady Fane'. She lived with him in a rented cottage on the Avon estate, which he managed for his mother.[1]

Fane, whose beautiful sister Harriet was the wife of Charles Arbuthnot* and the celebrated confidante of the duke of Wellington, had served with great distinction as a cavalry commander in the Napoleonic wars. Yet he had blotted his copybook by declining to join the army in Flanders in 1815 and so missing Waterloo.[2] In 1826 Wellington successfully urged on his ministerial colleagues Fane's claim to a vacancy in the order of the Bath, arguing that 'his services in the field were far superior to those of many even of those, some his juniors, who have obtained the order'; that it would be unjust 'to remember only his mistake', and that, 'with a view to the public interest', it was 'important that a man so capable of serving the public well should not feel himself disgraced, and in a manner under the necessity of keeping himself in the background'.[3] One of Wellington's first acts on becoming commander-in-chief in January 1827 was to appoint Fane to the colonelcy of the King's Dragoon Guards, worth £987 a year.[4] Two years earlier Wellington had named him as one of two generals best qualified for the command in Madras, but had doubted whether he would take it; if it was offered to him, Fane declined it.[5] In 1828 he applied to the home secretary Peel for the command in Ireland:

> I may explain, that I am no politician; and I hope I may add (without saying too much) that I should not be found wanting in temper, or in firmness, if placed in the situation I covet.

He was passed over for Sir John Byng*.[6]

In March 1829 Wellington as premier appointed Fane surveyor-general of the ordnance, at £900 a year. He was sent down to Sandwich to fill a vacancy on the government interest.[7] He was accused by a local clergyman of dissembling his views on Catholic emancipation and was challenged to pledge himself to oppose it. He denied having practised any deception, and at the nomination stated:

> No man living could be a more sincere and staunch Protestant than himself, but ... that question had now become ... political and not ... religious ... and the measures proposed by the government were calculated to protect the interests of the Protestant church, and to promote the welfare of all classes of society.

He was opposed at the last minute by an anti-Catholic Tory, but he easily prevailed in a truncated poll.[8] Had he failed, Lord Hertford might have accommodated him at Aldeburgh.[9] No trace of Fane's parliamentary activity has been found for the remainder of the 1829 session. In October the Ultra leader Vyvyan listed him among 'present government connections who will be

hostile' to a coalition ministry. In 1830 he voted with his colleagues against the transfer of East Retford's seats to Birmingham, 11 Feb., the enfranchisement of Birmingham, Leeds and Manchester, 23 Feb., and a reduction of judges' salaries, 7 July. He divided against Jewish emancipation, 5 Apr., 17 May, and the abolition of capital punishment for forgery, 7 June. On 2 Apr. 1830 he defended the employment of as many as 47 clerks in his department, which had to 'examine a great variety of details, even those of washing, and the emptying of everything that can be named – or rather that cannot be named here'. On the eve of the general election of 1830, faced with the prospect of a contest at Sandwich, he told Wellington:

> The opposition ... is such as, were I to meet it, would involve me in an expense which would be most inconvenient to me; and ... therefore I have notified to ... [Joseph] Planta* my objection to standing for that place ... I am, however, extremely desirous of continuing to serve under your administration, and shall do what I can to procure another seat, though I am not very sanguine in my expectations of success, excepting through government aid.

He was brought in on the treasury interest for Hastings.[10]

He was in the government minority on the civil list, 15 Nov. 1830, and left office on the change of ministry. He took a fortnight's leave to attend to 'public business', 23 Nov. 1830. Two months later the Irish viceroy Lord Anglesey warned the new prime minister Lord Grey against the possibility of Wellington's urging him to appoint Fane to the Irish command: he was 'capable enough; but high, assuming, a complete creature of the duke of Wellington, and he would be a complete spy from the enemy's camp'.[11] Fane questioned ministers about an arms contract with France, 21 Feb., and on 13 Apr. belittled their vaunted ordnance economies. Later that day he drew attention to the decrepit state of naval gun-carriages which, 'looking to the present state of Europe', was 'a matter of very deep importance'. He divided against the second reading of the reform bill, 22 Mar., and for Gascoyne's wrecking amendment, 19 Apr. 1831. He did not seek re-election at the ensuing general election.

A year later he applied to the Grey ministry for the governorship of the Cape of Good Hope:

> I have no desire to place myself in competition with any officer of *senior* standing in the army to myself, whose services may give him an equal claim for employment; but ... I solicit to be considered, only, before my name is passed over to the *advantage of a junior* ... I commanded the cavalry of the British contingent in France during

the greater period of our occupation of that country ... I am the only general officer, I believe, who belonged to the staff of that army who has not subsequently had the advantage of some profitable military employment; or who has not had some military employment over and above his regiment.

He was again ignored when the vacancy occurred.[12] In November 1834 Fane, who privately reacted to rumours that government planned to end military flogging with the comment that 'the army is gone if the power is taken away', was considered by his cousin the 10th earl of Westmorland as a candidate at the next election for Lyme Regis, where the family's traditional interest had been overturned. The notion was abandoned and soon afterwards, thanks to Wellington's brief return to power, he landed the potentially lucrative post of commander-in-chief in India. The Melbourne ministry confirmed his appointment and he set sail in May 1835, taking with him his son Henry as his aide-de-camp and his daughter Bella.[13]

He made a good impression in India. Macaulay found him to be 'a fine, spirited, soldierlike man'; and Mrs. Fanny Parks described him as 'a magnificent looking man with a good soldierlike bearing; one of imposing presence, a most superb bow and graceful bearing'.[14] In 1836 Bella reported to her aunt:

> You cannot think how popular my father is as commander-in-chief. It is said of him he has the interest of the army so thoroughly at heart and that ere long it will begin to recover the great injuries done it by that plague spot of India, Lord William [Cavendish] Bentinck*.[15]

Fane's nephew Henry Edward Fane, another of his aides, wrote home:

> I fear that we none of us properly respected him till he came to this country, and see the good he does and is doing every day, the work he does and the interest he takes and talent he displays in even the greatest trifle that comes through his department; which is no small quantity of work in an army of three hundred thousand men.[16]

During 1836 and 1837 Fane personally inspected every station under his command. The following year he prepared an army to go to the relief of Herat, besieged by the Persians, but he entirely disapproved of the governor-general Lord Auckland's aggressive policy, which precipitated the first Afghan war. He tendered his resignation, but in January 1839 the home government ordered him to remain until a suitable successor was found. He directed the offensive operations in Scind that year, but his health was breaking, and on his repeated requests to be relieved Sir Jasper Nicholls was appointed in his stead in August 1839.[17]

In his will of 7 Feb. 1828 Fane had left the Fulbeck estate to his son Henry, his household goods at Avon to Lady Fane and small annuities to his children Arthur and Bella. He revoked Arthur's legacy in 1833 following his marriage to a Wiltshire heiress.[18] His period in India dramatically improved his financial fortunes. Very soon he was 'wallowing in wealth', and he remitted some £50,000 to England between 1836 and 1839.[19] On going abroad he had 'left Lady F. with ample means for her wants', but later in 1835 her patent place was abolished without compensation, in what he considered 'a most rascally act of robbery and spoliation'. 'If it had happened before I came to India', he told Vere, 'it would have broken our backs'; as it was, he instructed his brother to arrange for Lady Fane's annual allowance of £200 to be increased to £500. To his annoyance Lady Fane, who would 'go about as a beggar woman, rather than apply for anything beyond that first arranged', refused to accept the extra money, but he insisted that it be paid into her account, which received arrears of £375 in April 1837. Later that year he withdrew his daughter's annuity in favour of a bequest of £5,000. In a codicil to his will, dated at Bombay, 20 Dec. 1839, he directed that all his money and securities in England should be invested for the benefit of Lady Fane for her life, and that £5,000 of the proceeds should go thereafter to Bella, to make her fortune £10,000.[20]

Fane left India on 1 Jan. 1840, after recovering from a serious illness and applying in vain for a baronetcy for his elder son in recognition of his own public services. He cherished hopes of reaching England alive, but his health soon collapsed.[21] He rallied during a short stay at Cape Town, but relapsed when the voyage was resumed and died off the Azores of 'water on the chest' in the small hours of 25 Mar. 1840; he was buried at sea later that day.[22] His will was proved on 22 May 1840 and his personalty sworn under £30,000.[23] He had inherited the Dorset and Hampshire estates from his mother in 1838, but she had entailed them, in default of his legitimate male issue, on his next brother the Rev. Edward Fane. The exchange of Fulbeck for Avon which he had been anxious for his son to make with Edward, who became head of the family, never took place.[24] Immediately after his death there was a stilted reconciliation between his children and Lady Fane.[25]

[1] *Miss Fane in India* ed. J. Pemble, 5; Lincs. AO, Fane mss 6/3/3, 5. [2] *Oxford DNB*. [3] *HMC Bathurst*, 598. [4] *Arbuthnot Jnl.* ii. 84. [5] *Wellington Despatches*, ii. 425; Buckingham, *Mems. Geo. IV*, ii. 214, 231-2. [6] Add. 40397, ff. 17, 19; *Arbuthnot Jnl.* ii. 146. [7] Wellington mss WP1/1007/14; 1035/53; 1048/39. [8] *Kentish Gazette*, 17, 20, 24, 27, 31 Mar., 3 Apr. 1829. [9] Add. 60288. f. 144. [10] Wellington mss

WP1/1123/24. [11] PRO NI, Anglesey mss D619/28C, p. 40. [12] Add. 40878, ff. 572, 574. [13] *Arbuthnot Corresp.* 169; *Wellington Pol. Corresp.* ii. 230, 490, 491, 809; Add. 40413, f. 299. [14] *Macaulay Letters*, iii. 155; *Miss Fane in India*, 28. [15] *Miss Fane in India*, 118. [16] Fane mss 6/3/17. [17] *Macaulay Letters*, ii. 197; *Miss Fane in India*, 141; H. E. Fane, *Five Years in India*, *passim*; Broughton, *Recollections*, v. 139-40; Fane mss 6/56; *Oxford DNB*. [18] PROB 11/1927/330. [19] *Miss Fane in India*, 95; Fane mss 5/37/14/5; 6/5/2. [20] Fane mss 6/4/3/1, 7, 9, 10, 13; PROB 11/1927/330. [21] Fane mss 6/5/7-13; 6/6/3, Fane to Lord Hill, 24 Nov. 1839. [22] *Gent. Mag.* (1840), ii. 426; Fane mss 6/5/ 16a. [23] IR26/1546/226. [24] PROB 11/1890/84; Fane mss 5/37/14/3, 7; 6/3/18. [25] Fane mss 6/5/17, 18, 20.

D.R.F.

FANE, Hon. Henry Sutton (1804–1857).

LYME REGIS   1826–1832

b. 13 Jan. 1804, 3rd but 2nd surv. s. of John, 10th earl of Westmorland (*d.* 1841), and 2nd w. Jane, da. of Richard Huck Saunders, MD. *educ.* Harrow 1818. *unm. d.* 7 May 1857.

2nd lt. 23 Ft. 1822, half-pay 1822; ensign and lt. 2 Ft. Gds. 1823; capt. 1825; capt. 34 Ft. 1825, maj. 1828, lt.-col. 1834; half-pay 1838; col. 1846; brevet col. 19 Ft. 1854.

Fane was the half-brother of the diplomat and former Member for Lyme Lord Burghersh, and became the younger of two surviving sons of the 10th earl of Westmorland and his second wife on the death of his brother Charles Saunders (1802-10). His mother was coheiress, with her sister Anne, wife of the 2nd Viscount Melville, through their father Richard Huck (who took the additional name of Saunders on his marriage in 1777 and died in 1785), to the estates of his wife's uncle, Admiral Sir Charles Saunders (*d.* 1775), former Member for Plymouth and Hedon.[1] Fane entered the 23rd Foot in July 1822 and exchanged into the Coldstream Guards late the following year, though he spent some time in Dresden, where he was said to be a sociable but idle student.[2] He became an unattached captain in October 1825, and in early 1826 accompanied the duke of Devonshire to Russia to attend the coronation of the new tsar. He was elected a freeman of Lyme Regis in August 1825 by gift, and at the general election in 1826 he was returned for that borough, in his absence abroad, by his father, who exercised complete electoral control there.[3] In politics he followed the lead of his father, the lord privy seal in the Liverpool administration. His parliamentary activities were sometimes confused with those of his father's cousin, Sir Henry Fane, and his own first cousin and colleague at Lyme, John Thomas Fane.

It was probably of Henry Sutton Fane that Hudson Gurney* wrote in his diary, 6 Mar. 1827, that the opponents of Catholic relief, including Westmorland, who left office at this time, 'had sent for Fane in *Vienna*' in their efforts to bring in votes; he was listed in the anti-Catholic majority that day. He voted against repeal of the Test Acts, 26 Feb., and Catholic relief, 12 May 1828. He divided against reducing the salary of the lieutenant-general of the ordnance, 4 July 1828. In February 1829 Planta, the Wellington ministry's patronage secretary, listed him as 'doubtful' on Catholic emancipation, but he was also considered as a possible mover or seconder of the address, for which Westmorland had instructed him to vote.[4] He duly divided for emancipation, 6, 30 Mar. He objected to the proposed disfranchisement of East Retford, 10 Apr., and, after several postponements, tried to move the writ, 7 May, arguing that although there was some evidence of corruption, it was unconstitutional to deprive the electors of their representation for so long a period and to make changes to the franchise. On 2 June 1829 he presented and endorsed two East Retford petitions for the restitution of its representation, but gained little support when he again moved the writ. He retorted to Peel, the home secretary, that it was 'a new doctrine, that the House of Commons could suspend the issuing of writs', and forced a division, in which he was teller for the minority of 44. He subsequently brought the whole matter to Wellington's attention.[5] Fane, who had joined the 34th Foot in December 1828, was obliged, for professional reasons, to travel with his regiment to Nova Scotia in late 1829, despite his father's attempts to extricate him so that he could attend Parliament.[6] His fellow officer Charles Richard Fox* described him in letters to Lord Holland, 6 Nov. and 1 Dec. 1829, as 'very *young* but very zealous, gentlemanlike and agreeable', and 'a very good-tempered, well disposed young man, very like ... [Lady Westmorland] and sometimes in manners, but he has I think some common sense'. On 10 Jan. 1830 Fox reported that Fane would soon return to England and exchange into another regiment and that he would like Holland 'to make his acquaintance, for he is clever and uncommonly good tempered, though a little in the "being bored" line which I like, you dislike. He however is not I think really so'.[7] Yet nothing came of Westmorland's request for a promotion for him and, although he may have had leave to attend Parliament, there is no evidence that he did so during the 1830 session.[8] He was returned unopposed at the general election that year, as he was again in 1831.

Fane was listed by ministers among their 'friends', but he was absent from the division on the civil list, 15 Nov. 1830. He voted against the second reading of the Grey ministry's reform bill, 22 Mar. 1831. He criticized ministers' changes to the bill, 14 Apr., when he called the reduction in the number of Members for Ireland and Scotland 'a national insult to these united kingdoms'. Arguing that the best system of representation was one which secured 'impartial justice, equal rights and equal laws', 19 Apr., he condemned the bill as extreme, ineffective and unrepresentative of the varied interests of the country, and concluded by declaring that 'I envy not that man his heart who concedes this bill, a bill founded on corruption and traffic, and directed to the basest passions of the people'. He duly voted for Gascoyne's wrecking amendment that day. He voted against the second reading of the reintroduced bill, 6 July. On 12 July, when he alleged that ministers had proposed the bill 'solely to relieve themselves from the difficulties in which their imbecility as ministers had involved them', he voted at least five times to adjourn the proceedings on it, though in the early hours of the following morning he admitted the absurdity of continuing to divide the House. He voted in favour of using the 1831 census to determine the boroughs in schedules A and B, 19 July, and to postpone consideration of the partial disfranchisement of Chippenham, 27 July. He was almost certainly the 'Mr. Fane' who made a perfunctory gesture of opposition to the abolition of one seat for Lyme, 29 July. He voted to censure the Irish government over the Dublin election, 23 Aug., and for issuing the Liverpool writ, 5 Sept. Although the speeches are credited to John Thomas Fane in the index to *Parliamentary Debates*, it was presumably he who objected to the £10 franchise, 26 Aug., the delegation of parliamentary powers involved in the appointment of boundary commissioners, 1 Sept., the unconstitutional removal of the franchise, 20 Sept., and the revolutionary character of the bill, 10 Oct. He voted against the third reading, 19 Sept., and passage of the bill, 21 Sept., and the second reading of the Scottish bill, 23 Sept. 1831.

He voted against the second reading of the revised bill, 17 Dec. 1831, and going into committee on it, 20 Jan., and was probably the Fane who spoke inaudibly against the inclusion of 30 boroughs in schedule B, 23 Jan. 1832.[9] He divided against the enfranchisement of Tower Hamlets, 28 Feb., and the third reading of the bill, 22 Mar. 1832. He was probably the 'Mr. Fane' who condemned ministers' hostile policy towards France, 26 Mar., advocated changes to the anatomy bill, 11 Apr., 11 May, and urged immediate consideration of the corn laws, 1 June. He made an angry speech against reform, 5 June, calling the now no longer independent House of Lords 'a stinking carcase, a very putrefaction, a stinking nuisance in the nostrils of the people'.

He criticized the £10 franchise as going beyond the real wishes of the people, and declared that

> I see below me some friends of mine, scions of the Whig aristocracy, who possess large domains, which they have derived from their ancestors and I fear they will live to see all our institutions overwhelmed in a common destruction, as happened in France.

Unless it was John Thomas Fane, he voted in the majority for Alexander Baring's bill to exclude insolvent debtors from Parliament, 27 June, and criticized giving undue power to Parliament to disfranchise boroughs, 6 Aug. It may have been he who made interventions on the cases of Alexander Somerville, 3 July, and Governor Darling, 1 Aug., increased expenditure, 6, 18 July, 8 Aug., and Greece, 6 Aug. He divided against the Russian-Dutch loan, 26 Jan., 12 July, and spoke in defence of Belgium, 16 July. Although he claimed to have supported the Maynooth grant in the past, he spoke and voted in the minority of eight against it, 27 July 1832.

As Westmorland 'could not be brought to the scratch' for him at Lyme, Fane left the House at the dissolution later that year.[10] In November 1834 Wellington reported that leave from the army might be obtained for him if he 'was in Parliament or likely to be in Parliament', and he was considered as a possible candidate for Lyme during the ensuing general election, but he never sat again.[11] After Westmorland's death in December 1841 he inherited £2,000 and came into Sir Charles Saunders's estates in Prince Edward Island. Thereafter he lived at Cotterstock Hall, near Oundle, Northamptonshire, the residence of his mother, who predeceased him by only six weeks. He died in May 1857, leaving his entire estate to his first cousin the 3rd Viscount Melville.[12]

[1] *Burke PB* (1930), 2457. [2] Wellington mss WP1/778/11. [3] Dorset RO, Lyme Regis borough recs. DC/LR B6/13; *Western Flying Post*, 12 June 1826. [4] Add. 40398, f. 87; Wellington mss WP1/994/24. [5] Wellington mss WP1/1023/27; 1029/5. [6] Ibid. WP1/1030/22; 1031/38. [7] Add. 51785. [8] Wellington mss WP1/1094/30; 1098/35; Add. 51786, Holland to Fox, 13 June 1830. [9] *The Times*, 24 Jan. 1832. [10] Lonsdale mss, Beckett to Lowther, 4 Dec. 1832. [11] *Wellington Pol. Corresp.* ii. 55, 230. [12] PROB 11/1958/142; 2254/536; 2095/461; *Gent. Mag.* (1857), i. 742; O. Barron, *Northants. Fams.* 109.

S.M.F.

FANE, John I (1751–1824), of Wormsley, nr. Watlington, Oxon.

OXFORDSHIRE   1796–8 Feb. 1824

b. 6 Jan. 1751, 2nd but 1st surv. s. of Henry Fane[†] of Wormsley and 3rd w. Charlotte, da. of Richard Luther of Myles's, Ongar, Essex; bro. of Francis Fane[†]. *educ.* Corpus Christi, Camb. 1768. *m.* 1 Dec. 1773, Lady Elizabeth Parker, da. of Thomas Parker[†], 3rd earl of Macclesfield, 2s. 5da.[1] *suc.* fa. to Oxon. estates 1777; bro. Francis to Essex estates 1813. *d.* 8 Feb. 1824.

Member, bd. of agriculture 1803, vice-pres. 1815-22.

Capt. Lewknor vols. 1803; lt.-col. commdt. S. Oxf. militia 1809.

According to a fulsome obituary notice Fane, who was returned unopposed for Oxfordshire for the seventh successive time at the general election of 1820

> never sacrificed a vote in Parliament at the shrine of ambition or self-interest; he never sought for, nor ever obtained, a place or pension for himself or his family ... He was uniformly the enemy of improvident expenditure, of partial and injurious grants, even to the highest personages of the state, of an unnecessary stretch of the prerogative, and of the improper exercise of that parliamentary power, which ministerial patronage gives to the government ... He was loyal to his king; a true but unostentatious patriot; and the kind, the sincere, the faithful friend of his constituents.[2]

In short, he was a typical independent county Member, basically inclined to give general support to ministers, but prepared to oppose them on specific issues on which he or his constituents felt strongly.

Fane, a prominent member of the board of agriculture, was one of the parliamentary contacts of the Central Agricultural Association, founded by George Webb Hall in January 1819 in an attempt to organize the agricultural interest into an effective pressure group. He was one of the Members who accompanied a delegation from the Association to the board of trade to put the protectionist case in February 1819. He may have abetted Webb Hall's attempt to take over the board of agriculture for use as a political instrument.[3] Certainly in April 1820 he wrote to Lord Hardwicke, president of the board, recommending Webb Hall, as 'a most zealous and active advocate on behalf of the agricultural interest', for appointment as its secretary in the place of the late Arthur Young.[4] (Webb Hall secured the post, but ministers ended his machinations by abolishing the board in 1822.) Fane attended the Association's London meetings in May 1820 and almost certainly voted for Sumner's successful motion for inquiry into agricultural distress on the

30th. He was named to the select committee the following day.

He voted against the Liverpool government on the appointment of an additional Scottish baron of exchequer, 15 May 1820. He attended but did not speak at the county meeting called to vote a loyal address to the king, 22 Jan., and voted in defence of ministers' conduct towards Queen Caroline, 6 Feb. 1821.[5] He divided with government on the state of the revenue, 6 Mar. (unless this was John Thomas Fane), parliamentary reform, 9 May, and Hume's call for economy, 27 June; but against them on compensation to the clerks of the Scottish admiralty court, 15 Feb., repeal of the additional malt duty, 21 Mar. (he did not vote when ministers mustered support to defeat it, 3 Apr.), the barracks grant, 31 May, and the payment of arrears to the duke of Clarence, 8, 18, 29 June, 2 July 1821.[6] He voted against Catholic relief, 28 Feb. 1821, 30 Apr. 1822, and criminal law reform, 23 May 1821.

Fane is not known to have spoken in debate in this period, but he presented several petitions for relief from agricultural distress in 1822, when he joined in the revolt of disgruntled Tory country gentlemen against the government.[7] He voted for Hume's amendment to the address, 5 Feb., and the call for more extensive tax reductions to relieve distress, 11 Feb., yet was listed in the government majority against the resolution condemning their proposed relief measures as inadequate, 21 Feb. He voted for relaxation of the salt duties, 28 Feb., admiralty reductions, 1 Mar., and, unmoved by ministerial attempts to restrain recalcitrant backbenchers, abolition of one of the joint-postmasterships, 13 Mar., 2 May. He was one of the diehard minority of 24 who voted for the protectionist solution of a 40s. fixed duty on imported corn, 8 May. He opposed reception of the Calcutta bankers' petition for the recovery of debts from the East India Company, 4 July 1822. Ministerial threats of resignation in May 1822 and the return of comparative agricultural prosperity the following year seem to have curbed Fane's rebelliousness. He voted with administration on the sinking fund, 3, 13 Mar., the assessed taxes, 10, 18 Mar., repeal of the Foreign Enlistment Act, 16 Apr., and the currency, 12 June 1823. He was in the minority of eight against the warehousing bill, 21 Mar. He was one of the anti-Catholic Members who voted for the production of papers relative to the Dublin Orangemen's theatre riot, 24 Mar., but he divided with ministers against inquiry into the legal proceedings against the miscreants, 22 Apr. 1823.

Fane, an 'urbane, affable, hospitable' country gentleman and benevolent landlord, died in February

1824. In accordance with his wishes, he was 'modestly borne to the grave by some of his labourers; thus carrying even to the gates of death the unostentatious character of his life'.[8] By his will, dated 12 Feb. 1822, he provided handsomely for his wife and children. His personalty was sworn under £80,000.[9]

[1] PROB 11/1685/291, correcting *HP Commons, 1790-1820*, iii. 724. [2] *Gent. Mag.* (1824), i. 181. [3] R. Mitchison, 'Board of Agriculture', *EHR*, lxxiv (1959), 63-64; D. Spring and T.L. Crosby, 'George Webb Hall', *JBS*, ii. (1962-3), 256-6; B. Hilton, *Corn, Cash, Commerce*, 99-100. [4] Add. 35632, f. 342. [5] *The Times*, 23 Jan. 1821. [6] HLRO, Hist. Coll 379, Grey Bennet diary, 22, 99. [7] *The Times*, 14, 23 Feb., 26 Apr., 22 May 1822; Hilton, 148; *Creevey Pprs.* ii. 34. (Creevey's comment on Fane's voting behaviour is misinterpreted and wrongly dated in *HP Commons, 1790-1820*, iii. 724.) [8] *Gent. Mag.* (1824), i. 181. [9] PROB 11/1685/291; IR26/999/354.

D.R.F.

FANE, John II (1775–1850), of Wormsley, nr. Watlington, Oxon. and 9 Great George Street, Mdx.

OXFORDSHIRE   8 Mar. 1824–1831

b. 9 July 1775, 1st. s. of John Fane I* and Lady Elizabeth Parker, da. of Thomas Parker†, 3rd earl of Macclesfield. *educ.* Dr. Samuel Glasse's sch., Greenford, Mdx. 1783;[1] St. John's, Camb. 1794; L. Inn 1796. *m.* 6 June 1801, Elizabeth, da. of William Lowndes Stone of Brightwell Park, Watlington, 4s. (1 *d.v.p.*) 5da. (3 *d.v.p.*). *suc.* fa. 1824. *d.* 4 Oct. 1850.
    Capt. commdt. Watlington troop, Oxon. yeoman cav. 1831; maj. Oxon. militia.
    Sheriff, Oxon. 1835-6.

Fane signed the requisition for an Oxfordshire meeting to vote a loyal address to the regent in the aftermath of Peterloo, but does not seem to have attended it.[2] He was one of the signatories of the protest issued by Oxfordshire Tories after their attempt to carry a loyal address to the king over the Queen Caroline affair had been thwarted by her supporters in January 1821.[3] On the death of his father three years later he succeeded to the family estates in Oxfordshire and the Ongar area of Essex.[4] He was not first in the field for the county seat which his father had occupied for almost 28 years and was in any case too ill to canvass; but when he came forward a rival who had started before him backed down. At the county meeting to select a candidate, he said that he 'should endeavour to tread in the steps of his beloved parent, and make his example the rule of his life'; and at his unopposed election he asserted that he would 'go into Parliament independently, and not attach himself to any party, but always keep in view the preservation

of our excellent constitution in church and state', and that he would 'pay regard to measures and not to men'.[5]

Like his father, he gave general support to the Liverpool ministry, but was not afraid to take an independent line on specific issues. He was in the minority for referring the reports of the Scottish judicial commission to a committee of the whole House, 30 Mar. 1824. He presented a Henley petition for inquiry into the prosecution of the Methodist missionary John Smith in Demerara, 4 June 1824, but may have voted with government against this on the 11th.[6] He presented an Oxfordshire parish petition for repeal of the house and window taxes, 4 Feb., and voted for repeal of the latter, 17 May 1825.[7] He voted with government for the Irish unlawful societies bill, 25 Feb. He divided against Catholic relief, 1 Mar., 21 Apr., 10 May, and the Irish franchise bill, 26 Apr. He presented a Banbury agriculturists' petition against alteration of the corn laws, 28 Apr.[8] He voted steadily against the grant to the duke of Cumberland in May and June 1825. He voted against ministers on the question of the president of the board of trade's salary, 10 Apr., and was in the protectionist minorities against the emergency admission of foreign corn, 8 May, and the corn bill, 11 May 1826.

At the general election of 1826 he became involved in a contest for the county (the first for 72 years), but his own seat was in no danger, for the intervention of a third man was inspired by dissatisfaction with the parliamentary conduct of the other sitting Member, Ashhurst. At the nomination Fane boasted of having kept his promise of conscientious independence. Pressed for a statement of his views on slavery, he routinely condemned it, but added that 'if the emancipation of the blacks was immediately and suddenly to take place, I think the heads of a good many whites would be *emancipated from their shoulders*'. He came second in the poll; his failure to top it was attributed to mismanagement and to the successful efforts of his supporters to ensure Ashhurst's return.[9] He presented several petitions against further alteration of the corn laws, 26 Feb., 19 Mar., and voted against the corn bill, 2 Apr. 1827.[10] He voted against the duke of Clarence's annuity, 2 Mar. He divided against Catholic relief, 6 Mar. On 4 May he was granted a fortnight's leave on account of the death of his daughter Georgiana the previous day. (He lost two other daughters in September that year and in November 1829.)[11] He was in the minority in favour of a separate bankruptcy jurisdiction, 22 May, but voted with the Canning ministry for the grant for Canadian waterways, 12 June 1827. That day he presented a Henley petition for repeal of the Test Acts.[12] He did not vote on this issue, 26 Feb. 1828, but he divided against Catholic relief, 12 May. The following day he was in the minority against the provision for Canning's family. He presented a Banbury petition against the new corn bill, 30 Apr. 1828. As expected by Planta, the Wellington ministry's patronage secretary, and the bishop of Oxford, he opposed Catholic emancipation in 1829.[13] He presented hostile petitions, 18 Feb., 10, 20 Mar. He voted against considering emancipation, 6 Mar., and on the 17th complained that 'the country had been taken by surprise ... [by] a measure which tended to subvert the constitution' and 'obliged so many to oppose a government which they would otherwise wish to support'. He was reported as saying that he was 'inclined' to support the bill to disfranchise Irish 40s. freeholders; but he was listed in the minorities of 17 against the second reading, 19 Mar., and of 20 for an amendment to permit reregistration, 20 Mar. He voted against receiving the report of the relief bill, 27 Mar., but was absent from the division on the third reading, 30 Mar. 1829.

Although the Ultra leaders did not count Fane as one of their group, emancipation largely alienated him from the ministry: Goulburn, the chancellor of the exchequer, observed in May 1830 that he 'more often votes with the Tories than with us'.[14] He voted for the amendment to the address, 4 Feb., and against the army estimates, 19 Feb. He paired against the enfranchisement of Birmingham, Leeds and Manchester, 23 Feb., and was given a week's leave to attend to urgent private business, 1 Mar. He presented Oxfordshire petitions complaining of agricultural distress and calling for repeal of the beer and malt duties, 16 Feb., 7 Apr., 6 May. He voted against government on the grant for the volunteers, 9 Mar., the treasurership of the navy, 12 Mar., the admiralty establishment, 22 Mar., the Bathurst and Dundas pensions, 26 Mar., and the ordnance estimates, 29 Mar. He divided against Jewish emancipation, 5 Apr. He presented a Henley petition for abolition of the death penalty for forgery, 6 May. He was in the opposition minorities on the public buildings grant, 3 May, the salary of the assistant secretary to the treasury, 10 May, privy councillors' emoluments, 14 May, and the grant for South American missions, 7 June. He voted against the second reading of the sale of beer bill, 4 May, presented a Wallingford petition against consumption on retail premises, 13 May, and on 21 June 1830 voted for Knatchbull's amendment to that effect.

Fane had to fight another contest at the general election of 1830, when he offered again for the county on 'independent principles'. At the nomination, he said that while he had opposed Catholic emancipation in an attempt to preserve the constitution, he would now 'lose my life rather than see it repealed'. He comfortably topped the poll.[15] Ministers listed him as one of the 'doubtful doubtfuls', with the subsequent endorsement of 'enemy'. He was absent from the division on the civil list which brought them down, 15 Nov. 1830. He presented petitions for the abolition of slavery, 3, 16, 25 Nov. 1830, 2 Mar. 1831. On 16 Mar. 1831 he presented a Chipping Norton petition in favour of the Grey ministry's reform bill, as he did one from Henley, 22 Mar. That day, perhaps in deference to constituency opinion, he voted silently for the second reading. On 24 Mar., however, he said that the measure would 'not benefit one man or any set of men' and would 'tend to destroy that which is the fundamental basis of the British constitution'; and on the 28th, while admitting that there was 'a strong, perhaps a popular, feeling in favour of reform', he denied that there was support for 'disfranchising ... the labouring classes' or reducing the size of the House. He voted for Gascoyne's wrecking amendment to the bill, 19 Apr. 1831. At the consequent dissolution, anticipating a victory for the reformers in Oxfordshire, he announced his retirement, on the plea that 'having stood two contests ... neither my circumstances nor constitution are equal to another canvass'.[16]

Fane, who served as sheriff of Oxfordshire in 1835, died at Wormsley in October 1850. By his will, dated 28 Mar. 1842, he left his wife an annuity of £500 charged on the Essex estates and set up trust funds for his surviving younger children.[17] The family estates, including property in Dorset which had come to him through his father's half-sister Mary Stapleton (d. 1835), passed to his eldest son John William Fane (1804-75), Conservative Member for Oxfordshire, 1862-8.

[1] *Heber Letters*, 19. [2] *Jackson's Oxford Jnl.* 30 Oct., 13 Nov. 1820. [3] *Oxford University and City Herald*, 27 Jan. 1821. [4] PROB 11/1685/291; IR26/999/354. [5] *Jackson's Oxford Jnl.* 14, 21, 28 Feb., 13 Mar.; *Oxford University and City Herald*, 13 Mar. 1824. [6] *The Times*, 5 June 1824. [7] Ibid. 5 Feb. 1825. [8] Ibid. 29 Apr. 1825. [9] Ibid. 16, 19-21 June; *Jackson's Oxford Jnl.* 17, 24 June 1826. [10] *The Times*, 27 Feb., 20 Mar. 1827. [11] *Gent. Mag.* (1827), i. 475; ii. 380; (1829), ii. 648. [12] *The Times*, 13 June 1827. [13] Add. 40343, f. 353. [14] Add. 40333, f. 99. [15] *Jackson's Oxford Jnl.* 3 July, 7, 14 Aug. 1830. [16] Ibid. 30 Apr. 1831. [17] PROB 11/2122/810; IR26/1868/557.

D.R.F.

FANE, John Thomas (1790–1833), of
Baltonsborough and Barton St. David, Som.

LYME REGIS   29 Mar. 1816–1832

b. 28 Apr. 1790, 1st s. of Hon. Thomas Fane[†] (d. 1807) of
Brympton, Som. and Ann, da. of Richard Lowe of Locko
House, Derbys. m. 10 Aug. 1816, Marianne Shrimpton,
da. of John Mills Jackson of Downton, Wilts., 1s. d. 23
Mar. 1833.
  Lt. 25 Ft. 1807; lt. 18 Drag. 1809; capt. 69 Ft. 1810;
capt. 87 Ft. 1811, Maj. de Meuron's regt. 1814, half-pay
1816; maj. 61 Ft. 1819; lt.-col. and insp. of militia, Ionian
Islands 1821; lt.-col. (half-pay) 22 Drag. 1824; ret. 1832.
  Clerk of privy seal 1814-d.

Fane entered the army in 1807, shortly after the
death of his father, another soldier and Member
for Lyme, under whose will he inherited £4,000 on
coming of age; he no doubt later succeeded to most
of his estate, which included personal wealth sworn
under £20,000.[1] Probably through the influence of
his father's brother, the 10th earl of Westmorland,
lord privy seal in Lord Liverpool's administration,
he was made a clerk of the privy seal in 1814. As the
son of a capital burgess of Lyme Regis, he was elected
to the corporation that year.[2] In 1816 Westmorland,
the patron of the borough, brought him in there, in
place of Lord Burghersh, and he was returned without
opposition at the following five general elections. In
the House, Fane, whose parliamentary behaviour
cannot always been distinguished from that of the
John Fanes, father and son, who consecutively represented Oxfordshire, was an inactive supporter of
Tory administrations.[3] In 1819 he joined a new regiment, which was based in Jamaica, so he may not have
been the 'Mr. Fane' who was granted a fortnight's
leave on urgent private business, 5 June 1820. He
was, however, named as a defaulter, 28 June, and was
excused, 4 July 1820, on the ground that he thought
the order to attend referred to John Fane.[4] As 'Thomas
Fane', he voted against the motion to censure ministers' conduct towards Queen Caroline, 6 Feb. 1821.
He divided against repeal of the additional malt duty,
3 Apr., parliamentary reform, 9 May, and Hume's
motion for economy and retrenchment, 27 June. On
23 July 1821 he was appointed a lieutenant-colonel and
made inspector of field officers of militia in the Ionian
Islands, which presumably explains his lack of parliamentary activity during the following two sessions.
He became a half-pay lieutenant-colonel in the 22nd
Dragoons in January 1824.

  Unless it was John Fane II, he voted against condemning the trial of the Methodist missionary John

Smith in Demerara, 11 June 1824. He voted for the
Irish unlawful societies bill, 25 Feb. 1825, and (as he
had on 28 Feb. 1821) against Catholic relief, 1 Mar., 21
Apr., 10 May, and the Irish franchise bill, 26 Apr., 9
May 1825. No trace of parliamentary activity has been
found for the following session, though he put in one
of his rare appearances at Lyme during the general
election of 1826.[5] It may have been of Fane's wife that
Philipp Von Neumann recorded, 2 Jan. 1827, that 'I
met a friend of mine, Mrs. Fane, who came to Madeira
for her husband's sake, who looks as if he needed it'.[6]
He divided against Catholic relief, 6 Mar., and was
granted a fortnight's leave because of illness in his
family, 29 Mar. 1827. He voted against repeal of the
Test Acts, 26 Feb., Catholic relief, 12 May, and reduction of the salary of the lieutenant-general of the ordnance, 4 July 1828. Listed by Planta, the Wellington
ministry's patronage secretary, as 'doubtful' on
Catholic emancipation in February 1829, he presented
an anti-Catholic petition from Lyme, 11 Feb., and
paired against the second, 18 Mar., and voted against
the third reading of the relief bill, 30 Mar. In October
1829 Westmorland, who had left the cabinet in 1827,
applied to the prime minister for a promotion for him,
as a steady and deserving supporter, but the following
August he expressed his annoyance that such a friend
of administration had not been assisted.[7] Fane voted
against the enfranchisement of Birmingham, Leeds
and Manchester, 23 Feb., and Jewish emancipation,
17 May 1830. He was listed by ministers among their
'friends', but was absent from the division on the civil
list, 15 Nov. 1830. He voted against the second reading
of the Grey ministry's reform bill, 22 Mar., and for
Gascoyne's wrecking amendment, 19 Apr. 1831.

  Fane, who received army half-pay of £200 and a
salary of £320 from his clerkship,[8] evidently experienced some personal disaster, probably in mid-1831,
which forced him into exile abroad. It apparently
related to his sinecure, as Lord Ellenborough noted, 20
June 1831, that Charles Jackson had 'called, in much
distress, Lord Durham [the lord privy seal] having
displaced him [as keeper of the records and assistant
clerk] in consequence of some pecuniary transactions
with Mr. Fane, who is his brother-in-law'.[9] In January
1832 king's bench ruled that Durham should admit a
deputy for Fane, as he had been appointed before the
Act requiring the holder of the office to carry out his
duties in person and was, in any case, unable to serve
because he was resident abroad.[10] His name does not
appear in any of the surviving opposition minority
lists on the reintroduced reform bill, and it was probably his cousin and colleague at Lyme, Henry Sutton
Fane, who made the anti-reform speeches attributed

to 'Mr. Fane' in that and the following session. He voted against the second reading, 17 Dec. 1831, and third reading of the revised reform bill, 22 Mar. 1832. It is unclear whether it was he or Henry Sutton Fane who voted for Waldo Sibthorp's amendment respecting Lincoln freeholders, 23 Mar., against the second reading of the Irish reform bill, 25 May, (as 'Colonel Fane') against going into the committees on the Irish party processions bill, 25 June, and crown colonies relief, 3 Aug., and for Alexander Baring's bill to exclude insolvent debtors from Parliament, 27 June 1832.

Fane, who was not brought forward for the one remaining seat for Lyme at the general election of 1832, died at St. Omer, France, in March 1833.[11] An unknown friend, who claimed to have long been a witness 'to his dreadful sufferings of mind and body', wrote to Fane's only child Augustus John (b. 1817), 14 Apr., transmitting his dying sentiments that the boy should take care of his mother and pay no regard to the accusations circulated by their enemies. Fane's mother Anne wrote to her grandson Augustus, 20 Apr. 1834, that he should ignore the 'reflections of those whose ill judging mode of life and most erroneous ideas of honourable and praiseworthy conduct have been the means of separating your parents and you from the society and intercourse of myself and family'. She insisted that there was no truth in the allegation that 'my unkind conduct and that of your father's family was the cause of his wretched situation' or 'that he died from grief and anxiety in consequence of neglect'.[12] By his will, dated 29 Oct. 1830, Fane left everything to his wife, who died at Boulogne, 15 Apr. 1836. Administration of the estate was subsequently granted in London, 14 Jan. 1837, and again, 22 Aug. 1840, to their son. He died, unmarried, 21 June 1840, and in August administration of his estate, worth only £200, was granted to his grandmother.[13]

[1] HP Commons, 1790-1820, iii. 726; PROB 11/1464/573; IR26/125/87. [2] Dorset RO, Lyme Regis borough recs. DC/LR B6/5, 11. [3] Black Bk. (1823), 154; Session of Parl. 1825, p. 463. [4] CJ, lxxv. 395. [5] Western Flying Post, 12 June 1826. [6] Von Neumann Diary, i. 145. [7] Wellington mss WP1/1051/5; 1086/13; 1091/8; 1094/30; 1098/35; 1132/29. [8] Black Bk. (1831), 440. [9] Three Diaries, 95. [10] The Times, 14 Jan. 1832. [11] Gent. Mag. (1833), i. 466. [12] Northants. RO, Westmorland (Apethorpe) mss W(A) 6/XIV. [13] PROB 6/216; 11/1859/157; Gent. Mag. (1836), i. 567; (1840), ii. 217.

S.M.F.

FANE, Vere (1785–1863), of 11 Nottingham Place, Mdx.

LYME REGIS   1818–1826

b. 5 Jan. 1785, 4th s. of Hon. Henry Fane[†] (d. 1802) of Fulbeck, nr. Grantham, Lincs. and Anne, da. and h. of Edward Buckley Batson, London banker, of Avon Tyrrell and Upwood, Dorset; bro. of Sir Henry Fane*. educ. Eton 1796. m. 2 June 1815, Elizabeth, da. of Charles Chaplin[†] of Blankney, Lincs., 1s. d.v.p. 4da. (2 d.v.p.). d. 18 Jan. 1863.
Mayor, Lyme Regis 1830-1.

Fane's father, the younger son of the 8th earl of Westmorland, bequeathed him £1,000 in East India stock and a sixth share in the proceeds of £1,882 invested in three per cent annuities.[1] His mother, whose slender means he slightly augmented, presumably used her family connections to start him on a career in banking. On hearing that he wished to resign his clerkship in Childs' bank, she wrote to him on 9 Feb. 1814 regretting that his profession 'has turned out so very unpleasant a one and that offers so distant a prospect of your profiting by it, till you are become so far advanced in life to have any enjoyment in what it may then produce'. Thinking that 'the precarious tenure of the pursuits you hint at appears to me somewhat objectionable', she advised him to consult his brother-in-law Charles Arbuthnot*, the Liverpool ministry's patronage secretary, about a possible place under government, or his own contacts about an opening in a mercantile house. Repeating her fear of the effect a future change of ministry might have on his income, 20 Mar. 1814, she gave the example of her husband, who had been deprived of his treasury clerkship in 1762, and recommended him 'to make your *fortune among the ladies*' as 'a much better pursuit for you than the one you are looking forwards to'.[2] He is not known to have taken office, but did marry into a Lincolnshire family the following year. He remained in banking, being a partner in Praeds and Company of 189 Fleet Street, London, from 1817 until his death.[3]

Fane became a freeman of Lyme Regis, the pocket borough of his cousin the 10th earl of Westmorland, the lord privy seal, by gift in 1813 and was elected a capital burgess in 1819.[4] Having replaced his eldest brother Sir Henry Fane as its Member in 1818, he was again returned unopposed at the general election of 1820.[5] He continued to support ministers in silence when present.[6] He voted against economies in revenue collection, 4 July 1820, repeal of the additional malt duty, 3 Apr., economy and retrenchment, 27 June 1821, more extensive tax reductions to relieve distress,

11, 21 Feb. 1822, and for the duke of Cumberland's annuity, 10 June 1825. He divided in defence of ministers' conduct towards Queen Caroline, 6 Feb. 1821, and against inquiry into Irish tithes, 19 June 1822, repeal of the Foreign Enlistment Act, 16 Apr. 1823, and condemning the trial of the Methodist missionary John Smith in Demerara, 11 June 1824. He voted against parliamentary reform, 9 May 1821, 20 Feb. 1823, and reform of Edinburgh's representation, 13 Apr. 1826. He divided against Catholic relief, 28 Feb. 1821, 30 Apr. 1822, 1 Mar., 21 Apr., 10 May, and the Irish franchise bill, 26 Apr. 1825. He was given two weeks' leave on urgent private business, 18 Feb., and was in the majority against the Leith docks bill, 20 May. He visited his constituency to dine with the corporation in the summer of 1825, but retired from the House at the dissolution in 1826 in favour of one of Westmorland's younger sons. He died in January 1863.

[1] PROB 11/1376/453. [2] Lincs. AO, Fane mss 6/4/1/13, 14. [3] O. Barron, *Northants. Fams.* 119; F.G. Hilton Price, *Handbook of London Bankers* (1890-1), 132. [4] Dorset RO, Lyme Regis borough recs. DC/LR B6/5, 11. [5] *HP Commons, 1790-1820*, iii. 726. [6] *Black Bk.* (1823), 154; *Session of Parl. 1825*, p. 463.

D.R.F.

FARDELL, John (1784–1854), of Eastgate, Lincoln and Holbeck Lodge, nr. Horncastle, Lincs.

LINCOLN 1830–1831

b. 4 May 1784, 1st s. of John Fardell, dep. registrar, archdeaconry of Lincoln and Eleanor Penelope, da. of John Hayward of Lincoln. *educ.* ?Louth g.s.; M. Temple 1817, called 1824. *m.* 26 Sept. 1809, Mary, da. of John Tunnard of Frampton House, nr. Boston, 2s. *suc.* fa. 1805. *d.* 5 Feb. 1854.
Dep. registrar, archdeaconry of Lincoln and registrar, archdeaconry of Stow 1805-21; clerk of common chamber and recvr.-gen.; clerk of fabric; coroner within their liberties, steward of galilee ct. and manorial cts. in Lincs. and Hunts., to dean and chapter of Lincoln 1806-21; chapter clerk and register 1810-21.
Steward, Lincoln 1836.

The Fardell family came originally from Northamptonshire, but had been settled in Lincolnshire since the early eighteenth century. John Fardell the elder entered the office of the deputy registrar at Lincoln. In 1767 he became one of the proctors in the consistory court and by 1774 was a notary public. He succeeded as deputy registrar in 1783 and held a number of separate offices under the bishop and his commissary in the archdeaconries of Lincoln

and Stow, as well as appointments under the dean and chapter. His position enabled him to lease and purchase church lands and secure his family's advancement.[1] His younger sons, Thomas and Henry, were educated at Cambridge and entered the church: Henry Fardell (1795-1854) married the eldest daughter of the bishop of Ely and was one of the notorious pluralists singled out by the *Black Book*.[2] John Fardell was destined to succeed his father in the registry, and in 1801 Fardell senior obtained a new patent of the Stow registrarship for their joint lives. No record of John's clerkship survives, but he was certainly involved with the business of the Lincoln consistory court by 1803, and succeeded to his father's offices on his sudden death in February 1805. Fardell senior's personal estate was valued at £25,000 and, after making provision for his two daughters, he left all his lands to his three sons as tenants in common and charged them with an annuity of £200 for his widow.[3] In July 1805 John Hodgson, the bishop's legal secretary and a family friend, urged Fardell to reply to a solicitor's inquiry, and wrote: 'You are the most silent young man I know, though you certainly have not that character amongst my young ladies, who insist upon it that your tongue seldom rested in their company in London'.[4] He was a notary public by January 1806 and was appointed to a number of offices under the dean and chapter in September. He married in 1809 and was appointed clerk to the dean and chapter the following year. He enrolled at the Middle Temple in 1817 but was not called to the bar until 1824; though listed as counsel until his death, he never practised. He was appointed registrar and actuary during the vacancy in the see of Lincoln which followed the translation of Bishop Pretyman to Winchester in 1820. In 1821, aged only 37, he sold his business as a proctor, notary and conveyancer to Robert Swan, a Lincoln attorney, for £7,000, and relinquished his other ecclesiastical offices in Swan's favour, though he secured the insertion of his elder son's life into the patents of the Stow registrarship.[5] In anticipation of his retirement he had written to Earl Brownlow, lord lieutenant of Lincolnshire, confident that his character and property in Lindsey and Kesteven entitled him to be made a magistrate and deputy lieutenant, but he had great difficulty in establishing his credentials. He tried again in 1821 with the bishop of Ely's support, but was again unsuccessful. He became a freeman of Lincoln by purchase in 1822. The following year he assured Brownlow of his support for the Liverpool administration: he had purchased his freedom with the 'express purpose of supporting those principles'. Even though he enjoyed an income of £3,000 a year, Brownlow again declined to admit him. In 1826, convinced that

Brownlow was prejudiced against him, he wrote in vindication of his character: his votes in the elections for Huntingdonshire and Lincolnshire were 'sufficient proof' of his attachment to the 'ministerial interest'. He had for some time acted as a general commissioner of taxes and was well acquainted with the Lincoln bench, but he was again disappointed in his aspirations. When two former lawyers were admitted to the commission in 1828 he was mortified to be excluded, particularly when his 'station in life and property in the county', as he told Brownlow, entitled him to be included. Neither Charles Chaplin, one of the county Members, nor any of Fardell's own county and ecclesiastical friends could persuade Brownlow to change his mind.[6] Like his father, Fardell was interested in the muniments of the dean and chapter. He was elected a fellow of the Society of Antiquaries in 1809 and subsequently admitted to that of Scotland. On a visit to Lincoln in 1825 his fellow antiquary the Rev. John Skinner sketched his collection of antiquities. He aspired to the life of a country gentleman, and in 1829 purchased the lordship of Greetham and 567 acres of land for £17,760. He had also come into possession of the advowson of Laceby. He possessed additional lands at Holbeck in the parish of Ashby Puerorum. He refurbished Holbeck Lodge, which became his country residence, and landscaped the grounds in the best Salvator Rosa taste.[7] Dr. Edward Parker Charlesworth of Lincoln, who knew him well, portrayed him as something of an amiable nonentity. On one occasion he told Sir Edward French Bromhead of Thurlby: 'I humour him in little points: his mind cannot grasp a large one, which saves me much trouble'.[8]

At the general election of 1830 the Lincoln independents, anxious to field a third man, solicited Montague John Cholmeley* to stand in opposition to Charles Waldo Sibthorp and Lord Monson's nominee. When he dithered they invited Fardell, whom they believed to be a reformer, to stand in his place. He agreed to do so, 'free and unshackled in political opinions'. As Charlesworth saw it, 'Jacky suffered himself to be dragged down in his carriage to do "third man" for the Blue committee, driven to their wits' end for somebody to pay the expenses they had incurred'.[9] He confirmed his previously pledged support for Sibthorp, even at the risk of ruining his own chances. The challenge seemed to be aimed at Monson's uncle Lord Mexborough*, but the Monson interest collapsed, and Fardell and Sibthorp were returned unopposed. He was described by Bromhead at the election as a supporter of 'public economy, moderate in his politics, and unconnected with any party'. Sir Charles Anderson of Lea depicted him as a 'good

natured man who will be sufficiently happy in franking letters at the old dame's *route* in the Minster Yard'.[10] He was a friend of Sir William Amcotts Ingilby, the senior county Member and a reformer, but his politics remained uncertain, and in October 1830 he gave a celebratory dinner for Sibthorp and the Tory corporation of Lincoln.[11] The Wellington ministry listed him among the 'good doubtfuls', but he voted against them in the division on the civil list which brought them down, 15 Nov. 1830. Yet he voted against the second reading of the Grey government's reform bill, 22 Mar., and for Gascoyne's wrecking amendment, 19 Apr. 1831. He was beheaded in effigy at Lincoln for these votes. He presented and endorsed the prayer of a petition against the register of deeds bill, 20 Apr. 1831. Before the dissolution Charles Tennyson* urged Gilbert John Heathcote* to stand for Lincoln, since Fardell would have a 'rough reception' and was hardly likely to 'make another attempt'. He apparently still had some support, but, arguing that the reform bill was too sweeping, he declined to contest the seat.[12]

Fardell kept up his antiquarian interests, and in 1833 was engaged in researching family history; but he told his friend Stacey Grimaldi, 'I shall have a labyrinth of difficulty to wade through before I shall be able to accomplish my object'.[13] In 1835 he presented Lincoln with a gas-illuminated clock to adorn the guildhall.[14] He was appointed steward of the city in 1836. He secured the reversionary interest to the valuable advowson of Sprotborough, near Doncaster for his elder son, the Rev. John George Fardell (1810-99). Anxious to avoid a dispute, but determined to 'protect he rights of the church', he settled a voluntary commutation of tithes there, and increased the value of the living from £625 to £700 a year.[15] In 1853 he sold the Holbeck estate to his younger son Charles for £11,000, and at about the same time disposed of much of his other Lincolnshire property, including the manor of Greetham and his estate at Wadddington for £24,000 and £17,000 respectively. He died of heart disease at his son's rectory in February 1854.[16] By his will, dated 22 Dec. 1853, he divided his remaining property equally between his sons.[17]

[1] 'Some Corresp. of John Fardell', *Lincoln Rec. Soc.* lxvi (1973), 45-50. [2] *Black Bk.* (1830), 25. [3] *Lincoln Rec. Soc.* lxvi. 50. [4] Lincs. AO Cor/R/5/40/ [5] *Lincoln Rec. Soc.* lxvi. 50. [6] Lincs. AO, Brownlow mss 4 BNL box 1, Fardell to Brownlow, 4 Feb., 23 May 1820; box 2, same to same, 15 Aug. 1821, 28 Feb. 1823, 15 July, 21 Aug. 1826, 23 Feb. 1828, replies, 19 Aug. 1826, 27 Feb. 1828, G. Gordon to Brownlow, 10 Nov. 1828; R.J. Olney, *Rural Society in 19th Cent. Lincs.* 43. [7] J. Varley, *Parts of Kesteven*, 98-99; D.M. Williamson, *Lincoln Muniments*, 10; J. Conway Waller, *Recs. of Parishes around Horncastle*, 11-12. [8] Sir F. Hill, *Georgian Lincoln*, 233. [9] Ibid. 234. [10] Ibid. 233-4; *Lincoln, Rutland and Stamford Mercury*, 30

July, 6, 13 Aug. 1830. [11] *Lincoln, Rutland and Stamford Mercury*, 22 Oct. 1830. [12] Lincs. AO, Ancaster mss XIII/B/6c, d; *Lincoln, Rutland and Stamford Mercury*, 8, 29 Apr.; *Stamford Herald*, 29 Apr. 1831. [13] Add. 34188, f. 554. [14] Sir F. Hill, *Victorian Lincoln*, 39. [15] J.G. Fardell, *Sprotborough*, 58. [16] *Gent. Mag.* (1854), i. 430. [17] PROB 11/2189/222; IR26/1995/226.

S.R.H.

FARQUHAR, James (1764–1833), of Johnston Lodge, Laurencekirk; Hallgreen, Inverbervie, Kincardine, and 13 Duke Street, Westminster, Mdx.

ABERDEEN BURGHS	5 Jan. 1802–1806
ABERDEEN BURGHS	1807–1818
PORTARLINGTON	1 Mar. 1824–1830

b. 1 Aug. 1764, 2nd surv. s. of John Farquhar (*d.* 1768), merchant, of Aberdeen and Rachel, da. of James Young, merchant, of Aberdeen.[1] *educ.* Aberdeen g.s.;[2] Aberdeen Univ. 1777-81. *m.* 19 May 1795, Helen, da. of Alexander Innes of Cowie, Kincardine, *s.p. d.* 4 Sept. 1833.

Proctor, Doctors' Commons 1788-*d.*; dep. registrar, diocese and archdeaconry of Rochester 1788-1805, admiralty ct. 1810-*d.*

Provost, Inverbervie; dir. Crown Life Assurance Co. c.1825-*d.*

Farquhar, who came from an Aberdeen mercantile family, was in successful practice as a proctor in Doctors' Commons. He was in partnership with Joseph Sladen at 19 Bennett's Hill until about 1820, when they were joined by John Irving Glennie. Since 1810, Farquhar had held the remunerative post of deputy registrar of the admiralty court, the duties of which were administered from his other office at 2 Paul's Bakehouse Court. His elder brother William (1762-1838) was in partnership as a merchant at 12 St. Helens Place, Bishopsgate Street with their youngest half-brother John Morice until about 1828. (Their mother, widowed in 1768, had married David Morice, an Aberdeen advocate, in 1773.)

James Farquhar, a general supporter of Lord Liverpool's Liverpool ministry, had surprisingly lost his seat for Aberdeen burghs, where he controlled Inverbervie, of which he was provost for many years, to the radical Joseph Hume in 1818. He never recovered his ground in the district. He sent a letter of apology and approval to be read at the Kincardineshire meeting called to vote a loyal address to the regent in the aftermath of Peterloo, 18 Nov. 1819.[3] At the general election of 1820 he came forward for the county, where his two purchased estates lay, and where he had been building up his strength for several years. He was confronted by a Whig, Sir Alexander Ramsay*

of Balmain, who was expected to beat him, while Lord Arbuthnott, the lord lieutenant, started his brother Hugh Arbuthnott* as a supporter of government. Lord Arbuthnott complained to one of the secretaries to the treasury that Farquhar, who was 'much disliked', had done 'much mischief', 'having come down and declared that he has the support of government, while I have a letter declaring that it has been refused to him'. In fact Lord Melville, the ministry's Scottish manager, had given Farquhar 'no assurance' when he personally requested ministerial endorsement; but he authorized the lord advocate Sir William Rae* to use his discretion from Edinburgh and informed Lord Arbuthnott that Farquhar's 'steady support in Parliament for a good many years gives him a reasonable claim upon us, and if he has the good wishes of yourself and other principal proprietors, I should hope he will succeed'.[4] Lord Arbuthnott continued to insist that only his brother had any chance of beating Ramsay, but Farquhar, who tried to get Hugh Arbuthnott out of the way by raising the prospect of his standing for Aberdeen Burghs, where he had influence in Inverbervie, resisted all Rae's efforts to get him to withdraw and transfer his votes to the Arbuthnotts. In the end Lord Arbuthnott withdrew his brother, but it turned out that he had made a secret agreement of mutual support with Ramsay. Melville, who blamed Lord Arbuthnott for what seemed almost certain to be the loss of a ministerial seat, instructed Rae to give full support to Farquhar, although after Ramsay assured Edinburgh ministerialists that he did not intend to go into systematic opposition, Melville let Farquhar know that if Ramsay won on this occasion and lived up to his promise, government 'must be wholly at liberty hereafter' to support him against Farquhar or any other man. Farquhar persisted, but was comfortably defeated by 12 votes in a poll of 52 freeholders.[5]

As provost of Inverbervie, he transmitted to the home secretary Peel an address of loyalty from the council for presentation to the king on his visit to Scotland, 12 Aug. 1822.[6] He found his way back into the House as a paying guest of the impoverished 2nd earl of Portarlington in March 1824. The contrast between himself and his late predecessor in the seat, the assiduous, talented and voluble radical political economist David Ricardo, could hardly have been more marked. Farquhar voted with government for the Irish insurrection bill, 14 June 1824. In December 1824 he sent on to Peel a letter from an unknown correspondent on the state of Ireland.[7] As previously, he was hostile to Catholic claims: he paired against them, 1 Mar., and voted against the relief bill, 21 Apr., 10 May 1825. He voted against the Irish franchise bill,

26 Apr. He was in the majority against the Leith docks bill, 20 May. He divided for the duke of Cumberland's annuity, 6, 10 June 1825, and with ministers on the Jamaican slave trials, 2 Mar., and against reform of Edinburgh's representation, 13 Apr. 1826. He renewed his contract with Lord Portarlington at the general election of 1826 and voted against Catholic relief, 6 Mar. 1827. He was in the minority, with Canning, the premier, against the disfranchisement of Penryn, 28 May, but was credited with a vote with the reformers against throwing the corrupt borough of East Retford into the neighbouring hundred, 21 Mar. 1828. Somewhat belatedly, he presented two Dunfermline petitions for repeal of the Test Acts, 2 Apr., and again divided against Catholic relief, 10 May 1828. The prediction of Planta, the Wellington ministry's patronage secretary, in February 1829 that Farquhar would vote 'with government' for their concession of emancipation proved to be wide of the mark, for he was in the hostile minorities of 6, 18, 30 Mar. He was one of the Members representing Irish constituencies who voted against Daniel O'Connell being allowed to take his seat without swearing the oath of supremacy, 18 May. He is not known to have contributed to debate in this period, but he presented a petition from the corporation of Aberdeen in support of the local improvement bill, 31 Mar. 1829. He was now listed among those who voted against the transfer of East Retford's seats to Birmingham, 11 Feb. 1830. He voted against the enfranchisement of Birmingham, Leeds and Manchester, 23 Feb.; but, in his last known vote before his retirement at the dissolution of 1830, he divided against the ministry for abolition of the Bathurst and Dundas pensions, 26 Mar. As delegate for Inverbervie at the 1830 general election, when it was reported that he had declined an invitation to stand for the burghs, he backed the successful ministerial candidate.[8]

Farquhar died at his London home in Duke Street in September 1833. By his will, dated 19 July 1833, he left his wife a life annuity of £1,500, and other legacies amounting to £11,000. He provided generously for a host of Farquhar, Morice, Young and Hadden relatives, as well as servants and employees, to the tune of over £64,000. He left £1,000 to be distributed among Aberdeen charities and £500 for the benefit of the poor of each of the two parishes in which his Mearns property was situated. His personalty was sworn under £140,000 within the province of Canterbury. He had previously devised the Hallgreen estate to his nephew (and partner since 1829) James Farquhar (1805-75), his brother's elder son; and the Johnston property to his nephew Alexander Gibbon (1793-1877), an advocate, the son of his sister Rachel Susan. He left his

brother's younger son, Thomas Newman Farquhar (1808-66), a solicitor, £15,000 'to compensate in some degree for the Scotch estate left to his brother'.[9]

[1] W. Johnston, *Descendants of James Young* (1894), i, 4-5. [2] Ibid. 92. [3] *Aberdeen Jnl.* 24 Nov. 1819. [4] TNA T64, Arbuthnott to Lushington, 24 Feb. 1820; NLS mss 11, f. 6; 1054, f. 177, 179. [5] NLS mss 11, ff. 6-19, 22, 28-40, 44, 55, 59, 62, 75; *Edinburgh Evening Courant*, 10, 17 Feb., 6 Apr.; *Caledonian Mercury*, 18 Mar., 6 Apr. 1820; Johnston, 93. [6] Add. 40349, f. 141. [7] Add. 40371, f. 125. [8] *Aberdeen Jnl.* 11, 18, 25 Aug. 1830. [9] *Gent. Mag.* (1833), ii. 552; PROB 11/1821/572; IR26/1321/566; Johnston, 88, 95.

D.R.F.

FARQUHAR *see also* **TOWNSEND FARQUHAR**

FARQUHARSON, Archibald (1793–1841), of Finzean, Banchory, Aberdeen.

ELGIN BURGHS   1820–1826

b. 6 Aug. 1793, o.s. of Archibald Farquharson of Finzean and 1st w. Christian Spring.[1] *m.* 16 Sept. 1814, Frances, da. of Francis Russel of Blackhall, Strachan, *s.p. suc.* fa. 1796. *d.* 14 May 1841.

Farquharson's father, the son of a merchant, succeeded to the Finzean estates in Aberdeenshire on the death of his second cousin Francis Farquharson in 1786. His first wife, this Member's mother, died in 1793. He subsequently married Mary Campbell of Islay, but died on 8 Mar. 1796. Farquharson's early life is obscure. At the general election of 1820 he was the late choice of the 6th earl of Kintore as his candidate for Elgin Burghs, where he and Colonel Francis Grant* operated a system of alternating nomination. In Grant's absence abroad his precarious interest in Elgin was under attack from the 4th Earl Fife* in a campaign marked by kidnappings and legal trickery. Farquharson received the votes of the delegates for Cullen (the returning burgh) and Kintore, while his opponent General Alexander Duff*, Fife's brother, got those of the Banff and Inverurie delegates. Rival delegates from Elgin voted for their respective candidates, but their votes were rejected as illegal by the returning officer, who declared Farquharson elected by Cullen's casting vote. Duff's petition was not pursued.[2]

Farquharson followed Kintore's opposition line of politics in the House, though he never joined Brooks's, but after an initial burst of activity before Easter 1821 his attendance fell away dramatically.[3] He was granted a month's leave on account of ill health, 1 June 1820. He voted to condemn the omission of Queen Caroline's name from the liturgy, 23, 26 Jan, presented an Inverurie petition for its restoration, 1 Feb.,[4] and divided for inquiry into the conduct of the sheriffs of Cheshire and Dublin at meetings in support of the queen, 20, 22 Feb.; but he was absent from the division on the opposition censure motion, 6 Feb. 1821. He was in a minority of 11 against the navy estimates, 2 Feb.[5] He voted to condemn the Holy Alliance's suppression of liberalism in Naples, 21 Feb., and for investigation of a complaint against chief justice Best, 23 Feb. He was in the majority for Catholic relief, 28 Feb. He voted to give Leeds a scot and lot franchise if it got Grampound's seats, 2 Mar. He divided for repeal of the tax on husbandry horses, 5 Mar., and the additional malt duty, 21 Mar., 3 Apr. He was in minorities on the revenue, 6 Mar., and the army estimates, 30 Mar., 6 Apr., when he took part in 'a desultory conversation',[6] 11 Apr. On 30 Apr. 1821 he was given six weeks' leave on urgent private business, and his next known vote was not until 24 Apr. 1822, when he was in Burdett's minority for remission of Henry Hunt's* gaol sentence. He voted for abolition of one of the joint-postmasterships, 2 May 1822. He attended the Aberdeen dinner held to applaud the parliamentary exertions of the radical Joseph Hume, 5 Sept. 1822.[7] In 1823 he divided for a reduction of £7,000,000 in taxes, 28 Feb., inquiry into the Irish church establishment, 4 Mar., amendments to the ordnance estimates, 10, 17 Mar., inquiry into the prosecution of the Dublin Orange rioters, 22 Apr., and Lord John Russell's parliamentary reform motion, 24 Apr. He was given a fortnight's leave on private business, 17 Feb., and presented a Forfarshire petition against interference with the corn laws, 5 May 1825.[8] His last known votes were against the duke of Cumberland's annuity, 2, 9, 10 June, and the grant for repairs to Lyme Regis cobb, 3 June 1825. He retired from Parliament at the dissolution in 1826, when Fife had gained the upper hand in the Burghs.

Farquharson died childless in May 1841. He was succeeded in the Finzean property by his uncle John Farquharson, who on his death in 1849 was succeeded by his son Francis.[9]

[1] A. Jervise, *Epitaphs and Inscriptions in NE of Scotland*, ii. 44. [2] NAS GD248/824/2/63, 64, 68, 90; *Inverness Courier*, 6 Apr. 1820. [3] *Session of Parl. 1825*, p. 463. [4] *The Times*, 2 Feb. 1821. [5] HLRO, Hist. Coll. 379, Grey Bennet diary, 11. [6] *The Times*, 7 Apr. 1821. [7] Ibid. 12 Sept. 1822. [8] Ibid. 6 May 1825. [9] Jervise, ii. 44.

D.R.F.

FARRAND, Robert (1792–1855), of 4 Catherine Court, Tower Hill, London.

HEDON	1818–1826
HEDON	1830–1832
STAFFORD	21 Feb. 1837–1841

b. 14 Mar. 1792,[1] illegit. s. of Christopher Atkinson† (d. 1819) of Holme Hale, Swaffham, Norf.; half-bro. of Albany Savile* m. Elizabeth Murray, s.p.[2] d. 2 Feb. 1855.

Like his father (before his temporary disgrace in 1783), the bastard Farrand was a corn factor. Although his business does not appear under his own name in the London trade directories until 1830, at 4 Catherine Court, he was corresponding from Fen Court, Fenchurch Street in 1823 and had long been active in the Swaffham area of Norfolk, where his father had acquired an estate.[3] At the general election of 1820 he again contested the venal borough of Hedon, where his father (who had died the previous year) had successfully put him up on his own interest in 1818, and was returned in second place. Unlike his legitimate half-brother Albany Savile, he never joined Brooks's, but he continued to vote generally with the Whig opposition to the Liverpool ministry on most major issues, especially those involving retrenchment, economy and tax reductions, in the 1820 Parliament, at least until 1824, when his attendance seems to have fallen away.[4] He voted for parliamentary reform, 20 Feb., 24 Apr. 1823, 26 Feb. 1824. On the Catholic question he changed sides, voting for relief, 28 Feb. 1821, but against Canning's bill to relieve Catholic peers, 30 Apr. 1822, and relief in general, 1 Mar., 21 Apr., 10 May 1825, despite having voted against the bill to suppress the Catholic Association, 15 Feb. 1825. His only known vote with government in this period was against repeal of the additional malt duty, 3 Apr. 1821. On 2 May 1825 he moved an unsuccessful amendment to allow corn to be removed from bond free of duty. He was named to the select committee on law merchant, 15 May 1823, and on 13 June gave evidence to the effect that a change in the regulations governing contracts with factors was desirable. He assisted John Smith* with the bill which he introduced on 18 June and corresponded with Lord Redesdale about the measure, which became law on 18 July 1823.[5] No trace of parliamentary activity has been found for 1826. At the general election that summer he was defeated at Hedon by two men backed by the Tory corporation and petitioned in vain; he later claimed in the House, 22 July 1831, that his vote for reform had cost him his seat.[6]

Farrand secured an unopposed return for Hedon at the general election of 1830, apparently with corporation approval.[7] The Wellington ministry listed him among their 'foes' and he divided against them when they were brought down on the civil list, 15 Nov. 1830. Yet he voted against the second reading of the Grey ministry's reform bill, 22 Mar. 1831. On the 28th he presented and endorsed East Riding petitions praying for more representatives. He divided for Gascoyne's wrecking amendment, 19 Apr. 1831. At the ensuing general election he was returned unopposed for Hedon, which faced disfranchisement, with the full backing of the corporation.[8] He voted against the second reading of the reintroduced reform bill, 6 July, and at least once for the adjournment, 12 July 1831. On the motion to disfranchise Hedon, 22 July, he argued that it deserved to be united with the hundred of Holderness to return one Member and complained of the East Riding's unfair treatment. He voted against the passage of the bill, 21 Sept., the second reading of the revised bill, 17 Dec. 1831, the enfranchisement of Tower Hamlets, 28 Feb, and the third reading, 22 Mar. 1832. His only other known votes were against government on the Russian-Dutch loan, 26 Jan., 12 July 1832.

At the 1832 general election Farrand offered as a Conservative for Stafford, but withdrew before the poll. Beaten there in 1835, he was successful in 1837. By then he was in possession of the Holme Hale estate, where he built a mansion house. His London business moved to 26 Mark Lane in about 1839; it was styled Farrand, Young and White from 1850. He died in February 1855, and his personalty was sworn under £3,000.[9]

[1] M.I. in G.A. Carthew, *Hist. Bradenham*, 194. [2] PROB 11/2206/276. [3] *HP Commons, 1790-1820*, iii. 94-96, 729; Add. 38744, f. 245; *Constable Corresp.* ed. R.B. Beckett, i. 181, 208, 249; ii. 278. [4] *Session of Parl. 1825*, p. 463. [5] *PP* (1823), iv. 44-46; Add. 38744, f. 244; *CJ*, lxxviii. 404, 479. [6] *Hull Advertiser*, 2 June 1826; G.R. Park, *Hist. Hedon*, 188-9. [7] *Hull Rockingham*, 7 Aug. 1830. [8] *Hull Advertiser*, 29 Apr. 1831. [9] IR26/2028/101.

M.P.J.C.

FAZAKERLEY, John Nicholas (1787–1852), of Stoodleigh, nr. Tiverton, Devon and 27 Upper Brook Street, Mdx.

LINCOLN	1812–1818
GREAT GRIMSBY	1818–1820
TAVISTOCK	1820–12 May 1820
LINCOLN	1826–1830
PETERBOROUGH	24 Nov. 1830–1841

bap. 19 Feb. 1787,[1] 1st s. of John Fazakerley (formerly Radcliffe) of Prescot, nr. Liverpool, Lancs. and Wasing,

Berks. and w. Catherine. *educ.* Eton 1799-1802; Christ Church, Oxf. 1805; Edinburgh Univ. 1807-8; European tour. *m.* 5 June 1822,[2] Eleanor, da. of Matthew Montagu[†] of Sandleford Priory, nr. Newbury, Berks., 2s. (1 *d.v.p.*) 3da. (1 *d.v.p.*). *suc.* fa. 1796. *d.* 14 July 1852.[3]

'Nobody to me [is] more agreeable than Fazakerley', Sydney Smith told Lady Holland in 1832.[4] Earlier that year Edward Littleton*, a fellow member of Grillion's Club, had described him as

> a man of more literary information, more acuteness, and power of argument, and withal of more extended and comprehensive views than most I know. Hence it is he [is] the intimate friend and correspondent of Lords Lansdowne and Holland, and most of the eminent men of that class of this day.[5]

Fazakerley, who had joined Brooks's in 1812, was a popular figure in Whig society. He was steadfast in his attachment to the tenets of mainstream Whiggery (for example, he applauded the choice of Tierney as leader in the Commons in 1818 as 'a rebuke to the Mountain');[6] but he was no man of action and made little mark in politics. At the general election of 1820 he would 'have nothing to do' with Great Grimsby, where his seat on Lord Yarborough's interest in the 1818 Parliament had cost him over £6,000.[7] He was returned by the 6th duke of Bedford, with whose son Lord John Russell* he was friendly, for Tavistock, to the surprise of Lord Morpeth[†], who thought he might have preferred 'a more independent seat, for he is by no means a violent Whig, nor to the level of the Russells'.[8] Within weeks, however, he was, as he told his Parisian correspondent Mrs. Pauline Graham of Drynie, '*libre et vagabond*', for Bedford was reluctantly obliged to turn out 'poor dear Faz' in order to accommodate Lord Ebrington, a rising star of opposition, who had lost his seat for Devon.[9]

Soon afterwards Fazakerley, whose health was indifferent at this time, sold his property at West Hill on the Isle of Wight, though 'not at half its value', as he told George Graham, 25 July 1820:

> One can't quite easily part with the old walls and trees and views to which one has been so long accustomed ... And now I meditate a scheme for seeing Italy and hearing some debates in the Parliament of Naples next winter.

He welcomed the rebellion there and the consequent 'discomfiture of the legitimates' of Europe, whom he wished 'no greater harm than to be obliged to govern by laws which secure the lives and properties of their subjects'. He reported that Queen Caroline was

> still a great favourite with the people, and even with those who have no doubt of her guilt she finds some mercy,

for they say she was so ill used that she could not help it ... I have little doubt of her conviction. There is an end to economy and reform of all sorts till this question is disposed of. No one will listen to any other subject.[10]

Fazakerley, who had acquired a Devon estate at Stoodleigh, did not in the event winter in Italy; he was at Bowood and Althorp at the turn of the year.[11]

In January 1822 he was at Nice, where he became engaged to the dwarfish and myopic Eleanor Montagu, 'one of the Portman Square constellation' of Tories with intellectual pretensions, whose sister Jane was married to Henry Goulburn*, the Irish secretary. He wrote 'jokingly' of the business to Graham:

The sun of Nice has melted two obdurate hearts and instead of going on as a bachelor into Italy as I intended I shall have to return to England to make preparations for submitting to the yoke of a little lady rather more diminutive even than your esteemed rib ... there is no great beauty and no money, so that at least I have proceeded on the hope of having discovered other excellent reasons for my choice ... it will take six or eight months at least to get money matters and my cursed estate put into proper order and in the meantime we wish to be as quiet as possible.[12]

Sir James Mackintosh* wrote sourly of this 'singular piece of news':

He is fastidious, indulgent to his own peculiarities and extremely susceptible to annoyance from disagreeable companions, and in short seemed a predetermined bachelor. He is to marry the daughter of a renowned bore and a member of a family so disagreeable that it seems needless to examine the character of any individual of it.[13]

George Agar Ellis* thought it a 'foolish' enterprise.[14] After making his way through France to 'settle my disorderly patrimony in preparation for matrimony', he arrived in London in early March, 'high in health and spirits, though somewhat thinner', according to Lady Holland, whose misgivings over the match proved to be unfounded: it was a happy one, and Eleanor Fazakerley, 'an amiable, pleasing little woman', in the words of Henry Edward Fox*, soon became a firm favourite in Whig circles.[15] Russell would have liked the vacant seat for the 2nd Earl Fitzwilliam's borough of Higham Ferrers which went to Lord Normanby in February 1822 to have been assigned to Fazakerley.[16] In March the Hollands pressed his pretensions to a vacancy at Lincoln, one of his former seats, on Brougham; but he, who had already encouraged his protégé John Williams* to start and complained to Lord Duncannon* that Lady Holland was 'working mischief', dismissed the idea as 'ridiculous'.[17]

In the late summer of 1822 Fazakerley, who observed to his friend Edward Davies Davenport* that he longed to see 'a great republic ... solidly established' in place of the Austrian monarchy, reluctantly tore himself away from 'ses bois et ses champs' at Stoodleigh, as his wife told Mrs. Graham, to go abroad with her.[18] They wintered at Nice, from where Fazakerley wrote to Lady Holland, 19 Feb. 1823, that he would be 'most unhappy if indignation against' the Franco-Spanish war 'does not break out in all possible ways in England', though he supposed that there was 'no chance of sweeping away the worst of our own Ultras in the storm'.[19] The Fazakerleys were in Switzerland in the summer and autumn of 1824, before moving to Rome for the winter. They made an excursion to Naples in the spring of 1825 and then travelled via Florence, Vienna, Salzburg and Prague to Germany, where they visited Berlin, Frankfort, Heidelburg and Baden Baden: Fazakerley, like his wife, had reservations about Germany, being 'glad to have seen it and to *have done with it*'. They returned to England by way of Strasbourg and Paris, where Mrs. Fazakerley fell temporarily ill, in August 1825.[20] Fazakerley, tempted by the notion of setting up as a gentleman farmer, was considering the purchase of another Devon estate at Courtlands, near Exmouth, which, unlike Stoodleigh, would be inhabitable in winter. His wife, whose tastes were essentially metropolitan, did not relish the prospect of rural immurement so far from her family in London, though she was ultimately ready to fall in with his wishes, as she told Fox:

He is a *little out* with me about my love of society and towns, which is only natural, as he cannot tell till he tries me whether I shall take to a life so different from what I was made for ... I am not afraid of his continuing dissatisfied with me, for I mean when once the die is cast to take to making butter and feeding chickens in good earnest. It would be too foolish with every *essential* happiness to throw it away because I do not exactly lead the life that suits my fancy.[21]

In late October, to the great relief of Eleanor, who perceived that it was 'a considerable privation to Faz, though the united opinions of all his friends had made him submit to think that it would not be a wise measure', he gave up the idea of buying Courtlands. They had already settled on Sidmouth for their winter quarters, and were resolved to wait a year or two before deciding what to do with the Stoodleigh estate, which was proving profitable, and where to settle permanently. There was, Mrs. Fazakerley told Fox, 'some chance of Faz's coming into Parliament, which delights me for many reasons'; and various unspecified schemes were considered during the following six months.[22] At the general election of 1826 he came forward for Lincoln on the Monson interest, under the aegis of Fitzwilliam, and after a sharp contest, in which national political issues seem to have played little part, he was returned with a Tory.[23]

Fazakerley, writing from Stoodleigh, his summer base, in August 1826, admitted to Lady Holland that 'I begin to acknowledge the inconvenience of the distance of Devonshire, and I should not be surprised if I made up my mind to sell what I have here, though it would cost me a pang'. Bedford commented to her two months later that 'the account of Faz is melancholy. He is wholly unfitted to be a country gentleman, and much as I should like to have him for a neighbour in Devon, I heartily wish for his own sake he would sell that estate'.[24] Despite suffering from what his wife described as 'the most abominable cold I almost ever knew him to have' and subjecting himself to a purgative 'calomel discipline', he went to London for the opening of Parliament in November.[25] He voted against the duke of Clarence's grant, 16 Feb., and for inquiry into the conduct of Leicester corporation, 15 Mar., and information on the Orange procession at Lisburn, 29 Mar. 1827. He divided for Catholic relief, 6 Mar. He was in the opposition minorities in the divisions on going into committee of supply, 30 Mar., and the Irish miscellaneous estimates and chancery delays, 5 Apr. Soon afterwards he went to Stoodleigh, but he was back in London by 28 Apr., when Lord Auckland told Lansdowne, who was contemplating throwing in his lot with Canning's administration, that Fazakerley had 'just been here with tears in his eyes entreating me to encourage you forward'.[26] He voted for the disfranchisement of Penryn, 28 May, but was in the government majority on Canadian water defences, 12 June. He presented petitions for repeal of the Test Acts, 30 May, 7, 15 June 1827.[27] At the end of the month he went with his wife to 'rusticate at Stoodleigh until October'.[28] He was thrown into despair by Canning's death, as he told John Evelyn Denison* in August:

I scarcely knew him ... but ever since the late struggle, all the opinions and principles which I value have been so bound up with Canning's existence and his power, that certainly no public event ever made me feel so comfortless and despondent. Indeed I cannot see hope in any direction, for if the king were to send for the best of the present men and desire them to form a government, I don't see how they could manage matters in the House of Commons. Wellington and Peel hang over me like a nightmare. I see no chance of escape. And then what is to become of Ireland and the whole of our foreign policy?

All this and the mortification which one feels at the triumph of those base people, his former colleagues.[29]

A few weeks later, rejoicing that 'the apolitical are still without the walls', he congratulated Thomas Frankland Lewis* on his appointment as financial secretary to the treasury in the Goderich ministry and exhorted him to 'be honest, and to use your influence ... to accomplish every practicable degree of retrenchment, and not to join the senseless and wicked cry of those who say there is no use in small savings':

The principle on which Canning professed to proceed, and on which Lord Lansdowne joined him, was that the old Tory fortress was not to be taken by storm, but that it was to be gradually and silently undermined by the effect of placing good men in situations of influence ... I think and from the beginning thought them so right in this that I believe no other system would have succeeded and that under any other mode of operating the church and king [party] would have scattered them to the winds.[30]

He had, however, no faith in Goderich's competence as premier and placed his 'hope, and confidence and comfort of every sort' in Huskisson, despite fears for his health.[31] The Fazakerleys left Devon at the end of October, visited Lansdowne at Bowood and moved on by way of Lymington to Brighton, where in December 1827 they were installed, as Lady Holland reported, in 'a *sheltered* spot beyond the Pavilion. They both dislike the roar of the sea and howl of the wind'.[32]

Fazakerley presented Lincoln petitions for repeal of the Malt Act, 8 Feb., and of the stamp duty on receipts, 25 Feb. 1828. He brought up petitions for repeal of the Test Acts, 21, 25, 26 Feb., when he voted for that measure. On 6 Mar. he presented a petition from the freeholders of Lincoln seeking the right to vote for the county. He voted against the proposal to sluice the delinquent borough of East Retford with the freeholders of Bassetlaw, 21 Mar. He voted for Catholic relief, 12 May. He divided against the Wellington ministry on civil list pensions, 20 May, the Irish assessment of lessors bill, 12 June, the archbishop of Canterbury's bill, 16 June, the garrisons grant, 20 June, the refurbishment of Buckingham House, 23 June, the additional churches bill, 30 June, and the ordnance estimates, 4 and 7 July. He presented a Lincoln petition for repeal of the Act restricting the circulation of one pound notes, 9 June, and one from Calne for the abolition of colonial slavery, 25 July 1828.

Fazakerley, who predicted to Littleton, 20 Sept., that 'these Brunswick clubs will drive the government to some decision' on the Catholic question, 'and as no government is likely to listen to their calls for blood, the decision can hardly fail to be right', took Sunning Hill, Berkshire as a winter residence that year.[33] Eleanor told Fox, 6 Dec. 1828, that

> we have no wandering plans at present and shall scarcely form any even of the most limited kind whilst Faz is in Parliament. A dissolution, however, from the king's health cannot be far off and then perhaps we may go abroad for a few months or a year.[34]

Fazakerley urged James Abercromby* to use his influence to try to restrain Sir James Graham* and Lord Althorp*, who had been speaking of 'open war if the duke [of Wellington] does not produce a measure' of Catholic emancipation. He subsequently expressed his hope that

> all the friends of civil and religious liberty will drop their differences and unite to press for measures of concession. It ought to be agreed to do this in an amendment [to the address] and to take a vote upon the first night, unless ministers announce their intention to do something, and I am ... anxious that this ground should be taken at once, and firm opposition proclaimed to any government that will not settle the question. If Althorp agrees in this view, and acts upon it stoutly from the first, everyone will rally behind him.[35]

He voted for emancipation, 6, 30 Mar., and presented a constituent's petition in its favour, 11 Mar. 1829. He brought up a Lincoln petition for repeal of the assessed taxes, 10 Apr. He voted for the transfer of East Retford's seats to Birmingham, 5 May, but was shut out of the division on Lord Blandford's reform motion, 2 June. He voted against the grant for the Marble Arch, 25 May, and to reduce the hemp duties, 1 June. He told Stratford Canning*, 10 May 1829, that after the passage of emancipation 'a languor and a want of interest' had overcome politicians: 'The Tories are gradually returning to their natural allegiance and the Whigs would require great provocation to act against ministers', especially as Peel as home secretary was 'as liberal on almost all subjects as he dares to be'.[36]

Fazakerley voted for the amendment to the address, 4 Feb., and on 12 Feb. 1830, expressing his 'entire concurrence' in the prayer of the Lincoln petition, presented by his colleague Sibthorp, for repeal of the assessed taxes and the malt duty to help relieve distress, called on ministers to reduce expenditure across the board. He voted with Hume for a remission of taxes, 15 Feb., and was in the opposition minorities on the estimates, 19 Feb., 1 Mar. He voted for the transfer of East Retford's seats to Birmingham, 11 Feb., 5, 15 Mar., and the enfranchisement of Birmingham, Leeds and Manchester, 23 Feb., but not for Blandford's

reform scheme, 18 Feb. He was one of the 27 opposition Members (he and Russell were examples of the 'wisest' among them, in the view of Graham) who met at the Albany, 3 Mar., and agreed to act under Althorp's leadership to seek reductions in expenditure and taxation.[37] He voted assiduously in support of the ensuing parliamentary campaign for economies, and was also in the opposition minority on British interference in the affairs of Portugal, 10 Mar. He voted for Jewish emancipation, 5 Apr., 17 May. He presented petitions against the Tiverton roads bill, 1, 2, 26 Apr., 3 May. 'Rather tired with the late sittings of the House', as his wife reported, he went to Stoodleigh 'to refresh himself in his woods' during the Easter recess.[38] When the House reconvened, he continued to divide steadily with the reviving Whig opposition on most major issues. He voted with O'Connell for revision of the Irish vestry laws, 27 Apr., and with Hume on the four-and-a-half per cent duties, 21 May, but was one of the handful of Whigs who divided with Fitzwilliam's son Lord Milton against repeal of the Irish coal duties, 13 May.[39] He voted for Russell's reform motion, 28 May, and for abolition of the death penalty for forgery, 7 June 1830.

At the general election a few weeks later Fazakerley abandoned Lincoln and canvassed Arundel on the interest of the 12th duke of Norfolk. His prospects initially appeared promising, but the intervention of a second Whig, which, as he explained to Milton, 'would have added both to the trouble and expense of the election', prompted him to withdraw, convinced that he had made the 'right decision'. He could not 'summon up courage' to stand for Pontefract, as Milton apparently suggested, and, writing from Stoodleigh, 24 July 1830, he observed:

> It is naturally very painful to me to separate from friends with whom I have so long engaged in the most interesting of all pursuits ... But the best things must have an end, and I shall content myself with observing from these remote fastnesses the progress which you all make in promoting the public good. In this almost unexampled relaxation of public morals, and I am sorry to think indifference in the constituent body, you will have a task more difficult than ever. The difficulties too of the country are becoming greater every day.[40]

Milton was not alone in regretting Fazakerley's absence from the next Parliament, reflecting that he and his father had 'the will, but not the means' to assist him. Charles Poulett Thomson* told him that 'I know of no one in the House amongst our common friends whose opinion I ranked so highly or on whose judgement I could so much rely as yours, and I shall badly miss the support I found in them'.[41] Fazakerley, who made a brief visit to Rouen in early August, welcomed the successful revolution in France.[42] A few weeks later his wife reported his retirement from Parliament to Fox:

I am sorry ... but I think his decision was only prudent under the circumstances ... This country (that is London) is abominably expensive, and we found that our income was not at all more than was absolutely necessary to live (though comfortably) yet *very quietly*, five months of the year in London; and therefore, when it was a question of sinking a considerable sum of money to come into Parliament, with no reasonable prospect of our common and unavoidable expenses doing anything but *increase*, we thought it high time to retreat and make the sacrifice in time. Faz dislikes London so much, that though of course sorry to lose the interest of politics and drop his intercourse with many friends whom he saw principally in the House, he does not much care about the matter, and I have already ceased to think about it.

They were undecided, she went on, whether to remain at Stoodleigh for the winter and spring, to take a house at Torquay or to go to Paris.[43] In the event, when Milton decided to retire from the House soon after the meeting of Parliament, he brought Fazakerley in for Peterborough in his room, to the pleasure of Althorp, who had considered his exclusion 'a great grievance' and regarded him as 'a very honest man and honest on the best principles', as well as 'a well judging man and one whose advice is of great value'.[44]

Fazakerley, whom Maria Edgeworth met and described as 'most agreeable' at about this time,[45] told Milton a week after his return that he believed that while the Grey ministry 'sets out with unexampled difficulties surrounding it on all sides', it was 'honestly and seriously intent on surmounting them': 'if ... [their] measures are as good as the promises which they have made, they may defy any opposition in Parliament, or appeal with confidence to the country'. Addressing the paramount question of reform, he admitted that he had not been 'hitherto, or rather I was not till within a few months, a strong reformer', but that

the last election, and the manner in which several counties broke loose from the old influence of aristocracy and property, convinced me of the necessity of dealing largely with this question: otherwise it was, I thought, clear that if the excitement went on at the next election, the 40s. freeholders throughout England would take the game into their own hands, return Members of extreme popular opinions for every county, and throw such a body into Parliament as would deprive any government of the power of controlling or shaping any measure of reform.

Had the late House of Commons acted differently on the questions of East Retford and the great towns, had the counties not acted as they did in many instances at the late election, and, to crown all, had ... Wellington not made so extravagant a declaration on the subject, the case might have been far different; but all these things together have produced a state of feeling with which, added to the real merit of the argument, it would be madness and folly to contend. The new government therefore very wisely at once announce a reform; and every one is very anxious to know what they will do.

For his own part, conceiving that 'the question concerns less the composition of the House of Commons, than the character and composition of the elective body', and that the principal object was 'to reconcile the middling classes to the parliamentary constitution', he favoured the abolition of 'decayed boroughs and transferring their rights to populous towns, fixing the right of voting at a reasonable amount of qualification'; opening 'close corporations' to 'resident householders rated at a certain sum'; disfranchising non-resident voters and 'the lowest of the scot and lot and potwallopers who are the people most open to bribery and profligate corruption', and making practical arrangements to reduce the cost of elections for counties, where he would raise the freeholders' qualification and give the vote to respectable copyholders and leaseholders.[46] Milton was in broad agreement with him, though he argued strongly against disfranchising all 'the lower orders'.[47] In reply, 10 Jan. 1831, Fazakerley confessed that, on the contrary, he would 'despair of any system which left a large part of the franchise in the hands of quite the lower orders', and argued that 'ballot will not prevent bribery and still less drunkenness'. At the same time, he hoped that Milton would

agree with me in thinking that almost any plan brought forward by this government ought to be supported by persons of our opinions. It is pretty certain to be a great improvement on the present state of things, and any government who will undertake such a measure has in my eyes so much merit and is sure to meet with so many difficulties, that it would require a very strong case to give me courage to vote against them. I feel this not only on the reform question, but generally, that we in our lives have never seen an administration so likely to do good and to act virtuously. Their own characters and the times are guarantees for their good conduct, so I shall go to London with a disposition to be among the most submissive of their adherents. It would indeed be most painful to find myself obliged to think even of acting otherwise.

He was in a dilemma over the recently revealed and 'frightful' list of sinecures and pensions: though reluctant to interfere with legal rights, he acknowledged that 'the proof of corruption here is so flagrant and the amount so enormous, and the whole system so flagitious, that I long to find in my own mind a plea for attacking them'.[48] Fazakerley, who was named to the select committee on the East India Company, 4 Feb. (and again, 28 June), was pleased with what Lansdowne, a member of the cabinet, hinted about the scope of their reform scheme.[49] He attended the debates on the English reform bill and voted silently for the second reading, 22 Mar., and against Gascoyne's wrecking amendment, 19 Apr.[50] Ludicrously, Holland had suggested to Grey, 4 Mar. 1831. that he 'might possibly do well as secretary at war' in the room of Williams Wynn; he was not appointed.[51]

Fazakerley was returned unopposed for Peterborough at the 1831 general election, but appears to have been an absentee, probably because of poor health, for most of the first session of the new Parliament, when the only known traces of his activity are his pairings on the ministerial side for the divisions on the second reading of the re-introduced reform bill, 6 July, and on details of the measure, 5, 9, 17 Aug. His friend Sir James Macdonald* told him, 14 Sept., that he 'ought not to hesitate' to go up for the third reading, and he was present to vote for the passage of the bill, 21 Sept.[52] The following day he was granted three weeks' leave on account of his daughter's illness. He went up from Stoodleigh to vote for the motion of confidence in the Grey ministry after the bill's defeat in the Lords, 10 Oct. A fortnight later he expressed to Milton his hope that the peers, having made their point, would be 'more tractable', especially if public opinion continued to run strongly in support of reform. Although he was a little concerned at the evidence furnished by the Dorset and Cambridgeshire by-elections of disaffection among the agricultural interest, despite its generous treatment under the reform bill, he attributed it largely to 'the fear of free corn'.[53] He developed a worry that there was 'some hitch with the king about the reform bill', on which Littleton reassured him.[54] He made the journey from Devon to vote for the second reading of the revised bill, 17 Dec. 1831. At the close of the year his wife, writing from Bowood, told Fox that their child was improving and that Fazakerley was 'quite well, though he still coughs'.[55]

He was much more assiduous in his attendance in the 1832 session, when he voted generally for the details of the reform bill, though he was one of the minority of 32 who opposed ratification of the £50 tenants-at-will franchise, 1 Feb. He divided for the third reading, 22 Mar. He voted with government

on the Russian-Dutch loan, 27 Jan., their policy on Portugal, 9 Feb., and the navy civil departments bill, 6 Apr. He presented a Peterborough petition against the general register bill, 31 Jan. He was added to the East India committee, 1 Feb., and named to that on slavery, 30 May. Kept in London during April by his wife's advanced state of pregnancy, he continued to fret about the reform bill's prospects in the Lords.[56] He voted for the address calling on the king to appoint only ministers who would carry it unimpaired, 10 May, the Irish bill, 25 May, and the Scottish measure, 1 June. He was in the majority in favour of making coroner's inquests public, 20 June. On 29 June 1832 he was given a month's leave to attend to urgent private business.

Fazakerley resisted attempts to get him to stand for the Northern division of Devon at the general election of 1832, when he came in again unopposed for Peterborough.[57] He headed the poll there in 1835 and 1837 and retired from Parliament at the dissolution of 1841, his last four years as a Member having been marred by wretched health, which drove him abroad.[58] He became something of a pundit on the poor laws and, as 'a sensible man and moderate Whig', in the words of Greville, supported the Grey and Melbourne administrations.[59] From the latter in 1835 he turned down offers of the government of Canada and, 'after a good deal of doubt', a special mission to Brussels, concluding that he was 'almost too old to begin so completely new a course of life'.[60] Widowed in 1847, he sold Stoodleigh and acquired a property at Burwood House, near Walton-on-Thames, Surrey, where he died in July 1852.[61] By his will of 4 Apr. 1845, amended after his wife's death by four codicils, he created a trust fund to provide for his daughters, his only surviving son and namesake, who entered University College, Oxford in 1852, aged 18, having been catered for by the terms of his marriage settlement. His personalty was sworn under £50,000, with a taxable residue of £42,872.[62]

[1] At Wasing (IGI, Berks.). His younger brother William, who entered Christ Church in 1807, was *bap.* at Wasing 1 Oct. 1788. [2] Add. 48215, f. 25. [3] Not 16 July as stated in *HP Commons, 1790-1820*, iii. 733. [4] *Smith Letters*, ii. 565. [5] Hatherton diary, 18 Jan. [1832]. [6] JRL, Bromley Davenport mss, Fazakerley to E.D. Davenport, 6 Oct. 1818. [7] Wentworth Woodhouse mun. F48/161. [8] Castle Howard mss, Morpeth to wife [13 Mar. 1820]. [9] Add. 48215, f. 11; 51654, Lady Holland to Mackintosh [3 Apr.]; 51667, Bedford to Lady Holland, 22 May [1820]. [10] Bromley Davenport mss, Fazakerley to Davenport, 4 Apr. 1820; Add. 48215, ff. 11, 13, 15. [11] *Edgeworth Letters*, 225, 228-9; *Lady Lyttelton Corresp.* 233. [12] Add. 48215, f. 19; 51576, Fazakerley to Lady Holland, 4 Jan.; 51687, Lansdowne to Holland, 21 Jan. 1822. [13] Add. 52445, f. 37. [14] Northants. RO, Agar Ellis diary, 20 Jan. [1822]. [15] Bromley Davenport mss, Fazakerley to Davenport, 25 Feb. 1822; *Lady Holland to Son*, 10;

Fox Jnl. 100, 122, 157, 194; Add. 48215, ff. 21, 25. [16] Add. 51679, Russell to Lady Holland [Jan. 1822]. [17] Add. 51562, Brougham to Holland [14 Mar.]; Bessborough mss, same to Duncannon [14 Mar. 1822]. [18] Bromley Davenport mss, Fazakerley to Davenport, 24 July, 28 Sept. 1822; Add. 48215, f. 27. [19] Bromley Davenport mss, Fazakerley to Davenport, 16 Nov. 1822; Add. 51576. [20] *Fox Jnl.* 194-5; Add. 52011, Mrs. Fazakerley to Fox, 1 Oct. [1824], 1, 12, 21 Feb. 1825; Bromley Davenport mss, Fazakerley to Davenport, 25 July 1825. [21] Add. 52011, Mrs. Fazakerley to Fox, 21 Feb., 7, 19, 29 Aug., 16 Sept.; 52017, Townshend to same, 30 Aug. 1825. [22] Add. 52011, Mrs. Fazakerley to Fox, 25, 31 Oct., 8, 11 Dec. 1825, 4, 8 Apr. 1826; 52017, Townshend to same, 30 Oct. 1825; Lansdowne mss, Lansdowne to Spring Rice, 27 Oct. 1825. [23] *Lincoln, Rutland and Stamford Mercury*, 5 May, 2, 9, 16 June; *The Times*, 2, 3, 5, 10, 12, 13 June 1826. [24] Add. 51576, Fazakerley to Lady Holland, 12 Aug.; 51669, Bedford to same, 15 Oct. [1826]. [25] Add. 52011, Mrs. Fazakerley to Fox, 24 Nov.; Surr. Hist. Cent. Goulburn mss Acc 304/67A, Goulburn to wife, 27 Nov. 1826. [26] Add. 52011, Mrs. Fazakerley to Fox [15 Apr. 1827]; *Canning's Ministry*, 267. [27] *The Times*, 31 May, 8, 16 June 1827. [28] Add. 52011, Mrs. Fazakerley to Fox, 2 July 1827. [29] Nottingham Univ. Lib. Ossington mss OsC 47. [30] NLW, Harpton Court mss C/416. [31] Hatherton mss, Fazakerley to Littleton, 29 Sept. 1827. [32] Add. 52011, Mrs. Fazakerley to Fox, 3 Nov. 1827; *Lady Holland to Son*, 72. [33] Hatherton mss. [34] Add. 52011. [35] NLS mss 24770, ff. 23, 29. [36] TNA FO352/10B/7. [37] Castle Howard mss, Graham to Morpeth [3 Mar. 1830]. [38] Add. 52011, Mrs. Fazakerley to Fox, 14 Apr. 1830. [39] Grey mss, Howick jnl. 13 May [1830]. [40] *Brighton Guardian*, 7, 14 July; *Lincoln, Rutland and Stamford Mercury*, 9 July; Add. 51813, Phillimore to Holland, 14 July 1830; Wentworth Woodhouse mun. G2/11, 18. [41] Castle Howard mss, Milton to Lady Carlisle, 25 July 1830; Add. 61937, f. 116. [42] Add. 51576, Fazakerley to Lady Holland, 11 Aug. [1830]; 61937, f. 114. [43] Add. 52011, Mrs. Fazakerley to Fox, 22 Aug. 1830. [44] Add. 61937, f. 120; Fitzwilliam mss, Althorp to Milton [14 Nov. 1830]. [45] *Edgeworth Letters*, 439. [46] Fitzwilliam mss, Fazakerley to Milton, 3 Dec. 1830. [47] Add. 61937, f. 120. [48] Fitzwilliam mss. [49] Lansdowne mss, Fazakerley to Lansdowne, 28 Jan. 1831. [50] Add. 51576, Fazakerley to Holland [4 Mar., 17, 19 Apr. 1831]. [51] Grey mss. [52] Add. 61937, f. 125. [53] Wentworth Woodhouse mun. G83/142. [54] Hatherton diary, 18 Nov. [1831]. [55] Add. 52011, Mrs. Fazakerley to Fox, 29 Dec. [1831]. [56] Wentworth Woodhouse mun. G83/149-52. [57] Duke Univ. Lib. Fazakerley mss, N. Fellowes to Fazakerley, 6 Sept. 1832. [58] Add. 52011, Mrs. Fazakerley to Fox, 3, 11, 23 Oct. 1839, 18 Dec. 1840, 6 Feb. 1842, 15 Sept. 1845; Bromley Davenport mss, Fazakerley to Davenport, 18 Mar., 14 July 1846. [59] Fazakerley mss, Sturges Bourne to Fazakerley, 4 Oct. 1832; *Three Diaries*, 319, 327; Add. 48215, ff. 47, 63; *Greville Mems.* iv. 23. [60] *Holland House Diaries*, 323; Add. 48215, f. 63; 61937, ff. 134, 135. [61] *The Times*, 16, 19 July 1852. [62] PROB 11/2157/629; IR26/1931/439.

D.R.F.

FELLOWES, Henry Arthur Wallop (1799–1847), of Eggesford, nr. Chudleigh, Devon.

ANDOVER   1831–1834

b. 29 Oct. 1799, 1st. s. of Hon. Newton Fellowes† (*d.* 1854) of Eggesford and 1st w. Frances, da. of Rev. Castell Sherard of Glatton, Hunts., rect. of Stainby and Gunby, Lincs. and Edmunthorpe, Leics. *educ.* Eton 1811; Trinity Coll. Camb. 1816, migrated to Trinity Hall 1818. *unm. d.v.p.* 15 Feb. 1847.

Fellowes was a nephew of the simple-minded 3rd earl of Portsmouth, who was certified by a commis-

sion of lunacy in February 1823. The proceedings, which were widely reported, revealed his obsession with bellringing, his compulsive attendance at funerals and, most notably, the fact that his wife's lover had shared their marital bed. It appears that this Member may have been the nominal petitioner, though his father, the earl's brother, was undoubtedly behind the suit.[1] As Member for Andover, 1802-20, his father had generally aligned himself with the Whigs, and he was classed as a Liberal when he resumed his parliamentary career in 1832 as Member for North Devon, where his principal residence lay. Until 1835 he remained steward of Andover, where the family had long possessed an interest, but he was so lax in the execution of his corporate duties as to be accused of deserting the borough.[2] This did not prevent his son standing at the general election of 1831, after the sitting Members had retired in the face of the corporation's conversion to parliamentary reform. On the hustings Fellowes claimed that he had always been a 'strenuous advocate' of this cause and pledged his 'firm and unflinching' support for the Grey ministry's bill. He was returned unopposed.[3]

Fellowes evidently missed the early part of the session, perhaps through illness, and is not known to have uttered a word in debate. He did not vote for the second reading of the reintroduced reform bill, 6 July, when he was noted as a supporter in a list of absentees in *The Times*, 8 July, and was also recorded as absent in divisions on the bill's details, 27, 28 July, 9 Aug. 1831. He eventually registered his presence with a vote against preserving the rights of freemen, 30 Aug. He divided for the bill's passage, 21 Sept., and Lord Ebrington's confidence motion, 10 Oct. He voted for the second reading of the revised bill, 17 Dec. 1831, gave steady support to its details, and divided for the third reading, 22 Mar. 1832. He was in the government majority on the navy civil departments bill, 6 Apr., but was absent from the division on the address calling on the king to appoint only ministers who would carry the reform bill unimpaired, 10 May. On 19 May he joined Brooks's, sponsored by Lord Gosford and 'Mr. Moreton'. He voted for the second reading of the Irish reform bill, 25 May, and with ministers on the Russian-Dutch loan, 20 July 1832.

Fellowes was returned unopposed for Andover at the general election of 1832 and was subsequently described as a 'moderate reformer and in general a supporter of ministers'.[4] He retired at the 1834 dissolution. His existence is not even mentioned in the family history, and he died intestate at Eggesford in February 1847, 'after a long and lingering illness'.[5]

His father never troubled to lay claim to his estate, administration of which was eventually granted in August 1854 to Fellowes's half-brother, Isaac Newton Fellowes, who had succeeded their father as 5th earl of Portsmouth that January.[6]

[1] *Genuine Report of Procs. in Portsmouth Case* (1823); *The Times*, 11 Feb.-1 Mar. 1823. [2] *Reg. of Unreformed Corporation of Andover* (Andover Local Archives Cttee. no. 7), unpaginated; Hants RO, Andover borough recs. 37M85 11/PE/56. [3] *Salisbury Jnl.* 2, 9 May 1831. [4] *Dod's Parl. Companion* (1833), 111. [5] Rev. E. Fellowes, *Fam. and Descendants of William Fellowes of Eggesford*; *The Times*, 18 Feb. 1847. [6] PROB 6/230/197.

H.J.S./P.J.S.

FELLOWES, William Henry (1769–1837), of Ramsey Abbey, Hunts. and Haverland Hall, Norf.

| HUNTINGDON | 1796–1807 |
| HUNTINGDONSHIRE | 1807–1830 |

b. 15 July 1769, 1st s. of William Fellowes[†] of Ramsey Abbey and Lavinia, da. and coh. of James Smyth of St. Audries, Som. *educ.* Charterhouse 1778-86; St. John's, Camb. 1786. *m.* 23 July 1805, Emma, da. of Richard Benyon[†] of Englefield House, Berks., 4s. (1 *d.v.p.*) 1da. *suc.* fa. 1804. *d.* 23 Aug. 1837.
   Maj. Hunts. militia 1797, 1808.

Fellowes, who remained attached to the Sandwich interest in Huntingdonshire, while portraying himself as an 'independent', attended the county meeting of condolence and congratulation to George IV, 4 Mar. 1820, and endorsed the loyal address. He begrudged voting thanks to the under-sheriff Samuel Wells, the radical attorney, and, so the rector of Buckden told Lord Milton*, displayed a narrow-mindedness 'which I should not have thought him capable of'.[1] He stood again for the county at the general election and was returned unopposed with the Whig Lord John Russell.[2] He continued to give general though not slavish support to the Liverpool ministry, but he was not a dedicated attender.[3] He voted against government on the appointment of an additional Scottish baron of exchequer, 15 May 1820. He presented petitions for relief from agricultural distress, 19 May 1820, 5 Mar. 1821.[4] He was granted a month's leave, 30 June 1820. He voted in defence of ministers' conduct towards Queen Caroline, 6 Feb., but declined to attend the county meeting called to petition against them on this issue, 30 Mar. 1821, pleading 'parliamentary duties' as his excuse.[5] He divided against Catholic relief, 28 Feb. 1821, 30 Apr. 1822, 1 Mar., 21 Apr. 10 May, and the associated Irish franchise bill, 26 Apr., 9 May 1825. He voted for repeal of the additional malt duty, 21 Mar., 3

Apr., but divided with administration against reduction of the grant for the adjutant-general's office, 11 Apr., and parliamentary reform, 9 May 1821. He mustered for the division against more extensive tax reductions to relieve distress, 21 Feb., but voted for abolition of one of the joint-postmasterships, 13 Mar., 2 May 1822. At his last rent day, according to the *Huntingdon Gazette*, he had given his tenants generous rebates. Even so, he refused to attend the county meeting to discuss distress, 3 Apr., as the requisitionists 'sought to introduce dangerous innovations under the name of reform'.[6] He presented a petition against revision of the corn laws, 9 May 1822.[7] He voted against inquiry into the borough franchise, 20 Feb., and reform of the Scottish electoral system, 2 June 1823. Although outmatched by a côterie of Whigs, he was the only dissentient to address the county reform meeting in March that year, when he criticized its promoters for their exclusion of agricultural distress from the agenda and countered John Bonfoy Rooper's* reference to the constitution's former purity with an allusion to Tudor despotism.[8] According to the *Gazette*, he presented and endorsed the prayer of a constituency petition against revision of the corn laws, 28 Apr. 1825; and the editor praised his 'attention to local business', for all their difference on 'the great political questions'.[9] He was a bailiff of the Bedford Level Corporation, and earlier in the session, according to another newspaper correspondent, his 'spirited opposition' to Lord William Cavendish Bentinck's proposed Eau Brink drainage bill had re-established his popularity among the fenmen.[10] He voted against the grant to the duke of Cumberland, 9 June, and was in the minority against restricting the use of spring guns, 21 June 1825. He divided with opposition against a separate salary for the president of the board of trade, 10 Apr., but voted against the reform of Edinburgh's representation, 13 Apr. 1826. He presented another petition against revision of the corn laws and divided against the government's plan to admit bonded corn, 8 May 1826.[11]

He had announced his intention of standing for the county at the next general election in December 1825.[12] His coalition with the Tory Lord Mandeville, the duke of Manchester's son, against Russell and his inconspicuousness in the House were easy targets for press ridicule in the approach to the election. According to the *Gazette*, he had sat in Parliament for more than a quarter of a century without giving one single vote in 'support of public liberty', or speaking against the infringement of the constitution.[13] Cavendish Bentinck described him to Milton as the 'very worst of Tories'.[14] Nothing came of reports that he would be transferred to the borough and that he was in line for a peerage at the dissolution. He duly offered for the county as an implacable opponent of Catholic relief, though according to Lady Mandeville he was uneasy about the contest, as he 'hates to spend money'. He nevertheless was an active canvasser and, so Russell complained to Lord Holland, 'gives away places in the excise in shoals, and then boasts of his opposition to any alteration in the corn laws'. He was barely able to secure a hearing at the nomination, but was returned with Mandeville after a four-day contest, at a cost of at least £6,692.[15]

Fellowes voted against Catholic relief, 6 Mar. 1827. He voted against relaxation of the corn laws, 2 Apr., but presented a petition for economy and retrenchment, 5 Apr. 1827.[16] He divided with Canning's ministry against the disfranchisement of Penryn, 28 May 1827. He voted against repeal of the Test Acts, 26 Feb., presented a hostile petition, 20 Mar., and paired against Catholic relief, 12 May 1828. He voted against the provision for Canning's family, 13 May, and the archbishop of Canterbury's estate bill, 16 June 1828. He presented a petition against Catholic emancipation, 11 Mar., and, as expected, voted steadily against it throughout March 1829. In his first known speech after 34 years in the House, 16 Mar. 1830, he defended himself against a charge of arbitrary conduct as a magistrate: he repudiated the accusations of George Goodwin, contained in a petition presented by Lord Nugent, and justified his refusal not to license an additional public house at St. Ives because there were already six there, not to mention 32 in the immediate neighbourhood. He presented petitions against the sale of beer bill (including one from St. Ives), 4, 11 May, and voted to amend the measure, 21 June. On 30 Mar. he moved the first reading of the divorce bill of his Norfolk neighbour Joseph Salisbury Muskett of Intwood Hall. He voted against Jewish emancipation, 17 May, and for the South American consular grant and against abolition of the death penalty for forgery, 7 June 1830.

He did not seek re-election at the ensuing general election, when he was apparently dropped on account of his unpopularity. Nevertheless he actively supported the Montagu candidates.[17] In 1831, however, he objected to his successor Lord Strathavon's platform of moderate reform, which, as he told Lady Sandwich, was 'very different from what I hoped', particularly as his pledge to vote only for disfranchisement offered no guarantee against his supporting other parts of the Grey ministry's reform bill. He was reluctantly won over shortly before the election, but only after

repeated assurances that Strathavon would support no more than schedule A. At the same time he told Lady Sandwich, 'I cannot yet believe that any person with any claim to the name of a gentleman can condescend to conciliate his opponents at the expense of his honour and integrity'.[18] Fellowes died in August 1837. In his will, dated 17 June 1837, and proved under a handsome £140,000, he directed that his funeral should be plain and of 'little expense'. He bequeathed to his wife his leasehold London house in Lower Berkeley Street, the interest on £45,000 and his Pennsylvanian stocks and shares. He devised £20,000 to each of his three younger children, and the residue of his estate to his second but eldest surviving son Edward Fellowes (1809-87), Member for Huntingdonshire, 1837-80, who was created Baron De Ramsey in 1887.[19] Some 2,000 mourners were reported to have witnessed his obsequies. The *Cambridge Chronicle* commented that 'it falls to the lot of but few men to go to the grave more sincerely lamented as a neighbour, friend, and landlord'.[20]

[1] *Huntingdon, Bedford and Peterborough Gazette*, 11 Mar.; Fitzwilliam mss, Maltby to Milton, 5 Mar. 1820. [2] *Huntingdon, Bedford and Peterborough Gazette*, 17 Mar. 1820. [3] *Black Bk.* (1823), 154; *Session of Parl. 1825*, p. 463. [4] *The Times*, 20 May 1820, 6 Mar. 1821. [5] *Huntingdon, Bedford and Peterborough Gazette*, 10, 31 Mar. 1821. [6] Ibid. 8 Dec. 1821, 6 Apr. 1822. [7] *The Times*, 10 May 1822. [8] *Huntingdon, Bedford and Peterborough Gazette*, 8 Mar. 1823. [9] Ibid. 30 Apr., 7 May 1825. [10] Ibid. 18 June 1825. [11] *The Times*, 9 May 1826. [12] *Huntingdon, Bedford and Peterborough Gazette*, 24 Dec. 1825. [13] Ibid. 28 Jan., 4, 25 Feb., 25 Mar., 15, 22 Apr. 1826. [14] Fitzwilliam mss 124/13. [15] Hunts. RO, Manchester mss ddM 21a/8, election expenses [1826]; ddM 49/15, Lady Mandeville to Lord F. Montagu, 23 May; Add. 51677, Russell to Holland, 23 June; *Huntingdon, Bedford and Peterborough Gazette*, 3, 10, 17, 24 June 1826. [16] *The Times*, 6 Apr. 1827. [17] *Huntingdon, Bedford and Peterborough Gazette*, 17 July; Fitzwilliam mss, Day to Milton, 16 July 1830. [18] Hunts. RO, Sandwich mss Hinch/8/49/1-3. [19] PROB 11/1887/226; IR26/145/86. [20] *Cambridge Chron.* 2 Sept. 1837.

S.R.H.

FENTON CAWTHORNE, John (1753–1831), of Wyreside Hall, Lancs.

LINCOLN	27 Jan. 1783–2 May 1796
LANCASTER	1806–1807
LANCASTER	1812–1818
LANCASTER	1820–1 Mar. 1831

b. 5 Jan. 1753,[1] 1st s. of James Fenton of Lancaster and Elizabeth, da. and event. h. of John Cawthorne of Wyresdale. *educ.* Queen's, Oxf. 1771; G. Inn 1792. *m.* 1 Aug. 1778, Frances, da. of Sir John Hussey Delaval†, 1st bt., of Doddington, Lincs., *s.p.* Took name of Cawthorne by royal lic. 15 May 1781 in compliance with wish of his mother's cos. John Lane of Hillingdon, Mdx.; *suc*. fa. 1791. *d*. 1 Mar. 1831.

Recorder, Lancaster 1791-6.

Col. Westminster regt. Mdx. militia 1791-6; brevet col. 1794-6.

Fenton Cawthorne's chequered parliamentary career included expulsion in 1796, after being cashiered by court martial for embezzling the Westminster militia regiment's funds. This also cost him the recordership of his native town of Lancaster. His personal interest there had been established through largesse and was strong enough to secure his unopposed return in 1806, and again in 1812, but he had been defeated in 1818 by the 10th duke of Hamilton's nominee, the Liverpool West India merchant John Gladstone*.[2] He rallied his friends afterwards at the Heart of Oak Club, promoted the adoption of a loyal address after the Peterloo massacre, 13 Sept. 1819, applied for Lord Lonsdale's protection, and saw off his Tory challenger, Thomas Richmond Gale Braddyll[†] of Conishead Priory, to come in unopposed with the nabob Gabriel Doveton in 1820, when Gladstone retired.[3] He confirmed his support for the 'constitution in church and state' on the hustings and afterwards at the *King's Arms*, where, on 18 Aug. 1820, he presided at the Heart of Oak Club anniversary dinner.[4]

Fenton Cawthorne had deserted Fox for Pitt in 1784, and opposed parliamentary reform, Catholic relief and any regulation of the slave trade, whose abolition had contributed to the decline of the port of Lancaster, in which he had a vested interest. Although ostracized by them, he had supported Lord Liverpool's administration in the 1812 Parliament, and did so again from 1820.[5] His 'few words' on the conduct of the Lancaster gaoler Higgins, the subject of a hostile petition from the radical prisoner Nathan Broadhurst, 5 July 1820, went unreported, as did his remarks on the vagrancy laws, 14 Mar. 1821.[6] He divided against Catholic relief, 28 Feb. 1821, 30 Apr. 1822 (paired), 1 Mar., 10 May 1825. He voted with administration on the Queen Caroline affair, 6 Feb., and the army estimates, 11 Apr., having cast a wayward vote for repealing the agricultural horse tax, 5 Mar. 1821. He presented and endorsed his constituents' petitions for equalization of the duties on East and West Indian sugars, 12 May 1823, and against the sale of beer bill, 7 May 1824, and brought up another that day complaining of 'certain tax gatherers'.[7] He divided for the duke of Cumberland's grant, 10 June 1825, and against Lord John Russell's electoral bribery resolutions, 26 May 1826. He had welcomed the return of the moderate Tory Thomas Greene in 1824 as Doveton's replacement, confirmed his own

candidature when a dissolution was anticipated in the autumn of 1825 and the political economist Francis Lee and the nabob Alexander Nowell* were manoeuvring against him, and prepared for a contest he could ill afford at the general election of 1826.[8] He was a trustee and director of the beleaguered Ground Rent Company, and on 3 June Charles Russell* warned his brother-in-law Greene:

> It is thought that Cawthorne will go to the wall, and within the walls too, for he is utterly ruined and penniless, and the only thing which has kept him out of gaol for years is privilege of Parliament. Of course he will do what he can, for he has nothing to lose and everything to [gain] ... It not infrequently happens that the mob, strange as it may appear, will stick by such a man, if, as is the case with Cawthorne, they like him, and enable him to give a great deal of trouble.[9]

He pleaded sickness, absented himself from the election and was returned unopposed with Greene.[10]

He received a month's leave on account of ill health, 27 Feb., another fortnight, 28 Mar. 1827, and is unlikely to have attended that session. He presented a petition against anatomy restrictions, 8 May, divided against Catholic relief, 12 May, and with the duke of Wellington's administration against ordnance reductions, 4 July 1828. That October he accompanied a Lancaster delegation to wait on the home secretary Peel during his north-western tour.[11] As the patronage secretary Planta predicted, Fenton Cawthorne opposed the concession of Catholic emancipation in 1829, presented hostile petitions, 2, 10, 20 Mar., and voted against it, 6, 30 Mar., although not, as the Lowthers had expected, on the 18th.[12] Begging a 'haunch of venison for Cawthorne' in September, Lord Lowther* told his father Lonsdale, 'it pleases him much and he is good humoured and always at command to vote or stay away either on great public questions or private business'.[13] He paired against Jewish emancipation, 17 May 1830. He had presented Lancaster corporation's petition against renewal of the East India Company's 'monopolistic' charter, 4 May, and he retained their support at the general election in July, when a campaign to unseat him as an ineffective Member failed, and polled in second place. He attended a celebration dinner at the *King's Arms*, 19 Aug. 1830.[14]

Ministers listed him among their 'friends', but he was absent from the division on the civil list when they were brought down, 15 Nov. 1830. He presented a petition from Leigh on the 25th for the abolition of colonial slavery. He was granted three weeks' leave on account of ill health, 21 Feb. 1831, and died in early

March at his London house in Hanover Street.[15] He was childless, and by his will, dated 2 July 1828 and proved under £100, 26 Aug. (resworn to £450, 2 Nov. 1831), he left everything to his wife (d. 1838). Wyreside was sold to Robert Garnett, the son of a Jamaica merchant, who had purchased most of Fenton Cawthorne's gaming rights in 1825.[16]

[1] N and Q (ser. 12), ii. 266. [2] HP Commons, 1790-1820, ii. 225-7; iii. 737-9. [3] Lancaster Gazette, 25 Aug., 11, 18, 25 Sept. 1819, 5, 19, 26 Feb., 4 Mar. 1820; The Times, 21 Sept. 1819; Lonsdale mss, Lowther to Lonsdale, 9 Feb. 1820. [4] Lancaster Gazette, 11 Mar., 26 Aug. 1820. [5] HP Commons, 1790-1820, iii. 737-9; New Tory Guide (1819), 159-61. [6] The Times, 6 July 1820, 15 Mar. 1821. [7] Ibid. 13 May 1823. [8] Lancaster Gazette, 1 June, 28 Oct. 1822, 8 Feb. 1823, 17, 24 Apr. 1824, 10, 17 Mar. 21 May, 22 Oct. 1825, 11, 18, 25 Feb.; The Times, 14 Feb. 1826. [9] Morning Chron. 11 July 1825; Bodl. MS. Eng. lett. c. 159, f. 44. [10] Lancaster Gazette, 3, 10, 24 June 1826. [11] Ibid. 18 Oct. 1828. [12] Lonsdale mss, Lowther to Lonsdale, 17 Mar. 1829. [13] Ibid. 10, 22 Sept. 1829. [14] Lancaster Gazette, 3, 24, 31 July, 7, 21 Aug. 1830. [15] Gent. Mag. (1831), i. 282. [16] PROB 8/224; 11/1789/451; Gent. Mag. (1838), ii. 669.

M.M.E.

FERGUSON, James (1735–1820), of Pitfour, Aberdeen and 36 St. James's Place, Westminster, Mdx.

BANFFSHIRE	22 Jan. 1789–1790
ABERDEENSHIRE	1790–6 Sept. 1820

b. 25 May 1735, 1st s. of James Ferguson of Pitfour, SCJ (Lord Pitfour), and Hon. Anne Murray, da. of Alexander, 4th Lord Elibank [S]. educ. Edinburgh Univ.; adv. 1757; grand tour 1758. unm. suc. fa. 1777. d. 6 Sept. 1820.

Rect., Aberdeen Univ. 1794-6.

In 1826, Henry Crabb Robinson recorded a typical example of the drollery which Ferguson inspired during his long and undistinguished parliamentary career:

Late at the Athenaeum. Hudson Gurney* was there. He related with great effect the experience of Ferguson of Pitfour, which he used to repeat when an old man, for the benefit of young Members: 'I was never absent from any division I could get at. I have heard many arguments which convinced my judgement, but never one that influenced my vote. I never voted but once according to my own opinion, and that was the worst vote I ever gave. I found that the only way to be quiet in Parliament was always to vote with the ministers, and never to take a place'.[1]

Ferguson, who had been aptly described in 1788 as 'a man of real good sense, but indolent', attended the Aberdeenshire county meeting which voted a loyal address to the prince regent in the aftermath of Peterloo, 22 Nov. 1819. He was approaching his 85th birthday when he secured his eighth consecutive return for the county four months later. There was no opposition.[2] Ministers would have counted on his continued loyalty, though they did not obtain his vote in the division on economies in revenue collection, 4 July 1820. The following day he gave qualified support to Hamilton's motion deploring the recent equalization of the Scottish and English malt duties: he 'could not agree that there should be no deviation from the old proportion of the duties, though he wished the duty to be somewhat lower in Scotland than in England'.

He was apparently 'in the habit, at the end of the parliamentary season, of entertaining at the British Coffee House those friends who had given him dinners during the session'; the duchess of Gordon called these gatherings 'the meeting of Pitfour's creditors'.[3] His 'many humorous sayings' provided a fund of affectionate anecdotes. Farington was regaled with a selection by Lord Lonsdale in 1817:

Speaking of his house at Pitfour ... he said, 'When you visit me there ask for what you want, and they will give you what they have' ... Appoplexy and Epylepsy being spoken of, and the characters of these diseases, Ferguson said, 'When men die it is called Appoplexy and when they live it is called Epylepsy'.[4]

It was 'apoplexy' which carried him off 'without a struggle' in September 1820. He was remembered as a man who 'enjoyed his claret at Bellamy's, till the call for the ministerial phalanx to descend', and as a benevolent landlord and keen promoter of agricultural and local improvement who 'left that a garden, which, when he came into his estate, was almost a desert'.[5] Administration of his effects, which were sworn under £600 within the province of Canterbury, was granted on 19 May 1821 to his nephew James Ferguson of Pitfour.[6]

[1] Crabb Robinson Diary, ii. 14. [2] Pol. State of Scotland 1788, p. 54; Aberdeen Jnl. 24 Nov. 1819, 22 Mar. 1820. [3] Broughton, Recollections, iii. 224. [4] Farington Diary, xiv. 5047. [5] Inverness Courier, 21 Sept. 1820; Gent. Mag. (1820), ii. 280. [6] PROB 6/197/230.

D.R.F.

FERGUSON, Robert (1769–1840), of Raith, Fife and 18 Portman Square, Mdx.

FIFESHIRE	1806–1807
DYSART BURGHS	1831–1832
KIRKCALDY BURGHS	1832–1834
HADDINGTONSHIRE	1835–1837
KIRKCALDY BURGHS	1837–3 Dec. 1840

b. 8 Sep. 1769,[1] 1st s. of William Ferguson (formerly Berry) of Raith and Jean, da. of Ronald Craufurd of Restalrig, Edinburgh; bro. of Sir Ronald Craufurd Ferguson*. *educ.* Edinburgh 1786; Glasgow Univ. 1788; adv. 1791. *m.* 20 Apr. 1808, Mary, da. and h. of William Hamilton Nisbet[†] of Dirleton, Haddington, div. w. of Thomas, 7th earl of Elgin [S], *s.p. suc.* fa. 1810. *d.* 3 Dec. 1840.

Ld. lt. Fife 1837-*d.*

Ferguson was a Whig landowner with substantial estates and political influence in Haddingtonshire, Fifeshire and Dysart Burghs, where, with the 2nd earl of Rosslyn, he returned his only brother and close confidant Sir Ronald. He was also the respected amateur geologist after whom the mineral Fergusonite is named. His parliamentary career as Member for Fifeshire had been curtailed in 1807 on account of the local unpopularity of Lord Grenville's administration, which he had supported, and the scandal of his acknowledged adultery with his future wife, the countess of Elgin.[2] Her first husband, his near neighbour the 7th earl, successfully sued him in both the English and Scottish courts that year for £10,000 in damages in one of the bitterest and most high profile divorce cases of the era. Elgin denied his ex-wife all contact with their children, and the attendant trauma was the rumoured reason why her marriage with Ferguson was childless.[3] Ferguson remained active in Whig and Foxite circles and was in France in 1819 when his candidature for Fifeshire was broached with a view to preventing the sitting Tory William Wemyss bequeathing the representation to his son. Although initially reluctant, he started late and polled second to James Wemyss in a three-man contest in 1820.[4] Outlining his political creed on the hustings, he affirmed his commitment to the 'constitution of 1688', reform and local interests, and declared 'extremes in politics – ultra Toryism and ultra Whiggism ... unsound'.[5]

While Sir Ronald remained a prominent opposition Member and advanced his military career in the 1820s, Ferguson concerned himself with county politics, business and legislation, especially the 1821 Dysart ferries bill and the collapse in November 1826 of Greenhill's Fife Ferry Company in which he had invested heavily, thereby suffering losses: he was a principal speaker at attendant county and trustees' meetings, 1825-8.[6] The parlous state of Elgin's finances also affected him under various settlements, and the 1829 Ferguson estate bill, authorizing trustees to sell his entailed estates (chiefly in Midlothian) was enacted to liquidate his debts and reduce his encumbrances. A bill filed in the court of session on 17 Aug. 1829 confirmed his 1817 holograph will in favour of

his brother.[7] He surprised the Edinburgh Whigs by supporting Lord John Hay* in Haddingtonshire and acquiescing in the return of Rosslyn's Tory son Lord Loughborough for Dysart Burghs at the 1830 general election, when Sir Ronald came in for Nottingham; but he declared unequivocally for reform at dinners afterwards in Fifeshire and Haddingtonshire.[8] He welcomed the Grey ministry's reform bill and wrote to James Brougham*, 20 Mar. 1831:

> Ministers must not give way. Better dissolve than yield one iota of importance. The conduct of some astonish me, and vex me. Our old friend Lord Rosslyn, where is he? Does he believe that ere long ... Wellington or P[eel will] govern the country? And to divide in the minority against your brother's most important [chancery] bills!!! And what is the meaning of this? There never was a moment which requires more firmness.[9]

At the general election in May 1831, precipitated by the bill's defeat, Ferguson rallied to Wemyss, the defeated 'reformer', in Fifeshire and co-operated with the town clerk of Kinghorn, Thomas Barclay, to secure his own return for the Burghs.[10] On the hustings he declared for the 'all-engrossing measure of reform in all its essential particulars' and praised the district's councils for endorsing it.[11]

Parliamentary reporters occasionally confused Ferguson, who was generally described as 'of Raith', with his brother 'the General', Robert Alexander Ferguson, Member for Londonderry, and the reformer Robert Cutlar Fergusson, Member for Kirkcudbright Stewarty. He generally supported the ministry with his brother and proved to be a steady voter and useful plain-speaking commentator for them on reform and Scottish issues.[12] Denis le Marchant[†], writing in February 1833, praised 'his simple straightforward manner and the earnestness with which he expressed himself' that commanded the attention of younger Members.[13] He voted for the reintroduced reform bill at its second reading, 6 July 1831, and consistently for its details. He took a pair for the first fortnight of September to 'conduct' his wife to Buxton, but agreed to 'return sooner if the report is brought up'.[14] Votes attributed to him on the Liverpool writ, 5 Sept., renewal of the Sugar Refinery Act, 12 Sept., and the disfranchisement of Appleby, 14 Sept., are therefore doubtful. He voted for the bill's passage, 21 Sept. Before dividing for the second reading of the Scottish reform bill, 23 Sept., he confirmed that country's support for the measure, defended the proposed £10 franchise and boldly denounced 'Scotch jobs':

> Some man has constantly stepped forward to undertake its political management, he got the patronage of the

country, and the English government never cared what became of Scotland provided he brought up his well-disciplined Members, and planted them in the back rows of the ministerial benches to do the ministerial biddings. I hope, however, that now the spirit of independence has arisen within us, as well as the wealth and intelligence, we shall all be different men.

He voted against the Tory amendment to give second county Members to Aberdeenshire, Ayrshire, Fifeshire, Forfarshire, Lanarkshire, Midlothian, Perthshire and Renfrewshire, 4 Oct., and for Lord Ebrington's confidence motion, 10 Oct. 1831. Deputizing for his fellow Whig Thomas Kennedy in the debate on the Irish yeomanry, 18 July, he described how 'these unfortunate Orange processions have found their way into Scotland' and should be legislated against. He contended that a free trade in corn, as advocated by Henry Hunt, would be ruinous to the landlord, the farmer and the agricultural labourer, 24 July. He added his voice as a member of the Pembrokeshire election committee to the clamour for the issue of a new writ there, despite the proven partiality of the sheriff and under-sheriff and the 'derogatory conduct of the assessor', 26 Sept. 1831.

He divided for the revised reform bill at its second reading, 17 Dec. 1831, steadily for its details and for its third reading, 22 Mar. 1832. *The Times* considered him a contender should further peerages be awarded to carry the bill, and he testified to Scotland's support for it 'as can be seen in their petitions, urban and rural', 2 Feb. 1832.[15] He voted for the address calling on the king to appoint only ministers who would carry the bill unimpaired, 10 May, for the second reading of the Irish reform bill, 25 May, and against a Conservative amendment to the Scottish measure, 1 June. When on the 4th Alexander Pringle countered his criticism of voting by superiorities, 'emblems of the old unconstitutional political workings in Scotland', by alluding to several he had sold, Ferguson admitted it and said that he had been short of money at the time. He added:

What does this high price prove, but, that, according to circumstances, these votes became valuable for political purposes ... [It is] another strong proof that they should cease to exist in future. Several years ago I possessed such votes in different counties in Scotland, but disliking their nature, I could not vote with satisfaction upon them, and gave them all up sold.

He failed to dissuade the reformer Hallyburton from dividing the House on a futile proposal to bar Scottish clergymen from voting in parliamentary elections, 6 June, and voted that day against Alexander Baring's bill denying insolvent debtors parliamentary privi-

lege. He welcomed the government's decision to abandon the Members' property qualification for burghs and criticized the Scottish coronation peers Lords Panmure (William Maule*) and Camperdown for advocating them, 27 June. When Banffshire petitioned for inquiry into Scottish municipal government, Ferguson spoke of it as a natural and immediate consequence of the enactment of reform and called on the lord advocate Jeffrey to propose it, as he would 'experience no great difficulty in carrying it through the House', 6 July. He divided with government on the Dublin election controversy, 23 Aug. 1831, and the Russian-Dutch loan, 12, 16, 20 July 1832.

Praising the Scottish master spinners and their employment practices, he spoke authoritatively against the precipitate passage of Hobhouse's factories regulation bill without adequate inquiry, 9, 20 Feb. 1832, although he voted for its committal that day. Heeding the alarm it had aroused in Kirkcaldy, he and his brother urged the House to 'legislate as simply as possible, with the least possible injury to the operative and employer, 7 Mar. He suggested extending the Scottish tithe system to Ireland, 'as it is impossible to maintain a church establishment that is inimical to the feelings of the great body of the nation', 8 Feb. He would have no truck with Hume's time-wasting division against including a reference to 'Almighty God' in the preamble to the Scottish cholera prevention bill, 16 Feb. He presented a petition in favour of the Haddington court house bill, 2 Mar., and several against the Edinburgh-Glasgow railway bill, 18 Apr., 25 June. On 28 June 1832 he published a letter declaring his personal support (and that of the reformers) for the candidature of Wemyss for Fifeshire at the first post-reform election.[16]

Standing as a Liberal, Ferguson was returned unopposed for the revamped Kirkcaldy district in December 1832.[17] He contested Haddingtonshire successfully in 1835, and on his defeat there in 1837 he resumed the Burghs seat.[18] He succeeded Rosslyn as lord lieutenant of Fifeshire that year and died at his London home in Portman Square in December 1840, only two days after the death of his stepson Lord Bruce. He is commemorated by the Raith monument designed by Robert Forest, and with his brother in Sir Henry Raeburn's portrait of 'The Archers'.[19] Sir Ronald was appointed Ferguson's executor, 24 Dec. 1840, but died before his succession to the estates under the holograph will was confirmed. His son Robert (Munro) Ferguson (1802-68), Liberal Member for the Kirkcaldy district, 1841-62, was sworn as Ferguson's heir, on inventoried goods valued at £4,181 7s. 1d., 25

Sept. 1846.[20] Paying tribute to the Fergusons in 1841, the Liberal lawyer Henry Cockburn wrote:

These two men showed what good may be effected by mere steadiness of principle and its honest exhibition; for without any superiority of knowledge, talent or original influence, public principle alone, fearlessly but temperately enforced on proper occasions, and softened by agreeable manners and very amiable acts, enabled them powerfully to advance the Scotch cause at a time when political independence had few attractions either for military officers or for country gentlemen. So long as Parliament was unreformed, the elder brother was exactly the man whom it was the object of the Scotch system to degrade by exclusion from the ... Commons, because, though a great landed proprietor, he dared to be in opposition. Yet he was returned, even then occasionally, and always since. A taste for science, however, and the personal superintendence of large estates always rescued him from the ordinary frivolities of wealthy idleness; and from his youth to his dying hour he did everything for the improvement of his countrymen that could be accomplished by active but candid co-operation with the Liberal party, and the promotion of all the local benefits which it is in the power of a judicious and resident landowner to diffuse ... The importance of two gentlemen of their character and station to the side they espoused can only be understood by those who acted in Scotch affairs before the reform bill emancipated the country.[21]

[1] IGI. [2] HP Commons, 1790-1820, ii. 596-7; iii. 741; [3] Trial of R. Ferguson ... for Crim. Con. (1807); Oswald of Dunnikier mss III/I; S.G. Checkland, The Elgins, 59, 61, 70, 71. [4] NAS GD51/1/198/10/77-80, 82, 86; Dundee, Perth and Cupar Advertiser, 18 Feb.; Bradford mss (History of Parliament Aspinall transcripts), Lady to Lord Newport, 27 Feb. 1820. [5] Scotsman, 25 Mar.; Caledonian Mercury, 3 Apr.; Oswald of Dunnikier mss VIA/2, election speeches, 1820. [6] Fife Herald, 3, 24 Mar. 1825; Caledonian Mercury, 14 Dec. 1826, 11 Oct. 1828; NAS GD164/1303/7, 15, 21; 1781/10. [7] Oswald of Dunnikier mss III/I, pprs. of 7th and 8th earls of Elgin; LJ, lxi. 259, 403, 458, 465, 588; CJ, lxxxiv. 373; NAS SC70/1/63. [8] Caledonian Mercury, 12 July, 6 Sept.; Fife Herald, 8, 22 July, 26 Aug., 9 Sept. 1830, 28 Apr. 1831; Add. 36554, f. 135. [9] Brougham mss. [10] Caledonian Mercury, 25, 28 Apr., 2, 12, 19 May 1831. [11] Ibid. 26 May; The Times, 31 May 1831. [12] G. Pentland, 'Debate on Scottish Parliamentary Reform, 1830-1832', SHR, lxxxv (2006), 118. [13] A. Aspinall, 'Le Marchant's Reports of Debates in the House of Commons, 1833', EHR, lviii (1943), 89. [14] Add. 34615, f. 159. [15] The Times, 19 Jan. 1832. [16] Caledonian Mercury, 2 July 1832. [17] Ibid. 20 Dec. 1832. [18] Scottish Electoral Politics, 15-16, 221, 226, 236-7, 268-9. [19] Gent. Mag. (1841), i. 315-16. [20] NAS SC70/1/63, 66. [21] Cockburn Jnl. i. 274-6.

M.M.E.

FERGUSON, Sir Robert Alexander, 2nd bt. (1796–1860), of The Farm, nr. Londonderry, co. Londonderry.

LONDONDERRY	1830–14 Mar. 1831
LONDONDERRY	2 Apr. 1831–13 Mar. 1860

b. 26 Dec. 1796,[1] 1st s. of Andrew Ferguson, MP [I], banker, of The Farm and Elizabeth, da. of Robert Alexander of Boom Hall, co. Londonderry. educ. Belfast Acad. (Mr. Bruce); King's Inns 1813; Trinity Coll. Camb. 1814; L. Inn 1815. unm. suc. fa. as 2nd bt. 17 July 1808. d. 13 Mar. 1860.

Sheriff, co. Tyrone 1825-6; mayor, Londonderry 1830; ld. lt. co. Londonderry 1840-d.; commr. of Irish land 1843.

Col. co. Londonderry militia 1839-d.

The obscure family of Ferguson was apparently Scottish in origin. A Dissenting minister of that name established himself in the north of Ireland, and his grandson John was a poor Londonderry surgeon or apothecary who, according to a later election squib, 'had the shop in the whole [sic] of the wal [sic] with three shillings worth of medicine'.[2] John's son Andrew (b. 1761), a well-to-do banker, married the Presbyterian daughter of the Londonderry merchant Robert Alexander, brother of the nabob Lord Caledon.[3] He was mayor of Londonderry, 1796-98, served as its Member on the Caledon interest, 1798-1800, and received a baronetcy, perhaps in belated compensation for the loss of his seat (which went briefly to his brother-in-law Henry Alexander[†]) after the Union, 7 Oct. 1801.[4] He died in an accident caused by his driving 'with incautious rapidity over a bridge wanting some repairs' in July 1808, when his younger son Harvey (d. 20 June 1824) survived unhurt.[5]

Ferguson,[6] who was presumably the chief beneficiary under his father's will, proved in Dublin in 1808, was a capital burgess of Londonderry and a leading member of the local gentry.[7] It was rumoured that he might come forward on the vestigial Caledon interest in the borough at the general elections of 1818 and 1820, but the seat was firmly in the hands of its Member Sir George Hill.[8] He was one of the requisitionists for the city and county meeting on 10 Jan. 1825, when he moved eight resolutions condemning the Catholic Association and prepared the hostile petition to Parliament. Having attended the Londonderry dinner in honour of the anti-Catholic county Member George Dawson, 28 Dec. 1825, he was present at the ceremonies on 12 Aug. 1828 when Dawson announced his conversion. His own opinions remained unchanged, however, and he chaired the meetings in September and October which established Brunswick Clubs for the county and the city, becoming president of both.[9] An influential figure, who interested himself in such local affairs as the county infirmary and purchased the city's shambles from the corporation, Ferguson was considered by the Beresfords in mid-1829 as a possible replacement for Dawson as their future candidate for the county.[10] However, on the announcement of Hill's appointment as governor of St. Vincent in April 1830 he immediately offered for the borough. An alderman since the previous year, he had been elected to serve as mayor from 2 Feb., and so resigned this office in April, although Hill's departure was in fact delayed until the dissolution later that year.[11] He seconded the resolution condemning higher duties on Irish stamps at the county meeting, 31 May, and was active at the similar city gathering, 4 June.[12] He successfully contested the borough, against another local Protestant, Captain Hart, at the general election in August 1830, although a petition was lodged alleging that he was technically still the returning officer and therefore ineligible.[13]

Considered 'pro-government' in Pierce Mahony's[†] analysis of the Irish elections, Ferguson was expected to follow the ministerialist line of the Beresfords and his brothers-in-law James and Josias Alexander, Members for Old Sarum. He was listed by the Wellington ministry among their 'friends' and divided in their minority on the civil list, 15 Nov. 1830. He was probably not the 'Sir Robert Fergusson' who criticized the new county Londonderry Member Bateson about the making of excessive observations on petitions, 10 Dec. 1830.[14] However, it was certainly he who, having attended several local meetings, presented Londonderry petitions from the Apprentice Boys against repeal of the Union, 4 Mar., and the merchants against alteration of the timber duties, 7 Mar. 1831.[15] His election was declared void a week later, and so he missed the division on the second reading of the Grey ministry's reform bill, which, according to Thomas Gladstone*, he would have voted against.[16] He was again opposed by Hart at the ensuing by-election, when, described as 'an old Tory', he pledged himself to vote for the bill in spite of his personal objections and so secured his return (albeit in the face of another petition).[17] He duly divided with ministers against Gascoyne's wrecking amendment, 19 Apr. 1831, which precipitated a dissolution. At the general election, when he rebuffed an address calling on him to oppose reform, he was once more returned after a contest against another local gentleman.[18]

Ferguson voted for the second reading of the reintroduced reform bill, 6 July, and against using the 1831 census to determine the boroughs in schedules A and B. He sided with opposition against the disfranchisement of Downton, 21 July, but otherwise, when present, divided with ministers for the bill's details. He spoke for the bill to establish lord lieutenants in Irish counties, 20 Aug., and commented on the value of the bishopric of Derry, 31 Aug. He voted with ministers for punishing those guilty of bribery in the Dublin election, 23 Aug., but in the minority for inquiry into how far the Sugar Refinery Act could safely be renewed with regard to West Indian interests, 12 Sept. He presented a Londonderry petition on the laws relating to the importation of flax seed, 11 Oct. 1831, and the following day moved for leave to introduce a bill to regulate the trade, but gave it up. He evidently missed the division on the second reading of the revised reform bill, 17 Dec. 1831, and it is not clear which way he voted on the Russian-Dutch loan, 26 Jan.; but he divided in the minority for inquiry into distress in the glove trade, 31 Jan. 1832. He voted for the disfranchisement of Appleby, 21 Feb., and although he sided with opposition against the enfranchisement of Tower Hamlets, 28 Feb., he paired for the third reading of the reform bill, 22 Mar. Having reported that the standing orders had been complied with in respect of the petition for the Londonderry improvement bill, 21 Feb., and advocated its cause at a local meeting on 4 May, he oversaw the passage of the bill that session.[19] He divided for Lord Ebrington's motion for an address calling on the king to appoint only ministers who would carry the reform bill unimpaired, 10 May, and the second reading of the Irish bill, 25 May. He voted against making permanent provision for the Irish poor by a tax on absentees, 19 June, against going into committee on the Irish party processions bill, 25 June, for the Irish tithes bill, 13 July, and against disqualifying the recorder of Dublin from sitting in Parliament, 24 July. He advised that the grant for the garrison at Londonderry should be used to rebuild the bridge there, 18 July. Reaping the benefit of his (as some said) cynical reform votes, he was returned for Londonderry as a Liberal at the general election in December 1832 after a bitter contest against Dawson.[20] He remained the representative of his native city until his death in March 1860, when his baronetcy became extinct.[21]

[1] Ex. inf. Stephen Lees. [2] Burke PB (1828), 224; PRO NI, Hart mss D3077/H/2/7; Newry Examiner, 30 June 1832. [3] E. Wakefield, Account of Ireland, ii. 179. [4] Col. Colby, Ordnance Survey of Co. Londonderry (1837), i. 85; HP Commons, 1790–1820, ii. 671. [5] Gent. Mag. (1808), ii. 749; Belfast News Letter, 22 July 1808, 2 July 1824. [6] Not to be confused with his near namesake Robert Ferguson* of Raith, Fife. [7] Index to Prerogative Wills of Ireland ed.

Sir A. Vicars, 165. [8]*HP Commons, 1790-1820*, ii. 672; *The Times*, 12, 17 Feb. 1820. [9]*Belfast News Letter*, 14 Jan. 1825, 15 Aug., 23, 30 Sept. 1828; *Belfast Commercial Chron.* 2 Jan. 1826. [10]PRO NI, Primate Beresford mss D3279/A/4/9, 28; S. Lewis, *Top. Dict. of Ireland* (1837), ii. 302. [11]*Belfast News Letter*, 21 Apr., 6 Nov. 1829, 9, 13 Apr. 1830. [12]Ibid. 4, 8 June 1830. [13]*Belfast Guardian*, 13, 17, 20, 24 Aug. 1830. [14]It was most likely Robert Cutlar Fergusson (or possibly Sir Ronald Craufurd Fergusson). [15]*Belfast News Letter*, 1, 8, 11 Feb. 1831. [16]St. Deiniol's Lib. Glynne-Gladstone mss 197, T. to J. Gladstone, 15 Mar. 1831. [17]*Belfast News Letter*, 1, 5, 15 Apr.; Grey mss, Howick to Grey, 4 Apr. 1831; PRO NI, Montgomery mss T1638/8/4. [18]*Belfast News Letter*, 10, 13 May 1831. [19]*Londonderry Sentinel*, 5 May 1832. [20]Ibid. 8, 15, 22 Dec. 1832. [21]Ibid. 16 Mar. 1860; *Gent. Mag.* (1860), i. 526.

S.M.F.

FERGUSON, Sir Ronald Craufurd (1773-1841), of Muirtown, Fife and 5 Bolton Street, Mdx.

DYSART BURGHS	1806–1830
NOTTINGHAM	1830–10 Apr. 1841

b. 8 Feb. 1773, 2nd. s. of William Ferguson (formerly Berry) of Raith (*d.* 1810) and Jean, da. of Ronald Craufurd of Restalrig, Edinburgh; bro. of Robert Ferguson*. *educ.* Edinburgh h.s. 1777-8; Berlin mil. acad. 1791-3. *m.* 4 Jan. 1798, Jean, illegit. da. of Gen. Sir Hector Munro[†] of Novar, Ross, 1s. surv. 1da. KCB 2 Jan. 1815; GCB 13 Sept. 1831; *suc.* bro. Robert to Raith 1840. *d.* 10 Apr. 1841.

Ensign 53 Ft. 1790, lt. 1791, capt. 1793; maj. 84 Ft. 1794, lt.-col. 1794; lt-col. 37 Ft. 1799; brevet col. 1800; maj.-gen. 1808; col. Sicilian regt. 1809; lt.-gen. 1813; col. 79 Ft. 1828; gen. 1830.

In 1841, the Edinburgh Whig lawyer Henry Cockburn recalled Ferguson and Lord Archibald Hamilton as 'the two most strenuous defenders of Scotland' in the Commons in the pre-reform era and wrote of Ferguson:

> The parliamentary struggles of this manly and disinterested soldier, unadorned as they were by eloquence, and consequently prompted by no ambition of display, and cheered at that time by very little hope of success, but proceeding solely from the impulse of right opinion and a gallant spirit, did honour to the whole army.[1]

A Foxite Whig, who as a commanding officer had received the thanks of both Houses for his services at Vimeiro in 1808 and a military knighthood in 1815, he had represented Dysart Burghs on the combined interest of his family and the 2nd earl of Rosslyn since 1806, defying successive attempts by the 2nd Lord Melville to restore the seat to government. Opposition proposed at the general election of 1820, when his brother Robert stood unsuccessfully for Fifeshire, was soon abandoned.[2]

A widower, Ferguson was a regular guest at Whig country houses, his brother's estate of Raith, near Kirkcaldy, and of his Whig friends in Edinburgh, but he lived mainly in London, where he associated with the Westminster reformers, including Francis Place. A supporter of George Tierney* for the party leadership in 1818, in the 1820 Parliament he attended assiduously, voted against administration in almost every major division and supported the 'Mountain' and Hume's campaigns for economy and retrenchment, becoming a respected spokesman for them on military matters. He divided silently for Catholic relief, 28 Feb. 1821, 1 Mar., 21 Apr., 10 May 1825. He maintained that Scotland was decidedly for concessions although its people were mainly Presbyterians, 28 Feb. 1825.[3] A radical publication of that year noted that he 'attended regularly, and voted with the opposition: speaks, not often, but to the purpose'.[4] Over half of more than 170 speeches credited to him, 1820-32, predate 1825, and most of the 17 attributed to him that year (1825) were on trade and commercial issues. 'Though ... not hostile to free trade' (he maintained that his views coincided with those of the political economist David Ricardo*), Ferguson appreciated the practical and political necessity of protecting the Scottish linen trade and supported Fifeshire petitions for an extension of the linen bounty, as an interim measure, at his constituents' request, 25 May, 8, 30 June 1820.[5] He criticized petitions against the 1823 Scottish linen manufacture bill entrusted to Hugh Lindsay, 15 May, silently presented others from Kirkcaldy, 7, 26 May, and made a point of thanking the president of the board of trade Huskisson 'for removing the vexatious enactments under which the trade had so long suffered', 9 May. He maintained on the 22nd that he was in 'correspondence with every part of Scotland where the linen trade was carried on but had not heard a single voice raised' against Huskisson's policies.[6] He brought up favourable petitions, 15 Mar., and protested at the 'hue and cry ... raised against the abolition of the bounties' in Ireland, 18, 22 Mar. 1824.[7] On foreign trade, 25 Mar. 1825, he referred again to his constituents' alarm at the removal of the bounties and his personal support for free trade, called for caution 'with respect to ... linens, especially coarse linen liable to be undersold by the German and New Orleans markets', and suggested lowering the duties on flax and hemp imports as palliatives. John Hobhouse* attributed his absence from the Westminster anniversary dinner, 23 May 1825, to his health (he felt unwell) and his obligation to hear a linen petition.[8] He presented petitions against and opposed the Tay salmon fisheries bill on behalf of his friends in Dundee, 12, 17 Mar., 3 May 1824, was appointed to the 1824 and 1825 select committees, and presented the Fifeshire linen manufacturers' petition against the abortive 1825 measure, 18 May.[9]

Taking a major role in the parliamentary campaign on Queen Caroline's behalf, he failed to persuade the leader of the House Lord Castlereagh to disclose details of the Milan commission's appointment and report, 24 June 1820. He moved for an address to the king for copies of the documents, 6 July, in a speech that reviewed events since the queen's departure for the continent in 1814, the motives for omitting her name from the liturgy and government inaction following the lord chancellor's 1818 visit to Milan, although statements 'contained in the green bag' must have been known to them. Castlereagh conceded ministerial responsibility, but condemned the motion as a 'waste of time' and it was easily killed. When, following the abandonment of the bill of pains and penalties, Castlereagh cited the motion's resounding defeat in an endeavour to rally support, 14 Jan. 1821, Ferguson countered that he 'had got rid of it by a mode peculiar to himself' and urged its reconsideration. He mustered with the queen's friends at Michael Angelo Taylor's* and at Brooks's, where he was a member of her subscription committee, presented petitions (from Culross, Burntisland and Kinghorn) and spoke for Hamilton's motion for restoration of her name to the liturgy, 26 Jan. 1821.[10] Yet, presenting a Kirkcaldy petition attaching distress and reform to the queen's cause, 31 Jan., he said that 'like other Scottish petitions, it said nothing of the liturgy, for he thanked God, there were no such trammels on divine worship in Scotland'. He now drew a sharp rebuke, which he ignored, from the lord advocate Sir William Rae, for warning that no credence should be given to professions of loyalty to the king's ministers adopted at Scottish public meetings.[11] He defended further expressions of support for the queen and criticized those loyal to ministers, 8, 13, 21, Feb. He refused to comment on a reference to the liturgy in a Dysart petition, 21 Feb.[12] When he failed to return from Taylor's supper table in time to vote on the issue (13 Feb.), the Grenvillite Commons leader Charles Williams Wynn observed: 'To our great amusement, Creevey, Ferguson, Wilson, Lambton and Sefton were shut out, and afterwards received the inquiries of their friends whether it was from scruples of conscience, or being unable to make up their minds, that they had abstained from voting'.[13] Ferguson's statement that he would not be 'bringing forward any motion' on the Milan commission, as he 'entertained no hope of doing any good in the state the House was', 21 Feb., drew an angry response from Castlereagh, whom he again chided for mishandling the queen's case, on

bringing up a Kirkcaldy petition, 12 Mar.[14] Before the coronation, which, to opposition cheers, he criticized as an extravagant, disruptive and useless pageant, 21 June, he outsmarted Londonderry (as Castlereagh had become) by asking for details of the queen's request to attend and to be crowned, creating an opportunity for her lawyer Denman to take the matter up, 30 June 1821.[15] He assisted Sir Robert Wilson* following his dismissal from the army for forcing a way through the City at the queen's funeral and, to cheers, described Wilson's treatment as an 'exercise of prerogative abused' in 'a base assassination of private character for the purposes of political intrigue', 13 Feb. 1822.[16] Praising his gallantry, he endorsed a proposal to restore him to his rank, 17 June 1825.

He voted for a scot and lot franchise for Leeds if it was awarded Grampound's seats and criticized the way in which the disfranchisement bill was handled by the committee chairman Brogden, 2 Mar. 1821.[17] He attended the reform dinner at the *London Tavern* with Sir Francis Burdett* and Hobhouse, 4 Apr.[18] He voted to disqualify civil officers of the ordnance from voting in parliamentary elections, 12 Apr., but missed the snap division on Lambton's reform scheme, 18 Apr. He voted for reform in England, 9 May 1821, 25 Apr. 1822, 20 Feb., 24 Apr. 1823, 27 Apr. 1826. He had supported Hamilton's campaign for Scottish parliamentary and burgh reform since 1817, and was appointed to the 1819-21 committees. He backed Hamilton's decision to confine his proposed inquiry into county representation to Scotland, 'because the two systems were wholly dissimilar in principle and in practice', and joined him in pressing for an extended property-based franchise, 25 May 1820, 10 May 1821. Ferguson's resignation in disgust from the burgh reform committee, 12 Mar. 1821, seems to have been deliberately timed to thwart the Grants' electoral objectives in Inverness.[19] However the explanation he gave and repeated when Hamilton, who dissented from it, brought up their report, 14 June, was that the committee's decision in 1819 to 'do more than ministers would allow' had caused subsequent ones to be packed with government supporters committed to protecting abuses, making his further attendance pointless. He supported Hamilton's proposal to refer the burgh reform reports to the whole House and complained that the remedial legislation planned by Rae ignored self-election and was too closely based on searches of 'old parchments and charters', 20 Feb. 1822. He exposed Rae's ignorance of the practice of holding annual burgh head courts when presenting a petition from Kinghorn against the burgh accounts bill, 17 June, and brought up another from Inverness,

28 June 1822.[20] He spoke, 9 Mar., and voted to reform Edinburgh's representation, 5 May 1823, 13 Apr. 1826, when, insisting that the question was 'short and simple', he described to the English Members how their Scottish counterparts were returned by 'small corporations' and parchment voters.

He knowingly placed his popularity at risk by opposing (in a minority of 17) the appointment of a select committee on the Scottish petitions against the additional malt duty, which he alleged was 'proposed not with reference to the merits of the measure itself, but as a boon to the Scotch Members to vote with the minister', 12 Apr. 1821. He spoke for the 'much needed' Scottish juries bill and criticized its Tory opponents (Sir George Warrender and William Douglas), 8 Feb., 18 May.[21] Supporting Hume on the estimates, he conceded his personal bias against disbanding the Cape regiment, 14 Mar., made the war secretary Lord Palmerston admit that the transfer of the 93rd Highlanders to the West Indies was badly timed, 11 Apr., and intervened and voted in small minorities on at least 15 further occasions, 16 Feb.-31 May. He spoke disparagingly of the duke of Clarence's grant, 30 June. He failed to persuade the Tory James Stuart Wortley to withdraw his libel allegations against the printer of the *Morning Chronicle*, 9 Mar., but made similar charges 'in a very good statement' on the 15th against the *Morning Post*, whose report of Creevey's quarrel with Warrender on 16 Feb. (for which he was their intermediary) could be traced to *John Bull*.[22] He contributed to proceedings on the paper's libel on the 'Mountaineer' Henry Grey Bennet, in which Londonderry's involvement was revealed, and was a minority teller for reprimanding its printer at the bar of the House instead of taking him into custody 11 May 1821. Grey Bennet thought Ferguson 'made a very good attack' that day, 'objecting to the wretches who had appeared at the bar being punished, but declaring his conviction that a person of rank and fortune was at the bottom of the whole proceeding'.[23] Edward Bootle Wilbraham* noted that Ferguson had himself been at risk of being 'shown up' in the inquiry and had 'gone to [Theodore] Hook and informed him that if he was he'd break his bones. The consequence of which has been that Sir Ronald has not been brought before the public'.[24] He refused to comment on petitions entrusted to him on behalf of the Fifeshire radicals John Hay, 21 Mar 1823, and Robert Gourlay, 29 Apr., 9 May, 5 July 1825, 26 Apr. 1826.[25] On slavery, he testified to the mass importation of slaves by Spain he had witnessed at Bahia, 26 June 1821.[26]

Ferguson condemned government's 'inadequate' relief proposals to combat distress, 11 Feb. 1822. His support for Hume in the resistance to the estimates was unstinting, but, safeguarding his military reputation, he qualified his vote for a 10,000-man reduction in the army with a warning that Ireland would be better served if insurrection was put down by regular troops, not the yeomanry, and he cautioned against spending to retain strategically vulnerable colonies captured in wartime, 4 Mar. He made the same point when criticizing 'abuse' of the Barbados revenues for electioneering and patronage purposes, 15 Mar.[27] On the ordnance estimates, 25 Mar., he explained that his dissatisfaction lay with the 'inadequacy and the types of cuts' ministers proposed, for example the dismissal of army surgeons and use of general practitioners unfamiliar with 'loiterers' to diagnose sickness, and the retention of the most expensive officers. He criticized the Edinburgh police bill as a ploy to 'place the whole power and authority of the police in the hands of the present superintendent, who had been detected in great fraud', 8, 12 Mar.[28] He pressed arguments voiced at the Fifeshire meeting the previous month against the malt tax and proposed changes to the excise duties inhibiting Scottish whisky exports, 6 May, and endorsed a petition from the Kirkcaldy and Firth of Forth ship owners for reductions in tonnage duty, lighthouse charges and consular and customs office fees to compensate for the losses they had suffered through the relaxation of the navigation laws, 4 June. Echoing Sir William Lemon's arguments for Cornwall, he pressed for concessions on the salt tax for the Scottish salt herring trade, 3, 11 June, and presented their petition for its abolition, 17 June 1822.[29]

Ferguson monitored the political manoeuvring following Londonderry's suicide in August 1822 from Raith, and he was hailed with Hamilton and Hume as a reformer when he attended civic dinners that Michaelmas in Perth and Dundee.[30] From Cantley on his way south, 19 Jan. 1823, he informed the opposition whip Lord Duncannon* that the Edinburgh Fox dinner that month had been one of the 'best ... which ever took place ... in Scotland' and that he was 'ready to start at an hour's notice'.[31] He made it clear in the House, 14 Feb., that despite their private friendship and his professional esteem for Lord Beresford, he would vote with Hume against his peacetime appointment as lieutenant-general of the ordnance (as an ally of the new foreign secretary and leader of the House George Canning) and did so, 19 Feb. Toeing the party line recommended by Brougham, who denounced Hume's unruly and factious opposition, Ferguson generally restricted his remarks to Scottish and commercial issues, many of them local, for the next two sessions. He exposed weaknesses in the government's policy on the spirit duties, 4 Mar., opposed their beer duties bill, 18 June, and as a spokesman for the distillers who were anxious to retain control over quality, he welcomed the deferral of the bill's clause empowering the excise to regulate (by closing the worm) the flow of spirits into the receiver, 30 June.[32] Supporting Hamilton's request for a copy of the royal warrant which had restored the old ruling oligarchy of Inverness to power at the last election, he delivered a complete vindication of Hume, whose criticism of Aberdeen council had been portrayed in debate as a general attack on the integrity of the Scottish magistracy. He tacked to it his own tenet that the 'right to intervene in the election of magistrates for a disfranchised burgh lay with the burgesses', 26 Mar. He endorsed the prayer of the Edinburgh reform petition for a £5 ratepayer franchise, 5 May 1823. He supported subscriptions for the Greek 'patriots' and for the Spanish refugees and deplored what he termed the 'rascality' that by 1824 was undermining Hume, Hobhouse and Lord Grey's brother-in-law Edward Ellice's* work as the funds' commissioners.[33] On 15 Apr. 1824 (and again, 10 Mar. 1826) he voted to end military flogging, although he perceived weaknesses in Hume's case for it. He admitted that he had 'administered corporal punishment himself' before seeing 'the folly of the thing', and confirmed that flogging was almost unknown in the best-disciplined regiments, 15 Mar. 1824. He criticized the additional churches bill as 'a useless application of public money', 9 Apr., and complained that 'the practice in these churches was to admit paupers free of charge and charge mechanics and persons in decent employ a shilling a year for a seat', 12 Apr., 14 June.[34] He brought up the Kirkcaldy ship owners' petition for the contentious London Oil Gas Company bill promoted by Ellice, 12 Apr., and several from Fifeshire against taxing strong beer and for equalization of the spirit duties, 6, 18 May.[35] Poking fun at Gascoyne for stating that his criticism of the hides and skins bill was full of holes, 14 Apr., he countered that the existing law fined a man for injuring his own property, and 'suppose by any unfortunate accident [Gascoyne] ... were to make a hole in his pantaloons, how would he like to be fined for misadventure'. He opposed the measure as a speaker and teller, 3, 5, 31 May.[36] He had been against proceeding with the government's Scottish judicature bill without the additional inquiry proposed by Hamilton, and he criticized the 'deceit' perpetrated by the lord advocate in promising consultation, 30 Mar. At the Fifeshire head court he confirmed that he had supported the cross-party measure rushed through at the fag end of the session, 5 Oct. 1824.[37]

Private, transport and utility bills preoccupied him in 1825, when Creevey, a pre-session guest at Raith and a diehard opponent of the scheme, deemed his frantic commitment to carrying the 1825 Liverpool-Manchester railway bill 'insane'.[38] He condemned the Edinburgh-Dalkeith railway bill as 'needless and objectionable', 16 May, and succeeded in wrecking it (by 63-29), 30 May. He opposed the Edinburgh-Leith water bill, 2, 4 May, and was a majority teller when it was killed (by 54-49), 3 June, and condemned as a job the Leith Docks bill carried by '14 or 15 Members with little knowledge of the seaports and their interests', who had voted without hearing the evidence, 11 May. He presented and endorsed a petition in favour of the St. Katharine's Docks bill from the seamen of Kirkcaldy, 22 Feb., and brought up others against withdrawing the protective tariff on imported rapeseed oil, 18 Apr., and re-enacting the combination laws, 9 May.[39] He supported inquiry into the Irish church and emigration, 13, 14 June, and was a minority teller for the spring guns bill, defeated by a single vote, 29 June. When a dissolution was anticipated in September 1825, Rosslyn's son and heir Lord Loughborough* and an unnamed government candidate started against him.[40] Adopting a higher local profile in 1826, Ferguson warned of damage to the Forth shipbuilding trade if promised reductions in the timber duties were delayed, 14 Feb., ordered returns on oil imports, 15 Feb., and pressed for details of any changes in the tobacco duties, 22 Feb.[41] He presented more than 20 petitions against introducing currency changes in Scotland in the wake of the 1825-6 banking crisis 1, 9, 16, 20 Mar., 13 Apr.;[42] one from Dundee in favour of the Lowestoft harbour bill, 23 Mar.,[43] and another for corn law revision, 10 Mar. 1826.[44] Endorsing the last, he explained that the petitioners wanted similar tariff structures for corn imports and manufactured goods, like silk, and expressed surprise that 'landlords had not got rid of their prejudices, which blinded them to their own interests on the question'. On the estimates, 3 Mar., he seconded Hume's proposal to abolish the entire yeomanry corps to secure a £25,000 saving, in a speech that confirmed his bias for regular troops and a plainly dressed cavalry 'without any of the fopperies of foreign troops or ... mustachios'. He refused to sanction the reductions Hume advocated in the 'highly skilled, expensive to train and difficult to replace' artillery, but paid tribute to his efforts 'during the last seven years to simplify the accounts of the public expenditure and render them intelligible', 6 Mar. At a stormy interview in London in early May, he demanded that Rosslyn (who obliged), should put a stop to Loughborough's hostile manoeuvring. He commenced his personal canvass the following week and overcame an attempt to unseat him at the general election of 1826.[45]

Henceforward Ferguson's name and that of the new Member for Kirkcudbright, Robert Cutlar Furgusson, an East India proprietor and judge, tended to be confused in parliamentary reports. Speeches on judicial and East Indian issues credited to Ferguson can be reattributed to Cutlar Fergusson, but ambiguities remain, especially on Scottish issues. Differing from Brougham and the Whig leaders, Ferguson naively supported Hume's amendment to the address, 21 Nov. 1826, 'because, as he conceived, it did not pledge the House to any opinion with respect to the topics introduced into it, but merely to take them into consideration'.[46] He had long recanted his early criticism of the duke of York's deployment of patronage, but he was nevertheless loudly cheered from the government benches when he echoed Calcraft's praise for the duke as commander-in-chief, 30 Nov. 1826. He presented petitions for outright repeal of the corn laws, 14, 15, 19 Feb.,[47] and voted for a 50s. pivot price, 9 Mar., against increased protection for barley, 12 Mar., and for the staggered introduction of a 10s. fixed duty on corn, 27 Mar. 1827. He divided against the duke of Clarence's annuity bill, 2 Mar., and voted for information on the treatment of the Lisburn Orange marchers, 29 Mar., and for inquiry into chancery delays, 4 Apr. 1827. He refused to deliver Brougham's acceptance when he was called out by Raikes at Brooks's, 4 Mar., and helped Wilson to secure his 'preventive' arrest, which they celebrated at Ellice's.[48] He divided for Catholic relief, 6 Mar. He expressed satisfaction with, 22 Mar., and presented petitions backing the salmon fisheries bill, 22 Mar., 22 May,[49] wholeheartedly endorsed the spring guns bill and urged a complete review of the game laws, 23 Mar. Remaining in opposition when Canning formed his ministry, he voted for the separation of bankruptcy and chancery jurisdiction, 22 May, and in a minority of ten for repeal of the Blasphemous and Seditious Libels Act, 31 May. He expressed support for the Edinburgh oil-gas bill, 23 May, but opposed its third reading, 1 June, after the arrangement between its sponsors had broken down. He also challenged the right of William Dundas (an interested party) to vote on the issue and joined in the fun provoked by Dundas's offer to give him his sole share by agreeing to accept it.[50] He voted to increase the number of visiting magistrates sanctioned by the Edinburgh bridewell bill, 11 June, and supported an unsuccessful bid to use the Dunbar harbour bill to boost the power of resident burgess on the council, 15 June.[51] In July 1827 he was a guest at private dinners attended by Canning.[52]

Ferguson voted to repeal the Test Acts which the Wellington ministry then opposed, 26 Feb. 1828. On the salmon fisheries bill, 7 Mar., he exposed the ignorance of its critic Lord Lowther (who had silenced Spring Rice) of the select committee reports. His appointment that month as colonel of the 79th Foot followed closely on Rosslyn's to the lord lieutenancy of Fifeshire (which his brother Robert coveted), and softened his opposition without changing his politics. Creevey wrote:

> We have an *event* in our family. Fergy has got a regiment, a tip-top crack one, one of those beautiful Highland regiments that were at Brussels, Quatre-Bras and Waterloo. But his manner of getting it is still more flattering to him and honourable to Lord Hill, backed, no doubt, as he must have been by the Beau [Wellington]. It has been the subject of a battle of ten days' duration between the king and Lord Hill. The former proposed Lord Glenlyon, the duke of Atholl's second son, married to the duke of Northumberland's sister, who has been in the king's household, and, as the king said, *had his promise* of a regiment (the 79th). On the other hand, the king has been known to say over and over again that Ferguson *never* should have a regiment in *his lifetime*, for various offences. He voted and spoke against the duke of York; he went to Queen Caroline's *in regimentals*; he moved for the Milan Commission ... and was voted against by Tierney and all the Whigs as being much too bad; and yet little Hill has carried him through ... I feel quite certain that Lady Conyngham's *sneers* and Sir Henry Hardinge's* fears were all connected with this then pending battle.[53]

Aligning as previously, he supported inquiry into chancery administration, 24 Apr., and to limit the crown's right to goods recovered under the customs and excise laws, 1 May. On the 5th he opposed the Aberdeen harbour bill as the work of a bankrupted corporation and

> because it has been altered from its original intention. It was at first introduced as for a new dock; now the dock is transformed into a 'floating harbour'. There is, perhaps, no great difference between the two. All I contend for is, that the parties should have the opportunity of attending to their own interest, by being allowed a proper share in the management of the harbour.

He or Fergusson spoke against introducing English poor law practices to Scotland, as broached by Thomas Kennedy, 6 May.[54] He voted for Catholic relief, 12 May. He was apparently 'shut out' from the division the Canning family's pension, 13 May, but, according to a time-wasting intervention which *The Times* attributed to him on the 20th, he had opposed it.[55] He voted in a minority of five to prohibit compensation payments under the archbishop of Canterbury's registrar's bill, 16 June, and cast critical votes on the cost of the Buckingham House refurbishment, 23 June, and ordnance expenditure, 4 July 1828. As the patronage secretary Planta had predicted, he voted for Catholic emancipation 6, 30 Mar. 1829. He criticized the use of inflammatory speeches, handbills and chapbooks to procure anti-Catholic petitions, 9 Mar., denounced the 'factious opposition raised' to emancipation in the House as the worst he had seen, 23 Mar., and when the Ultra Knatchbull disagreed, pointed to the anomaly of 'gentlemen who say that they will not believe Catholics on their oaths' taking 'so much trouble in framing oaths for them to take'. He provoked a similar altercation with Sir Robert Inglis and Wemyss over the hostile petition of the synod of Kirkcaldy, 30 Mar. He voted to permit Daniel O'Connell to sit without swearing the oath of supremacy, 18 May. According to *The Times*, he explained that though he was grateful to the ministry for carrying emancipation, he could not vote against transferring East Retford's seats to Birmingham under the disfranchisement bill, 5 May.[56] He kept a low profile pending the passage of his brother's Ferguson estate bill, which received royal assent, 19 June 1829.[57]

Ferguson apparently did not vote on the 1830 address. He presented petitions alluding to distress, 18 Feb., 18 Mar., but denied that it was universal in Scotland or that the 'agricultural interest in my part of the country is so depressed as it has been represented to be'. He poured scorn on Davies's proposal for a £213,000 saving in the army:

> In the course of a long parliamentary life, I have voted on nearly every occasion in favour of every proposition for economy; but as a military man, I have examined these army returns, and I am bound to say that, in my opinion, you cannot do with a single regiment of the line less than you have.

He endorsed expenditure on the Enfield ordnance factory, ridiculed contracting out and complained that the Birmingham guns he had seen 'on trial' were 'perfectly useless', 2 Apr. He voted to transfer East Retford's seats to Birmingham, 11 Feb., 5, 15 Mar., for Lord Blandford's reform scheme, 18 Feb., to enfranchise Birmingham, Leeds and Manchester, 23 Feb., and for Russell's general proposals, 28 May. He or Fergusson voted to prevent Members voting on bills in which they had a pecuniary interest, 26 Feb. He divided fairly steadily with the revived Whig opposition from 22 Mar., including for Jewish emancipation, 5 Apr., 17 May. He helped to carry the Dundee harbour bill enacted that session, 18 Mar., 19 May, and

brought up petitions against renewing the East India Company's charter from Kirkcaldy, 18 Mar., and Kinghorn, 6 May. In July 1830 the new king, William IV, promoted him to the rank of general.

Rosslyn's late withdrawal from their coalition and decision to return Loughborough for Dysart Burghs at the 1830 general election took Ferguson by surprise and left him without a seat.[58] The ensuing furore boosted his brother's interest in the constituency, and Ferguson was talked of as a likely challenger to John Stuart Wortley* in Perth Burghs and Robert Grant* and Jonathan Peel* at Norwich.[59] However, on Lord Holland's advice he contested Nottingham, where the local *Review* eulogized his credentials, and came in on the combined corporation and reform interests after a short poll.[60] According to his colleague Denman, he was 'received as a brother in every good political house' and 'not in the least affected by the run made against him'.[61] On the hustings, he stressed his good attendance record, opposition to slavery and support for reform, civil and religious liberties and retrenchment. He affirmed, when prompted, that he was an 'advocate of free trade in corn and opposed to the East India Company's monopoly'.[62] He spoke similarly when feted in Kirkcaldy, 3 Sept., but there he promoted Scottish electoral and burgh reform and praised Hume for encouraging petitioning. On ministers' health being proposed, he said:

> He was not to be understood to be in Parliament as a positive opposer of government. A long experience had given him reason to see that unconditional pledges either uniformly to support or uniformly to oppose ministers were among the worst guides of conduct it was possible to adopt.

Professing independence, he expressed gratitude to Wellington for the Test Acts' repeal and emancipation, but described his government, with the exception of Peel, as 'feeble' and 'quite contemptible. Still, weak men acting honestly, were better than rogues who had the talent to contrive mischief'.[63] They in turn counted him among the 'bad doubtfuls', but amended this to 'opposition'.

Ferguson was 'shut out' from the division on the civil list when the Wellington ministry was brought down, 15 Nov. 1830.[64] That evening, on presenting a petition for burgh and parliamentary reform he had solicited from Cupar (5 Nov.), he expressed astonishment at reports that Wellington had declared that he would 'oppose reform of any kind' and considered that 'the country was satisfied with the current system'.[65] He waited until the Nottingham reform petition was brought up on the 22nd to announce that the 'late elections had made him a convert to the ballot', and confirmed it in a letter of the 30th to the *Nottingham Review*, which kept his parliamentary conduct under close scrutiny.[66] According to the Tory Lord Ellenborough, who heard it from Beresford, Ferguson was passed over for the ordnance when Grey formed his ministry, but he later joined the military subcommittee chaired by Sir John Byng*, whom he denounced as 'incapable'.[67] He presented many Scottish and Nottingham anti-slavery petitions, 15, 19 Nov., 11 13, 20 Dec. 1830, 3 Feb. 1831. Making reform his priority, he expressed support for the ministerial Whigs pledged to it and joined Kennedy in presenting and endorsing reform petitions from the royal burghs, 13, 20, 23 Dec. 1830, 3, 8 Feb. 1831. He said that the Kirkcaldy one, which Loughborough presented and he had been asked to support, was a plea for emancipation, 'for in the present state of the franchise in Scotland the people are not actually represented' 23 Dec. 1830.[68] He endorsed pleas for the ballot in petitions from Dundee, 8 Feb., and hailed its successful deployment there in harbour commissioners' elections, 26 Feb. 1831. He discountenanced a demand for annual parliaments in the radical Basford petition, 8 Feb. Thomas Wood and his fellow anti-reformer Sir Charles Wetherell ridiculed Ferguson's claim that incorporations petitioning for the Scottish reform bill (he cited Kinghorn and Dundee) were willing to sacrifice their privileges to carry it, 16 Mar. He presented others, including one from the Glendale ward of Northumberland forwarded by his friend the Whig banker Charles Bigge, 19 Mar. He divided for the English reform bill at its second reading, 22 Mar., and against Gascoyne's wrecking amendment, 19 Apr. He had been assured of support at Nottingham when he visited the town with Denman, 11 Apr., addressed the public meeting that confirmed it following the dissolution, 27 Apr., and came in unopposed at the general election.[69] He had written to Holland, 22 Apr. 1831:

> As the good folks of Nottingham seem disposed to *stick* to me, I certainly intend to stick to them ... It is to your kind introduction that I owe my seat in the last Parliament, and I am not so *national* as to prefer a Scotch seat, to the representation of such a town.[70]

He also played a prominent part in his brother's election for Dysart Burghs and assisted the defeated reformer Wemyss in Fifeshire. He declared on the hustings at Cupar that he had no objection to the £10 vote and would 'go along with the whole bill, but ... had he prepared it, he would have gone much lower'.[71]

He voted for the reintroduced reform bill at its second reading, 6 July 1831, and steadily for its details.

Criticizing Henry Hunt, he spoke of the futility of declaring the bill unacceptable without the ballot when most people wanted it passed, 30 Aug. He became a grand companion of the Bath at the coronation in September. Edward Littleton* blamed him for the debacle over the dinner afterwards to the leader of the House Althorp:

> That right-down ass ... Ferguson, with whom Robert Grosvenor* has thought proper to concert proceedings, proposed the thing in such a way that it was impossible for us not to place in the chair Sir Francis Burdett, who was present, and whom we all wished to keep out of it! And then Sir Ronald, seeing the mischief he had done, wished to get out of it by a clumsy joke, saying that seeing they were both present he would vote for neither.[72]

Ill with rheumatism, which, with a liver complaint, had plagued him periodically since serving at the Cape, he could only pair for the reform bill's passage, 21 Sept. On 7 Oct. the *Nottingham Review* reported his continued absence from the House.[73] He divided for the revised reform bill at its second reading, 17 Dec. 1831, for its details and third reading, 22 Mar., and for the address calling on the king to appoint only ministers who would carry it unimpaired, 10 May 1832. He presented petitions against granting supplies until it became law from Haddington, 23 May, and Kirkcaldy, 5 June, when he also brought up one from Nottingham against the general register bill. He voted for the second reading of the Irish reform bill, 25 May, against opposition amendments to the Scottish measure, 1, 15 June, and against Alexander Baring's bill to deny insolvent debtors parliamentary privilege, 6 June. He divided with government on the Dublin election controversy, 23 Aug., the Liverpool writ, 5 Sept. 1831, the Russian-Dutch loan, 26 Jan., 12, 16, 20 July, relations with Portugal, 9 Feb., and the navy civil departments bill, 6 Apr. 1832. Ferguson joined Lord Morpeth in pressing for committee proceedings on transport and utility bills to be made public, 21 July 1831, and was personally involved, as a committee member, in the controversial defeat of the Durham (South Side) wet dock bill, 2 Apr. 1832.[74] He made it known that he 'imputed no blame' to the borough or county magistrates for the Nottingham reform riots and deplored the death sentences meted out to the offenders, 31 Jan., 1 Feb. He vehemently opposed Hunt's proposed inquiry into the conduct of the Nottingham gaoler, 22 June. He had voted against Hunt's motion for information on military punishments, 16 Feb., and resisted his demands for inquiry into Private James Somerville's case, 3 July 1832.

Ferguson attended the Nottingham reform festival in August 1832 and, standing as a Liberal, he topped the poll there at the general election in December and retained his seat for life.[75] He died, recalled as a brave soldier and politician, at his London home in April 1841, four months after his brother and before he had been confirmed as his heir.[76] His only son Robert Ferguson (1802-68), Liberal Member for the Kirkcaldy district, 1841-62, was sworn as his heir in 1843 and as his uncle's in 1846. In 1864 he succeeded to his maternal grandfather's estate of Novar and took the name of Munro before Ferguson.[77]

[1] *Cockburn Jnl.* i. 274-5. [2] *HP Commons, 1790-1820*, ii. 596-7; iii. 741-2; *The Times*, 7 Feb. 1809, 8 Apr. 1820; NAS GD51/1/198/10/86; NLS mss 11, f. 17; *Caledonian Mercury*, 25 Mar., 3, 6 Apr. 1820. [3] *The Times*, 1 Mar. 1825. [4] *Session of Parl. 1825*, p. 463. [5] *The Times*, 26 May, 9 June, 1 July 1820. [6] Ibid. 16 May 1823. [7] Ibid. 16 Mar. 1824. [8] Add. 36461, f. 91; 36467, f. 96. [9] *The Times*, 13, 18 Mar., 4 May 1824, 19 May 1825. [10] *Creevey Pprs.* ii. 2; HLRO, Hist. Coll. 379, Grey Bennet diary, 23. [11] *The Times*, 1 Feb. 1821. [12] Ibid. 9, 14, 22 Feb. 1821. [13] Grey Bennet diary, 19; Buckingham, *Mems. Geo. IV*, i. 122. [14] Grey Bennet diary, 26; *The Times*, 13 Mar. 1821. [15] *The Times*, 22 June 1821; Grey Bennet diary, 104, 114; *Geo. IV Letters*, ii. 934. [16] *The Times*, 14 Feb. 1822; *Russell Letters*, ii. 4. [17] *The Times*, 3 Mar. 1821. [18] Grey Bennet diary, 50. [19] NAS GD23/6/573/2. [20] *The Times*, 18, 29 June 1822. [21] Ibid. 19 May 1821. [22] Ibid. 16 Mar. 1821; Grey Bennet diary, 37-38; *Creevey's Life and Times*, 139, 140. [23] *The Times*, 11, 12 May 1821; Grey Bennet diary, 79. [24] *Colchester Diary*, iii. 251. [25] *The Times*, 22 Mar. 1823, 30 Apr., 10 May, 6 July 1825, 27 Apr. 1826. [26] Ibid. 27 June 1821. [27] Ibid. 16 Mar. 1822. [28] Ibid. 9 Mar. 1822. [29] Ibid. 4, 5, 12, 18 June 1822. [30] *Dundee, Perth and Cupar Advertiser*, 26 Sept. 1822. [31] Bessborough mss. [32] *The Times*, 5 Mar., 1 July 1823. [33] Add. 36460, f. 135. [34] *The Times*, 10, 13 Apr. 1824. [35] Ibid. 13 Apr., 7, 19 May 1824. [36] Ibid. 4, 6 May 1824. [37] *Caledonian Mercury*, 7 Oct. 1824. [38] *Creevey Pprs.* ii. 87-88. [39] *The Times*, 10 May 1825. [40] Creevey mss, Creevey to Miss Ord, 6 Sept. 1825. [41] *The Times*, 16, 23 Feb. 1826. [42] Ibid. 2, 10, 17, 21 Mar., 14 Apr. 1826. [43] Ibid. 24 Mar. 1826. [44] Ibid. 11 Mar. 1826. [45] NAS GD164/1770/3; 1779/12, 13; 1781/9, 12-14, 19; 1782/2, 3; *Caledonian Mercury*, 15 June; *Scotsman*, 5 July 1826. [46] *Geo. IV Letters*, iii. 1271; *The Times*, 22 Nov. 1826. [47] *The Times*, 15, 16, 20 Feb. 1827. [48] *Creevey Pprs.* ii. 106-7; *The Times*, 6, 8 Mar. 1827. [49] *The Times*, 23 May 1827. [50] Ibid. 2 June 1827. [51] Ibid. 12, 16 June 1827. [52] Add. 52447, ff. 77, 92. [53] *Creevey Pprs.* ii. 156-7. [54] *The Times*, 7 May 1828. [55] Ibid. 21 May 1828. [56] Ibid. 6, 8 May 1829. [57] *LJ*, lxi. 588. [58] Creevey mss, Sefton to Creevey, 2 July; Stair mss (History of Parliament Aspinall transcripts), Murray to Dalrymple, 2 July; *Fife Herald*, 8 July 1830. [59] Hopetoun mss, 167 f. 130; Add. 36554, f. 135; *Fife Herald*, 8, 15 July 1830. [60] Add. 51813, Denman to Holland [25 July and n.d.]; 51835, Ferguson to same, 30 July; *Nottingham Rev.* 23, 30 July; *The Times*, 2 Aug. 1830. [61] Add. 51813, Denman to Holland [3 Aug. 1830]. [62] *Nottingham Rev.* 30 July; *Caledonian Mercury*, 5 Aug. 1830. [63] *Fife Herald*, 9 Sept.; *Nottingham Rev.* 10 Sept. 1830. [64] *The Times*, 16 Nov. 1830. [65] *Fife Herald*, 11, 18 Nov. 1830. [66] *Nottingham Rev.* 27 Nov., 3 Dec. 1830. [67] *Three Diaries*, 24, 189. [68] *Dundee, Perth and Cupar Advertiser*, 9 Dec. 1830. [69] *The Times*, 7 May 1831; *Nottingham Rev.* 29 Apr., 4 May 1831. [70] Add. 51836. [71] *Caledonian Mercury*, 26 May; *The Times*, 31 May, 1 June 1831. [72] Hatherton diary, 15 Sept. 1831. [73] *Nottingham Rev.* 30 Sept., 7 Oct. 1831. [74] *Durham Chron.* 6 Apr. 1832. [75] *Nottingham Rev.* 10 Aug., 14 Dec.; *Fife Herald*, 20 Dec. 1832. [76] *The Times*, 10, 14 Apr.; *Fife Herald*, 15 Apr. 1841. [77] NAS SC70/1/63, 66; *Oxford DNB*.

M.M.E.

FERGUSSON, Robert Cutlar (?1770–1838), of Orroland, Kirkcudbright and Craigdarroch, Dumfries.

KIRKCUDBRIGHT STEWARTRY   1826–16 Nov. 1838

b. ?1770, 1st s. of Alexander Fergusson, adv., of Craigdarroch and Deborah, da. of Robert Cutlar, merchant, of Dumfries. *educ.* Edinburgh; L. Inn 1792, called 1797. *m.* 17 May 1832, Marie Josephine, da. of Gen. Augier, 1s. 1da. *suc.* fa. 1796. *d.* 16 Nov. 1838.

Standing counsel, Bengal 1813-18, king's adv. 1818-25.
Judge adv.-gen. July-Dec. 1834, Apr. 1835-Nov. 1838; PC 16 July 1834.
Dir. E.I. Co. 1830-5.

Fergusson belonged to an old Dumfriesshire family with an estate at Craigdarroch, near Moniaive, close to the border with Kirkcudbright Stewartry. His great-grandfather Alexander Fergusson (1685-1749), whose father was killed at Killiecrankie (1689) as a lieutenant-colonel in William III's army, married the celebrated Annie Laurie and was Whig Member for Dumfries Burghs, 1715-22. When his grandfather James Fergusson died in 1771, Craigdarroch passed to his son and heir Alexander (*b.* 1746), an eminent advocate and hero of Burns's ballad 'The Whistle', whose marriage to Deborah Cutlar (in Edinburgh, 23 July 1769) brought the Stewartry property of Orroland into the family. Craigdarroch was inherited by Robert Cutlar Fergusson on his father's death in a chaise accident, 30 Apr. 1796; and he was served heir to Orroland in 1810.[1] By then he had made his mark as one of the Friends of the People and the author of *The Proposed Reform of the Counties of Scotland Impartially Examined* (1792), though he did not belong to the contemporary Scottish reform societies.[2] After the death of his mother in 1792 Mrs. Maria Riddell informed the Edinburgh antiquary William Smellie that while Craigdarroch had 'sustained a sensible affliction', he had 'a source of happiness and comfort few parents can boast of in his eldest son, who seems everything that is amiable and accomplished'.[3] A year after his call to the English bar Fergusson was employed as fourth defence counsel in the trial for high treason of his friend John Allen and James O'Coigly, Arthur O'Connor, John Binns and Jeremiah Leary at Maidstone, 21, 22 May 1798. After the acquittal of all but O'Coigly, Fergusson became embroiled in the court room brawl which developed as O'Connor's friends tried to obstruct officers sent to rearrest him. With the earl of Thanet and three other men he was tried in king's bench for riot and other misdemeanours, 25 Apr. 1799, with the attorney-general Sir John Scott† (later Lord Eldon) leading for the crown. He and Thanet were found guilty, on very flimsy evidence. Fergusson was fined £100, sentenced to a year's imprisonment in king's bench gaol and bound over to keep the peace for seven years. He protested his innocence throughout and stated his case in his *Observations* on the business which he published as an appendix to an account of *The Whole Proceedings* (1799): he argued that the episode had demonstrated 'the necessity ... of a revision of our penal code, that a number of barbarous and bloody laws may be blotted from its pages'.[4] After his release, 9 June 1800, he emigrated to Calcutta, where he practised as a barrister and 'made more money than it was thought was ever before made at the [Bengal] bar'. He was reckoned to be earning about £25,000 a year during his period as attorney-general to the East India Company from 1818; and on his return to Britain in the summer of 1825 he was reputed to be worth 'near half a million'.[5] His brother had been surreptitiously canvassing the Stewartry on his behalf for a year, and Fergusson immediately declared his candidacy for the next election. The sitting Member General Dunlop had the support of the Liverpool ministry's Scottish manager Lord Melville and of the aristocratic Selkirk and Galloway interests; but he had neglected his position and was vulnerable to a spirit of independence among the resident proprietors, many of whom were willing to back Fergusson regardless of his politics, which were now somewhat uncertain. Although he seemed to have nailed his colours to the mast by joining the Whig bastion of Brooks's, sponsored by Lord Sefton* and Sir Ronald Ferguson*, on 25 Feb. 1826, he continued to do well; and at the general election in June he defeated Dunlop by one vote in a poll of 95 freeholders, despite having lost in the choice of praeses.[6]

Preservation of his seat in the short term required him to take a reasonably temperate line in the House, where he acted generally with the mainstream Whigs but eschewed blatant partisanship. He was a frequent and forceful speaker, whose didactic tone often irritated his opponents. On the address, 21 Nov. 1826, he declined to support Hume's radical amendment, declared his support for Catholic claims and on the corn laws said he was 'not prepared for a free import of grain ... although his opinion rather inclined that way'; he voted in the ministerial majority. The Whig leader Lord Grey (once a Friend of the People) was told by Lord Lauderdale that Fergusson's was 'considered a speech of great promise'. Grey commented to his son: 'I know him, from a very long acquaintance, to be a man of considerable talent; but these Scotchmen always puff one another, and I always take the accounts they give in such cases with considerable grains of allowance'.[7] According to John

Croker*, Fergusson soon afterwards ran into Eldon, now lord chancellor, who 'good humouredly recognized him, and congratulated him on ... [his] good fortune' in India.[8] He called for investigation of the bubble joint-stock companies, 5 Dec. 1826. He was one of the handful of Whigs who voted (after speaking) for the grant to the duke of Clarence, 16 Feb.; he did so again, 16 Mar. 1827.[9] On 1 Mar. he conceded that the 1815 corn law had failed, but said that 'the agricultural interest of Scotland' would be ruined by the government's proposed relaxation, even though he agreed with it in principle. His attempt to amend the scale was rejected, 9 Mar., and his amendment to alter the duty on oatmeal was rejected by 155 – 52, 19 Mar.[10] He voted silently for Catholic relief, 6 Mar. He expressed reservations about Shadwell's writ of right bill, 27, 30 Mar. On 5 Apr. he voted for inquiry into the Irish miscellaneous estimates and spoke and was a minority teller for information on chancery delays, denying that the motion was aimed at Eldon personally. He spoke and voted for the transfer of Penryn's seats to Manchester, 18, 28 May, but reserved his position on East Retford until the evidence was complete, 11, 22 June. He divided with Canning's ministry for the grant for Canadian water defences, 12 June. His own motion for inquiry into aspects of real property law in India was rejected, 21 June 1827.

Fergusson spoke, 8 Feb., and voted, 12 May 1828, for Catholic relief. He advocated repeal of the Test Acts, 11 Feb., and voted thus, 26 Feb., when he encouraged the supporters of Catholic claims to back it. He urged Lord John Russell not to jeopardize the measure by opposing Peel's qualifying clauses, 18 Mar. He again supported the production of information on chancery administration, 12 Feb. He thought giving East Retford householders the vote might answer, 22 Feb., but on 4 Mar. he admitted that the evidence of rooted corruption had 'completely changed' his view; he voted for transfer of the seats to Birmingham, 21 Mar., 27 June. He did not want the commission of inquiry into the defects of common law administration to be restricted as the duke of Wellington's ministry insisted, 29 Feb. He supported the salmon fisheries regulation bill, 20 Mar., but tried unsuccessfully to secure the exemption from it of the River Thurso, for the benefit of Sir John Sinclair† of Ulbster, 19, 23 June. On 25 Mar. he got leave to introduce a bill to deal with the liability of Indian real estate as an asset in the hands of trustees for the debts of a deceased owner. He introduced it on 16 May and it became law on 27 June (9 Geo. IV, c. 33). He condemned the corn bill, 31 Mar., 22 Apr., and supported an attempt to increase the protecting duty on barley and moved one of his own on oats, which was defeated

by 101-59, 28 Apr. He liked Kennedy's Scottish parochial settlements bill, 6 May, but not Davenport's proposal to empower magistrates to judge felony cases,
13 May. He 'regretfully' supported Hume's motion
for information on civil list pensions, 20 May, claiming that he had 'every wish' to support ministers, 'than
whom ... few ... have ever been placed in greater difficulties, both as regards foreign and domestic affairs';
he was a teller for the minority of 52. When he declared
that 'the whole agricultural interest of Scotland' would
welcome 'a protecting duty on wool', 13 June, Kennedy
rebuked him for presuming to speak for them. He had
a clause added to the Indian criminal justice bill, 7 July,
called for mitigation of excise penalties, 8 July, and
spoke and voted against government on the silk duties,
asserting that they had betrayed Indian producers, 14,
16 July 1828.

In early 1829 he got the backing of ministers for his
candidature for a vacancy in the East India Company's
direction. Lord Ellenborough, president of the board
of control, believed him to be 'the best man' and persuaded Wellington to support him:

> I hope to manage to conciliate Fergusson, and to bring
> him into our view as to the judicial administration of
> India. At any rate, as a member of the court of directors
> he is much more likely to take moderate and reasonable
> views than he is if excluded ... by our means. I do not
> believe we could exclude him, and we should only ...
> convert an independent man into an enemy.

In the event, he was crushed by Sir William Young, 20
Mar., polling less than 700 votes, despite having boasted
of over 1,100 promises. Ellenborough immediately
urged Planta, the patronage secretary, to implement 'the
adoption of measures for securing Fergusson's return
on the next vacancy'.[11] In the House, he divided silently
for Catholic emancipation, 6, 30 Mar.; but he opposed
on legal grounds Daniel O'Connell's bid to take his
seat unhindered, 18, 21 May. He welcomed the government's plan to simplify excise regulations, 31 Mar.
He pressed for action on East Retford, 10 Apr., and
spoke and voted for the Birmingham option, 5 May. He
asked ministers to reduce the punitive duties on Indian
silks, 13 Apr., but next day opposed Fyler's motion for
inquiry into the domestic industry and defended their
general policy of 'moderate protection'. He denounced
the government's Scottish gaols bill because it transferred financial responsibility from the burghs to the
counties, 5 May, and applauded its withdrawal, 27
May. He approved Kennedy's tailzies regulation bill as
'a measure of relief', 1 May. He thought Davenport's
palliative young offenders bill would increase crime,
12 May. He supported the proposed increase in

Scottish judges' salaries, 21 May, and dissented from
Brougham's criticisms, though he had reservations over
details. He presented and endorsed a Wigtownshire
fishermen's petition for continuance of the bounties, 2
June. He opposed Hume's 'most extraordinary' motion
for information on fees in Doctors' Commons, 5 June
1829, when he advocated inquiry by select committee into all aspects of the Indian judicial system. His
objection to Hume's motion on fees of the ecclesiastical
courts as 'novel, inquisitorial and mischievous' earned
him castigation as the opponent of 'reform in the abuses
of the courts', but he insisted that he favoured 'practical
and beneficial' change.

Fergusson was not in the House when it divided on
Knatchbull's amendment to the address, 4 Feb. 1830.
He was named on 9 Feb. to the select committee on the
East India Company (and its renewals, 4 Feb., 28 June
1831, 27 Jan. 1832), and a week later secured election as
a director. He voted for the transfer of East Retford's
seats to Birmingham, 11 Feb., 5 Mar., when he argued
that 'the influence of the peerage wants a counterpoise
in this House'. He voted for the enfranchisement of
Birmingham, Leeds and Manchester, 23 Feb. On 18
Feb. he expressed 'concurrence in most of the arrangements' outlined by Peel, the home secretary, for judicial reforms, but suggested reform of the privy council
court and, for Scotland, making more effective use of
the consistorial courts and the extension of jury trial
in civil cases. He recommended the exclusion of all
judges, not merely Welsh ones, from the Commons.
A belief that 'a considerable reduction of our military
force' should be made to facilitate tax remissions on
essentials led him to vote for a cut of 5,000 men, 19
Feb.; but on 9 Mar. he voiced satisfaction with most
of the government's recent economies. He preferred
inquiry by select committee to that by committee of
the whole House into the state of the nation, 18 Mar.,
when he exonerated ministers from the charge that
they were indifferent to distress, which he attributed
largely to the bank restriction of 1819. He sided with
the Bombay government in its clash with the supreme
court, 8 Mar. He criticized aspects of the administration of justice bill, 9 Mar., and of the ministry's
proposals for reform of the Scottish judicial system,
1 Apr.; but on 30 Apr. and 18 June he gave the latter
his general blessing, though he still cavilled at details,
especially the transfer of business from the commissary court to the court of session. His attempt to stop
this, 18 June, which was seen by some as an electioneering ploy, failed.[12] He gave 'cordial support' to the
principle of Brougham's scheme for the establishment of local courts in England and Wales, 29 Apr. He
spoke, 29 Apr., and voted, 17 May, for Jewish emanci-

pation. He divided against the public buildings grant, 3 May, and for inquiry into the commerce of Ceylon, 27 May, but otherwise took no part in the revived Whig opposition's onslaught on the government. He voted for abolition of the death penalty for forgery, 24 May, 7 June, when he asserted that repeal of the taxes on soap and candles would have been of more benefit to Scotland than that of the beer duty. Next day he rejected Attwood's nostrum of bi-metallism. On 17 June he spoke at length against the appointment of an additional chancery judge and stressed the need for a competent court of appeal to replace the privy council. When he said that compensation for the defalcation of the registrar of Madras should not come from India territorial revenues, 19 June, Brougham questioned the propriety of his and other Company directors voting on the issue; he put himself in the hands of the House. On 1 July 1830 he dismissed the West India interest's complaints against the ministry's sugar duties proposals, which he considered 'perfectly fair'.

Fergusson was returned unopposed for the Stewartry at the 1830 general election, after which ministers naturally counted him among their 'foes'. On 3 Nov. 1830 he said that

> the public business in this House cannot be carried out as it ought to be, unless a great change is made in the present system ... Many of the most important subjects are brought on after midnight, and thus it is that few matters of great interest meet with the discussion which they require. With the exception of ... [Hume], I have been earlier and later in this House than any ... Members ... I have lost a good deal of time ... listening to long discussions which could have no useful result ... [and] dull discussions on petitions.

He suggested that the orders of the day should be taken in strict rotation. Later that day he declined to vote for the amendment to the address, but criticized the latter's reference to the Belgians as 'revolted subjects' of the Netherlands. In response to Brougham's earlier call for repeal of the Union (3 Nov.), he defended it and blamed Ireland's problems on 'the unfeeling conduct' of many landlords. He welcomed Williams Wynn's bill to abolish the abjuration oath, 4 Nov. 1830, and advocated its extension to others, 4 Feb. 1831. He was in the majority against ministers on the civil list, 15 Nov. 1830, but four days later paid a personal tribute to Peel for his conduct in office. Observing that excessive expenditure on Windsor Castle and other projects had gone far enough, 6 Dec., he urged the new Grey administration to execute 'their three great avowed principles of non-interference with foreign powers, of moderate and satisfactory reform in

the Commons ... and, above all, of retrenchment in the public expenditure'. Next day he complained of the inattention of some Members to Kennedy's motion for leave to introduce three 'most important' tailzies regulation bills; but he thought they went too far and advised Kennedy to consult the Scottish judiciary. He liked Campbell's bill to establish a general registry of deeds, 16 Dec., and, goaded by the Ultra Wetherell, made a personal attack on Eldon, who for 25 years had presided over the 'oppressive and pernicious' chancery administration. He could see little benefit accruing from repeal of the coastal coal duties, 14 Dec. 1830. On the budget, 14 Feb. 1831, he regretted the abandonment of the controversial stock transfer tax and criticized the proposed tax by weight on raw cotton and that on steamboat passengers, which would hit the 'industrious poor'. He supported the Ultra Lord Chandos's attempt to reduce the sugar duties, 11 Mar. He presented and endorsed petitions for reform of the Scottish electoral system, 18 Dec. 1830, 3 Feb. 1831, when he argued that support for change was widespread and stated his personal wish to 'see the elective franchise extended ... but not so as not to maintain the political condition of the landed interest of Scotland'. Accused by Hunt of advocating reform purely to 'protect' it, he explained:

> The representatives of counties should be elected by landowners ... not ... by labourers ... I am an enemy to universal suffrage. I think that the possession of some property ... not of a large amount, should be required to enable a man to vote.

He supported Chandos's resolution on electoral corruption at Evesham, 17 Feb., and Benett's proposal to deal with venality at Liverpool, 21 Apr. As a Member returned 'by the independent votes of the freeholders against the influence of the government and the peerage', he spoke again for Scottish reform, 26 Feb. He approved the principle of the ministry's Scottish reform bill, 9 Mar., but criticized the preferential treatment given to the burghs and the 'extremely objectionable' proposal to enfranchise £10 householders in the counties. He voted for the second reading of the English bill, 22 Mar. On the ministerial modifications to their scheme, 13 Apr., he approved the decision not to reduce the size of the Commons by as much as first proposed, urged the claims of Dumfries, Inverness and Perth to separate representation and damned Hunt and his 'selfish' Lancashire working men, who were 'too ignorant to be entrusted with the franchise'. In another spat with Hunt next day, he deplored his 'dangerous' language in favour of universal suffrage. On 18 Apr. he said it was 'a matter of the most common notoriety' that borough seats were 'bought and sold like stalls in a market'. The following day he opposed Gascoyne's wrecking amendment to the English bill, which if carried would mean that Scotland would receive no additional Members, said that the 'baneful' influence of borough proprietors must be eradicated from the Commons, but hoped that 'beyond this bill Parliament will not go'. Presenting the petition of the Stewartry's commissioners of supply against the full extent of the reform plan, 20 Apr., he dissented from its reservations. At the general election precipitated by the success of Gascoyne's amendment he was challenged by a Tory anti-reformer, who initially bragged of his chances but gave up a week before the election.[13] Informing Lord Holland, a member of the cabinet, 17 May 1831, he reported that enthusiasm for reform was 'ferocious' in Scotland and predicted a ministerial gain of seven seats there.[14]

Fergusson opposed free trade in corn, 24 June, and said that there was little to be gained by trying to extend commercial links with China, 28 June 1831, when he denied an allegation that Company Members had been obstructive on the East India select committee. He reiterated his liking for the registry of deeds bill, 30 June, 21 Sept., deplored a Glasgow Protestants' petition against the Maynooth grant, 19 June, welcomed the government's stated intention of reforming Indian grand juries, 1 Sept., and argued that the president of the board of control should be made a 'permanent' official, 29 Sept. He was in minorities against issuing the Dublin writ, 8 Aug., and for printing the Waterford petition for disarming the Irish yeomanry, 11 Aug., but he divided with ministers on the Dublin election controversy, 23 Aug. He spoke and voted for the Liverpool disfranchisement bill, 5 Sept., was in a minority of 20 against the quarantine duties next day and on 12 Sept. spoke and voted for inquiry into the effects on the West India interest of renewing the Sugar Refinery Act. He blamed opposition partisans for inciting the election riots at Dumbarton, Dumfries and Stirling, 27 June. Supporting the second reading of the reintroduced English reform bill, 4 July, he admitted that it was more 'extensive' than what he would have proposed, but asserted that nothing less was now feasible and urged its passage 'while it yet may be adopted with safety, and before even greater concessions may be forced upon us'. He voted for the bill, 6 July, and gave general support to its details in committee, where he was a frequent contributor to the discussions. He denied being a 'pledged' supporter of the measure, 14 July, and next day, supporting schedule A, dismissed Agnew's notion of grouping the boroughs in it to return one Member

per district. He spoke and voted against government for the transfer of Downton from A to B, 21 July, and voted for the total disfranchisement of Saltash, 26 July. He opposed a Tory bid to add Salford to Manchester in schedule C, 2 Aug. He welcomed the enfranchisement of the metropolitan districts, 4 Aug., and the proposal to give eight counties three Members each, 12 Aug. He divided against the separate representation of Merthyr, 10 Aug. On the 17th he argued that only tenants in possession should be allowed a county vote as leaseholders, to avoid the temptation to create fictitious votes. He voted with ministers against Chandos's amendment to enfranchise £50 tenants-at-will, 18 Aug., but said on the 20th that in view of its success he would in future vote to keep urban and rural voters apart: thus he supported Davies's attempt to exclude parliamentary borough freeholders from the counties, 24 Aug. Next day he spoke and voted to deny weekly tenants the franchise in order to maintain the 'respectability' of the electorate. He criticized the proposed annual renewal of voters' lists, 3 Sept., and secured a change to the appeals procedure, 13 Sept. He voted for the third reading, 19, and passage of the bill, 21 Sept. He divided silently for the second reading of the Scottish reform bill, 23 Sept., and on 3 Oct. commended its principle as 'most excellent', having become reconciled to the franchise proposals, though he still wanted an increase in the number of county Members. He had objected to the proposed union of Peeblesshire and Selkirkshire, 3 Sept., but on 4 Oct. he felt obliged to vote against the ministerial decision to preserve their separate representation by throwing their respective chief burghs into them. He also spoke and voted that day for a Tory amendment to give the eight most populous Scottish counties two Members. He was one of 'the four principal men in the House at present' (the others being Sir Francis Burdett, Hume and O'Connell) who showed 'some strong interest' in the efforts of George Traill to secure separate representation for Orkney and Shetland.[15] He voted for the motion of confidence in the government after the English bill's defeat in the Lords, 10 Oct., and when Parliament was prorogued, 19 Oct. 1831, applauded the chancellor of the exchequer Lord Althorp's assurance that ministers were 'pledged' to bring forward one 'as full and efficient' in the next session.

On the address, 7 Dec. 1831, Fergusson condemned the recent 'riots and excesses' at Bristol and elsewhere, approved of the proclamation against 'illegal' political unions, which were incompatible with 'monarchical government', and said he would continue to support 'efficient reform', but he criticized the proposed enfranchisement of weekly tenants. He praised ministerial policy towards Belgium and France, but lamented their indifference to the fate of Poland, passed over in 'the silence of despair and death'. He voted for the second reading of the revised English reform bill, 17 Dec. 1831, and gave general but not undeviating support to its details. He again called for an increase in the Scottish representation and suggested allowing superiority holders to vote during their lives, 19 Jan. 1832. Next day he said that schedule A of the English bill embodied 'by far the most useful principle' of the measure. It is not clear whether it was he or Sir Ronald Ferguson who voted against government on the Russian-Dutch loan, 26 Jan.; but he was in their majorities on the issue, 12, 16, 20 July. On 27 Jan. he spoke and voted against the proposed division of most English counties, arguing that the enfranchisement of £50 tenants had made many of them vulnerable to control by 'large families'. He annoyed Lord John Russell by demanding more Scottish Members, but he replied in kind to the minister's tart remarks on reformers who opposed government. His failure to 'run quite straight with his party and his principles in the House of Commons just now' was attributed by Edward Littleton* to his being 'offended at not being made a privy councillor' on the strength of his services in India.[16] On 1 Feb. he spoke and voted in a minority of 32 for Heron's attempt to expunge the Chandos clause and divided against allowing borough freeholders to vote in counties. Next day he opposed Hunt's amendment for a borough householder franchise, though he thought he had a point in advocating rates as the best criterion; but when Vernon proposed this, 3 Feb., Fergusson concluded that it was impractical at present. He approved the amended registration clause because it took away much of overseers' powers, 8 Feb. He supported enfranchisement of the metropolitan districts, 28 Feb., and of the likes of Bradford, 2 Mar. He voted silently for the third reading of the reform bill, 22 Mar. He supported amelioration of the 'cruel system' of child labour in factories, 1 Feb., 7 Mar., when he also spoke and voted for Chandos's motion to reduce the sugar duties. He was in Hunt's minority for information on military punishments, 16 Feb. He recommended authorizing parishes to raise money to provide precautions against cholera, 15, 16 Feb. He approved the principle of the Irish Subletting Act amendment bill, 20 Feb., and on 28 Mar. called for intelligent reform of the 'monstrous' tithes system; Wetherell accused him of advocating confiscation and the abolition of episcopacy. He opposed and divided against the malt drawback bill, 2 Apr., but voted with ministers for their navy civil departments bill, 6 Apr. He pressed again for an increase in Scottish judges'

salaries, 10 Apr., complaining that 'the business and the voice of Scotland are not attended to in this House'. On 18 Apr. he moved for papers on the plight of Poland, whose cause he warmly espoused, arguing that its dismemberment by Russia contravened the Treaty of Vienna. He raised the subject again, 28 June, when his passionate language provoked some tetchy exchanges. He welcomed the government's scheme for interdenominational education in Ireland, 7, 21 May, 8 June. He voted for the address calling on the king to appoint only ministers who would carry reform unimpaired, 10 May. Supporting the second reading of the Scottish reform bill, 21 May, he explained that he was still not happy with the £10 franchise, which he had initially considered 'a species ... of revolution', and that he wanted an increase in the number of county Members; he voted for the Conservative Murray's motion to this effect, 1 June. He complained that the bill left Shetland effectively unrepresented, 6 June. On the 15th he moved to unite Port Glasgow with Greenock in order to remove its urban influence from Renfrewshire, but was defeated by 73-47. He divided with ministers that day on the case of Perthshire's border and also opposed a Conservative bid to transfer Kirkcudbright from the Dumfries to the Wigtown district. He may have voted to preserve Irish freemen's voting rights, 2 July. He supported the death penalty abolition bill and praised the work of Romilly and Peel in lessening the severity of the penal code, 30 May, and endorsed the forgery punishment mitigation bill, 31 July. He disliked Alexander Baring's bill to exclude insolvent debtors from the House, 6 June. He spoke and voted for inquiry into admissions to the Inns of Court, 17 July, but opposed as 'too partial' Hume's bill to ban the recorder of Dublin from Parliament, 24 July. He criticized the government's commercial policy towards Ireland as oppressive, 25 July 1832.

Fergusson, who belatedly married a French woman in May 1832, came in unopposed for the Stewartry in 1832, 1835 and 1837. He was judge advocate in Lord Melbourne's first and second ministries, but retired on account of 'bad health' shortly before his death in Paris 'of a consumption' in November 1838. He was buried at Craigdarroch, where he was briefly succeeded in due course by his only son and namesake (1836-59).[17] By his will, dated 10 Nov. 1836, he provided an annuity of £400 for his wife in addition to her jointure of £500 a year, increased his brother Henry's annuity from £500 to £700 and left the residue of his estate to his children. His personalty was sworn under £30,000 in the province of Canterbury.[18]

[1] *HP Commons, 1715-54*, ii. 29-30; *Faculty of Advocates* (Scottish Rec. Soc. lxxxvi), 69; *Scottish Nation*, ii. 197; *Gent. Mag.* (1796), i. 442. [2] H. Meikle, *Scotland and French Revolution*, 72, 111. [3] R. Kerr, *Mems. Smellie*, ii. 376-7. [4] *Oxford DNB*; *State Trials*, xxiv. 1191-1431; xxvii. 821-986. [5] *The Times*, 10 June 1800; *Oxford DNB*; *Croker Pprs.* i. 331. [6] NAS GD51/1/198/14/33, 34, 36, 37; *Glasgow Herald*, 16, 23, 26 June 1826. [7] *Geo. IV Letters*, iii. 1271; Grey mss, Grey to Howick, 24 Nov. 1826. [8] *Croker Pprs.* i. 331. [9] Add. 51784, Holland to C.R. Fox, 17 Feb. 1827. [10] *The Times*, 10, 20 Mar. 1827. [11] *Ellenborough Diary*, i. 322-3, 327, 328, 330, 400, 402, 406; *The Times*, 21, 23 Mar. 1829. [12] *Cockburn Letters*, 228-9. [13] *Caledonian Mercury*, 28, 30 Apr., 5, 12 May 1831. [14] Add. 51836. [15] Orkney Archives, Balfour mss D2/8/13, Traill to W. Balfour, 8 Oct. [1831]. [16] Add. 51573, Spring Rice to Holland, 27 Jan.; Hatherton diary, 29 Jan. [1832]. [17] *The Times*, 23 Oct., 18 Dec. 1838; *Raikes Jnl.* iii. 341; *Gent. Mag.* (1839), i. 94-95. [18] PROB 11/1905/19; IR26/1513/24.

D.R.F.

FERRAND, Walker (1780–1835), of Harden Grange, nr. Bingley, Yorks.

TRALEE	1831–1832

b. 5 June 1780, 2nd s. of John Ferrand (*d.* 1790) of Stockton and Barnard Castle, co. Dur. and Sarah, da. of Edward Dale, collector of customs, of Stockton. *m.* (1) 5 Sept. 1805,[1] his cos. Katherine Maria (*d.* 15 Feb. 1827),[2] da. and h. of Col. William Twiss of Myrtle Grove, Yorks., *s.p.*; (2) 13 Jan. 1829,[3] Margaret, da. of John Moss, banker of Liverpool, of Otterspool, Lancs., *s.p. d.* 20 Sept. 1835.

Ensign 2 Ft. 1799, lt. 1800, capt. 1804; capt. 67 Ft. 1806; capt. 128 Ft. (half-pay) 1807-*d.*

Lt.-col. Bradford local militia.

Ferrand, who was presumably named after his paternal grandmother's father George Walker, vicar of Stockton in the mid-eighteenth century, belonged to a Yorkshire family, though his immediate ancestors had resided in Durham. His elder brother Edward, who succeeded their father in 1790, resettled his branch of the family in the West Riding on inheriting, from his kinsman Benjamin Ferrand (*d.* 1803), the estate at St. Ives, near Bingley.[4] The neighbouring mansion of Harden Grange was apparently given over to the use of this Member, who spent heavily on building extensions and planting ornamental gardens.[5] He had entered the army in 1799, serving for a while on the continent, and retired on half-pay, having acted as a brigade major, in 1807. He married the daughter of another officer in 1805 and became a country gentleman, serving on the commission of the peace and in the Bradford local militia.

It is not known whether Ferrand had had earlier ambitions to enter Parliament, but he was returned unopposed for Tralee at the general election of 1831, presumably having purchased the seat from Sir Edward Denny*.[6] He voted against the second reading of the Grey ministry's reintroduced reform bill, 6 July, several times for adjourning the proceedings on it, 12 July, for using the 1831 census to determine the boroughs in schedules A and B, 19 July, and to postpone consideration of the partial disfranchisement of Chippenham, 27 July. He presented and endorsed the Kerry petition for the grant to the Kildare Place Society, 26 July. Although the speech was attributed to his near namesake Robert Farrand, it was no doubt he who on 5 Aug. called for the proposed constituency of Bradford to cover the full extent of the town and doubted that the bill's provisions would satisfy its inhabitants' demands for radical reforms. As 'Mr. Ferrand', he briefly urged higher penalties for trespass under the game bill, 8 Aug. He divided against the passage of the reform bill, 21 Sept., and the second reading of the Scottish bill, 23 Sept. He voted against the second reading of the revised reform bill, 17 Dec. 1831. Although he sided with ministers in the almost unanimous majority against limiting the polling in boroughs of under 1,200 voters to one day, 15 Feb., he divided with opposition against the enfranchisement of Tower Hamlets, 28 Feb., the third reading of the bill, 22 Mar., and the second reading of the Irish measure, 25 May 1832. His only other known votes were against the Russian-Dutch loan, 26 Jan., 12 July 1832. He was one of the original members of the Carlton Club that year.

He relinquished Tralee, where the late patron's heir had ambitions of his own, at the general election of 1832, when he probably did not attempt to stand again for the Commons. However, in January 1835 he was chosen by the agent of the former Tory cabinet minister Lord Westmorland, lord lieutenant of Northamptonshire, to offer at the last minute as a Conservative for Peterborough, where Lord Fitzwilliam, like his father before him, had a preponderating influence. He entered the town on the eve of the contest and put up a spirited fight, but finished in third place behind the sitting Liberal Members. In a parting address, he claimed to have received 281 votes (including 89 plumps) out of the nearly 600 electors polled and congratulated the independent electors on having commenced a campaign to liberate the borough. His charges of widespread intimidation were denied by his successful opponents Sir Robert Heron* and John Fazakerley*, who retorted that it was Ferrand, not he, who had resorted to irregular practices.[7] He voted for John Stuart Wortley* against the Liberal Lord Morpeth* in the by-election for the West Riding of Yorkshire in May 1835.[8]

Ferrand died, 'warmly attached to Conservative politics', in October 1835.[9] By his will, dated 4 Dec. 1834 with one codicil, he made provision for his second wife (d. 1846) and left his estate and personalty sworn under a total of £61,000 (in the provinces of Canterbury and York) in trust to the family.[10] Harden Grange and, on the death of Edward Ferrand in March 1837, St. Ives both passed to their sister Sarah, the widow of Currer Fothergill Busfeild (d. 1832) of Cottingley Bridge, whose elder brother William Busfeild of Upwood was Liberal Member for Bradford, 1837-51. Sarah's eldest son and heir William, who changed his surname to Ferrand in 1837 and lived at St. Ives (as Harden Grange was renamed), was Conservative Member for Knaresborough, 1841-7, and Devonport, 1863-6, and gained a considerable working class following as a prominent factory reformer.[11]

[1] *Gent. Mag.* (1805), ii. 874. [2] Ibid. (1827), i. 381. [3] IGI (Lancs.). [4] *Burke Commoners*, iv. 700; J. Foster, *Peds. of Yorks. Fams.* i *sub* Ferrand. [5] H. Speight, *Old Bingley*, 178, 361. [6] *Dublin Evening Post*, 12 May 1831. [7] *The Times*, 6, 7, 10 Jan.; *Northampton Mercury*, 10, 17, 31 Jan. 1835. [8] *Yorks. (W. Riding) Pollbook* (May 1835), 207. [9] *Bradford Observer*, 24 Sept. 1835; *Gent. Mag.* (1835), ii. 558. [10] PROB 11/1857/90; IR26/1415/86. [11] Speight, 361-2, 364-6; *Oxford DNB sub* William Ferrand.

S.M.F.

FETHERSTON, *alias* **FETHERSTON HAUGH**, **Sir George Ralph**, 3rd bt. (1784-1853), of Ardagh House, co. Longford.

Co. LONGFORD   15 Oct. 1819-1830

b. 4 June 1784, 1st s. of Thomas Fetherston[†], 2nd bt., MP [I], of Ardagh and Catherine, da. of George Boleyn Whitney of New Pass, co. Westmeath. *educ.* Newcome's, Hackney; Trinity Coll. Camb. 1801; L. Inn 1804. *m.* 22 Oct. 1821, Frances Elizabeth, da. of Richard Solly of Walthamstow, Essex, *s.p. suc.* fa. as 3rd bt. 19 July 1819. *d.* 12 July 1853.

Sheriff, co. Longford 1834-5
Maj. Longford militia 1810, lt.-col. 1833-d.

Fetherston, who was described by a local Tory in 1830 as a 'very proper man', continued to sit for county Longford on the interest of the dowager Lady Rosse, by whom he had been returned in 1819 as his father's successor with the backing of the other Member, Lord Forbes.[1] An indifferent attender, who is not known to have spoken in debate, when present he voted 'in general' with the Liverpool ministry, by whom he was listed as seeking promotions for Major Thomas Edgeworth of Kilshrewly, county Longford and one Tyrrell, who in 1817 had been placed on the assessor's list, as well as a clerkship for one Given.[2] He divided against economies in revenue collection, 4 July 1820, and in defence of ministers' conduct towards Queen Caroline, 6 Feb. 1821. He voted against Catholic relief, 28 Feb. 1821, 30 Apr. 1822, 1 Mar., 10 May, 21 Apr., and the Irish freeholders bill, 26 Apr. 1825. He was granted six weeks' leave on urgent private business, 4 May 1821. His only other known votes in the 1820 Parliament were with government against more extensive tax reductions, 11 Feb., but in the minority for inquiry into diplomatic expenditure, 15 May 1822, and the hostile majority for inquiry into the prosecution of the Dublin Orange rioters, 22 Apr. 1823.

At the 1826 general election he offered again, the Catholic press describing him as 'an Orangeman, though not perhaps of the extreme hue', and was returned unopposed.[3] He voted against Catholic relief, 6 Mar. 1827, 12 May 1828, and was granted a month's leave after serving on an election committee, 15 Mar. 1827. He divided against repeal of the Test Acts, 26 Feb. 1828. Speaking at the inaugural meeting of the Longford Brunswick Club, of which he was a founder member, 3 Nov. 1828, he stated that 'from his youth his principles were those which placed the House of Brunswick on the throne and he would carry those principles with him to the grave', denounced the 'evil counsels of designing demagogues', but called for 'firmness and moderation'.[4] He was part of the grand jury which, to the 'utter astonishment' of a local prosecutor, refused to indict an 'Orange mob' which had opened fire on Catholics at Ballymahon that month.[5] In February 1829 he was listed by Planta, the Wellington ministry's patronage secretary, as 'opposed' to emancipation but likely to support securities when the principle was carried. He presented hostile constituency petitions, 23 Feb., and voted accordingly, 6, 18, 23, 27, 30 Mar. 1829. He was granted a month's leave to attend the assizes, 8 Mar. 1830. His only other recorded vote was for repeal of the Irish coal duties, 13 May 1830.

At the 1830 general election he offered again, but Lady Rosse having put up a second candidate, shortly before the nomination he withdrew from the probable contest, boasting that 'in the worst of times I never courted popularity by a desertion of those principles which I conscientiously entertained, nor did I ever hesitate to oppose any measure which I thought injurious to the interests of my country'.[6] He died in July 1853.[7] His title and family estates passed to his brother the Rev. Thomas, and on his death the following month to his nephew Thomas (1824-69).

[1] NLI, Farnham mss 18613 (4), C. Fox to H. Maxwell, 22 June 1830; Add. 38575, f. 34. [2] *Black Bk.* (1823), 155; *Session of Parl. 1825*, p. 463. [3] *Dublin Evening Post*, 20, 22 June 1826. [4] *Westmeath Jnl.* 6 Nov. 1828. [5] *Dublin Evening Post*, 10 Jan.; *The Times*, 15 Jan. 1829. [6] *Dublin Evening Post*, 29 July 1830. [7] *Gent. Mag.* (1853), ii. 530.

P.J.S.

FFOLKES, Sir William John Henry Browne, 2nd bt. (1786–1860), of Hillington, King's Lynn, Norf.

NORFOLK	1830–1832
NORFOLK WEST	1832–1837

b. 30 Aug. 1786, o. surv. s. of Sir Martin Browne Ffolkes, 1st bt.*, and Fanny, da. and coh. of Sir John Turner, 3rd bt.†, of Warham. *educ.* Harrow 1801-3; Jesus, Camb. 1805. *m.* 21 Apr. 1818, Charlotte Philippa, da. of Dominick Geoffrey Browne of Castle Macgarrett, co. Mayo, 4s. (1 *d.v.p.*) 2da. *suc.* fa. as 2nd. bt. 11 Dec. 1821. *d.* 24 Mar. 1860.

Sheriff, Norf. 1828-9.

Ffolkes's father, who, with the acquiescence of the corporation, sat for King's Lynn on his wife's interest, intended that he should succeeded him in the borough's representation as an independent country gentleman. He shared his father's interest in Fenland development, and on his marriage to his kinswoman Charlotte Browne he settled at Congham Lodge, near King's Lynn, where his failure to support the borough's costly campaign against the 1818 Eau Brink Act angered the corporation, who accused him of putting his interests as a Marshland proprietor first.[1] He officiated at Norfolk Foxite dinners in 1820 and 1821 and declared his candidature for King's Lynn at the January 1822 by-election occasioned by his father's death, but was thwarted by the corporation's choice of another Whig with Marshland interests, Lord William Bentinck*, to whose locum Lord Titchfield he deferred, promising to '*stand a contest whenever an opportunity may occur, if the smallest hope of success can be entertained*'.[2] Assisted by his relations (his sister Lucretia and cousin James Browne*), he contested the borough unsuccessfully on the anti-corporation or independent interest in June 1822, March 1824 and at the general election of 1826, before relinquishing the attempt.[3] He remained an active Eau Brink commissioner and acquitted himself well as sheriff, 1828-9.[4] At the general election of 1830 he stayed away from King's Lynn, where he was put in nomination and defeated in a token poll; and, as requested by the yeomen, he stood with the sitting Member Thomas Coke for the county on the Whig interest, unseating the Tory Wodehouse without a

poll at a cost of £1,184 8s. 7d.[5] As at King's Lynn, he declared strongly for retrenchment and parliamentary reform, adding that he had no intention of mortgaging his estates, 'his family's future', or of soliciting preferment to finance a contest.[6] His friend Edmund Peel*, one of many surprised at the news, hoped that

> the measures of the ministry may be such as to allow you to give them your support in important matters. I trust I may not have the pain of seeing your name coupled with that of 'Newcastle' or Harry Inglis, for the mere purpose of overturning the duke of Wellington's government.[7]

Before Parliament met he addressed dinners at Great Yarmouth, King's Lynn, Norwich and Wisbech, and attended the county meeting requisitioned by his yeoman supporters to petition for repeal of the malt duties, 19 Oct. 1830.[8]

The ministry counted Ffolkes among their 'foes' and he divided against them on the civil list, 15 Nov. 1830. No parliamentary speeches by him are reported in this period, but he attended to local legislation and county business and presented and endorsed numerous Norfolk petitions against slavery, 9, 16 Nov., and the duty on coastwise coal, 13 Dec. 1830, 21 Feb. 1831, for a revision of tithes, 10, 21 Feb., 16 Mar., and for parliamentary reform, 10, 26 Feb., 2, 19, 21, 25, 28 Mar., 19 Apr. 1831. He voted for the Grey ministry's reform bill at its second reading, 22 Mar., and against Gascoyne's wrecking amendment, 19 Apr. 1831. His opposition to the 1831 Eau Brink bill (a casualty of the dissolution), which he presented petitions against, 23, 25, 29 Mar., pleased his friends in King's Lynn and the Marshland and, heeding their advice, he declared early for the county and solicited the support of the leading yeomen at the ensuing general election. Standing on his 'past conduct' as a reformer, he came in unopposed with Coke.[9]

On 29 June 1831 Ffolkes ordered returns of all criminal informations filed against justices of the peace in England and Wales since 1820. He voted for the second reading of the reintroduced reform bill, 6 July, and against adjournment, 12 July, and using the 1831 census to determine borough disfranchisements, 19 July. He generally gave steady support to its details, and his wayward votes against the proposed division of counties, 11 Aug., against granting county votes to freeholders in cities corporate, 17 Aug., and for Lord Chandos's amendment to enfranchise £50 tenants-at-will, 18 Aug., pleased his Norfolk supporters and were well received in the local press.[10] He voted for the bill's passage, 21 Sept., the second reading of the Scottish measure, 23 Sept., and Lord Ebrington's confidence motion, 10 Oct. He had been fêted at the

King's Lynn reform meeting, 1 Oct., and was again cheered when he spoke briefly at the county meeting as seconder of their address requesting the king to support the bill and the ministry, 19 Nov. 1831.[11] He voted for the revised bill at its second reading, 17 Dec. 1831, divided steadily for its details, and voted for the third reading, 22 Mar. 1832, and the address calling on the king to appoint only ministers who would carry it unimpaired, 10 May. He endorsed King's Lynn's petition of satisfaction at the restoration of the Grey ministry, 22 May, and presented another the next day from Diss requesting the withholding of supplies until the reform bill became law. He voted for the Irish reform bill at its second reading, 25 May, and against amending the Scottish measure, 1 June. He divided with government on the Dublin election controversy, 23 Aug. 1831 (but was absent from the division on the censure motion that day), the Russian-Dutch loan, 26 Jan., 16, 20 July, and relations with Portugal, 9 Feb. 1832.

Browne Ffolkes was appointed to the select committee on the use of molasses in breweries and distilleries, 30 June, and presented petitions against the practice from his constituents, 22 July, 2, 10 Aug. 1831. His minority vote for remission of the duties on quarantined vessels, 6 Sept. 1831, was welcomed in the Norfolk ports.[12] Marshland petitions against the Walpole enclosure and drainage bill were entrusted to him, 11 May, and he presented others for repeal of the duty on fire insurance, 23 May 1832. His votes for the immediate appointment of a select committee on colonial slavery, 24 May, and to make coroners' inquests public, 20 June, accorded with constituency opinion and assisted him at the general election in December 1832, when, after canvassing assiduously he came in unopposed for the new West Norfolk constituency with his fellow Liberal Sir Jacob Astley.[13]

He survived a contest in 1835 but was defeated at the general election of 1837 and declined requisitions to stand for King's Lynn in 1841 and Norfolk East in 1847.[14] He died at Hillington in March 1860, remembered as a competent Member of Parliament and able chairman of Swaffham quarter sessions, the Eau Brink commissioners, the Norfolk Estuary Company and the projected Lynn and Ely railway, in which he unwisely invested £20,000.[15] His will, dated 6 Apr. 1854, provided for his wife (d. 26 Dec. 1882), children and grandchildren. His eldest son Martin had predeceased him after being struck by lightning, 24 July 1849, and he was succeeded in the baronetcy and estates by his twelve-year-old grandson William Hovell Ffolkes(1847-1912), Liberal Member for King's Lynn, 1880-5.[16]

[1] H. Hillen, *Hist. King's Lynn* (1978), ii. 778-81. [2] *Norf. Chron.* 29 Jan. 1820, 13, 20 Jan., 22, 29 Dec. 1821; *Norwich, Yarmouth and Lynn Courier*, 12 Jan. 1822. [3] *Bury and Norwich Post*, 14 June; *Norwich Mercury*, 17 June 1826. See also KING'S LYNN; *Oxford DNB sub* Sir Edward West. [4] Norf. RO MC50/99; *Norwich Mercury*, 22 Jan., 4 June; *Huntingdon, Bedford and Cambridge Weekly Jnl.* 28 May 1825; Nottingham Univ. Lib. Portland mss PwJe 102, 490; Norf. RO NRS 7958, shrievalty accts. [5] Norf. RO NRS 8741; 8753; MC50/74/2-10; Add. 51593, Coke to Holland, 25, 30 July; *Norwich Mercury*, 24 July, 14, 21 Aug.; *The Times*, 4, 5, 9 Aug. 1830. [6] *Norf. Chron.* 31 July, 7 Aug.; *Norwich Mercury*, 31 July, 7 Aug. 1830. [7] Norf. RO NRS 8741, Peel to Ffolkes, 3 Sept. 1830. [8] *The Times*, 18, 25, 26 Oct. 1830. [9] Norf. RO NRS 8740; *East Anglian*, 26 Apr., 3, 10 May; *Norwich Mercury*, 30 Apr., 7 May; *The Times*, 9 May 1831. [10] *Norwich Mercury*, 20 Aug.; *Norf. Chron.* 20 Aug.; *East Anglian*, 23 Aug.; *Bury and Norwich Post*, 31 Aug. 1831. [11] *Norf. Chron.* 3 Oct., 21 Nov.; *Bury and Norwich Post*, 23 Nov.; *Norwich Mercury*, 26 Nov. 1831. [12] *The Times*, 3 Oct. 1831. [13] Norf. RO NRS 8740, memo. for abolition of slavery; *Norwich Mercury*, 26 May, 2, 17 June; *The Times*, 30 Oct., 20 Dec. 1832. [14] Norf. RO NRS 8753; MC50/74/21B; *The Times*, 8, 15, 19, 24 Jan. 1835, 6 Mar., 3, 17, 20, 21 July 1837. [15] *The Times*, 29 Mar.; *Lynn Advertiser*, 31 Mar. 1860; Hillen, ii. 597, 783. [16] *Gent. Mag.* (1849), ii. 331; (1860), i. 529.

M.M.E.

FFOLKES *see also* **BROWNE FFOLKES**

FIFE, 4th Earl [I] *see* **DUFF, James**

FINCH, George (1794–1870), of Burley-on-the-Hill, nr. Oakham, Rutland.

LYMINGTON	1820–25 May 1821
STAMFORD	1832–1837
RUTLAND	14 Feb. 1846–1847

b. 2 Sept. 1794, illegit. s. of George Finch, 9th earl of Winchilsea (*d.* 1826), and Mrs. Phoebe Thompson (formerly Thackray) of Brompton, Mdx.[1] *educ.* Harrow 1805-11; Trinity Coll. Camb. 1811; M. Temple 1817. *m.* (1) 7 June 1820,[2] Jane (*d.* 13 Feb. 1822),[3] da. of R.-Adm. John Richard Delap Halliday (afterwards Tollemache) of Cumberland Place, Mdx., *s.p.*; (2) 22 Oct. 1832, Lady Louisa Elizabeth Somerset, da. of Henry Charles Somerset†, 6th duke of Beaufort, 2s. 2da. *suc.* fa. to Burley 1826. *d.* 29 June 1870.

Sheriff, Rutland 1829-30.

In 1807, Joseph Farington recorded this bulletin from a recent visitor to Burley:

> Lord Winchilsea does not reside there much as it would be too expensive for his circumstances, but lives in a high style when he is there. He is a bachelor ... and very agreeable in his manners ... His Lordship visits a lady, Mrs. Thomson, who resides at Brompton at a beautiful villa ... but always returns at night to his house in South St. He has a son, 13 years of age, who is called Finch or Thomson, and was with him at Burleigh.[4]

Winchilsea, 'a nobleman of the old school', whose mother was governess to the royal family for 30 years, was a favourite of George III and held household posts as a lord of the bedchamber, 1777-1812, and groom of the stole, 1804-12. By seconding Charles Lennox in his duel with the duke of York in 1789 he incurred the lasting displeasure of the prince of Wales, and after the establishment of the regency he was seldom seen at Court.[5] His adopted son George entered Harrow in 1805 under the name of Thompson, but subsequently took that of Finch. He left Cambridge without taking a degree and his admission to the Middle Temple did not presage a legal career.

At the general election of 1820 he was returned for Lymington by its patron Sir Harry Neale*, who had served in the royal household with his father. On 6 June 1820 he took six weeks' leave of absence, but in 1821 he proved a reliable supporter of the Liverpool ministry, with whom he voted in defence of their conduct towards Queen Caroline, 6 Feb., and against repeal of the additional malt duty, 3 Apr., electoral disqualification of ordnance officials, 12 Apr., and parliamentary reform, 9 May. He voted for Catholic relief, 28 Feb. He is not known to have spoken in debate in this period and in May 1821 he vacated his seat for its previous occupant. (He was subsequently returned three times to the reformed House.) In February 1825 the prominent huntsman Lord Frederick Cavendish Bentinck* noted with approval that Finch had 'taken to the chase'.[6] On Winchilsea's death in 1826 the earldom passed to his Ultra Tory nephew George William Finch Hatton, but the bulk of his property was not entailed, and Finch was the major beneficiary of his will, inheriting Burley and other estates, together with 'a large fortune'.[7]

[1] P. Finch, *Hist. Burley*, i. 339: PROB 11/1716/468. [2] *Reg. St. George, Hanover Square*. [3] *Gent. Mag.* (1822), i. 284. [4] *Farington Diary*, viii. 3137. [5] *Raikes Jnl*. iii. 51-52. [6] Nottingham Univ. Lib. Portland mss PwL 11/1. [7] *Raikes Jnl*. iii. 51-52; PROB 11/1716/468.

D.R.F.

FINCHETT MADDOCK, John (?1775–1858), of 9 Abbey Square, Chester and Cae Gwyn, Caern.

CHESTER   18 May 1832–1832

b. ?1775, o.s. of Thomas Finchett, glover, of Chester and w. Elizabeth *née* Cooper. *m.* 18 Sept. 1803, Mary Francis, 1s. 4da. (3 *d.v.p.*).[1] *suc.* Richard Maddock to Richmond Hill, Caern. 1823 and took additional name of Maddock by royal lic. 12 Feb. 1824. *d.* 24 Jan. 1858.

Town clerk, Chester 1817-57.

No official record of the birth of Finchett, as he was first known, has been found, but he was raised and educated in Chester, where his family, previously from the Cheshire parish of Helsall, were established in trade by the early eighteenth century.[2] He was a schoolfellow and close correspondent of the Stockport poet Robert Farren Cheetham (1779-1800); and their 127 letters record how Finchett, who on 5 Feb. 1793 was articled as a clerk to the Chester notary Robert Baxter, forwarded poems to the Chester and Manchester newspapers and *Gentleman's Magazine* on Cheetham's behalf, occasionally, as requested, adding his own initials of J.F. He was perturbed by wartime censorship and the intolerance and drunkenness associated with politics in Chester, where what in 1796 he termed 'the rage and fury of a deluded aristocratical party' ran high. He was admitted as an attorney at Chester assizes in April and of king's bench on 5 May 1798, and passed 'nearly twelvemonths' in the office of his kinsman, the London attorney Thomas Finchett, at 2 Great Prescott Street, where he enjoyed 'clean lodgings' and visits to the Commons. The squalor of the West End disgusted him and he 'tired of London and revere it not for the professional improvement I am likely to acquire'.[3] He practised in Chester, where his marriage in 1803 to Mary, some six years his senior, created a stir,[4] and became treasurer to the militia volunteers and to the Tory Church and King Club, of which his brother-in-law Alderman Thomas Francis was secretary.[5] At the general election of 1812 he was an agent for Thomas Grosvenor*, whose cousin the 2nd earl Grosvenor sanctioned his permanent appointment in 1817 as town clerk; he had acted as deputy since 1813.[6] He testified at length before the parliamentary committees on the Chester election petitions of 1818 and 1820 which found for the Grosvenors, acted for their partisans on the corporation when civil actions were brought against them and joined the Cheshire and North Wales Whig Club established under Lord Grosvenor's presidency in 1821.[7] In June that year he inherited his father's Chester properties, which he sold for £2,100 in 1827.[8] He was also coheir and executor of the vindictive will of the attorney Richard Maddock of Horton, Tarvin, Cheshire and Richmond Hill, Caernarfon, in compliance with which he and his family, who inherited Richmond Hill (Cae Gwyn), took the additional surname of Maddock.[9]

Finchett Maddock brought his only son Thomas into his practice, and they were solicitors for the abortive 1831 Chester-Birkenhead and Chester-Tranmere railway bills and the 1832 Dee Bridge bill, which extended the completion time for the 'Grosvenor bridge' and remained under consideration when the death on 19 Apr. of the Whig reformer Foster Cunliffe Offley produced a vacancy in the representation of Chester.[10] The corporation opposed the candidature of the radical Whig Edward Davies Davenport* and put forward Finchett Maddock, who, after deferring briefly to Sir Charles Bulkeley Egerton, the unsuccessful candidate in 1826, defeated Davenport in a three-day poll. He issued no notices, but was belatedly described as a staunch supporter of the Grey ministry's reform bill.[11] He made no known parliamentary speeches, but he voted for the second reading of the Irish reform bill, 25 May, against a Conservative amendment to the Scottish measure, 1 June, and divided with government on the Russian-Dutch loan, 12 July 1832. That month his portrait was painted by William Jones and engraved by Charles Turner.[12]

Finchett Maddock's candidature for Chester as a Liberal in December 1832, when he campaigned for peace and retrenchment, and against slavery, monopolies and the corn laws, was vigorously opposed. 'The wealth and respectability of the city' backed him, but his detractors criticized his humble origins, mediocrity and connections with the Tories and a corrupt corporation, which, coupled with his abstemious refusal to spend on drink and rumours of his late resignation, contributed to his heavy defeat by two other Liberals.[13] He did not stand for Parliament again, but he was a founder member in 1834 of the Cestrian masonic lodge and remained town clerk until August 1857.[14] When he died at his residence in Chester's Abbey Square in January 1858, he was clerk to the magistrates (worth £500 a year), the Dee Bridge Trust, the assessed and income tax commissioners and several turnpike trusts, and acted for the Chester Junction Railway Company.[15] He was buried with his wife (d. 1839) in the family vault at Eastham, Cheshire. He left £105 to his daughter Elizabeth Rufford and the remainder of his estate to his son, who died unmarried, 5 Dec. 1892, having endowed the Finchett-Maddock exhibition at Oxford or Cambridge for pupils of the King's School, Chester, and devised the bulk of his estates, worth £39,120, to his business partner Henry Moss, who took the name of Finchett Maddock by deed poll, 13 Jan. 1893.[16]

[1] Cheshire and Chester Archives EDD 3913/12/2-3; P195/5/1. [2] Ibid. CR38/60. [3] Ibid. TCP7/1, corresp. of John Finchett and Robert Farren Cheetham, 1792-1801; Cheshire and Chester Archives H.S. 111. [4] Ibid. H.S.112-14, 130, 134. [5] Ibid. CR115/2. [6] Grosvenor mss 9/10/35-43; 9/12/8-9; Cheshire and Chester Archives AB/5, 2 May 1817. [7] Report of Procs. at Chester Election (1819); (1820); Report on Chester Corporation (1827); (1829); Grosvenor mss 9/126; Cheshire and Chester Archives TCC/141; TNA KB28/502; The Times, 6 Sept. 1821, 21 May 1827, 11 Oct. 1828. [8] Cheshire and Chester Archives CR38/59-60. [9] NLW wills

B/1824/105; The Times, 31 July 1815. [10] CJ, lxxxvi. 399, 425, 435, 481, 528, 547, 607; lxxxvii. 102, 199, 270, 331; Chester Chron. 8 Mar. 1831; Chester Courant, 27 Mar., 24 Apr. 1832. [11] The Times, 26 Apr.; Chester Chron. 27 Apr., 11, 18 May; Chester Courant, 1, 22 May 1832. [12] Cheshire and Chester Archives CR60/4/14. [13] Chester Chron. 28 Sept; The Times, 9, 18 Oct., 4 Dec.; Chester Courant, 13, 27 Nov., 4, 11, 18 Dec. 1832. [14] S.L. Coulthurst, Cestrian Lodge no. 425, pp. 9, 51 and passim; Cheshire and Chester Archives CB1, 14 Aug., 11 Sept. 1857. [15] Cheshire and Chester Archives TCP/7/92, 97, 232-9; The Times, 5 July 1847; Cheshire and Chester Archives CB1, 14 Aug. 1857; The Times, 29 Jan.; Chester Chron. 30 Jan. 1858. [16] Cheshire and Chester Archives P195/5/1, 2; G.L. Fenwick, Hist. Chester, 360; Chester Courant, 7 Dec. 1892; The Times, 16 Jan.; will proved 20 Jan. 1893.

M.M.E.

FINLAY, Kirkman (1773–1842), of Queen Street, Glasgow and Castle Toward, Argyll.

| GLASGOW BURGHS | 1812–1818 |
| MALMESBURY | 1818–20 June 1820 |

b. Apr. 1773, 2nd s. of James Finlay (d. 1790), merchant, of Glasgow and w. Abigail née Whirry of Whitehaven, Cumb. educ. Glasgow g.s. m. 7 Sept. 1795, Janet, da. of Robert Struthers, brewer, of Glasgow, 6s. (2 d.v.p.) 5da. (3 d.v.p.). d. 4 Mar. 1842.

Bailie, Provan 1801, Glasgow 1804; ld. provost, Glasgow 1812-14, 1818, pres. chamber of commerce 1812, 1816-17, 1823-4, 1829-30; rect. Glasgow Univ. 1819-20.

Lt. R. Glasgow vols. 1796, capt. 1797, maj. 1807.

Gov. Forth and Clyde Navigation 1814; dir. Glasgow Fire Insurance Co. 1803-11; dir. (extraordinary) Bank of Scotland 1821-d.

In 1795, when he was 21 and already embarked on his spectacularly successful entrepreneurial career, Finlay reproached himself in his diary for the 'petulancy of my temper':

The too great indulgence I received from my mother, and my early introduction to the world, where my abilities have been treated with more regard than they deserve, have given me a self sufficiency, a contempt for the opinions, conduct and amusements of others which I have long in vain endeavoured to correct. I believe, however, that I have got on the road to amendment, and I hope that upon every new inspection of my mind I shall find my respect for others increase. In companies and public assemblies my great ambition to shine and to appear a man of parts very frequently betrays me into many inconsistencies, and into an unpardonable loquacity. This fault I have formed many resolutions to amend [but] notwithstanding all my determination I find that my natural propensity is too great, and being flattered by the applause of the giddy, I very probably obtain a praise for spirit at the expense of sense.

In 1832 he let his fourth surviving son Alexander Struthers Finlay (1806-86), who was about to take his place in the Bombay trading house of Ritchie, Stewart and Company established by Finlay 16 years previously, into the secret of his success in commerce:

> I early saw the necessity for the most close attention to business ... I was as fair as I could be, also anxious to oblige and serve others, and in this way I was fortunate in obtaining the reputation of steadiness and attention at an age when these qualities are not always to be found ... There is nothing advances a mercantile man so much as character, and this is to be obtained not only by the greatest attention, industry and regularity of conduct, information and intelligence in business, but also by that friendly and obliging disposition of mind and behaviour which wins the good opinion and interest of all by whom you are surrounded.[1]

Finlay, a disciple of Adam Smith, was one of the pioneers of the expansion and diversification of Glasgow commerce after the collapse of the tobacco trade with America. From the 1790s he built up an extensive (and during the French wars illegal) network of trade in cotton goods to Europe and later to the Americas and the East, the latter after leading the Glasgow merchants' campaign against the East India Company's monopoly in 1812. His acquisition of cotton mills at Catrine, Ayrshire, Balfron, Stirlingshire and Deanston, Perthshire between 1792 and 1808 made him the leading manufacturer in Scotland. The Glasgow trading house of James Finlay and Company founded by his father developed branches in Heligoland, Dusseldorf, Gibraltar, London (Finlay, Hodgson and Company of 8 St. Helen's Place, Bishopsgate) and Liverpool, as well as Bombay. Finlay, a leading figure in the commercial and political life of Glasgow, and the independent and outspoken Member for its district of burghs in the 1818 Parliament, bought land at Achenwillan, Argyllshire, on the peninsula between the Firth of Clyde and Loch Fyne, for £14,050. He improved and added to the estate and, in what he later came to regret as an act of 'extravagant' folly inspired by 'pride and vanity', built the imposing residence of Castle Toward overlooking Rothesay Bay.[2]

In the 1818 Parliament Finlay had sat for Malmesbury as the nominee of the Whig 4th earl of Rosebery, who had bought the return from the boroughmonger Joseph Pitt*. At the 1820 general election he 'reluctantly' declined to stand for Glasgow Burghs, where the ministerialist Archibald Campbell* of Blythswood seemed impregnable.[3] He turned down a suggestion from the lord advocate, Sir William Rae*, who told Lord Melville, the Liverpool ministry's Scottish manager that he 'would go with us on all great questions', that he might try Stirling Burghs. There was support for him

also in Haddington Burghs, but in the event he came in again for Malmesbury.[4] He had turned alarmist in the wake of Peterloo, and at the Glasgow meeting of merchants and manufacturers, 11 Apr. 1820, he moved their resolution not to employ any person implicated in the recently thwarted radical insurrection and called for a union of 'firmness, prudence, assiduity and discretion' among employers to help 'eradicate the poison which had been so widely and deeply infused'.[5] In the House, 28 Apr., speaking from the government side, he confirmed the difficulties of 'the distressed population' of the Glasgow area and urged ministers to give financial aid 'unconditionally'. On 4 May he secured a return of information on Scottish spirit distillation, 1798-1818.[6] He was named to the select committee on the Scottish royal burghs that day. He divided against government on the civil list, 5, 8 May. On the 16th he presented and endorsed the petition of Glasgow chamber of commerce for 'the establishment of a free trade, and the removal of all restrictions upon commercial imports and exports' regardless of foreign reciprocity. Having recanted the support for protective corn laws which had landed him in trouble with the Glasgow mob in 1816, he argued that 'if it should be found that the history of our commercial policy was a tissue of mistakes and false notions ... that policy should be given up, and a permanent system of commercial regulations established in its stead'. He advocated also revision of the revenue and bankruptcy laws, inquiry into extents in aid and repeal of the usury laws. On 16 June 1820 he presented a petition from Grangemouth merchants involved in the timber trade for relaxation of the prohibitive duties on Baltic produce and applauded the government's advance of £500,000 to deal with hardship caused by Irish bank failures. He brought up the report of the committee on the Forth and Clyde Navigation bill.[7] Four days later he vacated his seat. In 1826 he told Hudson Gurney* that he 'might have done wrong in quitting Malmesbury, but [had] recovered health by it'.[8]

Finlay corresponded voluminously on commercial matters with the Liverpool merchant and ship owner John Gladstone, Member for New Woodstock in the 1820 Parliament, using him as a conduit to transmit his views to Canning, foreign secretary from September 1822, and his acolyte Huskisson, president of the board of trade from February 1823, when he replaced Canning as Member for Liverpool.[9] Huskisson valued his opinions as a friend of the liberalization of trade, consulted him on such matters and in the House, 25 Mar. 1825, when he proposed further tariff reforms, quoted a letter of 18 Feb. from Finlay, who 'unites to great practical knowledge a vigorous understanding', in favour of the 'sound principles of free commercial intercourse'.[10] After 'philosophising and world despising' at Castle Toward in early 1826 Finlay, who to Gladstone deplored the 'noise and nonsense' of Tory attacks on ministers' progressive commercial policy, gave evidence to the Commons select committee on Scottish and Irish small bank notes, 22 Mar., when he commended the current arrangement of 'a solid paper currency, convertible into gold'. A 'most interesting conversation' with Huskisson confirmed his admiration for the minister's 'fine ... system of mercantile policy'.[11] While he had no thoughts of coming in 'again for Glasgow [Burghs]' he evidently hankered after a return to the Commons and got Gladstone to sound Huskisson, who knew of a possible opening at the impending general election, provided Finlay favoured Catholic relief (which he did), but correctly guessed that it was probably too late to clinch a deal.[12] At the 1830 general election Finlay offered for Glasgow Burghs, 'from a persuasion', as he told Glasgow council, 'that I could better serve the great India and China questions *in* than *out* of the House', though Gladstone's son Thomas thought he 'runs considerable risk of injuring his health by going into Parliament', as he had been unwell recently.[13] He was sure of the backing of Dumbarton and Rutherglen, while the sitting Member Campbell of Blythswood could count on that of Renfrew. The election turned on the vote of Glasgow, the returning borough, where, after the council had divided 16-16, Provost Alexander Garden gave his casting vote for Campbell. As Glasgow's delegate he duly voted to the same effect at the election and returned Campbell with his casting vote. After the formalities Finlay, who at the Lanarkshire election had supported the unsuccessful Whig candidate Sir John Maxwell* as a man who would be 'unshackled by government' and so 'free' to promote open trade, said he would petition on the ground that Garden's decisive vote had been illegal. Anticipating success, he declared:

> Although watchful as a guardian of the public purse and of the liberties of the people ought to be, I can never allow myself to be considered as opposed to His Majesty's government, but quite otherwise ... I ... can never desire to place implicit confidence in any ministry, much less to become one of those blind adherents by whom ruinous measures are sanctioned and supported, and the grossest of all absurdities declared and voted.

He added that the duke of Wellington was the only member of the cabinet in whom he had confidence; that he would back Hume's campaign for economy and retrenchment and support 'slow and gradual' parliamentary reform, through the enfranchisement of large towns; that he now believed that the corn laws should be repealed, and that he favoured a cautious approach to the abolition of West Indian slavery and a complete end to the East India Company's trade monopoly.[14] Tom Gladstone regarded talk of his succeeding the dead Huskisson as Member for Liverpool in September 1830 as nonsense.[15] His petition was presented on 3 Nov. and the committee appointed on 2 Dec. 1830, when he was present to observe proceedings. He remained 'very sanguine of success', but was ostensibly 'unruffled' when the decision was given in favour of Campbell. Tom Gladstone reported that he 'feels confident of success on another occasion', but commented that 'whether he would be wise or not in availing himself of it is a question'.[16] Finlay tried again at the 1831 general election. At a meeting of the Glasgow Merchants' House, 4 May, claiming to be 'worn out and exhausted by the fatigues of a contested election', he praised the Grey ministry's reform scheme as 'statesmanlike, noble and extensive' and spoke of 'the advantage of reform in point of morality'. Backed only by Glasgow, he was beaten by the popular reform candidate Joseph Dixon.[17] The deaths of his fourth son Robert in Ceylon in 1830 and of his daughters Hannah and Caroline the following year hit him hard and increased his vulnerability to despondency and remorseful introspection. Lamenting his 'wild and inconsiderate outlay' on Castle Toward, he asked God's forgiveness for 'my rashness and folly, my neglectfulness and extravagance, my pride and vanity [which] rise up constantly before my eyes, and make every moment of my life a time of torment and misery'.[18] Tom Gladstone thought in June 1831 that he 'appears to stand well for Glasgow in the reformed Parliament', but he did not make any further serious bids for the seat, though he was noted as a possible Conservative contender in 1834. In 1837 he told his son that 'we have all been disappointed by the failure of our attempts to replace the Radical Member by a Conservative ... but the destructives have been too many for us on this occasion'.[19] He took a close interest in the early political career of the rising Conservative star William Ewart Gladstone[†], whom he encouraged to master the question of children's factory hours in order to 'infuse a little common sense into the shallow and thick-headed ones by whom you are surrounded'.[20] In a *Letter to Lord Ashley on the Cotton Factory System* (1833) he argued that the existing regulations, properly enforced, would give adequate protection to children and asserted that the 'visionary and impractical' ten hours campaign, got up by itinerant 'demagogues' and sustained by well meaning but misguided men such as Thomas Sadler* and Richard Oastler, would, if successful, 'paralyse and ultimately strangle' the cotton trade (pp. 3, 4, 19). He gave evidence to the Commons select committee on manufactures, commerce and shipping, 16 May 1833.[21] In 1840 he had to borrow £50,000 from the Royal Bank to save his rural mill communities from ruin.[22] Only four months before his death at Castle Toward in March 1842 he was consulted by William Gladstone, vice-president of the board of trade in Peel's second ministry, on the Scottish corn averages and the extent of distress.[23] He was buried in Glasgow Cathedral. His nephew George Finlay, the historian of Greece, recalled him as 'a man of cheerful disposition', whose 'talents were considerable' and 'judgements sound'; while the lawyer Sir Archie Alison, who met him in the early 1830s, reckoned him to be 'the most remarkable' of the Glasgow cotton traders, 'a man highly respected for his extensive mercantile information'.[24] By his will of 10 Jan. 1840 he left his wife an annuity of £1,000 and divided the residue of his estate among his six surviving children.[25] His business was carried on by his sons James, John, Thomas and Alexander, with James and Archibald Buchanan; but Thomas and James died in 1846 and 1847 respectively and Alexander, who came into possession of Castle Toward and was Liberal Member for Argyllshire, 1857-65, retired from trade in 1848. After the death of John in 1873 no Finlay was directly involved in the concern, which became a public limited company in 1909.[26]

[1] James Finlay and Company (Glasgow, 1951), 27-28. [2] Ibid. 5-15, 26-31, 127-8; Glasgow ed. T.M. Devine and G. Jackson, i. 201-2, 204, 224-5; PP (1833), vi. 35; Oxford DNB; HP Commons, 1790-1820, iii. 746-7. [3] Glasgow Recs. x. 539-40. [4] NLS mss 11, ff. 14, 17, 24. [5] P. Berresford Ellis and S. Mac A'Ghobhainn, Scottish Insurrection of 1820 (1989), 206, 208; Glasgow Herald, 14 Apr. 1820. [6] The Times, 5 May 1820. [7] Ibid. 17 June 1820. [8] Gurney diary, 22 Mar. [1826]. [9] Add. 38746, ff. 76, 79, 87, 90, 94, 96, 111, 113. [10] Add. 38746, f. 134. [11] Add. 38747, ff. 213, 215; St. Deiniol's Lib. Glynne-Gladstone mss 276, Huskisson to J. Gladstone, 25 Mar. 1826; R. Saville, Bank of Scotland, 296-7; PP (1826), iii. 57-71. [12] Gurney diary, 22 Mar. [1826]; Add. 38748, f. 38. [13] Glasgow Recs. xi. 382-3; Glynne-Gladstone mss 195, T. to J. Gladstone, 6, 8 July; Glasgow Herald, 2 July 1830. [14] Authentic Account of Glasgow Election (1830), 3-18; Glasgow, i. 262; Glasgow Herald, 6, 13, 27 Aug. 1830; Add. 38758, f. 226. [15] Glynne-Gladstone mss 196, T. to J. Gladstone, 17 Sept. 1830. [16] CJ, lxxxvi. 19, 139-40, 146; Glynne-Gladstone mss 196, T. to J. Gladstone, 2-8 Dec. 1830. [17] Glasgow Herald, 29 Apr., 6, 9, 13, 27 May 1831. [18] Finlay and Company, 127-8. [19] Glynne-Gladstone mss 198, T. to J. Gladstone, 1 June 1831; Scottish Electoral Politics, 226; Finlay and Company, 193. [20] Add. 44353, ff. 28, 167, 172, 176, 178. [21] PP (1833), vi. 35-45. [22] Glasgow ed. W. Fraser and I. Maver, ii. 104-5. [23] Add. 44358, ff. 203, 209; Glasgow Herald, 7 Mar. 1842. [24] Finlay and Company, 30; Sir A. Alison, Life and Writings, i. 344-5. [25] PROB 11/1960/249; IR26/1608/378. [26] Finlay and Company, pp. vi, 31, 33-37.

D.R.F.

FITZGERALD, Sir Augustine, 1st bt. (?1765–1834), of Carrigoran, co. Clare.

CO. CLARE	9 Aug. 1808–1818
ENNIS	28 Feb. 1832–1832

b. ?1765, 1st s. of Col. Edward Fitzgerald, MP [I], of Carrigoran and 1st w. Rachel, da. of Standish O'Grady of Elton and Cappercullen, co. Limerick; half-bro. of John Forster Fitzgerald[†]. educ. Trinity, Dublin, 23 Nov. 1781, aged 16. m. 15 Feb. 1796,[1] Elizabeth, da. of William Barton of Grove, co. Tipperary, s.p. suc. fa. 1814;[2] cr. bt. 5 Jan. 1822. d. 3 Dec. 1834.[3]

Ensign 8 Ft. 1785, lt. 1790, capt. 1791; capt. 5 Ft. 1791; maj. (half-pay) 107 Ft. 1795; brevet lt.-col. 1800; col. 1810; maj.-gen. 1813; lt.-gen. 1825.

Lt.-col. co. Clare militia 1803-d.

Like his father before him, Fitzgerald had sat for Clare as a pro-Catholic supporter of government with the backing of his stepmother's second cousin, the 1st Marquess Conyngham.[4] He had left the House in 1818 on account of sickness, but by May 1820 was said by Sir Edward O'Brien, Member for Clare, to be 'much improved in health'.[5] He seconded O'Brien's unsuccessful attempt to move a loyal address to the king at the county meeting in January 1821.[6] Owing to this, or perhaps rather to Lady Conyngham's influence over George IV, he secured a baronetcy, with remainder to his half-brother William, in 1822. He attended county meetings in Clare on the king's imminent visit to Ireland and agricultural distress in January 1823.[7] He travelled from Paris to London in May 1826, startling O'Brien, who intended to vacate his seat in favour of his son Lucius O'Brien*, by expressing an unexpected interest in standing, of which nothing eventually came.[8] He seconded William Vesey Fitzgerald for Clare at the by-election in mid-1828, when Daniel O'Connell defeated the newly appointed cabinet minister.[9] He became president of the county's Brunswick Club later that year and, on O'Connell being unseated, was mentioned as a possible candidate to oppose his re-election in July 1829.[10] He proposed Sir Edward O'Brien at the by-election in March 1831, when O'Connell's son Maurice was returned after a contest, and presented an address to the lord lieutenant, Lord Anglesey, on his visit to Ennis the following month.[11]

In February 1832, at the age of 66, he returned to the Commons on a vacancy for Ennis, the sitting Member and patron, Vesey Fitzgerald, having become an Irish peer.[12] (Ironically, he had unwittingly contributed to the embarrassing defeat of Vesey Fitzgerald, then chancellor of the Irish exchequer, in Clare in 1812.) He was sworn in, 28 Feb. He voted against the third reading of the English reform bill, 22 Mar., and for an unsuccessful attempt to give Lincoln freeholders a vote for the county the following day. He divided against the second reading of the Irish reform bill, 25 May, and to preserve the voting rights of freemen under it, 2 July. He was in the small opposition minorities against Crampton's amendment to the Irish tithes bill, 9 Apr., and the Irish party processions bill, 25 June. He was expected to join the Protestant Conservative Society of Ireland that summer.[13] He voted against government on the Russian-Dutch loan, 12 July 1832, and finally retired from Parliament, without apparently ever having spoken in debate, at the dissolution later in the year. He died in December 1834.[14] By his will, dated 24 June 1828, he left his property, including his house in Merrion Square, to his wife. His personalty within the province of Canterbury was sworn under £25,000, and that in Ireland under £27,076.[15] His half-brother John Forster Fitzgerald (d. 1877), was Liberal Member for Clare, 1852-7.

[1] *Gent. Mag.* (1796), i. 253. [2] Ibid. (1814), i. 415. [3] *Morning Chron.* 11 Dec. 1834. [4] *Hist. Irish Parl.* iv. 141-2; *HP Commons, 1790-1820,* iii. 749. [5] NLI, Inchiquin mss T23/2972, O'Brien to wife, 11 May 1820. [6] *Dublin Weekly Reg.* 20 Jan., 10 Feb. 1821. [7] *Dublin Evening Post,* 7, 18, 30 Jan. 1823. [8] Inchiquin mss 3627, O'Brien to wife, 2, 11, 15, 16, 18 May 1826. [9] *Clare Jnl.* 3 July 1828. [10] *Dublin Evening Mail,* 24, 27 Oct. 1828; *Dublin Evening Post,* 26 May, 16 June 1829. [11] *Clare Jnl.* 21 Mar., 7 Apr. 1831. [12] K. Sheedy, *Clare Elections,* 169-70. [13] NLI, Farnham mss 18611 (3), Lefroy to Farnham, 4 June 1832. [14] *Gent. Mag.* (1835), i. 220 gives date of *d.* as 4 Dec. [15] PROB 11/1842/84; IR26/1383/165.

D.R.F./S.M.F.

FITZGERALD, John (1775–1852), of Wherstead Lodge, nr. Ipswich, Suff. and Millburgh, Seaford, Suss.

SEAFORD 1826–1832

b. 25 Dec. 1775, 1st s. of John Purcell, MD, of Richmond Hill, Dublin and Eleanor, da. of John Fitzgerald of Little Island, co. Waterford. *educ.* Trinity, Dublin 1790; M. Temple 1792; King's Inns 1793, called [I] 1796. *m.* 16 May 1801, his cos. Mary Frances, da. and h. of John Fitzgerald of Little Island, Pendleton, Lancs. and Gayton, Staffs., 3s. 5da. (1 *d.v.p.*). *suc.* fa. 1806. Took name of Fitzgerald by royal lic. 3 Oct. 1818 following *d.* of fa.-in-law. *d.* 18 Mar. 1852.
Sheriff, Suff. 1824-5, co. Waterford 1838-9.
Lt.-col. E. Suff. vols.

The Purcells came to England at the Conquest and were settled in Ireland by 1172. John Purcell (?1740-1806), the father of this Member, studied medicine at Leyden and Edinburgh and had a successful practice as a physician in Dublin. In 1774 he married Eleanor Fitzgerald, whose family were descended from the 4th earl of Kildare and whose grandfather Edward (*d.* 1736) was the half-brother of Nicholas Fitzgerald, a prominent supporter of James II killed at the Boyne. They had five sons, John, Charles, Edward, Peter and Edward Carlton. Eleanor Purcell's brother, John Fitzgerald (1760-1818) not only inherited the family's Irish property from his father in 1784, but came into estates at Pendleton, near Manchester, and Gayton, near Stafford, through the will of his kinsman Richard Fitzgerald. With his wife Mary, daughter of Keane Fitzgerald of Totteridge, Hertfordshire, he had a son, John Charles, born in 1781, and a daughter, Mary Frances, born in 1779. Her first cousin John Purcell was called to the Irish bar in 1796, but never practised. He married Mary Frances Fitzgerald in 1801 and they made their home at the White House, Bredfield, near Woodbridge, Suffolk. (Mary's father had bought the neighbouring property of Boulge for them, but the widow of the previous owner continued to occupy the hall on a life interest and did not die until 1835.) The death without issue of Mary's brother in 1807 left her sole heiress to her father's great wealth in money and land; and she added to her assets in 1810 when she inherited the best part of her great-aunt Jane Joyce's estate of £700,000, plus the 3,000-acre manor of Naseby Wooleys, Northamptonshire.[1]

The couple had eight children in nine years, but they were ill-matched and came to lead largely separate lives. Purcell, an absent-minded, genial and gullible man, was fond of country life and pursuits. He was overshadowed and cowed by his domineering wife, whose trustees were careful to restrict his access to her money. Mary, a 'fine broad woman', who was reputed to have turned down an offer of marriage from Arthur Wellesley[†], was bored by children and Suffolk society. She eventually spent much of her time in London, playing the *grande dame*, giving opulent dinners at the family house at 39 Portland Place, mixing with painters, poets and actors and making ostentatious appearances at the opera. These developments lay mostly in the future when the Purcells went *en famille* to France in 1816 and took a house at St. Germain. Yet even then, while Purcell and the children returned to Bredfield for the summer Mary went on a European tour. They reassembled in Paris in 1817 and lived in the Rue d'Angoulême until the death of old John Fitzgerald, 6 Sept. 1818, brought them back to England. Mary, already worth an estimated £750,000, inherited a large fortune.[2] Purcell, who received £1,000 by his father-in-law's will, changed the family name to Fitzgerald, though he was under no legal obligation to do so.[3]

In 1823 the Fitzgeralds erected an obelisk at Naseby to mark the site of the Civil War battlefield. (It was in fact a mile away from the actual location and subsequently misled and infuriated Carlyle.)[4] While his wife spent increasing amounts of time in London and Brighton, travelling in an eye-catching yellow carriage pulled by black horses, Fitzgerald continued his life as a Suffolk squire. He served as sheriff in 1824-5, and at the end of his term of office moved the family home to another rented house at Wherstead, near Ipswich, previously occupied by the 1st Viscount Granville.[5] To realize his parliamentary ambitions he had already bought property at Seaford, including town houses and the adjacent Corsica Hall, which he rebuilt and named Millburgh.[6] At the general election of 1826 he was returned for the borough in conjunction with the son of Granville's friend and fellow Canningite Charles Ellis, the other patron, who was raised to the peerage as Lord Seaford. An unexpected opposition from two Norfolk Whigs was no more than an irritant.[7]

Fitzgerald presented a petition from Welford, Suffolk against any alteration of the corn laws, 20 Feb. 1827.[8] He voted for Catholic relief, 6 Mar., and in the largely Whig minority for the production of papers on the Orange procession at Lisburn, 29 Mar. When Seaford's son vacated his seat to accommodate Canning on his appointment as prime minister in April, Fitzgerald represented him at the election formalities and declared that 'it would be his pride, most cordially, yet disinterestedly, to support' his ministry; but he voted against it for the disfranchisement of Penryn, 28 May 1827.[9] In January 1828 Huskisson, explaining to Seaford his decision to take office under the duke of Wellington, said that Fitzgerald had behaved 'well' over it, unlike some other Canningites.[10] Seaford credited him with a good understanding of 'the whole subject of the poor laws', but he did not give the House the benefit of it in debate.[11] He voted for repeal of the Test Acts, 26 Feb., and Catholic relief, 12 May. After the resignation of Huskisson from the government Fitzgerald was one of the 'ejected liberals' who mustered in the House, 3 June 1828. In February 1829 the patronage secretary Planta numbered him among those Members 'opposed to securities' who would 'probably support' them rather than endanger the passage of Catholic emancipation, for which he duly divided, 6, 30 Mar. He voted to allow O'Connell to take his seat unimpeded, 18 Mar. 1829. His only other known vote in this Parliament was for Jewish emancipation, 17 May 1830.

At the general election that summer he and Augustus Ellis, who had resumed his seat on Canning's death,

were challenged at Seaford by two wealthy strangers. While their watchword was 'independence' from Lord Seaford's electoral domination, their intrusion was seen as part of the Wellington ministry's assault on the Canningite remnant. Attacked for failing to support the sale of beer bill, which 'brings relief to the poor man', Fitzgerald insisted that he had 'voted with ministers on the three readings' (even though the first and third were in fact uncontested); and claimed that 'unconnected with ministers, or with any party, I have generally supported the king's government, and feel myself as independent in Parliament as I do now in soliciting your suffrages'. One of his leading supporters made much of his 'liberality and benevolence' to the borough, where he had founded and endowed a free school and provided relief during recent outbreaks of fever. After topping the poll Fitzgerald slightly modified his explanation of his conduct on the beer bill, now claiming to have voted for the first and second readings, but to have taken a pair for the third: 'he always voted for the people, and wished ever to do so'.[12] On 7 Sept. 1830 he entertained 'nearly 200 persons of distinction' with food, fireworks and dancing at Wherstead, and the next day the parish poor were invited to dine there.[13]

Ministers listed him as one of 'the Huskisson party', and he was absent from the division on the civil list, 15 Nov. 1830. Of his attitude to the reform bill, his youngest son Edward Fitzgerald wrote, 15 Mar. 1831:

> My father set out against it at first, but is coming over, I think. The question with him, is not whether the bill is a good one, for he thinks it is; but whether he ought to vote for the disfranchisement of his own borough: wherein he certainly would not be its representative, because no borough would ever wish to be disfranchised.[14]

Fitzgerald paired against the second reading, 22 Mar., and voted for Gascoyne's wrecking amendment, 19 Apr. 1831. At the ensuing general election he was returned unopposed, having 'stated his belief that some reform, and an extensive reform too, was necessary, but [that] he did not approve of the disfranchisement of any borough, unless some corruption was proved to have taken place'.[15] He abstained from the division on the second reading of the reintroduced reform bill, 6 July 1831. A week later he presented and endorsed the Seaford electors' petition complaining of 'the injustice of their proposed disfranchisement':

> I am not opposed to reform and ... I shall not oppose the reform bill further than it may go to affect the interests of my constituents ... While I admit that this bill will be considered a great boon to the nation at large, I must ... say that it will be a bill of pains and penalties to my constituents and others.

Accordingly, he absented himself from all the major divisions on the reform bills. He was granted a fortnight's leave to attend to 'urgent business', 15 Sept., and was a defaulter, 10 Oct., the day of the motion of confidence in the Grey ministry. His only known vote in the 1831 Parliament was for the second reading of the Irish reform bill, 25 May 1832. In January that year he asked Seaford to use his influence with Lord Ripon, a member of the cabinet, to have him recommended to the premier for a baronetcy, of which he had had hopes as a supporter of the Canning and Goderich ministries in 1827: 'You will ... vouch for my principles being friendly to the present government, and that whatever interest I can command in either country is at its disposal'.[16]

In June 1832 Fitzgerald, who had been a prominent supporter of the reformer Sir Henry Bunbury* at the 1831 Suffolk election,[17] announced his candidature for the Eastern division of the county at the first election under the Reform Act:

> My politics are and ever have been those of an independent Whig. Unconnected with any government since the death of ... Canning, I have uniformly ... forwarded ... every measure the object of which was to remove civil or religious disabilities, to lighten the burthens or to better the conditions of my fellow subjects, especially by steadily upholding the agricultural interest, the basis of our national prosperity.[18]

Among the local reformers his credentials were highly suspect, and he was regarded as the creature of Sir Thomas Gooch* and the county Tories.[19] Attacked in the press for his failure to support reform, he claimed to have done so not only on the case of Penryn, but on those of East Retford and the enfranchisement of Birmingham, Leeds and Manchester; no evidence has been found to suggest that he was telling the truth. He said that he had opposed the first reform bill because it had proposed to reduce the number of English Members and explained that while he had approved of the final bill and 'never voted against a clause of it', he had been prevented from actively supporting it by his oath as a jurat of Seaford to defend the borough's chartered rights. He professed support for agricultural protection, economy and retrenchment, the government's pacific foreign policy and the abolition of slavery 'as soon as circumstances will permit'. In further public letters he denied having paired with the Wellington ministry on the civil list and stressed his anxiety to 'uphold the great agricultural interest' by resisting free trade and seeking a reduction of taxes.[20] Fitzgerald, who attended the first annual meeting of the East Suffolk Agricultural Association,

21 Sept., lay low for two months, perhaps expecting to walk over, and confirmed his candidature in late November 1832. When two Conservatives started on a platform of agricultural protection, he initially stood his ground, denying that Grey's ministry was 'inimical to the landed interest' and praising the premier as 'the most liberal and enlightened statesman of the present day'. It soon became obvious that he had no chance, and four days before the election he withdrew, advising his supporters to plump for the reformer Robert Newton Shawe, who had also been in the field since June.[21] Shawe was returned in second place; and at his celebration dinner Fitzgerald, whose campaign had typified his ineptitude and unworldliness, admitted his own 'disappointment', but rejoiced in 'the triumphant victory of political consistency and political principle over a confederated Tory aristocracy'.[22]

In the late 1820s he had begun to mine coal on the Pendleton estate, perhaps in a bid to assert and prove himself. The superintendent of operations was Robert Stephenson, the brother of George, whom Fitzgerald congratulated, 25 Sept. 1832, on receiving 'the joyful intelligence of you having reached the four foot seam'. The following year the colliery manager absconded with a quantity of money, as had the Naseby estate agent 'with something above £5,000' in 1830. Undeterred, Fitzgerald extended the enterprise in 1835 (the year he moved into Boulge Hall) by forming the Pendleton Colliery Company, which had the right to mine on adjacent land leased from the duchy of Lancaster. The undertaking, of which George Stephenson was a director, was expected to produce profits of £14,000 a year; but underground water was a persistent problem, and in August 1843 a flood wrecked the new mine. Edward Fitzgerald told Carlyle:

> My father, after spending £100,000 on a colliery, besides losses by everlasting rogues, runaway agents, etc., has just been drowned out of it ... So end the hopes of eighteen years; and he is near seventy, left without his only hobby! He may perhaps be able to let it out to a company at a low rent, that they may pump out the water. But he is come to the end of his purse. Naseby might have had many a draining tile but for that d——d colliery.[23]

Fitzgerald, whose son-in-law John Kerrich and friend Squire Jenney, investors in the company, were ruined by the flood, struggled on until 1848, when he filed for a petition of bankruptcy. His debts were put at over £130,000, and he proposed to pay £6,000 a year to his creditors, who included his wife and all seven of his surviving children, to the tune of £10,000 each. He was given protection under the Act.[24] As the case proceeded it emerged that his debts totalled £198,000, but that £138,000 of this was owed within the family, including a mortgage of £61,000 on the Pendleton works held by his wife's trustees. Her fortune was largely unscathed and, although the furnishings of Boulge had to be sold, the house itself was retained as part of her trust. By April 1849 she had formally separated from Fitzgerald, who was reputed to have kept a mistress in London. She took a house at Ham, Surrey, and initiated restoration work on the decrepit castle on Little Island (in the River Suir, two miles below Waterford). Fitzgerald stayed for a while at 39 Portland Place before moving to Regent's Park Terrace, Camden Town.[25] His affairs were close to settlement by late 1850, but the eventual outcome is not clear.[26] A broken man, plagued by recurrent bladder trouble, he died in March 1852, 'like', as Edward Fitzgerald told a friend as an afterthought three months later, 'poor old Sedley in Thackeray's *Vanity Fair*, all his coal schemes at an end': 'He died ... saying, "that engine works well" (meaning one of his colliery steam engines) as he lay in the stupor of death'.[27] Mary Frances Fitzgerald died at Brighton, 30 Jan. 1855, supposedly worth £1,000,000, though the personal estate devised in her will was sworn under £10,000.[28] The family estates, including Fitzgerald's Seaford property, passed to their eldest son John (1803-79), a highly eccentric and grossly fat lay preacher, who took the additional name of Purcell in 1858 and lived much at Castle Irwell on the Pendleton estate.[29] The second son, Peter Slingsby Fitzgerald (1807-75), became a Catholic, while Edward found fame, if not happiness, as the translator of the *Rubaiyat* of Omar Khayyam.

[1] *N and Q* (ser. 8), iv. 462-3; *VCH Lancs*. iv. 392-3; W.A. Copinger, *Suff. Manors*, vii. 239; R.B. Martin, *With Friends Possessed. A Life of Edward Fitzgerald*, 22, 26-27, 31. [2] *Letters of Edward Fitzgerald* ed. A. M. and A.B. Terhune, i. 13-14; Martin, 23, 25, 27, 29, 31-34, 36-40; A.M. Terhune, *Life of Edward Fitzgerald*, 2-3, 6-7, 10-12. [3] PROB 11/1608/409; IR26/743/632. [4] T. Wright, *Life of Edward Fitzgerald*, i. 62-63; *Northants. P and P*, iv. 168; *Fitzgerald Letters*, i. 92. [5] Martin, 32, 45; *Oakes Diaries* ed. J. Fiske (Suff. Recs. Soc. xxxiii), i. 291, 297; *Constable's Corresp*. ed. R. B. Beckett (Suff. Recs. Soc. x), iv. 70. [6] Martin, 41; M. A. Lower, 'Mems. Seaford', *Suss. Arch.Coll*. vii (1854),144-6. [7] W.D. Cooper, *Parl. Hist. Suss*. 48; *Brighton Herald*, 27 May, 3, 10, 17 June 1826. [8] *The Times*, 21 Feb. 1827. [9] *Courier*, 23 Apr. 1827. [10] Add. 38754, f. 234. [11] Add. 38755, f. 207. [12] *Brighton Guardian*, 7, 14, 21, 28 July, 4 Aug.; *Brighton Herald*, 17 July, 21 Aug. 1830. [13] *Bury and Norwich Post*, 15 Sept. 1830. [14] *Fitzgerald Letters*, i. 93. [15] *Suss. Advertiser*, 2 May 1831. [16] Add. 40878, f. 568. [17] *Ipswich Jnl*. 14 May; *Bury and Norwich Post*, 18 May 1831. [18] *Bury and Norwich Post*, 13, 27 June 1832. [19] CUL, Arcedeckne mss 1/5, Wood to Arcedeckne, 8 June, White to same, 11 June, Harland to same, 11 July 1832. [20] *Suff. Chron*. 30 June, 7, 14, 21 July, 4 Aug. 1832. [21] Ibid. 22 Sept., 24 Nov., 1, 8 Dec.; *Bury and Norwich Post*, 28 Nov., 5, 12 Dec. 1832. [22] *The Times*, 17, 20 Dec.; *Bury and Norwich Post*, 19, 26 Dec. 1832. [23] Add. 38781, ff. 45, 59, 70, 109, 116; Terhune, 178-80; Martin, 93, 133-4; *Fitzgerald Letters*, i. 92, 93, 398, 402; W. Axon, *Annals of Manchester*, 222. [24] Martin, 150; *Fitzgerald Letters*, i. 609, 612-13, 615-17; *The Times*, 5 Sept., 28 Dec. 1848. [25] Martin, 150-3; *Fitzgerald Letters*, i. 635-6; *The Times*, 3, 18 Jan., 27 Apr., 24 May, 22 June 1849. [26] *Fitzgerald Letters*, i. 671, 684; Martin, 161. [27] *Gent. Mag*. (1852), i. 531; Martin, 170; *Fitzgerald Letters*, ii. 57; iv. 193. [28] *Fitzgerald Letters*, i. 155; Martin, 189; PROB 11/2208/210; IR26/2028/137. [29] *Suff. Farming in Nineteenth Cent*. ed. J. Thirsk and J.Imray (Suff. Recs. Soc. i), 148; Axon, 372.

D.R.F.

FITZGERALD, Maurice, knight of Kerry (1774–1849), of Ballinruddery, nr. Listowel and Glanleam, Valentia Island, co. Kerry.

CO. KERRY   1801–1831

b. 29 Dec. 1774, 1st s. of Robert Fitzgerald, knight of Kerry, MP [I], of Ballinruddery and 3rd w. Catherine, da. of Lancelot Sandes[1] of Kilcavan, Queen's co. *educ*. Harrow 1786; Trinity, Dublin 1789; L. Inn 1792. *m*. (1) 5 Nov. 1801, Maria (*d*. 13 Nov. 1829), da. of David Latouche, MP [I],[2] of Marlay, co. Dublin, 6s. (4 *d.v.p.*) 4da. (1 *d.v.p.*); (2) Cecilia Maria, wid. of George Knight, *s.p. suc*. fa. 1781. *d*. 7 Mar. 1849.
     MP [I] 1795-1800.
     Commr. of customs [I] Aug. 1799-Feb. 1801; PC [I] 27 Jan. 1801; commr. of treasury [I] 1801-7; commr. of fisheries [I] 1819-30?; ld. of treasury July 1827-Jan. 1828; vice-treasurer [I] Mar.-Nov. 1830; ld. of admiralty Dec. 1834-Apr. 1835.
     Trustee, linen board [I] 1803.
     Capt. Feale cav. 1796; maj. Kerry militia 1797, lt.-col. 1801-*d*.; capt. commdt. Feale inf. 1805.

Like his kinsmen the White Knight (the 3rd earl of Kingston) and the knight of Glin (John Fraunceis Fitzgerald of Glin Castle, county Limerick), the 18th knight of Kerry, a Tory paladin, held his hereditary medieval title solely by traditional usage and in 1823 Peel, the home secretary, refused to recommend to the king that it be given formal recognition.[3] Nevertheless, this was how Fitzgerald was generally known (though not in parliamentary records), including in Kerry, where, as a child, he inherited the residual estates of his once Catholic ancestors from his father Robert, the 17th knight, who was Member for Dingle, 1741-81, and judge of the admiralty court, 1757-74. Even before coming of age, he gave up his hopes of a military career – he was, however, active in the militia – to represent his native county in the Irish Parliament.[4] He started out a ministerialist, but, as he much later recounted, his resentment at the failure of the Union (in the negotiations for which he took a part) to pave the way for Catholic emancipation led him to resign his junior government position:

The commencement of my life (public) was in the Pitt school, not that I agreed in his peculiar policy, but at the time he was the Conservative agent. My doctrines, though I never thought myself of importance enough to enounce them, were then impressed on my young mind by *Burke*. I have never swerved from them, and gave up a dear personal friendship with [Lord] Castlereagh* whilst he was in full power in deference to my more unqualified views on the Catholic question, the accomplishment of which he had taught me to expect from the Union. When on the formation of Mr. Fox's administration he expressed to me a wish that I should remain in office ... I declined, and was only induced under the controlling opinion of the late Lord [the 1st earl of] Kenmare ... my most powerful supporter as well as most particular friend, not to break my connection with a ministry from which he expected emancipation. The moment Lord Grey was removed [as foreign secretary in March 1807] ... that day, I ranged myself with the Whigs against the exclusive system of Perceval, resisting the earnest efforts of the duke of Wellington to keep me in office with full latitude on all points interesting to my constituents – he being then just appointed secretary to Ireland, an early and intimate friend of mine ... Then commenced my association with the Whigs, and during their 20 years of adversity I cordially acted as a party man, suppressing my differences of opinion, for barring religious freedom my sentiments much more accorded with their opponents, especially on parliamentary reform.[5]

He was elected to Brooks's in 1810 at the height of his opposition activism, but following the appointment of the Liverpool administration in 1812 he kept a lower political profile, save on the Catholic issue, his commitment to which he later claimed had cost him at least £40,000 in official salary.[6] This relative inactivity continued after the general election of 1820, when he was returned unopposed and spoke well at a dinner in his honour.[7]

In May 1820 it was reported by his friend and neighbour Daniel O'Connell* that he was still at Ballinruddery, but that he was 'coming into office with [the Grenvillite William Conyngham] Plunket*. I hope so as the poor fellow has a large family and a very small fortune much encumbered, and has been *a Patriot long enough, God knows*'.[8] On the death of Henry Grattan I in June, the knight, who led calls for a national monument to him, was narrowly passed over as the Irish Catholics' Commons spokesman in favour of Plunket.[9] Unless it was William Vesey Fitzgerald, one of the near namesakes with whom he may occasionally have been confused, he spoke for excluding the Dublin Member Thomas Ellis from the House as an Irish master in chancery, 30 June. He voted for Hume's motion for economies in revenue collection, 4 July, and, having supported the Irish tithes

bill on the 5th, he urged that imports of Irish spirits to Britain should remain free of duty, 6, 12 July 1820. That summer O'Connell noted that the knight, as 'a *decided* oppositionist', was deprived of county patronage, although two years later Goulburn, the Irish secretary, observed, in relation to the powers of Kerry magistrates to appoint constables, that he was 'always promoting some little job of his own'.[10]

In November 1820 he supported O'Connell's pretensions to become Irish attorney-general to Queen Caroline.[11] Early the following year, when he helped to suppress a loyalist county meeting in Kerry, he voted regularly in the opposition campaign on her behalf; as well as by making various minor interjections, to which he was prone, he condemned the brouhaha over the county Dublin meeting and the conduct of ministers, 22 Feb. 1821.[12] He divided against the renewal of the sugar duties, 9 Feb., and argued that an inquiry should be held into the Union duties prior to their being phased out, 16 Feb., when, as on a handful of other occasions that session, he voted with opposition for economies and tax reductions. He attacked the disorganized and sectarian state of Irish education on carrying his motion for relevant papers, 1 Mar., and the following day he divided for making Leeds a scot and lot (not £10 householder) borough if it received Grampound's seats. He had spoken and voted for Catholic relief, 28 Feb., and although he criticized the proposed state regulation of the Catholic clergy, 27, 28 Mar., he approved of the ensuing relief bill as 'a real act of union between the two countries'. He supposedly had to be cajoled into dividing for the third reading, 2 Apr., but was thanked for having come to the defence of O'Connell, whom he had kept informed of the content and progress of the ultimately unsuccessful bill.[13] The knight, who in September 1821 chaired a magistrates' meeting on local distress and agitation in Tralee, was delighted by the appointments of Plunket as Irish attorney-general and the pro-Catholic Lord Wellesley as lord lieutenant late that year.[14] No evidence of parliamentary activity has been traced during the 1822 session, which may have been why one contemporary radical source, perhaps misled by the fact that government majority lists were rarely printed, erroneously stated that he 'votes with the ministers'.[15]

He called for an immediate inquiry into the Dublin theatre riot, 24 Feb., and threatened to move for information on the activities of Orange societies, 26 Feb. 1823, when he voted in the minority for reducing the import price of corn to 60s.[16] He spoke – arguing for increased clerical residence, closer attention to education and the alteration of tithes – and voted for inquiry into the Irish church establishment, 4 Mar. The following day he strongly supported James Abercromby's motion condemning illegal Orange societies in a speech of which, according to George Agar Ellis*, 'the first half was excellent and quite eloquent, the last half ... equally low and in wretched taste'.[17] Deemed that year by the duke of Bedford to be, like Thomas Spring Rice, a possibly better sponsor of reforms to Irish tithes than Sir John Newport, he welcomed Goulburn's proposals provided they were put on a permanent and stable basis, 6 Mar.[18] He was granted a fortnight's leave, apparently to deal with disturbances in Kerry, 16 Apr., and the moderate Whig leader Lord Lansdowne regretted his absence that month over Catholic relief and in June over tithes.[19] He voted against the grant for Irish churches and glebe houses, 1 July, but congratulated ministers on the passage of the tithes composition bill, 4 July. He remained studiously neutral on the allegation of bribery against his colleague James Crosbie, 1 July 1823, and afterwards justified this privately to O'Connell:

> All matters now coming before the House are influenced by the physical exhaustion of Members, and this state favours the conservative principle of ministers, *viz.* 'to do nothing'. Such a system may in their foreign relations only produce contempt and degradation but applied to Ireland is calculated to engender civil war.[20]

Although encouraged to attend early in the 1824 session by his former guardian, the judge Robert Day, who was anxious to see him on good terms with his electoral allies in Kerry, he was not apparently present at its beginning.[21] He voted for inquiries into the Irish church establishment, 6 May, the state of Ireland, 11 May, and the trial of the Methodist missionary John Smith in Demerara, 11 June. He had been named to the select committee on the survey and valuation of Ireland (on 30 Mar.), one of several Irish committees to which he was appointed in this period, and he chaired its proceedings, 13, 14, 17, 19 May.[22] He divided against Irish clerical pluralists, 27 May, when he urged reconsideration of the Union duties, and the new churches bill, 14 June. He sprang to the defence of the Catholic Association, 31 May, when Christopher Hely Hutchinson* noted that he '*would* say something, which was not well received by the House, so that he was rather disconcerted and did not get out all he had intended'; he soon 'recovered himself', although he was again judged to be 'injurious and prolix' in vindicating the conduct of O'Connell.[23] He spoke and acted as a teller for the minority against the second reading of the Irish insurrection bill, 14 June 1824.

Until this time the knight of Kerry had lived mostly at Ballinruddery, which the poet Tom Moore, who had visited it in 1823, described as 'a mere cottage, but gentlemanlike and comfortable, and ... worthy of its excellent and high spirited owner'.[24] Now, however, the family switched its principal residence to Glanleam on Valentia Island, which, with its slate quarries, was already the centre of his economic ambitions. Among his plans for developing the area as a major port, the most grandiose was the formation of the American and Colonial Steam Navigation Company, to trade between the west of Ireland and Halifax, Nova Scotia.[25] Having failed to obtain a royal charter for this in 1824, despite lobbying his influential friends in London, he partly supervised the passage of a bill to establish it the following session (royal assent being granted on 22 June 1825) and obtained an amendment bill the following year (26 May 1826).[26] This particular venture was an expensive failure, but he continued to press the commercial and military potential of Valentia on successive governments and suggested other means of improving the state of manufacturing and transport in the south of Ireland.[27] As Alexander Nimmo of Killarney wrote to one correspondent, 31 Aug. 1824, the knight already had a local reputation as an indefatigable campaigner for such schemes as the improvement of Tralee harbour and for the implementation of effective public works programmes.[28] A rumour that he would soon be retiring from Parliament was denied in the press the following month.[29]

He opposed the suppression of the Association on the address, 4 Feb. 1825, subsequently informing O'Connell that he had been misreported in his minor criticisms of it and claiming that he had taken the course 'which appeared to me most judicious'.[30] He voted steadily against the Irish unlawful societies bill that month, including on the 21st, when he argued at length that it was not political repression but Catholic emancipation that would ensure lasting tranquillity. A supporter of O'Connell's parliamentary deputation to Westminster that session, he voted for Catholic claims, 1 Mar., 21 Apr., 10 May.[31] He presented a pro-Catholic petition from the Protestants of his county, 10 Mar., and insisted that his co-religionists fully approved of the relief bill, 10 May.[32] He supported the Irish bankers co-partnership bill, 15 Mar., measures to relieve the Irish poor, 22 Mar., the grant for assisted emigration, 15 Apr., and the assimilation of the British and Irish currencies, 12 May. He divided for criticizing chancery administration, 7 June, and against the grant for the duke of Cumberland, 9, 10 June 1825. He declined to attend the O'Connellite Dublin dinner,

2 Feb. 1826.[33] He commented on oppressive Irish market tolls, 16 Feb., and the problems of removing small Scottish and Irish bank-notes from circulation, 16 Mar. He advocated a non-sectarian system for Irish education, with religious schooling left to separate denominations, 20 Mar. He voted that day for Newport's amendment to the grant for Irish charter schools, and the next for regulation of the Irish first fruits fund. He divided for alteration of the representation of Edinburgh, 13 Apr., parliamentary reform, 27 Apr., and Russell's resolutions against electoral bribery, 26 May 1826.

The knight was considered certain of success in the violent Kerry contest during the general election of 1826, when his daughter Maria reported to her brother David in schoolgirl French that *'Papa se garde aussi tranquille que possible ... Tout là paroit très bien. Il dit que le grand chêne opposé aux fenêtres de l'étude est jeté à terre mais ce n'est que pour nous effrayer ... Il fut reçu le premier jour (samedi) très bien'*, and a 'great deal of applause and perspiration was lavished on him'.[34] He led throughout the delayed poll, being returned with another pro-Catholic William Hare at the expense of Crosbie. As well as urging emancipation, he promised not to accept office unless he could do so consistently with his opinions on religious liberty, and he was present at the county's gathering of Catholics at the end of July.[35] He complained to Peel about Major Wilcocks's conduct as head of the constabulary during the election riot, but Goulburn considered that he did this to protect his friend, the sheriff, who was really to blame.[36] That winter he sent several letters of advice and caution to O'Connell, who, although temperamentally indisposed to moderation, confided that 'there is no political man from whom I should be more happy to receive counsel or more grateful to for taking the trouble of giving it', while repeatedly pushing him towards closer co-operation with Lansdowne. After Liverpool's incapacitating seizure in February 1827 the knight wrote from his sickbed ('all *great* men must be ill, it seems') that O'Connell 'need not be alarmed as to the *colour* of the new [prime] minister', since either the Catholic sympathiser Canning, the foreign secretary, would be appointed or he would at least be able to strengthen his position in the cabinet.[37] He sided with ministers for the grant to the new heir presumptive, the duke of Clarence, 16 Feb., 16 Mar., stating on 19 Feb. that he did so simply on independent principles.[38] He emphasized that the Catholic priests were loyal to the state, 2 Mar., when, as on other occasions, he brought up pro-Catholic petitions from his county. He voted in the minority for relief, 6 Mar., and observed to O'Connell the following day that 'I was not san-

guine as to numbers and yet by no means prepared for the impression which this result has made on my mind', adding that 'I am so very ill that my attendance was difficult, and speaking out of the question'. He gave notice of a motion for producing official correspondence at the time of the Union, as a means of revealing the pledges then held out about emancipation, 7 Mar., and on the 9th alluded to another on the subject of Irish poor laws, which he does not seem to have pursued.[39] He took a month's leave to attend to urgent business, 19 Mar. 1827.

Yet he was in London during the protracted discussions which preceded the formation of the Canning coalition administration in April 1827. Thence, as the Whigs' main conduit to the Irish Catholic leader, he urged O'Connell to show 'the greatest forbearance', including by adjourning the Association

> with the double object of evincing confidence and disarming the prejudices which will be attempted to be inspired into the public feeling here, as against a ministry *'too Catholic'* ... The situation of the new ministry will be critical and their opponents (Tory) very powerful *in Parliament*. Do not let them wield no popery against it if possible.[40]

He attended the Whig meeting at Brooks's, 20 Apr., after which, believing that it was unnecessary to hold to the stipulation for an entirely pro-Catholic Irish administration, he was described as being among the 'shabby ones, anxious for place at any rate'.[41] The following day he wrote to a reluctantly receptive Lansdowne to beg him to restart the stalled negotiations with Canning and to take the home secretaryship, as, even with an anti-Catholic viceroy (provided he was a moderate), the Catholics were hopeful of practical progress being made in their favour. He also pointed out that O'Connell had begun to heed his requests for moderation, and it was in this light that he continued to urge O'Connell to swallow his public criticisms of the new ministers and warned him against counting on an entirely favourable government, since *'the thing is totally impossible. Do you think the king is to have no voice on that subject?'*[42] The knight's decision to give his backing to the Canning ministry was regretted by such anti-Catholic friends as Lord Londonderry.[43] Apparently reconciled to making no more than a token gesture in relation to his intended motion on the Union, which was to have opened the whole question of Catholic relief, he withdrew his notice for it, 7 May 1827.[44] That day he told Lord Chandos and other detractors in the Commons, that

> I stand here because I wish to lend my support to that party which is most adverse to the sentiments he expresses ... I stand here, further, to give my humble aid

to an administration which, however embarrassed by faction, I do believe contemplates the general welfare of the empire. Above all, I give it my support because I feel convinced that its real object is to promote the happiness of my own country.

He defended Protestant charter schools, 25 May, and denied that he had said Ireland would rebel if emancipation was not forthcoming, 6 June, but asked what progress emigration had made to alleviate Irish distress, 30 May, and complained about excessively high grand jury presentments, 6 June. He spoke and voted for the grant for water communications in Canada, 12 June.[45] Convinced that Canning and especially Lansdowne were acting in the best long term interests of Ireland, he attempted to persuade an increasingly impatient O'Connell to continue to 'keep all quiet', pleading that 'when therefore I give you *from the spot* the best counsel I can furnish, it is not because it is *palatable* to myself, however wholesome', and that 'I shall press and have pressed the policy we agree on in the strongest manner in my power'. In July, on Lansdowne finally becoming home secretary, he accepted an invitation to join the treasury board and justified himself to O'Connell by writing that the 'hostility of Tories suggests to any friend of Ireland to cling closely to the ministry which has ousted them and which will grow stronger from day to day, and from the establishment of adequate strength in them I augur every practical good to Ireland'.[46] He was re-elected unopposed for Kerry as an advocate of emancipation and Irish improvements that month, after which, at the request of O'Connell, who congratulated him on the favourable circumstances of his re-election, he supported his claim for a patent of precedence at the Irish bar.[47] He stayed in office on the appointment of Goderich in succession to Canning (who had acted as his own chancellor) in August, when Lord Francis Leveson Gower's* voluntary withdrawal saved him from losing his seat on the fully occupied board, another place now having to be found on the separation of the offices of first lord and chancellor of the exchequer.[48] He was disinclined to vacate during the ministerial crisis over the appointment of John Herries* to the latter position that month, and he considered the state of politics to be uncertain that autumn.[49] It was thought that the £1,000, presumably his salary, that he received would 'make a great impression upon the deficit of your affairs'.[50]

In January 1828 the knight, who afterwards claimed that he had, in fact, 'never augured much good' from the recent experiment of a liberal government, apparently told Rice that it was solely 'his desire to carry

Catholic emancipation which had induced him, though never a Whig in principles, to support a body pledged to its success'.[51] He evidently flirted with Wellington, the new premier, for, although the knight denied newspaper reports that he had been asked to stay on, the duke, who could not employ him, told him that 'it occurs to me that you would have remained in office from something you said to me some time ago'.[52] Moore, commenting on his reluctance to resign, recorded that 'he is a fine fellow notwithstanding and his only fault is having ever become Whig, as nature has written "Tory" on his chivalrous brow'.[53] He gave a silent vote for repeal of the Test Acts, 26 Feb., and for most of the session limited himself to making only minor interventions in debate. He oversaw the passage of the Tralee harbour bill, which benefited his constituents, that session and supported the unsuccessful Hibernian Joint Stock Company bill, which was anathema to O'Connell, 24 Apr.[54] Speaking in the Catholic debate, 8 May, he argued that Pitt had been pledged to carry the question at the time of the Union, arousing the House's impatience by reading several documents to this effect, and, as he put it afterwards to O'Connell, he 'endeavoured to give effect to the *terrors* of your Association'. The following day he was forced up to rebut Peel's aspersions that he had exaggerated the Catholics' case and should have left office on the death of Pitt in 1806. He voted in the majority for relief, 12 May, privately opining that 'I consider it almost certain that something practical must soon result from our triumph in numbers and still more in argument'.[55] Being 'unavoidably obliged to leave the House', he paired for making provision for Canning's family, 13 May. He attacked the finance committee, counterproductively as Croker thought, 16 May, and agreed that Irish prices should be included in calculations of the corn averages, 20 May. Although he had voted for transferring East Retford's seats to Birmingham on 21 Mar., he was seen leaving the House on this issue, which soon precipitated the resignation of the Huskissonites, 2 June, by Moore, who commented that he intended 'evidently to *shirk* the division – looked shy and awkward when we questioned him about it. It is to give Burdett for the *first* time (as he said) a suspicion of what *I* had long suspected – Fitzgerald's disposition to *rat*'.[56] He came to the assistance of Robert Wilmot Horton by speaking in favour of emigration and the encouragement of Irish agriculture, 24 June, when he spoke and was a minority teller for Newport's resolutions concerning abuses in the Irish church. He finally brought forward his motion of the previous year (ultimately withdrawn) for papers on the Union, 3 July, arguing, with reference to long quotations from pamphlets and speeches, that Pitt, Castlereagh and Cornwallis had promised to emancipate the Catholics and that the profound breach of faith that their failure so to do represented was the cause of Ireland's disturbed and disadvantaged condition. He spoke and presumably voted for the grants for the survey of Ireland and fortifications in Canada, 7 July, but divided in the minority against Fyler's amendment relating to the silk duties, which was carried with government support, 14 July, and he proposed alterations to the Irish butter trade bill, 15, 16 July 1828. He sought an interview with Wellington before leaving London that month and, back in Kerry, informed him that the 'excitement is general and the line of distinction between sects every day becoming wider, even where religious distinctions were before little known'. In two lengthy and highly alarmist letters that autumn, he warned the duke that Ireland was sliding towards civil war, with the Protestant gentry in disarray and 'the moral influence of the landlord, the magistrate, the laws ... fast dissolving'; he reckoned this an appalling situation which could only be rectified by the deployment of overwhelming military force and the immediate concession of Catholic relief, which he knew the prime minister already had in mind.[57] Among the other remedies he recommended were the more judicious handling of the Catholics' political leaders and the disfranchisement of the 40s. freeholders.[58]

He welcomed the announcement of emancipation in the House, 5 Feb., and in a letter to Wellington, 9 Feb. 1829, and was that month listed by Planta, the patronage secretary, as likely to be 'with government' on this (although a large cross was also entered against his name).[59] As he later recollected:

> I always expected Catholic concession from the duke of Wellington. I was laughed at for so thinking ... But that being once done, all bar to associating with his government on public principle was removed, at least to those thinking as I did on most other general questions of policy – foreign, domestic, colonial. But what determined me directly to support him was the arrangement of an opposition which availed itself of the vengeful feeling of the old Tories on the score of his Catholic crime and which I deemed an unworthy combination.

However, his plea to his Whig friends to support Wellington *en masse*, in order to prevent the duke being thrown back on the Ultras, met with scant success.[60] He, of course, divided for emancipation, 6, 30 Mar., speaking briefly in its favour, 9, 16, 23 Mar., and approving of the related Irish franchise bill on the 26th. At the bidding of O'Connell, he assisted in

his attempts to take his seat that session as Member for Clare, passing a conciliatory message to his beaten opponent, Vesey Fitzgerald, and informing the Speaker of the day on which he would make his appearance in the chamber.[61] He argued that O'Connell should be heard on his reasons for refusing to swear the oaths, 15 May, and should be allowed the benefit of the Emancipation Act, 18 May, when he was a teller for the minority for allowing him to take his seat unimpeded. He gave Wellington advice on the employment of the Irish poor and the Irish registration system that summer, when he again voiced alarm at the resurgence of religious conflict.[62] He attended the Tralee dinner on 19 Aug. 1829 in honour of O'Connell, but his, in O'Connell's view, misguided approbation of ministers was a growing cause of contention between them.[63]

The knight of Kerry failed to make much headway in pestering Wellington with his proposals for Irish public works schemes, which he forwarded with other unsolicited suggestions, including one about the county Limerick by-election, that winter.[64] Yet in January he informed the prime minister that he would publicly support his government with his speeches and votes, and he fulfilled this promise, 4 Feb. 1830, by speaking and dividing against Knatchbull's amendment to the address on distress.[65] He sponsored O'Connell on taking his seat that day, but criticized him for leaguing himself with English agriculturists who showed no interest in Irish affairs.[66] He asked to meet the duke to discuss the dangerous state of politics and expressed the hope that Lord Grey would likewise give in his adhesion to ministers.[67] He responded to complaints that he had denied that there existed distress in Kerry by a public letter to the editor of a Tralee newspaper, 15 Feb., and by an intervention in the Commons, 17 Feb., when he asserted that he had badgered government for relief measures.[68] His vote for Russell's motion for the enfranchisement of Birmingham, Leeds and Manchester, 23 Feb., was his last in favour of parliamentary reform. On 10 Mar. he informed the minister Charles Arbuthnot* that the Whigs, meeting at Lord Althorp's*, had agreed that they would support the introduction of an income tax if it was proposed by government.[69] Having secured Rice's approval for his ideas on public works being given preference over any extension of the poor laws to Ireland, he spoke for his motion for a select committee on the Irish poor, which met with ministerial concurrence, 11 Mar. 1830, and was named to it.[70] By the end of that month it had been decided that the knight would succeed Sir George Hill* as vice-treasurer of Ireland, with his son Peter as his deputy. Hill retreated to a colonial governorship, leaving his accounts in disarray, but his successor accepted it on the under-standing that it would become an 'efficient' parliamentary office and give him scope to pursue his legislative concerns about Ireland. Most of all it reflected his desire for a junction between Grey's friends and government, and his deep personal and political obligations to Wellington, to whom he nonetheless revealed his conviction that the ministry was already doomed.[71]

The knight, of whom his friend Sir James Willoughby Gordon* wrote at this time that 'a more upright, fair and honourable man does not exist', had Lansdowne's blessing for accepting this appointment, but not that of O'Connell.[72] The latter issued a denunciation of his conduct, although even this was not enough to disrupt his unopposed re-election for Kerry in April 1830, when he vindicated his allegiance to Wellington on the ground of gratitude over emancipation, explained the controversial proposed rises in Irish taxes and advocated public works as the best means of obtaining increased employment.[73] He took his seat, 10 May, when he defended the treasury's handling of the fee fund. Thereafter he divided with his ministerial colleagues, including against Jewish emancipation on the 17th, and limited himself to making minor contributions to debate, notably in relation to the civil government of Canada, 25 May, 11, 14 June. As he had done several times, so over emigration on 15 June he supported Wilmot Horton. He presented the Kerry petition against the increased Irish stamp and spirit duties, 7 June, and, although observing that 'no Irish representative is more exempt than myself from dependence on mere popular favour', he privately urged Wellington to abandon changes which were damaging his standing in public opinion.[74] It was said that the attitude of the knight, who was kept in London on official business until late July, on this issue would determine his fortunes at the general election that summer, but he was backed by O'Connell's brother John, who rallied his friends around him, and by the 2nd earl of Kenmare, who brought forward his brother William Browne, a Catholic, in tandem with him.[75] He was shouted down on the hustings, 13 Aug., but was returned after a contest, behind Browne, whose celebratory dinner in Killarney he attended.[76] That autumn he consulted on and improved his extensive plan for Irish public works, under which monies were to be vested in a system of commissioners, though he complained to Wellington that

> when I consider that at the age of 26 I stood in a relation of more consequence towards the Irish government, and certainly possessed more weight and influence than I do at 56 and that in that interval I am conscious that the recommendations which in my public capacity, whether in

or out of Parliament, I have given to the government are proved by bitter experience to have been as well founded as they were unsuccessful, I may be practised in being disappointed and it may be still my fate to be thwarted by those who know least of Ireland. I am however conscious of my own knowledge of the country and if anything can be available to take the population out of the hands of the revolutionists it is the immediate adoption of my plan.

Wellington, like Peel, gave it detailed consideration in October 1830, but decided that such advances of capital should remain under the direct control of government.[77]

The knight spoke in justification of the ministerial policies for non-interference abroad and against Irish agitation for repeal on the address, 2 Nov. 1830, when, according to his 'memorandum book', he was cheered by some Whigs, the 'general tendency' of whom, he believed, was 'to join the duke'.[78] The following day Croker recommended to Peel that he be encouraged to put himself forward as a government spokesman since he 'did very well last night on Ireland, and will do better when he gets confidence, for he still speaks under the restraint of recent Whiggism'.[79] Evidently accepting that a modicum of parliamentary reform was essential to quiet the inflamed mood of unrest in the country, on 5 Nov. he wrote boldly to Wellington to beg him not to resign if defeated on this (in the Commons on the 16th), as he seemed bent on doing, but rather, with the assistance of such moderate Whigs as Grey, to form a strong ministry as a mildly reformist bulwark against what would otherwise become an unstoppable force of radical extremism.[80] He was appointed to the select committees on the Irish poor, 11 Nov., and the civil list, 15 Nov., having of course sided with his colleagues in the division on this, which precipitated their resignation. He considered Peel's expression of relief on leaving office *'as giving way'*, but insisted on going out himself even though Wellington, with whom he remained in correspondence on Irish affairs, and others, such as John O'Connell, tried to persuade him to join Grey's ministry.[81] The new premier's warmth towards him was shown by his offer to do something for Peter Fitzgerald, who was deprived of his position, the vice-treasurership being transferred to John Smith, the clerk of Irish revenue, as a purely administrative office.[82] Having, in what Sir John Benn Walsh* thought a 'desultory harangue',[83] recommended that ministers take up his plan to provide for the relief of the poor by the advancement of loans, which had been largely approved by the last government, 9 Dec., he secured papers on his former office in order to demonstrate that it had been no sinecure and that he had earned his salary of £2,000 a year, 23 Dec. 1830.

The following month he took his concerns about the alarming state of Ireland and the worrying pressure for revolutionary reform to Grey and the home secretary, Lord Melbourne, but was gratified by their adoption of his idea for a department of public works and pleased by their suppression of the repeal agitation in Ireland.[84] In the House, he argued that no government schemes for relief would work unless taken up by the local gentry, 18 Feb., called for alteration of the first fruits fund as a means of strengthening the Irish church, 14 Mar., suggested the implementation of a permanently fixed duty on colonial trade, 18 Mar., and reiterated his opinions on Ireland's ills when speaking against the resort to the Insurrection Act in Clare, 13 Apr. Following the revelation of the ministry's reform proposals in early March, he appealed to Wellington to stem the tide of radicalism by coming to a compromise with 'the Whigs, who begin to desire a committee or some mode of mitigating their own proposition, and would gladly see the interposition of anyone who can prevent the collision of the extremes'.[85] He hoped that the weakened administration would resign if it lost its reform bill and duly voted against the second reading, 22 Mar.[86] Believing the measure a threat to the constitution, he refused to bring up the Kerry petition in its favour, which pleased Tory opinion in his county.[87] He objected to the use of the crown prerogative of delaying writs as an attack on the independence of Parliament, 30 Mar., and, in a private letter to Lord Brougham, 8 Apr., he condemned the principle of extending the franchise, which he feared would increase the influence of the masses at the expense of the propertied orders.[88] He complained that he had been unable to catch the Speaker's eye in any of the reform debates, 20 Apr., when he stated that he had divided for Gascoyne's wrecking amendment on the 19th because he was only in favour of there being more Irish seats if the number of English ones was increased in the same proportion. Like Peel and other Tories, on 21 Apr. 1831 he made what John Cam Hobhouse* described as a strong speech against the carrying of such a sweeping reform bill at a time of great upheaval and against the recourse to a dissolution as likely to cause additional unrest in Ireland.[89] Claiming to have opposed reform as long ago as 1797, although always amenable to the rectification of particular abuses, he boasted that he had nothing to fear from his constituents and declared that if they preferred a reformer, he would 'retire into private life with the satisfaction of having honestly and faithfully discharged my duty'.

The knight, who had already made public his wish to retire, declined Peel's offer of a seat on Lady Sandwich's interest at Huntingdon and at first decided not to stand again for Kerry at the general election of 1831, but he changed his mind on receiving a remonstrance from Kenmare and the leading Tory gentlemen.[90] He duly entered as an anti-reformer, but his hostile votes had already persuaded O'Connell, despite their former connection over emancipation, to turn him out, asserting that 'no man deserves such a fate better', and he prepared to employ the largely Catholic electorate against him in what was expected to be a severe contest.[91] Convinced that he would be deserted by the tenants of Kenmare, his main ally, and desirous of avoiding violent disruptions, the knight protested at the tactics used against him, but withdrew on the morning of the poll, leaving the way free for O'Connell, who gloated that 'we have completely defeated the knight. Perhaps there never was known a stronger instance of popular determination'.[92] He was, however, praised for his 'independence, integrity and ability' by his Kerry friends, whose gift of a service of plate was presented to him the following year.[93] Writing to Wellington in May 1831, he lamented that in England the government 'will have obtained a House of Commons so thoroughly Whig that it might as well sit at Brooks's Club as at St. Stephen's', and that in Ireland, with O'Connell at liberty to do his worst, the elections were a mockery, the 'mere nominations of mobs on the dictations of priests'.[94]

Reflecting the dismay and disgust of many of his fellow country gentlemen on the affairs of Ireland having effectively been placed in O'Connell's hands, he informed Smith Stanley, the Irish secretary, 30 May 1831, that he could no longer act as a magistrate, although he was endeavouring to restore some degree of order by providing employment on his Ballinruddery estate. On Smith Stanley replying in robust but amicable terms to his complaints, he responded on 6 June with a long *pièce justicative*, emphasizing the bitterness that he and his kind felt at the Irish administration's indifference to elections which 'involved a contest between menacing Catholic ascendancy and the last struggle for Protestant security', and regretting his own abandonment in Kerry. He also provided a summary of his personal journey back to Toryism and his growing desire for a fair coalition of his old and new friends, as well as stating that

> as to your measures I could not view them with prejudice, and for the individuals of the Whigs who came in you will do me the justice to believe that my prejudices could not be *against* them. But for that very reason it was incumbent on me to take a more distinct course. But on reform I could have no qualification. I am rootedly averse to it (not *rad*ically) and it has not been because the duke

of Wellington has opposed it so prominently, much as I estimate his practical good sense and am attached to him, but because I sincerely believe in extreme danger from the character and extent of what has been propounded.[95]

On 12 June 1831 he related similar concerns to Rice, who had advised him to withdraw with a view to resuming his seat at a later date, but, describing himself as 'an unpolitical (perhaps I should say an *impolitic*) person', he confided that 'it is a part of my physical nature that I shall not only be satisfied, but generally conscious of a sort of *exaltation* in the position I happen to be in for the moment, when nothing effecting the happiness of my family and friends is involved'.[96] He was surprised that summer that his son Peter was appointed a commissioner of public works, in belated compensation for the loss of his former post and apparently to the resentment of many ministerialists.[97]

In September 1831 the knight informed Wellington of his hostility to the reform bills, especially regarding his own country, for dealing with which, had the previous Parliament lasted a few days longer, he would have introduced a measure 'authorizing the crown to suspend the issue of writs of election to various counties in Ireland on the notoriety that no free elections could take place in them'.[98] At the time of the general election of 1832, when he backed his former colleague Browne for Kerry and did not – as O'Connell had conjectured he might – stand himself as a Conservative, he again despaired of the electoral chicanery which would result in a triumph for the repeal candidates, since, for him, their success portended the general spoliation of the Protestant ascendancy.[99] The following year he suggested using newspaper articles to counter government propaganda and in late 1834, when he rejoiced at the return of Wellington and Peel to office, he accepted a junior seat at the admiralty board, being employed, as he complained, 'to sign papers of mere form at Somerset House'.[100] He confidently expected to win back Kerry, but O'Connell, ridiculing his appointment by observing that 'the only ship he will ever command is the ferryboat to Valentia' and placing 'his *fame* on the issue', mobilized the Catholic tenants and their priests in a concerted bid to defeat him. The knight, who was confined to his London residence by illness, was therefore beaten into third place behind two repealers in a contest which bears comparison with O'Connell's victory in Clare in 1828.[101] His petition, alleging intimidation and clerical interference, was brought up, 10 Mar.; it was discharged, 11 June, but these issues were raised by Frederick Shaw* against O'Connell, 6 Mar., 15 May. Another petition

from him, complaining that he had not been allowed to prove any wrongdoing before the select committee on cases of intimidation, was briefly brought forward by Sir James Scarlett*, 19 Aug., when O'Connell's son John called his claims 'totally false'. Further discussion took place, with William Henry Ord defending the conduct of his committee, 21 Aug., and the (second) petition was at last allowed to lie on the table, 24 Aug. 1835, when the knight disputed Ord's argument in a letter to *The Times*.[102] He was introduced to the electors of Lambeth at a political dinner in December 1836 as their future Conservative candidate, speaking in praise of Wellington and Peel and damning radical reform proposals. Although he attended another such gathering early the following year, he withdrew, owing to a difference of opinion, before the general election of 1837, despite, as his son Peter recalled, his having 'had a considerable chance of success'.[103]

According to his fragmentary diary entry for 23 May 1838, he damned Wellington's compromise whereby the appropriation clause would be dropped from the Irish tithes bill in exchange for the passage through the Lords of the Irish municipal corporations and poor bills, and, referring to his endeavours in 1830, he criticized the latter measure in a public letter to Lord Melbourne, the prime minister, the following month.[104] Although declaring himself 'politically defunct' and 'renouncing all claim to political office', he welcomed Peel's resumption of power in 1841 and only broke his silence to correspond with him over parliamentary matters because of his concern about the effect of enforcing the poor rate in the already dangerous state of Ireland in 1843.[105] In his *Letter to Sir Robert Peel on the Endowment of the Roman Catholic Church of Ireland* (1845), which included an account of his involvement with Pitt at the time of the Union, he gave his endorsement to the premier's policies towards the Irish church. During that decade, when he was appealed to for vindication of O'Connell's conduct as a local landlord over his alleged use of the repeal rent to pay off arrears and his apparently neglectful treatment of his peasants, he continued to seek government support for his plans for Valentia and Irish public works in general.[106]

He died, still holding to a visionary belief that from his window at Glanleam he could 'see another Liverpool before me', in March 1849. His four eldest sons having predeceased him, he was succeeded in his heavily mortgaged estates and as 19th knight of Kerry by Peter George Fitzgerald (1808-80), who served as vice-treasurer of Ireland, 1841-6, and was created a baronet a few weeks before his death.[107] In his preface to his manuscript 'family record', Peter remembered his father as 'a man of considerable talent and special qualities quite remarkable', with a certain quiet charm and strength of character in adversity, adding that 'it could scarcely be said that he was a very steady or systematic man of business, but he had immense energy', much of which he devoted to practical attempts to improve Ireland.[108] He was reputed to be the last surviving Member of the Irish House of Commons, but this honour in fact belonged to Sir Thomas Staples (1775-1865).[109]

[1] Presumably not (although probably related to) the Lancelot Sandys (or Sandes) (d. 1728) who was Member for Portarlington, 1723-7 (Hist. Irish Parl. vi. 239). [2] So identified (and without the middle name 'Digges') as Member for Dundalk, 1761-8, Longford, 1768-83, Belturbet, 1783-90, and Newcastle, 1790-1800 (ibid. v. 62). [3] Add. 40355, f. 90. [4] JRL, Spring Rice coll. Eng. ms. 1189, p. 2. [5] Derby mss 920 Der (14) 124/3, knight of Kerry to Smith Stanley, 7 June 1831; 18th Cent. Irish Official Pprs. in GB ed. A.P.W. Malcomson, ii. 147. [6] Spring Rice coll. Eng. ms. 1189, p. 3. [7] General Advertiser or Limerick Gazette, 24 Mar. 1820; O'Connell Corresp. ii. 825-6. [8] O'Connell Corresp. ii. 840. [9] R.B. McDowell, Grattan, 218; O. MacDonagh, Hereditary Bondsman, 168. [10] O'Connell Corresp. ii. 847a; G. Broeker, Rural Disorder and Police Reform in Ireland, 155. [11] O'Connell Corresp. ii. 875, 878. [12] Dublin Weekly Reg. 27 Jan. 1821. [13] Dorset RO, Bankes mss D/BKL, Bankes jnl. 127 (2 Apr. 1821); PRO NI, Fitzgerald mss MIC639/11/6/32; O'Connell Corresp. ii. 895. [14] Dublin Evening Post, 25 Oct.; Lansdowne mss, Brougham to Lansdowne, n.d. [1821]. [15] Black Bk. (1823), 155. [16] The Times, 27 Feb. 1823. [17] Northants. RO, Agar Ellis diary. [18] Add. 51663, Bedford to Holland, n.d. [1823]. [19] Fitzgerald mss MIC639/11/6/51, 53. [20] Brougham mss, knight of Kerry to Brougham, 26 June 1823; O'Connell Corresp. ii. 1041. [21] Fitzgerald mss MIC639/11/6/58, 59. [22] PP (1824), viii. 135-50, 174-82. [23] TCD, Donoughmore mss D/43/62. [24] J.A. Gaughan, Listowel and its Vicinity, 284, 293; Moore Jnl. ii. 669. [25] A. Fitzgerald, 'Valentia and Knight of Kerry', in O'Connell: Education, Church and State ed. M.R. O'Connell, 80-84. [26] Fitzgerald mss MIC639/11/6/68-70; Wellington mss WP1/796/12; 800/5; 805/28; 807/19; 808/7; 812/5, 12; Add. 40374, f. 19; CJ, lxxx. 303, 521, 586; lxxxi. 76, 158, 164, 188, 318, 332, 337; O'Connell Corresp. ii. 1242, 1247. [27] Fitzgerald, 83; Wellington mss WP1/907/20; O'Connell Corresp. ii. 1480; Fitzgerald mss MIC639/12/6/109. [28] Fitzgerald mss MIC639/11/6/71. [29] Dublin Evening Post, 11 Sept. 1824. [30] O'Connell Corresp. iii. 1166. [31] Ibid. iii. 1178, 1183. [32] The Times, 11 Mar. 1825. [33] O'Connell Corresp. iii. 1278. [34] Dublin Evening Post, 10, 27, 29 June 1826; Spring Rice coll. Eng. ms. 1189, p. 51. [35] Dublin Evening Post, 6, 13 July; Freeman's Jnl. 4 Aug. 1826. [36] Add. 40332, f. 111; 40388, f. 299; 40389, f. 13. [37] O'Connell Corresp. iii. 1354, 1358, 1362, 1365; Fitzgerald mss MIC639/12/6/37. [38] Add. 51784, Holland to Fox, 17 Feb. 1827. [39] The Times, 3, 8 Mar. 1827; O'Connell Corresp. iii. 1369a. [40] MacDonagh, 235-6; O'Connell Corresp. iii. 1378. [41] Wentworth Woodhouse mun. G15/6; Creevey Pprs. ii. 112. [42] Lansdowne mss; Fitzgerald mss MIC639/12/6/36; O'Connell Corresp. iii. 1379-80, 1382. [43] Fitzgerald mss MIC639/12/6/52. [44] Colchester Diary, iii. 491. [45] The Times, 26, 31 May, 7, 13 June 1827. [46] O'Connell Corresp. iii. 1386-7, 1389-90, 1393-4, 1397, 1400. [47] Dublin Evening Post, 17, 24 July; Lansdowne mss, O'Connell to knight of Kerry, 30 July; latter to Lansdowne, 3 Aug. 1827. [48] Add. 38750, f. 231. [49] Palmerston-Sulivan Letters, 199; O'Connell Corresp. iii. 1420. [50] Fitzgerald mss MIC639/12/6/79. [51] Derby mss 124/3, knight of Kerry to Smith Stanley, 7 June 1831; NLI, Monteagle mss A/26 (NRA 19437). [52] Wellington mss WP1/914/16, 24; 915/45. [53] Moore Jnl. iii. 1116. [54] O'Connell Corresp. iii. 1455-7; Fitzgerald mss MIC639/12/6/92; CJ, lxxxiii. 72-73, 154, 189, 209, 262, 349, 392, 535. [55] O'Connell Corresp. iii. 1459. [56] Moore Jnl. iii. 1144. [57] Wellington mss WP1/941/15; 946/6, 35; 951/2; 955/16. [58] PRO NI, Anglesey mss D619/32A/2/142; Grey mss, Ellice to Grey, 27 Oct. 1828. [59] Wellington mss WP1/995/23. [60] Derby mss 124/3, knight of Kerry to Smith Stanley, 7 June 1831. [61] O'Connell Corresp. iii. 1474; iv. 1513a, 1524a, 1535, 1555a-b, 1563. [62] Wellington mss WP1/1017/8; 1027/2; 1033/7; 1035/72. [63] Kerry Evening Post, 22 Aug. 1829; O'Connell Corresp. iv. 1605, 1608. [64] Wellington mss WP1/1060/6; 1065/62; 1085/15; Fitzgerald mss T3075/18/31, 32. [65] Wellington mss WP1/1086/7; 1091/1. [66] Dublin Evening Post, 6, 9 Feb. 1830. [67] Wellington mss WP1/1093/1, 8; Grey mss, Durham to Grey [15 Feb. 1830]. [68] Western Herald, 22 Feb. 1830. [69] Add. 40340, f. 220. [70] Wellington mss WP1/1101/4, 7. [71] Ibid. WP1/1105/40; 1106/8; Spring Rice coll. Eng. ms. 1189, p. 3; Derby mss 124/3, knight of Kerry to Smith Stanley, 7 June 1831. [72] Taylor Pprs. 317; Fitzgerald mss T3075/18/36; O'Connell Corresp. iv. 1662a. [73] Dublin Evening Post, 17, 27 Apr.; Western Herald, 22 Apr.; Fitzgerald mss MIC639/9, knight of Kerry to Fitzgerald [Apr. 1830]; Wellington mss WP1/1108/34. [74] Wellington mss WP1/1115/19; 1119/1. [75] Fitzgerald mss MIC639/13/7/64, 75; Warder, 19 June; Western Herald, 8, 19, 22 July 1830. [76] Western Herald, 16, 19, 23 Aug. 1830. [77] Wellington mss WP1/1125/19; 1145/15; 1146/29; 1148/45. [78] Fitzgerald mss T3075/18/54. [79] Croker Pprs. ii. 73-74. [80] G.M. Trevelyan, Lord Grey of Reform Bill, 237; Fitzgerald mss T3075/18/54; Wellington mss WP1/1149/21; M. Brock, Great Reform Act, 128. [81] Fitzgerald mss T3075/18/54; MIC639/13/7/99; Wellington mss WP1/1152/5; 1154/36; 1156/8. [82] Fitzgerald mss MIC639/13/7/96, 105; R. B. McDowell, Irish Administration, 93. [83] NLW, Ormathwaite mss FG1/5. [84] Wellington mss WP1/1173/8, 37. [85] Fitzgerald mss T3075/18/60. [86] Wellington mss WP1/1179/2. [87] Kerry Evening Post, 30 Mar. 1831. [88] Brougham mss. [89] Broughton, Recollections, iv. 104. [90] Fitzgerald mss T3075/18/61, 63; MIC639/14/7/20-22, 24, 25; Western Herald, 17 May 1831. [91] Fitzgerald mss MIC639/14/7/3, 19, 26, 28-32; Western Herald, 28 Apr., 3, 5, 7, 10, 12 May 1831; O'Connell Corresp. iv. 1800, 1802; Wellington mss WP1/1184/9, 24, 31. [92] Add. 40402, f. 46; Fitzgerald mss MIC639/14/7/23, 36; Western Herald, 14, 17 May 1831; O'Connell Corresp. iv. 1810. [93] Western Herald, 19 May 1831; Kerry Evening Post, 14 Mar., 14 Apr. 1832. [94] Wellington mss WP1/1184/9; 1187/50. [95] Derby mss 124/3; Fitzgerald mss T3075/18/64. [96] Wellington mss WP1/1184/9; Monteagle mss 13371 (1). [97] Fitzgerald mss T3075/18/67; Wellington mss WP1/1187/50; Holland House Diaries, 28. [98] Wellington mss WP1/1196/31. [99] Ibid. 1239/10; Kerry Evening Post, 8 Dec. 1832; O'Connell Corresp. iv. 1943. [100] Wellington Pol. Corresp. i. 290; ii. 180-1, 227, 357, 679; Add. 40406, ff. 21, 116-19. [101] Wellington Pol. Corresp. ii. 679, 794; Add. 40410, f. 126; 40412, f. 23; Western Herald, 1, 8, 15, 22, 26 Jan., 2, 5 Feb. 1835; O'Connell Corresp. v. 2177-8, 2183-4, 2198, 2204-6; G.J. Lyne, 'O'Connell, Intimidation and Kerry Elections of 1835', Jnl. of Kerry Arch. and Hist. Soc. iv (1971), 74-97; K.T. Hoppen, Elections, Politics, and Society in Ireland, 36, 155-60, 391. [102] CJ, xc. 89-91, 327, 570, 578, 586; The Times, 22, 24 Aug. 1835. [103] The Times, 9 Dec. 1836, 1 Mar., 1 July 1837; Spring Rice coll. Eng. ms. 1189, p. 3. [104] D.C. Large, 'House of Lords and Ireland in Age of Peel', Irish Hist. Stud. ix (1955), 391; The Times, 28 June 1838. [105] Add. 40428, f. 100; 40478, f. 75; 40488, f. 9. [106] Fitzgerald, 85-86; O'Connell Corresp. vii. 3182; Add. 40573, ff. 127-50; 40586, f. 297. [107] Fitzgerald, 83, 86; Dublin Evening Post, 10 Mar.; The Times, 12 Mar. 1849; Gent. Mag. (1849), i. 423-4, 538-9; Oxford DNB. [108] Spring Rice coll. Eng. ms. 1189, pp. 2-4. [109] Hist. Irish Parl. iv. 155; vi. 325.

S.M.F.

FITZGERALD, Lord William Charles O'Brien (1793–1864).

CO. KILDARE   23 Mar. 1814–1831

b. 4 Jan. 1793, 3rd but 2nd surv. s. of William Robert, 2nd duke of Leinster [I] (*d.* 1804), and Hon. Emilia Olivia St. George, da. of St. George, 1st Bar. St. George [I]. *educ.* by Rev. John Smith at Woodnesborough, nr. Sandwich, Kent; Eton 1805-8; Christ Church, Oxf. 1810. *unm. d.* 8 Dec. 1864.

Fitzgerald, a contemporary of Lord John Russell* at Woodnesborough, had joined Brooks's, sponsored by Lord Holland, 16 Mar. 1813.[1] On coming of age the following year he had been seated for county Kildare on his family's dominant interest. At the 1820 general election he was again returned unopposed.[2] A regular but mostly silent attender, he continued to vote with the Whig opposition to the Liverpool ministry on most major issues, including economy, retrenchment and reduced taxation, although after 1825 he was frequently abroad.[3] During a debate on the conduct of the Dublin sheriff, 22 Feb. 1821, he made a 'single observation', which 'caused great cheering in the House' but was 'inaudible in the gallery'.[4] He voted for Catholic claims, 28 Feb. 1821, 1 Mar., 21 Apr., 10 May 1825. He divided for parliamentary reform, 9 May 1821, and inquiry into the Scottish royal burghs, 20 Feb. 1822. On 27 Mar. 1823 he spoke in support of a petition against the coal duties. At the 1826 dissolution he was in Paris and unable to leave owing to 'severe indisposition', but he was returned unopposed *in absentia* as 'a liberal'.[5] He was granted a month's leave after serving on an election committee, 19 Mar. 1827. He voted for Catholic claims, 6 Mar. 1827, 12 May 1828, and brought up a favourable petition, 7 May 1828. He presented petitions for Catholic emancipation, 16 Feb., 27 Mar., and divided accordingly, 6, 30 Mar. 1829. He presented one from the Kildare grand jury for the repeal of a road toll, 9 Apr. 1829. There is no record of any parliamentary activity in the 1830 session.

At the 1830 general election he rushed back from Italy in time for the nomination, where he promised to support reform and welcomed the 'wonderful and gratifying events' in France, which had delayed his journey home. He topped the poll after a two-day contest.[6] He was listed by the Wellington ministry among the 'bad doubtfuls' and voted against them on the civil list, 15 Nov. 1830. He presented a petition demanding equal treatment for Catholics and Protestants with regard to the Galway franchise, 9 Dec. 1830. He voted for the second reading of the Grey ministry's

reform bill, 22 Mar., and against Gascoyne's wrecking amendment, 19 Apr. 1831. At the ensuing dissolution he retired from Parliament, citing his 15 years' service.[7] In September 1859 Greville recorded passing a day with him 'seeing the town' of Dublin, where 'he took me over the old Leinster House, now the Royal Institution, and then to the bank to see the old House of Lords'.[8] He died unmarried at Harcourt Terrace, Dublin in December 1864.[9]

[1] Walpole, *Russell*, i. 13. [2] *Dublin Evening Post*, 9, 25 Mar. 1820. [3] *Black Bk.* (1823), 155; *Session of Parl. 1825*, p. 463. [4] *The Times*, 22 Feb. 1821. [5] *Dublin Evening Post*, 10, 17, 29 June 1826. [6] Ibid. 29 July, 10, 19, 21 Aug. 1830. [7] Ibid. 28 Apr., 3 May 1831. [8] *Greville Mems.* vii. 437-8. [9] *Gent. Mag.* (1865), i. 124.

P.J.S.

FITZGERALD *see also* VESEY FITZGERALD

FITZGIBBON, Hon. Richard Hobart (1793–1864), of Mount Shannon, co. Limerick.

CO. LIMERICK   1818–1841

b. 2 Oct. 1793, 2nd s. of John, 1st earl of Clare [I] (*d.* 1802), and Anne, da. of Richard Chapel Whaley, MP [I], of Whaley Abbey, co. Wicklow. *educ.* Harrow 1802; by Rev. John Smith at Woodnesborough, nr. Sandwich, Kent 1805. *m.* 11 July 1825 at Dunkirk (and again at St. James's, Westminster 9 Jan. 1826), Diana, da. of Charles Brydges Woodcock of Brentford Butts, Mdx., div. w. of Maurice Crosbie Moore of Mooresfort, co. Tipperary, 1s. *d.v.p.* 3da.; ?1s. illegit. *suc.* bro. John as 3rd earl of Clare [I] and 3rd Bar. Fitzgibbon [UK] 18 Aug. 1851. *d.* 10 Jan. 1864.

Usher and registrar of affidavits in chancery [I] 1810-36.

Ensign 1 Ft. Gds. 1808; capt. 2 Ceylon regt. 1811, ret. 1814; col. co. Limerick militia 1818-*d.*

Gov. co. Limerick 1818-31, ld. lt. 1831-48, 1851-*d.*

Fitzgibbon was the younger son of the heavyweight former Irish lord chancellor the 1st earl of Clare, one of the architects of the Union, and the only brother of the 2nd earl, who was described in 1813 by the bishop of Limerick as being 'without a particle of the fiery enterprising genius of his father', but 'a young man of much promise – a good scholar, mild and conciliatory in manner, with an excellent understanding; exceedingly popular in his county and … a respectable nobleman'.[1] A supporter of Lord Liverpool's administration, Clare returned his brother on his own interest for their native county in 1818, when Fitzgibbon, who already had a lucrative Irish legal sinecure, became governor and militia colonel of county Limerick. Both, unlike their father, favoured Catholic relief.[2] The inactive and mostly silent Fitzgibbon, who had already cast at least one wayward vote, made such a nuisance of himself by refusing to attend and raising patronage demands that on the eve of the general election of 1820 Charles Grant*, the Irish secretary, commented to the premier that he should no longer be regarded as a friend and that, if he was not in any case 'quite secure', he would 'not merit our support'.[3] However, he was elected by a sizeable majority after a contest, when he boasted of the number of his voters and claimed to be an independent.[4]

No evidence of parliamentary activity has been traced for that session, although on 19 Nov. 1820 Katherine Forester observed to the duchess of Rutland that 'I am sorry to hear Mr. Fitzgibbon is such a radical. Lord Clare seems quite the contrary'.[5] This was presumably in relation to the Queen Caroline affair, but he divided against censuring ministers' conduct towards her, 6 Feb., and his only hostile vote on the subject was on the decision of the sheriff of Dublin to suspend the county meeting, 22 Feb. 1821. He presented his county's petitions for relief from agricultural distress, 19 Feb., and for Catholic claims, 28 Feb., when he voted in this sense, and he commented adversely on the Catholic priests' petition got up in Limerick, 2 Apr.[6] He divided for making Leeds a scot and lot, not £10 householder, borough if it got Grampound's seats, 2 Mar. 1821, Russell's parliamentary reform motion, 24 Apr. 1823, and Newport's bill against non-resident voters in Irish boroughs, 9 Mar. 1826. He took six weeks' leave on urgent private business, 10 May 1821, and most likely did not return until the beginning of the following session, when he voted against the Irish habeas corpus suspension bill, 7, 8 Feb. 1822. He was appointed to the select committee on Limerick taxation, 23 May 1822. He was in the majority for inquiry into the legal proceedings against the Dublin Orange rioters, 22 Apr., and the minority against the committal of the Irish tithes composition bill, 16 June 1823. He brought up a petition from the weavers of Cashel for continuing the linen bounties, 22 Mar. 1824.[7] He divided for Catholic relief, 1 Mar., 21 Apr., 10 May 1825.

James Abercromby* reported to the duke of Devonshire, 6 Oct. 1823, that 'Fitzgibbon has gone off with a Mrs. Moore', the wife of Maurice Crosbie Moore, whom he wrongly identified as a daughter of Christopher Hely Hutchinson*. Referring to Fitzgibbon's mother, he continued

I should think Lady Clare would have a great contempt for such a proceeding. She will reasonably say, why could

they not follow my example who have been doing these things all my life and have always kept my place in society. I am however very sincerely sorry for Lord Clare, who has made himself a poor man for life by struggling to return his brother for the county of Limerick and here is the end of it, I suppose.[8]

Fitzgibbon, who presumably absented himself from Westminster for much of the following two years, and his mistress eloped to France and her husband subsequently began legal proceedings in Dublin in June 1824 and obtained a separation in the consistorial court, being awarded £6,000 in damages. His petition for a divorce was presented to the Lords, 7 Feb., and, after conclusive evidence had been heard on 26 Apr., the Act was passed, receiving royal assent on 27 June 1825.[9] The couple quickly married abroad, but in November, after unpleasant legal proceedings, their son Henry was ordered to be returned to the care of his nominal father Maurice Moore, who admitted he was acting purely out of vindictiveness.[10] By then Fitzgibbon had settled his quarrel over this with Clare, who was manoeuvring that autumn to secure his future re-election.[11] He signed the requisition for a pro-Catholic county Limerick meeting (which the sheriff refused to authorize) and spoke for emancipation at the Catholics' provincial meeting in Limerick, 24 Oct. 1825, but declined to attend the O'Connellite dinner in Dublin, 2 Feb. 1826.[12] Early that year Clare himself chose an unsuitable wife, Elizabeth Burrell, the daughter of Lord Gwydir, who was reluctant to reside at the grand house he had just constructed on his Limerick estate; Lady Williams Wynn commented that 'the entire uncontrolled indulgence in which she has passed some four or five and 30 years is a bad preparation for the little *travers* which must now and then occur in the best regulated marriages', and, indeed, they took the decision to 'unmarry' unofficially three years later, when Countess Granville cattily remarked: 'How amiable of Lord Clare to be sorry, if he is! I should be pleased never to see her again'.[13] Imitating the concern with Catholic relief and other Irish causes expressed by his seconder Thomas Spring Rice, who sat for Limerick city, Fitzgibbon was again returned at the head of the poll at the general election of 1826.[14] He called a meeting of magistrates to memorialize the lord lieutenant against the withdrawal of the military guard from the county gaol, 4 Dec. 1826.[15]

Fitzgibbon, who brought up several pro-Catholic petitions during the three ensuing sessions, voted for emancipation, 6 Mar. 1827, 12 May 1828, and, having been listed by Planta, the Wellington ministry's patronage secretary, as likely to be 'with government',

6, 30 Mar. 1829; however, he was in the minority for Duncannon's amendment to the related Irish franchise bill, to allow reregistration, on the 20th. He divided for repeal of the Test Acts, 12 May 1828, and Jewish emancipation, 5 Apr., 17 May 1830. He sided with opposition for reducing the salary of the lieutenant-general of the ordnance, 4 July 1828, to restrict the army grant to six months, 19 Feb., and for repealing the Irish coal duties, 13 May 1830. Clare, who was reported to be in improved spirits since his marital separation, successfully applied to be named governor of Bombay by Wellington, who commented that he 'must be well supported [as] he had not a strong mind', and refused him the order of St. Patrick. After some delay, he was finally elected to the post by the Company in March, with a view to travelling to India in the autumn.[16] The imminence of this appointment did not prevent Fitzgibbon voting with opposition for transferring East Retford's seats to Birmingham, 11 Feb., the enfranchisement of Birmingham, Leeds and Manchester, 23 Feb., and parliamentary reform, 28 May. He divided against the grant for public buildings, 3 May, and would have done so on the cost of repairs to Windsor Castle that day, had not the chancellor, Henry Goulburn, who thought his conduct 'rather too bad', conceded a select committee.[17] He deplored the increase in the Irish spirit and stamp duties in May, and brought up his county's petition against this on the 20th.[18] He was in the minority against abolition of the death penalty for forgery, 7 June 1830. He offered on the basis of his past services at the general election that summer and, with the prospect of another contest, Clare appealed to the Castle for support. But, reacting to the brothers' defence of their connection Peter Low of Lowtown and their hostile parliamentary votes, the Irish secretary, Lord Francis Leveson Gower, informed Clare that 'I do not see what any government can do more than abstain from interfering against him'.[19] However, the challenger dropped out and Fitzgibbon was returned unopposed.[20]

He was deemed to be 'pro-government' in Pierce Mahony's[†] analysis of the Irish elections, but, while Clare fulsomely expressed his allegiance to administration at the Company's parting dinner in his honour in August 1830 and remained loyal to the Tories, he was listed by ministers among the 'bad doubtfuls', and Planta wrote beside his name that 'he *should* support us – but will oppose'.[21] He voted for Daniel O'Connell's motion for repeal of the Irish Subletting Act, 11 Nov., and for a select committee on the civil list, which precipitated Wellington's resignation, 15 Nov. 1830. He divided for the second reading of the Grey ministry's reform bill, 22 Mar., and against Gascoyne's wrecking

amendment, which led to a dissolution, 19 Apr. 1831. Claiming that he had always supported the reform of abuses, he was again returned unopposed at the general election that spring, when no third candidate in the end emerged.[22] He voted for the second reading of the reintroduced reform bill, 6 July, at least twice against adjourning proceedings on it, 12 July, and steadily for its details. However, he brought up the Teignbridge Agricultural Association's petition against the division of counties, 14 July, and divided for Lord Chandos's amendment to enfranchise £50 tenants-at-will, 18 Aug. He was in the minority for printing the Waterford petition for the disarming of the Irish yeomanry. He voted for the passage of the reform bill, 21 Sept., the second reading of the Scottish bill, 23 Sept., and Lord Ebrington's confidence motion, 10 Oct. 1831.

He became lord lieutenant of Limerick that autumn, despite a remonstration from Rice, the treasury secretary, who noted that he 'cannot be invited by a single family in that county for his unfortunate marriage'.[23] In November he issued a circular insisting that in the new commission all magistrates would have to be active and resident, and he declined to attend the 'national council' on reform in Dublin early the following year.[24] He paired for the second, 17 Dec. 1831, and third readings of the revised bill, 22 Mar., and Ebrington's motion for an address calling on the king to appoint only ministers who would carry it unimpaired, 10 May 1832. He voted for the second reading of the Irish bill, 25 May, but for O'Connell's motion to extend the Irish franchise to £5 freeholders, 18 June. He presented Abington and Boher petitions against Irish tithes, 5 July, and divided for postponing this subject to the following session, 13 July. He was returned for county Limerick as a Liberal at the general election in December 1832 and sat until 1841. He succeeded his childless brother in 1851, but his only son John Charles Henry, Viscount Fitzgibbon, was killed at Balaklava in October 1854 and his peerages became extinct at his death in January 1864.[25]

[1] *Geo. IV Letters*, i. 333. [2] *HP Commons, 1790-1820*, ii. 668; iii. 758-9. [3] Add. 38283, f. 74; 38458, f. 298; 40296, ff. 23-24; *Black Bk.* (1823), 155; *Session of Parl. 1825*, p. 463. [4] *General Advertiser and Limerick Gazette*, 25 Feb., 21, 28, 31 Mar., 7 Apr. 1820. [5] Salop RO, Weld-Forester mss 1224/332/157. [6] *The Times*, 20 Feb. 1821. [7] Ibid. 23 Mar. 1824. [8] Chatsworth mss. [9] *The Times*, 9 June 1824; *LJ*, lvii. 19-20, 638-42, 759, 928, 1118. [10] *The Times*, 8-10, 17 Nov. 1825. [11] *Dublin Evening Post*, 15 Sept. 1825; Add. 40331, f. 237. [12] *Dublin Evening Post*, 6, 20, 27, 29 Oct. 1825; *O'Connell Corresp.* iii. 1278. [13] *Williams Wynn Corresp.* 339; *Arbuthnot Corresp.* 119; *Countess Granville Letters*, ii. 40. [14] *Limerick Chron.* 7, 24, 28 June, 1, 5 July 1826. [15] Ibid. 29 Nov., 6 Dec. 1826. [16] *Howard Sisters*, 122-3; *Ellenborough Diary*, ii. 50, 194-5, 209; Wellington mss WP1/1123/23; 1130/12. [17] Add. 40333, f. 101. [18] *Limerick Evening Post*, 7, 21 May 1830. [19] Ibid. 16 July, 3 Aug.; NAI, Leveson

Gower letterbks. Leveson Gower to Clare, 30 July, to Singleton, 30 July 1830; Add. 40297, f. 15. [20] *Limerick Evening Post*, 10 Aug. 1830. [21] *Ellenborough Diary*, ii. 347; *Three Diaries*, 92. [22] *Limerick Evening Post*, 29 Apr., 3, 13 May 1831. [23] Derby mss 920 Der (14) 117/8, Rice to Smith Stanley, 17 Sept. 1831. [24] *Dublin Evening Post*, 29 Nov. 1831, 10 Jan. 1832. [25] *Limerick Chron.* 12 Jan. 1864; *The Times*, 12 Jan. 1864; *Gent. Mag.* (1864), i. 386-7.

S.M.F.

FITZHARRIS, Visct. *see* **HARRIS**, **James Edward**

FITZROY, **Lord Charles** (1791–1865), of 49 Piccadilly, Mdx.

THETFORD   1818–1830
BURY ST. EDMUNDS   1832–1847

b. 28 Feb. 1791, 2nd. s. of George Henry Fitzroy[†], 4th duke of Grafton (*d.* 1844), and Lady Charlotte Maria Waldegrave, da. and coh. of James, 2nd Earl Waldegrave; bro. of Henry Fitzroy, earl of Euston* and Lord James Henry Fitzroy*. *educ.* Harrow 1802-5; Great Marlow. *m.* 25 Oct. 1825, Anne, da. of Lord George Augustus Henry Cavendish*, 2s. 2da. *d.* 17 June 1865.
    Ensign 1 Ft. Gds. 1807, lt. 1812, capt. 1812, maj. 1815, lt.-col. 1819; maj. 55 Ft. 1820, half-pay 1821; asst. adj.-gen. at Armagh 1830-2; sold out 1834.
    Vice-chamberlain July 1835-Apr. 1838; PC 1 July 1835.

Fitzroy, whose military and political careers and private life were blighted by his compulsive gambling habit, had served with distinction on the Walcheren expedition, in the Peninsula and at Waterloo. He was with the army of occupation in France when he and his elder brother Lord Euston were brought into Parliament in 1818 as the duke of Grafton's family Members for Thetford and Bury St. Edmunds.[1] A silent Whig, he had opposed the coercive legislation introduced after Peterloo, and he was again returned for Thetford at the general election of 1820, when his uncle Lord John Edward Fitzroy replaced Euston at Bury St. Edmunds.[2] The failure of his horse Swase to win the 1822 St. Leger completed his financial ruin, and he spent the next two and a half years abroad evading his creditors and his father's wrath.[3] Otherwise, he voted with the main Whig opposition to the Liverpool ministry in most major divisions in the 1820 Parliament and consistently with Hume and the 'Mountain' for economy, retrenchment and reduced taxation.[4] He backed the 1820-1 parliamentary and extra-parliamentary campaigns on behalf of Queen Caroline.[5] He divided for Catholic relief, 28 Feb. 1821, 1 Mar., 21 Apr., 10 May 1825, parliamentary reform, 9 May 1821, 13 Apr. 1826, and receipt of the radical Greenhoe reform petition, 3 June 1822. From Florence

and Venice in 1823 he expressed concern that his father had gained little by recently promoting the adoption of distress petitions advocating reform in Suffolk, and he welcomed Huskisson's appointment as president of the board of trade and the government's defeat on a motion for inquiry into the prosecution of the Dublin Orange rioters, 22 Apr.[6] In July 1824 Grafton relented and appointed lawyers to deal with his debts; and when he married in October 1825 Euston made Sholebrooke Lodge in Northamptonshire and the hunting in Salcey Forest available to him until his own heir came of age.[7] The Petre estate and interest in Thetford had been sold in 1822 to the financier Alexander Baring*, whose son William Bingham Baring became Fitzroy's colleague at the general election of 1826.[8]

He voted for Catholic relief, 6 Mar. 1827, 12 May 1828, to disfranchise Penryn, 28 May 1827, and to repeal the Test Acts, 26 Feb. 1828, and presented Thetford's petition for repeal of the Malt Act, 29 Feb. 1828. He repeatedly complained that their agreement of 5 June 1827 whereby Grafton underwrote his debts provided he assigned his entire income to him and his father-in-law, the Whig Member for Derbyshire, made parliamentary life unaffordable;[9] and his next known vote was on 1 July 1830, when he divided to delay on-consumption under the sale of beer bill. In an attempt to distance him from his gaming associates, Grafton had secured him an Irish posting under Sir Richard Hussey Vivian*, and he stood down at Thetford at the dissolution that month in favour of his younger brother.[10]

Fitzroy welcomed the appointment of Lord Grey's ministry and their reform bill. He wrote to the postmaster-general, the duke of Richmond, 5 May 1831, 'It is as well that the peers should have a certain majority for the bill dinned into their ears, that they may get used to the sound before reality comes before them'.[11] His father-in-law joined them in September as a coronation peer (earl of Burlington). By March 1832 Fitzroy had resolved to resign his command to return to England, ostensibly to assist his ailing in-laws at Burlington House.[12] Grafton reluctantly acquiesced in the arrangement and financed his election as Liberal Member for Bury St. Edmunds, where he topped the poll in December 1832. He retained the seat until 1847, the first dissolution after his father's death.[13] His appointment as vice-chamberlain in 1835 caused a stir, as did his dismissal in 1838 for voting against the Melbourne government on a slavery issue.[14] He failed to avoid bankruptcy and died at his wife's house, Elm Lodge, Hampton, Middlesex, in June 1865.[15]

[1] *Gent. Mag.* (1865), ii. 126; Suff. RO (Bury St. Edmunds), Grafton mss HA513/5/147-56; *HP Commons, 1790-1820*, ii. 295-6; iii. 765-6, 768. [2] *Bury and Norwich Post*, 15 Mar. 1820. [3] Grafton mss HA513/5/157-66, 171. [4] Ibid. HA513/5/18-121, 156. [5] *Bury and Norwich Post*, 22 Nov., 10 Dec. 1820. [6] Grafton mss HA513/5/161, 164, 166. [7] Ibid. HA513/5/18a, b, 172. [8] *Bury and Norwich Post*, 14 June 1826. [9] Grafton mss HA513/5/19-23, 79, 135. [10] *Bury and Norwich Post*, 28 July, 4 Aug. 1830. [11] W. Suss. RO, Goodwood mss 1433, f. 269. [12] Grafton mss HA513/5/196. [13] Suff. RO Acc 1396/22. [14] Grafton mss HA513/5/25-27, 79, 111, 181, 186-8; *Raikes Jnl.* ii. 142; *The Times*, 7, 8 Apr. 1838. [15] *Gent. Mag.* (1865), ii. 126; *Ipswich Jnl.* 24 June 1865.

M.M.E.

FITZROY, **Charles Augustus** (1796–1858), of Sholebrooke Lodge, Northants. and Stratton Street, Piccadilly, Midx.

BURY ST. EDMUNDS   1831–1832

b. 10 June 1796, 1st s. of Lord Charles Fitzroy[†] (*d.* 1829) and 1st w. Frances, da. of Edward Miller Mundy*. *educ.* Harrow, 1805-10. *m.* (1) 11 Mar. 1820, Lady Mary Lennox (*d.* 7 Dec. 1847), da. of Charles Lennox[†], 4th duke of Richmond, 3s. 1da.; (2) 11 Dec. 1855, Margaret Gordon (*née* Milligan), wid. of J.J. Hawkey, land agent, of Sydney, NSW, *s.p.* kntd. 1 June 1837; KCB 12 June 1854. *d.* 16 Feb. 1858.

Lt. Horse Gds. 1812, capt. 1820; maj. (half-pay) 1825; brevet lt.-col. 1825.

Mil. sec. Cape of Good Hope 1822, dep. adj. gen. 1825-31; lt.-gov. Prince Edward Island 1837; gov. Leeward Islands 1841-5, NSW 1846; gov.-gen. Australia 1850-5.

Fitzroy's father, a brother of the 4th duke of Grafton, on whose interest he had represented Bury St. Edmunds, was a general in the army and commander of the Ipswich garrison. His mother had died when he was a year old and his stepmother (*d.* 1810), the mother of his half-brothers and sister, was a sister of the Liverpool ministry's foreign secretary Lord Castlereagh*.[1] Fitzroy joined the Horse Guards and served as an aide-de-camp to Sir Richard Hussey Vivian* at Waterloo. He remained with the army of occupation in France and it was there that he met his first wife, who, following her father's traumatic death after being mauled by a bear near Ottawa in August 1819, had joined her brother, the 5th duke of Richmond, on his mission to Paris.[2] In 1822 the Fitzroys and their infant son Augustus Charles left for the Cape, where, as military secretary to the governor Lord Charles Henry Somerset[†], Fitzroy acted also as the wine taster, joint commissary of revenues and editor of the official *Cape Town Gazette*. His editorship terminated in 1824 amid allegations that he had deliberately exaggerated reports of rioting in Grahamstown in the 21 Feb. issue, two days after his controversial dismissal of the chaplain to the forces there, the Rev. William Geary, who duly instigated libel proceedings.[3] Fitzroy remained at the Cape until 1831, when, allegedly impoverished by maintaining a substantial household there, he returned to England to review his situation and claim part of his late father's estate. His wife was awarded an annual pension of £185 14s. in December 1830, after Richmond became the Grey ministry's postmaster-general.[4]

Fitzroy occupied Sholebrooke Lodge, Northamptonshire, vacant through the posting to Armagh of his cousin Lord Charles Fitzroy*, and at the general election of 1831 he contested Bury St. Edmunds, where his cousin Lord Euston had retired after voting against the ministerial reform bill. Unlike his half-brother Robert, who failed to come in for Ipswich, he declared firmly for the bill, despite its threat to Bury St. Edmunds's second seat, but made it clear that he would 'not pledge to vote for every clause in the committee'.[5] Assisted by his uncle Lord John Edward Fitzroy* and the borough recorder and putative candidate Robert Monsey Rolfe, he finished second in a four-cornered contest.[6] Lord Charles Fitzroy wrote, 'I am glad Charles Augustus is in Parliament and hope he may get something permanently useful to him through it'.[7] Fitzroy, a 'large burly man in robust health' who would 'never sit down to dinner without a fresh buttonhole', made no known speeches in the House.[8] He voted for the reintroduced reform bill at its second reading, 6 July 1831, consistently but sparingly for its details, and for its passage, 21 Sept. He voted for Lord Ebrington's confidence motion, 10 Oct. He divided for the revised reform bill (which restored the second seat to Bury St. Edmunds) at its second and third readings, 17 Dec. 1831, 22 Mar. 1832, and with government on the Russian-Dutch loan, 12, 20 July 1832. He presented his constituents' petition for the factories regulation bill, 26 Mar. 1832.

It had regularly been reported locally that Fitzroy was 'too ill' to attend reform meetings and dinners in Bury St. Edmunds, and he made way for Lord Charles Fitzroy at the 1832 dissolution.[9] He retained the use of Sholebrooke Lodge pending negotiations concerning his future career, in which Grafton and Richmond assisted. His hopes of returning to the Cape were dashed, and the colonial secretary Lord Glenelg rejected him for St. Helena, Van Diemen's Land and Prince Edward Island before he was appointed governor of the last in 1837. He turned down a posting to Jamaica in 1836 on health grounds.[10] His subsequent career benefited through his ability to curry favour with the 3rd Earl Grey and Lord Aberdeen and from his social skills.[11] He handled the dissolution of the legislative assembly in Prince Edward Island in 1838 with sensitivity, and his residence in Antigua was characterized by the speed with which he summoned and organized assistance following the earthquake of 1843.[12] His first wife's death in 1847 in a carriage accident in the driveway of Government House, Sydney, where he was governor of New South Wales, aroused much sympathy.[13] According to the *South Australian Register*, as the first Australian governor-general, 1851-5, the 'power he possessed, Sir Charles ... wisely allowed to slumber', and he successfully implemented the contentious 1850 Australian Colonies Government Act which established federal government. He saw censuses introduced, hostility to the return of convict transportation contained, a mint established in Sydney to regularize the 'gold rush' and the 'battle of the railway gauges' between Victoria and New South Wales resolved. Queen Victoria invested him as a knight commander of the Bath during her 1854 visit to Australia.[14] He died in London in February 1858, two years after returning with his second wife. Remarriage had put an end to his financial worries and speculation over his improper liaisons with women, but it posed problems in the execution of his will (proved on personalty of under £20, 30 Aug. 1858) as indentures to the settlement made on his first marriage, which favoured his three sons, had not been sworn. His property was subsequently sold and they each received about £1,000.[15]

[1] *HP Commons, 1790-1820*, iii. 765. [2] J.F.R. Browne, *Life of Lady Mary Fitzroy*, 5, 12. [3] Ibid. 23; *Dict. of S. African Biog.* ii. 238-9; *Recs. of Cape Colony*, xvii. 87, 267; xviii. 3, 9, 133, 143, 207, 214, 242; xix. 360; xx. 166; W. Suss. RO, Goodwood mss 1439, ff. 214, 331. [4] *The Times*, 31 Dec. 1829, 1 Jan. 1831. [5] *Ipswich Jnl.* 23 Apr. 7 May; *Bury and Norwich Post*, 27 Apr. 1831. [6] *Bury and Norwich Post*, 4 May; *Bury and Suff. Herald*, 4 May 1831. [7] Goodwood mss 1433, f. 269. [8] *Suff. Chron.* 7 May 1831; J.M. Ward, *Australia's First Governor General*, 22. [9] *Bury and Norwich Post*, 19 Oct., 16 Nov. 14 Dec. 1831, 11, 25 July; *Bury and Suff. Herald*, 10 Oct. 1832. [10] Goodwood mss 1439, ff. 214, 231, 277, 281; 1466, ff. 223, 281; 1477, f. 396; 1508, f. 210; 1511, f. 147; 1575, f. 313; 1890, f. 267; Browne, 30-31. [11] Ward, 3-5; *Oxford DNB*. [12] *Gent. Mag.* (1858), i. 449. [13] *The Times*, 21 Apr. 1848. [14] *S. Australian Reg.* 5 Feb. 1855; Ward, 14-21. [15] *Dict. of S. African Biog.*; Goodwood mss 1822, f. 408; *Illustrated London News*, 13 Mar. 1858.

M.M.E.

FITZROY, Henry, earl of Euston (1790–1863).

BURY ST. EDMUNDS	1818–1820
BURY ST. EDMUNDS	1826–1831
THETFORD	8 Aug. 1834–5 May 1842

b. 10 Feb. 1790, 1st. s. of George Henry Fitzroy†, 4th duke of Grafton, and Lady Charlotte Maria Waldegrave,

da. and coh. of James, 2nd Earl Waldegrave; bro. of Lord Charles Fitzroy* and Lord James Henry Fitzroy*. *educ.* Harrow 1802; Trinity Coll. Camb. 1808. *m.* 20 June 1812, at Lisbon, Mary Caroline, da. of Hon. Adm. Sir George Cranfield Berkeley† of Wood End, Suss., 3s. 2da. *suc.* fa. as 5th duke of Grafton 28 Sept. 1844. *d.* 26 Mar. 1863.

Cornet 7 Drag. 1809, lt. 1810, ret. 1819; cornet Northants. yeoman cav. 1813; col. E. Suff. militia 1823, W. Suff. militia 1830.

Ranger, Salcey forest 1811-44; hered. ranger, Whittlebury forest 1844-*d.*; recvr.-gen. profits of seals in q.b. and c.p. 1844-5.

Euston, a devout Anglican who did not share his brothers' love of gaming and the chase, had toyed with a military career and been suggested as a candidate for Suffolk and Northamptonshire, where he resided at Wakefield Lodge, before his father the 4th duke of Grafton returned him for Bury St. Edmunds in 1818.[1] He initially toed the political line drawn by Grafton and he was praised by the *Bury and Norwich Post* for opposing the malt tax, which affected local brewers and barley growers.[2] Alarmed by the Peterloo massacre, he wrote to his wife in September 1819:

> Parliament, it is clear, now is quite set aside by both parties. No one wishes for it, no one calls for it, and why? ... What an honest upright Parliament would do in a legal form, the reformers will do with or without your leave.[3]

He divided with his brother against the Liverpool ministry's repressive legislation that autumn, but caused a stir by criticizing Bury St. Edmunds as a corporation borough and stood down at the dissolution of 1820, when Lord Darlington's erstwhile Member for Ilchester, John Drage William Merest, threatened opposition.[4] Before canvassing the borough with his uncle Lord John Fitzroy, who took his place, he wrote to his wife:

> I ... hope he will be as well pleased as I am with the change, which indeed I am heartily, and not from any idle motive, whatever my friends may think ... We are all here deciders of our own actions, and if we think or consider at all, we must follow the dictates of our consideration, which is more likely to lead us right than the great wisdom of they that have not the same ... I may be blamed for changing my mind ... Humans are sometimes harder dealt with than animals: a fox who yields to circumstances and is obliged to deviate from his course is a good fox if he returns to it, but a poor human being who yields to circumstances is roughly dealt with and is given nothing but discredit.[5]

Out of Parliament he retained a high public profile. He joined his father in urging the adoption of a reform petition at the Suffolk county meeting, 10 Mar. 1821, but by 1823, when William Cobbett[†] was promoting radical reform in East Anglia, he privately doubted the 'utility or efficacy of petitioning on this score'.[6] He sponsored a subscription for the victims of arson attacks in Suffolk during the 1821-3 agricultural depression and attended throughout to Grafton's interests at Bury St. Edmunds and Thetford.[7] His support at the November 1822 Cambridge University by-election for the ministerial candidate Lord Hervey*, whose father was co-patron of Bury St. Edmunds, alienated the Whigs and was the subject of a hard-hitting editorial in *The Times*, which held him responsible for the defeat of the Whig lawyer James Scarlett*.[8] Declaring that he would 'make another trial' and 'secede as before' should he fail, Euston came in for Bury St. Edmunds with Hervey (Earl Jermyn) at the general election of 1826.[9] Speaking at the corporation feast in October, he urged the eastern division of Suffolk to subscribe adequately towards the county hospital in Bury St. Edmunds.[10]

Few records of Euston's attendance in 1826-7 survive, but he voted in the Whig minorities for inquiry into the Irish estimates, 5 Apr., and chancery delays, 5 Apr., and to disfranchise Penryn, 28 May 1827. After the duke of Wellington became premier, he intervened on the address to pay tribute to Admiral Codrington's victory at Navarino and criticized the government's failure to mark it with a vote of thanks, 31 Jan. 1828. He presented petitions for repeal of the Test Acts, 19 Feb., and voted thus, 26 Feb. Aligning as previously, he voted to limit the crown's right to goods recovered under the customs and excise laws, 29 Apr., and against abolishing the circulation of small bank notes, 5 June. He voted for Catholic relief, 12 May, and presented an anti-slavery petition from Bury St. Edmunds, 13 May 1828. As the patronage secretary Planta had predicted, he voted for Catholic emancipation, 6 Mar. 1829. He did not apparently vote on the 1830 address, from which mention of distress was omitted, and held aloof from the Suffolk meeting of 6 Feb. dominated by the Ultras, which petitioned for remedial measures.[11] However, he spoke and voted with Hume against the estimates 'in view of the distressed state of the country', 26 Feb. He voted to enfranchise Birmingham, Leeds and Manchester, 23 Feb., for O'Connell's radical and Russell's general reform proposals, 28 May, and steadily with the revived Whig opposition between 12 Mar. and 7 July, including for Jewish emancipation, 5 Apr., 17 May. Alleged charity abuse and the cost of poor relief were becoming major issues in Bury St. Edmunds, and Euston, who had been added to Slaney's 1828 committee, presented a petition favourable to the poor law

amendment bill from the guardians of Bury's incorporation of the poor, 4 May. He presented constituents' petitions for criminal law reform, 19 Feb., and equivalent duties on rum and corn spirits, 21 May. His return at the general election was unopposed, but his vote in O'Connell's minority of 13 on reform was criticized in the press and on the hustings, where he refused to give pledges and called for stringent economies 'on higher as well as lower salaries'.[12] He had declined an invitation to stand for Suffolk, where the Whig Sir William Rowley retired, and instead proposed his long-term rival for the seat, Sir Henry Edward Bunbury*, at the nomination meeting at Stowmarket, 6 Aug. 1830.[13]

Euston was listed among the Wellington ministry's 'foes' and divided against them when they were defeated on the civil list, 15 Nov. 1830. He afterwards relinquished his £400 army pension 'on moral grounds',[14] and endorsed the estimates proposed by the Grey ministry's secretary at war Williams Wynn, 14 Mar. 1831. He did not attend the Suffolk reform meeting, where Grafton declared unequivocally for the ministerial bill, 17 Mar.,[15] and he voted against its second reading, 22 Mar. Addressing his constituents, 28 Mar., after the pro-reform barrister Samuel Boileau had commenced canvassing against him, he declared that he

> opposed this bill, because I have thought it and still think it founded in injustice ... Parliament has no more just right to deprive the smallest borough of its rights, than the common law has to deprive the smallest individual of his life or rights unless he is found guilty of violating the laws of the country. At the same time, I consider Parliament has a right, and it is its duty, to correct the abuses of its representation in any just and legal manner it can; but not ... to cut the knot at once, and break through every barrier of law and justice to effect its object. I have another objection to the bill, which if not a legal infringement, I consider a violation of liberty, namely the diminishing the number of Members ... If you think them insufficient reasons for my having opposed the bill, you will do right to reject me as your representative. At all events, my only wish is to be chosen by the free will of the electors, whether they be the members of the corporation, or the inhabitants of the town.[16]

On 2 Apr. he announced that he would neither compromise his conscience nor seek re-election. He confirmed that he had 'never been for wholesale disfranchisement as a means of achieving reform or disfranchising a borough without a conviction of corruption', and expressed support for an extended franchise 'in every borough ... where that right is not already existing' and 'giving representatives to large and populous towns'.[17]

He voted for Gascoyne's wrecking amendment, 19 Apr. 1831, and retired at the ensuing dissolution.[18]

Euston was mooted for West Suffolk and Northamptonshire at the first post-reform election in December 1832, but remained out of Parliament until the death in 1834 of his brother Lord James Henry Fitzroy produced a vacancy at Thetford, which he was obliged to represent personally to sustain the Grafton interest there. He was unseated on petition in 1842, two years before succeeding to his father's titles and estates.[19] Ill and increasingly eccentric in later life, he died in March 1863 in the only room he occupied at Wakefield Lodge and was buried locally at Potterspury. His son, William Henry Fitzroy (1819-82), Liberal Member for Thetford, 1847-53, succeeded as 6th duke.[20]

[1] HP Commons, 1790-1820, iii. 767-8; B. Falk, Royal Fitzroys, 236. [2] Bury and Norwich Post, 23 June 1819. [3] Suff. RO (Bury St. Edmunds), Grafton mss HA513/6/215 [4] Oakes Diaries ed. J. Fiske (Suff. Recs. Soc. xxxiii), i. 250-1; Bury and Norwich Post, 1, 8, 15 Mar.; The Times, 6 Mar. 1820. [5] Grafton mss HA513/6/216. [6] Address to the Yeomanry of ... Suff. (Ipswich, 1821), 7, 25-28, 30; The Times, 23 Feb. 1821, 31 Jan.; Suff. Chron. 22 Apr., 4 May 1822; Fitzwilliam mss, Euston to Milton, 7 Dec. 1822. [7] Oakes Diaries, ii. 283; Suff. Chron. 22 Aug. 1822. [8] Suff. RO (Bury St. Edmunds), Hervey mss 941/1/1; The Times, 29 Nov. 1822. [9] Bury Gazette, 7 June; Suff. Chron. 17 June 1826. [10] Bury and Norwich Post, 11 Oct 1826. [11] Ibid. 27 Jan., 6 Feb. 1830. [12] Ibid. 4 Aug. 1830. [13] Suffolk Chron. 7 Aug. 1830. [14] The Times 4 Mar.; Suff. Chron. 5 Mar. 1831. [15] Bury and Norwich Post, 23 Mar. 1831. [16] Ibid. 30 Mar. 1831. [17] Ibid. 6 Apr.; The Times, 8 Apr. 1831. [18] Bury and Suff. Herald, 27 Apr. 1831. [19] The Times, 22 Oct. 1832, 7 Aug. 1834; Ipswich Jnl. 16 Aug. 1834; CJ, lxxxxvii. 255. [20] Bury and Norwich Post, 31 Mar., 7 Apr.; Gent. Mag. (1863), i. 657.

M.M.E.

FITZROY, Hon. Henry (1807–1859), of 24 Chapel Street, Mdx.

GREAT GRIMSBY	10 Aug. 1831–1832
LEWES	21 Apr. 1837–1841
LEWES	21 Nov. 1842–17 Dec. 1859

b. 2 May 1807, 2nd s. of George Ferdinand, 2nd Bar. Southampton (d. 1810), and 2nd w. Frances Isabella, da. of Lord Robert Seymour†. educ. Magdalen, Oxf. 1826.[1] m. 29 Apr. 1839, Hannah Meyer, da. of Nathan Meyer, Bar. de Rothschild, of London, 1s. d.v.p. 1da. d. 17 Dec. 1859. Cornet 4 Drag. 1827, lt. 1829, ret. 1831.

Ld. of admiralty Feb. 1845-July 1846; under-sec. of state for home affairs. Dec. 1852-Feb. 1855; PC 8 Feb. 1855; chairman of cttees. Apr. 1855-June 1859; first commr. of works June 1859-d.

A member of the cadet branch of the duke of Grafton's family, Fitzroy was the younger son of the

2nd Baron Southampton, who died when he was only three years old, leaving him as the heir presumptive to his elder brother Charles. They were raised by their 'austerely Calvinist' mother, who regularly administered severe physical punishments. Such a childhood left an indelible imprint and produced 'a certain timidity' in his character, though he 'stood well over six feet, with thick black hair, bright blue eyes and a ready smile'.[2] He joined the cavalry in 1829 but did not persevere in that line. At the 1831 general election he offered for Worcester as 'an advocate of moderate reform' opposed to the 'sweeping measures' proposed by the Grey ministry, but on being 'refused a hearing' in the city he withdrew; according to the local press he did so after discovering that 'the influence of the purse with which he was provided would nought avail him'.[3] When the sitting Tory Members for Great Grimsby, George Harris and John Villiers Shelley, were unseated on petition, 2 Aug. 1831, they vowed to introduce two anti-reformers at the subsequent by-election. Fitzroy and Lord Loughborough duly accompanied them to the borough, where they were warmly received. At his nomination Fitzroy told the electors that he professed the same principles as their unseated Members and accused his and Loughborough's opponents of being no more than nominees of the Whig Lord Yarborough, who had previously been able to control Great Grimsby's elections. He pipped Loughborough by one vote to top the poll.[4]

Fitzroy voted against ministers on the Dublin election controversy, 23 Aug. 1831. He divided to preserve the existing rights of freemen under the reform bill, 27 Aug., and in his maiden speech three days later argued against robbing 'these honest and incorrupt voters' of the franchise, citing the reduction of the electorate that would occur in Great Grimsby and the desire of freemen to pass on their rights to their children, which they valued 'as strongly as the higher classes do, the desire of transmitting their fortunes and their titles to their posterity'. He was in the minority for preserving the rights of non-resident freemen that day. He divided against the passage of the reform bill, 21 Sept. He was one of only seven Members who voted for Waldo Sibthorp's complaint of a breach of privilege by The Times, 12 Sept., when he also voted for inquiry into how far the Sugar Refinery Act could be renewed with due regard to the interests of the West Indian producers. He voted against the second reading of the revised reform bill, 17 Dec. 1831. When Great Grimsby's place in schedule B came before the House, 23 Feb. 1832, he followed Loughborough in defending the borough and its reputation, declaring that not only had its population increased significantly since

1821, but that it was likely soon 'to become one of the most important seaports in the kingdom'. He predicted that the bill would hand control of the borough to Yarborough, and in response to Robert Waithman, who suggested that Great Grimsby was 'notoriously corrupt', insisted that neither he nor his colleague had 'ever made a single promise of money to any voter'. He voted against the enfranchisement of Tower Hamlets, 28 Feb., the third reading of the reform bill, 22 Mar., and the second reading of the Irish measure, 25 May. He divided against ministers on the Russian-Dutch loan, 26 Jan., 12 July 1832.

At the 1832 general election Fitzroy unsuccessfully contested Northampton as a Conservative. He was defeated at Lewes in 1835, but returned at a by-election in 1837 and sat until 1841, when he was beaten but seated on petition. He remained a Member until his death. Initially a Conservative and a supporter of free trade, he gravitated to the Liberal party.[5] In 1838 he met Hannah Meyer Rothschild, the daughter of the Jew Nathan Rothschild, founder of the English branch of the family's banking interest, and reputedly Europe's richest man.[6] He soon asked for her hand, but the Rothschilds objected on religious grounds and asked Fitzroy to leave the country for six months to test Hannah's devotion to him. He went to Athens and Constantinople and on his return found her determined to marry him. Despite continued disapproval, tacit consent was given to the union, although only one family member, Hannah's brother, attended the wedding. There was no dowry, and her change of religion caused her to be disinherited. This came as a double blow, as Fitzroy's brother, on whom he depended for an income (his father not having provided for him), decided, at his wife's behest, to stop Fitzroy's allowance as he was marrying into a rich family: this led to the brothers not speaking for 14 years. Although his political career was successful and he served in administrations headed by Sir Robert Peel, Lord Aberdeen and Lord Palmerston, Fitzroy never achieved the high office he coveted. At the home office he was responsible for Acts regulating hackney cabs and for extending the jurisdiction of county courts.[7] He spent four years as chairman of committees in the House, working extremely long hours. This, it was said, together with the death of his invalid son, broke his health. He failed in his bid to be elected Speaker in 1857, but returned to a ministerial post at the board of works in June 1859. Plagued by constant ill health, he tendered his resignation in September, but Palmerston rejected his offer, saying, 'When I have got a good man in an office which requires a good man, I do not easily part with him. Therefore take your

time'. He went to convalesce in Brighton, but was confined to his bed for four weeks. He again offered his resignation, but before anything was done he died in December 1859, still heir presumptive to his brother. By his will, dated 11 Nov. 1858, he bequeathed all his real and personal estate to his wife, and directed that she should do as she saw fit 'for the benefit of herself and our daughter Blanche'.

[1] *Oxford DNB* continues to confuse this Member with his namesake (*d.* 1877), who attended Eton and Trinity Coll. Camb. (The same error in *DNB* is identified in *Alumni Cantab.* pt. 2, ii. 514.) *Oxford DNB* also gives a death date of 22 Dec. 1859, following *Gent. Mag.* (1860), i. 184. The correct date, as reported in *The Times*, 20 Dec. 1859 and Fitzroy's will, is 17 Dec. [2] R. Henrey, *A Century Between*, 11. [3] *Worcester Herald*, 30 Apr., 7 May 1831. [4] *Lincoln, Rutland and Stamford Mercury*, 19 Aug. 1831. [5] *Dod's Parl. Companion* (1847), 166. [6] Unless otherwise indicated, the rest of this biography is based on Henrey. [7] *Gent. Mag.* (1860), i. 184.

M.P.J.C./P.J.S.

FITZROY, Lord James Henry (1804–1834), of 47 Clarges Street, Piccadilly, Mdx.

THETFORD   1830–26 July 1834

b. 19 Apr. 1804, 3rd s. of George Henry Fitzroy†, 4th duke of Grafton (*d.* 1844), and Lady Charlotte Maria Waldegrave, da. and coh. of James, 2nd Earl Waldegrave; bro. of Lord Charles Fitzroy* and Henry Fitzroy, earl of Euston*. *educ.* Harrow 1816-19, Trinity Coll. Camb. 1821. *unm. d.* 26 July 1834.
    Cornet 10 Drag. 1822, lt. 1825, capt. 1826, half-pay 1829.

Fitzroy, whose mother died before his fourth birthday, was the 4th duke of Grafton's youngest son and a family favourite in whose progress his brothers took a keen interest. They were delighted when, in September 1823, he proclaimed his career in the cavalry a success.[1] However, he soon shared in his brother Lord Charles's misfortunes at the gaming table, and was substituted for him as Grafton's family Member for Thetford at the general election of 1830.[2] He was listed among the Wellington's ministry's 'foes' and voted against them with his brother Lord Euston on the civil list, 15 Nov. 1830, when they were brought down. He presented and endorsed an anti-slavery petition from the Wesleyans of Mildenhall, 19 Nov. 1830. Taking his father's line and differing from Euston, he voted for the Grey ministry's reform bill at its second reading, 22 Mar., and against Gascoyne's wrecking amendment, 19 Apr. 1831. At the ensuing general election he retained his seat for Thetford, which was then scheduled to lose a Member, and canvassed for his cousin Charles

Augustus Fitzroy*, who was substituted for Euston at Bury St. Edmunds.[3]

He voted for the reintroduced reform bill at its second reading, 6 July 1831, against adjourning its committee stage, 12 July, and sparingly until 10 Aug. for its details, including the complete disfranchisement of Appleby, 19 July, and St. Germans, 28 July, and partial disfranchisement of Dorchester, 28 July, and Sudbury, 2 Aug. 1831. No other votes by him have been found in this period. On 23 May 1832 he and his colleague Alexander Baring strenuously opposed Robert Grant's bill to transfer Thetford's assizes to Norwich. The revised reform bill restored its second Member to Thetford and, standing as a Liberal, Fitzroy retained his seat at the general election in December 1832.[4] He died intestate and deeply mourned in July 1834 after a feverish illness of ten days. Administration of his estate, sworn under £3,000, was granted to his father.[5]

[1] Suff. RO (Bury St. Edmunds), Grafton mss HA513/5/161, 164. [2] Ibid. HA513/5/135; *Norwich Mercury*, 24, 31 July 1830. [3] *Bury and Norwich Post*, 22 Mar., 4 May 1831. [4] *Bury and Suff. Herald*, 5, 19 Dec. 1832. [5] *Raikes Jnl.* i. 269; I.o.W. RO, Oglander mss OG/CC/406; *Ipswich Jnl.* 2, 16 Aug. 1834; PROB 6/211/198.

M.M.E.

FITZROY, **Lord John Edward** (1785–1856), of Half Moon Street, Piccadilly, Mdx.

THETFORD	1812–1818
BURY ST. EDMUNDS	1820–1826

b. 24 Sept. 1785, 6th s. of Augustus Henry Fitzroy[†], 3rd duke of Grafton (*d.* 1811), and 2nd. w. Elizabeth, da. of Very Rev. Sir Richard Wrottesley, 7th bt., of Wrottesley, Staffs., dean of Worcester; bro. of Lord William Fitzroy[†]; half-bro. of Lord Charles Fitzroy[†] and George Henry Fitzroy, earl of Euston[†]. *educ.* Harrow 1797-1803; Trinity Coll. Camb. 1803-5. *unm. d.* 28 Dec. 1856.

Fitzroy, a pro-Catholic Whig, had represented Thetford on the interest of his half-brother the 4th duke of Grafton in the 1812 Parliament, making way there in 1818 for his nephew Lord Charles Fitzroy*.[1] He returned to the Commons in 1820 as the family Member for Bury St. Edmunds, where a second nephew, Grafton's son and heir Henry Fitzroy, earl of Euston*, stood down and a contest seemed likely until the eve of the poll.[2]

Lord John was foreman of the special jury that declared the 3rd earl of Portsmouth insane (since 1809), 28 Feb. 1823. The law commissioners had rejected his plea for exemption from serving on

account of the 'great inconvenience which might result to him in the discharge of his public duties and as a Member'.[3] He divided fairly steadily with the main Whig opposition for economy, retrenchment and lower taxes between 5 May 1820 and 6 June 1825. He apparently did not vote on parliamentary reform in this period, nor did he attend the 1821 and 1822 Suffolk meetings with his relations, but he signed the reform petition proposed by Euston at Stowmarket, 10 Mar., and presented to the Lords by Grafton, 16 Apr. 1821.[4] He voted for Catholic relief, 1 Mar., 21 Apr. 1825. On 9 Mar. 1825, in his only reported speech, he successfully moved the second reading of the Metropolitan Fish Company bill, in which he claimed to have 'no private interest'. He made way for Euston at Bury St. Edmunds in 1826, but continued to subscribe to local causes and canvassed the borough strenuously on behalf of a third nephew, Charles Augustus Fitzroy*, at the contested election of 1831.[5] He died in London in December 1856, having bequeathed the bulk of his estate to his nephew, the 5th duke of Grafton (formerly Lord Euston), and provided annuities for his sisters Frances, Lady Churchill, and Lady Isabella Blachford.[6]

[1] *HP Commons, 1790-1820*, iii. 768. [2] Suff. RO (Bury St. Edmunds), Grafton mss HA513/6/216; *Oakes Diaries* ed. J. Fiske (Suff. Recs. Soc. xxxiii), ii. 250-1; *Bury and Norwich Post*, 8, 15 Mar. 1820. [3] Grafton mss HA513/4/132-3; *Ann. Reg.* (1823), 24-25; *The Times*, 11 Feb., 1 Mar. 1823. [4] *Ipswich Jnl.* 17 Mar.; *Suff. Chron.* 7, 21 Apr. 1821. [5] S. Tymms, *Handbk. of Bury St. Edmunds* (1854); *Suff. Chron.* 10 June 1826; *Bury and Norwich Post*, 27 Apr. 1831. [6] IR26/2094/20.

M.M.E.

FITZWILLIAM, **Charles William Wentworth**, Visct. Milton (1786–1857).

MALTON	1806–1807
YORKSHIRE	1807–1830
PETERBOROUGH	1830–4 Nov. 1830
NORTHAMPTONSHIRE	1831–1832
NORTHAMPTONSHIRE NORTH	1832–8 Feb. 1833

b. 4 May 1786, o.s. of William, 2nd Earl Fitzwilliam, and 1st w. Lady Charlotte Ponsonby, da. of William Ponsonby[†], 2nd earl of Bessborough [I]. *educ.* Eton 1796-1802. *m.* 8 July 1806, his cos. Hon. Mary Dundas, da. of Thomas Dundas[†], 1st Bar. Dundas, 4s. (1 *d.v.p.*) 6da. *suc.* fa. as 3rd Earl Fitzwilliam 8 Feb. 1833; KG 4 Nov. 1851. Confirmed by royal lic. 20 Aug. 1856 name of Wentworth bef. Fitzwilliam, assumed by his fa. 7 Dec. 1807. *d.* 4 Oct. 1857.

Capt. S.W. Yorks. yeomanry 1803.

High steward, Cambridge 1850-*d.*

Milton, a cherished only son born into the grand Whig aristocracy of a 38-year-old mother after almost 16 years of marriage, was heir to his father Lord Fitzwilliam's vast Yorkshire, Northamptonshire and Irish estates, which included extensive and expanding coal and iron mining enterprises in the area of south Yorkshire between Barnsley and Rotherham.[1] The mainspring of his existence was Evangelical religion, with its imperatives of duty and service. A devoted husband with a large family, he was one of the sober-minded and morally earnest 'Young Whigs' who spurned the casual attitude of the older Foxite generation, espoused the doctrines of the political economists and sought to preserve the supremacy of their order by adapting it to the demands of the rapidly changing state of British society. His closest associates in the party were his contemporaries Lord Althorp*, son of the 2nd Earl Spencer, Lord Tavistock*, son of the 6th duke of Bedford, and Lord Ebrington*, son of the 1st Earl Fortescue.[2] By 1820 Milton, whose 'hard Anabaptist nature', as Sydney Smith called it, was perfectly complemented by his thin, 'serious' face and dark brown fringe, which gave him the appearance of a Methodist preacher, had been a Member for over 13 years, most of them as the holder of one of the prestigious Yorkshire seats.[3] He carried some weight in the House, where his clear, 'matter-of-fact' oratory, though marred by the 'unpleasant monotony' of his voice, earned him a hearing. But his eccentricity, obstinacy and haughtiness, which masked a tormenting sense of his own unworthiness, made him an awkward political colleague, though Althorp valued his judgement highly.[4] With his 71-year-old father (whose dismissal from the lord lieutenancy in October 1819 for organizing a Yorkshire protest against Peterloo had boosted their county interest) in deteriorating health, Milton had assumed increasing responsibility for the family's estate, business and electoral concerns.[5]

At the general election of 1820 he made a tour of the West Riding manufacturing districts, during which he blamed excessive government tax-based expenditure for the prevalent distress, condemned ministers' recent repressive legislation, confirmed his hostility to 'any general reform', but expressed support for 'a partial reform', having specifically in mind Lord John Russell's* scheme to disfranchise the corrupt borough of Grampound in favour of an unrepresented large town. He was returned unopposed with his Tory colleague Stuart Wortley.[6] On 3 May 1820 he presented and endorsed a petition from Leeds woollen merchants and manufacturers for repeal of the duty on imported raw wool, which he said was 'in contradiction of every principle of political economy'. He wel-comed the London merchants' free trade petition, 8 May, when he argued that the root cause of distress was high taxation. This became his familiar refrain throughout the 1820 Parliament. On 25 May he admitted that the distress being endured by the agricultural interest was serious, but declared that they would be 'disappointed' if they relied on enhanced protection for relief. Convinced that the interests of agriculture and industry were inextricably linked, and anxious to atone for his 'sin' of supporting the 1815 legislation, he had become a dedicated opponent of the corn laws, though he was not yet quite committed to their total repeal.[7] His attempt to bring in a bill to repeal the duty on foreign wool was defeated by 202-128, 26 May. He spoke and voted with Brougham against the government's restriction of the remit of the select committee on agricultural distress, 30, 31 May.[8] The following day he fed the veteran Foxite Sir James Mackintosh*, who ungratefully described him in his diary as 'an excellent young man of feeble understanding who has risen from stammering to facility of utterance and who thinks the last such a wonderful attainment that his head has been turned by it'.[9] He spoke and voted against the 'green bag' inquiry into Queen Caroline's private life, 26 June, but in mid-July, when he was installed at Wentworth Woodhouse for the summer, he declined to present a Wakefield address to her, claiming that he would have done so if he had been in London, 'even if I felt that I could not make myself responsible for all its sentiments'.[10] Unlike Althorp, he subsequently became an active partisan for the queen, influenced by the farce of her trial before the Lords, and he subscribed to the collection for a service of plate.[11] The Whig 'Mountaineers' Grey Bennet and Creevey liked his speech in support of the opposition censure motion, 5 Feb. 1821.[12] He said that Trench, Member for Cambridge, who had denigrated the borough's petition for restoration of the queen's name to the liturgy, 6 Feb., was the representative not of the inhabitants but of the '200 burgesses' with the vote.[13] After casting his customary vote for Catholic relief, 28 Feb., on 2 Mar. he voiced his 'entire approbation' of Russell's bill to give Grampound's seats to Leeds, but, having the previous year taken soundings among the leading Yorkshire reformers,[14] argued that it would be safer to give the borough a ratepayer ('scot and lot') franchise than the proposed £10 householder arrangement. His amendment to that effect was rejected by 182-66. He had already confided to John Hobhouse* that 'reform was gaining ground in his mind';[15] and on 11 Mar. 1821 he explained to the Yorkshire Whig reformer Sir George Cayley† the reasoning behind his recent conversion to the cause, which had been inspired by the Commons' blatant disregard of public opinion on the queen's case:

> I never thought that there was any ground of complaint against the House of Commons or of suspicion that ... [it] did not fairly represent the public opinion of the nation ... This conviction of the consent between the ... Commons and the people made me an opponent of parliamentary reform, and so I should have continued if recent circumstances had not satisfied me that that consent is not as perfect as I had previously thought it ... When, as at present, there is a perfect *discordance*, we may be sure there is something wrong ... I am ready to admit that *the state of the constituent body* ... has its *share* in the production of ... [the problem] ... From the analysis which I have ... made of the House ... I am disposed to think that the evil originates in the numerous small boroughs, which ... are liable either to be corrupted or to be drawn within the influence of government by means of the immense patronage which ministers have at their disposal ... I am ready to support any plan for the removal of this cause which may appear to me coextensive with its share of operation and consistent with ancient principles and acknowledged rights ... The most constitutional and therefore the safest and most practicable plan would be, first, to extend the right of election to a given number of those communities known to the law and the constitution which have either lost or never enjoyed the ... franchise ... [and] second, to remove the obstacles which, as the law now stands, render the conviction of corrupt boroughs ... almost impossible.

He was trying to reach a clear and specific understanding on the issue which would enable him and his father, hitherto implacably opposed to reform, to join in the mooted county meeting. Nothing came of this, but on 30 Mar. he and Fitzwilliam attended the Huntingdonshire meeting. In deference to his father, he concentrated in his speech on the queen's affair and high taxation and stayed clear of reform, which was not mentioned in the petition which he formally proposed.[16] In the House, 17 Apr., on Lambton's reform motion, he gave a public explanation of his conversion, but declared that he could not support this scheme, which was 'pregnant with danger'. He was, however, listed in the minority of 43 who voted for the motion when ministers forced a premature division next day. He divided silently for Russell's general reform motion, 9 May, and Hamilton's for reform of the Scottish county representation, 10 May. He accused Austria and Russia of 'making the executive government too strong for the liberties of the people', 7 May. Grey Bennet thought that in his speech for inquiry into Peterloo, 15 May, when he urged 'protection of the lower orders in the security of their rights and privileges' in order to forestall revolution,

he 'made, as usual, some of the best remarks possible', but carped that he 'wants the power of fixing the attention of his audience'.[17] Milton, whose abiding fear was that heavy taxation would destroy the middle classes, called for a reduction of the pension list, 18 May.[18] He gave general approval to Scarlett's bill to reform the settlement laws for poor relief, 24 May. On the 30th he successfully moved for acceptance of the Lords' amendments to the Grampound bill, whereby its seats were given to Yorkshire, in order to achieve the main object, disfranchisement, although his strong personal preference was for Leeds. Next day he introduced a bill to allow polling for Yorkshire to be held in towns other than York, but it provoked considerable local opposition and he abandoned it.[19] He supported the grant of £6,000 to the duke of Clarence for the education of Prince George, 18 June, but opposed the payment of arrears, 29 June. Grey Bennet dismissed his speech in support of economy and retrenchment, 27 June 1821, as 'a feeble, indifferent effort'.[20]

Milton absented himself from the Commons for most of the 1822 session. Althorp, who did not press him to go up, could not agree with him in 'wishing to see our friends in administration', if only because the country's problems were so intractable that 'disgrace' would be inevitable.[21] He wanted to give 'unreserved and full support' to Russell's pending reform motion, but his father was very reluctant to allow this, as he explained to Lord Grey:

> I cannot bring myself to indifference, when I contemplate how much his influence and efficiency may be thrown away, when he becomes a prominent supporter of parliamentary reform, for from that instant he becomes the tool and slave of every worthless adventurer. He is born aristocrat, that is his station ... that enables him to defend the rights and liberties of the people; but ... he is impressed with the belief that these cannot be defended but by reform ... and that if his support of it does not meet with my concurrence, he must *quit* Parliament.

This was averted when Fitzwilliam discovered that Milton only wished to support the motion and not, as he had assumed, to second it. He waived his objections, though he still saw no sense in agitating the issue.[22] Milton accordingly gave a silent vote for the motion, 25 Apr. 1822. His only other known vote that session was for repeal of the salt tax, 28 June; and on 10 July 1822 he argued that tampering with the currency would not relieve agricultural distress and that £10,000,000 in taxes could easily have been remitted if ministers had had the will to act.

When Walter Fawkes[†] and other Yorkshire reformers revived plans for a county meeting to promote the cause in August 1822, Milton, advised by Althorp to involve himself 'as the reforming Member for the county', told Fawkes that as reform was 'the only subject' which disturbed his father's 'usual calmness' and it was essential that he should have 'tranquillity of mind' while undergoing operations on his failing eyes, he would keep out of it for the moment.[23] He did, however, chair the preparatory reform committee meeting at York, 4 Nov. 1822, despite his father's disapproval. Keen to ensure that the business remained in responsible hands, he attended and addressed the county meeting, 22 Jan. 1823, when he again explained his conversion and called for 'moderation and prudence'.[24] He presented and endorsed the 17,000-signature petition, 22 Apr. He spoke and voted for Russell's motion for inquiry into the parliamentary franchise, 20 Feb., and divided silently for his reform motion, 24 Apr. He urged Brougham not to goad ministers into going to war with France for the sake of Spain, but Althorp thought he took pacifism too far.[25] On 24 Feb., deprecating Grey Bennet's diatribe against the sinking fund and welcoming the 'spirit of enlarged policy' outlined by Robinson, the new chancellor of the exchequer, he remarked that 'it was so long since he had attended the House, that he hardly knew by whom he was supported, or to whom he was opposed'. Yet he complained that while ministers had at last admitted that 'the diminution of taxation was the ... only relief for the pressing distress of the people', Robinson's proposals were inadequate. Milton, who had now given up thick and thin attendance, described the divided Irish administration as 'a power capable of creating much mischief, but incapable of doing any good', 15 Apr. He spoke and voted for inquiry into their prosecution of the Dublin Orange rioters, 22 Apr., and on 12 May, deploring calls for renewal of the Insurrection Act, said that the Irish lower orders were 'a people to be governed by love and not fear'; he voted for inquiry into the current disturbances. He gave 'warm support' to Hamilton's motion for reform of the county representation of Scotland, whose unenfranchised 'middle class' were 'the most moral and virtuous in Europe', 2 June. Milton, whose mother had died in May 1822, was put out by his father's decision to marry, at the age of 75, the 73-year-old widow Lady Ponsonby in July 1823; but she lived only until September 1824.[26]

He voted for reform of Edinburgh's representation, 26 Feb. 1824. Calling for 'some modification' of the wool duties, 24 Feb., he approved Robinson's budget statement, but demanded more tax remissions and said that relaxation of the coastal coal duties unfairly favoured London. He supported motions for repeal of the window tax, 2 Mar., and the assessed taxes, 10 May, on the principle that 'the only chance there was of driving ministers to a general repeal of taxes was by voting for the repeal of every particular tax'; he would have preferred reduction of the beer and malt taxes. On 26 Mar. he said that the Halifax woollen merchants' and manufacturers' fear of foreign competition was 'unfounded': 'it was the duty of Members who held that their constituents were mistaken to endeavour to undeceive them'. He welcomed the government's liberal wool trade bill as 'one of the wisest measures that could be adopted', 21 May. He demanded full inquiry into the state of Ireland, lamenting 'the disregard of the upper orders ... for the opinion of the lower', 11 May; he was named to the select committee. His observations as a member of the select committee on the Combination Acts 'completely confirmed' his view that they should be repealed, while 'providing at the same time for the punishment of all acts of violence or intimidation'.[27] He disliked Stuart Wortley's game bill, as it was 'not the duty of Parliament to provide for the amusements of country gentlemen, but to legislate for the preservation of the morals of the country', 31 May 1824.

Milton, to the chagrin of Tierney, who was surprised that Fitzwilliam 'did not drive him up', missed the division on allowing the Catholic Association's lawyers to be heard at the bar, 19 Feb. 1825;[28] but he was present to vote against the bill to suppress the association, 21, 25 Feb. He voted for Catholic relief, 1 Mar., 21 Apr., 10 May, though on 19 Apr. he admitted that he was 'not blind to the corruptions of the Catholic church'. He disliked the bill to disfranchise Irish 40s. freeholders, but accepted it, 26 Apr., to secure emancipation and because it 'struck a blow at the oligarchy, of which he was a component part' and which was 'one of the great curses of Ireland'.[29] He condemned and was in Hume's minority of eight against an increase in the standing army, 7 Mar. He divided for relaxation of the corn laws, 28 Apr. 1825. He thought the government's promissory notes bill was unnecessary, but that Hume's wish to prosecute bankers who refused to pay in specie would make it pernicious, 27 Feb. 1826. He again damned the 'extravagant' army estimates, 3 Mar. Supporting a renewed attack on the corn laws, 18 Apr., he confessed to having transgressed by voting for them in 1815 but, repentant, contended that their unacceptable object was to secure 'high rents and large profits' for landowners. The protectionist Henry Bankes* considered his speech 'arrogant and offensive'.[30] He said that the emergency admission of bonded wheat would not help the distressed manufacturing workers, 2 May: 'the people of Lancashire might be considered the poor of England'. To the annoyance of Canning, the leader of the House, he carried by 109-60 a delaying amendment. He spoke and was a minority teller against the proposals, 8 May, when he said that they proved that the corn laws were 'only fit for the fair-weather state of the country'. His repeated calls for a grant of capital to relieve distress fell on deaf ministerial ears. He voted for Russell's reform motion, 27 Apr., and spoke and voted for his condemnation of electoral bribery, 26 May 1826.

Since 1823 Milton had been involved in the Yorkshire Whigs' discussions of their tactics for the next general election, when the county was to return two additional Members. He had acquiesced in the selection of his kinsman Lord Morpeth*, son of the earl of Carlisle, as his colleague, but the Tories' adoption in late 1825 of two anti-Catholics, at the expense of the pro-Catholic Stuart Wortley and Richard Bethell*, complicated matters and raised the spectre of a ruinous contest. In December 1825 Milton initially advocated dropping Morpeth, whose father had no money, but the West Riding Whigs persuaded him to change his mind and aim for a joint subscription of £70,000, of which he was prepared to provide £30,000. Reports that Carlisle would force Morpeth to withdraw prompted Milton, who thought this would wreck the entire Whig interest, to consider doing the same, as he could come in at no cost for Fitzwilliam's borough of Higham Ferrers. However, he confirmed his intention of standing on 30 Dec. 1825.[31] Morpeth retired the following month, but Milton persevered, though he still disliked the notion of being the only Whig Member, as attempts to put up the Leeds manufacturer John Marshal[b] seemed to be failing. In late May, with the dissolution imminent, he was persuaded to stand firm, and Marshall was at last got into the field for a joint campaign. At the Leeds Cloth Halls, 6 June 1826, Milton condemned slavery, advocated revision of the corn laws and supported the entitlement of West Riding manufacturers to a share in the county representation. Stuart Wortley's elevation to the peerage and Bethell's late retirement allowed Milton and Marshall to come in with the two anti-Catholic Tories, but their joint costs nevertheless exceeded £54,000. On the hustings, Milton asserted that 'the energies of this great people cannot be fully called into action until complete freedom be given both to opinion and industry'.[32]

He was heckled at a Doncaster farmers' meeting in August 1826, but persisted in his attack on the corn laws, which was now his political obsession, even though it set him at odds with his father and most Whig grandees.[33] Presenting petitions for their relaxa-

tion, 21 Feb. 1827, he said that they were 'founded in error' and advocated free trade, 'subject to a reasonable protection by a duty on importation proportioned to the exclusive taxation borne by the agriculturist'. He welcomed the government's corn bill as 'a great improvement', 1 Mar., but on the 9th complained that it did not go far enough and voted in the minority of 50 for a lower pivot price; he divided against increased protection for barley, 12 Mar. Grey privately deplored the 'language which Milton thinks it proper to hold' against the landed interest.[34] He supported Althorp's motion for the establishment of a permanent select committee to deal with election petitions alleging bribery, 26 Feb., when his amendments to Williams Wynn's alternative scheme were negatived.[35] He thought Althorp's proposed inquiry into county polls would be 'advantageous' and spoke and voted for investigation into Leicester corporation's alleged electoral malpractice, 15 Mar. He divided for Catholic relief, 6 Mar. When Scarlett, Whig Member for Peterborough on the Fitzwilliam interest, asked him if he should accept the new premier Canning's offer of the attorney-generalship, Milton advised him against it but left the decision to him:

> Your postscript ... intimates that the negotiations with Lord Lansdowne are resumed ... I think his acceptance of office would be a sufficient pledge for the agitation if not for the accomplishment of the Catholic question; but it appears to me that without some pledge to that effect ... the advocates of that measure ... cannot either hold office or accept favours from the new government ... [Canning's] sincerity ... I have never doubted, but ... it appears to me that ... [he] will ... acquiesce in the perpetuation, at least in the prolongation of a system of balance in the government from which no good can come. I regret this extremely, because I was in hopes that recent events would have brought the system to an end, and have disencumbered the nation, not only from Tory men, but from *Tory principles*. This, however, it seems is not to be the case, and the state of the *royal mind* is once more destined to mar the hopes of Catholics and to defer the tranquillization of Ireland.[36]

With Althorp and Tavistock, he refused to become actively involved in the Whig coalition with Canning, but in the House he declared his 'confidence' in the government, 2, 7 May, when he 'strongly opposed' inquiry into the grievances of the shipping interest as a retrograde step from reciprocity in trade. He had an open mind on the fate of the venal borough of Penryn, 8 May, but on the 28th, satisfied that 'gross corruption' had been proved, declared himself in favour of transferring its seats to a large manufacturing town in order to increase 'the influence of the inferior orders in the House', although his instincts were to 'proceed according to the wisdom of ancient times' by sluicing the borough. He supported repeal of the Blasphemy Act, 31 May, and next day, in view of the prevailing economic circumstances, gave ministers the benefit of the doubt on their cautious budget. Mackintosh was shocked by the 'severity' of his harsh comments on the Lords' emasculation of the corn bill, 18 June, which was 'increased in appearance by the *emphase* of his utterance as well as by the loud cheers of some of our zealots, but to be regretted on account of so good and kind a father who voted wrong'.[37] In mid-July Milton wrote to Lansdowne, now a member of Canning's cabinet, endorsing his decision to enter it, but warning him that

> to counterbalance the hatred and pertinacious activity of the Tories ... you must excite and draw into corresponding activity the zeal of those who, during the last session, have formed the only efficient support of government in the ... Commons, and ... this will be impossible unless they see a determination ... in *acts* to carry into effect the measures which they have so much at heart.

He specified the collective endorsement of Catholic relief by the cabinet and '*large scale*' reductions in expenditure and taxation. Lansdowne pleaded for restraint and time.[38] With Althorp and Tavistock, Milton was 'furious' at the instalment of the feeble Lord Goderich as Canning's successor and the appointment of the anti-Catholic Herries to the exchequer, which he attributed to the king's malign influence, and would have no part in supporting the ministry. They at length resolved on a line of 'strict neutrality'.[39] He was slightly mollified by the proposal to appoint Althorp to the chair of the planned finance committee, but remained determined to maintain an independent line.[40]

Milton was 'furious against' the duke of Wellington's ministry in January 1828 and told Scarlett, who wondered whether to stay in place, that

> no man, with even a tinge of Whig principles, can accept office without the ruin of his reputation ... It appears to me the very worst government I ever remember ... There is no vice belonging to a government which is not to be found in it; Tory principle, Court intrigue, tergiversations and coalitions of all sorts and sizes, a military commander at its head.[41]

Ministers considered him for the finance committee, but he was not appointed.[42] In the House, 18 Feb. 1828, he welcomed the inclusion of the Huskissonites in the government, but wished they had obtained 'more substantial guarantees' of liberal policies, hinted that they had sold themselves for power and

attacked Wellington as an anti-Catholic. He presented numerous Dissenters' petitions for repeal of the Test Acts, 20, 22, 25 Feb., and spoke and voted for that measure on the 26th. Two days later he goaded Peel, the home secretary, into losing his temper and leaving the chamber in a huff with pointed remarks on the 'idle false pretences' which he was adopting in a bid to thwart repeal. He felt himself to be entirely in the right.[43] He presented and endorsed pro-Catholic petitions, 28 Apr., 8, 9 May, and divided for relief, 12 May. He said that concession of the agriculturists' demands for protection against foreign wool would 'rebarbarize the country', 28 Apr. Next day he condemned the new corn bill as 'a decided compromise' and voted in the minority of 27 for Hume's radical amendment. His speech in support of the provision for Canning's family in recognition of the beneficial liberalism of his last five years, 13 May 1828, pleased Canning's relatives and friends.[44]

Delighted by the government's concession of Catholic emancipation, Milton, who, with Fitzwilliam, was sent 'to try their influence' in persuading O'Connell to 'submit' to the suppression of the Catholic Association,[45] praised them for achieving 'a victory over their own prejudices', 5, 10 Feb., 5 Mar 1829. He presented favourable petitions, including large ones from Sheffield (27 Feb.) and Leeds (16 Mar.), voted for the measure, 6, 30 Mar., and spoke for it, 18 Mar. He disliked the bill to disfranchise Irish 40s. freeholders, and on 20 Mar., arguing that it would enhance the power of great landowners, voted in the minority of 20 for Lord Duncannon's instruction concerning registration. Yet he made it clear that securing emancipation overrode his objections to details of its corollaries. Brougham was 'quite prepared' for this vote by Milton's advance warning, and thought the 'most conciliatory tone' of his speech tended to 'make his vote as little hurtful as was possible'.[46] Milton spoke and voted in favour of allowing O'Connell to take his seat without hindrance, 15, 18 May. He said the introduction of poor laws to Ireland would be disastrous, 7 May. He opposed any increase in the wool duty, 11 May, supported inquiry into the malt and beer taxes, 12 May, and on the 19th spoke and voted in a minority of 12 for Hume's motion for a fixed duty on corn imports and a bounty on exports. His only other known vote that session was against the grant for the marble arch, 25 May. Disgusted by the ministry's revelation of their 'cloven foot' in backing the anti-Catholic George Bankes* against a Whig in the Cambridge University by-election, he told Scarlett that he would personally boycott his re-election for Peterborough on his appointment as attorney-general.[47]

Milton did not resume attendance until mid-March 1830, so missing the reform divisions of February. Althorp failed to persuade him to go up to join in the attacks on Scarlett's use of *ex-officio* prosecutions and the government's foreign policy.[48] He was named to the East India select committee, 9 Feb. 1830 (and again, 28 June 1831, 10 Feb. 1832). He approved the proposed reduction in the leather tax, but would have preferred remission of the malt rather than the beer duty, 15 Mar. He divided with the reviving Whig opposition on most major issues from late April, having attended a meeting of 'about 35 of the best Whigs' at Althorp's rooms 'to consider public measures' on the 15th.[49] He called for further tax reductions, 30 Apr., and spoke and divided in a minority of 28 against the second reading of the sale of beer bill, 4 May. He presented many anti-slavery petitions in May, when he seconded Fowell Buxton's motion for 'entire abolition' at a Freemasons' Hall meeting, and voted for Jewish emancipation on the 17th.[50] He presented and endorsed a Leeds petition for economical and parliamentary reform, 11 May, and voted for Russell's reform motion, 28 May. He said that repeal of the Irish coal duty would not help the poor, as repeal of the coastal coal duties would not benefit manufacturers, 13 May. He did not want 'the wealthy to wallow in their emoluments' while the poor suffered, 14 May; Grey's son Lord Howick* (who found Althorp's reported wish to have Milton in office if the Whigs joined the ministry 'objectionable') considered this 'a bad speech'.[51] Milton attacked the corn laws, 25 May, and opposed inquiry into the currency, 8 June. On 26 June 1830, following the king's death, he postponed his planned motion on the corn laws.

With his father's health failing, he had decided to retire from the Yorkshire seat at the dissolution, and he stuck to this resolution despite the efforts of some county Whigs to persuade him to carry on. He endorsed Morpeth as his successor and trod carefully on the sensitive matter of the outsider Brougham's controversial candidature, but eventually acquiesced in it as popular support for him in the West Riding became irresistible. Yet he told Brougham frankly that he regarded it as 'an anomaly' and was determined that it should not become 'a precedent for disconnecting the representation of the counties from the[ir] landed or real property', which would open them to partisan ministerial intervention.[52] He declined an invitation to stand for Huntingdonshire, but supported the unsuccessful candidature of the Whig Rooper against two Tory aristocrats.[53] He had decided to return himself for Peterborough, which necessitated the removal of Scarlett, who was still in office. When

Scarlett found a berth at Malton on Fitzwilliam's interest it was reported that Milton was 'furious' at 'the old dotard having the weakness to yield'; but the truth was that Fitzwilliam made the offer of Malton without any solicitation from Scarlett. He accepted it, but when he was warned by Brougham that his holding a seat under the auspices of 'such determined opponents' of the ministry was 'a subject of general disapprobation', he placed himself in Milton's hands. Milton replied:

> It is ... true that your acceptance of office was with my father's approbation, and with my acquiescence ... Even at that period [June 1829] I had strong misgivings about the *principles* and *character* of a ministry led by the duke of Wellington and composed, in its other efficient parts, of Peel and Lord Aberdeen. I never could ... bring myself to believe that such a ministry was favourable ... to liberty ... and subsequent events (*vide* Portugal, *vide* Greece) have proved that I was not very far wrong ... With respect to *my mode of acting* ... there was nothing in it hostile to them. The Catholic question had been carried too recently to permit its advocates to turn around upon the ministers who had carried it, merely because they suspected their principles ... But it would be equally absurd to support a government for ever and aye because they had carried *one* good measure ... Those principles ... developed themselves gradually in the course of the last session. Very great ignorance too (in ... Wellington at least) upon commercial questions has been displayed, so that ... I left town with a pretty large stock of hostility ... Brougham therefore is not far wrong in his description of my present politics, though he makes the *bellum* rather more *internecinum* than perhaps I should ... But ... I am very far from building upon it the superstructure which Brougham seems to think I ought, or rather that *you* ought. Provided I can obtain, what I have obtained, the ample security which I enjoy in your assurance that parliamentary reform and an alteration of the corn laws will find in you an active supporter ... I am content.[54]

Milton was devastated by the death of his 43-year-old wife in premature (six months) labour on 1 Nov. 1830. He renounced public life for the sake of his children and vacated his seat a fortnight later, though the government evidently delayed his nomination to the Chiltern Hundreds until a 'second application' convinced them that he was in earnest. Had he stayed in the House, he would almost certainly have been offered a place in the Grey ministry.[55] On 5 Dec. 1830 he wrote to his successor at Peterborough, John Fazakerley, of his notion that an acceptable scheme of the reform which he now considered essential would be the disfranchisement of '20 or 30 of the smallest boroughs' in favour of 'an equal number of numerous elective bodies'. (He had communicated this to

Althorp, leader of the House, but had received no reply.) He explained that he would disfranchise not on the ground of corruption, which would require inquiry and was not confined to small boroughs, but on those of '*decay of population* and *poverty*'. He regarded 25 as a maximum because a greater number of suitable substitutes would be hard to find, as, 'with the exception of Manchester, Birmingham, Leeds and Sheffield, all the very large towns are *represented*'. He would add about five districts of London, including Marylebone and Lambeth. Keen to give 'the lower orders' an adequate share in elections, he favoured 'the old constitutional franchise' of scot and lot to any 'newfangled right'.[56] On 13 Dec. 1830 he wrote a letter to *The Times* correcting its 'somewhat exaggerated' report of the extent of his father's reduction of rents in 1822. The Tory alarmist William Fremantle* asked, 'Can anything demonstrate the power of the press or the submission to it more strongly than such a document from such a member of the aristocracy?'[57] At the end of 'this dreadful year' he wrote in his diary: 'I feel grateful to God for all his mercies but deeply humiliated, and I pray God it may work to my advantage'.[58]

On 28 Feb. 1831 he urged Lord Holland, a member of the cabinet, to be 'as careful of the public money as the porter at Holland House is of yours'.[59] At the Northamptonshire county reform meeting, 14 Apr., he expressed his 'strong approbation' of the ministerial scheme: 'by the general diffusion of the elective franchise, security would be given to property, and the due influence of every man brought into action'.[60] When Parliament was dissolved a week later, Milton tried unsuccessfully to persuade William Hanbury to stand as a reformer with Althorp against the other sitting Member, the Tory Cartwright. In reply to an invitation to stand himself from Wellingborough freeholders, he replied that 'no power on earth could induce me to engage as a candidate in a popular election, but I am far from saying that under certain circumstances I might not feel it a duty to obey the call strongly made upon me'. He maintained this stance, in which there was an element of subterfuge, refusing to canvass, appear on the hustings or pay costs. Althorp, horrified at the prospect of a contest, tried to block the move for a second reformer, but at the election meeting, 6 May, Milton was nominated *in absentia* and a second Tory, Knightley, was put up in response. Althorp, who stood accused, unfairly, of having betrayed Cartwright, vainly pleaded with Milton to show his face and exonerate him, especially 'as you have rather helped to bring me into the scrape by not at once refusing to let them put you up'. Milton would do no more than speak privately to Cartwright and Knightley and issue

an address. He deputed his 19-year-old son William Charles to represent him on the hustings. After a bitter 13-day poll Althorp and Milton were returned. By then Milton was in Ireland, visiting the family estates at Coolattin in Wicklow.[61]

He called for calm consideration of the Newtownbarry massacre and announced that he would bring on his corn laws motion in the next session, 23 June 1831. (He had recently composed an *Address to the Landowners of England on the Corn Laws*, but he delayed its publication until 1832 when reform was out of the way.)[62] Seemingly oblivious to the worry and expense which his conduct at the election had caused Althorp, who was additionally irked by his 'talking about the corn laws without any communication to me', he gave him a shabby return with some of his crotchety antics on the reform bill. He duly voted for the second reading of the reintroduced measure, 6 July, but two days later he gave notice of amendments to get rid of the county leaseholder franchise and to give the 21 new schedule D boroughs two Members each. The reformer Edward Littleton* considered this 'strange':

> He is an excessively proud, conceited, eccentric man, conceiving himself to be of another order of men, and ... 'one of those who inhabit a more elevated region, where they look down with contempt on the Thompsons and Johnsons in the vale below', and thus, unconscious of mischief, considers himself exempt from the ordinary rules and obligations of party men towards their leaders, whom he considers himself as patronising, not following.

At dinner on 10 July the cabinet ministers Russell and Graham

> ventured to rally him on his conduct, saying, 'Cartwright would have been a better Member for us'; and then proposed jocosely Mr. Cartwright's health, which we all drank in playful earnestness, amidst most malicious laughter; Milton trying all the while to stretch his muscles into a grin. As son as we went upstairs for coffee, he sat alone without speaking for an hour.[63]

According to Greville, Althorp called a meeting of ministerialists at which Milton

> made a speech just such as any opponent of the bill might make ... They were annoyed to the last degree, and the more provoked when reflecting that it was for him Althorp had been led to spend an immense amount of money, and compromise his character ... His obstinacy and impracticability are so extreme that nobody can move him, and Sefton told me that nothing could be more unsatisfactory then the termination of the meeting. I guess, however, that they will find some means of quieting him.[64]

The cabinet subsequently decided that Milton's proposal to give two Members to the schedule D boroughs was 'inadmissible'.[65] He tried to get Russell to explain the reasoning behind the contentious decision to disfranchise Appleby, 12 July, but did not press the matter;[66] and he defended the proposal, 19 July, when he divided with ministers against using the 1831 census to determine borough disfranchisement. He upheld the disfranchisement of Bere Alston, 20 July, but voiced doubts about that of Downton and St. Germans and voted against ministers on these points, 21, 26 July. He spoke for disfranchisement of the Looes, 22 July, when he presented and endorsed a Gloucester petition for repeal of the corn laws. Although he did not 'exactly approve' of schedule B, 27 July, he said he would support it and divided for the inclusion of Chippenham in it, against his better judgement. He did likewise on Dorchester, 28 July, Guildford, 29 July, and Richmond, 30 July, but he baulked at including Sudbury and voted accordingly, 2 Aug. He was in O'Connell's minority for swearing in the Dublin election committee, 29 July, but divided with government to punish the bribers, 23 Aug. He voted for the enfranchisement of Greenwich, 3 Aug., but next day, having voted for Littleton's motion to give Stoke two Members, moved his 'mischievous' amendment to give two to the schedule D boroughs. He denied that he was 'actuated by any hostility to the bill' or by want of confidence in ministers, and argued that

> in these towns [such as Bolton, Bradford, Brighton and Chippenham] the people are divided into parties very different from the parties in this House. They have each their local aristocracy and democracy; and let them have only one Member, and they will always be in collision.

He was defeated by 230-102, with a number of Tories in his minority.[67] On 5 Aug., when he voted for the enfranchisement of Gateshead, he said that it was wrong to regard county Members as the 'sole protectors of the agricultural interest'. He divided with government on the cases of Rochester, 9 Aug., when he exhorted them to look again at the Welsh representation, which as it stood would establish 'a system of oligarchical elections', and Merthyr, 10 Aug. He argued that measures other than the introduction of poor laws could be adopted to aid Ireland and denied Hunt's allegation that his father was an absentee Irish landlord, 10 Aug. He approved the division of the larger English counties, 11 Aug., but next day objected to the proposal to give an extra Member to the others, which he feared might open the way into Parliament for 'men ... of no great estimation, little interested in

the county'. He supported an unsuccessful amendment to give the Isle of Wight two county Members, 16 Aug. He voted with government on the county copyholder franchise, 17 Aug., but protested against the 'oligarchical tendency' of the proposed enfranchisement of leaseholders, and on the 18th tried in vain to have them excluded. That day he was in the ministerial minority against the Chandos amendment to enfranchise £50 tenants-at-will, but on the 20th he attacked the government's counter measure of allowing borough freeholders to vote in their counties as a response 'destitute of political wisdom'. The Tory Lord Ellenborough thought his hostile speech was 'as strong as any that could have been made by Croker'.[68] On 24 Aug., however, Milton enthusiastically supported the £10 borough householder franchise, contending that 'universal suffrage, kept within bounds by counteracting measures, is a most desirable form of constituency', and opposing an amendment for £5, which would guarantee 'uncontrolled universal suffrage'. That day he obtained three weeks' leave on account of a family illness and went into the country, but it seems that he did so in pique after receiving 'a letter of remonstrance' for his contrary behaviour from lord chancellor Brougham.[69] He went up to vote silently for the passage of the reform bill, 21 Sept., and renewed his furlough for three weeks on the 23rd. At a party meeting next day, according to Greville, he made 'a foolish speech, with prospective menaces and present nothingness in it'.[70] On 6 Oct. he refused to obey Lord Ebrington's* summons to London for a meeting to decide on the course of action if the Lords rejected the bill: his own notion was a popular campaign, managed by the Whig reformers, 'to pay no taxes till the bill is carried'. In a more reflective letter, 7 Oct., he expressed willingness to support the creation of '20 or as many peers as may be necessary to secure a majority', though he was worried about the almost inevitable 'creation of *poor peers*, who are as injurious to the constitution of the House of Lords as the rotten boroughs are to that of the House of Commons'. His preferred alternative parliamentary solution was 'a dissolution ... preceded by an address from the Commons to the king praying that he will not issue writs to boroughs in schedule A but that he will issue writs to the places in schedules C and D, taking no notice of schedule B'.[71] This nonsense, not surprisingly, was disregarded. He was absent from the division on Ebrington's confidence motion, 10 Oct., but at the Yorkshire county meeting, 12 Oct. 1831, he moved the petition to the Commons in favour of undiluted reform, explaining that although he had objected to details of the bill, 'when he considered the whole and the vast improvement effected, he was happy to take the whole bill'.[72]

Milton voted for the second reading of the revised reform bill, 17 Dec. 1831, and for the principle of schedules A, 20 Jan., and B, 23 Jan. 1832. He was in the government majorities on the Russian-Dutch loan, 26 Jan. (he paired on 12 July) and relations with Portugal, 9 Feb. He said that the division of some counties was a 'necessary evil', but he may have voted against it, 27 Jan., when he repeated his criticism of the three-Member counties.[73] On the presentation of petitions for protection of the glove trade, 31 Jan., he condemned 'the folly of the manufacturers in their expectation that they should gain anything by the adoption of a system of prohibition'. He spoke and voted in the minority of 32 for the unsuccessful attempt by Sir Robert Heron (who sat on his interest for Peterborough) to rescind the Chandos clause for enfranchising £50 tenants. He supported and divided for an amendment to give the borough vote to £10 ratepayers, 3 Feb. He joined Peel in welcoming ministers' concession of the vote to resident freeman by birth or servitude, 7 Feb.: 'although I am not desirous of giving them any paramount influence in the state, I do think there should be places where the very humblest classes should feel that they are in immediate connection with this House'. He voiced some doubts over the mechanics of the new electoral registration procedure, 8, 11 Feb. While he thought government were right to resist Hunt's call for retrospective inquiry into Peterloo, 10 Feb., he lamented how the episode had caused 'a separation of the lower classes ... from the upper' and, from a sense of obligation, voted in the minority of 31. He forecast that the abolition of Irish tithes would prompt landlords to increase their rents, 14 Feb. He defended the disfranchisement of the schedule A boroughs, including Appleby, 21 Feb., voted for the inclusion of Helston in B, 23 Feb., and spoke and divided for the enfranchisement of Tower Hamlets, 28 Feb., and Gateshead, 5 Mar. He was keen on the allocation of an individual seat to Merthyr, 9, 14 Mar. He voted silently for the third reading of the bill, 22 Mar. At the Brooks's party meeting to discuss the form of address to the king following ministers' resignation, 9 May, he 'spoke warmly' for a creation of peers to force reform through the Lords;[74] he voted for Ebrington's motion next day. In the debate which dashed the Conservatives' hopes of forming an administration to carry moderate reform, 14 May, he said that if Wellington did this he would be guilty of 'an act of public immorality'. On the reinstated Althorp's assurance that ministers had secured a guarantee of the passage of reform, 18 May, he abandoned at the last minute his planned motion

for an alternative 'strong address ... praying the king to make peers'. 'What a stormy debate it would have brought on', reflected John Campbell II*.[75] Milton paired for the second reading of the Irish reform bill, 25 May, and voted with government against an attempt to increase the Scottish county representation, 1 June. That day, confirming his notice of a corn law repeal motion for the 6th, he responded to pressure for disclosure of his views by saying that every measure 'that does not proceed on sounder principles than the present ... is vicious in its very foundation, and any superstructure that is built upon it must necessarily defeat the object'. In the event his motion lay dormant that session. On the Lords' amendments to the reform bill, 5 June, he observed that the peers would have been 'more prudent ... to be cautious' before rejecting a measure which did not directly affect them. He spoke and voted for extension of the Irish county franchise to 40s. freeholders, 13 June 1832. At a Northamptonshire celebration dinner, 28 June, he extolled the many virtues of 'popular government'.[76]

An advocate of a 'prudent and practicable' approach to the ultimate abolition of slavery, he stood for the Northern division of the county at the general election of 1832.[77] He topped the poll, but his father's death removed him from the Commons ten days after the new Parliament met.[78] He took his crusade against the corn laws into the Lords, but opposed further constitutional reform. He oversaw the Wentworth industrial enterprises with paternalistic prudence, but died unsure that he had lived a worthy life in October 1857.[79] He was succeeded as 4th earl by his second son William Thomas Spencer (1815-1902), having lost William Charles, at the age of 23, in 1835. He was assessed about then as an unimaginative 'man of highly respectable talents' and 'great moral courage'.[80]

[1] *Smith Letters*, ii. 750; G. Mee, *Aristocratic Enterprise*, 1, 23-25, 203; D. Spring, 'Earl Fitzwilliam and the Corn Laws', *AHR*, lix (1953-4), 288-9. [2] E.A. Wasson, *Whig Renaissance*, 47-52; P. Mandler, *Aristocratic Government in Age of Reform*, 30, 61, 88-91, 276; Spring, 289-90; B. Hilton, *Age of Atonement*, 238-40. [3] *Smith Letters*, i. 419-20; [J. Grant], *Random Recollections of Lords* (1836), 312. [4] Grant, 308-12; Wasson, 48-49. [5] E.A. Smith, *Whig Principles and Party Politics*, 349-52; *Althorp Letters*, 91-92. [6] *The Times*, 14 Mar.; Wentworth Woodhouse mun. WWM/F48/171; Fitzwilliam mss, Milton to Fitzwilliam, 20, 31 Mar. 1820. [7] Spring, 291-2. [8] Brougham mss, Brougham to Grey [1 June 1820]. [9] Add. 52444, f. 122. [10] *The Times*, 26 July 1820. [11] Wasson, 81; Fitzwilliam mss 102/12; *Althorp Letters*, 112; Add. 51562, Brougham to Holland [21 Dec.]; Bessborough mss, Grey to Duncannon, 25 Dec. 1820; *Wilberforce Corresp.* ii. 444. [12] HLRO, Hist. Coll. 379, Grey Bennet diary, 13. [13] *The Times*, 7 Feb. 1821. [14] Fitzwilliam mss, W. to G. Strickland, 31 May, Sir F.L. Wood to Milton, 1 June 1820. [15] Broughton, *Recollections*, ii. 140. [16] Fitzwilliam mss 731, p. 12; Smith, 363-7; *The Times*, 2 Apr. 1821. [17] Grey Bennet diary, 82. [18] Wasson, 115. [19] *CJ*, lxxvi. 402, 420, 434; *The Times*,

1, 7 June; Fitzwilliam mss, Yeoman to Milton, 9 June 1821. [20] Grey Bennet diary, 107. [21] Fitzwilliam mss, Althorp to Milton, 11 Mar. 1822. [22] Grey mss, Fitzwilliam to Grey, 24 Mar., 4 Apr.; Fitzwilliam mss, reply, 6 Apr. 1822; Smith, 368-9. [23] Fitzwilliam mss, Althorp to Milton, 9 Aug. 1822; 731, p. 43. [24] *The Times*, 7 Nov. 1822, 21, 24 Jan. 1823; Smith, 369-71. [25] Brougham mss, Milton to Brougham, 2 Feb.; Fitzwilliam mss, Althorp to Milton, 3 Feb. 1823. [26] Fitzwilliam mss 113/3, 4. [27] Ibid. 731, p. 77. [28] Grey mss, Tierney to Grey, 21 Feb. 1825. [29] Wasson, 146-7. [30] Dorset RO D/BKL, Bankes jnl. 157 (18 Apr. 1826); Wasson, 122-3. [31] Add. 76379, Milton to Althorp, 27 Dec. 1825; E. Baines, *Yorks. Election of 1826*, p. 16. [32] *Leeds Intelligencer*, 15 June; *The Times*, 23 June 1826; Smith, 374-6. See YORKSHIRE. [33] Wasson, 123-4. [34] Grey mss, Grey to Howick, 14 Mar. 1827. [35] Ibid. Howick to Grey, 2 Mar. 1827. [36] Wentworth Woodhouse mun. WWM G15/1; Fitzwilliam mss 731, p. 121. [37] Add. 52447, ff. 81-82; *The Times*, 19 June 1827. [38] *Canning's Ministry*, 346; Fitzwilliam mss, Lansdowne to Milton, 21 July 1827. [39] *Arbuthnot Corresp.* 89; *Creevey Pprs.* ii. 129; *Arbuthnot Jnl.* ii. 142; Add. 51677, Lord J. Russell to Holland, 16 Aug.; Lansdowne mss, Tierney to Lansdowne, 6 Sept., Spring Rice to same, 11 Sept.; Castle Howard mss, Abercromby to Carlisle, 14 Oct. 1827. [40] Hants RO, Tierney mss 31M70/66; Add. 38752, f. 164; Wasson, 153. [41] *Life of Campbell*, i. 453; Fitzwilliam mss 731, p. 135. [42] Add. 40395, f. 221. [43] Broughton, iii. 246; *Ellenborough Diary*, i. 45; Fitzwilliam mss, Milton to wife, 29 Feb. 1828. [44] Harewood mss, Lord G. Cavendish Bentinck to Lady Canning, 14 May 1828; TNA 30/29/9/5/67. [45] Grey mss, Ellice to Grey [12 Feb. 1829]. [46] Add. 51677, Lord J. Russell to Holland, 25 Dec. [1828]; 76371, Brougham to Althorp [24 Mar. 1829]; Fitzwilliam mss 731, p. 157. [47] Fitzwilliam mss 731, p. 167. [48] Ibid. Althorp to Milton, 20 Jan. 1830 [49] Salop RO 6003/6, 15 Apr. 1830. [50] *Buxton Mems.* 247. [51] Grey mss, Howick jnl. 13, 14 May 1830. [52] M. Brock, *Great Reform Act*, 97; Fitzwilliam mss 732, p. 12. See YORKSHIRE. [53] Fitzwilliam mss, Duberley, Maltby, Tavistock to Milton, 5 July 1830. [54] Nottingham Univ. Lib. Ossington mss OsC 75; Howick jnl. 27 July; Brougham mss, Scarlett to Brougham [26 July]; Fitzwilliam mss, same to Milton, 26 July, reply, 28 July 1830 (732, p. 9). [55] *The Times*, 6, 27 Nov. 1830; Wasson, 189. [56] Add. 61937, f. 120. [57] *The Times*, 17 Dec. 1830; Bucks. RO, Fremantle mss D/FR/139/20. [58] Mee, 5. [59] Add. 51836. [60] *The Times*, 16 Apr. 1831. [61] Fitzwilliam mss, Milton's memoranda, 13, 20, 21, 23, 26, 27 Apr., 2-4, 6 May; 732, pp. 25, 31; Althorp to Milton [6 May]; *Althorp Letters*, 155-6; Wasson, 214-17; Lincs. AO, Tennyson d'Eyncourt mss TdE H14/2, Milton to Tennyson, 21 May 1831; E.G. Forrester, *Northants. Elections*, 131-47 [62] Spring, 293. [63] Le Marchant, *Althorp*, 323; Hatherton diary, 10 July 1831; *Three Diaries*, 102-3. [64] *Greville Mems.* ii. 164. [65] *Holland House Diaries*, 11-12. [66] *Croker Pprs.* ii.129. [67] Hatherton diary, 4 Aug. [1831]; *Three Diaries*, 113. [68] *Three Diaries*, 121. [69] Le Marchant, 341-2. [70] *Greville Mems.* ii. 203. [71] Devon RO, Earl Fortescue mss 1262M/FC 87. [72] *The Times*, 14 Oct. 1831. [73] Add. 51573, Spring Rice to Lady Holland, 27 Jan. [1832]. [74] *Three Diaries*, 245. [75] Northants. RO, Agar Ellis diary, 18 May 1832; *Croker Pprs.* ii. 165; *Life of Campbell*, ii. 11. [76] *The Times*, 30 June 1832. [77] Northants. RO, Gotch mss GR 1216; Add. 57370, f. 98. [78] *Arbuthnot Corresp.* 176. [79] Spring, 293-300; Mee, 5-7, 13-22. [80] Grant, 307-8.

D.R.F.

FLEMING, John I (?1746–1829), of 104 Gloucester Place, Mdx.

GATTON	1818–1820
SALTASH	14 June 1820–1826

?*bap.* 2 Jan. 1747, s. of William Fleeming[1] of South Leith, Edinburgh and Helen, da. of William Cleghorn of Cramond. *educ.* ?Edinburgh. *unm. d.* 17 May 1829.

Asst. surgeon E.I. Co. (Bengal) 1768, surgeon 1771, head surgeon 1786; member, medical board 1786, pres. 1800-11; MD Edinburgh 1804; res. Nov. 1813.

Fleming, a former surgeon in the Indian medical service, was described at the time of his election as a fellow of the Royal Society in 1813 as 'a gentleman well versed in various branches of science and learning'. A large collection of Indian botanical drawings assembled by him was later purchased by the British Museum.[2] He was returned for Gatton in 1818 on the interest of Sir Mark Wood[†] as a supporter of Lord Liverpool's ministry, but his unreliable voting record meant that he was obliged to retire in 1820. He was returned unopposed for Saltash at a by-election that June on the interest of Michael George Prendergast, a former East India merchant, who had chosen to sit for Galway.

His votes are often difficult to distinguish from those of John Willis Fleming, Tory Member for Hampshire, but his record was apparently as inconsistent as before. He probably divided in the minorities against the aliens bill, 7 July, and the barrack agreement bill, 17 July 1820. He certainly voted to defend ministers' conduct towards Queen Caroline, 6 Feb. 1821. It is likely that he divided for Catholic claims, 28 Feb., as his namesake later voted against this measure. He may have voted with ministers against disfranchising civil officers of the ordnance, 12 Apr., and was definitely with them against Hume's economy and retrenchment motion, 27 June. However, he was almost certainly against them for the omission of arrears from the duke of Clarence's grant, 8, 18 June. It was presumably he who divided to abolish the death penalty for forgery, 4 June 1821. He voted against more extensive tax reductions, 11, 21 Feb., but for reduction of the number of junior lords of the admiralty, 1 Mar., and possibly for abolition of one of the joint-postmasterships, 13 Mar., and reduction of the navy victualling grant, 18 Mar. 1822. He may have divided against inquiry into the right of voting in parliamentary elections, 20 Feb. 1823. He probably voted for information regarding Catholic burials, 6 Feb., and was perhaps the 'J.S. Fleming' who voted to permit defence by counsel in felony trials, 6 Apr., and repeal of the usury laws, 8 Apr. 1824. He is less likely to have been the one who divided for the duke of Cumberland's annuity, 6 June 1825. It was said of him at this time that he 'appeared to attend frequently and vote sometimes with, and sometimes (though more rarely) against ministers'.[3] He retired at the dissolution in 1826.

Fleming died in May 1829 and in his will made bequests totalling £79,700 to 20 friends and relatives, leaving the residue to his 'dear friend' Thomas Wilkinson of Fitzroy Square; his personalty was sworn under £160,000.[4]

[1] Spelt thus in IGI (Scotland). In his will, Fleming stated that he was an orphan, brought up by his maternal uncle, John Cleghorn of Granton, Cramond. The IGI confirms that William Cleghorn had a son named John. [2] R. Soc. Certs. of Election, vi. 227; *Jnl. of Botany*, liv (1916), 301-2. [3] *Session of Parl. 1825*, p. 464. [4] PROB 11/1755/284; IR26/1193/200.

T.A.J.

FLEMING, John II (1781–1844), of North Stoneham, Hants.

HAMPSHIRE   1820–1831

HAMPSHIRE SOUTH   1835–10 Aug. 1842

b. 28 Nov. 1781,[1] o.s. of Rev. Thomas Willis, rect. of Bletchley, Bucks., and Catherine, da. of Col. West Hyde of Bucks. *educ.* Eton 1796; Corpus, Oxf. 1800. *m.* 18 Feb. 1813,[2] Christophena, da. of James Buchanan of Buchanan, Stirling, 4s. 4da. *suc.* fa. 1789; cos. John Fleming[†] to North Stoneham by 1813; took name of Fleming by Act of Parliament 7 July 1813. *d.* 19 July 1844.

Sheriff, Hants 1817-18.

Capt. S. Hants militia 1803, lt.-col. 1808.

Fleming, who was baptized John Barton Willis, was the great-grandson of Browne Willis (1682-1760), an eccentric Buckinghamshire antiquary.[3] He derived no direct benefit from the will of his father Thomas Willis, a Buckinghamshire clergyman, but as the reversionary heir of his cousin John Fleming (1743-1802), Member for Southampton, 1774-80, 1784-90, he acquired substantial estates at North Stoneham and Romsey, Hampshire, and Binstead, Isle of Wight.[4] This property had passed in the first instance to John Fleming's wife, who apparently did not long survive him, if it can be assumed that Willis was in residence by the time of his Hampshire militia appointment in 1803. He had certainly taken possession by 1813, when he complied with his benefactor's testamentary injunction on his heirs to take 'the name of ffleming [sic] exclusive of their own surnames ... and use the utmost endeavour by all proper means and methods to obtain an Act of Parliament to change their names'.[5] In spite of this, he was often referred to as John Willis Fleming or John Barton Willis Fleming, probably to facilitate identification, and his descendants used a hyphenated version of the name.

Fleming raised his profile as a Hampshire land-owner by the purchases of South Stoneham in 1819

and Chilworth in 1825. He resided at the former during the initial construction work on a vast new mansion at North Stoneham, built to the classical design of Thomas Hopper.[6] The 'gorgeous magnificence' of its interior furnishings was eulogized in an 1827 press report, and he lived, according to an admirer, 'in baronial splendour ... his purse ... always open to the poor and needy'.[7] He was certainly adept at securing maximum publicity for his philanthropic endeavours, in which the encouragement of self-reliance was a recurrent theme. The Hampshire Benefit Society, a contributory insurance scheme founded in 1824, was intended to restore 'that spirit of providence and personal exertion ... which the present miserable dependence upon the poor rate has of late years almost totally banished from the labouring classes'.[8] His aggressive promotion of this project, which duplicated existing provision, became a source of some local resentment against him.[9] Fleming came to political prominence at the outset of his Hampshire shrieval term in February 1817, when he ignored a requisition for a county meeting on distress in favour of another, to frame a loyal address. William Cobbett[†], the author of the former, protested that 'the little dull sheriff' did his utmost to stifle debate at the meeting, when he summarily declared the loyalist motion carried amid scenes of noisy chaos.[10] At the general election of 1820 he came forward for the county on a double vacancy. Thomas Freeman Heathcote, one of the retiring Members, had introduced him to the premier Lord Liverpool in October 1819 as

> a gentleman of very large fortune ... commanding a considerable influence in this county, which (though independent of any party) he has generally influenced in favour of the government and always in support of the constitution of his country.[11]

On the hustings he declared himself to be no enemy to 'temperate, safe and rational reform'. Many were impressed by his protestations of independence, but his essential ministerialism soon emerged after his unopposed return.[12] He became a close ally of the duke of Wellington, the Hampshire lord lieutenant, to whom he wrote advising against the appointment of an opposition supporter as chairman of the quarter sessions in March 1825. Later, in January 1833, he blamed himself for failures in the informal political vetting of appointments to the bench.[13]

Fleming seldom spoke in the House, though he was an accomplished enough orator out of doors. He was prepared to oppose ministers on occasions, often in deference to constituency opinion, but his votes in the 1820 Parliament are subject to confusion with those of John Fleming, Member for Saltash. It was probably the latter, who was more inclined towards opposition, who cast the votes against the aliens bill, 7 July, and the barrack agreement bill, 17 July 1820. The Hampshire Member chaired a local meeting of old Etonians later that month.[14] At a county meeting on the Queen Caroline affair, 12 Jan. 1821, he refused to comment on her exclusion from the liturgy and was hissed for his attempt to vindicate ministers' handling of the business.[15] He divided accordingly, 6 Feb. On the presentation of the meeting's petition, which he sought to denigrate, 26 Jan., he was accused of 'trying the patience' of the assembly by Alexander Baring. Given his later record it was probably he who voted against Catholic relief, 28 Feb., but it less likely that he was in the minority for mitigation of the punishment for forgery, 4 June. He presented a county petition complaining of agricultural distress, 19 Mar.[16] A local newspaper reported that he had voted for repeal of the additional malt duty, 21 Mar., and had paired for abolition of the tax on husbandry horses, 14 June, having been called away by the illness of one of his children.[17] If this was so, it was surely not he who divided for the omission of arrears from the grant to the duke of Clarence, 8, 18 June, and for economy and retrenchment, 27 June. To alleviate distress, he was said to have reduced rents by ten per cent in his audit of July 1821.[18]

Fleming introduced a yeomanry petition complaining of agricultural distress at the Hampshire quarter sessions in January 1822, but withdrew it after general exception was taken to his peremptory erasure of passages critical of the magistracy.[19] He was in government majorities against more extensive tax reductions to relieve distress, 11, 21 Feb., but voted for reduction of the salt duty, 28 Feb., and the number of junior admiralty lords, 1 Mar. Either he or his namesake was in the minorities to abolish one of the joint-postmasterships, 13 Mar., and for naval reductions, 18 Mar. He presented agricultural distress petitions from the New Forest, 23 Feb., and Romsey, 13 May, when he also presented one from Portsea against allowing Catholic peers to sit, in which sense he had probably divided, 30 Apr.[20] He presented two petitions against the poor removal bill, 30 May.[21] That month he distributed premiums to the most industrious labourers on his North Stoneham estate.[22] He voted to consider criminal law reform, 4 June, if it was this division to which he referred in a later speech.[23] He may have cast votes for repeal of the salt duty, 28 June, referral of the Calcutta bankers' petition to a select committee, 4 July, and in favour of a grant for printing government proclamations in Irish newspapers, 22 July, though he had suffered a double fracture of the arm in a carriage accident only days before the last. With the aid of an innovatory splint apparatus, he made a complete recovery.[24] He was reported to be too busy to attend the anniversary meeting of the Hampshire County Club, 7 Aug., but was present at Southampton races later that month.[25] In December 1822 he donated blankets to the poor of Southampton.[26] He announced a one quarter remission of rent and tithes in January 1823, and wrote off arrears of two years from one tenant, who was allowed to depart with his stock.[27] The general cry at the county meeting on 1 Mar. 1823 was against the 1821 Currency Act, but Fleming blamed economic distress squarely on foreign imports and described radical proposals to alter public credit arrangements as 'an act of robbery'.[28] He made little mark in the House that session, but may have divided against inquiry into the right of voting in parliamentary elections, 20 Feb, and was certainly in the ministerial majority against repeal of the Foreign Enlistment Act, 16 Apr. When he offered a further rent reduction to tenants in December 1823, he claimed to have voted to halve the assessed taxes, but if he did so it went unrecorded.[29]

Fleming's private efforts to persuade Peel, the home secretary, that the provisions of the Gaol Act would devastate the municipal finances of Portsea fell on stony ground in February 1824.[30] Assuming this to be evidence of his interest, it was surely he who was appointed to the select committees on prisons, 18 Mar., and county gaols, 12 Apr. 1824. He was unlikely to have voted for information on Catholic burials, 6 Feb., but may have been the 'J.S. Fleming' listed in minorities to permit defence by counsel in felony trials, 6 Apr., and for repeal of the usury laws, 8 Apr. He presented petitions for abolition of the duty on coals and excise licenses, 1, 22 Mar.[31] Although he went along with the demands for a reduction in assessed taxes made at a county meeting, 23 Apr., he claimed to detect signs of an upturn in the agricultural sector and defended the grant for additional churches, having lately contributed £100 towards one in Southampton.[32] He chaired the inaugural meeting of the Hampshire Benefit Society in December 1824, and was appointed to the select committee on friendly societies, 24 Feb. 1825.[33] The votes listed for 'J. Fleming' for suppression of the Catholic Association, 25 Feb., and against Catholic relief, 1 Mar., 21 Apr., 10 May, and the disfranchisement of Irish 40s. freeholders all accord with his known opinions, and it was probably he who divided in favour of the duke of Cumberland's annuity bill, 6, 10 June. He presented petitions for a repeal of assessed taxes from Southampton and Romsey, 4 Mar., having sent notice of the latter to his colleague Purefoy Jervoise. In a similar communication concerning the committee arrangements for the Portsea paving and lighting bill, 10 Mar., he confided his plans to leave London for a spell on account of his wife's health. On 20 Mar. he requested information on the progress of the Portsmouth canal bill and, anticipating 'sad disgrace if I do not attend', promised to be present for the second reading, which took place on 28 Mar.[34] He presented petitions from several Hampshire parishes against alteration of the corn laws, 28 Apr. 1825, and was probably responsible for votes against their relaxation in the following session, 8, 11 May 1826.[35] He presented petitions from Overton weavers against silk imports, 1 Mar., and both for and against changes to the law governing benefit societies, 14 Mar., 18 Apr. 1826.[36]

At the 1826 general election Fleming's proposer referred with approval to his opposition to Catholic relief, which he pledged to continue. He welcomed government endeavours to ease the tax burden but, in a reaffirmation of his support for the corn laws, blamed its recent deviation from 'good old commercial policy' for an economic downturn in the agricultural districts. When questioned on his attitude to progressive legislation, he claimed to have voted for reform of the customs and excise and the courts of equity, and for the disfranchisement of the corrupt borough of Grampound, but added that 'he was not for pulling the constitution to pieces'. Rumours of an opposition came to nothing and he was returned unopposed.[37] At Christmas he gave a dinner and fancy dress ball to the corporations of Southampton and Romsey.[38] He voted against Catholic relief, 6 Mar. 1827, 12 May 1828. He presented petitions against alteration of the corn laws from Petersfield and Fareham farmers, 29 Mar., and from county landowners, 18 June, and voted accordingly, 2 Apr. 1827.[39] On 28 May he divided for curbs on election expenses. He presented petitions for repeal of the Test Acts, 31 May, 11, 12 June 1827, but apparently did not vote on the issue, 26 Feb. 1828.[40] He presented petitions against the Malt Act, 28 Feb., and the friendly societies bill, 25 Apr. On 10 Apr. he spoke at a Romsey meeting against the use of boy chimney sweeps and extolled the virtues of mechanical alternatives.[41] Next month he went to Paris, having apparently abandoned plans for a similar trip the previous autumn.[42] On 8 May the foreign secretary Lord Dudley, an Oxford contemporary, had forwarded a letter of introduction to Lord Granville, the ambassador, in which he speculated that it was 'only to please his wife (who I am told is pretty; though I

never saw her) that he is going to trust himself for the second time in his life among our natural enemies'. He described Fleming as

> a genuine Tory gentleman of the old rock ... and as is often the case with English gentleman [he] has more sense than he shows for in conversation. I do not want you to introduce him to the 'Doctrinaires', nor will he want to *assist* at a meeting of the Academy. But some little civilities will not be thrown away upon him, and he will come back in charming humour for the rest of the session.[43]

As 'an approved Protestant', Fleming was paired with James Abercromby for a division on financial provision for Canning's family, probably that of 22 May.[44] In a letter of 30 May he expressed satisfaction at the Huskissonite secession from Wellington, now prime minister, who felt it unnecessary to take up his offer to return immediately.[45] No further parliamentary activity is recorded for 1828, when the recipients of his bounty included the Hampshire Agricultural Society, the countty hospital, the race meetings at Basingstoke, Southampton, Stockbridge and Winchester, the regattas at Southampton and Cowes and a grand ball at Winchester.[46]

The patronage secretary Planta listed Fleming as likely to vote 'with government' on their planned concession of Catholic emancipation in February 1829. He presented hostile petitions, 9 Feb., 4 Mar., when he indicated a new open-mindedness on the question and stated his confidence in Peel and Wellington. To the latter, he explained his intention to withdraw to Hampshire once he had redeemed his election pledge by voting against the introduction of the bill. This he did on 6 Mar., though he had further hostile petitions to present three days later.[47] By September he was sufficiently reconciled to emancipation to support the application of several Catholics to join the Hampshire bench.[48] He presented a silk thrower's petition for indemnity against foreign imports, 1 May, and, finding himself 'constantly assailed with complaints from all classes of my constituents', favoured Wellington with a lengthy protectionist diatribe, 26 Dec. 1829. He conceded that 'the extremely depressed value of commodities may be in a greater degree attributable to the contraction of the currency', but ascribed the sharp drop in his own income from timber sales purely to a glut of the foreign raw material, and warned that the healthy official trading figures did not tally with popular perception. To Wellington's assertion that agricultural distress was partly attributable to maladministration of the poor laws, he replied that this provision was already pared down 'as far as the necessities of the people will admit'.[49] Fleming's failure to oppose

Wellington any further came under scrutiny at a county meeting, 10 Mar. 1830. To disapprobation, he defended his vote of 23 Feb. against the enfranchisement of Birmingham, Leeds and Manchester on the score of his conscientious opposition to parliamentary reform, and claimed that the bare notice given to economic distress in the king's speech had been 'a mere verbal error'. He doubted if the general reduction in taxes demanded by the meeting was practicable, but as a man of principle he promised to support its petition, with which he expressed his 'entire concurrence' on its presentation, 16 Mar.[50] He voted against Jewish emancipation, 17 May. He presented an Isle of Wight petition against the sale of beer bill, 4 May, and voted to postpone permission for on-consumption, 1 July. Press reports stated that he viewed the measure as potentially ruinous to publicans, from which a sceptical commentator construed that he was merely anxious to preserve 'his magisterial influence in dispensing licensing favours'. It was claimed that from personal inclination he would have supported mitigation of the punishment for forgery, 24 May, but that he had abstained in deference to constituency opinion.[51] In a bid to promote his own social experiment of granting rent-free allotments in lieu of poor relief, he gave notice on 4 June of a bill to empower all parish officers to do the same, of which no more was heard.[52] He denounced calls for contingency plans to be made for a regency as 'disrespectful and precipitate' and politically motivated, 6 July 1830.

Before the general election of 1830 a rumour circulated that Fleming would stand for Southampton, where he possessed considerable influence, but in the event he offered again for the county.[53] Struggling to be heard from the hustings over the catcalls, he insisted that the aspersions lately cast on his attendance record were rooted in 'base and scandalous falsehood'. His equivocation over Catholic emancipation and his opposition to reform and economy were also held against him, but he was returned unopposed after attempts to mount an opposition ended in disarray. He prudently declined a chairing and was hanged in effigy by a mob.[54] At subsequent dinners he called for acceptance of the Catholic question as settled and hinted at support for a measure of partial relief to the Jews. He presented an Alton petition against slavery, 3 Nov. Listed among the 'friends' of the ministry, he voted with them in the crucial division on the civil list, 15 Nov. On 30 Nov. 1830 he was belatedly granted a week's leave on account of the disturbed state of his county. Incongruously clad in yachting attire, he had mustered the yeomanry eight days earlier to confront a riotous assembly of labourers at Portswood, before

joining his colleague Heathcote in Winchester.[55] That month he was involved in the formal re-establishment of the Romsey and Southampton yeomanry troop and other local militia forces.[56] The docility of his own workforce during the 'Swing' disturbances was ascribed by a sympathetic newspaper to their generous wages, to which were added incentive payments for marriage, sobriety, industry and church attendance and membership of the Hampshire Benefit Society.[57] The fire which caused damage of 'at least £4,000' to his North Stoneham residence on 20 Jan. 1831 was generally reported as accidental in origin, though this explanation was treated with scepticism by Cobbett.[58] On 3 Feb. Fleming presented a Hambledon petition in favour of a property tax, for which he had previously indicated his support.[59] He opposed the Grey ministry's reform bill from the outset and thought its success unlikely. On 4 Mar. he confidently told Wellington:

> Sir R. Peel's speech last night was decisive of the fate of this most revolutionary measure, and I trust also, although of less immediate importance, of the dismissal of the most daring, rash and incapable administration ever entrusted with the government of this country. Thank God they have been tried, and afforded a comparison of their abilities with those of their predecessors.[60]

Such was the clamour raised against him at a county meeting, 17 Mar., that his specific objections to the bill were inaudible.[61] He voted against its second reading, 22 Mar., and for Gascoyne's wrecking amendment, 19 Apr. 1831. At the ensuing general election he faced two reformers single-handed after the retreat of his colleague. In his address he attacked a ministry 'who have utterly failed in realising the economy and retrenchment so liberally professed before their accession to office', and despite being pelted on his canvass, assured Wellington that victory might be secured 'by a certain expenditure of cash', 28 Apr. Two days before the election he bowed to the inevitable and withdrew, but not before erroneously identifying one of his opponents as a government pensioner in an ungracious parting shot, for which he was later forced to apologize.[62]

Fleming continued to campaign against reform in Hampshire throughout the summer of 1831, but he deferred to Wellington's opinion that a formal declaration on the subject might do more harm than good, while his plans for a Southampton newspaper entitled *The Anti-Anarchist* came to nothing.[63] No trace has been found in the records of either House of the petition which he contemplated in November against the 'dangerous and illegal' political unions.[64] He had no notion of standing when a Hampshire seat became vacant by the resignation of Sir James Macdonald in June 1832, and told Wellington that he felt 'no ambition whatever to sit in the reformed House of Commons', 3 Sept., but he nevertheless stood for the Southern division of the county at the 1832 general election.[65] The Conservative whip Holmes was optimistic about his chances and he fought an aggressive campaign, targeting the anti-Dutch policy pursued by the foreign secretary Lord Palmerston, his principal opponent. He stressed his continued opposition to free trade and complained of the numerous 'anomalies' contained in the Reform Act.[66] After his defeat, he was active in the formation of the South Hampshire Conservative Association, and he topped the poll at the general election of 1835.[67] Palmerston, defeated on this occasion, hinted darkly at voter intimidation, and made the specific allegation that Fleming had offered tithe abatements exclusively to his supporters.[68] Rumours of his imminent elevation to the peerage proved to be unfounded, and he sat as a Conservative until his retirement in August 1842, when Peel, now prime minister, thanked him for his 'cordial support'.[69] In the meantime, he continued to take a close interest in elections for Southampton where, in the rhetoric of a radical candidate nearly 20 years after his death, he ruled the electors 'with a rod of iron'.[70] He co-ordinated the disruption of an anti-corn law meeting there in February 1842, and as a witness before an election committee later the same year successfully stonewalled an awkward line of questioning on local Conservative finances.[71]

In July 1843 Fleming embarked on a Mediterranean cruise, and from Naples informed Peel, 8 Apr. 1844, of his intention 'to proceed ... to Greece or Constantinople, and I hope also afterwards Syria and Egypt'.[72] He got no further than Piraeus, Athens, where he died on board his yacht of 'malignant fever', 19 July 1844.[73] An obituarist recorded that though he had cut down more than £300,000 worth of timber from his 15,000 acre Hampshire estate, he had 'left the whole as full as the land will bear'. His expenditure in the Southampton area was estimated at £18,000 per annum, and he was ritually acclaimed as a good landlord, though at an unspecified date his summary dispensation of notices to quit had been deemed worthy of investigation by the bishop of Winchester.[74] By his will, dated 25 Nov. 1842, Fleming left the Romsey great tithes to his wife and referred to provision from the sale of clerical livings for his two younger sons. But their annuities and those granted to his daughters and other relatives were not covered by his personal estate.[75] The cause of this difficulty was almost cer-

tainly his reported expenditure of £100,000 on North Stoneham, which was never completed.[76] In 1852 his eldest son John Browne Willis Fleming (1815-72), to whom the bulk of his landed property had passed, obtained a private Act of Parliament to permit the sale of entailed estate. South Stoneham became the residence of his second son Thomas James Willis Fleming (1819-90), Conservative Member for Winchester, 1864-5.

[1] *Ex. inf.* Stephen Lees. [2] *Gent. Mag.* (1813), ii. 1214. [3] IGI (Bucks.); *Berry's Hants Genealogies*, 126-8; *Oxford DNB.* [4] PROB 11/1191/217; *VCH Bucks.* iv. 278-9, 282. [5] PROB 11/1369/105; *VCH Hants*, iii. 479; iv. 453; v. 143, 151-2. [6] *VCH Hants*, iii. 468, 483; J. Vale, 'Country Houses of Southampton', *Procs. Hants Field Club*, xxxix (1983), 172, 180-1. [7] *Hants Telegraph*, 1 Jan. 1827, 20 Dec. 1830. [8] Wellington mss WP1/798/13. [9] *Hants Telegraph*, 19 June 1826. [10] *Pol. Reg.* 15 Mar.; *The Times*, 13 Mar. 1817. [11] Add. 38280, f. 103. [12] *Hants Telegraph*, 20, 27 Mar. 1820. [13] R. Foster, *Politics of County Power*, 30; Wellington mss WP1/814/22; WP4/5/1/2. [14] *Hants Telegraph*, 31 July 1820. [15] Ibid. 15 Jan. 1821. [16] *The Times*, 20 Mar. 1821. [17] *Hants Telegraph*, 26 Mar., 25 June; *Salisbury Jnl.* 2 July 1821. [18] *Hants Telegraph*, 9 July 1821. [19] Ibid. 28 Jan 1822. [20] *The Times*, 23 Feb., 14 May 1822. [21] Ibid. 31 May 1822. [22] *Salisbury Jnl.* 20 May 1822. [23] *Hants Telegraph*, 19 June 1826. [24] Ibid. 22, 29 July 1822, 14 July, 13 Oct. 1823. [25] Ibid. 12, 19 Aug. 1822. [26] *Salisbury Jnl.* 30 Dec. 1822. [27] *Hants Telegraph*, 2 Dec. 1822, 13 Jan. 1823. [28] Ibid. 3 Mar. 1823. [29] Ibid. 19 Dec. 1823. [30] Add. 40361, ff. 213, 217. [31] *The Times*, 2, 23, Mar. 1824. [32] *Salisbury Jnl.* 8 Mar.; *Hants Telegraph*, 26 Apr. 1824. [33] *Salisbury Jnl.* 6 Dec. 1824. [34] *The Times*, 5 Mar. 1825; Hants RO, Jervoise mss 44M69 G2/466/1-3. [35] *The Times* 29 Apr. 1825. [36] Ibid. 1, 15 Mar., 19 Apr. 1826. [37] *Hants Telegraph*, 19 June 1826. [38] *Southampton Herald*, 1 Jan. 1827. [39] *The Times*, 30 Mar., 19 June 1827. [40] Ibid. 1, 12, 13 June, 1827. [41] *Hants Chron.* 14 Apr. 1828. [42] *Palmerston-Sulivan Letters*, 202. [43] TNA 30/29/14. [44] Castle Howard mss, Abercromby to Carlisle, 17 May 1828. [45] Wellington mss WP1/934/25; 939/2. [46] Foster, 134. [47] Wellington mss WP1/1002/6,7. [48] Ibid. WP4/1/46. [49] Ibid. WP4/1/46,60,61. [50] *Hants Telegraph*, 15 Mar.; *Salisbury Jnl.* 15 Mar. 1830. [51] *Hants Telegraph*, 31 May, 7 June, 5 July 1830. [52] *Salisbury Jnl.* 3 May 1830. [53] *The Age*, 20 Dec. 1829; *Hants Advertiser*, 17 July; *Hants Telegraph*, 26 July 1830. [54] *Hants Telegraph*, 9 Aug. 1830. [55] Foster, 75-79. [56] Wellington mss WP4/2/2/36, 37. [57] A. Temple Patterson, *Hist. Southampton*, i. 154-5; *Hants Telegraph*, 27 Dec.; *Salisbury Jnl.* 27 Dec. 1830; *Portsmouth Herald*, 9 Feb. 1831. [58] *Portsmouth Herald*, 23 Jan.; *Hants Telegraph*, 24 Jan. 1831; Wellington mss WP4/3/1/3. [59] See *Hants Telegraph*, 15 Mar. 1830. [60] Wellington mss WP4/3/1/7; *Hants Telegraph*, 24 Jan.; *Hants Advertiser*, 12 Feb. 1831. [61] *Hants Telegraph*, 21 Mar. 1831. [62] Wellington mss WP4/3/4/18,19,21-23; *Portsmouth Herald*, 1 May; *The Times*, 9 May 1831. [63] Wellington mss WP1/1186/31; 1187/14,16; WP4/3/4/25, 26. [64] Ibid. WP4/3/4/46,47. [65] Ibid. WP4/4/2/50; 4/3/5. [66] *Arbuthnot Corresp.* 170; Southampton RO D/An 14,16-18. [67] Foster, 144-5. [68] *Palmerston-Sulivan Letters*, 259-61. [69] K. Bourne, *Palmerston*, 546; *Dod's Parl. Companion* (1835), 115; (1841), 152; Add. 40513, ff. 225-7. [70] Temple Patterson, ii. 39, 168. [71] Foster, 119-20; *PP* (1842), viii. 313-14. [72] Add. 40530, f. 419; 40542, f. 145. [73] *The Times*, 13 Aug. 1844; Vale, 180-1. [74] *The Times*, 13 Sept. 1844; Southampton RO D/S 1/1/22. [75] PROB 11/2006/755; IR26/1674/468. [76] *Gent. Mag.* (1844), ii. 544; Vale, 180-1.

H.J.S./P.J.S.

FOLEY, Edward Thomas (1791–1846), of Stoke Edith, Herefs. and 41 Curzon Street, Mdx.

LUDGERSHALL	1826–1832
HEREFORDSHIRE	1832–1841

b. 21 Dec. 1791, 1st s. of Hon. Edward Foley[†] of Stoke Edith and 2nd w. Elizabeth Maria, da. and h. of Thomas Hodgetts of Prestwood, Staffs.; bro. of John Hodgetts Hodgetts Foley*. *educ.* Brasenose, Oxf. 1809. *m.* 16 Aug. 1832, Lady Emily Graham, da. of James Graham[†], 3rd duke of Montrose [S], *s.p. suc.* fa. 1803. *d.* 29 Mar. 1846. Sheriff, Herefs. 1815-16.

Born into a Herefordshire and Worcestershire family which had produced several Whig Members for local seats, Foley was a first cousin of the 3rd Baron Foley and the eldest son of a immoral Foxite, whom he succeeded to a large estate at Stoke Edith in 1803.[1] In 1818 he declined to stand for Worcestershire, his father's old constituency, and before the general election in 1820 the retiring Member, William Henry Lyttelton, informed George Tierney*, the Whig leader, that 'Lord Foley has applied in vain to his cousin, Edward Foley (the *Bean*). However there is no great loss there to anybody'.[2] Similarly, Lord Beauchamp wrote to Sir Anthony Lechmere, 17 Feb. 1820, in relation to Herefordshire, where his first cousin Thomas Foley had sat until 1818 on the family interest:

> I cannot understand Edward Foley's motives. Lord Somers [the ministerial leader in the county] has had a letter from him declaring his intention of not offering himself. I think he never could have had a better opportunity.[3]

Instead, Foley, who according to Sir George Cornewall[†] was called 'silly filly' in London, gave his support to the Tory Member there, Sir John Geers Cotterell.[4] In fact, it was as a Tory that he entered the House, where his brother John, Member for Droitwich, was an inactive Whig. He purchased a seat, presumably on the Everett interest, at Ludgershall at the general election of 1826, and was returned there unopposed at the two subsequent elections.[5]

Foley voted against Catholic relief, 6 Mar., and the corn bill, 2 Apr. 1827. He again voted against Catholic claims, 12 May, and with the Wellington ministry against reduction of the salary of the lieutenant-general of the ordnance, 4 July 1828. Listed by Planta, the patronage secretary, in February 1829 as likely to be 'opposed to the principle' of Catholic emancipation, he voted steadily against it during the following month. He was not named as one of the Ultras by Sir Richard Vyvyan*, their leader, later that year, but he

remained somewhat disaffected. He paired for transferring East Retford's seats to Birmingham, 5 Mar., and voted against the beer bill, 4 May, and for amendments to restrict sales for on-consumption, 21 June, 1 July 1830. He divided against Jewish emancipation, 17 May. In September he was reckoned by ministers as one of their 'friends', but a query was entered beside his name on Planta's survey and he voted against them on the civil list, 15 Nov. 1830. He divided against the second reading of the Grey ministry's reform bill, 22 Mar., and for Gascoyne's wrecking amendment, 19 Apr. 1831. He voted against the second reading of the reintroduced bill, 6 July, and its passage, 21 Sept., and in letters to the press denied that he had voted with ministers against adjourning proceedings on the bill, 12 July, or paired for the partial disfranchisement of Dorchester, 28 July.[6] He was absent from the division on the second reading of the revised bill, 17 Dec. 1831, but voted against going into committee on it, 20 Jan., the enfranchisement of Tower Hamlets, 28 Feb., and the third reading, 22 Mar. 1832. His only other known votes were against the Russian-Dutch loan, 26 Jan., 12 July, and with the minority for inquiry into the glove trade, 3 Apr. He may have been the 'Mr. Foley' who presented Blockley and Foleshill petitions for relief of distress in the silk trade, 26 Mar.; if so, this was his only known verbal intervention in this period. Following the disfranchisement of Ludgershall, he started for Herefordshire as a Conservative at the general election of 1832. Described by his proposer as a 'man of real independence both in purse and spirit', and even praised by one of his Whig opponents, Sir Robert Price*, for his 'high character, and amiable and excellent disposition', he spoke in defence of agricultural protection and was elected unopposed.[7] He retired from the House in 1841 because of ill health and died in March 1846.[8]

[1] *HP Commons, 1790-1820*, iii. 781; PROB 11/1402/966. [2] *HP Commons, 1790-1820*, ii. 431; Hants RO, Tierney mss 48. [3] Worcester RO, Lechmere mss. [4] TNA C110/96 (ii), Cornewall to Jay, 9 Feb. 1820. [5] *Spectator*, 1 Jan.; *The Times*, 5 Aug. 1831. [6] *The Times*, 19 July, 2 Aug. 1831. [7] *Hereford Jnl.* 19 Dec. 1832. [8] *Gent. Mag.* (1846), ii. 98; *Worcester Herald*, 4 Apr. 1846.

S.M.F.

FOLEY, Thomas (1778–1822), of Newport House, Almeley, Herefs.

DROITWICH	30 Jan. 1805–1807
HEREFORDSHIRE	1807–1818
DROITWICH	16 Feb. 1819–11 Jan. 1822

b. 19 July 1778, o.s. of Hon. Andrew Foley[†] of Newport House and Elizabeth, da. and h. of Boulter Tomlinson of Cheltenham, Glos. *educ.* Westminster 1795; Christ Church, Oxf. 1796; L. Inn 1800. *unm. suc.* fa. 1818. *d.* 11 Jan. 1822.

Capt. Herefs. militia 1803, maj. 1804, lt.-col. 1805.

In 1819 Foley had resumed his seat for Droitwich on the family interest, headed since 1793 by his cousin the 3rd baron, filling the vacancy caused by the death of his father the previous year. Like him he was a zealous Whig. At the 1820 general election he and another of Lord Foley's cousins were returned unopposed.[1] Foley had been seriously ill in 1818, and a relapse may account for his absenteeism during this period, when he is not known to have voted or spoken in debate. He died at Newport House in January 1822.[2] By his will, dated 19 Oct. 1820 and proved under £12,000, he directed that all residue should pass to his sister Anna and brother William 'after my debts are paid', but he was declared 'insolvent'.[3]

[1] *Berrow's Worcester Jnl.* 2 Mar. 1820. [2] *Gent. Mag.* (1822), i. 93. [3] PROB 11/1658/315; IR26/905/481.

R.M.H./P.J.S.

FOLEY, Hon. Thomas Henry (1808–1869), of Whitley Court, Worcs. and 16 Bruton Street, Mdx.

WORCESTERSHIRE	1830–1832
WORCESTERSHIRE WEST	1832–16 Apr. 1833

b. 11 Dec. 1808, 1st s. of Thomas, 3rd Bar. Foley, and Lady Cecilia Olivia Geraldine Fitzgerald, da. of William Robert, 2nd duke of Leinster [I]. *m.* 16 July 1849, Lady Mary Charlotte Howard, da. of Henry Charles Howard*, 13th duke of Norfolk, 2s. 1da. *d.v.p. suc.* fa. as 4th Bar. Foley 16 Apr. 1833. *d.* 20 Nov. 1869.

Capt. gent. pens. (gent.-at-arms) May 1833-Dec. 1834, May 1835-Sept. 1841, July 1846-Feb. 1852, Dec. 1852-Feb. 1858, June 1859-July 1866, Dec. 1868-*d.*; PC 16 May 1833.

Recorder, Droitwich 1833-6; high steward, Kidderminster 1833-69; ld. lt. Worcs. 1837-9.

The Foleys, direct descendants of the Speaker (1695-8) of that name, were one of the leading Whig families in Worcestershire, where they controlled the representation of Droitwich and one of the county seats. Foley's grandfather the 2nd baron, an associate of Fox, was an 'inveterate gambler' who 'by a most rapid course of debauchery, extravagance and gaming' was said to have 'rendered one of the noblest fortunes in the kingdom abortive'. He was disinherited by the 1st baron, who had obtained a revival of the title

in 1776, in favour of Foley's father, himself 'a great sportsman' and winner of the Derby in 1806, the One Thousand Guineas in 1815 and the Two Thousand Guineas in 1818. In 1820 the 'foolish extravagance' of Foley's parents prompted an intervention by Lady Shelley and the duke of Wellington on behalf of their children, who were said to be 'often in great distress'.[1]

At the 1830 general election Foley, aged 21, offered for Worcester, but finding that he had 'not a chance' he started for the county, where the family seat was vacated for him by his Whig kinsman Sir Edward Winnington. Responding to concerns about his 'youth and inexperience', he promised that 'all public business shall have my most serious attention'. Rumours of a third candidate came to nothing and he was returned unopposed.[2] He was listed by the Wellington ministry as one of their 'foes', and divided against them in the crucial division on the civil list, 15 Nov. 1830. His father was appointed captain of the corps of gentlemen pensioners by the incoming Grey ministry. Foley presented petitions for the abolition of slavery 18, 23 Nov., 21 Dec. 1830. Granted five days' leave on urgent private business, 17 Mar. 1831, he spoke at a Worcestershire reform meeting the following day, promising to support the ministry's bill 'at every stage' and observing that the 'Commons should be the representatives of the people, not of the rich and wealthy few; and this bill will make it the House of the people, and not of a few boroughmongers'.[3] He presented reform petitions from the electors of Droitwich, noting that 'although the present measure will deprive them of part of their present privilege, they cordially approve of it', 19 Mar., and Stourbridge, 20 Apr. He duly voted for the second reading, 22 Mar., and against Gascoyne's wrecking amendment, 19 Apr. 1831.

At the ensuing general election Foley offered again, stressing the 'vital importance' of reform, which 'was calculated to preserve' and 'secure the rights of the people'. 'Very liberal subscriptions' were raised for him and the other reform candidate, Frederick Spencer, with whom he was accused of coalescing against the Tory Lygon. After a spirited week of polling he was returned in first place with a large majority. He was guest of honour at the dinner held to celebrate the return of two reformers for the county, 16 May, and a grand reform meeting held in Birmingham, 24 May.[4] He voted for the second reading of the reintroduced reform bill, 6 July, when, denying allegations that Spencer had 'disgraced and degraded' the 'honour and dignity' of the House by making anti-corn law election pledges, he insisted that they both owed their election solely to the prevailing 'feeling in favour of reform', and recounted how he had been 'drawn through every town in succession, and hailed with the warmest demonstrations of welcome, not because the interests of myself or my family were connected with those towns, but on account of the principles I profess'. He divided at least twice against adjourning the debates, 12 July, and gave steady support to the bill's details. He voted for its passage, 21 Sept., and Lord Ebrington's confidence motion, 10 Oct. He divided with ministers on the Dublin election controversy, 23 Aug. He presented a petition from the maltsters of Dudley against the use of molasses in breweries and distilleries, 5 Sept., and from Bromsgrove for placing the retailers of beer on the same footing as licensed alehouse-keepers, 28 Sept. 1831. Foley voted for the second reading of the revised reform bill, 17 Dec. 1831, and again generally supported its details, although he was in the minority of 32 against the enfranchisement of £50 tenants-at-will, 1 Feb. 1832. He divided for the third reading, 22 Mar. He presented a Worcestershire petition for exemption from the proposed division of counties, 27 Jan. He voted for Ebrington's motion for an address calling on the king to appoint only ministers who would carry the bill unimpaired, 10 May, and presented a Kidderminster petition for supplies be withheld until it was effected, 25 May. That day he divided for the second reading of the Irish bill. He voted against increased Scottish representation, 1 June. He divided with ministers on the Russian-Dutch loan, 26 Jan., 12, 16 July (as a pair), and relations with Portugal, 9 Feb., but was in the minorities for inquiry into the glove trade, 31 Jan., 3 Apr. He presented a petition from the silk throwers of Blockley and Foleshill complaining of distress and praying for relief, 26 Mar. 1832. At the end of that year he promised to support Charles Williams Wynn, Member for Montgomeryshire, if he stood against Charles Manners Sutton for the Speakership in the new Parliament.[5]

At the 1832 general election Foley came forward for the new division of Worcestershire West, where he was returned unopposed without being proposed or seconded, the crowd's cries of 'Foley and Lygon' being taken by the sheriff as sufficient. On the death of his father the following April he succeeded to the peerage. Although his father had insured his life for £200,000, providing 'the most formidable blow to the insurance offices', the legacy of both his and the 2nd baron's extravagance was such that Foley was forced to sell Whitley Court in 1837, for which he received £900,000 from Lord Ward, and retire to the more modest setting of Ruxley Lodge, near Esher, Surrey. He succeeded his father as captain of the gentleman pensioners, in which capacity he continued to serve under successive Whig and Liberal ministries from

Grey to Gladstone. He was one of five peers who protested against the Ten Hours Factory Act in 1847. Foley died at the Hotel Bristol, Paris, in November 1869. By his will, dated 7 Feb. 1854, his estates passed to his eldest son and successor in the barony, Henry Thomas (1850-1905).[6]

[1] *CP*, v. 537; *Shelley Diary*, 96. Wellington mss WP1/973/27 and 1007/15 also show that the duke assisted with promotions and introductions for Lord Foley's children. [2] Worcs. RO, Lechmere mss, Lady Gresley to Sir A. Lechmere, 11 July; *Worcester Herald*, 10, 17, 24, 31 July, 7 Aug. 1830. [3] Worcs. RO BA 3762 b. 899:31, Foley Scrapbk. iv. 172-8. [4] *Worcester Herald*, 30 Apr., 7, 14, 21 May; *The Times*, 28 May 1831. [5] NLW, Coedymaen mss 28, Williams Wynn to Phillimore [Dec. 1832]. [6] T.C. Turberville, *Worcs. in 19th Cent.* 24-25; *Gent. Mag.* (1833), i. 464; *CP*, v. 537-8.

P.J.S.

FOLEY *see also* **HODGETTS FOLEY**

FOLKESTONE, Visct. *see* **PLEYDELL BOUVERIE, William**

FORBES, Charles (1773–1849), of Newe and Edinglassie, Aberdeen and 3 and 9 Fitzroy Square, Mdx.

BEVERLEY	1812–1818
MALMESBURY	1818–1832

b. 3 Apr. 1773, 2nd but 1st surv. s. of Rev. George Forbes of Leochel and Katharine, da. of Gordon Stewart of Drumin, Banff. *educ.* ?Aberdeen Univ. *m.* 28 Feb. 1800, Elizabeth, da. of Maj. John Cotgrave, E.I. Co. service, wid. of William Ashburner, 4s. (1 *d.v.p.*) 2da. *suc.* fa. 1799; uncle John Forbes to Newe 1821; *cr.* bt. 4 Nov. 1823; served heir male general to Alexander Forbes, 3rd Lord Pitsligo [S], 1833. *d.* 20 Nov. 1849.

Rect. Marischal Coll. Aberdeen 1814-18, 1822, 1833; gov. Foundling Hosp. 1817-36, v.-pres 1836-d.

V.-pres. European Insurance Co. 1825, pres. 1829.

Descended from a cadet branch of the family of the Lords Forbes and, more recently, of that of the Forbes of Pitsligo, Forbes returned from India in 1811 and established himself at Newe, where he built a castle and acquired other lands.[1] He remained the senior partner in the leading agency house of Forbes and Company of Bombay and was a prominent member of the court of proprietors of the East India Company.[2] He acquired a seat in Parliament for Beverley in 1812 and transferred in 1818 to Malmesbury, where he was again returned unopposed as a paying guest of the patron Joseph Pitt* at the general election of 1820. A man whose 'essential kindness was almost unexampled', he was respected for the integrity of his opinions, yet he sometimes rendered himself ludicrous by the idiosyncrasies of his campaigning style. In politics he pursued a non-partisan, but not inconsistent, line, being a pro-Catholic supporter of the Liverpool ministry, who favoured some economies and legal reforms and was always hostile to extensive parliamentary reform. He was an active defender of the interests of the subcontinent and made frequent interventions in the House on aspects of Indian as well as Scottish affairs, serving on several select committees related to these and other matters.[3]

Forbes, who was granted one month's sick leave, 26 May 1820, made no known speeches or votes during that session. He supported the Aberdeenshire petition in praise of ministers' conduct towards Queen Caroline, 31 Jan., and voted in this sense, 6 Feb., but on the question of her grant, 1 Feb. 1821, he stated that

> many reasons had hitherto induced him to support the smaller, rather than the larger sum; but on further consideration, he had thought it advisable to give way to his feelings, which were, however, in this case, still in opposition to his sounder judgement.

He condemned the reduction of Britain's naval forces, 2 Feb. He voted against a proposal to disqualify civil officers of the ordnance from voting in parliamentary elections, 12 Apr., and reform of the Scottish county representation, 10 May. He sided with opposition for repeal of the additional malt duty, 21 Mar., 3 Apr., and divided for economies in the armed services, 30 Apr., 4, 25 May, and against further pensions from the four-and-a-half per cent Barbados fund, 24 May. According to Henry Grey Bennet's* diary for 4 June, Forbes, 'a staunch friend of the government', declared he would 'sit in the House to the last to stop the jobs they were in the habit of introducing at that period of the session'.[4] He voted for the third reading of the forgery punishment mitigation bill that day and divided for inquiry into the administration of justice in Tobago, 6 June. He complained that the duke of Cumberland was unfairly treated in the allocation of grants to members of the royal family, 6, 8 June, and voted against paying arrears to the duke of Clarence, 8, 18 June. He urged abolition of the agricultural horse tax and objected to the report on the East India Sugar Acts, 14 June, advocated compensation for General Desfourneaux, 15 June, and suggested economies in the Ophthalmic Institution, 10 July.[5] On the death of his uncle, the former Bombay merchant John Forbes, in June 1821, he formally succeeded to Newe and inherited part of his estate, which included personal wealth sworn under £350,000.[6]

Forbes voted against opposition motions for more extensive tax reductions to relieve distress, 11, 21 Feb., but for reducing the number of junior lords of the admiralty, 1 Mar. (when he supported the naval estimates), and abolition of one of the joint-postmasterships, 2 May 1822.[7] He vindicated the respectability of Aberdeen burgh, 20 Feb., was a teller for adding James Drummond to the select committee on foreign trade, 28 Feb. (when the House was counted out), and called for the restoration of Captain Romeo's pension, 25 Mar. He sided with opposition for reform of the criminal law, 4 June, and against the second reading of the Irish constables bill, 7 June. He was refused a hearing on the corn bill, 10 June, when he voted in the minority of 21 for permitting the grinding and export as flour of bonded corn.[8] He voted against inquiry into the lord advocate's conduct relative to the press in Scotland, 25 June, and on James Abercromby being cautioned by the Speaker not to prosecute any private quarrel as a result of the proceedings, 12 July, he made one of his favourite remarks, that Members should not say in the House what they were not prepared to repeat outside it. He sided with ministers for going into committee on the Canada bill, 18 July, and for the grant for government proclamations in the Irish newspapers, 22 July. He was appointed to the select committee on the petition from bankers in Calcutta, 4 July, and defended their right to seek redress from Parliament, 29 July. He brought up a petition from certain persons interested in remittances from India against further restrictions on sugar, 12 July, and only reluctantly withdrew his motion for an instruction, on the price at which to impose a duty, to the committee on the East India sugar bill, 25 July 1822.[9] That day he also complained of the lack of attention shown to Indian questions, and reiterated one of his standard arguments (which he had made, for instance, in the East India House, 12 June), that Indian interests were insufficiently represented in the Commons.[10]

He voted against parliamentary reform, 20 Feb., ridiculed Lord Archibald Hamilton's attempts to reform the Scottish burghs, 26 Mar., and divided against his motion for alteration of the Scottish representative system, 2 June 1823. He added his voice to those claiming that ministers had pledged themselves to appoint a select committee on the equalization of East and West Indian sugar duties, 3 Mar., when he described it as a question 'of paramount interest to the public at large'.[11] He divided against Hume's motions on the sinking fund, 3, 13 Mar., and other opposition motions for lower taxation, 10, 18 Mar. He voted against the production of papers on the plot to murder the Irish lord lieutenant, 24 Mar., and the grant for Irish churches and glebe houses, 11 Apr. He also sided with ministers against repeal of the Foreign Enlistment Act, 16 Apr., and inquiry into the currency, 12 June. He expressed the hope that Indian shipping and seamen would be placed on the same footing as their English counterparts, 21 May, and, having voted in the minority for inquiry into the sugar duties, 22 May, he again complained that the East Indian cause was unjustly neglected, 23 May. He voted for the second reading of the Scottish juries bill, 20 June, and spoke in its favour, 30 June. He raised objections to the New South Wales jurisdiction bill, 2 July, successfully moved an address for producing the instructions given to its governor, 3 July, and voted for an amendment to introduce trial by jury, 7 July.[12] His only other known votes that session were for receiving a petition of complaint against James Crosbie*, 1 July, and for further proceedings against Standish O'Grady, the Irish chief baron of exchequer, 9 July. In November 1823 he received the baronetcy which the king had promised him the previous year, and his tenants thereafter erected a cairn to him on Lonach hill in testimony of their 'affection and gratitude' for their 'highly distinguished and beloved landlord'.[13]

Forbes voted with ministers against the production of papers on Catholic office-holders, 19 Feb., and reform of the representation of Edinburgh, 26 Feb. 1824. He divided for permitting defence by counsel in felony cases, 6 Apr. Though not in favour of unrestricted freedom of the press in India, he called the existing limitations, especially the power of deportation, unnecessary and impolitic, 25 May; on this subject a *Letter to Sir Charles Forbes* and a *Second Letter* were addressed to him that year. He deplored the practice of Members voting in private bill committees and on the floor of the House when they had not heard the preceding debate, 27 May.[14] He spoke, and presumably voted in the minority, against the committal of the marine insurance bill, 3 June. He divided against condemning the trial of the Methodist missionary John Smith in Demerara, 11 June, and insisted on 15 June that

> missionaries, if not narrowly watched, would cause our expulsion, not only from the West, but from the East Indies. In that opinion he knew he was not singular: nay, he would venture to say, that the majority of the House were of the same sentiments, if they had only the candour to avow them.

He voted with ministers for the second reading of the Irish insurrection bill, 14 June. He cast aspersions on the negotiations conducted with the Dutch over the East Indies, 17 June, when he suggested that the sec-

retary of the board of control be granted a pension. He moved for papers to vindicate the conduct of the recorder of Bombay, 21 June 1824, but the previous question was passed against him.[15]

He intervened on the address, to attack the prosecution and incompetent handling of the Burmese war, 4 Feb., and criticized the failure of ministers to reduce duties on Indian commodities, 28 Feb. 1825. He divided for the Irish unlawful societies bill, 25 Feb. Named as a defaulter on the call on Catholic relief, 28 Feb., he was present to be excused, 1 Mar., when he explained that, although he had supported the moderately espoused cause for 13 years, he would not be bullied by the Catholic Association.[16] He therefore voted against the Catholics that day, as he did on 21 Apr., 10 May, and he also divided against the Irish franchise bill, 26 Apr. He expressed his disgust at the British aggression which had precipitated an unwinnable war in Burma, and his abomination of the practice of sending out Company ships singly and dangerously overloaded with troops, 7 Mar. He condemned Lord Amherst's suppression of the mutiny at Barrackpoor as 'one of the most barbarous murders that had ever been perpetrated', 24 Mar., and urged his replacement as governor-general. He added that the situation was exacerbated by the local press, which was 'the defender of tyranny and oppression, instead of being, as it was in this country, the detector of abuses', and concluded that 'as well as he could judge, India, at no former period, had been in so perilous a position'. He duly voted in the minority for information on the reorganization of the Indian army that day. Speaking in the court of proprietors, he said that 'he had observed that bills which concerned India were constantly introduced at a late period of the session and were regularly passed at a late hour of the night'.[17] In the Commons, he urged protection for the natives of India against the tyranny of their governors, 13 May, when he successfully moved two amendments to the East India judges bill. He asked that the increase in judges' salaries be extended to Scottish courts, 16 May, voted against the report stage of the Leith docks bill, 20 May, and drew attention to the cost of the production of the papers on Sierra Leone called for by Hume, 26 May.[18] He defended the grant for Cumberland, 27 May, 6 June, and voted in its favour, 30 May, 6, 10 June. He divided for the second reading of the St. Olave (Hart Street) tithe bill, 6 June, when he also made one of his not infrequent calls for government intervention to suppress the practice of burning Hindu widows. Annoyed by the general lack of discussion accorded to Indian issues, 7 June, he retorted to Canning, the foreign secretary, that 'he would venture to tell the right honourable gentleman that which his friends, perhaps, would be slow in telling him – that his wit was often misapplied and did much injury to the cause he would serve', and he divided in the minority for information on the appointment of the Rev. Bryse as clerk to the committee of stationery in Bengal. He voted to abolish flogging in the navy, 9 June, and for prior inquiry before agreeing a grant to encourage Irish emigration to Canada, 13 June. He favoured allowing Indians to serve on juries, 13 June, called the deportation of two men from Jamaica 'a case of greater oppression than any he had ever heard of in the East Indies', 16 June, and regretted that the House should rise without the production of further papers on Indian affairs, 1 July 1825.[19]

He repeated his concerns about India in the debate on the address, 3 Feb. 1826. He stated his opposition to government plans to alter the system of Scottish banks, 13 Mar., but, although he was against the idea of a select committee on small notes, 16 Mar., he declared that 'he approved so highly of the plain, downright, John Bull statements of the chancellor of the exchequer [Robinson] on most occasions, that he would not now oppose him'.[20] On 11 May he was added to the select committee on the petition of James Silk Buckingham*, whose cause he had supported at East India House.[21] Hudson Gurney* recorded in his diary, 7 May, that at a ministerial dinner at Canning's, '[William] Madocks* the radical reformer, Sir Charles Forbes and myself [were] the only ones not dead votes'.[22] He voted in the minority for the clause in the alehouses licensing bill to permit adjourned meetings for granting licences, 12 May, and against Lord John Russell's resolutions on electoral bribery, 26 May. He was returned unopposed with his son John for Malmesbury at the general election that summer, having presumably purchased both seats. One of the defeated Charles Palmer's* committee at Bath, he spoke at a dinner there in his honour, 21 June, when he praised his independence:

Being of no party, and anxious only to do my duty conscientiously towards my king and country, I think I may be permitted to say ... when a man enters that House, he ought to divest himself of all feelings and considerations, except those which may conduce to the welfare of the nation. Upon this principle I have endeavoured to act.[23]

Forbes contended for the impartial system of distributing patronage in the army to be extended to the navy, 30 Nov. 1826.[24] Detailing alleged abuses by a company in New South Wales, he called for inquiry into transactions relating to joint-stock companies,

5 Dec. 1826. John Macarthur junior reported to his mother that month that

Forbes has engaged to retract, in his place in the House of Commons, the observations he made against the company and has expressed his regret to me ... for any offence he may have given me from his supposed allusion to my family. This was all that could be desired. He is a very indiscreet and absurd old man to whom no one pays attention in the House, and he was certainly scarcely heeded, although deservedly so, at the time he made his observation.[25]

He spoke in praise of shipbuilding at Bombay, 12 Feb. 1827, and the following day urged an improvement in humane discipline on Company ships and the ending of impressment.[26] Amid cries of 'question', at the end of the debate on Sir Francis Burdett's motion on the 'necessity of taking into consideration the laws imposing civil disabilities' against the Catholics, 6 Mar., Forbes rose only to explain that two years before 'he had then thought that the time was not a fit one', but had now reverted to his former opinion. He asked for the word 'necessity' to be changed to 'expediency': Burdett concurred and Forbes voted in the minority for the amended motion. He sided with opposition for inquiry into the allegations against the corporation of Leicester, 15 Mar., but was in the majority for Clarence's annuity bill, 16 Mar. Having at East India House pledged to persist in bringing the mutiny at Barrackpoor before the Commons,[27] he again condemned it at length, on Hume's motion, 22 Mar., arguing that 'there was only one way to prevent mutiny among the native troops, and that was to do them justice and to use them well', adding that, 'if we wished to preserve our empire in India, we must establish it in the affections of the people, for it would be impossible to maintain it through their fears'. He ended by promising that, 'notwithstanding all that had been said of the danger likely to result from agitating this question, he should never cease, as long as he had a seat in that House, to bring under its notice, session after session, the massacre', and he duly divided in the minority for further information. He said a few words in favour of the grant to Protestant Dissenting ministers, 14 May, and the next day stated that he had the 'greatest confidence' in Huskisson's handling of Indian matters and therefore opposed the idea of a select committee on its commerce.[28] However, he divided against the Canning administration to consider separating bankruptcy jurisdiction from chancery, 22 May. He voted against the disfranchisement of Penryn, 28 May (when he also divided against Lord Althorp's election expenses bill), and again, 7 June, when he condemned ministers' change of heart on the subject. He made clear that day that whenever questions of this description came before the House, he invariably voted against them. He opposed them because he could never bring himself to punish partial, petty cases of alleged corruption, and leave the enormous ones untouched.

He declared that it would be fairer to introduce a general plan of reform, which he would then support, and he damned the hypocrisy of Members pretending that the representation was immaculate, and

> that they never heard of such a thing as paying for votes, that they never heard of places where, not merely money, but conscience was sacrificed, where candidates were bound down, on pain of forfeiting their seats, to vote, whatever the case might be, in favour of the minister.

He used very similar arguments in opposing the East Retford disfranchisement bill, since it was a case of 'punishing people, not because they were guilty, but because they were found out', 11 June, and he opposed the transfer of the seats to Birmingham, 'as manufacturing towns were the very hot-beds of corruption', 22 June, when he was teller for the minority against the bill's second reading. On the Preston election bill, 14 June, he again objected not to reform as such, but to 'this pettifogging mode of effecting it', and he suggested that every Member on entering the House should swear an oath that he had not obtained his seat by corrupt means. He presented an East Retford petition for the suppression of suttee, 16 June. He divided with ministers in favour of the grant to improve water communications in Canada, 12 June, and against the third reading of the Coventry magistracy bill, 18 June. He asserted that anyone found guilty of forging signatures on an election petition should be 'served with the same sauce' as Thomas Flanagan, 19 June 1827, but apparently voted in the minority of seven against his committal to Newgate.[29]

He paired in favour of Catholic claims, 12 May 1828. He may have been the 'Mr. Forbes' who defended the Bombay shipping interest, 19 May, and it was certainly he who spoke of his 25 years' experience of life in India when urging the inclusion of natives on grand juries, 22 May 1828. The duke of Wellington, the prime minister, dismissed out of hand a suggestion made that autumn that Forbes should be appointed president of the board of control.[30] In February 1829 he was listed by Planta, the patronage secretary, as likely to vote 'with government' on Catholic emancipation, and he duly did so, 6, 30 Mar. He supported the issue of the East Retford writ, arguing that it was unfair to leave the borough unrepresented, 5 May, and spoke against the tailzies regulation bill, 11 May. Accepting ministers' decision to delay the appointment of a select committee on Indian trade to the following session, 14 May, he urged that the House provide itself with fuller information, that the political and commercial aspects of the Company be separated and that the China (though not the Indian) monopoly be protected. He objected to the anatomy bill, 15, 18, 19 May, especially the dissection of corpses of members of the lower class without regard to the wishes of their relatives. He divided in the minority for allowing Daniel O'Connell to take his seat unimpeded, 18 May. He supported a petition in favour of the admission of Indians to juries and advocated the suppression of suttee, 5 June 1829. He reprobated the reforms of the Scottish judicial system, 1 Apr. 1830, when (as on 13 May) he suggested that the salaries of Scottish judges should be raised. He paired in favour of Jewish emancipation, 5 Apr., and voted for this, 17 May. He defended the interests of the subcontinent, 4 May, stating that 'the more I see of my own countrymen, the more I like the natives of India'. He expressed his approval of the Edinburgh petition against the capital penalty for forgery, 13 May, but again opposed changes to the legal system there, 27 May, favouring the retention of the 'old Scotch practice' of allowing majority verdicts in civil cases. He spoke and voted for inquiry into the commerce, revenue and expenditure of Ceylon, 27 May 1830. With his son, he was returned unopposed for Malmesbury at the general election that year.

Forbes was listed by ministers among the 'doubtful doubtfuls' and marked 'more yes than no'. He declared that despite the feelings of the House, 8 Nov. 1830, Wellington was worthy of respect for his military prowess and conversion to the cause of Catholic emancipation. He divided with ministers on the civil list, 15 Nov. 1830, when he teased Hume for his former dependence on Brechin burgh, and referred critically to the Perth Burghs election (as he did again, 8, 10 Feb. 1831). He was appointed to the select committee on the East India Company, 4 Feb. On Evesham, 17 Feb., he made his by now customary remarks against the disfranchisement of individual boroughs, and, in what Thomas Gladstone* described to his father John Gladstone* the next day as 'a foolish speech', he insisted that he could compile a lexicon of boroughs which Members knew to be corrupt. He told the chancellor, Althorp, that in 'endeavouring to benefit everyone, he pleased nobody', but in advising him to persist in his plan to tax steam vessels, he was the only Member not to be 'upon him' that day.[31] Wishing that every part of the empire was as prosperous as Scotland, he insisted that reform was unnecessary, 16 Feb., and he made the first of his vociferous declarations of staunch and defiant opposition to government's reform proposals 'as radically bad, and as tending to subvert the constitution', 7 Mar. He complained of the lack of discussion accorded the introduction of the Scottish reform bill, 9 Mar., and objected to the lemming-like character of the pro-reform petitions from that country, 14 Mar. Having again condemned reform, 18 Mar., he had a furious exchange with John Cam Hobhouse, who reminded him that he had often suggested the adoption of a general measure instead of piecemeal alterations, to which he answered that 'I always had, and always shall have, a wish for a general reform, but I have no wish for a revolution'.[32] He gave his support to Sir Robert Inglis's motion, 21 Mar., complaining of a breach of privilege by *The Times*, an editorial from which he had himself nearly brought before the House on the 3rd. He also stated that if the bill 'should be carried, I shall have no desire to enter the House so constituted, as it then must be; and I believe that in such an event seats will not be so much sought after, as formerly, by those men who have been the ornaments of the House'. He voted against the second reading of the bill, 22 Mar. He denounced the treatment of Durham city as a case of ministers 'taking care of their own household', 25 Mar., when he advised them to scrap the bill and start again rather than see it pulled to pieces in committee. He made a joke at the expense of Jeffrey, the lord advocate, who was unseated from Perth Burghs on petition, 28 Mar., saying that he would now discover the usefulness of those rotten boroughs condemned by Russell. He regretted the announcement that expenditure on shipbuilding at Bombay would soon cease, 28 Mar., and spoke in favour of Hutchinson's claim against the East India Company, 29 Mar. In evidence to the select committee on Indian affairs, 14, 18, 21 Apr., he argued that a separation of the Company's political and commercial functions would lead to better management and fewer abuses, and he urged the abolition of its monopoly.[33] On 12 Apr. he observed that the reform bill, which he would have preferred to have seen thrown out on the first night, had had an inflammatory effect in Scotland, the reform petitions from which he believed were not representative of opinion there. He divided for Gascoyne's wrecking amendment, 19 Apr., and congratulated ministers on withdrawing the bill, 21 Apr. 1831, when he hoped that they would also resign.

Forbes was elected for Malmesbury *in absentia*, despite an opposition, at the subsequent general election, and, expecting a short Parliament, he refused to pay as much as he had previously done for the seat.[34] He objected to the Canton merchants' petition for alteration of the laws relating to trade with the Chinese, 28 June, when he complained of the erratic attendance of Members on the Indian committee, to which he was reappointed that day. He was called to order by the Speaker when he attempted to ask a question on the duchy of Cornwall, 29 June. He voted against the second reading of the reintroduced reform bill, 6 July. On Hunt presenting a reform petition from Manchester, 8 July, he asserted that the bill would only lead to more radical measures, and he commented that the 'absurd' and 'utterly incomprehensible' £10 franchise 'will do incalculable evil, and among other things will operate as an inducement to people not to pay their rents'. However, that day he also urged giving the vote to women, as happened at East India House, and criticized the bill because 'it gives the elective franchise to one class, and there is no reason why it should not be given to the class immediately below'. He spoke for the issue of the Liverpool writ, 8 July. He voted at least five times to adjourn proceedings on the reform bill, 12 July, and, as Peel was leaving the House, he pointedly observed that he 'would fight under an able leader, if one could be found', his object being 'to throw out the bill and ministers too'.[35] He voted for using the 1831 census to determine the boroughs in schedules A and B, 19 July. He spoke and presumably divided in the minority against the lord steward bill, 20 July. He defended the representation of Beverley, 22 July, and Old Sarum, 26 July, voted to postpone consideration of the partial disfranchisement of Chippenham, 27 July, and vindicated the proceedings at recent Malmesbury elections, 30 July, when he also ostentatiously paraded his status as an independently elected Member. He denied that any unfair obstructions were being put in the way of the reform bill, 29 July, argued that it was not the slowness but the speed of its passage that provided grounds for complaint, 4 Aug., and briefly threatened to force a division against the House sitting on Saturdays, 5 Aug. 1831.

He sided with opposition against O'Connell's motion that the original Dublin election committee be sworn, 29 July 1831, and, having called for an inquiry, voted in the minority for postponing the writ, 8 Aug. He divided in the minority of six in favour of Hunt's motion for receiving the Preston petition on the corn laws, 12 Aug. He strongly advocated the provision of colonial constituencies, 16 Aug., claiming that Hume's proposal to introduce four Members for India was inadequate and that, if the existing bill passed, its interests 'would at once be cut off from any kind of representation in the House'. He voted in the majority against the second reading of the Irish union of parishes bill, 19 Aug. He was listed as voting with ministers for the prosecution of those guilty of bribery at the Dublin election, 23 Aug., but that day he also voted in the minority for Robert Gordon's motion to censure the conduct of the Irish government. He sided with opposition to preserve the existing rights of voting, 27 Aug., to allow non-resident freeholders to remain voters for their lives, 30 Aug., and to continue as electors the non-resident voters of Aylesbury, Cricklade, East Retford and New Shoreham, 2 Sept. He divided in favour of making legal provision for the poor of Ireland, 29 Aug. He presented and endorsed a petition from the natives of India to allow them to serve on grand juries, 1 Sept., when he noted that there would be insufficient seating for Members at the coronation. He remarked that it was 'a rather curious instance of inconsistency' that ministers had 'proposed uniting the Scottish counties whilst they are for dividing the English counties', 3 Sept. He spoke in favour of Hume's motion for a select committee on the discharge of small debtors, 6 Sept., and objected to the extension of the truck bill to Scotland, 13 Sept. He voted against the third reading, 19 Sept., and passage of the reform bill, 21 Sept. He complained of hasty progress on the Scottish bill, 23 Sept., when he voted against its second reading. He again opposed it, 26 Sept., and the following day asserted that

> the freeholders of Scotland have just as good a right to their superiorities as any Member in this House has to his estate, and the legislature would be as much justified in depriving the one of his superiorities as the other of his land, for the right to vote and the right to sell that privilege have ever been annexed to the land. By depriving the freeholder of his superiority, you deteriorate the value of the land to the extent of the superiority.

He assured the House that his tenants had no wish for the vote and promised that 'I will take care so to frame my leases that they shall not have a vote inflicted upon them. They shall not be liable to be carried away from their proper occupation, and from the care of their farms, to attend to elections'. On 4 Oct., when he said that the expressions 'the people' and 'property' were meaningless, he explained the system of superiorities, denied that he was a dealer in them and called for an increased county representation. He commented on the timing of the Irish reform bill, 27 Sept., supported maintaining the salary of the president of the board of control and praised the current governor-general, 29 Sept., spoke against the vestry bill, 30 Sept., agreed with the general register bill, 4 Oct., and opposed the bankruptcy court bill, 17 Oct. As a professed friend to the West India interest, he favoured the appointment of a select committee of inquiry, 6 Oct., and he supported the petition against the pilgrim tax in the East Indies, 14 Oct. On the Scottish exchequer court bill, 7 Oct., he stated that it would add to the destruction of 'our ancient institutions', told Peel that he had never set so bad an example, and asserted that 'I am opposed to all reform and a change in the laws of my country', the greatness of which he suspected would soon decline. He deprecated government intimidation of anti-reform independent Members, and the removal of office-holders who had voted against the bill, 20 Oct. 1831.

Forbes regretted that there was no mention of the East India Company in the king's speech, 6 Dec. 1831. He rejected the revised reform bill as 'nothing but an old monster with a new face', 12 Dec., and voted against its second reading, 17 Dec. 1831. He rose immediately after the lord advocate to oppose leave for the Scottish bill, 19 Jan. 1832, because of the extensive Scottish opposition to the county representation and the annihilation of the rights of freeholders. He voted against going into committee on the English bill, 20 Jan., when he called for further information, and declared that, should Peel persist in his opposition, 'I will remain by his side until seven in the morning'. He opposed the Vestry Act amendment bill as unnecessary and voted in the majority against its second reading, 23 Jan. On 27 Jan. he intervened on the general register bill, again condemned the Scottish reform bill and gave notice of a motion relating to the Deccan prize money, which, however, he did not press, 1 Feb. He was again reappointed to the select committee on the East India Company, 27 Jan., and was present at sittings of the subcommittee on its revenue affairs, to which he gave evidence on the opium trade at Bombay, 25 June.[36] He divided with Hunt on his amendments to give the vote to all tax-paying households, 2 Feb., and to exempt Preston from the £10 householder clause in the reform bill, 3 Feb. He was a founder member of the Carlton Club in March. He voted against the third reading of the reform bill, 22 Mar. He objected to the grant of a pension to the retiring chief baron of exchequer in Scotland, 10 Apr., when he supported Hutchinson's claim against the East India Company (as he did again, 14 June). He warned of the dangers of Russian expansion of its sphere of influence into Persia and India, 18 Apr., 7 Aug. 1832.

He gave his 'unqualified dissent' to the second reading of the Scottish reform bill, 21 May 1832, when he declared that

> however His Majesty's ministers, backed by the mob, may coerce this House, however they may coerce the votes of its Members, I tell them they shall not coerce me. I am well aware that my individual vote is of very little

importance on this occasion to any party in the House, but ... it is of some importance to me that I should preserve my own consistency and my own character, and I should be ashamed of myself if I could sit in this House and allow this bill to pass without giving it my most decided opposition.

He insisted that he would divide the House on it, but apparently decided against doing this at Sir George Murray's request. He voted against the second reading of the Irish bill, 25 May. He continued strenuously to oppose the Scottish bill in committee, 4 June, when he admitted that he had bought superiorities 'for the purpose of supporting my friends in both Houses', and 6 June, when he urged Scottish Members to 'fight every inch for the honour, independence, and dignity of their native country'. He opposed delay of the Indian juries bill, 18 June, voted for permanent provision to be made for the Irish poor by a tax on absentees, 19 June, and suggested an amendment to the coroners bill, 20 June. He divided in minorities for creating a system of representation for New South Wales, 28 June, and preserving the rights of freemen under the Irish reform bill, 2 July. He urged reduction of the duties on East Indian commodities to increase the prosperity of trade there, 3, 25 July, though he acknowledged the validity of the competing West India interests and did not persist in his motions knowing that government had the matter under consideration. He spoke against part of the tithes prescription bill, 5 July, asked whether ministers would withdraw the Irish tithes bill in return for the support of Irish Members on the Russian-Dutch loan, 9 July, and praised a Preston petition against the sending of troops to Ireland to enforce tithes, 3 Aug. His only other known votes were with opposition against the Russian-Dutch loan, 26 Jan., 12 July, when he was also teller for the minority for the order of the day for a call of the House. However, he argued that Britain was honour bound to pay the loan, 16 July, and presumably voted in this sense, 16, 20 July. He criticized the appointment of military governors of colonies, 23 July, objected to Hume's bill to disqualify the recorder of Dublin from sitting in Parliament, 24, 31 July, opposed the Aberdeen colleges bill, 1 and 3 Aug., and made suggestions about half-pay officers, 8 Aug. He supported the granting of compensation to Sir Abraham Bradley King, 3 Aug., to petitioners for Deccan prize money, 6, 7 Aug., and to the family of the Poona banker Outia for the illegal seizure of his property, 10 Aug. In his last known intervention in debate, 11 Aug. 1832, he said that he was not surprised if people had not paid their rates as Members had encouraged them to protest in this fashion, and it

was their own fault if they now found themselves disfranchised.

Forbes was once described as 'a perfect anomaly: as a politician, he is always wrong; as a private individual, full of good qualities'.[37] He left the House at the dissolution, and made no attempt to contest the remaining seat at Malmesbury at the general election in December 1832. He did not apparently seek another one elsewhere, until approached at the last moment by the Conservative interest in Middlesex, where he joined another opponent of Hume and George Byng*. He was given a hostile reception on the hustings, but achieved a respectable third place behind his Liberal opponents, and it was supposed that, if he had entered earlier, he might have been successful. At the declaration he managed to gain a hearing, and stated that

> he had been called all sorts of names, he had been loaded with abuse, but he treated the thing with contempt. His opponents might call him Tory, anti-reformer, Conservative, anything but Whig or Radical ... He had come forward, heart and purse, for the purpose of saving his country from the impending destruction which threatened it, to save it from the destruction which had been threatened to it by such men as Mr. Hume. All that remained of our religion or liberties he considered to be threatened ... He considered the reform bill, as he always had considered it, a revolutionary measure, the consequences of which we could not see. He trusted that the electors would consider that he had come forward only for the purpose of preserving them from the thraldom in which they were likely to be placed.[38]

He was considered as a possible Conservative candidate for Aberdeen or Edinburgh at the general election of 1835, but nothing came of this, and he never sat again.[39]

After a lengthy legal process he was finally denied his claim to the attainted peerage of Pitsligo, but was served heir male general in 1833.[40] He continued to be active in defence of Indian interests, both in private correspondence with ministers and in public, for instance in rebutting the bishop of London's speech in the Lords, 13 Aug. 1836, by writing to *The Times* that he had 'perfect confidence in the honour and veracity of the natives of India'.[41] On 6 Apr. 1840, at his house in Fitzroy Square, he was presented with an address, signed by over 1,000 of the principal native gentlemen and other inhabitants of Bombay, on the occasion of commissioning a statue of him, in appreciation of his continued efforts on their behalf.[42] He died suddenly in November 1849. His obituary notices praised him for his earnest endeavours in the cause of India, and his extraordinary generosity to Indian and British charities, 'which seemed neither limited in amount, nor confined to any particular locality or class, but in both respects were alike universal'.[43] His baronetcy and estate were inherited by his young grandson, his late son John's only son Charles (1832-52), and then by John's younger brother Charles (1803-77).

[1] A. Forbes, *Mems. of Fam. of Forbes of Freshfield*, 32-33; A. and H. Tayler, *House of Forbes*, 380-1. [2] C.H. Philips, *E.I. Co.* 243; *Oxford DNB*. [3] *HP Commons, 1790-1820*, iii. 785-6; *Highland Lady*, 391; *New Parl.* (1826), 17; *Oxford DNB*. [4] HLRO, Hist. Coll. 379, Grey Bennet diary, 96. [5] *The Times*, 7, 15 June 1821. [6] *Gent. Mag.* (1821), i. 574; PROB 11/1651/663; IR26/864/1225. [7] *The Times*, 2 Mar. 1822. [8] Ibid. 11 June 1822. [9] Ibid. 13, 26, 30 July 1822. [10] Philips, 250. [11] *The Times*, 4 Mar. 1823. [12] Ibid. 22 May, 1, 4 July 1823. [13] Add. 40304, f. 150; *Monuments and MI in Scotland* ed. C. Rogers, ii. 344. [14] *The Times*, 28 May 1824. [15] Ibid. 19, 22 June 1824. [16] Gurney diary. [17] *Debates at E.I. House*, ii. 264-5 (BL OIOC W.2073). [18] *The Times*, 14, 17, 27 May 1825. [19] Ibid. 8, 14 June, 2 July 1825. [20] Ibid. 14 Mar. 1826. [21] *Debates at E.I. House*, ii. 360-1, 457, 482. [22] Gurney diary. [23] *Bath and Cheltenham Gazette*, 2 June 1826. [24] *The Times*, 1 Dec. 1826. [25] Mitchell Lib. Sydney, Macarthur mss ML A 2911. [26] *The Times*, 13 Feb. 1827. [27] *Debates at E.I. House*, ii (pt. 2), pp. 81-82, 97-99, 122-3. [28] *The Times*, 15 May 1827. [29] Ibid. 15, 18, 20 June 1827. [30] Wellington mss WP1/964/29. [31] St. Deiniol's Lib. Glynne-Gladstone mss 197. [32] Wellington mss WP1/1179/2. [33] *PP* (1831), v. 139-59. [34] *Devizes Gazette*, 5, 19 May 1831. [35] Ibid. 14 July 1831; *Three Diaries*, 104. [36] *PP* (1831-2), xiv. 19, 273. [37] *The Times*, 5 Aug. 1831. [38] Ibid. 18, 19, 24, 25 Dec. 1832. [39] *Scottish Electoral Politics*, 225-6. [40] NLS mss 26.1.13; Forbes, 58-64, 82; Tayler, 374-6. [41] Add. 40874, ff. 146, 150; *The Times*, 26 Aug., 3 Sept. 1836. [42] *The Times*, 19 Aug. 1840. [43] Ibid. 22, 23 Nov.; *Aberdeen Jnl.* 28 Nov. 1849; *Gent. Mag.* (1850), i. 208-9; Tayler, 381; *DNB*; *Oxford DNB*.

S.M.F.

FORBES, George John, Visct. Forbes (1785–1836), of Kilren, co. Louth.

Co. Longford	1806–1832
Co. Longford	2 Apr. 1833–14 Nov. 1836

b. 3 May 1785, at Montpelier, 1st s. of George, 6th earl of Granard [I] (*d.* 1837), and Lady Selina Frances Rawdon, da. of John, 1st earl of Moira [I]. *m.* 4 Oct. 1832, Frances Mary, da. and h. of William Territt of Chilton, Suff., 2s. *d.v.p.* 14 Nov. 1836.

Lt. 108 Ft. 1794; capt. 74 Ft. 1795, half-pay 1804, brevet maj. 1805; capt. 8 garrison batt. 1809, lt.-col. half-pay 1812; a.d.c. to regent 1811-25; capt. de Meuron's regt. 1814; brevet col. 1815; maj.-gen. 1825.

Custos rot. co. Longford 1815, gov. 1831, ld. lt. 1831-*d*.

Trustee, linen board [I] 1818; comptroller of household to ld. lt. [I] Feb. 1828-Mar. 1829.

Sec. to order of St. Patrick 1828-*d*.

Capt. commdt. Longford inf. 1803; col. co. Longford militia 1824-*d*.

Forbes, of whom Thomas Creevey* observed that he had 'never seen a greater appearance of worth

and honour in any young man in my life', had joined Brooks's, sponsored by the duke of Devonshire, 16 Jan. 1805.[1] Following his return for county Longford on the family interest in 1806 he had sided with the Whig opposition, but by 1814 had gone over to the Liverpool government, who rewarded him with a place on the linen board in 1818 and a clerkship for one Allen the following year. At the 1820 general election he was returned unopposed with the additional support of Lady Rosse, whose Tory nominee he had assisted at the contested by-election of the previous year.[2] A poor attender, who is not known to have spoken in debate, he was described by the radical Whig Henry Grey Bennet* as a 'staunch friend of the government' in 1821 and as having 'voted always with ministers' by a radical commentary of 1823, but this was not invariably the case.[3] He divided in support of ministers' treatment of Queen Caroline, 6 Feb., but paired for inquiry into the conduct of the sheriff of Dublin at the meeting relating to the affair, 22 Feb. 1821. He voted for Catholic claims, 28 Feb. 1821, 1 Mar., 21 Apr., 10 May 1825. He divided against parliamentary reform, 9 May 1821. That August Lord Liverpool informed the home secretary Lord Sidmouth that Forbes wished his father to be promoted to a marquessate and had 'represented Lord Hastings, who is his uncle, as very anxious about it, and the king likewise disposed to favour it'. Liverpool advised Forbes that 'it must come recommended by' the Irish viceroy Lord Talbot, following which he

called on me a second time to express his disappointment at the king's not appearing to be friendly to the promotion, on the ground that Lord Forbes had not been a steady supporter of government. I told Lord Forbes that I must continue to refer the question to the lord lieutenant, but that as to his support of government I would certainly do him justice to the king when I had an opportunity. Now I wish it to be understood that the promotion ought in my judgement to depend upon the lord lieutenant's opinion of Lord Granard's claims compared with others. I have no desire to throw any obstruction in the way of it, nor am I disposed particularly to favour it.[4]

At the end of the year he was listed by ministers as 'out of sorts with the king' and 'the Irish government', and in January 1822 Talbot informed Gregory, the Irish under-secretary, that Forbes had written

to complain of Lord Granard not being included in the recent promotions in the Irish peerage, and says I had promised to name his wishes. I agree to this with this addition, 'if the subject was first mentioned by the government of England', or in other words that I would sanction the advancement if applied to by Lord Liverpool.[5]

Granard never received the promotion. Forbes voted against the Irish habeas corpus suspension bill, 7 Feb., but with ministers against further tax reductions, 28 Feb., and on the accounts, 13 Mar. 1822. He divided against inquiry into the prosecution of the Dublin Orange rioters, 22 Apr. 1823, and for the duke of Cumberland's annuity bill, 10 June 1825. That October 'a great portion' of Castle Forbes, the family seat, was destroyed by a fire, which

> without any alarm having been given, communicated to the bedroom of Lord Forbes. His lordship must inevitably have perished, were it not that a spaniel, which invariably slept in his room, fortunately awoke him before the flames had reached his bed ... Forbes had the presence of mind first to use a shot in order to arouse and alarm the servants, then to remove 25*lb* of gunpowder and ... secure a large chest of family papers.[6]

He declined to attend the Catholic Association dinner for the 'friends of civil and religious liberty', 2 Feb. 1826.[7]

At the 1826 general election Forbes, who was praised by the Catholic press as a 'liberal and emancipator', was returned unopposed.[8] During the violent contest in neighbouring Westmeath his coach was attacked by a mob and he was injured.[9] He voted for Catholic claims, 6 Mar. 1827. In February 1828 he was appointed comptroller of the household of Lord Anglesey, the Wellington ministry's Irish viceroy, who hoped that his re-election would be 'a bed of roses' and present 'no difficulty', as 'I really think we shall rally together a very choice establishment, which will give satisfaction at home and abroad'.[10] He was returned without trouble.[11] He presented constituency petitions for Catholic relief, 28 Apr., 8 May, and voted thus, 12 May, but was evidently not very hopeful of its passing the Lords, for that day Anglesey complained, 'I do not like to hear your doubts about carrying the question ... Unless the Catholics are downright mad they must in a short time obtain all they wish'.[12] In July Anglesey reported to Peel, the home secretary, that Forbes had 'just returned from the assizes' where he was 'in the habit of holding much intercourse with the priests and their flocks', who 'formerly were communicative and gave much useful intelligence', but were 'now all silent and reserved' and 'no money will tempt any of them to make a single disclosure'.[13] On Forbes being invited that November to chair a county meeting of Catholics 'as a liberal Protestant', Anglesey advised:

> If the address is moderate and not offensive, it will probably speak your own sentiments. If it is of a rougher character, you will be obliged either to put your name into a violent document or to state your objections to the meeting, or you must keep away, which is blinking the question.[14]

On finding that a vote of thanks was to be given to Daniel O'Connell* and the Association he 'withdrew altogether', warning Anglesey that the 'very violent and foolish high sheriff' intended 'to prevent the slightest impression of popular feeling' and the 'consequences of a collision of party under such circumstances' might 'lead to general insurrection throughout the country'.[15] 'You appear to have taken the true, manly course of avowing your sentiments, regardless of consequences', Anglesey replied.[16] He attended the meeting of the 'friends of civil and religious liberty' at the Rotunda, Dublin, 20 Jan. 1829.[17] He, of course, voted for the Wellington ministry's concession of Catholic emancipation, 6, 30 Mar., and presented favourable constituency petitions, 11, 20 Mar. On 5 June he wrote to Anglesey, who had gone into opposition following his recall as viceroy (when Forbes presumably resigned from the household), that he 'very much' regretted that Wellington's 'conduct towards you should have led to such a result', adding, 'that he now regrets it I have no doubt, feeling as he does that he is at the head of an administration which is far from steady, and knowing the importance of your support'.[18] Five days later Anglesey protested that a 'stranger on reading' his letter

> would suppose that *I* was the offending party and that ... Wellington would graciously condescend to forgive me for all offences ... What! Am *I* to stoop and show respect to a minister who first grossly deceives me and then publicly insults me, who misled me *purposely* in regard to his measures and then recalls me in a manner unprecedented in the annals of impertinence![19]

That October the Ultra leader Sir Richard Vyvyan* numbered Forbes among those who had voted in favour of emancipation whose attitude towards a putative coalition government was 'unknown'. On 16 Nov. Anglesey urged him actively to support the election of Lord Killeen* for county Meath, as 'it is most important that the most respectable of the Catholics should be in Parliament' and 'I do believe you are in *your heart Orange!!!*'[20] Forbes replied, 20 Nov.:

> I am not an Orangeman, but if I am to suffer the detestation of any class let it be from the well informed and high bred and not from such materials as the Catholic leaders of this country are composed of. I think O'Connell's conduct of the last three months has fully borne me out in the opinion I always held of him. Of Lord Killeen I hold a very different opinion [and] I quite agree with you in thinking that such men should be in Parliament to keep out such unprincipled men as O'Connell.[21]

Assuring Anglesey of the 'estimation in which your name is held by the respectable persons of Dublin',

7 Dec. 1829, he added that he had 'most sincerely advocated for Catholic emancipation because I believed the penal code was disgraceful to us as a nation. I wished justice to be done to the Irish Catholics, but God defend me from living with them'.[22] He was granted a month's leave on urgent private business, 22 Feb. 1830. He presented a constituency petition against the Irish stamp duties, 1 July 1830.

At the 1830 general election he initially held back from a potential contest, but following the withdrawal of his former colleague he came forward with the support of the local independents and government and was returned unopposed.[23] He was listed by ministers as one of their 'friends', but this was later queried and he was absent from the crucial division on the civil list, 15 Nov. 1830. He was granted a fortnight's leave on urgent private business, 6 Dec. 1830. On 24 Feb. 1831 Anglesey, the reappointed viceroy, urged Lord Melbourne, the home secretary, to allow Forbes to 'return instantly' to Ireland following the call of the House, as 'without him, the country will be in confusion, and if he stays with you, he will certainly oppose reform'.[24] (His father had recently moved to Paris, but retained his clerkship of the crown and hanaper, an Irish chancery sinecure worth £1,800 per annum, with the duties of which Forbes unofficially assisted as a deputy.)[25] On 18 Mar. he 'divided against' the Grey ministry on the timber duties, according to the Irish secretary Smith Stanley and the duke of Richmond, who advised Anglesey that he 'ought not to have voted against us' as 'it was a factious opposition, got up by ... Peel'.[26] 'I am provoked at Forbes to the last degree', Anglesey told Smith Stanley, 21 Mar.:

> How are we to make him lord lieutenant of Longford? Yet he is indisputably the only fit person. Could we appoint Lord Granard (who is thoroughly staunch) and who might make Forbes his vice lieutenant, giving the latter time to reflect on his follies before he got the higher charge? I am sadly vexed, but pray let it be understood that he has no situation in my household.[27]

Unrepentant, Forbes voted against the second reading of the English reform bill, 22 Mar., following which Lord Grey, in a reference to Granard's office, notified Anglesey that 'if Forbes has a principal, from whom he receives any emolument, I think he should be turned out', 24 Mar.[28] He divided for Gascoyne's wrecking amendment, 19 Apr. On 2 May 1831 Anglesey reminded Lord Holland, 'Do not forget that you may have Granard from Paris at a minute's notice. His son Forbes vexes me sadly. He is so good a man, so excellent a magistrate, and so unexceptionable as a lord lieutenant'.[29]

At the 1831 general election Forbes stood as an opponent of reform, having applied for Tory funds from Charles Arbuthnot* and assured Sir Henry Hardinge* that he would 'be safe with £1,000'.[30] He was returned in first place amid charges of a 'scandalous abandonment of principle' and 'betrayal' by the reform candidate Luke White*, a former supporter who had contributed £500 towards his previous election. Forbes demanded an immediate 'retraction' or 'the satisfaction due to a gentleman', which was refused until after the poll. Following the declaration, however, they were arrested and 'bound in recognizances in the sum of £5,000'.[31] 'I must say', observed Anglesey, 9 May

> that if White, who formerly served you most generously, was not duly and confidentially apprised by you of your intention to stand upon the principles you avow, there is sufficient ground for his feeling aggrieved, although I cannot think him justified in using the offensive language levelled against you in his address.[32]

On 14 May Anglesey added:

> I disapprove of his declining to explain or to meet you, I disapprove of the arrest, and I disapprove of your declining to meet him now *because* he declined to meet you then. God knows I have enough on hand, yet I should like to see the parties and to settle it for them ... Perhaps I ought not to have interfered at all, but having done so, I cannot leave things as they are. I have asked White to come and see me.[33]

Forbes voted against the second reading of the reintroduced reform bill, 6 July, but divided with ministers on the Dublin election controversy, 23 Aug. On 29 Aug. Holland complained in his diary that Forbes was one of those with 'anti-ministerial propensities' who retained influence with Anglesey, 'which I am told is too discernible in the disposal of small patronage'.[34] Clarifying the nature of their relationship, 3 Sept., Anglesey explained to Holland:

> I had Forbes as a sort of guide when I came over in 1828, and my firm belief was that he was a determined liberal. He supported the relief bill, and came in for Longford upon the Catholic interest. He turned around at the last election and was brought in by the opposite party. All this struck me forcibly, and I really felt that, after so strange a course, he would be better off out of my household, and so he felt also. Captain [John] Hart [deputy clerk to Granard in the hanaper office] is a natural brother.[35]

He divided against the reform bill's passage, 21 Sept. His appointment as the first lord lieutenant of Longford was condemned by O'Connell, who urged Lord Duncannon*, 4 Dec. 1831, to 'strike off the Tory lord lieutenants ... Lord Lorton, Lord Wicklow, Lord Forbes', who are 'your open enemies' and 'give these counties to your open friends'.[36] Later that month Anglesey, in an apparent warning, told Forbes, 'Do you really imagine that I sleep at my post, that have not my eye upon all?'[37] Unhappy with Forbes's list of deputy lieutenants, 14 Feb. 1832, Anglesey asked, 'Can you find some respectable Catholic to act as one, for I see you have some rare Orangemen amongst them?'; to which Forbes replied, 'We have not a Catholic proprietor in the county, with the exception of one who is under age ... added to which I do not think that the gentlemen whose names I returned would serve if one was appointed'.[38] He paired against the second reading of the revised reform bill, 17 Dec. 1831, and its third reading, 22 Mar. 1832. He was a founder member of the Carlton Club that month.[39] No other trace of parliamentary activity has been found for this session, and he is not known to have spoken in debate.

At the 1832 general election Forbes stood unsuccessfully for county Longford as a Conservative, but he was seated on petition the following year and survived a Liberal challenge in 1835. In October that year, after suffering an apoplectic seizure at Leicester, he was visited in Paris by Raikes, who noted that he was 'in a very precarious state of health and not likely to live long'. On 24 Aug. 1836 a commission of lunacy determined that he had 'been of unsound mind' since 29 Sept. 1835.[40] Forbes died v.p. in November 1836. A post mortem revealed that 'water had lodged itself on the brain'.[41] Raikes, who claimed 'in former years' to have 'lived in much intimacy with him, meeting constantly at Lady Sarah Bayly's house', recalled that he was 'a great friend of the late Tom Sheridan and Moore the poet, and a very amiable and unaffected character' who was 'much liked'.[42] His eldest son George Arthur (1833-89) succeeded to the family estates and his grandfather's United Kingdom barony in 1837.

[1] *Creevey Pprs.* i. 161. [2] *Dublin Evening Post*, 25 Mar. 1820. [3] HLRO, Hist. Coll. 379, Grey Bennet diary, 96; *Black Bk.* (1823), 156; *Session of Parl. 1825*, p. 464. [4] Add. 38289, f. 312. [5] PRO NI, Talbot-Gregory mss D4100/4/6. [6] *The Times*, 26 Oct. 1825. [7] *O'Connell Corresp.* iii. 1278. [8] *Dublin Evening Post*, 17, 20 June 1826. [9] *Westmeath Jnl.* 6 July 1826. [10] PRO NI, Granard mss T3765/J/11/8/32-33. [11] *Westmeath Jnl.* 27 Mar. 1828. [12] Granard mss J/11/8/43. [13] PRO NI, Anglesey mss D619/26/C/75-76 [14] Granard mss J/11/8/53. [15] Anglesey mss 32A/2/157; *Westmeath Jnl.* 28 Nov. 1828. [16] Granard mss J/11/8/55. [17] *O'Connell Corresp.* iv. 1507. [18] Anglesey mss 32/A/3/166. [19] Granard mss J/11/8/62. [20] Ibid. 8/64. [21] Anglesey mss 32/A/3/1/239. [22] Ibid. 1/251. [23] NAI, Leveson Gower letterbks. M. 738/194, Leveson Gower to Singleton, 7 July; *Dublin Evening Post*, 3, 19 Aug.; *Roscommon and Leitrim Gazette*, 14 Aug. 1830. [24] Anglesey mss 29B/66-7. [25] Granard mss J/1/7, J/11/11A. [26] Anglesey mss 31D/34; W. Sussex RO, Goodwood mss 486, ff. 26-27. [27] Derby mss 920 Der (14) 119/2. [28] Anglesey mss 28A-B/49. [29] Add. 51568. [30] NLI, Farnham mss 18606 (1), Arbuthnot to Lord Farnham, 6 May 1831. [31] Derby mss 920 Der (14) 121/2, Gosset to Smith Stanley, 26 Apr.; *Dublin Evening Post*, 12 May; *Roscommon and Leitrim Gazette*, 14 May 1831. [32] Granard mss J/11/8/74. [33] Ibid. 8/75. [34] *Holland House Diaries*, 41. [35] Anglesey mss 27/B/47-48. [36] *O'Connell Corresp.* iv. 1853. [37] Granard mss J/11/8/76. [38] Ibid. 8/77-78. [39] *The Times*, 10 Mar. 1832. [40] *Raikes Jnl.* ii. 245; *The Times*, 25 Aug. 1836. [41] *The Times*, 16 Nov. 1836; *Gent. Mag.* (1837), i. 202. [42] *Raikes Jnl.* iii. 73.

P.J.S.

FORBES, John (1801-1840), of 15 Harley Street, Mdx.

MALMESBURY   1826-1832

b. 15 Dec. 1801, 1st s. of Charles Forbes* and Elizabeth, da. of Maj. John Cotgrave, E.I. Co. service, wid. of William Ashburner. *educ.* ?Aberdeen g.s.; Magdalen, Oxf. 1821. *m.* 10 Dec. 1828, Mary Jane, da. of Henry Lannoy Hunter of Beech Hill, Berks., 1s. 5da. *d.v.p.* 26 Dec. 1840.
     Dir. E.I. Co. 1830-d.

Forbes, who always suffered from poor health, was the eldest son of the East Indian agent and proprietor, Charles Forbes of Bombay, and lived his life almost entirely in his father's shadow. Possibly born in India, he was sent to England in 1809, and educated in London under one Pearson.[1] His father followed two years later and took up residence at Newe, Aberdeenshire, so John may have been one of the 'John Forbes' listed as attending Aberdeen grammar school in the 1810s. He was probably associated with his father's Indian concerns, and evidently became a proprietor of East India stock soon after the death of his relation and namesake in 1821, as, in his will, he left £3,000 to his father 'by way of restoring to him the first vote he gave me in the India Company's affairs by appropriating one fifth of his legacy from my great-uncle amounting to £12,000 to that purpose'.[2] His father, who had been a Member since 1812 and had received a baronetcy in 1823, presumably bought him the second seat for his own borough, Malmesbury, from the proprietor Joseph Pitt* at the general election of 1826.

In the House he was an almost entirely silent Member, who, when present, contented himself with copying his father's independent line. He voted for Catholic relief, 6 Mar. 1827. He sided with opposition for inquiry into the allegations against the corporation of Leicester, 15 Mar., but divided in the majority for the duke of Clarence's grant, 16 Mar. He made his only known speech, 22 Mar., on the mutiny at Barrackpoor, one of his father's *causes célèbres*, when he considered that the papers called for were absolutely requisite, to show whether a case of sufficient necessity really did arise, for the dreadful massacre in which, not only 160 of the native soldiers lost their lives, but many women and children residing in their huts were sacrificed also.

Like his father, he voted that day in the minority for the production of information on this. He divided against the Canning administration to consider separating bankruptcy jurisdiction from chancery, 22 May, but voted against the third reading of the Penryn election bill, 7 June. He also sided with ministers in favour of the grant to improve water communications in Canada, 12 June, but with Hume against the committal to Newgate of Thomas Flanagan on a charge of forgery, 19 June 1827. In the unusual absence of his father, he voted for repeal of the Test Acts, 26 Feb., Catholic relief (for which his father paired), 12 May, a lower pivot price for corn imports, 22 Apr., and to condemn chancery delays, 24 Apr. 1828. Unless it was his father (riding another of his hobby-horses), he spoke in praise of shipbuilding at Bombay, 19 May. (A second speech credited to 'Mr. Forbes' on 22 May was certainly one of his father's.) In December 1828 he married the sister of a junior clerk at the board of control. Listed by Planta, the Wellington ministry's patronage secretary, in February 1829, as likely to be 'with government' on the Catholic question, he voted for emancipation, 6, 30 Mar. He divided in the minority for allowing Daniel O'Connell to take his seat without first swearing the oath of supremacy, 18 May 1829. He paired in favour of Jewish emancipation, 5 Apr., and voted for it, 17 May 1830. He registered another of the votes which he cast unaccompanied by his father, 7 June 1830, when he joined the majority in favour of abolishing the death penalty for forgery.

Forbes was elected to the court of directors of the East India Company in April 1830, one of only two connections of agency houses to be so represented, but he was out by rotation until the following year.[3] He was again returned unopposed for Malmesbury at the general election that summer. Listed by ministers among the 'doubtful doubtfuls' and marked, like his father, 'more yes than no', he would have divided in their favour, but was 'shut out' of the division on the civil list, 15 Nov. 1830. He divided against the second reading of the Grey ministry's reform bill, 22 Mar., and for Gascoyne's wrecking amendment, 19 Apr. 1831. With his father, who was soon to declare his decision not to stand again, he was elected for Malmesbury at the ensuing general election, despite a show of opposition.[4] He voted against the second

reading of the reintroduced reform bill, 6 July, to postpone consideration of the partial disfranchisement of Chippenham, 27 July, and against the third reading, 19 Sept., and passage of the bill, 21 Sept. He divided for Hunt's motion for receiving the Preston petition on the corn laws, 12 Aug., and with opposition on the Dublin election, 23 Aug. He voted against the second reading of the revised reform bill, 17 Dec. 1831, and going into committee on it, 20 Jan. 1832. Although not so listed in the *Journal*, he was apparently appointed to the select committee on the East India Company, 27 Jan., as he was named as being present at sittings of the subcommittee on its political affairs.[5] He divided with Hunt on his amendments to give the vote to all tax-paying households, 2 Feb., and to exempt Preston from the £10 householder clause in the reform bill, 3 Feb. He voted against the enfranchisement of Tower Hamlets, 28 Feb., the last of the only five known occasions on which his father was presumably absent. He voted against the third reading of the reform bill, 22 Mar., and the second reading of the Irish bill, 25 May. He divided in favour of permanent provision being made for the Irish poor by a tax on absentees, 19 June. His only other known vote was with opposition on the Russian-Dutch loan, 26 Jan., and he was listed as an 'anti-reformer absent' on this, 12 July. Sir Charles Forbes apparently made no provision for his son at the dissolution of 1832 and he never sat again.

He died at Ventnor, Isle of Wight, in December 1840, as a result of a 'rapid decline' caused by consumption. By his will, dated 30 May 1835 with one codicil, he left his library at Newe to his father, and the rest of his estate, which included personalty sworn under £9,000 in the province of Canterbury and at £5,092 in Edinburgh, in trust, to be divided among his children, who were all more or less consumptive.[6] His only son Charles (*b.* 1832), who succeeded to his grandfather's baronetcy in 1849, died unmarried at Madeira in 1852.[7]

[1] A. and H. Tayler, *House of Forbes*, 379, 381. [2] PROB 11/1945/331. [3] C.H. Philips, *E.I. Co.* 278, 336. [4] *Devizes Gazette*, 5, 19 May 1831. [5] *PP* (1831-2), xiv. 11. [6] Tayler, 380; PROB 11/1945/331; IR26/1574/269. [7] *Gent. Mag.* (1852), ii. 103.

S.M.F.

FORDE, Mathew (1785–1837), of Seaforde, co. Down and Coolgreany, co. Wexford.

CO. DOWN   9 May 1821–1826

b. 17 May 1785, 1st s. of Mathew Forde of Seaforde and Coolgreany and 1st w. Catherine, da. of William

Brownlow, MP [I], of Lurgan, co. Armagh. *educ.* Trinity, Dublin 1801; Magdalen, Oxf. 1804. *m.* (1) 9 May 1814, Mary Anne (*d.* 10 Sept. 1826), da. of Francis Savage†, MP [I], of Ardkeen and Hollymount, co. Down and 1st w., *s.p.*; (2) 27 Aug. 1829, Lady Harriet Savage, da. of Henry Thomas Butler, 2nd earl of Carrick [I], and 2nd w. and wid. of the same Francis Savage, *s.p. suc.* fa. 1812. *d.* 5 Aug. 1837.

Trustee, linen board [I] 1820.

Sheriff, co. Down 1820-1.

Lt.-col. R.N. Down militia 1806.

The Fordes, originally from Wales, settled in Ireland in the late sixteenth century and Mathew Forde of Dublin bought the estates of Coolgreany and Seaforde in 1637. He died childless in 1653 and was succeeded by his great-nephew Mathew Forde (*d.* 1709), Member for county Wexford in the Irish Parliament. His son and namesake (1675-1729), who migrated from Wexford to Down, where he built the original mansion house and the village at Seaforde, was Member for nearby Downpatrick, 1703-14. His youngest son, Colonel Francis Forde, served with distinction under Clive in India but was lost at sea in 1769 on his passage out to take up his duties as one of three supervisors of the East India Company's possessions; his son Robert was also a Member of the Dublin Commons. The eldest son, another Mathew (1699-1780), sat as Member for Bangor, 1751-60. In 1744 his neighbour Mary Delany described Seaforde as

a very pleasant place and capable of being made a very fine one; there is more wood than is common in this country and a fine lake of water with very pretty meadows. The house is situated on the side of a hill and looks down on his woods and water. The house is not a very good one, but very well filled; for he has *ten children*, the youngest about ten years old – but that's a *moderate family* to some in *this country*.

When the eldest son Mathew (1726-95), Member for Downpatrick from 1761 to 1776, married Elizabeth Knox, sister of the 1st Lord Northland, 'an agreeable young woman with ten thousand pounds fortune', in 1750, he received a generous settlement of £2,100 a year from his father. He was succeeded as head of the family by his only surviving son and namesake, the father of this Member, who rebuilt the house at Seaforde and in July 1804 drew the attention of the Irish government to subversive literature circulating in Downpatrick.[1]

In August 1811 Mathew Forde senior tried to secure the support of Lord Downshire for himself or his eldest son, who was normally styled Colonel Forde, as a candidate for Down at the next general election. He

boasted that he was 'the only gentleman in the county who would please all parties, and that he had no doubt of success without expense'; but Downshire and his electoral adviser were unimpressed, the latter remarking that 'in his own estimation he stands much higher than he does in that of any party or interest of weight in the county'. In the event he died seven months before the election of 1812 when his son, like most of the leading Down gentry, acquiesced in the agreement whereby Downshire and Lord Londonderry divided the representation between them.[2] In 1814 Forde married the only child of Francis Savage, who had sat for the county on the Downshire interest, 1801-12; three years after her death in 1826 he married her widowed stepmother. The Irish government considered him a potential Member for Downpatrick on a vacancy in 1815, but nothing came of this.[3] That year he applied to the Irish secretary Robert Peel* for appointment as a trustee of the linen board:

My pretensions in looking to it are having an extensive property on which I reside in the county of Down where the linen manufacture is carried on to a great extent, as also that one of my family has generally been a member of the board.[4]

He was unsuccessful on that occasion, but had his wish granted in 1820. At the general election that year he actively supported Edward Ruthven* in his unsuccessful candidacy for Downpatrick, where he might have stood himself.[5] As sheriff, he chaired the county meeting called to congratulate George IV on his accession and oversaw the uncontested return of Londonderry's son Lord Castlereagh, the foreign secretary, and Downshire's brother Lord Arthur Hill.[6]

On Londonderry's death the following year, which removed the new marquess from the county seat, Forde, whose own minor territorial interest amounted to just under 300 40s. freeholders, offered as an independent. His unopposed return in May 1821, with Downshire's blessing, had been prepared by him in advance through consultations with Castlereagh, apparently on the implicit understanding that he would make way in future for his nephew Frederick Stewart*, who would not be of age until 1826.[7] Castlereagh had earlier explained to his half-brother Lord Stewart (who succeeded him as 3rd marquess of Londonderry on his suicide the following year) that in backing Forde, he intended to

settle the county for your son [and] to conciliate the resident gentry by a liberal policy towards Forde, who, being connected with Francis Savage, has a considerable popular following; and with respect to general politics, though Forde may be less regarded as my Member

... I have every reason to believe that his politics will be friendly towards government and that he has no other than friendly feelings towards myself.[8]

However, Forde took an idiosyncratic line in the House, which he attended irregularly.[9] He sided with the Liverpool administration against more extensive tax reductions to relieve distress, 11 Feb., but with opposition on the same subject, 21 Feb. 1822. He divided for abolition of one of the joint-postmasterships, 13 Mar., and paired for this, 2 May. He voted for the relief of Catholic peers from their disabilities, 30 Apr. He welcomed the Irish tithes leasing bill as 'a stepping-stone to a full consideration of the whole question', 13 June, but was in the minorities for the replacement of tithes by a fair equivalent, 19 June 1822, and against the tithes composition bill, 16 June 1823. He voted against parliamentary reform, 20 Feb., and repeal of the Foreign Enlistment Act, 16 Apr., but for inquiry into the legal proceedings against the Dublin Orange rioters, 22 Apr., and to censure the lord advocate's dealings with the Scottish press, 3 June 1823.

On the presentation of a petition complaining of judicial discrimination against Catholics, 31 May, Forde asserted that 'justice was properly and impartially administered in Ireland', and he supported the claim of Belfast Academy for financial aid, 10 June 1824.[10] He voted in condemnation of the trial in Demerara of the Methodist missionary John Smith, 11 June. He divided for the Irish insurrection bill, 14 June 1824, and the Irish unlawful societies bill, 15, 25 Feb. 1825, when he declared that 'unless the [Catholic] Association be put down, the peace of Ireland cannot be preserved'. He was one of the new Irish county Members named to the inquiry into Irish disturbances, 17 Feb.[11] He voted against Burdett's successful motion for Catholic relief, 1 Mar., but in the debate on the relief bill, 19 Apr., announced 'in a very low tone of voice' that, like his cousin Charles Brownlow, Member for county Armagh, 'he had been lately made a convert to this cause', which he now 'earnestly supported'. He therefore voted, like several other previously hostile Irish Members, for the second reading of the relief bill, 21 Apr., to the delight of the pro-Catholic Lord Palmerston*.[12] On 9 May he explained that he supported the measure because he believed that, together with the allied proposals to reform the Irish franchise and make provision for the Catholic clergy, 'it would be the means of rendering Ireland permanently tranquil'.[13] He spoke briefly in its favour the following day before voting for the third reading, and he supported the franchise bill, 12 May 1825. He

seems to have been inactive in 1826, when he declined an invitation to attend the Catholic Association dinner for the 'friends of civil and religious liberty'.[14]

By early 1824, bolstered by his popularity in the constituency, he had expressed his reluctance to surrender his seat to another Londonderry nominee in the event of an early general election, and one of the marquess's advisers feared that a failed attempt to oust him would 'see Colonel Forde more firmly in his seat than ever'.[15] Intensive discussions that year and the next among their mutual friends eventually led to a declaration from a harassed Forde, who felt bound to stand again if requisitioned by his supporters, that, in recognition of his unopposed return in 1821, 'if Lord Castlereagh [as Frederick Stewart was now styled] is eligible at the dissolution, *I will not oppose him*'. Yet it was still felt that Forde would be likely to provoke a damaging contest, especially in the autumn of 1825 when a dissolution was again expected.[16] In March 1826, when he declined to give his small electoral interest in county Wexford to Lord Stopford*, he privately acknowledged

the difficult situation he stood in; that he would be well pleased to be clear of the business, if he could do so with credit; that he had no wish as far as he was individually concerned to oppose Lord C., but that he must be guided in a great measure by circumstances.[17]

At the general election, he initially stood his ground, informing the freeholders, 2 June, that he would stand against Castlereagh, who was still a few days short of his majority, or any stopgap candidate, but that his wife's illness prevented him from leaving London to canvass. However, with Londonderry determined to make a show of electoral strength and to postpone the contest as late as legally possible, so that its completion would fall after Castlereagh's 21st birthday, Forde eventually stepped aside. This outcome had long been expected, though one observer blamed his withdrawal, which he announced in a bitter address, 14 June 1826, on his pro-Catholic votes.[18] He refused to interfere in Downpatrick, where he claimed to own no qualifying properties, and, vociferously complaining that he had been forced out by an aristocratic coalition, held himself free to offer again for the county at some future date.[19]

Although he was present at the Down meeting to address the king on the death of the anti-Catholic duke of York, 1 Feb. 1827, he wrote approvingly to Downshire, 8 Feb. 1829, that he welcomed the Wellington ministry's emancipation bill and its decision to suppress the Association.[20] He made no opposition to Castlereagh's re-election on appointment to office that year, but, having objected to the increased Irish spirit and stamp duties at a county meeting in May 1830, he offered with the backing of the Independent Club, which he had had a hand in forming, at the general election that summer, in a vain attempt to open the representation.[21] He conducted a vigorous campaign to regain the seat, trying to split the supporters of the two main electoral patrons by (unsuccessfully) appealing for plumpers and second votes, and, influenced by the radical Presbyterianism of the Rev. Holt Waring, he advocated tax reductions, retrenchment and parliamentary reform.[22] Although he was said to have an 'immense interest' and to be popular as the antidote to that belonging to the absentee Londonderry, he fell behind Castlereagh, who topped the poll, and finished narrowly adrift of their ally Hill. He refused to be mortified by this result, which, at a dinner in his honour in September 1830, he blamed on the fact that a third of the electors were tenants on the estates of his two opponents (on his own there were reckoned to be 91 £10 freeholders).[23] At county Down meetings in January and March 1831 he supported petitions for reform, except for its call for triennial parliaments, and against repeal of the Union, the movement for which he considered to be the work of Daniel O'Connell's* 'mischievous agitators'.[24] Regretting the defeat of the Grey ministry's reform bill in April 1831, he nevertheless declined to enter as a reformer at the ensuing general election on the ground of illness; wisely so, in the view of one of his closest supporters.[25] There was some talk of his friends starting him again the following year, but he never re-entered Parliament.[26] He died, childless, in August 1837. He was succeeded by his next brother, the Rev. William Brownlow Forde (1786-1856), whose son and heir, Colonel William Brownlow Forde (1823-1902), sat as a Conservative for county Down, 1857-74.[27]

[1] *Hist. Irish Parl.* iv. 204-7; *Autobiog. and Corresp. of Mrs. Delany*, ii. 322, 574-5; Add. 35751, f. 48. [2] PRO NI, Downshire mss D671/C/12/100-3, 105; *HP Commons, 1790-1820*, ii. 643-4. [3] *HP Commons, 1790-1820*, ii. 646. [4] Add. 40248, f. 102. [5] PRO NI, Ker mss D2651/3/34, 36. [6] *Belfast News Letter*, 7, 21, 24, 28 Mar. 1820. [7] Ibid. 13 Apr., 11 May 1821; PRO NI, Castlereagh mss D3030/M/33; N/123-9; P.J. Jupp, 'Co. Down Elections', *Irish Hist. Stud.* xviii (1972), 187. [8] Castlereagh mss Q2/2, p. 256. [9] *Black Bk.* (1823), 156; *Session of Parl. 1825*, p. 464. [10] *The Times*, 1, 11 June 1824. [11] Add. 40373, f. 187. [12] Brougham mss, Mackintosh to Brougham, 16 Mar. 1825; Southampton Univ. Lib. Broadlands mss PP/GC/TE/171. [13] *The Times*, 10 May 1825. [14] *O'Connell Corresp.* iii. 223. [15] PRO NI, Cassidy mss D1088/45; Castlereagh mss N/130, 133, 146, 155. [16] PRO NI, Nugent mss D552/A/6/6/10-12, 16-19; Castlereagh mss N/147-50; Downshire mss C/12/315-17. [17] TCD, Courtown mss P33/14/91; Nugent mss A/6/6/20. [18] *Belfast Commercial Chron.* 7, 10, 19, 21 June; PRO NI, Londonderry mss D654/B4/2, Londonderry to

Castlereagh, 6, 15, 20 June; T1536/3A-C, P, Q; Castlereagh mss N/172, 174, 176; NLI, Farnham mss 18602 (19), Robinson to Maxwell, 12 June 1826. [19] PRO NI, Perceval-Maxwell mss G/1/36; Castlereagh mss N/184, 197, 201. [20] *Belfast News Letter*, 6 Feb. 1827; Downshire mss C/12/381. [21] PRO NI, Meade mss MIC259/2, Brush to Meade, 27 June 1829; 5, Forde to same, 8, 26 June; *Newry Commercial Telegraph*, 14, 21 May, 25 June, 6, 23 July; *The Times*, 20, 23 Aug. 1830; Perceval-Maxwell mss G/1/63, Jupp, 187, 202. [22] Castlereagh mss N/206-12, 216, 227, 239, 240, 250; *Newry Commercial Telegraph*, 17 Aug. 1830; *Narrative of Down Election* (1830), 18-21, 105-7; Jupp, 187-8, 206. [23] Add. 40338, f. 223; Durham RO, Londonderry mss D/LO/C/83/29; *Newry Commercial Telegraph*, 27 Aug., 21 Sept. 1830; PRO NI T761/19. [24] *Newry Commercial Telegraph*, 20 Jan., 29 Mar. 1831; PRO NI, Dufferin mss D1071/B/C/21/64. [25] *Newry Commercial Telegraph*, 29 Apr. 1831; Nugent mss A/6/6/43. [26] *Belfast Commercial Chron.* 23 July 1832. [27] *Downpatrick Recorder*, 12 Aug. 1837.

D.R.F./S.M.F.

FORDWICH, Visct. *see* **COWPER**, **George Augustus Frederick**

FORESTER, **Francis** (1774–1861), of Somerby House, Melton Mowbray, Leics. and 20 Sackville Street, Mdx.[1]

WENLOCK   1820–1826

b. 19 Aug. 1774, 5th s. of Lt.-Col. Cecil Forester† (*d.* 1774) of Ross Hall, nr. Shrewsbury, Salop and Anne, da. and coh. of Robert Townshend of Christleton, Cheshire; bro. of Cecil Forester† (afterwards Weld Forester). *m.* 22 July 1813, Lady Louisa Catherine Barbara Vane, da. of William Henry Vane†, 2nd earl of Darlington, 1s. 2da. *d.* 22 Oct. 1861.

Lt. 95 Ft. 1793, capt. 1794; capt. 46 Ft. 1796; capt. 15 Drag. Gds. 1799, maj. 1803.

Frank Forester, who was only three days old when his father died, was a cousin of George Forester† of Dothill and Willey Park, which his eldest brother Cecil, a personal friend of George IV as regent, inherited in 1811, giving him a controlling interest in the borough of Wenlock.[2] He was educated locally with John Cressett Pelham*,[3] whose love of hunting he shared, and was a founder member of the 'Four-in-Hand Club'.[4] Until he married a daughter of the wealthy Whig peer Lord Darlington, he pursued a military career, becoming a major in the cavalry, with whom he served in Portugal in 1808 and 1809, when they were defeated at Sahagun and Benevente and retreated to Corunna. At the general election of 1820 he came in for Wenlock for a single Parliament to replace Cecil, who retired in anticipation of a peerage, and whose sons were not yet of age.[5] The arrangement aroused little opposition, and the contest was for Wenlock's second seat.[6] Forester topped the poll throughout and said little of politics, but he expressed concern on the hustings for the depressed state of agriculture.[7] Afterwards, he was drawn into the local controversy concerning the votes cast at the election by Darlington's tenants.[8]

No speeches by Foster are reported and he appears to have been a poor attender who divided with the Liverpool ministry and against Catholic relief.[9] The death of his wife, 8 Jan. 1821, was a factor in his apparent failure to vote on the Queen Caroline case.[10] Darlington had voted against proceeding with it and signed the Lords' protest; but, despite early misgivings, Forester's brother, whose hopes of taking the title Baron Wenlock had suffered a setback, was anxious to demonstrate support for George IV.[11] Forester divided with government against the additional malt duty repeal bill, 3 Apr., to include arrears in the duke of Clarence's grant, 18 June, on retrenchment, 27 June 1821, and against more extensive tax reductions to relieve distress, 11 Feb., and abolishing one of the joint-postmasterships, 13 Mar. 1822. He voted against Catholic relief, which his brother the Rev. Townshend Forester, rector of Brosely and bailiff of Wenlock, vehemently opposed, 30 Apr. 1822, 1 Mar., 21 Apr., 10 May 1825.[12] He divided against inquiry into the lord advocate's treatment of the Scottish press, 25 June 1822, and in the ministerial majorities against repeal of the Foreign Enlistment Act, 16 Apr., and inquiry into the currency, 12 June 1823. He presented petitions from Wenlock against the hides and skins bill, 3 May, and the excise license duty, 6 May 1824.[13] His vote for the duke of Cumberland's annuity bill, 10 June 1825, was the last recorded for him before he made way for his nephew at the dissolution that month.[14]

In later life Forester let Somerby House and lived mainly in London, where he died, recalled as a sportsman, at his home in St. James's Place in October 1861. He left everything to his only son William Henry Forester (1819-91), who already received £4,000 a year under the will of his maternal grandfather the 1st duke of Cleveland.[15]

[1] Salop Archives, Weld-Forester mss 1224, box 337, property qualification of Forester as candidate for Wenlock in 1820. [2] G.T.O. Bridgeman, 'Some Account of Fam. of Forester', *Trans. Salop Arch. and Nat. Hist. Soc.* (ser. 2), iii (1891), 151-84; J.D. Nichol, 'Wynnstay, Willey and Wenlock', ibid. lviii (1965-8), 220-33; *HP Commons, 1754-90*, ii. 450-1; *HP Commons, 1790-1820*, iii. 790-1. [3] *Shrewsbury Chron.* 10 Mar. 1820. [4] *Gronow Reminiscences*, ii. 109. [5] Bridgeman, 177-83; H.T. Weyman, 'Members of Parliament for Wenlock', *Trans. Salop. Arch. and Nat. Hist. Soc.* (ser. 3), ii (1902), 350-2. [6] Weld-Forester mss, box 337, Procs. at Wenlock election, corresp. C. Weld Forester and Sir W. Williams Wynn, 25, 26, 28 Feb., R. Acton to C. Weld Forester, 1 Mar. 1820; *VCH Salop*, iii. 296-7; Nichol, 230-1. [7] *Shrewsbury Chron.* 25 Feb., 10 Mar. 1820.

[8] Weld-Forester mss, box 337, J. Scarth to C.W. Forester, 15 July 1820. [9] *Black Bk.* (1823), 156. [10] *Gent. Mag.* (1821), i. 186. [11] Weld-Forester mss 37/50-53; 332/144; Hull Univ. Lib. Forbes Adams mss DDFA/39/45, R. to B. Lawley, 14 July, 9 Aug., 26 Dec.; Add. 38369, f. 332; *Shrewsbury Chron.* 8 Dec. 1820. [12] Weld-Forester mss 332/180. [13] *The Times*, 4, 7 May 1824. [14] Weld-Forester mss 37/161, 165; Salop Archives, Blakemore mss 604, box 8, Lord Forester's letterbk. pp. 116-22; *Salopian Jnl.* 17 May 1826. [15] PROB 11/1960/243; *Lincoln, Rutland and Stamford Mercury*, 25 Oct.; *Gent. Mag.* (1861), ii. 693.

M.M.E.

FORESTER *see also* **WELD FORESTER**

FORTESCUE, Hon. George Mathew (1791–1877).

b. 21 May 1791, 2nd s. of Hugh Fortescue[†], 1st Earl Fortescue (*d.* 1841), and Hester, da. of George Grenville[†] of Wotton, Bucks.; bro. of Hugh Fortescue, Visct. Ebrington[*]. *educ.* Eton 1805. *m.* 19 Feb. 1833, Lady Louisa Elizabeth Ryder, da. of Dudley Ryder[†], 1st earl of Harrowby, 4s. (2 *d.v.p.*) 4da. (1 *d.v.p.*). *suc.* aunt Lady Grenville to Boconnoc, Cornw. and Dropmore Lodge, Bucks. 1864. *d.* 24 Jan. 1877.

Ensign 14 Drag. 1809, cornet 1809, lt. 1810; lt. 21 Drag. 1811; lt. 8 Drag. 1812; capt. 66 Ft. 1812; capt. 25 Drag. 1813; half-pay 1816-57.

Hugh Fortescue was briefly Member for Beaumaris before becoming 3rd Baron Fortescue in 1785, when he succeeded to Castle Hill, near Barnstaple, and large family estates in Devon. He received an earldom from Pitt in 1789, but followed the line of his wife's family, the Grenvilles, in politics, as did, at least initially, his sons Lord Ebrington and George Matthew Fortescue. The latter, although a sickly child, who was educated at Eton (and possibly Edinburgh University)[1], hankered after a career in the army, and his mother's brother Lord Grenville obliged by finding him a place in Lord Bridgwater's regiment in 1809. Later that year, however, Grenville wrote to Lord Fortescue that

I had entertained very sanguine hopes that regular exercise might at his exact time of life possibly develop the latent powers of his constitution and give him a degree of growth and strength necessary for what he has engaged in. [But this having failed] the great embarrassment certainly is how to occupy a mind so little disposed to study, and a body so unsuited to exercise – because we must not forget (with all the excellence of his nature and disposition) that idleness ever was the mother of all vice. Universities are out of the question – your own house, though so admirable in all he will see there of example, is not in other respects suited to give him that manliness of character and manners in which he is so deficient, and I see no recourse but travel, and even that by public events is greatly limited.

Although his 'radical weakness' and 'the unfortunate backwardness of his literary progress' might have curtailed his ambitions, Fortescue persisted with his military career. He exchanged regiments several times, mainly in order to avoid being sent on active service, but he seems to have visited India with the 8th Dragoons, and in 1816 his mother advised him that his health was not good enough to risk returning there.[2] After the war he undertook various travels in Europe, and embarked on a number of unfortunate love affairs. Henry Edward Fox* commented that he 'has a good deal of affectation, but I do not mind that much if he is otherwise agreeable'; and Maria Edgeworth wished that he 'were a lover of any of my friends – he is so agreeable melancholy and gentlemanlike'.[3]

Fortescue was elected to Brooks's, 7 May 1816, on the general admission of the Grenvilles. When, following a breach with the 2nd marquess of Buckingham, Ebrington retired from Buckingham borough in 1817, the seat was offered to Fortescue, who declined it. Buckingham's brother, Lord Nugent*, who sat as his nominee at Aylesbury, wrote to Ebrington, 30 May:

> I cannot but be glad that you are exempted from a worry which *you know* I should be most glad to be exempted from myself, I mean the worry of filling the seat of a man as the representative of his interest in Parliament, while you differ with him in views and opinions in almost every vote you give. I cannot but say that I am equally glad on George's account that he has had the manliness and proper feeling toward you and towards himself to forego the offer that was made, which, under the circumstances, might have been so alluring and so advantageous to him. It seems however to have been done, on all sides, handsomely and kindly.[4]

The duke of Bedford suggested his name to Lord Holland, 17 Aug. 1825, as a possible candidate for Exeter after the expected dissolution, but nothing came of it.[5] There may have been other attempts to have him returned to the Commons, but he had to wait until the general election of 1826, when an acquaintance of his,[6] the Whig Lord Grosvenor, brought him in for the seat which he had recently acquired at Hindon.

Fortescue divided against the duke of Clarence's annuity, 16 Feb., and for Catholic claims, 6 Mar. 1827. He voted to make 50s. not 60s. the import price for corn, 9 Mar., and against increased protection for barley, 12 Mar. He presented a South Molton petition in favour of the establishment of a mail to Ilfracombe, 29 Mar.,[7] when he voted for the production of information on the Irish government's handling of the Lisburn

Orange procession of 1825. The following day he voted to postpone the committee of supply. Like the staunch Whig Ebrington, in April he strongly favoured a junction between the new prime minister, George Canning, and the leader of the moderate Whigs, Lord Lansdowne, to whom he submitted his allegiance 'as a very unimportant member of the party'.[8] Ebrington agreed with his brother, in a letter of 12 Dec. 1827, that the Goderich ministry 'cannot go on without men [of] energy and unity of purpose among thems[elves] to oppose to the extravagant pretensions and personal slights and indifference if not dislike which they have to encounter from the king'.[9] Fortescue, who attended the House, 6 Feb. 1828, informed his friend Ralph Sneyd the following day of his doubts about Huskisson, who had '*almost* convinced me that he has acted honestly by his firmness in taking office under those who so bitterly hate both him and his departed friend', and how the duke of Wellington, the new prime minister, had denied that he had given him any 'pledges and stipulations'. By the following month, despite admitting to being 'so well reconciled' to his retirement from society that 'I bear with complacency the being uninvited even to Devonshire House, which ancient habit and Whig feeling would, were I asked, still incline me to go', he had decided that

> the duke's government will stand better than any other, in the present most strange and unmanageable state of both Houses; and I wish it may – for I believe that notwithstanding his education, and his character, formed on his long despotic rule, he is inclined to listen to and be guided by public opinion.[10]

He voted for repeal of the Test Acts, 26 Feb., and against extending East Retford into the hundred of Bassetlaw, 21 Mar. He voted for a pivot price for corn of 60s. not 64s., 22 Apr., and on 28 Apr., in his only reported speech in the House (and despite his earlier vote on the subject), he observed that

> much is said about the influence of the currency in favour of farmers, but the currency has no influence upon the poor rates or tithes. I trust that government will acquiesce in the proposed increase of [the protecting] duty [on barley], or the agriculturist must inevitably suffer.

He presented several pro-Catholic petitions, 1 May, and again voted for relief, 12 May. He divided for the second reading of the usury bill, 19 June, against the misapplication of public money on Buckingham House, 23 June, and for reducing the salary of the lieutenant-general of the ordnance, 4 July 1828.

That summer he visited the Channel Islands and attended the Cowes regatta, and in November 1828 he noted, in relation to Ireland, that 'though we may not approve *all* the acts of the [Catholic] Association, we must attach less blame to them than to their opponents'.[11] From Castle Hill, Fortescue reported to Sneyd, 3 Jan. 1829, that the 'thick-headed parsons and squires of these parts' had got up an anti-Catholic requisition, and condemned the prevailing 'deep-rooted, ignorant bigotry on this Catholic question'. He attended the subsequent county meeting, 16 Jan., and was disgusted by the Ultra attacks on the county Member Acland, which he thought would help secure him his seat at the next election. The following month he asserted that, contrary to reports in the press, the duke of Cumberland 'will vote against the [relief] bill, but will not join the violent opponents to it', and would then immediately return to Berlin, which he termed an 'act of peace'.[12] He was listed by Planta, the patronage secretary, among those 'opposed to securities' but otherwise 'pro' emancipation, and he duly sided with them on it, 6, 30 Mar. He divided in the minority in favour of allowing Daniel O'Connell to take his seat without swearing the oath of supremacy, 18 May. He voted against the grant for the marble arch sculpture , 25 May, and for a reduction in the hemp duties, 1 June 1829.

Fortescue, who in late 1829 was fearful about the 'stormy prospect' ahead, wrote to Sneyd, 11 Jan. 1830, to ask:

> Is the duke to snub us with the face he had when he prorogued us? If so, why did he defer any measure of importance to this session? His colleagues have learnt little wisdom in the interval and, Heaven knows, the difficulties of the country have not diminished. There was a notion among us Whigs of organizing ourselves into a party, to act under the joint leadership of Althorp and Brougham, but difficulties have arisen, as they were quite sure to do, and for the present the plan is abandoned. So we shall, I suppose, continue to support the government without sharing its responsibility, with the satisfaction of feeling that at any moment the very existence of the ministry is at our mercy.[13]

He voted for transferring East Retford's seats to Birmingham and against the East Retford bribery prevention bill, 11 Feb., paired in the same sense, 5 Mar., and divided against the third reading of the disfranchisement bill, 15 Mar. He voted for parliamentary reform, 18 Feb., 28 May, and the enfranchisement of Birmingham, Leeds and Manchester, 23 Feb. He may have been the 'Mr. Fortescue' who told Mrs. Arbuthnot, 17 Mar., that 'having people who were so entirely without the power of expressing themselves in Parliament did the government the utmost harm, and provoked those who were not in office but wishing to

be so and who felt their own superiority'.[14] He voted for restricting the grant for the army to six months, 19 Feb., inquiry into a revision of taxation, 25 Mar., and deducting the salary of the lieutenant-general of the ordnance from the estimates, 29 Mar. He divided for Jewish emancipation, 5 Apr., 17 May. He paired in favour of opposition resolutions relating to the affair at Terceira, 28 Apr., and for reducing the salary of the assistant secretary of the treasury, 10 May. He voted against grants for the Royal Military Academy at Woolwich, 30 Apr., and the South American missions, 7 June, and in favour of a return of privy councillors' emoluments, 14 May. He voted against capital punishment for forgery, 24 May, 7 June, and increasing recognizances for libel, 9 July 1830.

At the ensuing general election, Fortescue's mother wrote to him that

> I had so completely satisfied my mind that you would represent Hindon again that I fear I am not as grateful as I ought for being certified of it. But the truth is that not having heard from you so long I had half hoped that you had stood for another election where I should have been still more gratified by your success.[15]

He joined the rest of the family in urging Ebrington not to attempt another contest in Devon, but once he had chosen to offer, he accompanied him at the nomination meeting, 7 Aug., stood in for him on the hustings for three days, and presided at his subsequent celebration dinner.[16] On 14 Aug. he defended the conduct of the East India Company, saying that

> he had been in those parts, and knew something of the practical bearings of the subject; and he was quite sure, that the government of the East had much better be conducted as it now was, with some amendments, than to be thrown entirely into the hands of the ministers of the crown, to increase the extravagant patronage which they already possessed, and of which he feared they did not always make the purest use.

He spoke on several other occasions in the county, and made clear his belief in the need for religious toleration, parliamentary reform, changes in chancery administration, the abolition of slavery, alteration of the duties on foreign timber and alliance with the free states of Europe.[17] As he informed Lady Grenville, 27 Sept., the

> Devonshire election, of which the consequences, in the form of public dinners, etc., have been occupying a large part of the last six weeks, I was as little prepared for when I left London, as I was to take the prominent part in it that I found myself obliged to fill. Its result however has been so satisfactory – the indulgence with which I was listened to, and the attention I have since received, so very

flattering that I feel bound to devote myself more than I have hitherto done to county business.[18]

He was to have led the projected South Molton and Castle Hill troop of yeoman cavalry that was nearly raised during the rural disturbances of late 1830.[19]

Although, as Robert Grosvenor* reported to Fortescue, 20 Sept. 1830, his patron Grosvenor intended to rally to Wellington's administration if an amendment was moved to the address, Fortescue was listed by ministers among their 'foes', and he voted against them in the division on the civil list, 15 Nov., which brought about their resignation.[20] He presented an anti-slavery petition from the Dissenters of Bideford, 25 Nov. 1830, and was added to the select committee on the East India Company's affairs, 17 Feb. 1831. It may have been in this year that on 19 Feb. his mother expressed her hope that he would 'serve your country and *yourself* by *pairing*'.[21] In mid-March he attended on a private bill, but complained that the Commons had 'left me so little strength'.[22] He divided for the second reading of the Grey ministry's reform bill, 22 Mar., and against Gascoyne's wrecking amendment, 19 Apr. 1831. He retired at the ensuing general election, when he was present in Devon to see his brother re-elected.[23]

He sought seclusion at Weare Giffard, near Bideford, from where he wrote to Sneyd:

Will you believe it, that at this moment, 10 pm on Sunday [9 Oct. 1831] I am totally ignorant of the fate of the reform bill! For aught I know London may be in flames, the House of Lords abolished, the king's [?]ministers suspended and the affairs of the country conducted by a committee of public safety. Ebrington's zealous, forward and efficient support of the government and their measure may save our house in town – but for that I sometimes think that I might spare myself the trouble and expense of putting bookcases in my library here, my books being still in London, within reach of H.M. the Mob. The prominent part that Ebrington is taking, *conscientiously* taking, is matter of no small vexation to me, for differing as I do from him in all but one point, a desire that the bill should pass the Lords – *not* for the sake of its enactments, but for the peace of the country – we are obliged to observe an entire silence on the subject.

He also revealed that, although refusing to take any part in the recent Devon county meeting, he had attended it

because I could conveniently say that in the dilemma in which the government has placed us, the *least* evil would result from passing the bill, believing, as I do, that *somehow or other*, its provisions *will* be the law of the land.

In the midst of the disturbances that followed the bill's defeat, he attended a local meeting to preach peace. He also expressed his relief at being out of the Commons and that 'the opinions I entertain secure me I hope from a peerage'.[24] Sneyd, who teased him on his 'be-Devonment', disagreed with him over the actions of the Lords, but consoled him on his personal differences with his previously intimate brother.[25] Fortescue wrote to Lady Grenville from Castle Hill, 10 Mar. 1832:

I have nothing to take me to town, and I enjoy the prospect of passing the *whole* of the *half* of *this* spring as I passed the half of the last in this county, instead of abusing it in endeavouring to revolutionize the country in Parliament. How sincerely do I thank my stars that I am out of Parliament and therefore I have nothing to do with politics.[26]

Though confessing his hostility to the extent of reform, and his regret that there were not more moderate men in power, he approved of the sizeable majority in favour of the bill on its second reading in the Lords in May, which was

selon moi, the best thing that could have happened. If no peers are made (and I confess I am astonished after the reckless pace Lord Grey has been going, that none have been made), a bill may be formed out of the old one, such as even the *old Parliament might* have carried, had either temper or wisdom been shown by the ministers, and such as may preserve *for a time* some parts of the old constitution.[27]

In early 1833, after what he called a 'strange' affair, he married the youngest sister of Ebrington's late wife; and as Lady Dover noted

it seems to me *sans rime ni raison*, and the strangest end to all his sentimentality ... I suppose he thinks her youth makes it a fine thing to do, but then where there is youth without charm it ceases to have an advantage. I am glad for Lady Harrowby, who must like this sort of son-in-law.[28]

After the death of Lord Grenville in 1834, he settled at the former Pitt family estate of Boconnoc, which had been inherited by Lady Grenville. From there Sneyd reported to Lady Harrowby, 3 Nov. 1835, that

G. is in better condition physically and morally than I have seen him for long years. His settled prospects and the occupation and amusement present and future which the possession of this place opens to him, added to the influences of a happy home, seem effectually to have dispelled those wayward clouds that used to gather over his mind and weigh down his spirits.[29]

Fortescue, who took a minor interest in local affairs,[30] seconded the nomination of the Tory Lord Eliot for Cornwall East at the general election of 1837. He was given a very hostile hearing when he declared that

> I voted for the reform bill – I was a reformer when no place, no honours, nor advantages were to be had – and I am a reformer now – not perhaps, in the sense in which many of you hold that word; not certainly in the sense in which the honourable baronet holds it, who has with such talent addressed you, but a reformer, a conservator of all those institutions of our country which have placed us where we are.[31]

He also proposed Eliot for Cornwall East at the elections in July and September 1841.[32] He was himself solicited to stand on a possible vacancy for the county in 1843, but did not do so, and apparently never had ambitions to enter the House again, although he continued to be involved in local elections.[33] By the will of his father, who died in 1841, he gained a rent charge of £1,000 a year, in addition to his portion of £10,000.[34] On the death in June 1864 of Lady Grenville, whose will was proved in London, 4 Aug., he inherited her Cornwall and Buckinghamshire estates, personal wealth valued under £25,000, and a large collection of papers, which, like others in his possession, were partially published by the Historical Manuscripts Commission and later deposited in the British Library.[35] He revisited Holland House in 1855, when the 4th Lord Holland (as Fox now was) recalled that

> Fortescue was in my youth an habitué of this house, very handsome, and then an exquisite and dandy of that time, neither empty nor insolent. He was universally popular and justly so. I have not seen him for many years. Time has whitened his bushy hair, but otherwise, notwithstanding much illness, he is little altered.[36]

He died after a few days' sickness in January 1877, 'much and deservedly respected', his estate being inherited in turn by his two surviving sons, Cyril Dudley (1847-90), and John Bevill (1850-1938).[37]

[1] *The Times*, 29 Jan. 1877. [2] Add. 69046, ff. 94-98, 102-22; 69364, Lady Fortescue to son, 31 July [1816]; *HMC Fortescue*, x. 188, 304. [3] Add. 69050; 69364; *Fox Jnl.* 87, 181; *Edgeworth Letters*, 285. [4] Devon RO, Earl Fortescue mss 1262 M/FC 32; J.J. Sack, *The Grenvillites*, 174. [5] Add. 51663. [6] Keele Univ. Lib. Sneyd mss SC10/81. [7] *The Times*, 30 Mar. 1827. [8] Northants. RO, Agar Ellis diary, 26 Apr.; Lansdowne mss, Ebrington and Fortescue to Lansdowne, 27 Apr. 1827. [9] Add. 69364. [10] Sneyd mss SC10/83, 84. [11] Ibid. SC10/85, 86. [12] Ibid. SC10/87-89; G. I.T. Machin, *Catholic Question in English Politics*, 142-3; *Western Times*, 17 Jan. 1829. [13] Sneyd mss SC10/90, 91. [14] *Arbuthnot Jnl.* ii. 345. [15] Add. 69362. [16] Ibid. Lady Fortescue to son, 20 July; *Western Times*, 7, 14, 21 Aug.; *The Times*, 12, 14 Aug. 1830. [17] *Western Times*, 21 Aug., 4, 11, 25 Sept., 30 Oct. 1830. [18] Add. 69050, f. 146. [19] Earl Fortescue, *Yeomanry of Devon*, 42. [20] Add. 69366. [21] Add. 69362. [22] Add. 69050, ff. 150, 152. [23] *Western Times*, 14 May 1831. [24] Sneyd mss SC10/101, 102. [25] Add. 69364, Sneyd to Fortescue, 22 Oct., 6 Dec. 1831, 7 Jan. 1832. [26] Add. 69050, f. 160. [27] Sneyd mss SC10/103, 104. [28] Ibid. SC10/107, 108; *Howard Sisters*, 255. [29] Fortescue mss FC 39/78. [30] For example, see *Barclay Fox's Jnl.* ed. R.L. Brett, 167. [31] *West Briton*, 11 Aug. 1837. [32] *The Times*, 9 July, 24 Sept. 1841. [33] Add. 69366, Cholmondeley to Fortescue, 5 June 1843; 69367; Devon RO, Acland mss 1148 M/C/8/4. [34] PROB 11/1952/673; IR26/1576/646; *The Times*, 19 Oct. 1841, 4 July 1842. [35] *HMC 2nd Rep.* app. p. 49; *13th Rep.* app. iii; *14th Rep.* app. v; *HMC Fortescue*, vols. iii.-x. [36] Lord Ilchester, *Chrons. of Holland House*, 410. [37] Lord Clement, *Hist. Fam. of Fortescue* (1880), 137; *The Times*, 29 Jan. 1877.

S.M.F.

FORTESCUE, Hugh, Visct. Ebrington (1783–1861), of 11 North Audley Street, Mdx. and Castle Hill, nr. Barnstaple, Devon.

BARNSTAPLE	4 Aug. 1804–1807
ST. MAWES	22 July 1807–Feb. 1809
BUCKINGHAM	1812–8 May 1816
BUCKINGHAM	5 June 1816–9 June 1817
DEVON	1818–1820
TAVISTOCK	22 May 1820–1830
DEVON	1830–1832
DEVON NORTH	1832–1 Mar. 1839

b. 13 Feb. 1783, 1st s. of Hugh Fortescue†, 1st Earl Fortescue, and Hester, da. of George Grenville† of Wotton, Bucks.; bro. of Hon. George Matthew Fortescue*. *educ.* Eton 1793; Brasenose, Oxf. 1800. *m.* (1) 4 July 1817, Lady Susan Ryder (*d.* 30 July 1827), da. of Dudley Ryder†, 1st earl of Harrowby, 3s. (1 *d.v.p.*); (2) 26 July 1841, Elizabeth, da. of Piers Geale of Clonsilla, co. Dublin, wid. of Sir Marcus Somerville, 4th bt.*, *s.p.* *summ.* to Lords in his fa's barony as Lord Fortescue 1 Mar. 1839; *suc.* fa. as 2nd Earl Fortescue 16 June 1841; KG 12 July 1856. *d.* 14 Sept. 1861.
   Ensign 9 Ft. 1808.
   PC 1 Mar. 1839; ld. lt. [I] Apr. 1839-Sept. 1841; ld. steward of household July 1846-Mar. 1850.
   Ld. lt. Devon 1839-d.; high steward, Barnstaple and South Molton.
   Col. E. Devon militia 1816.

Ebrington, a man of 'sepulchral religiosity' with a 'tendency to carry conscientiousness to extremes', had severed his remaining connections with his Grenvillite relatives in 1817 and acted thereafter with the advanced section of the Whig party.[1] In 1820 he faced another severe contest against the Tories Bastard and Acland for the Devon seat which he had captured in 1818. He expressed disappointment in his address at Parliament's failure to enact 'reforms in our public expenditure' and reduce 'those burdens which press

... upon the people', justified his 'steady and conscientious' opposition to the Six Acts and reaffirmed his attachment to 'those great principles of religious liberty, which I have ever held to be inseparable from the cause of political freedom'. He retired after three days, ostensibly as a matter of honour after an accusation he had levelled against one of Acland's relatives of promoting a covert coalition with Bastard had been proved false, although he was at the bottom of the poll in any case. He was returned for Tavistock in May 1820 on the duke of Bedford's interest.[2]

He was a regular attender who continued to vote with the Whig opposition to Lord Liverpool's ministry on all major issues, including parliamentary reform, 9, 10 May 1821, 25 Apr. 1822, 20 Feb., 24 Apr., 2 June 1823, 13, 27 Apr., 26 May 1826. He paired for Catholic relief, 28 Feb. 1821, and divided against the Irish unlawful societies bill, 15, 21, 25 Feb., to hear the Catholic Association at the bar of the House, 18 Feb., and for relief, 1 Mar., 21 Apr., 10 May 1825. He observed in October 1820 that ministers seemed 'determined to drive matters to extremity between the king and the people' over the Queen Caroline affair, and in September 1821 he privately described Sir Robert Wilson's* dismissal from the army as a 'mean act of revenge for the victory gained over the ministers by the people at the poor queen's funeral'.[3] He attended the Devon county meeting on the Catholic question, 16 Mar. 1821, when he argued that concession posed no danger to the constitution and moved an unsuccessful amendment in favour of Burdett's relief bill.[4] He saw no justification for 'such frightful and oppressive measures' as the Irish Insurrection Act, 7 Feb., and acted as a minority teller against the Irish constables bill, which was 'subversive of everything like a free government', 7 June 1822. By 1824 it had become his practice to reside in Ireland for a few months each year, and in January 1825 he wrote that he intended to contribute to the 'Catholic rent'.[5] He was prepared to accept the Irish franchise bill, 9 May 1825, as it would 'conciliate to the cause of emancipation many persons who would otherwise remain hostile to it'. At a county meeting, 5 Apr. 1821, he moved the petition for relief from agricultural distress and reform, arguing that the only remedy was economy and retrenchment, which could never be achieved 'while the representation continued in its present corrupt state'. He personally favoured the disfranchisement of venal boroughs, the redistribution of 20 seats to large unrepresented towns, the opening of all close and corporation boroughs to the inhabitant householders, the removal of half the placemen from the Commons and triennial parliaments. He supported the resulting

petition in the Commons, 17 Apr. 1821.[6] He presented similar petitions from Tavistock and elsewhere in Devon, 6, 14 Mar., 22, 25 Apr., and expressed satisfaction with 'the diffusion of a liberal feeling throughout the country upon the subject', 9 May 1822.[7] Later that month at the Westminster election anniversary dinner he proposed the toast to the Member John Cam Hobhouse and prefaced his remarks 'with a handsome encomium, owning he had opposed me in [1819], had been in error and would never be in error again'.[8] He presided at the county meeting on reform, 11 Apr. 1823, and argued, with reference to events in Spain, that reform was essential to preserve popular liberties when 'there was abroad a combination of tyrants ... for the purpose of putting down that first right of every independent state'.[9] He presented the resulting petition, 2 June 1823. He favoured applying the whole of the sinking fund to tax reductions, 1 May 1822, and complained of the 'oppressive operation' of the coal duties, 29 Mar. 1824.[10] However, he reportedly 'stayed away' from the division on Lennard's motion on diplomatic expenditure, 16 May 1822, as a matter of 'good taste' towards his old Grenvillite allies.[11] He introduced a merchant seamen's wages recovery bill, 28 Apr., which gained royal assent, 26 May 1826. At the general election that summer he was again returned unopposed for Tavistock, although some radicals put his name forward for the county without his consent in order to force a token contest.[12]

He divided for Catholic relief, 6 Mar., and warned that unless something was 'speedily done for Ireland, much evil would follow', 13 Mar. 1827. He presented several petitions from Devon Dissenters for repeal of the Test Acts, 28 May, 6, 22 June.[13] He voted against increased protection for barley, 12 Mar., and for inquiry into Leicester corporation, 15 Mar., and Tierney's motion to postpone the committee of supply, 30 Mar. In April he assured Lord Lansdowne that if he joined Canning's coalition ministry, 'I, as a very humble member of the party which looks to you as its chief, shall feel bound to give ... my cordial and zealous support', while 'reserving ... my old opinions on parliamentary reform and possibly one or two other questions of general principle on which I may differ from you'.[14] Bedford, who wanted the Whigs to maintain their independence, was concerned that Ebrington and others 'talk of giving an unqualified support to Canning, solely to keep the intolerant ultras from returning', but when Ebrington offered to vacate his seat the duke expressed confidence in the 'integrity' of his political principles.[15] He voted against government for the disfranchisement of Penryn, 28 May, and thought a 'sufficient case' had been made for the disfranchisement of East Retford, 22 June. He supported the sale of game bill, 7 June, 'because he considered it to be the first step to greater improvements'.[16] In December 1827 he wrote to his brother that Lord Goderich's ministry could not survive 'without men [of] energy and unity of purpose among them' able to withstand 'the extravagant pretensions and personal slights ... from the king'. He was glad that Lansdowne had done 'one good service for the country by the dismissal of the yeomanry, which looks like an earnest of more constitutional feeling than we have seen for some time'.[17] He presented more petitions for repeal of the Test Acts, 21 Feb., and voted in this sense, 26 Feb. 1828. He divided for Catholic claims, 12 May, but concluded that the duke of Wellington's ministry had 'no intention' of acting, 12 June; he looked for ultimate success to 'the growing spirit of liberality ... within these walls' and to 'the union ... perseverance and ... power of the Catholics'. He voted for inquiry into the Irish church, 24 June. He divided against extending East Retford's franchise to Bassetlaw freeholders, 21 Mar., and to disqualify certain East Retford voters, 24 June, and argued that the seats should be given to a large manufacturing town, 27 June. He presented an inhabitants' petition against the Dartmouth harbour bill, 'as barefaced a corporation job as ever came under the notice of Parliament', 24 Mar. He voted to condemn delays in chancery, 24 Apr., and the misapplication of public money for building work at Buckingham House, 23 June. He divided against the small notes (Ireland and Scotland) bill, 16 June, and argued that 'by requiring security from the country bankers, we might have all the advantages of a paper currency without any of its dangers'. He voted for the usury laws amendment bill, 19 June. In October he applied to join the Catholic Association, explaining that while he had initially disapproved of its formation, and though his 'political opinions still differ in many respects from those ... expressed by some of its members', when he saw 'the British government and the Irish people' being 'menaced' by the Brunswick Clubs, he believed it was essential for 'the friends of religious liberty' to unite.[18] According to Lord John Russell*, Ebrington maintained in December 1828 that 'he should vote against any bill that disfranchised the 40s. freeholders, whatever else it might contain'.[19] It was said of him at this time that his 'spirits are much mended', after the death of his wife the previous year, and that 'he now mixes cheerfully in society, but there is still in him ... a morbid disposition to nourish sorrow'.[20]

Ebrington attended the county meeting on the Catholic question, 16 Jan. 1829, when he warned, as one who 'had a deep stake in both countries', that 'unless they contemplated the separation of Ireland from this country they must emancipate the Catholics'. He denied that emancipation would endanger the established church but argued that a reform of Irish tithes was needed.[21] He criticized the conduct of the meeting and the way signatures to the resulting anti-Catholic petition were obtained, 24 Feb., and claimed that a counter-petition showed that 'the property and respectability of the county are balanced upon the question'. Earlier that month, when it became clear that ministers intended to take action, he privately advised Daniel O'Connelb to dissolve the Association.[22] He offered his 'warm applause' to the government and praised the Association for helping to 'preserve peace and tranquillity in Ireland', by encouraging respect for the law, 19 Feb.; he duly voted for emancipation, 6, 30 Mar. He sponsored O'Connell's unsuccessful attempt to take his seat, 15 May,[23] and divided against the motion that he had to swear the oath of supremacy, 18 May. He voted to transfer East Retford's seats to Birmingham, 5 May, and for Lord Blandford's reform resolutions, 2 June. He divided against the additional grant for the sculpture of the marble arch, 25 May 1829. He voted for Blandford's reform plan, 18 Feb., the enfranchisement of Birmingham, Leeds and Manchester, 23 Feb., transfer of East Retford's seats to Birmingham, 5 Mar., O'Connell's secret ballot amendment to the East Retford disfranchisement bill, 15 Mar., and Russell's reform motion, 28 May 1830. He joined in the revived opposition campaign that session for economy and retrenchment. He divided for information regarding British interference in the affairs of Portugal, 10 Mar. He praised the 'temperate and very proper language' used in the Devon petition for tithes reform and believed that a settlement would be beneficial 'both to the clergy and to the agriculturists', 11 May. He voted that day to abolish the Irish lord lieutenancy. He presented a Tavistock petition for abolition of the death penalty for forgery, 13 May, and voted in this sense, 24 May, 7 June. He divided for Jewish emancipation, 17 May. He voted for Labouchere's motion on the civil government of Canada, 25 May, and reform of the divorce laws, 3 June 1830. At the end of the session a 'very large meeting' of opposition Members took place at Ebrington's house, where arrangements were made to act together in future under Lord Althorp's leadership.[24] Shortly before the dissolution that summer Ebrington offered to retire from Tavistock in order to avoid a possible conflict of opinion with his patron, as he felt that unless Wellington strengthened his cabinet 'I may eventually in the course of next session be driven into more decided opposition ... than I have been hitherto'. Although Bedford again returned him, he had already accepted a requisition to stand for the county and was returned at the head of the poll with Acland, ousting Bastard, in what he described as a 'battle of independence' which had 'taught a lesson to the bigoted and corrupt'.[25]

In his speech at a celebration dinner in August 1830, Ebrington acknowledged that 'the cause of religious liberty is indebted' to Wellington's government and that 'in consequence of such principles being acted upon ... I have been able, and hope still to be able, to give it my support'. He wished to see men of ability 'called into the high offices of state without regard to party', and a 'first step' taken towards 'that reform which is so necessary to the stability and welfare of the kingdom'. These comments caused some surprise to his Whig colleagues, and in a letter to Brougham he explained his meaning:

> That though I had seen much to condemn I had also seen much to approve in the measures of the present government, and that in various instances when I had opposed them I thought the fault was more in their incapacity than their ill intentions. That whilst the glorious events in France and the impression this had made throughout England must show them the necessity of adopting a more liberal system of foreign policy, I hoped that the accession of a new king quite free from all personal prejudices and petty jealousies would by enabling the duke ... and Mr. Peel to strengthen their government with abler and better colleagues ... afford me the satisfaction of giving them a more frequent support than that done hitherto. This I consider a fair exposé of the line of conduct which in conjunction with Althorp and others I pursued during the last session.[26]

Ministers listed him in September among their 'foes', but Russell was still encouraging him next month to move an address to the crown calling for their reinforcement.[27] He voted against them in the crucial civil list division, 15 Nov. It appears that he was 'not considered for office' in Lord Grey's ministry.[28] He presented numerous anti-slavery petitions in November 1830. He regretted the recent coercive measures introduced in Ireland, 11 Feb. 1831, but accepted that the state of the country made them 'absolutely requisite'. He warned that repeal of the Union would 'inevitably lead to a complete separation of the two countries', the 'ruin of Ireland' and the ultimate 'destruction of the British empire'. That day he presented petitions in favour of tithes reform and, 'as a sincere friend to the church', he urged the clergy to offer a speedy commutation, observing that in Devon there was 'such a degree of ferment on the subject as to occasion me

considerable alarm'. He presented a petition from the county reform meeting, 16 Feb., which he claimed would have received more signatures had it included the demand for the ballot, and similar ones from towns in Devon, 9, 11, 26, 28 Feb. On 2 Mar. he praised the government for its 'great and comprehensive, and safe, because efficient and full' reform bill, which appealed to 'the wealth, respectability and intelligence of the great body of the middle classes of England'. Speaking as one who was 'connected ... with the aristocratical parts of the constitution', he was 'not fool enough to wish to see them overthrown', but he was confident that their interests were 'perfectly reconcilable' with those of the middle classes. He admitted that in the past he had only supported a 'moderate' redistribution of seats, but he now recognized the need for a more extensive measure to give 'due preponderance to every interest of the state' and 'stem the torrent of corruption'. He was prepared to sacrifice shorter parliaments and the ballot so as not to endanger the bill, but warned that if it failed 'the confidence of the country will be altogether withdrawn from this House'. He presented petitions in favour of the bill from various parts of Devon, 19, 22 Mar., when he divided for its second reading. He voted against Gascoyne's wrecking amendment, 19 Apr. 1831. At the ensuing general election he stood again for Devon and was returned unopposed with Russell after Acland retired. He declared that he was for 'the whole bill', with only minor amendments possible in committee, argued that 'the number of Members for England ought to be diminished' and looked forward to the time when 'the race of borough mongers shall become extinct'.[29]

He divided for the second reading of the reintroduced bill, 6 July 1831, and steadily for its details in committee. It was apparently owing to his and Edward Littleton's efforts behind the scenes that the government stood firm and a successful division was achieved on the division of counties, 11 Aug.[30] He doubted the efficacy of Hume's plan to expedite the bill's passage and acquitted Althorp of the charge of 'slackness', 27 Aug. He voted for the third reading, 19 Sept., its passage, 21 Sept., and the second reading of the Scottish bill, 23 Sept. It was at this point that he emerged as a leading figure among the Whig backbenchers, although it is not clear to what extent he was acting on his own initiative, being put up to it by Thomas Macaulay (as the latter claimed),[31] or being manipulated by ministers. He, Littleton, Sir Francis Lawley and Edward Portman issued circulars summoning government supporters to a meeting at his house, 21 Sept., to consider what steps should be taken in the event in the bill's rejection by the Lords.

No specific decision was reached, but it was agreed that ministers should be persuaded not to resign; according to a Tory source Ebrington and Hume had wanted Members to pledge their support to the government 'through thick and thin, making it a condition that they should create peers'.[32] He was present at the county meeting to petition the Lords for the bill's speedy passage, 30 Sept., when he expressed the hope that William IV would if necessary 'exercise his prerogative for the benefit of the people' and declared that 'temper and perseverance must conquer'. However, shortly before the Lords' rejection of the bill on 8 Oct., Hobhouse found him to be 'somewhat fearful of popular tumult'.[33] That evening 'about 200' Members met 'under the auspices of Ebrington' at Willis's Rooms, where it was agreed to support his resolutions on the 10th proclaiming their 'firm adherence' to the bill and confidence in ministers.[34] In the ensuing debate he adopted a 'very moderate' tone and one Whig Member judged it to be a 'not very striking speech'. He called on the House to redeem its pledge to the country to 'support the cause of reform', and observed that the accession of Grey's ministry had helped to 'restore peace to the country' and 'allay the discontent of the middle classes'. He also praised the government for its tax reductions, reform of the game laws, chancery reforms and pacific foreign policy. Advising the people to remain orderly, the Commons consistent and ministers firm, he was confident that the reform bill would 'consolidate all the blessings which the British constitution can bestow upon a happy and united people'. The resolutions were carried by 329-198, which was regarded as 'a most opportune triumph' that had 'brought the ministry out from their defeat with flying colours'.[35] He thought it would be 'unjust to clog' Queen Adelaide's dower bill with conditions, in view of its connection with 'an illustrious personage to whom we owe so much gratitude', 22 July. He maintained that there was 'no ground whatsoever for tracing the distress in Ireland to the legislative Union', 16 Aug. He voted to punish only those guilty of bribery at the Dublin election and against the censure motion on the Irish administration, 23 Aug. He said that though 'a conscientious Protestant', he had always supported the Maynooth grant as 'affording to my Catholic fellow subjects a participation in the constitutional rights and privileges which I ... enjoy', 26 Sept. 1831.

Prior to the introduction of the revised reform bill Ebrington was in communication with Althorp, who promised to keep him informed of 'any changes we may make'.[36] He congratulated ministers on their 'equally as effectual, equally as desirable' measure, 12 Dec. 1831. At a cabinet dinner, 14 Dec., Althorp read a letter from him containing suggestions as to how the Irish representation might be increased and indicating that he 'felt it his duty to move' in the matter, but hoping that such a motion would 'in his hands ... be less injurious to the ministry than if taken up by a Member less disposed to consult their interests'.[37] He divided for the second reading of the English bill, 17 Dec. 1831, and steadily for its details. He advised Althorp to use Saturday sittings to overcome 'unnecessary obstructions' to the bill's progress, 2 Feb. 1832, and in an angry scene he repudiated Hardinge's insinuation that he was 'the organ of the mob'.[38] He admitted that a large creation of peers was 'a dangerous proceeding ... [which] I would much rather see avoided', 10 Feb., but considered the bill's defeat to be 'an evil of much greater magnitude'. It appears that during February he acted as an intermediary between Grey and the leader of the Tory 'Waverers', Lord Harrowby, his former father-in-law.[39] At the end of the month, according to Littleton, 'Ebrington and I pledged ourselves to ... die on the benches of the ... Commons sooner than allow town influence to be shut out of county elections'.[40] He divided for the bill's third reading, 22 Mar. It was rumoured the following month that he was on the ministerial list of proposed new peers.[41] On 9 May, when it became known that the ministry had resigned, Ebrington gave notice of a call of the House for next day, and that evening some 180 Members met at Brooks's to decide on the terms of his motion. He was reportedly pessimistic about the result of the impending division, fearing that 'the nominal friends of the ministry ... [were] more numerous than the real ones, and he was apprehensive of their falling away in the hour of trial'.[42] One Whig backbencher had 'never [seen] the House so excited and tumultuous' as it was on 10 May, and Ebrington, in the opinion of Denis Le Marchant, 'spoke better than I ever heard him'.[43] He argued that in a 'crisis so momentous' the House must leave the king in no doubt as to its feelings, and he denied that there had been any reaction in public opinion. The address, which was drawn up in 'far less strong' language than he personally would have used, implored the king to 'call to his councils only such persons as will carry into effect, unimpaired in all its essential provisions, that bill which has already passed this House'. It was carried by 288-208, a much smaller majority than had been achieved the previous October, which probably reflected the reluctance of some Whig Members to countenance the creation of peers, but it served an important purpose in helping to consolidate backbench resistance to the formation of an alternative government.[44] Amidst rumours that

Wellington was about to construct an administration and bring in his own reform measure, there was a meeting of Whig supporters at Brooks's, 13 May, when Ebrington advocated uncompromising opposition to '*any* bill the new ministers might propose'. He was reportedly dissatisfied with the decision to follow the more cautious line recommended by Althorp and Smith Stanley, and 'persisted in the intention of combining with Hume to bring the House to some very strong resolution condemnatory of the duke'. On 14 May he was 'loudly cheered' when he declared that it would be 'political immorality' for the Conservatives to support a bill sponsored by Wellington, and that if it was introduced he would feel free to press for other reforms which he had given up for the sake of the original bill.[45] Three days later he welcomed the reinstatement of Grey's ministry, which he hoped would allay 'the fearful alarm and excitement which prevailed' in the country, but it appears that he and Lord Milton would have moved an address to the crown had it not been made known that peers would be created if necessary.[46] He divided for the second reading of the Irish bill, 25 May, and paired against increased representation for Scotland, 1 June 1832.

He divided with ministers on the Russian-Dutch loan, 26 Jan., 12, 16, 20 July 1832. He was among a group of backbenchers which met the foreign secretary, Lord Palmerston, to hear his statement regarding Belgium, 5 Feb. Next day the chancellor of the duchy of Lancaster, Lord Holland, noted that Ebrington 'expressed his conviction that our friends in the Commons lamented their squeamishness about Russian loan, were anxious to retrieve the false step they had made, and disposed to uphold our Belgian negotiation and treaty and our union with France in a high tone'.[47] He spoke and voted in defence of Palmerston's conduct towards Portugal, 9 Feb., observing that Wellington's government had been guilty of 'something more than neglect of the interest of British subjects'. In presenting a petition from Poles resident in London condemning Russia's oppression of their country, 28 June, he warned that if Russia were 'allowed to pursue her career of restless ambition without remonstrance or opposition' there would be no 'permanent peace' in Europe. He criticized the Treaty of Vienna for 'trampling on the rights of ... smaller states', and trusted that 'should we unfortunately be obliged to draw the sword' against Russia it would be in alliance with France, 'on the side of free principles and free institutions'. He said he was unwilling to support coercive measures to enforce the payment of Irish tithes unless 'accompanied by some definitive arrangement' acceptable to the Irish people,

8 Feb.; he was apparently satisfied with Althorp's subsequent statement.[48] He described the position of the Irish church as 'pregnant with injury to the cause of religion', 8 Mar., and wished to see it reduced 'to a condition better proportioned to the wants of the Protestant inhabitants'. In July he was reportedly 'disgusted' with the behaviour of Irish Members, who were threatening to oppose the government unless they obtained a radical measure against the Irish church.[49] He promised his 'cordial and unqualified support' for Smith Stanley's tithes composition bill, 13 July, warning that if the present 'combination' against the payment of tithes succeeded an agitation against rents for absentee landlords would follow. It was necessary to 'bring back the lower classes from the gross delusion under which they labour', and he would endorse 'such measures as may be necessary to preserve ... the first principles of liberty, and the very foundations of the rights of property and of social order'. He repeated his call for reform of the Irish church and favoured the lay appropriation of surplus revenues, as 'I consider that the church was established for the benefit of the state and ... all its property is liable to be regulated by Parliament'. He presented a Devon petition against the government's plan for national education in Ireland, 11 May, but expressed his support for it and hoped to see the Irish people 'living together in charity and brotherly love, showing the fruits of a Christian, a moral and a literary education'. He voted with ministers on military punishments, 16 Feb., and the navy civil departments bill, 6 Apr. He urged Warburton to persevere with his anatomy bill, 11 Apr. He was named to the committee of secrecy on the Bank of England's charter, 22 May. He presented a ratepayers' petition against the Exeter improvement bill, 13 June 1832, but his amendment in favour of a wider franchise was defeated by 72-46.

At the general election of 1832 Ebrington was returned unopposed for North Devon as an advocate of 'Whig principles'.[50] In the first reformed Parliament he was 'the leading Whig backbencher in the Commons', being 'reckoned to control over 100 votes', and he was able to put pressure on Grey's ministry over such issues as Irish church reform, the reduction of sinecures and the abolition of slavery.[51] He sat until he was raised to the peerage in 1839, shortly before his appointment as lord lieutenant of Ireland. He succeeded to his father's title and estates in 1841.[52] He died in September 1861 and was succeeded by his eldest son Hugh Fortescue (1818-1905), Liberal Member for Plymouth, 1841-52, and Marylebone, 1854-9.

[1] B. Hilton, *Age of Atonement*, 238-9; J.J. Sack, *The Grenvillites*, 166, 173-4; E.A. Wasson, *Whig Renaissance*, 47; R. Brent, *Liberal Anglican Politics*, 38-39. [2] *Trewman's Exeter Flying Post*, 17 Feb., 16, 23 Mar., 18 May 1820. [3] Add. 51571, Ebrington to Lady Holland, 29 Nov. 1820, 25 Sept. 1821. [4] *Alfred*, 20 Mar. 1821. [5] Add. 51571, Ebrington to Holland, 16 Jan. 1825. [6] *Alfred*, 10, 24 Apr. 1821. [7] *The Times*, 7, 15 Mar., 23 Apr., 10 May 1822. [8] Add. 56545, f. 7. [9] *Alfred*, 18 Mar., 15 Apr. 1823. [10] *The Times*, 30 Mar. 1824. [11] Buckingham, *Mems. Geo. IV*, i. 325, 328-9. [12] *Trewman's Exeter Flying Post*, 15, 22 June 1826. [13] *The Times*, 29 May, 7, 23 June 1827. [14] Lansdowne mss, Ebrington to Lansdowne, 27 Apr. 1827. [15] LMA, Jersey mss 510/412, Bedford to Lady Jersey, 22 Apr.; Devon RO, Earl Fortescue mss 1262M/FC 83, Ebrington to Bedford, 8, 12 May, Bedford to Ebrington, 10 May 1827. [16] *The Times*, 8 June 1827. [17] Add. 69364, Ebrington to G. Fortescue, 12 Dec. 1827. [18] Earl Fortescue mss FC 84, Ebrington to Catholic Association, 12 Oct. 1828. [19] Brougham mss, Russell to Brougham, 15 Dec. 1828. [20] NLW ms 2796 D, Lady Williams Wynn to H.W. Wynn, 17 Dec. 1828. [21] *Woolmer's Exeter and Plymouth Gazette*, 17 Jan. 1829. [22] *Greville Mems.* i. 255. [23] D. Howell-Thomas, *Duncannon*, 139. [24] Earl Fortescue mss FC 86, Althorp to Ebrington, 29 Aug. 1830. [25] Ibid. Ebrington to Bedford, 6 July, reply, 7 July; *Western Times*, 24 July, 7-21 Aug. 1830. [26] *Western Times*, 21 Aug.; Brougham mss, Ebrington to Brougham, 25 Aug. 1830. [27] Earl Fortescue mss FC 86, Russell to Ebrington, 20 Oct. 1830. [28] P. Mandler, *Aristocratic Government in Age of Reform*, 126. [29] *Trewman's Exeter Flying Post*, 28 Apr., 12 May 1831. [30] Hatherton diary, 25 July, 11 Aug. 1831. [31] *Macaulay Letters*, ii. 100-1, 106. [32] Hatherton diary, 26 Sept. 1831; *Greville Mems.* ii. 201, 203; *Three Diaries*, 133. [33] Besley's *Devon Chron.* 1 Oct. 1831; Broughton, *Recollections*, i. 135-6. [34] *Greville Mems.* ii. 205-6; Cornw. RO, Hawkins mss 10/2171. [35] Broughton, iv. 138; Hawkins mss 10/2171. [36] Earl Fortescue mss FC 87, Althorp to Ebrington, 3 Nov. 1831. [37] *Holland House Diaries*, 93-94. [38] Hatherton diary, 2 Feb.; Add. 69364, Sneyd to G. Fortescue, 22 Feb. 1832. [39] *Greville Mems.* ii. 264-5. [40] Hatherton diary, 29 Feb. 1832. [41] *Greville Mems.* ii. 283. [42] M. Brock, *Great Reform Act*, 292-4; *Three Diaries*, 246. [43] Northants. RO, Agar Ellis diary, 10 May 1832; *Three Diaries*, 247. [44] *Greville Mems.* ii. 295; Brock, 292-4. [45] Brock, 299-301; *Three Diaries*, 251-4; Broughton, iv. 224. [46] Wasson, 243-4. [47] Hatherton diary, 5 Feb. 1832; *Holland House Diaries*, 125. [48] *Holland House Diaries*, 130. [49] Ibid. 197. [50] *Dod's Parl. Companion* (1833), 108. [51] Wasson, 189; Brent, 73-75; Mandler, 152; I. Newbould, *Whiggery and Reform*, 86-88. [52] The personalty was sworn under £70,000 (PROB 8/234; 11/1952/673).

T.A.J.

FOSTER, James (1786–1853), of Coton Hall, nr. Stourbridge, Worcs.[1]

BRIDGNORTH   1831–1832

bap. 11 May 1786, 3rd. s. of Henry Foster, ironmaster, of Stourbridge and Mary (*née* Haden), wid. of Gabriel Bradley, ironmaster, of Stourbridge. *unm. d.* 12 Apr. 1853.

Sheriff, Worcs. 1840-1

Foster was the youngest of seven children born to Henry Foster, an ironmaster of Cheshire yeoman stock, whose wife had inherited iron works and substantial property in Stourbridge on the death in 1771 of her first husband, a Quaker by descent, related to the Darbys of Coalbrookdale. Henry Foster died in 1793 worth an estimated £2,500, having entrusted

his property, tools, stock and articles of trade to his brothers James, William and Thomas, of Nantwich, Cheshire, directing them to pay his wife (*d.* 1813) £10 immediately and £45 a year, and to ensure that his children inherited in equal shares. He left his stepson, the ironmaster John Bradley (1769-1816), who is credited with bringing up his stepbrothers in the trade, £400, provided he relinquished all claim to his estate.[2] Their family partnership, John Bradley and Company of Stourbridge, which traded until 1982, flourished during the Napoleonic wars, and in 1802, when it was worth £8,000, Bradley held a one-third share, the Wellington wine merchant Thomas Jukes Collier another third, and the remainder was held equally by the six surviving Foster children. Bradley and James Foster, who also invested jointly in enterprises at Eardington and Hampton Loade, near Bridgnorth, had by 1813 bought out Collier and their siblings. Foster's technical treatise on iron production and a second partnership with Collier, who financed the development of John Wilkinson's former works at New Hadley, also date from 1813.[3] The Stourbridge firm, over which Foster assumed sole control on Bradley's death, and which Bradley's heir Henry Bradley joined, 1826-37, remained Foster's largest enterprise, and during his 12-year partnership with the engineer John Urpeth Rastrick, 1819-31, a railway and locomotives, including the *Agenoria* and *Stourbridge Lion*, were built at the works. Foster added mines, quarries and the Chillington works near Wolverhampton to his holdings, and by 1830 he was a leading figure at iron traders' quarterly meetings in Birmingham, Shropshire and the Black Country.[4] A pro-reform Whig opposed to monopolies and trade restrictions, he had supported Edward Littleton* in Staffordshire in 1820, and from 1826 he backed the political economist William Wolryche Whitmore* at Bridgnorth, where he became a freeman.[5]

Amid growing concern at the impotence of the ironmasters' lobby during the 1830 depression, Foster was requisitioned to stand for Wenlock at the general election that summer 'by members of the iron trade, and others ... convinced of the necessity of having some gentleman immediately connected with the manufacturing interests of this neighbourhood returned to represent them in Parliament'; a committee established in his interest in Wolverhampton raised £293.[6] He desisted in order to muster support for Wolryche Whitmore at Bridgnorth from the East India Association nationally, the Staffordshire and Shropshire iron trades and the manufacturing and commercial interests of Birmingham, Kidderminster, Wolverhampton and Stourbridge.[7] Seconding

Whitmore's nomination, Foster, who was heckled with cries of 'Tommy shops', said that the notion of separate landed and agricultural interests was 'absurd', and he endorsed his candidate's campaign against the East India Company and the Bank's monopolies and his support for retrenchment and lower 'public taxes'.[8] Trade remained depressed when Foster, who then employed some 3,000 men, addressed the 16 Mar. 1831 Dudley meeting of proprietors and occupiers of iron works and coal mines which petitioned for the Grey ministry's reform bill, and he supported similar petitions from Bridgnorth, Brierley Hill and Stourbridge.[9] At the general election precipitated by the bill's defeat, he came in unopposed with Wolryche Whitmore for Bridgnorth, where the Tory patron and Member Thomas Whitmore backed down and the absentee Catholic baronet Sir Ferdinand Richard Acton of Aldenham gave way to him.[10] He pledged to vote for the bill, and was fêted on his return to Stourbridge.[11] Shortly afterwards he paid the ironmaster Alexander Brodie's widow £1,300 for the Calcutts estate near Wenlock, which he later worked with neighbouring Madeley Court, purchased from the Whitmores for £1,200 in December 1827.[12]

Foster stayed at Batt's Hotel when in London on commercial or parliamentary business, attended the House rarely, made no known speeches and voted consistently for reform. He divided for the reintroduced bill at its second reading, 6 July, and against making the 1831 census the determinant for borough disfranchisements, 19 July 1831. He was one of the ironmasters delegated to present 'their complaint of the state of their trade' to Lord Grey, 21 July, of whom Littleton wrote: 'they took nothing by their motion of course. I was quite ashamed of taking them, and told Lord Grey so'.[13] Foster does not appear to have voted personally during the reform bill's committee stage, but he paired for its provisions for St. Germans, 26 July, Dorchester, 28 July, and Greenwich, 3 Aug., and against giving town and city freeholders voting rights in counties corporate, 17 Aug. He divided for the bill's passage, 21 Sept., the second reading of the Scottish measure, 23 Sept., and Lord Ebrington's confidence motion, 10 Oct. Industrial unrest prevented him from attending and voting for the second reading of the revised bill, 17 Dec. 1831,[14] but he divided for the schedule A, 20 Jan., and schedule B, 23 Jan., disfranchisements and paired for the enfranchisement of Tower Hamlets, 28 Feb. 1832. Writing to Whitmore's brother-in-law, the inventor Charles Babbage, 17 Feb., he remarked:

> The distresses in our trade from low prices have compelled me to get my head to work again, and I am going this summer to have my hands tied very full in the erection and contrivance of some additional machinery to economize the expenses of manufacturing iron, for unless that can be done, at present prices (with the determination of ministers not to alter the present currency laws) we ironmasters must all go into the *Gazette* [be bankrupted] together.[15]

He voted for the bill's third reading, 22 Mar., but was 'absent in the country' when the address requesting the king to appoint only ministers who would carry it unimpaired was adopted, 10 May. He divided with government on the Russian-Dutch loan, 12 July 1832. That summer, he patented a process he had developed at Chillington for transferring molten iron directly from the blast furnace to the puddling furnaces.[16]

Foster, who was reputedly brusque in manner and increasingly afflicted by deafness, did not stand for Parliament again, but he remained an active lobbyist for his trade, and from 1834 he was chairman of the Stourbridge and Kidderminster Bank, which became part of the Midland Group.[17] He died childless in April 1853 at Stourton Castle, near Stourbridge, which he had bought for £10,000 in 1833, and was buried with great pomp at Old Swinford.[18] His will, dated 19 Dec. 1849, was proved under £700,000 in London, £20,000 in York, and £14,000 in Dublin. He left his nephew and man of business William Orme Foster[†] (1814-99) iron works and mines valued at £153,000, and land and property worth an estimated £133,650 in Shropshire, Staffordshire, Worcestershire and Ireland, and provided for his unmarried sister Mary, who resided with him, John Bradley's daughters and other nieces and nephews. In 1867 Orme Foster, who was worth £2,588,000 at probate, 29 Sept. 1899, bought Thomas Whitmore's former estate of Apley Park. Foster's grandson William Henry Foster (1846-1924) represented nearby Bridgnorth as a Liberal, 1870-80, and as a Conservative, 1880-85.[19]

[1] Based unless otherwise stated on *Dict. of Business Biog.* (W.O. Foster) and N. Mutton, 'The Foster Family: A Study of a Midland Industrial Dynasty, 1786-1899' (London Univ. Ph.D. thesis, 1974). [2] PROB 11/798/206; 1604/228. [3] B. Trinder, *Industrial Revolution in Salop* (1981), 144. [4] London Univ. Lib. mss AL430/106; W.K.V. Gale, *Black Country Iron Industry*, 45, 70; Trinder, 143-4, 154; *VCH Salop*, xi. 292-5; N. Mutton, 'Forges at Eardington and Hampton Loade', *Trans. Salop Arch. Soc.* lviii (1965-8), 235-43. [5] *Wolverhampton Chron.* 1 Mar. 1820, 14 June 1826, 3 Oct. 1827; *The Times*, 9 Oct. 1826; Salop Archives, Bridgnorth Borough 4001/Admin/3/6, common hall bk. pp. 207-8. [6] *Wolverhampton Chron.* 20 Jan. 1830; London Univ. Lib. (Pprs. of John Bradley and Co.) mss 798/12/2 and *passim.*; Wolverhampton Archives DX/84/29. See WENLOCK. [7] *Wolverhampton Chron.* 14 July, 4, 11 Aug. 1830; Bridgnorth Borough 7/50, handbills; Add. 37185, f. 289. See BRIDGNORTH. [8] *Shrewsbury Chron.* 6 Aug. 1830. [9] London Univ. Lib. mss 798 23/2; *Wolverhampton Chron.* 23 Mar., 6 Apr.

1831. [10]*Shrewsbury Chron.* 22, 29 Apr., 6 May; *Salopian Jnl.* 11 May 1831; Bridgnorth common hall bk. pp. 401-3. [11] *Wolverhampton Chron.* 11 May 1831. [12]Salop RO 1649 [Alderman Jones's diaries], 10 July 1831; Apley estate recs. (NRA 11576); *VCH Salop*, xi. 38, 51-53, 62. [13]Hatherton diary, 21 July 1831. [14]J. Randall, *Severn Valley* (1862), 150-1; Trinder, 233-5. [15]Add. 37186, f. 254. [16]Reg. Patents (1832), no. 6300. [17]Add. 40351, f. 201; S. Griffiths, *Account of the Iron Trade* (1873). [18]*Berrow's Worcester Jnl.* 14, 21 Apr.; *Gent. Mag.* (1853), i. 673. [19]PROB 11/2172; IR26/1863/298; R.H. Trainor, *Black Country Elites*, 69, 128, 203.

M.M.E.

FOSTER, John (1740–1828), of Collon, co. Louth.[1]

CO. LOUTH   1801–17 July 1821

bap. 28 Sept. 1740, 1st s. of Anthony Foster, MP [I], of Collon, c. bar. exch. [I], and 1st w. Elizabeth, da. of William Burgh, MP [I], of Dublin. *educ.* by Rev. Dr. Richard Norris, Drogheda g.s.; Trinity, Dublin 1757; M. Temple 1759, called [I] 1766; bencher, King's Inns, Dublin 1784. *m.* 14 Dec. 1764, his cos. Margaretta, da. of Thomas Burgh, MP [I], of Bert, co. Kildare (she was cr. Baroness Oriel [I] 5 June 1790 and Viscountess Ferrard [I] 22 Nov. 1797), 5s. (4 *d.v.p.*) 1da. *suc.* fa. 1779; *cr.* Bar. Oriel [UK] 17 July 1821. *d.* 23 Aug. 1828.

MP [I] 1761-1800.

Chairman of ways and means [I] 1777-84; customer of Dublin 1779-84; PC [I] 9 July 1779, [GB] 6 Sept. 1786; chan. of exch. [I] Apr. 1784-Sept. 1785, July 1804-Feb. 1806, May 1807-July 1811; Speaker of House of Commons [I] 5 Sept. 1785-2 Aug. 1800; member, bd. of trade 1785-1800, Feb. 1802; first commr. of treasury [I] 1804-6, second commr. 1807-13, [UK] Sept. 1807-Jan. 1812; commr. of public recs. [I] 1810.

Trustee, linen board [I] 1784; vice-pres. bd. of agriculture 1803.

Custos rot. co. Louth 1798-1801, gov. 1798-*d.*

Capt. Collon inf. 1796.

Foster, who had sat undisturbed for Louth since the Union, had long aspired to a United Kingdom peerage as the last Speaker of the Irish Commons. After his unopposed return on his family interest at the 1820 general election Lord Camden advised him to apply again, explaining that as he had previously 'requested an audience of the prince regent, in which you laid before him your old claim and your anxious wishes, you would naturally repeat that request now that he is king'.[2] Foster accordingly notified Lords Liverpool, the premier, and Castlereagh*, the foreign secretary, of his renewed application and wrote to the king, 9 Apr. 1820

to express his humble hope that ... he may receive ... that accustomed and permanent mark of the approbation of the crown, which so many of his predecessors in the chair have received by an hereditary seat in the Upper House

... its having been the usual practice of the sovereigns of Great Britain to create new peerages on their accession ... Mr. Foster is now very near his eightieth year and hopes that this circumstance may excuse his anxiety.[3]

Assuring Foster that 'the mode of application has not been detrimental', 7 May 1820, Camden urged him to come to England to press his claims further.[4] Foster's son was also for 'pushing the matter' and against 'abandoning it', and complained 'that with the tenor of Lord Liverpool's letter before you no man in the kingdom has been so ill treated by the administration as you have'.[5]

Foster was named to the select committees on agricultural distress, 31 May 1820, 19 Mar. 1821. He called for repeal of the Union duties and the 'total removal of all obstacles to the commercial intercourse between England and Ireland', 8 June 1820. He spoke in support of a grant to prevent a run on the Irish banks, saying the 'necessity of an immediate remedy was obvious for the fact that eight banks had failed in the south-west of Ireland', 16 June. He condemned a move to prevent Irish masters in chancery from sitting in Parliament as an 'attempt to defeat the wishes, and to interfere with the franchises of the people of Dublin', who had returned Thomas Ellis, 30 June. That day he argued that 'it would be ingratitude to take away the bounties on linen from Ireland'. On 6 July he denied what had been had 'imputed to him' by William Smith, Whig Member for Norwich, insisting that he 'never could have been guilty of the absurdity of asserting' that the English Parliament 'could not legislate for the whole of the empire' and warning of the danger of 'setting the manufactures of one part of the country against those of another part, as if they had separate interests'. He seconded a motion for a grant to repair Banff and Peterhead harbours, 12 July 1820.[6] On 8 Jan. 1821 he organized a 'most numerous and highly respectable' county meeting at Drogheda to address the king and denounce the 'desperate attempts made in Great Britain to alienate the affections of the people from the constitution'.[7] He apparently did not vote on the Queen Caroline affair, 6 Feb., or Catholic relief, 28 Feb. He seconded a successful amendment for a select committee on the Newington vestry bill, 21 Mar., and secured returns of country bank notes, 28 Mar.[8] In his last known action in the House, he voted against repeal of the additional malt duty, 3 Apr. 1821.[9] He was one of George IV's coronation peers, for which Camden took much of the credit, although Castlereagh, whom he duly thanked, was also instrumental.[10]

Foster was described as 'the best gentleman-manager of nursery grounds, plantations, and woods' by the agricultural writer and Member for Cumberland, John Curwen. He 'entirely built' the 'remarkably neat village' of Collon, and 'in spite of the sterility of the soil', its 'elevated situation' and 'its uninterrupted exposure to the winds of the sea', his plantations there grew 'very luxuriantly'.[11] However, his 'relish for improving' and 'magnificent' style of living 'embarrassed his fortunes'. He died in August 1828, after a steady decline in his health.[12] He was succeeded by his only surviving son Thomas Henry Skeffington, who had replaced him as Member for Louth, 1821-24.

[1] See A. Malcomson, *John Foster*. [2] PRO NI, Foster mss D562/336, Camden to Foster, 2 Apr. 1820. [3] Ibid.; Add. 38284, f. 76. [4] Foster mss 336. [5] PRO NI, Chilham (Foster) mss T2519/4/1719, T. Skeffington to Foster, 11 June 1820. [6] *The Times*, 13 July 1820. [7] *Belfast Commercial Chron.* 17 Jan. 1821; Malcomson, 229. [8] *The Times*, 22 Mar., 29 Mar. 1821. [9] Malcomson, 350. [10] Foster mss 336, Camden to Foster, 6 July, reply, 9 July 1821. [11] J.C. Curwen, *Observations on the State of Ireland* (1818), ii. 292, 295-6. [12] *Gent. Mag.* (1828), i. 271, 290; Wellington mss WP1/949/18.

P.J.S.

FOSTER, John Leslie (?1781–1842), of Rathescar, co. Louth; 13 Merion Square, Dublin, and 107 Pall Mall, Mdx.

DUBLIN UNIVERSITY	1807–1812
YARMOUTH I.O.W.	4 Mar. 1816–1818
ARMAGH	1818–1820
CO. LOUTH	21 Feb. 1824–1830

b. ?1781, 1st. s. of Rt. Rev. William Foster, bp. of Clogher, and Catherine, da. of Rev. Henry Leslie, LLD, of Ballibay, co. Monaghan. *educ.* Trinity, Dublin 1 Mar. 1797, aged 16; St. John's, Camb. 1801; L. Inn 1800, called [I] 1803; to France 1802. *m.* 19 Aug. 1814, Letitia, da. of James Fitzgerald† of Inchicronan, co. Clare, 6s. 1da. *suc.* fa. 1797. *d.* 10 July 1842. Commr. bd. of education [I] 1813, 1824, inquiry into fees of law courts [I] 1814-18, fisheries [I] 1819; king's adv.-gen. ct. of admiralty [I] 1816; KC [I] 1816; second counsel to commrs. of revenue [I] 1818-28; counsel to commrs. of customs and port duties [I] 1819; bencher, King's Inns 1819; bar. of ct. of exch. [I] 1830; j.c.p. [I] 1841.
FRS 1819.

Foster, nephew and quondam secretary to the last Irish Speaker John Foster*, had been returned in 1818 for Lisburn, as the nominee of Lord Hertford, and also for Armagh, where he was accommodated by the Irish primate on condition with the Liverpool ministry that when his son William Stuart* came of age, he would be free to return him instead. Foster chose to represent Armagh, but at the 1820 general election was left stranded when the primate, who the former Irish secretary Peel had believed would 'never claim for his son the fulfillment of the promise', unexpectedly did so.[1] 'My retirement from the House of Commons was the result rather of accident than choice', he later reminded Peel, to whom he looked for advancement, adding, 'I have never been indisposed to return whenever circumstances should invite it'.[2] In 1822 he made a tentative pitch for the Irish solicitor-generalship, claiming that he had 'previously been thought of for the office and that it was probable that he would soon again be in Parliament', but the Irish secretary Goulburn advised Peel, now home secretary, against having both law officers in the Commons and noted that 'perhaps too Foster is not of calibre enough to be placed on the bench as a chief if a vacancy should occur, which is after all not very improbable'.[3] Backed by Stephen Rumbold Lushington*, the treasury secretary, who promised to do 'everything in my power to provide a seat for Leslie Foster', and Goulburn, who conceded that 'no man could be so well qualified to render useful assistance' on 'points of detail relative to Ireland', Peel put the case for finding him a seat to Lord Liverpool, 28 Nov. 1823, observing that 'the tithe bill must be amended, and Foster's assistance will be invaluable' and 'quite as useful on exchequer and revenue business'.[4] Liverpool concurred, telling Peel, 13 Jan. 1824, that there would 'certainly be a seat for Leslie Foster' either at Dorchester, 'if Warren vacates', or 'if not I should request Lord Galloway to return him' for Wigtown Burghs.[5] On 19 Jan., however, Foster apprized Peel of a likely opening on his family interest in county Louth, when the expected death of his aunt Lady Ferrard would elevate the sitting Member, his cousin Thomas Skeffington, to the Irish peerage.[6] As Goulburn notified Peel:

> Arrangements have long since been made for Leslie Foster's offering himself for the county and no effectual opposition is expected ... Under these circumstances Leslie Foster will not avail himself of Lord Liverpool's offer of a seat. He is however very grateful for the offer which has been made.[7]

On Skeffington's succession Foster duly came forward, citing the 'advantages Ireland would derive from the abolition of the protecting duties' and 'the improvement that the harbour of Dundalk was capable of'. He was returned unopposed.[8]

Foster was acknowledged by Sir John Wrottesley in the House to be 'undoubtedly a good authority, none better' on Irish affairs, 6 June 1828. John Denison, however, complained of his 'bold and unblushing way of stating facts, and Acts of Parliament, and authorities, with all minuteness ... while not once out of five times correct', 2 Apr. 1827. Recalling an 'incident illustrative of his influence as a legislative speaker', Richard Sheil*, in a satire for the *New Monthly Magazine* lampooning him as a 'walking encyclopedia', related:

> I was under the gallery of the House of Commons during the debate on the Catholic question in the year 1825. The House was full. Mr. Foster rose to speak, and the effect of his appearance on his legs was truly wonderful. In an instant the House was cleared. The rush to the door leading to the tavern upstairs, where the Members find a refuge from the soporific powers of their brother legislators, was tremendous ... The single phrase 'Mr. Speaker' was indeed uttered with such a tone as indicated the extent of the impending evil ... Mr. Foster takes exceedingly great if not very meritorious pains at his oratorical laboratory, and passes many a midnight vigil in compounding those opiates, with which, at the expense of his own slumbers, he lulls the House of Commons to repose.[9]

He spoke in support of compensating court officials for losses arising from the county courts bill, 26 Mar. 1824. He commended the Kildare Place Society for 'the utility of their labours' in correcting the 'misdirected education' of the Irish poor, 29 Mar., and was deemed by Liverpool to be suitable as a member of the education commission, but not 'the head', who 'must be an Englishman', 23 Apr.[10] He welcomed the commission's appointment, hoping that it would have 'an opportunity of revising the state of the schools in Ireland generally', 4 May, and was one of the members asked to resolve a dispute involving his cousin John McClintock* and the titular Catholic archbishop of Armagh, Dr. Curtis, that September.[11] Peel considered his many letters on the commission's proceedings to be 'very interesting' and came to 'entirely concur' in his belief that 'Parliament ought not to grant funds to the Roman Catholic prelacy for the separate education of Roman Catholics', given the 'impracticable' conditions which they laid down for any joint education of Catholic and Protestant children.[12] He warned that the usury laws repeal bill would 'raise the rate of interest in Ireland from six to eight or ten per cent' and have 'a most baneful effect', 8 Apr. He contradicted Hume's statements concerning the consumption of rum in Ireland, 9 Apr.[13] Denying the 'insignificance of the Protestant population of Ireland when compared with the Roman Catholics', he spoke and was a majority teller against inquiry into the Irish church, 6 May. He presented a Dundalk petition against the warehoused wheat bill, 7 May, but contended that 'in time of

dearth' it 'might be productive of the greatest advantage', 17 May.[14] He presented constituency petitions against the admission of foreign corn and from Irish attorneys complaining of their annual license duty, 11 May.[15] He warned of the 'difficulties' of extending exemption from oaths to 'separatist' sects, 13 May. He endorsed a petition from the maltsters of Wexford asking to be 'put on the same footing' with England, 17 May.[16] Giving evidence before the select committee on Irish disturbances (to which he had been appointed, 12 May), he called for measures to prevent the Irish peasantry 'multiplying on the spot where they were born, by introducing an improved mode of education among the people, by giving them superior notions of comfort, and by suggesting various lines of life in which they might better their condition by active pursuits, rather than staying inactive at home', 31 May 1824.[17]

Foster informed his sister that the foreign secretary Canning had been 'quite pleased to see him' at the opening of Parliament in February 1825, and was 'very anxious' for him to 'remain' and speak on the Catholic question, for which he was 'obliged to give up the Cavan assizes which is very vexatious'.[18] On 10 Feb. he condemned the Catholic Association for creating 'hatred on both sides', warning that it had 'awakened in one party an unfounded and artificial confidence' and in the other 'unfounded apprehensions'. He voted for the bill to suppress it, 15, 25 Feb., and was appointed to the select committee on the state of Ireland, 17 Feb. He gave evidence on this to the Lords inquiry, 18, 23, 25 Feb., when he contended that the 'operation of the Insurrection Act' had been 'extremely effectual in suppressing disturbance', and again, 20 May.[19] 'They examined me on oath for three days', he told his cousin Lord Farnham:

> While sitting on the stool of evidence and plied with all sorts of critical questions by members of the cabinet ... I could not help thinking of the old times in which you used so well to advise me not to commit myself. According to the new mode of proceeding in public affairs, when government must turn their friends inside out on the subject of abuses, they must at least make up their minds to their giving some inconvenient votes hereafter in Parliament in consistency with their sworn sentiments.[20]

He disapproved of appointing a 'paid officer as an assistant to the magistrates' in Ireland, 22 Feb. Speaking against Catholic claims, 28 Feb., he disclaimed any 'connection' with the Orangemen, whose existence he regretted, but insisted that the present state of tension was 'the very last moment when any change should be made'. Sir John Nicholl* considered it a 'smart performance on the state of Ireland', but Hudson Gurney* noted that he 'was by no means successful in a detail of Orange history somewhat of the oldest'.[21] (Giving evidence that month, Daniel O'Connell* confirmed that he had 'never heard that Mr. Leslie Foster was an Orangeman, nor do I believe that he is'.)[22] He divided against Catholic relief, 21 Apr., 10 May, but conceded that it was only the clergy, and not the Catholic laity or aristocracy, who were 'unfit to participate in the enjoyment of civil rights' on the grounds of 'security', 29 Apr. He endorsed the bill to disfranchise Irish 40s. freeholders, 26 Apr., and called for the disfranchisement of 'fraudulent holders in fee, as well as ... fraudulent leaseholders', 9 May. He presented a Dundalk petition against the cost of publicans' licenses, 1 Mar., and welcomed the grant of £8,000 to compensate his fellow education commissioners on their retirement, 15 Apr.[23] He recommended inquiries into the Irish butter trade, 22 Apr., and the admission of bonded corn, 2 May. He presented constituency petitions against any alteration of the corn laws and for special attention to the interests of millers, 28 Apr.[24] He was a minority teller against financial maintenance of the Irish Catholic clergy, 30 Apr. He approved the principle of assimilating the currencies of Great Britain and Ireland, 12 May 1825. He voted to receive the report on the salary of the president of the board of trade, 10 Apr., and against altering the representation of Edinburgh, 13 Apr. 1826.

At the 1826 general election Foster offered again, denying that he entertained 'hostile feelings towards my Catholic countrymen', whose emancipation 'conscience obliges me' to resist. The late intervention of the Catholic Association, whom he charged with adding 'all the terrors of another world to every art of intimidation that can be practised in this', produced a contest 'unparalleled in the parliamentary history of this or any other country'. He was narrowly returned in second place, having received, so the *Dublin Evening Post* asserted, 'a lesson' which 'will make him pause before he gives another vote against the emancipation of the Irish people!'[25] To Peel, however, he wrote:

> Many persons suppose that Catholic emancipation would abate the influence of the priests. My impressions to the contrary are only confirmed by what I have seen. If any candidate after the carrying of the measure should resist their notions of education, or their being provided with chapels or glebe houses, or ... any of their notions of aggrandizement, I am persuaded he would equally be denounced as an enemy ... and that all the same consequences would ensue ... The power of these priests is become so tremendous, and their fury in the exercise of it

so great, that I begin to fear a crisis of some kind or other is not far distant.[26]

Peel, in reply, doubted whether 'the late victory of the priests' would 'permanently add to their influence' or 'compensate the tenant for the estrangement of his landlord', but conceded the need for a thorough investigation of the 'spirit' of Irish popery.[27] 'The approaching effort which will be made in the new Parliament to force the [Catholic] question ... appears to me to make it of great importance that we should know the truth', he told Foster, 3 Nov., urging him to 'get, therefore, all the information that you have a legitimate claim to, as bearing upon the subjects of your [educational] inquiry', as 'when I see it inevitable, I shall (taking due care to free my motives from all suspicion) try to make the best terms for the future security of the Protestant'. On 6 Nov. 1826 Foster advised:

> The most practical safeguard would be a modification of the franchise. If the present election laws were to remain untouched, you would have at least sixty Catholic Members. And such Catholics! Sheil for Louth, and O'Connell for any southern county he might choose. Their presence in the House of Commons would be the least part of the mischief, a *bellum servile* would ensue all over Ireland ... The adoption of a principle that contribution of a certain amount to the county cess should be required to entitle the freeholder to vote ... would in its practical effects reduce the sixty Catholics to eight or ten, and secure that the latter should be gentlemen.[28]

He was appointed to the select committee on emigration, 15 Feb. 1827. He spoke against the bribery at elections bill, recommending better enforcement of the 'existing rules', 26 Feb. He endorsed a petition from 240 Irish millers against the importation of foreign flour the following day, and denounced one from the Catholic bishops of Ireland accusing Farnham of carrying out a 'crusade' to convert Catholics to Protestantism, 2 Mar.[29] He presented a Drogheda petition against Catholic relief that day, and voted thus, 6 Mar.[30] He was granted six weeks' leave to go the circuit, 8 Mar. He defended the report of his fellow commissioners on Irish charter schools, 5 Apr. He spoke as a member of the Penryn election committee, 18 May, and divided against its disfranchisement, 28 May. He criticized the costs of the Dublin Foundling Hospital and argued that 'the children reared in these establishments should, after they had arrived at a suitable age, be sent to New Brunswick, where there was at present a voracious demand for apprentices', 25 May. On 30 May 1827 he caused a stir by asserting that the 'population in various parts of Ireland was so dense, that the whole produce of the land was insufficient for its support', and contending that 'Irish landowners should take on themselves the charge of sending the superabundant population across the Atlantic'.[31]

Foster commended the Irish Subletting Act for preventing tenants from creating 'an unlimited population ... beyond what the land can possibly maintain', 19 Feb. 1828. He voted against repeal of the Test Acts, 26 Feb. He demanded compensation for Captain O'Reilly, whose money had been mislaid by the East India Company, 18 Apr., 22 May. He called for an extension of the Election Trial Acts consolidation bill to Ireland, where the 'state of law' was 'extremely defective', 21 Apr. He divided with the Wellington ministry on chancery delays, 24 Apr. Next day he welcomed their proposals to relax the corn laws, rejecting the 'apprehensions' of the agriculturists as 'absurd'. 'Although I have not before voted with ... ministers on any corn bill, I am now disposed to give them my support', he declared. He called for a petition against the Irish admiralty court to be referred to the commissioners of inquiry, anticipating that its allegations might 'not be well founded', 2 May. Resuming his opposition to Catholic claims, 9 May, when he again claimed to be 'no Orangeman' and to 'belong to no party', he warned that 'concession would only lead to fresh irritation'. 'If I could consent to change the vote I have constantly given on this subject', he added, no Member 'is more certain of an easy and inexpensive return'. He was a minority teller against relief, 12 May. He feared that the transfer of East Retford's seats to Birmingham would establish a precedent which would 'seriously injure, rather than serve the constitution', 19 May. He presented a petition from county Mayo complaining of distress, but warned of the 'utter hopelessness' of employing the population 'by advances of public money' and called for the removal of 'legal obstacles' to cultivation of the bogs, 5 June. That day he cautioned against 'any violent or extensive change' to bank note restrictions, in which he hoped Ireland and Scotland would soon follow England. He attacked the 'extravagant loss' incurred by post office steam packets to Ireland, urging ministers to 'transfer the excellent (160 horse power) vessels' from the Liverpool station to Holyhead, and so 'give to the Irish Members all the facilities of a shorter voyage', 6, 25 June. He opposed and was a minority teller against the assessment of lessors bill, 12 June. He denounced the usury laws repeal bill as 'a most flagrant delusion' which would allow 'properties to be brought to the market at the caprice of the money-lenders', 19 June. He did not think that professors should be admitted 'without some test' to the Belfast Academical Institution and considered it 'hardly fair that the salary of the chief justice of a court in Ireland should be less than that of a puisne judge in England', 23 June. The following day he dismissed proposals for inquiry into the Irish church as 'quite superfluous'. Speaking in support of the Irish registrar, 26 June, he asserted that 'there is no office in existence where half a million of deeds are so well registered'. He endorsed a Drogheda petition against the high taxes arising from its county status and advocated 'equalizing the rate on the county', 27 June. He voted against ordnance reductions, 4 July, and defended the grant for a 'correct map of Ireland', 7 July. He joined in calls for Robert Taylor to be punished for his lectures 'denying the truth of Christianity', 8 July. He voted with government on the silk duties, 14 July 1828.

Following the election of O'Connell for Clare that month, Foster joined his brothers-in-law Vesey Fitzgerald, president of the board of trade, and John Henry North* in advising Peel, again home secretary, of 'the danger' of leaving the question of his eligibility undecided until Parliament met.[32] He repeatedly warned that without a change in the Irish franchise there would be a landslide for the Catholic Association at the next election.[33] On 12 Dec. Peel wrote to consult him about 'the draft of a bill which you left with me in the summer', to 'limit the exercise of the 40s. franchise ... and correct some of the abuses of the system', 'a subject on which it might be necessary to write volumes to any one less thoroughly conversant than yourself in the ... details of the law and the practice of the right of voting in Ireland'.[34] In his reply, 16 Dec. 1828, Foster again recommended 'urgent and immediate' action, for otherwise 'at the very next general election you will have to deal with about 60 Radicals, the nominees of O'Connell ... who will sit fast in the House of Commons from the moment the Speaker takes the chair until the candles are put out'. The remedy, he insisted, was to abolish 'all franchises under £20 per annum' as 'a practical annihilation of whatever influence the Catholics now possess', and to counteract the 'system of fraud' by extending 'any new restrictions' to all types of freehold, 'whether arising from leasehold, or perpetuity, or fee simple'. Pre-empting criticism that his 'new system' would 'transfer much of the real power formerly exercised by the great proprietors to the minor gentry, the clergy, and the more opulent farmers', he pointed out that

the influence of the aristocracy is annihilated. The priests and the demagogues are in their place. The practical question seems to be whether we should not now aim at placing the power in the hands of that middle class, as the best course within our reach. The minor gentry of

Ireland are essentially Tory, rather than Whig. Very little of what is radical enters into their composition. They are also essentially Protestant. I should think that the government would have no reason to be dissatisfied with the representatives which this influence would return ... Few things could more powerfully conduce to the permanent tranquillity of Ireland than the taking the business of elections out of the hands of the lower classes. You would not merely allay the vague and restless passions of the peasantry but you would extinguish all the real hopes of the leaders of the Catholic Association. They are not dreaming of insurrection, legislate as you may, but they feed themselves with the expectation of their assured triumphs at the next general election. It is there they intend to make their fight and ... nowhere else. I have the sure means of knowing their private feelings upon this point and the adoption of either of the plans which we have considered would be a death blow to their hopes.[35]

Vesey Fitzgerald doubted that Foster's letter got 'rid of any of the difficulties', but was instructed by Peel to 'consider this most important delicate and difficult question conjointly' with him as part of a 'special committee' of four, which also included Farnham and George Dawson*.[36] On 25 Jan. 1829 Lord Ellenborough, a member of the cabinet, recorded in his diary that 'Peel told us he had seen Leslie Foster who was for a *settlement*, but strongly against paying the Roman Catholic clergy'. 'Foster consulting with the cabinet how Catholic emancipation may best be brought about!', he exclaimed, describing the following day how he was

brought through the park to the foreign office by Vesey Fitzgerald, and thence through all the dark passages to the cabinet-room, where we examined him as to the expediency of giving to the crown a power of prohibiting the exercise of the spiritual functions of any priest ... His evidence showed the inutility of the exercise of such a power.[37]

Speaking in support of the address, 6 Feb., Foster asserted that he was 'no Orangeman' and 'no Brunswicker', that 'for some time antecedent to the rise of the Brunswick Association' it had become his 'settled conviction' that 'an over-ruling necessity had arisen for attempting the settlement of the Roman Catholic question' and that owing to Wellington and his cabinet a 'far different course now lies before us' which, 'while it shall admit the Catholics to all civil privileges, shall do so upon Protestant principles, and accompanied with every measure which a reasonable Protestant can consider as a security'. These included the bill to suppress the Catholic Association, which the cabinet 'settled' with Foster and the law officers, 9 Feb., and for which he argued, 12 Feb., and the raising

of the qualification for the Irish county franchise from 40s. to £10, which he assured the House would offer 'a real and substantial security to the Protestant interest' and prevent 'the freeholder from being the tool of the landlord, or the slave of the priest', 20 Mar.[38] He, of course, voted for emancipation, 6, 30 Mar. He welcomed the special oath for Catholic Members, 23 Mar., but recommended tighter restrictions on Jesuits, 24, 27 Mar., when he argued that it was 'the duty of a Protestant legislature to meet and repress' their 'special obedience to the pope in respect of missionary labour'. On 26 Feb. he spoke in support of removing a 'tenant's right of pasture', which would assist in 'reclaiming the bogs of Ireland'. He was appointed to the select committee on the Irish estimates, 9 Apr. On 1 Sept. Peel asked him to 'write to me unreservedly and confidentially your opinion' on the 'great difficulty' of Irish education and Maynooth. In his reply, 12 Dec., Foster advised that 'any attempt which could be made at present to substitute a new system would involve all concerned in far more serious difficulties' and that 'any renewed agitation of the subject will call into violent action those feelings which, if not absolutely asleep, are at least in a sort of sullen torpor'. As Ellenborough put it, 14 Nov. 1829, 'he thinks the political and religious hostility of the two parties is subsiding. The chiefs alone keep it up. The adherents are gradually falling off. To open the questions of education, etc., now, would be to open closing wounds'.[39]

On 5 Feb. 1830 the Irish secretary Lord Francis Leveson Gower wrote to implore Foster 'to quit your fireside at Rathescar', explaining that while there was no 'inducement' to rival 'the late cabinet counsels of last year', they could offer

O'Connell on the second bench of the opposition and Newport pulling down the church. If this does not tempt you, I do not know what will. Seriously, if you can give us the benefit of your assistance, it never was more desirable or could be more appreciated.[40]

Foster duly attended and voted against parliamentary reform, 18 Feb., and the enfranchisement of Birmingham, Leeds, and Manchester, 23 Feb. In his last known speech, 19 Mar., he opposed inquiry into distress, claiming that it had been 'very much exaggerated' in Ireland where 'at no former period was there less', and declaring that 'there is no worse nostrum in the hands of political quacks, than that the distress of the country can be relieved by any addition to the currency'. He was granted a month's leave on urgent private business, 5 Apr. 1830.

At the 1830 general election Foster did not come forward, for it had long been agreed by Peel and

Leveson Gower that in view of the office which he had been 'lately compelled to resign', following the abolition of counsel to the revenue in January 1828, his claims to promotion were 'very much superior' to any others.[41] As Wellington had noted, the 'counsel to the commissioner of the revenue' was 'usually considered first for the post of solicitor-general or for the bench', and Foster 'receives a pension as compensation for his loss of office' which it 'is desirable to dispense with'.[42] On 5 Sept. 1828 Leveson Gower had written to Wellington

to offer a reason or two why I should prefer seeing Mr. Foster on the bench to the other alternative ... It is that Mr. Serjeant Lefroy* from the engagements, as I believe, of the late lord lieutenant, has at least a strong expectancy of promotion to the next vacancy ... [but] is a very strong Orangeman, and if he were to undergo any severe disappointment by the promotion of a gentleman of contrary politics I should fear the consequences on the minds of his Protestant friends. In the case of Mr. Foster no inconvenience of this nature could arise.[43]

Peel concurred, 3 Aug. 1829, observing that 'Foster's appointment to the bench would save the public ... £2,000 a year ... would satisfy him for the loss of his office, and would get rid of the embarrassment of a Louth election in his person', though he felt bound to 'express a doubt, however highly I think of Foster's abilities and acquirements, whether he would shine as a law officer of the crown'.[44] On 11 Aug. Leveson Gower, who was 'very confident that Foster will do better service on the bench than as solicitor-general', cleared the way with John Doherty*, another candidate, and by December 1829 Sheil considered it 'certain that an election will take place by the elevation of Mr. Foster to Baron McClelland's seat on the exchequer bench'.[45] However, Foster did not receive his 'hourly expected' commission until the following summer, by when it was clear that no writ would be moved for the vacancy owing to the king's 'alarming state of health'.[46] 'The next three judges are to be Joy, Leslie Foster and Sergeant Lefroy', O'Connell had earlier observed, 'what a prospect for the Irish people!'[47]

Foster's former associates continued to solicit his advice on Irish matters. In April 1832 Ellenborough sought 'information which your labour and knowledge have enabled you to acquire', in the hope of rendering the Grey ministry's Irish jury bill 'less objectionable and dangerous than I fear it is at present'. Thanking him for his 'very valuable opinion', 15 Apr., Ellenborough hoped 'we may be able to induce Lord Melbourne to put it off for this year ... it is now put off till after Easter'.[48] The following month Foster discouraged Ferrard from proposing postal voting in the Irish reform bill, observing that it 'would certainly give great protection in Ireland to tenants and assistance to the interest of landlord', but 'would be considered too great a departure from established principles'.[49] Foster, who moved to the court of common pleas in 1841, died on the circuit at Cavan in July 1842, after being 'seized with sudden illness' and 'having filled up and signed the codicil to his will'.[50]

[1] Add. 41295, ff. 131, 136, 146, 149, 155. [2] Add. 40357, f. 200. [3] Add. 40328, f. 1. [4] Add. 38195, f. 153; 40357, f. 305; 40339, f. 227. [5] Add. 40304, f. 214. [6] Add. 40360, f. 128. [7] Add. 40330, f. 11. [8] *Drogheda Jnl.* 25, 28 Feb. 1824. [9] *Sketches, Legal and Political* ed. M. Savage, i. 172, 183-6. [10] Add. 40304, f. 240. [11] *The Times*, 5 May 1824; Wellington mss WP1/800/24. [12] Parker, *Peel*, i. 344, 392-3. [13] *The Times*, 10 Apr. 1824. [14] Ibid. 8 May 1824. [15] Ibid. 12 May 1824. [16] Ibid. 18 May 1824. [17] *PP* (1825), vii. 241. [18] PRO NI, Foster mss D207/73/118, 121. [19] *PP* (1825), ix. 48, 93. [20] PRO NI, Foster Massereene mss D562/3457, Foster to Farnham, 8 Mar. 1825. [21] Merthyr Mawr mss F/2/8, Nicholl diary, 1 Mar.; Gurney diary, 1 Mar. 1825. [22] *PP* (1825), viii. 75. [23] *The Times*, 2 Mar., 16 Apr. 1825. [24] Ibid. 29 Apr. 1825. [25] *Dublin Evening Post*, 25 May, 8, 22, 24, 27, 29 June; *Drogheda Jnl.* 14, 17, 24 June, 5 July 1826. [26] Parker, i. 411-12. [27] RIA Dublin, J. L. Foster mss 23.G.39/1, Peel to Foster, 16 July 1826. [28] Parker, i. 423-4. [29] *The Times*, 28 Feb. 1827. [30] Ibid. 3 Mar. 1827. [31] Ibid. 26, 31 May 1827. [32] Wellington mss WP1/941/12. [33] Add. 40389, f. 266; 40322, f. 337. [34] Add. 40397, f. 372. [35] Ibid. ff. 384-94. [36] Add. 40322, f. 378; 40323, f. 31; N. Gash, *Secretary Peel*, 552. [37] *Ellenborough Diary* i. 321-3. [38] Wellington mss WP1/1004/19; *Ellenborough Diary*, i. 342. [39] Parker, ii. 127-32; *Ellenborough Diary* ii. 134; Gash, 607. [40] J.L. Foster mss 23.G.39/4. [41] Add. 40336, f. 266. [42] Wellington mss WP1/957/10. [43] Ibid. WP1/952/20. [44] Add. 40337, f. 99. [45] Ibid. f. 115; PRO NI, Anglesey mss D619/32/A/3/1/254, Mahony to Anglesey, 9 Dec. 1829. [46] *Belfast Guardian*, 11 June 1830. [47] *O'Connell Corresp.* iv. 1608. [48] J.L. Foster mss 23.G.39/4. [49] Foster mss T2519/4/2140, Foster to Ferrard, 30 May 1832. [50] *Gent. Mag.* (1842). ii. 424.

P.J.S.

FOSTER *see also* **SKEFFINGTON**

FOSTER BARHAM, Charles Henry (1808–1878), of Trecwn, Pemb. and Stockbridge, Hants.

APPLEBY   24 May 1832–1832

b. 16 May 1808,[1] 3rd s. of Joseph Foster Barham* (*d.* 1832) and Lady Caroline Tufton, da. of Sackville, 8th earl of Thanet; bro. of John Foster Barham*. *educ.* Charterhouse 1821-5; Christ Church, Oxf. 1827. *m.* (1) 20 Jan. 1836,[2] Elizabeth Maria (*d.* 1861), da. of William Boyd Ince of Ince, Lancs., *s.p.*; (2) 11 Feb. 1863,[3] Ellen Katherine, da. of Edward Taylor Massy of Cottesmore, Pemb., *s.p. suc.* bro. William to Trecwn 1840. *d.* 15 Aug. 1878.

Rect. Barming, Kent 1834-48; Kirkby Thore, Westmld. 1848-52.

Barham, as he was usually known, appears to have owed his brief appearance in the Commons to happenstance. According to his father's correspondence, plans were laid for him to visit Geneva after he left Charterhouse, but its uncertain whether he went or which of the three brothers was dangerously ill in September 1826.[4] Within a year of graduating from Oxford Barham was returned to Parliament for the doomed borough of Appleby in place of his uncle, Henry Tufton, who had succeeded as 11th earl of Thanet. His address was then given as Queen Anne Street, Marylebone, his father's London residence. He was sworn in, 1 June, and voted in the Grey government's majority on the Russian-Dutch loan, 12 July 1832. Perhaps deliberately, lest it should compromise his intended career in the church, no other parliamentary activity by Barham was reported. He plumped for the Liberal candidate, Thomas Law Hodges*, in West Kent at the elections of 1837 and 1847, but raised no objection to the return of the Conservative James Bowen for Pembrokeshire at the 1866 by-election.[5]

Barham, whose paternal grandfather had 'embraced many of the Moravian views of religion', became an Anglican deacon in 1833 and a priest the following year.[6] After the deaths of his eldest brother John in 1838 and his brother William in 1840, he succeeded to the encumbered Trecwn estate and the family's remaining property in Jamaica, which he disposed of together with certain properties in Kent, partly in order to cover William's bequests.[7] Thanet's death in 1849 made him the senior legitimate representative of the family, but he was not styled Lord Tufton, nor did he succeed to the hereditary shrievalty of Westmorland, which Thanet had attempted to devise to his illegitimate son.[8] The resultant controversy prompted legislation in 1849 which made office an annual appointment, as in other counties.[9] Barham gave up his Westmorland living in 1852 and retired to Pembrokeshire, where he and his first wife earned a reputation for beneficence. As a widower in 1863, he married a neighbouring landowner's daughter nearly thirty years his junior.[10] He died without issue at Trecwn in August 1878 following a period of prolonged ill health, having (by his will, dated 12 Aug. 1873, and proved, 12 Sept. 1878) left most of his personal estate to his widow. He was succeeded at Trecwn, where he failed to realize the high rental income he aspired to after renegotiating leases and settlements on farms and slate quarries in Buckett, Barnard's Well, Cilglynnau, Henry's Moat, Llanstinian, Maenclochog, Revel Fach and Temple Druid, by his sister Caroline's son, Francis William Robins (1841-1926), who, as required, took the name of Barham.[11]

[1] E.L. Arrowsmith, *Charterhouse Reg. 1769-1872*, p. 19 erroneously gives his birthdate as 16 May 1809. He was baptized at St. Marylebone, Mdx. on 17 June 1808 (IGI), and his birth was announced in *Gent. Mag.* (1808), i. 458. [2] IGI (Kent). [3] *The Times*, 14 Feb. 1863. [4] Bodl. Clarendon dep. c. 388, bdle. 1, Sir C. Hamilton to Joseph Foster Barham, 19 June [n.d.], 6 Sept. 1826. [5] F.F. Barham, *Foster Barham Genealogy*, 16; NLW, Llwyngwair mss 6780. [6] Beds. and Luton Archives MO2000/165; F.F. Barham, 15; Arrowsmith, 19. [7] A.H.F. Barham, *Descendants of Roger Foster*, 58-59; PROB. 11/1930/472; IR26/1538/533. [8] F.F. Barham, 16. [9] *The Times*, 16 Aug. 1849; R.S. Ferguson, *Cumb. and Westmld. MPs*, 334. [10] Arrowsmith, 19; IGI (Pemb.); *DWB*. [11] NLW, Williams and Williams mss (1) 1289, 12890, 2302-5, 4710-12, 5931-48, 6878, 6879, 7538, 7539, 7635-43; ibid. (3) 21633, 21933, 21934, 22195-97; *Pemb. Co. Hist.* ed. D. Howell, iv. 16; *Haverfordwest and Milford Haven Telegraph*, 21 Aug. 1878; A.H.F. Barham, 59; *DWB*.

H.J.S./M.M.E.

FOSTER BARHAM, John (1799–1838), of Trecwn, Pemb. and Stockbridge, Hants.

STOCKBRIDGE	1820–1826
STOCKBRIDGE	1831–1832
KENDAL	17 Feb. 1834–1837

bap. 16 Feb. 1799,[1] 1st s. of Joseph Foster Barham* and Lady Caroline Tufton, da. of Sackville, 8th earl of Thanet; bro. of Charles Henry Foster Barham*. *educ.* Eton 1814; Christ Church, Oxf. 1818. *m.* 14 Jan. 1834, Lady Katherine Grimston, da. of James Walter Grimston†, 1st earl of Verulam, *s.p. suc.* fa. 1832. *d.* 22 May 1838.
Sheriff, Pemb. 1834-5.

On first meeting Barham in 1833, Lady Salisbury described him as 'not good looking, nor the reverse: tall, with small eyes and a reddish face and rather tigerish in appearance'. As a friend of his betrothed, she subsequently came to regard him as 'a good sort of man'.[2] Barham (whose other surname was not often used) apparently left Oxford without taking a degree. He was brought in for Stockbridge at the 1820 general election by his father and, like him, aligned himself with the Whigs. An 'idle' Member, inaccurately described as a 'frequent attender' by a commentary of 1825, when present he voted with the opposition to the Liverpool ministry on most major issues, including economy, retrenchment and reduced taxation, although he and his father's voting records are often difficult to distinguish.[3] It is possible that he may have delivered some of the speeches by 'Mr. Barham' attributed to his father, though his youth and subsequent diffidence in the House argue against this. He divided for Catholic claims, 28 Feb. 1821, 21 Apr. 1825. He voted for parliamentary reform, 9 May 1821. No parliamentary activity has been found for 1824, but he was probably the 'J. F. Barham' who was named to a committee of the West India Planters and Merchants to apply to ministers for a reduction in the sugar duties, 25 June, and was present at its meetings, 14 July 1824, 16 Mar., 17 May 1825. He appears to have taken on the running of his father's West Indian estate by this time.[4] He voted against suppression of the Catholic Association, 15 Feb. 1825. No trace of parliamentary activity has been found for 1826. At that year's dissolution he retired from Stockbridge, where his father was in dispute with another patron, and although Thomas Creevey* recorded that he was in line to replace him at Appleby, on the interest of his maternal uncle, the 10th earl of Thanet, his father's intrigues to bring this about foundered.[5] He may have been the 'Pony Barham' who dined with Lady Holland (a cousin) in July 1826 and have been afflicted by a serious illness that September, if he was the son of Joseph Foster Barham referred to in contemporary correspondence.[6] When he contested Stockbridge at the 1830 general election on his father's revived interest (the management of which he had evidently assumed), it was as a friend of the Wellington administration, according to a friendly squib. He was defeated and his petition against the return was unsuccessful.[7]

At the 1831 general election he offered again for Stockbridge, which stood to be disfranchised by the Grey ministry's reform bill. He deplored this on the hustings, but professed himself to be a reformer in the broad sense and was returned unopposed.[8] He paired in favour of the second reading of the reintroduced reform bill, 6 July, voted against the adjournment, 12 July 1831, and gave general support to its details, though according to Lord Lowther* he took 'an active part' against the disfranchisement of Appleby, even if he did not vote thus, 19 July.[9] On 26 July he stayed mute on the subject of his own borough's extinction. He was in the minority for a committee of inquiry into the effect of the Sugar Refining Act on the West India interest, 12 Sept. He voted for the passage of the reform bill, 21 Sept., and Lord Ebrington's confidence motion, 10 Oct. He divided for the second reading of the revised reform bill, 17 Dec. 1831, the enfranchisement of Tower Hamlets, 28 Feb., and the third reading, 22 Mar. 1832. He was in the minority for a reduction in the sugar duties, 7 Mar. He presented a petition against the Holderness drainage bill, 18 Apr. He was absent from the division on the motion for an address calling on the king to appoint only ministers who would carry the reform bill unimpaired, 10 May, when he was listed as being 'in country'. He was in ministerial majorities for the second reading of the Irish reform bill, 25 May, and against Conservative amendments to the Scottish bill, 1, 15 June. He

paired with government on the Russian-Dutch loan, 16, 20 July. The balances in Barham's bank books had never looked healthy, and though the death of his father in September 1832 brought him estates in Pembrokeshire, Stockbridge and the West Indies, it does not appear to have left him financially secure. Shortly before her own death that November, his mother made over to him £12,000 in annuities.[10]

At the 1832 general election he answered the call of the reform party in Westmorland, to which he was connected via the earls of Thanet. A hostile report portrayed him as 'an admirable equestrian, and excellent shot, elegant and accomplished in his manners' but dismissed 'his qualifications as a Member for the county'. Aspersions were cast on his ability as a public speaker and an unsubstantiated rumour circulated that 'his private character is not what it ought to be'.[11] He was defeated by the established Lowther interest, but in December 1833 was invited to fill the vacancy at Kendal caused by the death of James Brougham*, whom he described in his address as 'a most valued and dear friend'. Pledged to continue his line of support for the Grey administration, he was returned unopposed.[12] He took time off from his canvass to get married to the daughter of the earl of Verulam, with whom he was, according to Lady Salisbury, 'desperately in love'.[13] The bride's mother was supposed to have observed in a more worldly vein that although the feeling was mutual, 'I am sure you would not wonder if you saw the diamonds'.[14] There was no opposition to his return in 1835, when he denied reports that he had gone over to the Conservatives. (He had abandoned his intention to contest the county again after a preliminary canvass.)[15] In January 1836 he recorded that he was 'under strict medical superintendence and shall be perhaps for some time to come', and the following month informed agents that he was too ill to present a petition, fearing that he would have to vacate his seat.[16] Shortly afterwards his mental health collapsed completely. When he was eventually certified by a commission, in the face of mounting concern from his constituency, 23 Mar. 1837, the jury determined that he had been of unsound mind since 21 Apr. the previous year.[17] This 'shocking calamity' was noticed by Lady Salisbury, 5 May 1836, when she reported that he was 'in confinement, and it is hoped he may not live'. His death in May 1838 was in her eyes 'a great blessing'.[18] Administration of his personal estate was granted to his widow, who had sought advice from Lord Brougham over anticipated difficulties from William Barham, her husband's brother and next of kin, a shadowy figure who appears to have died soon afterwards.[19] The estates in Pembrokeshire and the

West Indies were entailed on the next brother Charles (1808-78), briefly Member for Appleby in the 1832 session.[20]

[1] Reg. of Old Buckenham, Norf. (copy in Bodl. Clarendon dep. c.386), which gives his father's name as John, but is correct in other details. Other sources give his birthdate as January 1800, which would have made him an under age Member in 1820. [2] Gascoyne Heiress ed. C. Oman, 94-95, 97. [3] Black Bk. (1823), 137; Session of Parl. 1825, p. 449. [4] Inst. of Commonwealth Stud. M915/4; Bodl. Clarendon dep. c.389, passim. [5] Creevey mss, Creevey to Miss Ord, 20 Apr. 1826. [6] Lady Holland to Son, 43; Bodl. Clarendon dep. c.388, Sir C. Hamilton to Joseph Foster Barham, 6 Sept. 1826. [7] Bodl. Clarendon dep. c.369, bdle. 2, draft address [1830]; c.430, bdle. 4. [8] Salisbury Jnl. 8 May 1831. [9] Londsale mss, Lowther to Londsale, 22 July 1831. [10] Bodl. Clarendon dep. c.386; c.389, bdle. 14. [11] Westmld. Gazette, 10 Nov., 8, 22 Dec. 1832. [12] Bodl. Clarendon dep. c.382, bdles. 3, 4, passim; Kendal Chron. 11 Jan., 22 Feb. 1834. [13] Kendal Chron. 18 Jan. 1834; Gascoyne Heiress, 95. [14] Maxwell, Clarendon, i. 83. [15] Kendal Mercury, 3 Jan. 1835. [16] Bodl. Clarendon dep. c.382, bdle. 4, Barham to Nicholson, 24 Feb.; c.389, bdle. 16, same to Stanley, 28 Jan., to Richards, 18 Feb. 1836. [17] Ibid. c.382, bdle. 10, unnamed agent to Lady Katherine Barham, 14 Jan. and reply; The Times, 27 Mar. 1837; TNA C211/4/311. [18] Gascoyne Heiress, 202, 284; Gent. Mag. (1838), ii. 224, 234. [19] PROB 6/214/255; Brougham mss, Katherine Barham to Brougham, 26 Mar., 23 Nov., 2 Dec. 1838. [20] Haverfordwest and Milford Haven Telegraph, 21 Aug. 1878.

H.J.S./P.J.S.

FOSTER BARHAM, Joseph (1759–1832), of Trecwn, Pemb. and Stockbridge, Hants.

STOCKBRIDGE	22 Feb. 1793–3 Apr. 1799
STOCKBRIDGE	1802–1806
OKEHAMPTON	1806–1807
STOCKBRIDGE	1807–24 July 1822

b. 1 Jan. 1759, 1st s. of Joseph Foster Barham (formerly Foster) and Dorothea, da. and event. h. of Erasmus Vaughan of Trecwn. educ. ?Leipzig; G. Inn 1777. m. 26 July 1792, Lady Caroline Tufton, da. of Sackville, 8th earl of Thanet, 3s. 2da. suc. fa. 1789. d. 28 Sept. 1832.
  Capt. Stockbridge vols. 1798, lt. 1803, capt. 1804-6.

Foster Barham, a Welsh landowner and conscience-stricken West India proprietor, again returned himself on his own interest for Stockbridge at the 1820 general election. He took his seat on the opposition benches, as he later mentioned, 9 Mar. 1821, and though his attachment to the Whig cause had previously wavered, he sided with them against the Liverpool ministry on most major issues, including economy, retrenchment and reduced taxation, during his final years in the House.[1] The simultaneous return of his son John, with whom he was inaccurately classed as an 'idle fellow' by a radical commentary of 1823, presents problems of identification, but internal evidence

and this Member's seniority suggest that he delivered most of the speeches attributed to 'Mr. Barham' in debate. An obituary praised him as an 'acute and powerful speaker'.[2] Either he or his son voted against the appointment of an additional Scottish baron of exchequer, 15 May, but it was almost certainly he who was added to the select committee on the Welsh judicature, 1 June, and who spoke in support of its reform, 1 June 1820, when, after making a charge of corruption, he was obliged to deny that he meant to accuse John Lloyd, a Welsh judge. He moved for a list of practising Welsh attorneys, 9 June 1820, and was appointed to the revived committee, 21 Feb. 1821.[3] He defended the army ophthalmic establishment as a cost effective venture, 2 June, 10 July 1820. He divided against ministers on the Queen Caroline affair, 22 June 1820, 23, 26 Jan., but was apparently absent from the opposition motion censuring their conduct, 6 Feb. 1821. He divided for Catholic relief and objected to an 'illiberal, uncharitable, unchristian' passage in a hostile petition, 28 Feb.[4] He probably gave the vote to repeal the duty on husbandry horses, 5 Mar., as it was surely he who warned of the danger of famine in agricultural districts and called for economies in public expenditure and a revision of the corn laws, 7 Mar.[5] He spoke in defence of the Whig Morning Chronicle, which stood accused of a breach of parliamentary privilege, 9 Mar. It was possibly he who made a brief intervention concerning the size of proposed army reductions, 12 Mar., and divided for a figure of £10,000, 14 Mar.[6] On 4 May he denied that West India proprietors sought preferential treatment and objected to Henry Grey Bennet's assertion that they dealt in human flesh. He voted for parliamentary reform, 9 May, when, in a somewhat contrary speech, he claimed that tales of corrupt practice in his own borough belonged to a former era, and, according to one account, raised objections to the enfranchisement of large towns. (In an undated, apparently earlier memorandum, he had protested that all the schemes for parliamentary reform he had seen were based on 'a mistaken view of the nature of the constitution', which they would destroy.)[7] He was in the minority for reform of the Scottish county representation, 10 May. While he doubted the necessity of a bill to permit the humanitarian removal of slaves, he was content to allow it a second reading, 1 June. He voted for inquiry into the administration of justice in Tobago, but regretted that its mover, Lord Nugent, had descended to 'loose and unwarranted' accusations against planters and had to be persuaded to withdraw an amendment, 6 June.[8] On 25 June 1821 he made a stout defence of the West Indian sugar monopoly, arguing that the blame for the slave trade could not be laid exclusively at the door of the colonialists and contrasting the outcry at the maltreatment of slaves with the general indifference to the ritual immolation of Hindoo widows in India.

Foster Barham appears to have missed the early part of the 1822 session. On 1 Apr. he spoke in favour of the colonial trade bill, believing it 'absolutely necessary to do something for the colonial interest', and observing that 'as a proprietor himself ... he was absolutely compelled, by the pressure of the present situation, to deny his negroes (most unwillingly) many comforts and advantages to which they had been accustomed'.[9] He denied that the measure would revive the slave trade and again defended the West Indian sugar monopoly, wondering at the irony of East India men taking up the cry of free trade, 17 May. He welcomed Allen's initiative to consider previous select committee reports on the incorporation of the Welsh judicature into the English system, 23 May, but objected to the precipitate introduction of an alternative plan to reform existing arrangements, 30 May. Either he or his son voted against the new corn duties and in favour of a permanent bounty on wheat exports, 9 May, and paired for a motion blaming agricultural distress on the resumption of cash payments, 12 June. On 27 June he queried the value of legislation against the slave trade when other countries were of a different mind, and he assured Hume that the extent of economic distress in Trinidad was too great to permit any governmental economies, 5 July.[10] He took the Chiltern Hundreds, 24 July 1822.

Prior to this Foster Barham had agreed to sell his Stockbridge property to Lord Grosvenor, and he nominated the latter's chosen candidate as his successor, 30 July 1822.[11] According to Lord Lowther*, his West India estates had 'failed' and he was 'clamorous' for the repayment of a loan to his brother-in-law, Lord Thanet. There was indeed a sharp fall in his bank balance between 1821 and 1823 and he subsequently confirmed that financial difficulties had induced him to put Stockbridge up for sale.[12] This transaction was due for completion by the end of 1822, but dissolved into an acrimonious dispute which dragged on for eight years and sparked two electoral contests. Stung by attacks on his personal integrity, Foster Barham recalled in an undated letter:

He was 35 years in Parliament without even asking for an exciseman's post when his friends were in power ... Coming into a large West India estate which would be increased £10,000 per annum by the expenditure of £20,000 on negroes, which he had abundant means to purchase, [he] did however renounce that advantage when hardly anybody had scruples of the same sort.[13]

He had stressed his steady opposition to the slave trade in his 1823 tract *Considerations on the Abolition of Negro Slavery*, which envisaged a gradual shift to a wage economy in the West Indies and outlined plans for the compensation of planters and the education of slaves. It won praise from Sir James Mackintosh* and William Wilberforce*, who had long regarded Foster Barham as a worthy exception among planters and told him, 'if Mr. Pitt were now alive, he would be strongly tempted to carry your plan into execution'.[14] Lord Westmorland, by contrast, thought that the pamphlet was 'very ridiculous, but states well the West Indians' case'.[15] Foster Barham's attendance at meetings of the West India Planters and Merchants Committee was in decline by 1815, but he was appointed to committees on the renewal of the West India Dock Company charter, 15 Mar. 1821, 17 Apr. 1822.[16] He subsequently appears to have left the management of his West Indian estates to his son John.[17] The same applied to the Pembrokeshire estate, which, according to estimates for 1828, produced a modest annual return of £1,381.[18]

At the 1826 general election Foster Barham unsuccessfully intrigued to secure a seat for his son at Appleby, to which he was connected through Thanet. Commenting on this episode, Lord Kensington† was supposed to have remarked that 'he never touched anything without making a job out it'.[19] He was active on behalf of Henry Brougham* at that year's Westmorland contest, during which he stayed at his brother-in-law's seat at Appleby Castle, having the previous July failed to persuade Lord Lonsdale to compromise with his Whig opponent.[20] At a meeting of London-based Westmorland freeholders, 15 May 1826, he observed that the Lowther family's monopoly of the county representation appeared to substantiate the case for some degree of parliamentary reform, 'a process which I have always much deprecated', as he afterwards told John Beckett*, Lonsdale's son-in-law. He added that he had not come out expressly in support of Brougham at the meeting and objected that a Lonsdale acolyte had dismissed him as a West Indian *parvenu*, a comment from which the peer subsequently dissociated himself.[21] He was equally tetchy in his dealings over Stockbridge, 'the unexampled vexation and anxiety' of which he identified in September 1825 as the cause of his declining health, of which he complained steadily thereafter.[22] At some time in 1832 a doctor pleaded with his wife to dissuade him from a contemplated journey, but when he died at his sister's residence near Bedford that September, it was reportedly 'after an illness of only two days'. His wife Lady Caroline, 'one of the leaders of the *beau monde*', followed him five weeks later after being run over by a cab.[23] The residue of his personal estate, which was sworn under £16,000, 15 Oct. 1832, but resworn under £40,000, 5 July 1834, passed to his eldest son John, along with his town house in Queen Anne Street, Marylebone, and property in Pembrokeshire, Hampshire and Jamaica. In his will, dated 22 June 1832, he referred to the depreciation in value of the latter, and his consequent obligation to charge other estates with the provision for his wife and younger children. He left to his wife's discretion a bequest to his second son William, who may well have been the reprobate 'gentleman' of the same name convicted of an assault on a young woman in Regent Street in August 1832.[24]

[1] *The Times*, 10 Mar. 1821. [2] *Black Bk.* (1823), 137; *Session of Parl. 1825*, p. 449; *Gent. Mag.* (1832), ii. 573. [3] *The Times*, 10 June 1820. [4] Ibid. 1 Mar. 1821. [5] Ibid. 8 Mar. 1821. [6] Ibid. 13 Mar. 1821. [7] Ibid. 10 May 1821; Bodl. Clarendon dep. c.381. [8] *The Times*, 7 June 1821. [9] Ibid. 2 Apr. 1822. [10] Ibid. 28 June, 6 July 1822. [11] Bodl. Clarendon dep. c.388, bdle. 1; *Salisbury Jnl.* 5 Aug. 1822; Grosvenor mss 9/11/25. [12] Lonsdale mss, Lowther to Lonsdale, 11 Oct. 1822; Bodl. Clarendon dep. c.369, bdle. 2, address to Stockbridge inhabitants, Sept. 1825; c.389, bdle. 14. [13] See STOCKBRIDGE; Bodl. Clarendon dep. c.388, bdle. 1, Foster Barham to Sir C. Hamilton (draft). [14] Bodl. Clarendon dep. c.388, bdle. 2, Mackintosh to Foster Barham, 30 Nov. 1823, Wilberforce to same, 4 Dec. 1823. [15] Wellington mss WP1/773/14. [16] Inst. of Commonwealth Stud. M915/3, 4. [17] Bodl. Clarendon. dep. c.428, *passim*. [18] Ibid. c.372, bdle. 2. [19] Lonsdale mss, Lowther to Lonsdale, 18 Oct. 1825; Creevey mss, Creevey to Miss Ord, 20 Apr. 1826. [20] *Gent. Mag.* (1832), ii. 573. [21] *The Times*, 16 May 1826 (where the report identifies him as 'Mr. Barron'); Bodl. Clarendon dep. c.388, bdle. 2, Foster Barham to Beckett, Lonsdale to Foster Barham, 26 May 1826. [22] Bodl. Clarendon dep. c.369, bdle. 2; c. 388, bdle. 1, Hamilton to Foster Barham, *passim*. [23] Ibid. c. 369, bdle. 2, Dr. Maclure to Lady Caroline Barham [1826]; *Gent Mag.* (1832), ii. 573. [24] *The Times*, 15 Aug. 1832; PROB 11/1806/618; IR26/1281/731.

H.J.S./P.J.S.

FOSTER PIGOTT *see* **GRAHAM**

FOUNTAYNE WILSON, **Richard** (1783–1847), of Melton Hall, nr. Doncaster and Ingmanthorp, nr. Wetherby, Yorks.

YORKSHIRE   1826–1830

b. 9 June 1783, 1st s. of Richard Wilson of Rudding Hall and Elizabeth, da. of Very Rev. John Fountayne, DD, dean of York. *educ.* Eton 1799; Trinity Coll. Camb. 1800. *m.* Sophia, da. of George Osbaldeston† of Hutton Bushell, 4s. (2 *d.v.p.*) 5 da. *suc.* fa. 1786; maternal grandfa. 1802 and took additional name of Fountayne by royal lic. 20 July 1803. *d.* 24 July 1847.
  Sheriff, Yorks. 1807-8.
  Col. 1st W. Yorks. militia 1824-47.

Descended from Thomas Wilson, a Leeds merchant of the seventeenth century, Wilson's great-grandfather Richard Wilson was recorder of Leeds, 1729-61. His third son Christopher, this Member's grandfather, was bishop of Bristol, 1783-92, married a daughter of Dr. Edmund Gibson, bishop of London, 1720-48, and died 'extremely rich' in 1792.[1] Wilson's father apparently died *v.p.* in 1786, the same year as his mother, leaving him and his brother Thomas Charles as orphans.[2] Who raised them is unknown, but Thomas's death in 1801 left Wilson as the only surviving grandson of John Fountayne, the dean of York, who made him his heir and died on 14 Feb. 1802, bequeathing him Melton Hall. Wilson later inherited Fountayne's East Anglian estates from his aunt Catherine Judith Fountayne. In addition he possessed two large estates near Wetherby that had belonged to his father and a large amount of land in and around Leeds.[3] Thomas Creevey* reported in 1826 that Wilson was 'such a queer looking devil as ever you saw'.[4] He was made sheriff of Yorkshire in 1807, the year of the monumental county election, and it was later said that he had handled the occasion with 'sound discrimination and strict impartiality'.[5] In 1817, he presented the Leeds General Infirmary with 4,000 square yards of land on its south front, valued at £1,500, which was laid out as a garden and 'served materially to ornament the west entrance to the town'.[6] At a county meeting in October 1819 he backed Stuart Wortley, one of the Members, in opposing a petition to Parliament seeking to prevent prosecution of the organizers of the Peterloo meeting; but when he attempted to speak 'he was overpowered by clamour and compelled to desist'.[7] During the 1820 general election he was spoken of as a possible candidate for Yorkshire. Lord Hotham's* agent John Hall also reported, 5 Mar., that he 'came to Beverley, but would not oppose [George Lane] Fox, who had spent a great deal of money'.[8] At a county meeting in January 1823, Wilson again backed Stuart Wortley, this time against resolutions calling for parliamentary reform.[9] Later that year the Leeds tithes were commuted by payment of £14,000, half of which was paid by Wilson, the rest being raised by subscription.[10] When a Wetherby petition was set in motion against Catholic relief in April 1825, Wilson successfully asked the home secretary Peel to present it.[11] On 13 Apr. 1825 he chaired a Tadcaster meeting organized by local landowners, who drew up a petition that viewed 'with great anxiety and alarm' the efforts made by manufacturing and commercial interests to secure 'the removal of the present corn laws'.[12]

At a meeting of the Leeds Pitt Club in June 1825, Michael Sadler* proposed Wilson as a Member for the county at the next election, when four seats would become available. Thomas Tottie told the Whig county Member Lord Milton, 6 June, that the suggestion had been 'preceded by an insinuation that it was entirely without the knowledge of [Wilson's] personal intentions', but he believed Sadler to be

the puppet put forward on this occasion to try how the pulse beats towards an invitation ... to Mr. Wilson ... I need not tell your Lordship how skilfully and warily a certain family carry on their schemes of aggrandizement. I would not willingly cancel the worth of Wilson's gifts on several occasions to this town by referring them to merely as political purposes, but I cannot doubt that there is a strong infusion of that ingredient in the late donation of £7,000 towards the increase in this vicarage, with a view to the very thing now attempted.[13]

In the expectation of a dissolution, a meeting of Protestant freeholders was called in Leeds, 12 Nov., when it was decided that Wilson was 'a fit and proper person to represent the county'. Similar meetings throughout the West Riding endorsed this, and a requisition was started which he accepted, 1 Dec., promising 'to promote their interests and to protect and preserve, unimpaired, the Protestant church and government'. The Whig *Leeds Mercury* condemned him as 'a man of eccentricity and whim; totally unacquainted with and unfit for public business; destitute of talents, either as a speaker or a politician and fit to represent nothing in Parliament but his own money and his own prejudices'.[14] On 9 Dec. 1825 Lord Scarborough wrote to Lord Fitzwilliam explaining that he could no longer back Milton but would be transferring all his support to Wilson on account of the coincidence of their 'strict religious principles'. Wilson also received the backing of Miss Lawrence of Studley Royal, and over the succeeding months a number of Protestant committees were set up across Yorkshire to promote his campaign.[15] In May 1826 he issued an address promising to represent the 'great majority of the freeholders of Yorkshire' who were 'decidedly adverse to any further concessions of political power' to the Catholics.[16] Having joined forces with the Tory William Duncombe*, 6 June, he addressed the Cloth Halls of Leeds next day, when he argued that Catholics were 'unfit for performing the various duties connected with the legislature of a Protestant country like this', and pledged himself to support the abolition of slavery. Pressed on the corn laws, he called for 'a protecting duty on the importation of grain ... as would be alike consonant with the interests of the farmer and the manufacturer'. On leaving he was stopped by Edward Baines junior of the *Mercury*, who accused him of trimming on the corn laws and raised

the matter of the Tadcaster meeting. Wilson told him that he had not fully concurred in the resolutions passed there, but as chairman had been obliged to sign the resultant petition. Baines's intervention had the effect of sidetracking Wilson's campaign, and for the remainder of it he was forced to address the corn law issue instead of concentrating on his Protestant views. At the White Cloth Hall later that day he said he had 'no objection to a limited importation of foreign corn, which would serve as a check upon any exorbitant price which the farmer might demand', and on 8 June at Bradford he expressed 'rather more strongly his opinion that those laws ought to be revised'. Asked at Sheffield, 7 June, his opinion of parliamentary reform, he replied that he 'had never yet heard of a proposition for reform to which he could give his concurrence'. On his extensive canvass he only encountered strong opposition at Halifax, 10 June, and he was formally nominated at York, 12 June 1826. A contest was averted at the last minute and he was returned unopposed. At his celebration dinner Wilson admitted that he was 'fully aware' that he had been returned 'for no other reason' than to oppose Catholic emancipation.[17]

In the House he was a man of few words, but the presenter of a great number of petitions. He brought up some against Catholic relief, 11 Dec. 1826, 5 Mar., and voted thus, 6 Mar. 1827. He presented petitions for the protection of the landed interest, 14, 19 Feb., and against alteration of the corn laws, 20 Feb., 11 Apr. He was in the minority against the third reading of the spring guns bill, 30 Mar. He presented petitions for repeal of the Test Acts, 21 May, 12 June 1827, but voted against this proposal, 26 Feb. 1828. He divided with the Canning ministry for the grant to improve Canadian water communications, 12 June, and presented a Selby petition against the practice of suttee, 15 June 1827.[18] On 4 Mar. 1828 he brought forward a bill 'for the better recovery of small debts in several parishes in Yorkshire', which seems to have foundered.[19] That day he presented petitions from Beverley and Whitby against the stamp duty. He presented petitions against Catholic relief, 27 Mar., 24, 28 Apr., 30 Apr., and voted accordingly, 12 May. He presented a Woodhouse petition for limitations on the imposition of rates for church repairs, 8 July 1828. In February 1829 Planta, the Wellington ministry's patronage secretary, listed him among those 'opposed to the principle' of Catholic emancipation. He presented 12 petitions from various Yorkshire parishes against further concessions, 3 Mar., over 50 more in similar terms that month, and voted against the measure, 6, 18, 23, 27, 30 Mar. Despite his strong opinions on the subject, he made no recorded intervention in debate.

Along with the other Yorkshire Members, Wilson met the duke of Wellington to lobby for funds to help with repairs to York Minster, 26 Mar.[20] He presented a Harrogate petition for repeal of the house and window taxes, 4 May, and an individual's petition against the British Gas Light Company bill, 14 May 1829. In a letter to Lord Salisbury, 6 Aug., he was named by John Litton Crosby as one of those who had offered to help bail out the troubled Protestant paper, the *Morning Journal*.[21] In October 1829 he was one of the Tories listed by Sir Richard Vyvyan, the Ultra Commons leader, as 'strongly opposed to the present government'. He presented a petition from the landowners of Skelton against the Thirsk road bill, 24 Feb. 1830. Breaking his silence in debate, 4 Mar., he endorsed a petition against the Leeds and Selby railway bill, warning that it would destroy the towns along the Aire and Calder navigation canal and amounted to 'a direct attack upon the interests of the proprietors'. He presented a petition from the parish of Marrick complaining of distress, 16 Mar. He voted against Jewish emancipation, 17 May, and abolition of the death penalty for forgery, 7 June 1830. He retired from Parliament at the ensuing election.

Wilson died in July 1847 'after a long series of illnesses'.[22] By his will, dated 8 Apr. 1842, he devised Melton and the residue of his estate to his eldest surviving son Andrew, who had taken the surname of Montagu in 1826, and directed that £40,000, charged on his real estate, be divided equally between his other surviving son James and his five daughters. He left his wife £5,000 and an annuity of £1,500.[23]

[1] R.V. Taylor, *Biog. Leodinensis*, 200-2. [2] *Burke LG sub* Montagu; *Gent Mag.* (1786), i. 84. [3] PROB 11/1374/360; 2061/689; IR26/425/118. [4] Creevey mss, Creevey to Miss Ord, 7 Mar. 1826. [5] *Yorks. Gazette*, 31 July 1847. [6] Taylor, 424. [7] *Yorks. Gazette*, 16 Oct. 1819. [8] Wentworth Woodhouse mun. F49/72; Hull Univ. Lib. Hotham mss DDHO/8/2. [9] *The Times*, 24 Jan. 1823. [10] Taylor, 424. [11] Add. 40375, f. 389; 40376, f. 235. [12] *Yorks. Gazette*, 16 Apr. 1825. [13] Fitzwilliam mss. [14] *Yorks. Election 1826*, pp. 25, 42, 54; *Leeds Mercury*, 26 Nov. 1825. [15] Fitzwilliam mss 123/5; *Yorks. Election 1826*, pp. 60-62; Castle Howard mss, Strickland to Morpeth, 20 Dec. 1826. [16] *Yorks. Election 1826*. p. 72; *Leeds Mercury*, 27 May 1826. [17] *Yorks. Election 1826*, pp. 89-173. [18] *The Times*, 12 Dec. 1826, 15, 20, 21 Feb., 6 Mar., 12 Apr., 22 May, 13, 16 June 1827. [19] *Yorks. Gazette*, 8 Mar. 1828. [20] Wellington mss WP1/1004/35. [21] Hatfield House mss 2M/Gen. [22] *Yorks. Gazette*, 31 July 1847. [23] PROB 11/2061/689; IR26/1791/580.

M.P.J.C.

FOWNES LUTTRELL, **Henry** (1790–1867), of Hanover Street, Mdx.

MINEHEAD   12 Mar. 1816–2 Apr. 1822

b. 7 Feb. 1790, 2nd surv. s. of John Fownes Luttrell[†] (*d.* 1816) of Dunster Castle, Som. and Mary, da. of Francis Drewe of The Grange, Devon; bro. of John Fownes Luttrell*. *educ.* Eton 1805; Brasenose, Oxf. 1809; M. Temple 1813. *unm. suc.* bro. John 1857. *d.* 6 Oct. 1867.
    Commr. bd. of audit 1822-49.

Elected for the family borough of Minehead in succession to his father in 1816, Fownes Luttrell was again returned unopposed with his brother John in 1820. His political principles were expressed in a nomination speech on behalf of the Tory candidate for Somerset, Sir Thomas Lethbridge, whom he praised for his 'strong attachment to our invaluable constitution in church and state'.[1] He is not known to have spoken in debate during his Commons career. It was probably he who divided with the Liverpool ministry against economies in revenue collection, 4 July 1820. He voted in defence of their conduct towards Queen Caroline, 6 Feb., and against the disfranchisement of civil officers of the ordnance, 12 Apr., and parliamentary reform, 9 May 1821. As previously, he voted against Catholic relief, 28 Feb. 1821. Although he divided with government against more extensive tax reductions, 21 Feb., and abolition of one of the joint-postmasterships, 13 Mar., he voted for reduction of the salt duties, 28 Feb., and of the junior lords of the admiralty, 1 Mar. 1822. He vacated his seat in April 1822 after accepting a place worth £1,200 per annum. In 1857 he succeeded to the family's Dunster estate, one of the four largest in Somerset.[2] He died in October 1867 and was succeeded by his nephew, George Fownes Luttrell (1826-1910). His effects were sworn under £70,000, 30 Nov. 1867.

[1] *Taunton Courier*, 15, 22 Mar. 1820. [2] H. Maxwell Lyte, *Hist. Dunster*, i. 273-4.

T.A.J.

FOWNES LUTTRELL, **John** (1787–1857), of Dunster Castle, Som. and 225 Regent Street, Mdx.

MINEHEAD   1812–1832

b. 26 Aug. 1787, 1st s. of John Fownes Luttrell[†] of Dunster Castle and Mary, da. of Francis Drewe of The Grange, Devon; bro. of Henry Fownes Luttrell*. *educ.* Eton 1802; Oriel, Oxf. 1805. *unm. suc.* fa. 1816. *d.* 11 Jan. 1857.

Fownes Luttrell was the patron of Minehead, where he sat unopposed throughout this period, nominating his own colleague.[1] He continued to give general support to Lord Liverpool's ministry, but was evidently a poor attender. He was granted three weeks' leave for urgent private business, 21 June, but may have been present to vote with ministers against economies in revenue collection, 4 July 1820. He voted in defence of their conduct towards Queen Caroline, 6 Feb. 1821. He was allowed six weeks' leave for private business, 13 Feb., but was listed among the pairs against Catholic relief, 28 Feb. He voted against repeal of the additional malt duty, 3 Apr., parliamentary reform, 9 May, and mitigation of the punishment for forgery, 23 May 1821. With his younger brother, he divided with ministers against more extensive tax reductions, 21 Feb., and abolition of one of the joint-postmasterships, 13 Mar., but he voted in favour of reduction of the salt duties, 28 Feb., and of the junior lords of the admiralty, 1 Mar. 1822. He was in the minority against Canning's Catholic peers bill, 30 Apr. 1822. He divided with ministers against tax reductions, 3 Mar. 1823. He voted to suppress the Catholic Association, 25 Feb., and against Catholic relief, 1 Mar., 21 Apr., 10 May, and the Irish franchise bill, 26 Apr. 1825, in a session when he was said to have 'attended frequently and appeared to vote in general with ministers'.[2] However, he voted in the protectionist minorities against government measures for the emergency importation of foreign corn, 8, 11 May 1826. He divided against Catholic relief, 6 Mar., and was granted three weeks' leave, having served on an election committee, 21 Mar. 1827. He voted against repeal of the Test Acts, 26 Feb., and Catholic claims, 12 May 1828. In February 1829 Planta, the Wellington ministry's patronage secretary, listed him among those Members 'opposed to the principle' of Catholic emancipation who, once the principle was carried, would support any accompanying securities. He indeed voted against emancipation, 6, 18, 27, 30 Mar., and presented hostile petitions from Minehead and 'another place', 11 Mar. 1829.

After the general election of 1830 the Wellington ministry counted Fownes Luttrell among their 'friends', but he was absent from the crucial division on the civil list, 15 Nov. 1830. He voted against the second reading of the Grey ministry's reform bill, 22 Mar., and for Gascoyne's wrecking amendment, 19 Apr. 1831. He divided against the second reading of the reintroduced bill, 6 July, and to use the 1831 census for the purpose of scheduling boroughs, 19 July. He unsuccessfully moved that Minehead be transferred from schedule A to B, 22 July, complaining of its 'unjust and unconstitutional' treatment and lament-

ing the severance of a familial connection with the borough so ancient that 'I may almost consider it as a birthright'. He voted to postpone consideration of the partial disfranchisement of Chippenham, 27 July, and against the bill's passage, 21 Sept. He divided against the second reading of the revised bill, 17 Dec. 1831, the motion to go into committee, 20 Jan., and the enfranchisement of Tower Hamlets, 28 Feb. 1832. He made another futile attempt to save Minehead from total disfranchisement, 14 Mar., and voted against the bill's third reading, 22 Mar. He reportedly paired against the abolition of colonial slavery, 24 May, and the second reading of the Irish reform bill, 25 May.[3] He was in the minorities for inquiry into the glove trade, 3 Apr., and against the Russian-Dutch loan, 12 July 1832.

Deprived of his seat by the Reform Act, Fownes Luttrell offered in June 1832 for the new division of West Somerset, claiming to be in favour of a 'just arrangement' of tithes, prudent reductions in public expenditure, the protection of all property and encouragement for agriculture, 'the foundation of all our wealth and strength'. In a joint address with William Miles*, the farmers were urged to use the electoral power conferred by the Chandos clause to return candidates like themselves, 'the steady friends of agriculture, men of the old English stamp, neither warped by the flattery of political unions, nor tainted through foreign travel with revolutionary principles'.[4] His candidature provoked a number of ferocious character attacks, including accusations that he had persecuted Dissenters living on his estate, where he resembled 'a little rural tyrant, a petty despot in his own domain'. One extraordinary poster described scenes of moral depravity at Dunster Castle: 'a prostitute kept ... under the nose of his afflicted mother ... every servant prostituted to his lust. The wives of honest tradesmen assailed and seduced'; it was even claimed that his conduct had caused two husbands to commit suicide. By the time he withdrew, shortly before the poll, his expenditure had reached £5,000.[5]

Fownes Luttrell died in January 1857 and the Dunster estate passed to his brother Henry. His will, dated 14 Mar. 1855, instructed that £500 be paid to Mrs. Jane Richard, 'now residing with me and usually known as Mrs. Luttrell', who was also the beneficiary of a 'personal trust fund'.[6]

[1] H. Maxwell Lyte, *Hist. Dunster*, i. 272. [2] *Session of Parl. 1825*, p. 474. [3] *The Times*, 29 May; *Taunton Courier*, 30 May 1832. [4] Som. RO, Luttrell mss DD/L/2/23/136A, addresses, 11, 25 June, 4 July 1832 and n.d. [5] Ibid. 'an elector', 18 July, 'an independent elector', 30 July, address, 4 Dec., agents' bills; *Taunton Courier*, 28 Nov. 1832. [6] PROB 11/2248/215; IR26/2103/194.

T.A.J.

FOX, **Charles Richard** (1796–1873), of 1 Addison Road, Kensington and 33 South Street, Grosvenor Square, Mdx.

CALNE	1831–1832
TAVISTOCK	1832–1834
STROUD	1835–12 May 1835
TOWER HAMLETS	1841–1847

b. 6 Nov. 1796, illegit. s. of Henry Richard, 3rd Bar. Holland (*d.* 1840), and Lady Elizabeth Vassall, w. of Sir Godfrey Vassall[†] (otherwise Webster), 4th bt., of Battle Abbey, Suss., da. and h. of Richard Vassall of Jamaica and Golden Square, Mdx.; bro. of Henry Edward Fox*. *educ.* Eton 1808; M. Temple 1814. *m.* (1) 19 June 1824, Mary Fitzclarence (*d.* 13 July 1864), illegit. da. of HRH William, duke of Clarence (later William IV), of Bushey Park, Mdx., *s.p.*; (2) 16 Aug. 1865, Katharine, da. of John Maberly*, *s.p. d.* 13 Apr. 1873.

Midshipman RN 1809, res. 1813.

Ensign 85 Ft. 1815; lt. Royal W.I. Rangers 1818, half-pay 1818; lt. 85 Ft. 1819; capt. Cape corps 1820; capt. 15 Ft. 1822; capt. 95 Ft. 1824; maj. army (half-pay) 1824; maj. 85 Ft. 1825; lt.-col. army and half-pay 1827; lt.-col. 34 Ft. 1829; capt. and lt.-col. 1 Ft. Gds. 1830; half-pay 1836; col. army 1837; maj.-gen. 1846; lt.-gen. 1854; gen. 1863; col.-commdt. 57 Ft. 1865-*d*.

Equerry to Queen Adelaide 1830-1, to William IV 1831-2; a.d.c. to William IV 1832-7, to Victoria 1837-46. Surveyor-gen. of ordnance Dec. 1832-Dec. 1834, May-Sept. 1841, July 1846-June 1852; sec. to master-gen. of ordnance 1835-41.

Receiver-gen. duchy of Lancaster 1837-*d*.

Fox was descended from the notoriously corrupt paymaster-general Henry Fox[†], who held high office in the mid-eighteenth century and was created Baron Holland in 1763 (the title having been granted to his wife *suo jure* the previous year). He died in 1774, leaving an elder son Stephen, who also died that year, and his celebrated younger brother Charles James Fox[†], the great Whig leader. The peerage was inherited by Stephen's son Henry Richard, a minor, who was educated to adore his uncle's character and venerate his principles. Travelling on the continent in the mid-1790s, he made the acquaintance of Sir Godfrey Webster, who in 1795 adopted the surname of his wife Elizabeth Vassall, in place of his own; they had been married in 1786. Holland began a liaison with her in Florence, which continued after her husband's departure for England in 1795, and she gave birth to a son on 6 Nov. 1796 at Brompton Park House, where she had taken up residence with Holland after their return. Vassall, who obtained a decree of separation and £6,000 in damages in February 1797, divorced her

by an Act of Parliament, which received royal assent on 4 July 1797. Two days later Lady Vassall married Holland at Rickmansworth, and in 1800, when she inherited Jamaican estates by the will of her grandfather Florentius Vassall, they took the additional surname of Vassall before Fox.[1] The mentally unstable Vassall, who had resumed the name of Webster in 1797, committed suicide in 1800, when the baronetcy was inherited by his elder son Godfrey, Member for Sussex, 1812-20.

Charles Fox, who was acknowledged by Holland, nearly succumbed to a serious childhood illness in the winter of 1801-2.[2] He visited Spain with his parents from 1802 to 1804, and noted in the earliest of his numerous travel journals that 'we saw a fountain into which 36 noble moors had their heads chopped off'.[3] He toured Scotland, with the Rev. Henry Hartopp Knapp as a tutor, in 1807 and, having briefly attended Eton, accompanied the Hollands to Spain and Portugal from October 1808 to August 1809.[4] He was thus brought up, with the Hollands' other surviving children, Henry Edward, Mary and Georgina, in the febrile, intellectual and ardently Whig atmosphere of Holland House. Lady Holland, who directed her brilliant social circle with a mixture of heavy charm and forthright importunity, proved to be a difficult and demanding mother. Margaret Macaulay recollected in 1831 that 'her [first] son ... she was never kind to, and though she is very much attached to the second son, the heir to the title, she plagues him out of his life'.[5] Fox himself later remonstrated with her that 'you well know how you have been towards all your children for years and years, you know the things you have said to them, you know the jealousy you have shown of their being with him they loved above all'.[6] In contrast, by his father, a scholarly and amiable man, who was lord privy seal in the Grenville ministry, he was treated with patience, consideration and generosity, though he was occasionally teased (as 'Snarles') for his irritability.[7]

Evidently at his own request, Fox was allowed to join the navy in 1809. According to Lady Holland's journal for June 1810, Major-General Ronald Craufurd Ferguson*

acted the part of a real friend to our dear boy, he went out with him in the *Lively* and assumed a parental authority over him. He also, upon arriving at Cadiz, removed him from that ship and placed him with Captain Codrington of the *Blake*, where he now is, and is gone up to Minorca to escort the Spanish ships from Cadiz thither.

On 28 Dec. 1810, she wrote:

Hurrah! Huzza! A long and delightful letter from Charles, and a copious journal of all that has occurred since he sailed from Cadiz Bay, 7th August! ... Seems not so keen for *navy* as before; thank Heaven, if he should at the end of the year sicken of it![8]

He witnessed the hardships endured by seamen during his voyages in the Mediterranean, and was present at the siege of Tarragona in 1813.[9] In answer to Fox's censure of his dining with his political opponent Lord Wellesley, a pro-Catholic, in 1812, Holland rebuked 'my little Charles' for having

got a fancy that it is wrong to feel any good will to those whom one has once opposed, and that it is either foolish or wicked (I do not know which) to entrust a ship to a man who has a different opinion about the Virgin Mary and the sacrament from ourselves.[10]

Fox is not otherwise known to have held any but orthodox Whig views. In a letter to Henry, 1 Nov. 1813, he recounted a dream in which Charon had summoned the ancients for him to converse with, as well as Charles I ('a good man, but a bad king'), who was apparently 'condemned to go through the pain of being beheaded once every six years in the infernal regions, but that all the remaining time he lived in Heaven, and lived most cordially with Hampden and all the *honest* men who had opposed him in his mortal state'.[11]

Reports of Fox's poor progress in the navy eventually persuaded Holland to let him resign from it in 1813. He ruled out a career in the church, as he was 'fitted neither by habit nor temper to so dull, insipid and inglorious a life', but also forbade him from transferring to the army:

The absence, and occasionally the hardship of the army are as bad as those of the navy; the temptations to expense, the danger of bad company much greater, and, what I confess would weigh more strongly with me, your health more exposed to the consequences both of bad climate and intemperance and excess than any other profession. In short, I do not think you have constitution for the army and I do not believe that you would supply the defect by great caution and self-command, if you were exposed to the temptation.

He therefore insisted that Fox should study for the law, and he was admitted to the Middle Temple in January 1814 and placed under the Rev. William Manning, rector of Diss, later that year.[12] Despite admitting that 'your education hitherto has been somewhat irregular', Holland decided to take Fox with him on a tour of France, Switzerland and Italy at the end of July 1814.[13]

On 21 July 1815 Fox informed his father, who had withdrawn his opposition to his entering the army, that Lord Lauderdale had given him a commission in the 85th Foot at Chatham

so that I fear I shall not be in France this time. It is a mere skeleton having been very much cut up in America: however, any will do and they say a year's drilling in a marching regiment is a good thing. I am content and hope you will never have occasion to be otherwise with my conduct.

He also served at Liverpool and eagerly sought promotion, but with the war having ended, he found time to visit Naples, Venice, Munich and Brussels, partly, as he noted, in order to pursue his 'dearest LLL', Louisa Lloyd.[14] He was elected to Brooks's, 7 May 1816. In July 1817 he arrived in Corfu to take up his appointment as aide-de-camp to Sir Frederick Adam, with whom he subsequently travelled in Greece, Morea and Albania.[15] He laconically informed Holland, 17 Jan. 1818, that 'a canister of powder was good enough to explode under my nose and *scarify* my face to a great degree'. He had apparently been playing with it in his room, and was 'shockingly burnt', but luckily survived without losing his eyesight.[16] Back in England, he reported to his brother, 15 Aug. 1818, that

Sir John Osborn* *dit on* is to be made Lord Halifax, which will cause an election in our county [Bedfordshire]. Should I stand? I would to please the party, but that it would so much interfere with my military duties, and ... it is a prodigious *bore*.[17]

Nothing came of it. In January 1819 Sydney Smith commented that 'I scarcely ever saw a more pleasing, engaging, natural young man'; though two months later George Villiers, a nephew of the 2nd and 3rd earls of Clarendon, reported that 'that sweet woman, his mother, treats him like a dog and quite worries him out of his life'.[18] Fox, who had gained a lieutenancy in the Royal West Indian Rangers in late 1818, and a few weeks afterwards joined the half-pay list, exchanged back into the 85th Foot in 1819, and returned to Corfu.[19]

From there, 10 Sept. 1819, he congratulated Lord John Russell* on his *Life of Lord William Russell*, confessing that 'it has made me a far better being than I ever was before, because I am so used to hear such ultra-Whiggish sentiments that I had almost forgotten the rational and true principles of that party'.[20] He admitted to Henry, 6 May 1820, that 'I am not sorry to be out of the vortex of the elections for I hate them heartily',[21] and repeated to Holland, 17 May, that they 'are I think tiresome and (at least those I have seen) productive of ill blood and squabbles'. In a rare reference to politics in his letters to his father, 29 Aug., he expressed his admiration of his speech of 18 July on the aliens bill, which

> is an oppressive one and gives far too great power to the minister, for however necessary it may be to have such bills during the revolution and during our struggle against the gigantic power of France, it is quite absurd, quite ridiculous and illiberal to keep such force at this time.[22]

He complained to his brother, 24 Aug., that

> I don't quite understand your line of politics, and your excessive access of opposition. All parties are bad enough, but I do not think them worse than the usual quota of really honest men amongst them. I shall say nothing of the Queen [Caroline affair] ... except that it is a consolation that I hear a little less about her here (though more than I wish) than if in England.[23]

He lamented the 'alarming state' of the country to John Allen, 3 Sept., and hoped that 'all honest men will forget party, and leave off wrangling as to whose measures brought on the disaster, giving their minds to the best remedies'.[24] On 7 Dec. 1820 he told his brother that the 'queen's affair is nasty and uninteresting. Let me hear nothing about it I beg'.[25]

1820 had begun with Fox renouncing his love for Eliza Fitzclarence, one of the illegitimate daughters of the duke of Clarence with the leading actress Dora Jordan, the daughter of an Irish 'stage underling'. Not only had she spurned his advances, but the Hollands had refused to countenance the match, and Fox had had to submit to his father's wishes.[26] He then had a protracted period of illness and depression. As he wrote to Henry, 6 May:

> What do you mean by Oxford having faults for mind and body? Of the first I am no judge, but if by the latter you mean what I suspect, for God's sake take care and take warning from me who have been now ever since *December* confined to the house and, the greater part of the time, to my *room*, except three weeks, from *strictures*, the consequence of former follies, for follies they are, God knows ... I greatly fear that I shall not be quite recovered for many months, and these things bring on suppression of urine and *death*. You may guess under my circumstances what irritation, what vexation, I have endured and I do not exaggerate when I declare to you that I would sooner die than pass such another five months ... I cannot but warn you against indulging indiscriminately and if ever anything does happen to you to lay up at once and by no means ever use an *injection* in the first instance ... You will think I shall never have done writing, but the end is approaching and I must go to my bed. I am not fitted to live alone and to tell you how gloomily my time passes is impossible. Many *serious*, very *serious* reflections have passed in my mind, my dear Henry, and the prominent

and most painful one is that I have never acted from any religious principle and consequently have *never* done as I ought. You are too sensible, I hope, to laugh at what I say, but depend upon it unless a man *does* think upon those subjects he will like me have the bitterest reflections and reproaches of conscience.[27]

Eliza Fitzclarence married Lord Erroll late that year, which Henry feared would 'cost dear Charles a pang'.[28] After a lengthy correspondence and much useless speculation about various possible promotions, Holland informed Fox, 3 Sept., that the duke of York, the commander-in-chief, had obtained a captaincy for him in the Cape corps infantry.[29] He travelled extensively in Asia Minor, Turkey and Greece during the rest of 1820 and early 1821, and continued to collect coins, sometimes simply by scavenging among ancient ruins, a pursuit which had already engaged his fancy for some time.[30]

Henry Fox commented, 21 Apr. 1821, that Charles was 'lingering and dawdling' at Paris: 'provoking boy, he will get into her ladyship's black books even before arriving'.[31] After a few weeks in England, he embarked for Cape Town, and eventually joined his regiment at Grahamstown.[32] That year the Irish poet Tom Moore noted down some of Holland's lines on Fox, who apparently had a good memory: 'That he's like a palm tree, it may well be said, having always a cluster of dates in his head'. He also recorded that Lady Holland had 'forced Charles Fox into exile by her conduct to him'.[33] After much further consultation, Fox procured an exchange into the 72nd Foot, but this had to be abandoned when he learnt that, at Holland's request, he had already been gazetted into the 15th, and he accordingly returned to England in the autumn of 1822.[34] A good indication of the nature of Fox's relationship with his mother can be seen in his letter to Henry, 22 Dec. 1822:

> Mama said in her letter yesterday or the day before, after the usual '*financial lament*' ... 'neither Parliament for Henry nor promotion for you for years to be thought of', to which, after a scold for other offences, I daringly answered 'with regard to money for my promotion it will be time enough to refuse it when I ask it of you', which I think a just reply for she never gave me a fraction that I can recollect, except £20 to spend a month with at Paris ... However I am not in bad humour with her and only think it necessary and advantageous to my reason always to give her blow for blow as it prevents 'precedent of having her own way'.[35]

In 1823 he suffered a recurrence of his former illness, and Robert Vernon Smith* commented to Henry, 3 Mar., that

> your brother Charles complains dreadfully of his urethra and I believe submits to constant insertions and injec-

tions. If [only] he could make water as fast as he talks, and all secretions pass as glibly through his urethra, as secrets do through his throat.[36]

He himself confided to his brother from Ireland, where he spent the spring and summer, that he had not yet recovered from 'my swelled testicle', a 'most infernal complaint', and had 'spent a most melancholy two months, what with illness and other bothers'.[37] He informed Allen, 16 June 1823, that

> I hate Irish politics from my heart and never was in any country (not since Cape Town) where I felt less interest about what was going on. Both sides are so much more violent and absurd than any other parties elsewhere that it is unpleasant to talk upon the subject.[38]

Expecting a majority, Fox had to settle for a company in the 95th Foot in May 1824.[39] The following month, with his family's approval, he married Mary Fitzclarence, who, like her sisters, received a pension of £500 a year. She was 'a fine looking, brown girl with a pleasant countenance and manners', though Lady Holland feared she was 'a sickly subject' and had been in hopes that the 'roturier blood of the mother might have mitigated the royal constitutions'. On 31 Aug. she noted that

> dear Charles is very well in health, but getting into his usual restless way ... In that yesterday he was in one of *his ways*: got out of bed the wrong side. He does not like the notion of three days at Bushey, where she naturally likes to be. When he has been in harness a few months longer he will bear the restraint better. *En attendant*, though fond of her, he only considers her as an auxiliary to his medals and other possessions, not as a principal. But it will all do well; as she is very winning, and very firm, and sincerely fond of him.[40]

He left England with her in October, to take up his appointment as aide-de-camp to Lord Hastings, the new governor of Malta, and the following month York allowed him to purchase an unattached majority for £3,200. Having taken, at his father's request, a concerned interest in Henry's desponding state of mind and erratic character, he travelled home via Naples, Avignon and Paris in 1825, and took up residence at Dover as a major in his old regiment, the 85th Foot.[41]

Fox was ruled out, by the Whig adviser James Abercromby*, from taking advantage of a vacancy at the duke of Norfolk's pocket borough of Horsham, and instead was asked by Holland to attend the by-election there in March 1826 on behalf of his brother, who was still abroad. Holland soon afterwards apologized to Charles that 'I have not been unmindful about you for Parliament, but have not succeeded.

Something may turn up, but I have no money'.[42] At the general election later that year Holland asked him, 10 June, to attend the Bedfordshire election to support Lord Tavistock* and a possible second Whig candidate. He added that

> were so strange an event to happen as a call upon you in the town hall, I would have [you] simply say that your principles were those of civil and religious liberty, peace and reform, in short those of the person whose name you bear (the late Mr. Fox), that you were not conceited enough to imagine that in any quality but sincerity you could bear any resemblance to that person, and that you had never aspired to a seat in Parliament, still less to represent a county, but that if you were chosen you would do your best to do your duty, though it was unnecessary to add that if the freeholders could think of conferring such an honour upon you, it was quite out of your power to be at any expense.

On 26 June Holland wrote that 'we hear delightful accounts of your conduct and *speeches too* at Bedford'. Holland, who had forbidden Henry to marry Villiers's sister Maria Theresa, agreed with Charles, 29 June, that 'the main objection is to the connection not the individual', and urged him, 3 July 1826, to accompany Henry on a trip abroad to overcome his disappointment.[43] According to Henry's journal, Charles did join him for a while in Paris that year, when he described him as 'very amiable and agreeable, though for his own sake I regretted his coming, as he has no more prudence or foresight than a boy of 18'.[44]

By 1827 the Foxes had happily settled in Addison Road on the Holland estate in Kensington, in a mansion originally called Spectator House, but which became known as Little Holland House.[45] Fox regularly attended debates in the Commons in March and April, and took a close interest in the formation of Canning's ministry, vindicating his father's conduct in the negotiations. He wrote to Henry that the 'greedy looks of many Brooks's people was on the late resignations most amusing and continues to be so. I am really glad to have been in London at one of the great epochs, though I cannot say it has exalted my view of human nature'. He condemned Lord Grey's attack on his friends for adhering to government, and stated that

> there is much to be said, as Whigs, as to the propriety of joining Canning without any pledge for the Catholics and with the king decidedly hostile to them, however I think they have acted rightly in doing so and all the Catholics themselves were most eager for it.

At the end of May, complaining of having 'lost the skin off the roof of my mouth, which renders eating unpleasant and champagne *excruciating*', he added that the 'burst of interest and excitement about politics is now over', and he took little further notice of them that year.[46] Holland applied to his Whig colleague Lord Lansdowne, the new home secretary, and Clarence, the lord high admiral, for a promotion for Charles, and in August 1827 he was appointed to an unattached lieutenant-colonelcy on half-pay.[47] Later that year Holland admitted to Lansdowne:

> I wish that something could be done to turn his talents and good qualities (which without neutrality are not inconsiderable) to some object useful to his friends and profitable to himself, as he has nothing to do and not quite enough to live comfortably. He is, however, contented and happy.

Lansdowne responded positively, but nothing came of it, nor of a later application for a position in Ireland.[48] Holland praised Fox's interpretation of affairs, 3 Jan. 1828, writing that he was 'quite right (including Parliament) in all you say yourself. You err in nothing but too much humility and excess on that side is so rare that it is not only pardonable but amiable'. On 19 Jan. 1828 he observed that 'if you had been still at that d—d place Dover you might possibly have slipped into Parliament, for Bootle [Wilbraham]'s unpronounceable peerage vacates the seat'.[49]

Fox had to wait until July 1829 to return to active service, and then, despite preferring a regiment based in the Mediterranean, it was through the purchase of a commission in the 34th Foot, which was embarking for Halifax, Nova Scotia. He left England in September, and planned to stay in Canada until July 1830, and then to travel in the United States until April 1832.[50] However, the death of George IV in June 1830 put Fox's father-in-law on the throne as William IV, and he was anxious to bring his daughter home by having Fox transferred to the cavalry. He duly joined the Grenadier Guards soon after his return in September, and reluctantly took up his appointment as equerry to the queen, which he had been tempted to decline (as he had the offer of a Guelphic knighthood), professing no desire for 'court places and civil ribbands', and only acquiescing in the expectation of future promotions.[51] From the Tower, where he was on duty, he informed his brother, 12 Nov., that 'of our ministers, their conduct, the state of the feeling everywhere regarding them, I shall say nothing. *Je ne l'aurais jamais cru*! is all I can say'; and four days later he reported that 'the Tower has not been assaulted, though many of the great people wanted to make us think that it would'.[52] On the subsequent accession of the Whigs to office, Holland, who became chancellor of the duchy of Lancaster, applied to the new prime minister Grey, 18 Nov., for an appointment for Fox, claiming that

> the king likes him and would I know like to find him recommended and himself fortified in any favour, professional or not, that he is disposed to bestow on him. He has in truth promised to make him aide-de-camp, but it is without pay and in the spring 1832, and that is a long way off.

Having raised the possibility of a seat at the admiralty board, but instead pursuing an ultimately unsuccessful plan to have him appointed principal storekeeper of the ordnance, Holland again wrote to Grey, 27 Nov. 1830, informing him that

> *my* bringing Charles into Parliament is entirely out of the question. No doubt I should like to see him there but I have no means and even if I had, it would not be very pleasant on the eve of reform to engage for the first time in my life in purchasing seats. Should this circumstance lose Charles a place it will I believe cause very little disappointment to him. *He* scarcely expected it and is moreover much more indifferent to such matters than he ought to be.[53]

The king's anxiety not to arouse the jealousy of his sons, for whom no seats had been found, and a preference for giving the vacancy at New Windsor to Sir William Fremantle*, prevented Fox from coming in at an expected by-election there. He deferred to his father's judgment about his future, emphasizing that 'I do not want to be the means in any way of weakening the government and that if a more efficient person is thought of, I do not wish to press Lord Grey or make you do so and have it said that he sacrificed any body for your sake'. Holland was vexed that his son was left with only the equerryship, which in March the following year was transferred to the king's household.[54]

Nothing came of Holland's suggestion to Grey, 23 Apr. 1831, that Fox might fill the seat offered by John Calcraft* at Wareham.[55] Instead, on Macdonald's transferring to Hampshire, Lansdowne invited him to fill a vacancy at Calne, and despite an opposition, he was returned with Tom Macaulay, 2 May, when he spoke in favour of parliamentary reform and, although a stranger and no orator, 'gained much upon the affections of the people by his gentlemanly manner and deportment'.[56] Previously spoken of as a possible candidate for Bedfordshire, he attended the election, voting for Tavistock and his fellow Whig Peter Payne*; Holland believed he would have come in there free of expense, had he not already been committed at Calne.[57] Like her sisters, Mary Fox was granted the title and precedence of a marquess's daughter, 24 May. Recommending that ministers pay heed to the grievances of Sir John Doyle*, Fox stated in a letter to Holland, 6 July 1831, that

> I merely write this for the good of that government which I wish well to generally for its opinions and chiefly on your dear account, but which, as I said to Mama, will, when reform passes, fall to bits like an half-boiled pudding when taken out of the bag, unless they very much change their *manner*, their recklessness on many important points, and *above all their* nonchalance as to keeping the friends they have in good humour.[58]

He voted for the second reading of the reintroduced reform bill, 6 July, at least twice against adjourning proceedings on it, 12 July 1831, and steadily for its details. He divided in minorities for swearing the original Dublin election committee, 29 July, and postponing the writ, 8 Aug., and with ministers in favour of punishing only those guilty of corrupt practices there, 23 Aug. He paired against allowing town and city freeholders to vote in boroughs, 17 Aug., and two days later wrote to Henry that

> I have taken to pairing lately more than before you were here for it grows both tiresome and unwholesome. By the paper I see the government was beaten last night upon a question of detail of some importance [Lord Chandos's amendment to enfranchise £50 tenants-at-will], but I do not think it will hurt either them or the bill. Ireland is their present danger ... and this yeomanry business is full of great difficulty ... In short, I believe no one can foresee any thing but inconvenience and possible disaster whatever measures are pursued regarding that unhappy country.

A week later, he reported his inability to join his brother abroad:

> I hope when it gets (great tiresome beast as it is) into the House of Humbug then I [can] get away, *en attendant* I have only been able to get a pair for three days in next week to go and shoot at Ampthill ... [Mama] has taken my parliamentary attendance under her special care and talks to me in a tone on that head that would divert you and would make any one imagine that to *her* I owe my seat. You know me well enough to know the effect it has on me.[59]

He voted for the third reading of the bill, 19 Sept., and its passage, 21 Sept. When Sir Henry Hardinge attempted to place army half-pay officers on the same footing as naval ones in accepting civil offices, 7 Oct., Fox complained that he had 'made a most invidious distinction between the two services'. He voted for Lord Ebrington's confidence motion, 10 Oct. 1831. Later that month, at the king's request, he accompanied the Grand Duchess Hélène of Russia to Amsterdam.[60]

Margaret Macaulay recorded, 22 Nov. 1831, how Fox, by now an intimate member of the Court, had told her brother that

> he never saw the king in such humour and spirits, that the queen being away, he could now play a round game every night; whereas when she was there she liked to play a game called German fortresses, which he could not bear. Keeping the king in good humour and spirits seemed to be a question of great importance, Colonel Fox saying they must see what they could do to keep it up now the queen was come back, but he was afraid it would be rather difficult.[61]

He voted for the second reading of the revised reform bill, 17 Dec., and, approving ministers' handling of it, agreed with Allen, 28 Dec. 1831, that

> the better way was adopted, especially as it gave an opportunity of discussing each borough that was to be disfranchised, of which discussion, though God knows we had enough of it, the withholding of it, as by your plan would I conceive have been the case, would have been called injustice, and many of the places would have not been as convinced of their being impartially dealt with as they now must be.[62]

He voted against the production of information on Portugal, 9 Feb. 1832. He was added to the select committee on the East India Company, 16 Mar., and heard evidence given to its subcommittee on military affairs.[63] He apparently continued to pair,[64] but was present to vote for the partial disfranchisement of Helston, 23 Feb., and the enfranchisement of Tower Hamlets, 28 Feb. He informed his brother, 11 Mar., that he 'had been now three weeks suffering from a most irritating and persevering cough, but without a cold: it is so violent as to prevent my getting to sleep till generally five or six and has at last reduced me to keep my bed this day'. On 20 Mar. he wrote: 'think of my being up to speak last night in consequence of Croker quoting unfairly from my father's "Letter to a Neapolitan"!' He attended the debates on the third reading of the bill, and voted in its favour, 22 Mar.[65] He was in the minority for restoring the salary of the Irish registrar of deeds to its original level, 9 Apr. Making his maiden speech proper, 18 Apr., in praise of British and German support for the interests of Poland, he stated that

> the days of Frederick the Great are past; Germany now is no longer the Germany of those days; education has made there great progress; and I feel confident that all parts of that powerful and generous country will feel that she owes sympathy for Poland, in consequence of having formerly been a party in the shameful partition of that unfortunate and gallant country.

His father soon afterwards expressed himself 'delighted with Althorp's account' and that 'nothing escaped you at all disagreeable to government'; as well as 'satisfied with the report I have heard that you gave hopes of doing more'.[66] On 6 Apr. 1832 Greville noted that Fox had been proposed as one of the new peers, if they were needed to carry reform.[67]

On the dismissal of the Grey ministry, Francis Thornhill Baring* reported to his wife, 10 May 1832, that 'the king was hooted on going out of town last night, they say, and I know that Charles Fox and Lady Mary were hissed in one of his carriages'.[68] Fox immediately resigned his household office, and voted for Ebrington's motion for an address calling on the king to appoint only ministers who would carry the reform bill unimpaired, 10 May. He wrote to Henry from Addison Road, 15 May, that

my head has been really so addled and events have passed so rapidly that I have not had composure of mind sufficient to write even to you ... Living out here and sitting up in the House of Commons till 2, 3 or 4 with the excitement of these times I do assure you leave me hardly time to eat my dinner, besides mounting guard occasionally and being also shut up in a barrack yard ... I went on guard the day before yesterday. When relieved yesterday we went to the barracks and there found officers and men kept in, and they were not allowed to go out till 10 last night. However, at 4 o'clock out I went *of course* as a *legislator*, which supersedes all other duties. Well! What changes have occurred! Last night's was the most extraordinary debate I ever witnessed and so the oldest hands allow ... We shall hear the result today, but it is generally thought the duke of Wellington cannot form his cabinet on *reform principles*! ... I resigned my equerryship, a *great bore* as it takes away one *third* at least of my income ... but I could not do otherwise, feeling strongly as I do, and also respecting *Calne*. The king was kindness itself in his manner of taking it, as he always has been on all occasions towards me.[69]

Three days later he carried to his friends at Westminster the news that 'he had met Lord Grey on the stairs in the Palace, and Lord Grey in passing had said, "It is all right",' and the government was reinstated.[70] According to John Cam Hobhouse's* recollections, Fox confided to him that

a good deal of the late mischief had been caused by [William's eldest son] Lord Munster, whom he called a lover of money, not a politician. He had not spoken to the king for eight months, but ... helped to bring about the duke of Wellington's foolish effort. 'The other Fitzclarences are with us,' said Fox. 'Munster and [William's brother] the duke of Cumberland are now forbidden to talk politics at the Court. The king has no liking or disliking for ministers – a good old man, but

forgets what he says' ... Fox said to the king, 'By recalling Lord Grey, you have saved the country from civil war'. 'Yes,' said the king, 'for the present'.[71]

Holland recorded in his diary, 25 May, how Charles

while on guard at St. James's, was sent for by the king, whom he found at luncheon with his family and his sisters and who, rising, bade him kneel down immediately. He then told him to kiss hands and exclaimed, \"Now rise *Colonel* Fox and my aide-de-camp\". All this was done *de proprio motu*. Neither ministers, I, Charles, nor Sir Herbert [Taylor*, the king's secretary] were further aware of his intentions than from his having promised Charles himself, in 1830, that in March 1832, he would make him aide-de-camp.

A report had circulated that, as Edward Littleton* noted on 20 May, the king had said to Fox that

my equerries are my personal attendants, my minister has nothing to do with those appointments. If therefore you mean to continue equerry ... you must go out of Parliament. If you continue in Parliament you cannot be my equerry.

This having reached the press, Fox corrected it 'with great calmness and temper' by a paragraph in *The Times*, 26 May. The commander-in-chief, Lord Hill, resented the appointment because, as Lord Ellenborough commented, it automatically made Fox a colonel 'over the head of almost 700 lieutenant-colonels, some of whom had their lieutenancies for service at Waterloo'. At Hill's instigation and by the king's oversight, he was not gazetted colonel when the household appointment was announced. 'Not a little hurt and exasperated' by this, he almost decided to quit the army, but was swayed against this determination by his duty to the king as a soldier.[72] Holland recorded that William

is certainly much agitated and his manner as well as conduct are, by the account given me by Charles, so inconsistent and even incoherent as to raise some apprehensions in the minds of persons immediately about him. This is unpleasant. In Charles's affair he is at least friendly, just and candid, insists on his right of conferring and adhering to the appointment, and acquits ministers, me and Charles of any importunity, advice or application about it.[73]

Fox voted against increasing the county representation of Scotland, 1 June, and for the dismemberment of Perthshire, 15 June. His only other known votes in this Parliament were with ministers on the Russian-Dutch loan, 26 Jan., 12, 16 July, and he paired in this sense, 20 July 1832.

Following extensive negotiations that month, Fox was finally accommodated with a place at the ordnance, which he took up at the dissolution, when he left the one remaining seat at Calne to Lansdowne's elder son, Lord Kerry.[74] After hearing rumours about possible seats, including Lambeth, Rye and Shaftesbury, and having been seriously considered for Surrey East, he was returned, after a contest against a Benthamite radical, as 'the *town* Member' for Tavistock, with the duke of Bedford's candidate Lord William Russell*, at the general election of 1832.[75] He subsequently represented Stroud and Tower Hamlets as a Liberal, continued to hold office at the ordnance and received regular promotions in the army. Provided with almost nothing under the wills of his parents, he was denied his inheritance of the Bedfordshire estate at Ampthill by its sale, and resided in Addison Road throughout his life. After the death of his first wife, who for many years was housekeeper at Windsor Castle, he married a childhood sweetheart, Katharine Maberly.[76] Renowned as a numismatist, he edited *Engravings of Unpublished or Rare Greek Coins* in two parts (1856 and 1862), and at his death, after 'a long and tedious illness', in April 1873, his remarkable collection was sold to the Royal Museum in Berlin. In an obituary which emphasized his learning and benevolence, *The Times* averred that

> he did not take, like his father, a leading part in politics, but he inherited from both parents those social qualities for which his family has been distinguished for three generations. In him was combined the genial temperament of his father with that keen and rapid intuition of character which Lady Holland possessed in an eminent degree. His conversation had a peculiar charm; it was so fresh and original, so Horatian in its inexhaustible joyousness and playful irony, so frank and fearless in denouncing shams and conventionalities, and in upholding right against wrong.[77]

[1] Oxford DNB; The Times, 11, 22 Feb. 1797; LJ, xli. 333-4, 379. [2] Lady Holland Jnl. ii. 148-9. [3] Blair Adam mss 3/163 (NRA 9954). [4] Ibid. 3/164-6; Lord Ilchester, Home of Hollands, 225, 230, 235-6. [5] Mems. of Clan 'Aulay' (1881), 218. [6] L. Mitchell, Holland House and Hollands, 26. [7] For example, Add. 51786, Holland to Fox, 26 Nov. [1832]. [8] Lady Holland Jnl. ii. 259, 272. [9] Blair Adam mss 3/167-70; DNB. [10] Home of Hollands, 258-9. [11] Add. 52057. [12] Add. 51780, Holland to Fox, 1806-14; 51781, same to same, 29 June 1814; Home of Hollands, 259-61, 290. [13] Add. 51781, Holland to Fox, 29 June 1814; Blair Adam mss 3/171. [14] Add. 51781; Blair Adam mss 3/172-4. [15] Blair Adam mss 3/140-1, 174-5; Home of Hollands, 331. [16] Add. 51782; 51789, unknown to Lady Holland, 2 Jan. 1818. [17] Add. 52057. [18] Smith Letters, i. 309; Maxwell, Clarendon, i. 26. [19] Blair Adam mss 3/384. [20] Russell Early Corresp. i. 50. [21] Add. 52057. [22] Add. 51782. [23] Add. 52057. [24] Add. 52176. [25] Add. 52057. [26] DNB; Add. 51782, Fox to Holland, 4 Jan., 11 July, replies, 12 Sept., 1 Oct. 1820. [27] Add. 52057. [28] Fox Jnl. 40. [29] Add. 51782. [30] Blair Adam mss 3/142, 176-7; Add. 51789, Fox to Lady Holland, 21 Apr. 1814; 51966, Fox to Caroline Fox, 28 Mar. 1815. [31] Fox Jnl. 69. [32] Blair Adam mss 3/178-9. [33] Moore Jnl. ii. 482, 489. [34] Add. 51692, Lauderdale to Holland, 12 Dec.

1821; 51783, Holland to Fox, 7 Jan., replies, 12 Jan., 7 May 1822; 51831, Macdonald to Fox, 11 Dec., Tues. Sat. [n.d.] 1821; Lord Ilchester, Chrons. of Holland House, 30-31; Fox Jnl. 95. [35] Add. 52057. [36] Add. 52059. [37] Add. 52057, C.R. to H.E. Fox, 27 July, 10 Aug. 1823. [38] Add. 52176. [39] Add. 51783, Fox to Holland, 17, 23 Apr. 1824. [40] Blair Adam mss 3/181; Black Bk. (1823), 34; C. Tomalin, Mrs. Jordan's Profession, 310; Lady Holland to Son, 28, 30; Chrons. of Holland House, 41-42, 55. [41] Add. 51533, Hastings to Holland, 14, 16 Aug.; 51783, Holland to Fox [10 Aug.] 25 Oct. 1824; 51784, same to same, n.d., 29 Mar. 1825; 52057, C.R. to H.E. Fox, 13 Dec. 1824; ?3 July, 13 Aug., 11 Sept., 28 Oct. 1825; Lansdowne mss, Holland to Lansdowne, 29 Oct. 1824; Chrons. of Holland House, 41-42, 71; Blair Adam mss 3/182-3. [42] Add. 51574, Abercromby to Holland, 7, 17 Mar.; 51784, Holland to Fox, 5 Mar., 12 Apr.; 52057, C.R. to H.E. Fox, 19 Mar. 1826. [43] Add. 51784. [44] Fox Jnl. 225. [45] Survey of London, xxxvii. 105; Lady Holland to Son, 54; Add. 52011, Eleanor Fazakerley to H.E. Fox, 2 July 1827. [46] Add. 52058, C.R. to H.E. Fox, 6, 30 Mar., 27 Apr., 13, 31 May, 12 Oct. 1827. [47] Canning's Ministry, 247, 317; Add. 51784, Holland to Clarence [n.d.]. [48] Lansdowne mss, Holland to Lansdowne, 22 Oct.; Add. 51687, reply, 10 Nov. 1827; 51567, Anglesey to Holland, 2 Oct. 1828. [49] Add. 51785. [50] Ibid. Fox to Holland, 25 Dec. 1829; Chrons. of Holland House, 105; Blair Adam mss 3/186. [51] Add. 51575, Abercromby to Holland, 13 July; 51786, Holland to Fox, 13, 28 June, 1 July, 9 Sept., reply, 8 Sept. 1830; Chrons. of Holland House, 116-17; Russell Letters, ii. 213-14, 280; Blair Adam mss 3/187. [52] Add. 52058. [53] Grey mss; PRO NI, Anglesey mss D619/27A/87; Add. 51568, Anglesey to Holland [21 Nov.] 1830. [54] Grey mss, Taylor to Grey, 6 Dec.; Add. 51786, Holland to Fox, 18, 24, n.d. Nov., 16 Dec., replies, 28 Nov., 16 Dec. 1830. [55] Grey mss. [56] Devizes Gazette, 28 Apr., 5 May; Add. 51786, Fox to Holland, 2 May 1831. [57] The Times, 28 Apr. 1831; Anglesey mss 27A/114; Beds. Pollbook (1831), 48. [58] Add. 51786. [59] Add. 52058. [60] Lady Holland to Son, 123. [61] Mems. of Clan 'Aulay', 218. [62] Add. 52176. [63] PP (1831-2), xiii. 91. [64] The Times, 9, 10 Feb. 1832. [65] Add. 52058. [66] Add. 51786, Holland to Fox [c.19 Apr. 1832]; Lady Holland to Son, 134. [67] Greville Mems. ii. 283. [68] Baring Jnls. i. 97. [69] Add. 52058. [70] Three Diaries, 263. [71] Broughton, Recollections, iv. 236. [72] Holland House Diaries, 184-8, 191; Hatherton diary; Three Diaries, 269; Add. 51671, Bedford to Lady Holland, 31 May [1832]. [73] Holland House Diaries, 186-7. [74] Add. 51575, Abercromby to Holland, 21 July, 27 Nov.; 51644, Jeffrey to Lady Holland [20 July]; 51786, Holland to Fox, 21 [?22 July, ?11 Aug.] 1832. [75] Add. 51786, Holland to Fox, n.d., 22, 24, 25 Aug.; 51787, same to same, 12 Dec.; 51671, Bedford to Lady Holland [14, 15 Aug.]; 51724, Duncannon to Holland, 18 Aug.; E. Suss. RO, Rye corporation recs. 141/8; Devizes Gazette, 27 Sept. 1832; Wilts. Parson and his Friends ed. G. Greever, 109. [76] Chrons. of Holland House, 222-3, 289, 345-6, 426; PROB 11/1941/108; 2032/193. [77] The Times, 16, 21 Apr., 12 May 1873; Numismatic Chron. n.s. xiii (1873), 16-19; DNB; Oxford DNB.

S.M.F.

FOX, Hon. Henry Edward (1802–1859).

HORSHAM	17 Mar. 1826–5 Feb. 1827

b. 7 Mar. 1802, 2nd but o. surv. legit. s. of Henry Richard, 3rd Bar. Holland, and Elizabeth, da. and h. of Richard Vassall of Jamaica and Golden Square, London, div. w. of Sir Godfrey Vassall† (otherwise Webster), 4th bt., of Battle Abbey, Suss.; bro. of Charles Richard Fox*. *educ.* privately at home and by Rev. Matthew Marsh, rect. of Winterslow, Wilts. 1817-19; Christ Church, Oxf. 1819. *m.* 9 May 1833 at Florence, Lady Mary Augusta Coventry, da. of George William Coventry*, 8th earl of

Coventry, *s.p. suc.* fa. as 4th Bar. Holland 22 Oct. 1840; gt.-aunt Elizabeth Fox (wid. of Charles James Fox[†]) to St. Anne's Hill, Chertsey, Surr. 1842. *d.* 18 Dec. 1859.

Attaché to spec. mission to Belgium 1831; sec. of legation, Sardinia 1832-5; sec. of embassy, Austria 1835-7 and minister plenip. *ad int.* 1835-6; minister plenip. Germanic Federation (Frankfort) 1838, Tuscany 1839-46.

After meeting Fox at his parents' home in August 1832, when he was a 30-year-old bachelor just embarked on a belated diplomatic career, Macaulay wrote:

> He scarcely ever speaks in the society of Holland House. Rogers ... once said to me of him, 'Observe that man. He never talks to men. He never talks to girls. But, when he can get into a circle of old tabbies, he is just in his element. He will sit clacking with an old woman for hours together. That always settles my opinion of a young fellow.' This description is quite correct. Yet Fox's address is extremely polished, his person agreeable, and his mind, I believe, not uncultivated. He was, on this occasion, very courteous to me. But I despise his shallowness and instability.

Fifteen months later, when Fox was freshly married to Lady Augusta Coventry, 'a pretty little damsel, as red as a cherry and as plump as a partridge', Macaulay was more indulgent towards him:

> He is ... no favourite of mine. But I cannot deny that his powers of conversation are considerable, and his manners very sweet and courteous. Towards women – both his own wife and other men's wives – his manner is at once so respectful and caressing that I do not wonder at the havoc which he has made among the ladies. But he is lame and cannot walk without a stick, – a great drawback on his handsome face and figure.[1]

Fox's formidable, capricious and possessive mother, who was singularly devoid of normal maternal feelings, told him when he was 28 that his 'infirmity' – a slight deformity of the hip and spine which made him permanently lame – 'regulated all our plans and motions for years'.[2] In reality Fox, who was born two years after the death in infancy of the Hollands' first legitimate son, Stephen, was alternately neglected by his parents and overexposed to the pretentious wit and intellectualism of adult society at Holland House, which he grew to hate. He always admired and loved his father, but became increasingly alienated from Lady Holland. Above all, as an indolent, wilful, cynical young man, with, by his own admission, 'not a spark' of 'ambition', he resented his parents' assumption that as Charles James Fox's great-nephew he was destined, even morally obliged, to go into politics.

Sydney Smith pertinently observed to Lady Grey in 1823 that he would be 'nothing but agreeable; enough for any young man if he was not a Fox, and if the country did not seem to have acquired an hereditary right to his talents, and services'.[3]

'A clever and suprafine boy', as Smith put it, he was considered too delicate for public school and was educated at home, first by the Rev. Philip Shuttleworth, fellow and later warden of New College, Oxford, and between 1815 and 1817 by the ex-Catholic theologian Joseph Blanco White, who was advised by Holland that Henry 'above all requires constant attention and conversation to excite his diligence and to occupy and divert his mind'.[4] From the summer of 1817 until he went up to Oxford in October 1819 he spent periods with the Rev. Matthew Marsh, rector of Winterslow, near Salisbury. Smith applauded this turn of events in January 1818: 'Henry ... is a very unusual boy, and he wanted to be exposed a little more to the open air of the world'.[5] Fox never took to university life, though he was a voracious reader of books which interested him and took pleasure in the company of a small circle of college friends, notably William Henry Greville (younger brother of the diarist), George Howard* (grandson of the 5th earl of Carlisle) and John Stuart Wortley* (son of the Member for Yorkshire). He was one of the mass deputation which presented the University's loyal address to George IV, 26 Apr. 1820, when Holland commented jestingly to his elder illegitimate brother Charles:

> The king shook hands and spoke to him and he must be a good Whig indeed if such favour engrafted on an Oxford education does not infuse an alloy of Toryism ... He reads a *little* more than he did, but he has quite given up Greek and will not try for his degree, which with his parts and quickness a very little application would enable him to obtain.

Yet Fox wrote in his journal only three months later:

> Every day I live I am more and more persuaded not to meddle in politics; they separate the best friends, they destroy all social intercourse. And why? Is it for power? Is it for popularity? How unenviable they are separately! How seldom you see them combined; and most politicians have neither.[6]

After spending the summer of 1821 with his parents in Paris he fretted under 'the dull monotony of life at Holland House' in September; and in the Christmas vacation he suffered 'endurance vile' in the cold there, longing to return to the urban comforts of '*old smoky*'.[7] In March 1822 he persuaded his father to let him leave Oxford, but only after a 'sharp correspondence' which subsequently caused him a few stabs of filial guilt: he was surprised to feel 'every now and then a pang' of regret when he packed his bags and left the place '*for ever*' in early May.[8]

Fox was a ladies' man, drawn particularly to older, usually married, women for general gratification, but he also fell in love at the drop of a hat with pretty girls of his own age, and he was curiously eager to marry, perhaps to assert and secure his independence. In the summer of 1822, when he was in Edinburgh during the king's Scottish jaunt, he brought to a head a family row over his wish to marry Canning's daughter Harriet. His horrified parents would not hear of it, objecting ostensibly on the grounds of Fox's youth and their own meagre financial resources, and he reluctantly submitted to the veto.[9] He reflected at the end of the year that 'my own folly and impatience has only placed me in an awkward and not an advantageous position'. At that time Lord John Russell*, whom the Hollands had taken up almost as a surrogate son, interested and active in politics, warned Lady Holland:

I have no doubt of his abilities, but ... I have doubts whether he will do anything, partly because his father has done something, and partly from the straggling unsettled manner in which you bring up your sons. It is a sad thing that clever as he is, he is not able to take a common degree at Oxford ... As to his coming into Parliament I see no need for hurry. He is sure to be brought in by a friend in a short time. At 21 a young man either makes bad speeches or considers the House as a bore. Henry would probably go down after dinner, vote and then go to Almack's to praise Canning's fine speech. It is well he should feel anxious to come in before he does ... After all, however, he is one of the cleverest young men I ever saw and may do well if he is not spoilt by dowagers.[10]

In February 1823 Fox, having been advised by his mother to be 'careful of your health, take opening physics and wrap yourself up well', went with Stuart Wortley on a four month tour to Paris, Genoa (where he called on Byron), Pisa, Florence and Geneva. He acquired a taste for tobacco and for life in 'southern climes', noting that 'few are the charms that England offers me' and that he was 'greatly wanting in that satisfied, tranquil, imperturbable conviction that England is far superior to the rest of the world'.[11] Stuart Wortley was about to be returned to Parliament for his family's borough; and Holland tried to convince Fox of the 'attraction' of public service through participation in the work of Commons committees, where 'the whole business of this country' was done.[12] In London in the summer of 1823 he fell in love with Theresa, the daughter of George Villiers† (brother of the 2nd and 3rd earls of Clarendon), who had been

disgraced for embezzling public money as paymaster of marines. Their relationship became a close, though fraught one, but the Hollands refused to sanction a marriage, supposedly on the score of Theresa's youth and poor financial prospects.[13] In June 1824 Fox went abroad again, initially to Paris, from where Robert Adair†, an old family friend, who took him under his wing, assured Lady Holland that he was 'very well, very happy, and disposed to do anything that is proposed to him' and was 'not left to lounge about the boulevard, and fall into the abominable English society with which Paris abounds'.[14] Fox obtained his father's permission (with a caution about expense) to winter in Italy; but Holland's observation that a long absence might be 'an impediment to your coming into Parliament' prompted the following private reflection:

I am sorry to see his heart so bent upon my entering into politics, for which I have neither talents nor disposition ... If ... I felt any eagerness or strong opinion upon any subject I would not allow my vanity or fear of failure to overcome my opinions; but to be exposed to the reproach and contempt of half England for not supporting the fame of my name and family on a stage I am unwilling to appear on, and to which I have rather a repugnance, is still more hopeless. But with a wise and affectionate father I feel I should be wretched and unworthy of his tenderness if I were not to yield to whatever may be his wishes and try to fulfil his intentions, or at least allow him an opportunity of discovering his mistake by my own failure and disgrace ... I only possess a little quickness, which enables me to disguise my ignorance and to make the most of the little I do know. I have no steadiness, perseverance or application; I seize results and have not patience for details. This succeeds well enough in conversation; but in Parliament more depth and solidity is required, which I could only acquire by application and industry – efforts I am not capable of making except for something that deeply interests me, which Mr. Hume's economy, Lord John Russell's reform, or Mr. Wortley's game laws, do not in the least. I can conceive questions arising in which I willingly and earnestly should engage – the liberty of some continental country, the justice or injustice of some future war; but in these piping times of peace I cannot work myself up to the proper state of factious, peevish discontent, which I ought to cherish to become a worthy member of the opposition benches.[15]

If his parents were unaware of the depth of his aversion to a political career, they were soon enlightened, for in early October 1824 Russell reported to them the opinion of John Fazakerley*, with whom and his wife Fox had recently stayed at Lausanne:

'Henry Fox ... is most amiable and agreeable, quite unlikely, I think, to make any exertion in public life: he seems to lament that his family should expect such an effort from him, and if these are his feelings it is perhaps a pity that they should expose themselves to disappointment more acute than if the experiment had not been made'.

A few months later the veteran Whig Tierney confided to Lord Grey that he had 'no hope' of Fox's success in Parliament, for he 'has neither the energy nor the ambition which is necessary to call forth the talents he possesses'.[16]

Fox was ill with a deranged stomach at Venice, but reached Rome in November and moved on to Naples in January 1825.[17] From there he told Eleanor Fazakerley, his latest confidante, that he was so sick of hearing his father's 'balderdash' about the 'honour, distinction and delight of succeeding' in Parliament that he was 'ready to wish myself born a Provencal peasant without prospects or situation'; and a little later:

> The day alas! approaches when *bon que malgre* I am to become a steady voter and a red hot patriot foaming and spluttering about things I care not three straws for one way or another. But sufficient unto the day is the evil thereof.[18]

Indeed, at this very moment the 2nd Baron Yarborough was offering Holland, through a third party, to return Fox free of charge and unfettered by any 'unpleasant conditions' for Newtown, Isle of Wight, at the next general election.[19] Holland eagerly accepted, without consulting Fox, whose response when he was informed was dutiful but unenthusiastic.[20] Three weeks later he went to Malta to see his brother, and together they visited Corfu and Cephalonia, the siege of Missolonghi and Ibrahim Pasha's camp. Holland had written to Charles, 4 Apr.:

> His letters show some progress in knowledge and other improvement ... He is to come into Parliament ... I hope he shows in conversation or at least feels in his heart more pleasure at the prospect than he expresses in his letters. As to his politics I have no reason to believe he differs from me, and if he did ... I should not blame or interfere with him, but I do not like in a young one an *indifference* on such matters ... I am sometimes vexed at the prospect of a boy of so excellent an understanding, delightful manners and warm affections as Harry falling into a sort of indolent, pococurante philosophy which may make his life unprofitable to others and tedious and unsatisfactory to himself.[21]

Back at Naples in the summer he became stormily involved with Byron's former mistress Teresa Guiccioli and cultivated Lady Deerhurst, wife of the disreputable future 8th earl of Coventry, but remained emotionally though confusedly attached to Theresa Villiers, to the consternation of his parents, who when they found out precipitated a distressing correspondence.[22] Anticipating departure from Naples (where he had been '*very very* happy, more so than I ever expected to be again and more than I ever can be in future'), having been summoned to meet his parents in Paris, whence he was to return to England and Parliament, he moaned to Eleanor Fazakerley that 'I am about to open a door to all sorts of horrors'. He confided to her:

> My mind has long been made up – perhaps some time may intervene before I can carry my intention into execution – but my intention is to *pass my life* on this side of the Alps. I foresee that I shall not be able to settle *as I wish* in England ... I have no local attachments, no John Bull feelings, I hate the climate, dislike the manners and feel a most shameful indifference to the politics of the country.[23]

She tried to convince him that England had its merits and that he might be 'amused' by Parliament.[24] As it happened, a convenient riding accident, followed by some alarmingly 'violent palpitations' of the heart kept him in Naples until mid-December 1825, when he moved to Rome. At St. Peter's on the 23rd he was impressed by the 'mystery and solemnity' of Catholic church ritual, which 'hides the want of solidity of its foundation and leaves the imagination at work'.[25] He postponed his journey to Paris until the early spring of 1826, but was horrified by his father's casual written reference to the possibility of his being put up for Bedfordshire (where their Ampthill estate lay) at the impending general election:

> I hope ... [it] was merely a joke for ... I must openly decline any such honour. I have not health, inclination or opinions that would induce me to undergo the fatigue, odium and decision that is necessary for a county Member. If I come into Parliament (and you well know that I had *much much* rather not come in at all) I come in merely to please you and to satisfy or rather to disappoint your ambition by a display of total unfitness for an occupation for which I have no sort of inclination ... If there really was any notion or if you see it likely that such a notion should spring up for the convenience of the Russells, the Whitbreads, the Pyms or for the laudable diversion of annoying the adverse party I should take it particularly kind of you to baffle such intentions.

Holland assured him that it was not a 'serious design', but rebuked him for his dismissal of party obligations:

> As to your sneer of convenience to Russells, Whitbreads, etc. and at what you are pleased to call our indulgent and candid friends, I must say that it little becomes anyone

of our name who have derived so much consideration and even existence in the world from such connections to speak of them either as not worth having, or as not liberally bestowed upon us *when we deserve it*. We Foxes owe at least as much to party as party men owe to us.

Fox was conciliatory, but defended himself:

I do not see why I am to be called conceited because I cannot choose the same pursuits and inclinations. As to coming into Parliament ... I will do it as you wish it ... I did not mean to say I had any particular objection or pleasure in seeing the faults of our party more than of another.[26]

He set off for Paris in late February with 'painful and disagreeable feelings', which were intensified when, within minutes of his arrival on 6 Mar. 1826 he learnt that he was about to be returned on a vacancy for Horsham by the 12th duke of Norfolk; this, as he told Mrs. Fazakerley, 'cut sadly into some projects which I had and still fondly cherish'.[27] He was allowed to plead illness as his excuse for not going immediately to Horsham, where Charles stood in for him; but he was expected to take his seat after Easter. Tierney looked forward to introducing him, but when he was told by Holland, who consoled himself with the thought that at least his political views were 'quite reconcilable with [those of] an honest, independent Whig Member', of Henry's distressing 'indifference', he bemoaned the fecklessness of 'all the young ones'. Russell commented to Lady Holland that at most Norfolk 'must content himself with a lounger and be satisfied if Henry does not vote against his old Whig staunch opinions'.[28] Under pressure from his father, who allowed the 'clamour' of the party notables to overcome his and Lady Holland's worries about the Theresa Villiers affair, on which angry words were exchanged, Fox left Paris for England on 23 May. A handy three-week illness kept him away from Parliament, which was in any case dissolved on 2 June, and from the election formalities at Horsham on the 7th, when his brother again deputized for him. The Whig grandees were not amused.[29] He was, however, well enough to become 'once more entangled' with Theresa, which brought down on him the wrath of Holland, who swore that he would 'never consent to any connection' with her family and ordered Fox abroad again. He admitted that he had been wrong in his initial impression that Fox 'had not behaved with openness towards me', and concluded that while he had 'adhered to every promise', he had acted foolishly. Fox, 'sadly unhappy and agitated with a thousand apprehensions and doubts', reached Paris on 7 July, Lausanne on 1 Aug. and Italy in late September 1826.[30]

On 3 Oct. Holland wrote to Norfolk explaining that Fox would be unable to take his seat at the meeting of the new Parliament in November and placing it at his disposal. He informed Fox of this at the same time, but the following day was surprised to receive a letter from him in which he offered to return home and try to make a fist of Parliament if his parents would allow him to marry Theresa Villiers. Holland, keen to have him back, initially gave ground to the extent of promising that they would 'lay no restrictions with respect to your society or your time nor impose any conditions except that the discussion [of marriage] may not be renewed unless invited by me'. Norfolk assured Holland, who had informed him of Fox's possible return, that there was no need to do anything about the seat 'this side [of] Christmas'.[31] On receiving a letter of 30 Oct. from Fox in Rome, which contained a 'peremptory request for a decision', Holland gave way completely, and in his reply of 15 Nov. released him from his promise not to marry without parental consent and invited him to return home *entirely master of your own actions*, preferably in time to vote for Catholic relief, which he expected to come on early in 1827. To that end, he wished Fox to be at least as far north as Nice before Christmas. A fortnight later the Hollands were 'agitated' to receive an 'intemperate' letter from Fox announcing that he had ended his relationship with Theresa and intended to stay abroad and renounce Parliament, and asking Holland to apply for the Chiltern Hundreds for him. Holland, who rebuked him for using harsh words towards his mother, was irritated to learn that he had gone to Naples, but, claiming to want him to come home on account of 'my private comfort ... much more than idle dreams of your success in Parliament', advised him to reflect and reconsider. He declined to act over the Hundreds until he had had a rational reply and still pressed Fox to put himself within easy reach of London by the first week in February 1827, so that he could either vacate in time for a pro-Catholic successor to be returned or, if that was impractical, 'come over yourself to vote on that question even if you leave England and Parliament next day'.[32] On Christmas Day Fox wrote to Holland from Rome confirming that his decision to finish with Theresa – 'a victory of my reason over my inclinations' – was irrevocable and that he had 'no sort of intention under existing circumstances to return to England', and explaining that he had already written to Norfolk 'to relinquish my seat'. When his father still tried to persuade him to make himself available to vote on the Catholic question if necessary, he utterly refused, accusing Holland of stalling and of nursing 'in the bottom of your heart ... a hope that if I was in England and Parliament events might occur ... that would make me consent to remain in the House'.[33] A disappointed Holland finally accepted reality and secured the Hundreds for Fox on 5 Feb. 1827. He managed a wry joke:

> To be sure, your parliamentary career will be an odd one – in two Parliaments and never within the walls of the House. What a price among collectors your franks will fetch! My uncle's or Pitt's will be nothing to it.[34]

A few weeks later Fox, as he had doubtless been planning for some time, sought permission to marry Natalie Potocka, a young Polish aristocrat, who was supposed to have £60,000. His 'puzzled and confounded' parents reluctantly consented, but the affair soon petered out.[35] Fox, whose letters at this time showed an uncharacteristic interest in British politics (though Holland thought his 'speculations at a distance are often fanciful or false conjectures'), expressed a wish to 'enter the diplomatic line'. In January 1828 Lord Dudley, foreign secretary in the disintegrating Goderich ministry, offered Holland to give him an unpaid place as attaché at St. Petersburg, but Fox stipulated for somewhere in the warm South.[36] He stayed in Italy, taking up again with Teresa Guiccioli, and resisting his family's attempts to inveigle him into going home with 'threats, taunts, reproaches' and reports that his father was dying. Blaming his mother's bullying 'system', he became 'more resolved to remain away'.[37] He did pay a flying visit to England – 'a deplorable country ... for those who do not feel strong ambition and who have not vast wealth' – in late 1829, but was back in Rome by March 1830. Upset by the death of his latest confidante, Lady Northampton, 'the person on earth who cared most for me', he went to Naples for the summer and to England in November, arriving just as his father kissed hands as lord president in the Grey ministry. Closing his journal, he reflected:

> I look back upon life with much repentance. Not for the ambitious objects I have slighted, for had I attained them I should not have been happier, and had I failed in the attempt, which is more likely, I should have been mortified and miserable. But I have cruelly and wantonly played with the feelings of others, I have never believed anyone attached to me, and I have on that account ... determined not to be myself attached. My conduct towards Miss V., Mlle P., and Lady N. leaves me much to regret – especially the last two instances.[38]

Holland had 'nothing to ask for him' from the new premier, but dropped a hint about his diplomatic leanings.[39] Nothing came of notions of his being put up for Arundel or even Bedfordshire at the 1831 general election, or of an offer made through Lord Duncannon*, the government whip, of an unnamed 'certain' seat for

£1,200 a year.[40] The duke of Bedford, who had been particularly critical of Fox's conduct over Horsham, could not meet Holland's subsequent request to give him the vacant seat for Tavistock.[41] In July 1831 Adair took him as an attaché on his special mission to Brussels, and in February 1832, when it was suggested that he might go to the Lords if eldest sons were called up to force through the reform bill, he demurred, telling his father that 'the career which I have just begun has ever been the best suited to my habits and occupations, and I am very sincerely anxious to continue with it'. However, he was again 'wholly engrossed' with Teresa Guiccioli in Paris at this time, and in May 1832 he left Brussels, apparently unwell. Adair wrote frankly to Holland:

> I cannot guess at his future intentions ... Perhaps he has no fixed plan, but from what I see of him my notion is that except I were named to some mission in a warmer climate he would give the matter up ... the truth is that he does not like the business. He entered eagerly into it when he came here, but flagged very soon after the first excitement was over ... when he returns from any of his tours he never shows the least anxiety to know what has passed in his absence or even to put himself *en courant*. All this makes me afraid that diplomacy will never be a serious pursuit with him.[42]

A posting to Turin in September 1832 was more congenial to him. The following spring he married at Florence Lady Augusta Coventry (Lady Deerhurst's daughter), 'the very nicest little doll or plaything' Creevey had ever seen; he surmised that she was 'up to anything, as all Coventrys are'.[43] The marriage was happy enough, although there were two still-born children. In 1851 they adopted Marie, the illegitimate daughter of Victoire Magny of Soissons, who in 1872 married Prince Louis Liechtenstein. Fox subsequently served at Vienna, Frankfort and, most happily, at Florence, where the Conservatives kept him on in 1841 and did not recall him until July 1846, which ended his undistinguished career.[44] On his father's death in 1840 he succeeded to the peerage, but Holland's will had given his widow extensive powers, and he could not prevent her depredations of the more valuable contents of Holland House and the eventual sale of Ampthill; his mother's inherited Jamaican estates had been made virtually worthless by the abolition of slavery. Their relationship was poisoned by mutual suspicion and dislike until her death in 1845, when Fox got control of property worth about £7,000 a year and received a life annuity of £500. He carried out large-scale alterations and improvements to Holland House, which he financed by mortgages. He made a brief maiden speech in the Lords against the aliens bill, 17 Apr. 1848, but his health was already failing: he lost the sight of one eye and in his last years spent much time abroad.[45] He died, 'after a short but severe illness', at Naples in December 1859, and was buried there in the chapel erected by his wife, who survived him for almost 31 years. The barony of Holland became extinct. By his will, which was hastily drawn up the day before his death, he left all his property to his wife. His personalty was proved under £50,000 in February 1860.[46] His wife had become a Catholic in 1850 and Fox, who in 1841 had publicly denied a report of their conversion to Rome, may have followed suit on his death bed.[47]

[1] *Macaulay Letters*, ii. 182, 337, 339. [2] *Lady Holland to Son*, 85; *Lady Holland Jnl.* ii. 234-5, 244. [3] *Fox Jnl.* 190; *Smith Letters*, i. 395. [4] *Smith Letters*, i. 257; Add. 51645, Holland to White, 28 Aug. 1815. [5] *Smith Letters*, i. 283. [6] Add. 51749, Holland to C.R. Fox, 2 May 1820; *Fox Jnl.* 35. [7] *Fox Jnl.* 81, 97. [8] Ibid. 104, 116. [9] Ibid. 135-6, 137, 142-3, 151; Add. 51586, Tierney to Lady Holland, 26 Aug.; 51679, Lord J. Russell to same [Aug.]; 52011, Stuart Wortley to Fox, 16 Aug. [1827]. [10] Add. 51679, Russell to Lady Holland, 22 Dec. [1822]. [11] *Fox Jnl.* 157-67; *Lady Holland to Son*, 16, 23; Lord Ilchester, *Home of the Hollands*, 279; Add. 51667, Bedford to Lady Holland, 20 Apr.; 51783, Holland to C.R. Fox, 21 May 1823. [12] Add. 51748, Holland to Fox, 28 May 1823. [13] *Fox Jnl.* 173; Ilchester, *Chrons. Holland House*, 48; Add. 52011, Stuart Wortley to Fox, 2 [13] Oct. [1823]. [14] *Fox Jnl.* 190; Add. 51611, Adair to Lady Holland, 15 July [1824]. [15] Add. 51749, Holland to Fox, 27 Aug. 1824; *Fox Jnl.* 195-6. [16] Add. 51679, Russell to Lady Holland, 4 Oct [1824]; Grey mss, Tierney to Grey, 19 Jan. 1825. [17] Add. 51574, Abercromby to Holland [8 Nov.]; 51690, Lansdowne to Lady Holland, 14 Nov. [1824]; *Fox Jnl.* 196-202. [18] Add. 61937, ff. 1, 3, 5. [19] Add. 51832, Yarborough to unknown peer, 11 Feb. 1825; Wentworth Woodhouse mun. WWM/F33/64. [20] Add. 51749, Holland to Fox [c. 15 Feb.], reply, 5 Mar. 1825. [21] *Fox Jnl.* 205-11; Add. 51784. [22] *Fox Jnl.* 213-17; *Lady Holland to Son*, 29. [23] Add. 61937, ff. 24, 26. [24] Add. 52011, Mrs. Fazakerley to Fox, 25, 31 Oct. 1825. [25] *Fox Jnl.* 217-23; Add. 51586, Tierney to Lady Holland, 19 Dec.; 51679, Russell to same, 9 Nov.; 51749, Fox to Holland, 14 Dec.; 52011, Mrs. Fazakerley to Fox, 8, 11 Dec. 1825, 4 Jan. 1826; 61937, ff. 29, 31, 34, 36, 38. [26] Add. 51749, Fox to Holland, 15 Jan. [23 Feb.], reply, 28 Jan. 1826. [27] Add. 61937, ff. 41, 43; *Fox Jnl.* 223. [28] Add. 51574, Abercromby to Holland, 7 Mar.; 51584, Tierney to same, 12 Mar.; 51586, Tierney to Lady Holland [28 Mar.]; 51679, Russell to same, 26 Mar.; 51749, Holland to Fox, 6 Mar.; 51784, Holland to C.R. Fox, 5, 23 Mar.; 51833, Norfolk to Holland [11 Mar.]; 52057, C.R. to H.E. Fox, 19 Mar. 1826; 61937, ff. 43, 45. [29] *Fox Jnl.* 226-30; *Arbuthnot Jnl.* ii. 36; *Smith Letters*, i. 449-50; Add. 51598, Morley to Holland, 25 July, reply, 26 July, Lady Holland to Lady Morley, 26 June, Morley to Lady Holland, 1 July; 51749, Holland to Fox, 23 July, reply [July]; 51784, Holland to C.R. Fox, 27-30 June 1826; 61937, f. 53. [31] Add. 51749, Holland to Fox, 3, 4, 6 Oct.; 51833, to Norfolk, 3 Oct., reply, 8 Oct. 1826. [32] Add. 51749, Holland to Fox, 30 Oct., 15, 30 Nov., 1, 3 [17] Dec.; 51784, to C.R. Fox, 4, 18 Dec. 1826; 61937, f. 55. [33] Add. 51749, Fox to Holland, 25 Dec. 1826; 51750, Holland to Fox, 2, 5, 9 Jan., reply, 19 Jan.; 51833, Norfolk to Holland, 1, 14 Jan. 1827. [34] Add. 51750, Holland to Fox, 20, 26 Jan., 2, 5 Feb.; 51833, Robinson to Holland, 5 Feb. 1827. [35] *Fox Jnl.* 231; *Lady Holland to Son*, 61; Add. 51576, Mrs. Fazakerley to Lady Holland, 17 [Apr.]; 51750, Fox to Holland [c.

20 Feb.], reply, 9 Mar.; 52011, Eleanor Fazakerley to Fox [15 Apr.] 1827; 52447, f. 79. [36] Lansdowne mss, Holland to Lansdowne, 22 Oct. 1827; Add. 51834, Dudley to Holland 3 Jan. 1828; Ilchester, *Holland House*, 97-98; *Lady Holland to Son*, 67, 73. [37] *Fox Jnl.* 260-330, 343. [38] Ibid. 354-78; Ilchester, *Holland House*, 134. [39] Grey mss, Holland to Grey [18 Nov. 1830]. [40] Add. 51680, Russell to Lady Holland [?3 May]; 51724, Duncannon to Holland [Apr.]; 51836, Stuart to same, 24 Apr. 1831. [41] Add. 51663, Bedford to Holland [31 May 1831]. [42] *Holland House Diaries*, 18, 20, 49; *Lady Holland to Son*, 111; Ilchester, *Holland House*, 148; *Countess Granville Letters*, ii. 122. Add. 51604, Granville to Holland, 6 Feb.; 51610, Adair to same, 22 May 1832. [43] *Holland House Diaries*, 190, 192, 212; Ilchester, *Holland House*, 156-9; *Creevey Pprs.* ii. 268. [44] Ilchester, *Holland House*, 195-200, 219, 223, 248-9, 296, 307, 357, 400-2, 435; *Lady Holland to Son*, 157, 162-3, 167; *Von Neumann Diary*, ii. 247. [45] Ilchester, *Holland House*, 284-9, 292, 344-5, 367-71, 373, 376, 418; *Lady Holland to Son*, 189; Maxwell, *Clarendon*, i. 230; *The Times*, 8 Mar. 1841, 30 Mar. 1846. [46] Ilchester, *Holland House*, 419-20; *The Times*, 27 Feb. 1860. [47] Ilchester, *Holland House*, 299-300; *The Times*, 25 Oct. 1841. *Oxford DNB* suggests that a much earlier conversion may have 'influenced him in his refusal to take his ... seat for Horsham'; but this seems fanciful.

D.R.F.

FRANCO (afterwards **LOPES**), **Sir Ralph**, 2nd bt. (1788–1854), of Maristow House, nr. Plymouth, Devon; Market Place, Westbury, Wilts., and 76 Jermyn Street, Mdx.

WESTBURY	5 Dec. 1814–Apr. 1819
WESTBURY	1831–1837
WESTBURY	1841–1847
DEVON SOUTH	13 Feb. 1849–23 Jan. 1854

b. 10 Sept. 1788, o.s. of Abraham de Raphael Franco, coral merchant, and Esther, da. of Mordecai Rodrigues Lopes of Jamaica. *educ.* Tonbridge sch. ?1798; Winchester 1803; Brasenose, Oxf. 1807. *m.* 8 May 1817, Susan Gaisford Gibbs, da. of Abraham Ludlow of Heywood House, nr. Westbury, 6s. (1 *d.v.p.*) 1da. *d.v.p.*[1] *suc.* fa. 1799; uncle Sir Manasseh Masseh Lopes* by spec. rem. as 2nd bt. 26 Mar. 1831 and took name of Lopes by royal lic. 7 May 1831. *d.* 23 Jan. 1854.

Mayor, Westbury 1824-5, 1828-9, recorder 1831; dep. warden of stannaries 1852-*d.*

Capt. 4 Devon militia 1808; maj. N. Devon militia 1821.

Franco's ancestors were Portuguese Jews, who established mercantile houses in Leghorn, London and India. His grandfather Raphael Franco of 106 Fenchurch Street, who was the second son of Jacob, the second son of Moses Franco of Leghorn, died in 1781, having had with his wife Leah D'Aguilar (*d.* 1808), a son Abraham, one of several children who settled in Jamaica. Abraham married Esther Lopes (*d.* 1795), the daughter of a wealthy Jamaican sugar planter, and died at Lucknow in 1799, leaving one son.[2] Esther's brother Manasseh Lopes (later Masseh Lopes), who first entered Parliament in 1802, made this child, his nephew, baptized as Ralph Franco that year, his heir. He established him at his secondary Devon seat of Roborough, near Plymouth, and in 1814 brought him in for his pocket borough of Westbury, as a supporter of Lord Liverpool's ministry. In 1817 Franco married into an extended family of Westbury clothiers.[3]

A participant in Masseh Lopes's electoral intrigues, Franco 'retired of my own accord' in 1819 (as he told the House, 20 Jan. 1832), before his uncle's disgrace and imprisonment later that year. In July 1820 he pleaded with the prime minister for clemency to be shown to his aged patron, and apparently received a sympathetic response from Lord Sidmouth, the home secretary, for Masseh Lopes was released from gaol in September.[4] Franco does not appear to have been active in local politics. As mayor (an office he had probably filled several times) and one of the very few Westbury electors, he was present to assist in the tumultuous election of the home secretary Robert Peel, 2 Mar. 1829, on the resignation of Masseh Lopes in his favour.[5] By a special remainder, he succeeded his uncle, who died in March 1831, to the baronetcy which he had been granted in 1805. He was the executor and principal beneficiary of his will, and so came into most of his fortune, which was estimated at about £800,000.[6] He also took over the management of Westbury, as recorder, and, now a reformer, he turned out the anti-reform Member Sir Alexander Grant at the 1831 general election, when the other sitting Member sought a seat elsewhere. He returned himself and, after an apparent misunderstanding which occasioned a by-election, another reformer, Henry Frederick Stephenson.[7] Five days after his election he changed his name to Lopes, in accordance with his uncle's will.

In a long submission to Lord Brougham, the lord chancellor, 3 June 1831, Lopes set out his opinions on the Grey ministry's reform bill (under which Westbury, although originally scheduled for partial disfranchisement, was now, by a government amendment in April, to retain both its seats):

> Although a much interested individual in point of property, I am not one who has veered and twisted about with the growth and progress of this measure. My ground was taken from the first, as correspondences could show, and my opinions have been some time known to my friends, in as far as when the day arrived (which I will not be hypocritical enough to say I wished for) I should be among the foremost ready for personal sacrifice – that day is come, and if no one 'parts with his own' with more regret than I shall, there will be but little sorrow and annoyance at what is about to befall individuals.

He then listed his objections, beginning with the 'dangerous and pernicious' insinuation in the preamble that 'divers abuses' had 'long prevailed' in the return of Members. He attached most importance to the 'too low rate' of the borough qualification, and the 'undefined way in which the standard is to be estimated'. He added that

> anyone who has ever canvassed a scot and lot borough [as Lopes had at Newport, Cornwall, in 1818] can tell about privations the most destitute will undergo to keep themselves on the rate for the purpose of being voters. Numbers who ought to be receiving relief, are paying to the maintenance of the poor, that when the time of election comes round they may be reimbursed in a lump with interest that which they have put out in driblets.

He acknowledged the embarrassment it would cause ministers to rescind their promise, but warned that

> you may afterwards extend (and may be saved the trouble of doing it yourselves), but you never in a reformed Parliament will be able to contract the boundaries of the suffrage and if popular and external feeling has done much in enforcing the present state of things, it will be exerted in a tenfold degree to retain and secure it, and if it has influenced and dictated now, it will command upon any attempt at revision by putting an irresistible veto.

He therefore suggested a 'remedy or corrective':

> Let the £10 man have his vote, but let another who is higher rented or rated have two or more votes, rising according to a graduated scale. You thus preserve your own consistency, you keep faith to the public and you obviate the pernicious and overwhelming tendency of the £10 tide of voting. You give to property that due and just influence it ought to have, and rely upon it by doing this you will satisfy all parties, *high* and *low*, those *for* as well as those *against* reform, and you will give a feeling of security to thousands who are friendly to reform, but have a *deep, a rooted, though a silent dread* and apprehension of the £10 city and borough franchise.

Clearly drawing on his own experience at Westbury, he advocated giving ministers *ex-officio* membership of the Commons, so that

> if they happen to be representatives of any place let them have votes, like other Members, but if not, let them at least have place and voice, to expound, to advocate or to defend the measures of government. Suppose, by the by, when all private nomination is at an end, any minister in the middle of a Parliament changes his situation from a lower to a higher office and is obliged to appeal to his constituents, and they, possibly the voters of some insignificant borough, or of some place (as the case may be) where

popular feeling on any particular question is running high, and they chose to reject him. Is the king, for the mere caprice or hostility of *one* place, to be deprived of his paramount prerogative, the choice of his own ministers? Or is the country from the same cause to be deprived of the services of some high commanding and perhaps saving individual?

He also recommended a higher property qualification for Members, the prevention of any borough from being dominated by the neighbouring town with which it was to be amalgamated and the preservation of the 'nice balancing' of the agricultural, commercial and manufacturing interests.[8]

In the House, 6 July 1831, he rose, 'not ... under the advice, or as the representative of a numerous body of constituents, but impelled by my own feelings alone', to state that he was 'now willing to act up to the idea I have entertained from the first moment this subject has been discussed, that it is my duty to yield up and abandon every selfish and personal interest'. He put his arguments in favour of providing seats for ministers and safeguarding the agricultural interest, but stressed his support for the reintroduced bill, and voted for its second reading that day. He divided with ministers against using the 1831 census to determine the boroughs in schedules A and B, 19 July, but divided against the total disfranchisement of Downton, 21 July. He was listed as absent from the division on postponing consideration of the partial disfranchisement of Chippenham, 27 July. He paired in favour of removing one seat from Dorchester, 28 July, and the following day voted in this sense in respect to Guildford. He divided for the enfranchisement of Greenwich, 3 Aug., and paired for giving one seat to Gateshead, 5 Aug., and for combining Rochester with Chatham and Strood, 9 Aug. Unless it was Stephenson, he was reproved by the House, 10 Aug., for cheering Lord Althorp, the chancellor of the exchequer, in a 'marked manner'. He voted for the third reading of the bill, 19 Sept., and its passage, 21 Sept. He was granted three weeks' leave of absence because of illness in his family, 22 Sept. 1831.

Lopes paired in favour of the second reading of the revised reform bill, 17 Dec. 1831. Hoping to benefit from the widely expected peerage creations thought to be necessary to secure its passage through the Lords, he wrote to Brougham, 12 Jan. 1832, that

the much regarded relative whom I have succeeded, and to whom I am so deeply indebted, was persecuted, and with unreasonable severity punished, for the breach of those laws pronounced to be inherent in a system, now about to be abolished. It has been a source of pride to

me to have had an opportunity to vindicate his memory, by the voluntary and cheerful sacrifice I came forward to make at the call and under the emergencies of the government, and the country. Surely then, I may, I trust, be pardoned in saying, that I should feel an honest exaltation, if any act of mine could obliterate the painful feelings his sufferings occasioned, and the record of circumstances connected with them. And may I not, without invidious comparison, but rather in honour of him advance, that if he was made bitterly to atone for the liabilities to which he unguardedly subjected himself, the part I have taken, in an equal degree, gives me some title to a share in the honours about to be advanced to those who have promoted the question of reform, or have in that cause made any sacrifices of a personal nature.[9]

In fact, like his uncle, his hopes for a peerage were never fulfilled. On 20 Jan. he denied Croker's allegation that his selection of pro-reform Members for Westbury had influenced the government's decision, taken just before the dissolution, to allow it to retain its two seats. He voted to go into committee on the bill that day, and in favour of partially disfranchising the 30 boroughs in schedule B, 23 Jan. He divided against giving the vote to all £10 poor rate payers, 3 Feb., paired in favour of the enfranchisement of Tower Hamlets, 28 Feb., and voted for the third reading of the bill, 22 Mar. He spoke in praise of the foreign secretary Lord Palmerston's* conduct, 26 Mar., when he blamed the 'position in which we stand with regard to Portugal' on the 'tardy manner in which the late government interfered with a view to checking the practices of Dom Miguel'. He voted for Lord Ebrington's motion for an address calling on the king to appoint only ministers who would carry the reform bill unimpaired, 10 May. His only other known vote in this Parliament was with ministers for the Russian-Dutch loan, 26 Jan.; having been given six weeks' leave 'on account of a severe domestic affliction', 5 July, he was listed among the 'reformers absent' on this question, 12 July 1832.

Lopes declined to offer for one of the divisions of Devon and was returned unopposed as a Liberal for the remaining seat at Westbury at the general election of 1832.[10] He was elected to Brooks's, 4 May 1834. Defeated at Westbury in 1837, he again served as its Member in the 1841 Parliament and later represented Devon South as a Conservative. He died, after a long illness, in January 1854. Among his younger children was Henry Charles (1828-99), Conservative Member for Launceston, 1868-74, and Frome, 1874-6, who became a judge and was created Baron Ludlow in 1897. However, the Devon and Wiltshire properties and the baronetcy passed to his eldest son, Lopes

Massey Lopes (1818-1908), Conservative Member for Westbury, 1857-68, and Devon South, 1868-85, whose son, Henry Yarde Buller Lopes (1859-1938), Conservative Member for Grantham, 1892-1900, was created Baron Roborough in 1938.[11]

[1] *Gent. Mag.* (1832), i. 571; PROB 11/2188/218. [2] *Caribbeana*, v. 166; *W.I. Bookplates* ed. V. L. Oliver, 44; *Gent. Mag.* (1795), i. 348; (1799), ii. 1087; (1808), ii. 1045. [3] Sir R.C. Hoare, *Wilts. Westbury*, 34. [4] Add. 38286, ff. 92, 117. [5] Add. 40399, f. 25; *Keenes' Bath Jnl.* 9 Mar. 1829. [6] PROB 11/1785/283; IR26/1263/214; *Gent. Mag.* (1831), i. 465; (1833), i. 379. [7] *Devizes Gazette*, 14, 21, 28 Apr., 5 May 1831. [8] Brougham mss. [9] Ibid. [10] *Devizes Gazette*, 23 Aug. 1832. [11] *Plymouth, Devonport and Stonehouse Herald*, 28 Jan. 1854; *Gent. Mag.* (1854), i. 422-3.

S.M.F.

FRANK see SOTHERON

FRANKLAND, Robert (1784–1849), of Thirkleby Park, Yorks. and 15 Cavendish Square, Mdx.

THIRSK	31 Mar. 1815–12 Mar. 1834

b. 16 July 1784, 2nd but o. surv. s. of Sir Thomas Frankland[†], 6th bt., of Thirkleby and his cos. Dorothy, da. of William Smelt of Leases, Bedale, Yorks. *educ.* Christ Church, Oxf. 1803. *m.* 30 Nov. 1815, Louisa Anne, da. of Rt. Rev. Lord George Murray, bp. of St. Davids, 5da. (2 *d.v.p.*). *suc.* fa. as 7th bt. 4 Jan. 1831; cos. Robert Greenhill Russell* 1836, taking additional name of Russell 9 Feb. 1837. *d.* 11 Mar. 1849.
Sheriff, Yorks. 1838-9.

Frankland, who sat for the family borough of Thirsk throughout this period, made little mark in the House. He was an occasional attender who continued to vote with the Whig opposition to Lord Liverpool's ministry on all major issues. He divided against them on the civil list, 5, 8 May, and the additional Scottish baron of exchequer, 15 May 1820. He voted for restoration of Queen Caroline's name to the liturgy, 14 Feb., and inquiry into the conduct of the sheriff of Dublin, 22 Feb. 1821. He divided for Catholic relief, 28 Feb. If he was the 'Colonel Frankland' who was credited with a brief comment on the ordnance estimates, 18 Apr. 1821, this was his only known contribution to debate in this period.[1] He voted for more extensive tax reductions, 11 Feb., reduction of the junior lords of the admiralty, 1 Mar., abolition of one of the joint-postmasterships, 2 May, and reduction of the cost of the embassy to the Swiss cantons, 16 May 1822. He divided for Lord John Russell's reform scheme, 25 Apr., and Brougham's motion condemning the present influence of the crown, 24 June 1822. He

voted for abolition of the death penalty for larceny, 21 May, and reform in Scotland, 2 June 1823. He divided against the Irish unlawful societies bill, 15 Feb., and for Catholic relief, 1 Mar., 21 Apr. 1825. He voted against the duke of Cumberland's annuity bill, 6, 10 June 1825. No trace of parliamentary activity has been found for the sessions of 1824 or 1826.

He divided for Catholic relief, 6 Mar. 1827, 12 May, and repeal of the Test Acts, 26 Feb. 1828. He voted for the Wellington ministry's Catholic emancipation bill, 6, 30 Mar. 1829. That autumn the Ultra Tory leader Sir Richard Vyvyan* listed him among those supporters of emancipation whose sentiments were 'unknown' with respect to a putative coalition government. He voted for the transfer of East Retford's seats to Birmingham, 5 Mar., returns of privy councillors' emoluments, 14 May, and abolition of the death penalty for forgery, 7 June 1830. He was in the minority against Lord Ellenborough's divorce bill, 6 Apr. 1830. After the general election that summer ministers listed him among their 'foes', and he duly voted against them in the crucial division on the civil list, 15 Nov. 1830. He was absent from the divisions on the Grey ministry's reform bill, 22 Mar., 19 Apr. 1831. His only known vote on the reintroduced bill was with the minority in favour of counsel being heard on the hostile petition from Appleby, 12 July 1831. No evidence has been found to support the statement then made that he had 'voted for the bill in its former stages'.[2] He was named as a defaulter when the House was called over before Lord Ebrington's confidence motion, 10 Oct. 1831. He appears to have been absent from all the divisions on the revised reform bill of December 1831. He attended to vote with ministers on the Russian-Dutch loan, 12 July 1832.

At the general election of 1832 Frankland, who had succeeded to his father's title and estates the previous year, returned himself for the single Thirsk seat which had survived the Reform Act, but he retired from the House in March 1834. Two years later, on the death of his cousin and former colleague Sir Robert Greenhill Russell*, he inherited the Buckinghamshire estate of Chequers Court, which he initially intended to dispose of. Benjamin Disraeli[†] was reputedly prepared to bid £50,000 for it, but in the event the sale did not go ahead. Instead, Frankland Russell (as he now became), a gifted amateur artist who took an enthusiastic interest in architecture, enlarged the house and improved the estate. His friend Edward Buckton Lamb dedicated his study of *Ancient Domestic Architecture* (1846) to him, in recognition of 'the taste you have evinced in the desire to carry out ancient art in the spirit of the medieval periods'.[3] He died in March 1849. His title passed to his cousin Frederick William Frankland (1793-1878), but he left all his estates to his wife. In tribute to him, she had the church at Thirkleby rebuilt to designs by Lamb.[4]

[1] *The Times*, 19 Apr. 1821. [2] Ibid. 13 July 1831. [3] J.G. Jenkins, *Chequers*, 62-63. [4] *Gent. Mag.* (1849), i. 540; W. Grainge, *Vale of Mowbray*, 193; PROB 11/2093/386.

M.P.J.C.

FREMANTLE, Sir Thomas Francis, 1st bt. (1798–1890), of Swanbourne, Winslow, Bucks.

BUCKINGHAM   23 May 1827–3 Feb. 1846

b. 11 Mar. 1798, 1st s. of Adm. Thomas Francis Fremantle[†], RN, of Swanbourne and Elizabeth, da. and coh. of Richard Wynne of Falkingham, Lincs. *educ.* Eton 1811; Oriel, Oxf. 1816; L. Inn 1819. *m.* 27 Nov. 1824, Louisa Elizabeth, da. of Sir George Nugent, 1st bt.*, 5s. (1 *d.v.p.*) 6da. (1 *d.v.p.*). *suc.* fa. 1819; *cr.* bt. 14 Aug. 1821; Bar. Cottesloe 2 Mar. 1874; authorized by royal lic. to bear fa.'s title of baron of the Austrian Empire 4 Apr. 1822. *d.* 3 Dec. 1890.
  Sec. to treasury Dec. 1834-Apr. 1835, Sept. 1841-May 1844; sec. at war May 1844-Feb. 1845; PC 23 May 1844; chief sec. to ld. lt. [I] Feb. 1845-Feb. 1846; PC [I] 26 Mar. 1845; dep. chairman, bd. of customs Feb.-June 1846, chairman 1846-73.

Fremantle's father, a naval hero with a modest Buckinghamshire estate, died as commander-in-chief in the Mediterranean 'of an inflammation of the bowels', 19 Dec. 1819, at Naples, where he was buried on the 23rd. His third son Henry Hyde Fremantle, a midshipman in the *Glasgow*, followed him to the grave off the coast of Cephalonia three months later.[1] His eldest son Thomas Francis, recently come of age and down from Oxford, where he took a first in mathematics and a second in classics, inherited the Swanbourne property and the residue of personalty sworn under £3,000. He, his surviving brothers Charles Howe and Stephen Grenville, who had naval careers, and William Robert, who entered the church, and their three sisters were entitled by their father's will of 2 Mar. 1815 to share £10,000 on their mother's death; but this did not occur until 1857. Admiral Fremantle had in his will enjoined Thomas to submit himself 'entirely to be governed' by the 'advice and direction' of his uncle and trustee William Henry Fremantle, Member for Buckingham and confidant of the 2nd marquess of Buckingham, of whose small parliamentary squad he was the whipper-in.[2]

Fremantle began to study for the bar and stuck like glue to his uncle, who, with no children of his own, treated him generously and made him a long-term interest free loan to tide him over his immediate financial difficulties.[3] In the summer of 1821 he was designated for a baronetcy, in posthumous recognition of his father's services. For a month he negotiated with the authorities in an attempt to have the patent made out with a remainder to the male heirs of his father, to have him recognized as a baron of the Austrian Empire and to be given seniority in the list of baronets in accordance with his father's rank as a knight grand cross of the Bath (20 Feb. 1818). He secured only the first objective and considered mortgaging the Swanbourne estate for 'another £1,000' to pay fees and possible legal costs. He told his uncle that as well as having his father's and his own college debts to settle, 'besides the expense of fitting up Swanbourne last year and this', he was still being bombarded with fresh weekly bills, but that he was prepared to 'be content with a smaller income' in order to secure his object. His uncle may have assisted him again. He got royal licence to assume the Austrian barony in April 1822.[4] Buckingham, who was angling for a junction with the Liverpool ministry, had him in mind in June 1821, perhaps as his private secretary should he become Irish viceroy; but he thought there was little chance of his obtaining a salaried commissionership at one of the boards, as his uncle suggested.[5] Buckingham pressed him through his uncle to attend the county quarter sessions, 16 Oct., to help frustrate an attempt by his Whig brother Lord Nugent* and Robert Smith, the Whig county Member, to secure the placing of official advertisements in the new 'radical county newspaper', the *Buckinghamshire Chronicle*, 'in defiance of me'. Fremantle, who was on a tour which took him to Eaton Hall, the Cheshire home of his university friend Robert Grosvenor*, to Heaton Hall, near Manchester, owned by another of his Oxford set, Lord Wilton, and to Stoneleigh Abbey, Warwickshire, where his friend Chandos Leigh lived, was eager to comply, though he doubted the chances of actually suppressing 'so nefarious a publication'. He called on Buckingham at Stowe and duly attended at Aylesbury, where he was one of the majority of 33 (to 12) who vetoed putting advertisements in the *Chronicle*.[6] When Lord Wellesley and not Buckingham was made Irish lord lieutenant at the end of the year, Fremantle drafted but did not send (probably on William's advice) to Buckingham's uncle Lord Grenville a letter asking him to use his influence to persuade Wellesley to take him on as private secretary.[7] He then turned his attention to the place of chief clerk in the office of receipt of the exchequer, made vacant by a death, which was in Grenville's gift as auditor. His uncle approved the application, but warned him that although the office paid £1,000 a year it required 'constant unremitted attendance', was 'incompatible with Parliament' and, once obtained, must be 'your ultimatum'. As William expected, Grenville had already promoted the next clerk in line, but he thought no harm had been done.[8] When Buckingham was created a duke on his junction with government in January 1822 (William Fremantle was made a commissioner of the India board), Fremantle wrote sycophantic letters of congratulation to him and his son Lord Chandos, the other county Member.[9] In the early autumn of 1822 he devoted much time to executing 'a plan for the employment of the poor' in his parish, where most labourers were dependent on poor rates, by persuading initially reluctant farmers to employ them in return for a proportionate reduction in their rate assessments.[10] He displeased Buckingham in December 1822 by reportedly voting, as a member of the county finance committee, chaired by Chandos, to cut the remuneration of the high constables and by subsequently questioning Chandos's exercise of a casting vote. His uncle, passing on the rebuke, advised him to attend the next sessions to support the report, as the duke wished, but left it to him to decide whether or not to write to Buckingham. He did so, explaining that he had in fact voted against reduction and that his later conduct had been 'misrepresented', and avowing his undiminished zeal to play his part in the struggle 'between us and the radicals of the county'. The duke accepted the apology, but made it clear that he must toe the line in future. Fremantle, who had meanwhile been told by his uncle not to ask to be made secretary to Lord Clanwilliam as envoy to Prussia, duly obliged at the sessions of 14 Jan. 1823, when Buckingham's partisans carried the day. He had decided to let his chambers in Stone Buildings, Lincoln's Inn, which he could no longer afford, to go to Paris for six weeks and possibly to return to the continent that summer. He wrote to his uncle that 'even if I go on reading law, it is so much cheaper to live in lodgings' and 'I feel that I am very much behind hand with the rest of the world in travelling', while ' a little change of habits and diet would finally re-establish my health and spirits'.[11] In late March 1823 Buckingham told William Fremantle that if at the next general election he wished to retire from Parliament or find another seat, it was 'very probable that in that case I shall look to your nephew Tom'.[12]

In June 1823 Fremantle, recently elected to White's Club, received a modest windfall from the will of his great-aunt Mary Preston, who left him real estate near Bristol worth about £1,800 a year. His uncle waived his own claims on him for the moment and encouraged him to spend two years getting himself 'above the world in pecuniary circumstances'.[13] By October 1823 he was in France with his Catholic mother and sisters, learning the language by mixing in 'the secondary circles' of society in Paris and taking formal lessons. Of his health, he reported in January 1824 that 'I am better than I was, that is stronger (for I have no complaint in the world), yet every second night, I don't feel equal to going out, and am obliged to go to bed instead'. He returned to England at Easter 1824.[14] Keen to marry, he proposed to and was accepted by Louisa, the elder daughter of Buckingham's illegitimate cousin Sir George Nugent, the other Member for Buckingham. There were many difficulties, not least his uncle's 'displeasure' at this 'rash' step, which outlasted Nugent's dropping of his initial 'objections' and promise to 'give his daughter a liberal fortune', and greatly distressed Fremantle. The marriage eventually took place in late November 1824.[15] William Fremantle seems to have suspected an intrigue to have Thomas supplant him as Member for Buckingham; but the air was cleared and William observed that 'nothing could be more easy' than for the inactive Nugent to step aside. In June 1825 Buckingham told William Fremantle that he could not yet see 'daylight' in providing a seat for his nephew at the next general election, but that 'he stands first oars'.[16] The Fremantles were miffed when, in the autumn of 1825, Buckingham designated George Grenville Pigott* as his private secretary if he achieved his ambition of becoming governor-general of India; but William assured his nephew that 'your station in the county and the promise he has held out to you must compel him to look to you on parliamentary occasions'. He doubted the sincerity of Buckingham's 'declaration' to Fremantle's wife in the spring of 1826 that he in fact planned to take him rather than Pigott.[17] The duke could not find a seat for Fremantle at the 1826 general election, when his uncle and father-in-law again came in for Buckingham. A report in the *Chronicle* that at the dinner to celebrate Chandos's return for the county, 19 Aug., he had commended Chandos's recent 'spirited opposition' to Catholic relief (which Buckingham warmly supported) prompted him to write to the duke explaining that he had done no more than express his admiration for Chandos's political principles and resistance to 'new fashioned theories and speculative opinions', having in mind free trade and reform theories. His uncle talked him out of requiring the paper to publish a corrective paragraph.[18] In October 1826 Nugent's son George was authorized by Buckingham to offer Fremantle an unspecified seat in the Commons for £2,000, on condition of supporting Catholic relief, which he had himself turned down. Fremantle, having given up thoughts of the law, and painfully aware of 'the smallness of my income ... and the demands upon me which are daily increasing', could not afford it. Conscious that he was 'wasting in inactivity the best years of my life' and aching for money, he sounded his college friend Stephen George Lushington, a commissioner of customs and son of the secretary to the treasury, on his chances of obtaining a place at one of the public boards. On his father's advice Lushington told him that his case was 'a very desperate one', though Lord Grenville might be able to put in a word for him with Liverpool, and that his best hope of securing employment was 'to come into Parliament and serve the government there for two or three years'; even so, his connection with Buckingham, who had alienated ministers with his arrogance and importunity, would not advance his cause. His uncle endorsed this. Fremantle's desire for paid employment had been given added urgency by his inclusion at the head of a list of men nominated for the shrievalty of Buckinghamshire for 1827-8, which threatened him with 'impending ruin'. Nothing came of a bid to evade it by securing nomination as a gentleman of the privy chamber; but a direct request to the privy council office to be excluded was successful in February 1827.[19] His uncle thought the 'compliment' of his being placed in the chair at the January quarter sessions would enhance his prospects with Buckingham and Chandos.[20] In March 1827 he had a 'disagreeable' correspondence with his father-in-law over a solicitor's bill of £215 for drafting his marriage settlement, which he was obliged to pay.[21]

Next month, on the formation of Canning's ministry, William Fremantle, treasurer of the household since May 1826, found himself so much at odds with the duke, whose application for the government of India Canning had rejected, that he offered to resign his seat as soon as Buckingham required him to oppose the administration. He urged the duke not to spurn Fremantle, whom he encouraged to take the seat if it was offered to him. Fremantle was very keen, though wary of being 'placed on a side different from' his uncle's. When William informed the duke of this he was reprimanded for jumping the gun and told that 'to fill your seat, I shall probably look out for some person whose habits will enable him to be my organ in the House'. William informed Fremantle, observing that Buckingham's 'intention to get rid of his engagement to you if he can' was now clear and attributable largely to Chandos's pernicious influence. Fremantle agreed

and admitted to 'disappointment'; but he refused to play 'a dirty game' with Chandos to secure the seat, though he was prepared to discuss the situation with him. His uncle recommended him to 'soothe and court' Chandos.[22] When Fremantle met Buckingham at the quarter sessions, 24 Apr. 1827, the duke made it clear that he could not support Canning's ministry if the Lansdowne Whigs joined it and requested him to think carefully before committing himself to taking the seat should his uncle feel obliged to resign. William advised him to accept it if he was turned out. In a further inconclusive conversation with Buckingham on the 26th, Fremantle dismissed the duke's reservations about his entering political life at variance with his uncle and told him that 'having once made up my mind, I should decisively take my line with him and become his zealous partisan'. Later that day Chandos informed him that while he would not 'oppose his father's nomination', he would not attend the election or propose Fremantle if he intended to support Catholic relief. Fremantle said that he 'had considerable difficulties' on the question 'and that if I should come in *independently* I should refuse to pledge myself, but I was ready to support it if the duke, as of course he would, required it'. While he still believed that Buckingham would like to 'release himself from his engagement to me', he believed he felt that it was 'impossible, if I am willing to come in to his terms'.[23] On 29 Apr. Buckingham told William that he wanted him to vacate his seat and next day Fremantle, who was now laid up in London with 'a tiresome attack of illness', assured the duke that he 'willingly and thankfully' accepted it as his 'zealous partisan', even though he would 'rather avoid embarking in a decided line of opposition'.[24] Fremantle's continued indisposition delayed the moving of the writ until 17 May, and he was irritated by the duke's command that he and his father-in-law, at whose Buckinghamshire house he stayed after leaving London, should present themselves at Stowe on that day. He confided to his uncle that

this is very absurd, and will create delay. If he attempts to tie me down and extort promises which I consider derogatory and unusual, I shall rebel. I am willing to follow him and do his bidding, but he must place the same confidence in me he does in his other Members and act towards me in a manner usual under similar circumstances.

He nevertheless went to Stowe, where Buckingham talked of 'holding aloof and resting on his oars for the present, and abstaining from any strong demonstrations of opposition until we see what turn things may take'. He also learnt that the duke had forced Chandos and two other Buckingham burgesses to resign their gowns; and on visiting the borough he found that there was much hostility among the other burgesses to Buckingham's pro-Catholic stance. He had been advised by the duke 'not "to submit to be catechized by these fellows on the Catholic question, but to say that I should dispose of the question when it came before me"', though it was naturally understood that 'in accepting the seat, I was prepared to vote for the measure.'[25] He was confidentially warned by his uncle, who also sent him a canting retirement letter for communication to the bailiff and burgesses, of his belief that the duke was 'playing another game with Canning which may possibly but not probably end in his supporting him'. Confirmation of this came on 22 May, the day before the election, when Buckingham instructed Fremantle to tell his Members Carrington (St. Mawes) and East (Winchester) that it was 'advisable to hold off for the present, and abstain altogether from voting, neither supporting the government nor opposing it, and not to sit with Lord Chandos and appear to belong to his party'. He was also ordered to 'hint' to his uncle that the duke would like an audience of the king in order to explain 'his conduct, with a view to forming a juncture' with the ministry and to inform the duke's uncles Lord and Tom Grenville[†] that Canning had 'rejected every overture'.[26] The election, which was boycotted by the anti-Catholic burgesses, went smoothly, and Fremantle rejoiced to 'find myself in Parliament, notwithstanding sundry drawbacks in the tenure of my seat'. He had ignored a demand from 'a blackguard from the crowd' that he should support Catholic relief. He told his uncle that in their 'curious conversation' the duke had been 'full of complaints as usual'.[27] Three days after his election he was requested by the local Dissenting minister Barling to support Lord John Russell's motion next session for repeal of the Test Acts. He consulted Buckingham who, as well as urging him to go to Cheltenham or Leamington to seek a cure for his 'bilious disorganization of stomach', instructed him to answer by saying that he could not support the relief of Dissenters from their disabilities unless they showed 'a reciprocal disposition to conciliation ... towards the Catholics'. On 8 June he ordered Fremantle, who had not yet taken his seat, to alert his father-in-law and his other Members to a possible motion 'by a side wind striking at the Catholic question', but nothing came of this.[28] Fremantle was in the ministerial majority for the grant for improving Canadian water communications, 12 June 1827.

In mid-July Buckingham, who was about to go abroad for an extended period in an attempt to reduce his expenditure, assured George IV that he would 'support the king's government as long as the king supported it, meaning thereby that he had no connection with Canning', and that this was to 'regulate his votes in the House of Commons', with the exception of Chandos. 'You will see you are now to support the government', Fremantle was told by his uncle, who would not hear of his apparent offer to hand the seat back to him if he wished. Anxious to know how he was to steer his potentially tricky course, he consulted William, who was rather at a loss, having 'no confidence whatever' in Buckingham's 'acting up to his present declaration' and sure that as soon as Parliament met Chandos would 'assume the command over you all'. He thought a direct request to the duke for clarification might answer, but feared involving Fremantle with Chandos and was inclined to 'leaving the matter as is stands' in order to enable him to 'act the same part that Carrington does', which was tantamount to 'almost unconditional support of Chandos'. Fremantle evidently took this course, but his uncle warned him to be on his guard against Buckingham's 'continued system of ... double dealing'.[29]

In late November 1827 he accepted his uncle's offer to use his influence to have him named to the proposed finance committee, which would 'make you known and advance you'. John Herries[*], chancellor of the exchequer in the crumbling Goderich ministry, said he would bear Fremantle in mind, but he was not included when the committee was appointed under the aegis of the new Wellington administration in February 1828. William Fremantle was told that Sir Thomas had spoken 'extremely well and with great clearness and self command' on 'the poor laws'; but he 'did not know you had ever opened your lips' in debate, and no record of any such speech in 1827 has been found.[30] With Chandos and two other county magistrates Fremantle had promoted a scheme to invite Wellington and Peel to Buckingham in order to present the duke with an address commemorating his military glories. Fremantle was not invited by Chandos to the shooting party at Wotton which was to precede it, but his uncle advised him to swallow the insult, to remain silent, if, as seemed possible, Chandos used the occasion to air anti-Catholic views and to try to make Wellington's acquaintance. When Lord Nugent intervened to tell him that Buckingham had notified him of his wish to support the Goderich ministry unconditionally and that he could not therefore decently sit on the fence, having been returned by the duke as a supporter of relief, and so allow Chandos to undermine his father's interest in the borough, Fremantle put him down with a flat refusal to be bound by a second hand report of Buckingham's views and an assurance that the affair had always been intended to be strictly non-political. His uncle, reminding him that 'your only line is to keep well with Lord Chandos' and that 'as to what the duke writes or says or does, it ever proceeds from the momentary impression', and 'therefore you are only to look to what he may think on his return', entirely approved this line. The ceremony went off without controversy and Wiliam Fremantle was satisfied that his nephew had 'nothing more to complain of than an evident display ... of Lord Chandos's determination to keep you in the background', which would do him no harm with the duke when he returned: above all, 'you have not quarrelled with Chandos'.[31]

Fremantle agreed to present the petition from Barling's congregation for repeal of the Test Acts, which he did on 22 Feb. 1828, but he would not 'promise to support' Russell's motion and duly abstained on the 26th.[32] Eager to make a mark as a committee man, he was added to those on parochial settlements, 26 Feb., and Irish vagrants, 14 Mar., and named to those on the police of the metropolis, 28 Feb. (and again, 15 Apr. 1829), the Catholic land tax, 1 May, the Scottish gaols bill, 15 May, and the poor laws, 22 May 1828. He voted to sluice the corrupt borough of East Retford with freeholders of the hundred, 21 Mar., and with government against inquiry into chancery delays, 24 Apr., and reduction of the ordnance estimates, 4 July. He divided silently for Catholic relief, 12 May. On Slaney's labourers' wages bill, 23 May, he said that in Buckinghamshire wages were so low that they had often to be supplemented out of parish rates. He insisted that allegations against the conduct of St. Marylebone vestry stemmed from 'a most unjust prejudice ... raised in the public mind', 6 June 1828. The following month, after Parliament had risen, he received from Buckingham in Naples a letter directing him and his other Members, whom he was to contact, to take 'no decided step either in the support of the present government or of any opposition which may be formed against it'. In reply, 26 July 1828, he explained that Buckingham's 'friends' had 'endeavoured ... to adopt a moderate but consistent line', had 'given a general support to government, without surrendering our independence, or relinquishing our right to judge for ourselves' and had 'uniformly acted together'. He added that party conflict had largely been in abeyance, but that the Catholic question was approaching a critical point, 'when some measure must be taken either to grant the concession or to repress the rising spirit and power of the Catholic interest in Ireland'. Fremantle, who had lately bought the old manor house in Swanbourne village, said that he had

been in London without intermission from the opening of the session. I found the business of the House very interesting, and was constantly employed nearly every day on committees. I ... have I hope derived some benefit from a close attention to the forms and proceedings of parliamentary business.[33]

Towards the end of the year his uncle warned him to strive to avoid ' a participation in the feuds of Lords Chandos and Nugent, for neither party will let you be neuter, and you ... are really between two stools'.[34]

Fremantle evidently did not receive direct orders from Buckingham, but in mid-January 1829 he was shown by Bernard Morland, Member for St. Mawes, the duke's letter of 29 Dec. 1828 requiring his Members to do all they could do to secure Catholic relief and otherwise to 'give general support' to the government, reserving the right to exercise independent judgement, especially on foreign policy. At the same time he was 'trying to make terms' with the ministry and *offering himself* for office'. William Fremantle, seeing that the duke was playing 'his old game', advised Sir Thomas to 'vote for the Catholic question and on all other matters take Lord Chandos's wishes, for he is in fact the chief'. A letter of 21 Jan. from the duke to Fremantle's father-in-law expressing strong hostility to the government on the mistaken assumption that the recall of the Irish viceroy Lord Anglesey signified 'drawing the sword ... against the Catholic claims' was rendered irrelevant by the ministry's decision to concede them. Sir George Nugent thought Fremantle took 'a gloomy view of the situation of the [Grenvillite] party, as it is impossible the duke could have been ever on the point of abandoning those who were faithful to him in politics, or the Catholic question'. After consulting his father-in-law Fremantle, anxious to keep clear of the Grenville family squabble, was confirmed in his resolution to stay away from the anti-Catholic meeting promoted by Chandos at Buckingham, 21 Feb., when Lord Nugent clashed with his nephew.[35] Fremantle voted silently for emancipation, 6, 30 Mar. In the Easter recess he wrote to Buckingham in Rome to complain of Chandos's recent conduct and the duke's unhelpful silence:

My situation and that of all your friends has been one of pain and embarrassment ever since your departure – treated with slight and neglect ... as if we belonged to *a hostile party*, by those whom we wished to serve and oblige ... My residence in the county has been rendered so different from what it was a few years since that I can hardly believe so great a change should be effected without *any* fault of mine ... During your absence and with *all* your influence placed in other hands and used for other purposes ... not conducive to your real interests, I have always felt that resistance would not only be useless, but that it would be positively injurious ... I shall hope soon to learn your sentiments from your own lips ... If you are disposed to find fault with my conduct ... make allowances for the difficulties with which I have been surrounded ... I have make some sacrifices as your friend, and am ready to make more.

His uncle was 'not quite sure' that he had 'done right in writing to the duke', for 'if he is in a petulant humour and wants to discharge his bile he will answer you by some gross and unfounded and false assertions'. In fact Buckingham replied, 9 May 1829, unequivocally condemning Chandos's conduct on the Catholic question and disowning him as his spokesman or the leader of 'my political friends', and stating his wish to 'give general support to the government, but not to pledge ourselves further'.[36] In the House Fremantle, who was appointed to the select committees on vestries, 28 Apr. (and again, 10 Feb. 1830), and life annuities, 20 May, said transportation would be too harsh a sentence for a juvenile offending for a second time, 12 Mar. 1829. He presented petitions for local canal bills, 2 Apr., and one on behalf of Tyne and Wear colliery owners against using the duties on coal imports to defray the cost of the new London bridge approaches, 8 Apr. He spoke in this sense, 6, 8 May. On 10 Apr. he defended the archbishop of Canterbury's estate bill against radical attacks, which he said were 'more levelled against the church than against this bill'. He applauded Slaney's attempt to re-establish the principle of able-bodied employment by the parish, as the agricultural interest was 'in a state of pauperism', 4 May. He opposed the Smithfield Market bill, 11, 15 May. He approved of Byng's measure to make turnpike trusts rather than the parish responsible for the upkeep of bridge approach roads and was a teller for the minority of five, 12 May. He was forced to withdraw his opposition to the compulsory spending clause of the friendly societies bill, 15 May 1829.

Fremantle was apparently treated with more civility by Chandos, who was now embroiled with the disaffected Ultras, in the summer of 1829, when his uncle reckoned that 'it would be well for you to try and place yourself in the same boat with him', and he was 'sure to lead his father'. After a meeting with Chandos in late October, when Buckingham's return was imminent, William Fremantle warned Sir Thomas of Chandos's notion of having him put up for Aylesbury to aggravate Lord Nugent.[37] In reply to Fremantle's welcoming letter Buckingham wrote enigmatically of how 'many' of his 'old friends' had 'forgotten' him or 'proved ... how anxious they were to forget me'. William Fremantle advised him to ignore this 'insinu-

ation', which was probably aimed at others; and he was warmly received at Stowe in December 1829 and was invited to a ministerial junket there. His uncle, while warning him that if the duke immediately importuned ministers for a place he would get nothing, thought it was 'better to be on good and equal terms with him, than on confidential, which is so apt with him to lead to differences'.[38] Fremantle conceived the idea of volunteering his services to Peel, the home secretary, to move or second the address. His uncle approved but, aware that there would be trouble if he went behind Buckingham's back, made him consult the duke first. Buckingham vetoed 'so very decided a measure', which would 'commit him too much' to support the government unconditionally and so impede, as William Fremantle saw it, 'the same vacillating game he has always played'; but he felt that the answer as far as his nephew was concerned was 'perfectly satisfactory, as he talks of *us* and *we* which is all you can wish for, that is to be identified in his views and objects'.[39]

On the eve of the 1830 session Buckingham confirmed to Fremantle that 'my line must be *steady downright support* and instructed him to 'be upon the watch not to let any quirks or crotchets' of Chandos on 'currency, malt tax, etc. be considered as *mine*. Having twice voted for the principle of transferring East Retford's seats to Birmingham on 5 May 1829, he abstained, with Buckingham's blessing, from the division of 11 Feb. 1830.[40] He divided with ministers against Lord Blandford's reform scheme, 18 Feb., and the enfranchisement of Birmingham, Leeds and Manchester, 23 Feb. He dismissed Hume's plan for a tax to replace tithes, 8 Feb., and approved the notion of paying clerks of the peace by salary rather than fees, 17 Feb.; he was named to the select committee on this, 23 Feb. He asked to be placed on the East India select committee, but Peel, while claiming that it had been his 'particular wish' to do so, could not find room for him.[41] He was named to those on the sale of beer, 4 Mar., sheriffs' expenses, 9 Mar., the coal trade, 11 Mar., and superannuations, 26 Apr., and to the committee on the truck bill, 3 May. He assisted Chandos with his revised bill to reform the game laws, but after backing the motion for leave to introduce it, 22 Feb., had nothing to say on it in the House.[42] He supported the second reading of Lord John Russell's bill to reform St. Giles vestry, 2 Mar., and had Russell added to the committee on it, 17 Mar. He was in a vestry committee minority of two against Hobhouse's resolutions 'recommending a legislative measure founded on an elective principle', 31 Mar.[43] In the House next day he nevertheless supported the

St. Giles bill as a matter of urgent need, but on 2 Apr. he opposed Hobhouse's attempt to lower the voting qualification from £30 to £25 and was a teller for the minority against it. Joining in the successful opposition to the Avon and Gloucestershire railway bill, 12 Mar., he said that the interest of 'the landed proprietors deserved as much consideration as that of any other party concerned'.[44] He agreed with Portman that subsidized emigration offered a solution to the problems of poverty and high poor rates, 23 Mar., and he approved Slaney's poor law amendment bill, 26 Apr. He presented licensed victuallers' petitions against the sale of beer bill and voted in the minority of 28 against its second reading, 4 May. He voiced objections to details of the measure, 3, 4 June, when he was a minority teller for his proposed clause for notice of licensing applications to be displayed on church doors, which was rejected by 72-42. He divided for attempts to restrict the scope of the measure, 21 June, 1 July. He voted against Jewish emancipation, 17 May, and, with Peel, against the Galway franchise bill, 25 May. He defended the Millbank penitentiary experiment (of which he was one of the managing committee), 21 May, and demanded inquiry into the cost for counties such as Buckinghamshire of moving on Irish and Scottish vagrants, 26 May. He thought the beneficiaries of turnpike legislation should pay the customary parliamentary fees, 11 June, when, in the absence of its sponsor Littleton, he had the truck bill committed. On 23 June 1830 he was a majority teller with Littleton for its report stage.

He came in again for Buckingham at the general election of 1830. At a dinner celebrating Chandos's return for the county he praised his 'independent' conduct, while admitting their occasional differences of opinion.[45] Ministers listed him as one of their 'friends', and he was in their minority in the division on the civil list which brought them down, 15 Nov. 1830. In late January 1831 Buckingham informed him of his rooted hostility to the Birmingham and London railway bill; but his uncle, commenting that the duke was bound to change his mind, told him:

> As to keeping up any political connection with the present heads of the Grenville family with any view of either honour or advantage, it is past hope; all I should recommend is to take ample time in forming your decisions and this not till you see before you some other tangible station, etc. In the meantime the being in Parliament gives you the sort of intercourse and communication with current matters that must be an advantage.

Fremantle was by now mixing familiarly with the leaders and organizers of the Tory opposition.[46]

He refused to support the Grey ministry's game bill because Chandos's measure had been unfairly superseded, 15 Feb., and was not prepared to swallow Hobhouse's bill to open select vestries unless St. Giles was exempted, 21 Feb. He again defended Millbank penitentiary and claimed that two-thirds of its inmates became 'useful and honest members of society' on release, 17 Mar. On the 19th he said that a Northampton reform petition had not been unanimously adopted and, endorsing Buckingham corporation's petition against the reform bill, which unaccountably scheduled the borough for disfranchisement, contended that its actual population entitled it to retain one seat. He had privately raised this problem with Russell, who promised to look into it. (The borough was subsequently put in schedule B.) He voted against the second reading, 22 Mar., but next day presented a favourable petition from Kirkcudbright, while noting that the measure would destroy the privileges of the local authorities there. Buckingham, who believed 'ministers to be safely seated until the Birmingham [Political] Union is prepared to declare the republic', asked him to keep him furnished with 'the talk of the day'.[47] On 25 Mar. he called on the government to insist on Queen Adelaide taking a £50,000 outfit despite her husband's having turned it down. Raising the issue again, 28 Mar., Fremantle, who was told by his uncle for his 'private satisfaction' that this intervention had 'succeeded' at Windsor, denied that he had been 'set on by some other party', observed that Hume and his other detractors were 'not very friendly to a monarchical form of government' and warned William IV to beware of a reformed Parliament.[48] He divided for Gascoyne's wrecking amendment to the reform bill, 19 Apr. 1831.

Fremantle was again returned for Buckingham at the ensuing general election. His uncle, who judged in late July that he had managed 'extremely well' in staking his claim to Buckingham's interest there after reform was enacted, observed that

> so long as the duke is stout you are safe ... Though I despair of any advantage to you from the connection, yet on the whole it is the only line you can adopt, and the connection of the family is of such long standing and so well known that one cannot bear the feel of altogether breaking it up. Besides which I think your residence and station in Buckinghamshire give you the best possible claim and offer an advantage to the Grenville family, which must sooner or later tell.[49]

Fremantle voted against the second reading of the reintroduced reform bill, 6 July 1831. On the 11th he backed Chandos's endorsement of the Northampton electors' petition complaining of the use of the town barracks to accommodate out-voters in the reform interest, adding that at the general election 'influence of the most extraordinary kind has been exercised wherever the reform candidates have been opposed'. He voted at least twice for the adjournment, 12 July, demanded a clear statement of the criterion on which schedule A was based, 15 July, voted for use of the 1831 census as a basis for disfranchisement, 19 July, and suggested giving the schedule B boroughs two Members in order to 'protect them in a reformed Parliament', 27 July, when he divided against the inclusion of Chippenham. His uncle thought this speech was 'very good'.[50] He said that petitioners from the Manchester Political Union, 'so far from being satisfied with the [reform] bill, talk of correcting its anomalies in a reformed Parliament', 8 Aug. He did not see why me qualified to become Members should be exempted from serving as returning officers, 19 Aug. He expressed 'very strong objections' to the appointment of boundary commissioners, with dangerously extensive powers, and the inclusion among them of the Members Littleton and Gilbert, 1 Sept. Next day he moved to preserve the voting rights of freeholders of the sluiced boroughs of Aylesbury, Cricklade, East Retford and New Shoreham who lived more than seven miles away, and was a teller for the minority of 29. He objected to the grant for the salaries of Oxford and Cambridge professors, and as one of the derided 'amateurs' overseeing Millbank, once more defended the institution, 8 July. He was not happy with the introduction so late in the session of Hobhouse's vestry bill, 25 July. He suggested improvements to the game bill, 8 Aug., but failed in his bid to stop coach drivers and publicans selling game, 8 Aug. He protested at the 'levity' with which government supporters seemed to treat the Dublin election controversy, 20 Aug. He was named to the select committees on secondary punishments, 15 July (and again, 2 Feb. 1832) and ridding the House of its noisome atmosphere, 8 Aug. 1831. He was 'in good spirits as to the future' in mid-September, but Buckingham, disgusted with the 'sickening candour' with which the opposition leaders were 'now suffering the [reform] bill to pass unresisted', did not share his optimism. He signed the requisition of 13 Members urging Henry Bankes* to stand in the Dorset by-election.[51] He divided against the passage of the reform bill, 21 Sept. 1831. At this time he happily 'discovered' a financial windfall 'overlooked' by his father; his uncle declined his offer to use it to repay him.[52]

Fremantle's wife gave birth to their second son on 12 Dec. 1831, but at the duke's request he went up to vote against the second reading of the 'iniquitous'

revised reform bill, by which Buckingham was entirely reprieved, on the 17th.[53] He joined in opposition mockery of ministerial uncertainty as to whether the bill, once enacted, would become operative before the boundary bill reached the statute book, 23 Jan. 1832. He voted against the enfranchisement of Tower Hamlets, 28 Feb., said that the freeholders of Birmingham would be able to return one Member for Warwickshire as well as having £10 votes in their borough, 9 Mar., and divided against the third reading of the reform bill, 22 Mar. He was in the majority against the vestry bill, 23 Jan., and was a teller for the majority against printing a petition for the abolition of Irish tithes, 16 Feb. He divided against government on the Russian-Dutch loan, 26 Jan., 12 July. He predicted difficulties in raising local funds to implement cholera prevention, 14 Feb. He presented a Southwark petition against the London bridge approaches bill, 20 Feb. He saw no need to refer petitions against the general register bill to a select committee, 22 Feb., but he was added to this, 27 Mar. He was on the committees on the sheriffs' expenses bill, 7 Mar., and the highways bill, 11 May. He yet again defended Millbank against Hume, 13 Apr. On 20 June 1832 he presented a petition from the churchwardens and overseers of Winslow calling for the adoption of some means of setting unemployed paupers to work. He was mentioned as a possible member of the poor law commission, but nothing came of this.[54]

Fremantle became involved in but won a dispute with the duke of Buckingham over the expenses of his successful candidature for Buckingham at the 1832 general election, when he came second to a Liberal.[55] In August 1833 he became one of the trustees appointed to take responsibility for the duke's estates and personalty and satisfy his creditors. It was not a happy experience and he got out of it in 1835.[56] Peel made him financial secretary to the treasury on the formation of his first ministry in December 1834, and after the 1837 general election, as a man 'universally liked' and noted for 'discretion and straightforwardness', he was made Conservative chief whip.[57] He served briefly as secretary at war and Irish secretary in Peel's second administration but, obliged to vacate his seat by the hostility of the 2nd duke of Buckingham (as Chandos had become in 1839) to repeal of the corn laws in February 1846, he was made deputy chairman and then chairman of the board of customs, where he worked for 27 years before retiring at the age of 75. He was created a peer in 1874. He died at Swanbourne in December 1890. His eldest son and namesake (1830-1918) was Conservative Member for Buckinghamshire, 1876-85.

[1] *Oxford DNB*; *Gent. Mag.* (1820), i. 87, 568; *HP Commons, 1790-1820*, iii. 834-5. [2] PROB 11/1630/349; IR26/822/535. [3] Bucks. RO, Fremantle mss D/FR/138/5/5, 6. [4] Ibid. 49/1/1, 3, 29; 85/1A (vi) *passim*; *London Gazette*, 28 July 1821, 6 Apr. 1822. [5] Fremantle mss 51/5/11. [6] Ibid. 46/9/5, 9; 49/1/2. [7] Ibid. 138/2. [8] Ibid. 138/2/2-4, 6. [9] Ibid. 86/1/1-3. [10] Ibid. 46/10/43. [11] Ibid. 46/10/38, 46, 49; 86/1/8-10. [12] Ibid. 51/5/17. [13] *Gent. Mag.* (1823), i. 573; PROB 11/1672/374; Fremantle mss 138/5/5, 6. [14] Fremantle mss 49/1/26, 28; 138/14/9, 10. [15] Ibid. 46/11/103; 49/1/4. [16] Ibid. 46/11/118; 138/14/2; Buckingham, *Mems. Geo. IV*, ii. 152. [17] Fremantle mss 138/12/8, 9; 138/16/15. [18] *Bucks. Chron.* 26 Aug. 1824; Fremantle mss 138/18/6, 7, 9, 12, 13. [19] Fremantle mss 138/126/1-6, 8, 9, 16, 17. [20] Ibid. 138/21/1/2, 3. [21] Ibid. 138/26/11, 13, 14. [22] Ibid. 49/1/15, 16; 138/21/2/1-5, 7. [23] Ibid. 46/11/154; 49/12/13, 14, 17; 138/21/2/8. [24] Ibid. 46/12/109; 138/28/1. [25] Ibid. 46/9/2, 8; 49/1/8; 138/28/2. [26] Ibid. 46/10/48, 50; 138/21/2/9; 138/28/3. [27] Ibid. 46/10/40, 47; 138/21/2/10. [28] Ibid. 138/18/4, 5; 138/28/5. [29] Ibid. 138/21/2/12-14. [30] Ibid. 138/21/2/21; 138/22/1/2. [31] Ibid. 138/21/2/21-24; 138/22/2-6, 8. [32] Ibid. 138/18/1. [33] Ibid. 139/8/6, 7. [34] Ibid. 139/2/2-4. [35] Ibid. 139/10/4, 5, 7, 13, 14, 17, 21. [36] Ibid. 139/10/31, 33, 36. [37] Ibid. 139/10/47, 49, 55. [38] Ibid. 139/10/56, 57, 62, 64. [39] Ibid. 139/10/65, 66, 68, 69, 73. [40] Ibid. 139/14/9, 10; 139/20/21; *The Times*, 2, 4 May 1831. [41] Fremantle mss 139/14/11. [42] Ibid. 139/14/3. [43] Broughton, *Recollections*, iv. 14. [44] Fremantle mss 139/14/19. [45] *Bucks Gazette*, 28 Aug. 1830. [46] Fremantle mss 139/20/1, 5, 6, 8; *Three Diaries*, 54. [47] Fremantle mss 139/20/9. [48] Ibid. 139/20/11, 12. [49] Ibid. 139/20/29. [50] Ibid. 139/20/30. [51] Ibid. 139/20/31; Dorset RO D/BKL. [52] Fremantle mss 139/20/32. [53] Ibid. 130/5/9, 10. [54] Brougham mss, Slaney to Brougham, 28 June [1832]. [55] J.J. Sack, *The Grenvillites*, 23. [56] J. Beckett, *Rise and Fall of the Grenvilles*, 164, 171, 173-4, 175-6. [57] Add. 40405, ff. 47, 295; 40424, f. 37; *Wellington Pol. Corresp.* ii. 401; R. Stewart, *Foundation of the Conservative Party*, 120-1.

D.R.F.

FREMANTLE, William Henry (1766–1850), of Englefield Green, Egham, Surr. and Stanhope Street, Mdx.

ENNISKILLEN	31 July 1806–1806
HARWICH	1806–19 Feb. 1807
SALTASH	19 Feb. 1807–1807
TAIN BURGHS	7 May 1808–1812
BUCKINGHAM	1812–17 May 1827

b. 28 Dec. 1766, 4th s. of John Fremantle (*d.* 1788) of Aston Abbots, Bucks. and Frances, da. and coh. of John Edwards of Bristol. *m.* 21 Sept. 1797, Selina Mary, da. of Sir John Elwill[†], 4th bt., of Englefield Green, wid. of Felton Lionel Hervey, *s.p.* GCH 1827; kntd. 31 Oct. 1827. *d.* 19 Oct. 1850.

Ensign 66 Ft. 1782; lt. 105 Ft. 1783, capt. 1783; capt.-lt. 103 Ft. 1783, half-pay 1783-7; capt. 60 Ft. 1787; capt. 58 Ft. 1788, ret. 1789.

A.d.c. and priv. sec. to ld. lt. [I] 1782-3; jt. resident sec. [I] and jt. solicitor in England to revenue commrs. [I] 1789-1801; dep. teller of exch. 1792-1806; sec. to treasury Sept. 1806-Apr. 1807; PC 17 Jan. 1822; commr. bd. of control Feb. 1822-June 1826; treas. of household 1826-37; dep. ranger, Windsor Great Park 1830-*d.*

Lt. Bucks. yeomanry 1795, capt.-lt. 1797, capt. 1798, Mid. Bucks. 1803.

Fremantle, the confidant of the fat 2nd marquess of Buckingham and whipper-in of his slender Grenvillite Commons squad, who had a pension of £924 a year as quondam Irish revenue solicitor, was returned again for Buckingham's pocket borough at the 1820 general election. After the failure of his third party experiment, Fremantle had shared his wish for a union with the Liverpool ministry, on suitably favourable terms. He told Buckingham that all his Members had been present at the debate on the civil list, 8 May 1820, and that 'if we had voted against the government ... we would have diminished their numbers'.[1] He presented a petition for inquiry into the metropolitan water supply, 5 July 1820. He secured an inquiry into this problem, 6 Feb., and on 14 June 1821 introduced a regulation bill, which got nowhere.[2] Fremantle became 'quite low spirited' in the summer of 1820 over the popular clamour in support of Queen Caroline, from which he feared the 'subversion of all government and authority'. He wanted 'some volunteer establishments to be formed ... by the well-disposed and loyal who have influence, to check the torrent'. Buckingham, who fancied that the affair had so alienated the king from the Whig opposition that the beleaguered ministry had 'but one resource' for increasing its strength, namely the Grenvillites, urged Fremantle in Brighton and 'in all conversations with people about the Court' to spread the view that Caroline had 'put herself at the head of the radical party, and like it, *must be put down*'.Fremantle, who had the ear of the duke of York, privately considered the king's conduct 'abominable' and 'an excitement to popular hatred'.[3] After the abandonment of the bill of pains and penalties in mid-November he concluded that ministers would 'meet Parliament without change'; and he regretted the refusal of Lord Grenville, Buckingham's uncle, to take office ever again, when consulted by the king, 25 Nov. Fremantle dined with the king at Frogmore that evening, but gleaned little. Three weeks later he helped to get up a loyal address from his Surrey neighbourhood of Egham (two miles from Windsor). He was 'placed ... in great awkwardness' by the king's invitation that he and the 'principal persons' involved should present it and eat with him, as his coadjutors were 'all ... perfectly unfit' socially. He dined with the king a few days later, but 'nothing passed on the subject of politics', though he got the impression that ministers had decided to fight on the issue of the omission of the queen's name from the liturgy. He rejected, as likely to 'create suspicion', Buckingham's suggestion that he might contrive a meeting with the king in order to hint to him that the marquess was ready, as 'a channel of communication with others', to help save the day. On 28 Dec. 1820, having got rid of his address by sending it to the home secretary, he had an hour's audience of the king, whose 'increased hostility against the opposition, and more personally against Lord Grey' struck him forcibly. In mid-January 1821 Buckingham encouraged him to 'set ... [the] wheels rolling' with Princess Augusta to assure the king that if the government was defeated he could rely on the marquess, Lord Wellesley and a 'king's party' to form a ministry to keep out the Whigs.[4]

On 24 Jan. 1821 Fremantle told Buckingham that the Commons were 'evidently determined to support the ministers', who would struggle on, which vindicated 'our line of moderate and quiet support'. He had to inform the marquess, whose anger at Lord Castlereagh's* supposed attack on Grenville's part in the Milan commission of 1806 he tried to assuage, that while his cousin Charles Williams Wynn, the Grenvillite leader in the Commons, and their associate Joseph Phillimore were 'decidedly opposed to the opposition', he was *quite* satisfied' that there was almost no chance of the Whigs joining forces with the Grenvillites. Buckingham, still sore, at first ordered Fremantle to stay away from the division on the opposition censure motion, 6 Feb.; but at Grenville's prompting he subsequently directed him to vote with the government.[5] He was a teller for the majority for Catholic relief, 28 Feb., but Buckingham, whose son and heir Lord Temple, Member for Buckinghamshire, was hostile to it, did not share his optimism that the measure would pass the Lords. Both men welcomed 'the termination of the Neapolitan revolution'.[6] Fremantle voted silently against parliamentary reform, 9 May 1821.

A month later Buckingham, anticipating a ministerial reshuffle, ordered Fremantle to make to the duke of Wellington, a member of the cabinet, a 'strictly confidential' communication of his wish for a junction, on terms commensurate with 'what is due to the fair pretensions of myself, my family and those connected with me'. Fremantle, who wished 'to be placed at any one of the boards of treasury, admiralty or India', complied, but made the mistake of showing Buckingham's 'sacred' confidential letter to the 'half-Whig' Williams Wynn. He had his knuckles rapped, and promised to be more circumspect in future. He believed that an offer would be made during the recess and advised Buckingham to disregard Grenville and his other uncle Tom Grenville[†], 'who sit in their

libraries and fancy things and men as they were twenty years ago, and forget we are under a new reign, *and such a reign*'.[7] A 'strange' silence from ministers prompted Buckingham to press Fremantle to ask Wellington what was going on. When Fremantle, who believed that 'the government is so extremely weak and ... disunited ... that they don't know from day to day ... what will be their proceeding', saw Wellington on 4 July he learnt that the reshuffle had been postponed, but that changes, on which Buckingham would be consulted, were to be made before the next session. Dismissing the 'madness' of Williams Wynn's idea that the Grenvillites might rejoin the Whigs, he thought Buckingham should 'now hold yourself liberated from all connection with the government' but support 'the formation of any government that can rescue us from the danger of revolution'. At Buckingham's request, he communicated to Williams Wynn, Wellington and Liverpool a letter stating his wish to assist in the establishment of such a ministry, preferably involving Peel and Canning. By the end of the summer, with the queen dead, Fremantle could report that Liverpool and company were back in the king's good books.[8] In September he disputed Buckingham's pessimistic view that ministers would 'try to tide on another session' and conveniently failed to see Wellington, whom the marquess wished him to inform that he wanted to become first lord of the admiralty (where he would ask for Fremantle to be placed, with a privy councillorship), thinking that Buckingham was prostituting himself. At Brighton in October he gathered from John Croker*, the admiralty secretary, that on the king's return from Hanover an approach was almost certain to be made to the Grenvillites and Canning.[9] When Buckingham took umbrage in mid-November at the 'unpardonable' silence of ministers, Fremantle preached patience, arguing that they had to overcome the king's weakening resistance, though he agreed that if they did 'try and tide through another session' the best 'line should be to form a junction with Canning'. Hearing unofficially on the 21st that Buckingham was to be offered the lord lieutenancy of Ireland, with Williams Wynn as his secretary, Fremantle, who said that he would prefer the treasury or board of control to the admiralty if Buckingham did not head the latter, pressed him to accept; but the marquess replied that he would decline such an 'insulated' deal, as he had stipulated for a wider arrangement, with Williams Wynn in the cabinet.[10] On 27 Nov. Fremantle met Liverpool by invitation, to hear what he had to propose and relay the news to Buckingham. He suggested that the marquess would probably prefer cabinet office to the proffered dukedom, but in the event Buckingham took the latter and settled terms with the ministry. Part of the arrangement was Fremantle's being made a privy councillor, with a seat at one of the boards. Buckingham 'very earnestly' pressed for his appointment to the treasury, where his experience as secretary under Grenville, 1806-7, would be useful to the government, 'particularly in assisting Lord Londonderry in ... the management of the House of Commons'. Liverpool promised to do what he could to effect this, but Londonderry told an alarmed Mrs. Arbuthnot, wife of the patronage secretary, that it was 'quite nonsense to suppose for an instant' that Fremantle 'ever could have any confidential intercourse with him'. While Fremantle clearly coveted the treasury place, he professed at the turn of the year to 'care little' whether he landed there or at the board of control, which Williams Wynn was to head, and to be 'perfectly satisfied' as to Liverpool's good intentions.[11] When he and Williams Wynn were sworn of the privy council on 17 Jan. 1822 his destination remained undecided. According to Lord Bathurst, there was a ludicrous episode, as Fremantle

> was so anxious to identify himself that when Wynn said "I Charles Watkin Wynn", Fremantle said so too, until Greville [the clerk] explained to him that he was not Charles Watkin Wynn, but William Henry Fremantle; and that upon this occasion, as he was upon oath, he must submit to differing from the [Grenville] family.

Twelve days later Liverpool told him that he could not presently be accommodated at the treasury, but held out hopes for the future. (Williams Wynn reckoned that this was because Lord Anglesey was unwilling to allow his Member Berkeley Paget to vacate his seat for Milborne Port by being moved from the treasury to another post because he feared a contest there.) Fremantle was placed at the board of control. His initial pleasure at the junction was diminished, and he admitted to Buckingham that personally he was 'exceedingly sorry, and rather more so as I find I am to go to bed there with Phillimore', having 'thought I was entitled to a little better berth than he was'. Nor did he consider it 'the most creditable thing' for the Grenvillites 'that we should all be huddled up in a nest together'; Lord Grey duly noted that 'the whole patronage of India is surrendered to them'.[12]

Fremantle, who soon found himself on a bed of nails, presented a Buckingham farmers' petition for enhanced agricultural protection, 15 Feb. 1822.[13] Buckingham enjoined him at the start of the session to 'stick close' to the unpredictable Lord Chandos (as Temple was now styled) and to keep his other Members up to the mark. After the humiliating government defeat on the navy estimates, 1 Mar., Buckingham unhelpfully told Fremantle (and Williams Wynn) that ministers should resign to teach the recalcitrant country gentlemen a lesson.[14] On 11 Mar. Fremantle reported that the ministry's situation was 'precarious', though he believed it would survive thanks to 'the fear of the country gentlemen [of] bringing in the opposition'; but Buckingham, who had begun to complain of Williams Wynn's attitude towards him, thought 'things are gone too far for that'. Fremantle spoke against abolition of one of the joint-postmasterships, 13 Mar., and, like Buckingham, was pleased with the ministerial victory by 25 votes. He questioned the duke's comment that 'Irish affairs are going on very ill', as it was 'not thought so here'.[15] He delighted Buckingham by speaking and acting as a majority teller against reception of the Newcastle-upon-Tyne petition for the release of Henry Hunt*, parliamentary reform and inquiry into Peterloo, 22 Mar.; but was pestered by him to ask Canning, who was expected to go to India as governor-general, to take his godson George Pigott* with him. Buckingham eventually let him off the hook.[16] He then moaned about the king's 'deliberate and marked' affront in failing to respond to his request for the right of 'entrée' to his presence, as his gout made it 'impossible for me to bear the standing on hot carpets in hot rooms for two or three hours' at levees, hinting that he would break with Liverpool if not satisfied. Fremantle tried to convince him that there had been no intentional snub, merely an oversight, but he continued to fret about the matter, which seems to have been resolved in April.[17] Fremantle hoped that the Grenvillite William Plunket*, who had become Irish attorney-general in the junction with government, would not allow himself to be bullied by the Irish into raising the Catholic question in the House. Like Buckingham, who wrote a remonstrance, he deplored Canning's unilateral notice of a motion for a bill to relieve Catholic peers, which would embarrass Plunket and create a 'jumble'. Buckingham, affronted at not having been consulted, was inclined to order all his Members to abstain, but he reluctantly gave way when Grenville and Plunket indicated their intention of supporting the measure and Fremantle told him that 'whatever one may think of this question, it is not one that the public will go with you upon, in any measure of hostility to the government, much less of separation', which would lead only to 'another sixteen years of opposition'. Buckingham commanded him to attend and speak at the private meeting of leading pro-Catholics called for 16 Apr.; but when he arrived in London the day before he was informed by Williams Wynn that the gathering was restricted to Members who had been named to bring in the relief bill of 1821. He was obliged to keep out of it and to give Canning Buckingham's written exposition of his views.[18] On 7 May he croaked that 'every day lessens my confidence' in ministers, whose 'complete want of steadiness, and of an open, manly uniformity of conduct', notably on the problem of agricultural distress, gave him 'no hopes of its going on'. Buckingham encouraged him to let Wellington know that after the 'insults' heaped on him by cabinet ministers he was not prepared to 'expose myself to all the obloquy attending the support of these vacillating measures'.[19] The heavy defeat of attacks on diplomatic expenditure, including Henry Williams Wynn's[†] Swiss embassy, 15, 16 May, lifted Fremantle's spirits, though he was worried that failure to find a contractor for the deadweight pensions would put ministers at the mercy of the Bank. Buckingham considered 'both divisions as advantageous to you as your bad system of House of Commons tactics will allow'.[20] On 3 June Fremantle made one of his rare interventions in debate when successfully moving rejection of the Greenhoe reform petition on account of its 'insulting' language. A few days later Buckingham warned him that ministers' 'studied neglect and ill treatment' would 'very likely oblige me to break with government', and asked him to communicate this to Lord Londonderry and Wellington, who seemed 'better inclined ... than others of their colleagues'. He allowed Fremantle to vote for the aliens bill, which the duke and Williams Wynn were obliged by past votes to oppose, 19 July 1822. Fremantle sat the session out to the bitter and 'tedious' end and persuaded Buckingham not to extend feelers to 'so slippery and uncertain a man' as Canning, as there was 'no part of the government who wish for his connection'.[21]

After Londonderry's suicide in August 1822, however, Fremantle thought Canning would have to be admitted to the cabinet. He considered that his eventual appointment as foreign secretary and leader of the Commons strengthened the administration, but remained anxious to see Nicholas Vansittart* removed from the exchequer.[22] In mid-September Buckingham urged him to press his claim to either the admiralty or the Irish lord lieutenancy if a further reshuffle was necessitated by the removal of a cabinet minister to go in Canning's place to India; he wished Williams Wynn to be chosen. When Canning, who wanted to find room for William Huskisson*, told Buckingham that he and Liverpool had asked Williams Wynn to take the Speakership in the room of Charles Manners Sutton, whom they preferred for India, the duke refused to contemplate such an arrangement unless he himself was given a place in the cabinet, and ordered Fremantle

to put this to Liverpool. Fremantle declined to be drawn into 'any improper meddling' with Williams Wynn's interests and begged Buckingham, who was cross with him, to be patient. He was not very well at this time, suffering from 'attacks of uneasy sensations in the limbs', which his nephew and protégé Sir Thomas Francis Fremantle* attributed to 'derangement of the stomach' and 'mental uneasiness, caused by the variety of circumstances which contributed to annoy you during the last session'.[23] In early October Buckingham told Liverpool that if Williams Wynn took the chair he would give 'warm and active support' to the ministry as an individual, but renounce all his own pretensions and dissolve his '*official* connection with the government', which, he informed Fremantle, would require him to ask for the resignation of his seat if he wished to retain his office. In the event Williams Wynn turned down the chair and Lord Amherst was sent to India. A relieved Fremantle paid lip service to the probity of Buckingham's conduct, but advised him that his 'best' line 'for some time at least' was to stay 'quiet' and allow 'public discussion on men and parties and official situations to be diverted to other quarters', namely to Canning and his intrigues.[24]

Fremantle predicted that Canning would 'soon be leading' Liverpool, but hoped he would engineer the removal of Vansittart; and when this was accomplished in January 1823 he thought it had produced 'a much improved administration'.[25] Before the session began he was being bombarded with Buckingham's renewed complaints of senior ministers' incivility and inattention to him.[26] He reported that the first day, 4 Feb., had been 'most favourable to the government, and ... we are all in tip-top spirits'. Two weeks later he judged that Canning was doing 'remarkably well'. He disputed Buckingham's view that Lord Wellesley must be recalled from Ireland: 'such a complete victory to Orangeism ... would of necessity break up the government'. He privately believed that the peacetime appointment of a lieutenant-general of the ordnance, on which Hume made 'a desperate attack', 19 Feb., was 'an infernal job'.[27] Next day he divided against parliamentary reform. On 7 Mar., speaking as commanding officer of a corps of Buckinghamshire yeomanry, he repudiated Hume's criticisms of the force, arguing that 'the country was not very grievously taxed in paying £3 a man' for them. Thanking him for this, Chandos urged him to 'collect all the strength you can' to oppose Lord Cranborne's motion for inquiry into the game laws, 13 Mar., but there was no division.[28] Later that month Robert Plumer Ward, clerk of the ordnance and Member for Lord Lonsdale's borough of Haslemere, opened an unauthorized negotiation with Fremantle for an exchange of seats. It fell through, and Buckingham assured Fremantle that his seat was his for as long as he wanted it, but that if he decided at the next dissolution to retire or to look elsewhere his nephew Sir Thomas would probably be next in line for it.[29] At Brighton over Easter, when the king was ill, Fremantle found the scene 'glum and melancholy'. He moved on to Hastings and Eastbourne before returning to London, where he viewed with some disquiet the prospect of an attack on Plunket's use of *ex-officio* informations against the Dublin Orange rioters. As it happened the affair went off 'triumphantly', 15 Apr., though Fremantle was in the ministerial minority when Burdett carried a motion for a parliamentary inquiry, 22 Apr. Buckingham then threatened to break with ministers over their declarations of support for the Spanish liberals. He agreed that 'nothing can display greater weakness than the [official] papers', but argued that 'the feeling in the country is so strong in favour of neutrality and of the Spaniards, and also the feeling of Parliament, that ... the government will come out of the discussion triumphantly'. The duke spoke in favour of ministers in the Lords, 24 Apr. After the 'turbulent discussion' of Catholic relief, which he did not witness at first hand, 17 Apr., Fremantle concluded that the question 'is gone to the devil'.[30] At Buckingham's instigation he had at the end of May a 'confidential' talk with Wellington, who was willing to try to heal the rift between Williams Wynn and Canning; the duke was satisfied with the outcome. A month later Fremantle, who was incommoded by boils on his buttocks, but was apparently in the House to vote in the minority of 30 in favour of introducing jury trial to New South Wales, 7 July, reckoned that Canning had lost ground to Peel. As the session closed he judged that the government had emerged with 'more success altogether than one could have expected' and was encouraged by 'better accounts' from Ireland, where he had earlier feared 'a general insurrection'.[31] He agreed with Buckingham's observation that Canning 'only waits the opportunity of tripping us up' and that this was 'only to be resisted by a steady line of conduct on our parts, pursuing ... the system as it is now carrying on towards Ireland, until we see the opportunity, by the accordance of other members of the government, to meet him with a certainty of success'. That summer he had 'much intercourse' with the king, and assured Buckingham that '*we* are all in great favour with him'.[32] After recovering from a broken collarbone that autumn he was 'attacked by a repetition of the horrible boils' and 'endured agonies from one in the fleshy part of my thigh'.[33] When he informed Buckingham

in December 1823 of Wellington's illness and 'great difficulties arising from the state of our West India islands', where he anticipated a slave rebellion, he received a long moan about the admiralty's refusal to act as he and Chandos wished regarding a friend, an example of 'the general inattention and indisposition on the part of every individual of government since my friends belonged to it'.[34]

On the eve of the 1824 session Fremantle, whose damaged shoulder still disturbed his sleep and so produced 'a feeling of illness', told his nephew:

> I mean to be perfectly indifferent to all that passes in Parliament, but doubt when the scene commences whether I shall have philosophy enough to act up to my intentions. Everything promises at present an easy and quiet session, but when once the House opens I have always observed that business and difficulties arise which were never contemplated.[35]

He found the debate on the address, 3 Feb., when Canning and Peel explained their conduct on the Catholic question, 'flat and tiresome', but at the end of the month he reported that 'nothing can be going on more prosperously than the government is at present'. Though personally uneasy about the 'unpopular' proposal to grant £500,000 for building new churches, he saw that it was 'impossible now to surrender it without great damage to the character of the government'.[36] After the debate on amelioration of the conditions of West Indian slaves, 16 Mar., he reckoned that 'all real difficulties are completely put by for the session'; and he persuaded Buckingham to ignore Canning's attack on his Whig brother Lord Nugent* on the Spanish question, 18 Mar.[37] He reported rumours of Liverpool's imminent resignation in early May and speculated that Canning, his likely successor, would seek to recruit the Lansdowne Whigs. He thought the ministerial majority of 48 for the appointment of a select committee on the state of Ireland, 11 May 1824, was 'very bad', enjoyed the Whig Tierney's chastisement of the 'dirty and intriguing' Canning and believed that the committee would recommend an insurrection bill and that 'few of the Irish will be disposed to contend against its enforcement'. Yet he was concerned that the 'violent and objectionable' demands made in Irish Catholic petitions threatened to 'put the game completely in the hands of the anti-Catholics here'.[38] At the close of the session he observed that future developments depended 'entirely on Lord Liverpool's health', for he saw no chance of forming a stable administration without him.[39] In December 1824 Fremantle wrote to Buckingham, who agreed with him, that 'the prospect in Ireland is terrific', that Catholic emancipation conceded now 'would not cure the evil, and that the Irish Catholics' intemperance and disloyalty' had set back their cause and raised the prospect of repression. In this they were at odds with Williams Wynn, who thought emancipation must be carried at all costs. Fremantle predicted that the planned suppression of the Catholic Association would cause 'the whole mine ... [to] explode' and advised Buckingham, who wanted his own views made known to the king, not to commit himself prematurely.[40] He disbelieved rumours that Wellesley was to be sent from Ireland to India, but promised to urge Buckingham's pretensions to replace him in Dublin if the change took place.[41]

Fremantle approved of the early 1825 legislation to put down the Association, though he doubted its effectiveness. On the duke's uncles' preference for doing nothing he commented that 'it is very well to talk calmly and quietly in one's closet, of rebellion; but it won't do for a government to leave people to cut one another's throats'. His prediction that the motion to consider Catholic relief would be defeated in the Commons by 'many' votes was wide of the mark; it was carried by 13, 1 Mar., when he was in the majority.[42] That day he declared his opposition to Buxton's London Water Company bill, having concluded after his stint as chairman of the select committee that the existing companies were providing a decent service. He spoke at some length in defence of Amherst and the hierarchy of the Indian army over their handling of the Barrackpoor mutiny, 24 Mar. He was 'vexed ... very much' when Chandos brought up an anti-Catholic petition from Buckingham which offended his father, 18 Apr., but opted to remain silent on it.[43] He feared 'great dissension in the concoction and proceeding on the Catholic bill' and agreed with Buckingham, who was incensed by the duke of York's anti-Catholic rant in the Lords, 25 Apr., that the cause had been 'greatly damaged by its friends'. He went through the motions of voting for the relief bill, 21 Apr., 10 May, but saw the inevitability of its defeat in the Lords and concluded that 'nothing could have ended worse', for it had 'estranged the government' and 'created bad blood among them'. Anticipating an autumn dissolution, he observed on 17 June 1825 (when he was a government teller against an amendment to the judges' salaries bill) that

> the general belief prevails that the present state of things cannot last, and that Parliament will not meet again without some conclusion being come to with regard to the Catholic question ... I never can believe that Canning and those who support the Catholic question will allow any proceeding to be brought on in the last session of an expiring Parliament, which will ... raise a clamour in the

public mind and establish a No Popery Parliament ... I am quite satisfied that the king, duke of York and the high church party are determined to try the experiment of an anti-Catholic government.

The duke assured him of re-election for Buckingham 'if it is your *bon plaisir*'.[44]

Their relationship was soured soon afterwards as a result of the duke's asking him in late September 1825, after weeks of silence, to cajole Williams Wynn into getting the cabinet to nominate him to the directors of the East India Company as successor to Lord Amherst in India, claiming to have received from Liverpool and Canning an assurance that 'I have no competitor' and threatening to 'withdraw support from the government' if 'slighted'.[45] He thought Buckingham was degrading himself and told him as much, joining with Williams Wynn, who had a furious row with the duke, to insist that they 'could not stir in the business without appearing to recommend the recall of Lord Amherst', which was a matter for the Company, and that 'any interference or wish expressed on our part would be much more likely to injure that assist his objects'. He was 'hurt' to discover that Buckingham had offered the post of his private secretary to someone other than his nephew.[46] On 20 Oct. the duke, having been told by Liverpool that if Amherst was recalled Sir Thomas Munro would replace him, accused Fremantle of 'backing Wynn in all his paltry subterfuges, and supporting him in all his desertion of me', gave him a last 'opportunity of choosing between Wynn and me' and ordered him to leave Brighton to canvass the directors. A distressed Fremantle, who told his nephew that the affair must end in Buckingham's 'complete breach with the government' and consequently his own retirement, replied reminding the duke of his 'uniform and fervent display of attachment beyond all bounds to you and your family for upwards of forty years', protesting his innocence and refusing to budge from Brighton. Buckingham, who now claimed that going to India was essential for his health, wanted him to 'consult your own conscience and ask yourself have you taken yet one step to assist me'. On 1 Nov. Fremantle stated his case to Chandos, who abused Williams Wynn and warned him that Canning was trying to get rid of the Grenvillites and that if his father persisted in what was a hopeless cause he would accomplish Canning's object for him and destroy himself in the process. Although Chandos 'deprecated' his threat to resign his seat Fremantle wrote later that day to the duke offering to do so if he had forfeited Buckingham's confidence. The duke assured him that he wished to 'consider you as ... my oldest, my best, my warmest and steadiest friend', but Fremantle, nettled by an observation that the duke had 'felt very severely a want of exertion on a subject very dear to me', was still inclined to retire. Buckingham replied that the decision not to recall Amherst put an end to the matter, declared undiminished confidence in Fremantle and left the decision to him, but pointed out that his resignation would probably undermine Williams Wynn. Fremantle opted to stay in and put Buckingham on his guard against Canning; but he admitted to his nephew that although Buckingham was 'now perfectly satisfied of *my* conduct', he did 'not yet see daylight with regard to his future objects'.[47]

At the beginning of December 1825 Fremantle told Williams Wynn that Amherst's incapacity was now so notorious that there seemed to be no option but to replace him immediately with Munro, and argued that Buckingham's nomination 'at the present moment' would look like 'a job' and was certain to be rejected by the court of directors.[48] A few days later Buckingham told him that he had decided to lay his grievance before the king and to break with Williams Wynn now or in the spring, depending on the outcome. Although Fremantle knew that the directors very much wished to recall Amherst, while ministers did not, he was equally well aware that Munro was their chosen replacement. He confidentially told the duke this, but in response was ordered to inform Williams Wynn that unless he fully supported Buckingham's pretensions in the cabinet and his 'friends in office do the same and to the same extent out of cabinet', their political connection would terminate. Fremantle merely transmitted the duke's words to Williams Wynn by letter and protested to Buckingham that he had 'no right to demand' of him that he talk to Williams Wynn on the subject and so reveal to him 'my breach of duty in betraying the secret and official and government transactions necessarily confided in me'. Rebuked by Buckingham, who accused him of making things worse, he defended himself, but offered to do his best to 'promote a better understanding' with Williams Wynn.[49] As this problem remained unresolved, Buckingham seized on a report that Wellesley had told the cabinet that he was willing to go from Ireland to India and asked Fremantle to let it be known that he would acquiesce in this if he was appointed to Dublin, though, coming to suspect it as an intrigue by Williams Wynn to deprive him of India, he would refuse a cabinet place without office. Fremantle was advised by Williams Wynn that Liverpool had told Buckingham, in response to his direct enquiry, that there no truth in the Wellesley report. Yet almost immediately Buckingham, who had sent his statement of grievance to the king, complained to Fremantle of a conspiracy against him and directed him to promote 'the Irish exchange'. He then reprimanded Fremantle for indiscretion in this, renounced Ireland and said he would focus on India alone. Fremantle replied that he had in fact not mentioned the subject; and when Buckingham, trying to force the issue, urged him on 11 Jan. 1826 to 'throw out either to Canning or Lord Liverpool the possibility of your being obliged to opt between your place and ... seat ... supposing the breach between me and Wynn to continue', he frankly replied:

> The decisive step you have taken with regard to the government renders all further proceedings of your friends impossible. The statement you have laid before the king was handed over ... immediately to Lord Liverpool. I have also heard that it contained direct charges against some ... ministers ... [and] that these charges were more unexpected on the part of Lord Liverpool, because he had previously on the same day received a ... letter from you on the subject of Lord Wellesley without alluding in the slightest degree to the step you had taken ... The matter is much too serious for the intermeddling of any concern of my own ... I am ... perfectly prepared to follow the course you may direct by absenting myself [from Parliament] on the first day, and in this case, as I must decline Canning's invitation to hear the king's speech read, I shall previously notify to Lord Liverpool the resignation of my seat at the board of control. Believe me ... I shall consider this no sacrifice.

'Worried to death by these unpleasant transactions' and eager to 'get quit of office, although I give the full estimate of all its advantages', he told his nephew that 'the scabbard is thrown away, and I do not see how Lord Liverpool now could *even accept* his support'.[50] Buckingham backed down, assuring Fremantle that 'as my injuries are yet personal only, I do not wish my friends to consider them to the extent of affecting their present support of the government or, as far as my feelings are concerned, of preventing them from continuing to hold office under it'. Fremantle commented to his nephew that 'I cannot see how he can possibly extricate himself from the foolish and lamentable predicament in which he has placed himself without a complete separation from the government', though he conceded that the duke had been 'ill used' by 'the *folly and knavery*' of Williams Wynn. He deplored the 'complete hash' which the duke had created, thereby losing 'all chance of official appointment', and condemned Chandos for his part in the affair.[51] With Buckingham, apparently chastened, 'in a much more tranquil state', Fremantle wrote him a bland letter 'telling him the common occurrences of the day', 25 Jan. 1826, 'that he may not think I am caballing against him', but anticipated 'some unpleasant reply exacting some unpleasant duty which I cannot perform'. All he got was a threat that if Buckingham did not soon receive 'a satisfactory answer' to his remonstrance, he would 'demand an audience of the king, and if reparation is then denied me, I shall withdraw myself and my influence from government wholly and entirely'.[52]

Fremantle was soon in hot water again. He annoyed Buckingham by 'unnecessarily' speaking on the address, 3 Feb. 1826, in defence of Amherst's regime in India, holding out hopes of 'a successful termination of hostilities'. The duke conceded that as an official man he was bound to vote with his colleagues, but saw 'no obligation on you to play the orator, against the feelings of your oldest friend on the point above others on which he feels himself the deepest injured'. He demanded a 'promise to take no part, *by speaking*, on any subject connected with Lord Amherst's recall'; refusal would entail surrender of his seat. In an interview with Chandos set up by Buckingham, 7 Feb., Fremantle agreed to keep quiet on Amherst, but argued that he must be at liberty to speak on general Indian matters and said he would be 'extremely happy to be released from the very painful situation in which I was placed by my continuance in office'. Chandos was satisfied and waved aside his offer of resignation.[53] Fremantle, who is not known to have spoken in debate again, told his nephew a fortnight later that 'I am getting on better with the duke and Chandos, but in truth the whole matter rests now on a bed of candles which must blaze out shortly', for their object was to 'drive out Wynn and to continue friends with government'. He warned Chandos not to risk provoking a damaging reply from Canning by airing his father's Indian grievance in the House and, having talked to the duke's uncles, was satisfied that they at least were 'contented' with his recent conduct. Soon afterwards Buckingham reproached him for his failure to write and seeming to 'participate in your principal's avoidance of me'.[54] He only paired against condemnation of the Jamaican slave trials, 2 Mar. He accepted Buckingham's invitation to Stowe in mid-March, feeling that he had 'brought matters to a better bearing' with him. In early April, however, having been confidentially informed by the duke that he had made his personal peace with Williams Wynn and told him that 'we had much better continue our course together, whilst we think alike, but not necessarily in the same boat', and that he therefore required Fremantle's 'zealous assistance and advice' in order to 'ascertain what are the feelings of Lord Liverpool towards me', he wrote to his nephew:

I think the duke the most unaccountable man I ever knew. He cannot act straightforward ... [He wants me] to play a game separate and distinct from Wynn. This while I am in office I cannot and will not do. I know Wynn has told him distinctly that the step he took with regard to the king has so completely alienated the ministers from him ... that he [Wynn] cannot even if a vacancy occurred in India or Ireland promote ... the appointment of the duke ... What otherwise can he mean by his appeal to my zealous assistance ... but that I should interfere with somebody or do something to remedy the evil which his intemperance has created, and to place myself as an agent for the purpose in the room of Wynn ... I shall say ... that I am at his orders to quit office at a moment's notice from him, but that as long as I retain it, I must both publicly and privately uphold the conduct of my principal ... As to talking of a personal reconciliation and a political union, with separate interests and separate objects, it is really disgraceful and I will be no party to it ... As to Lord Liverpool and the government, from the king downwards with few exceptions, I believe they would be more delighted to get rid of the whole boutique of Grenvilles, and this I told him; and I [am] sure in his heart he thinks so ... [for] they get no support from them and are plagued individually by each for separate and excessive favours.

In fact he assured Buckingham of his continued loyalty, while reminding him that he was 'in the same boat with Wynn', promised to try to ascertain Liverpool's disposition, but advised him to 'leave matters to cool as they now stand, for nothing can remove the difficulties arising from your appeal to the king but a little time' and refused to approach the premier directly. Buckingham retorted that his connection with government through Williams Wynn was over, and that 'whether it is to continue under any other shape must depend upon the conduct of government towards me, which must be brought to an issue before the dissolution'.[55] Fremantle voted against reform of Edinburgh's representation, 13 Apr. Four days later he sent Buckingham a brief resume of Indian news and a comment that 'much damage has been done to the government by the indecisive folly' of bringing forward the question of the salary of the president of the board of trade (on which he had divided with his colleagues, 10 Apr.) Buckingham accused him of trying to conceal the approaching crisis in India and gave him an ultimatum:

Pray don't, if you wish our friendship to continue, act ministerially with me, because Wynn chooses to do so ... You only blind yourself by endeavouring to throw dust into my eyes. You said very truly at Stowe that my political strength could only be shown by bringing it forward *en masse*. That can only be done next Parliament by returning those who will look exclusively to *my* objects, and will exert themselves to gain them in every possible way. If you feel that you cannot do this, situated as you are with Wynn, and that you really wish to abide by me, my wishes would be that you should go to Lord Liverpool and try to exchange your situation for one at the treasury or admiralty.

A stunned Fremantle told Buckingham that he would resign his place immediately, being additionally motivated to do so by his wife's 'declining' health and his own 'advanced age' (he was not yet 60), but left it to the duke as to whether he should resign his seat. At the same time he reported his 25-year-old naval officer nephew Charles Fremantle's commitment on a capital charge of the aggravated rape of a female servant at his Portsmouth lodgings. As if he had never issued his ultimatum, Buckingham set about getting the young man 'out of the sad scrape', offering 'bail to any amount' and advising Fremantle 'at all hazards to buy off the evidence' in order to keep the scandal out of the press. Bail was granted and on Buckingham's advice a dubious attorney was employed to 'get rid of the evidence'. The 'unpleasant business' was successfully covered up, and in the course of time Charles Fremantle became an admiral.[56]

Fremantle, who was pleased with the 'great triumph against the reformers' in the heavy defeat of Russell's motion, 27 Apr., and evidently had not sought another place from Liverpool, was on 1 May 1826 offered, at the king's insistence, the vacant post of treasurer of the household (worth £904 a year). He accepted immediately (as he was bound to do), ascertained from the premier that it had no connection with recent dealings between the ministry and Buckingham and then informed the duke, expressing the hope that he could keep his seat. While Buckingham professed pleasure on Fremantle's behalf, he chose to interpret the appointment as a mark of royal and ministerial hostility to himself and advised Fremantle to weigh all the implications of potential conflict and embarrassment before deciding to continue as Member for Buckingham, and to consult Grenville and Chandos. Fremantle begged Buckingham to believe that his selection was no 'unfriendly act' and, bolstered by Grenville's opinion, argued that it did not change his situation as the duke's Member and that in the event of Buckingham's opposing the administration he would be obliged, as previously, to relinquish either his office or his seat. The duke initially agreed to retain him, but, on the pretext that returning him at a general election rather than a by-election (it having been decided to delay his formal appointment to avoid the inconvenience of two elections in a few weeks) altered the equation and said it was now essential for him to know 'the

footing on which I stand with government' before he brought in '*any official man*' whose loyalties might be divided. Ordered to clarify this, preferably in concert with Chandos, Fremantle saw the latter and persuaded him to tell his father that if he would not personally approach the king or Liverpool, Chandos would do so. The duke evidently agreed to communicate with Liverpool, but first insisted on Fremantle's procuring 'the fullest information' as well as fishing again for news of Amherst's possible replacement by Wellesley. Fremantle repeated his belief that Liverpool was not 'unfriendly' but that he would 'never enter into any engagement' about India or Ireland, and pointed out that his new place hardly betokened royal hostility. Buckingham continued to carp, stated his wish for 'a general and very slight expression of continued good disposition' from Liverpool and pronounced his own 'political career ... closed', declaring that after the elections he would 'go abroad, with every prospect blasted and feeling outraged'. Only a week before the dissolution (2 June) he charged Chandos to get Fremantle to seek an audience of the king 'distinctly to state the dilemma in which he is, and from which the king alone can rescue him', and complained that Williams Wynn's family had circulated a story that the king had 'treated the whole business as a subject of ridicule'. Fremantle refused to comply and denied that Buckingham was a laughing stock, but left the decision over the seat in his hands. Buckingham, advised by Chandos, who had earlier abused Fremantle for disloyalty, not to quarrel irrevocably with ministers, eventually offered on 26 May 1826 to return him again 'on condition that should I find myself obliged to separate from the government ... you will upon being called upon to do so, not hesitate to restore me my seat'. Fremantle accepted on these terms, which he considered `fair'.[57]

Fremantle was privately appalled by Chandos's arousal of anti-Catholic feeling in Buckinghamshire, which he attributed to a '*malady* of mind', and disgusted with his father's tame 'submission'. He also confided to his nephew Sir Thomas, who was anxious for employment, his view that Buckingham and Chandos had so exasperated ministers with their importunity and recalcitrance that 'the connection with him is now undoubtedly a hindrance instead of an advantage'.[58] He tried to convince Buckingham, who raised the subject again, that there was no chance of Amherst being soon recalled. On the eve of the opening of the new Parliament in November 1826 he encouraged the duke to bury the hatchet with Williams Wynn, but found him intractable as far as their political connection went and demanding humiliating terms for a personal reconciliation, which Williams Wynn could not accept. At the close of the year Buckingham was still harping on the possibility of Amherst's recall, and pestered Fremantle to find out how Liverpool and Williams Wynn regarded his pretensions. Fremantle told his nephew that Buckingham was 'in a very good *odour* with me but I think cross and out of humour', probably thanks to Chandos's mischief. He was relieved that he had no official role to play in the arrangement for the duke of York's funeral in January 1827.[59] At the end of the month he informed Sir Thomas that Buckingham 'now stands upon no foundation whatever', without a friend in power or opposition, and having 'alienated the king'. A week later the duke, hearing that Amherst had resigned, sent him a copy of his application to Liverpool for the post and asked him, 'as a proof of your personal friendship to me', to 'call upon Lord Liverpool and press my object'. Fremantle, who noted that this 'opens all the old *sores* and must drive him ... to a single insular independent opposition to both ministers and opposition', saw the premier on 10 Feb. Liverpool indignantly revealed to him that after all that had occurred in 1825-6, Buckingham had just before Christmas offered to coalesce with Canning to turn him out and that Canning had rejected this and made it known to the king and Liverpool. The premier sent Buckingham a flat refusal and Fremantle, warning him in advance, begged him not to respond 'without some days reflection'.[60] After a talk with Chandos, who argued that Buckingham was bound now to separate himself from the government, 12 Feb., Fremantle (at Chandos's request) wrote to the duke beseeching him not to take a precipitate step which could only destroy him by isolating him 'in hostility with the king, his ministers and the opposition, without the support of any one party, or even the concurrence of your own family, whereas by forbearing all public demonstration of hostility you disarm those who are now opposed to you, and place yourself in a situation to profit by future occurrences'. Buckingham agreed to the extent that he would not further 'annoy' the king, but he insisted on 'still trying to force the thing', as Fremantle observed, by writing to Wellington and sending Chandos to see Liverpool. The outcome was so 'repulsive' that the duke, who condemned Williams Wynn as a traitor, was tempted to take the final step, but he decided to wait until he heard from Wellington. Fremantle commented to his nephew that '*all the fat's in the fire* again' with regard to India and that while Buckingham had been 'unfairly used' by Williams Wynn in leading him to believe in 1825 that he would be made governor-general, he had no other case and was allowing Chandos to steer him 'to his political disgrace'.[61] Liverpool's incapacitating

stroke on 17 Feb., which in Fremantle's view raised 'insurmountable' difficulties, prompted Buckingham, who could scarcely conceal his delight, to 'consider this a complete change of ministry' and to stipulate that any communication to him and his 'friends' should be made directly and not through Williams Wynn. Fremantle privately doubted 'very much' that he would 'profit by occurrences ... under *any* contingency': 'I bless my stars every hour that I am out of his boutique and do not feel bound to follow his politics'. He entreated the duke not to take any hasty step, as whatever ministry emerged from the crisis was 'not likely to be a permanent one'. He was accused in return of having carried a 'message' to Williams Wynn and was required to 'pledge yourself to nothing' on the corn law question, on which the duke expected to clash with ministers. Fremantle denied the charge about Williams Wynn, but readily agreed not to commit himself on corn. After condemning Canning's proposals for relaxation of the laws, 1 Mar., as 'bare-faced robbery of the farmers', Buckingham told him that he would 'not support a government capable of treachery and ill usage which ... *may* be formed' and intimated that he would require Fremantle's 'support in the House ... on the question of *higher* protecting duties'.[62] He voted in the minority for Catholic relief, 6 Mar. 1827. Like the Duke, he was disgusted with Chandos's 'unfeeling joy' over 'a victory which is really a most calamitous event, for the numbers are so small that it cannot lead to settle or tranquillize the question'. He considered the duke's 'reasoning' on the corn question 'fallacious', but was prepared to 'satisfy him with my vote, which will go to oppose prohibition but admit (contrary to my own feelings but in accordance with his) a small increase of duties'.[63]

At the beginning of April 1827, as the ministerial uncertainty continued, Fremantle was ordered by Buckingham to confirm to Wellington that in the terms on which he and his squad had allied with the Liverpool ministry in 1822, Williams Wynn had not been specifically named as the recipient of the available cabinet place.[64] On 14 Apr. Buckingham summoned Fremantle and told him that Canning, the new premier, had rejected his application for India. After 'a warm conversation' Fremantle said that their opinions were now 'so perfectly different' that he would resign his seat whenever he was 'called upon ... to vote against the king's government'. He immediately notified Williams Wynn and warned Sir Thomas that although the duke had now made some difficulties about returning him in his place and 'things may change ... before he makes up his mind to decided opposition', he should be ready to accept the offer if it came. He was then reprimanded by the duke for mentioning the subject to Sir Thomas and told that he would probably return an experienced parliamentarian to be his 'organ'. Reporting this to his nephew, Fremantle observed that Buckingham, under Chandos's pernicious influence, was trying to squirm out of his earlier engagement:

> I feel perfectly satisfied ... that the duke has no earthly reason to complain of my conduct towards him in an one instance of my life, political or personal ... I am yet quite uncertain when he will decide on my retreat, and perfectly indifferent to it ... He has so destroyed his interest and power, by all the detestable intrigues he has been working through *underlings*, and is so misinformed and prejudiced by the rash and absurd conduct of Lord Chandos, that he is now left without an union political or personal ... I really and sincerely pity the duke, whose heart is naturally kind, and who can at times hear reason, and be convinced by it. Not so his son, who is now outrageous at being disappointed in getting rid of his father to India ... I sincerely love the duke of Buckingham and I respect and venerate his family, and I know he has been made the victim of this object and has been degraded by it.[65]

Fremantle advised his indignant nephew, 24 Apr., to stay cool and court Chandos, despite the duke's 'gross breach of promise'. That day Buckingham, now professing that 'I *cannot support Mr. Canning's government backed by the Whigs*', spoke to Sir Thomas at Aylesbury quarter sessions about the seat, without demanding an immediate answer, and informed Fremantle that it was up to him to decide whether or not to vacate. Next day Fremantle urged Sir Thomas to accept in principle, although he believed that the duke would 'pause before he gives me the order to vote against government', as 'my resignation of the seat will be at once the token of his decided hostility'. He also told Knighton, the king's secretary, of his wish 'if possible to secure ... [another] seat in order that I might now more fully evince my personal gratitude and devotion' to the king: he suggested arrangements by which he might be accommodated at New Windsor, 'where I am so well known, and where I think I could be of use to His Majesty by my constant residence in the neighbourhood'. On 28 Apr. Canning offered to find him a berth at the first opportunity, but next day expressed to Knighton dismay at a report that he was to be made first commissioner of woods and forests:

> It is impossible to appoint him to such an office without offending every man holding or hoping for privy councillor's office. He had never taken, nor can he take, any effective part in debate. The very fact of his being so nearly connected with the Court would *invite* attention to his department ... I wish Fremantle well ... but to put him

so forward ... would ... be invidious on his own account, and most inconvenient to the government.[66]

That day Buckingham ordered him to see Chandos about resigning his seat, which he would have to do, being 'hampered by your office', even if the duke's line was no more decided than one of '*not supporting*'. Fremantle duly did so and, 'without rancour or reproach', placed his seat, which his nephew had accepted, at the duke's disposal, though he kept to himself his belief that Buckingham's argument that Canning's coalition in office with the Lansdowne Whigs had 'injured' the Catholic cause was 'inconsistent with common reasoning'. As his last act as Buckingham's Member he was instructed to make it known that the duke had 'not joined Mr. Peel's opposition' and was acting unilaterally.[67] He vacated his seat on 17 May 1827, the more readily, as he confided to Sir Thomas, because he had discovered that Buckingham was 'playing another game with Canning which may possibly but not probably end in his supporting him'; he was 'determined ... not to be implicated'. Planta, the patronage secretary, assured him that he would 'take the earliest opportunity of finding' him a seat.[68]

In mid-July 1827 Fremantle rejected what was apparently his nephew's offer to return the seat to him:

> Nothing on earth should ever induce me once more to place myself in the unpleasant situation in which I found myself for the last three years ... I care very little about once more coming into Parliament, excepting as an occupation and coffee house. I have no reason to doubt the sincerity of Canning on the subject. If he does not fulfil his promise I cannot help myself, and I shall not further urge him as I do not wish to be under too great an obligation to him.

Canning's death and replacement by Lord Goderich, 'a personal friend', opened 'a fresh application' for him, but he still professed to be 'very indifferent about Parliament'. He was mentioned in ministerial circles as a possible candidate for Plymouth on the admiralty interest in mid-September, and in early October he half expected to be offered Hastings or Yarmouth, Isle of Wight, but nothing came of these speculations.[69] He was 'surprised' and delighted to be made a knight grand cross of Hanover that autumn.[70] As well as fulfilling his duties as a courtier, firmly in the king's confidence, and keeping his ear to the political ground, he sought to guide his nephew's tricky course between Chandos and Buckingham, especially during the latter's absence in Italy from August 1827 until November 1829. At the start of that year, when the duke was playing a double game towards the

Wellington ministry, he observed to Sir Thomas that the duke's

> conduct ... is of a piece with all he has done for the last ten years, never fixing to any one point, deceiving every party and every friend he deals with, and having no scruple of writing right hand and left, imagining that people would not show and compare his letters ... No party will have him ... I am really so hurt at all the duke has done (not as regards myself) but as affecting the great influence and power the Grenvilles possessed that I never think about it without putting myself in a passion.[71]

With the king's backing he had approached the ministry for a seat in its early days in 1828, but Wellington 'never encouraged him to hope that he would pay for a seat for him'. At the end of 1829 he renewed his application to Peel, the home secretary, rehearsing Liverpool's assurance of 1826 that as by taking the household post he had given up £600 a year, he would be catered for if he lost his seat for Buckingham, and Canning's 'promise ... followed by a personal excuse for not naming me to the first vacancy which occurred'. He now claimed to be 'anxious' to get back into the House, but because of the king's current hostility to the ministry nothing was done for him.[72] He was retained in his Court place by William IV, who evidently renewed his late brother's promise of support for the Castle seat at New Windsor in the event of a vacancy; but when this prospect arose in the early weeks of the Grey administration, an attempt by the king to insinuate Fremantle was thwarted.[73] Fremantle would soon have been in a fix, for he surely could not have swallowed the reform bill, which he considered 'the commencement of revolution' under 'the supremacy of the demagogue faction'.[74] He was 'vexed beyond measure' at the 'double dealing' of Buckingham and Chandos over Sir Thomas's candidature for Buckingham at the 1832 general election.[75] He left the household on the accession of Victoria. In the autumn of 1845 he tried to stir Peel's ministry, in which his nephew held office, into decisive action to secure the return of a Conservative for New Windsor.[76] Fremantle, who was widowed in 1841, died at Holly Grove, Windsor Great Park, his residence as deputy-ranger, in October 1850, 'after an illness of twenty three hours'. By his will, dated 7 Feb. 1847, he created a trust fund of £20,000 for the benefit of his niece Georgiana Fremantle and the children of his late nephew John Fremantle. He gave £1,000 each to his other three Fremantle nephews besides Sir Thomas, to whom, having helped him generously 30 years earlier, he left 400 shares in the Brighton and South Coast Railway (which realized £40,740), the residue of his personal estate and all his real estate, including property at Hardwick, near Aylesbury.[77]

[1] Buckingham, *Mems. Geo. IV*, i. 20. [2] Ibid. 6 July 1820; *CJ*, lxxvi. 40, 488. [3] Buckingham, i. 50-51, 59-61, 67, 71-72; Bucks. RO, Fremantle mss D/FR/46/11/31-33, 38, 39; 51/5/4. [4] Buckingham, i. 81-83, 88-89, 92-93, 97-99; Fremantle mss 46/11/37-39, 41; 46/12/37. [5] Buckingham, i. 111-16; Fremantle mss 46/11/42, 45, 46; 46/12/35, 36. [6] Buckingham, i. 140-1, 147-8; Fremantle mss 46/11/50; 46/12/34. [7] Fremantle mss 46/12/28-31; 51/5/11, 13; Buckingham, i. 161-5, 166-70. [8] Fremantle mss 46/11/52-54; 46/12/27; 51/5/14, 15; Buckingham, i. 171-8, 181-2, 194, 195-7. [9] Buckingham, i. 199-202, 211-13, 219; Fremantle mss 46/12/26. [10] Fremantle mss 46/11/57, 58; Buckingham, i. 225-8. [11] Buckingham, i. 231, 232-5, 237, 255-8, 263; Fremantle mss 46/11/59-61; 46/12/24, 25; 49/1/21; 138/2/2; *Geo. IV Letters*, ii. 969; *Hobhouse Diary*, 82; *Arbuthnot Jnl*. i. 133; Add. 38290, f. 155. [12] Harrowby mss XIV, f. 115; Buckingham, i. 264-6, 271-2, 275, 280, 281-2; *Hobhouse Diary*, 85; Grey mss, Tierney to Grey, 23 Jan.; Fitzwilliam mss, Grey to Fitzwilliam, 1 Feb. 1822; J.J. Sack, *The Grenvillites*, 190-1. [13] *The Times*, 16 Feb. 1822. [14] Fremantle mss 46/10/15, 17. [15] Buckingham, i. 294-7; Fremantle mss 46/10/19, 20. [16] Fremantle mss 46/10/21-23. [17] Ibid. 46/10/24-27; Buckingham, i. 307-8, 312, 316. [18] Buckingham, i. 298-9, 304-5, 308, 312-13, 314, 316-17; Fremantle mss 46/10/24-29, 56. [19] Buckingham, i. 322; Fremantle mss 46/10/32; 46/12/22. [20] Buckingham, i. 325, 337; Fremantle mss 46/12/79. [21] Fremantle mss 46/11/63; 46/12/77, 78. [22] Ibid. 46/10/36; Buckingham, i. 364, 372, 374. [23] Fremantle mss 46/10/43; 46/12/41, 74, 75; Buckingham, i. 379-80, 382-4. [24] Fremantle mss 46/12/72, 73; BL, Fortescue mss, Buckingham to Grenville, 3 Oct. 1822; Buckingham, i. 390-1. [25] Buckingham, i. 393, 417. [26] Fremantle mss 46/10/39; 46/11/68. [27] Buckingham, i. 423-5, 426, 433-4; Fremantle mss 46/11/71; 46/12/71. [28] Fremantle mss 46/11/78. [29] Lonsdale mss, Lowther to Lonsdale, 25 Mar. 1823; Fremantle mss 51/5/17. [30] Buckingham, i. 444-5, 447, 454-5, 456-9; Fremantle mss 46/11/80. [31] Buckingham, i. 456-9, 469, 475; Fremantle mss 46/11/81. [32] Fremantle mss 46/11/84; Buckingham, i. 481, 488-9; ii. 7-8. [33] Fremantle mss 46/87; 138/14/10. [34] Buckingham, ii. 21-22, 3334; Fremantle mss 46/11/88, 90, 91. [35] Fremantle mss 138/14/9. [36] Buckingham, ii. 42, 50, 51-52; Fremantle mss 46/12/66. [37] Buckingham, ii. 55; Fremantle mss 46/11/95, 96. [38] Buckingham, ii. 67-70, 75-76, 79; Fremantle mss 51/5/21. [39] Buckingham, ii. 91, 103; Fremantle mss 46/11/104; 51/5/22. [40] Buckingham, ii. 168-70, 178-9, 180-1, 182-3; Fremantle mss 46/11/111, 115, 122. [41] Buckingham, ii. 190-1, 195, 197-8; Fremantle mss 46/12/47. [42] Buckingham, ii. 202-4, 206-7, 208-12, 215-17. [43] NLW, Coedymaen mss, bdle. 18, Fremantle to Williams Wynn [18 Apr. 1825] (two letters). [44] Buckingham, ii. 225, 228-9, 238-40, 243-4, 250, 265, 267-8; Fremantle mss 46/11/118-18. [45] Coedymaen mss, bdle. 18, Fremantle to Williams Wynn, 28 Aug. 1825; Fremantle mss 138/12/8, 9. [46] Fremantle mss 46/12/64. [47] Ibid. 46/11/119; 46/12/ 56-61, 63, 67; 51/5/23; 138/12/5, 6. [48] Coedymaen mss, bdle. 18, Fremantle to Williams Wynn, 2 Dec. 1825. [49] Fremantle mss 46/11/120, 121; 46/12/50-54, 65; 138/12/2; Buckingham, ii. 286-9. [50] Fremantle mss 46/11/124-7; 46/12/46, 49, 80; 138/12/1; Buckingham, ii. 289. [51] Fremantle mss 46/12/81; 138/12/4. [52] Ibid. 46/11/128; 138/12/3. [53] Ibid. 46/12/43; 51/8/1. [54] Ibid. 46/11/131; 138/16/18. [55] Ibid. 46/12/83, 84; 138/16/15; Fremantle to Buckingham, 4 Apr. 1826. [56] Buckingham, ii. 297-300; Fremantle mss 46/12/85, 86; 51/5/26; 138/16/3, 4, 6, 7; Fremantle to Buckingham, 20 Apr., Buckingham to Fremantle, 9 July 1826. [57] Fremantle mss 48, Liverpool to Fremantle and reply, 1 May; 46/11/132-7; 46/12/87-94; 138/16/1; Sack, 207. [58] Fremantle mss 46/11/145; 136/16/1; 136/18/7; 138/26/4. [59] Ibid. 46/11/148, 149, 152; 49/1/24; 138/21/1/1, 3. [60] Ibid. 46/12/96, 98, 99; 138/21/1/5. [61] Ibid. 46/12/100-102; 138/21/1/8. [62] Ibid. 46/11/153, 155; 46/12/103-5; 138/21/1/9. [63] Ibid. 46/11/155; 138/21/1/10. [64] *Canning's Ministry*, 65, 69, 76; Fremantle mss 51/8/5. [65] *Canning's Ministry*, 123; Fremantle mss 46/12/107; 49/1/15, 16; 138/21/2/1, 3, 5. [66] Fremantle mss 46/11/154; 49/1/13-17; 51/11/6; 138/21/2/7, 8; *Canning's Ministry*, 274. [67] Fremantle mss 46/12/108-114; 138/21/1. [68] Ibid. 46/10/4, 47, 48, 50; 138/21/2/9, 10. [69] Ibid. 138/21/2/13-15, 17;

138/22/1/2; Lansdowne mss, Spring Rice to Lansdowne, 17 Sept. 1827. [70] Fremantle mss 138/21/2/19. [71] Ibid. 139/10/5. [72] Add. 40308, f. 307; 40399, f. 409; Wellington mss WP1/1065/61. [73] Grey mss, Taylor to Grey, 6 Dec.1830. [74] Fremantle mss 139/20/22-27. [75] Ibid. 49/1/12. [76] Add. 40575, ff. 17, 27, 29. [77] *Gent. Mag.* (1851), i. 92; PROB 11/2122/810; IR26/1868/560.

D.R.F.

FRENCH, Arthur I (1765–1820), of French Park, co. Roscommon.

Co. Roscommon   1801–24 Nov. 1820

bap. 6 Apr. 1765,[1] 1st surv. s. of Arthur French of French Park and Alicia, da. of Richard Magenis of Dublin. *m.* 8 Oct. 1764, Margaret, da. of Edmund Costello of Edmonstown, co. Mayo, 5s. 4da. *suc.* fa. 1799. *d.* 24 Nov. 1820.
MP [I] 1783-1800.
Trustee, linen board [I] 1795-*d.*
Gov. co. Roscommon 1819-*d.*
Capt. Elphin and French Park cav. 1796; commdt. French Park cav. vols. 1797.

French, whose ancestors had settled in county Galway in the fifteenth century, was first elected (apparently under age) in 1783 for county Roscommon, which his family had represented, almost continuously, since 1721. A friend of Catholic relief and an importunate supporter of successive governments, who had done well for his family out of the spoils system, he retained his county seat without opposition at the general election of 1820, despite being too ill to canvass.[2] He made no mark in the following session, which was his last, for he died in November 1820, 'after a severe indisposition of a few hours', supposedly brought on by overexertion in the hunting field. He left £18,000 to be divided among his younger children, having already provided for his eldest daughter Mary with £2,000 on her marriage. His eldest son and namesake succeeded him as head of the family and county Member.[3]

[1] *Hist. Irish Parl.* iv. 244. [2] Ibid. 244-5; *HP Commons, 1790-1820,* iii. 839-41; Add. 40296, f. 24; *Dublin Evening Post,* 9, 28 Mar. 1820. [3] *Dublin Evening Post,* 2 Dec. 1820; *Gent. Mag.* (1820), ii. 571; PROB 11/1644/333.

S.M.F.

FRENCH, Arthur II (?1788–1856), of French Park, co. Roscommon.

Co. Roscommon   16 Jan. 1821–1832

b. ?May 1788, 1st s. of Arthur French I* and Margaret, da. of Edmund Costello of Edmonstown, co. Mayo; bro.

of Patrick Fitzstephen French†. *educ.* Trinity, Dublin 3 June 1806, aged 18; Trinity, Oxf. 27 Apr. 1808, aged 19. *m.* 16 Apr. 1818, Mary Catherine, da. of Christopher McDermott of Creggah, King's Co., *s.p. suc.* fa. 1820; *cr.* Bar. De Freyne of Artagh 16 May 1839; Bar. De Freyne of Coolavin with spec. rem. to his bros. 5 Apr. 1851. *d.* 29 Sept. 1856.
Gov. co. Roscommon 1821-31, ld. lt. 1854-*d.*

French, whose first cousin and not he was the Dublin barrister of that name,[1] succeeded to his father's extensive Roscommon estates, with an annual rent roll of £18,000, in November 1820 and to the family seat for the county at an uncontested by-election early the following year.[2] His votes for inquiry into the conduct of the sheriff of county Dublin over the Queen Caroline affair, 22 Feb., and Catholic relief, 28 Feb., were praised at a Roscommon dinner in honour of his Whig brother-in-law Daniel Kelly of Cargins, 8 Mar. 1821.[3] But French, who divided against Maberly's motion on the state of the revenue, 6 Mar. 1821, for several years followed his father's example as an inactive supporter of the Liverpool administration and sought government patronage for his relatives as the price of that backing.[4] He commented on Irish education, 10 July, and, since in August 1821 he signed the requisition for a Roscommon meeting on the distressed state of his county and attended another on this the following year, it was probably he who thanked the English for providing relief for the West of Ireland, 30 July 1822. However, interventions on tithes, 15 May, 19 June 1822, may have been by his fellow Irishman Colonel Trench, Tory Member for Cambridge, with whom he was sometimes confused in the parliamentary records.[5] He sided with opposition in its majority for abolition of one of the joint-postmasterships, 2 May 1822, but divided against inquiry into chancery administration, 5 June 1823. He voted for inquiry into the state of Ireland, 11 May 1824. He divided against ministers on the Irish unlawful societies bill, 15, 21, 25 Feb. 1825. He voted for Catholic relief, 1 Mar., 21 Apr., 10 May, but against the related franchise bill, 26 Apr. He attended a meeting of the Catholics of county Roscommon in October 1825 and brought up their petition, 1 May 1826.[6]

French was returned unopposed at the general election that summer, when he proved very popular with the Catholic freeholders, whose meeting he again attended, 9 July 1826.[7] He voted for relief, 6 Mar. 1827. He divided for the committal of the duke of Clarence's annuity bill, 16 Mar., but with the protectionists against the corn bill, 2 Apr. 1827. He voted for repeal of the Test Acts, 26 Feb., and Catholic relief, 12 May 1828. Although he chaired the county meeting to address the departing lord lieutenant Lord Anglesey, 31 Jan., the following month he was listed by Planta, the Wellington ministry's patronage secretary, as likely to be 'with government' and he duly voted for Catholic emancipation, 6, 30 Mar., and to allow Daniel O'Connell to take his seat unimpeded, 18 May 1829.[8] He was in the minority against the bill to raise the Irish county franchise qualification, 19 Mar. 1829, and later that year his uncle George was removed as assistant barrister of Roscommon because of the conflict of interest that would arise through his supervising the new registration of freeholders.[9]

Outvoted at the meeting got up by his colleague Robert King's father, the Orangeman Lord Lorton, on the disturbed state of the county, 19 Nov., he convened another to express opposition to the proposal to invoke the Insurrection Act, 15 Dec. 1829. He signed the requisition for and moved the first resolution at the Roscommon meeting against the introduction of poor laws to Ireland, 30 Mar., and lodged this petition, 17 May 1830.[10] That year he usually joined in the opposition campaign for economies and tax reductions, although he was apparently in the majority against Hume's amendment to reduce judges' salaries, 7 July. He divided with O'Connell for abolition of the Irish lord lieutenancy, 11 May, information on the Doneraile conspiracy, 12 May, making Irish first fruits no longer nominal, 18 May, and repeal of the Irish Vestries Act, 10 June. He voted for abolition of the death penalty for forgery, 7 June, and against the administration of justice bill, 18 June. Well regarded by his constituents, he was in no danger at the general election that summer, when he was returned in conjunction with a leading local Catholic gentleman, the O'Conor Don, after nothing came of a threatened opposition. He joined the revamped Roscommon Election Club in August 1830 and the following month attended the celebrations of the county's independents.[11]

Listed by Pierce Mahony† among the 'neutrals' and by ministers among their 'foes', French was absent from the division on the civil list that led to Wellington's resignation, 15 Nov. 1830. He wrote to Lord Brougham, the new chancellor, 25 Dec. 1830, suggesting that, as he took 'an interest in this unlucky country', he might wish to rectify abuses in Irish chancery administration.[12] He divided for the second reading of the Grey ministry's reform bill, 22 Mar., and against Gascoyne's wrecking amendment, 19 Apr. 1831. Despite promising merely to maintain his consistent parliamentary conduct, he was returned slightly ahead of his colleague in a contest against an anti-reformer at the subsequent general election.[13]

He voted for the second reading of the reintroduced reform bill, 6 July, at least twice against adjourning proceedings on it, 12 July, and steadily for its details. He divided against the grant for civil list services, 18 July, and to print the Waterford petition for disarming the Irish yeomanry, 11 Aug., but for the Irish union of parishes bill, 19 Aug. He was in the ministerial majorities to punish those guilty of bribery at the Dublin election and against censuring the Irish administration over it, 23 Aug. (although he was also included in the minority on the latter division). He voted for the third reading, 19 Sept., and passage of the reform bill, 21 Sept., the second reading of the Scottish bill, 23 Sept., and Lord Ebrington's confidence motion, 10 Oct. 1831.

Having in December 1831 signed the requisition for a reform meeting in Roscommon, which he apparently did not attend, he presented its petition for making the alterations in Ireland as extensive as those proposed for England, 3 Feb. 1832.[14] He divided for the second reading of the revised reform bill, 17 Dec. 1831, the disfranchisement clauses, 20, 23 Jan., its details again, and the third reading, 22 Mar. 1832. He sided with government against producing information on Portugal, 9 Feb., but voted to restore the salary of the Irish registrar of deeds, 9 Apr., and, except when he divided for Crampton's amendment that day, he was frequently in small minorities for making ministers' Irish tithe reforms more extensive. He voted for Ebrington's motion for an address calling on the king to appoint only ministers who would carry the reform bill unimpaired, 10 May, and the second reading of the (in fact quite limited) Irish bill, 25 May, but for increasing the county representation of Scotland, 1 June, and O'Connell's amendment to enfranchise Irish £5 freeholders, 18 June. Apart from one for making coroners' inquests public, 20 June, his only other known votes were with ministers for the Russian-Dutch loan, 26 Jan., 12, 16 July. Deeply wounded by having been passed over for the lord lieutenancy of Roscommon the previous year, when Lorton had been appointed, he announced his retirement at the following dissolution, confessing that 'I cannot reconcile myself to support men who have treated me so badly, and I am determined private feeling shall never influence my public conduct'. On the hustings in December 1832, the new O'Conor Don* declared that, although he had been mostly silent in the Commons, 'his name stands enrolled on the side of freedom and of justice and of Ireland, in every division early or late, anticipated or unexpected', and in March 1833 the county approved an address of thanks to him at a special meeting.[15]

French was replaced by his younger brother Fitzstephen French, Liberal Member for Roscommon until 1873, who in 1833 exasperated Edward Littleton*, the Irish secretary, by using the grievance about the lord lieutenancy to demand further preferment for the family; pressure was later applied for a compensatory peerage.[16] A barony was awarded in 1839, when the spurious antiquity of the title was allowed on the basis of French's claim to be the seventeenth in lineal descent from Fulco De Freyne, whose family sprang from the 1st duke of Normandy.[17] As by the mid-1840s De Freyne was a childless widower, the title looked likely to become extinct, and O'Connell asked Lord John Russell's* government to fulfil the promise effectively evaded by Lord Melbourne, urging (not entirely accurately as to the Frenches' parliamentary service)

how suited this family is to a *permanent* peerage. There is the singular fact that for upwards of 160 years this family has represented their native county and that without intermission, always voting for the Liberal or Whig interest and being amongst the most active and continuous supporters of Catholic emancipation. They have more than once refused a peerage when offered by unfriendly parties, by parties adverse to the interests of Ireland. Lord Grey's government certainly treated the family very badly in appointing Lord Lorton, a virulent enemy, to the lieutenancy of the county instead of the then Mr. French, a steady supporter.[18]

Under the special remainder of the second creation, which was eventually granted in 1851, the 1st baron, who had become a member of Brooks's in 1840, was, after his death in September 1856, succeeded in turn by his brothers, the Rev. John (1788-1863), rector of Grangesilvia, county Kilkenny, and Charles (1790-1868), an army officer, through whom the title continued.

[1] *Al. Ox.* 1715-1886, ii. 495; *King's Inns Admission Pprs.* ed. E. Keane, P.B. Phair and T.U. Sadleir, 178. [2] S. Gibbon, *Recollections* (1829), 165; *Dublin Evening Post*, 2 Dec. 1820, 23 Jan. 1821. [3] *Dublin Evening Post*, 15 Mar. 1821. [4] *Black Bk.* (1823), 156; *Session of Parl.* 1825, p. 464; Add. 37301, f. 67. [5] *The Times*, 11 July 1821, 31 July 1822; *Dublin Evening Post*, 1 Sept. 1821, 18 June 1822. [6] *Roscommon and Leitrim Gazette*, 22 Oct. 1825; *The Times*, 2 May 1826. [7] *Roscommon and Leitrim Gazette*, 24 June, 22 July, 5 Aug. 1826. [8] *Roscommon Jnl.* 7 Feb. 1829. [9] Ibid. 11 July 1829. [10] Ibid. 21 Nov., 12, 19 Dec. 1829, 27 Mar., 3 Apr. 1830. [11] *Roscommon and Leitrim Gazette*, 24, 31 July, 7, 14 Aug.; *Dublin Evening Post*, 5, 10, 19 Aug., 25 Sept. 1830. [12] Brougham mss. [13] *Dublin Evening Post*, 5, 28 May; *Roscommon and Leitrim Gazette*, 14, 21 May 1831. [14] *Dublin Evening Post*, 24 Dec. 1831, 7 Jan. 1832. [15] Ibid. 8 Dec.; *Roscommon Jnl.* 21 Dec. 1832, 15 Mar. 1833. [16] *Three Diaries*, 354-5; *O'Connell Corresp.* vi. 2430. [17] J. D'Alton, *Mem. of Fam. of French*, 44; *CP*, iv. 114-15. [18] *O'Connell Corresp.* viii. 3256.

S.M.F.

FRESHFIELD, James William (1775-1864), of The Manor House, Stoke Newington and 9 Upper Wimpole Street, Mdx.

PENRYN	1830-1832
PENRYN AND FALMOUTH	1835-1841
BOSTON	22 Apr. 1851-1852
PENRYN AND FALMOUTH	1852-1857

b. 8 Apr. 1775,[1] 1st s. of James Freshfield of Chertsey, Surr. and w. Elizabeth. *educ.* Peterhouse, Camb. 1827; G. Inn 1827, called 1842. *m.* (1) 27 Feb. 1799, Mary, da. of James Blacket, 3s. (1 *d.v.p.*); (2) 22 Oct. 1821, Frances Jane Sims, *s.p. d.* 27 June 1864.
Attorney to Bank of England 1812-40.
Sheriff, Surr. 1849-50.

Freshfield was admitted as an attorney in 1795 and by 1805 he was a partner in the firm of Freshfield and Kaye, which developed 'an extensive practice in the City of London', acting as legal advisors to the West India Dock Company, the Royal Exchange Assurance Company and the Globe Insurance Company, of which he was a co-founder and eventual chairman. In 1812 he was appointed to the 'important and lucrative office' of attorney to the Bank of England.[2] He also became the private attorney of the Tory minister Robert Peel, and acted for another, Lord Ellenborough, in respect of his divorce bill. In 1823 he was 'entrusted with the conduct of the London merchants' petition to Parliament for an alteration in the law of principal and factor', and his address to a Commons committee was circulated by his clients.[3] He appears to have acted as an agent for prospective candidates seeking parliamentary constituencies.[4] In August 1825 he announced his intention of standing for the notoriously venal borough of Penryn and avowed his '*decided hostility* to what are termed Catholic claims', yet the following month his name was added to 'the list of candidates' for a peerage. His political ambitions suffered a setback shortly afterwards when it emerged that his partner, Charles Kaye, had made improper use of a client's stock; the partnership was dissolved and Freshfield lamented 'the loss of many thousand pounds'. He consulted Peel as to whether he should withdraw from Penryn or 'whether I might suffer more by not continuing to occupy a prominent station, from whence it might be inferred that I had sustained a greater shock than I have in credit and pecuniary consequence'. In the event, he withdrew shortly before the dissolution in May 1826 and introduced in his place the Bank of England director, William Manning*, for whose return he campaigned personally.[5] He indignantly repudiated the claims made by witnesses appearing before a subsequent Commons committee that he had supplied money with which to bribe the electors, and he told Peel that he hoped to represent the borough in the next Parliament if it was not disfranchised.[6] He expressed his 'respect and gratitude' in May 1827 for Peel's decision not to serve in Canning's coalition ministry. In May 1830 he welcomed the Commons' rejection of the Jewish emancipation bill, observing that this would 'materially remove an opinion prevalent that all ... vital principles are surrendered to the fear of being considered old fashioned, while the more active triumph in their work of destruction'.[7] At the general election that summer he was returned in second place for Penryn after a 'very smart' contest.[8]

The duke of Wellington's ministry regarded him as one of their 'friends', but he was absent from the crucial division on the civil list, 15 Nov. 1830. He presented an anti-slavery petition from Penryn Dissenters, 11 Nov. He informed Henry Brougham, 16 Nov., of his intention, 'unless his nerves should fail', of replying to the latter's complaint that he was being intimidated by the attorneys for promoting legal reform; Brougham's elevation as lord chancellor in the Grey ministry put an end to the matter.[9] He defended his profession from the imputation that its opposition to a general register of deeds was self-interested, 16 Dec. 1830. He condemned the 'gross injustice, the dire breach of faith' involved in the government's proposed tax on stock transfers, 11 Feb. 1831. He introduced jointly with the attorney-general Denman a Bankrupt Act amendment bill, 21 Feb., to rectify certain problems with the operation of the existing law; it passed, 9 Mar., but did not reach the Lords before the dissolution. He declared himself 'unfriendly and hostile in the highest degree' to the ministry's reform bill, 'a measure of revolution, calculated to destroy those institutions under which the country has flourished', 4 Mar., but said he was willing to support a 'safe and practical measure' such as that advocated by Lord Chandos. He presented a Penryn petition against the borough's partial disfranchisement, 21 Mar., and argued that its economic importance and 'improving circumstances' entitled it to retain two Members. He divided against the bill's second reading, 22 Mar., and for Gascoyne's wrecking amendment, 19 Apr. 1831. At the ensuing general election he was returned at the head of the poll.[10]

Reintroducing his Bankrupt Act amendment bill, 22 June 1831, Freshfield explained that it was 'confined to the remedy of a great and pressing evil' arising from an oversight in the existing legislation, which meant that the depositions of deceased witnesses ceased to be evidence of bankruptcy and persons who had purchased property from a bankrupt estate risked losing it through legal proceedings by the original owner; the bill, which incorporated suggestions from Brougham,[11] did not complete its report stage. He objected to Brougham's bankruptcy court bill in its present 'incomplete state', 12 Oct., and hoped that the House would not 'fall into the common error of the present day' of finding imperfections in 'institutions of great antiquity' and supporting drastic measures to reform them. He made several observations and suggestions for amendment, 14, 15 Oct., but stated on 17 Oct. that his objections to it 'seem to increase with ... consideration' and predicted that 'many material alterations' would soon be found necessary. He voted against the second reading of the reintroduced reform bill, 6 July, for five adjournment motions, 12 July, to use the 1831 census for the purpose of scheduling boroughs, 19 July, and to postpone consideration of Chippenham's inclusion in schedule B, 27 July. On 9 Aug. he moved an amendment to allow Penryn to retain two Members and its existing franchises, rather than being united with Falmouth. He accepted that Falmouth deserved separate representation but emphasized Penryn's 'increasing ... trade and commerce' and the fact that the population of the parish in which it was situated was over 4,000. He attached particular importance to protecting the rights of the scot and lot voters, who displayed an 'instinctive love of independence' although many were from the lower classes. He admitted that Penryn had gained a bad reputation, but insisted that the voters had struggled to make it an 'open borough' and maintained that 'no transactions have ever been proved ... that might not ... be charged upon any open borough in the kingdom'. However, he did not force a division. He voted against making proven payment of rent a requirement for voting in the boroughs, 25 Aug. He complained that the bill in practice 'limits the exercise of ... and provides for [the] annihilation' of the rights of freemen voters, 30 Aug., when he voted to preserve the rights of non-resident freemen. He voted to protect those of £5 non-resident freeholders in Shoreham, Cricklade, Aylesbury and East Retford, 2 Sept. He divided against the bill's third reading, 19 Sept., its passage, 21 Sept., and the second reading of the Scottish bill, 23 Sept. He protested against the attacks made by Members on the Lords for rejecting the bill, 18 Oct., and thought it was 'indefensible to hold up to odium' the bishops for doing their duty to king and country. He voted against the quarantine duties, 6 Sept., and for greater protection for the West Indian sugar interest, 12 Sept. 1831.

He emphasized the limited purposes of his reintroduced Bankrupt Act amendment bill, 15 Dec. 1831, and regretted that 'at different periods during the last session ... interested persons have found means, through some of the public journals, to arraign the justice of the measure and my motives in advocating it'; he denied that he had any personal interest in the matter. He mentioned that several suggested amendments had been adopted in committee, 18 May, and the bill passed, 26 July 1832, after he agreed to omit three clauses which had 'excited strong objections'. He warned Brougham that certain amendments could not be introduced without 'endangering the fate of the bill'; it gained royal assent, 15 Aug.[12] He defended 'the character' of the Bank in respect of certain bankruptcy cases, 10 July 1832, rejecting claims that it had acted 'oppressively' towards the creditors. He divided against the second reading of the revised reform bill, 17 Dec. 1831. On 23 Jan. 1832 he repeated his objections to the union of Penryn and Falmouth, which would be 'productive of nothing but disgust, confusion and disorder', because of the 'very considerable degree of jealousy' that existed between the towns, but his amendment to preserve Penryn's rights was negatived. He believed that enfranchising leaseholders and occupiers in the counties would operate 'most decidedly against' the agricultural interest, 1 Feb. He moved an amendment to allow the property conferring a £10 borough household vote to be held of more than one landlord, 3 Feb., observing that such tenants were 'less likely to be influenced'; but the leader of the Commons Lord Althorp argued that it might encourage the creation of faggot votes and it was negatived. He complained that the 1s. registration charge would be burdensome for many scot and lot voters and might 'furnish a temptation to bribery', 20 Feb., adding that 'the entire measure is calculated to multiply difficulties and add to the general expense of elections'. He voted against enfranchising Tower Hamlets, 28 Feb., and the bill's third reading, 22 Mar. Next day he proposed an amendment to better secure the rights of freemen voters whose qualification was based on birth, but Lord John Russell warned of its possible 'injurious effect' and it was negatived. He divided against the Vestry Act amendment bill, 23 Jan. He voted against ministers on the Russian-Dutch loan, 26 Jan., 12 July. He presented a petition from the Globe Insurance Company against the London Bridge approaches bill, 6 Mar. He divided for inquiry into the glove trade, 3 Apr. He was a majority teller for going into committee on the coroners bill, 7 May, but complained that the

principle of open court proceedings had been introduced by means of a 'sidewind', 20 June. He voted against inquiry into the inns of court, 17 July. On 1 Aug. 1832 he said that he was 'honoured' to present the first petition from the Incorporated Law Society, for better accommodation for judges in Serjeants' Inn, and expressed his belief that the new body would 'tend to raise the tone of my own branch of the profession'.

At the general election in December 1832 Freshfield was defeated at Penryn and Falmouth, but he represented the borough as a Conservative in three later Parliaments. He retired from legal practice around 1840 and became 'a considerable landed proprietor' in Surrey, but his sons and grandsons kept the firm of Freshfields going and they continued to act as attorneys to the Bank.[13] He died in June 1864. His elder surviving son, Charles Kaye Freshfield (1812-91), was Conservative Member for Dover, 1865-8 and 1874-85.

[1] *Ex inf.* Stephen Lees. [2] *Dod's Parl. Companion* (1838), 112; *Gent. Mag.* (1864), ii. 258-9; Boase, *Modern English Biog.* i. 1108. [3] Wellington mss WP1/1199/22; *Von Neumann Diary*, i. 205; *R. Cornw. Gazette*, 20 Aug. 1825. [4] Cornw. RO, Johnstone mss DD/J2/98, Freshfield to Hawkins, 6 Mar. 1826; Cent. Kent. Stud. Stanhope mss U1590/C130/9. [5] Add. 40381, f. 245; 40606, ff. 79, 87, 91, 97; *R. Cornw. Gazette*, 20 Aug. 1825, 20 May, 10, 17 June 1826. [6] *PP* (1826-7), iv. 371-484; *Canning Official Corresp.* 380-1; Add. 40396, f. 28. [7] Add. 40394, f. 90; 40607, f. 135. [8] *R. Cornw. Gazette*, 7 Aug. 1830. [9] Brougham mss, Freshfield to Brougham, 16 Nov. 1830. [10] *West Briton*, 6 May 1831. [11] Brougham mss, Freshfield to Brougham, 26 June 1831. [12] Ibid. same to same, 12 Aug. 1832. [13] *Gent. Mag.* (1864), ii. 258-9.

T.A.J.

FULLER MAITLAND (formerly MAITLAND), Ebenezer (1780–1858), of Park Place and Shinfield Park, Berks.; Stansted Mountfitchet, Essex, and 11 Bryanston Square, Mdx.

LOSTWITHIEL	1807–1812
WALLINGFORD	1812–1820
CHIPPENHAM	1826–1830

b. 23 Apr. 1780, o.s. of Ebenezer Maitland, merchant, of 13 King's Arms Yard, Coleman Street, London and Mary, da. of John Winter of Hanover Square, Mdx. *m.* 9 Dec. 1800,[1] Bethia, da. of Joshua Ellis of London, 4s. (1 *d.v.p.*) 8da. (2 *d.v.p.*). Took name of Fuller before Maitland by royal lic. 20 Nov. 1807, in accordance with the wish of his wife's aunt Sarah Fuller (*d.*1810). *suc.* fa. 1834; mother 1835. *d.* 1 Nov. 1858.
    Dir. S. Sea Co. 1815-*d.*
    Sheriff, Berks. 1825-6, Brec. 1831-2.
    Lt.-col. 2 Reading vols. 1804.

Fuller Maitland was descended from William Maitland (1635-81), a Presbyterian minister of the west of Scotland. His grandfather Robert Maitland (1713-89), uncle Robert Maitland (?1743-1810) and father, successful London merchants, were all buried in Bunhill Fields; and his father, a director of the Bank of England, 1798-1821, was chairman of the committee of deputies for the protection of the civil rights of the three denominations of Protestant Dissenters in 1813.[2] Fuller Maitland's own birth was registered at Dr. Williams's Library, and he was baptized at an Independent chapel in Carey street, but he evidently conformed to the Church of England in his adult life.[3] He apparently took no part in the family business, but he was well provided for by his father. His marriage to the granddaughter of William Fuller (d.1800), a London banker, brought him a substantial fortune, estimated at £500,000, when his wife's maiden aunt Sarah Fuller, William's only surviving heiress, died in 1810, leaving 'everything I possess' to the couple.[4] He invested some of his money in landed property at Shinfield, near Reading, and Stansted, near Bishop's Stortford.

As an inconspicuous and apparently silent Member for the venal borough of Wallingford, Fuller Maitland had given general support to the Liverpool ministry when present. In 1820 he stood again for Wallingford, having endorsed the principle of 'purity of election' expounded in a resolution adopted at a public meeting organized by the corporation. His colleague William Lewis Hughes, who looked askance at this manoeuvre, was joined by another Whig; and they polled enough shared votes to turn out Fuller Maitland, who was supported by every member of the corporation, but failed to fulfil his promise to petition.[5] In 1824 he acquired the property of Park Place on the Berkshire side of the Thames opposite Henley.[6] As revealed by the extensive correspondence with his local attorney Nathan Atherton, that year he also began tortuous negotiations to purchase houses in the burgage borough of Chippenham from his uncle John Maitland[†] and the other principal boroughmonger there.[7] According to 'Some memoranda on treating with Mr. Fuller Maitland' written by Atherton in June 1824, this was to be at the total cost of £34,000, on top of which he expected to meet the usual hefty expenses of both candidates at the next election.[8] He had been asked to stand for Reading, but declined in May 1825 on the ground that he was ineligible as sheriff of Berkshire; his name continued to be mentioned there, although nothing came of it.[9] Instead he announced that month that he would offer on his own interest for Chippenham, where he dined the electors and was considered secure as 'a gentleman of great fortune and high respectability'.[10] Threats of independent opposition and restiveness among the burgage holders forced him into increasingly anxious and costly management of the borough, through Atherton, over the following year, despite his private profession that 'I do not like to traffic in seats'.[11] But at the general election of 1826 he was returned unopposed, with a canny interloper Frederick Gye, at the expense of his supposed running mate John Rock Grosett*, who withdrew.[12] In his speech of thanks Fuller Maitland declared that 'it is not my habit to deal in professions', preferring to be 'judged by my actions'. He promptly promised to safeguard local interests and to assist his colleague in stimulating the town's depressed cloth manufacturing industry. He went on:

> The impressions of my mind lead me to support His Majesty's government, but thus far and no further; whenever I conscientiously in my heart believe that their measures are founded in wisdom, and dictated by sincerity. I shall enter Parliament perfectly unshackled ... I am ... a friend to civil and religious liberty, the advocate of religious toleration; but on ... Catholic emancipation ... I am not prepared to pledge myself ... I am a friend to the reform of the House of Commons, whenever any abuse shall be detected; but I never will consent to remove one single stone of that beautiful structure, which for so many ages has sheltered and protected us, until I can see some substitute brought forward equally safe and equally beautiful.

He professed his support for 'the slow and gradual, but effectual' abolition of slavery.[13]

Fuller Maitland voted against Catholic relief, 6 Mar. 1827. He remained a lax attender, but was almost certainly the 'P. Maitland' who voted in the Tory minority against the Coventry magistracy bill, 18 June. The following day he presented half a dozen petitions for repeal of the Test Acts, and he voted for that measure, 26 Feb. 1828, when he was in the chamber until the House broke up.[14] He again divided against Catholic relief, 12 May 1828; but his only known vote against emancipation in 1829, when he was omitted from analysis of Members' views drawn up by the Wellington ministry's patronage secretary Planta, was against considering the proposal, 6 Mar. He had been a defaulter the previous day, and again failed to appear, 10 Mar. 1829. His only other known votes were for Jewish emancipation, 5 Apr., and to reduce the grant for public buildings, 3 May 1830. He appears to have preserved his record of silence in debate.

At the general election of 1830 Fuller Maitland abandoned Chippenham, having sold his property there to Joseph Neeld*, perhaps because he had been stung by the size of the election bills and disadvantaged by the loss of Atherton's services.[15] Despite a rumour that he would stand for Wallingford, he stood for the single Member borough of Abingdon, where the economical reformer John Maberly was well entrenched. During his canvass he admitted his undiminished 'apprehension of the danger he conceived attendant on' Catholic emancipation; said that he had not yet encountered a scheme of parliamentary reform 'of which he cordially approved'; argued that 'trade was now more depressed than it was before the laws relating to it were meddled with'; professed support for tax reductions consistent with the dignity of the crown and the safety of the public creditor, and explained that he 'had not supported' the sale of beer bill because it interfered too much with the interests of publicans.[16] He was attacked on the hustings (in broiling heat) for his 'negative or neutral course' in the Commons, denounced as a monger of 'rotten boroughs' and accused of having 'asked for a treasury borough' before coming to Abingdon. He refuted the latter charge, while admitting that he had 'had a conversation with friends belonging to the treasury'. He did not repent his past association with close boroughs, pointed out that his declaration against corruption at Wallingford had cost him his seat and stood by his opposition to Catholic emancipation, which he hoped would 'answer the end intended'. He claimed not to have been 'wholly silent' in the House, where he had spoken to uphold the 'private or local interests' of Wallingford and Chippenham. He professed to believe that a measure of parliamentary reform was 'practicable', and said that he could support the scheme outlined by Maberly for the enfranchisement of 'populous unrepresented towns' at the expense of nomination boroughs, although he confessed that he did 'not quite comprehend it'. As for the tale that he had solicited votes from Dissenters by masquerading as one, he acknowledged his Dissenting background and connections, but insisted that 'I have always been a sincere member of the Church of England'. He was comfortably beaten by 65 votes in a poll of 253, and is not known to have made any further attempts to re-enter Parliament.[17]

Fuller Maitland had acquired a property at Garth, near Builth Wells, on the strength of which he served as sheriff of Breconshire, 1831-2. On the death in 1834 of his father, whose personalty was sworn under £35,000, he received a token legacy of 500 guineas, being already 'abundantly provided for'. His mother was the residuary legatee.[18] On her death the following year, worth £25,000, Fuller Maitland was her sole executor and residuary legatee, and his children received £1,000 each.[19] In 1848 he bought from

his distant kinswoman Elizabeth Agnes Maitland the Kirkcudbright estate of High Barcaple, part of which had once belonged to his grandfather.[20] Fuller Maitland died at Brighton in November 1858, leaving real estate in Essex, Middlesex and Kirkcudbright, plus the Clapham Common house inherited from his parents, to his eldest son William, his residuary legatee. His grandson William Fuller Maitland (1844-1932), of Stansted and Garth, an Oxford cricket blue, was Liberal Member for Breconshire, 1875-95.

[1] *The Times*, 10 Dec. 1800. Maitland ped. in *Misc. Gen. et Her.* (ser. 1), ii. 210, gives 9 Jan. 1800. [2] *Misc. Gen. et Her.* (ser. 1), ii. 207-9; Add. 38410, f. 290. [3] *Misc. Gen. et Her.* (ser. 1), ii. 210; IGI (London). [4] B. Flower, *Cautionary Hints* (1813), pp. viii, 9-12, 43-44; PROB 11/1516/542. [5] E.A. Smith, 'Bribery and Disfranchisement', *EHR*, lxxv (1960), 622-3; *Reading Mercury*, 21 Feb., 6, 13, 27 Mar.; *Jackson's Oxford Jnl.* 26 Feb., 11 Mar. 1820. [6] *VCH Berks.* iii. 162. [7] Wilts. RO, Bevir mss 1171/9. See CHIPPENHAM. [8] Bevir mss 15. [9] *Reading Mercury*, 23 May 1825. [10] Bevir mss 9, address, 28 May; *Salisbury Jnl.* 6 June; *Devizes Gazette*, 28 July 1825. [11] Bevir mss 9, Fuller Maitland to Atherton, 10 Oct., 5 Nov. 1825, 4 Feb., 27 Apr. 1826. [12] *Devizes Gazette*, 1, 8, 15 June 1826. [13] Ibid. 15 June 1826. [14] *The Times*, 20 June 1827; Bevir mss 9, Fuller Maitland to Atherton, 3 Mar. 1828. [15] Bevir mss 9, Fuller Maitland to Atherton, 15 Feb., 4 May 1827, Atherton to Fuller Maitland, 2 May 1828; *Devizes Gazette*, 1 July 1830. [16] *Berks. Chron.* 10, 17 July; *Reading Mercury*, 12, 19 July; *Jackson's Oxford Jnl.* 24 July 1830. [17] *Full Report of Abingdon Election, 1830*, pp. 4-7, 14-15, 21-22, 49-50, 59-64; J. Townsend, *Hist. Abingdon*, 159-60. [18] PROB 11/1837/582; IR26/1361/353. [19] PROB 11/1848/374; IR26/1392/235. [20] *Misc. Gen. et Her.* (ser. 1), ii. 208, 210.

D.R.F./S.M.F.

FYLER, Thomas Bilcliffe (1788–1838), of 19 Dover Street, Piccadilly and Teddington, Mdx.

COVENTRY   1826–1831

b. 12 Sept. 1788, 1st s. of Samuel Fyler, barrister, of Twickenham and 1st w. Mary, da. and h. of John l'Anson, barrister, of St. Margaret's, Westminster. *educ.* Winchester 1799-1806; Christ Church, Oxf. 1806; L. Inn 1810. *m.* 26 Nov. 1828, Dorothea Lucretia, da. of Lt.-Col. Alexander W. Light, 2s. 2da. *d.* 4 Mar. 1838. Capt. 5 Ft. 1813, half-pay 1814.

Fyler owed his middle name and much of his fortune to his great-grandfather Thomas Bilcliffe (*d.* 1773) of King Street, Westminster, a prosperous cabinet maker of Suffolk stock who bequeathed property in Dover Street and elsewhere to his daughters, Mary, the wife of George Fyler, an apothecary, and Elizabeth, the wife of James Chamness, with reversion to his only grandson, Fyler's father Samuel. In 1787 Samuel married his cousin Mary l'Anson, heiress to her barrister father John and uncle Sir Thomas Bankes l'Anson of Corfe Castle, Dorset.[1] Following her death, and before his remarriage, he safeguarded their children's parental and grandparental inheritances by indentures of 31 May 1800 and 30 Dec. 1802.[2] Small in stature and of a 'delicate constitution', Fyler trained but was not called as a barrister. He was seconded to the militia after joining the army in 1813, became an active Middlesex magistrate and divided his time between his Dover Street house and his brother James Chamness Fyler's Woodlands Park estate near Bagshot, Surrey. Contrary to reports in Coventry, which he contested successfully as a 'No Popery' Tory on the corporation interest in 1826, his election was not financed by a recent legacy from his father. Samuel Fyler (d. 1825) left his goodwill to the 'amply provided for' children of his first marriage and his dwindling fortune to those of his second.[3] Noting his brother James's constant presence, *The Times* commented that Fyler 'does not address the freemen, from want of ability'.[4]

Relieved not to be unseated on petition, Fyler, whose maiden speech on 13 Feb. 1827 against naval impressment failed to impress his constituents, initially played second fiddle to his colleague Richard Heathcote. He assisted as a speaker and minority teller against the Coventry magistracy bill, which the corporation opposed, and consistently criticized the measure as 'unwise, unconstitutional and unjust' and likely to 'aggravate the evils it was meant to cure', 8, 11, 13, 15, 18, 19 June. He attributed its passage through the Commons to the sharp practices deployed by its promoter Sir Charles Wetherell.[5] He voted against Catholic relief, 6 Mar., and increased protection for barley, 12 Mar., and for the award to the duke of Clarence, 16 Mar., the spring guns bill, 23 Mar., and government expenditure on the Canadian waterways, 12 June. He 'denied that the manufacturing towns were hotbeds of corruption' when the possible transfer of East Retford's seats to Birmingham was broached, 22 June,[6] and was sorry to see the Canning ministry's corn bill defeated in the Lords, 14 July. His parliamentary conduct was invariably closely scrutinized in the Coventry newspapers and, unlike Heathcote, he wrote to them regularly to answer his critics and publicize his achievements. On 15 and 19 June 1827 he claimed the credit for securing concessions to the Holyhead road bill, which had threatened Coventry's lammas lands.[7] In 1828 Fyler established himself as the spokesman of the Coventry silk trade and contributed frequently to discussions on a wide range of issues. He voted to repeal the Test Acts, 26 Feb., but against Catholic relief, 12 May, having defended the double land tax levied on Catholics, 21 Feb. He urged government action on corn law reform when presenting Coventry's petition, 21 Apr., and voted to lower the pivot price,

22 Apr. He spoke against limiting elections to 'seven, eight or ten days' under the borough polls bill, 21 Feb., but supported similar proposals in the amended measure, 6, 15, 23 May, and declared that he would vote for its third reading, 27 June. He divided with Hume for information on civil list pensions, 20 May, and for the second reading of the usury laws amendment bill, 19 June. He voted to disqualify certain East Retford voters, 24 June, and against the recommittal of the reintroduced disfranchisement bill, 27 June. He divided with the Wellington administration against ordnance reductions, 4 July 1828.

Overwhelmed by constituency business, especially petitions, he announced his intention to bring in legislation to repeal the 'Ribbon Act' (1827 Election Expenses Act), which Coventry held partly responsible for its depressed trade, 4, 19 Feb., 6 Mar., but, despite favourable petitions from the silk towns, he was refused leave for a bill by 91-9, 20 Mar. 1828. He pestered ministers, 25 Apr., presented hostile petitions, 1 May, 8 July, ordered returns, 12, 21 May, and lobbied the board of trade in protest at the belated renewal of the silk trades bill and for additional protection.[8] He complained of the disruption caused by piecemeal and short-term policies and accused government of making it impossible for the trade to compete in an international market, 16 June, 1 July. On the Customs Acts bill, 10 July, he conceded in committee that 'government could not have done otherwise than to have continued the large duties on foreign silks', but endorsed the former president of the board of trade Charles Grant's call for inquiry and spoke against forcing a division on Bright's amendment. He carried the bill's recommittal by 37-34, 14 July, and secured concessions in the implementation of *ad valorem* duties.[9] He renewed his plea for inquiry by select committee and criticized the reciprocity duties in further speeches and interventions, 15, 17, 18, 19, 25 July, when he reaffirmed his intention of seeking inquiry next session. He presented and endorsed petitions against the friendly societies bill, 21 24, 25 Apr., slavery, 9 June, the alehouse licensing bill, 19 June, and suttee, 1 July. Drawing heavily on his speeches against the 1827 Coventry magistracy bill, he opposed the corporate funds bill on behalf of the corporation, 12 June, 1, 8 July 1828.

As the Wellington ministry's patronage secretary Planta predicted, Fyler's hostility to Catholic emancipation in 1829 was undiminished; and he suspended his campaign against the silk duties pending its resolution. He disputed its promoters' claims that Catholic relief would 'produce harmony' in Ireland, 27 Feb.,

3 Mar., and presented and endorsed Coventry's anti-Catholic petition, 3 Mar., and another 15 Mar. He voted against the measure, 6, 18, 23, 26, 27, 30 Mar. Making silk again his priority, he confirmed the sorry plight of the Coventry weavers he had alluded to briefly on 16 and 27 Feb. in exchanges with the president of the board of trade Vesey Fitzgerald 7, 8, 9, 10 Apr., and prefaced his inquiry motion on the 13th by bringing up numerously signed petitions from Coventry and Macclesfield. In a 'very able speech',[10] tracing developments in the silk trade since the principle of free trade was conceded in 1824 and illustrated with statistics from official returns, he argued that

> free trade is beautiful in theory; yet I do not think that, in a country like this, which is altogether in an artificial state, groaning under a heavy load of taxation, oppressed by an enormous debt, and burdened with onerous poor rates ... there can be free trade with regard to manufactures, while in every other respect, there is a system of monopoly.

He accused ministers of experimenting with the livelihoods of the Coventry weavers. Vesey Fitzgerald hinted at concessions on drawbacks, which Alexander Baring and Huskisson opposed, and the debate was adjourned. Winding up before inquiry was rejected by 149-31 next day, Fyler refused to concede that a committee would delay remedial action: 'My constituents know, that if Parliament goes into the committee, the question will receive a full deliberation, which will satisfy and appease them'. He ordered further returns, 16 Apr., presented petitions criticizing the proffered drawbacks, 28 Apr., opposed the silk trades bill as a speaker and minority teller, 1 May, and criticized its principle and details at every opportunity, 1-8 May. Commenting on the Spitalfields riots, 2 June, he deplored the way in which the weavers had taken the law into their own hands, but also blamed ministers for failing to concede inquiry. He presented petitions against the truck bill, 11 May, and suttee, 3 June. He made his support for the anatomy bill conditional on its stipulating that dissection was not a punishment for crime, 15 May. In October 1829, contemplating a political realignment, the Ultra Commons leader Sir Richard Vyvyan listed him among the 'Tories strongly opposed' to the Wellington administration.

Fyler voted for Knatchbull's amendment criticizing the failure of the address to notice distress, 4 Feb., testified to its prevalence in agriculture and manufacturing in Warwickshire and Coventry, and, confirming his hostility to free trade, called for 'revision of the commercial code' and further retrenchment, 8, 9 Feb. 1830. He spoke similarly on presenting distress petitions from all branches of the ribbon trade, 12, 22

Feb., 11 Mar., and on Davenport's state of the nation motion, 16 Mar. Challenging the political economist Poulett Thomson, he maintained that a recent improvement in Coventry's silk trade was seasonal and nominal, 6 Apr. He supported the weavers' petition against shortening their traditional seven-year apprenticeship, 13 May, and tried in vain to legislate to abolish the concurrent system of half-pay apprenticeships, 13, 25 May, 11 June. Writing to his Coventry backers, he attributed his failure to a mistranscription in the printed bill by a 'fool of a [Commons] clerk'.[11] He testified to the continued depression in Spitalfields without endorsing the weavers' demand for parliamentary reform to alleviate it, 18 May 1830. Yet he saw nothing unconstitutional in enfranchising the manufacturing towns, and voted to transfer East Retford's seats to Birmingham, 5 May 1829, 11 Feb., 5, 15 Mar., to enfranchise Birmingham, Leeds and Manchester, 23 Feb., and for parliamentary reform, 28 May 1830. He voted to reduce the navy estimates, 1 Mar., and, except on Jewish emancipation, which he opposed, 17 May, he divided steadily with the revived Whig opposition for the remainder of that Parliament. He presented petitions, 30 Mar., 3 May, and voted to make forgery a non-capital offence, 24 May, 7 June. He brought up petitions from Coventry's influential directors of the poor against the liability of landlords bill, 24 May, and the poor removal bill, 18 June, and cast a hostile vote with the motley crew against the administration of justice bill that day. On the sale of beer bill, 30 Mar., he endorsed the Coventry licensed victuallers' hostile petition, and advocated further restrictions on on-consumption, 21 June, 1 July. Heathcote 'retired' at the general election that month, but his erstwhile supporters, whom he addressed, 5 July 1830, declared that 'Fyler was eligible for re-election after representing their views', and a bipartisan compromise secured his return after a token poll with the 1818-26 Whig Member, Lord Grey's brother-in-law Edward Ellice.[12]

The Wellington ministry listed Fyler among the 'violent Ultras' and he voted to bring them down on the civil list, 15 Nov. 1830. He cautioned against interpreting the tricolours displayed by the distressed Spitalfields weavers during the London trades procession as signs of disloyalty, 17 Dec. In the first of several speeches on the game laws, he approved the principle of Lord Chandos's bill, 7 Dec., but criticized its 'cumbersome clauses' and threatened to introduce a rival measure 'reducing the whole to the simple principle of trespass' should the new Grey ministry, in which Ellice was patronage secretary, fail to do so. For this he was soundly chastised 'from his own side of the House' by the Tory Thomas Wood, who could influence Coventry's London freemen. He declared his support for the leader of the House Lord Althorp's game bill, 14, 15 Feb. 1831. Responding to constituency pressure, he broached the question of half-pay apprenticeships on seconding Hobhouse's factories regulation bill, 15 Feb., and would not hear of extending its provisions to silk, where home working and small workshops prevailed, 15 Mar.[13] Uncertain and consulted only by the Political Union, whom he snubbed, he wrote to the town clerk of Coventry, 10 Mar., stating his views on the ministerial reform bill:

> Though a moderate, I am a very honest reformer, but consider the bill too sweeping and objectionable in many points, though on the other hand it contains many very excellent suggestions. I should be glad to hear your opinions of it. Is there any chance of a public meeting being held at Coventry? I think it should be.[14]

He confirmed overwhelming support for the measure and local concern over the voting rights of current apprentices when Ellice presented Coventry's favourable petition, 15 Mar., and disputed claims made by Hunt, to whom an alternative petition had been forwarded, that the weavers sought annual parliaments, the ballot and universal suffrage. Outlining his own stance, he declared for 'some disfranchisements and the enfranchisement of great towns', maintained that the bill tended to increase the power of the landed interest and added, 'Whether [it] ... should pass or not, I am satisfied that no minister could retain his place, even for a fortnight, who was not prepared to bring forward a sound constitutional, full and effective measure of reform'. He divided for the bill at its second reading, 22 Mar. His vote against Gascoyne's wrecking amendment, which his critics expected him to support, 19 Apr., surprised and confounded the Political Union and his Coventry supporters, to whom he had again written candidly of his reservations, fuelling a campaign to oust him.[15] Damaging reports that he had voted against the bill persisted.[16] In the House, 21 Apr., he explained that he had voted as a decided and sincere reformer who did not want to see the bill wrecked, criticized Hunt and claimed that he would have divided for the bill's details in committee had it been proceeded with. He issued notices, 22 and 27 Apr., and canvassed Coventry with his brother directly the dissolution was announced, forcing the corporation into a pretended neutrality.[17] Despite his many private and public protests at his treatment, bold speeches, expensive canvass and appeals to his 1826 supporters, he was defeated by the reformers Ellice and Henry Lytton Bulwer, who at a private meeting in London, 23 Apr. 1831, had tried to call his bluff

by insisting that he should declare immediately and unequivocally for the bill.[18]

Fyler rallied his supporters, 'the 1,151', at the *City Arms*, 4 May 1831, and, keeping this party together with dinners and newsletters, he mounted a costly but hopeless challenge at the general election of 1832.[19] Grant had recommended him to Grey for a baronetcy in September 1831, but Ellice forbade it.[20] He did not stand for Parliament again. He died in Torquay in poor health in March 1838, worth an estimated £4,000 at probate, leaving a widow and four young children, for whom he had nominated guardians and established a family trust. His widow subsequently married Herbert Hore of Pole Hore, county Wexford.[21]

[1]PROB 11/990/319; 1339/210. [2]Ibid. 11/1697/197; IR26/1041/254. [3] *Gent. Mag.* (1838), ii. 226; T.W. Whitley, *Parl. Rep. Coventry*, 277; *Coventry Herald*, 9, 23 June; *Coventry Mercury*, 26 June 1826; PROB 11/1697/197; IR26/1041/254. [4] *The Times*, 14, 21 June 1826. [5]Coventry Archives PA14/10/5, 20, 53, 59, 64, 65, 70; *Coventry Mercury*, 18 Feb.; *Coventry Herald*, 23 Feb.; *The Times*, 9, 12, 14, 16 June 1827. [6]Ibid. 23 June 1827. [7]*Coventry Mercury*, 24 June 1827; Whitley, 278. [8]*Coventry Mercury*, 15 June, 27 July 1828. [9] Coventry Archives PA14/10/52. [10]*Gent. Mag.* (1829), i. 360. [11]Coventry Archives PA14/10/55-57. [12]*Coventry Mercury*, 11, 18, 25 July, 1 Aug. 1830; Whitley, 280-85. [13]*Coventry Herald*, 11, 18, 25 Feb., 4 Mar. 1831. [14]Coventry Archives PA14/10/58. [15]*Coventry Herald*, 15 Mar., 1, 8, 15 Apr. 1831; Coventry Archives PA14/10/23. [16]*Midland Representative and Birmingham Herald*, 23, 30 Apr. 1831. [17]Coventry Archives PA14/10/23, 54. [18]Ibid. PA14/10/21, 22, 54, 55; Add. 36466, f. 410; *Coventry Mercury*, 24 Apr., 1, 8, 15 May 1831. [19]Whitley, 290-8; Coventry Archives PA17/76/8-10. [20]Grey mss, Grant to Grey, 1 Sept. 1831 [21]*Coventry Herald*, 16 Mar. 1838; PROB 8/231; 11/1895/313.

M.M.E.

FYNES (afterwards **FYNES CLINTON**), **Henry** (1781–1852), of Welwyn House, Herts. and Dean's Yard, Westminster, Mdx.[1]

ALDBOROUGH 1806–1826

b. 14 Jan. 1781, 1st s. of Rev. Charles Fynes, preb. of Westminster and perpetual curate of St. Margaret's, Westminster, and Emma, da. of Job Brough of Newark, Notts.; bro. of Clinton James Fynes Clinton*. *educ.* Southwell g.s. 1789-96; Westminster 1796-9; Christ Church, Oxf. 1799-1806; L. Inn 1808. *m.* (1) 22 June 1809, Harriott (*d.* 2 Feb. 1810), da. of Rev. Charles Wylde of Nottingham, *s.p.*; (2) 6 Jan. 1812, Katherine, da. of Rt. Rev. Henry William Majendie, bp. of Bangor, 2s. *d.v.p.* 9da. (2 *d.v.p.*). *suc.* kinsman Isaac Gardiner of Saffron Walden, Essex 1811; fa. 1827, having like him taken the additional name of Clinton by royal lic. 26 Apr. 1821. *d.* 24 Oct. 1852.

Fynes, who inherited property in Bedfordshire, Buckinghamshire, Cambridgeshire, Essex and

Middlesex from a relative in 1811, and purchased an estate in Hertfordshire the following year,[2] had sat for Aldborough since 1806 as the nominee of another distant kinsman, the 4th duke of Newcastle. However, he had long since abandoned any notion of making a mark in politics, and devoted most of this energy to preparing materials for a major work on Greek and Roman chronologies. As he noted at the end of 1819:

A government office, with duties to be performed in London, would impair my health, waste my spirits and withdraw me from that literature by which I am best able to be useful to myself or others: neither would it ultimately benefit my family, because an increased income would only bring with it an increased expenditure. I have no reason therefore for desiring such an office, were it within my reach. It would give me no pleasure, for I have examined my own mind, and find myself to be destitute of political ambition. As to the temporal welfare of my children, I shall best provide for it by a frugal management of that which I possess.

He allowed himself to be returned for the fifth time for Aldborough in 1820, after a contest, but lamented the fact that 'I have not looked into a book for this fortnight', observing that 'this interruption of my usual literary studies has been prejudicial to me ... without a literary object, my mind preys upon itself'.[3]

He continued to be an occasional attender who gave general support, when present, to Lord Liverpool's ministry. He attended the opening of Parliament and on 18 May 1820 presented a petition from the agent of his colleague Antrobus, requesting an extension of the time allowed for proving his property qualification, which had been challenged in a petition. In his only known contribution to debate, 25 May, he explained that Antrobus was in America and moved that his agent be permitted to swear to his qualification; this was agreed the next day. He was in his seat for over 12 hours for the debate on the Queen Caroline affair, 22 June, and voted with government against economies in revenue collection, 4 July 1820. He spent most of the remainder of the year at Welwyn, where the superintendence of building work disrupted his studies. On his fortieth birthday, 14 Jan. 1821, he wrote:

I have many causes for thankfulness to Providence ... I still possess better health, and more active powers of exertion, than I had any reason to expect three years ago ... I have good hopes of my chronology [of Greek literature], which proceeds towards a probable conclusion ... It is doubtless good discipline to press forwards ... But with my constitutional tendency to despond, it may be salutary sometimes to survey how much has been executed, that I may not be tempted to throw aside my task in despair.[4]

He was present for the renewed debates on the queen and voted in defence of ministers' conduct towards her, 6 Feb. He divided against Catholic relief, 28 Feb., because, as he privately noted, he 'could not agree to the manifest absurdity of giving to this sect that which would enable it to be mischievous again'.[5] He voted against a reduction in the army estimates, 11 Apr., parliamentary reform, 9 May, and Hume's economy and retrenchment motion, 27 June 1821. He divided against more extensive tax reductions, 11, 21 Feb. 1822, but attended only sporadically for the remainder of that session. He voted against relieving Catholic peers of their disabilities, 30 Apr. From June 1822 he spent six tranquil months at Bangor, where he made good progress with his literary projects, which he regarded as a 'duty' because they 'gradually bring me to a better understanding of the word of God', based 'not upon trust ... but upon ... reason and conviction', and because they 'enable me to become contented with my lot, to look with philosophical indifference upon the vain pursuits of ambition, and to appreciate justly the value of that safe mediocrity of station and fortune in which I am placed'.[6] He voted against repeal of the assessed taxes, 18 Mar., and the Foreign Enlistment Act, 16 Apr., and against inquiry into the currency, 12 June 1823. In 1824, when the first part of his *Fasti Hellenici* was published and well received, he divided against parliamentary reform, 26 Feb., and the abolition of flogging in the armed forces, 5 Mar., and mustered to support the aliens bill, 23 Mar. About this time Newcastle, who described Fynes as 'a man of great learning and abilities' who 'would do well in any situation', tried to secure him a place at one of the public boards, but the prime minister could not oblige. Fynes would have welcomed useful and lucrative employment, but had little difficulty in reconciling himself to the disappointment.[7] He voted for the Irish unlawful societies bill, 25 Feb., and against Catholic relief, 1 Mar., 21 Apr., 10 May 1825. No further votes have been found in his name, and he made way for his brother Clinton at the dissolution in 1826, when he wrote:

Called to a seat in the House of Commons in my twenty-sixth year, without solicitation, without preparation for it, I am now thrown back on to my original position, without a profession, without occupation, except such as I can create for myself; and at a period of life when it is too late to engage in a profession.

He had been, he reflected, 'as far as public speaking is concerned, an inefficient Member of Parliament'.[8]

Yet the biggest disappointment of Fynes's life was his failure to secure the head librarianship of the British

Museum in 1827, when he was passed over in favour of Henry Ellis, the long-serving keeper of printed books.[9] A later application by Newcastle on his behalf for the receiver-generalship of Nottinghamshire also came to nothing. He devoted himself after 1826 to his literary work: further instalments of the *Fasti Hellenici* were published in 1830 and 1834, his *Fasti Romani* appeared between 1845 and 1850, and the *Epitome of the Civil and Literary Chronology of Greece* in 1851. Newcastle regarded him as 'perhaps the best scholar of his day and very deeply read'.[10] After his death in October 1852 his work on Roman chronology was completed by his brother Charles, who recalled in the preface to his *Literary Remains* that the 'distinctive features of his character' were 'an ardent thirst for knowledge, an absence of ambition for worldly honours and distinctions, a profound reverence for the Most High, and an earnest desire to consecrate the labours of his intellect to His honour'. Fynes made provision for his wife and seven surviving daughters and directed that Welwyn be sold.[11]

[1] Based on H. Fynes Clinton, *Literary Remains* (1854). [2] Ibid. 45, 53; PROB 11/1518/23. [3] Fynes Clinton, 141, 147. [4] Ibid. 167-9. [5] Ibid. 26. [6] Ibid. 202. [7] Ibid. 205, 221-2; Nottingham Univ. Lib. Newcastle mss Ne2 F2/1/222; Add. 38299, f. 100. [8] Fynes Clinton, 247-8. [9] *Geo. IV Letters*, iii. 1446. [10] *Unhappy Reactionary* ed. R.A. Gaunt (Thoroton Soc. rec. ser. xliii), 15. [11] PROB 11/2163/904; IR26/1928/863.

D.R.F.

FYNES CLINTON, Clinton James (1792–1833), of Denton Hall, Lincs. and 58 Cadogan Place, Sloane Street and 7 Old Square, Lincoln's Inn, Mdx.

ALDBOROUGH   1826–1832

b. 13 Dec. 1792, 2nd s. of Rev. Charles Fynes (*d.* 1827) and Emma, da. of Job Brough of Newark, Notts; bro. of Henry Fynes*. *educ.* Westminster 1807; Christ Church, Oxf. 1811; L. Inn 1815, called 1818. *m.* 2 May 1825, Penelope, da. of Sir William Earle Welby†, 2nd bt., of Denton Hall, 1s. 4da. Like fa. and bro. took additional name of Clinton by royal lic. 26 Apr. 1821. *d.* 13 Apr. 1833.[1]

Recorder, Newark and Retford.

Fynes Clinton, a barrister on the Midland circuit, came from a family who were descended directly from the 2nd earl of Lincoln and thus were kinsmen of the 4th duke of Newcastle. He appears to have begun conducting legal work for the duke in 1823.[2] In May 1825 Newcastle recorded in his diary that Fynes Clinton had been to see him 'on business' and was 'much pleased with the near prospect of coming into Parliament',

which he did at the general election of 1826, when he replaced his brother Henry as one of the ducal nominees for Aldborough. At that time, Newcastle wrote to Fynes Clinton and his colleague, Sir Alexander Grant, that 'both have been of great service to me, both so intelligent and so active, that I do not fear the attack of any adversaries'.[3] Fynes Clinton subsequently worked closely with Newcastle's attorney William Tallents to prepare evidence to combat possible petitions against the return of the duke's Members for Aldborough and Boroughbridge, but these did not materialize.[4] In November 1827 Newcastle wrote of him that he was 'universally esteemed and looked up to as a lawyer' and was 'considered at this time as the most promising man at the bar', having 'more business than usually falls to young counsellors'; it seemed that 'if he lives he cannot fail to be seated on the woolsack'.[5]

Fynes Clinton divided against Catholic relief, 6 Mar. 1827. He was granted leave to go the circuit, 26 Mar., but returned to vote against the corn bill, 2 Apr. According to a newspaper report, it was he who declared his intention of opposing the Coventry election committee's report, 14 May.[6] He divided against the disfranchisement of Penryn, 7 June 1827. In presenting a petition from East Retford (another borough where Newcastle exercised influence) against disfranchisement, 8 Feb. 1828, he gave notice that he would move for the petitioners to be heard by counsel at the bar. He presented a further petition, 25 Feb., when he pointed to the inconsistency of the committee on the East Retford bill, who, having 'acquitted the electors of bribery' at the last general election, 'go on ... to fix upon them a general charge'. He explained to the House that he had been agent to Sir Henry Wright Wilson* at the election in question, 4 Mar., and maintained that he had promised no money to any freemen. He presented a petition from the Imperial Gas Company for a private bill to amend their regulating Act, 31 Jan. It was referred to a committee, which reported the next day, and resulted in his introducing a bill, 4 Feb., which secured a second reading, 8 Feb. However, despite his strenuous efforts it was rejected at the report stage, by 81-6, 25 Feb. He divided against repeal of the Test Acts, 26 Feb., and Catholic relief, 12 May. He voted with the duke of Wellington's government against reduction of the salary of the lieutenant-general of the ordnance, 4 July 1828. In presenting a Grantham petition against Catholic relief, 9 Feb. 1829, he observed that he had voted against this in the last two sessions and, 'notwithstanding the very great and unexpected changes which have lately taken place', he saw 'no reason why I should give a different vote this session'. He claimed that majority opinion at Oxford University was against concession, 4 Mar. Two days later, after voting against resuming the debate on the government's emancipation plan, he delivered a long and detailed speech in which he questioned the assumption that such a measure would pacify Ireland, maintained that it had never been the intention of their ancestors that the king, 'who must be a Protestant sovereign, should be surrounded with Catholic advisers', and asked, 'should we break in upon the principles of 1688, to purchase a short and precarious truce with the Catholics?' John Henry North, who spoke next, complimented his speech and acknowledged that 'both by the gravity of his manner and the evident sincerity with which he spoke his sentiments', he was 'entitled ... to the attention and consideration of the House'. Newcastle was delighted with his 'excellent speech', which had 'excited very great attention and ... gained to him a decided reputation', and felt he was 'sure to be a very distinguished object in Parliament'.[7] He divided against emancipation, 6 Mar., but cast no further recorded votes on this issue, though he presented hostile petitions from Aldborough, Boroughbridge and East Retford, 10 Mar. In July the Ultra leader Sir Richard Vyvyan*, writing to Newcastle about their attempt to oust Wellington and form a new ministry, observed that 'we must now look upon your relations Mr. Fynes Clinton and Mr. [Michael] Sadler*', who were 'both powerful men'.[8] That autumn Vyvyan counted Fynes Clinton among those Tories who were 'strongly opposed to the present government'. In January 1830 he informed Newcastle that 'some of our party are anxious to join with the Huskissons', a move that the duke would not hear of.[9] He voted for Knatchbull's amendment to the address on distress, 4 Feb., and spoke on this subject, 16 Mar. 1830. He consulted Lord Lowther* about the impending petition accusing Newcastle of electoral malpractice at Newark, and when it was presented to the Commons, 1 Mar., he declared that 'I never saw any petition ... so full of exaggerated statements and unfounded aspersions'; he was a majority teller for its rejection. Newcastle was pleased with his 'excellent speech'.[10] He presented two petitions from East Retford against disfranchisement, 4 Mar., and next day was granted a month's leave to go the circuit. He voted for reduction of the grants for public buildings, 3 May, and the establishment at Nova Scotia, 14 June. He presented an East Retford petition against the sale of beer bill, 6 May, and voted to prohibit consumption on the premises, 21 June. He divided against Jewish emancipation, 17 May, and the administration of justice bill, 18 June 1830. At the general election

that summer, when he worked with Tallents to organize the Newcastle interest at Newark, he was returned unopposed for Aldborough.[11]

The ministry listed him as one of the 'violent Ultras', and he duly voted against them in the crucial division on the civil list, 15 Nov. 1830. During the ensuing negotiations surrounding the formation of Lord Grey's ministry, Lord Palmerston* approached the Ultra leader Knatchbull, with Grey's permission, and suggested Fynes Clinton for a place; nothing came of it.[12] He was given leave to go the circuit, 4 Mar., but was present to vote against the second reading of the government's reform bill, 22 Mar. 1831. He presented a hostile petition from Aldborough, 18 Apr. 1831, and voted for Gascoyne's wrecking amendment the next day. He was returned again for Aldborough at the ensuing general election. In May 1831 Newcastle learned that, in the event of a vacancy for the Speakership of the Commons, the 'Peel party' intended to propose Henry Goulburn, with Fynes Clinton as their 'next ... choice'.[13] In a notable speech seconding Walsh's amendment to kill the second reading of the reintroduced reform bill, 4 July, Fynes Clinton warned that if Members were to be 'only the puppets of the popular will', there was 'an end to all freedom of discussion' and to 'public conduct of which calm inquiry and unbiased judgement are the guides'. He maintained that 'we are not merely sent here to re-echo the opinions of our constituents, but to do that which on our consideration and deliberation, may appear best for their interests'. While it was easy to 'point out and ... descant on the anomalies of the present system of representation', it was 'no difficult task to sketch out plans for their removal'. The 'real question', he believed, was whether reform would 'have the effect of producing an assembly more efficient, better calculated to discharge its functions'. The reformer Sir John Mackintosh, who followed him, was 'by no means surprised that the excellent speech we have just heard should have extorted from the House the applause with which [it] has been greeted', and remarked that Fynes Clinton's speeches 'leave no unpleasant impression but that of regret that he speaks so seldom'. Thomas Spring Rice, the treasury secretary, reported that he 'spoke as he always does, well', and observed that 'he is a lawyer and a gentleman and is formed of much better things than to play a second rate Tory'.[14] He divided against the second reading, 6 July, and for an adjournment motion, 12 July. He was granted ten days' leave to go the circuit, 13 July, and a further ten days owing to family bereavement, 16 Aug. He paired against the disfranchisement of St. Germans, 29 July, and voted to preserve the rights of non-resident freemen, 30 Aug., and those of the free-holders of East Retford and three other sluiced constituencies, 2 Sept. He argued that it would be better to extinguish Aldborough altogether than to destroy its established interest by extending its boundaries and placing it in schedule B, 14 Sept. He voted against the bill's passage, 21 Sept. 1831.

In October 1831 Fynes Clinton solicited the vacant recordership of Newark and the corporation, who were under Newcastle's influence, duly appointed him. This provoked an outcry in many quarters: a public meeting expressed condemnation of the selection of such a 'political partisan', and the duke received an anonymous letter threatening Fynes Clinton with a reception like Sir Charles Wetherell's* at Bristol. Flags were displayed bearing the legend 'No Clinton Rabble', and warnings were received that he would be assassinated. Writing to Tallents, he declared himself to be 'decidedly against any measures which have the appearance of timidity', and demanded that action be taken to deal with any attempted riot. Approaches were made to him to postpone the winter quarter sessions, but he refused, insisting that they be held at the regular time. He asked the home secretary Lord Melbourne to provide troops to quell any disorder, which was done. In the event, the sessions passed off quietly.[15] Fynes Clinton divided against the second reading of the revised reform bill, 17 Dec. 1831. He voted against going into committee, 20 Jan., and the enfranchisement of Tower Hamlets, 28 Feb., and paired against the third reading, 22 Mar. 1832. In May he was apparently one of a number of Tories who complained of a lack of communication from the leadership, before the breakdown of attempts to form a Wellington administration. According to Lord Stormont*, he had been 'endeavouring to bring over the duke of Newcastle' in support of such an enterprise.[16] He voted against government on the Russian-Dutch loan, 26 Jan., but with them against Hunt's motion regarding military punishments, 16 Feb. 1832.

Aldborough was disfranchised by the Reform Act and Fynes Clinton did not find another seat at the general election of 1832. He died in April 1833. According to an obituarist, his 'latter days were entirely engrossed by a diligent perusal of the sacred scriptures, in which he found his best support and comfort at his despairing hour'. The same writer noted that while 'his politics were strongly conservative ... his speeches in the House were delivered with a discreet and gentlemanly feeling which gained him universal respect'. Fynes Clinton left no will, but administration of his estate was granted to his wife; the personalty was sworn under £2,000.[17]

[1] According to his brother (H. Fynes Clinton, *Literary Remains* 299). *Gent. Mag.* (1833), i. 466, says the 11th. [2] *Unhappy Reactionary* ed. R.A. Gaunt (Thoroton Soc. rec. ser. xliii), 158, 160, 173. [3] Nottingham Univ. Lib. Newcastle mss Ne2 F2/1/36, 2/144. [4] Ibid. NeC 6719, 6723-6724; Notts. Archives, Tallents mss, Tallents to Newcastle, 11 July, 29 Aug. 1826. [5] *Unhappy Reactionary*, 15. [6] *The Times*, 15 May 1827. [7] *Unrepentant Tory* ed. Gaunt (Parl. Hist. rec. ser. iii), 77. [8] Cornw. RO, Vyvyan mss DD/V/BO/48, Vyvyan to Newcastle, 20 July, reply, 4 Aug. 1829. [9] *Unrepentant Tory*, 101. [10] Tallents mss, Fynes Clinton to Tallents, 23 Feb. 1830; *Unhappy Reactionary*, 63. [11] *Unhappy Reactionary*, 64. [12] Hatherton mss, Palmerston to Littleton, 17 Nov. 1830. [13] *Unrepentant Tory*, 153. [14] Add. 51573, Spring Rice to Lady Holland, 4 July 1831. [15] Tallents mss, corresp. between Fynes Clinton and Tallents, 4 Oct.-5 Dec. 1831; *Unhappy Reactionary*, 88-89. [16] *Three Diaries*, 257. [17] *Gent. Mag.* (1833), i. 466; PROB 6/209/220.

M.P.J.C.

GALLY KNIGHT, Henry (1786–1846), of Firbeck Hall, Yorks. and 69 Grosvenor Street, Mdx.

ALDBOROUGH	12 Aug. 1814–25 Apr. 1815
MALTON	1831–1832
NOTTINGHAMSHIRE NORTH	31 Mar. 1835–9 Feb. 1846

b. 2 Dec. 1786, o.s. of Henry Gally (afterwards Gally Knight), barrister, of Langold Park, Yorks. and Selina, da. of William Fitzherbert† of Tissington Hall, Derbys. *educ.* Eton 1799; Trinity Coll. Camb. 1805; tour of Spain, Sicily and the Near East 1810-11. *m.* 13 July 1825,[1] Henrietta, da. of Anthony Hardolph Eyre of Grove Park, Notts., wid. of John Hardolph Eyre, *s.p. suc.* fa. 1808. *d.* 9 Feb. 1846.

Sheriff, Notts. 1819-20.

Capt. S.W. Yorks. yeomanry 1808.

Gally Knight, a 'very bald-headed' man of 'middle height' who was 'rather stoutly made', had resigned his seat for Aldborough in 1815 because his support for Catholic relief put him at odds with the patron, the 4th duke of Newcastle.[2] He subsequently joined Brooks's, 7 May 1816, and became one of the Fitzwilliam circle of Whigs. In December 1820, however, he cautioned his friend Lord Milton*, Fitzwilliam's son, against the course the Whigs seemed embarked upon in the Queen Caroline affair. Although, unlike Milton, he believed the queen to be guilty, he warned against holding county meetings, which would 'increase the popular ferment', as 'they will appear to be party measures, they will not be free from violence [and] the discussion will wander from the question'. Instead, he recommended the sending of petitions from the counties 'signed by principal persons of all parties'.[3] Yet when a Nottinghamshire county meeting proposing a loyal address to the king was called in January 1821, Gally Knight suggested to the duke of Portland that he move an amendment criticizing the conduct of ministers. At the meeting, 25 Jan., he declared that the address as it stood meant 'nothing but the support of administration'. Despite attempts by Newcastle to prevent him, he proposed an amendment which gave 'an opinion as to the real cause of the present agitation and a hope that all further proceedings on the subject of the queen might be abandoned'. It was carried by a large majority and the meeting ended with three cheers for Gally Knight.[4] During the rumours of a dissolution in September 1825 Fitzwilliam offered to help him secure a seat for Grimsby, but he declined, telling Milton, 26 Sept., that 'many reasons ... dissuade me from wishing to return to Parliament. I have lately refused an offer of the same nature which makes it impossible for me to accept any other'.[5] However, he later told John Evelyn Denison* that he regretted his decision not to contest Nottinghamshire at the 1826 general election.[6] He maintained his pro-Catholic views and in 1828 wrote a pamphlet on the *Foreign and Domestic View of the Catholic Question*, in which he urged

> the Senate ... to bring back the cup of promise and send forth the fiat of justice ... I invoke the patricians of the state to wash the speck from their ermine and shake the dust from their robes ... Let your Majesty complete the glories of your reign with the pacific triumph of the restoration of Ireland.

It generated a hostile rejoinder from Abraham Bagnell, dedicated to Newcastle.[7] In March 1828, with the prospect of the East Retford franchise being extended into the hundred of Bassetlaw, Gally Knight 'ventured to make himself a candidate' for a future election by issuing an address.[8] A correspondent of his kinsman Sir Henry Fitzherbert thought it 'rather premature', for 'should not the bill pass into law, his canvassing becomes ridiculous', while Lord Wharncliffe considered it 'a strong reason for throwing East Retford into the arms of the Birmingham button makers'.[9] Gally Knight, realizing his error, attempted to withdraw it, but was too late to prevent its publication for a second week. On 20 July 1828 Newcastle noted, 'Knight has been so wavering that he has lost his chance and indeed he has made it over to Granville [Venables Harcourt] Vernon*', his brother-in-law.[10] Travelling through France in September the following year, Gally Knight informed his friend John Nicholas Fazakerley*:

> Since I have been abroad I have been mortified by the total change of the sentiments of the continent with regard to England, in consequence of the anti-liberal spirit in which our foreign policy has latterly been conducted ... Having had nothing else to do, I have given vent to my spleen in a letter to [the foreign secretary] Lord Aberdeen.

He asked Fazakerley to oversee its publication in England and wrote to him again, 19 Sept., explaining that his object was to 'shame them into a more liberal line of policy'.[11] When the letter appeared Lord Ellenborough, a member of the cabinet, dismissed it as 'a poor flimsy production' and 'a peacock's feather in the hilt of a Drawcansir's sword'.[12] Gally Knight, though, was pleased with its reception and urged Fazakerley to make sure that the leading Whigs received a copy. Like his earlier pamphlet this one also provoked a reply, from Sir James Wedderburn.[13]

Back in England for the 1830 general election, a correspondent of the *Nottingham Review* addressed a letter to him on behalf of the independent freeholders, inviting him to stand for the county. He declined, explaining to the *Nottingham Journal* that having been kept in suspense as to whether or not East Retford would be thrown into the hundred, and being under the impression that this would not be effected that session, he had accepted an invitation from St. Albans, where he was now pledged to come forward, with the backing of Lord Althorp*.[14] Writing to Milton, 21 July, he lamented:

> Bassetlaw exists. I will not say how I grieve not to go there where I should be amongst my friends and where I should probably be safe for life, but my new friends at St. Albans would think me shabby were I now to desert them, and the Whig cause and the Spencer interest would certainly go to the wall, were I to quit the field. Under those circumstances I feel myself bound in honour to remain at St. Albans and there abide my fate.[15]

Two weeks earlier, however, Althorp had advised his father that he had told Gally Knight 'not to persevere for the sake of preserving our interest, unless he thought it useful for himself to do so', as the family did 'not care about this interest'.[16] Despite Althorp's nominating him, by the second day it was clear he had little chance of success and he agreed to an early closure.[17] Harcourt Vernon was also defeated at East Retford, but Denison told Fazakerley that 'Gally would have carried Bassetlaw', 21 Aug.[18] Writing again to Milton, 12 Aug., Gally Knight observed:

> The sting lies in Bassetlaw, where they accuse me of losing the independent cause by my absence. I don't feel it is wholly the case, but it is most painful to me to know that those amongst whom I have lived, and am to live, think so ... All I long for now is quiet and calm for I have really felt stunned since my defeat ... Government did all it could against me, but the corruption of St. Albans did at least as much.

Adding his views on the Yorkshire election, for which Milton had asked, he added:

> I cannot say how much I regret [Henry Brougham] is come in for Yorkshire and I wish to heaven you had never resigned ... How I wish [John] Ramsden* would have declared ... It was shilli-shalliness and jealousies that opened the door to what I am sure no true Yorkshire man can like.[19]

He did not attend the Nottinghamshire county meeting in March 1831, but sent a letter 'highly approving' of the Grey ministry's reform bill.[20]

At the 1831 general election Gally Knight was returned unopposed for Fitzwilliam's pocket borough of Malton.[21] He proposed Denison for Nottinghamshire, 5 May.[22] Soon afterwards he went to Normandy where he spent the rest of that month and early June travelling with an architect with a view to publishing an account of the local buildings.[23] He was appointed to the select committee on the East India Company, 28 June 1831, and again, 1 Feb. 1832. In his maiden speech, 4 July 1831, he declared that 'this time last year I was no reformer', but that he now gave his 'unqualified support to the present bill', as

> when the franchise of East Retford was refused to Birmingham, when the petitions of the four great towns were uniformly disregarded, when I saw the safety-valve advisedly and resolutely nailed down, I despaired of the gradual process.

He voted for the second reading of the reintroduced reform bill, 6 July, and gave general support to its details, though he was in the minority for giving Stoke two Members, 4 Aug. He divided with ministers on the Dublin election controversy, 23 Aug. He was absent when the reform bill passed the House, 21 Sept., but present to divide for Lord Ebrington's confidence motion, 10 Oct. He voted for the second reading of the revised reform bill, 17 Dec. 1831, and again gave general support to its details, though he divided against Gateshead's inclusion in schedule D, 5 Mar. 1832. He voted for the third reading, 22 Mar., and the address asking the king to appoint only ministers who would carry the bill unimpaired, 10 May. He paired for the second reading of the Irish reform bill, 25 May, and against a Conservative amendment to increase Scottish county representation, 1 June. He divided with ministers on the Russian-Dutch loan, 26 Jan., 12, 16 July, when he declared that it would be 'extraordinary' if the House disregarded its obligation, and 20 July. Commenting on the situation in Portugal, 9 Feb., he urged that France be made 'aware that we should not permit a foreigner to take a further advantage of

opportunity than the reparation of injuries requires', but pleaded, 'let us not interfere', for 'by interference we have done enough harm already'. He was in the government majority later that day. In a speech which encompassed European affairs, 26 Mar., he declared that 'a good understanding' between England and France was 'essential to the peace of Europe'. On 13 Apr. he opposed a reduction in the number of royal palaces, deeming them 'appendages of the crown', and went on to argue for the establishment of a national gallery, the lack of which he considered a 'disgrace'. He looked forward to 'the complete extinction of slavery', 24 May. He condemned Russian interference in Poland, 28 June. He spoke and voted in favour of Sadler's proposal to introduce legal provision for the Irish poor, 19 June, and advocated an alteration of the Irish tithes collection system, 5 July 1832.

At the 1832 general election Gally Knight did not stand. He returned to the House at a by-election in 1835 as Member for Nottinghamshire North, a seat he held until his death, and soon became one of the 'Derby Dilly' who gravitated to the Conservatives.[24] James Grant observed of his speaking abilities in 1838:

> He has got a tolerable voice, but the evil of it is, he has got no ideas in the expression of which to employ it. He speaks seldom: in that he is wise ... He attempts none of the loftier flights of oratory: a most commendable resolution; for he never was destined to soar. He contents himself with giving utterance, two or three times a session, to thirty or forty sentences, not sentiments; and this done, he resumes his seat, with a look of infinite self-complacency, just as if he had thereby relieved his conscience of a burden which was pressing on it.[25]

His book, *An Architectural Tour in Normandy*, was published in 1836. That year he went to Messina to compile a companion volume, which was published in 1838 as *The Normans in Sicily*. In 1842-4 he published a two-volume work, *Ecclesiastical Architecture of Italy from Constantine to the 15th Century*. He was working on another architectural study when he died at his London residence, 69 Grosvenor Street, in February 1846.[26] By his will, dated 19 Mar. 1845, he provided a number of legacies for Harcourt Vernon and his family and directed that his Langold estate be sold for the benefit of his friend and neighbour Sir Thomas Wollaston White. He left his estates at Firbeck, Kirton and Warsop and his London house to his wife for her life, and ordered that after her death £6,000 from the sale of Firbeck should go to the ecclesiastical commissioners, with the remaining estates passing to Fitzherbert.[27]

[1] IGI (Notts.) [2] [J. Grant], *Random Recollections of Lords and Commons* (1838), ii. 110. [3] Fitzwilliam mss 102/9. [4] Nottingham Univ. Lib. Portland mss PwH 855-8; *The Times*, 29 Jan. 1821. [5] Fitzwilliam mss. [6] Nottingham Univ. Lib. Denison diary, 25 June 1826. [7] A. Bagnell, *Antiquated Scrupulosity contrasted with Modern Liberality: occasioned by H.G. Knight's ... "Foreign and Domestic View"* (1829). [8] *Nottingham Rev.* 28 Mar. 1828. [9] Derbys. RO 239M/F8651, 8656. [10] Nottingham Univ. Lib., Newcastle mss Ne2 F3/1/250. [11] Add. 61937, ff. 105, 107. [12] *Ellenborough Diary*, ii. 126. [13] Add. 61937, f. 111; J.W. Wedderburn, *A reply to H.G. Knight's Letter to the earl of Aberdeen* (1829). [14] *Nottingham Rev.* 2 July; *Herts Mercury*, 17 July; *Nottingham Jnl.* 24 July 1830. [15] Wentworth Woodhouse mun. G2/11. [16] *Althorp Letters*, 152. [17] *Herts Mercury*, 7 Aug. 1830. [18] Add. 61937, f. 114. [19] Wentworth Woodhouse mun. G2/11, 27. [20] *Nottingham Rev.* 17 Mar. 1831. [21] *Yorks. Gazette*, 30 Apr., 7 May 1831. [22] *Lincoln and Newark Times*, 11 May 1831. [23] *Gent. Mag.* (1846), i. 432. [24] R. Brent, *Liberal Anglican Politics*, 89. [25] Grant, ii. 106-7. [26] *Oxford DNB*; *Athenaeum*, 14 Feb. 1846. [27] *The Times*, 21 Feb. 1846; PROB 11/2033/203; IR26/1744/134.

M.P.J.C.

GARLIES, Visct. *see* **STEWART, Randolph**

GASCOYNE, **Isaac** (c.1763–1841), of Roby Hall, nr. Liverpool, Lancs. and 71 South Audley Street, Mdx.

LIVERPOOL   1796–1831

b. c.1763, 2nd. s. of Bamber Gascoyne† (*d.* 1791) of Bifrons, Barking, Essex and Mary, da. and coh. of Isaac Green of Childwall Abbey, Liverpool; bro. of Bamber Gascoyne†. *educ.* Felsted. *m.* 1 July 1794, Mary, da. and coh. (with her sis. Anne Jane, w. of John Dent*) of John Williamson, brewer, of Roby Hall, 3s. 3da.[1] *d.* 26 Aug. 1841.
Ensign 20 Ft. 1779; ensign 2 Ft. Gds. 1780, lt. and capt. 1784, capt. and lt.-col. 1792, brevet col. 1796; lt.-col. 16 Ft. 1799; maj.-gen. 1802; col. 7 W.I. Regt. 1805; lt.-gen. 1808; col. 54 Ft. 1816–d.; gen. 1819.

Since 1796, having previously been severely wounded serving in Flanders, Gascoyne had represented Liverpool, where his brother Bamber (whom he replaced) was lord of the manor. By 1820 he had acquired a reputation as an anti-Catholic Tory of moderate ability, who, placing constituency before party, spoke boldly on military, commercial and Irish issues with a view to retaining corporation and mercantile support. Assisted by the Liverpool True Blue Club formed in his interest after the 1818 contest, in 1820 he easily defeated his radical challengers, who accused him of soliciting payment for patronage, and polled second to George Canning as previously.[2]

His support for Lord Liverpool's administration in the 1820 Parliament was erratic. The presenter of at least 150 petitions and memorials forwarded to him through the Liverpool Parliament Office in Fludyer

Street, London (particularly during Canning's illnesses and absences abroad), he spoke frequently on a wide range of issues. He commanded ministers' attention on account of Liverpool's importance and by sheer perseverance, but he was rarely able to influence policy.[3] He divided against Catholic relief, 28 Feb. 1821, 30 Apr. 1822, 1 Mar., 10 May and the attendant franchise bill, 26 Apr. 1825. He was also an outspoken critic of relief, 30 June 1823, 6 May 1825.[4] A radical publication of that session noted that he 'attended occasionally and voted in general with ministers'.[5] He divided with them on the Queen Caroline affair, 6 Feb. 1821, and rejected the radicals' criticism of the conduct of the military at her funeral, 5, 6 Mar. 1822.[6] A general since 1819, his interventions in support of ministers on the army estimates (14 Mar., 11, 13 Apr, 1 May 1821, 4, 15 Mar. 1822, 20 Feb. 1824, 6 Mar. 1826) were authoritative, informative and calculated to disabuse their radical critics; but he joined them in faulting the secretary at war Lord Palmerston's proposals for relieving West Indian regiments, 4 Mar. 1825.[7] Though favourable to its principle, he criticized the complexity of the military and naval pensions bill, 3 May 1822. Making the welfare of army officers and their dependants his priority, he campaigned successfully following its passage to have payments in Ireland made in English pounds to prevent depreciation, 25 Mar., 28 Apr., 7, 22 May 1823.[8]

As a diehard opponent of the 1815 corn law on his constituents' behalf, he protested at the 'premature agitation' of the question by the agriculturists, 9, 12, 18, 30 May 1820, and tried vainly that day and the next to prevent the concession to them of a select committee on agricultural distress. His motion for selecting it by ballot was not seconded, and he promised to oppose any measure based on its recommendations, 31 May.[9] On 7 May 1821, when the committee was revived, he pointed to its members' differing views and predicted that the 'whole would come to nothing'.[10] He echoed the Liverpool merchants' pleas for easing commercial restrictions to relieve distress, 30 May, 17 Oct., and their reservations on the timber duties, 2, 5 June 1820. Stressing the high commercial cost of indecision, he criticized the vice-president of the board of trade Wallace and the timber trade committee for failing to announce the duties promptly, 14, 15 Feb., and backed the Canada merchants' petition against the ensuing bill, 4 June 1821.[11] Having held aloof from the 1818-19 debates on the currency, he registered his hostility to the resumption of cash payments and voted in the minorities for inquiry, 9 Apr. 1821, for withholding the Bank's fee pending disclosure of their management charges, 4 Mar. 1822, and against the Bank Charter Acts, 13 Feb. 1826. He divided with ministers on economy and retrenchment, 27 July 1821, and tax remissions, 11 Feb. 1822. Preferring concessions on salt to malt, he detailed the advantages to agriculture, fishing, manufacturing and the export trade of ending the salt tax, 28 Feb., 15 Mar., 1, 30 Apr., and voted for its gradual reduction, 28 Feb., and total repeal, 28 June 1822. His satisfaction with the conceded relaxation, 3 June, evaporated directly he realized that it did not apply to Liverpool's rock salt exports to Ireland, 14, 17 June.[12] He supported the government's relief package, 1, 24 May, but became a voluble critic of their corn bill, 13, 24 May, 3, 10 June, and was a teller for the majority, 3 June, and the minority, 10 June, for Canning's amending clause (proposed by their constituents) to facilitate the release of bonded corn for milling and export as flour, 4 Mar., 21 May.[13] Representing Liverpool shipping interests, he spoke, 6 May, and presented petitions against relaxing the navigation laws, 16 May, joined in the clamour for opening the China trade, 31 May, and sought assurances from government that vessels trading with the West Indies and newly independent South American states would be protected, 23 July, 5 Aug. 1822. According to *The Times*, the reply 'was in the nature of a puff to ministers' which satisfied neither Liverpool nor commercial interests.[14]

As Gascoyne had expected for some time, the president of the board of trade Huskisson replaced Canning as Member for Liverpool in February 1823. Playing 'second fiddle', he presented only a handful of minor petitions that session, and basked in Huskisson's inability to endorse the Liverpool tradesmen's petition for concessions on the window tax, 7 Mar.[15] He divided against government for inquiry into the prosecution of the Dublin Orange rioters, 22 Apr. 1823. Following Bamber's death in January 1824, his Liverpool interest passed to his son-in-law the 2nd marquess of Salisbury and Gascoyne looked increasingly to the clubs for support to safeguard his position.[16] In what must have been a disappointing session for him, he was unable to prevent a motion of complaint being brought against the recorder of Liverpool James Clarke as the absentee attorney-general of the Isle of Man, 1 Apr. 1824, and, outclassed by the Lancashire Member Lord Stanley's son Edward George Geoffrey Smith Stanley, he failed to defeat the Lancaster judges' lodgings bill, as part of Liverpool's campaign to become Lancashire's assize town, 2 Apr. He opposed the hides and skins bill on behalf of his constituents, 14 Apr., 18, 31 May, on the last occasion as a teller for a minority of one.[17] He paired against condemning the indictment in Demerara of the Methodist missionary John Smith, 11 June 1824.

Dissatisfied with ministers' policy on corn and heeding the artisans' demands for a cheap loaf, he was a minority teller for Whitmore's inquiry motion, 25 Apr., and proposed lowering the tariff on corn released from bond from 10s. to 8s., 2 May 1825, but the agriculturists scotched this for favouring importers. He exploited Huskisson's discomfiture over the shipwrights' dispute, stressed his own achievement in amending the 1799 Combination Acts and earned the gratitude of the artisans, who rewarded him with a gift of plate, by defending the right of the operatives to request wage increases to combat high corn prices and to strike, 3, 4 May, 29, 30 June 1825.[18] A ruse and hostile petitioning prevented him from carrying Creevey's 'devil of a railway' bill, the Liverpool-Manchester, that session, but he succeeded (by 88-41), 6 Apr. 1826, when, in his first major speech on a local bill, he conceded that certain property owners would be adversely affected and commended the project as a public measure, providing a vital additional means of transport which would benefit the Irish trade and 800,000 people.[19] He considered Liverpool's protest against Huskisson's decision to make London the sole entrepôt for foreign silk fully justified, 13 Apr.[20] On corn, he voted in Whitmore's minority to reduce agricultural protection, 18 Apr., disputed Sir Robert Wilson's claim that the decline in petitions signified indifference, 4 May, and pressed that day for immediate and more extensive inquiry than William Jacob's[†] and the prompt passage of the government's emergency bill. He voted for Lord John Russell's resolutions on electoral bribery, 26 May 1826, when, to the amusement of the House and the astonishment of his constituents, he said that he had never been obliged to 'pay, directly or indirectly, a single shilling for his seat'.[21] He did nothing to allay the dissatisfaction of the shipwrights with Huskisson at the general election next month and was returned with him after a short poll. He denounced the artisans' decision to put up his son Frederick, an army major, against Huskisson, fearing that it would encourage serious opposition to himself.[22]

On 30 Nov. 1826 Gascoyne described the half-pay list as 'not ... a matter of economy, so much as a matter of utility', and defended recent changes governing the sale of commissions. He presented heavily signed Liverpool petitions for 'free trade in corn', 8, 12 Mar. 1827, when, complaining of the 'vacillating conduct of ministers', he voted against increasing protection for barley.[23] His much publicized motion for a select committee on the distressed shipping industry, an attack on the recent relaxation of the navigation laws in general and Huskisson's 'Reciprocity Acts' of 1825 in particular, was announced, 21 Feb., postponed during Huskisson's illness and the uncertainty pending Canning's succession as premier following Lord Liverpool's stroke, and supported by petitions from the major ports. He bet £10 on a successful outcome. On 7 May, 'the great night of the shipping', he proposed it, prefaced by a long exposé of decline and trading losses compiled from board of trade statistics and the first hand accounts of Liverpool ship owners and merchants. Thomas Henry Liddell, one of Canning's private secretaries, seconded. Huskisson's compelling defence of his policies, delivered after Charles Poulett Thomson had prepared the ground, carried the debate; and 'floundering', Gascoyne sought refuge in withdrawal to avoid certain defeat.[24] According to Huskisson, he 'did not appear to have much knowledge of the business, which he rashly undertook ... He was full two hours upon his legs; but his statements were very confined and unimpressive'.[25] Gascoyne explained (in a rare surviving letter):

> Mr. Huskisson's reply, though not quite satisfactory, was conclusive. I was importuned by at least 20 Members not to divide and Mr. Liddell ... by my desire consulted the ship owners who had placed themselves under the gallery and their answer was that they left it to my discretion and thought a division must be unfavourable. Mr. Baring, Mr. Wodehouse, Mr. Ward, MP for the City, Alderman Thompson *cum multis aliis*, though they had *previously promised support*, recalled their promises and fairly told me they should vote against me. Mr. Curwen ... said he should redeem his promise and vote but *he was satisfied a committee was not now necessary*. Mr. Bernal and Mr. Bright, Hart Davis and others implored me not to divide and when Mr. Peel also spoke against the committee, his near *connections* found it *but consistent* that they should also vote against ... Thus deserted and bereft of the support I had really been encouraged to expect, I had no alternative but that of a very small minority, or withdrawing the motion.[26]

He divided against Catholic relief, 6 Mar. 1827 (and again 12 May 1828). On presenting Liverpool's petitions for repeal of the Test Acts, 7 June 1827 (some of the many he took charge of that session), he caused a furore by alluding to a 'tit for tat arrangement' by which both issues were postponed.[27]

Following Canning's death in August 1827, Gascoyne stood aloof from the controversy surrounding Huskisson's successive appointments as colonial secretary in the Goderich and Wellington ministries, and his Liverpool supporters did not oppose Huskisson's re-election in February 1828. Justifying his minority vote on East Retford, 21 Mar., he maintained that sluicing was no solution for electoral corruption and likely to extend it. He spoke and voted with government against ordnance reductions, 4 July. Overwhelmed by constituency business, especially petitions, he took charge of the abortive Liverpool elections bill sponsored by the corporation in the wake of the 1827 mayoral contest, 4, 11, 12 Feb., and, still insisting that that Liverpool elections were 'purer than in most populous towns and freer than anywhere in the United Kingdom', he opposed a rival Whig measure for extending Liverpool's franchise, 9 June.[28] Comparing the Mersey to the Thames, he justified proceeding with the corporation's dock bill as a public rather a local one in order to evade defeat on a technicality, 25 Feb. and overcame John Wood's objections, 23 May, to carry it with the attendant land bill and an extension to the Liverpool-Manchester railway bill that session. As previously (9 Mar. 1827), he called on government to legislate on poverty in Ireland, which invariably impacted on Liverpool, 14 Mar. 1828. His motion of 17 June for inquiry into the decrease of British seamen (resulting from Huskisson's 'liberal' policies) was an abysmal failure, for which he was castigated in the Liverpool press.[29] He had exploited the 'paper' loss to the mercantile fleet between 1826 and 1827 of 1,434 ships and 19,400 seamen, which, as Thomas Peregrine Courtenay stated in reply, was accounted for by the deliberate removal of non-existent crews and vessels from the shipping registers, as explained in the rubric. Undeterred, he ordered returns for his next attempt, 18 July 1828.

Gascoyne's hostility to Catholic relief in 1829 was, like Salisbury's, undiminished.[30] Refusing to be swayed by ministers' change of policy, he warned the home secretary Peel that his 'old arguments' would be used against him, 5 Feb., and promised to rally opposition to emancipation within and without doors, 6 Feb. He applauded Peel's decision to seek re-election for Oxford University in what Smith Stanley termed 'a foolish speech calling upon all who had changed their opinion in favour of the Catholics to follow his example', 17 Feb., spoke similarly, 20 Feb., and criticized ploys to procure massive petitions, especially by the inclusion of female signatories, 27 Feb.[31] He was forced to concede on presenting a 22,000-signature Manchester one, 2 Mar., that women were 'as much interested in this important subject as the other sex'. Although invariably well briefed, he had difficulty defending similar petitions, 4, 9, 16, 17, 19 Mar. Harrying ministers on each occasion, he divided against emancipation, 6, 18, 23, 27, 30 Mar. That day, he denounced the measure as an unconstitutional and short-term expedient introduced to seat Catholics in Parliament, which did nothing to pacify Ireland, and he demanded immediate legislation on Irish poverty. Heeding a recent personal request for support from Wellington, he added that he would oppose Peel on no other issues.[32] John Hobhouse* wrote in his diary that when he asked William Trant* and Gascoyne in April whether they were 'going up with Mr. [John] Halcomb† to present the so-called London and Westminster [anti-Catholic] address to the king, they looked silly'.[33] Gascoyne contributed effectively to discussions on Irish education, 9 Apr., and poverty, 7 May, and perceived the controversy generated by Daniel O'Connell's refusal to take the oaths as an opportunity to amend the Emancipation Acts, 19 May. He said he was in favour of O'Connell taking his seat, because he had been 'sacrificed' for private and party reasons, 21 May. He used the 'excitement and soreness' that emancipation aroused in Liverpool, where the Tories had recently fêted Peel and the Whig Henry Brougham* as his likely replacement, to 'strengthen himself'.[34] He carried the Liverpool (St. Martin's) church and Wallasey embankment bills, which were both vehemently opposed, 2, 3 Apr. Unlike Huskisson, who 'corrected' him in the House on most commercial issues except the East India Company monopoly, which they both opposed, 12 May, between 26 Feb. and 12 June Gascoyne testified repeatedly to the growing manufacturing distress in Lancashire, supported inquiry into the silk trade, 26 Feb., and restrictions on boot and shoe imports, 7 May, and voted to reduce the duty on hemp, 1 June 1829. Making a futile and ill-judged attempt that day to hijack the debate to propose a select committee on shipping, he explained: 'I do not want to do away with all the favourite principles of free trade, but I think we might modify them so as to save the ship owners from the consequence of the impositions we have put upon them'.

He divided for the Ultra Sir Edward Knatchbull's amendment criticizing the omission of distress from the address, 4 Feb., and, speaking on Edward Davenport's state of the nation motion, 16 Mar. 1830, he criticized John Irving and others who denied its existence. On 23 Mar. he contrasted prosperous Liverpool with its depressed hinterland and maintained that, though localized, distress merited inquiry. However, he deliberately distanced himself from Gooch and the agriculturists who pleaded for protection, and dismissed Davenport's comments on the currency as 'humbug'. As a committed opponent of the (Whig) property tax, he was happy to vote with government against inquiry into tax revision, 25 Mar. He was disappointed to be omitted by Peel from the East India select committee, protested that it ought to have been balloted, deplored any restriction of its

remit and mistrusted it to the last, 9 Feb., 8 July.[35] His exclusion from the select committee on the Irish poor, after seconding the motion for it in an inept speech, 11 Mar., was another embarrassment taken up by the Liverpool *Albion*, which also ridiculed his suggestion (9 Mar. 1830) that Irish immigrants should be required to have guarantors.[36]

Gascoyne saw nothing unconstitutional in enfranchising the manufacturing towns, and voted to transfer East Retford's seats to Birmingham, 5 May 1829, 11 Feb., and enfranchise Birmingham, Leeds and Manchester, 23 Feb. 1830. Commenting on the latter 'in view of Manchester's proximity to Liverpool', he explained that he 'could not agree' to its immediate implementation, nor to universal suffrage or radical reform, and 'I certainly am against increasing the number of Members in this House'. He quoted the 200 private and local bills he had presented over the past 30 years to substantiate his claim that county Members were 'not sufficient' and a seat for a populous town 'no sinecure'. When challenged, he attributed his differences with Tory colleagues to the implementation by them of liberal policies on free trade, currency reform and Catholic emancipation. He voted with the revived Whig opposition for reductions in official salaries, 10, 11 May, and to repeal the Irish coal duties, 13 May. Undeterred by favourable Liverpool petitions, he opposed the Jewish emancipation bill, 4, 17 May, when, denouncing the 'non-Christian exclusivity of Jewry', he moved the adjournment by which it was defeated with government backing. He cast a wayward vote on the consular services grant, 1 June, and supported inquiry into the government of Sierra Leone, 15 June (having broached it himself, 23 Feb. 1828); but he wanted its remit restricted to expenditure 'to avoid agitating the slavery question'. He was minority teller against the exchequer loan bill, 1 July. Later that day he protested at the high tariff and continuing differentiation in levies on East and West Indian sugars and claimed that their announcement had been deliberately delayed to deter petitioning. He refused to believe the charges against his 'personal acquaintance' General Darling as governor of New South Wales, 9 July 1830. Despite Whig and Tory manoeuvring, his ninth return for Liverpool at the general election in August passed uneventfully and he topped the token poll.[37] On the hustings, he repeated his call for an end to the East India Company's monopoly and the opening of the China trade and stressed his votes for retrenchment. Conceding that 'some reform' was necessary, he also alluded to his support for enfranchising large towns.[38] With Salisbury, he was at the opening of the Liverpool-Manchester railway when Huskisson was fatally injured, 15 Sept. 1830, and had similarly left his own carriage.[39]

The Wellington ministry listed Gascoyne among the 25 'violent Ultras' in the new Parliament, but he did not vote on the civil list when they were brought down, 15 Nov. 1830. Both Peel and the new Grey ministry, whom he urged to reappoint the East India select committee, 12 Nov., 10 Dec., conceded a place to him as a Liverpool Member, and he was named to it, 6 Feb. 1831.[40] The following day, he hosted a dinner for the Liverpool delegation lobbying for lower sugar duties.[41] He had tried to divert attention from the Nonconformists' anti-slavery petitions, 23, 25 Nov. 1830, and, as requested, he endorsed the Liverpool West India Association's petition for gradual abolition and compensation, presented by his new colleague William Ewart, 15 Dec. Urging immediate clarification, he now quipped that he had expected the matter to be settled by the new lord chancellor Brougham, 'but I find that the government have moderated the zeal of that noble personage. The wild elephant has been brought to by being led alongside the tame ones'[in the Lords].[42] He supported a similar petition from Dublin on his constituents' behalf, 29 Mar 1831.[43] He confirmed his opposition to Jewish emancipation, 15 Dec. 1830, and vehemently opposed Charles Williams Wynn's oaths in Parliament bill, 4 Feb. On 11 Feb. 1831, taking a mixed view of the budget, he made the chancellor Lord Althorp disclose that the penny duty on cotton was an additional one, faulted the concession on coal (having advocated total repeal, 22 Nov., 8 Dec. 1830) and criticized the proposed tax on stock transfers.

Concentrating on electoral reform, he spoke briefly on the Galway, 6 Dec., and Stamford, 14 Dec., election petitions, and complained that the rush to proceed with the Liverpool ones, lest Ewart vacate to evade scrutiny, was unjustified and prejudicial to their outcome, 20 Dec. 1830. He quizzed Russell closely over the government's intended reform bill when the disfranchisement of Evesham was discussed, 17, 18 Feb. 1831. Debilitating pain from a wartime head injury that periodically recurred kept him away from the House for the next three weeks. On 14 Mar., bringing up his constituents' petition for 'opening close boroughs, and giving the right of representation to large and populous towns', he approved the last tenet and said he hoped the House would 'not separate this session without coming to some resolution in favour of reform'. Discussing the ministerial measure, he suggested that Liverpool, with more £10 houses than the counties of Bedfordshire, Berkshire, Buckinghamshire

and Cambridgeshire combined, 'probably' merited additional representation. He saw no need to 'throw overboard 62 Members', as the bill proposed, and said he would oppose its details.[44] Two days later, 'confined to my room', he sought assistance on Liverpool business from the Parliament Office secretary William Wainwright, explaining that 'the exertion of Monday last [14 Mar.] threw me back considerably, chiefly in the necessity of wearing my hat, which had a material effect on my forehead by exciting its inflammation'.[45] Pleading illness, he paired against the reform bill at its second reading, 22 Mar. He made it known in mercantile circles that he approved the stance taken by John Gladstone* and the Liverpool anti-reformers and presented their 'moderate' petitions, 29 Mar., 12 Apr., when (as on 30 Mar., 13, 14 Apr.) he taunted Russell on his exclusion from the cabinet and criticized the bill on its minutiae and for transferring English seats to Scotland and Ireland in 'violation of the Acts of Union'.[46] On 30 Mar. he indicated that he would propose moving to give all towns with over 150,000 inhabitants and 20,000 electors four Members, as a means of appealing to committed reformers and thwarting the transfer of Members to Ireland, as the Ultras wished. Hampered by the delayed announcement of changes to the bill and restrained by the Tories, who complained that he had 'shipwrecked their opposition', he moved on 18 Apr., with Michael Sadler as his seconder, to instruct the committee 'that it is the opinion of this House, that the total number of knights, citizens and burgesses returned to Parliament for ... England and Wales, ought not to be diminished'. The tone of his speech was anti-Irish and the Irish secretary Smith Stanley and Russell were his bitterest critics.[47] Thomas Gladstone* informed his father that 'Gascoyne, never over able for such a task, was less so than usual ... from the state of his health, though improved', and the consensus was that the 'gasconade' was 'flat', but, as many on both sides had feared, he carried the division next day by 299-291, so wrecking the bill and precipitating a dissolution.[48] On the 21st, when John Benett, the Tory chairman of the Liverpool election committee, proposed legislating on their finding of 'gross bribery', Gascoyne warned of the danger of disfranchisement without inquiry and defended Liverpool and his conduct 'in a regular electioneering speech'.[49] He declared his candidature as a moderate reformer 'entirely independent' of party, 24 Apr. 1831, confident of backing from the 'lower ranks of freemen' who had requisitioned him, Salisbury and the opposition's Charles Street committee. His supporters' tactics were, however, no match for those of the reformers for Ewart and the former Canningite

John Evelyn Denison. 'Hooted and hissed', he polled a poor third.[50] The Whigs delighted in his drubbing.[51]

Despite speculation, Gascoyne, who was widely caricaturized in December 1831, when the revised reform bill left the number of Members unchanged, did not stand for Parliament again.[52] In February 1832 Thomas Gladstone observed that he looked 'many years younger ... thanks to being out of Parliament'.[53] He died of inflammation of the bowels at his London house in South Audley Street in August 1841, survived by his wife (d. 1849) and six children.[54] The Manchester mill owner Sir George Philips* recalled Gascoyne's gaming losses to the Liverpool Physician Dr. Bell, and the duel provoked by their subsequent public exchanges.[55] On 9 and 29 Nov. 1841, his wife, youngest son Charles and unmarried daughter Mary Anne testified to the authenticity of his will, a draft dated 1 Dec. 1836 confirming what he recalled of another deposited with his agents Cox and Company of Charing Cross, which, as he feared, had been 'mislaid'. By it he left everything to his wife, to whom probate on personalty under £7,000 was granted, 3 Dec. 1841.[56]

[1] Ex inf. Mary Elizabeth Allan. This source corrects references to Gascoyne having only one son in HP Commons, 1790-1820, iv. 9 and Oxford DNB. [2] Liverpool Mercury, 3, 10 Mar.; The Times, 18 Mar.; St. Deiniol's Lib. Glynne-Gladstone mss 128, H. to J. Gladstone, 8 Apr. 1820; Liverpool RO, election squib bk. (1820), 18, 23, 79, 126-8. [3] HP Commons, 1790-1820, iv. 9-10; W.O. Henderson, 'The Liverpool Office in London', Economica, xiii (1933), 473-9; Manchester New Coll. Oxf. Archives, William Shepherd mss vii, f. 5. [4] The Times, 27 Apr. 1825. [5] Session of Parl. 1825, p. 465. [6] The Times, 6 Mar. 1822. [7] Ibid. 15 Mar., 12 Apr., 2 May 1821, 7 Mar. 1826. [8] Ibid. 4 May 1822, 26 Mar., 29 Apr., 8 May 1823. [9] Ibid. 10, 19, 31 May 1820. [10] Ibid. 8 May 1821. [11] Ibid. 15, 16 Feb., 5 June 1821. [12] Ibid. 16 Mar., 1 May, 4, 15, 18 June 1822. [13] Ibid. 5 Mar., 2, 14, 22, 25 May 1822; Parl. Deb. (n.s.), vii. 874. [14] The Times, 7, 17 May, 1 June 1822. [15] Liverpool RO, Parliament Office mss 328/PAR2/97; Harewood mss WYL 250/8/73, Canning to J. Gladstone, 14 Sept. 1822; TNA 30/29/8/6/287; The Times, 8 Mar. 1823. [16] The Times, 27 Jan. 1824; C. Oman, Gascoyne Heiress, passim. [17] The Times, 24 Feb., 18, 23 Mar., 2, 9 Apr., 1 June 1824. [18] Parliament Office mss PAR3/26; The Times, 30 June, 1 July 1825; J. Picton, Memorials of Liverpool, i. 399-400. [19] The Times, 5 Feb., 16 Mar., 10 May 1825; Parliament Office mss PAR3/29; Glynne-Gladstone mss 350, passim; Creevey Pprs. ii. 87-88. [20] The Times, 14 Apr. 1826. [21] Liverpool Mercury, 2 June 1826. [22] Glynne-Gladstone mss 276, Huskisson to J. Gladstone, 30 May; Harewood mss 84, Huskisson to Canning, 12 June; Lonsdale mss, Holmes to Lonsdale, 13 June; Liverpool Mercury, 16 June 1826; E.M. Menzies, 'The Freeman Voter in Liverpool', Trans. Hist. Soc. Lancs. and Cheshire, cxxiv (1973), 94. [23] The Times, 9, 13 Mar. 1827. [24] Glynne-Gladstone mss 194, T. to J. Gladstone, 17, 22 Feb.; 276, Huskisson to same, 14 Apr.; The Times, 22, 26 Feb., 20, 24, 27 Mar., 4 May; Nottingham Univ. Lib. Denison diary, 3, 7 May 1827. [25] Glynne-Gladstone mss 277, Huskisson to J. Gladstone, 8 May 1827. [26] Ibid. 123, Gascoyne to J. Gladstone, 9 May 1827. [27] The Times, 5 June 1827. [28] Albion, 16 June 1828. [29] Liverpool Chron. 21 June; Albion, 23 June 1828. [30] Wellington mss WP1/993/77; 1002/1. [31] Derby mss 920 Der (14) 63, Lord Stanley to Smith Stanley [postmark 20 Feb. 1829]. [32] Brougham mss, Lord J. Russell to Brougham, 25 Mar.

[1829]. [33] Add. 56554, f. 5. [34] The Times, 10 Oct. 1828; Liverpool Chron. 21 Mar. 1829; Glynne-Gladstone mss 278, Huskisson to J. Gladstone, 11 June 1829. [35] Albion, 15 Feb. 1830. [36] Wellington mss WP1/1101/7; Albion, 15 Mar. 1830. [37] Add. 38758, f. 220; Albion, 5 July; Hatfield House mss, bdle. 3, Leigh to Salisbury, 9, 23 July, 5 Aug. 1830. [38] The Times, 4 Aug.; Albion, 7 Aug. 1830. [39] Hatfield House mss, bdle. 3, Leigh to Salisbury, 2 Sept.; C.R. Fay, Huskisson and his Age, 6; Albion, 20 Sept. 1830. [40] Add. 40340, f. 246. [41] Glynne-Gladstone mss 197, T. to J. Gladstone, 7, 12 Feb. 1831. [42] Ibid. 243, G. Grant to J. Gladstone, 18 Dec. 1830. [43] Ibid. 244, same to same, 29 Mar. 1831. [44] Gore's Advertiser, 5 Mar.; Glynne-Gladstone mss 197, T. to J. Gladstone, 14 Mar. 1831. [45] Parliament Office mss PAR7/127. [46] Glynne-Gladstone mss 197, T. to J. Gladstone, 22, 28 Mar. 1831. [47] Lonsdale mss, Lowther to Lonsdale, 3 Apr.; Glynne-Gladstone mss, T. to J. Gladstone, 14, 18 Apr. 1831; Brougham, Life and Times, iii. 111-2. [48] Add. 51573, Spring Rice to Holland [18 Apr.]; 51576, Fazakerley to same [18 Apr.]; Glynne-Gladstone mss, T. to J. Gladstone, 19 Apr. 1831; Broughton, Recollections, iv. 101. [49] Glynne Gladstone mss 198, T. to J. Gladstone, 22 Apr.; Gore's Advertiser, 28 Apr. 1831. [50] Glynne Gladstone mss 244, G. Grant to J. Gladstone, 23 Apr., 2-4 May; Hatfield House mss, bdle. 4, Leigh to Salisbury, 25, 27, 30 Apr., 2, 2 May; 2M/Gen. Arbuthnot to same, 5 May; Derby mss (14) 116/6, J. Winstanley to Smith Stanley, 25 Apr.; Creevey mss, Creevey to Miss Ord, 2 May; Liverpool Chron. 7 May 1831; Menzies, 95. [51] Creevey mss, Creevey to Miss Ord, 6 May; Grey mss, C. Grant to Grey, 7 May 1831. [52] Hatherton mss, Palmerston to Littleton, 14 May 1831; M.D. George, Cat. of Pol. and Personal Satires, xi. 16832. [53] Glynne-Gladstone mss 199, T. to J. Gladstone, 1 Feb. 1832. [54] Ann. Reg. (1841), Chron. p. 219. [55] Warws. RO MI 247, Philips Mems. i. 13. [56] PROB 8/234; 11/1955/802.

M.M.E.

GASKELL, Benjamin (1781–1856), of Thornes House, nr. Wakefield, Yorks. and Clifton House, nr. Manchester, Lancs.

MALDON	1806–4 Feb. 1807
MALDON	1812–1826

b. 28 Feb. 1781, 1st s. of Daniel Gaskell of Clifton Hall and Hannah, da. of James Noble of Lancaster. educ. Gateacre, nr. Liverpool; Manchester acad. 1796-7; by Rev. Thomas Belsham, Hackney, Mdx.; Trinity Coll. Camb. 1800; L. Inn 1804. m. 17 June 1807, Mary, da. of Joseph Brandreth, MD, of 68 Rodney Street, Liverpool, 1s. suc. fa. 1788; cos. James Milnes† to Thornes House 1805. d. 21 Jan. 1856.

Gaskell, a 'quiet' Lancastrian who had inherited a Yorkshire estate in 1805, was again returned unopposed for Maldon on the independent interest at the general election of 1820.[1] On his first venture on the hustings there in October 1806 one witness wrote that he was 'evidently quite inexperienced, but did not appear to want understanding or decision of character'.[2] Not known to have uttered a word in debate during his 14 years in the House, he continued to vote consistently with the Whig opposition to the Liverpool ministry; but he never joined Brooks's, and was far from being a thick and thin attender in this period.

He voted against administration on the civil list, 5, 8 May, the additional Scottish baron of exchequer, 15 May, and the investigation of Queen Caroline's conduct, 26 June. He divided against the aliens bill, 7 July 1820, 5 June 1822, 23 Mar., 2, 12 Apr. 1824. He was steady in support of Caroline, 23, 26 Jan., 6, 13 Feb. 1821. He voted for Catholic relief, 28 Feb. 1821, 1 Mar., 21 Apr., 10 May 1825. He only rarely voted for retrenchment, as on 15 Mar. 1821, 2, 15, 16 May 1822, 17 Mar. 1823, 10 Apr. 1826; but he opposed the royal grants, 8, 18 June 1821, 30 May, 2, 6, 9, 13 June 1825. He voted for parliamentary reform, 18 Apr., 9, 10 May 1821, 25 Apr. 1822, 26 Feb. 1824, 13, 27 Apr. 1826. He divided for reform of the judicial system, 9 May 1821, 26 June 1822, 7 June 1825, and for mitigation of the punishment for forgery, 4 June 1821. He voted for inquiry into Peterloo, 16 May 1821, and the remission of Henry Hunt's* prison sentence, 22 Mar., 24 Apr. 1822. He divided for a reduction in the number of placemen in the Commons, 31 May 1821, and to deplore the current influence of the crown, 24 June 1822. He was in the minority of 36 against the proposed corn duties scale, 9 May, and voted to relax protection, 18 Apr. 1826. He voted for inquiries into the government of the Ionian Islands, 14 May, the lord advocate's treatment of the Scottish press, 25 June, and the Calcutta bankers' complaints, 4 July 1822. He divided against the Irish constables bill, 7 June 1822, for inquiry into the state of Ireland, 11 May 1824, and against the Irish unlawful societies bill, 25 Feb. 1825. He was in the minorities condemning the prosecution of the Methodist missionary John Smith in Demerara, 11 June 1824, and the Jamaican slave trials, 2 Mar. 1826. He voted for the licensing of public houses, 27 June 1822, and tithe reform, 6 June 1825. He retired at the dissolution in June 1826, having given notice of this intention nine months earlier, when he stated that 'circumstances over which I have no control ... would probably interfere very much with the discharge of my duty'.[3]

Gaskell lived abroad, 1827-8, but thereafter led 'a life of quiet retirement and unostentatious goodness' at Thornes, where William Ewart Gladstone[†], the Eton and Christ Church friend of his only child James Milnes Gaskell (1810-73), Conservative Member for Wenlock, 1832-68, was a guest in 1829 and 1832. When Gladstone returned there in 1871 he experienced 'a vivid recollection of the place as it was associated with much kindness received and with my first stepping out from a very retired childhood and youth into the world'.[4] Gladstone was drawn to Gaskell's wife, who mothered and inspired him, by a common interest in religion.[5] Gaskell, whose brother Daniel was

Liberal Member for Wakefield, 1832-7, was widowed in 1845 and died intestate at Thornes in January 1856. Administration of his estate was granted to his son.[6]

[1] C.M. Gaskell, *An Eton Boy*, p. xii; PROB 11/1425/371; *Suff. Chron.* 11 Mar. 1820. [2] Essex RO, Bramston mss D/DLu 10/2/26. [3] *Colchester Gazette*, 3 Sept. 1825. [4] *Gladstone Diaries*, i. 257-60, 579-82; *Gladstone to his Wife* ed. A.T. Bassett, 189. [5] *Gladstone Autobiographica* ed. J. Brooke and M. Sorensen, i. 146-7, 149-50; Add. 44161, f. 39; 44355, f. 202; 44357, ff. 185, 205. [6] PROB 6/232/75.

S.K./D.R.F.

GIDDY *see* GILBERT

GIFFORD, Sir Robert (1779–1826), of 10 Whitehall Place, Westminster, Mdx.

EYE   16 May 1817–30 Jan. 1824

b. 24 Feb. 1779, yst. s. of Robert Gifford, grocer and general dealer, of Exeter, Devon and 2nd w. Dorothy. *educ.* at Exeter by a Dissenting minister; Alphington g.s. nr. Exeter; articled to one Jones, an Exeter att.; M. Temple 1800, called 1808. *m.* 6 Apr. 1816, Harriet Maria, da. of Rev. Edward Drewe, rect. of Willand, 4s. 3da. kntd. 29 May 1817; *cr.* Bar. Gifford 30 Jan. 1824. *d.* 4 Sept. 1826.
Solicitor-gen. May 1817-July 1819; att.-gen. July 1819-Jan. 1824; l.c.j.c.p. Jan.-Apr. 1824; sjt.-at-law 6 Jan. 1824; PC 19 Jan. 1824; dep. Speaker of House of Lords Feb. 1824-d.; master of rolls Apr. 1824-d.

Gifford, in the words of Horace Twiss*, was 'a lawyer of good abilities, and of still better fortune', whose rapid rise to eminence from humble origins was the more remarkable because, as his obituarist noted, 'his powers, though respectable, were not splendid, though solid, not profound'.[1] On his appointment as solicitor-general at the age of 38, which surprised many, John Campbell II* had observed:

> He has a slender share of political information, and will never make a great parliamentary orator, but he will be found useful as often as legal subjects are discussed in the House.[2]

At the general election of 1820 Gifford, 'a very vulgar but liberal and enlightened personage',[3] who had been promoted to attorney-general the previous July, was again accommodated in the seat for Eye which Lord Cornwallis habitually placed at the disposal of government. Soon afterwards he conducted the prosecution of the Cato Street conspirators and in the House, 9 May 1820, he successfully resisted, in what Henry Bankes* thought 'an extremely able and argumentative speech', an opposition attempt to expose the informer

George Edwards as the Liverpool ministry's *agent provocateur* in the affair.[4] He forced the withdrawal of a proposal to extend the scope of the insolvent debtors bill to crown debtors, 12 June. In response to Mackintosh's motion to exclude from the provisions of the aliens bill any persons entering the country to give evidence in the trial of Queen Caroline, 10 July, he protested against 'the doctrine of declaring the queen innocent and her accusers guilty' in advance. He was 'almost in tears' when he defended himself against an implied charge of neglect of duty over a libel on the queen, 25 July; and his denunciation of those who, under the 'hypocritical mask' of befriending her, were 'actively endeavouring to undermine the government, and to effect that which they had long had in view – a revolution', was seen as a symptom of government's unease.[5] His opening address before the House of Lords in support of the bill of pains and penalties, 19 Aug., was reckoned 'really wretched' even by ministerialists.[6] He spoke heatedly in the Commons against Hobhouse's motion for a prorogation, 18 Sept. On 27 Oct. 1820 he began his reply before the Lords and completely redeemed his reputation with a 'masterly' speech of 'acuteness, vigour and spirit'.[7] During Wetherell's attack on ministers' conduct towards the queen, 26 Jan. 1821, Gifford was 'rolling his eyes and mending his pen'. According to an opponent, his reply 'made no impression', but another observer thought he spoke 'very well and with great acuteness'.[8] He answered Burdett's personal attack on his role in the prosecution of the queen, 6 Feb. 1821.

Gifford, who divided against Catholic relief, 28 Feb. 1821, 30 Apr. 1822, defended the conduct of chief justice Best in fining Thomas Davison several times during his trial for blasphemous libel, 23 Feb., 7 Mar. 1821.[9] He moved a successful wrecking amendment against Curwen's patents protection bill, 22 Feb.,[10] and opposed Althorp's county courts rate bill, 15 Mar. He was hostile to Martin's bills to give prisoners charged with capital offences defence by counsel, 30 Mar., and to provide against cruelty to horses, 1 June. He justified the choice of Ilchester gaol for the incarceration of Henry Hunt*, 15 May, spoke against inquiry into the Peterloo massacre, 16 May, and deflected Whitbread's attempt to put a stop to prosecutions for blasphemous libel by the Constitutional Association, 3 July. He defended the 1815 commission of inquiry into the judicial system against charges of slowness and extravagance, 9 May, and opposed investigation of alleged delays in chancery, 30 May. He opposed Mackintosh's forgery punishment mitigation bill, 23 May, 4 June, arguing that the death penalty was an effective and necessary deterrent. He also

spoke against Mackintosh's dwelling house robbery bill, 4 June.[11] A report in December 1821 that he was to become chancellor of Ireland proved to be 'wholly without foundation'.[12]

Gifford rejected Hunt's allegations against the judges of king's bench and supported the Irish insurrection bill, 8 Feb. 1822. He saw no case to answer by the Lancaster gaoler for tampering with a Member's correspondence, 25 Feb.; advised against interference with the system of gaol deliveries, 27 Mar.; moved a successful amendment to throw out the Salford court extension bill, 13 May, but failed to defeat Martin's bill concerning the ill-treatment of cattle, 24 May. He conceded that the present structure of the Welsh judicature was defective, but could not acquiesce in its abolition, 23 May. He opposed Mackintosh's motion for criminal law reform, 4 June, because it would 'pledge the House to a measure which would cast a censure on the whole of the criminal law'; he professed willingness to dispense with capital punishment where it was demonstrably safe to do so, but upheld the established principle of leaving mitigation of prescribed punishments to the executive and crown. He moved the previous question but lost the division by 117-101. Encouraged by lord chancellor Eldon, he opposed Phillimore's Marriage Act amendment bill, 12 June, but failed to prevent the Lords' amendments to it being read a second time.[13] The following session (18 Mar. 1823) he introduced a modified measure in which Phillimore reluctantly acquiesced. He opposed abolition of the vice-chancellor's court, 26 June 1822.

He dismissed Hume's complaints on behalf of the Carliles over their prosecution and imprisonment for blasphemous libel, 26 Mar. 1823. He insisted on the legality of the Irish attorney-general's proceeding by *ex-officio* informations against the Dublin theatre rioters, 15 Apr.; and during the Commons inquiry into the affair, 8 May, warned of the dangers inherent in questioning witnesses on their duties as members of a grand jury, in defiance of their oath of secrecy. He opposed the abolition of punishment by whipping, 30 Apr., Mackintosh's resolutions for mitigation of the criminal code, 21 May, and his amendment to the larceny bill, 25 June. He thought the present system of nominating special juries could not be improved, 28 May; defended chief baron O'Grady against a charge of peculation, 17 June; objected to Lord Nugent's Catholic tests regulation bill, 18 June, and rejected allegations of improper conduct by the treasury in the case of Butt *v.* Conant, 19 June, when he declared that he would 'never be ashamed to stand up in Parliament to defend the decisions of any of the courts of law'.[14]

He opposed inquiry into the chancery and appellate jurisdictions, 4 June: there were no arrears in chancery, merely increased business, and measures were in hand to deal with the accumulation of Scottish appeals in the Lords. He voted against the Scottish juries bill, 20 June, and the usury laws repeal bill, 27 June. In his last reported speech in the Commons, on the bill appointing commissioners to investigate means of clearing arrears of appeals from Scottish courts, 10 July 1823, he replied to Brougham's personal vilification of Eldon. Gifford was widely seen as Eldon's subservient creature and his likely successor as chancellor. Many doubted his credentials, but Lord Tenterden thought him 'the fittest person to succeed': he was 'a good lawyer and a sound-headed man; warm rather than vigorous, and without dignity of person or manner'.[15]

In August 1823 Gifford was faced with the loss of his seat when Cornwallis, in failing health and desperate to provide for his daughters, sold his property at Eye to the Kerrison family, who stipulated that the seat occupied by Gifford must be vacated as soon as possible to accommodate Sir Edward Kerrison.[16] Ministers gave priority to finding Gifford another seat, but in November they were obliged to consider a reshuffle in the legal hierarchy by the retirement of Sir Robert Dallas as lord chief justice of the common pleas and the death of chief baron Richards. The obvious niche for Gifford, if he was to be moved, was the mastership of the rolls, but the incumbent, Sir Thomas Plumer[†], refused to retire. As a compromise Gifford took the common pleas, on the understanding that he was next in line for the rolls. He also became the first deputy Speaker of the Lords, an inquiry earlier in the year having recommended the creation of such a post to allow the hearing of Scottish appeals on five days a week instead of three, which made it necessary to provide a substitute for the chancellor when he was absent in court. As some peers objected to the notion of a commoner presiding over their sittings Gifford was offered a peerage. It was thought that he 'would rather have remained at the bar until he had amassed a larger fortune', but he accepted it to oblige Lord Liverpool. Nor could he have been oblivious to the inference that it had 'a great tendency' to smooth his path to the chancellorship.[17]

Gifford duly went to the rolls on Plumer's death later in 1824. According to Twiss, he was not entirely at ease there, although his diligence and acuteness would probably have enabled him to overcome his problems had he lived: 'in almost everything he did, there was visible a constraint, which seemed to result from a fear of getting beyond his depth and unwilling-ness that this depth should be too accurately sounded'. He was more comfortable with the appellate jurisdiction, which he discharged to general satisfaction.[18] It was still widely taken for granted that he was certain to succeed Eldon, but in 1826 Lady Grey reported that 'all the bar declare him incompetent, and he himself feels it'; and the home secretary Peel thought he would be 'a poor successor':

> He has no confidence in himself, no firmness of character. He was neither at a public school, nor at an university, which is a great misfortune to a man naturally of a timid character.[19]

Gifford, whose 'dashing, flaunting' wife, a clergyman's daughter, was said to have 'astonished' Edinburgh society in the autumn of 1825 'by her gaiety and *libre* conversation', did not live to claim the highest prize.[20] He contracted cholera soon after arriving at his Dover residence for a holiday and died there, aged 47, in September 1826, 'killed by his wife', who had 'insisted upon' his travelling when unwell.[21] Eldon remembered him for 'an uncommon kindness of manner, an unusual sweetness of temper, a strong judgement, a vast store of professional learning'.[22] An obituarist had this to say of him:

> His leading characteristic was good sense ... In the Commons ... he never shone ... His want of popular energy was here most apparent ... As a judge, he is entitled to great praise. Cool and dispassionate, scrutinizing, patient and impartial, he gained universal confidence ... his carriage was easy, his aspect mild without any admixture of weakness. His eye was quick and intelligent; his personal manner and address calm, frank and engaging.[23]

By his will, dated 14 Dec. 1820, he directed that all his real and personal estate should be sold and the proceeds invested for the benefit of his wife and children. His personalty was sworn under £50,000.[24] He was succeeded in the peerage by his eldest son Robert Francis (1817-72).

[1] Twiss, *Eldon*, ii. 506; *Gent. Mag.* (1826), ii. 367. [2] *Life of Campbell*, i. 346-7. [3] Keele Univ. Lib. Sneyd mss SC12/12. [4] Dorset RO D/BKL, Bankes jnl. 117 (9 May 1820). [5] Buckingham, *Mems. Geo. IV*, i. 53-54. [6] *Life of Campbell*, i. 381; *Fox Jnl.* 40-41; Grey mss, Grey to wife, 18 Aug.; Northants. RO, Agar Ellis diary, 19 Aug.; Bankes jnl. 119 (30 Oct. 1820). [7] *Life of Campbell*, i. 387; *Arbuthnot Jnl.* i. 47; Grey mss, Grey to wife, 28 Oct. 1820; NLS mss 1036, f. 70; Foss, *Judges of England*, ix. 20, [8] *Geo. IV Letters*, ii. 895; Add. 51574, Abercromby to Lady Holland [26 Jan.]; Castle Howard mss, G. Howard to Lady Morpeth, 28 [Jan.]; Bankes jnl. 122 (26 Jan. 1821); HLRO, Hist. Coll. 379, Grey Bennet diary, 5-6. [9] *The Times*, 8 Mar. 1821. [10] Ibid. 23 Feb. 1821. [11] Ibid. 5 June 1821. [12] BL, Fortescue mss, Williams Wynn to Grenville [5 Dec. 1821]. [13] Buckingham, i. 343. [14] *The Times*, 20 June 1823. [15] Buckingham, ii. 9; Lord Campbell, *Lives of Lord Chancellors*, viii. 32 and *Lives of Chief Justices*, iii. 296. [16] Add. 38296, f. 68; 40357, f. 305. [17] Add. 38298, f. 101; 38576,

f. 33; 40359, f. 147; 51574, Abercromby to Holland [Nov.]; 51654, Mackintosh to Lady Holland, 8 Nov., 19 Dec.; Buckingham, ii. 16-17; Twiss, ii. 476, 479, 508-9; *Hobhouse Diary*, 107-8; Grey mss, Ellice to Grey, 8 Dec. [1823]. [18] Twiss, ii. 507-8. [19] Buckingham, ii. 53, 90, 128; *Creevey Pprs*. ii. 95; Wellington mss WP1/848/24; 849/5. [20] Add. 51669, Bedford to Lady Holland, 21 Sept. [1826]. [21] Monypenny and Buckle, *Disraeli*, i. 386. [22] *Geo. IV Letters*, iii. 1251. [23] *Gent. Mag.* (1826), ii. 368-9. [24] PROB 11/1716/487; IR26/1084/565.

D.R.F.

GILBERT (formerly **GIDDY**), **Davies** (1767–1839), of Tredrea, Cornw.; Eastbourne, Suss., and 45 Bridge Street, Mdx.

HELSTON   26 May 1804–14 Apr. 1806

BODMIN   1806–1832

b. 6 Mar. 1767, o. surv. s. of Rev. Edward Giddy, curate of St. Erth, Cornw., and Catherine, da. and event. h. of John Davies of Tredrea, St. Erth. *educ.* Penzance g.s. 1775-9; by his fa. 1779-82; Donne's mathematical acad., Bristol 1782-5; M. Temple 1783; Pembroke, Oxf. 1785. *m.* 18 Apr. 1808, Mary Anne, da. of Thomas Gilbert of Lewes, Suss., 2s. (1 *d.v.p.*) 4da. (1 *d.v.p.*). *suc.* fa. 1814; wife's uncle Charles Gilbert of Eastbourne 1816 and took name of Gilbert 10 Dec. 1816. *d.* 24 Dec. 1839.

Sheriff, Cornw. 1792-3.

Member, bd. of agriculture 1808-22, vice-pres. 1815; pres. R. Soc. 1827-30.

Gilbert inherited his maternal grandfather's Cornish farm on the death of his father in 1814,[1] but financial security only came with his succession to a considerable estate near Eastbourne through his wife's uncle in 1816.[2] In addition to his literary and antiquarian interests, he was a 'first class mathematician' whose knowledge of the 'theory of mechanics' was such that he was frequently consulted by the leading engineers and industrialists of the day. As a public figure, he was the prototype of the 'new civil servant of Georgian and Regency England', a 'professional committeeman and ... administrative technician' who immersed himself in the details of practical issues, the solution of which helped to facilitate industrial development. He 'understood the role of the scientists' in dealing with these issues and in 1819 was appointed vice-president of the Royal Society. However, he was 'reluctant to face the social changes' that industrialization implied, and adhered to a conservative philosophy which he derived from Newton and Burke.[3] He had sat for Bodmin since 1806 on the 1st Baron De Dunstanville's interest and was returned unopposed for the fifth time in 1820, although he was considered sufficiently 'respectable' in Sussex landed circles to be mentioned as a possible candidate for that county.[4]

He continued to attend assiduously, giving general support to Lord Liverpool's ministry, making frequent contributions to debate and serving on several select committees each session. He declared himself a 'decided advocate for the principle of representation upon property rather than population', 19 May 1820, and warned that the transfer of Grampound's seats to Leeds would be the 'first step towards a new-fangled and dangerous system' that would 'speedily sweep away' the aristocracy and the monarchy. On 5 June he moved to extend Grampound's franchise to freeholders of the surrounding hundreds of Pyder and Powder and to remove it from those electors who were guilty of taking bribes, but the debate was adjourned. He was a minority teller for the second reading of the Sussex election bill, 23 June. He introduced the population of Great Britain bill, to conduct a census, 16 June;[5] it gained royal assent, 24 July. He introduced a turnpike trusts returns bill, to obtain an account of their funds and expenditure, 20 June, and argued that 'some measure of regulation' was needed to prevent the misapplication of money, 12 July;[6] it received royal assent, 24 July. He justified his metropolis turnpike roads bill, 30 June, on the ground that the roads around London were 'the very worst in the kingdom' because of the 'inefficiency of the small trusts' managing them. He wanted to see the construction and management of roads 'conducted upon the most scientific principles', and proposed that the trusts within a ten-mile radius of London be consolidated under new commissioners; his bill failed to get through committee. He was a majority teller against amendments to the Marriage Act amendment bill, 30 June. He explained that the minutes of the finance committee's inquiry into the audit office had excluded some evidence that might 'expose private differences without producing any sufficient result to the public', 12 July 1820, and argued that the office's staff should be increased. As a commissioner inquiring into the prevention of forged banknotes he commended the 'ingenuity of the plan now adopting', 1 Feb. 1821. He divided against the forgery punishment mitigation bill, 23 May. On the presentation of a Bodmin petition to restore Queen Caroline's name to the liturgy, 5 Feb., he mentioned that the corporation and 'every individual who was usually called a respectable inhabitant' had signed a loyal address to the king.[7] Next day he voted in defence of ministers' conduct towards the queen. He introduced a patents protection bill, 8 Feb.,[8] which failed its second reading, 22 Feb. He maintained that the present representative system reconciled 'the existence and co-action of a powerful democratic body with a monarchical form of government', 12 Feb., and moved the same amendment to the Grampound disfranchisement bill as in the previous session. According to a Whig diarist, 'the sense of the House' was so hostile that ministers did not dare support him, and he was defeated by 126-66.[9] He objected to the proposal that Grampound electors not convicted of bribery should be allowed to vote in the county, 2 Mar., as the 'respectability of the ... freeholders' would be tainted by association; he thought they should be connected instead with the neighbouring borough of Tregony.[10] He divided against Russell's reform resolutions, 9 May. In the debate on agricultural distress, 22 Feb., he expressed the hope that the government would not 'adopt so fatal an experiment' as a paper currency.[11] He voted against Maberly's resolution on the state of the revenue, 6 Mar., and repeal of the additional malt duty, 3 Apr. In reintroducing his metropolis roads bill, 27 Feb., he denied that he intended to place the turnpike trusts under government control, as 'there could be no surer mode ... of opening the door to jobs of all descriptions', and argued that his proposal to divide the trusts into three districts would help to achieve 'economy in procuring ... materials' and encourage the 'employment of scientific aid'. He complained of a petition from the trustees of certain roads requesting that they be heard by counsel, 11 Apr., observing that 'the whole opposition' to his bill 'arose from trustees and agents' rather than from 'any portion of the public', and that when he had agreed to refer the bill to a committee he had not expected to be 'placed under the necessity of attending to counsel or attorneys';[12] the bill was defeated at the report stage, 24 May. He divided against Catholic relief, 28 Feb., although the Grenvillite Charles Williams Wynn* claimed soon afterwards that he was 'completely turned' on the subject and likely to vote in favour; he did not.[13] He warned that the bill to abate the nuisance caused by steam engines would have 'very vexatious and ruinous consequences' for the Cornish mining interest, 30 Apr.,[14] but thought it might be applied to London and other urban centres, 7 May 1821. In a gloomy letter to a clergyman at this time, he remarked that 'my general principles of politics are not changed, but the circumstances of the times are changed around us and my anticipations are far from bright'.[15]

It was thought to be Gilbert who declared, 7 Feb. 1822, that he had 'no objection to some strong measures for ... putting down the present outrages' in Ireland, but warned that 'unless ... accompanied by measures of conciliation' they would merely 'increase the irritation that prevailed in that country'. Convinced that peace could never be achieved without the 'total abolition' of the tithes system, he argued

against giving 'extensive power' to the magistrates, as many of them were not 'respectable'; to opposition cheers, he maintained that 'in Ireland justice was bought and sold'.[16] He divided against more extensive tax reductions, 11, 21 Feb., and abolition of one of the joint-postmasterships, 13 Mar. He was reportedly shut out of the division on inquiry into diplomatic expenditure, 15 May.[17] He opposed a reduced duty on corn, 3 June,[18] and warned that the importation bill would not 'prevent foreign flour from being smuggled [for] home consumption', 10 June. He congratulated ministers for reducing the salt duty, 11 June, but thought it would be 'extremely beneficial to the agricultural interest' if it could be repealed. He stated, amidst laughter, that he would support a government proposal for repeal but not one emanating from other Members.[19] In supporting the Marriage Act amendment bill, 20 May, he gave examples to show that Parliament had passed bills with retrospective effect. He considered the laws requiring labourers to be paid in money rather than provisions to be 'inefficacious and unnecessary', 17 June, and was content to rely on 'the competition of trade' to protect their interests. He voted against inquiry into the lord advocate's conduct towards the Scottish press, 24 June, and referral of the Calcutta bankers' petition to a select committee, 4 July. He looked forward to the 'speedy' dismantling of London Bridge, which was 'disgraceful and dangerous', and its replacement with 'one which ... would be worthy of this great city', 12 July 1822.[20] That autumn he completed negotiations to assume the patronage of Bodmin jointly with the 3rd marquess of Hertford, the Tory lord warden of the stannaries.[21] He divided against inquiry into the borough franchise, 20 Feb., and reform in Scotland, 2 June 1823. He believed that an 'efficient sinking fund' would be 'productive of the best results to public credit' and was preferable to tax reductions, 3 Mar. He voted against further tax reductions that day, repeal of the duty on houses valued at under £5, 10 Mar., restriction of the sinking fund, 13 Mar., and repeal of the assessed taxes, 18 Mar. He divided in the minority for the usury laws repeal bill, 27 June. He defended the weights and measures bill, which aimed to 'establish a perfect theoretical standard', 21 Apr.[22] He voted against repeal of the Foreign Enlistment Act, 16 Apr., and inquiry into delays in chancery, 5 June. He divided in the minority to introduce trial by jury to New South Wales, 7 July 1823, when he supported an amendment to allow army and navy officers to judge cases. As chairman of the committee considering the London Bridge bill, he succeeded this session in overcoming government resistance to advancing the necessary loan.[23] On 18 Feb. 1824 he introduced a recovery of penalties bill, to facilitate the collection of fines imposed by magistrates and the execution of warrants; it gained royal assent, 31 Mar. He voted against the production of papers regarding Catholics holding public office, 19 Feb., and supported the Catholic marriages (England) bill, 13 Apr. He divided for the Irish insurrection bill, 14 June. He argued that repeal of the duty on salt would lead to its wider use in agriculture and industry, 23 Feb., and believed that repeal of the usury laws would be 'highly advantageous to the landed interest', 31 Mar., voting accordingly, 8 Apr. He supported the weights and measures bill, 25 Feb. He divided against reform of Edinburgh's representation, 26 Feb. He claimed that the ordnance survey of Britain had 'raised the country in the eyes of the scientific world', 27 Feb. He presented a Bodmin inhabitants' petition for inquiry into the trial of the Methodist missionary John Smith in Demerara, 27 May 1824.[24] He presented Penzance and Truro petitions in favour of the county courts bill, 24 Feb., and ones from Penzance and Bodmin for repeal of the coastwise coal duty, 24 Feb., 2 Mar. 1825.[25] He divided for Catholic relief, 21 Apr., 10 May. He welcomed the government's adoption of the quarantine bill, 13 May. He voted for the financial provision for the duke of Cumberland, 30 May, 6, 10 June. He advised that the West Looe burgesses' complaint about the infringement of their voting rights should be left to the courts, 20 June 1825.[26] He supported the home secretary Peel's plan to amend the law regarding theft from gardens and hothouses, 27 Apr., and voted against Russell's resolutions to curb electoral bribery, 26 May 1826. He was returned unopposed for Bodmin at the general election that summer.[27]

He considered the Tregony election return illegal, but did not blame the sheriff, 24 Nov. 1826. He presented two Sussex petitions against altering the corn laws, 19 Feb., 2 Apr.,[28] argued that the imperial measure should be retained to 'preserve ... uniformity', 8 Mar., and favoured 62s. as the pivot price, 21 Mar. 1827. He introduced a copyhold estates bill, to remove certain difficulties in the disposition of copyhold property by will, 19 Feb.;[29] it passed the Commons but not the Lords. He divided against Catholic relief, 6 Mar. He voted for the spring guns bill, 23 Mar. He supported the Sussex elections bill, 2 Apr., but advised its withdrawal as the select committee on county election expenses rendered it 'unnecessary', 9 May; he voted for Lord Althorp's resulting bill, 28 May. He presented a petition from the freeholders of the hundreds of Kerrier and Penwith, adjoining Penryn, for their inclusion in that borough rather than the transfer of its seats to Manchester, 12 June, but had little hope of success.[30] During the course of the year, Gilbert was embroiled in the manoeuvres to find a successor to Sir Humphry Davy as president of the Royal Society. He attempted to prepare the way for Peel's election, but encountered resistance from professional scientists such as Charles Babbage and William Herschell, who were opposed to the chair being filled by a gentleman amateur with political connections, and from Whig members of the council such as Henry Brougham*. Peel's friend John Wilson Croker* exclaimed that he had 'no patience with that fool Davies Gilbert', who was 'really a worthy man, but ... so timid and ignorant in anything that partakes of *business* that no reliance is to be placed on what he says, or what he will do'. In the event, Peel withdrew and Gilbert accepted the presidency as a compromise candidate, November 1827.[31] He introduced a customary tenures bill, to authorize the devising of real estates held in this form, 19 Feb. 1828; it failed to get into committee. He declared himself 'friendly' to the division of counties bill, 27 Feb. He voted against extending the East Retford franchise to Bassetlaw freeholders, 21 Mar., but supported a similar extension in the case of Penryn, 24 Mar., as it would include Penzance and Redruth; he denied that Cornwall was over-represented, pointing out that its boroughs currently only returned six Cornishmen. He believed there could be no 'grosser misapplication of corporate funds than to devote them to the election of MPs', 8 July, and voted for the corporate funds bill, 10 July. He argued that turnpike bills 'ought to be free from fees', 21 Apr., and wanted to see the 'greatest possible simplification of all ... roads bills'. On 5 June he presented a Penzance corporation petition against the alehouses licensing bill, which gave a concurrent jurisdiction to county magistrates, contrary to the borough's charter. He divided for the usury laws repeal bill, 19 June. He voted with the Wellington ministry against reducing the salary of the lieutenant-general of the ordnance, 4 July, when he said that he would not oppose the dissolution of the board of longitude, but thought it could still have done useful work. He saw 'little advantage' to Cornish miners in the revision of the lead duties, 15 July. He spoke 'warmly' of the need for a sinking fund to reduce the national debt, 17 July, and argued that a property tax, to which he would contribute 'cheerfully', must be levied to pay for it. He expressed a 'very deep interest' in the New South Wales bill, 20 June 1828, as that colony was 'destined to spread the English language' to the East. He thought 'trial by jury could not yet be introduced with safety', as there were too many recent convicts, but he favoured a representative assembly and the enfranchisement of all settlers and the sons of freed convicts. In February 1829 Planta, the patronage secretary, listed him as likely to side 'with government' for Catholic emancipation. His votes for the measure, 6, 30 Mar., may have been influenced by Hertford's decision to support it, although fears were expressed that this could cause problems with his constituents.[32] He advised George Byng to withdraw his county bridges bill and introduce a local one for Middlesex, as it might be 'inapplicable to other parts of the country', 25 Mar. He seconded the motion for a select committee on patents, 9 Apr., observing that patentees experienced 'many disadvantages ... under the existing law', but he warned Parliament to 'proceed cautiously' on the subject. He enquired whether the government would allow the London Zoological Society to extend its grounds, 19 May 1829. He divided against the enfranchisement of Birmingham, Leeds and Manchester, 23 Feb., and Jewish emancipation, 5 Apr., 17 May 1830. He favoured opening the British Museum reading rooms for 'as long as daylight lasts', 8 Mar., and believed it was 'impossible any institution can be better conducted'. He again introduced the population of Great Britain bill, 30 Apr., which gained royal assent, 23 June. John Cam Hobhouse* deplored his 'shabby' conduct in voting against Hume's motion on the vacation of offices following the demise of the crown, 3 May.[33] He objected to the government's plan to make the loss of weight of gold coins through usage fall on those who sent them to the mint for recoining, 4 June. He voted against reducing the grant for South American missions, 7 June, and judges' salaries, 7 July. He divided against abolishing the death penalty for forgery, 7 June. He urged that Cornish miners be exempted from the operation of the labourers' wages bill, 3 July, and while welcoming the concession on this point, 5 July, he warned that many workmen would lose their livelihoods if the truck system was abolished. He suspected that Littleton was 'acting upon the suggestion of some opulent manufacturers' in Staffordshire, who calculated that the bill's 'effect will be to raise the price of iron, in which they deal'. He was again returned unopposed for Bodmin at the general election that summer.[34] The continuing tensions within the Royal Society culminated in the publication of Babbage's *Reflections on the Decline of Science* (1830), which contained a personal attack on Gilbert's cliquish style of management and desire to maintain the body's social exclusivity. He decided in August 1830 to retire from the presidency and paved the way for the duke of Sussex to succeed him.[35]

Gilbert's sense of impending social danger was reinforced in the autumn of 1830 when hayricks on his Sussex estate were burned.[36] He was listed among the ministry's 'friends', but was absent from the crucial division on the civil list, 15 Nov. In December he wrote to Hertford that he would 'probably retire before another election', as he suspected that 'for many years to come this country will not be worth living in'.[37] He said he was now convinced that the truck bill would be 'most beneficial', subject to special provision for the mining districts, 14 Dec. 1830. He presented and endorsed Bodmin and Penzance petitions for repeal of the coal duties, 8 Feb. 1831. He divided against the second reading of the Grey ministry's reform bill, which proposed to reduce Bodmin's representation to one seat, 22 Mar. It was rumoured in early April that he had since been converted to the measure,[38] but he voted for Gascoyne's wrecking amendment, 19 Apr. 1831. At the ensuing general election he was returned unopposed for Bodmin after a hostile faction within the corporation decided not to force a contest.[39] He wrote to his old friend Josiah Wedgwood in June 1831 that he was 'fully convinced that changes great and important must come', as 'the condition is changed of the great mass of mankind', and conceded that 'the bases of all governments must be enlarged', though this should not be taken to 'extremes'.[40] He divided against the second reading of the reintroduced reform bill, 6 July, but was against the adjournment motion, 12 July, and the preservation of freemen's rights, 30 Aug. He favoured extending Fowey's boundary so that it might retain one Member, 21 July. He proposed the merger of East and West Looe, which were 'in fact one and the same place', and placing it in schedule B, 22 July, but did not force a division. He accepted that Bodmin's population meant it must remain in schedule B, 27 July, but insisted that it was 'neither a nomination nor a corrupt borough'. He proposed that one seat be given to Penzance, 6 Aug., on account of its size, wealth and respectability, and the fact that it was 'the capital of the district'; again he did not force a division. He said that when the reform agitation had begun he had taken a 'decided line' against it, 11 Aug., but admitted that his opinions had 'since somewhat changed'. He supported the bill 'to a certain extent', as he saw the need for increased county representation in order to 'counteract democratic influence'. He was 'favourable to the principle that county representation should be in the hands of country gentlemen' and hoped the additional seats created by the division of counties would prevent 'vexatious and expensive contests' caused by personal rivalries. On 19 Aug. he moved an amendment to clause 16 that 40s. freeholders should only have the vote if they were 'seized of an estate of inheritance' and that a £10 limit should apply to freeholders for life. His object was to 'draw a strong line between those who have real freeholds' and those with 'life leases' created 'merely for election purposes'. He agreed to withdraw after the leader of the House, Lord Althorp, promised to bring in a clause to this effect. He was appointed to the boundary commission, although 'some of the opposition' objected to him.[41] He was absent from the division on the bill's passage, 21 Sept. He voted against the censure motion on the Irish administration for using undue influence in the Dublin election, 23 Aug. He was granted ten days' leave for urgent business, 7 Oct. 1831.

He was absent from the division on the second reading of the revised reform bill, 17 Dec. 1831. Early in 1832 he wrote despairingly about the state of the country:

> Pestilence now actually beginning to rage ... and a servile war impending, with the view of obtaining objects beyond human reach, principally with the hope of attaining the products of labour without work and ... capital, and in addition to these evils, the gaudy iris of indefinite perfectibility dazzling the eyes of those who should see the true interests of mankind ... Oh Lord God, have mercy upon us.[42]

He thought it was 'evident' that the reform bill 'must pass', 1 Feb., and said he would not oppose it '*in toto*'. He wished to ensure that only those with 'such a stake in the country as will make them consider maturely the effects of any vote they may give' were enfranchised, and considered the £10 household franchise to be 'too low a qualification' in the large towns. He therefore moved, 3 Feb., to deduct the value of under-lettings from house valuations, as 'the lowest description of persons that can be imagined are those who take houses ... for the purpose of letting out into floors'. However, Althorp deemed this to be impracticable, and the amendment was negatived. He admitted that as an 'abstract mathematical question', Lieutenant Drummond's method of scheduling the boroughs (which reprieved both Bodmin's seats) was 'ingenious' and 'unobjectionable', 20 Feb. He was absent from the division on the bill's third reading, 22 Mar., and left the House before the division on Lord Ebrington's motion for an address asking the king to appoint only ministers committed to carrying an unimpaired measure, 10 May.[43] In the crisis debate of 14 May, he declared that having opposed the bill only once, 'on the metropolitan districts', and from his general parliamentary conduct, he could 'fairly claim to be considered one of the most independent Members'. He was 'persuaded that the ... country is decidedly in favour of the measure' and felt that if Wellington could only hold office by passing a similar bill, it was 'perfectly absurd' that Grey's ministry should not be reinstated and 'have the passing of it'. He was prepared to 'withdraw my opposition to the bill', and hoped the peers would do the same, in order to 'conciliate the nation ... establish peace and ... avoid all chance of a civil war'. This was regarded as a powerful and decisive expression of Conservative backbench opinion against the project to form an alternative government.[44] He noted in his diary, 7 June, that with the bill's passage 'the prescriptive constitution of England' was 'dead'.[45] He voted for Baring's bill to exclude insolvent debtors from Parliament, 27 June 1832.

Gilbert was unwilling to face a contested election and retired from Parliament at the 1832 dissolution. He continued to pursue his other interests, serving again as vice-president of the Royal Society, helping to form the British Association and publishing a four-volume *Parochial History of Cornwall*. His 'humility and diffidence' contributed to his subsequent obscurity, and it was said of him that 'he communicated largely to the wants of others from his own great stores of knowledge, and shone more by those reflected lights than by the direct diffusion of his rays'.[46] He died in December 1839 and left his estates to his only surviving son John Davies Gilbert (1811-54); his personalty was sworn under £18,000.[47]

[1] He was the residuary legatee of his father's estate, which was proved under £7,500 (PROB 11/1555/218; IR26/608/198). [2] The will was proved under £50,000 (PROB 11/1580/254; IR26/673/305). [3] A.C. Todd, *Beyond the Blaze: A Biography of Davies Gilbert*, 7-9, 11, 57-112, 168, 285. [4] E. Suss. RO, Ashburnham mss 3242, Egremont to Ashburnham, 24 Feb.; *West Briton*, 10 Mar. 1820. [5] *The Times*, 17 June 1820. [6] Ibid. 21 June, 13 July 1820. [7] Ibid. 6 Feb. 1821. [8] Ibid. 9 Feb. 1821. [9] HLRO, Hist. Coll. 379, Grey Bennet diary, 17. [10] *The Times*, 3 Mar. 1821. [11] Ibid. 23 Feb. 1821. [12] Ibid. 12 Apr. 1821. [13] Buckingham, *Mems. Geo. IV*, i. 142-3. [14] *The Times*, 1 May 1821. [15] Todd, 200-1. [16] *The Times*, 8 Feb. 1822. [17] Ibid. 16 May 1822. [18] Ibid. 4 June 1822. [19] Ibid. 12 June 1822. [20] Ibid. 13 July 1822. [21] Add. 60286, f. 238; Cornw. RO, Gilbert mss DD/DG/21, diary, 24 Sept., 22 Oct. 1822. [22] *The Times*, 22 Apr. 1823. [23] Add. 38294, f. 145; Todd, 203. [24] *The Times*, 28 May 1824. [25] Ibid. 25 Feb., 3 Mar. 1825. [26] Ibid. 21 June 1825. [27] *West Briton*, 9 June 1826. [28] *The Times*, 20 Feb., 3 Apr. 1827. [29] Ibid. 20 Feb. 1827. [30] Ibid. 13 June 1827. [31] Add. 40319, f. 266; 40394, ff. 235-86; Todd, 221-39. [32] Add. 60288, ff. 139, 163. [33] Add. 56554, f. 93. [34] *West Briton*, 7 Aug. 1830. [35] Todd, 240-66. [36] Ibid. 258. [37] Add. 60288, f. 331. [38] Macpherson Grant mss 361, J. Macpherson Grant to fa., 2-4 Apr. 1831. [39] Gilbert mss 23, diary, 30 Apr. 1831. [40] Todd, 267. [41] Hatherton diary, 1 Sept. 1831. [42] Todd, 270. [43] *The Times*, 14 May 1832. [44] *Greville Mems*. ii. 299; M. Brock, *Great Reform Act*, 301-2. [45] Gilbert mss 23, diary, 7 June 1832. [46] Todd, 7, 265-6, 272-3, 276-86; *Gent. Mag*. (1840), i. 208-11. [47] PROB 11/1922/94; IR26/1545/25.

T.A.J.

GILLON, **William Downe** (1801–1846), of Wallhouse, Linlithgow and Hurstmonceaux, Suss.

LINLITHGOW BURGHS	1831–1832
FALKIRK BURGHS	1832–1841

b. 31 Aug. 1801, o.s. of Lt.-Col. Andrew Gillon of Wallhouse and Mary Anne, da. of William Downe of Downe Hall, Dorset. *educ.* Richmond, Yorks. (Mr. Tate); Trinity Coll. Camb. 1819. *m.* 24 Oct. 1820, Helen Eliza, da. of John Corse Scott of Synton, Roxburgh, 2s. 3da. *suc.* fa. 1823. *d.* 7 Oct. 1846.

Gillon's ancestors had been in possession of the former monastic estate of Wallhouse, between Linlithgow and Bathgate, since the Reformation. John Gillon (*d.* 1650) and his son and namesake (*d.* 1695), who acquired property elsewhere in Linlithgowshire and in Midlothian, were Covenanters. The second John Gillon's grandson, another John, succeeded to Wallhouse in 1748. He was trained as an advocate and served as sheriff of Linlithgowshire, 1744-73. His younger brother Archibald Gillon became a merchant in London and left a son, John Gillon, who prospered in business there and in Dominica. On John Gillon of Wallhouse's death in 1775 he was succeeded by his second son Andrew, the father of this Member, his eldest son Alexander having predeceased him in 1769. Andrew Gillon obtained a commission in the 2nd Hussars (Royal Scots Greys) in 1778, attained the rank of major in 1794, was promoted to lieutenant-colonel in the army in 1798 and retired in April 1801. His Linlithgowshire estate was described in 1788 as a 'good' one.[1] His son William Downe Gillon was born in August, but his wife died eight days later; he never remarried. His first cousin, John Gillon of Dominica and Welbeck Street, Marylebone died in December 1809, leaving by his will of 18 July life annuities of £500 each to Andrew and William Downe Gillon and residual personal estate which he directed to be used for the purchase of landed property for the latter. Accordingly, the Sussex estate of Hurstmonceaux, near Hailsham was bought for him in 1819.[2] He did not take a degree at Cambridge and succeeded his father in 1823. In 1829 he became embroiled in a legal dispute with the commissioners for winding up the Edinburgh Shipping Company. The court of session twice ruled against him, and on 6 Dec. 1830 he appealed to the Lords. The case was eventually heard on 22 Sept. 1831, when his petition was dismissed and he was ordered to pay £150 in costs.[3] At the general election of 1830 Gillon, an 'athletic' man with 'a well developed forehead', stood for Linlithgow Burghs (as he had been planning to do for almost a year) against

a supporter of the Wellington ministry. He obtained only the vote of Linlithgow, the nearest burgh to his estate, to his opponent's three, and his subsequent petition against the return was unsuccessful.[4] At the general election of 1831 he tried again, as an avowed supporter of the Grey ministry's reform scheme, secured Lanark and Peebles as well as Linlithgow and was elected over a Tory amid scenes of popular celebration.[5]

Gillon's maiden speech, 30 June 1831, was against Alderman Wood's motion for a revision of public salaries to 1797 levels. He professed support for 'the most rigid economy consistent with the proper administration of the affairs of the country', but sought to expose the 'delusion' that vast savings could be made, which the Huntite radicals and the Tories were peddling, the latter in order to 'return to office, and again dip their hands into the pockets of the people'. He attributed agricultural distress to the 'iniquitous' currency settlement of 1819 and the burden of wartime taxation and declared his confidence in the sincerity of ministers' wish to economize. Later that day he expressed reservations about the possible sanction of the use of molasses in brewing and distilling, which he said would ruin Scottish whisky producers and damage the agricultural interest. He was, however, in the minority of 41 for Robinson's motion, seconded by Hunt, for a reduction in the grant for civil list pensions, 18 July. He voted for the second reading of the reintroduced English reform bill, 6 July, and at least twice against the adjournment, 12 July, and on the 22nd protested against 'the system of delay and irrelevant discussion ... pursued by the other side'. He gave steady support to the details of the measure throughout July and August. On 4 Aug. he presented and endorsed a petition from Linlithgow council deploring the 'great delays' in the progress of the bill and, moving that it be printed, asserted that the people of Scotland had a vested interest in the speedy passage of the English measure, for on this 'depends their own deliverance from a system which is an outrage and an insult to them'. He got into a minor scrape when he brought up a similar petition from the inhabitants of Linlithgow, 12 Aug., for inspection by the clerk revealed 'certain erasures', for which the Speaker demanded an explanation. Gillon confessed that he had made them to get rid of some 'strong' language. He grudgingly complied with the Speaker's order that he withdraw the now invalid petition, but began to rant about the 'earnest' support for reform in Scotland and was peremptorily silenced from the Chair. Next day Gillon, who apparently began his speeches 'in loud and distinct tones, and with considerable animation', but soon lapsed into a 'lower' register and a 'more languid' manner,[6] took issue with William James's passing reference to Members as 'the representatives of the people':

> Very few ... have a right the claim the title ... Most of them are mere dross, instead of being pure gold. They sit here as nominees of peers, as the Members for nomination and rotten boroughs. Instead of possessing independence, they are compelled to vote as their patrons direct them.

He said that if more Members could be allocated to Scotland without prejudicing England, he would gratefully accept them, but argued that as Scotland had been effectively unrepresented under the old system he was prepared to regard the 50 seats intended for it now as a 'boon'; he therefore supported the proposal to give some English counties three Members. When Joseph Dixon insisted that many Scots were disappointed in the bill and described him as one of those 'who cheer ... ministers on in the course that they have adopted', Gillon retorted that the people of Scotland desired above all that 'the bills should at once pass'. On 24 Aug. he explained that he had overcome his initial misgivings about the uniform £10 English borough franchise, which in some places would create almost universal suffrage, a desirable 'vent for popular feeling', but in others, especially the 'agricultural' towns, would confine the franchise to 'the aristocratic part of the community': overall, it would create an electorate comprising 'the respectable middle classes' and give them a stake in the new constitution. He opposed an attempt to exclude weekly tenants from the franchise, 25 Aug. He divided for the passage of the reform bill, 21 Sept., and the second reading of the Scottish measure, 23 Sept., when he played down the significance of the election riots of May; attacked Edinburgh councillors and their penchant for 'snug jobs'; declared that the history of the royal burghs presented an unexampled 'scene of corruption, petty tyranny, fraud, and demoralization'; called for 'a wholesome system of burgh reform' once parliamentary reform had been achieved, and hailed the reform bill as the instrument of 'a better system of representation, founded ... on the property and intelligence of the country'. In a public address to his constituents, 14 Sept., he had urged reformers to 'be true to yourselves and to that cause which we are pledged to support' and to petition the Lords to endorse the ministerial scheme and so ensure that 'we [shall] not have to sit down satisfied with a mockery of representation, or have our resources wasted and our rights as men despised'.[7] He applauded the lord advocate Jeffrey's statement of his determination that

'no rag or shred of the old system should remain', 27 Sept. On 4 Oct. he presented Lanark council's petition against the planned addition of Falkirk to the district and moved an amendment against the proposal to remove Peebles and Selkirk from it and throw them into their respective counties. He secured some Tory support, but ministers stood by the arrangement and defeated his amendment by 133-60. He then opposed the Tory Sir George Murray's attempt to secure eight additional county Members for Scotland, arguing that the bulk of the people were satisfied with the measure as it stood. After the defeat of the English reform bill in the Lords he wrote to Peebles council urging them and their counterparts in the other burghs to get up addresses to the king expressing their undiminished confidence in the government and 'unabated anxiety for the ultimate success of reform'.[8] He voted for the motion of confidence in the ministry, 10 Oct., and on 13 Oct. said to those Tories who accused them of having excited the people on reform that it was 'the system of misrule which those gentlemen ... supported that has led to the inevitable necessity of reform'. He was in the minorities for postponing the Dublin writ, 8 Aug., receiving the Waterford petition for disarming the Irish yeomanry, 11 Aug., and granting compensation to Lescene and Escoffery for their expulsion from Jamaica, 22 Aug.; but he divided twice with government on the Dublin election controversy, 23 Aug. 1831.

He paired for the second reading of the revised English reform bill, 17 Dec. 1831. He divided to go into committee on it, 20 Jan., again supported its details, and voted for the third reading, 22 Mar. 1832. On the reintroduction of the Scottish bill, 19 Jan., he denied that popular support for it had diminished and dismissed as 'scandalous' claims for compensation for loss of superiorities. He accused Scottish burgh Members 'closely connected with the agricultural interest' of obstinately resisting reform, 27 Jan. He did not vote in the division on the Russian-Dutch loan, 26 Jan. (nor in those of July), but he was in the government majorities on relations with Portugal, 9 Feb., and the navy civil departments bill, 6 Apr. He urged ministers to end the 'absurd and unjust' system of Irish tithes with an 'efficient' measure, 8 Feb.; he was in two small minorities against their tithes resolutions, 27 Mar. He got leave to introduce a bill to regulate the Scottish law of hypothec, relating to the purchase of grain, 9 Feb., but he abandoned it on 1 June. He emphasized his radical credentials with a number of votes and speeches. On 16 Feb. he voted to print the Woollengrange petition for disarming the Irish yeomanry and spoke and voted in the minority of ten for

Hume's amendment to omit reference to Providence from the Scottish cholera prevention bill. Next day he likened the plight of many agricultural labourers to that of West Indian slaves, claiming that in Sussex 'paupers are frequently harnessed together to draw loads', and backed Hume's call for repeal of the taxes on hemp and flax. On 15 Mar. he spoke and voted in the minority of 31 for Hunt's motion for inquiry into Peterloo, if only as a means of 'putting an end to that unconstitutional force ... the yeomanry', who had often been 'the mere tools of a Tory government'. Like a number of Scottish Members, he took strong objection to the ministerial proposal to reduce the malt drawback. He said it would encourage smuggling and illicit distillation, 17 Feb., and spoke and voted against the second, 29 Feb., and third reading, 2 Apr., of the bill, having failed in his bids to amend it in committee, 30 Mar. He presented Bathgate petitions in favour of the Edinburgh-Glasgow railway bill, 18 Apr., 11 May. On 10 May, after the resignation of ministers over the king's refusal to create peers to carry reform through the Lords, he informed Peebles council of the turn of events and exhorted them to promote petitions to the Commons for supplies to be withheld until reform was secured.[9] He presented a number of these, 21, 25 May, but on the first occasion was compelled to withdraw one from Bathgate because it was couched in unacceptable language. He divided for the address asking the king to appoint only ministers who would carry undiluted reform, 10 May. He said that news of the resignations would be greeted with 'horror and dismay' in Scotland, 11 May, but that the abuse of the bishop of Lichfield at a service in St. Bride's, Fleet Street 'disgraced the name of reformers', 15 May. He divided for the second reading of the Irish reform bill, 25 May. He denied that treasonable emblems had been flourished at the mass Edinburgh reform meeting, 1 June, when he again protested against the 'disfranchisement' of Peebles and Selkirk and voted against Murray's renewed bid to increase the Scottish county representation. He criticized the 'monstrous and impracticable' provision which required Scottish electors to register only in burghs which had a town clerk. On 15 June he voted with ministers against a Conservative amendment to the bill, but objected to their proposal to add Port Glasgow to the Dumbarton district and observed that 'no one change had been made to the bill except by ... ministers, and ... all bearing towards one side of the question'. He welcomed their abandonment of the proposed property qualification for Scottish burgh Members, which would ensure the return 'not as ... heretofore [of] Members who merely represented their own breeches' pockets, but Members representing the

feelings and opinion of their constituents'. Pressing them to drop the county Members' qualification also, he said:

> I am not aware of any magical property which the possession of land has in conferring knowledge and intelligence ... I have no interest except in land, but there is nothing I more desire than that I had another description of property ... I am glad we are to get rid of the aristocratic borough holders.

He divided against Baring's bill to exclude insolvent debtors from Parliament, 6 June, and in the minority of 23 for an amendment to the boundary of Whitehaven, 22 June. He was given a fortnight's leave to attend to urgent private business, 9 July 1832.

Gillon successfully contested Falkirk Burghs at the general election of 1832, came in unopposed in 1835 and 1837 and was defeated by a Conservative in 1841, when Benjamin Disraeli[†] gave him good riddance as a bore and 'a ruffian'.[10] He belatedly joined Brooks's in 1838 and employed his 'plain' but forceful oratory to promote church reform and other radical causes.[11] He died in October 1846, soon after selling the Hurstmonceaux estate to the Curteis family.[12] He was succeeded at Wallhouse by his elder son Andrew Gillon (1823-88).

[1] *Pol. State of Scotland 1788*, p. 230. [2] *Gent. Mag.* (1810), i. 89; PROB 11/1507/32; *VCH Suss.* ix. 134. [3] *LJ*, lxiii. 151, 196, 238, 407, 444, 993, 994. [4] [J. Grant], *Random Recollections of Lords and Commons* (1838), ii. 261; NAS GD224/581/4, C. Douglas to Buccleuch, 2 Oct. 1829.; *Glasgow Herald*, 23 July, 27 Aug. 1830; *CJ*, lxxxvi. 72, 333. [5] *Caledonian Mercury*, 23, 28 Apr., 26 May; NAS GD224/581/4, A. Pringle to Buccleuch, 2, 3, 4 May 1831. [6] Grant, ii. 257. [7] *Caledonian Mercury*, 17 Sept. 1831. [8] *Hist. Peebles* ed. J.W. Buchan, ii. 141. [9] Ibid. ii. 142. [10] *Disraeli Letters*, iii. 1172. [11] Grant, ii. 257-8. [12] *VCH Suss.* ix. 134; PROB 11/2048/35.

D.R.F.

GIPPS, George (1783–1869), of Howletts, Ickham, Kent.

RIPON   1807–1826

b. 29 Dec. 1783,[1] 1st s. of George Gipps[†] of Harbledown, nr. Canterbury and 2nd w. Sarah, da. of William Stanton, Spanish merchant, of Harbledown. *educ.* Charterhouse 1793; St. John's, Camb. 1801; L. Inn 1805. *m.* 3 May 1810, Jane, da. of John Bowdler of Hayes, 6s. (3 *d.v.p.*) 5da. (1 *d.v.p.*). *suc.* fa. 1800. *d.* 26 Apr. 1869.

Capt. Ashford regt. Kent militia 1809.

At the 1820 general election Gipps was again returned for Ripon by Miss Elizabeth Sophia Lawrence, his stepmother's niece. A 'frequent attender', he continued his independent ways in the

House.[2] He soon made a mark in the new Parliament as the apparently unwitting abettor of a piece of ministerial chicanery. In the debate on Holme Sumner's motion to refer petitions complaining of agricultural distress to a select committee, 30 May 1820, which government resisted, Gipps, encouraged by a suggestion from the Whig Henry Brougham, produced an amendment to restrict the inquiry to the task of establishing 'the mode best fitted for ascertaining the average price of corn'. Because of a technicality, the House was unable to divide on this proposal and, to ministers' dismay, the original motion was carried by 150-101. Next day Frederick Robinson, president of the board of trade (and Gipps's colleague at Ripon) forced through, against the protests of Brougham and others, a modified version of Gipps's amendment restricting the inquiry to investigation of the mode of calculating the averages in the 12 maritime districts.[3] Gipps declined to support Hume's motion accusing the authorities of connivance in the escape of a man arrested for issuing seditious placards, 17 Oct., but he deplored their failure to curb the recent 'activity with which placards of the most inflammatory nature had been circulated to excite the people to discontent'. He criticized Queen Caroline and justified the omission of her name from the liturgy, 1 Feb., voted with ministers in defence of their conduct towards her, 6 Feb., and spoke against the Whig attack on the sheriff of Cheshire for suppressing an address in her support, 20 Feb. 1821. He was absent from the division on Catholic emancipation, 28 Feb., but on 29 Mar. he 'professed himself ever to have been, and still to remain, a steady opposer' of the measure.[4] Although he voted with government against repeal of the additional malt duty, 3 Apr., he urged them to 'put their shoulders to the wheel' and find other means of raising £500,000 than by the tax on agricultural horses, 5 Apr., and the next day he voted to reduce the grant for the war office. He voted against the grant for the Royal Military College, 30 Apr., and the ordnance estimates, 14, 18 May, when his motion to reduce the grant for garrisons by £23,000 was defeated by 99-64. He quizzed ministers on the army extraordinaries and divided against them, 25 May, and on 31 May, after voting to reduce ordnance salaries, again moved for a substantial cut in the garrisons grant, which he lost by 94-68. He spoke and divided against the proposal to raise £200,000 by lottery, 1 June, and voted against the payment of arrears in the grant to the duke of Clarence, 8, 18 June 1821. Gipps thanked Hume for moving an amendment to the address demanding economies and tax reductions to relieve distress, 5 Feb., and duly voted for it, only to divide with ministers in defence of their

relief programme, 21 Feb. 1822. He could not have been entirely satisfied with it, for he voted for repeal of the salt duty, 28 Feb., having denied that in doing so he was 'actuated by any desire of popularity', spoke and divided for admiralty reductions, 1 Mar.,[5] and voted for abolition of one of the joint-postmaster-generalships, 13 Mar., 2 May, and against the public works grant, 29 Mar., and the naval and military pensions bill, 3 June. He was in the minority hostile to Canning's bill to relieve Catholic peers of their disabilities, 30 Apr., but in August 1822 the ministerialist John Wilson Croker* listed him among 'persons inclined' to Canning who would follow him if he went into opposition.[6]

Canning's adhesion to the ministry may have influenced Gipps, whose conduct was markedly less independent from this point. He spoke on the game laws, which he was disposed to defend, 13 Mar. 1823, and the same day voted with government on the national debt reduction bill, as he did against repeal of the foreign enlistment bill, 16 Apr. 1823. He cast wayward votes against the pensions bill, 14 Apr., and for inquiry into chancery delays, 5 June, and was one of the minority of 20 who 'remained in the House' in the division on Stuart Wortley's amendment approving British neutrality towards the French invasion of Spain, 30 Apr. 1823. His name appears in none of the surviving division lists of 1824, but he had a few words to say in debate. A leading supporter, with his father-in-law, of the building of new churches, he claimed that £500,000 was required for that purpose, 2 Mar. He had been appointed to select committees on the vagrancy laws, 14 Mar. 1821, 29 Mar. 1822, and in March 1824 he introduced a bill to provide for the better employment of agricultural labourers in winter, but it did not progress to a second reading.[7] He was added to the select committee on labourers' wages, 6 Apr. 1825, and was a member of those on poor returns, 30 Mar. 1824, 30 Mar. 1825, 16 Mar. 1826. He voted against Catholic relief, 1 Mar., 21 Apr., 10 May, and against the Irish franchise bill, 26 Apr. 1825. He was credited with a speech deploring the reduction of the wool duty, 25 Mar. 1825, but it was almost certainly delivered by Joseph Cripps.[8] It is not clear whether it was he or Cripps who proposed an amendment, defeated by 79-64, to the terms of the grant to the duke of Cumberland for the education of his son, 27 May, but Gipps was in the ministerial majority in favour of the award, 30 May 1825.[9] This was his last known vote, and he retired at the dissolution of 1826. He remained active locally, however, and in 1828 moved the motion against Catholic claims at the county meeting on Penenden Heath.[10] His nephew Henry Plumptre

Gipps, who unsuccessfully contested Canterbury as a Conservative in 1837, sat briefly for Canterbury in 1852 before being unseated on petition the following year.

Gipps died in April 1869. By his will, dated 16 May 1857, he made provision for his wife and seven surviving children, before leaving the residue and family estates to his eldest son George (1812-80).

[1] Not 18 Dec. as stated in *HP Commons, 1790-1820*, iv. 25. This and other genealogical information was supplied by Bryan Gipps of Egerton House, Kent. [2] *Black Bk.* (1823), 157; *Session of Parl. 1825*, p. 465. [3] Cf. B. Hilton, *Corn, Cash, Commerce*, 102, where Gipps's role is mistakenly allotted to Sir Robert Thomas Wilson. [4] *The Times*, 30 Mar. 1821. [5] Ibid. 2 Mar. 1822. [6] Add. 40319, f. 66. [7] *The Times*, 26, 31 Mar., 1, 7 Apr. 1824; *CJ*, lxxix. 325. [8] *The Times*, 26 Mar. 1825. [9] Ibid. 28 May 1825. [10] *Report of Speeches Delivered at the Kent County Meeting* (1828), 2-4.

D.R.F.

GISBORNE, Thomas (1789–1852), of Yoxall Lodge, Staffs.; 41 Grosvenor Place, Mdx., and Horwich House, Derbys.

STAFFORD	1830–1832
DERBYSHIRE NORTH	1832–1837
CARLOW	27 Feb. 1839–1841
NOTTINGHAM	5 Apr. 1843–1847

b. 20 Aug. 1789,[1] 1st s. of Rev. Thomas Gisborne of Yoxall, rect. of Cossington, Leics., and Mary, da. of Thomas Babington of Rothley Temple, Leics. *educ.* Trinity Coll. Camb. 1806. *m.* (1) c.1811, Elizabeth (*d.* 20 June 1823), niece of John and Edward Fyshe Palmer of Ickwell, Beds., 3s. (2 *d.v.p.*) 2da.; (2) 1826, Susan, wid. of Francis Dukinfield Astley of Dukinfield, Cheshire, *s.p. suc.* fa. 1846. *d.* 20 July 1852.

Gisborne came from an old Derby family, who had intermittently provided its mayors since the seventeenth century. His grandfather John had sat there briefly, 1775-6, before being unseated on petition. His father, who was appointed perpetual curate of Barton-under-Needwood, Staffordshire in 1783 and prebendary of Durham in 1826, was a distinguished theologian and social commentator, and one of the founders of Evangelicalism. He was closely associated with Dr. Johnson and William Wilberforce*, who frequently made Yoxall Lodge 'his ordinary summer residence'.[2] Although Gisborne was described after his death as a 'school fellow' of Robert Peel* at Harrow, where his father and two of his sons were educated, he does not appear in the published school registers.[3] As well as being the heir to estates in Derbyshire and Staffordshire, which included

church lands held under lease (his father's will was proved under £12,000), Gisborne had business interests as a 'coal, lime and sand merchant' at Mill Street and Port Street in Manchester.[4] Like his father, who resembled 'an itinerant preacher, with eyes that squint inward, and a mouth that constantly grins outward', Gisborne's physical appearance drew comment: Miss Edgeworth described him in 1831 as 'very oracular and squinting'.[5] In 1820 his sister Mary married the Derbyshire manufacturer William Evans, independent Member for East Retford. Gisborne's own marriages, first to Elizabeth Fyshe Palmer of Ickwell, and secondly to the widow Susan Astley, who on her first marriage in 1812 was Susan Fyshe Palmer of Ickwell, also connected him with Charles Fyshe Palmer, Whig Member for Reading.[6] These women were consanguineous, sharing the same uncles and aunts who left them bequests, but their parentage and relationship to one another is unclear.[7] Susan's first husband died of apoplexy at Gisborne's Derbyshire seat, Horwich House, in 1825, and she married Gisborne, whose first wife had died in 1823, the following year.[8]

In 1827 Gisborne addressed a pamphlet to the Rev. Henry Phillpotts in support of Canning and Catholic claims. Despite his 'absence from England' in Portugal, he claimed to have been 'an habitual reader of the debates in Parliament', and accused Phillpotts of 'unfairness' and 'perverse obstinacy' in his 'representations of Mr. Canning's recent conduct on the Catholic question'. 'I happen to have led a rambling life', he wrote:

> I have lived among agriculturists and among manufacturers; I have associated with the religious world and with the fashionable world; with men of letters and with men of pleasure; and I declare solemnly, that I have never met with a single man in any station, whose powers of mind rose above the most muddling mediocrity, who was not an advocate for concession to the Catholics.[9]

At the 1830 general election Gisborne offered for the venal borough of Stafford where, because of an initial lack of candidates, the price of votes had dropped. He declared his support for economy in public expenditure, free trade, parliamentary reform and the abolition of slavery, but defended his purchase of votes, saying he 'despised those who could behold iniquity in a poor man's disposing of that by retail, which the rich man could with impunity sell by wholesale'. 'Such persons', he contended, 'looked with a jealous eye on open boroughs like Stafford, which were accessible to gentlemen of fortune and principle, and not under the domination of any lord'. After a two-day poll he was returned in first place.[10]

Later eulogized by John Stuart Mill as 'one of the most consistent and earnest reformers in the House', Gisborne was nevertheless regarded as something of a 'rogue' by his maternal cousin Thomas Babington Macaulay, Whig Member for Calne. Speaking with a 'common-sense style of thoroughly Saxon diction' which was occasionally seasoned by a 'quaint and pithy joke', he was, according to Benjamin Disraeli[†] in 1840, 'sometimes a most rakehelly rhetorician' who 'produces great effects in a crowded House', especially when 'he is tipsy and is not prepared'.[11] He presented constituency petitions for the abolition of slavery, 9, 22 Nov., and voted for reducing the duty on wheat imported to the West Indies, 12 Nov. 1830. He had been listed by the Wellington ministry as one of their 'foes', and he divided against them on the civil list, 15 Nov. He was granted ten days' leave 'on account of the disturbed state of his neighbourhood', 23 Nov. 1830. On 11 Feb. 1831 he presented a petition from New Mills, Derby, for repeal of the duty on printed calico. He condemned the proposed appointment of a paymaster of marines, hoping it would not prove 'necessary to vote against' the Grey ministry on the issue, 25 Feb. That day he gave notice of his intention to introduce 'a bill to repeal the Small Note Act' and lift restrictions on the use of Scottish and Irish notes of under five pounds value in England. On 4 Mar. he resumed the adjourned debate on the Grey ministry's reform bill and spoke strongly in its favour. Linking the unreformed system to excessive taxation and profligate expenditure, he argued that it was Parliament's failure to economize which had produced 'the clamour in the country for reform', adding that under 'the present system of representation ... there are hardly any of the commercial class representing large boroughs' or 'professional class representing small boroughs'. On 15 Mar. he drew attention to 'the state of the law relative to diplomatic and consular pensions' and secured returns on the subject. Citing the 'five pensioned-off ambassadors from the Ottoman Porte', he asked whether 'such a state of things could have gone on if we had had a reformed Parliament'. He presented petitions in favour of the reform bill from Derby, 19 Mar., and Dukinfield, 24 Mar. He seconded the postponement of the Liverpool and Chester railway bill, 21 Mar., and presented a petition from the mortgagees of the Liverpool and Warrington road against the Liverpool and Manchester railway bill, 23 Mar. He divided for the second reading of the reform bill, 22 Mar., warned that 'without some concession to popular feeling' government 'could not be carried on', 24 Mar., when he declared himself to be 'unconnected with any party', and presented favourable petitions, 28 Mar., 18 Apr. 1831. Next day he voted against Gascoyne's wrecking amendment.

At the ensuing general election he was rumoured to be about to start for Derbyshire, where a vacancy had been created by the withdrawal of the Tories, but he was deliberately outmanoeuvred by the Whig Cavendish interest. 'We don't like him', wrote Lord Waterpark*, 'he is not a reputable person'.[12] He offered again at Stafford, claiming that he had 'been the first' to obtain 'from ministers a promise that the children and apprentices of burgesses should not lose their right' to the franchise. After a sharp contest he was returned in second place.[13] He was appointed to the select committees on the East India Company, 28 June 1831, 2 Feb. 1832. He presented a petition against the Manchester and Leeds railway bill from Manchester's surveyor of highways, 6 July 1831. He voted for the second reading of the reintroduced reform bill that day and gave generally steady support to its details, although he spoke and voted for giving two Members to Stoke-upon-Trent, not, as he put it, 'because I happen to be a Staffordshire man', but because of 'its vast importance as the sole manufactory of a peculiar description of ware', 4 Aug. He spoke on technical grounds for keeping Chippenham in schedule B, 27 July, and divided for the disfranchisement of Saltash, on which ministers offered no clear lead, 28 July. He reproached Warrender, Member for Honiton, for repeating his private conversations with other Members on the subject of reform, 29 July. In a brief speech on the game laws, 8 Aug., he argued for ascertaining 'who the trespasser is, else he may walk off'. He voted for postponing the issuing of the Dublin writ that day, and with ministers on the controversy, 23 Aug. On 11 Aug. he attacked Peel's idea of restricting the votes of urban annuitants to the boroughs, rather than extending them to the county, asking 'what would be more easy than for a few landed proprietors in ... a town to club their annuitant votes, and thus completely influence the return of the borough?' He was in the minority for printing the Waterford petition for disarming the Irish yeomanry the same day. He was elected to Brooks's, sponsored by Sir Francis Burdett* and General Ronald Ferguson*, 13 Aug. On 18 Aug. he voted in favour of the Chandos clause for enfranchising £50 tenants-at-will, stating his conviction that 'the period of the landlord's notice' and tenurial security would be sufficient to enable them to exercise their franchise freely, without fear of immediate eviction. When his Stafford colleague John Campbell objected to the enfranchisement of £10 householders who paid their rent weekly, on account of their susceptibility to proprietorial influence, 25 Aug., Gisborne pointed out that those who paid on less regular terms often had a clause in their leases 'to give up at a week's notice', owing to the fact that 'many manufacturers who are landlords do not know when they may have occasion to turn their houses into factories'. He voted for the passage of the reform bill, 21 Sept., and the second reading of the Scottish bill, 23 Sept. On 29 Sept. he was given a fortnight's leave on urgent business. He divided for Lord Ebrington's confidence motion, 10 Oct., and supported Campbell's stance against withholding a new writ for Liverpool, 12 Oct. On 8 Dec. 1831 he gave notice that he would introduce a bill to repeal the Small Note Act after the Christmas recess, but he did not do so.

Gisborne voted for the second reading of the revised reform bill, 17 Dec. 1831, and steadily for its details, though he demanded clarification of the restrictions on the electoral rights of beneficed copyholders, 1 Feb., and was in the minority for limiting polling in the boroughs to one day, 15 Feb. 1832. He divided for the third reading of the bill, 22 Mar. He voted with ministers on the Russian-Dutch loan, 26 Jan., 2, 16 July, when he disputed Peel's interpretation of the issue, arguing that 'the treaties make it imperative upon us to pay this money', and 20 July (as a pair). On 16 Feb. he was in the minority of 28 for information on military punishments. He secured returns on American mines, 22 Feb. He presented petitions against the factories regulation bill, 19, 28 Mar., when he was added to the select committee on it, 6 Apr. He asked if the chancellor of the exchequer intended to appoint a select committee on the Bank of England's charter, 23 Mar. On 30 Mar. he urged the necessity of Irish church disestablishment and 'justice in appropriation', parodying the government's attitude as one of 'we cannot coerce your minds, but we are the strongest, and, therefore, we will make you maintain our clergy', and demanding to know, 'is this mode of dealing consistent with justice, with equity, or even with sound policy?' He voted with ministers on the navy civil departments bill, 6 Apr., but was in the minority to reduce the Irish registrar's salary, 9 Apr., and absent from the division on the address asking the king to appoint only ministers who would carry the reform bill unimpaired, 10 May. He argued for inquiry into the whole subject of the currency, 22 May. He divided against the government's temporizing amendment on the abolition of slavery, 24 May. He voted against increasing the Scottish county representation, 1 June, but with O'Connell to extend the Irish county franchise to £5 freeholders, 18 June. He divided for making coroners' inquests public, 20 June. On 22 June he was severely admonished by other Members for having had the

House counted and adjourned during their absence the previous afternoon: he admitted that he had acted hastily and duly apologized, but when Torrens refused to let the matter drop the Speaker intervened to point out that Gisborne's action had been 'perfectly in order', though one 'not usually taken'. Later that day he requested clarification of the proposed polling places for Staffordshire, after the nomination venue for the southern division was moved from Walsall to Lichfield. He presented petitions from Yorkshire and Derbyshire on the subject of the Bank of England, 3, 5 July 1832, when he contended that distress had arisen 'from the injudicious system of our currency' and that 'the power now left to the Bank is too great'. Taking his lead from Hume, he protested against any government interference with friendly societies the following day.

At the 1832 general election Gisborne abandoned Stafford and stood for North Derbyshire, where, after a contest, he was returned with one of the Cavendishes. He was unopposed in 1835, but poor health forced him to stand down in favour of his brother-in-law Evans in 1837.[14] During his subsequent parliamentary career, which 'was broken and disjointed', he sat for Carlow and Nottingham and acted with the Radicals on issues such as slavery, church reform, the secret ballot and the currency. Although he 'took a leading and a vigorous part' in the campaigns of the Anti-Corn Law League, he 'personally farmed a considerable acreage' of his family's large estates, which passed to him in 1846, and corresponded with Peel, his Staffordshire neighbour, on drainage techniques. His articles on farming, which originally appeared in the *Quarterly Review*, were posthumously reprinted as a single volume in 1854. 'His single object', wrote its editor, 'was the advancement of the art of husbandry'. His other works included *Thoughts on an Income and Property Tax* (1852).[15]

Gisborne died at Yoxall Lodge in July 1852. By his will, dated 1 Aug. 1851, he left all his property, except personalty retained by his wife from her first marriage, to his first son, Thomas Guy Gisborne (1812-69). Fifty-five shares in the Manchester and Liverpool Railway which he had acquired from his late brother William, of the Ceylon civil service, passed to his nephew Frederick William. On the death of Anne, the niece of John Fyshe Palmer and wife of the Rev. Thomas Hornsby, he directed that her six children should each receive an equal share of £2,453 as a 'discharge of debt'. A codicil of 9 Dec. 1851 revoked a bequest to his other surviving son, John Bowdler, who had died that day at Torquay, 'aged 33'.[16]

[1] IGI. [2] T. Gisborne, *Abolition of Slave Trade* (1792); *The Duties of Men in the Higher Rank and Middle Classes* (1794); *Oxford DNB*; *Gent. Mag.* (1846), i. 643-6, 661; *Life of Wilberforce*, i. 278. [3] *Essays on Agriculture by the late T. Gisborne* (1854), p. vi. [4] IR26/1736/172. [5] *Countess Granville Letters*, i. 27; *Edgeworth Letters*, 557. [6] *Derby Mercury*, 11 June 1812. [7] PROB 11/1227/45; 1314/672; 1403/54; 1562/622; IR26/207/206; *N and Q*, clx. 399. [8] *Gent. Mag.* (1825), ii. 188. [9] Gisborne, *Letter to Phillpotts*, 3, 125, 154-7. [10] *Lichfield Mercury*, 16, 30 July; *Birmingham Jnl.* 31 July; *Staffs. Mercury*, 24, 31 July, 7 Aug. 1830. [11] *Mill Works*, vi. 212; *Macaulay Letters*, ii. 262; *Gent. Mag.* (1852), ii. 315; *Disraeli Letters*, iii. 1039. [12] C.E. Hogarth, 'Derbys. Parl. Elections of 1832', *Derbys. Arch. Jnl.* lxxxix (1969), 72-73. [13] *Lichfield Mercury*, 29 Apr.; *Staffs. Mercury*, 30 Apr., 7 May 1830. [14] Hogarth, '1835 Elections in Derbys.', *Derbys. Arch. Jnl.* xciv (1974), 51-52; 'Derbys. Elections, 1837-47', ibid. xcv (1975), 48. [15] IR26/1736/172; *Gent. Mag.* (1852), ii. 315; *Dod's Parl. Companion* (1833), 115; (1844), 177; Add. 40602, ff. 313-16; Gisborne, *Essays on Agriculture*, pp. v-ix, 125-7; *Oxford DNB*. [16] PROB 11/2163/920; IR26/1932/701; *Gent. Mag.* (1852), i. 207.

P.J.S.

GLADSTONE, John (1764–1851), of 62 Rodney Street, Liverpool; Seaforth House, Lancs., and 5 Grafton Street, Mdx.[1]

LANCASTER	1818–1820
NEW WOODSTOCK	1820–1826
BERWICK-UPON-TWEED	1826–19 Mar. 1827

b. 11 Dec. 1764, 1st s. of Thomas Gladstones (*d.* 1809), merchant and shopkeeper, of Leith, Edinburgh and Helen, da. of Walter Neilson, merchant, of Springfield, Edinburgh. *m.* (1) 5 May 1791, Jane (*d.* 16 Apr. 1798),[2] da. of Joseph Hall, merchant, of Liverpool, *s.p.*; (2) 29 Apr. 1800, Anne, da. of Andrew Robertson, provost of Dingwall, Ross, 4s. 2da. (1 *d.v.p.*). Dropped final 's' from name informally 1787 and by royal lic. 10 Feb. 1835. *cr.* bt. 18 July 1846. *d.* 7 Dec. 1851.

In 1820 Gladstone, a self-made Liverpool merchant prince of indomitable will, relentless energy, short temper and warm affections, had a business fortune of over £333,000, of which more than half was staked in the West Indies. He owned a Demerara sugar plantation, Success, worth £100,000, and had £150,000 invested in loans and his various trading partnerships. The following year he took over the European business of the Vreedenhoop plantation and, after a quarrel with his brother Robert, ended their East Indian commercial partnership and merged his East and West Indian companies into the firm of Gladstone, Grant and Wilson. If slave ownership sat uneasily with the Evangelical Anglicanism for which he had deserted his native Presbyterianism (he was a builder of churches and an active philanthropist), it did not show in his unabashed public stance on the issue, though the dichotomy troubled his beautiful and devoted second wife and sickly daughter Anne. A ship owner and investor in Liverpool urban property, he possessed the Litherland estate at nearby Seaforth, but was on the lookout for a landed base in Scotland. In Liverpool, to whose representation he aspired, he was the principal supporter of its Member Canning, his political hero since 1812, having then renounced his earlier association with the local Whigs and reformers opposed to the corporation's oligarchical rule, though he was no uncritical apologist for the latter. He was an effective and ruthless election manager in a city notorious for corruption, and made many enemies. He was valued for his commercial experience and expertise by Lord Liverpool's ministry (in which Canning was president of the board of control), whom he had supported silently as Member for the open and venal borough of Lancaster in the 1818 Parliament. He did not seek re-election there in 1820, when, after toying with the idea of challenging Gascoyne, the corporation-backed Member for Liverpool, he was recommended by Lord Liverpool to the 5th duke of Marlborough, who had asked him to name 'any eminent commercial person' for a seat for Woodstock, where he had the dominant interest. Gladstone was returned unopposed with an opportunist Oxfordshire Whig.[3] Marlborough was desperate for money, and evidently tried to persuade Gladstone to contribute £2,500 towards the payment of his local election debts. (He certainly sought a loan of £300 to meet an immediate emergency three months after the election.) Gladstone parted with no more than £877 to cover essential expenses.[4]

He was named to the select committees on the royal burghs' petitions, 4 May 1820 (and again, 16 Feb. 1821), highways, 16 May, and foreign trade, 5 June 1820; he was appointed to the latter in each of the following four years. On 19 June he testified to the select committee of inquiry into agricultural distress on frauds in taking the corn averages in Liverpool.[5] In May Marlborough asked him to 'summon what strength you can collect amongst our ministerial friends' to oppose the Western Union canal bill.[6] He divided with government against economies in revenue collection, 4 July. At a meeting of the Liverpool Canning Club in December 1820 Gladstone, who helped to persuade Canning not to resign his seat along with his place in the ministry over the Queen Caroline affair, denounced the campaign in her support as 'yet another radical conspiracy' against the established order, which if not checked would 'ere long terminate in revolution'. He was active in the concoction of a loyal address to the king.[7] In his maiden speech, 2 Feb. 1821, he defended Liverpool corporation against Creevey's attack on their resistance to the city's petition in support of Caroline; claimed that 'many gentlemen and merchants of Liverpool of great wealth and character ... approved of the measures of government', and said that the loyal address had been got up in a 'hole-and-corner' fashion solely because attempts to promote it openly had been 'put down by clamour'. On the navy estimates later that day he observed that the merchant navy was in an unprecedentedly flourishing condition. He voted in defence of ministers' conduct in the prosecution of the queen, 6 Feb. 1821.

On 9 Feb. he attributed agricultural distress largely to an excess of production over consumption, which was held down by low wages, and deprecated casual dissemination of the notion that there was a handy legislative solution. Denying a radical allegation that 'the friends of many Members of Parliament lived upon the taxes', he asserted that 'his support for the present ministers arose from his conviction' that their 'system ... was the best and safest for the country'. In the course of his speech, he was called to order for alluding to the previous night's debate.[8] He presented petitions against any alteration in the timber duties, 20, 26, 27 Feb.,[9] and on 16 Apr. expressed the approval of 'the commercial interest' for the government bill, complaining that he 'thought it extremely unfair to describe the ship owners as a class of men favoured and enriched at the expense of the community'. He voted, like Canning, for Catholic relief, 28 Feb. He was in the ministerial majorities on the state of the revenue, 6 Mar., repeal of the additional malt duty, 3 Apr., and the disfranchisement of ordnance officials, 12 Apr., when he was named to the select committee on the Scottish malt duty. On 29 Mar. and 2 Apr. he welcomed ministerial proposals to deal with abuses in taking the corn averages.[10] Called to give evidence to the Lords committee on foreign trade, 11 Apr., he put the case for opening the Indian trade and allowing private merchants to carry Indian goods to the Far East.[11] On Parnell's motion for inquiry into Anglo-Irish trade, 30 Apr., he urged the House to accept the ministerial assurance that the subject would be 'amply discussed' next session. He voted for the forgery punishment mitigation bill, 23 May, 4 June. He divided with ministers against the omission of arrears from the duke of Clarence's grant, 18 June 1821.

He did likewise against more extensive tax reductions, 11 Feb., and abolition of one of the joint-postmasterships, 13 Mar. 1822. He supported the prayer of petitions for removal of the restrictions on private trade to the East Indies, 3 May, and against the navigation bill (of which he disapproved), 6 May.[12] A supporter of a more open corn trade, he was in the minorities of 36 against the new duties, 9 May, and of 21 for Canning's clause to permit the grinding and export as flour of bonded corn, 10 June. He was attacked by the Liverpool radicals as an advocate of high bread prices. He was appointed to the select committee on mercantile law, 15 May, and called for steam packets to be equipped with more lifeboats, 21 May.[13] The prospect of Canning's going to India as governor-general seemed to open to Gladstone in the spring of 1822 the prospect of stepping into his shoes at Liverpool, though Huskisson, Canning's protégé at the board of trade, was an obvious rival. After Lord Londonderry's* suicide in August, when John Croker* named him as one of the Members who would follow Canning into opposition if he chose that option, Gladstone entertained him at Seaforth, chaired a Canning Club dinner in his honour, and urged him to take the foreign secretaryship. Canning did so and resigned Liverpool for a less demanding seat; but it was on Huskisson that his and the Liverpool Canningites' choice fell as his successor. Although Gladstone masked his private bitterness and disappointment and worked to secure Huskisson's unopposed return in February 1823, he vowed to have no more to do with Liverpool politics. He was unable, however, to stay out of them, and became Huskisson's mainstay in the constituency.[14]

Gladstone pressed on ministers in 1823 the need to reduce the British cotton industry's dangerous dependence on American raw material by increasing the duty on foreign imports and introducing a drawback for exports.[15] In the House, 26 Feb., he voted for Whitmore's proposal to reduce the corn import price to 60s.; but he sided with ministers against the repeal of £2,000,000 in taxes, 3 Mar., and of the Foreign Enlistment Act, 16 Apr., inquiries into the prosecution of the Dublin Orange rioters, 22 Apr., and chancery delays, 5 June, and Scottish parliamentary reform, 2 June. He welcomed the merchant vessels apprenticeship bill, which had 'the unqualified approbation of the ship owners', 24 Mar., and, in his last known speech in the House, supported its third reading, 18 Apr. 1823. He was consulted by ministers that session on the sugar duties.[16] In August he made Seaforth available to Huskisson as his base for a round of constituency engagements and in the following months he corresponded extensively with him on plans to remit Liverpool customs revenues.[17] In October 1823 he seconded the nomination of the first Whig mayor of Liverpool for time out of mind, and in February 1824 he spoke enthusiastically in support of the Greek cause at a meeting dominated by local Whigs and reformers.

The previous month Liverpool merchants and civic leaders had started a public subscription to recognize his services to the city; and he was presented with an elaborate service of plate the following autumn.[18]

In late 1823 Gladstone learnt of the August slave revolt in Demerara, which had been centred on his own plantation and been savagely put down. He sent reports from his agent to Huskisson, who expressed agreement with his view that the abolitionists were to blame and that the only safe way forward was that set out in Canning's resolutions of May 1823 in favour of amelioration in preparation for emancipation. Gladstone, who attempted to have enlightened practices and spiritual and moral improvement put into effect on his own plantations, was 'not sorry' to hear of the death in prison of the Methodist missionary John Smith, who had been arrested for incitement, 'as his release would have been followed by much cavil and discussion here'.[19] He had already entered into an extensive Liverpool newspaper controversy, under his customary pseudonym of 'Mercator', with the local abolitionist James Cropper.[20] He was placed on the West India Planters' standing committee, 10 Feb. 1824.[21] Gladstone, who was added to the select committee on artisans and machinery, 13 Feb., voted against reform of Edinburgh's representation, 26 Feb. 1824. He divided for repeal of the usury laws, 8 Apr. Later that month, to his own embarrassment and the fury of Huskisson, the latter's letter of 2 Nov. 1823 attacking the abolitionists, of which Gladstone had sent a copy to his brother-in-law Robertson, who had allowed it to be transmitted to Jamaica, was leaked to the press there and given publicity in Britain. Gladstone carried out a damage limitation exercise.[22] He of course voted with ministers on the Missionary Smith affair, 11 June 1824, when his name was kept out of the debates. Far from reducing his stake in the West Indies, he made major investments there in the next two years, when he bought Vreedenhoop for £80,000 and acquired property in Jamaica and Guyana. By 1828 he owned directly 1,050 slaves and was indirectly responsible for many more. He was an enthusiastic supporter of the Liverpool and Manchester railway scheme.[23] He was granted a fortnight's leave on account of ill health, 18 Feb. 1825, having recently taken a residence at Gloucester Spa, where the waters were supposed to be beneficial to his ailing wife and daughter.[24] He was named to the select committee on the export of machinery, 24 Feb. He was present to vote for Catholic relief, 1 Mar., 21 Apr., and paired for it, 10 May. From Gloucester, 6 July, he congratulated Huskisson on the close of a session which had been 'the most fruitful of good and important meas-

ures than any that ever preceded it'. His youngest son William Gladstone† found him at Gloucester 'looking well, but fatigued' at the end of August 1825.[25]

In March 1824 Gladstone had received the following letter from Marlborough:

I am sorry that the only request I have troubled you with on parliamentary matters since your election for Woodstock should meet with so determined a *refusal*. I cannot give up my opinion as to the question at issue, but as your opinion is as good as mine and mine *perhaps* as good as yours, there is an end to the matter. I confess I detest monopolies and will always support a competition, whether it may be between inn keepers or lamp lighters.

While it is not clear precisely what issue prompted this remonstrance (it may have been the beer duties bill) Gladstone, who absented himself from Liverpool but commissioned his son Robertson to act as a tour guide when Marlborough visited the city in December 1824, knew that he could not expect to come in again for Woodstock at the next general election.[26] In the autumn of 1825 he decided, after some deliberation, to accept an invitation to stand for the venal and open borough of Berwick, which seems to have originated with the London out-voters. One of the sitting Members, Sir John Beresford, a supporter of government, who had only recently established his interest there, planned to make way at the dissolution for his nephew Marcus Beresford. Gladstone kept an open mind as to whether he should stand separately or seek to coalesce with the Beresfords against the other sitting Member Sir Francis Blake, a Whig; but he told his Berwick contact R.A. Clunie that whatever course he adopted 'my great object would be to endeavour to bring those ... who approve of the public policy and conduct of His Majesty's present ministers *to draw together*'. On the eve of his first appearance in Berwick, 26 Oct., after a visit to Scotland, he was warned by his friend and correspondent Kirkman Finlay*, a Glasgow cotton merchant, to consider well 'the *certainty* of expense and the *uncertainty* of an unchallengeable future'.[27] In his initial address he claimed to be 'unfettered by any party', but praised the 'liberal and enlightened policy' pursued by ministers, 'by which our country has been raised to its present state of unexampled influence and prosperity'. A family illness at Gloucester obliged him to leave Berwick after a week's canvassing, but his supporters continued to promote his cause among the London and Northumberland out-voters.[28] The Beresfords were furious at his intervention and complained to Peel, the home secretary, who, fully taking their side, urged Liverpool to get Lushington, the patronage secretary, to 'do everything' to support their 'established interest'. While Liverpool agreed, he observed that 'though Gladstone is a supporter of government, he is a perfectly independent man, and one over whom we have never attempted to exercise any influence or authority. The Beresfords should be made to feel this'. To Lushington, whom he asked to exert government influence on their behalf, he commented that they had 'no right to dictate' to Gladstone, and that it was 'a pity that a seat could not be found for him in some other quarter'. Lushington, who complied, explained that

> we have no power of controlling Mr. Gladstone. He is independent of the government, and having no chance at Woodstock, thought it for his interest to close with an offer from Berwick. This he did without consulting me, and when he announced his departure for Berwick I warned him that he was embarking amongst a very troublesome and expensive set of constituents ... and I distinctly told him that the aid of government would be given in every possible way to the Beresfords. Even now I do not see that it is practicable to do more. If he had not voted for the Catholic question, it had been possible to find him a popular seat elsewhere at less expense, and little hazard.[29]

In December 1825 Gladstone, notwithstanding his recent criticisms of 'the cursed systems of country banking', which he largely blamed for the current commercial crisis, responded favourably to an approach from the Gloucester and Cheltenham bank of Turner, Turner and Morris, which had suspended payments, to invest £10,000 in a new partnership. While he was keen to set up the venture as an ideal example of what a sound and profitable country bank should be, he also thought it would enable him to 'establish for myself an important political interest' in Gloucester, which might be of use to himself or one of his sons. In the event he withdrew from the scheme after his potential associates, who were 'not altogether reconciled to the strictness of my system', had prematurely made it public.[30] He was still in Gloucester on 17 Feb. 1826, when he wrote to Huskisson of his qualms over the government's proposal to issue exchequer bills, which he feared would benefit and encourage the speculator rather than the 'regular merchant'.[31] He was named to the select committee on the Irish butter trade, 9 Mar., but may have spent most of the 1826 session in Gloucester, for his only known parliamentary activity was his appearance as a witness before the select committee on promissory notes, 26, 28 Apr.[32] He and his wife returned to Seaforth, after an absence of over 18 months, in late May 1826.

Chairing a Liverpool election meeting in support of Huskisson soon afterwards, he was given a hard time by a disgruntled ship's carpenter, who denounced Huskisson's support of the 1825 Combination Act. There was no substance to the usual rumours of his own candidature for the city.[33] He went to Berwick, where he faced a contest with Beresford and Blake, who eventually coalesced against him. On the hustings, he portrayed himself as an independent supporter of government. The local press reported him as opposing free trade in corn and criticizing the new Navigation Act, as well as taking a stance on slavery in accordance with the 1823 resolutions in favour of progressive amelioration combined with compensation for the proprietors when emancipation was effected. After a desperate and protracted contest, he beat Blake into third place by six votes in a poll of 860.[34] Recriminations soon started. Gladstone sought to correct in both Liverpool and Berwick what he considered to be a distorted report in the *Berwick Advertiser* of his hustings pronouncements on the corn and navigation laws. He insisted that while he had acknowledged the need to give fair protection to domestic agriculture and would never agree to 'a *permanent unrestricted* trade in foreign corn', he had advocated the adoption of a sliding scale of duties between fixed maximum and minimum prices, and pointed out that his strictures on the Navigation Act had had reference only to the British shipping industry's relationship with the Northern European powers. He had also to defend himself against an accusation of duplicity on the question of slavery, in that he had in a letter to a supporter in Berwick expressed support for the prayer of the borough's petition of February 1826 calling for immediate implementation of the resolutions of 1823, whereas in a letter of 5 Nov. 1823 to the *Liverpool Courier* (his organ) he had said that the Demerara revolt had awakened ministers to the folly of those resolutions, which had been forced on them by misguided and, in some cases, malevolent abolitionists. His retort was that while he had heartily supported the resolutions, and still did so, ministers had been compelled to adopt them, whereas if they had been left alone to deal with the slavery problem by administrative means, the uprising would never have taken place.[35] Gladstone, who felt that he had been duped into expecting a comparatively easy return, resented attempts to identify him as a partisan in the borough's politics, and was angered by the expectation that he would procure patronage for large numbers of those who had supported him, fell out with Clunie. He soon came to regret that he had ever become involved at Berwick, the more so when his return was petitioned against, 28 Nov. 1826, on the grounds of bribery, treating and reliance on illegal votes.[36] He paired for Catholic relief, 6 Mar. 1827, but was unseated by the

election committee on the 19th. William Gladstone*
loyally noted that Berwick had 'lost ... a representative
ten times too good for it'.[37]

A month later Canning, who probably found
Gladstone rather tiresome, was prime minister.
Gladstone, for his part, felt neglected by Canning,
complaining in a letter drafted to Huskisson but not
sent, 24 Mar. 1827, that he had been cool towards
him ever since becoming foreign secretary. Nothing
came of a rumour that Canning was to give him a
peerage. Nevertheless, he was a sincere well-wisher
to Canning's administration, and chaired a Liverpool
meeting in its support, 9 May, though he cavilled at some of his commercial policies and called
for 'the timely concession of the just claims of the
Catholics' to 'prevent Ireland from being deluged
in blood'.[38] Following Canning's death he remained
loyal to Huskisson, seconding his nomination on
his re-election for Liverpool after taking office in
the Wellington ministry in February 1828.[39] A year
later his daughter Anne died. He warmly welcomed
Catholic emancipation.[40] In December 1829, three
months after taking in his eldest son as a partner in
the Liverpool firm, from which Wilson departed,
he bought the Kincardineshire estate of Fasque for
£80,000. Because of his wife's poor health, which led
them to move to Leamington in search of a cure, they
did not take up permanent residence there until the
summer of 1833. Robertson Gladstone remained at
Seaforth to run the business and represent the family
in Liverpool affairs. At the general election of 1830,
when he again put his weight behind Huskisson at
Liverpool, Gladstone helped to secure the return
of his eldest son Thomas for Queenborough. After
Huskisson's death at the opening of the Liverpool and
Manchester railway in September (he had written to
Huskisson two weeks before the fatal event that 'I for
one cannot help thinking there is more made of this
railroad opening business than it deserves') he made a
final bid for his seat, but got nowhere.[41] He published
at this time *A Statement of Facts* on slavery, addressed
to Peel, in which he reiterated his customary warnings
of the dangers of ill-considered and precipitate abolition. In 1831 he investigated the possibility of standing for the district of burghs containing Leith, his
birthplace, when it was enfranchised by the Reform
Act, but nothing came of this. In the course of that
year he came to accept that a modicum of reform was
necessary, but at a Liverpool meeting to address the
king against the creation of peers, 21 Nov., he argued
that the borough property qualification was set too
low for safety.[42] The following year he encouraged
his son Robertson in the formation of a Conservative
Association in Liverpool, and was involved in the
launch of the *Liverpool Standard*. At the general election of 1832 Thomas was returned for Portarlington
and William embarked on his long and distinguished
political career as Conservative Member for Newark,
where his stern but doting father paid half his
expenses. Gladstone, who was widowed in 1835, stood
for Dundee as one who was 'liberally Conservative'
in 1837, but he was pelted with mud and stones and
humiliatingly beaten by the Liberal sitting Member.[43]
He published pamphlets against repeal of the corn
laws in 1839, 1841, 1843 and 1846. His third son John
Neilson, a naval officer, began a parliamentary career
as Conservative Member for Walsall in February 1841.
Gladstone accepted invitations to stand for Aberdeen
and the Leith district at the general election that year,
when he was almost 77, but neither scheme came to
fruition; and he rejected an invitation from Berwick
four years later. On leaving office in 1846 Peel, who
had promoted William Gladstone's early ministerial
career, offered a baronetcy to his father, dismissing his
punctilious scruples about acceptance because of his
conscientious opposition to repeal of the corn laws.[44]
Gladstone later admitted that Peel had been right to
carry that measure.

He substantially reduced his investment in the West
Indies after emancipation, which cost him between
£150,000 and £250,000. After experimenting with the
import of Coolie labour from Bengal to the Caribbean
as he concentrated more on trade with the East, he
sold Vreedenhoop in 1840 and largely wound up his
West Indian estates the following year, having earlier
transferred his Demerara assets to his children. He
invested heavily in domestic transport ventures. In
1843 he gifted £74,000 to his children. Five years later
he gave them a further £250,000 and made a will (8
Dec. 1848) to deal with the remainder. His surviving
daughter Helen, who had turned Catholic in 1842,
went through a phase of opium addiction and demen-
tia and died in continental exile, received a life interest
in £50,000, while the three younger sons were given
an additional £10,000 each. The Scottish estates had
already been made over to Thomas, whose stake in the
will amounted to £126,000, plus a quarter share with
his brothers in a residue of £216,000.[45] Gladstone was
described by William in the spring of 1851 as being
'very like a spent cannon ball, with a great and almost
frightful energy left in him'. In the autumn he went
into swift decline, and he died at Fasque in December
1851. His son wrote:

Though with little left either of sight or hearing, and only
able to walk from one room to another or to his brougham

for a short drive, though his memory was gone, his hold upon language even for common purposes imperfect, the reasoning power much decayed and even his perception of personality rather indistinct, yet so much remained about him as one of the most manful, energetic, affectionate, and simple-hearted among human beings, that he still filled a great space to the eye, mind, and heart, and a great space is accordingly left void by his withdrawal.[46]

He had more to say on his father, whose fortune at his death (about £600,000) was less than that of 'others who in native talent and energy he much surpassed':

> It was a large and strong nature, simple though hasty, profoundly affectionate and capable of the highest devotion in the lines of duty and of love. I think that his intellect was a little intemperate, though not his character ... He could not understand nor tolerate those who, perceiving an object to be good, did not at once and actively pursue it; and with all this energy he joined a corresponding warmth and ... eagerness of affection, a keen appreciation of humour, in which he found a rest, and an indescribable frankness and simplicity of character, which, crowning his other qualities, made him, I think (and I strive to think impartially), the most interesting old man I have ever known.[47]

[1] Based, unless otherwise stated, on S.G. Checkland, *The Gladstones* (1971). [2] Par. reg. St. Peter, Liverpool; *Gore's Advertiser*, 19 Apr. 1798. [3] Add. 38458, ff. 286, 325; 38290, f. 318; 64813, f. 46; St. Deiniol's Lib. Glynne-Gladstone mss 326, Blandford to Gladstone and reply, 5 Mar.; *Jackson's Oxford Jnl.* 4, 11 Mar. 1820. [4] *VCH Oxon.* xii. 404; Glynne-Gladstone mss 290, Marlborough to Gladstone, 8 June 1820. [5] *PP* (1820), ii. 154-6. [6] Glynne-Gladstone mss 290, Marlborough to Gladstone, 12 May 1820. [7] *Liverpool Mercury*, 15 Dec. 1820. [8] *The Times*, 10 Feb.; Glynne-Gladstone mss, T. to J. Gladstone, 14 Feb. 1821. [9] *The Times*, 21, 27, 28 Feb. 1821. [10] Ibid. 30 Mar., 3 Apr. 1821. [11] *LJ*, liv. 296-301. [12] *The Times*, 4, 7 May 1822. [13] Ibid. 22 May 1822. [14] *Gladstone to his Wife* ed. A. Tilney Bassett, 2-3; Add. 38743, ff. 154, 156, 162; 38744, ff. 70, 80, 115; 40319, f. 57; Glynne-Gladstone mss 290, Marlborough to Gladstone, 30 June 1822; *Liverpool Mercury*, 16, 23, 30 Aug. 1822; J.A. Picton, *Mems. Liverpool* (1907), i. 381. [15] Add. 38746, ff. 79, 96, 111, 113. [16] Add. 38744, ff. 149, 165, 172. [17] *The Times*, 30 Aug. 1823; Add. 38744, ff. 253, 283, 290, 311, 319, 323; 38745, ff. 1, 7, 16, 50, 75, 96, 101, 113, 166. [18] Picton, i. 388-91; *Liverpool Mercury*, 20 Feb. 1824; A.F. Robbins, *Early Public Life of W.E. Gladstone*, 34. [19] Robbins, 35-46; Add. 38745, ff. 77, 199. [20] Published as *Corresp. between John Gladstone and James Cropper on the Present State of Slavery* (Liverpool, 1824). See Add. 38745, f. 166. [21] *The Times*, 11 Feb. 1824. [22] Ibid. 27, 30 Apr., 3 May 1824; Add. 38745, ff. 263-85. [23] Add. 38746, f. 50; *Berwick Advertiser*, 13 May 1826. [24] Add. 38746, ff. 261, 271. [25] Add. 38747, f. 5; *Gladstone Diaries*, i. 6. [26] Glynne-Gladstone mss 290, Marlborough to Gladstone, 10 Mar., 8 Nov., 24 Dec. 1824. [27] Glynne-Gladstone mss 342, Clunie to Gladstone, 5 Oct., reply, 8 Oct., Finlay to Gladstone, 25, 30 Oct. 1825. [28] *Berwick Advertiser*, 29 Oct., 5, 12 Nov.; 3, 17 Dec.; *The Times*, 12 Nov. 1825; *Gladstone Diaries*, i. 16. [29] Add. 38195, f. 182; 38301, f. 12; 40305, f. 128; Wellington mss WP1/831/11. [30] Add. 38747, ff. 149, 176. [31] Add. 38747, f. 178. [32] *PP* (1826), iii. 473-9; (1826-7), vi. 511-20. [33] *The Times*, 5 June 1826; Picton, i. 398-9; *Gladstone Diaries*, i. 52-53. [34] *Gladstone Diaries*, i. 54-56; *Berwick Advertiser*, 10, 17,

24 June 1826. [35] *Berwick Advertiser*, 1, 8, 15, 29 July, 12 Aug.; Robbins, 49-51; Glynne-Gladstone mss 342, Clunie to Gladstone, 14, 19, 20 July, replies, 17, 19 July 1826 [36] Glynne-Gladstone mss 342, Clunie to Gladstone, 19 July, 7, 21 Aug., replies, 20 July, 3, 12 Aug. 1826; *Gladstone Diaries*, i. 64; Add. 38748, f. 208; Glynne-Gladstone mss 194, T. to J. Gladstone [14 Mar. 1827]. [37] *Gladstone Diaries*, i. 107. [38] Add. 38749, ff. 177, 207, 229, 315; *The Times*, 11 May 1827. [39] Add. 38750, ff. 210, 257; 38751, f. 17; 38756, f. 263; *The Times*, 6, 7 Feb. 1828. [40] Wellington mss WP1/1001/21; 1002/13. [41] Add. 38758, f. 226; *Gladstone Diaries*, i. 323-4; Add. 40401, f. 256; 44720, ff. 46-57. [42] Picton, i. 440. [43] *Gladstone Diaries*, ii. 306-7; *The Times*, 4, 10, 11 July, 1 Aug 1837. [44] Add. 40594, ff. 82, 84. [45] PROB 11/2151/301; IR26/1930/203. [46] *W.E. Gladstone* ed. J. Brooke and M. Sorensen (*Prime Ministers' Pprs.*), iii. 80-102; J. Morley, *Life of Gladstone*, i. 388. [47] Morley, i. 10, 19.

D.R.F.

GLADSTONE, Thomas (1804–1889).

QUEENBOROUGH	2 Dec. 1830–1831
PORTARLINGTON	1832–1834
LEICESTER	1835–1837
IPSWICH	3 June 1842–30 July 1842

b. 25 July 1804, 1st s. of John Gladstone* and 2nd w. Anne, da. of Andrew Robertson, provost of Dingwall, Ross. *educ.* Rev. Rawson's sch. Seaforth; Eton 1817; Christ Church, Oxf. 1823; I. Temple 1828. *m.* 27 Aug. 1835, Louisa, da. of Robert Fellowes[†] of Shottesham Park, Norf., 1s. 6da. (5 *d.v.p.*). *suc.* fa. as 2nd bt. 7 Dec. 1851. *d.* 20 Mar. 1889.

Ld. lt. Kincardine 1876-*d.*; lt. Kincardine rifles.

Gladstone, the eldest of the four sons of the wealthy Liverpool merchant John Gladstone, who had great political ambitions for them, enjoyed a happy childhood at Seaforth House, Lancashire, being especially close to his elder sister Anne, who was fated to die young, and to his younger brothers, Robertson and John Neilson Gladstone[†]. However, his upbringing was overshadowed by a domineering father and ineffectual invalid mother, and his early education both at home and the local school was strongly Evangelical.[1] He found Eton thoroughly alienating, partly because of the unfamiliar robustness of public school life and also because, beyond his intellectual abilities, he was put straight into the fourth form. He failed to live up to expectations, and loneliness led to increasingly unruly behaviour for which he was nearly expelled twice, much to the disgust of his parents. He eventually settled and took his brothers under his wing, but left having risen no higher than the fifth form.[2] At Christ Church he continued to make modest academic progress, perhaps in part because he was subject to frequent bouts of ill health.[3] In the Christmas vacation of 1824-5 he travelled to Paris, and he returned there the following summer, taking up the foreign secretary George Canning's offer of residence with the family of the British ambassador, where he was employed as a copyist. He completed his BA in 1827, but poor health led to a prolonged sojourn on the continent from the autumn of that year, which included visits to Paris, Florence, Naples, Rome and Milan.[4] Having finally recuperated, he intended to enter Lincoln's Inn in November 1828, but finding that he was too late to start the required legal dinners there, he instead enrolled at the Inner Temple, became the sole pupil of Serjeant Henry Alworth Merewether and began to attend lectures at University College. However, his languid nature and the attractions of London society, as a member of the Windham and Athenaeum Clubs, put paid to his putative legal career.[5] Although it was principally Robertson who assisted in his father's business activities, Gladstone occasionally reported news from the City and sometimes handled the family's affairs while he was resident in London. He also defended his father's business interests by monitoring the various political attempts to end colonial slavery, the existence of which he justified on commercial grounds.[6]

Gladstone had long been destined by his father for a political career, perhaps the more so as John Neilson was intent on pursuing advancement in the navy; and although he was already being eclipsed by his youngest brother, William Ewart Gladstone[†], their father was willing to use all his influence to get him into Parliament.[7] Gladstone himself exhibited an interest in politics from an early age, and followed his father in admiring Canning and William Huskisson*, with whom John Gladstone was associated at Liverpool. Congratulating his father on the outcome of the 1818 election there, the fourteen-year-old Gladstone recorded that 'I have read all Canning's speeches, and can safely say that I never admired anything of the sort half so much'. He followed his father's electoral and parliamentary affairs closely, and by 1827 he had begun to attend Commons debates and to report detailed accounts of political news and speculation to his father.[8] His illness, together with the death of Canning in August 1827 and the resignation of Huskisson in May 1828, which removed much of John Gladstone's influence, delayed his entry into Parliament. However, as George IV's death approached, he began to make enquiries for a seat that his father might purchase on his behalf.[9] One possibility was Chippenham where the proprietor, Joseph Neeld*, was looking for someone to be returned with himself, at an estimated cost of only £500, if a contest was avoided. Huskisson approved of this plan, and

suggested that Gladstone also follow up Edward John Littleton's* offer of a seat at Stafford, which could be had for under £4,000. He rejected this second option as he had no experience of fighting expensive elections. Through Huskisson, Gladstone was also offered Leominster cheaply, but he decided against it when it became clear that, in the unlikely event of success, the cost would be about £5,000, and that he would in any case be liable for at least £1,000. Huskisson and Sir Stratford Canning* urged him to accept another, unidentified, seat which was available for 5,000 guineas, but due to a misunderstanding he was just too late in applying for it. Commenting on the high price of seats, he wrote that 'the Catholic candidates added to the Protestants, who are of course as numerous as ever, make a material difference in the market and ... they offer very liberally'. He continued to follow up possibilities elsewhere, including in Ireland and Cornwall, until finally settling on Queenborough in mid-July 1830.[10]

Gladstone was introduced there by Merewether, who had previously acted as a legal representative of the freemen in their struggle to wrest control of the local fisheries from the select body of the corporation. A popular candidate was needed at the general election of 1830 to accompany John Capel* in his opposition to two men put forward on the ordnance interest, William Holmes* and Admiral Sir Philip Durham[†], who had threatened to pay whatever was necessary to win back both seats. Although Gladstone knew he would have to contribute to providing for the poor of the town, the estimated cost of £1,500 to £2,000 proved very enticing. Capel* undertook to support his candidacy by introducing him to the electors, and in addresses of 16 and 19 July Gladstone pledged himself to the cause of independence against both the ordnance and the select body.[11] As his list of freemen makes clear, he canvassed assiduously, even pursuing individual out-voters, and he also exploited his family's City and shipping influence and his father's 'venerable' reputation. While he calculated that he would be narrowly elected, he was also aware that he was not treating the freemen as lavishly as the other candidates.[12] At meetings in Queenborough, 23, 31 July, he agreed to forward an address of grievances against the select body if he were elected. On the hustings, 2 Aug., he attacked Durham for undermining the independence of the electors, and declared that he stood 'not as the opponent of government, but of the ordnance'.[13] He came fourth in the poll, with Holmes elected outright, and Durham and Capel* involved in a double return for the second seat. Gladstone's support from the independent burgesses was underlined when a meeting of resident freemen thanked him for his conduct during the contest, 3 Aug. 1830.[14]

The government candidates attempted to ward off a challenge to their election by having seats provided for Capel* and Gladstone elsewhere, but the latter was rightly suspicious of Holmes's hints to this effect, and anyway thought that a government seat 'would not quite suit'.[15] Capel* took charge of the campaign to overturn the result, and Gladstone was careful to co-operate with him, placing his colleague's hopes of success before his own.[16] Meanwhile he spent the autumn in Lancashire, and witnessed the fatal accident of Huskisson, whose loss he much lamented, 15 Sept. 1830.[17] He thought that there was sufficient support in Liverpool to warrant John Gladstone attempting to regain the seat, but his father was not finally convinced by his optimistic soundings.[18] He spent a good deal of his time in consultation with his legal advisers, Merewether and Henry Hall Joy, the electoral agents Comyn and Saunders, of 1 Queen Anne Place, Southwark Bridge, and Scott James Breeze, who was one of the leading independent burgesses and had chaired his committee. He was reluctant to stand alone, despite various calculations that by objecting to several non-residents he could establish a legal majority in the poll.[19] He therefore followed his father's advice to couple his cause to that of Capel*, whose property and popularity in the town would give him a controlling interest if the non-residents were excluded, although he did wonder whether Capel* would always wish to retain him as a colleague. They petitioned to be returned together, 9 Nov., and John Gladstone used his influence to secure the attendance of his friends in his son's favour.[20] Gladstone peremptorily refused to make a last minute deal with Holmes which would have given him one of the seats in return for paying his opponent's expenses. He was seated, 2 Dec., and was again congratulated by the freemen for his independence. He took his seat, 6 Dec. 1830, and immediately began what was to be an almost constant attendance in the House by listening to the decision on the Liverpool election.[21]

Elected as an independent, Gladstone was ambivalent in his attitude to Lord Grey's newly installed ministry. After the resignation of the duke of Wellington, he had written that

at the same time that all must feel the late administration's inadequacy to the task before them, I cannot but look forward with a want of confidence to their successor, unless the Huskisson party has a strong voice in the cabinet. We are now on the eve of a new era in the principles that govern this country; and who can say where the spirit of innovation will stop.

He wished that Sir Robert Peel*, whose speeches he much admired, was still in office. He objected to Tennyson's proposed bill to enfranchise men paying rates for three years prior to an election, because it would deprive property of its due influence. He was, however, summoned by Lord Althorp, the government leader, to attend the meeting of Parliament, 21 Jan. 1831.[22] He kept his father fully informed on business issues and promised to send him regular bulletins from the House. He reported on the progress of Thomas Fowell Buxton's intended anti-slavery motion and related matters, the West India planters' lobbying against the planned reductions in the sugar duties and the proceedings on the Liverpool by-election. Although initially in favour of the Liverpool and Leeds railway bill, he decided to oppose it because it conflicted with the interests of other lines. On 8 Feb. 1831 he wrote that 'although ministers have disappointed many in the House, I think they will also have conciliated many by their conduct'; but four days later he thought them foolish to risk weakening themselves over the abortive tax proposals in Althorp's budget, 'when the great question is so near at hand, and for which all their force will be required at *least*'.[23]

As early as 10 Feb. 1831 Gladstone had heard a rumour of what the schedules in the reform bill, though not the numbers in each, would be, and he was dismayed by the prospect that Peel might oppose it in its entirety and so cause its defeat. He intended to vote against Lord Chandos's plan to enfranchise Birmingham at the expense of Evesham if it came to a division, 18 Feb., but only because all those proved guilty of bribery there had been non-residents. He also thought the existing privileges of resident freemen ought to be continued for life. He was 'caught' on the Oxford election committee, 22 Feb.[24] Prior to Lord John Russell's statement on reform, 1 Mar., he agreed with his father on the gloomy prospects for the country if it was not carried; but he was staggered by the scope of the proposals, and wrote that 'were it not expediency, or perhaps necessity, I should not hesitate in aiding to damn so bold a change in our constitution'. He now hoped Peel might endeavour to scupper the bill with a view to introducing a more moderate measure of his own. He wished for concessions from government, but thought that if Peel moved for its immediate rejection, he would have to support him rather than appear to sanction such immense changes. He liked his father's idea of uniting boroughs, and wanted voters in disfranchised towns to be able to vote for county Members during their lifetimes. On 9 Mar. he recorded: 'I find a great many Members whose views are similar to mine; that is, who will not vote for the second reading, unless prospects of concession are held out by ministers'. He believed that rejection was preferable to the irrevocable adoption of hasty and large-scale reforms and claimed that he would assign his reasons if he felt compelled to vote against the bill's committal.[25] He was appointed to the Londonderry election committee, 8 Mar., and was in the majority of six which voted to unseat Sir Robert Ferguson, 14 Mar. He voted against reduction of the sugar duties, 11 Mar., partly in order to show sympathy with the West India planters who wanted their sugar to be admitted for use in British distilleries. He successfully avoided appointment to other committees in order to leave himself free to attend that on Liverpool. He voted in the majority against government on the reduction of the timber duties, 18 Mar. 1831. When Capel* presented an anti-reform petition from Queenborough that day, Gladstone, despite being unwilling to commit himself publicly, 'said something on the subject, but there was a noise in the House and ministers paid me no attention'. Because Queenborough was in schedule A, he knew he was unlikely to be returned again there, and this no doubt coloured his opinion of reform. He was, however, prepared to present a petition from Sheerness requesting that the two Queenborough seats be transferred to the whole Isle of Sheppey, if any was forthcoming.[26]

The government's indication that the reform bill would be revised in committee allowed Gladstone to support it, but he reported that its loss seemed certain. When its second reading passed by only one vote, 22 Mar. 1831, he recorded:

I voted in the majority and, if any one turned the balance more than another, *I did*, for up to the moment of the division itself I was in hopes that some person, in whom I could place confidence and who might have weight in the House, would pledge himself to bring forward a substantial but moderate measure of reform, and, if such had been the case, it would have decided me in voting, without hesitation, *against the bill*. As it was, in spite of my own feelings and *prejudices*, I could not make up my mind to do what was tantamount to saying 'I will have no reform'. And I consider that I am still as unpledged to the details of the bill as I was this time yesterday.

He was unable to speak in the debate because of the number of Members trying to get a hearing. He thereafter believed that the bill could only survive if it was substantially altered in committee.[27] In letters to the editor of the *Morning Herald*, 24, 26 Mar., he categorically denied any corruption in Liverpool elections involving Canning and Huskisson, which his father thought was imprudently overstating the case. With Buxton's motion imminent, Gladstone was active in circulating his father's *Statement of Facts* on slavery.[28] He was again summoned by Althorp, 7 Apr., in order to support the reform bill in committee. He regretted not having risen to correct Lord Morpeth's misrepresentation of his father's views on the ultimate emancipation of the slaves, 15 Apr. He objected to any reduction in the number of English and Welsh seats, and therefore voted for Gascoyne's wrecking amendment to this effect, 19 Apr. The next day he wrote that

I was the more reconciled to doing so because ministers had up to last night declared that they did not consider the point a vital one and because I could not see why it should be made so, unless they were sufficiently wrongheaded to be determined on having nothing but their own plan of reform.

He wanted Peel to become prime minister and hoped that moderate reform might still be pursued. He spoke in denial of any past electoral malpractice at Liverpool, 21 Apr. 1831.[29]

Gladstone's standing in Queenborough had considerably deteriorated in the past year. He was far less generous than Capel* in forwarding patronage applications, contributing to the alleviation of distress within the town or assisting in the freemen's legal proceedings. Although desirous of a settlement between the select body and the burgesses, he sided with the former and thought the actions of those rebellious fishermen who had violently extorted concessions at a court leet were indefensible. He was angered by repeated demands for charitable and other financial contributions, with which he only grudgingly complied. His reluctance was heightened by the realization that Capel's property and standing in the town made it highly unlikely that he would ever be returned if Queenborough became a single Member constituency; by the end of February 1831 he had decided to follow his father's advice and make no further outlay, since his hold on the borough was so weak.[30] He recognized that his vote in favour of the reform bill, and thus for disfranchising Queenborough, had ruined his chances, even with his supporters among the resident freemen. His subsequent vote against the bill was not enough to undo the damage, and Breeze candidly told him, 23 Apr., that 'the general feeling with regard to you is by no means favourable, so much so that I can by no means recommend you to come forward again as a candidate for this place'.[31] A quarrel had long been brewing between Capel* and the Gladstones over how they were to divide their election costs and the row was made public when one disaffected supporter, John Hall, alleged that Capel* had bought Gladstone's seat for him, at a cost of £2,000. Without government or

Capel's assistance, Gladstone's position was hopeless, and although rumours did circulate that he wanted to come forward again, he refused to pledge himself to the cause of parliamentary reform. Queenborough had cost John Gladstone an enormous outlay for so short a Parliament, and with a similarly brief one expected, neither father nor son had much enthusiasm for another immediate attempt. In April 1831 Gladstone did consider other possibilities, including Reigate, but by then it was too late.[32]

Even when he had ceased to be a Member, Gladstone occasionally attended the House on matters affecting his father. He was thoroughly disillusioned with the Whig ministers, whom he once described as a 'set of miserable wavering inconsistent asses', and he became one of the founder members of the new Conservative club, the Carlton, in March 1832. He spent much of his time preparing the ground at Portarlington, where he was returned as a Conservative at the 1832 general election. He never achieved security in any of his subsequent constituencies, and did not sit again after being unseated for electoral corruption at Ipswich in 1842.[33] Throughout his life he remained a staunch Conservative and Evangelical, and so came to differ, at times bitterly, with his brother William, the Liberal prime minister and high churchman. He inherited a 45,000-acre estate at Fasque from his father in 1851, and thereafter lived the life of a country gentleman and devoted himself to Kincardine affairs.[34] He died in March 1889, and was succeeded by his only son, John Robert (1852-1926).

[1] S. Checkland, *The Gladstones*, 91-93. [2] Ibid. 132-5, 138-9, 201, 409-11; *Gladstone Autobiographica* ed. J. Brooke and M. Sorenson, 23. [3] Checkland, 163-4, 167. [4] St. Deiniol's Lib. Glynne-Gladstone mss 192, T. to J. Gladstone, 18 May, 28 Nov., 14 Dec. 1824; 193, same to same, 2, 25 June, 6 July, 10 Oct. 1825; 194, same to same, 12 Oct., 26 Nov. 1827, 12 Jan., 18 Mar., 11 Apr., 7 May 1828; Checkland, 167-70. [5] Glynne-Gladstone mss 192, T. to J. Gladstone, 21 Nov. 1828; 452, Llewellyn to T. Gladstone, 28 Mar. 1829; 453, Magrath to same, 13 July 1830; 1360; Checkland, 231. [6] For example, Glynne-Gladstone mss 196, T. to J. Gladstone, 18-20 Nov. 1830; Checkland, 193-4. [7] Checkland, 167, 205. [8] Glynne-Gladstone mss 192, T. to J. Gladstone, 5 July 1818, 14 Feb. 1821; 193, same to same, 20 Mar. 1825; 194, same to same, 3, 17, 22 Feb., 12, 16 Mar. 1827. [9] Ibid. 195, T. to J. Gladstone, 5 May 1830; Checkland, 170. [10] Glynne-Gladstone mss 195, T. to J. Gladstone, 26, 28, 29 June, 3, 5-9, 12 July 1830. [11] Ibid. 195, T. to J. Gladstone, 12 July 1830; 1308; 1311. [12] Ibid. 195, T. to J. Gladstone, 19-23, 26-28 July, Pennall to T. Gladstone, 20 July; 453, Merewether to same, 20 July 1830; 1309. [13] *The Times*, 28 July, 3 Aug.; *Morning Chron.* 5 Aug. 1830. [14] Glynne-Gladstone mss 195, T. to J. Gladstone, 8 Aug. 1830. [15] Ibid. 195, T. to A. Gladstone, 4 Aug., to J. Gladstone, 5-7 Aug. 1830; *Kentish Gazette*, 21 Jan. 1831. [16] Glynne-Gladstone mss 195, T. to J. Gladstone, 6, 7 Aug. 1830. [17] Checkland, 232; Add. 38758, f. 292. [18] Glynne-Gladstone mss 196, T. to J. Gladstone, 17, 18, 20, 27, 28 Sept., 1, 2 Oct. 1830. [19] Ibid. 453, Merewether to Gladstone, 25 Aug. 1830; 521. [20] Ibid. 196, T. to J. Gladstone, 25-27 Oct., 3 Nov. 1830. [21] Ibid. 196, T. to J. Gladstone, 19, 20, 26 Nov., 3, 6, 7 Dec.; 1311, Queenborough freemen to T. Gladstone, 21 Dec.; *The Times*, 3 Dec. 1830. [22] Glynne-Gladstone mss 196, T. to J. Gladstone, 18 Nov., 8, 21 Dec. 1830; 544. [23] Ibid. 197, same to same, 5, 7, 8, 11, 12, 15-20, 22 Feb. 1831. [24] Ibid. 197, same to same, 10, 18, 22-24, 26 Feb. 1831. [25] Ibid. 197, same to same, 1-5, 8-10 Mar. 1831. [26] Ibid. 197, same to same, 9, 10, 12, 14-19, 21 Mar. 1831. [27] Ibid. 197, same to same, 11, 14, 19, 22-24 Mar. 1831. [28] Ibid. 197, same to same, 24-26, 28 Mar.; 454; *Morning Herald*, 25, 28 Mar. 1831; Checkland, 234. [29] Glynne-Gladstone mss 198, T. to J. Gladstone, 14, 16, 19-22 Apr. 1831; 454. [30] Ibid. 198, same to same, 8 Aug., 24 Nov., 3, 12, 16 Dec. 1830; 197, same to same, 22, 24, 26 Feb., 10 Mar.; 521, same to Capel, 2 Jan., to Breeze, 27 Jan. 1831. [31] Ibid. 197, T. to J. Gladstone, 24, 25 Mar. 1831; 521. [32] Ibid. 197, same to same, 17, 29 Mar.; 198, same to same, 22-24 Apr., 7 May 1831; 521, J. Gladstone to Capel, 15 July, 17, 19 Aug. 1830; *Maidstone Jnl.* 26 Apr. 1831. [33] Glynne-Gladstone mss 199, T. to J. Gladstone, 1, 6, 9, 11, 27 Feb., 12, 16, 19 Mar., 16, 19 Apr. 1832; 200; 522; Checkland, 238, 258-9, 285, 332. [34] Checkland, 240, 260-1, 358, 368, 375, 377-8; *Gladstone Autobiographica*, 17; *Fortunes Made in Business*, ii. 139-40.

S.M.F.

GLENORCHY, Lord *see* **CAMPBELL, John**

GLYNNE, Henry (1810–1872), of Hawarden Castle, Flint.

FLINT BOROUGHS   22 Sept. 1831–16 Feb. 1832

b. 9 Sept. 1810, 2nd s. of Sir Stephen Richard Glynne, 8th bt. (d. 1815), of Hawarden and Hon. Mary Neville, da. of Richard Aldworth Griffin (formerly Neville)†, 2nd Bar. Braybrooke; bro. of Sir Stephen Richard Glynne, 9th bt.* *educ.* West Bromwich 1819-23; Eton 1823-6; Christ Church, Oxf. 1828. *m.* 14 Oct. 1843, Hon. Caroline Lavinia Lyttelton, da. William Henry Lyttelton†, 3rd Bar. Lyttelton, 1s. *d.v.p.* 4da. (2 *d.v.p.*). *d.* 30 July 1872.

Rect. Hawarden 1834; rural dean, Mold 1851; canon St. Asaph 1855.

Glynne, the youngest Member elected to the Commons in this period, was intended for the church and to succeed his maternal uncle George Neville Greville to the lucrative living of Hawarden to which the Glynnes, as lords of the manor, had the right of appointment.[1] A 'plain, stolid, ordinary member of a handsome, witty, original family', he had lost his father to consumption at an early age and spent his childhood in London and at Hawarden and his grandfather and guardian Lord Braybrooke's residences in Berkshire and Essex. He followed his elder brother Stephen to Eton, of which he complained: 'This place is really so dull, I really have nothing to do, no football or anything'.[2] However, he enjoyed having Nicholas Vansittart's* old room there and recalled that 'Walker's lectures on experimental philosophy interested me very much'.[3] Writing to Stephen, 3 Feb. 1825, his headmaster, E.C. Hawtrey, noted: 'Henry is very well, but not as diligent as could be wished. Do not tell him this. No, perhaps a hint from you might be of great use'.[4] Braybrooke, anxious to overcome his dislike of 'mathematics and close subjects', had him tutored by one Hutchings at Hare Hatch until Christ Church would admit him.[5] He was an undergraduate there and a day over 21, when Sir Edward Pryce Lloyd's elevation to the peerage as 1st Baron Mostyn, 10 Sept. 1831, created a vacancy for Flint Boroughs, where his father had twice been defeated. His brother, a declared reformer, aspired to the representation but was disqualified as sheriff.[6] Glynne was therefore suggested as Stephen's locum, but his candidature proceeded only after his aunt Caroline, the wife of Paul Beilby Thompson*, had been assured by the bishop of London that becoming a Member of Parliament would not compromise his intended career in the church:

He [the bishop] says if he accepts it only while his brother is sheriff, and gets the Chiltern Hundreds the day he [Stephen] goes out of office, he (if he was in his diocese) would not object in any way to ordaining him. The *worst* that could happen would be to delay his taking deacon's orders a few months, which would make no difference as to the time of his becoming priest, and that no bishop could object to ordaining him if he makes no violent radical speech on the hustings or in Parliament ... The bishop said Henry being so young, and there being so long a time *after* he leaves Parliament before he is of age for orders is all in his favour of being in Parliament for this short period.[7]

A 'baby in apron strings', his candidature was made known to a select few on the eve of the election, and he was nominated and returned unopposed with great pomp, 22 Sept.[8] The marquess of Westminster observed to Stephen, 8 Oct.:

He will hardly submit to an academical examination after his political initiation. He will find the latter [by] a good deal the most difficult of task of the two in these desperate times. He intends, however, I fancy, to reverse the French proverb and *sauter pour mieux simuler* and have you to bear the brunt of the storms that are gathering on the political horizon.[9]

Though delayed, the return arrived in time for Glynne to honour his election promise by voting for Lord Ebrington's motion of confidence in Lord Grey's ministry, 10 Oct. 1831; and being summoned by the leader of the House Lord Althorp, he divided for the revised reform bill at its second reading, 17 Dec. 1831.[10] His relations had dissuaded him from 'moving at the head' of the Flintshire radicals at the 28 Sept. county meeting, and he made no known parliamen-

tary speeches.[11] He resumed his studies at Oxford before taking the Chiltern Hundreds in February 1832, so making way for his brother.[12] He graduated later that year, was ordained as planned and assisted Stephen, whose heir-at-law he remained, at subsequent elections. However, apart from church disestablishment and the proposed union of the dioceses of St. Asaph and Bangor, which he opposed, politics held little interest for him, and he used much of his stipend of £4,000 a year as rector of Hawarden to finance five national and three Sunday schools locally and to employ three curates.[13] He officiated with his uncle at the double wedding of his sisters Catherine and Mary to William Ewart Gladstone[†] and George William Lyttelton[†] in July 1839, and was married to Lyttelton's sister in 1843. He did not remarry following her death in childbirth in 1850, although his name was linked with a Miss Lowther and the daughter of a local pit owner, Miss Rose, who became a governess to his daughters and threatened to sue him for breach of promise.[14] Plans for Hawarden to pass to the Gladstones were in place before Glynne, who predeceased Stephen, died suddenly and intestate in July 1872, after being caught in a thunderstorm. He was buried at Hawarden and commemorated there by a sermon, elegy and memorial.[15] Administration of his estate was granted to his daughter Gertrude Jessy (*d.* 1940), from 1875 the second wife of the 2nd Baron Penrhyn.

[1] Flint RO, Glynne mss D/HA/1/7-8. [2] J. Marlow, *Mr. and Mrs. Gladstone*, 19-21; NLW, Glynne of Hawarden mss 3967-97, 4382. [3] St. Deiniol's Lib. Glynne-Gladstone mss GG23, H. to S. Glynne [undated]; Glynne of Hawarden mss 3909. [4] Glynne of Hawarden mss 4370, 4596. [5] Ibid. 4422, 4586, 4604; Glynne-Gladstone mss GG23, H. to S. Glynne, 1829. [6] *Chester Courant*, 29 Mar. 1831; Glynne of Hawarden mss 5397, 5398, 5406, 5409; NLW, Coedymaen mss 220, 221; Mostyn of Mostyn mss 8129, 8139-45; Warws. RO, Pennant mss CR2017/TP463/1. [7] Glynne of Hawarden mss 5402. [8] Mostyn of Mostyn mss 8134-8; Glynne of Hawarden mss 5392, 5396, 5401, 5410; Pennant mss CR2017/TP463/2; H. Taylor, *Historic Notices of Flint*, 191; Glynne mss D/HA/1251, 1252; *Chester Chron.* 23 Sept.; *Chester Courant*, 27 Sept. 1831. [9] Glynne of Hawarden mss 5408. [10] Ibid. 5391, 5394, 5395, 5403, 5407. [11] *Mem. and Letters of Sir Thomas Dyke Acland* ed. A.H.D. Acland, 32. [12] *Caernarvon Herald*, 18, 25 Feb., 3 Mar.; *Chester Chron.* 24 Feb., 2 Mar. 1832. [13] D.R. Thomas, *Hist. Diocese St. Asaph*, i. 363-4; Glynne mss D/HA/1255; Glynne-Gladstone mss GG23, H. to S. Glynne, 17 June 1839; GG30, S. to H. Glynne, 20 July 1836; Glynne of Hawarden mss 4657. [14] *Gladstone Diaries*, iii. 305; v. 465, 474-5, 516, 529; vi. 134, 298, 583; Add. 44239, f. 362. [15] Glynne mss D/HA/1/9, 17; *Chester Chron.* 3, 10, 17 Aug. 1872; *Gladstone Diaries*, viii. 187; Add. 40440, f. 105.

M.M.E.

GLYNNE, Sir Stephen Richard, 9th bt. (1807–1874), of Hawarden Castle, Flint.[1]

FLINT BOROUGHS	25 Feb. 1832–1837
FLINTSHIRE	1837–1841
FLINTSHIRE	23 May 1842–1847

b. 22 Sept. 1807, 1st s. of Sir Stephen Richard Glynne, 8th bt., of Hawarden and Hon. Mary Neville, da. of Richard Aldworth Griffin (formerly Neville)†, 2nd Bar. Braybrooke; bro. of Henry Glynne*. *educ.* Eton 1820-3; Christ Church, Oxf. 1825. *unm. suc.* fa. as 9th bt. 5 Mar. 1815. *d.* 17 June 1874.
    Sheriff, Flint 1831-2, ld. lt. 1845-*d.*

In 1815 Glynne, a descendant of the Glynllifon family and the Welsh princes, who had been groomed from birth to play a leading role in Flintshire politics, inherited the prestigious 7,000-acre Hawarden estate purchased by Sir John Glynne† in 1653 and the baronetcy conferred on Williams Glynne† eight years later.[2] His mother was a cousin of the 2nd marquess of Buckingham, and her Neville and Grenville connections brought close ties with the Delameres of Aston Hall, the Williams Wynns of Wynnstay and the Cholmondeleys of Vale Royal, who took a particular interest in the progress of the Glynne children following their father's early death from consumption.[3] Glynne's guardians, his maternal grandfather Lord Braybrooke and Sir William Earle Welby† of Denton Hall, Lincolnshire, and his maternal uncle George Neville Greville and other trustees, arranged his education and ensured that the estate, which was worth £9,320 13s. 8d. a year in 1823, benefited through enclosure and was not impoverished during his minority.[4] Even at Eton, where he excelled in academic subjects on account of his remarkable retentive memory, Glynne had demonstrated the passion for church music and architecture which made him the premier ecclesiologist of his age, and he prepared detailed descriptions of churches he visited in Wales, the south of England and France, on which he corresponded with Robert Champion Streatfield and others.[5] Lady Williams Wynn, however, found him at 17

> too quiet and slow to shine on the stage or indeed off it. He still retains that singular indisposition to mix or associate even with his schoolfellows when they visit him, and will, I fear, never be popular, though I must admit that his peccadilloes are all negative ones.[6]

His residence at Oxford, where he first met his future brother-in-law William Ewart Gladstone† and counted Sir Thomas Dyke Acland* among his closest friends, was minimal, and churches remained his main interest; but despite Braybrooke and Thomas Grenville's† concurrence that he should not risk his health by taking a degree, he gained a third in classics in 1828.[7] His coming of age that September was one of the great county celebrations he so dreaded, and he afterwards followed his family to France, where he spent over £17,000 on pictures and antiques.[8] He travelled extensively on the continent, but had returned to Hawarden before strikes and mob violence rocked the Flintshire coalfield in December 1830, when he was one of the first coal owners to panic and seek military assistance.[9] A poor horseman, who shunned the chase, he was dubbed 'the topographical baronet' by Mrs. Edward Stanley and cut a sorry figure as a militia captain; but his rents held up well, and, as sheriff, 1831-2, he assumed a high profile by fostering well-publicized work creation schemes and attending the Chester Cambrian Society St. David's Day celebrations, 1 Mar. 1831.[10]

He convened and chaired the Flintshire reform meeting at Mold, 21 Mar., where he declared for the Grey ministry's bill, and the county petitioned Parliament in his name to avoid delay.[11] The county seat was newly vacant through the death of Sir Thomas Mostyn, when the bill's defeat, 19 Apr., precipitated a dissolution. Glynne was disqualified as sheriff from standing and he remained 'neutral' when Mostyn's nephew and eventual heir, Edward Mostyn Lloyd Mostyn, took the county and his father, Sir Edward Pryce Lloyd retained the Boroughs at the general election in May 1831.[12] His 'solid religious principle and determination to act on it in spite of everybody' were considered remarkable for his age and when Lloyd's elevation to the peerage at the coronation produced a vacancy in Flint Boroughs, he co-operated with him to see off possible challenges from David Pennant and William Shipley Conway and celebrated his twenty-fourth birthday by bringing in his younger brother Henry, for whom he was substituted directly his term of office as sheriff expired in February 1832.[13] To the regret of his kinsman Charles Watkin Williams Wynn*, he repeatedly professed his support for reform, retrenchment, protection and the abolition of sinecures, which the marquess of Westminster warned might only work to his advantage in the short term.[14]

He took his seat, 26 Feb., and although he made no speeches of note, he voted as expected to enfranchise Tower Hamlets, 28 Feb., and Gateshead, 5 Mar., for the third reading of the revised reform bill, 22 Mar., and for Lord Ebrington's motion calling on the king to appoint only ministers who would carry it unimpaired, 10 May 1832. He divided for the second reading of the Irish reform bill, 25 May, and presented petitions that day from Denbighshire and Flintshire against the government's proposals for Irish education. Nonconformists welcomed his vote against the government amendment to Buxton's motion for inquiry into colonial slavery, 24 May 1832. Lloyd Mostyn correctly complained that Glynne neglected county meetings and chose not to confide in him, and noted his closeness to the Grenville family: 'Uncle Beilby [Paul Beilby Thompson*] with whom he is domiciled, *seems* to be his first adviser'.[15] He did not vote when party allegiance was tested on the Russian-Dutch loan in July 1832 and, like Thompson, he promised to support Charles Williams Wynn in preference to the Whig Littleton for the expected vacancy in the Speakership.[16] Rumours of a peerage for Glynne proved false, and the enlarged Flint District constituency returned him unopposed as a Liberal at the general election in December 1832.[17] There was however, 'an impression ... that Sir Stephen is returning to Toryism', and he later claimed that 'in supporting the reform bill I always considered it as a *final* measure'.[18]

As a Liberal Conservative, Glynne was returned *in absentia* for Flint Boroughs in 1834, defeated Lloyd Mostyn to take the county in 1837, but lost to him in 1841, when allegations that he was guilty of buggery coloured a particularly bitter campaign.[19] He was seated on petition, but, virtually bankrupted by the failure in 1845 of his Oak Farm coal and iron works, he stood down at the dissolution in 1847. (He failed to recapture the seat as an 'independent' in 1857.)[20] Although Glynne was an intensely private man, in 1845 his brothers-in-law prevailed on him to accept Peel's offer of the county lieutenancy, and in 1847 he became the first president of the Cambrian Archaeological Association. He also served on the committee of the Ecclesiological Society and contributed to its publications; archaeological notes on over 5,000 churches in England and Wales are attributed to him.[21] He died suddenly of a heart attack in Shoreditch High Street, London in June 1874, so extinguishing the Glynne baronetcy, and was buried at Hawarden, commemorated by an effigy by Matthew Noble. The Gladstones, who had invested heavily in the Hawarden estate and resided there with Glynne, saw to the arrangements and executed his will and the settlement of 16 Dec. 1867, by which Hawarden passed to his nephew William Henry Gladstone† (1840-91).[22]

[1] For a detailed account of Glynne's life see A.G. Veysey, 'Sir Stephen Glynne, 1807-74', *Flint Hist. Soc. Jnl.* xxx (1981-2), 151-70. [2] W.E.B. Whittaker, 'The Glynnes of Hawarden', ibid. iv (1906), 32-36; NLW, Glynne of Hawarden mss 140; *Oxford DNB*. [3] NLW ms 2792-8 *passim.*; Glynne of Hawarden mss 25, 4364, 4384-6, 4590. [4] Flint RO, Glynne mss D/HA/1/8; Glynne of Hawarden mss 140, 296-300, 3901-8, 3910-66, 3973-8, 3984, 4366, 4347, 4594, 4757, 5758. [5] Glynne of Hawarden mss 34, 56, 57, 4348, 4353, 4358-75, 4597; St. Deiniol's Lib. Glynne-Gladstone mss GG27, S. to M. Glynne, 22 July 1826; *Archaelogia Cambrensis* (ser. 3), v (1874), 249. [6] *Williams Wynn Corresp.* 306. [7] *Gladstone Diaries*, i. 265; Glynne of Hawarden mss 142, 4390, 4406, 4424, 4562, 4591, 4604-7, 4758; NLW ms 2795D, C. to H. Williams Wynn [1826]; *Mem. and Letters of Sir Thomas Dyke Acland* ed. A.H.D. Acland, 22, 33. [8] Buckingham, *Mems. Geo. IV*, ii. 379; *Williams Wynn Corresp.* 369-70; Glynne of Hawarden mss 142, 4423; NLW ms 2796D, Lady Delamere to H. Williams Wynn, 6 Oct. 1828. [9] NLW ms 2797D, Lady Williams Wynn to H. Williams Wynn, 17 Aug. 1830, Lady Delamere to same [23 Jan. 1831]; 4817D, C. Williams Wynn to same, 1 Sept. 1830; Glynne of Hawarden mss 4836. [10] Glynne of Hawarden mss 4763, 4769, 4770; *Chester Courant*, 4, 11, 18, 25 Jan., 1, 8, 15, 22 Feb., 1, 8 Mar. 1831; Veysey, 153-4. [11] *Chester Chron.* 18, 25 Mar.; *Chester Courant*, 22 Mar. 1831; *CJ*, lxxxvi. 456. [12] Mostyn of Mostyn mss 7904, 7905, 7910, 7912, 7914, 7949; *Chester Chron.* 22, 29 Apr. 1831; H. Taylor, *Hist. Notices of Flint*, 191. [13] *Acland Mem.* 32-33; Glynne of Hawarden mss 5391, 5392, 5404; Warws. RO, Pennant mss CR2017/TP463/1-2; Mostyn of Mostyn mss 265, Lloyd Mostyn to fa. [1832]; 8128-46; *Chester Chron.* 23, 30 Sept. 1831, 24 Feb., 2 Mar. 1832; *Chester Courant*, 27 Sept. 1831, 21, 28 Feb. 1832. [14] NLW, Coedymaen mss 220, 221; Glynne of Hawarden mss 5396, 5397, 5408. [15] Mostyn of Mostyn mss 265, Lloyd Mostyn to fa. 17 Mar.; Glynne-Gladstone mss GG37, S. to Mary Glynne, 4 Apr. 1832. [16] Coedymaen mss 234. [17] *Caernarvon Herald*, 7 Apr. 1832; *N. Wales Chron.* 1 Jan. 1833. [18] Pennant mss CR2017/TP433/10; Glynne mss D/HA/1258. [19] Glynne of Hawarden mss 4650, 5417; *Chester Chron.* 11 Aug. 1837, 21 May, 4 June 1841; Glynne mss D/HA/1/6; *Gladstone Diaries*, iii. 112, 122-6. [20] *CJ*, xcvii. 291, 296; S.G. Checkland, *The Gladstones*, 314, 353, 359-60; J. Marlow, *Mr. and Mrs. Gladstone*, 29, 48-49; Glynne mss D/HA/1/19-20. [21] Veysey, 157-66; Glynne of Hawarden mss 4706; Add. 40564, ff. 276-80; 40566, f. 133; E.A. Pratt, *Catherine Gladstone*, 19. [22] *Chester Chron.* 20, 27 June 1874; Glynne mss D/HA/1/9, 17; 2/7-8, 23, 27, 29-31, 34, 39; *Gladstone Diaries*, viii. 501-2, 533, 555; ix. 8, 147.

M.M.E.

GODSON, Richard (1797–1849), of Inner Temple and 22 Woburn Place, Mdx.

ST. ALBANS	1831–1832
KIDDERMINSTER	1832–1834
KIDDERMINSTER	1837–1 Aug. 1849

b. 1 June 1797, 2nd s. of William Godson (*d.* 1822), attorney, of Tenbury, Worcs. *educ.* Worcester (Mr. Simpson); Caius, Camb. 1814; L. Inn 1818, called 1821; I. Temple 1822. *m.* 11 Aug. 1825, Mary, da. and h. of James Hargreaves of Springfield Hall, nr. Lancaster, 3s. 1da. *d.v.p.*[1] *d.* 1 Aug. 1849.

QC 6 July 1841; bencher, L. Inn 1841; counsel to admiralty and judge adv. of fleet 1844-*d*.

Little is known of Godson's antecedents. His father William Godson was an attorney in practice at Tenbury, Worcestershire, and in 1809 was elected one of the county coroners.[2] Two of his sons,

Stephen and Septimus Holmes Godson, were articled to him in 1812 and 1815 respectively; the latter subsequently entered Gray's Inn and became a barrister in 1837. William Godson died 19 Aug. 1822. By his will, dated 4 July that year, he left all his property to his wife Margaret, who was presumably the mother of his surviving children. His personalty was sworn under £3,000.[3] Septimus Godson was heavily defeated in the election for coroner precipitated by his death.[4] Stephen Godson, who practised as an attorney at Worcester, married Susannah, the daughter of Robert Coker of Dorset, and died 9 June 1839.[5]

On his call to the bar in 1821 Richard Godson went the Oxford circuit. In December 1822 he completed a substantial *Practical Treatise on the Law of Patents for Inventions and of Copyright*, which was published the following year. At the Worcester Michaelmas sessions of 1830 he defended ten Kidderminster carpet-weavers brought to trial for their part in recent riots in the town. He secured several acquittals and reductions of charges, though he made it clear at the close that he did not condone their conduct, which had been 'of the most illegal description'. The weavers of Kidderminster subsequently presented him with a handsome hearth rug as a token of their appreciation of his efforts.[6] When the Grey ministry's reform bill proposed the enfranchisement of Kidderminster as a single Member constituency in March 1831, Godson accepted an invitation from potential electors to stand for the borough, where there was 'the greatest enthusiasm in his favour', at the first election after the bill became law. While on the circuit early the following month, he entered Kidderminster in a triumphal procession and made a public statement of his political principles. As 'one of the people to represent the people', he applauded the reform bill, which would restore 'the good old constitution' and ensure that 'the voice of the people was heard before wars were commenced and taxes imposed'. He predicted that from it would stem 'every species of reform which could be desired', notably elimination of the 'defects' in the church establishment, the abolition of commercial monopolies and the implementation of free trade. On the question of slavery, he revealed a personal embarrassment, explaining that on his marriage to a Lancashire heiress he had been 'forced to take possession of' a £50,000 mortgage on a West Indian estate:

> I scorn the idea of having property in my fellow subjects. The government may declare the black population free upon any conditions that may be thought reasonable; I only ask that the lives of the white people, resident on the islands, may be protected. I shall therefore vote for an emancipation which will protect our colonial possessions,

and the best emancipator is the man who is willing to sacrifice his own interests.

He wanted reform of the criminal code to produce 'cheap and good law, but no distressing imprisonments'.[7] At the general election three weeks later he stood as a reformer for the open and venal borough of St. Albans and was returned with another supporter of the bill after a contest against the Tory sitting Member.[8]

Godson, who never joined Brooks's, rose with self-confessed 'fear and trembling' in the debate on the second reading of the reintroduced reform bill, 5 July 1831. He had no regrets about having given on the hustings a so-called 'unconstitutional pledge' to support the whole bill: 'we will stick to this bill, and the whole of this bill; because, if we do not carry this reform, we shall have no reform at all'. He forecast that the benefits of the measure would be 'the removal of discontent and disaffection, and the establishment of confidence in the legislature'. He voted for it next day, and against the adjournment, 12 July. Two days later he was given leave to go the circuit, which prevented him from supporting the reform bill in committee for five weeks, though he arranged a pair for the divisions of 26, 28 July, 3, 5 Aug., and probably for others. He was present to divide with ministers on details of the bill, 17, 18, 20 Aug., 2 Sept. On 24 Aug. he presented a petition from the inhabitants of St. Albans for reduction of the borough householders' voting qualification from £10 to £5; it was alleged by his enemies that the petition was 'a hole and corner affair'.[9] He voted for the passage of the bill, 21 Sept., for the second reading of the Scottish bill, 23 Sept., and, after giving 'a sumptuous entertainment' to his St. Albans supporters, 7 Oct.,[10] divided for the motion of confidence in the ministry, 10 Oct. He was in the minority of 12 opposed to the grant of compensation to Lescene and Escoffery for their expulsion from Jamaica, 21 Aug.; but he sided with government on the Dublin election controversy, 23 Aug. He made a technical point in favour of the bankruptcy court bill, 14 Oct. 1831. Godson welcomed the 'improvement' effected by the ministerial amendments to the revised reform bill, 17 Dec.1831, when he voted for its second reading after arguing that it was not 'a party question' and claiming that 'I am not connected with ministers any more than I am with the opposition'. He voted steadily for its details and made an observation on the clause dealing with the appointment of returning officers, 24 Jan., but he was treated with disdain by ministers when he seemed to be suggesting that it was necessary in point of law to inquire into the usages of each borough before passing the measure, 16 Feb. 1832. He presented the petition of Kidderminster political union in favour of the bill, 27 Feb., when he got leave to go the circuit. He paired for the enfranchisement of Tower Hamlets, 28 Feb., and the third reading of the bill, 22 Mar. He voted with government on the Russian-Dutch loan, 26 Jan., but was in the minorities for inquiry into distress in the glove trade, 31 Jan., and the production of information on military punishments, 16 Feb. He preferred inquiry by select committee to Fyshe Palmer's proposed bill to regulate the office of sheriff and reduce its expense, 14 Feb. Godson presented a petition from the freemen of Stafford against the general registry bill, 13 Apr., and spoke of the 'many objections' to Cripps's coroners bill, 7 May, when he was a teller for the hostile minority. On 8 May he gave notice of four amendments which he intended to propose in committee on the death penalty abolition bill, which he welcomed, 30 May, as 'a good beginning for ameliorating the severity of the law'. He attended and spoke at the St. Albans meeting to address the king to reinstate the Grey ministry, 16 May.[11] He voted for the second reading of the Irish reform bill, 25 May, but was in minorities for amendments to extend the franchise to £5 freeholders, 18 June, and to do away with the payment of municipal taxes as a prerequisite of registration, 29 June. He spoke and voted against Baring's bill to exclude insolvent debtors from Parliament, 6 June, feeling that it was not designed to effect its object, however laudable. He secured an alteration to the boundary proposed for the enlarged constituency of St. Albans, 8 June. On 29 June Godson, who had voted in the minority against government's temporizing amendment on the abolition of slavery, 24 May, defended the loan of £1,000,000 to Barbados, Jamaica, St. Lucia and St. Vincent to deal with losses and damage incurred in recent hurricanes. Claiming that many Jamaican planters were 'reduced to ruin', he deplored the unnecessary 'rancour' of some zealous abolitionists and appealed to ministers to decide once and for all whether they wanted to retain British colonies in the West Indies:

> If they are worth having, they must be treated in a kindlier spirit, and the planters must be enabled to cultivate their estates, not less for their own sakes than for the sake of the slaves themselves, whose emancipation, nevertheless, I should be glad to see.

That day he was given a week's leave to attend the quarter sessions. He was initially listed among reformers absent from the division on the Russian-Dutch loan, 12 July 1832; but it was subsequently reported that he had voted in the opposition minority.[12]

Godson published a *Supplement* to his book on the law of patents in late 1832; in the preface (p. iv) he expressed the hope that next session an effort would be made to create 'a good code of laws for the better protection of inventions'. There was some notion in July that he might stand for both St. Albans and Kidderminster at the general election, but he opted for the latter alone, and was narrowly returned there in December 1832 after a contest with a fellow reformer.[13] He was defeated in 1835, but came in again in 1837, by which time he had become a free trade Conservative. He produced a second edition of his *Treatise*, which he dedicated to Lord Brougham, in 1840.[14] He took silk in 1841 and obtained a legal appointment from Peel in 1844, but continued to harbour an unfulfilled desire for something better.[15] He died at Springfield Hall 'from disease of the heart' in August 1849.[16] By his very brief will, dated 4 Oct. 1836, he left all his property to his wife.[17] Two of his sons, Arthur Richard and George St. Alban Godson, entered the church. His nephew Augustus Frederick Godson, the son of Septimus, was Conservative Member for Kidderminster, 1886-1906.

[1] *Gent. Mag.* (1825), ii. 270. His da. Gertrude Louisa died, 'aged 7', 13 Apr. 1834 (ibid. (1834), i. 666). [2] T.C. Turberville, *Worcs. in 19th Cent.* 56. [3] *Gent. Mag.* (1822), ii. 286; IR26/908/1343. [4] Turberville, 57. [5] *Gent. Mag.* (1839), ii. 102; (1844), i. 221. [6] Turberville, 270, 273; *Berrow's Worcester Jnl.* 2, 9 Sept., 21, 28 Oct. 1830. [7] Turberville, 50-51; *Berrow's Worcester Jnl.* 10 Mar.; *Worcester Herald*, 12 Mar., 9 Apr. 1831. [8] *The Times*, 28, 29 Apr.; *Worcester Herald*, 30 Apr.; *County Herald*, 30 Apr., 7 May 1831. [9] *Bucks Gazette*, 3 Sept. 1831. [10] Ibid. 22 Oct.; *County Herald*, 15 Oct. 1831. [11] *County Herald*, 19 May 1832. [12] *The Times*, 14 July; *Berrow's Worcester Jnl.* 19 July 1832. [13] *County Press*, 3, 14 July; *Worcester Herald*, 24 Nov., 15 Dec.; *The Times*, 14 Dec. 1832. [14] Brougham mss, Godson to Brougham, 1 May 1840. [15] Add. 40589, f. 229. [16] *The Times*, 3 Aug. 1849; *Gent. Mag.* (1849), ii. 318. [17] PROB 11/2104/927; IR26/1836/661.

D.R.F.

GOOCH, Thomas Sherlock (1767–1851), of Bramfield Hall and Benacre Hall, nr. Beccles, Suff.

SUFFOLK   20 Feb. 1806–1830

b. 2 Nov. 1767, 1st s. of Sir Thomas Gooch, 4th bt., of Benacre Hall and Anna Maria, da. of William Hayward of Weybridge, Surr. *educ.* Westminster 1781; Christ Church, Oxf. 1785; continental tour, home 1793. *m.* 11 May 1796, Marianne, da. of Abraham Whittaker of Stratford, Essex, 2s. 3da. *suc.* fa. as 5th bt. 7 Apr. 1826. *d.* 18 Dec. 1851.

Sheriff, Suff. 1833-4.

Capt. Suff. vol. cav. 1798, 1803; maj. commdt. 4 Suff. yeoman cav. 1809; lt.-col. commdt. 2 E. Suff. militia 1814.

By 1820, when to cries of 'No Gooch' he secured his sixth unopposed return for Suffolk, 'Gaffer' Gooch, an anti-Catholic Tory opposed to reform, had acquired a reputation as an able speaker and ready defender of the landed interest and Lord Liverpool's ministry.[1] His family, long established in the county, had purchased the Benacre estate in 1745, and were also major owners of land and property in Birmingham, where their tenants included the brassfounder Samuel Walker† and members of the Lloyd banking and iron-founding dynasty.[2] Gooch had been made a commissioner in the exchequer bills loan office in 1817, and benefited in Suffolk politics from the aristocratic oligarchy's preference for bipartisan representation, the interest of his brother-in-law, the former county Member Sir John Rous† (1st earl of Stradbroke), his personal wealth, and his father's reputation as a staunch Pittite.[3] The latter, who still occupied Benacre, was to die virtually bankrupt in 1826, having already sold out to Gooch to try to ensure that his mistress and three illegitimate children were provided for.[4]

Gooch seconded and served as teller for the motion for a select committee on the distressed state of agriculture, which government was forced to concede, 30 May 1820. He criticized attempts 'to separate the interests of agriculture from the interests of any other great branch of the national industry' and branded the 1815 corn law as 'defective' and 'totally inoperative', but he acknowledged that while agriculture needed protection the country needed taxes. He was appointed to the committee, 31 May, only to find its brief restricted to reviewing current methods of computing average corn prices: they recommended substituting one national for 12 regional averages and including Irish corn in returns.[5] Declaring that her guilt was 'as plain as the sun at noonday', he made much of his refusal in December 1820 to present the hundred of Lackford's address to Queen Caroline, agitated by the former under-secretary of war and Foxite Whig Sir Henry Bunbury*; and this, together with his readiness to consult the patronage secretary Arbuthnot about the growing distress and disaffection in Suffolk, pleased ministers.[6] He divided with them against censuring their handling of the queen's case, 6 Feb., repeal of the additional malt duty, 21 Mar., 3 Apr., and parliamentary reform, 9 May 1821. Although absent from the division on 28 Feb. 1821, he remained staunchly anti-Catholic, and opposed all concessions, 30 Apr. 1822, 30 June 1823, 1 Mar., 24, 26 Apr., 9, 10 May 1825.

On 5 Feb. 1821, he asked the leader of the House, Lord Castlereagh, whether ministers planned any measures to relieve agricultural distress that session. Told that a committee of inquiry might be permitted as a conciliatory measure, he moved successfully for one and was appointed to its chair, 7 Mar. Countering his critics in the press, he said that he did not perceive agriculture, distress or his committee as party matters, stressed the need for protective tariffs on grain imports, and criticized the chancellor Vansittart's optimistic interpretation of returns showing an increase in malt production, which derived solely from the abundance of barley in 1820, when the wheat crop had been poor.[7] Parliamentary commitments kept him away from the Suffolk county meeting convened to petition for reform as a means of alleviating distress, 16 Mar. Though not selected to do so, he seconded the petition when it was brought before the House, 17 Apr., claiming that he owed ministers nothing; however, he dissented from much of its prayer.[8] On the 21st, clearly disillusioned, he informed the Birmingham banker and future political unionist Thomas Attwood† that the recent currency change 'was *intended* to operate a total transfer of the landed rental of the kingdom into the hands of the fundholders'.[9] His decision to second the motion for repeal of the agricultural horse tax, which was carried against government, 14 June, surprised some Whigs like Thomas Coke I, who regarded him as a Member who 'for so many years always supported ... ministers, who had stood by them imposing every tax during this period, and in passing every bill brought in by them'.[10] Gooch replied that his object was simply to compensate for the failure of his committee (which the liberal Tory William Huskisson and the political economist David Ricardo had succeeded in dominating) to instigate any measures to afford 'effectual relief to agriculture this session'.[11] His vote was a token protest, and he seconded and was a majority teller for Henry Bankes's pro-government amendment to the address on public expenditure, 27 June.[12] He had presided at the Pitt dinner at the *London Tavern*, 28 May, and in July 1821 was instrumental in establishing the Suffolk Pitt Club.[13]

Gooch publicized his correspondence with the treasury, who agreed to concessions on taxing malted grain, but it was not enough to satisfy the radical Joseph Hume* or his critics at Foxite dinners in January 1822. On 29 Jan. the Suffolk agricultural distress meeting chastised him for 'colluding with ministers' by chairing the ineffectual 1821 committee, and for his votes.[14] He tempered criticism by calling on all parties to unite to combat distress and distanced himself from the 1821 report, but failed to prevent the adoption of a petition linking reform to its call for remedial action.[15] The former Whig Commons leader Tierney rightly predicted that the hostility to ministers demonstrated by Gooch and his allies that session was largely bluff and bluster.[16] He voted against an opposition motion for tax reductions to alleviate distress, 11 Feb., and on the 15th presented and commended a petition for unspecified palliative measures from Suffolk occupiers 'who he was glad to say ... did not mix up their case with politics'. He again disowned the 1821 report when Lord Londonderry (Castlereagh) moved for a select committee on agriculture, to which he was appointed, 18 Feb.[17] He stated that he would support cuts in the establishment and 'tax reductions consistent with the national interest' only, and he voted against Lord Althorp's resolutions criticizing the inadequacy of the government's relief proposals, 21 Feb., and against reducing the salt duties, 28 Feb. After failing to upstage the Whig Sir Matthew White Ridley by reviving the malt question, he divided with him against government to reduce the admiralty lordships from six to four, 1 Mar.; he similarly voted to abolish one of the joint-postmasterships, 13 Mar. The Whig banker Hudson Gurney* still counted him among the most ministerial of the squires; and, according to *The Times*, his presence on the opposition benches for the debates on the malt and salt duties, 4 Mar., aroused much mirth.[18] He presented but dissented from the plea for reform in the Suffolk distress petition, 7 Mar., drawing criticism from Thomas Barrett Lennard for claiming that it was entirely the work of the Whig aristocracy, and from James Macdonald (who had attended the Suffolk meeting), for failing to vote against the salt duties as his constituents had requested and been led to believe he would.[19] On 1 Apr. Gooch brought up the agricultural committee's report which he had written with Bankes. Based entirely on the 1821 evidence, it recommended a 70s. pivot price with fixed countervailing duties, and advocated an agricultural bank and closer scrutiny of bonded warehouses to dictate supply, prices and the opening and closure of ports. Its failure to scrutinize the grain market or recommend tax reductions were severely criticized in the press.[20] On the 29th, presenting a second petition adopted at the Suffolk county meeting, he confirmed the severity of the economic downturn and reasserted the case for prohibitive tariffs on imported corn, as markets were glutted and 'nothing satisfactory to the country' had been achieved; he again dissented from the petitioners' claim that reform would assist their cause. In this he was backed by Edmond Wodehouse, who attributed Suffolk's demands for reform to William Cobbett's[†] recent tour of the county.[21] Hume and others, however, sought to undermine Gooch's contribution by criticizing his voting record on taxation. He lamented party

divisions and defended ministers, when the debate on agricultural distress resumed, 8 May, for 'all they could do was to stem the torrent of mischief which was inundating the country and prevent fluctuation in prices by means of protection', and he repeated his refrain that although tax reductions were 'desirable' as a means of relief, it was necessary to 'keep faith with the public creditor'. He attended Londonderry's funeral in August 1822 and, according to Viscount Clive*, deliberately distanced himself from the dissatisfaction that many country gentlemen expressed with government that summer.[22] However, after Canning derided him in speeches at Liverpool, calculated to boost his claim to become foreign secretary and leader of the House, *The Times* cautioned: 'Apply not wit ... to such as Mr. Gooch and his associates. It is worse than meddling with *uncle Toby's* hobby-horse: "Ah! touch him, touch him, touch him – not"'.[23]

Gooch was appointed to the select committee on the game laws, 13 Mar., an issue discussed at the Suffolk reform meeting at Stowmarket, 4 Apr. 1823, when he was heckled for using ministerial patronage to procure the living of South Cove for his son Charles and clashed with Bunbury over his failure to support reform.[24] He voted with government against repeal of the Foreign Enlistment Act, 16 Apr., and divided against the usury laws repeal bill, 27 June. In August 1823 he rallied support at a Suffolk Pitt Club dinner.[25] He voted against abolishing flogging in the army, 5 Mar. 1824. On the 13th, referring to the 'great ability ... displayed by ministers', he seconded a successful spoiling amendment to the opposition's motion for information on the French evacuation of Spain and claimed that Britain had been correct not to interfere on behalf of the Spanish liberals.[26] He made numerous patronage applications to the home secretary Peel (on behalf of the inventor of the life buoy Captain Manby, the corporation of Beccles and others) and in February 1825 he used his influence with government to save John Thurston from becoming sheriff, an appointment that Bunbury then failed to avoid.[27] He raised no objection to the receipt of a contentious City of London petition for revision of the corn laws with which he disagreed, 25 Apr., and used it as bait to draw a response from Huskisson.[28] He spoke strongly against Whitmore's motion to remove protection, 28 Apr., now citing 60s. and 30s. a quarter as reasonable pivot prices for wheat and barley, and arguing that the 'present system ... with all its imperfections ... worked well and afforded the farmer a fair remunerating price', and that great reductions in taxation would be necessary if protection was to be abolished. Reports of his speech caused alarm in Suffolk, and in May he wrote to the local press to explain that 'all he admitted was that 60s. a quarter was the least possible remunerating price for wheat that a British grower could afford to accept', and reaffirmed his commitment to the 1822 rates.[29] He helped to secure a 5s. concessionary tariff on Canadian wheat, 2, 9 June 1825.[30] When the Staffordshire potteries petitioned for corn law repeal, 2 Mar. 1826, he insisted that '50-60s. a quarter' was 'no more than a fair remunerative price' and argued for protection as a means of encouraging corn growing to keep gold in the country in times of scarcity. He voted against the bill empowering the government temporarily to admit warehoused corn, 11 May. He opposed a cut in the grant for the yeomanry, 'the constitutional force of the country', 8 Mar. 1826. He was returned unopposed at the general election in June, although he encountered criticism and questions about his stance on the corn laws and the Holy Alliance. He maintained that he 'never let party interfere when he could render any service' and that his politics were 'unchanged and unchangeable'.[31] He had consulted Peel beforehand about a scheme, to which the duke of Richmond objected, for his eldest son Edward Sherlock Gooch[†] (1802-56) to be brought in for Aldborough at the next opportunity on his son-in-law Andrew Lawson's[†] interest.[32]

On 26 Feb. 1827 Gooch presented a series of Suffolk petitions for agricultural protection, deliberately and provocatively based on the president of the board of trade Huskisson's 1814 pamphlet promoting the 1815 corn law. He declared that he no longer sought 'total exclusion' and would be satisfied with a 70s. pivot price and 17s. duty.[33] He reiterated his protectionist principles in the corn debates of March following Lord Liverpool's stroke, claiming that while 'he wished to see the present administration continue in their places', he was 'not so chained down to any administration as not to give his vote against it if he disapproved of its measures'. He joined Sir Thomas Lethbridge and Sir Edward Knatchbull in doing so (for which the 'three baronets' were duly lampooned), 2 Apr., when, venting his spleen against political economists, he suggested using the latter as ballast for every vessel leaving the country after discharging its cargo of wheat. However, the baronets' attempt to discredit Canning in debate, 6 Apr., backfired.[34] On the 18th, at celebrations marking the return for Ipswich on petition of the anti-Catholic Tories Charles Mackinnon and Robert Adam Dundas, Gooch acknowledged that hitherto he had been 'a party man' and still saw advantage in a party system; but now that Canning headed the ministry he could no longer tell 'to what party I belong'. He declared that he remained duty bound to oppose all Catholic concessions, as he had done in the division on 6 Mar.[35] He described Canning as

a political cuckoo: he had laid his political egg, and his political friends have unconsciously nursed it into life and action, till at length, to prevent their necks being broken they have deserted their nests and flown away. All I can now hope is that the cuckoo having possession of the nest, he will not feather it to the exclusive advantage of his friends and the detriment of the country.[36]

Presiding at the 'spiritless' Pitt dinner at the *London Tavern*, 28 May 1827, he deplored Liverpool's political death and eulogized the duke of Wellington and Lord Eldon.[37]

Gooch welcomed Peel's return to the home office in Wellington's coalition ministry, but regretted Eldon's omission from the cabinet.[38] He was in Paris for his eldest son's wedding, 23 Jan. 1828, but, knowing that a new corn bill, for which John Drage Merest[†] and his Bury St. Edmunds allies lobbied, was in preparation, he sent Wellington a printed report from the Suffolk magistracy supporting his own contention that calculations should be based on prices received by the growers rather than on market prices. Wellington's polite but dismissive reply, 27 Mar., made it clear that the existing principle would be adhered to.[39] Undeterred, Gooch repeated his 'strong predilection in favour of the old law' when government introduced the new resolutions, 31 Mar., and presented and endorsed petitions from Suffolk reasserting his views, 25 Apr., 14 May. When the resolutions were read a second time, 29 Apr., he spoke against government, whom he attacked for not heeding the needs of the small landowner, took a swipe at the paternalism of the Whig aristocracy, and attributed current problems to a premature return to a metallic currency.[40] He was appointed to the committee of inquiry into the law on parochial settlement, 21 Feb., and supported the bill to regulate settlement by hiring, 29 Apr., stating that 19 out of 20 such cases brought before him as a magistrate depended on hiring and service. He presented petitions from Suffolk for repeal of the 1827 Malt Act, 28 Mar., protection for the woollen trade, 19 May, and the abolition of slavery, 30 May, 2, 10 June. Hume, noticing him in the House, 8 July, prompted general laughter by welcoming him back 'after a long absence'.[41] He brought up petitions against Catholic claims and the admission of Dissenters to high office, 25 Apr., and divided against Catholic relief, 12 May 1828. His diehard views remained unchanged when Wellington and Peel conceded emancipation in 1829. He promised to 'do my best to defeat it unless the bill contain more and fuller securities than I have at present reason to suppose it will', 10 Feb., presented hostile petitions that day and again, 12 Feb., 10, 27 Mar., and voted against the measure 6, 18, 23, 27, 30 Mar., but refrained from making a major speech on the issue. The chancellor of the exchequer Goulburn later confirmed his continued adherence to the ministry.[42]

Gooch appears to have had no difficulty in collecting his own rents but, recognizing his constituents' 'unparalleled distress', he stifled their proposals to meet 'by the hundred', signed the Suffolk Tories' requisition for a single county meeting and delayed his return to Parliament to attend it on 6 Feb. 1830. Wellington was informed that he proposed to moderate their petition; he also avoided voting on the omission of distress from the king's speech, 4 Feb. 1830.[43] On the hustings at Ipswich he concurred in the proposed petition's demands for protection, lower taxes, and 'the severest retrenchment in every department of the public expenditure' and described how his experience of the 1821 and 1822 agricultural committees had taught him to oppose free trade and distrust political economy. He attributed current difficulties to the precipitate return to the gold standard in 1819 and insufficient protection for agriculture. His promises to support repeal of the malt tax and retrenchment were interpreted as pledges to vote for them and cheered.[44] He presented distress petitions from five east Suffolk parishes calling for repeal of the taxes on beer and malt, 8 Feb., but merely testified to the 'genuine nature' of their grievances.[45] Bringing up the county petition, 5 Mar., he described himself as a 'declared supporter of administration' anxious to retain them in office, who deplored the omission from the king's speech of distress which was undeniable and should not be concealed. He repeated charges that ministers were too closely allied to free traders and that the protection afforded by the corn laws was totally inadequate for the small landowner, but Goulburn took solace from his pronouncement that the worst effects of the currency change were over.[46] When agrarian distress became an issue in the debate on the state of the nation, 19 Mar., he moved a wrecking amendment, but waived it for a government amendment to adjourn until the 23rd.[47] He presented petitions for repeal of the malt and beer duties and action against distress, 22 Mar., and when the debate was resumed, 23 Mar., declared that he would vote against the proposed inquiry. However, because 'it is the lower orders, the labouring and productive classes, who are suffering most severely', he pressed the need for tax reductions and suggested a modified five per cent property tax, but refrained from tabling it as an amendment. He introduced and was a majority teller for the Southwood Haven bill, from which Edward stood to profit, 3 May.[48] He presented a petition for equalization of the duties on rum and corn spirits, 12 May. He divided against Jewish emancipation, 17 May, and voted to make forgery a non-capital offence, 24 May. On the sale of beer bill, he voted for amendments granting magistrates greater licensing powers, 15 May, and to restrict on-consumption, 21 June 1830. He was still counted among the ministry's supporters at the dissolution.

His constituents, meanwhile, had failed to find proof that Gooch's promises of 6 Feb. 1830 were being translated into votes for economy and retrenchment, although, as the *Bury and Norwich Post* commented, 'whether he voted *against* the propositions, we have no means of ascertaining; for but few of the lists of "majorities" have made their appearance'. He also failed to dispel the damaging effects of allegations that he had used his position to acquire church livings for his son and sons-in-law and that he had put his party before his county and done nothing to 'endanger the permanency of the administration'.[49] Rous had died in 1827, the Tory 3rd marquess of Hertford refused to intervene, and at the general election Gooch lost his seat to one of his erstwhile supporters, Charles Tyrell, a liberal Tory prepared to sanction religious toleration and 'moderate reform', and ally of the Felixstowe merchant, the Tory Samuel Sacker Quilter, who, at the county meeting (6 Feb.) had accused Gooch of attending solely to the agricultural interest.[50] The patronage secretary Planta lamented Gooch's defeat, which he attributed 'to local matters and to his inattention to certain interests in the county'.[51] According to his partisan Lord Lowther*, 'Gooch's sin with his constituents was in abstracting himself from the government'.[52] He told his supporters:

> I carry with me into private life, the proud satisfaction of having, to the utmost extent of my abilities, promoted those measures which in my judgement have been best calculated to give stability and permanence to our valuable institutions in church and state; and to secure the prosperity of the British empire: and I can conscientiously say that in the discharge of my duty to my constituents in particular, and to the local interests of the county of Suffolk, I have ever most anxiously and unremittingly attended.[53]

Cobbett's 1830 lecture tour provided some justification for Gooch's claim 'that every art has been used by some itinerant orators to enrage the yeomanry of Suffolk against me'.[54] He retained considerable support among the Anglican clergy and the aristocracy, particularly in the eastern half of the county, but it had become impossible for him to obtain a hearing at public meetings, and he accordingly had to forego opportunities to stand for the county in 1831, when, recanting, he declared for moderate reform, and again for its eastern division in 1832.[55] He became sheriff in 1833 and chaired the quarter sessions until 1843. His patronage requests to Peel had little success, but he remained active in Conservative politics in Ipswich and in East Suffolk, which returned Edward as a Conservative in 1846. He died at Benacre in December 1851, leaving property in Birmingham, Norfolk and Suffolk to Edward, who succeeded him as 8th baronet and received £23,000 as residuary legatee.[56]

[1] *HP Commons, 1790-1820*, iv. 34-36; *Suff. Chron.* 26 Feb., 4, 11, 18 Mar.; *Ipswich Jnl.* 18 Mar. 1820; A. Mitchell, *Whigs in Opposition*, 79. [2] Birmingham City Archives mss 3449, 3609; [NRA 13644]. [3] *HP Commons, 1790-1820*, ii. 366-7; W.P. Scargill, *Peace of the County* (1830), 4-10. [4] *Bury and Norwich Post*, 12 Apr. 1826; PROB 11/1717/533; IR26/1085/708. [5] B. Hilton, *Corn, Cash, Commerce*, 102, 104. [6] *Bury and Norwich Post*, 15 Aug. 1820, 3, 10 Jan. 1821; *The Times*, 4 Sept. 1820, 5 Jan. 1821; Add. 38574, ff. 232, 235; *HMC Bathurst*, 490, 493-4. [7] *The Times*, 2 Mar. 1821; Mitchell, 79, 160. [8] *Ipswich Jnl.* 17, 31 Mar.; *The Times*, 21 Mar., 18 Apr. 1821. [9] C.M. Wakefield, *Life of Thomas Attwood* (1885), 81. [10] *The Times*, 15 June 1821. [11] J.E. Cookson, *Lord Liverpool's Administration*, 304-5; *Quarterly Rev.* xxv (1821), 466-70; Hilton, 104-9. [12] *The Times*, 28 June 1821; Hilton, 138-9. [13] *The Times*, 29 May; Essex RO, Barrett Lennard mss D/DL/C61, Barrett Lennard to fa. 20 May 1821; Suff. Coll. [BL 1034. m. 1.], f. 199. [14] *The Times*, 11, 16, 26 31 Jan. 1822; Hilton, 144. [15] *Ipswich Jnl.* 19, 26 Jan., 2 Feb. 1822; *Oakes Diaries* ed. J. Fiske (Suff. Recs. Soc. xxxiii), ii. 272; Mitchell, 162. [16] Grey mss, Tierney to Grey, 23 Jan. 1822. [17] *The Times*, 19 Feb., Hilton, 106-7. [18] Gurney diary, 28 Feb.; *The Times*, 5 Mar. 1822. [19] *The Times*, 8 Mar. 1822. [20] Ibid. 4 Apr. 1822; Hilton, 151. [21] *Cobbett's Rural Rides* ed. G.D.H. and M. Cole, i. 48. [22] *The Times*, 21 Aug.; Devon RO, Sidmouth mss, Clive to Sidmouth, 22 Aug. 1822. [23] *The Times*, 31 Aug., 2 Sept., 23 Nov. 1822. [24] *Ipswich Jnl.* 29 Mar., 5 Apr.; *The Times*, 7 Apr.; *Bury and Norwich Post*, 9 Apr. 1823. [25] *Bury and Norwich Post*, 27 Aug. 1823. [26] *The Times*, 14 Mar. 1824. [27] Add. 40356, f. 50; 40357, f. 261; 40363, f. 231; 40367, ff. 88, 102, 127, 174; 40373, f. 1. [28] *Arbuthnot Jnl.* i. 389; *The Times*, 26 Apr. 1825. [29] *Bury and Norwich Post*, 1 May 1825. [30] *Huskisson Pprs.* 181-5. [31] *The Times*, 9 June; *Bury and Norwich Post*, 14, 21, 28 June 1826. [32] Add. 40387, ff. 52-53. [33] *The Times*, 27 Feb. 1827. [34] G.I.T. Machin, *Catholic Question in English Politics*, 98-99; Nottingham Univ. Lib. Denison diary, 6 Apr.; *The Times*, 6 Apr. 1827; B. Gordon, *Economic Doctrine and Tory Liberalism, 1824-30*, pp. 4, 59; Mitchell, 187. [35] *The Times*, 26 Apr. 1827. [36] *Bury and Norwich Post*, 25 Apr. 1827. [37] *The Times*, 29 May 1827. [38] Add. 40375, ff. 15, 19. [39] Wellington mss WP1/925/51; *Bury and Norwich Post*, 18 Jan, 19 Mar.; *The Times*, 1 Apr. 1828. [40] Gordon, 65. [41] *The Times*, 9 July 1828. [42] Wellington mss WP1/1051/10. [43] *Bury and Norwich Post*, 27 Jan. 1830; Wellington mss 1083/13. [44] *Bury and Norwich Post*, 3, 10, 17 Feb. 1830. [45] *The Times*, 8 Feb. 1830. [46] Ibid. 6 Mar. 1830. [47] NAI, Leveson Gower letterbks. M. 736, Leveson Gower to Singleton, 20 Mar. 1830. [48] *Suff. Chron.* 24, 31 July, 7 Aug. 1830. [49] *Bury and Norwich Post*, 10 Feb., 31 May, 16, 30 June, 7, 14, 21, 28 July; *Suff. Chron.* 17 July 1830. [50] Add. 60288, f. 282; *Bury and Norwich Post*, 11, 18 Aug.; *The Times*, 12, 14 Aug. 1830. [51] Add. 40401, f. 125; Wellington mss WP1/1134/6. [52] Lonsdale mss, Lowther to Lonsdale, 12 Aug. 1830. [53] *Ipswich Jnl.* 14 Aug. 1830. [54] *Cobbett's Rural Rides*, i. 618; *Bury and Norwich Post*, 8, 15 Sept. 1830. [55] *The Times*, 28 Apr. 1831, 23 Jan., 15 July, 20 Dec. 1832; TNA 30/29/9/5/80; *Ipswich Jnl.* 4, 25 Feb.; CUL, Vanneck-Arc2/5, J. Wood to Arcedeckne [June-Dec.] 1832. [56] Add. 40494, ff. 301-3; 40569, ff. 152-4; *Bury and Norwich Post*, 24, 31 Dec.; *Illustrated London News*, xix (1851), 762; PROB 11/2147/119; IR26/1929/49.

M.M.E.

GORDON, Charles, Lord Strathavon (1792–1863), of Orton Longueville, Hunts.

EAST GRINSTEAD	13 May 1818–1830
HUNTINGDONSHIRE	1830–1831

b. 4 Jan. 1792, 1st s. of George, 5th earl of Aboyne [S], and Catherine Anne, da. and coh. of Sir Charles Cope, 2nd bt., of Brewerne, Oxon. *educ.* St. John's, Camb. 1812. *m.* (1) 20 Mar. 1826, Lady Elizabeth Henrietta Conyngham (*d.* 24 Aug. 1839), da. of Henry, 1st Mq. Conyngham [I], *s.p.*; (2) 9 Apr. 1844, Maria Antoinetta, da. of Rev. William Peter Pegus, 7s. (1 *d.v.p.*) 7da. (1 *d.v.p.*). *styled* Lord Strathavon 1794-1836, earl of Aboyne 1836-53. *suc.* fa. as 10th mq. of Huntly [S] and 2nd Bar. Meldrum [UK] 17 June 1853. *d.* 18 Sept. 1863.

Ld. of bedchamber 1826-30, in waiting 1840-1.

Ld. lt. Aberdeen 1861-*d.*

Capt. Hunts. yeoman cav. 1817.

Strathavon was again returned for East Grinstead in 1820 on the interest of his aunt, Lady Whitworth, widow of the 3rd duke of Dorset. He continued to support the Liverpool ministry, but was a very lax attender. He voted in defence of ministers' conduct towards Queen Caroline, 6 Feb., and against Catholic relief, 28 Feb. 1821, 30 Apr. 1822, 25 Apr., 10 May 1825. He paired against mitigation of the punishment for forgery, 23 May 1821. He voted against the abolition of one of the joint – postmasterships, 13 Mar. 1821. He was in the ministerial minorities against inquiry into the prosecution of the Dublin Orange rioters, 22 Apr., and the Scottish juries bill, 20 June 1823. His next recorded vote was for the Irish unlawful societies bill, 25 Feb. 1825. He divided against the Irish franchise bill, 26 Apr. 1825.

In March 1826 Strathavon married Lady Elizabeth Conyngham, the daughter of the king's mistress. He had first proposed to her in May 1824, according to Mrs. Arbuthnot, who commented: 'I think they will accept him. He is a very good natured rattle and I think, considering all her adventures, she will be fortunate to end in this manner'.[1] His offer was in fact refused, but he persisted and Lady Williams Wynn informed her daughter, 11 Dec. 1825: 'the Strathavon marriage is ... again at a hitch, Lord Aboyne saying that he has since the last time of asking paid £10,000 for his son's debts, and cannot therefore make his allowance what he then offered'. Later that month she reported the 'renewal of contracts', which had 'probably been facilitated by royal interference'.[2] Certainly the king took a lively interest in the match, suggesting in an enigmatic letter to Sir William Knighton that Lord Conyngham's 'great glee' at Lord Aboyne's final approval of the settlement was founded on his ignorance of some unspecified problems concerning it.[3] It was thought that Lady Elizabeth's fortune was £80,000. The family's Huntingdonshire residence at Orton Longueville was 'assigned' to them.[4] Williams Wynn implied that Strathavon was seriously ill at this time, but he recovered and was appointed a lord of the bedchamber after the marriage.[5]

He was returned again for East Grinstead in 1826 on the interest of the new patrons, Lords de la Warr and Plymouth. He voted against Catholic relief, 6 Mar. 1827, 12 May 1828, and repeal of the Test Acts, 26 Feb. 1828. He was in the Wellington ministry's majority against reduction of the salary of the lieutenant-general of the ordnance, 4 July 1828. Planta, the patronage secretary, expected him to vote 'with government' for their concession of Catholic emancipation in 1829, but he 'stayed away' (a report that he had divided in the hostile minority, 6 Mar., was false).[6] He voted against the transfer of East Retford's seats to Birmingham, 11 Feb., and Lord Blandford's parliamentary reform motion, 18 Feb. 1830. At the 1830 general election he confirmed earlier rumours by contesting his native Huntingdonshire, with the support of the Sandwich interest and the retiring Member William Henry Fellowes. George Day, a leading county Whig, informed Lord Milton*: 'I learn from Strathavon's agents that no expense will be spared, that success is their object and that they are reckless of money to attain it'. He was attacked by the independents as a servile Tory courtier, but he pointed out on the hustings that he had relinquished his bedchamber post on the death of George IV. He overcame the challenge of the Whig John Bonfoy Rooper* to finish in second place.[7] The Wellington ministry of course numbered him among their 'friends', but in early November Lady Granville reported that he would vote for reform in the anticipated confrontation on the issue.[8] However, he sided with government in the division on the civil list which brought them down, 15 Nov. 1830. The following day he presented a Petworth petition for the abolition of slavery. He was granted a month's leave of absence 'on account of the disturbed state of his county', 2 Dec. 1830. He presented a tradesmen's petition complaining of the duty on carts, 11 Feb. 1831. He was granted a further two weeks' leave to attend the assizes, 7 Mar. 1831. On his return, he voted for the second reading of the Grey ministry's reform bill, 22 Mar., before facing a county meeting called to discuss the question, 2 Apr. He there described himself as a 'friend to reform', but, to general disapproval, vowed to vote against the bill's third reading unless it was 'altered to meet the views

of all'.[9] He voted with ministers against Gascoyne's wrecking amendment, 19 Apr. 1831, and presented the county's reform petition, with which he had been reluctantly entrusted, 20 Apr. In debate the same day he concurred in Sir Richard Vyvyan's comments on the desirability of allotting more time for such presentations and the 'inconvenience' of lengthy discussions on the validity of individual petitions.

Strathavon's lukewarm support for reform brought about his political downfall at the 1831 general election, for it alienated the Huntingdonshire Tories while failing to convince the reformers. Rooper wrote to Milton, 'I am uncharitable enough to think we must attribute his vote on reform to an habitual subserviency to courts and ministers [rather] than to any regard for, or conviction of, the necessity of the measure'.[10] The lingering faint possibility of Whig endorsement for his candidature disappeared when in his address he pledged himself merely to 'support the bill as it corrects abuses', but to 'consent to nothing that will endanger the constitution in church and state'.[11] This statement was enough to placate Lady Sandwich, who had threatened to withdraw support, but not the duke of Manchester, who refused to exercise his influence in Strathavon's favour.[12] According to one report

> Lord Strathavon spoke rather violently at the close of poll ... with great bitterness against those who had deserted him, and said that other persons had run away from the fight in other places; but in this county, the freeholders should turn him out, and he would keep the poll open till they did so.[13]

He finished a distant third, and subsequently retired from public life.[14] His father became 9th marquess of Huntly in 1836.

Widowed in 1839, Strathavon remarried five years later. In 1848, on the occasion of Queen Victoria's visit to Alwyne Castle, the family seat in Scotland, his wife's half-sister, Lady Charlotte Guest, commented on his father

> old Lord Huntly, who has fitted up two rooms and taken up his residence there ... It was a melancholy sight. There in the house of his ancestors, now little more than a ghostly ruin, amidst the fine old property which he has so comparatively wrecked! ... His noble-minded son, struggling himself with poverty, coming up with his beautiful wife from their inn lodgings, to meet *there* on that almost haunted ground, which he holds only by the sufferance of reigning creditors and trustees. But some day, though the estate be crippled irremediably, it is to be hoped it will revive under Lord Aboyne's good rule and brave exertions.[15]

He succeeded to the marquessate in 1853 and died in September 1863, leaving his wife pregnant with their 14th child. He was succeeded in the peerage by his eldest son Charles Gordon (1847-1937).

[1] *Arbuthnot Jnl.* i. 317. [2] *Williams Wynn Corresp.* 331-2; Add. 52017, J.R. Townshend to H.E. Fox, 20, 29 Nov. 1825, 6 Jan. 1826. [3] *Geo. IV Letters*, iii. 1228. [4] *Huntingdon, Bedford and Peterborough Gazette*, 7 Jan.; Add. 52017, Townshend to Fox, 17 Jan. 1826. [5] *Williams Wynn Corresp.* 335. [6] Grey mss, Howick jnl. 10 Mar.; Gurney diary, 6 Mar. [1829]. [7] Fitzwilliam mss, Day to Milton, 23 June; *Huntingdon, Bedford and Peterborough Gazette*, 24, 31 July, 7, 14 Aug. 1830. [8] *Countess Granville Letters*, ii. 67. [9] *The Times*, 5 Apr. 1831. [10] Fitzwilliam mss, Rooper to Milton, 24 Apr. 1831. [11] *The Times*, 10 May 1831. [12] Hunts. RO, Sandwich mss Hinch/8/149/1-7; 161/1. [13] *The Times*, 10 May 1831. [14] *Huntingdon, Bedford and Peterborough Gazette*, 7, 14 May 1831. [15] *Letters of Lady Charlotte Guest* ed. Lord Bessborough, 219-20.

H.J.S.

GORDON, James Adam (1791–1854), of Naish House, Wraxall, Som. and Moor Place, Much Hadham, Herts.

TREGONY	1830–1831
TREGONY	25 Feb. 1832–1832

b. 16 Apr. 1791, o.s. of James Gordon[†] of Moor Place and Harriet, da. of Samuel Whitbread I[†] of Bedwell Park, Beds. *educ.* Harrow 1805; St. John's, Camb. 1809. *m.* 24 Sept. 1832,[1] Emma Katherine, da. of V.-Adm. Thomas Wolley of Clifton, Bristol, *s.p. suc.* fa. 1822. *d.* 4 Mar. 1854. Sheriff, Som. 1830-1; recorder, Tregony 1830.

Gordon's family had made their fortune in the West Indies in the eighteenth century and purchased plantations there and landed estates in England. On the death of his father (a Tory Member despite his marriage to a sister of the advanced Whig Samuel Whitbread) in 1822, he inherited property in Somerset and Hertfordshire, while the personalty, which was sworn under £100,000, was sold in order to purchase more land in England. A survey of his West Indian inheritance in 1824 showed that he owned 885 acres (with 460 slaves) in Antigua, 421 acres in St. Vincent and 112 in St. Kitt's.[2] He became laird of Knockspock and Terpersie, Aberdeenshire, in succession to a cousin in 1836.[3] At the general election of 1826 he offered for Tregony against the interest of the Whig patron, the 3rd earl of Darlington, and he was involved in a double return made by rival mayors. The Commons confirmed the election of his opponents, 29 Nov. 1826, and his petition was unsuccessful.[4] He subsequently purchased Darlington's property in the borough and was installed as recorder, 8 Apr. 1830.[5] His ambition was to be returned for Somerset and he canvassed the county in the summer of 1829. According to Henry Hobhouse

of Hadspen, he was 'nearly unknown' in the county and his politics were 'quite so', his father had 'cut his throat', his 'mother (who was Whitbread's sister) is deranged', and 'the young man himself has been under restraint'; his 'only pretension ... seems to be in the length of his purse'.[6] In the event, his appointment as sheriff in 1830 precluded him from standing at the general election that summer, and he returned himself and a friend for Tregony, despite local opposition.[7]

The duke of Wellington's ministry listed him as one of the 'good doubtfuls' with the additional note that he was 'a friend'. He voted with them in the crucial division on the civil list, 15 Nov. 1830. He divided against the second reading of the Grey ministry's reform bill, which proposed the disfranchisement of Tregony, 22 Mar., and for Gascoyne's wrecking amendment, 19 Apr. 1831. At the ensuing general election he retired and returned Charles Arbuthnot, son of the former Tory minister, in his place. However, this appears to have been a temporary arrangement and in February 1832 he required Arbuthnot to vacate, a decision that the latter's father deplored 'on public grounds', as 'it would have been wiser ... to have ... done it during the recess', and he had 'chosen the exact moment when it will produce the worst effect'. Gordon was returned at the resulting by-election, although he again faced local opposition.[8] He divided against the enfranchisement of Tower Hamlets, 28 Feb., and the third reading of the revised reform bill, 22 Mar. 1832. *The Times* listed him as having paired for increased Scottish county representation, 1 June.[9] It is not clear if he was the 'Hon. Capt. Gordon' who paired against ministers on the Russian-Dutch loan, 12 July 1832. He is not known to have spoken in debate. At the dissolution later that year he disappeared from the House along with Tregony.

Gordon died in March 1854. He left Stocks House, near Ware, Hertfordshire, and its surrounding estates to his wife, and instructed that the remainder of his property be sold to pay for a very large number of individual bequests and annuities, with the residue going to his wife. Knockspock and Terpersie passed to his nephew, Henry Percy Gordon (*d.* 1876), but the fate of his West Indian plantations is not known.[10]

[1] IGI (Herts.). [2] PROB 11/1655/195; IR26/904/282; V.L. Oliver, *Antigua*, ii. 22-28. [3] D. Wimberley, *Fam. of Gordon of Terpersie*, 17-18. [4] *West Briton*, 16 June 1826. [5] Ibid. 4 Apr. 1828, 9 Oct. 1829; *PP* (1835), xxiii. 650. [6] Dorset RO, Fox-Strangways mss D/FSI, box 332, Gordon to Ilchester, 27 Sept. 1829; Add. 40399, f. 310. [7] *West Briton*, 6 Aug. 1830. [8] Aberdeen Univ. Lib. Arbuthnot mss, Arbuthnot to son, 1 June 1831, 16 Feb.; *R. Cornw. Gazette*, 3 Mar. 1832. [9] *The Times*, 4 June 1832. [10] PROB 11/2193/451; IR26/1995/359; Wimberley, 17-18.

T.A.J.

GORDON, **James Edward** (1789–1864), of 5 York Street, St. James's Square, Mdx.

DUNDALK   1831–1832

b. 11 Mar. 1789, 3rd s. of James Gordon of Littlefolla, Fyvie, Aberdeen and Ann McDonald of Coclarachie, Abernethy, Perth. *m.* 25 Oct. 1836, Barbara, da. of Samuel Smith*, 2s. 1da. *d.v.p. d.* 30 Apr. 1864.
  Vol. RN 1804, midshipman 1806, master's mate 1810, lt. 1811, ret. 1815.

Gordon followed his elder brothers George and Peter into the navy, where he saw action in the Mediterranean and off the Spanish coast, before obtaining command of the *St. Lawrence*, a captured American schooner, 16 Nov. 1814. While carrying dispatches concerning the peace between Britain and the United States, 14 Feb. 1815, his vessel was taken after 'a desperate action' with the American privateer *Chasseur* in the Gulf of Florida. Gordon, who commended his captors' 'humane and generous treatment', was 'honourably acquitted' at his subsequent court martial in Bermuda, 21 Apr. 1815, but he retired from active service the next day on half-pay.[1] Thereafter Gordon, who had developed contacts with the Clapham Sect and the Glasgow Evangelical preacher Thomas Chalmers, busied himself with naval charities before turning his attention to the 'state of Popery' in Ireland, where he undertook numerous tours 'to obtain accurate information', particularly with regard to 'scriptural education' and 'the number of scholars under the Sunday School and Hibernian Societies'.[2] 'You may implicitly rely on any facts he states to you', John Maxwell Barry* informed the new home secretary Peel, 29 Dec. 1821, 'though perhaps you may not entirely agree in the conclusions he draws from them. He was, when he came over, a very strong advocate for Catholic emancipation, but his opinion is, I believe, now much changed'.[3]

On 13 Jan. 1824 Gordon, who had been campaigning steadily for a commission on Irish education, notified Peel of his 'perfect willingness to contribute the results of a four years investigation ... either on a commission or before a committee ... without regard to emoluments'. In March he reported his belief that 'there lives not in Irish society so immoral and disorderly a class of persons as the schoolmasters conducting the hedge and priests' schools'.[4] He protested at being passed over as a commissioner, 10 Apr. 1824, citing his 'intimate and particular acquaintance with the Roman Catholic and Protestant systems', his 'practical connection with the "local system" of the celebrated Dr. Chalmers' and 'the *liberality*' of his principles.[5] That

summer he and the Baptist Wriothesley Noel began another tour of 'about six months' for the Hibernian Society, with whose 'operations in Ireland' he professed an 'intimate acquaintance'.[6] The disruption of their meetings by the Catholic Association in September led to accusations in the House of their 'being the cause of general disturbance in Ireland', a charge which Gordon vigorously denied in a letter to Peel condemning the Association for spreading 'sedition, blasphemy and scurrilous invective', 21 Feb. 1825.[7] Speaking similarly before the commission on Irish education, 22 Feb., 12, 16 Apr. 1825, he praised the work of the Kildare Place Society, the London Reformation Society and the Hibernian and other Sunday school societies of which he was a member, but insisted that he had visited Ireland 'in a private capacity' to 'promote the moral improvement of the county' and not 'any institution in particular'.[8] A firm advocate of the need to proselytize the Irish Catholics, in May 1827 he established the British Protestant Reformation Society to 'attract popular attention to the errors of the Romish creed' and promote scriptural education in Ireland, where he continued to travel widely in his capacity as honorary secretary.[9] An admirer later recalled:

> The Lord raised up and sent forth a young naval officer, who had faith to believe that the sword of the spirit could cut its way through the sophisms of Papal superstition ... Ten of the best years of his life were chiefly spent in Ireland, in the attempt to render Protestantism aggressive.[10]

At the 1831 general election Gordon came forward for Dundalk as the nominee of the 3rd earl of Roden, vice-president of the Reformation Society, in order, asserted the Catholic press, 'to pour the last drop of bitterness into the cup of insult'. He was returned unopposed.[11] He is a 'strange selection' and 'so obnoxious to the Irish people', complained Richard Sheil*, who pledged to contest Dundalk at the next election.[12] Gordon has 'promised us ... to nail his flag to the mast for church and constitution and *not to be put down*, but I suppose Sheil will ... try to silence him', observed Charles Thackeray to the Irish primate, 4 June 1831.[13] In the House, 9 Sept. 1831, Gordon was described by the Grey ministry's Irish secretary Smith Stanley as 'chiefly remarkable for his over zeal on religious matters'. He asserted that a petition from the National Union presented by Hunt was illegal and called for a 'more vigorous method of dealing' with such 'atrocious incitements to rebellion', 28 June. Next day he contended that political unions were 'founded upon the jacobinical principles of the *Rights of Man*' and had no

other object than 'the subversion of the British constitution'. 'Gordon has begun to harangue us, and promises to be a bore of the first order', recorded Thomas
Macaulay.[14] He refuted allegations that he had identified Hume personally with 'seditious publications', 1
July, but pointed to the link between the societies he
'patronises and the publications in question'. He voted
against the second reading of the reintroduced reform
bill, 6 July. On the 12th he moved for an adjournment
of the debates, arguing that 'the House is not at the
present hour' able 'to give a favourable hearing to even
the most able and influential Members', which was
defeated 328-102, and voted again to the same effect at
least twice. Next day he denied any 'factious motives'
in his conduct, denounced the bill as 'revolutionary'
and destructive 'of every guarantee which is essential to the security of property and the existence of
society', remonstrated against the enfranchisement
of Dissenters and Catholics (warning that they would
'use the influence you give them against the church')
and ranted that the bill was supported by 'every
infidel' and 'all that is diseased, infected and degraded
in the country'. He divided for use of the 1831 census
to determine the disfranchisement schedules, 19 July,
and to postpone consideration of the inclusion of
Chippenham in B, 27 July. He voted against the bill's
third reading, 19 Sept., its passage, 21 Sept., and the
second reading of the Scottish bill, 23 Sept. 1831.

In a clash with Daniel O'Connell, 12 July 1831,
Gordon claimed that 'resistance to the payment
of tithes' in the south of Ireland had resulted in
'some most respectable clergymen' being 'starved
out of their localities'. He defended the work of the
Kildare Place Society, 14, 15 July, when, in response
to charges by James Grattan that he did 'not belong
to the country of which he speaks', he replied that
he had 'travelled through the length and breadth of
Ireland'. He denied that the Orangemen who had
fatally opened fire at Banbridge were guilty of murder,
as they had 'acted in self-defence', 18 July, and contrasted that event with 'the want of anxiety' shown
when murder was committed by Catholic priests,
3 Aug. He presented a petition from Dundalk ship
owners against 'excessive stamp duty upon policies
of insurance', 19 July. That day he moved unsuccessfully to print one from Glasgow Protestants against
the grant to Maynooth College, which he alleged promoted 'doctrines contrary to pure scripture', 5 Aug.
He condemned the 'indulgence' shown to the Rev.
Robert Taylor who stood accused of blasphemy, 22
July, and remonstrated that he had held up the religion of his country to 'contempt and abhorrence', 15
Aug. He repeatedly refuted O'Connell's allegations

that the Carlow grand jury had drunk anti-Catholic
toasts and, in a heated exchange with Sheil, that he
had personally stated 'that the Catholic peasantry
were still so bigoted to believe that their priests had
the power to turn them into hares or goats', 9 Aug.
'We gave Sandy Gordon a great dressing yesterday',
O'Connell boasted to a friend next day.[15] On 11 Aug.
he denounced a Waterford petition of protest at the
massacre at Newtownbarry for its 'charge against
the whole of the yeomanry' and, in a fracas which
prompted the intervention of the Speaker, protested
that Sheil had acted 'in an unparliamentary manner,
and his language is not that adopted in the society
of gentlemen'. He complained of a breach of privilege by publications describing Hunt as the 'opponent of the rights of the people' and himself as 'the
author of many ... blasphemous articles', 12 Aug.
He voted for the motion of censure against the Irish
government for using undue influence in the Dublin
election, 23 Aug. He rebutted O'Connell's 'inflammatory' assertions that the yeomanry's fatal action at
Newtownbarry was 'premeditated', 26 Aug, 9 Sept.,
3 Oct. He praised the Society for the Suppression
of Vice for checking 'the trade in licentious publications' and their 'advantageous effect on the morals of
society', 5 Sept. That day he voted against the issue
of the Liverpool writ. He moved unsuccessfully for
the printing of a petition from Newcastle-upon-
Tyne presbytery against the Maynooth grant and, in
another intemperate exchange of which the Speaker
despaired, regretted that 'he was not a match' for
O'Connell 'in the language of the fish-market', 9 Sept.
He again spoke and voted against the grant, 26 Sept.
On 9 Sept. he attacked Smith Stanley's proposals to a
create an Irish board of education and, in response to
charges by Henry Grattan that he was 'entirely ignorant of Ireland' and 'merely the nominee of a noble
Lord', retorted that he 'would rather be the nominee
of the footman of the noble Lord, than the nominee'
of O'Connell. He divided for inquiry into the effects
of the Sugar Refinery Act on the West India interest, 12 Sept. He threatened that 'if night after night
we are to have propositions for the abolition of the
property of the church', he would 'read the oath taken
by Members of the Roman Catholic persuasion', 14
Sept. He accused Catholic priests of inciting resistance to tithes and praised the 'Christian forbearance'
of the 'established clergy of Ireland', many of whom
'had been obliged to sell their libraries', 6 Oct. He
defended the wording of a petition which applied 'the
epithet "impious" to the Roman Catholic religion', 12
Oct. He postponed his motion on blasphemous and
seditious libels the following day, when he warned that

Westminster's 'refusal to pay parochial rates will soon be followed by a like refusal to pay the national taxes'. He welcomed a petition against the Indian pilgrim tax on the ground that 'all sanction to idolatrous ceremonies ought to be withheld by a Christian government', and objected to the 'equalization of religion in Lower Canada', which 'should remain a Protestant state', 14 Oct. He presented a Surrey petition against the proposed reform of Irish education, 17 Oct. 1831.

Gordon argued that reform petitions from political unions could not 'be admitted on any grounds of legislative distinction or of common sense', 16 Dec. 1831. He voted against the second reading of the revised reform bill the following day, opposed its details, and divided against the third reading, 22 Mar. 1832. On 18 May he admonished its supporters for appealing to the 'people out of doors' and predicted that 'the work of demagogues and incendiaries, and of political unions' would 'prove too strong for their masters', so that 'ere long a practical lesson may be applied to those who countenance their lawless proceedings'. He warned that radical publications were 'gradually maturing the people for the horrors of a rebellion' and pledged 'week after week, to bring them down to this House, and hold up their libels and calumnies to public observation', 21 May. He voted against the second reading of the Irish reform bill, 25 May, observing that he was 'one of those old-fashioned bigots who still stand up for Protestant ascendancy in Ireland'. He insisted that the measure would drive the Protestants who 'comprise 4/5ths of the population' into a 'collision with men to whom they are politically and religiously opposed', 6 June. He condemned an Edinburgh reform meeting as 'disgraceful', 1 June, and was in a minority of 39 to preserve the voting rights of Irish freemen, 2 July 1832.

He voted against government on the Russian-Dutch loan, 26 Jan., 12 July 1832 (as a pair). He welcomed the motion of Spencer Perceval for a general fast, 26 Jan., and following its ridicule in the press complained of a 'confederacy against the introduction ... into this House' of 'religious topics' and the 'lax and latitudinarian principles of the present day', 31 Jan. He argued that control over cholera outbreaks in Scotland should reside with 'the authorities in Edinburgh', 15, 16 Feb., when he demanded that the prevention bill include a reference to 'Almighty God', on which he hoped the House would divide 'in order that it may be known out of doors who are those who are enemies to the Christian religion'. He was in a minority of 13 against the anatomy bill, 27 Feb. He condemned petitions against the payment of Irish tithes as 'tissues of

misrepresentation', for which he was called to order by the Speaker, 15 Mar. He welcomed an Aberdeen petition against the 'rash and dangerous' Maynooth grant, 11 Apr., and presented others in similar terms from Stirling and Falkirk, 3 July, and Glasgow, 10 July. He was appointed to the select committees on public petitions, 9 May, and Irish outrages, 31 May. He complained of the 'prevailing neglect of the observance of the Sabbath by the example of persons high in authority', 14 June, and called for a select committee on the subject, 28 June, to which he was appointed, 3 July. He voted against permanent provision for the Irish poor through a tax on absentee landlords, 19 June. He spoke and voted against the Irish party processions bill, 25 June, declaring that he was 'as great an enemy to Orange processions' as the Catholics, but believed 'interference with them uncalled for' and 'imprudent'. He was not prepared to support the Scottish and Irish vagrants removal bill unless he succeeded in introducing 'a clause limiting the liability of the English parishes for casual poor', 4 July. He presented petitions from Brailsford for the abolition of slavery and the Maynooth grant, and for better Sabbath observance, 10 July, and one from St. Pancras for rescheduling parish meetings which fell on Sundays, 17 July. That day he was in a minority of two against inquiry into the inns of court. He seconded a motion for returns on cholera, which he believed had 'increased to an extent which ought to call for a daily report from the board of health', 23 July, and was in a minority of 16 against the bill to disqualify the recorder of Dublin from Parliament the following day. He spoke and was a minority teller against printing a 'most calumnious' petition against using troops to enforce Irish tithe payments, 3 Aug. 1832.

Throughout 1832 Gordon campaigned furiously against the new system of Irish education, on which he addressed *Six Letters on Irish Education* to Smith Stanley, denouncing its 'heaven-daring aggression upon the principles of the reformed faith' and '*desertion* of Protestantism in the moral contest in which it is at this moment engaged' (pp. 65-66). He accused the board of 'Roman Catholics, Churchmen, Presbyterians and Socinians' who had compiled the 'book of extracts from scripture for the instruction of the Protestant youth of Ireland' of being 'mutilators of the text of the Bible', 6 Mar., and over the ensuing months made good his threat of 14 Mar. to cover the table with petitions against the plan. He declared that the scheme was supported by 'the free thinker in religion, the radical in politics, and all that is morally infected, debased, and degraded in society', 28 Mar., and reproached ministers for adopting a system which was 'opposed not only to the intimations of the Bible itself, but to the very first principles of Protestantism', 4 Apr. He moved for returns of schools operating under the new scheme, 10 Apr., 5 July, and complained of the lack of opportunity to bring up further hostile petitions, 18 Apr. He praised the conduct of Mr. Synge of county Clare, a member of the Reformation Society, who had been 'fired at' because he 'felt it his duty, as a Protestant, to promote the education of the children on his estate', and declared that the 'influence of the priesthood is, at the present moment, directing the assassin's knife, and sending hundreds of persons to a premature grave', 21 May. He defended Chalmers for refusing to endorse 'a system of national education which was not founded on scriptural truth', 23 May, and proclaimed, 'If I am bigoted, I may claim the company of the established churches of England and Ireland, of the synod of Ulster, and of the kirk of Scotland', 5 June. He apologized 'for the frequency with which a sense of duty has compelled me to intrude myself upon the attention of the House on the momentous question of Irish education', 8 June, but vigorously denied being 'actuated either by feelings of religious bigotry or political partisanship', 5 July. He spoke and was a teller for the minority of 17 against the Irish education grant, 23 July, and declared that 'a more mischievously exclusive and party spirited system has never ... been introduced into any country under the name of national education', 28 July 1832. That month Macaulay described being in the Commons smoking room

> in the vilest of all vile company, with the smell of tobacco in my nostrils and the ugly, hypocritical, high-cheeked, gaunt, vulgar face of Lieutenant Gordon before my eyes ... That confounded, chattering, blackguard ... has just got into an argument about the church with an Irish Papist who has seated himself at my elbow, and they keep such a din that I cannot tell what I am writing. There they go. The lord lieutenant, the bishop of Derry, Macgee, O'Connell, your Bible meetings, your agitation meetings, the propagation of the gospel, Maynooth College, the seed of the woman shall bruise the serpent's head. My dear Lieutenant, you will not only bruise but break my head with your clatter. Mercy! Mercy!

A few days later he recorded a verse which was 'in the mouth of every Member':

> If thou goest in the smoking room,
> Three plagues will thee befall,
> The chlorate of lime, and the bacco-smoke
> And the captain who's worst of all,
> The canting sea captain,
> The lying sea captain,
> The captain who's worst of all.[16]

At the 1832 general election Gordon retired from Dundalk and, after an abortive canvass for Trinity College, Dublin, stood as a Conservative for Nottingham, where he was beaten soundly by two Liberals. He unsuccessfully contested Paisley at the by-election of March 1834. In a letter to the new premier Peel, in which he bemoaned his inability to secure a seat at the 1835 general election, Gordon praised the work of the *Record*, an Evangelical publication to which he was a frequent contributor, and offered a series of observations on religious reform originally intended for the duke of Wellington, in which he warned that Protestantism was 'the moral cement of the constitutional structure, destroy that cement and the venerable fabric becomes a dislocated and shapeless ruin'.[17] That year he helped to launch the Protestant Association, of which he was a central figure until 'symptoms of a very serious illness' forced him to retire from public life. Enjoying a temporary recovery of health in the 1840s, he wrote numerous letters to the *Record* calling for a repeal of Catholic emancipation, which later appeared as *British Protestantism: its present rights and duties* (1847).[18] In 1844 he condemned Peel, again prime minister, for his Dissenters' chapels bill, which he prophesied would place him, 'the Conservative government' and 'the nation under the ban of the Divine wrath':

> You are acting in complete ignorance of the moral guilt of the transaction to which you have but too hastily lent the sanction of your name and authority ... The unequivocal approbation of a handful of Socinian infidels will be found but a sorry compensation for the forfeited confidence and alienated feeling of all that is holy and righteous in the land.

Peel replied:

> Mr. Gordon would act more in conformity with the spirit of the religion which he professes were he less peremptory in imputing moral guilt to those who conscientiously differ in opinion from himself, and less presumptuous in undertaking to predetermine who are the proper objects of Divine vengeance.[19]

In his last known work, *Original Reflections and Conversational Remarks on Theological Subjects* (1854), Gordon warned his readers that Popery was 'the most malignant type of moral evil which has entered our world, and the deadliest foe to the Christian and constitutional liberty of British Protestantism' (pp. vi-vii).

Gordon died a widower and intestate at 20 Porchester Square, Bayswater, London, in April 1864. Administration of his estate was granted to his second son, the Rev. George Maxwell Gordon of Beddington, Surrey, a noted Protestant missionary in the Punjab.[20]

[1] C.O. Skelton and J. M. Bulloch, *Gordons Under Arms*, 179; W. O'Brien, *Naval Biog.* i. 410; G. Coggeshall, *Hist. American Privateers*, 367; E. Maclay, *Hist. American Privateers*, 298-300; E. Statham, *Privateers and Privateering*, 314-15. [2] J. Wolffe, *Protestant Crusade*, 34-35; Add. 40344, f. 205; 40356, ff. 94, 166. [3] Add. 40344, f. 205. [4] Add. 40360, f. 87; 40363, f. 89. [5] Add. 40364, f. 80. [6] Add. 40366, f. 255. [7] Add. 40373, f. 240. [8] *PP* (1825), xii. 707-8. [9] Wolffe, 35-59. [10] C.B. [Charlotte Ward], *Dawn and Sunrise: brief notes on the life and death of Barbara Sophia Gordon* (1860), 6-7. [11] *Dublin Evening Post*, 14 May 1831; Wolffe, 37. [12] *Sketches, Legal and Political* ed. M. Savage, i. 352; *Drogheda Jnl.* 24 May 1831. [13] PRO NI, Pack-Beresford mss D664/A/245. [14] *Macaulay Letters*, ii. 58. [15] *O'Connell Corresp.* iv. 1834. [16] *Macaulay Letters*, ii. 156-8, 160. [17] Add. 40413, f. 140. [18] Wolffe, 149, 221; *Dawn and Sunrise*, 8. [19] Add. 40546, f. 127. [20] *Gent. Mag.* (1864), i. 810; A. Lewis, *George Maxwell Gordon, the Pilgrim Missionary of the Punjab* (1889).

P.J.S.

GORDON, Sir James Willoughby, 1st bt. (1772–1851), of Niton, I.o.W.

LAUNCESTON   17 Mar. 1829–5 Apr. 1831

b. 21 Oct. 1772, 1st s. of Capt. Francis Gordon (formerly Grant), RN and Mary, da. of Sir Willoughby Aston, 5th bt.†, of Risley, Derbys. *m.* 15 Oct. 1805, Julia Lavinia, da. of Richard Henry Alexander Bennet† of North Court, Shorwell, I.o.W., 1s. 1da. KCB 2 Jan. 1815; *cr.* bt. 5 Dec. 1818; GCH 1825; GCB 13 Sept. 1831. *d.* 4 Jan. 1851.

Ensign 66 Ft. 1783, lt. 1789, capt. 1795, maj. 1797; lt.-col. 85 Ft. 1801; asst. q.m.g. at Chatham 1802; lt.-col. 92 Ft. 1804; mil. sec. to duke of York as c.-in-c. 1804-9; lt.-col. commdt. R. African Corps 1808, col. 1810; q.m.g. 1811-*d.*; maj.-gen. 1813; col. 85 Ft. 1815; col. 23 Ft. 1823; lt.-gen. 1825; gen. 1841.

Gordon, the author of *Military Transactions of the British Empire* (1809), saw active service in Ireland, the West Indies and at Gibraltar. He was present as a volunteer with Lord Hood's fleet at the siege of Toulon in 1793, witnessed the capture of French forces at Bantry Bay in 1796 and commanded the first battalion of the 85th Foot during the occupation of Madeira in 1801.[1] As military secretary to the duke of York he gave what Thomas Creevey* regarded as 'pompous, impudent evidence' to the Commons inquiry into the Mary Anne Clarke affair.[2] Lord Palmerston*, who as secretary at war clashed with Gordon on administrative matters, described him as 'a devilish clever active fellow, but inordinately vain and self-opinionated'. He was 'an old friend and frequent correspondent' of Lord Grey, whose father had been his commanding officer, and it is possible that in 1811 he aspired to Palmerston's place in the event of the regent appoint-

ing a Whig ministry. In 1812 he was sent to the Peninsula as Wellington's quartermaster-general, but 'his behaviour ... was so arrogant, and his role as the "particular friend and confidential informant" of the Whig opposition in England so disloyal, that he had to be sent back home' after a few months.[3] He was quartermaster-general at Horse Guards for the rest of his life and was awarded a baronetcy in 1818.

During the 1820s he became close to Wellington and corresponded with him on military matters even when the duke was out of office. He supplied private information regarding Grey's attitude towards the Goderich coalition ministry in 1827, and urged Grey in January 1829 not to move into opposition to Wellington's ministry, which he correctly believed was prepared to act on Catholic emancipation.[4] Two months later he was returned for Launceston on the interest of the 3rd duke of Northumberland, his wife's cousin, on the understanding that he would support the government. In his speech of thanks he declared that the Catholic question was 'one of a purely civil nature', that Catholics were 'worthy of being admitted to places of trust and power' and that as long as Protestantism was 'established on the genuine principles of the gospel' it would 'spread [and] triumph over every region of the globe'.[5] He duly divided for emancipation, 30 Mar. 1829. That summer he wrote to Wellington proposing his son as a candidate for Cambridge University.[6] He voted against the transfer of East Retford's seats to Birmingham, 11 Feb. 1830. In June he advised the premier of Grey's disinclination to join in with the opposition to his government.[7] At the general election in August he was again returned for Launceston.[8]

The ministry regarded him as one of their 'friends', but he was absent from the crucial division on the civil list, 15 Nov. Gordon, who is not known to have spoken in debate, presented anti-slavery petitions from Launceston Wesleyan Methodists, 5 Nov., and the inhabitants, 23 Nov., and one from the inhabitants for repeal of the coal duties, 17 Nov. 1830. On the formation of Grey's ministry he was offered the master-generalship of the ordnance, with the promise of a Grand Cross of the Bath and a colonial governorship 'when the opportunity occurs'. His appointment was apparently suspended owing to objections from the commander-in-chief, Lord Hill, who had not been consulted, but his eventual decision to decline the post was presumably influenced by a warning from Wellington that Northumberland would not allow him to keep his seat.[9] In March 1831 he informed Northumberland, who wished him to oppose the government's reform bill, that it was 'quite impossible for me as the senior officer upon the king's staff to vote against His Majesty's government under any circumstances whatever', and that he could only promise to 'keep away from the discussion'. He was indeed absent from the division on the second reading, 22 Mar., but was given 'notice to quit'; he resigned his seat, 5 Apr. 1831. He told Grey that he believed he had

> kept away one enemy from you by keeping my seat over the 2nd reading, and I should have been glad to have done the same till your measure had finally passed. I have convinced myself that it must pass in the main principle – the middle classes of this country will no longer endure that their property shall be at the disposal of the nominees of peers ... [In future] the business of the House of Commons will be conducted by those who have the greatest interest in the economical and efficient discharge of it, and not by professed party politicians, most of whom have no claim to such stations as the treasury bench, whether by birth, fortune, education or ability ... All this sort of cattle are in high excitement and flourishing about in all directions, but I think without method or connected power.

His request for a privy councillorship was not granted, but he later received a red ribbon.[10] In 1835 he unsuccessfully contested Newport, Isle of Wight (where he had a residence), as an 'independent' with Conservative leanings.[11] It was said of him by an obituarist that he was 'much esteemed for his urbanity and soldier-like qualities'.[12] He died in January 1851 and was succeeded by his only son Henry (1806-76), on whose death the baronetcy became extinct.[13]

[1] *Ann. Reg.* (1851), App. p. 248. [2] *Creevey Pprs.* i. 151. See Add. 49471-49517 for Gordon's papers, mainly on military matters. [3] *Palmerston-Sulivan Letters*, 78; K. Bourne, *Palmerston*, 105-7, 166; E.A. Smith, *Earl Grey*, 208. [4] *Canning's Ministry*, 129; Wellington mss WP1/897/5; 903/10; Add. 49479, ff. 61-66. [5] Wellington mss WP1/999/4; *West Briton*, 20 Mar. 1829. [6] Wellington mss WP1/1028/8. [7] Ibid. 1118/15. [8] *West Briton*, 6 Aug. 1830. [9] *Three Diaries*, 24-25; *Greville Mems.* ii. 71; Add. 49479, f. 84; Wellington mss WP1/1153/11; 1154/52, 59. [10] Grey mss, Gordon to Grey, 18, 29 Mar., 6 Apr. 1831; Add. 49479, f. 91. [11] Add. 35149, f. 158; 49479, f. 96; 49508, ff. 123-5. [12] *Ann. Reg.* (1851), App. p. 248. [13] PROB 11/2127/119; IR26/1897/86.

T.A.J.

GORDON, John (c.1776-1858), of Cluny, Aberdeen; 4 St. Andrew Street, Edinburgh, and 25 Jermyn Street, Mdx.

WEYMOUTH & MELCOMBE REGIS   1826-1832

b. c.1776, 1st s. of Charles Gordon of Braid, nr. Edinburgh and Joanna, da. of Thomas Trotter of Mortonhall, nr. Edinburgh. *educ.* Norwich sch.; St.

John's, Camb. 1797. *unm.* 2s. illegit. (1 *d.v.p.*) 2da. illegit. *d.v.p. suc.* fa. 1814. *d.* 16 July 1858.

2nd lt. R. Aberdeen light inf. 1800; lt. Aberdeen militia 1804, maj. 1808, lt.-col. 1820, col. 1836-*d.*

Although the family of the Gordons of Cluny had died out in the early eighteenth century, a spurious continuity was maintained by the purchase of the estate by John Gordon, 'the Curator' (?1695-1769). He, who was factor to the 3rd duke of Gordon and an Edinburgh merchant, established the family's Scottish propertied wealth, not least by his penuriousness. He was succeeded by his eldest son Cosmo Gordon (who died unmarried in 1800), of Kinsteary, Nairnshire, baron of the exchequer and Northite Member for Nairnshire, 1774-7, while his younger son Alexander (*d.* 1801) of Belmont, Tobago, acquired lucrative West Indian plantations. Their brother Charles, John's second son, was made a writer to the signet in 1763 and became a clerk to the court of session in 1788. He married, 8 Nov. 1775, 'Jackie' Trotter (*d.* 10 Aug. 1798), with whom he had at least six children. He greatly extended his estates, but suffered from the family vice of miserliness. It was later recorded that 'as he advanced in years his passion for saving became a perfect disease. He declined to move about for fear of incurring expense, and latterly he refused to get up out of bed on the ground that he could not afford it'. He died, 8 May 1814, leaving £12,000 to his son Alexander (of Great Myless, Essex), £10,000 to each of his three daughters, and Cluny and the rest of his property (which included personalty sworn under £30,000 in the province of Canterbury) to his eldest son John. He had embarked on a brief military career in 1800, travelled in Europe and the Levant, 1802-4, apparently in the company of the 4th earl of Aberdeen, and returned to England with Nelson's remains in 1805. He largely occupied himself with the management of his estates and, displaying a strongly litigious streak, was involved in three cases over them between 1815 and 1818.[1]

Through his sister Charlotte, widow of Sir John Lowther Johnstone†, Gordon wanted to obtain a seat at Weymouth, where the Johnstone family interest was managed by Masterton Ure* as trustee of the young 7th baronet.[2] As nothing came of a rumour in mid-1820 that Ure was to receive an appointment incompatible with a seat in Parliament, Gordon had to wait until the general election of 1826 to contest the borough.[3] He then offered, as a ministerialist and anti-Catholic, with Richard Weyland*, Charlotte's second husband, on the interest of the heir as distinct from that of the trustees, with whom the family were in dispute. He persisted in a bitter struggle, being a popular and able candidate, and one supporter noted that he liked his appearance 'very much – he looks a warm one'. He was finally returned in second place behind Thomas Fowell Buxton (the town Member), and ahead of Ure and his colleague Thomas Wallace, a junior minister.[4] A legal opinion against Gordon, alleging treating, obstruction and orchestrated violence, was prepared on behalf of the defeated candidate, but the matter was not pursued.[5] Gordon, who claimed that his election had cost him £40,000, complained to ministers about the summoning of the army to restore order during the contest.[6]

In the House, where he was usually distinguished from other Gordons by the title 'Colonel', he appears to have been an almost silent supporter of the Liverpool, Canning and Wellington administrations. He voted against the disfranchisement of Penryn, 28 May, and for the grant to improve water communications in Canada, 12 June 1827. He divided against inquiry into chancery administration, 24 Apr., and reduction of the salary of the lieutenant-general of the ordnance, 4 July, and for Fyler's amendment on the silk duties which was carried with government support, 14 July 1828. He divided against Catholic relief, 6 Mar. 1827, 12 May 1828, and in February 1829 was listed by Planta, the patronage secretary, as 'doubtful' on the government's new pro-Catholic policy. He duly divided against emancipation, 6, 30 Mar., and for Henry Bankes's amendment to prevent Catholics sitting in Parliament, 23 Mar. 1829, after which he received a vote of thanks from his constituents.[7] He was granted one month's leave on urgent private business, 12 Mar. 1830. In his only known speech, 29 Mar., he spoke as a professional soldier against the reduction of the ordnance grant by £1,200, urging that

> the army has great claims on the sympathy of the House and on the country; and I must say, it is beneath the talents of the great civilians here to enter the arena against the army, and strip for a contest with them about a petty sum like this.

He voted against abolition of the death penalty for forgery, 7 June 1830.

After Wallace's elevation to the peerage in February 1828, Gordon evidently gave his support to Weyland at the ensuing by-election, when his brother-in-law was defeated by the ministerialist candidate, Edward Sugden.[8] However, having that year become a trustee for his nephew, Sir George Frederic Johnstone†, he soon fell out with his sister, who accused him of trying to usurp the management of Weymouth. He came to a secret agreement with Sugden: that he should pay

his election expenses, providing he was allowed to sell two of the other three seats; that Sugden would endeavour to procure him a peerage, and that Weyland would be excluded. Sugden, who also gave him legal advice, acted as a cover for his purchase of property in the borough for £21,000. The news of this acquisition made him so unpopular that by early 1829 Gordon was obliged to come to terms with Ure.[9] He also began legal proceedings challenging Lady Johnstone's income under her late husband's trust.[10] He accompanied Sugden at the by-election in June 1829, following his appointment as solicitor-general. Stressing his continued independence, but strongly criticized for having abandoned the popular party, Gordon was returned unopposed for Weymouth with Ure, Sugden and Buxton at the general election of 1830.[11] He was listed by ministers among their 'friends', but was absent from the division on the civil list that precipitated their resignation, 15 Nov. A proprietor of East India stock, he may have been the 'John Gordon'[12] who attended the special meeting of the West India Planters and Merchants' Committee, 23 Nov. 1830, but he was not otherwise active on it.[13] He voted against the second reading of the Grey ministry's reform bill, 22 Mar., and for Gascoyne's wrecking amendment, 19 Apr. 1831.

An action for debt having been brought against him in late 1830 by his former agent James John Fraser, the summons to the court of session stated that Gordon

> has, for many years, been much concerned in political adventures, the main object of which was to raise him to the peerage; for which distinction he has constantly, but unsuccessfully, struggled, in a great variety of ways, and more particularly by attempting to get himself returned as a Member of Parliament to represent a Scotch county, he having become exceedingly unpopular in the borough of Weymouth.

He held property in several counties and was said to have been especially hopeful of succeeding his friend Lord Fife to the representation of Banffshire in 1827. Indicating his frustration at the failure of his ambitions, the summons also quoted him as saying that

> if the steady and zealous support which my predecessors and I have always given to the ministers of His Majesty's present government, and the increased support which, in future, I shall have it in my power to give them, is not enough, without the addition of £40,000 to put me on a level with the other candidates for royal favour, I will remain as I am.[14]

Incriminating correspondence between Gordon and Sugden, which was produced in court and published, initially in the *Caledonian Mercury*, created a good deal of criticism, which was exacerbated by Sugden and Fraser's self-justificatory remarks in the press. In response, a statement was issued that 'although not pretending to the quixotry of sacrificing his property solely to promote his nephew's advantage', Gordon was acting in Johnstone's long-term interests; and in a letter of 6 Apr. he denied being a party to the sale of seats.[15] Sugden's withdrawal, which cleared the path for Weyland, secured Gordon's return after a token contest at the general election of 1831, when he pledged himself to oppose the reform bill, which he considered to be 'too sweeping, too revolutionary'.[16] He plumped for the anti-reformer Bankes at the Dorset county contest,[17] and presumably supported the like-minded Charles Baring Wall* at the Weymouth by-election caused by Weyland's decision to sit for Oxfordshire.

Gordon voted against the second reading of the reintroduced reform bill, 6 July 1831. He was a teller for the minority on the second division to adjourn proceedings on it, 12 July, and divided at least three other times in this sense that night. He voted to postpone consideration of the partial disfranchisement of Chippenham, 27 July, and to censure the Irish government over the Dublin election, 23 Aug. He may, as 'R. Gordon', have voted for a select committee to inquire into how far the Sugar Refinery Act could be renewed with due regard to the West India interest, 12 Sept. He divided against the third reading, 19 Sept., and passage of the reform bill, 21 Sept., and against the second reading of the Scottish bill, 23 Sept. In the Dorset by-election that autumn he voted for the anti-reformer Lord Ashley*.[18] He paired against the second reading, 17 Dec. 1831, and voted against the third reading of the revised reform bill, 22 Mar., and the second reading of the Irish bill, 25 May 1832. He may have divided in favour of going into committee on Alexander Baring's bill to exclude insolvent debtors from Parliament, 27 June. His only other known vote was with opposition against the Russian-Dutch loan, 12 July 1832.

Johnstone, who had recently come of age, was elected for Weymouth with Buxton at the general election in December 1832, and there is no evidence that Gordon sought another seat.[19] He was said to have abandoned his parliamentary career in disgust after the unfortunate dispute with his agent, though he retained a small electoral interest in Scotland.[20] Instead he concentrated on consolidating his estates, purchasing Shiels and (for £65,000) Midmar near Cluny, and the islands of Benbecula, South Uist

and (for £150,000) Barra in the Hebrides. He was an assiduous, innovative and generous landlord, who largely rebuilt Cluny Castle, but he was fiercely criticized for his harsh treatment of his Hebridean tenants, many of whom underwent enforced emigration to Canada. Described as being 'above the middle size, and of a stout athletic make', he was 'possessed of a hardy constitution ... great intelligence and was very well bred', yet he too became eccentric in money matters, driving miles out of his way in order to avoid toll bars. He died, after a short illness, in July 1858, when he was reputed to be the 'richest commoner in the kingdom' of Scotland, leaving over £2,000,000.[21] By his will, dated 27 Apr. 1837, which was proved in London, 29 Aug. 1859, Gordon attempted to provide for his illegitimate children by his housekeeper and to create a distinct 'Gordon of Cluny' dynasty. In fact, his daughters Mary Steel and Susan had died in 1833 and 1856 respectively, and his younger son Charles on 27 Nov. 1857, so that the vast estates in Aberdeenshire, Banffshire, Inverness-shire, Midlothian and Nairnshire passed to his elder son John. He tried to break the terms of the entail and was challenged to the inheritance by his cousin, the eldest son of Alexander (*d.* 1839), Charles Henry Gordon (1816-95), which resulted in 20 years of litigation. John Gordon junior, an agricultural improver, died without issue, 22 July 1878, after which the estates descended through the family of Alexander's daughter, Maria Frederica Linzee.[22]

[1] J. M. Bulloch, *Gordons of Cluny*, 3-33, 41, 53-54; *Gent. Mag.* (1798), ii. 729; (1801), i. 92; (1858), ii. 310-11; *The Times*, 23 July 1858; PROB 11/1557/351; IR26/608/331. [2] The defeated candidate for Wootton Bassett at the general election of 1820 was probably John Gordon (1794-1843), Member for Athlone, 1818-20. [3] Northumb. RO, Middleton mss ZMI/S76/40/5, 8. [4] *Dorset Co. Chron.* 18, 25 May, 1, 8, 15, 22, 29 June 1826; Middleton mss S76/52/4, 7; Dorset RO D/ASH:B E20. [5] Dorset RO, photocopy 555. [6] E.S.L. Cosens, *Hist. Weymouth*, 82; Add. 40387, f. 229. [7] *Dorset Co. Chron.* 23 Apr. 1829. [8] *The Times*, 5, 6 Feb. 1828. [9] Ibid. 5, 6 Apr. 1831; [W. Carpenter], *People's Bk.* (1831), 374-7. [10] Brougham mss, Weyland to J. Brougham, 4 May 1829. [11] *Dorset Co. Chron.* 18 June 1829, 8, 15 July, 5 Aug. 1830. [12] Unless this was John Gordon (1774-1834), West India planter, of Wincombe Park, Dorset, Clifton, Glos. and Jamaica. [13] Inst. of Commonwealth Stud. M915, reel 4. [14] *The Times*, 12 Apr. 1831. [15] Ibid. 5, 6, 8, 9, 11, 13 Apr., 8 Aug. 1831. [16] *Dorset Co. Chron.* 5 May 1831. [17] *Dorset Pollbook* (1831), 27. [18] Ibid. (Sept.-Oct. 1831), 45. [19] The unsuccessful candidate for Banffshire was Colonel Thomas Gordon of Park, Banff. [20] See *Scottish Electoral Politics*, 125. [21] Bulloch, 34-40; *Gent. Mag.* (1858), ii. 310-11; *The Times*, 23 July 1858. [22] Bulloch, 4, 41-52.

S.M.F.

GORDON, Robert (?1786–1864), of Kemble House, nr. Cirencester, Glos.; Leweston House, nr. Sherborne, Dorset; Ashton Keynes, nr. Cricklade, Wilts., and 32 Bruton Street, Mdx.

WAREHAM	1812–1818
CRICKLADE	1818–1837
NEW WINDSOR	1837–1841

b. ?1786, o.s. of William Gordon, W.I. planter, of Auchendolly, Kirkcudbright and Anna, da. of Stephen Nash of Bristol, Glos., sis. and h. of Sir Stephen Nash of Leweston House. *educ.* Eton 1799; L. Inn 1803; Christ Church, Oxf. 1804. *m.* 11 July 1809, his cos. Elizabeth Anne, da. of Charles Westley Coxe[†] of Kemble House, 1da. *suc.* fa. 1802. *d.* 16 May 1864.
   Commr. of lunacy 1828-*d.*; commr. bd. of control June 1832-Dec. 1833, jt.-sec. Dec. 1833-Dec. 1834, Apr. 1835-Sept. 1839; sec. to treasury Sept. 1839-June 1841.
   Cornet Dorset yeomanry 1805, lt. 1808; capt. Wilts. yeomanry 1816.
   Sheriff, Glos. 1811-12.

'Bum' Gordon was how this Member was commonly known, at least behind his back, but the nickname is of uncertain derivation.[1] The imputation of idleness or inebriety would have been no more appropriate for him than for many politicians, though Edward Littleton* linked it to his character when he referred to Colonel Thomas Davies* and 'Bum Gordon [as] "damned *good-natured* fellows" proverbially'.[2] More speculatively, 'Bum' may have been a phonetic abbreviation of the contemporary pronunciation of the first syllable of bombast, as in Henry Brougham's* caricature of him as 'Bombastes Furioso', and he may well have boomed or hummed loudly while speaking in the House.[3] However, he probably just had a large posterior: according to one newspaper story, when Gordon asked the duke of Devonshire to add his name to a guest list, from which the duke of Wellington's had already been struck out, Devonshire

> was sorely puzzled. At length he hit upon the expedient of discharging the duke of Newcastle, and declared that he and the duke of Wellington would just make a proper place in the saloon to be filled up by Mr. Gordon. It is said that his grace chuckled at his cleverness, and some friends, who scarcely ever smiled before at any of his jokes, laughed outright at his grace's additional sally, which we do not repeat.[4]

Gordon was always in danger of appearing ridiculous, and, as Denis Le Marchant[†] later wrote, he

> was a contemporary of Sir Robert Peel*, like whom he had obtained the highest honours at Oxford, and he had equally the advantage of a large fortune and an early seat

in the House of Commons; but a love of ease and social pleasure, with an indifference to the higher branches of politics, always kept him in a position below both his pretensions and his abilities.[5]

Descended from the Gordons of Auchendolly, his grandfather and father were successful West India merchants, who acquired the plantations of Paisley and Windsor Lodge, Jamaica.[6] He presumably followed them into this business, and was perhaps one of the unidentified Gordons who attended meetings of the West India Committee (a 'Robert Gordon' was present on at least one occasion in 1816).[7] He almost invariably advocated lower duties on West Indian sugar and defended the practice of slave-owning. Through his parents and wife, he came into considerable property in the West Country, where he established himself as a local gentleman and magistrate. He was made a freeman of Gloucester in 1813, and was, for instance, a regular attender at the annual dinners of the Wiltshire Society in London.[8] He was returned for Wareham in 1812, and was elected in second place for the enlarged freeholder borough of Cricklade at the general election of 1818, when he voted for the Whig candidates Sir Samuel Romilly[†] and Sir Francis Burdett* in the contest for Westminster.[9] Having been returned unopposed for Cricklade at the following general election, the 16th earl of Suffolk, one of his Whig neighbours, commented to Lord Holland, 9 Mar. 1820, that 'though my acquaintance with Gordon is at an end, by his own fault I must say, yet I am always glad when a man of good and sound principles comes in'.[10] Although essentially a Whig opponent of the Liverpool administration, as seen in his generally hostile voting behaviour on legal, political and social issues, he had too independent a cast of mind and too great a sense of the self-righteousness of his own conduct to follow a consistent party line in Parliament. Like Joseph Hume, with whom he nevertheless also differed on occasion, he was one of the champions of economies and reduced taxation (almost always voting, sometimes as a teller, in this way, notably in the early 1820s) and, under all governments, he was relentless in his scrutiny of the estimates. A regular committee-man, he was very active in the House, making numerous minor interventions and frequently presenting petitions on local legislation and private matters.

   Gordon objected to the cost of the new post office, 3, 4 May, the funding of the African Company, 30 May, and the barracks grant, 6 June, 10 July 1820.[11] He divided against the appointment of a secret committee on the allegations against Queen Caroline, 26 June 1820. He signed the requisition for a Wiltshire county meeting on the affair, which he attended, 17 Jan. 1821. He afterwards reported to Holland that it had gone well, and in his own speech he explained

the trick of ministers to manage, as it was termed, the House of Commons, and described in so humorous a manner as to keep the meeting in constant roars of laughter the duties of the ministerial whipper-in, who had to keep the votes together. Fatal to the pay of the whipper-in was a good hunting week or a Newmarket meeting; for it was on those occasions alone, and not on any virtue in the House of Commons, that occasionally a beneficial measure passed, or a bad one was defeated. It was ludicrous, he said, to see the ministers secretly watching the door of the House of Commons, while the whipper-in was mustering the votes. On such occasions the ministers sat like 'tame hawks that sit and hear the very whispers curious'.

He declared that nothing but parliamentary reform would be of any benefit to the country, and praised opposition leaders for supporting it, revealing that he had quarrelled with them over their coalition with the Grenvillites and had feared that 'they had got tired of being so long nailed to the north wall of opposition; the cold of that chilly atmosphere had, however, he hoped sufficiently braced their nerves against the relaxing atmosphere of Courtly interest'.[12] He divided steadily in favour of the Whig campaign on Caroline's behalf during the first few weeks of the following session, and supported the Devizes petition against the removal of her name from the liturgy, 24 Jan. He voted against the sugar duties, 9 Feb., and denounced the rumoured offer of a bribe to government for renewal of the West India Dock Company's charter, 27 Feb. He unsuccessfully moved one of the delaying amendments in the committee of supply on the army estimates, 12 Mar., and urged further economies, 30 Mar., 13, 30 Apr., 14 May.[13] He voted to make Leeds a scot and lot, not a £10 householder, borough if it received Grampound's seats, 2 Mar., and was a steward at the *City of London Tavern* reform dinner, 4 Apr.[14] He was listed in both the minority for and the majority against disqualifying civil officers of the ordnance from voting in parliamentary elections, 12 Apr. He voted for parliamentary reform, 18 Apr., 9 May, reform of the Scottish county representation, 10 May, and to better secure of the independence of Parliament, 31 May. He came to the defence of the West India interest, 4 May, and was a teller for the majority against allowing James Stephen to give evidence against the slaves removal bill, 31 May 1821.

He apparently missed most, if not all, of the 1822 session, and was reported not to have voted 'for or against anything'.[15] It was not until the middle of the following year that he returned from a tour of the continent and resumed his parliamentary activities.[16] He divided to abolish the death penalty for larceny, 21 May, and against the usury bill, 27 June 1823. He paired in condemnation of chancery administration, 5 June, and was in the opposition majority for the Scottish juries bill, 20 June. He regretted the failure of the silk manufacture bill, 18 July 1823. On 20 Feb. 1824 Gordon supported ministers on the army estimates by justifying the cost of military defences in the West Indies, but, surprisingly, he joined his advanced Whig colleagues in calling for lower sugar duties as part of a general plan of free trade, 8 Mar. He voted for reform of the representation of Edinburgh, 26 Feb. He divided for abolition of flogging in the army, 5 Mar., and to consider the evils of naval impressment, 10 June. He asked whether it was worth retaining the civil and military establishments on the Gold Coast, 12 Mar., and urged free trade in silk, 22 Mar. He commented on the duties on salt and beer, 6 Apr., and rum, 8 Apr., and, although he had formerly objected to the grant for the building of new churches, he spoke of its necessity in 'a canting and hypocritical age', 9 Apr.[17] He voted in favour of inquiries into the Irish church establishment, 6 May, and the state of Ireland, 11 May, and against improper use of Irish first fruits revenues, 25 May, and Irish pluralities, 27 May. However, he sided with ministers for the Irish insurrection bill, 14 June. He divided against Brougham's censure motion on the trial of the Methodist missionary John Smith in Demerara, 11 June 1824.

He voted for hearing the Catholic Association against the Irish unlawful societies bill, 18 Feb. 1825, dividing against this measure at some or all of its stages. On the 24th he opposed leave for the introduction of a bear-baiting bill while there were more important issues before the House. As he had on 28 Feb. 1821, he voted for Catholic relief, 1 Mar., 21 Apr., 10 May 1825. Although he defended ministers' conduct on the Canadian waste lands bill, 15 Mar., he opposed the grant to the Irish linen board, 18 Mar. He claimed that a rise in the price of sugar would be of general benefit, 18 Mar., denied the allegation that planters had done all in their power to obstruct the amelioration of the condition of their slaves, 21 Mar., when he approved Huskisson's proposed warehousing system, and stated his approval of the West India Company bill, 16 May. He decided not to attend the Westminster reform dinner, 23 May, but told John Cam Hobhouse* that 'I have a right to be considered a zealous supporter, and you will not from my absence today infer any change in my public attachment or my private regard'.[18] He declared that children in cotton mills 'required the protection of the legislature as much as the slaves of the West Indies', 31 May, and voted for Hume's amendment to exclude magistrates who were factory owners from enforcing the combination laws, 27 June. He said he would vote against the Mauritius trade bill unless its implementation was postponed, 3, 6 June. He complained about customs officers being permitted to search individuals in foreign ships in order to prevent smuggling, 10 June, and objected to high duties on trifling articles of luxury, 17 June 1825, when he voted for Hobhouse's amendment to the judges' salaries bill.[19]

He condemned the government policy of restricting the circulation of country bank notes, 9, 10 Feb. 1826, because he thought that 'it would be impossible to pay in gold what had been borrowed in paper'. He voted against going into committee on the Bank Charter Acts, 13 Feb., and presented and endorsed a Cirencester petition critical of ministers' handling of the financial crisis, 14 Feb. He asked whether the report of the commissioners of inquiry into the courts in the West Indies would be acted on, 17 Feb. He agreed with Canning, the foreign secretary, that the impetus for the abolition of slavery should come from colonial assemblies and not Parliament, 1 Mar., though he presented an anti-slavery petition from Malmesbury, 20 Mar.[20] He divided for the bill to disfranchise non-resident voters in Irish boroughs, 9 Mar., to abolish flogging in the army, 10 Mar., and against the second reading of the corn importation bill, 11 May. He divided for reforming the representation of Edinburgh, 13 Apr., parliamentary reform, 27 Apr., and curbing electoral bribery, 26 May 1826. He was returned unopposed for Cricklade at the general election the following month. He brought up a Gloucestershire petition against alteration of the corn laws, 21 Feb., and divided against the second reading of the ministerial corn bill, 2 Apr. 1827.[21] He voted for inquiry into the allegations against the corporation of Leicester, 15 Mar., and for the production of information on the mutiny at Barrackpoor, 22 Mar., and the Orange procession and Lisburn magistrates, 29 Mar. He sided with opposition on the Irish miscellaneous estimates and chancery administration, 5 Apr. He voted for the disfranchisement of Penryn, 28 May, when he also, however, spoke and voted in the minority against Lord Althorp's election expenses bill. He voted with the Canning government for the grant to improve water communications in Canada, 12 June 1827.

He successfully moved for a select committee on the 'dreadful state of misery' in which pauper lunatics were kept in Middlesex, 13 June 1827. He chaired

its sittings on 11 occasions and presented the report, mostly written by himself on the 29th.[22] On 1 Jan. 1828 Thomas Spring Rice* informed Lord Lansdowne, the home secretary in the doomed Goderich ministry, that Gordon intended moving for a committee on the police and a bill founded on his lunacy report, to which Lansdowne replied next day that ministers would handle the former, but that Gordon could pursue the latter if he so wished.[23] He duly introduced his pauper lunatics bill for the construction of a new county asylum in Middlesex, 19 Feb., outlining allegations about the wrongful confinement of alleged lunatics under the signature of one doctor or apothecary; the appalling physical condition in which the lunatics were kept and the hopelessly inadequate level of medical attention; and the absence of inspection which made it extremely difficult for inmates who had recovered their sanity to secure their release. At Gordon's request, the motion was seconded by Lord Ashley,[24] and, in lending his support to the measure, Peel, who had recently returned to the home office, said that Gordon was 'fully entitled to the appellation of philanthropist for those exertions near which the suspicion of self-interest cannot come, for those exertions which can be prompted by nothing but pure humanity'. He defended the bill against various criticisms, 17, 25, 27 Mar., 1 Apr., and, on its rejection by the Lords, 6 June, reintroduced a replacement county lunatics asylum bill in the Commons that day. Although again much amended, this, and the lunatics regulation bill (which he had also first brought before the House on 19 Feb.) were given royal assent, 15 July.[25] Peel wished him to be president of the statutory commission of lunacy, but Gordon preferred to be named second in the list, announced in August 1828, leaving the honour to Lord Granville Somerset*.[26]

Gordon voted against the grant for 30,000 seamen, 11 Feb. 1828. He presented petitions against the Test Acts, 21 Feb., and divided for their repeal, 26 Feb. He chaired turbulent sessions of the committee on the East Retford disfranchisement bill, 3, 4, 7 Mar., and voted against the constituency being thrown into the hundred of Bassetlaw, 21 Mar. He reported from the committee on the Penryn disfranchisement bill, 24 Mar. He criticized the treatment of turnpike bills as private legislation and thus subject to heavy costs, 15, 21 Apr. He expressed his approval of the Scottish madhouses bill, 24 Apr. On the cities and boroughs poll bill, 28 Apr., 15 May, he noted that it excluded enlarged freeholder boroughs, in which he thought that the county authorities ought to be allowed to establish several polling places. He divided for establishing efficient control over proceedings by the crown for the recovery of penalties under the customs and excise laws, 1 May. He took exception to Lord Palmerston (who had just left office) presenting the Cambridge University anti-slavery petition, 3 June, stating his hope that the question would have been dealt with in a dispassionate and non-partisan fashion. Palmerston, although clearly riled, told the House that he would have been annoyed by the remarks of someone 'who sits on these benches', were he not 'accustomed to infuse an air of good humour into every subject with which he meddles'. Although Gordon admitted that he had already changed his view once on granting public money for church building, and had been castigated for it by his colleagues, he stated that he had reverted to his former opinion, 30 June, when he condemned the additional churches bill as riddled with drafting errors. He voted against its second reading that day, and twice acted as a teller for the minority for having it put off. He insisted that the condition of enslaved Africans had been improved, 3 July, objected to the practice of ministers presenting bills without stating the grounds for their introduction, 4 July, and praised the amended benefices regulation bill, 17 July 1828.

Gordon, who had divided in its favour on 6 Mar. 1827 and 12 May 1828, voted for Catholic emancipation, 6, 30 Mar., and stated his support for the Wellington administration on this, 9 Mar. 1829. He objected to the grant for Toulonese and Corsican emigrants, 13 Mar., supported Peel's justice of the peace bill, 25 Mar., and suggested that charity commissioners should be full-time paid employees, 2 Apr., when he called for further inquiry into official pensions. He thanked ministers for referring the Irish miscellaneous estimates to a select committee, 4 Apr., to which he was appointed, 9 Apr. At about this time he appears briefly to have become active on the West India Committee, his being the first signature on the requisition for a new standing committee, 8 Apr., and he was appointed to the new acting committee, handling the committee's daily administration, 8 May.[27] In the Commons he urged reduction of the duty on sugar, which he believed was an out-of-date wartime tax, 14 May, and objected to a motion against slavery, 3 June. He criticized the level of expenditure on Buckingham House, 11, 12 May, and voted against the grant for the marble arch, 25 May. On 14 May he expressed his annoyance at Vesey Fitzgerald's indignant objection to the supposedly angry manner in which he had complained about the duty on olive oil. He divided for O'Connell being allowed to take his seat without swearing the oath of supremacy, 18 May. He expressed his horror at the employment of children in factories, 19 May, and

moved the third reading of the cotton factories regulation bill, 4 June. He spoke against the Irish arms bill as an unnecessarily severe measure, 2 June, when he voted for parliamentary reform. In December 1829 Palmerston, who noted that Gordon 'travels about the continent with half a dozen carriages and all sorts of luxuries, and complains that he is ruined and cannot live in England', reported to Lady Cowper that 'he is all for paper currency and depreciating the standard, and what some people call equitable adjustment, which consists in robbing the fundholder, but then he has no stock and some land'.[28]

He was one of the members of a West India Committee delegation to Wellington in January 1830, after which he told Greville that 'they had all been shocked at the manner in which he had used them, that some of them had declared they would never go to him again'.[29] He introduced his lunatic licenses bill, 9 Feb., which passed that session, and supported Michael Angelo Taylor's lunacy bill, 2, 18 Mar. He voted for transferring East Retford's seats to Birmingham, 11 Feb., 5 May, and with Lord Howick against the East Retford bribery prevention bill, 11 Feb.; on 8 Mar. he explained that he would prefer the seats to be given to Birmingham, but, if that failed, he would vote for them being thrown into the neighbouring hundred. He divided for parliamentary reform, 18 Feb., 28 May, the enfranchisement of Birmingham, Leeds and Manchester, 23 Feb., and the ballot, 15 Mar. He paired for information on Portugal, 10 Mar., and urged ministers to lower the sugar duties to increase revenues, 19 Mar. Arguing that there was no reason to be alarmed by the state of Ireland, he spoke against the Irish constabulary bill, 30 Mar., and the arms bill, 2 Apr., 3 July, but he condemned abuses in the Irish admiralty court, 6 May. He presented petitions against the death penalty for forgery from Malmesbury, 12 May, and Cricklade, 3 July, and paired in this sense, 24 May, 7 June. He deprecated the fact that the king's West Indian sugars were no longer taxed, 21 May, and pleaded with ministers to relieve the distress of the West India merchants, 30 June, when he spoke against the sugar refinery bill and declared that their interest had been treated by government 'with the greatest contumely and neglect' that year. He served on two deputations from the West India Committee in June.[30] He divided in favour of reform of the divorce laws, 3 June 1830, and the next day provoked a furious reaction from Scarlett, the attorney general, by referring to the cost of the 'prosecutions, or rather persecutions, instituted by the treasury against the press'.[31]

Gordon, who voted for Knatchbull's amendment to the address on distress, 4 Feb. 1830, was a leading figure in the opposition campaign for economies and reduced taxation that session, during which he constantly probed ministers in depth and divided against them on financial questions. He infused unusual animation into the committee of supply, and according to Le Marchant

> Gordon's success was such that Lord Macaulay, then a young Member, speaking to me some years afterwards on the fleeting character of parliamentary distinction, observed that he used to listen with admiration to his speeches, thinking them eminently clever and persuasive, and hardly venturing to hope that he might one day speak as well.[32]

He questioned ministers about the number of full-pay army officers who were entitled to retain their salaries as well as accepting civil allowances for service in public offices, 11, 16, 17 Feb., withdrew a motion on this after receiving ministerial assurances that the matter would be investigated, 9 Mar., but expressed himself dissatisfied with the limited remit of the inquiry, 26 Apr. He emphasized the prevalence of distress, 18 Feb., warned that its existence in other countries had created 'a revolutionary spirit abroad', 22 Feb., and objected to an increase in the duties on spirits, which were the only 'resource for the unhappy' in such times, 23 Feb. Hobhouse detected him in an act of hypocrisy, privately observing that Gordon 'would not vote with us because he has an intimacy with the Bathurst family', his Gloucestershire neighbours, on the opposition motion to abolish the Bathurst and Dundas pensions, 26 Mar.[33] However, Gordon recommended the abolition of useless legal and financial offices, 1 Apr., 14 May, and the reduction of official salaries, 2, 30 Apr., 21 June. He spoke and was the teller for the majority against an amended clause in the poor law bill to provide education for children whose parents were unable to support them, 26 Apr. He rejected the attacks made on him and others who urged economies, 30 Apr., when he insisted that items in the estimates should be considered separately. On the motion to go into the committee of supply, 3 May, he berated Members for streaming out of the House and pointed out that, although 'eloquence and arithmetic never go well together', it was vital to scrutinize public expenditure, as 'we are not to consider, in these times, and under our present circumstances, what is useful or advantageous, but what is absolutely necessary'. He hinted that distress and reform were issues which would become linked in the public mind since 'the one consolation I have in seeing so many

Members without constituents support the government is that the subject must force itself into notice'. Sensing that he lacked enough support, he decided against moving for an impartial select committee to study the estimates in general, but his motion in the committee to refer the first item, the grant for public buildings, to such an inquiry was defeated by 139-123. He voted against the beer bill, 3 May, voiced objections to it on the instructions of his constituents, 3, 4, 14 June, and divided for amendments to prohibit its sale for on-consumption, 21 June, 1 July. He judged the labourers' wages bill to be 'weak and absurd', 11 June, and offered several amendments to it, 5 July, when, as he did on other occasions, he criticized the poor quality of drafting exhibited in government bills and disapproved of attempts to pass legislation late in the session. On 2 July, when opposition leaders were not supported by their followers in an attack on ministers in the committee of supply, Gordon 'came over to Herries and said he should vote with government'.[34] He was in the minority of two against the report of the select committee on repairs to Windsor Castle, 9 July, and spoke against it, 16 July 1830, when he asked for a review of committee procedures on private and public bills.

At the general election that summer, Gordon, who was again returned unopposed for Cricklade, attended the election at Gloucester, where he declared that 'I took great pains, in the last session, to reduce the expenditure of this country'. He told the electors that 'it is your business to send men to Parliament who will perform their duty, and to say this to your representatives, always attend a committee of supply, never be absent when any of the money of the people is to be voted away'. He questioned the candidates closely about their commitment to economies, and finally plumped for Edward Webb*.[35] He moved for papers on the pay of army officers in civil employment, 4 Nov., and the English pension list, 12 Nov. 1830. Deemed by ministers to be among their 'foes', he of course voted against them on the civil list, 15 Nov., and was evidently dismayed not to be invited to join the Grey ministry that succeeded them. Althorp, the new chancellor of the exchequer, wrote to Lord Milton*, 22 Nov., that Gordon was 'the most violent against us; he says that we are the most aristocratic administration that ever was formed, and that it is an insult to the people to have formed such a one in such times'.[36] Following Hobhouse's hint to government that there were too many 'anti-reductionists' on it, he and Gordon were added to the select committee on Members' salaries, 10 Dec.[37] The following day Gordon complained that pensions had been awarded under the new reign despite the absence of a legal pension fund, and later burst out that

> I observed that an honourable Member on the ministerial bench had a sneer on his countenance when I called on ministers to declare that they had nothing to do with the matter, as if it were utterly impossible that the present pure administration could make any kind of composition with its predecessors; but when I see what has been going on in Ireland, the pensions which have been created there, and the manner in which vacancies have been made and filled up, it is with regret I feel that the present government must be watched almost as closely as the last.

Althorp said that he took it in 'perfect good part', but on 13 Dec. 1830 there was a 'curious debate' with, as Lord Ellenborough put it, 'B. Gordon and others breaking ground against the new ministers'.[38] In fact Gordon denounced them for failing to abolish useless cabinet offices or to reduce the pension list; demanded that further economies be made, particularly in military expenditure, in order to relieve distress; and suggested, as he was frequently to do thereafter, that the estimates be voted a year in advance, and not merely sanctioned retrospectively.

Gordon chaired a reform meeting in Sherborne, 31 Jan. 1831.[39] He repeated his criticisms of government, 4 Feb., but Le Marchant noted that he and Sir Henry Parnell were 'two disappointed candidates for office, whose motives were too open to suspicion for their speeches to have any injurious effect'.[40] On 23 Feb. Gordon introduced a lunatics bill to consolidate and renew his Acts of 1828, and argued that 'although it has been my fate – perhaps I should say my choice – to cavil and discuss the estimates proposed by government', the measure was worth the expense; it was lost at the dissolution. He made light of his differences with Brougham, the lord chancellor, over it and the following day Macaulay's father Zachary wrote to Brougham that 'Gordon appears to have spared anyone the pains of drubbing him. Tom I believe would have been quite ready to do his best to make him regret any attack he might have made on you'.[41] He commented on the sinecure of paymaster of marines, 25 Feb., and naval half-pay and the tax on steam vessels, 28 Feb., when he told Sir James Graham* that the latter had said he was 'glad to see symptoms of returning kindness on my part; but I thought that nothing had ever fallen from me to make him suppose it was ever gone away. I am, however, a little pertinacious, more especially when I am not satisfied'. He presented Cricklade and Dursley reform petitions, 26 Feb., declaring that 'very little reform will be necessary if the system of voting by ballot be established. It is, in my opinion,

of itself preferable to any scheme of reform at present afloat'. He advocated relief for the beleaguered West India interest, 11 Mar., and asked ministers to delay their arrangements for the sugar duties, 14, 22 Mar. He attended a meeting of Whigs on reform at Althorp's, 17 Mar., when, according to Thomas Creevey*, 'that goose Ridley was the only untractable hound with the exception of a growl or two from "Bum" Gordon'.[42] He voted for the second reading of the reform bill, 22 Mar., and promised his support for it as a veteran reformer, 24 Mar., arguing that the purpose of the committee was 'not to throw out the bill, but to correct such of its details as well admit of alteration, without endangering the principle upon which it is founded'. He expressed his anger at ministers' refusal to agree to further inquiry into the civil list, 25 Mar., 12 Apr., when he declined to bother to oppose the reintroduced truck bill because it would be 'wholly inoperative and perfectly useless'. He paired in the minority against Gascoyne's wrecking amendment to the reform bill, 19 Apr. 1831, which precipitated a dissolution.

His name was mentioned as a possible reform candidate for Dorset, but at the general election Gordon was returned for Cricklade after a close contest, his colleague Philip Pleydell Bouverie being defeated by the supposed anti-reformer Thomas Calley. At a Malmesbury reform dinner, 30 May 1831, he spoke for the abolition of rotten boroughs and, although cautioning that there was much still to be done, he stated that 'the great blessing of reform would be that none but an honest ministry ever can hereafter govern the country'.[43] He reintroduced his lunatics bill, 27 June 1831, when he spoke against the army estimates and the confused accounts of the former vice-treasurer of Ireland. He praised government's inclination to do something to assist the West India interest, 30 June. He advocated economies that day and on several occasions during the following two months, dividing against ministers on public grants, 18, 25 July, 21 Aug. He voted for the second reading of the reintroduced reform bill, 6 July, at least twice against adjourning proceedings on it, 12 July, and for the disfranchisement of Appleby, 19 July. He presented and endorsed a Cricklade petition against the election being held in a church there, 20 July, and obtained a proviso in the reform bill to outlaw such practices, 6 Sept. He divided against government on the total disfranchisement of Downton, 21 July, and St. Germans, 26 July, when (according to his speech on 9 Aug.) he also voted for the amendment, in which ministers acquiesced, to salvage one of the seats at Saltash. He was listed as absent on the partial disfranchisement of Chippenham, 27 July, and Dorchester, 28 July. He condemned electoral corruption at Malmesbury, 30 July, and thereafter usually divided in favour of the bill's details, though he pointed out ministers' inconsistencies on the uniting of Penryn and Falmouth in schedule E, 9 Aug., and voted for Lord Chandos's amendment to enfranchise £50 tenants-at-will, 18 Aug. He was listed in minorities against printing the Waterford petition in favour of disarming the Irish yeomanry, 11 Aug., and for legal provision for the Irish poor, 29 Aug., and in the majority for the second reading of the Irish union of parishes bill, 19 Aug. 1831.

Having been named to the Dublin election committee, 29 July, he presented the report, 8 Aug. 1831, when he moved the writ for a new election and gave notice that he would raise the issue. During a heated debate on 23 Aug. he duly described the allegations made during the recent contest, though he was careful not to lay the blame on the unseated Members or Lord Anglesey, the lord lieutenant. His first and second resolutions, that there had been bribery and that this was contrary to election law, were agreed to, but the third, instructing the Irish law officers to prosecute those guilty of 'illegal and unconstitutional practices', was heavily criticized. Gordon agreed to withdraw it for a weaker resolution devised by the attorney-general, Denman, but this was also unsatisfactory to the House, so Denman introduced another, for prosecution only of those 'guilty of bribery'. This, Gordon considered a poor substitute for his original motion, which he then unsuccessfully moved as an amendment (it being lost by 147-224). The fourth resolution, alleging 'undue influence' by the Irish government, was dispatched by Smith Stanley, the chief secretary, who, in a strong speech, called it a 'direct censure' on the ministers with whom Gordon supposedly acted. Gordon confessed himself hurt by the unfavourable comments heaped on him by Members from both sides, but said it was his duty to persist. He was defeated by 207-66 in the second division, for which (as on the first) he acted as a teller. The next day Creevey wrote to Miss Ord that

> that spiteful Bum Gordon, from pure disappointment at not being treasurer of the ordnance, or some such officer, spent the whole night in attempting to spite Lord Anglesey, and was eventually beat by more than three to two; so far as it was it was mighty well, but a night was lost by it.[44]

Gordon, who defended his right to bring forward such a matter, 25 Aug., voted for Benett's amendment that there had been gross bribery at the Liverpool election, 5 Sept. 1831.

He spoke against the ministerial alteration to the reform bill to exclude electors of Cricklade who were freeholders from voting for the county of Wiltshire, 2 Sept. 1831, and the following day he criticized the decision to give the lord chancellor a veto over the choice of revising barristers. He called the Sugar Refinery Act one of the most objectionable laws he had ever known, 5 Sept., and warned ministers not to give the impression of being disposed to do injustice to the colonies, 7 Sept. He told the House, 22 Sept., when he called the measure flawed and impolitic, that if he had been present he would have voted in the minority for a select committee to inquire how far the Act could be renewed with regard to the West India interest, 12 Sept.;[45] he pressed strenuously for the matter to be dropped, 28 Sept., 13 Oct. He managed the committee and conference on the Lords' amendments to his lunatics bill, 26 Sept., and overturned a decision to transfer to the lord chancellor the power to appoint commissioners. Ellenborough recorded that 'Brougham is very angry about it – the government having been beaten by Bum Gordon to annoy Brougham', but the prorogation again intervened before the bill could be passed.[46] Gordon, who voted for the passage of the reform bill, 21 Sept., and the second reading of the Scottish bill, 23 Sept., was absent from the Commons on the call for Lord Ebrington's confidence motion, 10 Oct., but was excused on the 15th. He signed the requisitions for two Wiltshire reform meetings, and was probably present at them, 30 Sept., 28 Oct. 1831.[47] He voted for the defeated Whig candidate William Ponsonby* in the Dorset by-election that autumn, and at the turn of the year was listed among the prospective members of a putative Whig club in that county.[48]

He voted for the second reading of the revised reform bill, 17 Dec. 1831, and for the clause to partially disfranchise 30 boroughs, 23 Jan. 1832, when he divided for the vestry bill. He sided with opposition for inquiry into the glove trade, 31 Jan., and spoke in favour of this, 3 Apr. He again reintroduced the lunatics bill, 2 Feb., and, although substantially amended in both Houses, it passed that session, being given royal assent, 11 Aug.[49] He divided against giving the vote to all £10 poor rate payers, 3 Feb., but argued that the hereditary rights of freemen should descend through daughters as well as sons, 7 Feb. He pointed out the absurdity of levying taxes on pensions, 8 Feb., and recited details of how to make additional savings on the naval estimates, 13 Feb., when Rice accused him of taking 'great pleasure in finding fault'. He voted against the production of information on Portugal, 9 Feb. He was probably the Gordon who voted in the minority against the recommittal of the anatomy bill, 27 Feb. He divided for the enfranchisement of Tower Hamlets, 28 Feb., and Gateshead, 5 Mar., and for the third reading of the reform bill, 22 Mar. He asked ministers to postpone the debate on sugar, 29 Feb., voted in the minority against them for reduction of the duties on it, 7 Mar., and requested impartial inquiry into the sufferings of West Indian merchants, 9, 23 Mar. He again suggested ways of reducing expenditure, 26, 27 Mar., and on the 28th opined that

> if this be all that can be done in the way of economizing the public money, which the expense of the army calls for, I cannot help thinking that I and ... [Hume] and other gentlemen, have been wasting our time during the last 15 years in calling upon the Tory administrations to make reductions.

He voted for Ebrington's motion for an address calling on the king to appoint only ministers who would carry the reform bill unimpaired, 10 May, and the second reading of the Irish bill, 25 May 1832.

The following month Gordon joined the India board, on a salary of £1,200, and soon sowed the seeds of discord. As Macaulay wrote to his sisters, the

> history of it is this. Gordon, ... a fat, ugly, spiteful, snarling, sneering, old rascal of a slave-driver, is my colleague ... The appointment was, in my opinion, quite unjustifiable. He had always been a Whig, and a violent Whig. When the present ministers came in he asked for one of the under-secretaryships of state. They were all given. He became angry and, though he could not with decency oppose the reform bill, having always declared himself a zealous reformer, he gave the ministers all the trouble in his power. On their colonial policy, on their financial policy, on their commercial policy – nay, wherever a favourable opportunity offered, even on the details of the reform bill, he opposed and harassed them. It was not without much grumbling and reluctance that, on the night of Lord Ebrington's last motion, he voted for them. They have resolved, it seems, to buy him off and they have stopped his ugly, wide, grinning mouth with this commissionership. He brings into his new situation the same vile temper which he has always displayed in public life. Knowing nothing of the business of the office, he wishes to remodel it all. He has already quarrelled with Charles Grant* and with Hyde Villiers*, and wishes to draw me to his party. What chance he has of succeeding with me you may judge from this letter. I am opposed to him, not merely from dislike of his temper and from distrust of his principles, but also on public grounds. It is not merely by an envious, querulous, busy-bodyish disposition that he has been induced to act as he has acted. He differs from Grant and Villiers with respect to the policy which ought to be pursued towards India. We consider him as being, in fact, the creature of the directors, a friend of the China monopoly, a friend to the existing system of patronage. He as good as told me that he considered himself as placed at the board to be a check to Grant and Villiers.[50]

As expected, he was returned unopposed for Cricklade, 16 June 1832.[51] He was added to the select committee on the East India Company, 22 June, and sat on its subcommittee on revenue affairs.[52] He voted to make coroners' inquests public, 20 June, and thereafter, of course, with his colleagues, occasionally acting as a government teller. He defended the ministerial salaries of the lord privy seal and the postmaster-general, 27 July, but otherwise confined himself to making nondescript remarks, 25, 30 July, 4, 9 Aug. He was returned as a Liberal for Cricklade at the general election of 1832, later transferring to a seat for New Windsor, and continued to serve in minor office under Grey and Melbourne. He died 'aged 78' in May 1864, leaving everything to his unmarried only child Anna (1809-84), and was remembered as 'the Dorsetshire Joseph Hume'.[53]

[1] Grey mss, Howick jnl. 9 Mar., 3, 14 May, 14 June, 2 July 1830; *Three Diaries*, 34. [2] Hatherton diary, 5 Sept. 1831. [3] *OED*; *Macaulay Letters*, ii. 139. [4] *Devizes Gazette*, 28 June 1827. [5] Le Marchant, *Althorp*, 242. [6] K. Morgan, *Bristol and Atlantic Trade*, 185-6, 189, 191; *Sources of Jamaican Hist.* ed. K.E. Ingram, 696. [7] Inst. of Commonwealth Stud. M915/3, 4. [8] *Regs. of Freemen of Gloucester* ed. A.R.J. Juřica (Glos. Rec. Ser. iv), 208; *Devizes Gazette*, 31 May 1821, 20 May 1824, 11 May 1826. [9] *HP Commons, 1790-1820*, iv. 37-38; *Westminster Pollbook* (1818), 63. [10] Add. 51830. [11] *The Times*, 4, 5 May, 7 June 1820. [12] Add. 51831; *Devizes Gazette*, 11, 18 Jan. 1821. [13] *The Times*, 31 Mar., 14 Apr., 15 May 1821. [14] Ibid. 4 Apr. 1821. [15] *Black Bk.* (1823), 158. [16] *Devizes Gazette*, 7 Aug. 1823. [17] *The Times*, 7, 9 Apr. 1824. [18] Add. 36461, f. 88. [19] *The Times*, 7, 11, 18 June 1825. [20] Ibid. 18 Feb., 21 Mar. 1826. [21] Ibid. 22 Feb. 1827. [22] *PP* (1826-7), vi. 75-260. [23] Lansdowne mss. [24] G. Battiscombe, *Shaftesbury*, 37. [25] *CJ*, lxxxiii. 85, 122, 151, 208, 227, 411, 415, 421, 434, 498, 535. [26] Add. 40397, ff. 206, 210, 219. [27] Inst. of Commonwealth Stud. M915/4. [28] Countess of Airlie, *Lady Palmerston and her Times*, i. 169. [29] *Greville Mems.* i. 365. [30] Inst. of Commonwealth Stud. M915/4. [31] NLS mss 24770, f. 50. [32] Le Marchant, 242. [33] Add. 56554, f. 80. [34] *Ellenborough Diary*, ii. 301; Howick jnl. 2 July 1830. [35] *Gloucester Jnl.* 31 July 1830; *Gloucester Pollbook* (1830), 15. [36] Wentworth Woodhouse mun. [37] Add. 56555, f. 71. [38] *Three Diaries*, 34. [39] *Dorset Co. Chron.* 3 Feb. 1831. [40] Le Marchant, 271. [41] Brougham mss. [42] Creevey mss, Creevey to Miss Ord, 17 Mar. 1831. [43] *Dorset Co. Chron.* 28 Apr.; *Devizes Gazette*, 12, 19 May, 2 June 1831. [44] Creevey mss. [45] He was, nevertheless, credited with such a vote in the division list. [46] *CJ*, lxxxvi. 866-8, 874-5; *Three Diaries*, 135. [47] *Devizes Gazette*, 29 Sept., 27 Oct. 1831. [48] *Dorset Pollbook* (Sept.-Oct. 1831), 68; Dorset RO, Fox Strangways mss D/FSI 332, Parry Okeden to Ilchester, 28 Dec. 1831, 14, 21 Jan. 1832. [49] *CJ*, lxxxvii. 67, 70, 75, 157, 166, 172, 573-5, 584. [50] *Macaulay Letters*, ii. 139-40. [51] *Devizes Gazette*, 7 June 1832. [52] *PP* (1831-2), xi. 19. [53] *Gent. Mag.* (1864), i. 814.

S.M.F.

GORDON, Hon. William (1784–1858).

ABERDEENSHIRE   17 Oct. 1820–Aug. 1854

b. 18 Dec. 1784, 2nd s. of George Gordon, Lord Haddo (1st s. of George, 3rd earl of Aberdeen [S] and *d.* 1791), and Charlotte, da. of William Baird of Newbyth, Haddington. *educ.* Harrow 1795-7. *unm. d.* 3 Feb. 1858.

Entered RN 1797, lt. 1804, cdr. 1807, capt. 1810, r.-adm. 1846, v.-adm. 1854; c.-in-c. at Nore 1854-7. Ld. of admiralty Sept. 1841-Feb. 1846.

Gordon was six when his father, Lord Haddo, heir of the lascivious 3rd earl of Aberdeen, whose determination to provide for his several bastards created considerable problems for his legitimate successors, died suddenly in October 1791.[1] Lady Haddo quarrelled with Aberdeen and removed herself and her seven children, who included Gordon's elder brother George, now Lord Haddo and heir to his grandfather, from Gight Castle, Aberdeenshire, to London. On her death in October 1795, when Gordon and Haddo had entered Harrow School, the orphans were taken up by her friend Henry Dundas†, the premier Pitt's right hand man and manager of his ministry's Scottish interests. Gordon was started in the navy in July 1797. The following year Haddo, exercising his right under Scottish law, chose Pitt and Dundas as his and his siblings' legal guardians. On Lord Aberdeen's death in 1801 Haddo succeeded to the earldom and the entailed Aberdeenshire estates, but he inherited substantial debts and discovered that his grandfather had shown great ingenuity in providing money from the estates for his bastards. Gordon's nominal share of the spoils was £2,000, but he remained largely dependent financially on his brother, who was sometimes helped out by Dundas (now Lord Melville). Aberdeen embarked in 1801 on the distinguished diplomatic career which earned him election as a representative peer in 1806, a green ribbon in 1808 and a United Kingdom peerage (Viscount Gordon) in 1814, when, as ambassador to Austria, he signed the Treaty of Paris.[2] Gordon, whose next brother Alexander, lieutenant-colonel of the Scots Guards, was killed at Waterloo, served throughout the war on a variety of stations and achieved post rank at the Cape in 1810.[3] He was on the Aberdeenshire electoral roll by 1811 and attended the county meeting which voted a loyal address to the regent in the aftermath of Peterloo, 23 Nov. 1819.[4] On the death of the sitting Member in September 1820 he offered for the county on the interest of his brother Lord Aberdeen, now a prominent supporter of the Liverpool ministry, whose Scottish manager Lord Melville (Dundas's son), first lord of the admiralty, endorsed his candidature. A potential rival withdrew and Gordon, who declared that he would 'on all occasions be guided by constitutional principles', walked over.[5]

A reliable attender, he gave general but not undeviating support to the ministry.[6] He voted in defence of their prosecution of Queen Caroline, 6 Feb. 1821, and against parliamentary reform, 9, 10 May 1821, 20 Feb.

1823. He divided for repeal of the additional malt duty, 21 Mar., but spoke and voted against it when ministers forced the issue, 3 Apr. He cast wayward votes for partial repeal of the house tax, 10 Mar., against the grant for Irish churches and glebe hoses, 1 July, and, in a minority of 15, against the third reading of the trade reciprocity bill, 4 July 1824. He was absent from the division on Catholic relief, 28 Feb. 1821, but voted against the removal of Catholic peers' disabilities, 30 Apr. 1822, and relief in general, 1 Mar., 21 Apr. 1825. He presented constituency petitions against alteration of the timber duties, 26 Feb. 1821, for the free export of Scottish spirits, 29 Apr., and against the navigation bill, 6 May, and the stamp duties bill, 25 July 1822, and for relief from agricultural distress, 24 Feb. 1823.[7] Opposing inquiry into the royal burghs, 26 Mar. 1823, he said that whatever money had been spent by the magistrates of Aberdeen had been 'laid out for the benefit of the town'. He defended the system of naval promotions, 19 June 1823, the use of impressment as a matter of 'necessity', 10 June 1824, and the naval pensions arrangements, 21 Feb. 1826. He applauded the government's proposals to curb illicit distillation, 8 July 1823, 25 Apr. 1825.[8] He presented petitions from Aberdeenshire and Kincardineshire against relaxation of the corn laws, 28 Apr., 2 May 1825.[9] He was in a minority of seven for an amendment to the ministry's bank restriction scheme, 13 Feb. 1826, and in the following weeks presented and endorsed numerous petitions against interference with the Scottish banking system.[10] He said that 'no good' could come of the select committee on the circulation of small Scottish and Irish bank notes, 16 Mar. As a member of it, he concurred in Peel's report recommending no change for the time being;[11] and he extolled the virtues of the existing system in the House, 26 May. He presented Aberdeenshire anti-slavery petitions, 27, 28 Feb., 13 Apr., and one from there and another from Kincardineshire against any reduction of agricultural protection;[12] he probably voted against the second reading of the government's corn bill, 27 Apr. He spoke and voted against the spring guns bill, 11 May. He complained that the policy of reciprocity had seriously damaged British shipping interests, 13 May 1826. At the general election that summer he was returned unopposed for Aberdeenshire, where his resistance to the government's currency proposals had gone down well.[13]

Gordon presented and endorsed Aberdeenshire agriculturists' petitions against further interference with the corn laws, 21 Feb., brought up several more, 26 Feb., 23 Mar., and spoke and voted against the second reading of the corn bill, 2 Apr. 1827.[14] His attempt to amend the corn averages bill to include Irish returns in the calculations was defeated by 23-14, 31 May.[15] He divided against Catholic claims, 6 Mar., and Lord Althorp's election expenses bill, 28 May 1827. His duties as captain of the *Briton*, to which he was appointed in March 1827, apparently kept him away from Parliament in 1828, when his brother become, first, chancellor of the duchy of Lancaster, and then foreign secretary in the duke of Wellington's administration.[16] Planta, the patronage secretary, who had mentioned Gordon as a possible mover or seconder of the address, expected him to vote 'with government' for Catholic emancipation, and he duly did so on 30 Mar. 1829, having defaulted on a call of the House on the 5th.[17] Under instructions from his constituents, he opposed the Whig Kennedy's tailzies regulation bill in May 1829; he was a minority teller against its report on the 25th.[18] Paid off from naval service on 27 Apr. 1830, he voted with Peel and other ministers against the Galway franchise bill, 25 May, was a minority teller for an amendment to the Perth navigation bill, 28 May, and divided for the grant for South American missions, 7 June 1830. At the general election in August he was returned unopposed. He expressed some alarm over the revolution in France, for which he blamed the French king, but hoped there would not be a war.[19]

Ministers of course counted him as one of their 'friends', and he was in their minority on the civil list, 15 Nov. 1830. On 26 Feb. 1831 he gave credit to the Grey ministry's professed 'principles of economy, retrenchment and non-intervention', but said that 'they only follow in the steps of their predecessors' and warned that he was 'not prepared to support any great change in the established forms of the constitution by the adoption of theories which may shake the whole fabric'. He duly voted against the second reading of their English reform bill, 22 Mar., and for Gascoyne's wrecking amendment, 19 Apr.1831, after signing the Aberdeenshire anti-reform petition and denouncing the scheme in a public letter to his constituents.[20] At the ensuing general election he stood again, professing support for the 'temperate reform' of blatant abuses but condemning the ministerial plan as too dangerous. In a boisterous contest he defeated a reformer with reasonable comfort, but was shouted down by the unfranchised mob and forced to sneak away to avoid physical harassment.[21]

Gordon voted against the second reading of the reintroduced reform bill, 6 July, for use of the 1831 census to determine the disfranchisement schedules, 19 July, against the inclusion of Chippenham in B, 27 July, and against the passage of the bill, 21 Sept.

1831. He was in the Tory majority against issuing the Liverpool writ, 5 Sept. He voted against the second reading of the Scottish reform bill, 23 Sept., and on 3 Oct. 1831, while admitting that the Scottish representative system was 'not of a popular character', objected to the proposed increase in burgh Members and extension of the franchise to 'a class of persons ... which it is not desirable should continue to influence the return of Members'. He divided against the second reading of the revised reform bill, 17 Dec. 1831, the enfranchisement of Tower Hamlets, 28 Feb., and the third reading, 22 Mar. 1832. He voted against government on the Russian-Dutch loan, 26 Jan., 12 July. He voiced concern over the 'extensive' powers conferred on the authorities by the Scottish cholera prevention bill, 16 Feb., said that the malt drawback bill would encourage illicit distillation, 17 Feb., and thought the factories regulation bill should be referred to a select committee, 20 Feb. He voted against the second reading of the Irish reform bill, 25 May. On the Scottish measure, 22 June, he advocated the selection of a more central polling place for his county than Aberdeen; he preferred Dalkeith to Edinburgh for Midlothian, 27 June. He presented a clerical petition against the government's Irish education scheme, 8 June 1832.

At the general election of 1832 Gordon defeated, at considerable expense to his brother, his Liberal opponent of 1831.[22] He resigned his place at the admiralty in Peel's second ministry in order to vote against repeal of the corn laws in deference to the wishes of his farming constituents.[23] He held his county seat until his appointment to the Nore command in 1854, when Aberdeen was prime minister. He died a bachelor at Exmouth in February 1858.

[1] *Gent. Mag.* (1791), ii. 971. [2] M.E. Chamberlaine, *Lord Aberdeen*, 18, 20-21, 25, 79-81. [3] *Gent. Mag.* (1858), i. 340. [4] *Pol. State of Scotland 1811*, p. 12; *Aberdeen Jnl.* 24 Nov. 1819. [5] *Aberdeen Jnl.* 13 Sept., 18 Oct. 1820; NAS GD51/1/198/1/23; 51/5/749/1, pp. 279-80. [6] *Black Bk.* (1823), 158; *Session of Parl. 1825*, p. 465. [7] *The Times*, 27 Feb. 1821, 30 Apr., 7 May, 26 July 1822, 25 Feb. 1823. [8] Ibid. 9 July 1823. [9] Ibid. 29 Apr., 3 May 1825. [10] Ibid. 25, 28 Feb., 17, 21, 22 Mar., 8, 15, 19, 22, 29 Apr. 1826. [11] Nottingham Univ. Lib. Acc. 636, Denison diary, 19 May [1826]. [12] *The Times*, 28 Feb., 1 Mar., 14, 19 Apr. 1826. [13] *Aberdeen Jnl.* 28 June 1826. [14] *The Times*, 22, 27 Feb., 24 Mar. 1827. [15] Ibid. 1 June 1827. [16] *Gent. Mag.* (1858), i. 340. [17] Add. 40398, f. 85. [18] *Aberdeen Jnl.* 6 May 1829. [19] Ibid. 7 July, 25 Aug. 1830. [20] Ibid. 23 Mar., 13 Apr. 1831. [21] Ibid. 27 Apr., 25 May 1831; Wellington mss WP1/1184/25. [22] Chamberlaine, 256-7. [23] Parker, *Peel*, iii. 336; *Disraeli Letters*, v. 2051; *Dod's Parl. Companion* (1847), 172-3.

D.R.F.

GORDON CUMMING, **Sir William Gordon**, 2nd bt. (1787–1854), of Altyre, Forres and Gordonstown, Elgin.

ELGIN BURGHS   1831–1832

b. 20 July 1787, 3rd but 1st surv. s. of Sir Alexander Penrose Cumming (afterwards Cumming Gordon†), 1st bt., of Altyre and Gordonstown and Helen, da. of Sir Ludovick Grant, 7th bt., of Castle Grant, Elgin; bro. of Charles Lennox Cumming Bruce*. *m.* (1) 11 Sept. 1815, in Zurich, Eliza Maria (*d.* 20 Apr. 1842),[1] da. of John Campbell† of Shawfield and Islay, Argyll, 7s. (1 *d.v.p.*) 6da. (1 *d.v.p.*); (2) 19 Dec. 1846, Jane Eliza, da. of William Mackintosh of Geddes, Nairn, 1s. 2da. *suc.* fa. as 2nd bt. 10 Feb. 1806. *d.* 23 Nov. 1854.

Provost, Nairn 1820-1, 1830-1.

Gordon Cumming (who reversed the order of the surnames affected by his father in order to avoid obscuring his clan name) became heir to the family's Elginshire estates on the death at sea in December 1800 of his elder brother George (*b.* 1774) on his way home from civil service with the East India Company in Bengal. (Another brother, Alexander Penrose, had died an infant in 1780.)[2] He succeeded his father, who had received a baronetcy from Pitt, in 1806, at the age of 18. In early 1824 his first cousin Colonel Francis William Grant, Tory Member for Elginshire, strongly recommended him to the Liverpool ministry for the vacant lord lieutenancy of Nairnshire, as the possessor of 'the political influence of the burgh of Nairn' and 'an old proprietor in the county', but he was passed over because he had 'no residence in the county'.[3] He was reckoned to have sustained 'ten thousand pounds worth of damage' to his Altyre property in the destructive floods of 1829.[4] At an Elginshire county meeting called to petition for reform of the Scottish representative system, 22 Dec. 1830, he seconded his younger brother Charles Cumming Bruce's unsuccessful amendment calling for moderation. He helped to promote an Elginshire petition against the Grey ministry's reform bills in April 1831.[5] At the general election the following month he secured his brother's return for Inverness Burghs and got the backing of Grant and his kinsman Lord Fife* to ensure his own unopposed return for the Elgin district.[6]

He voted against the second reading of the reintroduced English reform bill, 6 July, and at least three times for the adjournment, 12 July. Next day Lord Ellenborough ran across him at the Tory opposition's Charles Street headquarters.[7] He divided with them for use of the 1831 census to determine the borough disfranchisement schedules, 19 July, and against the inclusion of Chippenham in B, 27 July; but he was credited with a vote for the disfranchisement of St. Germans, 26 July.[8] He was in Daniel O'Connell's minority of ten for swearing the Dublin election committee, 29 July. He voted against the passage of the reform bill, 21 Sept., and the second reading of the Scottish measure, 23 Sept. In his only reported Commons speech, 3 Oct. 1831, he denounced the proposed electoral junction of Elginshire and Nairnshire. He was absent from the division on the second reading of the revised English reform bill, 17 Dec. 1831, and his only known votes in the 1832 session were against the enfranchisement of Tower Hamlets, 28 Feb., the third reading of the reform bill, 22 Mar., and the government's navy civil departments bill, 2 Apr. He was given six weeks' leave to deal with urgent private business, 3 July 1832. He stood down at the dissolution in December and 'did not again aspire to senatorial honours'.[9]

Gordon Cumming, whose first wife was the daughter of the authoress Lady Charlotte Bury, died at Altyre in November 1854. He was succeeded by his eldest son Alexander Penrose (1816-66), an army officer.

[1] M.E. Cumming Bruce, *Fam. Recs. of Bruces and Cumyns*, 476. [2] Ibid. 474-5; *Gent. Mag.* (1801), i. 275. [3] Add. 40361, f. 9. [4] *Edgeworth Letters*, 449. [5] *Inverness Courier*, 29 Dec. 1830; *Cockburn Letters*, 303. [6] *Inverness Courier*, 26 Apr., 4, 25 May, 1 June 1831; *Wellington Pol. Corresp.* i. 144. [7] *Three Diaries*, 104. [8] *The Times*, 28 July 1831. [9] *Gent. Mag.* (1855), i. 81.

D.R.F.

GORE *see* **ORMSBY GORE**

GORE LANGTON, **William** (?1760–1847), of Newton Park, nr. Bath, Som.; Dean House, Oxon., and 12 Grosvenor Square, Mdx.

SOMERSET	21 Sept. 1795–1806
TREGONY	30 Jan. 1808–1812
SOMERSET	1812–1820
SOMERSET	1831–1832
SOMERSET EAST	1832–14 Mar. 1847

b. ?Dec. 1760, 1st s. of Edward Gore of Barrow Court, Som. and Barbara, da. and h. of Sir George Browne of Kiddington Park, Oxon., wid. of Sir Edward Mostyn, 5th bt., of Talacre, Flint. *educ.* New Coll. Oxf. 19 Oct. 1776, aged 17. *m.* (1) 21 July 1783, Bridget (*d.* 5 Dec. 1793), da. and h. of Joseph Langton of Newton Park and took additional name of Langton 9 Aug. 1783, 3s. (1 *d.v.p.*)

1da.; (2) c.1800,[1] Mary, da. of John Browne of Salperton, Glos., 2s. (1 *d.v.p.*) 2da. *suc.* fa. 1801. *d.* 14 Mar. 1847.
Lt.-col. Oxf. militia 1782, col. 1798.

Gore Langton's ancestors were prominent figures in the City of London who had established themselves in Somerset in the seventeenth century. In 1801 he inherited his father's Barrow Court estate along with other scattered properties in Somerset, Gloucestershire and Wiltshire, having already received unspecified properties as a marriage settlement.[2] However, it was his acquisition by marriage of the Newton Park estate that enhanced his standing in the county sufficiently for him to become one of its representatives. He was an active Member of the Whig opposition before 1820, joining Brooks's Club, 11 May 1816, but his consistent support for Catholic relief alienated many of his constituents and created an opportunity for his old rival, Sir Thomas Lethbridge*, to campaign against him. At the dissolution in 1820 he sent a letter from Paris announcing his decision not to stand again, although he defended his record in 'protecting the properties and liberties of my fellow subjects and ... opposing the encroachments of preponderating influence'.[3] He continued to take an active part in Somerset politics, being one of the freeholders who signed an address urging the county meeting in January 1823 to consider petitioning for parliamentary reform; he would have moved the resolutions on this subject at the second meeting that month had he not caught a cold attending the first.[4] In August 1830 he nominated Edward Sanford at the county election, commending him as one who would 'support the rights and liberties of the people, with truth and independence'.[5] The following April he was requisitioned by the freeholders of Bath to stand for the county, free of expense, as a supporter of the Grey ministry's reform bill. He welcomed the opportunity to 'assist in carrying into effect that important measure', which he had advocated throughout his career, but said this was 'his only motive in coming forward at this time of life' and that once reform was accomplished 'he hoped he should again be permitted to retire into private life'. He also supported triennial parliaments. He was returned unopposed with Sanford and promised to 'fearlessly do my duty towards my king, my country, and the constitution' and 'show myself on all occasions the faithful guardian of the public purse'.[6]

He divided for the second reading of the reintroduced reform bill, 6 July 1831, and generally supported its details. However, he voted against the division of counties, 11 Aug., repudiated the insinuation that he was therefore not a sincere reformer, 16 Aug., and protested against these 'odious and obnoxious clauses' which would remove 'all the honour and ... benefit of county representation', 2 Sept., when he added that 'nothing on earth should induce me to become a candidate for a division of a county'. He voted for the bill's third reading, 19 Sept., its passage, 21 Sept., and Lord Ebrington's confidence motion, 10 Oct. He divided for the second reading of the revised bill, 17 Dec. 1831, and generally supported its details, including the provision limiting to two days the interval between county nominations and elections, 11 Feb. 1832, as he thought a longer period would mean 'we shall never have a *bona fide* county election ... there will be too much temptation for candidates to hang back in order [to] take their opponents by surprise'. However, he moved an amendment for the counties to remain undivided and return four Members each, 27 Jan., warning that the ministerial plan would be 'highly injurious to the future independence of counties'. He feared that the power of large landed proprietors would increase and that of 'the gentleman of small independent property' diminish, while 'those small independent freeholders, who were at once the honour and the security of this country, will be altogether destroyed'. His 'Whig crotchet', as one minister privately described it, was defeated by 215-89.[7] He also voted with the minorities to enfranchise £10 ratepayers, 3 Feb., and against Helston remaining in schedule B, 23 Feb. He divided for the bill's third reading, 22 Mar., expressed 'deep regret' at the resignation of ministers, 9 May, voted for Ebrington's motion for an address asking the king to appoint only ministers committed to carrying an unimpaired measure, 10 May, and presented Shepton Mallet and Bath petitions for withholding supplies until it was carried, 18 May 1832.

He voted in the minorities to print the Waterford petition for disarming the Irish yeomanry, 11 Aug., and inquire into the 'most objectionable' corn laws, 15 Sept. 1831. He observed that such a 'large and numerous body of my constituents' had expressed their hostility to the general register bill that he felt it was his 'duty to oppose it by every means in my power', 20 Sept. He was granted three weeks' leave 'on the public service', 26 Sept. He supported petitions against the importation of French gloves, 15, 16 Dec. 1831, and voted for inquiry into the trade, 31 Jan., 3 Apr. 1832. He divided against ministers on the Russian-Dutch loan, 26 Jan., and was absent from the divisions on this issue in July. He voted with them on the navy civil departments bill, 6 Apr. He reportedly paired for Buxton's anti-slavery motion, 24 May.[8] He expressed his 'utter indignation and horror' at the tsar of Russia's conduct towards the Poles, 9 July 1832.

In the summer of 1832 Gore Langton accepted a requisition to offer for the new Eastern division of Somerset, explaining that the 'warm interest' thus shown had dissuaded him from carrying out his declared intention of retiring at the dissolution; he was returned at the head of the poll.[9] In fact, he continued to sit, as 'one of the oldest reformers in the House ... in favour of the ballot and the immediate abolition of slavery', until his death in March 1847, 'aged 87'.[10] He left his Somerset estates to his grandson, William Henry Powell Gore Langton (1824-73), Conservative Member for West Somerset, 1851-59, 1863-73.[11] His eldest son from his second marriage, William Henry Gore Langton (1802-75), was Liberal Member for Bristol, 1852-65.

[1] *Smith Letters*, i. 49. [2] The will was sworn at the 'upper value': PROB 11/1357/318; IR26/51/79. [3] Wilts. RO, Benett mss 413/485, Poole to Benett, 20 Feb.; *Taunton Courier*, 15 Mar. 1820. [4] *Bristol Mirror*, 25 Jan., 1 Feb. 1823. [5] Ibid. 7 Aug. 1830. [6] Ibid. 30 Apr., 7, 14 May 1831. [7] Add. 51573, Rice to Lady Holland 24 Jan. 1832. [8] *Keenes' Bath Jnl.* 4 June 1832. [9] *Bristol Mirror*, 14 July, 8 Sept., 22 Dec. 1832. [10] *Dod's Parl. Companion* (1833), 132-3; *Gent. Mag.* (1847), i. 545. [11] PROB 11/2057/499; IR26/1778/383.

T.A.J.

GOSSET, William (1782-1848), of Round Ward, nr. Truro, Cornw. and 64 Harley Street, Mdx.

TRURO   5 June 1820-1826

b. 18 Jan. 1782, in Jersey,[1] 4th surv. s. of Matthew Gosset (*d.* 1799) of Bagot and 2nd w. Margaret, da. of Thomas Durell of Jersey. *m.* 23 July 1808,[2] Gertrude Martha, da. of Ralph Allen Daniell[†] of Trelissick, nr. Truro, 1s. 3da. kntd. 3 May 1831; KCH 1831. *d.* 27 Mar. 1848.

2nd lt. R. Engineers 1798, 1st lt. 1801, 2nd capt. 1805, capt. 1809; brevet maj. 1814, lt.-col. 1816; lt.-col. R. Engineers 1817 (on half-pay 1817-21), col. 1837; maj.-gen. 1846.

Sec. of legation to Barbary States 1813; sec. to master-gen. of ordnance 1827-8; priv. sec. to ld. lt [I] 1828-9; under-sec. [I] 1831-5; sjt.-at-arms to House of Commons 1835-*d.*

Gosset belonged to a French Huguenot family who had fled to Jersey after the revocation of the Edict of Nantes. His great-uncle Isaac Gosset (1713-99) settled in London and made a name for himself as the creator of exquisite wax models, specializing in cameo portraits; his son, also Isaac (1745-1812), attended Oxford University and became a celebrated biblical scholar and bibliophile.[3] Gosset's father, who remained in Jersey and died intestate in 1799, worth £5,000,[4] had at least three sons with his first wife Elizabeth Hilgrove: the eldest, Matthew (*d.* 1843), obtained the

office of viscount of Jersey. As secretary to William A'Court's[†] special mission to the Barbary States in 1813, Gosset made himself familiar with the fortifications of Algiers; and in 1816, as major commandant of the engineers in Lord Exmouth's punitive expedition against the dey, he distinguished himself in the taking and destruction of an enemy frigate.[5] In 1808 he had married the daughter of Ralph Daniell, Member for West Looe, 1805-12, and a leading figure in the affairs of Truro. He settled in the area and at the general election of 1818 was put up for the borough on Lord Yarmouth's* interest against the dominant Falmouth interest, in harness with Sir Richard Hussey Vivian; they were defeated by one vote and their petition was discharged.[6] They tried again at the general election of 1820, when Vivian topped the poll but Gosset was involved in a double return with the Falmouth candidate. He petitioned to be seated but failed to enter into recognizances. The election for the second seat was then declared void and at the subsequent by-election in June 1820 Gosset, who boasted of his 'independent' backing, prevailed by a majority of two votes; he survived a subsequent petition.[7]

He was an occasional attender who gave general support to Lord Liverpool's ministry. He almost certainly divided against economies in revenue collection, 4 July 1820. He voted in defence of ministers' conduct towards Queen Caroline, 6 Feb. 1821. He divided against Catholic relief, 28 Feb. He voted against repeal of the additional malt duty, 3 Apr., parliamentary reform, 9 May, the omission of arrears from the duke of Clarence's grant, 18 June, and Hume's economy and retrenchment motion, 27 June. On the army estimates, 25 May 1821, he observed that there had been no recent increase in the pay of inspectors of the Channel Islands militia.[8] He divided against more extensive tax reductions, 11 Feb., and abolition of one of the joint-postmasterships, 13 Mar. 1822. He defended the way in which he, as the officer in charge, had handled the transfer of the late queen's coffin to the boat at Harwich, 6 Mar. He had more to say in defence of the Jersey militia, 22 Mar., but his observations on the ordnance estimates, 28 Mar., were inaudible to the reporters.[9] He voted against relieving Catholic peers of their disabilities, 30 Apr. 1822. He presented Truro petitions against the hawkers and peddlers bill, 24 Mar. 1823, and the coastwise coal duties, 13 Feb. 1824.[10] He voted against repeal of the Foreign Enlistment Act, 16 Apr. 1823. He divided for the Irish unlawful societies bill, 25 Feb. 1825, when he was granted a week's leave to deal with urgent private business. He returned to vote against Catholic relief, 1 Mar., 21 Apr. 1825. It was said of him at this time that he 'attended seldom, and voted with ministers'.[11] He retired from Parliament at the dissolution in 1826.

Gosset was taken up by the 1st marquess of Anglesey, who appointed him his secretary as master-general of the ordnance in Canning's ministry and employed him as his private secretary during his first spell as Irish viceroy under the duke of Wellington in 1828.[12] That year Gosset obtained modest civil list pensions for his only son and two female relatives.[13] Anglesey, who described him as 'honest, zealous, indefatigable [and] industrious to a degree', secured his appointment as under-secretary at Dublin Castle when he returned to Ireland as viceroy on the formation of Lord Grey's ministry. Gosset, who was knighted soon afterwards, came to exercise very considerable influence, and he played an important part in managing the Irish elections in 1831, including that for Dublin. However, his blatant Orange bias made him a *bête noir* of Daniel O'Connell*.[14] In 1835 the second Melbourne administration, anxious to implement a change of direction in Irish policy, removed him, under the 'gloss' of resignation. Attempts to provide him with a colonial or revenue place were unsuccessful, but, to the pleasure of William IV, who considered him 'a useful and loyal man', he was appointed serjeant-at-arms to the Commons.[15] He became embroiled in the protracted privilege case of Stockdale *v.* Hansard.[16] He died in harness in March 1848 and left all his property to his wife, who died the following year.[17] His son Ralph Allen Gosset (1809-95), who had been appointed as his assistant in 1835, rose to become deputy serjeant-at-arms in 1854 and serjeant in 1875; he had a turbulent time in the 1880 Parliament with Bradlaugh and the Irish Home Rulers.[18]

[1] L.M. May, *Charlton*, 64. [2] IGI (Cornw.). [3] *Gent. Mag* (1799), ii. 1088-9; (1812), ii. 596-7, 669-70; (1848), i. 547; *Procs. Huguenot Soc.* iii (1888-91), 540-68; xxi (1965-70), 273-9; xxii (1970-6), 504; G.R. Balleine, *Biog. Dict. of Jersey*, 298-9. [4] PROB 6/175/221. [5] *Gent. Mag.* (1848), i. 547; Balleine, 302; *Ann. Reg.* (1816), Hist. p. 102; W. Porter, *Hist. R. Engineers*, i. 392; Add. 41534, f. 267; 41535, f. 4. [6] *R. Cornw. Gazette*, 20 June 1818. [7] *West Briton*, 17 Mar., 2, 9 June 1820. [8] *The Times*, 26 May 1821. [9] Ibid. 29 Mar. 1822. [10] Ibid. 25 Mar. 1823, 13 Feb. 1824. [11] *Session of Parl. 1825*, p. 465. [12] *Canning's Ministry*, 166; Mq. of Anglesey, *One-Leg*, 184; *O'Connell Corresp.* iv. 1508; *Greville Mems.* i. 231. [13] *Extraordinary Black Bk.* (1832), 537. [14] Anglesey, 245; *New Hist. Ireland*, v. 181, 205; Derby mss 920 Der (14) 121/1/2, Gosset's letters to Smith Stanley, 1831; Add. 36467, ff. 1, 12, 77, 80, 107; *O'Connell Corresp.* v. 2001, 2025, 2121, 2123; Walpole, *Russell*, i. 262-3; *O'Connell Corresp.* v. 2033, 2035; *Holland House Diaries*, 300, 317. [16] Balleine, 303-4. [17] *Gent. Mag.* (1848), i. 547; PROB 8/241 (15 Apr. 1848); 11/2073/311. [18] Balleine, 299-301.

D.R.F.

GOUGH CALTHORPE, Hon. Arthur (1796–1836), of 13 Chapel Street, Grosvenor Square, Mdx.

BRAMBER	8 Mar. 1825–1826
HINDON	1826–1830

b. 14 Nov. 1796, 6th s. of Henry Gough Calthorpe†, 1st Bar. Calthorpe (*d.* 1798), and Frances, da. and coh. of Gen. Benjamin Carpenter; bro. of Hon. Frederick Gough Calthorpe*. *educ.* Harrow 1810-13; Oriel, Oxf. 1817. *unm. d.* 5 Mar. 1836.

The life of Gough Calthorpe, the 1st Baron Calthorpe's youngest son,[1] was blighted by illness, most notably recurrent deafness. This may explain his apparent inability to settle to any activity as a young man: his sojourn at Oxford lasted just a year, while in 1823 he was reported to be studying law, but he evidently did not pursue it.[2] Similar incapacity marked his parliamentary career, which began when he was returned on a vacancy for Bramber in 1825 on his brother the 3rd baron's interest. He is not known to have spoken in debate. He divided for Catholic relief, 21 Apr., 10 May 1825. His other recorded votes in this Parliament were with the Whig opposition to Lord Liverpool's ministry, for revision of the corn laws, 28 Apr. 1825, 18 Apr. 1826, and inquiry into delays in chancery, 7 June 1825. At the 1826 general election he exchanged seats with his brother Frederick and was returned for Hindon. That autumn he travelled in Ireland, from where he complained that he was 'by no means so strong since I came' and 'very much deafer than before'. Frederick subsequently reported that his brother would miss the opening of the new Parliament, as his doctor had recommended that he should remain in the Irish coastal town of Howth, 'for the benefit of the air in consequence of a severe bowel complaint that he had had and also in the hope of the air improving his ears. He writes rather out of spirits and says, poor fellow, he can be of no use ... to anybody'. While in Ireland, his Evangelically inspired support for ecclesiastical reform led to his being considered 'the very bathos of low church'.[3] Following his return he divided for Catholic relief, 6 Mar. 1827, 12 May 1828, and repeal of the Test Acts, 26 Feb. 1828. Either he or his brother voted for inquiry into the Irish church, 24 June. He divided against extending East Retford's franchise to Bassetlaw freeholders, 21 Mar. 1828. In February 1829 Planta, the patronage secretary in the duke of Wellington's ministry, listed him as being 'with government' for Catholic emancipation, but no trace of parliamentary activity has been found for that session. He divided for the enfranchisement of Birmingham, Leeds and Manchester, 23 Feb., and to transfer East Retford's seats to Birmingham, where his family held property, 5 Mar. 1830. He voted with the revived Whig opposition for reduction of the admiralty estimates, 22 Mar., a revision of taxation, 25 Mar., deduction of the lieutenant-general's salary from the ordnance estimates, 29 Mar., and to condemn British interference in Portugal's internal affairs, 28 Apr. He voted to abolish the death penalty for forgery, 24 May 1830. He retired at the dissolution that summer. He died 'near Paris' in March 1836; no will has been found.[4]

[1] His father left him £7,000 in his will in 1798, to be paid on his coming of age (PROB 11/1306/316). [2] Hants RO, Calthorpe mss 26M62/F/C 60, 193. [3] Ibid. F/C 19, 58. [4] *Gent. Mag.* (1836), i. 447.

H.J.S.

GOUGH CALTHORPE, Hon. **Frederick** (1790–1868), of Grosvenor Square, Mdx.

HINDON	1818–1826
BRAMBER	1826–1831

b. 14 June 1790, 4th s. of Henry Gough Calthorpe[†], 1st Bar. Calthorpe (*d.* 1798), and Frances, da. and coh. of Gen. Benjamin Carpenter; bro. of Hon. Arthur Gough Calthorpe*. *educ.* Harrow 1803-8; Christ Church, Oxf. 1808. *m.* 12 Aug. 1823, Lady Charlotte Sophia Somerset, da. of Henry Charles Somerset[†], 6th duke of Beaufort, 5s. (2 *d.v.p.*) 6da. Discontinued surname Calthorpe by royal lic. 14 May 1845. *suc.* kinsman John Gough to Perry estate 29 July 1844; bro. George as 4th Bar. Calthorpe 27 Sept. 1851. *d.* 2 May 1868.
  Commr. of lunacy 1828-31.
  Sheriff, Staffs. 1848-9.

Gough Calthorpe, whose family was linked by marriage and political ties to William Wilberforce* and other prominent Evangelicals,[1] was returned again for Hindon in 1820 by his brother George, 3rd Baron Calthorpe. He was a silent Member but a fairly regular attender, who acted with the Whig opposition to Lord Liverpool's ministry on many issues. However, he continued to exhibit a markedly independent spirit. He voted for parliamentary reform, 25 Apr. 1822, 24 Apr. 1823, but against the disfranchisement of ordnance officials, 12 Apr. 1821, and reform of Edinburgh's representation, 13 Apr. 1826. He divided for Catholic claims, 28 Feb. 1821, 1 Mar., 21 Apr., 10 May, but also for the Irish unlawful societies bill, 25 Feb. 1825. He voted in defence of ministers' conduct towards Queen Caroline, 6 Feb. 1821. While he usually divided for opposition economy and retrenchment motions, including Hume's, 27 June 1821, and Brougham's

on distress, 11 Feb. 1822, he voted with government against Maberly's motion on the state of the revenue, 6 Mar. 1821, more extensive tax reductions, 21 Feb., and repeal of the salt duties, 28 June 1822, and for the duke of Cumberland's annuity, 30 May 1825. He presented a petition from Suffolk, where his family owned land, for relief from agricultural distress, 7 Mar., and was named to the subsequent select committee, 16 Mar. 1821 (and again, 18 Feb. 1822). In voting for inquiry into the currency, 9 Apr. 1821, he was presumably influenced by the connection between his family, whose West Midlands estates included part of Birmingham, and local manufacturers and agriculturists who were campaigning against the resumption of cash payments.[2] He toured Ireland later that year.[3] It was said of him in 1825 that he 'attended frequently and voted both with and against government'.[4] On his marriage in 1823 Wilberforce commented that 'he is eminently blessed with the qualities ... best calculated to preserve an unclouded conjugal atmosphere and from all I hear providence has rewarded his virtuous celibacy by giving him a partner singularly fitted both for producing and enjoying domestic happiness'.[5] At the general election of 1826 he exchanged seats with his brother Arthur and was returned unopposed for Bramber.

He divided for Catholic relief, 6 Mar. 1827, 12 May 1828, and repeal of the Test Acts, 26 Feb. 1828. He voted against extending East Retford's franchise to Bassetlaw freeholders, 21 Mar. Either he or his brother voted for inquiry into the Irish church, 24 June 1828. He divided for Catholic emancipation, 6, 30 Mar., and against obliging Daniel O'Connell to swear the oath of supremacy before taking his seat, 18 May 1829. He voted to reduce the grant for the sculpture of the marble arch, 25 May. He divided for the transfer of East Retford's seats to Birmingham, 5 May 1829, 5 Mar. 1830. He voted with the revived Whig opposition to abolish the Bathurst and Dundas pensions, 26 Mar., condemn British interference in Portugal's internal affairs, 28 Apr., reduce the grant for public buildings, 3 May, inquire into privy councillors' emoluments, 14 May, and reduce the grant for South American missions, 7 June. He divided for Jewish emancipation, 5 Apr. He voted against Lord Ellenborough's divorce bill, 6 Apr., and for reform of the divorce laws, 3 June. He divided for abolition of the death penalty for forgery, 24 May, 7 June. He voted to prohibit on-consumption in beer houses, 21 June, and for the abolition of slavery, 13 July 1830. He was again returned for Bramber at the general election that summer.

The duke of Wellington's ministry regarded Gough Calthorpe as one of the 'bad doubtfuls', and he voted against them in the crucial civil list division, 15 Nov. 1830. He divided for the second reading of the Grey ministry's reform bill, 22 Mar., and against Gascoyne's wrecking amendment, 19 Apr. 1831. Reportedly irked by this, his brother replaced him with an anti-reformer at the ensuing general election, and there is no evidence that he sought to re-enter the Commons.[6] He succeeded to his brother's title and estates in 1851, and presided over a buoyant period in the family's fortunes arising from the expansion of Birmingham and the resultant soaring value of his Edgbaston and Perry properties. However, his role in Birmingham's development has been assessed as 'ornamental', as his 'shy and retiring' nature prevented him from taking a prominent part. In the Lords he was an occasional participant in debates on philanthropic and religious issues, and he espoused a 'Palmerstonian' brand of politics.[7] He died in May 1868 and was succeeded by his eldest son, Frederick Henry William Gough Calthorpe (1826-93), Liberal Member for East Worcestershire, 1859-68, and then in turn by his other two surviving sons.

[1]*Gent. Mag.* (1868), i. 777-8. His father left him £7,000 in his will in 1798, to be paid on his coming of age (PROB 11/1306/316). [2]B. Hilton, *Corn, Cash, Commerce*, 92. [3] Hants RO, Calthorpe mss 26M62/F/C 8. [4]*Session of Parl. 1825*, p. 454. [5]Calthorpe mss F/C 91. [6]*Brighton Gazette*, 5 May 1831. [7]D. Cannadine, *Lords and Landlords*, 129, 134-5, 141-3, 153-7.

H.J.S.

GOULBURN, Henry (1784–1856), of Betchworth, Dorking, Surr.[1]

HORSHAM	26 Feb. 1808–1812
ST. GERMANS	1812–1818
WEST LOOE	1818–1826
ARMAGH	1826–1831
CAMBRIDGE UNIVERSITY	1831–12 Jan. 1856

b. 19 Mar. 1784, 1st s. of Munbee Goulburn of Amity Hall, Jamaica and Portland Place, Mdx. and Hon. Susannah Chetwynd, da. of William Chetwynd[†], 4th Visct. Chetwynd. *educ.* by Dr. Moore at Sunbury, Mdx. c. 1791-3; Trinity Coll. Camb. 1801. *m.* 20 Dec. 1811, Jane, da. of Matthew Montagu[†] of Sandleford Priory, Berks., 3s. (1 *d.v.p.*) 1da. *suc.* fa. 1793. *d.* 12 Jan. 1856.
Under-sec. of state for home affairs Feb. 1810-Aug. 1812, for war and colonies Aug. 1812-Dec. 1821; plenip. for negotiating peace with USA July 1814; PC 10 Dec. 1821; chief sec. to ld. lt. [I] Dec. 1821-Apr. 1827; chan. of exch. Jan. 1828-Nov. 1830, Sept. 1841-July 1846; sec. of state for home affairs Dec. 1834-Apr. 1835.
Capt. duke of Gloucester's vol. inf. 1803-7.

By 1820 the saintly, sober, 'cockeyed' Goulburn had completed ten years as a junior minister in the Tory administrations of Perceval and Lord Liverpool.[2] Well regarded by his superiors, especially his departmental chief, the colonial secretary Lord Bathurst, he had acquired a reputation for diligence, efficiency and reliability and was on terms of intimate friendship with Robert Peel*, the Tories' coming man, whose hostility to Catholic claims he shared and in whose shadow he was content to walk.[3] Reserved and unimaginative, though not without humour, he was a self-consciously poor speaker. He had purchased a modest Surrey estate near Dorking, was happily married to a devoted if neurotic woman and doted on his four children, particularly his eldest son Harry (*b.* 1813). From his shady father, who had died when he was seven, he had inherited the substantial Amity Hall plantation in Jamaica. The ownership of slaves sat uneasily with his deep Evangelical commitment (though he was no religious zealot); and on discovering in 1818 through his brother Frederick, the bungling manager of the estate, that they were suffering inhumane conditions, he tried to improve matters and became an advocate of amelioration and gradual abolition. As his Jamaican income had fallen to barely £2,000 a year, slightly less than his under-secretary's salary, he was obliged to be financially prudent.[4]

At the general election of 1820 he was returned again for West Looe on the Buller interest. In the House (where he frequently acted as a government teller) he claimed 'a very considerable diminution of the expense' of the Ionian Islands staff, 2 June, and stated that the information requested by Lord John Russell would exonerate ministers from the charge that they had betrayed Parga by returning it to Turkey, 29 June. He believed that the king would get the better of Queen Caroline, 'his *worse* half', if he showed his face more; and in December 1820, explaining the government's determination not to concede restoration of the 'guilty' queen's name to the liturgy, he sounded the influential county Member Littleton for a hint of how the 'country gentlemen' felt.[5] He paired against Catholic claims, 28 Feb., moved an amendment to prevent Catholics becoming colonial governors, which was beaten by 163-120, 27 Mar., and denounced the measure as a 'danger ... to the Protestant establishment', 2 Apr. 1821. His handling of departmental business included a defence of the cost of Mediterranean garrisons, 14 Mar., replying to Creevey's motion alleging misuse of the Barbados four-and-a-half per cents, 24 May, and opposing inquiry into the administration of justice in Tobago, 6 June, and Maitland's regime in the Ionian Islands, 7 June. A few days later he called on

Croker, secretary to the admiralty, to express regret at Peel's refusal to return to office at the board of control. Croker, who noted that he 'wishes that we should keep altogether', recorded that they 'laughed about his refusing [in 1818] to go to Ireland [as chief secretary] on account of the expense', while the present idle incumbent Charles Grant was 'laying by £4,000 a year out of it'.[6] He remained uneasy at the possible consequences of the king's ill humour with Liverpool, but joked to Bathurst that whoever informed him of the queen's death in August 1821 'stands a chance of being made a *baronet*'. He backed the premier's successful bid to moderate the commander-in-chief the duke of York's scheme for severe reductions in the colonial military establishment, and in October 1821 turned his mind to the problem of relieving distressed West Indian colonies by relaxing restrictions on their foreign trade.[7]

In late November 1821 the cabinet decided, as part of the impending coalition with the Grenvillites and replacement of Lord Sidmouth as home secretary by Peel, to appoint the duke of Wellington's pro-Catholic and mercurial brother Lord Wellesley lord lieutenant of Ireland, '*provided a very capable* secretary could be found'. After Huskisson had turned it down, Goulburn was reckoned to be the 'best' choice, with his staunch Protestantism seen as an additional recommendation in view of Wellesley's bias. He agonized for more than 24 hours, ostensibly, as he told Bathurst, on account of financial worries, 'considering my own circumstances and the little prospect of improvement in West Indian affairs'. Yet he also had severe reservations, which he kept to himself, about taking on 'one of the most difficult and laborious offices under the government' in harness with the 'dilatory and inefficient' Wellesley, who would take 'the whole credit' for any success, while 'the whole labour of the administration must necessarily devolve upon me'. He fretted too that William Plunket*, who was to be made Irish attorney-general, 'might occasion embarrassment' by being so prominent a champion of Catholic claims. The entreaties of Liverpool and Lord Londonderry*, the offer of an annual pension of £1,000 (doubled in 1825) for long service at the colonial office and his confidence that he could rely on Peel for support and advice overcame his misgivings.[8] The appointment of Goulburn, 'the most sincere and therefore the most bigoted opponent of the Catholic claims', perturbed Lord Grenville, and his alarm was conveyed to Liverpool by his nephew Charles Williams Wynn*, who was destined for a cabinet place in the reshuffle. (Williams Wynn's cousin Lord Buckingham, head of the Grenvillite squad, was des-

perate for a share of power and his personal reward of a dukedom, and therefore not inclined to complain.) Liverpool allowed Williams Wynn to reserve his right to promote the Catholic cause and publicly criticize Goulburn's appointment if necessary.[9] Goulburn and Peel's friend William Vesey Fitzgerald*, though a pro-Catholic, welcomed his appointment as that of 'a man of courage and honour ... who will not think it enough to court the Catholic demagogues and to be praised by the Catholic press'; while the anti-Catholic backbencher Henry Bankes believed him to be an essential counterbalance to Wellesley:

> He possesses very good sense, great industry, considerable practice in business ... together with a clear and unaffected manner of explaining everything which belonged to his departments. His private character is excellent, and even exemplary, his habits of life temperate, orderly and becoming his circumstances, which were confined rather than affluent.[10]

After briefing meetings with Peel and Liverpool, Goulburn arrived in Dublin on 20 Dec. 1821, to begin what proved to be over five years' hard and harassing labour. One of his enduring problems was Wellesley's idleness and inefficiency, as he later wrote:

> It was very difficult to get an opinion or direction from him without on his part much previous deliberation and conference with others. Written papers sent to him were detained indefinitely and to obtain with respect to them any written authority was impossible. My whole official intercourse with him when I was in Dublin was by personal interviews, and those only occurred after repeated postponement on account of real or pretended indisposition and never except after waiting always one and not infrequently as many as three hours in his anteroom. The interviews generally resulted in my having permission to take the course which I might in conversation have suggested. When I was in London I rarely heard from him and I was compelled to take in Parliament in concert with ... [Peel] that line ... which I judged expedient ... To myself he was kind and considerate. He readily listened to the objections which I had ... occasion to offer to appointments ... and often sacrificed his personal feelings in deference to representations of which he admitted the justice.[11]

On the other hand, he received steady support from Peel and got on famously with William Gregory, the experienced under-secretary at Dublin Castle.[12] A month after his arrival Williams Wynn reported to Buckingham that his 'regular and constant manner of doing business is very much *pronee* by the Orange party, contrasted with the indecision and idleness of Grant, though they allow that abstinence from

wine is a new and dangerous feature in an Irish secretary'. Daniel O'Connell* and the Catholic agitators, of course, regarded him as 'our mortal enemy'.[13]
Goulburn went to England in February 1822, when
his wife's illness distracted him, for the opening of
Parliament and his necessary re-election, which, as
he confided to Peel, presented him with additional
anxieties:

> I am ruined already by non-payment of rents, by the
> decay of my West India property and by an office which
> does not pay its expenses. But ... I do not think I could
> in fairness to the government say that I would have
> nothing to do with West Looe, which would be ... to
> put myself out of Parliament. I am therefore compelled
> to run into this new expense and can only endeavour to
> restrict it with in certain limits ... I think Arbuthnot* [the
> patronage secretary] ought to know how I am situated
> and whether if I fail at Looe I have any chance of being
> returned elsewhere; if not ... I shall retire into *private* life,
> and I hope before I am quite a bankrupt.[14]

He was opposed by and defeated a wealthy adventurer, whose subsequent petition was unsuccessful; he
presumably got some assistance from the treasury. In
his absence the Irish insurrection and habeas corpus
suspension bills were pressed through the Commons
by Londonderry.[15] His first reported speech on Irish
business was in reply, described as 'heavy and ambiguous' by the Whig Sir James Mackintosh* and as 'very
poor indeed' by Williams Wynn, to Newport's call for
'remedial measures', 22 Apr., when he gave an assurance that ministers had matters in train.[16] He spoke
in similar terms, 29 Apr., before making a flying visit
to Dublin, where Wellesley concurred in his plans to
establish a regular police force, purge incompetent
magistrates (in which he made good progress that
year) and effect a temporary adjustment of tithes.[17]
On 16 May he got leave to introduce a bill to provide
for the employment of the Irish poor in a subsidized
programme of road building, which became law on
the 24th. His police bill encountered strong opposition, but in discussions with 'leading Irish Members'
he conceded some modifications and prevailed in
his argument that the measure was a 'necessity'; it
received royal assent on 5 Aug. and represented, as
Goulburn believed, 'the foundation successfully laid'
of a regular police force.[18] He introduced a bill to facilitate the leasing of tithes, which became law on 6 Aug.
On 17 June he assured Vesey Fitzgerald in the House
that the authorities were doing all possible to relieve
Irish distress, and next day, asking Gregory for facts
and figures, he moaned that 'I am persecuted nearly to
death both in and out of Parliament, and am supposed
to be the most inhuman and unfeeling of men because

I have not given an assurance that the government of
Ireland can or will feed the people'.[19] The urgent need
for additional relief overcame his doctrinal aversion to
large-scale government intervention, and he secured
an extra grant of £100,000, 21 June. He opposed as
'subversive' and defeated by 72-65 Hume's proposals
for the reform of Irish tithes, 19 June. Carrying extension of the Insurrection Act, 15 July, he claimed that
without it 'open insurrection and rebellion would have
broken out'. He defended the Canada bill, 18 July, and
opposed inquiry into the government of Trinidad,
25 July 1822.

Back in Ireland by 11 Aug., he remained fearful of
'a renewal of insurrection'. He ended direct distress
relief on 1 Sept., but continued the public works programme in the hardest-hit areas.[20] The Whig James
Abercromby*, visiting Ireland at this time, suspected that there was 'no harmony' between Wellesley
and Goulburn, who 'appears to be quite oppressed
by his office'.[21] In early November 1822 he heeded
Peel's advice to keep out of the current contest for
the vacant seat for Cambridge University (which he
coveted), in order to avoid an awkward clash with
Liverpool's nephew Lord Hervey*, but he laid down
his marker for the next opportunity.[22] Encouraged by
Peel, he worked throughout the autumn on the 'difficult' problem of tithes.[23] He and his wife, who narrowly missed serious injury from a flying bottle, were
in the Dublin New Theatre Royal when the Orange
demonstration against Wellesley occurred, 14 Dec.
1822; but he was dismayed by what he considered the
viceroy's overreaction and the subsequent ill-judged
prosecutions of the miscreants, which he believed
had scotched any hope of reconciling Protestants to
a moderate tithes reform. He came close to resigning,
but was talked out of it by his wife, whose anxiety that
the promotion of his friend Frederick Robinson* to
the exchequer in February presaged a wider reshuffle which would exclude him, he had to quell. He
was obliged to announce in the House, 5 Mar. 1823,
that the government intended to introduce a general
measure to outlaw all illegal societies, including
Orange organizations; he duly did so on 7 May.[24]
He was in Dublin when Barry moved for papers on
the prosecutions, 24 Mar., and shared Peel's view of
Plunket's 'injudicious' explanation, though the composition of the small minority led him to hope that
when the issue was renewed 'we shall not have one
English country gentleman as furiously or as generally against us as I at one time imagined'. Yet he was
far from confident of defeating Brownlow's motion
for information, 15 Apr., when he defended Plunket
and denied any rift between himself and Wellesley;

he gave Plunket full credit for his 'admirable' speech, which enabled the orders of the day to be carried. He regarded the success of Burdett's motion for a parliamentary inquiry, which he spoke against, 22 Apr., as 'more matter of regret than surprise', as ministers were 'beaten by the defection of all the English country gentlemen who usually support'.[25] On 10 Feb. he refuted Vesey Fitzgerald's charge that his 1822 Tithes Leasing Act was 'impracticable', but conceded that 'it might not have been as efficient as he could have wished'; and on 6 Mar. he got leave to introduce a bill to provide for a temporary composition of tithes and one to establish a permanent commutation. Both were attacked by the Protestant hierarchy and the second had to be ditched; but the composition measure, which Goulburn guided through the House in May and June, became law on 19 July 1823. During the winter recess he monitored its initial operation and, after consultation with Peel, obtained leave to bring in an amending bill, 9 Mar. 1824, when the Whig George Agar Ellis* was 'inclined to call out with Lord Byron, "I wish he would explain his explanation"'. This became law on 17 June 1824 and, with the earlier legislation, helped to improve the lot of the Irish poor.[26] He successfully opposed Hume's motion for inquiry into the Irish church and tithes, 4 Mar. 1823, as 'a precedent, pregnant with the utmost danger to every kind of property'; but Agar Ellis considered this defence to be 'mere general declamation'.[27] He resisted more effectual levying of Irish first fruits revenues, 10 Apr., renewed the Insurrection Act to guard against the 'state of insubordination' still prevalent locally, 12 May, and opposed abolition of the lord lieutenancy and inquiry into Irish education, 25 June, and referral of the Irish Catholics' petition complaining of bias in the administration of justice to the judicial commission, 26 June 1823. To O'Connell, Goulburn, 'a man of miserable intellect and only the more virulent on that account', had become the 'rancorous ... supporter of all the abuses in the church and in the corporations and ... the Orange lodges'; but in Liverpool's eyes he was 'not only invaluable in himself, but just the man to be secretary' to Wellesley, as 'his purity and correctness of character make amends for the defects of the other'.[28] Back in Dublin by late August 1823, he concluded that 'the state of the country is at the present moment better than it has been at any time since my arrival'. Despite worries about scarcity, his optimism continued through the winter, though he believed that continued outrages in Cork and elsewhere were 'clear indications that the spirit of disturbance is not subdued and that the disposition of the people is not altogether reformed'; he reckoned that Ireland would

require its current military force of 20,000 for the foreseeable future.[29]

Goulburn saw off Newport's motion for information on Catholic burials, 6 Feb., and Grattan's for returns of Catholic office-holders, 19 Feb. 1824. Aiming to seize the initiative from opposition, he got leave on 16 Feb. to introduce a bill to enforce Irish clergy residence, which became law on 21 June, and on 26 Feb. a brief one to amend the previous year's Church Rates Act, which reached the statute book on 16 Mar. He objected to the principle of the Catholic bishops' petition for separate funding for education of the Irish Catholic poor, 9 Mar., defended the grant for Protestant charter schools, 16 Mar., and, acquiescing in Newport's proposal for the establishment of a commission of inquiry into education, 25 Mar., paid lip service to the virtues of interdenominational instruction.[30] In early April, when there was a groundless rumour that he was to resign, he was discommoded by one of his habitual colds, but he was able to go to Dublin for the Easter recess. There he discussed the growing threat of the Catholic Association with Wellesley.[31] On 4 May he opposed a motion for an advance of capital to Ireland, which would raise unrealistic hopes. Next day he beat by 26-10 a proposal to reduce the Irish militia. In his long reply to the Whig motion for inquiry into the state of Ireland, 11 May, he 'stopped short in the middle' and 'could not go on and was obliged to sit down, having lost the thread of his argument'. Mrs. Arbuthnot, who felt that he 'lends no assistance in getting rid of abuses and the notorious *jobbings* that go on in Ireland', expected him to suffer 'numberless jests'.[32] He defeated by 87-71 a new attack on first fruits revenues, 25 May. After recovering from a sprained ankle he secured continuation of the Insurrection Act, 14 June 1824.

Later that summer he had private talks with Orange leaders in a bid to discourage lawlessness among the rank and file and made a tour of the supposedly distressed areas around Limerick, Killarney and Tralee, from which he returned to Dublin 'very agreeably disappointed ... in ... the condition of the people'. He could not detect anything politically sinister behind the foreign secretary Canning's visit to Ireland.[33] The mounting influence of the Association and the electoral potential of the Catholic clergy convinced him that repressive action was necessary, though he dissociated himself from the hysteria of the Protestant extremists, believing that there was no danger of 'immediate and combined insurrection', but rather of 'a sudden ebullition of fanatical fury in particular places'. In concert with Peel he overcame

Wellesley and Plunket's reluctance to move against the Association, but in the event the cabinet decided on a bill to outlaw all illegal societies, which Goulburn sought leave to introduce, 10 Feb. 1825.[34] He was very nervous beforehand, but felt that he had performed creditably (though Agar Ellis deemed his speech 'confused'), and he steered the measure through the Commons with comparative ease.[35] He acquiesced in the introduction of Newport's Irish vestries bill and Parnell's justices regulation bill, reserving his right to oppose later, 22 Feb. He took the same line on Grattan's poor relief bill, 22 Mar., and Newport's measure to curb pluralism, 14 Apr. He was a teller for the minorities against Catholic claims, 1 Mar., 26 Apr., having spoken briefly against the second reading of the relief bill, 25 Apr., after his initial post-midnight attempt on the 19th had been silenced by the adjournment. He opposed the 'securities' of disfranchising the Irish 40s. freeholders, 26 Apr., and payment of the Catholic clergy, 29 Apr. He voted against the third reading of the relief bill, 10 May, was pleased by the narrowness of the majority and was relieved by its subsequent defeat in the Lords, believing that the peers' hostility accurately reflected popular opinion. He told Gregory that had the majority been 'very small, or but little more than the bishops', he would have expected Liverpool, Peel, Lord Eldon and other anti-Catholic ministers to resign in order to allow 'an experiment to be made by those who thought they could conduct it as to Catholic emancipation with adequate securities'. As it was, he was reconciled to staying in office as long as Liverpool and Peel remained. Fresh rumours that he was about to be replaced by Robert Wilmot Horton* came to nothing. [36] He opposed Spring Rice's motion for information on Irish religious animosities, 26 May, and persuaded Newport to withdraw his for the prosecution of individuals found guilty of abuses in running Protestant charter schools, 9 June 1825. He terminated the proceedings of the Irish select committee by carrying a short report leaving all major problems to government, and on the potentially troublesome education report hinted that they were willing to experiment cautiously with reform. His subsequent line that mixed education should only be implemented on a limited scale was adopted as official policy.[37] When a dissolution was expected in September he predicted 'some severe and unpleasant contests' and numerous adverse results in the Irish counties.[38] The domestic conflict between Wellesley's new American Catholic wife and his bastard son and secretary Edward Johnston aggravated Goulburn, but he failed to persuade Liverpool to recall Johnston to his post in the London stamp office. He did scotch Wellesley and

Plunket's notion of reviving 'private communication' with leading members of the Association and, with Peel's help, Plunket's unscrupulous bid to have his son made dean of Clogher. He had remained a contender for Cambridge University, and in November 1825, when a canvass took place, confirmed his candidature for the general election now expected next early summer. The situation was awkward, for the sitting Member Lord Palmerston, the pro-Catholic secretary at war, intended to stand, as did his anti-Catholic colleague William Bankes, while the other serious candidate was the Trinity man John Copley*, the anti-Catholic attorney-general. Goulburn was 'very angry' with Copley for intervening and confessed to Peel that if the treasury were to back him, as was being hinted, 'I shall think that I am very ill used'. In mid-December 1825 he made a short visit to Cambridge to show his face and Peel, though careful not to interfere with Palmerston, did what he could to dispel the idea that the government preferred Copley.[39]

On another trip to Cambridge in early February 1826 Goulburn told Jane that he was 'pretty sure' that even if he could not defeat Bankes this time he could establish an impregnable position for the next. Anticipating a comparatively quiet session on Irish matters, he predicted a difficult time over the prevailing distress and the consequences of the recent financial crash, especially as 'Hume, Hunt and Cobbett have like seagulls who portend a storm come from their ... hiding places and begun the one to talk of economy and retrenchment, the others to assemble and harangue the people'. Privately, he could not see why the cabinet 'turned a deaf ear' to agitation for an issue of exchequer bills to relieve commercial distress; he criticized Canning's folly in staking the government's existence on resistance to this and Liverpool's 'obstinacy'. The Bank's intervention to advance money to businessmen on security of their goods 'relieved' him and enabled him to soothe Jane's anxieties about his possible loss of office.[40] He announced on 16 Feb. that he would legislate on Irish subletting and church rates. As an amendment to Newport's motion that day, he got leave to introduce a bill to regulate rates, which became law on 31 May. His subletting bill, which in practice merely facilitated evictions, was presented on 10 Mar. and received royal assent on 5 May.[41] He agreed to the appointment of a select committee on Irish tolls and customs, 16 Feb. He stalled on education, 7, 20 Mar., when he defended the Kildare Place Society and said that action had been taken to correct abuses in the charter schools. He reserved his future response to Spring Rice's bill to improve local jurisdiction and Newport's to prevent episcopal unions, but would not countenance the latter's measure to disfranchise non-resident Irish freemen, 9 Mar. On 2 Mar. he supported the government amendment against intervention to overturn the verdicts in the Jamaican slave trials, as one who had 'had the misfortune to succeed to a property' there. His object, he told his wife, had been to 'impress upon the House how much more useful it was to attack the system than the individuals who administered it'. He was now 'satisfied that slavery ought to be abolished as soon as it can be done with consistency and due regard to the interests of the slaves', but he expected abolition to spell 'ruin' for all West Indian proprietors. Though fatigued by the demands of his Cambridge University campaign, select committee work and Commons duties, he claimed to be 'quite well'.[42] His Easter visit to Dublin alarmed him with evidence of impending economic collapse and renewed famine, and he secured modest grants to relieve hardship in Dublin and Drogheda.[43] He defeated Whig amendments to his church rates bill, 21 Apr., and objected to O'Connell's petition calling for the removal of the aged Lord Norbury as Irish chief justice, 5 May 1826. On the 'very serious' unemployment riots in Lancashire in late April, he commented to Jane that they exhibited 'the folly which always animates the lower orders under such circumstances of destroying the machinery by which we have created so great a demand for the manufactures of the country and the labour of the people'. His hopes of an early end to parliamentary business were dashed when the cabinet got themselves into a 'scrape' by proposing, 'very imprudently' as he thought, the emergency admission of warehoused foreign corn, which 'aroused against them a great many of their best friends'.[44]

Goulburn was assured of a seat for Harwich on the treasury interest at the general election, but decided to persevere at Cambridge, even though he knew he had no chance. An invitation to contest Dublin did not seriously tempt him, but on 19 May 1826, a fortnight before the dissolution, he accepted the offer (which had been on the cards for almost a year) of the archbishop of Armagh, the primate of Ireland, to return him unconditionally for Armagh city in recognition of his 'services' to the Irish church. He 'very readily' accepted, reflecting that by placing Harwich at the government's disposal he would give himself 'a good claim another time'.[45] Thus insured, he stood the poll at Cambridge in order to establish his future position whenever Copley, who came in with Palmerston, was promoted to the bench. In fact, he finished a distant last, 71 votes below Bankes, whose 'superior tactics' he privately acknowledged. He remained confident of eventual success, but some thought that

many Protestant voters blamed him for letting in Palmerston.[46] Concluding that the overall result of the elections meant that 'we shall have a very blackguard set in the next Parliament', he checked that all was 'in good order' at Betchworth and made courtesy calls in Cambridge before rejoining his family in Dublin in early July 1826.[47] The Cambridge election had cost him £1,500, which he could barely afford, and damaged his relations with Palmerston. He was additionally worried by a scandal involving his brother Frederick as governor of New South Wales and the problem of providing for his profligate brother Edward.[48]

He had gone to Ireland expecting the worst, resigned to the continuance of Johnston's bad influence over Wellesley and Plunket's petulance, and filled with 'forebodings as to the wretched state' in which the country was likely to be placed by autumn famine, which 'make me almost wish that I had nothing to do with it'. Peel authorized the expenditure of £4,000 to contain the current fever epidemic and £3,000 to relieve distress, but their worst fears about the harvest were not realized.[49] Goulburn was above all alarmed by 'the state of party feeling' and bitter religious divisions, which suited O'Connell's 'mischievous' game, and the increasing electoral power of the Catholic priesthood. He gave Peel a requested review of the military force at the disposal of the Irish government at the end of October: he reckoned that the existing one was adequate as long as reserves were available, and commented that 'our divisions are no longer political', as 'the language of the priests is more directed against the Protestant religion than against the Protestant ascendancy'.[50] He had the 'great annoyance' of having to cross to London for the preliminary session of the new Parliament, where he rebuked Spring Rice for his partisan tone on the Catholic question, 6 Dec. 1826, and saw 'many new faces and very few that I was acquainted with'.[51] Back in Dublin, he was alarmed by the 'unexpected' transfer of troops from Ireland to Portugal, but was reassured of contingent reinforcements by Peel, who urged him to consider the matter of whether to proceed against the new Catholic Association, on which Wellesley was prevaricating. Goulburn was against prosecution and persuaded Wellesley to take he same line, which settled the issue, though George Dawson*, Peel's undersecretary, criticized his 'apathy'.[52]

Goulburn returned to the Irish office on 10 Feb. 1827, but was rendered largely *hors de combat* for the best part of a fortnight by his customary cold, exacerbated by a deranged stomach. The news of Liverpool's stroke and political death, which he received while discussing business at Peel's on 17 Feb., initially filled him with gloom, as he anticipated the immediate 'break-up' of the ministry, the formation of a new one to concede Catholic emancipation and his own necessary resignation with Peel, as he told Jane:

> That I shall regret office I cannot deny as it has enabled me to contribute more to your comforts and to those of my family and friends. Independently of those considerations, I shall not regret having more time to enjoy your company and to attend to the education of my boys.

Her hysterical reaction to the prospect of his loss of office and income led him to adopt a calmer tone, holding out renewed hope of things continuing as they were, but he entreated her to reconcile herself to a possible change of circumstances. He now reckoned on a likely Commons majority against Catholic relief, in which case he 'saw no reason why the government might not go on'. Having failed to find anything new to say on the question, he spoke briefly against Burdett's unsuccessful motion, 6 Mar., when he said that as Irish secretary he had been obliged to treat Catholics 'in a more indulgent manner than he should otherwise have done'. He made himself so hoarse that he was speechless and distressed for three days.[53] On the prevalent notion that a compromise concession of some Catholic claims might be made in return for 'an assurance of no further agitation of the question', he told Gregory that he was not indisposed to it, though he insisted that 'the Parliament, privy council and bench must be exclusively Protestant'. In slightly improved health, he prepared to pay back Newport for 'some of those absurd speeches which he made in my absence', 15 Mar., but the chance did not arise, and instead he opposed inquiry into the electoral malpractice of Leicester corporation. Still plagued with stomach trouble (Dr. Warren attributed his indigestion to 'foulness of the bowels which irritates the stomach and makes it refuse to do its duties properly' and purged him with blue pills), he resisted Brownlow's motion for copies of his correspondence with the Lisburn magistrates about the Orange procession, 29 Mar., and Newport's on the laws regulating the repair of Irish churches, 3 Apr., when he denied personal bigotry and defended his record in office. He still hoped that the existing government might be preserved, though he had 'doubts how the principles of both parties can be brought to coincide on some important points'.[54] When Peel, Wellington, Eldon and others resigned rather than serve in Canning's coalition with the Lansdowne Whigs, Goulburn followed suit and placed his office at Canning's disposal.[55] Copley's appointment as

lord chancellor opened Cambridge and he offered again, but after a discouraging canvass he withdrew, 'the expense of a second contest being very ill accommodated to an out of office income'. On his return to London he found William Lamb* in possession of the Irish Office, and on 1 May he took his place in the House with Peel 'on the second row between the treasury bench and the bar'. He regarded the presence of Brougham and Burdett behind the treasury bench as 'a tolerable indication that nothing but cowardice prevents the introduction of the Whigs into the government at the present moment'; they were to 'come in at the end of the session'.[56] He supported the Penryn disfranchisement bill to 'mark his sense of the existing corruption', 7 June, and reserved his opinion on East Retford until the evidence had been presented, 11 June. He opposed the Coventry magistracy bill as 'destructive of chartered rights', 8 June, and voted with government against it, 11, 18 June, as he did for the grant for Canadian water defences, 12 June 1827. During the ministerial negotiations which followed Canning's death in August he enjoyed the discomfort of the Lansdowne Whigs over Herries's appointment to the exchequer under Lord Goderich; and on Wellesley's removal from the Irish lord lieutenancy he remarked that tranquillity there would 'not be attained by those who profess to support the Roman Catholics while they do not go the full length of the priesthood or demagogues'.[57] From the opposite perspective, Newport told Lord Holland, 15 Aug. 1827, that Lamb had already 'gained much credit by his readiness of access and conciliatory manners, in both of which qualities (exclusive of his narrow minded bigotry) Goulburn was decidedly deficient, and his self-sufficiency even in communication with the adherents of his party was extreme'.[58] Goulburn regarded the destruction of the Turkish fleet at Navarino as 'an unjustifiable attack on a friendly power'.[59] In January 1828 Wellington, commissioned to form a ministry after Goderich's collapse, offered Goulburn an unspecified cabinet place, which he accepted, anticipating 'an office of hard work' and welcoming the duke's apparent disposition to reunite 'all those who acted under Lord Liverpool'.[60] He got the chancellorship of the exchequer, for which he had no obvious qualifications. The appointment, which was dictated by political considerations, in that the Huskissonites, whom Wellington took in, would not accept the retention of Herries at the exchequer, raised many eyebrows and spawned a conspiracy theory that it was of Huskisson's devising.[61] In practice, Goulburn was scarcely less financially ignorant than his treasury colleagues Wellington and Dawson (financial secretary);

and while he was required to speak with punishing frequency on ministerial economic policies, these emerged from a collective cabinet effort superintended by the duke. Goulburn's personal inclination, determined in part by his Evangelical commitment, was for preservation of the revenue producing tax base and avoidance of deficit financing and a large national debt, with tax reductions to be implemented only sparingly.[62] The snobbish second generation peer Lord Ellenborough, a senior member of the government, noted that neither Goulburn nor Herries, being 'of the class of under-secretaries', looked 'as if they belonged to a cabinet' when it first assembled.[63]

Goulburn, who inevitably caught 'a very severe cold' before February was out, derided Hume's notion of establishing a dozen separate finance committees on the 15th and outlined the aims of the recently appointed committee, on which he of course sat and where he narrowly failed to carry his proposal for a specific annual sum to be set aside for debt reduction'.[64] He voted with Peel against repeal of the Test Acts, 26 Feb., but in cabinet subsequently seemed to Ellenborough to be 'rather for and against it'. He accepted Huskisson's compromise on the corn laws, drafted resolutions as a basis for further discussion and was Wellington's emissary to Grant, president of the board of trade, who wanted further relaxation.[65] He refused to consider repeal of the lucrative stamp duty, 11 Mar., but promised to consider that on marine insurances, 25 Mar. On the 12th he carried a resolution to repeal the Act empowering the national debt commissioners to grant life annuities and on the 14th introduced an enabling bill, which became law on 9 May. He defended his Irish Vestry Act against Hume's attack, 20 Mar., and opposed Davies's borough polls bill 31 Mar. He presented and endorsed anti-Catholic petitions, 21, 29 Apr., and voted silently in that sense, 12 May. He dismissed Harvey's motion for parliamentary control over crown excise prosecutions, 1 May, and next day, on the advice of Croker, dropped his amendment to extend a provision of the Test Acts repeal bill to Ireland. His speech proposing the financial provision for Canning's family, 13 May, was condemned as 'miserable', 'cold' and 'received as coldly' by Canning's nephew Lord George Cavendish Bentinck*.[66] He was against repeal of the usury laws, 20 May, Hume's call for full disclosure of civil list pensions, 20 May, and transfer of the malt tax to beer, 23 May. The king and Ellenborough were keen for him to replace the departed Huskisson at the colonial office in May, but Wellington vetoed this on account of his being compromised on the slavery issue.[67] On 3 June he obtained leave to introduce a bill to restrict the circulation in England of small Scottish and Irish bank notes, which became law on 15 July and completed the currency system adopted in 1819. He denied his alleged involvement in malversation in the Leinster police establishment, 12 June, and opposed inquiry into the Irish church, 24 June. He got rid of a resolution deploring the decline of British shipping, 17 June, and defended the 'misrepresented' additional churches bill, 30 June, but abandoned it for the session, 8 July. He resisted as 'a bad economy' the Whig proposal to abolish the place of lieutenant-general of the ordnance, 4 July, though in cabinet beforehand he had been inclined to concede it.[68] His first cautious budget statement, 11 July, identified a genuine surplus revenue of £3,000,000 to be applied to reduction of the sinking fund, boasted of the ministry's achievements on retrenchment and presented an optimistic view of the economy's general health. Strong opposition forced him reluctantly to withdraw his bill to cut the cost of pensions by imposing, as the finance committee had recommended, a superannuation scheme for public servants funded by deductions from salaries, 14 July 1828. He effected it the following year, partly by decree.

In September 1828 he obtained a Welsh judgeship for Edward.[69] He continued the search for economies in public expenditure that autumn. He was appalled by the bad timing of Dawson's public assertion that the Catholic question must be settled forthwith, but perceived its essential truth.[70] According to Mrs. Arbuthnot, he was held in high regard by Wellington at the beginning of 1829, when he was one of the six Protestant ministers who told the king on 13 Jan. that immediate action was necessary: 'a good dinner in a very warm room' gave him 'a cold and a pain in my leg'.[71] In cabinet, 17 Jan., he 'begged it might be understood that he reserved himself for the details, before he divided in favour' of emancipation; and next day he 'talked of the advantage of doing away with the [Irish] lord lieutenant at some not too distant time'. He was one of the small group who drafted the king's speech and, after George IV had endorsed it, 27 Jan., he was deputed to inform the Irish primate, to whom he additionally explained his personal reasons for supporting concession and offered to resign his seat if necessary. He told Gregory that it 'has been a choice between tremendous difficulties' and asked to be given 'credit for honesty of intention, and a desire to do what was best for the country'.[72] He announced his conversion in the House when presenting several hostile petitions from Irish clerics, 12 Feb., arguing that 'a disunited administration and a divided Parliament are likely to prove much more prejudicial to the interests of the Protestant church' than emancipation with adequate securities. In cabinet he now backed the disfranchisement of Irish 40s. freeholders. Hampered by a streaming cold and an obvious lack of enthusiasm, he spoke flatly for the relief bill, 17 Mar. 1829, explicitly placing himself in the same boat as Peel.[73]

On 13 and 20 Feb. 1829, when the Whig Lord Howick* thought he 'cut a most laughable figure, clearly not knowing what to say', he maintained under questioning that there was no need to reappoint the finance committee.[74] He opposed amalgamation of the two London ordnance establishments, 2 Mar., increasing the interest rate on British compensation claims against France, 4 May, reduction of the malt and beer duties, 12 May, repeal of the agricultural horse tax, 13 May, when he presaged intended revision of the assessed taxes next year, and inquiry into East Indian trade, 14 May. Bankes thought his second budget statement, 8 May, when he boasted of another surplus and continued retrenchment, but ruled out tax cuts, was 'very clear and intelligible'.[75] Goulburn also completed his abandonment of the sinking fund and announced his plan to convert unfunded into funded debt by giving holders of £3,000,000 in exchequer bills incentives to take four per cents instead. The obscurity of this part of his speech was deliberate and designed to lay the ground for a more ambitious conversion scheme, which it was 'the practice of the time' to keep from the public.[76] He defended the interim measure, 14, 22 May. He justified the cost of Nash's London improvements and the refurbishment of Buckingham House, 12 May, but he set an excess limit of £150,000 on the latter, 25 May 1829. He, Peel and Vesey Fitzgerald were charged with investigating the condition of the Irish poor and the feasibility of introducing a regular system of poor relief.

On the address, 4 Feb. 1830, he peddled the official line that distress was local and temporary. He upheld the currency settlement of 1819, 5, 11 Feb., when he opposed the transfer of East Retford's seats to Birmingham, unable to see 'any deficiency in the adequate representation of commerce or manufactures'. He defeated by 184-69 Hume's demand for large tax remissions, an implied censure of himself, 15 Feb. Opposition observers were contemptuous of all these performances, especially the last two; and Lord Holland described him as 'an encumbrance not an assistance' to Peel in debate.[77] He outlined savings of £1,300,000 in public expenditure, 19 Feb., and on the 23rd announced his intention to hold an inquiry into the beer trade, with a view to opening it. He secured the appointment of a select committee, 4 Mar., and on

8 Apr. brought in a bill to effect its recommendations, which he steered through, in significantly amended form, against strong opposition in June. He denied Davies's charge that he had shown partiality to Nash in the last investigation, 2 Mar. He opposed inquiry into the Irish church, 4 Mar., and admitted its defects but claimed that it had been improved, 27 Apr., when he replied to O'Connell's attack on the Vestry Act and defeated by 177-47 his motion for an amendment bill. The cabinet decided that Davenport's planned motion on the state of the nation must be resisted, and on Peel's insistence Goulburn brought forward his budget statement to pre-empt it. In cabinet he proposed 'a modified property tax' on 'landed property, all fixed property, and the funds as well as all offices', but not on 'the profits of trade', to finance repeal of the beer tax, temporary remission of the hop duty and reduction of the sugar duties. Wellington and a majority of his colleagues compelled him to abandon the property tax. On 15 Mar. he revealed this to the Commons, before detailing his plan to cut the beer, cider and leather taxes, further reduce the four per cents and, in order to claw back revenue, increase the Irish stamp duties (he was forced to abandon this contentious measure) and the Irish and Scottish spirit duties and tax Irish tobacco. Howick conceded that the plan was 'upon the whole satisfactory' and 'a good beginning'.[78] He refused the Ultra Lord Chandos's request for reduction of the coffee duties to assist the West Indian colonists, 19 Mar. He spoke for the continuation of the treasurership of the navy as a separate office, 22 Mar., and on the 25th beat by 167-78 Poulett Thomson's motion for inquiry into a revision of taxation. Next day he explained his scheme to reduce the four-and-a-half per cents. He spoke against abolition of the Bathurst and Dundas pensions on which ministers were defeated, 26 Mar. On 5 Apr. he spoke, 'ill', as Agar Ellis thought, and with 'a purling stream of language ... full of phrased nothings and gentle shufflings', as Richard Monckton Milnes† described it, and voted against Jewish emancipation. He attributed the government's 'embarrassing' defeat, on an issue to which he claimed to be indifferent, partly to the ostentatious abstention of Dawson, Holmes and other official men.[79] His and Wellington's attempt in the prolonged negotiations with the bank over renewal of its charter to secure a relaxation of restrictions on joint-stock banks ended in failure.[80] He secured the appointment of a select committee on superannuations and saw off 'Bum' Gordon's bid to widen its scope, 26 Apr. In Peel's absence on account of his father's death, 3-17 May, the already overworked Goulburn was in charge of the Commons. On 3 May he was forced by

the prospect of defeat to withdraw the vote of money for Windsor Castle repairs with an assurance that he would set up a committee to determine its full and final cost. Informing Peel, he observed that 'the state of the king's health and the prospect of an early dissolution' were encouraging 'the country gentlemen who usually support us' to please their constituents by questioning all government expenditure. However, Wellington fully approved his decision.[81] He made O'Connell withdraw his motion for information on persons executed under the Irish Constables Act, 4 May, had a 'heavy' but successful evening on the miscellaneous estimates, 10 May, and easily defeated Hume's call for abolition of the Irish lord lieutenancy, 11 May, Spring Rice's motion for repeal of the Irish coal duties, 13 May, and Graham's for a return of privy councillors' emoluments, 14 May, when Howick felt he missed a chance to expose the exaggerations in the opposition case.[82] He expressed support for gradual progression towards abolition of the death penalty for forgery and did not oppose Slaney's motion for inquiry into employment fluctuations in the manufacturing districts, 13 May. He defeated a motion for inquiry into the tobacco duties, 25 May, and declined to repeal those on soap and candles, 7 June, when he defended the grant for South American missions. On 11 June he successfully resisted reduction of the grant for consuls abroad. He opposed Smith Stanley's Irish ecclesiastical leases bill as a violation of church property, 16 June, and the following day defeated proposals for inquiry into the conduct of the church commissioners and interference with the merchants seamen's fund. He ran into trouble on the expiring West Indian sugar duties. Faced with Grant's notice of a motion for a general reduction, he concocted a scheme to impose a temporary sliding scale of duties on coarser sugars and to recoup revenue by raising the duty on Irish and Scottish spirits and rum, which he explained after defeating Chandos's motion for substantial reductions, 14 June. Initial optimism that the plan would take soon evaporated, however, and on 21 June he made a poor fist of defending it against Howick's onslaught. Forced by lack of time to give in, he had the humiliation on 30 June 1830 of having to concede a 'temporary' reduction in the duties.[83]

Thomas Creevey* heard that at the levee to kiss the new king's hand, 26 June, the myopic William IV, when Goulburn's turn came, said '"I can't make out who you are. You must tell me your name, if you please"'.[84] He was being widely criticized for failing to give Peel adequate support in debate, was known to aspire to the Speakership and was therefore the subject of speculation that summer.[85] He reconnoitred

Cambridge University, but concluded that he had no chance. He was returned *in absentia* for Armagh, even though some, including the primate, now doubted his suitability in view of the furore which his stamp duties proposals had provoked and his turnaround on Catholic emancipation; his election did not go down well with the inhabitants.[86] Goulburn was with Peel and Wellington in late September 1830, when they decided to try to attach Palmerston and his friends to the ministry; the negotiations failed.[87] On 5 Oct. he presented to the cabinet his scheme to transfer to the consolidated fund all the salaries previously partly paid out of the civil list and to make savings of £28,000 in the diplomatic service. The king's objections obliged him to modify the plan.[88] In the House, where he thought 'the general feeling is against us', he brought forward his proposals for a 'considerable saving' in the list, 12 Nov., in a speech which even ministerialists considered at best 'indifferent' and others 'wretched'. He opposed Parnell's motion for inquiry as 'an infraction of the inalienable prerogative of the crown', 15 Nov. 1830, when the government's defeat ended his 20-year tenure of office (interrupted only for eight months in 1827-8).[89] Two weeks later he told Gregory:

I am by no means sorry for a change which has released me from a mental and bodily labour which was I felt beyond my strength to bear and which must necessarily have been increased by the determination of the opposition to use every mode of vexatious delay which the forms of the House permitted in order to wear out its opponents.

Alarmed by the 'species of servile war raging in some parts of the country', he organized farmers of the Betchworth area to deal with any 'Swing' disturbances, but also got neighbouring squires to make more generous contributions to poor relief. He continued his regime of domestic stringency, and to prepare Harry for Cambridge placed him with the leading Evangelical Henry Venn Elliott in Brighton.[90] Arbuthnot was inclined to exclude Goulburn, 'whom he destines for the Chair', from the Tory leaders and managers' early consultations on organizing the party in opposition; it is not clear whether or not he participated.[91] In the House, he defended the Irish Protestant clergy, 18 Nov., and opposed a radical motion for returns of church rates, 25 Nov. He denied having when in office misled the Commons as to the cost of the Canadian Rideau canal project, 6 Dec., and promised the Grey ministry 'fair play' in scrutiny of their plans to reduce public salaries, 9 Dec.; he was named to the select committee. He argued that day that Hodgson's requested return of English borough freemen would 'afford no useful information'. On 16 Dec. 1830 he interrupted Hume's boast of his consistent devotion to 'reform in everything' with a cry of 'Hear, hear', which prompted Hume to denounce him as 'the defender of every extravagance and ... abuse'. Goulburn retorted that Hume had gone back on his initial support of the sale of beer bill in order to advance his prospects of election for Middlesex.

He concerted with Herries and Sir George Murray, 3 Feb. 1831, on opposition tactics that evening in the Commons, where in the event 'little or no business' came up. He told his wife:

As to reform all that passed ... showed the difficulty in which ... [ministers] were in respect to it. The petitions mostly prayed for ballot, universal suffrage, etc., as a means of attaining other objects subversive of the present state of our society, and if the government mean not to go these lengths they will not gain anything in the opinion of those who now cry out boldly for reform and whom it is their object and interest to pacify. I rather apprehend that they will go as far as they can in accordance with popular opinion ... They are popular for the moment and they do not see that ultimately they must either resign ... or adopt every unjust measure which the people or rather the mob of England or Ireland may think fit to clamour for.

He had been persuaded by Wellington not to raise the question of British relations with France and subsequently prompted the duke to veto any Tory parliamentary initiative on foreign policy.[92] He was pleased with the opposition's 'capital' performance on 4 Feb., when he and Calcraft pointed out 'some of the leading fallacies' of the ministerial civil list proposals and enjoyed 'crowing over them for their change of opinion'. A visit to the City the following morning revealed to him 'a great doubt whether the change of government has been for the better', and he reflected that 'the talents of the government appear as much obscured by office as ours used to be', that the 'damp' which Peel's absence had caused had been 'removed by the operation of last night', that 'we shall be able to beat them in debate as well as in information' and that 'if we do but manage our proceedings with temper and discretion we shall have the feeling of the country soon with us'.[93] He was appointed to the select committees on the East India Company, 4 Feb., and public accounts, 17 Feb. He had a satisfying evening on 11 Feb. when, 'evidently prepared', he shredded the budget of his successor, Lord Althorp, 'furiously declaiming' against the proposed tax on stock transfers and repeal of the duty on printed calicos. He welcomed the abandonment of the transfer tax, 14 Feb., but argued that the budget's basic flaw

was that it reserved 'no surplus whatever of revenue beyond expenditure for the redemption of the national debt'. Once more plagued with 'the remains of a cold', he told Jane that ministers would 'learn by experience the folly of taking off old taxes, to which the people are accustomed, for the sake of present relief, while they impose new burdens in another quarter which from being new is not so readily borne'.[94] He acquiesced in the reference of the Windsor Castle and Buckingham House projects to a select committee (to which he was appointed), 15 Feb., but reserved his future right to defend himself if blamed retrospectively. He briefed Ellenborough on the cotton duties, 17 Feb., and four days later joined him and a few other Tories in hearing the grievances of a deputation of ship owners disgruntled with the timber duties proposals.[95] According to a government backbencher, he took notes as Sir James Graham laid out the navy estimates, 25 Feb., but 'shrunk from the battle'.[96] He reiterated his criticisms of the new tax plans, 21, 28 Feb., 10 Mar., and on 11 Mar. urged Althorp to stop dithering on the timber duties and attacked his proposal to reduce those on sugar. He joined in the opposition assault on the former, 18 Mar., and enjoyed their victory.[97] He endorsed the Irish secretary Smith Stanley's resistance to Ruthven's bid to relieve small occupiers from the potato tithe and defended his own Composition Act, 22 Feb. He deplored the implication of Newport's motion on Irish first fruits, 14 Mar., and criticized the government's advance of capital to Ireland, 30 Mar. He supported their proposal to grant £10,000 a year to the crown for civil contingencies, 25, 28 Mar., 14 Apr., when he claimed that it differed little from his own abortive plan; but on 30 Mar. 1831 he condemned the salaries committee's recommendation that no future pensions should be granted without parliamentary consent as 'an invasion of the constitution and an inroad on the dignity of the crown'.

Goulburn's first reaction to the government's reform scheme, 1 Mar. 1831, was to write to Jane from the House:

Never was any measure conceived with greater wickedness. It is evident that the Whigs mean to leave office and to make it untenable for any successor; and to do this they leave a question which will be the foundation of perpetual agitation if rejected and of revolution if carried ... The cowardice of the representatives of populous places will prevent many who will vote against it afterwards from opposing the first introduction and under these circumstances we shall reserve our strength until the second reading.

'Almost as tired as if I was in office' as a result of attendance on committees and in the House, he continued to hope that the reform bill would be rejected at that stage, and was in any case sure that if it got through it could be emasculated in committee. He convinced himself that there was little popular enthusiasm for reform, despite 'the government making every effort to have the mob on their side', though he lamented that 'the respectable classes of society' were 'cowardly as well as alarmed and unwilling to come forward'. He had 'no fear of the bill passing even if the second reading be carried', as there was 'an incipient apprehension among some of the middling orders who have property'.[98] His own contributions to the reform debates were limited to a brief attack on the bill as a 'monstrous and violent' measure which would raise and disappoint 'extravagant expectations' and reduce the monarchy to dependence on the Commons, 9 Mar., an assertion that the Irish proposals would endanger the Union, 24 Mar., and a defence of the Cambridge University anti-reform petition, 30 Mar. He voted against the second reading of the English bill, 22 Mar., and surmised that despite the majority of only one for it 'the responsibility of a dissolution is one which the government may not be willing to take upon themselves however convenient it may be to them to get rid of the present House'. He was pleased to find Peel and Herries 'in good heart, determined to resist the bill most manfully', in early April. He regarded Russell's abandonment of the proposed reduction in the number of Members as 'an indication of a change of purpose' which would be 'a great encouragement to the timid and wavering on our side' and delighted in the radical Hunt's assertion that most of 'the lower orders' in the manufacturing areas were hostile to the bill. He divided for Gascoyne's successful wrecking amendment, 19 Apr. 1831, and told Ellenborough next day that 'if ministers did not go out, the bill was lost'.[99]

At the ensuing general election Goulburn stood for Cambridge University with Peel's brother William, professing support for 'temperate' reform, as the culmination of a month-long campaign against Palmerston, the foreign secretary, and the other sitting Member, the Whig William Cavendish, organized by the resident anti-reformers. They won comfortably, inflicting on the ministry its only defeat in a large open constituency. Goulburn, who had been ready if beaten to 'hail the tranquillity of private life and freedom from attendance in the House of Commons as a great blessing', occupied the seat for the rest of his life. His friends opened a subscription to defray his £2,000 costs. Attacks on his ownership and alleged maltreatment of slaves, which he had prepared himself to refute, led to a protracted public dispute with Zachary Macaulay.[100] Immediately afterwards he told

Wellington that he now accepted the necessity of some measure of just reform based on enfranchisement rather than disfranchisement, but the duke, discounting the notion of 'a reaction among the lower orders', thought the Tories 'should consent to no violation of principle, of justice or of property'.[101] Three weeks later Goulburn urged Peel to exert himself more decisively in the new Parliament to secure

> a perfect understanding and concert among all who are opposed to the government measure of reform. We must not be scrupulous as to little differences ... Without it, I much fear that the false opinion circulated by the government of your disinclination to combine with others in opposition to the bill will gain ground, that men will think the bill likely to be carried as it is and will be inclined to make good their individual interests and to secure a certain popularity under the new constitution rather than endeavour by patient and continued resistance to save the actual constitution ... We have a good force and I think may do a great deal if we can direct it properly and in a body.

Peel professed willingness to co-operate in opposition to reform, however futile, but refused to promote any alternative scheme or to countenance renewed 'party connection with the Ultra Tory party'.[102]

On 16 June 1831 Goulburn took his seat in the Commons, where he 'saw many new faces, not very good looking nor yet so bad as I expected', and concluded after a conversation with the radical Member John Maberly that 'our best course undoubtedly will be to endeavour to break the connection between the radicals and the present government', though he had 'no hope' of success, as the ministers were 'more radical than the radicals'. Later that day he attended the small opposition meeting which decided to adopt Planta's Charles Street house as a party headquarters.[103] On 22 June he joined temperately in criticism of the omission of any reference to providence in the king's speech. He objected to Hume and Hunt's imputation of nepotistic corruption to all who dispensed patronage, 28 June, when he secured the addition to the renewed select committee on the king's printers of two Members 'not so directly opposed to me on all political questions'. He was named to the select committee on the use of molasses in brewing and distilling, 30 June, and defended the Sale of Beer Act, while admitting that its 'inconveniencies' in practice had been greater than anticipated and that if it could be shown to have 'tended to the democratisation of the lower classes' legislation would be necessary. He ridiculed the radical alderman Wood's call for a return of salaries to 1797 levels and refuted Graham's charge that the late ministers had 'fled from the helm of affairs'. He and Dawson left the House before the division, 'shabbily', as Littleton saw it, 'because they would not swell the ministerial majority'.[104] Goulburn welcomed the proposed repeal of the coastal coal duties, but criticized Althorp for neglecting the revenue, 1 July, berated Hunt for his attack on the grant for Oxford and Cambridge professors' lectures, 8 July, and tried to exploit ministerial differences on the wine duties, 11 July. He took exception to Hume's assertion that the Wellington ministry had blindly upheld the Protestant ascendancy in Ireland, 18 July. He voted against the second reading of the reintroduced reform bill, 6 July, and concluded optimistically that the 'express reservation' made by 'several' of its supporters of 'their opposition on a further stage' meant that 'the majority ... will be as small as can be necessary for carrying the bill'.[105] On 19 July, when he voted for use of the 1831 census to determine the disfranchisement schedules, he contended that the proposal to disfranchise Appleby was inconsistent with the reprieve of Reigate. He denied that Bishop's Castle was corrupt, 20 July, and on 22 June argued in vain for East Looe, Lostwithiel, Minehead and Petersfield to be allowed to keep one Member. Illness put him out of action until 3 Aug., when he denounced the enfranchisement of Greenwich and the other metropolitan districts and deplored Hobhouse's thinly veiled threat to the Lords. The previous day he had found the Tory committee 'in good heart' and discerned 'a growing opinion from the tone of the papers and some members of the government that they are not quite united on reform'.[106] On 5 Aug. he voiced concern at the powers given to the boundary commissioners, backed Croker's attack on the enfranchisement of Gateshead and insinuated that the generous treatment of County Durham smacked of gerrymandering in favour of Lord Durham, a member of the cabinet and one of the authors of the bill. He said more on this, 9 Aug., maintaining that Sculcoats, near Hull, deserved separate representation if Gateshead did. Later, on the proposal to unite Rochester with Chatham, he again alluded to the treatment of Durham, and a cheer from some Tories provoked the radical Tom Duncombe to launch a savage personal attack on him. The House was 'in a state of great excitement for about two hours'. Although Goulburn stayed silent, he consulted friends 'as to whether he should notice the matter out of the House', but Duncombe was eventually brought to apologize and the Speaker intervened to ensure that the affair went no further.[107] Undeterred, Goulburn implied partiality in the configuration of the Pembroke Boroughs, 10 Aug., when he enjoyed ministers' discomfiture in a discussion on the Irish poor, in which they were 'attacked and abandoned by all their friends

as being a government that did nothing though they promised everything', and their enforced withdrawal of a botched clause of the reform bill. He told Jane, 'I think the opinion of their incapacity is gaining ground among their friends, many of whom though still voting with them let out their complaints in no very measured language'.[108] He was named to the select committee on the charges of civil government, 12 Aug., but a recurrence of illness kept him away from the hot and putrid House until 29 Aug., when he praised the work of the Irish board of charitable bequests. Next day he voted to preserve the voting rights of existing non-resident freemen. Continued ill health prevented him from accepting Peel's invitation to Drayton for shooting in early September.[109] He returned to the Commons on the 12th and made several interventions on details of the reform bill in the following week: he denounced the proposal to deprive three county towns, including Guildford, of a Member, 15 Sept. That day he criticized ministers for not meeting Hunt's motion for repeal of the corn laws with a direct negative and repeated his fear that their wine duties plans would damage relations with Portugal. He condemned the Irish public works bill as a measure intended 'merely to increase the patronage of the government', 16 Sept., and exchanged heated words with Smith Stanley. He divided against the passage of the reform bill, 21 Sept., and the second reading of the Scottish bill, 23 Sept. He voted with government against inquiry into the 'trumpery and iniquitous' allegations of the Deacles, 27 Sept., and anticipated 'the rejection of the [reform] bill by a large majority in the Lords'.[110] He spoke in favour of inquiry into the effects of renewal of the Sugar Refinery Act on the West India interest, 28 Sept., and said the ministerial proposal for the appointment of a select committee on those colonies was 'an absolute delusion', 6 Oct., when he supported the prayer of an Irish clergyman's petition for the proper enforcement of tithes collection. He condemned the abolition of the Scottish exchequer court, but was not listened to, 7 Oct. On 10 Oct., when he was listed as home secretary in a putative moderate reform ministry, he made what was generally reckoned to be a listless speech against the motion of confidence in the government.[111] He joined in the attack on Russell over his 'whisper of a faction' indiscretion, 12 Oct., applauded the attorney-general Denman's assurance that the government would take stern action against rioters, 13 Oct., and clashed with Burdett over the acceptability of the Birmingham Political Union's petition for the creation of peers to carry reform, 19 Oct. 1831. A few days later he sent Wellington a paper on the national finances and picked a hole in Althorp's calculations.[112]

Goulburn, who told Harry on 30 Nov. 1831 that the next session would be stormy, as 'the state of the country and of all our concerns foreign and domestic is such as to call forth every latent feeling of bitterness and hostility', pressed Peel to come to London for 'consideration and concert'.[113] In the House, 15 Dec., he acquiesced in (and was named to) the select committee on Irish tithes, but carped at ministers for prevaricating on the issue; he was named to the West India select committee that day. He voted against the second reading of the revised reform bill, 17 Dec. 1831. In the Christmas recess he tried to interest Peel in an alternative moderate bill drafted by the barrister Hildyard, but Peel dismissed the idea and argued that it was preferable to try to modify the government's measures. Goulburn thought that as 'the majority of the House of Commons' would 'vote as they are bid' there was no hope of achieving this:

> My view is ... to get the bill again rejected if possible. A second year's consideration would be invaluable to the country ... I am daily more convinced that this reform is not desired except by those who are to gain by it, and I therefore think that all we can do in the way of encouraging resistance to it either in our House or in the Lords ought to be done ... It is ... bad policy in us to do anything which looks like encouraging an idea that we think the bill as it is must pass.[114]

On 17 Jan. 1832 he secured a return of income and expenditure designed to give Althorp 'credit for a blunder in the arrangement of his budget, a deficiency of £1,000,000'.[115] He spoke and voted against going into committee on the reform bill, 20 Jan., and on the 23rd (when he was in the majority against Hobhouse's vestries bill) protested that it was impossible to consider the proposals for individual boroughs without the boundary commissioners' recommendations to hand. On 25 Jan. he concerted with Peel and Herries the 'plan of operation' for prosecuting their 'good case' against the Russian-Dutch loan next day, as part of their campaign to exploit 'a growing opinion in the public mind of the incompetency of the government to conduct any real business'. He did not speak in the debate, 26 Jan., when ministers scraped by with a majority of only 20 'despite every effort made by them to procure attendance'; but he privately contrasted 'the adverse feeling entertained towards them' with 'the enthusiasm with which the duke of Wellington's health was received' at a Burns Night dinner. Earlier that evening he had listened uneasily as his Irvingite friend Spencer Perceval had intemperately called for a day of general fast and humiliation. He said he would vote with Perceval if he divided the House, but when Althorp repeated his assurance that ministers

intended to name such a day he prevailed on Perceval to withdraw his motion. He was 'grieved' by Perceval's demented rant against Godless ministers, 20 Mar., when he tried in vain to shut him up. He subsequently in private impressed on Perceval and his wife 'the extreme danger of underlying imaginations as to being directed by the Holy Spirit ... but with very little success'.[116] He said the proposed division of counties would set the agricultural and manufacturing interests at odds, 27 Jan. On supply, 6 Feb., he indulged in some 'bitter ... invective' against Althorp's financial management; he told Jane that he was 'much approved and what I said received no answer'.[117] Busy in the mornings with his work on the West India committee, he continued to criticize details of and point out anomalies and inconsistencies in the reform bill: he voted against the enfranchisement of Tower Hamlets, 28 Feb., hinted at political bias in the preferential treatment given to Whitby over Dartmouth, 9 Mar., and complained of the disfranchisement of Minehead and enfranchisement of Merthyr Tydvil, 14 Mar. He was inclined to give ministers' plans for Irish tithes reform general support 'in order to enforce payment of what is due to the Irish clergy', but he found their declarations on the subject, 14 Feb.

> very embarrassing to their future measures and still more embarrassing from the mode in which they were taken up by the radicals to those who like myself were disposed to give them real and effective assistance in tranquillizing the country. But they are weak and foolish in all their proceedings, doing what is right so as to make it appear wrong and raising resistance to themselves by a foolish desire of conciliating radical support. I have increased my cold.[118]

He divided with government against Hunt's motion for information on military punishments, 16 Feb. He endorsed Althorp's refusal to repeal the soap tax, 28 Feb., but supported Chandos's call for a greater reduction in the sugar duties to relieve the West Indians, 7 Mar. He voted against the third reading of the reform bill, 22 Mar., and afterwards claimed 'victory' in argument for its opponents and urged the Lords to throw it out. He opposed the malt drawback bill, 30 Mar., 2 Apr., when he outlined his general but qualified support for the government's tithes reform plans. He was a founder member of the Carlton Club in March. He spoke against the navy civil departments bill, 6 Apr., and continued to try to show up ministers' financial incompetence, believing that 'the more we damage them now the better'.[119] He presented and supported a petition against the new Irish education scheme, 8 May 1832.

After the Lords had rejected the reform bill, 7 May 1832, he speculated about the 'awful questions' of peerage creations or ministerial resignation, but concluded that 'the solution ... depends not on our will so much as on far higher powers'. He at first considered it 'impossible' that the Conservatives could 'take office to carry such a reform bill as will satisfy the people and what is worse the king's pledges on the subject' and foresaw only 'ruin': 'in the maze in which we are we have no hope but in God's guidance and superintendence'. He doubted the wisdom of Wellington's determination 'not to desert' the king if called on, for he could not imagine how he could form a viable government 'with such a House of Commons and under such circumstances as those in which the Whigs have placed us'. He followed Peel's example in refusing Wellington's request to serve in a Conservative reform ministry, clear in his mind that moderate reform was now a chimera, that such an attempt could lead only to inflamed passions and 'yet more violent measures' and that 'a united opposition to the bill' led by Peel afforded a far better chance of modifying it. The notion that if Manners Sutton resigned from the Chair to lead the Commons or even head a government Goulburn could succeed him was dismissed by the reformers, who had no doubt that the House would not elect him as its Speaker.[120] Even on 14 May 1832 Goulburn did 'not despair yet of a [Conservative] government able to go on'; but the humiliating Commons debate of that evening convinced him that the game was up, though he fretted that the Conservatives had abandoned the king to 'men who, having no regard for monarchy and no feeling for existing institutions, will not be very merciful in their triumph and will for a time march uncontrolled upon the revolutionary road which they have opened for themselves'.[121]

Goulburn was named to the select committee on the Bank's charter, 22 May 1832, and its proceedings occupied much of his time in the following three months. He voted silently against the second reading of the Irish reform bill, 25 May. He objected to details of the boundaries bill, 7, 8 June. He quizzed Althorp on the state of the finances, 4 June. On the 18th he got leave to introduce a bill to amend the 1827 Irish Union of Parishes Act, which became law on 17 July. He opposed the births registration bill, 20 June, voted for Baring's measure to exclude insolvent debtors from Parliament, 27 June, defended the Irish Protestant clergy, 28 June, and stressed the importance of securing their entitlement from tithes when calling on Irish Catholics and Protestants to bury the hatchet, 29 June. He voted against government on the Russian-Dutch loan, 12 July, and spoke thus, 16 July. He divided

against Harvey's attempt to open the Inns of Court, 17 July. On the 23rd he spoke and voted against the Irish education plan, arguing that if the Protestant scriptures were jettisoned 'we may have able talkers, able leaders of political unions and able agitators, but we shall not have good citizens, good subjects or good Christians'. Next day he opposed Hume's motion to exclude the recorder of Dublin from the House. He mocked Althorp's financial incompetence, 27 July. On 30 July 1832 he denounced the bribery at elections bill as 'calculated to encourage conspiracies' and seconded the motion of thanks to Manners Sutton on his supposed retirement from the Chair. Wellington wanted Goulburn to stand for the Speakership in the next Parliament, but when Peel, who had been solicited to support the better qualified Williams Wynn, sought his views but rather discouraged him, he gave up the idea, professing that 'what feelings of ambition I may have had are gone and I only remain in public life because God has cast my lot there and because I consider it the duty of every man to use his best endeavours in the station in which he finds himself to arrest the progress of evil; in other words, to check the frantic career of the government'.[122]

Goulburn, as Peel's faithful lieutenant, remained a leading Conservative politician for almost 20 years. He was home secretary in Peel's first administration and, having been narrowly defeated for the Speakership in 1839, an able and supportive chancellor of the exchequer in his second. The death of Harry from consumption in 1843 was a blow from which he never fully recovered. Peel's death in 1850, when he acted as a pallbearer and executor, caused him great anguish.[123] He died at Betchworth 'after a very short illness', in January 1856. By his will, dated 30 Jan. 1855, he left all his real estate to his elder surviving son Edward, his residuary legatee, and charged it with annuities of £200 for his wife (who died in 1857) and £100 for his daughter Lydia. He left £3,200 to be invested for his wife's benefit.[124] In 1846 Croker, reflecting on Goulburn's being compelled to 'eat his words ... in silence' by Peel's decision to repeal the corn laws, described him as 'a most excellent and honourable man, with high principles, both moral and political'.[125]

[1] See B. Jenkins, *Henry Goulburn, 1784-1856. A Political Biog.* (1996); *Oxford DNB.* [2] *Arbuthnot Corresp.* 233; *Creevey Pprs.* ii. 212. [3] *Peel Letters*, 32. [4] Jenkins, 99-102; *HP Commons, 1790-1820*, iv. 44-45. [5] *HMC Bathurst*, 485; Hatherton mss, Goulburn to Littleton, 19 Dec. 1820. [6] *Croker Pprs.* i. 189. [7] *HMC Bathurst*, 503-8, 517-19. [8] Ibid. 522-4; *Croker Pprs.* i. 217-18; *Hobhouse Diary*, 80; Harrowby mss 14, f. 104; Add. 38290, ff. 98, 119; Surr. Hist. Cent. Goulburn mss Acc 304/68/1, pp. 58-60 (Goulburn's ms mem.). [9] Buckingham, *Mems. Geo. IV*, i. 235, 239, 247-8, 250, 252; NLW, Coedymaen mss 946; *Arbuthnot Jnl.* i. 129-30. [10] Add. 40322, f. 1; Dorset RO, D/

BKL, Bankes jnl. 131 (Dec. 1821). [11] Jenkins, 132-5; Buckingham, i. 255; Goulburn mss 68/1, pp. 61-64; *Arbuthnot Jnl.* i. 157-8. [12] Jenkins, 135; *Arbuthnot Corresp.* 26; Add. 40328, ff. 1, 9, 12; *Mr Gregory's Letter-Box* ed. Lady Gregory, 173. [13] Buckingham, i. 274; *O'Connell Corresp.* ii. 949. [14] Add. 40328, ff. 14, 31. [15] Goulburn mss 68/1, pp. 67-70; Add. 37298, f. 158. [16] Add. 52445, f. 78; Coedymaen mss 636. [17] *Arbuthnot Jnl.* i. 158; Jenkins, 144-5; Add. 40328, f. 69. [18] Add. 37299, ff. 207, 213, 238; Goulburn mss 68/1, pp. 75-76; Jenkins, 145-6. [19] *Mr Gregory's Letter-Box*, 189-90; Jenkins, 150-1. [20] Add. 40328, f. 109; Jenkins, 152. [21] Castle Howard mss, Abercromby to Morpeth, 1 Sept.; Lansdowne mss, same to Lansdowne, 7 Oct. 1822. [22] Add. 40328, ff. 184, 194. [23] Add. 40328, ff. 129, 147, 149, 266, 288, 293; 40329, ff. 10, 19, 29. [24] Add. 40328, ff. 300, 306; 40329, ff. 1, 5, 7, 10, 17, 19; Lansdowne mss, Spring Rice to Lansdowne, 1 Feb.; Goulburn mss 67, Goulburn to wife, 4, 12, 26 Feb., reply [Feb. 1823]; Jenkins, 140, 153-6. [25] Add. 37301, ff. 14, 29; 40329, ff. 49, 54, 56. [26] Add. 40329, ff. 131, 172; Buckingham, ii. 13-14; Northants. RO, Agar Ellis diary, 9 Mar. [1824]; Jenkins, 157-8. [27] Agar Ellis diary, 4 Mar. [1823]. [28] *O'Connell Corresp.* iii. 1080; *Arbuthnot Corresp.* 44. [29] Add. 40329, ff. 117, 137, 199, 203, 218. [30] Jenkins, 160. [31] Add. 40330, ff. 29, 39, 59; 40363, f. 235. [32] *Arbuthnot Jnl.* i. 311; Jenkins, 160. [33] Add. 40330, ff. 93, 101, 105, 108; N. Gash, *Secretary Peel*, 388; Jenkins, 162. [34] Add. 40330, ff. 207, 237, 246, 275, 304, 312, 316, 319; 40331, ff. 5, 19, 36, 48, 65; Parker, *Peel*, i. 346-7, 352-8; Buckingham, ii. 208; Jenkins, 164-6; Gash, 389-94. [35] Goulburn mss 67, Goulburn to wife, 11, 19, 21 Feb.; Agar Ellis diary, 10 Feb. [1825]; Broughton, *Recollections*, iii. 84-85; Add. 37303, f. 196; Jenkins, 165-6. [36] *Mr Gregory's Letter-Box*, 223-5; *O'Connell Corresp.* iii. 1205, 1207, 1219, 1229; Jenkins, 167-8. [37] Add. 40331, f. 154; Jenkins, 169-71. [38] Add. 40331, ff. 143, 147. [39] Add. 40331, ff. 233, 246, 275; 40384, ff. 130, 228; BL, Herries mss, Goulburn to Herries, 26 Nov.; Hants RO, Calthorpe mss 26M62/F/C938. [40] Goulburn mss 67A, Goulburn to wife, 24, 25 Feb., 2 Mar. 1826. [41] Jenkins, 171-2. [42] Goulburn mss 67A, Goulburn to wife, 2, 3, 9 Mar. 1826. [43] *Huskisson Pprs.* 202-3; Jenkins, 173. [44] Goulburn mss 67A, Goulburn to wife, 29, 30 Apr., 4 May 1826. [45] Ibid. 67A, Goulburn to wife, 17, 20 May 1826; Add. 40381, f. 267; 40387, f. 107. [46] Goulburn mss 67A, Goulburn to wife, 24 May [11], 15, 16 June; Add. 37303, f. 146; Rutland mss (History of Parliament Aspinall transcripts), Lord C. Manners to Rutland, 18 June [1826]; *Colchester Diary*, iii. 441. [47] Goulburn mss 67A, Goulburn to wife, 21, 25 June 1826; Add. 40332, ff. 44, 46. [48] Jenkins, 176-7. [49] Add. 40332, ff. 44, 46, 76; Jenkins, 177-8. [50] Parker, i. 416-18, 420-2; Add. 40332, ff. 52, 65, 127, 174; Jenkins, 178-80. [51] Add. 40332, f. 170; Goulburn mss 67A, Goulburn to wife, 20, 25, 27 Nov. 1826. [52] Parker, i. 428-32; Add. 40332, ff. 209, 211, 219, 227, 241; 40390, f. 281; Jenkins, 180. [53] Goulburn mss 66A, Goulburn to wife, 5, 10, 13, 15, 17 [18], 20-25 Feb., 5, 8 Mar. 1827; *Mr Gregory's Letter-Box*, 225-7; *Canning's Ministry*, 8. [54] *Mr Gregory's Letter-Box*, 227-8; Add. 37305, f. 53; Goulburn mss 66A, Goulburn to wife, 20, 22 Mar. 1827. [55] *Mr Gregory's Letter-Box*, 228-9. [56] Add. 40332, ff. 317, 319; *Mr Gregory's Letter-Box*, 230-2. [57] Add. 40332, f. 324; *Mr Gregory's Letter-Box*, 234. [58] Add. 51833. [59] Goulburn mss 66A, Goulburn to wife, 14 Nov. 1827. [60] *Peel Letters*, 104-5; Goulburn mss 67B, Goulburn to wife, 11 Jan. 1828. [61] Parker, ii. 29; Lonsdale mss, Lowther to Lonsdale, 19, 21, 23 Jan.; *Croker Pprs.* i. 403; Herts. Archives, Panshanger mss D/Elb F78, W. to F. Lamb, 28 Feb. 1828. [62] Keele Univ. Lib. Sneyd mss SC12/85; P.J. Jupp, *British Politics on Eve of Reform*, 83, 137; Jenkins, 191. [63] *Ellenborough Diary*, i. 3, 31. [64] Add. 40395, f. 22; Goulburn mss 66A, Goulburn to wife, 29 Feb. 1828; Jenkins, 193. [65] *Ellenborough Diary*, i. 46, 52; Add. 40333, f. 8; Jenkins, 194-5. [66] Harewood mss, Cavendish Bentinck to Lady Canning, 14 May 1828. [67] *Ellenborough Diary*, i. 118-19. [68] Ibid. i. 153. [69] Wellington mss WP1/952/6. [70] *Wellington Despatches*, iv. 652-3; Jenkins, 200-1. [71] *Arbuthnot Jnl.* ii. 229; Goulburn mss 67B, Goulburn to wife, 16 Jan. 1829; Jenkins, 202. [72] *Ellenborough Diary*, i. 300, 305; *Croker Pprs.* ii. 12; PRO NI, Primate Beresford mss T2772/2/6/12; Parker, ii. 89. [73] *Ellenborough Diary*, i. 348-9, 358, 388; Jenkins, 203. [74] Grey mss, Howick jnl. 20 Feb. 1829. [75] Bankes jnl. 167 (8 May 1829). [76] Le Marchant, *Althorp*, 232; Jenkins, 205. [77] Howick jnl. 5, 11, 15 Feb.; Grey mss, Durham to Grey, 12 Feb.; Add. 51785, Holland to C.R. Fox, 20 Feb. 1830. [78] *Ellenborough Diary*, ii. 203-4, 209-12; Howick jnl. 15 Mar. 1830; Jenkins, 208-10. [79] Agar Ellis diary, 5 Apr. [1830]; Reid, *Monckton Milnes*, i. 95; Add. 40333, f. 88. [80] Jenkins, 207-9, 213-14; Wellington mss WP1/1111/42. [81] *Ellenborough Diary*, ii. 237; *Arbuthnot Jnl.* ii. 355; *Croker Pprs.* ii. 60; Add. 40333, f. 101. [82] Add. 40333, f. 99; 40400, f. 170; Howick jnl. 14 May 1830. [83] *Ellenborough Diaries*, ii. 269-70, 274-5, 280; Howick jnl. 21 June 1830; Jenkins, 212. [84] *Creevey Pprs.* ii. 212. [85] *Baring Jnls.* 64; *Ellenborough Diary*, ii. 290, 291, 306; *O'Connell Corresp.* iv. 1688; *Arbuthnot Jnl.* ii. 366, 395; Sir James Graham mss (IHR microfilm XR 80), Palmerston to Graham, 25 July 1830. [86] Primate Beresford mss T2772/2/6/20; PRO NI, Pack-Beresford mss D664/A/184, 192, 207, 208. [87] *Arbuthnot Jnl.* ii. 389, 395; *Peel Letters*, 125; *Lieven Letters*, 249; Coedymaen mss 1028. [88] *Ellenborough Diary*, ii. 383; Wellington mss WP1/1148/51. [89] *Ellenborough Diary*, ii. 416, 427, 431; *Arbuthnot Jnl.* ii. 401; Agar Ellis diary, 12 Nov. 1830; *Baring Jnls.* 70; *Life of Campbell*, i. 486. [90] Jenkins, 218-19. [91] *Three Diaries*, 23; Add. 40340, f. 250. [92] Goulburn mss 67B, Goulburn to wife [4 Feb. 1831]; *Three Diaries*, 42, 46-47; Wellington mss WP11175/12, 15 [93] Goulburn mss 67B, Goulburn to wife [5 Feb. 1831]; Wellington mss WP1/1175/12; *Three Diaries*, 46. [94] Add. 51569, Ord to Holland [11 Feb.]; Le Marchant, 280-3; *Three Diaries*, 8, 50; Goulburn mss 67B, Goulburn to wife [15 Feb. 1831]. [95] *Three Diaries*, 53, 55. [96] *Baring Jnls.* 82. [97] Goulburn mss 67B, Goulburn to wife, 19 Mar. 1831. [98] Ibid. 67B, Goulburn to wife, 2, 3, 9, 16, 17, 19 Mar. 1831. [99] Ibid. 67B, Goulburn to wife [22, 23 Mar.], 12, 13 Apr. 1831; *Three Diaries*, 82. [100] *Three Diaries*, 72, 91; Goulburn mss 67B, Goulburn to wife [2 May 1831]; Jenkins, 226-7. [101] Wellington mss WP1/1184/23. [102] Add. 40333, f. 116; Parker, ii. 187-8. [103] Goulburn mss 67B, Goulburn to wife, 17 June 1831; *Three Diaries*, 93. [104] Hatherton diary, 30 June [1831]. [105] Goulburn mss 67B, Goulburn to wife, 7 July [1831]. [106] Ibid. 67B, Goulburn to wife, 2 Aug. 1831. [107] Hatherton diary, 9 Aug.; Goulburn mss 67B, Goulburn to wife [12 Aug. 1831]; *Peel Letters*, 137. [108] Goulburn mss 67B, Goulburn to wife [11 Aug. 1831]. [109] Parker, ii. 188; Jenkins, 221-2, 230. [110] Goulburn mss 67B, Goulburn to wife, 28 Sept. 1831. [111] *Three Diaries*, 148; Le Marchant, 356; Cornw. RO, Hawkins mss 10/2172. [112] Wellington mss WP1/1198/41. [113] Jenkins, 231; Parker, ii. 195-6. [114] Add. 40333, ff. 118, 120; Parker, ii. 196-9. [115] *Arbuthnot Corresp.* 161. [116] Goulburn mss 67B, Goulburn to wife, 25 [27 Jan.], 21 Mar. [Mar.] 1832. [117] Add. 51573, Spring Rice to Lady Holland, 6 Feb. [1832]; Goulburn mss 67B, Goulburn to wife [7 Feb. 1832]. [118] Goulburn mss 67B, Goulburn to wife, 13-15 Feb., 7, 14 Mar 1832. [119] Ibid. 67B, Goulburn to wife, 11 Apr. 1832. [120] Goulburn mss 67B, Goulburn to wife, 8-11 May; 68/1, pp. 81-83; W. Suss. RO, Goodwood mss 1486, pp. 199-200; *Wellington Despatches*, viii. 306; *Three Diaries*, 248, 250-1; *Croker Pprs.* ii. 159, 163; Hatherton diary, 12 May 1832. [121] Goulburn mss 67B, Goulburn to wife, 14 May 1832; *Von Neumann Diary*, i. 272; Jenkins, 234-5. [122] Wellington mss WP1/1236/16; Jenkins 238-9. [123] Jenkins, 299-300, 348-9. [124] PROB 11/2227/111; IR26/20632/101. [125] *Croker Pprs.* iii. 60.

D.R.F.

GOULD see **MORGAN**

GOWER see **LEVESON GOWER**

GRAHAM (afterwards **FOSTER PIGOTT**), **George Edward** (1771–1831), of Chayley, Suss. and Bryanston Square, Mdx.

KINROSS-SHIRE	16 Sept. 1819–1820
KINROSS-SHIRE	1826–1830

b. 3 Nov. 1771, 3rd. s. of John Graham (*d.* 1785) of Yatton, Som., member of supreme council, Bengal, and Mary, da. of William Shewen, collector of customs, of Swansea, Glam. *educ.* Harrow 1779-85. *m.* 5 July 1794, Mary, da. and h. of Rev. John Foster, DD, headmaster[1] of Eton, 3s. 3da. Took names of Foster Pigott 12 Mar. 1827. *d.* 5 Nov. 1831.

Cornet 3 Drag. 1788, lt. 1791; capt. 22 Drag. 1794, ret. 1795; lt.-col. S. Lewes vols. 1803; commdt. centre regt. Suss. militia 1810.

A former army officer with East Indian connections, Graham had had to wait until the death in 1819 of his uncle Thomas Graham of Kinross to come in for that county, and sat only briefly as an unobtrusive supporter of Lord Liverpool's administration and their Scottish manager Lord Melville before the representation transferred to Clackmannanshire at the dissolution in 1820.[2] Kinross-shire again returned him unopposed as a 'church and state' Tory in 1826, but he remained an inconspicuous Member for whom no speeches or major select committee appointments were reported. He was listed in the majority and the minority on Catholic relief, which he almost certainly voted against, 6 Mar. 1827.

The death on 5 Feb. 1827 of his wife's uncle, the Rev. William Foster Pigott of Eton College, a wealthy pluralist and royal chaplain, invoked a settlement of 23 Aug. 1815 giving Graham and his wife joint possession of the Cambridgeshire estate of Abington Pigotts, held since before 1500 by the family of Foster Pigott's late wife Mary (*d.*1815). Graham accordingly assumed the names Foster and Pigott, 12 Mar., executed Foster Piggott's will (dated 20 Mar. 1820 and sworn under £25,000) and settled with his family in Cambridgeshire, where he authorized timber sales and improvements at Abington Hall and became an active magistrate and promoter of the Society for the Propagation of the Gospels.[3] As Colonel Pigott, he voted for the grant to the duke of Clarence, 16 Mar. 1827, against repealing the Test Acts, 26 Feb., and Catholic relief (as a pair), 12 May, and to repeal the usury laws, 19 June 1828. The Wellington ministry's patronage secretary Planta predicted that he would vote 'with government' for Catholic emancipation in 1829, but he divided resolutely against it, 6, 18, 26, 27, 30 Mar. Before standing down at the dissolution in

1830, when Clackmannanshire became the returning county, he presented Kinross-shire's petition against the additional duty on corn spirits, 6 May, and divided against Jewish emancipation, 17 May. He started early but failed to offer for Kinross-shire in 1831. He died at Abington Hall in November 1831, having bequeathed everything to his wife (*d.* 1858). His personalty was sworn under £2,000.[4]

[1] Not provost as stated in *HP Commons, 1790-1820*, iv. 48. See *Oxford DNB sub* Foster. [2] *HP Commons, 1790-1820*, iv. 48. [3] PROB 8/220; 11/1723/184; *The Times*, 12 Mar. 1827, 25 Jan., 31 Dec. 1828; *Windsor and Eton Express*, 24 Mar. 1827. [4] *Gent. Mag.* (1831), ii. 474; PROB 8/225; 11/1800/319.

M.M.E.

GRAHAM, James, mq. of Graham (1799–1874).

CAMBRIDGE	4 Feb. 1825–1832

b. 16 July 1799, 2nd but 1st surv. s. of James Graham†, 3rd duke of Montrose [S], and 2nd w. Lady Caroline Maria Montagu, da. of George Montagu†, 4th duke of Manchester; bro. of Lord Montagu William Graham*. *educ.* Eton 1811; Trinity Coll. Camb. 1817. *m.* 15 Oct. 1836, Hon. Caroline Agnes Horsley Beresford, da. of John, 2nd Bar. Decies [I], 3s. (2 *d.v.p.*) 3da. (1 *d.v.p.*). *suc.* fa. as 4th duke of Montrose [S] and 4th Earl Graham [UK] 30 Dec. 1836; KT 12 Mar. 1845. *d.* 30 Dec. 1874.

Vice-chamberlain of household Feb. 1821-Apr. 1827; PC 23 Feb. 1821; commr. bd. of control Feb. 1828-Nov. 1830; ld. steward of household Feb.-Dec. 1852; chan. of duchy of Lancaster Feb. 1858-June 1859; postmaster-gen. July 1866-Dec. 1868.

Ld. lt. Stirling 1843-*d.*

Chan. Glasgow Univ. 1837-*d*; pres. Highland and Agric. Soc. [S] 1845-9.

Col. Stirling, Dunbarton, Kinross and Clackmannan militia 1827-*d*; maj.-gen. R. Co. of Archers [S].

Graham's father was a man of some ability. His political career ended with Pitt's death, but he was reappointed master of the horse, at £1,260 a year, in 1807, while continuing to draw £2,000 annually from his sinecure place as lord justice general of Scotland. He was a zealous protector of his electoral interests in Stirlingshire and Dunbartonshire, though perhaps inclined to overrate their strength.[1] In February 1821 Graham, who had been conventionally educated, was made vice-chamberlain of the household, at £1,159 a year, and a privy councillor. Five months later, on the eve of the coronation, Lord Hertford offered his resignation as lord chamberlain; but the prospect of Graham having to perform his official duties at the ceremony was averted when Hertford was persuaded to attend. George IV wished to replace Hertford with Lord Conyngham, husband of his latest concubine, but the premier Lord Liverpool and his colleagues would not have it. Nor were they willing to acquiesce in the king's alternative scheme of making Montrose lord chamberlain and giving the mastership of the horse to Conyngham.[2] While this dispute remained in deadlock Montrose took umbrage at lack of government support for his interest in recent by-elections for Dunbartonshire and Stirlingshire. He threatened to resign his lord lieutenancy of both counties and to veto the future appointment of Graham; but he was evidently persuaded to change his mind, even though Lord Melville, the government's Scottish overlord, did not think he had 'the slightest cause of complaint'.[3] Towards the end of the year Montrose was made lord chamberlain and replaced as master of the horse by the duke of Dorset, while Conyngham was accommodated as lord steward.[4]

Graham was mentioned as a possible candidate for the vacant Cambridge University seat in October 1822, but nothing came of this.[5] In February 1825 he was brought forward on a vacancy for Cambridge on the controlling interest of his kinsman the 5th duke of Rutland. (The 2nd duke, whose daughter had married Graham's grandfather, the 2nd duke of Montrose, was their common ancestor.) Graham was described by his proposer as a young man who, 'despising the frivolities of fashionable life', had 'devoted himself to the attainment of that knowledge, which might be useful to him'. Although there was no opposition, he had to contend with much barracking from the unfranchised residents who made up the bulk of his audience. He declared:

I ... congratulate you on the present state of the nation. If we look around us we shall see a greater degree of prosperity than this country has ever before enjoyed. Our commerce and revenue are increasing, whilst our debt and taxes are decreased; and in the king's speech ... His Majesty hopes there will be a still further reduction of taxation. After the great reductions which have already been made, when we see another reduction of taxation in contemplation, we have cause to congratulate ourselves ... I do not see why I should withhold my support from those persons under whose management the country has arrived at its present prosperity.[6]

He voted for the Irish unlawful societies bill, 25 Feb., and against Catholic relief, 1 Mar., 21 Apr., 10 May, and the Irish franchise bill, 26 Apr. 1825. He was in the ministerial majorities on the duke of Cumberland's grant, 30 May, 2, 6, 10 June 1825. He presented a Cambridgeshire petition against alteration of the corn laws, 17 Feb.,[7] and divided with government in defence of the Jamaican slave trials, 2 Mar. 1826.

He stood again for Cambridge at the 1826 general election, when he admitted on the hustings that the country was less prosperous than at the time of his first return:

He doubted not it would shortly rise from its depression with redoubled vigour. The stagnation which now prevails has arisen from overtrading and speculation; but still trade is the bulwark and support of the kingdom; and as the floods which overspread the land bring mischief in the first instance, although they ultimately fertilize the soil, so we may hope that what causes evil today will tomorrow produce riches and abundance.

He was returned with another ministerialist after a token contest.[8] He voted against Catholic relief, 6 Mar., and was in the minority against the spring guns bill, 30 Mar. 1827. He and his father resigned their household posts on the formation of Canning's ministry the following month, feeling it 'absolutely impossible', as Graham told the king, to give him 'firm and decided support'.[9] He was granted a week's leave, 14 May 1827, having served on an election committee. He was in Italy when he was appointed to a place at the India board in the duke of Wellington's administration in February 1828, and his younger brother represented him at the formalities of his quiet re-election for Cambridge.[10] His father was reinstated as lord chamberlain, but at the end of April was rapped on the knuckles by Wellington for giving a proxy vote against repeal of the Test Acts and defending his action in a blustering letter.[11] Graham did not take his seat until 29 Mar. 1828. He voted against Catholic relief, 12 May (his father abstained in the Lords). He presented the Cambridge petition for the abolition of slavery, 17 June, and voted with his colleagues on the ordnance estimates, 4 July 1828. Although he presented Cambridge parish petitions against the Catholic claims, 2 Mar., he declared his support for the Irish franchise bill, 20 Mar. 1829: it would put an end to the 'system of gross deceit and evasion' manipulated by the priests, and was the necessary price to be paid for the 'great boon' of emancipation, for which he cast silent votes, 6, 30 Mar. (His father sent proxy votes for it, 4, 10 Apr., giving the lie to an earlier rumour that, influenced by the king and his son-in-law, the 10th earl of Winchilsea, he 'had changed back'.[12]) Graham was appointed to the select committee on the East India Company, 9 Feb. 1830. He was in the government majorities against various schemes of parliamentary reform, 11, 18, 23 Feb. The previous month Lord Ellenborough, his chief at the India board, had noted that Wellington had told him that he had had some conversation last year at Belvoir with Lord Graham upon Indian affairs, and had been quite surprised to find how much he knew. He had thought he only knew how to comb his hair.

Ellenborough harboured a notion of promoting him to 'first commissioner', which would 'force him to come forward' and demonstrate these hitherto unsuspected talents. Nothing came of it, but Graham spoke in defence of Sir John Malcolm* against an opposition attack on his conduct as governor of Bombay, 4 Mar., and Ellenborough was assured that he 'was unembarrassed and did well'.[13] His only other known votes in this session were against Jewish emancipation, 5 Apr., 17 May 1830. On the accession of William IV, when Montrose resigned his household place, Ellenborough recorded that 'Peel seems to think that Lord Graham is dissatisfied and unfriendly. It seems he has been heard complaining of vacillation, etc., on the part of the government, and does not attend well'.[14]

Graham was returned unopposed for Cambridge at the general election, though his platitudinous speech of thanks was shouted down.[15] According to Ellenborough, he did not think the ministry irrevocably doomed by Wellington's declaration against parliamentary reform.[16] He was in their minority on the civil list, 15 Nov. 1830, and went out of office with them. He did not object to an extension of time for the petitioner against his brother's return for Dunbartonshire to enter into recognizances, 30 Nov., and presented the Cambridge anti-slavery petition, 8 Dec. 1830. He was named to the renewed East India committee, 4 Feb. 1831. Five weeks later, he gave 'a bad account of the spirit of the House of Commons' in the debates on the Grey ministry's reform bill: he 'feared the second reading would be carried, nor did he expect much would be done in committee'.[17] He voted against the second reading, 22 Mar., and for Gascoyne's wrecking amendment, 19 Apr. 1831. The enthusiasm for reform in Cambridge posed no electoral threat to Graham, who declared his 'insuperable objections' to the bill, which was 'revolutionary and republican in its principles, subversive of vested interests and the rights of corporations, and destructive in the end of the monarchy itself'. While he claimed that he would have supported 'a moderate and rational system of reform' to enfranchise large manufacturing towns and reduce bribery, he promised 'constant ... determined and uncompromising opposition' to the 'wild and dangerous bill'.[18] In fact, he did little more than go through the motions of resistance to the reintroduced bill, voting silently against its second reading, 6 July, for use of the 1831 census as a basis for

disfranchisement, 19 July, and against its passage, 21 Sept. Graham, who voted against the second reading of the Scottish bill, 23 Sept., claimed (wrongly) to know that ministers 'expect and hope' to be beaten in the Lords on a 'preliminary point before the second reading' and had the king's blessing for a creation of peers.[19] He divided against the final bill on the second reading, 17 Dec. 1831, going into committee, 20 Jan., the enfranchisement of Tower Hamlets, 28 Feb., and the third reading, 22 Mar. 1832. His only other known votes were against government on the Russian-Dutch loan, 26 Jan., 12 July 1832. He did not seek re-election at the 1832 general election.

He succeeded to the peerage in 1836. When Peel formed his second ministry in September 1841 Graham sent him a whining letter expressing his 'mortification' at his 'utter neglect' in being passed over for office. Peel was unmoved, but later propitiated him with the lord lieutenancy of Stirlingshire and a green ribbon.[20] For all this, he broke with Peel over repeal of the corn laws, and subsequently held office in all Lord Derby's administrations. As postmaster-general he concluded postal conventions with America, China and India, and effected improvements in mail contracts with the East.[21] 'Rather a practical man of business than an orator', he died at Cannes, where he had gone 'for the benefit of his health', 30 Dec. 1874, 38 years to the day after his father.[22] As his first two sons had predeceased him, he was succeeded as 5th duke of Montrose by the only surviving one, Douglas Beresford Malise Ronald Graham (1852-1925). His widow, who was 19 years his junior, twice remarried, the second time in 1888 at the age of 70. She died in 1894.

[1] Oxford DNB. [2] Geo. IV Letters, ii. 940-2; HMC Bathurst, 502-3; Arbuthnot Jnl. i. 110; Hobhouse Diary, 68-69. [3] Devon RO, Sidmouth mss, Melville to Sidmouth, 7 Sept. 1821. [4] Arbuthnot Jnl. i. 125, 126; Hobhouse Diary, 81. [5] Hants RO, Calthorpe mss 26M62/F/C127. [6] Cambridge Chron. 14, 21, 28 Jan., 11 Feb. 1825. [7] The Times, 18 Feb. 1826. [8] Cambridge Chron. 2, 16 June 1826. [9] Geo. IV Letters, iii. 1312, 1313; Canning's Ministry, 153, 260; Colchester Diary, iii. 485. [10] Wellington mss WP1/914/38; 915/56; Cambridge Chron. 8, 15 Feb. 1828. [11] Geo. IV Letters, iii. 1492; Wellington Despatches, iv. 410-12. [12] Arbuthnot Jnl. ii. 259. [13] Ellenborough Diary, ii. 158, 205. [14] Arbuthnot Jnl. ii. 367; Greville Mems.ii. 2; Ellenborough Diary, ii. 300. [15] Cambridge Chron. 16, 30 July, 6 Aug.; Cambridge and Hertford Independent Press, 7 Aug. 1830. [16] Ellenborough Diary, ii. 416. [17] Three Diaries, 67. [18] Cambridge Chron. 29 Apr. 1831. [19] Arbuthnot Corresp. 149. [20] Add. 40487, ff. 339, 341; 40525, ff. 114, 116; 40530, ff. 377-84. [21] Oxford DNB. [22] The Times, 1 Jan., 13 Aug. 1875.

D.R.F.

GRAHAM, Sir James, 1st bt. (1753–1825), of
Kirkstall, nr. Leeds, Yorks. and Edmond Castle, nr.
Carlisle, Cumb.[1]

COCKERMOUTH	1802–10 July 1805
WIGTOWN BURGHS	9 Aug. 1805–1806
COCKERMOUTH	1806–1812
CARLISLE	1812–21 Mar. 1825

b. 18 Nov. 1753, 2nd s. of Thomas Graham (d. 1807) of
Edmond Castle and 2nd w. Margaret, da. of Thomas
Coulthard of Scotby, Cumb. educ. L. Inn 1780. m. 17
June 1781, Anne, da. of Rev. Thomas Moore of Kirkstall,
2s. 3da. suc. to Kirkstall in right of his w. on d. of her only
bro. Thomas 1784; cr. bt. 3 Oct. 1808. d. 21 Mar. 1825.
Recorder, Appleby 1812-d.
Dir. Westminster Life Insurance Co. 1813.
Vol. London and Westminster light horse 1794-1802.

Graham, a successful and well-connected London
lawyer, had been brought in for the Lowther borough
of Cockermouth in 1802, transferring in 1812 to his
home city of Carlisle, where he was invariably treated
as a Lowther nominee despite his largesse and local
influence. He had purchased alternative interests
at Ludgershall, represented by his Whig son and
heir Sandford Graham*, and Weymouth, which in
1817 had returned his son-in-law and political ally
Augustus John Dalrymple*.[2] Although opposed at
Carlisle at the general election of 1820, Graham's
return on the Tory (Yellow) interest was never in
doubt, and he topped the poll in a violent three-man
contest.[3] As in 1818, he could not dictate the outcome
of the election at Weymouth, and his support for the
Lowthers in Cumberland and Westmorland was a
factor in Dalrymple's return for their Appleby seat.[4]

Graham spoke and voted sparingly on party issues
after 1820. He sat on numerous select committees as
hitherto and attended closely to issues affecting his
high society associates, Carlisle constituents, Yorkshire
estates and the metropolis. He presented Matthias
Attwood* and William Thompson's* successful
petition alleging an invalid return for Callington, 1
May 1820.[5] He opposed the Cork harbour bill, 12
June, backed a clause exempting the Aire and Calder
Navigation Company from poor rate charges, 13 June,
and spoke briefly against the extra post bill, 13 July.[6]
On 10 July he argued in vain against issuing a warrant
for the detention of Sir William Manners†, on whose
interest he had unsuccessfully contested Ilchester
in 1802. He secured a second reading for Lord
Exmouth's son Captain Pownall Pellew's* divorce
bill, 14 July 1820.[7] Summoned by the Lowthers,

he voted in defence of the Liverpool government's
conduct towards Queen Caroline, 6 Feb., having
paired against inserting her name in the liturgy, 26
Jan. 1821.[8] He divided against Catholic relief at their
request, 28 Feb.[9] He presented an agricultural distress petition that day from Buckinghamshire and one
from Carlisle, which he endorsed, for leave to build
and appoint clergy to new churches, 13 Mar.[10] He
attempted to justify the Carlisle magistrates' decision
to call in the military at the 1820 by-election, 15 Mar.,
and was appointed on the 30th to the select committee on privileges to which it had been referred. His
motion to kill the Blackfriars Bridge bill was carried by
the Speaker's casting vote, 3 Apr., but one for hearing
counsel against the metropolitan roads bill failed,
11 Apr.[11] Next day he opposed further inquiry into
the Lyme Regis franchise as a speaker and majority
teller with Lord Lowther, 12 Apr. He presented and
endorsed petitions from St. Marylebone backing the
metropolitan magistrates bill, 1 May, and Scarlett's
poor bill, 24 May, from Whitehaven for a reduction
in the coastwise coal duty, 30 May, and from Peckham
for legislation to prevent cruelty to animals, 20 June.[12]
He was a majority teller for the wharf buildings bill,
28 May. He testified to Carlisle's strong support for
Curwen's proposal to repeal the tax on husbandry
horses, 8 June.[13] He defended the ministry's decision
to include arrears in the duke of Clarence's award, 18
June. His wife, in whose right he held the Kirkstall
estate, died on 28 Aug. 1821.

Graham promoted the contentious Highgate chapel
bill, 26 June, 5 July, presented petitions against the beer
bill, 18 July, and was a majority teller for the Orphans'
Fund bill, 22 July 1822, but cast no reported votes that
session.[14] He presented and endorsed petitions from
London and Carlisle against the coastwise coal duties,
27 Mar., for repeal of the Insolvent Debtors Act, 11
Apr., and for the abolition of West Indian slavery, 12
May, and was a minority teller with Lord Chandos for
amending the Kettering road bill, 2 May 1823.[15] After
apparently failing to vote on the prosecution of the
Dublin Orange rioters, 24 Mar., 22 Apr., he deferred
to ministers during the inquiry and abandoned his
proposed adjournment motion, 23 May.[16] Poor health
caused him to spend the recess with Sandford at
Short Grove, near Saffron Walden, and in November
1823 he arranged to transfer half his canal shares to
Dalrymple for £5,000.[17] Returning late to London for
the 1824 session on account of illness,[18] Graham presented petitions from Carlisle and elsewhere for abolishing colonial slavery, 16, 23 Mar., equalization of the
spirit duties, 19 Mar., and removal of the prohibition
on wool exports, 26 Mar., and against the hides bill,

17 May.[19] Attending to his private concerns, he condemned the Hammersmith road bill as useless and unnecessary, 13 Apr., opposed the Islington improvement bill as minority teller in both divisions, 25 May, and spoke and was a majority teller against hearing counsel on the Equitable Loan Society bill, 25, 26 May 1824.[20] Poor health precluded further parliamentary attendance and he died at his residence in Portland Place in March 1825.[21] His will, dated 4 July 1822, was proved on 25 May 1825 under £45,000, adjusted to £40,000 in the province of Canterbury and £9,000 in York. It confirmed and extended the provisions he had made in 1807 for his children and provided small bequests for his nephews and servants. He was succeeded in the baronetcy and to the Ludgershall estates by Sandford, and left his daughter Anne his shares in the Equitable Loan Insurance Company and the Westminster Life Insurance Company.[22]

[1] See W.H. MacKean, *The Grahams of Kirkstall.* [2] Lonsdale mss, Lowther to Lonsdale, 31 July 1827, 25 Oct. 1829; *HP Commons, 1790-1820,* ii. 91-94; iv. 48-50. [3] Lonsdale mss, Hodgson to Lonsdale, 6 Feb.; Brougham mss, Pearson to Brougham, 7 Feb. 1820. [4] Castle Howard mss, Morpeth to wife, 7 Mar. 1820; Northumb. RO, Middleton mss ZM1/S76/34/2-7; 35/5. [5] *The Times,* 2 May 1820. [6] Ibid. 14 July 1820. [7] Ibid. 15 July 1820. [8] Lonsdale mss, Lowther to Lonsdale, 27 Jan. 1821. [9] Ibid. same to same, 23 Feb. 1821. [10] *The Times,* 1, 14 Mar. 1821. [11] Ibid. 4, 12 Apr. 1821. [12] Ibid. 2, 25, 31 May, 21 June 1821. [13] Ibid. 9 June 1821. [14] Ibid. 27 June, 6, 18, 23 July 1822. [15] Ibid. 12 Apr., 13 May 1823. [16] Ibid. 24 May 1823. [17] Cumbria RO (Carlisle), Hodgson mss D/Hod/2/25, Graham to Hodgson, 25 June, 18 Nov. 1823. [18] Add. 51562, Brougham to Holland [1 Mar. 1824]. [19] *The Times,* 17, 20, 24, 27 Mar., 18 May. 1824. [20] Ibid. 26, 27 May 1824. [21] Lonsdale mss, Lowther to Lonsdale, 21, 22 Mar. 1825. [22] PROB 11/1699/259; IR26/1041/301.

M.M.E.

GRAHAM, James Robert George (1792–1861), of Netherby, Cumb.[1]

KINGSTON-UPON-HULL	1818–1820
ST. IVES	1820–7 May 1821
CARLISLE	1826–15 Dec. 1828
CUMBERLAND	16 Jan. 1829–1832
CUMBERLAND EAST	1832–1837
PEMBROKE BOROUGHS	20 Feb. 1838–1841
DORCHESTER	1841–1847
RIPON	1847–1852
CARLISLE	1852–25 Oct. 1861

b. 1 June 1792, 1st s. of Sir James Graham†, 1st bt., of Netherby and Lady Catherine Stewart, da. of John Stewart†, 7th earl of Galloway [S]. *educ.* by Rev. Walter Fletcher at Dalston, Cumb.; Westminster 1806; Christ Church, Oxf. 1810; continental tour 1812-15. *m.* 8 July 1819, Fanny, da. of Col. James Campbell (formerly Callander) of Craigforth, Stirling and Ardkinglas, Argyll, 3s. 3da. *suc.* fa. as 2nd bt. 13 Apr. 1824; GCB 15 Apr. 1854. *d.* 25 Oct. 1861.

First ld. of admiralty Nov. 1830-July 1834, Dec. 1852-Mar. 1855; PC 22 Nov. 1830; sec. of state for home affairs Sept. 1841-July 1846.

Rect. Glasgow Univ. 1838-40.

Prov. Grand Master Cumb. Masons 1827-60, Cumb. and Westmld. Masons 1860-*d.*

According to Harriette Wilson, who once took him to the opera, Graham was 'a beauty: a very Apollo in form, with handsome features, particularly his teeth and eyes; sensible too and well educated'.[2] His Scottish mother, a devout Evangelical, had influenced his religious views, while clandestine assignments entrusted to him in 1813 and 1814 as private secretary to Lord William Cavendish Bentinck*, the permanent envoy in Sicily, intensified his political ambitions and mistrust of Lord Liverpool's administration.[3] Deferring to his Tory father and Lord Carlisle, he did not contest Cumberland, but came in for Kingston-upon-Hull in 1818 on the Fitzwilliam interest, espousing 'genuine Whig principles' of economy, peace, religious freedom and 'a moderate reform of Parliament'. His early speeches failed to impress, but he divided steadily with opposition and became a reliable supporter of Henry Brougham* and the Whig aristocracy against the Tory Lowthers in Westmorland and Cumberland, where he took a prominent part at the Peterloo meeting of 13 Oct. 1819.[4] His prospects of a second return for Hull at the general election of 1820 were good but beyond his means. Dissension among the Whigs in Cumberland, where John Curwen's* candidature threatened Lord Morpeth's† return, troubled him, and he turned down requisitions to stand for Carlisle or the county and distanced himself from the fray by going to support John Cam Hobhouse* in Westminster and contesting St. Ives, where he topped the poll.[5] Informing the Whig Sir James Mackintosh* of Morpeth's defeat, 30 Mar., James Abercromby* noted that Graham was 'also a great sufferer, for his pretensions to represent either Carlisle or the county are strong ... and now he finds both the city and county filled to his exclusion'.[6] In August 1820 Graham chaired the first Cumberland Independence dinner.[7] He divided steadily with the main Whig opposition in the Commons and supported the 1820 and 1821 parliamentary campaigns on Queen Caroline's behalf.[8] He received a month's leave on account of illness in his family, 22 Feb., and divided for the additional malt duty repeal bill, 21 Mar.,

3 Apr.; his 'radical' speech at the Cumberland agricultural distress meeting, 5 Apr. 1821, was acclaimed by the Whigs.[9] His vote for inquiry into costs in the naval dockyards, 7 May 1821, was his last that Parliament. His seat for St. Ives had been under threat since Sir Walter Stirling[†] had petitioned against his return, alleging bribery, 9 May 1820. His election was confirmed, but he lacked the money to defend fresh charges and vacated. It emerged that his opponents had relied on perjured evidence.[10]

Out of Parliament, Graham read widely, studied the works of David Hume, John Locke, and the political economists Adam Smith and David Ricardo*, and initially spent more time with his wife and children at Croft Head near Longtown, Cumberland, where he relieved his ailing father of much of the management of their neglected 26,000-acre Netherby estate, which had a gross rental of £17,946 in 1818.[11] He 'scouted' Curwen's proposals for a county meeting in March 1822 to petition for an additional protective duty on corn, believing it 'could yield no benefit to the farmer', and informed Brougham:

> I ever have been and ever shall be opposed to high prices attained by any such exaction. *If it were of use*, I am most ready to join in a petition for a large reduction in our overgrown establishments, and for a correspondent diminution in the taxes, which sustain them. The reduction is most requisite in the civil list and expenses of the collection of the revenue, for these are at once the causes of the most corrupt influence and the most profligate expenditure. The relief likewise is certain and immediate, for the taxes might be instantly taken off to the amount of the reduction, and, not withstanding all the jargon on the subject of prices, it is clear that taxation curtails the demand of the consumer and the net profit of the grower. I say, *if it were of use*, I am ready to petition; but ... I never again will join in a petition to Parliament which does not mention the necessity of some reform in the representation, because to me it appears worse than delusion to address a body with the air of confiding hope, from which I expect nothing but scorn, contumely and evil. The ... Commons constituted as it now is, seems to me the greatest curse of this unhappy country, for it keeps up the semblance of free government when the reality is torn from us and lost. The petition of this year would say no more than the petition of last, and would be treated with the same indifference and contempt. The country people also are weary of meeting and petitioning in vain. Annual attendance destroys the novelty, and, with it, the interest of these proceedings; and thus by frequent repetition it diminishes their importance ... Retrenchment of expense and reduction of taxes must advance together and at equal paces; for I confess I am an advocate for a clear surplus [of] revenue, thinking it of the most importance to the landed interest that credit should be maintained.[12]

On succeeding his father in April 1824 he contemplated selling out and becoming a merchant banker with the ill-fated Pole, Thornton, Downe and Company, a scheme he had been considering since 1822, but the Bristol banker James Evan Baillie* dissuaded him.[13] He appointed John Yule as his steward, oversaw his work closely and in 1825 borrowed £45,000, in addition to the £55,000 recently raised by his father, to improve the estate. To economize, he closed Netherby, took a cottage at Sidmouth, Devon, and various London lets and returned to Cumberland only for the races and agriculturists' meetings, where he drew on the expertise of his schoolfellow William Blamire*, Curwen, the Tory churchman John Rooke of Akehead and Joseph Saul of Greenrow, and formulated his own theories.[14] He remained in correspondence with Brougham and the Cumberland Whig hierarchy, but turned down their offer of support at the Carlisle by-election of March 1825, and when a dissolution was anticipated that summer, he refused to declare 'prematurely' for Cumberland in order to create a diversion to assist Brougham's Westmorland campaign.[15] He stood for 'troublesome' Carlisle on the 'Blue' interest at the general election of 1826 with a view to strengthening his position in the county, and topped the poll in a violent contest.[16] The Tory *Carlisle Patriot*, in which he had inherited his father's shares, dismissed him as a 'good-looking gentleman; clever, but too irritable ... a rash and inconsistent politician'.[17] A report that he 'disgraced himself' afterwards by taking a group of Carlisle weavers to support Brougham in the Westmorland election was unfounded.[18] His pamphlet *On Corn and Currency* was published that month, favourably reviewed in *The Times*, and generated replies from William Jacob[†] and William Cobbett[†]. It ran to at least four editions and established him as a landowner who 'understood' that 'the alternative evils of redundancy and scarcity, unsteady prices and uncertain rents are the inevitable consequences of the present system of our corn laws'. He also opposed all monopolies 'whether East Indian, West Indian or Bank interests'. Despairing of the way the government had handled distress in 1822, he suggested remedying it through retrenchment, 'free importation with an ample protecting duty', joint-stock banking, pound notes, currency reform and a tax on incomes.[19] Writing to Lord Holland, 29 Oct. 1826, shortly before leaving Netherby for Parliament, he warned that it would be impossible to stifle discussion of the plight of the distressed manufacturing districts and concluded:

> If the country gentlemen were half as honestly resolved to enforce a reduction of expenditure and of establish-

ments [as the urban working classes] some hopes of averting a serious convulsion might still remain, but the knowledge of flagrant abuses on the one hand, weighed with bitter suffering, and on the other, the boldest adherence to the corrupt system without the least regard to consequences, would seem to lead inevitably to some fatal crisis, which may shake even property itself.[20]

He criticized the ministry's projected emigration schemes to relieve distressed manufacturing districts like Carlisle as 'contrary to the spirit of our laws, and opposed to many of our most ancient regulations', 7 Dec. 1826. Next day, the colonial under-secretary Horton replied that the matter remained unresolved and would be decided by a select committee on emigration. (Graham was appointed to it, 15 Feb. 1827.)[21] His intention, he later informed Edward Davies Davenport*, had been to 'experiment' preparatory to raising the currency question, in order to 'overcome that fear of my audience' which had marred his previous performances in debate.[22] He hectored ministers on matters of concern to Carlisle, such as alehouse regulation, 13 Dec. 1826, 21 Feb., 21 Mar., the billeting of troops, 16 Feb., and machinery exports, 19 Mar. 1827. By prior arrangement with the home secretary Peel, he presented petitions of complaint against the deployment of troops there at the general election, 3 Apr.[23] Rejecting inquiry by the privileges committee whose report on a similar Carlisle petition in 1820 had not been implemented, he called for the establishment of an adequate civil force under the Carlisle police bill, and carried it in the teeth of opposition from the Tory corporation, 14 June.[24] He presented two Carlisle petitions for corn law revision, 19 Feb., and divided for a 50s. pivot price, 9 Mar.[25] He voted against the duke of Clarence's grant, 16 Feb., and divided for Catholic relief, 6 Mar., for inquiry into Leicester corporation, 15 Mar., for the spring guns bill, 23 Mar., and for inquiry into the conduct of the Lisburn Orange magistrates, 29 Mar. He voted to delay supplies until the ministerial crisis following Lord Liverpool's stroke was resolved, 30 Mar., and for inquiry into chancery arrears, 5 Apr. (and 14 Apr. 1828). Returning from a visit to Cumberland, 28 Apr. 1827, he confirmed his allegiance to the 3rd marquess of Lansdowne, who delayed joining the new Canning ministry as minister without portfolio until 20 May:

> If it be your wish that I should support the new administration, I am only desirous that it should be known I do so as your follower ... It is possible that owing my seat to a popular election I may be compelled by a sense of duty to give an occasional vote in favour of particular measures, which it may not be expedient for a minister of the crown directly to sanction.[26]

He spoke, 18 May, and voted, 28 May, for the disfranchisement of Penryn, and for Lord Althorp's bill limiting election expenses, 28 May, and presented constituents' petitions for Catholic relief and repeal of the Test Acts, 7 June.[27] He pleased his relations and other Scottish Whigs by moving their amendment to the Edinburgh bridewell bill and carrying it (by 68-56), 11 June.[28] He cast a majority vote for the Canadian waterways grant, 12 June. Writing on the 29th to Rooke, whose pamphlet *Free Trade in Corn, the Real Interest of the Landlord*, he was now instrumental in publishing, he observed:

> The recent struggle of parties has been highly injurious to the public interests; and never was a session less productive of solid advantage to the community. I am not pleased with the present position of affairs; and I fear that for some time the government will be disorganized and public attention dedicated to the character and conduct of men without much reference to measures. Every day's additional experience convinces me more and more of the soundness of our views respecting the currency; the bill of 1819 lies at the foundation of all our difficulties. Corn laws, customs regulations, emigration reports and relief to the manufacturers, all are but the fringes of this one great first cause, on which our difficulties and our fate depend.[29]

He dined with the Whig leaders at Charles Tennyson's*, 8 July 1827, and, after sounding opinion at Boodles, left with his family for Switzerland, so distancing himself from Carlisle, where his brother-in-law Wilfrid Lawson lost narrowly to a Tory at the by-election in August.[30] When he returned in September Canning was dead, Curwen close to death, Lord Goderich premier and Lansdowne home secretary.[31] John Herries's* appointment as chancellor of the exchequer, which in conversation with Lord Grey's son-in-law John Lambton* in Lyons he had dismissed as impossible, dismayed him and he informed Lady Holland that he despaired for their friends still in office.[32] He found 'some excellent reasoning backed by strong facts' to commend in Davenport's letter to Huskisson that month.[33] By October Abercromby found him 'very agreeably impressed with the state of things' and preparing to contest Cumberland.[34] Assessing his potential as a lobbyist for Scottish interests early in 1828, Henry Cockburn cautioned that he had yet to establish himself in debate and as a man of business:

> Graham has sometimes occurred to me, because he would probably work, is connected with Scotland, with the great advantage of being [in] England, is judicious, steady but moderate, and perfectly well disposed. But no one can appreciate the fitness of any person for the situation

of representative for Scotland, without knowing his weight in the House; and as to Sir James's I know nothing.[35]

He kept a high profile throughout the 1828 session, querying the expenditure proposals of the duke of Wellington's new administration, attending to the ailing Curwen's constituency business and matters affecting Scotland and the Borders. He voted, 26 Feb., and presented a petition from South Shields for repeal of the Test Acts, 2 Apr., and brought up others, 24, 30 Apr., and divided for Catholic relief, 12 May. He promoted bills for the better regulation of elections and turnpikes and made the campaign to retain one and two pound notes issued by country banks his own. In July the radical Whig John Hobhouse* described him as a 'favourite', who 'has £15,000 a year and the prettiest woman in London for a wife, and is besides really a clever, painstaking, and prepossessing man', and 'foremost' with Edward [Smith] Stanley* 'of the *youngsters*'.[36]

Graham refused to accept that the appointment of a finance committee by Wellington precluded investigation into official salaries and moved successfully for detailed returns, 27 Feb. 1828. His speech seconding Hume's motion for information on the 'profligate' sale of commissions by half-pay officers embarrassed the secretary at war Lord Palmerston, 12 Mar.; but his questions to George Bankes on the remit of the select committee on public works were confused and inappropriate, 24 Mar. He was pre-empted in his plan to expose abuses in the Irish registry of deeds by the Irish secretary William Lamb, 27, 31 Mar.[37] 'Though not wedded to any general theories', he harried Horton over emigration and the attendant passenger regulation bill, 4 Mar., before deciding to support a similar measure promoted by government, 25 Mar. He saw no justification in opposing the navy estimates as the Russo-Turkish war precluded reductions, 16 May. Following the Huskissonite secession, his hostility to the ministry became more marked. He forced a division, which he lost (by 70-38), on the governor of Dartmouth's salary, 20 June, and voted to reduce the payment to the Cork Institution, 20 June, and in condemnation of the Buckingham House expenditure, 23 June. Realizing that ministers intended imposing the salary reductions recommended by the finance committee on clerks and dockyard labourers, but not on political officers, he encouraged Althorp to press for a reduction in the salary of the lieutenant-general of the ordnance and supported him with a 'very good speech', 4 July. Hobhouse, who disliked it, thought it 'personal and sarcastic, and not without point'.[38] He

voted against the grant for North American fortifications, 7 July. He voted against sluicing the franchise at East Retford, 21 Mar., opposed the disqualification bill as a minority teller, 24 June, and voted against recommitting the disfranchisement bill, 27 June. Lord Lowther strenuously opposed the freeholder registration bill he introduced on 10 Mar. as a measure to 'diminish the expenses of elections, rescue the voter from the trammels of predominant influence, increase the facilities of voting, and, *pro tanto*, to enlarge the elective franchise', and although he carried its second reading (by 32-17), 25 Mar., it was repeatedly deferred and killed by adjournment, 13 June.[39] He divided for the corporate funds bill, 10 July 1828.

Perpetuating the assumption that Graham was the author of Rooke's *Free Trade in Corn*, on 27 Mar. *The Times* recommended it 'to all legislative landowners ... as a sedative to their alarms and a text book for their speeches on the approaching discussion of the corn laws'.[40] In the House, Graham pressed the president of the board of trade Charles Grant for information on average taking and urged the inclusion of Scottish and Irish data in the statistics, 3 Apr. He voted for a reduction from 64s.-62s. in the corn pivot price, 22 Apr., and highlighted the anomaly of Manx flour imports, 28 Apr. Criticizing the intended restriction of low denomination bank notes to Scotland under the promissory notes bill, he announced a counter-measure, 5 May, which he reformulated as an amendment for inquiry by select committee, 22 May. Supported by petitions from Carlisle, 23 May, and backed by the former Canningite Thomas Henry Liddell, he led the unsuccessful opposition to the government's measure, 'a premature, a theoretical remedy for an evil which is not yet in existence', 3 June. He quoted from Hume, Locke and Alexander Baring* and urged the Members who had voted with Peel in 1819 to join him in rejecting Ricardo's theories. He criticized the failure to introduce joint-stock banking uniformly following the 1825-6 collapse and accused ministers of trying to tackle the currency that 'flows' from a bad system rather than the system itself. He did 'not wish to be understood as being enamoured of a paper currency, in the abstract', but deemed it the only safe one then viable. He failed (by 82-17) to prevent an adjournment, which gave Peel time to intervene and allege that his speech had been riddled with misquotations, 5 June. He had corresponded with Lord Lauderdale and the Scottish bankers throughout, and remained convinced that the measure was 'unnecessary and unfair' to England and 'delusive' to Scotland and Ireland. He added that a law that prohibited him from banking with a Scottish house made that currency a 'contraband of war'.[41] Taking charge of legislation on Scottish vagrants and customary tenures, 19, 20 Feb., 11, 14 Mar., he refused in both cases to bow to ministerial pressure to agree to a pre-committal withdrawal or postponement. He moved the second reading of the Wakefield-Ferrybridge canal bill in Lord Milton's absence, 3 Mar., but failed to prevent its defeat (by 179-91 and 110-105) at the hands of Lord Lowther and his fellow shareholders in the Aire and Calder Canal Company. He brought up Carlisle's petition for repeal of the 1827 Malt Act, asked Peel if remedial legislation was planned, 17 Mar., and spoke briefly on coroners' fees, 3 Apr. Motivated by difficulties encountered when renewing the Carlisle and Bampton roads bill, and with the Longtown Act about to expire, he introduced a General Turnpike Act amendment bill to simplify procedures, 23 May, but it was thrown out by the Lords. His amended bill, introduced, 10 July, received royal assent, 15 July 1828.[42] (On 27 Feb. 1829 the select committee confirmed his premise that 'once established a trust ceases to be a speculation', and he overcame Hume's objections to the new fee structure they recommended.) His advocacy of a clause in the alehouse licensing bill giving county magistrates concurrent jurisdiction with city and borough magistrates incensed the Whig Member for Chester, Lord Belgrave, 19 June, while his endorsement of the Hull ship owners' distress petition, 24 June, was seen as a ploy to revive the currency question. He divided for the assessment of lessors bill, 12 June, and inquiry into the Irish church, 14 June. As 'a warm friend to the church establishment', he called the additional churches bill 'injudicious' and voted against its second reading, 30 June. He presented petitions from Cumberland and elsewhere requesting the abolition of colonial slavery, 17, 19, 24 June, 10 July 1828.

Predicting possible ministerial blunders following O'Connell's return for county Clare, he wrote on 15 July to urge Smith Stanley to 'take the field in force' and grasp a 'golden opportunity of forming a party in the ... Commons on some broad and intelligent principle, without any reference to leaders in the ... Lords and without any direct compact with Brougham'.[43] Meanwhile, commenting on speculation that Graham might be won over to widen the government's base, the Tory John Croker* informed Peel:

Personally, I know nothing of him and what little I have heard from the Lowthers has not prepossessed me in his favour; but he speaks remarkably well with a natural flow of words and a great deal of good sense. Once or twice he has left the violents to vote and even speak with us and I suppose [he] might be induced to come over under the shadow of Calcraft. I doubt whether in real powers he be

second to Stanley, but (at worst) he is the next to him at that side of the House.[44]

Abandoning the immediate prospect of minor office, Graham helped Althorp, Brougham and Smith Stanley to dictate the pace of Peel and Wellington 'conversion' to Catholic emancipation in the closing months of 1828. The rise of the Brunswick Clubs alarmed him:

This appeal to club law is insane on the part of the aristocracy: the reaction is certain; conflict is the tendency; religion will infuse only the venom of its hatred, but redress of civil wrongs will be the cry; and the appeal to numbers and to physical force is madly made by the weaker party. Brunswickers will be met by reformers, No Popery by Dissent from the church establishment, the government, feebly hesitating, will be overborne and a convulsion ensue, which may shake the whole fabric.[45]

Directly Curwen died, 11 Dec. 1828, Graham vacated Carlisle and declared his candidature for Cumberland, whereupon the Tory *Cumberland Pacquet* commented waspishly:

His corn law dreamings the farmers ... justly consider inapplicable to men who are awake and have their senses about them. His party pledges and connections are certainly not of a kind best calculated to secure his independence; the trading politicians, for their own special purposes, are understood to have obtained too great an ascendancy over his inexperience'.[46]

Abercromby also had reservations about Graham, 'who has almost an undue importance in the House'. Fears that the Lowthers would intervene or Lord Carlisle (as Morpeth had become) seek to regain a Cumberland seat for his son proved unfounded and he was unopposed, 16 Jan. 1829.[47] On the hustings he said he would be 'ashamed of myself, could I be capable of paring down my political sentiments to suit the views of party', opposed all 'jobs' and 'unnecessary outlay', and pressed for reductions in public expenditure, 'unnecessary places' and taxation. Elaborating, he described himself as

an adherent of that small party still remaining in the ... Commons who maintain the rights and privileges of the people in opposition to the power and influence of the Court; and although I consider party as the best depository of public principles, by the power it has in holding men to their professions, I am no advocate of faction and can never be made the tool of any party.

He expressed qualified praise for Wellington, whose concession of Catholic emancipation he endorsed, and condemned the violence of the Catholic Association and the Brunswick Clubs.[48] The strength of anti-

Catholic feeling in Cumberland surprised him. When their hostile petitions were presented, 4 Mar., he attributed them to undue Lowther influence, praised the political realism of Peel and referred to the favourable petitions he was due to present on 9 Mar.[49] He divided for emancipation, 6, 30 Mar., objected to Hume's time-wasting interventions on the Irish franchise bill, 25 Mar., and voted to permit Daniel O'Connell to sit without taking the oath of allegiance, 15 May. He voted to transfer East Retford's seats to Birmingham, 5 May. Presenting a protectionist petition from the landowners of Leath ward, he confirmed their distress, but he refused to join them in attributing it to cheap wool imports and declared that he would campaign afresh for a review of currency and banking, 11 May. He endorsed petitions from Carlisle and Cockermouth against renewal of the East India Company's monopoly and high corn prices, 12 May. He was 'altogether' opposed to the settlement by hiring bill, 3 May, and harboured doubts over the friendly societies bill, 15 May, but he strongly supported the anatomy regulation bill that day, including the use of unclaimed pauper corpses. He called for 'some public tribunal' to deal with the French claims, 5 June 1829.

Speculation that he would be offered a place by Wellington remained unfounded.[50] He appreciated that 'the duke's position is critical ... but it is not the confusion of a beaten army, without a leader and without a plan'.[51] Illness severely curtailed his activities during the recess, but with a view to 'producing a splash' he promoted the adoption in Cumberland of a contentious distress petition calling for 'a reversal of the measures adopted since 1819 ... the strictest economy in the public expenditure and the repeal or reduction of ... taxes, such as the duties on malt and beer, which press most grievously on the poor'. At the county meeting, 26 Jan. 1830, he also expressed qualified support for the government and pressed them to act on the currency as they had on emancipation.[52] He voted for Knatchbull's amendment regretting the omission of distress from the king's speech, 4 Feb., and led the subsequent attack on the government's failure to implement the economies recommended by the 1828 finance committee. He announced that he intended moving to reduce official salaries to their 1797 levels on presenting the Cumberland distress petition, 8 Feb., voted next day to limit the estimates to six months, and introduced his resolutions in a celebrated two-hour speech when the supply committee reported on the 12th.[53] He prefaced his call for retrenchment from official salaries downwards by reiterating his criticism of the Small Notes Act and attributed currency depreciation and rising prices to

the 1797 Bank Restriction Act. He criticized the 1819 Bank committee for interpreting inflation solely in terms of gold prices, excused his own vote to restore the gold standard to youth and the influence of Ricardo, and described how shortfalls in agricultural profits and rents contributed to the distress of the labourers. Deliberately excluding the privy purse and the royal household, he specifically targeted colonial governors' salaries, expenditure on public debt management (£11,500,000 in 1797; £27,366,000 in 1828) and excise profits. Outbid by the treasury secretary George Dawson's conciliatory counter-resolutions promising inquiry and a £1,000,000 tax reduction, he did not force a division, and there were signs of resentment in Whig ranks at his rapid promotion.[54] He voted to cut taxes, 15 Feb., presented the lead workers of Alston's distress petition, 16 Feb., and proposed and was appointed to a select committee on the emoluments of clerks of the peace, 23 Feb. His wife's illness rendered it uncertain to the last whether he would be able to introduce his motion condemning the 'unnecessary' office of navy treasurer, 12 Mar. 1828.[55] A veiled attack, as incumbent, on the erstwhile Canningite Thomas Frankland Lewis*, it exposed a 'schism' among the Whigs, for Althorp, Brougham and Lord John Russell deemed it too hostile to government.[56] To the secretary at war Hardinge, it was a regrettable sign that Graham 'thought under the present circumstances he could be a more considerable man out of office than he would be in a subordinate situation' under Wellington.[57]

He dissociated himself from Davenport's intended motion on the state of the nation, 3 Mar. 1828, and stayed away, like Morpeth and Smith Stanley, from the Whig meeting that day which invited Althorp to become leader 'for one definite object, namely the reduction of expenditure and of taxation'. Althorp's friends in turn (he reported to Smith Stanley) tested his loyalty with 'a sort of motion respecting the treasurership, from which the sting of censure has in great measure been extracted: if I move it in this shape they will support it; if in my own, I conclude they will move it as an amendment'. Biding his time, he consulted Littelton, Palmerston 'and others', ordered returns, 5, 9 Mar., and voted for information on the interference of British troops in Portugal, 10 Mar. Supported by Grey's son Lord Howick, but not Althorp, and with Huskisson in his minority, his motion criticizing ministers for missing an opportunity to save the treasurer's £3,000 salary failed by 188-90, 12 Mar.[58] He divided with the revived Whig opposition against the Bathurst and Dundas pensions, 26 Mar. Moving to abolish the office of lieutenant-general of the ordnance from 'a quarter of the House where the principal friends of ministers have of late been found', he acknowledged that 'the character of an economical reformer is at all times obnoxious ... and that its being joined to that of a parliamentary reformer, will not render it more acceptable', and lost by 200-124, 29 Mar. Continuing, as he did until 6 July, to divide with opposition, he prepared to introduce a motion hatched by Edward Littleton and Lord Wellesley and originally drafted by Huskisson with Hume in mind, for an account of all privy councillors' emoluments, excluding the royal family.[59] Its announcement, 30 Apr., angered the chancellor of the exchequer Goulburn and added bite to Graham's interventions on the navy pay bill, 3 May, French claimants, 6 May, and supply, 10 May. Its execution on the 14th confirmed him as one of the most talented politicians out of office and the best speaker on finance.[60] Defining retrenchment and value for money as his objectives, he stated that his patience had been exhausted by repeated referrals to ineffective select committees and called for inquiry into the continued receipt of public money by 113 out of 169 privy councillors, whom he called 'birds of prey'. He censured in particular payments to the former ordnance office clerk Penn, and Lords Cathcart, Melville and Rosslyn. Challenged by the Whig General Grosvenor, he conceded that at the start of the session the currency question had been the only major issue separating him from government and attributed his growing disaffection to their refusal to implement the reductions recommended by the finance committee. Hobhouse (no doubt irked by Graham's refusal to support an inquiry motion targeting the Irish solicitor-general John Doherty*, 12 May) considered defeat by 232-174 'a poor minority for such a question on the eve of a dissolution' and suspected Graham of having 'more than a public motive for his present virulence against government' and taunts at opposition.[61] Howick thought

> it would ... have been better had he confined himself more strictly to the subject. Superannuations had nothing to do with it. He also exaggerated his case most amazingly, which, as it happened, was all in our favour, but if it had been exposed, as it might have been, would have told very much against him.[62]

He presented petitions and agitated for concessions on the Clyde navigation bill, 17, 21, 26, 28 May, 10 June, Scottish paupers, 21 May, lead imports, 25 May, and the corn laws, 26 May. According to Lord King, 'he got a great victory' over Peel on the four-and-a-half per cent Barbados and Leeward Island duties, which the minister promised to place under parliamentary control, 4 June.[63] His follow-up motion was timed out.

He 'spoke well' and failed by only 118-99 to procure a reduction in the grant for South American missions, 7 June, and by 121-98 to cut that for consular services, 11 June 1830.[64]

Graham divided for Lord Blandford's reform proposals, 18 Feb., the transfer of East Retford's seats to Birmingham, 11 Feb., 5 Mar., the enfranchisement of Birmingham, Leeds and Manchester, 23 Feb., inquiry into Newark's petition of complaint against the duke of Newcastle's electoral influence, 1 Mar., and Lord John Russell's parliamentary reform motion, 28 May 1830. He voted to reform the divorce laws, 3 June, and to abolish the death penalty for forgery, 24 May, 7 June. He moved for correspondence on the 1829 Greek blockade and accounts of civil list pensions, 8 June. His recent dealings with Huskisson encouraged speculation, and he still considered an overture to Grey from the Wellington ministry likely when he attended an opposition meeting at Althorp's for the first time, 4 July. As he and Smith Stanley had hoped, they resolved to 'go into regular opposition' in the next Parliament should the Wellington administration 'do no better'.[65] According to Charles Arbuthnot's* informant, Graham had 'declared that he was a Whig, and that he certainly should not leave his party; but that he had been in contact with Huskisson on matters of business, and that this he intended to continue'.[66] Assessing the session in a letter to Rooke, 21 June 1830, he expressed regret that the currency question had 'not been touched'.[67] He passed on information about Hull to Palmerston at the dissolution in July and came in unopposed for Cumberland, where he resisted pressure to stand with a second Whig. The increasingly radical Carlisle Journal regretted that there were Tories among his pre-election dinner guests at Dalston and Whitehaven and complained that he had 'trimmed his sails' to please both parties. In his speeches he approved the French revolution, promised to support 'further reduction in taxation [and] moderate but effective reform in the representation', including opening more polling stations, the enfranchisement of copyholders and customary tenants, a redistribution of corrupt borough seats and a £10-20 borough franchise.[68] He neither approved of nor was party to the electoral pact between Brougham, Lonsdale and Lord Thanet, which left Westmorland undisturbed, and maintained with the benefit of hindsight that he had been prepared to make way for Brougham at Carlisle in 1826, to give him an 'honourable retreat' from Westmorland.[69]

Before Parliament met, he assumed an interest in the Scottish representation with a view to joining Brougham in pressing for reform in the new Parliament. He predicted that Wellington would 'yield' only 'to the extent of conferring the elective franchise on some of the larger towns'.[70] He regarded any arrangement between him and the former Canningites as 'political suicide' for the latter, notwithstanding the precondition of 'total reconstruction' they imposed, and discussed opposition tactics with Huskisson on the eve of the ill-fated opening of the Liverpool-Manchester Railway, 15 Sept. 1830.[71] He saw Huskisson's death as a temporary 'God-send' for Wellington and corresponded frequently afterwards with Lord Durham (as Lambton had become), the Lansdowne Whigs and Brougham, to whom he wrote that a

> junction of the Whigs with Palmerston and the Grants, if it took place, should precede the meeting of Parliament; and ... the leading principles on which the new party is formed should be announced to the public, comprehending, as it were, the scheme on which the government would be conducted if the duke were removed from power; and in my humble judgement this scheme should include a substantial measure of parliamentary reform, a reduction of salaries and of establishments, a review of the taxation of the country in the sum of [Sir Henry] Parnell's* admirable book, law reform on your model, commutation of tithes and a better provision for the working clergy ... by a new valuation of tithes and first fruits; and the abolition of the feudal game laws, substituting in their stead the right of property. In a word the new party should stand pledged to the *maximum* of reform consistent with the safety of our present form of government, and believe me this maximum after all will be found the minimum with which public opinion will rest content. A pledge also should be given not to accept office separately. A leader should be chosen, and constant attendance promised when notes by his desire are sent. Something of this sort should be done before the fight begins; for the duke has no chance unless from divisions and disorganization among Members.[72]

Mistrusting him still, in October Edward Ellice* suspected that Graham was the author of *The Answer*, an influential pamphlet which independently reviewed the state of the parties and suggested coalition.[73] Liaising with Howick and encouraged by the Tory renegade Sir George Warrender*, he tested the response of the Whig hierarchy and Palmerston's friends to Brougham's reform scheme, which deprived each rotten borough and certain small boroughs of one Member in order to enfranchise the large towns. It suggested an inhabitant householder franchise.[74] The Whigs at Althorp's, 31 Oct., backed it, and Graham persuaded Brougham, who hosted a pre-session dinner, 7 Nov., not to move it as an amendment

to the address, but as a motion for inquiry, scheduled for 16 Nov., three days after the Whig muster, in order to give it a realistic prospect of success.[75] Hobhouse, who was present, wrote in his diary that Graham also reported [from Palmerston] that the Huskissonites were 'prepared to go to any lengths, so far as excepted turning out the administration. That they would vote for enfranchising the great towns and would assent to Brougham's motion if vaguely worded'.[76] According to Howick, Grey had recently convinced Graham that 'the plan of taking only one seat from each of the rotten boroughs will never answer'.[77] Launching into outright opposition directly the cancellation of William IV's visit to the City was announced, 8 Nov., Graham deplored Wellington's anti-reform declaration and accused him of being 'too fond of running alone' and too 'obstinately attached to that policy which he thinks is right'. Two days later he alarmed ministers by proposing a motion censuring their appointment of the dean of Durham Dr. Phillpotts to the see of Exeter while holding the lucrative Durham living of Stanhope *in commendam*.[78] Targeting the civil list, he stated that he would vote for nothing before receiving the returns he had ordered on 6 June. He presented petitions for the abolition of colonial slavery from Cumberland and Westmorland, 10, 11, 15 Nov., and, bringing up another for parliamentary reform that day from Lonsdale's borough of Cockermouth, he urged the reform of Scottish representation. He voted to bring down the ministry on the civil list, 15 Nov. 1830, and, after much haggling, he postponed his motion on Phillpotts, 17 Nov. He was an intermediary for the Whigs and Huskissonites in negotiations pending the formation of Grey's reform ministry, in which he was passed over for the home office, declined the war office and accepted the admiralty with cabinet rank and a seat on the privy council. He became one of the main government speakers in the Commons. Abercromby (and the new lord chancellor Brougham) considered Graham and Smith Stanley 'Lansdowne's props', and Abercromby was one of the few to approve Graham's 'prematurely high' appointment.[79] The caricaturist 'HB', in 'Drawing for the Twelfth Cake', caricatured Graham saying, 'Who ever thought of seeing me first lord of the admiralty?'[80] Predicting his failure, Greville traced his conduct over the previous decade and commented: 'it is one thing to attack strong abuses and fire off well-rounded set phrases, another to administer the naval affairs of the country and be ready to tilt against all comers, as he must do for the future'.[81] With the paymaster Lord John Russell and the commissioner of woods and forests Lord Duncannon, he was one of the committee, chaired by the lord privy seal Durham, to whom Grey entrusted the task of preparing the ministerial plan of reform. Cartoonists depicted him as the brakeman on the reform coach.[82]

Graham's re-election was unopposed, 8 Dec. 1830, and afforded him an opportunity to ascertain the views of the radical Member for Carlisle William James on the ballot and annual parliaments.[83] Left to manage the House in its leader Althorp's absence, 20 Dec., his response to the 'sharp and most rancorous' attack by Dawson on government's overhaul of Irish legal appointments was found wanting.[84] Next day he presented his constituents' petitions against colonial slavery and the coastwise coal duties with others for Scottish parliamentary and burgh reform. That had been largely entrusted to Henry Cockburn, solicitor-general for Scotland, and Thomas Francis Kennedy, Member for Ayr Burghs, with whom he liaised to ensure a uniform tax qualification.[85] He refused to be provoked by Hume into discussing the civil list when Josiah Guest questioned Mrs. Arbuthnot's entitlement to a £1,200 pension, 23 Dec. 1830, nor would he resurrect the currency question in response to a written plea from Western.[86] Despite the furore generated by the president of the board of trade Charles Grant's threatened resignation over the civil list allowance for Queen Adelaide's clothes, on 24 Jan. 1831 Graham wrote confidently to Morpeth that

> *excepting the corn laws*, there is hardly one great subject in our domestic policy, which we shall not be prepared to deal ... Croker and the underlings breathe fury. Peel and the duke pretend moderation; but with the latter forbearance is only caution, and boundless hostility is common to the crew ... I like my colleagues and we are firmly united. If we fail, show me the government that can save the country'.[87]

Making light of opposition by Calcraft and Hunt, he defended the civil list in what the Wellington ministry's president of the India board Lord Ellenborough considered 'a very high Tory speech', 4 Feb., and commended the stock transfer tax proposed in Althorp's budget, 14 Feb.[88] His hasty, waspish defence of Palmerston's foreign policy and the cost of policing Ireland, 18 Feb., haunted him, for he fell victim to Peel's invective and Sir George Murray and North pounced on his use of the term 'demagogues' for 'certain agitators' seeking repeal of the Irish Union, and accused him of preaching 'English supremacy'. The issue escalated and was resolved only after William Macnamara*, acting for The O'Gorman Mahon*, who treated the remark as a personal slander, met Althorp (as Graham's representative), 20 Feb., and agreed to 'be satisfied' by an 'explicit' Commons statement.

Graham apologized when Daniel O'Connell revived the issue, 21 Feb.[89] To make matters worse, when opposing Lord Chandos's motion for inquiry into the distressed West Indian colonies that day, Graham contradicted his colleagues (Grant and Poulett Thomson) and 'stood alone' in contending that this 'would not obstruct the committee of supply'. He added, 'I have made too many of these motions myself to know that it is intended to be and would be considered in the nature of an indirect but intelligible censure upon government'. He later defended Althorp's decision to give priority to tax reductions on candles and coastwise coal in a 'tight' budget (21 Feb.). According to Ellenborough, 'it was said at the levee' that he 'tendered his resignation' afterwards; but Greville wrote that 'Graham declared a vote against ministers would make them resign'.[90] In February 1831 he was said to be preparing to 'eat his words'.[91]

In view of the king's close interest in the navy and the need for retrenchment, Graham consulted the Tory Admiral Hotham and Sir Samuel Pechell* on naval matters, and Palmerston on developments in the Mediterranean and the Scheldt, and read Wellington's secret evidence to the finance committee on the defence of the Canadian colonies before drafting his estimates.[92] On 24 Jan. 1831 he informed Grey that he was disposed to 'ask for 22,000 seamen and 10,000 marines' and that he would promise not to exceed that number 'without the consent of Parliament', or, in case of an emergency, 'without a frank statement of the excess and of the cause of it, so soon as Parliament shall reassemble'.[93] With the king's approval, he moved for £1,081,600 to finance them, 25 Feb.[94] His speech, in which he also trailed his scheme for separating the navy and victualling boards, helped to restore his reputation and government morale, for he demonstrated that he could deploy naval expertise and expose previous malpractice to advantage. For example, he dismissed and deflected questions from Hume, the Tory admirals and the comptroller of the navy Sir Thomas Byam Martin, a personal friend of the king, on the escalating cost of the Bermuda garrison and Robert Torrens's* appointment as deputy adjutant-general of marines.[95] He refused to be provoked by opposition taunts over the reorganization of the marines, the exclusion of warrant officers from court, and the half pay, 28 Feb. However, as the reform bill crisis deepened, and with a negligible majority to rely on, he struggled to see through the mutiny bills, 7 Mar., and estimates, 21, 23, 25, 28 Mar. 1831, despite being 'up to his business to a remarkable degree'.[96]

Conservative by comparison with Duncannon and at least initially more pragmatic than Russell, his 'two *sine qua nons*' for the reform bill became a uniform £10 voter qualification in the boroughs and the principle of disfranchisement; but he also, at different times, advocated the ballot and quinquennial elections, registration, short polls, increased county representation and enforcing a residence qualification. He initially recommended a £20 franchise.[97] Dealing primarily with registration, he liaised fairly effectively with his colleagues on the committee and deliberately summoned Durham to the cabinet meeting, 28 Jan. 1831, when Althorp sought to lower the householder voting qualification to £10.[98] Hardinge expected him to try to secure a compromise.[99] He presented reform petitions from Cumberland and elsewhere, 9, 26, 28 Feb.[100] With a sense of impending doom, he informed Grey on 17 Feb. that he doubted 'whether the draft of any one of the three bills is complete' and that modifications had yet to be agreed. He urged their discussion 'in the cabinet clause by clause', in the presence of Russell, Duncannon, the lord advocate Jeffrey and the attorney-general Denman, warning that 'without some such preparation I anticipate disaster and we have already suffered much from the imperfect discussion of great questions in the cabinet before they have been brought forward in the House'.[101] He called for patience when information remained unavailable two days after the bill's introduction, 3 Mar. Promoting the bill, 8 Mar., he tried to justify it according to Charles James Fox's[†] premise that 'the best system of representation was one which secured to the country the largest number of independent voters, and the worst was one which embraced the largest number who, from being in dependent circumstances, were incapable of deliberation and act as they were commanded'; but his speech was apologetic, statistical, and according to the Whig Sir Henry Bunbury* 'failed sadly', and gave the impression that he cut 'a sorry figure in Parliament'. He struggled to overcome the opposition's taunts that his £5,000 salary was a 'privy councillor's emolument', and his speech was memorable only because of a misapplied simile which, as the Tory admiral Sir Joseph Yorke promptly noticed, inadvertently likened the bill to a foundering ship.[102] He was confident of carrying the second reading, but 'anxious as to its fate in the committee; if it be emasculated there, it will fail to produce the healing effect which is the real benefit it is calculated to bestow'.[103] He introduced several favourable petitions, 19 Mar. To his embarrassment, his attempt to dismiss the anti-reformer Sir Robert Inglis's breach of privilege allegation against *The Times* was scotched by Charles

Williams Wynn, who had resigned as secretary at war rather than support the reform bill. Deputizing for Althorp, Graham failed to restore order when feuding over reform petitions disrupted the House, 29 Mar., and his poor response to Peel's speech for Gascoyne's wrecking amendment was said to have contributed to the bill's defeat, 19 Apr. 1831.[104] He predicted a government victory at the ensuing general election, 'for the voice of a united people is irresistible'.[105] He sent Sir Edward Troubridge* and Joseph Marryat* to contest Sandwich on the admiralty interest and eventually settled on Byam Martin and George Elliot[†] for Plymouth.[106] He correctly anticipated a hard struggle in Cumberland, where the Lowther-controlled press were unstinting in their criticism of the budget, naval reforms and his parliamentary conduct; but he failed to appreciate that the momentum to field two reformers there was unstoppable.[107] Forced to revise his plans to 'stand alone', his return at the top of the poll was engineered by Blamire, who defeated Lord Lowther and was elected with him.[108] His hasty condemnation on the hustings of the Whig renegade Scarlett's return for Cockermouth, as the Lowthers' replacement for his cousin Lord Garlies, almost resulted in a duel and fuelled his hatred of a partisan press, which he assuaged by selling his shares in the *Carlisle Patriot* and investing in the Whig *Whitehaven Herald*.[109] Reassuring him that the incident had not cost him the king's confidence, the duke of Richmond quipped, 'it would be inglorious to be shot by a special pleading lawyer, who knows but little of the law of honour'.[110] He failed to tempt his uncle Lord Galloway out of retirement to support reformers in the Scottish peerage elections.[111]

He attended the pre-session reception at Lansdowne House, 27 May 1831, and, before Parliament met, he authorized additional dockyard provisioning and dispatched Codrington's squadron to the Mediterranean, a frigate to the Tagus and guardships to Ireland, where, he advised Smith Stanley

> no government can allow its people to starve according to the most approved rules of political economy: only be it observed that the necessity of such extraordinary aid proves the urgency of taking into consideration some scheme for the relief of the poor by local assessment.[112]

He moved the adjournment in Althorp's absence, 14 June, and met his colleagues regularly over the next week to discuss alterations to the reform bill.[113] Resisting pressure from the shires to waive the division of counties, he upheld the right of the aristocracy to a voice in the representation of county divisions as a counterpoise to the increased 'democratic influence' created by the enfranchisement of large towns, and advised Grey:

> No more important change can be made in our original measure; none which will more justly excite the alarm of the aristocracy. If the £10 qualification for cities and boroughs be sacred, this countervailing arrangement of the subdivision of counties cannot be reversed without seriously affecting the whole measure.[114]

On 27 June, responding to criticism from Lord Mahon, who attributed the dissolution to his failure to carry the army and navy supplies (28, 29 Mar.), he explained that the discovery of a surplus fund had rendered voting them through unnecessary. He afterwards defended the ministry's Irish policy. Francis Thornhill Baring* noted that his reply 'showed more pluck than last session'.[115] Presenting the navy estimates, 28 June, he explained that they were unchanged and emphasized that he sought 1,000 fewer men than his predecessors, 'soon to be 2,000 fewer' through natural wastage and his policy of appointing officers to one vacancy in three, to reduce the half-pay list. He left it to the radicals, whom he ignored, and the naval experts, whom he addressed deferentially, to quibble over the details. Keen to preserve cabinet unity, he countered rumours that Palmerston was about to defect, defended public salaries when these were criticized by Hume, 30 June, and justified the arduous timetable the reform bill imposed, 8 July, and the wine duties, 11 July.[116] Challenged by Robert Gordon over consular salaries, 18 July, he admitted, without elaborating, that he had indeed considered the system unsound. A week later, when the grants for Newfoundland and Sierra Leone were voted, 25 July, he turned Gordon's comments on the benefits of running on the estimates according to the French practice to good effect, and he refused to be drawn by Hunt's questions about the Dover packet boats, 27, 29 July. He failed to prevent Thomas Wyse obtaining leave for bill to establish a national education system in Ireland, 8 Aug. Writing to Robert Shapland Carew* on the 15th for advice on a suitable preparatory school for his eldest son, he conceded that Irish affairs pressed 'most grievously' on government.[117] Returning to the House, 30 Aug., after an absence of about ten days caused by a fever, he was unable to reply to questions about Brazil and the whereabouts of the American squadron without Palmerston's assistance. Byam Martin's failure to support him on reform and admiralty matters had troubled him for some time;[118] and in September he risked the wrath of William IV by refusing to reinstate Lord Dundonald, to authorize naval expansion or to sack Torrens, who, at a City

common hall, had uttered a rash threat to abolish the Lords unless they backed reform, 21 Sept.[119] In each case, he ensured that he had the consent of the cabinet before informing the king of his decision.[120] He acquiesced in Palmerston's policy of giving tacit support to the rebel Dom Pedro in Portugal, and joined him and Smith Stanley in declaring against Brougham's call for wholesale peerage creations at the coronation to safeguard the bill.[121] Privately, he had already recommended his brother-in-law Lawson for the honour.[122] He naturally divided for the reform bill in crucial divisions and helped to vote through its details when present, but he spoke only to justify the inclusion of Workington in the new Whitehaven constituency, which the Lowthers opposed, 6 Aug., 1 Sept., and the award of three rather than four Members to Dorset, 13 Aug.[123] After the bill's passage, 21 Sept., he carried a 'vote' for a further £27,000 for the Royal Clarence dockyard at Gosport without a division, 30 Sept., but his utterances on naval half-pay, 7 Oct., and chain cables, 13 Oct. 1831, were censured in the press.[124]

He initially regarded the reform bill's defeat in the Lords as a resignation matter, and wrote to Grey, 8, 17 Oct., pressing for proof of the king's loyalty in the prorogation speech that month and requesting the dismissal of Byam Martin and Lord Howe from his department for failing to support reform.[125] Palmerston thought he would 'not be sorry to see ... [the revised bill] a good deal mitigated'.[126] Official business in Plymouth prevented him attending the cabinet, 17, 19 Nov., when they revised their strategy on reform and left the peerage question open. He accordingly set out his case for a single and prompt mass creation of peers, in a memorial he sent to Grey, 26 Nov.[127] Althorp, the only other cabinet member authorized to read it, write to Grey on the 25th:

> Probably ... Graham will save us the trouble of having many more difficulties to contend with. For if he goes out on the grounds that he has now taken [immediate peerage creations] the people will desert us because we have not followed his advice and the peers, knowing that we have not secured the power of creating as many as we like, will be totally unmanageable.[128]

He sent a letter of support to the 15 Nov. Cumberland reform meeting, and his protest to the sheriff over the *Carlisle Patriot*'s subsequent misrepresentation of the reformer Philip Howard's* speech elicited a vicious response from the Lowther newspapers. They also exploited the recent appointment of his brother Fergus Graham as postmaster of Carlisle.[129] Croker thought he 'seemed zealous for' the revised reform bill introduced on 11 Dec.,[130] and he was depicted in caricature smiling 'sardonically' when Smith Stanley demolished Croker's arguments against it at its second reading, 17 Dec. 1831. He afterwards conveyed Lord Huntingdon's proxy to Grey.[131] Alerted by Littleton to 'misplaced' reports of his 'inattention to Members in the House', he said it was 'owing to his being jaded to death with official business before he could come down ... and promised amendment'.[132] During the Christmas recess, he tried in vain to persuade Garlies to allow his name to be put forward for a peerage.[133] He was rumoured to have declined to retire with a peerage to make way for Althorp at the admiralty when ministerial changes were contemplated in February 1832.[134] In March, when Brougham wanted Althorp called up to assist him in the Lords, Graham, like Smith Stanley, threatened resignation on account of the additional work it would give him.[135]

He divided with his colleagues on the Russian-Dutch loan, which he privately conceded he would have attacked in opposition, 26 Jan., 12, 16, 20 July 1832.[136] He brought in the quarterly estimates successfully, 13 Feb., maintained a show of force in the Tagus and the Scheldt and planned a complete overhaul of his department under the navy civil departments bill, which ended civil appointments and replaced the admiralty, navy and victualling boards with separate departments for accounts, stores, victualling, physicians and surveying, each controlled by an admiralty lord, making an estimated annual saving of £20,000 in salaries and £10,000 in messengers' fees.[137] According to Littleton, on 9 Feb.

> a party of eight or ten met at the admiralty in consequence of a suggestion of mine ... to hear an explanation of his plan of reduction of the navy civil establishment ... We were all charmed with Graham's expose, and urged him to introduce as part of his plan a curtailment of the right to sit in Parliament now belonging to the lords of the admiralty ... to three. He promised to consult the cabinet and the king. I expect a great effect from his statement.[138]

He forwarded the draft bill to William IV that day, requested his opinion on the anticipated charge that it created placemen by replacing the commissioners with admiralty lords, and warned that Clerk, Cockburn, Croker and Byam Martin, 'a weight of authority and of official experience' were against it.[139] He obtained leave for the bill, which had his predecessor Lord Melville's tacit approval, despite their objections, 14 Mar.[140] He carried the preamble (by 118-50), 6 Apr., and the bill received royal assent, 1 June. The revelation by *The Times*, 15 Feb., that a commissioned officer, Admiral Sartorius, had assumed the command of Dom Pedro's fleet, publicized a disciplinary matter

raised repeatedly since December 1831 by the king, who considered it a contravention of his prerogative. Graham, supported by Grey and most of the cabinet, objected to implementing the Foreign Enlistment Act in the case.[141] When questioned by Yorke, 17 Feb., he argued that that Sartorius was unpaid and his conduct unauthorized. To opposition taunts, he confirmed on 19 Mar. that Sartorius had been dismissed from the navy for being absent without leave. He spoke briefly against abolishing the sixpenny monthly levy on merchant seamen for Greenwich Hospital, 8 Mar., and dealt adequately with Clerk's criticism of his strategy and office practices on moving the estimates, 16 Mar. 1832. Showing a 5,000 reduction in manning and a saving of £983,000, they were carried without a division on the 26th.

Convinced that it was both prudent and the king's wish, in cabinet, 4 Mar., he again recommended creating peers sooner rather than later to avert a second Lords defeat.[142] Before they considered Durham's proposals on the 11th, he wrote to Grey suggesting 50 as a suitable number, he voted with Grey and Russell against precipitate action to avoid the risk of being obliged to resign.[143] He lay 'on the floor at the end of the House of Lords opposite the throne, all night' to hear the Lords debate, 10 Apr., and was a party to the subsequent negotiations with Lord Wharncliffe at Newmarket.[144] When the bill's defeat on 7 May put a ministry headed by Wellington in contemplation, he resigned with his colleagues and commenced his Cumberland canvass in anticipation of a dissolution. He was reinstated, 16 May.[145] He was appointed to the committee of secrecy on the Bank of England's charter, 22 May, and to the select committee on the West Indian colonies, 30 May, from which he reported, 6 Aug., notwithstanding Burge's objections. According to the abolitionist Thomas Fowell Buxton

> Graham came into the committee ignorant of the subject and indifferent about it. I am much mistaken, if he did not leave it convinced of the policy, or rather the necessity of a rapid emancipation. He made the best of chairmen.[146]

He struggled to overcome Hume and Byam Martin's criticism of the navy estimates, 29 June, and announced 'after further scrutiny' that he had waived his objections to half-pay naval officers receiving their salaries while on coast guard duty, 8 Aug., and justified the admiralty's inaction in the case of the deserter Popjoy's compensation claim, 11 Aug. 1832. He went to Goodwood for the races directly the king's prorogation speech was agreed and to the Isle of Wight on the admiralty yacht.[147] In December Denis Le Marchant† echoed the general criticism of Graham, who was accused of 'giving his best patronage to the Tories':

He certainly is a very timid, irresolute man. He speaks in the House as if he was under an awful sense of his responsibility, which is singular, as he was remarkably bold and splashing when on the opposition side. No man ever was more changed by the move. In private life he is agreeable, mild, courteous and well bred, and more modest than perhaps beseems a cabinet minister ... He has not much general information but he is well skilled in figures and very practical in his views. Lord Althorp does not approve of his opposition to Peel's bill, but I fear Ld. A. could not write so well on the subject as Graham has.[148]

Patronage requests, Torrens's unauthorized absence, voter registration and resignation threats by Brougham and Smith Stanley, which he tried to avert, preoccupied Graham before the general election that month, when he stood jointly as a Liberal for Cumberland East with Blamire and came in unopposed, advocating 'some protection for agriculture', and was criticized over the 'economy', 'retrenchment' and 'the Dutch war'.[149]

He resigned from the cabinet with Smith Stanley in April 1834 over the Irish church question, kept his Cumberland seat at the general election of 1835, but lost it in 1837 following his defection to the Conservatives with the 'Dilly'. Seats were found for him at Pembroke Boroughs, Dorchester and Ripon in the next three Parliaments. As rector of Glasgow University, 1838-40, he organized the Scottish Conservatives and opposed the church seceders. 'Frenetic' as home secretary 'Paul Pry' in Peel's second ministry, he had to contend with social unrest, Chartism and the campaign for Irish home rule. He resigned with Peel from the Carlton Club over the repeal of the corn laws, came in for Carlisle as a Liberal in 1852 and returned to the admiralty as first lord in Lord Aberdeen's coalition ministry. He resigned, embittered, from Palmerston's administration in 1855 rather than face inquiry into the Sebastopol defeat, in which he was implicated. He remained an important political figure and a Liberal until he died of a heart attack at Netherby in October 1861. He had been predeceased in 1857 by his wife, and was succeeded in the baronetcy and estates by his eldest son Frederick Ulric Graham (1820-88). His will was proved in London, 12 Nov. 1861.[150] Devout and an Evangelical to the last, he was also a leading freemason. He rarely attended personally to the business of his province, but his funeral at Arthuret was celebrated with full Masonic honours.[151] Heeding the contemporary condemnation he evoked, Graham's obituarists recalled him as a fluent but pompous debater and able and hard working administrator and statesman whose 'frequent changes of party prevented him from enjoying the confidence of any'.[152] Historians, however, have contrasted his personal shortcomings with his pragmatism and analytical grasp of policy and management, and portrayed him as a major force in creating and dismantling ministries.[153]

[1] See T.M. Torrens, *Life and Times of Sir James Graham* (1863); H. Lonsdale, *Worthies of Cumb.* ii (1868); C.S. Parker, *Life and Letters of Sir James Graham* (1907), whose annotated partial transcripts of Graham's correspondence contain many inaccuracies; A.B Erickson, *Political Career of Sir James Graham* (1952); J.T. Ward, *Sir James Graham* (1967). [2] *Harriette Wilson's Mems.* (1929 edn.), 68, 70. [3] *Oxford DNB.* [4] *HP Commons, 1790-1820*, iv. 53-54; *Carlisle Jnl.* 16 Oct.; *The Times*, 18 Oct. 1819. [5] Brougham mss, Graham to Brougham, 7 Feb.; Castle Howard mss, Morpeth to wife, 8 Feb., 7, 9, 11, 14 Mar.; Northumb. RO, Middleton mss ZM1/S76/29/4; 35/1-5; Add. 52444, f. 99; Ward, 37-38. [6] NLS mss 5319, f. 195. [7] *The Times*, 10 Aug. 1820. [8] Sir James Graham mss (IHR microfilm XR 80), 1, bdle. 1, Graham to Lyndhurst, 21 Aug.; *Whitehaven Gazette*, 13, 20 Nov. 1820. [9] *The Times*, 10 Apr. 1821. [10] Ward, 40-41; TNA E197/1, p. 285. [11] Ward, 41-42. [12] Brougham mss, Graham to Brougham, 3 Mar. 1822. [13] Sir James Graham mss 1, bdle. 2, W. Vizard to Graham, 20 Dec. 1822; Torrens, i. 164-5. [14] Ward, 50-62; Sir James Graham mss 1, bdle. 2, Graham-Yule corresp.; *Carlisle Jnl.* 11 Aug., 29 Sept. 1821; D.J.W. Mawson, 'Agricultural Lime Burning: The Netherby Example', *Trans. Cumb. and Westmld. Antiq. and Arch. Soc.* (ser. 2), lxxx (1980), 137-51; D. Spring, 'Netherby under Sir James Graham', *Agricultural Hist.* xxix (1955), 73-81. [15] Lonsdale mss, Lowther to Lonsdale, 22 Mar.; *Carlisle Jnl.* 26 Mar., 2 Apr.; Brougham mss, Graham to Brougham, 25 July, 22 Aug. 1825, W. Brougham to Graham, 16 Feb. 1826. [16] Sir James Graham mss 1, bdle. 2, Graham to Yule, 5, 15, 18 May; *Carlisle Jnl.* 6, 13 May, 10, 17, 24 June; *The Times*, 16 May 1826. [17] Reading Univ. Archives, Printing coll. (Folio 324.4285 SQU), Carlisle Elections, ff. 28-33; *Carlisle Patriot*, 10, 17 June 1826. [18] Lonsdale mss, Beckett to Lonsdale, 25 June 1826. [19] Sir James Graham mss 1, bdle. 2, Graham to Yule, 15 May; *The Times*, 12 July 1826; B. Hilton, *Corn, Cash, Commerce*, 270. [20] Add. 51542. [21] *The Times*, 9 Dec. 1826. [22] JRL, Bromley Davenport mss, Graham to Davenport, 31 Dec. 1826. [23] *The Times*, 14 Dec. 1826, 17, 22 Feb., 20, 22 Mar. 1827; Add. 40318, f. 1. [24] *CJ*, lxxxii. 122, 315, 427, 558. [25] *The Times*, 20 Feb. 1827. [26] *Canning's Ministry*, 266. [27] *The Times*, 8 June 1827. [28] *Cockburn Letters*, 172; *The Times*, 12 June 1827. [29] Sir James Graham mss 1, bdle. 2, Graham to Rooke, 29 June 1827. [30] Broughton, *Recollections*, iii. 208; Lonsdale mss, Lowther to Lonsdale, 22, 26 July; *Carlisle Jnl.* 28 July, 18 Aug. 1827. [31] Lonsdale mss, Lowther to Lonsdale, 10 Sept. 1827. [32] Add. 51542, Graham to Lady Holland, 10 Sept.; 69366, Greville to Fortescue, 15 Sept. 1827. [33] Bromley Davenport mss, Graham to Davenport, 21 Aug. 1827. [34] Castle Howard mss, Abercromby to Carlisle [Oct. 1827]. [35] NLS mss 24749, f. 42. [36] Broughton, iii. 283. [37] Northants. RO, Agar Ellis diary, 24 Mar. 1828. [38] Broughton, iii. 283. [39] *CJ*, lxxxiii. 139, 153, 202, 431. [40] *The Times*, 27 Mar. 1828. [41] Wellington mss WP1/940/18. [42] Sir James Graham mss 1, bdle. 2, Graham to Yule, 17 May 1828; *CJ*, lxxxiii. 364, 382, 477, 509, 517, 537, 534. [43] Sir James Graham mss 1, bdle. 2, Graham to Smith Stanley, 15 July 1828. [44] Add. 40320, f. 51. [45] *Palmerston-Sulivan Letters*, 211-12; Add. 51542, Graham to Holland, 4 Nov.; 51564, Brougham to Lady Holland, 13 Aug.; Sir James Graham mss 1, bdle. 2, Graham to Brougham, 8 Oct. 1828; NLS mss 24770, ff. 23, 29. [46] *Cumb. Pacquet*, 16 Dec. 1828. [47] Castle Howard mss, Abercromby to Carlisle, 14 Dec., Lady Carlisle to same, 19 Dec.; Lonsdale mss, Lowther to Lonsdale, 15 Dec.; *Cumb. Pacquet*, 23, 30 Dec. 1828, 6

Jan. 1829. [48] Lonsdale mss, Abercromby to Lonsdale, 21 Jan., Benn to same, 24 Jan.; *Carlisle Jnl.* 17 Jan. 1829. [49] Lowther to Lonsdale, 4 Feb.; *Cumb. Pacquet*, 3, 17 Feb. 1829. [50] *Arbuthnot Jnl.* ii. 290, 293. [51] *Ellenborough Diary*, ii. 18-19, 60; NLS mss 24770, f. 35. [52] Brougham mss, Graham to Brougham, 6 Oct. 1829, Crackenthorpe to same, 9 Feb. 1830; Lonsdale, iv. 287; *Carlisle Jnl.* 23, 30 Jan.; *Cumb. Pacquet*, 26 Jan. 2 Feb.; Lonsdale mss, bdle. on 1830 Cumb. meeting. [53] Grey mss, Durham to Grey, 8 Feb. 1830; Nottingham Univ. Lib. Portland mss PwH 149; Brougham, iv. 8. [54] Grey mss, Ellice to Grey, 11 Feb., Howick jnl. 12 Feb., Durham to Grey, 13 Feb. 1830; *Greville Mems.* i. 37; *Arbuthnot Jnl.* ii. 334. [55] Howick jnl. 11, 12 Mar. 1830. [56] Keele Univ. Lib. Sneyd mss, Littleton to Sneyd, 24 Feb. 1830; A. Mitchell, *Whigs in Opposition*, 222-8. [57] *Ellenborough Diary*, ii. 201. [58] Castle Howard mss, Graham to Morpeth [3 Mar.]; Howick jnl. 12 Mar. 1830; Mitchell, 227; *Arbuthnot Jnl.* ii. 344. [59] Hatherton mss, Huskisson to Littleton [May 1830]. [60] Add. 51564, Brougham to Lady Holland [13 May] 1830; *Croker Pprs.* ii. 62; Ward, 85; N. Gash, *Secretary Peel*, 613-15; Hopetoun mss 167, f. 142; Wellington mss WP1/1166/8; Broughton, iv. 8; *Greville Mems.* ii. 77. [61] Add. 56554, f. 98; Broughton, iv. 21. [62] Howick jnl. 13-15 May 1830 [63] NLS mss 24770, f. 50. [64] Howick jnl. 7, 12 June 1830. [65] Ibid. 28 June 1830; Broughton, iv. 36. [66] Add. 40340, f. 226. [67] Sir James Graham mss 1, bdle. 3. [68] Ibid. Palmerston to Graham, 25 July, 4 Aug.; Castle Howard mss, Graham to Morpeth, 31 July; *Carlisle Jnl.* 31 July, 7, 14 Aug.; Hants RO, Carnarvon mss 75M91/L3, H. Howard to Lady Porchester, 9 Aug.; Lonsdale mss, Lowther to Lonsdale, 16 Aug. 1830. [69] J.R. McQuiston, 'Lonsdale Connection and its Defender' *Northern Hist.* xi (1975), 176; Brougham mss, Graham to Brougham, 16 Aug. [1830]. [70] Add. 61937, ff. 116, 118; Brougham mss, Graham to Brougham, 1 Sept. 1830; *Cockburn Letters*, 239-42. [71] Sir James Graham mss 1, bdle. 3, Huskisson to Graham, 26 Aug.; Brougham mss, Graham to Brougham, 1, 7 Sept. 1830. [72] Brougham mss, Graham to Brougham; Grey mss, Durham to Grey, 4 Oct.; Lansdowne mss, Macdonald to Lansdowne, 22 Oct. 1830. [73] Grey mss, Ellice to Grey, 28 Oct. 1830. [74] Sir James Graham mss 1, bdle. 3, Warrender to Lansdowne, 21 Sept.; Howick jnl. 7 Nov. 1830; Mitchell, 242-3. [75] Brougham mss, Graham to Brougham, 1 Nov.; Sir James Graham mss 1, bdle. 3, same to same, 2 Nov.; Add. 51564, Brougham to Lady Holland [8 Nov.]; Broughton, iv. 60; Agar Ellis diary, 2 Nov. 1830; Mitchell, 243-4. [76] Add. 56555, f. 45. [77] Howick jnl. 6 Nov. 1830. [78] Wellington mss WP1/1150/20, 23; 1151/9; R.N. Shutte, *Life of Phillpotts* (1863), i. 283-9; Grey mss, Grey-Van Mildert corresp. Oct.-Dec. 1830. [79] *Oxford DNB*; Northumb. RO, Blackett-Ord (Whitfield) mss 324/A/36; Erickson, 78-80; *Greville Mems.* ii. 75, 75; Ward, 96; Add. 51575, Abercromby to Holland, 19 Nov. 1830. [80] M.D. George, *Cat. of Pol. and Personal Satires*, xi. 16395. [81] *Greville Mems.* ii. 88. [82] D. Howell-Thomas, *Duncannon*, 143-5; Reid, *Lord Durham*, i. 216; M. Brock, *Great Reform Act*, 136. [83] Carlisle Elections, ff. 202-4; *Carlisle Jnl.* 27 Nov., 11 Dec. 1830. [84] Add. 51569, Ord to Lady Holland, 21 Dec. 1830. [85] Gash, *Politics in Age of Peel*, 39; *Cockburn Letters*, 274-5. [86] *Arbuthnot Corresp.* 140; Sir James Graham mss 1 bdle. 3, Western to Graham, 26 Dec. 1830. [87] Castle Howard mss, Graham to Morpeth, 24 Jan. 1831; Lambton mss, same to Durham, 27 Jan.; Sir James Graham mss 1, bdle. 3, Palmerston to Graham, 31 Jan.; TNA GD30/29, Holland to Granville, 1 Feb. 1831. [88] *Three Diaries*, 46; *Greville Mems.* ii. 112-13. [89] *Three Diaries*, 54; *The Times*, 22 Feb.; *Cumb. Pacquet*, 1 Mar. 1831. [90] *Three Diaries*, 58; *Greville Mems.* ii. 118. [91] St. Deiniol's Lib. Glynne-Gladstone mss, 197, T. to J. Gladstone, 17, 19 Feb. 1831. [92] Ward, 123; Sir James Graham mss 1, bdle. 4, Graham to Palmerston, 11 Jan. 1831; Wellington mss WP1/1157/8, 12; 1173/2. [93] Sir James Graham mss 1, bdle. 4, Graham to Grey, 24 Jan. 1831. [94] Ibid. same to same, 28 Jan., 2, 4 Feb.; Brougham mss, Graham to Brougham, 7 Mar. 1831. [95] PRO NI, Anglesey mss D619/27, Smith Stanley to Anglesey, 28 Feb. 1831; Add. 34614, f. 119; *Baring Jnls.* 82. [96] Gurney diary, 28 Mar. 1831. [97] NLW, Coedymaen mss 476; Lansdowne mss, proposals for the English, Irish and Scottish bills, 15 Jan. 1831; Brougham mss, Russell to Brougham, 15 Nov. 1837. [98] Lansdowne mss, Duncannon, Durham, Graham and Russell to Grey, 14 Jan.; Lambton mss, Graham to Durham, 27 Jan. 1831. [99] TNA 30/12/7/6. [100] *Carlisle Jnl.* 5 Feb. 1831. [101] Sir James Graham mss 1, bdle. 3, Graham to Grey, 17 Feb. 1831. [102] *Bunbury Mem.* 160; Glynne-Gladstone mss 197, T. to J. Gladstone, 9 Mar.; NLS mss 24748, f. 120; *Three Diaries*, 65-66; *Greville Mems.* ii. 127; *Russell Letters*, ii. 328; Agar Ellis diary, 25 Mar. 1831. [103] Add. 51542, Graham to Holland, 15 Mar. 1831. [104] Hopetoun mss 167, f. 257; *Baring Jnls.* 85. [105] Southampton Univ. Lib. Broadlands mss, Graham to Palmerston, 18 Apr. 1831; E.A. Wasson, *Whig Renaissance*, 212. [106] Sir James Graham mss 1, bdle. 5, memo. 22 Apr. 1831. [107] *Cumb. Pacquet*, 15 Feb.-29 Mar.; Sir James Graham mss 1, bdle. 5, Browne-Graham corresp. 4 Apr.-1 May, Graham to Rev. E. Stanley, 11 Apr.; *The Times*, 28, 29 Apr. 1831. [108] Sir James Graham mss 1, bdle. 5, Graham to Grey, 5 May; 80/29, bdle. re Cumb. Election, Blamire-Graham corresp. 25 Apr.-1 May and undated; *The Times*, 10-12, 24 May 1831; Northumb. RO, Hope-Wallace mss ZHW/2/14. [109] Wellington mss WP1/1207/1; *Greville Mems.* ii. 147; *The Times*, 30, 31 May, 2 June; Sir James Graham mss 29, bdle. re. Cumb. Election, Wilson to Graham, 31 May, 1, 2 June, Graham to Rooke, 18 June 1831; A. Aspinall, *Politics and the Press*, 367. [110] Sir James Graham mss 1, bdle. 5, Richmond to Graham, 2, 3 June 1831. [111] Ibid. Graham to Galloway, 20 May 1831. [112] *Macaulay Letters*, ii. 16; Sir James Graham mss 1, bdle. 5, Graham to Grey, 5, 7 June, to Stanley, 31 May, 6 June 1831; Ward, 112. [113] Sir James Graham mss 1, bdle. 5, Richmond to Graham, 2 June; *Cockburn Letters*, 288; Hatherton diary, 29 June 1831. [114] Sir James Graham mss 1, bdle. 5, Graham to Grey, 17 June 1831. [115] *Baring Jnls.* 88. [116] Hatherton diary, 29 June 1831. [117] TCD, Shapland Carew mss 4020/28. [118] Sir James Graham mss 1, bdle. 5, Graham to Grey, 28 June 1831. [119] Brougham mss, Graham to Brougham 21 Sept.; Sir James Graham mss 1, bdle. 6, Graham to Grey, 25 Sept. 1831. [120] *Holland House Diaries*, 51, 54, 60; Sir James Graham mss 1, bdle. 6, Graham to Grey, 28 Sept. 1831. [121] *Holland House Diaries*, 51, 59; Herts. Archives, Panshanger mss D/Elb, Palmerston to Melbourne, 3 Sept. 1831. [122] Sir James Graham mss 1, bdle. 6, Graham to Grey, 22 Aug.; 29, bdle. re Cumb. Election, Graham-Lawson corresp. 25, 29, 31 Aug. 1831. [123] See Wasson, 234 on Graham's relative silence in debate. [124] *The Times*, 22 Oct. 1831. [125] Sir James Graham mss 1, bdle. 6, Graham to Grey, 8, 17 Oct., Smith Stanley to Graham, 27 Oct. 1831. [126] Broadlands mss PP/GC/RI/11. [127] *Holland House Diaries*, 80-81; Add. 51542, Graham to Lord Holland, 14 Nov. 1831; Sir James Graham mss 2, bdle. 1. [128] Add. 76373. [129] *Carlisle Jnl.* 19 Nov. 1831, 7 Jan. 1832; *Carlisle Patriot*, 19 Nov., 10 Dec.; Sir James Graham mss 29, bdle. re Cumb. Election, Mounsey-Graham corresp. Oct.-Nov. 1831. [130] *Croker Pprs.* ii. 141-2. [131] George, xi. 16834; Sir James Graham mss 2, bdle. 9, Grey-Graham corresp. 10-21 Dec. 1831. [132] Hatherton diary, 25 Dec. 1831. [133] NLS Acc 6604/1, J. Stewart to Garlies, 20 Dec. 1831, 3 Jan. 1832. [134] *Three Diaries*, 189; Hants RO, Malmesbury mss 9M73/403, Clive to Malmesbury, 4 Feb. 1832. [135] Add. 75941, Althorp to Lord Spencer, 17 Mar. 1832. [136] Hatherton diary, 29 Jan. 1832. [137] Sir James Graham mss 2, bdle. 9, Graham to Grey, 6, 7, 13 Dec. 1831. [138] Hatherton diary, 9 Feb. 1832. [139] Sir James Graham mss 2, bdle. 12, Graham to king, 9 Feb. 1832. [140] Ibid. Melville to Graham, 30 Mar. 1831. [141] Ibid. Graham to Grey, 21 Dec. 1831; *Holland House Diaries*, 103, 106. [142] Brougham mss, Graham to Brougham, 9 Jan. 1832; *Holland House Diaries*, 144. [143] *Holland House Diaries*, 152; Sir James Graham mss 2, bdle. 10, Graham to Grey, 10 Mar. 1832. [144] *Three Diaries*, 221; *Baring Jnls.* 94; Sir James Graham mss 2, bdle. 12, Graham to Grey, 22 Apr. 1832; *Greville Mems.* ii. 290-1. [145] Sir James Graham mss 2, bdle. 13, Graham to Saul, 11 May, to Lawson, 11 May, Palmerston to Graham, 14 May; *Croker Pprs.* ii. 169; *Grey-William IV Corresp.* ii. 418. [146] Brougham mss, Buxton to Brougham, 2 Aug. 1832. [147] Sir James Graham mss 2, bdle. 14, Graham to Smith Stanley, 29 July, 16 Aug. 1832. [148] *Three Diaries*, 288-9; Add. 51563, Brougham to Holland Sept. 1832; Broughton, iv. 257. [149] Sir James Graham mss 2, bdle. 14, Graham to Wood, 8 Sept., to Smith Stanley 3 Nov.; *Cockburn Letters*, 428;

Brougham mss, Graham to Brougham, 19 Nov., 6, 18 Dec.; *Cumb. Pacquet*, 25 Dec. 1832; Gash, *Politics in Age of Peel*, 324. [150] Lonsdale, ii. 258. [151] K.W. Bond, *New Hist. of Freemasonry in Province of Cumb. and Westmld.* (1994 edn.), 66-68. [152] Ward, pp. xi-xiv; *The Times*, 26, 28 Oct.; *Gent. Mag.* (1861), ii. 681-2. [153] A.P. Donajgrodzki, 'Sir James Graham at the Home Office', *HJ*, xx (1977), 97-120; *Oxford DNB*.

M.M.E.

GRAHAM, Lord Montagu William (1807–1878), of 25 Grosvenor Square, Mdx.

DUNBARTONSHIRE	1830–1832
GRANTHAM	1852–1857
HEREFORDSHIRE	18 Dec. 1858–1865

b. 2 Feb. 1807, 3rd but 2nd surv. s. of James Graham[†], 3rd duke of Montrose [S] (*d.* 1836), and 2nd w. Lady Caroline Maria Montagu, da. of George Montagu[†], 4th duke of Manchester; bro. of James Graham, mq. of Graham*. *educ.* Eton 1820. *m.* 14 Feb. 1867, Hon. Harriet Anne, da. of William Hanbury[†], 1st Bar. Bateman, wid. of Capt. George Astley Charles Dashwood, *s.p. d.* 21 June 1878. Ensign and lt. 2 Ft. Gds. 1825, lt. and capt. 1830, ret. 1840.

Lord William Graham (as he was always known) had an ornamental career in the Guards. In February 1828, when only just of age, he stood in for his absent elder brother during the formalities of the latter's re-election for Cambridge on being appointed to junior office in the duke of Wellington's ministry.[1] At the general election of 1830 he stood for Dunbartonshire, where his father had a significant interest. He and his Whig opponent, John Campbell Colquhoun[†] of Killermont, obtained 30 votes each, but Graham was returned by the casting vote of the praeses. He declared that he would 'continue the firm and consistent advocate of those principles of the constitution which his family had espoused', but said he would 'always be the friend of any improvement which could with safety be carried into effect'. Campbell Colquhoun's attempt to unseat him on petition was unsuccessful.[2]

The ministry regarded Graham as one of their 'friends', and he duly voted with them in the crucial division on the civil list, 15 Nov. 1830. On the presentation of a Dunbartonshire petition calling for parliamentary reform, 26 Feb. 1831, he alleged that it had been 'carried by a majority of two or three only, notwithstanding ... the most strenuous exertions ... made by the persons who got up the meeting'. He divided against the second reading of the Grey ministry's reform bill, 22 Mar. He did not attend the county meeting six days later, when an amendment con-

demning the bill was carried by his supporters,[3] but he presented and endorsed the resulting petition, 14 Apr., when he more or less openly accused ministers of being 'biased by political predilections' in framing their measure. In reply to the lord advocate's assertion that most of the genuine landed proprietors of Dunbartonshire favoured reform, Graham insisted that they were overwhelmingly hostile to it. He voted for Gascoyne's wrecking amendment, 19 Apr. He presented a Dumbarton ship owners' petition against the proposed alteration of the timber duties, 16 Mar., and one from the county meeting against the proposed tax on steamboat passengers, 14 Apr. 1831. He offered again for Dunbartonshire at the subsequent general election and maintained that he had 'done my duty in opposing a measure which, from its sweeping tendency, I conceived to be dangerous to the general welfare of Scotland, and from its particular details injurious to the interests of landed proprietors'. He defended his earlier observations on the balance of opinion in the county and denounced ministers, who were 'confessedly incapable of understanding and explaining their own measure', a 'rash and perilous experiment', 'full of glaring errors and mistakes', which they had tried to force through 'under the threat and penalty of immediate dissolution'. At the same time, he professed willingness to accept 'judicious and temperate alterations' and 'all safe extension of the franchise to persons of property and respectability'. He defeated Campbell Colquhoun, a supporter of reform, by five votes in a poll of 51. On leaving the court house he and his minders were pelted with missiles by the infuriated Dumbarton mob and forced to take refuge in a private house, hiding under bed clothes; they luckily escaped detection when the rioters broke in. Eventually an escort of shipwrights secured him a perilous passage through the angry crowd to a small boat, which took him to the safety of a steamer moored in the Clyde.[4]

He divided against the second reading of the reintroduced reform bill, 6 July, but his only other known vote against it was on its passage, 21 Sept. 1831. Two days later he voted against the second reading of the Scottish bill, after presenting a Dunbartonshire petition against the proposal to unite the county with Buteshire (it was subsequently allowed to retain its separate representation). He was absent from the division on the second reading of the revised reform bill, 17 Dec. 1831, but was present to vote against the enfranchisement of Tower Hamlets, 28 Feb., and the third reading, 22 Mar. 1832. His only other recorded votes in this period were against government on the Russian-Dutch loan, 26 Jan., 12 July. He presented a petition for continuance of the duty on foreign tapioca,

11 July 1832. He did not stand at the general election later that year.

Graham received £10,000 on his father's death in 1836 and became entitled to an annuity of £800 when his mother died in 1847.[5] He re-entered the House as a Conservative in 1852. He married at the age of 60 but died childless in June 1878, leaving all his property to his wife.[6]

[1] Cambridge Chron. 8, 15 Feb. 1828. [2] Edinburgh Evening Courant, 5, 8, 10 July, 5, 19 Aug. 1830, 10 Mar. 1831. [3] Ibid. 2 Apr. 1831. [4] Ibid. 25, 28 Apr., 19, 21 May 1831; J. Irving, Bk. of Dunbartonshire, i. 332-3. [5] PROB 11/1873/107. [6] The Times, 25 June, 16 Aug. 1878.

D.R.F.

GRAHAM, Sandford (1788–1852), of Kirkstall, nr. Leeds, Yorks.; Edmond Castle, nr. Carlisle, Cumb., and 1 Portland Place, Mdx.

ALDEBURGH	13 Apr. 1812–1812
LUDGERSHALL	22 Dec. 1812–25 Apr. 1815
LUDGERSHALL	1818–1826
LUDGERSHALL	1830–1832

b. 10 Mar. 1788, 3rd but o. surv. s. of Sir James Graham*, 1st bt., of Kirkstall and Anne, da. of Rev. Thomas Moore of Kirkstall. educ. Eton 1802; Trinity Coll. Camb. 1806. m. 22 Apr. 1819, Caroline, da. of John Langston† of Sarsden House, Oxon. 5s. (2 d.v.p.) 3da. (1 d.v.p.). suc. fa. as 2nd bt. 21 Mar. 1825. d. 18 Sept. 1852.

Since 1812, with one interruption, Graham had represented Ludgershall on the interest of his father, Tory Member for Carlisle. Despite their political differences, Graham, who in late 1819 had signed the requisition for a Wiltshire meeting on Peterloo and the county constitutional declaration condemning it, was again returned unopposed at the general election of 1820.[1] On 17 Apr. he wrote to James Atkinson to apologize for his inability to attend a dinner for the defeated Whig candidate in Westmorland, Henry Brougham*, stating that

no man can be more friendly to the cause of independence wherever it may be assisted than myself ... but the kind of connection which has subsisted so long between the family of Lowther and my father, and the friendship which I have long experienced from that family from my earliest years, would render it highly indelicate in me to take a decided part on the occasion of the present contest.[2]

Almost entirely silent in the House, he voted against the Liverpool ministry on the civil list, 5, 8 May, and the appointment of an addition baron of exchequer in

Scotland, 15 May, and continued to act regularly with the Whigs, notably in their campaign for lower expenditure and taxation in the early 1820s.[3] He divided with opposition on the Queen Caroline affair, 26 June 1820, as he did consistently in the early weeks of the following session. He voted to censure the conduct of the Allies over Naples, 21 Feb., and to receive the petition of Thomas Davison complaining of ill treatment by Justice Best, 23 Feb. 1821. He was shut out of the division on parliamentary reform, 18 Apr., and was listed as an absentee on this, 9 May, but voted for the bill to secure the independence of Parliament, 31 May. He divided to repeal the Blasphemous and Seditious Libel Acts, 8 May, against the author of an article in *John Bull* being imprisoned for breach of privilege, 11 May, and for the forgery punishment mitigation bill, 23 May, 4 June 1821. He sided with opposition on Sir Robert Wilson's* removal from the army, 13 Feb., the outrage against Robert Waithman*, 28 Feb., and the remission of Henry Hunt's* sentence, 24 Apr. 1822. In what was presumably his maiden speech, 25 Feb., he acquitted the post office of all blame in the charging of Members for petitions sent with their ends sealed.[4] He voted for parliamentary reform, 25 Apr., and to condemn the influence of the crown, 24 June 1822. He divided for repeal of the Foreign Enlistment Act, 16 Apr., and inquiry into the legal proceedings against the Dublin Orange rioters, 22 Apr. 1823. He voted for information on ministers' conduct towards France and Spain, 17 Feb., reform of the representation of Edinburgh, 26 Feb., to refer the reports on Scottish courts to a committee of the whole House, 30 Mar., and in condemnation of the trial of the Methodist missionary John Smith in Demerara, 11 June 1824. During February and March 1825 he voted steadily against the Irish unlawful societies bill. As he had on 28 Feb. 1821, he divided for Catholic relief, 1 Mar., 21 Apr., 10 May. In March he succeeded to his father's title, the residue of a personalty sworn under £45,000, and the family estates, which included the manor and lordship of Ludgershall.[5] He divided against the duke of Cumberland's annuity, 2, 9, 10 June, and to abolish flogging in the navy, 9 June 1825. He voted against going into committee on the Bank Charter Acts, 13 Feb., and for compelling country banks to make monthly returns of the number of notes in circulation, 7 Mar. 1826. Although he now controlled at least half the representation in Ludgershall, at the general election of 1826 he presumably sold his seat to another Whig, George Agar Ellis.

At the general election of 1830 he displaced Agar Ellis to come in unopposed on his own interest.[6] He was listed by the duke of Wellington's ministry among their 'foes', and duly voted against them on the civil list, 15 Nov. 1830. He divided for the second reading of the Grey ministry's reform bill, 22 Mar., and against Gascoyne's wrecking amendment, 19 Apr. 1831. He again returned himself at the ensuing general election. He divided in favour of the second reading of the reintroduced bill, 6 July, and frequently for its details. Supporting the suppression of rotten boroughs on the motion for the disfranchisement of Ludgershall, 22 July, he stated with heavy irony that 'as the patron of this borough has determined to give his support to the bill, I, as the nominee, am obliged to obey him'. He divided with government on the Dublin election controversy, 23 Aug., the passage of the reform bill, 21 Sept., the second reading of the Scottish bill, 23 Sept., and Lord Ebrington's confidence motion, 10 Oct. He voted for the second reading of the revised bill, 17 Dec. 1831, the disfranchisement of Appleby, 21 Feb., and the enfranchisement of Tower Hamlets, 28 Feb. 1832. He divided for the third reading of the reform bill, 22 Mar., and paired for Ebrington's motion for an address calling on the king to appoint only ministers who would carry the bill unimpaired, 10 May. His only other known votes were for the Russian-Dutch loan, 26 Jan., 16, 20 July 1832. Graham, who was fond of inviting people to breakfast 'in order to observe their habitual appearance', left Parliament at the dissolution that year and died in September 1852. He was succeeded by his three surviving sons consecutively: Sandford (1821-75), on whom the Kirkstall estate had been settled during his lifetime, Lumley (1828-90) and Cyril (1834-95), on whose death the baronetcy became extinct.[7]

[1] *HP Commons, 1790-1820*, iv. 55; *Salisbury Jnl.* 6 Dec. 1819. [2] Brougham mss. [3] *Black Bk.* (1823), 158; *Session of Parl. 1825*, p. 465. [4] *The Times*, 26 Feb. 1822. [5] PROB 11/1699/259; IR26/1041/301. [6] Northants. RO, Agar Ellis diary, 4 June 1830. [7] *Gent. Mag.* (1852), ii. 526; W.H. MacKean, *The Grahams of Kirkstall*, 14-15.

S.M.F.

GRANT, Alexander Cray (1782–1854), of 6 Whitehall Gardens, Westminster, Mdx.

TREGONY	1812–1818
LOSTWITHIEL	1818–1826
ALDBOROUGH	1826–1830
WESTBURY	1830–1831
CAMBRIDGE	23 May 1840–13 Mar. 1843

b. 30 Nov. 1782, 1st s. of Sir Alexander Grant, 7th bt., of Malshanger House, nr. Basingstoke, Hants and Sarah,

da. and h. of Jeremiah Cray of Ibsley. *educ.* St. John's, Camb. 1799; L. Inn 1799. *unm. suc.* fa. as 8th bt. 24 July 1825.[1] *d.* 29 Nov. 1854.

Member of assembly, Jamaica 1810-11; agent, Antigua 1819-20, St. Christopher 1820-3, Nevis 1823-6.

Chairman of ways and means 1826-31;[2] commr. bd. of control Dec. 1834-Apr. 1835; commr. public accts. 1843-*d.*

Lt. Mdx. vols. 1803; recorder, East Retford 1827.

Grant's grotesque physiognomy earned him the universal nickname of 'Chin'.[3] In 1829 Charles Baring Wall* wrote to Ralph Sneyd: 'Do you know why Sir Alexander Grant is like Paul Pry? Because he is always searching (Sir Chin)'.[4] He was the heir to two Jamaican plantations, the Albion and the Berwick, with 700 slaves, which, after he came into full possession on the death of his father in 1825, brought him a clear profit of £9,000 in bad years and four times that in good.[5] One of his younger brothers, Ludovick (*d.* 1851) and Robert Innes (1794-1856), was receiver of the four-and-a half per cent sugar duties; and the latter was head of the family's London West India agency (later styled Grant and Kemshead) at 46 Lime Street.[6] Although Grant, a stalwart of the West India planters and merchants' committee and, in his own words, an 'enthusiastic politician and zealous partisan', was a slightly preposterous figure, he could not have been a complete idiot, for Peel, who had no patience with fools, was generally indulgent towards him.[7]

Before his own unopposed re-election for Lostwithiel as a supporter of the Liverpool ministry on the Mount Edgcumbe interest in 1820, Grant sent his friend William Vesey Fitzgerald* a budget of election news.[8] He voted against economies in revenue collection, 4 July 1820, and in defence of ministers' conduct towards Queen Caroline, 6 Feb. 1821. He voted against Catholic relief, 28 Feb., 30 Apr. 1822, 1 Mar., 21 Apr. 1825. He was in the ministerial majorities on the revenue, 6 Mar., and against repeal of the malt duty, 3 Apr., the disfranchisement of ordnance officials, 12 Apr., parliamentary reform, 9 May, reduction of the barracks grant, 31 May, and the omission of arrears from the duke of Clarence's grant, 18 June 1821. He voted against more extensive tax remissions, 11, 21 Feb., reduction of the salt tax, 28 Feb., abolition of one of the joint-postmasterships, 13 Mar., and inquiry into the lord advocate's dealings with the Scottish press, 25 June, and for the aliens bill, 19 July 1822. He was named to the public accounts committee, 18 Apr. An infrequent speaker, he said 'a few words' on the agency for Jamaica, 5 July 1822.[9] He divided against parliamentary reform, 20 Feb., 2 June, tax reductions, 3 Mar., and repeal of the assessed taxes, 18 Mar., and of the Foreign Enlistment Act, 16 Apr. 1823. On 27 May 1823 he presented a petition complaining of distress from the council of St. Kitts, for which he was currently the London agent.[10] That year he bought the lease of one of the old houses in Whitehall Gardens, Westminster, and with Peel, who purchased the adjoining one and abandoned a tour of inspection in August when he spotted '"The Chin" perched upon the wall of his house', produced a plan for the redevelopment of the site. In November 1824 Grant, who had two houses built for £15,000 on his plot and sublet one to Charles Long*, obtained a crown lease. He lived at 6 Whitehall Gardens from 1825 until 1828, when he sold the house to Cuthbert Ellison* and moved to 1 Carlton Gardens.[11]

He attended a general meeting of West India planters and merchants, 10 Feb. 1824,[12] but the only traces of his parliamentary activity that session are a brief comment on the sugar duties, 8 Mar., and a vote in defence of the prosecution of the Methodist missionary John Smith in Demerara, 11 June. He voted for repeal of the usury laws, 8 Feb., and for the Irish unlawful societies bill, 25 Feb. 1825. On 21 Mar. he defended the West India proprietors, denying that it was 'their object to make the greatest quantity of profits from their estates' and claiming that they wanted only 'a fair return' and that they gave 'a proper attention to the condition of the slaves'. He voted against the bill to disfranchise Irish 40s. freeholders, 26 Apr., and paired against the third reading of the Catholic relief bill, 10 May. He voted for the duke of Cumberland's grant, 30 May, 2, 6 June 1825. He divided with government on the Jamaican slave trials, 2 Mar., and the salary of the president of the board of trade, 10 Apr. 1826. At the general election two months later he was returned for Aldborough by the strongly anti-Catholic 4th duke of Newcastle, to whom Peel had recommended him, and who noted, after concluding terms, that he was 'a right man in every respect and it will be agreeable to be connected with him as our political views on all points are similar'. Grant ended up paying £1,145.[13]

On 24 Nov. 1826 Grant, who in August had been prompted by the sudden death of his cook, 'a strong looking woman under 40', to 'reflect upon the uncertainty of our tenure', was nominated as chairman of ways and means in the room of James Brogden. Henry Goulburn* reported to his wife next day that a ministerial dinner party had 'laughed a little' at the 'Chin's' elevation.[14] He remained chairman for the duration of the 1826 Parliament and its successor. On 5 Dec. 1826 he testily explained, in response to an allegation by

Attwood, that his own direct concern in a joint-stock company formed to promote the trade of the Sandwich Islands had lasted for only a few weeks the previous year. Out of the chair, he obtained a return of information on the slave trade, 6 Dec. 1826.[15] He voted against Catholic relief, 6 Mar., and for the Clarence annuity bill, 16 Mar. 1827. He voted with Canning's administration against the disfranchisement of Penryn, 28 May, 7 June, 28 May, for the grant for Canadian canals, 12 June, and against the Coventry magistracy bill, 18 June. He divided for the election expenses bill, 28 May. During the ministerial crisis which followed Canning's death in August 1827 he kept Peel abreast of political developments in London and visited him twice at his holiday retreat at Maresfield, Sussex.[16] Soon after the formation of the duke of Wellington's ministry early in 1828 Grant confirmed to Lord Ellenborough, the lord privy seal, the accuracy of a report that 'the [anti-Catholic] Tories were more dissatisfied at Lord Eldon's not having been consulted than at his not being in the cabinet'.[17] He voted against repeal of the Test Acts, 26 Feb., and paired against Catholic relief, 12 May. On 5 Mar. and 17 June he deplored the abolitionists' persistent misrepresentation of the planters, who had invested capital in the West Indian colonies 'on the public faith': 'I am not an advocate for the existence of slavery, but I cannot consent to have my property taken out of my pockets at the instance of other people'. He was a teller for the majority for an amendment concerning turnpike bill fees, 21 Apr. In August 1828 Vesey Fitzgerald, in search of a safe seat to escape from O'Connell's harassment in county Clare, complained to Peel that the gossiping Grant had talked out of turn on the subject and 'does and will continue to do irreparable mischief by affecting people's confidences and assuming to be trusted'.[18]

Five months later Ellenborough reported him as fishing in vain for information on the government's intentions on Catholic emancipation. Planta, the patronage secretary, assumed that he would swallow it, but he voted silently against it, 6, 18, 30 Mar. He was a teller for the majority against Otway Cave's motion on slavery, 4 June 1829. He divided against the transfer of East Retford's seats to Birmingham, 11 Feb., and the enfranchisement of Birmingham, Leeds and Manchester, 23 Feb. 1830. He voted against Jewish emancipation, 5 Apr., 17 May, and the Galway franchise bill, 24, 25 May. On the 18th he welcomed ministers' promise to investigate West Indian distress and urged them to give some immediate relief by 'remedying the extreme inequality of the pressures of the [sugar] duties'; he was chastised by Goulburn, the chancellor of the exchequer, for not speaking to the question. He attended the meeting of West India Members on the rum duties, 2 June, and on the 14th joined in calls on Lord Chandos to drop his motion on the sugar duties in order to give ministers a chance to elucidate their proposals, which he welcomed in principle. He voted against abolition of the death penalty for forgery, 7 June, and any reduction of judicial salaries, 7 July. On 20 July 1830 he protested against the abolitionist Fowell Buxton's appeal to the electors to reject all candidates tainted by connection with slavery, argued that the amelioration resolutions of 1823 had not pledged Parliament to emancipation and demanded 'fair and equitable consideration of the interests of private property'.

At the 1830 general election Grant, who had apparently offered, unsuccessfully, £130,000 for the borough of Gatton and its seats the previous November, was jettisoned by Newcastle because 'he does not suit me'.[19] He was returned for Westbury on the Lopes interest. Ministers of course listed him among their 'friends' and he was in their minority on the civil list, 15 Nov. 1830. In January 1831 he was reported to be 'most melancholy' on account of 'West Indian affairs or some such matter looking ill, and the chair slipping from under him'.[20] He presented an individual's petition in favour of the Grey ministry's reform bill, 14 Mar., but voted against its second reading, 22 Mar., and for Gascoyne's wrecking amendment, 19 Apr. 1831. At the ensuing general election Sir Ralph Franco*, patron of Westbury, turned him out as 'an anti-reformer'; and although opposition managers were 'most exceedingly anxious' to find him another seat, none was forthcoming.[21] On 19 Aug. 1831 Peel told his wife:

> Yesterday I paid a visit to ... Grant [in Carlton Gardens]. I found him suffering from influenza but evidently in a great fuss about something else. He was sitting in his dining-room, the folding doors open and both rooms set out in the smartest order. He had all the appearance of sitting for company. At length he said that in a few moments he expected Lord Howden, who was about to treat for his house, that he had asked £30,000 for house, furniture and stables, and that Lord Howden had offered £25,000, not for himself, but for ... Lord Goderich ... The Chin was very much disposed to accept the offer, and I have little doubt that he did so.[22]

He eventually did, and by 1834 he was living in lodgings at 16 Grosvenor Street. In October 1831 he privately denounced the 'anti-reformers' in the Lords as 'fools' for summarily rejecting the reform bill rather than giving it a second reading and using their numerical superiority to force modifications in com-

mittee.[23] At the end of 1832 he asked ministers to give his brother 'the option of continuing to conduct the business' of the four-and-a-half per cent duties when the plan to bring them under the aegis of the board of customs had been matured.[24]

Grant was horrified by the government's scheme for the emancipation of the slaves in 1833, complaining in private and as a planters' delegate to ministers that the proposed compensation settlement was 'robbery': he reckoned that he was fairly entitled to £90,000 rather than 'the miserable £15,000 which is now talked of, but by no means assured'.[25] At the general election of 1835 he stood for Grimsby, utterly confident of success and buoyed by Peel's fulfilment of his wish to be appointed an unpaid commissioner of the India board in his new ministry. His defeat astonished and mortified him and, whining that Peel's friendship was 'perhaps the only object of my life in which I have not experienced *bitter disappointment*', he pleaded to be made a privy councillor. Peel could not gratify him, but was personally kind to him that summer.[26] He was one of the Conservatives' 'red-tapers and second rate officials' beaten at the 1837 general election (at Honiton);[27] but he won a by-election at Cambridge in May 1841 and was successful there at the general election the following year. He then embarrassed and irritated Peel by asking, ludicrously, to be made chairman of ways and means in the new Parliament.[28] In 1842, lamenting 'the utter destruction of my income' (presumably by emancipation), he implored Peel to find him a job abroad to relieve him from 'the misery and humiliation of living in a community in which *I feel that I have lost caste*'. Unable to carry out his scheme to retire to Jamaica because of 'the *exorbitant demands*' of his insurance companies, and ill with worry and shame, he solicited an excise place later that year. Peel could not accommodate him, but in March 1843 made him a commissioner of public accounts, which ended his parliamentary career and, with its annual salary of £1,200, made him 'indebted' to Peel 'for the bread I eat'; he was pathetically grateful.[29] He died in harness in November 1854. By his brief will of 22 Oct. 1842, in which he moaned that 'a series of untoward and irresistible events of ruin and most unfair treatment has reduced me from high expectations and affluence to that state of fortune that the payment of my debts will leave but a small surplus to my successor', he devised all his property to his sole executor, Harry Spencer Waddington† of Cavenham Hall, Suffolk in return for his 'unparalleled friendship and confidence for 40 years'. Waddington renounced probate, which was granted to Grant's brother Robert, his successor in the baronetcy. Grant's personalty was sworn under

£3,000; but annotations on the estate duty register indicate that there was no real estate and that he died 'insolvent'.[30]

[1] *The Times*, 28 July 1825 and IR26/1042/684. *Burke PB* and other standard sources incorrectly give 26 July. [2] *HP Commons, 1790-1820*, iv. 59 erroneously gives 1826-32. [3] M. D. George, *Cat. of Pol. and Personal Satires*, xi. 16219; *Disraeli Letters*, iv. 538X; *Peel Letters*, 46; *Arbuthnot Corresp.* 192. [4] Keele Univ. Lib. Sneyd mss SC17/52. [5] Add. 40403, f. 255; PROB 11/1703/484; IR26/1042/684. [6] Add. 40403, ff. 110, 113; *Black Bk.* (1823), 158-9. [7] Inst. of Commonwealth Stud. M915/4; Add. 40414, f. 328. [8] NLI, Vesey Fitzgerald mss 7858, pp. 167-70. [9] *The Times*, 6 July 1822. [10] Ibid. 28 May 1823. [11] N. Gash, *Secretary Peel*, 270-1; *Peel Letters*, 46; *Survey of London*, xiii. 184-5, 193-4, 196; Add. 40345, f. 75; 40605, f. 168, 171. [12] *The Times*, 11 Feb. 1824. [13] Nottingham Univ. Lib. Newcastle mss NeC F2/1/139-41; 6971b; 6973; 6975-7. [14] Add. 40606, f. 254; Northants. RO, Agar Ellis diary, 24 Nov. 1826; Surr. Hist. Cent. Goulburn mss Acc 304/67A. [15] *The Times*, 7 Dec. 1826. [16] Gash, 450; Parker, *Peel*, ii. 10-11, 13, 19, 22; Add. 40394, ff. 169, 180, 196, 212, 216, 219. [17] *Ellenborough Diary*, i. 18. [18] Add. 40322, f. 278. [19] PRO NI, Hill mss 642/242; Newcastle mss NeC 2 F3/1/245. [20] Add. 40320, f. 173. [21] NLI, Farnham mss 18606 (1), Arbuthnot to Farnham, 5 May 1831. [22] *Peel Letters*, 131. [23] Broughton, *Recollections*, iv. 145. [24] Add. 40403, ff. 110, 113. [25] Add. 40403, f. 255; *Wellington Pol. Corresp.* i. 45, 72-73, 75, 80, 226, 281; *Greville Mems.* ii. 349-50; *Three Diaries*, 293. [26] Add. 40404, f. 336; 40406, f. 198; 40409, f. 166; 40414, ff. 328, 332; *Peel Letters*, 156. [27] *Disraeli Letters*, i. 643. [28] Add. 40486, f. 216; 40488, ff. 19, 23; 40489, f. 29; *Greville Mems.* iv. 415. [29] Add. 40506, ff. 330, 332; 40517, ff. 239, 242, 244; 40525, f. 414; 40545, ff. 258, 262. [30] PROB 11/2204/30; IR26/2028/2.

D.R.F.

GRANT, Charles (1778–1866), of Waternish, Skye and Glenelg, Inverness.

INVERNESS BURGHS	4 Nov. 1811–1818
INVERNESS-SHIRE	1818–11 May 1835

b. 26 Oct. 1778, at Kidderpore, Bengal, 1st s. of Charles Grant[†] of E.I. Co. and Jane, da. of Thomas Fraser of Balnain, Inverness; bro. of Robert Grant*. *educ.* privately by Rev. John Venn and Rev. Henry Jowett;[1] Magdalene, Camb. 1795, fellow 1802-5; L. Inn 1801, called 1807. *unm. suc.* fa. 1823; *cr.* Bar. Glenelg 11 May 1835. *d.* 23 Apr. 1866.

Ld. of treasury Dec. 1813-Mar. 1819; chief sec. to ld. lt. [I] Aug. 1818-Dec. 1821; PC [I] 19 Sept. 1818; PC [GB] 28 May 1819; vice-pres. bd. of trade Apr. 1823-Sept. 1827, pres. Sept. 1827-June 1828; treas. of navy Sept. 1827-Feb. 1828; pres. bd. of control Dec. 1830-Dec. 1834; sec. of state for war and colonies Apr. 1835-Feb. 1839.

Vol. London and Westminster light horse 1801-13.

Grant, a lanky, sandy-haired man with a long, lugubrious pale face, which the American artist Newton likened to 'a first sitting to a painter – large outline and extreme whiteness', was described by Tom Macaulay*, who greatly liked him, as 'a languid politician', but '*d'ailleurs le meilleur des hommes*'. Macaulay's sister Margaret depicted him in 1832 as

> the perfect model of a gentleman. High-minded, and most highly principled, intellectual, cultivated, with a retiring manner and a countenance expressive of all these qualities, and of something more interesting still. It might be the expression of a very elevated and refined mind that regarded with contempt the struggles and paltry objects of the men who surround him and that had itself suffered much from the necessity of bending to the drudgery and details of life and sometimes to its littlenesses.[2]

He had talent and was capable of stirring oratory, but he was notoriously idle and a by-word for unpunctuality.[3] The product of an Evangelical upbringing by his formidable father, a member of the Clapham Sect, he was nevertheless 'very liberal and tolerant' and a staunch supporter of Catholic claims.[4]

His natural charm and 'amiable disposition' went down well in Ireland, where he had succeeded Peel as chief secretary in 1818; but his administrative shortcomings were made all the more blatant by his predecessor's efficiency, and in the disturbed state of the country he eventually became something of a liability.[5] In late 1819 his liberal instincts prompted him to urge on the premier Lord Liverpool a substantial application of public money to promote employment of the Irish poor, but the English treasury was hostile and nothing was done.[6] As agrarian violence and disorder worsened in the west in the winter of 1819-20, Grant found himself at odds with the lord lieutenant, Lord Talbot, and the home secretary, Lord Sidmouth, in opposing any significant increase in the military presence, preferring the use of an expanded police force, supported by troops as necessary, though he conceded at the end of February that things were so bad in Galway that if Parliament had not been on the verge of dissolution following the death of George III it would have been 'well worth trying to pass the Insurrection Act'. His views generally prevailed, but Sidmouth was vexed by his failure to keep the home office fully informed of developments.[7] His re-election for Inverness-shire, where he had been returned in 1818 in succession to his father, was not challenged. Giving thanks, he defended the government's recent legislation to curb popular unrest, fomented by 'doctrines nearly allied to those principles which had the disastrous merit of convulsing France with revolution and Europe with war', and attributed the tranquillity of the Highlands to the influence of religion and the benevolence of a resident gentry.[8]

Grant defended the size of the viceroy's salary, 17 May 1820. He acquiesced in the introduction of Parnell's bill to regulate the removal of Irish paupers from England, 14 June, when he joined in tributes to the dead Henry Grattan I*, though the Whig Member Sir James Mackintosh thought he 'spoke ill'.[9] He welcomed the government's advance of £500,000 to relieve distress caused by Irish bank failures and praised the 'temper and patience' of the people, 16 June. When Peel's friend James Daly moved for inquiry into the Irish disturbances and the need for additional powers, Grant, in 'a Whiggish speech much applauded' by opposition (whose Commons leader George Tierney commented to Mackintosh that Grant 'never would be a speaker'), described the Insurrection Act as 'the worst mode of meeting the evil' and argued that two centuries of British injustice could only be redressed by conciliation.[10] He allowed Parnell to introduce a bill to reform Irish tithes, 5 July; Mackintosh reckoned that 'the furious Orange faction in Ireland are straining every nerve to drive ... [him] out of office'.[11] By September 1820 he had changed his attitude towards the Irish peace preservation force, whose 'frightful' increase in size and cost had dampened his enthusiasm; but his plan for an alternative rural police force made no progress. In early January 1821 he had to report to Sidmouth that Ireland exhibited 'many symptoms of the disorders incident to a country without an adequate system of civil authority', but Talbot saw no cause for alarm and nothing new was done.[12]

Grant led the ministerial opposition to Lord John Russell's motion for inquiry into the conduct of the sheriff of Dublin at a meeting in support of Queen Caroline, which was defeated by 124-90, 22 Jan. 1821. His speech of 28 Feb. in support of Catholic relief as part of the Union settlement originally envisaged by Pitt was 'much cheered'; the radical Whig Henry Grey Bennet* thought it 'excellent' and, though 'bad, coarse and vulgar in manner', indicative of 'a vigorous and comprehensive understanding, with a large stock of sound and honest principles'.[13] Next day he promised a bill to implement the recommendations of the Irish education commissioners, but none was forthcoming. On 12 Mar. he asserted that Ireland was 'in a state of tranquillity', yet argued that reduction of its military establishment must be gradual. Although he moved the reduced grant of £20,000 for Irish Protestant charter schools, 15 June, he admitted that it did not have his 'unqualified approbation' and that Hume was right to say that the schools had 'completely failed'. He said he would reconsider the size of the grant for publishing Irish government proclamations, 28 June 1821.

After doing his duty during the king's visit to Ireland in August 1821, Grant found time to attend and chair the Inverness-shire Michaelmas head court, where steps were taken to strengthen his interest.[14] On his return to Ireland he found Munster in a state of turmoil, which threatened to run out of control. In late October John Croker*, secretary to the admiralty, who had earlier joked with the hard-up Henry Goulburn* about the idle Grant's 'laying by £4,000 a year out of' a post which Goulburn had turned down for financial reasons in 1818, told the Grenvillite William Fremantle* that

Ireland was going to the devil, in consequence of Grant's indolence. I said, 'Surely he is a Catholic, and that suits our views'. His answer was, 'Yes, that's true; but he thinks of nothing but devotion; he is a Saint, and can and will do no business whatever. The government of Ireland must be changed, or the country will go to the devil'.[15]

Talbot, having reluctantly acquiesced in Sidmouth's insistence on an increase in the Irish military force, called out, with the home secretary's approval, 3,000 members of the Ulster yeomanry. He did not consult Grant, who, fearing that their notorious Orangeism would make matters worse, cancelled the orders to the Ulster units. Sidmouth was furious, and although Talbot at first backed Grant, he partially gave way to pressure from London. Grant, however, remained resolutely opposed to using the yeomanry.[16] In early December 1821 Thomas Wallace II*, vice-president of the board of trade and head of the revenue commission, told Liverpool that there was 'a loud clamour against Grant' in Ireland, which he considered unjustified; but by then the cabinet had decided to recall both him and Talbot as part of a general reshuffle which involved taking in the Grenvillites and replacing Sidmouth with Peel. According to Liverpool, Talbot, who was succeeded by Lord Wellesley, blamed Grant for this humiliation. Grant's successor was the staunch Protestant Goulburn. He was seen to be 'in absolute disgrace', and Liverpool did nothing to soothe his wounded feelings beyond assuring him that while there were 'insurmountable difficulties at the present moment in the way of any official proposal', he would be given another office at 'the earliest opportunity'. He may have been offered a place at the India board under the Grenvillite Charles Williams Wynn* in January 1822, but if so he declined it, preferring to meet the anticipated parliamentary call for inquiry into Irish affairs 'in an independent character than as an office man'.[17]

In the House, 7 Feb. 1822, he reluctantly acquiesced in the introduction of the Irish insurrection bill, to mark his confidence in the pro-Catholic Wellesley, but he called for remedial measures, including a 'complete revision' of tithes, on which he subsequently sought reliable information. Goulburn thought he gave the ministry 'a very fair and honourable support', but the backbencher Hudson Gurney perceived the speech as being 'dead against' them.[18] Grant voted with government against more extensive tax reductions, 21 Feb. At a cross-party meeting of a few leading advocates of Catholic relief, 16 Apr., he was inclined to think that 'the general motion had better have been brought forward', but he deferred to the opinion of William Plunket*, the Irish attorney-general, in favour of postponement.[19] He made a splash on 22 Apr. with his speech (later published) on the Irish Whig Newport's motion for inquiry into the state of Ireland, which he opposed as an implied censure of the government, while agreeing with virtually all Newport had said: he urged Irish landlords to assist tenants to improve and advocated reform of the 'cardinal evil' of tithes collection and of the police, magistracy and education, to be executed in 'a spirit of persevering kindness'. Williams Wynn told the duke of Buckingham, who was impressed by Grant's effort, that it was

> excellent, better than I ever before hard from him, but I do not believe ... any ... lord lieutenant would like him as a secretary, as his warmest friends admit his inefficiency and idleness. His total neglect of his correspondence with this country, after repeated friendly admonition, was really inexcusable.

Yet Mackintosh, who regarded the 'heavy speech' as 'an able and liberal dissertation', thought he acted 'shabbily' in voting against the motion.[20] Grant breakfasted with the Whig Thomas Spring Rice* on 9 May, when Maria Edgeworth noted the 'sense and goodness, feeling and indolence in his face'.[21] On 7 June he made what Mackintosh considered 'a most wise, eloquent and honest speech' against the second reading of the government's Irish constables bill, which he condemned as unconstitutional; the measure was significantly modified.[22] He objected to the grant of £10,000 for the erection of the Scottish national monument on Calton Hill at a time when several Highland parishes had no church, 16 July, but he divided with government for the Canada bill, 18 July 1822.

There was speculation that Grant, one of the 'dissatisfied', as Croker called him, would receive office when Canning rejoined the ministry as foreign secretary in August 1822, but nothing came of it.[23] At the Inverness-shire Michaelmas head court, which he chaired, he tried to assuage alarm over the impending reduction in the barilla duty, explained that he

and other Scottish Members had at least persuaded ministers to delay it for three months and promised to continue monitoring the problem.[24] He rejected the Holland House Whig Whishaw's attempt to entice him to stand for the current vacancy for Cambridge University, being 'determined to adhere to his Scotch county'.[25] In January 1823 his father reflected that the recruitment of Canning, who had 'many friends of his own, throws the reappointment [to office] of Charles, which at one time was thought certain and even near, into more distance and obscurity, especially as it is not easy to allot an office suitable to that which he last filled'. In mid-March, however, he was made vice-president of the board of trade, in place of Wallace and under Canning's friend William Huskisson*, at a salary of £2,000. He was unable to escape from departmental duties to attend his quiet re-election on 11 Apr. 1823, when his father stood in for him.[26] In the House, 22 Apr., he and Williams Wynn mutually glossed over the difficulty created by the latter's assertion on the 17th that the Grenvillites had only joined the ministry on the understanding that there would be a more tolerant attitude towards Catholics in Ireland, which had seemed likely to produce ministerial embarrassment.[27] Grant was in the largely Whig minority for an amendment to the Irish county treasurers bill, 2 May. He failed to persuade Huskisson that his proposed preferential treatment of the West India interest on the sugar duties infringed the 'sound doctrine that monopoly should be the exception, and non-monopoly the principle' of commercial policy; he voted in the minority of 34 for inquiry, 22 May.[28] He bestowed 'pains' on the 'county subjects' of a tolls bill and the barilla duties, the recent reduction of which he condemned in the House, 5 June, as 'a gross act of injustice to the kelp manufacturers'.[29] Next day he welcomed the government's tithes composition bill, which would 'go far to alleviate one of the greatest evils with which Ireland was afflicted'; but he objected to an aspect of the compulsory clause. He defended the silk trade bill and was a majority government teller for it, 9 June. He was in the minority for repeal of the usury laws, 27 June, and secured the third reading of the reciprocity bill, 4 July. He chaired the county meeting of 24 July 1824, when he was thanked for his protection of local interests in roads, distilling and kelp. A fortnight later he informed Liverpool from Inverness that while bad weather threatened the harvest and rents were 'ill paid ... most sensible persons think there are appearances of better times and of general improvement'.[30] He was in Vienna in late November 1823 when he got news of his father's death, 31 Oct. He rushed back to London in nine days and proved the will, under £60,000, on

12 Jan. 1824; he did not greatly profit by it. In the following months he tried to arrange the sale of the Skye estate of Waternish, but this was not accomplished until late in 1831. He bought for £85,000 the estate of Glenelg on the west coast of Inverness-shire.[31] With an eye to his constituency interests, he secured in February 1824 his appointment as a commissioner of the Caledonian Canal and of Highland churches. He communicated to James Grant of Bught, his confidant in Inverness, news of the proposed reduction of the wool duties; and after consulting Bught he decided that it would be 'as well' if he did not take the chair of the select committee on salmon fisheries (30 Mar. 1824), which might create 'situations of delicacy with my constituents', but he took an active part on it. In April he wrote 'public letters' on a variety of topics to the county conveners' meeting.[32] In the House, 9 Mar., he said that the Dublin Kildare Place Association was not guilty of Protestant proselytism, but on 15 Mar. 1824 he again expressed his 'powerful objections' to the Protestant charter schools, though he was not prepared to vote against the grant. He acknowledged the 'many vexatious and useless regulations which fettered the linen trade of Ireland', 19 Mar., and defended the wool duties bill, 21 May 1824. In August, when Huskisson's absence abroad obliged him to stay in London to mind the shop, he failed to convince Liverpool of the need to interfere to prevent the 'fictitious' rising price of oats from reaching the level at which the ports had to be opened.[33] The threat of 'competition' for his seat that autumn prompted him to confirm his intention of offering at the next general election and to take steps to strengthen his position.[34]

Grant voted for Catholic claims, 1 Mar. 1825. He favoured state provision for the Irish Catholic clergy and the disfranchisement of 40s. freeholders as essential adjuncts of the relief bill, for which he voted, 21 Apr., 10 May, after speaking for it.[35] He conceded that Parnell had proved that the regulations governing the Irish butter and linen trades had 'led only to fraud and collusion', 15 Mar. He warned against uneven interference with Irish charitable institutions, which might 'collect in Dublin all the pauperism and profligacy of Ireland', 18 Mar. Bught's son, a spectator in the gallery, thought he 'spoke very indifferently' when backing Huskisson's advocacy of 'the removal of our restrictive system' from commerce, from which 'gradually rising benefits' would follow, 25 Mar.[36] He endorsed Huskisson's motion for inquiry into the problems created by Hume's repeal of the Combination Acts, 29 Mar. A month later he made a point of attending the Inverness-shire annual general meeting to safeguard his electoral prospects.[37] In the Commons, 19 May, he

praised the Whig Thomas Kennedy's work on salmon fisheries, but doubted that there was time to legislate that session. He explained and defended the quarantine laws bill, 3 June, and on 9 June 1825 commented that the revelation of 'enormities' in the management of the charter schools proved that the system 'must ultimately work out its own destruction'. In December 1825 he covertly mustered his leading county supporters to resist an attempt to promote a declaration of opinion on the corn laws, which he perceived was 'meant chiefly as an attack on me'. Leaving aside this aspect, he argued that it would be

> truly most unwise and impolitic in the agriculturists to be the first to come forward ... They are now in possession of what they wish to retain, and their true policy is to abstain ... from unnecessarily exciting any passion ... For ought they know ... nothing may be done ... But if they make a tumult ... they will infallibly excite a counter-spirit ... and if the public mind be inflamed, it is not easy to foresee the necessity to which ministers may even reluctantly be driven.

His supporters succeeded in preventing the adoption resolutions for enhanced protection, 13 Dec. 1825. A renewed attempt by his opponents to raise the issue in the new year was also thwarted.[38]

Grant defended the government's promissory notes bill, 13 Feb. 1826, stressing the need to 'place our currency on a firm and solid basis' in order to restore confidence after the winter's banking crash. He did not interfere in the county meeting called to petition against meddling with the Scottish banking system, 8 Mar., but had 'no difficulty in presenting the petition', 16 Mar., when he concluded privately that 'the currency question is as well disposed of for the session as could have been expected' by its being referred to a select committee; he declined to serve on this in view of the strong feelings in Scotland on the subject. He 'very much approved the principle' of restricting the issue of small notes, but questioned 'the expediency of pressing it at this moment'.[39] He opposed and was a government teller against Ellice's motion for inquiry into the silk trade, 24 Feb., blaming manufacturers for rash speculations and arguing that an end to prohibition would stimulate domestic production. The Scottish Whigs Henry Cockburn and Leonard Horner sought his assistance in the promotion of parochial schools in March; he was sympathetic, but encountered 'obstacles in certain quarters' of 'the high authorities'.[40] In April he urged Peel not to 'take a decided line against' a Scottish law reform bill brought in by his Whig friend John Peter Grant.[41] He was a majority teller against inquiry into manufacturing distress, 2 May, and on the 13th, answering Hume, maintained that relaxation of the navigation laws and commercial tariffs had benefited shipping and trade. He voted against reform of Edinburgh's representation, 13 Apr. 1826 (as he had against parliamentary reform in general, 9 May 1821). At the general election of 1826 he faced opposition from an anti-Catholic (two other contenders having cried off); but after protracted legal wrangling over the composition of the roll the challenge was easily defeated.[42] He asserted himself to frustrate his rival's bid to have a score of voters enrolled at the Michaelmas head court.[43]

Grant was unable to prevent what he considered to be a premature county meeting on the corn laws in January 1827 and, feeling bound by 'official duty' to keep 'silence' on ministers' plans, he did not communicate on the subject. The meeting merely set up a monitoring committee.[44] In the House, where he was in the minority for Catholic relief, 6 Mar., he defended the government's proposals, 1 Mar., and, obliged by Huskisson's illness to 'work double tides', piloted them through, defeating various amendments, 8, 9, 19 Mar., but conceding one on the 23rd for use of the imperial rather than the Winchester measure. A county meeting, 20 Mar., resolved that the protection it offered was inadequate.[45] Grant duly presented the petition, 2 Apr., but, moving the second reading of the corn bill that day, he argued that it aimed to secure uniformity of price, protection for farmers and independence of foreign supplies, and 'deprecated nothing more than the overthrow of this measure by the landed aristocracy', warning that 'a starving population would listen to no terms'. He carried the third reading, 12 Apr. By then he had agreed to retain his office in Canning's new ministry. On 30 May 1827 he told the House that a delegation of distressed Norwich weavers had shown 'intelligence', but he had rejected their request for the local regulation of wages as 'delusive'. It was fancifully reported in mid-July that he had 'got a fancy to become secretary of the treasury'.[46] On Canning's death three weeks later, which he described as a 'most melancholy event ... of deep and deplorable misfortune to the country and the world, he wrote to Huskisson, who was abroad:

> On the political consequences ... we can at present say nothing ... The rumour is that the duke of Wellington will be sent for ... I wish you were here, and so do all of us.[47]

He was promoted to the presidency of the board of trade, with a seat in the cabinet, in Lord Goderich's administration; but some observers questioned his competence.[48] Grant, who blamed the intrigues of the anti-Catholic lord chancellor Lyndhurst for the col-

lapse of the ministry in January 1828, was one of the 'triumvirate', with Lords Dudley and Palmerston*, asked by Huskisson to decide whether he could honourably sit in Wellington's cabinet with John Herries*, whose objections to Lord Althorp's proposed chairmanship of the finance committee had precipitated the fatal crisis. Grant concurred in the view that there was no difficulty, provided that Herries was removed from the exchequer; and on this basis he agreed to serve in the ministry as president of the board of trade, though he was concerned that 'the four places which among them dispose of the whole of the domestic patronage of the country are to be held by decided anti-Catholics' and that Huskisson was 'too easily satisfied' by the duke's assurances on this score.[49] He was reluctant to go to Inverness for his re-election, 28 Feb., pleading pressure of business, and he was relieved to be reassured by Bught that his attendance was not necessary.[50]

Lord Ellenborough, a member of the cabinet, thought Grant would vote for repeal of the Test Acts, given the chance, but he was not in the division on 26 Feb. 1828, when it was carried against the government.[51] His silence on the front bench began to attract adverse comment, and his intransigence over the government's modified corn bill, which he was expected to propose in the Commons, came close to destroying Wellington's uneasy coalition with the Huskissonites in March. He initially joined Huskisson in suggesting a scale similar to that of 1827, but Wellington held out for enhanced protection. A compromise was reached, but Grant continued to oppose it unilaterally, arguing that he stood pledged to the 1827 measure and that the new one increased the pivot price. A further compromise was effected, but Grant, in great mental turmoil, prevaricated and absented himself from the cabinet, despite remonstrances from Huskisson, who saw that he would be obliged to resign if Grant did so, and Wellington and Peel. On 25 Mar., three days before he was due to lay the resolutions before the House, his previous day's letter of resignation was read to the cabinet. Ellenborough and Wellington's confidante Mrs. Arbuthnot thought he would be no loss. Later on the 25th Grant wrote to Huskisson proposing an entirely new scale, which Huskisson forwarded to Peel, who saw Grant the following day but, like Huskisson, made 'nothing of him'. On the 27th Huskisson warned Grant, who was also lectured by Palmerston on the folly of wrecking the government over such an issue, that the king had been informed of the crisis and had reacted with 'extreme annoyance'. He begged Grant to see sense and put forward the plan as an 'award between conflicting interests, fears and prejudices, which you offer as a peace-making', but Grant refused to meet him and contended that ministers were about to propose a measure 'discreditable to them'. Huskisson replied that when he saw the king the next day he would communicate to him his 'conviction that our retirement will be received in the first instance with shouts and throwing up of hats by all who are hostile to liberal politics, and afterwards, when the ground of it is to be explained, with incredulous astonishment and ineffable ridicule by every other class of men in the state'. He went to see the king at Windsor on the afternoon of the 28th. At the same time Wellington sent Goulburn, the chancellor of the exchequer, to Grant to learn his 'final determination'. His response was that he was 'too unwell' to move the resolutions that evening, but would do so on the 31st. Peel hastily sent this news to Huskisson, who received it while in audience with the king. The immediate crisis was thus averted.[52] Ellenborough thought Grant would be conveniently 'indisposed' on 31 Mar., but he duly moved the resolutions, presenting them as a compromise modification of the 1827 measure but not disguising his basic disapproval of them, and concluding with 'a studied panegyric' of Canning, which, as Croker noted, was 'not well taken by the Ultra Tories, though cheered by the rest of the House'. Ellenborough, who considered this 'a foolish flourish', sensed Wellington's disappointment that Grant and the other Huskissonites had not resigned.[53] Grant rejected as 'founded in misconception' the request of Cumbrian lead miners for additional protection against foreign ore, 1 Apr., and dismissed calls for wage regulation in the silk industry, 21 Apr., 1 May. In committee on the corn duties, 22 Apr., he lamely explained the apparent contradiction between his earlier statement that the measure was 'intermediate' and his current line that it was 'permanent' by saying that it was temporary in the sense that experience of its harmless operation would pave the way for the 'introduction of a better measure'. He and Huskisson were inclined to adopt an amendment proposed by John Benett which gave more protection at lower prices, but Wellington would not wear it and it was defeated by 230-32 on 25 Apr.[54] Grant got rid of protectionist amendments for barley, oats and rye, 28 Apr., and next day crushed by 139-27 Hume's proposal for a fixed duty. He gave an assurance that ministers had no intention of raising the duty on foreign wool, 5 May. He spoke and voted for Catholic claims, 12 May. During these weeks he cut a forlorn figure: for example, Herries told Mrs. Arbuthnot, 21 Apr., that it was 'impossible' that he 'should continue in office, that he did nothing, everything he says dies in his hands

and ... he either always is, or pretends to be, ill, and ... for his own sake he had better retire'.[55] Grant seemed inclined to side with Huskisson in favour of granting the Canning pension for two lives, and he joined Huskisson, Dudley and Palmerston in trying to curb Wellington's hostility to Russia. By the second week of May Wellington, according to Mrs. Arbuthnot, was 'broken-hearted about his cabinet' and 'deeply' sorry that he had taken in the Huskissonites. Grant he considered 'obstinate and useless', though he was 'seldom there, and takes little part'.[56] The fatal illness of his eldest sister kept him from the division on East Retford, 19 May, when Huskisson and Palmerston voted in the minority against throwing the borough into the hundred of Bassetlaw. When Wellington eagerly took at face value Huskisson's hasty offer of resignation, it was thought at first that Grant might 'stay'. His sister died on 23 May, and in his 'great affliction' he had 'taken no step' by the 26th; but next day he sent in his resignation to the premier, joining Huskisson, Lord Palmerston and William Lamb as one of 'the ejected liberals' who mustered in the Commons, 3 June.[57] Yet ten days later he explained his personal perspective to Bught:

I do not consider myself as personally bound to ... Huskisson, and should not have resigned merely because he did. But the question was one of deeper influence ... [and] of principle. The mere circumstance of East Retford is insignificant, except as it gave an occasion for the explosion of a long brooding event ... The point at issue for Lord Dudley and me was merely whether we should resign now or six weeks hence. If this division about Retford had never taken place, still I believe that at the end of the session the same result would have happened. Under this impression, not hastily formed, but produced by actual observation and experience, I have acted ... with regret and reluctance ... after full deliberation and consultation I felt I had no alternative.[58]

He acquiesced in the government's continuance of the sugar duties for a year, 9 June, but said that they must be soon reduced to stimulate consumption. He presented a Ross-shire agriculturists' petition for an increased duty on foreign wool, one from Gallowshields woollen manufacturers to the opposite effect, and one from Skye for a bounty on herrings, 13 June. On 17 and 24 June he defended his own and Huskisson's relaxation of commercial restrictions and urged Members to consider the question on 'great and general principles' and not 'narrow notions ... unsuitable to the enlightened period in which we live'. He voted in the minority against the East Retford disfranchisement bill, 27 June. On the customs bill, 10 July, he supported Poulett Thomson's amendment for an *ad valorem* duty of 30 per cent on East Indian silk pieces; and he spoke and voted against the proposed duties, 14 July, when he secured an amendment limiting their duration and opposed the superannuation allowances bill, which would injure 'real, official, working agents' in government departments. On 15 July he presented the Inverness-shire petition for protection against foreign wool imports and declared his hostility to the Irish butter trade bill. He again insisted on the 'soundness' of Huskisson's principles when arguing that the silk trade had not been damaged by their application, 18 July. He defended the French trade treaty of 1826, 25 July. On 28 July 1828, when Bught's son reported that he had found him giving 'no indication of bad health as I was led to imagine' and 'not very decided' in his holiday plans, he was prevented from moving for returns of information by the appearance of Black Rod.[59]

In December 1828 he went with Palmerston, Lamb, Goderich and Thomas Frankland Lewis* to confer with Huskisson at his Sussex home.[60] On the address, 6 Feb. 1829, he made what one observer reckoned 'a capital speech' welcoming the government's concession of Catholic emancipation. His speech in support of the measure, 6 Mar., when he equated the Catholic Association with 'the people of Ireland', was also a success.[61] He said that he disliked the disfranchisement of Irish 40*s*. freeholders, 19 Mar., but unlike Huskisson and Palmerston he was not prepared to jeopardize emancipation by opposing it.[62] Supporting a pro-Catholic petition from Edinburgh, 26 Mar., he admitted that there was 'a strong feeling' against emancipation in 'many parts of Scotland'; and, learning that 'some Invernessians have done me the honour to burn me', he asked Bught to report on local feeling, though he himself was satisfied that

> the events of this session have been extraordinary, indeed unexampled. There never has been a more wonderful revolution. To those who have always supported emancipation ... it is in many views gratifying, though I certainly cannot respect or admire sudden conversions. The effect ... has I think been to shake all trust in public men and confound all notions of right and wrong. The general notion is that ... [Peel's] character will not recover.

Bught assured him that respectable county opinion favoured emancipation.[63] He voted to allow Daniel O'Connell to take his seat unhampered, 18 May. He supported the prayer of a London East India merchants' petition for a reduction of the duty on manufactured silks, 13 Apr., and next day backed ministers' resistance to inquiry into the silk trade, arguing that the 'restrictive system' had been unsustainable. He

divided for the transfer of East Retford's seats to Birmingham, 5 May. On 25 May he proposed substantial reductions in the sugar duties and was a teller for the minority of 60. He presented a constituency petition in favour of Kennedy's tailzies regulation bill, 27 May, and called for a reduction in the tobacco duty, 1 June 1829. In October Sir Richard Vyvyan*, the Ultra leader, discussing the possibilities for a coalition government with Palmerston, observed that as Grant was 'too much identified with free trade' he could be 'got out of the way' by being made governor of Jamaica.[64]

Grant returned to London from an Italian tour, where he was 'detained by illness at Rome', in mid-January 1830, 'well' and 'strengthened for my parliamentary duties'.[65] Taking his seat with Huskisson and Palmerston 'in their old places below the gangway' on the government side of the House, he voted for the amendment to the address, 4 Feb. Next day, 'with great spirit and effect', according to Lord Holland, he backed Palmerston's attack on the government's support of despotism in Portugal and Greece; Grey's son Lord Howick* considered his speech 'excellent'.[66] His effort on 11 Feb., explaining his intended vote for the transfer of East Retford's seats to Birmingham to allay the 'great excitement in the public mind' produced by ministers' refusal of 'the just and reasonable demands of the people', was also reckoned to be 'very good', indeed 'very brilliant'. John Evelyn Denison*, with whom he and his brother concerted with Huskisson and Palmerston a line of 'strict independence', keeping 'clear of all factious opposition' and scrutinizing 'measures on their own merit', reported that Grant was now 'quite at the top of the tree in the estimation of the House'.[67] However, he 'defended ministers weakly', as Howick saw it, against Hume's motion for large tax remissions, 15 Feb.[68] He voted silently with them against the Ultra Lord Blandford's reform scheme, 18 Feb., but divided for the enfranchisement of Birmingham, Leeds and Manchester, 23 Feb., and investigation of the Newark petition complaining of the duke of Newcastle's electoral interference, 1 Mar. He voted with opposition on relations with Portugal, 10 Mar., taxation, 25 Mar., the Bathurst and Dundas pensions, 26 Mar., and abolition of the post of lieutenant-general of the ordnance, which he condemned as 'useless', 29 Mar. He voted for his brother's unsuccessful bid to secure Jewish emancipation, 5 Apr., 17 May, in the minority of 16 against Ellenborough's divorce bill, 6 Apr., and for reform of the divorce laws, 3 June. On 28 Apr., in what John Hobhouse* described as 'a bitter and eloquent speech', he moved a condemnation of ministerial policy towards Portugal as exemplified by their ordering the interception at Terciera of a ship of pro-queen refugees; but many Whigs 'kept away' and the division was 'poor'.[69] He voted for repeal of the Irish coal duties, 13 May, and returns of privy councillors' emoluments, 14 May. He was 'satisfied' to remain silent after Brougham's rousing speech for abolition of the death penalty for forgery, 24 May, and voted thus, 7 June.[70] He divided for Labouchere's resolutions on Canada, 25 May, though he had welcomed the ministerial statement of policy. He did not vote for Russell's parliamentary reform motion, 28 May. He would not support the Ultra Lord Chandos's motion for reduction of the sugar duties to benefit the West India interest before the government's plan was revealed, 14 June. He presented London and Glasgow merchants' petitions for equalization of the East and West Indian duties, 15 June. On the 21st, setting aside his own preference for an *ad valorem* duty, he supported Huskisson's amendment to reduce the West Indian duty to 20s.[71] He welcomed the 'important concession' of 24s. as 'the first step towards a better arrangement', 30 June. He presented a petition for action against profanation of the Sabbath, 5 July 1830.

At about this time Wellington made an overture to Lord Melbourne (as Lamb now was), who replied that he would not join the ministry alone. The duke indicated that he had no objection to Palmerston, but, according to Charles Arbuthnot* and Ellenborough, he deemed Grant to be 'quite out of the question'. When Melbourne said that he would not come in without Huskisson and Grey the matter ended.[72] At the general election precipitated by the death of George IV, the government made a dead set against Grant and his brother, whom they succeeded in depriving of his seat for Inverness Burghs. Grant was challenged by John Norman Macleod* of Dunvegan, on whose behalf 'all the power of government' was exerted. Throughout the protracted canvass Grant remained confident, having retained the support of Bught and other influential freeholders, despite their divergence in politics, while Macleod's blatant partisanship alienated others. At the election, 27 Aug. 1830 (the last to be held in the kingdom), Grant's nominee won the contest for praeses by nine votes, which prompted Macleod to give up. Before his formal return Grant defended his political conduct since 1828, denied that he had gone into systematic opposition and dismissed allegations of his neglect of local interests.[73] His success delighted the Huskissonites (as one of whom he was listed by ministers) and some leading Whigs.[74] His views following Huskisson's death, 15 Sept., when initial feelers were put out to Melbourne and Palmerston by the Whigs and when, twice in October, Wellington

sought to recruit Palmerston, are not entirely clear. Ostensibly he agreed with Palmerston and Melbourne that a formal junction with the Whigs would be 'highly inexpedient', though cordial co-operation on acceptable issues was desirable, and that they should on no account join the ailing ministry without a total reconstruction, including the admission of Whigs to the cabinet. Yet when Lord Clive* renewed Wellington's overture at the end of October Grant, who had hastened to London from Scotland (where he had earlier declined an invitation to stand for Liverpool in Huskisson's room),[75] told Palmerston that he had misgivings about rejecting it out of hand. In the event he fell into line, and a week later agreed with Palmerston and the other Commons Huskissonites to support Brougham's forthcoming reform motion if it was 'vaguely worded'. James Abercromby* reported from Edinburgh soon afterwards that if Grant *'was* stout and firm', he had 'been unfortunate in conveying a contrary impression' and that 'his silence and that of his friends confirmed that impression, and if he does not forthwith show himself, he will be held in little estimation by the best people here'.[76]

In the House, 8 Nov. 1830, Grant deemed the government's proposed colonial trade bill 'a wise measure', though he had some qualms about its effect on Canada. He was in the minority of 39 for a reduced duty on wheat imported by the West Indian colonies, 12 Nov. He divided against government on the civil list, 15 Nov., and was appointed to the select committee. Joining Grey's ministry with Palmerston, Melbourne and Goderich (to whom he gave way in their competition for the colonial secretaryship), he became president of the board of control – an inappropriate office for one who was notoriously 'not a man of business'. He was reckoned to be the only member of the cabinet who 'believes there is a soul'.[77] His re-election *in absentia* was uneventful, after Macleod had failed to muster support for a challenge.[78] In January 1831 he was reported to be 'reading very hard' in order to master his departmental brief, as he knew 'nothing of India'.[79] He secured the reappointment of the select committee on the East India Company, which he chaired, 4 Feb. He defended the chancellor of the exchequer Althorp's controversial stock transfer tax, 11 Feb., speaking 'very well', as Brougham's secretary Denis Le Marchant† thought, 'but without the earnestness or authority which at the moment was so much wanted'.[80] He had to explain its withdrawal, 14 Feb. Next day he presented half a dozen petitions for the abolition of slavery. On 21 Feb. he concurred in Lord Chandos's motion for due consideration of the West India interest, which the first lord of the admiralty

Sir James Graham treated as one of confidence in the ministry, but said he would oppose it because it would obstruct the progress of supply. He was reckoned by some ministerialists to have gone 'out of the way to make a blunder and to make the public believe that disunion reigns in our camp'. Holland, a member of the cabinet, commented a week later that Grant, 'though an able, honest and amiable man, is somewhat whimsical and has not ingratiated himself with his colleagues by the manner or reason with which he urges any difference of opinion he entertains'. Grant indicated that he was 'decidedly opposed' to a proposed government amendment to the colonial trade bill affording enhanced protection and 'must vote against it'; but he was evidently appeased, for he supported the measure, 1 Mar.[81] He presented reform petitions from Inverness and Peebles, 28 Feb. He had been 'advisedly' reported to be 'disposed to go great lengths' on reform, yet there were false rumours in early March that he was about to resign.[82] On 21 Mar. he defended the English reform bill as a timely concession, observing that 'by the delay of a just measure we have only sown the seeds of agitation, which have brought forth an abundant harvest'. He of course voted for the second reading the next day and was in the ministerial minority against Gascoyne's wrecking amendment, 19 Apr. 1831. Criticism of his performance persisted: Agar Ellis reckoned that he had 'failed lamentably in speaking and courage', while Holland conceded that he 'certainly ... takes little pains to ingratiate himself with his colleagues or to assist us in the House', though he would be 'very sorry if we part with him, first because I have a very good opinion of him and secondly because he is a staunch friend of peace and in my judgement perceives the right method of preserving it'.[83] At the ensuing general election Grant was initially challenged by a moderate reformer, who soon gave up, so rendering academic his loss of Bught's active backing on account of his support for reform. Returning thanks, he contended that the ministerial scheme was 'final in its intention' and that 'the time had come when reform was no less just than it was expedient'.[84]

According to Thomas Creevey*, who dismissed Grant as a 'canting puppy', 'a despondent Grey' remarked 'with the greatest innocence' at Lady Sefton's, 6 July 1831, '"Everybody told me there was nothing to be done without the two Grants, and they have never been worth a farthing"'.[85] He voted for the second reading of the reintroduced reform bill that day, divided steadily for its details and voted for its passage, 21 Sept. He had nothing to say on it, however, and Macaulay suspected that he was 'not very hearty' in the cause.[86] He secured the reappointment of the

East India select committee, 28 June, when he promised to consider the difficulties of British merchants at Canton. In cabinet, 21 July, he 'seemed ... to concur' in Holland's argument for British participation in mediation between Russia and Poland. Two days later he and others warned Grey of the 'dangers and impropriety' of maintaining an armed yeomanry in Ireland after the Newtownbarry incident; and on 15 Aug., at a cabinet meeting called by himself, he 'deprecated in an elaborate paper all countenance given to the Irish yeomanry' and 'ended ... by rather a strange conclusion *to do nothing at all*, but to allow the yeomanry silently to expire'.[87] In the House, 1 Sept., he announced that he planned to legislate to allow native Indians to serve on grand juries and to introduce jury trial there. He spoke and voted for the second reading of the Scottish reform bill, 23 Sept. On the 29th he accepted the finance committee's recommendation of a cut from £5,000 to £3,500 in his salary. In mid-September Sir James Macdonald* began to wonder if Grant was 'equal to the crisis' of reform.[88] He of course voted for the motion of confidence in the ministry, 10 Oct., and on 12 Oct. 1831 he deplored the 'unnecessary heat' generated on both sides in the debate on recent political meetings and processions. Smith Stanley, the Irish secretary, had 'no notion' of Grant's views on the political situation in late October, but three weeks later the opposition whip William Holmes* heard that he and Melbourne had 'taken fright at these political unions'.[89]

In cabinet in December 1831 Grant and Holland argued unsuccessfully for the inclusion of Catholics on the Irish tithes committee. Grant was also inclined to give additional Members to Ireland. Ellenborough heard that he had 'done nothing' on Indian business, and a government supporter commented that he had been conspicuously the least successful senior minister.[90] He did not attend the Commons when the revised reform scheme was introduced, 12 Dec., but was present to vote for the second reading of the English bill, 17 Dec. 1831.[91] He was 'decisive' in favour of a creation of peers if it proved necessary to force reform through the Lords, arguing in cabinet, 2 Jan. 1832, that 'we were not justified in having gone so far if we did not go through with our measure'; but two months later Palmerston reported that he was 'decidedly adverse *to any creation* at present, and disposed to be guided by circumstances'.[92] Littleton noted that he arrived at a dinner at Grillion's, 25 Jan., 'with characteristic punctuality, half an hour after we had sat down, as we had all foretold he would, and was greeted with much laughter'.[93] In the House, 28 Feb., he supported the enfranchisement of the metropolitan districts and challenged a Conservative assertion that an infusion of 'democracy' had destroyed the Roman Empire. He divided silently for the third reading of the reform bill, 22 Mar. Renewing the East India select committee, 27 Jan., he reviewed its progress and secured the appointment of eight subcommittees to expedite matters. He spoke for the Scottish cholera prevention bill, 15 Feb., supported a Whig motion for inquiry into the silk trade and dismissed Attwood's currency fixation, 1 Mar., and defended the government's Irish education scheme, 6 Mar. He naturally voted for the address calling on the king to appoint only ministers who would carry reform unimpaired, 10 May. He voted for the second reading of the Irish reform bill, 25 May, and against a Conservative amendment to the Scottish measure, 1 June. On 4 June, endorsing the enfranchisement of Scottish £10 owners, he said that although he sacrificed 'much' as a landowner by supporting reform, as an individual he would 'gain more than I lose'. He presented a constituency petition for relief of the West Indian colonies and one from the inhabitants of Singapore for the establishment of an independent judiciary there, 17 May. On the Lords' amendments to the English reform bill, 5 June, he said that Grey, far from being the 'criminal' depicted by Mackworth Praed, had saved the country from disaster, and admitted that he had changed his own mind on reform 'because of the changed circumstances of the times and of the advance of knowledge of every kind among the people'. On 29 June 1832 Macaulay, who had recently become a commissioner of the India board, told his sister:

> I have begun work with an energy which makes poor Charles Grant stare. It was with something of an oath that he received two reports which I have drawn up within twenty four hours on cases which occupied a cart load of paper ... The president seemed really to think me a conjuror.[94]

It was later said that Holmes 'frequently used to send a note' to Grant 'to tell him to come to his place' in the House for divisions.[95]

At the general election of 1832 Grant beat Macleod, as he did narrowly in 1835. On the formation of Melbourne's second ministry that year he was appointed colonial secretary and created Lord Glenelg. He oversaw the total abolition of slavery, but his political career ended in humiliation in 1839 when he was effectively sacked for his inept handling of the Canadian rebellion. He was compensated with a commissionership of land tax and a pension of £2,000 a year.[96] Princess Lieven considered him 'a charming man of high capacity', while Hobhouse unconvincingly contended that 'he was not lazy', but 'too scru-

pulous and critical as to what he wrote'. Macaulay observed that he had 'a mind that cannot stand alone', rather 'a feminine mind ... always turning, like ivy, to some support'.[97] He spent his last unhappy years living with Brougham in the south of France. He died a bachelor at Cannes in April 1866.

[1] H. Morris, *Charles Grant* (1904), 195. [2] *Highland Lady*, 273; Add. 52447, f. 74; *Macaulay Letters*, ii. 266; Margaret Macaulay, *Recollections*, 235. [3] *Three Diaries*, 307; *Holland House Diaries*, 213; *Greville Mems.* i. 356. [4] B. Hilton, *Age of Atonement*, 226; *Macaulay Letters*, ii. 144. [5] *O'Connell Corresp.* iii. 1394; Lord Teignmouth, *Reminiscences*, i. 170; N. Gash, *Secretary Peel*, 367; G. Broeker, *Rural Disorder and Police Reform in Ireland*, 105-6; B. Jenkins, *Era of Emancipation*, ch.5. [6] B. Hilton, *Corn, Cash, Commerce*, 84-85; Add. 38282, ff. 43, 74, 314. [7] Broeker, 110-16; Add. 38458, f. 298. [8] NAS GD23/6/745/124, 127-9, 131; *Inverness Courier*, 9 Mar., 13 Apr. 1820. [9] Add. 52444, f. 151. [10] Broughton, *Recollections*, ii. 129; Hatherton diary, 28 June [1820]; Add. 52444, f. 180. [11] Add. 52444, f. 187. [12] Broeker, 117-19. [13] Hunts. RO, Manchester mss M10 A/3/35; HLRO, Hist. Coll. 379, Grey Bennet diary, 28; Northants. RO, Agar Ellis diary, 28 Feb. [1821]. [14] NAS GD23/6/745/151; *Inverness Courier*, 4 Oct. 1821. [15] *Croker Pprs.* i. 189; Buckingham, *Mems. Geo. IV*, i. 213. [16] Broeker, 119-22; PRO NI D4100/3/12, Gregory to Talbot, 21 Nov. 1821. [17] Gash, 367; Buckingham, i. 227-8, 273; *HMC Bathurst*, 522, 525; *Hobhouse Diary*, 80-81; Add. 38290, ff. 108, 113; 38743, f. 60; 51574, Abercromby to Holland [Dec. 1821]; NLW, Coedymaen mss 615; Lansdowne mss, Mackintosh to Lansdowne, 28 Dec. 1821, Spring Rice to same, 28 Jan. 1822. [18] Add. 37298, f. 158; TCD, Jebb mss 6396/147, 149; Gurney diary, 7 Feb. 1822. [19] Buckingham, i. 314; Add. 51586, Tierney to Lady Holland, 16 Apr. 1822. [20] Buckingham, i. 317-18; Bucks. RO, Fremantle mss D/FR/46/10/31; Add. 52445, f. 78; Agar Ellis diary, 22 Apr. [1822]. [21] *Edgeworth Letters*, 402. [22] Add. 37299, f. 238; 52445, f. 87; Broeker, 145-6. [23] *Huskisson Pprs.* 142; Add. 40319, f. 57; 51586, Tierney to Lady Holland, 23 Aug. [1823]; 52445, f. 104. [24] *Inverness Jnl.* 3 Oct. 1822. [25] Add. 51659, Whishaw to Lady Holland, 25 Oct. 1822. [26] NAS GD23/6/745/154, 155; Buckingham, i. 417; *Inverness Courier*, 20 Mar., 17 Apr. 1823. [27] *Arbuthnot Jnl.* i. 229. [28] Hilton, *Corn, Cash, Commerce*, 199; Add. 38744, f. 204. [29] NAS GD23/6/745/156. [30] *Inverness Courier*, 3, 31 July 1823; Add. 38296, f. 96. [31] PROB 11/1680/21; IR26/998/17; Add. 51659, Whishaw to Lady Holland, 3 Dec. [1823]; NAS GD23/6/746/53, 54, 57; *Inverness Courier*, 21 Dec. 1831. [32] Add. 40361, ff. 40, 41; NAS GD23/6/746/59, 60, 64-66. [33] NAS GD23/6/746/72; Add. 38299, f. 59. [34] NAS GD23/6/583/5; 600/1-3; 746/73; *Inverness Courier*, 28 Oct. 1824. [35] *Colchester Diary*, iii. 384. [36] NAS GD23/6/583/8. [37] *Inverness Courier*, 4 May 1825; NAS GD23/6/746/76, 77. [38] NAS GD23/6/606/1-4; 746/79, 82, 83, 88-90, 92; *Inverness Courier*, 30 Nov., 14 Dec. 1825. [39] NAS GD23/6/746/91-93. [40] *Cockburn Letters*, 136, 139. [41] Add. 40363, f. 188. [42] NAS GD23/6/611; 746/95-98; *Inverness Courier*, 21 June, 12 July 1826. [43] NAS GD23/6/746/100; *Inverness Courier*, 4 Oct. 1826. [44] NAS GD23/6/106/3; 746/103; *Inverness Courier*, 17, 24 Jan. 1827. [45] NAS GD23/6/583/18; 746/108; *Inverness Courier*, 28 Mar. 1827. [46] *HMC Bathurst*, 638. [47] NAS GD23/6/746/113; Add. 38750, f. 15. [48] *Huskisson Pprs.* 225; *Countess Granville Letters*, i. 421, 428-9; Add. 38750, f. 22; Wellington mss WP1/896/3; Coedymaen mss 201; NAS GD23/6/746/115; *Hobhouse Diary*, 142. [49] Add. 38754, ff. 124, 133, 148, 150, 182; 40395, f. 9; Bulwer, *Palmerston*, i. 216-18; TNA 30/29/9/3/36; Southampton Univ. Lib. Broadlands mss BR 23AA/5/2. [50] NAS GD23/6/746/115, 117-19; *Inverness Courier*, 6 Feb., 5 Mar. 1828. [51] *Ellenborough Diary*, i. 35, 46. [52] Add. 38755, ff. 155, 160, 178, 180, 182, 187, 202, 205, 256, 265, 271, 271-83; 40396, ff, 85, 87; *Arbuthnot Jnl.* ii. 167, 171, 175, 177, 179; *HMC Bathurst*, 653; Bulwer, i. 232, 235, 239-46; *Ellenborough Diary*, i. 51-53, 55-58, 60-61, 64-72; Hilton, 287-9; N. Gash, *Secretary*

Peel, 465-9. [53] *Ellenborough Diary*, i. 73-74; *Arbuthnot Jnl.*, ii. 179; *Croker Pprs.* i. 415; Cent. Kent. Stud. Stanhope mss U1590 C355, Pusey to Mahon, 8 Apr. 1828. [54] *Ellenborough Diary*, i. 90-91; Hilton, *Corn, Cash, Commerce*, 290. [55] *Arbuthnot Jnl.* ii. 180-2. [56] *Ellenborough Diary*, i. 97-98, 103-4; Bulwer, 227. [57] *Croker Pprs.* i. 420; Add. 38756, ff. 127, 185, 247; *Ellenborough Diary*, i. 106-9, 113, 118-19, 122; *Gent. Mag.* (1828), i. 571; *Palmerston-Sulivan Letters*, 205; TNA 30/29/9/5/71. [58] NAS GD23/6/746/120. [59] NAS GD23/6/58 3/20. [60] K. Bourne, *Palmerston*, 293. [61] Suff. RO (Bury St. Edmunds), Hervey mss Acc 941/56/60; Nottingham Univ. Lib. Denison diary, 6 Mar. [1829]. [62] Bourne, 296. [63] NAS GD23/6/746/121. [64] *Palmerston-Sulivan Letters*, 234. [65] NAS GD23/6/746/122. [66] Bourne, 307; Add. 51785, Holland to C.R. Fox, 7 Feb.; Grey mss, Howick jnl. 5 Feb. 1830. [67] Howick jnl. 11 Feb.; Agar Ellis diary, 11 Feb.; Grey mss, Durham to Grey, 12 Feb.; Nottingham Univ. Lib. Ossington mss OsC 74; Add. 51785, Holland to C.R. Fox, 20 Feb. 1830. [68] Howick jnl. [69] Broughton, iv. 18; Agar Ellis diary, 28 Apr. [1830]. [70] NLS mss 24748, f. 89. [71] Howick jnl. 21 June [1830]. [72] Broadlands mss PP/GMC/33; Add. 40340, f. 226; *Ellenborough Diary*, ii. 306; Bulwer, i. 361; Agar Ellis diary, 18 July [1830]. [73] *Ellenborough Diary*, ii. 305; Add. 38758, f. 214; 40309, f. 151; 40340, f. 226; NAS GD23/6/583/23-26; 746/123, 125-7; Wellington mss WP1/1130/49; 1134/11; 1139/19; *Inverness Courier*, 7, 14 July, 25 Aug., 2 Sept. 1830. [74] Add. 38758, f. 267; 51670, Bedford to Lady Holland, 2 Sept. [1830]. [75] *Inverness Courier*, 6 Oct. 1830. [76] Broadlands mss PP/GMC/35, 42, Grant to Palmerston, 31 Oct., reply, 1 Nov.; Bourne, 322-3, 327; Agar Ellis diary, 1 Oct.; Brougham mss, Agar Ellis to Brougham, 4 Oct.; Add. 51580, Carlisle to Lady Holland, 17 Oct.; 51670, Bedford to same, 11 Oct.; Castle Howard mss, Abercromby to Carlisle, 10 Nov. 1830. [77] *Three Diaries*, 23; Hatherton mss, Littleton to R. Wellesley, 19 Nov. 1830; Ward, *Letters to 'Ivy'*, 366. [78] NAS GD23/6/746/128, 129, 131; *Inverness Courier*, 8 Dec. 1830, 5 Jan. 1831. [79] *Three Diaries*, 40. [80] Le Marchant, *Althorp*, 283. [81] *Three Diaries*, 56; *Greville Mems.* ii. 118; *Baring Jnls.* i. 81-82; Add. 76382, Poulett Thomson to Althorp, 22 Feb.; TNA 30/29, Holland to Granville, 24 Feb.; St. Deiniol's Lib. Glynne-Gladstone mss 197, T. to J. Gladstone, 24 Feb. 1831. [82] *Croker Pprs.* ii. 104; *Lieven Letters*, 297; *Greville Mems.* ii. 123; Glynne-Gladstone mss 197, T. to J. Gladstone, 10 Mar. 1831. [83] Agar Ellis diary, 25 Mar.; TNA 30/29, Holland to Granville, 14 Apr. 1831. [84] NAS GD23/6/614/8; *Inverness Courier*, 27 Apr., 4, 11 May, 1 June 1831. [85] *Creevey Pprs.* ii. 234. [86] *Macaulay Letters*, ii. 91. [87] *Holland House Diaries*, 30. [88] Add. 61937, f. 125. [89] Sir James Graham mss (IHR microfilm XR 80), Smith Stanley to Graham, 27 Oct.; Aberdeen Univ. Lib. Arbuthnot mss, Holmes to Mrs. Arbuthnot, 18 Nov. 1831. [90] *Holland House Diaries*, 91, 94; *Three Diaries*, 161; *Baring Jnls.* 91. [91] *Croker Pprs.* ii. 141. [92] *Holland House Diaries*, 109, 145; *Three Diaries*, 202. [93] Hatherton diary. [94] *Macaulay Letters*, ii. 143. [95] *Three Diaries*, 307. [96] *Greville Mems.* iv. 122-3, 125; *Holland House Diaries*, 390; *O'Connell Corresp.* vi. 2589; *Oxford DNB*. [97] *Lieven Letters*, 276; Broughton, v. 97-98; *Macaulay Letters*, ii. 328.

D.R.F.

GRANT, Sir Colquhoun (?1763–1835).[1]

QUEENBOROUGH   1831–1832

b. ?1763.[2] *m.* 7 Aug. 1810,[3] Marcia, da. of Rev. John Richards of Long Bredy, Dorset, 1s. *d.v.p.* 2da. (1 *d.v.p.*). KCB 2 Jan. 1815; KCH 1816; GCH 1831; *suc.* Francis John Browne† to Frampton, Dorset 1833. *d.* 20 Dec. 1835, aged 72.[4]

Ensign 36 Ft. 1793, lt. 1795; lt. 25 Drag. 1797; capt. 9 Drag. 1800; maj. 28 Drag. 1801; lt.-col. 72 Ft. 1802; lt.-col. 15 Drag. 1808-16; a.d.c. to prince regent 1811-14;

brevet col. 1811; maj.-gen. 1814; col. 12 Drag. 1825; col. 15 Drag. 1827-*d.*; lt.-gen. 1830.

Groom of bedchamber to duke of Cumberland 1815-*d.*

Grant's origins are obscure. He was said to be descended from the Grants of Gartenbeg, but no trace of him has been found in the published pedigrees of that family. According to Elizabeth Grant of Rothiemurchus, he was the son of a wadsetter and was 'but poorly reared'.[5] He apparently made a belated entry to the army on the outbreak of war. He served first in India, where he was present at Seringapatam in 1799, and later in Ireland as a captain of dragoons. He commanded the 72nd Highlanders at the Cape in 1806 and was wounded. He exchanged into the 15th Hussars in 1808 and led them with distinction in the retreat from Corunna. The regiment was deployed in the English Midlands during the Luddite disturbances, but returned to the Peninsula under Grant's leadership in January 1813. He commanded cavalry brigades at Morales, where he was again wounded, at Vitoria and Waterloo. During the 1820s he served as a general officer on the Irish staff.[6]

Grant canvassed the government borough of Queenborough, in tandem with the independent Member John Capel, at the general election of 1830, but was 'frightened out of the field' by the prospect of an expensive contest.[7] Having been applied to by the freemen, he and his fellow anti-reformer Capel were returned, without having coalesced, for that borough after a contest at the general election the following year.[8] He voted against the second reading of the Grey ministry's reintroduced reform bill, 6 July, and in the opposition minority in favour of using the 1831 census to determine the boroughs in schedules A and B, 19 July 1831. In his only known speech, 26 July, he deplored the disfranchisement of Queenborough on the 'arbitrary and unjust principle' of population, and declared that his 'chief object in wishing for a seat' had been to 'express' his hostility to reform. He voted against the partial disfranchisement of Chippenham, 27 July, the passage of the bill, 21 Sept., and the second reading of the Scottish bill, 23 Sept. He paired in favour of terminating the Maynooth grant, 26 Sept. He voted against the second reading of the revised reform bill, 17 Dec. 1831, and going into committee on it, 20 Jan. 1832. He paired for the division against the registration clause, 8 Feb. He voted against the enfranchisement of Tower Hamlets, 28 Feb., and the third reading of the reform bill, 22 Mar. His only other known votes were against government on the Russian-Dutch loan, 26 Jan., 12 July, and with the majority against the production of information on the extent of corporal punishment in the army, 16 Feb. He did not stand for Parliament at the 1832 general election.

Soon afterwards he inherited the principal Dorset estate of his wife's sister's husband Francis Browne of Frampton, near Dorchester, who died in March 1833 at the Weymouth house which Grant was then occupying. Browne left £10,000 and his property at Abbotsbury and Litton in remainder to Grant's younger daughter Charlotte Augusta, but she died in Brussels a few months later.[9] Grant subsequently acquired a London house at 9 Grosvenor Square. He was unwell for 'some time' early in 1835, but in May came forward as a Conservative for Poole, whose Whig sitting Member had been made a peer. While his back was turned, his only surviving child Marcia Maria eloped from London with Richard Brinsley Sheridan[†] (?1809-88), grandson of the dramatist, with whom Grant had forbidden her to have any intercourse. The affair became the talk of the town, and a furious Grant hurried back to 'consult his lawyer' and 'shoot Miss Grant's favourite horse'. A kinsman stood in for him at Poole, where he was narrowly beaten by the son of the former Member. Convinced that the elopement had been organized by Sheridan's celebrated sisters Helen Blackwood, Caroline Norton and Lady Seymour, he charged the husbands of the two latter with complicity in 'the disgraceful plot that has been fatal to my pride and happiness'. He accepted Norton's protestation of innocence, but fought a bloodless duel with Seymour on 29 May 1835. It was thought that he would prosecute the entire Sheridan clan for conspiracy, but in the event he soon became reconciled to his son-in-law, with whom he reached an agreement over the disposal of the estate on 16 Oct.[10] In his will, executed a week later, he devised Frampton to Marcia, his residuary legatee, who took the names of Grant and Browne before Sheridan the following year. Grant died of 'dropsy in the chest' in December 1835. His personalty was sworn under £60,000. On the strength of the Dorset property Sheridan sat as a Liberal for Shaftesbury, 1845-52, and Dorchester, 1852-68.[11]

[1] Not to be confused with Lt.-Col. Colquhoun Grant (1780-1829), the duke of Wellington's chief intelligence officer (*Oxford DNB*). [2] Possibly the son of John Grant who was baptized, 23 Dec. 1763, at Boleskine, Inverness, or the son of Evan Grant, who was baptized there in June 1764 (IGI). [3] *Reg. St. George, Hanover Square*, iii. 13. [4] *Gent. Mag.* (1836), i. 545. [5] *Highland Lady*, 108. [6] *DNB*; Mq. of Anglesey, *One-Leg*, 125, 135, 138, 143, 146, 359, 364; Add. 40334, f. 221; 40350, f. 18. [7] St. Deiniol's Lib. Glynne-Gladstone mss 195, T. to J. Gladstone, 12 July; *Maidstone Jnl.* 13, 20 July 1830. [8] Glynne-Gladstone mss 521, Capel to T. Gladstone, 1 Apr.; 198, T. to J. Gladstone, 3, 8 May; *Maidstone Gazette*, 3 May; *Maidstone Jnl.* 10 May 1831. [9] J. Hutchins, *Dorset* (1868), ii. 298; *Gent. Mag.* (1833), i. 465-6; ii. 191; PROB 11/1815/271; IR26/1312/289; *HP Commons, 1790-1820*, iii. 281. [10] J.G. Perkins,

Mrs Norton, 67-69; *Malmesbury Mems.* i. 66; *Creevey's Life and Times*, 407-8; *Lieven-Palmerston Corresp.* 86; *Raikes Jnl.* ii. 112; *The Times*, 18, 19, 21-23 May, 1 June 1835. [11] *Gent. Mag.* (1836), i. 545; PROB 11/1856/25; IR26/1415/40; *DNB*; *Oxford DNB*.

D.R.F./S.M.F.

GRANT, Francis William (1778–1853), of Castle Grant, Elgin and Cullen House, Banff.

ELGIN BURGHS	1802–1806
INVERNESS BURGHS	1806–1807
ELGINSHIRE	1807–1832
ELGIN AND NAIRNSHIRE	1832–10 Apr. 1840

b. 6 Mar. 1778, 4th but 2nd surv. s. of Sir James Grant[†], 8th bt. (*d.* 1811), of Castle Grant and Jean, da. and h. of Alexander Duff of Hatton Castle, Aberdeen; bro. of Lewis Alexander Grant[†]. *m.* (1) 20 May 1811, Mary Anne (*d.* 27 Feb. 1840), da. of John Charles Dunn of Higham House, Suss. and St. Helena, 7s. (3 *d.v.p.*) 1da.; (2) 17 Aug. 1843, Louisa Emma, da. of Robert George Maunsell of Limerick, *s.p. suc.* bro. Lewis as 6th earl of Seafield [S] 26 Oct. 1840. *d.* 30 July 1853.

Rep. peer [S] 1841-*d.*

Lt. 1 (Strathspey) fencibles 1793; capt. 97 Ft. 1794; maj. (perm. rank) Fraser's fencibles 1795, lt.-col 1796; lt.-col. (perm. rank) Argyll fencibles 1799, half-pay 1802-25; brevet col. 1809.

Col. Inverness militia 1803-13; ld. lt. Inverness 1809-*d.*; provost, Nairn, Elgin and Forres on various occasions up to 1818.

Colonel Grant, a strait-laced, congenitally shy man, had been acting head of his Strathspey clan since 1811, when his imbecile bachelor elder brother Lewis had succeeded their father in the baronetcy and their cousin James Ogilvy (7th earl of Findlater) as 5th earl of Seafield.[1] Although he was a generally steady supporter of the Liverpool ministry, he was disgruntled because he had again been passed over in the brevet promotion of 1819, as his friend Francis Nicoll, principal of St. Andrews University, explained to Lord Melville, the government's Scottish manger, at the end of the year:

Colonel Grant is virtually the representative of two very old families and at the head of perhaps the first property in the north of Scotland ... which after the expiring of the existing leases will not be worth less than £50,000 a year. He is therefore galled exceedingly at finding men of his own clan passing over his head in the army, whilst he can neither get forward nor be allowed to quit the profession ... He is met in every corner of the society in which he moves by superior officers and new made knights who of course take precedence of him.

Nicoll suggested that if the promotion could not be awarded, Grant would be more than satisfied with the rank of the younger children of an earl, which would have been his by right had his father outlived and succeeded Findlater, being conferred on himself and his sisters. He remained a colonel for the rest of his life, but was given the precedence he coveted in 1822.[2] In August 1819 he had taken his wife abroad for the sake of her health, and they were in Italy when George III's death in late January 1820 precipitated a dissolution. His friends and agents in Elginshire quickly secured declarations of support for his re-election from the leading county proprietors, including the 4th Earl Fife*, who was seen as a potential threat.[3] Although he was still absent at the time of the election, Grant was returned unopposed, for the fourth consecutive time, and he sat unchallenged for the rest of this period. Fife attacked his precarious controlling interest in the burgh of Elgin, but was unable on this occasion to secure the return of his brother for Elgin Burghs.[4]

Grant continued to support the ministry, but he was an indifferent attender.[5] In 'a maiden speech' (after 18 years in the House), 16 May 1820, he objected 'as a military man' to any reduction in the grant for the cavalry. He was given a month's leave to deal with urgent private business, 30 June. On 3 July he was examined by the select committee on the Scottish royal burghs, and admitted, in vague and evasive testimony, that he had 'probably' in 1818 been provost of Nairn and of Cullen and a councillor of Elgin and Forres; he also stated that he had expended £3,000 of his own money on the erection of a new harbour at Cullen. The committee's report noticed 'the very extraordinary facts' disclosed by Grant, apparently infringing the setts of three of these burghs, which required councillors to be residents, but blamed such 'culpable irregularity' more on the defects of prevailing practice than on Grant himself. He was not pleased, and wrote to the revived committee in 1821 claiming that the sett of Forres did not require residence; that no sett for Nairn had ever been seen; that the sett of Elgin did require residence, but that long practice had dispensed with this for the provost, and that his position as praeses of Cullen was purely honorary. The committee resolved, 5 Mar. 1821, that his conduct was 'not liable to the imputation of irregularity' and conceded that the remarks in the previous year's report had been 'founded on an inaccurate view of the evidence' and should not have been published. At the same time, they reprimanded Grant and invited him to apologize for 'expressions which imply an [unwarranted] imputation on a member of the last committee [not named]'. Grant subsequently gave a satisfactory explanation.[6] He voted in defence of ministers' conduct towards Queen Caroline, 6 Feb., and on the revenue, 6 Mar., but cast wayward votes for repeal of the additional malt duty, 21 Mar., 3 Apr. He had previously opposed Catholic claims, but he voted to concede them, 28 Feb. 1821, 1 Mar., 21 Apr. and (as a pair) 10 May 1825. He received another six weeks' leave for urgent business, 5 Apr. 1821. He was in the ministerial majorities against abolition of one of the joint-postmasterships, 13 Mar. 1822, and reform of the Scottish electoral system, 2 June 1823, in defence of the trial in Demerara of the Methodist missionary John Smith, 11 June 1824, and for the Irish unlawful societies bill, 25 Feb. 1825. He divided for repeal of the usury laws, 17 Feb. 1825. He presented an Elginshire petition against relaxation of the corn laws, 3 May 1825.[7] He was abroad with his ailing wife for most of the 1826 session.[8]

In February 1828 Grant, who was largely a cipher in the 1826 Parliament, applied to the new premier, the duke of Wellington, for a United Kingdom peerage, to be annexed to the Scottish earldom of Seafield to which he was heir presumptive. Melville, a member of the cabinet, endorsed his claim, but the duke was unwilling to add to the large number of creations since 1826.[9] Grant paired for Catholic relief, 12 May 1828, and as expected voted 'with government' for emancipation, 6, 30 Mar. 1829. His only other known vote in that Parliament was against the enfranchisement of Birmingham, Leeds and Manchester, 23 Feb. 1830. Immediately after the death of George IV in late June 1830, Melville told Wellington that Grant, who had an important role to play in the forthcoming elections for Inverness-shire and Inverness Burghs, where ministers were trying to oust the Huskissonite Grant brothers, was still sore at his failure to obtain a British peerage, to which he had strong claims. Melville had to inform Grant that as the new king had no intention of creating new peers 'at present', Wellington could do nothing for him for now, but gave him reason to have hope for the future:

> The duke is not a person to forget a friend or leave him in the lurch when it may be in his power to serve that friend. As for myself, I have no motive to disguise ... the opinion which I have already expressed to yourself, that with reference partly to the Scottish earldom to which you or your children will succeed, and partly to your own situation in the country and to your steady support for so many years, you have ... a preferable claim ... to any other person in Scotland, and as far as I may have an opportunity of advising or influencing, I shall act upon that opinion.[10]

Grant refused to support Charles Grant* in Inverness-shire, as 'from the line of politics opposite to mine which he and his brother have adopted it is quite impossible that I can [do so] consistently with the terms upon which I am with the present government [and] my approbation of their measures', and worked to secure clan support for the unsuccessful ministerial candidate.[11]

After the elections ministers of course listed him among their 'friends', and he was in their minority in the crucial division on the civil list, 15 Nov. 1830. The following day he renewed his peerage application, but three weeks later Melville told him that it had been 'quite impossible' to act on it as Wellington had already resigned.[12] He divided against the second reading of the Grey ministry's English reform bill, 22 Mar. He was 'angry' with John Morison, Member for Banffshire, for abstaining on a flimsy pretext, and promoted an opposition to him at the 1831 general election.[13] He voted for Gascoyne's wrecking amendment to the reform bill, 19 Apr., and next day presented a petition against Scottish reform from the freeholders, commissioners and heritors of Elginshire. At his own election he claimed to be 'a friend to rational reform', but condemned the ministerial scheme as 'too extensive and sweeping'. He divided against the second reading of the reintroduced English reform bill, 6 July, for use of the 1831 census to determine the disfranchisement schedules, 19 July, against the inclusion of Chippenham in schedule B, 27 July, and against the passage of the measure, 21 Sept. He voted against the second reading of the Scottish reform bill, 23 Sept., and on 3 Oct. pleaded with ministers to reconsider the proposed annexation of Nairnshire to Elginshire for electoral purposes, which he deemed a 'gross ... injustice'. He voted against the second reading of the revised English reform bill, 17 Dec. 1831, going into committee on it, 20 Jan., the enfranchisement of Tower Hamlets, 29 Feb., and the third reading, 22 Mar. 1832. His only other known votes in this period were against government on the Russian-Dutch loan, 26 Jan., and the malt drawback bill, 2 Apr., after presenting hostile Elginshire petitions, 20, 26 Mar. He helped to secure an amendment to the registration clause of the Scottish reform bill, 5 June. He was given a month's leave on urgent private business, 3 July 1832.

Grant, still professing support for moderate reform, was returned unopposed as a Conservative for Elgin and Nairnshire at the 1832 general election.[14] As soon as Peel came to power in late 1834 he renewed his peerage claim, but to no avail.[15] He retired from Parliament after the death of his first wife in 1840 and later that year succeeded his brother as 6th earl of

Seafield. A generous promoter of local improvements, he was a Conservative representative peer from 1841 until his death at Cullen House in July 1853.[16] He was succeeded by his eldest surviving son John Charles (1815-81), who was created Baron Strathspey in the United Kingdom peerage in 1858.

[1] HP Commons, 1790-1820, iv. 64-66, 70-72. [2] St. Andrews Univ. Lib. Melville mss 4587, 4589. [3] NAS GD248/824/2/12, 14, 15, 19, 21; Melville mss 4614. [4] NAS GD51/1/198/17/14; GD248/824/2/25, 36, 54. [5] Black Bk. (1823), 159; Session of Parl. 1825, p. 466. [6] PP (1820), iii. 5-6, 59-62; (1821), vii. 71. [7] The Times, 4 May 1825. [8] NAS GD248/824/6/4, 9, 11. [9] Wellington mss WP1/917/22; 918/5; 920/48. [10] Ibid. WP1/1121/39; NLS mss 2, f. 173. [11] NAS GD23/6/659/1, 2; Macpherson Grant mss 690, Grant to G. Macpherson Grant, 6 July; Castle Howard mss, Abercromby to Lady Carlisle, 10 July 1830. [12] NAS GD51/1/194. [13] Macpherson Grant mss 361, J. to G. Macpherson Grant, 2/4, 19 Apr. 1831. [14] NAS GD23/6/659/8; Inverness Courier, 19, 26 Dec. 1832. [15] Add. 40405, f. 300. [16] Sir W. Fraser, Chiefs of Grant, i. 476-9; Gent. Mag. (1853), ii. 308.

D.R.F.

GRANT, John Peter (1774–1848), of The Doune of Rothiemurchus, Inverness.

GREAT GRIMSBY	1812–1818
TAVISTOCK	27 Mar. 1819–1826

b. 21 Sept. 1774, o. s. of William Grant, MD, of Lime Street, London and Elizabeth, da. and event. h. of John Raper of Twyford House, Essex and Thorley Hall, Herts. educ. privately; Edinburgh h.s.; Edinburgh Univ. 1790; adv. 1796; L. Inn 1793, called 1802. m. 2 Aug. 1796, Jane, da. of Rev. William Ironside of Houghton-le-Spring, co. Dur., 2s. 3da. (1 d.v.p.). suc. fa. 1786; uncle Patrick Grant to Rothiemurchus 1790; kntd. 30 June 1827. d. 17 May 1848.
  Puisne judge, Bombay 1827-30, Bengal 1833-48.
  Capt. commdt. Rothiemurchus vols. 1797, maj. commdt. 1801, 1803; lt.-col. commdt. Strathspey vols. 1808.

Grant, who squandered his inheritance and fell short of his aspirations in politics and the law, was described by his daughter Elizabeth as 'a little sallow brisk man without any remarkable feature', but with 'a charm in his manner' which many found irresistible. As a family man, he was 'active' and 'very despotic when called on to decide, yet much beloved'; and he was 'ever exceedingly reserved ... on all matters of personal feeling'. Always dapper in his dress, he was 'to the last very nervous under ridicule'.[1] By 1820, when he was sitting for Tavistock through the good offices of its patron, the 6th duke of Bedford, he was beleaguered by financial problems, which were largely the product of the high cost of obtaining his seat for Grimsby in the 1812

Parliament, but were worsened by his general carelessness about money and the well-meaning domestic incompetence of his long-suffering wife, who endured a 'thickly shadowed life, none of it ... really happy'.[2]

At the time of the dissolution in 1820 there were reports in Grimsby, where the expected sale of his property had not yet taken place, that he would stand again.[3] In the event, Bedford once more accommodated him at Tavistock. In the new Parliament, where he was appointed to the select committee on the Scottish burghs, 4 May 1820, he continued to act with his Whig friends, although he did not vote with them in the divisions on the Queen Caroline affair, 22, 26 June. On 3 July he pressed the Liverpool ministry to clarify the confusion over the late king's personal estate. He was a steady opponent of the aliens bill, protesting against the 'monstrous power' which it conferred on government, 10 July, and failing in a bid to mitigate its severity, 11 July 1820. On the Irish spirits intercourse bill next day, he pointed out the 'extreme absurdity' of the current tangle of legislation on the subject.[4] According to his daughter's recollections, the extent of his financial difficulties began to emerge that summer, though the full and horrible truth remained concealed for a while longer. A decision was taken for the family to abandon Edinburgh, where Grant was making little headway in his renewed attempt to succeed at the Scottish bar, and to return once for all to their Highland home at Rothiemurchus. A trust deed was executed, and Grant's elder son William Patrick gave up his legal career to devote himself to the management of the property and take responsibility for total debts of over £60,000. Grant himself was to 'proceed as usual; London and the House in spring, and such improvements as amused him when at home'.[5]

He made a nuisance of himself at the Inverness county meeting of 4 Jan. 1821, called by local ministerialists to deplore disaffection and vote a loyal address to the king. He complained that insufficient notice had been given by its promoters, an unrepresentative clique, denied the 'existence of sedition and blasphemy' implied in the address, and asserted that 'the present agitation in the country was chiefly owing to the ill-advised measures against the queen'. He managed to have the address amended to state that the county was untainted by any 'spirit of disaffection, of irreligion, or of immorality'. He subscribed to the sentiments of the concluding paragraph, which applauded the 'vigour and wisdom' of government, only in so far as they could be taken as referring to 'constituted authorities in a general sense', for he did not believe that the present ministers were endowed

with either quality: 'on the contrary, they had betrayed in their proceedings imbecility and indecision, and the very reverse of wisdom'.[6] He went up early to join in the parliamentary campaign on behalf of the queen in the first weeks of the 1821 session and was an opposition teller in the division on the omission of her name from liturgy, 23 Jan. He spoke of the 'strong feeling' in her support throughout Scotland, 31 Jan., when he defended the Edinburgh petition in her favour and said that few of those who had attended the Inverness meeting had an acre in the county. He supported Hamilton's motion for a copy of the 'most absurd and preposterous' order in council to the Scottish church on the subject of the liturgy and was a teller for the minority of 35, 15 Feb. On the complaint against the sheriff of Dublin, 22 Feb., he argued that the Commons could not responsibly leave protection of the right of petitioning to the courts. He had more to say on this theme when supporting reception of Davison's petition against chief justice Best the following day.[7] He was again appointed to the select committee on the Scottish burghs, 16 Feb. 1821, but on 22 Mar. he was excused from further attendance. He voted in protest against the suppression of the liberal regime at Naples, 21 Feb. He voted for Catholic relief, 28 Feb., and paired against Peel's amendment to the relief bill, 27 Mar.[8] He voted to make Leeds a scot and lot borough if it received the seats taken from Grampound, 2 Mar., but he was not in the minorities for parliamentary reform, 18 Apr., 9 May. He was a supporter of economy, retrenchment and reduced taxation in most of the major divisions of the session, but was not one of those who joined Hume in hounding ministers on these issues. He secured accounts of the national debt, 1, 20 Feb., and of the medical expenses of the army, 6 Mar.[9] He welcomed the Lords' report on the timber duties, 9 Feb., and presented a petition from an individual who had been ruined by the alteration in them after sinking capital in a mechanical saw, 27 Mar.[10] On 16 Apr. he unsuccessfully proposed the imposition of fixed duties on Baltic and Canadian produce, arguing that the duties constituted a tax of £600,000 and that 'the principle of free trade ought to be acted upon'. He promised to raise the matter next session, 30 May. He insisted that the army, even allowing for the requirements of the new colonies and the burden imposed by 'the continued misgovernment' of Ireland, could be reduced by one eighth, 14 Mar. Supporting repeal of the usury laws, 12 Apr., he stated that distress arose from 'the preposterous theory of a legislative interference with money dealings, which was not applied to any branch of commerce'. Later that day he agreed to the proposal to refer petitions on the Scottish malt duty to a select committee, even though it was 'brought forward under very suspicious circumstances'. He was a teller for the minority of 31 for equalizing the interest on Irish treasury and English exchequer bills, 30 May. He opposed proceeding against the Whig *Morning Chronicle* for breach of privilege, 9 Mar., and supported Maxwell's slave removal bill, 31 May, 1 June.[11] He favoured inquiry into the administration of justice in Tobago, 6 June, when he was a teller for the minority;[12] but he refused to support Hume's motion on the conduct of Sir Thomas Maitland* in the Ionian Isles the following day. On the Scottish juries bill, 14, 16 Feb., he claimed that judges had arrogated to themselves an illegal power to pass sentences of transportation. He expressed reservations about the proposals to regulate the court of session, 15, 26 Feb., when he helped to persuade Creevey to drop his wrecking amendment to the resolutions concerning the Scottish admiralty court.[13] He drew attention to the 'good effects' of the fact that Scottish sheriffs were 'actually barristers, and actually administering justice', 27 Mar.[14] He accused government of deliberately fomenting unrest in Scotland, 16 Apr. 1821.

Grant did not go up for the 1822 session until after Easter, when he voted for remission of Henry Hunt's* sentence, 24 Apr., reform, 25 Apr., and to condemn the increasing influence of the crown, 24 June. He voted for measures of economy, 2, 3, 15, 16 May, 28 June, 5 July. He divided for criminal law reform, 4 June, and inquiry into Irish tithes, 19 June, and spoke and voted in favour of limiting the duration of the Irish insurrection bill, 8 July.[15] He was a teller for the minority for inquiry into the lord advocate's dealings with the Scottish press, 25 June. On 7 May he stated that agricultural distress in Scotland, which was felt most severely by breeders of sheep and cattle, would not be cured by 'any such hopeful projects as ... ministers had lately unfolded'.[16] After presenting a hostile petition from Inverness, he endorsed Hamilton's criticisms of the Scottish burghs accounts bill, 17 June, when he was unsuccessful with two amendments, rejected by 53-35 and 71-44.[17] He approved the changes made by Kennedy to his Scottish juries bill and demanded to know when Inverness, disfranchised in 1818, would have its sett restored, 28 June.[18] He advised Hamilton to give up his motion for repeal of the Scottish cottage tax, which ministers had promised to investigate, 9 July 1822.[19] On the occasion of the king's visit to Scotland the following month, he wrote from Edinburgh to his family of 'the ludicrous state of bustle and expectation of the sedate and sober citizens of the Scottish metropolis, and the whimsi-

cal affectation [by George IV] of a sort of highland costume, with about as much propriety in the conception and execution as if it had taken place in Paris or Brussels'. According to his daughter, he supplied the king with some rare Glenlivet whisky and 100 ptarmigan, a gesture which may have stood him in good stead a few years later.[20]

Grant was a staunch supporter of his clan's electoral interest in Inverness-shire, and on 11 Apr. 1823, as praeses of the meeting, he proposed the re-election of Charles Grant after his appointment as vice-president of the board of trade.[21] Again a late arrival for the session, he divided against the naval and military pensions bill, 18 Apr., for inquiry into the prosecution of the Dublin Orange rioters, 22 Apr., and to abolish punishment by whipping, 30 Apr. He voted for reform, 24 Apr., presented and supported an Edinburgh petition for reform of its representation, 5 May, and spoke and voted for general reform in Scotland, 2 June, when he contrasted the oligarchical system in force there with the 'popular representation' enjoyed in England. Next day he spoke in censure of the lord advocate's conduct in the Borthwick case and was a teller for the minority. He voted for inquiries into chancery arrears, 5 June, the currency (in a minority of 27), 12 June, when he encouraged Phillimore not to delay his bill to remove restrictions on the celebration of marriage by Catholic priests, and the coronation expenses, 19 June. He divided to recommit the silk bill, 9 June, and objected to an increase in the duty on post horses, 12 June, but supported the temporary raising of the barilla duties, 13 June.[22] He was in a minority of 26 against the beer duties bill, 17 June. On 18 June he deplored the apparent lack of concert between the lord advocate and English ministers which had delayed the Scottish commissaries and juries bills. He moved an adjournment on the third reading of the former because of the lateness of the hour, 19 June, and joined in objections to one of the Lords' amendments, 18 July. He was listed as having paired for the second reading of the juries bill, 20 June 1823, although he was also reported as speaking on it.[23] Grant appears to have been absent from Parliament for the whole of the 1824 session, during which proposals were drawn up for the liquidation of his debts.[24] He was a defaulter on a call of the House, 28 Feb. 1825, but attended and was excused the next day, when he voted for Catholic relief, as he did again, 21 Apr., alluding to Scotland's long history of toleration, and 10 May. He voted for repeal of the assessed taxes, 3 Mar., and of the beer duties, 23 May. He opposed the Metropolitan Fish Company bill because it gave 'a chimerical Company' advantages which were not enjoyed by regular fishermen, 9 Mar., and called for legislation to regulate joint-stock companies to prevent fraud, 18 Mar., though he admitted that the problem was a knotty one, 29 Mar. He spoke and was a minority teller against the Leith docks bill, 20 May. He successfully moved a wrecking amendment against the Edinburgh waterworks bill, 3 June, but got nowhere with his complaints that the Scottish partnership societies bill would expose the House to 'absolute ridicule', 22 June.[25] On 5 May he sought leave to introduce a bill to amend the Act of 1701 concerning wrongous imprisonment in Scotland, in a long speech which he subsequently polished and had published. Ministers did not oppose it, but hinted at reservations. Grant presented the measure, 18 May, and saw it through its second reading on the 20th, but it was printed at the report stage, 2 June, and abandoned for the session on the 17th.[26] He welcomed the government's proposal to revise the Scottish laws concerning sedition and blasphemy, 5 May, and called for Scottish judges to be placed and paid on the same basis as English, 19 May.[27] The following day he was a teller for the minority of 29 for Brougham's motion to make puisne judges immovable. He criticized the fees exacted in courts as a 'severe tax' on litigants, 27 May.[28] He supported Williams's attempt to increase judges' retirement pensions, 2 June, noting that in Scotland especially many were currently tempted to stay on the bench into very old age; and he voted to reduce the proposed new salaries, 17 June. Alarmed that the Scottish shooting and stabbing bill made throwing vitriolic acid a new capital offence, he moved a killing amendment against its third reading, 20 June, but withdrew it on being assured that the measure was only temporary. He said that ministers' promise that Prince George would be educated in England was not sufficient in itself to persuade him to support the grant, 27 May, and he voted against the duke of Cumberland's annuity bill, 2, 6, 9, 10 June. He was in small minorities against the grant for repairs to Lyme Regis Cobb, 3 June, for information on the appointment of the clerk of stationery in Bengal, 7 June, and for Hume's amendment to the combination bill concerning intimidation, 27 June. He voted against government on chancery delays, 7 June 1825. Grant's financial problems were, if anything, increasing. His daughter recalled the sad occasion of her sister Jane's marriage in December 1825 to the old and ugly Colonel Pennington, whose fortune was discovered to be 'much smaller than had been expected'. (The marriage in fact 'turned out well'.) 'My poor father, the unhappy cause of our sorrows, did look heart broken when he gave that bright child of his away'. Soon afterwards Pennington had to bale out

William Grant, who was arrested and imprisoned in Edinburgh for a debt of his own. A gloomy winter was spent at Rothiemurchus, with unpaid tradesmen's bills in Inverness creating difficulties in making ends meet. At about this time Elizabeth Grant and her sister Mary began to write stories for the monthly magazines to supplement the family's income.[29]

On his belated arrival at Westminster Grant voted against government on the salary of the president of the board of trade, 10 Apr. 1826. On 13 Apr. he called for reform of Edinburgh's representation as 'a special case of corruption and abuse'. He discountenanced 'radical reform', but argued that 'it would be impossible even to govern Scotland otherwise than as a province or a colony, until she obtained something like a fair representation'; he was a teller for the minority. He voted for Russell's general reform motion, 27 Apr., and his resolutions against electoral bribery, 26 May. He expressed qualified approval of the bank charter amendment bill, 14 Apr., thinking that ministers had probably made the best bargain they could, though they had perhaps 'not done enough for the permanent advantage of the country'. He was added to the select committee on Scottish and Irish promissory notes, 17 Apr. He presented a petition against any alteration of the Scottish banking system, 28 Apr., and, on the committee, voted with Peel to that effect the following month.[30] He spoke in the same sense in the House, 4 May, when he said that the Paisley petitioners for an end to the paper currency as a means of relieving distress were deluding themselves. He objected to the Scottish bankers bill, 12 May. He reintroduced his wrongous imprisonment bill, 19 Apr., but on the 28th agreed to abandon it for the year.[31] He voted for the introduction of defence by counsel in felony trials, 25 Apr., and, though friendly to the principle of the spring guns bill, 28 Apr., was against making all deaths caused by them cases of manslaughter. He was in the minority of 13 for reducing the salaries of Irish prison inspectors, 5 May, and voted for investigation of James Silk Buckingham's* petition touching press freedom in India, 9 May; but he was one of the Whigs who divided against the revised corn bill, 11 May 1826.

Bedford required the Tavistock seat for his brother at the general election the following month and Grant, who was prominent in support of Charles Grant* in the contested election for Inverness-shire, failed to find a berth elsewhere.[32] 'This enforced retirement', as his daughter recalled, 'closed the home world' to him, for 'without this shield his person was never safe' from his creditors. Grant, who was told in December 1826 that it was next to impossible to raise money on the security of his Morayshire property and the following month executed a deed entitling his four younger children to shares in the sum of £6,000 settled on them by his marriage contract, seems to have spent several months skulking on the continent and in London.[33] In the summer of 1827 salvation of a kind was forthcoming in the shape of his appointment as a puisne judge at Bombay. He owed it to the influence of Charles Grant, a member of the Canning and Goderich ministries, although his daughter liked to think that recollection of his favour to George IV in 1822 had played a part. Sir James Mackintosh* saw him at Grant's, 18 June, and wrote: 'There is something very attractive in the good nature which in spite of some demerits endears poor Rothiemurchus to his family'.[34] In the weeks leading up to his departure in late September 1827 he was still on the run from the bailiffs, and he had the humiliation of having to be smuggled on board the ship off the English coast with his younger son (for whom he had obtained a place in the Bengal civil service) after hiding at Boulogne. He reached what he called his 'splendid exile' in February 1828.[35] Within months Grant, who as a result of deaths was for a time the sole judge of the Bombay supreme court, became embroiled in a bitter dispute with the new governor, Sir John Malcolm*, over the rights of jurisdiction which he claimed for the court. The quarrel became personal and scandalous and reached a head when Grant peremptorily closed the court in April 1829. His daughter later noted that this rash act 'put him in the wrong at the end', and reflected that it was all too typical of him:

> There is a bee in the bonnets of the Grants. As a race they are very clever, very clear headed, and very hard working. Under rule and guidance, they do well, none better ... When they make their own work, they make a mill of it – they can't sit idle and they never appear to consider the consequences of their impulsive acts.

The government promoted Dewar, the advocate-general, to chief justice over the head of Grant, who was further mortified by Malcolm's probably deliberate leaking of the description of him by Lord Ellenborough, the president of the board of control, as 'a wild elephant'. He conveniently ignored an official order recalling him to explain his conduct, but resigned in September 1830.[36] He moved to Calcutta and spent three years practising at the bar there, before, thanks to Charles Grant, president of the board of control under Lord Grey, he was appointed a puisne judge of the Bengal supreme court.[37] He retired in early 1848, at the age of 73, but died at sea on his way home in May and was buried in Edinburgh. By his brief will,

written on board the *Earl of Hardwicke* on his departure from India, 16 Mar. 1848, he confirmed the deed of appointment of 1827 regarding his younger children and all settlements made by way of life assurances for providing for his wife. He referred to the sale of all his household goods in Scotland by the trustees for the payment of his debts, and left to his wife the commemorative silver plate which he intended to buy with money given to him for the purpose by Sir Jamsetjee Jeejebhoy and other native inhabitants of Bombay. His personalty was sworn under a paltry £450.[38] His second son, John Peter Grant (1807-93), had a distinguished career as an Indian administrator and was governor of Jamaica, 1866-74.[39]

[1] *Mems. of a Highland Lady* ed. A. Tod (1988), i. 10, 11, 31, 83, 119. [2] Ibid. ii. 156, 203. [3] Grimsby Pub. Lib. Tennyson mss, Daubeny to Tennyson, 11 Dec. 1819, 5, 12, 16, 20, 26 Feb., Veal to same, 23 Feb. 1820. [4] *The Times*, 12, 13 July 1820. [5] *Highland Lady*, ii. 150, 152, 155-6, 193. [6] *Inverness Jnl.* 5 Jan. 1821. [7] *The Times*, 24 Feb. 1821. [8] Ibid. 29 Mar. 1821. [9] Ibid. 2, 21 Feb., 7 Mar. 1821. [10] Ibid. 28 Mar. 1821. [11] Ibid. 1 June 1821. [12] Ibid. 7 June 1821. [13] Ibid. 16, 27 Feb. 1821. [14] Ibid. 28 Mar. 1821. [15] Ibid. 9 July 1822. [16] Ibid. 8 May 1822. [17] Ibid. 18 June 1822. [18] Ibid. 29 June 1822. [19] Ibid. 10 July 1822. [20] *Highland Lady*, ii. 165-6. [21] *Inverness Courier*, 17 Apr. 1823; NAS GD23/6/583/18. [22] *The Times*, 13 June 1822. [23] Ibid. 19-21 June, 19 July 1823. [24] NRA [S] 0102, p. 69. [25] *The Times*, 4, 23 June 1825. [26] *CJ*, lxxx. 380, 435, 448, 463, 472, 484, 551. [27] *The Times*, 6, 20 May 1825. [28] Ibid. 28 May 1825. [29] *Highland Lady*, ii. 191-6. [30] *The Times*, 28 Apr.; Nottingham Univ. Lib. Denison diary, 14 May [1826]. [31] *CJ*, lxxxi. 259, 261, 272, 303. [32] *Inverness Courier*, 12 July 1826. [33] *Highland Lady*, ii. 199; NRA [S] 0102, pp. 42, 71. [34] Add. 52447, f. 81. [35] *Highland Lady*, ii. 199-213, 222; NRA [S] 0102, pp. 42, 43. [36] *Oxford DNB* (Malcolm); Wellington mss WP1/961/9; 970/18; 1008/25; 1024/12; 1025/9; 1038/19; 1039/22; 1061/3; 1139/4; *Ellenborough Diary*, i. 327; ii. 82, 144-5, 174-5, 441-2; *Highland Lady*, ii. 256-7, 281, 283; Add. 41964, f. 7. [37] *Highland Lady*, ii. 283; NRA [S] 0102, pp. 56, 81-84, 98; W.S. Seton Karr, *Grant of Rothiemurchus*, 2; *Macaulay Letters*, iii. 165. [38] *Highland Lady*, ii. 283; *Gent. Mag.* (1848), ii. 335; PROB 11/2093/351; IR26/1834/260. [39] *Oxford DNB*.

D.R.F.

GRANT, Robert (1780–1838).

ELGIN BURGHS	1818–1820
INVERNESS BURGHS	1826–1830
NORWICH	1830–1832
FINSBURY	1832–June 1834

b. 15 Jan. 1780, at Kidderpore, Bengal,[1] 2nd s. of Charles Grant† of E.I. Co. and Jane, da. of Thomas Fraser of Balnain, Iverness; bro. of Charles Grant*. *educ.* privately by Rev. John Venn and Rev. Henry Jowett;[2] Magdalene, Camb. 1795, fellow 1802; L. Inn 1801, called 1807. *m.* 11 July 1829, Margaret, da. of Sir David Davidson of Cantray, Nairn, 2s. 2da. kntd. 20 Aug. 1834; GCH 1834. *d.* 9 July 1838.

Commr. of bankrupts 1815-30; sjt.-at-law, duchy of Lancaster 1827-30; PC 24 Nov. 1830; judge adv.-gen. Dec. 1830-June 1834; commr. bd. of control Dec. 1830-June 1834; gov. Bombay 1834-*d*.

Grant, a commissioner of bankrupts from 1815, was fatter and marginally less indolent than his elder brother Charles, who relied on him for moral support in his frequent moments of indecision, but he remained in his political shadow.[3] On his return for Elgin Burghs on the interest of Colonel Francis Grant*, acting chief of his clan, in 1818, one observer described him as 'a good declaimer' who was unlikely to succeed in the Commons.[4] When George III's death in January 1820 precipitated a dissolution, he initially held little hope of being retained in his seat, as it was Lord Kintore's turn to nominate the Member; but he declined an offer of government backing elsewhere from Lord Melville, the Liverpool ministry's Scottish manager, preferring to rely on the 'moral certainty' of his eventual return for Inverness Burghs, where his father, whom he consulted, was cultivating an interest. He was anxious for an early privy council decision on the disputed municipal sett of Inverness, which was currently disfranchised, to advance his cause, but nothing could be immediately done. When an unexpected threat arose to his interest, Kintore considered adopting Grant as his candidate for the Elgin district, but this ended in smoke.[5] Grant continued to press the lord advocate to intervene to secure a 'final resolution' of the Inverness case, and in August 1822 the privy council authorized the re-election of the old council and so restored the burgh's electoral voice, which virtually ensured his return to the next Parliament.[6] In late October 1822 he started for the vacant Cambridge University seat, having been put up by his friends on the spot and sent for from Scarborough; Lord Liverpool's pro-Catholic nephew Lord Hervey* was already in the field. The young Tom Macaulay*, an undergraduate, considered Grant 'a man qualified to represent the literature of the country, to do honour to its established system of education and to exhibit in his public conduct, the elegance ... manliness and ... liberality which our academical institutions are intended to produce'; but a more experienced Whig, John Whishaw, considered him 'a respectable man, but very much a Saint and entirely devoted to ministerial politics'. Yet the Whig Sir James Mackintosh* was keen on him as 'one of the most moderate (I may even say liberal) of Tories' and a likely supporter of 'the Irish politics of his brother', whose pro-Catholic and conciliatory line had contributed to his humiliating removal from the Irish secretaryship a year earlier.[7] On 2 Nov. Grant explained to his friend Lord Calthorpe

that although he was 'almost certain' to come in for Inverness Burghs at the next general election, he could expect to retain that seat for no more than two consecutive Parliaments, and was eager to get back into the House as soon as possible:

Since I enter into Parliament as a business, as part of my system of life, I must look forward ... and, acting on the supposition ... that life is spared to me until the average period, must provide if possible that I may not be again left in the lurch ... and may not either suffer the inconvenience (which, suffered a second time, would be irreparable) of completely cutting up my course of life, or purchase an exemption from it at an expense which neither I nor any member of my family could ever have well endured, but which we are now less able to endure than ever ... The next general election ... is not likely to take place at least for three [years] ... So long a delay ... must swallow up ... the best years of life. Even if I considered not myself but my family, I must think of [Charles], abandoned by every public connection and standing in the House of Commons without a single friend. To him, in his present situation, it must be important to have at least one supporter on whom he can rely.

In response to Calthorpe's criticism that 'some more explicit statement' of his 'political sentiments' was required than was contained in his first circular (the work of his friends), he said that he had thought it best to let it be assumed that 'I am of my brother's politics'. If more was wanted, he was

perfectly willing to have it given out that my politics are those of an independent person, willing to support government, and from principle inclined to uphold establishments; yet ready, in a clear and strong case, to take his own line resolutely, and at all events not to vote against his conscience ... I would vote with government where I could ... Where I could not, I would rather stay away than vote against them; but ... in a third class of cases, I would even vote against them rather than stay away ... I should not choose to pledge myself in any way. Even *did* I pledge myself, that pledge must be partly contingent, depending on what may be the future conduct of government, which surely (and especially after the recent change [Canning's return to office]) cannot be considered as altogether a *given quantity*.[8]

The intervention of the Whig James Scarlett* and the anti-Catholic William Bankes* dished Grant, who ungraciously withdrew four days before the election. Macaulay, like Charles John Shore, felt that he had damaged himself by his equivocation on the Catholic question:

He not only shrank from explanation ... but in his circular letter of resignation he absolutely complained of being considered as a supporter of the claims and represented the unfairness of attacking, on that ground, a person who had never spoken on the subject, and who had merely given one silent vote on it.[9]

A threat to his position in Inverness Burghs in 1824 petered out, and by early 1825 the seat seemed 'as secure as anything human can be'.[10] That year he composed *A View of the System and Merits of the East India College at Haileybury*, a defence of its monopoly on the training of Company writers based on his speech before the court of proprietors, 27 Feb. 1824. It was published in 1826, when he was duly returned unopposed for Inverness Burghs at the general election in July.[11]

Grant, whose brother had been vice-president of the board of trade since April 1823, was named to the select committee on the Arigna Mining Company, 5 Dec. 1826, and wrote and presented its report, 3 Apr. 1827.[12] He opposed inquiry into the Devon and Cornwall Mining Company, 15 May. He was appointed to the select committee on electoral malpractice by Northampton corporation, 21 Feb. He voted silently for Catholic relief, 6 Mar. His brother remained in office under Canning, and Grant divided with government against the disfranchisement of Penryn, 28 May, and Lord Althorp's election expenses bill, 28 May, and for the grant for Canadian water defences, 12 June, when he spoke in the debate.[13] He opposed proceeding that session with the salmon fisheries bill, 11 June, and 'as a friend to toleration' supported William Smith's Dissenters' marriages bill, 19 June 1827.[14]

Charles Grant joined the duke of Wellington's ministry as president of the board of trade with his associates Huskisson and Lord Palmerston* in January 1828, and Robert was put up to second the address on the 29th, when John Croker* thought he did 'very well', but was 'nothing remarkable'.[15] He was considered for the finance committee, but was not appointed to it.[16] He was named to the committees on Irish education and the Scottish entails bill, 11 Mar. He presented an individual's petition against the salmon fisheries bill, 17 Mar., when he gave guarded support to the government's tithes commutation bill. During the cabinet crisis of March, when his brother's intransigence over the proposed modification of the corn laws threatened to end in his and Huskisson's resignations, the latter appealed to Grant to try to persuade Charles to 'yield something'.[17] He paired with the minority for Fyler's bill to lift the ban on the distribution of ribbons at elections, 20 Mar. He presented an Inverness-shire petition for continuance of the fisheries bounties, 18 Apr. He was named as a coadjutor in the preparation of the lord advocate's bill to improve

the Scottish prison system, though he had some reservations about the plan, favouring compulsion or at least an initial government grant to expedite the erection of new gaols. He was named to the committee on the measure, 15 May, and promoted and presented on 5 June a petition for effective reform from Inverness council.[18] He divided for Catholic relief, 12 May. When his brother resigned with the other Huskissonites at the end of the month, Grant was duly listed as one of the 'rump of the Canning party'. He advocated the removal of restrictions on Europeans' commercial intercourse with the Indian interior, 16 June, but next day opposed inquiry into the European inhabitants of Calcutta's call for repeal of the local stamp duties. He voted against the bill to extend the franchise at East Retford to the freeholders of Bassetlaw, 27 June. He divided with government on the ordnance estimates, 4 July, but spoke and voted against their proposed *ad valorem* duty on silks, 14 July 1828, as he had 'long viewed with indignation the manner in which the legislature trifles with the feelings and interests of the inhabitants of India'.

On 10 Feb. 1829 he argued that Peel, the home secretary, had failed to justify the introduction of a bill to outlaw the Catholic Association, but said he would accept it in order to secure 'the great blessings' of Catholic emancipation; the Whig George Agar Ellis* thought his speech was 'admirable'.[19] He did even better with his speech of 18 Mar. in favour of emancipation and invoking Canning's memory, which, as his brother reported to their chief supporter in Inverness, James Grant of Bught, 'covered him with glory'.[20] He voted to allow Daniel O'Connell to take his seat unhampered, 18 May. He was named to the select committees on Scottish entails, 27 Feb., vestries, 28 Apr., and the registrar of Madras scandal, 5 May. He advocated wholesale reform of the system of trial and imprisonment for debt, 19 Feb., and supported Spring Rice's bill to clarify the law touching the right of executors to claim the undisposed parts of a heritor's personal estate, 10 Mar. He approved of Brownlow's measure to promote the drainage of Irish bogs, 26 Feb., and the ministerial bill to assimilate Irish and English regulations on tobacco cultivation, 12 Mar., when he said that prohibition should be ended. He privately considered the new Scottish gaols bill to be no improvement on its predecessor and believed that 'until some more mature and better concocted measure can be brought forward the legislature had better be quiet'.[21] He presented hostile petitions from the councils of Inverness and Nairn, 12 May, Banff, 13 May, and Forres, 27 May, when, as a member of the committee on the bill, he told the House that he had tried to render it more efficient to its purpose. He was not sorry when it was abandoned for the session. Reporting this to Bught, he claimed not to have disregarded his wish to be furnished with full details of parliamentary proceedings relevant to his constituency, but he jibbed at the suggestion that he should send the complete daily votes of the House to Inverness.[22] He voted for the transfer of East Retford's seats to Birmingham, 5 May, and called for an independent commission to investigate British citizens' claims on the French government, 28 May 1829. In July he married Maggie Davidson of Cantray, whom Macaulay considered to be 'a fool'.[23]

Grant joined his brother in voting for Knatchbull's amendment to the address, 4 Feb. 1830. He was named to the select committees on the East India Company, 9 Feb., and vestries, 10 Feb., and added to that on manufacturing employment, 3 June. After discussing the matter with Charles and John Denison*, he voted for the transfer of East Retford's seats to Birmingham, 11 Feb. (and again, 5 Mar.), the enfranchisement of Birmingham, Leeds and Manchester, 23 Feb., and investigation of the allegations of the duke of Newcastle's interference at Newark, 1 Mar., but divided against Lord Blandford's reform scheme, 18 Feb.[24] As a spectator in the Lords, 13 Feb., he pronounced Wellington's speech on Greece to be the work of 'a great man'.[25] He supported, in what Lord Ellenborough, president of the India board, considered 'a moderate tone, but disingenuous' speech, a motion for information on the dispute between the government of Bombay and the supreme court, 4 Mar.; he voted in the minority of 15 on the 15th.[26] He divided with the revived opposition on all major issues in March. He supported the printing of the evidence in Ellenborough's divorce case for the sake of 'the moral welfare of the country', 1 Apr., and opposed the enabling bill on the ground of 'a moral incapacity' to accept it, 6 Apr.; he was in the minority of 45 for reform of the divorce laws, 3 June. He had presented and endorsed the petition of 597 London Jews for removal of their disabilities, 22 Feb., and on 5 Apr. he moved for leave to introduce a bill to effect this, speaking 'admirably for an hour and a half', as Agar Ellis saw it. Ministers opposed him, but Peel's absence and some bungling by the whips enabled him to carry the division by 115-97, to Wellington's great fury.[27] On 17 May, when Grant expressed willingness to support Quaker emancipation, the second reading was opposed by Peel and defeated by 228-165. He voted for his brother's motion on the Terceira incident, 28 Apr., and for repeal of the Irish coal duties, 13 May, and a return of privy councillors' emoluments, 14 May. He paired for abolition of the death penalty for forgery offences, 24 May and 7

June, and inquiry into the civil government of Canada, 25 May. On 30 Apr. he brought in a bill to reform bankruptcy administration, which had a second reading on 11 May but made no further progress. He presented petitions against the Scottish inventory duty and for a tax on West Indian rum equivalent to that on Scottish spirits, 26 May. On 24 June he argued that the government's chancery regulation bill was 'immature and ill digested'; he was twice a minority teller against it that day. On 2 July he gave notice of a motion to the effect that Parliament should not be dissolved before a possible regency had been provided for, should William IV die before Princess Victoria came of age. He moved an address to the king before 'a very thin' and 'noisy and inattentive' House, 6 July 1830, but was humiliatingly beaten by 247-93.[28]

The government made a dead set at the Grants at the ensuing general election, but failed to keep them out of the new Parliament. In normal circumstances Robert could have expected to come in again for the Burghs, where Inverness had the return, but he had caused 'offence' there and discovered that Bught and his colleagues on the council had transferred their support to a ministerialist.[29] He gave up, returned to England and, after considering the possibilities there with Huskisson, went, on the advice of the Whig Henry Brougham*, to contest the open borough of Norwich with the local Quaker Richard Gurney. He declared his support for a 'liberal, tolerant and enlightened' domestic policy and an 'energetic and honourable' foreign one, and for retrenchment, reduced taxation and 'every measure for the correction of public abuses and for obtaining a practical reform in the representation of the people'. To the delight of the Whigs, he and Gurney won a signal victory over two ministerialists, one of whom was a brother of Peel.[30] Ministers of course listed him as one of 'the Huskisson party'. As such, he was included in autumn speculation as to whether they would join Wellington or the Whigs.[31]

On 11 Nov. 1830 he presented Norwich Dissenters' petitions for the abolition of slavery. He divided in the majority against government on the civil list, 15 Nov. He was initially assigned to the post of judge advocate, worth £2,500 a year and with membership of the privy council, in the Grey ministry, where his brother was president of the board of control, but there arose a possibility that he would be offered the secretaryship at war in order to accommodate Mackintosh as judge advocate. When Charles gave him the 'option', however, he preferred the latter post. He received his patent on 4 Dec. 1830 and resigned his commissionership of bankruptcy. He also took a place at his brother's board.[32] By then he had been safely re-elected for Norwich, where a threatened challenge evaporated, having borrowed £1,200 from Edward Littleton* for the purpose. (He had turned down the offer of a subscription from some grateful Jews in the summer.)[33] He presented more anti-slavery petitions, 10, 18 Dec. 1830, 29 Mar. 1831, and one for emancipation from metropolitan Jews, 15 Dec. 1830, when he gave notice for 17 Feb. 1831 of a motion, which was subsequently deferred. He asked for ministers to be given a fair trial of the sincerity of their promise to reduce pensions and salaries, 13 Dec. 1830. He was appointed to the renewed East India select committee, 4 Feb. 1831 (and again, 27 Jan. 1832). He presented a Norwich petition for repeal of the coastal coal duties, 14 Feb. 1831. Ellenborough reckoned that he spoke 'miserably' on the 18th, when he appealed to Irish Catholic Members to be 'less warm' in their agitation for repeal of the Union and again asked the House to give ministers time.[34] There was a false report in early March that he had resigned in protest at the scope of the ministerial reform scheme;[35] but on the 7th he spoke at length for it, admitting that his 'early opinions were very much against' reform, attributing his conversion to the recent French revolution and the success of reformers in open constituencies in 1830 and arguing that to 'grant what is just and reasonable' was the best way of 'deflating extravagant hopes and expectations'. The Whigs William Ord* and Lord Durham respectively described his speech as 'capital' and 'very clever in some parts', while even the Tory Thomas Gladstone* conceded that he did 'very well'.[36] Grant presented and endorsed reform petitions from Norwich and Peebles, 19 Mar., voted for the second reading of the reform bill, 22 Mar., tried to portray the hostile Cambridge University petition as one in favour of 'moderate reform', 30 Mar., and divided against Gascoyne's wrecking amendment, 19 Apr. 1831. At the ensuing general election he and Gurney won a crushing victory over two prominent anti-reformers.[37]

Grant dismissed opposition complaints at the omission of any reference to Divine Providence in the speech from the throne, 22 June 1831. He voted for the second reading of the reintroduced reform bill, 6 July (when Lord Grey complained at a dinner party that 'the two Grants' had 'never been worth a farthing' in their contribution to the ministry),[38] and divided steadily for its details. He opposed hearing counsel on the case of Appleby, 12 July, and on the 20th, defending his hustings criticism of aristocratic influence over the return of Members, said he wanted the representatives of the people to form 'a House of Commons and not an out-house of the peers'. He conceded that in

some large constituencies a poll would take longer than two days, 5 Sept. He presented petitions for the Norwich poor bill, 13 July, and was in the two ministerial majorities on the Dublin election controversy, 23 Aug. He voted for the passage of the reform bill, 21 Sept., after stating that it would 'produce a vast and much required infusion of the popular mind and feeling into this House' and oblige Members to be more responsive to their constituents' opinions and interests. He voted for the second reading of the Scottish reform bill, 23 Sept., repudiated a Tory allegation that 'parchment votes' had secured his brother's return for Inverness-shire, 3 Oct., presented a Hamilton householders' petition for that burgh's enfranchisement, 6 Oct., and of course voted for the motion of confidence in the government, 10 Oct. He approved the principle of Brougham's bill to reform chancery administration, 13 Oct., and supported its details, 14, 17 Oct. 1831, when he said that in his 15 years as a commissioner he had earned an average of £394. At the end of the month Lord Holland urged Brougham to press on Grey Grant's replacement by Mackintosh, who would be just as 'active and useful in the Commons ... as Robert Grant, who only makes two or three good speeches in a session'. Grey had evidently considered offering him the chief justiceship of Bengal, but nothing came of this, as Brougham was sure he would not take it.[39]

Grant sat in the gallery for the introduction of the revised reform bill, 12 Dec. 1831.[40] He voted for the second reading on the 17th, supported its details and spoke and voted for the third reading, 22 Mar. 1832. He was naturally in the government majorities on the Russian-Dutch loan, 26 Jan., 16 (when he spoke) and 20 July, and relations with Portugal, 9 Feb. Macaulay had some private fun at his expense by amusing his sisters with 'all sorts of parodies on *Watt's Hymns* about the sluggard, of which Mr. R. Grant, with his laziness, his fat, and his padding, was the hero'. According to Margaret Macaulay, who noted in mid-February rumours that ministers were still unsuccessfully trying to tempt Grant to go to India in order to bring her brother into office

> two or three nights since, Tom, in endeavouring to get up to some high benches in the House, stumbled over Mr. R. Grant's legs, as he was stretched out half asleep as usual. Being roused, he made many apologies in the usual manner, and then added, oddly enough, 'I am very sorry, indeed, to stand in the way of your mounting'.[41]

Grant defended courts martial as 'efficient and impartial', 2 Apr., and opposed Hunt's motion for the suspension of army flogging, 19 June, when he said that the authorities were working towards its abolition. On 3 Apr. he got leave to introduce a bill to fix the Norfolk assizes at Norwich, which passed its second reading by 44-13, 23 May, and received royal assent on 23 June (2 and 3 Gul. IV, c. 47).[42] He of course divided for the address calling on the king to appoint only ministers who would carry reform unimpaired, 10 May, but he was credited with a vote for the Liverpool disfranchisement bill, 23 May, and only paired for the second reading of the Irish reform bill, 25 May. He voted against increasing the Scottish county representation, 1 June, and defended the proposed £10 franchise there, 4 June. He deputized for his sick brother on an Indian question, 14 June. On 21 July 1832 he presented and endorsed another emancipation petition from London Jews and promised to pursue the issue.

At the general election of 1832 Grant, whom Macaulay had come to regard as 'a regular twaddle', topped the poll for the new metropolitan constituency of Finsbury.[43] His Jewish emancipation bills of 1833 and 1834 foundered in the Lords. In June 1834 he accepted the governorship of Bombay and a knighthood. He died intestate at Dalpoorie in July 1838, after contracting a fever, and was buried at Poonah.[44] Administration of his estate, which was sworn under £7,000, 17 June 1839, was granted to his widow, but his affairs were found to be in an 'embarrassed state'.[45] His brother published an edition of his hymns as *Sacred Poems* in 1839.

[1] H. Morris, *Charles Grant* (1904), 70. [2] Ibid. 195. [3] Margaret Macaulay, *Recollections*, 230; Lord Teignmouth, *Reminsicences*, i. 298; *Macaulay Letters*, ii. 328. [4] *Life of Campbell*, i. 351. [5] NAS GD23/6/745/123, 127; GD51/1/198/17/14, 15; 198/29/9; 51/5/749, pp. 177-9. [6] NAS GD23/6/573/1, 2. [7] *Macaulay Letters*, i. 181; *Cambridge Chron.* 2 Nov.; Add. 51653, Mackintosh to Holland, 27 Oct.; 51659, Whishaw to Lady Holland, 25, 29 Oct. 1822; Buckingham, *Mems. Geo. IV*, i. 392. [8] Hants RO, Calthorpe mss 26M62/F/C 545. [9] *Colchester Diary*, iii. 262; *Cambridge Chron.* 22 Nov. 1822; Teignmouth, i. 302-3; *Macaulay Letters*, i. 223. [10] NAS GD23/6/746/66, 75, 78; Add. 39193, f. 68. [11] *Inverness Courier*, 7, 21 June, 5 July 1826; NAS GD23/6/610. [12] Add. 36463, f. 303; *The Times*, 4 Apr. 1827. [13] *The Times*, 13 June 1827. [14] Ibid. 12 June 1827. [15] *Croker Pprs.* i. 406. [16] Add. 40395, f. 221; Keele Univ. Lib. Sneyd mss SC17/26. [17] Add. 38755, f. 203. [18] NAS GD23/6/573/5. [19] Northants. RO, Agar Ellis diary, 10 Feb. [1829]. [20] Grey mss, Howick jnl. 18 Mar. 1829; *Greville Mems.* i. 274; *Ellenborough Diary*, i. 399; NAS GD23/6/746/121/1. [21] NAS GD23/6/573/6, 7. [22] Ibid. 6/573/8. [23] *Macaulay Letters*, ii. 204. [24] Nottingham Univ. Lib. Ossington mss OsC 74. [25] *Greville Mems.* i. 373. [26] *Ellenborough Diary*, ii. 205. [27] Agar Ellis diary, 5 Apr. 1830; Add. 40400, f. 154; *Arbuthnot Jnl.* ii. 349. [28] Howick jnl. 11 July 1830; *Arbuthnot Jnl.* ii. 370. [29] *Ellenborough Diary*, ii. 305; NAS GD23/6/573/9, 10; 6/583/22, 23; *Inverness Courier*, 28 July 1830. [30] St. Deiniol's Lib. Glynne-Gladstone mss 195, T. to J. Gladstone, 20 28 July; *Inverness Courier*, 4 Aug.; *Ellenborough Diary*, ii. 333; Brougham mss, Mackintosh to Brougham, 31 July; Chatsworth mss, Brougham to Devonshire [21 Sept. 1830];

Add. 61937, f. 116. [31] *Arbuthnot Jnl.* ii. 391; Castle Howard mss, Abercromby to Carlisle, 26 Sept.; Brougham mss, Agar Ellis to Brougham, 4 Oct. 1830. [32] Grey mss, Lansdowne to Grey [19 Nov.], C. Grant to same, 19 Nov.; Add. 51562, Brougham to Holland [22 Nov]; Lincs. AO, Tennyson d'Eyncourt mss 2 TdE H89/60; Brougham mss, R. Grant to Brougham, 4, 6 Dec. 1830. [33] Hatherton mss, Grant to Littleton, 24 Nov., Littleton to R. Wellesley, 26 Nov. 1830; Add. 51836, Goldsmid to Holland, 28 June [1831]. [34] *Ellenborough Diary*, 54. [35] Ibid. ii. 64. [36] Add. 51569, Ord to Lady Holland [7 Mar.]; Grey mss, Durham to Grey [7 Mar.]; Glynne-Gladstone mss 197, T. to J. Gladstone, 8 Mar. 1831, [37] *Three Diaries*, 90. [38] *Creevey Pprs.* ii. 234. [39] Brougham mss, Holland to Brougham, 27 Oct.; Add. 51563, reply [1 Nov. 1831]. [40] *Croker Pprs.* ii. 141. [41] Macaulay, ii. 230, 233-4. [42] Brougham mss, Grant to Brougham, 26 Feb. 1831. [43] *Macaulay Letters*, ii. 266; *The Times*, 22 June, 7 Nov., 12, 13, 21 Dec. 1832. [44] *Oxford DNB*; *Gent. Mag.* (1838), ii. 658-9. [45] PROB 6/215/32; *Holland House Diaries*, 389.

D.R.F.

GRANT *see also* **MACPHERSON GRANT**

GRANT SUTTIE (formerly **SUTTIE**), **Sir James**, 4th bt. (1759–1836), of Balgone and Prestongrange, Haddington.

HADDINGTONSHIRE 21 Mar. 1816–1826

b. 10 May 1759, 1st s. of Sir George Suttie[†], 3rd bt., of Balgone and Agnes, da. of William Grant[†], Lord Prestongrange (SCJ). *educ.* Glasgow Univ. 1777; adv. 1781; L. Inn 1777, called 1785. *m.* 14 Apr. 1792, Catherine Campbell, da. of James Hamilton of Bangour, 1s. 2da.[1] *suc.* fa. as 4th bt. 25/26 Nov. 1783; aunt Janet Grant, countess of Hyndford, to Prestongrange and took name of Grant before Suttie 1818. *d.* 20 May 1836.

Lt. Haddington fencible cav. 1794, capt. 1796.

Addressing the Haddingtonshire meeting called to vote a loyal address to the regent and condemn sedition, 26 Oct. 1819, Grant Suttie, the Tory Member since 1816, gave an assurance that 'he should consider it his duty ... to attend in his place on the first day ... [of the emergency session] to support such measures as [ministers] might think most expedient in the present crisis'.[2] At the general election of 1820 'the slow moving Suttie' was challenged by Lord Tweeddale's brother Lord John Hay*, who claimed to have the backing of the Liverpool ministry. Lord Melville, their Scottish manager, authorized Grant Suttie, who had appealed to him, to 'contradict the assertion'. He defeated Hay by a single vote.[3] Immediately afterwards, he renewed an application for patronage for two supporters.[4] Although he continued to support ministers he was a lax attender.[5] He voted against economies in revenue collection, 4 July 1820. He was in the government majorities on the Queen Caroline affair, 6 Feb., the revenue, 9 Mar., the additional malt duty,

3 Apr., and the disfranchisement of ordnance officials, 12 Apr. 1821. He voted against Catholic relief, 28 Feb. 1821. He took periods of leave to attend to private business, 19 Apr., and because of ill health, 14 May 1821. His only known vote in the 1822 session was against the relief of Catholic peers, 30 Apr. He divided with administration on the sinking fund, 13 Mar., and against inquiry into the prosecution of the Dublin Orange rioters, 22 Apr. 1823. He took six weeks' sick leave, 14 Feb. 1825, but was present to vote against Catholic claims, 21 Apr., 10 May. He was in the minority for the Leith docks bill, 20 May 1825. He voted against reform of Edinburgh's representation, 13 Apr. 1826. He is not known to have spoken in debate during his ten years as a Member, but he presented protectionist petitions, 12 May 1824, 28 Apr. 1825.[6] He was in the minority against relaxation of the corn laws, 8 May 1826. At the dissolution the following month he abandoned the county to Hay.

On 4 June 1830 Charles Stuart Cochrane, a long-term visitor to Grant Suttie's neighbourhood who was peeved not to have been invited to Balgone, denounced him to Sir Edward Troubridge* as 'stupid and stingy', and added that his unmarried daughter 'is turned Methodist' and was 'ugly enough to take the veil'.[7] At the general election that summer Grant Suttie's only son and successor George (1797-1878) stood for the county but lost to Hay, who had the support of the Wellington ministry. Grant Suttie, who initiated a major reconstruction of the mansion house at Prestongrange, died in May 1836.[8]

[1] *Edinburgh Mar. Reg.* (Scottish Rec. Soc. liii), 767. In both *Burke PB* and *CB* she is named as Katherine Isabella. [2] *The Times*, 6 Nov. 1819. [3] NAS GD51/1/198/9/22-24, 28; 51/5/749, pp. 186-7; NLS mss 11, ff. 14, 24, 79; *Longs of Longville* ed. R.M. Howard, ii. 446. [4] NAS GD51/1/198/9/29. [5] *Black Bk.* (1823), 196; *Session of Parl. 1825*, p. 486. [6] *The Times*, 13 May 1824, 29 Apr. 1825. [7] NMM, Troubridge mss MS 84/070, box 3/1. [8] *Trans. E. Lothian Antiq. Soc.* x (1966), 98-110.

D.R.F.

GRATTAN, Henry I (1746–1820), of Tinnehinch, co. Wicklow and Moyanna, Stradbally, Queen's Co.[1]

MALTON	23 Apr. 1805–1806
DUBLIN	1806–4 June 1820

bap. 3 July 1746, o. s. of James Grattan of Dublin, KC, MP [I], and Mary, da. of Thomas Marlay, MP [I], of Marlay Abbey, co. Dublin, c.j.k.b. [I]. *educ.* Ball's sch., Ship Street and Young's sch., Abbey Street, Dublin; Trinity, Dublin 1763; M. Temple 1767, called [I] 1772. *m.* Dec. 1782, Henrietta, da. of Nicholas Fitzgerald of

Greensborough, co. Kilkenny, 2s. 2da. *suc.* fa. 1766. *d.* 4 June 1820.
MP [I] 1775-97, 1800.
PC [I] 19 Sept. 1783-6 Oct. 1798, 9 Aug. 1806-*d.*

Grattan, 'a small bent figure, meagre, yellow and ordinary', with a large head, jutting chin and shrill voice,[2] was one of the parliamentary giants of his day; but when, at the age of 73, he was again returned unopposed for Dublin at the general election of 1820, his life was near its end. He had fallen seriously ill with a chest complaint the previous autumn on a family excursion to the Wicklow mountains and was unable to go to London for the emergency session of 1819. He wrote to Justice Day, 19 Nov.:

> I have been attacked by an occasional difficulty of breathing, which is teasing though not painful, and presents to the mind the idea of stifling; however, I am better. The radicals I do not think will destroy liberty; but it is only because they will not succeed, for their proposition would put an end to freedom; first by anarchy, and then by a military government, the necessary result of anarchy.[3]

He went to Dublin for his election in March 1820, but was too weak to attend the hustings, where his second son and namesake stood in for him.[4] Improving spring weather somewhat revived him, and in April he became increasingly anxious to make an early appearance in the new Parliament, as he told his son:

> I wish to take my seat and speak on two subjects, reform and the Catholics. I fear that the radicals will put down the principles of liberty. The government and the House of Lords on the one side, the radicals on the other, would put down all freedom. The Lords have no right to interfere with the Commons in their efforts to amend their representation; the boroughs should be reduced ... On the other question, I would strive to do something for the country; it is a monstrous thing that one sect should proscribe another.

In the middle of the month his son recorded that

> he grew very restless and impatient; his appetite was nearly gone, but his strength revived occasionally and surprised everyone. He said he would go to ... [Dublin] and see some of the leading friends of the Catholics, and then to London by slow journeys – 'for though I cannot speak I can make the motion. I owe it to the public good, to the interests of the body that has trusted me, and to my own memory. I have the motion in my mind – two resolutions, one declaring the determination to uphold the Protestant religion, the other to grant their liberties to the Catholics. I will do it. I am not without hope. It may lay the ground for some future measure'.[5]

Against the advice of his Dublin doctors, he insisted on going to Westminster, and through his son got his friend Sir Henry Parnell to give notice on his behalf, 28 Apr., that he would submit a motion on Catholic relief on 11 May. His health took a turn for the worse, and on 30 Apr. he received the sacrament. He survived, but in early May was in such a bad way that he had to give up his London plan for the time being. Under instruction, Parnell postponed his motion to the 25th, holding out a hope that Grattan would be able to attend by the end of the month.[6] He rallied slightly, and on 12 May went to Dublin, determined to receive a deputation of Catholics, who had implored him not to go to London, and then to do precisely that. In his formal written response to the Catholics (he was too ill to speak), 13 May, he advised them to maintain the connection with Britain to 'keep clear of every association with projectors for universal suffrage and annual parliaments', and to accept emancipation on 'terms that are substantial and honourable'. He concluded:

> I shall go to England for your question, and should the attempt prove less fortunate to my health, I shall be more than repaid by the reflection that I make my last effort for the liberty of my country.[7]

He left Dublin, accompanied by his son, on 20 May, reached Liverpool the following day and, too feeble to travel by road, made his slow way to London by canal, on a specially prepared boat. He arrived, with his legs in an advanced state of mortification, on 31 May. He continued to talk of taking his seat and moving his resolutions, and even contemplated a literal swansong in the House in the style of Chatham; but his friends talked him out of the idea.[8] He died at his lodgings in Baker Street in the early evening of 4 June 1820. Lord Holland later wrote that he died 'almost at the moment when the queen's triumphant arrival extinguished for a time all interest about ... [the Catholic] question more effectually than the death of its ablest advocate'.[9] Moving the new writ for Dublin, 14 June, the Whig Sir James Mackintosh, in the absence of Sir John Newport, paid tribute to Grattan as 'the founder of the liberties of his country', who had 'all the simplicity of genius', and read his death bed declaration in favour of emancipation under the British connection. He was followed by the heavyweights Lord Castlereagh, Charles Grant, Wilberforce and Vesey Fitzgerald; while the Irish Whig backbencher Wrixon Becher communicated Grattan's dying exhortation to the Catholics to steer clear of radical politics. Mackintosh's nervousness was increased when he received just before he rose 'an angry letter from Brougham complaining that I should do that for Grattan which I thought in general a bad practice and which we had agreed not to do for Romilly'. He replied that it was too late to back

out and stressed, as he did in his speech, 'the difference between a recent death where the praise might be natural and a death some time before the motion when it must seem cold and studied'. He believed that he made a 'strong impression on the House'.[10] Nine years later, however, Holland, who had 'unfeigned respect' and 'the greatest admiration' for Grattan, 'a really *great* man', reckoned that these orations 'fell flat and unimpressive from the frequency of such exhibitions and the indifference and dislike of the House not to the object of the panegyric but to the unparliamentary practice of such funeral orations', which neither Pitt nor Fox had received.[11] At the request of a number of leading Whigs, who signed a memorial to his family drawn up by the poet Rogers, Grattan was buried in Westminster Abbey, next to Fox, on 16 June 1820.[12] In one provision of his will, he directed that if all his four legitimate children died without surviving issue, the Queen's County estate which he had bought with the sum of £50,000 voted to him by the Irish Parliament in 1782 in acknowledgement of his services to the country should revert to the public in trust to form a foundation 'for the annual support of unprovided gentlewomen, daughters of poor and meritorious citizens of Dublin'.[13] His son and biographer Henry failed to come in for Dublin in his room, but he did so in 1826 and sat for Meath, 1831-52. His elder son James represented county Wicklow, 1821-41.

Mackintosh considered Grattan, as whom there was 'nobody so odd, so gentle, and so admirable', to be 'a great thinker'; but, like other contemporaries, he recognized the essential artificiality of his unique oratory, which had 'a taint of that disposition to antithesis and point which gives such a littleness to style'; it was, as Thomas Creevey* remembered it, 'highly ornamental'.[14] A few months after Grattan's death Tom Moore was told by Canning that

> for the last two years, his public exhibitions were a complete failure, and that you saw all the mechanism of his oratory without its life. It was like lifting the flap of a barrel-organ, and seeing the wheels. That this was unlucky, as it proved what an artificial style he had used. You saw the skeleton of his sentences without the flesh on them; and were induced to think that what you had considered flashes, were merely primings, kept ready for the occasion.[15]

Lady Bessborough thought him 'clever and ... affected', and Lord Colchester wrote that 'his conduct ... in the United Parliament had been uniformly wise and useful; his eloquence always fantastic, and often ridiculous'.[16] Brougham credited him with 'a rare union of the moderation which springs from combined wisdom and virtue, with the firmness and the zeal which are peculiar to genius'.[17] Sir Jonah Barrington had 'never met any man who possessed the genuine elements of courage in a higher degree than Mr. Grattan, in whom dwelt a spirit of mild, yet impetuous bravery, which totally banished all apprehensions of danger'.[18] Sir George Philips*, who knew him well, remembered him with affection and admiration:

I do not think you could be with him for an hour or two without hearing from him some remarks so original either in thought, or expression, as no one but himself could make ... There was a strange want of correspondence between his manners and his mind. His manner was obsequious, and to strangers it would appear finical and affected; but simplicity was the real character of his mind, which was of a lofty and powerful order. He was a man of genius, incapable of doing anything mean or unworthy of himself, or of omitting to do what he conceived his duty to his country required of him, whatever risk, misrepresentation, or danger it might expose him to.[19]

[1] See R. B. McDowell, *Grattan. A Life* (Dublin, 2001); *Oxford DNB*. [2] Sir J. Barrington, *Personal Sketches*, i. 351; McDowell, 33. [3] H. Grattan, *Life and Times of Henry Grattan*, v. 541. [4] Ibid. v. 542; *The Times*, 8 Feb.; *Dublin Evening Post*, 8, 10 Feb., 11, 16, 18 Mar. 1820. [5] Grattan, v. 544-5. [6] Ibid. v. 545-8. [7] Ibid. v. 548-9; McDowell, 217-18. [8] Heron, *Notes*, 118; Add. 52444, ff. 123-4. [9] Grattan, v. 550-4; *The Times*, 6 June 1820; *Gent. Mag.* (1820), i. 563; Holland, *Further Mems.* 282. [10] Add. 52444, f. 151. [11] Add. 51741, Holland to Caroline Fox [16 June 1820]; Hants RO, Tierney mss 75b. [12] *The Times*, 17 June 1820; *Von Neumann Diary*, i. 25. [13] *The Times*, 4 July 1820; *Gent. Mag.* (1820), i. 640. For rumours that he had fathered a dozen bastards see McDowell, 243 (n. 76). [14] *Mackintosh Mems.* (1835), ii. 140-1, 353; *Creevey Pprs.* ii. 183. See also McDowell, 160-1. [15] *Moore Mems.* ii. 160-1. [16] *Leveson Gower Corresp.* ii. 466; *Colchester Diary*, iii. 141. [17] *Hist. Sketches* (1839), i. 260. [18] Barrington, i. 346. [19] Warws. RO MI 247, Philips Mems. i. 282, 286.

D.R.F.

GRATTAN, Henry II (?1787–1859), of 84 St. Stephen's Green, Dublin and Moyrath, co. Meath.

DUBLIN	1826–1830
CO. MEATH	11 Aug. 1831–1852

b. ?1787, 2nd s. of Henry Grattan I* (*d.* 1820) and Henrietta, da. of Nicholas Fitzgerald of Greensborough, co. Kilkenny; bro. of James Grattan*. *educ.* privately; Trinity, Dublin 17 May 1804, aged 16½; M. Temple 1807; King's Inns 1807, called [I] 1811. *m.* 5 Oct. 1826, Mary O'Kelly, da. of Philip Whitfield Harvey, newspaper proprietor, of Grove House, Portobello, co. Dublin, 4s. *d.v.p.* 7da. *suc.* bro. James to Tinnehinch, co. Wicklow 1854. *d.* 16 July 1859.

The younger son and namesake of the great Irish Patriot, who represented Dublin at Westminster from 1806, Henry Grattan junior was destined to live in his father's shadow and he never escaped it. Having graduated from Trinity in 1808, he was in attendance at parliamentary debates and privately taking his father's part, by the following year. 'Law books be damned', he once wrote to his brother James, who had entered the army, but although he neglected his legal studies, he did qualify and apparently practice at the bar, at least for a while. With a lively mind and a fiery temperament, he exhibited a youthful indignation at Ireland's dependent status, but, as he recounted to James, 9 Aug. 1810, his father prevented him making his political debut at a Dublin meeting for repeal of the Union:

I thought it would be a measure useful to him among his constituents; that it might make me and him popular, however he differed from me ... I had some idea of embarking in the question and rising or falling with it; but there is so little spirit that the measure of repeal I fear would not be supported at all. My father of course will not advance.

He added, with characteristic hyperbole, that 'an Irishman of ambition dies in Ireland, he droops in England ... We have become a province drained of every particle of spirit ... By God the Irish mind is debased'; and later opined that, between foolish Catholics and tyrannical Protestants, the Irish of his own type were without a country of their own, being 'half colonists, half indigent adventurers, men on garrison duty'. His kindly father tended to tolerate such outbursts, confiding to James, 7 Oct. 1811, that Henry's politics 'are more violent than mine and he argues with too much acerbity, of that he will mend'.[1] However, he courted celebrity, as well as his father's disapproval, with at least one controversial publication, *Faction Unmasked or a Letter to the Roman Catholics of Ireland* (1815), which was widely attributed to him.[2] Some anonymous journalistic pieces in the *Dublin Evening Post*, vindicating his father against the aspersions of the Catholics, involved him in a threatened prosecution at the hands of Saurin, the high Protestant Irish attorney-general.[3]

Grattan, who was considered a possible successor at Dublin if his father resigned the seat, stood in for him at the general election of 1820, when he also backed Richard Wogan Talbot* for the county, and, as his factotum, accompanied him on his last journey to England.[4] On his father's death in early June, when he fought a bloodless duel with Lord Clare and took exception to the speed with which the new Dublin writ was issued, Grattan immediately offered as his political heir, particularly on behalf of the Catholics.[5] But he was defeated by the corporation and ministerialist candidate Thomas Ellis, an extreme anti-Catholic, in a vicious contest, after which he condemned the intimidation practised on the freemen and promised to uphold the independence of the borough, especially in regard to its freeholders, although he did not pursue his petition.[6] He was admitted a freeman of the smiths' guild in October 1820 and in January 1821 joined in the condemnation of the sheriff's conduct at the county Dublin meeting the previous month.[7] He collected materials for his father's life, but the poet Tom Moore rejected the proposal of writing his biography, finding them insufficient and reflecting too much the son's limited memory and taste.[8] In its place he edited a collection of his *Miscellaneous Works* and the four volume *Speeches of the Right Honourable Henry Grattan* (both 1822), dedicated to the people of Ireland, in which he commented that his father's life 'was *one continued, gentle, moral lesson*' in defending liberty, to 'teach us perseverance and firmness, in upholding the freedom and the rights of our country; protecting her against her own inconstancy and guarding ourselves against the fallibility of human nature'.[9]

In the early 1820s Grattan maintained a high profile in Dublin, where he was criticized for opposing calls for repeal of the Union as untimely at a meeting of the merchants' guild, 14 Oct. 1822, concurred in the condemnation of the Orange theatre rioters late that year and made himself an expert on the vexed local issue of corporation taxation.[10] He also cultivated interests in several other counties, for instance Monaghan, where he was believed to be registering freeholders in 1822, and Cavan, where he spoke at a county meeting in January 1823.[11] In January 1824 his less excitable brother James, Member for Wicklow, recorded in his journal:

> Henry writes long complaints of the state and neglect of Ireland ... He is quite too hasty, so about tumult and the inquiry, and conduct of [William] Plunket* in filing *ex-officio* [informations against the theatre rioters] he said *he was glad he was roused* and he was wrong ... He mismanages his private affairs with an apparent contempt of family ... [which] does not serve his credit; and his imprudence and misjudgement has lost him the city, and to the family, and has put him to great expense. He also writes complaints about the tithe bill ... His opinion is really good for nothing.[12]

He announced his future candidacy for Dublin by an address, 27 Nov. 1824, and was considered certain to stand on the independent interest during electoral speculation the following summer. Yet he had his detractors, like Henry Westenra, the wavering ministerialist Member for Monaghan, who in January 1825 remarked that 'as to my voting for Grattan, it is a thing I should deplore. His politics appear to me to be childish, and the character of the man would not bear one out in the voting for him as my friend'.[13]

By a campaign of registering dubious Catholic freeholders and, according to Richard Sheil*, a blatant attempt to woo corporators' wives at the Dublin tabinet ball, Grattan, who appealed constantly to his father's principles, put himself in a strong position as the only liberal candidate at the general election of 1826, when he seconded the pro-Catholic Robert Henry Southwell in the Cavan contest.[14] Ellis was now disqualified from standing and, after Sir Robert Shaw* had unexpectedly withdrawn, Grattan was returned for Dublin with the corporation's anti-Catholic champion George Moore, whom he accused of reviving religious discord.[15] In October he married at St. Peter's, Dublin, the daughter of Philip Whitfield Harvey, who had died, 'in principle a pure Whig', 6 Aug. 1826. Since 1802 Harvey had been the proprietor of the *Freeman's Journal*, a liberal Dublin daily, and the paper now passed to Grattan as part of his wife's marriage portion.[16] Although it naturally gave its new owner good coverage, Grattan probably had only a limited editorial role: for instance, in January 1827, when Daniel O'Connell* applauded his election victory at a national meeting of Catholics, he printed a statement disclaiming all knowledge of a recent article attacking Trinity College. Nevertheless, he often had to bear the brunt of criticisms of the *Journal*, and in late 1827 he apparently fought a duel with Thomas Newcomen Edgeworth, who had taken offence at one of its paragraphs.[17]

Grattan was said to have done well in speaking against the address, 21 Nov. 1826, when he was a minority teller for his own amendment for including mention of Irish grievances and promising their redress, which was defeated by 135-58.[18] Thereafter, like his brother (from whom he was distinguished as 'Henry Grattan' rather than 'Mr. Grattan'), he was very active in promoting Catholic claims, for which he presented many petitions, and advancing numerous Irish causes, as well as undertaking a large amount of constituency business. He warned ministers that Ireland would not be satisfied without Catholic relief, 6, 8 Dec. 1826, and, having (as he was frequently to do) differed with his colleague over a hostile Dublin petition, 5 Mar., voted for emancipation, 6 Mar. 1827.[19] He spoke for introducing poor laws to Ireland, 9 Mar., to condemn the system of stipendiary magistrates there, 16 Mar., and for reducing excessive church taxes, 3 Apr. He divided for the production of information on the mutiny at Barrackpoor, 22 Mar., the Orange procession and Lisburn magistrates, 29 Mar., and chancery administration, 5 Apr. He voted for Tierney's amendment to postpone the committee of supply, 30 Mar., and for a select committee on the Irish miscellaneous estimates, 5 Apr. He obtained leave for a bill to afford greater protection to Catholic places of worship, 10 Apr., but did not proceed with it. The following day he complained of discrimination against Catholics in the administration of justice.[20] He was in minorities for separating bankruptcy jurisdiction from chancery, 22 May, and against committing Thomas Flanagan to Newgate, 19 June. He was admitted to Brooks's, sponsored by Lords Fitzwilliam and Duncannon*, 30 May 1827.

He used the presentation of petitions to complain about the Irish Subletting Act, 25 Feb., and discrimination against Catholics in education, 28 Feb. 1828. He voted for repeal of the Test Acts, 26 Feb. He continued to raise matters connected with Dublin, such as the appointment of juries, 5 Mar., and the admission of Catholics to the corporation, 11 Mar. Having seconded Parnell's motion for production of the treaty of Limerick as inconsistent with the penal laws, 6 Mar., he spoke forcefully for Catholic relief, 12 May. Declaring that 'I plead not only for their rights but for your security', he emphasized that there should be equal treatment for all and suggested, in what became one of his favourite themes, that an alienated Ireland might one day go the way of the American colonies; he divided in the majority that day. He remonstrated against government inaction over distress in Ireland, 5 June, pointed out a misapplication of public money there, 12 June, and supported his constituents' attempts to abolish the coal duties, 20, 27 June. He unsuccessfully moved to include the protection of Catholic chapels under the Irish malicious injuries bill, 16 June; he wrote to O'Connell that 'I tried all I could but in vain. Government is incorrigible', adding that 'I hope the Catholics will not fall *into the trap* of securities and veto'.[21] He voted against the grant for the Society for the Propagation of the Gospels, 6 June, and for inquiry into the Irish church, 24 June, and was in minorities against considering excise licenses for cider retailers, 26 June, the additional churches bill, 30 June, and Fyler's amendment in the committee on the silk duties, 14 July 1828. He signed the Protestant declaration in favour of the Catholics that autumn and the requisition for the Dublin meeting of the friends of civil and religious liberty in January 1829.[22]

Grattan congratulated the Wellington administration on its decision to grant Catholic emancipation, 5 Feb. 1829, and brought up numerous Dublin parish and other favourable petitions that session. He rebutted his colleague's insistence on the unsympathetic attitude of public opinion in relation to hostile petitions from county Dublin, 3 Mar., Dublin corporation, 13 Mar., and the Protestants of Ireland, 17 Mar., and deplored the invidious distinctions drawn between Protestants and Catholics in parliamentary debates, 12 Mar. He voted for emancipation, 6, 30 Mar., but, as he had made clear he would, 10 Mar., he spoke and divided against the franchise bill, 19 Mar., when he argued that no proof had been advanced as to the delinquency of the 40s. freeholders either among the Catholics, who he said were not dominated by their priests, nor among the Protestants of the North. The following day he was in the minority for Duncannon's amendment to allow reregistration, but on the 26th he objected to Moore's attempt to extend the franchise bill to boroughs as a ruse to disfranchise the Catholics altogether. He briefly raised a query about whether O'Connell would be permitted to take his seat, 23 Mar., and voted to allow him to do so unimpeded, 18 May.[23] He spoke for the Maynooth grant, 22 May. Sending £50 towards O'Connell's renewed electoral campaign in county Clare, 26 June 1829, he commented that 'his return last year was a master stroke of Irish policy and the country is greatly indebted to him for his exertions'.[24]

No stranger to journalistic confrontations, Grattan fell foul of the law late in 1829, when the *Freeman's Journal*, despite its support for emancipation, was one of the papers made an example of by the Irish secretary Lord Francis Leveson Gower, who wished to suppress the publication of inflammatory and libellous press comment. He was obliged to remain in Dublin during the early part of the following year, and was eventually convicted, without punishment, in May 1830. He parted company that year with the *Journal*, which was said to have declined considerably because of inefficient management during his proprietorship; it picked up thereafter under Patrick Lavelle.[25] Grattan apparently left Ireland on the 20th and the first votes that can safely be attributed to him that session were those for abolition of the death penalty for forgery, 24 May, 7 June, information on Canada, 25 May, and both O'Connell's and Lord John Russell's motions for parliamentary reform, 28 May. Having promised his constituents that he would join his colleague in strenuously opposing the increased Irish stamp and spirit duties, he did so in the House, 28 May, and at a meeting of Irish Members on this subject, 29 May.[26] He divided against reform of the divorce laws, 3 June, the grant for South American missions, 7 June, and the government amendment to increase recognizances under the libel bill, 9 July. He advocated the virtues of Irish landlords being resident on their estates, 4, 7 June, complained about the distressed state of Ireland, 21 June, remarked that the proposed tax increases would only exacerbate the situation, 29 June, and urged greater expenditure on public works to provide relief, 2, 7, 13 July 1830.

Although praised by the *Freeman's Journal* for his parliamentary exertions and championing of liberal causes, Grattan was forced on to the defensive at the general election of 1830, when he suffered from a relative lack of mercantile credibility and was challenged by a coalition of Moore and Frederick Shaw*, the recorder.[27] He boasted of his conduct in promoting the independence and economic interests of Dublin on the hustings, but trailed throughout the ensuing contest and blamed his defeat on corporation intimidation and other sharp practices; he entered a petition to this effect, but again failed to pursue it.[28] He was belatedly thought of as a candidate for county Meath, where he was briefly proposed from the gallery, and by that winter he had announced his future candidacy there.[29] Vehemently opposed to the Irish administration's attempt to suppress the current agitation for repeal of the Union, he chaired the Dublin inhabitants' meeting in its favour, 25, 26 Jan. 1831.[30] Mentioned as a possible candidate for Clare, he in fact contested Meath, with O'Connell's backing, at the general election that spring, when he declared his principles to be those of 1782, 'Ireland and Independence', but was defeated by the pro-reform sitting Members Lord Killeen and Sir Marcus Somerville.[31] The latter's death provided another opportunity for Grattan, who backed the reform candidates in the contemporaneous Dublin by-election, and he was duly elected for Meath in August 1831, with the support of O'Connell and the priests, after a one-day poll; the Irish administration, which had opposed him, considered his speech hinting that misgovernment might provoke popular revolution on the recent French example to be inflammatory and put his success down to Catholic intimidation.[32]

Like his brother, Grattan, whom Robert Gordon had intended to call on to respond in his place to allegations of fraudulent freeholder creations in Dublin borough, did not vote on the resolutions relative to the Dublin election, 23 Aug. 1831. The first evidence found of parliamentary activity that session was on 29 Aug., when he objected to excessive church taxes and voted for making legal provision for the Irish poor. The following day he spoke of the difficulties of registering freeholders and divided against preserving the voting rights of Irish freemen. In addition to numerous minor interventions, he handled business relating to Dublin (such as the coal meters establishment, 2 Sept.) and Meath (such as the Navan Catholics' petition for the redistribution of church revenues, 9 Sept.), and constantly raised matters concerning the other eight counties in which he claimed (on 20 Mar. 1832) to own properties. He condemned Orange outrages perpetrated by the Irish yeomanry, 31 Aug., and called for its total disbandment, despite being himself an officer in it, 7, 9 Sept. His clashes with James Gordon, Member for Dundalk, 9 Sept., Sir Richard Vyvyan, Member for Okehampton, 13 Sept., and Frederick Shaw (on the subject of improper electoral influence), 21 Sept., illustrated the acerbity he often resorted to in debate. He voted for transferring Aldborough from schedule B to schedule A, 14 Sept., but for the third reading, 19 Sept., and passage of the Grey ministry's reintroduced reform bill, 21 Sept., the second reading of the Scottish bill, 23 Sept., and Lord Ebrington's confidence motion, 10 Oct. He welcomed the Irish secretary Smith Stanley's bills to amend the Whiteboy Act, 22 Sept., and to reform Irish grand juries, 29 Sept., but continued to oppose his arms bill, 23 Sept., and to raise complaints against the Irish yeomanry, 3 Oct., police, 4 Oct., magistrates, 5 Oct., and clergy, 6 Oct. He defended Maynooth College and its grant, 26 Sept., and urged greater attention to Irish affairs in general, 27 Sept. He intervened acrimoniously about the Dublin election, 12 Oct. 1831, and the following day, when he stated that he opposed government as far as Ireland was concerned, he was silenced by the Speaker during an attack on Sir Charles Wetherell, the former attorney-general.

Grattan, who signed the requisition for a Meath county meeting on reform in October, spoke in its favour at the Navan dinner held in his and Killeen's honour, 28 Nov., and at the county Dublin meeting, 3 Dec. 1831.[33] He paired for the second reading of the revised reform bill on the 17th and chaired a Dublin meeting to consider the gloomy state of Ireland, 31 Dec. 1831.[34] He voted in the minority for Heron's amendment against enfranchising £50 tenants-at-will, 1 Feb., but otherwise generally divided in the majority for the details, as for the third reading of the reform bill, 22 Mar. 1832. He sided with ministers over Portugal, 9 Feb., and on 27 Feb. was credited with being in favour of recommitting the anatomy bill, which he wished to see extended to Ireland. Frequently raising cases concerning tithes and bringing up Irish petitions for their total abolition that session, he voted to print the hostile Woollen Grange petition, 16 Feb., and condemned Smith Stanley's interim report on the subject as premature and misconceived, 17 Feb., 8 Mar., when he was in the minority to postpone this debate. He made extensive criticisms of government's tithes resolutions and voted for amendments to them, 27, 30 Mar., when he unsuccessfully moved for tithes to be levied in greater accordance with the wishes of the Irish people, and on 16 Apr. he repeated his argument that church revenues from them should be used to benefit the poor. He objected to Smith Stanley's Irish subletting bill, 20 Feb., defended the Irish lord chancellor Plunket's use of patronage relative to the post of secretary to the master of the rolls, 22 Feb., 6 Mar., when he quarrelled violently with the Donegal Member Edward Conolly over the Kildare Place Society, and thanked the corporation of London for taking a greater interest than its counterpart in Dublin in the affairs of Ireland, 16 Apr., 4 July. He was absent from the division on Ebrington's motion for an address calling on the king to appoint only ministers who would carry reform unimpaired, 10 May; he was presumably in Dublin because on 1 June, when he attacked the corporation for its Protestant exclusiveness, he stated that he had attended the inhabitants' meeting to petition for withholding supplies until reform had been carried. He criticized the additional seat proposed for Dublin University, 23 May, 13 June, and welcomed widening its franchise by giving the vote to the masters of arts, 9 July. He said the Irish reform bill was not sufficiently extensive, but was in the majority for its second reading, 25 May. He urged the adoption of lower qualifications for freeholders, 13 June, and leaseholders, 18 June, and divided for giving the vote to £5 freeholders, 18 June, and against making electors liable to pay municipal taxes before being allowed to vote, 29 June. He remonstrated against Catholic ceremonies being covered by the Irish party processions bill, which he otherwise supported, 14, 19 June, and reprobated Dublin corporation for maintaining its dominance by means of creating Protestant freemen, 25 June, 2 July. Having warned ministers that it would be impossible to enforce future collections of tithes, 14 June, he spoke and voted against the tithes bill, 13 July, when he was vituperative in his exchanges with Smith Stanley and pessimistic in his assessment of the intentions of the Protestant ascendancy. He divided to make permanent provision for the Irish poor by a tax on absentees and to suspend flogging in the army, 19 June, to open coroner's inquests to the public, 20 June, and to establish a system of representation for New South Wales, 28 June. He divided with government for the Russian-Dutch loan, 26 Jan., 12, 16 July 1832.

Grattan, who was returned unopposed for Meath with Maurice O'Connell* at the general election of 1832, was later described by James Grant as tall, sallow and gentlemanlike in appearance and to be a reasonably good speaker, although

> there is always an abundant infusion of burning liberalism in his speeches. It is impossible for him to give expression to half a dozen sentences without getting into a downright passion ... He is by far the best specimen of a wild Irishman ... in the House.

Grant also commented that Grattan 'has much of the attachment to his native country which blazed in the breast of his illustrious father, but unhappily he has not a tithe of the talent'.[35] His *Memoirs of the Life and Times of Henry Grattan*, which appeared in five volumes between 1839 and 1846, was passionate but undistinguished in style, displaying more of a righteous filial affection for, than a balanced historical understanding of, his father's life and principles.[36] A Repealer, he was defeated in Meath in 1852 and died in July 1859, when his estates were apparently divided between his two married daughters Henrietta, the wife of Charles Langdale, who inherited the Grattan family residence of Celbridge Abbey, county Kildare, and Pauline, the wife of Thomas Arthur Bellew of Mount Bellew, county Galway, who changed his name to Grattan Bellew.[37]

[1] NLI, Grattan mss 2111; R.B. McDowell, *Grattan*, 189-90, 195; A.P.W. Malcomson, *John Foster*, 356. [2] Grattan mss 27805, James to Henry Grattan, 10 May; *Pprs. of Denys Scully* ed. B. MacDermot, 531. [3] R.L. Sheil, *Sketches of Irish Bar* (1854), i. 353-4. [4] *Dublin Evening Post*, 3, 29 Feb., 30 Mar.; *Dublin Jnl.* 17 Mar. 1820. See HENRY GRATTAN I. [5] Northants. RO, Agar Ellis diary, 31 May, 6 June; *Dublin Evening Post*, 8, 10, 13, 22 June; Grattan mss 27805, address [June], O'Grady to Grattan, 5 July 1820. [6] *Dublin Evening Post*, 27, 29 June, 1, 6, 8 July 1820. [7] Ibid. 16 Nov. 1820, 20 Jan. 1821. [8] McDowell, 221. [9] *Grattan Speeches* ed. H. Grattan, vol. i, pp. iii-iv, xxxv-xxxvi. [10] *Dublin Evening Post*, 15 Oct., 30 Nov. 1822, 6 Jan., 15, 20 May 1823, 15 Feb., 4 Mar. 1824; *O'Connell Corresp.* ii. 982. [11] PRO NI, Rossmore mss T2929/3/20; *Strabane Morning Post*, 21 Jan. 1823. [12] Grattan mss 5777. [13] *Dublin Evening Post*, 30 Nov. 1824, 8 Aug. 1825; Rossmore mss 3/104. [14] Sheil, i. 352, 354-5; *Newry Commercial Telegraph*, 23 June 1826. [15] *Dublin Evening Post*, 6, 10, 13, 24 June 1826. [16] *Freeman's Jnl.* 7 Aug., 6 Oct. 1826; A. Aspinall, *Politics and the Press*, 116. [17] *Freeman's Jnl.* 2, 19 Jan.; *Dublin Evening Mail*, 16 Mar., 7, 21 Nov. 1827. [18] Castle Howard mss, Abercromby to Carlisle [22 Nov. 1826]. [19] *The Times*, 7, 9, Dec. 1826, 6 Mar. 1827. [20] Ibid. 11, 12 Apr. 1827. [21] *O'Connell Corresp.* iii. 1461. [22] *Dublin Evening Post*, 7 Oct. 1828, 8 Jan. 1829. [23] *Greville Mems.* i. 280. [24] *Dublin Evening Post*, 2 July 1829. [25] B. Inglis, *Freedom of Press in Ireland*, 171, 188-9, 240; *Westminster Rev.* (1830), i. 88-89. [26] *Dublin Evening Post*, 15, 18 May, 1 June; *Warder*, 29 May, 5 June 1830. [27] *Freeman's Jnl.* 5, 27, 30 July, 3, 4 Aug.; *Dublin Evening Post*, 6, 13, 20, 29 July, 3 Aug. 1830. [28] *Dublin Evening Post*, 5, 7, 10, 12, 14, 28 Aug. 1830. [29] Ibid. 2 Nov.; *Westmeath Jnl.* 19 Aug.; *Drogheda Jnl.* 21 Aug. 1830. [30] *Dublin Evening Post*, 11, 27 Jan. 1831. [31] Add. 51572, Darnley to Holland, 8 Feb.; Derby mss 920 Der (14), Gosset to Smith Stanley, 16 Mar.; *Dublin Evening Post*, 28 Apr., 14, 17 May 1831. [32] *O'Connell Corresp.* iv. 1834; *Dublin Evening Post*, 14, 16 July, 6, 11, 18 Aug.; *Freeman's Jnl.* 10-13 Aug.; PRO NI, Anglesey mss D619/31D/52; Derby mss 119/2, Anglesey to Smith Stanley, 10

Aug.; 121/2, Gosset to Earle, 11 Aug. 1831. [33] *Dublin Evening Post*, 20 Oct., 1, 6 Dec. 1831. [34] *The Times*, 4 Jan. 1832. [35] [J. Grant], *Random Recollections of Commons* (1837), 337-8. [36] McDowell, 221-2; Malcomson, 398. [37] *Evening Freeman*, 19 July; *The Times*, 20 July 1859; *Gent. Mag.* (1859), ii. 202.

S.M.F.

GRATTAN, James (1785–1854), of Tinnehinch, co. Wicklow.

Co. WICKLOW 9 Feb. 1821–1841

b. 7 Apr. 1785, 1st s. of Henry Grattan I* and Henrietta, da. of Nicholas Fitzgerald of Greensborough, co. Kilkenny; bro. of Henry Grattan II*. *educ.* privately; Trinity, Dublin 1803-8; ?King's Inns 1809. *m.* 7 Aug. 1847, Lady Laura Maria Talmash, da. of Sir William Manners, 1st. bt.[†], Lord Huntingtower, of Buckminster Park, Leics., *s.p. suc.* fa. 1820. *d.* 21 Oct. 1854.
Cornet 20 Drag. 1810; lt. 9 Drag. 1811, half-pay 1814. PC [I] 1841.

In his recollections of the Commons published in 1838, James Grant observed that Grattan was

> hardly known in the House as a speaker; but the circumstance of his being the son of the celebrated Henry Grattan, is of itself sufficient to entitle him to a brief notice. He does not address the House above once or twice in the course of a session, and then only briefly ... He talks with great fluency; he never appears to be at a loss for words, but his style is by no means polished. His ideas are of an inferior order; they never, even by accident, rise above the common-place. Occasionally he repeats himself, and at other times he is not so very explicit as he might be. In his manner he has nothing of the vehemence of his brother, the present Henry Grattan ... When about to speak, he puts his hat under his left arm, and in that position retains it during the time he is on his legs ... Grattan is pretty regular in his attendance on his parliamentary duties: when an Irish question is before the House, you may calculate as safely on his presence as on that of the Speaker himself, or the clerks at the table.[1]

Grattan, the keeper of a substantial but mostly illegible political journal, joined Brooks's, sponsored by Lord King, 14 Apr. 1810, shortly before entering the army.[2] He served on the Walcheren expedition and in the Peninsula, and was a noted society associate of Colonel Fitzgerald and the princess of Wales.[3] In June 1820 either he or his brother Henry fought a bloodless duel in Hyde Park with Lord Clare after making 'offensive' remarks about Clare's late father at a public meeting in Dublin.[4] Writing to Henry shortly before their father's death that month, he reported that old Grattan 'is quite sick of all politics and, as you said,

he seems to be making his peace with all parties. I feel more disposed to declare war with them ... We must get him in good humour as the Catholics plague him and he is not inclined to do anything this year'.[5] He voted for Henry, who stood unsuccessfully as their father's successor, in the ensuing Dublin by-election.[6] In early 1821 he came forward on a vacancy for county Wicklow as the nominee of the 2nd Earl Fitzwilliam, promising to pursue the same 'principles and conduct' as his father, and was returned unopposed.[7]

A regular attender, he voted with the Whig opposition to the Liverpool ministry on most issues, especially economy, retrenchment and reduced taxation.[8] He voted for Catholic relief, 28 Feb. 1821, 1 Mar., 21 Apr., 10 May 1825, and in his maiden speech, 26 Mar. 1821, called for an end to the Protestant 'monopoly of place, which had already existed for too long'. He divided for parliamentary reform, 18 Apr., 9 May 1821, 25 Apr. 1822, 24 Apr. 1823, 27 Apr. 1826, and to reform the representation of Scotland, 10 May 1821, 2 June 1823, and Edinburgh, 26 Feb. 1824, 13 Apr. 1826. On 5 Feb. 1822, in response to the address, he complained that the Union 'had not produced the benefits which the people of Ireland had been taught to look for' and that it would be 'in vain' to govern Ireland or collect rents by military force. Recording the day's events, he observed:

> I went on about Ireland, her state, her government, etc., etc., as I had written it out. Committed an error, lost my head for a moment till the House grew impatient, the Speaker got up and called them to order. I recovered a little but *not sufficiently* ... It was a bad business ... I might have concluded shorter ... There were a few *hears*.[9]

He spoke and voted steadily against the Irish insurrection bill thereafter, warning ministers that 'they might hang and shoot, but the evil will still go on', 7 Feb. He called for the abolition of Irish potato tithes, 15 May, and voted against the tithes leasing bill, 19 June, 8 July 1822, when he was a minority teller. That month he fought another duel 'in consequence of a political dispute' with a Captain O'Grady.[10] At the end of the year Grattan and Henry were observed by Daniel O'Connell* speaking at the meeting of Catholics called to vote an address to the Irish viceroy Lord Wellesley.[11] He urged ministers to act 'vigorously' against Orange societies and 'their violent proceedings', 6 Mar. 1823. He wanted the beer duties bill to be extended to Ireland, 24 Mar., when he was in the minority of 32 for information on the alleged plot to murder Wellesley. He voted for inquiry into the related legal proceedings, 22 Apr., briefly examined a witness, 5 May, and warned that a premature cessation of the investigation would 'produce great mischief in Ireland', 26 May. He welcomed and was a majority teller for the Irish joint tenancy bill, 28 May. He seconded and voted for a motion for inquiry into Dublin disturbances, 24 June 1823. He spoke and voted for information on Catholic burials, 6 Feb. 1824. On the 19th he moved for returns of the number of Irish Catholic office-holders, alleging discrimination against their appointment to positions they were competent to hold, but was defeated by 38-11. On 9 Mar. he presented a petition from the Irish Catholic bishops against grants for Protestant societies and their 'indiscriminate use of the Bible'. Lord Clancarty was 'dismayed' to learn of it and warned the duke of Wellington that the Catholics were adopting titles which had 'no sanction or legality'.[12] Grattan argued that it was too early to alter the Irish Tithes Composition Act, 9 Mar., 3 May, when he protested that the proposed amendments were 'completely in favour of the ecclesiastical party'. He was a minority teller to condemn Irish church pluralities, 27 May, and spoke and voted against the new churches bill, 14 June. He was a minority teller against the Irish magistrates' indemnity bill, 15 June 1824. He defended the Catholic Association, 10 Feb. 1825, although next day he said that 'he himself did not belong to it because he could not justify all its actions'. He denounced the bill to suppress it as 'nothing less than an Orange ... declaration of war against the Catholics', 11 Feb., and voted accordingly, 15, 21, 25 Feb. That month he was one of the Members who met the Association's leaders.[13] He defended the grant for Irish charities as a 'great portion of this was for education', but criticized that for the linen board, where 'situations were given away upon a system of favouritism', 18 Mar. On 22 Mar. he obtained leave to introduce a bill to relieve the Irish poor, which left it optional for parishes to collect subscriptions and assess to relieve distress. It was read a first time, 15 Apr., but was postponed for three months, 17 June, and went no further. He argued that the grant for Irish emigration to the Canadas was a failed 'experiment', 15 Apr. He condemned the bill to disfranchise the Irish 40s. freeholders which accompanied emancipation as 'unconstitutional and monstrous', 26 Apr., was reported by Henry Bankes* to have been in that day's hostile minority (although he does not appear in the known division lists), and voted against it, 9 May, when he asserted that if the freeholders were unfit to vote, they were also unfit to be emancipated.[14] O'Connell reported to his wife:

Young Grattan has behaved on this bill exceedingly ill. I gave him a strong hint to that effect when I saw him ... after the debate. In his speech he said "*I do not think this bill will cure the remedy*"!!! Only think ... of such

blockheads being the persons who govern and make laws for us.[15]

Grattan presented and endorsed a petition against the bill, 12 May 1825. He believed the 'most extraordinary instances of abuse' had taken place in the collection of Irish church rates and called for 'some plan for education of the peasantry', 16 Feb. 1826. Following objections by other Irish Members, he waived his amendment for a clause in the Irish church rates bill enabling parishes to assess for relief of the poor, 25 Apr., but tried again two days later, when it was negatived without a division. He voted for Lord John Russell's resolution against electoral bribery, 26 May 1826.

At the 1826 general election, when Henry was returned for Dublin, Grattan offered again for county Wicklow, speaking at the nomination in defence of his recent poor law proposals and attacking the junior minister George Dawson* for his attempts to stir up an Orange opposition. He was returned unopposed.[16] On 6 Dec. 1826 he disputed the allegations of George Moore, the other Dublin Member, that Catholic priests excommunicated their political opponents. He clashed with the junior minister Wilmot Horton over his Irish emigration plans the following day and 7 Feb. 1827, when he contended that the 'enormous sums' involved in promoting his 'hobby' would be better spent in making people 'comfortable at home'. He denied that the Protestants of county Wicklow were opposed to Catholic claims, urged the Association to 'persevere' with their 'lawful and laudable purposes' and defended the Irish clergy's involvement, 2 Mar. He voted for relief, 6 Mar. 1827. On 9 Mar. he denied that poor laws would make Ireland 'infinitely worse', but agreed not to press for their introduction 'in opposition to the declared hostility of so many Irish Members'. He presented a petition from the Catholic bishops against the 'system of proselytism' by Irish Protestant schools, 19 Mar. He believed the use of spring guns in Ireland would be 'productive of the most lamentable results to the innocent', 27 Mar. He divided for information on the Lisburn Orange procession, 29 Mar. He seconded a motion against the 'intolerable' building of Protestant churches in Ireland with Catholic taxes, 3 Apr. On 10 Apr. he was granted a month's leave after serving on the Northampton election committee. On 28 May he argued that 'no line of conduct would better serve the Catholic cause than that of supporting the new Canning ministry. He attended a Dublin meeting for the construction of a canal from Dublin to Galway, 29 Nov. 1827.[17] He presented petitions for Catholic relief, 4, 20 Feb., 31 Mar.,

1 May, and voted thus, 12 May 1828. He argued that 'in its present shape' the Irish Subletting Act would 'do serious injury', 19 Feb. He divided for repeal of the Test Acts, 26 Feb. He seconded a motion against the parochial settlements bill, which 'would exclude all the poor Irish from Scotland', 14 Mar. He presented and endorsed a petition for Irish poor laws that day and 1 Apr., when he called for 'a proper system of relief' which 'would not partake of the evils' of the English one. He repeatedly urged their introduction thereafter. On 25 Mar. he brought in a bill to make lessors liable for parochial and county assessments in all future Irish lettings. He moved and was a teller for its second reading, 12 June, when it was defeated by 39-21. He complained of 'great abuses' in the expenses of the Irish constabulary, 30 May, 12 June, said that the Irish promissory notes bill would 'drive all the gold out of Ireland', 20 June, and divided for inquiry into the Irish church, 24 June 1828.

On 3 Mar. 1829 Grattan spoke of 'the exertions of the Catholic Association' in bringing about the Wellington ministry's concession of emancipation, for which he voted, 6, 30 Mar., and presented many petitions. He condemned the disfranchisement of the 40s. freeholders, criticizing those who 'by proposing the bill in 1825' had 'afforded a precedent' and warning that the registration requirements would turn the new minimum £10 freehold qualification into a £20 franchise, 26 Mar. He presented a petition from the Catholic clergy against the relief bill's restrictions on monasteries, 7 Apr. He presented and endorsed one from the Catholic bishops for a national system of Irish education, 9 Apr. He voted for the transfer of East Retford's seats to Birmingham, 5 May. He denied that colonization would alleviate Irish distress, 7 May 1829. He was not conspicuous in the House during the 1830 session, when he voted for alteration of the Irish vestry regulations, 27 Apr., information on the conduct of the Irish solicitor-general in the Doneraile conspiracy, 12 May, repeal of Irish coal duties, 13 May, the second reading of the Jewish emancipation bill, 17 May, for Irish first fruits to cease to be nominal, 18 May, and for parliamentary reform, 28 May. He condemned additional Irish newspaper duties, 10, 17 May, demanded a 'uniform and equal system' of Irish poor laws, 17 May, and supported Sadler's motion for their introduction, 3 June. He feared that the Scottish and Irish poor removal bill would prevent the poor from obtaining employment in England, 26 May, and welcomed its postponement, 4 June 1830.

He was returned unopposed for county Wicklow at the 1830 general election, when he stressed his support

for emancipation and tax reductions and efforts to improve the condition of the Irish poor.[18] On 9 and 19 Nov. 1830 he defended the running of Fitzwilliam's estates in county Wicklow against the attacks of O'Connell, insisting that recent notices to quit had only been served on his tenants 'to comply with the provisions of the Subletting Act'. (Fitzwilliam's agent later noted that as a result, the tenantry could no longer be relied on to support Grattan in a contest.)[19] He spoke and voted for repeal of the Subletting Act, 11 Nov., when he complained that the 'greater part' of the committee appointed to consider Irish poor laws were hostile to their introduction. He repeatedly urged the necessity of a 'modified system of poor laws' thereafter. Ministers had, of course, listed him among their 'foes' and he voted against them in the crucial division on the civil list, 15 Nov. He defended the Irish grand jury system, 9 Dec. 1830. On 22 Feb. 1831 he resumed his opposition to subsidized emigration from Ireland. He presented a petition from the Wicklow Union for the alteration of tithes and secured information on irregularities which had occurred there over church pluralities, 15 Mar. He welcomed the corporate funds bill, 28 Mar. He considered the military force in Ireland 'sufficient' and hoped ministers would not resort to the Insurrection Act to suppress disturbances, 13 Apr. He voted for the second reading of the Grey ministry's reform bill, 22 Mar., hoped it would 'allay the agitation for repeal of the Union', 29 Mar., and divided against Gascoyne's wrecking amendment, 19 Apr. 1831.

At the ensuing general election he stood as a reformer and was returned unopposed.[20] He voted for the second reading of the reintroduced reform bill, 6 July, and gave generally steady support to its details, though he was in the minority for the disfranchisement of Aldborough, 14 Sept. 1831. On 4 Aug. he berated the anti-reformers for 'repeating, night after night, not the same arguments, for arguments I cannot call them, but the same statement of facts, which have been answered over and over again'. He voted for the third reading, 19 Sept., and passage of the measure, 21 Sept., the second reading of Scottish bill, 23 Sept., and Lord Ebrington's confidence motion, 10 Oct. He condemned the yeomanry for their part in the Newtownbarry affray, 23 June, and warned that the Irish people would not be satisfied until a full investigation had been held, 1 July. He spoke and voted for printing the Waterford petition for disarming the Irish yeomanry, 11 Aug. He demanded that some of the revenues of the Irish church be appropriated for the relief and employment of the poor, 12 July, 14 Sept. He attacked James Gordon for his Protestant speeches against a national system of Irish education, 15 July, 5 Aug. He voted in the minority of 41 for civil list reductions, 18 July, and against the grant to the Society for the Propagation of the Gospels, 25 July. On 8 Aug. he called for inquiry into the Dublin election and voted in the minority to postpone the issue of a new writ. He introduced a bill to exclude all Irish recorders from sitting in Parliament, 10 Aug., but at its second reading, 12 Aug., agreed to defer it until after the Dublin election. On 23 Aug. he again demanded investigation of the Dublin election petition, but he did not vote in either of the divisions regarding the punishment of those guilty of corruption.[21] He welcomed the appointment of lord lieutenants of Irish counties and suggested that clergymen should be barred from the magistracy, 15 Aug. Next day he called for the establishment of an Irish board of trade, believing it would help mitigate agitation for repeal. He spoke and voted for legal provision for the Irish poor, 29 Aug. On 2 Sept. he introduced a bill to provide poor relief in certain cases, which foundered owing to a technical problem with its first clause and went no further.[22] He divided for inquiry into the conduct of the Winchester magistrates during the arrest of the Deacles, 27 Sept. 1831.

Grattan voted for the second reading of the revised reform bill, 17 Dec. 1831, again supported its details, and divided for the third reading, 22 Mar. 1832. He argued for abolition of the system of Protestant freemen in Ireland and reform of the Irish registration system, 19 Jan., and presented a petition for preserving the peculiar franchise of Galway, 16 Feb. He did not vote in the division for an address calling on the king to appoint only ministers who would carry reform unimpaired, 10 May. He voted for the second reading of Irish reform bill, 25 May, but spoke regularly for more Members to be given to Ireland and criticized its registration details, 6, 13 June, when he warned it would 'create dissatisfaction', and 6, 9 July. He demanded revision of the disfranchisement of 40s. freeholders, 13, 29 June, was in the minority for O'Connell's motion to extend the franchise to £5 freeholders, 18 June, and welcomed the enfranchisement of 20 year leaseholders, 25 June. He divided against the liability of Irish electors to pay municipal taxes before they could vote, 29 June 1832. Grattan warned that the present system of Irish tithes would result in 'the downfall of the Protestant religion' and was appointed to the select committee on the issue, 15 Dec. 1831. On 14 Feb. 1832 Lord Ellenborough reported that Lord Grey had told Lord Rosslyn that 'Grattan alone held out' against the committee's report, unless it contained 'a distinct pledge that "the name and

character of tithes" should be done away'.[23] He voted to print the Woollen Grange petition for their abolition, 16 Feb. He advocated inquiry into the Subletting Act, 20 Feb., and argued that Irish juries should be placed on the same footing as English ones, 22 Feb. He insisted that nothing would satisfy the Irish people except the 'future appropriation of the immense revenues of the Irish church', 8 Mar. He divided against the Irish tithes bill that day and steadily thereafter, calling it 'mad and mischievous', 30 Mar., and predicting that it would provoke 'riots and disorders', 6 Apr. On 5 July he unsuccessfully moved for abolition with compensation and urged the establishment of a fund to promote religion and charity. He protested that the reimposition of the Insurrection Act would be 'a most illegal and destructive method of keeping the peace', 31 Mar., and demanded inquiry into the causes of disturbances, 23, 31 May. He voted with ministers for the navy civil departments bill, 6 Apr., but was in the minority against the Irish registry of deeds bill, 9 Apr. He welcomed the new Irish education plan that day and 8 June. On 5 June he presented and endorsed a Dublin petition complaining of the absence of the recorder on parliamentary duty. He divided against Alexander Baring's bill to exclude insolvent debtors from Parliament, 6 June. He spoke and was a minority teller for a tax on absentee landlords to provide permanent provision for the Irish poor, 'not so much for the relief of the poor, as by way of check upon the rich', 19 June, and welcomed the Scottish and Irish vagrants removal bill, 28 June. He divided for coroners' inquests to be made public, 20 June. He voted with government on the Russian – Dutch loan, 12 July and (as a pair) 16 July 1832.

Grattan was returned in second place for county Wicklow as a Liberal at the 1832 general election and sat there until his defeat in 1841. In a letter to *The Times*, 3 Aug. 1835, he denied trying to prevent the public from visiting his father's property, explaining that he had been obliged to put in a gate and keeper 'in consequence of the conduct and disreputable character of many who frequented there'. He married at the age of 60 and died childless in October 1854, when the family estate passed to his brother Henry, Liberal Member for county Meath, 1831-52.[24]

[1] [J. Grant], *Random Recollections of Lords and Commons*, ii. 283-85. [2] See NLI, Grattan mss 3847-53, 5775-9, 14136-63. [3] *Oxford DNB*; Broughton, *Recollections*, ii. 50-51. [4] *The Times*, 7 June 1820. [5] Grattan mss 27805. [6] *Report of Proceedings at Election ... for City of Dublin* (1820), 96. [7] *Dublin Evening Post*, 20 Jan., 13 Feb. 1821. [8] *Black Bk.* (1823), 159; *Session of Parl. 1825*, p. 466. [9] Grattan mss 14132. [10] *The Times*, 6 July 1822. [11] *O'Connell Corresp.* ii. 982. [12] Wellington mss WP1/788/12. [13] *O'Connell Corresp.* iii. 1172.

[14] Dorset RO D/BKL, Bankes jnl. 154 (26 Apr. 1825). [15] *O'Connell Corresp.* iii. 1224. [16] *Dublin Evening Post*, 6, 22 June 1826. [17] *O'Connell Corresp.* iii. 1432. [18] *Dublin Evening Post*, 27 July, 12 Aug. 1830. [19] Fitzwilliam mss, Chaloner to Milton, 14 Jan. 1831. [20] *Dublin Evening Post*, 12 May 1831. [21] *The Times*, 26 Aug. 1831. [22] *O'Connell Corresp.* iv. 1838. [23] *Three Diaries*, 195. [24] *Gent. Mag.* (1854), ii. 624.

P.J.S.

GRAVES, Thomas North, 2nd Bar. Graves [I] (1775–1830), of Bishop's Court, nr. Exeter, Devon and Thanckes, Cornw.

OKEHAMPTON	1812–1818
NEW WINDSOR	16 Feb. 1819–1820
MILBORNE PORT	1820–June 1827

b. 28 May 1775, 1st s. of Adm. Thomas Graves[†], 1st Bar. Graves [I], of Thanckes and Elizabeth, da. and coh. of William Peere Williams of Cadhay, Devon. *educ.* Eton 1788-92; Univ. Coll. Oxf. 1794; I. Temple 1792. *m.* 27 June 1803, Lady Mary Paget, da. of Henry, 1st earl of Uxbridge, 5s. (1 *d.v.p.*) 7da. (1 *d.v.p.*). *suc.* fa. as 2nd Bar. Graves [I] 9 Feb. 1802; kntd. 20 Aug. 1821. *d.* 7 Feb. 1830.

Comptroller of household to duke of Sussex 1804-*d.*; ld. of bedchamber 1813-27; commr. of excise 1827-*d.*

Ensign, E. Devon militia 1794, lt. 1795, capt. 1796; maj. Devon yeomanry 1802, lt.-col. 1823.

Graves, a fat and impoverished courtier, was a target for the low wit of the youngest of his five brothers-in-law, Berkeley Paget*, who reported in 1811:

Mon petit Graves is solely occupied during the morning in instructing ladies in cotillons and in the evening in dancing them. Waltzing also engages his attention. I do flatter myself we shall see him one of these days on the stage. Though in size somewhat similar one cannot well compare him to Shakespeare's elephant in *Troilus and Cressida*. "The Elephant hath joints, but none for courtesy, His legs are for necessity, not for flexure".

A year later, Paget 'heard that the Fat Man had so seriously shaken his huge carcase that he could never hunt again', which 'would be a fortunate event not only for himself, but his horse'. Graves was said to have reacted furiously when Sir John Burke* mocked him after his attempt at an elegant *entrechat* at a ball at Almack's deposited him on the floor, warning that 'if you think I am too old to dance, I consider myself not too old to blow your brains out'. Another of the Paget brothers, Charles, viewed Graves with some distaste, describing him as 'an exemplification in his own person of the sentiment, which he told me he was confident pervaded the breast of mankind in general, *self-interest and self-enjoyment*'. Charles later wrote:

Of his integrity I never had any opinion, if it *suited his purpose* to lie. I therefore never have confided him with anything, though I have always been on the best terms with him on account of his good humour and companionable qualities. But I don't suppose the man exists, who *respects* or *esteems* him. The main support of his character has been his connection with us.[1]

He had sat for Okehampton on the Savile interest and New Windsor on the Castle interest, and in 1820 was returned for Milborne Port by his eldest brother-in-law Lord Anglesey.

He naturally continued to support Lord Liverpool's ministry but, as before, he was an indifferent attender. He was granted a month's leave for private business, 23 June 1820. He voted to defend ministers' conduct towards Queen Caroline, 6 Feb. 1821. He divided against repeal of the additional malt duty, 3 Apr., and disfranchisement of ordnance officials, 12 Apr. In a noisy debate on the army estimates, 11 Apr., he denied William Smith's allegation that he and his cronies 'at the lower part of the House' were only there to heckle Joseph Hume.[2] In October 1821 he applied, though his wife, for a United Kingdom peerage, but Liverpool held out no hope of his obtaining one in the foreseeable future.[3] He divided against more extensive tax reductions, 11 Feb., and dissociated himself and most people of 'rank and fortune' from the Devon petition on that subject, which advocated parliamentary reform, 25 Feb. 1822.[4] He voted against reduction of the salt duties, 28 Feb., and abolition of one of the joint-postmasterships, 13 Mar. When ministers mustered votes against a civil list inquiry, 15 May, he was 'brought down in all haste' and in full uniform from the theatre, where he had attended the king, only to be shut out of the division.[5] He divided against the removal of Catholic peers' disabilities, 30 Apr., and inquiry into the lord advocate's conduct towards the Scottish press, 25 June 1822. Shortly afterwards he accompanied George IV on his visit to Scotland and featured in a comical report of the levee at Edinburgh:

Lord Graves ... told all the men as they entered that they must *kiss hands*. Some who had had the benefit of a grammar school made violent attempts to kiss both in lettered obedience, others who were more elegant and *degages* in their manner, kissed their own hands to the king as they passed him bowing, and at last the king was obliged to order Graves to say '*kiss the king's hand*'.

That autumn Lord John Russell* heard that Graves was 'out of favour' with the king.[6] He voted against repeal of the house tax, 10 Mar., inquiry into the prosecution of the Dublin Orange rioters, 22 Apr., Scottish parliamentary reform, 2 June, and inquiry into delays in chancery, 5 June 1823. Later that year he sought relief from the pressing financial problems created by his large family by asking the king to intervene to secure him a 'lucrative' office, but George IV declined to interfere with government patronage and threw him on the mercy of ministers.[7] He voted against the motion to condemn the prosecution of the Methodist missionary John Smith in Demerara, 11 June 1824. He divided against Catholic relief, 21 Apr., 10 May, and defended Anglesey from criticism of his recent declaration of hostility to it in the current disturbed state of Ireland, 26 May 1825. He voted against the Irish franchise bill, 26 Apr. He divided for the Cumberland annuity bill, 2, 6, 10 June 1825. His name appears on Charles Tennyson's* list of the majority against the third reading of the spring guns bill, 27 Apr. 1826.[8] He was returned unopposed for Milborne Port at the general election that summer.

He divided against Catholic relief, 6 Mar. 1827, after Lord Lowther* had urged the king's private secretary to exert royal pressure on Graves and a fellow courtier to set an example and so 'render the loyal Protestants an effectual support.[9] That June he secured an excise place, which removed him from the House. He was thought to be in line for a United Kingdom peerage at the end of the year, but the honour eluded him.[10] For some time he lived apart from his wife, who was provided with a grace and favour apartment at Hampton Court, although financial necessity rather than marital breakdown may have caused their separation. In January 1830 London society gossip was dominated by a luridly publicized tale that Graves had caught his wife and the infamous duke of Cumberland *in flagrante* at Hampton Court and was 'bent on a divorce'. Lady Graves, it was claimed, had been discovered 'once before with the duke of Cambridge, though the matter was then hushed up'.[11] The following month Graves created a 'prodigious sensation' by cutting his throat, apparently unable to live with the insinuation that he had been bribed to connive in his wife's adultery. A hastily summoned inquest returned a verdict of suicide 'in a sudden fit of delirium', and in the press Cumberland was vilified as Graves's murderer. Most observers dismissed the story of Lady Graves's infidelity as a complete fabrication, concocted by Cumberland's political enemies, and the duke himself vigorously protested his innocence in private. Yet there were some, including Lord Durham, who were prepared to vouch for the fact of Graves's 'discovery' and to attribute his act of self-destruction to his

having been forced 'by the king's command' to make a 'disgraceful and humiliating retraction' of his allegation.[12] Whatever the truth of the matter, at least one contemporary of Graves, John Douglas*, who had known him since their Oxford days, recalled him with affection: 'a more honourable, kinder hearted man does not exist'.[13]

[1] *Paget Brothers* ed. A. Paget, 199, 249, 291, 312-13; *Gronow Reminiscences*, ii. 298. [2] *The Times*, 12 Apr. 1821. [3] Add. 38290, f. 46. [4] *The Times*, 26 Feb. 1822. [5] Ibid. 16 May 1822. [6] *Creevey's Life and Times*, 158; Add. 51679, Russell to Lady Holland, c.20 Oct. 1822. [7] *Geo. IV Letters*, iii. 1132. [8] Norf. RO, Gunton mss 1/21. [9] *Geo. IV Letters*, iii. 1289. [10] Fitzwilliam mss, Grey to Fitzwilliam, 15 Dec. 1827. [11] Bodl. MS. Eng. lett. c. 160, f. 119; *Greville Mems*. i. 362. [12] *Gent. Mag.* (1830), i. 268; *The Times*, 9-12 Feb.; *Greville Mems*. i. 371-2; *Geo. IV Letters*, iii. 1577 and app. pp. 505-8; *Von Neumann Diary*, i. 202, 204; *Lieven Letters*, 212-13; *Arbuthnot Jnl*. ii. 333, 358; *Dyott's Diary*, ii. 70; Grey mss, Durham to Grey, 17 Feb. 1830. [13] Rutland mss (History of Parliament Aspinall transcripts), Douglas to Rutland, 12 Mar. 1830.

D.R.F./T.A.J.

GREENE, Thomas (1794–1872), of Slyne and Whittington Hall, Lancs.

| LANCASTER | 20 Apr. 1824–1852 |
| LANCASTER | 12 Apr. 1853–1857 |

b. 19 Jan. 1794, o.s. of Thomas Greene of Slyne and Whittington and Martha, da. and coh. of Edmund Dawson of Warton. *educ.* Lancaster g.s.; Oriel, Oxf. 1811; G. Inn 1811, called 1819. *m.* 30 Aug. 1820, Henrietta, da. of Sir Henry Russell, 1st bt., of Swallowfield, Berks., 3s. 2da. (1 *d.v.p.*) *suc.* fa. 1810. *d.* 8 Aug. 1872.

Bencher, G. Inn 1838; chairman of ways and means 1841-7; commr. for completion of Palace of Westminster 1848-1852.

Sheriff, Lancs. 1823-4.; constable, Lancaster Castle 1865-*d.*

Greene, whose family had held land in Slyne and Hest Bank since the reign of James I, was raised in Lancashire and London, where his barrister father had chambers in Gray's Inn and a house in Bedford Square.[1] His death (worth £80,000) in December 1810, before arrangements for Greene's Oxford education were finalized, added to his mother's grief, for she intended Geeene to be a 'reading man' and feared that without 'a tutor of zeal and perseverance' he would drift into idleness.[2] Her brother-in-law, the barrister William Long of Marwell Hall, Hampshire, soon secured Greene's admission to Oriel, where he became a lifelong friend of the future canon of St. Paul's, James Ednell Tyler, and gained a third in classics. Slyne had been entrusted to his father's brother-in-law Robert Bradley, with whose son, Robert Greene Bradley, Greene trained as a barrister and special pleader.[3] He was called in 1819, but probably never practised. After returning from a 12-month continental tour in August 1817 (the first of three for which his journals survive),[4] he oversaw the management of his north Lancashire estates, including the development of Hest Bank Quay, and became an active member of Lancaster Pitt Club and the Lancashire grand jury. He took a London house in Seymour Street after his marriage in 1820 and visited Parliament regularly, taking a particular interest in procedures and private bills.[5] He had projected himself as a prospective 'church and state' Member when Lancaster met to address the regent after Peterloo, 13 Sept. 1819, but he delayed his candidature until the death in April 1824 of the sitting Member Gabriel Doveton produced a vacancy. His considerate treatment of his tenants following the collapse in 1822 of Worswick's Lancaster Bank and his successful campaign as sheriff, 1823-4, to keep the assizes at Lancaster, secured him the corporation's backing and the tacit support of the Whig 12th earl of Derby, and his return was unopposed, despite hostile manoeuvring by the Whig 10th duke of Hamilton. On the hustings, Greene approved the policies of Lord Liverpool's administration, but insisted that he was 'not devoted to party and would always vote conscientiously, even if he should differ with them'.[6] His annual income of £4,000 was already stretched by loans to his impecunious brothers-in-law Whitworth and Francis Whitworth Russell, and he appears to have financed his 'lavish' election entertainments through consol sales. He also postponed (to 1830) the outright purchase of land surrounding Whittington Hall, near Kirkby Lonsdale, which he renovated as his country seat. When Parliament was in session he rented various London properties or stayed with the Russells at 27 Charles Street.[7]

In his early parliamentary career Greene tacked between the Tories and Whigs to retain the local support by which he made his seat his own, and gained respect through his endeavours to overhaul tithes legislation by replacing the plethora of local and private Acts with a permissive one tending to a general commutation. The 1824 Cockerham tithe bill that he promoted was shelved, 31 May, but a Lancaster one entrusted to him, 4 June, received royal assent on the 17th. He voted against condemning the indictment in Demerara of the Methodist missionary John Smith, 11 June, an emotive issue on account of Lancaster's many Dissenters and declining West India trade. He divided for the Irish insurrection bill, 14 June 1824, to outlaw the Catholic Association, 25 Feb. 1825, and

against relief, 1 Mar., 21 Apr. He voted for the duke of Cumberland's grant, 30 May, 2, 10 June, and against the spring guns bill, 21 June. His maiden speech on 2 Mar. was an endorsement of the petition he presented against the Liverpool-Manchester railway bill, and showed his thorough knowledge of the locality and understanding of legal precedents. It also drew a barbed reply from the president of the board of trade Huskisson, who had reluctantly supported the measure as a Liverpool Member. He presented a protectionist petition from Kirkby Lonsdale against relaxation of the corn laws, 28 Apr., spoke and was a majority teller against amending the church lands exchange bill, 21 June, and was instrumental in carrying private bills that session to protect the Peruvian Mining Company, the Arigna Iron and Coal Company, the Cornwall Mining and Smelting Company and the Atlantic and Pacific Junction and Ship Canal Company.[8] Invited and briefed by the leader of the House Canning, he seconded the address, 2 Feb. 1826, in an erudite endorsement of government commercial and foreign policy, and called for the establishment of joint-stock banks and additional legislation restricting small bank notes.[9] He chaired the anti-Catholic Estcourt's London committee when he came in for Oxford University that month and rallied in defence of lord chancellor Eldon in the Commons, 21 Apr.[10] Obliged from the outset to deny reports that he was standing down at Lancaster, he sought the assistance of Charles Russell* and Henry Russell as speechwriters at the general election in June, and saw off his challengers to come in unopposed, with Hamilton's grudging acquiescence.[11]

Greene was absent from the division on Catholic relief, 6 Mar., but voted for information on chancery arrears, 5 Apr. 1827. Little is known of his political allegiance during Canning's premiership, but he congratulated Derby's grandson Edward George Geoffrey Smith Stanley* on his appointment as the Goderich ministry's colonial under-secretary, and accepted a summons from Huskisson, as their leader in the Commons, to attend in 1828.[12] He presented the Lancaster Dissenters' petitions for repeal of the Test Acts, 20, 25 Feb. 1828 (as previously, 6 June 1827), and voted thus, 26 Feb. He divided with the duke of Wellington's ministry against investigating chancery arrears, 24 Apr., and against Catholic relief, 12 May, and ordnance reductions, 4 July 1828. His tithes commutation bill, in essence a redraft of one he had agreed to postpone in 1827, was his main preoccupation that session. He had introduced it, 1 Feb. 1828, after prior consultation with the lawyers William Fuller Boteler and Henry Brougham*, and he felt unjustly treated when the home secretary Peel wrecked it with a restrictive amendment, 17 Mar.[13] On 6 June he brought up the Lancaster West India planters' petition against legislative change and for inquiry into the condition of slaves. He waited on Peel, as expected, during his north-western tour in October 1828, and took a house in New Street for the 1829 session.[14] The patronage secretary Planta correctly considered his support for the concession of Catholic emancipation 'doubtful'. He spoke of the alarm it had provoked in the North on introducing a hostile petition from Ulverston, 12 Feb., and presented and endorsed others, 2, 10 Mar., when Smith Stanley, representing the Lancaster emancipationists, disputed his statements.[15] Lancaster corporation, however, passed a resolution thanking Greene for accurately representing their views, 13 Mar.[16] He divided against the relief bill, 6, 18, 23, 27 Mar., denounced it that day and on the 30th as a threat to the Protestant establishment, but praised English Catholics, 27 Mar. He gave his vote to Peel against the Ultra Inglis at the Oxford University by-election. He brought up petitions against the truck bill, 28 Apr., and butlerage on wine imports, 25 May. Greene saw nothing unconstitutional in *ad hoc* enfranchisements of manufacturing towns, and voted to transfer East Retford's seats to Birmingham, 5 May, 2 June 1829, 5, 15 Mar. 1830. He divided against Lord Blandford's reform proposals, 18 Feb., but voted to enfranchise Birmingham, Leeds and Manchester, 23 Feb. 1830. The tithes bill he introduced, 8 Feb., conceded the 21-year rule on which his last one had foundered, but still attracted criticism and had to be abandoned.[17] On 22 Mar. he presented several petitions against the St. Helens-Runcorn Gap railway bill. He voted against abolishing the death penalty for forgery, 7 June, and to restrict on-consumption under the sale of beer bill, 1 July, to which he also recommended adding a clause clarifying the law on drunkenness, but Brougham scotched the proposal. He voted against an amendment to the administration of justice bill reducing judges' salaries, 7 July 1830. A severe inflammation of the trachea had kept him away from the House for six weeks from April to June and it frustrated his hopes of canvassing early at the general election that summer, when his colleague Cawthorne's local opponents forced a poll. Accused on the hustings of neglecting constituency interests, Greene made illness the excuse for his 'poor' voting record and claimed that, though absent from the published lists, he had voted against the Bathurst and Dundas pensions, 26 Mar. 1830, 'at great peril to his health'. He defended his conduct as a local Member and, taking the same line as Charles Russell, he called for the enfranchisement of the

manufacturing towns and 'measures to do away with the need for violent reform' and end the East India Company's trading monopoly.[18]

Ministers listed Greene among their 'friends', but he was absent when they were brought down on the civil list, 15 Nov. 1830. Adopting a higher local profile, he presented numerous Lancashire petitions for the abolition of colonial slavery, 3 Nov., 17, 21 Dec., and against the truck system, 21 Dec., and urged inquiry into tithes, 13 Dec., and abolition of the tax on printed calicoes, 17 Dec. 1830. He brought up petitions opposing the Liverpool-Leeds and Liverpool-Chorlton railway bills, 15, 28, 29 Mar., and alterations in the timber duties, 17 Mar., and in favour of the Warrington-Newton railway bill, 15 Apr. Greene, like Russell, accepted reform as inevitable, but he kept a pragmatic silence on the issue until after the Lancaster by-election of 14 Mar. 1831, when Hamilton's nominee Patrick Stewart was returned unopposed as a reformer.[19] As requested by the Lancaster meeting, 15 Mar., he joined Stewart on the 19th in endorsing its petition in favour of the Grey ministry's reform bill, expressed relief that his constituents shared his views and said that although he was unwilling to 'pledge myself to the whole of the details', he 'fully approved' the principle of the bill.[20] He divided for it at its second reading, 22 Mar., and against Gascoyne's wrecking amendment, 19 Apr. His ecclesiastical lands exchange bill (a redraft of the 1825 measure) became a casualty of the dissolution. Having circulated his 1830 election speech as proof that he was 'no reformer of convenience or recent convert', he contested Lancaster as a 'moderate reformer' at the general election in May 1831, and came in unopposed with Stewart. On the hustings he called for the enfranchisement of the manufacturing towns and a property-based franchise and praised the bill as a means of preventing more sweeping reforms. He confirmed his opposition to the ballot and colonial slavery, but conceded that immediate abolition was unsustainable.[21]

Greene divided for the reintroduced reform bill at its second reading, 6 July, and supported it fairly steadily in committee, where his wayward votes for the enfranchisement of borough freeholders in counties corporate, 17 Aug., and £50 tenants-at-will, 18 Aug., and his commitment to denying votes to weekly tenants and lodgers, 25 Aug. 1831, confirmed his conservative approach to reform. He insisted that his vote for the amendment preserving freemen's voting rights, 30 Aug., was 'in full accordance with the best principle of the bill' and that the gradual extinction of the freeman vote would soon halve the Lancaster electorate. Later that day, ostensibly to avoid the 'complication' of divided parishes, he suggested amending the seven-mile residence rule by including an entire parish within its remit if 'any portion' was within the limit, but the bill's architect Lord John Russell would have none of it. He divided for the bill's passage, 21 Sept., and Lord Ebrington's confidence motion, 10 Oct. He voted for the second reading of the revised reform bill, 17 Dec. 1831. Finding Lord Althorp's summons to attend on 20 Jan. 1832 inconvenient, he wrote to Estcourt on the 13th seeking a pair and to sound him on his proposal for a bill giving all illegitimate children, wherever born, the parish of settlement of their mother. (He did not proceed with it.)[22] He received ten days' leave on account of illness in his family, 23 Jan. 1832. From 8 Feb., with the exception of the Gateshead enfranchisement, 5 Mar., he divided steadily for the bill's details, its third reading, 22 Mar., and the address calling on the king to appoint only ministers who would carry it unimpaired, 10 May. He voted for Alexander Baring's bill to deny insolvent debtors parliamentary privilege, 27 June, and with government on the Russian-Dutch loan, 12, 20 July.[23] The Irish secretary Smith Stanley approved his candidature for Lancaster, and requesting his support in the new Lancashire North constituency at the general election in December 1832, he added that the general opinion was that 'though not a supporter of Lord Grey's government in the sense in which that word is generally used, you had always supported measures of reform, both before and during his administration'.[24]

Greene reintroduced his ecclesiastical corporations bill on 22 June and 9 Dec. 1831, but he no longer had the full support of the archbishop of Canterbury and it did not progress beyond its first reading.[25] He fully endorsed petitions he introduced against the factory bill from the proprietors and employees of Lancaster's Dolphinholme spinning mill, 30 July, 8 Aug. 1831, 7, 14 Mar. 1832, when, citing an erroneous report in *The Times*, he insisted that he opposed the employment of young children.[26] He presented Lancaster's petition for the anatomy bill, 23 Feb. As one of the visiting magistrates, he refuted allegations by the radical Nathan Broadhurst and his fellow petitioners of maltreatment in Lancaster gaol, 27 Mar., and justified the practice of putting prisoners to work and opening their mail on grounds of economy and security. He objected to receiving petitions from debtors imprisoned at Lancaster, because they had approached the House before informing the magistrates of their grievances, 4 Apr. 1832.

The Whig *Lancaster Herald* had repeatedly taken Greene to task for appealing to both sides in his speeches at corporation and reform meetings, 1831-2, and it scrutinized his conduct closely throughout the protracted canvass at the 1832 general election, when his pro-reform votes and judicious declarations against the ballot, slavery, monopolies, and opposition to removing the assizes and to capital punishment for non-violent crimes enabled him to see off a second Liberal and secure an unopposed return with Stewart.[27] He reverted to Conservatism soon afterwards.[28] His appointment as chairman of ways and means in 1841 was made by Peel on Stanley's recommendation and with bipartisan support.[29] The consequent 'distraction' from constituency business, his endorsement of corn law repeal and involvement with the troubled Lancaster Joint-Stock Banking Company almost cost him his seat in 1847, and he was defeated in 1852, after devoting the previous four years to overseeing the completion of the new Houses of Parliament.[30] He was re-elected in 1853 but retired in 1857. He died at Whittington in August 1872 after a long illness, and was succeeded there by his eldest son and residuary legatee Dawson Cornelius Greene (1822-87).[31] By his will, dated 30 July 1869 and proved in London, 4 Sept. 1872, his widow (*d.* 1882) received an additional £400 a year drawn on his Southwark property, his second son Thomas Huntley Greene (1823-87) £10,500 in stocks, and his youngest son Henry Aylmer Greene (1827-77) £14,000.[32]

[1] *VCH Lancs.* viii. 138. [2] PROB 11/1518/20; IR26/167/153; Lancs. RO, Dawson Greene mss DDGr C9, bdle. 1, Martha Greene to Mrs. Long, 12, 22 Dec. 1810, 1 Jan. 1811. [3] Dawson Greene mss C9, bdle. 1, Martha Greene to Mrs. Long, 18 Feb. 1812, 30 Jan. 1816; C10, E. Coppleston to Greene, 1 June 1821. [4] Ibid. C8, bdle. 3; C9, bdle. 1, Martha Greene to Mrs. Long, 8 Oct. 1816; F5, *passim*. [5] Dawson Greene mss A5; C7, bdle. 2; Lancs. RO HS3 (1820-4); *VCH Lancs.* viii. 94-95, 137. [6] *The Times*, 21 Sept. 1819; Dawson Greene mss C7, bdle. 2, Greene to Bradley, 29 Feb. 1820; HLRO, Thomas Greene mss GRE/4/1-7; *Lancaster Gazette*, 1 June, 19 Oct. 1822, 29 Mar., 5 Apr., 31 May 1823, 3, 10, 17, 24 Apr.; *The Times*, 24 Apr. 1824. [7] Dawson Greene mss A5; C10, Greene to Wheeler, 18 July, 13, 20 Oct. 1824, 23 Mar. 1825; C20, W. to H. Russell, 28 Jan. 1822 and *passim*; *VCH Lancs.* viii. 246. [8] *The Times*, 22 Mar., 29 Apr., 22 June 1825. [9] Greene mss 4/8-11. [10] *Morning Chron.* 8-10, 13, 15, 17, 20 Feb. 1826; Glos. RO, Sotherton Estcourt mss D1571 X 27. [11] *Lancaster Gazette*, 10 Mar., 7, 21 May 1825, 18, 25 Feb., 10, 24 June 1826; Bodl. Ms. Eng. lett. c. 159, ff. 36-46; Greene mss 4/12. [12] Derby mss 920 Der (14) box 61, Greene to Smith Stanley, 29 Oct. 1827; Greene mss 4/14. [13] *The Times*, 7, 23 June; Brougham mss, Greene to Brougham, 31 Dec. 1827; Greene mss 4/13, 15. [14] *Lancaster Gazette*, 18, 25 Oct. 1828; Herefs. RO, diaries of John Biddulph of Ledbury [Biddulph diary] G2/IV/J55, 27 Feb.; Derby mss (14) box 63, Greene to Smith Stanley, 3 Mar. 1829. [15] Derby mss (14) box 63, T. Higgin to Smith Stanley, 28 Feb.; Greene mss 4/16. [16] *Lancaster Gazette*, 21 Mar. 1829. [17] *Sunday Times*, 7 Mar.; *Lancaster Gazette*, 3 Apr. 1830; R.H. Jago, *Letter to T. Greene* (1830). [18] Bodl. Ms. Eng. lett. c. 160, f. 165;

Lancaster Gazette, 3, 10, 17, 24, 31 July, 7 Aug. 1830. [19] Bodl. MS. Eng. lett. d. 153, f. 24. [20] *Lancaster Gazette*, 26 Mar. 1831. [21] Ibid. 30 Apr., 7 May, *Lancaster Herald*, 7 May 1831. [22] Sotherton Estcourt mss D1571, f. 209. [23] *The Times*, 14 July 1832. [24] Greene mss 4/20, 25. [25] Ibid. 4/17, 18. [26] *The Times*, 8 Mar. 1832. [27] Greene mss 4/21; *Lancaster Herald*, 1, 15, 22 Oct., 5 Nov. 1831, 23 June, 29 Sept.; *Lancaster Gazette*, 14 July, 15 Sept., 20, 27 Oct.; *The Times*, 11, 13 Dec. 1832. [28] Greene mss 4/23, 27-31, 37. [29] Ibid. 4/64-70. [30] Derby mss (14) box 65/8, Greene to Stanley, 25 Sept., 3, 24 Nov. 1841, 19, 23 Aug. 1844, 8 Nov. 1847; Greene mss 4/40-60. [31] *Lancaster Gazette*, 10, 17 Aug.; *The Times*, 12 Aug.; *Lancaster Guardian*, 7 Sept. 1872. [32] IR26/2732/742.

M.M.E.

GREENHILL RUSSELL, Robert (1763-1836), of Chequers Court, Ellesborough, Bucks. and 4 Stone Buildings, Lincoln's Inn, Mdx.

THIRSK   1806–1832

b. 1763, o. surv. ch. of Rev. John Russell Greenhill, LLD, rect. of Fringford, Oxon., and Elizabeth, da. and h. of Matthew Noble of Sunderland, co. Dur. *educ.* Westminster 1773; Christ Church, Oxf. 1780; L. Inn 1780, called 1790. *unm. suc.* fa. 1813; to estates of the late Sir George Russell, 10th bt., of Chequers Court and took additional surname of Russell by sign manual 13 May 1815; *cr.* bt. 15 Sept. 1831. *d.* 12 Dec. 1836.

Russell continued to occupy one of the Thirsk seats throughout this period under the patronage of his uncle Sir Thomas Frankland†, and later of his cousin and fellow Member Robert Frankland. He was a less diligent attender than in the past, but continued to vote with the Whig opposition to Lord Liverpool's ministry on all major issues. He divided against them on the civil list, 5, 8 May, and the barrack agreement bill, 17 July 1820. He voted against Wilberforce's resolution urging Queen Caroline to compromise, 22 June 1820, for the restoration of her name to the liturgy, 23, 26 Jan., 14 Feb., and to condemn ministers' conduct towards her, 6 Feb. 1821. He divided for Catholic relief, 28 Feb. He voted for repeal of the additional malt duty, 3 Apr., and of the Blasphemous and Seditious Libels Act, 8 May 1821. He divided for Sir Robert Wilson's motion complaining of his removal from the army, 13 Feb. 1822. He presented a petition from the farmers of Ellesborough complaining of agricultural distress, 19 Feb. He voted for more extensive tax reductions, 21 Feb., abolition of the one of the joint-postmasterships, 14 Mar., 2 May, inquiry into the duties of officers of the board of control, 14 Mar., and reduction of the cost of the embassy to the Swiss cantons, 16 May. He divided for Lord John Russell's reform scheme, 25 Apr., and against the aliens bill, 5 June 1822. He voted for repeal of the Foreign Enlistment Act, 16 Apr., Russell's reform motion, 24 Apr., and reform

in Scotland, 2 June 1823. He divided for inquiry into the state of Ireland, 11 May 1824. He paired for Catholic claims, 1 Mar., and voted for it, 10 May 1825. He divided against the duke of Cumberland's annuity bill, 10 June 1825. There are no recorded votes for the 1826 session.

He divided for Catholic relief, 6 Mar., and against Canning's coalition ministry for the disfranchisement of Penryn, 28 May 1827. He voted for repeal of the Test Acts, 26 Feb., and Catholic relief, 12 May 1828. That summer, and again two years later, he applied unsuccessfully to the prime minister, the duke of Wellington, for the restoration of the Russell family baronetcy.[1] He divided for the government's Catholic emancipation bill, 6, 30 Mar., and the transfer of East Retford's seats to Birmingham, 5 May 1829. His only known vote in the next session was for Jewish emancipation, 17 May 1830. After the general election that summer the ministry listed him as one of their 'foes', but he was absent from the crucial division on the civil list, 15 Nov. 1830. He presented several anti-slavery petitions, 23 Nov. 1830. He divided for the second reading of the Grey ministry's reform bill, 22 Mar., and against Gascoyne's wrecking amendment, 19 Apr. 1831. He voted for the second reading of the reintroduced bill, 6 July, and three of its details, but he presented a hostile petition from his constituents, 14 July 1831. On the motion that Thirsk be included in schedule B, 30 July, he made his only known speech in this period, in which he explained that while he 'agreed generally in the principle of the bill', he believed that Thirsk's economic importance entitled it to return two Members. He also dwelt on an 'irregularity' in the 1821 census return, but did not press his objections to a division. He voted for the bill's passage, 21 Sept., the second reading of the Scottish bill, 23 Sept., and Lord Ebrington's confidence motion, 10 Oct. He voted to punish only those found guilty of bribery at the Dublin election and against the motion accusing the Irish administration of using undue influence, 23 Aug. He divided for the second reading of the revised reform bill, 17 Dec. 1831, three of its details, and the third reading, 22 Mar. 1832. He voted for an address asking the king to appoint only ministers committed to carrying an undiluted measure, 10 May, and for the second reading of the Irish bill, 25 May. He divided with ministers on relations with Portugal, 9 Feb., and voted or paired with them on the Russian-Dutch loan, 12, 16, 20 July. He voted to make coroners' inquests public, 20 June 1832.

With Robert Frankland filling the one remaining seat at Thirsk after the Reform Act, Greenhill Russell, who had been awarded a baronetcy in the coronation honours of 1831, retired at the dissolution in 1832. He died in December 1836, when his title became extinct. He left his Chequers estate, which he had 'modernized with great taste', to his 'old and valued friend' Frankland; his personalty was sworn under £140,000.[2]

[1] Wellington mss WP1/946/25; 1139/21. [2] *Gent. Mag.* (1837), i. 204; G. Lipscomb, *Bucks.* ii. 198; PROB 11/1871/36; IR26/1460/242.

M.P.J.C.

GREGSON, John (1793–1860), of 18 Bedford Row and 1 Cumberland Street, Portman Square, Mdx.

SALTASH   1830–17 Feb. 1831

?b. 30 Nov. 1793, illegit. s. of John Gregson of Sunderland and Jane Carr of Durham.[1] adm. attorney 25 Nov. 1816. *?unm. d.* 9 Dec. 1860.

This Member has been erroneously identified elsewhere as John Gregson (1805-79) of Burdon and Murton, Durham, a barrister practising on the northern circuit, who succeeded his father and namesake to the family estates a few miles south of Sunderland in 1840.[2] In fact, he was almost certainly the illegitimate son of one John Gregson (then of Sunderland), who was born in 1793 but only 'received into the church' at St. Nicholas, Durham, on 15 Mar. 1801. Unfortunately, it has not proved possible to identify Gregson's father with absolute certainty: he may also have been the father of the John Gregson of Burdon mentioned above, a Durham attorney and sometime deputy registrar of Durham chancery court, whose marriage to Elizabeth Allgood, 15 Sept. 1800, could conceivably have had a bearing on the churching of the illegitimate John Gregson; but another likely candidate is John Gregson (1770-1835), of St. Oswald, Durham, the son of the Rev. John Gregson of nearby Brancepeth, who married Elizabeth Harrison of Bishopwearmouth at St. Nicholas, Durham, 1 Nov. 1795, and had three legitimate sons.[3] This Member was articled to the Sunderland attorney Robert Davison in August 1810, transferred to William Grey of 2 Holborn Court, Gray's Inn, London, 'for the remainder of the term', 9 Feb. 1815, and was admitted an attorney in king's bench in November 1816. By the following year he was in partnership with William Whitton at Verulam Buildings, Gray's Inn, and subsequently at Bedford Row. In the 1820s he became the attorney of William Russell* of Brancepeth and was involved in managing his client's borough interests at Bletchingley and Saltash.[4] At the general election of 1830 he was returned by Russell for Saltash, but

this was merely 'a temporary arrangement' until the political situation became clearer.[5]

In acknowledgement of Russell's opposition politics, the duke of Wellington's ministry listed Gregson as one of their 'foes', but while he had intended to vote against them in the crucial division on the civil list, 15 Nov. 1830, he was by some mischance shut out of the lobby.[6] Before he was able to make any mark in the House, he was obliged to vacate his seat for Philip Crampton, the Irish solicitor-general in Lord Grey's ministry.[7] Gregson evidently took sole charge of the Bedford Row practice following Whitton's death in 1832, and this remained the case until about 1856, when John D'Urban became his partner. In 1850 he was acting as attorney to the 3rd marquess of Londonderry.[8] According to his death certificate, he died of 'homiplegia' in December 1860, 'aged 67'. He left two-thirds of his real and personal estate to D'Urban and the remainder to D'Urban's sister Elizabeth Jane, for whom he had already made some provision by a separate deed.

[1] IGI (Durham). [2] W.P. Courtney, *Parl. Rep. Cornw.* 163; G.P. Judd, *Members of Parliament, 1734-1832,* p. 212. There is a detailed genealogy of this family in *Burke LG.* [3] These speculations are based on information contained in the IGI and the library of the Society of Genealogists. The will of John Gregson (d. 1840), of Burdon, proved at Durham and summarized in the death duty register (IR26/1548/651), makes no mention of any illegitimate children. According to the index of wills (IR27/237), details of the estate of John Gregson of South Shields (as he was at the time of his death in 1835) were registered at IR26/1415/159, but no such entry was in fact made. [4] Lincs. AO, Tennyson D'Eyncourt mss Td'E H1/105; H98/24. [5] Ibid. 2 Td'E H89/8; Brougham mss, Durham to Brougham, 7 Sept. 1830. [6] *The Times,* 18 Nov. 1830. [7] NLS, Ellice mss, Ellice to Russell, 25 Dec., reply, 27 Dec. 1830. [8] Surr. Hist. Cent. Goulburn mss, box 45, Hardinge to Goulburn, 11 Nov. 1850.

D.R.F.

GRENFELL, Pascoe (1761–1838), of Taplow House, Bucks and 19 Charles Street, St James's, Mdx.

GREAT MARLOW   14 Dec. 1802–1820

PENRYN   1820–1826

b. 3 Sept. 1761, 1st s. of Pascoe Grenfell, commissary to the States of Holland, of Marazion, Cornw. and Mary, da. of William Tremenheere, attorney, of Penzance. *educ.* Truro g.s. 1777. *m.* (1) 26 Aug. 1786, his cos. Charlotte (d. 2 May 1790), da. of George Granville, otherwise Grenfell, of Kentish Town, Mdx.,[1] 2s. 1da.; (2) 15 Jan. 1798, Hon. Georgiana St. Leger, da. of St. Leger, 1st Visct. Doneraile [I], 2s. 10da. (3 *d.v.p.*). *suc.* fa. 1810. *d.* 23 Jan. 1838.
  Dir. R. Exchange Assurance Co. 1789-1829, gov. 1829-*d.*

Grenfell had prospered as the associate and partner in the copper trade of the Williams family, to whom he owed the seat for Great Marlow which he had occupied as a Grenvillite Whig and loquacious financial pundit since 1802. His partnership with Owen Williams, the other Member for Marlow, in the London copper agency at Castle Baynard wharf, Upper Thames Street continued, and he operated profitable smelting concerns in the Swansea area of South Wales.[2] Shortly before the dissolution in 1820 he learned that his seat was required by Williams for his own son. Grenfell sought assistance from his mentor Lord Grenville, who proved unwilling to appeal directly to Lord Liverpool's ministry for electoral support for a man who, while he had supported the recent repressive legislation and 'declared [his] hostility to the visionary projects of change in our constitution now afloat under the specious name of parliamentary reform', was in general their opponent. Nevertheless, Grenville gave his written blessing and authorized such discreet use of it as seemed appropriate. Grenfell, whose rumoured candidature for Hull came to nothing, kept this letter in reserve for a possible bid for the Court interest at Windsor, but looked first to the open and venal Cornish borough of Penryn, having been promised the limited influence of the Tory Lord De Dunstanville. He supposed that his credentials 'as a Cornishman, and a considerable purchaser of the produce of the Cornish mines' gave him a 'fair' chance.[3] He comfortably topped the poll, reportedly without resorting to bribery.[4]

He continued to attend regularly and acted with the Whig opposition on many issues, although his record on economy and retrenchment motions was mixed and he remained lukewarm about parliamentary reform. He divided for Catholic relief, 28 Feb. 1821, 1 Mar., 21 Apr., 10 May 1825. On 28 Apr. 1820 he secured a return of bank notes in circulation, as he did in successive sessions of the 1820 Parliament.[5] He condemned the 'most disgraceful manner' in which the £5,000,000 issue of exchequer bills had been conducted, 31 May, but changed his tune, 9 June, when he approved it, though he criticized (as was his wont) the 'delusion' of the current sinking fund system. In moving, as he did every year, for an account of public balances in the Bank of England and its administrative charges, 13 June, he professed to hope that 'the warfare between the Bank ... and himself was over', now that the Advances Act of 1819 had significantly reduced its holdings. Yet he argued that further reductions could be effected, and throughout this Parliament he persisted in his personal crusade against the Bank's exorbitant profits from its public transactions.[6] He

blamed recent Irish bank failures on the 'false system of paper currency', 16 June. He endorsed the prayer of the London merchants' free trade petition, 8 May. He reaffirmed his aversion to the 'wild theory' of parliamentary reform, 19 May, but supported the proposed disfranchisement of Grampound, though he disliked the idea of giving its seats to Leeds rather than to a county; he spoke to the same effect, 6 June 1820.[7] At the London merchants' meeting in support of Queen Caroline, 24 Jan. 1821, he moved the vote of thanks to the lord mayor.[8] He admitted that his objections to parliamentary reform had been 'considerably shaken' by the government and the House's disregard of public opinion in the matter, 31 Jan., and as 'a moderate man' he promised to support any acceptable 'moderate plan of reform'. He explained that he approved the Grampound disfranchisement bill because it 'applied a proper punishment to an acknowledged abuse', 12 Feb. However, he did not vote for Lambton and Russell's general reform motions later that session. He opposed Burdett's demand for inquiry into Peterloo and stood by his votes for the Six Acts, 15 May. He resumed his attack on the 'delusive' aspect of the sinking fund, 1 Feb., but defended the 1819 currency settlement, 22, 27 Feb., 28 Mar.[9] He took up his familiar refrain that 'the only sinking fund that could ever be applicable to the reduction of the [national] debt, must be the surplus of the income over the expenditure of the country', 3 Apr. On the third reading of the cash payments bill, 12 Apr., he borrowed from the late Frank Horner[†] to describe the transactions between the Bank and government as 'a scene of rapacity on the part of the directors, and of extravagance and profligacy on the part of the chancellor of the exchequer'. He seconded Parnell's motion for inquiry into trade with Ireland and called for assimilation of the two currencies, 19 Apr. He was a teller for the small minority who wished to permit Catholics to become directors of the Bank of Ireland, 13 June. Although he advocated 'every description of rigid retrenchment' to 'restore public tranquillity', 12 Feb., he voted for the duke of Clarence's grant, 18 June. He opposed Curwen's plan to tax stock transfers, 5 Mar., and voted against repeal of the additional malt duty, 3 Apr. He was a stern critic of the 'unwarranted' grant of £20,000 to Desfourneaux for losses sustained at Guadeloupe, 8, 13, 21, 28 June, when he moved and was a teller for a successful amendment to reduce it to £3,500.[10]

Grenfell was in the opposition minority on the address, 5 Feb., yet voted with ministers against more extensive tax reductions, 11, 21 Feb. 1822. He gave 'hearty support' to admiralty reductions, 1 Mar., and called for repeal of the 'most objectionable' salt tax,

1 Apr., 30 May, 2 June.[11] Infuriated by the proposal to pay the Bank for handling the conversion of the navy five per cents, 4 Mar., he moved a nullifying amendment which was defeated by 76-39; he had more to say on this, 7, 8, 11 Mar., though he considered the plan itself to be 'fair and just'.[12] He brought up and endorsed a Berkshire petition against renewal of the Bank's chartered monopoly, 31 May. He failed to persuade the chancellor to include revision of the sinking fund in the remit of the select committee on public accounts, 18 Apr.[13] He dissented from Hume's call for abolition of the fund, 25 July, but conceded that it operated injuriously in time of war. He gave guarded approval to the government scheme for military and naval pensions, 1 May, but secured the adoption of an amendment to empower the national debt commissioners to use their funds to buy those annuities, 3 June. He largely dissented from the arguments of a Cornwall agriculturists' distress petition, 22 Apr., maintaining that difficulties were localized and that the economy was reviving. He welcomed Bennet's alehouses licensing bill, 14 May, and regretted ministers' abandonment of the warehousing bill, 21 June 1822.[14] He warned Maberly and Hume that he 'by no means concurred' in their proposals for draconian tax remissions, 24 Feb., and he voted accordingly, 3 Mar. 1823. He condemned the coastwise coal duties, 10, 24 Mar.[15] He supported the national debt reduction bill and dismissed Ricardo's property tax 'crotchet', 11 Mar. He divided with ministers for the debt reduction bill, 13 Mar., and against repeal of the assessed taxes, 18 Mar. He was now a relentless opponent of the bill to entrust management of the dead weight military pensions fund to the Bank, which would be made thereby 'a jobber and speculator in public securities'; he unsuccessfully divided the House against it, 11, 14, 18 Apr.[16] He voted with government in the controversy over the prosecution of the Dublin Orange rioters, 24 Mar.[17] He advocated Catholic emancipation, 16 Apr. He divided for Scottish parliamentary reform, 2 June, and paired for inquiry into arrears in chancery, 7 June 1823. He presented a constituency petition against the coal duties, 9 Feb., and pressed for their repeal, 23 Feb., 29 Mar. 1824.[18] He exhorted ministers to support repeal of the usury laws, 16 Feb., 31 Mar. He attended the London merchants' meeting which petitioned for revision of the corn laws, 13 Apr.[19] On 25 Feb. he obtained leave by 78-30 to introduce the St. Katharine's Docks bill, which some irregularities forced him to reintroduce, 22 Mar.; he carried its second reading by 74-55, 2 Apr. He explained that reports of the scale of housing clearance required had been grossly exaggerated, 15 Apr., but the weight of petitioning against the bill

blocked its progress that session. He supported the South London Docks bill, 3 May.[20] He approved the West India Company bill provided it did not harm the slaves, 10 May. Though 'a friend to liberal principles', he opposed the marine insurance bill as a threat to the chartered rights of Lloyds and his own Royal Exchange Assurance Company, 17, 27, 28 May, 3, 11, 14 June.[21] He was named to the select committee on the private business of the House, 27 May, after applauding Hume's exposure of an unsatisfactory system which was 'a complete denial of justice'. He presented and endorsed a Falmouth petition condemning the prosecution of the Methodist missionary John Smith in Demerara, 10 June, explaining that 'he was neither a Methodist nor a fanatic, and most certainly not a Saint', but that as a Christian he considered the slaves 'the most wretched of the human species'. He voted in the ministerial majority for the Irish insurrection bill, 14 June. He called for 'great public officers' to be provided with adequate pensions, 21 June 1824.

On 15 Feb. 1825 Grenfell expressed support for the bill to suppress the Catholic Association, which 'impeded the pure stream of justice', but he raised eyebrows with his 'fervent prayer' for successful Irish Catholic resistance to their being 'oppressed, injured, insulted [and] trampled upon' by the Protestant majority. Six days later he recanted and opposed the measure. He carried the second reading of his reintroduced St. Katharine's Docks bill by 119-30, 22 Feb., though his own vote was subsequently disallowed after he admitted being a subscriber to the scheme. He said he wanted Members with vested interests in opposing private bills to be prevented from voting on them, 23 Feb., 10 Mar. He steered the docks bill through the Commons and it gained royal assent, 10 June.[22] He spoke and was a majority teller for the London and Westminster oil gas bill, 22 Feb.[23] He objected to the practice of giving joint-stock companies and their officials mutual suing powers, 28 Feb., and called for regulation of 'these speculations', 29 Mar. He introduced a bill to empower the Royal Exchange Company to grant mortgages, 10 Mar.; it became law, 2 May.[24] Having been one of a small deputation who lobbied ministers on their plans to reduce the copper duties, he applauded the 'liberal principles' which lay behind this, 11 Mar., but advised caution.[25] He divided for revision of the corn laws, 28 Apr. He approved the government's plan to assimilate the English and Irish currencies, 12 May. He called for 'some remedy' for the chaos produced by repeal of the combination laws, 31 May.[26] In October 1825 he was one of a number of supporters of Catholic relief who advised the Catholic Association not to petition on the subject in the forthcoming session of Parliament.[27] About this time he informed his constituents that he would not offer at the next general election, as he stood no chance of success without resorting to illegal practices.[28] On the address, 2 Feb. 1826, Grenfell, the words doubtless sticking in his throat, praised the Bank directors for their 'liberal' intervention to deal with the recent financial crisis. Yet a week later he could not resist criticizing the Bank's profits and inordinate remuneration for its public services. He largely accepted the emergency legislation on banking and the currency, 20, 27 Feb., though he privately confessed to Grenville a recent 'inclination' towards a silver standard.[29] He was named to the select committee on Irish and Scottish small notes, 16 Mar., and was a dissentient from its chairman Peel's report recommending no change.[30] He urged ministers to encourage the Bank to make its notes as difficult to forge as possible, 21 Mar. He demanded an end to the prohibition on the export of machinery, 5 May. On 2 Mar. Lord John Russell noticed in the House Grenfell's earlier address to his constituents and invited him to support his bill to prevent electoral bribery: the reply was that he had said nothing to 'prevent him from opposing ... any innovation, founded upon an undefined, speculative plan of parliamentary reform'. Nevertheless, Grenfell was a minority teller for Newport's motion to disfranchise non-resident Irish borough voters, 9 Mar., and he would have voted for reform of Edinburgh's representation, 13 Apr., but was shut out;[31] he spoke and voted for Russell's resolution condemning bribery, 26 May. He denounced the court of chancery as 'a curse to the country', 18 Apr., and was ranting at the inadequacy of the government's bill to reform it, 31 May 1826, when the arrival of Black Rod silenced him and ended his parliamentary career.

In 1829 Grenfell fell out with Owen Williams, who vowed 'never [to] make it up with' him, over the conduct of the copper business, apparently on account of the large sums which the 'overbearing' Grenfell had borrowed without consulting him. Williams had by then withdrawn from the enterprise, which continued as Pascoe Grenfell and Company.[32] Grenfell addressed the London merchants' meeting called to express support for the Grey ministry's reform bill, 25 Mar. 1831.[33] At the general election five weeks later, when he was almost 70 years old, he was prevailed on to stand for Buckinghamshire as a supporter of the 'healing and comprehensive measure', in an attempt to turn out Grenville's Tory great-nephew Lord Chandos. His refusal to spend any money and squabbles with the other reform candidate left him hopelessly adrift in third place and, amid recriminations, he gave up after four days' polling.[34] At a meeting of London merchants and bankers to address the king, 13 Oct. 1831, he moved the resolution deploring the reform bill's defeat in the Lords.[35] The following month he was an intermediary in negotiations for a compromise on reform between ministers, the Tory 'Waverers' in the Lords and Horsley Palmer, the governor of the Bank, but one interested observer reckoned that his 'dictatorial temper' contributed to their collapse.[36] He died in January 1838 and, having quarrelled with his eldest son, his will instructed that all his real estate be sold for the benefit of his second son, Charles Pascoe Grenfell (1790-1867), Liberal Member for Preston, 1847-52, 1857-65, who became head of the copper business.[37]

[1] *Gent. Mag.* (1784), ii. 798; PROB 11/1126/79. [2] J.R. Harris, *Copper King*, 154, 182-4; Add. 58977, f. 164. [3] Add. 58977, ff. 165, 167, 169, 171; Wentworth Woodhouse mun. F49/24, 57, 59; Hants RO, Tierney mss 31. [4] *West Briton*, 25 Feb., 3, 10, 17 Mar. 1820. [5] *The Times*, 29 Apr. 1820. [6] Ibid. 14 June 1820, 21 Feb., 21 Mar., 3, 19 May 1821, 12, 13 Feb., 5, 8, 9, 11 Mar., 1, 3, 7-9, 15 May, 21 June 1822, 10 Feb., 25 Mar. 1823, 11 Feb. 1824, 24 Feb., 6, 11 May 1825, 3 Feb., 29 Apr. 1826. [7] Ibid. 7 June 1820. [8] Ibid. 25 Jan. 1821. [9] Ibid. 28 Feb., 29 Mar. 1821; HLRO, Hist. Coll. 379, Grey Bennet diary, 28. [10] *The Times*, 9, 14, 22, 29 June 1821. [11] Ibid. 2 Apr., 31 May, 4 June 1822. [12] Ibid. 5, 8 Mar. 1822. [13] Ibid. 19 Apr. 1822. [14] Ibid. 22 June 1822. [15] Ibid. 11, 25 Mar. 1823. [16] Ibid. 15 Apr. 1823; J.H. Clapham, *Bank of England*, ii. 89. [17] Buckingham, *Mems. Geo. IV*, i. 446. [18] *The Times*, 10 Feb. 1824. [19] Ibid. 14 Apr. 1824. [20] Ibid. 26 Feb., 23, 31 Mar., 3, 16 Apr., 4, 12 May 1824. [21] Ibid. 28 May 1824. [22] Ibid. 10, 25 Mar., 14, 20, 22, 23 Apr. 1825. [23] Ibid. 23 Feb. 1825. [24] Ibid. 11 Mar. 1825. [25] NLW, Vivian mss 1019. [26] *The Times*, 1 June 1825. [27] Harewood mss WYL 250/8/87. [28] Buckingham, ii. 282-3. [29] Fitzwilliam mss 124/8/1; Add. 58977, f. 186. [30] Nottingham Univ. Lib. Denison diary, 14 May [1830]. [31] *The Times*, 15 Apr. 1826. [32] Vivian mss 1120, 1122. [33] *The Times*, 26 Mar. 1831. [34] Add. 37185, f. 538; Bucks. RO, Fremantle mss D/FR/139/20/23; Creevey mss, Creevey to Miss Ord, 6 May; *The Times*, 16 May 1831. [35] *The Times*, 14 Oct. 1831. [36] Sheffield Archives, Wharncliffe mss, Palmer to Wharncliffe, 16 Nov., A. Baring to same, 4 Dec. 1831. [37] *Gent. Mag.* (1838), i. 429; IR26/1481/76.

D.R.F.

GRENVILLE, George, 2nd Bar. Nugent [I] (1788–1850), of Lilies, nr. Aylesbury, Bucks.

BUCKINGHAM	30 Jan. 1810–1812
AYLESBURY	1812–1832
AYLESBURY	1847–26 Nov. 1850

b. 31 Dec. 1788,[1] 2nd s. of George Grenville†, 1st mq. of Buckingham (*d.* 1813), and Lady Mary Elizabeth Nugent (*cr.* Baroness Nugent [I] 26 Dec. 1800), da. and coh. of Robert Nugent†, 1st Earl Nugent [I]; bro. of Richard Temple Nugent Grenville, Earl Temple†. *educ.* Brasenose, Oxf. 1804. *m.* 6 Sept. 1813, Anne Lucy, da. of Hon. Vere Poulett† of Addington House, Bucks., *s.p. suc.* mother by spec. rem. as 2nd Bar. Nugent [I] 16 Mar. 1812; GCMG 12 Aug. 1832. *d.* 26 Nov. 1850.

Ld. of treasury Nov. 1830-Nov. 1832; ld. high commr. to Ionian Islands 1832-5.

Cornet 2 Bucks. yeomanry 1803, lt.-col. 1813.

Nugent was even fatter than his elder brother, the 2nd marquess of Buckingham, but not remotely as obnoxious. Habitually dressed in top hat, tail coat and spurred boots, and scurrilously credited with a taste for prostitutes, he was personable, 'accessible and affectionate', possessing what Miss Edgeworth, who thought he looked 'like a humorous Irishman', called 'a kind of offhand dashing cleverness'. According to the painter Haydon, his 'manners' were 'graceful and commanding' and he was 'cultivated and entertaining'.[2] He was perennially short of money, even though he received a life annuity of £1,500, raised on the family's Wotton estates (where his residence of Lilies lay) by the terms of his father's will. A legacy of £10,000 was never paid to him, nor did he take advantage of the bequest of an estate at Gosfield, Essex. His brother, who gave him £500 a year, had subsidized his returns for Aylesbury in 1812 and 1818, but by the latter date they had diverged politically, with Nugent remaining attached to the Whig opposition while Buckingham, the head of a small parliamentary squad, had turned alarmist and was gravitating towards a junction with the Liverpool ministry. Their only common political bond was their zealous support for Catholic claims.[3] Nugent was, as Daniel O'Connell* noted in 1825, 'no great orator'; and another contemporary commentator, who praised him as 'a steady, courageous and consistent politician', observed that when he strove for 'oratorical effect', there was 'a certain clumsiness of elaboration ... in his arrangement and delivery'.[4]

He was returned unopposed for Aylesbury at the general election of 1820, and for the last time Buckingham paid his expenses.[5] Anti-Catholicism was rife in the borough, and seven weeks later Nugent, whose independent colleague Rickford was opposed to relief, published *A Letter to the Electors of Aylesbury on the Catholic Question*, in which he explained and defended his position. In the House, which he attended with fair regularity, though by no means fanatically, he continued to act with the advanced wing of opposition. When his nephew Lord Temple, Buckingham's son, presented a Buckinghamshire petition for relief from agricultural distress, 12 May 1820, he endorsed its complaint against the burden of poor rates, but dissented from its demand for enhanced protection and attributed current difficulties to 'an immense [national] debt and a fictitious paper currency'. On 2 June he denounced the maintenance of a large standing army in peacetime and declared that 'if complaints

of taxation were to be met by enlarged establishments ... we should move on in a circle till some final rupture took place between the crown and the people, the issue of which must be either to confirm disaffection, or to establish a military government'. His proposal to reduce the army by 15,000 men, 14 June, when he was a minority teller, was defeated by 101-46. He voted against Wilberforce's compromise resolution on the Queen Caroline affair, 22 June, and on the 25th opposed the appointment of a green bag committee, protesting that pro-government newspapers 'teemed with paragraphs calculated to excite prejudices subversive of public justice'; he was a teller for the minority, 26 June. He supported the prayer of a Protestant Dissenters' petition for repeal of the Test Acts, 13 July, when he spoke and was a minority teller against the barrack agreement bill. As his brother saw it, his 'politics encourage all sorts of violence' at Aylesbury in support of Caroline; and on 16 Aug. 1820 he waited on her in London with the loyal address which he had helped to promote.[6]

He joined in the opposition's parliamentary campaign in support of the queen early in 1821, but his brother's confidant William Fremantle* gathered that he was 'discontented' with the leaders' 'milk and water' approach.[7] He spoke of Caroline as a wronged though sometimes badly advised woman, 24 Jan. At the Aylesbury protest meeting, 29 Jan., he said that the government majority against restoration of her name to the liturgy conclusively proved the need for parliamentary reform, best 'effected by firmness and moderation' in conjunction with economical reform, tax remissions, liberalization of trade and army reductions.[8] He presented the petition, 31 Jan. He spoke in the same sense in the House, 5 Feb., tried unsuccessfully to persuade the duke of Devonshire to contribute to the subscription for the queen, 14 Feb., and attended her Brandenburgh House dinner, 17 Feb.[9] On 16 Feb. he seconded Hume's motion for presentation of the ordnance estimates in detail. He brought up and supported the petition of over 8,000 English Catholics for relief, 28 Feb., when he divided in the majority; Buckingham blamed his 'violence' for Temple's hostility to Catholic claims.[10] Nugent had a favourable petition from the archdeaconry of Bath 'read at length' and was a teller for the majority for the second reading of the relief bill, 16 Mar. He presented a petition from the four English Catholic peers (Norfolk, Shrewsbury, Petre and Arundel), 23 Mar., and argued that no part of the Catholic service was 'exclusive', 26 Mar.[11] He was a steward of the *London Tavern* reform dinner, 4 Apr., when he declared that 'reform was rendered indispensable by the great corruption which had crept in, by the change of property which had taken place, but above all by the intelligence and virtue of the British people', in whose hands lay 'the first principle of reform'.[12] He divided silently for Lambton's and Russell's reform motions, 18 Apr., 9 May. His bid to have the proprietor of *John Bull* reprimanded rather than gaoled for breach of privilege, 11 May, was defeated by 109-23. He voted to abolish capital punishment for forgery offences, 23 May, 4 June. His motion for inquiry next session into alleged abuses in the administration of justice in Tobago was rejected by 105-66, 6 June 1821.

At the October quarter sessions he unsuccessfully opposed with his vote his brother's ban on the placing of official advertisements in the new 'radical' paper, the *Buckinghamshire Chronicle*, though he 'had the good taste to remain silent' when the issue was debated. He got up a protest, ostensibly to try to reverse the decision, but in reality to bolster the Whig cause in the county. Buckingham, for whom blood was thicker than water, confided to Fremantle that Nugent's 'conduct is *hourly* getting so violent and so insane that I fear things will come to an explosion e'er long between us. Nothing but the greatest exertions on my part have prevented this for a long while past'.[13] Nugent was keen to contradict a false report that he had subscribed to the fund to support Sir Robert Wilson* after his dismissal from the army (which he voted to condemn, 13 Feb. 1822); but in January 1822, as his brother's junction with the government, which earned him a dukedom, neared completion, his maternal uncle Lord Carysfort wrote to his paternal uncle Lord Grenville:

> The only drawback ... is that poor Lord Nugent now appears quite separate from his family ... He is so good humoured and agreeable that it is impossible not to be very much concerned for him ... [He] has even lately been acting very absurdly. I am, however, convinced that there might be a chance, not of his immediate reformation, yet with management of his coming round in a little time ... I ... know ... that he has really great love for his brother, and is grieved at being told that he is following a course that persisted in must separate them entirely at last.[14]

Nugent voted for the amendment to the address, 5 Feb., and was one of the diehard opponents of the suspension of habeas corpus in Ireland, 7, 8 Feb. 1822. He addressed a meeting of distressed Aylesbury agriculturists, 9 Feb., and presented their petition for economies, reduced taxation and reform, 15 Feb., when he claimed that most of them were opposed to enhanced protection and a return to a paper currency.[15] His vote for Creevey's motion for inquiry into the board of

control, an attack on the Grenvilles, 14 Mar., was considered 'the height of folly' by Fremantle, a member of the board, and a 'personal' slight by Buckingham, who also complained that on 27 Feb. he had 'sat unmoved in the House ... to hear' Grey Bennet 'abuse and falsify his father's memory' over the sinecure tellership of the exchequer.[16] Nugent presented an Aylesbury reform petition, 25 Apr., before voting for Russell's motion.[17] His fellow Whig Member Sir James Mackintosh thought his speech on Canning's bill to relieve Catholic peers, which he disliked but voted for, 30 Apr., was 'clumsy and tedious'.[18] He voted with opposition on diplomatic expenditure, 15 May, but next day had the 'good taste', as Fremantle put it, to stay away from the attack on his cousin Henry Williams Wynn's† embassy to the Swiss Cantons; Buckingham sourly remarked that he and Lord Ebrington, who also abstained, had 'just recollected that they too were Grenvilles, a fact they seemed entirely to have forgotten'.[19] They both attended the Westminster anniversary purity of election dinner, 23 May.[20] Nugent was in small minorities against the Irish insurrection bill, 8 July. On 25 July 1822 he supported Wilberforce's motion for inquiry into the state of the Cape, Mauritius and Ceylon and the administration of justice in the Leeward Islands. At the end of the year his wife fell seriously ill, and in January 1823 she was moved to Lilies 'in a sort of carriage made on purpose for invalids'.[21]

Nugent divided for inquiry into the parliamentary franchise, 20 Feb., Russell's reform motion, 24 Apr., and reform of the Scottish representative system, 2 June 1823. He was preoccupied that session with the Catholic question. On 28 May he secured leave for a bill to place English Catholics on the same footing as Irish in respect of their right to vote and hold office. It had a second reading on 18 June. Liverpool and Peel, the home secretary and leader of the parliamentary Protestants, gave it their blessing on condition that Nugent divided it into two bills, one dealing with the franchise and the other with offices, in which Peel wished to include swearing the oath of supremacy. Both passed the Commons in early July, but they were scuppered in the Lords on the 9th. Buckingham complained that his own vote and proxy 'were lost by George never holding the slightest communication'.[22] Nugent voted for inquiry into the Dublin disturbances, 24 June, and to refer the Irish Catholics' petition alleging bias in the administration of justice to the judicial commission, 26 June 1823. That summer he went to Spain to fight with the liberals. He was bitterly disappointed by the recall of the British minister from Seville and was back in England in October 1823, after the surrender of the Constitutionalists.[23] He divided for the production of information on Catholic burials, 6 Feb. 1824. On the 17th he attacked the government's 'most hostile' attitude, disguised as neutrality, to Spain, and moved for the relevant papers. The Whig George Agar Ellis* considered the motion 'foolish', and an amendment endorsing ministerial policy was carried by 171-30. Nugent's subsequent amendment, proposed to record his views, was negatived.[24] When Russell took up the Spanish issue, 18 Mar., Canning, the foreign secretary, included in his reply some mockery of Nugent's military enterprise as 'a most enormous breach of neutrality', making much of his journey in 'the heavy Falmouth coach', equipped with 'a box of most portentous magnitude' containing 'full uniform of a Spanish general of cavalry, together with a helmet ... scarcely inferior in size to the celebrated helmet in the Castle of Otranto'. The House was convulsed with mirth, but by all accounts Nugent, whose 'large person' was painfully conspicuous, as no one was sitting near him, 'took it with perfect good humour'.[25] He spoke against the aliens bill, 5 Apr., and was a teller for the minority to limit its duration, 12 Apr. He voted for an advance of capital to Ireland, 4 May, and inquiry into that country, 11 May. He presented petitions for repeal of the leather tax, 27 May, and the abolition of slavery, 4 June; he voted to condemn the prosecution in Demerara of the Methodist missionary John Smith, 11 June 1824.[26] That autumn he went to the Morea to assist the Greek independents.[27]

He deplored the bill to suppress the Catholic Association, 4, 18 Feb., and was a teller for the minorities against its introduction, 15 Feb., and for his own wrecking amendment, 21 Feb. 1825, when he said that 'the right of free discussion was the only plank ... left to the despairing Catholics'.[28] He divided for relief, 1 Mar., attended the pro-Catholic dinner for O'Connell at Norfolk House, 6 Mar., presented three favourable petitions, 18 Apr., and next day presented and endorsed the English Catholics' petition.[29] He was a teller for the majority for the second reading of the relief bill, 21 Apr., yet according to Buckingham was 'heartily sick of his party but does not know how to shake it off' and 'out of humour with everybody'.[30] On 10 May he presented a pro-Catholic petition before voting for the third reading of the bill.[31] After its defeat in the Lords he signed the declaration of Protestant peers with Irish property got up by his brother, which impressed on ministers the need for emancipation but asked Irish Catholics to shun violence. At the end of the month Fremantle informed the duke that Nugent

states himself *as authorized* to tell all the opposition, and every being interested in the Catholic question, that

you are no party to any compromise that may have been made in the cabinet, and that you entirely condemn the proceedings ... of government. I mention this that you may guard your brother against such a declaration on your part, because you must see how deeply it will affect [Charles Williams] Wynn's* situation.

Williams Wynn, president of the board of control, later complained to Buckingham of his using Nugent as a messenger to convey his sentiments to the opposition; but the duke convinced him that Nugent had exceeded his brief, and Williams Wynn intervened to curb his indiscretion.[32] Nugent voted for inquiry into the corn laws, 28 Apr., and against the duke of Cumberland's grant, 30 May, 2 June, when he was a minority teller, and 10 June. He presented petitions from Leighton Buzzard for revision of the licensing laws, 4 May, and from the resident freemen of West Looe for inquiry into the borough's franchise, 20 June 1825.[33] In November he publicly denied having any connection with the dubious Swennappe Mining Company, but Fremantle thought he had made a 'terrible *hash*' of his explanation and that he would 'not make the public believe him, more particularly as he seems to have been engaged in other shares which he has disposed of'.[34] In December 1825 he let Lilies 'for the purpose of getting a little money in his pocket' and took '*two* adjoining houses' in Aylesbury, which, Fremantle commented, would 'make a pleasant residence'.[35]

On 17 Jan. 1826 Nugent chaired and passionately addressed a Buckingham meeting to petition for the abolition of slavery and to form an Anti-Slavery Society, of which he became president. He spoke in the same sense at Chipping Wycombe, 1 Feb., and Aylesbury, 19 Apr., and presented and supported petitions, 6, 16 Feb. He applauded the government's stated intention of abolishing slavery as soon as possible, 2 Mar., when he was a teller for the minority for inquiry into the Jamaican slave trials.[36] He was named to the select committee on the slave trade at Mauritius, 9 May. He was in minorities of 24 and 19 against the promissory notes bill, 20, 27 Feb. He divided for the abolition of flogging in the army, 10 Mar., and for defence by counsel in felony trials, 25 Apr., when he withdrew his motion for a bill to secure the independence of West Indian judges on an assurance that ministers had the matter in hand. He voted for Russell's reform motion, 27 Apr., and investigation of James Silk Buckingham's* allegations of curbs on press freedom in India, 9 May 1826, when he was put on the select committee. At the general election the following month he adopted a 'purity of election' stance, on the model established by Sir Francis Burdett* in Westminster, declining to stand unless invited to do so by his constituents (as he duly was) and refusing to canvass or spend money. His brother thought he was inviting trouble, but promised to get his 'friends' to vote for him if there was a contest. He was angered when Nugent directed 'the *cap of liberty* to be hoisted upon the tops of his colour staves', apparently 'in spite of the remonstrances even of his radical friends'. There was no opposition to his return, after which he declared that with the spread of popular intelligence, 'the mask of corruption' was 'wearing out', and said that the Whig party had been 'promoting measures of salutary reform, by the gradual influence which their unceasing and patient efforts have had and will continue to have over the measures of government'. At a dinner to celebrate his election he said that if a body of his constituents amounting to half the number of those who had signed the requisition inviting him to stand should indicate dissatisfaction with him, he would resign his seat. He asserted his conscientious right to support Catholic relief, in the face of majority opinion in the borough, and referred to the damage to family harmony which his adherence to liberal principles had entailed. He professed anxiety to inform and enlighten his constituents, and published later in 1826 a new edition of his *Plain Statement* in support of Catholic claims.[37]

Nugent, whose correspondence with a local clergyman defector from the Catholic cause appeared in the county press, presented and endorsed the English Catholics' relief petition, 2 Mar., and voted in the minority, 6 Mar. 1827.[38] He divided for relaxations of the corn import tariff, 9, 27 Mar., and inquiries into the electoral interference of Leicester corporation, 15 Mar., and the Barrackpoor mutiny, 22 Mar. He called for an end to army flogging, 12 Mar. Supporting Lord Althorp's motion for a select committee on county polls (to which he was named), 15 Mar., he raised the problem of non-resident freemen and suggested their registration, as in Ireland. He collected information on this subject, was added to the select committee on borough polls, 14 May, and on 29 June sought leave to introduce a registration bill, but was persuaded to drop it.[39] He divided for the spring guns bill, 23 Mar., for information on the Lisburn Orange procession, 29 Mar., and to withhold supplies until the ministerial crisis following Liverpool's stroke was resolved, 30 Mar. When Canning, the new premier, turned down Buckingham's request to be made governor-general of India, the duke told Nugent that any member of his family maintaining amicable relations with Williams Wynn, who had stayed in office, was no longer his

friend; but Nugent was 'inclined to think that in ... a very short time' his brother 'would come round and be again a supporter of government'.[40] In the House, 7 May, he declared his support for the new ministry, if only to keep out the anti-Catholic Tories, while reserving his position on reform and repeal of the Test Acts. He presented petitions for the latter, 22, 30 May, 8, 19 June, claiming that most of his Dissenter constituents favoured Catholic relief. He attended and addressed the Westminster anniversary dinner, 23 May.[41] He called for general religious toleration at an Aylesbury Independents' meeting to petition against the Acts, 26 May.[42] In June he gave Mackintosh 'a sad account of his brother's conduct and condition and of the absurd violence of his nephew' Lord Chandos (formerly Temple).[43] At the Aylesbury anniversary celebration of his election, 15 June, he attacked the late ministers as a reactionary faction who had sought 'only to chill, to neutralize and taint' every liberal measure, justified his support of Canning, urged Dissenters to make common cause with the Catholics and spelled out his guiding principles of economy, reform, the abolition of slavery and religious toleration. He 'answered for the Romans' when Lord John Russell and others contemplated the formation of a society to promote the last object.[44] His claim to employment in the Goderich administration was one of the Whig objects which Lord Holland thought 'time alone can accomplish'.[45] Sending William Fremantle's nephew Sir Thomas Fremantle, Member for Buckingham, an extract of a letter from the duke asking him to support the ministry, 9 Dec. 1827, Nugent, who had declined his brother's offer to take him on his extended money-saving retreat to Italy because he wanted to be on the spot to uphold the Catholic cause against Chandos, pressed him not to participate in the planned fête for Wellington and Peel at Buckingham on the 15th, which he believed would have a blatant political and anti-Catholic slant. When Fremantle, one of its promoters, told him to mind his own business and that the ceremony was to be non-political, Nugent admitted that he had jumped to the wrong conclusion. William Fremantle, urging Sir Thomas to keep well in with Chandos in the duke's absence, warned him against 'mingling' with Nugent, who had 'the most perverted judgement with the first rate ability', was 'as little to be depended on for firm and steady support as his brother', could 'never be friends' with Chandos and was 'always playing a false and unprofitable game' with the duke.[46]

Nugent presented petitions from Aylesbury and 5,000 English Catholics in favour of repeal of the Test Acts, 25 Feb. 1828, and next day spoke and voted for that measure. He was not happy with the declaration inserted by Peel in the subsequent bill. He opposed throwing East Retford into the hundred of Bassetlaw, 21 Mar., 2, 24, 27 June. On the Penryn disfranchisement bill, 24 Mar., he stated his preference for six months' imprisonment to a £50 fine for bribery offenders. He challenged the contention that slaves were legal property and that their owners had a right to compensation in the event of abolition, 6 Mar. On the 10th he unsuccessfully moved to limit the infliction of corporal punishment in the army to cases of drunkenness, theft, fraud and assault. He was a teller for the majority for a bill to restrict the use of ribbons at elections, 20 Mar., when he approved the principle of Ross's bill to regulate the admission of borough freemen but said it would achieve little, whereas his own registration bill 'took a more extended sweep'. He secured leave for this measure, which aimed to break attorneys' 'undue monopoly of knowledge' and stop excessive creations for electoral purposes, 22 May. He made changes to it and, moving its second reading, 19 June, said he would not press it further that session, as he wanted it to be altered to accommodate local rights and customs. A wrecking amendment was carried against it. He presented petitions for Catholic relief from 14,000 English and Scottish Catholics, 7 May, and the freemen of Sudbury, 19 May; he voted for relief, 12 May. He supported the provision for Canning's family, 20 May, when he voted against the Wellington ministry on civil list pensions, as he did on the cost of Buckingham House improvements, 23 June, inquiry into the Irish church, 24 June, the additional churches bill, which he spoke against, 30 June, and the ordnance estimates, 4 July. At the Aylesbury anniversary dinner, 2 May, he proclaimed that 'the seed which had been sown in Westminster' had been 'resown in Aylesbury, and had shot up into a rich and glorious harvest ... under the patient and virtuous husbandry of the middle class'. He expressed his lack of confidence in the ministry and again exhorted Dissenters to join in the campaign for Catholic emancipation.[47] He presented a Newport Pagnell petition against the Malt Act, 25 July 1828. In September he went to Ireland, visited O'Connell and was given a public dinner by the friends of civil and religious liberty at Waterford, where he made what William Fremantle considered 'a foolish speech ... going out of his way unnecessarily to abuse the king'.[48] On his return in October he published a letter to his constituents condemning Chandos's promotion of a county Brunswick Club and arguing that Catholic emancipation was essential to save Ireland from anarchy. On 6 Nov. he chaired a meeting of the supporters of the Aylesbury British School for Boys and expounded on the moral and political benefits of universal education.[49] In December 1828 he submitted a 'plan' for dealing with the Catholic question to Lord John Russell, who did 'not think ... [it] practicable, and if not practicable folly to attempt'.[50]

Nugent had successfully defied Chandos to call a county meeting on the issue, and in early February 1829, when the ministry's decision to concede emancipation was announced, he was fortified by receipt of a letter from Buckingham giving him 'positive directions to prevent his tenants from attending any county or other meetings' and promising 'his whole support at Aylesbury' against Chandos's machinations.[51] In the House, 13 Feb., he praised Peel for his change of mind, presented an Oxford petition for emancipation and said he would not offer any 'captious objection' to the bill to suppress the Catholic Association. On the 16th he countered Chandos's presentation of dozens of hostile petitions from Buckinghamshire with an assertion that majority opinion there was favourable, and presented petitions in that sense, including that of the duke of Norfolk and 18,000 English and Scottish Catholics; Chandos observed that his seat might be at risk next time. He decided to attend the anti-Catholic meeting of the three hundreds of Buckingham got up by Chandos, 21 Feb., but failed to persuade Sir Thomas Fremantle and his colleague Sir George Nugent to join him. He had a furious row with Chandos when opposing the resolutions and stating his brother's views.[52] He said the Dover anti-Catholic petition was unrepresentative, 3 Mar., asked Peel if English and Scottish Catholics were to be placed on the same footing as Irish concerning the oath of supremacy, 5 Mar., voted for emancipation next day and said it would have a 'tranquillizing effect' on Ireland, 13 Mar. He presented and endorsed favourable petitions, 17, 27 Mar., and divided for the third reading of the relief bill, 30 Mar. He assisted O'Connell in his bid to take his seat without swearing the oath and voted thus, 18 May.[53] He voted for the transfer of East Retford's seats to Birmingham, 5 May, and to issue a new writ, 2 June, when he paired for Lord Blandford's reform scheme. He urged the continuation of the investigation into West Indian judicial systems, 25 May 1829, when he was again at the Westminster dinner.[54] Chandos threatened to get up an opposition to him at Aylesbury at the next general election, and on Buckingham's return home towards the end of the year William Fremantle wondered how he would steer his course between his warring brother and son.[55]

Nugent divided again for the transfer of East Retford's seats to Birmingham, 11 Feb., 5, 15 Mar. 1830, when he announced that he had 'lately become a convert' to the secret ballot before voting in O'Connell's minority of 21 for it. Supporting Blandford's reform plan, even though he did 'not understand the details', 18 Feb., he stated his preference for triennial parliaments and a significant extension of the franchise. He voted for the enfranchisement of Birmingham, Leeds and Manchester, 23 Feb., and for Russell's reform motion, 28 May. He pointed out to Hume that taking the number of voters at the last contested election would not furnish an accurate assessment of the English borough electorate. At an Aylesbury meeting, 24 Feb., he predicted that Birmingham, Leeds and Manchester would have two Members each before the year was out, for the cause of reform was 'advancing with a giant's stride', sustained by 'the increasing intelligence ... [and] education of the people'. He attributed distress to 35 years of national overspending, dismissed currency nostrums and advocated rigid economy. He also called on landlords to rescue labourers from the pauperism to which their selfishness had driven them.[56] He supported Lord Ellenborough's divorce bill, 1 Apr., and voted for reform of the laws of divorce, 3 June. On the St. Giles vestry bill, 2 Apr., he argued for a compromise voting qualification of £20. He attended a meeting of 'about 35 of the best Whigs' at Althorp's, 15 Mar., and divided with the revived opposition on most major issues that session.[57] He voted for Jewish emancipation, 5 Apr., 17 May, and to end the death penalty for forgery offences, 24 May, 7 June. He was a teller for the two minorities on the address to the new king, 30 June, and for Brougham's motion for the immediate abolition of slavery, 13 July. After presenting a petition from the labouring poor of Ashenden against the practice of paying a portion of wages from the poor rates, 6 Apr., he secured leave to bring in a bill to improve parish provision for the employment of the poor and to eradicate the 'roundsman' system. After its second reading, 10 May, the bill was referred to a select committee; but it was got rid of, 9 July 1830. Four days later, on hearing of his brother's appointment as lord steward of the household in the room of Lord Conyngham, he amused Lady Williams Wynn by remarking that it was comical to think of the strait-laced duchess of Buckingham replacing Lady Conyngham, George IV's mistress for nine years.[58] At the general election later that month Nugent offered himself for Aylesbury in defiance of stories that he was to be challenged on account of his support for Catholic emancipation, but he again refused to canvass. After

his unopposed return he restated his political principles of 1826 and boasted of his lifelong attachment to the Whigs, 'the party for liberty', as against the Tories, who stood for 'thraldom'.[59]

Nugent did not share Lord Holland's keenness to save the lives of Polignac and the other French ex-ministers, feeling that Britain owed them nothing, though as an opponent of 'all capital punishments', who thought 'the killing of a man is at best but a bungling sort of way of obtaining reparation for any mischief he may have done or intended', he was willing to back the campaign.[60] He supported Williams Wynn's bill to abolish some parliamentary oaths, 4 Nov. 1830. He helped to vote the government out of office on the civil list, 15 Nov., and next day presented a Bridport reform petition. On 19 Nov. he said that repeal of the Union would not curb the influx of Irish paupers and secured leave to reintroduce his bill to promote the employment of the labouring poor. On 17 Dec. 1830, having been made a lord of the treasury in the Grey administration and re-elected for Aylesbury, where he promised to work for 'severe retrenchment to lighten those burdens which years of unmeaning senseless profusion have cast on the people', he deferred the second reading to allow adjustments to be made. The measure got no further.[61] He announced that ministers hoped to make savings in the cost of official printing and gave an assurance of free access for solicitors to inmates of Aylesbury and Warwick gaols, 10 Feb. 1831. He presented reform petitions from Aylesbury and elsewhere, 28 Feb., and of course divided for the second reading of the reform bill, 22 Mar., and against Gascoyne's wrecking amendment, 19 Apr. He presented anti-slavery petitions, 28 Mar. At the 1831 general election he seconded the nomination of the reformer John Smith* for the county and, having proclaimed in his address that the dissolution had put 'the cause of reform ... once more ... in the hands of the people', was returned in second place for Aylesbury after a contest forced by an anti-reformer, who received support from his brother and nephew's 'pocket votes'. He attacked Chandos for his intervention and said that in future he would canvass in person.[62]

On 23 June 1831 Nugent got leave to introduce a bill to abolish 40 customs and excise oaths, which received royal assent a week later (1 and 2 Gul. IV, c. 4).[63] He was named to the select committee on the East India Company, 28 June. As an official man, he of course voted for the second reading of the reintroduced reform bill, 6 July, solidly for its details, occasionally as a ministerial teller, and for its third reading, 19 Sept., and passage, 21 Sept. He was in the majorities on the Dublin election controversy, 23 Aug., and the Liverpool writ, 5 Sept. There was a false report at that time that he was to be made a coronation peer.[64] On 10 Oct. he hosted with a breakfast at Lilies the inaugural meeting of the Aylesbury Independent Union, planted a tree of reform, deplored the Lords' rejection of the reform bill and urged its supporters to be 'firm ... watchful [and] ... constant' but to avoid violence, which would be 'playing the game of your enemies ... a disappointed and desperate faction'. He went immediately to London to divide for the motion of confidence in the ministry. At an Aylesbury dinner, 17 Nov. 1831, he condemned self-styled 'moderate reformers' and declared that 'the £10 franchise must be nailed to the mast'.[65]

Nugent, whose *Memorials of John Hampden*, his hero, was published in December 1831 (Tom Macaulay* found it 'dreadfully heavy'),[66] voted for the second reading of the revised reform bill on the 17th. He was a steady supporter of its details, though he was credited with an unlikely vote against the enfranchisement of Gateshead, 5 Mar., and he divided for the third reading, 22 Mar. 1832. He was in Hobhouse's minority for vestry reform, 23 Jan. Declining to reintroduce his labourers' employment bill because it might be construed as a government measure, 17 Feb., he called for action on the problem; he welcomed Burrell's bill, 18 May. He presented a bill to establish a general registry of births, 6 Mar., but it provoked great opposition and lapsed on 6 July. He approved the principle of Sadler's factories regulation bill, 16 Mar., when he was placed on its committee, but was afraid of its hindering British manufacturers. He was a teller for the majority for the Irish tithes bill, 16 Apr. He presented a petition for abolition of the death penalty for non-violent crimes, 8 May. He voted for the address calling on the king to appoint only ministers who would carry reform unimpaired, 10 May. At an Aylesbury meeting on the 15th he defended ministers' resignation following the temporary success of 'a base and filthy intrigue', denounced the duke of Wellington and company and urged his audience to 'be at your post, in firm, compact and sustained union'.[67] Reinstated with his colleagues, he voted for the second reading of the Irish reform bill, 25 May, and paired against a Conservative amendment to the Scottish one, 1 June. He voted to make coroners' inquests public, 20 June 1832. At the Chipping Wycombe by-election that month he appeared on the hustings to back Grey's son against the enigmatic Benjamin Disraeli†, whose comment in defeat that the 'nearest thing to a Tory in disguise was a Whig in office' he interpreted as a personal insult. A duel was averted by the intervention of mediators.[68] The impecunious Nugent had apparently

solicited the war secretaryship on the resignation of Sir Henry Parnell* in January, but he was deemed by Althorp to be quite 'unfit' for it. Yet he was regarded as a deserving case, whose 'services at the treasury can easily be supplied', and he was offered the government of the Ionian Islands (partly because it would stop him applying for domestic posts which were beyond his abilities).[69] He jumped at it. Macaulay told his sisters that he would go

as soon as a ship has been built large enough to carry him out. I recommend that the vessel which is to bring us Cleopatra's needle from Egypt should carry his Lordship to Corfu. I should think that the machinery which will raise an obelisk of ninety feet long might be sufficient to embark and disembark even the portly frame of a Grenville.[70]

An attempt by the Conservatives, who had his seat in their sights, to secure the immediate issue of the writ so that a by-election could be fought on the old franchise was thwarted, and he remained Member until the dissolution on 3 Dec. 1832. By then he was well on his way to Corfu, having issued four months earlier a valedictory address urging his constituents to elect a reformer and arguing that the farmers' demand for high protecting corn duties was 'fraught with a fatal fallacy'. His bid to ensure his replacement by the reformer Thomas Hobhouse†, which so enraged Buckingham that he withdrew Nugent's annual allowance, ended in defeat by a Conservative.[71]

Nugent, whose *Legends of the Library at Lilies*, a joint production with his wife, was published in 1832, improved the revenues of the Ionian Islands before resigning in 1835 on the formation of a Conservative ministry supported by his brother and nephew. He was 'hardly treated' by the Liberal party leaders on his return, being passed over as a candidate for Marylebone in 1836 and 1838.[72] He was defeated at Aylesbury, now in Conservative hands, in 1837, when he published a pamphlet advocating the secret ballot, and 1839. His *On the Punishment of Death by Law* (1840) put the case for the abolition of capital punishment and his *Letter to the Chairman of the Committee of the Anti-Corn Law League* (1842) explained why he had withdrawn from it as a Marylebone delegate. That year he unsuccessfully contested Southampton. After travelling in Greece, Egypt, the Holy Land and Syria, 1843-4, and recording his observations in *Lands, Classical and Sacred* (1845), he succeeded at Aylesbury in 1847, after repeal of the corn laws had removed the major issue which had dished him there.[73] Nugent, who lost his wife in 1848, sat until his death at Lilies in November 1850, after three weeks' torture from 'low fever and erysipelas'.[74] In his will, dated 25 Oct. 1848, after his wife's death, he listed debts of about £14,000 and noted that his £10,000 patrimony had been transferred by Chandos (now 2nd duke of Buckingham) to a firm of solicitors as security for a mortgage without his knowledge or consent. He left Lilies and the residue of his personal estate to his 'sister-in-law' Mrs. Vera Connel, who since his wife's death had lived with him 'like a sister', with remainder to Lucy Henrietta, eldest daughter of his kinsman Sir George Edward Nugent of Westhorpe. He left freehold fields at Weedon for use as allotments by the poor. His affairs were found to be in great disarray.[75]

[1] Bucks. RO, Spencer Bernard mss PFE 4/9a. [2] Gent. Mag. (1851), i. 92; M.D. George, Cat. of Pol. and Personal Satires, x. 14416, 14689, 14828, 14831; Edgeworth Letters, 491; Lord Nugent, Mems. of Hampden (1854), p. liv. [3] J.J. Sack, The Grenvillites, 8-9, 25, 166, 168, 174; J. Beckett, Rise and Fall of the Grenvilles, 91, 111, 121, 149; HP Commons, 1790-1820, iv. 86-88. [4] O'Connell Corresp. iii. 1203; Nugent, p. xlv. [5] The Times, 9, 13 Mar. 1820. [6] Bucks. RO, Fremantle mss D/FR/46/11/31; The Times, 17, 25 Aug. 1820. [7] Buckingham, Mems. Geo. IV, i. 111. [8] The Times, 8 Feb. 1821. [9] HLRO, Hist. Coll. 379, Grey Bennet diary, 13, 20, 23. [10] Fremantle mss 46/12/34. [11] The Times, 17, 24, 27 Mar. 1821. [12] Grey Bennet diary, 50; The Times, 5 Apr. 1821. [13] Fremantle mss 46/9/5/1; 46/9/9; Althorp Letters, 116; R.W. Davis, Political Change and Continuity, 60-62. [14] BL, Fortescue mss, Carysfort to Grenville, Sunday [Jan. 1822]; Buckingham, i. 218. [15] The Times, 12 Feb. 1822. [16] Buckingham, i. 294; Fremantle mss 46/10/20, 24. [17] The Times, 26 Apr. 1822. [18] Add. 52445, f. 83. [19] Buckingham, i. 325, 329. [20] Add. 56545, f. 7. [21] Fremantle mss 46/10/49. [22] G.I.T. Machin, Catholic Question in English Politics, 42-43; Colchester Diary, iii. 280; Buckingham, i. 472, 474; Fremantle mss 46/11/84. [23] Nugent, p. xxx. [24] Northants. RO, Agar Ellis diary, 17 Feb. [1824]. [25] Ibid. 18 Mar. [1824]; TNA 30/29/9/5/22, 23; Harewood mss, Canning to wife, 20 Mar.; Hatherton diary, 18 Mar. [1824]; Life of Wilberforce, v. 217. [26] The Times, 28 May, 5 June; Bucks. Chron. 26 June 1824. 1824. [27] Nugent, p. xi. [28] The Times, 19 Feb. 1825. [29] O'Connell Corresp. ii. 1182, 1203. [30] Fremantle mss 46/11/116. [31] The Times, 11 May 1825. [32] Buckingham, ii. 257-9, 265, 267, 268. [33] The Times, 5 May, 21 June 1825. [34] Ibid. 3, 7, 9, 10 Nov., 1 Dec. 1825; Christ Church, Oxf. Phillimore mss, Fremantle to Phillimore, 24 Nov. 1825; NLW, Coedymaen mss 954. [35] Fremantle mss 138/12/2. [36] Bucks. Chron. 21 Jan., 4 Feb., 25 Apr.; The Times, 7, 17 Feb., 3 Mar. 1826. [37] Bucks. Chron. 3, 10, 17, 24 June, 15 July; The Times, 12 July 1826; Fremantle mss 46/11/138; 51/5/25; 138/21/1/5; Davis, 81. [38] Bucks. Chron. 24 Feb., 3 Mar. 1827; Canning's Ministry, 32. [39] Creevey mss, Creevey to Miss Ord, 10 Dec. 1826; Wilts. RO, Marlborough (Burke) mss 124/1/74/1, 2; The Times, 30 June 1827. [40] Sack, 210; Fremantle mss 49/1/13. [41] Add. 56550, f. 177; The Times, 24 May 1827 [42] The Times, 23, 31 May, 8, 20 June; Bucks. Chron. 2 June 1827. [43] Add. 52447, f. 76. [44] Bucks. Chron. 23, 30 June; Add. 51677, Russell to Holland, 14 Oct. [1827]. [45] Lansdowne mss, Holland to Lansdowne, 4 Sept. 1827. [46] Fremantle mss 138/21/2/21, 23; 138/22/6, 8; 138/22/3/1. [47] Bucks. Chron. 31 May 1828. [48] Bucks. Chron. 20 Sept., 11 Oct. 1828; O'Connell Corresp. iii. 1492; Fremantle mss 139/2/1. [49] Bucks. Chron. 25 Oct., 15 Nov. 1828. [50] Add. 51677, Russell to Holland, 25 Dec. [1828]. [51] Fremantle mss 139/2/3; 139/10/3, 4. [52] Ibid. 139/10/21; The Times, 24 Feb. 1829. [53] O'Connell Corresp. iv. 1559. [54] Add. 56554, f. 17. [55] Fremantle mss 139/10/ 47, 55, 56, 62, 64. [56] Bucks Gazette, 27 Feb. 1830. [57] Salop RO 6003/1, Slaney diary, 15 Apr. 1830. [58] Williams Wynn Corresp. 376. [59] Bucks Gazette, 24 July, 7 Aug.; Add. 51835, Nugent to Holland, 5 Aug. 1830. [60] Add. 51835, Nugent to Holland, 17 Sept. 1830. [61] Bucks Gazette, 4, 11 Dec. 1830; Fremantle mss 139/14/72. [62] Bucks Gazette, 23 Apr., 7, 14, 21 May 1831; Fremantle mss 139/20/23. [63] Nugent, p. li. [64] Coedymaen mss 218. [65] Bucks Gazette, 15 Oct., 19 Nov. 1831. [66] Macaulay Letters, ii. 110; Disraeli Letters, i. 188. [67] Bucks Gazette, 19 May 1832. [68] Disrali Letters, i. 203; The Times, 3 July; Bucks Gazette, 7 July 1832. [69] Add. 76373, Althorp to Grey [30 June 1832]. [70] Macaulay Letters, ii. 159; George, xi. 17206. [71] Bucks Gazette, 4, 11, 18, 25 Aug., 1, 8, 15, 22 Sept., 29 Dec. 1832; Sack, 26; Davis, 111-12. [72] Nugent, pp. lv-lxi; Holland House Diaries, 350, 352. [73] Nugent, pp. lxvi-lxviii; Davis, 136-7, 143-6, 159-60. [74] Nugent, p. lxxiii; Gent. Mag. (1851), i. 92. [75] PROB 11/2129/224; IR26/1909/182; Disraeli Letters, v. 2087.

D.R.F.

GRENVILLE *see also* **TEMPLE NUGENT BRYDGES CHANDOS GRENVILLE**

GRESLEY, Sir Roger, 8th bt. (1799–1837), of Drakelow, near Burton-on-Trent, Staffs.

DURHAM	1830–8 Mar. 1831
NEW ROMNEY	19 Mar. 1831–1831
DERBYSHIRE SOUTH	1835–1837

b. 27 Dec. 1799, 1st and o. surv. s. of Sir Nigel Bowyer Gresley, 7th bt., of Drakelow and 2nd w. Maria Elizabeth, da. and h. of Caleb Garway of Worcester. *educ.* Christ Church, Oxf. 1817. *m.* 2 June 1821, Lady Sophia Catherine Coventry, da. of George William, 7th earl of Coventry, 1 da. *d.v.p. suc.* fa. as 8th bt. 26 Mar. 1808. *d.* 12 Oct. 1837.

Groom of bedchamber to duke of Gloucester 1823-34. Sheriff, Derbys. 1826-7.

Capt. Staffs. yeoman cav. Sept. 1819, Worcs. militia Dec. 1819.

A handsome, well-connected and ambitious linguist and author, consumed by an overriding ambition to enter and succeed in Parliament, Gresley claimed direct descent from the Norman Roger de Toeni, whom the Conqueror had rewarded with the manor of Castle Gresley, part of the Drakelow estate, equally divided between Derbyshire, Leicestershire and Staffordshire. Sacrificing his unentailed estates to his passion for politics and high society, from 1825 he 'parcelled out' land, mineral rights and tithes 'in such a manner that by annual sales it should last him for life; but he died a comparatively young man'.[1] He had succeeded his father in the baronetcy at the age of eight and his eccentric mother, the heiress of Worcester glove and porcelain manufacturers, her kinsman John Ross, bishop of Exeter,[2] and his uncle by marriage the Rev. William Gresley (1760-1829), the head of the Netherseal branch of the family and the representative of his trustees, disagreed over his upbringing. He consequently became a ward of chancery under the guardianship of Lord Beauchamp, Tory Member for Worcester, 1806-16, an experience which dictated his politics and inspired his 1829 novel *Sir Philip Gasteneys: a Minor*.[3] He drafted his first publication, *A Monody on the Death of Princess Charlotte* (1818), while at Oxford, where Arthur Hill Trevor*, Lord Deerhurst* and his brother John Coventry were his gaming companions and friends. Permitted to 'wander where he pleased', he refused to return to Oxford after a riding accident in November 1818 placed his health at risk, and joined the cavalry and militia in Staffordshire and Worcestershire, where, at Severn Stoke, he courted Deerhurst's sister Sophia, two years his junior. A restraining order from chancery, 27 Mar. 1820, merely delayed their marriage (which her father condoned and his mother opposed) until June 1821, when Gresley, now of age, had returned from a continental tour.[4] Their only child, Sophia Editha, born on 4 Oct. 1823, after Gresley had joined the duke of Gloucester's household, died the following month, and he spent most of the next year in Italy, where he became a regular visitor.[5]

He had made known his desire for a seat on joining the Tory Derby True Blue Club in 1820, but by-elections in Derbyshire in 1822 and Staffordshire in 1823 provided no opening for him.[6] Uneasy at being suggested for Wells in February 1825 by Deerhurst, whom he had hoped to succeed as Member for Worcester on his mother's and Lord Coventry's interests, he canvassed and spent money at East Retford and Evesham before the general election of 1826. He also employed agents to monitor his prospects at Derby, which as sheriff in 1826 he had to decline, and at Stafford and at Lichfield, where his father had been defeated in 1798. Nothing had come in July 1825 of his own Lichfield canvass, but after trying Evesham, he stood there as an independent in 1826, proposed by his half-sister's brother-in-law, the recorder Theophilus Levett of Winchnor, to whom he had refused to give way.[7] Defeated by the combined Anson-Vernon interest in a tumultuous contest, he retired after seven days, dined his supporters and briefly considered petitioning.[8] Heeding the advice of Hill Trevor and his agents, he declined to contest Stafford in December 1826 and returned to Italy, having first suspended chancery proceedings to have his mother declared a lunatic. She, in addition to making unhelpful interventions on his behalf in Worcester, had run up £800 in debts during twelve months' residence with her servants at the *Hen and Chickens* inn in Berwick-upon-Tweed, 'establishing an electoral interest'.[9] On 10 Dec. 1826 Gresley was cleared of defrauding a gaming-house keeper, to whom he had given a bad cheque when under age.[10] His life, according to numerous references in *The Times*, was subsequently one of constant litigation over tithes and his laxity in honouring family settlements and his mother's debts.[11] Briefed on ministerial negotiations by Gloucester, he published an anti-Catholic pamphlet dedicated to Peel in 1827 and another in 1828.[12] His anti-papal essay, *Life of Pope Gregory VII*, based on Italian material, was not published until 1832. Ever in pursuit of a seat, he moved in the highest circles, entertained lavishly like a man on £20,000 not £8,000 a year, toured the North-East with Hill Trevor and Lord Londonderry's party during the duke of Wellington's 1827 visit, and joined them in Paris in 1828.[13] His cousin William Dyott, who fretted over his extravagance, observed: 'There is a lively vivacity about Sir Roger, with great fluency of language, and, like many men [he] prizes his talents rather higher than the generality of the world will admit'.[14] Sir Henry Hardinge*, the Wellington ministry's secretary at war, praised his 'talents and bias and disbursement' and offered his assistance; but enquiries made in Canterbury, Maldon, Orford and Newcastle-under-Lyme, where his brothers-in-law Richard Heathcote* and the Rev. Thomas Levett had influence, proved unfruitful.[15] Tregony, Weymouth and Lymington were suggested and investigated by his London lawyers after he appealed to and pledged support for Peel as incoming home secretary in January 1828.[16] Obliged to raise £40,000 to meet the cost of bills and a spate of high profile prosecutions involving his mother, whom Sir Robert Inglis* had proved insane, he remained in Italy when Catholic emancipation was conceded in 1829.[17] He entertained his old Christ Church friends at Drakelow in January 1830. One of them, Sir John Benn Walsh*, observed:

> Drakelow is a curious old house. We dined in an immense parlour, quite out of proportion to the rest ... Additions he is making ... are in excellent taste, and will greatly improve it. They are built in the style ... [of] the old manor house of Queen Elizabeth. We walked ... over his stables, which are excellent. Sir Roger appears to live at a great expense, and must be deeply injuring his fortune. However, he has less cause for regret, as it seems unlikely, if Lady Sophia lives, that he will ever have children ... Poor Sir Roger. It is a strange wild scrambling life he is leading.[18]

Aligning himself politically with Sir Edward Knatchbull* and the Ultras, he procured a hostile memorial on distress from Derbyshire that month, which Gloucester criticized and refused to present.[19] He was rebuffed at Leominster in February 1830, but at the general election in July he contested Durham (where Hardinge vacated) on the Londonderry interest, having first tested the ground at Derby,

Lichfield, Newcastle-under-Lyme, Stafford and Worcester.[20] Lampooned as a stranger and writer of cheap fiction, he owed his victory after a four-day poll to Hill Trevor's assistance, a heavy purse and a late rally prompted by the Whig Lord Durham.[21] On the hustings in Durham, 2 Aug., and afterwards in Derby, 6 Aug., where he seconded the Tory Francis Mundy's* nomination for the county, he pledged allegiance to 'church and state' and called for 'retrenchment in every department'.[22] He donated a buck for the True Blue Club dinner in Lichfield, 24 Aug. 1830, to mark his success.[23] He used his frank to publicize his return and inform his friends that he had 'changed the spelling of his name from Gresley to *Greisley*', and was styled thus when he became a fellow of the Antiquarian Society, 9 Dec. 1830.[24]

The Wellington administration listed Gresley among the 'violent Ultras', but he divided with them when they were brought down on the civil list, 15 Nov. 1830, a vote he claimed the Ultras never forgave.[25] Edward Strutt*, who had heard his Derby speeches, attributed it to 'the promise of a regiment' to Lord Londonderry.[26] A petition against his return was certain when he made his maiden speech on the address, 3 Nov. 1830. He welcomed its support for the 'constitution and existing laws and institutions ... without manifesting any bigoted indisposition to salutary and necessary reforms'. He refuted 'captious' suggestions that the government were indifferent to the 'extensive and prevailing' distress and expressed confidence in their economic policies as the best means of alleviating it. However, he added a plea for greater retrenchment to his endorsement of a Sunderland petition for repeal of the coastwise coal duty, 16 Nov. A grand ball graced by the duke of Devonshire and the Londonderrys marked his 31st birthday and the completion in December 1830 of his improvements at Drakelow, which Greville, visiting three years later, faulted as 'a miserable place, with the Trent running under the windows and Lord Anglesey's land close to the door'.[27] On 4 Feb. 1831 Gresley criticized the Grey ministry's civil list proposals as overgenerous and unsustainable and promised to vote against them and against reform should he remain a Member. Furious to be unseated on petition, 8 Mar., he effected an exchange with Hill Trevor, who vacated New Romney, and he was returned there on Sir Edward Dering's* interest the following week.[28] He upheld the Ultra Inglis's complaint of a breach of privilege by *The Times* in misreporting his speeches and complained that he was another 'victim' of the practice, 21 Mar. He divided against the Grey ministry's reform bill at its second reading, 22 Mar., and for Gascoyne's wrecking amendment, 19 Apr., having presented and briefly endorsed an anti-reform petition from Durham, 15 Apr. 1831. By the dissolution on the 23rd arrangements were in place for him to contest Newark on the interest of the Ultra duke of Newcastle, who had applied to the Tory opposition's management committee in Charles Street committee for a second man.[29] He came third, after fighting an excellent and costly campaign, and the duke privately praised his 'very considerable talent ... quickness and ... spirited and steady determination not to be surpassed: very few men would have persevered as he has done with the same energy and alacrity'.[30]

Gresley declared his candidature for Derbyshire at the first post-reform election in June 1831 and announced that he had 'abandoned all hope of a successful opposition to the bill'. *The Times* seized on his 'conversion'.[31] He toyed with attempting Newark in September 1831 and Tewkesbury in February 1832, having wisely refrained from attempting Derbyshire prematurely in September 1831.[32] He commenced his canvass of Derbyshire South directly the Tory Sir George Crewe desisted in March 1832 and, though soundly defeated in a violent contest in December, his pragmatism on reform and support for retrenchment, protection and tithe revision reunited the local Conservatives, who returned him in 1835.[33] He vainly asked Peel, with typical hyperbole, if he could move the 1835 address, and made what Dyott and others termed 'a sad ass of himself in Parliament'. With defeat certain, he retired on health grounds at the 1837 dissolution, nine months after suffering paralysis in a riding accident.[34] He died suddenly and without issue that October having, by his will, dated 2 May 1837 and proved under £14,000, 24 Apr. 1838, entrusted his estates to Lords Chesterfield and Castlereagh* and provided for his widow (*d.* 1875), who retained Drakelow House for life and in 1839 married Henry William des Voeux.[35] He was succeeded in the baronetcy and entailed estates by his first cousin, the Rev. William Nigel Gresley (1806-47) of Netherseal, a descendant of the 2nd baronet.

[1] F. Madan, *Gresleys of Drakelow*, 126. [2] *Gent. Mag.* (1808), i. 554; *Oxford DNB sub* Ross. [3] Madan, 124, 127; PROB 11/1893/241; IR26/1481/139. [4] Derbys. RO, Gresley of Drakelow mss D77/36/1, corresp. 1819-21; D77/36/11, *passim*; D77/44/1, E. Morton to Lady Gresley, 6 Nov. 1818; Hatherton diary, 18 Dec. 1819; *The Times*, 28 Mar. 1820; Madan, 128; *Gent. Mag.* (1821), i. 562. [5] *Gent. Mag.* (1823), ii. 567; Gresley mss D77/41/1, Gloucester to Gresley, 7 Oct. 1823; D3999/2; *Dyott's Diary*, i. 354. [6] *Derby Mercury*, 31 Jan. 1821, 27 Nov. 1822; Gresley mss D77/4/1, Fowler to Gresley, 7 July 1823. [7] Gresley mss D77/36/2, J. Coventry to Gresley, 17 Feb., Theophilus Levett to same, 1 June, R. Lloyd to same, 11 June, Gresley to Deerhurst, 19 Feb., to Manning, 19 Feb.; D77/36/4,

G.W. Lloyd to Gresley, 8 Apr. 1826; D77/41/1, Gresley to Thomas Levett, 23 Nov. 1825; D3038/1/5; *HP Commons, 1790-1820*, ii. 358-60; *Dyott's Diary*, i. 368, 377; *Staffs. Advertiser*, 27 Aug. 1825, 10 June 1826; *Worcester Herald*, 13 May-10 June 1826. [8] *Staffs. Avertiser*, 17, 24 June; *The Times*, 18 June; *Dyott's Diary*, i. 379-80; Gresley mss D77/36/4, M. Lister to Gresley, 7 Aug. 1826. [9] Gresley mss D77/36/3, *passim.*; D77/36/4, Hill Trevor to Gresley, 24 Sept., 8 Nov. [Dec.]; D77/36/5, J.T. Law to same, 8 Nov.; D77/36/6, S. Brampton to same [1826]; *The Times*, 2 Sept., 10, 11 Nov.; *Berwick Advertiser*, 25 Nov. 1826. [10] *The Times*, 11 Dec. 1826. [11] For example, Gresley *v.* Collins (*The Times*, 20 July 1826, 18, 29 July, 20 Nov. 1833) and Woodyatt *v.* Gresley (ibid. 1, 8 Aug. 1826); Gresley mss D77/36/7, corresp. of W.Y. Alban, W. Heelis and W.E. Mousley with Gresley, 1830. [12] Gresley, *Letter to ... Peel on Catholic Emancipation* (1827) and *Letter to ... John, Earl of Shrewsbury in reply to ... Reasons for Not Taking the Test* (1828); Gresley mss D3999/2. [13] *Countess Granville Letters*, ii. 19; *Von Neumann Diary*, i. 187. [14] *Dyott's Diary*, ii. 39. [15] Gresley mss D77/36/4, H.M. Levett to Gresley, 27 Nov.; D77/36/5, same to same, 29, 30 Nov., R.E. Heathcote to same, 30 Nov., Hardinge to same, 6 Dec. 1827; D77/37/9, Lushington to same, 17 Apr., J. Benbow to same [Nov.] 1827; D/3038/2/2. [16] Add. 40395, f. 101; Gresley mss D77/37/10, Mousley to Gresley, 29 Jan., Benbow to same, 5 Aug.; D77/37/11, same to same, 15 Feb. 1828. [17] *The Times*, 5, 18 Feb., 11, 26 Aug., 4 Sept., 31 Oct. 1828, 12, 23 Feb., 25 Apr., 8 June, 12 Nov. 1829; Gresley mss D77/36/6, 8, *passim*; D3999/2. [18] NLW, Ormathwaite mss FG1/5, pp. 11-13. [19] Add. 40412, f. 25; *Derby Mercury*, 20 Jan. 1830; Gresley mss D3999/2. [20] Gresley mss D77/36/7, T. Hale to Gresley, 6 Feb., Moulsey to same, 26 May; D77/38/5, same to same [27 June] [July], Durham to same, 2 July; St. Deiniol's Lib. Glynne-Gladstone mss 195, T. to J. Gladstone, 28 June; Worcs. RO, Lechmere mss, Lady Gresley to Sir A. Lechmere, 3, 11 July; *Ellenborough Diary*, ii. 299; *Lichfield Mercury*, 30 July 1830. [21] *Procs. at Durham City Election* (1830); *The Times*, 27 July, 7 Aug. 1830. [22] *Derby Mercury*, 11 Aug. 1830. [23] *Dyott's Diary*, ii. 87. [24] Ormathwaite mss G37, f. 16; Gresley mss D77/36/7, pprs. 9, 10 Dec. 1830. [25] Add. 40412, f. 25. [26] Derby Local Stud. Lib. Strutt mss, Strutt to wife, 19 Nov. 1831. [27] *Dyott's Diary*, ii. 100; *Greville Mems*. iii. 6. [28] Strutt mss, Strutt to wife, 9 Mar. 1831. [29] Notts. Archives, Tallents mss, Newcastle to Tallents, 23 Apr.; Nottingham Univ. Lib. Newcastle mss Ne2 F4/1/18. [30] Newcastle mss NeC 4529, Tallents to Newcastle, 27 Apr.; 4530/1, Gresley to same, 25, 26 Apr.; Ne2 F4/1/22-24; *The Times*, 28 Apr., 3 May; Tallents mss, Gresley to Tallents, 5 May 1831. [31] *The Times*, 10 June 1831. [32] Tallents mss, Tallents to Newcastle, 22, 25 May, 6 June, 27 Nov. 1831; Add. 40402, f. 183. [33] Gresley mss D77/38/5, election pprs. Mar.-Dec. 1832; Derbys. RO D239M/F8936, G. Meynell to Sir H. Fitzherbert, 10 Mar. 1832; J. Wrigley, 'Derby and Derbys. during Great Reform Bill Crisis', *Derbys. Arch. Jnl.* ci (1988), 140-7; *Derby Mercury*, 24 Aug. 1831, 11 July, 21 Nov., 19, 26 Dec. 1832; *Dyott's Diary*, ii.153-4. [34] Add. 40412, f. 25; *Dyott's Diary* ii. 193; Heron, *Notes*, 214; *Derby Mercury*, 19 July 1837. [35] *Derbyshire Courier*, 21 Oct. 1837; PROB 11/1893/241; IR26/1481/139.

M.M.E.

GREVILLE, Sir Charles John (1780–1836), of 15 Chesterfield Street, Mdx.

WARWICK	17 May 1816–1831
WARWICK	1832–15 May 1833
WARWICK	1835–Aug. 1836

b. 5 Apr. 1780, 3rd but 2nd. surv. s. of George Greville†, 2nd earl of Warwick (*d.* 1816), and 2nd w. Henrietta, da. of Richard Vernon† of Hilton, Staffs. *educ.* Winchester 1790-3. *unm.* KCB 2 Jan. 1815. *d.* 2 Dec. 1836.

Cornet Warws. fencibles 1795, lt. 1795; ensign 10 Ft. 1796, lt. 1796, capt. 1799; capt. 81 Ft. 1803; maj. 38 Ft. 1803, lt.-col. 1805; brevet col. 1813; col. 12 British Brigade at Paris 1815; maj.-gen. 1819; col. 98 Ft. 1832; col. 38 Ft. 1836-*d*.

A career soldier, whose bravery during the Napoleonic Wars was always praised on the hustings, Greville had been substituted for his elder brother Henry as the Castle or 'church and state' Member for Warwick following the latter's succession as 3rd earl of Warwick in 1816, and his return in 1820 was assured.[1] As hitherto, in the Parliament of 1820 he adopted Lord Warwick's anti-Catholic Tory line, giving silent support to Lord Liverpool's administration.[2] He divided against Catholic relief, 28 Feb. 1821, 30 Apr. 1822, 1 Mar., 21 Apr., 10 May 1825, the attendant franchise bill, 26 Apr., and to outlaw the Catholic Association, 25 Feb. 1825. He voted against parliamentary reform, 9 May 1821. He refused to present Warwick's radical address to Queen Caroline in January 1821 and refrained from voting on the issue.[3] He divided with government on the revenue and taxation, 3 Apr., 28 May, 27 June 1821, 11, 21 Feb. 1822, and for repeal of the Foreign Enlistment Act, 16 Apr. 1823. He voted in their minority against inquiring into the prosecution of the Dublin Orange rioters, 22 Apr. 1823, and paired against inquiry into chancery arrears, 5 June 1824, and the president of the board of trade's salary, 10 Apr. 1826.[4] He voted to retain capital punishment for forgery, 23 May 1821, and against condemning the indictment in Demerara of the Methodist missionary John Smith, 11 June 1824, and the Jamaican slave trials, 2 Mar. 1826. A bid to make him mayor of Warwick (after he became an alderman in 1822) and so to disqualify him from standing there in 1826 failed, and he was returned unopposed with the independent John Tomes, the victor at the recent by-election. On the hustings he paid tribute to his late colleague Charles Mills and explained that his recent reluctance to present anti-slavery petitions derived from his conviction that although slavery was 'barbaric and the disgrace of Christians and civilized Europe, West Indian interests should be protected'.[5]

Greville's recorded activity in the 1826 Parliament is minimal. He voted against Catholic relief, 6 Mar. 1827, 12 May 1828. Following his brother's appointment (on the recommendation of the duke of Wellington's ministry) as a lord of the bedchamber in March 1828, he also voted with them on chancery delays, 24 Apr., and ordnance reductions, 4 July 1828. The patronage secretary Planta predicted that he would go 'with government' for Catholic emancipation in 1829, but he merely refrained from voting. He presented a petition for the Warwick-Napton canal bill, 27 Mar. 1829. In 1830, when Warwick's absence from the Upper House early in the session gave rise to concern,[6] Greville presented his constituents' petitions for measures to alleviate distress, 8 Mar., and against the administration of justice bill, 13 May, and abolition of the death penalty for forgery, 7 June, and divided against Jewish emancipation, 5 Apr., 17 May. His brother touted him in vain for a colonelcy that month, and although nothing came of it, at the dissolution in July Wellington suggested him as a suitable replacement for O'Neill as constable of Dublin Castle.[7] Greville had resigned as a Warwick alderman in 1827 and his return at the general election of 1830 was not at risk. However, reflecting the growing tension between the corporation and the independents, who had forwarded their own addresses of condolence and congratulation to William IV, his speech on the hustings eulogized the late king, and he refused to be drawn on retrenchment, reform or slavery.[8]

The ministry counted him among their 'friends', but he did not divide on the civil list when they were brought down, 15 Nov. 1830. He received ten days' leave after serving on the Calne election committee, 30 Nov. He presented a Warwick petition for reform and the ballot as requested, 28 Feb., but declined to endorse it, and his vote against the Grey ministry's reform bill at its second reading, 22 Mar. 1831, provoked a vigorous campaign to oust him.[9] Appealing to the self-interest of the lower orders, who, he claimed, would be disfranchised by the measure, he made it known that 'his vote against the reform bill was actuated by the more immediate effect it will have upon the representation of ... Warwick'. He canvassed personally there in April, during the Easter recess, and returned to Westminster to vote for Gascoyne's wrecking amendment, 19 Apr. 1831, by which the bill was lost.[10] His claim to be a 'moderate reformer' was unconvincing, and reformers nationwide delighted in his subsequent defeat 'at his brother's castle gate' after a riotous five-day poll.[11]

Greville was promoted colonel of the 98th Foot in 1832 and topped the poll at Warwick at the general election that year, but was unseated on petition, 15 May 1833, after malpractices by his brother and agents were exposed.[12] Standing as a Conservative, he regained his seat in 1835, but resigned the following year on account of failing heath. He died, colonel of his old regiment, the 38th Foot, in December 1836, recalled in prose and verse as a strict but popular dis-

ciplinarian and 'no drawing room soldier'.[13] His will, dated 1 Feb. 1836, took the form of a personal letter to his brother and sisters, the main beneficiaries, and was proved under £25,000, 27 Dec. 1836.[14]

[1] HP Commons, 1790-1820, iv. 97; Warwick Advertiser, 19 Feb., 4, 11 Mar. 1820. [2] Black Bk. (1823), 159; Session of Parl. 1825, p. 466. [3] Warwick Advertiser, 30 Dec. 1820, 13 Jan. 1821. [4] The Times, 12 Apr. 1826. [5] Warwick Advertiser, 2 Nov. 1822, 10, 17 June 1826; PP (1835), xxv. 661; P. Styles, 'Corporation of Warwick', Trans. Birmingham Arch. Soc. lix (1935), 115. [6] Wellington mss WP1/1105/10. [7] Ibid. 1113/5; 1117/36; 1131/20. [8] Warwick Advertiser, 19 May 1827, 24, 31 July, 7 Aug. 1830; Styles, 116. [9] Warwick Advertiser, 5 Feb., 5 Mar. 1831. [10] Ibid. 26 Mar.; The Times, 14 Apr. 1831. [11] Warwick Advertiser, 30 Apr., 7 May; Creevey mss, Creevey to Miss Ord, 4 May; Brougham mss, G. Phillips to Brougham, 5 May 1831; VCH Warws. viii. 503. [12] The Times, 6 Oct., 15 Dec. 1832, 20 May 1833. [13] Warwick Advertiser, 10 Dec. 1836; Warws. RO, Lucy [of Charlecote] mss L6/1719; Gent. Mag. (1837), i. 203. [14] PROB 11/1870/715; IR26/1418/759.

M.M.E.

GREY, Hon. Charles (1804–1870), of Sheen, Surr.

CHIPPING WYCOMBE   26 June 1832–1837

b. 15 Mar. 1804, 2nd s. of Charles Grey[†], 2nd Earl Grey (*d.* 1845), and Mary Elizabeth, da. of William Brabazon Ponsonby[†] of Bishop's Court, co. Kildare; bro. of Henry George Grey, Visct. Howick*. *m.* 26 July 1836, Caroline Eliza, da. of Sir Thomas Harvie Farquhar, 2nd bt., 2s. (1 *d.v.p.*) 4da. *d.* 31 Mar. 1870.

2nd lt. Rifle Brigade 1820; lt. 23 Ft. 1823; capt. 43 Ft. 1825; maj. unattached (half-pay) 1828; maj. 60 Ft. 1829; lt.-col. unattached (half-pay) 1831; lt.-col. 71 Ft. 1833; half-pay 1842; col. army 1846; maj.-gen. 1854; col. 3 Ft. 1860; lt.-gen. 1861; col. 71 Ft. 1863-*d.*; gen. 1865.

Priv. sec. to fa. as first ld. of treasury Aug. 1832-July 1834, to Prince Albert 1849-61, to Queen Victoria 1861-*d.*; jt.-keeper of privy purse 1866-*d.*

Grey's father preferred him to his elder brother Lord Howick and, remembering his own misery at Eton, had him educated privately and carefully at their Northumberland home at Howick, where a relaxed regime gave him a happy boyhood, although idleness was not tolerated and much stress was laid on duty and obligation.[1] Lord Grey was unhappy with his choice of an army career (in the tradition of his grandfather), believing that the law would serve him better, but obtained for him a commission in the Rifle Brigade in November 1820, when he told Grey's mother:

This, I conclude, will give him pleasure. It inspires me only with melancholy, in thinking that with the talents and advantages of education he possesses, the highest distinctions of the state as well as reputation and fortune are within his power and that he abandoned them for a profession in which he will too probably live uncomfortably and die a beggar. I am afraid however that the die must now be considered as cast, and I have only to pray that he may never find reason to repent his choice.[2]

When Grey went to Ireland with his regiment in 1821 his father, commenting that 'though the army is your profession ... you are not to consider yourself precluded from other things', namely diplomacy or Parliament, exhorted him to read Demosthenes and Homer.[3] The following year Lord Holland's son Henry Fox*, a guest at Howick, found him to be 'clever, and agreeable from his boyish high spirits'.[4] His father bought him a captaincy in the 43 Foot in 1825 and, after a spell near Edinburgh, where he was urged to take advantage of its 'opportunities for improvement', and assisting in Lord Howick's unsuccessful bids to secure the Northumberland county seat in the spring of 1826, he was on active service in Portugal from November that year until the end of 1827.[5] Lord Grey purchased him a half-pay majority for £1,400 in 1828, when he was an aide-de-camp to Lord Anglesey as lord lieutenant of Ireland in the Wellington ministry.[6] After Anglesey's recall and the concession of Catholic emancipation, he was stationed with his regiment at Limerick, whence he went to Ennis in August 1829 to witness the county Clare by-election which saw the final return of Daniel O'Connell. He formed the erroneous opinion that 'O'Connell and his set are very well disposed to be quiet and conciliatory'.[7] By April 1830, when he was still in Ireland, he was anxious to secure promotion; but it was not until July 1831, by which time his father, an enthusiastic practitioner of nepotism, was in power as the head of the reform ministry, that he obtained a half-pay lieutenant-colonelcy.[8] For most of that year he was abroad, spending time at Gibraltar and sailing to Turkey in his sailor brother Frederick's ship.[9]

In June 1832 he was sent by his father's ministry to contest a vacancy for Chipping Wycombe on the interest of the largely Whig corporation. According to his opponent Benjamin Disraeli†, whose father lived at nearby Bradenham, and who, having failed to obtain government backing, stood on an ostensibly radical platform, Grey was provided with two treasury minders, and on his first appearance in the borough 'made a stammering speech of ten minutes from his phaeton'. Though completely outshone on the hustings by the flamboyant Disraeli, Grey, who at the nomination praised his father as a veteran reformer, denied being a government nominee, said that he would 'never' support the ballot or triennial parliaments and advocated economy, retrenchment and 'a total and effectual alteration' of Irish tithes, had a

comfortable victory.[10] He took his seat on 2 July and was in the government majorities on the Russian-Dutch loan, 12, 16, 20 July 1832, but is not known to have spoken in debate in the six weeks before the Parliament was dissolved. He was his father's private secretary from that time until the end of his premiership in 1834. He successfully contested Chipping Wycombe at the general elections of 1832 and 1835, but retired from Parliament, where he made no mark, in 1837. He found his metier as a dedicated and discreet private secretary first to the Prince Consort, of whose *Early Life* he published an account in 1867, and then to Queen Victoria. He paid homage to his father with his reverential *Life and Opinions of the 2nd Earl Grey* (1861). He suffered a paralytic stroke on 26 Mar. 1870 and died without regaining consciousness five days later at his apartment in St. James's Palace.[11] His elder son Charles had died in 1855, but the survivor, Albert Henry George (1851-1917), succeeded Howick as 4th Earl Grey in 1894.

[1] E.A. Smith, *Lord Grey*, 92, 137-9; *Oxford DNB*. [2] Grey mss, Grey to Lady Grey, 9 Nov. 1820; Smith, 142-3. [3] Smith, 143. [4] *Fox Jnl.* 145. [5] Grey mss GRE/B22/1/4-30, 41-70. [6] Smith, 143-4. [7] Grey mss B22/1/72, 73. [8] Ibid. B22/2/7. [9] Ibid. D1A. [10] *Bucks Gazette*, 16, 23, 30 June 1832; *Disraeli Letters*, i. 201. [11] *The Times*, 1 Apr. 1870.

D.R.F.

GREY, Henry, Visct. Howick (1802–1894).[1]

WINCHELSEA	1826–1830
HIGHAM FERRERS	1830–1831
NORTHUMBERLAND	1831–1832
NORTHUMBERLAND NORTH	1832–1841
SUNDERLAND	17 Sept. 1841–17 July 1845

b. 28 Dec. 1802, 1st. s. of Charles Grey†, 2nd Earl Grey, and Mary Elizabeth, da. of William Brabazon Ponsonby† of Bishop's Court, co. Kildare; bro. of Hon. Charles Grey*. *educ.* by Rev. James Morton 1809-18; Trinity Coll. Camb. 1818. *m.* 9 Aug. 1832, Maria, da. of Sir Joseph Copley, 3rd bt., of Sprotborough, Yorks., *s.p. styled* Visct. Howick 1807-45; *suc.* fa. as 3rd Earl Grey 17 July 1845; KG 1863; GCMG 1869. *d.* 9 Oct. 1894.

Under-sec. of state for war and colonies Nov. 1830-Apr. 1833; for home affairs Jan.-July 1834; sec. at war Apr. 1835-Aug. 1839; PC 18 Apr. 1835; sec. of state for war and colonies June 1846-Feb. 1852.

Ld. lt. Northumb. 1847-77.

Howick was named after his childless great-uncle, Sir Henry Grey, to whose Northumberland estate of Howick his father, leader of the Foxite Whigs, succeeded in 1808. A highly intelligent, difficult and obstinate boy (qualities that, according to the Whig lawyer Henry Brougham*, he used to 'great harm' as an 'underling' in his father's administration), he lacked the warmth and good looks of his next brother Charles, their father's favourite. It was also Howick's misfortune that his tall, slender form, 'carroty hair' and slight lameness were readily caricatured.[2] He was tutored privately under close parental supervision before going up to Cambridge, where, as president of the Union in 1822, his debating companions included Thomas Babington Macaulay* and Winthrop Mackworth Praed*.[3] Certain that the personal antipathy of George IV (who never forgave him for fathering a child with the duchess of Devonshire), precluded his return to office, Grey looked to Howick from an early age to realize his ambitions; and directly the 'insanity' of the sitting Whig Thomas Wentworth Beaumont manifested itself in August 1823, he initiated negotiations to bring him in for Northumberland at the earliest opportunity.[4] Howick was three months short of his majority and touring Switzerland with Charles when alerted to the scheme, of which he wrote:

I hardly know whether I ought to be pleased or not at the effect which you tell me this event may produce on my own prospects ... but at the same time I cannot but feel considerable diffidence in myself and consequently a good deal of uneasiness at the idea that there is a possibility of my being called so soon into a situation where so much will be required of me.[5]

Making his acquaintance in August 1824, John Cam Hobhouse* 'thought little of him when I first saw him', but gradually appreciated his 'original and decisive turn of mind', liberal opinions and 'perhaps future distinction'.[6] Howick's aloofness towards the squires at Newcastle-upon-Tyne races that month and the magistrates and county gentry the following year annoyed his Whig sponsors in Northumberland and blighted his prospects. The squires and ship owners also disliked his flirtation with political economy, and his parents' residence at Dartmouth during his mother's illness reduced his chance of success. Beaumont's repeated refusal to stand down and the intrigues of rival candidates added to the uncertainty.[7] In the absence of his father and with his brother-in-law John Lambton* too ill to advise him, on 2 Feb. 1826 Howick declared his candidature for the Northumberland seat unexpectedly made vacant by the death of the Tory Charles John Brandling. He thus embarked on what, in view of his pre-poll 'retirement' the following week, proved to be a costly but successful attempt to prevent the return of the Canningite Henry Thomas Liddell*,

by supporting the anti-Catholic Tory Matthew Bell*. The by-election also gave Howick a platform to launch his canvass for the general election in June, and enabled his friends to check the aspirations of the former Member and Whig renegade Sir Charles Monck of Belsay Hall.[8] Overawed at the prospect of making his first major public speech at the nomination at Alnwick, 21 Feb., he wrote to Grey, 14 Feb.:

My great difficulty is what to say with regard to my political opinions, as there are so few questions of any importance on which one can commit oneself without inconvenience. I fear it is impossible to express an opinion in favour of parliamentary reform in however guarded a manner. The Catholic question it would also I think be dangerous to touch upon. I have seen in canvassing very strong indications of a general feeling that something should be done for the slaves in the West Indian islands. Would there be any objection to my avowing a similar opinion? I think I might also say something in favour of the commercial policy which ministers seem inclined to adopt, though this must also be done with caution, not to alarm the farmers and landlords about the corn laws.[9]

Initial reports of his reception, 'statesmanlike' neutrality and speech, in which he defended the 'constitution of 1688' and advocated Catholic emancipation, moderate reform and an abolition of slavery 'consistent with the rights of property and the well-being of the slaves', were encouraging.[10] However, as James Abercromby* predicted, 17 Mar., and George Tierney* later confirmed, his prospects were poor, and plans were laid to seat him elsewhere.[11] Tierney fretted over the cost to Grey and Howick's want of energy, but deemed him an eager young man 'who possesses many requisites for a debater in Parliament', and said he would 'not be surprised if he succeeds in the House'.[12] Contrary to his agents' predictions, the doubts expressed by Charles, who assisted with the canvass, were realized, and Howick was easily defeated in a four-cornered contest at the general election. The first to retire, he spent £19,213 in addition to his by-election costs, and the whole was financed by the sale of Ulgham Grange for £40,000 in 1827.[13] Lord Darlington meanwhile had returned him for Winchelsea, where Thomas Creevey* deputized.[14]

Howick, whose conduct was monitored closely for Grey by his brother-in-law Edward Ellice*, who had lost his Coventry seat,[15] made what Abercromby termed 'rather a bad beginning' by differing from Brougham and the Whig leaders and voting in Hume's minority on the address, 21 Nov. 1826.[16] He explained to his father, who in reply criticized Brougham and warned him against Hume, that

I was a good deal puzzled how to vote, as after the House was cleared for the division Brougham said that he should vote against Hume's amendment and afterwards propose that which Mr. Grattan had intended to move. It appeared to me that it would have been better not to move any, as it was universally agreed that there was nothing objectionable in the address, but if any addition was to be made to it I most decidedly preferred Hume's as I did not see why the House should pledge itself to take into consideration one or two of the topics he brought forward and not others, as they appear to me to be all of great importance, and as he explained that by the words 'free trade in corn' he only meant that the importation should not be *prohibited* though it might be subject to a duty, I did not think his amendment went to bind us to any particular line of conduct hereafter. Most people, however, were of opinion as you may see by the numbers. We were only 24 for the first amendment and 58 for the second.[17]

Pressed by Grey to attend constantly and 'serve a regular apprenticeship till you have made yourself thoroughly master of all the forms and proceedings of the House', he formed a close friendship with Charles Wood*, who in 1829 became his brother-in-law. Like Ellice, Howick was one of Grey's most reliable political informers during his frequent absences from London, and the regular recipient of his advice.[18] An inhibited speaker, rarely satisfied with his performance, he 'took advantage of a sparsely attended House to say a few words against the vote for the military college', 20 Feb. 1827, 'principally to get over the awkwardness of a first appearance' and because he felt that there was 'no more necessity for having officers educated at the public expense than lawyers or clergymen'. Grey wrote that his observations were 'very proper' and 'sensible'.[19] His vote against the award to the duke of Clarence, 16 Feb., however, troubled Grey, who was concerned at the political capital made of the issue while the succession to Lord Liverpool as premier was uncertain. Heeding his advice, Howick declined to vote on the issue, 3 Mar., and stated that he 'did not choose to join in what I thought a useless and vexatious opposition with Hume and his associates'.[20] He took a particular interest in the 26 Feb. debate on Lord Althorp's proposal for a standing committee on election petitions and, encouraged by Grey, learnt much about tactics and procedures as the Whig Sir Francis Blake's* nominee on the Berwick-upon-Tweed committee.[21] He divided for Catholic relief, 6 Mar., but the anti-Catholic majority that day, Burdett's speech and inaccurate reporting of the debate dismayed him.[22] More of a free trader than Grey, who complained to Princess Lieven that he voted 'in every division with *les hommes des principes*', he 'contended that fluctuating duties work ill for the landed interest' and resisted

pressure from Ellice and Lambton to toe the line on the corn laws.[23] 'Convinced that a much meaner approach to a sound system' was necessary than what ministers proposed, he praised Whitmore's resolutions, which Grey deplored, and divided with him for a 50s. pivot price, 9 Mar. To Grey's relief, he disputed Whitmore's tenet that 'landlords had been repaid (for their investment) by the high price of grain'.[24] He voted against increased protection for barley, 12 Mar., and for the staggered introduction of a fixed 10s. duty, 27 Mar. He voted in the minorities for inquiry into Leicester corporation, 15 Mar., the spring guns bill, 23 Mar., and the Lisburn Orange magistrates, 29 Mar. He voted with Tierney to delay supplies during the ministerial uncertainty, 30 Mar., and again on the Irish estimates and chancery arrears, 5 Apr. Privy to Grey's fears that the Whigs would be seduced and betrayed by Canning, he fully acquiesced in his decision to remain in opposition during Canning's premiership, although his intended mentor Lord Lansdowne and Tierney took office and Lambton returned from Italy to support them.[25] As yet Darlington's endorsement of Canning did not jeopardise his seat.[26] Adopting a high profile when the new ministry was tested, he was a teller for the minority for removing bankruptcy jurisdiction from chancery, 11 May, and voted for the disfranchisement of Penryn, 28 May. Grey was 'very glad' to learn that he had spoken and voted in the minority of ten for repeal of the stamp duty on small publications, 31 May, a motion which by invoking the Six Acts was deliberately calculated to 'distress' the Whigs.[27] He did not interrupt his continental tour on account of Canning's death in August 1827 and was expected to oppose the Goderich ministry, which Grey's erstwhile allies adhered to and to whom Lambton owed his elevation to the peerage as Baron Durham.[28]

Howick wrote to Grey from Paris in January 1828 for clarification of the confused ministerial situation and, acting on his advice, he refrained from deliberate hostility to the Wellington ministry until after the Huskissonite secession in May.[29] He naturally voted against them for repeal of the Test Acts, 26 Feb., for which he presented a petition, 18 Mar.; and he presented a petition, 25 Apr., and voted for Catholic relief, 12 May. On East Retford, which he agreed merited disfranchisement, 10 Mar., he maintained that the problem of bribery was widespread and had to be dealt with, for it was notorious that nine-tenths of borough Members were 'returned by bribes of money or money's worth'. He made his support for the disfranchisement bill conditional on the failure of the sluicing amendment and voted accordingly, 21 Mar. He also opposed its revival, 2 June, and objected to changes in its details, 27 June. Speaking that day, he toyed with the notion of giving its seats to the county instead of the hundred, but instead he took up a suggestion in Lord John Russell's speech and proposed an amendment transferring them to Yorkshire, which he lost by 95-17. His views on corn law reform were unchanged and, warning of the dangers of 'extreme protection' and 'gambling speculations on the price of corn', he voted for the gradual introduction of a fixed 10s. duty, 29 Apr. When Lord Cleveland (Darlington) afterwards criticized his vote against the award to Canning's family, 13 May, and bade him refrain from hostility towards the ministry, Grey fully endorsed his decision to offer to vacate his seat and approved the 'honourable compromise' whereby he kept it.[30] Joining in the opposition's criticism of the finance committee of which he had been a member, on 16 May he complained that they had been asked to consider revenues before establishments and attacked the master of the mint Herries and chancellor of the exchequer Goulburn, whose estimates he now criticized; Herries accused him of 'constitutional ignorance'. He clashed with Calcraft before voting against the civil list pensions, 20 May, supported inquiry into the circulation of small bank notes, 3 June, and seconded Hume's amendment to the promissory notes bill, 16 June. He spoke and voted in condemnation of the Buckingham House expenditure, 23 June, to reduce the salary of the lieutenant-general of the ordnance, 4 July, and against the grant for North American fortifications, 7 July 1828, when he harassed ministers in a vain attempt to delay the vote on the Canadian waterways grant.

Howick toured Scotland during the recess.[31] He was shooting at Woburn in January 1829 when he learnt of Wellington and Peel's decision to concede Catholic emancipation.[32] Cleveland directed him to 'abstain from *supporting* any question which could be described as an attack upon or hostile to the government, except as to the affairs of Ireland', and he was glad to find Lord Holland, whom he met at the Fox dinner, 7 Feb., 'apparently less indisposed towards the duke than I feared'.[33] He attended the House almost daily, paid social calls most mornings, enjoyed the theatre and frequented Brooks's, to which he had been admitted, 10 Feb. 1824, and the Travellers' Club, where he often dined and played billiards or cards. He considered the emancipation proposed 'as complete and satisfactory as one could possibly wish', admired Peel's speech on introducing it, 5 Mar., and was relieved when the opposition meeting at Burdett's that day resolved not to oppose the attendant franchise bill:

Whatever objections I may have to the principle on which it is done and the manner of doing it, I am inclined to believe that the result will be the obtaining a more independent body of electors in Ireland and that it is not impossible it may lead to the substitution of a more reasonable qualification than the present technical freehold in England. It seems at least a favourable opportunity of exposing the absurdity of the existing system.

He paired for emancipation, after failing to dissuade George Moore from moving factiously for adjournment, 6 Mar., and quibbled at the Ultras' delaying tactics before pairing again, 9, 17, 20 Mar. Supporting the franchise bill that day, he found that he could make 'little or no use' of his prepared draft and complained that the only part of his speech listened to was his impromptu response to Lord George Cavendish Bentinck. Already ill with a severe cough, he was treated by Sir Henry Halford two days later and was absent from the House until June. Sounded meanwhile as a candidate for Cambridge University (where he went to support the Whig William Cavendish*), he told Ellice that he wished 'nothing to do with it, as, in the first place I am convinced I should have no chance of success, in the next, though my present seat is not very secure or altogether satisfactory, I should gain little by the change, as it is not likely with my opinions I will remain long in public life without offending such a body of constituents as the senate of Cambridge'. On 2 June he presented a petition for inquiry into the English universities and the established church in Ireland, divided for Lord Blandford's reform proposals and, 'quite put out by the inattention of the House', tried to repeat what he could recall of his March 1828 speech before voting against issuing the East Retford writ. Bored and unwell, he went to Ascot races, 18 June, and attended the Fox dinner at Greenwich on the 27th. He cancelled his planned continental tour on medical advice because of a severely ulcerated throat and returned to Howick, where he read widely, worked on a new speech and resolutions on East Retford and infuriated his father by applying to the duke of Northumberland's agent for permission to shoot at Long Houghton and Renington. Leaving Alnwick on 16 Dec. 1829 with his sister Georgiana, he attended Rainhill locomotive trials, toured the commercial and manufacturing districts of Liverpool, Manchester, the Black Country and Birmingham and visited Lord Dacre at The Hoo and the duke of Bedford at Woburn, whence he returned to London with Lord John Russell, 3 Feb. 1830.

Cleveland's adhesion to the ministry, hinted at in June 1829, was confirmed, 12 Jan. 1830, and Howick's tenure at Winchelsea remained in doubt until a compromise permitting him to sit unimpeded until the general election was effected a few hours before the address was moved, 4 Feb.[34] With Grey now a contender for office to bolster the ailing administration, Howick was 'very much at a loss how to vote, as I did not wish to give a triumph to the enemies of government, while I could not pretend to deny the universality of distress'. Refusing to be ruled by Durham, he divided 'with government', after first expressing broad agreement with Althorp, who opposed them, and stating that he would defer judgement until the details of the ministerial retrenchment proposals were known. He cautioned against clamouring for a depreciation of the currency or the appointment of a finance committee. Denis Le Marchant[†] held him responsible, by example, for 'saving the government from a signal defeat'.[35] Following the advice of his uncle Grey of Falloden to 'speak continually on all trifling questions in the House of Commons', he gained in confidence that session, and to his father's delight became 'fully launched' as one of the best prospects among the young Whigs.[36] Determined to move his East Retford resolutions despite Grey's misgivings, he was prevented from doing so by his late arrival in the House, after the amendment proposing the transfer of its seats to Birmingham had been moved, 11 Feb. He nevertheless delivered much of his intended speech, which questioned the justification for treating it as an individual disfranchisement case rather than a general bribery and corruption issue, before voting for the amendment, pressed for a select committee on bribery as a step towards reform, and failed (by 55-154) to prevent the introduction of the disfranchisement bill, which he criticized as *ex post facto* law.[37] Elated by his performance, he defended the landed interest when the Essex distress petition was presented next day and ridiculed the Colchester Member Daniel Whittle Harvey's plea for rent-control legislation. Newly fitted with 'artificial teeth', he seconded Hume's resolutions for tax reductions with a short critique of finance committees and currency reform, 15 Feb.[38] Advocating 'nothing but a thorough reform', he voted for Blandford's proposals, 18 Feb., but he privately ridiculed them as 'a mere schoolboy's declaration with a few good sentences in it' and 'a tissue of nonsenses'. He voted to reduce the army estimates 'against my original intention, principally on account of an excellent speech of Labouchere's', 19 Feb. Writing to Grey that day, Althorp, to whom Howick had confided his dislike of Huskisson, noted his 'rapid improvement ... readiness in reply and perfect command of words [that] are putting him on the first scale of debating speakers'.[39] He voted for the enfranchisement of

Birmingham, Leeds and Manchester, 23 Feb., inquiry into Newark's petition of complaint against the duke of Newcastle, on which he regretted speaking, 1 Mar., and Russell's reform motion, 28 May.[40] Unwell with a cold, he paired for the transfer of East Retford's seats to Birmingham, 5 Mar., and divided silently against the disfranchisement bill, 15 Mar. 1830.

At Grey's request he attended the Whig meetings at Althorp's rooms on 3 and 6 Mar. which invited Althorp to become leader 'for one definite object, namely the reduction of expenditure and of taxation' and resolved not to unite with another party. He recorded that 'very little was done as a great many of those who were present were irreconcilably adverse to a property tax, without which it does not appear to me that much can be done'.[41] Perturbed when Grey justified opposition to the tax, warned of the danger of proceeding without Huskisson and detailed Brougham and Althorp's shortcomings as party leaders, he discussed politics at length with Wood and called on Lord Fitzwilliam, 11 Mar.[42] He harried ministers on the estimates, 8, 9 Mar., and was a speaker and minority teller for Graham's motion criticizing the recent appointment of a treasurer of the navy, 12 Mar., when Canningite resentment at the veiled attack on the incumbent Thomas Frankland Lewis* ensured that Peel had the 'best of the debate'. Howick, failing to comprehend this, wrote: 'I thought myself better than I ever did before, but I suppose it was not so, as not a soul paid me the slightest compliment and I have generally had more than I deserved.'[43] He deemed Goulburn's financial statement, 15 Mar., 'upon the whole satisfactory' and a 'good beginning', and resented having to listen to Davenport's 'tiresome and stupid' speech on the state of the nation, to which he was expected to reply, 16 Mar. Doing so, he repeated his 4 Feb. statement that the ministry were 'upon the whole ... entitled to our thanks', criticized Davenport's obsession with the currency, which he conceded was 'neither economical nor secure', and angered Herries by declaring that the banking system required investigation. He joined in the general clamour before voting against the navy estimates, 22 Mar., and for inquiry into tax revision, 25 Mar., and paired against the Bathurst and Dundas pensions, 26 Mar. Being busy in committee on the Glasgow railway bill, where he was hampered by his ignorance of Scottish law, he spoke only briefly in justification of his vote to abolish the office of lieutenant-general of the ordnance, 29 Mar. 1830. He paired for inquiry into the management of crown land revenues next day and stayed at Woolbeding, The Hoo and Hatfield during the Easter recess.

Undeterred by speculation that Wellington was strengthening the ministry, he divided against reforming Irish vestries, 27 Apr., for information on British interference in Terceira, 28 Apr., and for economies, 30 Apr., 3 May, but he deplored Hume and O'Connell's repeated attacks on the estimates, 30 Apr. 1830. He attended at Althorp's, 1 May, and afterwards discussed the currency and political economy, on which Alexander Baring coached him, with Charles Poulett Thomson at Brooks's. To his relief Grey, who returned to London on 5 May after a ten-month absence, was 'getting quite as much inclined to oppose the duke as I can be'. He criticized the grants for colonial churches and the Canadian legislature, 10 May, voted for reductions in official salaries, 10, 11 May, and to repeal the Irish coal duties, 13 May, when he was peeved to find that his like-minded colleagues Fazakerley, Milton, Poulett Thomson, Ridley and Michael Angelo Taylor had voted for them on principle, as had been his own intention before hearing Althorp and Acland's counter arguments. Grey, now contemplating heading a Whig-Huskissonite coalition, was prepared in the event of office to offer him a lordship of the treasury, which pleased him greatly, notwithstanding his preference for the post of undersecretary at the home office. Preoccupied with the hackney coach committee, he voted silently for returns of privy councillors' emoluments, 14 May, and in his journal criticized the gross exaggerations in its mover Graham's speech, which 'nine tenths of the public' would believe. His hostility to the government had increased and he approved Brougham's proposal to obstruct money votes, although he deplored the precedent it set by 'taking the only nights in the week the ministers have for public business'. He voted for Jewish emancipation, 17 May, and to abolish the death penalty for forgery, 24 May, 7 June, and held ministers directly responsible for its defeat in the Lords, 20 July. His 'half-prepared' speech on Labouchere's resolutions on the civil government of Canada had been in train since he ordered papers on 5 Mar., and he was bitterly disappointed with his fudged and lacklustre performance, which added nothing to the debate, 25 May. He succeeded in engaging Peel in discussion on the grants for South American missions, 7 June, and consular services, 11 June, and resolved to take the sense of the House on them again. He revised his speech on the currency with Wood and Hammick before speaking against Attwood's proposals, 8 June, but could add little on depreciation to what Herries and Baring said and so concentrated on their differences on the Promissory Notes Act and pressed for its repeal. On 14 June he voted to cut the grants for

Nova Scotia and Prince Edward Island and failed by a disappointing 46-145 to halve that for the Society for the Propagation of the Gospels. He wrote afterwards that he had been 'too busy playing billiards at the Travellers'' to revise his speech and 'totally threw away the very best opportunity of making an effective speech ... that year' by delivering a 'weak and confused statement'. He considered Huskisson's 'excellent' speech on the sugar duties 'fatal to the ministry', 21 June, and rebuked O'Connell for promoting instability by suggesting that the Irish people should apply to the banks for gold, 24 June. He deliberately avoided legal debates, but regretted his inability to speak effectively against the increased recognizances proposed under the libel law amendment bill, 9, 20 July. Speculation about Grey's appointment to office and a junction with the Huskissonites revived following the king's death, and Howick was heartened by the increased opposition attendance at Althorp's, 4 July 1830, when they resolved to go into outright opposition next Parliament should Wellington 'do no better'. At the meeting he disputed Althorp's decision to proceed with Robert Grant's motion on the regency on the 6th without forcing a division and infuriated Brougham, who had a bill prepared. He wrote of the ensuing debacle, in which 'we were only 93 to 246', that Brougham's speech was 'most clever and amusing though not much to the purpose, certainly not such a display as to warrant his leading us into such a scrape in order to satisfy his vanity by making it'. At the general election he took an interest in developments in Durham and in Northumberland, where Beaumont replaced Liddell, saw suggestions that he should stand for Southwark, Surrey or Hull quashed by his father, and was substituted by Fitzwilliam for his uncle Frederick Ponsonby at Higham Ferrers, which was 'better than being out of Parliament, though a disagreeable way of coming in, as I cannot bear turning him out'.[44]

Brougham's speeches following his Yorkshire victory and presumption in speaking for the Whigs in *The Result of the General Election* and *Country Without a Government* annoyed Howick, although he conceded the need to co-operate with the disaffected Tories and Huskisson to overthrow the ministry. Despite his previous criticism, he viewed Huskisson's death on 15 Sept. 1830 as 'a great loss at the moment'. Aware through Holland and Grey of the obstacle it presented to recruiting Lord Palmerston* and Lord Melbourne, who had 'little confidence in *Althorp* and less in *HB*', he welcomed Palmerston's rejection of an overture from Wellington in October and acted afterwards with Graham to test the reaction of the Huskissonites and the Whig hierarchy to Brougham's moderate reform scheme. The Whigs at Althorp's backed it, 31 Oct., but in private on 6 Nov. Howick, as his father's emissary, and Graham agreed that it would 'never answer'. They sounded Althorp and Palmerston and were instrumental in persuading Brougham next day that to succeed he should move for inquiry only and delay doing so until 16 Nov., three days before the next Whig muster.[45] On 2 Nov., Howick stated that he would have considered the address 'very satisfactory had it not been for the passage relating to Belgium and the absence of anything about reform'. Privately, he considered Althorp's reply 'injudicious', Blandford's amendment 'almost as long as a pamphlet and still more absurd' and O'Connell's speech impressive. On 5 Nov. he drew out Peel by reiterating his opinion that ministers had resisted reform and underestimated the likelihood of war in the Netherlands. When the Whigs went into outright opposition following the cancellation of the king's visit to the City, 8 Nov., he considered it only a matter of time before Wellington was 'turned out either by a vote or by the king', and he attributed his defeat on the civil list, 15 Nov. 1830, to which he contributed, and announced personally to Grey, Durham and Holland, to Tory votes.[46] Lampooned as one of Grey's family administration, with his uncles Ellice and Ponsonby and brothers-in-law Barrington, Durham and Wood, he was passed over for the war office and became deputy, at £2,000 a year, to the amenable Lord Goderich at the colonial office: 'a place which though there is an immense deal to do and I am rather afraid of it I think I shall like very much as the business is some of it of an important and interesting kind'.[47]

Speaking officially for the first time, 6 Dec., he confirmed his 1827 vote against the Canadian waterways grant on announcing its continuation, and warned Hume, who requested returns on colonial pensions, against relying on the editor of the *Sydney Monitor*'s inaccurate statistics, 23 Dec. 1830. He presented and endorsed anti-slavery petitions, 7 Dec. 1830, and wrote optimistically to Charles that day of their father's prospects of securing reform and preventing an Anglo-French war, but predicted strong opposition in the Commons after Christmas.[48] His defence of the chancellor Althorp's decision to end the protective tariff on Cape wine, 14 Feb. 1831, which he repeated at subsequent meetings with the wine merchants, did little to allay their hostility to the measure and the ministry, and Althorp may have stifled his interventions on the budget.[49] He introduced his Canada bill confidently and with candour, 18 Feb., drawing heavily on the review of Canadian papers he had prepared in opposition. His conduct towards Goderich's

predecessor Murray, whose 1829 and 1830 bills had been timed out, was conciliatory throughout and he avoided apportioning blame for the breakdown in relations between the colonial legislatures and Parliament and the archaic methods of fixing and financing official salaries. He proposed adding 14 members to the Canadian legislative council, forbade the judges from interfering with its operations and provided for pensions and salaries by means of a civil list until the Canadians had complete budgetary control. Responding to the clamour generated by the 'Swing' riots, he sounded his colleagues and members of the 1827 committee preparatory to introducing a bill to facilitate subsidized emigration, 22 Feb.[50] Fierce opposition inside and outside Parliament ensured that it became a casualty of the dissolution.[51] He presented papers on slavery and manumission, 10, 25, 28 Mar., and pressed Buxton to postpone his abolition motion, 29 Mar. When it came on, 15 Apr. 1831, he rejected a suggestion that the matter be taken over by the colonial office, criticized the Jamaican legislature and their Acts and declared against precipitate abolition, as not in the best interests of the slaves, and likewise against letting the proprietors' compensation claims stand in the way of emancipation. He stated that an order in council similar to Canning's in 1823 was in preparation, but gave nothing away when Peel pressed for details. The West India merchant Thomas Gladstone* thought it 'disgraceful that such principles should activate a person in his office and acting in the House as a principal'. Brougham, claiming to represent the abolitionists, was also disappointed; but to the Quaker John Gurney, who discussed it with Grey, Howick's speech deserved 'praise for its honesty and feeling as well as its talent', although 'the old premier seemed to think that his son had been carried by his zeal rather too far'.[52]

Howick predicted that the popular clamour for reform would frighten opposition into accepting the ministerial bill as an alternative to revolution, and although he acknowledged that the scale of the changes proposed on 1 Mar. 1831 had astounded even the Whigs, he remained optimistic of its success.[53] He intervened to support Russell, 3 Mar., and, using his East Retford notes, replied at length three days later to Warrender's 'measure of spoliation' speech with what William Ord* termed 'an impudent one', in which he conceded that reform was popularly sought 'as a means of providing against misgovernment and extravagance', but said it could 'afford no immediate relief'.[54] Warning of the 'ruinous consequences' of rejecting the measure, he added:

The real wisdom ... of this plan consists in its apparent boldness. I admire it because it leaves nothing behind it for future strife or future concession; whereas had it been framed on a contrary principle, and left half of these rotten boroughs in existence, or taken only one Member from each of them, instead of a final settlement, we should have had ... a payment on account ... a short and hollow truce.

He presented favourable petitions from Stockport and Alnwick, 15 Mar. Greville noted that he was now in high spirits and pleased with the popularity of the bill in Northumberland, where the Whigs invited him 'to propose himself (at the proper time)' and formed an association 'for the purpose of bringing him in free from expense'.[55] He anticipated that the single vote majority for the second reading, 22 Mar., would make it impossible to carry the bill in that Parliament, took heart from ministers' reception at the Guildhall banquet, 4 Apr., the success of the younger William Chaytor, a reformer, at the Durham by-election and the furore generated by Wellington's anti-reform speech. With his tenure at Higham Ferrers in doubt, he also hoped to profit from hostility in Northumberland to the anti-reformer Bell, although he was unwilling to 'burn my fingers with another contest'.[56] He silenced the critics of the northern coal owners' cartel, 28 Mar. At the dissolution he solicited the support of Portland, the Whig grandees Carlisle and Tankerville and the first lord of the admiralty Graham as custodian of Greenwich Hospital interest, and announced his candidature for Northumberland, where, standing jointly with Beaumont, he saw off a challenge mounted by the duke of Northumberland through Bell, whose retirement left them unopposed.[57] The Newcastle barrister James Losh complained that his 'address is cold, very cold, if his manners prove as much so when he arrives he will damage us greatly'.[58] Cautioned specifically by Grey against using 'any of the vulgar and hackneyed terms of *rotten boroughs, borough mongerers*, etc.', he stated on the hustings, 9 May:

For four long years was the miserable question of East Retford ... suffered to hang on, detaining public business, leading to the breaking up of one administration, and greatly weakening another, and all for the purpose of determining whether certain persons had been guilty of an offence which is of every day practice. When we entreated them to institute a similar examination into every borough in the kingdom, and not to waste their time on an isolated case ... we pleaded in vain ... But happily we failed in our endeavours, and I rejoice that we did so because to those two discussions and the repeated exposure of the effects of the system, I attribute much of the feeling for reform which now exists in the country.

He censured Members who had failed to vote to transfer East Retford's seats to Birmingham yet now claimed to be 'moderate reformers', and defended the provisions of the bill.[59] When Lord Stormont called him to account in the House, 21 June 1831, for failing to intervene when the 'sovereignty of the people' was toasted before 'the king' at his election dinner, he blamed his supporters' ignorance on 'a matter of form'. Ponsonby, for whom he had neglected to find a seat, berated him in an acrimonious correspondence over the next eight months and protested at being treated like a 'sucked orange'.[60]

The 1831 Parliament proved to be a testing and formative one for Howick, who in addition to dealing with the slavery question was charged with preparing and handling bills reforming commerce and the colonial legislatures. He clashed frequently with the Worcester Member Robinson, an expert on the Newfoundland trade, who harried him over the government's proposals for the legislature, 27 June, when he admitted that ministers had no plans to tackle slavery that session. Admonished by anti-reformers and radicals for failing to demonstrate reductions in his departmental budget, 1 July, he was obliged to defend each sum voted, 8, 18, 25 July, when opposition made the grant to the Society for the Propagation of the Gospels their particular target. He revived the Canada revenue bill unchanged, 27, 28 June, and carried its third reading without a division, 19 Aug. Forced to speak on slavery by Burge, whose request for returns he resisted, 17 Aug., he defended his department and the government's conduct, cited evidence to support his view that circumstances were now right for the emancipation of crown slaves in Mauritius and refuted suggestions that emancipated slaves would become chargeable on the colonies. He presented the Mauritius petition for reduction of the duty on West Indian sugar, 18 Aug., and rejected a request for papers on the compensation paid to Lescene and Escoffery, two coloured free men expelled from Jamaica, but he failed to kill the issue when it was revived in committee of supply, 22 Aug. With pressure to carry the reform bill mounting, he could disguise neither his irritation nor poor knowledge of the fisheries and French rights when Robinson proposed a constitutional legislative assembly for Newfoundland, 13 Sept., forcing Althorp to intervene to suggest the concession of a select committee. He defeated the West India lobby's request for inquiry into the impact of the Sugar Refinery Act by only 125-113, 28 Sept., and in a bid to regain the initiative and stave off future defeat, he conceded inquiry into West Indian colonies only and sat on the select committee appointed on 6 Oct. He was a government teller for the sugar refinery bill when it was carried (by 130-96), 7 Oct., and (49-12) on the 13th. Advised by Wood to say nothing that might revive the church patronage issue and excite the bishops, he expressed sympathy for but evaded discussion on the Assembly of Lower Canada's petition complaining of the mode of selecting legislative councils, stating only that his department had the matter in hand, 14 Oct.[61] He naturally divided steadily for the reintroduced reform bill, but spoke only to express irritation at the time-wasting tactics of its opponents, 11 Aug. He cited the precedent of East Retford in justification of the government's decision to issue a new writ for Liverpool and claimed that the reform bill rendered further inquiry superfluous and that bribery prosecutions should be referred to the courts, 8 July. When the Irish government was implicated in corruption at the Dublin election, he embarrassed Grey and prompted calls for his resignation by refusing to vote in the majority by which inquiry was stifled, 23 Aug., but he divided with his colleagues later that day against the censure motion.[62] He of course voted for Lord Ebrington's confidence motion, 10 Oct., and was prepared to see reform forced through with new peerages and made more extensive and radical. He approved his father's decision to keep him in the Commons (and was to refuse a similar offer in 1839).[63] He divided for the revised reform bill at its second reading, 17 Dec. 1831, and being 'sick of town', spent the Christmas break shooting with Littleton in Staffordshire.[64] In 1832 he voted silently with his colleagues on reform, the Russian-Dutch loan, 26 Jan., 12, 16, 20 July, relations with Portugal, 9 Feb., and the navy civil departments bill, 6 Apr.

Briefed thoroughly beforehand by the colonial office clerk Hay, he fended off criticism from Hume and others of his departmental budget, 7, 17, 22 Feb. 1832, persuaded Goderich to refer the contentious issue of Canadian church patronage to the cabinet and discussed schemes to reform the colonial agencies with his colleague Thomas Hyde Villiers* of the India board.[65] Faced with renewed pressure from Burge and Lord Chandos to act to combat the severity of the Jamaican insurrection and West Indian distress, 17 Feb., 7, 9, 15, Mar., 13 Apr., he could do little more than appeal to the order in council of 5 Nov. 1831 and other papers currently before the House and repeat the mantra that relief was conditional on the recalcitrant assemblies obeying the orders. He was lucky to survive a close (148-134) division on the sugar duties bill, 7 Mar., but Althorp's interventions and his own commanding speech, which drew heavily on Canning and Huskisson's dispatches, secured its passage by 169-27 on the 23rd. He resigned with his colleagues

and prepared to defend his Northumberland seat when the reform bill's defeat in the Lords on 7 May put a ministry headed by Wellington in contemplation, and plans were also laid that month to return him for Northumberland North at the first post-reform election.[66] As the threat to the reform bill evaporated and reports of colonial distress increased he was tested in the House almost daily on slavery, the New South Wales legislature bill, which the radicals exploited to revive the complaints against the former governor Charles Darling, 25 June, 5, 23 July, and the crown colonies relief bill, which as he had cautioned when directed to announce it as a 'vague statement of intent' in December 1831, risked 'if not defeat, a victory which will not be a great deal less injurious to government'.[67] When on 22 May Althorp asked him to persuade Fowell Buxton to put off his motion for the immediate appointment of a select committee on slavery, he resisted doing so on private and public grounds, convinced of the merits of a mixed committee of West Indians and abolitionists, and replied, 23 May:

> If we cannot agree with him now as to the form of his motion, there will be still less chance of our being able to do so later in the session, when it will be absurd to propose an inquiry and he will therefore if he brings forward the subject at all be compelled to ask the sanction of the House to some distant proposition ... My own situation I feel to be peculiarly embarrassing. Not only do I entertain the strongest opinion that it is the duty of the government and of Parliament to take the earliest possible measures for putting an end to a system which I cannot doubt to be one of the most shocking cruelty and injustice, but I am also publicly pledged to this opinion in a way which must prevent my retracting or disguising it. In a debate last year I expressly stated that if I should be convinced that immediate emancipation would be safe, that it would conduce to the interests of the slaves themselves, I should hold it to be the bounden duty of this country to adopt that measure without the delay of a single day, leaving it to be settled afterwards in what proportion the loss should fall upon this country and upon the colonists. The motion which Buxton proposes does not go one step beyond this ... A division in which Buxton should be on one side and the government on the other would thus be no less embarrassing to myself than I believe it would be injurious to the government. The best way ... would in my opinion be to agree upon the terms in which a committee might be moved for tomorrow, the other to get the motion postponed till next session.[68]

He was party to Althorp's vain attempt on the morning of the 24th to badger Buxton into agreeing to postponement. His independently minded speech that evening, which Buxton praised as 'capital and giving such a testimony to the speech of last year as delighted me', advised against precipitate action, but expressed confidence that inquiry would yield a solution, attributed the lack of progress since 1823 to previous ministerial procrastination, maintained that slave mortality had decreased and sugar exports increased in the crown colonies which, unlike Jamaica, had obeyed the order in council, and recommended the appointment of a committee 'not to establish the evils of slavery but to plan for its abolition'.[69] He was named to it, 30 May. Finding that distress petitions from the crown colonies contradicted his speech that day, he changed tack and placed his confidence in his department's proposals for colonial legislatures, which he brought in on 7 June. He also presented an anti-slavery petition from Alnwick that day and quashed an attempt to institute inquiry into the alienation of crown lands in New South Wales and Van Diemen's Land. He crushed by 65-26 a proposal to give New South Wales a system of representation, 28 June. His defence of the colonial estimates, 23 July, was competent on all points save the grant for the Society for the Propagation of the Gospels, which, as he had directed with cabinet backing the previous November, was discounted preparatory to abolition. Sorely tested in committee on the crown colonies relief bill, 3 Aug., by the colonial agents, to whom no 'formal' relief was promised, and the radicals, who maintained that the principle of the 5 Nov. 1831 order in council was being undermined, he defended his department's actions, highlighted the selective use of documents and statistics by the bill's critics on both sides and maintained that aid was justified although acceptance of emancipation was 'patchy'. He carried the division (by 51-20), but was again bombarded with questions when the report was brought up on the 8th. He married Sir Joseph Copley's daughter Maria the following day and took no further part in proceedings on the bill, which received royal assent, 16 Aug.[70] He had supported the Monkwearmouth railway bill at his constituents' request, 14 Feb., and presented petitions from the Northumberland magistracy and quarter sessions against the locally unpopular general registry bill, 22 Feb. 1832, and tried that day to allay its critics fears that only Members favourable to it would be appointed to the committee.[71] Talk of making him secretary at war revived when the Irish secretary Smith Stanley threatened resignation; but the Conservative Charles Arbuthnot* observed that 'it is thought he could not venture upon a new election for Northumberland and his temper is so bad that Lord Grey would hardly dare to put him at the war office'.[72]

Howick almost certainly colluded with the Conservative Lord Ossulston to secure an unopposed return for Northumberland North at the 1832 general election, when he refused to spend or stand jointly with the Liberal John Culley, and was outshone by Ossulston's proposer Liddell on the hustings.[73] Temperamentally unsuited to working in the shadow of Smith Stanley, who replaced Goderich as his principal in January 1833, he resigned over slavery in May after failing to persuade his father's cabinet to give precedence to his scheme for precipitate emancipation.[74] Reinstated as home under-secretary in January 1834, he resigned with Grey six months later. He became war secretary in Melbourne's 1835 cabinet, but left it in 1839 with a reputation as a difficult, divisive, haughty and impatient colleague, after he had been thwarted in his ambition to become leader of the House and had seriously undermined the policies of Lord Glenelg (as Charles Grant had become) and Poulett Thomson.[75] Defeated by two Conservatives in Northumberland North in 1841, after bringing down the government on the Irish franchise bill, he was accommodated at Sunderland, which he represented until he succeeded his father as 3rd Earl Grey and *de facto* leader of the Liberals in the Lords in 1845.[76] He came to terms with Palmerston's appointment as foreign secretary and served with him as colonial secretary in Russell's first administration, instituting surprisingly conciliatory and farsighted constitutional reforms. John Campbell II*, then chancellor of the duchy of Lancaster, found him 'intrepid, vigorous, disinterested and sincere', but recalled:

> He certainly was very ill-tempered and wrong headed. I had myself unavoidable quarrels with him in the House of Commons when he was under-secretary of state and I was attorney-general. Since July 1846 I must say that he has conducted himself in the cabinet with uniform moderation and courtesy. He has occasionally expressed his opinion with vivacity, but without giving just cause of offence and without offending anyone.[77]

Excluded from Lord Aberdeen's coalition ministry in 1852, he was a constant critic of all parties for the next 40 years and declared for the Conservatives in 1880, when his nephew and heir, Charles's son Albert Henry George Grey (1851-1917), came in for Northumberland South as a Liberal. He died without issue at Howick in October 1894, predeceased in 1879 by his wife. His will was proved in London, 8 Feb. 1895, by his nephew the 4th earl, to whom he had already made over his estates.[78]

[1] There is no comprehensive published biography of Grey, but his *Colonial Policy of Lord John Russell's Administration* (1853), *Parl. Government Considered* (1858) and *Corresp. of William IV with Earl Grey* (1867) provide a partial and selective review of his own and his father's administrative careers. [2] E.A. Smith, *Lord Grey*, 137;

Brougham mss, autobiog. fragment; M.D. George, *Cat. of Pol. and Personal Satires*, x. 15131-3; [J. Grant], *Recollections of House of Commons* (1837), 223; *Pencillings of Politicians* (1839), 115-16. [3] *The Times*, 13 Oct. 1894; *Oxford DNB*. [4] Smith, 139-42. [5] Grey mss. [6] Broughton, *Recollections*, iii. 77-78. [7] Grey mss, J. Lambert to Grey, 22 Mar. 1824, 7 June 1825, 22 Jan. 1826, Lambton to Howick, 25 Aug. 1824, to Grey, 30 Nov., 16 Dec. Howick to same [21 July, 6 Aug., 15, 21, 25 Sept., 16, 21 Oct., 16, 18 Nov., 1 Dec. 1825], replies, 10 Sept. 1824, 10 Sept.-20 Nov. 1825; *Durham Co. Advertiser*, 13 Aug.; Creevey mss, Creevey to Miss Ord, 6 Sept. 1825. [8] Grey mss, Howick to Grey, 2 Feb.-9 Mar., replies 4 Feb.-14 Mar., Lambert to Grey, 3 Feb., Ellice to same, 2 Feb., 2 Mar.; *The Times*, 7, 10, 14 Feb.; Creevey mss, Creevey to Miss Ord, 11, 12 Feb. 1826. [9] Grey mss. [10] Ibid. Creevey to Grey, 21 Feb., reply 23 Feb.; Fitzwilliam mss 124/9, Grey to Fitzwilliam [22, 23 Feb.]; Add. 51784, Holland to C.R. Fox, 5 Mar.; *Durham Chron.* 23 Feb. 1826; *Diaries and Corresp. of James Losh* ed. E. Hughes (Surtees Soc. clxxiv) [hereafter *Losh Diaries*, ii], 41. [11] Add. 51574, Abercromby to Holland, 17 Mar.; 51584, Tierney to same, 10 Apr., 4-5 May; 51586, Tierney to Lady Holland [28 Mar.]; 51663, Bedford to same, 9 May; Add. 51833, Yarborough to Brocklesby, 20 Mar.; Creevey mss, Creevey to Miss Ord, 17 Apr. 1826. [12] Add. 51586, Tierney to Lady Holland, 18 Apr. 1826. [13] Add. 30111, f. 231; Grey mss, C. Grey to Grey, 9 Mar., 20 May, 2 June, Lambton to same, 29, 31 May, 3 June, Lambert to same, 31 May, 2, 7 June, election accts. (1826-7); *Baring Jnls.* i. 48; NLS, Ellice mss, Grey to Ellice, 7 Feb. 1827. [14] Grey mss, Darlington to Grey, 7 June; Creevey mss, Creevey to Miss Ord, 11 June 1826. [15] Grey mss, Ellice to Grey, 17 Aug. 1826-10 July 1830. [16] Castle Howard mss, Abercromby to Carlisle [22 Nov. 1826]. [17] Grey mss, Howick to Grey, 22 Nov., reply 24 Nov. 1826. [18] Smith, 142; Grey mss, Howick to Grey, 28 Nov., 9, 13 Dec. 1826. [19] Grey mss, Howick to Grey, 22 Feb., reply 23 Feb. 1827. [20] Ibid. Grey to Howick, 19, 28 Feb., reply, 3 Mar. 1827. [21] Ibid. Howick to Grey, 2-20 Mar., replies, 14, 23 Mar. 1827. [22] Ibid. Howick to Grey, 6, 7 Mar. 1827. [23] *Lieven-Grey Corresp.* i. 39. [24] Grey mss, Howick to Grey, 12, 16, 31 Mar., replies, 14, 22 Mar. 1827. [25] Ibid. Grey to Howick, 19 Feb.-23 Mar.; Lansdowne mss, Grey to Lansdowne, 16, 17, 27 Apr. 1827. [26] Grey mss, Darlington to Grey, 19 Apr. 1827; *Creevey Pprs.* 464. [27] *Geo. IV Letters*, iii. 1341; Ellice mss, Grey to Ellice, 1 June 1827; A. Mitchell, *Whigs in Opposition*, 202. [28] Grey mss, Howick to Grey, 22 Sept. 1827; *Arbuthnot Jnl.* ii. 142. [29] Grey mss, Howick to Grey, 21 Jan. 1828; Smith, 249. [30] Grey mss, Cleveland to Grey, 17 Mar., 4 Apr. and undated, replies, 21, 23 May, Howick to Cleveland, 21 May, reply 22 May 1828. [31] Ibid. Howick to Grey, 11 Aug. 1828. [32] Unless otherwise stated, the following account of Howick's career, Jan. 1828-Nov. 1830, is based on his jnl. (Grey mss). [33] Grey mss, Cleveland to Grey, 27 Jan. 1829. [34] Ibid. Howick to Grey, 2 June 1829, 22 Jan., 4 Feb., Cleveland to same, 12 Jan., reply, 16 Jan., same to Howick, 12 Jan., 4 Feb., Grey to Howick, 5 Feb., Durham to same, 5 Feb., Grey to Holland, 9 Feb.; Ellice mss, Grey to Ellice, 6, 11 Feb.; Creevey mss, Sefton to Creevey, 30 Jan. 1830. [35] Grey mss, Grey to Howick, 5 Feb. 1830; Le Marchant, *Althorp*, 233-4. [36] Ellice mss, Grey to Ellice, 17 Feb.; Add. 51670, Bedford to Lady Holland, 20 Feb.; 51681, Lord W. Russell to Holland, 10 May; 51785, Holland to C.R. Fox, 20 Feb.; 52176, J. Allen to same, 4 Apr. 1830; *Lieven-Grey Corresp.* i. 441, 445. [37] Grey mss, Grey to Howick, 10 Feb., Howick to Grey, 12 Feb., Durham to same, 12 Feb. 1830; J.R.M. Butler, *Passing of Great Reform Bill* (1914), 66-67. [38] Grey mss, Howick to Grey, 15 Feb. 1830. [39] Grey mss. [40] Ibid. Howick to Grey, 2 Mar. 1830. [41] Ibid. Howick to Grey, 2, 3, 6 Mar.; Castle Howard mss, Graham to Morpeth [3 Mar.] 1830. [42] Grey mss, Grey to Howick, 9, 14 Mar. 1830. [43] Ibid. Grey to Howick, 15 Mar., Graham to same [Mar. 1830]. [44] Grey mss, Durham to Grey, 9 Mar., Macdonald to same 14, 15 July, Wood to Howick [21 July]; BL, Althorp mss, Althorp to Spencer, 7 July 1830. [45] Brougham mss, Brougham to Graham [Oct.]; Add. 51564, same to Lady Holland [8 Nov] 1830; Broughton, iv. 60; Mitchell, 242-4. [46] A. Aspinall, *Lord Brougham and the Whig Party*, 184. [47] *Three Diaries*, 25; *Greville Mems.* ii. 75; Grey mss, Durham to Grey, 19 Nov., Howick to C. Grey, 24 Nov. 1830. [48] Grey mss. [49] *Three Diaries*, 58; Le Marchant, 282. [50] Grey mss, Hay to Howick, 3, 29 Jan., Wood to same [Jan.], Graham to same, 3 Feb., Poulett Scrope to same, 21 Feb. 1831. [51] Ibid. Richmond to Howick, 3 Feb., 3 Apr.; *Durham Chron.* 19 Mar. 1831; H.J.M. Johnston, *British Emigration Policy, 1818-1870*, pp. 163-4. [52] St. Deiniol's Lib. Glynne-Gladstone mss 198, T. to J. Gladstone, 16 Apr.; Grey mss, Brougham to Howick [Apr. 1831]; *Buxton Mems.* 266. [53] Grey mss, Howick to C. Grey, 31 Jan. 1831; *Lieven-Grey Corresp.* ii. 178. [54] Add. 51579, Ord to Lady Holland [7 Mar. 1831]. [55] *Greville Mems.* ii. 129; Grey mss, Headlam to Howick, 8, 10, 26 Mar. 1831; *Losh Diaries*, ii. 111, 189, 193. [56] Fitzwilliam mss, C.H. Dundas to Fitzwilliam, 29 Mar.; Grey mss, Howick to C. Grey, 4 Apr. 1831. [57] *Geo. IV-Grey Corresp.* i. 234; Grey mss, Headlam to Howick, 24, 25 Apr., Howick to mother, 2 May; *Newcastle Chron.* 30 Apr., 7 May; Add. 51569, Ord to Lady Holland 1 May 1831; *Lieven-Grey Corresp.* ii. 218; George, xi. 16648. [58] Brougham mss, Losh to Brougham, 5 May 1831. [59] Grey mss, Grey to Howick, 1 May; *Newcastle Chron.* 14 May 1831. [60] Grey mss, Ponsonby to Howick, 20, 30 May, 6 Sept. [31 Oct.], 28 Dec., Howick to Milton, 26 May, reply 30 May 1831. [61] Ibid. Wood to Howick, 5 July 1831. [62] *Greville Mems.* ii. 185; *Three Diaries*, 122. [63] Smith, 270-1; Southampton Univ. Lib. Broadlands mss, Palmerston to Richmond, 8 Nov. 1831; Wilts RO, Hobhouse mss, Hobhouse to wife, 25 Jan. 1832; *William IV-Grey Corresp.* ii. 195. [64] Hatherton diary, 21-26 Dec. 1831. [65] Grey mss, Howick to Hay, 17 Nov. 1831, replies, 6, 10, 31 Jan. 1832, Villiers to Howick, 19 Dec. 1831, 4 Feb. 1832. [66] *Newcastle Chron.* 19, 26 May 1832; *Losh Diaries*, ii. 133. [67] Grey mss, Althorp to Howick [Dec. 1831], Howick to Goderich [Feb. 1832]. [68] Ibid. Howick to Althorp, 23 May 1832. [69] *Buxton Mems.* 287, 290. [70] *Raikes Jnl.* i. 61. [71] *Losh Diaries*, ii. 135. [72] *Croker Pprs.* ii. 150; Aberdeen Univ. Lib. Arbuthnot mss 3029/1/2/45. [73] *Losh Diaries*, ii. 172-3; Grey mss, Howick to C. Grey, 31 Aug., 4 Sept.; *Newcastle Jnl.* 22 Dec. 1832. [74] Add. 52011, Eleanor Fazakerley to H.E. Fox, 29 Mar. 1833; *Holland House Diaries*, 207; *Greville Mems.* ii. 371-2. [75] Smith, 308-24; R. Brent, *Liberal Anglican Politics*, 288. [76] *Newcastle Chron.* 10 July 1841; M.J. Turner, 'Reform Politics and the Sunderland by-election of 1845', *Northern Hist.* xxxviii (2001), 83-106. [77] *Life of Campbell*, ii. 208. [78] *The Times*, 10, 13, 15 Oct. 1894, 13 Feb. 1895.

M.M.E.

GRIFFITH, John Wynne (1763–1834), of Garn, Denb.

DENBIGH BOROUGHS 1818–1826

b. 1 Apr. 1763, o.s. of John Griffith of Garn and Jane, da. and coh. of John Hughes of Weeg, Caern. and Cae'r Berllan, nr. Llanrwst, Denb. *educ.* Trinity Hall, Camb. 1781. *m.* 16 Feb. 1785, Jane da. of Robert Wynne of Garthmeilio, Corwen, Merion. and Plasnewydd, Henllan, Denb., 9s. (5 *d.v.p.*) 4 da. (3 *d.v.p.*). *suc.* fa. 1791. *d.* 13 June 1834.

Burgess, Denbigh 1784, councilman 1794, alderman 1803, 1806, 1819; recorder 1817-*d.*

Capt. Denb. vols. 1798, maj. 1803; lt.-col. centre regt. Denb. militia 1808.

Griffith, who regularly served as chairman of the Denbighshire bench, had come in for Denbigh Boroughs in 1818 on the Biddulph interest (then in minority), his candidature having been suggested and endorsed by Denbigh corporation, of which he was recorder, William Shipley, dean of St. Asaph, and William Hughes* of Kinmel Park, and sanctioned by the county Member, Sir Watkin Williams Wynn of Wynnstay.[1] He outpolled the 5th Earl De la Warr's cousin, Frederick West, heir to the rival Llangollen and Ruthin Castle interests, by 131-92, to retain the seat at the general election of 1820. A widower since 1814, his dependence on the widowed Mrs. Biddulph and his votes against the Six Acts were criticized and lampooned during the canvass, and in his victory address he acknowledged his debt to his patron and declared his determination to vote as he saw fit.[2]

He proved as hitherto to be a staunch member of the Whig opposition 'Mountain' to the Liverpool ministry, and also divided unstintingly with Hume until 1824, often in very small minorities.[3] He spoke only on issues connected with agriculture, on which he took an independent line. Hunting, agricultural improvements and botany remained his principal interests, and he counted Dr. William Withering and his sister Charlotte Botfield of Norton Hall, Northamptonshire among his closest friends. He visited both in the summer of 1820, and also toured the Wynnes' Merioneth estates, whose revenues he controlled.[4] His son Edward had kept him informed of developments in Denbigh's contributory borough of Holt, where in July the Wests failed to take control of the corporation; and he attended meetings at Chirk Castle before chairing the Denbigh Michaelmas dinner, where his recent support for the parliamentary campaign on behalf of Queen Caroline was criticized. He refused to be drawn, arguing that his independence dictated that his votes be determined by what he heard in debate.[5] He took his daughter Harriet to watch the queen's procession to St. Paul's in November, after the case against her was dropped.[6]

Tierney requested his attendance in the Commons by 25 Jan. 1821. He continued to support the parliamentary campaign on the behalf of the queen, but although present for most of the debate, he apparently left before the division on her allowance, 31 Jan., having received news that his son George had been captured by Neapolitan bandits and held to ransom.[7] He divided for Catholic relief, 28 Feb. 1821, but not subsequently. He voted to make Leeds a scot and lot borough if it received Grampound's seats, 2 Mar., and for parliamentary reform, 10 May 1821, 25 Apr. 1822. The West and Kenyon interests gained control of Holt at Michaelmas 1821 and, concerned with the Morfa Rhuddlan enclosure, the projected route of the Holyhead road through his estates, and Charlotte Botfield's illness, he delayed his return to London until

March 1822, making one of many visits to Norton Hall on the way.[8] He had not voted to repeal the agricultural horse tax, 5 Mar., or the additional malt duty, 3 Apr. 1821, and his sons warned him repeatedly in the spring and summer of 1822 that it was politically imperative that he should campaign strenuously for action to combat distress.[9] He presented Denbigh's distress petition, 11 Mar.,[10] and endorsed the Ruthin tanners' petition against the leather tax which he presented, 29 Apr. When the agriculture committee reported, 8 May, he attributed 'the embarrassments experienced by the agriculturists' to the 'change in the value of the currency, and the increased pressure of taxation from the payment of taxes by a medium of increased value', and, complaining that poor rates fell disproportionately heavily on land compared with other forms of wealth, divided for large tax remissions. He voted in the minorities for a permanent 18s. bounty on wheat exports and against the new corn duties, 9 May, and divided for repeal of the salt duties, 3 June. He voted that day to receive the radical Greenhoe petition linking parliamentary reform and agricultural distress. He voted for a gradual resumption of cash payments, 12 June 1822, and inquiry into the currency, 12 June 1823. Debating the Irish Butter Act, he suggested a tariff of 10s. on imports, 20 June 1822.[11]

The line of the Holyhead road over Bryn-y-Garn had been settled to his liking, but he was annoyed during the recess to find that the Williams Wynns now denied him the gaming rights he had enjoyed for 40 years over the Llansannan hills. Trusteeship of the Plasnewydd estate, which had formed part of his marriage settlement, involved him in preparations for further chancery litigation early in 1823.[12] He was granted a fortnight's leave, 10 Apr., on account of the death of a near relation. He divided steadily with opposition from May until July. In November 1823, when his son George was comptroller, he attended the Llanrwst hunt.[13] Votes to repeal the leather tax, 18 May, and in condemnation of the indictment in Demerara of the Methodist missionary John Smith, 11 June (for which he had introduced a petition, 28 May), and against the Irish insurrection bill, 14 June 1824, are the only records of Griffith's attendance that session. He joined most of the corporation and county squires at Shrewsbury assizes in August to hear the Jones v. Williams case, which cast doubt on the chartered right of Denbigh magistrates to delegate power; and he was kept busy by Plasnewydd business on account of the 'violent behaviour' of his relation William Wynne, who came of age, 9 Oct. 1824.[14] Illness, for which he was granted two months' leave, 15 Feb., and a further month, 14 Apr., delayed Griffith's return to London in 1825, and he played no part in the passage of the Denbigh-Pentre Foelas road bill. However, he divided against the duke of Cumberland's annuity bill, 27 May, 2, 6, 10 June, and for inquiries into chancery delays, 7 June, and the Irish church, 14 June. He voted for the St. Olave tithe bill, 6 June, and was probably the B. Griffith in the minority for trial by jury under the combination laws, 27 June 1825. Anticipating a dissolution before Robert Myddelton Biddulph* came of age (26 June 1826), Denbigh corporation met at Mrs. Biddulph's request, 7 June 1825, and made Griffith 'the first offer'. There was no guarantee of Chirk Castle funding, and his response is not known.[15] He voted against reviewing the Bank Charter Acts in the wake of the 1825-6 crisis, 13 Feb., and to add a clause enforcing payments in specie to the promissory notes bill, 27 Feb. 1826. Although present to vote for reductions in the army estimates, 2 Mar., he failed to divide that day on the Jamaican slave trials, on which opinion in Denbigh was divided. He voted for regulation of the Irish first fruits revenues, 21 Mar. He stood down at the dissolution in June 1826, when Myddelton Biddulph remained marginally under age and Joseph Ablett of Llanbedr Hall represented their interest in a violent and costly contest against West, which produced a double return. 'After an illiberal attempt to obstruct his purpose, which he repelled with suitable spirit [Griffith] moved a vote of thanks to the assessor'.[16]

Griffith, whom Lady Delamere described as 'the greatest bore in England or Wales (with a constant and alternate flow of words *out* of his mouth and brandy *into* it)', remained an active spokesman in county and borough politics.[17] He mediated between Chirk Castle and Denbigh corporation over property sales in April 1828 and offered the freedom of Denbigh to the duke of Sussex at the eisteddfod that September (conferring it in 1832).[18] At the sessions, 15 July 1829, and county meetings, 22 Sept. 1829, 15 Apr. 1830, he led Denbighshire's opposition to the justice commission's proposals to abolish the Welsh judicature and court of great sessions, which threatened the existing county based assize system.[19] He nominated Myddelton Biddulph for the Boroughs in 1830 and 1831 and supported him for the county in 1832.[20] With John Madocks of Glan-y-wern, who came in for the Boroughs in 1832, he organized and addressed meetings on distress in March 1830 and parliamentary reform in 1831, when he offered to stand for the county himself should Madocks decline. In the event, and much to his sons' relief, he was persuaded to be content with exacting an election promise from Sir Watkin Williams Wynn to heed his constituents' support for

reform.[21] His own support for it was tempered by his fears that Wrexham would dominate the post-reform Denbigh Boroughs constituency, a development he tried to counter by lobbying Welsh pro-reform Members and encouraging Abergele and Llanrwst to petition for contributory borough status.[22] He used his standing in the county and connections as a former Member to further his sons' careers in the law and the church.[23] Several months at Leamington Spa in 1832 failed to halt the decline in his health and he died a lingering death at Garn in June 1834.[24] His will (proved under £3,000) incorporated complex trust arrangements based on an agreement of April 1833 concerning his Llanfynydd lands, and unresolved Plasnewydd business. Edward Lloyd of Cefn and Robert John Mostyn of Calcot Hall renounced trusteeship and probate was granted to Griffith's eldest surviving son, George, a barrister on the Chester circuit, who also succeeded to Garn and the recordership of Denbigh. The other main beneficiaries were Harriet, whose husband John Price of Brynbella had recently been bankrupted, and his sons Edward, Frederick and William.[25]

[1] *HP Commons, 1790-1820*, ii. 495; iv. 112-13. [2] NLW ms 1498 A, ii. 17; *The Times*, 15 Apr. 1819, 1 Mar. 1820; NLW, Chirk Castle mss C/78-85; NLW, Garn mss (1956), W. Hughes to Griffith, 19 Feb. 1819, W. Shipley to same, 2 Jan., C. Biddulph to same 4, 22 Feb., G. Griffith to C. Williams, 4 Apr. 1820; *Cambrian*, 15 Jan.; *Chester Chron.* 25 Feb., 3, 10, 17 Mar.; *N. Wales Gazette*, 9, 23 Mar. 1820. [3] HLRO, Hist. Coll. 379, Grey Bennet diary, 11. [4] Garn mss (1956), C. Botfield to Griffith, 26 June, 13, 27 July, 6 Sept. 1820. [5] *Chester Chron.* 7 Apr., 30 June, 6 Oct. 1820; Garn mss (1956), E. to J.W. Griffith, 25 June, 17 Sept. 1820. [6] T.A. Glenn, *Fam. of Griffith of Garn and Plasnewydd*, 132. [7] Garn mss (1956), Tierney to Griffith, 4 Jan. 1821; Glenn, 132, 332-42. [8] *Chester Chron.* 12 Oct. 1821; Garn mss (1956), C. Botfield to Griffith, 5, 27 July, B. Botfield to same, 20, 25 Aug., 1, 10, 26 Sept., 21, 25 Oct. 1821, 5, 14, 15 Jan., 19 Mar., 22 May 1822, H. Stoddart to same, 22 Jan., J.W. to G. Griffith, 27 Feb., 9 Mar. 1822, corresp. with office of woods and forests, Jan. 1822-July 1823, *passim*. [9] Garn mss (1956), R. to J.W. Griffith, 1 Apr., G. Griffith to same, 20 June, J.W. to G. Griffith, 10 June 1822. [10] *The Times*, 12 Mar. 1822. [11] Ibid. 21 June 1822. [12] Garn mss (1956), J.W. to G. Griffith, 5, 27, 29 Apr., 16 May, C.W. Williams Wynn to Griffith, 11, 17, 25 Aug. 1822, corresp. with G. Bridges, Frowd, J. Heaton, G. Rose, J. Saul and 'Richards, Clarke and Nares', *passim*. [13] *N. Wales Gazette*, 4 Dec. 1823. [14] *The Times*, 29 May, 16 Aug.; NLW ms 14984 A, ii. 25-27; Garn mss (1956), J. Saul to Griffith, 24 Sept, 25 Nov. 1824. [15] Garn mss (1956), J. Copner Williams to Griffith, 7 June 1825. [16] Ibid. J.W. to G. Griffith, 24 June; *Chester Courant*, 27 June 1826. [17] NLW ms 2796 D, Lady Delamere to H. Williams Wynn, 20 Aug. 1828. [18] Chirk Castle mss E/3487-8; *Shrewsbury Chron.* 12, 18 Sept. 1828; C.J. Williams, 'Denbigh Borough Recs.' *Trans. Denb. Hist. Soc.* xxv (1976), 185. [19] Garn mss (1956), J. Edwards to Griffith, 11 Sept., J. Copner Williams to same, 13 Sept. 1829; *Chester Courant*, 22 Sept. 1829, 6, 20 Apr. 1830; *Shrewsbury Chron.* 25 Sept.; *N. Wales Chron.* 15 Oct. 1829. [20] *Chester Courant*, 23 Feb., 3, 10 Aug. 1830, 3 May 1831; *N. Wales Chron.* 11 Mar., 12 Aug. 1830, 1 Jan. 1833; *Caernarvon Herald*, 7 May 1831; UCNW, Mostyn of Mostyn mss 7878; NLW ms 2797 D, F. to H. Williams Wynn, 9 May 1831. [21] *Chester Courant*, 22, 29 Mar., 5 Apr., 10 May 1831; Garn mss (1956), W. Owen to Griffith, 1 Jan., Madocks to same, 4, 7, 9 May, W. to G. Griffith, 5

May 1831. [22] Mostyn of Mostyn mss 7871-2. [23] Garn mss (1956), C.W. Williams Wynn to Griffith, 21 Mar. 1831, W. to G. Griffith, 14 Nov., Denman to Dinorben, 28 Nov. 1832, Sir W. Williams Wynn to Griffith, 31 Dec. 1833. [24] Garn mss (1956), W. to G. Griffith, 15 Feb., 15 May, 4 July, J.W. to G. Griffith, 24 May 1832; *Caernarvon Herald*, 21 June 1834. [25] Garn mss (1956), R.J. Mostyn to J. Vaughan Horne, 20 June, E. Lloyd to same, 30 June 1834; PROB 11/1844/167; IR26/1383/91; *CJ*, lxxxiii. 484; lxxxiv. 400; Glenn, 133.

M.M.E.

GRIFFITH WYNNE, Charles Wynne (1780–1865), of 39 Portman Square, Mdx.; Voelas, Denb., and Cefnamlwch, Caern.

CAERNARVONSHIRE   1830–1832

b. 4 Mar. 1780, 1st. s. of Hon. Charles Finch[†] and Jane, da. and h. of Watkin Wynne of Voelas. *educ.* Westminster 1795; Brasenose, Oxf. 1797, fellow, All Souls 1800-12; L. Inn 1799. *m.* 14 May 1812, Sarah, da. and coh. of Rev. Henry Hildyard of Stokesley, Yorks., 4s. (1 *d.v.p.*) 4da. Took names of Griffith and Wynne by royal lic. 26 June 1804; *suc.* mother to Voelas and Cefnamlwch 1811; fa. 1819. *d.* 22 Mar. 1865.
Sheriff, Caern. 1814-15; Denb. 1815-16.

This Member's father, the 3rd earl of Aylesford's second son, sat briefly for Castle Rising and Maidstone after marrying a Welsh heiress five years his senior, who was destined to inherit her father's Denbighshire estate and the 4,200 acres of their kinsman John Griffith of Cefnamlwch (*d.* 1794).[1] Finch, as he was first known, was brought up in London and attended Westminster School before going up to Oxford in May 1797. His withdrawal from Brasenose College six month later was attributed to his parents' separation. This, his mother declared in her will (of 11 June 1798) 'was not promoted be me'. She subsequently lived in Mill Hill, Middlesex, and her Denbighshire home, Lima, over-looking the Conway Valley near Pentre Foelas, while his father resided in Hill Street, Berkeley Square. Eighteen months after entering Lincoln's Inn, Finch was admitted to All Souls, remaining there until he married, shortly after inheriting his mother's estates. He had taken the names of Griffith and Wynne in 1804 as her heir presumptive. His mother's brother-in-law, Thomas Assheton Smith I* of Vaenol, and his co-executors renounced probate and Griffith Wynne found that providing for his younger brother and sisters as she had directed rendered Lima, Llanfynydd and their Spytty holdings virtually insolvent by 1820. Lima was reserved for his sisters until they married, and he raised his own family in Coleshill, Warwickshire, which, with his father's share in other properties that had formerly belonged to his maternal grandmother Lady Charlotte Seymour, reverted to him in 1819.[2]

The Griffith family of Cefnamlwch had a con-trolling interest in Aberdaron, near the borough of Nefyn, and had dominated the representation of Caernarvonshire, 1715-41, but the Assheton Smiths, who hoped to do the same, had failed to secure the seat for more than the Parliament of 1774.[3] Griffith Wynne controlled approximately 160 Caernarvonshire votes, but paid little attention to the county's politics before 1825, when Assheton Smith as lord lieutenant backed the campaign to oust the sitting Member Sir Robert Williams. Canvassing as Assheton Smith's repre-sentative with the chairman of the county magistrates John Edwards of Nanhoron, Griffith Wynne assisted and nominated the anti-Catholic Lord Newborough of Glynllifon when he deprived Williams of the seat in 1826, and it was subsequently alleged that he had only refused the nomination himself because he had a large family to support.[4] He responded sparingly and equivocally to the 1828 justice commissioners' inquiries into the administration of justice in Wales, whose subsequent proposals to change the assize dis-tricts were locally resented.[5] At the dissolution in 1830 he announced his candidature for Caernarvonshire, where his cousin Thomas Assheton Smith II had succeeded his father in 1828 and wished to try his strength. Newborough and Sir Robert Williams were abroad for health reasons and he came in unopposed.[6] He had recently shown 'much liberality to his tenants' and refused to support the marquess of Anglesey's brother Sir Charles Paget* in Caernarvon Boroughs, where he assisted the Ultra, William Ormsby Gore*.[7] At Michaelmas 1830 the yearly rental on his estates totalled almost £8,542: £4,037 from Cefnamlwch, £3,106 from Voelas and £1,398 from his English holdings.[8]

The Wellington ministry listed Griffith Wynne among their 'friends', but, like Assheton Smith, whose political line he toed, he was absent when they were brought down on the civil list, 15 Nov. 1830. He made no reported parliamentary speeches and freely admit-ted that he was 'no orator' when, with Newborough and Ormsby Gore, he addressed the January 1831 county meeting which petitioned for repeal of the coastwise duties on coal and slate. He agreed to support the peti-tion despite his misgivings that 'it would go before Parliament at rather an unseasonable time to ask for the repeal of a tax' (the coal duty was conceded in April).[9] He divided against the Grey ministry's reform bill at its second reading, 22 Mar., and for Gascoyne's wreck-ing amendment, 19 Apr. 1831. Assheton Smith chose not to stand at the ensuing election, so Griffith Wynne hurried to Caernarvonshire where he was returned unopposed, sponsored by Edwards of Nanhoron and

Newborough. He promised on the hustings to 'consult his constituents' and attend to their 'individual interests'.[10] He divided against the reintroduced reform bill at its second reading, 6 July, for an adjournment, 12 July, and to make the 1831 census the criterion for borough disfranchisements, 19 July 1831. Illness prevented him voting again during the bill's committee stage or at its passage, 21 Sept. 1831. Proposing a toast to him at the Caernarvon Michaelmas dinner, the pro-Paget Whig, Thomas Parry Jones Parry, explained that Griffith Wynne was 'prevented by illness from mixing much in public life', and 'by attendance to his duties in Parliament he had suffered so much that his physicians had been obliged to tell him that it was as much as his life was worth to continue his exertions'.[11] He divided against the revised reform bill at its committal, 20 Jan., and third reading, 22 Mar., having also voted against enfranchising Tower Hamlets, 28 Feb. 1832. He divided against the Irish reform bill at its second reading, 25 May, and for Alexander Baring's bill to deny insolvent debtors parliamentary privilege, 27 June. He voted against government on the Russian-Dutch loan, 26 Jan., 12 July. With Assheton Smith and Ormsby Gore out of Parliament, it had fallen on Griffith Wynne to represent their interests in the select committees on the contentious Ffestiniog railway and Caernarvon roads bills, which were both enacted, 23 May 1832.[12]

Throughout the summer of 1832, Ormsby Gore and the Tory *North Wales Chronicle* made much of Griffith Wynne's 'attention to his parliamentary duties', claiming again that they had ruined his health, making it the reason for retirement after warming the Caernarvonshire seat for Assheton Smith. At his election dinner in December, Assheton Smith proposed a toast to 'his cousin', who he hoped 'had given satisfaction'.[13] Ever the caretaker Member and party man, Griffith Wynne gave his Boroughs votes in 1832 to the Conservative, Nanney.[14] He did not stand for Parliament again. 'Ready to promote the material comfort and moral welfare of all within his influence', he divided his time between Denbighshire and his London house in Portman Square, where he died in March 1865. He was buried at the church he had built and endowed in Pentre Foelas.[15] His successor at Voelas and Cefnamlwch, his eldest son Charles (1815-74), Liberal Conservative Member for Caernarvon Boroughs, 1859-65, had inherited Stokesley in 1860 and assumed the names Wynne Finch in lieu of Griffith Wynne shortly before his second marriage in 1863. Griffith Wynn's will of 1 Aug. 1855 confirmed previous settlements and provided for family Members, but disinherited his son John Henry

Griffith Wynne (1819-93) under a codicil dated 5 July 1864.

[1] *HP Commons, 1754-90*, ii. 424. [2] PROB 11/1531/120; 1623/571; IR26/543/97; 782/1033; Gwynedd Archives, Caernarfon, Poole mss 6328, 6329. [3] K. Evans, 'Caernarvon Borough', *Trans. Caern. Hist. Soc.* vii (1947), 57-61, 65; P.D.G. Thomas, 'Parl. Rep. Caern. in 18th Cent.' ibid. xix (1958), 42-53; xx (1959), 77-83. [4] Gwynedd Archives, Caernarfon, Glynllifon mss 4328; *N. Wales Gazette*, 22, 29 June 1826; UCNW, Plas Newydd mss i. 393. [5] *PP* (1829), ix. 400-1. [6] Plas Newydd mss i. 393, 479, 465; *N. Wales Chron.* 1, 8, 22, 29 July, 5, 12, 19 Aug. 1830. [7] *N. Wales Chron.* 18 Feb., 25 Mar. 1830; Plas Newydd mss i. 463, 490. [8] NLW, Voelas and Cefnamlwch mss 3. [9] *Caernarvon Herald*, 22 Jan. 1831. [10] Plas Newydd mss i. 577; *Caernarvon Herald*, 30 Apr., 7 May 1831. [11] *Caernarvon Herald*, 1 Oct. 1831. [12] *CJ*, lxxxvii. 51, 58, 135, 286, 304, 331-2. [13] *Caernarvon Herald*, 14 July, 11 Aug.; *N. Wales Chron.* 17 July, 14 Aug., 25 Dec. 1832. [14] Plas Newydd mss iii. 3617. [15] *Caernarvon and Denbigh Herald*, 1 Apr. 1865.

M.M.E.

GRIMSTON, James Walter, Visct. Grimston (1809–1895).

St. Albans	1830–1831
Newport	12 July 1831–1832
Hertfordshire	1832–17 Nov. 1845

b. 22 Feb. 1809, 1st s. of James Walter Grimston[†], 2nd Bar. Verulam, and Lady Charlotte Jenkinson, da. of Charles Jenkinson[†], 1st earl of Liverpool. *educ.* Harrow 1823-7; Christ Church, Oxf. 1827. *m.* 12 Sept. 1844, Elizabeth Joanna, da. of Richard Weyland*, 3s. 3da. (1 *d.v.p.*). *suc.* fa. as 2nd earl of Verulam 17 Nov. 1845. *d.* 27 July 1895.
Ld. in waiting Mar. 1852-Jan. 1853, Feb. 1858-June 1859.
Pres. Camden Soc. 1873.
Ld. lt. Herts. 1845-92; capt. cmmdt. Cashio yeomanry 1831; lt.-col. Herts. yeoman cav. 1847-64.

Grimston's father had sat for St. Albans on the family interest (the borough lay only two miles from the Grimstons' seat at Gorhambury) from 1802 until 1808, when he succeeded as 2nd Baron Grimston. He also held an Irish viscountcy (Grimston), a Scottish barony (Forrester) and a baronetcy (Luckyn). In 1807 he married the half-sister of Lord Hawkesbury[†], who as 2nd earl of Liverpool and prime minister obtained for him the earldom of Verulam in 1815. He successfully applied to Liverpool for the vacant lord lieutenancy of Hertfordshire in 1823, when he acknowledged 'the most happy connection it has been my good fortune to have engaged in with your family'.[1] An anti-Catholic Tory, he had sufficient parts for Lord Ellenborough to suggest him to the duke of Wellington as a possible replacement for Lord

Anglesey as viceroy of Ireland in December 1828. Yet Lord Bathurst advised the duke that 'Lord Verulam has certainly a very large head and the public give him the credit therefore of having a very thick one. I am afraid it would not do'. He was passed over for the duke of Northumberland, to the disappointment of Lord Palmerston*, for one, who considered him to be 'more a man of the world'.[2] Verulam was surprised by the government's decision to concede Catholic emancipation soon afterwards, and uneasily spoke and voted against the 'odious bill' in the Lords, though the affair did not permanently alienate him from Wellington.[3]

Grimston, his eldest son, was an accomplished sportsman, and was captain of cricket at Harrow in 1827. On his coming of age in February 1830, when he was still at Oxford, his father wrote affectionately, if awkwardly to him:

> Many happy returns of this day to you, my dear fellow. You know how well I wish you, and as it is more than I can attempt to express, I will not attempt to do it ... I hope you will find the wine good which I have sent ... and that you will have a merry evening, without incurring a headache tomorrow, or any of the other *disagreables* attendant on excess.[4]

At the general election six months later Grimston offered for St. Albans, where support had been mobilized for his long-anticipated candidature. He made much of his local connections and, while admitting that he was a political novice, stated in his first address that 'the line adopted by my family has met my perfect approbation; I despise a subservient adulation of a minister, as much as I deprecate a restless and systematic opposition'. Both the sitting Members retired, but two other candidates, including one sent down by the Whig opposition, came forward. On the hustings, Grimston said that, like his father, he would 'support the ministry while they do right, but no further'. He easily topped the poll.[5]

Ministers of course numbered Grimston as one of their 'friends', and he was chosen to move the address at the opening of the new Parliament, 2 Nov. 1830, when, amongst the customary platitudes, he observed:

> The awakening spirit of the age, and the keen eye of the politician, looks to improvement ... to that degree of reform which may be necessary not to break in upon (God forbid!), but to keep up the spirit of the ancient constitution under the present aspect of affairs. I am glad ... to perceive, that ministers have felt this, and have acted upon it without fear of what imputations might be cast upon them.

He declared his 'decided support' for government on the strength of his 'deliberate judgement upon public

affairs'; but he failed to rally to them for the division on the civil list which brought them down, 15 Nov. 1830. He presented a petition from the householders of St. Albans for the ballot, 26 Feb. 1831, but sent his excuses for non-attendance at the borough reform meeting two days later.[6] He voted silently against the second reading of the Grey ministry's reform bill, 22 Mar., and for Gascoyne's wrecking amendment, 19 Apr. He presented a petition from subscribers to the London and Birmingham railway scheme to have their names erased from the contract, 9 Apr. 1831.

Grimston stood again for St. Albans at the 1831 general election, when his father made a written appeal to the electors, which paid lip service to the need for moderate reform, but condemned the 'revolutionary tendency' of the government bill, a 'reckless and sweeping invasion of property and rights'. He was challenged and humiliatingly defeated by two strangers, standing as its uncompromising supporters.[7] According to Lady Holland, the marquess of Salisbury was the prime mover behind a late bid to get Grimston returned for the county, where the sitting Members were seeking re-election as reformers; his father was supposed to have acquiesced in it 'with reluctance and remonstrance'. A canvass proved so discouraging that at the nomination Grimston had to back down, admitting that he 'had no prospect of success, owing to the general feeling in favour of reform, a measure to which he was conscientiously opposed'. He complained that 'the appeal was now made to the passions and not to the feelings of the people, many of whom had not seen or read a line of the bill'.[8]

In June 1831 Grimston's mother incurred the displeasure of Lord Melbourne, the home secretary and a Hertfordshire neighbour, for introducing politics into the affairs of the yeomanry by expressing the hope, when presenting colours to the Cassio troop at Gorhambury, that they would protect the country from the possible consequences of 'the restless and innovating spirit of the times'. He asked Wellington to keep his political adherents in check; but the duke, though sharing his concern at Lady Verulam's indiscretion, thought Melbourne should himself take the matter up with her husband.[9] A few weeks later Grimston was returned on a vacancy for Northumberland's pocket borough of Newport, but he made no mark in this Parliament, which he seems to have attended spasmodically. His only known votes against the reintroduced reform bill were for use of the 1831 census as a basis for disfranchisement, 19 July, and against its passage, 21 Sept. He voted for inquiry into the problems of

West Indian sugar producers, 12 Sept. He divided against the revised reform bill on its second reading, 17 Dec. 1831, the enfranchisement of Tower Hamlets, 28 Feb., and the bill's third reading, 22 Mar. 1832. In January 1832 his father and Salisbury got up a county address, described by Greville as 'a moderate reform manifesto', against the creation of peers to force the reform bill through the Lords, which they presented to the king at Brighton on the 16th, after travelling overnight.[10] (Verulam opposed the bill in the Lords, 13 Apr., 7 May, but on the return of the reform ministry to office he abandoned his resistance, though he declined to comply with the 'extraordinary' request of the king, with whom he had another audience on 16 May, to join in a declaration to that effect in the House. After consulting Wellington, he went to Newmarket races, bored 'to death' with 'the state of politics' and unable to see any 'way of extricating the country from the disasters which threaten it'.)[11] Grimston's only other known votes in this Parliament were against the vestry bill, 23 Jan., and against government on the Russian-Dutch loan, 26 Jan., 12 July 1832.

At the general election of 1832 he was returned in third place for Hertfordshire, having declared his opposition to 'the dictation of political unions'.[12] His father was made a lord of the bedchamber in Peel's first ministry.[13] Grimston, whose younger brother Edward Harbottle Grimston (1812-81) sat for St. Albans as a Conservative from 1835 to 1841, when he took holy orders, retained the county seat until he succeeded to the peerage in 1845. In a departure from his usual practice, Peel appointed him lord lieutenant of Hertfordshire in immediate succession to his father.[14] He died in July 1895, and was succeeded as 3rd earl of Verulam by his eldest son, James Walter Grimston (1852-1924), Conservative Member for the St. Albans division of Hertfordshire, 1885-92.

[1] Add. 38575, f. 172. [2] Wellington mss WP1/972/29; 973/12; 975/36; *Wellington Despatches*, v. 357, 377; *Palmerston-Sulivan Letters*, 227. [3] Herts. Archives, Verulam mss D/EV F54, Verulam's diary, 5, 7, 9, 10 Feb., 3, 4, 14 Apr. 1829. [4] Ibid. F308, Verulam to Grimston, 22 Feb. 1830. [5] *Herts Mercury*, 3, 10, 31 July, 7, 14 Aug. 1830. [6] *County Herald*, 5 Mar. 1831. [7] Verulam mss F308, Verulam's address [Apr.]; *County Herald*, 30 Apr., 7 May; *Bucks Gazette*, 7 May; Creevey mss, Creevey to Miss Ord, 30 Apr. 1831. [8] TNA 30/29, Lady Holland to Granville [5 May]; *County Herald*, 7, 14 May; *Bucks Gazette*, 14 May 1831. [9] *County Herald*, 11 June; *The Times*, 14 June 1831; Wellington mss WP1/1187/31; 1191/12; *Wellington Despatches*, vii. 472-3. [10] *Greville Mems*. ii. 236-7, 257; Verulam mss F55, Verulam's diary, 11, 14-16 Jan. 1832; Wellington mss WP1/1213/22; *Wellington Despatches*, viii. 162-4. [11] Verulam mss F55, Verulam's diary, 16-18 May 1832. [12] *County Press*, 26 June, 22, 29 Dec. 1832. [13] Add. 40407, ff. 112, 169. [14] Add. 40581, ff. 289, 291.

D.R.F.

GROSETT, John Rock (?1784–1866), of Lacock Abbey, nr. Chippenham, Wilts. and Spring Garden and Petersfield, Jamaica.

CHIPPENHAM   1820–1826

b. ?1784, 2nd[1] but o. surv. s. of Schaw Grosett, merchant, of Clifton, Glos. and Mary, da. of Thomas Rock, merchant, of Bristol. m. (1) 19 Feb. 1810, his 1st cos. Mary Spencer (d. 31 Oct. 1820), da. of Edward Shirley of Cockthorpe Hall, nr. Witney, Oxon.,[2] at least 4s. (3 d.v.p.) at least 2da. d.v.p.; (2) 20 July 1825, Christina Maria de Kantzow,[3] at least 1s. d.v.p. suc. fa. 1820. d. 22 Sept. 1866.
   Cornet 13 Drag. 1804, lt. 1805, ret. 1807.
   Member of assembly, Jamaica 1831-44; member of council.

The Grosetts, whose rare surname had several variants, are believed to be descended from Alexander Grosier or Grosiert, a Frenchman who served in Charles I's army and then settled in Scotland. His son Alexander, who was described as a merchant of Bo'ness, Lanarkshire, and formerly of Rotterdam, married Christian Cochran, and was granted lands in Logie, near Dunfermline, Fife, in 1711. In 1717 these were inherited by his son Archibald Grosett, who married Euphemia, daughter of James Muirhead of Bredisholm, Lanarkshire. Their third son, James, a Lisbon merchant, who was 'a gentleman of reputation' and 'a rising man that way', married Donna Leonora de Miranda of the house of Cordova.[4] He took the additional surname of Muirhead by royal licence in 1753, when he purchased Bredisholm, but his son died without issue and it was through his elder brother Alexander that the family of Grosett Muirhead (later Steuart Grosett Muirhead) continued.[5] The eldest son, Walter, who married Dinah Devlieger in 1729 and succeeded Archibald in 1739, was collector of customs at Alloa. He took an active part against the Jacobite rebels in 1745, and, despite being accused of corruption, later became collector at Glasgow and an inspector-general of customs in Scotland.[6] In 1760 he was succeeded by his eldest son, James, a lace merchant of Gerrard Street, Westminster. He sold the property at Logie, and had many children with his wife Elizabeth, including another Walter, who retired from the navy with the rank of rear admiral in 1846.[7]

Schaw, a younger son of Walter Grosett of Alloa, was born in 1741 and was probably involved in the family's Portuguese interests. On 13 Mar. 1783 he married Mary Rock (1755-1807), and on the same day her sister, Hannah Spencer Rock (1759-1808), married Edward Shirley of Cockthorpe Hall. The brides became coheiresses to the Jamaican plantations of their grandfather John Spencer (*d.* 1768) on the decease of their brother John Spencer Rock, and of their mother Hannah (in 1797), who after the death of their father Thomas Rock in 1772, had married, 13 July 1773, Henry Shirley (*d.* 1812) of Upper Wimpole Street, another Jamaican planter. John Rock Grosett, who spent some of his youth in Lisbon and served briefly in the army in England, consolidated this inheritance in 1810 by marrying his orphaned first cousin, Mary Spencer Shirley. Apart from the provision which was made for his unmarried sister Hannah Spencer, Grosett succeeded to his father's entire estate, which included personal wealth sworn under £18,000, in April 1820. However, like his father, he also experienced prolonged legal problems over his West Indian possessions, and he had to set aside £10,000 for his younger children in order to leave the properties to the eldest at his death.[8] He rented Lacock Abbey, which was described by the poet Thomas Moore as a 'remarkably curious old place', and it was there that, to his 'inexpressible grief', his first wife, 'a woman of the greatest virtue and piety', died, aged 36, in October 1820.[9]

He may have been introduced to Chippenham by another wealthy Jamaican planter and one of its former Members, James Dawkins. Indeed, it was on the interest of John Maitland, another former Member, who had purchased Dawkins's property there and usually controlled one of the seats, that he first stood at the general election of 1818. Despite an active and favourable canvass, he was beaten into third place.[10] Grosett, who never seems to have displayed any firm party allegiance, split for Paul Methuen[†] and John Benett* against the ministerialist William Pole Long Wellesley* at the Wiltshire election of 1818, but switched to the Tory interloper John Dugdale Astley*, against Benett, at the following year's by-election.[11] He made an agreement with Maitland to pay a total of £4,000 for being elected free of other expenses, and was returned unopposed for Chippenham at the general election of 1820.[12] It was probably not Grosett but William Gosset who, as 'Col. Grossett', voted against Hume's motion for economies in revenue collection, 4 July. He spoke in commendation of the Devizes Bear Club at its annual dinner, 11 Aug. 1820, and was a regular attender at meetings of this and the Wiltshire Society, another charity.[13]

He declined to present the Chippenham address to Queen Caroline while she was under trial, because he thought it would prejudge the issue, and he voted in defence of ministers' conduct towards her, 6 Feb. 1821.[14] He did not vote in the division on Catholic claims, 28 Feb., but made a brief intervention against the relief bill, 23 Mar., citing the *Journal* of the Irish Commons for 1642 to show that the Elizabethan oath did exclude Catholics from the House. He presented and supported a Chippenham petition against their claims, 26 Mar., on the grounds that they aimed at political power and not merely toleration.[15] He divided against Hume's bill to disqualify civil officers of the ordnance from voting in parliamentary elections, 12 Apr., and was possibly the 'W. Grosset' who voted against parliamentary reform, 9 May 1821. He chaired a meeting of local inhabitants, 23 Jan. 1822, at which it was decided to establish the Chippenham Savings Bank, and was appointed as one of its presidents.[16] He was added to the standing committee of the West India Planters' and Merchants' Committee, 22 Mar., and was thereafter a regular attender at its sittings, at least during the parliamentary session.[17] He voted for the remission of the remainder of Henry Hunt's* gaol sentence, 24 Apr., against the Catholic peers bill, 30 Apr., and for Western's motion condemning the resumption of cash payments, 12 June. As a local magistrate he attended the inquest on the two men killed during the Chippenham riots in September 1822.[18] He presented anti-Catholic petitions from Chippenham and two Wiltshire parishes, 25 Feb., 15 Apr. 1823, and St. Vincent petitions complaining of distress and the equalization of East and West Indian sugar duties, 19 Mar., 22 May.[19] He sided with opposition on the ordnance estimates, 17 Mar., inquiry into the legal proceedings against the Dublin Orange rioters, 22 Apr., and parliamentary reform, 24 Apr. 1823.

In January 1824 a young cousin of his, Walter Grosett, died in Jamaica 'from a fever caught in performing militia duty in repressing the late conspiracy among the slaves'.[20] Despite being active in defence of West Indian interests, Grosett presented a Chippenham anti-slavery petition, 1 Mar., but when another was brought up, from Melksham, 15 Mar., he protested that it had been 'handed about' by a Methodist parson rather than approved at a public meeting.[21] He justified the seizure of several men in Jamaica, 21 May, arguing that they had raised money for missionary work but had used it to arm rebellious slaves, and on 16 June 1825 he reiterated his belief that 'the persons might be guilty' and 'denied that they were entitled to be provided for'. He voted against condemning the trial of the Methodist missionary John Smith in Demerara, 11 June 1824. In the same month he published a pamphlet, *Remarks on West India Affairs*, in which he criticized anti-slavery societies for inflaming public opinion:

Mr. Buxton's motion of last session [15 May 1823], and above all the workings of a party in this country have produced infinite mischief, by unsettling the mind of the negro population and by the infusion of false and exaggerated expectations.

Fearing revolution, as had occurred in the French islands, he asserted the planters' legal right to own slaves and praised the foreign secretary Canning's 'eloquent speech' of 16 Mar. 1824, which had argued that practical improvements in their conditions could only realistically come from their proprietors. He agreed with George Watson Taylor's* defence of slavery at the Devizes Bear Club dinner, 27 Aug. 1824, when he emphasized the colonial contribution to England's naval expertise.[22]

He divided against Catholic relief, 1 Mar., 21 Apr., 10 May, and the related Irish franchise bill, 26 Apr., and brought up another hostile constituency petition, 24 Mar. 1825.[23] In July he married into the de Kantzow family, relations by marriage and commercial associates of the Grosetts in Portugal.[24] In the autumn he was appointed provincial grand master of Wiltshire, and he later praised freemasonry as an 'object worthy of cultivation and encouragement, as it unites men in one common bond of union, affection and good fellowship'.[25] He voted in the minority of 39 against going into committee on the Bank Charter Acts, 13 Feb. 1826, and presented another Chippenham anti-slavery petition, 17 Feb.[26] He told the House, 1 Mar., that it 'seemed to pass over entirely the state of slavery in which many of the natives of the East Indies were held; a slavery which was more abject and degrading than that in the West Indies'; and the following day he divided against condemning the Jamaican slave trials. His last recorded votes were against alteration of the representation of Edinburgh, 13 Apr., and resolutions to curb electoral bribery, 26 May 1826. Under his agreement with Maitland, Grosett was obliged to withdraw if his patron sold his property in Chippenham. However, when he proposed to convey his burgages to his nephew, Ebenezer Fuller Maitland*, who intended to stand himself, Grosett claimed to have forgotten the terms of the arrangement, having said on 26 May 1824 that 'he did not consider himself precluded from standing for Chippenham if the people chose to elect him'. A settlement was nevertheless reached, on the same financial basis as before, when it was decided that Fuller Maitland would stand on his own interest, while Grosett would offer in place of William Alexander Madocks, on the interest of Anthony Guy, who was in the process of selling control of the other seat to Fuller Maitland.[27] Grosett was considered to

be 'a most amiable man in private life' and assiduous in his attention to Chippenham affairs, but neither his popularity, nor Guy's, was proof against the entry, at the general election of 1826, of an independent candidate, Frederick Gye*, who promised to revitalize the town's depressed cloth industry. Having been politely requested to stand aside, he bowed to the inevitable and issued an address stating that he would 'rather sacrifice my own advantage, than, after the handsome manner in which you have addressed me, be the supposed cause of any injury to you'.[28] He is not known to have sought a seat elsewhere and never sat in the Commons again.

By the late 1820s he had ceased to live at Lacock, although he retained property in Chippenham and served as a magistrate and deputy lieutenant of Wiltshire.[29] He attended the West India Committee's meetings until 1829.[30] He signed the Wiltshire anti-Catholic declaration early that year and was present at the Wiltshire Society dinner, 19 May 1830, but he must soon afterwards have left England to settle in Jamaica.[31] He was elected to the assembly there, for the constituency of St. George, at a by-election, 11 Nov. 1831, and was returned at four subsequent general elections.[32] He was also for many years a member of the island's council, and served as custos of St. George. He must have resided there for most of the rest of his life, as the Wiltshire freemasons complained that absence abroad and ill health had led him to neglect the duties of his office, which he left in 1847.[33] It was also there that he suffered the deaths of his children, Mary Henrietta, John Schaw and Hannah Teresa, in 1833, and Albert Henry (at Clifton) and Edward Walter, in 1838, while the only known child of his second marriage, Charles Walpole, died in 1852.[34] He died in September 1866, aged 82, at Chew Magna, Somerset, where he was then living.[35] By his will, dated 23 July 1859, which was proved in London, 1 Nov. 1866, provision was made for his wife if she recovered from her 'mental malady', and everything else was left to his only surviving child, Frederick Rock Spencer Grosett. He, however, died intestate, aged 50, 17 Feb. 1868, before he could execute his father's will, and administration of their joint estate was eventually granted, 14 July 1869, to Frederica Theresa Henrietta, Countess de Maricourt of Versailles.[36]

[1] *W.I. Bookplates* ed. V. L. Oliver, 46. [2] *Reg. St. Marylebone, Mdx.* ix. 16. [3] *Reg. St. George Hanover Square,* iv. 35. [4] G.F. Black, *Surnames of Scotland,* 330; A. Nisbet, *System of Heraldry,* ii. (1742), 268; W. Stephen, *Hist. Inverkeithing and Rosyth,* 203-4. [5] *Burke LG* (1886), ii. 1316; PROB 11/980/292. [6] IGI (London); *Grosett ms* ed. D. N. Mackay (1917); *Faithful narrative of many enormous frauds and abuses* (1747); *James Grosett, appellant* (1763) [BL 516.m.19.(77)].

[7] IGI (London); Stephen, 204; W.R. O'Byrne, *Naval Biog.* i. 436. [8] IGI (Clackmannan, London); *Reg. St. George Hanover Square*, i. 344; *Gent. Mag.* (1797), ii. 1073; (1806), i. 586; (1807), ii. 1078; (1808), i. 367; (1812), ii. 594; (1820), i. 476; PROB 6/182/449; 11/983/421; 1543/215; 1629/279; IR26/822/388; *MI of Jamaica* ed. P. Wright, 2940a; *Caribbeana*, ii. 185; *Sources of Jamaican Hist.* ed. K.E. Ingram, i. 398. [9] *Moore Mems.* ii. 282; *Salisbury Jnl.* 6 Nov. 1820; *Bristol Cathedral Reg.* ed. C.R. Hudlestone, 49. [10] *Salisbury Jnl.* 15 June 1818; Oldfield, *Key* (1820), 29-30. [11] *Wilts. Pollbook* (1819), 84. [12] Wilts. RO, Bevir mss 1171/9, electoral agreement, 'Grosett', n.d.; *Bath Jnl.* 21 Feb.; *Salisbury Jnl.* 20 Mar. 1820. [13] *Devizes Gazette*, 17 Aug. 1820, 31 May 1821. [14] J.A. Chamberlain, Chippenham, 111. [15] *The Times*, 27 Mar.; *Devizes Gazette*, 29 Mar. 1821. [16] *Devizes Gazette*, 31 Jan. 1822. [17] Inst. of Commonwealth Stud. M915/3, 4. [18] *The Times*, 14 Sept. 1822. [19] Ibid. 26 Feb., 20 Mar., 16 Apr., 23 May 1823. [20] *Gent. Mag.* (1824), i. 647; *MI of Jamaica*, 2939. [21] *The Times*, 2 Mar.; *Devizes Gazette*, 18 Mar. 1824. [22] *Devizes Gazette*, 2 Sept. 1824. [23] *The Times*, 25 Mar. 1825. [24] PROB 11/1364/663; IR26/56/85. [25] F.H. Goldney, *Hist. Freemasonry in Wilts.* 12-13; *Devizes Gazette*, 7 Aug. 1828. [26] *The Times*, 18 Feb. 1826. [27] Bevir mss 1171/9, 'Mem. in London', May; 'Mem. relative to purchase of Mr. Guy', Nov.; electoral agreement, 12 Nov. 1824. [28] *Devizes Gazette*, 28 July 1825, 15 June, 26 Oct.; *The Times*, 25 Mar., 3 June 1826. [29] Wilts. RO, Ross mss 1769/93; *Gent. Mag.* (1866), ii. 698. [30] Inst. of Commonwealth Stud. M915/4 [31] Glos. RO, Sotheron Estcourt mss D1571 X114, Long to Bucknall Estcourt, 8 Feb. 1829; *Salisbury Jnl.* 24 May 1830. [32] *Members of Assembly of Jamaica* ed. G. Robertson, 37, 53. [33] Goldney, 13-15, 69-70. [34] *Gent. Mag.* (1833), i. 479; (1838), ii. 227; *MI of Jamaica*, 1425, 2938, 2940; J. H. Lawrence-Archer, *MI of British W.I.* 122. [35] *Gent. Mag.* (1866), ii. 698. [36] IR26/2467/892; *The Times*, 22 Feb. 1868.

S.M.F.

GROSVENOR, Richard, Visct. Belgrave (1795-1869).[1]

CHESTER	1818–1830
CHESHIRE	1830–1832
CHESHIRE SOUTH	1832–1834

b. 27 Jan. 1795, 1st. s. of Robert Grosvenor†, 2nd Earl Grosvenor, and Hon. Eleanor Egerton, da. and h. of Thomas Egerton†, 1st Bar. Grey de Wilton (afterwards 1st earl of Wilton); bro. of Hon. Robert Grosvenor*. *educ.* Westminster 1806-12; Christ Church, Oxf. 1812; European tour 1815-17. *m.* 16 Sept. 1819, Lady Elizabeth Mary Leveson Gower, da. of George Granville Leveson Gower†, 2nd mq. of Stafford, 4s. (2 *d.v.p.*) 9da. (1 *d.v.p.*). *styled* Earl Grosvenor 1831-45. *suc.* fa. as 2nd mq. of Westminster 17 Feb. 1845; KG 6 July 1857. *d.* 31 Oct. 1869.

Ld. steward of household Mar. 1850-Feb. 1852; PC 22 Mar. 1852.

Ld. lt. Cheshire 1845-68.

Capt. R. Flints. militia 1818; maj. commdt. Flints. yeomanry 1831.

Belgrave was heir to the vast wealth of the Whig Lord Grosvenor, who in this period increased his influence by completing the lavish refurbishment of his family seat, Eaton Hall, near Chester, and deploying the proceeds from property developments on his Ebury estate in Belgravia, Mayfair and Pimlico, Middlesex, to purchase the Dorset estates of Gillingham and Motcombe (1822-8), Moor Park, Hertfordshire (1829), and controlling interests in the boroughs of Shaftesbury, Dorset (1820), and Stockbridge, Hampshire (1822-5).[2] In 1818 Grosvenor had brought him in for Chester, where his power to return both Members was strongly challenged. Despite criticism of his failure to vote against the repressive measures adopted after the Peterloo massacre, he topped the poll there in a violent contest in 1820.[3]

Belgrave's attendance could be erratic, but his votes and occasional speeches echoed his father's support for Queen Caroline, parliamentary reform and Catholic relief. In 1825 a radical publication noted that he had 'attended frequently and voted in opposition to government'.[4] He divided steadily with the Whig moderates on most major issues, including economy and retrenchment, and he was careful to attend to and represent constituency interests. At Chester, 9 Jan. 1821, he successfully proposed the resolutions for a loyal address and petition criticizing ministers' conduct towards the queen, which he presented to the Commons on the 26th. He was present at the Cheshire county meeting that terminated in chaos when his father moved a similar address, 11 Jan., signed the ensuing protest, and steadily supported the parliamentary campaign on the queen's behalf.[5] Defending his father, he made what the radical Whig Member Grey Bennet considered 'a very good speech' on presenting the Cheshire protest, 9 Feb. In it he explained that the original requisition included freeholders and inhabitants, emphasized the danger of a corrupt meeting chaired by a corrupt sheriff acting 'in excess of his powers' and alleged that the affray had been deliberately engineered by members of the ministerialist Cholmondeley family.[6] He spoke similarly when Creevey moved unsuccessfully to censure the sheriff's conduct, 20 Feb., but as the Grenvillite leader Charles Williams Wynn* observed, he deliberately went away without voting.[7] He paired, 28 Feb. 1821, and divided for Catholic relief, 1 Mar., 21 Apr., 10 May, and, watched by his wife, he confirmed his support for it on presenting a hostile petition from Chester, 25 Apr. 1825.[8] He voted for parliamentary reform, 9 May 1821,[9] 20 Feb., 2 June 1823. He criticized the house tax, 5 Apr. 1821, 2 Mar. 1824, but condoned that on glasshouses, 5 Apr. 1821.[10] He seconded Burdett's abortive amendment against the tobacco duties bill, which the Chester trade opposed, 18 June, and supported inquiry into the Llanllechid quarry leases on the 21st.[11] He was elected an alderman of Chester in October 1821 and became a founder member that month of the Cheshire Whig Club.[12] He enjoyed hunting, ice hockey and skating on the frozen River Dee, and remained at Eaton at the start of the 1822 session.[13] In May his brother Robert joined him in the House as their father's Member for Shaftesbury. Belgrave presented Chester's petitions for the small debts bill, 17 Apr., and criminal law reform, 3 June, and voted for the latter, 4 June. His admission to Brooks's, which Lord Grosvenor had recently joined, 8 May 1822, was proposed by Lords Holland and Lansdowne. Presenting the Chester tobacco manufacturers' petition, 12 June, he endorsed their claims that tobacco consumption had fallen and smuggling increased as a result of higher duties, and alleged that this had cost the treasury £55,000 in lost revenue.[14] During the recess he visited Stockbridge, where Lord Grosvenor had recently purchased the Barham interest.[15] He and his brother Robert were talked of but not put forward as candidates for Dorset at the February 1823 by-election.[16]

Belgrave presented a Chester petition against the Insolvent Debtors Act, 17 Mar. 1823.[17] His eldest son Gilbert, a sickly infant who died aged nine months, was born on 10 Apr. Belgrave himself received a fortnight's leave on account of ill health, 15 Apr., after undergoing surgery for haemorrhoids.[18] Touring the North in August, he and his wife stayed at Castle Howard, where Lord Morpeth[†] thought Lady Elizabeth 'very pretty and good humoured and cheerful, he emulating a Jew in appearance, but good natured'.[19] He presented Chester petitions against the hides and skins bill, the malt, beer and excise licence duties, and the proposed house tax reassessment, 26, 29 Mar., and for the abolition of colonial slavery, 5 Apr., 4 May 1824.[20] He endorsed the Shrewsbury brewers' petition against increasing the duty on malt, 6 May.[21] He voted in condemnation of the indictment in Demerara of the Methodist missionary John Smith, 11 June, having presented petitions advocating it, 28 May 1824.[22] During the recess he was a guest of Lansdowne's at Bowood, 'where the company included the Hollands, Lord Ellenborough and Lord John Russell*'. Staying afterwards with his wife's aunt, the duchess of Beaufort, at Badminton, he visited Longleat and Fonthill.[23] Belgrave could no longer mask his political differences with his colleagues in the Cheshire Whig Club, whose professed creed included triennial parliaments, and, rather than subscribe to it, he resigned before the annual dinner on 9 Oct., stating in an open letter:

I have always felt averse myself to attendance at political clubs and periodical meetings; but it is a great additional objection to my mind where, as in the present instance, it is attempted to form a precise standard of principles, particularly at a time when most political differences are rather differences of degree, than of principle.[24]

The duke of Bedford thought it the work of 'a foolish conceited young man' and 'as shabby and dirty a letter as I ever read'. He wrote to Lord Holland, 31 Oct. 1824: 'I see Lord Belgrave has *ratted*. It was always supposed he would, but I am afraid it will annoy Lord Grosvenor'.[25] Holland saw 'nothing that a general Whig has to apprehend in it', but added, 'how far a Cheshire Whig has to complain of his writing any, or he has to complain of the Cheshire Whigs for exacting tests and printing creeds unnecessarily, must depend on what has passed in that sapient district'.[26] Belgrave presented a tobacco growers' petition for lower duties, 18 Feb. 1825. Commenting on the quarantine bill, 19 May, he expressed astonishment that Members could contend that plague was not contagious. He paired against the duke of Cumberland's annuity bill, 6 June 1825. Reports in September that he had killed an Irishman in a duel were entirely unfounded.[27] The birth on 13 Oct. of his heir Hugh Lupus was marked by private and public celebrations, and Grosvenor increased his annual allowance by £1,000 in consequence.[28] Before the dissolution in 1826, he criticized the government's corn importation bill as 'inexpedient' and unlikely to afford relief to the manufacturers 8, 11 May.[29] After 'a desperate struggle', he and his absent brother Robert topped the poll at Chester at the general election in June at an estimated cost of £20,000, and he hinted at the chairing that his family were unlikely to contest both seats in future.[30]

Belgrave habitually suffered from bouts of earache and temporary deafness, and his absence for this reason from the division on Catholic relief, 6 Mar. 1827, encouraged speculation in the anti-Grosvenor *Chester Courant* that his indisposition was 'affected'. This the partisan *Chester Chronicle* naturally denied.[31] He confirmed that the Chester anti-Catholic petition that he presented on 7 May was 'numerously and respectably signed', adding that he regarded emancipation as the 'most effectual means of diminishing the influence of the pope in this empire'; but he cautioned the new Canning ministry against proposing it prematurely.[32] In October 1827 the Goderich ministry turned down Grosvenor's application for a marquessate.[33] Tierney, their master of the mint, included Belgrave in his November 1827 list of possible members of the finance committee, but he was not appointed to it and is not known to have resumed his parliamentary duties before April 1828. His views on the repeal of the Test Acts, which his father and Robert openly supported, are unknown. He presented Chester petitions against the friendly societies bill, 18 Apr., and the alehouse licensing bill, 7 May, which, as it compromised the authority of corporation magistrates in Cheshire, he spoke strongly against, 21 May, 19 June. He divided for Catholic relief, 12 May. He objected to routing the Irish mail through Liverpool, instead of Chester and Holyhead, 6 June. He voted against the Buckingham House expenditure, 23 June 1828, and presented Chester's anti-slavery petition that day.

A riding accident, in which his wife was 'violently concussed', delayed Belgrave's return to London for the 1829 session, and on 3 Feb. the *Chester Courant* reported that he had privately informed his supporters on the corporation that the Grosvenors 'would no longer press for both seats in Chester'.[34] He did not vote 'with government' for Catholic emancipation as the patronage secretary Planta had predicted, but he contributed £50 to Peel's Oxford University election fund.[35] He endorsed the locally contentious Cheshire constabulary bill, 13 Apr., and, true to his promise to the Chester meeting of 29 Jan.,[36] he endorsed their petitions against the Dee Ferry road bill, 4 May 1829. He stayed away from the Cheshire county meeting, 25 Feb. 1830, when Grosvenor's Member for Shaftesbury, Edward Davies Davenport, carried a controversial petition claiming that distress emanated from currency change.[37] He presented petitions from Chester for criminal law reform, 28 Apr., and against the poor law amendment bill, 6 May, and another that day from Covent Garden backing the proposed Waterloo Bridge road scheme, which was conducive to Lord Grosvenor's Belgravia development. He divided fairly steadily with the revived Whig opposition in May and June, including for parliamentary reform, 28 May, and paired for abolishing capital punishment for forgery, 3 June. Conscious of the surprise which his opposition to the Jewish emancipation bill would cause, he spoke of his resentment at seeing the measure 'brought forward under the banner of Roman Catholic emancipation' and of his conviction that a race who 'through the medium of religion choose to establish themselves as a separate people' could not show 'the same attachment to country', 17 May.[38] Attending to local interests, on 18 May he presented and had the tobacco manufacturers' petition referred to the select committee on tobacco cultivation, of which (since 14 May) he was a member, and he presented and endorsed Chester's petition against renewal of the

East India Company's charter, 4 June. As requested by the corporation and county magistrates, he presented petitions, 6 May, and liaised closely with the lobbying committee appointed to oppose the administration of justice bill's proposal to abolish Cheshire's palatine courts. He advocated concessions and criticized the bill's details, 27 May, 5 July, but confirmed his support for its principle, 2, 7 July, as promoted by his friend Lord Cawdor, and he was later credited (amid allegation of ratting) with securing concessions in the law on evictions.[39] Before the 1830 dissolution he declined to join Hume's Middlesex committee and announced his candidature for Cheshire, where Davies Davenport's retirement had produced a vacancy, 30 June.[40] He set out for Eaton on 9 July after a preliminary canvass in London.[41] No effort was spared on his behalf and his rivals, including Edward Davies Davenport, who was also nominated, desisted, making his return with the sitting Tory Wilbraham Egerton a formality. Nevertheless, his speeches failed to satisfy those who questioned his recent commitment to the palatine courts, free trade and reform, and the *Chester Courant* warned:

> He is neither Whig nor Tory; reformer nor anti-reformer; free trader nor for restrictions; he has made up his mind on all great national questions, yet publishes his ignorance to the world. To sum up in a few words, his lordship appears anxious to be all things to all men ... If he fails to satisfy, the freeholders will oust him despite the might of his purse.[42]

Notwithstanding Lord Grosvenor's recent commitment to strengthening the ministry, they listed Belgrave among the 'doubtful doubtfuls'. He presented anti-slavery petitions, 10 Nov., and warned against prematurely condemning the disgraced dean of Chester Phillpotts, 11 Nov., but he was absent when the government were brought down on the civil list, 15 Nov. 1830. He presented petitions from the Catholics of St. Nicholas, Galway for equality with Protestants, 19 Nov., and from Cheshire for the abolition of slavery and of the civil list, 22 Nov. He expressed his hostility to the truck system, 13 Dec. Addressing a party dinner in Chester, where Robert's re-election following his appointment by Lord Grey as comptroller of the household was opposed, he spoke of the unrest generated by the 'Swing' riots and promised to do everything in his power to ensure that the constitution was upheld and property protected, 20 Dec. He commanded the Flintshire yeomanry during the disturbances in the North Wales coalfield that winter, but nothing came of his plans to raise an additional cavalry troop in Cheshire.[43] He moved the first reading of the Hyde, Werneth and Newton waterworks bill, 21 Feb., and secured leave to introduce the Grosvenor Chapel bill, 21 Mar. 1831. Later that day he moved the second reading of the second Liverpool-Chester railway bill and presented a petition against the first bill. He presented others favourable to the local courts bill, for amending the rules governing savings bank deposits and for the abolition of slavery, 22 Mar. As the sole diner at Grillion's, 1 Mar., Belgrave wrote in their record book: 'Unanimous for reform – in the club. No ballot'.[44] He divided for the second reading of the ministerial measure, 22 Mar., which his father had endorsed at the Cheshire meeting on the 17th,[45] presented a favourable petition, 15 Apr., and voted against Gascoyne's wrecking amendment, 19 Apr. 1831. At the ensuing general election there was talk of making him a peer, but he came in unopposed for Cheshire where a contest was averted by the retirement of two anti-reformers.[46] Edward Stanley, the future Baron Stanley of Alderley, whom Grosvenor had returned for Hindon, commented:

> He has come out of it well ... He has refused any coalition with the two others and has been abused by both; he has persisted in it from the first to the last that he came forward to represent the county, not as the champion of reform, and has not lent himself to the popular enthusiasm at all, but gone on, with his imperturbable smile, through all the excitement, cautious to an extreme of committing himself – provoking some by his coolness, yet forcing them to have a respect for his consistent firmness, and here in his speech he stated how it was his attachment to the constitution that induced him to vote for the measure that was to restore and preserve it, but gave in to none of the unqualified expectations, telling them in short, what they were not to expect from it; and there is a simplicity in all he does and says that carries conviction of his honesty with it.[47]

He divided for the second reading of the reintroduced reform bill, 6 July, against adjournment, 12 July, and to disfranchise Appleby, 19 July, and Downton, 21 July 1831. He paired for its details, 26 July-17 Aug. On 28 July he presented a petition from Congleton seeking separate enfranchisement. He cast a wayward vote for withholding the £10 borough vote from weekly tenants and lodgers, 25 Aug. He assumed the courtesy title Lord Grosvenor when his father became marquess of Westminster at the coronation, and returned from a short family holiday at Hoylake to vote for the bill's passage, 21 Sept.[48] He received three weeks' leave on urgent private business, which included yeomanry duties, 27 Sept. Congratulating Sir Stephen Glynne* on his brother Henry Glynne's return as his locum for Flint Boroughs, he observed:

So you have addressed the course I have thought wisest to follow and professed yourself a reformer. It may be the safest line for the country in its present state to pursue, but I own I have great fears for the result and have never hesitated to avow that I think the ministers have pressed their measure much too far.[49]

At the Cheshire reform meeting which protested at the bill's defeat in the Lords, 25 Oct., he reaffirmed his disapproval of 'parts of the bill' and thanked the freeholders for approving his conduct.[50] He, like Robert, was inconvenienced when Sir Watkin Williams Wynn terminated their pairing arrangement, and he failed to divide for the second reading of the revised reform bill, 17 Dec. 1831. He voted to proceed with it in committee, 20 Jan., where, differing from Robert, he divided against its provisions for Helston, 23 Feb., and Tower Hamlets, 28 Feb. 1832. He conceded that the Cheshire anti-reform declaration was 'respectably signed', 19 Mar. He voted for the bill's third reading, 22 Mar., but was absent when the House divided on the address requesting the king to appoint only ministers who would carry it unimpaired, 10 May. He presented several Cheshire petitions calling for the withholding of supplies pending its passage, 4 June 1832. He divided with government in both divisions on the Dublin election controversy, 23 Aug. 1831, and on the Russian-Dutch loan, 16, 20 July 1832.

He presented petitions from Cheshire's grand jury for repeal of the Beer Act, 14 July 1831, and favourable to the bill amending it, 4 June 1832, and brought up others that day against the general registry and factory regulation bills. When in February 1832 Edward Clarke, Samuel Adlam Bayntun's* former valet, was charged at Bow Street with forging Lord Belgrave's frank, his lawyers vainly maintained that Belgrave no longer existed and Grosvenor's testimony was sought.[51] As a spokesman for the depressed Cheshire silk trade, Grosvenor sought the establishment of a select committee to consider and 'devise some better protection against foreign competition', 17 Feb., and refused to desist from doing so because of disagreements between the Spitalfields, Macclesfield and Coventry trades, 21 Feb. Introducing his motion, 1 Mar., he spoke of the distress caused by the 1824 and 1826 regulations, the poor rate fluctuations and the decline from 10,229 to 3,622 in the number of employed silk workers, which induced him to advocate protection notwithstanding his prior commitment to free trade. A committee was conceded, but the balance between free traders and protectionists and the likely inclusion of the wealthy merchant and political economist James Morrison, to which Grosvenor objected, proved divisive. The impasse was resolved after ministerial intervention, but Grosvenor failed to prevent Morrison being added to the committee, 5 Mar. Before casting a wayward vote for inquiry into smuggling in the glove trade, 3 Apr., he said that he felt bound to do so because of the close analogy with silk, and, making light of initial 'irritations', he praised its members' work. Differing from its presenter, Wilbraham, he alleged that the county petition against the Cheshire Constabulary Act was the work of Edward Davies Davenport alone and that the Act was popular with the magistracy, 10 July. He presented a petition from the overseers of Stockport against the vagrants removal bill, 13 July 1832.

Grosvenor took charge of arrangements at Eaton during Princess Victoria's visit in October 1832. Through a late coalition with Wilbraham, he came in for the new constituency of Cheshire South as a Liberal after a severe contest in December.[52] He retired rather than risk defeat in 1834 and did not stand for Parliament again.[53] He embarked on a lengthy continental tour with his family and subsequently settled at Motcombe House, near Shaftesbury, where he controlled his father's business affairs. After succeeding as 2nd marquess in 1845, he purchased and made Fonthill his principal residence. He died there of a malignant carbuncle in October 1869.[54] Famed for his enormous wealth, the excellent care he took of it, and his patronage of the arts, charities and the Turf, he was also remembered as an advocate of corn law repeal and promoter of legislation for juvenile offenders and as lord steward of the household and a privy councillor during Lord John Russell's administration, for which he was rewarded with the garter in 1857.[55] He was succeeded in the marquessate, to entailed estates in Cheshire, Flintshire and London valued at £4,000,000, and his £750,000 personal fortune by his eldest surviving son Hugh Lupus Grosvenor (1825-99), Liberal Member for Chester, 1847-69, and from 1874 1st duke of Westminster.[56]

[1] Access to the Grosvenor papers, privately held at Eaton Hall, is gratefully acknowledged. For detailed accounts of Grosvenor's life see G. Huxley, *Lady Elizabeth and the Grosvenors* and *Victorian Duke*; and M.J. Hazelton-Swales, 'Urban Aristocrats' (London Univ. Ph.D. thesis, 1981). [2] *HP Commons, 1790-1820*, iv. 114-15; *Oxford DNB* sub Robert Grosvenor, (1767-1845). [3] *HP Commons, 1790-1820*, iv. 115-16; *Chester Chron.* 11, 17 Mar. 1820; *Report of Procs. at Chester Election* (1820). [4] *Session of Parl. 1825*, p. 450. [5] *The Times*, 6, 10, 13, 15, 18, 27 Jan.; *Chester Courant* 9, 16, 30 Jan.; *Chester Chron.* 12, 19 Jan. 1820. [6] *The Times*, 10 Feb.; *Chester Courant*, 13 Feb. 1821; HLRO, Hist. Coll. 379, Grey Bennet diary, 17. [7] *The Times*, 21 Feb. 1821; NLW, Coedymaen mss 629. [8] *The Times*, 19 Feb., 26 Apr. 1825; Huxley, *Lady Elizabeth*, 15. [9] Huxley, *Lady Elizabeth*, 89. [10] *The Times*, 6 Apr. 1821. [11] Ibid. 19 June 1821. [12] *Chester Chron.* 12 Oct.; *Chester Courant*, 11 Sept., 2, 9, 16 Oct. 1821. [13] Huxley, *Lady*

Elizabeth, 24. [14] *The Times*, 18 Apr., 13 June 1822. [15] Grosvenor mss 9/12/20. [16] Dorset RO D/BKL, Bankes mss, J. Bond to H. Bankes, 15 Feb. 1823. [17] *The Times*, 18 Mar. 1823. [18] Huxley, *Lady Elizabeth*, 46. [19] Bodl. MS. Eng. lett. c. 439, f. 154; Add. 51579, Morpeth to Lady Holland, 14 Aug. [1823]. [20] *The Times*, 27, 30 Mar., 6 Apr., 5 May 1824. [21] Ibid. 7 May 1824. [22] Ibid. 29 May 1824. [23] Huxley, *Lady Elizabeth*, 46-48. [24] *The Times*, 13, 25 Oct.; *Chester Courant*, 15 Oct. 1824. [25] Add. 51663; 51668, Bedford to Lady Holland, 24, 26 Oct. [1824]. [26] Lansdowne mss, Holland to Lansdowne, 29 Oct. 1824. [27] *The Times*, 13, 17, 19 Sept. 1825 [28] *Chester Chron.* 14, 21, 28 Oct. 1825. [29] Huxley, *Lady Elizabeth*, 83. [30] Grosvenor mss 9/10/78; *The Times*, 12, 14, 23 June; NLW ms 10804 D, C. Williams Wynn to Buckingham, 24 June; *Chester Chron.* 30 June 1826; *Procs. at Chester Election* (1826). [31] Huxley, *Lady Elizabeth*, 24; *Chester Courant*, 13 Mar.; *Chester Chron.* 16 Mar. 1827. [32] *The Times*, 8 May; *Chester Chron.* 11 May 1827. [33] Lansdowne mss, Dudley to Lansdowne, 11 Oct. 1827. [34] *Chester Courant*, 3, 10, 17 Feb. 1829. [35] Ibid. 3 Feb.; *Chester Chron.* 6 Feb. 1829; Keele Univ. Lib. Sneyd mss SC10/89. [36] *Chester Chron.* 6 Feb. 1829. [37] *Chester Courant*, 26 Jan.; *The Times*, 28 Jan.; *Chester Chron.* 29 Jan. 1830. [38] *The Times*, 18 May; *Macclesfield Courier*, 29 May 1830. [39] Cheshire and Chester Archives QCX/1/2. [40] Add. 36466, f. 170; *Chester Chron.* 2 July 1830. [41] *Macclesfield Courier*, 10 July 1830. [42] Grosvenor mss 12/1-9; *Macclesfield Courier*, 24, 31 July, 7, 14 Aug.; *Chester Courant*, 27 July, 31 Aug.; *Stockport Advertiser*, 5, 12 Aug. 1830. [43] *Chester Chron.* 3, 10, 17, 24 Dec. 1830; *Chester Courant*, 18 Jan. 1831. [44] P.M.G. Egerton, *Annals of Grillion's Club*, 54. [45] *Chester Courant*, 15, 22 Mar.; *The Times*, 21 Mar. 1831. [46] PRO NI, Anglesey mss, Holland to Anglesey, 29 Apr.; Grosvenor mss 12/1, 12, 13; *The Times*, 5, 29 Apr., 5, 14, 18 May; *Macclesfield Courier*, 30 Apr.; 7, 14, 21 May 1831. [47] *Mems. Edward and Catherine Stanley* ed. E. and C. Stanley (1880), 284-5. [48] *The Times*, 23 Sept. 1831; Huxley, *Lady Elizabeth*, 52. [49] NLW, Glynne of Hawarden mss 5408. [50] *Macclesfield Courier*, 29 Oct. 1831. [51] *The Times*, 1, 4, 8 Feb. 1832. [52] Huxley, *Lady Elizabeth*, 82-109. [53] *The Times*, 14 Jan. 1835; *VCH Cheshire*, ii. 153. [54] *The Times*, 20, 26 Feb., 14, 19 May 1845, 2 Nov. 1869; Add. 40560, ff. 146-52. [55] *The Times*, 21 Feb. 1846, 2 Nov. 1869, 25 Feb. 1870; Add. 43251, f. 283; *Oxford DNB*. [56] *The Times*, 22 Nov., 24 Dec. 1869, 1, 4 Jan. 1870.

M.M.E.

GROSVENOR, Hon. Robert (1801–1893).[1]

SHAFTESBURY	30 Apr. 1822–1826
CHESTER	1826–22 Jan. 1847
MIDDLESEX	3 Feb. 1847–15 Sept. 1857

b. 24 Apr. 1801, 3rd. s. of Robert Grosvenor†, 2nd Earl Grosvenor (*d.* 1845), and Hon. Eleanor Egerton, da. and h. of Thomas Egerton†, 1st Bar. Grey de Wilton; bro. of Richard Grosvenor, Visct. Belgrave*. *educ.* Westminster 1810-16; Christ Church, Oxf. 1818; L. Inn 1821. *m.* 17 May 1831, Hon. Charlotte Arbuthnot Wellesley, da. of Henry Wellesley†, 1st Bar. Cowley, 5s. (1 *d.v.p.*) 2da. *styled* Lord Robert Grosvenor 1831-57; *suc.* fa. to Moor Park, Rickmansworth, Herts. 1845; *cr.* Bar. Ebury 15 Sept. 1857. *d.* 18 Nov. 1893.

Comptroller of household Nov. 1830-Dec. 1834; PC 1 Dec. 1830; groom of stole to Prince Albert 1840-1; treas. of household July 1846-July 1847; commr. health of the metropolis 1847-50, clerical subscriptions 1864-1865, ritual 1867-70.

Grosvenor was born at Millbank House, Westminster, and named after his father, one of the wealthiest noblemen in England.[2] He was educated at Eton and Oxford and embarked on a tour of the continent with his brother Thomas in the summer of 1819, only to return in haste in September for the wedding of their eldest brother Lord Belgrave, Member for Chester. His new sister-in-law thought him 'full of entertainment and fun ... a most amiable creature and easy friend'.[3] Within a week of his coming of age in 1822 his father returned him on a vacancy for his 'new' borough of Shaftesbury.[4] Lord Grosvenor acted with the Whig opposition and Robert and Belgrave voted with them to abolish one of the joint-postmasterships, 2 May, and reduce embassy costs, 15, 16 May, and for criminal law reform, 4 June 1822, for which he presented a Shaftesbury petition that day.[5] Disappointed in love, he set out for the continent in July and remained abroad until December 1823.[6] His father had considered putting him or Belgrave forward for Dorset at the February 1823 by-election, but desisted.[7] On 1 Sept. 1823 his mother wrote to him:

> Your father has been long grumbling at your beguiling us with continual plans of removal and giving us directions to write to other places while you have been dawdling ... at Naples and I have been seriously uneasy, fearing that your heart was in danger, that you were severely exposed to temptation and had no friend at hand to admonish you.[8]

He was admitted to Brooks's, 25 Feb 1824, proposed by Lords Morpeth[†] and Derby, and voted with Belgrave for repeal of the window tax, 2 Mar., against renewing the Aliens Act, 2 Apr., for inquiry into the Irish church, 6 May, and the state of Ireland, 11 May, and in condemnation of the indictment in Demerara of the Methodist missionary John Smith, 11 June 1824. He divided for Catholic relief, 1 Mar., 21 Apr., 10 May, and paired against the duke of Cumberland's annuity bill, 6 June 1825. Mrs. Arbuthnot had speculated in March that he was 'the cause' of Isabella Forester's broken engagement with Lord Apsley*.[9] Before leaving for Russia as an unofficial member of the duke of Devonshire's ambassadorial delegation to the coronation of Tsar Alexander, he presented an anti-slavery petition from Shaftesbury, 21 Mar.,[10] and voted against administration on the president of the board of trade's salary, 7, 10 Apr., and for corn law revision, 18 Apr., and parliamentary reform, 27 Apr. 1826.[11] His kinsman General Thomas Grosvenor made way for him at Chester at the general election in June, when he was returned *in absentia* after a severe contest.[12]

Grosvenor remained lax in his attendance. He divided for Catholic relief, 6 Mar. 1827, and on the 8th presented a Chester petition against the importation of foreign flour. He voted to postpone the vote of supply pending resolution of the ministerial uncertainty following Lord Liverpool's stroke, 30 Mar., and his application for a week's leave that day was ridiculed and rejected. He was named as a defaulter, 5 Apr., but excused. He voted for the disfranchisement of Penryn for electoral corruption, 28 May. He presented constituents' petitions for repeal of the Test Acts, 6 June, and against the alehouse licensing bill, 18 June 1827.[13] That month he tried to counter strong local opposition to his family's support for Catholic relief by publishing a pro-emancipation pamphlet, which he also defended in the correspondence columns of the *Chester Chronicle*.[14] He presented and endorsed Chester's petitions for repeal of the 1827 Malt Act, 15 Feb., and of the Test Acts, 25 Feb., for which he voted, 26 Feb. 1828. He confirmed his support for Catholic relief on presenting favourable petitions from the Catholics of Chester and Piddington, 29 Apr., and divided for it, 12 May. He voted for more effective control over the crown's excise recovery proceedings, 1 May, and against the Buckingham House expenditure, 23 June 1828. He divided for Catholic emancipation, 6, 30 Mar. 1829. On 13 Apr. he set out on a fact-finding tour of the Eastern Mediterranean, where he was privy to the negotiations between the Russians and Turks. After visiting consulates in the Greek Islands, Constantinople, Malta, Tunis and Tripoli, he prolonged his travels by taking a passage to Cadiz, where on 12 June 1830 he wrote informing his mother that he would return forthwith via Barcelona and Paris:

> I know not what may be my father's intentions with regard to me at the ensuing elections. You do not ask me to return home, but I think from the tenor of your correspondence that you do not forbid me altogether to do so. You have had no opportunity of writing to me since the king's health declined so rapidly, and, after due consideration, I do not think I shall be doing my duty towards my father if I do not at least put it in his power to make what use of me he shall think fit, in case of His Majesty's demise.[15]

Lord Grosvenor put him forward alone for Chester, where he arrived to canvass on 24 July 1830. His 'three year sojourn on the continent' was severely criticized, but his return with the Tory Sir Philip Grey Egerton was unopposed and he assisted in Belgrave's successful canvass of the county.[16] An edition of his travel journal was published afterwards to raise funds for Chester infirmary.[17]

The Wellington ministry listed Grosvenor among their 'foes', and he was perturbed when Lord

Grosvenor, who had been admitted to the privy council, 22 July 1830, directed him to 'vote with the duke' if an amendment was moved and to 'join no factious opposition'. Writing in confidence to his friend George Fortescue, whom Grosvenor had brought in for Hindon, he observed:

My opinion is daily becoming less and less favourable to the duke's way of going on, and I have almost arrived at the conclusion that he ought to be turned out. My father says he is sick of party and looks with aversion upon any junction with extreme *droite*; I begin to think party is almost essential to the carrying on of the affairs of state and I think nothing so bad as that desultory half-and-half sort of opposition which characterized our proceedings during the last Parliament.[18]

Though listed as absent from the division on the civil list by which the Wellington ministry were brought down, 15 Nov. 1830, he subsequently claimed that he had been paired with Lord Charles Vere Ferrers Townshend, who voted in person against it.[19] His appointment as comptroller of the household, at £800 a year, in Lord Grey's administration was a surprise and caused Lord Bathurst to speculate that it might be a ploy to silence his father's probing questions in the Lords.[20] Presenting anti-slavery petitions from Chester, 25 Nov., he dissented from their prayer for immediate abolition and echoed Warburton's plea 'that the condition of the negroes should be first so gradually improved as to render freedom a benefit, and not a curse'. His re-election was opposed by the 'popular' party in Chester, who denounced him 'not only as the son of a peer who is a notorious and powerful boroughmonger, but a pensioner upon the public purse, and as a man who has been deficient in the performance of his public duties'. He defeated their absent nominee Foster Cunliffe Offley* in the ensuing poll.[21] Addressing his supporters at a party dinner, 20 Dec. 1830, he reiterated his belief that slavery should be abolished gradually and spoke strongly in favour of parliamentary reform, but did not disguise his reservations on the merits of the secret ballot.[22] He 'inadvertently omitted to take the oaths before taking his seat', and a second by-election was held, 15 Mar. 1831, when his return was not opposed. A bill indemnifying him from payment of a penalty fine of £500 for each day he had sat since his re-election had been carried unanimously and received royal assent, 11 Mar.[23] He presented the Chester printers' petition for repeal of the stamp duties on newspapers, 19 Mar. Indicating that his support for reform, on which he corresponded with the anti-reformer Bickham Estcott†, had strengthened since he and Egerton had issued an equivocal joint statement, 5 Mar., he presented their constituents'

petition in favour of the ministerial reform bill and emphasized that Chester was 'a Tory town' loyal to the king and constitution and that support for the petition had been unanimous.[24] He divided for the reform bill at its second reading, 22 Mar. Presenting the Cheshire reform petition the next day, he declared his

determination to support ministers in every part of the bill. By this measure ministers propose to redeem their pledges, not by instalments, but to the full amount. If ministers should yield up a single essential point, I will not continue to give them my support.

He voted against Gascoyne's wrecking amendment, 19 Apr. 1831. Chester returned him and the reformer Cunliffe Offley unopposed at the ensuing general election, and he maintained that he had also been requisitioned to stand for two other counties.[25] He briefly assisted Belgrave in his canvass of Cheshire before returning to London for his wedding to Wellington's niece Charlotte, which had been 'approved' by his colleagues at Grillion's.[26] Lord Wellesley informed her father, who was then ambassador in Vienna: 'I think you will be satisfied with the connection. Mr. Grosvenor appears to me to be an excellent man of very good manners and steadiness of conduct. I believe the whole family to be very amiable and worthy'. The duke, who also lent them Stratfield Saye for their honeymoon, gave the bride away.[27]

Grosvenor voted for the reintroduced reform bill at its second reading, 6 July, against adjournment, 12 July 1831, and sparingly for its details. He criticized its opponents for using the Manchester-Leeds railway bill to delay its progress, 21 July, and, to expedite it, he commended ministers for uniting Chatham with Rochester and Strood, 9 Aug., and appointing half-pay officers as boundary commissioners, 1 Sept. Informing *The Times* that his name had been erroneously omitted from the government minority against enfranchising £50 tenants-at-will, 18 Aug., he stated that it was 'the third time it has occurred ... I do not wish to spend my nights in the dense atmosphere of the House ... without having the credit of doing my duty'.[28] He assumed the style Lord Robert Grosvenor when his father became marquess of Westminster at the coronation. Edward Littleton* privately blamed him, through his association with Sir Ronald Craufurd Ferguson*, for the election of Sir Francis Burdett* to chair the reform dinner at Stationers' Hall in honour of Lord Althorp* and Lord John Russell*.[29] He voted for the bill's passage, 21 Sept., and Lord Ebrington's confidence motion, 10 Oct. He presented a Chester petition against the importation of foreign flour, 6 Sept., and Cheshire's reformers now openly approved his conduct.[30] Summoned by circular, he divided for the revised reform bill at its second reading, 17 Dec. 1831, after Sir Watkin Williams Wynn terminated their pairing arrangement, but seems to have failed to do so in January 1832.[31] He divided for the bill's provisions for Appleby, 21 Feb., Helston, 23 Feb., and Tower Hamlets, 28 Feb., and its third reading, 22 Mar., and for the address calling on the king to appoint only ministers who would carry it unimpaired, 10 May. On the 13th the Speaker advised him how, if necessary, he should deliver the monarch's response.[32] He voted against a Conservative amendment to the Scottish reform bill, 1 June. He divided with government in both divisions on the Dublin election controversy, 23 Aug. 1831, and on the Russian-Dutch loan, 26 Jan., 12, 16, 20 July, and helped to 'kill off' William Evans's abortive motion claiming that Britain had a right under the treaties of 1814 and 1815 to interfere to prevent Russian aggression in Poland, 7 Aug. Attending to constituency concerns, he pressed for the appointment of a select committee on the general register bill and was appointed to it, 22 Feb. He said he would prefer to see a duty levied on Russian tallow than an excise duty on soap, 28 Feb., and endorsed Lord Sandon's testimony to the growing unpopularity in Northern England of the grants to Irish charter schools, 16 Mar. He presented petitions from Chester for and against the government's proposals for Irish education, 18 June, and against the vagrants removal bill, 3 July 1832.

Grosvenor presented Chester's civic address to Princess Victoria when she opened the Grosvenor Bridge over the Dee, 16 Oct. 1832, and she sponsored his daughter Victoria Charlotte at her christening next day.[33] His return for Chester as a Liberal in December 1832 was assured, although the borough was polled, and he now proved 'indefatigable in his exertions' on Belgrave's behalf in the gruelling contest for Cheshire South.[34] He remained Member for Chester until his election for Middlesex in 1847, and a Liberal until Gladstone conceded Home Rule in 1886, when he defected to the Unionists. He served with distinction as a health commissioner, travelled extensively with his family and became the chief lay spokesman for the Evangelical party in the Lords, to which he was elevated in 1857. He died in November 1893 at his London home in Park Street, recalled as a church reformer, inaugural member and president of the Association for Promoting a Revision of the Prayer Book and a Review of the Acts of Uniformity, and as the author of many tracts and pamphlets.[35] His eldest son Robert Wellesley Grosvenor (1834-1918), Liberal Member for Westminster, 1865-74, succeeded him

in the peerage and to Moor Park (the Hertfordshire estate bequeathed to him by his father), and his other surviving children inherited the bulk of his personal fortune.[36]

[1] Access to the Grosvenor papers, privately held at Eaton Hall, is gratefully acknowledged. For Grosvenor's later letters and speeches see E.V. Bligh, *Lord Ebury as a Church Reformer* (1891). [2] *HP Commons, 1790-1820*, iv. 114-15; *Oxford DNB sub* Robert Grosvenor (1767-1845). [3] G. Huxley, *Lady Elizabeth and the Grosvenors*, 17; Keele Univ. Lib. Sneyd mss SC10/81-90. [4] M.J. Hazelton-Swales, 'Urban Aristocrats' (London Univ. Ph.D. thesis, 1981), 445; Grosvenor mss 9/11/48; *The Times*, 12 Nov. 1822. [5] *The Times*, 5 June 1822. [6] Bodl. MS. Eng. lett. c. 439, ff. 1-123. [7] *The Times*, 14 Feb. 1823; Grosvenor mss 9/9/10, 24, 46, 47; 9/10/94; 9/11/40-43; 9/13/7. [8] Bodl. MS. Eng. lett. c. 439, f. 156. [9] *Arbuthnot Jnl.* i. 384. [10] *The Times*, 22 Mar. 1826. [11] Add. 52017, Townshend to H.E. Fox, 29 Apr. 1826. [12] *Chester Chron.* 19 May; *Procs. at Chester Election* (1826). [13] *The Times*, 9, 31 Mar., 7, 19 June 1827. [14] *Chester Chron.* 1, 8 June 1827. [15] Bodl. MS. Eng. lett. c. 440, ff. 1-84; Ms. Eng. Misc. c. 667-8; *Greville Mems.* i. 324. [16] *Chester Courant*, 6, 13, 20, 27 July; *Chester Chron.* 9 July, 6, 13 Aug. 1830; Grosvenor mss 12/1. [17] *Extracts from Jnl. of Lord R. Grosvenor* (1831). [18] *Greville Mems.* ii. 8; Add. 69366, Grosvenor to Fortescue, 20 Sept. 1830. [19] *Chester Chron.* 10 Dec. 1830. [20] Bodl. MS. Eng. lett. c. 441, ff. 8-11; Add. 76373, Althorp to Grey [?19 Nov. 1830]; Wellington mss WP1/1156/7. [21] *Chester Courant*, 7, 21 Dec.; *Chester Chron.* 3, 10, 17 Dec. 1830; Derby mss 920 Der (13) 1/161/27. [22] *Chester Chron.* 24 Dec.; *Chester Courant*, 28 Dec. 1830. [23] *Chester Chron.* 11, 18 Mar.; *Chester Courant*, 15 Mar. 1831; *CJ*, lxxxvi. 353, 355-6, 359, 363. [24] Bodl. MS. Eng. lett. c. 441, ff. 1-4; *Chester Chron.* 18, 25 Mar.; *Chester Courant*, 22 Mar. 1831. [25] *Chester Courant*, 10 May 1831. [26] *Chester Chron.* 20 May 1831; P.M.G. Egerton, *Annals of Grillion's Club*, 55. [27] Bodl. MS. Eng. lett. 441, ff. 92-93. [28] *The Times*, 20 Aug. 1831. [29] Hatherton diary, 15 Sept. 1831. [30] *Chester Courant*, 18 Oct. 1831. [31] Bodl. MS. Eng. lett. c. 441, ff. 4-7; NLW ms 2797 D, Sir W. to H. Williams Wynn, 18 Dec. 1831. [32] Bodl. MS. Eng. lett. c. 441, ff. 13-14. [33] Huxley, 42. [34] *Chester Chron.* 28 Sept.; *The Times*, 18 Oct., 4 Dec.; *N. Wales Chron.* 18 Dec. 1832; Huxley, 103-5. [35] *The Times*, 19 May 1845, 24 July 1861, 20 Oct. 1891, 20, 23, 24 Nov. 1893; Bodl. MS. Eng. lett. c. 441, ff. 51-53; R. Grosvenor, *Leaves From My Jnl.* (1851); *On the Revision of the Liturgy* (1859); *The Only Compromise Possible in Regard to Church Rates* (1861); *On the Amendment of the Act of Uniformity* (1862); *The Laity and Church Reform* (1886); *Quis Custodiet Ipsos Custodes?* (1877); *Auricular Confession and Priestly Absolution* (1880); J. Hildyard, *The Ingoldsby Letters on the Revision of the Book of Common Prayer* (1860, 1861). [36] *The Times*, 5 Mar. 1894.

M.M.E.

GROSVENOR, Thomas (1764-1851), of Stocking Hall, Leics. and Grosvenor Street, Hanover Square, Mdx.

CHESTER	20 Feb. 1795-1826
STOCKBRIDGE	1826-1830

b. 30 May 1764, 3rd but 2nd surv. s. of Thomas Grosvenor[†] of Swell Court, Som. and Deborah, da. and coh. of Stephen Skynner of Walthamstow, Essex. *educ.* Westminster 1773. *m.* (1) 6 Apr. 1797, Elizabeth (*d.* 26 July 1830), da. of Sir Gilbert Heathcote[†], 3rd bt., of Normanton, Rutland, *s.p.*; (2) 15 Oct. 1831, Anne, da. of

George Wilbraham[†] of Delamere Lodge, Cheshire, *s.p. suc.* fa. to property in Walthamstow 1795. *d.* 20 Jan. 1851.

Ensign 3 Ft. Gds. 1779, lt. and capt. 1784, capt. and lt.-col. 1793, brevet col. 1796; brigadier (local rank) 1800; maj.-gen. 1802; lt.-col. 7 W.I. Regt. (half-pay) 1802-7; col. 97 Ft. 1807; lt.-gen. 1808; col. 65 Ft. 1814-*d.*; gen. 1819; f.m. 1846.

Mayor, Chester 1810-11.

At the general election of 1820 Grosvenor, a devotee of the Turf and professional soldier, who drew £1,241 a year from the army, secured his eighth successive return for Chester on the interest of his cousin the 2nd Earl Grosvenor. The close contest was marked by his pronouncements against the 'diabolical' Cato Street conspirators and his fortuitous escape when the mob overturned his carriage into the River Dee.[1] A petition against his return was dismissed.

He remained a very poor attender who voted infrequently and confined his few remarks to military matters. Like his colleague, Grosvenor's heir Lord Belgrave, he cast a critical vote with the Whig opposition against the appointment of an additional Scottish baron of exchequer, 15 May 1820. On 26 June he was granted a week's leave on urgent private business. He kept aloof from the controversies surrounding the duke of Wellington's visit to Chester in December 1820 and the Queen Caroline case and is not known to have voted in 1821. That October a Chester common hall refused to elect him an alderman.[2] He voted to reduce the Swiss embassy's costs, 16 May, for criminal law reform, 4 June, and against the aliens bill, 5 June 1822. His other known votes this Parliament were for postponing the award to the Irish Protestant charter schools, 15 Mar. 1824, against outlawing the Catholic Association, 18 Feb., and for Catholic relief, 1 Mar., 21 Apr., 10 May 1825. Drawing on his close connections with the banker Andrew Drummond of Cadland and Joseph Foster Barham*, Grosvenor had been party to Lord Grosvenor's negotiations for the purchase of Shaftesbury (1820) and Stockbridge (1822-5) and, after consulting his brother Robert and nephew Richard Edward Erle Drax Grosvenor*, he cautioned against offering his young nephew Lord Robert Grosvenor* as a candidate at the 1823 Dorset by-election.[3] He made way for him in 1826 and successfully contested Stockbridge with George Wilbraham before joining in the campaign at Chester.[4]

Grosvenor spoke in defence of the conduct of Lord Charles Somerset[†] as governor of Cape Colony, 7 Dec. 1826. During the ministerial uncertainty following Lord Liverpool's stroke, he voted with his relations to postpone the vote on supply, 30 Mar., and refer the Irish miscellaneous estimates to a select committee, 5 Apr. 1827. He welcomed the Canning ministry's decision to adopt a vote of thanks to the army in India and spoke highly of its commanders and of Wellington as commander-in-chief, 8 May 1827. He divided for Catholic relief, 12 May 1828, and for emancipation, 6, 30 Mar. 1829. Differing from Belgrave, he voted, 5 Apr., 17 May, and spoke, 16 June 1830, in favour of Jewish emancipation. In April Wellington passed him over for the vacant governorship of Blackness Castle.[5] He criticized the Whig Sir James Graham's inquiry motion on privy councillors' emoluments, 14 May, as 'nothing more than a vexatious and agitating question', but welcomed Trant's attempt to revive the case of the Irish admiralty judge Sir Harcourt Lees, 24 June. His speech defending General Darling, whose conduct as governor of New South Wales was criticized by Hume, 9 July 1830, was his last before he retired at the dissolution. His wife died, 26 July 1830, and, despite the initial disapprobation of his relations, in October 1831, at the age of 67, he married his former colleague Wilbraham's sister, then 'aged 40 and said to be an old maid, disagreeable, cross, and peevish', upon whom £15,000 was settled.[6] He informed the duke of Rutland:

> I cannot live alone; and have been so fortunate to find a gentle lady that takes pity on my singleness ... The fact is (I speak for my humble self) I have done with all politics and public men and business. I shall shut my eyes to all newspapers and *I must* open them on something.[7]

He became a field marshal in 1846 and died at his residence, Mount Arrarat, Richmond, Surrey, in January 1851, having bequeathed his land in Gloucestershire, Suffolk, Cambridgeshire and Surrey and almost all his personal estate to his widow.[8]

[1] *HP Commons, 1790-1820*, iv. 116-17; Sheffield Archives, Wharncliffe mss WhM/T.E4; Add. 52444, f. 92; *Chester Chron.* 3, 17, 24 Mar.; *The Times*, 14, 15 Mar.; Dorset RO, Bankes mss D/BKL, diary of Mrs. Henry Bankes, 22 Mar. 1820. [2] *Chester Courant*, 2, 9, 16 Oct. 1821. [3] Mss *penes* (in 1998) Major Maldwin Drummond, OBE, JP, DL, Hon. DSc, of Cadland House, Fawley, Southampton SO45 1AA; Bodl. Clarendon dep. c. 430, bdle. 2; Grosvenor mss 9/9/24; 9/10/94; 9/11/39-42. [4] *Narrative of Procs. at Chester Election* (1826), 3-6. [5] Wellington mss WP1/1111/48. [6] G. Huxley, *Lady Elizabeth and the Grosvenors*, 19; Cheshire and Chester Archives, Wilbraham of Delamere mss DDX/82/1. [7] Draft in Grosvenor mss 10/4. [8] *Oxford DNB*; *The Times*, 22 Jan. 1851; PROB 8/244; 11/2127/121.

M.M.E.

GROSVENOR *see also* **ERLE DRAX GROSVENOR**

GUEST, **Josiah John** (1785–1852), of Dowlais House, nr. Merthyr Tydfil, Glam.

HONITON	1826–1831
MERTHYR TYDFIL	1832–26 Nov. 1852

b. 2 Feb. 1785, 1st s. of Thomas Guest, ironmaster, of Dowlais and Jemima, da. of Thomas Phillips of Shiffnal, Salop. *educ.* Bridgnorth g.s.; Monmouth g.s. *m.* (1) 11 Mar. 1817, Maria Elizabeth (*d.* 14 Jan. 1818), da. of William Ranken, late of E.I. Co., *s.p.*; (2) 29 July 1833, Lady Charlotte Elizabeth Bertie, da. of Albemarle Bertie†, 9th earl of Lindsey, 5s. 5da. *suc.* fa. 1807; *cr.* bt. 14 Aug. 1838. *d.* 26 Nov. 1852.
Sheriff, Glam. 1819-20.

Guest's family had been farmers in Shropshire until the mid-eighteenth century, when his grandfather John Guest moved to Merthyr Tydfil, where he became the manager of, and later a partner in, the Dowlais iron works. His father also managed the company and on his death in 1807 Guest inherited his freehold property, a one-sixteenth share in Dowlais and a one-fifth share of the residue.[1] He assumed the management of the company and, following the death of his uncle William Taitt in 1815, became the principal shareholder. He took a keen interest in developments in geology, chemistry and engineering and their practical application to his business, and under his auspices the annual output of Dowlais expanded from 12,500 tons in 1815 to over 70,000 tons in the 1840s, when it was 'supplying the railways all over the world', employing 7,000 people and making profits of £50,000; he became the sole proprietor in 1849. He was also a partner in a country bank with branches in Cardiff and Merthyr.[2] At the general election of 1826 he was returned at the head of the poll for the venal borough of Honiton, which he had canvassed 18 months earlier, declaring himself to be 'a friend to civil and religious liberty' who would go to Parliament 'free and unshackled' and 'steer clear of all parties'.[3]

He acted with the Whig opposition to Lord Liverpool's ministry, voting against the duke of Clarence's annuity bill, 2 Mar., for a reduced level of agricultural protection, 9 Mar., inquiry into Leicester's corporation, 15 Mar., and inquiry into the Irish miscellaneous estimates and information regarding delays in chancery, 5 Apr. 1827. He divided for Catholic relief, 6 Mar. He was granted ten days' leave for urgent business, 19 Mar. He voted against Canning's ministry to disfranchise Penryn, 28 May 1827. He joined Brooks's Club, 6 Feb. 1828. He opposed the duke of

Wellington's ministry by dividing against the grant for 30,000 seamen, 11 Feb., to postpone the grant to the Society for Propagating the Gospels in the colonies, 6 June, and reduce civil list pensions, 10 June. He voted against the grant for the Royal Cork Institution, 20 June, and to condemn the misapplication of public money for work on Buckingham House, 23 June. He presented several petitions for repeal of the Test Acts and voted accordingly, 26 Feb. He divided for Catholic claims, 12 May. He voted for a lower pivot price for the corn duties, 22 Apr., and a 15s. duty, 29 Apr. He voted against going into committee on the small notes (Ireland and Scotland) bill, 16 June 1828. He divided with the ministry for Catholic emancipation, 6, 30 Mar. 1829, and presented several favourable petitions. He obtained a second reading for the Merthyr magistrates bill, 13 Mar., which received royal assent, 1 June. He introduced a bill to establish a corn market at New Ross, county Wexford, 13 Mar.; it was committed but made no further progress. He voted for Lord Blandford's reform scheme, 2 June, and Hume's proposed table of fees in the ecclesiastical courts bill, 5 June 1829. He divided for Knatchbull's amendment to the address on distress, 4 Feb., and tax reductions, 15 Feb. 1830, and steadily in the revived opposition's campaign for retrenchment that session. He voted to transfer East Retford's seats to Birmingham, 11 Feb., and enfranchise Birmingham, Leeds and Manchester, 23 Feb., and paired for Russell's reform motion, 28 May. He was granted one month's leave for urgent private business, 3 Mar. He voted to abolish the Irish lord lieutenancy, 11 May, and for Labouchere's motion on the civil government of Canada, 25 May. He presented a Honiton petition to abolish the death penalty for forgery, 25 May, and paired in this sense, 7 June. He voted for reform of the divorce laws, 3 June 1830. At the general election that summer he was returned unopposed for Honiton after declaring that he had done his utmost to 'stem the torrent of corruption and extravagance' and reduce taxation, and that his aim was to 'secure the stability of our free institutions'.[4]

The ministry of course listed Guest among their 'foes', and he voted against them in the crucial civil list division, 15 Nov. 1830. He presented a Merthyr ironworkers' petition for repeal of the corn laws, 19 Nov. 1830, one from Honiton for repeal of the coal duty, 7 Feb. 1831, and several that winter for the abolition of slavery. On 23 Dec. 1830 he drew attention to the 'great number of abuses' in the system of granting civil list pensions and maintained that they could only be awarded for the monarch's lifetime, unless renewed by Parliament, and that they should only be given for 'actual [public] service'. His motion for an address to the king for the production of the warrant authorizing the pension to Harriet Arbuthnot, the wife of a Tory ex-minister, was agreed. John Charles Herries* informed Mrs. Arbuthnot that the motion had taken the opposition 'somewhat by surprise'.[5] Guest gave notice of a motion for a select committee to investigate civil list pensions, 7 Feb. 1831, but this did not come on, and his intended resolution declaring that many of them had been 'improperly granted and ought to be inquired into', announced on 20 Apr., was overtaken by the dissolution. He obtained a return of the pensions paid from the consolidated fund, 11 Feb. His motion for an account of all civil and military sinecures was withdrawn because of the problem of definition, 22 Feb. He complained of the 'enormous sums' being spent on fortifications in the colonies, 10 Feb., and was a minority teller for reduction of the garrisons grant, 14 Mar. He obtained a return of those employed in the customs department receiving more than £1,000 per annum, 25 Feb. 1831. He maintained that 'nineteen-twentieths of the people' of Honiton favoured parliamentary reform and that 'this feeling pervades the country generally', 21 Dec. 1830. In presenting a Merthyr petition for reform and the ballot, 7 Feb. 1831, he observed that Glamorgan was underrepresented by comparison with many English counties. He presented a Swindon petition for economy, retrenchment and reform, 9 Feb., and reform petitions from Merthyr and Brecknock, 16, 19 Mar. He divided for the second reading of the Grey ministry's reform bill, 22 Mar., and against Gascoyne's wrecking amendment, 19 Apr. 1831. At the ensuing general election he offered again for Honiton, where he claimed that an 'odious oligarchy' had thwarted reform in order to resist economy and retrenchment, and while expressing regret that the borough stood to lose one of its Members he was confident that his constituents were 'too generous to set up selfish views in opposition to a great national benefit'. He was mistaken, and came bottom of the poll.[6]

Guest had been the principal speaker at a public meeting in Merthyr, 8 Apr. 1831, when he had called for the town's enfranchisement, and he was involved in the subsequent campaign for this objective which was achieved in March 1832. He immediately announced his intention of offering for the new borough, and he was returned unopposed in December 1832 as 'a reformer ... in favour of free trade, a revision of the corn laws, the abolition of monopolies, the ballot and a commutation of tithes'. His position as a large employer enabled him to exercise 'a kind of industrial feudalism' at Merthyr and by the 1840s he was described as 'a Whig'.[7] His marriage in 1833 to the

daughter of an impecunious peer and the award of a baronetcy by Lord Melbourne's government in 1838 'symbolized the recognition of industrial success by the aristocracy', and in 1846 he purchased Canford Manor in Dorset for over £350,000. He was described as 'a man of great mental capacities, a good mathematician and a thorough man of business, not without a taste for the refinements of literature', who 'took a comprehensive view of his social duties'.[8] He died in November 1852 and was succeeded by his eldest son, Ivor Bertie Guest (1835-1914), who was created Baron Wimborne in 1880. His business interests at Dowlais were divided between his sons, who retained control of the company until it was merged with Keen and Nettlefold of Birmingham in the 1890s.[9]

[1] The personalty was sworn under £12,500 (PROB 11/1466/663; IR26/126/119). [2] Gent. Mag. (1853), i. 91-92; Diaries of Lady Charlotte Guest ed. Lord Bessborough, 5-7; A. Birch, Hist. British Iron Industry, 67-74, 289-95. [3] Trewman's Exeter Flying Post, 15, 22 June 1826. [4] Western Times, 10 July, 7 Aug. 1830. [5] Arbuthnot Corresp. 140. [6] Trewman's Exeter Flying Post, 28 Apr., 5, 12 May 1831. [7] D. Wager, 'Welsh Politics and Parl. Reform, 1780-1832', WHR, vii. (1974), 441, 445-7; Dod's Parl. Companion (1833), 119; (1843), 160; N. Gash, Politics in Age of Peel, 199-200; R. Grant, Parl. Hist. Glam. 47-50. [8] Birch, 289-95; Gent. Mag. (1853), i. 91-92. [9] PROB 11/2165/26; IR26/1962/13; Birch, 171; C. Erickson, British Industrialists, 150.

T.A.J.

GUISE, Sir Berkeley William, 2nd bt. (1775–1834), of Highnam Court, Glos.[1]

GLOUCESTERSHIRE	7 Feb. 1811–1832
GLOUCESTERSHIRE EAST	1832–23 July 1834

b. 14 July 1775, 1st s. of Sir John Guise, 1st bt., of Highnam and Elizabeth, da. and h. of Thomas Wright of Laurence Lane, London. educ. Eton 1791; Christ Church, Oxf. 1794. unm. suc. fa. as 2nd bt. 2 May 1794; to Guise fam. estates of Elmore Court and Rendcomb, Glos. on d. (1807) of his cos. Jane, w. of Rt. Rev. and Hon. Shute Barrington, bp. of Durham. d. 23 July 1834.

Verderer and dep. warden, Forest of Dean 1801-d.; sheriff, Gloucester 1807, mayor 1818.

Capt. N. Glos. militia 1798; lt.-col.commdt. 1 R.E. Glos. militia 1809.

Guise, whose landed estates in Gloucestershire reputedly yielded £7,000 per annum,[2] was again returned unopposed for the county in 1820 as the representative of the 'independent' freeholders, with the Tory Lord Edward Somerset. He affirmed his opposition to 'lavish expenditure', blamed the 'present system of enormous taxation' for economic distress and expressed his 'decided opposition' to the Six Acts.[3]

He continued to vote steadily with the Whig opposition to Lord Liverpool's ministry on all major issues, including parliamentary reform, 9 Mar., 9, 10, 31 May 1821, 25 Apr. 1822, 24 Apr., 2 June 1823, 27 Apr. 1826. He paired for Catholic relief, 28 Feb. 1821, and divided for it, 1 Mar., 21 Apr., 10 May 1825. However, he rarely spoke in debate. He presented numerous Gloucestershire petitions for relief from agricultural distress in 1820, 1821 and 1822.[4] He attended the county meeting to agree an address to the king calling for the dismissal of ministers, 30 Dec. 1820, when he denounced the recent proceedings against Queen Caroline and the government's 'ill advised and impolitic measures', which had 'reduced the country to its present situation of difficulty and distress'; he presented petitions in support of the queen, 24, 26 Jan. 1821.[5] He was listed as a steward of the City of London Tavern reform dinner, 4 Apr. 1821. He was granted a week's leave for urgent private business, 18 Apr. 1822. He hoped that a grant would be made to erect a statue in honour of Edward Jenner, 19 Mar. 1823. He presented a Gloucestershire woollen manufacturers' petition against imported wool, 16 Feb., and three in favour of repealing the wool duty, 25 Mar. 1824.[6] He presented petitions from Cheltenham for repeal of the house tax, 1 Mar., and Clifton for repeal of all assessed taxes, 6 May 1824; more followed in 1825 and 1826.[7] He was a majority teller for the second reading of the Cheltenham waterworks bill, 25 Mar. 1824, supported the second reading of the Severn Valley railway bill, 28 Apr., and presented a Severn fishing proprietors' petition against the salmon fisheries bill, 18 May 1825.[8] He presented petitions against the importation of silk, 15, 23 Feb., and voted for inquiry into the trade, 24 Feb. 1826.[9] At the general election that summer he was again returned unopposed for Gloucestershire, after pledging his adherence to 'the same independent principles which have hitherto actuated me'.[10]

He presented Gloucestershire petitions in favour of agricultural protection, 22 Feb., and voted against the corn bill, 2 Apr. 1827.[11] He divided against the Clarence annuity bill, 2 Mar., and for Catholic relief, 6 Mar., the spring guns bill, 23 Mar., and inquiry into the Irish miscellaneous estimates, 5 Apr. He voted against Canning's ministry to remove bankruptcy jurisdiction from chancery, 22 May, and to disfranchise Penryn, 28 May 1827. He presented numerous petitions for repeal of the Test Acts in 1827 and 1828 and voted in this sense, 26 Feb. 1828. He divided for Catholic claims, 12 May. He voted against extending East Retford's franchise to Bassetlaw freeholders, 21 Mar., and for reduction of civil list pensions, 10 June 1828. In presenting a Clifton petition against

further concessions to the Catholics, 27 Feb. 1829, he expressed the hope that 'if any measure of relief ... be proposed, it may be guarded effectually by securities'. He presented three Gloucestershire pro-Catholic petitions, 4, 16 Mar., and voted for emancipation, 6, 30 Mar. He presented a Cheltenham petition for repeal of the house and window taxes, 20 Feb., and voted to reduce the grant for the sculpture of the marble arch, 25 May 1829. He divided for Hume's tax cutting amendment, 15 Feb., inquiry into the revision of taxation, 25 Mar. 1830, and steadily in the revived opposition campaign for retrenchment that session. He was present at the meeting on 3 Mar. when Lord Althorp agreed to lead the Whigs for this purpose.[12] He voted for the enfranchisement of Birmingham, Leeds and Manchester, 23 Feb., the transfer of East Retford's seats to Birmingham, 5 Mar., and Russell's reform motion, 28 May. He paired for Jewish emancipation, 17 May. He urged the Commons to reject the Avon and Gloucestershire railway bill, 12 Mar., alleging that the promoters had not kept faith with the Bristol and Gloucestershire Railway Company. He voted for reform of Irish vestries, 27 Apr., and abolition of the lord lieutenancy, 11 May. He presented Stroud and Nailsworth petitions against the death penalty for forgery, 3 May, and voted accordingly, 24 May, 7 June. He presented a Stroud publicans' petition against on-consumption in beer houses, 3 May, and voted in this sense, 21 June. He supported a Gloucestershire woollen manufacturers and operatives' petition against the truck system, 10 May. He divided for Labouchere's motion on the civil government of Canada, 25 May. He successfully moved that the Lords' amendments to the Sheffield waterworks bill be agreed, 26 May, and made two minor interventions on details of the Dean Forest bill, 11 June 1830. At the general election that summer he was again returned unopposed, after declaring his support for 'the interests of the people, the liberty of the ... press and a moderate reform in the Commons', and pledging his 'unqualified opposition' to any interference in France's internal affairs.[13]

The duke of Wellington's ministry of course listed Guise among their 'foes', and he duly voted against them in the crucial civil list division, 15 Nov. 1830. He presented numerous anti-slavery petitions in November and December 1830 and others for repeal of the assessed taxes, 9 Feb., and reform or abolition of tithes, 9 Feb., 2, 16 Mar. 1831. He voiced his 'strongest objections' to the vestries bill, 28 Feb. He presented several petitions in favour of the Grey ministry's reform bill, 19, 23 Mar., divided for the second reading, 22 Mar., expressed confidence that it would 'remedy great evils without creating any new mischief', 24 Mar., and voted against Gascoyne's wrecking amendment, 19 Apr. 1831. At the ensuing dissolution a requisition was organized in Gloucestershire pledging support for Guise and another reformer, Henry Reynolds Moreton, and they were returned unopposed after Somerset retired. Guise declared that the reform bill 'may already be regarded as carried', condemned the rotten boroughs as 'unconstitutional and pernicious', argued that reform was needed in order to relieve the burden of taxation and concluded that the bill would 'not only contribute to the happiness and prosperity of the people, but strengthen the hands of ministers and secure the stability of the throne'.[14]

He said he was not opposed to the Dean Forest bill, 27 June 1831, but observed that 'as the tumults which lately took place ... are a great deal connected with the boundaries of the forest, and with the imaginary rights of the people', it was desirable to revive the local courts in that district. He divided for the second reading of the reintroduced reform bill, 6 July, and generally supported its details, though he voted for Lord Chandos's amendment to enfranchise £50 tenants-at-will, 18 Aug. In a letter to a local supporter, 25 Aug., he added:

I am very apprehensive that ... giving the 40s. freeholders in towns a right to vote for the county will in various counties entirely overturn the agricultural interest ... I therefore supported Col. Davies's motion to prevent the 40s. freeholders in borough[s] ... from voting for counties, but to grant them a right for voting for the town in which their property is situated ... Unfortunately Webb [Member for Gloucester] and self were in a minority last night upon that point, which I think is very injurious to the landed interest. I think it also very unfair as those towns will not only send representatives for the commercial and manufacturing interest, but will also have a great preponderating interest in returning Members for those counties ... which I have mentioned.[15]

He divided for the bill's passage, 21 Sept., and Lord Ebrington's confidence motion, 10 Oct. He arrived late for the county meeting to petition the Lords for reform, 28 Sept., but made a brief speech denying that the country had become apathetic on the subject. At a subsequent dinner in Cheltenham he declared that while the bill was 'not ... entirely without defects', these were 'very trifling'.[16] He divided with the minority against the compensation offered to Lescene and Escoffery for their illegal removal from Jamaica, 22 Aug. Next day he voted to punish only those guilty of bribery at the Dublin election. He said he had been asked by some Bristol inhabitants to support the vestries bill and did so 'with all my heart', 30 Sept. He divided for the second reading of the revised

reform bill, 17 Dec. 1831, and generally supported its details, but he voted against the proposed division of counties, 27 Jan., and for the amendment to prevent borough freeholders from voting in counties, 1 Feb. 1832. He divided for the third reading, 22 Mar., and Ebrington's motion for an address asking the king to appoint only ministers committed to carrying an unimpaired measure, 10 May. He argued unsuccessfully that Wotton-under-Edge rather than Thornbury should be the nomination place for West Gloucestershire, 22 June, when he voted in the minority for Blamire's amendment to the boundaries bill concerning Whitehaven. He informed *The Times* that he had paired for the second reading of the Irish reform bill, 25 May.[17] He voted against ministers on the Russian-Dutch loan, 26 Jan., but was absent from the divisions on this issue in July. He voted with the minority for inquiry into the glove trade, 31 Jan., but with government on relations with Portugal, 9 Feb. He warned that if the Purton Pill railway bill was carried the Commons would be 'guilty of a positive breach of faith' towards two other railway companies, 22 Mar. He was in the minorities for the abolition of slavery, 24 May, and permanent provision for Irish paupers from a tax on absentees, 19 June. He voted to make coroners' inquests public, 20 June 1832. At the general election later that year he was returned at the head of the poll for East Gloucestershire, promising the 'same attachment to liberal principles'.[18] He sat until his death in July 1834 and was succeeded by his brother, Major General Sir John Wright Guise (1777-1865).[19]

[1] The family seat but 'not his residence, as he generally lives, when in the county, at Rendcomb near Cirencester' (*Diary of a Cotswold Parson* ed. D. Verey, 23). [2] *Farington Diary*, xv. 5259. [3] *Gloucester Jnl.* 20 Mar. 1820. [4] *The Times*, 19, 20 May 1820, 21 Feb., 1 Mar. 1821, 14, 19, 26 Feb., 27 Apr. 1822. [5] *Gloucester Jnl.* 1 Jan.; *The Times*, 25, 27 Jan. 1821. [6] *The Times*, 17 Feb., 26 Mar. 1824. [7] Ibid. 2 Mar., 7 May 1824, 18, 26 Feb. 1825, 9 Mar. 1826. [8] Ibid. 29 Apr., 19 May 1825. [9] Ibid. 16, 24 Feb. 1826. [10] *Gloucester Jnl.* 5, 19 June 1826. [11] *The Times*, 23 Feb. 1827. [12] Castle Howard mss, Graham to Morpeth [3 Mar. 1830]; A. Mitchell, *Whigs in Opposition*, 226-7. [13] *Gloucester Jnl.* 7 Aug. 1830. [14] Ibid. 23, 30 Apr., 7, 14 May 1831. [15] Glos. RO, Clifford mss D149/52, Guise to Clifford, 25 Aug. 1831. [16] *Gloucester Jnl.* 1 Oct. 1831. [17] *The Times*, 29 May 1832. [18] *Gloucester Jnl.* 21 July, 22 Dec. 1832. [19] PROB 11/1836/512; IR26/1353/516.

T.A.J.

GUNNING, Sir Robert Henry, 3rd bt. (1795–1862), of Horton, Northants.

NORTHAMPTON 1830–1831

b. 26 Dec. 1795, 1st s. of Sir George William Gunning[†], 2nd bt., of Horton and Elizabeth Diana, da. of Sir Henry Bridgeman, 5th bt.[†], of Weston Park, Staffs. *educ.* Eton

1806-11; Trinity Coll. Camb. 1813. *unm.* 1s. 2da. illegit. *suc.* fa. as 3rd bt. 7 Apr. 1823. *d.* 22 Sept. 1862.

Capt. Brackley and Chipping Warden yeoman cav. 1831.

Sheriff, Northants. 1841-2.

Gunning's family were originally from Cornwall, but his grandfather, a career diplomat, was created a baronet and purchased Horton in 1778. His father, Member for Wigan, 1800-2, Hastings, 1802-6, and East Grinstead, 1812-18, was a steady friend of the Liverpool ministry and had been expected to come in for one of Lord Bath's seats at the 1820 general election, but was passed over.[1] Gunning, who shared his politics, succeeded him in 1823, becoming one of the most prominent of Northamptonshire's gentry. In February 1826 Northampton's Tory corporation, who were seeking to oust the incumbent Whig Members, asked Gunning to come forward as a ministerial candidate at the approaching general election. He initially declined, probably fearing the cost of a contest, but after the corporation had pledged to contribute £1,000 towards his expenses he resolved to stand.[2] In his address he promised to 'strenuously oppose' the admittance of Catholics to office, because it was 'likely to lead to most injurious consequences', and to pay strict attention to local interests.[3] Illness, however, prevented him from canvassing until 8 June 1826, and he was absent for much of the polling. After a violent contest he was left in third place behind the sitting Members, for which he blamed 'circumstances that are well known [which] prevented you putting forth your real and entire strength'.[4] On 1 Feb. 1827 Lord Althorp, Whig Member for the county, noted that Gunning had failed to attend a county meeting to move an address of condolence to the king on the death of the duke of York.[5]

At the 1830 general election Gunning offered again for Northampton as a supporter of the Wellington ministry. Pressed for his views on parliamentary reform, he declared that he had 'always been equally reluctant blindly to support antiquated institutions, or rashly to depart from the system of our ancestors', and that he would only support gradual and moderate change, for example the transfer of seats from places where the 'elective franchise has been grossly abused' to 'some large unrepresented town'. After another fierce contest he was returned in second place, but because of his poor health his brother Henry was chaired in his stead.[6] He presented a Hackleton petition for the abolition of slavery, 4 Nov. 1830. He had been listed by ministers among their 'friends' and he duly voted with them on the civil list, 15 Nov. In his first known

spoken intervention, 15 Dec. 1830, he endorsed a Northampton petition for repeal of the assessed taxes presented by his Whig colleague, saying, 'I know of no taxes which press so heavily on the country'. On 15 Mar. 1831 he was urged by the corporation to support a Northampton petition endorsing the Grey ministry's reform bill, to which he promised to give 'every attention'.[7] He voted against its second reading, 22 Mar., telling his constituents a few days later that he had 'most unhesitatingly' opposed the measure because it was 'fraught ... with the greatest danger to the country', and he could not 'as an honest man, vote one way while I think another'. A Northampton meeting passed a resolution condemning his votes 'on the only two questions of importance', 28 Mar., and the pro-reform *Northampton Free Press* predicted that 'Sir Robert may bid his friends goodbye ... when the next election arrives'.[8] In response his friends circulated a letter approving his conduct, which received over 500 signatures.[9] He attended the Northamptonshire reform meeting at the shire hall in Northampton, 13 Apr., but when, after a two hour delay caused by a boisterous crowd, the sheriff adjourned the meeting to the market place, he joined other anti-reformers in complaining that the move outside was unprecedented and withdrew to an inn to draw up a letter of protest.[10] When Althorp presented the resulting pro-reform petition, 19 Apr. 1831, Gunning objected to the way in which the meeting had been conducted and claimed that the letter of complaint expressed the real feelings of the county. He voted for Gascoyne's wrecking amendment to the reform bill that day.

At the ensuing general election he offered again, insisting that the question at issue was not 'reform or no reform', but the specific ministerial bill. On the hustings he reiterated his pledge to support a degree of reform, complained that the people had lost sight of the 'beauties and excellencies' of the existing representative system, and protested at the proposed reduction of English Members and increase of Irish. After coming third in the poll he demanded a scrutiny, which lasted 15 days, but did not alter the result.[11] His petition against the return, alleging bribery and corruption by both his opponents, was presented, 4 July, but withdrawn next day in favour of one against his nearest rival.[12] On 18 July 1831 he published a letter announcing that he was abandoning this one also, on account of the inconvenience it would cause his friends, the expense and the likelihood of an election as soon as the reform bill had passed.[13]

In the event Gunning did not seek election again. He had been named as sheriff of Northamptonshire in 1825, but declined to serve.[14] He filled the post in 1841. He died in September 1862. Although he never married he had a son and two daughters with a Mary Anne Whitlock. By his will, dated 24 Aug. 1860, he directed that she should be allowed to reside for life in the London house which he had provided for her in Upper George Street, Bryanston Square, and left her an annuity of £200. He bequeathed small annuities to his children. His brother, the Rev. Sir Henry John Gunning (1797-1885), who succeeded him as 4th baronet, was his residuary legatee.

[1] *HP Commons, 1790-1820*, iii. 119-20.   [2] J.C. Cox, *Recs. Northampton*, ii. 510; Add. 40385, f. 240. [3] *Northampton Mercury*, 3 June 1826. [4] Ibid. 17, 24 June 1826. [5] *Althorp Letters*, 135. [6] *Northampton Mercury*, 17, 31 July, 7, 14 Aug. 1830. [7] *Northampton Free Press*, 22 Mar. 1831. [8] Ibid. 29 Mar. 1831. [9] *Northampton Mercury*, 2 Apr. 1831. [10] *The Times*, 16 Apr. 1831. [11] *Northampton Free Press*, 3, 10, 31 May 1831. [12] *CJ*, lxxxvi. 610, 621, 672, 676. [13] *Northampton Free Press*, 19 July 1831. [14] *London Gazette*, 5, 19 Feb. 1825.

M.P.J.C./P.J.S.

GURNEY, Hudson (1775–1864), of Keswick, Norf.

SHAFTESBURY	1812–19 Feb. 1813
NEWTOWN I.o.W.	3 June 1816–1832

b. 19 Jan 1775, 1st s. of Richard Gurney, banker and brewer, of Keswick and North Repps, Norf. and 1st w. Agatha, da. and h. of David Barclay of Youngsbury, Herts.; half-bro. of Richard Hanbury Gurney*. *educ.* at Youngsbury by Dr. Thomas Young and John Hodgkin. *m.* 27 Sept. 1809, Margaret, da. of Robert Barclay† of Urie, Kincardine, *s.p. suc.* fa. 1811. *d.* 9 Nov. 1864.
  Sheriff, Norf. 1835-6

Gurney was the nominal head of a Norfolk banking family, but preferred the languid society of literary London to business.[1] He was brought up a Quaker, but disowned in 1803, when, after a narrow escape from internment in France, he contributed to a government war chest.[2] A renowned antiquarian and bibliophile, who claimed to have read all 15,000 volumes in his library, he was a fellow of the Royal Society and the Society of Antiquaries from 1818 and a vice-president of the latter, 1824-46.[3] Among his own verse works were the free translations *Cupid and Psyche* (1798) and *The Orlando Furioso* (1808), and the classically inspired *Heads of Ancient History* (1814). His *Observations on the Bayeux Tapestry* (1817) put the case for the authenticity of its subject. All his grander literary plans fell victim to his guilt-wracked indolence. In August 1832 his cousin Amelia Opie reported a typical scene, in which he bemoaned 'his useless-

ness, and how he had thrown away, and was throwing away life'. She provided an illustrative recollection of the occasion when 'his uncle Joseph said to him when the clock struck *twelve* one day and he had thought it was only *eleven*, "Ah, Hudson, with thee it will *always* be the *eleventh hour*!"'.[4] Yet for all his self-proclaimed underachievement, he managed to accumulate a large fortune through his partnerships in his family's Norwich bank and the brewing concern of Barclay, Perkins and Company.[5]

In Parliament Gurney was an independent, whose disposition to side with the Whig opposition to the Liverpool ministry generally weakened as the period wore on. He was noted as a pundit on fiscal matters, with a reputation as an awkward customer, which, he once insisted, stemmed only from a tendency to see both sides of every question. Nonetheless, much of his fundamental thinking was at odds with the rationalist *zeitgeist*: for example, his avowed preference for first impressions over second thoughts. For the doctrines of Jeremy Bentham and his philosophic radical associates he reserved the utmost contempt:

> The greatest enjoyment of the greatest number, the slang of the Benthamites, this is nonsense. It is the well-being of the whole community, the greatest advancement of the species with the least injustice to the less fortunate. Otherwise, supposing warm human flesh to be the greatest of luxuries, twelve men being round a table, the eleven would have the right to cut the twelfth into collops, and eat him raw.[6]

His diaries show him to have been an assiduous attender of debates, to which he made regular contributions. Being susceptible to colds which rendered him virtually inaudible, he was not the most forceful of speakers and was frequently critical of his own performances, which, he once lamented, too often meandered towards anti-climax.[7] Before the 1820 dissolution he entertained doubts as to whether he even wished to continue as a Member, but in the event he was returned again on the interest of Sir Fitzwilliam Barrington for Newtown. As he observed to his friend and fellow antiquary Dawson Turner, 22 Mar., the arrangement was made, 'as that market goes, not unfairly, and in its *manner* peculiarly handsomely'. He went on:

> I was always as you know extremely anxious to see Parliament. I *have* seen it and I also now see that whoever goes there as a free man must dig deeply into his own fortune, that is to say, he will be 20 or 30 [thousand pounds] the worse man for it after 10 or fifteen years. I shall go on whilst I can afford it and sit ... for some time longer perhaps, but I shall *now* quit at any time without

much regret, for it has answered my object. My part in the drama of life is mainly that of spectator. Less and less I ambition turmoil, and rejoice in being a quiet man.[8]

Writing to his half-sister Anna, 17 Mar., Gurney reckoned that the returns had augmented the number of neutrals like himself.[9] Yet as he informed Turner, 11 Apr. 1820, he was quite decided that 'a change of administration is a thing infinitely to be desired', as the incumbents were so tainted by association with the post-war economic depression 'that they never can get the country out of the horrible state into which it has fallen'. In such circumstances, his dilemma was

that every motion comes forward on a specific allegation ... [which] ... is nine times out of ten disproved. Then let the *effect* of the *division* be what it may, how can *I* vote against my opinion *on the thing before me*? If any man would move straightforward an address to the king to change his ministers I would vote with him, but I still feel that I should be compelled to vote with any administration whether I liked them or not oftener than against them, because government must be oftenest right in *detail*, and 'tis the detail that is generally before the House of Commons.[10]

Gurney, who privately deplored the 'vile innovations' of the new throne and crown used by the king at the opening of Parliament, voted for investigation of new sources of revenue for the civil list, 5 May, and was present for the debates on the budget and the Queen Caroline affair in June 1820. Events conspired to prevent him from delivering an intended speech on the corrupt borough of Grampound, 28 June, and on 5 July he missed a Norwich petition on account of unexpected visitors, with a complaint that so far, 'this whole session has been to me very unprofitable'.[11] He recommended clemency for Henry Swann*, the former Member convicted of electoral corruption with Sir Manasseh Masseh Lopes*, 11 July, and thought that refusal to print an individual's reform petition, even though it was not a 'sensible composition', would set a dangerous precedent, 25 July. He supported a motion for the liberation of one Franklin, incarcerated for the distribution of seditious placards, 17 Oct. On 16 Sept. he had offered Turner a diagnosis of the nation's ills, which he ascribed to the abolition of the property tax, overprotective corn laws, commercial restrictions and the reversion to a gold standard in 1819. But he perceived a vital bulwark against revolutionary chaos in the fact that 'no country in the world ever had so great a proportion of persons with something to lose'. On the Queen Caroline affair, 8 Oct., he marvelled that everyone seemed prepared 'to go to loggerheads for a madman and a bitch', yet was sanguine as to the

outcome, 'if she be whitewashed, which I suppose she must be'.[12] By 25 Oct. 1820 he was convinced that 'the bill [of pains and penalties] *must* stop', having witnessed a popular demonstration of support for the queen of such decorum as did 'more credit to the English nation that can be weighed down by an ass of a king, a b-d of a queen and fools of ministers'.[13]

On 2 Feb. 1821 Gurney complained to Turner of the superficial nature of much parliamentary debate and, noting the lack of oratorical power on the treasury bench, remarked: 'I think they must be *hooted* out, if not out *voted*'.[14] He joined the Whig opposition's campaign in support of the queen during the early part of the session, though by 6 Feb., when he voted for their censure motion, he regarded them as a spent force, and he only paired for the restoration of her name to the liturgy, 13 Feb. He voted to condemn the revocation of the liberal constitution of Naples by the Holy Alliance, 21 Feb. On 28 Feb. he braved the 'tremendous cold' to vote for Catholic relief. He did not divide for repeal of the additional malt duty on 21 Mar., which he felt would 'take off enough money to embarrass the finances, and not enough to give any sensible relief'.[15] He spoke in favour of transferring Grampound's seats to Yorkshire, 12 Feb., 2, 5 Mar., and privately expressed delight that the principle of granting Members to unrepresented towns had apparently gained broad acceptance.[16] He praised the British Museum and its staff, 16 Feb., 11 Apr. Although Gurney opined to Turner, 17 Mar. 1821, that the general extent of agricultural distress had been 'greatly exaggerated', he admitted its impact in Norfolk and Suffolk. For this he blamed the 1819 Bank Act, from which he had foretold these consequences as a witness before the committee which had recommended it.[17] Yet he supported ministerial proposals for a swifter implementation of its provisions, 19 Mar. He was, as he boasted to Turner, among the mixed bag of '27 malcontents' who voted for an inquiry into the currency, 9 Apr., when he supported Alexander Baring's prescription of a bimetallic standard, allied to a revaluation of the sovereign at 21s.[18] On 17 May he informed Turner of his intention, despite some qualms, to vote for the second reading of the usury laws repeal bill. He continued to divide for the proposal in subsequent sessions of the Parliament, though in a letter to his cousin and banking partner Joseph John Gurney in February 1822 he indicated a wish to retain certain safeguards against exploitative interest rates.[19] Gurney voted for mitigation of the punishment for forgery, 23 May, and inquiry into the government of the Ionian Isles, 7 June 1821, 14 May 1822. He expressed his 'cordial, entire and universal abhorrence' of Scarlett's proposals to reform the poor laws, in which he detected the unwelcome influence of Malthusian theories, and defended existing arrangements on practical and moral grounds, 8 June, 2 July 1821.[20] His vehemence on the latter occasion brought calls for explanation, which he gratified only to the extent of disclaiming personal hostility.[21] He supported investigation of Robert Owen's social experiment at New Lanark, though he believed that it 'tended to destroy all individuality', 26 June. He voted for the omission of arrears from the grant to the duke of Clarence, 18 June, 2 July. At one time he had been an enthusiast for the French Revolution, and he was distressed by intelligence of the death of Buonaparte, 4 July, noting that 'the *littleness* of our *insults* to him after he fell into our hands, in denying him his rank, etc., etc., disgraces this county for ever'.[22] During the summer recess he suffered something akin to existential angst, telling Turner, 28 Aug. 1821, 'I lie in bed in the morning and do nothing ... go to the bank and do nothing, and come home, and sit up late because I am used to it, doing nothing'. His state of mind was not improved by failing eyesight.[23]

Gurney thought the king's speech to be 'poor, worn out, commonplace', and the subsequent exchanges even less inspiring, 5 Feb. 1822. By his own account, he voted against the Irish insurrection bill and the suspension of habeas corpus, 7 Feb., and for Sir Robert Wilson's protest against his removal from the army, 13 Feb. 1822, after being persuaded by his 'perfect' defence.[24] (On 16 Oct. 1820 he had been baited by his lifelong friend Lord Aberdeen for seeming to take Wilson seriously.)[25] He told Turner that the government's package of measures to relieve agricultural distress amounted to 'utter delusion', 13 Feb., yet was listed in the ministerial majority on the issue, 21 Feb. 1822, though his diary records that he left the House without voting.[26] According to other entries he was in the majority against reduction of the salt duty, 28 Feb., and was purposely absent from the division on its repeal, 28 June. Although he voted against ministers for a reduction in the number of junior lords of the admiralty, 1 Mar., he admitted to himself that while the measure might be expedient, it was not justified 'on a large view of things'.[27] He expressed private doubts as to the sanity of David Ricardo*, the leading political economist, 1 Mar., and pointedly told the House that the Bank of England experienced difficulties only when 'interfered with by theorist and speculators', 8 Mar.[28] His punchy speech in support of abolition of one of the joint-postmasterships, 13 Mar., suggests that his inclusion by one source in a list of those who opposed it was an almost certainly an error. Nor, it appears, did he vote as listed in the majority against

the renewed motion, 2 May, when he noted that he left the House without voting. Conversely, his intervention on behalf of the brewers in a debate on the malt duty, 20 Mar. 1822, was apparently noticed only by himself.[29]

Having finally caught the Speaker's eye on 3 Apr. 1822, Gurney pronounced that agricultural distress was 'entirely' a product of the Bank Act.[30] For relief, he rejected a large remission of taxes as financially irresponsible, but suggested the replacement of selected duties with a property tax, 8 May. To Turner, he compared the ministerial relief package to ideas propounded by William Cobbett†, noting that the 'drift' of their policy was 'to increase the circulation and thereby raise prices and float things generally, still holding the Bank to pay in gold, which I do not see to be possible'.[31] He voted for inquiry into the resumption of cash payments, 12 June, when he observed that while the alteration of a circulating currency might not conform to the soundest fiscal principles, it had been adopted in many countries with no ill effects, and made brief interjections on the small bank notes bill, 20 June, 8 July.[32] On 17 Apr. and 12 May he spoke in support of a bill for the recognition of Unitarian marriages. He intentionally abstained on a motion for parliamentary reform, 25 Apr.,[33] and paired in favour of the Catholic peers bill, 30 Apr. On 16 May he opposed a tax on absentee landlords on the same libertarian principles on which he based his objections to the cruelty to animals bill the same day.[34] He spoke against government plans to fund military and naval pensions, 1 May, 24 May, when he was amused to find himself in a minority with Hume and Ricardo, though it was his Whiggish half-brother Richard who was named in the published list.[35] That day he spoke against remission of the Irish window tax. He opposed protective measures for its butter trade, 20 June, and supported the introduction of an Irish poor law, 24 July. Although he voted steadily against the renewal of the Aliens Act, he complained of opposition exaggerations of its effects, 1 July. Sir James Mackintosh, his principal target, recorded that he 'disclaimed voting' that day, but this does not tally with Gurney's own account, nor with the published lists.[36] He denounced the proposed national monument in Scotland as 'a bald, meagre and miserable imitation of the Parthenon' and a thorough waste of money, 5, 16 July. On 11 July he was privately concerned that he might have been considered 'somewhat forward ... as though I make no long speeches I have had something either to attack or defend almost every day for the last week or two'.[37] He quizzed Peel, the home secretary, on arrangements for obtaining passports, 19 July, and defended the work of the record commission, 24 July. With a notable lack of foresight, he told Turner that Canning was a 'great ass' for declining the governor-generalship of India, 'for the sake of three years in the House of Commons', and predicted that he would 'die a beggar and be forgotten in ten', 17 Aug. 1822.[38]

Although Gurney was assured by Aberdeen of the government's determination to maintain a neutral stance over the Franco-Spanish conflict, he dreaded the effect of a popular outcry and was dismayed by the bellicose tone of many speeches at the opening of Parliament, 4 Feb. 1823, telling Turner that 'our going to war about their quarrels appears downright madness, unless we are willing to face a bankruptcy'. While he thought the conduct of the French amounted to 'madness and wickedness', he nevertheless opposed repeal of the Foreign Enlistment Act, 16 Apr.[39] He drew attention to the privations of the regular soldier in a debate on the mutiny bill, 14 Mar. He again aired his concerns about the investments used to fund military and naval pensions, 18 Apr., and absented himself from a debate on parliamentary reform, 23 Apr., though he did vote for reform of the Scottish representative system, 2 June.[40] He denigrated a Norfolk petition for reform as the work of Cobbett and as having emanated from 'a very good humoured meeting: everybody was laughing', 24 Apr. Cobbett must have brooded on this insult, for he referred to this episode over two years later and to Gurney as 'the Hickory Quaker'.[41] Although he agreed that whipping was overused as a punishment in prisons, he did not vote against it, 30 Apr.[42] He argued that legislation was unnecessary to render Quaker affirmations admissible in a criminal court, 8 May, and suggested that a simple alteration in the wording of the Act of Supremacy would allow Catholics to conform and thereby remove their disabilities at a stroke, 28 May. He argued for the formal enfranchisement of Catholics, 30 June. He spoke against an increase in barilla duties, 5, 13 June, and opposed the silk manufacture bill as an interference in labour relations, 11 June, 18 July. He welcomed a grant to the British Museum to house the library of George III, 20 June, 1 July.[43] On the latter date he was in a minority for the reception of a petition alleging corruption against James Crosbie, Member for Kerry. He proposed an amendment effectively exonerating O'Grady, the Irish chief baron, from similar charges, but did not press it, 9 July. He spoke and voted for the introduction of trial by jury to New South Wales, 7 July 1823. Earlier that month he had commented that Robinson's first budget statement as chancellor of the exchequer was 'very encouraging' and the 'improvement from Vansittart inconceivable', and by the autumn of 1823 he believed that if the country

remained at peace, as far as commerce was concerned, 'we seem to see our way before us'.[44]

Early in 1824 Gurney moved his London residence from Gloucester Place, Marylebone, to the 'much more convenient situation' of St. James's Square.[45] On 2 Mar. he informed Joseph John Gurney of his 'almost daily attendance' on the select committee on artisans and machinery, to which he had been added, 18 Feb., and observed:

> The people examined ... render it very interesting. We had a little touch from the lord mayor of Dublin today, which convinces me there is more *cruelty* as well as *oppression* in Ireland than in the *West Indies*.[46]

With a degree of prescience, he urged the Bank to issue figures for its notes in circulation and so reduce the chance of public alarm triggering financial panic, 19 Feb. In private, he hoped that ministers would stand firm for freer trade against the vested interests of the silk industry, 5 Mar.[47] Either he or his half-brother voted for repeal of the window tax, 2 Mar. Having evidently overcome his earlier doubts, he spoke for remission of the remaining salt duties, 6 Apr. He contributed briefly to a debate on the British Museum, 29 Mar.,[48] and queried details of the marine insurance bill, 28 May, and the new churches bill, 4 June. He voted to end flogging in the military services, 15 Mar., and for inquiry into the Irish church establishment, 6 May, and paired for inquiry into the trial of John Smith, the Methodist missionary accused of inciting rebellion among slaves in Demerara, 11 June 1824. He divided against the Irish unlawful societies bill, 11 Feb., and voted for Catholic relief, 1 Mar., 21 Apr., 10 May 1825, though it was his private belief that 'the Catholics are in a worse position as to getting what they want than they have been for years'.[49] He confessed himself 'puzzled' by the accompanying measure to disfranchise Irish 40s. freeholders and did not vote on it, 26 Apr.[50] Likewise, he left the House before a division on Members' rights of voting on bills in which they had a pecuniary interest, 10 Mar., but not before he had cited the experience of his half-brother with an unnamed railway company as an illustration of the attempts of speculators to buy parliamentary influence.[51] He deprecated the clamour for re-enactment of the combination laws which, he insisted, had been shown not to work, 29 Mar., 4 May. He would countenance only a limited relaxation of the quarantine regulations, 30 Mar., and in a hit at fashionable anti-contagionist theories of disease, observed that it was 'curious to see how extremes meet; and that the ultra-philosophers of Westminster have at last arrived at the wisdom of the Turk'. Either he or his half-brother voted for a revision of the corn laws, 28 Apr. He defended the grant to the duke of Cumberland for the education of Prince George, 30 May. He spoke and voted for a prohibition on spring guns, 21 June. He defended country bankers against a petition complaining of the non-redemption of notes, but gave a portentous warning that 'the immense mass of paper engagements' created a real danger that 'any domestic alarm, founded or unfounded' could precipitate a run on the banks, 27 June 1825.

By the time Parliament reassembled in 1826 such an event had indeed occurred and the survival of Gurney's own house was, according to its historian, partly thanks to his prudent avoidance of any overissue of notes.[52] In debate after the crash, he agreed that some change to currency regulation was necessary, 2, 9 Feb. He 'somewhat doubtingly' joined Baring's minority against the government proposals, 13 Feb., but he spoke strongly against the inclusion of the Bank in the proposed ban on the circulation of small notes and moved its exemption, which was lost by 66-7.[53] Convinced that without a replacement for the lost circulation commercial operations would grind to a 'standstill', he tried again the following day, when his motion was negatived without a division. On 17 Feb. ministers agreed to a nine-month delay in the implementation of the legislation, apparently after a delegation of Norwich bankers had threatened a £500,000 run on the Bank. Gurney, who was heavily implicated in this manoeuvre by John Hobhouse* and Greville,[54] welcomed this concession, 22 Feb., when, as he admitted to his uncle Joseph Gurney, he was greeted with considerable hostility, not least from Robinson, even though he insisted that ministers had not been held to ransom. Four days later he reported that there were still 'anxious faces' in the City, for which he could discover no definite cause.[55] He opposed an attempt to make the instant payment of notes in gold a legal obligation and argued that the publication of circulation figures, however desirable, should remain voluntary, 21, 24, 27 Feb., 7 Mar. He deprecated interference in the Scottish banking system, 14, 16 Mar., and counselled against modelling the Bank's new charter on its counterpart in Ireland, 14 Apr. He dismissed a petition complaining of the non-payment of country banknotes (including those of his own concern) as another production of Cobbett, 2 May. Baffled by Hume's 41 resolutions on finance, 4 May, he fled the House.[56] On 26 May he revived the notion of a bimetallic standard and suggested augmenting the circulation with 'government paper', by which a subsequent diary entry suggests he probably meant exchequer bills.[57] He presented a Norwich petition for revision of the corn laws, 2 Mar., and paired accordingly, 18 Apr.[58] He spoke in favour of a separate ministerial salary for the president of the board of trade 'for the sake of a fling at the Whigs', 7 Apr., and reckoned himself the only independent Member to vote with government on this three days later. His personal wish for John Copley's* appointment as lord chancellor, which he privately believed would be 'a greater reform than Lord John Russell's', 9 Apr., further illustrated his move away from the Whig opposition, as did his attendance at a ministerial dinner, 7 May.[59] He called for financial remuneration for the Westminster high constable and displaced settlers in Cape Province, 19 May. On 26 May 1826 he caused a stir by opposing Russell's resolutions against electoral bribery with the assertion that 'there was not a Member in the House who did not pay for his seat, either in meal or malt'. To demands for an explanation, he answered that he had merely intended to highlight the practical absurdity of the existing law.

At the 1826 general election he was returned again for Newtown, as he informed his sister, Agatha Hanbury, 'without demur on either side, and whilst I can go on and do not break'.[60] That November he was irked to be named to an appeals committee.[61] He repeated his calls for an overhaul of the regulations governing joint-stock company partnerships, 5 Dec. 1826, 15 May 1827. On 6 Dec. 1826 he failed to get a hearing in a debate on the export of machinery, when he was seemingly disturbed to detect a reaction against free trade.[62] He supported inquiries into the electoral activities of the corporations of Northampton, 21 Feb., and Leicester, 15 Mar. 1827. He voted for Catholic relief, 6 Mar., the defeat of which he ascribed to a divided cabinet, though on 13 Feb. he had recorded his strong suspicion that 'this is a very bad House of Commons, raw boys and fools'. To add to his despondency, he was appointed to the Dublin election committee, 'the worst in the whole session', 21 Mar.[63] He voted to ban spring guns, 23 Mar. Following the formation of Canning's ministry, he commented, 13 Apr., 'it comes to a total split, the two old parties again ... Canning and Peel, for Pitt and Fox. I am sorry for it. But *our* men are worth a thousand of the old two'. Retrospectively, he considered Canning to have been 'the greatest man of *my* time' (12 Mar. 1831), but on 3 May 1827 he referred to his supporters as 'an ill-assorted, ungainly multitude', though he was equally scathing about their Tory opponents.[64] He presented a petition for deletion of the declaration against transubstantiation from the parliamentary oaths, 9 May. He spoke against a bill to extend the jurisdiction of Warwickshire magistrates to Coventry, 22 May, 1, 8 June. He opposed measures to curb fraudulent votes and expenditure at elections on the grounds that similar legislation had failed in Ireland, 23, 28 May. That day he abstained from the division on the fate of the corrupt borough of Penryn, as he approved neither of its disfranchisement nor its enlargement.[65] He spoke against a petition from Norwich weavers for Parliament to set wage levels, 30 May, when he urged that a proposal to sanction Unitarian marriages be extended to all Dissenters. He opposed the use of criminals' bodies for dissection, 20 June, and called for information on the case of an alleged lunatic detained in Cold Bath Fields prison, 2 July 1827.

On 8 Feb. 1828 Gurney recorded a conspiracy theory propounded by Wilson, that John Herries*, as chancellor of the exchequer, had plotted the collapse of the Goderich ministry at the instigation of the Court, to which he added his own speculation on the existence of a 'stockjobbing connection' involving the royal household. At a Lords debate three days later, he noted the oratorical inexperience of the duke of Wellington, the new premier, and the 'pompous speechifying fashion of delivery' in general use.[66] In the Commons he made short interventions on the undermanning of naval vessels, 12 Feb., and the life annuities repeal bill, 25 Mar. He paired for repeal of the Test Acts, 28 Feb., and complained of changes in the oath made by a Lords' amendment, 2 May. On 12 May he paired for Catholic relief, thereby, as he told his half-sister Anna, avoiding 'three tremendously crowded and boring nights', though 'here my good luck ends, as I shall have to sit through the committee as there pairing is impossible'.[67] He argued against the appointment of a select committee on the reintroduction of small notes, believing that it would now serve no purpose, 3 June, but objected to a ban on the circulation of Scottish notes in England as detrimental to cross-border trade, 16, 27 June. He opposed compulsory returns of note issues, as country bankers had 'already enough to dispirit them in the way of their business', 26 June, and was concerned at the possibility of runs on the new savings banks, 10 July. On 20 June he supported a legislative assembly for New South Wales. He spoke against a voters' registration bill, 19 June, and the disfranchisement of named electors in the corrupt borough of East Retford, 24, 27 June, but welcomed a bill to prevent the misappropriation of corporate funds for electoral purposes 8, 10 July, and promised to reintroduce it if ministers failed to adopt it, 17, 18, 19 July 1828. (On 29 June 1829 he reported having received 'remonstrances' for his failure so to do, but would undertake only to ensure that the matter was not forgotten.) He was in the ministerial majority against ordnance reductions, 4 July, and presented

a petition from 500 government clerks against cuts in their superannuation allowances, 14 July 1828.

Gurney was absent from the opening of the 1829 session, but reckoned that the announcement of the government's decision to concede Catholic emancipation had given 'general satisfaction'. He considered that the decision of Peel, again home secretary, to resign his seat for Oxford University reflected 'greatly to his honour', 8 Feb., and mused on the irony that Wellington had turned out to be 'the most pacific minister we ever had'.[68] He spoke against an anti-Catholic petition from Norwich, 19 Feb., and alleged that many such 'had been got up by misrepresentations and culpable delusions practised on timid, unthinking people', 10 Mar. He was unimpressed by the case made in the House by opponents of emancipation, for which he voted, 6, 30 Mar.[69] He spoke for the issue of the writ for East Retford, saying that the borough had been punished enough by its lengthy trial, 10 Apr., 7 May, but was listed in the minority for the transfer of its seats to Birmingham, 5 May, which he apparently preferred to extension into the hundred. He was sceptical of Hobhouse's attempt to reform select vestries and warned him by letter that 'people being accustomed to old grievances and old abuses do not much care for them, but are sorely annoyed when they are travelled in a new place'.[70] In debate, he cast doubt on the accuracy of allegations in some anti-slavery pamphlets, 3 June. Next day he denounced the prayer of a petition for reductions in taxation and government expenditure as a recipe for national bankruptcy. His opposition to the Currency Act surfaced once more, though he declared that if a paper currency was again to be issued, it should not be in the hands of private banks. In December 1829 Aberdeen, now foreign secretary, jokingly upbraided Gurney for his 'grumbling and croaking' about public affairs.[71] The following month he was reported by Joseph John Gurney to be 'in a rather morbid and irritable state' as a result of his half-brother's siring of an illegitimate child.[72] He abstained from voting on the address, 4 Feb., but privately expressed unease at government complacency over economic distress.[73] This he informed the House, 19 Mar., was 'very great', though he felt unable to support the reflationary measures proposed by Western and fell back on his familiar call for an alteration in the currency.[74] In view of the king's grave illness, he regarded cavils at the cost of Windsor Castle repairs as distasteful, 3 May. He divided for Jewish emancipation, 17 May. On 7 June he divided for the grant for South American missions and spoke and voted in favour of ending the death penalty for forgery. He was in the minorities for restrictions to the provisions of the sale of beer bill, 21 June, 1 July. He was content to leave the law governing the payment of wages in kind as it stood, 12 June, 1, 5, 9 July, but was more receptive to the measure of reform introduced in the next Parliament, 15 Dec. 1830.

Addressing his sister Agatha in plaintive mode, 4 June 1830, Gurney remarked, 'I go on in much the old way, attending the H. of C. to no purpose and not doing *anything* to any purpose. I believe my going on in Parliament is now a foolish thing, and that it would be better to retire'.[75] At the 1830 general election he was again returned unopposed for Newtown. Ministers listed him among their 'foes', with the endorsement 'doubtful', and he was absent from the crucial division on the civil list, 15 Nov. He was bitterly critical of the reluctance of 'the opulent among the Irish' to shoulder a share of the tax burden, 23 Nov., but opposed a call for a return of bankrupt Irish magistrates, 15 Dec. 1830. On 18 Feb. 1831 he presented an Isle of Wight petition for parliamentary reform. When the Grey ministry's scheme of reform was introduced on 1 Mar. he was privately unhappy with the proposed reduction in the Members for the Island, for which, despite representing a pocket borough, he clearly regarded himself as a spokesman. His other immediate objections to the bill were the additional representation it gave to Ireland and to the metropolitan districts, which he feared would 'return the *worst* of representatives ... radicals, knowing nothing, and representing no interest whatsoever'.[76] Yet the Whig Denis Le Marchant† reported hearing him say that it was 'an honour to the age for any administration to propose a measure like this, but there is no chance of their getting the House to pass it. No one but Cromwell could ever have done that'.[77] Gurney afterwards adopted a quirky stance of opposition to the bill that led one contemporary radical publication to describe him as 'a strange, unintelligible kind of person'.[78] Many of his votes on the measure are uncertain, probably as a result of hostility to the collusion of Members in the reporting of proceedings, which he made clear in a complaint of breach of privilege on 7 Sept. Plagued by a cold, he failed to get a turn in debate before the division on the second reading, 22 Mar., on which, according to the published lists, he abstained.[79] Yet two days later he indicated in debate that he had actually voted in favour, in order to permit further discussion of the bill, but with no commitment to support it any further. He cast doubt on the prerogative right of the crown to disenfranchise any borough, 30 Mar., but, in redemption of his earlier pledge, welcomed the provisions to prevent the abuse of corporate funds, 14 Apr. Taken as a whole he assessed the bill as 'a radical reform which threat-

ens to sap and undermine all the institutions of the country', 15 Apr., and it seems clear that he voted for Gascoyne's wrecking amendment, either in person or as a pair, 19 Apr. 1831.

He had negotiated an unfettered return with his patron before the ensuing general election, though again he expressed a readiness to give up.[80] 'I am become old and effete', he told his half-sister Anna, 16 Mar.:

> I think it is quite right for me to retire from the arena of strife, where *I* can join with *no* party. I am not strong *enough* to make *fight* for *moderate compromises*. In short, ineffective to argue and bawl.

Two days before, however, his thoughts had taken a different turn:

> The House of Commons closes all my time to *very* occasional and *infrequent* purpose, but it is living in a very stimulant and amusing society under the pretence of business and giving an interest in interesting oneself in a world of things from day to day which otherwise one's attention would not be called to. If I were a wise man, or an industrious, I should be much better out of it, but as I am neither, I do not feel *sure* whether I shall employ myself much more profitably.[81]

He was concerned at the storm that might be provoked by a last-ditch opposition to the bill, and at a meeting of the Royal Society in May, expressed satisfaction that the elections had at least provided a positive indication of public opinion. He replied to an attack by the duke of Sussex and privately derided his assumption that the bill would mark the end of aristocratic influence in the Commons.[82] He left the House before the vote on the second reading of the reintroduced bill, 6 July, when the Commons was 'hot beyond human endurance, Wetherell bothering beyond human sufferance'.[83] He was listed in the majority against an adjournment, 12 July, but expressed his hope that the House would carefully attend to the claims of individual boroughs for reprieve the following day. He spoke up for Aldeburgh, 14 July, Appleby, 19 July, and his own borough, whose burgage franchise could not, he argued, be taken away on the score of its tiny population, 22 July. Although he opposed total disfranchisements, he did not carry out his threat to move for all boroughs to retain one Member, 14 July. In debate the following day he held Bentham responsible for the extra-parliamentary campaign in favour of the bill. The approval of schedules A and B caused Gurney to rethink his opposition to the enfranchisement of the metropolitan districts, and he voted to give two Members to Greenwich, 3 Aug., when he repeated his warning concerning their probable character. He was unable to present a petition for an extra Member for the Isle of Wight owing to the loss of his voice, 12 Aug, but did so four days later.[84] He wished the boundary commissioners to be vested with wide powers of investigation, 1 Sept., and defended their actions, 21 Sept. He injected a note of levity with an anecdote about a peer's attempt to vote at a Kent election, 6 Sept., and spoke against the disfranchisement of crown officers, 14 Sept. Regarding allegations of improper patronal interference at Hertford, he offered the all-purpose remedy of 'an improved state of the morals of the people', 21 Sept. The same day, to no great effect, he quoted a statute of Richard II in support of his claim that the schedule A disfranchisements were unconstitutional. Sources disagree as to whether he then voted against the passage of the bill, or absented himself from the division. On other matters, he welcomed proposals for a new road north from Waterloo Bridge and called for similar improvements in other parts of the capital, 23 June, 11 July. He supported the issue of the Liverpool writ, 8 July, and voted against a motion condemning the borough for gross bribery, 6 Sept. In November 1831 he welcomed the establishment of a museum in Norwich as an indication of 'the spread of scientific inquiry ... which one much wants to balance the unsettlement and fury of political ignorance'.[85] A letter from Aberdeen the following month indicates that he was in trepidation of another crisis in the banking system.[86]

Gurney apparently abstained on the second reading of the revised reform bill, 17 Dec. 1831. He deemed the allocation of a separate Member to the Isle of Wight to be the minimum requirement, 1 Feb., and divided in favour of the enfranchisement of Tower Hamlets, 28 Feb., but considered that despite such improvements as the retention of freemen's rights, the new bill still contained 'most of the injustice of the former', 20 Mar. 1832. That day he added a warning that 'the nearer you approach to universal suffrage, the more you place the numerical majority of persons working to acquire property in power over the minority who possess it'. He was absent from the divisions on the third reading of the bill, 22 Mar., and the motion calling on the king to appoint only ministers who would carry it unimpaired, 10 May. He was in the minority against the malt drawback bill, 2 Apr., but he paired with ministers on the Russian-Dutch loan, 12, 16 July, and voted with them, 20 July. He thought an inquiry into non-resident clergy was unnecessary, 8 May, and deemed a bill to reduce sheriffs' expenses 'a most ridiculous piece of legislation', 20 July. On the bribery at elections bill, he warned of the need for

great care in framing definitions and oaths, 30 July, 9 Aug. He was sarcastic about its provision for the disfranchisement of errant boroughs, even 'though our next Parliament is to be so pure and honest', 6 Aug. The same day he used the attempts of English liberals to frame a constitution for Greece as an opportunity for another glance at Bentham and his acolytes. He admitted that a reformed Parliament was likely to be more competent than 'this self-condemned one' to judge demands for modifications to the Reform Act contained in a Westminster petition, 11 Aug. 1832. The same day he stood by the government's insistence on the secrecy of proceedings in the Bank's charter committee.

On 25 Dec. 1832 Gurney was reported by Amelia Opie to be 'cheered' on the subject of general politics.[87] However, he did not seek a replacement for his abolished seat either at the elections then taking place or subsequently, having long before announced his unsuitability to represent a populous place. He contented himself with the observation that

> no person hates party more than I do. Perhaps my time in the House of Commons ... was the precise period in which neutrality was easiest, and the moment of my leaving ... that in which neutrality was to become next to impossible. I have during the time I have been there lived well with everybody. It is very possible in these times that I may live better with everybody for being out.[88]

At the same time he resigned his partnership in the Gurneys' bank, a step he had meditated for a decade. His lack of appetite for business apparently coincided with the social prejudices of his wife 'Mag', though he was sensible enough of its lucrative benefits, observing on one occasion that during all but the most severe social upheavals, 'the banker holds the bag to those who have something to put in it'.[89] He evidently felt the loss of his two greatest concerns, noting in his diary, 2 Jan. 1833, 'I am too old for balls. I am too blind to know people, too deaf to hear them, and too husky in the throat to make them hear me'. But he found suitable occupation in the rebuilding of Keswick in 1838 and in literary and antiquarian pursuits. In 1831 he had published a *Memoir of the Life of Thomas Young*, as an introduction to his late tutor's Egyptian dictionary, and in 1847 he added *Letter to Dawson Turner, on Norwich and the Venta Icenorum*, which endeavoured to prove that the city had been the headquarters of the Iceni tribe. The task of editing the remainder of his voluminous notes for publication was too much for his well-ingrained habits of procrastination. He seldom rose before midday, a habit acquired from parliamentary sittings which he never broke.[90] In 1835 he was apparently involved in his half-brother's vain election bid for East Norfolk and he remained abreast of political developments.[91] He was untroubled by Chartist agitation in May 1839, being convinced that 'the mass of the people are very sick of reforms and movements'; but his tirade against sections of the anti-slavery lobby in August that year upset his kinswoman Anna Gurney, who commented that 'with all Hudson Gurney's kindness it is odd that he should allow prejudice to becloud his benevolence and good sense'.[92] In 1843 he was struck down by serious illness, from which he never fully recovered. Aberdeen attempted to rally him, 14 Feb. 1844, observing that 'your views of men and things are never very sanguine, and I hope that in your own case you have taken rather too gloomy a prospect'.[93] When Gurney wrote to Brougham on 14 July 1850 he had been 'almost confined for seven years', though his subsequent remarks indicate that his capacity for reflective self-denigration was undiminished:

During a very useless and sole life I have been either reading or dreaming over history, in some shape or other, and I have lived to see everything happen which was impossible, and everything in the world's story which had been supposed to have passed, proved to have been all wrong, so that I am arrived at my second childhood, in the comfortable conviction that I can comprehend *nothing*, and that the march of intellect and of discovery should appear to have involved everything, in every direction, in inextricable confusion.[94]

In August 1862 he ventured far enough outdoors to check the progress of the harvest, but 'had great difficulty in getting back again'.[95] He died at Keswick in November 1864, having outlived his wife by nine years.[96] By his will, dated 6 June 1860 with six codicils, his entire landed estate passed to John Henry Gurney (1819-90), the son of his cousin and banking partner Joseph John Gurney, Liberal Member for King's Lynn, 1854-65. Out of his personalty, which was sworn under £1,100,000, Gurney left £120,000 to his first cousin Daniel Gurney (1791-1880) of North Runcton, Norfolk, the family historian, about whose scholarship he had often been churlish.[97] He bequeathed the same sum, for investment in land, to John Gurney (1845-87), later of Sprowston Hall, Norfolk, the grandson of Samuel Gurney, another first cousin. Smaller sums were distributed among his many cousins in the Barclay and Gurney families and to deserving causes in his Norfolk locality. Gurney had once written: 'I am not aware of having ever in my life taken advantage of any man, or of having persecuted anyone. I have been very guarded of individually injuring anyone, or of standing in anyone's way'.

The impressive attendance at his funeral at Intwood, and the warm tributes to his philanthropic humanity in obituary notices, suggest that in this respect at least, he had gone some way towards meeting his own expectations.[98]

[1] W.H. Bidwell, *Annals of an East Anglian Bank*, 55. [2] Soc. of Friends Lib. 'Dict. of Quaker Biog.'; Bidwell, 69. [3] *Gent Mag.* (1865), i. 108. [4] Soc. of Friends Lib. Gurney mss 2/36. [5] Bidwell 58-59, Norf. RO, Gurney mss RQG 520. [6] *Oxford DNB*; Bidwell, 147-9. [7] Gurney diary (in the possession of D. Q. Gurney, Esq. of Bawdeswell Hall, Norf.), 1 July. 1821 and *passim*. [8] Trinity Coll. Lib. Camb. Dawson Turner mss DT2/K1/30. [9] Norf. RO, Gurney mss 401/158. [10] Dawson Turner mss K1/31. [11] Gurney diary. [12] Dawson Turner mss K1/32, 34. [13] Gurney diary. [14] Dawson Turner mss K2/1. [15] Norf. RO, Gurney mss 401/121, 122, 161. [16] *The Times*, 5 Mar. 1821; Dawson Turner mss K2/2. [17] Dawson Turner mss K2/3; B. Gordon, *Political Economy in Parl.* 37, 42. [18] Dawson Turner mss K2/4, 5. [19] Ibid. K2/8; Bidwell, 158-9. [20] *The Times*, 9 June, 3 July 1821. [21] Gurney diary. [22] Ibid.; V. Anderson, *Friends and Relations*, 237. [23] Dawson Turner mss K2/12, 15. [24] Gurney diary. [25] Norf. RO, Gurney mss 334/48. [26] Dawson Turner mss K3/3. [27] Gurney diary. [28] Ibid. [29] Ibid. [30] Ibid. [31] Dawson Turner mss K3/6. [32] *The Times*, 21 June 1822. [33] Gurney diary. [34] *The Times*, 17 May 1822. [35] Norf. RO, Gurney mss 402/10. [36] Add. 52445, f. 90; Gurney diary. [37] Dawson Turner mss K3/9. [38] Ibid. K3/10. [39] Ibid. K3/13,14; K4/3; Gurney diary. [40] Gurney diary. [41] *Cobbett's Rural Rides* ed. G.D.H. and M. Cole, i. 327. [42] *The Times*, 1 May 1823; Gurney diary. [43] *The Times*, 2 July 1823. [44] Gurney diary; Dawson Turner mss K4/9. [45] Soc. of Friends Lib. Gurney mss 2/1, Anna Gurney to her uncle, 14 Jan. 1824. [46] Ibid. 2/102. [47] Gurney diary. [48] *The Times*, 30 Mar. 1824. [49] Gurney diary, 15 Feb., 14 Mar. 1825 [50] Ibid. [51] Ibid. [52] Bidwell, 152-3. [53] Gurney diary. [54] Broughton, *Recollections*, iii. 126. In *Greville Mems.* i. 156-7, the editors, apparently incorrectly, identify the chief protagonist as Samuel Gurney. See F. W. Fetter, *Development of British Monetary Orthodoxy*, 133. [55] Bidwell, 154-7, 185. [56] Gurney diary. [57] Bidwell, 105-6. [58] *The Times*, 3 Mar. 1826 [59] Gurney diary. [60] Norf. RO, Gurney mss 574/3. [61] Gurney diary. [62] Ibid. [63] Ibid. [64] Ibid. [65] Ibid. [66] Ibid. [67] Norf. RO, Gurney mss 402/57. [68] Gurney diary. [69] Ibid. [70] Add. 36465, f. 110. [71] Norf. RO, Gurney mss 334/61. [72] Soc. of Friends Lib. Gurney mss 3/520. [73] Gurney diary. [74] B. Gordon, *Economic Doctrine and Tory Liberalism*, 132. [75] Norf. RO, Gurney mss 576/5. [76] Gurney diary. [77] *Three Diaries*, 14. [78] [W. Carpenter], *People's Bk.* (1831), 271-2 [79] Gurney diary. [80] Ibid. 2 Apr. 1831. [81] Norf. RO, Gurney mss 402/87; 576/16. [82] Gurney diary, 24 Apr., 5 May 1831. [83] Ibid. [84] Ibid. 12 Aug. 1831. [85] Add. 46126, f. 351. [86] Norf. RO, Gurney mss 334/63. [87] Soc. of Friends Lib. Gurney mss 1/350. [88] Bidwell, 146-7. [89] Ibid. 173-4, 181-5; Anderson, 283. [90] Bidwell, 197, 223; Add. 37966, f. 110. [91] Norf. RO, Gurney mss 334/78. [92] Soc. of Friends Lib. Gurney mss 2/105, 3/95. [93] Bidwell, 221; Norf. RO, Gurney mss 334/109. [94] Brougham mss. [95] Soc. of Friends Lib. Gurney mss 2/108. [96] *Gent. Mag.* (1865), i. 108-10. [97] Anderson, 288, 291. [98] Bidwell, 225, 247-9; *Gent. Mag.* (1865), ii. 108-10; *The Times*, 11 Nov. 1864.

H.J.S./P.J.S.

GURNEY, Richard Hanbury (1783–1854), of Keswick and Thickthorne, Norf.

NORWICH	1818–1826
NORWICH	1830–1832

b. 2 Aug. 1783, 2nd *s.* of Richard Gurney, banker and brewer, of Keswick and North Repps, Norf. and 2nd

w. Rachel, da. of Osgood Hanbury of Holfield Grange, Coggeshall, Essex; half-bro. of Hudson Gurney*. *m.* 17 May 1830, Mary, da. of William Jary of Burlingham, Norf., div. w. of Joseph Salisbury Muskett of Intwood Hall, Norf., 1 illegit. da. *suc.* fa. as partner in Norwich bank 1811. *d.* 1 Jan. 1854.

Gurney, a keen agriculturist, popular sportsman and 'lapsed Quaker', who admitted spending £80,000 on electioneering for himself and his friends, was a member of the Quaker banking dynasty and a partner in the Norwich and Yarmouth banks. The banker and natural leader of the Norwich 'Blue and White' party, he had contested the city successfully on their interest at the general election of 1818, and they returned him unopposed and 'without *ruinous* expense' with his fellow Whig, the Dissenters' parliamentary spokesman William Smith, in 1820.[1] On the hustings and in his addresses, he testified to his opposition to Lord Liverpool's administration and wasteful taxes, expressed disquiet at the recent Cato Street conspiracy and 'wild visionary schemes of reform' and called for support for the monarchy.[2] Unlike his halfbrother, with whom his votes and rare utterances tend to be confused, Gurney, whose love of the chase, firm commitment to his business interests and tendency to gout kept his attendance spasmodic, was a proreform Whig and professed political devotee of Lord Althorp*.[3] He divided with opposition on the Queen Caroline case, 22, 26 June 1820. On 23 Nov. 1820, at the Norwich common hall which addressed her, he spoke of the damage caused to the royal family by her prosecution and called for parliamentary scrutiny of the Milan commission.[4] According to Hudson, at whose house he stayed, Gurney arrived for the session on 23 Jan. 1821

> too late for the division ... [and] much resembling a bear poked with a cudgel, to do his duties of dancing to a hand organ. The honourable Member on his hind legs, however, seems in much better spirits, and to have lost much of his discomfiture today, as he stays to vote on Friday.[5]

Though 'sick of the queen's case', he divided with her partisans, 26 Jan., 6 Feb., before resuming his country pursuits, returning reluctantly to vote for the additional malt duty repeal bill, 3 Apr.[6] He received a month's leave to deal with urgent private business, 19 Apr., and the remaining votes attributed to him that session (23 May, 7, 18, 21 June and 2 July 1821) were almost certainly cast by Hudson.

Gurney divided with opposition on distress, 11 Feb., and the dismissal of Sir Robert Wilson* from the army, 13 Feb., and paired for large tax concessions, 8 May 1822. He voted for remission of Henry Hunt's* gaol sentence, 24 Apr., parliamentary reform, 25 Apr., and inquiries into the government of the Ionian Isles, 14 May, embassy costs, 15, 16 May, and the conduct of the lord advocate towards the Scottish press, 25 June, having also voted against the naval and military pensions bill, 24 May, and the aliens bill, 14 June 1822. He arrived for the 1823 session on 10 Feb., but on the 28th Hudson wrote that 'there seems nothing in Parliament which would withdraw him from the foxes – even if he liked it better than he does'.[7] He received a fortnight's leave on account of ill health, 15 Apr.,[8] and votes against the naval and military pensions bill, 18 Apr., and for inquiry into the prosecution of the Dublin Orange rioters, 22 Apr. 1823, may have been misattributed to him. He divided for repeal of the taxes on windows, 2 Mar., and leather, 18 May, against permitting the export of long wool used in the Norwich worsted trade, 21 May, and in condemnation of the indictment in Demerara of the Methodist missionary John Smith, 11 June 1824. He divided for Catholic relief, 1 Mar., 21 Apr., 10 May 1825. According to Hudson Gurney's diary, he also voted against the attendant Irish franchise bill, 26 Apr., but he is not named in the usual lists.[9] He voted to repeal the assessed taxes, 3 Mar., and to consider corn law reform, 28 Apr. 1825. Summoned to Norwich shortly before the December 1825 banking crisis, he dealt adroitly with the repercussions of the failure of Day's bank and took over much of their business.[10] Heeding local interests, he voted in the minority for the appointment of a select committee on the silk trade petitions, 24 Feb. 1826, and returned to London for three days in March but spent 'the first in the City and the House, the second in bed and the third hobbling'.[11] He voted for parliamentary reform, 27 Apr. 1826. His announcement two days later that he was standing down on health grounds at the dissolution also referred to differences with his supporters, whose commitment to free trade and a return to the gold currency he did not share.[12] His retirement surprised his relations and left his party little time to find an alternative candidate at the general election, when his nomination *in absentia* was discounted.[13] Family correspondence attributed his decision to misgivings over the Norwich and Lowestoft Port bill and the growing anti-Catholicism of the Norwich mob, for his health soon recovered at Cheltenham and he retained 'a great leaning for a borough if one should offer'.[14]

Out of Parliament, Gurney devoted his time to rural pursuits and banking.[15] In October 1829 he caused a sensation by eloping with Mary, the estranged wife of Joseph Salisbury Muskett of Intwood Hall, who in March 1818 had unsuccessfully brought a *crim. con.* action against him at Thetford assizes.[16] Mary was now heavily pregnant, and the bill by which her divorce from Muskett was secured received royal assent, 3 May 1830, five months after the birth of her daughter with Gurney. It followed successful high profile proceedings brought by Muskett in December 1829 in the consistory count and in king's bench, which on the 21st found Gurney guilty of *crim. con.* and awarded Muskett damages of £2,000 with costs.[17] Several newspapers erroneously reported that the adulterer was Hudson Gurney.[18] According to their cousin and partner, the Quaker minister Joseph John Gurney, since January 1830 Gurney had been

> at the bank daily; received by everybody as if nothing had happened. I have myself taken the line of silence on the sorrowful event, and of strictly confining our communications to matters of business, in which he continues to be useful and effective. He seems fully resolved to settle in the neighbourhood of Norwich, not being able it appears, to endure living elsewhere. He has been looking at Easton where Micklethwaite used to live, but does not like it. It is melancholy to me to see the standard let down, and a little questionable whether one ought to be so far mixed up with him as we necessarily are on the immediate management of the business. Yet I see for the present no alternative. He looks worn, and by no means happy. Yet I fear it is his unsettlement which grieves him, rather than his sin.[19]

Gurney and Mary, the daughter of a well-to-do Norfolk yeoman, were married at St. Marylebone church on 17 May 1830.[20] His candidature for Norwich at the general election in July, when he was also talked of the county, discomfited the Quakers on moral grounds, but they nevertheless welcomed his return with the Huskissonite Robert Grant.[21] Not surprisingly, he had to endure many jibes about 'muskets' and wife-stealing during the contest.[22] His speeches advocated reform, retrenchment and moderate tax reductions, and he cited the lengthy depression in the Norwich textile industry in justification of his earlier reservations on free trade.[23]

The Wellington ministry counted Gurney among their 'foes' and he divided against them when they were brought down on the civil list, 15 Nov. 1830. At the by-election following Grant's appointment as the Grey ministry's judge advocate, he expressed confidence in the government and voiced his concern at the escalating rioting in Norfolk, 30 Nov. 1830.[24] He gave 'general support' to the 'radical' resolutions adopted at the Norwich reform meeting, 19 Jan. 1831, but called for forbearance and public backing for the min-

istry in their difficult task of securing the passage of a reform bill in an unreformed House. Nevertheless, he promised to oppose them 'if I shall find them at any time guilty of a job, or taking to themselves what of right belongs to the people'.[25] He presented a petition from the Norwich parish of St. Michael at Plea for repeal of the assessed taxes, 4 Feb., and was awarded a week's leave for urgent private business after serving on an election committee, 14 Mar. He voted for the ministry's reform bill at its second reading, 22 Mar., and against Gascoyne's wrecking amendment, 19 Apr. 1831. Although absent and unable to canvass on account of a bad attack of gout, he came in again for Norwich with Grant at the ensuing general election, defeating the anti-reformers Michael Sadler* and Sir Charles Wetherell* in a 'costly and vexatious' poll.[26]

Gurney voted for the second reading of the reintroduced reform bill, 6 July, and against adjourning its consideration in committee, 12 July 1831. He generally supported its details, but cast wayward votes against the division of counties, 11 Aug. (according to the local press),[27] against giving freeholders in cities like Norwich county votes, 17 Aug., and for the enfranchisement of £50 tenants-at-will, 18 Aug.[28] On 15 Sept. he explained that he wished

> to support the present administration in every way I possibly can, but I cannot vote with them against my conscience, and therefore I have been against them on particular clauses. Since my election I have been amongst my constituents, and I declare that they have never said, do this, or do that, but have left me quite unfettered; and unfettered I shall remain, notwithstanding anything that may be said by opposition.

He divided for the bill's passage, 21 Sept. At the Norwich common hall on the 29th, which petitioned the Lords in its favour, he said he 'sincerely wished such a measure had been carried 30 years ago', saving 'upwards of £800,000 a year' in unnecessary taxes, and discussed prorogation, peer creation and withholding supplies as possible strategies to ensure its passage.[29] When they met on 18 Oct., following its defeat, he said he hoped that the next bill would be introduced in the Lords to lessen the strain on Members, and urged the populace 'to be peaceable in the interests of reform' and to 'combine together firmly and steadily and the day is your own'.[30] He was cheered at the Norfolk county meeting, 19 Nov.[31] He voted for the revised reform bill at its second reading, 17 Dec. 1831, fairly steadily for its details, and for its third reading, 22 Mar. 1832. Illness prevented him from voting on the address requesting the king to appoint only ministers who would carry it unimpaired, 10 May, and he remained unwell on the 14th, when he addressed the Norwich meeting that petitioned for withholding supplies until it became law.[32] He voted for the second reading of the Irish reform bill, 25 May, and divided with government on the Russian-Dutch loan, 12 July 1832.

Standing as a Liberal, Gurney was defeated 'mainly on malt' at Norwich, where bribery prevailed, at the general election in December 1832, and in East Norfolk in 1835 and 1837.[33] He did not offer subsequently, but as a substantial Norfolk landowner, he opposed repeal of the corn laws in 1846.[34] His recurrent attacks of gout and paralysis caused his family great concern, but they did not prevent his success in business. He died in January 1854, the senior partner in the bank of Overend, Gurney and Company. His nephew Daniel Gurney recalled him as 'a person of great strength, both of body and mind, full of sterling sense and kindly feeling, but neither his education nor early associations led to a complete development of either'.[35] His will, dated 8 Nov. 1851, provided for his wife (who died 2 Dec. 1857, worth £40,000), servants and relations, but the main beneficiary was his only daughter Mary (Jary), who in 1846 had married her cousin John Henry Gurney, Liberal Member for King's Lynn, 1854-65; Gurney's Norfolk and Sussex estates devolved on their issue.[36] She died in Paris, 19 Oct. 1872, having in 1860 made over her principal interests in the estate to her husband, whom she had left for her groom, William Taylor.[37]

[1] HP Commons, 1790-1820, iv. 120; Norf. RO, Gurney mss RQG 357/3; 401/3; 402/69; 571/41; 572/2, 3; Hants RO, Calthorpe mss 26M62/F/C219; W.H. Bidwell, Annals of an East Anglian Bank, 139-41, 143; D.E. Swift, 'J.J. Gurney and Norwich Politics', Jnl. of Friends' Hist. Soc. xlix. (1959), 50, 53. [2] Norf. Chron. 4, 11 Mar. 1820. [3] Gurney mss 402/69. [4] Bury and Norwich Post, 29 Nov.; The Times, 1 Dec. 1820. [5] Gurney mss 401/160. [6] Ibid. 401/161; 402/6. [7] Ibid. 402/21. [8] Gurney diary, 15 Apr. 1823. [9] Ibid. 26 Apr. 1825. [10] Gurney mss 402/16; Bidwell, 152-3; Norwich Mercury, 24, 31 Dec. 1825. [11] Gurney mss 402/37. [12] Norwich Mercury, 6 May 1826. [13] Gurney mss 402/40; Gurney diary, 9 June; Add. 40387, f. 248; The Times, 12 June 1826. [14] Gurney mss 334/58; 574/3. [15] Soc. of Friends Lib. Gurney mss Temp 434/3/452. [16] Norf. Chron. 21 Mar. 1818. [17] The Times, 12, 22, 29 Dec. 1829; LJ, lxii. 38, 49, 73, 108-11, 167, 173, 176, 280, 303; CJ, lxxxv. 243-4, 340, 350. [18] The Times, 2 Mar. 1830. [19] Soc. of Friends Lib. Gurney mss Temp 434/3/520. [20] Norf. Chron. 22 May 1830. [21] Surr. Hist. Cent. Howard of Ashtead mss 203/31/53; Soc. of Friends Lib. Gurney mss Temp 434/3/526a; Bidwell, 189. [22] The Times, 19, 30 July; Norwich Election Budget (1830), 38-48. [23] Norwich Mercury, 17, 24, 31 July, 7 Aug. 1830. [24] Ibid. 4 Dec. 1830. [25] Ibid. 22 Jan.; The Times, 24 Jan. 1831. [26] Bidwell, 189; The Times, 28 Apr., 2 May; Norwich Election Budget (1831), passim. [27] Norwich Mercury, 20 Aug. 1831. [28] The Times, 19 Aug. 1831. [29] Norwich Mercury, 1 Oct. 1831. [30] Ibid. 22 Oct. 1831. [31] The Times, 21 Nov. 1831. [32] Ibid. 16 May 1832. [33] Norf. RO, Gurney mss 402/9a, 99; The Times, 13, 14 Dec. 1832; Norwich Mercury, 7, 14 Jan. 1854; Bidwell, 195, 341, 400. [34] Norwich Mercury, 7 Jan. 1854. [35] Soc. of Friends Lib. Gurney mss Temp 434/1/78, 147; 2/431; 3/ 45, 76, 72, 113, 217, 713; A.J.C. Hare, Gurneys of Earlham, i. 29; Gent. Mag. (1854), i. 320-1. [36] PROB 11/2186/113; 2261/893; IR26/1994/93; 2097/954; Soc. of Friends Lib. Gurney mss Temp 434/3/231-6, 877; Norf. RO, Gurney mss 287, 288. [37] Soc. of Friends Lib. Gurney mss Temp 434/2/57; Norf. RO, Gurney mss 284/432-3.

M.M.E.

GYE, Frederick (1780–1869), of 38 Gracechurch Street and 141 Fleet Street, London, and Wood Green, Mdx.

CHIPPENHAM   1826–1830

bap. 4 Dec. 1780, 2nd but 1st surv. s. of William Gye, printer and bookseller, of Bath, Som. and w. Mary Batchelor. *m.* 7 July 1804, Sarah Dicks of Bath, 1s. 2da. (1 d.v.p.).[1] *suc.* fa. 1802. *d.* 13 Feb. 1869.

Gye's family origins are obscure, though they probably came from the West Country where the surname was a common variant of Guy; he may, for instance, have been related to one Waldern Gye, a Bath apothecary, who died in 1760.[2] His father, William Gye, was born in 1750 and worked in his father's printing works at 4 Westgate Buildings, Bath, before opening an establishment at 13 Market Place. An active and successful printer and bookseller, and sometime publisher of the *Bath Courant*, he was highly respected for his attempts to improve the conditions of the city's poor.[3] It was through his efforts that a clause setting out summary fines for using seditious language was incorporated into the rules of all the local trades' benefit societies, which allowed magistrates to issue them with licenses.[4] His greatest philanthropic endeavours were connected with the relief of the prisoners in the county gaol at Ilchester, of which he was once described as the agent, and which he visited every week with food, clothing and money. He issued trade tokens, and when they were redeemed in his shop, it was his custom to point out the inscription on them ('Remember the debtors of Ilchester gaol') in order to elicit donations.[5] He died of an apoplectic fit in 1802, and was remembered for his 'strict integrity and unblemished reputation'. His wife Mary, whom he had married in 1774, inherited his printing and stationery business, which was managed by her and then by their third son, Henry, who also had an outlet in Clare Street, Bristol.[6]

Frederick Gye, the third of 13 children, was educated at Chippenham and apparently came to like the town during his sojourn there.[7] He probably worked initially in the family business, but he settled in London and in 1807 entered a partnership with Giles Balne, a master printer, of 7 Union Court, Broad Street. They established their printing and stationery office at 38 Gracechurch Street the following year, and continued to operate from there, despite its being destroyed by fire in 1820.[8] Gye had a contract with Thomas Bish, the lottery agent, for printing state lottery tickets, some of which on one occasion passed into his hands and won him a prize of £30,000.[9] With the proceeds he established in 1817 at 44 Southampton Row the London Wine Company, which moved to 141 Fleet Street in 1822. The following year, in partnership with Richard Hughes, he founded the London Genuine Tea Company, marketing a high quality and well-packaged product. The provincial wholesale tea trade was run from Fleet Street, and shops were opened at 8 Charing Cross, 148 Oxford Street and 23 Ludgate Hill.[10] His most renowned venture was his management of the famous Vauxhall Gardens, which he purchased with Bish and Hughes in 1821, for £28,000. Reopened under the title of 'The Royal Gardens, Vauxhall', with the approval of George IV, 3 June 1822, they then entered on a period of expansion and improvement. As well as promoting major refurbishment and the construction of several new arenas for ballet, concerts, fireworks and all manner of performing artists, he also presented special events, such as a spectacular re-enactment of the battle of Waterloo in 1827.[11] His theatrical zeal was not universally popular, however, and following complaints from local residents, he was forced to attend the Surrey sessions, 18 Oct. 1826, when he protested that the dark walks had by then been suitably lit, that improper women and disorderly dancing had never been allowed, and that the gardens should be permitted to remain open past midnight.[12]

Perhaps because of his earlier connection with the town, Gye accepted the invitation of a deputation from Chippenham to stand on the independent interest at the general election of 1826. He initially eschewed financial inducements, and, in an address, 25 Mar., promised to raise the matter by petition if he were defeated. But he did reluctantly engage in treating, and it was asserted that he 'has not a leg to stand upon; nor would all the champagne in his cellars in Fleet Street afford him one'.[13] He soon made more explicit his promise to procure sales of cloth in order to provide employment for the town's distressed workers, and by early June he had actually purchased large quantities of wool so as to restart production in the factories. One of the sitting Members, John Rock Grosett, therefore retired in his favour, and Gye was duly elected unopposed.[14] At a dinner, 13 June, he declared that

> although strictly independent in his political creed, he should enter the House of Commons with a strong

feeling in favour of the present [Liverpool] administration, because he considered that they had obtained, and justly deserved, the confidence of the country.

In Bath, where he was 'universally known and respected', he was praised for having overturned the long established 'burgage-tenure-thraldom' at Chippenham.[15] He fulfilled his pledge by purchasing one of the largest businesses in his constituency, and on his next visit, in May 1827, he reiterated his promise to keep the inhabitants fully employed.[16] He was largely inactive in the House, where he is not known to have spoken, except in presenting two constituency petitions for repeal of the Test Acts, 7 June 1827, 22 Feb. 1828.[17] He voted for this, 26 Feb. 1828, and for Jewish emancipation, 17 May 1830, but against Catholic relief, 6 Mar. 1827, 12 May 1828 and steadily throughout March 1829. His only other reported votes were against transferring East Retford's seats to Birmingham, 11 Feb., to abolish the death penalty for forgery, 7 June, and for prohibiting the sale of beer for on-consumption, 21 June 1830. He was thought to be opposed to the New Sarum poor bill that session.[18]

Possibly because his cloth concerns were a failure and, as one election poster put it, 'cash is scarce (on the Surrey side of the water)', but mainly because the borough had completely fallen under the control of a single patron, Gye withdrew from Chippenham at the dissolution in 1830.[19] He offered instead for Berwick, and asked Thomas Gladstone*, who described him as 'an inferior sort of person', for a 'few lines of introduction or recommendation' from his father, John, a former Member.[20] He claimed to have elicited such support, but as a stranger he failed to gain widespread acceptance in his attempt to oust the Whig Sir Francis Blake. He was depicted as a 'commercial gentleman of the highest respectability', but had to defend his character on the hustings, 31 July, when he stated that

> in nine cases out of ten I have gone into the House of Commons not knowing how I should divide. I confess I have generally divided on the same side as Colonel [Marcus] Beresford: but whenever I have on any occasion differed from the ministers, I have fearlessly divided against them.

He also stressed that a port required an active Member resident in London, and boasted that he had been in trade for 27 years and was still 'a man of business and always at my post'. He was disappointed in his promises and withdrew from the contest.[21] He did not sit in the Commons again, although he was approached by the reformers of Shaftesbury in 1831.[22]

Always anxious to extend his multifarious business interests, Gye proposed a plan to increase the number of horse-drawn carriages in London in 1828 and was also the owner of the Portugal Hotel in Fleet Street. He had a brief association with the *Mirror of Parliament*, taking it over from Henry Winchester*, but reportedly 'lost a good deal of money by it'.[23] However, the Vauxhall Gardens remained his principle concern. Among his innovations in the 1830s were the introduction of illuminations and optical illusions, ascents by the Great Nassau balloon, and day-time opening. But not all them were successful, as was proved in 1837 by the unfortunate death of Robert Cocking, whose experimental parachute failed to operate properly on his descent from a balloon. Gye was also faced by mounting financial problems. His printing business seems to have been dissolved soon after 1830, his wine company failed in 1836 when a speculation was made in what turned out to be a bad vintage of port, and a number of wet seasons contributed to the decline of Vauxhall Gardens, which closed for the last time under his management, 5 Sept. 1839. He and his partners were declared bankrupt in May 1840, with debts of about £20,000, and the tea company and gardens were sold.[24] He retired to Brighton, where he died of influenza in February 1869, leaving what property he had to his daughter Letitia Scalding Gye (*b.* 1810). Her twin brother and Gye's only son, Frederick, who had managed the Vauxhall Gardens for his father in the 1830s, and had later become the proprietor of the Royal Italian Opera, Covent Garden, and one of the leading theatrical impresarios of the nineteenth century, died as the result of a shooting accident, 4 Dec. 1878. His eldest son Ernest (?1839-1925), one of several successful children, was also an operatic manager, and married the celebrated singer Madame Albani.[25]

[1] IGI (London, Som.); *Gent. Mag.* (1853), ii. 102. [2] PROB 11/856/238. [3] W. Longman, *Tokens of 18th Cent.* 57-58; P.J. Wallis, *18th Cent. Book Trade Index*, 18; *Census of British Newspapers and Periodicals* ed. R.S. Crane and R.B. Kaye, 118. [4] S. Poole, 'Radicalism, Loyalism and "Reign of Terror" in Bath', *Bath Hist.* iii (1990), 123. [5] Longman, 58; J.S. Cox, *Ilchester Mint*, 68; *Gent. Mag.* (1807), ii. 723; *Printers' Reg.* 6 Jan. 1879. [6] Longman, 58-59; PROB 11/1383/823. [7] *Keenes' Bath Jnl.* 30 Oct. 1826. [8] W.B. Todd, *Dir. of Printers*, 9, 86. [9] H.S. Edwards, *Lyrical Drama*, ii. 15-17. [10] *Oxford DNB*. [11] Ibid.; *The Times*, 14 Mar. 1822; W. Wroth, *London Pleasure Gardens*, 316-22; J.G. Southworth, *Vauxhall Gardens*, 21-22, 61-69, 92-110. [12] *The Times*, 18, 19, 26 Oct. 1826. [13] *Keenes' Bath Jnl.* 27 Feb., 3 Apr.; *The Times*, 25 Mar. 1826; Wilts. RO, Bevir mss 1171/9, address. [14] *Devizes Gazette*, 27 Apr., 8, 15 June; *The Times*, 3 June 1826. [15] *Bath Herald*, 17 June; *Bath Gazette*, 20 June 1826. [16] *Devizes Gazette*, 3 Aug. 1826, 31 May 1827. [17] *The Times*, 8 June 1827. [18] Wilts. RO, Peniston mss 451/59, Peniston to Baker, 2 Apr. 1830. [19] Wilts. RO 740/49; G19/1/43. [20] St. Deiniol's Lib. Glynne-Gladstone mss 195, T. to J. Gladstone, 26 June, 27 July 1830. [21] *Berwick Advertiser*, 10, 31 July, 7 Aug. 1830. [22] Dorset RO, Rutter

mss D50/3, Chitty to Gye, 13 Apr., reply, 23 Apr. 1831. [23] Wellington mss WP1/937/6; *Hist. of 'The Times'*, i. 428; J. Grant, *Great Metropolis* (ser. 2), ii. 217. [24] *Oxford DNB*; *The Times*, 27 May, 22 July, 9 Nov. 1840, 5 June 1841. [25] *DNB*; *Oxford DNB*; Edwards, i. 17-30; Sir H. Keppel, *Sailor's Life under Four Sovereigns*, iii. 25-26; *The Times*, 6 Dec. 1878, 13 June 1925.

S.M.F.

HALDIMAND, William (1784–1862), of Ashgrove, nr. Sevenoaks, Kent and 38 Grosvenor Street, Mdx.[1]

IPSWICH   1820–23 Feb. 1827

b. 9 Sept. 1784, 2nd surv. s. of Anthony Francis Haldimand (*d.* 1817), merchant, of 51 St. Mary Axe, London and Jane, da. of J[oshua] Pickersgill, merchant, of 5 Adams Court, Broad Street, London. *unm. d.* 20 Sept. 1862.
   Dir. Bank of England 1809-24, Guardian Fire and Life Assurance 1821-8.

Haldimand came from a Swiss merchant family of Yverdon, with branches in Turin and London, where in 1765 his father became a partner in Zachary, Long and Haldimand of Poultry, a firm specializing in Piedmontese and Italian silks, before establishing his own business in St. Mary Axe in 1769. William was the 11th of his 12 children, and his mother died in 1785 shortly after his brother Frederick's birth. He grew up in the City, received his early education at home with his sisters and, at 16, entered his father's counting house, where he soon showed an aptitude for finance.[2] His father had inherited the estate of an uncle, the distinguished soldier Sir Frederick Haldimand (1718-91), and his business, in which Haldimand and his only surviving brother George became partners in 1806, when they traded as A.F. Haldimand and Sons of Bearbinder Lane, benefited from the family's matrimonial ties with the banking and merchant families of Abrie, Aubergenois, Aubert, Bertrand, Bird, Devos (Doors), Long, Matthews, Mills and Morris.[3] George's marriage in 1807 to Charlotte, daughter of the London alderman and East India Company agent John Prinsep†, furthered Haldimand's entry into fashionable society, and at 25 he became a director of the Bank of England, where his expertise in the foreign exchanges was valued.[4] His father died in 1817, having willed that his estate, which included property in Italy, Switzerland and Clapham Common, should be divided between his four surviving children and their Saunders cousins. The partnership of A.F. Haldimand and Sons of Cateaton Street, to which Charles Morris and Anton Louis Prevost had been admitted, was required to continue trading for at least a further two years, and Haldimand was to have an additional £14,200 immediately, as he had 'not yet married' and received a settlement.[5] Haldimand was known to favour a graduated scale of ingot payments and in 1819 was called before the parliamentary committee on the resumption of cash payments. Being frequently in Paris on business he had observed the regular traffic in French stock among 'travelling gentlemen' and estimated that Britons then held some £10,500,000 in foreign loans. He therefore concluded that 'the spell of capital export was over and that the stage of interest import was setting in'.[6] He was a leading signatory of the City address of condolence to the king on the death of George III.[7]

At the general election of 1820 Haldimand, who claimed to be 'unconnected with party', stood with Thomas Barrett Lennard* as a Whig or Yellow candidate at Ipswich, where the interest cultivated by Henry Baring* in the borough since 1818 was available to him.[8] Barrett Lennard described him as 'a good looking, rich, gentlemanly man', who favoured religious toleration, was friendly to triennial parliaments and abhorred lavish expenditure. It was agreed that in the House Haldimand would 'look to finance' and Lennard 'to other matters'.[9] The political economist David Ricardo* observed:

> I should be glad to have some enlightened commercial men added to ... the House ... I hope that Haldimand will succeed at Ipswich. He is brother to Mrs. Marcet and appears to be a clever man. He is rich, and has much influence amongst his brother merchants.[10]

Money was vital in a contest against the Ipswich bankers, Crickitt and Round, and Haldimand, who, after a severe contest, was returned at an estimated personal cost of £30,000, profited by bringing down four Bank of England directors to support him.[11] The chairing was postponed until July, pending Barrett Lennard's successful petition against Robert Crickitt's return, but Haldimand, who was briefly the target of a counter-petition, presented on 11 May 1820, took his seat immediately and adopted a lower profile in A.F. Haldimand and Sons, which in turn was compensated for by admitting James Morris and John Lewis Prevost as partners.[12]

Except for a couple of rogue votes, Haldimand divided steadily and unstintingly with the main Whig opposition to Lord Liverpool's ministry during his first four years in Parliament, and consistently with Hume and the 'Mountain' for economy, retrenchment and reduced taxation until 1823. He spoke only on trade and finance. The strong 'No Popery' cry in Ipswich had deterred him from declaring for Catholic emancipation until his election was assured, and he

voted only to receive information on Catholic burials, 6 Feb. 1824, and paired against the Irish unlawful societies bill, 15 Feb., and for Catholic relief, 10 May 1825.[13] A radical publication of that year noted that he 'attended frequently, and voted with the opposition'.[14] He voted to disqualify civil officers of the ordnance from voting in parliamentary elections, 12 Apr. 1821, for reform in England, 18 Apr., 9 May 1821, 25 Apr. 1822, 24 Apr. 1823, and Scotland, 26 Feb. 1824, and to receive the radical Greenhoe reform petition, 3 June 1822. He subscribed to Queen Caroline's cause and silently supported the 1820-1 parliamentary campaign on her behalf.[15] He was admitted to Brooks's Club 10 May 1821, sponsored by Lord Lansdowne and Edward Ellice*. During the 1821 recess he paid his dues at Ipswich, where the bailiwick elections proved costly and local charities expected over £200 per annum from each Member.[16] His vote to censure the conduct of the Holy Alliance towards independent states, 20 June 1821, was recalled in November when A.F. Haldimand and Sons underwrote a £3,000,000 loan to the Danish government.[17]

Haldimand voted for the amendment to the address, 5 Feb., and Brougham's resolution calling for unspecified tax reductions, 11 Feb., but with the ministerial majority against Lord Althorp's criticizing their relief proposals, 21 Feb. 1822. Forced to justify his vote to his Ipswich constituents, he explained that he regarded abolition of the sinking fund, which Althorp suggested, as dishonourable to the creditors of the state, of which he as a banker was one.[18] He was added to the select committee on agrarian distress, 23 Feb. He voted in the minority of 25 for a 20s. duty on wheat, 9 May. Drawn into the debate on Western's motion attributing distress to the currency changes, 12 June 1822, he defended the Bank and his own role in the resumption of cash payments in his maiden speech, and pointed out, 'in a very low tone of voice', that it was 'too late to propose the reconsideration of that measure'.[19] He justified the accumulation of gold by the Bank prior to resumption, arguing that 'so long as the Bank was ready to pay its notes in gold, the House had no reason to complain whether there were five millions more or less of their notes in circulation'. Ricardo agreed, but he criticized the Bank for not increasing their issues so as to operate on foreign exchanges and prevent large importations of gold and thus implied that Haldimand's judgement had been at fault. Opposing the military and naval pensions bill, 11 Apr. 1823, when government carried the division by 55-44, he disputed the chancellor of the exchequer Robinson's interpretation of the agreement between the government and the Bank, which was due to expire in July 1828, and he maintained that the bill (which he again divided against, 14 Apr.), 'was a mere delusion, intended to throw dust in the eyes of two classes of persons: those who desired a reduction of taxation and those who wished to support public credit by means of a sinking fund'. He had supported the London merchants' 1820 campaign for trade deregulation and he robustly defended free trade and faulted protectionist arguments in petitions from Sudbury and other silk towns opposed to the repeal of the Spitalfields Act, 21 May 1823.[20] He criticized the East India Company's monopoly and spoke similarly against 'that artificial support which was erroneously called protection', 5, 8, 19, 22 Mar. 1824, but he now conceded the case for a two-year adjustment period and allowances for stock-in-hand, while tariff changes affecting silk were phased in. He had a stake in the proposed St. Katharine's Docks, which he commended as a public benefit, and, amid strong opposition from directors of the London Dock Company, he spoke for the bill to establish it and was a majority teller for its second reading, 2 Apr. 1824. He presented anti-slavery petitions from Ipswich, 5 May 1823, and Clavering, 19 Mar. 1824, on which, as a slave proprietor, he made no comment; nor did he vote for inquiry into the indictment in Demerara of the Methodist missionary John Smith, 11 June, after presenting Ipswich's petition for it, 31 May 1824.[21]

Rallying Ipswich's London freemen at the *Paul's Head*, Cateaton Street, 4 Feb. 1824, following a recent visit to France and Switzerland, he denounced the Holy Alliance, as he had done in 1821, criticized ministers for failing to curb its 'despotic intentions' and praised liberal Spain. He argued that 'only by returning men of independent principles to Parliament' like himself, might the country 'resume its commanding power' and signified his intention of seeking re-election.[22] According to Prevost, as contractors in 1821 and 1823 A.F. Haldimand and Sons had been 'much interested in the Spanish loans which were being negotiated, and in order to get the earliest possible information employed special couriers between London and Paris and had their own clippers in the Channel'. On 3 May 1824 they found it necessary to publish a letter in *The Times* advising clients of a delay in half-yearly dividends, as their agents, Ardoin, Hubbard and Company, had not been paid by the Spanish government.[23] Haldimand was shouted down at the bailiffs' election at Ipswich, 8 Sept. 1824, and charged with holding 'republican principles'; and his absences abroad for 'health reasons' in 1825 and 1826 encouraged rumours that the cause was financial and the sufferer his business.[24] He was granted a month's leave on

account of ill health, 18 Feb., and again, 14 Apr. 1825. He had resigned as director of the Bank in 1824, but he remained with Guardian Assurance and in 1825 negotiated successfully with the 2nd Earl Grosvenor, Seth Smith and William Cubitt for a 99-year lease on Belgrave Square, where he had 49 houses built: 16 to be owned by George Haldimand, 14 by himself, eight by Prevost, four by Smith and three by Cubitt.[25] He went to Ipswich for the 1825 bailiwick elections and, unlike Barrett Lennard, sought a second return at the next general election despite the additional financial burden imposed by the corporation's October 1825 ruling that Members should bear the full cost of future borough elections. He stipulated that he would not underwrite the return of two Whigs.[26] He is not known to have voted in 1826, but speaking briefly on the navigation laws, in response to Alexander Baring, 13 May, he called for such tax reductions as would enable British merchants to compete with foreigners in world markets, and close scrutiny of the post-war tax burden which left government expenditure at £60,000,000 a year. He had commenced his Ipswich canvass in April by apologizing for his poor attendance, depositing £5,000 at Henry Alexander's bank, and introducing the political economist and editor of the *Globe* Robert Torrens as his colleague; but poor health caused him to return to Aix-les-Bains before the election, leaving his brother George, his friend Richard Raikes, and business colleagues to campaign on his behalf.[27] Denounced as a republican, atheist and absentee, he was returned at great cost with Torrens but they were ousted on petition, 23 Feb. 1827.[28]

Haldimand remained abroad. The partnership of A.F. Haldimand and Sons was liquidated, 31 Dec. 1827, and their affairs left entirely in the hands of Morris, Prevost and Company.[29] In 1828 he settled at Denantou near Lausanne, where he had retained property and citizenship rights and he used his fortune to aid the Greek insurgents; to endow a hospital for the poor at Aix; to establish an Anglican church at Ouchy (although, as a religious sceptic 'he hardly visited it'); and to purchase *rentes* to strengthen the new Orleans dynasty in France.[30] His best known act of largesse was the endowment of an asylum for the blind at Lausanne at an estimated cost of £24,000. This became his life's work.[31] It was rumoured that he would stand for Nottingham in 1830 and 1831, but he did not do so.[32] In 1845 he became active in Swiss politics as a liberal committed to a free market in Europe and religious freedom.[33] He died without issue at Denantou in September 1862, predeceased in 1852 by his brother George, and was buried in the church at Ouchy.[34] His will, which was proved in London, 7 Nov. 1862, provided for the Lausanne asylum and all his relations, the principal legatees being his nephews and nieces Frank Marcet, James and Jane Morris, Sophia Romilly and Alexander Prevost. He had donated General Sir Frederick Haldimand's papers to the British Museum in 1857.[35]

[1] Draws on A. Hartman, *Gallerie Beruhmter Schweizer der Neuzeit*, 2 vols. (1868-71). [2] Ibid.; A. Prevost, *Hist. Morris, Prevost and Company*, 1-6. [3] *Oxford DNB* sub Sir Frederick Haldimand; *Gent. Mag.* (1791), i. 586; Prevost, 6; *Misc. Gen. et Her.* (n.s.), iv. 369. [4] *Gent. Mag.* (1807), ii. 1171; J.H. Clapham, *Bank of England*, ii. 68. [5] *Gent. Mag.* (1817), ii. 474; PROB 11/159/630; IR26/713/1194; Prevost, 6. [6] B. Hilton, *Corn, Cash, Commerce*, 42, 48, 49, 64, 88, 89; Clapham, ii. 67-69; I.P.H. Duffy, 'Discount Policy of Bank of England during Suspension of Cash Payments, 1797-1821' *EcHR* (ser. 2), xxxv (1982), 67-82. [7] *The Times*, 1, 6 Mar. 1820. [8] Ibid. 22, 28 Feb., 4 Mar.; Essex RO, Barrett Lennard mss D/DL/C60, St. Vincent to Barrett Lennard, 20 Feb. 1820; Suff. RO (Ipswich), J. Glyde, 'Materials for Parl. Hist. Ipswich', ff. 87-90; and *New Suff. Garland*, 435-54. [9] Essex RO, Barrett Lennard mss C58/90, 91. [10] *Works and Corresp. of Ricardo* ed. P. Sraffa, viii. 163. [11] *Ipswich Jnl.* 4, 11 Mar.; *Morning Chron.* 13-15, 21, 24 Mar.; *The Times*, 15, 21 Mar. 17 Apr. 1820; Glyde, *New Suff. Garland*, 453. [12] *Morning Chron.* 12 May, 14, 15 June; *The Times*, 8 July 1820; Prevost, 6. [13] *Suff. Chron.* 18 Mar. 1820. [14] *Session of Parl. 1825*, p. 467. [15] *The Times*, 12, 16 Aug. 1820. [16] *Suff. Chron.* 8, 15 Sept.; *The Times*, 11 Sept. 1821; Barrett Lennard mss C61, Lennard to fa. 30 Oct. 1821; O41/1-3. [17] *The Times*, 19 Nov. 1821. [18] *Suff. Chron.* 13 July; *Ipswich Jnl.* 20 July 1822. [19] *The Times*, 13 June 1822. [20] Ibid. 31 May 1820, 22, 23 May 1823. [21] Ibid. 20 Mar., 1 June 1824. [22] Ibid. 5 Feb. 1824. [23] Prevost, 7-8. [24] *The Times*, 13 Sept. 1824; Glyde, 'Materials for Parl. Hist. Ipswich', ff. 96-100. [25] Prevost, 8; *Survey of London*, xl. 35-44. [26] *Ipswich Jnl.* 10, 17 Sept.; *Bury and Norwich Post*, 7 Sept. 1825. [27] *Suff. Chron.* 29 Apr. 8, 13, 20, 27 May, 3, 10, 17 June; *The Times*, 5 June 1826. [28] *Ipswich Jnl.* 24 June 1826, 24 Feb. 1827. [29] *London Gazette*, 1 Jan. 1828; Prevost, 7. [30] Hartman; *Oxford DNB*. [31] W. de la Rive, *Vie de Haldimand*. [32] Add. 51813, Denman to Holland [July 1830]. [33] Hartman. [34] PROB 11/2137/634; *Gent. Mag.* (1851), ii. 332; (1862), ii. 510. [35] IR26/2291/949; Add. 21631-895.

M.M.E.

HALL, Benjamin (1802–1867), of Abercarn and Llanofer Court, Mon.[1]

MONMOUTH	3 May 1831–18 July 1831
MONMOUTH	1832–1837
MARYLEBONE	1837–1859

b. 8 Nov. 1802, 1st. s. of Benjamin Hall[†] of Abercarn and Hensol Castle, Glam. and Charlotte, da. of Richard Crawshay, ironmaster, of Cyfarthfa Castle, Glam. *educ.* Westminster 1814; Christ Church, Oxf. 1820. *m.* 4 Dec. 1823, Augusta, da. and coh. of Benjamin Waddington of Llanofer, 2s. *d.v.p.* 1 da. *suc.* fa. 1817; *cr.* bt. 16 Aug. 1838; Bar. Llanover 29 June 1859. *d.* 27 Apr. 1867. Pres. bd. of health Aug. 1854-July 1855; PC 29 Nov. 1854; first. commr. of works and public buildings July 1855-Feb. 1858.

Sheriff, Mon. 1826-7, ld.-lt. 1861-*d.*

Hall was the eldest of seven children born to Benjamin Hall, the dean of Llandaff's barrister son, and the wealthy ironmaster Richard Crawshay's daughter Charlotte. Until 1808, when Crawshay bought the 3,000-acre Abercarn estate for the family, he was raised in London, where he and his brothers later became townboys at Westminster with their maternal cousin Richard Franklen, whose father managed his kinsmen the Grants' Glamorgan estate of Gnoll Castle. In 1810 Hall's father 'Slender Ben', then Member for Totnes, inherited an equal share (three eighths) with Crawshay's son William in the Cyfarthfa works, the remaining two passing to Crawshay's nephew Joseph Bailey.[2] Unlike Bailey, he resisted selling out to Crawshay until 1817, when, dying of consumption and £100,000 in debt after purchasing Hensol Castle, Glamorgan and his election for that county in 1814, he did so for £60,000, with an additional £30,000 for his share in the Hirwaun works.[3] His fortune was 'wholly exhausted', but Hall's mother (*d.* 1839), who in 1821 married Samuel Hawkins of the Court Herbert family, received Abercarn for life and £2,200 a year; and a trust fund provided Hall, who inherited fully at 21, £1,000 a year at 18, and £10,000 for each for his siblings.[4]

Hall's relationship with Hawkins was frosty, and after Oxford, where the archbishop of York's sons, Charles and George Vernon*, became his lifelong friends, he and Franklen toured Wales in 1821 and Scotland and the Lake District in 1822, whence they were summoned back following his brother Henry's death.[5] His marriage to Augusta Waddington, upon whom Llanofer was settled, was planned well before Sir Charles Morgan* of Tredegar presided at his coming of age celebrations in November 1823. They were married by his grandfather the following month and took Nieuport House, Almeley, Herefordshire. At over six foot four, and of the Crawshay build, Hall had already earned the nickname 'Big Ben', later given in his honour to Parliament's clock.[6] As sheriff of Monmouthshire in 1826, he sold Hensol to William Crawshay junior for £27,500 and purchased Court Lettice, near Llanofer, and The Mardy prior to returning to Abercarn, which his mother vacated.[7] Reports that he would contest Monmouth in the anti-Beaufort interest that year were quickly discounted.[8] The Halls joined the Tredegar party at the Brecon eisteddfod that autumn and Augusta, who in 1834 took the bardic name 'Gwenynen Gwent', embarked on the passionate promotion of Welsh culture, language, and traditions for which, as Lady Llanover, she became renowned.[9] In January 1828 she inherited Llanofer, where Hall engaged Thomas Hopper to build a new mansion.[10]

William Booth Grey of Dyffryn, Aberdare and Sir Ronald Craufurd Ferguson* sponsored his admission to Brooks's, 17 Feb. 1829, and in June that year the 6th duke of Beaufort vainly recommended him to the duke of Wellington for a baronetcy, describing him as 'a young man of considerable fortune in Monmouthshire', whose father was 'known to [Lord] Liverpool but died before the honour had been conferred'.[11] He and his family spent the next year on the continent, often in the company of his sister-in-law Frances and her husband Christian, Baron Bunsen, the future Prussian ambassador. At the 1830 general election they risked the perils of the revolution in France to return to England, where Hall had directed the London attorney Vizard (who recommended him to the Broughams) to find him a good seat, preparatory to attacking the 'Beauforts in Monmouthshire next turn'.[12]

Addressing the Monmouthshire reform meeting he had promoted to the Morgan family's annoyance, Hall publicized his intention of opposing Beaufort's sons as anti-reformers at the next opportunity, 17 Mar. 1831.[13] He defined himself as 'a staunch reformer, wholly averse to annual parliaments and still more so to universal suffrage', and asked:

Are the wishes of those who represent the whole wealth and importance of the county to be spurned and set at naught by the two great houses of Beaufort and Tredegar? ... If the Members do not agree with their constituents they must be ousted in favour of men that will.[14]

He chaired the meeting at Usk, 11 Apr., that adopted William Addams Williams* of Llangibby Castle as the reform candidate for Monmouthshire and, confirming his candidature for Monmouth afterwards, he pledged support for the Grey ministry's reform bill, economy, retrenchment and the 'abolition of all sinecures and ill-merited pensions'. He canvassed the Morgan stronghold of Newport, 20 Apr.[15] The Loyal and Patriotic Fund contributed £500 to his costs, and despite concern at his overreliance on Newport and its new freemen, sanctioned by his attorney Thomas Philips, acting for his partner-at-law the town clerk Thomas Prothero, he remained active and confident throughout.[16] On the hustings, he reaffirmed his support for reform and retrenchment and appealed to the anti-Beaufort lobby, but denied authorship of a scurrilous attack on Beaufort family sinecures, printed in the *Spectator*, 30 Apr. 1831. He outpolled the duke's heir Lord Worcester* by 168-149 and was chaired and fêted.[17] Hall presented petitions from the anti-Beaufort parties in Monmouth, Newport and Usk seeking provisions 'to disqualify persons created burgesses upon no claim of right from hereafter voting', 4 July 1831. He divided for the reintroduced reform bill at its second reading, 6 July, and against adjournment, 12 July 1831.[18] He was unseated on the 18th, after Worcester's petition challenging the legality of 73 of his Newport votes, alleging bribery, and confirming the rights of the Monmouth and Usk burgesses was upheld.[19] He had had no opportunity to demonstrate his considerable debating skills, but authorized the *Monmouthshire Merlin* to announce that he had been present and voted with ministers in all divisions on the reform bill, and that his attendance had averaged ten hours a day, with one 16-hour session.[20]

Hall addressed reform meetings in October and December 1831, stewarded at the Monmouthshire assembly at the *Angel* in Abergavenny, 16 Jan. 1832, and in July announced his candidature as a Liberal for Monmouth Boroughs, where he defeated Worcester at the general election in December, but only narrowly avoided having to defend a petition.[21] After another costly contest and petition in Monmouth in 1835, in 1837 he chose to stand for Marylebone, which he represented continuously until raised to the peerage in 1859 on the recommendation of Lord Palmerston*, in whose ministry (as commissioner of works) he had promoted the 1855 Act establishing the metropolitan board of works.[22] Though a life-long Anglican, Hall, who died at his London home in Great Stanhope Street in April 1867 after a long and painful illness, championed the cause of ecclesiastical reform, including the use of the Welsh language in the Principality's churches and the admission of Dissenters to Oxford and Cambridge.[23] His sons having predeceased him, the barony was extinguished, and he left everything to his wife, who in 1896 was succeeded by their daughter, Augusta Charlotte, wife of the Catholic squire John Arthur Edward Herbert (formerly Jones) of Llanarth Court, Monmouthshire and mother of Ivor Caradoc Herbert, Liberal Member for Monmouthshire South from 1906 until his elevation to the peerage in 1917 as Baron Treowen.[24]

[1] A detailed sketch of Hall's life is available in a series of articles by M. Fraser in *NLWJ*, xii (1961-2), 1-17, 250-87; xiii (1963-4), 29-47, 209-34, 313-28; xiv (1965-6), 35-52, 194-213, 285-300, 437-50; xv (1967-8), 72-88, 113-26, 310-24, 389-404; xvi (1969-70), 23-42, 105-22, 272-92. [2] M.S. Taylor, *Crawshays of Cyfarthfa Castle*, 26-27; Fraser, *NLWJ*, xii. 1-9. [3] J.P. Addis, *Crawshay Dynasty*, 40, 158, 173; Fraser, *NLWJ*, xii. 9-13; *HP Commons, 1790-1820*, iv. 123-4. [4] PROB 11/1596/479; IR26/711/776; Addis, 153. [5] Fraser, *NLWJ*, xii. 252-63. [6] J. Bradney, *Mon. Co. Hist.* i (2b), 386; NLW, Bunsen and Waddington mss 1/78, 119; Fraser, *NLWJ*, xii. 255, 263-87; xiii. 29-32. [7] Taylor, 46; Fraser, *NLWJ*, xiii. 32; *Mon. Co. Hist.* ii (2b), 385; *Mon. Merlin*, 2 Apr. 1831. [8] *Courier*, 5, 15 June; *Morning Chron.* 10 June; *The Times*, 10 June 1826; NLW, Tredegar mss 57/45. [9] H.M. Vaughan, *S. Wales Squires*, 128-35; Fraser, 'Lady Llanover

and her Circle', *Trans. Hon. Soc. Cymmrodorion* (1968), 170-96; *Oxford DNB sub* Hall, Augusta. [10] Fraser, *NLWJ*, xiii. 35-38. [11] Wellington mss WP1/1023/7; 1029/4. [12] Fraser, *NLWJ*, xiii. 40-42; Gwent RO D/43/2358, 2782-6; Bunsen and Waddington mss 2/42; *Life and Letters of Baroness Bunsen*, i. 342; Brougham mss, J. to H. Brougham, 27 Aug. 1830. [13] D. Williams, *John Frost*, 59-65; Gwent RO D/949/221; *The Times*, 11 Feb.; *Mon. Merlin*, 12 Feb., 12, 19, 26 Mar. 1831; Fraser, *Presenting Mon.* xii (1961), 8-10. [14] *Mon. Merlin*. 26 Mar. 1831. [15] Ibid. 9, 16, 23 Apr.; *Cambrian*, 16, 23 Apr. 1831. [16] *Mon. Merlin*, 7 May 1831; C. Williams, 'The Great Hero of the Newport Rising: Thomas Philips, Reform and Chartism', *WHR*, xxi (2003), 488-92. [17] *Mon. Merlin*, 14 May 1831. [18] Ibid. 9 July 1831; *CJ*, lxxxvi. 613. [19] *Mon. Merlin*, 14 May, 16 July; *Cambrian*, 14 May, 23 July; *The Times*, 19 July 1831; NLW, Sir Leonard Twiston Davies mss (Twiston Davies mss) 4113, 4137-41, 4169, 4175, 4235, 5294, 5934, 5994; *CJ*, lxxxvi. 537, 645, 655. [20] *Mon. Merlin*, 23 July 1831. [21] Gwent RO D/749/211-35; *Mon. Merlin*, 1, 8 Oct., 26 Nov., 10 Dec. 1831, 21 Jan., 23 June, 7 July, 24 Nov., 8, 15, 22 Dec. 1832; C. Williams, 492-4; D. Williams, 67-73; Twiston Davies mss 6077. [22] C. Williams, 494-7; M. Cragoe, *Culture, Politics, and National Identity in Wales, 1832-1886*, pp. 126-7; *Oxford DNB*. [23] B. Hall, *Letter to Archbishop of Canterbury on State of Church* (1850); *Letter to Rev. C. Phillips* (1852); *Illustrated London News*, 4 May; *Gent Mag.* (1867), i. 814; Fraser, *NLWJ*, xvi. 281-7. [24] *Oxford DNB*.

M.M.E.

HALLYBURTON, Hon. Douglas (1777–1841), of Hallyburton House, Forfar.

FORFARSHIRE (ANGUS)   31 Jan. 1832–1841

b. 10 Oct. 1777, o.s. of George Gordon, 4th earl of Aboyne [S] (*d.* 1794), and 2nd w. Lady Mary Douglas, da. of James, 14th earl of Morton [S]. *m.* 16 July 1807, Louisa, da. and h. of Sir Edward Leslie, 1st bt., MP[I], of Tarbert, co. Kerry, *s.p. suc.* to Forfar estates of cos. Hon. Hamilton Douglas Hallyburton of Pitcur 1784 and assumed name of Hallyburton. *styled* Lord Douglas Gordon Hallyburton and granted precedence as yr. son of mq. by royal lic. 24 June 1836–*d. d.* 25 Dec. 1841.

Ensign 1 Ft. Gds. 1793; capt. 113 Ft. 1795, 22 Ft. 1796, 1 Ft. Gds. 1798; maj. army 1803; lt.-col. 1810; maj. Corsican rangers (half-pay) 1810-26.

Hallyburton, as this Member became on inheriting his cousin's extensive Forfarshire estates and taking the name of his maternal grandfather James Hallyburton of Pitcur, was a brother-in-law of William Beckford[†] of Fonthill and half-brother of George Gordon, 5th earl of Aboyne (from 1836 9th marquess of Huntly, a Tory representative peer, 1796-1806, 1807-18, and father of Lord Strathavon*). A shrewd soldier, landowner and bank director who counted Henry Brougham*, Lord Lansdowne and the duke of Sussex among his personal correspondents and friends, his military career included service in Austria, whence he returned with dispatches from Colonel Crawford in 1796, and seven years (1803-10) as an assistant to the quartermaster-general in Ireland, which equipped

him well to develop his substantial interests in banking and transport in Dundee and Ireland.[1] A regular speaker and sponsor of Whig causes at county meetings, he presided at the election of the Foxite William Maule for Forfarshire at the general election of 1826, and of the Wellington ministry's colonial secretary Sir George Murray for Perthshire in 1830. He nominated the Grey ministry's lord advocate Francis Jeffrey for Perth Burghs at both elections in 1831.[2] He had himself been considered for Forfarshire in 1807, before Lord Melville ruled him out as a supporter of Catholic relief. Writing to lord chancellor Brougham, 17 Mar. 1831, of his aspirations, he observed:

> Perhaps you would ask me do I wish to come into Parliament. My answer would be, not very violently. I feel no *necessity* on the subject. Twenty years ago, had circumstances been propitious, I should have felt differently, but having turned the corner of 50, I am apt to think it is rather late to begin a parliamentary life, with much hope of satisfaction to oneself, or benefit to others. If elected and in health, I would transact the essential business of my constituents honestly and zealously. This much I think I may say, without any breach of modesty; but this is not all I should have aspired to, had events brought me in to Parliament at a fresher period of my life. If it becomes a question of *duty*, however, the case is entirely changed, and personal considerations ought then to be kept as much as possible out of sight.[3]

He staked his claim to the post-reform Dundee constituency the following month, and at the Forfarshire meeting on 16 May he took the lord lieutenant, Lord Airlie, to task for refusing to convene reform meetings, promoting hostile petitions and sponsoring his brothers Donald Ogilvy* and William Ogilvy* as anti-reform candidates.[4] In September 1831 he abandoned his consultations with the boundary commissioner Sir John Dalrymple[†] and his canvass of Dundee, where his refusal to support a precipitate repeal of the corn laws and defence of Huskisson's policies had left him trailing behind the radical George Kinloch[†], and contested Forfarshire 'under the auspices' of Maule, whose elevation to the peerage as Lord Panmure at the coronation had created a vacancy.[5] Although outpolled by Donald Ogilvy, his subsequent petition alleging partiality by Airlie succeeded.[6]

In his maiden speech, 8 Mar. 1832, Hallyburton endorsed a petition from Arbroath for repeal of the hemp duties and used statistics to demonstrate that doing so would boost the Forfarshire trade to the detriment of their Russian and German competitors without diminishing exchequer revenues. He divided steadily for the details of the revised reform bill and voted for its third reading, 22 Mar. He voted for the address calling on the king to appoint only ministers who would carry it unimpaired, 10 May, and staked his claim to the extinct Halyburton [*sic*] peerage as the sole surviving male descendant of his grandfather Lord Morton, when peerage creations were mooted.[7] He testified to the strong pro-reform minority in Perthshire when the county's anti-reform petition was presented, 23 May, but admitted his failure to carry one there endorsing the government's proposals. He divided for the Irish reform bill at its second reading, 25 May, and against Murray's amendments for increasing the Scottish county representation, 1 June, and adding certain Perthshire parishes to Clackmannan and Kinross, 15 June. On 6 June he seconded an abortive proposal to bar Scottish clergymen, whose virtues he extolled, from voting in parliamentary elections in order 'to keep the character of the clergy ... free from all political taint or secular feelings'. He maintained that the proposal was consistent with the principle of the bill, accorded with 'the feelings' of the Scottish people and merely extended the resolution (in clause 36) denying votes to sheriffs and sheriff's clerks. He voted against Alexander Baring's bill to exclude insolvent debtors from Parliament the same day. He divided with government on relations with Portugal, 9 Feb., the navy civil departments bill 6 Apr., and the Russian-Dutch loan, 12, 16, 20 July, but voted with other Scottish Members against the third reading of the malt drawback bill, 2 Apr. 1832.

Hallyburton was returned unopposed for Forfarshire as a Liberal at the general election of 1832, defeated a Conservative there in 1835 and sat undisturbed until his retirement on account of ill health in 1841.[8] To curb speculation about his increasing debility, his physician had informed *The Times* that 'the malady is corporeal, weakening the powers of speech as well as the muscular powers generally, but unaccompanied by anything like mental derangement in the proper and usual sense of the word'.[9] Known as Lord Douglas Gordon Hallyburton following his half-brother's succession as marquess of Huntly, he died in London on Christmas Day that year, recalled as a lifelong Whig and promoter of the Perth-Dundee railway. He was buried in Kensal Green cemetery.[10] His will, of which his nephew and successor as Member for Forfarshire, Lord John Frederick Gordon Hallyburton (*d.* 1878), was the main beneficiary, was proved under £100 in London, 16 June 1842, and £27,000 in Ireland in 1843. Probate was confirmed at Forfar sheriff's court, 25 Jan. 1856, over four years after the death of his widow and when proceeds from the sale of the Irish estates had been reinvested in Scottish property as Hallyburton had directed.[11]

[1] *Gent. Mag.* (1842), i. 324; Brougham mss, Hallyburton to Brougham, 17 Oct. 1829. [2] *The Times*, 5 July 1826; Brougham mss, Hallyburton to Brougham, 25 Aug.; *Stirling Advertiser*, 27 Aug. 1830; *Kelso Mail*, 13 Jan., 6 June; *Perthshire Courier*, 26 May 1831. [3] *HP Commons, 1790-1820*, ii. 541; Brougham mss. [4] NAS GD16/34/387/8/12-17; *Dundee, Perth and Cupar Advertiser*, 14 Apr.; *Perthshire Courier*, 2 June 1831. [5] *Dundee, Perth and Cupar Advertiser*, 23, 30 June, 15, 22 Sept. 1831, 2 Feb. 1832; Brougham mss, Hallyburton to Brougham, 22 Aug. 1831. [6] *Perthshire Courier*, 29 Sept., 6 Oct. 1831; NAS GD16/34/387/8/66; Dundee City Archives, Camperdown mss GD/Ca/Tin Box EC/12/11. [7] Brougham mss, Hallyburton to Brougham, 29 Mar. 1832. [8] *Scotsman*, 15, 22 Dec.; Add. 51837, Panmure to Holland, 22 Dec.; *Dundee, Perth and Cupar Advertiser*, 27 Dec. 1832. [9] *The Times*, 7, 8 June 1841. [10] *Perthshire Courier*, 6 Jan.; *Gent. Mag.* (1842), i. 324. [11] PROB 11/1964/407; IR26/1613/662; NAS SC47/40/23; SC70/1/74.

M.M.E.

HALSE, James (1769–1838), of St. Ives, Cornw. and 25 Half Moon Street, Mdx.

St. Ives	1826–1830
St. Ives	1831–14 May 1838

bap. 28 Jan. 1769,[1] s. of John Halse and w. Johanna. *m.* 14 Apr. 1800, Mary, da. of Thomas Hichens of St. Ives, *s.p. d.* 14 May 1838.

Lt.-col. commdt. St. Ives vols. 1803.

Halse, who was apparently descended from a 'historian of Cornwall of the same name', settled in St. Ives around 1790, established himself as an attorney and became town clerk and an alderman. He was also 'one of the most enterprising and successful adventurers in mines' of his day, and he 'derived a large part of his substantial fortune' from the Wheal Reeth tin mine, which he had reopened. His other main venture was the St. Ives Consols tin mine, which he opened in 1818 and used to build an electoral interest by creating the village of Halsetown, within the borough boundary, to accommodate his workers.[2] He had for some years been the champion of the 'independent' interest and at the general election of 1820 he returned both Members, but his bitter rival, Sir Christopher Hawkins of Trewithen, retaliated by harassing him and his supporters with a 'constant succession of prosecutions'; Halse was acquitted of bribery charges in 1821. At the general election of 1826 he was returned in second place behind Hawkins, after another bitter contest.[3]

He was a silent Member whose occasional votes exhibited independent Tory leanings. He divided against Catholic relief, 6 Mar., and for the spring guns bill, 23 Mar. 1827. He was granted six weeks' leave for urgent business, 'having served on an election committee', 30 Mar. He voted against Canning's ministry for the separation of bankruptcy jurisdiction from chancery, 22 May, but with them for the grant to improve water communications in Canada, 12 June 1827. He divided for repeal of the Test Acts, 26 Feb., but against Catholic relief, 12 May 1828. He voted with the duke of Wellington's ministry against abolition of the office of lieutenant-general of the ordnance, 4 July, but divided for the corporate funds bill, 10 July 1828. In February 1829 Planta, the patronage secretary, correctly predicted that he would side 'with government' for Catholic emancipation. He voted accordingly, 6 Mar., but was in the largely Whig minority for allowing Daniel O'Connell to take his seat without swearing the oath of supremacy, 18 May 1829. He divided against Jewish emancipation, 17 May 1830. He was presumably the 'James Hulse' who voted for the grant for South American missions and against abolition of the death penalty for forgery, 7 June 1830. At the general election that summer he was defeated at St. Ives by the new interest established by Wellington's nephew, William Pole Long Wellesley*.[4]

By the time of the 1831 general election Halse had reasserted his position and he was returned unopposed in conjunction with the reformer Edward Bulwer Lytton.[5] He divided for the second reading of the Grey ministry's reintroduced reform bill, 6 July, the inclusion of Gateshead in schedule D, 5 Aug., and the proposed division of counties, 11 Aug. 1831. However, he voted for counsel to be heard on Appleby's case against disfranchisement, 12 July, and the disfranchisement of Saltash, 26 July. It is not certain whether he divided against the bill's passage, 21 Sept., or was absent. He presented a St. Ives petition for repeal of the stamp duty on marine insurance policies, 11 Aug. He voted with ministers to punish only those guilty of bribery in the Dublin election, 23 Aug., but divided against the Maynooth grant, 26 Sept. He was allowed a month's leave for urgent business, 5 Oct. He was absent from the division on the second reading of the revised reform bill, 17 Dec. 1831, but voted against the enfranchisement of Tower Hamlets, 28 Feb. 1832.[6] He was absent from the divisions on the third reading of the bill, 22 Mar., and Lord Ebrington's motion for an address asking the king to appoint only ministers committed to carrying an unimpaired measure, 10 May. He divided against the second reading of the Irish bill, 25 May. He voted against ministers for immediate consideration of the abolition of slavery, 24 May, permanent provision for the Irish poor by a tax on absentees, 19 June, and on the Russian-Dutch loan, 12 July 1832.

At the general election of 1832 Halse was returned for St. Ives, now a single Member borough, as a 'reformer'. He sat until his death in May 1838, by which time he was a 'Conservative'.[7] He left the residue of his estate to his nephew, Edwin Ley, the recorder of St. Ives; his personalty was sworn under £70,000.[8]

[1] IGI (Cornw.) [2] 2 Dod's Parl. Companion (1838), 118; Gent. Mag. (1838), ii. 214; Parochial Hist. Cornw. ii. 260, 271; D. Barton, Hist. Tin Mining in Cornw. 66; C. Noall, St. Ives Mining District, i. 64-66. [3] West Briton, 17 Mar. 1820, 6 Apr. 1821; The Times, 15, 16 June 1826. [4] West Briton, 13 Aug. 1830. [5] R. Cornw. Gazette, 26 Mar., 7 May 1831. [6] The Times, 29 Feb. 1832. [7] Dod (1833), 120; (1838), 118. [8] PROB 11/1900/594; IR26/1487/533.

T.A.J.

HAMILTON, Lord Archibald (1770–1827), of Chapel Street, Mdx.

LANARKSHIRE   1802–4 Sept. 1827

b. 6 Mar. 1770, 2nd s. of Lord Archibald Hamilton[†] (from 1799 9th duke of Hamilton [S] and 6th duke of Brandon [GB], who d. 1819) and Lady Harriet Stewart, da. of Alexander, 6th earl of Galloway [S]. educ. Harrow 1776; ?Eton 1785; Christ Church, Oxf. 1788; L. Inn 1790, called 1799. unm. 1 illegit s. d. 4 Sept. 1827.[1]
    Col. Lanark militia 1800-2; rect. Glasgow Univ. 1811-12.

Hamilton, whose elder brother Alexander succeeded their father as 10th duke of Hamilton in December 1819, was one of the handful of Scottish Foxite Members who had defied the Tory hegemony created by Henry Dundas[†]. He did not, however, belong to the set of Edinburgh Whigs dominated by Henry Cockburn and Francis Jeffrey*, though he maintained communications with them. He had been raised and educated in England, and London was his habitual milieu.[2] The 'miracle' of his unexpected success in securing by 149-144 the appointment of a select committee, which he chaired, to investigate the anachronistic municipal government of the Scottish royal burghs, 6 May 1819, had crowned his two-year campaign as the parliamentary spokesman for their reform; and at the Glasgow Fox birthday dinner, 24 Jan. 1820, one of the toasts was to 'Lord Archibald Hamilton and the speedy reform of the Scottish burghs'.[3] At the general election in March he was returned for Lanarkshire, unopposed after the withdrawal of a rival, for the sixth consecutive time. Portraying himself as the representative not merely of the freeholders but of the unfranchised inhabitants, he said he would 'endeavour to reconcile the interests and the feelings of the higher and of the other classes of society, by supporting the claims of the former to a just authority, and of the latter to their constitutional rights'.[4]

In the House he continued to vote with his Whig friends on most major issues, though he was not a thick and thin attender in this period and was not conspicuous in the campaign for economy and retrenchment. On the address, 28 Apr. 1820, he urged on the Liverpool ministry 'the necessity of attending to the distress' of western Scotland, where 'many persons ... were in such an absolute state of destitution that they looked on their existence as a burden which they could scarcely support'. He suggested subsidized emigration to save unemployed handloom weavers from catastrophe and restore tranquillity to the Glasgow area. On 4 May he had the royal burghs select committee reappointed: 12 of its 21 members survived from 1819, but the newcomers were predominantly ministerialists. He presented petitions for reform, 13, 30 June, and brought up the report, which recommended change, 14 July.[5] His motion of 15 May condemning the appointment of Sir Patrick Murray[†] as an additional Scottish baron of exchequer, in defiance of the judicial commissioners' recommendation of abolition, was only beaten by 189-177; but 'some mismanagement afterwards' between him, Brougham and the opposition leader Tierney rather ruined the effect of this 'success'.[6] Ministers announced that a new vacancy would not be filled, 24 June, but on 14 July Hamilton was obliged to correct the impression given in a *Morning Chronicle* report that he had accused them of appointing Murray in order to remove him as an 'inconvenient' candidate for Perthshire.[7] He secured a return of the current freeholders' rolls of the 33 Scottish counties with a view to basing a reform motion on them, 25 May, when he indicated that he would allow existing freeholders to continue voting but would advocate extension of the franchise to men 'possessed of considerable property'. His sister Lady Anne Hamilton was a lady-in-waiting to Queen Caroline and rode in her carriage on her entry to London with Alderman Matthew Wood* on 6 June.[8] That day in the House Hamilton said that ministers had 'long prosecuted her with ignominy and insult' and 'now brought forward what was tantamount to a charge ... against her'. He opposed and was a minority teller against Wilberforce's compromise resolution, 22 June, when his amendment for insertion of her name in the liturgy was crushed by 391-124. He got peevish with the leader of the House Lord Castlereagh for refusing to disclose how government intended to provide for Caroline, 3 July. The chancellor of the exchequer Vansittart suggested that they were willing to offer a temporary allowance of 6*d*. per bushel on malt made from bigg, 5 July, but Hamilton

rejected this as inadequate and went ahead with his motion condemning the recent equalization of the Scottish with the English duties, which was defeated by 53-43. He opposed the aliens bill, 7 July, and on the 25th denied that his criticism of ministers' conduct towards Caroline was done 'with a view of inflaming anyone either in or out of doors'. On 17 Aug. Thomas Creevey* reported how, in the Lords' examination of Caroline, 'Lady Anne Hamilton waits behind the queen, and ... for effect and delicacy's sake, she leans on her brother Archy's arm, though she is full six feet high, and bears a striking resemblance to one of Lord Derby's great red deer'. Lady Granville commented that Hamilton, who was very deaf, 'sat by his sister ... and insisted upon her repeating to him all that was going on, which put this amiable virgin in a somewhat awkward predicament'.[9] Two days later she reported a ludicrous episode at dinner when Lord Erskine

> began by abusing the bareness of the soil in Scotland, and said that some Ayrshire sheep coming to London were terrified at the sight of the trees when they arrived in England. Lord Archibald, who instead of sheep heard men, exclaimed, 'They were impostors, depend upon it, they were impostors', and [was] irritated by the shouts of laughter, and never listening to Lord Erskine bawling out, 'Sheep, Lord Archibald, sheep'.[10]

In the Commons, 21 Aug. 1820, Hamilton gave 'reluctant' support to Osborne's unsuccessful amendment for the prorogation of Parliament, in opposition to Tierney.

According to the advanced Whig Henry Grey Bennet*, at a party meeting at Burlington House, 22 Jan. 1821, it was arranged that Lord Tavistock would give notice of a motion of censure on ministers' conduct towards the queen for the 26th, and Hamilton of one for an address to the king calling for restoration of her name to the liturgy for the 29th. Before the House met the following day, a reluctant Tavistock was persuaded by Lord Sefton* to let Hamilton's motion take precedence; and, after eight new Members had been sworn in, Hamilton gave notice accordingly for the 26th. On 24 Jan. Tavistock gave notice of his censure motion for 5 Feb. (Grey Bennet reckoned that the party meeting had 'passed off unanimously', but some ministerialists got the impression that the subsequent disagreement between the 'obstinate' Hamilton and Tavistock had occurred there.)[11] A speech by Alderman William Heygate later on the 24th, to the effect that while he deplored the omission of the queen's name from the liturgy he was not prepared to vote for an address for its restoration, induced Hamilton to let it be known that he would now move a resolution that the omission was 'ill advised and expedient', in the hope of 'catching the votes of those friends of the ministry' who felt like Heygate. Lord Harrowby, a member of the cabinet, thought that this was 'a very foolish motion, for it has in it nothing practical, and as a censure it is too weak'.[12] So it proved. Lushington, the secretary to the treasury, recorded, 26 Jan.:

> The speech of Lord Archibald was bald and bad. He laboured ineffectually and made no impression upon the House. He evaded the legal part of the question and attempted to justify the nothingness of his own motion by referring to the more extensive one of Lord Tavistock; at the same time most inconsistently prating about the numerous petitions for the restoration ... whilst his own motion leaves her completely in the lurch.[13]

The young Whig George Howard*, a spectator in the gallery, thought Hamilton was 'as dull, heavy and injudicious as was possible to be'; and Grey Bennet heard that he 'made ... by no means a good speech'.[14] The motion's defeat by 310-209 greatly disappointed the Whigs and knocked the heart out of their parliamentary campaign on the queen's case.[15] Hamilton's motion for production of the order in council to the general assembly of the Church of Scotland concerning the queen (which Castlereagh had denounced as 'a disgrace to the order book' of the Commons) was rejected by 102-35, 15 Feb. Two days later he was a dinner guest of the queen at Brandenburgh House.[16] On 16 Feb. he secured the reappointment of the royal burghs select committee, which was composed of all but two of the men named to it the previous year. He presented and had referred to it petitions from Inverness, 16 Mar., and Edinburgh, 2 Apr., but by now he had little influence over it, informing his fellow Scottish Whig Thomas Francis Kennedy*, 6 Mar., that it 'goes on worse and worse' and that the Edinburgh reformers' 'compromise' of their case had proved 'most *injurious* to the cause'.[17] He later claimed in the House (20 Feb. 1822) that the attendance had dwindled to 'four or five placemen', Joseph Hume and himself; his allies Ronald Craufurd Ferguson and John Peter Grant certainly abandoned the inquiry in disgust.[18] The dominant ministerialists refused to take parole evidence, and when Hamilton returned from ten days' leave of absence on 'urgent private business' (voting in the Stirlingshire by-election) on 1 June 1821, he found that in his absence a 'meagre and imperfect' report had been drafted by the lord advocate, Rae, and Lord Binning, a member of the India board, who had easily overcome Hume's resistance. He dissented from it when he formally presented it,

14 June 1821. He divided for Catholic relief, 28 Feb. 1821, 1 Mar., 21 Apr. and (as a pair) 10 May 1825. He spoke and was a teller for repeal of the additional malt duty, 21 Mar., 3 Apr., when he praised Lord Fife* for sacrificing his household place on the issue, though he declined to vote for Creevey's motion condemning Fife's dismissal, 6 Apr. On 22 Mar. he thanked Hume for his 'unwearied exertions in promoting retrenchment and economy', and he seconded his amendment for ordnance reductions, 6 Apr. He supported and was a minority teller for Baring's motion for inquiry into the 1819 Bank Act, stressing the need to 'return to a sound currency', 9 Apr. He did not attend the City reform dinner, of which he was named as a steward, 4 Apr.;[19] nor did he vote for Russell's parliamentary reform motion, 9 May. Next day, in a thin House, which prompted him to be brief, he moved for consideration next session of the state of the Scottish county representation and the need to 'effect some extension of the number of voters and to establish some connection between the right of voting and the landed property'; he was a teller for the minority of 41 (to 53). On 18 May he accused Rae of writing to the authorities of Scottish counties to get up petitions against Kennedy's Scottish juries bill.[20] He presented and endorsed a petition from a Lanarkshire county meeting in favour of Owen's New Lanark scheme, 4 June;[21] and he supported inquiry into the experiment, 26 June. He opposed the appointment of Thomas Frankland Lewis* to the Irish revenue commission, 15 June. He called the duke of Clarence's grant 'improper' and 'the claim for arrears unpardonable', 25 June, and on 2 July 1821 tried unsuccessfully to have recorded in the *Journals* the observation that it should not be taken as a precedent for the other royal dukes.

From a London '*yet thin* of MPs', 31 Jan. 1822, Hamilton informed Kennedy:

> I see no prospect, from talking with those who are here, of much *concert*, nor of any chance of procuring a *new* head to our discordant body; but then the warmth of the country gentlemen, even of many of the Tories, will form a new feature in the opening of the session, and will probably *force* on important divisions *early* ... I shall no doubt move *something* about the burgh concern, and shall again also attack our *county* representation.[22]

He supported the amendment to the address calling for economies, 5 Feb., alleging that 'the supporters of ministers cast wholly out of their view the inability of the people to pay the oppressive taxes which weighed them down'. On 18 Feb. he sought leave to introduce a bill to abolish the inferior commissary courts of Scotland, as recommended by the judicial commissioners. Even though Rae asked him to defer to the pending government bill, he persisted, but his motion was negatived. On 22 Feb., admitting that he had taken up the cause of burgh reform unaware of 'the time or the labour it would require', he proposed referring the reports of the three select committees to a committee of the whole House. He condemned the measure being planned by Rae to regulate the burghs' accounting methods and prevent non-residence by magistrates as 'quite inadequate' to reform the 'incurably noxious system' which prevailed. He disclaimed 'any inclination to ... wild and extensive changes' and said he wished to 'produce some community of interest and feeling ... between those who govern and those who are governed': in 'large and populous burghs' he would restore the guildry and let them elect the dean of guild and a portion of the council; open the corporation to all men of property and allow them to elect their own deacons, who would choose some of the council; empower the councillors thus chosen to elect the remainder annually and have magistrates go out of office every one to three years. Rae opposed the motion, which was defeated by 81-46. Hamilton duly resisted the ministerial bill, 22 Feb., and presented hostile petitions, 17, 22 Apr., 3, 13, 20, 30 May.[23] When the measure was divided into two, 17 June, he denounced that dealing with accounts (which became law on 29 July) as inadequate. Chairing a Brooks's Club dinner to mark the secession of the duke of Buckingham and Charles Williams Wynn*, who had joined the ministry, 6 Mar., he proposed the first toast, to 'the purification of the club'.[24] He called for the application of 'adequate relief' to worsening agricultural distress, 17 Apr., and presented a Lanarkshire petition to that effect, 7 May.[25] He voted silently for Russell's reform motion, 25 Apr., and reception of the Greenhoe reform petition, 3 June. He spoke for abolition of one of the joint-postmasterships, 2 May, and against the aliens bill, 5 June. He supported and was a minority teller for Western's motion for inquiry into the currency, 12 June, though he disavowed any wish to alter the standard or repeal the 1819 Act. His attempt to prevent the second reading of the tithes leasing bill was defeated by 64-22, 8 July; and next day he dropped a motion for a bill to repeal the Scottish cottage tax when Vansittart promised to deal with it. He condemned the government's conduct towards Greece in her struggle with Turkey as 'partial and oppressive', 15 July 1822, when he protested against the surreptitious passage of the Irish insurrection bill.

In December 1822 Cockburn, appalled at Kennedy's talk of leaving Parliament, observed that on such issues as the Scottish juries bill Hamilton (like

Hume and Ferguson) was 'ignorant and ... slight'.[26] He secured returns of the number and residences of royal burghs councillors, 19 Feb. 1823, and next day said that agricultural distress in Scotland was very severe.[27] He voted for Russell's motion for inquiry into the English borough franchise, 20 Feb., and his general reform scheme, 24 Apr. He opposed the national debt reduction bill as a probable bar to further tax reductions, 14 Mar.[28] He spoke and voted for information on the Dublin theatre riot, 24 Mar. His motion for a copy of the privy council warrant reinstating the suspended council of Inverness was rejected by 49-31, 26 Mar. The following day he expressed concern at the ministerial attitude to the French invasion of Spain and deplored their support of 'the projects of the Holy Alliance for so many years past'. He objected to the grant for Irish churches and glebe houses, 11 Apr. On the 30th he was a teller for the minority of 20 in the snap division on Spain, having been shut in, according to Brougham, as a result of his deafness.[29] Opposing the Irish insurrection bill, 12 May, he argued that 'the House should now be disposed to investigate the cause of these disorders and avoid, if possible, the beaten track of severity'. His motion of 2 June for future consideration of reform of the Scottish county representation prompted an exodus of Members who had been anticipating a debate on the game bill. He detailed the small total nominal electorate of about 2,400, explained how parchment superiority voters outnumbered genuine freeholders in most counties and complained that sheriffs, who were crown appointees, had too much power, citing the hostile conduct towards himself of the sheriff of Lanarkshire in 1818. The defeat of the motion by only 152-117 was 'the best ever known on a reform question' and was received with 'loud cheers from the opposition benches'.[30] When Binning defended the sheriff of Lanarkshire, 18 June, Hamilton stuck to his guns and also accused the sheriff of Stirlingshire of party bias.[31] He was a teller for the minority for information on the Borthwick episode, 3 June, and was again in Western's small minority on the currency, 12 June. Next day he welcomed the government's decision to raise the barilla duties as marking the end of their 'vacillating policy'. He divided the House twice against the Scottish commissaries bill, 18 June, protested next day at Rae's practice of smuggling through this and other Scottish legislation 'without discussion' and again forced a division against it, 30 June, even though he approved its object.[32] On 18 July he had one of the Lords' amendments concerning fees negatived.[33] He paired for the Scottish juries bill, 20 June. He presented anti-slavery petitions, 24 June and 10 July 1823.[34]

Hamilton was in Lord Nugent's minority of 30 who voted to condemn Britain's policy on Spain, 17 Feb. 1824. He divided silently for reform of Edinburgh's electoral system, 26 Feb., having earlier written to George Sinclair*, a candidate for Caithness, to applaud his public declaration for reform and 'expose of ministerial profligacy and insolence'.[35] He objected to details of the silk trade bill, 18, 22 Mar. On 30 Mar., in what George Agar Ellis* thought a 'dreadful, dull, long' speech, he proposed referring the 12 reports of the Scottish judicial commissioners to a committee of the whole House, aiming to force Rae to explain 'what could be said in defence of the total neglect of the reforms recommended'.[36] He was defeated by 124-76. He presented a large Glasgow inhabitants' petition for the abolition of West Indian slavery and indemnification for the planters, 6 Apr., and presented and endorsed one from Lanark for the free export of Scottish spirits to England, 4 May. He condemned Kennedy's Scottish poor bill out of hand, 14, 24, 25 May, and forced him to withdraw it.[37] He got leave to introduce a bill to facilitate the recovery of small debts in Scotland, 10 June, and had it printed, 14 June 1824. He brought it in again, 7 Mar. 1825, steered it through the Commons and saw it become law on 22 June 1825 (6 Geo. IV, c. 48).[38] His health was beginning to collapse, and his only known votes in the 1825 session, besides those for Catholic relief, were against the Irish unlawful societies bill, 15, 21, 25 Feb. On petitions for repeal of the Combination Acts, 3 May, he cited some examples from Lanarkshire, Renfrewshire and Stirlingshire of union violence and intimidation against workmen who had been willing to take lower wages. He spoke and was a majority teller against the Leith Docks bill, 20 May. He called for a reduction of the duty on soap and candles, 7 June 1825. In late September he was at Worthing, 'unable to report any amendment of my *complaint*', but claiming that 'my *health* is *quite good*'. He reckoned to have 'thought little' about politics 'for some time past': 'so unsatisfactory do I think the *termination* of Whig labours and Whig party, that I shall take all those matters *goute a goute*, and no more *draughts* of them'.[39]

Hamilton failed to get a straight answer from the chancellor Robinson as to whether the proposed restriction of small bank notes was to apply to Scotland, 6, 20 Feb. 1826. He supported Hume's unsuccessful attempt to empower magistrates to force banks to pay in specie, 27 Feb. Next day he sent an open letter to the praeses of the Lanarkshire county meeting called to petition against interference with the Scottish banking system (4 Mar.), in which he promised to defer to the general 'repugnance' to the plan evinced in Scotland.[40] He supported the third reading of the promissory notes bill, 7 Mar., not as a perfect solution, but because it would 'tend in some degree to amend the defects of the present system of country banking'. He presented the Lanarkshire petition, 14 Mar., and was named to the select committee on the issue as it affected Scotland and Ireland, 16 Mar. On the 22nd he cautioned the House against sanctioning the formation of new joint-stock companies 'after the dishonest practices which had been committed by many of the companies who obtained charters last year'. He spoke and voted for reform of Edinburgh's electoral system, 13 Apr., but was absent from the division on Russell's reform motion, 27 Apr. He thought Littleton's scheme to regulate private bill committees would create 'a tribunal to arraign the conduct of Members', 19 Apr. He presented petitions from Glasgow tailors for repeal of the corn laws, 21 Apr., and from Glasgow and Campsie for the abolition of slavery, 19 May 1826.[41]

When he offered again for Lanarkshire at the general election in June 1826, he wrote:

> Many of my political opinions, which met with strenuous opposition for several years, have recently been carried into effect, particularly a reduction of taxes, so long and so injuriously withheld, and a return to metallic currency, so long and so fatally suspended.

He was too unwell to attend his unopposed election on the 20th, when his brother the duke stood in for him at the celebration dinner.[42] At the Lanarkshire county meeting on distressed local handloom weavers, 23 Sept., he dismissed cheaper corn and emigration as solutions and called for 'a diminution of public expenditure and an invariable currency'.[43] His last reported speech in the House was a passionate plea for ministers to intervene to rescue the unemployed weavers of Glasgow and Lanarkshire from their 'state of destitution, hopelessness and helplessness', 5 Dec. 1826. He paired for Catholic relief, 6 Mar., and was granted a token fortnight's sick leave, 3 May 1827. On 30 July he told Lord Holland, who was on the lookout for a villa for him, that 'my views have now extended to the banks of the Thames, where I could take *air* in a boat without fatigue'. Though tortured by 'this hot weather', he claimed to be 'going on well';[44] but he died at his residence in the Upper Mall, Hammersmith, in early September 1827. By his will of 13 Dec. 1826 Hamilton, who had had an illegitimate son with his cousin Lady Augusta Murray (daughter of the 4th earl of Dunmore and later married to the duke of Sussex) and enjoyed the sexual favours of the promiscuous countess of Oxford of 'Harleian Miscellany' notoriety, left £20,000 to his brother and £3,000 to Lady Anne.

He bequeathed sums ranging from £2,000 to £5,000 to various Murrays, Augustus and Emma D'Este (the children of Sussex and Lady Augusta) and two of Lady Oxford's children. His personalty was sworn under £70,000.[45]

[1] Not 28 Aug. as stated in *HP Commons, 1790-1820*, iv. 132. [2] *Cockburn Jnl.* i. 275. [3] *Cockburn Mems.* 308; *CJ*, lxxiv. 409; *Glasgow Herald*, 28 Jan. 1820. [4] *Glasgow Herald*, 31 Mar. 1820. [5] *The Times*, 14 June, 1 July 1820; *CJ*, lxxv. 146, 452. [6] Add. 30123, f. 157. [7] *The Times*, 14, 15 July 1820. [8] *Hobhouse Diary*, 24. [9] *Creevey Pprs.* i. 309; *Countess Granville Letters*, i. 156. [10] *Countess Granville Letters*, i. 158. [11] HLRO, Hist. Coll. 379, Grey Bennet diary, 1, 2; *The Times*, 24, 25 Jan. 1821; *Colchester Diary*, iii. 201; *Arbuthnot Jnl.* i. 65-66; *Hobhouse Diary*, 48; Add. 38742, f. 171. [12] *Hobhouse Diary*, 48; Harrowby mss, Harrowby to Sandon, 26 Jan. 1821; Add. 43212, f. 180. [13] *Geo. IV Letters*, ii. 895. [14] Castle Howard mss, Howard to Lady Morpeth, 28 [Jan. 1821]; Grey Bennet diary, 5. [15] *Arbuthnot Jnl.* i. 65; *Hobhouse Diary*, 48; Add. 38742, f. 171. [16] Grey Bennet diary, 5. [17] *The Times*, 17 Feb. 17 Mar., 4 Apr. 1821; *Cockburn Letters*, 18-19. [18] *CJ*, lxxvi. 160, 194. [19] *The Times*, 4, 5 Apr. 1821. [20] Ibid. 19 May 1821. [21] Ibid. 5 June 1821. [22] *Cockburn Letters*, 40-41. [23] *The Times*, 18, 23 Apr., 4, 14, 21, 31 May 1822. [24] HLRO, Moulton Barrett diary, 6 Mar. [1824]. [25] *The Times*, 18 Apr., 8 May 1822. [26] *Cockburn Letters*, 72. [27] *The Times*, 20, 21 Feb. 1823. [28] Ibid. 15 Mar. 1823. [29] Add. 40687, f. 1. [30] Northants. RO, Agar Ellis diary, 2 June 1823; *Cockburn Mems.* 379. [31] *The Times*, 19 June 1823; Add. 40356, f. 337. [32] *The Times*, 20 June 1823 [33] Ibid. 1 July 1823. [34] Ibid. 25 June, 11 July 1823. [35] NAS GD136/519/7. [36] Agar Ellis diary, 30 Mar. [1824]. [37] *The Times*, 7 Apr., 15, 25 May 1824. [38] Ibid. 15 June 1824, 8, 19 Mar., 23 June 1825; *CJ*, lxxx. 168, 586. [39] Add. 51570, Hamilton to Holland, 20 Sept. [1825]. [40] *Glasgow Herald*, 6 Mar. 1826. [41] *The Times*, 22 Apr., 20 May 1826. [42] *Glasgow Herald*, 9, 23, 26 June 1826. [43] Ibid. 25 Sept. 1826. [44] Add. 51570. [45] PROB 11/1730/540; IR26/1130/739.

D.R.F.

HAMILTON, Hans (1758–1822), of Sheephill Park, co. Dublin.

Co. Dublin	1801–22 Dec. 1822

bap. 19 July 1758,[1] 1st s. of James Hamilton of Sheephill and Holmpatrick, dep. prothonotary of k.b. [I], and 1st w. Hannah, da. and h. of William Phillips of Dublin. *m.* (1) 18 June 1787,[2] Sarah (*d.* 9 Feb. 1805), da. of Alderman Joseph Lynam, banker, of Dublin, 2da. (1 *d.v.p.*); (2) 30 Mar. 1807, Anne, da. of Hugh Henry Mitchell, MP [I], of Glasnevin, 1s. 4da. *suc.* fa. 1800. *d.* 22 Dec. 1822.[3]

Cornet 2nd Regt. of Horse [I] 1777, lt. 1780; capt. 5 Drag. 1783, ret. 1789.

MP [I] 1797-1800.

Sheriff, co. Dublin 1803-4, gov. 1813-*d.*, custos rot. 1821-*d.*

Commdt. Fingal and Balbriggan yeomanry.

Hamilton, whose grandfather James had sat for Newry and Carlow between 1723 and 1760, came in for county Dublin shortly before the Union, which he opposed.[4] The dearest object of his life was an Irish peerage, for which he thereafter pestered suc-

cessive governments; these he mostly sided with at Westminster, though he slowly became a supporter of Catholic relief.[5] In June 1818 he was regarded as having a 'promise' of the next creation, but he was passed over for George Canning† (Lord Garvagh) in October and for Sir John Cradock (Lord Howden), a former Member of the Dublin Parliament, a year later. When he was again returned for county Dublin, on the basis of his territorial interests, after a contest at the general election of 1820, the Liverpool administration merely noted that he had 'had expectations' of a peerage.[6] It was observed that he slipped away from the county Dublin meeting held in support of Queen Caroline, 30 Dec. 1820, apparently approving of the sheriff's controversial attempt to curtail the proceedings. He voted in defence of ministers' conduct towards her, 6 Feb., and earned more local criticism by his failure to speak on the hostile constituency petition, 22 Feb. 1821, when he was not listed in the minority for Lord John Russell's motion for inquiry into this affair.[7] He divided for Catholic relief, 28 Feb. He voted against John Maberly's resolution on the state of the revenue, 6 Mar., and repeal of the additional malt duty, 3 Apr. 1821. Soon afterwards he was appointed custos rotulorum of his county. He was named to the select committee on Dublin local taxation, 20 Mar. 1822, but a few weeks later it was reported that a severe illness had prevented his attending Parliament.[8] No further votes have been found and he is not known ever to have spoken in debate.

Earlier that year he had complained to the cabinet minister Lord Sidmouth that his repeated applications for church preferment for his brother had been ignored:

> I have supported the present administration for upwards of twenty years and that during that time I have derived very little advantage from the patronage of the crown is not less certain ... My brother has been recommended for promotion ... these twelve years, yet he has been constantly overlooked, and being unconscious of having done anything to forfeit the confidence of government, I feel satisfied that your lordship will upon this occasion recommend my brother to Lord Wellesley for early promotion.[9]

Whether he got satisfaction from the Irish viceroy on this matter is not clear. If not, he was doubly disappointed, for he died a commoner shortly before Christmas 1822, 'after a most painful and tedious illness'.[10] His son James Hans Hamilton (1810-63) represented county Dublin from 1841 to 1863, when he was succeeded as Conservative Member by his only surviving son Ion Trant Hamilton (1839-98), who occupied the seat until 1885 and was raised to the peerage as Baron Holmpatrick in 1897.

[1] IGI. [2] Ibid. [3] *Dublin Weekly Reg.* 28 Dec. 1822. [4] *Hist. Irish Parl.* iv. 336-7, 343-4; G. Hamilton, *Hist. House of Hamilton*, 971. [5] *HP Commons, 1790-1820*, iv. 133-4. [6] Add. 38279, ff. 146, 367; 38286, f. 46; 40296, f. 29; 40298, f. 14; *Dublin Weekly Reg.* 4, 11, 18, 25 Mar., 1 Apr. 1820. [7] *Dublin Evening Post*, 30 Dec. 1820, 2 Jan., 27 Feb. 1821. [8] Ibid. 11 May 1822. [9] Add. 40296, ff. 28-29; 40297, f. 51; 40344, f. 187. [10] *Dublin Evening Post*, 9 Nov., 24 Dec.; *The Times*, 26 Dec. 1822.

D.R.F./S.M.F.

HAMILTON, Thomas, Lord Binning (1780–1858), of 5 Chesterfield Street, Mdx. and Tynninghame, Haddington.

ST. GERMANS	1802–1806
COCKERMOUTH	17 Jan. 1807–1807
CALLINGTON	1807–1812
MITCHELL	5 Dec. 1814–1818
ROCHESTER	1818–1826
YARMOUTH I.o.W.	1826–24 July 1827

b. 21 June 1780, o.s. of Charles, 8th earl of Haddington [S], and Lady Sophia Hope, da. of John, 2nd earl of Hopetoun [S]. *educ.* Edinburgh Univ. 1796; Christ Church, Oxf. 1798. *m.* 13 Nov. 1802, Lady Maria Parker, da. and h. of George Parker†, 4th earl of Macclesfield, *s.p. cr.* Bar. Melros 24 July 1827; *suc.* fa. as 9th earl of Haddington [S] 17 Mar. 1828; KT 25 Oct. 1853. *d.* 1 Dec. 1858.

Commr. bd. of control July-Nov. 1809, June 1816-Feb. 1822; PC 29 July 1814; ld. lt. [I] Dec. 1834-Apr. 1835; first ld. of admiralty Sept. 1841-Jan. 1846; ld. privy seal Jan.-July 1846.

Hered. keeper of Holyrood park 1828-43.

Capt. E. Lothian yeomanry 1803; lt.-col. Haddington militia 1808.

Binning, who had been returned on the government interest for Rochester in 1818, stood there again at the general election of 1820 and, despite rumours of other candidates coming forward, was returned unopposed.[1] Originally a Pittite, he was closely connected with George Canning* and had served under him at the India board since 1816. He was an active Member, especially on Scottish affairs, and when in office of course voted steadily with Lord Liverpool's administration, frequently acting as a teller. He was named to the select committee on Rochester bridge, 16 June 1820, one of several such appointments in that Parliament. He obtained leave to bring in a bill to allow the East India Company to raise a corps of volunteer infantry, 14 June, and spoke in its favour, 16, 19 June. He defended the barracks grant, 12 July.[2] He was one of the deputation nominated by a meeting of freemen in Rochester to carry their address to Queen Caroline, 21 July.[3] He thought that the case against her was 'clearly made out, to my mind so clearly that I think, had I been a peer, no doctrine of expediency could have prevented me from voting stoutly for the bill' against her, but he rightly judged that the government would survive the affair.[4] Canning resigned over the issue in December 1820, but he successfully overcame Binning's reluctance to remain in office and disapproved of his having hinted to the prime minister that he might, albeit assigning other reasons, soon follow his example.[5] Noting that he was to be temporarily replaced by Charles Bathurst*, Canning commented in a letter to his wife, 5 Jan. 1821, 'how Binny will fume!'[6]

Binning argued that Scottish county meetings in support of ministers were genuinely representative of opinion there, 31 Jan. 1821, and he was a teller in defence of their conduct towards the queen, 6 Feb., and against printing the hostile Nottingham petition, 20 Feb. He denied Denman's allegation that Canning was guilty of corruption, 9 Feb., and was thanked by him for delivering such a swift rebuke.[7] He acted for Sir George Warrender, who had taken offence at Creevey's personal attack on him in the Commons, 14 Feb., and after several hours of discussion the following evening he managed to settle the row; according to Henry Grey Bennet*, he made 'a very good statement' condemning libellous newspaper accounts of the disagreement, 15 Mar.[8] He spoke in favour of reforming the system of Scottish juries, 14 Feb., but against taking their nomination out of the hands of judges, 18 May. As in the previous year, he was appointed to the select committee on Scottish burghs, 16 Feb., and on the presentation of the report, which he had helped to concoct, 14 June, he stated that it contained all that was necessary to satisfy the demands of reformers. He voted in favour of Catholic claims, 28 Feb., and against the forgery punishment mitigation bill, 23 May. He justified ministerial policy on the burning of Hindu widows, 20 June. He spoke in favour of reducing the grant of £20,000 to General Desfourneaux, 28 June, when he unsuccessfully moved that it should be lowered to £5,000 rather than to the eventually agreed figure of £3,500.[9] He vindicated the court of session and its president, his cousin Charles Hope†, against the criticisms of Hume, whom he forcefully 'took to task' without, however, persuading the House of the disinterestedness of his defence, 10 July 1821.[10]

In October 1821 Henry Lawes Long of Hampton Lodge, Surrey, who was on a visit to Tyninghame, described Binning as 'a thin under jawed fellow' and 'one of the pleasantest men I ever met'.[11] By December Binning, like William Sturges Bourne*, had decided to resign from the India board. He had reportedly refused to serve under its new president, Charles Williams Wynn*, but he disclaimed any intention of wishing to embarrass Canning or the administration. On 21 Dec. he wrote to William Huskisson*, who objected to their retirement, that

it is surely a very simple question whether it be or be not worth our while, being in no sense dependent upon office and the youngest of us being in his 42nd year, to continue in so disagreeable a situation, there being absolutely no such probability of escaping from it by promotion, as any reasonable man could rely upon, however sanguine his disposition might be. A general arrangement is made and we take that natural opportunity, in perfect good humour, to make our bow, fully intending to be in our places and give as constant a support as we did before.[12]

He duly voted with ministers against more extensive tax reductions to relieve distress, 11, 21 Feb., repeal of the salt duties, 28 Feb., 28 June, and abolition of one of the joint-postmasterships, 13 Mar. 1822. He was appointed to the select committee on agricultural distress, 18 Feb. On 1 Mar. he went up to the wife of the former Whig Commons leader Tierney in the ventilator above the chamber and 'told her, with perceptible pleasure, that the ministers would be heartily thrashed', as they were, on the opposition bid to suppress one of the junior lordships of the admiralty.[13] However, he defended the conduct of his former department on the issue of Hindu widows, 14 Mar. He presented petitions for relief from the shoemakers of Rochester, 24 Apr., and the coach proprietors and innkeepers on the London to Dover road, 19 July.[14] He was a teller for the second and third readings of Canning's bill to allow Catholic peers to sit in Parliament, 30 Apr., 10 May. He voted with government for the Canada bill, 18 July 1822.

On leaving office, Binning's involvement in debates on Scottish affairs increased markedly. He spoke against providing an account of the fee fund of the court of session, 12 Feb. 1822. He opposed Lord Archibald Hamilton's motion for inquiry into the royal burghs, 20 Feb., as he thought that it was designed to achieve by stealth a general parliamentary reform, which he trusted 'would always be steadily resisted by this House', and that details of lord advocate Rae's intended bill should have been heard first. He defended the burghs accounts bill, 17 June,

on the ground that it remedied abuses that had crept in without trenching on existing charters, and was a teller for its third reading, 18 July.[15] He again spoke, 'wretchedly' as Sir James Mackintosh* recorded, against altering the system of jury nomination, 20 June.[16] He unsuccessfully sought the postponement of James Abercromby's motion on Rae's conduct in the allegedly partial prosecution of Borthwick, 13 June, and was a teller for the majority against inquiry into it, 25 June. When Abercromby presented Borthwick's petition, 28 June, Binning stated that his close friend John Hope (son of Charles), who was also implicated, would co-operate with any inquiry, but he begged the House to keep an open mind until both sides had been heard. He failed to stop Hope's printed letter of protest to Abercromby being voted a breach of privilege, 9 July, but he again defended his conduct, 12 July. On 17 July he claimed that Hope had vindicated himself in his evidence before the House that day and that his letter should be judged a pardonable transgression; the matter was not pursued further.[17] He brought up a petition in favour of the bill for a national monument in Edinburgh, 1 July, and in unsuccessfully moving that it should be referred to the committee, 5, 15 July, defended the allocation of £10,000 for building a new church there as an integral part of the plan. The House approved his motion to compel a majority of the members of the council of every burgh to reside within three miles of it, 19 July 1822.[18]

In August 1822 Binning was listed by John Wilson Croker* as one of the Members closely connected with Canning, but he did not follow his chief when he returned to office as foreign secretary in September. Canning thought that Binning had been quite right to refuse his offer of an under-secretaryship as it would have meant resigning his seat.[19] He divided with ministers against inquiry into the right of voting in parliamentary elections, 20 Feb., and on the sinking fund, 3 Mar. 1823. He was given a fortnight's leave on urgent private business, 14 Apr., but was back to vote against inquiry into the legal proceedings against the Dublin Orange rioters, 22 Apr. On the presentation of a pro-reform petition from Edinburgh, 5 May, he denied that its 7,000 signatures made it representative of opinion there and declared that 'he was no friend to partial, or temperate, or moderate or any other kind of reform'. He spoke and voted against reform in Scotland, 2 June, because it lacked any popular demand, had enormous implications if applied to England and would mean interfering with the Act of Union. When the Borthwick case was raised, 3 June, he again defended Hope's conduct. He spoke in support of increasing the duty on barilla in order to encourage the production of kelp, 13 June. On the same day he attempted to present a petition from the sheriff depute of Lanarkshire, and when he introduced the matter again, 18 June, he rebutted Hamilton's allegations that the petitioner had been guilty of misconduct during the 1818 election for that county.[20] He spoke and was a teller against the Scottish juries bill, 30 June 1823, when he also voiced his support for extending the vote to Scottish Catholics.

He presented and endorsed a petition from the distillers of Scotland for equalizing the duties on Irish and Scottish spirits, 25 Feb. 1824. George Agar Ellis* reckoned that he spoke 'feebly', 26 Feb., on his reiterating his former arguments against reforming the representation of Edinburgh; in a long contribution, he stressed his view that any changes which did more than ameliorate minor blemishes in the constitution would be contrary to chartered rights and would upset the whole elective franchise of the country.[21] He voted to repeal the usury laws, 27 Feb., and abolish flogging, 5 Mar. He spoke in favour of changes to the game laws, 25 Mar., though he was concerned that the transfer of the ownership of game from the lord of the manor to the landowner was an invasion of property rights. On 1 Apr. he urged the lifting of duties on charitable legacies. He spoke and was a teller against inquiry into the Scottish courts of justice, 30 Mar., and on 17 June he declared that the Scottish judicature bill would thrust down the throats of his countrymen a measure second only in significance to the Act of Union. He continued to voice his opposition to the Scottish juries bill, 4 May, and unsuccessfully moved its recommittal, 24 May. He paired with Agar Ellis on the opposition motion for repealing the assessed taxes, 10 May.[22] He was appointed to the select committee on the disturbances in Ireland, 11 May, and voted for the second reading of the Irish insurrection bill, 14 June. He divided with ministers against condemning the prosecution of the Methodist missionary John Smith in Demerara, 11 June. He argued for an increase in official pensions, particularly in his former department, 12 June, and for the restoration of attainted Scottish peerages, 14 June 1824.[23] That summer Huskisson, a fellow invalid, privately observed that Binning, who was unable to decide when and where he would recuperate, was as 'fidgety as usual' and 'finds a constant occupation in watching and nursing his dyspeptic organ'.[24]

Binning again voted for repeal of the usury laws, 8 Feb. 1825. He was named to the committee to consider a petition to light Rochester with gas, 14 Feb., and, following one of the corporation's requests for assistance,

he was involved with the passage of the subsequent bill.[25] He was reappointed to the select committee on Ireland, 17 Feb., and voted for the Irish unlawful societies bill, 25 Feb. He divided for Catholic relief, 1 Mar., and the second reading of the relief bill, 21 Apr., when he stated that opinion had shifted to the view that it would calm, not inflame, Ireland. He added:

> The best security of the church was the truth of its doctrines. In these he believed, as well as in the respectability of its ministers; and, if they but broke away the disadvantages under which it laboured, by the handle which it furnished its enemies, they would thereby give it more security, than could be given to it by all the laws now in existence or which might be hereafter enacted.

He also advocated disfranchisement of the 40s. freeholders and payment of the Catholic clergy in order to ensure its success. On 2 May he denied that he had said that the destruction of the Protestant church in Ireland would be no great evil, as had been reported in the Edinburgh papers. He voted for the bill's third reading, 10 May, and was disappointed by its defeat in the Lords.[26] He spoke against limiting the application of the duke of Cumberland's grant solely to expenses incurred within Great Britain, 27 May, and voted for it, 30 May, 6, 10 June. He had something to say on Carlile's petition for greater freedom of religious discussion, 2 June. He spoke in favour of the spring guns bill, 21 June, attempted to move an amendment to allow their use in gardens and orchards, 23 June, and had this agreed, 29 June 1825, when he also voted for the bill's second reading.[27] He travelled on the continent late that year and early the next and made no recorded votes or speeches in the 1826 session. One local paper reported in September 1825 that he had decided to withdraw from Rochester at the next dissolution and that the 'motives which have led him to this determination are, we believe, wholly unconnected with politics'. At the general election of 1826 he was returned unopposed as a government supporter for Yarmouth, presumably on the interest of Lord Yarborough for the Worsley Holmes trustees.[28]

In early 1827 Binning, described by Charles Percy* as one of 'Canning's toads',[29] was convinced that his chief would succeed the ailing Liverpool, especially as he had been declared by the Whigs to be the *undoubted lord of the ascendant*. On the Catholic question, he wrote that

> the industry of the Protestant runners is immense ... They are industriously circulating the opinion that we who vote for the Catholics, but are friends of the government, ought to pray most heartily that we may be beat, because in that event the necessary ministerial

arrangements will be made with ease, whereas, if we conquer, the government must break down. This is most mischievous and is but too likely to tell.

He voted for relief, 6 Mar., but was not unduly alarmed by the effect of its defeat on Canning's prospects, and later denied that the new prime minister had been forced to accept restrictions on the issue as a pre-condition for entering office.[30] He voted for the spring guns bill, 23 Mar., and was named among those appointed to prepare a bill to regulate parochial settlements in Scotland, 3 Apr. He spoke in favour of the propagation of the gospels in Canada, 14 May, provided that due allegiance to the imperial government was also inculcated, and on the importance of maintaining the position of the Scottish church there, 15 June. He presented a petition from Haddington against being taxed for the expenses of the Dunbar harbour bill, 21 May, and proposed as an amendment to the bill, 15 June, that five burgesses of Dunbar be made additional trustees; Lord John Hay, who believed Binning's motives were 'to go against his near political friends, to overthrow the Maitlands', attacked him effectively in the Commons at some point in May and privately commented that 'before this took place he was in the habit of going through all the committees of which he was a member and bullying them into his own views'.[31] He voted against the disfranchisement of Penryn, 28 May, 7 June 1827, arguing that it was wrong to punish the whole electorate for the corruption of a minority.

Of Canning's demands during minor ministerial changes the previous year, Mrs. Arbuthnot had written that 'Binning is the new person he would bring in of his own friends, which is fair enough'.[32] William Ord* reported to John Nicholas Fazakerley*, 17 Apr. 1827, that Binning had been made a commissioner of woods and forests, but although he was also considered for a place at the treasury, he was not given any office under Canning. However, Lord Melville's resignation opened the way for him to take over the role of Scottish manager, and he wrote to his close friend Charles Bagot that 'Canning has put the concerns of Scotland into my hands and I am to be peered this session'. This provoked a horrified outcry from various Scots, especially the Whig Members, and Abercromby convinced Canning of the necessity of letting Scotland be governed

by the ministry or by some known and responsible part of it, specially assigned to the duty by constitutional office, instead of handing us over as a province to some proconsul and taking no more thought of us.

In the face of this attack, Binning withdrew his pretensions and on 30 Apr. he asked Canning 'to dispose of me *absolutely*. I have no wish for the thing if it is not to be a clear and decided advantage to you. It could in such case only produce *misery* to me'.[33] Nevertheless, in the following months he advised ministers on Scottish affairs, and attempted to have Hope promoted from solicitor-general to lord advocate and given a seat in Parliament. In July 1827 Binning was raised to the British barony of Melros, partly in order to bolster the new ministry's debating strength in the Lords. He set about organizing the attendance and support of the Scottish peers for the forthcoming session. He declined to try to mediate between Canning and the duke of Wellington in July 1827, and was shocked by the premier's death the following month.[34]

He succeeded his father as 9th earl of Haddington in March 1828 and in June was listed by Lord Palmerston* as a 'Liberal'. He voted for Catholic emancipation, 4, 10 Apr. 1829. He maintained a close friendship with Huskisson and much regretted his death in September 1830.[35] He was one of the leading 'Waverers' on parliamentary reform and, like Lords Harrowby and Wharncliffe, voted against the second reading of the Grey ministry's reform bill, 7 Oct. 1831, but in favour of the second reading of its revised version, 13 Apr. 1832. In November 1834 he pledged his support for the caretaker Wellington administration, in which he served as lord lieutenant of Ireland. He thereafter became a leading Conservative, held senior office under Peel and supported him over repeal of the corn laws.[36] His ministerial career surprised many, and Richard Monckton Milnes† commented that his appointment as first lord of the admiralty in 1841 was 'not much to the satisfaction of those who remember that Canning, his great friend and patron, never saw anything in him worthy of official distinction and gave him a peerage without a place'.[37] He had many intellectual interests and numbered Sir Walter Scott and Baron Bunsen among his friends. He died in December 1858, after a brief attack of jaundice. The barony of Melros became extinct, but he was succeeded in his Scottish earldom and estates by his second cousin, George Baillie (1802-70), of Mellerstain, Roxburgh, and Jerviswood, Lanark, who was a Conservative representative peer, 1859-70.[38]

[1] *Kentish Gazette*, 25 Feb., 3 Mar.; *Morning Chron.* 8 Mar. 1820. [2] *The Times*, 15, 20 June, 13 July 1820. [3] *Kentish Gazette*, 25 July 1820. [4] Add. 38742, f. 131; A. Aspinall, *Lord Brougham and Whig Party*, 118. [5] Haddington mss, Canning to Binning, 14, 28 Dec., Binning to Liverpool, 20 Dec.; TNA, Dacres Adams mss, Courtenay to Adams, 21 Dec. 1820. [6] Harewood mss WYL250/8/26. [7] Haddington mss, Canning to Binning, 19 Feb. 1821. [8] *Creevey's Life and Times*, 139-40; HLRO, Hist. Coll. 379, Grey Bennet diary, 37-38. [9] *The Times*, 19 May, 21, 29 June 1821. [10] Grey Bennet diary, 116. [11] *Recs. and Letters of Fam. of Longs of Longville*

ed. R.M. Howard, ii. 444, 454. [12] Add. 38290, f. 225; 38411, f. 81; 38743, ff. 73-77, 82; Haddington mss, Canning to Binning, 1, 22 Dec. 1821; Buckingham, *Mems. Geo. IV*, i. 273. [13] Add. 52445, f. 60. [14] *The Times*, 25 Apr. 1822. [15] Ibid. 13 Feb., 18 June 1822. [16] Add. 52445, f. 88. [17] *The Times*, 14, 29 June, 10, 13 July 1822; NLS mss 3895, f. 28; Add. 38743, f. 183. [18] *The Times*, 2, 16, 20 July 1822. [19] Add. 38744, f. 10; 40319, f. 57; Haddington mss, Canning to Binning, 14, 20 Sept., reply [?17] Sept.; Harewood mss, Canning to Granville, 21 Sept. 1822; Bagot, *Canning and Friends*, ii. 157-8; A. Aspinall, 'Canningite Party', *TRHS* (ser. 4), xvii (1934), 207. [20] *The Times*, 14, 19 June 1823; Add. 40356, f. 337. [21] Northants. RO, Agar Ellis diary. [22] Ibid. [23] *The Times*, 25 May, 14 June 1824; Add. 38576, f. 49. [24] TNA 30/29/9/3/10, 11. [25] Medway Archives and Local Stud. Cent. Rochester city recs. RCA/A5/2, 70. [26] *Edinburgh Evening Courant*, 25 Apr. 1825; Sir W. Fraser, *Mems. of Earls of Haddington*, i. 316-17; Bagot, ii. 280-4. [27] *The Times*, 3, 24 June 1825. [28] Fraser, 317-18; *Maidstone Jnl.* 6 Sept. 1825. [29] Keele Univ. Lib. Sneyd mss SC12/79. [30] *Canning's Ministry*, 31, 42, 117; Bagot, ii. 375-6, 378-80, 383. [31] *The Times*, 15, 22 May, 16 June 1827; NLS mss 3436, ff. 153, 159; 14441, f. 24. [32] *Arbuthnot Jnl.* ii. 18. [33] Duke Univ. Lib. Fazakerley mss; NLS mss 24749, f. 35; *Canning's Ministry*, 111, 261, 278; *Cockburn Mems.* 417; *Cockburn Letters*, 153-63. [34] Add. 38750, f. 275; 38752, ff. 75, 176, 276; 38753, f. 71; *Canning's Ministry*, 314; Haddington mss, Canning to Binning, 28 June 1827; Bagot, ii. 385, 408, 422; NLS mss 3618, f. 126. [35] Bulwer, *Palmerston*, i. 278-9; Add. 38755, ff. 24, 158; 38756, ff. 150, 156; 38758, f. 282. [36] Wellington mss WP1/1216/24; *Wellington Pol. Corresp.* ii. 152; Fraser, 326-55. [37] Reid, *Monckton Milnes*, i. 270; *Greville Mems.* iv. 416. [38] NLS mss 3893, f. 120; 3896, f. 129; 3899, f. 29; Fraser, 317-18, 356-60; *The Times*, 3 Dec. 1858; *Gent. Mag.* (1859), i. 92; *Oxford DNB*.

S.M.F.

HAMILTON *see also* DALRYMPLE HAMILTON

HAMLYN WILLIAMS, Sir James, 3rd. bt. (1790–1861), of Edwinsford, Carm. and Clovelly Court, nr. Bideford, Devon.

CARMARTHENSHIRE	1831–1832
CARMARTHENSHIRE	1835–1837

b. 25 Nov. 1790, 1st. s. of Sir James Hamlyn Williams†, 2nd bt., of Edwinsford and Clovelly and Diana Anne, da. of Abraham Whitaker, merchant, of Stratford, Essex. *educ.* Winchester 1802-6. *m.* 15 Feb. 1823, Lady Mary Fortescue, da. of Hugh Fortescue†, 1st Earl Fortescue, 3da. *suc.* fa. as 3rd bt. 3 Dec. 1829. *d.* 10 Oct. 1861.
Lt. 7 Drag. 1810, capt. 1813, maj. 1821, ret. 1823.
Sheriff, Carm. 1848-9.

The Williamses of Cwrt Derllys and Edwinsford were descendants of the Welsh warrior Eidio Wyllt, whose history 'illustrates the survival of an ancient family of "uchelwyr" and ... its progression from the ranks of rural freeholders to the vanguard of Carmarthenshire's county families in post-Tudor days'. In May 1797, on the death of Hamlyn Williams's paternal grandmother Arabella, control of the 10,000-acre estates passed to the Hamlyns of Clovelly. His father accordingly took the name and

arms of Williams in 1798 and in 1811 succeeded to the Hamlyn baronetcy first conferred on his grandfather in 1795, as the Williams baronetcy had lapsed.[1] With Lord Dynevor's support, they had represented Carmarthenshire in the Red or Tory interest from 1793 until his father's retirement in 1806 to avoid an expensive contest. He did not stand again, but he maintained his interest, strove to acquire a reputation as an improving landlord and was annoyed at not being consulted when Dynevor's heir took the seat in 1820.[2]

Hamlyn, as he was first known, spent his childhood at Clovelly and in London, with occasional holidays at Edwinsford. Unlike his younger brothers, he was educated at Winchester, whence on 5 Mar. 1805 he wrote to the Edwinsford agent David Thomas requesting 'a ham and a fowl or two in a little parcel'. His father forbade it, adding:

He has everything that he ought to have, and he is very apt to send to shops and all other places to get things in my name ... We must look sharp after him. He is a wag.[3]

His father kept him 'under my eye' when he left school, and he was tutored privately before joining the army, where he served with distinction in the Peninsula as an aide-de-camp to Sir William Henry Clinton*, receiving medals for his bravery at Orthez and Toulouse.[4] He chose to be known as Hamlyn Williams on attaining the rank of major and remained in the army until shortly after his marriage to one of Lord Ebrington's* sisters, which strengthened his ties with the Whig moderates and the Grenvillite Williams Wynns* of Wynnstay, Denbighshire.[5] He enjoyed hunting in Carmarthenshire, corresponded with landowners on whose estates he wished to shoot, and in November 1825, sure of the support of Colonel Sackville Gwynne of Glanbran, J.G.H.G. Williams of Llwynywormwood and Thomas Foley of Abermarlais, he consulted the leading Blue or Whig magnate, the 2nd Baron Cawdor, in confidence about his prospects should he start for the county. His kinsman by marriage, Cawdor's agent Richard Bowen Williams, who acted as intermediary, advised Cawdor:

I should be inclined to hope that if he could secure any considerable part of the interest which supported his father ... he might have a good chance, especially if he could add to that any great proportion of the Blue interest ... [but] there must be a great mass of small freeholders of which I know nothing ... How would old Lewis of Llysnewydd act? ... What would [Hughes] of Tregib do?

Williams also thought Hamlyn Williams's 'own notion ... not to canvass previously but to make a start on the day of the election' ill-advised and actively discouraged the attempt in 1826.[6] In about 1827 Hamlyn Williams assumed responsibility for Edwinsford, which with Cwrt Derllys was worth £7,000 a year, considered buying adjoining farms, and by coming to the aid of William Lewes junior when he was in financial difficulties in 1828, secured the vital political interest of Llysnewydd.[7] 'The first of the shooting on my best partridge grounds' remained of paramount importance to him and in March 1829 Gwynne, as the presiding magistrate at Llandovery, cautioned him privately against bringing prosecutions which 'could not fail to produce an impression in the county which you would find very much against you in case of your becoming a candidate'.[8] Although a signatory to an open letter approving Cawdor's plan to abolish the Welsh courts of great sessions, he was able to avoid attending public meetings on this divisive issue in the autumn of 1829 on account of his father's illness and death.[9] With his brother Charles, he helped to secure Ebrington's election for Devon in 1830, when he was also pleased to learn that the Carmarthenshire Member George Rice Trevor's parliamentary conduct was unpopular and his prospects of representing the county had improved.[10] As foreman of the Carmarthenshire grand jury, 11 Mar. 1831, he ensured that they adopted a petition for reform and 'total repeal of the assessed taxes, the duty on malt, and the adoption of a proper system of economy by abolishing all sinecures and removing all placemen', which Trevor would be unable to endorse.[11] Moving the resolution backing the Grey ministry's reform bill at the Carmarthenshire meeting, 29 Mar., he urged all reformers to support it to avoid civil war and explained that although he wanted triennial parliaments and voting by ballot, which the bill failed to provide, he would give it 'full support', as unanimity was essential.[12] Trevor was known to be prepared to resign rather than support the bill and Hamlyn Williams and another reformer, Rees Goring Thomas of Carmarthen, commenced canvassing well before the dissolution in April 1831, precipitated by its defeat.[13] Thomas made way for him (as the stronger candidate) and he was returned unopposed as a staunch reformer, 'unshackled and unconnected to any party', at a cost of £817 17s., and chaired 'on the chair of his great ancestor Sir Nicholas Williams†'.[14] Grasping the significance of the ministry's decision to give Glamorgan a second Member, he promised to press for another two Carmarthenshire Members, one for the county and one for its mining districts. He said that he favoured 'the total and immediate abolition of slavery', would vote to repeal the taxes on malt, soap

and candles and reduce the assessed taxes, and do his utmost 'to oppose the efforts of placemen' and 'end all sinecures and pensions'.[15]

Hamlyn Williams attended the county meeting, 8 June, and presented its petitions for a second county Member and separate representation for Llanelli and Kidwelly, 24 June 1831.[16] He divided for the reintroduced reform bill at its second reading, 6 July, and steadily for its details, but cast a wayward vote for the total disfranchisement of Aldborough, 14 Sept. He spoke briefly against delaying consideration of the Carmarthen election petition, 29 July, and presented further petitions from his county calling for landowners to be given £10 votes, 30 July, and for additional representation, 4 Aug. He divided for the bill's passage, 21 Sept., the second reading of the Scottish reform bill, 23 Sept., and Ebrington's confidence motion, 10 Oct. 1831. The bill's defeat in the Lords led to further petitioning and fears of unrest in Carmarthenshire, but Hamlyn Williams remained in London.[17] He voted for the revised reform bill at its second reading, 17 Dec. 1831, consistently for its details, and for its third reading, 22 Mar. 1832. Carmarthen petitioned for the creation of additional peers to pass the bill and, after voting for the address calling on the king to carry it unimpaired, 10 May, Hamlyn Williams wrote to the attorney George Thomas: 'I trust that you and my friends at Carmarthen will be of opinion that the ... Commons has done its duty'.[18] He divided for the Irish reform bill at its second reading, 25 May, against a Conservative amendment to the Scottish measure, 1 June, and against Alexander Baring's bill denying insolvent debtors parliamentary privilege, 6 June. He divided with government on the Dublin election controversy, 23 Aug. 1831, the Russian-Dutch loan, 26 Jan., 12 July, information on Portugal, 9 Feb., military punishments, 16 Feb., and the navy civil departments bill, 6 Apr. 1832, and considered himself a constant supporter of Lord Grey; but, true to his abolitionist principles and his pledge to his constituents, he voted against the government's restrictive amendment to Fowell Buxton's motion for the appointment of a select committee on colonial slavery, 24 May 1832. Attributing blame to previous administrations, he had called for a reduction in civil list expenditure, 18 July,[19] and he voted against the grant for the Society for the Propagation of the Gospels in the colonies and criticized the award to improve the Canadian waterways as 'nothing but a disgraceful job', 25 July 1831. He divided with the radicals against the compensation proposed for Escoffery and Lescene for their wrongful removal from Jamaica, 21 Aug. 1831, and to reduce the barrack grant, 2 July 1832. The only private petition he presented was against the Hartlepool docks railway bill, 2 Apr. 1832.

Hamlyn Williams felt he had fulfilled his pledges to his constituents and hoped for an unopposed return for the new two Member Carmarthenshire constituency at the general election in December 1832, when Trevor stood as a Conservative, but Cawdor was unwilling knowingly to sanction one-and-one representation and fielded a declared Liberal against 'Independent' Hamlyn Williams, whose late bid for Red support failed, leaving him bottom of the poll.[20] The Whig Lewis Jones had warned his agent (David Davies of Froodvale) in August 1832:

Sir James Williams must know or ought to know his political interests better than I can presume to do, but in my humble opinion, if he should throw the weight of his influence into Trevor's scales or even remain neutral when a reform candidate shall be in the field, he will commit political suicide.[21]

Standing as a Liberal endorsed by Cawdor, he came in for Carmarthenshire with Trevor in 1835, but the independent squires failed to bring him in in 1837, when his support for the ballot went 'too far' for Cawdor, who had gravitated to the Conservatives, and he did not stand again.[22] In retirement he completed the hobby drives at Clovelly and Edwinsford, was appointed to the honorary office of gamekeeper for the manors of Caio, Mallaine and Talley in 1845, and served as sheriff of Carmarthenshire. He died and was buried privately at Clovelly in October 1861. It was erroneously reported that he was succeeded in the baronetcy by his brother, Rear-Admiral Charles Hamlyn, but he had predeceased him and the baronetcy lapsed.[23] By his will, which was remarkable for its detail and 'unusual dimensions', he left an estate with all its chattels and mineral rights to each of his daughters: Clovelly to Susan Hester Fane, Cwrt Derllys to Edwina Augusta Davie and Edwinsford to Mary Elinor Drummond. He made bequests to his orphaned godson, James George Glyn Shaw of Blackheath, and his widow (d. 1874), whose life interest in his Upper Grosvenor Street house was to pass to his nephew and executor, Gerard James Noel (1823-1911), Conservative Member for Rutland, 1847-83.[24]

[1] F. Jones, 'Williams of Edwinsford' (pt. i), *Trans. Hon. Soc. Cymmrodorion* (1986), 63, 66-98; (pt. ii), ibid. (1987), 9-42. [2] *HP Commons, 1790-1820*, ii. 488-91; iv. 139; v. 580-1; Sir F.D. Williams Drummond, *Annals of Edwinsford*, 5, 9, 38; Carm. RO, Dynevor mss 161/5; NLW, Edwinsford mss 3057. [3] Edwinsford mss 2980, 2990, 3010a, 3012, 3015-17, 3056, 4135. [4] Ibid. 3030; Williams Drummond, 16; *Carmarthen Jnl.* 25 Oct. 1861. [5] *Williams Wynn Corresp.*, 317. [6] Edwinsford mss 3056, 3059, 3061; Carm. RO, Cawdor mss 2/209. [7] Edwinsford mss 3057, 3061-7, 3083, 4143, 4163. [8] NLW, Dolaucothi mss 3962; Edwinsford mss 3068. [9] *PP* (1829), ix. 388; *Gent. Mag.* (1830), i. 80-81. [10] *The Times*, 12, 16 Aug.; *Carmarthen Jnl.* 13 Aug. 1830; Edwinsford mss 3072. [11] *Carmarthen Jnl.* 25 Mar. 1831. [12] Ibid. 1 Apr. 1831. [13] Ibid. 22 Apr. 1831. [14] Ibid. 29 Apr., 6, 13 May 1831; Dolaucothi mss 3963; Carm. RO, Plas Llanstephan mss 924, 925; NLW ms 13477 C, pp. 18-20; Edwinsford mss 3834. [15] *Cambrian*, 13 May; *Carmarthen Jnl.* 13 May 1831. [16] *Carmarthen Jnl.* 10 June 1831. [17] Ibid. 16 Sept., 14, 28 Oct., 25 Nov. 1831. [18] Ibid. 4 May 1832; NLW, Highmead mss 3186. [19] *The Times*, 19, 20 July 1831. [20] Plas Llanstephan mss 924, 925; Dolaucothi mss L3125, 3126, 3964, 3965, 3968-73, 4148-52; Dynevor mss 161/5; Highmead mss 3155; Edwinsford mss 4148-52; NLW ms 1172 E, ff. 29, 36; *Carmarthen Jnl.* 28 Dec. 1832. [21] NLW ms 1172 E, f.37. [22] M. Cragoe, 'Carm. Co. Politics, 1804-37', *Carm. Antiquary*, xxx (1994), 75-79; Dolaucothi mss L3974-80; Highmead mss 3158, 3188-92. [23] Williams Drummond, 16; *Gent. Mag.* (1861), ii. 577; *Carmarthen Jnl.* 18, 25 Oct. 1861. [24] IR26/2309/44-52; *Welshman*, 7 Feb. 1862.

M.M.E.

HANBURY TRACY, Charles (1777–1858), of Toddington, nr. Winchcombe, Glos. and Gregynog, nr. Newtown, Mont.

TEWKESBURY 1807–1812
TEWKESBURY 23 Jan. 1832–1837

b. 28 Dec. 1777, 3rd s. of John Hanbury† (d. 1784) of Pontypool Park, Mon. and Jane, da. of Morgan Lewis of St. Pierre, Mon. educ. privately by David Williams;[1] Rugby 1790; Christ Church, Oxf. 1796. m. 29 Dec. 1798, his cos. Hon. Henrietta Susanna Tracy, da. and h. of Henry Leigh, 8th Visct. Tracy [I], 6s. (2 d.v.p.) 3da. Took additional name of Tracy by royal lic. 1 Jan. 1799; cr. Bar. Sudeley 12 July 1838. d. 10 Feb. 1858.
Sheriff, Glos. 1800-1, Mont. 1804-5; ld. lt. Mont. 1848-d.
Lt.-col. Montgomery vol. legion 1803.

Hanbury Tracy, who acquired extensive estates in Gloucestershire, Montgomeryshire and Shropshire through marriage, and who displayed 'peculiarly polished' manners, was an amateur architect of some distinction. In 1819 he began work replacing the damp and dilapidated seventeenth century house at Toddington with an imposing Gothic mansion of his own design, which incorporated some of the features of Magdalen College, Oxford, and was considered by contemporaries to be an architectural success. It took almost 20 years to complete (although it was ready for occupation by 1833) and cost around £150,000, some of which he raised by mortgaging his copyhold rights on the Pontypool estate belonging to his elder brother Capel Hanbury, and by sales of timber from his own land.[2]

He had sat for Tewkesbury, an open borough about eight miles from Toddington, in the 1807 Parliament, and acted with the advanced wing of the Whigs before standing down in 1812 on account of ill health. He counted Sir Francis Burdett* and John Cam Hobhouse* among his friends.[3] His politics remained constant, and in December 1830 he signed the requisition for a Montgomeryshire county meeting to petition for parliamentary reform. However, at the general election of 1831 a sense of personal loyalty prevented him from opposing the veteran Member, Charles Williams Wynn, despite the latter's vote against the Grey ministry's bill. He assured Williams Wynn of his continued good wishes, but said he was powerless to prevent the local reformers from moving against him and intended simply to keep away:

> With the sentiments I have always professed on the subject of parliamentary reform, with the impossibility of declaring myself otherwise than friendly to the bill and as regretting the necessity that ministers were under of dissolving Parliament, I hardly know how I could enter the field as *your champion* and apprehend that my appearance in Montgomeryshire, whilst it would be embarrassing to myself, would be anything but useful to your cause.[4]

In any case, he had accepted a requisition to stand for Tewkesbury as a supporter of the reform bill, which he considered essential to the 'welfare and tranquillity' of the country. He was beaten into third place by a well-entrenched opponent of the measure, but was reckoned to have laid the foundation for future success for himself or one of his sons.[5] He also served on the committee working for the reformer Henry Reynolds Moreton*, who had started for Gloucestershire, and at the election he nominated Sir Berkeley William Guise, the pro-reform sitting Member. He celebrated the rout of the Tories, called for 'a free and fair representation in Parliament', warned against the duplicity of 'sham friends' of reform and declared his support for 'the whole bill', in the belief that 'reform is now absolutely necessary for the safety of the nation and to restore the confidence of the people in their government'. He defended the dissolution on the ground that Lord Grey had 'found it impossible to carry on the government, in consequence of the many wheels of corruption with which he has been embarrassed in the machinery of the House of Commons and in every department of the state'.[6] In September 1831 Williams Wynn, on hearing that Hanbury Tracy was to join in 'fanning the flame' of reform in Montgomeryshire by supporting the proposed county meeting to petition the Lords in support of the bill, commented that until he saw him 'actually take part against me I will not believe it possible that he can forget his obligation to me'. What this referred to is not clear, but Hanbury Tracy evidently took no active part in the proceedings.[7] That month

it was reported that he had been offered the vacancy for the venal borough of Wallingford created by the elevation to the peerage of the patron, his old friend and political associate William Hughes. In the event, his eldest son Thomas Charles, who had changed his surname to Leigh, successfully contested the seat.[8] Hanbury Tracy's chance at Tewkesbury came somewhat earlier than expected with the death in early January 1832 of the pro-reform sitting Member John Martin; he was returned unopposed at the resulting by-election.[9]

He took his seat on 26 Jan. and divided with ministers on the Russian-Dutch loan later that day, as he did again, 12, 16, 20 July 1832. He is not known to have spoken in debate in this period, but he presented a petition in support of the Purton Pill railway bill, 1 Feb. He voted with ministers on relations with Portugal, 9 Feb. He divided steadily for the details of the revised reform bill, its third reading, 22 Mar., and Lord Ebrington's motion for an address asking the king to appoint only ministers committed to carrying an unimpaired measure, 10 May. He voted for the second reading of the Irish bill, 25 May, and against a Conservative amendment to the Scottish bill, 1 June. He may have been the man, named as C.H. Truby or Treby, who divided against Hume's call for information on military punishments, 16 Feb. He voted with government for the navy civil departments bill, 6 Apr. He was in the minority against restoring the salary of the Irish registrar of deeds to its original level, 9 Apr. He voted to make coroners' inquests public, 20 June 1832.

Hanbury Tracy was returned for Tewkesbury at the general election of 1832 'after a severe struggle' and sat as an advocate of 'Whig principles' until his retirement in 1837.[10] He received a coronation peerage in 1838. He added to his reputation as an architect with his work on the reconstruction and modernization of Hampton Court, Herefordshire, but his proposed alterations in 1844 to Barry's plans for the new Houses of Parliament were rejected.[11] He died in February 1858 and was succeeded by his eldest son Thomas Charles Leigh (1801-63), to whom he left all his landed property. His expenditure on Toddington contributed to the crippling financial problems experienced by his successors.[12] His second son, Henry Hanbury Tracy (1802-89), was Liberal Member for Bridgnorth, 1837-8.

Chron. 24 Sept. 1831. ⁹ *Gloucester Jnl.* 7, 14, 28 Jan. 1832. ¹⁰ *The Times*, 14 Dec. 1832; M. Stenton, *Who's Who of British MPs, 1832-1885*, p. 382. ¹¹ *The Sudeleys*, 228-32; Add. 40543, ff. 357, 365; 40545, f. 322. ¹² *The Sudeleys*, 253-67.

D.R.F./T.A.J.

HANDCOCK, Richard (1791–1869), of Moydrum Castle, co. Westmeath.

ATHLONE 1826–1832

b. 17 Nov. 1791, 1st s. of Richard Handcock, MP [I], 2nd Bar. Castlemaine [I], of Moydrum and Anne, da. of Arthur French of French Park, co. Roscommon. *m.* 17 Apr. 1822, Margaret, da. of Michael Harris of Dublin, 3s. (1 *d.v.p.*) 2da. *suc.* fa. as 3rd Bar. Castlemaine [I] 18 Apr. 1840. *d.* 4 July 1869.

Rep. peer [I] 1841-*d*.

Handcock, whose uncle William, created Baron Castlemaine in 1812, was governor and sole proprietor of Athlone, served in alternate years from 1816 to 1826 as sovereign and vice-sovereign of the family controlled corporation on a salary of £100 per year, a position which had been held since 1798 by his father, who succeeded to the barony in 1839.¹ Following a campaign by the town's inhabitants against the corporation's 'tolls and customs', which they denounced as a hindrance to 'prosperity and trade', Handcock came forward at the 1826 general election promising to address 'the grievances of which the public complain'; he was returned unopposed.² He immediately began negotiating a new agreement between the corporation and the town's inhabitants, which was finalized on 16 Oct. 1826.³ A petition against his return was presented, 8 Feb., but he presented another successfully challenging its authenticity, 13 Mar. 1827.

Handcock signed the Irish landed proprietors' petition against Catholic relief in February, voted thus, 6 Mar. 1827, 12 May 1828, and brought up hostile petitions, 28 Apr., 1 May 1828.⁴ He was granted a month's leave on 'urgent business', 5 Apr. 1827. He divided against repeal of the Test Acts, 26 Feb. 1828. He was in a minority of 24 against going into committee on Irish and Scottish small bank notes, 16 June 1828. He presented petitions against the Wellington ministry's concession of Catholic emancipation, 18 Feb., 2 Mar. 1829. Next day he denied the assertion of Brownlow, Member for County Armagh, that the recent election to the representative peerage of Lord Dunalley* rather than Lord Castlemaine (who in 1828 had privately solicited the support of the premier, the duke of Wellington, citing his 'influence' in Westmeath and 'the return of his nephew' for Athlone), demonstrated

the Irish aristocracy's support for emancipation, observing that '33 peers voted for my noble relative out of about 80'.⁵ He divided against emancipation, 6, 18, 23, 27 and (as a pair) 30 Mar. He had been expected by Planta, the patronage secretary, to support securities after emancipation had passed, but he was a teller for the minority of 16 who voted to raise the Irish freehold qualification from £10 to £20, 26 Mar. 1829. He was granted a month's leave on urgent private business, 10 Mar. 1830. He divided with opposition for repeal of the Irish coal duties, 13 May, for accounts of privy councillors' emoluments, 14 May, and to reduce the grant for Prince Edward Island, 14 June. He secured returns of expenditure on Irish public works, 4 June. He voted for abolition of the death penalty for forgery, 7 June 1830.

At the 1830 general election he was returned after a token contest with an outsider.⁶ He was listed by the Wellington ministry as one of the 'moderate Ultras', and was absent from the crucial division on the civil list, 15 Nov. 1830. He voted against the second reading of the Grey ministry's reform bill, 22 Mar., and for Gascoyne's wrecking amendment, 19 Apr. 1831. At the ensuing general election he offered again for Athlone, promising to oppose the 'revolutionary' bill 'on all occasions' and to 'maintain the rights, liberties and franchises of this corporation'. He defeated a reformer with a majority of 30 votes 'of the old freemen'.⁷ On 4 July 1831 he endorsed and 'bore testimony to the weight and respectability' of an anti-reform petition from Westmeath. He voted against the second reading of the reintroduced reform bill, 6 July, to adjourn, 12 July, for use of the 1831 rather than the 1821 census, 19 July, and against the partial disfranchisement of Chippenham, 27 July. He paired against the bill's passage, 21 Sept., and divided against the second reading of the Scottish bill, 23 Sept. He was in a minority of 13 for the reduction of salaries to 1797 levels, 30 June, and voted for the cessation of the Maynooth grant, 26 Sept. He was absent from the division on the second reading of the revised reform bill, 17 Dec. 1831. He welcomed a petition concerning the unrest in Westmeath, declaring that it was 'in such a state of insubordination that the laws, as now constituted, are not strong enough', and urged government to 'adopt some measures to stop the progress of crime', 15 Mar. 1832. He divided against the third reading of the reform bill, 22 Mar., and was in the minority of 27 for Waldo Sibthorp's amendment concerning Lincoln freeholders, 23 Mar. He voted against the second reading of the Irish reform bill, 25 May. He divided against ministers on the abolition of slavery, 24 May, and the Russian-Dutch loan, 12 July, but voted for their Irish tithes bill, 13 July 1832. He was a founder member of the Conservative Society of Dublin established that summer.[8]

At the 1832 general election he stood unsuccessfully as a Conservative for Athlone and he was defeated in Westmeath in 1837. Following his succession in 1840 as 3rd Baron Castlemaine he pressed his claims to the Irish representative peerage, but finding that it had 'been arranged that ... Lord Caledon should come in' on the first vacancy, he informed Sir Robert Peel, 6 Mar. 1841, that he was 'not willing to create any division' and would 'withdraw', adding that 'in doing so, I hope I shall be considered on the next vacancy, trusting that *past* services and that my endeavours to recover what we have at present lost in Westmeath and Athlone, will not be forgotten'.[9] He was duly elected a representative peer in July 1841 and served until his death in July 1869. He was succeeded in the Irish barony by his elder surviving son Richard (1826-92).

[1] *PP* (1835), xxvii. 326-7. [2] *Westmeath Jnl.* 8, 22 June 1826. [3] *PP* (1835), xxvii. 332. [4] Add. 40393, f. 3. [5] Wellington mss WP1/914/49. [6] *Kilkenny Moderator*, 11 Aug. 1830. [7] Ibid. 30 Apr. 1831; *Westmeath Jnl.* 12 May 1831. [8] NLI, Farnham mss 18611 (3), T. Lefroy to Farnham, 4 June 1832. [9] Add. 40429, f. 138.

P.J.S.

HANDLEY, Henry (1797–1846), of 7 Charles Street, Mdx. and Culverthorpe Hall, nr. Sleaford, Lincs.

HEYTESBURY	3 Aug. 1820–1826
LINCOLNSHIRE SOUTH	1832–1841

b. 17 Mar. 1797, 3rd but 1st surv. s. of Benjamin Handley, attorney and banker, of Sleaford and Frances, da. of Jacob Conington of Boston, Lincs. *educ.* Charterhouse 1805; Eton 1811; Christ Church, Oxf. 1815; L. Inn 1816. *m.* 15 Oct. 1825, Hon. Caroline Edwardes, da. of William Edwardes[†], 2nd Bar. Kensington [I], 2s. 8da.; 1s. illegit. *suc.* fa. 1828. *d.* 29 June 1846.

This Member's father, Benjamin Handley of Sleaford (*b.* 1754), was descended from an old Nottinghamshire family, being the youngest son of William Handley (1719-86) of Newark, a mason, who married Sarah, the daughter of Benjamin Farnworth of Sutton, a Newark stationer. He, who married into a Boston gentry family, had a son Benjamin, who was born late in 1785, but this child must have been dead by 1791, when another son of his was baptized Benjamin.[1] This Benjamin, a lieutenant in the 9th Dragoon Guards, drowned in 1813, when his boat was upset in Lisbon harbour. Another Benjamin Handley (1784-1858), a captain in that regiment, who only

narrowly survived the same accident, was the second son of William Handley (1746-98), the eldest son of William Handley of Newark.[2] Promoted to the rank of major in 1816, he became Member for Boston in 1832, while his elder brother William Farnworth Handley was elected for Newark in February 1831.[3]

Henry Handley, the last of seven children, was briefly educated at Oxford and Lincoln's Inn, but apparently did not take his degree or practice as a barrister. Shortly after the end of the 1820 session, he was returned for Heytesbury, presumably by purchase, in place of one of the brothers of Sir William A'Court[†], the proprietor. In the House he occasionally registered wayward votes, but generally sided with the Liverpool administration. He divided in defence of their conduct towards Queen Caroline, 6 Feb. 1821. He voted against Catholic claims, 28 Feb. 1821, and the Catholic peers bill, 30 Apr. 1822. He divided against repeal of the additional malt duty, 3 Apr., and parliamentary reform, 9 May, but for the forgery punishment mitigation bill, 23 May 1821. He voted against more extensive tax reductions to relieve distress, 11, 21 Feb. 1822. Opposing reduction of the salt duties, 28 Feb., he declared, in a maiden speech which was ridiculed by the radical John Wade,[4] that

> notwithstanding the wild speculations which had been propagated, he could not think taxation the cause of, nor parliamentary reform the remedy for, the distress which existed. He was thoroughly convinced that the distress was almost solely and exclusively to be ascribed to excessive production.

Nevertheless, he voted in the majorities for reducing the number of junior lords of the admiralty, 1 Mar., and abolishing one of the joint-postmasterships, 2 May, and in the minority for total repeal of the salt duties, 3 June 1822. He divided against inquiry into the right of voting in parliamentary elections, 20 Feb., and reform of the Scottish representative system, 2 June 1823. He voted in the minority for reducing the import price of corn to 60s., 26 Feb., but against repealing certain taxes, 3, 16 Mar. He voted against repeal of the Foreign Enlistment Act, 16 Apr., yet divided with opposition for inquiry into the legal proceedings against the Dublin Orange rioters, 22 Apr. He voted for the advanced Whig Sir William Amcotts Ingilby[*] at the Lincolnshire by-election in late 1823.[5]

Handley divided against the usury bill, 27 Feb. 1824. He was in the minority for an advance of capital to Ireland, 4 May. He was a teller for the majority for the West India Company bill, 10 May. He objected to the warehoused wheat bill, 17 May, saying that it would be beneficial to the president of the board of trade William Huskisson's Liverpool constituents, but would not help the general cause of agriculture, 'since it would hold out an encouragement to foreign countries to deluge the British market with their corn'. He moved a wrecking amendment against its second reading, but withdrew it after further debate. He divided against condemning the trial of the Methodist missionary John Smith in Demerara, 11 June 1824. He voted against Catholic relief, 1 Mar., 21 Apr., and the Irish franchise bill, 26 Apr., and paired against the third reading of the relief bill, 10 May 1825. In committee on the corn laws, 2 May, he agreed with Huskisson's proposal for a 10s. duty on bonded corn, but did 'not approve the plan for importing wheat from Canada at the intended low duty'. He voted against the grant for the duke of Cumberland, 30 May. He was in the majority for the spring guns bill, 21 June 1825. His only other known votes in this Parliament were against the corn importation bill, 11 May, and for resolutions to curb electoral bribery, 26 May 1826. He left the House at the dissolution that summer.

Handley, who until then had lived in Sleaford, took up residence at Culverthorpe Hall at about the time of his marriage in 1825.[6] Three years later, on the death of his father, who was deputy recorder of Boston, 1817-26, he inherited property in Lincolnshire and Nottinghamshire and the bulk of his estate, which included personal wealth sworn under £20,000. He also came into his father's share of the Sleaford and Newark bank of Peacock, Handley and Company, which he had founded in the 1790s.[7] Handley began to take a serious interest in agricultural affairs and, although he professed to be a reformer, he retained much of the political outlook of a country gentleman and ministerialist. Along with his cousins, he may have been considered for the vacancy at Newark in 1829, and it is possible that he assisted in the promotion of their ambitions there and in Boston during the following years.[8] In late 1829 he offered a premium of £100 for the invention of a steam plough, and it was reported that he had 'expected ere this to have seen the wonder-working powers of steam applied to general agricultural purposes, and that locomotive engines would have smoked in our fields, even before they had established themselves on our roads'.[9]

He signed the requisition for a Lincolnshire meeting to complain about agricultural distress, and, when the sheriff refused to give his permission, chaired an informal meeting, 8 Jan. 1830, which agreed to petition the Commons for a reduction of the beer and malt taxes.[10] At the general election that year he was approached to stand with Amcotts Ingilby against the ministerial Member, Charles Chaplin, but he felt obliged to decline.[11] He again put his name to a requisition for a county meeting, at which, 8 Oct. 1830, he seconded the motion for a petition against the malt tax. He observed that

> it was impossible for the present system to continue long; the voice of the people must prevail; there was some ground of hope from the present House of Commons; they enjoyed a greater share of popularity; and he hoped those ministers who were rather for increasing than lessening the burdens of the people, would meet with something like a serious opposition.[12]

In seconding the nomination of Amcotts Ingilby at the general election of 1831, he explained that

> reform was once a wild and indefinite term; it comprised every change from the man who lent a tardy and unwilling vote to the disfranchisement of some petty detested borough, to him who went to the daring length of universal suffrage; thanks to His Majesty's ministers, we have now a certain test by which we can separate the metal from the dross: will you support the bill, aye or no!

He made clear his own support for the Grey ministry's reform bill, 'which I believe firmly, while it secures the liberty of the people, will give support to the crown and stability to the established institutions of the country'.[13] In November 1831 he signed the requisition for a county meeting on reform, which he silently attended.[14] Once the reform bill had passed, he offered for the Kesteven and Holland division of Lincolnshire, declaring in an address, 22 June 1832, that the reasons for his former refusal no longer existed: 'the provisions of the bill, which essentially affect the regulations of county elections, alike diminish the inconvenience of the voter and the unavoidable expenses of the candidate'. He advocated further economies, agricultural protection and the abolition of slavery.[15] He was promised the support of the former prime minister Lord Goderich, and, 'highly beloved by the gentry, and farmers and tradespeople', he was considered 'certain of his election'. He was duly returned unopposed at the general election of 1832 and sat until 1841 as a Liberal, though he concentrated his efforts on defending the agricultural interest.[16]

According to James Grant, Handley, 'a respectable speaker, but nothing more', was

> a tall, stout, good-looking man. He has a jolly, countrified countenance, with a complexion redolent of health. His face is full, and his features are regular and pleasing. His hair is of a light brown, and he sports a pair of whiskers of which any Spanish Don might be proud.[17]

He died in June 1846, dividing his estate among his numerous children, but revoking the annuity that he had previously intended for Henry Handley Farrell, the natural son of one Mary Farrell, because he had 'wilfully abandoned' his profession.[18] His elder legitimate son, Henry Edwardes (1835-92), of Barrowby Cottage, Grantham, was a lieutenant in the 2nd Dragoon Guards, and the younger, the Rev. Edward (1842-1904), was rector of Clipsham, Rutland and Winthorpe, Nottinghamshire.

[1] G.Y. Hemingway, 'Handley Fam.' (typescript, Newark Mus.), 57-58; IGI (Lincs.). [2] Hemingway, 63; The Times, 17 May 1813. [3] The two cousins called Benjamin Handley have sometimes been confused; for example, Burke LG (1937), 1043. [4] Black Bk. (1823), 160-2. [5] Lincs. Pollbook (1823), 75. [6] Hemingway, 64-65. [7] Ibid. 58-61; Gent. Mag. (1828), i. 477; PROB 11/1744/472; IR26/1166/610. [8] See NEWARK. [9] Devizes Gazette, 24 Dec. 1829. [10] Lincoln Herald, 11 Dec. 1829, 15 Jan. 1830. [11] Ibid. 6 Aug. 1830; Boston Gazette, 3 July 1832. [12] Lincoln Herald, 1, 15 Oct. 1830. [13] Ibid. 13 May 1831. [14] Ibid. 11, 25 Nov. 1831. [15] Boston Gazette, 3 July 1832. [16] Add. 40879, f. 49; The Times, 30 June, 17 Nov., 19 Dec. 1832; Hemingway, 66-68; N. Gash, Politics in Age of Peel, 179. [17] [J. Grant], Random Recollections of Lords and Commons (1838), ii. 138-40. [18] Gent. Mag. (1846), ii. 205; PROB 11/2043/729.

S.M.F.

HANDLEY, William Farnworth (1780–1851), of North Gate, Newark, Notts.

NEWARK   21 Feb. 1831–1834

b. 9 Oct. 1780, 1st s. of William Handley of Newark and Ann, da. of John Marshall of Pickering, Yorks. unm. suc. fa. 1798. d. 4 Dec. 1851.
  Lt. Newark vols. 1798, capt. 1803.
  Sheriff, Notts. 1822-3.

Handley belonged to a family long prominent in Newark, where his father was a banker (until 1791) and brewer and had a share in a cotton mill. He entered the family business, succeeded his father to his urban property in 1798 and in 1801 became a partner with his younger brother John (1782-1856) in the brewery, which had a branch at Gainsborough, Lincolnshire. They were partners in the Newark branch of the Sleaford bank of Peacock, Handley and Kirton.[1] Handley was a leading supporter of the united (Newcastle-Middleton) interest at Newark, and after the 1826 election was consulted over the proposed eviction of recalcitrant tenants.[2] He subsequently purchased most of the Newark property (two dozen houses) of Sir Jenison Gordon of Haverholme Priory, Lincolnshire, a friend of his uncle Benjamin Handley of Sleaford.[3] At the rowdy Newark by-election of March 1829 he appealed from the hustings for

order when the anti-Catholic Michael Sadler* was nominated.[4] At the 1830 general election he proposed the Middleton sitting Member Willoughby.[5] When Willoughby resigned in February 1831 Handley, after an initial demur, accepted an invitation from 400 electors to stand against the reformer Wilde, with Lord Middleton's tacit support and the duke of Newcastle's blessing. At the nomination he declared his support for every practical measure of reform and reduced taxation, but when questioned declined to support the ballot, arguing that the Grey ministry's intention 'to propose so full and fair a reform' made it unnecessary. He opposed further interference with the currency. He comfortably beat Wilde.[6]

Handley, who is not known to have spoken in debate in this period, voted for the second reading of the reform bill, 22 Mar., but with opposition for Gascoyne's successful wrecking amendment, 19 Apr. 1831. Abused in Newark for his desertion of ministers, he defended his behaviour in an explanatory handbill:

> Though a supporter of the reform bill, I did think that the number of Members for England and Wales ought not to be diminished, but that other large and populous towns, beyond those contemplated by ministers, should have the elective franchise conferred upon them.[7]

Standing for Newark at the subsequent general election, he retained the support of Middleton but, anxious to avoid an expensive contest following the collapse of the united interest, he was prevailed on to coalesce with Newcastle's nominee Gresley in order to keep out Wilde. The unnatural coalition did not last long, and Handley incurred Newcastle's wrath for his 'treachery' in declining to ensure that his second votes went to Gresley. Censured again on the hustings for his equivocation over reform, he refuted the imputation of having hindered the progress of public business by supporting the call for an adjournment, 21 Apr., and, though guarded over his paradoxical association with Newcastle's nominee, he pledged himself to 'support the bill in all its stages'. He was returned in second place with Wilde.[8]

Handley voted for the second reading of the reintroduced reform bill, 6 July 1831, and for most of its details. He was in the minority for the postponement of a new writ for Dublin, 8 Aug., but voted twice with government against charges of improper interference in the election, 23 Aug. He voted for the third reading and passage of the reform bill, 19 and 21 Sept., and the second reading of the Scottish reform bill, 23 Sept., but took three weeks' leave on account of ill health, 28 Sept., and so missed the division on the confidence motion, 10 Oct. He voted for the second reading of the revised reform bill, 17 Dec. 1831, was again a steady supporter of its details and divided for the third reading, 22 Mar. 1832. He voted with ministers on the Russian-Dutch loan, 26 Jan., 16, 20 July, and relations with Portugal, 9 Feb., but was in the minority for inquiry into the glove trade, 31 Jan. He presented a Newark petition against the general register bill, 6 Feb. He divided for Lord Ebrington's motion for an address calling on the king to appoint only ministers who would carry reform unimpaired, 10 May. He cast wayward votes for the Liverpool disfranchisement bill, 23 May, and against government's temporizing amendment to Fowell Buxton's motion for the immediate abolition of slavery, 24 May. He voted for the second reading of the Irish reform bill, 25 May, and against Conservative amendments to the Scottish bill, 1, 15 June. He voted for making inquests public, 20 June 1832.

Handley was returned for Newark as a Conservative at the general election of 1832 and retired from Parliament in 1834. Elected to Newark town council in 1836, he remained a prominent figure in borough politics.[9] He died a bachelor in December 1851.

[1] G.Y. Hemingway, 'Handley Fam.' (typescript, Newark Mus.), 29-30, 36. [2] Notts. Archives, Tallents mss, Tallents to Newcastle, 15, 23 Sept. 1826. [3] Ibid. same to same, 10 Oct. 1826. [4] Nottingham Jnl. 7 Mar. 1829. [5] Ibid. 7 Aug. 1830. [6] Tallents mss, Tallents to Newcastle, 5 Feb., Handley to same, 8 Feb., reply, 9 Feb.; Nottingham Univ. Lib. Newcastle mss Ne2 F3/1/318, 320; Nottingham Jnl. 26 Feb. 1831. [7] Lincoln and Newark Times, 27 Apr. 1831. [8] Newcastle mss Ne2 F4/1/18, 22; NeC 4527-9, 4531, 4533; Tallents mss, Tallents to Godfrey [May]; Lincoln and Newark Times, 27 Apr., 4 May 1831. [9] Add. 44358, f. 100.

S.R.H.

HANMER, Henry (1789–1868), of 7 Devonshire Place, Mdx. and Stockgrove Park, Soulbury, Bucks.

WESTBURY   1831–24 June 1831

AYLESBURY   1832–1837

b. 30 Apr. 1789,[1] 5th s. of Sir Thomas Hanmer, 2nd bt. (d. 1828), of Bettisfield Park, Flints. and Margaret, da. of George Kenyon of Peel Hall, Lancs. educ. Rugby 1799; Peterhouse, Camb. 1807. m. 27 Jan. 1815, Sarah Serra, da. of Sir Morris Ximenes of Bear Place, nr. Maidenhead, Berks., s.p. suc. aunt Arabella Hanmer to Stockgrove 1828; KH 1833. d. 2 Feb. 1868.
  Cornet R. Horse Gds. 1808, lt. 1810, capt. 1813, maj. and lt.-col. 1826, ret. 1832.
  Sheriff, Bucks. 1854-5.

The Hanmer family, among whose members was the early eighteenth-century Speaker, Sir Thomas Hanmer, had long established interests in Flintshire and some, of more recent date, in Buckinghamshire. Hanmer's father, who succeeded his father, Walden Hanmer, former Member for Sudbury, in 1783, was an active improver of his estate at Bettisfield, where he otherwise lived a very retired life until his death in October 1828. Hanmer served in the Peninsula under the duke of Wellington, notably at Vitoria and Pamplona, where he was aide-de-camp to Sir Robert Hill, and he received a silver war medal with two clasps.[2] In late 1818 he asked his brother-in-law, the 2nd Lord Kenyon, to solicit Lord Liverpool, the prime minister, for a place following the death of Colonel Edward Disbrowe†, vice-chamberlain to the late Queen Charlotte, but no appointment was forthcoming.[3] He was refused promotion in 1824, but in 1826 he was allowed to purchase his majority and a lieutenant-colonelcy in the army. Four years later he filed a criminal information against John Jebb for circulating allegations that he had profited by purchasing horses on his own account in order to resell them to his regiment at a higher price.[4] Under the will of his uncle, Edward Hanmer, who had died in 1821, he inherited an estate near Leighton Buzzard and the residue of personal wealth sworn under £12,000 on the death of his widow in 1828, and thereby gained an electoral interest in the neighbourhood.[5] In 1830 he applied for the knighthood that he had declined in 1814, after he had commanded the bodyguard which escorted Louis XVIII on his visit to London. This was refused, but he was created a knight of Hanover in 1833.[6]

At the general election of 1831 he was returned for Westbury with its patron, Sir Ralph Lopes, on the understanding that he would support parliamentary reform;[7] but on only the fourth sitting day of the session, 24 June, he vacated his seat and was replaced by Henry Frederick Stephenson, an ardent reformer. In the Commons, 20 Jan. 1832, John Wilson Croker, who was perhaps misled by the fact that Hanmer had been erroneously listed among the absentees on the second reading of the reintroduced reform bill, 6 July 1831, said that Lopes had removed him for voting against reform, a statement which Lopes did not deny. There were in fact no divisions during Hanmer's short spell in the House, but whatever the truth of this particular allegation he was evidently turned out because of his Tory, anti-reform views. In July 1832 Lord Chandos* chose him as his candidate for a vacancy at Aylesbury, which was expected on the appointment of Lord Nugent as commissioner of the Ionian Islands. He issued an address in defence of the agricultural interest and hostile to free trade in corn. He supposedly had a successful canvass, but was reported to have said, on leaving the town, that 'he had already paid quite as much as it was worth for the interest the marquis of Chandos possesses in the borough'.[8] In the event no vacancy occurred before the general election in December, when, after a renewed canvass, he spoke against extravagant expenditure and attacks on the property of the established church. Challenged on the hustings about his conduct in Parliament, he made clear that he had not voted on the reform bill, which he had opposed, and that he had 'resigned his seat rather than abandon his principles'. He was elected as a Conservative with William Rickford*, against the Liberal Thomas Benjamin Hobhouse†, at a cost of £5,000.[9] A member of the Carlton Club and a magistrate in Bedfordshire, Berkshire and Buckinghamshire, he retired from the House in 1837. He died in February 1868, leaving his residual estate to his nephew, Wyndham Edward Hanmer (1810-87), the second son of his eldest brother Thomas, who succeeded as 4th baronet in 1881.

[1] IGI (Flints.). [2] Lord Hanmer, *Mem. of Parish and Fam. of Hanmer*, 206-7; R. Gibbs, *Hist. Aylesbury*, 290-1. [3] Add. 38274, f. 236. [4] Wellington mss WP1/799/5; 800/3; 865/27; *Gent. Mag.* (1826), i. 558; *The Times*, 5 May 1830. [5] PROB 11/1648/506; 1754/224; IR26/1197/166. [6] Wellington mss WP1/1108/26. [7] *Devizes Gazette*, 5 May 1831. [8] NLS mss 3870, f. 75; *Bucks Gazette*, 28 July; *Bucks. Herald*, 28 July, 4 Aug. 1832; R.W. Davis, *Political Change and Continuity*, 111-12. [9] *Bucks. Gazette*, 10 Nov., 15 Dec.; *Bucks. Herald*, 15 Dec. 1832; Add. 40486, f. 194.

S.M.F.

HARBORD, Hon. Edward (1781–1835), of Henbury House, nr. Wimborne Minster, Dorset and Gunton Hall, Norf.[1]

GREAT YARMOUTH	1806–1812
SHAFTESBURY	1820–1 Aug. 1821

b. 10 Nov. 1781, 3rd but 2nd surv. s. of Harbord Harbord†, 1st Bar. Suffield (*d.* 1810), and Mary, da. and coh. of Sir Ralph Assheton, 3rd bt., of Middleton, Lancs.; bro. of Hon. William Assheton Harbord†. *educ.* Aylsham, Norf. 1787; Neasden; Eton 1793; Christ Church, Oxf. 1799; Northern tour (Denmark, Russia, Prussia) 1800; L. Inn 1802. *m.* (1) 19 Sept. 1809, Hon. Georgiana Venables Vernon (*d.* 30 Sept. 1824), da. and h. of George Venables Vernon†, 2nd Bar. Vernon, 2s. 1da.; (2) 12 Sept. 1826, Emily Harriott, da. of Evelyn Shirley of Ettington, Warws., 7s. (1 *d.v.p.*) 1da. *suc.* bro. as 3rd Bar. Suffield 1 Aug. 1821. *d.* 6 July 1835.
Military sec. Gen. Decken's mission to Portugal Aug.-Sept. 1808.
Chairman, q.s. Norf. 1821-*d.*
Capt. Blickling rifle vols. 1803; lt.-col. 1 regt. E. Norf. militia 1808-21.

Harbord, a slight but athletic figure with an increasingly religious cast of mind, was politically at odds with his ministerialist elder brother, who succeeded their father as 2nd Baron Suffield in 1810. He resigned his seat for Great Yarmouth in 1812, but at the general election of 1818 stood unsuccessfully as an independent for Norwich, which his father had represented for 30 years.[2] The Quaker Joseph John Gurney of Earlham Hall, who got to know him at this time, commented that although his family was connected with 'the high party in church and state', Harbord was 'a friend to public improvement, especially adverse to all kinds of warfare, opposed to capital punishment, and zealous for the administration of prison discipline'; in the last cause he was a collaborator of another Norfolk country gentleman, Thomas Fowell Buxton*. Harbord joined Gurney in condemning corruption in Norwich municipal politics in March 1819, but later that year was privately reprimanded by him for making his laudable benevolent intentions the subject of ordinary daily conversation.[3] He condemned the Peterloo massacre, distancing himself at the same time from the radical Henry Hunt*, and declared that he held himself independent of Tory or Whig allegiances at the Norfolk county meeting in October 1819. This provoked Suffield, whose wife was the sister-in-law of the foreign secretary Lord Castlereagh*, into disowning him.[4] Abandoned by the Purple and Orange party (supporters of Lord Liverpool's administration) in Norwich, he withdrew his pretensions there at the general election of 1820.[5] Instead, he accepted the invitation of the Whig Lord Grosvenor to come in, as 'a *brother reformer*', for his newly acquired borough of Shaftesbury. Assured by Grosvenor that he would 'be at liberty on all occasions to use your entire discretion' and would not be displaced simply to suit the convenience of the patron's family, he was duly returned unopposed and without expense, under the wing of his colleague Abraham Moore.[6]

An assiduous attender and latterly a reasonably capable speaker, Harbord was credited with having voted with the Whig opposition in almost all known division lists during his second spell in the House. According to Buxton's later recollection, he was

> most diligent in all his parliamentary duties; I remember one session he never missed a division but once, when he was dining with me, and a division took place without his being aware of it, which he much lamented. He was perhaps the only man in the House of Commons at that time who could say as much.[7]

He commented on the 'impolicy' of the barrack system, 16 June, opposed capital punishment, 30

June, supported the New South Wales duties bill, 3 July, and pointed out the urgency of assisting Irish paupers, 10 July 1820.[8] He criticized conditions at the gaol in Norwich, 5 July, and later that year published his proposals for the erection of a replacement in his *Remarks Respecting the Norfolk County Gaol*.[9] He divided against the appointment of a secret committee on the Queen Caroline affair, 26 June. In a letter to his friend and later biographer Richard Mackenzie Bacon, 17 Aug., he condemned ministers' conduct over this and expressed his fears of queenite unrest. He added that 'I *did not miss* a division during the last session of Parliament, excepting the last, and that took place after I had left town', and that he had ('but I disdained party') on one occasion sided with government; possibly this was on Wilberforce's compromise motion on the queen, 22 June, when he was not listed in the minority.[10] His constituents entrusted him with an address to her in July and a petition in her support in October.[11] Replying publicly to the reformers of Middleton, who had invited him to support the queen on the same platform as William Cobbett[†] and John Cartwright, 11 Oct., he made it clear that they were the 'leaders of a particular party [which] would alone be with me sufficient reason for not acting in connection with them'. Cobbett replied angrily to this snub by quoting in his *Political Register* an extract from the forthcoming *Links of the Lower House*, which exposed Harbord's aristocratic connections and repeated the canard that he had received £5,000 under his father-in-law's will in order to buy a parliamentary seat.[12] Harbord dismissed his political enemies in a letter to Bacon, 12 Nov. 1820, as 'poor misguided radicals', though he had earlier warned him that '*reform* can alone prevent revolution'. At about this time he was shown round the site of Peterloo by a leading Manchester magistrate, who temporarily convinced him that he and his colleagues had acted precipitely out of pure terror.[13]

Harbord, who in December 1820 avowed that 'a revolution must ensue if the present ministers continue in office' and in February 1821 contributed £50 to the subscription for the dismissed army officer Sir Robert Wilson*, an advanced Whig, continued to vote regularly with opposition.[14] He complained of political subjects intruding into sermons on the queen's case, 13 Feb. He divided for Catholic relief, 28 Feb. He seconded the motion for the appointment of a select committee on the vagrancy laws, 14 Mar., and secured another on the sale of bread, 15 Mar.; he served on these and was added to the select committee on another of his main interests, gaols, 21 Mar. He spoke 'a few words' on education in Ireland, 1 Mar., and the

army estimates, 30 Mar., but their substance went unrecorded.[15] He was scathing in his attack on the game laws, 5 Apr., when he was teller for the minority for inquiry into them, and backed investigation of Ilchester gaol, 11 Apr. He warned of the dangers of extra-parliamentary forces pledged to revolution and urged the House to reform itself 'from within', 18 Apr., and voted for Lambton's reform proposals that day; he again divided for parliamentary reform, 9 May, and alteration of the Scottish county representation, 10 May. He presented and endorsed petitions for inquiry into the yeomanry's actions at Peterloo, 15 May, voted in the minority for this, 16 May, and, on the barrack grant, 28 May, declared himself 'decidedly averse' to measures of public intimidation.[16] He praised the vagrancy bill, asserting that it was the duty of a civilized society to relieve those in need, 24 May, spoke and voted for the forgery punishment mitigation bill, 4 June, and in the poor law debate, 7 June, argued the government ought to promote an increase in the population rather than encourage vice and misery as a check to its increase.[17] He opposed paying the arrears on the grant to the duke of Clarence, 8 June, and, after Hume had declined to press this to a division, moved an amendment against the arrears, which was lost by 119-43. He reverted to this topic, 29 June, and made his last known interventions in the House, 2 July 1821.[18]

He inherited his peerage in August 1821 and soon made plans to revamp Gunton, but his late brother fulfilled his promise by bequeathing the unentailed properties to his widow. He resigned his command of the local militia, in protest over Peterloo, but accepted the chairmanship of the quarter sessions.[19] As testimony to his independent conduct in Parliament, his constituents at Shaftesbury, at the suggestion of Grosvenor's political opponents, awarded him a gold snuff box. Thanking them, he promised to continue in the Lords along the same political course.[20] At the Norfolk meeting on agricultural distress, 12 Jan. 1822, when he advocated relief measures and parliamentary reform, he was reported as declaring that 'he didn't belong to any party ... by party in this instance he meant *faction*, understanding *faction* to be founded on men, party on principle'. Yet, while remaining hostile to ministers, in March 1822 he wrote to Bacon that 'I do not desire a change of ministers ... a Whig ministry would be as hostile to reform as the present'.[21] In the Lords, where he continued to promote his favourite causes, he campaigned almost single-handedly for the abolition of colonial slavery. He died, from the effects of a fall from his horse, in July 1835.[22] He was succeeded as Baron Suffield in turn by the first surviving sons of each of his two wives: Edward Vernon (1813-53), a huntsman and gambler, who was one of the defeated Liberal candidates for Norwich at the general election of 1834, and Charles (1830-1924), a soldier and courtier.

[1] Based on R.M. Bacon, *Mem. of Bar. Suffield* (1838). [2] *HP Commons, 1790-1820*, iv. 147-9. [3] *Mems. of J.J. Gurney* ed. J.B. Braithwaite, i. 154-8; *Buxton Mems.* 64; Bacon, 118. [4] *The Times*, 1 Nov. 1819; Bacon, 85-95. [5] Bacon, 95-100, 110; *HP Commons, 1790-1820*, ii. 295. [6] Norf. RO, Gunton mss GTN/1/3, Grosvenor to Harbord, 7, 9, 10 Feb.; 1/7, Moore to same, 5 Mar.; 1/9, Suffield to Harbord, 20 Feb. 1820; Bacon, 101-4, 110-11. [7] Bacon, 118-20. [8] *The Times*, 22 June, 4, 11 July 1820. [9] Bacon, 126-7. [10] Ibid. 121-3. [11] *Salisbury Jnl.* 10, 17 July, 21 Aug.; Gunton mss 1/7, Gillingham to Harbord, 5 Oct. 1820. [12] Bacon, 43, 124-6, 130-1; *Pol. Reg.* 4, 11 Nov. 1820; *Links of Lower House* (1821), 16. [13] Bacon, 124. [14] Ibid. 131-3. [15] *The Times*, 2, 31 Mar. 1821. [16] Ibid. 16 May 1821. [17] Ibid. 8 June 1821. [18] Ibid. 3 July 1821. [19] Bacon, 139-42; PROB 11/1331/885. [20] Bacon, 144-9; Gunton mss 1/14, Jones to Suffield, 8 Sept.; *Salisbury Jnl.* 10 Sept. 1821. [21] Bacon, 151-2, 164; *The Times*, 14 Jan. 1822. [22] Bacon, 506-12; *The Times*, 1, 8 July 1835; *Gent. Mag.* (1835), ii. 317-20; *DNB*; *Oxford DNB*.

R.M.H./S.M.F.

HARCOURT *see* **VERNON**, **George Granville Venables**

HARCOURT VERNON (formerly **VERNON**), **Granville Venables** (1792–1879), of Grove Park, Notts.

ALDBOROUGH	4 May 1815–1820
EAST RETFORD	1831–1847

b. 26 July 1792, 7th but 6th surv. s. of Rt. Rev. and Hon. Edward Venables Vernon (afterwards Harcourt) (*d.* 1847), abp. of York, and Lady Anne Leveson Gower, da. of Granville Leveson Gower†, 1st mq. of Stafford; bro. of George Granville Venables Vernon* (afterwards Harcourt). *educ.* Westminster 1805; Christ Church, Oxf. 1810; L. Inn 1811, called 1817. *m.* (1) 22 Feb. 1814, Frances Julia (*d.* 5 Feb. 1844), da. and coh. of Anthony Hardolph Eyre† of Grove Park, 5s. (4 *d.v.p.*) 1da. *d.v.p.*; (2) 22 Nov. 1845, Hon. Pyne Jessie Brand Trevor, da. of Henry Otway, 21st Bar. Dacre, wid. of John Henry Cotterell, *s.p.* Took name of Harcourt before Vernon (his fa. having suc. to Oxon. estates of William Harcourt†, 3rd Earl Harcourt) 15 Jan. 1831. *d.* 8 Dec. 1879.

Chan. dioc. York, 1818–*d.*; official principal, chancery ct. of York 1818–*d.*[1]

This Member's father, the archbishop of York, was a younger son of George Vernon, who adopted the surname Venables Vernon (the usual form for his offspring) and was created Baron Vernon in 1762; his third wife was the sister of the 1st Earl Harcourt and their daughter, the archbishop's sister, married the 2nd Earl. On the death of the childless 3rd Earl Harcourt in June 1830, the headship of the family descended to the archbishop's nephew, the 4th Baron Vernon, but the entail was cut off in favour of the archbishop, who inherited his first cousin's Oxfordshire estates and changed his name early the following year. The archbishop's eldest son George Granville Venables Vernon, who represented Lichfield, 1806-31, likewise adopted the surname Harcourt and subsequently sat for Oxfordshire on the family interest there. However, his younger brother Granville, this Member, who had sat for Aldborough from 1815 to 1820, seems, like some of his other siblings, to have dropped Venables and taken the surname of Harcourt Vernon (although, confusingly, both he and his brother were occasionally referred to as 'Vernon Harcourt').[2] He had been given the sinecure of official principal of the chancery court of York in 1818 by his father, who was later criticized for distributing such places within his numerous family. At that time the income was under £1,000 a year, but by May 1830, when he gave evidence before the ecclesiastical commissioners, it averaged £1,200 per annum, of which £200 was used to pay his deputy.[3]

Vernon's increasingly overt connection with the Whigs was probably what lost him his seat at the dissolution in 1820, since the electoral patron of Aldborough, the 4th duke of Newcastle, was a Tory and anti-Catholic. His marriage drew him into East Retford politics, and, like his wife's brother-in-law Lord Manvers, he complained to Newcastle, who had a dormant interest there, about the outrageous proceedings at the general election of 1826.[4] When the enlarged borough was again contested in 1830, Vernon offered as an independent in place of another brother-in-law, Henry Gally Knight*, who attempted to win St. Albans. Newcastle, who privately deprecated the standing and performance of 'Venomous Vernon', brought forward Arthur Duncombe and connived with Manvers for the return of the latter's heir Lord Newark, so Vernon, who had refused to countenance treating, was forced to resign on the third day of the poll.[5] According to an early report, he had been confident of success, but John Evelyn Denison* put his defeat down to 'personal unpopularity and bad management'.[6] However, the local Whig paper reported that his retiring speech 'filled his very opponents with compunction' and secured his promise of future support.[7] He was the principal speaker at the East Retford reform meeting in March 1831, and stood again as an uncompromising advocate of reform at the general election that spring, when he was 'enthusiastically placed at the head of the poll', being returned with Newark at Duncombe's expense.[8]

In the Commons his appearances may occasionally have been mistaken not only for those of his brother, but also of Lord Vernon's heir George John Venables Vernon, who came in for Derbyshire. He made a forthright speech in favour of the Grey ministry's popular and extensive reform bill, 5 July 1831, declaring that he 'hailed the advent of reform as that of a tutelary deity' and 'regarded its avatar as the approach of an era of safety and of regeneration'. He duly voted for its second reading the following day, and generally for its details thereafter, though he divided for Lord Chandos's amendment to enfranchise £50 tenants-at-will, 18 Aug. On 2 Sept. he supported government's amendment of the proposition to place Aylesbury, Cricklade, East Retford and New Shoreham on the same footing as other boroughs, thereby preventing the freeholders from having a double franchise. He sided with ministers on the Dublin election, 23 Aug., but on the 29th he reproached the House for resolving to suspend the Liverpool writ, arguing that the extension of the borough's franchise under the reform bill would be a sufficient safeguard against future bribery. Convinced of the futility of delay, he moved a new writ, 5 Sept., considering that it was 'unnecessary and inexpedient to take up the case of a particular borough' and being determined to achieve by the reform bill that 'which at so great an expense was done for East Retford alone'. He acted as a teller in the subsequent division, which was lost by 41 votes, but succeeded in securing the writ, 12 Oct., when he was one of the majority tellers. He divided for the passage of the reform bill, 21 Sept., the second reading of the Scottish bill, 23 Sept., and Lord Ebrington's confidence motion, 10 Oct. 1831.

Harcourt Vernon presented a reform petition from Misterton, 7 Dec., and paired for the second reading of the revised reform bill, 17 Dec. 1831. Having spent part of the Christmas recess investigating the anticipated operation of the £10 qualification clause in a sample of 80 parishes, he proposed an amendment to enfranchise all £10 ratepayers, 3 Feb. 1832, an expedient which had 'the merit of making the burden coextensive with the privilege'; he was a teller for the minority of 184 (to 252). Styling himself one of the reform bill's 'cordial friends', he otherwise voted for its details, and the third reading, 22 Mar., but apparently missed the division on Ebrington's motion for an address calling on the king to appoint only ministers who would carry it unimpaired, 10 May. He suggested two minor improvements to the anatomy bill, 27 Jan., and divided against the production of information on Portugal, 9 Feb., but for inquiry into Peterloo, 15 Mar. He voted with government for the Russian-Dutch

loan, 26 Jan., but was listed among the reformers who were absent on this, 12 July 1832. He continued to sit for East Retford in the reformed Parliament and, although he later abandoned the Liberals over Irish church appropriation, he retained his seat until his retirement in 1847. His eldest son, Granville Edward (1816-61), was Member for Newark, 1852-7. On his death in December 1879 Harcourt Vernon was succeeded by his only surviving child, the Rev. Edward Hardolph (1821-90), prebend of Lincoln.[9]

[1] His brother, Rev. Leveson, was chan. of the cathedral of York. [2] E.W. Harcourt, *Harcourt Pprs.* xiii. 225. [3] *Black Bk.* (1832), 126-7; *PP* (1831-2), xxiv. 115-16; (1877), lxix. 15. [4] *Unhappy Reactionary* ed. R.A. Gaunt (Thoroton Soc. rec. ser. xliii), 49. [5] Ibid. 65-68; *Nottingham Jnl.* 24 July, 14 Aug. 1830. [6] Castle Howard mss, Lady Caroline Lascelles to Lady Carlisle [24 July 1830]; Add. 61937, f. 115. [7] *Nottingham Rev.* 13 Aug. 1830. [8] Ibid. 6 May; *Nottingham Jnl.* 26 Mar.; *The Times*, 9 May 1831; *Unhappy Reactionary*, 79, 82. [9] *Nottingham Jnl.* 9, 13 Dec. 1879.

S.R.H./S.M.F.

HARDINGE, Sir Henry (1785–1856), of Ketton, co. Dur. and 16 Sackville Street, Mdx.[1]

DURHAM	1820–1830
ST. GERMANS	1830–9 Dec. 1830
NEWPORT	17 Dec. 1830–1832
LAUNCESTON	1832–May 1844

b. 30 Mar. 1785, 3rd but 2nd surv. s. of Rev. Henry Hardinge (*d.* 1820) of Ketton, rect. of Stanhope, co. Dur., and Frances, da. of James Best of Park House, Boxley, Kent. *educ.* Durham sch.; R.M.C. 1806-7. *m.* 10 Dec. 1821, his cos. Emily Jane, da. of Robert Stewart[†], 1st mq. of Londonderry [I], wid. of John James, sec. of embassy and minister plenip. to the Netherlands, 2s. 2da. KCB 2 Jan. 1815; *suc.* fa. to Ketton (by purchase) 1828; GCB 1 July 1844; *cr.* Visct. Hardinge 2 May 1846. *d.* 14 Sept. 1856.

Ensign (army) 1798; lt. 4 Ft. Gds. 1802, 47 Ft. (half-pay) 1803; capt. 57 Ft. 1804, dep. q.m.g. Portuguese army 1809-14, maj. 1809; lt.-col. 40 Ft. 1814; capt. and lt.-col. 1 Ft. Gds. 1821, half-pay 1827; maj.-gen. 1830; col. 97 Ft. 1833; lt.-gen. 1841; col. 57 Ft. 1843-*d.*; c.-in-c. army Sept. 1852-July 1856; gen. 1854; f.m. 1855.

Clerk of ordnance Apr. 1823-May 1827, Jan.-May 1828; PC 30 May 1828; sec. at war May 1828-July 1830, Aug. 1841-July 1844; chief sec. to ld. lt. [I] July-Nov. 1830, Dec. 1834-Apr. 1835; gov.-gen. Bengal June 1844-8; master-gen. of ordnance Mar.-Sept. 1852.

Hardinge, an affable and able tactician, negotiator and administrator who established himself as the duke of Wellington's military and political aide-de-camp, was a direct descendant of the Civil War baronet,

Sir Robert Hardinge of King's Newton, Derbyshire, and a grandson of the clerk of the Commons (1731-48) and junior treasury secretary (1752-8) Nicholas Hardinge[†] (1699-1758). The latter's marriage in 1738 to the 1st Earl Camden's sister Jane presaged a close connection with the Pratt family and their kinsmen the Stewarts of Mount Stewart, county Down, which was strengthened by Hardinge's marriage in 1821 to the 1st marquess of Londonderry's next youngest daughter. She was also the widow of Camden's grandson. He passed much of his early childhood at The Grove, near Sevenoaks, Kent, but was educated in Durham, where his father was rector of Stanhope, worth £5,000 a year, and had a small estate at Ketton. School annals record that he 'used to be sent up the buttresses of the cathedral and on other dangerous expeditions in search of birds' eggs'.[2] Intended with his brothers George Nicholas, Richard and Frederick for a military career, he joined the Queen's Rangers with a commission at the age of 13, and for the next six years served with them in Canada, where his exploits included rescuing Lord Grey's future brother-in-law Edward Ellice* from a gang of robbers.[3] He attributed his subsequent success to the tuition of General Jarry at the Royal Military College, 1806-7, and Sir William Beresford's[†] decision to make him a deputy quartermaster-general in 1809. A distinguished veteran of the Peninsular war, he fought in all the major battles: under Wellington at Rolica and Vineiro (1808); with Sir John Moore[†], whom he tended when he was fatally wounded at Corunna (1809); at Albuera (1811), where the campaign historian Napier credited him personally with saving the day; and at Salamanca (1812), Vitoria (1813), the Pyrenees, Nivelle, Neve and Orthes (1814). Wellington seconded him to the staff of the Prussian Field Marshall Blücher for the Waterloo campaign, with the local rank of brigadier general, and his left hand was shattered by French fire at Quatre Bras, 16 June 1815, and amputated. Knighted and granted a £300 disability pension, he remained with the Prussian army of occupation until 1818.[4]

Hardinge returned to Durham in 1819 to test the political ground for his cousin Lord Charles William Stewart[†], the foreign secretary Lord Castlereagh's* half-brother, who was keen to revive the Vane Tempest (Wynyard) interest of his second wife and unseat her uncle by marriage, the Whig veteran Michael Taylor*. Though failing in the latter, Hardinge came in for Durham unopposed with government backing at the general election of 1820, after the sitting ministerialist Richard Wharton[†] was persuaded to vacate to contest the county.[5] He informed his aunt and future mother-in-law Lady Londonderry:

Though I do not intend to allow myself to be excited into any blindness of the difficulties I shall have to encounter in this new career, opposed to greater experience and more ready talkers than myself, yet I can unaffectedly say that I rather like the difficulties the better in proportion as I come in closer contact with them, and you may depend that as long as I can stir tongue or limb or any faculty I shall do my best endeavours to carry the point we have so earnestly at heart.[6]

As one of Castlereagh's family Members, 1820-2, Hardinge co-operated closely with David Ker, Thomas Wood and his lifelong confidant, and brother-in-law from 1821, Lord Ellenborough. He sent regular reports of debates to Lady Londonderry and shared in the allocation of Durham patronage during Stewart's absences abroad.[7] He thwarted schemes to illuminate the United Services Club and the Guards Club when Queen Caroline's prosecution was abandoned in November 1820, secured the 'expulsion' of *The Times* (then a Whig paper) from the latter and divided against censuring ministers' conduct of the affair, 6 Feb. 1821. He predicted, correctly, that the clamour it generated would be brief.[8] A lifelong advocate of religious toleration, he divided for Catholic relief, 28 Feb. 1821, 1 Mar., 21 Apr., 10 May 1825, but privately expressed 'unease' at

any material interference with the Protestant establishment in church and state. The fears of Popery I despise, but the innovation may tend to encourage a sort of combined assault of all the Dissenters.[9]

He voted against parliamentary reform, 9 May 1821, 2 June 1823, and in the ministerial majorities on economy and retrenchment, 4 July 1820, 27 July 1821, and against the malt duty repeal bill, 3 Apr. 1821.

By confining himself to military matters, on which he could demonstrate his professional expertise, Hardinge quickly acquired a reputation as a clear and businesslike speaker.[10] Drawing on personal experience and the 1817 finance committee report, he made an erudite defence of the army estimates, including the decision to retain seven Guards battalions, in his maiden speech, 14 Mar., and criticized attempts to secure reductions, 15 Mar., 11, 30 Apr., 1, 2, 21 May 1821.[11] He voted against disqualifying civil ordnance officers from voting at parliamentary elections, 12 Apr., and to retain capital punishment for forgery, 23 May. He paid an electioneering visit to Durham with Stewart and the Staffordshire Member Littleton in October 1821, and when he married in December he took a house in Grosvenor Place and arranged to purchase South Park, near Penshurst, Kent.[12] He divided steadily with government in 1822 and, clashing frequently with Hume, he doggedly defended the army estimates, including the cost of the Guards' table at St. James's, commissions, the promotion system and the grant to the Military College, 4, 6, 15, 22, 28 Mar.[13] Drawn into the political manoeuvring which followed the suicide of the 2nd marquess of Londonderry (Castlereagh) in August 1822, he found his patronage requests blocked after Stewart, as 3rd marquess, resigned his Austrian embassy and threatened to head a breakaway family party. He made a parliamentary tribute to his half-brother, a peerage with reversion to the issue of his second marriage and the colonelcy of the Londonderry militia the price of his continued support for government.[14] Trusted by Londonderry to 'feel and act as I do', Hardinge countered newspaper criticism of Castlereagh, declined to second the 1823 address and, backed by Wellington and the 1st Marquess Camden, secured a promise of the 'Derry regiment' and the titles of Earl Vane and Viscount Seaham for Londonderry, who had yet to return from the continent.[15] Contemplating war and a return to active service following the French invasion of Spain, he wrote to him, 24 Jan. 1823: 'Emily has spoilt me for the profession, but I detest politics, and would consent to be quiet for the rest of my life if the demands of my family did not point out exertion as a duty'.[16] No reports survive of his parliamentary attendance until March 1823, after Londonderry had confirmed his support for ministers.[17] He divided with them on taxation, 3, 18 Mar., and defended the grant to the Military College, 7 Mar. His appointment as clerk of the ordnance, reporting to Wellington as master-general, was gazetted on 5 Apr. 1823, a week after Londonderry's peerage.[18] Wynyard and Brancepeth (Russell) agents co-operated to see off a challenge to his re-election that month, a two-day poll engineered by the Whig county Member Lambton.[19]

Hardinge's competent presentation of the ordnance estimates, 27 Feb. 1824, when he carried the divisions against a 10,000-man reduction (by 89-19) and cutting the barrack grant (by 95-57), and his reply to Hobhouse were cheered and earned him the praise of the foreign secretary Canning.[20] A motion to reduce his salary failed, 9 Mar.[21] He brought in the mutiny bill and robustly defended military flogging, 5, 11, 15 Mar., as he was to do throughout his career, for he believed that the object of military punishment was 'not only ... the repression of crime, but effecting that object in the shortest possible time'. He intervened to support the secretary at war, Lord Palmerston, when the conduct of the Guards was criticized, 17 Mar., and took charge of the barrack amendment bill on the 25th.[22] Implicated by association in Londonderry's

five-month dispute with William Battier of the 10th Dragoons, he briefed Wellington on the matter and was Londonderry's second when it culminated in a much caricatured bloodless duel at Battersea, 12 May. Battier's subsequent insults and criticism were effectively silenced.[23] Attending to Durham business, he presented a petition for repeal of the coastwise coal duties, 23 Feb., tried unsuccessfully (with Thomas Wood) to have the Tees and Weardale railway bill, to which Londonderry objected, thrown out, 3 May 1824, and opposed the 1825 measure.[24] His vote against condemning the indictment in Demerara of the Methodist missionary John Smith for encouraging slaves to riot, 11 June 1824, was the subject of a hostile editorial on the 19th in the Whig *Durham Chronicle*. He spent much of that summer and the next with his wife and children at Muddiford, near Chichester, where their guest Mrs. Arbuthnot noted that Wellington had a high opinion of him.[25] He made light of opposition to the ordnance estimates, which included a £650 increase in his salary (to £1,836), 4 Mar., justified the use of troops for the Irish survey (as a member of the select committee), 7 Mar., and reproved Hume for overburdening his department with requests for printed returns, 23 June 1825.[26] His defence of the conduct of the first commissioner of woods and forests Arbuthnot and Wellington as trustees of the Deccan prize money deflected blame on to the governor of Madras Sir Thomas Hislop and was not well received, causing Canning to intervene, 1 July 1825; but he fared better on the 5th, when he made the claimants' lawyers the scapegoats.[27] A radical reviewer of the session noted that he 'spoke occasionally and with considerable force and animation'.[28] He justified the cost of renewing ordnance stores and artillery, upgrading barracks and maintaining the Woolwich establishment, but refused to give details of the Canadian expenditure, 6 Mar. 1826.[29] He voted against condemning the Jamaican slave trials, 2 Mar. 1826, and, heeding the comparisons made between them and courts martial, he submitted a memorial to Wellington recommending concessions on military flogging based on the Prussian two-tier punishment system that restricted it to the lower, non-commissioned ranks. The duke of York, as commander in chief, rejected the scheme.[30] Nothing came of an early flurry of opposition to his return for Durham, but his placeman status, want of patronage and failure to endorse the campaign against colonial slavery were all severely criticized at the general election in June. On the hustings he expressed his admiration for Pitt and support for Catholic relief.[31] Afterwards, he mediated between Londonderry and his eldest son Lord

Castlereagh, Member for county Down, on patronage and estate matters.[32]

Defending his department, Hardinge sidestepped Warburton's allegation that they had been supplied with inferior timber by their contractors by promising an internal investigation, 8 Dec. 1826; and prompted by the opposition later that day, he criticized the conduct of Colonel Bradley in refusing to recognize Colonel Arthur as his commander-in-chief in Honduras. He spoke similarly, 14 Feb. 1827.[33] On the estimates, 9, 16 Feb., he easily overcame criticism of the Irish survey and the barrack grant, but found Alexander Baring's criticism of the Canadian expenditure difficult to counter.[34] He defended the practice of awarding the best Sandhurst students free commissions, 19 Feb. Endorsing military flogging 'applied with leniency', 12 Mar., he cited a report by the governors of Millbank penitentiary stating that 'an error had been committed in abolishing corporal punishment' there and said that the armies in the Peninsula had found it a useful alternative to capital punishment.[35] He divided for Catholic relief, 6 Mar. His conduct following Liverpool's stroke was dictated by Londonderry, and he resigned with him in April when Canning's succession as premier was confirmed.[36] He continued to meet the Canningite Littleton socially and privately hoped to see Wellington remain at the ordnance or become commander-in-chief. Even so, he handled the official transfer to Lord Anglesey for the duke and prepared to defend him in the Commons.[37] On 7 May, as one of the few pro-Catholic Tories in opposition, he protested that Caning and his ministers had sacrificed Catholic relief to their desire for office, criticized the Lansdowne Whigs for abandoning the Catholics to support Canning despite his opposition to reform and challenged Henry Brougham to justify this 'monstrous' union of Whigs and Tories. He divided against their Coventry magistracy bill, 11 June 1827. In July Londonderry consulted him about a possible realignment in Durham politics when, as anticipated, Lambton became a peer. He suggested that if their city seat was also to be retained, a Wynyard-Lambton pact afforded the best prospect of securing Londonderry's son Viscount Seaham's future election for the county. He deliberately ruled himself out as a locum there, because he was a lackland without independent means.[38]

Hardinge was in London when Canning died in August 1827, and consulted John Calcraft*, John Croker*, Lord Falmouth, John Herries*, Littleton, Sir James Macdonald*, Robert Peel* and Sir Herbert Taylor* during the ensuing political negotiations,

of which he sent Londonderry, Ellenborough, Peel and Wellington detailed reports.[39] He advised Wellington against accepting the incoming premier Lord Goderich's offer to appoint him the army's commander-in-chief as it would make him the 'cat's paw and stalking horse' of the ministry, and said that he hoped to see him head an alternative ministry supported by Ellenborough, Grey and Lansdowne, not 'the Wilsons, Broughams and Burdetts', preparatory to a Tory realignment.[40] Croker recalled that Goderich was prepared to 'make room' for Hardinge at the ordnance, but no offer was made and Hardinge insisted that he would not have been 'neutralized' thus.[41] He regarded Goderich's administration from the outset as miserable, short-lived and 'trumped up ... from within their own interior', as the 'king cannot brook flying for refuge to any of his old friends', Ellenborough or Grey.[42] He accompanied Wellington on his October 1827 tour of the North-East and sent reports to London of his rapturous reception.[43] Preferring 'a coalition with the *High* Whigs to the *Low* Tories', he urged Londonderry to negotiate a formal pact with Lambton as a matter of urgency and plotted to bring down the ministry over the Navarino episode directly Parliament met.[44] Beforehand, he was a go-between for the chancellor of the exchequer Herries and Londonderry in the negotiations leading to the formation of Wellington's administration in January 1828.[45] Informing Londonderry, before visiting Peel at Drayton, of its likely Whig element and his hopes of office, 8 Jan., he admitted that he 'would rather see the Whigs a little more compromised and degraded and the Canning party and principles more completely shown up than to come into office now'. With a county by-election, through Lambton's peerage, imminent, he suggested conciliating William Russell* there to ensure his 'neutrality in case of a re-election for the city ... without compromising your right to oppose any Whig county Member hereafter'.[46] By the 15th, heartened by the 'fury' of the 'place-hunting Whigs' and the 'stiff Whigs' delight at their misfortune', he conceded the impolicy of including Grey (as an opponent of the Six Acts and the Foreign Enlistment Act) in the ministry 'even if he could get over his Catholic difficulty'. He also saw the necessity of retaining 'treacherous and cunning' Huskisson to boost their debating strength in the Commons and to avoid a straight 'peace and Tories, or war and Whigs' division.[47] When Londonderry, who was refused the Paris embassy and the Irish lord lieutenancy, publicly denounced the coalition and Hardinge's '*ungrateful, indirect and selfish*' support for it, he made a virtue of his return to the 'drudgery of the ordnance' to accommodate

Wellington, after hoping for something better. He also praised the duke's 'politic and able game' in declaring a 'necessary' amnesty, while working to restore the *'great Tory party'*.[48] To appease Londonderry, whom Lambton now encouraged to join opposition and deny him his Durham interest, he wrote:

> I felt it would have been dishonourable in me, pending a difficult negotiation where secrecy was most important, to divulge to you as a political leader, information not derived from being your Member (and which from day to day I might have, either from the duke or his confidants) being bound down to secrecy in the little that I did know. If you conceive that I ought as your Member to have divulged what I heard under such conditions of secrecy, your sense of what my obligations are essentially differ from the ideas I entertain of my duties, and as the moment is approaching when you can exercise your political power, and I must receive or decline a new obligation, I am bound in honour to take care that there should be no misunderstanding between us as to the terms.[49]

Reviewing the political situation on the 25th, he argued against an 'Ultra' or anti-Catholic government and claimed that the Canningite rump had been 'rendered innoxious':

> Huskisson is no longer at the head of trade, nor does he lead the House or represent the government. I consider him destroyed as a leader to do mischief. The Ultra Tories hate him, the Canningites loathe him, the Whigs are as bitter as gall against him, and as in a few weeks he will have been so vituperated that he cannot withdraw, he is *scotched*, and will not long survive as his reserves are weak. If he had joined the Whigs or held himself in balance at the head of the Canningites and a large independent class of economical disciples, he would have been an oracle on every discussion. He and [Lord] Dudley are done, quite done, for mischief, whilst in matters of business Huskisson is very able and must follow in principle the will of the cabinet. Meanwhile, he is the bridge over which can pass a class of Whigs who are anxious to join our ranks ... I may be wrong, but the Tory anger will evaporate when they see the government strong.[50]

Londonderry belittled his achievements as a constituency Member but acquiesced in his re-election, and he easily outpolled the anti-Catholic protectionist Alexander Robertson*, put up against him by Durham's London freemen.[51] He had agreed to resign immediately should Londonderry go into opposition.[52]

The ordnance estimates which Hardinge presented on 22 Feb. 1828 were subject to scrutiny by the finance committee and not seriously opposed. He testified before the committee on eleven occasions, 19 Mar.-23 May, always demonstrating his military expertise and credentials for promotion.[53] In the House, 16 May, he attributed departmental delays to time spent before the committee, and the refusal of its Whig chairman Sir Matthew White Ridley to grant him a copy of his evidence. He divided with his colleagues in government against repealing the Test Acts, 26 Feb., and voted for Catholic relief, 12 May. He defended the northern coal owners' 'vend' and the Clarence railway bill when Londonderry's interests were invoked to expose divisions in the ministry, 9 May. The Huskissonite resignations that month facilitated his appointment as secretary at war in place of Palmerston but without cabinet rank. A proposal to make him Irish secretary, for which the Arbuthnots, Ellenborough and Wellington considered him well suited, was dropped lest his appointment during Anglesey's viceroyalty should give the Irish administration 'too military a tone'.[54] He infuriated Londonderry, who received nothing, by offering to meet the estimated £8-10,000 cost of a Durham by-election.[55] With his angry acquiescence and the co-operation of Lord Durham (Lambton), he canvassed assiduously, spent £4,000, and with Thomas Wood as intermediary, he persuaded his rival William Chaytor† to retire on the eve of the poll.[56] On the hustings he stated that he was 'no Ultra but a Tory in the rational sense of the word: a supporter of Peel's criminal law reforms, repeal of the Test Acts, now it was law, and Catholic relief'; and that Chaytor had been hoodwinked into standing by the London attorney Ralph Lindsay.[57] He afterwards sold the lease on his Grosvenor Place house, worth £650 a year, and rented 11 Whitehall Place.[58] With ministerial backing, the contentious Hardinge estate bill, which facilitated land sales (including his own purchase of Ketton) under the wills of his father and uncle Sir Richard Hardinge (d. 1826), to whose estates and baronetcy his elder brother Charles had succeeded, received royal assent, 15 July, and the Londonderry estate bill did so on the 25th.[59] Presenting the army estimates, 13 June, he showed respect to their military critic Davies and poured scorn on the complaints of Hume, with whom he sparred again on the 20th, before carrying the division on the garrison grant (by 70-38). He carried the award to the Royal Cork Institution (by 66-26) that day and avoided a division on the disembodied militia through the timely interventions of Wood, as colonel of the Middlesex regiment. He was questioned closely on military pensions, in which the finance committee recommended reductions, 23 June, and performed well when harried over individual awards, 23 June, and Colonel Bradley's case, 3 July. In several exchanges with Sir Henry Parnell, William Bankes, John Maberly and Ridley, he confirmed his testimony to the finance committee and defended government's decision to overrule them by retaining the office of lieutenant-general of the ordnance, 4 July, when they carried the divisions by 204-95 and 163-43.[60] Insisting that the 'opinion of the finance committee was a qualified opinion', he was instrumental in defeating further attempts to secure ordnance reductions, 7 July (by 120-9 and 125-51), and similar motions on the 8th, when pensions, the barrack grant and Canadian fortifications were in contention. He presented and endorsed the ordnance clerks' petition against the salary reductions proposed in the superannuation bill, 14 July 1828. As he had proved to be one of the government's best debaters in the Commons that session, the president of the India board Ellenborough and the chancellor of the exchequer Goulburn tried to persuade him to speak on 'finance and subjects unconnected with his office' with a view to leading the House should Peel fail, but he dismissed the idea as 'visionary'.[61] During the recess he devised and circulated a military pension scheme calculated to reward long service, yield long-term savings and boost the colonial labour force by promoting early discharge and assisted passages. He also proposed further militia reductions, a restructuring of guards' salaries and all half-pay and pressed again for a two-tier punishment system to reduce military flogging.[62]

He was anxious to see the Catholic question resolved following Anglesey's recall, privately ridiculed the Bruswick clubs and considered

the O'Connells and the Sheils the most alarmed of the croakers, and that the really formidable question is the power of the priests, with the 40s. freeholders, to take the representation out of the hands of the gentry and aristocracy ... If 60 Irish agitators were seated in the House of Commons no government could be carried on.[63]

He welcomed Wellington and Peel's decision to concede emancipation in 1829, dissented from the prayer of the hostile petition he presented, 16 Feb., and divided for the measure, 6, 30 Mar. Despite the high cost, he insisted on printing the army and ordnance estimates in detail to avoid misrepresentation.[64] He peppered his speech on presenting them with extracts from his testimony to and the reports of the finance committee, 20 Feb. As again, 23 Feb., 2 Mar., Maberly, Alexander Baring and Sir Hussey Vivian were his severest critics. The House was 'nearly empty' and Hume the challenger when he carried the mutiny bill, which Wellington had again refused to amend, 10 Mar.[65] As Wellington's seconder in his bloodless duel with the Ultra Lord Winchelsea, 21 Mar., Hardinge negotiated the terms with Lord Falmouth and directed

proceedings in Battersea Fields, having ensured that the duchess of Wellington's physician, Dr. John Hume, would be present.[66] He later dominated the 1830-2 select committees on the militia and, assisted by Wood, he defended their cost, a 'real diminution' of £32,080, 4 May 1829. The government's weakness in the Commons troubled him and with Londonderry, to whom he had become reconciled during his daughter's illness in November 1829, 'nibbling at the Cumberland faction', he warned Wellington that the 50 votes lost to the Tories since February 1827 amounted to a difference of 100 in a bad division and suggested trying to recruit Lord Chandos*, Sir James Graham* and Herries and decided that he would not stand for Durham again.[67] Ignoring the Ultras' protests, he defended the dismissal for 'positive disobedience' of soldiers who had refused to fire a salute in honour of a Catholic saint in Malta, 12 July. The Ultra leader Sir Richard Vyvyan* listed him as 'hostile' to a putative political realignment in October 1829.

As trustees of his marriage settlement, his brother Richard and Londonderry permitted Hardinge to raise £9,000 to purchase and extend his London house in December 1829.[68] Sounded by Ellenborough that month, he stressed his ineligibility to succeed Lord William Cavendish Bentinck* as governor-general of Bengal.[69] Pre-session talks with Peel and Chandos confirmed his doubts over the king's loyalty to Wellington, but, according to Ellenborough, ministerial majorities on the address, 4 Feb., East Retford, 11 Feb., and the enfranchisement of Birmingham, Leeds and Manchester, 23 Feb., allayed his misgivings.[70] At Peel's insistence, he postponed the army estimates to 19 Feb., to permit revision, but even so his figures differed embarrassingly from Goulburn's and Davies made the 'paltry £213,000' overall saving a test case of the government's commitment to act on distress.[71] The amendment restricting the vote to six months was easily defeated, but Hardinge faced continued pressure from the royal household over unpopular changes in the Guards' pay scheme, and from opposition on supply. Harried increasingly by Hume, he explained details, defended policy and carried divisions (by 122-38, 118-42 and 83-23), 22 Feb., and fared better, 5, 8 Mar., but on the 9th his majority was reduced to 104-59. He carried the mutiny bill, 12 Mar., but refused to have it printed. Though hard pressed in debate, he defeated an attempt by the revived Whig opposition to combine the offices of master and lieutenant-general of the ordnance (by 200-124), 29 Mar., and carried the grants for the Enfield ordnance factory (by 80-40), 2 Apr., and the Woolwich academy (by 131-59), 30 Apr. Ellenborough's divorce bill, which he steered through the Commons, proved time-consuming, and he prepared a major speech on the Terceira incident, which was 'not wanted', 30 Apr.[72] He moved for and was named to the select committee on superannuations, 26 Apr.[73] He corrected several points in Graham's case for disclosing information on privy councillors' emoluments, 14 May. He divided against Jewish emancipation, 17 May, voted against making forgery a non-capital offence, 7 June, and helped to secure the grant for the Canadian waterways that day. He voted in the minority against the Galway franchise bill, 25 May. Mediating with ministers that month, when Castlereagh, a junior admiralty lord, threatened resignation over the Irish stamp duties and Londonderry vacillated between Grey and the Ultras, he made it clear that his first obligation was to Wellington, although he disliked his 'harsh and ill tempered' treatment of officials.[74] To spare Londonderry a by-election, he made his acceptance of the Irish secretaryship he was offered on 23 May, in an exchange with Lord Francis Leveson Gower (with an extra £2-3,000 in salary and allowances), conditional on its deferral until the death of the ailing George IV.[75] Intervening on 8 July 1830, he criticized attempts to draw the war office into the scandal surrounding Darling's conduct as governor of New South Wales. Preoccupied with preparations for Ireland and the ministry's weakness in the Commons, where the sugar duties, Irish estimates and the regency bill posed problems, he privately suggested transferring the premiership to Peel, promoting Thomas Frankland Lewis* and making offers to Edward Smith Stanley* and Palmerston, but not Huskisson.[76] To assist Londonderry and acting with Thomas Wood, he promoted the candidatures of Sir Roger Gresley* for Durham and Castlereagh for county Down at the general election, and came in for St. Germans as a treasury nominee.[77]

Hardinge's letters from Ireland in August 1830 were optimistic. He found the 'routine' at Dublin Castle 'less dry than the war office', was delighted with the secretary's Lodge, and worked well with his principal the duke of Northumberland and the Protestants. Except for sporadic anti-Unionism and rioting in county Cavan, he thought the Irish elections had gone satisfactorily, with only two or three seats lost and no serious prospect of revolution.[78] However, faced with removing Lord O'Neil as joint-postmaster general, mounting hostility to the Union, trouble at Newry, a hostile press and the heightened demands of Daniel O'Connell* and Richard Sheil*, whom ministers were anxious to prevent acting in concert, he found little time to develop or implement the poor law, education, land and legal reforms discussed in cabinet before his

departure. He proposed a £57,000 reduction in the Irish civil list and prepared to mount a show of force, should the proclamation of 19 Oct. 1830 prohibiting Anti-Union Association meetings fail.[79] He returned to London for pre-session discussions on the 24th, three days before his correspondence challenging O'Connell to a duel (which was declined) was printed in the London newspapers.[80] Wellington had notified him of the overture made to Palmerston, but deeming parliamentary reform 'in one word revolution' and any coalition with its Whig advocates unlikely to last the session, he saw little prospect of strengthening the ministry and wrote despondently to Ellenborough that 'Peel, having gained as much reputation as he can hope to retain, is vigilantly looking out ... for an honourable pretence to withdraw, and will not boldly state what measures are practicable and necessary to strengthen the government in the Commons'.[81] On the address, 2 Nov., he 'had to come to the rescue of the knight of Kerry and speak for the proclamations for putting down the Anti-Union Society and the Volunteers', which he did by asserting that it was intended to prohibit the spread of Anti-Union Associations, not the right to hold public meetings, and promising to treat arguments against the Union 'with candour and respect'.[82] He claimed that accounts of distress were 'overcharged', but said that the action recommended by the previous session's select committee on the poor was essential.[83] As directed by the cabinet, he introduced seven of the 19 Irish bills planned that session, 4-12 Nov. 1830: on census taking, courts of conscience, constabulary, grand juries, sheriffs and subletting. He candidly told Wellington, for whose life he feared after he declared against reform, that a minority vote or a small majority against Brougham's proposal on the 16th would be a resignation matter, and he considered the cancellation of the king's visit to the City, 8 Nov., 'the end of the government'.[84] He divided with his colleagues when they were brought down on the civil list, 15 Nov. 1830. After the change of ministry Greville observed: 'Peel, Lyndhurst and Hardinge are three capital men for the foundation of a party – as men of business superior to any three in this cabinet'.[85]

Though saddened by Peel's initial refusal to lead a Tory opposition and by the tactics of the incoming ministers, Hardinge responded positively to a barrage of questions on Ireland from O'Connell and others over the next few days and expressed respect for his successor as Irish secretary Smith Stanley, to whom he wrote privately, after dining with the king, 22 Nov.:

So far from intending opposition, I consider Irish affairs relating to great questions of domestic policy to be no fair field for party politics. Our common object should be to ameliorate the condition [of Ireland] ... Without hesitation I place this record of my position in your hands, requesting you to be assured that I shall be more inclined to be one of your coadjutors, than to impede useful measures for the unworthy object of opposition.[86]

As one of the Tories' leading spokesmen, he was brought in for Northumberland's pocket borough of Newport after forfeiting his St. Germans seat. He was also a regular guest at dinners where policy and tactics were discussed and became Wellington's most voluble defender in the Commons.[87] Drawing on correspondence with Henry Phillpotts, he upheld the duke's contentious decision to appoint him to the see of Exeter while holding the living of Stanhope *in commendam*, 22 Nov.[88] He defended the late ministry's record on retrenchment, 23 Nov., and on 6 Dec. 1830 set out the strategic military case for spending on the Rideau canal and Canadian fortifications, without which 'you will render the United States a powerful maritime state ... and your influence as a maritime state would decline'. Though initially critical of the ministry's civil list, he welcomed the slight increases in the estimates in response to French military activity,[89] and generally confined his quibbling and comments to minutiae, 21, 28 Feb., 14, 23, 30 Mar., 13 Apr. 1831, when he naturally denounced the proposed abolition of the office of lieutenant-general of the ordnance. An ardent anti-reformer, Hardinge remained on good terms with William IV and fostered the belief in Tory circles early in 1831 that the cabinet moderates, Goderich, Charles Grant, Palmerston and Williams Wynn, would insist on a 'minimum of reform' or wreck the ministry, and that the king would not consent to a dissolution.[90] Confident also that the Ultras would be won over, he boasted to the first lord of the admiralty Graham, who held him in high esteem, that the Tories could turn out ministers 'when they pleased, and were quite ready to take the administration on anti-reform principles'.[91] On 3 Mar., in a speech cribbed largely from Ellenborough, as was often the case on reform,[92] he queried the proposed increase (four to ten) in the representation of county Durham under the ministerial bill and protested at its revolutionary nature. Called to order by Hobhouse, he repeated:

Its tendency [is] most revolutionary ... I say that it is calculated to pull the crown off the king's head; and I do hope, that if leave should be given to introduce this bill ... [Lord John Russell] will, before we come to the second reading of it, introduce a clause by which the House of Lords may be passed by, in order that they may not irritate the country by the rejection of it.

He spoke similarly on endorsing Inglis's complaint against *The Times*, 21 Mar., when his assertion that he sat as freely for Newport as he had for Durham prompted furious replies from 'Cornubiensis' and others.[93] He voted against the reform bill at its second reading, 22 Mar., when his prediction that it would be carried by two votes was almost confirmed.[94] He repeatedly harried ministers for details of the Irish measure, 21, 22, 23 Mar., and denounced it the next day for 'standing the population-property argument on its head' and ending Protestant representation by opening the 24 close boroughs retained at the Union. His several hostile interventions, 30 Mar.-20 Apr., demonstrated more temper than efficiency, and with his hopes of a regiment dashed, he now despaired over his party's poor prospects of resuming office and his lack of income.[95] 'Mad with rage' when the bill's defeat, to which he contributed, 19 Apr., precipitated a dissolution, 22 Apr., denying the Tories a chance of office as 'moderate reformers', he crossed the House on hearing a gun salute and told ministers, 'the next time you hear those guns they will be shotted, and take off some of your heads'.[96] A leading Member of the opposition's Charles Street committee at the ensuing election, he again declined Londonderry's invitation to stand for county Durham and came in for Newport, which was designated for disfranchisement, and declared his intention of trying Northumberland's neighbouring schedule B borough of Launceston 'next time'.[97] He was Peel's second when Hobhouse's Westminster election speech, which they later agreed was misreported, almost provoked a duel, and tried to assuage Hobhouse's annoyance at being prevented by Charles Ross* from proceeding with his vestry bill.[98] Taken aback by the size of the ministerial majority, which he had estimated at no more than 50, and convinced that 'they will persevere in annihilating the Tory [party]', he rallied support for Peel before Parliament met and was at the meeting of Tory leaders, 16 June 1831, that formally made Charles Street their party headquarters (the precursor of the Carlton Club). An important political go-between for the Conservatives, as they were now coming to be styled, he was active in election management and promoting a partisan press.[99] Sharing Peel's disappointment at their election losses, he had written from Penshurst, 19 May 1831:

I hear the king passes his time in crying and drinking sherry. He told a friend of ours that he was aware his name had been used during the election most improperly, that the bill must be greatly modified and that he *knew* Lord Grey *repented* that the measure was so strong. Having borrowed a force to carry a party triumph, they now begin to find the day of reckoning very embarrassing ... [Sir Robert] Wilson* says that the more respectable part of the cabinet want to throw off the radicals and compromise matters with the Tories by great concessions in the new bill, that Brougham and Lord Grey have lately had violent altercations ... However, we really know very little of what is passing in the enemy's camp. That they will persevere in annihilating the Tory [party], however, I have not the slightest doubt, and in the king's drooping state [they will] risk anything to secure their power during the ministry.[100]

He endorsed a petition for continued enfranchisement from Durham's Gateshead, South Shields and Sunderland freemen and called for their children's voting rights to be enshrined in law, 22 June 1831. He divided against the reintroduced reform bill at its second reading, 6 July, but for its committal, 12 July, and criticized its provisions for Tavistock, Newport, Launceston and Appleby in several obstructive interventions during the following week, and again, 11 Aug. He objected to the partial disfranchisement of Chippenham, 27 July, and pressed for the incorporation of Newport in a two Member Launceston constituency, 22, 29 July, and the addition of Rye to Winchelsea, 30 July. Littleton attributed his fury at the introduction of Saturday sittings to expedite progress, 29 July, to the clash with Londonderry's Saturday breakfast parties.[101] Stressing his local knowledge, Hardinge welcomed the decision to award two Members to Sunderland and one to South Shields, objected to Gateshead's separate enfranchisement as 'a piece of extravagance' and joined Thomas Wood in pressing Merthyr's claims, 5, 9, 10 Aug. He predicted that the government's defeat on Lord Chandos's amendment for enfranchising £50 tenants-at-will, 18 Aug., would 'do much good in putting forward the Tories as the successful advocates of the landed interest' and hoped for further successes or narrow defeats, which, tactically, he preferred.[102] On the Dublin election controversy, he intervened 8, 25 Aug., to defend the Irish administration and their local supporters, who had been backed by the Charles Street committee.[103] Ellenborough noted on 2 Sept. that Hardinge looked forward to the prospect of war over Belgium and a chance to command an army division, but nothing materialized. Furthermore, his decision to join Peel's shooting party at Drayton and his absence from the coronation that month annoyed the king, who denied him military preferment until the reform bill became law.[104] Reporting on 12 Sept. to Peel (whom he urged to return to London) on a Charles Street meeting and arrangements to transfer the reform bill to the Lords, where they hoped to defeat it at the second reading,

he said that no opposition to the Scottish reform bill was intended in the Commons and speculated over the cause of Calcraft's suicide and possible peer creations.[105] He protested at the inappropriate use of the House as a court of appeal in the Deacles v. Baring case, 19 Sept., and divided against the reform bill at its third reading that day, and its passage, 21 Sept. He voted against the second reading of the Scottish reform bill, 23 Sept. He had discussed the likely Lords defeat, the ministerial confidence motion agreed at Lord Ebrington's and plans for a dissolution, peer creation and the bill's reintroduction with Ellenborough and Hobhouse, who observed, 22 Sept., 'Hardinge comes to get what he can out of me. Of course I tell him no lies, nor no truths, except such as I think he ought to propagate'.[106] He contributed to the speculation that a coalition or Conservative reform ministry would be appointed following the bill's defeat in the Lords and canvassed for the anti-reformers at the October by-elections in Cambridgeshire and Dorset. He wrote to Lord Clive* and other likely supporters of the 'Waverer' Lord Wharncliffe's cross-party initiative, which he monitored closely in November and December 1831, to promote the new Conservative party's policies and its call for 'general declarations throughout the country against the bill, but in favour of moderate reform'.[107]

In the House, 4 Oct. 1831, he made an unfavourable comparison between the preparations made in London to combat insurrection in November 1830 and those in the wake of the reform bill's likely defeat. Following this, he carried a pistol in his pocket, took steps to protect Wellington and criticized the mob attacks on Londonderry and fellow anti-reformers in debate, 12 Oct. He also denounced the alleged dealings of Russell and the chancellor of the exchequer Lord Althorp with Thomas Attwood† and the political unionists, 15 Oct.[108] He divided against the revised reform bill at its second reading, 17 Dec. 1831, and committal, 20 Jan. 1832.[109] His bitter personal criticism of Ebrington and Russell, and accusations that ministers reintroduced Saturday sittings to carry the bill to the timetable dictated by the unions and the mob, 2 Feb., demonstrated what Littleton termed 'one of those glaring faults of temper or rather excitement, which have so continually exposed him to censure in the House'. His remarks so damaged his reputation that he did not speak on the English reform bill again.[110] He voted against the enfranchisement of Tower Hamlets, 28 Feb., and the bill's third reading, 22 Mar. He was briefed on the former foreign secretary Lord Dudley's conversations with the king in April 1832 and privately considered the bill redeemable by good management, with concessions possible to exclude borough voters from county constituencies, and on three Member counties and the metropolitan districts. When Grey briefly resigned and a ministry headed by Wellington was contemplated in May, he agreed to support a 'hybrid' bill and serve as Irish secretary under Lord Rosslyn. However, as he had realized from the outset, without Peel the scheme was unworkable.[111] Provoked, as intended, by derogatory comments from Ebrington and Lord Milton into defending Wellington's conduct, 14 May, he claimed that he had received no formal offer of office and denounced reform as a 'dangerous and revolutionary measure' in need of mitigation. His attempts to clarify his remarks were shouted down. Peel backed his protest at *The Times*'s hostile coverage of the 'rout' that day, but nothing came of it.[112] He voted against the second reading of the Irish reform bill, 25 May, and quibbled over its £20 voter clause, 25 June. He regretted Peel's absence from the Pitt dinner, 30 May, at which he rallied with Londonderry for Wellington. He now wagered five guineas 'that the king will not have created 20 peers before 1 July and that Grey and his government will be out by 1st September'.[113] He denounced Russell's 'obnoxious' bribery bill as unworkable and criticized him for making opposition the scapegoat for its loss, 30 July. He divided against government on the Russian-Dutch loan, 26 Jan., 12 July 1832, and declared his intention of doing so again on the 20th.

On military matters, he raised no objection to the estimates for the ordnance, if his guidelines had been adhered to, 27 June 1831, 29 Feb. 1832. However, he repeatedly criticized the army estimates proposed by the secretary at war Parnell, held Althorp personally responsible for failing to execute his reforms on half-pay, and defended his own policies, 27, 28 June, 25 July, 22 Aug., 7 Oct. 1831. He 'refused to have anything to do with the military subcommittee'.[114] He considered the increased army estimates proposed by Parnell's successor Hobhouse, 17 Feb. 1832, entirely justified and said that the imminent expiry of the Mutiny Act would moderate his criticism of details to expedite progress. In several interventions that day, he defended the Conservative Lord Hill's decisions as commander-in-chief, criticized Russell's conduct as paymaster and argued that the army should be spared the cost of militia and yeomanry pensions. Backing Hobhouse, he would have no truck with the savings recommended by Parnell and the radicals, especially the abolition of free places at Sandhurst, 28 Mar., 4 Apr. 1832.[115] His statement on 28 June 1831 that his army pay was 'barely the interest of the money I gave for my commission' silenced even Hunt and, as indi-

cated (25 Aug., 15 Sept., 7 Oct. 1831), he revived his 1828-9 army half-pay and promotion schemes. He failed to have the half-pay concessions introduced by Graham for naval officers extended to the army, 7 Oct. 1831, 16 Mar. 1832. On 2 Apr. he embarrassed Hobhouse by interrupting proceedings on the mutiny bill to introduce a pension bill, which he justified in a detailed speech based on his official papers. However, heeding objections from Hobhouse, who pointed to anomalies in his statistics, he withdrew his proposals so that the mutiny bill could proceed and they agreed a compromise measure, 4 Apr.[116] On the cholera bill, he argued forcibly, on economic, humanitarian and military grounds, for the immediate barracking of troops and improvements to their accommodation to reduce the risk of infection, 13, 15 Feb. Requesting ordnance returns 'to keep the system in check', 2 July, he praised Beresford and Wellington's management and stressed the advantages of retaining the factories. He joined its presenter Hume in endorsing the former sergeant armourer and Swan River settler Beasmore's petition for compensation, 9 July, pointing out that his plight had unearthed the system of pension fraud, which he had acted to end. Despite the embarrassment caused, he opposed Peel's brother-in-law George Dawson's call for further spending on the Culmore forts and Londonderry bridge, in line with his previous policy, 18 July 1832. Deputizing for Peel, he forced Hume to make useful disclosures on the authorship of the *Republican*, 29 June, 1 July, and on 13 Oct. 1831 he thanked Wetherell for his valiant opposition to the reform bill and Brougham's 'jobbing' chancery bill, which he also opposed effectively himself, 27 July 1832.[117] He defended the grant to the Hiberian Society's Protestant schools, 22 Aug. 1831, joined in the criticism of the increasing deployment of troops to keep the peace in Ireland, 29 Feb., and sent Smith Stanley a copy of the military memorial he had drafted as Irish secretary, with a note authorizing him to forward it to Grey, 17 Mar. 1832.[118] He objected to the tone of several Irish anti-tithe petitions, 10 Apr., 14 June 1832.

Hardinge took charge of the Irish borough elections for the Conservatives at the general election in December 1832. On Wellington's advice, he declined nomination for Durham South and stood by his decision to contest the single Member borough of Launceston (to which Newport had been added), narrowly defeating a Liberal there after a desperate seven-month campaign.[119] The victor again in 1835, he was unchallenged in 1837 and 1841. Appointed an army colonel in 1833, he combined high military and political office and helped to heal the breach between

Wellington and Peel, in whose 1834-5 administration he served (as he had feared, without distinction) as Irish secretary.[120] His military expertise and outstanding success as secretary at war in Peel's second ministry made him the natural choice in 1844 to replace the 'incompetent' Ellenborough as governor-general of Bengal during the Sikh Wars. Before he relinquished the government to Lord Dalhousie in 1848, his achievements in underpinning the British victories at Mukudi and Ferozesha (1845) with a raft of social and educational reforms, and in fostering a non-Muslim buffer state in the Punjab were rewarded with a viscountcy, sustained by a £3,000 annual pension for himself and his next two heirs, when the Treaty of Lahore was ratified in 1846.[121] His appointment as master-general of the ordnance in March 1852 created a permanent breach with Londonderry, who had coveted it.[122] That September he succeeded Wellington as commander-in-chief, becoming the last 'political general' to be put in charge of the army. He relinquished his command after suffering a stroke in July 1856, and died at Penshurst that September. Queen Victoria praised his 'valuable and unremitting services', and he was recalled as a popular 'brave, good *religious* veteran ... spirited debater and a clearheaded man of business'. But he was implicated in some of the army's shortcomings in the Crimean War.[123] He was buried with full military honours at Frodcomb, Kent.[124] He was succeeded in the peerage and estates by his elder son Charles (1822-94), Conservative Member for Downpatrick, 1851-6, and himself an amputee following a boating accident in 1842, and left bequests to his widow (d. 1865) and other family members.[125]

[1] See W. Broadfoot, *Career of Maj. G. Broadfoot ...compiled from his papers and those of Lords Ellenborough and Hardinge* (1888); C.S. Hardinge, *Visct. Hardinge* (1891); *Letters of Visct. Hardinge ... to Lady Hardinge and Sir Walter and Lady James, 1844-1847* ed. B.S. Singh (Cam. Soc. ser. 4, xxxii); V. Kumar, *India under Lord Hardinge* (1978). [2] *Durham Sch. Reg.* ed. C.S. Earle and L.A. Body, 63; *Gent. Mag.* (1856), ii. 646-9. [3] Hardinge, 12. [4] *Hardinge Letters*, 4-6; Hardinge, 13-29; *Gent. Mag.* (1856), ii. 646-9. [5] Cent. Kent. Stud. Camden mss UB40 C530/1; Dorset RO, Bond mss D/BoH C15, Jekyll to Bond, 8 Feb.; Add. 51959, Londonderry to Miss Fox [Feb.]; *Tyne Mercury*, 15 Feb.; *Newcastle Courant*, 19 Feb., 4 Mar. 1820; Add. 38458, f. 294; A.J. Heesom, '"Legitimate" versus "Illegitimate" Influences: Aristocratic Engineering in Mid-Victorian Britain', *PH*, vii (1988), 289-90. [6] Camden mss C530/1. [7] Add. 38289, f. 49; Camden mss C530/1-8. [8] Camden mss C530/5-8; *Gronow Reminiscences*, ii. 212. [9] Camden mss C530/8. [10] Add. 39775, f. 77. [11] *The Times*, 15 Mar.; 2, 3, 22 May 1821. [12] Hatherton diary, 10 Oct.-2 Nov. 1821; *Hardinge Letters*, 6. [13] *The Times*, 16, 23 Mar. 1822. [14] Add. 38291, f. 122; 40313, ff. 1-9; Wellington mss WP1/846/9; *Arbuthnot Corresp.* 31. [15] Blickling Hall mss (History of Parliament Aspinall transcripts), Londonderry to dowager Lady Londonderry, 14, 29 Dec. 1822, 20 Feb. 1823; *Arbuthnot Corresp.* 40; Wellington mss WP1/754/26, 30; 762/17, 23;

764/2; 766/12. [16] Blickling Hall mss. [17] Add. 38292, f. 381; Wellington mss WP1/766/12; *The Times*, 8 Mar.; Blickling Hall mss, Londonderry to dowager Lady Londonderry, 2 July 1823. [18] *The Times*; 8 Mar.; *Gent. Mag.* (1823), i. 366. [19] *Tyne Mercury*, 1, 8 Apr.; Lincs. AO, Tennyson d'Eyncourt mss T d'E H88/24, Russell to Tennyson [Apr.]; Blickling Hall mss, Londonderry to dowager Lady Londonderry, 23 Apr. 1823. [20] Add. 56548, f. 56; Wellington mss WP1/785/16; 786/1; 939/1. [21] *The Times*, 10 Mar. 1824. [22] Ibid. 18, 26 Mar. 1824; P. Burroughs, 'Crime and Punishment in the British Army, 1815-70', *EHR*, c (1985), 545-71, especially 565. [23] Wellington mss WP1/790/10; 791/6; 792/7, 8, 10, 13; 793/19, 23; *The Times*, 10, 11, 17, 24, 27 May 1824; M.D. George, *Cat. of Pol. and Personal Satires*, x. 14661-4. [24] *The Times*, 24 Feb., 4 May 1824, 5 Mar. 1825. [25] *Arbuthnot Jnl.* i. 333. [26] *The Times*, 8 Mar., 24 June 1825. [27] Ibid. 2, 6 July 1825; Wellington mss WP1/822/11; *Arbuthnot Jnl.* i. 405. [28] *Session of Parl. 1825*, p. 467. [29] Wellington mss WP1/848/22. [30] Ibid. WP1/872/3, 4; *Wellington Despatches*, iii. 198-201; J.R. Dinwiddy, 'The Early 19th Cent. Campaign Against Flogging in the Army', *EHR*, xcvii (1982), 308-31. [31] *Durham Chron.* 21, 28 Jan., 10, 17 June 1826. [32] Durham CRO, Londonderry mss D/Lo/C83/3(1). [33] *The Times*, 9 Dec. 1826, 15 Feb. 1827. [34] Ibid. 10, 17 Feb. 1827. [35] Ibid. 13 Mar. 1827. [36] Add. 40313, f. 13; *Durham Chron.* 21 Apr. 1827. [37] *Arbuthnot Jnl.* ii. 88, 96; Wellington mss WP1/887/23, 28; 888/10; *Canning's Ministry*, 116, 150, 166, 196, 283. [38] Londonderry mss C83/3(1). [39] Ibid. C83/4-6; Wellington mss WP1/895/10, 13, 15, 16, 22, 25; Add. 40313, f. 15; TNA 30/12/7/6, Hardinge to Ellenborough, 13 Aug. 1827; N. Gash, *Secretary Peel*, 450. [40] Londonderry mss C83/4; TNA 30/12/7/6, Hardinge to Ellenborough, 13 Aug. 1827. [41] *Croker Pprs.* i. 388 [42] TNA 30/12/7/6. [43] Aberdeen Univ. Lib. Arbuthnot mss, Hardinge to Mrs. Arbuthnot, 28, 30 Sept., 6 Oct. 1827; Londonderry mss C83/7, 8. [44] Londonderry mss C83/10 (1-4); Arbuthnot mss, Hardinge to Mrs. Arbuthnot, 7 Nov. [Dec.]; Derbys. RO, Gresley of Drakelow mss D77/36/5, Hardinge to Gresley, 6 Dec. 1827. [45] Londonderry mss C83/11, 12; Wellington mss WP1/913/8. [46] Londonderry mss C83/12. [47] Ibid. C83/13 (1), 182. [48] Camden mss C528/10; Arbuthnot mss, Hardinge to Mrs. Arbuthnot, 18 Jan., to Arbuthnot, 24 Jan. 1828; *Arbuthnot Corresp.* 103; Londonderry mss C83/16. [49] *Ellenborough Diary*, i. 11; Londonderry mss C83/15-17. [50] Londonderry mss C83/25. [51] Ibid. C83/14, 19, 177; *Durham Co. Advertiser*, 1, 8, 15 Feb., 1 Mar. 1828. [52] Londonderry mss (History of Parliament Aspinall transcripts), Hardinge to Londonderry, 24 Jan. 1824. [53] *PP* (1828), v. 31-84, 95-119, 128-40; *Ellenborough Diary*, i. 86; *Arbuthnot Jnl.* ii. 174. [54] *Ellenborough Diary*, i. 111-12, 118-19, 122-4, 126; Broughton, *Recollections*, iii. 270; Wellington mss WP1/980/30; *Arbuthnot Jnl.* ii. 189-91; *Russell Letters*, i. 89. [55] Wellington mss WP1/934/24; 979/13; *Ellenborough Diary*, i. 130-1; *Arbuthnot Corresp.* 106; Londonderry mss C83/179; C113/92. [56] Londonderry mss C83/22, 23, 180, 181; C86/5; *Pprs. of Sir William Chaytor, 1771-1847* ed. M.Y. Ashcroft (N. Yorks. Co. RO Publications, 1 (1993 edn.)), 122-3; Add. 38757, f. 91. [57] *Durham Chron.* 14 June 1828. [58] Macleod of Macleod mss, Hardinge to wife, 10 Mar. 1828. [59] *CJ*, lxxxiii. 453, 470, 506, 535; *LJ*, lx. 123, 482, 539, 654. [60] *Arbuthnot Jnl.* ii. 196; *Russell Letters*, i. 89. [61] *Ellenborough Diary*, i. 158, 160, 177. [62] Ibid. i. 241, 264, 291; Surr. Hist. Cent. Goulburn mss D/319/45, Hardinge to Goulburn, 3 Sept.-12 Nov. 1828; Wellington mss WP1/957/14; 1005/9/4. [63] TNA 30/12/7/6, Hardinge to Ellenborough, 11 Sept.; Londonderry mss C83/2(a); Arbuthnot mss, Hardinge to Mrs. Arbuthnot, 30 Sept. 1828. [64] Goulburn mss D/319/45, Hardinge to Goulburn [1828]. [65] Grey mss, Howick jnl. 10 Mar. 1829; *Ellenborough Diary*, ii. 23. [66] Wellington mss WP1/1003/30, 31; 1004/2-6, 8, 15, 16; 1007/28, 29; Howick jnl. 22 Mar. 1829; *Ellenborough Diary*, i. 403-6; George, xi. 1596, 1597. *Greville Mems.* i. 276-7, incorrectly gives the location as Wimbledon and Joseph Hume as the physician. [67] Londonderry mss C83/2; Wellington mss WP1/988/26; *Arbuthnot Corresp.* 120; *Arbuthnot Jnl.* i. 279-80, ii. 290; *Ellenborough Diary*, ii. 55, 60, 63; Londonderry mss (History of Parliament Aspinall transcripts), Londonderry to Hardinge, 6 July 1829. [68] Londonderry mss

C83/27, 184. [69] *Ellenborough Diary*, ii. 142-3, 207. [70] Ibid. ii. 73, 173, 177-8, 191, 201 [71] *Arbuthnot Corresp.* 131; *Arbuthnot Jnl.* ii. 344-5; Howick jnl. 19 Feb. 1830. [72] *Ellenborough Diary*, ii. 224, 231. [73] Goulburn mss D/319/45, Hardinge to Goulburn, 16 Mar. 1830. [74] *Arbuthnot Jnl.* ii. 359-60; Wellington mss WP1/1113/18. [75] Wellington mss WP1/1117/58, 70; 1121/29; *Ellenborough Diary*, ii. 260; Londonderry mss C83/29; *Gent. Mag.* (1830), ii. 173. [76] *Ellenborough Diary*, ii. 275, 289-90, 297-8, 305-6, 316. [77] Londonderry mss C83/30; Wellington mss WP1/1126/24; 1130/47; 1131/15. [78] Add. 40313, ff. 17A-21; PRO NI, Fitzgerald mss MIC/639/13/78, 99; *Arbuthnot Corresp.* 136; *Ellenborough Diary*, ii. 348-9; Wellington mss WP1/1136/23. [79] Add. 40313, ff. 23-139; P. Jupp, *British Politics on Eve of Reform*, 101; Wellington mss WP1/1136/26; 1140/28; 1146/16; M. Staunton, *Hints for Hardinge* (Dublin, 1830); *Ellenborough Diary*, ii. 388-9, 391-2, 397, 399. [80] *Ellenborough Diary*, ii. 399, 402; *The Times*, 27, 29 Oct. 1830. [81] TNA 30/12/7/6, Hardinge to Ellenborough, 5 Sept. 1830; George, xi. 16299. [82] Howick jnl. 2 Nov. 1830. [83] Howick jnl. 2 Nov. 1830. [84] *Ellenborough Diary*, ii. 416-18, 423. [85] *Greville Mems.* ii. 73. [86] Ibid. ii. 441; *Croker Pprs.* ii. 76; *Arbuthnot Jnl.* ii. 404; Derby mss 920 Der (14) box 116. [87] *Greville Mems.* ii. 113; *Three Diaries*, 15, 27, 32, 45, 60, 63, 66. [88] Wellington mss WP1/1151/19; 1153/9, 25; 1154/38. [89] Broughton, iv. 82-83. [90] TNA 30/12/7/6, Hardinge to Ellenborough [10 Jan. 1831]; *Three Diaries*, 40, 73. [91] PRO NI, Anglesey mss D619/31D/24, Smith Stanley to Anglesey, 25 Feb.; *Three Diaries*, 61; Hatherton diary, 1 Dec. 1831. [92] *Three Diaries*, 67. [93] *The Times*, 21, 26 Mar. 1831. [94] *Three Diaries*, 68. [95] Ibid. 59; *Baring Jnls.* i. 85; Broughton, iv. 98. [96] *Three Diaries*, 81-82; Broughton, iv. 106; Granville mss (History of Parliament Aspinall transcripts), Holland to Granville, 22 Apr. [1831]. [97] *Three Diaries*, 68, 85-9; Wellington mss WP1/1186/2; Londonderry mss C83/32, 33; *Cornubian*, 6 May; *Western Times*, 7 May 1831. [98] Add. 40313, ff. 145-50; 56554, f. 94; Broughton, iv. 110-11; [99] Londonderry mss C83/33; Creevey mss, Creevey to Miss Ord, 6 May; Add. 57370, Arbuthnot to Herries, 25 May 1831; *Three Diaries*, 92-94, 125, 203-4; Wellington mss WP1/1199/15; *Arbuthnot Corresp.* 161. [100] Add. 40313, ff. 151-2. [101] Hatherton diary, 29 July 1831. [102] Arbuthnot mss, Hardinge to Mrs. Arbuthnot, 19 Aug. 1831. [103] *Three Diaries*, 125. [104] Ibid. 110, 127, 191; N. Gash, *Sir Robert Peel*, 21-22; P. Ziegler, *William IV*, 194; *Greville Mems.* ii. 170; Wellington mss WP1/1202/31; 1203/19; *Holland House Diaries*, 151. [105] Hatherton diary, 8 Sept. 1831; *Three Diaries*, 125; Add. 40413, ff. 155-9. [106] *Three Diaries*, 132-3; Wilts. RO, Hobhouse mss 145, Hobhouse to wife, 23 Sept. 1831; Broughton, iv. 133. [107] Dorset RO, Bankes mss D/BKL, address to Henry Bankes, 15 Sept.; Hants RO, Carnarvon mss M91/L12/9; *Arbuthnot Corresp.* 151; NLW, Ormathwaite mss FG/1/6, pp. 7-9; Wellington mss WP1/1201/2; Powis mss (History of Parliament Aspinall transcripts), Hardinge to R. Clive, 24 Oct. 1831; *Three Diaries*, 147-8, 157, 160-1. [108] Broughton, iv. 142; *Greville Mems.* ii. 209. [109] *Three Diaries*, 178. [110] Hatherton diary Feb.; Add. 51573, Spring Rice to Lady Holland [n.d.]; 51676, Lord G.W. Russell to Holland, 3 Feb.; 69364, Sneyd to Fortescue, 22 Feb. 1832; *Russell Letters*, iii. 8. [111] Wellington mss WP1/1224/2; NLW, Coedymaen mss 795; Londonderry mss C83/178; W. Suss. RO, Goodwood mss 1486, f. 100; *Three Diaries*, 248-51; *Croker Pprs.* i. 137; ii. 163. [112] *Three Diaries*, 254-5, 258; *Croker Pprs.* i. 165; *The Times*, 15 May 1832. [113] Arbuthnot mss, Arbuthnot to son, 30 May; *John Bull*, 3 June 1832; *Three Diaries*, 230-1; Londonderry mss C83/58. [114] *Three Diaries*, 189. [115] Add. 56556, f. 108. [116] Broughton, iv. 208-9. [117] *Arbuthnot Corresp.* 151. [118] Derby mss 920 Der (14) box 116. [119] *Three Diaries*, 266, 276; George, xi. 17290; Londonderry mss C83/201; Wellington mss WP1/1232/1; 1239/7; Add. 40313, ff. 162-6; *Falmouth Packet*, 15 Dec.; *Cornubian*, 18 Dec. 1832. [120] *Greville Mems.* iii. 114; T.K. Hoppen, 'Politics, the Law, and the Nature of the Irish Electorate, 1832-50', *EHR*, xcii (1977), 747, 759, 766. [121] *Hardinge Letters*, 5-15, 172; *The Times*, 8, 22 Apr. 1846; A. Hawkins, 'Parliamentary Government and Victorian Political Parties, 1830-1880', *EHR*, civ (1989), 638-669. [122] Mq. of Anglesey, *One-Leg*, 387. [123] Add. 39775, ff. 77, 110; *The Times*, 16, 25, 27 Sept.; *Durham Co. Advertiser*, 3 Oct. 1856; *Oxford DNB*. [124] *The Times*, 2, 3 Oct. 1856. [125] PROB 11/2241/843; IR26/2069/1040.

M.M.E.

HARE, Hon. Richard (1773–1827).

CO. CORK   1812–24 Sept. 1827

b. 20 Mar. 1773, 1st s. of William, 1st Visct. Ennismore and Listowel [I] (*d.* 1837), and 1st w. Mary, da. of Henry Wrixon of Ballygiblin, co. Cork. *educ.* ?Eton 1783-8; Oriel, Oxf. 1792. *m.* 10 June 1797, Hon. Catherine Bridget Dillon, da. of Robert, 1st Bar. Clonbrock [I], 5s. 2da. *styled* Visct. Ennismore 1822-d. *d.v.p.* 24 Sept. 1827.
MP [I] 1797-1800.
Trustee, linen board [I] 1824-d.

Hare, considered 'our worst Irish politician' by the Whig Thomas Spring Rice*, and noted for his 'false impressions' and 'artifice' by Lord Donoughmore, continued to sit for county Cork on his family interest with the support of the independent 'high church' Protestant gentry.[1] A mostly silent Member who attended 'very seldom', when present he generally voted with the Liverpool ministry, but he complained frequently of their insufficient attention to his patronage requests.[2] (In 1819 Peel, the Irish secretary, had urged Lord Liverpool to grant his request for an earldom for his father, citing his 'marked attachment' to government and retention of his seat at the 1818 election, despite the 'desertion' to opposition of his former ally the 3rd earl of Shannon.)[3] On 4 Feb. 1820 Hare informed Liverpool that owing to the government's 'neglect' of his supporters in county Cork, 'should a contest again arise, the results might be very different':

> I have received no advantage whatsoever. The promotion of my father, the only family object I had in view, and the *only* favour I asked for some years, has been deferred to so indefinite a period, that it has lost considerably as to its importance, [he] being considerably advanced in life ... In other matters, likewise, I have only experienced disappointment from numerous applications made to me by those who incurred much trouble and expense in my support ... I should feel that I was wrong, were I not to state ... the causes for disaffection which have occurred, and which must naturally effect a change in the sentiments of one who has every possible wish ... to be a strenuous supporter of your lordship.

Liverpool replied, 21 Feb.:

> If you have met with either neglect or inattention ... I very much regret it. Upon the only point which has reference to myself, a promotion in the peerage ... I never

concealed from you that your father's promotion could not take place *individually*, but ... whenever any promotion was made to the Irish peerage ... With respect to the other considerations ... they are wholly new to me and I can do no more than inquire about them. But I have no hesitation in saying that you are fully entitled to every degree of favour and consideration from government, to which any friend ... under similar circumstances can have claim.[4]

At the 1820 general election attempts to get up an opposition came to nothing and he was again returned unopposed.[5] He endorsed a petition to the king for a pension from the mother and sister of the late General William Hume, deputy assistant commissary in Demerara, 4 Apr.[6] He was granted six weeks' leave on urgent private business, 23 June 1820, 13 Mar. 1821. He voted against disqualifying civil officers of the ordnance from voting in parliamentary elections, 12 Apr., and parliamentary reform, 9 May. Presenting a constituency petition complaining of agricultural distress, 7 May, he 'strongly urged the necessity of devising some speedy measure of relief'.[7] He voted for the third reading of the forgery punishment mitigation bill, 4 June. He was in the majority against the omission of arrears from the duke of Clarence's grant, 18 June 1821. On his father's elevation to an Irish earldom, he assumed the title of Viscount Ennismore, 5 Feb. 1822. He brought up a county Wexford petition against the distress resulting from tithes, 26 Apr., for which he blamed the 'exorbitant rents ... demanded by the middle men', 20 May.[8] He voted against relieving Catholic peers of their disabilities, 30 Apr. He was appointed to the select committees on Irish grand jury presentments, 3 May, and the Irish linen trade, 18 May 1822. He obtained returns of county Cork convictions under the Irish Insurrection Act, 21 Apr., and advocated harsher measures, warning that 'it was necessary to strike terror into the lower orders' or a 'formidable rebellion would break out', 12 May 1823.[9] That year he applied at least twice to Liverpool for an East India Company cadetship for his nephew William Boldero.[10] He presented constituency petitions against repeal of the Irish linen bounties, 6, 7 May, and one from Youghal against slavery, 19 May 1824.[11] He was appointed to the select committee on the Irish Insurrection Act, 11 May, and voted for its second reading, 14 June. He divided against condemnation of the trial in Demerara of the Methodist missionary John Smith, 11 June 1824. He divided for suppression of the Catholic Association, 15, 25 Feb. 1825. That day Daniel O'Connell* recorded that Ennismore had asked him 'a few' questions in the select committee on the state of Ireland, to which he had been appointed,

17 Feb.[12] He voted to consider Catholic claims, 1 Mar., but on 19 Mar. stated that he 'intended to vote against the second reading' of the relief bill, as the clauses he had hoped for, 'providing for the Catholic clergy and regulating the franchise', had not been included. He was not listed in the divisions on the second, 21 Apr., or third reading, 10 May, but later informed the Tory *Cork Constitution* that he had been 'omitted' from the latter's hostile minority.[13] He presented constituency petitions against alteration of the corn laws, 28 Apr., 3 May 1825.[14]

At the 1826 general election he offered again, saying that there was insufficient time for a personal canvass. Criticized by the *Southern Reporter* for his 'extraordinary' failure to vote 'for or against' relief, 'upon which every man must ere now have formed an opinion', he replied, 18 June:

It is true that I did not vote in the first division, because other enactments were proposed as accompaniments to the measure, and I wished to know, before giving my vote, the precise nature of these and whether they were to be adopted. I afterwards found that they were neither to be included in the bill nor to accompany it [and] I therefore voted against the bill ... In Parliament I twice stated most fully my reasons for the line of conduct which I pursued [which] renders your misstatement the more extraordinary.

'Surely the noble lord does not mean to convey that he either stated reasons or spoke at all!', retorted the paper, adding that as 'the names exactly correspond with the numbers' in the voting lists, 'we think his memory has been somewhat treacherous on this matter'. Ennismore reaffirmed his account at the hustings, when, during the course of a lengthy 'catechising' by John Boyle, editor of the *Freeholder*, he declared that he 'would support any measure accompanied by securities, but ... not ... simple emancipation'. Declining to comment on the 'private family matter' of whether he had tried to 'dissuade' his eldest son William from standing as a supporter of emancipation in county Kerry, he observed, 'I yield to him the right of his own judgement', whereupon he was accused of 'denying to the Catholics that right which you allow to your son'. The opposition having withdrawn owing to the state of the registry, he was returned unopposed, 'a little shaken' and regarded as 'shuffling' on the 'great measure'.[15]

In November 1826 he urged Liverpool to attend to his request for a baronetcy for Arthur Blennerhassett of Ballyseedy, county Kerry.[16] On 6 Mar. 1827 he appeared with his son William, Member for Kerry, in the minority for Catholic claims, but that day he was listed by Planta, the patronage secretary, as a 'Protestant' and he was later added to the hostile majority by *The Times*.[17] He died *v.p.*, 'suddenly' of a 'violent attack of apoplexy', in September 1827, it being observed that there were 'those who believed that his lordship would, at no distant day' have been found 'acting in concert' with his son.[18]

[1] Lansdowne mss, Spring Rice to Lansdowne, 2 Sept. 1825; TCD, Donoughmore mss D/27/1; *Southern Reporter*, 17 June 1826. [2] *Black Bk.* (1823), 154; *Session of Parl. 1825*, p. 462. [3] Add. 38195, f. 97. [4] Add. 38282, f. 371; 38283, f. 100. [5] *Dublin Evening Post*, 9, 11, 14, 16 Mar. 1820. [6] Add. 38380, f. 148. [7] *The Times*, 8 May 1821. [8] Ibid. 27 Apr., 21 May 1822. [9] Ibid. 22 Apr. 1823. [10] Add. 38411, ff. 126, 232. [11] *The Times*, 7, 8, 20 May 1824. [12] *O'Connell Corresp.* iii. 1176. [13] *Cork Constitution*, 26 May 1825. [14] *The Times*, 29 Apr., 4 May 1825. [15] *Southern Reporter*, 17, 20, 22 June; *Cork Constitution*, 22 June 1826. [16] Add. 38301, f. 97. [17] Add. 40398, f. 311; *The Times*, 6 Mar. 1827. [18] *Southern Reporter*, 25 Sept. 1827; *Gent. Mag.* (1827), ii. 366.

P.J.S.

HARE, Hon. William (1801–1856).

Co. Kerry	1826–1830
St. Albans	9 Feb. 1841–Aug. 1846

b. 22 Sept. 1801, 1st s. of Richard Hare, Visct. Ennismore* (*d.* 1827). *educ.* Eton 1817; St. John's, Camb. 1820. *m.* 23 July 1831, Maria Augusta, da. of V.-Adm. William Windham (formerly Lukin) of Felbrigg Hall, Norf., wid. of George Thomas Wyndham of Cromer Hall, 5s. (1 *d.v.p.*) 6da. *styled* Visct. Ennismore 1827-37; *suc.* grandfa. as 2nd earl of Listowel [I] 13 July 1837; KP 29 Apr. 1839. *d.* 4 Feb. 1856.

Ld.-in-waiting to Victoria Feb. 1840-Sept. 1841, Aug. 1846-Mar. 1852, Oct. 1853-*d.*

Sheriff, co. Cork 1834-5; v.-adm. Munster 1838-*d.*

Although this Member's family fortune had been made in county Cork, for which his father was the anti-Catholic Tory Member from 1812, it owned large estates in county Kerry, especially around Listowel, from which his grandfather, whose seat was at Convamore, county Cork, took his title on being elevated to an earldom in 1822.[1] Hare made his political debut there by attending the county Catholics' meeting in Tralee, 28 Mar. 1824, when he admitted he was a stranger, but argued that his presence proved his sympathy with their cause, and he canvassed Kerry that August.[2] Although his father's hostility made him suspect with the largely Catholic voters, Hare offered for the county, with the backing of the key aristocratic interests, at the general election of 1826, when he insisted on his long-standing pro-Catholic views. Relying heavily on his family's territorial interest, he benefited from the extreme and highly partisan disturbances, during which James Crosbie, one of the sitting Members, physically attacked his father, and was eventually returned behind the other, the knight of Kerry, after a contest.[3] He survived a petition.

Hare declared his approval of Catholic relief as a means of tranquillizing Ireland on presenting the favourable Listowel petition, 9 Feb., and he brought up the Kerry petition to the same effect, 27 Feb. 1827.[4] He privately informed Daniel O'Connell* that month that it was his 'intention to pursue the course I have adopted with steadiness and zeal, unabated by any trivial circumstances and unaccompanied by injudicious or compromising conduct'; he was one of the ministerialists who O'Connell insisted should show their commitment by backing their fellow pro-Catholic Canning, the foreign secretary, in his ambition to form an administration following Lord Liverpool's seizure.[5] He duly voted for Catholic relief, 6 Mar., when his father was listed in both majority and minority lists. He seems to have been very inactive in Parliament and at the Kerry by-election in July he was criticized as an inadequate interloper by O'Connell's brother John.[6] His father died suddenly, 24 Sept. 1827, after which he assumed the courtesy title of Lord Ennismore. He joined Brooks's, 1 Mar., and divided with opposition for censuring chancery administration, 24 Apr., and against the suppression of small Scottish and Irish bank notes, 5 June 1828. He introduced the Hibernian Joint Stock Company bill, 17 Mar., attempted to move its second reading, 22, 24 Apr., and finally secured this on the casting vote of the Speaker, acting as a teller in its favour, 1 May, but the measure was not proceeded with.[7] Declaring that he had been sent to Parliament by his Catholic electorate to advance their claims, he spoke fulsomely for conceding them, particularly as a means of ending violence and oppression and to safeguard economic prosperity and constitutional government, 12 May 1828, when he voted in the majority for relief. He was considered a possible mover or seconder of the address by Planta, the patronage secretary, in January 1829, and was expected to be 'with government' for emancipation the following month, when he was part of the Kerry deputation which carried the county address to the departing lord lieutenant, Lord Anglesey.[8] He duly divided silently in its favour, 6, 30 Mar. 1829. He made no other known votes or speeches during that or the following year, although he was among the Irish Members who met to oppose the increased Irish stamp and spirit duties in May 1830. He resigned at the dissolution that summer, explaining that circumstances prevented his offering again.[9]

In July 1831 Ennismore married Maria Augusta, the daughter of a distinguished naval officer, who was defeated at the Sudbury contest that year; his late brother-in-law and namesake William Windham† of Felbrigg Hall had been a leading Portland Whig and Pittite minister. She, whose first husband of nearly four years' standing had died in February 1830, was the sister of the Liberals William Howe Windham, Member for Norfolk East, 1832-4, and Charles Ashe Windham, who occupied the same seat, 1857-9.[10] Ennismore, who inherited his grandfather's peerage in 1837 and was an official in the royal household for many years, was Conservative Member for St. Albans, 1841-6. He died in February 1856 and was succeeded in his title and estates by his eldest son William (1833-1924), an army officer, who was awarded the United Kingdom barony of Hare in 1869.[11]

[1] J.A. Gaughan, *Listowel and its Vicinity*, 298. [2] *Dublin Evening Post*, 13 Apr., 19 Aug. 1824. [3] Ibid. 10, 15, 27, 29 June, 1, 8, 13 July; *Freeman's Jnl.* 20 June, 5, 7 July 1826; Gaughan, 301-3, 307-8. [4] *The Times*, 28 Feb. 1827. [5] *O'Connell Corresp.* iii. 1363-4. [6] *Dublin Evening Post*, 24 July 1827. [7] *O'Connell Corresp.* iii. 1455. [8] Add. 40398, f. 86; *Dublin Evening Post*, 21 Feb. 1829. [9] *Western Herald*, 17 May, 15 July 1830. [10] *Gent. Mag.* (1826), ii. 171; (1830), i. 380; (1831), ii. 171; (1833), i. 269-70. [11] *The Times*, 5, 6 Feb.; *Southern Reporter*, 6, 8 Feb. 1856.

S.M.F.

HARRIS, George (1787–1836), of York Chambers, St. James's, Mdx.

GREAT GRIMSBY   1830–2 Aug. 1831

b. c.1787, 2nd s. of Thomas Harris (*d.* 1820) of Putney Hill, Wimbledon, Surr. *m.* 29 Nov. 1821, Anna Maria, da. of John Woodcock of Fern Acres, Bucks., 1s. 1da. CB 4 June 1815. *d.* 27 Oct. 1836.
    Midshipman RN 1801, lt. 1805, cdr. 1806, capt. 1807.

Harris's father 'came of a respectable family, and was brought up in trade'. In August 1767, in conjunction with three partners, George Colman the dramatist, William Powell and John Rutherford, he bought the patent of Covent Garden theatre for £60,000. During the first season a 'violent quarrel' arose between Harris and Colman 'in consequence of the pretensions of Mrs. Lessingham, an actress with whom Harris lived'. Powell sided with Colman and barricaded the theatre against Harris and Rutherford, who forcibly broke it open: litigation and a pamphlet war between the two sides ensued. The matter was settled in Colman's favour in July 1770 (Powell having died in the meantime), but he resigned from the theatre in 1774, and Harris became chief manager, which post he retained

until he passed control to his elder son Henry a few years before his death in 1820.[1]

Harris did not follow his father and brother but pursued a distinguished naval career. He took part in a successful attack on a flotilla off Boulogne in 1801 and the capture of four Spanish frigates, 5 Oct. 1804. He served in the Mediterranean, 1805-7, before being posted to the East Indies in 1808. Off Java in August 1810 he captured a total of 17 armed Batavian boats, five pirating proas and 35 Dutch trading vessels. Under his captaincy a flotilla of 16 French boats was destroyed in May 1811, and the following August he led the capture of the French fortress at Sumanap on the Isle of Madura. Here he succeeded in persuading the sultan to ally himself with the British, an action described by Admiral Stopford as a 'masterstroke of policy' which 'essentially contributed to the final reduction of Java'. On 3 Apr. 1813 Harris captured the *Grand Napoleon*, an American schooner with four guns, and on 11 May he took the *Revenge*. In 1814 he commanded 800 seamen and marines who overran the five batteries protecting the entrance to the River Gironde, destroying all their cannon. For this achievement he was made a companion of the Bath.[2] On 28 Nov. 1823 he was brought to court martial at Plymouth, charged with 'delaying the public service' through delays in conveying Sir Edward Thornton, the new ambassador, to Lisbon. Harris conducted his own defence, and the court received unsolicited letters of commendation from eight vice-admirals and from Admiral Lord Exmouth, who described him as 'an officer of zeal, talent, and ability'. Harris was 'most honourably acquitted', 2 Dec. 1823, the blame being apportioned to Thornton.[3]

At the 1830 general election Harris came forward for Great Grimsby on the Tory interest, promising to bring forward a second candidate, Colonel Mayne of Boulney Court. Mayne canvassed with him, 14 July, but soon withdrew, whereupon Harris, who considered his election certain, introduced another friend.[4] A contest ensued and Harris was returned in second place.[5] The Wellington ministry listed him among their 'friends', but he voted against them in the crucial division on the civil list, 15 Nov. 1830. He presented a Grimsby petition for the abolition of slavery, 7 Mar., and made his maiden speech, deploring the proposed partial disfranchisement of Great Grimsby, when presenting a petition from the town against the Grey ministry's reform bill, 21 Mar. 1831. He voted against its second reading next day and for Gascoyne's wrecking amendment, 19 Apr. During discussion of the navy estimates, 25 Mar., Admiral Sir Joseph Yorke questioned the cost and effectiveness of chronometers for ships and made reference to the loss of the *Thetis*. Harris defended its captain, and said that as Yorke well knew, 'if the current be strong, as it proved to be in this case, and the weather thick, twenty, even fifty chronometers would not have saved the ship'. That day he asserted that more clerks, rather than fewer as suggested by Hume, were required by the dock yards. Harris announced his intention of standing for Great Grimsby as an anti-reformer at the 1831 general election, and promised to introduce his likeminded friend John Villiers Shelley as his colleague.[6] They again faced two candidates in the pro-reform interest, but Harris and Shelley triumphed, Great Grimsby's fate under the reform bill being the deciding factor. Their opponents promised to petition against the return.[7] Three days after his victory, 5 May 1831, Harris, 'in the presence of hundreds of spectators', laid the foundation stone of his rope and canvass factory, which was inscribed, 'To commemorate the victory achieved by the independent freemen ... over every conjoined influence that could be opposed to them'. The building was to be the largest in Great Grimsby and was expected to employ two or three hundred people in producing goods from raw materials imported from New Zealand. (In a debate on the supplies, 8 July 1831, he asserted that the production of rigging by convicts would be best performed in New Zealand, 'from whence a better commodity in the shape of hemp or flax than is now in use could be obtained'.) He told the crowd that he had taken out patents in France and Holland for similar factories, but assured them that he intended this to be his 'principal station'.[8]

Harris voted against the second reading of the reintroduced reform bill, 6 July, and for the attempts to adjourn the debate on it, 12 July. During discussion of the use of the 1821 census to determine the disfranchisement schedule, 14 July, he pointed out that Great Grimsby now had over 4,000 inhabitants and more than 300 houses, and was therefore entitled by the principles of the bill to retain both its Members. He highlighted its ancient privileges, said the freemen had never abused their rights, and denied that it was a nomination borough, citing his own election as proof of its independence from the interference of Lord Yarborough. He challenged his former Whig colleague to say whether he had been the free choice of the people or a nominee when he had represented the borough, and warned ministers to be cautious in their interference unless they could prove that Great Grimsby deserved to lose a representative. He brought up the subject again during a debate on the civil list, 18 July, when he asked Lord Althorp, chancellor of

the exchequer, whether or not the pensions under discussion were monarchial grants. He called for consistency, complaining that as disfranchising the freemen of Great Grimsby would nullify a grant of the sovereign, 'the pensions of the rich shall be continued' while those 'of the poor freemen of Grimsby shall cease'. He voted for use of the 1831 census to determine borough disfranchisements, 19 July, and against considering Chippenham's inclusion in schedule B, 27 July. Next day, in committee on Great Grimsby's place in the schedule, he again doggedly defended the borough. Heckled throughout, he was applauded by Waldo Sibthorp for the way in which he had expressed his 'contempt for the titters and ungracious gesticulations' of ministerial supporters. As the question was being put, Harris leapt to his feet and asked if any of the former Members for the borough in the House had a good word to say for it. Although none did, this tactic caused a delay as an argument on procedure ensued, and the question was deferred. Unfortunately for Harris, before it was reconsidered he and his colleague were unseated on petition for treating and barred from offering at the ensuing by-election, 2 Aug. 1831. Three days later they issued a defiant address promising to 'bring down two gentlemen as staunch as ourselves to your interests'.[9] Welcomed on their arrival by 'three-fourths of the populace' that day, they brought with them Lord Loughborough and Henry Fitzroy, who triumphed over two reformers at the poll.[10]

In June 1832 William Maxfield, one of the defeated candidates, canvassed the borough in readiness for the first post-reform election. Advised of his activities by Alderman Edward Brown, Harris issued an address announcing his own candidature, 3 July. On 30 Aug. he informed Brown that he would be in Great Grimsby to canvass as soon as possible, but that he had to go to France to complete negotiations over his proposed factory there, otherwise he might lose 'many thousands of pounds'. He continued:

> I cannot but reflect and ask myself the question: is it possible that a Mr. Anybody under the interest of a government, who have mercilessly taken from the borough half its privileges, can succeed against a man who has for these two years past watched with fatherly affection over its prosperity; endured all the trouble incidental on three elections, and a petition, to say nothing about expense, and who besides that, has expended so much money in and about the borough? ... I will not suppose he will prove successful.

Harris, however, did not persevere, and Maxfield defeated Loughborough.[11] The rope factory initially prospered, but it was in trouble by 1836, when it closed, causing a decline in Great Grimsby's prosperity and population.[12] Harris died at Devonport in October that year. By his will, dated 13 Oct. 1836, and proved under £8,000, he instructed that all his freehold property at Great Grimsby and his personal estate was to be sold and the proceeds invested to provide for his children until they reached the age of 21. He appointed William Gregory of Marston, Cheshire as their guardian.[13]

[1] *Oxford DNB sub* Thomas Harris; *Cuttings relating to Covent Garden Theatre*, i. 27; *Gent. Mag.* (1820), ii. 374. [2] J. Marshall, *R. Naval Biog.* ix. 286-92. [3] G. Harris, *Minutes of Court Martial*, 83. [4] *Grimsby Pollbook* (Skelton, 1830). [5] *Lincoln, Rutland and Stamford Mercury*, 6 Aug. 1830. [6] *Grimsby Pollbook* (Skelton, May 1831). [7] *Lincoln, Rutland and Stamford Mercury*, 6 May 1831. [8] *Hull Advertiser*, 13 May 1831. [9] *Grimsby Pollbook* (Skelton, Aug. 1831). [10] *Hull Advertiser*, 12 Aug. 1831. [11] *Grimsby Pollbook* (Palmer, 1832). [12] E. Gillett, *Hist. Grimsby*, 213. [13] PROB 11/1878/373; IR26/1453/253.

M.P.J.C./P.J.S.

HARRIS, James Edward, Visct. FitzHarris (1778–1841), of Heron Court, Hants.

HELSTON	1802–18 May 1804
HORSHAM	10 Oct. 1804–1806
HEYTESBURY	1807–1812
WILTON	11 Nov. 1816–21 Nov. 1820

b. 19 Aug. 1778, at St. Petersburg, 1st s. of James Harris[†], 1st earl of Malmesbury, and Harriet Maria, da. of Sir George Amyand[†], 1st bt., of Carshalton, Surr. *educ.* Eton 1791; Christ Church, Oxf. 1796; continental tour 1799-1800. *m.* 17 June 1806, Harriet Susan, da. of Francis Bateman Dashwood of Well Vale, Lincs., 3s. *suc.* fa. as 2nd earl of Malmesbury 21 Nov. 1820. *d.* 10 Sept. 1841.

Précis writer, home office and private sec. to sec. of state for home affairs July 1801-July 1802; ld. of treasury May 1804-Feb. 1806; under-sec. of state for foreign affairs Mar.-Aug. 1807; gov. I.o.W. Aug. 1807-*d.*

Cornet, Woodley vol. cav. 1798-1805; maj. commdt. Loyal Henley vols. 1801; capt. 2 Wilts. militia 1803, lt.-col. 1804.

FitzHarris, a reluctant politician from the outset, had sat in the Commons almost continuously since 1802, his career owing more to the reputation of his father, the outstanding Pittite diplomat Lord Malmesbury, than to any merit of his own. He became even fonder of a life of rural retreat at Heron Court after the untimely death of his wife in 1815, although the increasingly frail health suffered by Malmesbury, the lord lieutenant, forced him to be active on Hampshire business.[1] He had a pension of £1,200, in addition to his salary of £1,379 as governor of the Isle of Wight.[2] In a letter full of alarm at the recent discovery of the Cato Street conspiracy, he reported to his father, 27 Feb. 1820, that his governorship precluded him from interfering at the imminent general election. However, this habitual self-effacement did not prevent him from privately expressing his support for the ministerialist candidates John Fleming* and Henry Combe Compton[†], against the Whig George Purefoy Jervoise*.[3] To his father's satisfaction, he moved the formal address of condolence and congratulation to George IV at the Hampshire meeting on the eve of the county election.[4] Referring to Jervoise's expected success, the moderate Whig Lord Lansdowne commented to FitzHarris, 10 Mar., that 'I am afraid you will see some recruits in this Parliament whom we neither of us should approve of, [as] the spirit of reform has really ... taken a root in the public mind'.[5] That day, putting in an appearance at the patron Lord Pembroke's request, he was again returned unopposed for the pocket borough of Wilton (of which he had been a burgess since 1800).[6] He had taken the government whip in the previous Parliament, and the Liverpool administration would have counted on his support, when present.[7] However, no further evidence of parliamentary activity has been traced, and he was granted a month's leave on urgent private business, 19 June 1820.

Condemning ministers' failure to stifle the explosive issue of how to deal with Queen Caroline, FitzHarris complained to Pembroke, 21 July 1820, that had they done so, 'we should have been now enjoying (comparatively with last year) something like tranquillity, instead of being, as is my decided opinion, upon the *very verge* of ruin'. Explaining that 'God knows I give no preference to either of the two parties; *I don't know which to think the worse of*', he nevertheless argued that, since the king could not enter any prosecution with '*clean hands*', the parliamentary charges made against the queen were unjustifiable. As the leader of the House, Lord Castlereagh, had 'notified an intention of *enforcing an attendance*', FitzHarris felt obliged to inform his patron that 'if I am called on to vote, it would be in *opposition to the line of proceeding* unhappily adopted by the government', and that, as this might place him in conflict with Pembroke, he wished to vacate his seat. Pembroke, responding with equal civility, 5 Aug., urged him to defer his resolution, thinking 'the present moment the most improper for a man to withdraw himself from either House of Parliament', and adding that 'I am far from supposing you to be bit by radicals and still less to be influenced by fear of them, but perhaps I may suspect you of being bit by a love of solitude which often misleads the best heads and the best hearts'. Desperately concerned that the gains recently made against the forces of radicalism had been thrown away and that bloodshed and anarchy were inevitable, FitzHarris repeated his criticisms of ministers in a letter of the 7th, but seems to have heeded Pembroke's calming response, dated 12 Aug. 1820, in which he pointed out that FitzHarris could always abstain, that 'never was it my wish or intention to shackle you with my opinions', and that a secession would be liable to misinterpretation.[8]

FitzHarris recorded in his letterbook his astonishment at the arrival at Heron Court of Sir George Cockburn*, 30 Sept. 1820, with instructions from the king that he should immediately cross to the Isle of Wight and organize a loyal address from Newport. Obeying such a direct command, albeit against his better judgement, he informed Cockburn, 2 Oct., that he was convinced that, given 'the present disturbed state of the public mind', such an attempt could only be counterproductive.[9] Summoned to attend Parliament on 16 Oct., he privately remarked that '*I must* be under the necessity of declining'.[10] He inherited his father's earldom in November 1820, which relieved him of this embarrassment, although the following month Pembroke recommended that he should process the necessary legal paperwork, if only to prevent 'such an awkward circumstance as your being obliged to answer to a call of the House of Commons, should one take place previous to the issue of your writ of summons to the House of Lords'.[11] He was not a total recluse thereafter, since he spoke occasionally in the Lords, where he was one of the 22 'stalwarts' who voted against the third reading of the Grey ministry's reform bill, 4 June 1832. Yet, having put the family estates back into some kind of order, shooting and the study of nature remained his governing passions. His shooting journals, meticulously recording over 40 years of dedicated slaughter, were considered by Lord Beaconsfield as 'the most extraordinary example of patience and a sturdy character he ever saw'; extracts were later published.[12] Although eclipsed politically by his father and eldest son, who succeeded him as the 3rd earl in September 1841 and served in Derby and Beaconsfield's cabinets, he was not without substance. His heir, who judged that 'the insincerity of politics was little suited to his susceptible feelings of morality and honour', later recalled that, 'with all this devotion to sport, he read everything, ancient and modern; and, having lived with clever men and in anxious times ... his conversation was most amusing and instructive'.[13]

[1] *HP Commons, 1790-1820*, iv. 156-9; Hants RO, Malmesbury mss 9M73/195. [2] *Red Bk.* (1821), 176. [3] Malmesbury mss 330;

415, FitzHarris to Fleming, 12 Feb., to Palmerston, 27 Feb. 1820. [4] Ibid. 195, p. 508; G2459, Malmesbury to FitzHarris, 9, 16 Mar. 1820. [5] Ibid. 401. [6] Ibid. G2459, Malmesbury to FitzHarris, 8 Feb.; G2538, Pembroke to FitzHarris, 5 Feb., 2 Mar.; 376, acct. bk. 11 Mar. 1820; Wilts. RO, Wilton borough recs. G25/1/22, f. 242. [7] Malmesbury mss 402. [8] Ibid. 404; 415. [9] Ibid. 415. [10] Ibid. G2342, FitzHarris to Sturges Bourne, 11 Oct. 1820. [11] Wilts. RO, Pembroke mss F4/22, p. 221. [12] *Half a Century of Sport in Hants* ed. F.G. Aflalo (1905), pp. vi, vii, xvi, xxv, xxxi, xxxii. [13] Ibid. p. xxxvi; *Gent. Mag.* (1841), ii. 539; *Malmesbury Mems.* i. 2, 11-12.

D.R.F./S.M.F.

HARRIS, John Rawlinson (1774–1830), of Winchester Place, Southwark, Surr.

SOUTHWARK   1830–27 Aug. 1830

b. 8 Oct. 1774,[1] o. surv. s. of John Harris, hatter, of 56 Cannon Street, London and Ann, da. of Simon Warner, coal factor, of East Lane, Rotherhithe.[2] *m.* 23 Apr. 1814, Ann Durrant, da. of William Quincey, timber merchant, of Holland Street, Blackfriars Road, London,[3] 3s. *suc.* fa. 1819. *d.* 27 Aug. 1830.

Harris belonged to a Quaker family, who originally came from Fordingbridge, Hampshire. His grandfather Robert Harris (1709-91) married one Elizabeth Cross 'of London' in 1739, was established by 1752 as a retail hatter in Cannon Street and later retired to Wandsworth.[4] His father became a partner in the family firm in 1766, and in turn Harris was involved at the same level from 1798. The following year, according to a local history, the firm purchased premises in Southwark which doubled as Harris's private address.[5] By 1811 they were described in trade directories as 'hat makers', and in 1817 their manufactory occupied five houses. Following the death two years later of his father, who made him the sole residuary legatee of personal estate sworn under £30,000,[6] Harris entered into partnership with a cousin, John Warner. It appears that his parents had been disowned by their Quaker meeting in 1811, and the same fate befell him in 1814 when he married an outsider in a church. He was afterwards 'greatly esteemed' as chief warden of St. Saviour's, Southwark Cathedral.[7] He made much of his local connections when contesting his native borough at the general election of 1830; his eleventh-hour candidacy was reportedly championed by the licensed victuallers. He disavowed party labels, but professed an abhorrence of slavery and support for a 'moderate and temperate reform, and economy in the public expenditure'. Pressed to elaborate, he advocated the enfranchisement of populous places and a general extension of voting rights, and denied that he was 'a trimmer and a friend to the ministry for the time being'. Although his surprise return at the head of the poll, after a five-day contest, was ascribed by newspapers to his popularity among the 'potwallopers', the duke of Wellington's ministry regarded it as a gain for them. His colleague, Sir Robert Wilson, who had not previously heard of him, gathered that he was 'distinguished by his private acts of benevolence' and 'belonged to that class that "did good by stealth and blushed to find it fame"'. A 'splendid cavalcade' followed the election, and at his celebratory dinner Harris was feted as a 'decided enemy to jobbing and a friend to the liberty of the press'.[8]

The excitement proved too much for Harris, and before he could take his seat he died, 27 Aug. 1830, following 'a short illness, which terminated in a typhus fever, supposed to have been occasioned by the fatigue and anxiety attendant on the election'.[9] His wish to be laid to rest in the Quaker burial ground at Bunhill Fields was not respected, and he was interred at St. Saviour's, Southwark. He left all his freehold estates, consisting of 42 houses in Southwark and other property in London and Essex, to his eldest son and heir to the family business, John Quincey Harris (b. 1815); his personalty was sworn under £50,000.[10]

[1] Soc. of Friends Lib. London and Mdx. birth reg. [2] Ibid. Mins. London Two Weeks Meeting, vol. 9, p. 209. [3] The Times, 25 Apr. 1814. [4] T. Collins, Richard of the Square Mile, 12-18; GL MIC 616; PROB 11/1209/428. [5] Gent. Mag. (1819), ii. 477; Collins, 16; W. Rendle and P. Norman, Inns of Old Southwark, 363. [6] PROB 11/1624/20; IR26/825/20. [7] Soc. of Friends Lib. Mins. London Six Weeks Meeting, vol. 18, p. 316; Mins. Southwark Meeting, 1809-16, pp. 310, 381, 397, 422; Pendle and Norman, 363. [8] The Times, 31 July, 2-6, 13, 17 Aug.; County Chron. 10 Aug.; Baldwin's Weekly Jnl. 14 Aug. 1830; Add. 40401, ff. 132, 140. [9] Gent. Mag. (1830), ii. 283. [10] PROB 11/1776/557; IR26/1229/441; GLRO X14/124.

H.J.S.

HARRISON BATLEY, Charles (?1787–1835), of Bramley Grange, nr. Leeds, Yorks. and 13 Chapel Stairs, L. Inn, Mdx.

BEVERLEY   1826–1830

b. ?1787, 1st s. of Charles Harrison of Ripon, Yorks. and w. Isabella Charnock.[1] educ. Trinity Coll. Camb. 1805; fellow, St. Catharine's, Camb. 1810; L. Inn 30 Jan. 1810, 'aged 22', called 1813. m. 25 May 1822, Anna, da. of John Baines, surgeon, of Masham, nr. Ripon, wid. of John Lodge Batley of Masham, 2da. Took additional name of Batley by royal lic. 10 May 1822. d. 1 Aug. 1835.
  Recorder, Ripon by 1819-d.

Harrison Batley belonged to a family of minor Yorkshire gentry. From 1813 until his death he was a practising equity draftsman on the northern circuit; and by 1819 he was recorder of Ripon, his native town.

His marriage to the widow Anna Batley (whose father was a cousin of Edward Baines, proprietor of the Leeds Mercury) brought him wealth and an extra name.[2] When he offered for the venal borough of Beverley at the general election of 1826, with the blessing of the retiring Member George Lane Fox, he was described as 'a gentleman of independent fortune'. He professed qualified support for revision of the corn laws, provided there remained 'a protecting duty, alike advantageous to the grower and consumer'. He promised to resist 'further concessions to the Roman Catholics, owing as they do allegiance to a foreign power'. He was returned in second place after a contest which was reckoned to have cost him about £3,000.[3]

An active and conscientious Member, he opposed reception of the petition of Robert Taylor praying for Deists to be sworn in courts of justice 'upon the works of nature', 29 Nov. 1826, arguing that 'a person who did not believe in our Saviour ought not to be tolerated in a British House of Commons'. On 6 Dec. 1826, seconding a motion by Spence, Member for Ripon, for information on the pending business of the equity courts, he 'rejoiced at the prospect of seeing the equity side of the exchequer thrown open to the public' and declared that under lord chancellor Eldon the administration of chancery was 'perfect'.[4] He was 'quite satisfied' that bankruptcy jurisdiction should remain in chancery, 13 Mar. 1827. He thought a proposal to establish a committee of appeal for private bills was 'impolitic', 15 Feb. 1827. He welcomed the home secretary Peel's three bills designed to mitigate the severity of the criminal law, 23 Feb. He voted against Catholic relief, 6 Mar., and endorsed the hostile petition from Beverley corporation, 22 Mar.[5] He was in the minorities for a reduced import price of 50s. for corn, 9 Mar., and against increased protection for barley, 12 Mar. From his place on 'the hinder ministerial benches' he supported Lord Althorp's motion for inquiry into ways of reducing the cost of county elections, which he wanted to be extended to the boroughs, 15 Mar. He was in the Canning ministry's minorities against the disfranchisement of Penryn, 28 May, 7 June, and the Coventry magistracy bill, 18 June 1827. On 31 Jan., 25 Feb., 3, 4, 7 Mar. 1828 he contended that the evidence of corruption at East Retford was not damning enough to justify its disfranchisement. Nor was he prepared to see Penryn disfranchised because of the delinquency of 150 electors, 24 Mar. He supported Davies's bill to limit the duration of borough polls, 21 Feb., 23 May, when he said that 'protracted elections are the source of every evil that can be imagined'; but he voted against Fyler's bill to lift the restriction on the use of ribbons at elections and an attempt to introduce a measure to control the admission of borough freemen, 20 Mar. He voted against repeal of the Test Acts, 26 Feb., and Catholic relief, 12 May, having presented and endorsed a hostile petition from his constituency, 24 Apr. He brought up one from Beverley merchants and traders for repeal of the stamp duty on receipts, 4 Mar., and advocated this step, 11 Mar. He divided with the Wellington ministry against inquiry into chancery delays, 24 Apr., and reduction of the ordnance estimates, 4 July, and for the silk duties, 14 July. On 22 May he spoke warmly in support of the proposed provision for the family of Canning, whose 'indisputably brilliant services' had put the country in his debt. He presented a Beverley petition against restriction of the circulation of one pound bank notes, 6 June, and divided for revision of the usury laws, 19 June. He thought William Smith's proposal to insert provision for punishment by hard labour would defeat the object of Peel's offences against the person bill, 6 June. He spoke and voted for the third reading of the corporate funds bill, asserting that their application to 'electioneering purposes' was 'wholly irreconcilable to the freedom of election' 10 July. He suggested an amendment to the alehouses licensing bill, 19 June 1828.

Harrison Batley made it clear that he supported the bill to suppress the Catholic Association not 'because it is the precursor' of emancipation, but because it was 'necessary for the support of our government in Ireland', as the association was 'unconstitutional' and 'treasonable', 12 Feb. 1829. He remained convinced that the 'uppermost object of ambition in the Catholic mind is to make its own religion the dominant hierarchy'. Unaccountably, Planta, the patronage secretary, reckoned that Harrison Batley would side 'with government' for the concession of emancipation; but he was one of its diehard opponents in the lobbies. He presented and endorsed a constituency petition against it, 4 Mar., arguing that the question 'affects the security and comfort of our homes and our altars' and stressing that his sentiments were entirely in harmony with those of his constituents; he sent a written assurance of this to the mayor of Beverley.[6] He spoke vigorously against emancipation, 6 Mar., accusing Peel of a betrayal and fearing that 'we are pulling down the adamantine pillar in the temple of the constitution'. He brought up and endorsed an anti-Catholic petition from a large meeting of 'the respectable inhabitants' of Beverley, 16 Mar., and said he would have resigned his seat had he found himself at odds with the petitioners. On 23 Mar. he suggested but eventually withdrew an amendment to the relief bill designed to safeguard Church of England prop-

erty. He spoke against allowing O'Connell to take his seat unhindered, 18 May. He opposed the transfer of East Retford's seats to Birmingham, 5 May 1829, 11 Feb., when he professed willingness to give representation to great commercial and trading interests, but not by an act of injustice, 5, 15 Mar. 1830. He was in the minority for issuing a new writ for the borough, 2 June 1829. He voted against Lord Blandford's reform scheme, 18 Feb., but for Lord John Russell's proposal to enfranchise Birmingham, Leeds and Manchester, 23 Feb. 1830. He declared his 'decided opposition' to the secret ballot as 'a most fatal blow to the independence' of the Commons, 23 Mar. He presented Beverley petitions against renewal of the East India Company's trade monopoly, 16 Mar., and for the Leeds and Selby railway bill, 17 Mar. He voted against government to get rid of the Bathurst and Dundas pensions, 26 Mar., but refused to support the opposition motion of 'censure' on the Terceira episode, 28 Apr. He spoke and voted against Jewish emancipation, 5 Apr., and was in the majority against it, 17 May. He was an opponent of Lord Ellenborough's divorce bill, 1, 6 Apr. He presented constituency petitions against the bill to open the beer trade, 6 Apr., 6 May, and spoke and voted for amendments to it, 1 July. He divided to abolish capital punishment for most forgery offences, 24 May, 7 June, when he was in the ministerial majority for the grant for South American missions. He spoke for reform of the insolvent debtors courts, 14 May, but, as a chancery barrister, asserted that the proposal to appoint an additional judge there was 'unnecessary', 17 June. He voted against Hume's attempt to reduce judicial salaries, 7 July, but spoke and voted against the ministerial amendment to increase libel recognizances, 9 July. He was in Brougham's minority of 27 for the abolition of colonial slavery, 13 July 1830.

Harrison Batley retired from Parliament at the 1830 dissolution. He died, 'aged 49', at St. Omer in August 1835.[7] No will or administration has been found.

[1] According to IGI (ancestral file). [2] J. Fisher, *Hist. Masham*, 394. [3] *Hull Rockingham*, 2 June; *Hull Advertiser*, 16 June; *Yorks. Gazette*, 3 June; Hull Univ. Lib. Hotham mss DDHO/8/4, Hall to Hotham, 1, 10, 24 June 1826. [4] *The Times*, 7 Dec. 1826. [5] Ibid. 23 Mar. 1827. [6] Beverley Lib. DX 24/25 (4 Mar. 1829). [7] *Gent. Mag.* (1835), ii. 667.

M.P.J.C./D.R.F.

HART, **George Vaughan** (1752–1832), of Kilderry House, co. Donegal.

CO. DONEGAL 1812–1831

b. 1752, 4th but 2nd surv. s. of Rev. Edward Hart (*d.* 1793), rect. of Desertegny, co. Donegal, and Elizabeth, da. of Rev. John Ramsay, rect. of Stranorlar, co. Donegal. *m.* 22 July 1792, Charlotte, da. of John Ellerker of Ellerker, Yorks., 7s. (2 *d.v.p.*) 5da. (3 *d.v.p.*). *suc.* uncle Henry to Kilderry 1790; e. bro. John to Ballynagard, co. Londonderry 1816. *d.* 14 June 1832.

Ensign 46 Ft. 1775, lt. 1777, capt. lt. 1779; capt. 55 Ft. 1779; maj. 75 Ft. 1787, lt.-col. 1795, col. 1798; maj.-gen. 1805; lt.-gen. 1811; gen. 1825.

Dep. paymaster-gen. of the forces, Bombay 1788-90, Madras 1791-2, India 1792-5.

Gov. Londonderry and Culmore 1820-*d.*

Lieutenant-General Hart, who had made money in India and inherited valuable estates in his native county, represented Donegal from 1812 with the backing of the 1st marquess of Abercorn and the Castle interest. Emulating his ancestor Henry Hart (*d.* 1623), whose family had originally come from the West country, he was appointed governor of Londonderry and Culmore Fort at a salary of over £300 in January 1820 and continued to seek government patronage.[1] A steady supporter of the Liverpool administration, he was again returned for Donegal at the general election that spring, when he condemned the harsh enforcement of the Irish distillery laws for causing local distress.[2] He rode this hobby horse in the Commons, 7 June, presented the Templemore petition against the Illicit Distillation Act, 21 June, and criticized the chancellor's proposals on the subject, 7, 14, 17, 18 July.[3] He voted for a select committee on the Union duties, 14 June, and urged conciliation not augmented military forces as the best means of pacifying Ireland, 29 June 1820.

Hart, who divided against condemning ministers' conduct towards Queen Caroline, 6 Feb., voted against Catholic relief, 28 Feb. 1821, 20 Apr. 1822. He again favoured inquiry into Anglo-Irish trade, 30 Apr., and supported reducing the Irish window duties, 16 May, but he withdrew his bill to allow commissioners of excise to licence small Irish stills on receiving assurances from ministers, 13 June, and sided with them against Hume's motion for economy and retrenchment, 27 June 1821, and Brougham's for more extensive tax reductions to relieve distress, 11 Feb. 1822.[4] He could not resist blaming the distillery laws for the continuing unrest in his comments on the Irish constables and insurrections bills, 7 June, 15 July.[5] Crossing from Ireland for the forthcoming parliamentary session, 24 Dec. 1822, he was the victim of what he described as a 'gross, malignant and on my part totally unprovoked assault', during which he was knocked down senseless by a savage punch to the back of his neck. This was apparently perpetrated by the employees of the Bangor ferry, 'or their accomplices',

who had tried to extort excessive fares from him and his fellow passengers.[6]

He testified to the good conduct of the Irish yeomanry, 10 Mar., when, as on the 13th and 18th, he voted against tax reductions, though he commented that a higher duty on barilla would benefit the North of Ireland on bringing up a petition from the kelp manufacturers of Donegal to this effect, 13 June 1823.[7] He was listed in minorities for information on the plot to murder the Irish lord lieutenant, 24 Mar., and against the Irish tithes composition bill, 16 June. He was in the ministerial minority against the Scottish juries bill, 20 June, but divided for the introduction of trial by jury in New South Wales, 7 July 1823. He voted against inquiry into the trial of the Methodist missionary John Smith in Demerara, 11 June, and, having divided for the Irish insurrection bill on the 14th, he suggested that Irish towns be enclosed with walls so that the well-disposed would be able to prosecute agrarian trouble-makers without fear of retribution, 18 June 1824. He voted for the Irish unlawful societies bill, 15 Feb., and against Catholic relief, 1 Mar., 21 Apr., 10 May 1825. Promoted a full general later in May, he divided for the duke of Cumberland's annuity bill, 2, 6 June 1825. He supported inquiry into Scottish and Irish promissory notes, 16 Mar., and voted for receiving the report on the salary of the president of the board of trade, 10 Apr., and against alteration of the representation of Edinburgh, 13 Apr. 1826.[8]

Promising to continue his exertions on behalf of his constituents, Hart was again returned for Donegal at the general election of 1826 and in October he spoke at the Belfast dinner in honour of the leading anti-Catholic Lord George Beresford*, who had been defeated in county Waterford.[9] He signed the Protestant petition from the Irish noblemen and gentlemen early the following year and, having presented hostile petitions from his own county, 26 Feb., 2, 13 Mar., he voted in this sense, 6 Mar. 1827.[10] He was granted three weeks' leave, 4 May 1827, on account of the illness of his wife, who died on the 20th. Despite advocating the payment of Catholic clergy, if only as a means of preventing improvident and fertile marriages, 19 Feb., Hart, who sided with the Wellington government against inquiry into chancery administration on 24 Apr., again divided against Catholic claims, 12 May 1828. Illness prevented him attending the meeting that autumn for the establishment of a Brunswick Club in Donegal, but he became a vice-president of the one in Londonderry.[11] Listed by Planta, the patronage secretary, as 'opposed to the principle' of emancipation, he voted, 6 Mar., presented Donegal petitions, 11, 16 Mar., and paired against it, 27, 30 Mar. 1829. He divided against allowing Daniel O'Connell to take his seat unimpeded, 18 May 1829, and Jewish emancipation, 5 Apr., 17 May 1830. He voted against amendments to the Galway franchise bill, 24 May, and abolition of the death penalty for forgery, 7 June, and supported his county's petition against the increased Irish spirit duties, 14 June 1830, when he brought up and endorsed Londonderry corporation's petition to the same effect.

Brushing aside rumours that he would retire at the dissolution in 1830, he issued a circular to his supporters in which he dwelt on his 18 years' tenure of the representation as 'a connection which has become dearer to me in proportion to its continuance and which it is impossible for me voluntarily to abandon'.[12] He was present in Londonderry to witness his eldest son John's unsuccessful attempt to win the borough seat as an independent at the general election, when he was returned unopposed for the last time for Donegal.[13] He was listed by ministers among their 'friends' and duly divided with them on the civil list, 15 Nov. 1830. He was absent from the division on the second reading of the Grey ministry's reform bill, 22 Mar. 1831, but John Hart, who unsuccessfully stood for Derry as an avowed reformer at a by-election the following month, insisted that his father would have voted for it had he not been unwell.[14] Hart himself, who in his last known speech urged a grant of money to Ireland to provide employment and relieve distress, 30 Mar., evidently favoured only a moderate degree of reform, and even attended a meeting of Irish Members who had been in the minority on the 22nd in order to become better informed. Following his vote for Gascoyne's wrecking amendment, 19 Apr. 1831, his younger son and namesake informed John that their father, who 'merely wishes the Members to be removed from the lesser to the more popular towns', had done so because he feared that 'if the English Members alone were to be reduced, and the Irish remain as they are ... [the dominant] anti-Union party would become fearfully strong'.[15]

Professing an 'ardent affection' for his county, Hart initially offered again for Donegal at the general election of 1831, when John failed to win a seat for county Londonderry. However, with his own popularity doubtful (one radical opponent described him as 'universally scouted'), he withdrew on the pretext of old age, rather than risk a contest with two genuine reformers.[16] Considered a brave soldier, faithful Member and loving paterfamilias, Hart, who was said to have refused a baronetcy, died at Kilderry in

June 1832.[17] By his will, dated 12 Jan. 1832, he left the bulk of his estates and personal wealth sworn under £13,000 in Ireland to John Hart (1798-1838), who issued an address to the freeholders of Donegal at the general election in December 1834, but never sat in Parliament. The will stipulated that his eldest son could only succeed if he had *not* married the daughter of a Westminster tailor named James Fisher, as this 'connection would disgrace himself and his family'; but, almost certainly because no such marriage had taken place (though he acknowledged a natural son), Kilderry and other properties were inherited by him.[18]

[1] *HP Commons, 1790-1820*, iv. 161-2; Add. 40296, ff. 28-29; 40381, f. 133. [2] *Black Bk.* (1823), 162; *Session of Parl. 1825*, p. 467; *Enniskillen Chron.* 6 Apr. 1820. [3] *The Times*, 22 June, 8, 15, 18, 19 July 1820. [4] Ibid. 17 May, 14 June 1821. [5] Ibid. 8 June 1822. [6] Add. 40354, f. 10. [7] *The Times*, 14 June 1823. [8] Ibid. 17 Mar. 1826. [9] *Strabane Morning Post*, 13 June, 4 July; *Belfast Commercial Chron.* 17 July, 16 Oct. 1826. [10] Add. 40392, f. 5; *The Times*, 27 Feb., 3, 14 Mar. 1827. [11] *Belfast News Letter*, 30 Sept.; *Enniskillen Chron.* 2 Oct. 1828. [12] PRO NI, Hart mss D3077/C/8/11; *Belfast News Letter*, 27 July 1830. [13] *Belfast Guardian*, 13 Aug.; *Enniskillen Chron.* 26 Aug. 1830. [14] *Belfast Guardian*, 5 Apr. 1831. [15] Hart mss H/2/5, 13. [16] *Dublin Evening Post*, 26 Apr., 5 May; *Belfast News Letter*, 29 Apr., 10 May 1831; PRO NI, Anglesey mss D619/33B/3. [17] H.T. Hart, *Fam. Hist. of Hart of Donegal*, 48; *Londonderry Sentinel*, 16 June 1832; *Gent. Mag.* (1832), ii. 180-1; *DNB*; *Oxford DNB*. [18] *Londonderry Sentinel*, 27 Dec. 1834; Hart mss F/16/21; H/2/5; PROB 11/1809/763; IR26/1294/769; Hart, 114-16. This corrects the erroneous statement that John Hart was so disinherited in *HP Commons, 1790-1820*, iv. 162.

S.M.F.

HARTOPP, George Harry William Fleetwood (1785–1824), of Doe Bank, Sutton Coldfield, Warws.

DUNDALK   29 June 1820–31 Mar. 1824

b. 20 Aug. 1785, 1st s. of Sir Edmund Cradock Hartopp†, 1st bt. (*d.* 1833), of Four Oaks Hall, Atherstone, Warws. and Anne, da. and h. of Joseph Hurlock, gov. Bencoolen. *educ.* Christ Church, Oxf. 1804. *unm. d.v.p.* 31 Mar. 1824.

Hartopp, whose father had represented Leicestershire, 1798-1806, assumed the additional name of Fleetwood in acknowledgement of his lineal descent from the Cromwellian General Charles Fleetwood (*d.* 1692), whose estates had devolved on his mother. At Oxford he was considered an 'elegant scholar, and of studious turn of mind'.[1] He came in unopposed on a vacancy for Dundalk on the controlling interest of the Jocelyn family in June 1820. That October he proposed Francis Lawley* in the Warwickshire by-election.[2] A poor attender, who is not known to have spoken in debate, he voted in support of the Liverpool ministry on the Queen Caroline affair, 6 Feb., and the revenue, 6 Mar. 1821. He divided for Catholic relief, 28 Feb. 1821. He was in a minority of 26 for information on the expense of foreign embassies, 25 Mar., and voted for inquiry into the prosecution of the Dublin Orange rioters, 22 Apr., but divided with government against Scottish parliamentary reform, 2 June 1823.

Hartopp died intestate and *v.p.* at Mitcham, Surrey in March 1824, having taken 'cold during his parliamentary attendance' from 'want of attention to warm clothing'. His estate and 'funded goods' passed to his father.[3]

[1] *Gent. Mag.* (1824), i. 463. [2] *Warwick Advertiser*, 28 Oct. 1820. [3] *Gent. Mag.* (1824), i. 463; IR26/219/142.

P.J.S.

HARTY, Robert Way (1779–1832), of Merrion Square East, Dublin and Prospect House, Roebuck, co. Dublin.

DUBLIN   1831–8 Aug. 1831

b. 27 Dec. 1779, 4th s. of Timothy Harty (*d.* 1799) of Kilkenny and Mary, da. of John Lockington. *m.* 21 Mar. 1807, Elizabeth, da. of John Davis of Eden Park, 4s. 3da. *cr.* bt. 15 Sept. 1831. *d.* 10 Oct. 1832.
 Common cllr., Dublin 1804-11, sheriff 1811-12, sheriff's peer 1812-22, alderman 1822-*d.*, ld. mayor 1830-1.

Harty was the youngest of four brothers, of whom the eldest, William, was a Dublin physician and the other two, John and Joseph, were officers in the 33rd Foot. A hosier, with business premises at 9 Westmoreland Street and 7 Lower Ormond Quay, he built up a considerable private fortune and, having in 1804 been elected to the common council as one of the representatives of the hosiers' guild, of which he was a freeman, he gradually gained a high position in the corporation of Dublin, on which his brother-in-law Alderman Thomas McKenny, his sister Susannah's husband, was one of the few prominent Whigs. As sheriff, in 1812 he gave great offence by empanelling an impartial jury to try the Catholics who were being prosecuted by government.[1] He moved the resolutions praising the late Member Henry Grattan at a meeting of Dublin electors, 13 June, and in the corporation he seconded the unsuccessful amendment in favour of adopting his son and namesake, rather than Thomas Ellis*, as the prospective candidate, 19 June 1820; he voted for Henry Grattan* junior in the by-election that month.[2] He was expected to have made himself unpopular by speaking against the motion for

the corporation to petition against the Catholic peers bill, 22 May 1822, but, after this question had been postponed, he surprisingly beat the anti-Catholic Sir Nicholas Brady by one vote (53-52) in the aldermanic election that day.[3] Nothing came of a rumour in June 1827 that, like other disgruntled aldermen, he might resign in protest at the corporation's failure to elect its sheriffs that year.[4] On 22 Jan. 1830 he was in the minority of eight aldermen for the admission of the respectable Catholic merchant Ignatius Callaghan to the freedom.[5]

Harty's nomination as lord mayor elect was confirmed by 79-19 in the common council, 23 Apr. 1830.[6] He complained about the general neglect of Ireland at the Dublin meeting to petition against the increased Irish stamp and spirit duties in May, and in July he led the delegation which unsuccessfully called on the former county Londonderry Member George Robert Dawson* to stand for the borough as a pro-Catholic, commercial and government candidate.[7] He was listed among the aldermen who opposed the return of the recorder Frederick Shaw* for the city at the general election that summer, when he was reported to have voted for Nicholas Leader* in the Kilkenny contest.[8] He was sworn in as lord mayor, 30 Sept., when his civic dinner, in the presence of the duke of Northumberland, the lord lieutenant, was notable for the attendance of radicals such as Richard Sheil* and the fact that the usual Orange toast to the 'glorious memory' was omitted.[9] He presented the corporation's loyal address to the new king, in person, 27 Oct., but the custom of conferring a baronetcy was not adhered to on this occasion.[10] Refusing to comply with the O'Connellite requisition for a meeting to petition for repeal of the Union, 3 Dec. 1830, he told the deputation that delivered it that

> though, in common with my fellow citizens, I was decidedly opposed to the enactment of the legislative Union, I cannot now, after a lapse of nearly 30 years, recognize in its repeal a measure of such practical and unmixed good as could compensate for the unequivocal mischief that must ensue from reviving and maintaining a continued state of agitation in the public mind, after its most recent and salutary subsidence.[11]

His neighbour, Mrs. O'Connell, reported to her husband two days later that his

> speech was most impertinent and he deserves to be well humbled. How glad I am I did not visit the lady mayoress. I waited to know how he would act after his return from London. His head has been turned by the compliments there paid to him and he forgets that he was once one of the people and glad to have their support.[12]

In February 1831 and subsequent months, he convened meetings to organize the provision of relief for the poor of Dublin and the West of Ireland.[13] He supported parliamentary reform at the meeting of inhabitants which he chaired, 15 Mar. 1831, but was unable to prevent the corporation petitioning against the Grey ministry's reform bill the following month.[14]

After what he described as 'a restless night – no sleep till day break', Harty yielded to the request of his friends and offered for Dublin as a reformer, with Louis Perrin*, against the sitting Members George Moore and Frederick Shaw, the corporation's candidates, at the general election of 1831.[15] Although he was attacked in the Tory press as 'vulgar, illiterate and wholly uneducated', with no credibility in commercial circles, he was described by the lord lieutenant Lord Anglesey, who pleaded with the prime minister to secure him a baronetcy 'in case it should be necessary to engage him to withdraw in order to secure Perrin's return', as 'most respectable in every way'.[16] Having advocated reform as a cure for the stranglehold of the boroughmongers and denied that any parliamentary vote he might give for the reform bill would conflict with his corporation oath to uphold the rights of the freemen, he was elected in first place, narrowly ahead of Perrin, after a severe contest, and he again advocated reform at their election dinner, 31 May 1831.[17] The high level of his expenses, which one observer put at over £7,000, apparently caused him to differ with his colleague and the Irish government.[18] The following month the Irish secretary Smith Stanley wrote to Anglesey about Harty's request for a baronetcy, stating that 'he seems in an awkward position, as he is universally called *Sir Robert* and he keeps saying that his patent is not yet made out. If there be no intention of making him, he will be furious'. Anglesey replied that Harty was 'an energetic and independent character [who] has stood up against very pernicious corporation abuses and has stood manfully forward at a very critical moment', but denied either having promised a baronetcy or £5,000 towards payment of his election expenses. Under further pressure from Smith Stanley, who related that Harty had received groundless assurances of its bestowal from members of the lord lieutenant's entourage, Anglesey made the case for awarding a baronetcy to Lord Grey, who was not unsympathetic.[19]

Harty raised the issue of Irish distress, which he said was caused by high taxation and landlord absenteeism, on the address, 22 June 1831, when he doubted whether charitable action and the possible introduction of poor laws, although welcome in themselves, would be sufficient to provide relief; with his strong accent and Irish colloquialisms, this maiden speech and later ones were cruelly ridiculed in the *Dublin Evening Mail*.[20] He defended the agricultural interest on the subject of West Indian sugar duties, 30 June, 20 July, and supported the Dublin wine merchants' petition against higher duties, 12 July. He urged that Irish revenues should be retained for expenditure there, 5 July, but welcomed the grant for paying salaries to the commissioners of public works in Ireland, 22 July, when he was active in the committee on the Dublin and Kingstown railway bill.[21] He voted for the second reading of the reintroduced reform bill, 6 July, at least twice against adjourning proceedings on it, 12 July, for using the 1831 census to determine the disfranchisement schedules, 19 July, and generally for its details. Said to be almost unregarded in the Commons, he made a last minute appeal to the Dublin election committee to allow him to call more witnesses, but was unseated by it, 8 Aug., and so disqualified from offering again at the ensuing by-election.[22] Before leaving London that month, he pestered Smith Stanley about receiving at least £4,000 in expenses, a disagreement which had still not been resolved when he wrote again to Smith Stanley in October 1831, and his outstanding baronetcy, which, because he had been found guilty of bribery, Grey was now unwilling to sanction.[23]

Harty, whose locum Alderman Richard Smyth had had to suppress censure motions against him in the corporation, 22 July 1831, was much criticized for his 'sham baronetcy' on his return to Ireland the following month, but finally received it, under cover of the coronation honours, in September.[24] On 16 Sept. he chaired the grand Dublin meeting to petition the Lords in favour of the reform bill, the last major act of his mayoralty, which ended on the 30th.[25] With only one dissentient, the common council voted to disfranchise him for absenting himself from his official duties without permission, but this was overruled in the court of aldermen, 14 Oct. On a separate charge, that he had voted in the Commons against compensation to the leading corporator Sir Abraham Bradley King for the loss of his patent as king's stationer in Ireland (on 11 July), he explained in a public letter to the sheriffs, 21 Oct., that he had brought pressure to bear in King's favour on several Members during the debate, at the end of which he had intended to speak, but had instead been accidentally locked in for the division. However, King resentfully insisted, in a printed reply, 3 Nov., that Harty had promised him his vote and had betrayed him as a friend. Thereafter he was almost ostracized by the mostly Tory corporation; for instance, the grand jury decided to dispense with its usual dinner that term out of personal hostility against him.[26] He attended reform meetings in Dublin in May and June and was involved in the Liberal registration campaign there in August 1832, when he was rumoured to be canvassing himself, although not as a repealer.[27] Harty was reported by Sheil to be

a good-humoured, rosy-faced, blue-eyed person, with a prompt and ready smile, accompanied, however, with a consciousness of that dignity which £50,000 and a baronetcy, the reward for his honourable services as lord mayor, are calculated to impart.[28]

He died of cholera in October 1832, when he was remembered for his 'great ingenuousness of manners and natural uprightness of mind'.[29] He was succeeded in his title consecutively by his eldest son, Robert (1815-1902), and his youngest, Henry Lockington (1826-1913).

[1] Burke PB (1930), ii. 1192; R.L. Sheil, Sketches of Irish Bar (1854), ii. 361. [2] Dublin Evening Post, 15, 22 June 1820; Report of Procs. at Election for Dublin (1820), 78. [3] Dublin Evening Post, 23 May 1822; Cal. Ancient Recs. Dublin, xvii. 456. [4] Dublin Evening Post, 12 June 1827. [5] Ibid. 23 Jan. 1830. [6] Warder, 24 Apr. 1830; Cal. Ancient Recs. Dublin, xviii. 411-12. [7] Dublin Evening Post, 15, 18 May, 27, 29 July 1830. [8] Morning Reg. 4, 12 Aug. 1830. [9] Dublin Evening Post, 30 Sept., 2, 5 Oct.; The Times, 4 Oct. 1830. [10] Cal. Ancient Recs. Dublin, xviii. 485-91. [11] Dublin Evening Post, 7 Dec. 1830. [12] O'Connell Corresp. iv. 1739. [13] Dublin Evening Post, 8 Feb., 2 Apr., 7, 11 June 1831. [14] Ibid. 10, 15, 17 Mar. 1831; Cal. Ancient Recs. Dublin, xviii. 494. [15] Derby mss 920 Der (14) 121/2, Gosset to Smith Stanley, 26 Apr.; Dublin Evening Post, 26, 28 Apr., 3 May 1831. [16] Dublin Evening Mail, 27, 29 Apr., 2 May 1831; PRO NI, Anglesey mss D619/28C, pp. 106-8. [17] Dublin Evening Post, 7, 10, 12, 14, 17, 19, 21 May, 2 June 1831. [18] PRO NI, Young mss D2930/8/39; Dublin Evening Mail, 30 May 1831. [19] Anglesey mss 28C, pp. 135-8; 31D/43, 44, 46; Derby mss 119/2, Anglesey to Smith Stanley, 29 June 1831. [20] Dublin Evening Mail, 27 June, 29 July 1831. [21] Dublin Morning Post, 25 July 1831. [22] Dublin Evening Mail, 1, 10 Aug. 1831. [23] Anglesey mss 31D/55, 57; 33D, pp. 76-77; Derby mss 119/2, Harty to Smith Stanley [Oct. 1831]. [24] Dublin Evening Mail, 25 July, 29 Aug., 2, 9 Sept. 1831. [25] Dublin Evening Post, 13, 15, 17, 20 Sept. 1831. [26] Ibid. 18 Oct., 10 Nov.; Dublin Evening Mail, 4, 7, 11 Nov. 1831. [27] Dublin Evening Post, 15 May, 5 June, 21, 28 Aug. 1832; O'Connell Corresp. iv. 1914. [28] New Monthly Mag. (1831), ii. 3. [29] Morning Reg. 12 Oct.; Warder, 13 Oct. 1832.

S.M.F.

HARVEY (afterwards SAVILL ONLEY), Charles (1756–1843), of Stisted Hall, Essex and 22 Great George Street, Mdx.

| NORWICH | 1812–1818 |
| CARLOW | 1818–1826 |

b. 20 Dec. 1756, 3rd s. of Alderman Robert Harvey (d. 1816), merchant, banker and twice mayor of Norwich, and Judith, da. of Capt. Anthony Onley, RN, of Staverton and Catesby, Northants. educ. Lynn; Caius, Camb. 1772;

M. Temple 1774, called 1780. m. (1) Mar. 1783, Sarah (d. 12 Mar. 1805), da. of John Haynes of Twickenham, Mdx., 1s. 3da.; (2) 27 Mar. 1817, Charlotte Haynes, his first w.'s sister, s.p. suc. mat. uncle Rev. Charles Onley of Stisted Hall and took name Savill Onley by royal lic. 14 Dec. 1822. d. 31 Aug. 1843.

Bencher, M. Temple 1783; steward, Norwich 1783; recorder 1801-26.

Capt. Norwich vol. inf. 1797, maj. 1803, lt.-col. 1804, col. 1807-8.

Chairman, Penclawdd Copper Co. 1815; manager, Grand Junction Canal Co.

Harvey came from a leading family of Norwich corporators who, as a friend reminded the home secretary Peel in 1825 when soliciting a position for his distinguished elder brother, Lieutenant-Colonel John Harvey of Thorpe Lodge, Norfolk, had 'always been attached to government'.[1] He continued to sit unopposed for the 'comeattible borough' of Carlow placed by the 1st earl of Charleville at treasury disposal, provoking local anger that an 'Englishman and a stranger' had again been 'chosen to represent' a town 'which he never saw!!'.[2] Harvey, described in a radical publication as 'one of the Irish Members' who 'scarcely ever attend', continued to give general support to the Liverpool ministry when present.[3] He presented a Norwich petition for repeal of the wool duties, 1 May 1820. On 1 June he successfully moved that Henry Swann* be brought to the bar for questioning by the Penryn election committee, of which he was a long-serving member.[4] He was granted a week's leave on urgent business, 3 July 1820. He voted in support of ministers' conduct towards Queen Caroline, 6 Feb. 1821. He divided for Catholic claims, 28 Feb. 1821, 1 Mar., when he was erroneously listed by Hudson Gurney* as one of those who 'came over', 21 Apr., 10 May 1825.[5] He voted against repeal of the additional malt duty, 3 Apr., and military reductions, 11 Apr. 1821. He presented multiple petitions from the coach masters and farmers of Essex against the metropolis roads bill, 18 May 1821.[6] He divided against more extensive tax reductions, 11 Feb. 1822. By the death of his uncle, the Rev. Charles Onley, whose surname he assumed, he obtained 'possession of a very fine estate in Essex' later that year.[7] He voted against Hume's amendment to the national debt reduction bill, 13 Mar., and inquiry into the currency, 12 June 1823. He spoke briefly and was a minority teller against the second reading of the Bristol and Taunton canal bill, 30 Mar. 1824.[8] He divided for suppression of the Catholic Association, 15 Feb. 1825. He voted for the duke of Cumberland's annuity bill, 10 June 1825, and against reform of Edinburgh's representation, 13 Apr. 1826.

At the 1826 dissolution he made way for Charleville's son Lord Tullamore. The following year he offered as the 'county candidate' for a vacancy at Maldon, professing hostility to Catholic relief, but he caused 'a most extraordinary sensation' by retiring on the ground that he had been lured into standing by 'representations which he had subsequently discovered to be false'.[9] It was later said of him that he lacked 'the energy which distinguished ... [and] animated the conduct' of his brother John, but that in 'cheerful sociality' they had 'greatly resembled each other'.[10] Harvey died at Stisted Hall in August 1843. By his will, dated 11 July 1838, he left his daughters large annuities and his wife his leasehold London house in Great George Street. The remainder of his estate passed to his only son Onley Savill Onley (1795-1890).[11]

[1] Add. 40372, f. 257; *Gent. Mag.* (1842), i. 452.   [2] *Ramsey's Waterford Chron.* 4, 21 Mar. 1820. [3] *Black Bk.* (1823), 162; *The Times*, 2 May 1820. [4] *The Times*, 2 June 1820. [5] Gurney diary, 1 Mar. 1825. [6] *The Times*, 19 May 1825. [7] *Gent. Mag.* (1843), ii. 546. [8] *The Times*, 31 Mar. 1824. [9] Ibid. 4 Dec. 1827. [10] *Gent. Mag.* (1843), ii. 546. [11] PROB 11/1987/715; IR26/1654/665.

P.J.S.

HARVEY, Daniel Whittle (1786–1863), of Feering House, Kelvedon, Essex and 7 Great George Street, Mdx.

COLCHESTER	1818–30 June 1820
COLCHESTER	1826–1834
SOUTHWARK	1835–16 Jan. 1840

b. 10 Jan. 1786, 1st s. of Matthew Barnard Harvey (*d.* 1820), merchant and banker, of Witham, Essex and a da. and h. of John Whittle of Feering House. *educ.* I. Temple 1810. *m.* 23 May 1809, Mary, da. and h. of Ebenezer Johnston of Stoke Newington, Mdx., 1da. *d.* 24 Feb. 1863.
Common councilman, London 1808-18; registrar, metrop. public carriages 1839-40; commr. of police, City of London 1839-*d.*

Harvey, a tall, handsome man, with a 'jovial rollicking nature', and 'an orator born', was reckoned by 'many persons' in 1832 to be 'the best speaker in the House', but he was 'damaged in character'. The establishment regarded him as 'a scoundrel' and 'vile', although his cleverness and fluency were acknowledged.[1] A Unitarian by upbringing, an Essex attorney by profession and the possessor of a modest maternal estate at Kelvedon, he had a propensity for getting into scrapes. Above all, he bore the stigma of having been

found guilty of stealing deeds and misappropriating money in 1809; and it was not until 1834 that a parliamentary inquiry exonerated him. This scuppered his application to be called to the bar in 1819, when he aspired to the recordership of Colchester, where, after two unsuccessful bids, he had secured his return at the general election of 1818 on the independent, anti-corporation interest, with the financial backing of a relative and the support of the large Dissenting element in the electorate.[2] As a self-styled champion of the people, he espoused a moderate radicalism, of which church reform was a key component. He made enemies easily and had as little time for Whigs as for Tories. Like most contemporary radicals, he was by nature outspoken, truculent and self-righteous; but his exclusion from the bar embittered him and gave a rancorous edge to his politics.

At the general election of 1820, soon after the death of his bankrupt father, Harvey stood again for Colchester, where the late intervention of a third man forced a contest. He condemned the Six Acts as 'most serious innovations' inflicted on the constitution by 'a most profligate and daring administration' and claimed that he had attended the House on 77 of the 82 nights of the last session. He topped the poll and promised to continue to act 'by those principles which marked the ... Revolution in 1688'.[3] He divided with the opposition to the Liverpool ministry on the civil list, 5, 8 May, and called for 'close' scrutiny of such expenditure, 18 May 1820. He voted against the appointment of an additional Scottish baron of the exchequer, 15 May, questioned the utility of Lord Althorp's insolvency bill, 5 June, and voted to reduce the army, 14 June, and the barrack establishment, 16 June, when he criticized grants for the secret service fund and demanded a revision of barristers' fees. He supported the bill to give Colchester quarter sessions and was a teller for the minority for its second reading, 20 June.[4] He divided against government on the Queen Caroline affair, 22, 26 June 1820. Four days later his election was declared void on a technicality arising out of his having let a freehold house in Brighton, which was deemed to have invalidated his property qualification. He did not stand at the ensuing by-election, but recommended and backed the successful Whig candidate and promised to offer at the next opportunity.[5] He spoke at a Colchester meeting to celebrate the abandonment of the bill of pains and penalties, 19 Dec. 1820.[6]

In November 1821 he vainly pleaded his case for admission before the benchers of the Inner Temple, who gave his alleged transgressions as the reason for his rejection. His immediate appeal to the judges was also unsuccessful, and after their decision, 1 Feb. 1822, he published a *Letter to the Burgesses of Colchester* stating his case and seeking to link local radicalism with his persecution. At the Essex county meeting on distress, 21 Mar. 1823, he moved but was prevailed on to drop an alternative petition calling for parliamentary reform, an 'equitable distribution' of taxation, retrenchment and a commutation of tithes.[7] In October 1822 he had established the London-based *Kent and Essex Mercury*; and four months later he became the owner of the *Sunday Times*, which he turned into a mass-circulation radical organ. In the autumn of 1823 he was convicted on an *ex-officio* information for libel, following the publication in both papers of articles insinuating that the king was insane. He was fined £200, sentenced to three months in king's bench prison and bound over for five years on security of £2,000. On the day he was sentenced he was also involved in a dubious civil action brought by one Revett over a loan. Harvey later claimed that the Essex Whigs spitefully blackballed his application to join their Maldon Independent Club. Soon after his release he disposed, profitably, of his newspaper concerns, but he revived them in 1833 with the purchase of the *True Sun*.[8]

At the general election of 1826 Harvey, who 'avowed himself the advocate of parliamentary reform' but advised the London out-voters of Maldon (where he was accused by the local Whigs of introducing the successful Tory candidate) that 'before electors ventured to complain of non-representation, they should reform themselves', offered again for Colchester, 'unfettered by party engagements or family compact'. For financial reasons he and his leading supporters were anxious to avoid a contest, and in the event he came in unopposed with the new corporation nominee, Sir George Smyth. On the hustings he declared that he 'could not be a Tory, a Whig he could not be, his object was to recognize the interests of the people'. He promised that he would 'never vote for' Catholic relief, which was anathema to most of the electors and on which he had accordingly abstained in the 1818 Parliament, 'unless required to do so by his constituents'. He called for a gradual move towards free trade and a redistribution of taxation.[9] He voted for the amendment to the address, 21 Nov. 1826. He secured returns of information on conveyancers' fees and poor rates, 29 Nov., and of excise prosecutions, 1 Dec., when he urged the people to petition heavily for repeal of the corn laws.[10] He presented Essex petitions to this effect, 9, 12, 16 Feb., and rebuked the representatives of the 'landed interest' for their intemper-

ance on the issue, 13 Mar. 1827.[11] He was in Hume's minority for a small fixed duty, 27 Mar. He called for a full inquiry into reform of real property law, 14, 27 Mar., and suggested the establishment of a septennial committee to monitor the military estimates, 20 Feb., when he was in a minority of 15 on those for the army. He voted against the duke of Clarence's grant, 16 Feb., 2, 16 Mar. On the 22nd, when he also voted for papers on the Barrackpoor mutiny, he explained that unlike 'the party tacticians on his side', who had opposed the grant because Clarence was not the heir apparent, he had done so 'on the broad principle that the general financial affairs of this country required a speedy, sincere and effectual supervision, with a view to a real and unsparing system of retrenchment and economy'. He dismissed the government's bill to separate bankruptcy from chancery administration as a piece of futile tinkering, 27 Feb., and on 13 Mar. secured a return of bankruptcy fees to prove his contention that the lord chancellor pocketed £30,000 a year. He abstained on the Catholic question, 6 Mar., letting it be known in Colchester that he felt that emancipation would 'operate as a measure of perpetual exclusion' to the Protestant Dissenters, whose release from the restraints of the Test Acts should have priority.[12] In the House, 23 Mar. (when he voted for the spring guns bill), he asserted that most Dissenters, who formed the 'greater part' of his constituents, 'found it difficult to reconcile the security of spiritual freedom, with the bondage and superstition of Catholic dominion'. On 22 May he said that 'if the Catholics gained an ascendancy in Parliament, they would be decidedly opposed to Protestant toleration'.[13] He voted for information on the Lisburn Orange procession, 29 Mar., but was not in the opposition minority for a speedy resolution of the ministerial crisis next day. On 5 Apr. he voted for inquiry into the Irish miscellaneous estimates and tried to get returns of recently completed and pending chancery and bankruptcy business. Replying to the debate, he denied any personal animosity towards Lord Eldon, but accused Wetherell, the attorney-general, of having defended the Cato Street conspirators in 1820 purely to spite the lord chancellor. His motion was beaten by 132-66. On 22 May he attacked the Canning ministry for abandoning urgently needed chancery reform. He thought there were grounds for inquiry into the involvement of Wilks, Member for Sudbury, in the Devon and Cornwall Mining Company, 9 Apr. He examined witnesses in the Penryn election inquiry, 18 May. He presented ten Essex petitions for repeal of the Test Acts, 7 June, and said that the government's arrests on mesne process bill was unlikely to effect 'a cheap and expeditious mode of recovering debts', 15

June.[14] He voted against the Coventry magistracy bill, 18 June 1827.

On 5 Feb. 1828 Harvey disputed the notion that Catholic emancipation would tranquillize Ireland and, with reference to the duke of Wellington's accession to power, said that he would support 'any government that will steadily fix an undeviating eye on financial reform'. He demanded a clear statement of intent from ministers, 11 Feb., when he was in Hume's minority of 15 on the navy estimates. He presented petitions for repeal of the Test Acts, 22 Feb., 12, 25 Mar., and voted for that proposal, 26 Feb.; he made light of the 'very sententious' hostile Colchester petition presented by Smyth, 17 Mar. He believed that the complaints of debtors in Horsham gaol warranted investigation, 28 Feb. He deplored the 'irresponsible power' of licensing proposed to be given to magistrates, 29 Feb., 1 Apr. He examined witnesses in the East Retford inquiry, 3, 7, 10 Mar., when he accused Lord Fitzwilliam of 'unconstitutional' interference there, divided against sluicing the borough with the freeholders of Bassetlaw, 21 Mar., and said that such a clear case of corruption deserved punishment, 27 June. He thought Ross's proposed bill to regulate the admission of freemen would be 'inoperative', 20 Mar., and seconded an unsuccessful attempt to add to the bill transferring Penryn's representation to Manchester a requirement for Members to forswear bribery before taking their seats, 28 Mar. He liked some aspects of Davies's borough polls bill, but felt that the restriction to six days was too short for places more than 20 miles from London, 15 May. He presented constituency petitions against the Malt Act, 22 Feb., 12 Mar. When bringing up a mass petition for wage regulation or revision of the corn laws, 21 Apr., he argued that 'no principle can be more flagrant than that the landed interest should be supported and upheld at the expense of the labouring classes' and that ministers must either 'refuse the aristocracy their monopoly in corn' or jettison 'impracticable' free trade theories. He voted for lower protecting duties on corn, 22, 29 Apr. In early March he offered his services to lord chancellor Lyndhurst as a member of the forthcoming commission of inquiry into the common law, but he was ignored; Peel, the home secretary, privately felt that 'many people would decline to act ... with him' in view of his shady reputation.[15] On 5 Mar. Harvey obtained returns to support his contention that the structure of the expensive and so far unproductive commission of inquiry into charities required reform. He objected to the bill extending to Scotland and Ireland the right of barristers to perform the functions of attorneys in court, 2 Apr. He spoke and voted for inquiry into chancery administration, 24 Apr., denouncing the existing system as 'monstrously hideous, vicious ... deformed ... odious ... dangerous ... ruinous ... unequal, cruel, and oppressive'. He presented many petitions against the friendly societies bill, 22 Apr., 1 May, when his motion to establish more efficient control over crown prosecutions for the recovery of excise penalties was defeated by 146-39. He again abstained on the Catholic question, 12 May. He pressed Peel to go further with his bill to facilitate the recovery of small debts, 22 May, when, in what Canning's nephew Lord George Cavendish Bentinck* condemned to Canning's widow as a 'blackguard speech', he opposed the financial provision for her and said that Canning had easily seduced the unprincipled Lansdowne Whigs in 1827.[16] He thought the Colchester petitioners against a restriction on the circulation of small paper bank notes were deluded, 3 June, and reiterated his view that without 'a system of rigid, strict and honest economy on the part of government', all economic tinkering would be useless; he favoured Hume's proposal for quarterly returns from banks, 26 June. He spoke, 5 June, and voted, 16 June, against the archbishop of Canterbury's bill and opposed the Irish registrar's bill, objecting to the imposition of charges on the enrolment of deeds, 17, 26 June. Although he wanted relaxation of the usury laws, he believed that the compulsory clause negated Poulett Thomson's measure, 19 June. Next day he condemned the repeated reference of expenditure reductions to the finance committee as 'a blind' and voted against the Irish estimates. He spoke and divided for postponement of the additional churches bill, 30 June. On 1 July he presented a Colne hand-loom cotton weavers' petition for wage regulation, dissented from the idea of a minimum wage and expounded his argument, which he rehearsed ad nauseam for the rest of this period, that to make free trade effective and fair it was essential to lower the burden of taxation on the labouring classes and to introduce a graduated property tax. John Hobhouse attacked him 'for abusing ... the political economists' and reflected that Harvey was a 'sad dog, totally unprincipled and reckless of what he says'.[17] He spoke in the same sense at a meeting of the Colchester Independent Club in London, 14 Oct. 1828.[18]

At a Colchester meeting of his supporters, 2 Feb. 1829, when the government's concession of Catholic emancipation was rumoured, Harvey, stripped now of his excuse of Dissenters' exclusion, said that he would 'find it much less difficult to vote for the abolition of all church establishments, than countenance the introduction of the Papal system'; he promised to oppose any 'measure of unregulated concession' and to resign his seat if he found himself at odds with his constituents.[19] In the event he supported emancipation, although his vote to consider it, 6 Mar., was his only one on the issue. That day he admitted that the hostile petitions presented by Smyth expressed 'the universal sentiments of the population of Colchester and its vicinity'; but he insisted on his right to act as 'a representative of the people, and not merely ... the deputy of a borough'. At the same time, he argued that only redistribution of Irish church revenues would permanently pacify Ireland, a theme to which he recurred on 10 Mar., when he offered to give up his seat if required and denied being 'an enemy to a national church establishment', and on the 16th, when he presented a Colchester petition for 'religious liberty'. He presented a Walworth Dissenters' petition against all church establishment and Catholic emancipation, 26 Mar. Securing returns of crown lands revenues, 24 Feb., with a view to moving for their reform, he lamented, not for the last time, 'the suppression of the finance committee'. He criticized the size of the grant for Windsor Castle repairs, 13 Mar.; clashed with the chancellor of the exchequer, Goulburn, over the cost of the Charing Cross improvements, 7 Apr., when he presented an Essex silk-workers' relief petition; repeated his usual economic arguments after the budget statement, 8 May; drew attention to the escalating cost of the refurbishment of Buckingham House, 12 May; voted against the grant for the marble arch, 25 May, and avowed that 'we cannot go on, under the pressure of taxes of a war aspect, with a contracted peace currency', 12 June. He opposed the St. Martin's (Liverpool) church bill as a 'misapplication of a public fund', 2 Apr., and on 10 Apr. denounced the archbishop of Canterbury's bill as an 'example of indifference to the real wants of the church'. He was one of the five Members who attended the annual Westminster purity of election dinner, 25 May.[20] On 5 June he attacked the excessive size of barristers' fees and 'the system of tyranny and oppression now exercised by the Inns of Court' over admissions, complained that 'we are now going to be sent to our homes, without having done anything for the people' and criticized the terms of the charities inquiry bill. He later sent Wellington his plan to streamline the charities commission and revived in the press the issue of his exclusion from the bar, which he had tried unsuccessfully to bring before the law commissioners.[21] In a letter excusing himself from attendance at a meeting of the London Colchester Independent Club because his indifferent health 'renders it imperative that I avoid as much as possible hot rooms', 3 July 1829, he ignored the Catholic question and bragged of his

parliamentary efforts to expose 'the quackery of the times'.[22]

On his way to Yorkshire to investigate crown lands in the Malton area in November, Harvey stopped at Newark to survey the duke of Newcastle's property held on an expiring crown lease; the duke, who wrongly assumed that he had church property in his sights, privately dismissed him as 'a clever man, but utterly devoid of any principle'.[23] At a constituency meeting to petition for repeal of the beer and malt taxes, at which his enemy Western, the Whig county Member, spoke, 19 Dec. 1829, he proposed but did not press an alternative petition making expenditure reductions and a redistribution of taxation the priorities. At the quarterly meeting of the London Independent Club, 5 Jan. 1830, when he was pressed to declare his intentions for the forthcoming session, he warned that asking 'the aristocratic combination' who dominated Parliament to reform the 'system of plunder' would be 'like calling upon the inhabitants of Bedlam to establish a code of rationality', and said that he would concentrate for the moment on appropriation of church and crown lands revenues and the reform of charities. At the Essex county meeting, 11 Feb., he proposed and easily carried an amended petition for parliamentary reform, tax revision, the abolition of sinecures and unmerited pensions, a reduction of public salaries, an equitable adjustment of tithes, simplification of the poor laws and the overthrow of monopolies.[24] When Western presented it to the Commons next day Harvey, who had voted for the amendment to the address, 4 Feb., mocked his currency fixation and endorsed the petition's reform agenda. Soon afterwards the Whig Lord Holland remarked that if Harvey could 'get a decent character or shake off the very bad one he always carries about him he would I am told be a first rate man'.[25] In fact Harvey had already done himself more harm by setting up as a parliamentary agent in partnership with the pleader Sir William Sydney: they had advertised their services to country agents for the management of private bills, in return for a share in the profits. Peel, apprised of this during the recess, said that he would 'not be sorry if there is a good case against ... Harvey', but would be 'surprised if so very clever and plausible a rogue shall have laid himself open'.[26] When Littleton raised the matter in the Commons, 19 Feb. 1830, Harvey admitted and defended his involvement, but agreed to abide by the House's decision. Littleton proposed a resolution forbidding Members from the management of private bills for pecuniary reward, 26 Feb., when Harvey expressed contrition but, on the advice of Hobhouse, moved an amendment that no Member could vote in committee on any measure in which he had a direct interest. He was defeated by 174-27, with Hume his only significant supporter.[27] He had voted for Hume's call for a revision of taxation, 15 Feb., and he divided fairly regularly for economy and retrenchment that session. He spoke on these subjects, 15 Mar. (when he welcomed repeal of the leather and beer taxes, but demanded abolition of 'the horrid tax upon bread'), 22, 23 Mar., 14 June. He paired for the enfranchisement of Birmingham, Leeds and Manchester, 23 Feb., and voted for reception of the Newark petition complaining of Newcastle's electoral interference, 1 Mar., and Russell's reform motion, 28 May. At the Essex by-election in mid-March, when he supported as an independent Wellington's wastrel nephew William Pole Long Wellesley*, but, after his late withdrawal, backed the less extreme of two Tories, he declared, during a long rant:

> I will give my support to the duke of Wellington whenever I think fit, yet I should be sorry to see the Whigs in office tomorrow, for I think they have abandoned every sound principle of policy. So long as the people were ignorant of the nature of parliamentary reform ... they were eternally professing to be its advocates. Now that the people understand it ... a change takes place.[28]

Yet in the House, 15 Mar., he emphasized his hostility to the secret ballot and universal suffrage, which were 'suitable adjuncts of a simple scheme of [republican] government'. On the 30th he moved for inquiry into crown lands revenues, which he put at £20,000,000 a year, with a view to their appropriation for public use; he was beaten by 98-46. The Tory backbencher Henry Bankes referred to him on this occasion as 'crafty attorney and very good speaker'.[29] He voted for Jewish emancipation, 5 Apr., 17 May, and for abolition of the death penalty for forgery offences, 24 May, 7 June. He called for urgent inquiry into the debtors' laws, 29 Apr., but on 14 May approved the ministerial proposal to allow offenders who could pay 10s. in the pound to be released from gaol. He supported and was a minority teller for Hume's attempt to wreck the Rother Levels drainage bill, 10 May. He voted for abolition of the Irish lord lieutenancy, 11 May, backed O'Connell's demand for inquiry into the Cork conspiracy trials next day, when he was in the minority of 12, and divided for better use of Irish first fruits revenues, 18 May. He championed the right of Barrington, the Irish admiralty court judge accused of peculation, to be heard in his own defence, alleging that the Wellington ministry had reneged on their predecessors' promise to let him off, 13, 20, 22, 25 May. He voted for reform of the laws regulating divorce, 3

June, and in Hume's minority of 14 for inquiry into the conduct of the church commissioners over St. Luke's, 17 June. He had a bad tempered exchange with Scarlett, the renegade Whig attorney-general, 4 June, when he exposed the large fees paid to the law officers for their nominal involvement in charity cases; he put the annual 'spoliation and robbery' arising from charities in general at £1,000,000. He spoke and voted against the creation of three new judgeships by the Welsh judiciary bill, 18 June, and on the 24th dismissed Wetherell's bill to reform the 'curse and torment ... and ... terror' that was chancery as 'wholly inadequate'. Presenting the London-based Colchester freemen's reform petition, 5 July 1830, he proclaimed that the only way to advance the cause was for voters to return its advocates at the impending general election. In his address to Colchester that day he wrote that 'the progress of national improvement depends mainly upon the people, for great as is the power of the boroughmongers, it is yielding to the mighty current of public opinion, by which it must eventually be swept away, provided the people are true to themselves'. He stood by his 'rational political creed'. His conduct on Catholic emancipation had cost him some support, and a rival London club had been established in an attempt to throw him out. Harvey, who again supported Long Wellesley for the county and was a persistent and angry critic on the Chelmsford hustings of the Whig and Tory coalition which defeated him, comfortably saw off their challenge and topped the poll. He admitted to having spent £25,700 on his Colchester campaigns since 1812. At his celebration dinner, 8 Sept. 1830, he castigated the 599 freemen who had shown such 'want of thought and political principle' as to vote for his two opponents, denied being an enemy to the church and state establishments and expressed regret at the bloody events in France.[30]

On complaints that petitioning was out of hand, 3 Nov. 1830, he told the House, 'Diminish the taxes, alter their character, abolish slavery, and grant reform, and there will be but few subjects left to petition upon'. Moving again for information on crown lands revenues, 5 Nov., he applauded the government's proposal to appropriate some hereditary ones for public use. He welcomed their statute of frauds bill, but deplored the halting progress of legal reform, 9 Nov. As one of their 'foes' he helped to vote them out of office on the civil list, 15 Nov. Four days later he urged agricultural landlords to reduce their rents to pre-war level and the clergy, as regarded tithes, to 'practise that forbearance, humanity and economy which they preached once a week'. He presented a Colchester anti-slavery petition, 23 Nov. Approving the Grey ministry's motion for inquiry into a reduction of official salaries 'as a pledge of great and long-desired reform', 9 Dec., he said that 'although I am sitting among those who may be considered hostile ... if that government does what I expect ... I shall feel it my duty to support them'. He called for the repeal of stamp duty on freemen's admissions, 9 Dec.; agreed to withdraw his notice of a motion for information on the proportion of borough electors to populations in deference to the government's planned reform bill, 13 Dec.; welcomed Littleton's measure to end truck payments, 14 Dec.; urged a repeal of assessed taxes, 17 Dec., and said he would accept the secret ballot if the 'general feeling of the public' favoured it, though he still believed that it was not an essential ingredient of reform, 21 Dec. 1830. On 10 Feb. 1831 Harvey unsuccessfully contested the London aldermanic vacancy for Portsoken against the disreputable reformer Scales. He demanded a scrutiny but abandoned the business a fortnight later.[31] He approved the ministry's proposed tax on stock transfers, though he would have preferred a comprehensive property tax, 11 Feb. He presented and endorsed an Essex parish petition for tithe reform, 16 Feb. At the Essex county reform meeting, 28 Feb., he announced that he had now taken his seat on the treasury benches to support ministers not as Whigs but as the professed advocates of reform and economy, and stated that he favoured

> an efficient reform, and such a one as will conserve the present form of government. I am an enemy to ... radical reform ... because its advocates know not what the consequences would be. You cannot have universal suffrage and the ballot, unless you are prepared to overthrow the monarchy and the aristocracy ... We must have a reform which shall make large concessions, but which requires evidence of property and intelligence.[32]

On this basis he supported the ministerial reform bill, 4 Mar., being prepared to do so even though its proposed disfranchisement of freemen would harm his own electoral interests. On 9 Mar. he pointed to the belated popular awareness of 'the pervasion of the means, and of the mismanagement of the resources of the nation' by the privileged elite as the catalyst for the irresistible demand for reform, and indignantly repudiated the allegation of John Tyrell, the Tory county Member, that he had promoted republicanism at the county meeting. At the second Essex reform meeting, 19 Mar., he declared that reform would pave the way for 'a regulation of the church' and 'cheap and speedy law'.[33] He voted for the second reading of the bill, 22 Mar., having denied Tyrell's charges that he supported it 'as affording the foundation for a lever,

by which revolutionary measures may be raised' and that he was an enemy of the church, earning a rebuke from the Speaker for his vehemence. He divided against Gascoyne's wrecking amendment to the bill, 19 Apr. 1831. At the ensuing general election he stood for Colchester as its uncompromising supporter and was returned, after a contest forced by the corporation, with his erstwhile independent opponent of 1830, as the general enthusiasm for reform forged an uneasy alliance between them. His diatribe on the hustings included an attack on supposed corporation peculation; and in his victory address he vowed to continue his parliamentary crusade for 'checking that system of fiscal spoliation and political corruption ... which has well nigh thrown us into the hands of despotism'.[34] At the county election he enthusiastically supported Western and Long Wellesley as reformers and on 9 May 1831 he led a cavalcade of Colchester voters into Chelmsford.[35]

Harvey, who impressed Littleton with the 'justness and beauty' of his private observation on the paucity of 'great men' in the House, that 'there is too much light for luminaries',[36] voted for the second reading of the reintroduced reform bill, 6 July, and on the 8th condemned 'the hollowness of the sympathy which those who have always been the strenuous defenders of the rotten boroughs now manifest for the labouring classes' threatened with disfranchisement. Objecting to hearing counsel on behalf of Appleby, 12 July, he disclaimed 'the imputation of being one of the marshalled majority who are to be led out of the House at the nod or command of any man or ministry' and proclaimed himself 'the advocate of the rights of the people'. He stated his willingness to set aside his reservations about certain aspects of the measure, 15 July, and gave its details generally steady support; but he thought a case had been made out for reprieving Chippenham from the loss of a Member, 27 July, and duly voted for inquiry. He said that Maldon was expensive to contest but not corrupt, 29 July, defended the enfranchisement of Gateshead, 5 Aug., opposed Hume's attempt to do away with actual payment of rent as a requirement for the borough franchise, 25 Aug., when they squabbled childishly, and disputed his assertion that popular opinion was turning against the measure because it did not go far enough, 30 Aug. That day he spoke and voted for the disfranchisement of non-resident freemen, but he urged ministers to abolish the stamp duty on their admissions. He was in the minority for the disfranchisement of Aldborough, 14 Sept. He divided for the passage of the bill, 21 Sept., and for Lord Ebrington's confidence motion, 10 Oct., and on 12 Oct. accused those 'feeble' reformers who sought to impede the Liverpool writ of wishing to 'canonize a system of nomination'. He had the Waterloo Bridge New Street bill, the potential cost of which perturbed him, sent to a select committee, 11 July. Next day he condemned as an outrage the bishop of Londonderry's possession of a 90,000-acre estate, considering that the people were 'weighed to the earth by fiscal oppression'. On 18 July, when he voted to reduce the grant for civil list services, he criticized the cost of printing parliamentary papers and of the largely ineffectual law commission. He rebuked Irish Members for harassing ministers over the question of disarming the yeomanry, 11 Aug., arguing that they could not 'remedy ... by a single statute the misgovernment of centuries'; and he voted with administration on the Dublin election controversy, 23 Aug. He briefly attacked the corn laws, 13 Aug., and objected to the steam vessels regulation bill, 19 Aug. He said that if there was no inquiry into the apparent 'plunder' of public money by the Irish vice-treasurer, 'all our speeches can be considered no more than a joke', 31 Aug., supported the Irish public works bill, 16 Sept., and called for the application of English and Irish church revenues to relief of the poor, 26 Sept. Next day he spoke and voted for inquiry into the Deacles' allegations against William Bingham Baring*, which he said raised important issues:

> As long as I have a seat in this House, I will always be ready to raise my voice in behalf of the poor, however much such conduct may displease those gentlemen whose arithmetic is puzzled in counting their millions, and whose enormous fortunes are accumulated at the expense, and almost by the destruction, of their poor fellow countrymen.

He presented a Brighton traders' petition for the easier recovery of small debts, 4 Oct., approved, with some reservations, Campbell's general register bill and supported Sadler's measure to improve the condition of the labouring poor, 11 Oct., and welcomed the ministry's bankruptcy reform bill, 14, 17 Oct. 1831.

Harvey successfully discouraged plans to call Colchester meetings to petition the Lords both before and after the bill's defeat there and declined an invitation to the Maldon Independent Club's anniversary dinner in November unless their slight to him was renounced, which it was not.[37] However, he helped to promote a county meeting, 10 Dec., when he spoke at length and with great animation for reform, economy, repeal of the corn laws and church and tithe reform. He read, but did not press, after a furious row with Long Wellesley, in which they almost came to blows, an address to Lord Grey encouraging him to use all possible means to carry reform. His performance further alienated Western and the county Whigs.[38] In the Commons, 14 Dec., he replied to a personal attack on him for his 'public execration' of the church with the observation that the bishops' participation in the defeat of the reform bill had given 'the real foes of the church ... a strong ground of attack'. He voted for the second reading of the revised bill, 17 Dec. 1831, and divided silently for its details and for its third reading, 22 Mar. 1832. He was keen to see the general registry bill improved by submission to professional advice, 19 Jan., 7 Feb., 6 Mar.; he was added to the select committee on it, 27 Mar. He divided with government on the Russian-Dutch loan, 26 Jan., and the affairs of Portugal, 9 Feb., but he was in Hunt's minority of 31 for inquiry into Peterloo, 15 Mar. He secured a return of intestates' effects administered by the crown, which involved the appropriation of large sums, 28 Feb. He wanted the rights of the poor to be better protected in enclosure bills, 19 Mar. He thoroughly approved the ministerial scheme for non-sectarian Irish education, 9 Apr. He voted for the address calling on the king to appoint only ministers who would carry reform bill undiluted, 10 May, and on the 15th blamed the recent disturbances on 'the irritating language of anti-reformers' and 'the conduct of the episcopal bench'. He tried to present an address from Colchester expressing gratitude for the passage of the bill, 14 June, but it was ruled inadmissible. He was in O'Connell's minority for the enfranchisement of Irish £5 freeholders, 18 June 1832.

Harvey voted for the immediate abolition of slavery, 24 May, for coroners' inquests to be made public, 20 June, for the bill to exclude insolvent debtors from the House, 27 June, and to give representation to New South Wales, 28 June 1832. On 14 June he moved for leave to empower king's bench to compel the benchers of the Inns of Court, in certain cases, to admit men as students and barristers, denouncing their 'odious despotism', enforced by 'irresponsible and secret tribunals'. He referred directly to his own case in his reply. The motion was opposed by government and beaten by 68-52. In a preface to the published version of his speech, which was separately issued as *A Letter ... to his Constituents* (30 June 1832), he alleged that ministers had, as 'a remnant of the original bar conspiracy', treated him in a 'treacherous manner' by reneging on their offer, which he had accepted, to make him secretary of the revived charities commission. He complained that when the commission had been belatedly established in December 1831 lord chancellor Brougham had tried to fob him off with mere membership of it and that a subsequent proposal to make him its solicitor had been vetoed by the treasury. He viewed this and official resistance to his bid to open the Inns as part of a personal vendetta:

> Had I served the Tories with a tithe of the zeal with which I have sacrificed my health, my time, and my fortune in the cause of their opponents, I should not have been repaid by the treachery of professional advisers, nor insulted by the tender of heartless sympathies (p. 13).

He abstained from the division on the Russian-Dutch loan, 12 July, explaining in a letter to the press that while he 'could not adopt the construction of the treaty as urged by the government', he 'was not prepared to sanction an amendment, being in fact a vote of censure'.[39] The attorney-general, Denman, did not resist his motion for an address directing the law commissioners to examine the Inns' admissions policy, 17 July; but Wetherell did so, and the House was counted out when it divided 26-2 for the motion. Denman assured Harvey that he would nevertheless lay the matter before the commissioners, 18 July. That day he conceded the validity of Hunt's assertion that the Reform Act's requirement for borough voters' rates to be paid by the 20th to qualify them would disfranchise many and encourage bribery; but he argued that it was 'obligatory upon every friend of freedom to gave the bill fair play' and that 'if the extended representation does not secure better government, the ballot will not achieve the object desired'. He was in the minority for a more radical reform of Irish tithes than that proposed by government, 24 July. On 30 July, when he criticized the £10,000 salary awarded to the lord chancellor, he had a clause inserted in the electoral bribery bill requiring Members to swear their innocence before taking their seats. He hinted at a potential fraud over the emoluments of excise commissioners and announced that next session he would propose the funding of national education from the resources of charities and inquiries into crown duchy revenues and chancery administration, 1 Aug. Recurring to the problem of urban ratepayers' registration, 9, 15 Aug. 1832, he criticized their own 'supineness', but suggested that disfranchisement would be limited and localized.

At the general election of 1832 Harvey, frustrated in his bid to come in for the Northern division of Essex, was again returned for Colchester, but only in second place. He had to defend himself against Western's allegations that to spite his Whig enemies he had leagued himself with Conservatives there, at Harwich and Maldon and in the county.[40] A founder of the Radical Westminster Club in 1834, he remained 'an *eccentric* politician.'[41] He abandoned Colchester to the

Conservative in 1835 and came in for Southwark. In November 1839, beset with financial problems of his own making, he accepted from the second Melbourne administration, who were anxious to be rid of him, 'the mess of potage' of the commissionership of the newly established City police force, thereby deserting 'his rightful sphere' for 'an uncongenial occupation'. Harvey, who was reckoned by one commentator to have been 'as great an orator as Burke', died in harness at his official residence, 26 Old Jewry, in February 1863, from 'a carbuncle in the mouth' which had led to erysipelas. He was given an imposing police escort to his grave in the grounds of the Unitarian chapel at Hackney.[42] No will or administration has been found.

[1] *Gent. Mag.* (1863), i. 662; *Pol. Economy Club* (1921), 231; *Greville Mems.* iii. 58; Harewood mss, Lord G. Cavendish Bentinck to Lady Canning, 27 May 1828; Nottingham Univ. Lib. Newcastle mss Ne2 F3/1/180; Bodl. MS. Eng. lett. c. 159, f. 40. [2] Add. 38458, f. 331; *Oxford DNB*; Grey mss, Howick jnl. 5 June [1830]; C.F. Smith, 'Daniel Whittle Harvey', *Essex Rev.* xxiv (1915), 25-30; *PP* (1834), xviii. 331-839. [3] *Procs. at Colchester and Essex Elections* (1820), 11, 14, 39. [4] *The Times*, 12, 31 May, 17, 21 June 1820. [5] Smith, 29; *Suff. Chron.* 8, 15 July; *County Chron.* 18 July 1820. [6] *Suff. Chron.* 23 Dec. 1820. [7] *Colchester Gazette*, 22 Mar. 1823. [8] M.E. Speight, 'Politics in Colchester' (London Univ. Ph.D. thesis, 1969), 207-8; Smith, 135; *Oxford DNB*; *The Times*, 31 Oct., 1, 21 Nov. 1823; *Speech of Whittle Harvey ... in vindication of his conduct*, 27 Nov. 1832, p. 6. [9] *Kent and Essex Mercury*, 16, 23 May; *Colchester Gazette*, 27 May, 3, 10 June 1826; Bodl. MS. Eng. lett. c. 159, ff. 38-42. [10] *The Times*, 30 Nov., 2 Dec. 1826. [11] Ibid. 13, 17 Feb., 14 Mar. 1827. [12] *Colchester Gazette*, 17 Mar. 1827. [13] *The Times*, 23 May 1827. [14] Ibid. 8, 16 June 1827. [15] Ibid. 21 May 1828; Add. 40396, f. 45. [16] Harewood mss, Cavendish Bentinck to Lady Canning, 27 May 1828. [17] Add. 56552, f. 116. [18] *The Times*, 15 Oct. 1828. [19] *Colchester Gazette*, 7 Feb. 1829. [20] Add. 56554, f. 17. [21] Wellington mss WP1/1030/26; *The Times*, 11 Aug. 1829. [22] *Colchester Gazette*, 11 July 1829. [23] *The Times*, 6 Nov. 1829; Newcastle mss Ne2 F3/1/180, 208. [24] *Colchester Gazette*, 26 Dec. 1829, 9 Jan., 13 Feb. 1830. [25] Add. 51785, Holland to C.R. Fox, 20 Feb. 1830. [26] Add. 40399, ff. 397, 399. [27] Add. 56554, f. 68. [28] *Colchester Gazette*, 13 Mar. 1820. [29] Dorset RO D/BKL, Bankes jnl. 169. [30] *Colchester Gazette*, 10, 17, 24, 31 July, 7 Aug., 11 Sept.; Speight, 190-2, 233-5; Essex RO, Barrett Lennard mss D/DL O42/3, Harvey to Wright, 6 July 1830; *Essex Co. Election* (1830), 12, 16-17, 25-30, 91-93. [31] *Colchester Gazette*, 12, 26 Feb. 1831; A.B. Beaven, *Aldermen of London*, i. 188, 242. [32] *Colchester Gazette*, 5 Mar. 1831. [33] Ibid. 26 Mar. 1831. [34] Ibid. 30 Apr., 7 May 1831. [35] *The Times*, 6, 7, 9 May; *Colchester Gazette*, 14 May 1831. [36] Hatherton diary, 26 July [1831]. [37] *Colchester Gazette*, 24 Sept., 15 Oct.; Barrett Lennard mss C62, Harvey to Barrett Lennard, 15 Nov. 1831. [38] *Colchester Gazette*, 26 Nov., 17 Dec.; Barrett Lennard mss C60, Western to Barrett Lennard, 21 Dec. 1831. [39] *The Times*, 17 July 1832. [40] *Speech of Harvey ... in vindication of his conduct*, 27 Nov. 1832. [41] *Disraeli Letters*, iii. 415; *Arbuthnot Corresp.* 181, 194; *Greville Mems.* iii. 136-7. [42] *The Times*, 15, 20 Nov. 1839, 25 Feb. 1863; *Oxford DNB*; Smith, 133-4, 137-8; *Gent. Mag.* (1863), i. 662-3.

D.R.F.

HARVEY, Sir Eliab (1758–1830), of Rolls Park, Chigwell, Essex and 8 Clifford Street, Mdx.

MALDON	27 May 1780–1784
ESSEX	1802–1812
ESSEX	1820–20 Feb. 1830

b. 5 Dec. 1758, 4th but 2nd surv. s. of William Harvey† (*d.* 1763) of Chigwell and Emma, da. and coh. of Stephen Skynner of Walthamstow, Essex. *educ.* Westminster 1768; Harrow 1770-5. *m.* 15 May 1784, Lady Louisa Nugent, da. and coh. of Robert Nugent†, 1st Earl Nugent [I], 2s. *d.v.p.* 6da. *suc.* bro. William Harvey† 1779; KCB 2 Jan. 1815; GCB 11 Jan. 1825. *d.* 20 Feb. 1830.

Midshipman RN 1771, lt. 1779, cdr. 1782, capt. 1783, r.-adm. 1805, v.-adm. 1810, adm. 1819.

Cdr. Essex sea fencibles 1798-9.

Admiral Harvey, a hero of Trafalgar, whose volcanic temper had landed him in serious trouble and ended his active naval career in 1809, at the age of 50, was a reformed gambler turned skinflint. A veteran Pittite, who found routine parliamentary business boring and the expenses and obligations of a county Member burdensome, he had given up his Essex seat on financial grounds in 1812.[1] At the general election of 1820, however, he offered in the room of the retiring Tory Member and was returned unopposed with the advanced Whig Western. At the nomination, when a late bid to start another Blue to run with him failed, he said that

> the times were so alarming, that ... nothing but a signal defeat should drive him back ... He was ... not alarmed with fear and trepidation, but ... [had] a manly and decided determination to meet the radicals and their crew when called upon ... They found themselves opposed neither to friend nor enemy; their hand grenades, daggers, or the midnight murders of innocent men going to their dinners; there were none of these things on board ships; they fought like men, not like assassins ... He was *church and king* to the backbone, and a king's man he would be for ever.[2]

Harvey presented petitions against, 11 May, and for, 16 June 1820, the bill to divide the Essex sessions between Colchester and Chelmsford. He spoke against it and was a teller with Western for the hostile majority, 20 June.[3] He joined in calls for a grant of money to the innovative naval architect Seppings, 9 June. On 1 July his long-suffering wife, on whom he habitually vented his spleen, told their daughter Louisa, the wife of William Lloyd of Aston Hall, Shropshire, that he was 'wrapped up in the House of Commons and can give his mind to no one other thing'.[4] He voted with the Liverpool ministry against economies in revenue collection, 4 July 1820, and in defence of their conduct towards Queen Caroline, 6 Feb. 1821. He demanded an increase in the marine force, 2 Feb. He opposed the metropolis roads bill, 27 Feb., 27 Mar., 24 May.[5] On 28 Feb. he presented the archdeaconry of Essex's petition against Catholic claims and voted accordingly; he 'sat up all night to be in a minority' against a clause of the relief bill, 23 Mar.[6] The committee on the state of London Bridge (12 Feb.) – he was keen for a new one to be built – also kept him busy that month.[7] He divided with government on the revenue, 6 Mar., but was in the majority for repeal of the additional malt duty, 21 Mar., and did not vote when ministers had this rescinded, 3 Apr.[8] He voted with them on the army estimates, 11 Apr., and against the forgery punishment mitigation bill, 23 May 1821. That November he was willing to do what little he could to promote his son-in-law's aspirations to a seat for Shropshire (which were frustrated), but warned him against involvement in a contest and that 'the manner in which debates and the public business are conducted is tedious beyond belief (excepting upon the public questions)'. He subsequently told Lloyd that in their correspondence on the matter he had

> mistaken my party principles, for a most decided party man I am, and notwithstanding I claim to be as independent as any Member in the House of Commons ... I am *church* and king, and moreover I *belong* to several Pitt Clubs ... The expenses of being chosen and attending Parliament even without an opposition are by no means trifling, including the attendance at county meetings, subscriptions to public charities and other institutions ... and the times by no means favourable to country gentlemen collecting such monies as may reduce them ... It is right to bring these things under your consideration for there is no passport to happiness in this life beyond our own fireside.[9]

Harvey voted against more extensive tax reductions to relieve distress, 11, 21 Feb., but divided against government for admiralty economies, 1 Mar., and abolition of one of the joint-postmasterships, 13 Mar., 2 May 1822. He presented and endorsed a petition from Essex grand jury for more frequent gaol deliveries, 27 Mar. On 1 Apr. he confirmed Western's statement of the 'great extent' of agricultural distress in the county, and he presented parish petitions calling for relief, 22 Apr., when he dissociated himself from Western's currency fixation, and 3 May.[10] At the Whig-inspired county meeting to petition for relief, 8 May, he argued that taxation and the metallic currency were less damaging than his colleague reckoned; but in the House, 17 May, he admitted the respectability of the gathering.[11] He was in the minority of 24 for a 40*s.* fixed duty on corn imports, 8 May. He voted against Canning's bill to relieve Catholic peers, 30 Apr. He presented a West Ham churchwardens' petition against the poor bill, 30 May, and seven from Winchester publicans against the beer retail bill, 17 July.[12] He was in the ministerial majority for the aliens bill, 19 July 1822. The death on 2 Mar. 1823 of his only surviving son William (whose elder brother had been killed at Burgos in 1812) devastated Harvey, created a 'house of misery' at Rolls and made his temper even fouler than before.[13] No votes of his have been found for that session, but he presented clerical anti-Catholic petitions, 17 Apr., and the Essex agricultural distress petition, 2 May.[14] In early November 1823 his wife went to Paris with their unmarried daughters. Anticipating with dread his arrival later in the month, she told Louisa, 'I wish the admiral would stay away as it is such good fun without him'. He duly arrived, 'very disagreeable [and] dreadfully shabby', and proceeded to find 'faults with everything' and make everyone miserable. He returned to England on 28 Jan. 1824, 'so out of spirits', as his wife reported, 'that it was quite uncomfortable to us all'; he took 'a little frightful dog' as his noisy travelling companion.[15]

He presented several Essex petitions for repeal of the coastwise coal duties in February 1824.[16] His only known vote of that session was in the majority against the production of information on Catholic office-holders, 19 Feb. He presented Colchester and Romford anti-slavery petitions, 17 Mar.[17] To the dismay of his wife, who thought he 'looks ill', he rejoined her in Paris in early April and went on to be 'very disagreeable ... to us all and to everybody and everything'. On 3 May, shortly before he went back to England, Lady Harvey told Louisa that his 'temper is really so bad that I am annoyed to death and worried out of my life with him'; she was tempted to leave him.[18] He presented a petition for the easier recovery of small debts, 24 May.[19] He brought up a Romford petition for inquiry into the prosecution of the Methodist missionary John Smith in Demerara, 1 June, but he did not vote in that sense on the 11th.[20] Opposing Hume's motion for an investigation of naval impressment, 10 June, he said that 'no probable good could arise from ... inquiry into a law of the land, which policy and long experience had fully justified'. He supported the Norfolk assizes bill, 10 June 1824, 24 Feb. 1825. Next day he presented a Hornchurch petition against the coal duties and voted for the Irish unlawful societies bill.[21] He presented the Essex archdeaconry's anti-Catholic petition, 28 Feb.;[22] and on 15 Mar. he complained that it had been 'received with an uproar and clamour which was more worthy of a bear garden than of the House of

Commons'. He divided against Catholic relief, 1 Mar., 21 Apr., 10 May, and the Irish franchise bill, 26 Apr. He opposed the Metropolitan Fish Company bill, 15, 16 Mar.[23] He presented an Essex agriculturists' petition for the better prevention of the theft of grain, 18 Apr., and one from Rochford against interference with the corn laws, 28 Apr.[24] On the warehoused corn bill, 13 May 1825, he approved Holme Sumner's suggestion of a specific limitation on annual Canadian imports.

Early in 1826 his wife complained that Harvey was 'in one of his dreadful talking humours', having 'been ill', and was `cross and ... stingy'.[25] He presented petitions for the more effective recovery of small debts, 7 Feb., from Essex silk weavers against foreign imports, 23 Feb., and from Saffron Walden for the abolition of slavery, 13 Mar.[26] He thought the provisions of the Scottish steam vessels regulation bill should be extended to the rest of the kingdom, 9 Mar. He was in the minorities against the emergency admission of foreign corn, 8, 11 May 1826, but announced on the 12th that he 'would not persevere in the opposition'. At the general election the following month he came in again unopposed with Western, after quoting 'Humpty Dumpty' to illustrate the 'danger in tampering with established institutions' and assuring the electors that 'they might rely upon his exertions to prevent the further encroachments of the Catholics'.[27]

In mid-November 1826 a furious Harvey joined his wife at Brighton, where he reprimanded her for leaving Chigwell on 'a whim' and putting him to expense. Two months later she reported that 'at present his occupations are quarrelling with his servants ... and swearing dreadfully ... and *saving* money'.[28] He presented Essex petitions against interference with the corn laws, 16, 27 Feb., 15 Mar., and voted in the protectionist minority against the corn bill, 2 Apr. 1827; he later told his daughter that 'the corn question bears a better appearance and the harvest [is] delightful'.[29] He presented anti-Catholic petitions, 2 Mar., 31 May, and paired against relief, 6 Mar. He brought up Dissenters' petitions for repeal of the Test Acts, 30 May 1827, 19 Feb. 1828, but did not vote for that measure, 26 Feb. 1828.[30] He divided in the minority of 58 for a 60s. pivot price for corn imports, 22 Apr., and presented and endorsed a Chelmsford agriculturists' petition for enhanced protection, 28 Apr. He condemned the 'bad and mischievous' Maldon tolls bill, 24 Apr. He brought up petitions from wealthy East London sugar refiners in favour of the East London railway bill, 1 May, and from the corporation of Saffron Walden against the alehouses licensing bill, 2 May. He presented a Saffron

Walden petition against Catholic claims, 6 May, and voted thus, 12 May 1828. Six months later his wife told Louisa that he was 'in perfect *health*, but never by any chance in good humour, and is a constant fidget, scolding his servants or talking about his own health and eating'; and that he 'looks thin and his eyes [are] staring out of his head and [he has] a *settled* furious cross countenance ready to fly at and eat up everyone'. On Christmas Day 1828 she wrote:

> The admiral is sadly out of sorts. His temper is so irrita-
> ble that he has given warning to five servants ... [He] has
> *actually* scraped up all his money to lend out at interest,
> depending on some interests of former sums he has lent,
> which are due to him now and which he has not received,
> which adds to his horrid temper ... He has not one guinea
> in his banker's hands ... He has scraped up ... £35,000 ...
> and he is so proud of it, he is always boasting to me of the
> large sum he has put out.[31]

As expected, he opposed Catholic emancipation when the Wellington ministry conceded it in 1829. Presenting and endorsing a hostile petition from Saffron Walden, 17 Feb., he declared that 'my opinion is strengthened, not relaxed, as to the propriety of maintaining the constitution as it now stands'. He presented many hostile Essex petitions in the following six weeks, said that the 'most dangerous' measure was 'very much worse than I could possibly have imagined it would be', 6 Mar., and accused Peel of betraying his followers, 12 Mar. He voted against emancipation, 6, 18 Mar., and paired against it, 23, 30 Mar. He brought up petitions against the East London waterworks bill, 25 Mar., 13 Apr., and 1 May, the Thames Watermen Act, 4 May, and the metropolitan roads bill, 11 May. In his last known speech in the Commons, 13 May 1829, he urged Western to withdraw his motion for repeal of the tax on husbandry horses because ministers had promised to review the assessed taxes.

Reports of Harvey's death in early November 1829 were only slightly premature, for he died 'suddenly' at Rolls in February 1830, four days after the marriage of his daughter Emma to Colonel William Eustace, 'so that the bridal apparel had not lost its freshness when it was exchanged for sable mourning'.[32] On the face of it he 'cut up well': by his will of 9 June 1818 and a codicil of 7 Feb. 1830, proved under £120,000, he left £10,000 to each of his six daughters, to be raised by the sale of his town house in Clifford Street and of real estate at West Ham, Wanstead, Leyton and North Weald. His assets were put at £110,627 and his debts at £25,000. There were, however, protracted disputes and litigation among his children.[33] Rolls House, the main seat of his family for over 160 years, passed

to Louisa Lloyd and her husband and their male descendants, while Harvey's manor of Abbess Roding went to his daughter Elizabeth and her husband Thomas William Bramston of Skreens, whose father briefly succeeded the admiral as county Member.[34]

[1] *HP Commons, 1790-1820*, iv. 165-6; *Farington Diary*, iv. 1287. [2] Essex RO, Gunnis mss D/DGu C1/2/3, Harvey to da. Louisa Lloyd, 10 Mar.; *Suff. Chron.* 11, 18 Mar. 1820; *Procs. at Colchester and Essex Elections* (1820), 45-46. [3] *The Times*, 12 May, 16, 21 June 1820. [4] Gunnis mss Z2. [5] *The Times*, 28 Feb., 28 Mar., 25 May 1821. [6] Ibid. 1 Mar.; *Colchester Gazette*, 3 Mar.; Gunnis mss Z1, Harvey to Louisa Lloyd [24 Mar. 1821]. [7] Gunnis mss Z1, Harvey to Louisa Lloyd, 15 Mar. 1821. [8] Ibid. Z1, Harvey to Louisa Lloyd, 22 Mar. [1821]. [9] NLW, Aston Hall mss 460, 461. [10] *The Times*, 23 Apr., 4 May 1822. [11] Ibid. 9, 18 May 1822. [12] Ibid. 18 July 1822. [13] *Gent. Mag.* (1823), i. 285; Gunnis mss Z3, Lady Harvey to Louisa Lloyd [Mar. 1823]. [14] *The Times*, 18 Apr., 3 May 1823. [15] Gunnis mss Z3, Lady Harvey to Louisa Lloyd, 13, 26 Nov., 30 Dec. 1823, 25, 30 Jan. 1824. [16] *The Times*, 17, 19, 21, 26, 27 Feb. 1824. [17] Ibid. 18 Mar. 1824. [18] Gunnis mss Z3, Lady Harvey to Louisa Lloyd, 5, 9, 15, 28 Apr., 3, 8 May 1824. [19] *The Times*, 25 May 1824. [20] Ibid. 2 June 1824. [21] Ibid. 11 June 1824, 25, 26 Feb. 1825. [22] Ibid. 1 Mar. 1825. [23] Ibid. 17 Mar. 1825. [24] Ibid. 19, 29 Apr. 1825. [25] Gunnis mss Z4, Lady Harvey to Louisa Lloyd, Tuesday [1826]. [26] *The Times*, 8, 24 Feb., 14 Mar. 1826. [27] *Colchester Gazette*, 3, 16 June 1826. [28] Gunnis mss Z4, Lady Harvey to Louisa Lloyd, 16 Nov. 1826, Jan. 1827. [29] *The Times*, 17, 28 Feb., 16 Mar.; Gunnis mss Z1, Harvey to Louisa Lloyd, 2 Aug. 1827. [30] *The Times*, 31 May 1827. [31] Gunnis mss Z4, Lady Harvey to Louisa Lloyd [Nov.], 25 Dec. 1828. [32] *Colchester Gazette*, 14 Nov. 1829, 27 Feb. 1830; *Gent. Mag.* (1830), i. 170, 365-6. [33] NLS mss 2272, f. 67; PROB 11/1768/175; IR26/1227/75; Gunnis mss C8, E. Williams to W. Lloyd, 26 Oct. 1831; Z1, Louisa Lloyd to Harvey [1823]. [34] *VCH Essex*, iv. 5, 24, 28, 190.

D.R.F.

HAWKINS, Sir Christopher, 1st bt. (1758–1829), of Trewithen, Probus, Cornw. and 31 Argyll Street, Mdx.

MITCHELL	21 June 1784–16 Apr. 1799
GRAMPOUND	28 July 1800–1807
PENRYN	1818–1820
ST. IVES	26 May 1821–20 Feb. 1828

bap. 29 May 1758, 2nd but 1st surv. s. of Col. Thomas Hawkins[†] of Trewithen and Anne, da. of James Heywood of Austin Friars, London. *educ.* M. Temple 1768; Eton 1769-73. *unm.*; 1da. *suc.* fa. 1770; *cr.* bt. 28 July 1791. *d.* 6 Apr. 1829.

Sheriff, Cornw. 1783-4.
Recorder, Tregony 1796, Grampound 1804, St. Ives.
Maj. commdt. Tregony and Grampound vols. 1798.

Hawkins, who had inherited 'extensive estates and several profitable mines' from his father at the age of 12, became the 'great Cornish borough Leviathan', returning at various times one or both Members for

Grampound, Helston, Mitchell, Penryn, St. Ives and Tregony. However, he never obtained the peerage that he coveted, presumably because of the prosecution in 1807-8 for bribery and corruption at Penryn, which almost led to his expulsion from the Commons. By 1820 his electoral influence had 'greatly diminished', and though he returned one Member for Mitchell at the general election that year, his candidates for Helston and St. Ives were defeated and he lost his own seat at Penryn. His bitter rival Francis Basset, 1st Baron De Dunstanville, observed: 'Poor Sir Christopher beaten everywhere, and to render his mortification complete, everyone laughs at it'. In fact, he partially rebuilt his interest at Penryn, and in May 1821 he was returned unopposed at a by-election for St. Ives, where he was lord of the manor.[1]

He was an occasional attender who gave continued support to Lord Liverpool's ministry. He voted against Hume's economy and retrenchment motion, 27 June 1821, and more extensive tax reductions, 11, 21 Feb. 1822. He divided against repeal of the Foreign Enlistment Act, 16 Apr., and inquiry into the prosecution of the Dublin Orange rioters, 22 Apr. 1823. He presented a St. Ives petition for repeal of the coastwise coal duty, 16 Feb. 1824.[2] He voted against the motion condemning the trial of the Methodist missionary John Smith in Demerara, 11 June, and for the Irish insurrection bill, 14 June 1824. He was named as a defaulter, 28 Feb., but attended next day to divide for Catholic relief, and did so again, 10 May 1825. He was granted one month's leave for urgent private business, 28 Mar., and voted for the financial provision for the duke of Cumberland, 30 May 1825. That autumn he attempted to obtain from the foreign secretary, Canning, a place for one of his Trelawny nephews, but this was deemed to be impossible without causing offence to Turkey.[3] In January 1826 he published a pamphlet on the Catholic question in order, so he told John Cam Hobhouse*, to 'justify myself to my friends and many of my constituents, who think differently from me'. He argued that Catholics sought only the 'toleration granted to all dissenting from the Church of England', and that they shared 'an interest with the Protestants in supporting the state and in attachment to the constitution', which gave them the same protection under the law. He believed that Catholic peers, many of whose titles dated 'from the earliest times of our history', and who were 'associated with the liberties of our country', should not be excluded from Parliament, and that Catholics should be allowed to hold public office with appropriate safeguards. He recognized that English resistance to emancipation was based on 'fear and even dread of Popery', but regarded

the opposition from the Irish church as being 'of a personal and selfish nature'. He was convinced that provided the Catholics did not 'frustrate their wishes by ... over zeal or indiscretion', their claims could 'no longer be resisted'.[4] He voted against the motion condemning the Jamaican slave trials, 2 Mar. 1826. At the general election that summer he was returned at the head of the poll for St. Ives.[5]

Hawkins divided for Catholic relief, 6 Mar., and was granted one month's leave, 'having sworn off', 6 Apr. 1827. He addressed the House on the Penryn election bill, 18 May, but was 'totally inaudible in the gallery'. He presented a Cornish petition for repeal of the Test Acts, 7 June 1827.[6] In January 1828 he acknowledged a letter from Peel, leader of the Commons in the duke of Wellington's new government, and promised to attend at the start of the session, but in the event he vacated his seat the following month and installed Charles Arbuthnot, an office-holder, in his place.[7] A bachelor, he died of erysipelas in April 1829, when his title became extinct. He instructed that his property at St. Ives and in other specified Cornish parishes be sold to pay his debts, and left the remainder of his estates, including Trewithen, to his nine-year-old nephew, Henry Hawkins. He provided £20,000 for his 'adopted daughter Christiana Dutton', who was 'aged about 18 years' and 'residing at Miss Smallwell's'. His personalty was sworn under £30,000.[8]

[1] E. Jaggard, Cornw. Politics in Age of Reform, 48-54; The Times, 4 Mar.; Carew Pole mss CC/M/53, De Dunstanville to Pole Carew, 18 Mar. 1820; West Briton, 1 June 1821. [2] The Times, 17 Feb. 1824. [3] Add. 36461, f. 253. [4] Ibid. f. 383; West Briton, 13 Jan. 1826. [5] West Briton, 16 June 1826. [6] The Times, 8 June 1827. [7] Add. 40395, f. 126; West Briton, 29 Feb. 1828. [8] Gent. Mag. (1829), i. 564; PROB 11/1755/291; IR26/1197/285; West Briton, 10 June 1831.

T.A.J.

HAWKINS, **John Heywood** (1802–1877), of Bignor Park, nr. Petworth, Suss. and 16 Suffolk Street, Pall Mall, Mdx.

MITCHELL	1830–1831
TAVISTOCK	13 July 1831–1832
NEWPORT I.o.W.	1832–1841

b. 21 May 1802, 1st s. of John Hawkins and Mary Esther, da. of Humphrey Sibthorp† (afterwards Waldo Sibthorp) of Canwick Hall, Lincs. educ. Eton 1815; Trin. Coll. Camb. 1820. unm. ch. illegit. suc. fa. 1841. d. 27 June 1877.

Hawkins came from an old Cornish family. His grandfather Thomas Hawkins (?1724-66), the only son of Christopher Hawkins of Trewinnard, near St. Erth, succeeded in 1738 to the Trewithen estate, near Probus, of his uncle Philip Hawkins, and sat for Grampound in the 1747 Parliament. With his wife Anne, the daughter of James Heywood, a merchant, of Austin Friars, London, he had four sons, of whom two died in youth or early manhood. The elder surviving son, Christopher Hawkins, inherited Trewithen and was created a baronet in 1791. He sat for four Cornish boroughs, including St. Ives from 1821 to 1828. His younger brother, John Hawkins, born in 1761, was educated at Helston, Winchester, Trinity College, Cambridge and Lincoln's Inn, and travelled extensively in Germany, Italy, Hungary, Greece, Crete and Turkey in the period 1787-98. He was something of a polymath, with particular interests in mineralogy, in which he excelled, botany, horticulture, archaeology and geology. He assisted John Sibthorp, sherardian professor of Botany at Oxford, in the collection of material for his *Flora Graeca*, published posthumously from 1806 by his trustees. He was a fellow of the Royal Society and the Geological Society of London and a founder of the Horticultural Society in 1804. He had a stake in the Ionian Islands and contributed essays to Walpole's *Memoirs relating to European and Asiatic Turkey* (1817) and *Travels in Various Countries of the East* (1820). A man of means, he bought in 1806 the property of Bignor Park on the Sussex Downs, where the remains of a Roman villa were discovered in 1811. In 1824 he bought a 'complete marine residence', Berkeley House, at Littlehampton, into which he moved for a few years from 1826 when, with the aid of a legacy of £8,000 from his uncle John Heywood of Coventry Street, London (*d.* 1822), he had the mansion house at Bignor rebuilt in Neo-Greek style.[1]

With his wife, Sibthorp's niece, John Hawkins had two sons, this Member, and Christopher Thomas Henry Hawkins, who was not born until 1820. By then John Heywood Hawkins, who was physically unprepossessing, having developed into 'a tall ungainly young man with a squinting eye', was at Cambridge, where, as his father reported in 1823, he showed a keen interest in architecture and pursued his 'passion for the study of antiquities'.[2] In 1828, when his father praised his 'very uncommon knowledge of architecture and ... great taste for picturesque gardening', which were of considerable assistance in the Bignor project, he went on an architectural tour, which took him to Cambridge, Durham (where he visited Whitfield, the home of his Cambridge contemporary and friend William Heny Ord[†], son of the Whig William Ord[*]) and the Lake District.[3] On the death of Sir Christopher Hawkins the following year his principal Cornish estates passed,

by the terms of his will of 1823, to Hawkins's younger brother.[4] In early 1830 he spent some time in London, devoting himself to 'painting, play-going, dining and political economy'.[5]

At the general election in August 1830 he was returned unopposed for Mitchell, where his father, as trustee for his younger son, had assumed the right of nomination to one seat which Sir Christopher had shared with the Tory 1st earl of Falmouth.[6] One observer heard that he had come in 'merely to get the best price after the meeting [of Parliament], and without regard to party', but this was not the case.[7] Almost immediately after his election Hawkins went to Paris to examine buildings and pictures. To his father, 13 Aug. 1830, he wrote that 'the conduct of the people' in the recent upheaval was 'beyond all praise', and ventured the opinion, formed after talks with members of 'the middle classes, who now rule the roost here', that 'an *hereditary legislative* peerage can[not] any longer exist in France'. In September he began 'as much of my projected tour in Normandy as the late political drama of Paris has left me time for'.[8] The Wellington ministry listed him among the 'good doubtfuls', but he was absent from the division on the civil list, 15 Nov. 1830. In February 1831 he joined Brooks's, sponsored by Lord Althorp[*] and one of the Ords, and he voted for the second reading of the Grey ministry's reform bill, by which Mitchell was to be disfranchised, 22 Mar. Opposing Gascoyne's wrecking amendment, 19 Apr., he delivered a maiden speech of stunning virtuosity, in which he asserted that 'we shall give no small confirmation of that charge of legislative incapacity which is now ringing in our ears, if we neglect to repair our House while it is still summer, because the winter hurricane is not yet upon the horizon', and called on the Commons to 'inscribe ourselves on the page of history as the first recorded example of power correcting its own usurpation'. John Cam Hobhouse[*] recorded that he 'spoke with great fluency and precision during nearly an hour, gaining every moment on his audience until the House became quite silent', and made 'certainly by far the best first speech I ever heard in Parliament'.[9] The elder Ord, informing Lady Holland that Hawkins, who '*squints* horribly and is hideous', was 'rather a protégé of mine', reported that 'the best judges are all in ecstacies about it', as 'the most beautiful speech in our favour that ever was heard'.[10] Thomas Spring Rice[*] privately applauded his 'superior abilities and exquisite taste and eloquence', which had brought him a 'complete' triumph.[11] Sir Henry Bunbury[*], who correctly assessed Hawkins as 'one of those retiring, scientific men that will be disinclined to speak often', considered it 'the best speech that has been delivered' during the debates on the bill.[12] Thomas Gladstone*, an Etonian contemporary of Hawkins, was sure that 'no speech but Peel's first has yet been so much cheered', though he suspected, rightly, that 'it must have been written out for the press', and thought that his 'manner is not impressive, or the effect would have been still greater'.[13] James Hope Vere* also perceived that while the speech was 'well delivered', it was 'evidently ... all previously wrote and committed to memory'.[14] Anne Sturges Bourne heard from her father that 'the ministers were charmed, and at Lansdowne House ... [Hawkins] was pointed out as the lion of the night, the Mr. H. who made *the* speech'.[15]

At the 1831 general election Hawkins paid the price of his support for reform when Falmouth, on the pretext that he had violated the terms of the electoral pact and sacrificed his younger brother's future interests, put up a second Tory against him at Mitchell and secured his defeat.[16] Ministers wanted to provide him with a seat in the new Parliament, if possible. Four days before the Mitchell election Althorp had suggested to him that he 'might be brought in for Liverpool free of expense', but he deemed this to be 'impossible', though he was ready to accept any offer without strings.[17] He let it be known that he 'could not pay a farthing' and 'would not sacrifice a particle of independence', and heard that Lord Grey 'said, at a dinner party, that I was to be returned'.[18] Towards the end of May he received an offer from the 6th duke of Bedford of the seat for his borough of Tavistock which was about to be vacated by his son Lord John Russell, who had also been returned for Devon. Bedford, who would have brought in Lord John's brother Lord George William Russell* if he had wanted the seat, was responding to a 'movement' among the leading electors in favour of Hawkins as a man of promise and martyr to the reform cause; but he had the ultimate power of determining who was returned. Hawkins was at pains to establish that he could sit for Tavistock not only free of expense, but politically 'responsible to no one', as he had been in the previous Parliament, and would have been in the new had he come in again for Mitchell:

Under these circumstances of perfect independence, it was my intention to ... sacrifice all points of minor importance for the purpose of supporting a ministry of whose good intentions I am satisfied, and who, I believe, will, if they continue in office, do more good in the long run than any ministry that could be formed; but without knowing what their opinions and intentions are on any of the great questions that might be brought forward after this [reform] bill, I feel an insuperable objection to enter

Parliament without an entire discretion as to how far I may see fit to carry that support and without a power to act as I please upon any measure which may seem to me to be of too great importance to the public welfare to be considered as a mere party question.

Bedford gave him satisfactory assurances on both points.[19] When they met in London to settle matters, the duke took to Hawkins, though he could not resist indulging in a joke at the expense of his unfortunate physiognomy, commenting to his son and Lady Holland that while he hoped that he would 'answer people's expectations' in the House, he was sure that they would 'be convinced that it is on public grounds alone that I have brought him in, and not *pour ses beaux yeux!*'[20] Hawkins went to Tavistock on 12 July and was returned unopposed the following day after addressing the inhabitants 'at some length', chiefly on the reform bill. In the course of his speech he said that

the boroughmongering system had been a dirty job under William Pitt; a difficult one under George Canning; but impossible to continue under the present administration ... He did not mean to tell the poor man that the bill would give him a twopenny loaf for a penny, or that the pint pot would in future contain a quart, nor did he mean to say that the man who went to bed badly shod at night, would awake in the morning and find a new pair of shoes at his bedside; but ... the effects of the bill would tend to promote education among the lower classes, and from the increase of labour materially benefit them.

He called for the abolition of slavery, an end to the cycle of 'famine and rebellion' in Ireland, which was barely controlled by 'the military and the gibbet', and a redistribution of clerical incomes and tithe reform.[21]

He took his seat in time to vote in the minority of 41 for a reduction in the civil list grant, 18 July 1831. The following day he divided with ministers against the opposition proposal for the 1831 census to be used to determine the disfranchisement schedules of the reform bill, and he voted steadily for the details of the measure during the next seven weeks, at the end of which he told his father that 'the enemy are tired out. Their opposition has been gradually waxing faint'. He anticipated that the 'factious and loquacious propensities' of the Irish Members would produce lengthy debates on their reform bill.[22] He voted twice with government on the Dublin election controversy, 23 Aug. He was one of a 'small party' of ministerialists who dined at Althorp's at the end of the month, and he attended the coronation with Macaulay, a new friend, 8 Sept.[23] On the third reading of the reform bill, 19 Sept., he tried to repeat his oratorical success of April with a long and florid set piece dismissing the objections raised to the measure and accusing its opponents, in predicting 'revolution', of 'holding up the consequences of their own obstinacy as a warning to mankind'. His condemnation of their appeals to the 'vulgar motives of personal fears and private interests' in the Lords provoked cries of protest and a dressing from Alexander Baring, and he was forced to make a partial retraction. The effort was generally reckoned to have been 'a failure', which, as Bunbury saw it, 'lowered him from the scale on which his first speech had seemed to place him'. Charles Williams Wynn* reported that Hawkins had 'only strung together a number of antitheses and flowers of rhetoric which faded almost as they budded'; and Hudson Gurney* dismissed it as 'poor gossip slip-slop, got by heart, poorly delivered'.[24] Perhaps chastened by this setback, Hawkins kept his mouth shut for the remainder of the 1831 Parliament. He voted for the passage of the reform bill, 21 Sept., and for the second reading of the Scottish measure, 23 Sept. The defeat of the reform bill in the Lords came as no surprise to Hawkins, who attended the party meeting which agreed to support Lord Ebrington's motion of confidence in the ministry and duly voted thus, 10 Oct. Remaining in London until the prorogation, he initially thought that ministers had little choice but to resort to a creation of peers to carry the bill. Moreover, he believed that

> the best thing that could be done now for the future stability of the Upper House, would be to infuse some new blood into it. As for the bishops, it is useless trying to save them. They must either quit the House of Peers, or the Church of England, before ten years are out.

He was sure that the king could be relied on, if only because he 'likes popularity'; and he had faith in the ability of Thomas Attwood† and the other 'clever men' leading the mass reform movement to prevent serious unrest: 'the affair is *not* in the hands of the mob, but of the middling classes, and therefore all will go well', he told his father. He was, however, a little alarmed by the Derby and Nottingham riots and by reports that 'the people are becoming very impatient about the reform bill'. As he now saw it, the ministry's 'very awkward dilemma' was rooted in the fact that while the Lords, deluding themselves that there had been a 'reaction' against reform in the country, might be willing to swallow 'a considerable measure', it was clear to everyone else that 'the introduction of a less efficient (that is, less democratic) bill, by the present ministry, would place us in imminent danger of an insurrection, and that the resignation of the ministry would produce one instantly'. Yet if ministers forced through, by a creation of peers, a measure ostensibly

'but a little more efficient' than that which the peers would take willingly, they would appear to be guilty of 'great tyranny'.[25]

Hawkins voted for the second reading of the revised reform bill, 17 Dec. 1831. He thought it gave 'great satisfaction to the reformers' while offering enough concessions to 'afford an excuse for any repentant Tory to withdraw his opposition'. He believed that 'the anti-reformers, both in Parliament and out, consider the passing of the bill as inevitable', though they were 'thoroughly frightened at the state of the country, as they well may be'.[26] He was therefore surprised by the 'appearance of an obstinate resistance on the part of the enemy' given by their dividing against going into committee on the bill, 20 Jan. 1832, when he of course sided with ministers. A week later, however, he concluded that opposition had resigned themselves to the bill's passage through the Commons and were 'inclined to direct their attacks from different quarters'.[27] He attended and voted steadily as the measure went through committee, though he was in the minority of 32 who voted to expunge the provision for the enfranchisement of £50 tenants-at-will, 1 Feb.[28] He told his father that he had been 'anxious to speak' on the third reading, for which he voted, 22 Mar. 1832, 'not for any sense of ability in doing so, but as a farewell to the question', but that he failed to catch the Speaker's eye on the second night, and on the third 'sat still in compliance with Althorp's desire to conclude the debate'.[29]

Hawkins was keenly interested in the government's plan for the revision of Irish tithes, which, he wrote in December 1831, 'if it be anything better than one of those milk and water expedients which are unfortunately the characteristic of Whig policy', would isolate Peel, ending 'the little appearances of coquetry which still remain' between the ministry and him, enrage the more reactionary Tories and so ensure 'a more unflinching support from the radicals and the press'. When the proposals were unveiled in March 1832, he was largely satisfied, and pleased with ministerial hints that 'English tithes will not much longer remain an assessment of the gross produce'. Yet he was annoyed by the 'inexcusable' threats of Irish Members to press for more radical change, which he thought would 'seriously embarrass the progress of the reform bill in the House of Lords'.[30] He did not vote in the division on the Russian-Dutch loan, 26 Jan. 1832, when he privately criticized the 'miserable mismanagement' of ministers in the Commons and thought them lucky to have escaped defeat;[31] but he was in their majorities when the issue was raised again,

12, 16, 20 July. On 27 Jan. he was named to the select committee on the East India Company, 27 Jan., whose investigations he professed to find 'most entertaining' and informative.[32] He voted with government on the question of interference in the affairs of Portugal, 9 Feb., and for the navy civil departments bill, 6 Apr.; but on 16 Feb. he was in Hume's minority of 28 for information on military punishments, and he rejoiced at being involved in the 'glorious division' of 2 Apr., when Hume's motion to abolish flogging in the army, as modified by Burdett (whose suggested exceptions Hawkins thought 'judicious', as it was 'a case in which it is as well to proceed cautiously') was defeated by only 11 votes.[33] He deplored Hunt's 'factious and popularity-hunting' opposition to Warburton's anatomy bill, which he stayed at his post in mid-April 1832 to support as a measure 'of great importance as a matter of principle'.[34]

He witnessed the debates in the Lords on the reform bill and flattered himself that the narrow success of the second reading 'removes ... the last opportunity of provoking popular disturbances', as 'no damage done to the bill in committee is likely to cause a riot'. At the same time, he thought that there was now 'only a choice between a creation of peers, or a compromise', fearing that abandonment of the provisions creating the new metropolitan constituencies, which the Tories hated, would 'give most offence to the lower classes', especially in London.[35] He voted for the motion calling on the king to appoint only ministers who would carry the bill unimpaired, 10 May. The following day, writing to his father on the current crisis, he discounted the notion that Peel or Wellington would come in to effect reform and asserted that for the moment, at least, the people were 'inclined to keep the peace', under the direction of the unions:

It is the ultimate consequence of this event which appears to me most pregnant with difficulty. We had already made the political unions our masters; we are now about to owe our safety to them. They will exhibit more forbearance than bodies of men have ever yet shown, if they do not rule us for some years to come with a rod of iron. Of course, we shall have no more of this bill as a final measure. The House of Lords have now proved that which the anti-reformers have been asserting all along, that, as at present constituted, they are a body whose existence is incompatible with a House of Commons freely elected by the people. As we cannot avoid, much longer, seeing a House of Commons so elected, the inference is obvious. The only choice will be between a senate elected for life, or continual creation for the purpose of carrying the successive reforms which the advance of the public mind will render necessary. This was, in truth, the last throw of the hereditary peerage; and they have

played it away even more childishly than their worst enemies could have hoped.[36]

He presented a Tavistock petition for the supplies to be withheld until reform had been secured, 23 May, and voted for the Irish, 25 May, and Scottish reform bills, 1 June. He was still attending the House in the dog days of early August 1832, when he reported that Smith Stanley had 'wisely' abandoned his bill to reform the administration of justice in Ireland.[37]

At the general election of 1832 Hawkins successfully contested Newport, Isle of Wight, where he had canvassed in June, after being approached by the leaders of the 'popular party' there. On 1 Aug. he told his mother that the local Tories 'affect to be much shocked at the radicalism of my opinions'; but he wondered how they would react when William Henry Ord, who stood and came in with him after Robert Torrens* had transferred his attention to Bolton, made known his views: 'Poor things, they don't know what radicalism is, yet!'[38] A supporter of the ballot, who was later said to have been 'regarded with disfavour by most of the leaders of the Whig party', he was returned again after contests in 1835 and 1837 (on the former occasion by one vote), but retired from Parliament in 1841, soon after succeeding his father to Bignor and property in Lancashire.[39] He died, leaving no legitimate issue, at 76 Regent's Park Road, London in June 1877. By his will, dated 3 Dec. 1862, he left most of his property to his brother, who succeeded him at Bignor. He bequeathed £1,000 to his bailiff and the rest of his ready cash and invested money to one Sarah Hawkins of 3 St. James Terrace, Regent's Park, formerly Sarah Dallin of Dartmouth, with remainder to their surviving illegitimate children. His personalty was sworn under £25,000, 22 Oct. 1877, and resworn under £35,000 in 1903 after the death of Christopher Hawkins, when the family estates passed to the Johnstone family, descendants of their married sister Mary Anne.

[1] *Oxford DNB*; *I am, my dear Sir* ed. F.W. Steer, pp. ix-xiv; *Hawkins Pprs.* ed. F.W. Steer, pp. v-vi; *Letters of John Hawkins and Samuel and David Lysons* ed. F.W. Steer, pp. v-vii; PROB 11/1654/140; Add. 39782, f. 257. [2] Add. 56555, f. 125; *I am, my dear Sir*, 36. [3] *I am, my dear Sir*, 60; Cornw. RO, Hawkins mss 10/2149-55. [4] PROB 11/1755/291; *I am, my dear Sir*, p. xv. [5] Hawkins mss 10/2157. [6] *West Briton*, 30 July, 13 Aug. 1830. [7] Add. 51835, Goodwin to Holland [Aug. 1830]. [8] Hawkins mss 10/2158, 2160. [9] Add. 56555, f. 125. [10] Add. 51569, Ord to Lady Holland [19 Apr. 1831]. [11] Add. 51573, Rice to Holland [19 Apr. 1831]. [12] *Bunbury Mem.*, 160-1. [13] St. Deiniol's Lib. Glynne-Gladstone mss 198, T. to J. Gladstone, 20 Apr. 1831. [14] Hopetoun mss 167, f. 257. [15] Hants RO, Sturges Bourne mss F9/6. See also *Three Diaries*, 83 and *Baring Jnls.* i. 85. [16] *West Briton*, 6, 20 May, 3, 10 June; *The Times*, 12 May 1831. [17] Cornw. RO, Johnstone mss

DD/3/2142/6, 7. [18] Add. 76382, Poulett Thomson to Althorp, 11 May 1831; Hawkins mss 10/2162. [19] *Russell Letters*, ii. 340, 341-2; Hawkins mss 10/2162; Add. 51663, Bedford to Holland, Tuesday [June 1831]. [20] *Russell Letters*, ii. 343, 346, 351; Add. 51670, Bedford to Lady Holland, Sunday [?17 July 1831]. [21] Hawkins mss 10/2163; *Plymouth, Devonport and Stonehouse Herald*, 16 July 1831. [22] Hawkins mss 10/2165, 2166. [23] *Macaulay Letters*, ii. 31, 89, 97; Hawkins mss 10/2167. [24] *Bunbury Mem.* 163-4; NLW, Coedymaen mss 220; Gurney diary, 19 Sept. [1831]. [25] Hawkins mss 10/2169-72. [26] Ibid. 2175, 2176. [27] Ibid. 2178, 2179. [28] Ibid. 2180-5, 2195. [29] Ibid. 2190. [30] Ibid. 2175, 2176, 2184, 2187. [31] Ibid. 2179. [32] Ibid. 2185. [33] Ibid. 2191. [34] Ibid. 2192. [35] Ibid. 2193, 2194. [36] Ibid. 2198. [37] Ibid. 2207, 2208. [38] Ibid. 2200, 2201, 2203, 2205-6, 2209-13; *The Times*, 8, 14 Dec. 1832. [39] *The Times*, 6 July 1877; *Gent. Mag.* (1841), ii. 322-3; PROB 11/1955/807.

D.R.F.

HAY, Adam (1795–1867).

LINLITHGOW BURGHS	1826–1830

b. 14 Dec. 1795, 7th but 3rd surv. s. of John Hay (*d.* 1830), banker, of Edinburgh and Haystoun, Peebles, and Hon. Mary Elizabeth Forbes, da. of James, 16th Lord Forbes [S]; bro. of Sir John Hay, 6th bt*. *m.* 23 Mar. 1823, Henrietta Callender, da. of William Grant of Congalton, Haddington, 4s. (1 *d.v.p.*) 5da. (1 *d.v.p.*). *suc.* bro. as 7th bt. 1 Nov. 1838. *d.* 18 Jan. 1867.

Hay entered the Edinburgh banking house of Forbes, Hunter and Company, in which his father was a partner. On his marriage in 1823 his father gave him £3,000.[1] At the general election of 1826 he was returned for Linlithgow Burghs after securing the support of Lanark, Linlithgow and his family's stronghold of Peebles, the returning burgh. He was reported to have been 'not unmindful of the distressed operatives' of Lanark, 'for whose relief he subscribed very liberally'.[2] He presented but dissented from the prayer of a Linlithgow petition against further relaxation of the corn laws, 26 Feb., and brought up one from Perthshire for protection against foreign wool imports, 6 June 1827.[3] He was given three weeks' leave on account of a family illness, 23 Mar. He was in the minorities of 37 for the separation of bankruptcy administration from chancery, 22 May, and of 16 against the Coventry magistracy bill, 11 June. Although he was reckoned to be one of the 'sworn allies' of the former minister and Scottish manager the 2nd Viscount Melville, who had resigned rather than serve in Canning's coalition ministry, he divided with government for the grant for Canadian water defences, 12 June 1827.[4] He was unable to comply with the new Wellington administration's request for his attendance at the opening of the 1828 session, but assured Peel, the home secretary, of his 'determination to support the line of politics, and party, you might think most likely to benefit the nation'.[5] He was in their major-

ity against chancery reform, 24 Apr. He presented petitions for repeal of the stamp duty on merchants' receipts, 22 Feb., and restrictions on wool imports, 16 May. As expected, he voted with government for Catholic emancipation, 6, 30 Mar. 1829. He presented constituency petitions against the Scottish gaols bill, 12 May 1829. He voted against Lord Blandford's parliamentary reform scheme, 18 Feb., and the enfranchisement of Birmingham, Leeds and Manchester, 23 Feb., and for the grant for South American missions, 7 June, but was in the majority against ministers for abolition of the Bathurst and Dundas pensions, 26 Mar. 1830. He presented petitions for repeal of the leather duties, 11 Mar., against renewal of the East India Company's charter, 17, 30 Mar., and for an increased duty on rum, 12 May 1830. To the surprise of one local observer, he announced his retirement from Parliament when the king's death the following month precipitated a general election.[6]

Hay duly became a partner in Forbes, Hunter and Company and an original member of the Edinburgh board of the Glasgow Union Bank which when it absorbed the firm in 1838.[7] He succeeded his unmarried brother John to the family's baronetcy and Peeblesshire estates in November that year. He died at Cannes in January 1867.[8] He was succeeded by his second but first surviving son Robert Hay (1825-85).

[1] *Hist. Peebles* ed. J.W. Buchan, ii. 369; PROB 11/1777/606. [2] *Caledonian Mercury*, 15, 26 June, 6 July; *Glasgow Herald*, 7 July 1826 [3] *The Times*, 27 Feb., 7 June 1827. [4] *Arniston Mems.* 333. [5] Add. 40395, f. 143. [6] Hopetoun mss 167, f. 148. [7] R. Saville, *Bank of Scotland*, 283, 400, 501. [8] *Gent. Mag.* (1867), i. 384.

D.R.F.

HAY, Lord John (1793–1851).

HADDINGTONSHIRE	1826–1831
NEW WINDSOR	1847–Feb. 1850

b. 1 Apr. 1793, 3rd s. of George, 7th mq. of Tweeddale [S] (*d.* 1804), and Lady Hannah Charlotte Maitland, da. of James, 7th earl of Lauderdale [S]. *m.* 2 Sept. 1846, Mary Anne, da. of Donald Cameron of Lochiel, Inverness, *s.p.* CB 17 Feb. 1837. *d.* 26 Aug. 1851.

Entered RN 1804, lt. 1812, cdr. 1814, capt. 1818, r.-adm. 1851.

Ld. of admiralty July 1846-Feb. 1850; commodore-superintendent, Devonport dockyard 1850-*d.*

Hay's father, the first surviving and possibly illegitimate son of John Hay of Newhall, Haddingtonshire, and Dorothy Hayhurst, daughter of a Lancashire labourer, was an officer in the naval service of the

East India Company. In 1787, two years after marrying a daughter of the 7th earl of Lauderdale, he succeeded his first cousin once removed as 7th marquess of Tweeddale and to the family's Haddingtonshire property at Yester, near Giford. He became lord lieutenant of the county in 1794 and a Scottish representative peer two years later. In 1802 he and his wife went to France for the benefit of his health. They were detained on the renewal of war and died within three months of each other at Verdun in 1804. Tweeddale was succeeded as 8th marquess by his 16-year-old eldest son George, an ensign in the 85th Foot. He rose rapidly through the ranks, served as aide-de-camp to Wellington in the Peninsula and was badly wounded at Busaco and Vitoria and again at Niagara when commanding the 100th Foot in America. A representative peer from 1818 until his death, he received a green ribbon in 1820 and was appointed lord lieutenant of Haddingtonshire in 1823. His younger brother Lord John Hay nominally entered the navy in December 1804, aged 11. From 1805 until the end of the French war he was 'constantly employed on active service', initially in the Mediterranean. On a cutting-out expedition from the *Seahorse*, 16 May 1807, he was severely wounded in both thighs, and his left arm was so badly mangled by a cannon ball that it had to be amputated at the shoulder. He shared in the capture of a Turkish frigate, 6 July 1808. In 1811, backed by his uncle, the 8th earl of Lauderdale, he petitioned the regent to be promoted to lieutenant while still six months short of the required minimum age of 19, but the admiralty would not permit this and he had to wait until May 1812.[1] He served in the West Indies, 1812-14, and subsequently at Lisbon, in the Channel and on the Halifax station. He achieved post rank in December 1818 but was unemployed for 14 years thereafter.[2]

In December 1816 Tweeddale, probably at Lauderdale's behest, declared Hay a candidate for Haddingtonshire at the next election, supposedly as a supporter of the Liverpool administration. Friends of the ministerialist sitting Member Sir James Grant Suttie ensured that he was detained abroad, and he was withdrawn at the 1818 general election.[3] At the county meeting called to vote a loyal address to the regent in the wake of Peterloo, 26 Oct 1819, when Tweeddale moved the resolution condemning sedition, Hay proposed the vote of thanks to the chairman.[4] He stood against Grant Suttie, who had the support of government, at the general election of 1820, but lost by one vote in a poll of 77.[5] His petition claiming a majority of legal votes was rejected. In September 1823 the radical Whig John Cam Hobhouse*, who married Hay's sister Julia in 1828, described him as

'a very intelligent, shrewd man indeed, a little formal at first'.[6] He came forward for Haddingtonshire at the 1826 general election and walked over. He later claimed that he had stated that he could not support government on the Catholic question;[7] and he voted for relief, 6 Mar. 1827. Not known to have spoken in debate in this period, he presented constituency petitions against relaxation of the corn laws, 27 Feb., 2, 9 Apr., and voted in the minority of 98 against the corn bill, 2 Apr.[8] He divided for the spring guns bill, 23 Apr. He was one of the 'combinationists', as he called them in a letter to Tweeddale, who went 'with Peel' on his retirement from office rather than serve with Canning that month. He told his brother on the 27th that the new ministry might prove to be 'formidable' and that 'party spirit runs high in town', so that it was 'hardly safe to open one's mouth'. A week later he praised Peel's 'manly and honest' explanation of his conduct and informed Tweeddale that he was one of the 'number of Members' who had 'decided not to vote for the Catholic question as long as Canning is at the head of administration':

> Some tell me I am very inconsistent ... but I feel justified in doing so when I know that the king was obliged to give a pledge to the bishops in order to get them to support the government that he would never grant the claims. It is in my opinion highly improper to place the king in that situation ... Canning has a desperate game to play ... If he loses there is an end to his political career and he must die like a dog.[9]

In mid-May 1827 he dined with Peel, who noticed that he was the only Scottish Member among the 30 guests, which prompted Hay to speculate that 'in the event of his coming into office again I ... shall have a good and useful friend in him'. He reported that Lauderdale was 'not ... pleased with my taking so decided a part' and wanted to bracket him with his sons Lord Maitland and Anthony Maitland and 'hold us up to the government as his Members, but that would never suit me'. He added that during his attendance on a private bill committee he had frequently 'come into competition' with the Canningite Lord Binning, 'the would-be manager of Scotland', over burgh reform, which Hay was willing in theory to accept, provided the Scottish counties were reformed also.[10] He duly supported Wellington's administration, in which Peel was home secretary, from January 1828, though he voted in the majority for repeal of the Test Acts, 26 Feb. He presented two petitions from Haddington for repeal of the stamp duty on receipts, 31 Mar., and one from his county against interference with the corn laws, 28 Apr. He voted for Catholic relief, 12 May. He was in the minority of 54 against the financial provision for Canning's family, 13 May, and the ministerial majority on the ordnance estimates, 4 July 1828. In January 1829 he was considered as a possible mover or seconder of the address, which would announce the proposed concession of Catholic emancipation.[11] He was not selected for this task, but he voted for the measure, as expected, 6, 30 Mar. His only known votes in the 1830 session were against the enfranchisement of Birmingham, Leeds and Manchester, 23 Feb., and for Jewish emancipation, 5 Apr. He presented Scottish petitions against the additional duty on corn spirits, 6 May 1830.

Three days later he told his brother, who was in Geneva, that uncertainty over the king's survival had 'paralyzed' political affairs, that 'considerable alterations in the formation of the government' were likely and that the Whigs, who 'sit with their mouths open and will take any scraps however trivial that the duke may throw out', could probably be seduced. At the end of the month, however, he reported that Lord Grey and the Whigs remained in 'decided opposition', that the Huskissonites were inclined to back them and that the estranged Ultra Tories were unpredictable: if they all joined forces against Wellington, 'his government could not stand a day'.[12] By then he was certain of being opposed in Haddingtonshire at the anticipated general election by Grant Suttie's son. He feared for his chances unless Wellington could be got to '*tell*' Lord Melville, the Scottish manager, that 'he does not wish me to be opposed'. Wellington intervened, and when Parliament was dissolved following the king's death Melville made it clear that the government preferred Hay, who had 'steadily supported them'.[13] At the election, when Grant Suttie persisted, Hay's supporters carried the vote for praeses and he was victorious by ten votes in a poll of 74. He laughed off the criticism of Sir George Warrender* that his lack of a personal property stake in the county made him unfit to represent its agricultural interest. He claimed to have supported the promotion of 'free and liberal principles' and to have backed Wellington's ministry 'from principle': 'he was under no pledge to ministers, and his support depended entirely on the character of their measures'. His boast that 'in all great questions of principle, he had as often voted against as for ministers' is not substantiated by the evidence of the surviving division lists. He reported his success to Wellington and promised continued support, and in reply was congratulated 'most sincerely'.[14]

Ministers duly listed him as one of their 'friends'. On 4 Nov. 1830 he told Tweeddale that 'things begin to look better' and that 'the government party' expected a majority of 60 – the minimum for credibility, he thought – against Brougham's anticipated reform motion, though 'everyone regrets more than ever the decided tone of the duke [against reform], as he has left ministers no retreat in the event of being beat in the Commons'. Five days later he deplored the efforts of some Members of Parliament and 'many blackguards outside of it' to 'cry down the government', and approved their decision to advise William IV not to attend the City dinner. As for the reform showdown on the 15th, he had

> much fear they will not be strong enough to resist the fury of opponents supported as they are by a lawless mob. I wish them joy if they (the Whigs) succeed, but I doubt their courage to execute one plan they have in view at the moment. Place is all they want, and having got that they will throw all liberal opinions overboard and rule with a rod of iron, as Whigs and Jacobins have always done.

On 14 Nov. he dined with Wellington, who was 'in great spirits', with 'about 30 of the Commons'.[15] He was in the ministerial minority on the civil list next day. As the Grey ministry was being formed, he reported the 'very bad news' that 84,000 Birmingham workers had 'struck for higher wages' and reflected that 'the new people will find it much easier to make speeches than to keep peace in the country'.[16] By the following week, when he had taken his place 'on the opposition bench' with 'Peel and Co.' (in his own case, next to Dan O'Connell, whom he found 'a most agreeable fellow'), he was beginning to consider the implications of the 'extensive change' to the Scottish electoral system which ministers were expected to propose:

> I am most anxious to know the opinion of the county, as I must shape my course accordingly. Whatever the freeholders of Scotland may say to it they may rest assured that a reform bill will be carried in the Commons by five to one ... I have always thought that as long as things were allowed to remain as they are in England, Scotland ought to be left alone, but if a change of the system took place in one part of the kingdom the same reform must be applied to the whole.

When Lord Maitland told him in December 1830 that he would jeopardize his seat if he supported reform and that 'my friends had said I was for going all lengths', he kept his counsel, but informed Tweeddale:

> In one respect that is true ... [but] I have never failed to qualify my opinions, so that *if I am compelled* to entertain the question, I shall advocate and support that which I think most sure to maintain the aristocracy in their present position and at the same time ensure the country a lasting repose. It is the opinion of every man I am in

the habit of speaking to that if reform is refused to the present government a revolution will follow. In Scotland I believe the people do not care much about it; but ... in [England] ... nine tenths are in favour of it.

He believed that any reform should be 'simple and extensive', as 'a half measure will not do': he favoured the retention of existing voting rights combined with a £40, perhaps £20, franchise in the counties and a £10 qualification in the burghs. Dismissing the notions of both 'moderate' and 'radical reformers', with which his brother furnished him, he was anxious to preserve the power of the crown and the authority of the nobility, which in Scotland could be done by enfranchising 'the yeomen' in order to 'encourage them to make common cause with the aristocracy'.[17] But the day after the government's reform scheme was unveiled on 1 Mar. 1831, he wrote to his brother:

> I will vote most decidedly against ... [this] most unreasonable and unjustifiable plan ... It would not leave a vestige of the constitution behind it. Although I had ... modified my opinions ... after hearing ... [those] of others and particularly those who send me to Parliament ... I was prepared to go beyond them from a conviction that something was absolutely necessary to conciliate the country, or rather the reformers ... I was willing to give the large towns representatives, also to have extended the franchise ... The general opinion is that government will be in a minority of *100*, some think *150*.

On 10 Mar. he alerted his brother to the proposed £500 property qualification for Members in the Scottish reform bill, which would 'be a most effectual way of throwing me overboard', and advised him, on the assumption that the measure would eventually become law, to consult Lauderdale as to its likely effect on their county interest. He was inclined to 'give it up with a good grace' in favour of Lauderdale's son-in-law James Balfour* at the next dissolution, quite apart from the consideration that under naval regulations he was obliged 'in the course of two or three years' to make an offer of active service to avoid forfeiting his promotion to rear-admiral.[18] He divided against the second reading of the English reform bill, 22 Mar., and was 'astonished' at its being carried by one vote. Sure that the Parliament 'cannot live three months longer', he was keen to retire when the dissolution came. He suggested to Tweeddale that the best line to take would be to inform the Haddingtonshire freeholders that 'the aspect of affairs in Europe renders it probable that the navy may shortly be called into active service', which would prevent him from fulfilling his duties as Member. He accordingly addressed the county in these terms, 7 Apr., and a week later Balfour declared

his candidature as an opponent of the reform bills.[19] Hay voted in the majority for Gascoyne's wrecking amendment to the English bill, 19 Apr. 1831, and retired when Parliament was dissolved a few days later.

He was appointed to the *Castor* frigate in September 1832 and from then until 1840 was active in command of a small squadron off the northern coast of Spain during the civil war. He frequently led combined naval and marine forces on land and was involved in the relief of Bilbao in December 1836.[20] He was made a lord of the admiralty in Lord John Russell's* first ministry in 1846 and was returned to Parliament as a Liberal for New Windsor. He retired in 1850 to take charge of Devonport dockyard, where, as 'a man of strict habits, and stern inflexible justice', he sought to root out corruption and favouritism. His death in harness in August 1851, shortly after being promoted to rear-admiral, earned him a public funeral.[21]

[1] *Gent. Mag.* (1851), ii. 427; Add. 45044, ff. 107-13, 116, 117. [2] *Oxford DNB.* [3] *HP Commons, 1790-1820*, ii. 543. [4] *The Times*, 6 Nov. 1819. [5] NAS GD51/1/198/9/23, 29; 51/5/749/1, pp. 186-7; *Caledonian Mercury*, 23 Mar. 1820. [6] Broughton, *Recollections*, iii. 26. [7] *Caledonian Mercury*, 12 Aug. 1830. [8] *The Times*, 28 Feb., 3, 10 Apr. 1827. [9] NLS mss 14441, ff. 20, 22. [10] Ibid. f. 24. [11] Add. 40398, f. 86. [12] NLS mss 14441, ff. 44, 63. [13] NLS mss 2, f. 151; 14441, f. 63; Hopetoun mss 167, f. 155; Wellington mss WP1/1132/26; *Caledonian Mercury*, 17 July 1830. [14] *Caledonian Mercury*, 12 Aug. 1830; Wellington mss WP1/1133/38. [15] NLS mss 14441, ff. 74, 78, 91. [16] Ibid. f. 89. [17] Ibid. ff. 82, 104, 110, 116. [18] Ibid. ff. 96, 114. [19] Ibid. ff. 100, 102, 119; *Edinburgh Evening Courant*, 14, 16 Apr. 1831; Wellington mss WP1/1182/9. [20] Wellington Pol. Corresp. ii. 858; *Holland House Diaries*, 354; *Oxford DNB.* [21] *Gent. Mag.* (1851), ii. 428.

D.R.F.

HAY, Sir John, 6th bt. (1788–1838).

PEEBLESSHIRE 9 Aug. 1831–1837

b. 3 Aug. 1788, 3rd but 1st surv. s. of Sir John Hay, 5th bt., banker, of Edinburgh and Hon. Mary Elizabeth Forbes, da. of James, 16th Lord Forbes [S]; bro. of Adam Hay*. *educ.* adv. 1811. *m.* 6 Oct. 1821, Anne, da. of Capt. George Preston, *s.p. suc.* fa. as 6th bt. 23 May 1830. *d.* 1 Nov. 1838.

Hay's grandfather James Hay, the son of John Hay of Haystoun, near Peebles and his first wife Grisel Thompson, was a physician in Edinburgh. His younger brother Adam Hay served in the army, 1747-68, and was Member for Peeblesshire, 1767-8 and 1775, when he died deep in debt. Dr. James Hay, who had succeeded his father in 1762, bought Adam's estate of Soonhope and acquired other Peeblesshire property. In 1804 he claimed the baronetcy of

Hay of Smithfield, dormant since the death of his grandfather's degenerate third cousin, Sir James Hay, 3rd baronet, in about 1683; and on 9 Nov. 1805 he established before a jury in Peebles that he was entitled to assume it.[1] His son John Hay, born in 1755, was in 1774 apprenticed in the Edinburgh banking house of Sir William Forbes of Pitsligo, his sister Elizabeth's husband. He became a partner in the firm of Forbes, Hunter and Company in 1782, married into the Scottish aristocracy in 1785, built a house at Kingsmeadows, Peebles and accumulated much property in the burgh. He succeeded to the assumed baronetcy in 1810 and was one of the 'quiet country gentlemen set' of Edinburgh society.[2]

His eldest surviving son John Hay was bred to the Scottish bar, but achieved no distinction there. He was in Greece in April 1819 and so out of contention for an opening for Linlithgow Burghs. He succeeded to the baronetcy and entailed estates in May 1830.[3] On a vacancy for Peeblesshire in the summer of 1831 he offered, without disclosing his views on parliamentary reform, and came in unopposed.[4] He voted with the Tory opposition to censure the Irish administration's interference in the Dublin election, 23 Aug. 1831. He divided against the third reading, 19 Sept., and passage, 21 Sept., of the Grey ministry's English reform bill, and the second reading of the Scottish bill, 23 Sept. On 4 Oct. he denounced this as 'a ten-pronged fork, of vulgar fashion' and condemned the proposal to throw the burgh of Peebles into the county. He secured returns of information on excise duties on spirits, 7, 10 Oct. He was absent from the division on the second reading of the revised English reform bill, 17 Dec. 1831, but voted against going into committee on it, 20 Jan., and the third reading, 22 Mar. 1832. He divided against government on the Russian-Dutch loan, 26 Jan., and was in the minority of 41 against the malt drawback bill, 2 Apr. He repeated his objection to the arrangement for Peebles, 1 June, made a suggestion for rewording the £10 freeholder clause of the Scottish reform bill, 'a gratuitous insult to the gentry of Scotland', 4 June, and supported an attempt to debar Scottish clergymen from voting, 6 June. He was given a month's leave to attend to urgent private business, 29 June 1832.

Hay's confidence in his chances of being returned for Peeblesshire at the 1832 general election proved to be justified, and he sat for the county as a Conservative until his retirement in 1837.[5] He died in Rome in November 1838, and was succeeded in the baronetcy by his next surviving brother Adam Hay.

[1] HP Commons, 1754-1790, ii. 598; Hist. Peebles ed. J.W. Buchan, ii. 336-41, 360-6. [2] Hist. Peebles, ii. 130, 134, 136, 366-8. R. Richardson, Coutts and Co. (1901), 87, 93, 97, 105; Highland Lady, 308; Scott Jnl. 316; PROB 11/1777/606. [3] HP Commons, 1790-1820, ii. 612; PROB 11/1777/606; IR26/1229/538. [4] Caledonian Mercury, 16 July, 11 Aug. 1831; The Times, 19 July 1831. [5] Add. 40879, f. 253.

D.R.F.

HAYES, Sir Edmund Samuel, 3rd bt. (1806–1860), of Drumboe Castle, co. Donegal.

Co. Donegal   1831–30 June 1860

b. 2 July 1806, o.s. of Sir Samuel Hayes, 2nd bt., of Drumboe and Elizabeth, da. of Sir Thomas Lighton, 1st bt., MP [I], of Merville, co. Dublin. educ. Trinity, Dublin 1823. m. 3 July 1837, Emily, da. of Hon. Hercules Robert Pakenham*, 3s. (1 d.v.p.) 10da. suc. fa. as 3rd bt. 16 Sept. 1827. d. 23 June 1860.
  Sheriff, co. Donegal 1830-1.

Hayes's great-grandfather Challis (or Charles) Hayes of Bridgwater, Somerset, who married Deborah Holditch of Totnes, Devon, was vice-consul in Lisbon, where he was murdered by his servant in 1737. His only son Samuel, who worked as a London surgeon, married the heiress Mary Basil and so gained the valuable estate of Drumboe in the north of Ireland. As Member for Augher, 1783-90, he was an inactive opposition Whig, but he was awarded an Irish baronetcy on 27 Aug. 1789, and, presumably through his friendship with Lord Abercorn, he served as joint-governor of Donegal, 1789-1800. Following the general election of 1797 he quarrelled with one of the county Donegal Members, Alexander Montgomery, who apparently alleged that Hayes was 'an old pintle farrier: his father was kept on charity and his mother was a Brazil mulatta slave'. A duel ensued, in which Hayes was slightly wounded twice without hitting his opponent. On his death in 1807 he was succeeded by his only son and namesake, an army officer, who also became a governor of their county. In 1803 he had married the eldest daughter of Sir Thomas Lighton, who began life as a Strabane trader but made a fortune in India, represented Tuam, 1790-7, and Carlingford, 1798-1800, as a ministerialist and ended his days a wealthy Dublin banker.[1]

On the death of his father, who had signed the anti-Catholic petition of the Irish noblemen and gentlemen earlier that year, Hayes inherited Drumboe Castle and the baronetcy in September 1827.[2] He moved the resolution for the subscription to fund the Donegal Brunswick Club at the county meeting on 25 Sept. 1828, and spoke in defence of the Protestant constitution at another, 5 Jan. 1829.[3] As sheriff, he presided at the Donegal election in 1830, when he explained that he would have resigned this office to stand against the sitting pro-Catholic Member Lord Mount Charles had he not believed that a stout Protestant would have come forward. At the general election the following spring, when he was praised in the Ultra press as an 'estimable and upright young gentleman', he successfully contested Donegal with another anti-Catholic landowner against two reformers.[4] He voted against the second reading of the Grey ministry's reintroduced reform bill, 6 July, and to postpone consideration of the partial disfranchisement of Chippenham, 27 July 1831. He made his maiden speech, defending the independency of the magistracy, on the Irish lord lieutenants bill, 15 Aug. He divided against issuing the Liverpool writ, 5 Sept., and for inquiry into the effects of the renewal of the Sugar Refinery Act on the West India interest, 12 Sept., when he was listed in the minority against committing the truck bill. He voted against the third reading, 19 Sept., and passage of the reform bill, 21 Sept., and the second reading of the Scottish bill, 23 Sept. He divided against the Maynooth grant, 26 Sept. 1831, 27 July 1832.

Hayes signed the requisition for and was present at the abortive anti-reform meeting in county Donegal, 14 Jan. 1832, when he was described by a radical paper as a 'brainless booby'; on the 17th, at the Protestant meeting in Dublin, he denounced the Catholic priesthood for having orchestrated the disturbances which led to its cancellation.[5] Having missed the division on the second reading of the revised reform bill, 17 Dec. 1831, he voted against the enfranchisement of Tower Hamlets, 28 Feb., and the third reading, 22 Mar., and for Waldo Sibthorp's amendment on Lincoln freeholders, 23 Mar. He divided for the Liverpool disfranchisement bill, 23 May, and Alexander Baring's bill to exclude insolvent debtors from Parliament, 25 June. He voted against the second reading of the Irish reform bill, 25 May, and to preserve the voting rights of Irish freemen, 2 July. He brought up many petitions, 4 Apr., 25 June, 2, 27 July, against the ministerial plan for Irish education, against which he spoke and voted, 23 July. He condemned the Irish tithes bill as destructive to the established church, 30 Mar., and voted against Crampton's amendment to it, 9 Apr., although he divided in the majority for the introduction of another bill, 13 July. He was naturally expected to join the Protestant Conservative Society of Ireland that summer.[6] His speech (and vote) against the Irish party processions bill as a blatantly partial measure, 25 June, was praised in Ulster, although following its withdrawal he used his position as grandmaster of the Orange Order in Donegal to urge restraint prior to the marches on 12 July.[7] His only other known votes in this Parliament were with opposition against the Russian-Dutch loan, 26 Jan., 12 July. A founder member of the Carlton Club in March, Hayes was returned unopposed for Donegal as a Conservative at the general election of 1832 and sat for the rest of his life. He died in June 1860 and was succeeded in turn by his two surviving sons, Samuel Hercules (1840-1901), an army officer, and Edmund Francis (1850-1912), on whose death the baronetcy became extinct.[8]

[1] *Hist. Irish Parl.* iv. 387; v. 94; *Intro. to Abercorn Letters* ed. J.H. Gebbie, 201-2. [2] Add. 40392, f. 5; PROB 11/1749/708. [3] *Enniskillen Chron.* 2 Oct. 1828; *Impartial Reporter*, 15 Jan. 1829. [4] *Enniskillen Chron.* 26 Aug. 1830, 2 June; *Strabane Morning Post*, 3, 24 May; *Impartial Reporter*, 5 May 1831. [5] *Ballyshannon Herald*, 13, 20 Jan.; *Newry Examiner*, 18 Jan.; *Enniskillen Chron.* 26 Jan. 1832. [6] NLI, Farnham mss 18611 (3), Lefroy to Farnham, 4 June 1832. [7] *Ballyshannon Herald*, 6 July; *Londonderry Sentinel*, 7 July 1832. [8] *Ballyshannon Herald*, 29 June 1860.

S.M.F.

HAYES *see also* PARNELL HAYES

HEATHCOTE, Sir Gilbert, 4th bt. (1773-1851), of Normanton Park, Rutland and Durdans, nr. Epsom, Surr.

LINCOLNSHIRE	1796-1807
RUTLAND	1812-1841

b. 6 Oct. 1773,[1] 1st s. of Sir Gilbert Heathcote†, 3rd bt., of Normanton and 2nd w. Elizabeth, da. of Robert Hudson of Teddington, Mdx. *educ.* Newcome's acad. Hackney; L. Inn 1786. *m.* (1) 16 Aug. 1793, Catherine Sophia (*d.* 28 Apr. 1825), da. of John Manners† of Grantham Grange, Lincs., 3s.; (2) 10 Aug. 1825, Charlotte Eldon of Park Crescent, Portland Place, Mdx., 1s. *suc.* fa. as 4th bt. 2 Nov. 1785. *d.* 26 Mar. 1851.

Capt. Rutland yeoman cav. 1794-1801; maj. commdt. Folkingham and Bourne vols. 1801.

Sheriff, Rutland, 1795-6.

Heathcote, a veteran reformer and a member of Brooks's since 1804, continued to sit unchallenged for Rutland by dint of his large landed stake in the county and with the connivance of the 2nd marquess of Exeter. At the general election of 1820, when his eldest son Gilbert John was returned for Boston, he was too ill to attend the formalities, and his younger son Edward Lionel stood proxy for him.[2] He continued to act, on an independent basis, with the Whig opposition to the Liverpool ministry, but he was a notably lax attender in this period. He voted against the aliens bill, 7 July, and the barrack agreement bill, 13 July 1820.

He divided for restoration of Queen Caroline's name to the liturgy, 26 Jan., 13 Feb., and to censure ministers' conduct towards her, 6 Feb. 1821. He voted for Catholic relief, 28 Feb. He paired for repeal of the additional malt duty, 3 Apr., was credited with presenting a Boston petition for amelioration of the criminal code, 4 May,[3] and voted for barrack reductions, 31 May 1821. He attended to vote for the amendment to the address, 5 Feb., large tax reductions, 21 Feb., and admiralty economies, 1 Mar. 1822. His only known votes in the next three years were for parliamentary reform, 25 Apr. 1822, 24 Apr. 1823. He presented an Oakham anti-slavery petition, 23 Mar. 1824.[4] He was a defaulter on a call of the House, 28 Feb. 1825, when he received a request from Sir Francis Burdett to attend the imminent division on Catholic relief, 'a question I think you have much at heart', and a warning that he would be 'taken into custody if not in your place'.[5] He attended and was excused next day, and duly voted in the majority for relief. He paired for relief, 21 Apr., 10 May. He divided for a repeal of assessed taxes, 3 Mar. 1825. No trace of activity has been found for the 1826 session.

At the general election that summer he declared his intention to pursue an independent course, 'voting as my judgement best points out', professed to be a 'friend to both agriculture and commerce' and, under questioning, denied having voted to reduce protection for domestic corn producers:

> He always wished corn to be at a moderate price, but yet not so low as to withhold remuneration from the farmer. He thought corn might be too high as well as too low, as he did not wish to starve the poor ... He did not often vote with the administration, but ... when he thought they were right he would not vote against them ... He thought government the best judges of what is for the most general benefit of the country, even better than the collective body of the agriculturists.[6]

He presented a Perth petition in favour of agricultural protection, 26 Feb. 1827.[7] He paired for Catholic relief, 6 Mar. On 30 May 1827 he was a teller for the minority of two against the second reading of the sale of game bill. He presented a petition for repeal of the Test Acts, 21 Feb., and voted accordingly, 26 Feb. 1828. On 24 Apr. Burdett wrote to advise him of the forthcoming division on Catholic relief, and he attended to vote for it, 12 May 1828.[8] He divided for the Wellington ministry's concession of emancipation, 6, 30 Mar. 1829, and on the 25th praised the home secretary Peel for his 'noble part' and urged the opponents of the measure to 'adopt more moderate language towards their Roman Catholic fellow-citizens', who would be

'faithful and loyal subjects of the Protestant king'. He did not attend the Rutland county meeting called to petition for relief from distress and parliamentary reform, 27 Feb., but he presented and endorsed the petition, 23 Mar.1829, and urged ministers to 'turn in their minds the possibility, at least, of affording relief', though he was 'not wishing to thwart the intentions of government'.

At the general election of 1830 he was criticized for his absence from the February county meeting, but he dismissed the charge that he was hostile to the agricultural interest as 'groundless':

> On all great questions of national policy he had done his duty, but he could not consent to injure his health and waste his time for the mere purpose of swelling the ranks of any set of men actuated by motives of party. He believed the present government to be as good as we could obtain.

He added that he had refused to support one of the revived opposition's motions for economy because it went too far, but claimed to favour judicious 'economy and retrenchment', though he refused to give 'any pledges as to how he might feel it right to vote'.[9] Ministers listed him among their 'foes', but he was absent from the division on the civil list which brought them down, 15 Nov. 1830. He presented anti-slavery petitions, 17 Nov., 15 Dec. 1830. He was granted a fortnight's leave on account of ill health, 14 Feb., but was present to vote for the second reading of the Grey ministry's reform bill, 22 Mar. 1831. He paired against Gascoyne's wrecking amendment, 19 Apr. 1831. He was too ill to attend the hustings at the ensuing general election. At a celebratory dinner he was described by Gilbert John as a 'staunch and unflinching supporter of reform'.[10] On 2 July 1831 Lord Grey told the patronage secretary Ellice that although there was 'no person to ... whom I should have greater pleasure' in obliging, he was afraid that there were 'almost insurmountable difficulties' in the way of fulfilling his request for army promotion for his Edward Lionel.[11] Heathcote voted for the second reading of the reintroduced reform bill, 6 July, and for a few of its detailed provisions, 19, 27, 28, 29 July. He was in the minority for the disfranchisement of Saltash, 26 July. From early August he paired on the ministerial side, having been forced by 'a cold' to seek a cure at Broadstairs.[12] He was absent from the division on the passage of the bill, 21 Sept., but turned up to vote for Lord Ebrington's motion of confidence in the ministry, 10 Oct. He divided for the second reading of the revised reform bill, 17 Dec. 1831, its details, 20, 23 Jan., 3, 8 Feb., and its third reading, 22 Mar. 1832. He was absent from the division on the address asking the king to appoint only ministers who would carry undiluted reform, 10 May 1832.

Heathcote continued to sit for Rutland until his retirement in 1841. A keen devotee of the Turf, he had purchased the estate of Durdans, near Epsom, in 1819, and subsequently became perpetual steward of Epsom races; his colt Amato won the Derby in 1838.[13] He died in March 1851 and was succeeded in the barony and family estates by Gilbert John.

[1] TNA 30/8/136, f. 220 suggests 5 Oct. [2] *Drakard's Stamford News*, 3, 24 Mar. 1820. [3] *The Times*, 5 May 1821. [4] Ibid. 24 Mar. 1824. [5] Lincs. AO, Ancaster mss 3ANC 9/7/57. [6] *Drakard's Stamford News*, 16 June 1826. [7] *The Times*, 27 Feb. 1827. [8] Ancaster mss 3ANC 9/7/58. [9] *Boston, Louth, Newark, Stamford and Rutland Champion*, 10 Aug. 1830. [10] Ibid. 3, 10 May 1831. [11] Ancaster mss 3ANC 9/10/44. [12] *Boston, Louth, Newark, Stamford and Rutland Champion*, 4 Oct. 1831. [13] *VCH Surr*. ii. 497; *Surr. Arch. Coll*. xliv. 21; xlviii. 9.

S.R.H./D.R.F.

HEATHCOTE, Gilbert John (1795–1867), of Stocken Hall, Rutland.

BOSTON	1820–1830
BOSTON	1831–1832
LINCOLNSHIRE SOUTH	1832–1841
RUTLAND	1841–26 Feb. 1856

b. 16 Jan. 1795, 1st s. of Sir Gilbert Heathcote, 4th bt.*, and 1st w. Catherine Sophia, da. of John Manners† of Grantham Grange, Lincs. *educ.* Westminster 1808-12; Trinity Coll. Camb. 1814. *m.* 8 Oct. 1827, Hon. Clementina Elizabeth Drummond Burrell, da. of Peter Robert Drummond Burrell†, 2nd Bar. Gwydir, 1s. 2da. *suc.* fa. as 5th bt. 26 Mar. 1851; *cr.* Bar. Aveland 26 Feb. 1856. *d.* 6 Sept. 1867.
Capt. Rutland yeoman cav. 1819, maj. 1820; hon. col. R. South Lincoln militia 1857.
Ld. lt. Lincs. 1862-*d.*

Heathcote, whose father, probably one of the largest landowners in south Lincolnshire, sat as Whig Member for Rutland, entered Westminster school in January 1808: he was placed in the Upper 4th and 'so I am not a fag', he told his mother.[1] He left in 1812 and according to an obituary spent some time at Edinburgh University, though no record of his admission has been found. At Cambridge he was assigned a tutor but appears neither to have matriculated nor taken a degree. He was admitted to Brooks's, sponsored by the duke of Devonshire, 25 Feb. 1816, and two years later, according to Lady Williams Wynn, was 'very well spoken of, and very *gros parti* of course'. Nothing came

of a proposed marriage to Lady Catherine Osborne in 1818, even though the dowager duchess of Leeds was reported to be delighted by the prospect.[2]

At the 1820 general election he came forward for the venal borough of Boston, where the family's influence had been revived, replacing his friend Peter Robert Drummond Burrell on the Blue, or Whig interest. He was too ill to canvass, but headed the poll with a record majority after a two-day contest. His universal popularity, so the Rev. Thomas Kaye Bonney informed Sir Gilbert, more than guaranteed his future return, provided he did not mind the 'common expense attending it'. His costs, including bribes to freemen, amounted to almost £4,000 and, on the advice of the banker William Garfit, his agent and the nominal head of the Orange party, were settled unobtrusively. He was eager to make himself acquainted with Boston's affairs and told Garfit of his willingness to be of 'any service to the freemen', though he was all too soon aware of their rapaciousness. In line with Sir Gilbert's wishes, he made a concerted effort at economy, but the uncertainty surrounding the petition against the return of his absentee colleague Henry Ellis undermined his determination not to spend more money before the next election. At the declaration he declared it his first duty to be the 'organ of his constituents' and pledged himself to a 'punctual attendance' at Westminster.[3]

A regular attender, who took a keen interest in Boston's commercial and local affairs, he voted with the Whig opposition to the Liverpool ministry on most major issues, including economy, retrenchment and reduced taxation.[4] In July 1820 he told Garfit that although he deplored the proceedings against Queen Caroline, he wished to remain 'entirely unpledged', since every Member would be called on to act as a juryman. He nevertheless backed and presented Boston addresses to her at Brandenburgh House, 27 Aug., 27 Nov. 1820, and joined in the opposition campaign in her support.[5] In his maiden speech, 26 Jan. 1821, he presented and endorsed a Boston petition calling for restitution of her rights, deprecated ministers' prosecution of the divorce to the exclusion of every other 'natural object', and censured them for bringing the monarchy into disrepute. In line with a request from Garfit, he moved for information on bonded corn, 15 Feb., and was 'very much amused, though but little flattered' at being mistaken by more than one reporter for Edward Curteis, Member for Sussex, some 33 years his senior. It may have been his father who divided for Catholic relief, 28 Feb. 1821, for he was ill with a cold at about this time, though he told Garfit that he was 'able to attend the House very regularly'.[6] But it was certainly he who voted thus, 1 Mar., 21 Apr., 10 May 1825. He voted for repeal of the additional malt duty, 21 Mar., 3 Apr., and presented a petition from Lincolnshire for economy and reduced taxation, 6 Apr. 1821.[7] When his new colleague Colonel Johnson presented and endorsed a Boston petition in support of Lambton's anticipated reform scheme, 17 Apr., he declared himself a 'sincere friend' to reform, but not without reservations: he was opposed to sudden constitutional changes and warned the House that impracticable reform measures raised hopes which could not be satisfied. Yet he voted for Lambton's measure, 18 Apr., Russell's proposal, 9 May 1821, inquiry into the Scottish burghs, 20 Feb., parliamentary reform, 25 Apr. 1822, 20 Feb., 24 Apr., 2 June 1823, 27 Apr. 1826, and reform of Edinburgh's representation, 26 Feb. 1824. Throughout 1821 he made a number of representations to the treasury on behalf of his constituents and was in close contact with Garfit over local issues. On one occasion, having read one or two pamphlets, he told him of his decided opposition to Brougham's proposal for the education of the poor.[8]

Heathcote moved for further information on bonded grain, 13 Feb. 1822. On 28 Feb. he presented and endorsed a Louth petition for agricultural relief, observing that neither their industry nor the remission of rent could save Lincolnshire's farmers from 'utter ruin' and ascribing distress to excessive taxation. He brought up a Lincolnshire petition for reduced taxation and parliamentary reform, 25 Mar., but was reported to have offended many of his constituents by not attending a county reform meeting at Lincoln in April.[9] In his reply to William Tuxford, one of Boston's leading Blues, he apologized for his unintentional absence and appealed with 'perfect confidence' not only to his attention to constituency affairs, but also to his voting record. He presented petitions on behalf of his father's Rutland constituents against Ricardo's proposed fixed duty on corn, 14 May, and the poor removal bill, 31 May, and a Gainsborough petition for repeal of the salt tax, which he endorsed, 17 June 1822.[10] He brought up Boston petitions against the Insolvent Debtors Act, 19 Feb., and the General Turnpike Act, 15 Apr. 1823. He appears to have suffered from ill health towards the close of the session, but had completely recovered by late August when, according to the *Boston Gazette*, his constituents were 'delighted by his urbanity'. When Charles Anderson Pelham succeeded his father as 2nd Baron Yarborough in September he was eager for Heathcote to replace him as county Member, since, as he told him, 'your public political conduct exactly agrees with

my opinion'. Yarborough, who set his face against the candidature of Sir Robert Heron*, assured Heathcote that Sir William Amcotts Ingilby, the only viable choice as far as he was concerned, would stand down in his favour. As leader of the county Whigs Yarborough was confident of success and assured Heathcote that many of the Tories would find it difficult to fault his conduct. Pressed for an immediate decision in early October, Heathcote declined to stand without a decisive answer from his father. Heron, who withdrew before the publication of Amcotts Ingilby's first address, was angered by Yarborough's dictation and urged Heathcote to oppose Amcotts Ingilby, 16 Oct. 1823. Heron wrote again three days later but could not prevail on him to stand, despite his assurance of an 'easy victory'. Yarborough finally gave Amcotts Ingilby his interest in early December, telling Sir Gilbert, whom he had replaced as county Member in 1807, that nothing would have given him greater pleasure than to have endorsed his son's candidature, since 'from what I know and hear from all quarters so excellent a private and public character [as] he would have succeeded'.[11]

Heathcote pressed government to reduce the duty on excise licences, 4 Mar. 1824, and next day moved for further information on bonded corn. He presented a Boston petition for the abolition of slavery, 15 Mar. According to Lady Williams Wynn, 31 Mar., he was all set to marry Lady Emma Brudenell, a daughter of the 6th earl of Cardigan, but broke off the engagement and was immediately challenged to a duel by her quarrelsome and loose-living brother Lord Brudenell*. When they met, Brudenell, who ironically had formed an association with Elizabeth Johnstone, a married relative of Heathcote's mother

> fired first and the other of course would not return it, so there it ended, the brother only requiring him to sign a certificate that he had no reproach to make to Lady Emma, which he said he was most ready to do, never having thought of making the slightest imputation on her. The story told is, that it is all connected with Lady Emma's 'first fault', or rather to go still higher, with the strong fancy which her mother took originally for Mrs. Johnson, between whom and her daughters, she formed the strictest intimacy. To the continuance of this intimacy under the existing circumstances, Heathcote vehemently objected as far as regard his fiancée, and at last got her to promise to drop it, in spite of which, however, he found that she continued a private correspondence, and taking fright at such a palpable breach of faith, he declared off.

Lady Williams Wynn added that Lady Derby, in conversation with Thomas Creevey*, had commented that

Heathcote, after receiving Cardigan's shot, ought to have said 'Now, my Lord, I must beg of you to receive *my* shot for your conduct to my cousin!'. 'Damned fair, I think', was Creevey's reply.[12] Shortly afterwards Robert Wilmot Horton* informed Lord Granville that 'Heathcote comes to the House of Commons but looks wild and conscious and I understand many people cut him. I must say that I think as he has been shot at for his jilting it is enough'.[13] Apparently unperturbed, he unsuccessfully objected to the licensing clause of the game laws amendment bill on the grounds that it discriminated against the smaller landowner, 1 Apr. 1824. He presented a Boston maritime petition in favour of the St. Katharine's Docks bill, 3 Mar., and accordingly opposed its recommitment, 24 Mar. He supported repeal of assessed taxes, 3 Mar., but cautioned Members against bowing to public pressure for abandonment of the sinking fund which, in time of war, had enabled government to 'arm the troops, and raise the necessary supplies'. On 25 Apr. he urged the free trader William Whitmore not to press for inquiry into the corn laws, since 'the subject was now agitating the country in an alarming degree'. In the ensuing debate, 28 Apr., he presented a petition against their revision on behalf of his father's constituents. He took a leading part in opposition to the second reading of the cruelty to animals bill, 11 Mar., explaining that he had heard the evidence of the bill's proponents and, in particular, of the 'many injuries inflicted, on a bear baited at the Westminster pit', but on investigation he had found a healthy animal 'grown too fat for exercise'. He challenged Members, eager to hear the 'casuistry by which the question was evaded', whether it was more cruel to bait a bear with two dogs than to hunt a stag with a pack of hounds, and argued that if Parliament banned bear-baiting yet allowed stag-hunting and other rural sports to continue, it might well be said that they had 'one law for the poor and another for the rich'. His wrecking amendment was carried by a majority of 18 that day. He opposed the introduction of legislation to increase the scale of fines for the ill-treatment of animals, 24 Mar., and was particularly averse to leaving punishment to the discretion of magistrates. That day he was a majority teller against amending the Cruelty to Animals Act. On the mistaken assumption that he would not stand again for Boston at the next general election George Agar Ellis, then Member for Seaford, sought to replace him during the rumours of a dissolution in the autumn of 1825.[14]

Heathcote spent some time at Belvoir Castle, in company with Lord and Lady Exeter, as a guest of the 5th duke of Rutland in early February 1826. Speaking in committee on the navigation laws, 14 Feb., he alleged that the commercial treaties with La Planta and Colombia had caused redundancies in the British shipping industry. On 21 Feb. he secured information on the number and tonnage of ships entering British ports. He deprecated the frequent discussions of the Scottish currency, since it undermined what little confidence remained, 6 Mar. He deplored the divisive language of recent petitions against the corn laws, 10 Mar., observing that those from the 'lower orders', who were suffering from the 'pressure of distress', were entitled to respect, but when petitioners, such as the magistrates of Arbroath, referred to the laws as the 'bread tax, the landlords' tax and the job of jobs', they were sowing the seeds of discord. He presented petitions from Boston for the abolition of slavery, 21 Mar., and from Sunderland shippers against the Reciprocity of Duties Act, 17 Apr., when he argued that the relaxation of the navigation laws, which allowed British and foreign ship owners to trade on equal terms, was detrimental to British shipping. He obtained information on the tonnage of British and foreign ships entering home ports, 26 Apr. He presented a Boston corn merchants' petition against the bonded corn bill, 5 May, when he warned that the decision to admit foreign corn would upset the market. Elaborating, 8 May, he did not oppose the release of bonded corn to relieve distress, but questioned ministers' consistency after their defeat of a proposal to reduce agricultural protection on 18 Apr. He opposed the measure as an expedient adopted in response to 'outrage and clamour' and was a teller for the minority of 58 in the subsequent division, 8 May. He presented a Boston petition against revision of the corn laws, 9 May 1826.

At the 1826 general election he offered again for Boston and topped the poll after a two-day contest. Before the campaign he drew up a budget to curb expenses, but at the same time told Garfit 'not to do less than the Pinks'. On the hustings he boasted that during the last six years he had voted on all the 'great political questions'. He had been returned unpledged in 1820, but trusted that henceforward 'I shall be known by my zealous exertions to secure the rights and privileges of the freemen'. Alluding to the remarks of his ministerialist colleague Neill Malcolm, he accepted that government had done 'much for the good of the people', but he wished them to do more, and called on Malcolm to support the campaign for reduced taxation. He ended by urging those freemen with county votes to support Amcotts Ingilby.[15] Heathcote presented a Boston petition for inquiry into the corn laws, 12 Feb., and voted for Catholic claims, 6 Mar. 1827. On 14 Mar. he endorsed a Hull petition for relief for the shipping industry, arguing that the merchant navy was the 'keystone' of the nation's prosperity and observing that Boston's trade in British vessels had decreased by a third, while foreign shipping had nearly trebled.[16] He sought clarification of Sweden's monopoly restricting the import of salt and hemp to her own merchantmen, 23 Mar., obtained information on the strength of the merchant navy, 27 Mar., and presented petitions for protection of the shipping industry, 2, 3 May.[17] He voted for information on the Lisburn Orange procession, 29 Mar., and chancery delays, 5 Apr., and for inquiry into the Irish estimates that day. That month his industry on behalf of his constituents was applauded by the *Gazette*.[18] He was added to the select committee on borough polls, 3 May. He despaired at an intervention challenging Canning over vacancies in his new administration during the debate on the shipping interest, 4 May, and, aware of the impossibility of securing a fair hearing while the composition of the new ministry remained in doubt, called for an adjournment, as 'there never was a time when the spirit of party was so high, [but] there never was a question brought before the House which required more temperate and less of party feeling'. On the introduction of the bill for the recovery of small debts, 23 May, he called for the abolition of 'unjust' acquittal fees in magistrates' courts and trusted that Peel, though out of office, would continue his programme of legal reforms which had 'gained him so much credit'. He voted for the disfranchisement of Penryn, 28 May. He was a minority teller against going into committee on the game laws, 8 June. He presented petitions from Rutland and Boston for repeal of the Test Acts, 11, 12 June.[19] He obtained information on British maritime trade with Scandinavia and the Baltic, 15 June 1827. In early autumn news of his engagement to the eldest daughter of Drummond Burrell, now 2nd Baron Gwydir, was all over London. Lady Williams Wynn, anxious to see him settled and 'off our shoulders', told Fanny Williams Wynn, 5 Sept., that he was once more on the 'brink of matrimony'. The Gwydirs, she added

will not lose sight of him till the knot is actually tied fast. It has been for sometime the height of their ambition to catch him, having to them, the particular merit of near neighbourhood in addition to all other general ones, so that I think he will hardly slip away.[20]

Under the terms of the marriage settlement, 25 Sept. 1827, lands in Lincolnshire and Rutland, worth over £7,480 a year, were set aside to provide him with an annual rent charge of £4,000, as well as a jointure of between £2,000 and £3,000 for his wife, then still a minor. They were married at Drummond Castle, Perthshire, and the celebrations at Boston, according

to the *Gazette*, were marked by scenes of 'drunkenness and depravity'.[21]

Heathcote presented petitions for repeal of the Test Acts, 22 Feb., but did not vote for it, 26 Feb. 1828. He secured an account of the preceding year's maritime trade, 24 Mar. He endorsed a petition on the depressed state of the wool trade, citing the 'extreme anxiety' that prevailed among farmers and landowners and stating that in some instances the price of wool had fallen by 30 per cent, 17 Apr., and presented petitions for an import duty on wool next day and 28 Apr. He presented petitions against the revised corn duties, 17, 22 Apr., when he declined to explain his objections to the existing scale because of the late hour, and for greater agricultural protection, 24, 25 Apr. Speaking at length in defence of the agricultural interest, 28 Apr., he argued that the agriculturists were the 'best judges of their own interests' and vilified those political economists and advocates of the manufacturing interest who professed to know better. That day he complained that the price of freight had not been sufficiently considered in determining British and foreign corn averages. He presented a Boston petition against Catholic claims, 30 Apr., but voted for relief, 12 May. He divided against provision for Canning's family next day. On 23 May he opposed a call for information on Millbank penitentiary as the relevant statistics were already before the House. He presented but declined to endorse the prayer of the Lincolnshire wool growers' petition, 3 June, on the ground that their call for protection was too extreme, but he stressed the need for inquiry and hoped that the Wellington ministry would pay more attention to the wool trade. He voted to restrict the circulation of small notes in Scotland and Ireland, 5 June, and presented a petition from Welsh lead miners against the import of foreign ore, 9 June. He presented additional petitions from wool growers, 17, 23 June, and took the opportunity of presenting another, 4 July, to argue the case for further protection. He deprecated the desultory discussion of the usury laws, 15 May, and on 19 June refuted the argument that they had had a 'ruinous effect on trade'. He sneered at the political economists' devotion to the open market which, 'according to the strictest and best approved rules of the art', would ruin the agricultural interest. On 24 June he protested that the question of financial reform had often been improperly introduced into debate and pledged himself against further opposition to currency reforms during the present session. As a spokesman for the shipping interest, however, he reiterated their grievances in the face of competition from cheaply freighted foreigners. He appreciated the impossibility of effecting a remedy at this late stage, but accepted the assurance of ministers that the maritime interest would be investigated during the recess. He presented petitions for the abolition of slavery, 30 June, and the cessation of £1 notes, 1 July. On 4 July he presented a petition from the coroner of Bury St. Edmunds for increased travel expenses and, later in the same sitting, denounced the practice of introducing important bills at 'one or two o'clock in the morning'. He voted to abolish the governorship of Dartmouth garrison, 20 June, and to reduce the salary of the lieutenant-general of the ordnance, 4 July 1828.

In late February 1829 he was listed by Planta, the Wellington ministry's patronage secretary, among Whigs 'opposed to securities' to accompany the concession of Catholic emancipation, for which he voted, 6 Mar. 1829. He rejected the claims of Colonel Sibthorp, the Tory Member for Lincoln, that the county was hostile to the measure, 9 Mar., when he brought up two favourable petitions, and 20 Mar., when he condemned the practice of smuggling covert and unrepresentative petitions into the House and expressed his belief that the majority of freeholders were content to leave the issue to government. On 25 Mar. he urged Byng to withdraw his proposal to indemnify counties against the expense of repairs to roads adjoining public bridges, since it would be lost during the present session. He secured information on the volume of exported and imported wool, 25 Mar. He was in the minority for the transfer of East Retford's seats to Birmingham, 5 May, justifying his vote not only on the account of Birmingham's economic importance, but also from a wish to extend the 'rights of the people', 7 May. He spoke against the issue of a new writ that day, though he was aware that many of his Whig friends still wished to save the old constituency, saying that he preferred the respectable freeholders of Bassetlaw to the 'corrupt and degraded' voters of East Retford and that it was ridiculous to suppose that the former were under the thumb of the Ultra Tory duke of Newcastle, whose influence there was no more than that which 'ought fairly to belong to property'. He endorsed a Cumberland petition for agricultural relief and, referring to the dramatic fall in the price of long wool, argued for inquiry, 11 May. Certain that ministers would not revise the corn laws, 14 May, he declared his opposition to Hume's proposal for inquiry, largely because any discussion would pose a threat to public order, especially in the aftermath of the disturbances in Cheshire and Lancashire. Expanding on this theme, 19 May, he declared that the operation of the existing regulations had proved 'adequate' in the face of high prices and repudiated the claim that the laws were responsible for manufactur-

ing distress. On 15 May he presented and endorsed a Lincolnshire petition in support of the Smithfield market bill and urged Members not to disregard the evidence of 'practical men'. Reiterating his opposition to reform of the usury laws, 25 Mar., he called on the friends of the landed interest to back government in opposing the proposal. He supported a call to permit tobacco cultivation in England as a means of relieving rural unemployment, 1 June 1829.

Heathcote was absent for much of the 1830 session on account of his wife's serious illness and was described as an 'idle Member' in a subsequent radical commentary.[22] On 15 Feb. Lord Valletort* urged him to attend the division on Hume's proposal for retrenchment 'if you really wish the government well', but he did not appear more regularly until after the Easter recess, though his friend Lord Exeter kept him abreast of proceedings.[23] He presented a Boston petition for relief from agricultural and commercial distress, 16 Mar., when he told the House that graziers were the class of agriculturists most badly affected by the fall in land prices. Speaking in support of reduced taxation, 17 Mar., he endorsed the proposal to increase Irish taxes to offset the shortfall, as in the aftermath of emancipation it was 'not unreasonable' that Ireland should bear her 'fair share' of the burdens of the United Kingdom. On 19 Mar. he spoke against repeal of the malt tax because it would increase the profits of the 'great brewers', and applauded ministers' attack on the 'evil folly' of the brewers' monopoly, endorsing their proposal to abolish the beer tax: 'It is by cheap prices alone, that the great mass of the people can be relieved'. He spoke accordingly in support of the second reading of the sale of beer bill, 4 May, but objected to its discussion in committee, 3 June, as many Members had left the chamber on the understanding that it would not be debated at such a late hour. He presented and verified the respectability of a Boston petition for reform of the criminal code, 26 Apr. That day, reaffirming his opposition to the usury laws amendment bill, he declared that in the present state of the economy, which favoured the moneyed interest, it was unjust to allow financiers to charge 'unlimited interest', and was a teller for the minority against the second reading. He was assiduous in his subsequent opposition to the bill and spoke against it at length, 6 May, 15 June. He sneered at the petition for relief from the aldermen and livery of London, 17 May, reminding Members that City retailers maintained prices at an 'abominable' level, irrespective of the reduction in wholesale prices. He voted to abolish the sugar duties, 21 May. Echoing his father's objections to the Northern roads bill, he declared his opposition to its public subsidy and presented a petition and voted against it, 3 June. He argued that the labourers' wages bill was 'dangerous and injurious', 11 June. On 7 July he acknowledged that he had not been 'sufficiently active' in supporting the revived opposition's campaign for economy and retrenchment, but vowed to demand 'efficient reforms' from ministers in the event of his re-election, and spoke and was in the minority of 11 for the reduction of puisne judges' salaries. He voted against increased recognizances in cases of blasphemy, 9 July 1830.

At the 1830 general election Heathcote offered again for Boston, where the local reformers had persuaded the radical reformer John Wilks I* to stand. Addressing the freemen, 30 June, Heathcote repudiated criticisms of his lax attendance, saying he had regularly attended to his parliamentary duties for over ten years with the exception of the last four months, in consequence of the dangerous illness of his wife, and even then he had gone up to present petitions and 'since the Easter recess I have attended more regularly and voted on at least 30 important questions'. Questioned over his absence from Graham's proposal to reduce privy councillors' emoluments, 14 May, he pleaded ill health, assuring the freemen that otherwise he would have voted for it. Perceiving his position to be untenable, he withdrew, 13 July, and made strenuous efforts to find a seat elsewhere.[24] Brougham had no regrets about his retirement in view of his poor record of attendance.[25] He declined Protheroe's invitation to replace him at Evesham, 15 July, because 'I did not think it would succeed, and the event proved I was right'. Charles Tennyson* encouraged him to come forward for Lincoln following his own decision not to stand, 14 July, saying, 'Your name would be all-sufficient'. After consultation with Sir Gilbert among others, however, he decided not to try his hand, 27 July. Grantham, where his father was supposed to have some influence, was another possibility, but he declined to pursue this, 19 July, since 'I should have turned out my uncle Lord Huntingtower†'. William Denison* was sorry that he might be out of Parliament, for 'independent of losing a friend, the country wants ... men of your firm principles, and upright conduct', and urged him to consider either Beverley or Hull, but only as a third man. He communicated with Denison's attorney at Beverley as well as with Sykes, the sitting Member for Hull, but Beverley was ruled out following the freemen's requisition to Sykes, and he had little enthusiasm for the expense and inconvenience of Hull. Almost as a last resort Charles Western* encouraged him to consider standing for Ipswich, but this he also rejected on the ground of expense. In early November

the 2nd Earl Grosvenor, aware of his ambition to return to Parliament, informed him of the possibility of obtaining a seat at Wells, but no vacancy occurred.[26]

On 20 Mar. 1831 Tennyson once more recommended him as a candidate for Lincoln in the event of the passage of the Grey ministry's reform bill, saying he had no ulterior motive but merely wished to assist 'such a man as yourself' to find a seat. Heathcote was formally asked by the freemen to stand as a reformer, 26 Mar., but was warned by Garfit that any association with them would prejudice his chances at Boston. He was mentioned by the *Boston Gazette*, 5 Apr., as a likely candidate for the southern division of Lincolnshire in a reformed Parliament, and was encouraged by Heron to declare himself as such. In reply to Heron, 2 Apr., he explained:

> My first wish is that there may be no dissolution, the second is that if there is, some man may be *found* to come forward to support reform. I have no money to spare nor *any wish* to be the other man, but I would put myself to inconvenience and stand by the cause if no one else will do so. It is on these terms only that I asked your help. I know my political opinions are not popular, but still I think the county at large would not like the return of one opposed to reform. Be assured I will make no offer of myself till the last moment, but will invite others to come.

Rumours of his candidature for the reformed county were well received, but Sir Gilbert was adverse to his 'coming in' to the short Parliament which would ensue in the event of the reform bill being rejected, though it was quite possible that an opportunity might present itself, but this was quite different from actively 'seeking' one. He accordingly refused to have any truck with negotiations over an unspecified borough, 3 Apr., but agreed to speak privately with Lord Saye and Sele whenever the chance occurred. He was opposed to any public declaration over the southern division, but suggested that an anonymous advertisement might be placed in the local papers, requesting the freeholders to reserve their votes. Heron persistently urged him to declare himself in order to ward off Chaplin, one of the county Members, as a refusal at this stage would 'weaken a future claim'. At the same time the revival of the Orange interest at Boston and his growing popularity there, not least because he had always paid bribes, gave rise to speculation about his real intentions. He was certainly interested in the possibility of standing there and keen to improve his chances. To add to the mystery he told Johnson, who had declared for the southern division, 16 Apr., that he had long considered doing so himself, and that the almost unanimous offers of support 'confirm me in this intention'. The defeat of the bill, however, made this aspiration academic. Yarborough's eldest son requested his support at the nomination for the county, in recognition of his considerable influence in south Lincolnshire. Shortly after the dissolution, 22 Apr., he was invited to canvass Grantham, as a successor to Sir Montague Cholmeley, but was almost immediately advised not to appear once Colonel Hughes, unseated on petition in 1820, had declared himself. On 25 Apr. he offered as a reformer for Boston, where it was reported that the freemen had determined to secure his return. At the nomination he affirmed his loyalty to the king and respect for the privileges of peers, but said his first duty was to the people, the 'source of all legitimate power', and argued that reform would give 'stability to the throne, happiness to the people, and knit together all classes'. Pressed for his views on retrenchment, he promised to strive to reduce the 'shameful profligacy' which had crept into the revenue. After a violent two-day contest he was returned with Wilks. Shortly afterwards he defended Sir Gilbert's reputation as a reformer and stood in for him at the Rutland election and subsequent celebratory dinner.[27]

Heathcote, in company with other Lincolnshire Members, took some interest in the progress of the Fordingham drainage bill in June and July 1831.[28] On 29 June Lord Durham promised to acquaint his ministerial colleagues with his communication on county polling districts. He secured returns of the number of brigs and frigates in the navy, 20 July. He voted for the second reading of the reintroduced reform bill, 6 July, and gave generally steady support to its details, though he was in the minorities against the disfranchisement of Appleby, 19 July, and the partial disfranchisement of Guildford, 29 July. In the debate on the proposed division of Lincolnshire, 20 July, he sneered at Sibthorp's 'impudent assertion' that it would thereby become a 'nomination county' and, with obvious impatience, explained to Sadler, the duke of Newcastle's nominee for Aldborough, the circumstances which safeguarded the county's independence. He voted for the passage of the reform bill, 21 Sept., and next day was granted a fortnight's leave on account of family illness. He divided for the second reading of the revised reform bill, 17 Dec. 1831, again supported its details, and voted for its third reading, 22 Mar. Like Sir Gilbert, he was absent from the division on Lord Ebrington's motion for an address calling on the king to appoint only ministers who would carry it unimpaired, 10 May. He divided with ministers on the Russian-Dutch loan, 26 Jan. He obtained information on convictions under the game laws, 20 Mar. He presented petitions against the Nocton and

Branston drainage bill, 11, 21 May. On 23 July 1832 he warned that reduced woad duties would inflict 'considerable injury' on the Wiltshire growers. Having privately represented their case to the board of trade he pressed Poulett Thomson, the vice-president, for an explanation but the reply failed to placate him and, much to the annoyance of a number of Members, he asserted that growers would be ruined for the 'sake of conformity'.

Heathcote's future at Boston was by now uncertain. Garfit told him candidly, 19 June 1832, that his prospects were not good, that he could count on the old freemen, but otherwise could not calculate with 'anything like certainty', and there had been 'much more dissatisfaction' with his failure to vote in the second half of the session, particularly as he was known to be in London. 'Both the Pink [Tory] and Blue [Whig] party do not fail to talk of it and we do not know what to say in reply', Garfit reported. As to his qualms over election expenses, 'the large fortunes of both your families are so magnified here that the people consider the expense to you a mere trifle and I fear there is no means of making them think otherwise'. He was already under threat. Benjamin Handley[†], deputy recorder until 1826 and a 'most violent radical', according to a prominent Newark election agent, had given notice of his ambition to replace him in late May 1831, when it was supposed that he would opt for the county. Out of step with the aspirations of the Boston Political Union and criticized for not being 'sufficiently industrious and decided', he readily accepted a requisition from the freeholders of South Lincolnshire, 26 June 1832. He had previously tested the ground and began his canvass almost at once.[29] At the 1832 general election he was returned unopposed. He sat unchallenged as a moderate reformer until 1841, when opposition from both parties forced him to abandon the seat and he replaced Sir Gilbert as Member for Rutland.[30] He succeeded his father in 1851 and was created a peer in 1856, when the vacancy was filled by his only son Gilbert Henry Heathcote (1830-1910), Liberal Member for Boston since 1852. Heathcote died in September 1867. By his will, dated 10 Aug. 1863, he made provision for his daughters in addition to their entitlement under any marriage settlement, and to his wife bequeathed £20,000 and a life interest in his leasehold house at 10 Belgrave Square. She became suo jure Baroness Willoughby d'Eresby when the abeyance of that barony was terminated in her favour, 13 Nov. 1871, and took the name of Heathcote Drummond Willoughby by royal licence, 4 May 1872. The residue of his estate was entailed on his son, who in 1888 became 22nd Lord Willoughby d'Eresby and joint-hereditary great-chamberlain as a descendant of the extinct dukedom of Ancaster. He was created 1st earl of Ancaster in 1892, when he was one of the few remaining noblemen who possessed over 100,000 acres in the United Kingdom.[31]

[1] Lincs. AO, Ancaster mss 3ANC9/7/39. [2] *Gent. Mag.* (1867), ii. 534; *Williams Wynn Corresp.* 227. [3] *Boston Gazette*, 7, 14 Mar. 1820; Ancaster mss XIII/B/10r, v. [4] *Black Bk.* (1823), 163; *Session of Parl. 1825*, p. 467; Ancaster mss XIII/B/10h, j, l, v. [5] Ancaster mss XIII/B/10aa, bb, jj; *Boston Gazette*, 29 Aug., 3 Dec. 1820. [6] Ancaster mss XIII/B/10b, o. [7] *The Times*, 7 Apr. 1821. [8] Ancaster mss XIII/B/10n. [9] *The Times*, 14 Feb., 1, 26 Mar. 1822. [10] Ibid. 15 May, 1, 18 June 1822. [11] Ibid. 20 Feb., 16 Apr., 7 June; *Boston Gazette*, 2 Sept. 1823; Ancaster mss XIII/B/4c-f; B/10t. [12] *The Times*, 5, 6, 16 Mar., 2 Apr. 1824; *Williams Wynn Corresp.* 309; J. Wake, *Brudenells of Deene*, 429. [13] TNA 30/29/9/6/2. [14] *The Times*, 4, 25 Mar., 29 Apr. 1825; Ancaster mss 3ANC9/10/9, 10. [15] *The Times*, 22 Feb., 7, 11, 18, 22 Mar., 18, 27 Apr., 10 May; *Boston Gazette*, 16 May, 13, 20 June 1826; Ancaster mss 3ANC9/10/27; 14/58, 129. [16] *The Times*, 13 Feb., 15 Mar. 1827. [17] Ibid. 3, 4, May 1827. [18] *Boston Gazette*, 3 Apr. 1827. [19] *The Times*, 13, 16 June 1827. [20] *Williams Wynn Corresp.* 363. [21] Ancaster mss 5ANC2/B/1-2; *Boston Gazette*, 16 Oct. 1827. [22] [W. Carpenter], *People's Book* (1831), 277. [23] Ancaster mss 3ANC9/10/29, 30. [24] *Boston Gazette*, 29 June, 6, 13, 20 July 1830. [25] Brougham mss, Brougham to Denman [Sept. 1830]. [26] Ancaster mss 3ANC9/10/38-40; 14/168, 170-71; XIII/B/5a, c-h, j-l, q-v, x, y, aa-cc. [27] Ancaster mss XIII/B/a-g, i, j, l-r; *Boston Gazette*, 5, 26 Apr., 3, 31 May; *Stamford Champion*, 10 May; *Drakard's Stamford News*, 3 June 1831. [28] Ancaster mss 3ANC9/13/3, 7. [29] Ancaster mss 3ANC9/10/43; 13/63; 14/193, 194, 205; *Boston Gazette*, 26 June, 3 July 1832. [30] P. Salmon, *Electoral Reform at Work*, 156-62. [31] *Gent. Mag.* (1867), ii. 534; IR26/2502/1117; Sir F. Hill, *Victorian Lincoln*, 66.

S.R.H./P.J.S.

HEATHCOTE, Richard Edensor (1780–1850), of Longton Hall and Apedale Hall, Staffs. and 9 Bolton Street, Mdx.

COVENTRY	1826–1830
STOKE-UPON-TRENT	1835–5 Feb. 1836

b. 25 Oct. 1780,[1] 1st s. of Sir John Edensor Heathcote of Longton Hall and Anne, da. of Sir Nigel Gresley, 6th bt., of Drakelow, near Burton-on-Trent, Staffs. *educ.* Westminster 1796; Christ Church, Oxf. 1799; L. Inn 1802. *m.* (1) 16 Aug. 1808, his cos. Emma Sophia (*d.* 13 Sept. 1813), da. of Sir Nigel Bower Gresley, 7th bt., 2s. (1 *d.v.p.*) 1da. *d.v.p.*; (2) 13 Dec. 1815, Lady Elizabeth Keith Lindsay (*d.* Sept. 1825), da. of Alexander, 23rd earl of Crawford [S] and 6th earl of Balcarres [S], 2da. (1 *d.v.p.*); (3) 19 June 1838, Susan Cooper, 3s. (2 *d.v.p.*). *suc.* fa. 1822. *d.* 3 May 1850.

Heathcote's father, who was knighted on his appointment as sheriff of Staffordshire in 1784, was the eldest son of Michael Heathcote of Buxton, Derbyshire, and his heiress wife Rachel (*née* Edensor) of Hartington. He had prospered as a barrister, pur-

chased the mansion (1778) and manor (1784) of Longton with its potteries and coal seams and married the eldest daughter of Sir Nigel Gresley of Drakelow, whose estates and influence extended into Derbyshire, Leicestershire and Staffordshire. The eldest of their ten children, at least two of whom were deaf and dumb, Heathcote excelled academically, graduated in classics at Oxford and was intended for the bar or the church, but preferred country pursuits.[2] In 1808 he married his cousin Emma Gresley, on whom property in Castle Gresley, Ashby-de-la-Zouch, Lichfield and Newcastle-under-Lyme was settled. He leased Condover Park near Shrewsbury, where Emma died in September 1813, shortly after giving birth to their fourth child.[3] Following his marriage in 1815 to Lord Crawford's daughter, he lived mainly in London, but he leased Lord Combermere's Staffordshire estate at Rugeley after embarking on a £5,000-rebuilding programme at Longton, which he inherited, 'dilapidated and encumbered', in October 1822.[4] When a vacancy at Newcastle-under-Lyme in July 1823 coincided with one for Staffordshire, which his absent cousin Sir Roger Gresley* aspired to, Heathcote was invited to offer for Newcastle as an anti-reformer opposed to Catholic relief, but stood as a champion of the local independent party, favourable to both. Writing to the *Staffordshire Advertiser*, he explained:

> I told my friends most distinctly that I was no advocate of reform in its common and hackneyed sense, but only so far as I believed it to be perfectly safe and consistent with the preservation of our ... form of government ... All that I contended for was that where abuses were obvious, and the correction of them was practicable, they might in all cases be corrected and removed with an honest and steady hand ... My property, my connections, and the political conduct of my family, which had always been most loyal and disinterested, as well as my own on many trying occasions, might, I thought, afford them a sufficient guarantee, that I should never be the person to desire change of a violent and dangerous kind ... I should equally, I said, disguise my real sentiments, were I to describe myself entirely favourable or entirely hostile to the claims of the Roman Catholics. I differed alike with that party, which would resist all concessions *in limine*, and with that, which would remove at once all restraint and concede all that is asked without looking to consequences, or requiring any countervailing safeguards.[5]

He attributed his defeat by John Evelyn Denison to his 'late start' and urged his supporters to challenge the corporation through the courts.[6] His prospects at Newcastle were soon scotched by the sitting Member Wilmot Horton, a junior minister, whose letters to the home secretary Peel cast doubt on Heathcote's allegiance to Lord Liverpool's administration and criticized his conduct; and also by his forfeiture of the Kinnersley interest.[7] In November 1827, when a by-election was anticipated at Newcastle, he was unable to muster sufficient support for a realistic challenge by Gresley.[8]

Heathcote was widowed for the second time in September 1825, and unlike Gresley (who had been defeated at Lichfield), he did not scour the country in search of a seat at the 1826 general election. Probably on the Staffordshire Member Littleton's recommendation, he started late on the corporation interest at Coventry where the corporation had advertised for a 'No Popery' Tory opposed to free trade, and topped the poll with Bilcliffe Fyler, so defeating the sitting Whigs.[9] His speeches and addresses professed allegiance to church and state and stressed his Black Country roots, commercial concerns and hostility to all 'jobs': he 'would neither systematically oppose, nor systematically support the government'.[10] Reports of his 1823 defeat and pro-Catholic sympathies were belatedly circulated and, with a petition on behalf of the former Members pending, the press made great play of his involvement in prosecutions of the poor for nutting.[11] Initially more astute and knowledgeable than Fyler, Heathcote's advice and contacts helped to secure the election petition's defeat, but his differences with his sponsors and a hostile press made him an ineffective Member and a convenient scapegoat when the corporation failed to secure amendments to bills and tariff concessions.[12] Not surprisingly, some confusion occurred between him and the three Heathcote Members for Boston, Hampshire and Rutland. His voting record was pro-Catholic and essentially Whig. He spoke almost exclusively on matters affecting Coventry and should probably not be credited with interventions on behalf of the ship owners, 4 May, 15 June 1827, 24 Mar. 1828. No speech can safely be attributed to him after May 1829. He paired for Catholic relief, 6 Mar., and voted for inquiry into the Barrackpoor mutiny, 22 Mar. 1827. Representing the corporation, he vainly opposed the Coventry magistracy bill, which extended the county justices' jurisdiction to the borough, in speeches and as a minority teller, 22 May, 8 June, presenting hostile petitions, 23, 31 May, and by moving adjournments and repeatedly forcing divisions, 11, 15, 18 June, when the third reading was eventually carried by 65-55.[13] He voted in the Canning government's majority for the Canadian waterways grant, 12 June 1827. Having missed the start of the 1828 session through illness,[14] he presented protectionist petitions from the wool producers of Cargill, Perthshire, 18 Apr., and Caernarvonshire, 17 June, the landowners of Cargill, 24 Apr., and the leadminers of Dolwyddelan and Betws-y-Coed on the Caernarvon-Denbigh border, 9 June 1828. He spoke and voted against the Customs Acts bill, 1 May, 4 July, and divided for Catholic relief, 12 May, and for information on civil list pensions, 20 May. He may have been the Heathcote named as minority teller for postponing the usury laws repeal bill, 19 June 1828. The Wellington ministry's patronage secretary Planta considered his support for Catholic emancipation in 1829 'doubtful', but he declared for it, 3 Mar. When Coventry's hostile petition was brought up by Fyler that day, he condemned the means by which rival petitions 'Against Popery' and 'For Popery' had been got up and signatures presented as poll results: '3,915:903 – Majority for the Protestant Ascendancy 3012'. He spoke similarly on presenting the pro-Catholic petition, 9 Mar. He voted for emancipation, 6 Mar. (but not on 30 Mar.), and to permit Daniel O'Connell to sit without swearing the oath of supremacy, 18 May. He divided against the locally unpopular silk trade bill, 1 May, and voted to transfer East Retford's seats to Birmingham, 5 May 1829. His brother Henry's death, 5 May, his own purchase of the Fenton Spring coal seam, 1 Nov. 1829, and the disclosure that year of bad investments by his father preoccupied him, and he received a month's leave on account of family illness, 8 Mar. 1830.[15] His poor attendance and failure to press the cause of the distressed Coventry ribbon weavers prompted calls for his immediate resignation, and 1,600 signed a memorial to this effect.[16] Spurning it, he announced, 4 Apr. 1830:

> I have no intention of relinquishing my seat for Coventry, previous to a dissolution ... nor any desire to occupy it one day afterwards. In the meantime I shall take leave to exercise my own discretion as to the period when my attendance in the House may be most likely to promote the interests of my constituents or the public.[17]

From 28 Apr. 1830 he divided steadily with the revived Whig opposition, including for Jewish emancipation, 17 May. Later that month both Coventry papers carried critical reviews of his recent votes.[18] He stood down at the 1830 dissolution.

A prominent figure at Staffordshire meetings in 1831 and 1832, Heathcote overcame his initial reluctance to support the Grey ministry's reform bill, declared for the ballot and triennial parliaments and unsuccessfully contested the new Stoke constituency as a Liberal in 1832. He prevailed there in January 1835, but retired a year later.[19] Deterred by encroaching industrialization, which he had promoted, from living at Longton, he and his third wife settled at Apedale Hall. He died in May 1850 near Geneva, where he had gone for health reasons, having bequeathed everything except his entailed estates to his widow.[20]

[1] IGI (Staffs). [2] E.D. Heathcote, *Fams. of Heathcote*, 198-9; Potteries Mus. Hanley, Heathcote of Longton Hall mss [NRA 36839] D4842/11/1/22-32; *VCH Staffs.* viii. 230. [3] *Gent. Mag.* (1813), ii. 403; Derbys. RO, Wilmot Horton mss D3155/7157-60, 7167, 7168; IGI (Staffs). [4] *VCH Staffs.* viii. 229; Heathcote mss 11/2/10-12, 34-36; PROB 11/1666/84; IR26/957/145; *Dyott's Diary*, ii. 96. [5] Derbys. RO, Gresley of Drakelow mss D77/41/1, Fowler to Gresley, 7 July; *Staffs. Advertiser*, 19 July 1823. [6] *Staffs. Advertiser*, 26 July, 2, 9 Aug. 1823; J.C. Wedgwood, *Staffs. Parl. Hist.* 48; C. Hardy and I. Bailey, 'Downfall of Gower Interest in Staffs. Boroughs', *Colls. Hist. Staffs.* (1950-1), 278-81. [7] Add. 40357, ff. 114, 190A; 40369, f. 70. [8] Gresley mss D77/36/4, Mrs. Levett to Gresley [27, 29, 30 Nov.]; 36/5, Heathcote to same, 30 Nov.; D3038/2/2, Tomlinson to same, 26 Nov. 1827. [9] *The Times*, 12-17, 19, 21, 28 June; *Coventry Herald*, 23 June; *Coventry Mercury*, 25 June 1826. [10] *Coventry Herald*, 9 June; *Coventry Mercury*, 12 June 1826. [11] *Globe*, 9 Oct.; *The Times*, 13 Oct.; *Coventry Herald*, 13 Oct.; *Coventry Mercury*, 15 Oct., 26 Nov. 1826. [12] Coventry Archives PA14/10/5, 62-65; *Coventry Herald*, 9, 16 Mar. 1827. [13] *The Times*, 24 May, 1, 16, 19 June 1827. [14] *Coventry Herald*, 9 May 1828. [15] Heathcote mss 11/2/27, 29, 36. [16] *The Times*, 1 Mar.; *Coventry Mercury*, 28 Mar., 4 Apr. 1830. [17] *Coventry Mercury*, 11 Apr. 1830. [18] *Coventry Herald*, 28 May; *Coventry Mercury*, 30 May 1830. [19] *Staffs. Mercury*, 16 June, 17 Nov., 15 Dec. 1832, 10 Jan. 1835; Wedgwood, 87, 90, 92, 96. [20] *VCH Staffs.* viii. 231; PROB 8/244; 11/2129/208.

M.M.E.

HEATHCOTE, Sir William, 5th bt. (1801–1881), of Hursley, nr. Winchester, Hants.[1]

HAMPSHIRE	1826–1831
HAMPSHIRE NORTH	1837–17 Mar. 1849
OXFORD UNIVERSITY	7 Feb. 1854–1868

b. 17 May 1801, o.s. of Rev. William Heathcote, preb. of Winchester and rect. of Worting, and Elizabeth, da. of Lovelace Bigg Wither of Manydown, nr. Basingstoke, Hants. *educ.* by Rev. Edward Meyrick at Ramsbury, Wilts.;[2] Winchester 1813; Oriel, Oxf. 1818; fellow, All Souls 1822-5, hon. fellow 1858-*d.*; I. Temple 1822. *m.* (1) 8 Nov. 1825, Caroline Frances (*d.* 3 Mar. 1835), da. of Charles George Perceval†, 1st Bar. Arden, 3s. (1 *d.v.p.*) 1 da.; (2) 18 May 1841, Selina, da. of Evelyn John Shirley*, 4s. (1 *d.v.p.*) 4da. *suc.* fa. 1802; uncle Sir Thomas Freeman Heathcote†, 4th bt., of Hursley as 5th bt. 21 Feb. 1825. *d.* 17 Aug. 1881.

PC 8 Aug. 1870.

Sheriff, Hants 1832-3; chairman, Hants q.s. 1838.

Capt. N. Hants yeoman cav. 1824-7, 1830, maj. 1831.

The branch of the Heathcote family to which this Member belonged was distantly related to the baronets of Normanton Park, Rutland and had been seated at Hursley since 1718. Heathcote's grandfather and namesake had represented Hampshire, 1790-1806, and his uncle Sir Thomas Freeman Heathcote, who

had succeeded as 4th baronet in 1819, from 1808-20.[3] Following the death of his father, a Hampshire clergyman, 29 Mar. 1802, the infant Heathcote was brought up at Manydown, the residence of his maternal grandfather Lovelace Bigg Wither (*d.* 1813), whom he described in an autobiographical fragment as 'the kindest of parents and most venerable of men'. In 1809 he was sent to an 'excellent private school' in Wiltshire, before transferring in 1813 to Winchester, where his mother took a house in the cathedral close. An able, delicate child, he won a gold medal for his poem 'Antigone' in 1817, and took a first class degree at Oriel in 1821. His tutor, the high churchman John Keble, was an abiding influence, and held the living of Hursley from 1835 until his death in 1866. In 1819 Heathcote toured northern England and Scotland with his college contemporaries Arthur Perceval, a nephew of Spencer Perceval, the late prime minister, and later chaplain to George IV, and James Wentworth Buller*. He 'heartily enjoyed' his later travels with Perceval through France, Switzerland, Italy and Germany in 1822, if only for the confirmation they provided for his notions of national superiority. Having acquired a particular antipathy for Italians, he subsequently declared that he 'never wished to leave England again'. In the autumn of 1822 he was elected a fellow of All Souls and commenced his study of the law under the supervision of his cousin John Awdry, an experience which confirmed his belief that 'one may extract amusement from anything'.[4]

Heathcote's preparation for the bar was interrupted by the sudden death of his uncle in February 1825, when he succeeded to the baronetcy and to Hursley. Keble offered commiserations on his being 'called at once to a post in society so full of temptations and burdens', the latter of which became readily apparent when it emerged that Freeman Heathcote had left the bulk of his disposable property, including land in Ireland, to the son of his butler, whom he had adopted. The family historian attributes this to resentment at the rejection of his offer to do the same for his nephew, though he had taken a sufficiently avuncular interest in his educational progress, and probably framed his will on the basis of an overestimation of the intrinsic value of the Hampshire estate, which was seriously damaged by the collapse in the market for timber.[5] With the sole exception of a silver vase, Heathcote was required to purchase all the furniture and fittings, valued at £10,000, as well as adjacent non-entailed land 'essential to the comfortable enjoyment of the property', which was worth some £80,000.[6] He raised the money 'in different ways ... having, at the time of Sir Thomas's death, no more than £3,000 belonging to me'. (His father's will had been sworn under a meagre £2,000.)[7] Thus preoccupied, he did not take up residence until after his marriage in November 1825 to Perceval's sister Caroline, a 'deeply religious spirit'.[8] His elevation to the county bench and admission to the freedom of Southampton during 1826 confirmed his accession to the county elite.[9] A 'good horseman', he was already a captain of the yeomanry, in whose activities he found 'that pleasure and relaxation which other men find in field sports, for which he had no taste'.[10] In January 1826 he became vice-president of Hampshire Agricultural Society, and he acted as steward of Winchester and Southampton races during the summer.[11]

In anticipation of a general election, Heathcote announced his candidacy for Hampshire in October 1825.[12] He secured the support of George Purefoy Jervoise, the opposition-inclined retiring Member, as well as the evident acquiescence of the Liverpool government, to whom he was expected to offer general support, though his brief hustings speech in 1826 contained nothing more than a ritual affirmation of independence and a frank admission of his political naivety.[13] He was returned unopposed, as he reported to Awdry, 21 June, 'with perfect unanimity and good humour'.[14] In late December 1826 he chaired a meeting in support of the establishment of a public library in Winchester.[15] For the ensuing session of Parliament he took a house in Old Palace Yard, Westminster.[16] He voted against Catholic relief, 6 Mar. 1827, 12 May 1828. On 28 Mar. 1827 he was granted a month's leave on urgent business after serving on an election committee. He evidently shared the hostility to Canning and his ministry evinced by Perceval, who on 8 May urged him to look to the Lords as a bulwark against Catholic emancipation and 'not be cast down at the appearance of public affairs'.[17] He had returned to Hursley by 27 June, when Keble wrote to complain of the creeping secularism of 'the age', noting that 'there never was a time when an honest man might be more useful in Parliament, and I am glad you are in it'.[18] In the light of economic conditions, Heathcote granted a 15 per cent rent remission to his tenants in April. He attended a meeting of the Hampshire Agricultural Association in July.[19] He presented petitions for repeal of the Test Acts, 7, 8 June 1827, 21, 28 Feb., and voted thus, 26 Feb. 1828.[20] His popularity with the Dissenters was evident at the following general election, though in later years he supported the retention of university entrance tests and lost precious estate income by his absolute refusal to take non-Anglican tenants.[21] On 16 June he was in a minority against restricting the circulation in England

of Scottish and Irish small banknotes. That August he was listed as a subscriber to the King's College, London fund.[22] He seconded the sole candidate for the vacant Hampshire coronership, 1 Oct., presided at a meeting of the county Horticultural Society, 10 Oct. 1828, and was nominated as a visiting magistrate for lunatic asylums later that month.[23] He presented petitions from Hampshire parishes against the Wellington ministry's concession of Catholic emancipation, 4 Mar., when he also brought up one from the clergy of Surrey and Hampshire, 12, 25, 30 Mar. 1829. As Planta, the patronage secretary, had anticipated the previous month, he voted steadily against the measure, 6, 18, 27, 30 Mar., for which he was commended by a Gosport meeting, 6 Apr.[24] That month he granted another rent reduction to his tenants and presented a trophy for the best piece of home-spun cloth at a meeting of the Hampshire Agricultural Society.[25] He was in a minority for protection of the silk trade, 1 May. At a Southampton meeting of the Society for the Propagation of the Gospels in the colonies, 23 Apr., he ventured the opinion that the 'benign influence of our apostolical church should be commensurate with the extent of our national domination'.[26] He was in the minority of 14 against the Maynooth grant, 22 May. The Ultra leader Sir Richard Vyvyan*, with whom he had resided in London for a spell in 1826, visited him in October, and reckoned him to be 'strongly opposed' to the administration.[27] It has been suggested that Heathcote, who named a son after Vyvyan the following year, may have acted as a go-between in his negotiations with Lord Palmerston* for the formation of an alternative ministry.[28]

At his estate audit of November 1829 he announced another remission in rents and hoped for 'brighter prospects' for farmers.[29] He distributed blankets and foodstuffs in his locality in January 1830, when it was reported that his 'extensive charitable donations are frequently acknowledged with gratitude by the poor'.[30] He was surely the 'Heathcote' present at the Ultra Tory meeting referred to on 15 Feb. by Sir Edward Knatchbull, for whose amendment to the address on distress he had voted, 4 Feb.[31] He presented Hampshire petitions complaining of distress, 22, 23, 26 Feb., 4 Mar., when he named Wellington as the only prominent non-signatory of one from Kingsclere and demanded an 'effectual remedy' for what he perceived as a permanent problem, and 5, 16 Mar., when he asserted that 'nothing short of a serious reduction' of taxation 'would have the effect of relieving the country'. He spoke in similar terms at a county meeting, 10 Mar., when his votes for military reductions, 19, 22 Feb., were applauded, but he cautioned that there were 'a great many difficulties to overcome' on parliamentary reform, against which he had divided, 18 Feb. A demand for this featured in the meeting's petition, with which he nonetheless expressed his 'entire concurrence' on presenting it, 16 Mar.[32] According to a local press report, he was in the majority against the Bathurst and Dundas pensions, on which ministers were defeated, 26 Mar.[33] He was in minorities for the reduction of grants for official salaries, 10 May, South American missions, 7 June, and the Nova Scotia establishment, 14 June. He divided against the second reading of the sale of beer bill, 4 May, presented hostile petitions that day and 11 May, and voted in favour of amendments to restrict on-consumption, 21 June, 1 July. He voted against Jewish emancipation, 17 May 1830.

The rumblings of opposition prior to the general election of 1830 were not directed at Heathcote, who was returned unopposed after a bland profession of 'perfect independence'.[34] He attended a meeting of the Hampshire Horticultural Society, 10 Sept., and dined with his tenants, 4 Oct.[35] He presented anti-slavery petitions, 5 Nov. Ministers listed him as one of the 'violent Ultras', and he duly voted against them in the crucial division on the civil list, 15 Nov. Having arrived in Winchester at the height of the 'Swing' disturbances, 20 Nov., he secured a vulnerable militia arsenal, organized civil defences until the arrival of military reinforcements, and confronted an armed group of labourers near the city, of whom the ring-leaders were arrested.[36] The family historian recounts that a number of his tenants, concerned at the possibility of reprisals, spontaneously formed themselves into a personal bodyguard, which became the nucleus of a revived militia troop.[37] It is certain that the yeomanry were re-established under his local command, a move he applauded as 'the only good result' of the riots.[38] In his response to the official inquiry, he noted the 'extraordinary' number of skilled workers who had been involved in the disorder, which he interpreted as 'evidence that a revolutionary spirit has been infused into the people, in some parts at least'.[39] This viewpoint was echoed in his subsequent alarmist response to parliamentary reform, though Lord Ellenborough reported him to be one of the Ultras who were 'neuter' on the subject, 9 Feb. 1831.[40] He presented a Gosport petition for reform, 10 Feb., and another, from the same place, welcoming the Grey ministry's reform bill, 19 Mar., with which it was surmised locally that he did not concur.[41] At a county meeting two days before, he had complained that the bill was biased against the agricultural interest and gave an excessive representation to Ireland, before concluding, amid hisses, that it

'might lead to good, but he feared it would not'.[42] He offered the House a less circumspect prediction that it would bring 'the most serious evils to the country' and 'severe retribution' on the government, 22 Mar., when he voted against the second reading. But he conceded that public opinion was overwhelmingly in its favour, for which he blamed 'the indifference of the House of Commons to the distresses of the people', 29 Mar. He signed a Hampshire declaration against the bill and divided in favour of Gascoyne's wrecking amendment, 19 Apr. 1831.[43]

At the ensuing general election Heathcote declined a contest against two reformers, among them his neighbour and friend Charles Shaw Lefevre, who paid him a generous tribute on the hustings.[44] He had no regrets, telling Awdry, by now a Bombay judge, 10 Aug., 'I am enjoying myself this summer much more than I should had I still been a Member of Parliament, working away at the reform bill in St. Stephen's, a place with which I have done as I hope forever'. On 30 Oct. 1831 he reflected on his own part in recent political upheavals:

> I helped, as you saw, to turn out the late government ... Bitterly as I now deplore the existence of the present, I do not think, with the lights I then had, I could have done differently. Of course I was prepared and wished for a Whig government, but I do not think, on any ordinary principles of calculation, it was on the cards that they would have exhibited so complete a want of principle as ... these people have managed to do.[45]

For a time his public work was confined to his locality, where he promoted allotment schemes and helped to finance the rebuilding of churches.[46] In June 1832 he inaugurated a prize at Winchester school 'to promote a knowledge ... chiefly of the principles of the Christian religion, as defined by the Church of England'.[47] That February he had reluctantly accepted the office of sheriff, which disqualified him from standing for either Hampshire division at the general election. Wellington surmised that he would not have done so in any case, but noted that there was 'no man better qualified to represent the county with such claims to its confidence', 7 Oct. 1832.[48] Heathcote did not officiate at the election, having lately been concussed in a riding accident sustained on a yeomanry exercise, which left him permanently prone to headaches.[49]

In the post-Reform Act period Heathcote sank further into despondency over public affairs. He told Awdry, who had hitherto inclined towards the Whigs, 11 Apr. 1833, that

> the progress of the revolution (of which the reform bill was, in my opinion, the first act) has been so much more

rapid than I anticipated, and the measures of government so much more violent and unprincipled, that ... I should think that you must doubt whether you were not a little hasty in distinguishing in your last letter ... between Lord Grey and [Henry] Hunt*, at least if you supposed Lord Grey to be the *less* revolutionary character of the two.

He railed against the proposed reform of the municipal corporations and at the number of 'low men' in the Commons, 9 Feb. 1834, and in a letter to the antiquary, the Rev. Philip Bliss, expressed 'satisfaction' at William's IV's dismissal of the Melbourne administration, which had been 'so unprincipled and incompetent', 17 Dec. 1834.[50] The Whigs, he informed Awdry, 11 Mar. 1836, 'have proceeded on *theories* more or less supported by general reasoning, rather than on the safe foundation of English precedent and experience', and should have followed the lead of Burke, not Fox. He regarded Buonapartist despotism as the inevitable consequence of the shift towards democracy, yet expressed 'no partiality' for Wellington or Peel, and in the course of a diatribe against centralization, criticized the latter's 'French police'. At the general election of 1837 he allowed himself to be nominated for North Hampshire and was returned unopposed with Shaw Lefevre. This distinction was, he told Awdry, 'so hateful to me that I am not willing to enlarge on the subject'. He was far more gratified at becoming chairman of the quarter sessions the following year.[51] He was classed as a Conservative, a term he derided as an example of 'the cant of the day', and opposed repeal of the corn laws in 1846.[52] Three years afterwards he retired, citing 'continued ill health', but he recovered sufficiently to accept an invitation to succeed Sir Robert Inglis* as Member for Oxford University in 1854.[53] Two years later the American author Richard Henry Dana visited Hursley, 'a large brick house ... [which] cannot be called handsome, but ... is ... convenient and stately'. He was captivated by 'the delightful countenance and delicate manners' of his host, who had hitherto 'never had a contested election, either for Oxford or Hampshire, though often chosen in the middle of high party feeling, and he is not a compromise man, but a decided Tory and Tractarian'.[54] Heathcote's biographer asserts that he was Shaw Lefevre's preference to succeed him as Speaker, while Lord Derby certainly considered him as a fallback candidate for the colonial office in 1858, but he remained a backbencher until failing health forced his final retirement at the dissolution of 1868.[55] He continued to regard public events as a progressive erosion of the natural order. In a revealing aside to Sir John Coleridge, Keble's biographer and a judge in king's bench, he bemoaned the descent of political leadership to 'the worst and most unprincipled stratum of English society, viz. the so-called middle classes', 11 Oct. 1858.[56] In 1870 he was sworn a member of the privy council 'in recognition of his long life of public usefulness'.[57]

Heathcote died at Hursley in August 1881. He was eulogized by Coleridge as 'a perfect specimen of the old-fashioned, high bred, highly cultivated country gentleman', and by his neighbour the 4th earl of Carnarvon, as 'the highest product of a class and school of thought that is fast disappearing'.[58] Behind the mask of gentility, his biographer perceived that he was 'an abidingly anxious, if not an unhappy man'. Much of his personal life was as vexatious to him as the trend of public affairs. His first wife died in March 1835 after a routine operation, and her loss was followed by that of his youngest son from his second marriage, a great favourite, in June 1858. His eldest son William Perceval Heathcote (1826-1903) joined the army against his wishes, lived beyond the means of the family and adopted the creed of his wife, an Irish Catholic.[59] Even worse, William Arthur Heathcote (1853-1924), his eldest grandson and the heir presumptive to the baronetcy, became a Jesuit priest, while another, George Wyndham Heathcote (1855-1930), was a navy deserter. Both grandsons were specifically excluded from Heathcote's will of 22 July 1881, by which his widow received an annuity of £1,000 in addition to her marriage settlement and a life interest in Hursley, which was directed to be let thereafter to an Anglican. The residue was applied to the preservation of his Hampshire estate, which stretched to over 14,000 acres in 1883, but was broken up and sold before the turn of the century.[60]

[1] See F. Awdry, *A Country Gentleman of 19th Cent.* (1906). [2] Ibid. 199. [3] E.D. Heathcote, *Heathcote Fam.* 116. [4] Awdry, 7-30, 64-65, 149, 199-200; Hants RO, Heathcote mss 63M84 234/11, 12, 14. [5] Awdry, 23, 31; Heathcote, 143; Heathcote mss 234/18, 21, 22. [6] Awdry, 33, 96, 201-2; PROB 11/1698/203; IR26/1045/322. [7] Awdry, 202; PROB 6/178/396. [8] Awdry, 33, 36-37. [9] Wellington mss WP1/824/3; 848/15; *Southampton Corporation Jnls. 1815-35*, p. 41. [10] Heathcote, 144; Awdry, 129. [11] *Hants Telegraph*, 23 Jan., 22 May, 31 July 1826. [12] Ibid. 10 Oct. 1825. [13] Ibid. 24 Oct. 1825; 12, 19 June 1826; *Hants Chron.* 19 June 1826; Wellington mss WP1/829/3. [14] Awdry, 35-36. [15] *Hants Telegraph*, 1 Jan. 1827. [16] Awdry, 202. [17] Heathcote mss 480/1, 2. [18] Awdry, 38-40. [19] *Hants Telegraph*, 23 Apr., 30 July 1827. [20] *The Times*, 8, 9 June 1827. [21] *Hants Telegraph*, 6 Sept. 1830; Awdry, 96, 113, 160. [22] *Hants Chron.* 4 Aug. 1828. [23] Ibid. 6, 13, 30 Oct. 1828. [24] Ibid. 13 Apr. 1829. [25] Ibid. 6, 20 Apr. 1829. [26] Ibid. 27 Apr. 1829. [27] Awdry, 41; B.T. Bradfield, 'Sir Richard Vyvyan and Fall of Wellington Government', *Univ. of Birmingham Hist. Jnl.* xi. (1968), 148. [28] K. Bourne, *Palmerston*, 302. [29] *Hants Chron.* 9 Nov. 1829. [30] *Hants Telegraph*, 18 Jan. 1830. [31] Bradfield, 152. [32] *Hants Telegraph*, 15 Mar. 1830. [33] *Hants Chron.* 5 Apr. 1830. [34] *Portsmouth Herald*, 8 Aug.; *Hants Telegraph*, 9 Aug. 1830; Wellington mss WP4/4/3/20. [35] *Hants Telegraph*, 13 Sept.; *Hants Chron.* 4 Oct. 1830. [36] R. Foster, *Politics of County Power*, 77-79; *Baring Jnls.* i. 74;

Wellington mss WP4/2/2/2,4,11,12. [37] Heathcote, 145. [38] Awdry, 46-47. [39] Foster, 70-71. [40] *Three Diaries*, 49. [41] *Hants Telegraph*, 13 Dec. 1830, 14 Mar. 1831. [42] Ibid. 21 Mar. 1831. [43] *Hants Chron.* 18 Apr. 1831. [44] Wellington mss WP4/3/4/19; *Hants Chron.* 2, 9 May 1831. [45] Awdry, 43-48. [46] Heathcote, 146, 152. [47] Add. 34571, f. 114. [48] Wellington mss WP4/4/1/10; 4/3/20, 24. [49] Awdry, 49-50; *Hants Chron.* 17 Dec. 1832. [50] Add. 34571, f. 404; Awdry 49-50, 52-53. [51] Awdry, 66-71. [52] Ibid. 71-72; *Dod's Parl. Companion* (1847), 182. [53] Awdry, 89, 103, 107. [54] C.F. Adams, *Richard Henry Dana*, 86, 95-96. [55] Awdry, 93, 161-3; *Victoria Letters* (ser. 1), iii. 371; *The Times*, 12 Oct. 1868. [56] Awdry, 121. [57] *The Times*, 22 Aug. 1881. [58] Ibid. 22, 24 Aug. 1881; Heathcote mss 500. [59] Awdry, 6, 59, 86, 92, 119. [60] Heathcote mss 498; *The Times*, 29 Oct. 1881; *VCH Hants*, iii. 407, 420, 449; iv. 413, 492.

H.J.S./P.J.S.

HEBER, Richard (1774–1833), of Hodnet, Salop; Marton, Yorks., and Pimlico Lodge, Mdx.

OXFORD UNIVERSITY   24 Aug. 1821–Feb.
                                                              1826

b. 5 Jan. 1774, 1st s. of Rev. Reginald Heber of Hodnet, rect. of Malpas, Cheshire, and 1st w. Mary, da. and coh. of Rev. Martin Baylie, rect. of Wrentham, Suff. *educ.* Dr. Glasse's sch. Greenford, Mdx. 1783-90; Brasenose, Oxf. 1790. *unm. suc.* fa. to Hodnet and Marton 1804. *d.* 4 Oct. 1833.

Sheriff, Salop 1821-2.

Capt. Hodnet vols. 1803; col. Craven Legion 1804.

Heber's father, who was ordained in 1753, was a fellow of Brasenose until 1766, when he succeeded his elder brother to Hodnet and became a rural clergyman. Marton, the family's original property, did not come into his possession until the death of his brother's widow in 1803. His first wife died soon after Richard Heber's birth and he married again in 1782: the first child of this union was Reginald Heber (1783-1826), later bishop of Calcutta. Richard Heber's bibliomania, which became the mainspring of his life, manifested itself during his schooldays, when his father, frequently irked by his 'debts contracted with booksellers', tried to curb it:

> I cannot say I rejoice in the importation of the cargo of books you mention from abroad, we had before enough and too many, ten times more than were ever read or even looked into. Of multiplying books ... there is neither end nor use. The cacoethes of collecting books draws men into ruinous extravagancies. It is an itch which grows by indulgence and should be nipped in the bud.[1]

At Oxford Heber refined his literary tastes, continued to collect books and earned some reputation as a scholar and *littérateur*. He was a frequent attender at debates in Parliament in the 1790s. He toured Scotland in 1799 and the West of England in 1800, when he

formed a lasting friendship with Walter Scott, whose literary circle he joined: he was later a member of the Roxburghe Club and a contributor to the *Quarterly Review*. He visited France in 1802 and returned before war broke out to busy himself with the volunteers. His father's death in 1804 brought him a handsome inheritance which gave him full rein to indulge his bibliomania.[2] He was a notably generous lender of books to his wide circle of friends.

Heber first appeared as a candidate for Oxford University in the premature canvass of 1805. He went to the poll in 1806 but came a poor third. He was involved in another abortive canvass in 1814, when he was handicapped by doubts as to his firmness on the Catholic question. Suspicions were aroused by his silence on the issue and memories of his support for Lord Grenville in the contest for the chancellorship in 1809. He satisfied his former tutor, who catechized him on the subject, that he was a 'true and steady church and kingman'.[3] The same difficulty arose in the summer of 1821, when he disputed a vacancy with Sir John Nicholl*, a leading opponent of Catholic relief. Heber enjoyed some Whig support, while the premier Lord Liverpool and the home secretary Lord Sidmouth were reported to be 'very favourable' to his pretensions. On the other hand, the assets of his 'popular manners, his great library, his genuine Toryism and his assiduous canvass of near 15 years' were offset by the 'great cry' raised against him by 'the high churchmen', who were said to 'accuse him of travelling in stage coaches, of living at a brewery, of associating with the opposition, and of being favourably disposed towards the Catholics'.[4] Heber assured one correspondent that he was 'no emancipator', his half-brother, though personally in favour of relief, publicized Richard's 'determined hostility' to it, and his committees issued a statement to the same effect, which quelled the doubts and enabled him to establish a decisive lead.[5] The Tory Sir Thomas Fremantle† thought he would 'make a very good Member'; and the Canningite John William Ward* commented that Heber, 'a gentleman and a scholar', was 'likely to act honestly and independently':

> His own notions, for I take him to be a Tory, will naturally lead him to support the government of the day; but he will be content to consider the honour the University has done him as the *end*, and not as a mere stepping-stone to selfish objects of a lower order; he will not sell piecemeal a mark of confidence so honourably and freely conferred upon him.[6]

Despite his reputation for wit and wisdom, Heber signally failed to distinguish himself in the Commons, where his performance was 'by no means answerable to the expectations of many of his constituents'.[7] He divided with government against more extensive tax reductions to relieve distress, 21 Feb., but voted for relaxation of the salt duties, 28 Feb., and admiralty economies, 1 Mar. 1822. It was rumoured in Oxford that he was to make his *début* on Canning's motion to relieve Catholic peers, 30 Apr., but he settled for a silent hostile vote.[8] He voted against the salt duties, 28 June, but for the aliens bill, 19 July. On the Irish estimates, 22 July, he voted against the grant for glebe houses but in favour of that for the publication of government proclamations. When speculating which way Canning would jump after Lord Londonderry's death, John Wilson Croker* included Heber among Members 'inclined' to him who would probably follow him if he went into opposition. Heber wrote a congratulatory letter to Canning when he became foreign secretary.[9] In 1823 he divided more regularly with ministers: against inquiry into the borough franchise, 20 Feb., for the sinking fund, 3, 13 Mar., and against repeal of the Foreign Enlistment Act, 16 Apr., inquiry into the prosecution of the Dublin Orange rioters, 22 Apr., and reform of the Scottish county representation, 2 June. His only known wayward votes were for the recommittal of the silk bill, 9 June, and to incorporate jury trial in the New South Wales bill, 7 July. His only recorded vote in 1824 was against the production of a list of Catholic office-holders in Ireland, 19 Feb., and he was confined with a sprained ankle in March.[10] Next month, in correspondence with the home secretary Peel, his fellow Member for the university, he suggested the addition to the county courts bill of a clause to safeguard the ancient privileges of Oxford and Cambridge.[11] On 14 May 1824 he presented a Magdalen College petition against the St. Katharine's Dock bill.[12]

Heber was an *habitué* of Holland House, and Lady Holland had this to say of him in 1822: 'His memory is quite remarkable, and his ready application of verses and stories smart and brisk. He is a valuable inmate to help on conversation'.[13] In 1823 her son Henry Edward Fox* wrote:

> He is good-natured and has acquired a good deal with all his book-collecting and reading, but is rather in the Oxford style of humbug, which is so very odious. I rather like him. He is very much given to drinking and eating, which his *friends*!!! say has deadened his understanding.[14]

Heber was a founder member of the Athenaeum Club and, early in 1825, Lady Holland noted:

> This activity has done him harm at Oxford, as they complain of his drawing off members from the University

Club – indeed I fear Heber is not popular at Oxford, as he keeps no house nor has spoken in Parliament.[15]

This was true. In May 1825 the provost of Oriel encouraged Heber to allay the growing dissatisfaction with his anonymity in the House by the 'trifling sacrifice' of giving 'some *public* evidence of attention to the political feelings of the University'; but he merely cast silent votes against the Catholic relief bill, 1 Mar., 10 May. He also voted for the bill to suppress the Catholic Association, 25 Feb., and against regulation of the Irish franchise, 26 Apr. On 28 July 1825 he left for the continent, and the following month he informed his half-sister Mrs. Cholmondeley that he had decided to resign his seat:

> Towards this I have been turning onward for some time and the impending dissolution seemed the proper moment to decide. Not taking an *active* part in its proceedings, I found the House somewhat of a fag and a bore and the time it took up unprofitably spent. All things considered, I do not think I shall repent my resolution.[16]

The true reason for Heber's precipitate retreat from English public life was less innocent. At some time in 1825, probably in July, he made sexual advances at the Athenaeum to two young men, including the son of his agent, one Fisher, who threatened to bring charges against him. The affair was brought to Peel's notice by Robert Wilmot Horton*, a close friend of Heber's half-brother, who had 'the strongest suspicions' that Reginald Heber had gone to India in 1823 'in consequence of his having *obtained* some sort of knowledge' of Richard's moral laxity. Heber's friend, Henry Hobhouse, Peel's under-secretary, was enlisted in their attempt to prevent the episode from bringing 'irretrievable ruin' on Heber and in the process 'leaving an almost ineffaceable stain upon his own caste in society'. Heber had at first protested his innocence and determination 'to abide the result'; but eventually he '*admitted* enough' for Hobhouse to advise him to leave the country and take steps to vacate his seat at the dissolution (which was expected in the autumn). He reluctantly complied and by 4 Aug. 1825 was at Calais, whence he wrote to Hobhouse, promising to deal with the matter of his seat, but asking whether he might return for a short while to settle some private business. Hobhouse's reply gave him nothing for his comfort:

> I think the object of those with whom I have recently communicated respecting you is to prevent your retaining the place you have filled in English society; and that if that object can be attained without recourse to legal proceedings, there is no disposition to take those steps, to which they would otherwise recur. Under these circumstances you must judge for yourself of the prudence of

visiting England, taking into the account that since your departure the facts have (I believe) been imparted to Mr. F[isher] ... If you resolve on running the risk, there are cogent reasons, why *I* should neither be party nor privy to the fact of your being here.

He promised not to return 'at *present*', but still prevaricated about his seat. Hobhouse believed he would do nothing about it unless forced to, but was disinclined to exert himself further in the affair. Peel persuaded Hobhouse to reconsider and, agreeing that 'a man who has so disgraced himself' ought to leave Parliament 'both for the sake of himself and the public', he pressed Heber to act. Heber, who was now in Antwerp, 'submitted to the self-abasement suggested to him' and sent letters of resignation, to be forwarded to the Oxford authorities when a dissolution was announced, which ascribed his retreat to 'tedium and a wish to be able to devote his time more exclusively to literary pursuits'. Hobhouse was evidently able to use them to avert a renewed threat, presumably from Fisher, to expose the truth.[17]

The dissolution was postponed, and Heber's resignation was formally submitted in January 1826, when it became 'the topic and wonder' of the moment. Peel, replying to his former tutor's inquiries, blandly replied that 'Heber was so listless last session, and appeared to have such a horror of anything which might by possibility call him up in the House of Commons, that I am hardly surprised at his resignation'.[18] Although there were those who surmised that there was something 'not pleasant' behind it, and Lady Holland had some knowledge of 'Heber's scandalous life', his resignation was generally put down to his awareness of the increasing dissatisfaction in Oxford with his ineptitude as a Member.[19] Lord Dudley (as Ward had become) assured Lord Aberdeen that 'the history of it is simply this, that he could not muster nerves for a single anti-Catholic speech, and was forced by his inconceivable want of moral courage to sacrifice a seat which had cost him 20 years' canvass'.[20] A further convenient blind to the truth was provided by the recent bankruptcy of the leading London bookseller Thomas Thorpe, with whom Heber was thought to have had 'very expensive speculations' which might have caused him 'pecuniary embarrassment'.[21] In May 1826 speculation about the reason's for Heber's flight and retirement was intensified by the publication by Edward Shackell, the owner and editor of *John Bull*, of observations that Heber would not return to England for some time, 'the backwardness of a foreign climate being found more congenial at this season of the year' (7 May); and that the 'complaint, for which ... [he] remains on the conti-

nent, is stated to be occasioned by an over-addiction to *Hartsthorn*'. This was a clear insinuation that Heber's suspiciously close relationship since 1821 with Charles Henry Hartsthorne, a clergyman's son who was 29 years his junior, was a homosexual one and lay behind his withdrawal. Heber himself shrugged off the innuendo, but Hartsthorne, who was also abroad, was summoned home by friends in August 1826 and advised to bring a criminal charge of libel against Shackell. Heber declined Hartsthorne's request to come home to refute the slur, but offered financial aid for the suit. In king's bench, 18 and 28 Nov. 1826, a rule absolute was given against Shackell. The libel action was heard on 20 Oct. 1827, when Shackell, despite his contrition and admission that he had not verified the original story, was found guilty. On 27 Nov. 1827 he was fined £500 for his libel.[22] In the immediate aftermath of the appearance of the insinuations in *John Bull*, Scott was shocked to be told that Heber's retirement was as a result of 'his having been detected in unnatural practices':

> God, God, whom shall we trust? Here is learning, wit, gaiety of temper, high station in society and complete reception everywhere all at once debased and lost by such a degrading bestiality.

Soon afterwards Scott got wind of the intervention of Hobhouse, who had 'detected a warrant for ... [Heber's] trial passing through the [home] office': 'the fairest outsides so often cover the foulest vices'.[23] Later in 1826 Lady Spencer told her husband:

> Abercromby told me yesterday an anecdote about Heber which ... I think proves him to be mad. During the Fonthill sale he was invited to reside at Mr. Bennet's ... and one night after a supper, where he had drunk immoderately, he ... found his way to Miss Bennet's room, and actually assaulted this very pretty young woman so that on her running for protection to her mother's apartment, it was judged fitting to turn him out of doors the next morning.[24]

There was speculation that Heber would 'take orders and slip himself into his own living', but he did not return to England until 1831 and even then, according to an obituary notice, 'not into the society which he had left; for rumours had been in circulation degrading to his moral character'.[25] His health and spirit were wrecked and he lived in exclusion at Pimlico, though to the last he indulged his passion for book collection, which did eventually enmesh him in some financial difficulties. His friend Thomas Dibdin was shocked by 'the emaciated frame, flurried discourse, and uncertain movements of his later years', in contrast to the charm and gaiety of his heyday, when Scott had called him 'Heber the magnificent'.[26] He died at Pimlico in October 1833. Alexander Dyce wrote that he breathed his last *without a friend to close his eyes, and ... broken-hearted*.[27] His will, hidden on a bookshelf, was not found for three months. It was proved under £60,000 on 13 Jan. 1834 by his sole executrix Mrs. Cholmondeley, who received a life interest in all Heber's estate, reckoned to be worth £200,000. The will made no provision for his books, which filled to bursting eight houses in England and Europe. They were disposed of in a series of sales in London, Paris and Ghent, 1834-7, which realized slightly less than £67,000.[28]

[1] *Heber Letters*, 25, 33, 52. [2] Ibid. 53, 55, 79, 87, 91, 99, 113-31, 137-41, 158. [3] Ibid. 213-15, 244-5; *HP Commons, 1790-1820*, ii. 329. [4] *Althorp Letters*, 115; Add. 51659, Whishaw to Lady Holland, 16 July 1821. [5] *Heber Letters*, 288-91; Add. 52011, J. Stuart Wortley to H.E. Fox, 25 July 1821; A. Heber, *Life of Reginald Heber*, ii. 47. [6] Bucks. RO, Fremantle mss D/FR, Sir T. to W.H. Fremantle, 2 Sept. 1821; Ward, *Llandaff Letters*, 289. [7] *Gent. Mag.* (1834), i. 107. [8] *Heber Letters*, 301. [9] Add. 40319, f. 66; Harewood mss, Heber to Canning, 16 Sept. 1822. [10] Add. 40363, f. 34. [11] Add. 40364, f. 179. [12] *The Times*, 15 May 1824. [13] Lord Ilchester, *Chrons. of Holland House*, 31. [14] *Fox Jnl.* 154. [15] Ilchester, 56. [16] *Heber Letters*, 328-31. [17] Add. 40380, ff. 227-31, 234-6, 257, 258, 315; 40381, ff. 166, 169, 220, 284, 310. This episode is overlooked in *Oxford DNB*. It is coyly hinted at by A. Aspinall in *Parl. Affairs*, xiv (1960-1), xiv. 396, 446-50. See also L. Crompton, *Byron and Greek Love*, 46, 357. [18] Add. 40342, ff. 297, 303. [19] *Williams Wynn Corresp.* 341, 343; Add. 51586, Tierney to Lady Holland, 3 Mar.; 51659, Whishaw to same, 26 Jan.; Castle Howard mss, Abercromby to Carlisle, 26 Jan. 1826. [20] Add. 43231, f. 171. [21] Add. 51749, Holland to H.E. Fox, 8 Feb. 1826; Hopetoun mss 167, f. 12. [22] *The Times*, 20, 29 Nov. 1826, 22 Oct., 23 Nov. 1827; *Oxford DNB*. [23] *Scott Jnl.* 162, 170-1. [24] Add.75938, Lady to Lord Spencer, 8 Nov. 1826. [25] *Williams Wynn Corresp.* 343; *Ann. Reg.* (1830), App. to Chron. p. 246. [26] T.F. Dibdin, *Reminiscences*, 429-45. [27] P. Fitzgerald, *The Book Fancier*, 230. [28] *Gent.Mag.* (1834), i. 105-9, 196; *The Times*, 18 Jan. 1834; *Oxford DNB*.

D.R.F.

HELY HUTCHINSON, Hon. Christopher (1767-1826), of Benlomond House, Downshire Hill, Hampstead, Mdx.

| CORK | 8 Jan. 1802-1812 |
| CORK | 1818-26 Aug. 1826 |

b. 5 Apr. 1767, 5th s. of John Hely Hutchinson (formerly Hely), MP [I], provost of Trinity, Dublin (*d.* 1794), and Christiana, da. of Abraham Nixon of Money, co. Wicklow, h. of her gt.-uncle Richard Hutchinson of Knocklofty, co. Tipperary (cr. Baroness Donoughmore [I] 16 Oct. 1783); bro. of Hon. John Hely Hutchinson†. *educ.* Trinity, Dublin 1784; L. Inn 1789, called [I] 1792. *m.* (1) 24 Dec. 1792, Anne Wensley (*d.* 30 Mar. 1796), da. of Sir James Bond, 1st bt., MP [I], of Coolamber, co. Longford, 1s.; (2) 1 Oct. 1818, Anne, da. of Hon. and

Very Rev. Maurice Crosbie, dean of Limerick, wid. of John Brydges Woodcock, 2s. 2da. illegit. *d.* 26 Aug. 1826. MP [I] 1795-6.

Vol. army 1799, lt.-col. 1801.

'Kit' Hely Hutchinson, a 'violent declaimer' noted for his long speeches of 'monotonous energy', had in 1818 regained his seat on the family interest for Cork, where he was known locally as 'the Papist' on account of his support for unqualified Catholic emancipation. His elder brothers Richard, 1st earl of Donoughmore, and John, Baron Hutchinson, both inveterate place-hunters, had long since abandoned any attempt to control him, it being well known that they had 'no influence', but still regularly came to his rescue financially, especially following his second marriage to a spendthrift mistress in 1818.[1] On 6 Feb. that year he had joined Brooks's, sponsored by Lords Hutchinson and Grey.

At the 1820 general election he offered again for Cork amidst expectation of a contest, in which, as Charles Arbuthnot* observed, he 'must, of course, be opposed' by the Liverpool ministry.[2] ('His conduct has been so atrociously violent in the last session and his adhesion to Catholic emancipation without modification or restriction', that it induces 'me to make every effort in my power against him', remarked one elector.)[3] Conscious of the 'thousands' already spent by his family on his seat, on 2 Mar. he told Donoughmore that he was 'quite ready and willing' to decline 'should you and John ... decide that I should do so', for

> though I feel as I ought most grateful for that expenditure ... I never considered the seat for Cork worth *money*, but only (considering that I was an idle man) worth my own exertions, of which I have not been sparing, to recover if possible for the family, what in a great degree was lost perhaps by my own conduct in Parliament.[4]

He persevered, appealing to the 'Protestant electors' to contribute their 'essential' votes to those of the Catholic freeholders, and after a six-day contest was returned at the head of the poll.[5] Pressed at the nomination, he declared himself 'a friend to reform, but the decided enemy of annual parliaments and universal suffrage'. It may have been his condemnation of 'unfortunate' remarks made by the defeated candidate Gerard Callaghan* about the new king's likely death causing another election that prompted a duel with Callaghan's brother Patrick, near the Lough in Cork, 7 Apr.[6] Donoughmore was informed:

> After the first exchange of shots it was supposed that neither had taken effect and the pistols were again put into the hands of the parties, when Daniel Callaghan,

perceiving blood dripping from Christopher's hand, exclaimed that his brother could not fire at a wounded man. Christopher instantly replied that it was a mere scratch. He felt no pain ... and was ready to 'go on'. Daniel Callaghan then said, 'My brother is perfectly satisfied'. The Callaghans then left the ground and the affair terminated ... Christopher is as well as ever he was, except the great apprehension he feels lest Mrs. Hutchinson should think of coming over, which makes him not a little uneasy.[7]

It was later remarked that after the Callaghans had halted proceedings, Hely Hutchinson 'held up his hand in derision, with a finger hanging to it', and exclaimed, 'What sir, is your ... honour satisfied by a scratch like that?'[8] On 10 Apr. 1820 Daniel O'Connell's* wife wrote to her husband:

> I ... cannot divest myself of a dread that a man so delicate as Hutchinson will fall victim to the illness which must proceed from the amputation of his finger. What on earth was the cause of this unfortunate business? The stupid papers give no detail ... I hope ... your letter ... will give me a more satisfactory account of our patriot ... Hutchinson is honest and that is his fault. *They* would wish to put him out of the way ... I anxiously entreat of you ... to take care of yourself. I know your friendship for Hutchinson.[9]

A few days later *The Times* reported that 'one of the fingers of the left hand ... has since been amputated, but we understand he is going on well'.[10]

An assiduous attender, Hely Hutchinson voted with the advanced wing of opposition on all major issues, especially economy, retrenchment and reduced taxation.[11] He warned that repeal of the Irish linen duties would have the 'worst effects', 2 June 1820. He dismissed an army medical board's criticism of Sir William Adams of the Opthalmic Institution that day, 10, 12 July, when, after exonerating the *Morning Chronicle* from a supposed 'misrepresentation' of his views, he was called to order for proceeding to offer another 'high encomium' on Adams.[12] He was granted a fortnight's leave on account of family illness, 5 June. He criticized the regulations governing the Irish spirit trade, 15, 18 July, when he unsuccessfully moved for information on Irish distillers, who were about to be driven 'completely out of the market', and campaigned steadily for their reform thereafter.[13] In a speech in which the 'impatience of the House ... long prevented him from being heard', he defended the role of his brother Lord Hutchinson as the king's envoy to Queen Caroline at St. Omer, denounced the 'highly censurable' conduct of ministers in the affair and argued and voted against proceeding by a select committee, 22 June. On 17 July he condemned the

'imprudent agitation of this question', saying that although he was 'a sincere friend to the liberty of the press, to economy' and 'the reform of every abuse', of which the 'greatest' was the state of the representation, he 'would most strenuously resist any attempt made to overawe Parliament'. Lord Hutchinson and Donoughmore's support for ministerial measures against the queen made him temporarily unpopular in Cork, from where an agent expressed a hope that his 'conduct when Parliament meets will set all to rights', and assured him, 'Your Cork friends are not the men to quarrel with you because your brothers are personal favourites with a king', 11 Dec. 1820.[14] He voted with opposition in her support, 26 Jan., 6, 14 Feb. 1821. He opposed a petition for repeal of the Union duties, 16 Feb., explaining that many commercial 'engagements' depended on their continuation, 30 Apr. He voted for Catholic claims, 28 Feb., but denounced the accompanying securities as 'useless, dangerous and unwarrantable', despite the unpopularity this might cause him in Cork and the pleas of friends who had 'deprecated his opposition as injurious to the Catholic cause', 27, 28 Mar.[15] 'We got through all the clauses', Joseph Phillimore informed Lord Buckingham next day

> but Hutchinson opened a broadside upon us, which in the earlier stages of the bill might have sunk the whole concern, inasmuch as he characterized the second bill (now consolidated with the first) as a bill of pains, penalties, degradation, etc., imposed on the Roman Catholic clergy. The attack, however, recoiled upon the promoter of it, and the discussion was so conducted as to assist the bill.[16]

'I don't think that Hely Hutchinson will do you any harm', Buckingham replied.[17] 'The Irish Catholics have been betrayed by their representatives and ... pretended friends in Parliament, with the exception of Kit', who 'has heard ... the ... protests ... of the clergy', observed Lord Hutchinson, 29 Mar.[18] On 2 Apr. Hely Hutchinson announced that he would abstain from voting on the bill's third reading, as it had been 'rendered almost valueless' by the oaths required of the Catholic clergy. 'Hutchinson and Maurice Fitzgerald, declaring their disapprobation of these regulations, and agreeing with the opinions expressed by the priests, were hardly prevailed upon by their friends to give their vote', observed Henry Bankes* that day.[19] On 15 Mar. Hely Hutchinson praised Hume's campaign against the 'excessive and extravagant' estimates but disavowed any party motives for having 'joined in', explaining that he 'acknowledged no leader' except the 'distresses of the people'.[20] He remonstrated against the 'disgraceful' detention of Buonaparte at St. Helena, 29 Mar. He made an 'able speech' at the

London Tavern parliamentary reform meeting, 4 Apr., and voted accordingly, 18 Apr., 9 May 1821, 25 Apr. 1822 (as a pair), 20 Feb. 1823, 24 Apr., 2 June 1823.[21] On 4 May 1821 he denounced Britain's 'blind' foreign policy towards the Holy Alliance, the 'tyrants of the continent', who were ruining the 'liberties of the world', and moved unsuccessfully for inquiry. In what Henry Brougham* dreaded would be a speech by 'Kit Hutchinson upon the world in general', he 'launched' into a motion and was a minority teller for an address to the king against the interference of the Holy Alliance with independent states, 20 June.[22] Henry Grey Bennet* described it as:

> a long set speech, very tiresome and heavy, travelling over every part of the subject and doing justice to none, the principle good and sound, although at times somewhat extravagant and rather tending to embroil us in foreign disputes ... The numbers were for the motion (which was remarkably ill drawn up, and as awkwardly worded as it could be) 28 to 117.[23]

Speaking in similar terms, he charged Lord Castlereagh*, the foreign secretary, with abetting the Alliance's 'system of tyranny', 29 June 1821, and of lending his 'best support to the unholy cause of slavery and injustice', which if he 'knew anything about foreign affairs, he must be well aware of', 5 Feb. 1822. He demanded repeal of the 'disgraceful and insulting' Seditious Meetings Act, 8 May 1821. Ignoring interruptions by coughing, he defended the *John Bull* journalist Collier against charges of a breach of privilege, 11 May.[24] He objected to the appointment of Irish revenue commissioners by the crown, 18 June 1821.

Hely Hutchinson condemned the 'severe measures' to suppress Irish disturbances outlined in the king's speech, 5 Feb., and demanded inquiry into the causes of unrest, warning that 'hanging, transporting, imprisoning or scourging those unhappy people' would have no effect while 'grievances existed', 7 Feb. 1822. That day he was a minority teller against the suspension of habeas corpus and the Irish insurrection bills, against which he campaigned and voted steadily thereafter. He divided for inquiry into the Scottish royal burghs, 20 Feb. He was granted three weeks' leave on urgent private business, 27 Mar. He demanded abolition of the 'intolerable' Irish potato tithes, 15 May, welcomed the appearance of the Irish tithes bill 'without committing himself', 14 June, but voted for Newport's amendment to it, 19 June, when he observed that 'a pledge of the House to reduce the calamitous abuses of the tithe system would be attended with the most beneficial results'. He praised ministers for their remission of the Irish window tax and relief of the leather tax, but regretted that there had not been further salt tax reductions, 24 May. He divided against the second reading of the Irish constables bill, 7 June. He was appointed to the select committee on the Irish linen trade, 17 June, and warned that any loss of its protection would be 'detrimental', 21 June. On 15 July 1822 he implored the House to condemn the 'barbarous ferocity' of the Turks against the Greeks and criticized ministers for their 'degraded' and 'unmanly' inaction in foreign policy. He welcomed their firmer stance in the king's speech, 5 Feb. 1823, but believed that 'stronger language' would have 'struck terror into the congregated despots of the continent', which was 'looking up to the conduct of this country'. 'I am grateful that you approve of the few words I said on the address', he informed Donoughmore, 13 Feb., adding that for the next week he had been confined to his house 'by sore eyes and pains in the head'.[25] On 12 Feb. he endorsed Hume's motion for withholding the supplies and demanded inquiry into public expenditure. He criticized and obtained papers on the French imprisonment of John Bowring, 28 Feb. He voted for inquiry into the Irish church, 4 Mar. 1823, 6 May 1824, 14 June 1825. He refuted the allegations of a petition condemning the conduct of Irish Jesuits, 5 Mar. 1823. Next day he announced that 'having for years maintained an angry opposition against government with respect to Irish affairs', he 'felt it his duty, now that he saw' their 'anxiety to do everything that was right and proper', to support the Irish tithes bill. He attacked the crown's 'despotic' power to dismiss officers without court martial and called for the reinstatement of his 'dear and valued friend' Sir Robert Wilson*, whose 'exertions on the day of the queen's funeral had prevented the spilling of blood', 14 Mar. On the 28th Lord Hutchinson commented that 'Kit, I see by the Cork paper, is on the city grand jury of Cork, though I have not heard one word from him since his arrival in Ireland'.[26] Writing to Donoughmore, 4 Apr., Hely Hutchinson observed that O'Connell had 'seemed much surprised a few days since when I asked him if he had heard that the [Catholic] question was not to come on. Since, I have not seen him'.[27] On 22 Apr. his uncharacteristic absence from the House the previous week was attributed to 'a severe feverish cold'.[28] He voted for inquiry into the prosecution of the Dublin Orange rioters that day, but protested at the interference of government and unsuccessfully moved for a six-month extension, 26 May. He spoke and was a minority teller against the Irish joint tenancy bill next day. He complained that the inquiry into the conduct of chief baron O'Grady of the Irish exchequer court had heard insufficient evidence, 17 June, and was a teller for the minority of 19 against going into committee, 2 July, and for the majority of 38 to terminate proceedings against an individual whom he believed 'to be innocent', 9 July. He voted for inquiry into Dublin disturbances and demanded one on the state of Ireland, 24 June 1823, for which he divided, 11 May 1824. He feared that Hume's proposal to abolish the Irish viceroy would occasion 'great mischief', 25 June 1823. He spoke and was in the minority to refer the Catholic petition complaining of the administration of justice in Ireland to the grand judicial committee, 26 June 1823. 'I was ably supported by Hutchinson', Brougham told O'Connell next day.[29]

Hely Hutchinson voted for information on Catholic burials, 6 Feb., and presented a petition against the Catholic burials bill, with which he disagreed, 1 Apr. 1824. He divided for returns of the number of Irish Catholic office-holders, 19 Feb. Next day he warned that without concessions, the Irish people 'might at length' be driven to 'dangerous extremities'. He opposed a motion for papers on ribbon men as 'injurious to the best interests of Ireland', 11 Mar. He was in the minority against the grant for Protestant Irish charter schools, 15 Mar., but welcomed that to the Royal Cork Institution as a 'great boon', 19 Mar., and defended that given to the Kildare Place Society, 29 Mar. He warned that Irishmen engaged in coarse linen manufacture would be 'reduced to starvation and driven to acts of outrage' by repeal of the linen bounties, 18, 22 Mar., 3 May, and was a teller for the minority of 26 against the third reading of the related customs bill, 27 May. On 23 Mar. he defended his use of the 'strongest language' in 'reprobation of the miscalled Holy Alliance' and condemned the aliens bill as 'unnecessary' and part of the same 'system of tyranny'; he complained of the bill's 'injustice' to emigrants who had sought asylum in England, 5 Apr. Next day Canning, the foreign secretary, informed his wife that 'Hutchinson announced last night that on ... the third reading he should answer my speech point by point', but in the event he was prevented 'by indisposition' from speaking or voting as intended, 12 Apr.[30] He argued and was in the minority of 33 for an advance of capital to Ireland, 4 May. Next day he could not see why the Irish militia should be a third more numerous than the English and was in the minority of ten for its reduction. He divided for proper use of Irish first fruits revenues, 25 May, and against Irish church pluralities, 27 May. On the 31st he defended the actions of the Catholic Association, saying that 'if they had transgressed' the law it was 'the fault of government, which had driven them to such a state of madness that they were likely to injure their cause through excess

of zeal', and rebuked Sir Frederick Trench for his 'unqualified libels' on the Irish Catholics.[31] 'As usual I was wretchedly reported in yesterday's papers', he informed Donoughmore two days later, but

I was quite guarded and inoffensive to anybody and was well heard ... In reference to that part of Trench's speech against O'Connell, I said that I desired to repeat to O'Connell what I had years before said in the House, namely that I was happy to avow him as one of my friends ... The *Chronicle* in its wisdom adds, 'my *dearest* friend'.

Donoughmore replied that he was 'most happy that he had taken up O'Connell's cause so manfully'.[32] On 10 June he presented a Cork petition for Catholic relief, of which he was convinced many Protestants now saw the necessity, and contrasted the Association, whose 'proceedings were public', with the closed Orange societies, which 'were illegal in their constitution and purpose'. Explaining to Donoughmore why he 'did not vote on the insurrection bill' that month, he observed that 'the general feeling and wish in Ireland being for it, I did not consider I should have been justified in outraging those who must judge the matter much better', 16 June 1824.[33]

On 20 Jan. 1825 Lord Hutchinson complained to his brother Francis that Hely Hutchinson's wife had 'wanted to purchase a house in London and furniture with £3,200 ... [of] my money ... in Kit's name', adding

I tire of having the most disagreeable discussions with poor Kit ... He is entirely under the dominion of that terrible woman and it becomes absolutely necessary for me to endeavour to restrain her, or she would ruin by her extravagance her husband and her children.[34]

Hely Hutchinson deprecated the suppression of the Association, which had 'done more than any previously constituted body to promote the tranquillity of Ireland', 4 Feb., remonstrated against the 'crying injustice' of a hostile Protestant petition, 15 Feb., and presented and endorsed a supportive one from Cork, 24 Feb. 1825. He voted accordingly, 15, 21, 25 Feb., when he ignored attempts to shout him down, saying hecklers 'would only compel him to remain ten times longer on his legs', and questioned the wisdom of insulting seven million Irishmen in the current state of foreign affairs. On 18 Feb. he voted for allowing the Association to be heard at the bar of the House. That day O'Connell reported arriving at the Commons, '*into which* and under the gallery Kit Hutchinson conducted us with the permission of the Speaker'.[35] He divided for Catholic claims, 1 Mar., 21 Apr., when he welcomed a favourable petition, but castigated the accompanying measure to disfranchise the Irish 40s. freeholders as an 'unnecessary' security, 22 Apr., and was a teller for the minority against it, 26 Apr., when, to 'loud symptoms of impatience', by which he 'would not be silenced', he doubted that Irish freeholders were prone to 'more corruption' than English ones and demanded an inquiry. He 'rejoiced' at the bill's subsequent lapse, but 'regretted' that this was owing to the failure of emancipation, 27 May. He insisted that the distress of the Irish poor would not be alleviated by emigration schemes but by 'finding employment for its population', 18 Apr. Next day he was appointed to the select committee on the Irish linen trade. On 12 Sept. 1825 he apologized to Lord Hutchinson, who the previous month had succeeded as 2nd earl of Donoughmore, for what had 'passed the other night' between them with respect to his wife:

> I am quite ashamed of myself for the violence of my conduct ... but you have not scrupled to abuse her to everyone in the most unqualified terms ... At one time the charge you brought against her was that she had bought furniture, in the intent of taking a house, in which I assured you and am still convinced, she was perfectly right ... Another charge, that of our having kept improper company and of improper scenes having passed in Bulstrode Street ... is false and barbarous ... Anne is represented as having such unbounded influence over me, that I am not responsible for anything ... I had not the most remote idea of troubling you ... but to my simple enquiry where my son had gone, you dragged me and mine before your judgement seat ... and pronounced sentence of *condemnation*.[36]

Hely Hutchinson complained of ministers' inattention to Ireland, 3 Feb., and contended that a 'greater degree of misery and degradation' existed there 'than in any other portion of the world', 16 Feb. 1826. Replying that day to a letter from Michael Bruce* expressing concern for his health, he declined to 'retire' and 'be quiet':

> Although I may continue to strut a little longer on the stage of public life as unprofitably to the community and to my family as heretofore, yet, there my lot having cast me, I think I should continue a zealous labourer, at least for a short while longer.[37]

He protested that the 'system of government was too expensive', 15 Feb., and that going into committee on the estimates without an account of the financial state of the country was 'absurd', 17 Feb. He was appointed to the select committees on Irish tolls, 21 Feb., and the Irish butter trade, 9 Mar. He spoke and was in the minority for the disfranchisement of Irish non-resident borough voters that day, but hoped that

'no existing interests' would be disturbed 'without giving all parties concerned the fullest opportunity of being heard'. On the 10th he urged withdrawal from Sierra Leone, where the 'deadly maladies by which it was infested' necessitated sending two officers to each appointment, which was a 'wanton waste of human existence'. He denied that the Catholic clergy neglected the scriptural education of their flocks, 20 Mar. On 10 Apr. 1826 he was 'accidentally locked out' of the division on the salary of the president of the board of trade, which he had intended to oppose.[38] Next month his son John, Member for Cork, 1826-1830, attributed the 'melancholy state' of his 'health' to the 'baneful influence of a certain person, who cares not what misery and wretchedness she may inflict on him, provided she can obtain her wild and wicked ends', adding that 'from the moment she perceived she could not govern Lord Donoughmore as she pleased, she resolved to bring about a rupture and ... at length affected it'.[39] That June Donoughmore commented that 'poor Kit was very ill'.[40]

At the 1826 general election he offered again, regretting that his health would prevent him leaving London and deputing John to act for him. Rumours of a contest came to nothing and he was returned unopposed *in absentia*.[41] On 20 July 1826 the *Southern Reporter* prematurely announced his 'long expected' death, but in their apology two days later insisted that his 'illness was unlikely to be conquered'.[42] He lingered for another five weeks, an obituarist paying tribute to the

> assiduity of his attendance in Parliament ... as attested by the record of his name in all the divisions which have taken place ... upon great questions of foreign and domestic policy ... So paramount was his sense of public duty ... that, contrary to the urgent remonstrances of his medical friends, he insisted upon quitting Brighton last spring to take an active part in the business of the Irish committees, an effort so much beyond his strength as to produce the fatal relapse which followed.[43]

Donoughmore privately lamented that 'poor Kit was so wild a politician and so much under the influence of his crazy wife, that he never could have been of use either to himself or to anybody else', and later noted that 'Kit and his family have cost me an enormous sum, owing to his folly and the perverse wickedness of his wife'.[44] Addressing the Cork electors 'for the last time' from his 'deathbed', in a letter dated two days before his demise but which appeared posthumously, Hely Hutchinson urged the claims of his son for the vacancy 'about to be created', hoping that it would not cause the 'revival of party feuds'. After 'one of the most severely contested' elections 'ever known to have taken place in Cork', John was returned as his successor.[45]

[1] *Session of Parl. 1825*, p. 470; D.O. Madden, *Revelations of Ireland*, 201-2, 221. [2] *Dublin Evening Post*, 26 Feb., 9 Mar. 1820; Add. 38458, f. 308. [3] NLI, Vesey Fitzgerald mss 7858/14. [4] TCD, Donoughmore mss D/43/45. [5] I. D'Alton, *Protestant Society and Politics in Cork*, 134-5. [6] *Dublin Evening Post*, 4 Apr.; *The Times*, 14 Apr. 1820. [7] Donoughmore mss D/43/46. [8] Madden, 208. [9] *O'Connell Corresp.* ii. 836. [10] *The Times*, 14 Apr. 1820. [11] *Black Bk.* (1823), 166; *Southern Reporter*, 31 Aug. 1826. [12] *The Times*, 13 July 1820. [13] Ibid. 19 July 1820. [14] Donoughmore mss D/33/49, 51, 54. [15] *The Times*, 29 Mar. 1821. [16] Buckingham, *Mems. Geo. IV*, i. 145. [17] Christ Church, Oxf. Phillimore mss, Buckingham to Phillimore, 30 Mar. 1821. [18] Donoughmore mss F/13/29. [19] Dorset RO D/BKL, Bankes jnl. 127. [20] *The Times*, 16 Mar. 1821. [21] Ibid. 5 Apr. 1821. [22] Bessborough mss F 53, Brougham to Duncannon, 18 June 1821; Lonsdale mss, Beckett to Lowther, 20 June 1821. [23] HLRO, Hist. Coll. 379, Grey Bennet diary, 102. [24] *The Times*, 12 May 1821. [25] Donoughmore mss D/43/53. [26] Ibid. F/13/80. [27] Ibid. D/43/55. [28] *The Times*, 22 Apr. 1823. [29] *O'Connell Corresp.* ii. 1035. [30] Harewood mss WYL 250/8/27; *The Times*, 13 Apr. 1824. [31] *The Times*, 1 June 1824. [32] Donoughmore mss D/43/62. [33] Ibid. D/43/64. [34] Ibid. F/13/105. [35] *O'Connell Corresp.* iii. 1169. [36] Bodl. Bruce MS. Eng. c. 5753, ff. 74-80. [37] Ibid. ff. 81-84. [38] *The Times*, 13 Apr. 1826. [39] Bruce MS. Eng. c. 5753, f. 90. [40] Donoughmore mss F/13/151. [41] *Southern Reporter*, 6, 13 June; *Cork Constitution*, 6, 15 June 1826. [42] *Southern Reporter*, 20, 22 July; *Cork Constitution*, 27, 29 July 1826. [43] *The Times*, 28 Aug.; *Southern Reporter*, 31 Aug. 1826. [44] Donoughmore mss F/13/155; G/7/6. [45] *Southern Reporter*, 31 Aug., 30 Dec. 1826; *Gent. Mag.* (1826), ii. 370-1.

P.J.S.

HELY HUTCHINSON, John I (1787-1851), of Palmerston House, Dublin.

Co. TIPPERARY	1826-1830
Co. TIPPERARY	1831-29 June 1832

b. 1787, 1st. of Hon. Francis Hely Hutchinson, MP [I], and Frances Wilhelmina, da. and h. of Henry Nixon of Belmont, co. Wexford. *educ.* Trinity, Dublin 1803, aged 16. *m.* (1) 15 June 1821, Hon. Margaret Gardiner (*d.* 13 Oct. 1825), da. of Luke, 1st Visct. Mountjoy [I], 1s. 1da. *d.v.p.*; (2) 5 Sept. 1827, Barbara, da. of Lt.-Col. William Reynell of Castle Reynell, co. Westmeath, 1s. 3da. *suc.* fa. 1827; uncle John Hely Hutchinson†, Bar. Hutchinson, as 3rd earl of Donoughmore [I] and 3rd Visct. Hutchinson [UK] 29 June 1832; KP 8 Apr. 1834. *d.* 14 Sept. 1851.

Ensign 1 Ft. Gds. 1807, lt. and capt. 1812, half-pay 1819.

PC [I] 17 Nov. 1834; commr. for charitable donations and bequests [I] 1844-51.

Sheriff, co. Tipperary 1822-3, ld. lt. 1832-*d.*

Hely Hutchinson was portrayed by Richard Sheil* in 1831 as 'what is commonly called a "good fellow", who does not set up any claims to eminent faculty, but whose title to good sense is beyond dispute'. Dubbed 'the Captain' by his family in order to distinguish him

from his cousin and namesake, Member for Cork, 1826-1830, but more widely known as 'Lavalette' Hutchinson, he had followed his uncle General Lord Hutchinson into the army in 1807 and served in the Peninsula, where he was present at Corunna.[1] A veteran of Waterloo, he was afterwards with the occupying forces in Paris, where, together with Sir Robert Wilson* and Michael Bruce*, he was put on trial for assisting the escape of General Lavalette, Buonaparte's postmaster-general, whom he concealed in his lodgings overnight and next day accompanied to the border. Acquitted of treason but found guilty of an illegal act, he and his accomplices, whose 'humanitarian' motives had evoked the sympathy of the press, were sentenced to three months' imprisonment with costs, the 'very lightest sentence that the law could allow', and publicly admonished by the prince regent. Following his return to England in August 1816 he was deprived of his commission but soon reinstated. He retired from the service in 1819.[2] Shortly before the 1820 general election Lord Hutchinson informed Hely Hutchinson's father Francis that 'when at Knocklofty', the family seat of their eldest brother Richard, 1st earl of Donoughmore, 'I discovered that John had some dream about the county of Tipperary. Put that out of his head. He would not have the slightest chance'.[3] Rumours that he would come forward on the 'independent interest' for Clonmel came to nothing.[4] In February 1822 he was appointed sheriff of county Tipperary, much to the dismay of Lord Hutchinson, who complained, 'He is not fit for it. The present state of the country must call for great energy and exertion on the part of that officer, of which he is quite incapable'.[5] That November he refused an application by Lord Glengall, Donoughmore's main political rival, for a county meeting to draw up a petition for the commutation of tithes.[6] In March 1823 Lord Hutchinson advised Francis that Knocklofty was 'falling down' and proving 'ridiculously expensive', and predicted that 'your son with his encumbrances ... would never be able to live here' on his succession to the earldom.[7]

At the 1826 general election Hely Hutchinson came forward for a last minute opening in Tipperary with the support of Lord Hutchinson, now 2nd earl of Donoughmore. 'His gallant delivery of Lavalette has gained him the unqualified praises of British soldiers', observed the local press. 'You don't seem quite to approve of John's offering', Donoughmore told Francis, 18 June, but 'his election is secure and ... it would have been ... a dereliction of duty towards my family, if I had not seized this opportunity'. At the nomination he declared his support for Catholic emancipation and the abolition of slavery and denounced attempts by the Glengalls to 'barter' the representation. 'He did very well and is on the hustings at least as good a speaker as needs be', Donoughmore conceded.[8] After an eight-day contest he was returned in second place.[9] A lax and mostly silent Member, Hely Hutchinson's votes in the 1826 Parliament were subject to confusion with those of his cousin, whose campaign he assisted at the 1826 Cork by-election, incurring criticism from Donoughmore for 'spending immense sums of money'. Deputizing for him at the declaration, Hely Hutchinson stated, 'I am convinced that if all of us had been in Parliament last session we would have been found among the firmest supporters of ... government'.[10] Commenting on the cousin's return, Donoughmore told Francis, 'He will be of great use to the Captain, as they both mean to live together in London. John will read Acts of Parliament and public papers and communicate his knowledge to your son, who would never take the trouble of doing so himself'.[11] He joined Brooks's, sponsored by Donoughmore and Lord Cowper, 24 Feb. 1827. He voted for Catholic claims, 6 Mar. 1827, 12 May 1828, and presented a favourable Tipperary petition, 28 Feb. 1828. He was granted a month's leave on urgent business after serving on an election committee, 15 Mar. 1827. That month, following Lord Liverpool's incapacitation by a stroke, Donoughmore told him:

> You must certainly always continue an opposition man ... but ... you should be on your guard against [Lord] Castlereagh* [whose] father Lord Londonderry ... hates Canning ... I would do anything in my power to weaken the present government and to strengthen the opposition. If you have any doubts ... you had better consult [James] Abercromby* ... As for your father's dream, that you can never support any government till there is a cabinet favourable to the Catholics, it is quite out of the question.[12]

On 31 Mar. his cousin informed him that the landlady of their lodgings at 10 Mount Street was 'anxious to know whether you mean to come over by the beginning of May'.[13] Following the appointment of Canning as premier his cousin added, 21 Apr., 'It is absolutely necessary that you should come over here for the meeting of Parliament. You owe it to your constituents and yourself not to be absent during the present eventful crisis ... So put yourself in motion without delay'.[14] He was appointed to the select committee on Irish grand jury presentments, 6 June 1827. Either he or his cousin voted for repeal of the Test Acts, 26 Feb., against the public expenditure on Buckingham House, 23 June, and for ordnance reductions, 4 July 1828. He presented constituency petitions against the

Irish Subletting Act, 30 Apr., and the Irish butter bill, which he 'strongly urged' ministers to abandon as 'it would cause great inconvenience', 7 July. His public refusal that summer to attend a Munster provincial dinner for the friends of civil and religious liberty and associate with leaders whose 'depraved ingenuity' was driving Ireland towards a 'state of insurrection', and his condemnation of their 'unconstitutional' mode of demanding pledges and getting up declarations, provoked the wrath of the Catholic Association, which launched a campaign against his family. 'I rather regret young Hutchinson giving so many reasons in his letter to the Munster people, but nothing ever was so annoying to anyone who really wishes well to the Catholics as their attacks upon the Hutchinsons *en masse*', observed Henry Brougham* to Wilson, 12 Aug. 1828. He 'incurred ... a good deal of popular disrelish by writing what was certainly a very incautious letter of admonition', Sheil later remarked.[15] He presented petitions for Catholic emancipation, 17 Feb., 30 Mar., and voted accordingly, 6, 30 Mar. 1829. On 21 Feb. he vainly urged Donoughmore to come over from Ireland, explaining that the 'absence of all our names from the Protestant declaration has already been remarked' on, and although 'I do not care one farthing what the Catholics feel ... I would not allow the rascals the gratification of complaining that we had become lukewarm in their cause, at the very moment of its triumph'.[16] He presented and endorsed a Tipperary petition against militia reductions, criticizing the lack of provision for those 'persons who during the war had been employed in recruiting', 24 Mar. 1829. It was probably he rather than his cousin who voted for the transfer of East Retford's seats to Birmingham, 11 Feb. 1830, for during his subsequent election campaign he claimed to have opposed ministers on this issue. (A subsequent vote, however, was attributed to his cousin, 5 Mar.) He was granted a month's leave on account of family illness, 9 Mar. On 13 Mar., in a letter copied to the duke of Wellington, Donoughmore advised Hely Hutchinson that ministers had 'a strong claim' to the family's support since their settlement of the Catholic question, which 'may even have placed an obligation' on them.[17] Either he or his cousin was nevertheless in the minorities for repeal of the Irish coal duties, 13 May, returns of privy councillors' emoluments, 14 May, and the second reading of the Jewish emancipation bill, 17 May. He presented Tipperary petitions against the Irish Vestry Act, 28 May, and the regulations governing Irish medical appointments that day and 10 June. He voted against abolition of the death penalty for forgery and was in the majority for the grant for South American missions, 7 June 1830.

At the 1830 general election he offered again for Tipperary. Denounced on the hustings as an enemy of Daniel O'Connell*, and criticized for being 'either absent' or a 'ministerial hack', he retorted that ministers were 'entitled to credit' for having passed the 'great measure' of emancipation, but denied being among their ranks, citing his votes on the East Retford and Galway bills. After a seven-day contest in which he complained of 'gross misrepresentations of his public conduct' and intimidation by a 'hireling mob' he was defeated, to the delight of O'Connell, who welcomed the 'glorious victory over the last of the fallen Hutchinsons'.[18] His 'imprudence cost him the county', Sheil remarked of his earlier skirmish with the Catholic leaders, adding, 'he did not regret it, but it grieved old Lord Donoughmore to the heart'.[19] Notwithstanding his statements to the contrary, he was listed by Henry Brougham* as one of those who had backed 'the duke in the last session'. An attempt to seat him on petition came to nothing.[20] At the 1831 general election he offered again as a supporter of the Grey ministry's reform bill, amid reports that he was 'hated' and had 'no chance' but was prepared to spend 'on a most liberal scale'. On the hustings he again denied having been 'a supporter' of the Wellington ministry but admitted having assisted them on 'minor questions' following emancipation. After the late withdrawal of another candidate he was returned unopposed. At the declaration he promised to 'resign should any difference arise between my constituents and myself on any question on which their wishes shall be strongly expressed' and to earn their 'good opinion' by a 'strict attention to my parliamentary duties'.[21] Rumours that he would 'very shortly' succeed Donoughmore, who, on the day after his election suffered 'a fresh attack' and was not expected 'to last the week', came to nothing.[22]

Hely Hutchinson voted for the second reading of the Grey ministry's reintroduced English reform bill, 6 July, and gave generally steady support to its details, though he was in the minorities for the disfranchisement of Saltash, 26 July, and Aldborough, 14 Sept. 1831. He divided with ministers on the Dublin election controversy, 23 Aug. He voted for the bill's third reading, 19 Sept., its passage, 21 Sept., and Lord Ebrington's confidence motion, 10 Oct. Following the bill's rejection by the Lords, Donoughmore instructed him to tell 'Grey that you and I have gone great lengths in supporting the present plan of parliamentary reform, but as to going any further no human power shall ever induce us to consent', 30 Nov.[23] There was evidently some notion of his going to the Lords to

support the bill, for on 16 Dec. 1831 Donoughmore commented:

> It is not desirable certainly to pay money for a new peerage, when in the course of nature you must be one very soon. However, if Lord Grey requires it I certainly would accept. At the same time I would tell him fairly that you considered it as doing him a great act of kindness, because it could be no object to you to pay £600 or £700 for a peerage, when you were on the eve of being one without expending any money ... I differ very much with you about the reform bill. I think the alterations are most material ... but ... I am quite of your opinion about O'Connell. I think that he has been used ill and foolishly by the government.[24]

Hely Hutchinson, who was repeatedly urged by Donoughmore 'to go over and attend your duty in Parliament', divided for the second reading of the revised reform bill, 17 Dec. 1831, but was absent from the third reading, 22 Mar., and the division on the address calling on the king to appoint only ministers who would carry reform unimpaired, 10 May 1832.[25] Early that year he appears to have assumed management of the family estates. On 8 Jan. Donoughmore, who was by now 'very ill indeed', wrote:

> In the name of God exert yourself by a little business or I shall be disgraced ... I wish you knew more about my affairs, or rather of your own ... You say nothing about the new tenants. I suppose you have not time to take into your consideration such trifling matters. They may hereafter prove of great consequence to you and your family.[26]

That month Hely Hutchinson refrained from informing Lord Anglesey, the Irish viceroy, about Donoughmore's determination to resign as lord lieutenant of Tipperary in protest at the government's plans to appoint Anthony Ryan, a former member of the Association, to the magistracy. 'You managed the business as well as it could be done', Donoughmore later conceded, urging him, however, to treat government 'with the same indifference they treated me', 24 Jan., and, following a volte face by Anglesey on the issue, to 'break off contact with Dublin Castle' 2 Feb.[27] He voted for the second reading of the Irish reform bill, 25 May. Commenting on the rumours of peerage creations to ensure the passage of reform that month, Donoughmore observed, 'If you choose to be a peer, it would be a foolish act. I don't see how you could pledge yourself to the imbecile party ... I assure you, you must be a peer in the course of a few months'.[28] Hely Hutchinson duly succeeded as 3rd earl the following month and took over as lord lieutenant of Tipperary shortly thereafter.[29] On 19 Aug. 1832 Grey informed him of the 'advancement' of his 'brothers and sisters to the honorary rank of the younger sons and daughters of earls'.[30] He was made a knight of St. Patrick and a privy councillor in 1834 and appointed one of the commissioners of charitable donations and bequests in Ireland by the Peel ministry in 1842, having become a Conservative in about 1839. He died 'from an attack of paralysis' in his '64th year' at Palmerston House, Dublin in September 1851. He was succeeded in the earldom by his eldest son Richard John (1823-66), vice-president of the board of trade, 1858-9, and president, 1859, in the Derby administration.[31]

[1] R. Sheil, *Sketches, Legal and Political* ed. M. W. Savage, ii. 340-1; TCD, Donoughmore mss F/13/155, 157. [2] *The Times*, 17, 19, 20 Jan., 17 Feb., 22, 27 Apr., 2 Aug. 1816; *Raikes Jnl.* iii. 47; *Gent. Mag.* (1851), ii. 539. [3] Donoughmore mss F/13/26. [4] *Dublin Evening Post*, 11 Mar. 1820. [5] Donoughmore mss F/13/36. [6] Ibid. F/13/105. [7] Ibid. F/13/83. [8] *Southern Reporter*, 17, 20, 24 June 1826; Donoughmore mss F/13/152, 153. [9] *Southern Reporter*, 29 June 1826. [10] Ibid. 30 Dec. 1826; Donoughmore mss F/13/162; G/6/33; G/7/6. [11] Donoughmore mss F/13/155. [12] Ibid. G/7/7. [13] Ibid. G/6/15. [14] Ibid. G/6/20. [15] *Tipperary Free Press*, 18 Aug. 1830; Add. 30115, f. 87; Sheil, ii. 341. [16] Donoughmore mss E/361-362. [17] Wellington mss WP1/1101/9. [18] *Tipperary Free Press*, 18, 21, 25, 28 Aug. 1830; *O'Connell Corresp.* iv. 1713. [19] Sheil, ii. 341. [20] NLI, Wyse mss 15024 (2), Scully to Wyse, 13 Sept., 3, 16 Oct. 1830. [21] *Tipperary Free Press*, 4, 7, 14 May 1831; Wyse mss 15024 (11), Egan to Bianconi, 2 May; 15024 (11), Maher to Wyse, 4 May 1831. [22] Wyse mss 15024 (11), Marshal to Wyse, 13 May 1831. [23] Donoughmore mss G/7/23. [24] Ibid. G/7/25. [25] Ibid. G/7/24. [26] Ibid. G/7/29-31. [27] Ibid. G/7/34, 38A, 38B, 42, 47. [28] Ibid. G/7/76. [29] *The Times*, 5 July 1832. [30] Donoughmore mss G/6/24. [31] *Oxford DNB.*; *The Times*, 15 Sept. 1851; *Gent. Mag.* (1851), ii. 539-40.

P.J.S.

HELY HUTCHINSON, John II (c.1795–1842), of Benlomond House, Downshire Hill, Hampstead, Mdx.

CORK   29 Dec. 1826–1830

b. c. 1795, 1st s. of Hon. Christopher Hely Hutchinson* and 1st w. Anne Wensley, da. of Sir James Bond, 1st bt., MP [I], of Coolamber, co. Longford. *unm. suc.* fa. 1826. *d.* 1842.

Hely Hutchinson, son of Christopher, quasi-radical Member for Cork, 1802-12, 1818-26, was 'a great favourite' with his uncle John, Lord Hutchinson, who 'almost entirely directed the course of his education'. In November 1823 he was in Florence, where his father's eldest brother Richard, 1st earl of Donoughmore, sent him a letter of introduction to the duke of Devonshire at Rome.[1] He evidently shared his uncle's disapproval of his father's second wife, to whose 'baneful influence' and 'wild and wicked ends' he attributed the 'melancholy' state of his 'poor father's health' in May 1826, when

he reluctantly agreed to deputize for him at the Cork general election.[2] In August 1826 he came forward for the vacancy caused by the death of his father, who two days before dying had appealed to the electors to support him, saying 'I know him to be talented and extremely well informed'.[3] He secured the backing of Lord Hutchinson, now 2nd earl of Donoughmore, who agreed to make it 'a family object' to have him in Parliament:

> He is a much more capable man than I took him to be, has a great deal of concealed energy about him and can throw off his indolence, whenever he is roused to exertion ... He ... is quite a different man, of more reflecting mind, of ten times the understanding, than his father ever was, and will never adopt but rational and moderate views.[4]

Commenting on his rebuttal of another candidate's complaints to the press about the seat becoming 'inheritable property', in which he expressed a 'natural aversion to engage in newspaper controversy', Donoughmore remarked, 'John's answer' does 'admirably' and 'very few men could write a paper of that kind'.[5] Pressed on the hustings, he explained that he was a 'decided opponent' of any concession to the Catholics that did not provide 'for the security and inviolability of Protestantism', and promised to support the abolition of slavery and 'moderate reform', though he deprecated 'radical reform' with its 'annual parliaments and universal suffrage'. After a severe and protracted contest he was returned *in absentia* on the tenth day.[6] He was too ill to attend the declaration, when his cousin and namesake, Member for county Tipperary, spoke on his behalf:

> He goes into Parliament belonging to no party ... It has been asserted that whoever might be minister of England my relative would be in the ranks of opposition. So far from that being the case, I am convinced that if all of us had been in Parliament last session we would have been found among the firmest supporters of ... government.[7]

Donoughmore later blamed Hely Hutchinson 'more than anybody else' for the high expenditure incurred, 'entirely contrary' to his 'express instructions', during the election, adding, 'I do not think that John will make an efficient Member ... [for] his mind is rather for writing than for speaking'.[8]

Hely Hutchinson's votes in this Parliament were subject to confusion with his cousin's, but those which mistakenly appeared with the initials of his father were surely his. He was listed as such in the opposition minority against the grant to the duke of Clarence, 16 Feb. 1827. He presented Cork petitions for Catholic claims, 2 Mar., 2 Apr., and voted thus, 6 Mar. 1827,

12 May 1828.[9] On 7 Mar. 1827 he joined Brooks's, sponsored by Donoughmore and Lord Clifden. He presented a petition from the flour millers of Shallaghan, county Tipperary against the importation of foreign flour, 19 Mar. 1827, next day telling his cousin, 'I presented a petition from your d—d millers, but the House would not listen to my tale of their woes'. He presented a similar Cork petition, 29 Mar.[10] That month, following Lord Liverpool's incapacitating stroke, Donoughmore urged his nephews 'to do anything ... to weaken the present government and to strengthen the opposition', but if in doubt to 'consult [James] Abercromby* ... and tell him I desired you to do so'.[11] Hely Hutchinson divided for information on the Barrackpoor mutiny, 22 Mar., and the Lisburn Orange procession, 29 Mar., and against the supplies next day. On 21 Apr., after Canning's accession as premier, he urged his cousin

not to be absent during the present eventful crisis, where it is said that the Tories, or as they will henceforth be, the opposition, mean to make a great rally and to turn out the new ministry. I do not know whether any or what arrangements will be made with the Whigs but I am at present all for supporting the new minister if he be inclined to play a fair and open game with respect to Ireland.[12]

He presented Cork petitions against the salmon fisheries bill, 11, 22 May, 8 June.[13] He was in the ministerial majority (as C.H. Hutchinson) for the grant to improve water communications in Canada, 12 June. On 16 June 1827 he informed Donoughmore of having

just heard that it is the intention of ministers to bring in another corn bill ... Although I have not spoken, I have certainly not been idle during this session as I have been a very regular attendant on committees and my constituents have continued to keep me continually employed.[14]

He presented and endorsed petitions for Catholic claims, 21 Feb. 1828, when, in his maiden speech, he warned that 'matters could not remain' as they were, condemned the withholding of rights 'guaranteed' by the treaty of Limerick and argued that by 'removing this discontent', 'capital would flow into Ireland' and 'indolence ... poverty and wretchedness' would disapppear. Either he or his cousin voted for repeal of the Test Acts, 26 Feb., and to censure public expenditure on Buckingham House, 23 June. He presented a Cork petition for repeal of the local coal duties, arguing that it was necessary to afford 'every possible facility to the internal trade of Ireland', 12 Mar., and against the stamp duty on receipts, 14 Mar. Following reports about his admission to the Cork Brunswick Club, he assured Donoughmore, 6 Apr.:

You need be under no alarm with respect to my belonging to the Orange Club as I had the honour of being blackballed yesterday ... The Catholics were not opposed to my being put up, as the feeling was that if I were admitted, it would completely break up that establishment ... I never dreamt of such a thing as forming a connection with the violent party, but I still think that much is to be done by coming into contact with those who are most violently opposed to me.[15]

On 16 June he was in the minority against the archbishop of Canterbury's appointment of a registrar. He divided against the additional churches bill, 30 June, and for ordnance reductions, 7 July 1828. (It was probably he rather than his cousin who had voted the same way three days before.) That autumn he travelled widely on the continent.[16]

Hely Hutchinson voted for the Wellington ministry's concession of Catholic emancipation, 6, 30 Mar., and presented a favourable petition, 17 Mar. 1829. He divided to allow Daniel O'Connell to take his seat unhindered, 18 May. In July 1829 Lord Francis Leveson Gower*, the Irish secretary, informed him that Donoughmore's 'application for command of the county of Cork militia' had been unsuccessful, but hoped there would be 'some other opportunity' of 'obliging' their family.[17] It was probably his cousin who voted for the transfer of East Retford's seats to Birmingham, 11 Feb., but a similar vote was firmly attributed to him, 5 Mar. 1830. He divided for the enfranchisement of Birmingham, Leeds and Manchester, 23 Feb. He presented Cork petitions against the Clyde navigation bill, 23 Mar., and the assimilation of Irish stamp duties, which would 'utterly destroy the newspaper press of Ireland', 17 May. Either he or his cousin voted for repeal of the Irish coal duties, 13 May, information on privy councillors' emoluments, 14 May, and Jewish emancipation, 17 May. He presented a petition from Cork distillers for a reduction of Irish spirit duties, 18 June 1830.

At the 1830 general election he offered again for Cork, proclaiming his 'complete independence' from the other candidates. Peel, the home secretary, advised Leveson Gower that he did 'not know' what his politics were.[18] Six days before the nomination he unexpectedly withdrew, citing the growth of the city's 'corruption' and the settlement of the Catholic question, which his family had 'long' supported. 'As long as there was a great public principle' at stake, he explained, 'there was some justification for contributing to the public benefit', but 'now that is has become a question of mere personal ambition, I do not think myself justified in submitting ... to an unlimited expenditure of money'.[19] By the end of December 1830 he had decamped to Paris, from where he sent Donoughmore regular accounts of the aftermath of the July revolution, conjecturing that a similar 'crisis must take place in England', and complained that the Grey administration's neglect of Irish affairs would lead to repeal of the Union.[20] 'I quite agree with you in your estimate of our present ministry', he told Donoughmore, 28 Mar. 1832:

They are collectively and individually incapable, and advance from blunder to blunder from one month's end to the other ... I hear nothing certain as to the fate of the [reform] bill. I have long considered it as too extensive a change, but after all it matters little, as I am convinced that we are rapidly advancing towards ... a revolution in England.[21]

He died unmarried in 1842.

[1] TCD, Donoughmore mss D/27/5. [2] Bodl. Bruce MS. Eng. c. 5753, f. 90; *Southern Reporter*, 13 June 1826. [3] *Southern Reporter*, 31 Aug. 1826. [4] Donoughmore mss F/13/155. [5] *Southern Reporter*, 17, 19 Oct. 1826; Donoughmore mss F/13/158. [6] *The Times*, 21 Dec.; *Southern Reporter*, 23, 30 Dec. 1826. [7] *Southern Reporter*, 30 Dec. 1826. [8] Donoughmore mss G/7/6; F/13/163. [9] *The Times*, 3 Mar., 3 Apr. 1827. [10] Ibid. 20, 30 Mar. 1827; Donoughmore mss G/6/11. [11] Donoughmore mss G/7/7. [12] Ibid. G/6/20. [13] *The Times*, 12, 23 May, 9 June 1827. [14] Donoughmore mss E/353. [15] Ibid. E/357. [16] Ibid. E/359-60, 371. [17] NAI, Leveson Gower letterbks. M. 736/204, 213; Wellington mss WP1/1030/29. [18] Add. 40338, f. 218. [19] *Southern Reporter*, 22, 31 July 1830. [20] Donoughmore mss E/371, 374-6. [21] Ibid. E/386.

P.J.S.

HENEAGE, George Fieschi (1800–1864), of Hainton Hall, nr. Louth, Lincs.

GREAT GRIMSBY	1826–1830
LINCOLN	1831–1834
LINCOLN	1852–Feb. 1862

b. 22 Nov. 1800, 1st s. of George Robert Heneage of Hainton Hall and Frances Anne, da. of George Ainslie, gov. Eustatius and Dominica. *educ.* Eton 1817; Trinity Coll. Camb. 1818. *m.* 17 Jan. 1833, Frances, da. of Michael Tasburgh of Burghwallis, Yorks., 2s. 1da. *suc.* fa. 1833. *d.* 11 May 1864.
Sheriff, Lincs. 1839-40.

Heneage, by all accounts an 'oddity', was commonly known as 'Fish' among the Lincolnshire gentry, presumably on account of his middle name.[1] A member of an ancient county family who could trace their origins to the time of William Rufus, his ancestor John de Heneage had been granted the manor of Hainton

by Edward III, and the family had resided there, with one minor interruption, ever since. Thomas Heneage (*d.* 1553) was private secretary to Cardinal Wolsey and subsequently master of Henry VIII's household, while his nephew and successor George Heneage (*d.* 1595) was Member for Great Grimsby. Heneage's great-grandfather Thomas Henry had married a daughter of Roboaldo Fieschi, count de Lavagna, in Genoa in 1728. Whether or not the family's Catholicism dates from this time is unclear, but they were certainly Catholics when his grandfather, also George Fieschi, married a daughter of the 8th Lord Petre in 1755.[2]

Heneage's uncle, Thomas Fieschi Heneage, was married to the sister of the Whig Lord Yarborough, who headed the Blue party at Great Grimsby and had been Member for Lincolnshire before succeeding his father in December 1823, when he was replaced by Sir William Amcotts Ingilby. The county Whigs, however, were divided over him, and immediately after the by-election it was rumoured that Heneage would be brought forward next time, as he 'stood innocent of the various managements' and although

he is a very unpopular man now, yet he has a very good understanding and he loves application and ... when he has anything to do he will do it well ... despite his slowness ... Perhaps Lord Yarborough does not know his merit.[3]

In 1825, however, it was settled with Yarborough that Heneage should start for Great Grimsby, where his family had 'always commanded about 20 votes'.[4]

At the 1826 general election Heneage, who had renounced his Catholicism, duly came forward, amid confusion about whether he was supported by Yarborough or his close friend Charles Tennyson, the retiring Member, an opponent of Yarborough. He was joined by Charles Wood of Hemsworth, Yorkshire, and they canvassed together. Their opponents made much of Heneage's former religion in a virulently anti-Catholic campaign, but the Blues were never in any danger and Heneage was returned in second place behind Wood.[5] A few weeks afterwards he and Tennyson went as a party to Cambridge to receive their masters' degrees.[6] He joined Brooks's, 28 Feb., sponsored by Yarborough and the duke of Norfolk. He voted for Catholic relief, 6 Mar. 1827, 12 May 1828, and brought up multiple favourable petitions, 29 Apr. 1828. He divided for inquiry into Leicester corporation, 15 Mar., to go into committee on the spring guns bill, 23 Mar., and for information on the Orange procession and the Lisburn magistrates, 29 Mar. 1827. Next day he voted for Tierney's amendment to postpone going into committee of supply. He divided against the corn bill, 2 Apr. 1827. He voted for repeal of the Test Acts, 28 Feb. 1828. He was appointed to the select committee on the Catholic land tax, 1 May. He presented a Great Grimsby petition against the Spirituous Liquors Act, 28 Mar., and divided for information on chancery delays, 24 Apr., and improved recovery of penalties under customs and excise laws, 1 May. He voted against the use of public money for Buckingham House, 23 June, and the additional churches bill, 30 June 1828. In February 1829 Planta, the Wellington ministry's patronage secretary, predicted that he would divide 'with government' for their concession of Catholic emancipation, but he cast no known votes on the issue. He divided for Daniel O'Connell to be allowed to take his seat unhindered, 18 May. He voted for the transfer of East Retford's seats to Birmingham, 5 May 1829, 23 Feb., 5 Mar. 1830. He was in the minorities for referral of the Newark petition against the duke of Newcastle to a select committee, 1 Mar., and information on the interference of British troops in the internal affairs of Portugal, 10 Mar., and thereafter voted steadily with the revived opposition for economy and reduced taxation. He presented petitions in favour of the Leeds and Selby railway bill, 25 Mar., and divided for abolition of the death penalty for forgery, 24 May, 7 June 1830.

At the 1830 general election Heneage offered again for Great Grimsby in alliance with Wood, with whom he canvassed and hosted a dinner for the corporation and gentlemen of the borough. After another contest he was defeated in third place.[7] At the 1831 dissolution he came forward for Lincoln as a reformer, with the support of its reform committee and Thomas George Corbett, the defeated candidate in 1826. Reporting on his canvass, the *Lincoln, Rutland and Stamford Mercury* commented:

> Though a fluent speaker, Mr. Heneage has a rapidity and indistinctness of utterance, together with a weak voice, unfavourable for producing effect. Many of his sentences appeared not to reach his hearers ... He was however received with much applause.

Following the retirement of a second reform candidate he and the Tory sitting Member, a close acquaintance, were returned unopposed.[8] He voted for the second reading of the Grey ministry's reintroduced reform bill, 6 July, against the adjournment, 12 July, and generally for its details, though he voted for Lord Chandos's amendment to enfranchise £50 tenants-at-will, 18 Aug. 1831. He divided against the Irish union of parishes bill next day, and with ministers on the Dublin election controversy, 23 Aug. He voted for the

reform bill's passage, 21 Sept., but was absent from a call of the House, 10 Oct. and did not vote for Lord Ebrington's confidence motion that day. He presented a Lincoln petition for the bill, 14 Dec., voted for the second reading of the revised measure, 17 Dec. 1831, again supported its details, and divided for the third reading, 22 Mar. 1832. When his colleague attempted to alter the proposed boundary between the north and south of Lincolnshire next day, Heneage objected, saying that the boundary had 'given general satisfaction to the parties interested' and that he felt it his 'duty to oppose the amendment', which was defeated. He voted for the address calling on the king to appoint only ministers who would carry reform unimpaired, 10 May, and presented a Lincoln petition for withholding supplies until it passed, 24 May. He divided for the second reading of the Irish reform bill, 25 May, and paired against a Conservative amendment to increase the Scottish county representation, 1 June. He was in the minority of 19 for Tennyson's attempt to alter Stamford's boundaries, 22 June 1832. He voted with ministers on the Russian-Dutch loan, 26 Jan., 12, 16 July, and relations with Portugal, 9 Feb. On 8 Mar. he seconded Amcotts Ingilby's motion for the production of papers on the unexpected disbandment of the north and south Lincolnshire militias, asserting that he could not 'at all understand on what ground the dismissal took place ... with no cause assigned but the cold weather', which 'is generally expected at Christmas'. He conceded that it was unlikely that anything useful would be gleaned from the documents, however, and the motion was eventually negatived without a division. He divided for coroners' inquests to be made public, 20 June 1832.

At the 1832 general election he offered again for Lincoln as a Liberal and topped the poll. He retired at the 1834 dissolution, when he was rumoured as a candidate for North Lincolnshire but did not stand. The previous year he had married Frances Tasburgh, 'a Catholic who lives near Doncaster', who is not at all pretty, but on a very large scale'.[9] Whether he resumed the religion himself is unknown. Heneage successfully contested Lincoln as a Liberal Protectionist, following which he supported Lord Derby's Conservative administration.[10] He voted to censure free trade in November 1852, but returned to the Liberal ranks after Derby's fall. With his position at Lincoln insecure, in February 1862 he took the Chiltern hundreds in order to contest what he thought would be a safe seat for Great Grimsby.[11] However, he lost by 12 votes and retired from politics. Commenting on his character in 1849, Colonel Charles Weston Cracoft of Hackthorn Hall observed:

What a singular being George Heneage [is] ... sometimes apparently in a trance and dead as it were to all around him, and then starting up, making some absurd observation, and then laughing the most curious laugh at his own wit ... However, with all his oddities Heneage is a clever man, exceedingly well read, and can converse well on most subjects.

Heneage's aunt Mrs. Hoare, however, considered him 'the greatest bore she knew'.[12] Heneage died 'of water on the chest after an illness of three weeks' in May 1864.[13] By his will, dated 14 Jan. 1858, he bequeathed his Brackenborough estate in Lincolnshire, £20,000 and income from £14,000 in stocks and securities to his younger son Charles, and gave his daughter Georgiana Mary £20,000 to double her marriage portion. The remaining estates passed to his eldest son Edward (1840-1922), Liberal Member for Lincoln, 1865-8, and Great Grimsby, 1880-92, 1893-5, who was created Baron Heneage in 1896.

[1] Sir F. Hill, *Victorian Lincoln*, 16. [2] *Gent. Mag.* (1864), ii. 813; *Oxford DNB sub* Sir Thomas Heneage. [3] Suff. RO (Ipswich), Barne mss HA53/359/88, E.M. Boucherett to Mary Barne, 24 [Dec.] 1823. [4] Wentworth Woodhouse mun. F33/64, 67. [5] E. Gillett, *Hist. Grimsby*, 201; *Grimsby Pollbook* (Skelton, 1826); *Hull Advertiser*, 10 Mar., 28 Apr.; *Lincoln, Rutland and Stamford Mercury*, 16 July 1826. [6] Lincs. AO, Tennyson D'Eyncourt mss Td'E H98/32. [7] *Hull Advertiser*, 23 July 1830. [8] *Lincoln, Rutland and Stamford Mercury*, 29 Apr. 1831; *Boston Gazette*, 3 May 1831. [9] Hill, 16. [10] *Dod's Parl. Companion* (1852), 197. [11] Hill, 33. [12] Ibid. 16. [13] *Louth and North Lincs. Advertiser*, 14 May 1864.

M.P.J.C./P.J.S.

HEPBURNE SCOTT, Henry Francis (1800–1867), of Mertoun House, Berwick.

ROXBURGHSHIRE   8 May 1826–1832

b. 1 Jan. 1800, 2nd but 1st surv. s. of Hugh Scott[†] (afterwards Hepburne Scott) of Harden, Roxburgh (confirmed as 6th Lord Polwarth [S] 26 June 1835) and Henrietta, da. of Hans Moritz, Count von Brühl of Martinskirk, Saxon envoy to London; bro. of Francis Scott[†]. *educ.* St. John's, Camb. 1818. *m.* 11 Nov. 1835, Georgina, da. of George Baillie[†] of Jerviswoode, Berwick, 2s. 3da. *styled* master of Polwarth 1835-41; took name of Hepburne before Scott as heir-at-law to fa.'s cos. James Hepburne (*d.* 1793) of Humbie, Haddington in Dec. 1820; *suc.* fa. as 7th Lord Polwarth [S] 28 Dec. 1841. *d.* 16 Aug. 1867.
Rep. peer [S] 1843-*d.*; ld. in waiting Feb.-Dec. 1852, Mar. 1858-June 1859, July 1866-*d.*
Ld. lt. Selkirk 1845-*d.*
Capt. Roxburgh yeomanry 1824; commdt. Selkirk militia 1855; lt.-col. Roxburgh and Selkirk vol. rifle corps 1861.

Scott, as he was generally known, despite taking the name of Hepburne, had become heir to his fam-ily's estates in Berwickshire, Roxburghshire and Selkirkshire by the death in 1804 of his brother Charles Walter Scott. The parliamentary career of his father, who briefly represented Berwickshire, had been curtailed in 1784 by a political and dynastic dispute over the succession to the Polwarth peerage and estates, from which the will of his grandfather, the 3rd earl of Marchmont, had barred him, but he remained an influential political figure in the Borders with his cousin Sir Walter Scott.[1] Born in Brighton, near the Petworth estate of his mother's half-brother, the 3rd earl of Egremont, Scott was educated and sent to Cambridge with his brother William, 16 months his junior, their father's favourite.[2] After stewarding at Kelso races in September 1822, he spent most of the next 15 months with his mother's relations in Berlin, Dresden and Frankfurt, and another six in Lausanne under the tutelage, with Sir John Dalrymple[†], of a Monsieur Leigneux. He kept a journal throughout.[3] During his absence the Lords confirmed the Scotts' rival Sir William Purves Hume Campbell in possession of the Marchmont estates in Berwickshire and his father waived his prior claim to government assistance there at the next election. This, and astute canvassing by his relations, served Scott well when the sudden death of Sir Alexander Don produced a vacancy for Roxburghshire in April 1826.[4] The major interests of the Tory 5th duke of Buccleuch and 7th marquess of Lothian and the Whig 2nd earl of Minto backed him, the Liverpool administration's Scottish manager Lord Melville endorsed his candidature, and he saw off his challengers, Sir William Francis Eliott of Stobbs Castle, and Sir John Scott Douglas of Springwood Park, to come in unopposed.[5] Recommending him to Buccleuch's guardian Lord Montagu, Sir Walter Scott wrote: 'A good honest lad he is and a plain speaking one and I think has no vacillation in his character'.[6] His father granted him £400 a year drawn quarterly on Coutts towards his London expenses.[7] After celebrating he informed Lothian:

I have got one election over, and did not stick in my speech of thanks, but did not contrive to say all I wanted to say at dinner. I have a most uncommon headache this morning, which comes of drinking without being drunk. We dined 103 and finished 19 dozen kegs and some bottles of wine. I shall be with you in a few days when you shall have a full account of the proceedings.[8]

Minto's support and Scott's election speech, or rather the absence from it of a protectionist statement on corn, fuelled Tory speculation that he was a covert Whig, and this was further encouraged by his arrival in London 'too late' to vote on corn law reform and

Scottish banking. On his father and Melville's advice he did not over-react to the reports. Scott Douglas's attempt to exploit them failed and, having cast a solitary known vote against Lord John Russell's electoral bribery resolutions, 26 May, Scott was returned unopposed at the general election in June 1826.[9] In addresses and on the hustings he asserted his independence and confirmed that he would support Lord Liverpool's ministry if he deemed their policies satisfactory.[10] That summer he and his brothers hunted otters at Sir Walter Scott's Abbotsford estate and were guests of Buccleuch for the shooting at Drumlanrig.[11]

Scott, who corresponded regularly on political issues with his father, Buccleuch, Lothian and Minto, made no significant reported speech in the House before 1831. Canning summoned him in September 1826 to vote for the admission of foreign corn, and after discussing it at length with his father, who cautioned him against concerning himself with the theories of the political economists, he divided uneasily for the Liverpool ministry's corn bill, 9 Mar. 1827, and corresponded regularly with the leaders of the Union Agricultural Society on the subject.[12] To his father's relief he divided against Catholic claims, 6 Mar. 1827, 12 May 1828, with government for the award to the duke of Clarence, 16 Mar. 1827, and against repealing the Test Acts, 26 Feb. 1828.[13] As the Wellington ministry's patronage secretary Planta had predicted, Scott voted for Catholic emancipation, 6, 30 Mar., but he presented anti-Catholic petitions from Kelso and elsewhere, 12, 16 Mar. 1829. The following session he voted against Lord Blandford's reform proposals, 18 Feb., the enfranchisement of Birmingham, Leeds and Manchester, 23 Feb., and abolition of the death penalty for forgery offences, 7 June, having presented a favourable petition from Hawick, 14 May. He presented one supporting the Northern roads bill from Roxburghshire's freeholders, justices and commissioners of supply, 24 June 1830. He was unopposed at the general election that summer,[14] when his main concern was the death of his brother George, taken ill while touring the continent with their brother Francis.[15]

The Wellington ministry counted Scott among their 'friends' and he divided with them on the civil list when they were brought down, 15 Nov. 1830. He wrote to his mother next day:

It is impossible [not] to feel most anxious as to what the turn of public affairs may now be and I am not without great hopes that all may turn out for the best, as the Whig government which the turbulent people of the country are calling out for must now come in and they will hardly be able to do anything very violent with the strong opposition which will necessarily watch their motions. I believe many of those who voted against the government were sincerely voting for it when they found they were in a majority which they did not in the least expect and had only intended ... a bit of populism in voting against government on a finance question. Peel, I am convinced, was glad of it and rather intended he should be beat on a question of retrenchment rather than reform.[16]

His letters to relations that month reveal a certain disillusionment with the 'bore' of parliamentary life and his opposition to reform,[17] of which he wrote entertainingly to his sister Anne, the wife of George Baillie of Jerviswoode, 4 Nov. 1830:

We have been through long nights talking a great deal and doing nothing and from all appearance shall go on doing so. I begin to dread that I shall not emerge till very near Xmas and London is truly detestable. It is such a change from being out all day to be now cooped up in the heated atmosphere of the House and when out to trudge about the hard pavement ... I have little amusing to write about unless I give you a full description of how beautiful and elegant the Miss Riddells looked in celestial blue gowns and white feathers in the House of Lords and how I escaped without speaking to them, dreading the hatred of their bright eyes. I have [seen] few of our relations. The last I beheld was poor [Sir George] Murray who at all times is not over beautiful and yesterday while attempting to make a speech in the House looked more as if a letter of his name had been transposed than ever. He did not by any means succeed and I do not think will attempt it often again. He spoke in favour of reform and I am sorry he did, as at the time heard it was uncalled for and I think he will be sorry he has committed himself on it so soon. Last year he was quite against it. I shall today try and dine [with] Lord Egremont as I am tired of bad mutton in the hot coffee room of the ... Commons and must now set out to bespeak a place at the peer's table. His house is most wonderfully improved by a little paint and paper and when the floors are washed will look not look so uninhabitable as it used to do.[18]

A campaign to replace Scott with a reformer was under way before the county meeting at Jedburgh, 25 Jan., determined to test him and Lothian by asking them to present and endorse their reform petition, which Scott refused to do, 29 Jan. 1831.[19] Inspired by his correspondence and dinners with Sir Walter Scott, who delighted in their exchanges and predicted that he would 'do remarkably well if he can get rid of his bashfulness', he publicly condemned the Grey ministry's reform bills as too sweeping and hosted a meeting of 'some of the Scotch Members' in his room, 12 Mar.[20] Afterwards, he reported to Lothian:

We have decided that it is not desirable on the main question that we should have any further discussion on the Scotch bill on its being read a first time, reserving our opposition until the second reading which I trust will never take place, as should the English bill be lost, the Scotch one will go along with it. At the same time, Sir George Clerk or someone is to state on the first reading the silence of [the] Scotch on the general question was not from any feeling of assent, but because *he* the lord advocate had neglected to explain the measure so as to make it comprehensible. Nor did he make it much more so, when, at the end of the debate, we called on him for further explanations and after making a speech of three quarters of an hour he pressed some of the most important points. We certainly ought to petition against the measure, but at the same time it will require some caution to ascertain if there is a sufficiently strong feeling amongst the commissioners of supply and farmers to induce them to petition against what at first sight may appear to be for their advantage or at least a boon or rather bait held out to them. If the farmers dislike the measure it would be *most desirable* that we should have *petitions from every parish*. Both sides talk with great confidence of carrying the question, but I still think we are safe, but I fear not with a greater majority than 30. There are many who have not yet made up their minds and every exertion is making to sway votes both in public and private. We have been over the list of Scotch Members with care and I am sorry to say there are 16 in favour and I fear it will be difficult to bring them over.[21]

Despite the robust tone of his letters to Sir Walter Scott, by the 15th his confidence that the English bill would be lost at its second reading had evaporated, although 'in conversations I always talk of it as being certain of a majority of 50', and he was convinced that 'some measure of reform' would have to be conceded.[22] He did not attend the rival Roxburghshire reform meetings, 21, 22 Mar., but his letter to the former criticized the ministerial measure as badly timed, a promoter of urban-rural divisions, a sop to popular clamour and a violation of vested corporate interests. He condemned the creation of leaseholder votes as destructive of landlord-tenant relations and a step towards the ballot – tenets which he and Francis ensured were incorporated in a petition adopted by the Roxburghshire anti-reformers, 21 Mar., which Scott presented on the 29th.[23] After voting against the second reading of English bill, 22 Mar., he described to Lothian how

on the last man walking in and numbers declared I confess I felt as if my nearest relation was dead, a sort of shock I could hardly have conceived it possible to feel on a division in the House and it was evident enough I was not the only one, for many were so, I may almost say *overcome* as hardly to be unable to speak ... I do not know what

is to be the fate of the Scotch bill. The second reading stands for tomorrow and I understand there is a count before it in which case it must stand over till after Easter. I want it debated, as I am sure we can show more bad then ... and that nothing explains a measure so fully to the country as a debate in the House.[24]

He disputed Hume's claims that reform petitions like the Renfrewshire one were unsolicited and the people of Scotland almost universally favourable to reform, 25 Mar., and he spoke again of the popular urban clamour for the ministerial bill and the opposition of the 'wealth and intelligence of Scotland' to it, when Hunt presented the radical New Lanark petition, 14 Apr. He voted for Gascoyne's wrecking amendment, 19 Apr. 1831. Backed by Buccleuch, Lothian and Melville, he defeated the reformer Sir William Eliott at the ensuing general election after a bitter and violent campaign, and supported anti-reformers in neighbouring constituencies.[25]

It had been mooted on the hustings that Scott, whose father had resubmitted his claim to the Polwarth barony, was disqualified from standing as a Scottish peer's eldest son, but the House rejected Eliott's petition to this effect, 22 July 1831.[26] Nevertheless, what Scott termed 'this confounded peerage case', which was unexpectedly postponed *sine die*, 1 Sept., obliged him to campaign for Buccleuch's brother Lord John Scott as his likely replacement and undermined his authority in the constituency, especially after it was put about that his father's intention had been to unseat him as 'unsatisfactory' and bring in William, who had qualified as a barrister.[27] On 25 Aug. 1831 *The Times*'s survey of anti-reformers in the 1831 Parliament noted that Scott was 'only known as the reported dependant of the duke of Buccleuch'. His private papers reveal that he prepared far more speeches on reform in 1831-2 than he was able to deliver and that although present, he frequently chose not to vote.[28] He presented a petition from Lauder for the £10 burgh franchise before dividing against the second reading of the reintroduced English reform bill, 6 July, and voted to postpone consideration of the partial disfranchisement of Chippenham, 27 July, and against disfranchising non-resident freeholders of Aylesbury, Cricklade, East Retford and New Shoreham, 2 Sept. He divided against the bill's passage, 21 Sept., the second reading of the Scottish bill, 23 Sept., and against the second reading of the revised English reform bill, 17 Dec. 1831. He and his father tried to rally the Roxburghshire anti-reformers during the Christmas recess and to procure a petition on the lines of the hostile Berwickshire one, but it foundered through lack of support from Buccleuch's agents.[29] Disillusioned, Scott accepted an invitation to go shooting 'for ten days or so' from 10 Jan. 1832 with his friend Charles Baring Wall*, in order to meet Lord and Lady Henry Thynne*.[30] He voted against the reform bill's committal, 20 Jan., enfranchising Tower Hamlets, 28 Feb., and probably the third reading, 22 Mar. 1832.[31] On 2 Mar. he upbraided the Scottish Members on the ministerial side of the House for maintaining that the Scottish people were satisfied with the 'proportion of representation assigned to Scotland ... compared with ... England'. His was one of several Scottish abstentions on the third reading of the malt drawback bill, 2 Apr. He divided against the Irish reform bill at its second reading, 25 May, but no votes or speeches by him on the revised Scottish measure were reported. He divided with opposition on the Russian-Dutch loan, 26 Jan., but not subsequently, and in the majority for Alexander Baring's bill to exclude insolvent debtors from Parliament, 27 June. He had started for Roxburghshire as an 'independent' in April and issued notices, 17 June, but, with success unlikely and his father unwilling to spend, he desisted two days later and canvassed for Lord John Scott, the defeated candidate at the December 1832 general election.[32]

From October 1832 Scott's major concern was his work as Sir Walter Scott's executor, which included plans to save Abbotsford and Scott's collections and to commemorate him with a monument.[33] A 'firm Conservative', he did not stand for the Commons again, but, after succeeding his father in the Polwarth barony in 1841, he made his interest available to his brother Francis, Conservative Member for Roxburghshire, 1841-7, and Berwickshire, 1847-59, sat as a representative peer for almost a quarter of a century and served as a lord-in-waiting to Queen Victoria during Lord Derby's ministries.[34] He died at Mertoun House in August 1867, having been predeceased in 1859 by his wife, a sister of his brother-in-law George Baillie Hamilton, 10th earl of Haddington. He was recalled as a militia leader, county lord lieutenant, elder of the Scottish church and breeder of Leicester cattle. His elder son Walter Hugh Hepburne Scott (1838-1920) succeeded him in the barony and estates.[35]

[1] HP Commons, 1754-90, iii. 412-13; HP Commons, 1790-1820, ii. 522-5; M. Warrender, Marchmont and Humes of Polwarth, 101, 107; Caledonian Mercury, 28 Mar. 1822. [2] Illustrated London News, 31 Aug. 1867; NAS GD224/580/3/1/43. [3] NAS GD157/1735; 2354/1; 2411/1-15. [4] NAS GD157/1413-15; 2961/1/8; Perthshire Courier, 11 Apr. 1823. [5] Scott Jnl. i. 154-9, 166; Scott Letters, ix. 502-3, 510; x. 2, 3, 7, 63; NAS GD40/9/322/4, 5; 328/9/1; GD51/1/198/24/21-25, 28, 29; GD157/2961/1/8-11; 2967/5; 2968/1-8, 12; Berwick Advertiser, 22 Apr., 13 May 1826. [6] Scott Letters, ix. 502-3. [7] NAS GD157/2065/2. [8] NAS GD40/9/327/1. [9] NAS GD40/9/307/4; 322/6/1, 2; GD157/2962/37; 2963/4; 2964/1-3; 2965/3; 2967/2-9; 2968/9-11; Scott Letters, x. 63. [10] Kelso Mail, 8, 22 June, 3 July 1826. [11] Scott Letters, x. 86; NAS GD157/2967/10. [12] NAS GD157/2494/1-3; 2499; 2500; 2504; 2960. [13] NAS GD157/2502. [14] Berwick Advertiser, 21 Aug. 1830. [15] NAS GD157/2511; 2976/2-4. [16] NAS GD157/2411/18/1. [17] NAS GD157/2411/16, 17; 2550/9, 10. [18] NAS GD157/2550/8/1-3. [19] Kelso Mail, 17, 27 Jan., 3, 7 Feb. 1831; NAS GD40/9/327/2; GD157/2981/1, 2. [20] Scott Jnl. ii. 134, 135, 139; Scott Letters, xi. 456, 483-4. [21] NAS GD40/9/327/3. [22] NAS GD157/3010; Scott Jnl. ii. 153-4. [23] NAS GD157/2981/4-9; Kelso Mail, 17, 24 Mar., 11 Apr. 1831. [24] NAS GD40/9/327/4. [25] NAS GD40/9/318/7-18; 327/6; GD157/2411/19; 2412; 2978/1-14; 2981/1, 2, 11; 2985-8; GD224/580/3/1/3/9-11; Scott Jnl. ii. 170; Kelso Mail, 23 May 1831. [26] Kelso Mail, 25 July 1831. [27] NAS GD40/9/327/7-10; 345/1; GD224/580/3/1/13-24, 37-38, 54, 55; The Times, 2 Sept. 1831. [28] NAS GD157/3010. [29] NAS GD224/507/1/18-20; 508/3/2/1-6; Kelso Mail, 19, 22 Dec. 1831; Cockburn Letters, 377-8, 382. [30] NAS GD157/2411/21. [31] Kelso Chron. 30 Mar. 1832. [32] NAS GD40/9/327/11-14; GD157/3002/1-3; 3010; GD224/580/3/2/7-16; The Times, 31 Dec. 1832. [33] NAS GD40/9/327/16. [34] NAS GD157/1417, 1418, 1473, 1477; Ann. Reg. (1841), Chron. pp. 240-1. [35] Ann. Reg. (1859), Chron. p. 469; Kelso Mail, 17 Aug. 1867.

M.M.E.

HERBERT (formerly **CLIVE**), **Edward**, Visct. Clive (1785-1848), of Powis Castle, nr. Welshpool, Mont. and Grafton Street, Mdx.

LUDLOW   1806-16 May 1839

b. 22 Mar. 1785, 1st s. of Edward Clive†, 2nd Bar. Clive [I], afterwards 1st earl of Powis, and Lady Henrietta Antonia Herbert, da. of Henry Arthur Herbert†, 1st earl of Powis; bro. of Robert Henry Clive*. educ. Eton 1799-1802; St. John's, Camb. 1803. m. 9 Feb. 1818, Lady Lucy Graham, da. of James Graham†, 3rd duke of Montrose [S], 5s. 4 da. (1 d.v.p.). Took name of Herbert in lieu of Clive 9 Mar. 1807 according to will of his mat. uncle George, 2nd earl of Powis (d. 1801); suc. fa. as 2nd earl of Powis 16 May 1839; KG 12 Dec. 1844. d. 17 Jan. 1848.
    Commr. new bishoprics 1847-d.
    Maj. commdt. Ludlow yeomanry 1807-28; lt.-col. commdt. S. Salop yeoman cav., R.E. Mont. yeomanry 1828-d.
    Bailiff, Ludlow 1807-8; Bishop's Castle 1808-9
    Ld. lt. Mont. Apr. 1830-d.

Lord Clive, who as a well-connected Tory and close personal friend of Lord Palmerston* played an important part in party negotiations in this period, was heir to the extensive Powis Castle and Walford estates and the electoral influence of his father the earl of Powis, lord lieutenant of Montgomeryshire and Shropshire and holder of the largest interest in the increasingly troublesome boroughs of Bishop's Castle, Ludlow and Montgomery.[1] He had been brought in for Ludlow at the first general election after coming of age and, like Powis, in accordance with whose wishes he invariably acted, he had generally supported the Liverpool administration as an anti-Catholic Tory. His few known speeches, cautious and pertinent, but impaired by dull delivery, marked the allegiance of Powis's four to six Members. Since his marriage in 1818 Clive had made his home at Powis Castle in Montgomeryshire, where, as in Shropshire, he regularly promoted the Powis interest at county and borough meetings, the assizes and social functions. He had tacitly supported the unsuccessful candidate, Panton Corbett*, his steward at Llanfyllin and Welshpool, at the 1819 Shrewsbury by-election; and his eldest daughter was christened Emma Favoretta after Corbett's wife and daughter, 9 Feb. 1820.[2] At the general election of 1820 Clive and his brother Robert narrowly avoided a contest against Edmund Lechmere Charlton† at Ludlow and assisted in the return for Bishop's Castle of a local barrister, Edward Rogers of Stanage Park, and the government whip William Holmes.[3] Powis's arrangement with his son-in-law Sir Watkin Williams Wynn* held firm in Montgomeryshire, where Williams Wynn's brother Charles held the county seat and a distant relation, the home office under-secretary Henry Clive, the borough of Montgomery. Corbett came in for Shrewsbury, and after nominating the sitting Whig Sir John Kynnaston Powell for Shropshire, 11 Mar. 1820, Clive proposed the addresses of condolence and congratulation to George IV.[4]

Mindful of constituency pressures, he helped to push through legislation on the Montgomeryshire bridges and the Pool, Oswestry and Ludlow roads early in the new Parliament.[5] His estate bill, which received royal assent, 8 June 1820, also affected his brother Robert, sisters Henrietta Antonia, the wife of Sir Watkin Williams Wynn, and Charlotte Florentia, duchess of Northumberland. It substantially changed his parents' marriage settlement and the post-enclosure sales and exchanges it facilitated strengthened Clive's interest in Bishop's Castle and the Montgomeryshire boroughs of Llanfair Caereinion, Llanfyllin and Welshpool.[6] In January 1821 the patronage secretary Arbuthnot considered Clive 'breast high' with government on the Queen Caroline affair,[7] and he promoted the Shropshire loyal address at the county meeting, 10 Jan., when he boldly and humorously dismissed its opponents' charge that its real purpose was to demonstrate support for ministers.[8] He divided with them against the opposition censure motion, 6 Feb. 1821. He was granted a month's leave on urgent private business, 20 Feb. He divided against Catholic relief, 28 Feb. 1821, 30 Apr. 1822, 1 Mar., 21 Apr., 10 May 1825, but according to Charles Williams Wynn, he voted for the attendant Irish franchise bill, 26 Apr. 1825.[9] He divided against the malt duty repeal bill, 3 Apr.,

abolition of the death penalty for forgery offences, 23 May, and a call for economy and retrenchment, 27 June 1821. His brother moved the address, 5 Feb., and they divided against more extensive tax cuts, 21 Feb., and abolition of one of the joint-postmasterships, 13 Mar. 1822. At Ludlow, 1 Mar., Clive tried to moderate the agriculturists' distress petition and, addressing the contentious Shropshire meeting on the 25th, he attributed the economic downturn to the transition from a wartime to a peacetime economy, overproduction and rising imports. His jibe against absentee gentry who spent their incomes on the continent was loudly cheered, but few shared his confidence in the sinking fund and current ministerial policy.[10] In June he became party to an agreement between Sir Watkin Williams Wynn and the 1st Baron Forester for the future representation of Wenlock.[11] After conversing with George Holme Sumner* and Thomas Gooch* at Lord Londonderry's* funeral in August, he informed the former home secretary Lord Sidmouth, who was sounding opinions, that the country gentlemen were unlikely to welcome the return of Canning to high office. Writing again, 13 Sept. 1822, when Canning's appointment as foreign secretary and leader of the House seemed assured, he expressed regret at

> the course which Lord Liverpool appears to be taking, because I think it will not be the *most satisfactory* which can be adopted to the country, and will I think tend to weaken the hand of government in the … Commons upon many occasions. At the same time many reasons may readily occur to render the steps now taken less objectionable than they would have been some months ago.[12]

According to the Williams Wynns, Clive, who attended the meeting of leading Protestants in the Commons at Henry Bankes's house, 28 Apr. 1823, soon regretted his failure to endorse the candidature of the Tory Member for Wenlock, William Lacon Childe, at the December 1822 Shropshire by-election, so letting in the eccentric Whig John Cressett Pelham.[13] He voted against repeal of the Foreign Enlistment Act, 16 Apr., in the government's minority against inquiry into the prosecution of the Dublin Orange rioters, 22 Apr., and their majority against inquiry into chancery arrears, 5 June 1823.[14] In September he was called on to intervene to prevent a potential breach of the Wenlock agreement.[15] Powis did not encourage the anti-slavery movement in Shropshire and, writing in confidence to Palmerston, 30 Dec. 1823, Clive criticized the government's West Indian policy:

> I wish with all my heart that Wilberforce, Bastard and Co. were sent out to the West Indies themselves, and that a portion of Mr. Buxton's brewery profits were commuted

for the losses of the W.I. proprietors into assets for their relief from the effects which their pseudo-philanthropy ... is likely to occasion. Surely government will not allow these proceedings, which appear to me to be little better than a second edition of American wisdom and will be the means of placing the West India islands under American protection. It will render the islands more unprofitable to the owners than at present and render it probable a change of masters may be of advantage to them.[16]

He paired against condemning the indictment in Demerara of the Methodist missionary John Smith for encouraging slaves to riot, 11 June 1824.[17] He also paired (with the Whig George Agar Ellis) against inquiry into the state of Ireland, after listening to most of the debate, 11 May.[18] In September he hosted a grand eisteddfod at Powis Castle.[19] Writing to the home secretary Peel concerning the Shrewsbury house of industry, 21 Oct. 1824, he commented on the recent improvement in agriculture, but warned that any attempt 'to touch the corn laws again ... at this time is ... much to be deprecated and will be productive of much discontent'.[20]

Clive tried to quell strong local opposition to legislation for Shrewsbury's poor, the Ludlow and Severn railroad and the Brithdir enclosure in 1825. He was granted a fortnight's leave on urgent private business, 15 Feb., and was at Ludlow the following day, when it was decided to abandon the railroad bill, in view of the failure of Prodgers' bank.[21] Errors in the Shrewsbury poor bill promoted by Corbett and the premier's half-brother Cecil Jenkinson prompted Clive to become a majority teller against it, 2 May 1825, and he ensured that the revised measure was enacted in 1826. The Montgomery poor bill that he had sponsored received royal assent, 10 June 1825.[22] Conscious of its effect on Lord Kenyon's family, he suggested amending the 'frivolous' writs of error bill to permit compensation to be paid for loss of judicial fees, 17 June.[23] In September 1825 he presided at the assizes and Pool junction canal meetings at Welshpool.[24] He voted against condemning the Jamaican slave trials, 2 Mar., and was named to the select committee on slave trading in Mauritius, 9 May 1826. He presented Lord Glengall's petition against extending the provisions of the spring guns bill to Ireland, 20 Apr., and brought up the report on the Liverpool-Birmingham canal bill, 25 Apr.[25] He and his brother saw off a challenge from Lechmere Charlton, who forced a poll at Ludlow at the general election in June, and their interest also prevailed at Bishop's Castle and Montgomery.[26] Corbett topped the poll at Shrewsbury, but nothing came of Thomas Frankland Lewis's* aspirations in Radnorshire, which Clive encouraged.[27]

He was named to the select committee on the troubled Arigna Mining Company in which Palmerston and several of his friends in government had invested, 5 Dec. 1826, and divided against Catholic relief, 6 Mar. 1827. As Canning realized, he was bitterly opposed to the government's corn importation bill,[28] and although this put him at odds with ministers whom he had supported for almost 20 years, he proposed a resolution calling for protection and the restriction of imports to Canada and Ireland, 8 Mar. 1827. To loud cheering, he attributed increasing agricultural distress to currency reform and the poor harvest, and ended with a call for 'some protection' and currency regulation. However, he withdrew his proposal after Sir Edward Knatchbull, the chancellor of the exchequer Robinson and Peel spoke against it.[29] He presented a protectionist petition from Woodbridge, 16 Mar.,[30] and he and his colleagues divided against the corn bill, 2 Apr. On 12 June the Whig Sir James Mackintosh* confidently described Powis and his sons as 'friends of Mr. Canning' as prime minister, but their allegiance was neither tested nor confirmed.[31] Holmes was asked to ascertain Powis's attitude to the Goderich ministry, and by October he thought their initial hostility had 'disappeared', but the king cautioned 'that the great aristocracy of the country' were still 'against the principle of [reforming] the corn laws'. Goderich accordingly informed Clive that the king was prepared to make his father a knight of the garter to secure his support. During their negotiations Powis affirmed that he 'had no sort of hostile feeling towards the government', but he declined the ribbon, as 'he was not prepared to pledge himself to that uniform support which the acceptance of such an honour would necessarily require'.[32] There was talk of offering Powis a barony with remainder to Robert Clive and calling Clive to the Lords when the duke of Wellington formed his administration in January 1828; but, Powis, possibly influenced by the dismissal from the cabinet of Charles Williams Wynn, was 'hostile' and 'aloof'.[33] Assessing the impact of the 'explosion' in Goderich's former cabinet in letters to Palmerston, 13-19 Jan. 1828, Clive, who knew of his negotiations with the duke of Wellington at Apsley House with Lord Dudley, Charles Grant* and William Huskisson*, 18 Jan., advised him and his Canningite colleagues to remain in office under the duke

because I believe at this moment in the country no two men can be found equally qualified at home or abroad to give confidence ... I regret particularly your objection to Peel as premier ... Depend upon it, whatever may be the result of the Catholic question (upon which we, you and I, differ, and which I consider only as an Irish and Whig bugbear) the less you all who wish to carry that question put yourselves in a way to force it, the more you will injure your cause.[34]

Clive neither voted nor presented petitions for repeal of the Test Acts, but he continued to attend the House and, according to the lord privy seal Lord Ellenborough, he was 'very much distressed' by the controversy provoked by the former chancellor Herries's statement on 21 Feb., which revealed the insensitivity with which Wellington had made appointments to the exchequer, the India board, the board of trade and the colonial office.[35] Calling for a '*full*' investigation, he staunchly defended his family's record at Ludlow when the inhabitants' petition for inquiry into alleged appropriation of funds by the corporation was presented and withdrawn by Sir Francis Burdett, 21 Apr. He divided against Catholic relief, 12 May, but, according to Palmerston, he already conceded privately that the 'Protestants are beat, that public opinion is against them'.[36] He cast a wayward vote against the small notes bill, 5 June, having first notified Wellington, through whom he sought patronage, of his intention and enclosed a copy of his memorandum advocating the adoption of a local paper currency to remedy fluctuations in the money supply.[37] He presented a petition for repeal of the 1827 Malt Act, 9 June, and divided with government on the customs duties bill, 14 July 1828. That summer he was elected to the Roxburghe Club.[38]

Northumberland replaced Lord Anglesey as Irish viceroy in January 1829, and on the 28th Peel invited Clive (who had last done so in 1812) to move the address announcing the concession of Catholic emancipation. Ellenborough considered his acceptance, dispatched on the 30th after consultation with Powis and Robert Clive, to be 'an excellent letter'. He wrote:

The Catholic question, as it is called, has been for some months in such a state as rendered it imperative upon the government to negotiate some decisive measures with a view to its final adjustment. The country could no longer have borne to be agitated from one extremity to the other while the administration remained neutralized upon it. Impressed with these sentiments, and feeling that the time is arrived when some legislative measure is indispensable, entertaining also a sincere conviction that to no two persons can I with more safety apply for submitting to Parliament measures likely to secure a *safe* and *satisfactory adjustment* of this question than the duke of Wellington and yourself, and having your assurance that the king has consented to allow the subject to be introduced into the speech for opening Parliament, I do not hesitate, although I would have preferred a more quiet observation of your measures, to answer your call.[39]

Clive incorporated these points in his speech, 5 Feb., when, drawing on the evidence of the past six months, he denounced the Catholic Association, pledged support for a Protestant constitution and professed to be 'fully persuaded' that emancipation would 'contribute essentially to the tranquilization of Ireland'. He alluded also to recent diplomatic and military successes in Greece, Portugal and Spain.[40] He voted for the Catholic relief bill, 6, 30 Mar. Powis divided for it in the Lords, 9 Apr., but Ludlow petitioned against it, 9 Mar. 1829.[41]

Powis suffered a 'paralytic attack' in January 1830, and pending his recovery Clive presided over 'difficult' county meetings on the route of the Holyhead road through Shropshire and cleared the debt on the loan for the Pool house of industry.[42] Arrangements were also now made, through Sidmouth and Wellington, for him to take over the lord lieutenancy of Montgomeryshire from Powis.[43] He presented Shropshire petitions for relief from distress and repeal of the malt duties, 8 Mar. As a member of the 1817, 1820 and 1821 select committees on the Welsh judicature, Clive had tended to favour its abolition, but when the 1830 administration of justice bill which effected it proposed partitioning Montgomeryshire and altering the court of great sessions circuits, he presented and strongly endorsed the hostile petition of the sheriff and grand jury (of Montgomeryshire) against any alteration, 8 Apr., and urged ministers, especially the attorney-general Scarlett, to attend seriously to its suggestions.[44] He divided against Jewish emancipation, 17 May. He joined the Shropshire Member Rowland Hill in opposing amendments to the Ellesmere and Chester canal bill that day, and presented a petition from Ludlow against the sale of beer bill. He had chaired several local meetings on the Birmingham Junction canal bill in 1829,[45] and, on his suggestion hostile petitions were referred to the committee on the measure, 11 Mar., which found its solicitor Thomas Eyre Lee guilty of failing to comply with the standing orders. Clive presented Lee's petition requesting representation by counsel, 19 May, and ensured that he was heard at the bar of the House, 20 May, but his vindication of Lee failed to prevent the adoption of a resolution condemning his negligence.[46] Clive is not known to have attended the House in the interval between his mother's death, 3 June 1830, and the dissolution precipitated by that of George IV.[47] At the ensuing general election, Charles Williams Wynn and Henry Greville belatedly persuaded Lechmere Charlton to stand down at Ludlow on payment of £1,125 and a promise that Clive would not oppose inquiry into the franchise, and he and his brother came in unopposed.[48]

A threat of opposition soon evaporated at Bishop's Castle, where the bishop of Worcester's son Frederick Cornewall replaced Holmes.[49]

At Mrs. Arbuthnot's suggestion, before Parliament met Wellington entrusted to Clive a negotiation with Palmerston, who he hoped would join and thereby strengthen his ministry; but Palmerston declined to come in alone, they failed to reach an understanding on India and reform and the scheme failed.[50] On 21 Oct. 1830 the patronage secretary Planta formally requested the support of Powis's Members, but, while they agreed to vote 'to keep the duke in', they were 'very unwilling' to vote against reform, 'thinking the public feeling so strong'.[51] They divided with government when they were brought down on the on the civil list, 15 Nov. 1830. Charles Williams Wynn was appointed secretary at war in the Grey ministry, and Clive assisted him in Montgomeryshire at the ensuing by-election in December. However, his 'want of face in attempting to supersede the resolutions of the requisitionists by such silly amendments' at the attendant reform meeting on the 13th was criticized and he was shouted down for expressing doubts that the ministry would promote reform and for asserting that distress was 'beyond the reach of government'.[52] He enrolled over 1,000 special constables in Montgomeryshire during the January 1831 disturbances,[53] and, having served on an election committee, on 7 Mar. was granted a fortnight's leave to attend the assizes at which the miscreants were tried. He and Powis's other Members voted against the government's reform bill at its second reading, 22 Mar. Clive attended an opposition dinner at Ellenborough's, 27 Mar., but, as Thomas Creevey* noted, by the 30th he and Robert had 'opened negotiations with the government. They profess to see the reform bill *must* be carried, and all their anxiety is to see Lord Grey continue minister, as the man of all others to save the country'.[54] Creevey's impressions were confirmed in the detailed report of their negotiations which the foreign secretary Palmerston sent to Lord Grey, 8 Apr., after talks with the Williams Wynns' cousin Lord Tavistock* had stalled.[55] However, as the patronage secretary Ellice informed Grey, unconfirmed reports also circulated that the Clives 'have placed themselves at the head of a party who are to declare for a moderate but extensive reform'.[56] Clive dreaded 'the dissolution of Parliament upon the bill', fearing that it would 'array the upper and lower classes against each other' and 'perpetuate the differences of the moment', encouraging extremism and weakening the ties between the country gentlemen and the aristocracy. However, he refused to support an unmodified bill, and Palmerston told him 'with all the unreserve of an old friend' not to waste time

unless he saw a prospect of being able to bring himself, and others, to support the fundamental and essential principles of the bill, because, whether the government would or would not agree to modifications, on condition of receiving such support as would enable them to carry the bill (upon which question I gave no opinion) yet it is quite certain that it would be impossible for them to abandon its principles.[57]

Clive contributed £100 to the fund for disseminating publicity against the bill, 16 Apr., and he his colleagues voted for Gascoyne's wrecking amendment by which it was lost, 19 Apr.[58] He presented petitions against the Ellesmere and Chirk road bill, 30 Mar., 12 Apr. 1831. Despite the strong undercurrent of support for reform, Ludlow, Montgomery and Bishop's Castle, where the anti-reformer John Lewis Knight replaced Cornewall, were not contested at the general election that month.[59] In a widely publicized address 'to the burgesses of Ludlow', the Clives claimed that they were 'not opponents to reform', but objected to those parts of the bill

> which reduced the number of English representatives in the House of Commons; established one right of voting in all cities and boroughs, to the extinction, either immediately or eventually, of existing rights; destroyed to a sweeping extent, old and established franchises, and placed in the hands of select bodies of the privy council decisions respecting county divisions, and the extent and power of boroughs which ought, we submit, only to be settled by the open and scrutinizing examination of Parliament. Being satisfied that great risk would have ensued to the constitution, and that the country would have had reason bitterly to lament its effects, from which no retrograde movement would have preserved it, if the bill had passed into law, we opposed its progress. We are at the same time ready to admit in accordance with public opinion, that alteration in the state of the representation was called for.

The conditions under which they would support reform remained vague.[60] Nominating Charles Williams Wynn, who defeated a reformer in Montgomeryshire, Clive defended a Member's right to vote as he saw fit and pointed to the inconsistencies of the bill, which left the Welsh counties underrepresented, enfranchised £10 voters in the boroughs, but made no equivalent provision for agricultural tenants.[61] When Shropshire returned two anti-reformers, he intervened swiftly to stifle allegations that he had persuaded the reformer William Lloyd to retire early by promising him his support at the next election.[62]

He helped to secure the passage of the 1831 Ludlow roads bill, and presented a petition against the Birmingham-Basford railway bill, 29 June 1831.[63]

He had hoped that a division on the second reading of the reintroduced reform bill could be prevented; but Peel rejected the notion as divisive and 'absolutely impossible' to achieve and warned that 'no successful opposition could be made ... if there was that acquiescence in the principle of it, which must be inferred from consent to the second reading'.[64] Accordingly, he and his colleagues divided against it, 6 July. He voted for adjournment, 12 July, and intended voting to make the 1831 census the criterion for English borough disfranchisements, 19 July, but Knight's inappropriate defence of Bishop's Castle, whose disfranchisement the bill proposed, so exasperated him that he left the House early.[65] He and his colleagues failed to divide on the schedule A disfranchisements, but they voted against the partial disfranchisement of Chippenham, 27 July, and the bill's passage, 21 Sept., and Powis contributed to its defeat in the Lords, 8 Oct. A critical editorial in *The Times* maintained that as county lord lieutenants, neither he nor Clive should have thus defied the king.[66] Asked by Edward John Littleton* in November whether 'he would like to have his castle and park within the borough of Welshpool or excluded' under the boundary bill, he declined to express any preference 'as he had not been honoured by being consulted about any of the boroughs in his neighbourhood'.[67] He had recently presided at Tory dinners in Bishop's Castle, Ludlow and Montgomery's contributories of Llanfyllin, Machynlleth and Welshpool, but he had little influence in Llanidloes and Newtown, which were to form part of the group.[68] With Alexander Baring* and Lord Chandos* he engaged in pre-session discussions with the earl of Harrowby, who still deemed 'compromise practicable if coldly and temperately gone into', even though negotiations between Grey and Lord Wharncliffe had ceased; and he ensured that the Williams Wynns, Frankland Lewis, the 2nd earl of Malmesbury and the Grenvilles were kept fully briefed.[69] As they intended, the neutral speech which Clive made when the revised bill was introduced, 12 Dec. 1831, showed little allegiance to Peel and caused a great stir, for he congratulated ministers candidly on their conciliatory tone and the modifications made, before calling for further changes, particularly in the £10 householder qualification and the provisions for metropolitan counties.[70] Members crossed the House to congratulate him, and Littleton commented:

> Lord Clive friendly! Lord Clive, the Tory son-in-law of the duke of Montrose, the brother-in-law of the Tory duke of Northumberland, the son of the Tory borough monger, Lord Powis. This was a blow to Peel he had little expected.[71]

As Lord Lowther* perceived, there was 'no truth in the assertion' that the Clives had 'gone over', and Clive spent the 14th 'seeing Peel, whom I had to hunt out, Lord Melbourne, Lord Hill and Briding [Bridgeman], and endeavouring to see the duke of Wellington, who was not well enough'.[72] He and his brother deliberately left town before the division on the second reading, 17 Dec., and he attributed erroneous reports that they had paired against it to the *Globe and Traveller* and its former editor Robert Torrens*.[73] Reviewing his position in a letter of 23 Dec. to the discomfited and increasingly sceptical Charles Williams Wynn, whom he also saw at Powis Castle and Wynnstay during the Christmas recess, he stated:

> It is nothing to see how the bill has originated. There it is. The die is cast. I have resisted as far as I could, and will do so again if such alterations as I think necessary are not made in it. ... I will concur in endeavouring to amend it in the House of Commons in committee, but unless the metropolitans are ousted, unless schedule B is mitigated in its effects (I consider schedule A as lost, a borough or two perhaps may be rescued from the flames), I must as heretofore vote against the third reading. The collision of the two Houses ... must be put an end to if possible ... I saw Palmerston the day before I left London and told him distinctly that my future vote depended upon their future conciliatory proceedings ... Harrowby rather wished me to speak more in detail on the second reading. I said no, I want to see what government will do before I give in my ultimatum, and I also wished to advise with you and Frankland Lewis before I get into particulars. Frankland Lewis approves of my course. I have reason to think Lord Cowley does so and I believe several of the supporters of government. [Alexander] Baring's decidedly for settlement.[74]

He paired against government on the Russian-Dutch loan, 26 Jan., and, as Grey knew they would, he and his colleagues voted silently against the enfranchisement of Tower Hamlets, 28 Feb., and the reform bill's third reading, 22 Mar. 1832.[75] On 7 June he defended ministers' decision to make Church Stretton the chief polling town for the new South Shropshire constituency. He was a minority teller against the London-Birmingham railway bill, 28 Feb., and had all the Buckinghamshire, Hertfordshire and Middlesex Members added to the committee, 29 Feb., but despite a tenacious struggle he failed to prevent its passage, 18 June. He was appointed to the committee on the sheriffs' expenses bill, 7 Mar., and brought in a second Newport roads bill, 26 Mar. 1832. The *Spectator*, in its review of Shropshire Members that autumn, described Clive as a sagacious, clear-headed man of business, with perhaps the most insinuating address and plausible exterior of any Tory leader in the kingdom; and although no debater, is a formidable parliamentary tactician. The reform bill, by rendering the tenure of his Welsh borough interest precarious, by enfranchising Ludlow and disfranchising Bishop's Castle, has struck a heavy blow on the unconstitutional influence of this active politician.[76]

At the general election of 1832 Clive unexpectedly topped the poll at Ludlow, where Robert Clive's defeat was a severe blow to their interest, mitigated by his subsequent return for South Shropshire.[77] Their candidate was returned for the Montgomery district, but unseated on petition, and control of the constituency remained difficult and costly.[78] Clive retained his Ludlow seat for the Conservatives until his succession as 2nd earl of Powis in 1839, but failed to bring in Henry Clive as his replacement. An active Conservative, he was made a knight of the garter on Peel's recommendation in 1844 and supported repeal of the corn laws in 1846.[79] That year he mounted a successful campaign to prevent the proposed union of the sees of Bangor and St. Asaph, and in January 1847 he was appointed to the royal commission on new bishoprics. In August that year he was defeated by Prince Albert in the election for the chancellorship of the Cambridge University. He died as a result of a shooting accident in January 1848, when his second son Robert Henry's gun misfired. He was commemorated through the 'Powis exhibitions' to assist Welsh students at Oxford and Cambridge, who were intended for the church.[80] His eldest son Edward James Herbert (1818-91), Conservative Member for Shropshire North, 1843-8, succeed to his titles and estates. He left his London house in Portland Place to his wife and daughters for life and provided for his children.[81]

[1] [T. Wright], *Charters and Grants to the Town of Ludlow*; Salop Archives, Ludlow Borough LB3/1/986-7; *The Times*, 13 Sept. 1819; Add. 28730, ff. 41-152. [2] Salop Archives 1066/122, diary of Katherine Plymley, 9 Feb. 1820. [3] Salop Archives, Ludford Park mss 11/1001; Salop Archives, Clive-Powis mss 552/22/67; *Shrewsbury Chron.* 25 Feb., 3, 17 Mar. 1820. [4] *Shrewsbury Chron.* 11, 18 Feb.; *Salopian Jnl.* 15 Mar. 1820. [5] *CJ*, lxxv. 137, 149-50, 147, 171, 216, 222, 251, 306, 374, 432. [6] *LJ*, liii. 68, 91, 95, 145, 159, 267, 274; *CJ*, lxxv. 349, 359, 418, 423; NLW, Powis Castle mss 4398, 6185, 22119; Clive-Powis mss 552/4401-5, 6049, 6790-6843, 8466, 9506-12. [7] Add. 57370, f. 23. [8] *Salopian Jnl.* 3, 10, 17 Jan.; NLW, Coedymaen mss 611. [9] Buckingham, *Mems. Geo. IV*, ii. 242. [10] *Salopian Jnl.* 6, 13, 27 Mar.; *Shrewsbury Chron.* 8, 29 Mar. 1822. [11] Salop Archives 1224, box 337, Sir W. Williams Wynn to Forester, 10 June, and draft reply, private memo. made in London, 17 June, J. Pritchard, jun. to sen. 18 June; NLW ms 2794 D, Lady Williams Wynn to H. Williams Wynn, 18 June 1822. [12] Devon RO, Sidmouth mss, Clive to Sidmouth, 22 Aug., 13 Sept. 1822. [13] N. Gash, *Secretary Peel*, 411; NLW ms 2794 D, Sir W. to H. Williams Wynn, 4 June 1823. [14] Gash, 411. [15] Salop Archives, Weld Forester

mss 1224, box 337, Williams Wynn to Forester, 21 Sept., and reply, 25 Sept., Clive to Forester, 27 Sept.; NLW ms 2794 D, Sir Watkin to H. Williams Wynn, 1 Oct. 1823. [16] Southampton Univ. Lib. Broadlands mss BR22(i)/1/26. [17] Plymley diary 1066/133, 20 June 1824. [18] Northants. RO, Agar Ellis diary, 11 May 1824. [19] Plymley diary, 1066/134, 6 Sept. 1824. [20] Add. 40369, f. 112. [21] NLW, Glansevern mss 13559; *Hereford Jnl.* 16 Feb.; *Salopian Jnl.* 27 Apr. 1825. [22] *CJ*, lxxx. 12, 342, 417, 452, 466, 518; lxxxi. 391; *The Times*, 23 Apr., 3 May 1825. See SHREWSBURY. [23] *The Times*, 18 June 1825. [24] *Shrewsbury Chron.* 30 Sept. 1825. [25] *The Times*, 21, 26 Apr. 1826. [26] Clive-Powis mss 552/22/82-85 and uncatalogued; Ludlow Borough LB7/1847, 1894; *Hereford Independent*, 28 Jan., 4, 11, 18, 25 Feb., 4, 11, 18, 25 Mar., 29 Apr., 24 May; *Shrewsbury Chron.* 14 Apr., 2, 9, 16 June; *Salopian Jnl.* 21 June 1826; *VCH Salop*, iii. 290. [27] *Shrewsbury Chron.* 23 June 1826; NLW, Harpton Court mss C.595. [28] *Geo. IV Letters*, ii. 1292. [29] *The Times*, 9 Mar. 1827. [30] Ibid. 17 Mar. 1827. [31] Add. 52447, f. 79. [32] Lansdowne mss, Spring Rice to Lansdowne, 25 Oct.; Bucks. RO, Buckinghamshire mss, Geo. IV to Goderich, 23, 28, 30 Nov. 1827 and replies; *Geo. IV Letters*, ii. 1430, 1433. [33] Powis mss (History of Parliament Aspinall transcripts), Holmes to Powis, 17 Jan.; Lonsdale mss, Lowther to Lonsdale, 22 Jan. 1828. [34] Broadlands mss PP/GMC/19, 21, 22, 24. [35] *Ellenborough Diary*, i. 38. [36] Broadlands mss BR23AA/5/3. [37] Wellington mss WP1/936/1; 947/19; 980/22. [38] *Oxford DNB*. [39] *Ellenborough Diary*, i. 305, 312, 325, 329; Add. 40283, f. 101; 40398, f. 105; Powis mss, Peel to Clive, 28 Jan. 1829. [40] Nottingham Univ. Lib. Denison diary, 5 Feb.; *The Times*, 6 Feb. 1829; Gash, 557. [41] *Salopian Jnl.* 11, Feb., 4 Mar. 1829; Add. 40399, f. 41; NLW, Aston Hall mss C.5330. [42] Wellington mss WP1/1085/2; *Salopian Jnl.* 13, 20 Jan. 1830; Powis Castle mss 6998. [43] Wellington mss WP1/1086/4; 1088/19; 1090/35; 1091/22, 24; 1098/25. [44] *Salopian Jnl.* 31 Mar. 1830 [45] Ibid. 21, 28 Jan., 4 Feb. 1829. [46] *The Times*, 21 May; *Salopian Jnl.* 26 May, 2, 9 June 1830. [47] *Salopian Jnl.* 9, 16 June 1830. [48] *Greville Mems.* ii. 16; *Hereford Jnl.* 11 Aug. 1830. [49] Clive-Powis mss 552/22/91; *Salopian Jnl.* 4 Aug. 1830 [50] Wellington mss WP1/1143/65; 1147/19; Broadlands mss PP/GMC/36, 38, 42; BR23AA/5/3; Powis mss, Wellington to Clive, 30 Sept., reply, 1 Oct., Clive's memos. Oct., 10 [Nov.]; Hatherton mss, Palmerston to Littleton, 12 Oct. 1830; Gash, *Secretary Peel*, 643, 645; *Arbuthnot Jnl.* ii. 389-90; *Greville Mems.* ii. 63; *Palmerston-Sulivan Letters*, 14-15. [51] Powis mss, Planta to Clive, 21 Oct. 1830; *Ellenborough Diary*, ii. 426, 433. [52] *Shrewsbury Chron.* 10, 17 Dec.; *Salopian Jnl.* 15, 22 Dec.; *N. Wales Chron.* 23 Dec. 1830; Aston Hall mss C.1097; Glansevern mss 14045-7. [53] *Salopian Jnl.* 5, 12 Jan.; *Shrewsbury Chron.* 7, 14, 21 Jan. 1831; Glansevern mss 8779. [54] *Three Diaries*, 74; Creevey mss, Creevey to Miss Ord, 30 Mar. 1831. [55] Grey mss, Palmerston to Grey, 8 Apr. 1831. [56] Ibid. Ellice to Grey, 6 Apr. 1831. [57] Ibid. Palmerston to Grey, 8 Apr. 1831. [58] *Three Diaries*, 79. [59] *Shrewsbury Chron.* 28 Jan., 6 May; *Salopian Jnl.* 2 Feb., 6, 27 Apr., 11 May; *The Times*, 3 Feb.; *Hereford Jnl.* 16 Mar. 1831. [60] *Salopian Jnl.* 27 Apr.; *Shrewsbury Chron.* 29 Apr. 1831. [61] *Shrewsbury Chron.* 6, 13 May; *The Times*, 10 May; *Salopian Jnl.* 11 May 1831. [62] *Salopian Jnl.* 11, 18 May 1831. [63] *CJ*, lxxxvi. 588, 677, 685, 717. [64] Powis mss, Peel to Clive, 4 July 1831. [65] Le Marchant, *Althorp*, 381. [66] *The Times*, 31 Oct. 1831. [67] Hatherton diary, 30 Nov. 1831. [68] *The Times*, 4 Nov.; *Chester Courant*, 6 Dec. 1831. [69] Hants RO, Malmesbury mss 9M73/403; Coedymaen mss, bdle. 19, Clive to C. Williams Wynn, 9 Dec., Williams Wynn to T. Grenville, 11 Dec. 1831. [70] *Croker Pprs.* ii. 141; Add. 51573, Spring Rice to Holland [12 Dec.]; *Holland House Diaries*, 93; Le Marchant, 381; *Salopian Jnl.* 14 Dec. 1831. [71] NLS mss 24762, f. 49; Hatherton diary, 12 Dec. 1831. [72] Coedymaen mss, bdle. 19, Clive to C. Williams Wynn, 23 Dec. 1831. [73] *Cockburn Letters*, 367; *Three Diaries*, 168; Coedymaen mss 224; bdle. 19, Clive to Williams Wynn, 23 Dec. 1831. [74] Powis mss, C. Williams Wynn to Clive, 20, 25 Dec.; Coedymaen mss, bdle. 19, Clive to Williams Wynn, 23 Dec. 1831; NLW ms 2797 D, Sir W. to H. Williams Wynn, 15 Jan. 1832. [75] Grey mss, Ellice to Grey [2 Mar. 1832]. [76] *Spectator*, 27 Oct.; *Salopian Jnl.* 2 Nov. 1832. [77] *Shrewsbury*

Chron. 29 June, 6 July, 28 Sept., 14, 21, 28 Dec.; *Hereford Jnl.* 19, 26 Dec.; *Salopian Jnl.* 19, 26 Dec. 1832; Coedymaen mss 183, 235; *The Times*, 4, 15 Jan. 1833; *VCH Salop*, iii. 336. [78] NLW ms 2797 D, Sir W. to H. Williams Wynn, 15 Jan. 1832; Glansevern mss 14037; B. Ellis, 'Parl. Rep. Mont. 1728-1868', *Mont. Colls.* lxiii (1973), 74-95. [79] Add. 40423, f. 106; 40485, f. 77; *The Times*, 10 May 1839; Gash, *Politics in Age of Peel*, 144, 193-4; *VCH Salop*, iii. 314, 336-9. [80] *Gent. Mag.* (1848), i. 428-32; *Palmerston-Sulivan Letters*, 296; *Shropshire Conservative*, 22, 29 Jan. 1848. [81] PROB 11/2047/337; IR26/1813/229.

M.M.E.

HERBERT, Hon. Edward Charles Hugh (1802– 1852), of Tetton, Som.

CALLINGTON 1831–1832

b. 30 Mar. 1802, 2nd s. of Henry George Herbert[†], 2nd earl of Carnarvon (*d.* 1833), and Elizabeth Kitty, da. of John Dyke Acland[†] of Pixton, Som.; bro. of Henry John George Herbert, Lord Porchester*. *educ.* Eton 1814; Christ Church, Oxf. 1820. *m.* 19 June 1833,[1] Elizabeth, da. of Rev. Thomas Sweet Escott, rect. of Brompton Ralph, Som., 2s. (1 *d.v.p.*). *d.* 30 May 1852.

Capt. W. Som. yeoman cav. 1829.

Herbert was the younger son of Lord Porchester, Whig Member for Cricklade since 1794, who in 1811 succeeded his father as 2nd earl of Carnarvon and to the extensive family estates at Highclere, on the Hampshire and Berkshire border. Like his elder brother, Lord Porchester, he was educated privately, produced quantities of juvenile verse and proceeded to Eton, whence he once reported to his father that

> cricket is going on like fury ... There is a boy who has had his eye nearly cut out from a blow by a cricket ball, another with an arm nearly broke, another with a leg everything but broke and another with a hand cut in two, besides the bruises that are given and received every day.

He had a spell at Oxford and travelled on the continent, notably in 1826 and 1828. He was admitted to Brooks's, 12 May 1827, sponsored by the 5th Earl Cowper and his father. From Paris, 5 Mar. 1828, he expressed his surprise at the size of the majority on Lord John Russell's motion for repeal of the Test Acts, 28 Feb.[2] He took up residence at Tetton, under an inheritance from his mother's family, and became active in the Somerset militia. He attended the by-election at Rye in February 1830 to hear the 'speechifying' of his brother's friend, Philip Pusey, who was unseated on petition. In July he was recommended by John Willis Fleming, Member for Hampshire, as a magistrate of that county, and he was duly appointed the following year.[3]

Like Carnarvon and Porchester, by about 1830 he had abandoned the Whigs, particularly because of their commitment to extensive parliamentary reform.[4] No doubt attempts had previously been made to find him a seat in Parliament, but he was not returned until the general election of 1831, when Alexander Baring, who transferred to Thetford, brought him in for Callington, apparently at a cost of under £1,000.[5] He made no known speeches in the House. He voted against the second reading of the Grey ministry's reintroduced reform bill, 6 July 1831, and at least once for adjourning debate on it, 12 July. He divided in favour of using the 1831 census to determine the boroughs in schedules A and B, 19 July, and postponing discussion of the partial disfranchisement of Chippenham, 27 July. He voted in the minority for appointing a select committee to consider how far the Sugar Refining Act could be renewed with due regard to West India interests, 12 Sept. He presented a Hampshire petition against the Hundred Act, 21 Sept., and divided against the passage of the reform bill that day. He voted against the second reading of the revised bill, 17 Dec. 1831, the enfranchisement of Tower Hamlets, 28 Feb., and the third reading, 22 Mar. 1832. His only other known votes were against the second reading of the vestry bill, 23 Jan., and the Russian-Dutch loan, 26 Jan., 12 July 1832. He was deprived of his seat by the Reform Act and left the House at the dissolution in December 1832.

At the Somerset West election that month he was given a very unruly reception when he attempted to nominate the Conservative Bickham Escott, who soon became his brother-in-law and was Member for Winchester, 1841-7.[6] According to his brother, now 3rd earl of Carnarvon, 8 July 1833, the Conservative whip William Holmes* 'thinks Herbert might come forward for Bridgwater and is going to write to him. I said we had no money, but he says money is not wanted, but that is a Holmes speech'.[7] Nothing came of it. Active in the Conservative interest of his relation Thomas Dyke Acland, son and namesake of the 10th baronet, at the general election of 1837, Herbert proposed him for Somerset West in a speech which condemned the 'brilliant but delusive expectations' excited by reform and praised Conservative principles as the true support of the country.[8] Of Herbert's sickly wife, Carnarvon admitted that 'I own I cannot see her actual state without considerable uneasiness. She has cough, what appears to be a very decided flush, and an expression of eye which I do not like, and after dinner today her hand was feverish and her pulse as I thought very wrong'. Her 'hectic flush' proved to be consumption, of which she died in July 1840 in Italy, where her husband had taken her to recuperate.[9] Herbert's nephew, the 4th earl, who witnessed his death in May 1852, recalled that he was

a man of considerable powers, but his natural gifts were marred by an inability to pursue anything consistently and steadily to its end. He was kindly and agreeable, and in early life a great walker and swimmer, as well as a good shot; later he used to shut himself up in retirement, which, so far as books and writing were concerned, ended in little.[10]

Acland, in a letter to his father, lamented: 'Dear Herbert, his was a gentle fine-strung mind, very generous and noble, and I believe humble and earnestly devout; believing strongly, and the more strongly for having his faith much tried'.[11] His heir, his only surviving child Edward Henry Charles (b. 1837), a diplomat, was murdered by brigands in Greece in 1870.[12]

[1] Hants RO, Carnarvon mss 75M91/F10/34. [2] Ibid. B11/1, 2, 4-6; E10/1C; E11/10; E14/50; F1/1; F10/16-32; H6/5. [3] Ibid. H2/1, 2; Earl of Carnarvon, Herberts of Highclere (1908), 78; Wellington mss WP4/2/1/9; Hants RO, q. sess. recs. Q27/3/293. [4] Carnarvon mss H5/3. [5] Ibid. B24/60; L12/7; The Times, 8 Aug. 1831. [6] Taunton Courier, 19 Dec. 1832; Ped. of Escott of Som. (1928). [7] Carnarvon mss J3/20. [8] Ibid. F5/1; F6/14; F9/4, 14; Taunton Courier, 12 July, 2 Aug. 1837. [9] Carnarvon mss E43/86; J3/35, 36, 38. [10] Ibid. J9/3; Carnarvon, 78; Taunton Courier, 9 June 1852. [11] Mem. and Letters of Sir Thomas Dyke Acland ed. A.H.D. Acland, 172. [12] The Times, 7 May 1870.

S.M.F.

HERBERT, Henry John George, Lord Porchester (1800–1849), of Pixton, Som.

WOOTTON BASSETT   1831–1832

b. 8 June 1800, 1st s. of Henry George Herbert†, 2nd earl of Carnarvon, and Elizabeth Kitty, da. of John Dyke Acland† of Pixton; bro. of Hon. Edward Charles Hugh Herbert*. educ. Eltham, Kent (Rev. J. Smith) 1812; Streatham, Surr. (Rev. Reynold Davis) 1812;[1] Eton 1814; Christ Church, Oxf. 1817. m. 4 Aug. 1830, Henrietta Anna, da. of Lord Henry Thomas Howard Molyneux Howard*, 3s. 2da. suc. fa. as 3rd earl of Carnarvon 16 Apr. 1833. d. 10 Dec. 1849.
Lt. W. Som. yeoman cav. 1823, maj. 1824, lt.-col. 1831.

Porchester seems to have caught a passion for continental travel from his father and, according to his heir, he inherited his mother's 'amiable and romantic, but rather unpractical temper'. He was also given an early introduction to politics by his father, with whom he attended debates in both Houses in 1812. Educated at private schools before going to Eton, he 'had a natural power of words and a singularly correct

taste in writing', and his time at Christ Church was 'marked by constant evidence of ability, but unfortunately without the continuous exertion necessary to success'.[2] He gave up all thoughts of taking his degree because of ill health, but created quite a stir in the university with his verse Letter to the Oxford Spy from the Bigwig's Friend (1818), in reply to James Shergold Boone's Oxford Spy. It sold very well, being made 'a complete party thing', and Porchester wrote that 'I have been accused of being the author but there is not the least well-founded suspicion of the truth, indeed I think all danger of discovery is pretty well passed'. Among his closest friends were Philip Pusey*, who later married his sister Emily, and Viscount Mahon, his future colleague at Wootton Bassett.[3] His first tour, from 1819 to 1821, took him to France, Switzerland and Italy, and according to his son's recollections

he gravitated by a sort of instinct towards the centres of political disturbance ... Nor was he content to remain a spectator. His interest and enthusiasm were aroused, and he more than once made himself an actor, even at the imminent risk of his life. At Nice he harangued on one occasion a revolutionary mob in French; at Genoa he nearly lost his life in the midst of an émeute.[4]

Travelling in the Peninsula in the early 1820s, when he considered himself 'extremely fortunate in visiting it at this moment of fermentation', he and Pusey were arrested by Catalan guerrillas as suspected government spies. John Nicholas Fazakerley* noted that, among other travellers' disappointment with the Spanish 'Liberales', 'I hear Lord Porchester's reprehensions of their proceedings cited with loud exultation'. He exploited this incident in his historical poem The Moor, which was published in 1825 and reprinted in 1827. In a lengthy preface on the Spanish constitution, he dwelt on the need for the due representation of property, but laid the blame for the failure of the reforms of the Cortes on the 'injudicious moment selected for carrying them into effect, the unjust and clumsy means by which they were effected and the contempt of circumstances that should regulate the application of all general rules'.[5]

He visited Scotland in 1825, and it was probably that year that his father suggested he should write a pamphlet on the Catholic question. Nothing came of rumours that a 'ring-fence match' would take place between Porchester and his cousin, a Miss Morton (probably one of the daughters of the 4th Baron Ducie), or of an engagement to Lady Georgiana North, daughter of the 3rd earl of Guilford.[6] Sir Walter Scott described him as a 'young man who lies on the carpet and looks poetical and dandyish ... fine lad too'. Mahon generally praised his verses, though he execrated some in 1829, and the poet Thomas Moore recorded that he had once dined next to Porchester, 'whose modesty evidently prevented him from entering into conversation with me; a rare quality in a young lord, and imputable solely to his poetry'.[7] His tragedy *Don Pedro, King of Castile*, which was allowed by the lord chamberlain, 16 Feb. 1828, opened at the Drury Lane theatre, 10 Mar., and according to one review

> was heard throughout very favourably and was announced for repetition on Saturday, amidst mingled applause and disapprobation ... It is an extremely able production, exhibits considerable powers of thought and expression, and adds to the reputation which Lord Porchester's literary and poetical talents have already so deservedly gained him.

The play's success led his friends to publish it, though the author was in fact absent in southern Spain.[8] A narrative of his travels there, 1827-8, was eventually published under the title *Portugal and Galicia* (1836), but the more immediate result was *The Last Days of the Portuguese Constitution* (1830), the costs of which he agreed to underwrite. This pamphlet, which Charles Greville thought was 'very well done', sought to defend the Portuguese attempt to establish a constitutional form of government, and condemned the interference of Britain which had contributed to its downfall:

> The vehement denunciation of arbitrary principles, the eloquent advocacy of national rights and the enthusiastic cheers of our assenting Parliament are forgotten almost as soon as they are uttered, while the prayers of thousands, ruined by our vacillating policy, are heard with indifference or rejected with contempt.[9]

Porchester rejoiced at the acquittal of Queen Caroline in 1820.[10] He was elected to Brooks's, 24 Feb. 1824, sponsored by his father. In the autumn of 1825, when a dissolution was expected, he was rumoured to be a possible candidate for Southampton, but nothing came of this.[11] He scrupulously opposed being returned to Parliament by one of Carnarvon's friends, preferring to come in on some popular interest rather than risk any form of dependence. In spite of poor health, he was anxious to succeed at the general election of 1826, but hoped that the £2,200 put down by his father, whose financial resources were limited, was not going to be used to buy him a seat at Tiverton, where 'I am so intimate with the Harrowbys and I cannot bear the appearance of turning on my friends the moment it becomes my interest'. He was also wary of accepting a seat through the influence of Lord Lansdowne:

> I feel that in deference to my father's opinions and the active part he takes in politics I can get only into the Commons on a Whig interest and though a borough from a friend, by giving me the power of resigning at pleasure, leaves me comparatively unfettered, still such an opportunity may not present itself. I trust in the actual state of parties I may be able to work well with the moderate opposition, but if I should be fettered beyond the line of conduct which I mention to you could not with credit to myself come so into Parliament.[12]

In the end he stood a contest against the Buller interest at East Looe, but was defeated, despite receiving the support of 41 householders who considered themselves entitled to vote, and his petition failed.[13] Soon afterwards he was elected a burgess of Wilton, where his father was recorder, though he was not sworn until 1829.[14]

He approved Carnarvon's decision to decline household office in Canning's ministry in 1827, and wrote to his sister Harriet from Lisbon, 7 Feb. 1828, of the succeeding government that

> after Lord Goderich's first tremors the dissolution of the cabinet was not an event that could surprise me, though recent accounts rather led me to expect that the administration would have become more purely Whig. There appears to be something in the composition of a Whig which unfits him for office as this is their second trial and second failure, nor do they appear to have managed matters brilliantly while in power. This Navarino affair seems to have [been] sadly foolish and injurious to the foreign policy of England. It might probably have been altogether prevented if ministers had sent an overpowering instead of an equal force against the Turks. Poor Canning was a splendid but a dangerous politician and his Whiggish associates readily caught the mantle which he dropped.[15]

Porchester, whose allowance in 1830 was £1,000 per annum, sought a seat at the general election of that year, and Mahon informed Pusey that he seemed

> to feel a little delicacy about pushing his parliamentary views from the idea that they would interfere with mine. Now it is very far from certain that we are nibbling at the same hook, but if even we are, you who have seen more of these things must see that his feeling however amiable is quite mistaken and unfounded, and I depend on your not allowing him to flag in his exertions.[16]

He evidently failed to gain an opening in one of Lord Grosvenor's boroughs or at Chippenham.[17] Instead, he again forced a contest on an independent interest, this time at Petersfield, where he opposed the dominance of Hylton Jolliffe*. Apart from agreeing to be liable for his expenses, all he was obliged to do was to declare in favour of reform. He advocated moderate changes, plus lower taxation and expenditure to relieve distress, 30 July; the following day he urged the electors to emancipate themselves from their proprietor. His chances were initially good, but his own pessimism proved to be justified when only six of his 163 votes were allowed and a petition was lodged.[18] Meanwhile he was busy with his much delayed wedding, 4 Aug., when his father gave him the estate at Pixton, and with other election matters.[19] George Agar Ellis* informed Lady Carlisle, 8 Aug., that Porchester stood for Hampshire (where the main family estates lay), 'which with a dying father seems to me foolish'.[20] He was in fact nominated in his absence and without his approval, but was certain to have been defeated; Sir Thomas Baring* relayed his refusal, and Sir James Macdonald* said that he had declined because it was 'no joke for any man to stand forward as a candidate for the representation of a large and populous county, with the whole host of government influence against him'.[21]

In November 1830 Porchester fully sympathized with his father's indignation at not being offered a position in the newly appointed Grey administration, and believed that he should have no connection with it and should 'enter into a temperate opposition to government when he can do so without departing from his own political views'.[22] Carnarvon, who was hostile to reform, advised his son not to commit himself too soon on the question and to be careful with whom he chose to sit in the House if he were elected. Yet Porchester, utterly opposed to any extensive alterations, signalled his further disillusionment with the Whigs in an apocalyptic letter to Mahon, 22 Jan. 1831:

> Wherever I go I hear one pervading feeling of discontent towards existing institutions and I fear a restless desire for extensive changes. That the present administration has hurried on the march of events I have no doubt – moderate reforms would have satisfied the country for some time had they been dextrously proposed ... I question much whether the gale that will eventually sweep aristocracy from the face of this country has not set in. If the falling interest of the great borough holders can be transferred to the land in a great measure and not so much to the towns the balance may yet be maintained and we landed aristocrats may hope to preserve for a short time longer some share of our former influence but I think we are in imminent danger of shipwreck.[23]

He was unable to attend the Hampshire county meeting on reform, 17 Mar., because he had to attend the Petersfield election committee, which eventually decided against him, 22 Mar. His worries about the final expenses and the possibility, if seated, of being turned out in the near future, were shown to have been unnecessary. He responded to reports that ministers had intended to make him an offer of employment, and might yet do so, by siding with his father against them, though he claimed that Carnarvon had treated him badly.[24] Mahon asked Pusey, 2 Apr., to use his influence to help Porchester, who was 'very anxious about his prospect of getting into Parliament'. A story that he might stand in earnest for the county at the general election of 1831 proved to be false. Instead, by now (like his father) a stern opponent of the ministerial reform bill, he found a seat at Wootton Bassett on the interest of the Villiers family. It seems likely that Pusey, who was defeated at Rye, was the intermediary in the matter, since Henry Howard, Member for New Shoreham, reported to his sister, Lady Porchester, 25 May, that her husband should give up the seat 'if Pusey chose to take advantage of it', and there was evidently some disagreement between them over paying the £1,500 a year which it cost.[25]

Porchester's literary expertise and continental experiences were used to great effect in his speech (which was later printed) against the second reading of the reintroduced reform bill, 4 July. In one typically rhetorical passage he declared:

> I have no parliamentary interest to defend; I bring to the consideration of this great question no party animosity; I stand here a decided but a reluctant opponent of His Majesty's ministers; for born and bred a Whig, every early sympathy, every political prejudice, every personal partiality was enlisted on their side; and between the period when ... ministers accepted office and pledged themselves to introduce a measure of reform, and the time when they actually redeemed that pledge, I did hope, most fervently did I hope, that if I had a seat in this House during the period of its discussion, I might be enabled to give it a humble, but a sincere and conscientious support. But to the measure which they did actually introduce, to the measure which they have shown themselves determined to carry through the House with no essential modifications, to this bill which will leave us little of our ancient constitution but the name, I must offer, however feebly, however unwillingly, my most unflinching opposition.

He condemned it as inexpedient, inconsistent and dangerous in its exclusion of men of property (including tenants-at-will) from the franchise, and of men of talent from the House. He instead commended the British constitution for its Burkean virtues of stability and the capacity for gradual evolution, in contrast to various experiments tried in Europe, where 'they did not understand the secret but powerful influences which cement so many naturally discordant elements, and they overlooked the hidden springs which keep our machine in constant and comparatively harmonious movement'. His speech met with immediate and general acclamation: according to John Cam Hobhouse*, he was 'rapturously cheered' and was 'applauded and congratulated by all'. Lord Ellenborough, who found Porchester 'very intelligent but strangely awkward', thought it 'full of historical illustration and good reasoning, well delivered, fluent, correct to a *fault* in language, and eloquent'.[26] Towards the conclusion of the debate (after which Porchester voted against the bill), 6 July, Sir Robert Peel and Lord John Russell both called it the best maiden speech they had ever heard, a sentiment which was widely echoed in private, including by the Speaker. Carnarvon gloried in his son's triumph, and the 3rd earl of Clarendon wrote to 'express the sincere gratification, which, on many accounts, I have felt in having been instrumental to your obtaining a situation in which you have already so eminently distinguished yourself'.[27] He voted at least once with ministers against adjourning proceedings on the bill, 12 July. Ellenborough suggested that he should take an active part in attacking its details, but he generally gave it only a silent opposition, for instance by voting for using the census of 1831 to determine the disfranchisement schedules, 19 July.[28] Defending the rights of the voters of Wootton Bassett, 26 July, he repeated his arguments against such an over-extensive and ruinous measure, and stated that he had 'heard the successive extinction of the devoted boroughs with the same feeling with which I should hear a knell tolled over a parted friend'. He voted for postponing consideration of Chippenham's case, 27 July, and made minor interventions against intemperate debate, 28, 30 July. He divided against the bill's passage, 21 Sept., and the second reading of the Scottish bill, 23 Sept. He attended the opening day's debate on the second reading of the bill in the Lords, 4 Oct., and began to doubt that it would be thrown out, which, however, it was, with Carnarvon voting in the majority, 7 Oct. He 'tried to speak but could not' on Lord Ebrington's confidence motion, 10 Oct. 1831, and in a letter to Harriet the following day declared that 'the Whigs still talk of perseverance in this blasted measure, the king is an ass and deserves the fate of Charles the 1st, and the people ought to be governed with a rod of iron'.[29]

At Peel's request and with only a day's notice, he moved the wrecking amendment against the second reading of the revised reform bill, 16 Dec. 1831.[30] William Ord* called his speech a 'tiresome declamation', while Thomas Spring Rice* thought that, by being 'long, tedious and discursive', he had lost his former reputation.[31] Yet his wife, who heard it from the ventilator, recorded that the House

gave him deep and continued attention, but his speech had not many of those claptraps for applause, which draw forth constant cheering, but was very well received, and I hear Peel's attention was rivetted. There was certainly great novelty and strength in the argument, and many of the ministerialists said it was quite refreshing to hear a speech from those benches, so free from party spirit or bitterness. Lord Althorp paid him a handsome compliment, and I find all his own party were much pleased.[32]

Though welcoming some of the alterations, Porchester particularly condemned the unbalancing of the borough and county franchises, which he claimed would exacerbate the already perilous danger of property being overturned by revolution. He duly voted against the bill, 17 Dec. 1831, but the amendment was lost by 324-162. He voted against going into committee on the bill, 20 Jan., and the enfranchisement of Tower Hamlets, 28 Feb. 1832. He was a founder member of the Carlton Club, 10 Mar. In the last of his three major speeches in the Commons, 22 Mar., he forecast a continual struggle between the agricultural and the newly created urban interests, a succession of unstable ministries which would invariably be subject to fluctuations in popular opinion, and the likelihood of well-intentioned liberal reforms giving way to anarchy. He voted against the bill's third reading that day. In early May he waited anxiously to see if his father, who had voted for Lyndhurst's wrecking amendment, 7 May, would be offered a position under the duke of Wellington; he was, and Porchester might himself have been given one. His wife, who knew of his objections to that idea, wrote that

it is now understood, that the *same* bill is to be taken up by the Tories, so that anti-reform speech must be eat up forthwith, which Lord P. and Mr. [Edward Charles Hugh] Herbert think a most bitter dose, but Pusey House swallows it entire without one wry face.

She, who also lived 'in dread of Lord Porchester's getting into some quarrel', as 'men will not measure their language now', noted that he was one of those who vainly endeavoured to persuade Peel to accept office.[33] He rose to correct a misinterpretation of a comment made by his father the previous day in the Lords, 15 May, and divided against the second reading of the Irish bill, 25 May. He voted for going into committee on the bill to exclude insolvent debtors from Parliament, 27 June. His only other known votes were for the majority against the vestry bill, 23 Jan., and against the Russian-Dutch loan, 26 Jan. (when he told Ellenborough that 60 or 70 of 'our friends' were not present), 12 July 1832.[34]

Porchester declined to offer for Hampshire at the by-election in June 1832, when Baring's success scuppered a plan to have him returned for the Northern division of the county in place of Charles Shaw Lefevre at the general election later that year. Porchester's candidacy was approved by Wellington and other leading Tories, and Carnarvon had once suggested a similar plan, but, as he explained:

> It would now be an act of aggression on his part provoking an almost certain contest, and his resources would not make it wise in him to provoke such a contest, and my father having been smarted by two Hampshire contests, besides one nearly as expensive at Cricklade, in the last years of his life left me with an entailed estate and no command of money.[35]

He decided to stand instead on Joseph Pitt's* interest for Cricklade, the earl's former seat, but thought his chances very doubtful.[36] He issued an address, 3 Dec., against reform, alteration of the corn laws and extensive changes to the established church, and in favour of the abolition of slavery and further economies.[37] However, the reformers were in the ascendant and the revising barristers came down heavily against his likely supporters. As Porchester told Mahon, 1 Dec., he withdrew on the day before the nomination because of his hopeless position, being

> beaten after a most strenuous canvass of the hundreds and having entertained but four days before my resignation very sanguine hopes of success. Three fourths of the property of the hundreds were in my favour. My canvass through the country was very prosperous. We had a majority of the old rights with us but were swamped by the new £10 constituency in the towns, which were hostile to me almost to a man.

In a final address, 12 Dec. 1832, he repeated his claim that 'by far the largest portion of the respectability and property of the hundreds is warmly exhibited in my cause', but his 'serio-comic lucubrations' were ridiculed in an anonymous reply. According to his wife, it was the opposition of their relation Lord Suffolk which sealed his fate, and he recognized that the family interest there had entirely disappeared.[38] Mahon, expressing his grief at the dismal general election results for the Conservatives, called Porchester's a 'melancholy failure'. He himself commented, on the West Somerset election, that Bickham Escott† was 'beat by so immense a majority as fully to prove the inexpediency on his own account of coming forward', especially since Escott was 'weak in numbers not only because he was a Conservative, but because he was Escott'.[39] Porchester inherited his father's title and estates in April 1833, and resumed his travels, first in

Italy and, in the late 1830s, in Greece.[40] He continued to pursue his humanitarian interests, for instance as president of the Society for the Prevention of Cruelty to Animals, and he spoke as a Conservative in the Lords, being described by Greville in 1846 as 'one of the cleverest of the Protectionists'. He died, after a long period of declining health, in December 1849.[41] He was succeeded as 4th earl of Carnarvon by his eldest son, Henry Howard Molyneux (1831-90), who remembered him as

> refined, cultivated, poetical; words followed thoughts with remarkable facility, both on paper and in conversation; his fund of anecdote was unusual, and the charm of his graceful and unpremeditated conversation was, as I have often heard, very great ... His early friends seem always to have preserved an affection for him and to the hour of his death he influenced and drew strangers to him. It was in fact an eminently honourable, loyal and chivalrous character.[42]

[1] Hants RO, Carnarvon mss 75M91/E1. [2] Ibid. H3/4, 6; Earl of Carnarvon, *Herberts of Highclere* (1908), 54-57; Sir A. Hardinge, *Life of 4th Earl of Carnarvon*, i. 4-6. [3] Add. 60993, ff. 27-32; Carnarvon mss E4/1-18; Carnarvon, 57-58. [4] Add. 60993, ff. 37-56; Carnarvon mss E4/18-31; Carnarvon, 58-63; Hardinge, i. 6-7. [5] Lord Porchester, *The Moor* (1825), pp. xxiv, lxxviii-lxxix, 320-34; JRL, Bromley Davenport mss, Fazakerley to Davenport, 24 July 1822; Add. 51831, Porchester to Holland, 19 Dec. 1821; Som. RO, Herbert mss DD/DRU/5/6; Carnarvon, 66. [6] Carnarvon mss E4/32-40, 43; N9/1; *Williams Wynn Corresp.* 346; Add. 51690, Lansdowne to Lady Holland, 14 Mar. [1826]. [7] *CP*, iii. 47; Berks. RO, Pusey mss D/EBp C1/4; *Moore Mems.* v. 174. [8] Add. 42889, f. 226; *Lady Holland to Son*, 78; *The Times*, 11 Mar. 1828; Lord Porchester, *Don Pedro* (1828), p. vii; Pusey mss C1/7; Carnarvon mss E4/59-69,73-76; E11/32. [9] Add. 46611, f. 88; *Greville Mems.* i. 371; Lord Porchester, *Last Days of Portuguese Constitution*, 109-10. [10] Add. 60993, f. 43. [11] *Southampton Herald*, 26 Sept. 1825. [12] Herbert mss 5/6, Porchester to Harriet Herbert, n.d. [1825], 25, 26 Mar. 1826; Carnarvon mss E4/46; H4/6. [13] *West Briton*, 16 June 1826; Carnarvon mss E4/54, 56, 58; E10/1C. [14] Carnarvon mss E3/1, 4; Wilts. RO, Wilton borough recs. G25/1/22, ff. 317, 323. [15] Carnarvon mss B17/6, 7; H4/8. [16] Cent. Kent. Stud. Stanhope mss U1590 C130/9, Mahon to Stanhope, 31 May 1830; Pusey mss C1/14. [17] Add. 51578, Carlisle to Holland, 10 July; Stanhope mss C353, Porchester to Mahon, 17 Aug. 1830. [18] Carnarvon mss E4/28-30, 92; F2/4; L12/2-4; Herbert mss 5/7, 'Procs. at election at Petersfield'; *Hants Telegraph*, 2, 9 Aug. 1830. [19] Hardinge, i. 11; Carnarvon mss H2/3-4; L27/2; Add. 27925, f. 129. [20] Castle Howard mss. [21] *Hants Chron.* 9 Aug.; Stanhope mss C353, Porchester to Mahon, 17 Aug. 1830; Carnarvon mss B10/1; E4/80; L17/1. [22] Carnarvon mss B17/8-19; E4/85, 86A; E11/34; E12/1; J3/17. [23] Ibid. E4/93; J3/18; Stanhope mss C353. [24] *Hants Chron.* 21 Mar.; Carnarvon mss E4/81, 96, 99; E43/6; H4/12; L14/2, 3; M3, Lady Porchester to Lady H. Howard, 26 Mar. 1831. [25] Carnarvon mss L3; L12/6, 7; *Salisbury Jnl.* 4 Apr.; *Devizes Gazette*, 28 Apr.; Pusey mss C1/38; Keele Univ. Lib. Sneyd mss, Mahon to Sneyd, 5 May 1831. [26] Broughton, *Recollections*, iv. 119; *Three Diaries*, 99, 102. [27] Wellington mss WP1/1187/50; *Greville Mems.* ii. 159; *DNB*; Add. 58992, f. 167; Herbert mss 5/6, Nosworthy to Lady Porchester, July; Clarendon to Porchester, 19 July 1831. [28] *Three Diaries*, 106. [29] Carnarvon mss L12/9, 10, 14. [30] Stanhope mss C318/2, Mahon to Lady Stanhope, 16 Dec. 1831. [31] Add. 51569, Ord to Lady Holland [16 Dec.]; 51573, Rice to same [16 Dec. 1831]. [32] Carnarvon mss M3, Lady Porchester to Lady

H. Howard, 17 Dec. 1831. [33] Ibid. H5/2-4. [34] *Three Diaries*, 184. [35] Carnarvon mss E4/99; Wellington mss WP1/1229/24; WP4/4/1/15; 2/58; 3/5, 11-17. [36] Stanhope mss C353, Porchester to Mahon, 16 Aug. 1832. [37] Herbert mss 1/37; *Devizes Gazette*, 6 Dec. 1832. [38] *The Times*, 29 Nov., 15 Dec.; *Devizes Gazette*, 20 Dec. 1832, 3 Jan. 1833; Stanhope mss C353; Carnarvon mss B23; L12/15; M3, Lady Porchester to Lady H. Howard, n.d. [39] Pusey mss C1/25; Carnarvon mss B8/19. [40] Carnarvon, 63-67; Hardinge, i. 15, 18-25; Earl of Carnarvon, *Athens and the Morea* (1869). [41] Hardinge, i. 25; Carnarvon mss E41; Herbert mss 1/19, 20; *Greville Mems.* v. 290; *The Times*, 11 Dec. 1849; *Oxford DNB*. [42] Carnarvon, 53-54, 70, 75; Hardinge, i. 37-38.

S.M.F.

HERON, Sir Robert, 2nd bt. (1765–1854), of Stubton Hall, nr. Grantham, Lincs.[1]

GREAT GRIMSBY	1812–1818
PETERBOROUGH	30 Nov. 1819–1847

b. 27 Nov. 1765, o. surv. s. of Thomas Heron of Chilham Castle, Kent, recorder of Newark, and 1st w. Anne, da. of Sir Edward Wilmot, 1st bt., of Chaddesden, Derbys. *educ.* by Rev. John Skynner at Easton, nr. Stamford, Lincs. 1773; L. Inn 1775; St. John's, Camb. 1783; grand tour 1784-5. *m.* 9 Jan. 1792, Amelia, da. of Sir Horatio Mann†, 2nd bt., of Linton, Kent, *s.p. suc.* fa. 1794; uncle Sir Richard Heron, 1st bt., MP [I], as 2nd bt. 18 Jan. 1805; uncle Rev. Robert Heron to Grantham estate 1813. *d.* 29 May 1854.[2]

Maj. Kesteven vol. cav. 1798; lt.-col. commdt. Grantham vols. 1803, Loveden militia 1808.

Sheriff, Lincs. 1809-10.

Heron, who had a 'thin saturnine face and Roman cast of countenance',[3] was an intelligent but quirky Lincolnshire squire, eternally frustrated in his ambition to represent his county in Parliament. A Whig in politics, who had joined Brooks's as Member for Grimsby in 1813, he was returned on a vacancy for Peterborough on the Fitzwilliam interest in November 1819 and sat there for the remainder of his career. In his curious *Notes*, first published in 1850, in which he mixed political comments with trite observations on his menagerie of exotic creatures at his Stubton estate, he portrayed himself as a man of honour and independent principles, implacable in his detestation of Tory reaction and corruption, but critically detached in his view of the Whig leaders, who seem to have taken little notice of him. In the House in this period he was an occasional and usually terse speaker, but he was not a thick and thin attender and he rarely lingered at Westminster after early June.

At the general election of 1820 he thought better of renewing his candidature for the county, where his unsuccessful intervention in 1818 had damned him in the eyes of the Whig sitting Member Anderson Pelham. His bid to have proceedings adjourned from the 'ferociously hostile' county hall to the yard, where he hoped to find a more receptive audience, was blocked by the sheriff. At Peterborough he was reported to have 'made a very forcible appeal' for support for Queen Caroline's rights. In the autumn he helped to promote an organized attempt to ensure the future electoral independence of Lincolnshire.[4] He privately noted that 'the violence of the ministerial party is beyond measure increased' by the Cato Street outrage, but felt that their 'calumnies ... upon ... those who support the Whig principles' did not 'make much impression on the country'. He voted with opposition on the civil list, 5, 8 May 1820, and on the 12th attacked ministers for paying lip service to 'economy' while 'fixing the civil list at the highest rate at which it has ever been'. He divided against the appointment of an additional Scottish baron of exchequer, 15 May, for inquiry into military expenditure, 16 May, and against the aliens bill, 1 June. Irritated by the Whig leaders' 'far too great complaisance ... towards the new reign' and 'the repeated postponement of all important business', and 'weakened by a most severe dysentery of two days', he got a fortnight's leave, 19 June, and went to Stubton. He voted against the appointment of a secret committee on the queen's conduct, 26 June, and for economies in revenue collection, 4 July, and again against the aliens bill, 7 July. He pressed for Sir William Manners† to be brought to book for his evasion of the Grantham election inquiry, 5, 7, 10 July 1820.[5] He remained sickened by the opposition hierarchy's 'subservient feeling' towards George IV, which, with 'the hope of succeeding to a tottering administration', had 'made all attempts hopeless to oppose the extravagance of ministers'.

Heron was no less disgusted with the government's 'base subserviency ... in lending themselves apparently against their opinions, to the illegal persecution of the queen'; and at Sleaford sessions in January 1821 he discountenanced a loyal address got up by the Tory lord lieutenant Brownlow. He voted to condemn the omission of the queen's name from the liturgy, 23, 26 Jan., and on 2 Feb., without consulting Tierney, the Whig leader, gave notice of a motion for the 8th for its restoration. The matter was subsequently taken out of his hands, but he voted for the opposition censure motion, 6 Feb., and for restoration to the liturgy, 13 Feb., and presented and endorsed petitions in support of Caroline, 12, 13 Feb.[6] On the address, 24 Jan., he called for interference to safeguard the liberal regime at Naples against 'that most happy piece of royal blasphemy, the Holy Alliance'. He was given a month's leave to deal with urgent private business, 26 Feb., and again, 19 Apr.; and he was absent from the division on the Catholic question, 28 Feb. He voted, when present, for economy, retrenchment and lower taxation; and at the end of the session noted that the zealous efforts of Hume and a few others had 'forced upon ministers a very considerable reduction in all departments ... though very far below the necessities of the country'. He presented and supported distress petitions from Great Grimsby, Lincoln and Stamford, 3, 6 Apr.[7] He called Onslow's plan to repeal the usury laws 'a bill for more speedily ruining the young nobility and gentry', 12 Apr., when he voted for the disfranchisement of ordnance officials and presented and endorsed an Alford parliamentary reform petition.[8] He divided for inquiries into Peterloo, 16 May, and the administration of justice in Tobago, 6 June, and for the forgery punishment mitigation bill, 23 May. On 28 May he 'protested against the unconstitutional increase of barracks in a time of profound peace'. He was a teller for the minority against the Postage Act amendment bill, 17 May. He considered Scarlett's poor bill inadequate for its object and joined in calls for its postponement, 8 June 1821;[9] he was a conscientious guardian and visitor of a 'house of industry' at Stubton, though he was 'no friend to the principle'.

He voted for the amendment to the address, 5 Feb., and doggedly against the suspension of habeas corpus in Ireland, 8 Feb. 1822. He divided for more extensive tax reductions to relieve distress, 11, 21 Feb., when he queried the cost of the coronation,[10] supported Creevey's attack on the 1817 Civil Offices Pensions Act, 27 Feb., and voted sporadically for economy, retrenchment and tax remissions after Easter. He opened proceedings at the Lincolnshire county distress meeting, 29 Mar., calling for a return to 'an entire prohibition of the importation of foreign corn' except in emergencies, and demanding substantial economies.[11] In the House, 29 Apr., he said that the sufferers from distress in both agriculture and manufacturing were being fobbed off with 'miserable expedients'. He blamed excessive taxation, aggravated by the unforeseen effects of the 1819 currency settlement, and saw no solution but 'a reduction of the interest of the national debt'.[12] At the end of the session he privately criticized Hume's 'eternal interference on every question ... in attempting trifling savings', which had diverted attention from 'more important questions'. He voted in protest at Sir Robert Wilson's* dismissal from the army, 13 Feb., for inquiry into the Scottish burghs, 20 Feb., and for remission of Henry Hunt's* gaol sentence, 24 Apr. 1822. Believing that government must sooner rather than later submit to the

growing 'popular voice' for parliamentary reform, at the Lincolnshire county meeting, 19 Apr., he opposed the ballot and universal suffrage, but advocated 'substantial and effective reform' of the Commons. He voted for Russell's reform motion, 25 Apr. 1822, after endorsing the Lincolnshire petition.[13]

He felt no sorrow at the suicide of Lord Londonderry*, 'the constant supporter of foreign tyranny, and the bitter enemy of every liberal principle'. He voted against the appointment of a lieutenant-general of the ordnance in peacetime, 19 Feb., for large tax remissions, 28 Feb., and against the naval and military pensions bill, 18 Apr. 1823. He divided for repeal of the Foreign Enlistment Act, 16 Apr. He declared his support for Catholic claims, 17 Apr., when he was a teller for the minority for adjourning the debate. He voted for inquiry into the prosecution of the Dublin Orange rioters, 22 Apr., and chaired the investigation in committee of the whole House; the home secretary Peel praised his 'impartiality and ability', 27 May. He called for an end to the 'degrading' punishment of whipping, 30 Apr. He voted for inquiry into the state of Ireland, 12 May. He divided for inquiry into the parliamentary franchise, 20 Feb., having promoted and chaired the thinly attended Lincolnshire reform meeting, 2 Jan., encouraged by the example set in Yorkshire. At the better supported meeting of 26 Mar. he deplored extremism, advocated triennial parliaments and a householder franchise, expressed continued doubts about annual parliaments and the ballot and attacked Lord Sidmouth's pension and the 'cold-blooded' Londonderry's collaboration with 'the tyrants of Europe'.[14] He endorsed the petition in the House, 22 Apr., voted for Russell's reform motion, 24 Apr., and reform in Scotland, 2 June 1823. While privately admitting the failure of the reform campaign in the country, he reckoned it was 'gaining ground' in the Commons. He credited Robinson, the new chancellor of the exchequer, with giving 'some satisfaction to the country by a diminution of taxes'; but he remained suspicious of Canning, Londonderry's successor as foreign secretary, doubting the sincerity of his professions of support for 'liberal ideas'. He subsequently came to believe that Canning had wanted to intervene on behalf of Spanish liberals and conceded that his 'internal policy is certainly far superior to anything the Tories have ever given us before'. When Anderson Pelham succeeded his father as Lord Yarborough in September 1823 Heron 'felt in some measure bound to offer' for Lincolnshire, although he was 'not in a situation to incur the heavy expense of a contest'. The unforgiving Yarborough, who alleged that Heron had 'materially hurt the old Whig interest' in 1818 and was widely disliked, would have none of it and backed Sir William Amcotts Ingilby*. Heron, who deluded himself that 'had I persevered, I might have been successful', withdrew and initially seemed to support Ingilby, but, later claiming to suspect him of covert Toryism, he soon turned against him, tried unsuccessfully to persuade Gilbert John Heathcote* to stand and in the end gave vigorous support to the independents' reluctant nominee Sir John Thorold, who was overwhelmingly defeated. Personal spite seems to have motivated him at least as much as principle.[15]

Heron opposed Martin's motion for inquiry into bull-baiting as 'a petty and trumpery' attack on 'the amusements of the people', 25 Feb. 1824. Next day he voted for reform of Edinburgh's representation. On 27 Feb. he spoke and voted against the ordnance estimates and opposed and was a minority teller against interference with the usury laws; he again divided against this, 17 Feb. 1825. He voted to accuse lord chancellor Eldon of a breach of privilege, 1 Mar., and for repeal of the window tax, 2 Mar. 1824, when, 'as a country magistrate', he welcomed Hume's call for information on their activities. He was forced to drop his motion for leave for a bill to end the need for military officers to pay fees for the renewal of their commissions on a demise of the crown. 4 Mar. Back at Westminster after Easter, he voted to reduce the Irish militia, 5 May, for inquiries into the Irish church establishment, 6 May, and the state of Ireland, 11 May, and for proper use of Irish first fruits revenues, 25 May. He divided for a repeal of assessed taxes, 10 May, and suggested an amendment to the savings banks bill, 18 May.[16] He presented a Peterborough petition condemning the prosecution of the Methodist missionary John Smith in Demerara, 1 June, and voted in that sense, 11 June 1824.[17]

He divided steadily against the bill to suppress the Catholic Association in February 1825, and on the 15th 'defended the people of England from the calumnious charge of being hostile to the Catholic concession'.[18] He voted for relief, 1 Mar., 21 Apr., 10 May, and presented favourable petitions, 19 Apr. He was privately not happy with Burdett's 'doubtful' compromise of the question and attributed its defeat in the Lords 'chiefly ... to the violent opposition of Lord Liverpool'. He wanted Stuart Wortley's game bill to be limited to the legalization of sales, 17 Feb. He was a teller for the majority for the St. Katharine's Docks bill, 22 Feb., but voted against the Leith Docks bill, 20 May, and presented a petition against the Greenock Docks bill, 2 May.[19] His own measure to amend the regulations governing public sewers got nowhere.[20]

He brought up a constituency petition in favour of the county courts bill, 25 Feb.[21] He voted for revision of the corn laws, 28 Apr., repeal of the window tax, 17 May, in Brougham's minority of 29 for making puisne judges immoveable, 20 May, and against the duke of Cumberland's grant, 27, 30 May, 6 June 1825. At the close of the session he reflected that 'the more liberal commercial system introduced by ministers and the acknowledgement, by Canning, of the new South American states', had 'weakened the opposition, and even diminished the inclination to oppose'.

Consulted at the end of 1825 'on a proposed association of the agricultural interests in Lincolnshire', he 'did not much approve', but unwisely 'advised a county meeting' in the depths of winter. It was 'miserably attended', 23 Dec., when he carried 'a moderate petition' for better protection for domestic farmers, though he praised the government's current 'liberal course of policy' on free trade. The association was duly formed, but Heron resolved to keep out of it, because 'I neither agree with them in approving the present corn laws, nor approve their applying the terms of gross misrepresentation to their antagonists, on a fair subject of difference of opinion'.[22] In the event, he voted against the government's emergency corn importation proposal, 11 May 1826, though on the 17th he suggested that it would be largely inoperative, while criticizing the agricultural Members for tamely acquiescing in it. He voted against ministers on the Jamaican slave trials, 2 Mar., and the army establishment, 3, 7 Mar., declaring on the first occasion that 'every shilling that went to the support of volunteer cavalry [was] thrown away'. He believed that the government's measures to deal with the financial crisis missed the point by ignoring 'the forcible diminution of the national debt'; and on 7 Mar., when he was in two small minorities against the promissory notes bill, he asserted that 'the only measure which would give relief to the country was an immediate and extensive curtailment of the public expenditure'. He voted for the disfranchisement of non-resident Irish borough voters, 9 Mar., and Russell's reform motion, 27 Apr. He voted to abolish flogging, 10 Mar. On 21 Apr. he opposed the infliction on Ireland of 'the additional misery of a system of poor laws'. He threatened to bring in a bill to legalize the sale of game, 4 May, but did not do so.[23] He was in the minority for investigation of a complaint of curbs on press freedom in India, 9 May 1826.

Heron's difference of opinion with his friend Lord Milton*, Lord Fitzwilliam's son, on the corn laws was openly acknowledged and did not affect his re-election for Peterborough in June 1826, when he condemned the Peterloo massacre, advocated Catholic relief, the abolition of slavery and reform and demanded enhanced agricultural protection.[24] In the county he opposed the adoption by the independents of the increasingly radical William Augustus Johnson*, whose candidature came to nothing and, in Heron's view, irreparably damaged the cause. He spoke and was a teller for the minorities of 39 and 15 against the Clarences' annuity bill, 2, 16 Mar. 1827. He voted for Catholic relief, 6 Mar., and privately blamed its unexpected defeat on 'the zealous interference' in the 1826 elections of the 'experienced jobber' Lushington, secretary to the treasury. He voted for inquiry into Leicester corporation's electoral malpractice, 15 Mar., and for information on the Lisburn Orange procession, 29 Mar. He supported the spring guns bill, 23 Mar. He was not in the opposition minority for supplies to be withheld until the ministerial crisis following Lord Liverpool's stroke was settled, 30 Mar. He divided against the corn bill, 2 Apr. He was 'anxious to support' Canning as premier, 'less from personal reliance on his character, than from an earnest desire to exclude those [Tories] who are opposed to him'; but he felt that Brougham went too far in throwing himself 'into the arms' of the 'cunning' Canning. He took his seat 'on the left hand of the Speaker', with Milton, the Russells and 'many more staunch Whigs, ready to support ministers when we can, but unwilling to pledge ourselves to them'. He voted for the disfranchisement of Penryn, 28 May 1827.

Heron initially hoped that the duke of Wellington, at the head of an administration shorn of the 'violent jobbers' and supported by the Huskissonites, had 'seen the necessity of acting on better principles', though he was worried by the aspect of foreign affairs in early 1828. He called for abolition of the 'worse than useless' yeomanry corps, 25 Feb. Next day he presented petitions and voted for repeal of the Test Acts, and he divided for Catholic relief, 12 May. He was in the opposition minorities against the financial provision for Canning's family, 13 May, and for information on civil list pensions, 20 May. That day he acquiesced in the introduction of Poulett Thomson's bill to amend the usury laws, but he remained hostile to their total repeal. On 21 May 1828 he supported Estcourt's licensing bill because village alehouses encouraged 'profligacy among the labouring classes'. He welcomed Catholic emancipation, a 'great and salutary measure' which he attributed to 'the just fears of ministers', though he considered it 'ungracious to consent to the immediate disqualification of the 40s. freeholders' and 'irksome ... to be obliged to consent

to exclude' O'Connell; he was in the minority on this, 18 May, having voted for emancipation, 6 Mar., and paired for it, 30 Mar. 1829. He disputed the balance of county opinion on the issue with Waldo Sibthorp, Tory Member for Lincoln, 16 Feb., 12, 16, 20 Mar., praised Peel's 'noble conduct', 17 Feb., and presented favourable petitions, 4 Mar. He divided for the transfer of East Retford's seats to Birmingham, 5 May (and again, 5 Mar. 1830). He liked the government's proposal to improve the regulations governing justices of the peace, 11 May 1829.

When the sheriff of Lincolnshire refused to call a county meeting to petition for repeal of the beer and malt taxes, Heron and three other magistrates arranged one for 8 Jan. 1830, when he moved a censure of the sheriff and argued that 'long, decided and radical economy', especially in the military establishment, would pay for the repeal. He was satisfied with the outcome, though 'a good deal ashamed' of his 'coadjutors of the ... [Ultra] faction, with their tirades against free trade, toleration, etc.', and felt that it would have been wiser to confine the campaign to the malt tax.[25] In the House, 22 and 26 Feb. 1830, when he endorsed the petition, he repeated his demand for 'a system of rigid retrenchment and economy'. He voted in that sense, 22 Feb., 1, 12, 22 Mar. He divided for the enfranchisement of Birmingham, Leeds and Manchester, 23 Feb., and condemned the recent *ex-officio* prosecutions of the press for libel, 2 Mar. He spoke up for the Irish labourers who habitually went to Lincolnshire to assist in harvesting, 9 Mar. On the 26th he moved to get rid of the pensions of £400 and £500 paid to sons of Lords Bathurst and Melville, causing a commotion when he referred to the late Lord Melville's 'equivocal services' as virtual viceroy of Scotland in Pitt's heyday. He carried the question by 139-121, inflicting on the ministry its first defeat, and was widely applauded.[26] He was granted a month's leave to deal with urgent private business, 30 Mar. On his return, he voted for abolition of the Irish lord lieutenancy, 11 May, regulation of Irish first fruits revenues, 18 May, for information on privy councillors' emoluments, 14 May, and the civil government of Canada, 25 May, and for reform, 28 May. He divided for Jewish emancipation, 17 May, and condemned the northern roads bill, 20 May 1830. Summing up 'a most extraordinary session, there being no man who has authority to keep the House of Commons in order', he wrote:

Ministers have no secure majority, for whenever the old opposition and the Ultras can agree on any subject, they must be left in a minority. The duke of Wellington has certainly done more for the country than any former minister, but it is not enough to meet the necessities of the times; the country begins to be tired of his despotism ... The gratitude the old opposition has felt for the carrying the Catholic bill has more than once saved the administration; but this is fast wearing out, and their only safeguard now is the fear of their successors.

Heron, who rejoiced at the death of the 'faithless, worthless, heartless' George IV and believed William IV to be 'a foolish, well meaning man' in Wellington's pocket, was prevented by a 'recent severe indisposition' from canvassing his constituents at the 1830 general election, which 'passed off very satisfactorily' at Peterborough.[27] Aware that the elections had been 'unfavourable' to the government (who of course listed him among their 'foes'), he now felt that reform, once an 'almost hopeless' prospect, was 'certain and approaching' and that 'the longer delayed, the more it will be radical'. After Huskisson's death Heron acknowledged his abilities but deplored the 'extravagant praise' wasted on a man of 'such profligate public conduct'. At a county meeting called to petition for economies and tax reductions, including repeal of the malt duty, 8 Oct., he condemned the Ultras, 'a faction ... with Lord Eldon at its head and Michael Sadler* at the tail, and aided by the *virtues* of the duke of Cumberland', who were fomenting unrest in Ireland.[28] He presented 15 anti-slavery petitions, 12 and 15 Nov. 1830, when he helped to vote the ministry out of office on the civil list.

He was confident that their successors, mostly 'honest and able men', would 'redeem their pledges' for 'parliamentary reform ... retrenchment, and non-interference', though he was concerned that the impatience of the 'extreme radicals' might upset the apple cart. He advocated reform at the county meeting, 28 Jan., and endorsed its petition in the House, 26 Feb. 1831, when he approved its call for adoption of the secret ballot but urged ministers to make this a separate measure.[29] He had belatedly presented and supported the Lincolnshire petition of the previous autumn, 8 Feb. He presented one from Epworth in favour of the ministerial reform bill, 21 Mar., voted for its second reading the next day and was in the minority against Gascoyne's wrecking amendment, 19 Apr. At the ensuing general election he denounced 'the rage and vexation of the anti-reformers in the House of Commons, and the disorderly conduct of the Tory Lords in the Upper House'.[30] Committed 'body and soul' to the measure, he tried unsuccessfully to persuade Gilbert Heathcote to offer for the county, where in the event he nominated, by request, Yarborough's son, whom he had helped to persuade to stand in order to frustrate Johnson; he backed Heathcote at Boston.[31]

Heron voted for the second reading of the re-introduced reform bill, 6 July, and at least twice against the adjournment, 12 July 1831; but he evidently took a pair for about the next four weeks. He was present to vote for the combination of Rochester with Chatham and Strood, 9 Aug., and the enfranchisement of Merthyr as part of a district, 10 Aug., when he dismissed Waldo Sibthorp's assertions that the bill would annihilate the agricultural interest. He said that Boston would be a 'most inconvenient' polling place for the southern division of Lincolnshire, 12 Aug., and he later approved the choice of Sleaford, 24 Jan. 1832. He voted against the enfranchisement of £50 tenants-at-will, 18 Aug., for the third reading, 19 Sept., and passage of the bill, 21 Sept., and for the second reading of the Scottish measure, 23 Sept. 1831. He voted against government in favour of disarming the Irish yeomanry, 11 Aug., but with them in the first division on the Dublin election controversy, 23 Aug. He voted for the motion of confidence in them, 10 Oct. 1831.

'After much consideration', Heron promoted a county meeting to address the king in support of the government, 18 Nov. 1831. He anticipated significant 'improvements' in the new reform bill, attacked 'demagogues' who 'thwarted public business', but conceded that any republicans returned to the House would be 'a set off against despotism'. Although an alternative 'Huntite' series of resolutions was also carried, Heron considered the affair 'as attended with complete success'.[32] He paired for the second reading of the revised reform bill, 17 Dec. 1831,[33] but was present to vote to go into committee on it, 20 Jan. 1832. He argued that the proposed division of Lincolnshire would not create 'nomination' constituencies, 24 Jan.; but he feared that the enfranchisement of tenants-at-will might ultimately have that effect in other counties. His attempt to expunge the Chandos clause, 1 Feb., was crushed by 272-32. He voted steadily for the other details of the measure and divided for its third reading, 22 Mar. He voted with ministers on the Russian-Dutch loan, 26 Jan. (he paired for them on this issue, 12, 16 July), and relations with Portugal, 9 Feb. He was privately critical of the king's 'weakness' during the crisis of May; and on Lord Grey's restoration to power relied on 'the resolution of an enlightened people' and 'the support of a reformed House of Commons' to frustrate the future machinations of the Tory 'faction which has so long misruled the country to its own profit'. He voted against a conservative amendment to the Scottish reform bill, 1 June, but on 13 June 1832 he tried to deprive Dublin University of one of its two Members; he got 97 votes against 147.

Heron, who described the first reformed House of Commons as 'a very honest, but a very ignorant and a most disagreeable one', retired from Parliament, at the age of 81, in 1847. Four years later, closing his *Notes*, he boasted:

I can reflect on my conduct, both public and private, with honest satisfaction; and as in nearly forty years [*sic*] spent in the House of Commons, I have neither received nor asked any favour from any administration, I think the merit of disinterestedness cannot be refused me.

He had unwisely described Croker as 'one of the most determined jobbers', and Croker avenged himself by savaging the work in the *Quarterly Review* as a 'farrago of nonsense and libel' written by a 'crazy simpleton'.[34] Macaulay could only hope that Heron was 'a better zoologist than politician'.[35] He died suddenly in the library at Stubton in May 1854. By his will, dated 14 Jan. 1854, he devised the estate to one George Neville, his residuary legatee, and directed his executors to sell the rest of his real estate.[36]

[1] Based, unless specified otherwise, on Heron's *Notes* (Grantham, 1851 edn.). [2] *HP Commons, 1790-1820*, iv. 191, following *Gent. Mag.* (1854), ii. 74, gives 26 May. [3] Sir F. Hill, *Georgian Lincoln*, 227. [4] *Lincoln, Rutland and Stamford Mercury*, 18 Feb., 10, 17 Mar., 20 Oct.; *Drakard's Stamford News*, 10 Mar. 1820. [5] *The Times*, 6 July 1820. [6] Ibid. 3, 13 Feb. 1821. [7] Ibid. 4, 7 Apr. 1821. [8] Ibid. 13 Apr. 1821. [9] Ibid. 9 June 1821. [10] Ibid. 22 Feb. 1822. [11] Ibid. 6 Apr. 1822. [12] Ibid. 30 Apr. 1822. [13] *Lincoln, Rutland and Stamford Mercury*, 26 Apr. 1822. [14] *The Times*, 14 Dec. 1822, 9 Jan., 28 Mar. 1823. [15] Fitzwilliam mss 113/1; 114/2-5; vol. 731, p. 57; Lincs. AO, Ancaster mss 3 Anc 9/10/4; XIII/B/4a-e; *The Times*, 26, 27 Nov., 1, 4 Dec. 1823; *Lincs. Election Procs.* (1824), 20-22. R.J. Olney, *Rural Society and County Government in 19th Cent. Lincs.* 148. [16] *The Times*, 19 May 1824. [17] Ibid. 2 June 1824. [18] Ibid. 16 Feb. 1825. [19] Ibid. 3 May 1825. [20] Ibid. 23 Feb. 1823; *CJ*, lxxx. 111, 147, 533. [21] *The Times*, 26 Feb. 1825. [22] *Lincoln, Rutland and Stamford Mercury*, 30 Dec. 1825. [23] *The Times*, 5 May 1826. [24] *Huntingdon, Bedford and Peterborough Gazette*, 27 June 1826. [25] *The Times*, 11 Jan.; *Lincoln, Rutland and Stamford Mercury*, 15 Jan. 1830. [26] Northants. RO, Agar Ellis diary, 26 Mar. [1830]; M.D. George, *Cat. of Pol. and Personal Satires*, xi. 16076, 16077. [27] *Huntingdon, Bedford and Peterborough Gazette*, 31 July 1830; Wentworth Woodhouse mun. WWM/F132/25. [28] *Lincoln, Rutland and Stamford Mercury*, 15 Oct. 1830. [29] *The Times*, 3 Feb. 1831. [30] Ibid. 7 May 1831. [31] Ancaster mss XIII/B/6i-n, q, r; *The Times*, 11 May 1831. [32] *The Times*, 21 Nov. 1831. [33] Ibid. 22 Dec. 1831. [34] *Quarterly Rev.* xc (1852), 206-25. [35] *Macaulay Letters*, v. 159. [36] PROB 11/2202/923; IR 26/2001/1072.

D.R.F.

HERRIES, John Charles (1778–1855), of 11 Great George Street, Mdx.[1]

HARWICH	10 Feb. 1823–1841
STAMFORD	1847–Aug. 1853

b. Nov. 1778, 1st s. of Charles Herries (*d.* 1819), merchant, of 4 Jefferies Square, London and w. Mary Ann Johnson. *educ.* Cheam, Surr.; Leipzig Univ. *m.* 8 Feb. 1814, Sarah, da. of John Dorington, clerk of fees of House of Commons, 3s. (1 *d.v.p.*) 3da. *d.* 24 Apr. 1855.

Jun. clerk, treasury 1798-9, under clerk of revenue 1799-1805, asst. clerk 1805-11; priv. sec. to Nicholas Vansittart* as sec. to treasury 1801-4, to Spencer Perceval* as chan. of exchequer 1807-9 and first ld. of treasury 1809-11, to William Wellesley Pole* as chan. of exchequer [I] July-Oct. 1811; registrar and sec. to Order of Bath 1809-22; commissary-in-chief 1811-16; auditor of civil list 1816-23; revenue commr. [I] 1821; sec. to treasury Feb. 1823-Sept. 1827; PC 17 Aug. 1827; chan. of exch. Sept. 1827-Jan. 1828; master of mint Feb. 1828-Nov. 1830; pres. bd. of trade Feb.-Nov. 1830; sec. at war Dec. 1834-Apr. 1835; metropolitan improvement commr. 1842-51; pres. bd. of control Feb.-Dec. 1852.

Cornet London and Westminster light horse vols. 1803, lt. 1804, capt. 1809.

Herries, the grandson of a minor Dumfriesshire laird, rose from the obscurity of a treasury clerkship to become chancellor of the exchequer, but acquired a probably undeserved reputation as a 'rogue'.[2] His father, the younger brother of Sir Robert Herries, founder in 1770 of the London bank of Herries and Company of St. James's Street, was a Spanish merchant, with premises in the parish of St. Mary Axe. More importantly for the career of his eldest son John Charles, he was a leading figure in the London and Westminster light horse volunteers, of which he was appointed lieutenant-colonel in 1794 and colonel in 1797. Under his command the corps reached a high pitch of efficiency, attracted a large number of politicians and City figures and enjoyed the patronage of George III.[3] The failure of the finance house of Boyd, Benfield and Company in July 1798 irrevocably ruined Colonel Herries, who was declared bankrupt and left penniless. His regimental colleagues subscribed to buy him a life annuity of £1,000, and in 1799 the king conferred pensions of £300 a year on his wife and £150 on each of his three daughters.[4] The disaster robbed John Charles, who was educated mostly in France and Germany, of a potentially handsome inheritance; but on the death in 1819 of his father, 'my dearest friend and companion', who was buried in Westminster Abbey and left personal estate sworn under £6,000, he wrote that it had 'operated to increase … [his] happiness … by terminating at the age of 54 all the painful cares and solicitudes of a mercantile career, which though externally splendid, had in reality been attended with more of disappointment than success'.[5] The colonel's influential contacts had enabled Herries to be placed as a junior treasury clerk at £100 a year in July 1798. Able and industrious, he was promoted to under clerk in the revenue department (£200) in January 1799 and to assistant clerk (£300) in August 1805. He executed much of the work spurned by his idle departmental chief and in 1800 drafted financial resolutions to be used by the prime minister Pitt (who did not thank him) in the Commons. During the Addington ministry he was employed as private secretary by the secretary of the treasury Nicholas Vansittart*, a light horse volunteer. In 1803 he published a translation of Gentz's book *On the State of Europe before and after the French Revolution* and a defence of ministerial financial policy against William Cobbett's[†] strictures, *A Reply to Some Financial Misstatements*.[6] In March 1805 he was seconded to Ireland to assist Vansittart as Pitt's chief secretary. He returned to England on Pitt's death in January 1806 and in December was offered by the Grenville administration a customs place at Buenos Aires worth £1,000 a year, but this was thwarted by the government's fall three months later. Vansittart did not join the Portland ministry, but Colonel Herries persuaded the chancellor of the exchequer Spencer Perceval, treasurer of the light horse, to employ Herries as his private secretary at an additional £300 a year. His career flourished under Perceval, who valued him highly. In 1809 he obtained the sinecure post of secretary to the Order of the Bath, nominally valued at £144 a year but capable of realizing as much as £7,000 in fees, which he held for over 13 years. When Perceval became prime minister in October 1809 he retained Herries, whose undisguised Tory and anti-Catholic partisanship made him obnoxious to some of the Whig opposition, as his private secretary.[7] In 1811 he published anonymously *A Review of the Controversy respecting the High Price of Bullion, and the State of our Currency*, an attack on the 'visionary' theories of the 1810 bullion committee report.[8] In June 1811 he was sent to Dublin as private secretary to the new chancellor of the Irish exchequer, William Wellesley Pole*, the duke of Wellington's brother, having declined to become a lord of the Irish treasury. In his absence Perceval, who told the regent that Herries was 'one of the best men of business ... [I] ever knew', asserted his authority to secure his appointment to a vacant comptrollership of army accounts. He never took it up, for in late August Perceval agreed to press for him to succeed the retiring James Willoughby Gordon* as commissary-in-chief, at £2,700 a year, notwithstanding the prior claim of a candidate backed by the regent and Wellington. He got his way, and Herries was installed in the commissariat's Great George Street office in October 1811.[9]

As commissary he continued Gordon's attempts to reduce the jobbery and administrative inefficiency which had long bedevilled the department, seeking to improve the supply lines for Wellington's Peninsular army. He now defended the bank restriction as an incentive to the importation of capital. Crucially, from 1814 he organized the successful financing of the invasion of France and defeat of Buonaparte through large infusions of French money into the war chest. In this enterprise he worked closely with the German Jewish financier Nathan Rothschild of New Court, London, whose firm supplied the bullion and established their massive fortune in so doing. Herries also involved in these transactions his friend Baron Limburger, a Leipzig tobacco merchant, whose wife was (before her marriage) the reputed mother of the illegitimate daughter whom Herries had fathered during his student days. (It is possible that the Limburgers were blackmailing him.) While some of the Rothschilds' methods were highly dubious and they had hastily to cook the books at the end of the war, there is no convincing evidence that Herries acted corruptly, by contemporary standards. Yet he undoubtedly profited significantly from his association with the Rothschilds: he was a regular participant in and beneficiary of lucrative post-war loans to European governments. There was inevitably 'strong suspicion' in some quarters that he had feathered his nest by jobbing in the stock market, as Edward Littleton* noted, 21 Dec. 1835: he 'certainly never inherited any fortune [and] can now spend £10,000 a year. I have never heard any of his friends account for his wealth by any other means than that he turned the early information his office gave him to good account'.[10] In 1814 Herries wrote of 'the extraordinary pressure of business which the treasury have gradually accumulated upon me, a great deal of it only remotely connected with the duties of this office'; and by 1815 the prime minister Lord Liverpool had come to rely heavily on his advice on financial policy.[11] When the commissariat was wound up in October 1816 he was granted a pension of £1,350 a year (£1,200 when holding office) and, on Liverpool's insistence, became the first auditor of the civil list at a salary of £1,500. In the Commons, 8 May 1817, the advanced Whig Henry Grey Bennet* attacked the preferential treatment of Herries, who he alleged had merely kept 'in motion' Gordon's reforms and now received '£1,200 for doing nothing and £1,500 for doing little'. Vansittart, now chancellor of the exchequer, and Lord Castlereagh, the foreign secretary, defended Herries and extolled his services, and the motion was defeated by 93-42. Yet he was uncomfortable in the auditor's job, and on the eve of the general election of 1818 he wrote sourly to an unknown correspondent:

We go on grumbling here against our masters, with whom ... no persons ... are really satisfied ... I cannot perceive that they make up in worth what they lack in talent. As the government is now constituted I hope I shall never be called upon to connect myself more closely ... with it. Some changes that would bring forward younger and better statesmen would alter my inclination ... In the meantime I will gradually withdraw from all extra work for these men and pursue my own way of living, which inclines to domestic enjoyment ... Many very respectable men are retiring from the ... Commons, from the absolute want of any attachment to the government ... These men will I fear be mostly succeeded by reformers and Jacobins, for there is but little management used in supplying these vacancies at the great House.[12]

He welcomed the recommendations of the 1819 committee on the resumption of cash payments, though he dissented from the principles espoused in their report.[13] He remained 'dissatisfied and disgusted' with his 'irksome' job as auditor, which he privately complained involved little more than 'checking the consumption of eggs and butter and tallow candles, or the expense of close stools in the royal household'. He was also sick of the 'odium to which I have been exposed for holding it in conjunction with my compensation allowance', an arrangement which he had been forced into by Liverpool's belief that 'the civil list was one of the most dangerous points under his administration' and that Herries was 'peculiarly qualified to defend it'. The death in February 1821 of his wife of seven years, a savage blow, inclined him to retire on his pension if he could not get a more congenial office. He indirectly made this known to Liverpool, who he knew had resisted all notions of moving him, but he was persuaded to remain as auditor until a suitable replacement was found. Meanwhile he agreed to become a member of the Irish revenue commission, which was formally constituted on 10 July 1821, standing third of five under the chairmanship of Thomas Wallace*, vice-president of the board of trade. The commission's powers were enhanced in 1822, when Herries drew up its report recommending merger of the British and Irish revenue collecting machinery.[14] In August Herries retired from the Bath sinecure in favour of his brother William and urged Liverpool to remove him from the auditorship as soon as possible. Liverpool and Wallace were keen to have him in Parliament, and as part of the ministerial reshuffle in February 1823, which saw the replacement of Vansittart at the exchequer by Frederick Robinson*, Herries succeeded Stephen Rumbold Lushington* as junior (financial) secretary to the treasury, while Lushington took over from Charles Arbuthnot* as patronage secretary. Reckoned to be 'highly delighted with his new office', he was returned for Harwich on

the treasury interest with Canning, the new foreign secretary, as his colleague.[15]

In his first reported speech, 18 Mar. 1823, Herries (a government teller in at least 36 divisions in the 1820 Parliament) opposed repeal of the window tax and argued that although there was some localized distress 'the general state of the country' did not justify tax cuts and interference with the sinking fund. He resisted an attempt to legalize the off-sale of small quantities of beer by public brewers, 28 May, and defended the government's beer duties bill, 13 June. His relationship with the Rothschilds enabled him in October 1823 to broker their contract for settlement of the £2,500,000 Austrian loan, which he explained to the House, 24 Feb. 1824.[16] His other occasional contributions to debate included a defence of the silk trade bill, 19 Mar., the moving of a successful wrecking amendment against Maberly's land tax redemption bill, 14 June 1824, and opposition to motions for repeal of the beer duties, 5 May, and the window tax, 17 May 1825. He divided silently against Catholic relief, 1 Mar., 21 Apr., 10 May 1825. Later that year he took 'unauthorized' steps to promote the candidature of the Protestant attorney-general Sir John Copley* for Cambridge University, to the detriment of the pro-Catholic sitting Member and war secretary Lord Palmerston.[17] In 1841 he recalled that during his five years service under Liverpool 'the general financial business of the country devolved mainly upon me'. He had a leading share in consolidation of the customs regulations.[18] He was at the heart of the treasury's resistance to the liberalizing tariff reforms promoted by Huskisson at the board of trade and Canning; and in April 1825 he told Mrs. Arbuthnot, the confidante of Wellington, a member of the cabinet, that Huskisson's 'indecent presumption and haste in altering the trading laws was creating great alarm and dissatisfaction among the merchants of the City' and that 'Rothschild had ... told him that the consequence of admitting foreign goods was that all the gold was going out of the country'. Herries and Vansittart (now chancellor of the duchy of Lancaster as Lord Bexley) tried unsuccessfully that autumn to persuade Robinson not to deflate the economy and to raise the cash needed to redeem exchequer bills by borrowing from the Bank or, preferably, getting the Bank or Rothschild to buy up bills. Herries believed that the delay in advertising exchequer bills contributed to the panic and bank crash of 1825-6. His arguments converted Wellington, who helped to convince Liverpool (reckoned to be 'afraid' of Huskisson) that the Bank must be allowed to continue to stamp small notes until October 1826. In negotiations with the Bank in February Herries secured its agreement to lend distressed merchants up to £3,000,000 on security of their goods, which greatly alleviated the crisis.[19] He defended ministerial policy in the House, 8, 15 Feb. 1826. On the 21st, opposing Hume's obstructive amendment on the navy estimates, he insisted that they had 'observed the most rigid economy in every department' and 'carried reductions to the utmost extent'. He replied to Maberly's resolution on the sinking fund, 10 Mar. 1826.

Herries came in unopposed for Harwich at the general election in June 1826. Later that year he oversaw ministerial efforts to relieve the silk workers of Lancashire and Cheshire.[20] In the House, 19 Feb. 1827, he refuted Hume's allegations of discrepancies in the army estimates. At the end of the month he told Sir William Knighton, the king's factotum, with whom he had developed close links through his involvement in the financing of the projected Windsor Castle and Buckingham House improvements and Nash's London developments, that he considered Liverpool to be politically dead after his stroke and that he was 'pursuing my own laborious vocation without looking to the right hand or the left', being 'not in the following of any party'.[21] Canning, in temporary charge of affairs, found Herries 'much mistaken' about the strength of Tory backbench hostility to the proposed relaxation of the corn laws; and Herries and Lushington were accused by some pro-Catholics of using unscrupulous methods of persuasion to help produce the narrow majority against Catholic claims (in which Herries of course voted) on 6 Mar. At about this time he circulated a memorandum advocating the appointment of a finance committee, but Wellington thought it would 'not answer'.[22] Herries told Mrs. Arbuthnot that when he talked with Knighton on 25 Mar. he found him

> in a state of the greatest possible distress ... pledged to make Canning minister, but now feeling that it is impossible or at least most highly inexpedient ... He asked Herries whether in his opinion Canning was fit to be minister ... Herries ... said he was in a subordinate situation and would not presume to give an opinion. Sir William pressed him and at least he said that ... [Canning] *was not* fit, that if he was at the head of affairs he would, from his indiscretion, the violence of his temper and his want of management, get the government into perpetual scrapes, that age and long official habits had not corrected these faults ... [which] rendered him wholly unfit.

Yet Herries, whom Canning 'courted and flattered up to the eyes', decided to remain in office under him, even though his natural affinity was with Peel and the other anti-Catholic seceders; he claimed that 'any junction with the [Whig] enemy' was the Rubicon which *I* cannot pass'. When he saw the Lansdowne Whigs being admitted piecemeal to office and discovered 'more and more how much ... Canning had been for a considerable time implicated' with them, he grew disgruntled, but it was too late to escape. His suggestion, derived from a notion of Robinson (now Lord Goderich), that he might be put at woods and forests, which 'would be agreeable to the king', while continuing to transact 'a great deal of important [treasury] business ... in Parliament', was dismissed by Canning.[23] Herries, who remained in the confidence of Copley (now lord chancellor as Lord Lyndhurst), produced a memorandum for Canning (chancellor of the exchequer as well as first lord of the treasury) arguing that it was vital to apply only a real annual surplus to reduction of the national debt, that economies must be made and that a finance committee was required.[24] In the House, 11 May, he said that the miscellaneous estimates had been 'brought down to the lowest possible standard'. He welcomed George Bankes's bill to exempt Catholics from a double assessment of land tax, 23 May, and was in the Tory minorities against the disfranchisement of Penryn, 28 May, and the Coventry magistracy bill, 18 June 1827. In mid-May he complained to his cousin that 'the whole of the treasury, deliberative and executive, having rested entirely on my shoulders, Canning has not yet bestowed the least attention upon his office', and predicted that the imminent completion of the junction with the Lansdowne Whigs (who Canning assured him he had agreed to oppose parliamentary reform and to keep the Catholic question open) would 'sooner or later relieve me of the trouble and fatigue of this office'. He told Mrs. Arbuthnot at the end of June that 'the government are not in a comfortable position'.[25] A few days later he informed Canning that having 'for some time past experienced a gradual failure of health and strength' he needed to be relieved of 'the weight of my present duties, either by being out of office altogether or placed in an office requiring less labour and attention', such as vice-president of the board of trade or commissioner of woods and forests: there he 'might perhaps be able to render you more assistance in your financial arrangements ... and more particularly in preparing the materials for the finance committee and attending to its proceedings'. Canning, he learnt from Planta, the patronage secretary, interpreted this as a 'solicitude' for an immediate move, and he was anxious to assure the premier that he had only specified alternative places in order to make it clear that he was not angling for 'an honorary sinecure such as the paymastership'. He refused to take a seat at the treasury board, where he would be 'wholly lost and out of my natural place ... in the working class of politicians'. He suggested 'as the best course under the circumstances' that his intention to leave the treasury should 'remain secret' until Canning's 'other general arrangements' with the Whigs had been completed, and that he should be allowed to go at around the end of July, 'leaving the whole question of future employment to time and circumstances hereafter'. As he wished that 'it should be clearly understood in all quarters that the motives for my retirement are wholly unmixed with any feelings of discontent or estrangement with respect' to Canning, he added that admission to the privy council, which had been coupled with the offer of a lordship of the treasury, would 'help most distinctly to mark the character' of his retirement. Arbuthnot, one of the seceders, assured him that although it had been 'no secret' that he had 'first intended to throw up office if the Whigs came in', there were 'valid grounds' for his 'remaining ... rather than be the cause of embarrassment in your particular department of the king's government'; but he warned Herries that his taking another office in conjunction with the Whigs would damage him in the eyes of his former Tory colleagues and jeopardize his chances of employment if they came in again. Arbuthnot then said as much to Peel, reporting that Herries 'tells me that Canning and the Whigs are ... wide asunder, that Canning's time is passed in resisting their encroachments and that ... the two parties are so much at variance that sooner or later they must split'. In mid-July, after Canning had acquiesced in Lansdowne's appointment as home rather than foreign secretary, Herries told Arbuthnot, who still did not know which way he would jump, that the premier was 'on the declivity of a hill, and ... was hurried forward without being able to stop himself'. At this juncture Herries explained his situation to his cousin, writing from Montreal, the Kent residence near Sevenoaks which he rented from Lord Amherst:

> I have been completely knocked up by the fatigues which the peculiar circumstances of the late session heaped upon me ... I was not only weary but sick of all that was going on and vexed that ... I was unable without dealing fairly by the public service to withdraw myself from the mess ... I am now getting better, but ... a long interval of relaxation is indispensably necessary for my complete restoration ... I have given warning to Canning that I cannot face the double work of my station ... He wants me to take some situation in which I may have more honour and more ease, so as to be able to assist him in finance and in Parliament. I have discouraged these propositions, but I have assured him that I will endeavour as much as possible to meet his convenience in the mode and time of my ultimately giving up my present office.

Two weeks later he welcomed Arbuthnot's news of a friendly meeting between Wellington and the king:

> The more good feeling between them is maintained the greater will be the facility for getting things right again when the proper opportunity arrives. I am quite confident that the new friends cannot long continue so ... The special imprudence and fiery temper of some of the leaders must inevitably lead to a violent separation ... The possession of the government during the remainder of the present reign ... by the Tories will then depend upon the prudence of their management at that juncture ... I am getting out of my trammels, but using my best endeavours to do so without creating inconvenience or embarrassment to anyone. I shall give every assistance in my power to prepare for the difficult arrangements which we have to make in the next session, upon the successful execution of which the stability of the government, let who will be at the head of it, must materially depend.

Arbuthnot, wishing that Herries would 'not try to lessen ...[ministers'] difficulties', showed this letter to Wellington and Peel, who doubted the 'correctness' of his prediction of a fatal split. By 5 Aug 1827 Herries, whose impending resignation was now public knowledge, was on the verge of embarking on an extended European tour, though he feared that the ailing Canning's death in the immediate future would 'embarrass me exceedingly'.[26]

As Canning lapsed towards his death in the small hours of 8 Aug. 1827, Herries was persuaded by Lyndhurst and Planta to postpone his departure.[27] Later that day the king invited Goderich to form a ministry on the same basis as Canning's and suggested the appointment of the Canningite William Sturges Bourne*, already in the cabinet as commissioner of woods and forests, as chancellor of the exchequer. Goderich complied, but Sturges Bourne was unwilling to take on the office. Herries, who considered his resignation to have been accepted by Canning, was not initially inclined to involve himself further in office with 'Whigs and Radicals'. When Wellington's confidant Sir Henry Hardinge* saw him in London on 9 Aug. he found him

> looking very ill ... He says he must for the present resign, as he is completely done up and must be abroad. He said he did not know until lately the extent of the intrigue and dirty work that had been going on ... He thinks he will for the present decline on the score of health, but support as a looker-on ... He advocates oblivion of the past, but rather as it regards Tories *in*, and did not say anything distinct as to the policy of a mixture of Whigs.[28]

On 10 Aug. Goderich called twice on Herries, who 'assured him that he might consider me as remaining attached to his administration', but told him that his wish to leave the treasury still held and, when sounded about the exchequer, to which the king had suggested appointing him, recommended Huskisson. He then went into the country.[29] On the 12th he was called to London by Planta, who told him that Goderich wanted him to take the exchequer. Next day he met separately Lyndhurst and Goderich, who pressed him to take the post as 'the king's appointment' before going on his holiday. Herries wrote to his sister Isabelle that evening:

> I am put in a most perplexing and uncomfortable situation, by that which to most men would be a subject of great exultation ... The government is to remain unchanged except that two Tories, Charles Grant* and myself, are to be introduced ... while no new Whig is to come in. The Whigs it is said are to be kept down. But it is a weak government, and can hardly go on. Ought I to run the risk of going down with it ... or ... without any good reason to allege throw away the opportunity of advancement and the favour of the king by refusing? ... If I refuse ... I must do so upon the ground that *I cannot resolve in the present state of my health to take upon me so heavy and anxious a charge* ... Pray let me have a line ... stating your opinion, on ... the supposition that *though really unwell enough to justify a refusal*, I am yet in a state to *hope to be soon well enough to justify an acceptance*. So that ... the acceptance or refusal must spring in my own mind from political feelings.

Hardinge commented to Wellington that although Herries had 'openly stated' that Goderich's ministry 'won't stand the first week of the session', he had 'blown so often hot and cold that I think he will not refuse the bait'; but Mrs. Arbuthnot thought it would be 'strange' if he accepted.[30] In the event, after a restless night Herries, who was expected to go to Windsor on the morning of the 14th to kiss hands, informed Goderich that he wished not to take the office and wrote to Knighton declining it on the ground of ill health.[31] Later that day he received via Knighton a personal message from the king urging him to reconsider, which he felt obliged to do, though when he accepted on the morning of the 15th he sought and obtained permission from Goderich to go abroad with the option of relinquishing the office should his health not improve. Arbuthnot remarked sourly that Herries, who had always regarded Goderich 'with the most sovereign contempt' and was himself 'a good secretary' but had 'the farthest from an enlarged mind', was probably 'ashamed of himself' for swallowing the lure and had 'signed his death warrant as a public man'. Goderich's weakness and indecision threw matters into chaos. Unknown to Herries, and having

been quizzed by Lansdowne and the Whig George Tierney*, master of the mint, about the approach to him, he had offered the exchequer to Palmerston, who was willing to take it, with Herries replacing him as war secretary outside the cabinet. He confessed his quandary to Herries, who on the 15th urged him to make use of his earlier formal refusal and prepared to go abroad. The king vetoed Palmerston, insisted that Herries was the 'fittest person', sent Goderich an open letter to Herries commanding him to accept the office and directed that Herries was to attend at Windsor on the 17th to accept the seals. When Goderich saw Herries on the 16th he did not show him this letter, but admitted that his appointment had now become a bone of contention with the cabinet Whigs and hinted that he would like Herries to step aside. Herries retorted that it behoved Goderich, as prime minister, to stand up to the king and asked him to advise George to let him retire.[32] When Goderich belatedly showed Herries the king's open letter on the morning of 17 Aug. they agreed that it was 'impossible to oppose any further resistance', and Herries went to Windsor. There took place a bizarre episode, in which Lansdowne and Tierney, aware of mounting Whig rank and file hostility to Herries as a Tory partisan and anti-Catholic bigot, the supposed creature of Knighton and the king and a suspected stock jobber, told Goderich that they would resign if he was appointed. They were also disgruntled over the king's refusal to admit Lord Holland to the cabinet, and Tierney, an old enemy of Herries, argued that he was not of sufficient parliamentary calibre to lead the Commons should Huskisson's health give way. Herries was informed of this by Goderich, who urged him not to accept the seals until he had seen the king again. Herries duly informed the king of all that had passed between him and Goderich, declined to take the seals and persuaded the king to see Goderich. At this interview the king agreed to postpone a decision until Huskisson, leader of the Canningites and earmarked for the colonial secretaryship, returned from his European holiday. Yet he still made it clear to Herries that the exchequer seals were his, and had him sworn a member of the privy council. Palmerston reported that before his audience 'poor Herries [looked] like a victim about to be cast into a den of lions ready to devour him', but he discounted the Whig belief that he would allow George and Knighton free rein over the contentious royal finances, as he was 'an honourable man' who, setting aside his poor health and awareness of his unpopularity with the Whigs, would

> 'really be an excellent man for the office', being 'a very intelligent, clearheaded man ... of strict integrity', and

who if he had 'not at present perhaps the scope of mind which belongs to a cabinet situation' might develop it with time.[33]

In an interview with Goderich, Lyndhurst and the Whig cabinet member Lord Carlisle, 21 Aug., the king stressed, for the benefit of Lansdowne and Tierney, that while he was willing to await Huskisson's arrival, he had no intention of admitting Holland to the cabinet and was determined to have Herries.[34] The Canningite Lord Howard de Walden, foreign office under-secretary, warned Huskisson that Herries, 'a creature of Knighton's', did '*not* stand well in the world', that 'people *do not* like him as a cabinet minister and moreover there are some awkward stories about his connection with Rothschild'. The duke of Devonshire was informed that Herries was regarded in the City as being 'in Rothschild's power' and likely as chancellor to 'betray the cabinet secrets to a stock jobber'. On 24 Aug. the *Morning Chronicle* alleged that Whig objections to Herries's appointment were grounded on these suspicions; but, as Lansdowne perceived, these slurs made it 'more difficult for him to recede', especially as there was 'nothing that can be substantiated'. With Goderich's blessing and endorsement Herries, now 'determined to press for his appointment ... in order to prevent any imputation being cast on his character', wrote to *The Times* (27 Aug.) to repudiate the allegations, though Lyndhurst talked him out of suing the *Chronicle*.[35] On 25 Aug. he told Isabelle that matters were no further forward and that at a requested interview with Goderich he had encountered

again a scene of unmanly perplexity. I could not learn from him what his real intentions were ... It appeared quite clear, however, that the Whigs had threatened to resign if my appointment were persisted in, and he threw out some indistinct hints of his own disposition to resign if *they* did. I told him I could not understand his feelings in that respect ... He seemed puzzled by this, but he said there were circumstances which I did not know, and which he could not explain to me ... The king is come to town and I much suspect the affair will thereby be brought to a crisis. Either the Whigs will give way, or he will turn them out ... The Whigs are disseminating lies about me.[36]

Palmerston felt that the Whigs would be mad to resign over Herries's appointment, while Henry Brougham*, anxious to keep out the old Tories and secure the party's hold on power, thought they should swallow it if he 'satisfactorily' denied, when questioned directly, that 'he ever made a farthing' by stock jobbing with Rothschild. Holland, however, stressed to Lansdowne

'the utter impossibility of undertaking the business of the House of Commons with a finance minister whose views and principles are unknown to you' and argued that the rumours about his connections, even if false, were 'an additional inconvenience' to an appointment 'only recommended by Court favour or Court intrigue'.[37] When Huskisson arrived on 28 Aug. Herries, now 'quite passive in the whole of this business', as he told Isabelle, kept out of his way; he condemned the 'vacillating' Goderich and thought the Whigs could 'hardly do otherwise' than resign. Huskisson saw the king on the 29th, declined to take the exchequer himself and suggested the temporary appointment of Sturges Bourne as a way out of the mess. Next day Herries met Goderich, Huskisson, Lyndhurst and Sturges Bourne and was presented with a compromise arrangement, whereby he would become president of the board of trade with management of the finance committee, on the understanding that he would eventually replace Sturges Bourne at the exchequer. To Huskisson's fury, he refused to submit to what he considered a humiliation; in any case, Sturges Bourne declined to take the exchequer. After Huskisson had consulted Lansdowne, however, Sturges Bourne seemed to change his mind, but Herries would not give way. In a later talk with Lansdowne and Huskisson he was 'nearly won over', as the latter saw it; but Sturges Bourne's final retraction put matters 'more at sea than ever'.[38] Herries joined Lansdowne in vainly urging Huskisson to take the exchequer, while he stayed at the treasury for the time being. At Windsor on 31 Aug., when Herries, Goderich, Lyndhurst, Huskisson and Sturges Bourne were present, the king insisted on Herries's appointment, but he still did not take the seals, and it was agreed that Goderich and the king should exhort Lansdowne not to wreck the government. The offer of some concessionary junior Whig places and the king's personal appeal induced Lansdowne to give way, and Tierney reluctantly complied, though he remained deeply dissatisfied.[39] Herries, whose appointment was also 'a bitter pill' to Holland and others, kissed hands on 3 Sept. 1827 and later that month went abroad for four weeks. Before leaving he told his relatives that while he 'should certainly have been much better satisfied to have been left alone ... so many compensatory circumstances have occurred to counterbalance the vexations ... that I do not feel I ought to complain'. He claimed, with some justice, that 'I was most unwillingly drawn into the field of contention of which I was the chief object and at last almost the victim'.[40]

His part in the episode which wrecked Goderich's government four months later was perhaps less innocent. In cabinet in late November 1827 he joined Tierney in opposing Huskisson and Lansdowne's wish to back the Russian plan to invade Moldavia and Walachia. According to Mrs. Arbuthnot, in a 'long conversation' with her husband he

> told the same story as [William] Holmes* of the dissensions in the cabinet ... He said the king and Knighton are very hostile to the Whigs and are quite resolved to turn them out if they get into any difficulties. If this does occur, they are determined to send for ... [Wellington]. He said Lord Goderich was laughed at and despised by everybody ... He was positive there must be a break-up ... He added that, if war was determined on, *he would retire* (the only part of his story I don't believe).

When informed of this by Arbuthnot, Peel commented:

> I distrust all that is said to you by Herries, except so far as it is confirmed by other circumstances. As he has waded up to his chin through the widest part of *the Rubicon*, he is naturally ashamed of himself. That we should have lived to see the day, when instead of mending the blunders in the malt bill, he, *Herries*, backed by *Tierney*, is giving peace to Europe by resisting the invasion of Moldavia and Walachia![41]

On 28 Nov. Herries was informed by Huskisson that the leading Whig backbencher Lord Althorp, whom ministers wished to cultivate, was being considered as chairman of the finance committee. The idea had originated with Tierney, who had already secured Goderich's approval and now revealed to Herries that Althorp had accepted in principle. Herries, by all accounts, 'concurred without qualification'. Next day he told Huskisson that he had had second thoughts, considering Althorp to be a 'dangerous reformer'. On the 30th Huskisson heard from Planta that Herries was 'very sore' and was falsely alleging that he had only found out about the proposal from a backbencher and that the arrangement had been covertly made. Huskisson ordered Tierney to stop considering names for the committee with anyone outside the cabinet and wrote to Herries arguing that Althorp would be 'safer' in the chair than as a member of the committee. As Herries did not raise the issue when they met in cabinet on 3 Dec., Huskisson assumed that the 'misconception' had been removed and the matter was in abeyance. Tierney did continue to negotiate covertly with Althorp, which gave Herries the semblance of a genuine grievance and a handy pretext for his next move.[42] Goderich's renewed attempt to secure the admission of Holland to the cabinet, the deterioration of Herries's relationship with Huskisson and his desire, which was partly inspired by pressure from Rothschild, to protect City interests against a reform-

ing finance committee prompted him to try to break up the ministry. He and Lyndhurst were in communication with Knighton, whom the lord chancellor asked to notify the king of Herries and Bexley's likely impending resignations on 20 Dec. Next day Herries wrote to Goderich tendering his resignation on the ground that the arrangement with Althorp, on a matter central to his concerns as chancellor of the exchequer, had been made behind his back. Huskisson, who believed that Herries was up to his neck in Knighton's intrigues (a suspicion validated by Herries's letter to Knighton of 31 Dec. 1827 assuring him that he and Lyndhurst saw 'matters quite in the same light'), offered to resign, but was talked out of it, though he insisted on going out if Althorp was not made chairman. Herries would not back down and on 7 Jan. 1828 he rejected a last attempt by the dithering Goderich to persuade him to 'yield'. In a conversation that day with Hardinge, intended to be relayed to Wellington and Peel, he said that the king ignored Lansdowne, 'disliked Tierney and despised Goderich', criticized Huskisson and denounced Tierney as 'an old rogue'. Next day the tearful premier told the king that he could not go on. He was dismissed from office and Wellington sent for.[43] Herries's ostensible role in the collapse of the ministry was soon common knowledge, but opinions varied as to the rights and wrongs of his conduct; even some Whigs thought he had been badly treated, but most condemned the 'odious little clerk' for conspiring to upset the applecart.[44] Herries himself, naming Brougham as the chief culprit, privately attributed the government's collapse to the Whigs' attempts to force Holland into the cabinet: Goderich 'felt himself dying of Whig poison and seized the occasion to induce the king out of pure compassion to end his miseries'.[45]

The recall of Wellington and Peel did not advance his political career. Wellington's initial notion to make him chancellor of the duchy of Lancaster was unacceptable to the king, who did 'not like' his removal from the exchequer, though he was agreeable to his being appointed president of the board of trade. Meanwhile Herries brokered a deal with Rothschild to lend money, guaranteed by the new ministry, to Dom Miguel.[46] Huskisson, whom Wellington was keen to take in, regarded Herries as 'the stumbling block', and after negotiations with the duke and consultation with his allies Lord Dudley, Palmerston and Grant, he agreed on 17 Jan. 1828 to take office only if Herries was removed from the exchequer, having decided that they could not reasonably insist on his exclusion from the cabinet. Wellington, who despised Herries, had no problem with this: Huskisson stayed at the colonial office, the duchy went to Lord Aberdeen and the exchequer to Henry Goulburn*, and Herries replaced Tierney ('a good epigram', thought Huskisson) at the mint, a cabinet office with 'no departmental influence'. It was in fact 'almost a sinecure', hardly appropriate for a man of his financial expertise and administrative experience, especially in view of Goulburn's ignorance of financial questions.[47] Herries made an 'unlucky' start, for the premature disclosure in the *Morning Chronicle* of 19 Jan. of the membership of the new cabinet was (incorrectly as it turned out) attributed to his having passed on the information to the advanced Whig John Maberly*, a former army contractor with whom he had a curious relationship. The fault lay with Herries's clerk, who had been indiscreet, but Wellington rapped Herries's knuckles and lectured him on the importance of cabinet confidentiality.[48] John Croker* found him 'feeling ... that he is degraded' in his peripheral office, away from 'his Martello tower' of finance, but was convinced by his lamentation that he 'must be what he is or nothing', for 'he alone could not set up a Tory opposition' and he 'could not join the Whigs'. At his first sighting of Herries at a cabinet dinner, 22 Jan. 1828, the second generation peer Lord Ellenborough, lord privy seal, described him as 'a plain, ordinary-looking, clerk-like man, full of information' but, as one of 'the class of under-secretaries', appearing out of place in a cabinet.[49]

In the House, 6 Feb. 1828, Herries squabbled with Hume over the accounts for exchequer bill payments. He advised Peel, the home secretary, on the most acceptable composition of the finance committee, to which he was appointed, 15 Feb. He was very active on it, gave evidence to it and drew up its fourth report, which belatedly endorsed the policy of tariff reform.[50] On 12 Feb. he complained to Ellenborough that in his explanation of the collapse of his ministry in the Lords the previous evening Goderich had omitted some pertinent facts (a view shared by Huskisson, though from a different perspective).[51] In the Commons, 18 Feb., Herries followed Huskisson in giving his side of the story: he dismissed Goderich's allegation that the sole cause of the break-up had been his clash with Huskisson over the chairmanship, denied having intended, still less plotted, to wreck the ministry and read in full his correspondence with Goderich between 21 Dec. 1827 and 7 Jan. 1828, in order to demonstrate the late premier's feebleness. The initial impression on both sides of the House was favourable, and his speech, though delivered in a 'very low' tone, was cheered. But Tierney tellingly exposed some of the inconsistencies in his statement, particularly his three-week silence on the chairmanship,

while Tom Duncombe, radical Member for Hertford, anxious to make a splash, associated him with 'a secret influence behind the throne' (Knighton) and a 'master of unbounded wealth' (Rothschild) and called on Wellington to ensure that the national finances would no longer be 'controlled ... by a Jew' or patronage dispensed 'by the prescription of a physician'. Brougham also attacked Herries to good effect on the 19th.[52] While on his feet admitting the 'injurious effects' of the 1827 Malt Act, 21 Feb., Herries tried to vindicate himself, insisting that Goderich had left him in ignorance of Huskisson's threat to resign until it was too late and repeating 'barefacedly' but not elaborating on his allegation that there had been a deeper 'plot' to destroy the government. He was roughly handled by Brougham, Sturges Bourne, Charles Williams Wynn and Macdonald and emerged very considerably 'damaged', as Hardinge reported and Peel was supposed to believe.[53] He divided silently against repeal of the Test Acts, 26 Feb., and Catholic relief, 12 May, having presented a hostile Harwich petition, 9 May. He now cut a somewhat forlorn figure in the House and in the cabinet, where he kept out of the arguments about the corn laws. Mrs. Arbuthnot noted on 29 Feb. that he 'never utters, and last night there was a laugh of derision when he was named as a minister'.[54] He replied to criticism of expenditure on royal residences and repudiated Sir James Graham's insinuation that he would take a biased view of it on the finance committee, 24 Mar. He also backed Goulburn's refusal to postpone the grant of £2,000,000 for the sinking fund and defended the conduct of the Canning and Goderich ministries on life annuities. He opposed Harvey's motion for more effective control over crown excise prosecutions, 1 May, and on the 16th said that John Wood's 'garbled statement' on the national finances was 'erroneous'. In April Mrs. Arbuthnot had suspected him of hankering after the idle Grant's job at the board of trade; and when Grant and the other Huskissonites resigned in the last week of May the king suggested moving Goulburn to the colonial office and giving Herries the exchequer. Wellington ruled this out, ostensibly on the ground that their necessary re-elections would remove them from the House at a 'very inconvenient' moment and interrupt Herries's work on the finance committee. On 28 May Herries appealed directly to the premier for a move:

> The office which I now fill is a mere sinecure and ... such as might be held by any person who, by high rank or influential connections, though unqualified by official ability or experience, might add to the strength of your government. My only means of being in any degree useful ... must consist in the efficient discharge of some public

duties; and I ... feel myself out of my proper position so long as I occupy an office suited to the station and influence which I do not possess, and unsuited to the exercise of any little ability which I may have acquired ... I feel it to be right, now that you are about making a new distribution of ... offices ... candidly to state that it would have given me more satisfaction if ... it would have accorded with your arrangements to place me in a situation of more labour and responsibility.

Wellington entreated him to 'be satisfied, and have patience, and be assured that you must rise eventually to offices of more business', and meanwhile to make the most of his freedom from departmental duties, which allowed him to 'assist the government on a variety of subjects'.[55] In the House, 30 May, Herries defended the compensation to the revenue commissioners. He supported the second reading of Poulett Thomson's usury laws amendment bill, 19 June, and led the ministerial reply to Taylor's charge of misappropriation of public money in the liquidation of British claims on France, 23 July. On 11 July he refuted Hume's allegation that Canning had 'misled' the Commons on the sinking fund, dissociated himself from the view of some other members of the finance committee that ministers should abandon attempts to reduce the national debt and lost his temper with Hume. He defended the national debt reduction bill, 17 July 1828.

He was consulted on the question of renewal of the Bank's charter in September and was briefly ill in November.[56] At the close of the 1828 session he had told Mrs. Arbuthnot that Peel was 'fully aware that it was necessary to settle the [Catholic] question', though he did not foresee that he would concede emancipation while in office.[57] He acquiesced in the decision on the ground of political expediency, as he explained in the House on presenting Harwich corporation's hostile petition, 10 Feb. 1829, when he emphasized that ministers remained determined to 'preserve inviolate the Protestant establishments', a line which he asked a constituent to disseminate in the borough. He had to defend himself in the face of some local disgruntlement in March.[58] Keen on securities, he voted silently for emancipation, 6, 30 Mar., but according to Ellenborough was in the minority of 20 for an amendment to the Irish franchise bill, 20 Mar. Greville recorded that in mid-March he made it clear to the Whig opposition that hostilities would resume once emancipation was carried, for ministerial 'policy was conservative, that of the Whigs subversive'.[59] He explained items of supply, 2 Apr., and said that he favoured equalization of the Irish and Scottish malt duties, 14 Apr. He was named to the select commit-

tees on the Irish miscellaneous and militia estimates, 9, 10 Apr. At this time Ellenborough, now president of the board of control, who did not trust Herries on domestic financial matters, suggested to Wellington that he might advantageously be made governor of Bombay. The duke doubted that Herries would go, but 'evidently thought it would be a very good thing if he would'. Yet when Ellenborough broached the idea he suggested to Herries that he might go out 'as a sort of chancellor of the exchequer to the governor-general' of Bengal, with a remit for 'general management of the finances of India' and the prospect of being able to line his pockets with £5,000 to £7,000 a year. Herries dismissed the notion. Mrs. Arbuthnot thought he was 'a great fool' to do so, for he was '*nul* altogether in his present situation', whereas 'if he had come back in three years having shown himself to be an able financier, he might have looked with confidence to the post of chancellor of the exchequer'.[60] He defended the silk trade bill, 1 May, backed Goulburn's arguments for the redemption of exchequer bills, 8 May, replied at length to Maberly's attack on the application of £3,000,000 to reduction of the debt, 11 May, and on 22 June 1829 got rid of motions for returns of Anglican archdeacons and Leicester corporation's expenditure. The government's deficiencies in debating talent in the Commons, where Herries was deemed to be virtually 'mute', prompted Hardinge to press Ellenborough to revive the Indian project 'with the view of opening the mint' to a speaker, but he refrained, as Herries had 'said his domestic circumstances made it impossible, and the duke did not seem to like it at all'. He found Herries 'rather hostile to the continuance' of the East India Company's trade monopoly.[61]

In October 1829 Herries accompanied Bexley to his swearing-in as high steward of Harwich and got away without trouble on the score of his support for Catholic emancipation.[62] In January 1830 he was promoted to replace the ailing William Vesey Fitzgerald* as president of the board of trade. He was commended to Wellington by Lord Bathurst as 'a man of business and experience, neither a decided enemy nor vehement friend to ... free trade'; but Wallace, his former chief in the Irish revenue commission, commented privately that he would be 'of no use in the House', did 'not particularly understand the business' and was 'above all' disqualified by 'the total want of all *public confidence* which attaches to him'. The mint could not be disposed of satisfactorily and Herries, who was quietly re-elected for Harwich, retained it.[63] On 15 Feb. he opposed Hume's motion for large tax remissions and economies, arguing that the current distress was beyond the reach of legislation and that Hume's assertion that £8,500,000 could be saved was 'decla-mation'. But on 9 Mar. he assured Hume that vacan-cies in public offices would not be filled unnecessarily. His performance in leading the ministerial reply to Palmerston's motion for information on relations with Portugal, 10 Mar., was reckoned 'pitiful' by the Whigs; and Mrs. Arbuthnot noted that in the debate on the state of the nation, 16 Mar., when he rambled, quoted statistics and called for 'patient endurance', he spoke

so woefully ill that nothing else has been talked of ... He seems to have quite broken down and been unable to express himself ... Pushing on Herries has done the duke's government more harm than anything ... [Wellington] is aware, I think, what a mistake he made when he promoted him ... I am surprised at Herries's failure, for no doubt he understands all subjects of trade and finance better than anyone, is a very hard headed, shrewd man, and it seems surprising that such a man should be so utterly incapable of putting his ideas into words. Lord Althorp told ... Arbuthnot that, upon the finance committee, nobody gave so much or such valuable information as he did, or proved so clearly how perfectly informed he was upon every subject of finance.[64]

In cabinet Herries, who did not believe that the reduc-tion of import duties on foreign goods had caused distress, joined Goulburn and Peel in arguing for the imposition of a property tax in order to reduce the indirect tax burden 'on the shoulders of the middling and labouring classes', a policy which he had intended to promote when chancellor. They were overruled by Wellington and a majority of the cabinet.[65] He allowed Littleton's bill to abolish truck payments to be brought in, 17 Mar., and was one of the committee to whom it was referred, 3 May; he defended it as 'indispensably necessary', 23 June, 5 July. He was named to the select committees on superannuations, 26 Apr., and Sierra Leone, 15 June. He opposed Poulett Thomson's motion for inquiry into a revision of taxation, 25 Mar., and next day promised Hume and Maberly that the government were heeding the recommendations of the finance committee to cut the cost of pensions for public servants. He said the damage done to British shipping by foreign competition had been exaggerated, 2 Apr., but on the 8th announced that he intended to close a loophole which allowed Baltic timber imported via Canada to evade full duty. He resisted inquiry into the state of the shipping interest, deploring 'vague assertions hostile to our commercial policy', 6 May. He said ministers would try to alleviate distress in the West Indies, 18 May, and defended their sugar duties proposals, which he foresaw would have to be modi-fied, 21 June. He had a bad tempered exchange with 'Bum' Gordon on the subject, 30 June.[66] He opposed

currency reform, 8 June, warning that departure from the 1819 settlement would presage 'a political relapse' and that if the dual standard was restored 'tomorrow's sun would not set without having witnessed panic, ruin and convulsion'. He spoke for the sale of beer bill, 1 July. Criticism of his inadequacies as a parlia-mentary speaker, especially his inability to assist Peel in general debate, persisted and mounted: Lyndhurst, for example, considered him 'worse than *nul* for he was contemptible'. With Sir George Murray*, the colonial secretary, he was being considered for removal by the time of the 1830 dissolution, but Wellington could not 'see a way to provide' for them, particularly Herries who, as Arbuthnot observed, was generally recognized as being 'valuable in a subordinate situation, but ... misplaced where he is'.[67] After his unopposed return for Harwich Herries predicted that

there will be no considerable change in the relative numbers of the principal parties in the House, but I fear the radical party will be more influential, and radical reforms of all kinds more in favour ... The business of the government, whether in yielding to these demands or resisting them, will be most difficult, and to satisfy the two factions, the conservative and the subversive, or either of them, if it pursues a prudent course, will be quite impossible.[68]

Since April he had been involved in negotiations with the United States for the removal of restrictions on trade between America and the British West Indian colonies. A settlement was concluded before the new Parliament met, and on 8 Nov. 1830 Herries explained his proposals, which he again defended on the 12th as no departure from free trade principles. When Mrs. Arbuthnot asked John Doherty* 'whether, putting aside the dullness of the speech, there was much infor-mation in it, he said I was supposing an impossible case for that he would defy anyone to attend to him'.[69] He had advised Peel in June on the prospect of opposi-tion to the civil list for the new reign;[70] and on 15 Nov. 1830 he opposed Parnell's motion for inquiry, arguing that there was already 'ample information'. He was of course in the ministerial minority in the division, which brought them down; he was named to the select committee.

As the Tory men of business considered how to organize the party in unfamiliar opposition to the Grey ministry, Arbuthnot initially wished to exclude Herries 'as a cabinet minister'. Ellenborough reflected that he '*never should*' have been one, but felt 'it would be difficult to set him aside', especially as he was 'an able and practised man of trade and finance'. When Herries called on him a few days later to urge prompt action to secure the services of a daily newspaper, Ellenborough was 'rather embarrassed'; but in the event he became one of the small opposition press management committee. Herries, who was described by Mrs. Arbuthnot in January 1831 as 'the most active of the late government', despaired of doing much with the provincial press, fearing that 'we have so completely let go of all the lines of this machinery that we shall have difficulty in getting hold of them again'. While Wellington was encouraging, Peel was reported to be averse to 'attempts to get hold of the press', which inclined Herries to suggest a temporary suspension of this work, as 'it would be most unadvisable to adopt any measures in which he did not concur', though he remained convinced of the 'necessity for some exertion on our part to obtain a voice for our party, the conservative'. On a visit to Drayton in the third week of April he found Peel

> much as usual, extremely circumspect in all that he says and does, but acting very indifferently the character of a country gentleman indifferent to office and politics. He is ... much more hearty in the anti-ministerial cause than he acknowledges ... I made no impression on him with respect to the press: at least, he would come to no conclusion ... My habits of intimacy with him are not such as would have warranted me in pressing any subject much upon him. Upon the whole ... I think he is very well disposed, and will pursue a firm and prudent line in the ensuing session ... But he must cultivate his party with more warmth, or he will lose it.

In the end the committee had to fall back on the *Morning Post*, and the *Albion* was recruited under the auspices of the shady McEntaggart.[71] On 17 Dec. 1830 Herries told Ellenborough that he believed that ministers 'would have a large majority on pounds, shillings and pence questions', but 'would not carry the House with them on any question of general policy'.[72] In the Commons that day he acquiesced in their postponement of his colonial trade bill, but insisted that it was sound in principle and, in reply to Whig allegations that it restored protection, said that America was 'altogether wrong' and Britain 'altogether right' in the dispute. On 20 Dec. he confirmed that the late ministry had planned to reduce the barilla duties, but condemned ministers for doing so without consulting Parliament; he thought opposition 'showed up the new board of trade'. With his few companions on the opposition front bench, he was taken unaware by radical attacks on the existing civil list pensions, to which ministers did not react, 23 Dec., and, disregarding the inclination of Croker and others to stay quiet, he criticized them 'for abandoning by their silence the cause of the monarchy and the just rights and privileges of

the crown' in the face of 'unconstitutional trash'. His intervention got a response from Sir James Graham, first lord of the admiralty, to the effect that the government would uphold the principle of non-interference with the royal prerogative to bestow pensions; and Herries told Mrs. Arbuthnot (whose own pension was under scrutiny) that

> it appears to have had a good effect ... I saw no evil spirit in the House ... beyond a cowardly desire of many of the Members to curry favour with their constituents by manifestations of anti-corruption, as they are pleased to call it ... The ministry looked dull and black.

He heard that there were 'symptoms of schism among them on the subject of reform', and at the turn of the year claimed to know from 'the *most unquestionable authority*' (probably Maberly) that there was 'serious dissension in the enemy's camp'.[73] He went with Croker to Wellington's at Stratfield Saye, 27 Jan., and at a Tory meeting at the Athenaeum, 2 Feb. 1831, was 'elected leader ... for tomorrow' in Peel's absence, but no material business came on.[74] He declined to censure ministers for treasury intervention on the barilla duties, 7 Feb., but warned them as to their future conduct. He presented an Ashburton petition for tithe reform, 11 Feb., and one from Galway landowners against reduction of the barilla duties, 25 Feb. He urged the chancellor of the exchequer Lord Althorp, whose first budget was under fire, to make a speedy decision on the cotton duties, 16 Feb.; he was said to be confident that opposition would 'beat the government out of all their taxes'.[75] On 17 Feb. he secured from Parnell clarification of the remit of the public accounts select committee, to which he was appointed. He discussed West Indian affairs with Peel and others, 19 Feb., and two days later received a deputation of ship owners aggrieved at the ministerial timber duties proposals. He and Goulburn were 'beset by deputations and individual applications for advice and assistance' from the commercial interest.[76] On 18 and 22 Mar. he denounced ministers' conduct on the timber duties as 'a political trick' designed to effect 'a great change in the policy of the country' which would wreck British interests in the Canadian trade. It was said that Grey 'complains of his House of Commons treasury bench suffering such men as Herries to roll them in the kennel without reply'.[77] He concurred 'substantially' in the principle of the revised colonial trade bill, 11 Mar., but claimed it as his own, before having a shouting match with Hume, who accused him of 'ignorance'. He was involved in attempts to effect a reconciliation (vital as he saw it) between Peel and the Ultras to combat the government's reform scheme, which he believed would seal the Tories' 'political extinction' if carried; but as their emissary he made little initial impression on the leader.[78] He voted silently against the second reading of the reform bill, 22 Mar. According to Tom Macaulay*, 'Mammon' Herries, as Sydney Smith called him, 'looked like Judas taking his neck cloth off for the last operation' when the ministerial majority of one was revealed.[79] Two weeks later he had recovered his spirits and Goulburn found him (and Peel) 'in good heart, determined to resist the bill most manfully and to do all that may be most likely to effect its rejection'. He commissioned one Nelson Coleridge to 'get up a pamphlet dissecting the bill clause by clause' and promoted the sale of 30,000 'anti-reform tracts', commenting to Ellenborough that 'good tracts may be circulated as well as bad if good men will be as active as bad always are'. He was confident of success on Gascoyne's wrecking amendment against decreasing the number of English Members, for which he duly voted, 19 Apr. 1831.[80] He was sure of being returned by the corporators of Harwich at the ensuing general election, despite a canvass by two reformers, but as he and his colleague George Dawson left the borough after a reconnaissance, 23 Apr. 1831, their carriage was stoned. Precautions were taken to avoid trouble on election day a week later, when Herries, defying an angry audience of non-voters, attacked the government and their reform scheme, though he professed to favour moderate reform.[81]

Arbuthnot asked him, at Wellington's behest, to exert himself to 'get up our friends' for 'the fullest possible attendance' on the first day of the new Parliament. He was requested by some party understrappers to seek the approval of Wellington and Peel for a non-party dinner to rally anti-reformers. He did so, though he doubted the wisdom of the idea, to which Wellington had no objection but which Peel dismissed. Herries, who was unable to accept Peel's invitation to join Holmes and Planta at Drayton, now detected among the opposition rank and file a stiffening resolve to oppose reform.[82] He was at the small party meeting of 16 June 1831 when it was decided to subscribe to subsidize the adoption and use of Planta's Charles Street house as a permanent headquarters.[83] He voted against the second reading of the reintroduced reform bill, 6 July, for use of the 1831 census to determine the disfranchisement schedules, 19 July, and against the partial disfranchisement of Chippenham, 27 July; but he was 'not at all well' that summer and had little to say in debate on the measure. He was informed that his 'silence' was causing 'a good deal of surprise and perhaps misunderstanding' among Harwich corporation, whose petition against the bill he presented on

11 July.[84] He argued that Cockermouth was entitled to retain two Members, 28 July, and Guildford likewise, 15 Sept. He welcomed the government's plan to encourage coal exports, but criticized the tax on raw cotton, 1 July. He harped on ministerial divisions over the wine duties, 11 July, and condemned their proposals as an infraction of the treaty with Portugal, 22 Aug. He voted against issuing the Liverpool writ, 5 Sept., and next day contended that the Bank of Scotland had been given too much power by the terms of the renewal of its charter. On 15 Sept. he made what he considered 'a smart attack' on the wine duties bill, but felt it was 'no use to divide', as he told Mrs. Arbuthnot:

I do not recover from my black fit. The indications of the last few days make me more gloomy. The government are now evidently prepared for defeat in the Lords upon the [reform] bill, and as evidently determined to carry it through ultimately at all hazards ... I have written ... to the duke to let him know this. The wine duties are a hopeless case ... We had a poor attendance, and their troops were well marshalled and ready to stand by them, thick and thin ... Luckily Peel was not there. If he had been ... he would have thrown us overboard. No person who has not seen this House of Commons can form a notion of it. We who have ... can judge somewhat of the character and composition of the future reformed House.[85]

He voted against the passage of the reform bill, 21 Sept., and the second reading of the Scottish measure, 23 Sept. Being 'pledged' on the sugar duties, he was 'induced to stay away' from the debate of 30 Sept.[86] On 6 Oct. he complained of the appointment of a select committee on the West Indian colonies so late in the session. From Sussex in mid-October he informed Wellington that the local farmers who had supported reform in the summer were now signing hostile petitions, which he thought augured well for the prospects of securing a modification of the reform bills. A month later he passed on to Wellington and the home office reports of the arming of the Birmingham Political Union.[87] Soon afterwards he suggested to Peel that the government's 'excellent' proclamation against the unions and rumoured 'proposed concessions in the new modification of the measure of reform must create an entire division between them and the radicals' and so drive them to 'lean for support on the Tories and moderate reformers'. He approved Peel's 'judicious' refusal to enter into any understanding with the 'Waverer' peers, but deluded himself that if ministers made even 'half the concessions' which were being reported, 'we may retort on Lord John Russell his quotation, "The Lord hath delivered them into our hands"'.[88]

The revised reform bill, against the second reading of which he voted, 17 Dec. 1831, brought him back to reality; a few days later Arbuthnot told his wife, 'I have not called on Herries as he would kill me with croaking'.[89] He helped to muster as strong an opposition attendance as possible for the start of the 1832 session and voted against going into committee on the reform bill, 20 Jan.[90] He had for several months been working up a strong case against government for continuing to pay interest on the Russian-Dutch loan after the separation of Belgium from Holland. With high hopes of a 'very strong' division, he moved resolutions condemning the waste of £5,000,000, 26 Jan. For a while ministers seemed likely to be beaten, but a spirited intervention by Palmerston, the foreign secretary, who threatened their supporters with resignation, enabled them to carry the previous question by 239-219 and to defeat Herries's third resolution by 238-214. The reformer John Hawkins attributed their narrow escape also to 'the bungling way in which Herries laid down his resolutions, which ... bound many of those who voted for them to a more decided opinion on the meaning of the treaty than they intended to give'.[91] He presented but dissented from a Ludlow glovers' petition for the restoration of protection, 31 Jan., though he thought they were entitled to have their grievances investigated. He voted against the enfranchisement of Tower Hamlets, 28 Feb. Two weeks later Mrs. Arbuthnot reported that 'Herries for the first time is cheerful', having told her that 'the government is lower and lower', that 'even Joe Hume says the Whigs have done more jobs and follies in one year than the Tories did in thirty' and that there was a belief that Grey would resign if the Lords rejected the bill.[92] He divided against the third reading, 22 Mar. In early May he provided Ellenborough with 'an account of the particular interests of each place in schedules C and D', though he had 'little hopes' of the opposition peers being able to use it to force a modification of the bill. When Wellington was invited to form a ministry after the government's resignation Herries did not immediately refuse to take part, but it soon emerged that he had no intention of doing so.[93] Just after the reinstatement of the Grey ministry Benjamin Disraeli[†] sat between Peel and Herries, a member of the Conservatives' English election committee, at dinner, and was astonished to discover that 'old grey headed financial Herries turned out quite a literary man'.[94] He was named to the committee of secrecy on the Bank's charter, 22 May. He voted for Alexander Baring's bill to exclude insolvent debtors from Parliament, 27 June, and to preserve the voting rights of Irish borough freemen, 2 July. On 4 June he welcomed the temporary suspension of Russian-Dutch loan payments, but accused ministers of shifting the ground of their defence. When Althorp moved to consider the question, 12 July, Herries proposed an amendment condemning the continued payments as illegal, but it was defeated by 243-197. Further attacks on 16 and 20 July, when he did not speak, were beaten by 191-155 and 191-112; and after the latter division Macaulay wrote:

> Old Croker, when we shouted, looked heavenly blue with rage –
> You'd have said he had the cholera in the spasmodic stage.
> Dawson was red with ire as if his face was smeared with berries.
> But of all human visages, the worst was that of Herries.[95]

On 7 Aug. 1832 he seized on ministers' tardy concession of an extension of the time to allow potential urban voters to pay their rates as proof that the Reform Act could not be 'final'.

Herries predicted the Conservative debacle at the 1832 general election, when he topped the poll at Harwich, as he did in 1835 and 1837.[96] He remained prominent on the Conservative side of the House and was secretary at war in Peel's brief first administration. In 1841 he stood for Ipswich, but defeat there cost him a place in the second, to his bitter chagrin.[97] He resurfaced as Protectionist Member for Stamford in 1847 and was president of the board of control in Lord Derby's 1852 government. He retired from Parliament, at the age of 74, in 1853. He died intestate at his home at St. Julian's, near Sevenoaks, 'after a very short illness', in April 1855. Administration of his estate was granted on 6 June 1855 to his elder surviving son Charles John (1815-83).[98]

[1] See *Mem. of Public Life of John Charles Herries* by his son Edward (1880), a reply to slurs which was 'not intended for a complete biography' (Intro. p. 8), and *Oxford DNB*. [2] See, e.g., Northants. RO, Agar Ellis diary, 10 Jan. [1828]; Hatherton diary, 21 Dec. 1835. [3] *Colchester Diary*, i. 135; *Farington Diary*, iii. 1028. [4] *Hist. Rec. Light Horse Vols.* (1843), 109-15; *Farington Diary*, iii. 1033; *Prince of Wales Corresp.* ii. 593. [5] Add. 57447, memos. 3, 7 Apr. 1819; *Gent. Mag.* (1819), i. 381, 485; PROB 11/1616/223; IR26/784/391. [6] D. Gray, *Spencer Perceval*, 315. [7] *Colchester Diary*, ii. 219; Herries, i. 20-22. [8] B. Hilton, *Corn, Cash, Commerce*, 38. [9] Gray, 325-6; *Prince of Wales Corresp.* viii. 3097, 3148. [10] Hilton, 38; Herries, i. 23-64; N. Ferguson, *House of Rothschild, 1798-1848* (2000), 9, 86-89, 97, 103-4, 154; R.W. Davis, *English Rothschilds*, 30-34; Gray, 325-30; J.E. Cookson, *Lord Liverpool's Administration*, 25; Hatherton diary. [11] Herries, i. 64, 114-19; *HMC Bathurst*, 345-6. [12] Add. 57418, Herries to 'Dear Sir', 8 June 1818. [13] Hilton, 45; Add. 57445, memo. 1 May 1819. [14] BL, Herries mss, Herries to cos. R. Herries, 25 May 1821; *Croker Pprs.* i. 208; Herries, i. 118-19. [15] Add. 38291, f. 185; 38743, f. 263; 57367, Herries to Liverpool, 3 Aug. 1822; Herries mss, Arbuthnot to Herries [20 Jan.]; Lonsdale mss, Long to Lonsdale, 2 Feb. 1823. [16] Add. 38297, ff. 26, 36, 52, 54, 140, 198; 38747, ff. 10, 21; 57367, Liverpool to Herries, 29 Oct., 7 Nov. 1823. [17] K. Bourne, *Palmerston*, 243; *Palmerston-Sulivan Letters*, 179. [18] Add. 57447, memo. [Sept. 1841]; Hilton, 183. [19] *Arbuthnot*

Jnl. i. 390-1, 426; Hilton, 211-14, 217, 222, 225-6; Add. 57402, Robinson to Herries, 16, 18 Sept. 1825. [20] Hilton, 84. [21] *Geo. IV Letters*, iii. 1278, 1288. [22] Ibid. iii. 1292; *Canning's Ministry*, 50. [23] *Canning's Ministry*, 133; *Arbuthnot Jnl.* ii. 108; Herries, i, 124-6. [24] Add. 57419, Lyndhurst to Herries [4 May 1827]; Hilton, 252; Herries, i. 139-44. [25] *Canning's Ministry*, 309; *Arbuthnot Jnl.* ii. 129; Herries, i. 126. [26] Herries, i. 131-6; *Canning's Ministry*, 340, 347, 360, 365, 371; *HMC Bathurst*, 638; Lansdowne mss, Herries to Canning, 2 July; Add. 57370, Arbuthnot to Herries, 5, 31 July 1827. [27] Herries, i. 150-2. For accounts of the events of 8 Aug.-4 Sept. 1827 see A. Aspinall, 'Goderich Ministry', *EHR*, xlii (1927), 533-43; A. Mitchell, *Whigs in Opposition*, 204-5, and Bourne, 265-8. Palmerston's inaccurate retrospective account in Bulwer, *Palmerston*, i. 182-5 is corrected by Herries, i. 153-236. [28] Add. 57419, T.P. Courtenay to Herries, 9 Aug. 1827; *Wellington Despatches*, iv. 75; *Palmerston-Sulivan Letters*, 191. [29] *Geo. IV Letters*, iii. 1381, 1386; *Wellington Despatches*, iv. 77, 79. [30] Add. 57419, Herries to sister, 13 Aug. [1827]; *Wellington Despatches*, iv. 90; *Arbuthnot Jnl.* ii. 136. [31] *Geo. IV Letters*, iii. 1391; *Wellington Despatches*, iv. 94. [32] *Palmerston-Sulivan Letters*, 192-3; *Geo. IV Letters*, iii. 1392; *Wellington Despatches*, iv. 97-98. [33] *Palmerston-Sulivan Letters*, 193-6; *Greville Mems*. i. 184; *Huskisson Pprs*. 226-30; BL, Althorp mss, Tavistock to Spencer, 15 Aug.; Add. 38750, f. 39; 51677, Lord J. Russell to Holland, 16 Aug.; Harrowby mss, Sturges Bourne to Harrowby, 19 Aug. 1827; TNA 30/29/9/5/53. [34] Chatsworth mss, Carlisle to Devonshire, 21 Aug.; Add. 40340, f. 191; 51586, Tierney to Holland, 22 Aug.; Hants RO, Tierney mss 31M70/37c. [35] Add. 38750, f. 75; 40394, f. 202; 51687, Lansdowne to Holland, 24 Aug.; 57419, Hill to Herries, 24 Aug.; Chatsworth mss, Young to Devonshire, 22 Aug.; Castle Howard mss, Lady Carlisle to Morpeth [25 Aug.] 1827. [36] Add. 57419. [37] *Palmerston-Sulivan Letters*, 198-9; Chatsworth mss, Brougham to Devonshire [26 Aug.]; Lansdowne mss, Holland to Lansdowne, 27 Aug. 1827. [38] Add. 38750, ff. 145, 149, 152, 158; 51586, Tierney to Lady Holland, 30 Aug., 57419, Herries to sister, 30 Aug.; NLW, Coedymaen mss 199; *Huskisson Pprs*. 233-5; TNA 30/29/9/5/56; Lansdowne mss, Sturges Bourne to Lansdowne, 31 Aug. 1827. [39] Add. 38750, ff. 152, 156, 188; 51584, Tierney to Holland, 1 Sept.; 51586, to Lady Holland, 31 Aug.; 51687, Lansdowne to Holland, 2, 5 Sept.; Lansdowne mss, Goderich to Lansdowne, 31 Aug.; Holland to same, 3 Sept. 1827; *Palmerston-Sulivan Letters*, 200; A. Aspinall, *Politics and the Press*, 219; *Arbuthnot Jnl.* ii. 140-1. [40] *Arbuthnot Jnl.* ii. 143; Lansdowne mss, Holland to Lansdowne, 3 Sept.; *Creevey Pprs*. ii. 128; Add. 57419, Herries to W. Herries, 8 Sept.; Herries mss, same to R. Herries, 8 Sept. 1827. [41] Herries, ii. 3-7; *Arbuthnot Jnl.* ii. 149-50; *Arbuthnot Corresp.* 93; *Von Neumann Diary*, i. 180; *Wellington Despatches*, iv. 168. [42] Add. 38753, f. 199; Tierney mss 4, 85a, b; Herries, ii. 15-17; Add. 75938, Lady to Lord Spencer, 14, 15 Dec. 1827; E.A. Wasson, *Whig Renaissance*, 153-4. [43] *Arbuthnot Jnl.* ii. 152-3, 155; *Wellington Despatches*, iv. 168-71, 181-2; *Geo. IV Letters*, iii. 1447, 1451; *Croker Pprs*. i. 397; *Huskisson Pprs*. 268-9; *HMC Bathurst*, 650-1; Durham CRO, Londonderry mss D/Lo/C83/11, 12, 83; Add. 38753, ff. 45, 159, 167, 185, 199, 223, 242, 282; 38754, f. 24; Lansdowne mss, Goderich to Lansdowne, 4, 8 Jan. 1828; Wellington mss WP1/913/8; Tierney mss 85b; Herries, ii. 44-57; Hilton, 243-5; Aspinall, 'Goderich Ministry', 551-5. [44] *Arbuthnot Jnl.* ii. 157; *Howard Sisters*, 98-99; *Von Neumann Diary*, i. 182; Add. 36464, f. 166; 40395, f. 9; Herts. Archives, Panshanger mss D/Elb F78, W. to F. Lamb, 11 Jan. 1828; *Greville Mems*. i. 196-8. [45] Add. 57447, memo. [1828]. [46] *Wellington Despatches*, iv. 187, 192, 195; *HMC Bathurst*, 652; Parker, *Peel*, ii. 29; *Geo. IV Letters*, iii. 1463. [47] *Arbuthnot Jnl.*, ii. 159; Bulwer, i. 218-19; Herries, ii. 59-61; Add. 38754, ff. 124, 126, 162; 40395, f. 21; Tierney mss 85a; Lonsdale mss, Lowther to Lonsdale, 19 Jan. 1828; Southampton Univ. Lib. Broadlands mss BR23AA/5/1. [48] Wellington mss WP1/914/40; *Wellington Despatches*, iv. 212; *Croker Pprs*. i. 405. [49] *Croker Pprs*. i. 403, 405-6; *Ellenborough Diary*, i. 2-3. [50] Add. 40395, ff. 219, 221; Herries, ii. 90-101; Hilton, 257. [51] *Ellenborough Diary*, i. 30-31; Add. 38755, f. 30. [52] *Ellenborough Diary*, i. 34-35; Hatherton diary, 18, 19 [Feb.]

1828; *Geo. IV Letters*, iii. 1504; Broughton, *Recollections*, iii. 245; Bagot, *Canning and Friends*, ii. 433-4; Keele Univ. Lib. Sneyd mss SC12/86; TNA 30/29/9/5/62; M.D. George, *Cat. of Pol. and Personal Satires*, ix. 15515, 15522. [53] Hatherton diary, 21 [Feb.]; Agar Ellis diary, 21 Feb. [1828]; *Lady Holland to Son*, 74; *Ellenborough Diary*, i. 38; Bagot, ii. 435; *Greville Mems*. i. 206; Nottingham Univ. Lib. Portland mss PwH 146/1-3; Heron, *Notes*, 170. [54] *Arbuthnot Jnl.* ii. 166; *Ellenborough Diary*, i. 46, 47, 52. [55] *Arbuthnot Jnl.* ii.181-2; *Ellenborough Diary*, i. 118-19; *Wellington Despatches*, iv. 462, 473-4. [56] Wellington mss WP1/952/17; 969/30. [57] *Arbuthnot Jnl.* ii. 200. [58] Add. 57419, Herries to Cobbold, 17 Feb., to [unknown], 14 Mar. 1829. [59] *Ellenborough Diary*, i. 349, 358, 402; *Greville Mems*. i. 270. [60] *Ellenborough Diary*, i. 398; ii. 12-13, 19; Add. 57410, Ellenborough to Herries, 19 Apr. 1829; Herries, ii. 105-8; *Arbuthnot Jnl.* ii. 291-2. [61] Bulwer, i. 335; *Ellenborough Diary*, ii. 63, 72. [62] Devon RO, Sidmouth mss, Bexley to Sidmouth, 22 Oct. 1829. [63] *Greville Mems*. i. 353-4; *Arbuthnot Jnl.* ii. 328; *Countess Granville Letters*, ii. 57; *Wellington Despatches*, vi. 401; Northumb. RO, Middleton mss ZMI/5/77/3/1; Lonsdale mss, Lowther to Lonsdale, 25 Jan., 4 Feb. 1830. [64] Grey mss, Howick jnl. 10, 16 Mar.; Agar Ellis diary, 10 Mar. 1830; *Howard Sisters*, 125; *Arbuthnot Jnl.* ii. 345-6. [65] Wellington mss WP1/1164/11; *Ellenborough Diary*, ii. 212-15; Herries mss, Herries to R. Herries, 8 Mar. 1830. [66] *Ellenborough Diary*, ii. 274-5. [67] *Arbuthnot Jnl.* ii. 356, 366, 372-3; *Ellenborough Diary*, ii. 290; *Baring Jnls*. 64; Add. 40340, f. 228. [68] NLW, Harpton Court mss C/430, Herries to Lewis, 19 Aug. [1830]. [69] Herries, ii. 111-14; Wellington mss WP1/1108/7; 1111/28; 1117/40; *Arbuthnot Jnl.* ii. 401. [70] Add. 40400, f. 217. [71] *Three Diaries*, 23, 26, 27; *Arbuthnot Jnl.* ii. 411; Aspinall, *Politics and the Press*, 329-30, 334; R. Stewart, *Foundation of Conservative Party*, 68-69, 76; Aberdeen Univ. Lib. Arbuthnot mss, Herries to Mrs. Arbuthnot [21], 31 Dec. 1830, 3, 26 Jan. 1831; Add. 57370, Arbuthnot to Herries, 24, 26, 28 Dec. 1830, 6 Jan. 1831. [72] *Three Diaries*, 36. [73] Arbuthnot mss, Herries to Mrs. Arbuthnot [21 Dec. 1830], 3 Jan. 1831; *Arbuthnot Corresp.* 140; *Three Diaries*, 37-38. [74] *Three Diaries*, 42, 45, 47; Surr. Hist. Cent. Goulburn mss Acc 304/67B, Goulburn to wife [4 Feb. 1831]. [75] *Arbuthnot Corresp.* 143. [76] *Three Diaries*, 54, 55; *Greville Mems*. ii. 119. [77] Broughton, iv. 96. [78] *Three Diaries*, 57, 63; *Greville Mems*. ii. 126; *Arbuthnot Jnl.* ii. 416; *Arbuthnot Corresp.* 145; *Macaulay Letters*, ii. 11, 33. [80] *Arbuthnot Corresp.* 145; *Three Diaries*, 75-76; Goulburn mss 67B, Goulburn to wife, 12 Apr. 1831. [81] *Colchester Gazette*, 30 Apr., 7 May 1831. [82] Add. 40402, f. 89; 57370, Arbuthnot to Herries, 25 May; 57402, Peel to same, 2 June 1831; Wellington mss WP1/1187/2. [83] *Three Diaries*, 93. [84] *Three Diaries*, 115; Aspinall, *Politics and the Press*, 336; Add. 57420, C.D. to Herries [18 Aug. 1831]. [85] *Arbuthnot Corresp.* 149. [86] *Three Diaries*, 138. [87] Wellington mss WP1/1199/7; 1201/30; Herries, ii. 160. [88] Add. 40402, f. 125; Parker, ii. 194-5. [89] *Arbuthnot Corresp.* 156. [90] Add. 40402, f. 175; *Three Diaries*, 175. [91] *Three Diaries*, 180, 184, 185; Add. 57447, memo. [Sept. 1841]; Cornw. RO, Hawkins mss 10/2179. [92] Arbuthnot mss 3029/1/2/44. [93] *Three Diaries*, 237, 244, 250-1; *Croker Pprs*. ii. 163; *Wellington Despatches*, viii. 306. [94] *Three Diaries*, 266; *Disraeli Letters*, i. 192. [95] *Macaulay Letters*, ii. 155. [96] Herries, ii. 161-2. [97] Parker, *Graham*, i. 308; Add. 57447, memo. [Sept. 1841]. [98] PROB 6/231/391.

D.R.F.

HERVEY, Frederick William, Earl Jermyn (1800–1864).

BURY ST. EDMUNDS   1826–15 Feb. 1859

b. 15 July 1800, 1st s. of Frederick William Hervey†, 5th earl and 1st mq. of Bristol, and Hon. Elizabeth Albana Upton, da. of Clotworthy, 1st Bar. Templetown[I]†. *educ.* Eton 1814; Trinity Coll. Camb. 1819. *m.* 9 Dec. 1830,

Lady Katherine Isabella Manners, da. of John Henry, 5th duke of Rutland, 4s. (2 *d.v.p.*) 6da. *styled* Lord Hervey 1803-29 June 1826; Earl Jermyn 30 June 1826-59; *suc.* fa. as 2nd mq. of Bristol 15 Feb. 1859. *d.* 30 Oct. 1864.

Treas. of household Sept. 1841-Aug. 1846; PC 6 Oct. 1841. Hered. steward, Bury St. Edmunds 1823; col. W. Suff. militia 1846-*d.*

Lord Hervey, as he was known until 1826, was raised in London, Suffolk and France, where his family resided for long periods in peacetime, pending the completion of extensions and refurbishments to their mansion at Ickworth and London house in St. James's Square, a process delayed by reduced revenues from rents.[1] His early education was entrusted to the family tutor, the Rev. Dr. Samuel Forster, a former head-master of Norwich Grammar School.[2] A nephew by marriage of Lord Liverpool, he was intended for a political career, and his father, a Grenvillite who returned a Member for Bury St. Edmunds, duly sent him to the premier in September 1820 for 'your guid-ance rather than your assistance'.[3] To Lord Grenville, Bristol explained, 17 Nov. 1820:

> I had indeed hoped that my son might have followed in the same steps and looked to you as the leader of his party, but if I have been disappointed in this wish I have at least the satisfaction of thinking that on my part there has been no reserve, on yours no misconception.[4]

Hervey had canvassed the corporation of Bury St. Edmunds at the general election of 1820 as 'persona-tor' for his uncle, General Arthur Percy Upton, the locum during his minority, and would probably have been returned there directly he came of age in 1821 had Upton then been offered the command of a 'good infantry regiment'.[5] In the event and with no afforda-ble vacancy for the county of Suffolk likely, he offered for the prestigious Cambridge University seat at the November 1822 by-election as a pro-Catholic, anti-slavery ministerialist. Bristol, assisted by his relations, the foreign secretary Canning and the East Anglian aristocracy of all parties, launched a powerful cam-paign on his behalf, which deterred other govern-ment candidates from proceeding to a poll. Liverpool, although supportive, was among the many who con-sidered his bid premature.[6] He wrote to his sister-in-law Lady Erne, 12 Nov.:

> If my advice could have been asked before the step was taken, I think I should have advised against it, because I think difficult to resist the argument that no man ought to be a Member for the university who has not besides an excellent character in the university (which Hervey has), established his reputation in the world.[7]

Hervey's defeat by the anti-Catholic Tory William John Bankes was seen as damaging to the Whigs and to ministers, and variously attributed to his 'untried' status, fears that the constituency would become a treasury seat, and the split in the pro-Catholic vote between him and the Whig lawyer James Scarlett*.[8] His partisan Robert Grant*, who had withdrawn before the poll, dismissed him as a 'pleasing and prom-ising youth'.[9] In 1825 he was included in the duke of Northumberland's delegation to Paris for the corona-tion of Charles X.[10] He came in unopposed for Bury St. Edmunds in 1826.[11]

Now as Earl Jermyn, the courtesy title of the mar-quessate awarded to his father in June 1826,[12] he sig-nified his political allegiance to Canning directly Liverpool suffered a stroke in February 1827, but adopted a low parliamentary profile and, ostensibly on health grounds, spent much time between 1826 and 1830 in France.[13] He voted for Catholic relief, 6 Mar., against inquiry into electoral irregularities at Leicester, 15 Mar., and for the duke of Clarence's annuity bill and the spring guns bill, 23 Mar. 1827. As a member of the Berwick-upon-Tweed election com-mittee, he vexed his fellow Canningite John Gladstone, who claimed he was unseated thereby, by voting to find him guilty of treating, 19 Mar.[14] He did not attend the call of the House when the Fowey election petition was brought up, 6 Apr. As requested by his father and Canning as prime minister, he quashed reports of his candidature for the Cambridge University seat made vacant by Copley's appointment to the woolsack.[15] According to his notices, he was 'unwilling to owe his election to the accidental division of the interests hostile to the Catholic claims', but did not rule out his future candidature.[16] Lord Lansdowne, a member of Lord Goderich's ministry, again suggested him for the seat in September 1827.[17]

Jermyn voted to repeal the Test Acts, when the duke of Wellington's new coalition ministry, to which Huskisson belonged, opposed it, 26 Feb., and for Catholic relief, 12 May 1828. He presented peti-tions from Bury St. Edmunds against the malt duties, 17 Mar., and from West Suffolk for equalization of the sugar duties and the abolition of colonial slavery, 9 July. Following the Huskissonite resignations, he mustered in the Commons with the 'ejected liberals', 3 June.[18] He voted to repeal the usury laws, 19 June, and for concessions in the silk duties, 14 July. In his maiden speech, 3 July 1828, for Fitzgerald's motion for production of the correspondence between the English and Irish governments at the time of the Union, he suggested that the Catholics had acquiesced in it because of expectations generated concerning their future treatment, as Pitt had 'held out to the higher ranks the prospect of getting into Parliament, to the lower the idea of some effectual relief, and to the clergy ... a competent provision'. He grudgingly welcomed Peel and Wellington's decision to concede Catholic emancipation in 1829, and wrote to his father, whose long political career overshadowed his own, 9 Feb.:

Most of my friends here, Wortleys, etc., were very hard upon Peel ... and maintained that he ought to have gone out. I fought the other side stoutly. Still, I cannot help feeling a *lack* of *confidence* in men who have waited for the storm to burst, before they would believe that a storm was coming, who have been watching the gathering of the clouds for years, *in vain*; and who though warned and admonished, urged and entreated, would yet take no warning ... Even the vulgar herd may well believe in the storm, when it begins to pelt, but the man who pretends to the character of a *statesman* ought surely to watch the signs of the times; and to provide against future dangers, when precautions may yet avail. I very much fear that we may yet have some difficulties of detail ... The reports which circulate of the intentions of government to propose some *very violent measure* of interference with the elective franchise ... fill my mind with some nervous sensations. For, however disposed one may be to swallow all trifling and subordinate objections, and to throw aside over-nice and critical curiousness ... yet, there must of course be limits to forbearance and a point where constitutional principle may be too daringly outraged. Besides ... there is another very material question, which is this: how far it is worthwhile to risk the loss of all the healing, salutary and conciliatory tendency of the measure of *concession*, by an over-anxiety to court the ultra Protestant part of the community. Still, I confess, I see very strongly the importance of waiving all minor objections, and giving a hearty support to government as the best means of carrying the great question ... I shall therefore be disposed to do almost anything to avoid an awkward hitch. ... Not a word has yet been said about the elective franchise by anyone. (1st) My view would be to leave the *bona fide* 40s. freeholders exactly as they are. (2nd) To disfranchise *no one*, having a *life* interest in a freehold, till the period of his registration expires ... (3rd) The [franchise] qualification ... *in virtue of a life interest* (or lease for a life) might be raised to that point, *and no further*, which would be necessary to get rid of the *perjury* so frequent at Irish elections and to place some check upon the mischievous practice of *subdividing property*, which Irish landlords adopt for electioneering purposes. The *preamble of the Act* should recite these as grounds for legislating. To take away the franchise upon other grounds would I think be most unjust and unconstitutional, a measure of violence and of gross tyranny, not to say a very dangerous precedent ... It appears to me that *it is hardly safe* to have a large mass of your population entirely stripped of all constitutional

vent for their wishes and feelings ... Voting at elections is *a habit* with a great proportion of the population in Ireland ... A sudden change of habit *may* produce general dissatisfaction, the effects of which it would be difficult to calculate: especially as I fear there is no thought of acting upon the policy of Pitt and Burke!! in regard to a *provision for the Roman Catholic clergy*. I fear that ... Pitt is not held in such estimation by our wiseacres in the cabinet of today, or by my lords the bishops ... You see what I am afraid of. *Disfranchisement* upon a large scale; *dissatisfaction* (if not disaffection) upon a large scale; *unpaid priests* sympathizing with the people, holding correspondence perhaps with lay agitators in Dublin ... no *peace* civil or religious, no cordial union between landlord and tenant, rich and poor, which I verily believe would be restored if concession was made graciously and property left to find its natural level and to assume its ascendancy.

He reassured Bristol the following day that he would do all he could to support Wellington publicly and he voted to consider emancipation, 6 Mar.[19] He presented a petition from Bury's guardians of the poor endorsing the parochial settlement bill, 3 Mar. He voted to transfer East Retford's seats to Birmingham, 5 May 1829. Despite murmurs of discontent among the corporation at his recent poor attendance and support for the government's adjustments to the corn laws, which he hailed as the 'best means of reconciling the conflicting interest of the country', his return for Bury St. Edmunds at the 1830 general election was unopposed.[20]

Jermyn was listed by ministers among the 'bad doubtfuls' and was absent when they were brought down by the division on the civil list, 15 Nov. 1830. When he married the Tory duke of Rutland's daughter £10,000 was settled on her, but some observers, though approving the connection, considered their financial circumstances 'constrained'.[21] Jermyn declared promptly with his father against the Grey ministry's reform bill, by which Bury St. Edmunds was scheduled to lose a Member, and voted against it at its second reading, 22 Mar., and for Gascoyne's wrecking amendment, 19 Apr. 1831. Notwithstanding the hostility of the mob, who threw stones and denied him a hearing, he topped the poll at Bury St. Edmunds at the ensuing general election.[22] He voted against the second reading of the reintroduced reform bill at its second reading, 6 July, to make the 1831 census the criterion for English borough disfranchisements, 19 July, and against taking a seat from Chippenham, 27 July. He paired (probably in the majority to include Dorchester in schedule B), 28 July. He divided against the bill's passage, 21 Sept. His father was a voluble contributor to its Lords' defeat in October, and afterwards Jermyn organized and circulated the Suffolk anti-reformers' petition and address to the king.[23] Undeterred by its restoration of the second seat to Bury St. Edmunds, he voted against the revised reform bill at its second reading, 17 Dec. 1831, and committal, 20 Jan., against enfranchising Tower Hamlets, 28 Feb., and the third reading, 22 Mar. 1832. He divided against government on the Russian-Dutch loan, 26 Jan., and voted for Baring's bill to deny insolvent debtors parliamentary privilege, 27 June. On 3 July 1832 he thwarted an attempt by the Ipswich Member Wason to introduce a bill transferring the Suffolk summer assizes from Bury St. Edmunds to Ipswich.

Standing for Bury St. Edmunds at the general election in December 1832 as a self-styled 'liberal reformer opposed to parliamentary reform', Jermyn, who stressed his local connections and support for Catholic relief, the East Retford disfranchisement bill and the anti-slavery campaign, maintained that he intended 'no party hostility towards the government of Lord Grey'. He succeeded in splitting the Liberal vote to finish in second place.[24] He retained the seat for the Conservatives until he succeeded his father in 1859, and served as treasurer of the household in Peel's second ministry. He died at Ickworth in October 1864.[25] His son Frederick William John Hervey (1834-1907) succeeded him as 3rd marquess.

[1] *Oxford DNB* (Hervey, Lord Arthur Charles); Suff. RO (Bury St. Edmunds), Hervey mss 941/59/2; Add. 38265, f. 25; D.E. Davy, *Excursions through County of Suff. 1823-4* ed. J. Blatchley, 41. [2] *Gent. Mag.* (1865), i. 99. [3] Add. 38287, f. 332. [4] Add. 58993. [5] *Oakes Diaries*, ed. J. Fiske (Suff. Recs. Soc. xxxiii), ii. 250-1; *Bury and Norwich Post*, 15 Mar. 1820; Suff. RO (Bury St. Edmunds) 1641/13; Hervey mss 941/56/71, Upton to Bristol, 6, 13 July 1821. [6] Hervey mss 941/11/1/11A; Lonsdale mss, Lowther to Lonsdale, 12 Nov.; Dorset RO, Bankes mss D/BKL, Canning to H. Bankes, 23 Nov. 1822. [7] Sheffield Archives, Wharncliffe mss WhM/693/807. [8] Hervey mss 951/56/3; 59/1; *The Times*, 16, 23, 28 29 Nov. 1822. [9] Hants RO, Calthorpe mss 26M62/F/C545. [10] Hervey mss 941/59/1, Northumberland to Jermyn, 13 Feb.; *The Times*, 16 Mar., 9 May 1825. [11] *Oakes Diaries*, ii. 310-11. [12] Add. 38371, ff. 162, 168. [13] Hervey mss 941/59/2. [14] St. Deiniol's Lib. Glynne-Gladstone mss 277, J. Gladstone to Huskisson, 24 Mar. 1827. [15] *Palmerston-Sulivan Letters*, 187. [16] *Suff. Chron.* 2 June 1827. [17] Bucks. RO, Buckinghamshire mss, Lansdowne to Goderich, 17 Sept. 1827. [18] A. Aspinall, 'Canningite Party', *TRHS* (ser. 4), xvii (1934), 225; *Palmerston-Sulivan Letters*, 205; *Colchester Diary*, iii. 567-8. [19] Hervey mss 941/56/60. [20] *Bury and Norwich Post*, 28 July, 4 Aug. 1830. [21] Hervey mss 941/56/59, 60, 59/6; Suff. RO (Bury St. Edmunds) HA507/4/34. [22] *Bury and Suff. Herald*, 9, 23 Mar., 27 Apr.; *Bury and Norwich Post*, 4 May 1831. [23] *Bury and Norwich Post*, 12 Oct., 14 Dec. 1831; Hervey mss 941/11B, 11C; 56/24. [24] *The Times*, 15 July; *Bury and Suff. Herald*, 28 Nov., 19 Dec. 1832; W.P. Scargill, *A Reformer's Reasons for Voting for Earl Jermyn*; Hervey mss 941/2/1-3; 3/1-22. [25] *Gent. Mag.* (1865), i. 99.

M.M.E.

HEYGATE, William (1782-1844), of Chatham Place, Blackfriars, London; Holwood, Kent, and Southend, Essex.

SUDBURY   1818-1826

b. 24 June 1782, 1st s. of James Heygate, hosiery manufacturer, later banker, of Hackney, Mdx. and Southend and Sarah, da. of Samuel Unwin of Sutton-in-Ashfield, Notts. *m.* 19 May 1821, Isabella, da. of Edward Longdon Mackmurdo of Upper Clapton, Mdx., 4s. *cr.* bt. 15 Sept. 1831; *suc.* fa. 1833. *d.* 28 Aug. 1844.

Common councilman, London 1809-12, sheriff 1811-12, alderman 1812-43, ld. mayor 1822-3, chamberlain 1843-*d.*

Dir. Eagle Insurance 1811-14, Grand Surr. Dock Co. 1813-*d.*, Phoenix Fire Office 1819-42, Pelican Office 1823-*d.*, South Sea Co. 1823-9, 1832-*d.*, W.I. Dock Co. 1824-30, Revisionary Interest Soc. 1825-*d.*; commr. exch. bill loan office 1823-*d.*

Heygate, whose family owned estates in Essex and Leicestershire and property in London's Aldermanbury, was a City alderman and partner in his father's Leicester bank of Pares and Heygate. Prominent as a Merchant Taylor, company director and founder member of the Hampden Club to promote parliamentary reform, he had declined to contest London as a Whig moderate in 1817, but came in for the venal borough of Sudbury on the interest of the predominantly Tory corporation at the general election of 1818, and topped the poll there in 1820.[1] Taking an independent line, he had distinguished himself as an opponent of the resumption of cash payments by the Bank of England, supported burgh and criminal law reform and pressed in vain for three-year restrictions to the 1819 blasphemous libels and seditious meetings bills.[2]

Heygate spoke in favour of transferring Grampound's franchise to Leeds, 12 Feb. 1821,[3] and voted for reform, 9 May 1821, and against Catholic relief, 28 Feb. 1821, 1 Mar., 21 Apr., 10 May 1825.[4] His commitment to promoting his views on finance and measures affecting his London and commercial interests tended to make his parliamentary conduct unpredictable and when he defended or amended his early stance as an anti-bullionist he was frequently at variance with all parties. He voted with the Whig opposition for deferring the civil list report, 8 May, on tax collection, 4 July 1820, and against the war office grant, 6 Apr. 1821; but with government against the additional malt duty repeal bill 3 Apr. 1821. He considered the decision to prosecute Queen Caroline 'impolitic' and detrimental to the country and 'all parties' concerned; but, once commenced, he said that he wished her trial to proceed until the evidence on both sides had been heard, 18 Sept. 1820.[5] In common council, 21 Nov., he expressed delight at the abandonment of the bill of pains and penalties, but opposed the queen's proposed procession through the City to a service of thanksgiving at St. Paul's, and was one of the 'seven wise aldermen' (and was lampooned as such) who refused, as a magistrate, to sanction it.[6] On 8 Dec. 1820 he signed the corporation's loyal address to the king, deprecating the 'torrent of impiety and sedition' which the episode had produced.[7] Presenting a petition from Sudbury censuring ministers and calling for the restoration of the queen's privileges, 24 Jan. 1821, he created a stir by declaring that she had 'rendered herself unworthy of any mark of grace or favour by her scandalous letter to the king and ... treasonable answers to the addresses' from Nottingham and Cripplegate.[8] He insisted that he was 'no supporter of ministers, nor an enemy to the queen', and his condemnation of Lord Archibald Hamilton's 'milk and water' motion regretting the omission of her name from the liturgy, 26 Jan., as 'a measure ill advised and inexpedient', whose 'maxims were true in the abstract but mischievous in the application', dismayed the Whigs, who had deliberately refrained from requesting that her name be restored, in a bid to 'capture his vote'.[9] He divided with government against a motion censuring their handling of the affair, 6 Feb. 1821.

Demonstrating a diehard attachment to the views he had expounded in 1819, he maintained that the resumption of cash payments was responsible for the depressed state of trade and agriculture, and said that he would oppose any increase in corn prices or tax on mercantile capital, 30 May 1820.[10] In the committee of ways and means, 9 June, he praised Pitt's wartime sinking fund, but spoke against issuing £17 million in bills to repay the Bank under the government's consolidated loan scheme, 'as this would of necessity produce a reduction of the circulating medium, which must be attended with increased distress throughout the country'; the political economist Ricardo and the radical Hume insisted that he was mistaken. He spoke again of the folly of the loan and proposed, but could find no seconder for a resolution 'regretting, in the fifth year of peace, the adoption of any measures tending to augment the public debt, and recommending such a system of economy as should eventually lessen the burdens of the people', 19 June. He stressed the monetary causes of the depressions in trade and agriculture, when the Birmingham merchants' petition was presented, 9 Feb. 1821, and now maintained that 'there should be an option of paying in either silver or gold' to facilitate foreign trade and assist

the Bank. He interpreted the 1821 bank cash payments bill as a currency question, voted in his fellow banker Alexander Baring's minority of 27 for inquiry, 9 Apr., and complained that the bill would create an acute shortage of specie and induce country banks to withdraw their small notes, thereby reducing forgeries while increasing the incidence of highway robberies, 9, 13 Apr. On 14 May 1821, shortly before his marriage, he received six weeks' leave to attend to urgent private business and is unlikely to have returned to the House that session.

He voted with ministers against more extensive tax reductions, 11, 21 Feb., and spoke against repealing the tax on salt, 28 Feb., but cast a wayward vote for a reduction in the junior admiralty lordships, 1 Mar. 1822.[11] Although 'no advocate for [Henry] Hunt*', he expressed regret at the commissioners' findings at Ilchester gaol and thought his treatment and conditions there merited immediate redress, 4 Mar. His speech opposing the vote of thanks to the court of proprietors of the Bank at their dinner, 21 Mar., was deliberately omitted from but made the subject of a hostile editorial in *The Times*, correcting his 'vulgar error' that the Bank had 'greatly contracted its issues on the resumption of cash payments'. In the version printed on the 23rd (*The Times* claimed there were two different ones) he blamed Peel and the select committee for the shortcomings of the 1819 Act and exonerated the Bank's directors, who 'had been so often violently attacked and feebly defended in the ... House'.[12] When the agriculture committee report was considered, he criticized and voted against the leader of the House Lord Londonderry's relief proposals, 9 May, and said that he was 'most inclined' to favour Curwen's, but would 'vote for no plan which did not contain a clause to remit the duty in the event of the price of corn raising so high as to indicate the approach of scarcity'. He indicated that his preferred concession would have been repeal of the window tax, 24 May. He complained that he was shut out from the division on the cost of the Swiss embassy, 15 May, a veiled attack on the Grenvillite accession, which government supporters were summoned to oppose.[13] Backing the Essex county Member Western's motion for inquiry into the resumption of cash payments, 12 June, he conceded that much of his opposition to the 1819 Act derived from its timing, the predominance of bullionists on the committee, and their adherence to a 'false theory ... that gold was the exact index of the depreciation of our currency'; but he remained convinced that distress was partly attributable to the premature restoration of the gold standard. Notwithstanding his support for Western, he expressed reservations on the use of silver as an alternative, 12 June, 10 July. He presented a petition against the Highgate chapel bill, 5 July,[14] and divided with government for the aliens bill, 19 July 1822.

Following his election as lord mayor of London, 28 Sept. 1822, Heygate equipped himself with lavish livery, and wrote to Lord Liverpool requesting the baronetcy he thought his rank, lineage and property merited

> because, however frequently I have both in and out of Parliament supported at critical moments the great measures of your ... administration, believing them to be wise and just, I am not aware that I have ever asked or received for myself or for any of my connections a single favour of any kind from ... government.[15]

Partly on account of the precedent it might set and tensions between the City and the king, who had declined to attend civic functions, his request was refused, as was his application as retiring mayor in September 1823, which the duke of York, the godfather of his first-born son, had endorsed.[16] The common council and corporation commended Heygate as a popular and diligent mayor and he had written:

> I need not impress upon your lordship how laborious, responsible and frequently unpleasant are the duties which are performed by the aldermen of the City of London (as magistrates, sheriffs and mayors) not only without any expense to the public but with a great sacrifice, in *general* of money and always of time, nor the importance and at the same time the difficulty of procuring men of property, education and respectable situation in life to take upon themselves the offices. It is now, I believe, ten years since a magistrate of London had the distinction of the baronetage. In that time, and indeed very recently, it has been conferred frequently on merchants, Bank directors, etc., whose fortune and standing have not been superior to those of many of the aldermen and who have *shrunk* in many instances from undertaking a public duty. I am far indeed from wishing to question the disposal of honours of the crown, but I am quite sure your lordship would regret that it should be imagined (as it is beginning to be) that a laborious and gratuitous public duty should operate rather as a bar than as a recommendation to them and this at a time when it has just been so largely augmented by the legislature ... I may perhaps appear to ... attach too much importance to a mere distinction, but it is desirable to me holding an official situation in the City for various reasons. Were I to relinquish that, it would be of little or no value.[17]

He had supported the establishment of a parliamentary reform subcommittee of the common council, 23 Jan., but corrected reports that he had voted in Lord John Russell's minority for reform, 20 Feb. 1823, when he was 'absent through indisposition'.[18] He convened a meeting of City merchants, bankers and traders to petition for changes in the legislation governing insolvent debtors, and presented the 1,600-signature petition, which called for restrictions on the powers of detaining creditors, 27 Mar.[19] He brought up others against the London Bridge bill, 14 May, 16, 20 June, and criticized it as a measure which empowered government at the corporation's expense by deploying £150,000 from the consolidated fund, 16 June, and granting the treasury the right to appoint an engineer, 20 June. He failed to kill it that day (by 4-71), or to carry a rider authorizing the corporation to choose an engineer (by 16-78). He briefly expressed his support for the government amendment commending 'strict neutrality' before the House divided on Macdonald's motion censuring their failure to intervene on behalf of liberal Spain, 30 Apr.; while in the City, he consulted the corporation's lawyers and investigated the legality of common council's resolutions committing funds to the Spanish and Greek loans, on which opinion was divided, 13, 23 June.[20] He beat London's boundaries with great pomp the following month, and presided over the Auxiliary Missionary Society's meeting there, 24 Sept.[21] At the sheriffs' dinner, 30 Sept. 1823, he paid tribute to their guest speakers, Canning and Huskisson.[22]

He deprecated any interference with the wartime sinking fund, 10 Feb., and denied reports on 4 Mar. that he had supported the government's resolutions for a national debt reduction bill, which he had opposed 'as inconsistent with the former pledges of Parliament in passing the original Acts', 3 Mar. 1824.[23] He presented protectionist petitions from Sudbury's silkworkers against repeal of the Spitalfields Acts, 21 May, but failed to kill the measure by adjournment or to secure its recommittal for tradesmen's evidence to be heard, 11 June 1824.[24] (He supported inquiry into the silk trade on his constituents' behalf, 24 Feb. 1826.) He was in the small minority against permitting long wool to be exported, 21 May 1824. Overcoming his dislike of the assessed taxes, 'which brought the people in more direct collision with government' (4 Feb. 1825), he declared that he would not vote for their repeal lest the sinking fund be endangered, 10 May 1824, but he voted to reduce taxation on houses and windows, 3 Mar. 1825, 'under [the] conviction that even without it ministers would be able to reduce the expenditure to the limits of the income'.[25] He considered the usury laws 'salutary' despite their flaws and, 'although indisposed', 27 Feb., he spoke and was a minority teller against their repeal, which he criticized as 'necessary only to satisfy the lawyers', 31 Mar. 1824.

He maintained that the current laws served the landed interest by limiting the size of the national debt, but conceded that supplementary legislation to regulate 'penalties and forfeitures' was necessary, 31 Mar., 8 Apr. He received leave to introduce a remedial bill, 26 May 1824, but abandoned it after a second repeal bill was defeated, 17 Feb. 1825.[26] His stake in the Grand Surrey Dock Company and the West India Dock Company made him a natural advocate of reduced tariffs on waterborne and coastwise coal, 12 Feb. 1824, and an opponent of the bill authorizing the construction of the rival St. Katharine's Docks, which he criticized as unnecessary and condemned as 'one of those projects which had grown out of the high price of stocks, which, if stocks fell again, would disappear like the South Sea Bubble', 2 Apr. 1824. With his fellow directors John Smith and William Manning, he spoke and presented petitions to the Commons against it, 25 Feb., 2 Apr., 3, 6, 12, 17, 28 May, 2 June 1824, and again, 22 Feb., 11 Mar. 1825, when he complained that the select committee had been packed with the bill's supporters.[27] He similarly opposed the South London Dock Company bill, 28 May, 2 June 1824.[28] He presented anti-slavery petitions from Sudbury, 16 Mar. 1824, 21 Feb. 1826, and Chichester, 29 Mar. 1824, and divided for Brougham's motion criticizing the indictment of the Methodist missionary John Smith in Demerara, 11 June 1824, but voted against condemning the Jamaican slave trials, 2 Mar. 1826. He supported reform of London's tithes, as lord mayor, and in the House, 14 Feb. 1825, and called for inquiry into the operations of turnpike trusts in the metropolis, 17 Feb. 1825.[29] He voted against the duke of Cumberland's annuity bill, 30 May, 10 June 1825. A radical publication classified him as a Member who had 'attended very infrequently' that session and 'voted in general with ministers: a fastidious speaker'.[30] Heygate's bank survived the 1825-6 crisis, and speaking on the proposed Bank Charter Act, 13 Feb. 1826, he poured scorn on Horne Tooke, Ricardo, McCulloch and pamphlet writers and political economists generally, and was criticized by the home secretary Peel for arguing that the measure posed a threat to country banks. Commenting privately on the disappointing contribution of the bankers to the debate, George Agar Ellis* noted that Heygate had been 'unbearable'.[31] Hume criticized him the next day for 'abusing the system of political economy' through his opposition to free trade, but, undaunted, he continued to call for 'the amount of notes in circulation to be laid before the public' and demanded that £1 notes be issued on government security rather than that of the Bank of England or any other bank, 27, 28 Feb.,

7 Mar. He praised the report of the select committee on banking in Scotland and Ireland and commended both systems, 26 May. As seconder, he tried to adjourn proceedings on Hume's state of the nation motion 'to prevent the premature conclusion of the debate' on a 'most interesting' subject, 4 May 1826.

It was reported when Heygate visited his ailing father on the continent in the autumn of 1825 that he would stand down at Sudbury at the dissolution, and he did so in June 1826, despite the failure of his canvass at St. Albans.[32] The £8,000 he expended in Sudbury between 1818 and 1826 ensured that he was requisitioned when the corporation were short of candidates in 1828 and 1830, and he started there as a Conservative in 1837, but retired before polling commenced.[33] The duke of Wellington as premier rejected his application for a baronetcy in June 1829, but he became a coronation baronet in 1831, partly through the intervention of the king, who noticed his omission from a list resubmitted by Lord Grey, from which he had been excluded to dampen aldermanic rivalry in the City.[34] He suffered financially after it emerged that his brother James, who was dismissed as a partner in 1830, had embezzled funds from the family bank, which was sold soon after his father's death in 1833.[35] Heygate now moved to the family estate he inherited at Roecliffe, Leicestershire, but he remained committed to metropolitan politics, was talked of as high bailiff of Southwark in 1842, and defeated Sir John Pirie (by 2,374-1,910) to become chamberlain of London, 17 May 1843.[36] Sponsoring him, his friend of over 40 years Matthew Wood* noted that he was 'never tied down to any administration and he always enlightened both sides by his admirable financial speeches in Parliament'.[37] He died at Roecliffe in August 1844, possessed of estates in Essex, Derbyshire, Leicestershire and London, and was succeeded as 2nd baronet by his barrister son Frederick William Heygate (1822-94), Conservative Member for county Londonderry, 1859-74. He willed that following his wife's death his property should be divided fivefold between his four sons, allowing two shares to the eldest.[38] His second son William Unwin Heygate (1825-1902) represented Leicester, Stamford, and Leicestershire South as a Conservative.

[1] HP Commons, 1790-1820, iv. 192-3; Suff. RO (Bury St. Edmunds), Sudbury borough recs. EE501/7, 8; Bury and Norwich Post, 8, 15 Mar. 1820. [2] B. Hilton, Corn, Cash, Commerce, 47, 66; HP Commons, 1790-1820, iv. 192-3. [3] The Times, 13 Feb. 1821. [4] Ibid. 4 May 1825. [5] Ibid. 19 Sept. 1820. [6] Ibid. 20, 22 Nov., 2 Dec. 1820; M.D. George, Cat. of Pol. and Personal Satires, x. 14014. [7] Gent. Mag. (1820), ii. 560. [8] The Times, 25 Jan. 1821. [9] Arbuthnot Jnl. i. 65-66; Colchester Diary, iii. 201; HLRO, Hist. Coll. 379, Grey

Bennet diary, 7; Add. 43212, f. 180; Harrowby mss, Harrowby to Sandon, 26 Jan.; Castle Howard mss, G. Howard to Lady Morpeth, 28 Jan.; *The Times*, 27, 30 Jan. 1821. [10] *The Times*, 31 May 1820; Hilton, 93. [11] *The Times*, 4 Mar. 1822. [12] Ibid. 22, 23 Mar. 1822. [13] Ibid. 16 May 1822. [14] Ibid. 6 July 1822. [15] Ibid. 30 Sept., 26 Oct., 6 Nov. 1822; CLRO, LOL/AC/13/001/20; RMD/CE/10/083; Add. 38291, f. 156. [16] Add. 38291, f. 164; 38296, ff. 296-8; *The Times*, 23 Oct., 30 Nov. 1822. [17] *The Times*, 20 Dec. 1822, 11 Nov. 1823; Add. 38296, ff. 291-3. [18] *The Times*, 24, 31 Jan., 10 Mar. 1823. [19] Ibid. 21 Feb., 28 Mar. 1823. [20] Ibid. 1 May, 14, 24 June, 8 July 1823. [21] Ibid. 24 July, 25 Sept. 1823. [22] Ibid. 1 Oct. 1823. [23] Ibid. 4, 10 Mar. 1824. [24] Ibid. 27 May 1824. [25] Ibid. 11 May 1824. [26] Ibid. 27 May 1824, 18 Feb. 1825. [27] Ibid. 18 May 1824; R. Harris, 'Political economy, interest groups, legal institutions and repeal of the Bubble Act in 1825', *EcHR*, l (1997), 675-96. [28] *The Times*, 29 May, 3 June 1824. [29] Ibid. 11, 25 Feb. 1823, 15, 18 Feb. 1825. [30] *Session of Parl.* 1825, p. 468. [31] Keele Univ. Lib. Sneyd mss SC8/79. [32] Add. 76135, Kinder to Spencer, 6 Jan. 1826. [33] *Ipswich Jnl.* 15, 29 Oct. 1825; *Colchester Gazette*, 10 June 1826; 'Sudbury borough' (ms *penes* A.T. Copsey in 1991); NLW, Ormathwaite mss FG1/5, pp. 77, 82, 83; G35, f. 98; *The Times*, 12 Dec. 1837. [34] Wellington mss WP1/1023/24; Grey mss, Taylor to Grey, 4 Sept., Ellice to same [Oct. 1831]. [35] *The Times*, 18 Sept. 1830; Derbys. RO, Pares mss D5336/2/6/5, 10, 19; 3/571/7/1-53; Derbys. RO, Wilmot-Horton mss D3155/C6688. [36] *The Times*, 29 July, 19, 20 Oct. 1842, 11-13, 16, 19 May 1843; B.R. Masters, *Chamberlain of the City of London, 1237-1987*, pp. 66-67, 73, 113. [37] *The Times*, 10 May 1843. [38] Ibid. 30 Aug., 24 Sept. 1844; *Gent. Mag.* (1845), i. 543; GL mss 12,011, f. 137; PROB 11/2005/1707.

M.M.E.

HEYWOOD, Benjamin (1793–1865), of Claremont, nr. Pendleton, Lancs. and 26 Dover Street, Mdx.

LANCASHIRE   1831–1832

b. 12 Dec. 1793, 1st s. of Nathaniel Heywood, banker, of Manchester, Lancs. and Ann, da. of Thomas Percival, physician, of Manchester. *educ.* by Rev. Edward Lloyd at Fairfield, Warrington, 1803-6; Rev. John Corrie in Birmingham 1806-9; Glasgow Univ. 1809-11. *m.* 22 Oct. 1816, his cos. Sophia Anne, da. of Thomas Robinson of Woodlands, Lancs., 6s. 2da. *suc.* fa. 1815; uncle Benjamin Arthur Heywood to Claremont 1828; *cr.* bt. 9 Aug. 1838. *d.* 11 Aug. 1865.

Heywood was a direct descendant of the ejected Dissenting minister Nathaniel Heywood of Ormskirk (1633-77). His grandfather Benjamin (*d.* 1795), father Nathaniel (1759-1815) and uncle Benjamin Arthur Heywood (1755-1828) had prospered as bankers, while another uncle, Samuel Heywood (1753-1828), was a Welsh judge. Born in Manchester, he spent his childhood in Liverpool and Everton, received a Dissenter's private education and studied at Glasgow University with his lifelong friend John Kenrick, before joining the Manchester branch of the family bank, Heywood Brothers and Company (of Manchester and Liverpool) in 1811. A partner from his coming of age in December 1814, he succeeded his father as head of the Manchester branch four months later, and became

head of the firm, one of the first to introduce variable interest rates and current and deposit accounts, following the death in 1828 of Benjamin Arthur Heywood, a prominent Liverpool Whig and the corporation's banker.[1] As a well-known Manchester Unitarian and philanthropist, he frequented Cross Street Chapel, was treasurer of the Literary and Philosophical Society and the founding president in 1825 of the Manchester Mechanics' Institute.[2] He entertained William Huskisson* at Claremont during his 1829 visit to the area, and considered sponsoring a 'commercial man' for Lancashire when John Wilson Patten was substituted for the ailing Ultra John Blackburne at the general election of 1830.[3] At the dissolution in April 1831, after attempts to persuade Wilson Patten to declare for the Grey ministry's reform bill and Lord John Russell* to stand had failed, he agreed to be requisitioned by the 'select few' as a reformer, 25, 28 Apr., to deter the Huntite Political Unions and uninvited outsiders from offering.[4] Supported by a coalition of wealthy Liverpool and Manchester Dissenters, merchants and reformers, he declared for the 'whole bill', secured the support of reform committees in the manufacturing towns, and possibly by agreeing to stand down at the first post-reform election, persuaded his fellow reformer Lord Sefton's* heir Lord Molyneux†, who had started late, to defer to him.[5] Russell approved his candidature, Wilson Patten desisted rather than risk defeat and he came in unopposed with the sitting Whig Lord Stanley.[6] On the hustings he criticized the corn laws and all trade monopolies, especially that of the East India Company, and declared for reform and against slavery.[7] Praising Wilson Patten at the dinner afterwards, he said he hoped the 'passing of the bill would be the means of restoring him again to Parliament'.[8] Commenting on the result, the duke of Wellington's confidante Mrs. Arbuthnot complained: 'in Lancashire they threw out Mr. Wilson Patten, who they acknowledge is the best county Member they ever had, and take a Mr. Heywood, a banker who knows nothing of Parliament or anything but his shop'.[9] Heywood addressed the Manchester reform dinner in honour of the king's birthday, 28 May, and stewarded at the races there before Parliament met. According to his brother Thomas, he turned down an invitation to move the address, but agreed to join Brooks's, doing so, 9 July 1831.[10]

Heywood, who never ceased to regard his return as a tribute to the popularity of reform, not himself, was undermined and criticized throughout his parliamentary career by certain Lancashire radicals and anti-reformers, whose speeches and unstamped news sheets disputed his right to sit 'unfettered'.[11] He was goaded into making his maiden speech on 8 July by Henry Hunt, the presenter of a 19,409-signature Manchester petition calling for repeal of the corn laws, annual parliaments, universal suffrage and the ballot. Hunt knew that Heywood thought the last too extreme and exploited this to justify his claim that the working classes were dissatisfied and disappointed with him for failing to live up to the radical promises on his election banners.[12] He divided for the reintroduced reform bill at its second reading, 6 July 1831, and, except for a vote for the total disfranchisement of Saltash, which ministers no longer pressed, 26 July, he divided steadily for its details. He ably contradicted its opponents' arguments against the proposed Lancashire enfranchisements, notably the decision to award Salford its own Member, 2 Aug. 1831. The Tory *Manchester Herald* reprimanded him for speaking similarly, 28 Feb. 1832.[13] He voted for the bill's passage, 21 Sept., the second reading of the Scottish reform bill, 23 Sept., and Lord Ebrington's confidence motion, 10 Oct. Afterwards he returned briefly to Lancashire where he and his friends failed to prevent the adoption of Huntite resolutions at mass meetings in the manufacturing towns which petitioned in protest at the bill's defeat in the Lords, and at political union meetings.[14] Although Heywood had secretarial help throughout, he privately expressed consternation at the mountain of constituency mail demanding replies by return which he received daily, in addition to the demands of his bank. He also calculated that the House had sat after midnight, which he found tiring, on 85 of the 123 days he attended in 1831.[15] He divided for the second reading of the revised reform bill, 17 Dec. 1831, consistently for its details, and cited statistics for Manchester to counter claims made by Sir James Scarlett for the anti-reformers, that the £10 householder vote would produce unmanageably large electorates in the great towns, 3 Feb. 1832. He voted for the bill's third reading, 22 Mar., and the address calling on the king to appoint only ministers who would carry it unimpaired, 10 May. Next day, seconding the Preston Member John Wood's motion to bring up the controversial Manchester petition for withholding supplies pending its passage, he expressed himself 'satisfied that no measure of reform of less efficiency will give satisfaction to the country without at once acceding to the wishes of the people'. He announced on 17 May that he would refrain from presenting similar petitions; but criticism of his failure to present the first Manchester petition himself induced him to bring up those from Heywood, Manchester, Oldham, Rochdale, Royton and Todmorden on the 23rd.[16] He divided for the second reading of the Irish reform bill,

25 May, and against Conservative amendments to the Scottish measure, 1, 15 June. He presented Salford's petition requesting extension of the English bill's provisions to Ireland, 25 June 1832.

Heywood divided with administration on the Dublin election controversy, 23 Aug., and in the minority for issuing the Liverpool writ, 5 Sept. 1831. His progovernment vote on the Russian-Dutch loan, 26 Jan. 1832, was criticized as unnecessary in the Tory press, and the foreign secretary Lord Palmerston afterwards ensured that he was briefed in person on the Belgian question.[17] He divided with government on Portugal, 9 Feb., against Hunt's call for inquiry into Peterloo, 15 Mar., and for the navy civil departments bill, 6 Apr., and the Russian-Dutch loan, 12, 16, 20 July, but with Hunt for information on military punishments, 16 Feb. He voted to make coroners' inquests public, 20 June 1832. He brought up a petition for renewal of the Sugar Refinery Act from Manchester Chamber of Commerce, 12 Aug. 1831. Cautioning against rushing through changes in the settlement laws that day, and again on the 17th, he warned that the interests of the manufacturing districts risked being subordinated to those of the agricultural areas. Making reform his priority, he confirmed that he considered the corn laws 'impolitic in principle and pernicious in practice', but he thought Hunt's advocacy of repeal was 'founded on a fallacy and supported by calamitous attacks on men whose motives he cannot appreciate', 15 Sept. 1831.

Heywood was named to the select committee on the East India Company, 27 Jan., and the committee of secrecy on the Bank of England's charter, 23 May 1832. His commercial skills and local knowledge as a Lancashire Member were, as he realized, factors in his appointment to the select committee on the silk trade, 5 Mar., four days after drawing on evidence from Congleton, Macclesfield and Manchester to endorse the vice-president of the board of trade Poulett Thomson's claims that reports of distress generated by foreign competition were exaggerated (1 Mar.).[18] Before being named on 16 Mar. to the select committee on the factory bill (against which he presented and endorsed petitions 7, 9 and 16 Mar.), he explained that he considered the measure in its 'present shape' to be 'wholly inoperative', damaging to trade and to the working classes, but intended voting for its second reading with a view to amending it, as 'some legislative interference to restrict children's working hours' was necessary. He handled the Manchester improvement bill, 5, 26 Mar., and brought up numerous petitions on local legislation and private bills on his constituents' behalf. He 'wholly endorsed' the Dissenters and

Unitarians' petitions he presented in favour of the Maynooth grant, 25 June, 2, 9, 16 July. On bringing up hostile petitions, 28 June, 2, 5, 9, 21 July 1832, he also made a point of testifying to local concern and the high cost to Liverpool and the county of implementing legislation for the removal of Scottish and Irish vagrants. Arrangements for him to campaign jointly with Stanley in the event of a dissolution had been in place since a ministry headed by Wellington was contemplated in May, and his retirement, which was announced after the reform bill received royal assent in June and justified on health grounds, caused surprise.[19] Refusing to reconsider, he informed his committee, 22 June 1832:

> I have suffered more in health than is externally apparent ... My more immediate connection with the commercial interest has led to my being named on so many committees that from noon until after midnight during five days in the week I am chiefly within the walls of the ... Commons. The confinement is very oppressive, and to one representing a large constituency is not likely to be materially lessened in the first reformed Parliament.[20]

A lifelong Liberal and correspondent of Henry Brougham*, he proposed opening temperance rooms to rival the public houses after their party did badly in Lancashire in 1837, and assisted his brother James, Member for Lancashire North, 1847-57, at elections.[21] In 1838 Lord Melbourne rewarded his loyalty with a baronetcy. He chaired the committee of Manchester College at York, 1832-34, and was president, 1840-2, when it returned to Manchester.[22] A widower since 1847, he retired from the bank, where five of his six sons had become partners, in 1860, and died at Claremont in August 1865. He was succeeded in the baronetcy and to his estates by his eldest son Thomas Percival Heywood (1823-97), for whom, with other family members, he made ample provision.[23]

[1] T. Heywood, *Mem. of Benjamin Heywood*, 5-39; T.S. Ashton, 'Bills of exchange and private banks in Lancs.' *EcHR*, xv (1945), 25-35. [2] J.T. Slugg, *Reminiscences of Manchester*, 173, 262; Brougham mss, Heywood to Brougham, 17 Feb. 1825, 29 Aug. 1828; LSE Lib. Archives Division, Coll. Misc. 0146, Potter mss, letterbk. iv, f. 39. [3] *Lancaster Gazette*, 29 Aug. 1829; Add. 38758, f. 2; *The Times*, 9 Aug. 1830; M.J. Turner, *Reform and Respectability*, 290-1. [4] *Manchester Guardian*, 12, 19 Mar.; *Manchester Times*, 26 Mar., 16, 23 Apr., 21 May 1831. [5] *Manchester Guardian*, 23, 30 Apr.; Creevey mss, Creevey to Miss Ord, 30 Apr., 4 May; Hatfield House mss, bdle. 4, Leigh to Salisbury, 27 Apr.; Brougham mss, W. Shepherd to Brougham [1831]. [6] Add. 51680, Russell to Lady Holland [May]; *The Times*, 6 May; *Manchester Times*, 7 May 1831. [7] *Lancaster Herald*, 7, 14 May 1831. [8] *Manchester Herald*, 18 May 1831. [9] *Arbuthnot Jnl.* ii. 421. [10] *Manchester Herald*, 1 June 1831; Heywood, 75-80. [11] *The Times*, 3 Aug. 1831; 'A Letter from one of the 3,730', 24 Mar. 1832 and *passim*.; Heywood, 89. [12] *Manchester Herald*, 11, 18 May; *Poor Man's Guardian*, 16 July 1831; Heywood, 86.

[13] *Manchester Guardian*, 24 Sept. 1831; *Manchester Herald*, 7 Mar. 1832. [14] *Manchester Guardian*, 15, 22 Oct., 26 Nov., 3 Dec.; *The Times*, 30 Nov. 1831. [15] Heywood, 82, 86. [16] *Manchester Herald*, 14 May; *Wheeler's Manchester Courier*, 19 May 1832. [17] *Manchester Herald*, 1 Feb.; Hatherton diary, 5 Feb. 1832. [18] Heywood, 86-88, 100; *Manchester Guardian*, 10, 17 Mar. 1832. [19] *Manchester Guardian*, 12 May, 23 June; *John Bull*, 1 July 1832. [20] Heywood, 94-101. [21] Brougham mss, Heywood to Brougham, 29 July 1837 and *passim*. [22] *Roll of Students entered at the Manchester Academy* (Manchester, 1868). [23] *Manchester Guardian*, 14 Aug. 1865.

T.A.J.

HILL, Lord Arthur Moyses William (1792-1860).

Co. Down   **26 Feb. 1817-1 Aug. 1836**

b. 10 Jan. 1792, 2nd *s.* of Arthur Hill†, 2nd mq. of Downshire [I] (*d.* 1801), and Mary, da. of Hon. Martyn Sandys, 2nd *s.* of Samuel, 1st Bar. Sandys (she was *cr.* Baroness Sandys 19 June 1802); bro. of Lord Arthur Marcus Cecil Hill† and Lord George Augusta Hill*. *educ.* Eton 1802. *unm. suc.* mother as 2nd Bar. Sandys 1 Aug. 1836. *d.* 16 July 1860.

Cornet 10 Drag. 1809, lt. 1810, capt. 1813; capt. 21 Drag. 1814, maj. (half-pay) 1815; a.d.c. to duke of Wellington 1815; capt. 2 Drag. 1816; brevet lt.-col. 1819; maj. 2 Drag 1825, lt.-col. 1832, col. 1837; half-pay 1837; maj.-gen. 1846; col. 7 Drag. Gds. 1853-8; lt.-gen. 1854; col. 2 Drag. 1858-*d.*

Register, chancery [I] 1794-1800.

Hill's father, who sat for Down in the Irish Parliament until he succeeded as 2nd marquess of Downshire in 1793, was a staunch opponent of the Union and committed suicide in 1801.[1] Hill, a career army officer, served directly under the duke of Wellington in the Peninsula. He joined Brooks's in 1812 and at a by-election in February 1817 was brought in as a Whig for Down by his elder brother, the 3rd marquess.[2] He was again returned unopposed at the general election of 1820 alongside the foreign secretary Lord Castlereagh, with whose family the Hills usually shared the representation, although differing in politics.[3] Described by Harriette Wilson as 'fat' and as having 'something comical about his manner, which I thought amusing enough', Hill was evidently considered something of a card.[4] In 1821 Lady Williams Wynn observed, wrongly as it turned out, that he was certain to marry Lord Hertford's daughter Frances Maria, since their relationship had 'begun at Brighton and has been vigorously followed on since'.[5] Three years later, having taken up residence at his recently widowed aunt Lady Salisbury's house at 20 Arlington Street in order to provide her with company, Thomas Creevey* reported that 'Atty is as good as any play in his description of a late dinner at

Little Sussex's. He was invited for the express purpose of destroying all formality in the other visitors, who were exclusively royal'.[6]

Hill was not a thick and thin attender, but in the first four sessions of the 1820 Parliament he divided with the Whig opposition to the Liverpool ministry on most major issues and voted regularly for reduced expenditure and taxation. He divided to make Leeds a scot and lot, not a £10 householder borough on the disfranchisement of Grampound, 2 Mar., and for parliamentary reform, 25 Apr. 1822, 24 Apr. 1823. He voted for Catholic relief, 28 Feb. 1821, and against the Irish habeas corpus suspension, 7 Feb., and insurrection bills, 8 Feb., 8 July 1822. He paired for the forgery punishment mitigation bill, 23 May 1821. He voted for inquiries into Irish tithes, 19 June 1822, the legal proceedings against the Dublin Orange rioters, 22 Apr., and the state of Ireland, 12 May 1823. He divided for inquiries into the Irish church establishment, 6 May, and the state of Ireland, 11 May 1824, and to secure the proper use of Irish first fruits revenues, 25 May 1824, his only known votes that year. He attended to vote against the Irish unlawful societies bill, 15, 18, 21, 25 Feb., and for Catholic relief, 1 Mar., 21 Apr., 10 May 1825. He presented petitions from Downpatrick in favour of the Catholics, 3 Mar., from Newry against alteration of the corn laws, 29 Apr. 1825, and from Bandon and elsewhere to abolish slavery, 8 May 1826.[7]

In February 1825 the Rev. Mark Cassidy, one of Lord Londonderry's supporters, remarked that the brother of the unpopular but powerful Downshire 'is not much known, personally rather liked than disliked, but not respected; the general opinion is that he would fill the character of *nobody* as well as of the Member of the county Down'.[8] At the general election of 1826, when the Stewart family's disaffected stopgap Member Mathew Forde withdrew, Hill was returned with Londonderry's son Lord Castlereagh, the nephew of the former holder of that title, after an artificially extended contest.[9] He again voted for Catholic relief, 6 Mar. 1827. He divided for the duke of Clarence's annuity bill, 16 Mar., but to postpone the committee of supply, 30 Mar. 1827. He was 'dreadfully wounded' in a fall from his horse, 25 Jan. 1828, and was not reckoned to be out of danger until April.[10] He was therefore excused attendance on the Westmeath election committee, 18 Apr., and paired for Catholic relief, 12 May 1828. He voted for Catholic emancipation, 6, 30 Mar. 1829. He divided for parliamentary reform, 18 Feb., and the enfranchisement of Birmingham, Leeds and Manchester, 23 Feb. 1830. He voted for repeal of the Irish coal duties, 13 May, but against Jewish emancipation, 17 May. He brought up petitions against the increased Irish stamp and spirit duties from Down, 14 June, and Bleris and Hillsborough, 1 July 1830.

Hill was involved in a severe contest in Down at the general election of 1830, when Forde's independent candidacy threatened to displace him. On the hustings he defended the government's record, especially on emancipation, refused to commit himself on reform and denied collusion with Castlereagh, now a junior minister. He trailed behind Forde until the sixth day of the poll, but finished narrowly in second place and in his address of thanks attacked the Down Independent Club for having misled many freeholders.[11] He was listed by ministers among their 'friends' and divided in their minority on the civil list, 15 Nov. 1830. Apparently after discussions within the family, he, like his brother George, now Member for Carrickfergus, divided for the second reading of the Grey ministry's reform bill, 22 Mar., and against Gascoyne's wrecking amendment, 19 Apr. 1831. Although he declined to bring up the county's radical reform petition, his conduct was deemed to have stood him in good stead at the ensuing general election. He offered as a reformer, apparently in alliance with the independent candidate William Sharman Crawford[†], but nevertheless maintained a tacit understanding with Castlereagh and, having drawn support from both sides, was elected with the latter by a substantial majority.[12]

Hill divided for the second reading of the reintroduced reform bill, 6 July, and the disfranchisement of Appleby, 19 July, and St. Germans, 26 July 1831. Thereafter he was apparently absent, but he paired for the partial disfranchisement of Dorchester, 28 July, and the enfranchisement of Greenwich, 3 Aug., and Gateshead, 5 Aug. Nothing came of speculation that he would get a coronation peerage in September.[13] He voted for the passage of the reform bill, 21 Sept., and Lord Ebrington's confidence motion, 10 Oct. He divided for the second reading of the revised bill, 17 Dec. 1831, to include 56 boroughs in schedule B, 20 Jan., against giving the vote to all £10 ratepayers, 3 Feb., to enfranchise Tower Hamlets, 28 Feb., and for the third reading, 22 Mar. 1832. He voted with ministers against the production of information on Portugal, 9 Feb., but in the minority for printing the Woollen Grange petition for the abolition of Irish tithes, 16 Feb. His last recorded vote was for the address calling on the king to appoint only ministers who would carry the reform bill unimpaired, 10 May. He had been given the lieutenant-colonelcy of the Scots Greys in March and in July he took command of the regiment at Birmingham. From there he issued a moderate address and was returned unopposed for Down at the general election of 1832.[14] In August 1836 he was removed to the Lords by the death of his mother, whose barony had a special remainder in favour of her younger sons, and thereafter he acted with the Conservatives. Sandys died in July 1860, at his mother's family's former residence of Ombersley Court, Worcestershire, where he was much esteemed for his amiable character. His title and estates passed to his next younger brother Lord Arthur Marcus Cecil Hill (1798-1886), Liberal Member for Newry, 1832-4, and Evesham, 1837-52.[15]

[1] Hist. Irish Parl. iv. 418-22. [2] HP Commons, 1790-1820, iv. 196. [3] Belfast News Letter, 7, 24 Mar. 1820. [4] Harriette Wilson's Mems. (1929), 399, 401. [5] Williams Wynn Corresp. 265. [6] Creevey's Life and Times, 197. [7] The Times, 4 Mar., 30 Apr. 1825, 9 May 1826. [8] PRO NI, Cassidy mss D1088/45. [9] Newry Commercial Telegraph, 6, 13, 30 June 1826; PRO NI, Downshire mss D671/C/2/237/1. [10] Newry Commercial Telegraph, 1 Feb., 18 Apr. 1828; Downshire mss C/12/341. [11] Newry Commercial Telegraph, 2 July, 3, 17, 20, 24, 27 Aug. 1830. [12] Ibid. 5 Apr., 3, 10, 13, 17, 20, 24 May 1831; Downshire mss C/2/449, 451. [13] Belfast News Letter, 6 Sept. 1831. [14] Ibid. 31 July; Newry Commercial Telegraph, 11, 21 Dec. 1832; Wellington mss WP1/1239/27. [15] The Times, 21 July; Berrow's Worcester Jnl. 21 July 1860; Gent. Mag. (1860), ii. 190.

S.M.F.

HILL, Lord George Augusta (1801-1879).

CARRICKFERGUS   1830-1832

b. 9 Dec. 1801, 5th but 4th surv. s. of Arthur Hill†, 2nd mq. of Downshire [I] (d. 1801), and Mary, da. of Hon. Martyn Sandys, 2nd s. of Samuel, 1st Bar. Sandys (she was cr. Baroness Sandys 19 June 1802); bro. of Lord Arthur Marcus Cecil Hill† and Lord Arthur Moyses William Hill*. m. (1) 21 Oct. 1834, Cassandra Jane (d. 14 Mar. 1842), da. of Edward Knight (formerly Austen) of Godmersham Park, Kent, 2s. 1da.; (2) 11 May 1847, her sis. Louisa Knight, 1s. d. 6 Apr. 1879.
   Cornet R. Horse Gds. 1817, lt. 1820; capt. 1825; capt. 8 Drag. 1825; a.d.c. to c.-in-c. [I] 1830; maj. (half-pay) 1830; maj. 47 Ft. 1838, ret. 1838.
   Comptroller, household of ld. lt. [I] 1833-4.
   Sheriff, co. Donegal 1845-6.

Hill was the youngest brother of the 3rd marquess of Downshire and Lord Arthur Moyses Hill, Member for Down. He entered the army in May 1817, serving initially in the duke of Wellington's regiment, and transferred to the Royal Irish Dragoons in 1825. At the general election of 1826 he was proposed for Carrickfergus, where Downshire was a minor landowner, but withdrew after a token contest, stating that he had been unaware of the nomination, in favour of the sitting Member Sir Arthur Chichester.[1] He evi-

dently served with his regiment on peacekeeping duties in the north of Ireland and in December 1828 he deplored the dismissal of the lord lieutenant Lord Anglesey.[2] In April 1830 he became aide-de-camp to Sir John Byng*, commander of the forces in Ireland, but he obtained his majority and joined the half-pay list, 6 July.[3] This was with a view to canvassing at Carrickfergus, where a family member was required to head the revived opposition to Lord Donegall's interest. At the general election he defeated Chichester after a severe contest, surviving a subsequent petition, and was returned as a supporter of Wellington's administration.[4]

Hill was listed by ministers among their 'friends', but was absent from the division on the civil list that led to their resignation, 15 Nov. 1830, and subsequently followed his brothers in adhering to Lord Grey's coalition government. He declined to present the Carrickfergus petition for radical parliamentary reform, but voted for the second reading of the reform bill, 22 Mar., and against Gascoyne's wrecking amendment, 19 Apr. 1831.[5] He was again returned for Carrickfergus after another of the Chichesters had failed to push his candidacy to a contest at the general election in May.[6] He divided for the second reading of the reintroduced reform bill, 6 July, and steadily for its details. He sided with ministers in their majorities on the Dublin election controversy, 23 Aug., but was listed in the minority for making legal provision for the Irish poor, 29 Aug. He divided for the passage of the reform bill, 21 Sept., and Lord Ebrington's confidence motion, 10 Oct. He voted for the second reading of the revised bill, 17 Dec. 1831, again for its details, and the third reading, 22 Mar. 1832. He divided for Ebrington's motion for an address calling on the king to appoint only ministers who would carry the reform bill unimpaired, 10 May, and the second reading of the Irish bill, 25 May. He voted with ministers for the Russian-Dutch loan, 26 Jan., 12, 16, 20 July, and against producing information on Portugal, 9 Feb. 1832.

Hill, who made no known parliamentary speeches, issued an address from Paris, 11 Oct. 1832, in which he boasted of his assiduity in attending on the reform question and announced his retirement on account of ill health. He returned to Ireland in time to assist the return of his brother Lord Arthur Marcus Hill for Newry at the general election of 1832, but apparently never sought to re-enter Parliament himself.[7] By 1833 he had been appointed comptroller in the reappointed Anglesey's viceregal household and he continued in office under his successor Lord Wellesley until the following year.[8] He exchanged into the 47th Foot, 23 Mar. 1838, but sold his commission the following day. That year he was apparently provided by his family with sufficient funds to buy an extensive estate at Gweedore in Donegal. There he devoted the rest of his life to agricultural improvements, notably by suppressing the prevalent 'rundale' system, in which the available land was divided into small cultivated patches. His *Facts from Gweedore*, which went through five editions between 1845 and 1887, played a large part in the bitter public debates about the effects of Irish landlordism. The Commons select committee on destitution in Gweedore and Cloughaneely, to which he gave evidence, 23, 24 June 1858, was critical of his actions, and he was gradually borne down by the weight of local resistance to his well-meaning endeavours.[9] Thomas Carlyle, who visited him in 1849, described Hill as 'a man you love at first sight, handsome, gravely smiling; [with] thick grizzled hair [and] military composure'. He died at his then residence of Ballyane House, Ramelton, in April 1879, leaving his estate to his eldest son, Arthur Blundell George Sandys Hill (1837-1923), another army officer.[10]

[1] *Belfast Commercial Chron.* 17 June 1826. [2] PRO NI, Downshire mss D671/C/348/4, 5. [3] *Belfast News Letter*, 16 Apr. 1830. [4] Ibid. 30 July, 6, 10, 13 Aug. 1830; Downshire mss C/1/611; PRO NI, Londonderry mss T1536/30. [5] *Belfast Guardian*, 4 Feb. 1831. [6] *Belfast News Letter*, 29 Apr., 6 May 1831. [7] Ibid. 13 Nov. 1832; *Newry Commercial Telegraph*, 4 Jan. 1833. [8] W.A. Maguire, *Downshire Estates in Ireland*, 11; *Wellington Pol. Corresp.* i. 297. [9] *Facts from Gweedore* ed. E.E. Evans (1971), pp. v-xviii; Maguire, 19, 236; *Donegal Hist. and Society* ed. W. Nolan *et al.* 547-82; J. Bardon, *Hist. Ulster*, 279-80; *PP* (1857-8), xiii. 89, 381-401. [10] *Facts from Gweedore*, pp. vi, xviii; *Belfast News Letter*, 9 Apr.; *The Times*, 11 Apr. 1879.

S.M.F.

HILL, Sir George Fitzgerald, 2nd bt. (1763–1839), of Brook Hall, co. Londonderry.

Co. LONDONDERRY	14 Jan. 1801–1802
Co. LONDONDERRY	1802–1830

b. 1 June 1763, 1st s. of Sir Hugh Hill, 1st bt., of Brook Hall and 2nd w. Hannah, da. of John McClintock, MP [I], of Dunmore, co. Donegal, wid. of John Spence of co. Leitrim. *educ.* Londonderry; Trinity, Dublin 1780; L. Inn 1780, called [I] 1786; continental tour. *m.* 10 Sept. 1788, Jane, da. of Hon. John Beresford† of Abbeville, co. Dublin and Walworth, co. Londonderry, *s.p. suc.* fa. as 2nd bt. 31 Jan. 1795. *d.* 8 Mar. 1839.
  MP [I] 1791-8.
  Clerk of the parl. [I] 1798-1800; commr. of treasury [I] 1807-17; PC [I] 24 Dec. 1808, [GB] 31 May 1817; vice-treas. [I] 1817-30; gov. St. Vincent 1830-3, Trinidad 1833-*d.*

Recorder, Londonderry 1792-*d.*; trustee, linen board [I] 1801.
  Capt.-commdt. Londonderry yeomanry legion 1796; lt.-col. co. Londonderry militia 1800, col. 1822-30.

Hill, who had sat for Coleraine and Londonderry in the Irish Parliament in the 1790s, was returned to the Westminster Parliament for Londonderry for the sixth consecutive time at the general election of 1820. He continued to manage the affairs of the borough, of which he was a burgess and the recorder, on behalf of his influential relations by marriage, the Beresfords. Receiving £2,265 a year in compensation for the loss of his clerkship of the Irish Parliament, from 1817 he also had a salary of £1,500 as vice-treasurer of Ireland. In 1820 Lord Liverpool's administration noted that he had had 'immense local patronage'.[1] As an active member of the payroll vote, he of course continued to divide regularly with government, and often spoke, introduced legislation and acted as a teller, especially on Irish financial and commercial business; he regularly sat on select committees on Irish matters and frequently presented petitions from his constituency. An Orangeman, who served at least once on the committee of the Grand Orange Lodge, he remained opposed to Catholic relief, but steadily refused to sanction Protestant excesses.[2]

Hill commented on the need for relief after the failure of banks in Ireland, 16 June, and asked the chancellor about the scope of the promissory notes bill, 14 July 1820. He objected to the Irish master in chancery Thomas Ellis being excluded from the House, 30 June, and presented a Dublin petition to this effect, 12 July, when he attempted to point out a breach of privilege.[3] He read the Londonderry corporation's address to the lord lieutenant, Lord Talbot, on his visit to the city, 15 Sept. 1820. He moved the loyal address at a borough meeting, 4 Jan. 1821, when he justified the ministry's record on the whiskey duties.[4] He spoke and divided against Catholic claims, 28 Feb., insisted that the House be called over on this question, 2 Mar., and criticized the relief bill, 16, 23, 27, 28 Mar., 2 Apr.[5] He opposed the Irish tithes leasing bill, 15 Mar., and moved the wrecking amendment against its third reading, 10 May.[6] In November he complained that the Irish government had ignored his memorial deploring vilification of the yeomanry.[7] The corporation of Londonderry presented him with a piece of plate at a dinner in his honour, 28 Dec. 1821.[8]

During 1822, partly as the result of his own suggestions, further consolidation took place in the residual Irish financial administration, and Hill became responsible, for example, for the functions of the Irish paymaster-general.[9] At the beginning of that session he wrote confidentially to Peel, the new home secretary, that 'the country gentlemen and agriculture will give rather general trouble, I apprehend, and I rather hope will consume the most time'.[10] He voted against the Catholic peers bill, 30 Apr. He secured the appointment of a select committee on the Irish linen trade, 18 May, and brought up its report in favour of further encouragement for the industry, 17 July 1822, when he clashed with Brougham about the 12th of July celebrations in Londonderry.[11] After the suicide of Lord Londonderry*, the foreign secretary, that autumn, Hill petitioned for and received the colonelcy of the county Londonderry militia, much to the fury of the 3rd marquess, now head of the rival Stewart interest in the county, who claimed that Hill was 'a ruined man' without 'parliamentary ability, influence or property', denounced him for his 'jobbing and mean conduct' and threatened to stir up an opposition against him in his borough.[12] Ministers, who declined to dismiss Hill from office, put enormous pressure on him (until July 1823) to resign the colonelcy, but he steadfastly refused to do so, despite thereby incurring their and the king's displeasure.[13] He vindicated his conduct by appealing to the reversion which the late marquess had given him, emphasizing his desire to consolidate the Beresfords' interests and promising to act amicably with the Stewarts over militia patronage and county politics.[14]

Defending the grant for the Irish yeomanry, 10 Mar. 1823, Hill observed that its officers had ended their involvement in Orange processions. He was among the 'violent Orangeists' who opposed Brownlow's motion censuring the legal proceedings against the Dublin theatre rioters, 15 Apr., when Lord Milton complained that he was retained in office in spite of his Orange principles.[15] He divided against the compromise motion for an inquiry, 22 Apr., but asked several questions during its sittings in May. On 28 Apr. he attended the meeting at Henry Bankes's* house to hear Peel's proposals on the Catholic question, and in May he gave Mrs. Arbuthnot 'a deplorable account of the state of Ireland' and predicted imminent rebellion.[16] He praised the Irish viceroy Lord Wellesley's efforts to suppress sectarian disorder, 25 June, and in August 1823, when he informed Peel of the state of unrest in the North of Ireland, he attended a county Londonderry meeting about an outrage in Maghera.[17] He defended the grant to Irish Protestant charter schools, 15 Mar., commented on the linen laws, 19 Mar., and defeated an attempt to reduce the Irish militia establishment, 5 May 1824.[18] He was forced to withdraw the bill relating to Derry

Cathedral, 10 May, but expressed his wish that a trust might be formed for its repair, 18 May, 17 June. He seconded Croker's motion for a return of the number of inhabitant householders and freeholders in Ireland, 19 May, hoping that it might lead to the suppression of small freeholders.[19] Writing in November 1824 to his friend George Dawson, the county Londonderry Member and junior minister, he wryly suggested that he should receive the vacant Indian governorship and commented that

> the Popish proceedings are more audacious every hour. Protestants stare at each other and say, what are we to expect? Shall we take a part and express our sentiments? This I have been now frequently asked. My reply has been that the House of Commons is the fit place for any exertion I can make, declining thereby to promote any public meeting by active interference. This causes speculation: 'Is Sir George afraid of Lord Well[esley], maybe he knows that Peel and Liverpool are relaxing, etc., etc., etc.'[20]

Hill was, however, present at the city and county Londonderry anti-Catholic meeting, 10 Jan. 1825, when he attacked the radical Francis Horner for agitating the issue of Catholic freeholders being allowed to attend.[21] He related to Peel that he had sought to prevent any aspersions being cast against the Irish government at the meeting, and in a long and unreserved letter of the 23rd he stressed the overwhelming, if currently latent, power of the Catholics and the readiness of moderate Protestants to 'compromise for future security', for instance on the basis of the bill which it was rumoured that Canning, the foreign secretary, would introduce.[22] The following month he appealed, on the strength of his long experience, for a place on the select committee on the state of Ireland, but Peel refused on the ground that room could not be found for him and Dawson, whom he had already chosen.[23] Having justified the conduct of his county's magistrates relating to marriages performed by Catholic priests, 8 Feb., and presented the hostile Londonderry petition, 10 Feb., he voted for the Irish unlawful societies bill, 25 Feb., and against Catholic relief, 1 Mar., 21 Apr., 10 May, and the attendant franchise bill, 26 Apr. Yet, in private he was apparently prepared to seek concessions, as according to Daniel O'Connell's* letter to his wife, 4 Mar., 'a great Orangeman from the North, Sir George Hill, but his name should not appear in print, has just announced that a number of the English supporters of the ministry are going in a body to Lord Liverpool *to insist* that he should no longer oppose emancipation'.[24] Amongst other legislative initiatives that year, he again chaired an inquiry into Irish linen and secured the passage of a bill to regulate the trade. After a session in which he admitted having been 'almost a passive observer of what passed', he reported to Peel in July that the Protestants were sulky at being deprived of opportunities to demonstrate while Catholic processions were left unhindered.[25] In September 1825, forecasting sweeping gains for the pro-Catholics in the expected election that autumn and the future ruin of the Protestant community in Ireland, he lamented to him that 'to have comfort or means of peace in Ireland you must either give up the establishment and make room for us in England or concur in your cabinet to act together in resisting the *extent* of concessions sought for'.[26]

Hill's official duties in Dublin prevented him attending the ceremonies in Londonderry on 18 Dec. 1825, but he was present to denounce the Catholic Association at a dinner in honour of Dawson there on the 28th. He presented the city's anti-Catholic address to the duke of York, 23 Feb. 1826.[27] He brought up Londonderry petitions relating to imports of butter and Irish banknotes, 7 Apr., when he explained the duties attached to his office and defended its annual expenses.[28] His interest in Dublin was thought to be useful to Croker in his contest for the University at the general election of 1826, when he was again elected for Londonderry, where his portrait was donated to the corporation hall.[29] As Dawson reported to Peel from the city, 22 June, Hill was 'doing his best here to keep up a proper feeling of attachment to the government, and a determination to be firm in supporting a Protestant constitution. Poor fellow, I wish his means were better, for he has a generous heart and affectionate disposition'.[30] Underlining his regret at the success of the Catholic cause, Hill told Peel, 6 July, that he was not sanguine that the Protestants would show restraint on the 12th and that 'the present state of things cannot be endured: the Romans are united as one man, and common safety will justify counter-association against the chance or dread of commotion'.[31] He continued to believe that government would have to act against the Catholic Association, and he spoke in condemnation of its activities at dinners in Londonderry, 3 Oct., and Armagh, 5 Oct. 1826.[32]

On 21 Oct. 1826 Hill sent Dawson a long appraisal of the state of public opinion:

There are some republicans in Belfast and a few in Derry who have no religion and would coalesce with any mixture which would promote confusion and dissolve the Union; these are not numerous. There are a few also who wish well to monarchy and church but who would sacrifice for repose; these would emancipate (bless the term) to procure quiet. There are also some selfish dealers, who, governed by dread of losing Popish customers for their

articles of sale, will not offend (as they say) by taking a part against the Romans. And I regret to add that there are a few good men, honest sincere fellows, who are persuaded that Peel and Goulburn [the Irish secretary] are playing a game which permits the manifestation of such energy, power and determination on the part of the Romans as they (P. and G.) calculate will prove to John Bull that resistance to the Popish measure is both absurd and inadmissible, thus providing for themselves and the Protestant part of the cabinet excuse nay approbation for relinquishing further opposition.

Emphasizing that 'for 36 years I have slaved in these quarters in the North and although highly stationed officially, I have sacrificed my means to the performance of political duty', he bleated that 'I ought therefore to have my retirement provided for if any colour of truth belongs to a serious contemplation of our ministers to require their official friends to relinquish their Protestant principles'.[33] Feeling duty bound to inform Peel of his opinions, he wrote at length on 2 Nov. 1826, beginning with what he termed the 'common' and 'incontrovertible' observation that 'the state of Ireland under the government of Great Britain can not be permitted to remain as it is'. He expatiated on his previous analysis and, stressing that Ulster Protestants were convinced that government intended to let the situation deteriorate until emancipation became inevitable and that the extremists could not in any case impede its passage, he urged the cabinet to come to a united decision in favour of a limited form of concession in order to prevent Ireland from becoming 'a Popish country'. For his own part he stated that 'I will not make these admissions in public, in doing so I should be called recreant; on the contrary I will continue to act in co-operation with those who are zealous against the Roman claims'.[34] He duly attended the county Londonderry anti-Catholic meeting the following day.[35]

In February 1827 Hill forwarded to Peel the anti-Catholic petition, which he had himself signed, from the Irish nobility and gentry, and supplied him with information about Brownlow's censure motion on the handling of the Lisburn Orange march.[36] In the House he clashed with Brownlow over a petition from the Catholics of county Londonderry, 2 Mar.[37] He and Dawson were tellers for the majority of four against Catholic relief, 6 Mar. He defended the lord lieutenant's decision to appoint a stipendiary magistrate in county Waterford, 16 Mar., insisted that the Irish government was attempting to suppress Orange outrages, 11 Apr., and denied that Irish landowners were expelling their paupers to England, 30 May.[38] Having stayed in office under Canning, he divided against the disfranchisement of Penryn, 28 May, for the grant for improved water communications in Canada, 12 June, and against the Coventry magistracy bill, 18 June. In October it was known to the Goderich ministry that Hill 'was desirous of going out of office and out of Parliament, but that his affairs were much deranged, and that he could not do so except by "commutation for some minor government"'. The Whig supporters of the administration hoped that he might be eased out in order to provide for Sir John Newport*, but nothing came of it.[39] Hill presided at the dinner on 18 Dec. 1827 to celebrate the shutting of the gates of Londonderry.[40]

As a member of the duke of Wellington's government, he divided against repeal of the Test Acts, 26 Feb. 1828. He presented the petition from the Irish Society against the salmon fisheries bill, 7 Mar., and was a teller for the majority for his wrecking amendment, 20 Mar. He supported the Hibernian Joint Stock Company bill as a means of increasing investment in Ireland, 22 Apr., but failed to have it referred to a select committee, 24 Apr., 2, 6 May. He voted against Catholic relief, 12 May. He spoke in favour of the additional churches bill, 30 June, and defended the conduct of the Londonderry magistrates towards Orange processions, 8 July. Aware of the state of alarm in Ireland, he returned there after the session, 'determined to endeavour to moderate Protestant feeling' and to urge his friends to place their trust in whatever ministers should decide to do. However, as he confided to Wellington, 'many whom I thought I could influence reject my advice to be moderate and patient, pointedly asking me "if I too was going to betray them"'.[41] Chairing the Londonderry dinner on the anniversary of the lifting of the siege, 12 Aug., he spoke in praise of the Protestant constitution, but was unable to restrain the anger demonstrated against Dawson's ill-fated declaration in favour of the Catholics. He wrote to Wellington and Peel in mitigation of Dawson's offence, pleading that he and Dawson had both expressed considerable sympathy with the cause of their Protestant fellow countrymen, who felt threatened by the disarming of the yeomanry.[42] In a further letter to Peel, 20 Aug., he urged him not to resign if the cabinet decided to emancipate the Catholics.[43] Absenting himself in Dublin on the excuse of official business, he kept his distance during the formation of Brunswick Clubs in Londonderry that autumn and missed the anti-Catholic county meeting on 4 Dec. 1828; but he did write to the press to rebut the widely held presumption that Dawson had been speaking on behalf of the government.[44]

Planta, the patronage secretary, listed Hill as likely to vote 'with government' for emancipation, and it was known that he would not quit his place.[45] He duly divided for the Catholics, 6 Mar., much to the surprise of some observers.[46] Bringing up the hostile petitions from the county and corporation of Londonderry, 16 Mar., he explained his own change of heart on the grounds that it had been advanced by administration as a national measure and was a step made unavoidably necessary by the need to avoid further perilous unrest in Ireland. He voted for the third reading of the emancipation bill, 30 Mar., and for allowing O'Connell to take his seat unhindered, 18 May 1829. He continued to serve ministers as a teller, although Wellington was anxious to replace him with the knight of Kerry*.[47] He was reckoned to be overoptimistic in his assessment that the Northern Protestants were reconciled to emancipation, but it was thought likely he would 'get off well' when he returned to Ulster that summer.[48] Although Hill had not always been considered a suitable figure to manage the Beresfords' interest in the county, he drew up a detailed analysis of their support on the registers there in July 1829.[49] He remained loyal to Dawson, whom the connection intended to ditch in favour of another candidate, and Henry Barré Beresford commented to Archbishop Beresford that

> I feel much for him. His heart is with us if he was independent, but situated as he is with government, he endeavours naturally to soften public feeling in city and county, for of course the subsiding of that feeling is of great moment to him as Member for Derry, as also for the government with whom he acts; you of course must be aware that the people of the county through delicacy to him (for whom they all feel as I do) do not speak so plainly as to me, but he has heard plain facts to my knowledge and will hear more.[50]

Hill helped to prevent any overt display of Protestant anger on 12 Aug. and later that month was given a dinner with Dawson by Londonderry corporation. He repeatedly stressed to the heads of the Beresford family that his 40 years' experience as 'an active political agent', centred on his 'head quarter of politics' at Brook Hall, gave credit to his requests for their standing by Dawson, who had government support, but in September he reluctantly broke with them altogether.[51] Lord Beresford considered his arguments and behaviour 'absurd', and Hill received short shrift when he attempted to argue that Dawson should be found a bolthole at Coleraine or elsewhere.[52] He was, however, congratulated by Peel for his efforts 'to conciliate the good will and the support of all reasonable and well judging men' in Londonderry in December 1829.[53]

Hoping for a more lucrative appointment, Hill initially reacted cautiously to Wellington's offer of the governorship of St. Vincent in January 1830, but in March, haunted by fears of financial disaster, he resigned the vice-treasurership in order to take it up.[54] In the meantime, he continued to side with administration, being a teller against Lord Blandford's amendment to the address, 5 Feb. He voted against transferring East Retford's seats to Birmingham, 11 Feb., and the enfranchisement of Birmingham, Leeds and Manchester, 23 Feb. He spoke in defence of the Irish yeomanry, 22 Feb. He divided against Jewish emancipation, 5 Apr., 17 May. He commented on the Galway franchise bill, 26 Apr., and voted for it, 24, 25 May. His last recorded vote was against abolition of the death penalty for forgery, 7 June, and his only other known speeches were in vindication of the conduct of the corporation of Londonderry, 23 Mar., 23 June 1830.

In expectation of his departure abroad, Hill made no attempt to stand for Londonderry at the general election of 1830. However, in daily expectation of being arraigned for debt, he even suggested to the Beresfords, who wanted nothing to do with him, that he could be returned as a locum for Coleraine, where he was also a corporator; he had hopes of a similar retreat in England.[55] Barré Beresford, who rented Brook Hall as his base in county Londonderry, noticed that Hill was 'in wonderful spirits' in August, but in late September he commented, 'Poor fellow. He is low enough ... What a hand he has made of himself'.[56] His governorship was not gazetted until August, when he made haste to leave the country, and he thereafter enjoyed a salary of £4,000. Because she would have been left with nothing in the event of being widowed, Lady Hill obtained a pension of £467, one of the last acts of the Wellington administration.[57] As was announced in the Commons on 6 Dec. 1830, his old office was absorbed into the treasury in London and made a non-political appointment. However, problems arose because his 'desperate and unprincipled inattention to money dealings' had extended to his official functions, and his accounts were found to be in disarray and heavily in arrears.[58] Questions were raised in the House, 27 June, and on 31 Aug. 1831, on the motion to defray a charge of £5,534 relating to the office, it was revealed by the treasury secretary Rice that Hill had not sent in his accounts since 1825, that no vouchers or receipts existed for lawyers' invoices totalling £10,000 a year and that Hill still personally owed £2,180. Other criticisms were raised and although Dawson, for example, came to his defence, he was fortunate to escape a motion for an address

calling on the king to have him recalled or his salary docked. A return was ordered of his accounts and emoluments, 7 Sept., but no further action was taken against him because in October his family, with assistance from the Beresfords, finally paid off the amount of the defalcation.[59] Neither did Hill escape the charge of peculation in relation to the defective corporation of Londonderry, as one of the city's radicals, James Edwards, informed the Irish secretary, Smith Stanley, 17 Oct. 1831, that 'during Sir George Hill's political career he derived, although the public did not, much advantage from the manner in which the functions of the corporation were exercized'.[60]

Hill, who observed to Goderich, 28 Aug. 1832, that 'I rejoice to be out of Ireland and to have abandoned politics', was in April 1833 transferred to Trinidad, where the following year there was an uprising by the semi-emancipated slaves.[61] His reputation, including his conduct as vice-treasurer, was blackened by the author of a vindictive pamphlet, in which Hill was depicted at a dinner 'enlivening the scene by the exhibition of several acts of tomfoolery, and aiding in keeping up the disgusting revel by the spouting of his usual maudlin orations'.[62] He died and was buried in Trinidad in March 1839, when comments on his 'considerable irritability of character' and lack of energy were again given an airing.[63] No will has been traced, but his title and remaining Brook Hall property passed to his nephew George Hill (1804-45), a barrister and Londonderry corporator, who had served under him as deputy vice-treasurer of Ireland until 1830.

[1] Add. 40296, ff. 29-30; 40298, ff. 28-29; *The Times*, 21 Feb. 1821; *Hist. Irish Parl.* iv. 422-3; *HP Commons, 1790-1820*, iv. 196-8. [2] PRO NI, Leslie mss MIC606/3/J/7/21/4. [3] *The Times*, 13, 15 July 1820. [4] *Belfast News Letter*, 22 Sept. 1820, 12 Jan. 1821. [5] *The Times*, 3, 17, 24, 28 Mar. 1821. [6] Ibid. 16 Mar., 11 May 1821. [7] PRO NI, Talbot-Gregory mss D4100/3/12. [8] *Belfast News Letter*, 4 Jan. 1822. [9] PRO NI, Hill mss D642/162; A/22/1-28; R.B. McDowell, *Irish Administration*, 92. [10] Hill mss A/14/22. [11] *The Times*, 18 July 1822. [12] Add. 38291, f. 152; 38295, f. 172; Cent. Kent. Stud. Camden mss U840 C504/5; PRO NI, Stewart-Bam mss D4137/B/2/5; Norf. RO, Blickling Hall mss, Londonderry to wife, 2 July 1823. [13] Add. 37301, f. 232; 40304, f. 84; Wellington mss WP1/766/13; 767/2, 11; 768/4; 770/5; *Arbuthnot Jnl.* i. 244-7. [14] Hill mss A/21/1-3, 7, 12; Wellington mss WP1/763/23; 768/14. [15] Buckingham, *Mems. Geo. IV*, i. 451; H. Senior, *Orangeism in Ireland and Britain*, 203. [16] N. Gash, *Secretary Peel*, 411; *Arbuthnot Jnl.* i. 235. [17] Add. 40357, f. 294; 40358, f. 44. [18] *The Times*, 16 Mar. 1824. [19] Ibid. 20 May 1824. [20] Hill mss A/18/7. [21] *Belfast News Letter*, 14 Jan. 1825. [22] Add. 40372, ff. 189, 195. [23] Add. 40373, ff. 175, 177; Hill mss A/14/25; *HP Commons, 1790-1820*, iv. 196-7. [24] *O'Connell Corresp.* iii. 1180. [25] Add. 40380, f. 318. [26] Add. 40381, f. 208. [27] *Belfast Commercial Chron.* 2 Jan., 27 Feb. 1826. [28] *The Times*, 8 Apr. 1826. [29] Add. 40319, f. 171; *Belfast Commercial Chron.* 7 Aug. 1826. [30] Add. 40387, f. 212. [31] Ibid. f. 300; Parker, *Peel*, i. 412; Gash, 397; Senior, 220-1. [32] Add. 40388, f. 318; Hill mss 208; *Belfast Commercial Chron.* 11, 16 Oct. 1826. [33] Hill mss 208. [34] Add. 40389, f. 221; Parker, i. 424-6; Senior, 221. [35] *Belfast Commercial Chron.* 11 Nov. 1826. [36] Add.

40392, ff. 3, 5, 13, 76. [37] *The Times*, 3 Mar. 1827. [38] Ibid. 12 Apr., 31 May 1827. [39] Lansdowne mss, Macdonald to Lansdowne, 21 Oct. [1827]. [40] *Belfast Guardian*, 25 Dec. 1827. [41] Wellington mss WP1/947/24. [42] Ibid.; Add. 40397, f. 238; *Belfast News Letter*, 15 Aug. 1828. [43] Add. 40397, f. 250. [44] *Belfast News Letter*, 3, 10 Oct., 12 Dec. 1828. [45] *Ellenborough Diary*, i. 321. [46] See, for example, Gurney diary. [47] *Ellenborough Diary*, ii. 19. [48] PRO NI, Primate Beresford mss D3279/A/4/10, 12. [49] Ibid. A/4/14; PRO NI, Pack-Beresford mss D664/A/24, 106. [50] Primate Beresford mss A/4/16, 22; Hill mss 221B. [51] *Londonderry Chron.* 26 Aug. 1829; Primate Beresford mss A/4/32, 36, 39, 43; Pack-Beresford mss A/97. [52] Pack-Beresford mss A/98-101, 119, 122. [53] Hill mss 246, 247. [54] Wellington mss WP1/1087/3; 1090/45; 1105/4; Hill mss A/23/5; *Belfast News Letter*, 9 Apr. 1830. [55] Pack-Beresford mss A/161, 162, 170, 171, 179, 184. [56] Ibid. A/164; PRO NI, Carr Beresford mss T3396, H.B. to Lord Beresford, 30 Sept., 4 Oct. 1830. [57] *London Gazette*, 20 Aug. 1830; *Black Bk.* (1832), 543; Wellington mss WP1/1156/13; 1163/11. [58] Hill mss A/23/4-27; McDowell, 93. [59] Wellington mss WP1/1189/3; Hill mss A/23/13. [60] Derby mss 920 Der (14) 126/9. [61] Add. 40388, f. 64; *The Times*, 25 Sept. 1834. [62] S. Hodgson, *Truths from West Indies* (1838), 86-87. [63] *Londonderry Sentinel*, 11 May 1839; *Gent. Mag.* (1839), ii. 89.

S.M.F.

HILL, Rowland (1800–1875), of Hawkstone, Salop.

SHROPSHIRE	18 Oct. 1821–1832
SHROPSHIRE NORTH	1832–10 Dec. 1842

b. 10 May 1800, 1st s. of Col. John Hill of Hawkstone and Elizabeth Rhodes, da. of Philip Cornish, surgeon, of Exeter, Devon. *educ.* Harrow 1813; Oriel, Oxf. 1818. *m.* 21 July 1831, Ann, da. of Joseph Clegg of Peplow Hall, Salop and h. of her grandfa. Arthur Clegg of Irwell Bank, Lancs., 2s. *suc.* fa. 1814; grandfa. Sir John Hill†, 3rd bt., as 4th bt. 21 May 1824; uncle Sir Rowland Hill† as 2nd Visct. Hill 10 Dec. 1842. *d.* 3 Jan. 1875.

   Cornet R. Horse Gds. 1820-4.

   Cornet N. Salop yeoman cav. 1814, lt. 1816, lt.-col. commdt. 1824-72; col. Salop militia 1849-52; lt.-col. commdt. Salop yeoman cav. 1872-*d.*

   Ld. lt. Salop 1845-*d.*

Hill was born at Hawkstone, into a family renowned for their Protestantism and military service, who had long shared in the representation of Shrewsbury and Shropshire. He was baptized at Hadnal, 10 Oct. 1800, and educated by private tutor and at Harrow, which he entered in September 1813 with his brothers John and Richard Frederick. His father, the heir to Hawkstone, served with the duke of York in Flanders and died, 27 Jan. 1814, having entrusted the care of his seven children to their deeply religious mother and their paternal grandfather Sir John Hill, a former Tory Member for Shrewsbury. Their father's unmarried brother Rowland Hill, the hero of the battles of Aboukir (1801), Talavera (1809), and Almaraz (1812), who represented Shrewsbury from 1812 until his elevation to the Lords as Baron Hill in 1814, also took a keen inter-

est in their progress, and in 1816 he secured a special remainder to his nephews on his titles. Hill graduated in law with distinction in 1820 despite concern for his health, and was subsequently bought a commission in the Blues and introduced to estate business.[1] His coming of age in May 1821 was a county occasion;[2] and he wrote of his life in London at this time:

> I dine out whenever I am invited, which is four or five times a week, when I am not, I find a friend, perhaps Frank Needham*, and dine at a coffee house; in short I go to every party and every dinner I can and when I can find nothing to do by invitation I am obliged to take care of myself.[3]

Shortly afterwards, on the advice of the Rev. Henry Pearson, dean of Salisbury, he set out for the continent with John Roger Kynnaston, the heir to Hardwick, and, passing through France, the Low Countries, Germany and Switzerland, reached Turin, where on 21 Sept. he learnt of the death on 24 Aug. of the Shropshire Member John Cotes and of the canvass organized by his grandfather on his behalf.[4] He returned immediately, arrived shortly before the nomination on 15 Oct. and was elected unopposed on the 18th.[5] Congratulating his mother, the Rev. Reginald Heber, the future bishop of Calcutta, observed:

> You are now, I trust, convinced that he needs nobody to speak for him and I am happy to express a hope ... that when he has acquired more confidence in his own powers, and is less afraid of the sound of his own voice (a terrifying sound, as I well know it to be, in the case of all young beginners) he will in *this* as well as the other and far more essential requisites of good sense, high honour and attention to his duties, be a valuable Member of the House of Commons. I own I consider it a great advantage and, if properly employed, a great blessing to a young man of high expectations to be early in life initiated in the duties of a responsible and laborious situation; to have an object held up to him in the present life distinct from and superior to the amusements which, at his age, too often constitute the whole round of existence; to have an honourable and conscientious stimulus for exertion ever present and to find himself compelled, in the most agreeable and, at the same time, the most cogent manner, to the *practical* study of the rights, the duties and the interests of his country. Some of the *greatest* men of my acquaintance have had their characters in a great degree formed in the House of Commons, and, while I have every confidence that Rowland's services will be long beneficial to and approved by his constituents, I cannot but hope that his early entrance there may be in the highest and most important sense of the words a source of happiness and blessing to himself.[6]

Hill's election owed much to Lord Hill's popularity as a military leader, and he was expected to act 'with government'.[7] He divided with them on distress, 11 Feb., and taxation, 21 Feb., and against reducing the salt duty, 28 Feb. 1822. He kept aloof from the controversy surrounding the Shropshire distress meeting of 25 Mar., but he confirmed the severity of the agriculturists' plight when presenting their petition for remedial measures, 25 Apr.[8] He presented petitions for tax reductions from the Shropshire ironmasters, 24 Apr., and the tanners of Whitchurch, 1 May.[9] He voted against Catholic relief, 30 Apr. 1822, 1 Mar., 21 Apr., 10 May, and the attendant Irish franchise bill, 26 Apr. 1825. His family acquiesced in the return of the Whig eccentric John Cressett Pelham at the Shropshire by-election in December 1822.[10] Ostensibly because as a soldier he was obliged to wear military dress, Hill was passed over as a possible mover of the address in February 1823.[11] He voted against inquiry into voting rights, 20 Feb., and the tax cuts sought by opposition, 10 Mar., but cast a wayward vote for inquiry into the prosecution of the Dublin Orange rioters, 22 Apr. 1823. At Canning's request, he moved the address, 3 Feb. 1824, confident that he would secure its 'unanimous approbation'.[12] He praised post-war achievements in commerce, manufacturing and finance; spoke as an agriculturist of the recent gradual 'amelioration' of distress; defended the government's foreign policy, especially its neutrality towards Spain, and attributed their proposed increase in military expenditure to the state of the West Indies, where 'a steady and calm investigation will prove that the true interests of the colonists are inseparably connected with the moral improvement and meliorated condition of the slave population; and that the chief cause of the military augmentation will soon cease to exist.' According to *The Times*, 4 Feb.:

> In consequence of the low and faltering tone of voice ... only a few occasional words reached the gallery. After expressing a full sense of his inability to discharge the duty which he had devolved upon him, and bespeaking ... the full indulgence of the House, he glanced hastily at the various topics which the royal speech embraced, and concluded by moving the address, which was as usual an echo of it.

William Wilberforce, who was present, however, assured Mrs. Hill by letter on the 9th

> that your son acquitted himself in such a way ... as to have produced in all who were present (at least all whose good opinion is worth having) a very favourable impression of his talents, and a still more favourable one of his moral character ... His very modesty may have made him send you a less favourable report of his performance than was just, and therefore I am the more desirous of stating to you the truth of the case.[13]

Hill is not known to have spoken or voted again that session, but he presented the Whitchurch petition for repeal of the 'regulations relating to hides and skins', 3 May.[14] He resigned his commission on succeeding his grandfather in May 1824 to the baronetcy and 14,000-acre Shropshire estates, which, though worth £19,581 a year, were encumbered by £94,000 in mortgages and charged with providing over £5,000 in annuities; he received nothing as residuary legatee.[15] He voted against admitting foreign corn, 8 May 1826. His return at the general election in June, when he chose to speak of his relations rather than his politics, was not opposed.[16]

Hill presented Shropshire petitions against amending the corn laws, 19 Feb., and against Catholic claims, 2 Mar., which he divided against, 6 Mar. 1827.[17] Having served on the Kilkenny election committee, he was awarded three weeks' leave on urgent business, 23 Mar. Lord Hill declined the Goderich administration's offer of the ordnance in December 1827, but offered his support to the new Wellington administration in January 1828 and in February was appointed commander-in-chief.[18] Hill is not known to have voted or presented petitions on the repeal of the Test Acts, but he presented several for repeal of the 1827 Malt Act, 29 Feb., and voted against Catholic relief, 12 May 1828. The patronage secretary Planta predicted that he would vote 'with government' for Catholic emancipation in 1829, but he remained '*as firm as a rock*' against it, and expressed regret at Peel and Wellington's decision to concede it when presenting a hostile petition from the diocese of Marchia, 16 Feb. According to his mother, he expected that 'the Catholics will gain their cause and that in a division a hundred votes will not be found on the other side'.[19] He presented and endorsed the Shropshire anti-Catholic petition before voting against the introduction of the relief bill, 6 Mar., divided against it on the 18th, but did not vote on its third reading, 30 Mar. He presented petitions against militia reductions, 4 May, and renewal of the East India Company's charter, 22 May 1829. He voted against transferring East Retford's seats to Birmingham, 11 Feb., Lord Blandford's reform proposals, 18 Feb., and the enfranchisement of Birmingham, Leeds and Manchester, 23 Feb. 1830. He presented petitions for repeal of the malt duties, 26 Feb., 2 Mar., against the truck system and renewal of the East India Company's charter, 2 Mar., and for abolition of the death penalty for forgery offences, 27 Apr. As a shareholder in the Birmingham and the Ellesmere Canal Companies,[20] he presented a petition against the Trent and Mersey canal bill, 3 May, and on the 17th moved the third reading of the rival Ellesmere and

Chester canal bill. He divided against Jewish emancipation the same day. His return at the general election in August was unopposed.[21] In October 1830 he entertained his regiment at Hawkstone following their exercises at Market Drayton.[22]

The Wellington ministry counted Hill among their 'friends' and he divided with them on the civil list when they were brought down, 15 Nov. 1830. He led the yeoman cavalry against the rioting colliers at Chirk Bridge, 5 Jan. 1831, and afterwards assisted the lord lieutenant, Lord Powis, in quelling incendiarism.[23] He voted against the second reading of the Grey ministry's reform bill, 22 Mar., and for Gascoyne's wrecking amendment, 19 Apr. He presented several anti-slavery petitions, 23 Mar. Now projecting himself as a moderate reformer and supporter of the enfranchisement of large towns, he engaged in an arduous and costly canvass at the general election in May 1831 and topped the poll in a four-man contest.[24] However, many squires found him 'wanting' as a Member and were disturbed by his decision to assist Cresett Pelham, a recent convert to Toryism, in preference to his kinsman by marriage, the moderate reformer William Lloyd of Aston Hall, who retired in third place.[25] Hill voted against the second reading of the reintroduced reform bill, 6 July 1831, and was afterwards said to be 'in despair ... upon the subject of politics'.[26] He divided against the partial disfranchisement of Chippenham, 27 July, and the bill's passage, 21 Sept., knowing that Lord Hill, who subsequently abstained, would not support it in the Upper House.[27] Like Powis's Members, he chose not to divide on the second reading of the final bill, 17 Dec. 1831, but voted against considering it in committee, 20 Jan., the enfranchisement of Tower Hamlets, 28 Feb., and the third reading, 22 Mar. 1832. He divided against the Irish measure at its second reading, 25 May. Although disappointed, he took a pragmatic view of Wellington's failure to form a government that month.[28] He divided against administration on the Russian-Dutch loan, 26 Jan., 12 July. Afterwards he and his young wife, the heiress Ann Clegg, set out on a tour of the Lake District.[29] She had been a regular guest at Hawkstone since being orphaned at the age of 13 in 1828 and made the ward of her grandfather, the Manchester merchant Arthur Clegg, who, 'supposing himself to be on the point of death', had her wedding to Hill, which was conducted privately at Irwell Bank, 21 July 1831, brought forward.[30] Clegg died, 22 Sept., and, by his will, dated 3 Aug. 1831 and proved on 25 Feb. 1832 under £180,000, his estates were entrusted to the Hills and Edward Lloyd of Nanhoron, for the use of Ann and her heirs. Hill also gained control of the bulk of her

fortune and the Peplow estate.[31] The marriage should have remained unannounced for about a year or until Ann was 18, but it was soon the talk of Shrewsbury, where it was said that a local surgeon and corporator, Dr. Duggard, had demanded £2,000 from the Hills for arranging it. Writing in March 1832, William Mostyn Owen of Woodhouse surmised that

> the general opinion is that if his [Duggard's] *hands are very dirty* Mrs. Hill's are not *quite clean*. A more disgraceful transaction has certainly seldom taken place, and at all events poor silly Sir Rowland is as completely sold as any slave or beast of burthen, and whatever he gains in money will lose, and ought to lose, in character.[32]

In May 1832 Sir James Scarlett* and Sir Edward Sugden* as counsel advised the immediate announcement and registration of the marriage. A settlement followed, 11 Aug. 1835.[33]

Hill's return for the North Shropshire constituency as a Conservative was assured at the general election of 1832 notwithstanding the bitter contest for second place.[34] He represented the constituency until December 1842, when he succeeded to the viscountcy awarded in August to his uncle. They had hoped for an earldom; and in a letter of complaint to the premier Peel, Hill defended his own silence in the House, stressed his family's military record and loyalty 'to church and king from time immemorial' and included among his achievements educating and purchasing commissions for his brothers.[35] He died at Hawkstone in January 1875 after a long illness and was buried in the family vault at Hodnet. He was remembered as a pioneer of eland farming and improver of smallholdings, and for his great skills as a sportsman, militia commander and county lord lieutenant, to which office he had succeeded the absentee duke of Sutherland in 1845.[36] He left £30,000 to his younger son Jeoffrey and was succeeded in the peerage, baronetcy and 16,500-acre estates, mortgaged to the Bridgnorth banker John Pritchard with assets of £25,000 and liabilities of £23,200, by his elder son Rowland Clegg Hill (1833-95), who died insolvent. Hill's widow died in Brighton in 1891, worth £9,203.[37]

[1] Salop Archives, Rev. J.C. Hill mss 549/121-2. [2] *Shrewsbury Chron.* 11 May 1821. [3] Rev. J.C. Hill mss 811/1. [4] Ibid. 549/123; 811/2-27; *Shrewsbury Chron.* 14, 21, 28 Sept.; *Salopian Jnl.* 10 Oct. 1821. [5] Salop Archives 1066/125, diary of Katherine Plymley, 15, 18 Oct.; *Salopian Jnl.* 17, 24 Oct.; *Shrewsbury Chron.* 19 Oct. 1821; E. Sidney, *Life of Lord Hill* (1845), 326. [6] Rev. J.C. Hill mss 549/125. [7] NLW, Aston Hall mss C.460-1. [8] *Shrewsbury Chron.* 1, 8, 15, 22, 29 Mar.; *The Times*, 26 Apr. 1822. [9] *The Times*, 25 Apr., 2 May 1822. [10] Ibid. 18 Nov., *Salopian Jnl.* 4 Dec. 1822. [11] *Arbuthnot Corresp.* 43. [12] Salop Archives, Bygott mss 731/11/88-89; Salop Archives 6001/3055, p. 35. [13] Sidney, 330.

[14] *The Times*, 4 May 1824. [15] *Gent. Mag.* (1824), ii. 278; Bygott mss 731/5/3/46; 731/5/5/231/1; 731/5/5/246-7; 731/10/4-8; 731/11/28; PROB 11/1689/471; IR26/1004/893. [16] Salop Archives 1066/137, Plymley diary, 12 June; *Shrewsbury Chron.* 16, 23 June 1826. [17] *The Times*, 20 Feb., 3 Mar. 1827. [18] Sidney, 331-4; Wellington mss WP1/914/25. [19] Rev. J.C. Hill mss 811/49. [20] Bygott mss 731/10/4-8. [21] Sidney, 342; *Shrewsbury Chron.* 6, 13 Aug. 1830. [22] E.W. Gladstone, *Shropshire Yeomanry*, 86-87. [23] Rev. J.C. Hill mss 549/354, diary of Catherine Kenyon, 3-11 Jan.; *Salopian Jnl.* 5, 12, 19, 26 Jan., 9 Feb., 16 Mar., 6 Apr.; *Shrewsbury Chron.* 7 Jan., 4 Feb. 1831. [24] Salop Archives qD45/13; Aston Hall mss C.1248, C.5326-7; Rev. J.C. Hill mss 811/51; *Salopian Jnl.* 4, 11, 28 May, 22 June 1831. [25] Aston Hall mss C.527; C.5329; Rev. J.C. Hill mss 811/52; *Shrewsbury Chron.* 3 June 1831. [26] Rev. J.C. Hill mss 811/54. [27] Sidney, 351-2. [28] Rev. J.C. Hill mss 811/36. [29] Ibid. 811/29-35. [30] Aston Hall mss C.527; C.5298; Rev. J.C. Hill mss 811/28, 55; Bygott mss 731/11/910. [31] PROB 11/1795/74; IR26/1283/106. [32] *Corresp. of Charles Darwin* ed. F. Burkhardt and S. Smith, i. 190-1, 211-12. [33] Bygott mss 731/11/97. [34] Rev. J.C. Hill mss 549/47/1; 811/54; Aston Hall mss C.5332; Wellington mss WP1/1229/18; *Darwin Corresp.* i. 254-5; Salop Archives qD45/10; *Shrewsbury Chron.* 15 June, 6 July 1832; *Bygones*, Nov. 1897, p. 169; *VCH Salop*, iii. 139, 319. [35] Add. 40499, f. 135; Bygott mss 731/11/664-7. [36] *Ann. Reg.* (1875), p. 129; *The Times*, 4 Jan. 1875; Bygott mss 731/11/90; 731/14/5-7; Add. 40576, ff. 227-36; *VCH Salop*, iii. 139; iv. 226-7. [37] IR26/1664/60; 2895/94; Bygott mss 731/5/5/60; *VCH Salop*, iv. 208-10.

M.M.E.

HILL TREVOR, Hon. Arthur (1798–1862), of Whittlebury, Northants.

NEW ROMNEY	1830–11 Mar. 1831
DURHAM	1831–1832
DURHAM	1835–1841
DURHAM	5 Apr. 1843–14 July 1843

b. 9 Nov. 1798, 1st and o. surv. s. of Arthur Hill Trevor, 2nd Visct. Dungannon [I], and Hon. Charlotte Fitzroy, da. of Charles Fitzroy†, 1st Bar. Southampton. *educ.* Harrow 1812-17; Christ Church, Oxf. 1817. *m.* 10 Sept. 1821, at Leghorn, Sophia, da. of Col. Gorges Marcus Irvine of Castle Irvine, co. Fermanagh, *s.p. suc.* fa. as 3rd Visct. Dungannon [I] 14 Dec. 1837. *d.* 11 Aug. 1862.

Rep. peer [I] 1855-*d.*

Sheriff, Flints. 1855-6.

The Brynkinalt estate, on the Denbighshire, Flintshire and Shropshire borders, of Speaker Sir John Trevor (1637-1717) had devolved on Trevor's great-grandfather Arthur Hill of Belvoir (the younger brother of the 1st Viscount Hillsborough) through his mother, the Speaker's daughter Anne. A Member of the Irish Parliament and chancellor of the Irish exchequer, 1754-5, he took the additional name of Trevor in 1759, was created Viscount Dungannon in 1765 and was succeeded in 1771 by his grandson, Hill Trevor's father, a first cousin of the duke of Wellington and supporter of the Londonderry interest in county Down.[1] Hill Trevor was born and raised in London with his younger brother Charles Henry, their father's favourite, who died on 18 Sept. 1823, after falling while leading the field at Stapleton Park races.[2] Since their marriage in September 1821 Hill Trevor and his wife had lived at Whittlebury, the seat of his late uncle Lord Southampton, and they were included in the circle of the 3rd marquess of Londonderry, a brother of Southampton's widow. An anti-Catholic Tory, he assisted Londonderry politically in Ireland, was one of Wellington's entourage during his 1827 tour of Northern England, and managed the London out-voters when his close friend and sporting companion since their Oxford days, the Ultra Sir Roger Gresley, successfully contested Durham on the Londonderry interest at the general election of 1830. Hill Trevor tried his luck at Sudbury, where he was the 'phantom third man', and came in for New Romney as the paying guest of Sir Edward Dering*.[3]

He was named on the Wellington ministry's list of 'violent Ultras' in the Commons, but divided with them when they were brought down on the civil list, 15 Nov. 1830, a vote, according to Gresley, who acted similarly, the Ultras never forgave.[4] A bold public speaker later described by the Conservative election manager Francis Bonham* as 'one of the cannon balls of the Tory right',[5] Hill Trevor supported the West India interest on slavery and defended the proprietors' rights to compensation in his maiden speech, 23 Nov., and again, 15 Dec. 1830. The following day, he embarrassed Lord Grey's administration by calling for the prosecution of William Cobbett†, as the publisher of the *Political Register* of 11 Dec., for malicious and seditious libel and inciting the 'Swing' rioters.[6] Pursuing the issue, he pressed for a ruling by lord chancellor Brougham and highlighted Cobbett's attack on the 'oppressive upper classes', the church as a collector of tithes and the decision to try the rioters by special commission. Determined to kill the motion, the leader of the House Lord Althorp stirred up comments and allegations from Hill Trevor's maiden speech, imputing that slaves were better clothed, fed and lodged than the distressed labourers, whereupon Hill Trevor briefly defended himself and withdrew his motion on John Croker's advice. He set out his views on reform in an open *Letter to the duke of Rutland*, 30 Jan. 1831, which called for a dissolution in view of the extensive changes proposed by ministers and the radical Ultras, advocated retrenchment, and defended the established church. In the House, 21 Feb., he warned that his *bête noir* the select vestries bill would 'throw the preponderating influence of the more populous parishes into the hands of a class of persons very ill calculated to possess such overwhelming power', causing frequent and tumultuous elections and increasing party acrimony. Held to account by Gresley, after he was unseated on petition, 8 Mar., he vacated in his favour at New Romney, and lost to the reformer William Richard Carter Chaytor in a seven-day poll at Durham. On the hustings he defended his parliamentary conduct, appealed to the self-interest of the freemen facing disfranchisement and promised to stand at the general election, which, as he predicted, took place 'in a few short weeks'.[7] He then narrowly avoided a contest through the enforced withdrawal of the Whig veteran Michael Taylor and was returned (with Chaytor) as an advocate of rational and constitutional reform and guardian of vested rights, committed to wrecking the ministerial reform bill.[8]

On the address, 21 June 1831, Hill Trevor maintained that reform was necessary, but that its advocates exaggerated the bill's popularity: 'the election result would have been different had people had time to think'. He presented a petition against disfranchisement from Durham's London freemen, 23 June, and pleaded their cause in his speech against the second reading of the reintroduced reform bill, 5 July (printed in the Tory *Durham County Advertiser*, 15 July). It rehearsed the anti-reformers' usual complaints and ridiculed the enfranchisement of the fluctuating populations of the resorts of Brighton and Cheltenham. He divided accordingly, 6 July, and remained one of the bill's severest and most frequent critics. He opposed its committal and protested at the use of Saturday sittings to expedite its progress, 12 July; argued that the 1831 census should be the determinant of borough disfranchisement, 19 July; and presented and endorsed a hostile petition from the out-voters of Newcastle-upon-Tyne, 20 July. He also objected to the partial disfranchisement of Chippenham, 27 July, the proposed division of counties, 16 Aug., and the definition of 'resident voters', 17 Aug. He spoke against lowering the borough voting qualification from £10 to £5 and recommended raising it to £20, 24 Aug., and joined in the fray later that day when the Newcastle-upon-Tyne Member Hodgson suggested including work premises in the assessment. Although generally averse to co-operating with the bill's radical opponents, he divided in Henry Hunt's small minority against making proven payment of rent a qualification for borough voters, 25 Aug. He voted to preserve existing voting rights, 27, 30 Aug., and failed (by 31-151) to carry an amendment that day safeguarding for life the voting rights of existing non-resident freemen. He withdrew another, extending the residence qualification from seven to 20 miles, amid scenes of great

confusion, 13 Sept. He divided against the bill at its third reading, 19 Sept., and passage, 21 Sept., having entered a 'formal protest' on the 20th concerning the manner in which it had been carried, and condemned it as 'the forerunner of revolution'. After witnessing the assault on Londonderry for contributing to its Lords defeat, he blamed the press for inciting reform riots in Derby, London and Nottingham, 11, 12 Oct., and took up the case of the queen's chamberlain Lord Howe, who had been dismissed on account of his hostile vote, 13, 18 Oct. He chaired the Northamptonshire anti-reform dinner at Brackley in November 1831.[9]

On the address, 6 Dec. 1831, Hill Trevor criticized the 'most ambiguous and unsatisfactory' statements on Belgium and Portugal, the failure to suggest remedies for domestic unrest and the dubious tenet that Irish tithes could be reformed 'consistently with the safety of the established church'. He professed himself 'unpledged' on reform, pending revelation of the details of the revised bill, but warned that unless it had been drastically changed he would strenuously oppose it. He only paired against its second reading, 17 Dec., and spent the following week hunting and discussing tactics with Londonderry and his Durham agents at Wynyard, where, conceding the futility of outright opposition to reform, they resolved to press for the enfranchisement of the nearby town of Stockton-on-Tees.[10] He voted against the proposed enfranchisement of Tower Hamlets, 28 Feb., and the bill's third reading, 22 Mar. 1832. He welcomed the incorporation of Lord Chandos's clause extending the county franchise to £50 tenants-at-will, 1 Feb., and quibbled only over the minutiae of borough voting, 2, 6, 7, 23 Feb. He presented and endorsed Stockton's petition for enfranchisement, 7 Feb., and, ignoring the objections of Croker, who proposed pressing Merthyr's superior claims, 2 Mar., he moved to substitute it for Gateshead, 5 Mar. He argued that the exchange would redress the imbalance in representation between North and South Durham and justified its enfranchisement by citing its 9,000 population, 600 £10 householders, 300 40s. tenements and increased annual customs revenue, which ranked it above Cheltenham and Brighton. The proposal, however, was opposed on both sides of the House and negatived without a division.[11] Hill Trevor failed to vote on Merthyr that day, and renewed his protest at the discrepancy in North and South Durham representation when the enfranchisement of South Shields was approved, 7 Mar., and again at the third reading, 21 Mar. He now added the uniform borough franchise and the destruction of property, religious establishments and the monarchy to his litany of complaints against the bill, 'which under the gilded form of bestowing equal representation ... is, in fact, leading the way to as bloody and fearful a revolution as the pages of history can unfold'. When a ministry headed by Wellington was contemplated, he called for government action to stop the Birmingham Political Union sitting permanently until the reform bill became law, 7 May, and denounced the ministerial resignations and threatened peerage creations, 18 May 1832. He had criticized the foreign secretary Lord Palmerston's* Belgian policy, 11, 18 Aug. 1831, and divided against government on the Russian-Dutch loan, 26 Jan., 12 July, and maintained that the papers before the House exonerated Britain from repayment, 20 July 1832.

Hill Trevor ridiculed Hunt's arguments against the yeomanry grant, 27 June, and vehemently opposed the radicals' campaign on behalf of the imprisoned Deist Robert Taylor, 22 July, 15 Aug., 5, 7 Oct. 1831, when (as on the 18th) he defended his prosecution for blasphemy and denounced his Commons supporters. He supported Chandos's demand for higher fines for unlicenced shooting, 8 Aug. He presented petitions and added his voice to the clamour for greater restrictions on licensing and on-consumption under the 1830 Beer Act, 17, 29 Aug. 1831, 7, 17 May, and implicated it in the recent rise in crime, 8 May 1832. His amendment to curtail opening hours was rejected by 111-12, 31 May 1832. He voted in the minority of 11 against the Irish union of parishes bill, 19 Aug. 1831, and criticized the ministry's decision to withdraw the grant from the Protestant Kildare Place Society while continuing that for Catholic Maynooth College, 6, 11 Apr. 1832. He seconded and was a minority teller for Waldo Sibthorp's complaint against the pro-reform *The Times*, 12 Sept. 1831. Having opposed the vestries bill as a minority teller, 5 Oct., he instigated proceedings against *The Times* for misreporting its passage, but withdrew them after engaging Hume, John Campbell I and Hobhouse in time-wasting discussion, 13 Oct., when he was also a minority teller against the sugar refinery bill. Ridiculed by the radicals, he denounced the licentious press and argued for an increase rather than the reduction they sought in the newspaper stamp duty, 7 Dec. 1831, 9 Mar. 1832. His stance on capital punishment was dictated by his abhorrence of nocturnal crime, and he failed to vote for the 'severe restriction of the death penalty' which he advocated, 26, 27 Mar., 17 May. He deemed the anatomy bill 'an insult to the poor whom it pretends to protect' and criticized the clause permitting the dissection 'like murderers' in cases of hospital death, 11 May. He presented petitions and joined in the clamour against the general register bill, 27 Jan., 2, 8 Feb., and was a minority teller against its committal, 22 Feb.

In a partially successful bid to obtain concessions, he threatened to divide the House on a motion to appoint all English county Members to the committee and refuted suggestions that hostile petitions were 'got up by a few interested landlords', 6 Mar. He opposed the measure to the last, 18 July. Petitions against the Hartlepool Dock, 13 Mar., and Sunderland (South Side) Dock bills, 14 Mar., were entrusted to him, and he was a majority teller against the South Shields and Monkwearmouth railway bill, 26 Mar. Though of the committee, he chose not to attend for the crucial division by which the Sunderland Dock bill was lost, 2 Apr.[12] He defended the Durham gaoler Prouchard when his alleged misconduct was made the subject of a radical petition, 11 Apr. 1832.

Hill Trevor visited Durham directly the reform bill became law and spent the summer of 1832 in Ireland.[13] Defeated by two Liberals at the general election in December, he retained a high profile in the city and, backed by Londonderry's Conservative Association, he came in 1835, when his support for Peel's government was 'not absolute', and again in 1837.[14] 'His tall thin person appearing perpendicularly' to speak in debate often provoked 'scenes of uproar and confusion'.[15] Plagued by rumours that he had mistreated his dying father, from whom he had long been estranged, he went to Ireland when he succeeded him in 1837 to put his Down, Kilkenny and Queen's County estates in order, so provoking a temporary breach with Londonderry for neglecting Durham.[16] He stood down in 1841 and was considered for Shropshire North in 1842, but his estates were deemed too peripheral.[17] Unseated on petition after defeating the free trader John Bright[†] at the 1843 Durham by-election, he did not stand there again, despite being requisitioned, and he correctly predicted the defeat of Londonderry's son Adolphus in 1852.[18] Following his election to the Lords in 1855 as an Irish representative peer, he divided his time between Ireland, where he was County Grand Master of the Orange Order in Antrim, Brynkinalt, and his London house in Grafton Street, where he died without issue in August 1862, so extinguishing the viscountcy.[19] His views on church and municipal reform in Wales and Ireland, education, religious toleration, rural crime, the House of Lords and divorce survive in several political tracts and letters to *The Times*. He also wrote the unremarkable *Life and Times of William, Prince of Orange* (1835-6). He left everything to his widow (*d.* 1880), and as his father had willed, the estates passed to his nephew, the 3rd marquess of Downshire's son Lord Arthur Edwin Hill (1819-1911), Conservative Member for County Down from 1845 until his elevation to the Lords in 1880 as Baron Trevor.

[1] *Oxford DNB.* [2] *The Times,* 15, 22 Sept. 1823. [3] NLW, Ormathwaite mss G35 f. 121. [4] Add. 40412, f. 25. [5] A.J. Heesom, *Durham City and Its MPs,* 25. [6] Add. 51578, Carlisle to Holland, 18 Dec. [1830]. [7] *Durham Co. Advertiser,* 11, 18, 25 Mar.; *Durham Chron.* 9 Apr. 1831; H. Klieneberger, *Durham Elections,* 30-33. [8] *The Times,* 26 Apr.; *Durham Co. Advertiser.* 29 Apr., 6 May 1831; Wellington mss WP1/1182/25; 1184/3; Klieneberger, 33. [9] E.G. Forrester, *Northants. Co. Elections and Electioneering,* 146. [10] *Durham Co. Advertiser,* 23 Dec. 1831; Durham CRO, Londonderry mss D/Lo/C108/6. [11] T.J. Nossiter, *Influence, Opinion and Political Idioms in Reformed England,* 22, 59. [12] *Durham Chron.* 6 Apr. 1832. [13] Londonderry mss C146/42, 60; *John Bull,* 24 June 1832; *Pprs. of Sir William Chaytor, 1771-1847* ed. M.Y. Ashcroft (N. Yorks. Co. RO Publications, 1 (1993 edn.)) [hereafter *Chaytor Pprs.*] 175. [14] Londonderry mss C146 (11), (48-50), (67); Derbys. RO, Gresley of Drakelow mss D77/36/8(iii); *Chaytor Pprs.* 182; *The Times,* 15 Dec. 1832. [15] [J. Grant], *Recollections of Lords and Commons* (1838), ii. 101. [16] Londonderry mss C107/2, 17, 19; PROB. 11/1892/157; IR26/1477/185. [17] *VCH Salop,* iii. 320. [18] *The Times,* 22 July 1843; Durham Univ. Lib. Wharton mss 848-54. [19] *The Times,* 13 Aug.; *Belfast Weekly News,* 16 Aug.; *Cat. of Sale at Brynkinalt* (1862).

M.M.E.

HOBHOUSE, John Cam (1786–1869).[1]

WESTMINSTER	1820–1 May 1833
NOTTINGHAM	23 July 1834–1847
HARWICH	1 Apr. 1848–Feb. 1851

b. 27 June 1786, 1st s. of Sir Benjamin Hobhouse[†], 1st bt., of Westbury College, Glos., Cottles House, Wilts. and Whitton Park, Twickenham, Mdx. and 1st w. Charlotte (*d.* 25 Nov. 1791), da. of Samuel Cam of Chantry House, Bradford, Wilts. *educ.* at Lewin's Mead, Bristol by Dr. John Prior Estlin; Westminster 1800; Trinity Coll. Camb. 1803. *m.* 28 July 1828, Lady Julia Tomlinson Hay, da. of George, 7th mq. of Tweedddale [S], 3da. (1 *d.v.p.*). *suc.* fa. as 2nd bt. 14 Aug. 1831; *cr.* Bar. Broughton 26 Feb. 1851; GCB 23 Feb. 1852. *d.* 3 June 1869.

Sec. at war Feb. 1832-Mar. 1833; PC 6 Feb. 1832; chief sec. to ld. lt [I] Mar.-May 1833; chief commr. of woods and forests July-Dec. 1834; pres. bd. of control Apr. 1835-Sept. 1841, July 1846-Feb. 1852.

Capt. R. Cornw. and Devon Miners 1812-13.

Hobhouse's father, the younger son of a prosperous Bristol merchant, acquired from the father of his first wife a stake in a Bath bank and in 1800 bought a £33,000 share in the London porter brewery of Whitbread's. After his marriage he became a Unitarian. As Member for Bletchingley, 1797-1802, Grampound, 1802-6, and Hindon, 1806-18, he was initially a moderate Foxite reformer, but subsequently attached himself in office and opposition to his close friend Henry Addington[†] (Lord Sidmouth), whose appointment as home secretary in 1812 confirmed his support of the Liverpool ministry, from whom he received a baronetcy. He was appointed to the non-profit making office of first commissioner for liquidat-ing the Carnatic debts in 1806, and held the post until 1829.[2] John Cam Hobhouse, the eldest son of what became a large family, lost his mother when he was five and never warmed to his father's second wife, a stern and penny-pinching Unitarian. He was raised and initially educated in that faith, but he subsequently conformed. His five years at Westminster School introduced him to the House of Commons as an observer of debates. At Cambridge, where he resented being a 'humble' pensioner, he founded a Whig Club and the Amicable Society and formed an intimate friendship with Byron, which dominated and shaped much of his life for the next 20 years.[3] He accompanied Byron on his tour to Portugal, Spain, Albania, Greece and Turkey, 1809-10, some of which he described in his *Journey through Albania* (1813). After a brief period at home, when his father paid off his £5,000 debts on condition that he applied for a militia captaincy (he served briefly in Ireland, 1812-13), he followed the track of the French and German armies through Germany. An ardent admirer of Buonaparte, he witnessed the restoration of the Bourbons in Paris in May 1814. He was best man at Byron's ill-fated marriage in January 1815, returned to Paris when Buonaparte escaped from Elba and, after the Hundred Days, learned that his soldier brother Benjamin had been killed at Quatre Bras. His hastily written book on the Hundred Days, in the form of *The Substance of Some Letters written by an Englishman resident at Paris,* criticized the Bourbons and the threat to liberty posed by the Holy Alliance. It was savaged by John Wilson Croker* in the *Quarterly Review* and landed its French printer and translator in jail. In the summer of 1816 he rejoined Byron at Villa Diodati, on Lake Geneva. They subsequently went to Venice and Rome, where Hobhouse stayed for over a year, researching for his companion volume (*Historical Illustrations*) to Canto IV of *Childe Harold's Pilgrimage,* which was published in the spring of 1818.[4]

Hobhouse was by now a familiar figure in high Whig society, but his political sympathies, though rooted in the Foxite tradition, were with the liberal 'Young Whigs' rather than the tired and cynical older generation of grandees. He was particularly friendly with Lord Tavistock*, the heir of the duke of Bedford, who introduced him to his Russell brothers, John George Lambton* and Edward Ellice*. He was also on close terms with the lawyer Henry Bickersteth, one of the Westminster reform activists. He first showed evidence of political ambitions by canvassing Cambridge University in 1814, but he was warned off by the Whigs and withdrew his pretensions in 1817. He joined Brooks's Club on 11 May 1816,[5] but also belonged to the Rota Club of gentleman reformers. By 1818 he knew Sir Francis Burdett, the patrician radical Member for Westminster, who, with Bickersteth, initially encouraged him to harbour hopes of standing for the second seat there at the general election if he would declare for annual parliaments and universal suffrage. He was willing to do so, but he received no further backing, possibly because his father's Tory politics and office were anathema to the radical tailor Francis Place, the prime mover of the Westminster reformers. Hobhouse served on the committee for Burdett and his friend Douglas Kinnaird[†], the radical aristocratic banker, in the bitter contest with a ministerialist and the Whig legal reformer Sir Samuel Romilly[†]. Kinnaird had to retire on the third day, and Romilly beat Burdett into second place. To Byron, Hobhouse, who believed that he might have come in without undue trouble, condemned the 'iniquity on the part both of Tories and Whigs', and reported that by canvassing for single votes for Burdett 'I am on the list of proscribed made out by Tierney, Brougham and Co. and the other cubs at H[olland] House'. He reckoned that had he secured 'a seat in the den' he would have abjured his 'Whig principles altogether', as it was 'impossible to bear the arrogance, selfishness and surliness of a party that has elected Bruffam for their bully'.[6] When Romilly's suicide in November 1818 threw Westminster open again, Hobhouse, who was still on good terms with Tavistock and the younger Whigs, ranged himself behind Kinnaird, the choice of Place and the reformers, knowing that he was so unpopular with the Whigs that he could hardly hope to come in quietly. He discovered that the Whigs would not tolerate Kinnaird, but that if he himself stood half would back him and half stay neutral. He seems to have acted honourably by Kinnaird, who eventually and reluctantly stood down, and was taken up by the reformers. During the two months which elapsed before the election in February 1819, Hobhouse had to steer a careful course between Whigs and reformers. He had a few scrapes, but by the first week in February seemed assured of success. On the 9th, however, he was betrayed by overconfidence, and probably by a genuine desire to distinguish himself from the Whig hacks, into condemning the party's insipid reform views in a speech at the *Crown and Anchor*. He might have got away with this indiscretion, but it was compounded by Place's publication of the report of the Westminster committee (which Hobhouse had tried to keep under wraps, though he was ultimately powerless to do so) which, reflecting all his unbridled hatred of the Whigs, exposed the corruption which they had resorted to in Westminster and condemned them for

abandoning the cause of reform. The Whigs put up the barrister George Lamb[*], a younger son of Lord Melbourne, at the last minute. At first Hobhouse tried a moderate and ambivalent line on reform in a bid to appeal to respectable electors, but this did not take, and as Lamb forged ahead in the poll with the overt support of the government and the Court, he became increasingly strident in his denunciations of the Whigs and so branded himself as a radical, though he remained a Whig at heart, albeit one who espoused the 'principles ... of the Whigs of 1798 in contradistinction to the Whigs of 1819'. He was beaten by 604 votes in a poll of 8,364.[7]

Hobhouse, who told Byron in April 1819 that 'the Whigs are down and dead for ever', contributed the weighty *Defence of the People* to the ensuing pamphlet war between radicals and Whigs. After the Peterloo massacre he joined Burdett in speaking at the protest meeting in Palace Yard, 2 Sept., and later published a *Supplicatory Letter to Lord Castlereagh*, condemning in advance the anticipated repressive legislation. This he followed with *A Trifling Mistake in Lord Erskine's Recent Preface*, a furious attack on ministerial policies, to which Place added 'a thundering note'. He signed the requisition for a county meeting in Wiltshire, where some of his father's property lay, and the subsequent protest against the sheriff's refusal to grant it.[8] On 8 Dec. he addressed the Westminster meeting called to demand inquiry into Peterloo, denounce the Six Acts and press for reform: he castigated reactionary lawyers and predicted the certain triumph of 'moral resistance' by the people.[9] His last pamphlet, particularly its observation that only the military authorities and their troops prevented 'the people from walking down to the House, pulling out the Members by the ears, locking up their doors, and flinging the keys into the Thames', was drawn to the attention of the Commons, and he was pronounced guilty of a breach of privilege and sentenced, by a majority of 65, to confinement in Newgate. He went quietly, but obtained a hearing in king's bench, where chief justice Abbott refused to accept his argument that the Speaker's warrant was illegal, 5 Feb. 1820. He published a lengthy protest in *The Times*, 8-15 Feb. His imprisonment (which was genteel enough, with plenty of visitors) had made him a national radical hero; and he received and publicly responded to a supportive address from 'the electors of Westminster', where his prospects of success at the general election precipitated by George III's death had been greatly enhanced.[10] He was due for release on the day of dissolution, 28 Feb., but for three weeks beforehand, guided, coached and occasionally lectured by Place, he prepared himself to stand with Burdett, ostensibly in response to the invitation of the electors. Lamb's candidature was at length confirmed. Hobhouse's liberation made him feel 'quite queer'. On 2 Mar. he went with Burdett (who was facing a trial for seditious libel) to a *Crown and Anchor* meeting called to celebrate his release. He seemed to one reporter 'to have suffered from his ... imprisonment', but he was warmly received, and in what he considered a 'good' speech, with 'two or three capital hits', he attacked his prosecutors and denounced the spy system and military oppression, but noticed favourably Whig exertions 'in the cause of a thorough reform of Parliament' at Norwich, Edinburgh, Newcastle, Bristol and York, though he insisted that the impetus for change must come from 'the people'. His father, unperturbed by his radicalism, generously gave him £500 to cover some of the unavoidable legal expenses of a Westminster election.[11] On the hustings (which Burdett attended for the first time in his career as Member for Westminster), Hobhouse seized an immediate initiative by reading out, to great effect, a letter of Lamb to an elector in which he solicited ministerial support and referred to the supporters of his radical opponents as 'the lower orders'. He established a handsome early lead over Lamb, who failed to get significant government backing, and although he had a few anxious moments when Lamb gained some ground in the later stages, he finished the 15-day poll in second place, 446 ahead of Lamb. He had 'cried like a child' on learning of Burdett's conviction at Leicester assizes towards the end of the contest, and his delight in his own success was a little 'dampened' by it. He reflected that he had been returned 'without great family, or fortune, or friends, or any help except from my own exertions on behalf of reform ... to represent the constituents of Fox and Burdett, the most enlightened, the most independent, and the most numerous body of electors in the kingdom'; but he declined to exult too much 'until I know what I have done to justify the great expectations raised of me': 'I am sure I have gained character by this election. I hope I shall lose none in the House of Commons'.[12] To Byron, who mistakenly thought he was hand in glove with such extremists as Henry Hunt[†] and William Cobbett[†], he again condemned the Whigs and asserted that 'the proudest of all politicians and the most uncondescending is the man of principle, the real radical reformer'.[13] On the hustings on the last day he defined 'radical reform' as 'reform on those principles which have been maintained by the best men, in the best periods of our history', aimed at 'the rooting up of ... [the] tree of corruption'. This encouraged Ellice to argue to a sceptical Lord Grey, the Whig leader, that there was room for some

sort of accommodation with the likes of Hobhouse and Burdett on reform, which must form an essential part of the party's programme in opposition and, if it came to pass, in power.[14] The Commons clerk Hatsell predicted that Hobhouse would 'probably bring the ... Commons into some difficulty, and himself into the Tower'; while, according to Mrs. Arbuthnot, the duke of Wellington was prepared to give some credence to a story that Hobhouse had shown an 'inclination to place himself at the head of any revolutionary government', as the Cato Street conspirator Thistlewood was reputed to have asked him to do earlier in the year.[15]

Hobhouse, a short, stocky man, with a prominent Roman nose on the Wellingtonian model, and 'a pensive cast' to his face,[16] entered Parliament just short of his 34th birthday, outwardly confident but given to self-doubt. His keeping a daily diary for the bulk of his adult life attests to his strong and not always healthy inclination to introspection; and on 15 Nov. 1821 he noted that 'my difficulty is a sort of nervous sensibility about reputation which may go far to preventing my having a reputation'.[17] He was in a not entirely enviable situation, for Place hoped to groom and direct him as an efficient 'man of business', attentive to constituency business and supportive of the interests of working people; but his ties to the Whigs had not been irrevocably cut, and as a Member in opposition he was obliged, both by necessity and desire, to co-operate with at least the more progressive elements of the party. Place constantly cajoled and lectured him, but ultimately was disappointed in him and washed his hands of him. Throughout the 1820 Parliament he divided steadily with the extreme left of the opposition to the government, missing only a handful of significant divisions. He was an exemplary attender (unlike Burdett, who pleased himself more often than not) and by his own lights took great pains with constituency business in committees, promoting legislation and taking up the cases of aggrieved groups and individuals, though he frequently found it tedious. He was in the Commons to hear the debate on the address, 27 Apr., when he thought Tierney, the Whig leader there, was 'very bad' and was prepared to second an amendment had Burdett moved one. He witnessed the execution of Thistlewood and the conspirators, 1 May, and was impressed by their dignified deportment. Next day he was 'horror-struck' when Brougham *defended* the employment of government spies and 'had half a mind to get up and attack' him, but held his peace.[18] On 9 May he made his maiden speech for inquiry into the spy system, having 'swallowed half a dozen glasses of wine and a biscuit' beforehand: he 'scarcely said a word of what I had got ready, confining myself chiefly to answer'. He was complimented privately by Lambton, Sir Robert Wilson* and David Ricardo*, and decided that 'what I said was not bad'. The independent Tory Member Henry Bankes thought he spoke 'fluently and well', and the 'Young Whig' Lord Althorp* reported that the debut was 'a very promising one'. The most remarkable feature of the debate, however, was Canning's violent denunciation of Burdett and insulting designation of Hobhouse as 'his man'.[19] On 11 May Hobhouse was perturbed to discover that a petition had been lodged against his return, but the Whigs disavowed it and, after a fortnight of anxiety he was relieved when the 'foolish and vexatious job' lapsed for want of recognizances, 26 May.[20] He presented and endorsed a petition for redress from inhabitants of Oldham injured by troops, 12 May.[21] On the 19th he welcomed Lord John Russell's Grampound disfranchisement bill as a small step towards reform, 'putting in the claim of radicals as not being *bigots*'; Russell thanked him when he sat down.[22] At the Westminster purity of election anniversary diner, 23 May, he delivered what he considered 'a *lively* speech', promising to 'go all lengths that he could constitutionally go' to promote reform, and giving the health of Lambton and success to his reform motion planned for 6 June.[23] Place cajoled him into preparing a speech for this, pointing out that it would 'afford to you an opportunity to place yourself high above both the factions'. He duly collected materials and studied them, but he was still finding his feet in the Commons and was uncomfortable at the prospect: 'this new occupation completely upsets me and whatever little sense and spirit I had seem quite evaporated. I know not if I shall ever shake off this incubus which oppresses me whenever I enter or think of the House of Commons'. On 2 June he and Burdett dined with Middlesex freeholders to celebrate the return of the Whigs George Byng and Samuel Charles Whitbread (Hobhouse had played an active part in bringing in the latter), but he concluded that 'the people feel no interest in ... anything Whiggish'. He went to the Commons 'in a great agitation at contemplated speech' on the 6th, and 'felt a load off my mind' when the king's message regarding the return of Queen Caroline obliged Lambton to postpone his motion. On his way from the House he saw her coming over Westminster Bridge 'in an open lumbering landau'.[24] Supporting Lord Nugent's motion to reduce the standing army by 15,000 men, 14 June, he said he would 'have voted for disbanding the whole army' and that ministers seemed to aspire to 'governing by the sword'. This elicited 'a great cheering' from the government benches, but Hobhouse felt

he had spoken 'pretty well and very strongly'.[25] He objected to the £40,000 grant for annual law charges because the 'money had been expended in the prosecution of political opinions', 16 June. On the 26th he spoke and voted against the 'green bag' inquiry into the queen's conduct abroad, but the Whig Sir James Mackintosh* thought it was a 'miserable' effort.[26] He attended and addressed a Westminster meeting to address the queen, 4 July, when he 'spoke well, I think, at least produced an effect', and 'took care to say that whether the queen was innocent or guilty she had been ill treated and the ministers were guilty', as this was 'the just as well as the safest method of putting the question'. On the 6th he, Burdett and the high bailiff of Westminster presented the address to the queen at her 'little lodgings' in Portman Street, where he was touched and impressed by her dignified bearing. 'We don't care a fig about her guilt as they call it', he told Byron, adding that Brougham 'says he has Bergami's b____x in a bottle'.[27] On 11 July, opposing the East India volunteers bill, he proclaimed that

> though it was the fashion to insist that the people were inflamed by demagogues ... they had never entertained any such designs as to warrant ministers advocating [such] measures ... The standing army was 92,000 men, while Cromwell had been able to keep down a disaffected population with not more than one third of the force. New barracks were constructing in all directions ... Government had so long talked of the phantom of disaffection, that they now believed in its existence as children frightened into a notion of the reality of ghosts.

Next day he spoke for an hour, without consulting his notes, against the 'odious ... unconstitutional' aliens bill. He thought 'the thing was well done for a bumpkin', though Henry Grey Bennet* said he was 'too loud', and 'to mortify whatever little vanity I might feel' he discovered that the speech was 'reported very shortly in all the papers' next day. He had heard from Byron that that there was not 'the smallest doubt' about Caroline's very 'public' adultery with Bergami in Italy, but this did not deter him from asserting at the end of his speech that 'all the proceedings against ...[her] are stained with injustice of the deepest dye'. His motion was defeated by 69-23.[28] He seconded Bright's motion for reception of an individual's petition calling for reform of the 'corrupt' Commons, 15 July, but bowed in the end to the Speaker's ruling that it was inadmissible.[29] On 21 Aug. he went to London from his father's Middlesex home at Whitton to second Lord Francis Osborne's amendment for an immediate prorogation rather than an adjournment to 18 Sept. He was disappointed when Osborne, abandoned by Tierney and Brougham, did not divide and reflected that if he 'had been an old Member' he would have done so, as 'we should have divided 40 at least and with them some of the best men in the House'.[30] On 18 Sept. he secured 12 votes to 66 for his amendment for an address for a prorogation. Grey Bennet reported that he 'began well, but [was] too didactic', but Hobhouse felt he had 'succeeded'.[31] He chaired a meeting of ladies of London, Westminster and Southwark which addressed the queen, 26 Sept. In the House, 17 Oct., disgusted with the feebleness of the Whig amendment to the ministerial motion to adjourn until 23 Nov., he persuaded Lord Folkestone, John Calcraft and James Scarlett to take 'a very different tone' and added a few words of protest of his own. Afterwards he found Tierney indifferent towards the queen and cynical about the prospects of turning out the ministry.[32] He went to the House on 23 Nov. 'upon a scheme of catching the miscreants', and was involved in the rowdy scenes in which the few Members on the opposition benches 'fairly hooted the Speaker and [Lord] Castlereagh out of the House'.[33] He had had 'a long interview' with the queen on the 16th, when he congratulated her on the abandonment of the prosecution, but still saw trouble ahead. Unlike Burdett, he attended and addressed Westminster parish meetings in her support, and one chaired by Russell at the *Freemasons' Tavern*, 17 Nov., when it was agreed that it would 'be a farce to change ministers without reform'. He was at Caroline's thanksgiving in St. Paul's Cathedral, 29 Nov. He thought 'curious' a letter from Grey which Ellice showed him on 7 Dec. 1820, asking whether he should 'pledge himself to reform' if invited by the king to form a ministry, and concluded either that Grey was 'a cautious man' or 'perhaps he really wants to know what Burdett and myself, and others, who he knows herd with Ellice, say on these subjects'.[34] At the end of the year he was alarmed by a succession of fainting fits, but on Christmas Day Burdett urged him to join him at Bath: 'the great thing of all is change of scene and being away from eternal applications, frequently unreasonable and annoying'.[35]

In the first week of January 1821 Hobhouse got the sheriff of Wiltshire to put his name to the requisition for a county meeting in support of the queen. When Paul Methuen[†] expressed a fear that he would go to Devizes 'to preach radical doctrines', Hobhouse assured him that he would 'not speak unless the Whigs said anything about blasphemy and sedition, in which case nothing should prevent me from censuring such odious and pernicious hypocrisy'. Before going on the hustings, 17 Jan., he had some talk with his Whig acquaintance Lord Lansdowne and agreed that he and Burdett, who was also there, would not make them-

selves 'prominent'. In the event they remained silent until they were called on to speak after the main business had been transacted, and 'did not say ... much ... about reform'. He and the Whigs thought the meeting was 'excellent'.[36] On 26 Jan. he presented petitions in support of the queen before supporting Hamilton's motion on the omission of her name from the liturgy, arguing that the affair had strengthened the case for parliamentary reform and vowing to 'contribute all in his power' to the task of removing ministers. He denied having called Arthur Onslow 'an idiot'. The treasury official Stephen Rumbold Lushington[*] told the king that Hobhouse had spouted 'the cream of all he has [been] spluttering for the last five months'; and even Grey Bennet deemed the speech a failure, though the young Whig George Howard[*] reckoned it was a 'very fair' effort.[37] He reported to Byron as the campaign on behalf of the queen ended in smoke that 'the opposition [are] completely outnumbered in Parliament and [there is] no chance whatever of a change'.[38] He brought up more petitions in support of the queen, 13 Feb., when he threw in Castlereagh's teeth his declaration of 1792 in favour of reform of the Irish Parliament and asserted that the Commons 'must ultimately adopt a radical reform'. In consultation with Place he drafted the Westminster electors' public address of support to Burdett on his imprisonment, chaired the meeting at which it was adopted, 12 Feb., when he noted that there was 'not a Whig there', and led the deputation which presented it to Burdett outside Newgate prison, 21 Feb.[39] Supporting inquiry into Davison's complaint against Justice William Best[†], 23 Feb., he said that 'the ermine with which a judge was clothed did not invest him with fallibility'. He voted for Catholic claims, 28 Feb., and for the subsequent relief bill. He did not vote for a proposal to make Leeds a scot and lot borough if it got Grampound's seats, 2 Mar., but on the 5th, when Russell abandoned the measure, which now proposed to give the seat to Yorkshire, he said that 'although a radical reformer, I should support the bill even in its present wretched form' and was 'much cheered' when he replied to some earlier taunts about Westminster electors by Alexander Baring. He spoke to the same effect on 19 Mar., when he again lashed Baring.[40] On 9 Mar. he denied the power of the House to commit to gaol the printer of the *Morning Chronicle* for breach of privilege. The Speaker called him to order for this, but he 'went on and made a decent short speech', divided in the minority of 33 and then in Creevey's minority for reducing the number of placemen in the House, when 'many of the opposition voted against us'.[41] He was busy on committees on the Newington vestry and the supply of water to the metropolis, and on 21 Mar. went to Court with an address to the king for the dismissal of ministers: George did not speak to him, but was 'gracious as far as smiling and bowing went'.[42] He was 'employed about getting up a reform dinner in the City of London' to presage Lambton's reform motion 'and to show that we radicals will help the Whigs when the Whigs will do anything'. He attended and spoke 'well but too long' at the gathering, 4 Apr., having drawn up all the toasts and 'contrived to mention all the MPs present'.[43] He seconded and was a minority teller for Creevey's motion for inquiry into distress, 6 Apr., and on the 12th secured 33 votes (to 82) for his proposal to refer the Lyme Regis petition complaining of Lord Westmorland's electoral interference to the committee of privileges. Unable to forget Canning's 'insult' on the occasion of his maiden speech and another more recent one in a debate on the Catholic question, and feeling that he owed it to his maligned constituents as well as to himself to show 'moral courage' by replying, he 'got up a portrait of a political adventurer as a contrast to the demagogue whom Canning is so fond of letting fly at, and ... connected it with parliamentary reform by showing how much such a being is caressed in Parliament'. He obtained the approval of Burdett (who was still in gaol) and delivered his attack as the conclusion of his long speech in support of Lambton's reform scheme, 17 Apr. Canning appeared to be discomfited, and Hobhouse received many congratulations. It was expected that Canning would respond in the resumed debate next day, but he did not do so, and after the premature division, from which Hobhouse, Lambton and many of the reformers were shut out, left the chamber. Hobhouse, who regarded this episode as an 'important' one in his parliamentary career, recalled in his old age that Canning never thereafter 'repeated his first incivilities' and was often 'pointedly commendatory'. At the time he told Byron:

> I *bray'd* to some tune ... The effect in and out of Parliament has been such as you would wish ... Had I not had provocation the attempt would have been imprudent, but as it was I have been told on all hands, Whigs and Tories, that I was quite right. I was sensible that it would be either a complete hit or a complete miss. It was not the latter.[44]

He voted silently for Russell's reform motion, 9 May, but was absent from the division on reform of the Scottish county representation next day. On the 15th he presented petitions from people wounded at Peterloo before seconding and speaking for 'an hour or more' in support of Burdett's motion for inquiry. He recorded that he was 'loudly cheered by the opposition during the speech' and, 'for the first time' since

he had entered the House, received 'several rounds of applause' when he finished. Mackintosh 'shook hands' with him.[45] At the Westminster anniversary dinner, 23 May, he read parts of letters of support from Grey Bennet, Nugent, Dr. Stephen Lushington* and Thomas Barrett Lennard* and argued that the reform cause was flourishing. He privately thought the description by which he was introduced – 'the man who dares to attack apostacy when sheltered by power' – was 'ridiculous', as Caning was not in office 'when I let fly at him'. Later that day he voted for mitigation of the punishment for forgery, and found himself, 'oh rare, in a majority'.[46] He advocated repeal of the vagrancy and combination laws and restrictions on emigration, 7 June, condemned the Constitutional Association and the system by which 'prosecutions might be suspended over the heads of innocent men to eternity, 14 June, and on the issue of Hunt's treatment in Ilchester gaol, 21 June, 'remarked upon the zeal with which all functionaries were defended' in the House. He raised the case of his constituent William Benbow, a bookseller, who had been imprisoned by the action of the Association, and got the attorney-general to promise to investigate it, 3, 4 July. On 10 July he urged ministers to recommend a royal pardon of all 'political prisoners' to mark the coronation.[47] He wrote in his diary, 27 June:

> I find politics a most engrossing pursuit, and the more I see of them the more I am convinced that men of ordinary capacities are best qualified for them. A great eagerness to excel creates a fastidiousness which is fatal to excellence, and, generally speaking, the study of passing events irritates too much to improve the intellectual faculty.[48]

In August he was involved in the disorder which occurred during the funeral procession of the queen (who he thought had 'died of a broken heart in the common sense of the term') and was outraged by the subsequent dismissal of Sir Robert Wilson from the army, observing to Byron that 'we have a pretty set of fellows over us, have we not?'[49] In December 1821, after spending much of the autumn in the country with Burdett, he went, for the first time since 1814, to Tavistock's Bedfordshire home at Oakley, noting that 'politics have lately kept ... Tavistock and myself more asunder than in former days', but that 'nothing could be kinder than his reception of me'.[50]

In January 1822 Hobhouse told Place that he was 'almost inclined to think that there should be a meeting called in Westminster' to petition for reform, relief from distress and inquiry into Peterloo, but Place, as usual, had anticipated him, and bombastically advised him as to the best approach. The meeting took place on 13 Feb., when Hobhouse, following Burdett's familiar line, declared that 'without reform, he ... looked to no retrenchment'.[51] He supported the prayer of the petition in the House, 15 Feb. On the address, 5 Feb., he seconded Burdett's amendment to postpone further consideration of it and asserted that 'the nation was not afraid of the revolutionary plunderer, but of the tax-gathering plunderer ... who came to drag the beds from under them, and to reduce them to the last stage of poverty and wretchedness'. Tierney did not want a division and, according to Hobhouse, Burdett would have 'given way', but he 'insisted on dividing'. The minority was 58, and that on Hume's subsequent amendment 89 (to 171), with a number of leading 'country gentlemen' in the majority, which convinced Hobhouse that 'we do not seem likely to mend much by the agricultural distresses'.[52] He spoke forcefully for the remission of Hunt's sentence, 8 Feb., 1, 22 Mar., 24 Apr., and for inquiry into the conduct of the military at the queen's funeral, 28 Feb. On the same subject, 6 Mar., when Lord Londonderry (Castlereagh) 'called the queen's friends a faction', he 'answered very warmly', observing that some who had tried to exploit her for their own ends were 'a factious cabal' and speaking out for the poor and rootless, 'this despised portion of the people'. He was told that the speech was 'the best I ever made in Parliament', but thought it 'was not', though 'it had a good deal of effect and was loudly cheered'.[53] He attended the 'dull' and 'dear' dinner at Brooks's to celebrate the secession from the club of the Grenvillites, who had just joined the ministry.[54] In mid-April he received a lecture from Place, in reply to his observation that he had 'blushed' when his name had been coupled with Burdett's at the Middlesex election dinner, 11 Apr., when he had said that 'parliamentary corruption' was at the 'root' of the country's problems:

> Why do you show such want of proper confidence in yourself? ... I will tell you my opinion ... and it is not mine alone ... that you are by far the better minded man of the two, and capable of much more as a legislator for the good of your country ... You appear to be guided altogether too much by Sir Francis, not that he is unfit to take as a guide but because it evidently prevents you from exercising or putting out all your power. It is well to have a man to consult occasionally, but he who does not take opinions from others cautiously, and satisfy himself by his own cogitations, will never progress much in real knowledge. If you were to turn seriously to work, on all the great points of legislation and political economy, I am sure you would make a great display and do us most important services. Ricardo has a pamphlet in the press which will be well worth your attention.

Hobhouse resented Place's insinuation that he was 'lazy', responding that 'I can work hard enough when there is anything to do, but the den is a damper to industry'. Place denied having meant to imply idleness: 'I give you credit for being industrious, but I am sometimes sorry to see that you despond. I never do ... I do not make any charge against you, but I do desire to furnish motives to induce you to go far beyond "the limit which it is not given to go"'.[55] Hobhouse voted silently for Russell's 'excellent and appropriate' reform scheme, 25 Apr., when the anticipated personal attack by Canning did not materialize. He voted for Canning's bill to relieve Catholic peers, 30 Apr., and on 3 May noted that 'ministers continue to develop their great schemes' for relief of distress, 'which neither they nor any one else seem to believe can do any good'; but after the crushing defeat in the division on the Swiss embassy, 16 May, he wrote that 'the opposition are now as low as ever'.[56] He annoyed Place by suggesting to him, partly at Burdett's behest, that the annual Westminster dinner might be brought forward a day to 22 May in order to enable a number of Whig Members, including Lambton and Tavistock, to attend, which they could not do on the 23rd, adding that 'perhaps, on this occasion, when the scoundrels are tottering, it might be worth while to strain a point in order to show a union between public men'. Place would have none of it, reminded him that 'we stand on high ground', above party, and said that 'the reason on which you ground the proposal appears to me the best of all reasons for not adopting it', in that, as Burdett had always preached, it was best for the cause of popular liberty to allow the present ministers to persist in their folly and incompetence and so eventually to 'bring the nation to its senses', and to 'refrain from assisting to change them for another set, not one jot better but more artful and more likely to deceive the people'. When Hobhouse subsequently expressed a hope that 'radical reform' would not be toasted because it would 'offend the Whigs', Place damned him in a letter to the Westminster activist Puller, who was inclined to agree with Hobhouse: 'If the toast be an insult, so will be ... [his] speech ... Oh dear, *our* Members, *our radical reform Members*, are to talk poor driveling party stuff *to please the Whigs*, while other Members [such as Hume and Ricardo] ... come to the dinner on purpose to talk ... boldly ... of *radical reform*, and thus leave our Members, or at least one of them, far behind'. Hobhouse, to whom Tavistock had confided his fanciful notion of having Burdett installed as leader of the opposition in the Commons, attended the diner on its appointed day, and noted the presence of a score of opposition Members, including the 'young Whig' Lord Ebrington, who surprised him by giving his health, prefaced by 'a handsome encomium, owning he had opposed me in Westminster, had been in error and would never be in error again and trusted Westminster would never be divided again'. He felt that he 'spoke ill', but thought the meeting would almost certainly prevent the intervention of a Whig candidate at the next general election and might 'also assist Tavistock's project' (which came to nothing a week later).[57] Hobhouse went to a Southwark electors' diner with Lambton, 18 June, but he was at a low ebb when he confided to his diary on his 38th birthday, 27 June:

My body and mind have undergone a change for the worse during the last year. My attendance in the House ... has certainly broken my health, and I have nothing in the way of parliamentary exertion to show for it this session ... I ... feel something very like decay of the poor faculties which I think used to put me formerly something, but not much, above par. My memory is very much shattered, and I have not the same power of application which I used to possess ... Perhaps a reform of habits altogether might bring me back to a tolerable condition ... I feel confident that I shall not live much longer [he survived for another 47 years], so what I intend to do in this world I must do quickly ... I find I hate politics more than ever, but I cannot conceal from myself that one of the causes is that I am not qualified for making ... a 'figure' in the ... Commons. I am too afraid of failing ever to succeed. An honest man in Parliament, however, I can be – I think I may add, I will be. If the Westminster men are not contented with that, let them turn me out. I trust I shall be able to bear that which will be no disgrace.[58]

On 1 July he 'took some pains' with a speech against the aliens bill, 'this misshapen offspring', for which he got 66 votes (to 142). Mackintosh thought he spoke 'readily, sharply and fairly, but in a manner both vulgar and dull'.[59] He had postponed his planned motion for repeal of the house and window taxes, a matter of particular concern in Westminster, until ministers revealed their own proposals; but he considered these inadequate, and on 2 July 1822, having been coached by Place, he spoke for an hour and a half, and, while there were no more than 'from 15 to 25 present at any time', he thought the division of 59-146 was 'all things considered' a 'good' one and that his 'pains were not thrown away'.[60]

Three weeks later he went to Italy with his brother Edward and two sisters. He ran Byron to earth in Pisa, 15 Sept., bade farewell to him (for the last time) on the 20th and went to Florence and Rome. He returned to England via Venice, from where he 'had a look at the Congress of Verona', and Paris, where he dined with Constant and met Lafayette.[61] He attended the opening of the new session, 4 Feb. 1823, with 'an amendment in my pocket declaring abhorrence of Holy Alliance and of [the French] invasion of Spain', but decided, with the concurrence of Russell and others, not to move it, as the mover of the address was 'very decided against the interposition of France'. He and other 'radicals' dined with the Speaker at his 'first opposition dinner', 9 Feb.[62] He voted for inquiry into the borough franchise, 20 Feb., and information on the municipal government of Inverness, 26 Mar., hailed 'the great progress which the cause of reform was now making in the country', 16 Apr.,[63] and divided for Russell's reform motion, 24 Apr., and reform of the Scottish electoral system, 2 June. On 24 Feb. he supported the prayer of a Southwark petition for repeal of the Foreign Enlistment Act and praised ministers for their 'prudence' in relation to the Franco-Spanish conflict.[64] Five days later he went to Holland House for the first time since 1818: he was well received and became a regular visitor thereafter.[65] He said on 24 Feb. that despite ministerial concessions on the window tax he would persevere with his intended repeal motion. He presented and endorsed a constituency petition to that effect, 4 Mar. He urged ministers to reform the Insolvent Debtors Acts, 18, 21 Mar., and presented a Westminster tradesmen's petition for the more effectual recovery of small debts, 24 Apr.[66] On 18 Mar. he was infuriated when Canning 'let out at last that Spain and France were almost sure of war, and that we should not agree *in hostilities* in support of the Spanish liberals'. When William Plunket, a Grenvillite Whig who had defected to become Irish attorney-general, was called by the Speaker to propose Catholic relief, 17 Apr., Hobhouse joined Burdett, Sefton, Grey Bennet and others in walking out of the chamber in protest. On Macdonald's motion for papers on the Spanish problem, 28 Apr., he 'spoke for an hour and ten minutes ... for war, at least for preparing war'. Although he was 'far from well and left out some of my best points', he 'heard afterwards that it was the best speech I had ever made'. In his reply next day, Canning was 'very complimentary' to Hobhouse.[67] At the Westminster anniversary, 23 May, when he took the chair in the absence of the poorly Burdett, he had Ebrington on his right and Lambton on his left, was toasted by Thomas Coke* of Norfolk, who recanted his 'error' in opposing him in 1820, and in his speech 'appealed to [the] electors whether or not I was not right in saying [in the Commons, 28 Apr.] they would have supported a war against France for the liberties of Europe'; he 'had a most unequivocal reply'.[68] He called for reform of the method of striking special juries, preferring a ballot to nomination by the crown office, 28 May. He supported Hume's attempt to secure inquiry into the cost of the coronation, 11 June, and raised the case of one Butt, claiming recompense for false imprisonment, 19 June, but receive short shrift from the solicitor-general. He said that the partial reduction of the window tax had greatly disappointed many Westminster shopkeepers, 19 June.[69] He objected to the proposal to house the king's library in the British Museum, 'a piece of patchwork', arguing that a location in Whitehall would be more appropriate, 20 June, 1 July.[70] He presented petitions for repeal of the Combination Acts, 25 June, and the abolition of slavery, 30 June.[71] In Burdett's continued absence, he presented on 16 July 1823 a 'radical reform' petition from the freeholders and inhabitants of Somerset, arguing that 'everything which had passed during the present session ... had tended to show the necessity of a reform' and claiming that almost one third of the membership of the Commons had now voted for it.

Hobhouse took a leading part in the organization of support for the Spanish liberals and was a founder member in June 1823 of the Spanish committee, which received 'no encouragement whatever from the grandees'. The cause ended in defeat and disappointment.[72] He had long been an enthusiast for Greece, and in March 1823 was involved in the formation of the Greek committee set up to help the rebels against Turkish oppression, in whose cause Byron made his fateful journey to Greece as the agent of the committee in July. In this, too, disillusionment and bad feeling awaited Hobhouse, but he threw himself zealously into the committee's work.[73] Having been 'recommended to travel and amuse myself', he went in early September to North Wales, Cheshire (staying with local Whig Members) and from Liverpool by steamboat to Glasgow. He was the guest of Lord Glenorchy* at Auchmore, where he met Lord John Hay*, brother of the marquess of Tweeddale. Saddened to hear of the early sudden death of Ricardo, he visited Edinburgh in the last week of September and made his way to Burdett's Kirby hunting lodge in Leicestershire by way of Lambton Castle (where he encountered Brougham, incongruous in a party of 'racing men'), the home of Walter Fawkes† at Farnley and Newstead Abbey, Byron's ancestral home, which was under renovation.[74] He contributed an initial £10 to the London Mechanics' Institution, about which Place was enthusiastic, but they had slightly differing views as to its usefulness. However, he subscribed an additional £100 in January 1825.[75]

On the address, 4 Feb. 1824, Hobhouse criticized France for an 'open breach of faith' towards Spain and said that the anti-Greek proclamation issued by Sir Thomas Maitland†, governor of the Ionian Islands, seemed to have been 'written in a drunken frolic'. He informed Byron soon afterwards that 'Parliament has begun very slackly, and the session promises to be exceeding dull and peaceful, very much to my satisfaction, who have been and still am in a very queer way with affections of the head which the doctors call stomach and which may be anything'. He added that 'the ministers certainly are popular, and the agricultural asses have amazed all the opposition in the rising bushels of their corn doles'.[76] On 19 Feb. he warned of the 'injurious consequences' of introducing treadmills into prisons and supported Grattan's motion for information on Catholic office-holders, urging the 'more liberal' ministers to overcome the Irish secretary Goulburn's objections. Next day he spoke and voted, in Hume's minority of ten, for reducing the army by 10,000, observing in his diary that 'no one cares' that 4,000 soldiers had been added and that even Holland, worried about his West Indian plantations, 'approves the augmentation'. He was in a minority of eight on the same issue, 23 Feb. On the 27th he drew attention to the army barracks in King's Mews, Charing Cross, a source of irritation and anxiety to the residents, and condemned the increase in expenditure on 'this system of planting a military force throughout the country'.[77] His motion to reduce the barrack grant to £90,000 was negatived, 9 Mar. He suggested two amendments for the benefit of his constituents to Althorp's bill for the easier recovery of small debts, 23 Feb.: creditors should be able to renew their demands every two years and to sue away from debtors' places of residence. That day and on 16, 23 Mar., 5 Apr. he presented petitions for repeal of the Combination Acts.[78] He divided for reform of Edinburgh's representation, 26 Feb. On 2 Mar. he presented two petitions for repeal of the assessed taxes before speaking for an hour and 40 minutes in support of his own motion for remission of the window tax. He later wrote that he 'did the first quarter of an hour well off hand', but that 'when I began to look at my papers I began to boggle and am afraid my speech sounded very badly, although it was not a bad one'. He got 88 votes to 155, 'nearly 30 more than I did in 1822', but still felt that 'on the whole the attempt is what is called a failure'.[79] He spoke, 11 Mar., and was a teller for the minority of 47, 15 Mar., in favour of ending army flogging. He presented and endorsed a petition from inhabitants of Westminster for reduction of taxes, using the surplus of the sinking fund, and reform of the 'misrule' in Ireland. He saw 'some plausibility' in the reform scheme (repeal of the Bribery Acts, the sanctioning of the open sale and purchase of seats and the enfranchisement of large towns) outlined by his constituent Worgman in a petition, 17 Mar., but could not endorse it overall. At the request of constituents affected by the provisions of the silk bill, he supported the prayer of their petition for compensation for stock in hand, but made it clear that he approved the general principle of the measure. Next day he delivered what he thought was 'a strong speech' against the introduction of the aliens bill. 'Several friends' asked him not to divide, but Lambton said he would if Hobhouse did not, and they obtained a respectable minority of 70 (to 131).[80] As a member of the committee on the home secretary Peel's county courts bill, he objected on 26 Mar. to its giving the appointment of 70 new posts to the crown, but conceded that it would correct some abuses in the process of recovering small debts. He condemned the proposal for subsidizing the building of new churches, 5, 9 Apr., when his wrecking amendment was defeated by 148-59, declaring on the first occasion that the money would be better spent 'in buying up rotten boroughs'. He spoke briefly against any future promotions on the judicial bench, 13 May. Next morning he was woken by the arrival of a note from Kinnaird informing him of Byron's death at Missolonghi, which put him into 'an agony of grief'. As one of the executors he proved the will in July and oversaw arrangements for the burial of Byron's remains at Hucknall, Nottinghamshire on the 16th. It was on his advice that Byron's memoirs were destroyed.[81] He was 'totally at a loss' as to what to say to the Westminster electors at the anniversary dinner, 24 May, as the 'times [are] so changed in appearance, that except the necessity of reform which is an axiom [there is] nothing to enforce'. He found the presence of the Greek deputies 'a God-send', but felt unable 'to refer to Greece as I otherwise would', as 'the very word stuck in my throat'. He warned 'the people of England against being deluded by the temporary prosperity which they enjoyed at this moment' and concentrated on foreign affairs. Next day he returned to the Commons, where he 'fought the Islington improvement bill'.[82] He opposed the third reading of the Equitable Loan Company bill, the object of which was 'private profit', 1 June, and called for an end to naval impressment, 10 June. He obtained only 14 votes (to 52) for his attempt to kill the Irish insurrection bill, 18 June, when he said that as long as the cabinet remained divided on the Catholic question nothing could or would be done for Ireland. On 24 June 1824 he exposed the privations of debtors in Horsemonger Lane gaol and recommended a curb on magistrates' powers of committal.

On his 38th birthday he lamented Byron's death and wrote that 'I have sunk into a complete valetudinarian, so much so that I quite wonder that I have been able to do the little I have done in the ... Commons this year, where I learn that my constituents think that I have made progress instead of going back or standing still, and I learn generally that my good Westminster friends are contented with me'. Yet he found that 'everything palls upon me, and the prospect that by the common course of nature, myself, and those of whom I am fond, cannot add, but must lose gradually the capacity for enjoyment, makes me look with distaste upon what may remain of existence'. That day he received a letter of thanks from the inmates of Horsemonger Lane, where the magistrates had relaxed the rules, but he reflected that 'if they were justified by my real conduct and character', the thanks 'might reconcile a man fond of praise to the weight of existence'.[83] He was inclined to honour Byron's memory by going to Greece as an agent of the committee, but disagreements with Hume and the advice of Burdett and Ellice, who persuaded him that he would be better employed at home, changed his mind. With the secretary John Bowring, he contributed a survey of Byron's activities in Greece to the July 1824 issue of the new *Westminster Review*. Even though the enthusiasm of most members of the committee waned rapidly, Hobhouse remained a believer and devoted much time and energy to the cause in the next two years, but, through no fault of his own, to little effect.[84] In the autumn of 1824 he toured the northeast of England, where he met and befriended Grey's son Lord Howick*. As a guest at Lambton Castle he encountered Grey himself, who, 'owing probably to his acquaintance with my father ... was ... particularly kind and talked on political subjects without reserve': 'he several times talked to me with great despondency on the want of public spirit in England'. Hobhouse did not, however, think much of that 'very wag' Creevey. On his return to London he called 'by appointment' on Byron's former lover Lady Caroline Lamb, who gave him 'a ridiculous account of the attempt lately made to confine her as a madwoman'. He continued to write articles for the periodical press in defence of Byron's reputation.[85]

When he opposed bringing up the report of the address, 4 Feb. 1825, he deplored the proposed suppression of the Catholic Association, damned Plunket, protested at the size of the standing army and called for support for the Greeks, but applauded the liberalization of commercial policy and 'the improvement of ministers'; he detected unusual 'symptoms of great irritation on all sides of the House'.[86] He spoke for allowing the Catholic Association to present its case at the bar and said the bill to put it down was 'pregnant with danger to the best interests of the country', 18 Feb. Three days later Daniel O'Connell*, in London as one of the Catholic deputation, described Hobhouse on first acquaintance as 'a direct-minded, honest man'.[87] Resuming his campaign, on behalf of his constituents, against the house and window taxes, he presented a petition for their repeal, 28 Feb., and said the inhabitants of Westminster were far from satisfied with the ministerial proposal to reduce them, 2 Mar. At the Westminster meeting called to petition for repeal, 24 Mar., he was attacked by Hunt as the son of a sinecurist, with reference to Sir Benjamin's office as a Carnatic commissioner. He retorted that Hunt's charge was 'as false as his own conduct to the public', that his father had never taken public money for doing nothing and that his salary of £1,500 was paid jointly by the creditors of the nabob and the East India Company.[88] It was not until 17 May that he moved for repeal of the window tax, securing 77 votes to 114. He voted for Burdett's successful motion to consider Catholic claims, 1 Mar., and for the relief bill, 21 Apr., 10 May, though he had misgivings on account of his 'great dislike' of the associated bill to disfranchise the Irish 40s. freeholders. When Brougham denounced the latter, 26 Apr., Hobhouse 'had my doubts what to do' and, not wishing to 'appear to abandon Burdett', yet 'unable to support the principle' of the bill, he abstained. On 9 May he begged Lambton not to vote against the relief bill on account of his hostility to the disfranchisement measure.[89] He criticized fraudulent joint-stock companies, 28 Feb., and on 16 Mar. spoke 'well' for an hour and 20 minutes against the second reading of the Peruvian Mining Company bill, but did not divide the House, reflecting later that this effort 'has cost me a great deal of trouble and will bring much individual resentment against me'.[90] On 9 Mar. he warmly welcomed Peel's juries regulation bill as 'the most salutary reform that could be found in our statute books'. He explained, 15 Mar., that he had initially wanted to support Frederick Trench's Thames Quay scheme, but that his interested constituents' protests had now convinced him of its 'utter impracticability'. He had reservations about the salary of £800 proposed by Peel's police magistrates bill, 21 Mar. He asserted that putting the planned National Gallery in the British Museum would be 'like uniting the Jardin des Plantes with the Musee', 28 Mar., when he failed again to persuade ministers to remove the barracks from King's Mews. He objected to the proposed increase in judicial salaries, 16 May, 17 June, when his wrecking amendment was lost by 74-45. He could see

nothing to recommend Twiss's assessors at elections bill, 21 June. Warned by one of the Westminster activists that Burdett's advocacy of Catholic claims had upset some of his constituents and that most of the stewards of the 18th anniversary dinner (23 May) did not wish O'Connell to attend, Hobhouse asked Lord Killeen*, who refused, and then Maurice Fitzgerald* 'to keep him away'. In the event the toast to Catholic emancipation was given and O'Connell did turn up (to speak 'shortly and well'), but Hobhouse, who thought his own effort was poor, though he was 'as well received as ever', was pleased to record that 'the whole meeting went off well' and that 'the cause of religious freedom must be a gainer by it'.[91] A week later he dined at Lansdowne House for the 'first time since political squabbles in Westminster'.[92] His genuine humanitarianism prompted him in 1825 to make his first attempt to legislate to reduce the hours of child and juvenile labour in cotton factories. He tried unsuccessfully to interest Peel in improving his father's Act of 1819, but under pressure from 'the poor operative deputies from Manchester' decided to go ahead himself, though he wanted 'some one to do it more likely to succeed'. On 5 May he obtained leave to introduce a bill to reduce the working day to 11 hours for children under 16 and to give Peel's Act teeth by empowering magistrates to summon witnesses and prevent magistrates who were mill owners or their sons from acting as inspectors. He carried its second reading, 16 May, but Peel recommended him to restrict the measure to making his father's Act operative. On 31 May he explained that he had altered his measure to limit hours to 12 a day, Monday to Friday, and nine on Saturday. The bill became law as 6 Geo. IV, c. 63; and in 1829 Hobhouse carried through a bill to improve enforcement of the regulations (10 Geo. IV, c. 51).[93] In late June 1825 Place bombarded Burdett and Hobhouse with information pertaining to the ministerial bill partially to reinstate the combination laws after the practical failure of Hume's botched repeal measure of the previous year. Hobhouse thought they had put up 'a stout fight' against it (he spoke at length against a penalty clause, 27 June) and they succeeded in securing 'some material amendments'; but when he told Place that 'not much harm is done' by the passage of the measure, Place predicted that 'not a single association of workmen will exist in six months' except illegal ones and warned that 'the working people will not quietly submit to the tyranny and degradation this Act will bring upon them'.[94] In his end of term birthday lucubrations, Hobhouse wrote:

> I have taken a much less active part in public affairs this year than last, but I have been more employed in private

business connected with my constituents than at any former period ... My health on the whole has been better than during the last year, but I have still symptoms about me that convince me I shall be an invalid all my life. As to my intellect, it is certainly decaying, either from bad habits of living, or from my total neglect of any literary studies that might tend to brace and invigorate my mind ... By losing my friend Byron I have lost one of the most powerful motives to exertion and ... I am daily more careless of what I may do or what may be said of my doings.[95]

At Place's pressing request, he went to London to attend the inaugural meeting of the Western Literary and Scientific Institution, which involved 'the sons of respectable tradesmen and merchants in Westminster', in November 1825, but Burdett, with whom he was staying at Kirby, after a period with Ellice in Norfolk, developed a convenient attack of 'gout'. Hobhouse subscribed £25 to the venture.[96]

He 'tried to understand this great question' of the banking and currency crisis of 1825-6 and decided that ministers were 'right' in their response;[97] but he saw reason to change his mind, and voted in a minority of 24 against a detail of their promissory notes bill, 20 Feb., and supported Hume's attempts to require country banks to hold deposits equal in amount to that of notes issued, 24, 27 Feb., when he said that ministers had abandoned 'correct principles' and that 'unless something was done to strike at the root of the present banking system, the country would be exposed to the constant recurrence of those evils under which it now suffered'. He spoke and voted, with Hume, for reduction of the army estimates, 3, 6 Mar., making another protest against the King's Mews barracks, and on 7 Mar proposed a once for all reduction of the army to 77,000: he got 34 votes to 106. He opposed the introduction of a bill to regulate steam vessels in Scotland, 9 Mar., and obtained leave to bring in a bill for the erection of a new gaol in Westminster, 13 Mar. He carried its third reading, 26 Apr., and it became law on 5 May.[98] Supporting Russell's bill to curb electoral bribery, 14 Mar., he said that the standing orders against the interference of peers were routinely flouted and 'it was well known that many ... who sat in that House were only representatives of their own money'. He then endorsed Hume's denunciation of army flogging, against which he had voted in a minority of 47 on 10 Mar. Place briefed him at length on the question of special jury selection in London and the proposed government sponsored improvements to the Charing Cross area, and he presented a petition for compensation from householders of St. Martin-in-the-Fields, 10 Apr.[99] Later that day he opposed receiving the report on the separate ministe-

rial salary of the president of the board of trade, and in the course of his speech declared that while 'it was said to be very hard on His Majesty's ministers to raise objections', he thought it was 'much more hard on His Majesty's opposition'. He thus originated a phrase which passed into common political usage, though thanks, he said, to the typical 'happy spirit of blundering' to which Hume was prone, the initial credit went to Tierney.[100] He spoke and was a minority teller for reforming Edinburgh's representation, 13 Apr. When Peel gave notice that the Aliens Act would not be renewed, 20 Apr., Hobhouse thanked him, for which he was rebuked by 'some of my friends'. He remained determined to give ministers credit 'when I felt they did right', if 'only because I feel their omnipotence, and how completely Parliament would stand by them even if they did wrong'. On 27 Apr. he spoke for an hour and a half in support of Russell's reform scheme, arguing that all reformers should endorse the transfer to 'the opulence, the industry, the importance of such towns as Manchester and Birmingham' of the 'rights now thrown away upon, and shamefully bartered by, the penniless, idle, insignificant vote-sellers of such boroughs as Orford'. He noted Hume's absence, produced an analysis by type of constituency of the voting of Members, 1821-2, to prove his case that the existing system bolstered the government and declared that he wanted 'real popular control over the measures of government, which alone can ... save us from a relapse into the miseries inseparable from a corrupt and delusive system of representation'. The speech was considered a great success by Russell and many Whigs, and Hobhouse had it published as a pamphlet; but privately he doubted 'that I should do any permanent good by this exposure' of the system. He thought the agriculturists were 'foolish' to make such an 'outcry' against the government's 'trifling' proposal for the emergency admission of bonded corn, which he supported, though he felt that ministers had been 'most shuffling' and might have produced a better 'settlement' of the corn law issue. On 19 May he urged government to aid the Greeks, especially as the French were assisting Turkey. He then 'sat out' a long debate on slavery and divided in the minority of 38 for abolition, 19 May, but did not think the abolitionists' cause was 'gaining ground amongst the really influential part of the community', while in the Commons it was 'losing ground'.[101] At the 'thinly attended' Westminster anniversary dinner, 23 May, he 'spoke well but too long', as he thought, about reform and Greece.[102] He was in the chamber for the debate on Russell's resolutions against electoral bribery, 26 May 1826, but did not vote in the majority for them.[103]

On the eve of the dissolution Hobhouse was perturbed to learn that 'nothing was doing in Westminster' towards his and Burdett's re-election and was angered by a paragraph in the *Morning Herald* accusing them of 'remissness in attendance', which in his case, saving the absence on 26 May, was 'absurd in the extreme'. Matters were put in train by Place and Kinnaird, but Hobhouse was 'much displeased' when Kinnaird allowed reporters to remain at a poorly attended meeting which resolved to invite them to be nominated, and which thus looked like a closed cabal, and 'more so still' by the resolutions' opening attack (Place's work) on the 'two political factions that had so long kept Westminster without a real representative'. He and Burdett were 'resolved we would not attack the Whigs and would say so publicly if required'. He remonstrated with Kinnaird and called very late at night on Place, who thought his agitation was largely unwarranted. Place oversaw and co-coordinated from his home subsequent proceedings and persuaded Hobhouse and Burdett to take no notice of the 'factions' remark in their answer to the formal invitation. An attempt to put Canning in nomination ended in farcical failure, and Burdett and Hobhouse were returned unopposed in under an hour. At the nomination, Hobhouse made light of the accusations against him and asserted that while reform was essential, the bribery resolutions were 'nugatory' and 'delusive'. Place meanwhile, had recorded his view that he and Burdett were 'little if any better than mere drawling Whigs' and that as Members they were now 'inefficient and almost useless'.[104] Holland and Ebrington asked Hobhouse to go to Nottingham to support the Whig Lord Rancliffe*, but he was unable to do so, explaining that not only was he ineligible to vote, having declined to accept the offered freedom at the time of Byron's funeral, but he was fully committed to helping Whitbread in Middlesex and then 'the Bedfordshire reformers', if required.[105] On 5 July he went with his brother Thomas Benjamin to Germany, Switzerland, Austria and Italy (Milan and Genoa), returning via Toulon, Marseilles and Paris, where he obtained authorization from the local Greek committee to act with Colonel Stanhope in the disposal of their funds for the support of the expedition being planned by Lord Cochrane†, whom he had seen in Marseilles. But when he got back to London on 12 Nov. 1826 having decided, though there seemed to be no urgency as far as the opening of Parliament was concerned, that it was 'as well to be in the way', he found the Greek cause there mired in scandal and stories of mismanagement and corruption. He was also greeted by a long letter from Place on the subject of special jury selection.[106]

He divided in the minority of 24 on the address, 21 Nov. 1826. He praised Waithman for exposing the Arigna Mining Company scandal and ministers for backing him, 5 Dec., and on 8 Dec., not for the first or last time, pressed in vain for an indication of when the Charing Cross improvements were to begin.[107] In the first week of December he received from Place an extraordinary long letter, a sequel to an earlier conversation, in which the tailor frankly told him that in Westminster 'a general opinion prevails that you want habits of business', yet at the same time offered to entrust him rather than the more dependable Hume with the case of an aggrieved constituent provided he was willing to go into it patiently and effectively. Hobhouse, unamused, wrote a lengthy and spirited defence of his parliamentary conduct, contending that he believed it had been satisfactory to all reasonable electors, admitting that he had no wish or inclination to follow Hume's example of incessant, often misdirected and perverse activity to create an impression of efficiency, and reminding Place that he had never portrayed himself as 'a man of business'. He showed his reply to Burdett, who approved it and remarked that 'I would do without Westminster much better than Westminster could do without me', but 'on second thoughts' he resolved not to send it. He mentioned the episode to Brougham, who 'laughed at the "habits of business"'.[108] Hobhouse spent some time with Tavistock in January 1827. He 'did not stay to vote against the duke of Clarence's additional pension', 16 Feb., 'having walked down to the House ... with ... Althorp, and agreed with him that it would be inexpedient to do so unless too large a sum was proposed'. However, he subsequently decided that the grant was too large, and he voted in the minority of 39 against the annuity bill, 2 Mar.[109] When Peel outlined his plans for consolidation of the criminal code, 23 Feb., Hobhouse was fulsome in his praise, observing the he had 'laid the basis for being a great man, by showing himself to be a good one'. On the 26th he supported Althorp's motion to legislate against electoral bribery, though he 'did not think that any good would be effected by this or any other temporary expedient', and backed Hume's bid to end army flogging. He spoke in the same sense on the mutiny bill, 12 Mar. He voted silently for Catholic relief, as proposed by Burdett, 6 Mar., but found himself in a minority.[110] He presented a Westminster shoemakers' petition for free trade in corn, 8 Mar., and voted for reduced protection, 6, 9 Mar., when he denounced the government, 'wretched and disjointed' since Liverpool's stroke, as 'not worth twopence'.[111] He voted for inquiry into the electoral activities of Leicester corporation, 15 Mar., information on the Barrackpoor mutiny, 22 Mar., and to withhold supplies until a settled administration was in place, 30 Mar., though he considered it an empty gesture.[112] He seconded Hume's motion for a select committee on debtors' gaols and the operation of the relevant laws, but advised him that finding a solution would not be 'as easy as ...[he] seemed to think'. On 5 Apr. he got himself into a tangle by rising in anger to 'declaim' against lord chancellor Eldon but, wrongly thinking the debate was on the master of the rolls Copley's chancery amendment bill (it was in fact on Harvey's motion for information on chancery delays) made much of Copley's absence. Canning raised 'a great laugh' by insinuating that Hobhouse was drunk, which he was not, but did not overdo the sarcasm. Nevertheless Hobhouse 'felt very uncomfortable and went home' without voting, but 'scarcely slept a wink'.[113] He presented and endorsed a petition from shareholders in the County Fire Office complaining of their treatment by the vice-president of the board of trade Wallace in the revenue inquiry.[114] During the Easter recess he suffered again 'under a smart attack of my old complaint in the head', but was 'pretty well' by the time Canning's appointment as prime minister and the coalition in office with him of the Lansdowne Whigs were confirmed. He had already predicted to Tavistock, who wanted 'to sail in the same boat with me', that 'Canning would be the cause of a disunion between the Whigs, and that having heard that Peel was going abroad, I thought I should follow his example, for my occupation was over'. On 30 Apr. Burdett informed him that he had decided to 'sit behind the treasury bench' and support the ministry 'as a choice of evils'. Hobhouse 'told him that I could not bring myself to sit behind the arch-enemy of the reformers, and that having no confidence at all in ... Canning, I could not take a step which would make it appear that I had confidence in him'. He added that he would 'vote for Canning when he was right' and that 'he would derive a more respectable support from the opposition on their own benches than when considered as mere appendages to the treasury bench'. Next day Burdett assured Hobhouse that 'seeing his going behind the treasury bench gave me so much pain, he should keep his old seat but make a declaration in favour of ministers'; but he broke his word when the House assembled, and even tried to persuade Hobhouse to cross the floor with him. Hobhouse seated himself 'on the second opposition bench'.[115] He presented petitions on assorted constituency business, 9, 14, 21 May, and on the 22nd, prompted by Place, brought up and endorsed one from Newcastle seafarers for an end to impressment.[116] He voted for inquiry

into bankruptcy administration, 22 May, spoke and voted for the disfranchisement of Penryn, making it clear that he would not swallow its sluicing, 28 May, and was in Hume's minority of ten for repeal of the Blasphemous and Seditous Libels Act, 31 May. At the Westminster anniversary dinner, 23 May, when Cobbett and Hunt created a near riot by denouncing Burdett for supporting Canning, Hobhouse considered himself 'the principal sufferer, for what between the vociferation of our friends and the clamour of Cobbett and company I could not get a hearing for the first time since I have been known in Westminster'. He 'bore the disappointment calmly enough until I heard Cobbett calling me names, upon which like a silly fellow I took up a steward's wand and threatened to knock him down'. He reckoned the shambles 'a partial defeat' for the Westminster reformers, but next day was told by Burdett that he had 'a very erroneous impression of the meeting' and ordered to keep his mouth shut about it.[117] He had a long talk with the Hollands on 'the prospects of the new government', 30 May, and was struck by the 'short and simple statement' with which Canning introduced his cautiously optimistic budget next day. He presented Westminster petitions on arrests for small debts and various building projects, 7 June, and on the 11th the petition of the householders of Rye complaining that the franchise had been 'surreptitiously taken from them' by the treasury interest. He was tempted to answer Hume's attack on the report of credit for Portugal, 10 June, but 'did not like the appearance of being more a ministerialist than I am, particularly more a Canningite'. He tried in vain to secure alterations to the bill regulating arrests for debt on mesne process, 16, 18 June, when he divided against the Coventry magistracy bill but voted 'for the government corn bill'. He decided that accepting Canning's invitation to dine with him on 2 July 1827, the day of prorogation, would 'compromise my independence', and so turned it down.[118]

By this time, after further setbacks and scandals, one of which had more or less exhausted his patience with Hume, Hobhouse was thoroughly disillusioned with 'anything connected with the Greeks'.[119] At Whitton in mid-July, he was relieved and pleased to find from Burdett that he would not destroy himself by accepting the peerage on which Canning had had him sounded. As Canning lay dying at Chiswick House in early August, he twice called to enquire after him. He was saddened by his death, but decided (unlike Hume, 'the impudent fool') to stay away from the public obsequies, for he had hardly known and never quite trusted the man.[120] During a stay with Burdett in Derbyshire in September, Hobhouse courted his daughter Sophia.

Burdett gave his blessing to a proposal of marriage, but after several weeks she turned him down. Soon afterwards he began a furtive and tormented affair with the wife of a Wiltshire acquaintance.[121] His autumn travels included a November sojourn with Ellice at Dawlish, where they received the news of the destruction by the Allies under Admiral Codrington of the Turkish fleet at Navarino, 'an important event' which in the end 'saved Greece'.[122] On 18 Dec. 1827 he wrote to Place mocking the tottering Goderich ministry, but received a reply expressing the hope that the ministerial incompetence would long continue, so that 'the people' would be roused at last to work out their own salvation, and 'abusing the aristocracy, and saying the people now were too wise to care for any public man much'. Hobhouse answered him forcefully, arguing that it was wrong to say that the ruling classes derided 'the march of intellect', which they either feared or encouraged, according to their political stance, and telling Place

> frankly that ... public men have very little encouragement to try to please what you call the people ... It is expected they should, without the least regard to times and seasons, be always doing something ... although it is morally impossible under the present system that their exertions however assiduous should produce any immediate or speedy effect, yet they are blamed ... for having done nothing ... The first person who when in office adopts some of their recommendations and carries them into effect robs them of all the praise ... Any coarse unfeeling pretender, with no other merit than having a strong digestion and a bad heart, laborious about trifles, and trifling about matters of real import, envious, dishonest, and unfair, impatient and intriguing and except for his own purposes altogether impracticable ... can at any time, by bidding higher and stooping lower, make himself a favourite with a good many of those who ought to know mankind a little better than they do.

Place insisted that 'the fault is not at all in the people, but in the [public] men themselves', and in the same breath asked Hobhouse to give his name and secure those of his father, Burdett and Bedford as stewards for the Mechanics' Institution's approaching anniversary jamboree.[123] At the turn of the year, when he was at Whitbread's home at Southill, Bedfordshire, he heard that Burdett had formally withdrawn his support from the Goderich administration, and on 2 Jan. 1828 wrote to Burdett 'telling him I was uneasy at having taken no line by speaking my opinion last session, and that I felt inclined to do so next. I told him there was no fear of my being too active. My propensity was repose, as it is with most men'. Burdett replied that he would 'do as I do, sink or swim'. Hobhouse, who received a circular requesting his attendance at

the opening of the session from Huskisson, the leader of the Commons, could 'not see how the government is to stand', on 4 Jan., but still doubted 'whether it is wise to lend a hand to its destruction'. When he sought Place's advice on this, he received the unhelpful reply that it was 'of no importance whatever' whether the ministry stood or fell, though at least there could never again be an unadulterated 'Castlereagh and Eldon administration'.[124] When Tavistock showed him a letter from Althorp 'declining all concert and combination for an organized opposition' and one from Holland complaining of 'the distrust of the administration by their own Whig friends', Hobhouse sent him 'a long letter ... showing how little Lord Holland's letter applied to us' and arguing that Lansdowne was to blame for any 'want of union'. On 8 Jan. Burdett arrived at Southill and urged Hobhouse to 'take a line [on] the first day', but he responded by saying that 'I foresaw there was little chance of united action for any purpose'. Next day came the news that Goderich had finally thrown in the towel and the duke of Wellington (for whom Hobhouse had a genuine admiration as a man and leader of men) was forming a ministry, which might include Huskisson and his Canningite group as well as Peel. Hobhouse wrote to Place to say that if Wellington was 'really resolved to name liberal ministers and to try liberal measures, I think it would be unwise as well as unfair to oppose his administration at once without giving it every trial'. He got a scathing reply, in which Place again denounced all party politicians and mocked Hobhouse's implication that Peel and Wellington were 'liberal', observing, fatuously, that the former 'would make a despotism', while the duke 'would cut the throats of anyone who stood in the way of his supreme ignorance'. Hobhouse, exasperated with Place's obsessive obduracy, replied that 'with your views about public men you must be supremely indifferent to the event now brewing, except indeed that you would naturally prefer the worst cabinet that could be chosen', adding that for himself he 'should like to see the Whigs, such as Lord Althorp and the duke of Bedford fairly tried, and if they would do nothing we should then know that good will could do nothing, for I certainly believe they are sincere in their professions'. Place's retort was that the real cabinet would be Wellington, the king's confidant Knighton, Rothschild and his creature John Charles Herries*, and that Althorp and Bedford were 'names, nothing, or little more than nothing now', who 'might go into the cabinet quietly as a couple of old women', but who had no 'particular claim to the support of the people'.[125] On a more realistic plane of action, Hobhouse continued to correspond with Tavistock, Althorp and other

Whig 'watchmen', and by 24 Jan. 1828 had concluded with them that 'now our course is clear, we all go into regular opposition, and may do the only good the Whigs ever can do; by acting separately and watching the government'.[126]

He was still 'hesitating' as to what to do on the opening day:

> My natural inclination leads me to be silent, but it will not do for a Westminster Member always to look on ... Yet if Huskisson has already liberalized ... [the] administration – which is just probable – I think this ministry is as good as the last; nay, better, inasmuch as it does not compromise the character of reformers; and though the resigning ministers may attack Huskisson, I do not see why I should.

On the address, 31 Jan., he asked Lord Palmerston, the foreign secretary, whether ministers intended to present Admiral Gore's report on Navarino to the House and move a vote of thanks to Codrington. He accepted Palmerston's explanation that it would not be necessary to bring up the report, but not his statement that no thanks would be proposed, and gave notice of a motion to that effect for 14 Feb. Althorp and Wilson discouraged him as the day approached, but he went ahead, 'with beating heart and throbbing temples', in a 'very full' House. He spoke for almost two hours, was heard 'well' and received many 'compliments' when he sat down. Having made his point successfully, he submitted to Burdett's advice and withdrew the motion at the end of the debate. He received much subsequent praise, but later wrote that had he realized how many 'friends' would object to the proposal, he would not have made it.[127] On 26 Feb. he presented petitions for repeal of the Test Acts before voting in the unexpected majority for that measure. On 28 Feb. he complained that he had been listed, without his authority, as a member of the committee of the Covent Garden vestry bill, which a majority of his constituents did not want him to support. He questioned Peel on the progress of the commission of inquiry into the supply of water to the metropolis, agreeing with him that private speculators should pay for the surveys, and as a member of the committee on alehouse licensing seconded Escourt's motion for leave to bring in a regulatory bill, 14 Mar. On 28 Mar. he told Peel that the report of the water supply commissioners was 'anything but satisfactory', in that they appeared to have restricted themselves to the condition of current supplies and ignored the question of remedial measures to improve quality. Place later introduced him to one of the managers of a project to supply the city with 'pure water'.[128] Hobhouse voted against sluicing East

Retford into the hundred, 21 Mar., and supported Althorp's freeholders registration bill, 25 Mar. Place sent him an enormous manuscript of his projected work on 'morals and manners', commenting that 'with your talents, your quickness, and aptitude in all respects for pursuing the inquiry in which you are engaged, the *whole* truth might be worked out, had you the doggedness which I lament you have not'. Hobhouse's heart must have sunk when he opened this packet. Place also pressed him to research and expose to the House, in reference to Peel's plans for a revamped metropolitan police force, the wretched and corrupt 'former state of this establishment'.[129] He presented and endorsed many petitions against Courtenay's friendly societies bill, a source of 'great consternation' among his constituents, 25 Mar., 1, 15, 18, 22 Apr., and welcomed its abandonment, 28 Apr. He said that the Marylebone select vestry bill, for which he had presented the original petition, was much needed on account of existing abuses, 31 Mar. He presented a petition complaining of inequitable rate assessments by the select vestry of St. James's, Westminster, and noted that returns relating to St. Martin's which he had earlier requested had not yet been furnished. On 22 Apr. he demanded to know why ministers had changed their minds on the corn bill since last year and divided for a pivot price of 60s. Next day at the drawing room he chided Huskisson about this, but denied being 'angry' with him, though he retained his view that Huskisson was 'a shabby, unprincipled man'.[130] Hobhouse divided in Hume's minority of 27 for a fixed 15s. duty, 29 Apr., and presented and endorsed a Westminster free trade petition, 19 May. He supported the prayer of a petition against the Lambeth Bridge bill, one of several 'wholly unnecessary' such projects, 28 Apr. He voted silently for Burdett's motion to consider Catholic claims, 12 May, and against the pension for Canning's family next day, for he did not 'know what Canning has ever done to entitle him to a national reward after his death'. On 17 May he was 'in a private room' for the first time with Wellington at Lord Belgrave's* diner party, but they did not converse. He divided in the minority against sluicing East Retford after the 'long and angry' debate which led to the resignation from the government of the Huskissonites, 19 May.[131] He denounced Millbank penitentiary as 'a most useless charge on the country', 23 May. He made no effort to recruit Members for the Westminster anniversary dinner, postponed to 26 May by Epsom races, mainly because he 'did not like to ask them to come and run the risk of meeting the ruffian Cobbett'. In the event, only three other Members attended and, while Hunt attacked Burdett, both he and Hobhouse (who was still fretting about his health, noting increasing deafness and the fact that 'my right side is not so active as my left') were 'very well received'. The topics of his speech were 'the reported change of ministry and the little chance of the king choosing a good administration when the Parliament was no representative of the people'.[132] At dinner at Devonshire House, 28 May, he asked Lord Alvanley to let Wellington know that in the present state of the Commons a 'bigoted old Tory government' could not survive, and that 'in order to avoid these repeated changes it would be necessary to fall in with the general disposition of the times and liberalize his government'. In the House, 30 May, he rose 'half out of breath' and deprecated ministerial instability, said that the choice of the soldier Sir George Murray* as colonial secretary 'might be a good' one, but that it needed to be long-term, and stated his hope of seeing 'a ministry acting upon good principles ... at last permanently appointed'. Yet he felt that these observations 'fell flat because they were not factious, and because I did not fall in with the foolish notions about a military cabinet'. In a conversation on 1 June, he found that Grey, like himself, 'did not approve of our going at once into strong opposition', which would 'only strengthen the ministry'.[133] Place alerted him to the fact that the borough polls bill would significantly increase the basic expenses of Westminster elections, and he raised this problem in the House, 6 June, when the bill's sponsor Thomas Davies said he was willing to exempt Westminster and agreed to postpone the third reading.[134] On 2 June he said that he would rather return to corruption than sluice East Retford and wished that 'we had done with this unlucky subject'; and on 27 June, when he argued that the seats should go to a large town, he declared that the only thing left to do that session was to 'knock up the bill'. Next day he agreed with Hume that the duties on malt and beer should be reduced to encourage the consumption of beer rather than gin. He spoke and voted in a minority of 28 against the grant for the Society for the Propagation of the Gospels, 6 June, and on the 20th divided in minorities of 38 and 22 against details of the miscellaneous estimates. He called for the abandonment of the additional churches bill and voted to condemn the waste of public money on Buckingham House refurbishment. Having again been pressed on the matter by Place, he tried in vain to get an answer from ministers as to the timing of the projected Charing Cross improvements, 25 June. Place rapped his knuckles for declining to move for returns of St. Martin's rate assessments to be printed on the ground that they were too voluminous.[135] When Daniel Harvey, 'a sad dog', presented a petition from Colne handloom weavers for wage regulation, 1 July, Hobhouse rebuked him for his 'very exalted tone' in 'abusing ... the political economists' and accusing other opposition Members of indifference to distress, and applauded Peel's stated willingness to back the liberalization of trade. He thought he performed 'well'. Later that day he supported Burdett's motion for inquiry into the metropolitan water supply and was named to the select committee.[136] He voted for abolition of the post of lieutenant-general of the ordnance, 4 July, but privately recorded his envy of Sir James Graham and Edward Smith Stanley, wealthy young men and 'foremost of the *youngsters*' on the opposition benches, and mused that 'I must rouse myself, or these folks will beat the old stagers out of the field'.[137] On 16 July 1828 he unsuccessfully urged ministers to accept Poulett Thomson's amendment to the customs bill to confirm their adhesion to 'a more liberal and generous system of policy'.

For several weeks Hobhouse had been courting Hay's consumptive sister Julia, and on 30 May 1828 he found himself 'in a most ridiculous embarrassment' at Grosvenor House between his married lover and the 'lady ... who I wish to be my wife'. On 25 June he spent the night with his lover 'in a way which I shall not record though I shall never forget it', and next day made a successful offer of marriage to Lady Julia. On the 27th her uncle Lord Lauderdale gave his blessing, and told him that her crown pension would lapse on the marriage and that she 'had no fortune'. Next day he terminated his relationship with his lover, 'in the best way I could', but 'had a dreadful scene and wished myself at the bottom of the sea', though he felt that he had 'nothing to charge myself with on the core of duplicity', having 'always told what I thought might happen'. By the marriage settlement, Lady Julia was to have 'nearly £2,000 a year if I die before her, which I shall most assuredly'. (Hobhouse in fact was to be a widower for the last 34 years of his life.) At the wedding by special licence at 3 Cumberland Place, 28 July, when Hobhouse was 42 and his bride ten years his junior, she fainted twice and had 'not quite recovered' when they arrived at Whitton for the first part of their honeymoon. On 12 Aug. 1828 they left for the continent and made their way to Naples, Rome and Florence, returning by way of Genoa, Turin and Paris, where Hobhouse met Burdett, and arriving in London in the first week of February 1829. Soon afterwards they moved into their new house at 21 Charles Street, Berkeley Square, where Hobhouse quickly impregnated Julia with their first child.[138]

On his passage from Calais he met the Huskissonite Palmerston. On the announcement, 5 Feb. 1829, of the government's plan to concede Catholic emancipation, he found 'our friends quite in ecstasies and satisfied' and inclined to treat the recommendation to suppress the Catholic Association as 'nothing, a mere formality'. He entered his own 'humble protest' against this, 12 Feb., but said he would not oppose it, and called on ministers to 'say they staked their government on it, as the only way of determining the wavering peers'. He praised past Whig champions of emancipation to counteract the tributes paid to Canning. On 20 Feb. he defended Peel and Wellington against an Ultra's charge of 'political apostacy', and on the 23rd said that petitioners against emancipation from the rural deanery of Gloucester were in error in stating that the measure had been 'repeatedly rejected' hitherto by the Commons. He voted silently for emancipation, 6, 30 Mar., pairing off for the committee stages of the relief bill, though on the latter day he was so angered by the Ultra Wetherell's 'perversions of history' that he shouted a corrective rebuke 'across the table'. On the 19th he asserted that what the Surrey Member Charles Pallmer had presented as the anti-Catholic petition of householders of London and Westminster was not representative of opinion in his constituency. He was one of the 100 or so Members who accompanied Peel to the Lords with the bill 31 Mar., and he attended the debates there. He had come to distrust O'Connell, 'a strange compound' who 'did not know his station', and did not vote for allowing him to take his seat unimpeded, 18 May, although he was evidently in the chamber during the debate.[139] In Burdett's absence through illness, Hobhouse chaired the 22nd Westminster anniversary dinner, 25 May, which proved to be a rowdy affair. He described the events in his diary:

> The king's health was given and God save the king. Here the first disturbance began, for Hunt grumbled and Cobbett would not stand up. Then I gave reform and Hunt ... complained that I gave it without comment. I said nothing. Sturch then proposed Burdett's health and someone hissed ... Hunt ... made a speech against the toast. I kept silent pretty well. Cobbett spoke. The accusations were that Burdett had not voted against the building of palaces, that he had not voted against disfranchising the [Irish] 40s. freeholders and finally not voted against [the] ... anatomy bill! ... I put the question whether the health of Burdett should be drunk. Almost all the company rose and when I put the contrary only five or six held up their hands ... The health was drunk with the greatest enthusiasm ... Alexander Dawson* gave my health ... and I rose and met with a most cordial reception. The speech I made completely overthrew the enemy and gave a portrait of Cobbett which the company

recognized at once ... When I sat down Hunt shook his fist at me of which I took no notice.

He was astounded to find in *The Times* of 27 May 'an attack on me for praising Cobbett's talents', and wrote a letter of remonstrance to the editor Barnes, who replied on 30 May 'praising me up to the skies and offering to explain his former paragraph'; he was unimpressed.[140] On 2 June 1829 he spoke and voted in the minority of 40 for the Ultra Lord Blandford's reform scheme, not as a step towards preventing another ministerial 'betrayal', but as one towards necessary change, particularly the eradication of nomination boroughs. Howick thought that 'unluckily' the speech was 'meant to be for us, but ... turned out against us'.[141] Hobhouse divided that day in the minority of 44 for issuing a new writ for East Retford.

It was in this session that he first brought seriously before the House the problem of vestry reform, a subject of particular interest in Westminster, where there were several closed vestries whose wasteful and self-interested management of parochial affairs had provoked resentment among many of the parishioners. It was an issue in which Place took a close interest, and he supplied Hobhouse with materials and advice in his usual overbearing and didactic fashion.[142] On 28 Apr. 1829 Hobhouse moved for the appointment of a select committee of inquiry into vestries in England and Wales in a speech which gave detailed examples of the most glaring abuses, including those in Westminster and the wider metropolis, where he wanted select vestries to be abolished. There was a 'thin' House and there was little response. Peel, in what Hobhouse thought a 'shabby speech', challenged his allegations of malpractice, arguing that popularly elected vestries would become chaotic, but he conceded the inquiry in so far as it went to investigate abuses in parochial expenditure. Hobhouse replied that he was averse to 'open' vestries, but wished to modify 'the elective principle' and extend the provisions of the Act of 1819 to the metropolis. He chaired the committee's deliberations during May, clashing frequently with William Sturges Bourne, who he believed 'will attempt to bring my inquiry to nothing'. He intended to present the report on 12 June, 'but did not' do so until the 19th. He also introduced that session bills dealing with the Westminster vestries of St. James and St. Paul. He lost the former on its third reading by 83-61, 21 May, noting that 'the opponents rode off on my general measure'. He got the St. Paul's bill through the Commons and solicited support for it in the Lords from Grey, Lord King and Lord Durham (as Lambton now was). It became law on 22 May 1829.[143]

In late November 1829 Hobhouse told Brougham that he saw no reason to oppose the ministry, for 'the only fault I found was that ... Wellington had inferior associates where he might have the best men in the country'. Accordingly, he was one of the oppositionists who with little 'hesitation' divided with government against Knatchbull's amendment to the address, 4 Feb. 1830. He thought he saw next day, when Burdett, possibly drunk, delivered a 'philippic' against the government which he noted 'embarrasses me for I differ from him altogether and shall be obliged to say so', that his vote on the address had 'rather displeased some of my Whig cronies'.[144] He voted to transfer East Retford's seats to Birmingham and for some punitive action, 11 Feb., when he forced the second division, and on 5 Mar., when he said 'a few words' in favour of O'Connell's proposal to incorporate the ballot in the bill.[145] He was 'in woeful health', but attended dutifully, agreeing with Tavistock that the government was too feeble to carry 'bad measures' and that they should generally support 'the duke, with his wings clipped', though it would be gratifying to see him bring in some 'better' men.[146] He divided with Hume for major tax cuts, 15 Feb., and next day decided not to speak on Greece, as he 'should have taken a different view of the subject from all my friends and might have been misunderstood not only in England but elsewhere'. He recorded that Palmerston confided to him his belief that Greece could not possibly 'stand alone'. On 18 Feb. he delivered what Howick thought 'an exceedingly amusing speech' on Blandford's reform plan, though 'by some unaccountable confusion' he and other Whigs divided for this rather than for the general resolution proposed by Brougham. Speaking for Davies's motion to delay the army estimates, 19 Feb., he wanted 'to give a reason why I did not like voting with the Ultra Tories', but 'got confused because I did not like to say harsh or personal things of them'. On 22 Feb. he 'sat up till near two ... voting in Hume's four minorities against the army estimates'.[147] Next day he voted silently for Russell's motion to enfranchise Birmingham, Leeds and Manchester, only to find in the *Morning Journal* of 24 Feb. 'a charge of my having voted with ministers'. He stormed round to the office and secured the promise of a correction. He was told 'by many' that his speech in support of the Newark petition complaining of the duke of Newcastle's eviction of electorally recalcitrant tenants had '*floored*' his opponents, but he believed that 'the speech was distasteful to many and was not well listened to with the complacency with which I usually meet'. He was pleased when Burdett paid 'a compliment to the duke of Wellington and his government', 2 Mar.[148] He was

at the small meeting of 'the party' at Althorp's rooms, 6 Mar., when he spoke in support of the proposal 'to announce that a certain number of men were acting together for reduction of taxation'. He recommended 'some sort of communication for this object only with the Huskissonians and the [Ultra] Tories', but was overruled, though he subsequently explained that he was 'averse to any coalition for the purpose of turning out ministers, who I preferred to all the world except the gentlemen present'. He did not attend the meeting on 16 Mar.[149] He divided against government on relations with Portugal, 10 Mar., and against the appointment of a treasurer of the navy, 12 Mar.[150] He moved and was a minority teller for a wrecking amendment to the East Retford sluicing bill, 15 Mar., when he voted in O'Connell's minority of 21 for the adoption of the ballot. That day he passed on a petition from licensed victuallers against free trade in beer to Alderman Thompson, because he was 'a party concerned' as a result of his father's interest in Whitbread's.[151] He agreed with Althorp that inquiring into the state of the nation, as Edward Davenport proposed, 18 Mar., 'meant nothing less than depreciating the currency'. He admired the eloquence of Burdett's speech in the resumed debate, 23 Mar., but thought he 'talked sad nonsense' about prices and was provoked by the implied 'threat' of his observation that 'he wondered how any [man] could meet his constituents who voted against the inquiry' into staying on to divide with government. He supported reception of a Drogheda petition for repeal of the Union presented by O'Connell, 22 Mar., but privately deemed him guilty of hypocrisy. He voted for inquiry into taxation, 25 Mar., and to reduce the ordnance estimates, 29 Mar. His speech for abolition of the Bathurst and Dundas pensions, 26 Mar., was 'extremely well received during the delivery and loudly cheered at the close', but he thought that attribution to it of the opposition majority was misguided; he expected that the female Bathursts, who had recently called on Julia, would not do so again.[152] He voted for Jewish emancipation, 5 Apr., 17 May 1830, though on the first occasion he was 'angry' at the government's feebleness in allowing the proposal to be carried against them.[153]

On 10 Feb. 1830 Hobhouse secured the renewal of his select committee on vestries and had the minutes of evidence from the 1829 investigation printed. He failed to persuade Russell to postpone the St. Giles's vestry bill, 2 Mar., and on the 16th presented a hostile petition from that parish and St. George's, Bloomsbury, moved to have it referred to the committee on the bill and wore down the Speaker's resistance to this on a point of order. He seconded Hume's unsuccessful bid to reduce its voting qualification from £30 to £15, 1 Apr., and brought up more hostile petitions next day.[154] Meanwhile, he worked hard at his own committee, 16 Feb.-25 Mar., receiving little support from opposition members of it in his battle with Sturges Bourne, Charles Ross and Sir Thomas Fremantle. He gave evidence himself from Bristol, 11 Mar. Place was disappointed that the 1829 report had not recommended democratic involvement in parochial government, and bombarded Hobhouse with advice and information as the committee's proceedings drew towards their end. Hobhouse, who presented the new report at half past two on the morning of 2 Apr., when there was 'only one other Member in the House', struggled to prepare a bill during the Easter recess, which he spent with his brother at Send, near Guildford. He admitted that he was 'a good deal embarrassed with technical difficulties, as also the necessity of making the provisions apply to all parishes, small as well as large, rural as well as metropolitan'. He had been obliged to abandon, 'very much against my own inclinations', the 'great principle of giving every rate payer one vote and no more'. He expected that the measure would 'satisfy nobody', but Place, though 'well aware' of his 'difficulties', thought he was 'decidedly wrong in endeavouring to make the bill palatable to the House'. He introduced it on 12 May 1830 and had it read a second time and referred to a committee upstairs on the 20th, with a view to its being printed and held over till next session. It was mutilated there, with plural voting reinstated and the voting qualification for parishes outside London doubled to £20. Hobhouse commented that it was 'a very ungracious task and by no means a labour of love'. The dissolution put an end to the business for the moment.[155]

Hobhouse divided steadily with the revived opposition in the second part of the 1830 session. He was in O'Connell's minorities for reform of Irish vestries, 27 Apr., 10 June. On 28 May he spoke and voted for O'Connell's radical parliamentary reform scheme, declaring his recent conversion to the ballot, and Russell's more moderate plan. Like most opposition Members, he voted for the government's sale of beer bill, 4 May, and would not submit to constituency pressure from licensed victuallers to 'make a stand against selling on the premises'.[156] He complained again about the King's Mews barracks, 30 Apr. On 3 May he divided the House on the issue of giving public access to St. James's Park from Waterloo Place and obtained 123 votes to 139. He presented and endorsed parish petitions for the construction of a new road northwards from Waterloo Bridge, 6, 11 May, and on 4 June criticized ministers for not giving

active support to 'this great national improvement'. He condemned as 'monstrous' the principle of the bill for the removal of Scottish and Irish paupers, whereby the cost was to fall on the relevant parish, 26 May. He voted with O'Connell for papers on the Cork conspiracy trials, 12 May, but after reporters had been cleared from the gallery 'took care to state that I did so not in order to inculpate the [Irish] solicitor-general [John Doherty*] but only on principle'.[157] He spoke and voted against the grant for South American missions, 7 June, and paired that day for abolition of the death penalty for forgery. On the 8th he protested against the 'disgraceful negotiations' which had damaged the Greek cause. He brought up and supported the prayer of a petition of Strand householders for compensation for the chaos created by the slow progress of demolition for the Charing Cross improvements, 21 June. He said that in the next Parliament he would legislate again to tighten the restrictions on child labour in cotton factories, 5 July. Next day he divided with opposition on the regency question, but was 'vexed at voting', which he would not have done had he not been present at the meeting at Althorp's to discuss the matter. When 'we made such a wretched figure' in the division he told Althorp that his prediction of humiliation had been fulfilled. On 7 July he took Hume to task for his 'foolish and stale fallacy' in appealing to electors to return a majority of independent Members at the impending general election, pointing out that 'without some essential change in the system ... [his] object can never be obtained'.[158] He spoke and voted against the libel law amendment bill, 9 July, and was in Brougham's minority of 27 for the abolition of colonial slavery, 13 July 1830.

In early May 1830 Burdett, without consulting Hobhouse, agreed to chair a meeting, ostensibly of the electors of Westminster, got up by James Silk Buckingham† to publicize his grievance against the East India Company. Hobhouse remonstrated with Burdett and made him contact Place to organize a requisition to legitimize the meeting. Hobhouse's brother Henry was a candidate for the East India Company direction, but he felt that this should not deter him from attending, as 'I must fill my own place in Westminster, though I wish Buckingham at the bottom of the sea, for it is a farce and no good will be done to anybody'. On the day of 'the confounded meeting', Burdett developed a convenient illness, and Hobhouse was forced to take the chair. He had 'enough to do to keep the peace', but reckoned that Hunt's 'sly allusions to the Carnatic claims and to younger sons of the aristocracy going to India' evoked no reaction in the audience. In his own speech, he declined to pledge himself 'at all on the matter'.[159] At the sparsely attended Westminster anniversary dinner, 24 May, he explained that he and Burdett had made no parliamentary initiatives on reform because they wished to give new recruits such as Blandford their head. He noted the absence of the disgruntled publicans and reflected that 'unless reform receives some fresh support in Westminster I may as well withdraw myself'. A fortnight later he discovered that one of the leading Westminster activists had 'been intriguing against me amongst my friends'.[160] For over a week from 15 June he was preoccupied with and aggravated by his efforts, which were eventually successful, to secure the 'very shabby shuffling' Hume's nomination for Middlesex at the approaching election. At one point it was suggested that he might stand there (and come in 'without opposition'), but he ruled this out.[161] On 25 June, the day before George IV died, he and Tavistock 'had a great deal of talk on politics' and 'agreed as to the strange inconsistency and weakness of Lord Grey's general conduct, sometimes coquetting with ministers, and then undoing all previous courtship by unreasonable hostility'. A week later he was told by Julia that Lauderdale wished to 'sound me through her brother whether or not I would accept office under the duke of Wellington': 'very likely indeed', he commented in his diary. In mid-July he was 'very much' inclined to agree with Burdett that at the start of the next session they should declare their 'decided' support for the ministry.[162] Matters were well in train for their re-election, but Hobhouse was now very jaundiced about his situation in Westminster: he had replied to the preliminary invitation to stand again, 2 July, in 'terms very measured and without any expressions of gratitude, which I cannot say I feel'. Rumours of opposition persisted, but they came to nothing. On 16 July Hobhouse attended a 'reform meeting' promoted by the radical Colonel Leslie Grove Jones, where he again remonstrated with Hume and confirmed his conversion to the ballot, only to be traduced, as he saw it, in the *Morning Chronicle*. A black man asked him 'whether I was *for* or *against* radical reform', and 'after a great deal of uproar' Hobhouse 'referred him to my speech on O'Connell's motion'. He wrote the Middlesex freeholders' requisition to Hume and his reply, but left the 'common' committee work to Henry Warburton*, who 'cannot write'. On 18 July he was told by his wife's brother Lord Tweeddale that he had heard from ministers that 'there was a wish that I should join the administration, and also take a high place, having liberty however to vote for reform of Parliament and to act in that respect as before'. He gave the same reply as he had to Hay earlier in the month:

Namely that I did not see how such an arrangement was possible, but that it was time enough to give the answer when the proposal was made. I also said that unless Burdett and two or three other independent influential men took the same step, I could be of no use to the government. I should only ruin my own character and not help them.

But when Tweeddale told him that ministers wanted him to replace Goulburn as chancellor of the exchequer, Hobhouse 'burst out laughing' and realized that the whole thing was 'a hoax'. He added that 'if I did support ministers' he would prefer to 'do so without office, or at least with only honorary office', but Tweeddale said 'that would be of no service'. Next day Hobhouse attended a 'very satisfactory' public meeting in Marylebone at which he 'put to rights the misconceptions' about his vestry bill. When Parliament was dissolved on 24 July he wondered if 'my public life is at an end', as the hostile press continued to stir up trouble, but on the 30th the 'astounding and glorious news' of the revolution in France 'drove the thought of tomorrow's election out of my head'. There was no opposition, but his and Burdett's reception was 'anything but flattering', especially from the publicans and 'two or three little knots of malcontents' who hurled cabbage stalks. Hobhouse reckoned that Burdett took the brunt of the criticism and that he was heard in comparative silence as he defended his record in the House and attention to local interests, though there were a few ignorant cries alluding to his support for the anatomy bill and his vestry measure. When all was over, he did not share Burdett's purblind view that all had gone off 'very well', and reflected that 'we cannot in the common sense of the word be called the popular Members for Westminster'.[163]

Hobhouse, who went to assist Hume in the 'odious' Middlesex election before going to join Julia and their infant daughter at Eastbourne, was increasingly enthused by the progress of events in France and, with Burdett, contemplated a visit. Burdett irritated him by including a 'rhodomontade' about France in his address of thanks, having previously agreed to say nothing, which obliged Hobhouse to alter his own address accordingly. On 11 Aug. 1831 he discovered from the papers that Burdett had allowed Buckingham to get up a dinner in Westminster to celebrate the French revolution without consulting the local reformers. Hobhouse alerted the latter, chided Burdett and tried to have it put off, but this proved to be impossible. He went to London for it, 18 Aug., concerted plans beforehand with Burdett and was relieved when it 'went off admirably', with Colonel Jones outmanoeuvred.[164] He shared some of Burdett's alarm at 'the outcry beginning to be raised against the new aristocracy' in France and changed his mind several times about going to Paris. In the end he followed Burdett's example and decided not to go, but, having moved to Brighton on 17 Sept., he wrote for *The Times* an article, signed 'An Old Subscriber', in which he attacked 'the great mass of those who call themselves the Whig party' for failing to support Louis Philippe, defended the new regime and criticized, out of personal pique, Cobbett and Dr. Bowring of the *Westminster Review* for jumping on the French bandwagon; it was published on 7 Oct. 1830.[165]

He spent three weeks with his brother at Send, which intensified his new found 'love of a country, that is an idle life'. Strongly inclined to move an amendment to the address, on 30 Oct. 1830 he went to London in order to take the oath and his seat (with Brougham). He found that 'Brougham and the party are furious against the duke'. Next day he heard from a British officer who had witnessed the fighting horrific tales of 'the atrocities' committed by Dutch soldiers against the civilian population of Belgium after the rising: these included the rape of women 'before their husbands and fathers' and cold blooded killing. The provisional Belgian government sent its representative Vanderweyer to consult with Hobhouse in the first week of November, and the reference in the king's speech to the Belgians as 'revolters', 2 Nov., prompted him next day to give notice for the 12th of a motion for an address to the king on non-interference in Belgian affairs.[166] On 5 Nov. he said that Wellington's declaration against all reform had completed the alienation of the House and country, deplored the prospect of war held out in the address and declared that he must now oppose the government 'systematically'. He conceded that some of O'Connell's activities in Ireland were indefensible, but asserted that he had drawn 'a dreadful picture' of the state of that country. Next day at Brooks's Durham, assuming that the government was doomed, asked him 'whether I would take office under Lord Grey', to which Hobhouse replied that 'a reforming ministry might be joined by any reformer'. On the 7th he dined with Brougham, Graham, Althorp, Smith Stanley, Howick, James Brougham*, Lord Morpeth*, Sir James Macdonald* and Thomas Denman* to discuss tactics. Before they had got far, Thomas De Vear, the chairman of the Westminster committee, and another man arrived to ask if there should be a constituency meeting on Belgium and reform. Hobhouse referred the question to his companions, who voted five to four in favour. Hobhouse, who was against, communicated the result to De Vear, but in the event no meeting took place. It was proposed that Hobhouse

should second Brougham's planned reform motion, 'but it was thought better to try and procure' Edward Littleton. On a report that Palmerston and the liberal Tories would support a 'vaguely worded' reform motion but had declined to 'give a positive answer' concerning Hobhouse's Belgian one, he was pressed to give precedence to Brougham. He 'told them that my constituents naturally expected that I should make some effort ... that my character to a certain degree had been compromised by my previous silence, but that if I could be convinced it would be better for the case of reform that the first division should take place on Brougham's motion I would yield, but I must have another day given up to me'. Brougham offered to give him his 'slavery day'. Hobhouse reckoned that nothing was absolutely settled, but promised a final answer next day. According to his diary, he was for Brougham's 'dealing in generalities and confessing fairly that he did so in order to extract from the House the opinion whether or not the old system should be persevered in', but he added that 'the people would not be satisfied except *all* nomination [boroughs] were done away with'. He 'ventured to expostulate with Brougham on his eulogy of the aristocracy and begged him to have recourse to no such topic in his reform speech, not because the sentiment was incorrect, but because the people did not like to hear one of their principal champions recite the language of the corruptionists'. He left the meeting, where he 'took care to declare more than once that I was no Whig', convinced that 'these men are utterly ignorant of the state of the country, and will persevere deliberating on the miseries of petty political factions till the storm burst over them, and all is lost with them and the country'. In the House, 8 Nov., he insisted that there was no 'disaffection' among the people of the metropolis sufficient to warrant ministers' decision to cancel the king's visit to the City. At the request of Althorp and Brougham, he agreed to postpone his motion on Belgium to 18 Nov., but in doing so made some observations on the base intentions of the Holy Alliance.[167] His brother-in-law Hay criticized him privately for 'blackguarding' Wellington in the House.[168] On 13 Nov. he attended a large party meeting at Althorp's, where Brougham expounded his reform plan and Hobhouse recommended him to 'say as little as possible ... for fear of frightening the moderate reformers'. He divided in the decisive majority against the government on the civil list, 15 Nov. 1830, and immediately afterwards 'unwisely', as he later admitted, asked them if they intended to resign, but Brougham stepped in to prevent any unpleasantness. He regarded their resignation next day as '*le commencement de la fin*', but on the 17th was peeved to learn that some Whigs affected to be angry with him 'for pushing ministers' on the 15th.[169]

On 18 Nov. 1830, when Grey was forming his ministry, Hobhouse withdrew the notice of his motion on Belgium, 'as it would have been absurd to bring it forward in the present state of the House', quite apart from the fact that the Belgians now seemed to be 'contented with the assurances of the Allies'. He had qualms about the letter of support to Grey which Burdett, who had seen the new premier the day before, showed him before sending it, but did not press the issue. Next evening he found a note from Durham, the lord privy seal, who had told him earlier in the day that Grey 'based his administration on reform ... and next on retrenchment', indicating that the prime minister 'would like to see me the next day'. He duly presented himself at Downing Street at 12.30 on the 20th, but, after seeing only Howick, who asked if he wanted to see his father, was left alone for an hour and a half. He was on the verge of stalking out when Howick returned and expressed 'surprise' at his still being there. Hobhouse explained about Durham's note, and when Durham himself appeared begged him not to let Grey know he was there but to tell him he had called because he had been invited and was always at Grey's disposal. He thought that Howick and Durham 'seemed much annoyed', but he 'bore this accident, as I suppose it was ... with equanimity ... though of course I could not help being inwardly annoyed'. Before he left Durham confided to him that Grey, who had 'the highest possible opinion' of his 'capacity', had wished to know 'whether there was any situation' which he would like. Hobhouse did not respond, and resolved to act as if the 'strange misadventure' had arisen from Grey's forgetfulness in the press of business, rather than an attempt 'to entrap me into an apparent acquiescence in the new government' or a calculated snub.[170] On 21 Nov., at Brooks's, he concurred in criticism of Grey's shameless nepotism in his ministerial appointments, especially that of his brother-in-law Ellice as patronage secretary, but agreed with Tavistock that 'Grey ought not to meet any difficulties from us, especially on personal grounds'.[171] He presented petitions from South Shields for reform of the church establishment, from the parish authorities of St. Clement's against the Metropolitan Police Act and from individuals for repeal of the house and window taxes, 2 Nov. He also gave notice that after the Christmas recess he would reintroduce his vestry bill. He was less than pleased when a deputation from metropolitan parishes voiced to him their objection to 'the essential clause' of his measure, 3 Dec.: 'so all my labour has been in

vain – the fate of most men who try to reconcile contending interests'.[172] After the appointment of the select committee on public salaries, 9 Dec., when he thought there was 'a great deal of nonsense talked', he told Charles Wood*, Grey's secretary, that he 'did not much like the constitution of the committee as being composed too much of anti-reductionists', and next day Althorp had him and 'Bum' Gordon added to it.[173] On 13 Dec., in 'a sort of profession of faith', he conceded that the Wellington ministry had gone 'as far as the corrupt system of this House and of the constitution of the government allowed them' in economy and retrenchment, but said that the duke's fateful declaration against reform had revealed his ignorance of the recent dramatic change in public opinion, which was

> running in a current which cannot be opposed by the present government ... [or] by any who may follow them. I have no doubt that the present ministers mean well ... I have had the felicity of knowing them privately, and I see what is their course in their public duty ... Having every reason to repose confidence in them, I will not withhold it (till I see grounds for believing that I am mistaken) and thus run the risk of embarrassing measures which, I think, will tend to the common good.[174]

He supported the prayer of the City petition for repeal of the coastwise coal duties, 14 Dec., but dissented from Wilson's view that this could only be financed by the introduction of a property tax. He was 'angry, more than was wise', when two Westminster activists 'called to remonstrate' with him for not presenting a St. John's parish petition for vestry reform the previous night. He then went to the Middlesex county reform meeting at Hackney, where he proposed the third resolution, for a householder and ratepayer suffrage (making clear his personal preference for universal), called for confidence to be placed in the new ministers on reform and retrenchment and silenced ignorant criticism of his father's supposed sinecure. He was 'well received', but thought 'the Middlesex men' were in much the same bad humour as his 'Westminster friends, though Heaven knows the cause of their discontent'. He was concerned that Jones and the extremists were 'evidently hostile to us, and ... to the whole frame of society'. He duly presented and endorsed the St. John's vestry reform petition next day, explaining that at the behest of his constituents he had restored his original provision for a single vote for every qualified ratepayer, and intended to let the measure stand or fall as it was. He had a satisfactory meeting on the subject in St. James's, 17 Dec., and noted that 'the good folks were much pleased, and so they ought to be!' He promised to send Place a copy of the bill as soon as it was drafted.[175] On the Middlesex reform petition, 21 Dec., he put the case for the ballot, which would safeguard electors against the exercise of 'undue influence', attacked the Tory opposition for asserting that ministers had held out unattainable expectations to the country and argued that 'the old appellations of Whig and Tory should be forgotten, and the only distinguishing title of parties now should be Reformers and anti-Reformers'. On 23 Dec. 1830 he mentioned to Althorp, now chancellor of the exchequer and leader of the Commons, with whom had 'a long talk ... on currency', that at his recent re-election the war secretary Charles Williams Wynn had 'declared against parliamentary reform', but Althorp persuaded him not to mention it in the House. He had take a lease for eight weeks on a house at 1 Herring Court, Richmond, Surrey, where he spent most of the recess, working on his vestry bill and reading the second volume of Moore's *Life of Byron*, with which he was not much enamoured. He attended a meeting of parochial delegates at the *Freemasons' Tavern*, 20 Jan. 1831, when his bill was 'discussed clause by clause', and he then 'framed it exactly to their wishes, but told them honestly it had no chance of passing'. He privately thought that 'if we are to have capital punishment at all' he could think of no 'malefactors more deserving of it' than the 'Swing' rioters recently convicted before the special commissions. He was willing to chair a meeting of the Westminster liverymen of London in favour of the candidature of Waithman for the chamberlainship, which was being opposed by Hume, but this project was abandoned.[176] On 1 Feb. 1831 he received from Althorp an invitation to a 'parliamentary dinner' next day, but he made an excuse, 'as I considered it a meeting of Members notoriously supporting the administration, amongst which number I do not choose to be ranked. I am a friend but no follower, nor ought a Member for Westminster to be'. He felt 'certain that the ministers or their retainers would be glad enough to secure me or anyone by the cheapest of favours'. He declined another such invitation on 13 Feb. 1831.[177]

He brought in his new vestry bill, which was far more radical than the previous one, on 8 Feb. 1831. He defended it on its successful second reading, 21 Feb., and had it committed, reported and printed, 28 Feb., but it was overtaken by the early dissolution. On 14 Feb. he advocated a 'graduated property tax' and said that many of Althorp's budget tax proposals, especially the controversial stock transfer tax, would 'not have the effect intended'. He accompanied a deputation of calico tradesmen to Althorp, 23 Feb., noting that he 'did not seem to know much about the matter but ... did not give in' to their demands.[178] On 17 Feb.

he introduced a bill to restrict the factory hours of apprentices under 18 to eleven and a half per day. It was referred to a select committee, 14 Mar., but lapsed with the dissolution.[179] On 15 Feb., at the salaries committee, he witnessed the examination of Brougham, now lord chancellor. In the House he made a speech, 'not a bad one', on the 'extravagant tastes' of George IV and the 'enormous expense' of Windsor Castle and Buckingham House refurbishments. He thought the disastrous budget would have brought the ministry down but for anticipation of the reform scheme and Brougham's projected chancery reforms.[180] He presented and endorsed several reform petitions, 14 Feb., and said that the ballot was 'absolutely and indispensably necessary', 26 Feb. He (and the rest of 'the Mountain', as he later recalled) 'cheered long and loud' when Russell revealed the government's reform proposals to an astonished House, 1 Mar., but both he and Burdett thought there was 'very little chance of the measure being carried, and that a revolution would be the consequence'. Nor did they think that Place and the Westminster reformers would be satisfied with it, especially the proposed £10 borough franchise, but they were pleasantly surprised to find next day that Place was 'charmed with the reform of ministers, and says that all our friends are equally so'. In the House, 3 Mar., after rebuking Sir Henry Hardinge for calling the scheme 'revolutionary', he delivered a major speech in its support and, apologizing to Peel 'for my exultation on the day of his being beaten out of office', appealed to him to 'become a reformer'. At the Westminster reform meeting got up by Place, 4 Mar., Hobhouse was involved in the turn of events by which Place's resolutions in favour of the ballot and short parliaments were thrown out for an address to the king and a petition to Parliament 'simply in support of ... ministers' and their plan; this episode was not forgotten by the more extreme Westminster activists. When Greville congratulated him on the success of his Commons speech, 7 Mar., he asked him 'if he thought it would be carried', and Hobhouse replied that 'he did not like to think it would not, for he was desirous of keeping what he had, and he was persuaded he should lose it if the bill were rejected'. On 5 Mar. he dined at the Speaker's 'at a mixed ministerial party', for the first time ...[since] I had been in Parliament'.[181] On 6 Mar. Williams Wynn indicated that he must resign because he could not support the reform scheme. Next day, when a paragraph appeared in the *Chronicle* stating that Hobhouse was to replace him, Durham asked him, supposedly on behalf of Grey, whether he would accept office if it was offered to him. Hobhouse confirmed his wholehearted support for the reform

bills, said he would 'consider myself much complimented by any proposal' from Grey and that he would
have to consult 'two or three' leading Westminster
men, but 'doubted very little their acquiescence'. He
begged Durham to keep this confidential and not to
give Grey the impression that he was soliciting a place.
He later reflected:

> Had I wished to make office my object I ought to have
> taken a different course and said at once that if the
> place was offered to me I would take it. But I have by
> no means made up my mind to do any such thing and
> moreover I am not quite sure that Lord Durham is a safe
> man. Perhaps the place might not be offered to me and
> ... [Durham] might give out that I applied for it. Under
> these circumstances I took the prudent as well as the
> honourable course.

In fact Durham, with the blessing of Althorp, wrote
that night to Grey urging 'the great advantage of
securing Hobhouse', whose appointment and re-
election for Westminster would 'show that in practice
the government would find no difficulty in getting
the re-election of their members for populous places'
in a reformed Parliament. He added that taking him
in would be 'very gratifying to a numerous party to
whom as yet you have show no attention and who have
supported us most manfully even before our reform
bill', and would bring some much needed 'energy'
and 'power of speaking' to the treasury bench. He
also made the dubious assertion that 'as a man of business you could not find one more efficient'. On 9 Mar.
Hobhouse was bullied by Burdett, who decided at the
last minute that he could not go, into taking the chair at
a dinner given to 'the Polish would-be envoy Marquess
Wielopolski', 'an untimely and useless parade' which
Burdett, with his usual 'indiscretion', had sanctioned
without consulting anyone else. The event passed
off 'with less than the usual nonsense talked'. On 12
Mar. Durham told Hobhouse that he had secured the
approval of Grey and Althorp to offer him the war secretaryship, but that the 'unlucky Polish dinner' had
made it 'impossible' to appoint him, as 'the Russians
would take it as a decided proof of hostility to them'.
Hobhouse explained the circumstances, but Durham
said that there was nothing to be done, though the fuss
might 'blow over' by the time Williams Wynn formally resigned after the second reading of the English
reform bill. Hobhouse wrote in his diary next day:

> I made as light of the business as possible and never told
> him whether or not I would have accepted the place ...
> It is true that I had foreseen when I went to the dinner
> that such an uncalled for demonstration of opinion might
> stand in the way of this appointment ... but I resolved to
> go at all risks ... Nevertheless I cannot but think that the

dinner is made the pretext and cannot be the real cause
of the exclusion. There must be some objection to me
for any office or for this particular office quite independent of my expressed opinions in favour of the Poles ...
However, whatever may be the cause I ought not to be
dissatisfied with the result for I maintain my independence and run no risk of showing myself unfit for business. Add to this my health is much on the decline and
a constant attendance at the Horse Guards would have
hastened the decay.[182]

He dined at Downing Street with Althorp, 12, and
Grey, 'an over-anxious man, more in manner perhaps
than in action', 19 Mar. Place tried to involve him
in the newly formed Parliamentary Candidates
Society, of which his brother Thomas was a committee member, but he seems not to have responded. He
presented and endorsed Westminster petitions for the
reform bills, 15, 19, 28 Mar. He divided silently for the
second reading of the English bill, 22 Mar.[183] After the
debate on the civil list, 25 Mar., when ministers 'got
into a hobble' by proposing more than recommended
by the select committee, he noted that 'nothing but
reform can give these men a chance of keeping their
ground'. On the 30th he accused Goulburn of giving 'a
false notion' of what had been decided by the salaries
committee. That day the appointment of Sir Henry
Parnell as war secretary was confirmed, and Hobhouse
observed privately that 'he is a much better man *there*
than I should have been; but I am a better man in the
House, at least so far as speaking goes'.[184] On 3 Apr.,
when he again dined with Grey, he had 'a long talk'
with Durham, who said that he had been passed over
for the war secretaryship because 'I should be obliged
to explain government proceedings on Westminster
hustings or to Westminster committees, but made no
mention of the Polish dinner'. He then

> told me I might do anything ... He wished me to come
> forward again on the reform bill and show how service-
> able I could be to the government. I told him that a man
> out of office had not the same right to defend govern-
> ment nor the same opportunity as one in place and that I
> had no scruple in saying that under Lord Grey I should
> have no objection to serve, in a proper situation. As for
> the secretaryship at war, it was ... the most unfit place for
> me. Lord Durham said, 'Oh, it was only *pour commencer*,
> you would not stop there'. He again urged me to take a
> prominent part in the ensuing debates, and confessed the
> inability of the present treasury bench. I talked very con-
> fidentially with him, but not more so than was prudent
> ... I see no reason why a man like myself should not
> accept office or even should not endeavour to obtain it,
> after witnessing such unequivocal proof of honesty in the
> government.[185]

Hobhouse, who received Althorp's circular letter requesting attendance after Easter and thought that 'that rogue and fool' Hunt was 'playing into the hands of the Tories, by stating that the people are beginning to be against the bill', 'spoke for the first time in my life from behind the treasury bench' when refuting William Bankes's allegation that political partiality had secured the preservation of Lansdowne's borough of Calne, 15 Apr.[186] He voted against Gascoyne's successful wrecking amendment to the reform bill, 19 Apr., and witnessed the angry scenes in the Commons when Peel lost control of himself as Black Rod arrived to summon Members to the Lords for the dissolution, 22 Apr.[187] His re-election with Burdett, adroitly stage managed by De Vear and the committee, was a triumph. At the Westminster meeting called to address the king and thank him for dissolving Parliament, 26 Apr., they were 'received as in the old time, and gave the boroughmongers a dressing'. They went in procession 'in an open barouche' to the Covent Garden hustings, 2 May, when torrential rain did not dampen 'the utmost good humour' of the crowd, though it drowned much of his speech.[188] Hobhouse was active in the promotion of the Loyal and Patriotic Fund to assist reformers at the elections, but his involvement inevitably entailed a clash with Place, who badgered him to put the case for paying £100 to Colonel George De Lacy Evans* for his unsuccessful attempt, encouraged by Hobhouse, to dish Hunt at Preston, and John Nicholson for his abortive intervention at Dover.[189] On 3 May, as he was preparing to go to Cambridge to vote in the University election, he was informed by Hardinge that Peel had taken exception to some of his remarks in his *Crown and Anchor* speech on 26 Apr. and wanted satisfaction. The affair was settled amicably by their intermediaries.[190] He rejoiced in the reformers' success at the elections, which he celebrated with Burdett and their supporters at the Westminster anniversary dinner, 23 May 1831, when a 'festival' atmosphere prevailed.[191]

Hobhouse received Althorp's letter requesting attendance on 21 June 1831 a week later, but by then his life had been clouded by the first serious symptoms of the consumption which was to kill Julia in 1835. An 'all but fatal' verdict was pronounced on her by the doctors in mid-June, but this was kept from her, and she recovered to a degree as the summer wore on. But when he attended the Commons for the re-election of the Speaker, taking a seat on the 'bench behind the treasury', 14 June, he was thinking 'of home' and 'how changed [it had become] since I was last in ... [the] House'. To add to his worries, his father was dying in his 'house of sickness and sorrow' at 42

Berkeley Square. Hobhouse decided that he had to act as if he had 'nothing but politics' on his mind and to 'plunge into the business of the session' as a necessary 'distraction'.[192] He reintroduced his amended cotton factories regulation bill, 4 July. It generated much controversy, and in the end he altered it to apply only to factories where children under 18 had a 12-hour day: it also prohibited night work for persons under 21 and obliged employers to keep a record book of hours. It became law on 15 Oct. 1831 (1 & 2 Gul. IV, c. 39), but disappointed provincial factory reformers. Hobhouse explained and defended his conduct in a letter to the *Leeds Mercury*, 5 Nov. 1831.[193] He announced that he would probably reintroduce his vestry reform bill, 30 June, and, after consulting parish meetings of his constituents, he did so on 29 July. In committee on it, 30 Sept., he resisted Althorp's amendment to require a two-thirds majority for decisions, but was beaten by 67-37. However, when he complained that those who had 'most wished' him to bring in the bill would now probably 'ask me to withdraw it', Althorp agreed to a compromise of three-fifths. Hobhouse accepted two years as the time limit for lawful requisitions, but forced Vyvyan to withdraw his amendment to restore plural voting according to wealth and a bid to impose a £20 qualification for Bristol. He carried the third reading by 38-8, 5 Oct. The measure emerged not entirely unscathed, but 'changed ... part clumsily and partly for the better' from a House of Lords distracted by reform and became law 20 on Oct. 1831 (1 & 2 Gul. IV, c. 60). It now applied to open as well as closed vestries, represented a significant step towards the democratization of local government and was Hobhouse's most lasting achievement as a politician: he thought it 'a very great reform'.[194]

He voted for the second reading of the reintroduced reform bill, 6 July 1831. On the 9th he attended the 'very splendid' Mansion House banquet in honour of Russell. Worried about Julia, he took a pair and left the House before the protracted series of divisions on the opposition motions for adjournment, 12 July. He voted fairly steadily for the details of the disfranchisement and enfranchisement clauses, 19 July-5 Aug., but did not speak until 3 Aug., when, cajoled by Althorp into removing his 'muzzle', he delivered from 'the third bench behind the treasury' what Littleton thought was 'a good speech' for the enfranchisement of Greenwich. In the course of it he urged the Lords to ponder well the consequences of rejecting a measure passed by the Commons and endorsed by overwhelming public support. He later wrote that this 'effort' was 'by far the most successful I had ever made' and contributed towards the government's unexpectedly large majority on the potentially vulnerable case of the metropolitan districts.[195] On 10 Aug. he voted against joining Merthyr Tydvil with Cardiff and 'said a few words to put down' Sir Edward Sugden, who talked of reform Members being 'dragged to the vote'. He was, however, alarmed by 'dissensions ... among our friends' on Ireland, and told Althorp 'what I thought of Stanley's tone' towards O'Connell and Richard Sheil*. As he left the House he received a note from Julia telling him that his father was 'much worse', and next day he arranged to obtain a fortnight's leave of absence. His father died on the 14th, and was buried in the vault of St. Mark's chapel, North Audley Street on 22 Aug. By his will of 17 Feb. 1830 Hobhouse, now of course a baronet, succeeded to the landed estates and received a share of his mother's marriage settlement of £14,000 and a £25,000 share in Whitbread's. He proved the will at about £230,000 on 27 Aug., and in 1832 benefited as residuary legatee to the tune of £109,093. He realized that if the brewery continued to prosper, the Whitbread shares would 'ensure me a large income, larger than I know what to do with', but he counted 'on nothing in these uncertain times' and partook 'a little in the panic which the Tories are sedulously raising'. On 3 Sept. he was at a 'very dull' dinner at Althorp's in Downing Street.[196] On 7 Sept. he stayed in the Commons to see the reform bill come out of committee. He attended and addressed a Westminster meeting to petition the Lords to pass it, 21 Sept., and voted for the passage of the measure through the Commons later that day. He accompanied Russell to the Lords with the bill, 22 Sept., voted for the second reading of the Scottish bill, 23 Sept., and attended the dinner to ministers at Stationers' Hall on the 24th. He signed the requisition for the Wiltshire reform meeting, 30 Sept. 1831.[197]

Having assured Ebrington that he would not use 'violent language' in debate if the Lords rejected the bill, he joined his family at Brighton on 7 Oct. 1831 and learned of the defeat next day. On the 10th he went to London, where he attended the mass Westminster meeting at the *Crown and Anchor*, 'the largest meeting I ever saw there', and, borrowing the words of Thomas Attwood[†] of the Birmingham Political Union, 'preached patience'. He went to the House to vote for Ebrington's confidence motion, but he thought young Macaulay's speech went 'somewhat near the wind on the intimidation side' and told him so. When he attended Court to present various metropolitan electors' addresses to the king in support of the ministry and reform, he was 'surprised on going into the streets to find the shops shut and a great many ill-looking and ill-dressed people standing about': 'there

was something in the look and manners of the crowds' which he 'did not like'. On the 13th he chaired a parish meeting of St. George, which was attended by the Tory 'Waverer' Lord Wharncliffe. In the House that day he dismissed a Tory's complaint that householders of St. James's had breached privilege by threatening to withhold payment of rates and taxes until reform was secured.[198] On 11 Oct. 'my friend Place', who did not trust Grey and his colleagues to persevere with reform, sent him a long letter reprimanding him for 'having preached patience to the people yesterday'. Hobhouse replied that he too had 'occasionally very great apprehensions', but he thought Place's 'gloomy' prognostications of a revolution were unfounded and that 'the instinctive good sense and good feeling of the great mass of the community' would prevent convulsion. He reiterated his faith in 'the intentions of ministers', not doubting 'their resolution or capacity to do what is right, so far as reform is concerned'. On 17 Oct. Grey's letter to Hobhouse promising 'an equally efficient reform bill in the next Parliament' was published in the press, but this did not satisfy Place and 'the impatient metropolitans', who organized of a deputation of delegates to wait on Grey and badger him on standing firm, which did not please the harassed and irritable premier. Hobhouse could understand their anxiety, but was privately appalled.[199] He maintained his deliberately moderate stance as the provincial reform riots raged, steering clear of Place's National Political Union, in which Burdett unhappily embroiled himself, and the short-lived Westminster Reform Association, which was killed off by the government's proclamation of 5 Nov. He foresaw 'a squabble amongst our Westminster friends, which, if reform does not take place, will probably break them up and cost me my seat'. He professed to be 'more than indifferent, for I think I should like an honest excuse for quitting public life – at least as M.P. for Westminster. I know I have done my duty, and if others do not think so, I cannot help it'.[200]

Hobhouse had 'a terribly tedious drive' from Hastings to London for the introduction of the revised English reform bill, 12 Dec. 1831. He thought Russell's speech was 'not well done', but was pleased to find that the measure was 'neither more nor less than the old ... in all its essential principles, and ... more radical, if anything'. His 'friends' pressed him 'very much' to speak in the debate on the second reading, 17 Dec., but he cast a silent vote. He supplied Smith Stanley with materials for his crushing attack on Croker that evening.[201] On 15 Dec. 1831 he obtained leave to bring in a bill to remove a practical difficulty in the way of implementation of his Vestry Act, in that 'parochial taxes' had not been properly defined. On 22 Jan 1832 he went to London for the session and settled in his father's Berkleley Square house, which he had rented from his stepmother for her lifetime. He explained his vestry amendment bill when moving the second reading, 23 Jan., asserting that as it stood the Act was inoperable, but it was 'violently' opposed by a number of Members, including, to his surprise a 'tipsy' George Lamb, and rejected by 44-40, with a number of senior ministers in the majority. He complained in his diary that they 'knew nothing of the state of the question'. Hume supported him and attacked ministers, but not without expressing a '*regret*' to Hobhouse that he had not waited for 'a larger House'. In practice, the loss of the bill proved to be largely immaterial.[202] Hobhouse evidently missed the divisions on the principles of schedules A and B of the reform bill, 20, 23 Jan. According to Greville, who got it from the 'Waverer' Lord Harrowby's son Lord Sandon*, he spoke to the latter after the angry debate on the 23rd and 'said how anxious he was they should come to some understanding, and act in a greater spirit of conciliation, and talked of a meeting of the moderate men on either side'. Before he voted with government on the Russian-Dutch loan, 26 Jan., he was assured by Place that there was much 'apathy' and 'disgust' among 'the people'. On the 28th Macdonald and Macaulay told him that the government 'could not stand with the present treasury bench' and that he 'must come into office'; he agreed that 'ministers did seem to want assistance'.[203] On 29 Jan. the full cabinet decided that Parnell had to be dismissed as war secretary for failing to vote on the Russian-Dutch loan and that the place should be offered to Hobhouse, though there was some apprehension that the king's 'exhortation to abstain from popular names seems to threaten some obstacle'. Holland believed that Hobhouse was 'as unlikely a man to be intractable in office as any I know and more likely to run the career, though with superior talents and taste, of his father from demagogue to ministerialist, from ministerialist to placeman, and from placeman to courtier, than to embarrass any government he is connected with [by] any austere notion of retrenchment or any visionary plans of reform'. Grey wrote to the king (at Brighton) seeking his sanction for the offer to be made, stressing that Hobhouse was well qualified to 'defend the measures connected with the establishment of the army against the attack which will be directed against it, more especially by ... Parnell'. He conceded that Hobhouse had 'been formerly engaged in active scenes of popular contention', but said he had 'the strongest assurances that his present views are moderate and just, that he

disapproves of many of the measures of the candidates for popular favour, which he has proved by refusing to belong to the Westminster Union' and that he could be relied on not to rock the boat. The king readily gave his blessing, noting Hobhouse's recent conspicuous moderation and his 'advantage of being of an old and respectable family'.[204] On the morning of 31 Jan. Althorp summoned Hobhouse to Downing Street and made him the offer. His immediate response was that he needed a little time to consider and to consult his leading supporters in Westminster. Althorp assented, told him confidentially that ministers 'would carry the reform bill but were not likely to be permanent' and added that the offer came with the approval of all the cabinet and the sanction of the king. When Hobhouse said that this office was 'the least agreeable place he could offer me', Althorp agreed, but said it was 'a high office, and they had no other to give'. He brushed aside the problem of Hobhouse's commitment to oppose army flogging and doubts as to his capacity for administration. An hour later Durham reiterated all this, observing that 'the office would only be a step to a more important position, and that no one would be promoted over my head'. Hobhouse, who was inclined to accept, though not without misgivings, interpreted this as an assurance that he was to get the first cabinet office that came vacant. He consulted Burdett, who was decidedly in favour of acceptance, De Vear, who took the same line and said 'Westminster will be pleased', and Place, who was less enthusiastic but concluded that 'it would do good to the people'. He accepted the offer in the evening. Next day he saw Grey, who read him part of the king's letter, gave him 'some hints as to the nature and duty of my office' and urged him to 'keep up a good understanding' with the commander-in-chief Lord Hill and the officials at Horse Guards.[205] Hobhouse, who was advised by Tavistock to preserve his health under the weight of departmental business by 'taking a trot on the roughest bone-shaker you can get, for an hour, at least, every morning', included in his draft reply to the formal invitation from Westminster the phrase 'an administration determined and as I have every assurance able to bring ... [the reform plan] to a happy conclusion', but he showed it first to Althorp, who advised him to omit the reference to 'ability'. He asked him 'several important questions and got satisfactory answers'. At his swearing-in and kissing of hands, 6 Feb., when the king was 'very, very kind' and spoke fondly of his father, he seemed to Holland to be 'mightily tickled with his appointment and honours'. His re-election, 8 Feb., went off quietly. In his speech of thanks, he said he would back ministers 'so long as they were supporting reform and support them as I had the popular cause ... *not by halves* but without caviling at little faults, constantly and unremittingly'. He remained (rightly as it turned out) doubtful as to 'my being any great accession' to government 'as active debater and man of business in Parliament', and felt that 'too much is expected of me, that is certain'.[206] Raikes saw his appointment as 'a bold ... measure'. In the House, 10 Feb., Hunt expressed his pleasure that there was now a minister 'who knows what it is to be sent to gaol'; and Littleton recorded a ludicrous episode at the Speaker's dinner, 11 Feb., when Hobhouse turned up 'in his new official uniform. Some one said, "Hobhouse, who made your coat?" The attorney-general answered for him, "Place"'. Hardinge interpreted his appointment as a sign that 'the ministers are sure of the king and mean to use him to create peers'.[207] In fact, Hobhouse came close to resigning on this very issue less than a week after his formal appointment. He had been alarmed on 5 Feb. by Durham's hint that 'all was not right as to the bill', and told him that 'I had a character to lose, and if I had been deceived as to the resolution of carrying the bill, I had also deceived my constituents and the public', and 'added that I would quit office the moment I knew there was any hesitation'. Other members of the cabinet reassured him, but he remained aware of 'doubts on the great question of creating peers' to carry the bill through the Lords, and on 11 Feb. Howick surprised him by telling him that his father was decidedly averse to 'swamping the peerage'. He asked Hobhouse to see Grey and to make him aware of 'the consequences of rejecting the bill'. Hobhouse, who would have preferred a party meeting for this purpose, wondered if Grey had taken up reform 'as a toy which he might break or lay down again'. He went to Burdett, who, 'equally shocked', advised him to 'resign office instantly, upon discovering that there was any intention of risking the bill'. At the Speaker's dinner later that day he urged on Charles Grant*, a member of the cabinet, the 'necessity of creating peers at once' and said he would see Grey next day and resign if he was 'not assured that the bill was to be carried'. On the 12th he first saw Durham, who informed him that he had told Grey that he too would resign unless the bill was made safe in the Lords. But what Durham said of Grey's views did not seem to tally with Howick's account, and Hobhouse, perplexed, went to Althorp to seek 'some positive reassurance in regard to carrying the reform bill'. Althorp assured him that he and Brougham would resign if there was no moral certainty of carrying the measure, but that ministers wished if possible to avoid a large creation. Hobhouse retorted that this was not possible

and insisted on having 'an engagement which could not be violated'. A further long talk with Althorp, who impressed Hobhouse with his unaffected sincerity, did not entirely appease him, but on 13 Feb. Durham gave him 'a satisfactory account of a correspondence now going on between the king and Lord Grey' on the issue. Yet nine days later Durham was 'again in the greatest alarm at the delay in making peers', and Hobhouse 'begged ... [him to] let me know in time to save myself, for as the coach was to be upset I should certainly jump off first'. Graham, first lord of the admiralty, gave him a desponding view of the state of play, 2 Mar., but Althorp made light of this. On 3 Mar., however, he was more pessimistic, and inclined to resign if the bill went to its second reading in the Lords without a prior guarantee of a creation. Hobhouse pressed Althorp to 'abide by this determination' in order to try bring his wavering cabinet colleagues into line. That day he wrote to Thomas Kennedy*, who had recently taken office:

> Our country's prospects ... at present ... are most gloomy, and I do not conceal from myself that those who are on the street side of the door are more enviable than the inmates of a tottering house. But I am sure that both of us have done what is right ... To be a public man at all is to be exposed to some, and indeed in these times no little danger, and the difference between our peril and that of less apparent politicians is hardly worth a thought.[208]

In the House, 13 Feb., Hobhouse, in his official capacity, defended the grant of £1,000 for a survey of the metropolitan water supply and denied Hume's charge that it was 'a job and a juggle'. His only known votes on details of the reform bill were on the cases of Appleby, 21 Feb., Tower Hamlets, and Gateshead, 5 Mar. He clashed with Sugden and Wetherell over their obstructive resistance to the measure, 16 Feb. On 10 Mar. it was rumoured that if Althorp was sent to the Lords to handle the bill there, Smith Stanley would become chancellor of the exchequer and Hobhouse replace him as Irish secretary. This speculation continued for three weeks, and Hobhouse himself was aware of it.[209] On 10 Mar. Althorp informed him that he had failed to persuade the cabinet to secure a promise of a creation of peers before the second reading and that he was considering whether or not to resign. Hobhouse 'went away pondering my own position, whether I ought to resign now, for I see the bill is to be risked'. He told Ellice on 12 Mar. that the ministers were 'mad' not to insist on a creation, and next day was informed by Durham and Russell of the continuing disagreement within the cabinet and uncertainty as to the fate of the bill in the Lords.[210] On 22 Mar. 1832 he delivered a major speech of one and a half hours in support of the third reading of the bill:

> I made a strong attack on Peel and his party and put them into a violent rage, but although I was a great deal cheered and some of the speech was good, yet I was not pleased with myself. Nor did my colleagues much like it. I hear from ... Howick ... that ... Grey liked it, and Macaulay praised it ... It was not so good as I could have made it had I not been really very unwell and forgot some of my best points.

Althorp considered it 'too much a hustings speech'.[211]

Hobhouse was uncomfortable in his office. Tavistock warned him that he would 'find it difficult to keep pace with Graham' at the admiralty, but that 'we shall look to you for great reductions' and a reform of 'the expensive and complicated machinery by which our army is governed'. He accepted Hobhouse's disclosure that the unsettled state of Ireland and the continent made it impossible to reduce the size of the army at present, but welcomed his enthusiasm for administrative reform and retrenchment.[212] On 16 Feb. 1832, before Hobhouse appeared in the House, Hunt moved unsuccessfully for information on military flogging and alluded to his absence. Later Hobhouse, goaded by Wetherell, reaffirmed his hostility to flogging, but said he would have opposed Hunt's motion because he had given no reason for furnishing the information. Having 'crammed' himself intensively, he brought in the army estimates for the first quarter of the year, 17 Feb. He explained that he was not personally responsible for them, but agreed with his predecessor that the army could not be reduced and pointed out that the total estimate was £684,000 less than in 1820. Hume carped and quibbled, but Hobhouse, who now discovered that 'there was no arguing with this gentleman', stuck to his guns; he was reasonably pleased with his performance. He came up with a scheme for reducing the colonial force and some other minor reforms and enlisted Althorp's aid in selling it to Grey. But when he presented the plan to Hill and Lord Fitzroy Somerset*, the military secretary at the war office, as the proposal of the cabinet, he ran into trouble, for Hill complained to Althorp, who rebuked Hobhouse for going 'a little too far' in taking this approach. Goderich, the colonial secretary, also went bleating to Althorp, and Hobhouse, 'highly indignant', replied uncompromisingly and half expected to be turned out. He felt as though he had been appointed on a whim and left to 'sink or swim'. On 7 Mar. he tackled Grey directly on the colonial reductions, but the premier peremptorily dismissed him with the observation that no cuts were possible. A week later, at the levee, he got the king's back up with suggestions for change, including making Sandhurst self-supporting, and irritated Hill with a sarcastic remark.[213] On 28 Mar. he dined at four with Althorp 'on his leg of mutton' and went down to the House to bring in his own army estimates for the next year, with 'not above 30 Members present'. He explained that recent events in the West Indies and elsewhere had scuppered his plans for reductions. He was criticized by 'shabby' Parnell, Davies, Hume and Hunt, and supported by Althorp and Hardinge, whose 'very civil' speech he appreciated. In his reply he said that he was 'in rather a hard situation' and disputed Parnell's claim to have left him a 'plan of reduction'. He concluded privately that 'though I did my best, I was in no very pleasant predicament', and admitted that he found Parnell's 'suggestions ... in many respects quite reasonable, and I did not know what answer to give to them'. On 2 Apr. he replied to Hardinge's criticism of army pension arrangements and gave an assurance that he was keen to improve the provisions for soldiers now serving abroad but also to prevent fraud. In committee on the mutiny bill, Hunt proposed to omit corporal punishment. Hobhouse 'felt very uncomfortable, but felt it best to tell the exact truth', namely that 'I was as much against flogging as ever, that all the authorities I had consulted were on the other side, and that as I did not frame the mutiny bill I could not help the continuance of the practice'. Hardinge made 'something like an attack' on him, observing that he was the responsible minister, and Hobhouse again 'felt in a very unpleasant predicament, which I had foreseen when I took office, for though not in fact the framer of the mutiny bill I am in form the minister who ought to defend it, and if I cannot defend it I ought to give up my office'. To his surprise and relief, for he 'hardly' knew 'how I could have brought myself to vote against him', Hunt did not divide the House.[214] On 4 Apr. 1832 Hobhouse told Hardinge that he had looked into the pensions commutation problem and found that while he had 'a fair ground of complaint', there were extenuating circumstances to absolve the war office from blame.

He was told by Althorp on 28 Mar. that the king had agreed to a creation of peers, but on 4 Apr. 1832 that all was 'gloomy' and uncertain again. He witnessed the second reading debates in the Lords, 9-14 Apr. After the bill's defeat in committee, 7 May, and the king's refusal of the cabinet's request for peers to be made, he of course resigned with his colleagues, taking formal leave of the king on the 14th. He voted for Ebrington's motion for an address calling on the king to appoint only ministers who would carry undiluted reform, 10 May, but thought it best as an ex-minister to stay away from the Westminster protest meeting, 11 May.

He attended the party meeting at Brooks's, 13 May, when it was decided not to press the issue further in the Commons for the moment. He remained in touch with Place, who kept him abreast of popular feeling, and on 18 May, when the Grey ministry was virtually reinstated but some 'uncertainty' remained, wrote him a letter to the effect that while the run on gold had ceased as soon as Grey was sent for, any hitch which led to the appointment of Wellington as premier would provoke renewed panic and probably 'a commotion in the nature of a civil war, with money at our command'. Whether Hobhouse showed this letter to members of the cabinet is not clear, and the crisis was resolved later that day.[215] When Hunt and Hume moved for an address to the king to suspend army flogging for a year, 19 June, Hobhouse answered that he remained personally opposed to it and had secured a 'diminution of punishment' by reducing the number of lashes from 300 to 200 for regiments and from 500 to 300 for brigades. Hunt divided the House and Hobhouse had a majority of 37 to 15, which included 'some of my old friends'.[216] He went to the Westminster anniversary dinner, which Burdett pronounced to be the last one, 27 June, and when he spoke was 'much better received than I thought any placeman could be', with 'no hints about flogging'. A libellous letter in the *Examiner* a few days later which accused him of 'receiving perquisites and sharing public plunder with a near relation' tempted him to prosecute, but Burdett, Place and the home secretary Lord Melbourne talked him out of it.[217] The case of Alexander Somerville, a private in the Scots Greys who had been court martialled and sentenced to 100 lashes ostensibly for insubordination, but according to Hume, who raised the case in the House, 3 July, for having expressed reforming views, caused Hobhouse more aggravation. He secured a court of inquiry, which censured the commanding officer responsible and gave Somerville an honourable discharge, but he felt that he got no credit for this and that Hume treated him less than candidly in the House, 6, 20 July, 8, 9 Aug.[218] Hunt moved for returns on flogging, 24 July, and Hobhouse 'amended and then granted them', which had never been done before. When De Lacy Evans, who had an eye on the Westminster seat, proposed a substantial reduction in the army establishment, 26 July, Hobhouse moved the previous question. He was 'manfully' backed by Althorp, but 'did not feel quite comfortable as many of Evans's suggestions were such as I approved'. The motion was withdrawn, but Hobhouse believed that the episode 'although very unjustly will be made a handle against me'.[219] He expressed surprise when Sadler presented a petition from factory workers

claiming to have been victimized by their employers for testifying before the committee on the factories bill, 30 July, but conceded that it warranted investigation. He carried a vote of £50,000 for commutation allowances to Chelsea pensioners, 3 Aug. On the 8th he brought forward his clause in the Appropriation Act granting half-pay officers permission to hold civil offices. He felt that Hume's opposition to this 'act of justice' was 'most unfair', but 'got through the business well'. On 9 Aug. he regretted Althorp's decision to drop his proposed remedial measure to deal with the problem of voter registration in the large towns and metropolitan seats, where, as Evans had been arguing for some time, thousands of householders faced disfranchisement as a result of being late with their rate payments. He attended the Westminster electors' meting on the issue next day and presented and endorsed its petition, 11 Aug. 1832, claiming that there would be 3,500-4,000 registered electors in Westminster, where the true figure should be 18,500. He was not entirely satisfied with Althorp's assurance that in practice the problem would not be serious, but also accused Evans of grossly exaggerating it. He reflected that it was a 'queer finale to the session – the secretary at war against [the] chancellor of the exchequer'.[220]

Hobhouse fell out with Hume over the latter's support of the Radical John Roebuck[†] against his brother Henry at Bath at the 1832 general election. This completed his fall from grace with Place, who washed his hands of him and publicly condemned him as a traitor to radical reform. He sought re-election for Westminster, with Burdett, but refused to pledge himself to a radical reform programme. Place and the more radical Westminster activists took up Evans (though De Vear remained loyal to the sitting Members), and Hobhouse was returned in second place, 2,344 ahead of Evans. According to Denis Le Marchant[†], he was 'in immense exultation at his success' and 'complained of Place the tailor in no uncertain terms, and did not lavish less abuse upon Hume'. At the end of March 1833 he replaced Smith Stanley as Irish secretary. He was re-elected unopposed, but a month later not only resigned his new office over his colleagues' refusal to support repeal of the house and window taxes, but put his Westminster seat on the line. This time Evans, assisted by the intervention of a no-hope Conservative, turned him out.[221] He came in for Nottingham in 1834 and served in the Liberal ministries of Melbourne and Russell. A combative Commons performer, better 'in attack than defence', he was rather harshly described in 1836 by Ellice as 'a good fellow, but without courage or influence'.[222] As Holland had predicted, his career in many respects echoed that of his father, though he remained a man of liberal views, and he was made a peer in 1851. He died in June 1869 and was buried in Kensal Green cemetery.

[1] See R.E. Zegger, *John Cam Hobhouse: a Political Life, 1819-1852* (1979) and M. Joyce, *My Friend H* (1948). As Lord Broughton, he had five vols. of *Some Account of a Long Life* privately printed, 1865-7. His daughter Lady Dorchester published portions of this, together with extracts from his daily diaries, as *Recollections of a Long Life*, 6 vols. (1909-11). This (cited hereafter as Broughton), has been drawn on, and the unpublished diaries (Add. 56540-56557) have been selectively used. [2] *HP Commons, 1790-1820*, iii. 209-12; Zegger, 34-37. [3] For his letters to Byron, 1808-24, see *Byron's Bulldog* ed. P.W. Graham (1984). [4] Zegger, 37-52; Joyce, 117; Broughton, i. 5-348; ii. 1-99. [5] Not 1818, as stated in Zegger, 54. [6] *HP Commons, 1790-1820*, ii. 275-8; *Byron's Bulldog*, 231-47. [7] *HP Commons, 1790-1820*, ii. 278-82; Zegger, 55-72; Joyce, 117; Broughton, ii. 103-6; *Byron's Bulldog*, 263. [8] *The Times*, 3 Sept.; *Devizes Gazette*, 11 Nov., 9 Dec. 1819. [9] Zegger, 72-78; *Byron's Bulldog*, 266, 272-3; *The Times*, 9 Dec. 1819. [10] Zegger, 77-79; Broughton, ii. 115-16; *Colchester Diary*, iii. 101; *The Times*, 21 Dec. 1819; *Byron's Bulldog*, 280-3; Lincs. AO, Tennyson D'Eyncourt mss H108/5. [11] Add. 27843, ff. 11, 16, 22; 36458, ff. 133, 180, 182, 184, 185; 56541, ff. 3-4, 6-9; Broughton, ii. 118-22; *The Times*, 3 Mar. 1820. [12] Northants. RO, Agar Ellis diary, 9 Mar.; *The Times*, 10 Mar. 1820; Add. 56541, ff. 12-21; Broughton, ii. 121-3. [13] *Byron's Bulldog*, 286-7. [14] *The Times*, 27 Mar.; Grey mss, Ellice to Grey, 7 Apr. 1820. [15] *Colchester Diary*, iii. 125; *Arbuthnot Jnl.* i. 17. [16] [J. Grant], *Random Recollections of Commons* (1837), 215. [17] Zegger, 31. [18] Broughton, ii. 125-7. [19] Add. 51541, f. 34; Dorset RO D/BKL, Bankes jnl. 117 (9 May 1820); *Althorp Letters*, 107; NLW, Coedymaen mss 935. [20] Add. 56541, ff. 35-37. [21] *The Times* 13 May 1820. [22] Broughton, ii. 128. [23] Add. 56541, f. 37. [24] Add. 36458, f. 309; 56541, ff. 38-39. [25] Add. 56541, f. 42. [26] Add. 52444, f. 177. [27] *The Times*, 5, 7 July 1820; Add. 56541, ff. 48-49; *Byron's Bulldog*, 296. [28] Add. 56541, f. 62; M.W. Patterson, *Sir Francis Burdett and his Times*, ii. 518. [29] *The Times*, 17 July 1820. [30] Add. 56541, f. 73. [31] Ibid. ff. 73-74; Brougham mss, Grey Bennet to Brougham [19 Sept. 1820]. [32] Add. 56541, f. 83-85. [33] Patterson, ii. 514-15. [34] Ibid. ii. 520; *The Times*, 18, 28 Nov. 1820; *Geo. IV Letters*, ii. 884. [35] Add. 47222, f. 59. [36] Add. 51686, Lansdowne to Holland, 11 Jan.; 51687, same to Lady Holland, 18 Jan.; 51831, Gordon to Holland [c. 18 Jan.]; 56541, ff. 131, 133; *Devizes Gazette*, 11, 18, 25 Jan. 1821. [37] Broughton, ii. 140; *Geo. IV Letters*, ii. 895-6; HLRO, Hist. Coll. 379, Grey Bennet diary, 5; Castle Howard mss, Howard to Lady Morpeth, 28 [Jan. 1821]. [38] *Byron's Bulldog*, 304. [39] Add. 56542, ff. 1-2; *The Times*, 22 Feb. 1821. [40] Broughton, ii. 141. [41] Add. 56542, f. 8. [42] Ibid. ff. 11-12. [43] Ibid. ff. 11, 14; Broughton, ii. 145; Grey Bennet diary, 50. [44] Broughton, ii. 145-50; *Von Neumann Diary*, i. 58-59; *Greville Mems.* i. 117. [45] *The Times*, 16 May 1821; Add. 56542, f. 28. [46] *The Times*, 24 May 1821; Add. 56542, ff. 29-30. [47] *The Times*, 8, 15, 22 June, 4, 12 July 1821. [48] Broughton, ii. 152. [49] *Hobhouse Diary*, 73; Add. 30109, f. 264; *Byron's Bulldog*, 315, 318. [50] Broughton, ii. 174. [51] Add. 36459, f. 213; *The Times*, 14 Feb. 1822. [52] Add. 56544, f. 60. [53] Ibid. f. 70. [54] Broughton, ii. 179; HLRO HC. Lib. Ms 89, Moulton Barrett diary, 6 Mar. [1822]. [55] *The Times*, 12 Apr. 1822; Add. 27837, f. 205; 36459, f. 239, 243; G. Wallas, *Francis Place* (1908), 153. [56] Broughton. ii. 183-6. [57] Add. 27843, ff. 347-50; 56545, ff. 4-8, 12; *The Times*, 24 May 1822. [58] Broughton, ii. 188-9. [59] Add. 52445, f. 90; 56545, ff. 25-26. [60] Add. 56545, ff. 26-27. [61] Broughton, iii. 1-10. [62] Ibid. ff. 10-11; *Byron's Bulldog*, 326; Add. 52444, f. 112. [63] *The Times*, 17 Apr. 1823. [64] *Creevey Pprs.* ii. 64. [65] Broughton, iii. 15. [66] *The Times*, 25 Feb., 5, 22 Mar., 25 Apr. 1823. [67] Broughton, iii. 20-21. [68] Add. 56548, f. 2; *The Times*, 24 May 1823. [69] *The Times*, 20 June 1823. [70] Add. 56548, f. 7. [71] *The Times*, 26 June, 1 July 1823. [72] Add. 36460, f. 123; 56548, f. 7; Broughton,

iii. 21-22; Zegger, 118-20. [73] Zegger, 120-5; *Byron's Bulldog*, 328-52. [74] Broughton, iii. 24-30. [75] Add. 27823, f. 350; 27824, f. 25; 36460, ff. 155. [76] *Byron's Bulldog*, 344, 347. [77] Add. 56548, ff. 55-56. [78] *The Times*, 24 Feb., 16, 24 Mar., 6 Apr. 1824. [79] Add. 56548, ff. 56-57. [80] Ibid. f. 62. [81] Broughton, iii. 35-71. [82] Add. 56548, ff. 92-93; Broughton, iii. 44; *The Times*, 25 May 1824. [83] Broughton, iii. 54-56; Add. 56549, f. 4. [84] Broughton, iii. 46-47, 55, 72-76. [85] Ibid. iii. 77-85. [86] Add. 56549, f. 83. [87] *O'Connell Corresp.* iii. 1172. [88] *The Times*, 28 Feb., 3, 25 Mar. 1825; Add. 36461, f. 51. [89] Broughton, iii. 96-97. [90] Add. 56549, f. 102. [91] Ibid. ff. 122-4; Broughton, iii. 101; *The Times*, 24 May 1825. [92] Broughton, iii. 104. [93] Ibid. iii. 95, 99; Zegger, 170-2. [94] Add. 36461, ff. 130, 141, 147; Broughton, iii. 111. [95] Add. 56549, f. 141. [96] Broughton, iii. 119-20; Add. 27824, ff. 392, 397, 399, 447; 36461, f. 263. [97] Broughton, iii. 125. [98] *The Times*, 14 Mar., 27 Apr. 1826. [99] Add. 36462, ff. 49, 67; *The Times*, 11 Apr. 1826. [100] Broughton, iii. 129-31. [101] Ibid. iii. 132-5. [102] Add. 56550, f. 79; *The Times*, 24 May 1826. [103] Broughton, iii. 135. [104] Add. 27843, ff. 390-3, 396-7, 404, 408-13; Add. 36462, f. 235, 238; 56550, ff. 84-94; Broughton, iii. 137; *The Times*, 10 June 1826. [105] Add. 36462, ff. 271, 275; 51569, Hobhouse to Holland, 18 June [1826]. [106] Broughton, iii. 145-58; Zegger, 127-9; Add. 36463, f. 19; 37949, f. 175. [107] *The Times*, 9 Dec. 1826. [108] Add 36463, ff. 66, 75, 79, 83; 56550, ff. 117-18. [109] Broughton, iii. 161-6, 169; Add. 51784, Holland to C.R. Fox, 17 Feb. 1827. [110] Broughton, iii. 173-6. [111] *The Times*, 9 Mar. 1827. [112] Broughton, iii. 180. [113] Ibid. iii. 180-1. [114] Add. 36463, ff. 311, 313, 329. [115] Add. 37949, f. 456; Broughton, 185-8; NLS mss 14441, f. 20. [116] *The Times*, 10, 15, 22, 23 May 1827; Add. 36463, f. 407. [117] Add. 47222, f. 191; 56550, ff. 176-8; Broughton, iii. 195-6; *The Times*, 24 May 1827. [118] Broughton, iii. 198-9, 201-5; *The Times*, 8, 12, 16, 19 June 1827. [119] Zegger, 134. [120] Broughton, iii. 209-18. [121] Joyce, 196-7. [122] Broughton, iii. 223-5. [123] Add. 35148, f. 3, 6; 36464, f. 114; Broughton, iii. 229. [124] Broughton, iii. 230-3; Add. 36464, f. 173. [125] Broughton, iii.233-6; Add. 35148, ff. 9, 10, 13; 36464, ff. 173, 179, 185. [126] Add. 36464, ff. 166, 176, 182; Broughton, iii. 236-7. [127] Broughton, iii. 327-8, 242-5; *Ellenborough Diary*, i. 35; Hatherton diary, 14 Feb. [1828]; Keele Univ. Lib. Sneyd mss SC17/36. [128] Add. 36464, f. 354. [129] Ibid. ff. 283, 298. [130] Broughton, iii. 257. [131] Ibid. iii. 260-2. [132] Add. 56552, f. 101-2; Broughton, iii. 271; *The Times*, 27 May 1828. [133] Broughton, iii. 273-5. [134] Add. 36464, f. 356. [135] Ibid. iii. ff. 369, 372. [136] Add. 56552, f. 116. [137] Broughton, iii. 283. [138] Ibid. iii. 280-300; Add. 56552, ff. 104-5, 114-15, 122-3; 56553, ff. 140-2; Joyce, 197-201. [139] Add. 56553, ff. 142-6, 152-6; 56554, f. 159; Broughton, iii. 301-21. [140] Add. 56554, ff. 17-20; *The Times*, 26, 27 May 1829. [141] Grey mss, Howick jnl. 2 June [1829]. [142] See Zegger, 143-5; Add. 37949, f. 223. [143] Add. 56554, ff. 8, 10-12, 15-17, 19, 21, 22, 24; Broughton, iii. 320. [144] Broughton, iv. 3, 7-8; Howick jnl. 4 Feb.; *The Times*, 6 Feb. 1830; Add. 47223, f. 38; 56554, f. 60. [145] Add. 56554, ff. 62, 71. [146] Add. 36466, ff. 12, 31; 56554, f. 64. [147] Add. 56554, ff. 64-67; Broughton, iv. 9. [148] Add. 56554, ff. 67, 70-71. [149] Ibid. ff. 71-72, 75. [150] Broughton, iv. 12. [151] Add. 56554, ff. 75-76. [152] Ibid. ff. 76, 78-80; Broughton, iv. 13. [153] Broughton, iv. 16. [154] Add. 56554, f. 83. [155] See Zegger, 145-52; Add. 35148, ff. 42, 44, 49, 52, 53, 58; 36466, f. 94; 56554, ff. 61, 64, 67, 68, 70, 73, 74, 76, 83, 88-89, 94, 101, 114, 118, 119; Broughton, iv. 22, 27. [156] Add. 56554, f. 93. [157] Ibid. f. 98. [158] Broughton, iv. 36-38; Add. 56554, ff. 131. [159] Add. 56554, ff. 95-98. [160] Ibid. ff. 104, 113; *The Times*, 25 May 1830. [161] Broughton, iv. 28-30; Add. 36466, ff. 161, 163; 56554,f. 120. [162] Broughton, iv. 31; Add. 56554, f. 129, 133. [163] Add. 56554, ff. 127-8, 131, 133-6, 138; 56555, ff. 2-4; Broughton, iv. 43; *The Times*, 2 Aug. 1830. [164] Wilts. RO, Hobhouse mss 145/2/b, Hobhouse to wife, 2, 4 Aug. 1830; Add. 47222, f. 253; 56555, ff. 5-6, 8, 10-14; Broughton, iv. 44, 46. [165] Add. 56555, ff. 17-19, 21, 28-29; Broughton, iv. 48, 52-54; Zegger, 138-40. [166] Add. 36815, f. 50; 56555, ff. 28-31, 33-35; Broughton, iv. 55-56; *Arbuthnot Corresp.* 200. [167] Add. 51564, Broughton to Lady Holland [8 Nov.]; 56555, ff. 35-47; Broughton, iv. 57-66; Howick jnl. 7 Nov.; Agar Ellis diary, 7 Nov.; Chatsworth mss, Brougham to Devonshire [8 Nov. 1830]. [168] NLS mss 14441, f. 78. [169] Add. 56555, ff. 50, 52; Broughton, iv.

66-70. [170] Add. 56555, ff. 57-61; Broughton, iv. 70-72. [171] Add. 56555, ff. 62, 66. [172] Broughton, iv. 75. [173] Add. 56555, f. 71. [174] Broughton, iv. 76; Add. 56555, f. 74. [175] Add. 37950, f. 103; 56555, ff. 74-76; *The Times*, 16 Dec. 1830. [176] Add. 56555, ff. 77-79, 80, 85-87; Broughton, iv. 80-81. [177] Broughton, iv. 81, 84. [178] Ibid. iv. 84; Add. 56555, f. 97. [179] Add. 56555, f. 128. [180] Broughton, iv. 85-86. [181] Ibid. 86-91; Add. 51569, Ord to Lady Holland [3 Mar.]; 56555, ff. 100-2; *The Times*, 5 Mar. 1831; Wallas, 257-9; *London Radicalism* ed. D.J. Rowe (London Rec. Soc. v), 13-14; *Greville Mems.* ii. 126-6 [182] Add. 56555, ff. 104-9; Grey mss, Durham to Grey [7 Mar. 1831]. [183] Broughton, iv. 93-97; *Three Diaries*, 69; Add. 36464, ff. 294,299; 56555, f. 110, 114. [184] Broughton, iv. 98. [185] Ibid. iv. 99; Add. 56555, ff. 119-20. [186] Add. 36466, f. 311; 56555, ff. 122-3; Wilts. RO, Malmesbury (Burke) mss 124/1/175. [187] Broughton, iv. 101-8. [188] Ibid. iv. 109-10; Add. 36466, f. 316; 56555, ff. 131-2; *The Times*, 27 Apr., 3 May 1831. [189] Broughton, iv. 109; Add. 36466, ff. 333, 345, 354, 385, 405, 410; 56555, ff 132-3. [190] Broughton, iv. 110-12; Add. 40402, ff. 23-34. [191] Broughton, iv. 113; Add. 56555, f. 140; *The Times*, 24 May 1831. [192] Add. 36464, f. 374; Broughton, iv. 113-15; Add. 56555, ff. 143-63. [193] Add. 56555, f. 169; Zegger, 174-8. [194] Broughton, iv. 133-5, 144, 145; Add. 56556, ff. 12, 14. See Zegger, 153-6. [195] Broughton, iv. 119-28; Add. 56555, f. 163; Hatherton diary, 3 Aug. [1831]. [196] Broughton, iv. 129-30; Add. 56555, ff. 176, 179-80, 183-91; PROB 11/1789/467; IR26/1261/505. [197] Broughton, iv. 130-3; Add. 56555, ff. 191-4; *The Times*, 22 Sept.; Hobhouse mss 145/2/b, Hobhouse to wife, 24 [Sept.]; *Devizes Gazette*, 29 Sept. 1831. [198] Broughton, iv. 135-43; Add. 56556, ff. 5, 7-9; *The Times*, 11, 14 Oct. 1831. [199] Broughton, iv. 144-5, 147-9; Add. 35149, ff. 83-89; 36466, 422; 56556, ff. 6, 13-14; Wallas, 276-7; *Holland House Diaries*, 70. [200] Broughton, iv. 146-53; Add. 56556, ff. 16-27. [201] Hobhouse mss 145/2/b, Hobhouse to wife, 13, 17 Dec. 1831; Broughton, iv. 153-7; *Greville Mems.* ii. 230. [202] Broughton, iv. 161; Add. 56556, ff. 44-45; Zegger, 155-6. [203] *Greville Mems.* ii. 241-2; Broughton, iv. 165-5. [204] *Holland House Diaries*, 121-2; *Grey-William IV Corresp.* ii. 164-5, 173. [205] Broughton, iv. 165-9; Add. 56556, f. 52; 75941, Althorp to Spencer, 31 Jan.; Hobhouse mss 145/2/b, Hobhouse to wife, 31 Jan., 1 Feb. 1832; *Grey-William IV Corresp.* ii. 177-8, 180-1. [206] Broughton, iv. 169-73; Add. 47223, f. 49; 56556, ff. 55, 59-61; *Holland House Diaries*, 126; *The Times*, 9 Feb. 1832. [207] *Raikes Jnl.* i. 9; Hatherton diary, 10 Feb. [1832]; *Three Diaries*, 191, 194. [208] Broughton, iv. 170, 174-81, 184-5, 188-93; *Cockburn Letters*, 389-90. [209] *Three Diaries*, 211, 217; *Baring Jnls.* i. 92-93; Aberdeen Univ. Lib. Arbuthnot mss 3029/1/2/45; Add. 56556, f. 110. [210] Broughton, iv. 194-6. [211] Add. 56556, f. 102-3; *Three Diaries*, 215. [212] Add. 47223, ff. 52, 57. [213] Broughton, iv. 181-7, 193-4, 201-3; Add. 47226, f. 146; Zegger, 194-6. [214] Add. 56556, ff. 108-9, 111. [215] Broughton, iv. 209-10, 212-13, 218-34; Add. 27794, f. 278; 35149, f. 150; Wallas, 315-17, 320; Zegger, 191-3. [216] Add. 56556, f. 159 [217] Add. 56557, ff. 1-4; Broughton, iv. 244; *The Times*, 28 June 1832. [218] Broughton, iv. 246-7; Add. 56557, ff. 15, 16; Zegger, 197-8. [219] Add. 56557, ff. 11-12. [220] Ibid. f. 15. [221] Zegger, 198-208; *Three Diaries*, 284, 286. [222] Grant, 213; Reid, *Lord Durham*, ii. 109.

D.R.F.

HODGES, Thomas Law (1776–1857), of Hemsted Place, Benenden, Kent.

KENT	1830–1832
KENT WEST	1832–1841
KENT WEST	1847–1852

b. 3 June 1776, 1st. s. of Thomas Hallett Hodges of Breedy, Dorset and Dorothy, da. of William Cartwright of Marnham, Notts. *educ.* Tonbridge 1783; Harrow 1786; L. Inn 1793; Emmanuel, Camb. 1796. *m.* 16 Feb. 1802, Rebecca, da. of Sir Roger Twisden, 6th bt., of Bradbourne Park, nr. Maidstone, Kent, 5s. (4 *d.v.p.*) 6da. (3 *d.v.p.*).[1] *suc.* fa. 1801. *d.* 14 May 1857.

Capt. W. Kent militia 1798, maj. 1804, ret. 1805.

Hodges was a member of a gentry family which had long resided in Dorset and Gloucestershire. His great-grandfather, Thomas Hodges of Breedy, had a son Thomas, who married a Miss Hallett and died in 1771 while governor of Bombay. His son, Thomas Hallett Hodges, who was born in 1754, married in 1775, and in 1780 purchased an estate in Kent, where he was appointed sheriff in 1786 and deputy lieutenant in 1793.[2] Hodges, the eldest of seven children, was made captain of Harrow, which, he informed his father, 'during a laborious process of eight years, I have had continually before my eyes, and has been no small spur to my industry'.[3] He was an 'indulgent master' to his fag, Lord Althorp*, and Denis Le Marchant† recorded that, 'one of the best specimens of the old English country gentleman', 'even after the lapse of many years, Mr. Hodges could not speak of him to me without emotion'.[4] Having entered Lincoln's Inn in 1793, he was admitted to Emmanuel College, Cambridge, as a pensioner in 1794, but did not matriculate until 1796, taking his degree in 1799. In April 1798 he was given command of a new supplementary company of the West Kent militia, and served with them during the rebellion in Ireland until July 1799. His diary recorded his official duties and social life, as well as his fear that because of religious divisions and agricultural backwardness

it will require many years even of the most profound peace completely to restore cordiality to this country. If a person has never been in Ireland, he can have no conception of the deplorable condition of the lowest orders, their wretchedness and misery is only equalled by their extreme ignorance and brutal savagery.

He therefore welcomed peaceable Union, as a means of improving the well being of the poor and reconciling them to government from England.[5] After coming into a valuable inheritance from his father, he concentrated on ameliorating the condition of his own labourers and gained a reputation as an agricultural improver.[6] He consolidated his position within the local gentry by marrying into the Twisden family, and he took a principal part in enforcing his wife's claim to a £10,000 portion from her grandfather, Sir John Papillon Twisden, which was ordered by chancery, 6 Mar. 1804. Several of his daughters also married into well-to-do neighbouring families, and he gradually expanded his local influence as he became increasingly active in county affairs.[7]

Although Hodges voted for the ministerial candidates, Sir William Geary[†] and Sir Edward Knatchbull[†], for Kent at the 1802 general election, he always claimed to be a reformer.[8] No doubt he was strongly influenced in this by his maternal uncle, the radical John Cartwright, who in 1814 sent him his pro-reform epistles with the injunction

> not only to give them your attention, but to read with the pen in your hand, noting particularly such arguments as do not convince. Although the final effect on your mind may not be complete till you shall have gone through the series, yet, by criticizing each letter as it appears, and putting down your remarks in writing, you will best make yourself master of the question.[9]

He nominated Geary, who, although independently minded was certainly not the Whigs' preferred candidate, at both the 1812 and 1818 general elections, but in 1820 he proposed a Whig, William Philip Honywood[*], and thereafter consistently adopted an ardently Whig, occasionally radical, stance in politics.[10] He refused to stand for Maidstone in 1820 and, although he had acted as a steward at a reform meeting in 1811, he declined Cartwright's invitation to do so at his gathering on Spain, Naples and Portugal in September 1820. He argued that those who knew him in Kent

> will never doubt the rectitude of my principles, nor shall they ever have reason to be ashamed of my conduct. For whenever the time of action comes I shall be found on the side of those who defend civil liberty. I have prescribed this for my own conduct, but I have not confidence enough in my own abilities to stand forward as a leader, and therefore I shall decline such posts at public meetings, and content myself with doing my duty as well as I can when the crisis arrives.[11]

He signed the requisition for a county meeting on the Queen Caroline affair in late 1820. He spoke in favour of one about distress at a meeting of agriculturists in Maidstone, 13 Dec. 1821, and supported a petition calling for relief and reform when it finally took place, 11 June 1822.[12] Having appeared at least once before a select committee of the Commons (to give evidence on Gibbon's charity school at Benenden, 6 Nov. 1818), he attended the committee on the encouragement of emigration, 27 Apr., 4 May 1826, when he described his own successful scheme for giving financial incentives to potential local emigrants, thereby reducing the number of dependent paupers and the poor rates.[13] A rumour briefly circulated that he would offer for Kent at the 1826 general election, but he again nominated Honywood.[14] He advocated petitions for continued protection at meetings in Maidstone, 20 Mar., 29 Apr. 1828.[15] After repeated interruptions from the Brunswickers at the county meeting on the Catholic question, 24 Oct., he was eventually given a brief hearing, in which he moved an unsuccessful pro-Catholic amendment that the best way to support the Protestant establishment would be by allowing ministers to decide on the issue and suppressing the Catholic Association. In a letter complaining of his treatment, 29 Oct., he reiterated his concern over the desperate state of the poor in Ireland and urged the introduction of poor rates there.[16] He was a steward at the anti-Brunswick dinner at Maidstone, 22 Dec. 1828, when he called for the removal of the grievances of the Irish Catholics, argued that they did favour reform, else he would not have supported their claims, and stated that reform was the 'great panacea for all the evils under which the country labours'. He spoke in favour of reform and against tithes at a county meeting, 12 Mar. 1830.[17]

Both the Tory Sir Edward Knatchbull, son and namesake of the former Member, and Honywood offered again at the general election in 1830, but the Whigs were dissatisfied with the latter, who was non-resident and in poor health, and approaches were made to Hodges. He was initially diffident, telling one correspondent, 9 July, that he was 'thoroughly aware of what must be expected and required of any man who is placed in that situation, and therefore I cannot think of voluntarily putting myself forward as a candidate'. However, he promised to discharge his duties 'diligently and conscientiously' if Honywood resigned and he received enough promises of support.[18] Although a meeting in Hodges's favour broke up without even appointing a chairman, 2 Aug., Honywood was evidently persuaded to withdraw shortly before the election. Lord Darnley informed Lord Holland, 4 Aug., that he had 'left the field open to a very respectable successor, Mr. Hodges, a good and liberal politician', while his son, Lord Clifton[*], told Honywood of his delight at having 'so efficient and valuable a man as Hodges in your place'.[19] On the hustings, 9 Aug., Hodges advocated economies and reform, declared that he would never have stood had Honywood been able to continue and promised to be as active and impartial in handling county business as Knatchbull, with whom he was duly elected unopposed, at very little expense.[20] At a dinner in Hawkhurst, 8 Sept., he spoke against involvement in a foreign war, and at another in Rochester, whose corporation had agreed to make him an honorary freeman, he pledged himself to work on behalf of the city and the county, taking '*spectemur agendo*' ('let us be judged by our deeds') as his motto, 20 Oct.[21] The Wellington ministry listed him among its 'foes' in September. That autumn his tenants refused to pay their rents because of the prolonged distress, and, as a magistrate, he was involved in attempts to quell the 'Swing' riots that subsequently occurred.[22] In his maiden speech, made on the first day of the session, 2 Nov., he noted that the 'disturbed condition of Kent is a matter of general notoriety. It is occasioned by the general distress of the labouring population of the country'. He added that nothing but a great remission of taxation would solve the problem, which could only be effected by a reformed Parliament, thus linking the two issues which were to dominate his activities in the Commons. The following day he made the first of several motions for returns of the poor rates, and from then on he brought up numerous local petitions. He presented and endorsed one from Tenterden complaining of distress, 11 Nov., and others from Hawkhurst and Goudhurst against the malt duty, 15 Nov., when he voted against government on the civil list. He brought up, and fully concurred with, a Kentish petition for agricultural relief and the abolition of tithes, 6 Dec. In evidence before a Lords select committee on the poor laws, 7 Dec., he defended his experiment in encouraging emigration, but argued that distress, which was largely caused by over-population, was nevertheless acute and had led to a number of disturbances in his neighbourhood.[23] He presented and endorsed four other Kentish petitions in favour of relief and reform, 10 Dec. 1830, when he argued that the appointment of a new ministry under Lord Grey had had a good effect by calming the minds of the people. On the 11th he corrected a misinterpretation of this speech, by denying that he had said that magistrates had refused to carry out their duties under the former government.

Hodges, who was elected to Brooks's on the nomination of Althorp, the chancellor, 12 Feb. 1831, continued to be highly active in presenting various county petitions for reduced taxes and reform throughout the session. He endorsed all their demands, including that for vote by ballot, except those for universal suffrage and repeal of the Union. He and Knatchbull led a Kentish deputation to Althorp at the treasury, 26 Feb., to request the abolition of the malt duty.[24] On presenting the east Kent reform petition, 28 Feb., he claimed that he had already brought up between 20 and 30 such petitions from Kent, and was 'convinced, that the tranquillity of that county, of the whole kingdom, depends upon the nature and successful issue of that great question'. He lodged a Greenwich petition for the town to be separately represented, 10 Mar., when

he agreed with Hume that the system for balloting the militia was most objectionable. On 15 Mar. he declared that

> the reform bill will have a most beneficial effect, by destroying the aristocratical influence which has too long prevailed in this House and by conferring the elective franchise on a class of individuals whose property will make them feel an interest in the welfare of the country.

He stated that the feeling of Kent was 'decidedly in favour' of it, 17 Mar., and duly voted for its second reading, 22 Mar. At another county meeting on the subject, 24 Mar., when he revealed that he had been unable to catch the Speaker's eye in the preceding debate, he argued that the bill would lead to the 'moral and political amelioration' of the people and would prevent anarchy.[25] On presenting the ensuing petition to the House, 25 Mar., he commented on the marked lack of opposition it had met with, even from Maidstone freemen who faced disfranchisement. He brought up the reform petition of the sheriff of Sussex, 18 Apr., and voted against Gascoyne's wrecking amendment, 19 Apr. Despite fears of a contest in Kent, he offered again, 22 Apr., and there were few doubts about his success. He united his interest with Thomas Rider, another reformer, and they canvassed together in several parts of the county, before Knatchbull finally withdrew.[26] On 11 May he spoke of his ambition to finish the work of reform, even if the bill itself was not perfect, and indicated that as a delegate he would be bound to follow his constituents' wishes and to vote in its favour. He was again returned very cheaply and without opposition.[27] Although sceptical about its immediate benefits, he spoke in praise of the bill at reform dinners in Rochester and Cranbrook, 8, 10 June 1831.[28]

He objected to the London coal bill, 1 July 1831, because it threatened to extend the boundaries of the city into Kent. He voted for the second reading of the reintroduced reform bill, 6 July, and on the 11th attended the meeting at which Althorp asked Whig Members to support government silently on reform, 11 July, though, according to Edward John Littleton*, he was one of the county Members 'urging his crotchet' against the division of counties.[29] He later told his constituents that 'during the late memorable parliamentary campaign, I was favoured with good health, so that I was never absent an hour from the debates', and 'when we came to the voting, which after all is the most essential point, I was always at my post'.[30] He did, indeed, divide regularly with ministers on the bill's details, though he voted against the total disfranchisement of Saltash, 26 July, when they allowed it to retain one seat. He voted for the enfranchisement of Greenwich, 3 Aug., believing, 'from the number and respectability of the inhabitants, that it will produce a most unobjectionable constituency'. He spoke and voted in favour of uniting Rochester with Chatham and Strood, 9 Aug., when he commented that 'considerable disgust' had arisen in Kent over the delays to the bill. Although it was the feature he liked least, he stated, 11 Aug., that 'as the country has demanded the whole bill, I am bound to preserve the consistency of the measure and to vote for the division of counties'. The price of his acquiescence, however, was his support for Lord Chandos's amendment to enfranchise £50 tenants-at-will, 18 Aug., which he argued would increase the constituency of counties diminished by the enfranchisement of large towns, and 'carries the principle of the bill into more effectual operation'. He added that

> when I consider the class of people whom it is proposed to benefit, when I consider the large proportion of the county rates and poor rates which they sustain, I must say that I consider it nothing but an act of justice to confer the elective franchise upon the renting tenantry of England.

He denied that opinion in Kent had turned against the bill, 30 Aug., or that he had pledged himself to his constituents to support it, 15 Sept. As he had on 18 Mar., he urged the 'absolute necessity' of the establishment of a modified system of poor laws in Ireland, 12 Aug., 26 Sept. He voted against ministers on Sadler's motion on the subject, 29 Aug., but with them on the Dublin, 23 Aug., and Liverpool elections, 5 Sept. He helped to prepare and bring in a bill to amend the laws relating to sewers, 17 Aug., advocated relief of agricultural distress, 13 Sept., and spoke, 16 Sept., and voted in defence of the Deacles, 27 Sept. He divided for the third reading, 19 Sept., and passage of the bill, 21 Sept., the second reading of the Scottish bill, 23 Sept., and Lord Ebrington's confidence motion, 10 Oct. He signed the requisition for the Kent county meeting on 30 Sept. 1831, when he advocated reform and claimed that he would have introduced an amendment similar to Chandos's, had it proved necessary.[31]

He voted for the second reading of the revised reform bill, 17 Dec. 1831, its committal, 20 Jan. 1832, and again for many of its details. He spoke in favour of reducing the malt duty at a meeting in Maidstone, 5 Jan., and waited on Althorp with a delegation of Kent and Sussex hop-growers to request the reduction or postponement of the hop duties, 20 Mar.[32] He denied that landlords had too much influence over their tenants and indicated that he would vote for

the retention of Chandos's amendment, 1 Feb., but he divided with ministers against the production of information on Portugal, 9 Feb. He presented a petition complaining about the poor laws, but refused to endorse its demand for increased emigration unless a system of poor relief was first extended to Ireland, 3 Feb. He urged the use of more national resources to combat the spread of cholera, 14 Feb., and was in the minority of 13 against recommitting the anatomy bill, 27 Feb. He spoke in favour of continuing the informal arrangements which had developed for handling the enormous number of reform petitions coming before the House, 23 Feb., and advocated the inclusion of Ramsgate in the constituency of Sandwich, without forcing a division against ministers, 14 Mar. He voted for Hunt's motion for inquiry into Peterloo, 15 Mar., and for Buxton's for a select committee on colonial slavery, 24 May, to which he was named, 30 May. He voted for the third reading of the reform bill, 22 Mar., Ebrington's motion for an address calling on the king to appoint only ministers who would carry it unimpaired, 10 May, the second reading of the Irish bill, 25 May, and against increasing the representation of Scotland, 1 June, when he agreed that consideration of the corn laws should be postponed to the following session. He voted in minorities against the Liverpool disfranchisement bill, 23 May, Baring's bill to exclude insolvent debtors from Parliament, 6 June, and for a system of representation for New South Wales, 28 June. He divided for making permanent provision for the Irish poor by a tax on absentees, 19 June, and to make coroners' inquests public, 20 June. He voted with ministers for the Russian-Dutch loan, 26 Jan., 12, 16, 20 July, but against them on the Greek loan, 6 Aug. At a series of dinners to celebrate the success of reform that autumn, he defended his conduct in Parliament, repeatedly rebutted Tory criticisms that he was hostile to the agricultural interest and argued against excessive taxation and colonial slavery.[33]

At the general election of 1832 he was elected at the top of the poll for Kent West, which remained his seat for much of his life.[34] He published his *Minutes of Evidence* before parliamentary committees and the *Use of Pearson's Plough* in 1833, and he became chairman of the Maidstone quarter sessions and deputy lieutenant of Kent. He died in May 1857. His monument in Benenden Church recorded that 'a true patriot, a kind and liberal landlord, an unfailing friend of the poor, faithful in every relation of public and private life, he served his generation according to the will of God'. He was succeeded by his eldest son, Thomas Twisden Hodges (1804-65), who sat as a Liberal for Rochester, 1835-7 and 1847-52.[35]

[1] Sir J.R. Twisden, *Fam. of Twysden and Twisden*, 421-2. [2] Ibid.; IGI (Notts.); *London Gazette*, 15 Jan. 1793. [3] Cent. Kent. Stud. Twisden mss U49 C13/86, 91, 93. [4] Le Marchant, *Althorp*, 32. [5] Add. 40166, f. 68; J. Bonhote, *Hist. Recs. of W. Kent Militia*, 167, 177, 180-6. [6] PROB 11/1360/465; IR26/53/78; *Cobbett's Rural Rides* ed. G.D.H. and M. Cole, i. 213; iii. 990. [7] Twisden, 417-19, 423-4; *Gent. Mag.* (1857), i. 735. [8] *Kent Pollbook* (1802), 240. [9] Twisden mss C13/5. [10] *Kentish Chron.* 16 Oct. 1812, 23 June 1818, 21 Mar. 1820. [11] Ibid. 14 Mar. 1820; Twisden mss C13/7. [12] Cent. Kent. Stud. Stanhope mss U1590 C190/1, Knatchbull to Stanhope, 14 Dec.; *Kentish Chron.* 2 Jan., 21 Dec. 1821, 14 June 1822. [13] *PP* (1819), vol. x. pt. a. 371-3; (1826), iv. 133-42, 182-7; Wellington mss WP1/864/23. [14] *Kentish Chron.* 20, 23 June 1826. [15] Ibid. 25 Mar.; *Kentish Gazette*, 2 May 1828. [16] *Kentish Chron.* 28 Oct. 1828; *Report of Speeches at Kent County Meeting* (1828), pp. xi-xii, 30-32. [17] *Kentish Chron.* 9, 30 Dec. 1828, 16 Mar. 1830. [18] Twisden mss C13/151. [19] *Kentish Chron.* 3 Aug.; *Kentish Gazette*, 6 Aug. 1830; Add. 51572; Cent. Kent. Stud. Honywood mss U221 O3. [20] *Maidstone Jnl.* 10 Aug. 1830. [21] Ibid. 14 Sept., 26 Oct. 1830; Medway Archives and Local Stud. Cent. Rochester city recs. RCA/A1/6, 621. [22] J. L. and B. Hammond, *Village Labourer*, 254; M. McNay, *Portrait of Kentish Village*, 25-26; Cent. Kent. Stud. Knatchbull mss U951 C14/3. [23] *PP* (1831), viii. 334-45; T.L. Hodges, *Letter to Poor Law Commissioners* (1843), 2-8; *Three Diaries*, 30. [24] *Kentish Chron.* 1 Mar. 1831. [25] *Maidstone Jnl.* 29 Mar. 1831. [26] Ibid. 5, 12, 26 Apr., 3, 10 May; *The Times*, 30 Apr.; *Kentish Chron.* 3 May 1831. [27] *The Times*, 12, 28 May; *Maidstone Jnl.* 17 May 1831. [28] *Maidstone Jnl.* 14 June 1831. [29] Hatherton diary. [30] *Maidstone Jnl.* 8 Nov. 1831. [31] Ibid. 4 Oct. 1831. [32] Ibid. 10 Jan.; *Kentish Gazette*, 23 Mar. 1832. [33] *Kentish Gazette*, 22 June; *Maidstone Jnl.* 17, 31 July, 28 Aug., 18 Sept.; *Kentish Chron.* 31 July 1832. [34] *Maidstone Jnl.* 18 Dec. 1832. [35] F. Haslewood, *Parish of Benenden*, 2-5; Twisden, 449-50; Cent. Kent. Stud. Cranbrook deeds U78 T335.

S.M.F.

HODGETTS FOLEY, John Hodgetts (1797–1861), of Prestwood Park, Staffs.

DROITWICH	14 Feb. 1822–1834
WORCESTERSHIRE EAST	1847–13 Nov. 1861

b. 17 July 1797, 2nd *s.* of Hon. Edward Foley† (*d.* 1803) and 2nd *w.* Elizabeth Maria, *da.* and *coh.* of John Hodgetts of Prestwood; *bro.* of Edward Thomas Foley*. *educ.* Christ Church, Oxf. 1815. *m.* 20 Oct. 1825, Charlotte Margaret, *da.* of John Gage of Rogate Lodge, Suss., 1s. Took name of Hodgetts before Foley by royal lic. 14 Apr. 1821. *d.* 13 Nov. 1861.

Hodgetts Foley's father, the second son of the 1st Baron Foley and a reprobate Foxite, had sat for Droitwich, 1768-74, and Worcestershire, 1774-1803, on his family's interest, headed since 1793 by the 3rd Baron, Hodgetts Foley's cousin and his sponsor at Brooks's, 7 Feb. 1817. By his father's will (proved 14 Dec. 1803), on the death of his mother in 1810 Hodgetts Foley's guardianship passed to his uncles Andrew Foley, Member for Droitwich, 1774-1818, and Sir Edward Winnington, Member for Droitwich, 1807-16, and for Worcestershire, 1820-30.[1] At the 1820 general election he was considered 'much fitter

in all respects' than his elder brother Edward to fill the vacancy which had arisen on the family interest in Worcestershire, but being 'unluckily abroad' and 'never here in England', there was 'great reason to think he also would decline'.[2] In February 1822, however, following the death of his cousin Thomas Foley, Hodgetts Foley came forward for the vacancy at Droitwich. Reports that Lord Foley would no longer be able to 'bring in' a second family member proved unfounded and he was returned unopposed.[3]

A regular attender, Hodgetts Foley (who was sometimes confused with his predecessor in the House) divided steadily with the Whig opposition to the Liverpool ministry on most major issues, including economy, retrenchment and reduced taxation, but is not known to have spoken in debate.[4] He voted for parliamentary reform, 25 Apr. 1822, 27 Apr. 1826. He voted against suppression of the Catholic Association, 15 Feb. 1825, but was one of the few Whigs who divided against Catholic claims, 1 Mar., 21 Apr., 10 May 1825. At the 1826 general election he was re-elected unopposed.[5] He was granted a month's leave on urgent business after serving on an election committee, 16 Mar. 1827. He voted against Catholic relief, 6 Mar. 1827, 12 May 1828, but for repeal of the Test Acts, 26 Feb. 1828. He divided for reductions in the corn duties, 22 Apr. 1828. In February 1829 Planta, the Wellington ministry's patronage secretary, predicted that he would be opposed to securities to counterbalance Catholic emancipation. He voted to consider it, 6 Mar., paired against the second reading of the relief bill, 18 Mar., but voted for the third reading, 30 Mar. On 16 Mar. 1829 he presented a hostile petition from a parish in Herefordshire. He divided against government on the affair at Terceira, 28 Apr., and the civil government of Canada, 25 May 1830. He voted for abolition of the death punishment for forgery, 7 June, and for an amendment to the sale of beer bill prohibiting on-consumption, 21 June 1830.

At the 1830 general election Hodgetts Foley was again returned unopposed.[6] He was listed by the Wellington ministry as one of their 'foes', but was absent from the crucial division on the civil list, 15 Nov. 1830. He was granted leave for three weeks on urgent business, 2 Dec. 1830, and a fortnight on account of ill health, 14 Feb. 1831. He voted for the second reading of the Grey ministry's reform bill, 22 Mar., and against Gascoyne's wrecking amendment, 19 Apr. 1831. At the ensuing general election he was again returned unopposed.[7] He voted for the second reading of the reintroduced reform bill, 6 July, against the adjournment, 12 July, and gave generally steady support to its details, although according to *The Times* he paired with his fellow Whig Member for Droitwich, Sir Thomas Winnington, for use of the 1831 rather than the 1821 census to determine the disfranchisement schedules, 19 July. In a letter to that newspaper about a subsequent division, however, he complained of having been mistakenly included in a list of those who had voted for the enfranchisement of Greenwich, 3 Aug., when he had paired in that sense with the Tory Lord Holmesdale.[8] He divided for the third reading of the bill, 19 Sept., its passage, 21 Sept., and Lord Ebrington's confidence motion, 10 Oct. He voted for the second reading of the revised reform bill, 17 Dec. 1831, again supported its details and divided for the third reading, 22 Mar. 1832. He voted for the address calling on the king to appoint only ministers who would carry the bill unimpaired, 10 May. He divided with government on the Russian-Dutch loan, 26 Jan., 12, 16 July 1832 (as a pair).

At the 1832 general election Hodgetts Foley was returned unopposed for Droitwich, which lost one Member by the Reform Act. Following his defeat there in 1835, against which he petitioned unsuccessfully, he was out of Parliament until 1847, when he was returned on the family interest for Worcestershire East. He died 'suddenly' in November 1861, leaving no will.[9] Administration of his estate passed to his only son Henry John, Liberal Member for Staffordshire South, 1857-68.

[1] PROB 11/1402/966. [2] Hants RO, Tierney mss 48. [3] Grey mss, Tierney to Grey, 23 Jan. 1822. [4] *Black Bk.* (1823), 155; *Session of Parl. 1825*, p. 464. [5] *Worcester Herald*, 10 June 1826. [6] Ibid. 17, 31 July, 7 Aug. 1830. [7] Ibid. 7 May 1831. [8] *The Times*, 21 July, 8 Aug. 1831. [9] *Gent. Mag.* (1861), ii. 698.

P.J.S.

HODGSON, Frederick (?1795-1854), of 15 James's Place, Mdx.

BARNSTAPLE	8 Mar. 1824-1830
BARNSTAPLE	1831-1832
BARNSTAPLE	1837-1847

b. ?1795, 2nd s. of Mark Hodgson, brewer, of Bromley-by-Bow, Mdx. and w. Mary. *m.* 31 July 1831, Amelia Catherine, da. of John Erskine, *s.p. suc.* fa. 1810; bro. George Hodgson 1816. *d.* 30 Mar. 1854.

Hodgson's grandfather, George Hodgson, founded the family brewery at Bow in 1752 and by the early nineteenth century, under his father's management, it had established a dominant position in the export trade to India. 'Hodgson's India Ale' became

'a generic name', although a rival professed to dislike its 'thick and muddy appearance' and 'rank bitter flavour'.[1] On Mark Hodgson's death in 1810 trustees were appointed to run the company on behalf of his sons George and Frederick, the residuary legatees of his estate, until they came of age; his personalty was sworn under £90,000.[2] However, George's early death in 1816 left Frederick as sole heir to the brewery, and directories of 1817 list him as the head of the company.[3] The Burton brewers, Allsopp and Bass, moved into the Indian market during the 1820s, gradually undermining Hodgson's supremacy, but his company still accounted for nearly one-third of the strong ale exported to Bengal in 1832-3. He was 'known as "brown stout" from his size and dark complexion', as well as from the fame of his brewery.[4] In 1838 he formed a partnership with Edward Abbot, who had taken control of the brewery by 1845. For some years, until 1838, he and one Thomas Drane were partners in a London mercantile firm in Leadenhall Street.

Hodgson was abroad when a sudden vacancy occurred for the venal borough of Barnstaple in March 1824, but he was returned at the head of the poll thanks to the exertions of his friends.[5] He presented a Barnstaple brewers' petition against the beer duties bill, 21 May, and voted against the measure, 24 May 1824.[6] He divided with Lord Liverpool's ministry against the motion condemning the trial of the Methodist missionary John Smith in Demerara, 11 June 1824. He voted for the Irish unlawful societies bill, 25 Feb., and against Catholic claims, 1 Mar., 21 Apr., 10 May, and the Irish franchise bill, 26 Apr., 9 May 1825. He divided in the minority to relax the corn laws, 18 Apr. 1826. At the general election that summer he was returned for Barnstaple at the head of the poll, declaring himself to be a 'Tory', though 'strictly independent, inasmuch as fortune ... rendered the pecuniary assistance of the ministry to him unnecessary'.[7] He divided against Catholic claims, 6 Mar. 1827, 12 May 1828. He voted against increased protection for barley, 12 Mar. 1827. He informed *The Times* that he had not voted against repeal of the Test Acts, 26 Feb. 1828, 'being confined at home by indisposition'.[8] In February 1829 Planta, the Wellington ministry's patronage secretary, predicted that he would side 'with government' for Catholic emancipation, and he voted accordingly, 6, 30 Mar. On 16 Feb. he introduced the Stratford-le-Bow vestry bill, to increase the number of vestrymen, regulate the appointment of parish officers and provide better poor relief; it passed but was defeated in the Lords. He introduced a revised bill, 26 Mar., which gained royal assent, 13 Apr. He presented a London and Westminster butchers' petition against the Smithfield market bill, 2 Apr. 1829. He divided against the enfranchisement of Birmingham, Leeds and Manchester, 23 Feb., and Jewish emancipation, 17 May 1830. He presented a Barnstaple petition for repeal of the coastwise coal duty, 12 May. He voted in the minority to prohibit sales for on-consumption in beer houses, 21 June 1830. Early in July he announced that he would not stand for Barnstaple at the impending general election, but gave no reason for his decision.[9] Later that month he successfully applied for the honorary appointment of gentleman of the privy chamber, which the home secretary Peel, possibly unaware of his decision to retire, supported on the ground of his 'very constant and uniform support in the ... Commons'.[10]

In May 1831, on arriving at Dover from the continent, Hodgson was 'gratified to learn by the newspapers that ... *unsolicited by me*' he had again been returned for Barnstaple at the head of the poll, after a faction in the borough, determined to force a contest, had nominated him and given the impression that he was a moderate reformer.[11] In fact, he divided against the second reading of the Grey ministry's reintroduced reform bill, 6 July. He voted for an adjournment motion, 12 July, and to use the 1831 census for the purpose of scheduling boroughs, 19 July, postpone consideration of Chippenham's inclusion in schedule B, 27 July, and preserve the voting rights of non-resident freemen, 30 Aug. However, he informed *The Times* that he had voted for the proposed division of counties, 11 Aug., despite his overall hostility to the measure.[12] He voted against the bill's passage, 21 Sept. He divided against the second reading of the revised bill, 17 Dec. 1831,[13] the enfranchisement of Tower Hamlets, 28 Feb., and the third reading, 22 Mar. 1832. He voted against the Vestry Act amendment bill, 23 Jan. He divided against ministers on the Russian-Dutch loan, 26 Jan., 12 July. He was a minority teller against appointing a select committee on the general register of deeds, 22 Feb., but his name was added to it, 27 Mar. 1832. He did not offer for Barnstaple at the general election later that year, but he was returned in 1837 and sat as a Conservative until his defeat in 1847.[14] In November 1841 he applied to Peel for a baronetcy, explaining that his claim was 'entirely political', based on five 'severe and very expensive contests' at Barnstaple and his consistent support, 'with the exception of the Poor Law Amendment Act', for 'all the great measures advocated by yourself whether in or out of office'. He added that he had 'ample fortune to support the rank' and intended to retire from business shortly; since he had 'no family, the honour ... would die with me'. However, Peel was unwilling to

recommend any new creations.[15] Hodgson died in Paris in March 1854, 'in his 59th year', and left the residue of his estate to his wife. An obituarist wrote that 'his frank and manly bearing ... disarmed the hostility of his political opponents' and that in his contests at Barnstaple 'he dispensed his bounties from his ample purse with a profusion that has seldom been exceeded'.[16]

[1] *N and Q* (ser. 7), vi. 417; P. Mathias, *Brewing Industry*, 190-2; T. Gourvish and R. Wilson, *British Brewing Industry*, 90-91. [2] PROB 11/1514/421; IR26/162/142. [3] He was the residuary legatee of George's estate; the personalty was sworn under £70,000 (PROB 11/1583/436; IR26/678/614). [4] E. Yates, *Recollections*, 8-9. [5] *Trewman's Exeter Flying Post*, 4, 11 Mar. 1824. [6] *The Times*, 22 May 1824. [7] *Syle's Barnstaple Herald*, 13 June 1826. [8] *The Times*, 6 Mar. 1828. [9] *N. Devon Jnl.* 8 July 1830. [10] Add. 40309, f. 153; Wellington mss WP1/1128/12; 1137/5. [11] *N. Devon Jnl.* 5, 19 May 1831. [12] *The Times*, 13 Aug. 1831. [13] Ibid. 22 Dec. 1831. [14] *Dod's Parl. Companion* (1838), 124. [15] Add. 40494, ff. 385-8. [16] PROB 11/2189/290; IR26/1999/283; *Gent. Mag.* (1854), i. 652; *N. Devon Jnl.* 6 Apr. 1854.

T.A.J.

HODGSON, John (1806–1869), of Elswick House, Northumb.[1]

| NEWCASTLE-UPON-TYNE | 1830–1834 |
| NEWCASTLE-UPON-TYNE | 27 July 1836–1847 |

b. 30 July 1806, 1st. s. of John Hodgson of Elswick and Sarah, da. and coh. of Richard Huntley of Friarside, co. Dur. *educ.* by Rev. James Birkett at Ovingham, Northumb. 1814-19; Durham sch. 1819-23; Trinity Coll. Camb. 1823. *m.* 31 Jan. 1833, Isabella, da. and coh. of Anthony Compton of Carham Hall, nr. Berwick-upon-Tweed, Northumb., *s.p. suc.* fa. 1820; Elizabeth Archer Hinde to Stelling Hall and Ovington Lodge, Northumb. 7 Mar. and took additional name of Hinde by sign manual 11 Aug. 1836. *d.* 25 Nov. 1869.
Sheriff, Northumb. 1849-50.

Hodgson was a direct descendant of William Hodgson, who was sheriff of Newcastle-upon-Tyne in 1474, and heir to the manor and 800-acre Tyneside estate of Elswick on the city's outskirts, purchased in 1717 by his paternal great-grandfather, a prosperous linen draper. His father (*d.* 1820) had exploited the estate's mineral wealth, built a new mansion, and resited Elswick village to facilitate smelting and coal extraction. At Cambridge, Hodgson's 'superfine black dress and white linen always told more of the student than the squire' and he excelled in Latin, palaeography and 'Border anecdotes', on which he later became an expert. He acquired Elswick and an independent income of £500 on coming of age in 1827, and made his first foray into Newcastle politics the following year as an opponent of the proposed route of the Newcastle-Carlisle railway and promoter of the Scotswood suspension bridge.[2] Capitalizing on local dissatisfaction with the sitting Whig Sir Matthew White Ridley and the Tory Cuthbert Ellison's dread of a contest, at the general election of 1830 he came in unopposed for Newcastle, on his 24th birthday, after an arduous ten-week canvass. He was the preferred candidate of the low freemen and condoned by the shipping interest, but their spokesmen warned him on the hustings that he was 'on trial'.[3] At his election and dinners he declared against free trade and promised to promote the coal and carrying trades, a gradual abolition of slavery, repeal of the Septennial Act and a 'moderate' reform of Parliament that 'did not interfere with vested rights ... without giving an indemnity to those who may suffer by the change'.[4]

The Wellington ministry listed Hodgson among the 'good doubtfuls', but he divided against them on the Irish Subletting Act, 11 Nov., and when they were brought down on the civil list, 15 Nov. 1830, having, by his own testimony, lost confidence in them on account of their 'warlike' king's speech.[5] He presented anti-slavery petitions from Newcastle and beyond, 8, 10, 12, 15, 18 Nov., endorsed, 15 Nov., and presented, 2 Dec., others for repeal of the coastwise coal duties, and soon established himself as a ready debater attuned to local mercantile interests. Speculating that the recent sharp rise in freeman admissions in Newcastle, where he had financed some 300 creations, was replicated elsewhere, he ordered detailed returns of admissions for every borough to 'discover the amount of stamp duty paid with a view to repealing that tax', 7 Dec. 1830, but he withdrew his request, when asked to so by the Grey ministry's chancellor of the exchequer and leader of the House Lord Althorp.[6] Two days later he received a drubbing from the home office under-secretary George Lamb and the anti-reformers John Croker and Sir Charles Wetherell for proposing a similar motion targeting local enrolment fees. In a well-received speech at the Newcastle reform meeting, 21 Dec. 1830, he expressed qualified support for the government as promoters of peace, retrenchment and reform, and acknowledged that differences with his constituents on the latter were a resignation matter. He called for the enfranchisement of the northern industrial towns, the abolition of rotten boroughs, the enfranchisement of resident householders and for compensatory votes 'where they lived' for non-resident freemen, and refused to sanction the ballot.[7] Anticipating an early dissolution, he publicized his candidature at the next election, 5 Jan. 1831, and before Parliament recon-

vened sought the support of the individual Newcastle guilds for his intended 'vote of conscience' for reform.[8] He expressed support for his constituents' petition for the ministerial reform bill, but criticized its failure to give South Shields separate representation, 7 Mar. He divided for its second reading, 22 Mar., and against Gascoyne's wrecking amendment, 19 Apr. On introducing the burgesses' petition requesting its amendment to safeguard freemen's rights, 28 Mar., and again at the Newcastle mayoral dinner, 6 Apr., he said he would move amendments at its committee stage for a seven-mile rule and six months' residence qualification.[9] On 15 Apr. the Newcastle barrister James Losh informed lord chancellor Brougham that Hodgson claimed 'he was one of the 20 Members who would be content to give up all opposition to what is called disfranchisement, provided persons now apprentices and the sons of freemen above 15 years of age were allowed to vote [for] life'.[10] He refused to be goaded into endorsing the hostile South Shields petition he presented, 20 Apr. Like his colleague Ridley, with whom he was returned unopposed as a reformer at the general election in May, he had upheld the interests of the Newcastle manufacturers by speaking out against the barilla duties bill, 7 Feb., and the coastwise coal duties, 11, 23 Feb., and refuting charges of price-fixing by the northern coal owners, 23 Feb. He welcomed the treasury's concession on the Greenwich Hospital levy, 28 Mar. 1831.[11]

Hodgson brought up petitions criticizing details of the reintroduced reform bill from the 'free brothers' of Morpeth, 1 July, and from Manchester, 5 July 1831. He divided for its second reading, 6 July, and against adjournment, 12 July, but in committee his support for it was erratic and tempered by his defence of vested rights. He voted to retain the 1821 census as the determinant of borough disfranchisement, 19 July, but cast wayward votes against disfranchising Appleby, 19 July, Downton, 21 July, and St. Germans, 26 July 1831. He voted for the schedule B disfranchisements, 27, 28, 29 July, 2 Aug., to enfranchise Greenwich, 3 Aug., and Gateshead, 5 Aug. (whose entitlement to representation independently of Newcastle he defended in speeches on 4, 5, 9 Aug.), and to unite Rochester with Chatham and Strood, 9 Aug. He voted to retain Merthyr in the Cardiff group of boroughs, 10 Aug. He dissented from the prayer of the Newcastle anti-reformers' petition presented by Ridley, 20 July, but upheld its complaint that the rate assessment provisions for tradesmen with separate shops and residences was inadequate, 13, 24 Aug. He voted against the anti-reformers' proposals to extend the county franchise to freeholders in counties corporate, 17 Aug., and borough copyholders and leaseholders, 20 Aug., but for Lord Chandos's clause enfranchising £50 tenants-at-will, 18 Aug. He presented and endorsed the Coventry apprentices' petition for continued enfranchisement, 13 July, and urged the preservation of existing voting rights, 27, 30 Aug., but voted for the government's amendment disfranchising non-resident freeholders in the hundreds of New Shoreham, Cricklade, Aylesbury and East Retford, 2 Sept. He divided for the bill's third reading, 19 Sept., and passage, 21 Sept., the second reading of the Scottish reform bill, 23 Sept., and Lord Ebrington's confidence motion, 10 Oct. Returning afterwards to Newcastle, he defended his independent conduct as a reformer in speeches at the mayor's dinner, 19 Oct., and publicly at the reform meeting, 25 Oct.[12] He divided for the revised reform bill at its second reading, 17 Dec. 1831, and steadily for its details. He answered criticism of its polling provisions, 7, 15 Feb., and struggled to overcome the anti-reformers' attempts to ridicule his justification, on geographic and commercial grounds, of the separate enfranchisement of Gateshead (in preference to Merthyr), 5 Mar., South Shields, 7 Mar., and Whitby, 9 Mar. 1832. He welcomed the belated decision to award Merthyr separate representation by denying Monmouthshire a third Member as a fair adjustment of town and county representation, 14 Mar. South Shields and Westoe's petitions protesting that the boundary commissioners had underrepresented their population were brought up and endorsed by him, 20 Mar. He divided for the reform bill's third reading, 22 Mar., and the address requesting the king to appoint only ministers who would carry it unimpaired, 10 May. Undeterred by the complaints of the political unionists and the town's guilds, Newcastle's reformers commended Hodgson's conduct. He endorsed their petition for 'such measures as would effectively secure' the reform bill's passage, 21 May, and divided for the Irish reform bill at its second reading on the 25th.[13] On the Scottish measure, he voted in the minority for a Conservative amendment to increase the county representation, 1 June 1832. He divided with government on the Dublin election controversy, 23 Aug. 1831, the Russian-Dutch loan, 26 Jan., 20 July, and relations with Portugal, 9 Feb., but cast wayward votes on the sugar refinery bill, 12 Sept. 1831, for inquiry into the glove trade, 31 Jan., and for the immediate appointment of a select committee on colonial slavery, 24 May 1832. He voted against disqualifying the recorder of Dublin from sitting in Parliament, 24 July 1832.

Confirming his support for retrenchment, Hodgson voted to reduce public salaries to 1797 levels, 30 June, and against the civil service grant, 18 July 1831. He divided against compensating two free coloured men, Louis Lecesne and John Escoffery, for their deportation from Jamaica, 22 Aug. He voted for the Irish union of parishes bill, 18 Aug., and to make absentee landlords liable for the Irish poor, 29 Aug., but against the Maynooth grant, 26 Sept. He presented petitions and joined in the clamour against the locally contentious general register bill, 21 Sept., 4 Oct. On 14 Dec. 1831, to the acclaim of the liberal *Tyne Mercury*, he announced that he would move to exempt the Northern circuit counties from its provisions.[14] Backed by further hostile petitions, he refuted the arguments of the bill's promoter, Edward Littleton, and stated that a government, like Grey's, which had 'obtained office through the force of popular opinion' should not sanction this unpopular measure, by which they stood to gain nothing but 'an immense quantity of patronage', 27 Jan. 1832. He was a minority teller against its committal, 22 Feb., protested at the exclusion of its opponents from the select committee, 6 Mar., and was consequently added to it on the 27th. He presented and endorsed the merchants and manufacturers of Newcastle's petitions for the repeal of stamp duty on marine insurance policies, 26 Sept. 1831 (and others for reductions in the duties on soap and its ingredients, 23 Jan. 1832). Taking charge of the South Shields and Monkwearmouth railway bill, in which his relations and political allies had vested interests, 10 Feb., he carried its second reading (by 55-9) on the 14th in the teeth of opposition from the county Durham Member Sir Hedworth Williamson and the engineer Stephenson. He defended it robustly, 2, 6, 22, 26 Mar., but failed (by 37-22) to have its defeat referred to an appeal committee, 26 Mar.[15] Co-operating with the Durham Member William Chaytor, he backed the Hartlepool docks and railway bill, 13 Mar., and presented petitions against the Sunderland (North side) docks bill, in which Williamson had a proprietorial interest, 23 Mar., 4 Apr. His conduct as a member of the select committee on the rival Sunderland (South side) wet docks bill became the subject of breach of privilege allegations following its defeat there by ten votes to seven in select committee, 2 Apr.; and he candidly conceded the part he had played in transmitting their division list to the local attorneys responsible for its publication, 16 Apr. He upheld the attorneys' conduct when they appeared before the House, 7 May.[16] He supported Ridley's motion to abolish the merchant seamen's levy, 8 Mar., and was a spokesman with him for Newcastle interests when the customs duties bill was considered, 25 July 1832.

After a difficult canvass in which his refusal to support the ballot and his equivocal stance on corn law reform and the Bank of England's monopoly were major issues, Hodgson, a Conservative standing as a self-declared Liberal, outpolled the political unionist Charles Attwood to retain his Newcastle seat at the general election of 1832.[17] Defeated in 1835, he became vice-chairman of the North Shields Railway Company, before he was returned for Newcastle as a Conservative at the 1836 by-election caused by Ridley's death. He retained his seat until 1847, when his intended successor, his brother the railway entrepreneur Richard Hodgson (1812-79), Conservative Member for Berwick-upon-Tweed, 1837-47, and Tynemouth, 1861-5, was defeated.[18] He had sold Elswick, and moved with his mother (d. 1858) to Stelling Hall near Hexham, formerly the estate of Elizabeth Archer Hinde, having in compliance with her will (dated 13 Oct. 1835 and proved in Newcastle, 11 May, and London, 16 May 1836) taken the additional name of Hinde, purchased the remaining sixth of the estate and consolidated the whole in 1837 by means of a private Act. Now devoting himself to antiquarian studies, Hodgson published the *Pipe Rolls for Cumberland, Durham and Westmorland* (1847), *The Foundations of British History Explored* (1852), an introductory volume to his late namesake's *History of Northumberland* (1858), and *Simeon of Durham's Works* (1868). He was also a regular contributor to the transactions of the Newcastle Society of Antiquaries, of which he was vice-president.[19] He died intestate and without issue at Stelling Hall in November 1869 and was buried in the family vault at Bywell St. Peter.[20] His widow (d. 1879) having renounced probate, administration of his personal estate, which was thrice sworn (under £20,000 in Newcastle, 20 Dec. 1869, £16,000 and £2,000 in London in 1870) before he was ruled 'insolvent' for estate duty purposes, passed to Richard, who, as heir by right of his wife (Hodgson's widow's sister) to Carham Hall, assumed the name of Huntley. Stelling Hall reverted to Hodgson's younger brother, the Rev. Thomas Hodgson (b. 1814), who accordingly took the names of Archer and Hinde.[21]

[1] Draws on R. White, *Biog. Notice of John Hodgson Hinde*, reprinted from *Archaeologia Aeliana* (n.s.), vii (1873), and R. Welford, *Men of Mark 'Twixt Tyne and Tweed*, ii. 522-8. Bywell (Northumb.) MI incorrectly gives Hodgson's year of death as 1809. [2] IR26/829/1435; Welford, ii. 523-5; *Diaries and Corresp. of James Losh* ed. E. Hughes (Surtees Soc. clxxi) [Hereafter *Losh Diaries*, i], 151; ibid. (cclxxiv) [Hereafter *Losh Diaries*, ii], 34. [3] Tyne and Wear Archives, Ellison of Hebburn mss DF/ELL/A66, *passim*; Northumb. RO, Ridley (Blagdon) mss ZRI25/59, *passim*; P.D. Brett, 'Newcastle Election of 1830', *Northern Hist.* xxiv (1988), 101-23. [4] *Newcastle Chron.* 5 June-14 Aug. 1830; Northumb. elections [BL J/8133.i.13.], ii. 627, 635, 681-3, 723-9, 643, 761. [5] *Newcastle Chron.* 28 Dec. 1830. [6] Ellison of Hebburn mss A66, Sorsbie to Ellison, 20 June; Ridley (Blagdon) mss 25/59, Shadforth to Ridley,

24 June 1830. [7] Northumb. RO, Blackett-Ord (Whitfield) mss NRO324/A/36, W.H. Ord to fa. [23 Dec.]; *The Times*, 29 Dec. 1830. [8] *Tyne Mercury*, 11, 25 Jan., 1 Feb. 1831. [9] Ibid. 5, 12 Apr. 1831. [10] *Losh Diaries*, ii. 191. [11] *Tyne Mercury*, 26 Apr., 3 May; *The Times*, 4 May 1831. [12] *Tyne Mercury*, 25 Oct., 1 Nov. 1831. [13] *Newcastle Chron.* 12, 19 May; *Tyne Mercury*, 15 May; *The Times*, 26 May 1832. [14] *Tyne Mercury*, 27 Dec. 1831. [15] Ibid. 21 Feb. 1832. [16] *Durham Chron.* 16, 30 Mar., 6, 13, 20 Apr.; *Tyne Mercury*, 10, 17 Apr. 1832. [17] *Tyne Mercury*, 31 July-18 Dec.; *Newcastle Courant*, 8-22 Dec. 1832. [18] *Losh Diaries*, ii. 228; *Public Dinner to Hodgson* (1835); *Tyne Mercury*, 19, 26 July; Blackett-Ord (Wylam) mss ZBK/C/1/B/2/10, Ord to Blackett, 3 Aug. 1836. [19] IR26/1420/341; *Gent. Mag.* (1836), ii. 319; C.M. Fraser, 'John Hodgson, County Historian', *Archaeologia Aeliana* (ser. 5), xxiv (1996), 171-86. [20] *Tyne Mercury*, 3 Dec.; *Hexham Herald*, 4 Dec. 1869; J.C. Hodgson, *Hist. Northumb.* vi. 141-3; *Burke LG* (1871, 1886, 1906) has Stella Hall. [21] IR26/1293/616; 3349/1556.

M.M.E.

HODSON, James Alexander (1788–1832), of Grove-within-Upholland, nr. Wigan, Lancs.

WIGAN   1820–21 Feb. 1831

b. 1 Sept. 1788, 1st s. of James Hodson of Ince and Jane, da. of Jarvis Johnson.[1] *educ.* Reading; Peterhouse, Camb. 1804. *m.* c. 1809, Sarah, at least 3s. (1 *d.v.p.*) 3da. (1 *d.v.p.*).[2] *d.* 24 Nov.1832.
    Lt. Wigan vol. light horse 1819.

Hodson belonged to a prominent Wigan family, who had established a strong position in the corporation by the last decade of the eighteenth century. His father James, who was probably the man of that name who served as mayor three times between 1784 and 1790 and was a patron of St. George's chapel of ease, 1781-4, was dead by 1806. Like his brother John Hodson[†], the beneficiary at the general election of 1802 of a coup against the established aristocratic interests, he was involved in cotton manufacture.[3] His sons James Alexander and John Johnston (?1791-1869) appear not to have been, and were conventionally educated at Cambridge and Oxford respectively.[4] John took holy orders and died as rector of Yelvertoft, Northamptonshire. When their uncle John Hodson, who had no children, retired from the representation of Wigan at the dissolution in 1820, James came forward in his room. He was returned with Lord Lindsay, the son of the 6th earl of Balcarres, the Hodsons' new electoral ally, after a contest forced by an abortive bid to revive the Bradford interest.[5]

As was noted in a radical publication of 1823, Hodson supported the Liverpool ministry when present, but he was a lax attender, who is not known to have spoken in debate.[6] He voted in defence of ministers' conduct towards Queen Caroline, 6 Feb. 1821. He divided against Catholic relief, 28 Feb. 1821, and

Canning's bill to relieve Catholic peers of their disabilities, 30 Apr. 1822. He voted against reducing the barracks grant, 28 May 1821, and abolition of one of the joint-postmasterships, 13 Mar. 1822. He lost an infant daughter on 19 Dec. 1822. His wife gave birth to another on the 30th, but died, 'in her 34th year', on 8 Jan. 1823.[7] No trace of parliamentary activity by Hodson has been found for the ensuing session. He divided for repeal of the usury laws, 8 Apr. 1824, 8 Feb. 1825. He presented a petition from the clergy and magistrates of Wigan against the beer bill, 11 May 1824.[8] He voted against the motion condemning the prosecution of the Methodist missionary John Smith in Demerara, 11 June 1824. He was granted a fortnight's leave on account of ill health, 21 Feb. 1825. He divided against Catholic relief, 21 Apr., 10 May. He presented a Wigan petition against alteration of the corn laws and for protection of the flour trade, 4 May.[9] He voted for the duke of Cumberland's grant, 30 May, 2, 6, 10 June 1825. A radical survey of that session commented that he had 'attended occasionally, and voted with ministers'.[10] He divided against the opposition motion on the Jamaican slave trials, 2 Mar., and reform of the representation of Edinburgh, 13 Apr. 1826.

Hodson was returned unopposed for Wigan at the general election of 1826.[11] It seems likely that poor health increasingly interfered with his attendance. He voted against Catholic relief, 6 Mar. 1827, 12 May 1828. On the death of his uncle that year he became entitled to the interest on £8,000 invested for the benefit of himself and his children.[12] Planta, the Wellington ministry's patronage secretary, predicted in February 1829 that he would vote 'with government' for Catholic emancipation, but he presented a hostile petition from Hindley, 4 Mar., and divided against the proposal, 6 Mar. His Wigan colleague James Lindsay, cousin of the 7th earl of Balcarres (as Lord Lindsay had now become), who supported it, reported from London four days later that Hodson had 'vacillated half a dozen times since he came here'.[13] He presented the Wigan anti-Catholic petition, 17 Mar., and voted in the hostile minorities of 18, 23, 30 Mar. He presented a Wigan petition against the East India Company's trade monopoly, 13 May 1829. He was granted a month's leave on account of ill health, 26 Feb. 1830. He presented a constituency petition against the sale of beer bill, 3 May, and voted against its second reading, 4 May, and for an amendment to prohibit sales for on-consumption, 21 June. He voted against Jewish emancipation, 17 May, and the Galway franchise bill, 25 May 1830.

Before the general election of 1830 he expressed an inclination to retire from Parliament, but he was persuaded by Balcarres and Lindsay to stand again. A contest was forced by local dissidents who wished to challenge the existing right of election and put up two businessmen of advanced views. Hodson, who pledged himself under constituency pressure to oppose renewal of the East India Company's charter, apparently had no prior knowledge of the surprise intervention of his cousin John Hodson Kearsley*, who nominated himself and attacked Lindsay. Hodson and Lindsay were returned.[14] Ministers listed him among their 'friends', but he never took his seat in the new Parliament. On 3 Nov. 1830, when the petition against his and Lindsay's return was presented to the Commons, he told Balcarres, who later claimed that Kearsley had already canvassed Wigan, that he still wished to retire, more particularly as 'I have been confined to my bed almost ever since the last election and am only just able now to get down stairs'.[15] On 15 Nov. his formal notification that he would not personally contest the petition was accepted by the House, and Kearsley was given permission to act in his stead, 6 Dec. 1830. As soon as his return was confirmed by the election committee, 21 Feb. 1831, he took the Chiltern Hundreds; Kearsley replaced him at the ensuing by-election.

Hodson, who owned property in Wigan but lived at Upholland, four miles to the west, and had a share in the thriving Kirklees colliery, died in November 1832.[16] By his will, dated 25 Dec. 1830, and proved at Chester under £12,000, 13 Dec. 1832, he directed that a total of £22,500 be raised for the equal benefit of his four younger children. His eldest daughter Sarah received £2,500 in addition to the sum settled on her on her marriage to John Woodcock in 1829. His eldest son and residuary legatee James Alexander Hodson (1813-89) was the principal beneficiary.[17] His second son John Fowden Hodson (b. ?1815) was educated at Merton College, Oxford and took the name of Hodges in 1844 after succeeding to the Oxfordshire property of his maternal uncle Frederick Richard Hodges of Henley-upon-Thames.[18]

[1] Lancs. RO, All Saints, Wigan par. reg. [2] IGI (Lancs.); Gent. Mag. (1810), i. 389; (1823), i. 93. [3] HP Commons, 1790-1820, ii. 239; iv. 212; G.T.O. Bridgeman, Hist. Church and Manor of Wigan (Chetham Soc. n. s. xviii), 781. [4] W.D. Pink and A.B. Beavan, Parl. Rep. Lancs. 239 and W. Bean, Parl. Rep. Six Northern Counties, 463 incorrectly suppose James Alexander Hodson to have been the son of the Member for Wigan. [5] Liverpool Mercury, 18 Feb., 3, 10 Mar. 1820. [6] Black Bk. (1823), 164. [7] Gent. Mag. (1823), i. 81, 93. [8] The Times, 12 May 1824. [9] Ibid. 5 May 1825. [10] Session of Parl. 1825, p. 468. [11] Liverpool Mercury, 16 June 1826. [12] Lancs. RO, John Hodson's will. [13] NLS, Crawford mss 25/1/435. [14] Ibid. 25/13/353; 40/7/28;

Liverpool Mercury, 16, 23, 30 July, 6 Aug.; *Manchester Guardian*, 31 July, 7 Aug. 1830. [15] Crawford mss 25/13/352, 354. [16] Bridgeman (Chetham Soc. n. s. xvii), 647, 654; D. Anderson and A.A. France, *Wigan Coal and Iron*, 64-66. [17] Lancs. RO, Hodson's will; IR26/1294/819; *Gent. Mag.* (1829), ii. 558. [18] *Gent. Mag.* (1843), ii. 444.

S.R.B./D.R.F.

HOLDSWORTH, Arthur Howe (1780–1860), of Mount Galpin, Dartmouth and Widdicombe, Devon.

DARTMOUTH	1802–24 Dec. 1819
DARTMOUTH	26 Jan. 1829–1832

b. 26 Nov. 1780, 1st s. of Arthur Holdsworth† of Widdicombe and Elizabeth, da. of Robert Holdsworth, merchant, of Dartmouth. *educ.* Eton 1796. *m.* (1) 8 Feb. 1803, Elizabeth Were (*d.* 1804), da. of Richard Hall Clarke of Bridwell, 1da.; (2) 16 July 1807, Catherine Henrietta, da. of John Eastabrook of Okehampton, 3s. 1da. *suc.* fa. 1787.[1] *d.* 14 May 1860.[2]

2nd lt. Dartmouth vols. 1798; lt.-col. Coldridge vols. 1803, Dart and Erne yeomanry 1813.

Gov. Dartmouth Castle 1807-d; mayor, Dartmouth 1821-2, 1824-5, recorder 1832.

Holdsworth, head of the family which dominated Dartmouth life for over a century before the Great Reform Act, was a man of several parts: politician, pamphleteer, inventor, artist, governor of Dartmouth Castle and indefatigable exploiter of the spoils system on behalf of his relatives.[3] After vacating his Dartmouth seat in December 1819, supposedly to attend more closely to 'business', he remained the leading figure in the borough's municipal and electoral affairs. He moved the address of congratulation and condolence to George IV at a town meeting chaired by his kinsman Henry Joseph Holdsworth, 28 Feb. 1820.[4] At a meeting on 27 Dec. 1820 he proposed a loyal address to the king and drew a parallel between 'the popular party of the present day' and the Independents of 1648, warning that 'unless something is effectually done to arrest in its progress that tide of impiety and sedition, that is flowing through the country and finding its way into the most remote branches of society, England must soon be lost'. He had his speech published and asked the printer to distribute copies 'in all parts of this and the adjoining counties ... any of the cities, watering places and libraries where you know your men, and particularly to Dock and Plymouth'.[5] Three months later, at a Devon county meeting, he moved a petition against Catholic claims, of which he was an unyielding opponent, declaring that 'he could not conceive that Roman Catholics were the most fit to legislate and advise in a Protestant establishment'.[6] In the spring of 1826 he published a *Letter to the Members for Devon*, in which he defended the landed interest against charges of monopoly and called for the corn law question to be settled, observing that 'keeping it alive ... tends only to paralyse the exertions of the farmer from a fear of the uncertain state of future markets, and to give the manufacturing labourer a mischievous weapon with which to amuse himself when it suits the purpose of his employer to discharge his men and leave them to the parish for their support'. He attended the Devon meeting to petition against Catholic emancipation, 16 Jan. 1829, when he attacked Lord Ebrington, Whig Member for Tavistock, for flirting with the Catholic Association. After a particularly tedious historical review of the issue, he asserted that 'it was to the Bible that they were indebted for their liberties ... Did not the priests, who were in obedience to the pope ... endeavour to suppress that sacred book by every means in their power?'[7] Ten days later he returned himself for Dartmouth on a vacancy created by the death of one of the sitting Members. He promised continued zeal in the promotion of local interests and remarked that the 'failure' of some of his past endeavours had been 'occasioned in great measure by the violent dispositions of some men, who are ever found ready to maintain or support opposition'.[8]

He took his seat on 19 Feb. 1829. That month Planta, the Wellington ministry's patronage secretary, listed him as being 'opposed to the principle' of Catholic emancipation, and he proved to be one of its diehard opponents. On the presentation of the hostile Devon petition, 24 Feb., he said the meeting had been 'as well conducted and as orderly as could be expected from an assembly of 16,000 persons'. He presented and endorsed various hostile petitions and divided against emancipation, 6, 18, 23, 27, 30 Mar. He insisted that 'those who are anxious for the church and state remaining as they are should be allowed the opportunity of expressing their opinions', 9 Mar., but was persuaded to drop his attempt to alter the form of the proposed oath so that Members would have to swear to resist the pope's temporal authority. Peel, who pointed out the dangers of thereby admitting its existence, also dismissed his worries over potential problems arising from the appointment of chaplains to Catholic Speakers and naval captains, 24 Mar. 1829. It is not clear whether it was he or Thomas Houldsworth, Member for Pontefract, who defended county magistrates against Hume's attack and had something to say on the county bridges bill, 25 Mar. 1829. He complained that Portman's friendly societies bill would 'take the jurisdiction now possessed by them out of the hands of all the cities and boroughs in the country', 15 May. He presented a Dartmouth petition for repeal of the coastwise coal duties, 22 May. He or Houldsworth criticized a detail of the justice of the peace bill, 27 May, and argued against a fixed duty on corn imports, 1 June 1829. The following month he applied to government for the crown living of Stokenham, made vacant by the death of his brother Charles (and which his brother Robert, vicar of Brixham, did not want), for his nephew Henry Taylor, son of the recorder of Dartmouth. Wellington reluctantly complied, though he moaned to Planta that he had had someone else in mind and that it was 'too much that I should be obliged to give my own patronage for the purpose of government and that I can get nothing even to set that free'.[9] In October 1829 the Ultra leader Sir Richard Vyvyan* listed Holdsworth among the 'Tories strongly opposed to the present government'. However, he is not known to have cast any hostile votes in the 1830 session. He was appointed to the select committee on the London coal trade, 11 Mar., after expressing the hope that a national inquiry would follow. He presented a constituency petition for repeal of the coastwise duties, 16 Mar., and secured a return of information, 30 Mar. Opposing inquiry into the state of the nation as futile and deceitful, 19 Mar. 1830, he argued, on the strength of his recent visit to the industrial areas of West Yorkshire, that 'the distress lies in the middle class ... not in the lowest of all'. He thought a general investigation of the banking system might be beneficial, as 'the present depression mainly depends on the want of confidence and credit which exists among small traders and persons engaged in agriculture'. He was returned again for Dartmouth at the general election that summer, defying an attempt by his local rival John Henry Seale† to poll the inhabitant ratepayers.[10]

Ministers listed Holdsworth among their 'friends', and he voted with them in the crucial civil list division, 15 Nov. 1830. Three days later he successfully objected to the reception, while inquiry into Seale's election petition was pending, of a Dartmouth ratepayers' petition claiming the right to vote and advocating parliamentary reform. The election committee confirmed him in his seat, 30 Nov. He presented a Brixham petition for repeal of the coastwise coal duties, 23 Nov., and was given a week's leave on account of the disturbed state of his neighbourhood, 6 Dec. 1830. He voted against the second reading of the Grey ministry's reform bill, 22 Mar., and for Gascoyne's wrecking amendment, 19 Apr. 1831. At the ensuing general election he was returned unopposed for Dartmouth, though his declaration of continued opposition to

reform reportedly earned the 'disapprobation' of many of his audience.[11] He divided against the second reading of the reintroduced reform bill, 6 July, and for Gordon's adjournment motion, 12 July 1831. He was in the opposition minorities for use of the 1831 census to determine the disfranchisement schedules, 19 July, and to postpone consideration of the partial disfranchisement of Chippenham, 27 July. He complained that the bill would 'bestow a preponderating influence upon the towns over the rural electors', 17 Aug. Although he was granted three weeks' leave on account of family bereavement, 15 Sept., he was present to vote against the bill's passage, 21 Sept. He voted to censure the Irish government for interference in the Dublin election, 23 Aug., and for inquiry into the state of West Indian sugar producers, 12 Sept. He was absent from the division of 17 Dec. 1831 on the second reading of the revised reform bill, by which Dartmouth, hitherto unmolested, was condemned to lose one Member. He joined in calls for confirmation of its assignment to schedule B to be postponed, 23 Feb. 1832, claiming that the recent disappearance of a local tax collector had caused a large defalcation in its return of assessed taxes, which would otherwise have been sufficient to warrant its retention of both seats. When Lord John Russell, who disputed this, suggested that Dartmouth's commerce was in decline, Holdsworth replied that while the Newfoundland traffic had dwindled, the coastal trade was buoyant and increasing. He made further unavailing protests against the borough's loss of a seat, 2, 14 Mar. He voted against the enfranchisement of Tower Hamlets, 28 Feb., and the bill's third reading, 22 Mar. His only other known vote was against ministers on the Russian-Dutch loan, 12 July 1832.

Holdsworth did not stand for Dartmouth at the 1832 general election, when the extended franchise made a gift of the borough to Seale.[12] As he explained to Peel, when encouraged to stand two years later by Conservative party managers:

> The expenses which I incurred when I before represented the place, added to the treatment which I personally received from the late government had driven me to give up all idea, for the present, of attempting to recover it ... Justice to my family required that I abstained from entering into a contest ... and I felt confirmed in the propriety of this decision from a consciousness that if the contest terminated successfully I had not the means of supporting the situation as I ought to do.

Yet he professed willingness to try to recover the seat if Peel would give him 'any situation, however laborious, which would sanction an open avowal of connection with the government and ... enable me to maintain my post as I ought to do'. Peel had nothing for him, and he conceded Dartmouth to Seale at the 1835 general election.[13] Shortly before this, he had solicited from Peel a commissionership of tithes under planned legislation, explaining that 'I feel it of real importance to my family that whilst the energies of my mind and body continue, I should if possible fill some public situation which may keep up my connection with the world'; he was again unsuccessful.[14] He encountered frustration in other respects, including his failure in 1841 to have Dartmouth rather than the admiralty's choice of Falmouth established as the packet station for the new West Indian mail service.[15] In 1840 he published *Campaign of the Indus*, an edition of letters to him from his son Thomas, a lieutenant in the 2nd Foot serving in Bombay, and three years later he sought to explain to a doubtless fascinated public the *Advantages which may be derived from working low-pressure marine engines by expansion*. Among his several inventions was a system of water-bulkheads for preventing and combating fire in ships, for which he pursued a claim for compensation against the admiralty.[16] He died in May 1860 and was succeeded by his eldest son, Arthur Bastard Eastabrook Holdsworth (1808-75), formerly a captain of dragoon guards.

[1] PROB 11/1158/451. [2] According to the probate reg. *Gent. Mag.* (1860), i. 646 says the 13th. [3] P. Russell, *Dartmouth*, 120, 145, 150-2. [4] *Alfred*, 7 Mar. 1820. [5] A.H. Holdsworth, *Speech at Dartmouth* (Exeter, 1821); Wilts. RO, Simpson mss 130/75, Holdsworth to Flindell, 11, 17 Jan. 1821. [6] *Alfred*, 20 Mar. 1821. [7] *Woolmer's Exeter and Plymouth Gazette*, 17 Jan. 1829. [8] Ibid. 31 Jan. 1829. [9] Wellington mss WP1/1031/10; 1042/63; 1048/2. [10] *Woolmer's Exeter and Plymouth Gazette*, 31 July 1830. [11] *R. Devonport Telegraph*, 30 Apr., 7 May 1831. [12] Ibid. 15 Dec. 1832. [13] Add. 40405, ff. 131, 134; 40406, f. 71. [14] Add. 40418, f. 155. [15] Add. 40490, ff. 316-23; Holdsworth, *Dartmouth: the advantages of its harbour* (1841). [16] Russell, 152.

D.R.F./T.A.J.

HOLFORD, George Peter (1767–1839), of 15 Bolton Street, Mdx. and Weston Birt, Glos.

BOSSINEY	12 Jan. 1803–1806
LOSTWITHIEL	1807–1812
DUNGANNON	1812–1818
HASTINGS	1818–1820
QUEENBOROUGH	1820–1826

b. 1767,[1] 2nd s. of Peter Holford, master in chancery, of Lincoln's Inn Fields, Mdx. and Weston Birt and Anne, da. of William Nutt of Buxted, Suss. *educ.* Harrow 1780; St. John's, Camb. 1784; L. Inn 1788, called 1791. *m.*

1802,[2] Anne, da. of Rev. Averill Daniell of Lifford, co. Donegal, 1s. surv. 3da. *suc.* fa. to Weston Birt 1804. *d.* 30 Apr. 1839.

Sec. to bd. of control May 1804-Feb. 1806, Apr. 1807-Jan. 1810.

Vol. London and Westminster light horse 1798-1800.

Holford, a ministerialist lawyer and active philanthropist, who could not be accommodated at Hastings at the general election of 1820, was mentioned by the premier Lord Liverpool to Lord Bath, 29 Feb. 1820, as

the person I should have been most disposed to recommend to your lordship if you had had an opening ... He is one of the oldest friends I have in the world, has been nearly 20 years in Parliament and is particularly useful in the House of Commons from the attention that he gives to all business which is connected with public charities and institutions ... [He] is one of the Members in whom the respectable part of the House have most confidence in matters of this nature, and this consideration is of the more importance as he is a steady friend to the established church.[3]

In the event he was returned for the ordnance borough of Queenborough and continued steadfastly to support the ministry, appearing in almost all surviving government division lists. After the suicide in August 1822 of his close friend Lord Londonderry*, whose executor he was, he opined to his heir, 29 Oct., that 'we who are attached to your brother, should avoid anything like an expression of hostile feelings towards his successor', and, in a bid to mollify him towards the new foreign secretary, stated that his own line would be

to support Canning as the head of the government in the House of Commons, so long as I shall continue to have a seat in the House, a period which however is not likely to extend beyond the present Parliament.[4]

In December 1822 Londonderry, who counted Holford as a placeholder, doubted that he would abandon government to join his putative third party.[5]

Holford voted against the forgery punishment mitigation bill, 23 May 1821. He divided against the Catholic peers bill, 30 Apr. 1822, and Catholic relief, 1 Mar., 21 Apr., 10 May 1825. He was a teller for the minority against the ill-treatment of cattle bill, 24 May, and complained of the vagueness of its provisions, 10 June 1822. He joined in requests for Henry Grey Bennet to withdraw his alehouses licensing bill, 27 June 1822.[6] When Lord Eldon, the lord chancellor, mentioned Holford in 1824 as a possible candidate for an undisclosed office, the home secretary Peel replied that he 'would not be of much service. At least, his uniform support of the government would detract from his weight'.[7] After incurring a fine for non-attendance on a jury during a parliamentary session he asked if exemption was not an automatic right for Members, 20 Feb. 1826, and was satisfied the following day, when the committee of privileges reported that it was. He introduced a bill to regulate the Indigent Blind School, 24 Feb., which passed into law on 5 May 1826.[8]

Holford's main interest was in prisons, particularly the recently built penitentiary at Millbank, of which he was a governor. He described it as an essential alternative to transportation for short-term prisoners, replied to attacks on its cost and rejected the notion that it should be open for public inspection, 16 June 1820. He defended additional grants for it, 19 June 1820, 28, 31 May 1821; on the last occasion he 'spoke in high terms of the order and discipline of this establishment'.[9] In 1821 he published his *Thoughts on the Criminal Prisons of this Country*, which advocated the separation of different categories of offenders and an increased role for prison chaplains, in the belief that 'religion is the most powerful engine that can be applied to the human mind'. This, like subsequent pamphlets, was published by the Philanthropic Society, of which he was a vice-president. In the *Edinburgh Review* Sydney Smith praised Holford's 'good sense' but criticized his lapse into 'the usual nonsense about "the tide of blasphemy and sedition"'. Maria Edgeworth commented that

> Mr Holford's connections with Lord Londonderry he alludes to as if Mr. Holford were a sycophant flattering for patronage for some nephew or son. Nothing *can* be more false. Mr. Holford is a man of large fortune who uses it for benevolent purposes and wants no patronage for any creature.[10]

He was named to select committees on gaols, 16 Mar. 1821, prison laws, 5 Mar. 1822, 18 Mar. 1824, the metropolis police, 14 Mar. 1822, and Scottish prisons, 14 Apr. 1826. In 1822 he published *A Short Vindication of the General Penitentiary at Millbank*, which refuted allegations that its regime was lax. He moved a successful amendment to the bill for consolidating prison laws, 21 June 1822, to prevent justices from compelling prisoners who took the county food allowance to work before trial. In his speech, published as a pamphlet in 1824, he condemned the original clause as a 'monstrous injustice ... departing from the broad distinction between punishment and safe custody', which ran counter to 'the humane presumption of English law in favour of innocence'.[11] He also denied the right of authority to subject a prisoner to educational or moral improvement without his consent, an argument apparently inconsistent with his reply to Sir John Newport's criticism of compulsory attendance at Anglican service for prisoners and the practice of employing only Anglican prison officers, 24 Mar. 1823: 'It was thought fit that the officers should set an example to prisoners in attendance upon divine service, and that they could not do so unless they were members of the English church'.[12]

Holford, who was appointed to select committees on Millbank penitentiary, 14 May 1823, 1 Mar. 1824, defended the conduct of its management committee when information was demanded regarding an outbreak of disease among the inmates and cuts in their diet, 28 Apr. 1823. He subsequently admitted, in his second *Vindication* (1825), which denied that the regime was too harsh, that the committee had been wrong in bowing to outside pressure to reduce the diet. During further discussions on the Millbank epidemic, 9 July, he denied allegations that the prison's riverside location was responsible for the outbreak, a view he elaborated in his third *Vindication* (1825).[13] On 10 July 1823 he moved that extracts from the committee's minutes be placed before the House to illustrate the adequacy of the allowance for a prisoner on bread and water. He supported a grant to defray the cost of moving officers and prisoners from the penitentiary because of the epidemic, 1 Mar. 1824. His 1825 pamphlet *The Convict's Complaint in 1815 and the Thanks of the Convict in 1825* consisted of two pieces of verse, one bemoaning conditions aboard a hulk, the other eulogizing the healthy discipline of the penitentiary. An apparent dilemma for Holford surfaced in the preface, where he claimed that at Millbank 'punishment of the offender is subservient to his amendment', whereas in *Thoughts on the Criminal Prisons* he had written that 'punishments are instituted not for the reformation of offenders (although [that] is certainly desirable ...) but for the protection of the public and to deter others'. When approving another grant, 10 Mar. 1826, he denied a charge of excessive use of solitary confinement and enthused over the health and general condition of the prisoners.[14] His 1826 critique, *Statements and Observations Concerning the Hulks*, focused mainly on the necessity of separating prisoners.

As anticipated, Holford retired from the House at the dissolution in 1826. He spent some time in his wife's native Ireland in late 1828, an experience which confirmed him in his heartfelt opposition to Catholic relief and his belief in the need for a policy of repression. An alarmist, he held similarly reactionary views on parliamentary reform which, he informed Lord

Bristol two years later, would 'probably have no other effect than to make the House of Commons, which is already too popular, still more of a bear garden'.[15] In 1828 he published *An Account of the General Penitentiary at Millbank* and in 1830 a *Letter to the Editor of the Quarterly Review*, in which he denied that the penitentiary had been a failure and complained of the lack of government support. As he explained to Bristol, to whom he described the Commons as 'the great coffee house of the nation':

My letter, though addressed to the editor of the *Review*, is in part intended as a brief for such Members of Parliament as may be inclined to protect the penitentiary from unmerited abuse in the ensuing discussion upon the miscellaneous estimates, an occasion in which we are regularly assailed by the gentlemen who think imprisonment a mere question of pounds, shillings and pence ... and weakly defended, or rather attacked in another way, by the government, for we have no friends in the ... [home] office, being considered there as rivals not auxiliaries.[16]

A valetudinarian, he hoped that Gloucestershire would not be disturbed at the general election of 1830, but confessed that if it was, 'I shall leave the battle to those who are younger than I am, and have more landed property to make it proper to them to take a part in struggles for county representation, than has fallen to my lot'.[17] He died in April 1839.[18] His surviving son and heir, Robert Stayner Holford (1808-92), who had succeeded his immensely wealthy uncle Robert (this Member's brother) the previous year, became an art and plant collector, and was Conservative Member for Gloucestershire East, 1854-72.[19]

[1] A.T. Lee, *Hist. Tetbury*, 219. [2] Ibid. [3] Add. 38283, f. 149. [4] Londonderry mss. [5] Norf. RO, Blickling Hall mss, Londonderry to wife, 14, 29 Dec. 1822. [6] *The Times*, 28 June 1822. [7] Add. 40315, ff. 133-5. [8] *The Times*, 25 Feb. 1826. [9] Ibid. 29 May, 1 June 1821. [10] *Edgeworth Letters*, 270. [11] *Substance of Speech of George Holford* (1824). [12] *The Times*, 25 Mar. 1823. [13] Ibid. 11 July 1823. [14] Ibid. 11 Mar. 1826. [15] Suff. RO (Bury St. Edmunds), Hervey mss 941/56/59, Holford to Bristol, 31 Aug., 15 Oct. 1828, 2 Aug.; 56/60, same to same, 9 Nov. 1830. [16] Ibid. 56/60, same to same, 23 Apr. 1830. [17] Ibid. 56/59, same to same, 12 July 1830. [18] *Gent. Mag.* (1839), ii. 318. [19] Ibid. (1838), ii. 444-5, 678; *HP Commons, 1790-1820*, iv. 215-16; *Oxford DNB sub* Robert Stayner Holford.

H.J.S.

HOLMES, William (?1777–1851), of 10 Grafton Street, New Bond Street and Vine Cottage, Fulham, Mdx.

GRAMPOUND	17 Mar. 1808–1812
TREGONY	1812–1818
TOTNES	1818–1820
BISHOP'S CASTLE	1820–1830
HASLEMERE	1830–1832
BERWICK-UPON-TWEED	1837–1841

b. ?1777, 5th s. of Thomas Holmes, brewer, of Farnhill, co. Sligo and Anne, da. of Harloe Phibbs of co. Sligo. *educ.* Trinity, Dublin 6 Apr. 1795, aged 17. *m.* 24 Oct. 1807,[1] Helen, da. and coh. of John Tew of Dublin, wid. of Rev. Sir James Stronge, 1st bt., rect. of Tynan, co. Armagh, 1s. *d.* 26 Jan. 1851.

Lt. 4 Ft. 1799, 69 Ft. 1800; capt. 3 W.I. Regt. 1803-7. Treas. of ordnance June 1818-Nov. 1830. Agent, Demerara 1818-33.

By 1820 'Black Billy' Holmes, a coarse, foul-mouthed Irishman and self-confessed 'ministerial hack', was firmly established as the chief government whip.[2] Unusually, he had no direct connection with the treasury, having been installed in 1818 in the place of treasurer of the ordnance, worth £1,200 a year. He had, by his own admission, done well for his family out of the spoils system, and he owned property in Demerara, for which he was colonial agent.[3] Although he performed his functions efficiently enough to retain the confidence and friendship of leading Tory ministers in this period, he was, as two men who knew him well put it, noted for 'his habitual irregularity' and 'a certain carelessness in his habits': the minor errors and omissions which litter his letters are sufficient testimony to this shortcoming.[4] He was, too, notoriously indiscreet and garrulous, surprisingly so for a man in his position, and there was about him an unmistakable impression of rascality, or worse. At the general election of 1820 he was 'supplanted' at Totnes by John Bent and was initially reported to be at a loss for a seat.[5] In the event he stood for Bishop's Castle on the Clive interest, which had lost one seat to a radical at a by-election the previous year. He told Arbuthnot, the patronage secretary, 21 Feb., that the Clives' opponent was so well entrenched that 'at present I have scarcely a hope' of success; but he and his colleague were involved in a double return, the inquiry into which confirmed them in their seats and re-established the Clive interest.[6] Holmes was a government teller in the divisions on the Barbados pension fund, 25 Mar. 1822, and the beer duties bill, 17 June 1823. He made no known contributions to debate in the 1820 Parliament, but he presented petitions from Bishop's Castle against the beer retail bill, 22 May, and from Dingwall for the abolition of slavery, 21 June 1824.[7]

Holmes voted against Catholic claims, 28 Feb. 1821, but, aware from his calculations that the relief bill would pass the Commons, was reported by a friend of the measure to have become 'quite indefatigable in the use of every means, fair and foul, to induce Members to vote against us'. It was said that Lord Castlereagh, the government leader in the House, 'promised to insist on checking' this 'activity'.[8] He voted against Canning's bill to relieve Catholic peers, 30 Apr. 1822, and Catholic claims, 1 Mar., 21 Apr., 10 May 1825, though the pro-Catholic Edward Littleton* seized on his private admission that 'he begins to think the cause [of resistance] must be abandoned'.[9] He was a teller for the minority against the bill to disfranchise Irish 40s. freeholders, 26 Apr. 1825. In June 1821 he held out to the Grenvillites the prospect of the government reshuffle which brought them into office six months later.[10] He advised Canning on the choice of a mover and seconder of the address on the eve of the 1823 session.[11] He was an occasional attender at meetings of the committee of West India planters and merchants in this period.[12] He was returned unopposed for Bishop's Castle at the general election of 1826.[13]

As expectations rose that the Catholic question would be carried in the new Parliament, Charles Long* told Lord Lonsdale, an opponent of their claims, in February 1827 that he had 'desired Holmes to be upon the alert. He says he has to ascertain the intentions of about 130 who are quite new to the question'. Holmes duly voted against relief, 6 Mar. 1827, when Lord Binning* complained that 'that Irish rascal Black Holmes' was helping to propagate the notion that if the motion was successful the stricken Liverpool ministry would collapse.[14] He retained his place and his whipping duties under Canning, apparently after consulting Lord Powis, his electoral patron, who encouraged him to believe of the new ministry that 'their reign will be as ephemeral as their projects will be evanescent'.[15] He voted against the disfranchisement of Penryn, 28 May, and the Coventry magistracy bill, 18 June 1827. The following month he relayed to Arbuthnot, for the edification of Peel and the other seceding ministers, tales of the tensions and disagreements between Canning and his Whig colleagues, and in particular let it be known that Whig backbench supporters of the ministry had 'refused to receive treasury notes, and that they never would attend unless they were summoned by Lord Duncannon*'.[16] During the ministerial turmoil which followed Canning's death he kept Wellington and Peel fully apprised of developments, though some of his information, such as his report that Lord Lansdowne had never tendered his resignation and that the king had vetoed Lord Holland's admission to the government, was inaccurate.[17] Keen to see the restoration of a thoroughgoing Tory government, he rejoiced in Wellington's appointment as commander-

in-chief; but to Mrs. Arbuthnot in early September he expressed reservations, which he was not alone in harbouring, about Peel's fitness as a party leader:

> My own opinion is that the government will blow up on some point of government or principle long before Parliament meets. The Portuguese, Greek and army reduction measures afford a fine prospect of difference of opinion, and if the Tories will only take up a position on the neutral territory, and form a corps of observation without (in the first instance) going into decided opposition, they will soon overthrow these people. A regular Tory opposition cannot be formed, because there is no leader. Peel, though able, honest and high-minded, is too selfish, too proud and haughty in his manners to have a personal following, and he is disliked by the king ... You may rely upon it, that whenever this government drops, the duke of Wellington will be sent for and not Peel.[18]

Yet according to the junior Lansdowne Whig minister Spring Rice, Holmes spoke in late October 'with the utmost confidence of [ministerial] parliamentary strength next year'.[19] Peel suspected that Holmes had been kept on by Lord Goderich purely to 'obtain a majority in the House of Commons *against* the Roman Catholic question', which he and his senior colleagues 'professed to support'.[20] At the turn of the year Holmes, who was said to be 'very much in the confidence' of lord chancellor Lyndhurst and Herries, the chancellor of the exchequer, kept the Arbuthnots abreast of the disintegration of the ministry: he was openly scathing of their 'total want of principle and their unblushing rapacity and jobs'.[21]

Anticipating the formation of Wellington's ministry, in which he remained *in situ*, Holmes, though uncertain as to whether the Huskissonites would join it, was sure, as he told Powis, that 'the Whigs have no chance under any circumstances'.[22] He voted against repeal of the Test Acts, 26 Feb. 1828, and the following day presented a Bishop's Castle petition for repeal of the Malt Act. He was in the government majorities against inquiry into chancery delays, 24 Apr., and ordnance economies, 4 July. On 6 Mar. 1828, while going from the House to dine in the company of his wife and Croker, he 'caught a pickpocket with his hand in his pocket' in Cockspur Street, but 'let him off' after his show of penitence.[23] On a more serious note, he 'bitterly' complained to Mrs. Arbuthnot later that month of Peel's priggish 'conduct which, he says, disgusts the Tories in the House to such a degree that they will not stay and vote'. He also told her that on being shown by Planta, the patronage secretary, an 'impudent' note from four aristocratic backbenchers protesting against over zealous whipping, he urged him to 'send the note back with a list of the sums pocketed by the families of these four gentlemen', but that the 'good natured' Planta preferred to ignore it.[24] Although he voted against Catholic relief, 12 May 1828, he admitted to Powis that 'some settlement must be come to on this subject as things cannot rest where they now are, and we Protestants are clean beat after a fair stand-up fight in the Commons'. He was glad to see the back of the Huskissonites at the end of the month: 'I trust in God we never shall have any more of these cursed new light people in power. The duke of Wellington is firm, and says he will carry on his government with clerks and appeal to the country if necessary.'[25] He was clearly discomfited by the government's decision to concede Catholic emancipation in 1829. Croker suspected that he had 'feigned illness' to avoid the dinner at Peel's to hear the king's speech, 4 Feb.; and his friend Lord Lowther* reported later in the month that he was 'so dejected and melancholy, he has been but twice in the House of Commons and swears he will not go again until after all this business is passed'.[26] On 1 Mar. he went to Westbury to enforce the arrangement by which Sir Manasseh Masseh Lopes made way for Peel, just ousted from Oxford University. Informing Planta of Peel's election and a narrow escape from an embarrassing Ultra Protestant challenge the following day, he moaned that he had to endure the 'cursed bore' of dinner with Lopes in his draughty house before he could escape back to London.[27] He cast no known vote on emancipation,[28] but doubts persisted as to his attitude to the issue, as Lord Althorp* explained to Brougham, 10 Mar.:

> I ... told Arbuthnot that Holmes was using very dangerous language, saying to Phillimore, for instance, that he had compared his list with Chandos, and made out they [the anti-Catholics] would divide 180 on the second reading. He answered me it was impossible, for that Holmes was with us, and that not an hour before he had been with the duke, and him as eager for carrying the measure as they were. I told him that Phillimore was undoubtedly a credible witness, and that I could not doubt that he had quoted Holmes correctly. He said, 'I will take care of him, then'.[29]

Holmes was a teller for the majority for the anatomy regulation bill, 18 May 1829.

At the end of the session he visited Ireland, but Wellington's letter of 2 July 1829 asking him to intercede in the Cork by-election on behalf of Colonel Hodder reached him in Dublin too late. On his return to London he gave Peel 'an account of Ireland satisfactory as far as the upper classes are concerned'.[30] In November 1829 the Ultra leader, Sir Richard Vyvyan*, speculating on the possibility of forming a coalition government, observed that Holmes would have no difficulty in serving in it, as he was 'always faithful to the ministry for the time being'; and Holmes was the conduit for the duke of Buckingham's invitation to Wellington to visit him at Stowe that month.[31] He was with Planta at his Sussex home at Fairlight in January 1830, when the company were hugely amused by a report in the *Standard* of a change of government.[32] According to Greville, Holmes and the other whips feared 'for a long time' that government would be beaten on Knatchbull's amendment to the address, 4 Feb. 1830, and were mightily relieved when two dozen Whigs rescued them. A week later, however, he and Planta told Lord Ellenborough that 'the temper of the country gentlemen is much improved', and they were 'quite in spirits again' as a result.[33] Holmes voted against Lord Blandford's reform motion, 18 Feb., and the enfranchisement of Birmingham, Leeds and Manchester, 23 Feb. After Peel's excellent speech on the question of the treasurership of the navy, 12 Mar., Holmes and Sir Henry Hardinge* told Mrs. Arbuthnot that although his 'odious' manners were still a problem, if he continued in his recent 'spirited' fashion, they 'should soon have a good stout party'.[34] Holmes found himself in a scrape when Robert Grant's motion for leave to introduce a Jewish emancipation bill was carried by 18 votes, 5 Apr. Goulburn, the chancellor of the exchequer, accused him of leaving the House 'some time before the division', thereby helping to create an impression among the government's customary supporters that ministers were indifferent about the outcome. It emerged that Holmes had in fact 'paired off early in the day' – the first time he had done so for five years – because, as he explained to an angry Planta in his own defence, he had 'a sore throat'; but he claimed to have remained on the scene until after midnight, 'giving you all the assistance in my power'. He attributed the defeat to the poor showing put up in debate by Goulburn and other opponents of the measure, and to the question having been unexpectedly brought on in Peel's absence. At the same time, he admitted a failure by the party managers, in which he implicated Planta, to make clear at an early stage 'the determination of government to oppose the measure': 'I shall never pair off as long as I live again, and on the second reading we shall get rid of it. I am *very very* sorry I was absent last night'. Mrs. Arbuthnot, who was inclined to blame Holmes alone for the fiasco, believed that he had been 'spoiled by the duke and has got his head turned'; and she advised Wellington that 'he would do him immense mischief if he was not *set down*': 'The duke, who was very angry about the Jews, promised to remonstrate with him'.[35]

The bill was duly thrown out on its second reading, 17 May, when Holmes, who at the beginning of the month had told Ellenborough that 'the friends of government were rather more disposed to come down, and he could on any great question get 300', voted in person against it.[36] He presented a petition from Bishop's Castle publicans against the sale of beer bill, 24 May, and voted for the grant to South American missions and against abolition of the death penalty for forgery, 7 June 1830.

On the dissolution the following month Holmes's only son, Thomas Knox Holmes, who had recently come of age, was encouraged by Lord Chandos* to stand for Wendover; but when the patron, Lord Carrington, announced his adhesion to government, Holmes went in pursuit of his son and intercepted him before he could enter the borough. His stepson Sir James Stronge got nowhere in a reconnaissance of county Tyrone.[37] Holmes was returned for Haslemere on the interest of the 1st earl of Lonsdale, whose son Lowther recommended the arrangement partly because Holmes would be able to assist him with local private bills and obtain preferment for some of the electors.[38] He also stood with Sir Philip Durham† for Queenborough on the interests of the ordnance and the corporation against the independent sitting Member, John Capel, and his colleague Thomas Gladstone, and apparently deployed every available device of electoral chicanery. Holmes topped the poll, but Durham and Capel were tied in a double return for the second seat. Although Holmes was constantly expected to vacate to exercise his option on Haslemere, he did not do so, to the annoyance of Gladstone, who at one point commented, 'How inveterate a liar he is'. When the joint petition of Capel and Gladstone was considered under the auspices of the new Grey government, Holmes and Durham offered no defence, and the independents were seated.[39]

Holmes, who had been standing next to Spencer Perceval† when he was assassinated in the lobby of the Commons in 1812, was the closest person to Huskisson when he had his fatal accident on the Liverpool and Manchester railway, 15 Sept. 1830.[40] He was at Drayton with Wellington, Lord Aberdeen, Goulburn and the Arbuthnots a week later, when he passed on Lord Clive's* hint that Lord Palmerston* semed keen to rejoin the government.[41] It fell to Holmes, who had admitted that he 'knew nothing at all about' some 100 Members when Parliament met, to interrupt Wellington's dinner party to inform him of the ministry's defeat in the Commons, which he had apparently seen coming, on the civil list, 15 Nov. 1830. He was of course in the minority. It was said that he

was 'thunderstruck' when the duke, having assumed that government had won by 28, 'began by complaining of the smallness of the majority'. Greville heard that he 'implored' Wellington to resign immediately. He went out with him, and, writing to Powis a few days later, claimed that 'relieved from office, and poor as I am', he felt happier than he had done since the break-up of the Liverpool ministry, though he hoped that the new government would be short-lived, and believed that the opposition 'should still have equal numbers in the House of Common'[42] As for his poverty, he was the recipient of a civil list pension of £500 a year, controversially given to him by Wellington on 16 Nov., 'after he *virtually* was out'. The duke was satisfied that he had 'well defended' the grant when it was criticized in the Lords, 13 Dec.; but it is not clear whether its being nominally conferred on Holmes's son was a response to the continued carping which it provoked.[43] Holmes was one of the ex-ministers who in the week immediately after Wellington's fall formed a committee – the Charles Street gang, as it became known – to organize and direct the operations of the Tory opposition to the Grey ministry. They also concerned themselves with management of the press, and Holmes introduced to them and vouched for the honour and reliability of a plausible Irishman, George McEntaggart, for whom he had secured ministerial work earlier in the year in his capacity as editor of the *Courier* and a self-styled press agent. In doing so, he unwittingly stored up a peck of future troubles for himself and the committee.[44]

In early January 1831 Holmes was the 'standard bearer' at Apethorpe of a pledge of support from Buckingham to Lonsdale if the latter would put himself at the head of the opposition, and later in the month he was Peel's guest at Drayton.[45] He shared in the 'high spirits' of the leading Tories who thought ministers had 'damaged themselves very much' with their civil list proposals, and in mid-February was boasting, with Herries, that 'they will beat the government out of all their taxes'. He 'very discreetly' and effectively intervened with the West India committee to have the sting taken out of the effects of Peel's resistance to Chandos's motion of 21 Feb. for increased protection for colonial sugar producers.[46] After the introduction of the ministerial reform bill, which he had at one point predicted would never materialize, he was busy with Planta and Francis Bonham* counting heads: early calculations of a majority of 40 or more against the measure proved to be well wide of the mark.[47] Holmes voted in the minority against the second reading, 22 Mar. A fortnight later he had 'recovered his spirits', as Ellenborough perceived, and, in bullish mood, advised Peel, who consulted him on the point, not to risk defeat on the motion to go into committee on the bill, but to throw everything into Gascoyne's amendment against any reduction in the number of English Members, for which he was rightly confident of securing a good attendance. He duly voted for the amendment, 19 Apr. 1831. Returned unopposed for Haslemere at the ensuing general election (though there were apparently men at Sandwich willing to support him if Wellington gave him his blessing), he went to Cumberland to assist Lowther in his unsuccessful contest there.[48]

Holmes, who sent out 266 notes for attendance at the Commons in early June 1831, was present at the meeting of opposition leaders and organizers which resolved to rent Planta's former house in Charles Street as a permanent party headquarters. He took over management of the general fund, which now included the press fund.[49] He voted against the second reading of the reintroduced reform bill, 6 July. His only known vote in committee was for use of the 1831 census in determining the borough disfranchisement schedules, 19 July, and he is known to have taken a pair on the 27th, when the fate of Chippenham was voted on; but he told Mrs. Arbuthnot in late August, when he was busy organizing the annual opposition fish dinner at Greenwich and predicting that 'we shall yet damage the bill most seriously in our House' (while remaining utterly confident of its defeat in the Lords), that

> wherever I am, our young ones run away. I had hoped that with the loss of my office I should have had some rest, but in the whole course of my parliamentary life I have never fagged as hard as I have done in the last six months.

He expressed a devout wish that the cholera would sweep through Downing Street, but had the decency not to vote for the motion condemning the Irish government's 'shameful and open' interference in the Dublin election, 23 Aug., 'as, God knows, I have done twice as much in that way as Lord Anglesey did, but not in so bungling a manner'.[50] He voted against the issue of the Liverpool writ, 5 Sept., and for inquiry into the effects of the Sugar Refinery Acts on West Indian producers, 12 Sept. He was livid at the abortive division against the third reading of the reform bill, in which he voted, 19 Sept: Littleton met him 'immediately afterwards, swearing and abusing everybody in a manner that rendered it dangerous to speak to him'. He wrote to Mrs. Arbuthnot in pique:

> I am still suffering from violent cramps in my left leg. I scarcely get any sleep from it, and I cannot lay up for a few days. I go every morning to Charles Street, where I am obliged to answer one hundred foolish questions put to me daily, and at four I go to the House, where I remain till two o'clock the next morning.

He was satisfied with the opposition showing of 236 against the passage of the bill, 21 Sept., when he was 'thirteen hours in the House, and never, I believe, sat down. I remained in the lobby and kept our people well together'.[51] He voted against the second reading of the Scottish reform bill, 23 Sept. He assisted in calculating numbers for the clash in the Lords, where he predicted a majority of 40 against the bill (it was in fact 41). Through Edward Ellice*, the patronage secretary, he made sure that the state of play in the Upper House was brought in advance to the attention of Lord Grey, perceiving that the likely size of the hostile majority would deter him from seeking a creation of peers to carry the bill. Holmes was also busy with the demands of the crop of by-elections which occurred in the autumn of 1831, and went in person to Cambridge in late October to liaise with Lowther in organizing the Tory campaign for the county, which ended in a rare defeat. He had earlier told Mrs. Arbuthnot: 'I wish I was out of this vortex of hurry and confusion. I am tired to death, and nothing enables me to go on but the certain conviction that the Lords will do their duty well'.[52] On 13 Oct. 1831 he presented a petition from some Staffordshire farmers calling for the county franchise under the reform bill to be extended to non-freeholders who were rated at the same level as borough householders, and one from Wigtownshire against the use of molasses in brewing. The next day he secured an adjournment of proceedings on the Wallingford election petition, so that the defeated Tory candidate could change his surety.

Holmes, who was detained in London in November 1831 by his son's illness, mistakenly told Wellington, who passed on the information to ministers, that steps were being taken in London to provide the Birmingham Political Union with arms.[53] He reported that the government had 'taken fright' at the unions and that there was 'not that general cordiality of sentiments in the cabinet which existed some time ago'. He feared and warned Peel that ministers would 'humbug' the 'Waverer', Lord Wharncliffe, whom he saw after his discussions with them on the possibility of reaching a compromise; and, with Herries, he indicated the bulk of the party's approval of Peel's discouraging response to Wharncliffe's feelers.[54] Towards the end of the month he was put to work to muster the opposition for the fullest possible attendance in both Houses at the meeting of Parliament on 6 Dec. He informed

Mrs. Arbuthnot, 23 Nov: 'I have enough to do, and I believe I am destined never to enjoy another day's shooting. I have received this morning 22 letters from persons begging me to pair them off'. It was primarily at the suggestion of Holmes, who, as well as thinking that 'nothing more can be done with the press at present', considered the Charles Street house too cramped for a party headquarters, that the committee decided at the turn of the year to seek 'a much larger house and turn it into a sort of club': the outcome was the formation of the Carlton Club the following spring.[55] He voted against the second reading of the revised reform bill, on which opposition divided only 162 to 324, 17 Dec. 1831.

An attack of gout prevented him from visiting Drayton in early January 1832, but his close contacts with Ellice enabled him to keep Peel informed of developments on ministers' negotiations with the king at Brighton for a possible creation of peers to carry the reform bill, which he was eventually inclined to believe had not gone well. He wrote to Mrs. Arbuthnot, 11 Jan.:

> I have this day received 26 letters from MPs, most of whom write to ask, will not the 1st of February do as well as the 20th of January?, and I have to answer all these stupid inquiries, or they will not come ... I never am able to finish my letters before seven o'clock. I am very anxious to have a good attendance at the meeting of Parliament, because I am convinced that there never was any period, since these people came into power, in which they felt themselves so embarrassed as they do at this moment, and particularly from what has taken place at Brighton.

The following day he had to remonstrate with Peel, who was not disposed to come up until the last minute:

> Your letter has alarmed me beyond measure ... I have been working hard for the last month to endeavour to procure an attendance of our friends for the 20th ... and I shall not be prepared to tell our friends what course we are to take, unless I hear from you ... They all look up to you, and if you are not here to guide us I shall be obliged to run out of town on the 17th to avoid the questions and angry looks of those I have summoned to town when they find that their chief is not here.[56]

He was in the opposition minority of 99 against going into committee on the bill, 20 Jan. Three days later he voted in the majority against reform of select vestries. He voted against government on the Russian-Dutch loan, 26 Jan., when they had a majority of only 24; but he was furious with the Tory peer Lord Wynford for raising the issue in the Lords, 2 Feb., when Lord Brougham gave him such a drubbing that his motion

had to be humiliatingly withdrawn: according to Denis Le Marchant†, he loudly denounced Wynford in the lobby of the Lords as 'a dotard and asked whether anything could have been more egregiously silly after the success they had had in the Commons to court a battle in the very place where the superiority of their enemies lay'.[57] Soon afterwards Raikes recorded the story of a so-called 'joke' by Holmes: when James Morrison, Member for Ipswich, a wealthy silk merchant, 'asked him if he could get him a *pair* for the evening, "Of what", said Holmes, "gloves or stockings?"'[58] Holmes voted against the enfranchisement of Tower Hamlets, 28 Feb., and the third reading of the reform bill, 22 Mar. On 2 Apr. he voted against the malt drawback bill, and next day he dismissed Hume's objections to details of the Highbury Place road bill and was twice a teller for minorities against his amendments. He presented a petition from subscribers to the London and Birmingham railway project who wished to pull out of their commitment, 4 Apr. He was in the minority of 13 against Crampton's amendment to the Irish arrears of tithes bill, 9 Apr. Holmes, who expected that peers would 'eventually be made', counted on a government majority of five for the second reading of the reform bill in the Lords, and an opposition one of about 25 in committee: he rather underestimated the opposition strength in both cases.[59] In mid-April Ellenborough noted that the treasury had 'called upon Holmes to pay a sum of £1,000 lost by the peculation of his nephew', Alexander Erskine Holmes, a junior clerk to the secretary to the ordnance board, and that opposition leaders intended to raise the sum for him out of their own pockets. The following month it emerged that Holmes's son was one of the investors in the unsuccessful *Albion* newspaper who were losing money hand over fist; and Arbuthnot was concerned that Holmes might well have 'cause to be angry' at Wellington's refusal to help bale it out.[60] Holmes, who had by this time become a hanger-on of the duke of Cumberland, joined Goulburn in convincing Croker of the futility of his attempt to persuade Peel to set aside his objections to forming a government after the dismissal of the reform ministry. On their reinstatement, he referred 'aptly enough' to recent events as 'the interlude of the duke of Wellington'. He was a member of the committee formed by the opposition in late May to manage the forthcoming English elections.[61] He voted against the second reading of the Irish reform bill, 25 May. He was named to the select committee on the abolition of slavery, 30 May. He divided against government on the Russian-Dutch loan, 12 July, and was in the minority of 17 against the Irish education grant, 23 July. He was a teller for the minority against going into committee on the crown colonies relief bill, 3 Aug. 1832.

Holmes, who was at Walmer Castle and Drayton in October 1832, harboured some misplaced optimism about Conservative prospects in the English and Irish elections. For himself, Haslemere was disfranchised, and he told Peel, 17 Nov., that

> I have abandoned all hopes of coming into Parliament, unless something unexpected turns up at the eleventh hour. The fact is, I am not able to encounter the expense of a contest; but you may rest assured that whatever assistance an individual out of Parliament can give to a party will be constantly at your command.[62]

Peel seems to have taken little interest in Holmes's personal fate or his electoral management activities, which were apparently being engrossed by Bonham. Writing to the latter for an intimation of his 'hopes for future returns', 4 Oct., Arbuthnot urged him not to tell Holmes 'that I have asked you the question as he would fancy that I have doubted him'.[63] On the other hand, Hardinge thought it was desirable that he should be found a seat on account of 'the great importance of his services and abilities'.[64] The wretched McEntaggart had been obtaining money from Herries to help him out of financial difficulties during the earlier part of the year, and in November 1832 he revealed himself in his true colours by threatening to expose the activities of the Charles Street committee unless he was paid money which he claimed he was owed for services rendered. Holmes suddenly proved to be very elusive to both McEntaggart and Herries, who was baffled and irritated by his conduct; and it was not until February 1833 that he was brought to broker a meeting between the two men.[65] It is tempting to believe that the following veiled reference by Arbuthnot in a letter to Herries, 30 Dec. 1832, was to Holmes, although the internal evidence is not conclusive:

> It is no new thing that our friend gains nothing by his communications with the enemy, and that he gives a great deal for that nothing. He is garrulous in the extreme. He has a great notion of his own *savoir faire*; and I was quite aware that he had received great personal obligations. I could not help talking to the duke [of Wellington] about him. The duke said that he was so aware of his not being safe that he made a point of saying nothing to him that there could be harm in repeating ... You see therefore that you are not single in your opinion about our friend ... I certainly do not, any more than you, accuse our friend of treachery, but he is very loose. I hope he does not learn more than the duke fancies.

Certainly Holmes's notorious intimacy with Ellice raised doubts about his reliability, though Ellice himself reckoned that the Conservatives had not 'the slightest reason' for such suspicions.[66]

Without a seat in the first reformed Parliament, Holmes, who became increasingly intimate with Cumberland, without being blinded to his deficiencies as a politician, nevertheless remained involved in party management.[67] However, he was enmeshed in financial difficulties, and he steadily fell out of favour with the Conservatives. He did himself great damage in the continuing saga of McEntaggart, whose claims went to legal arbitration in March 1834. Despite much previous bluster about his intention to expose McEntaggart as a liar and 'smash' him, he testified against his own side, to the effect that he had from the start encouraged McEntaggart to expect remuneration for his services, though he admitted that he had done so without the sanction of Herries or any other member of the committee. As a result, the arbitrator awarded McEntaggart £333 and costs, to the disgust of Herries, who thought that there had all along been 'something mysterious and unaccountable in ... [Holmes's] conduct about this man', apparently because he had a blackmailer's hold over him and members of his family.[68] According to Greville, who considered Holmes to be 'a low blackguard, and, however shrewd and active, a bad confidant and *fidus Achates* for the duke [of Wellington] to have taken up', he colluded with ministers to deprive Peel and Wellington of the opportunity of forming a government on Grey's retirement in July 1834. Seven months later Greville wrote of Holmes, who found no seat at the general election of 1835 under the auspices of a Conservative government, that 'though I hear of him sometimes as a volunteer correcting lists and interesting himself about their affairs, he no longer runs about the offices like a tame cat, nor is domesticated at Apsley House as formerly'.[69] In January 1836 Arbuthnot wrote to Peel:

> With regard to Holmes, the duke, talking to me privately about him, said that he was the most difficult person to deal with he knew; that he took good care not to tell him anything which ought to be secret; but that he would continue somehow or other to get into the house, to question the secretary, or if that would not do he would examine the servants. I mention this to you, because I remember once telling you how much the duke was on his guard in respect to him, and you see that he continues to be so.[70]

Holmes tried his luck at a by-election for Berwick in May 1835, but found 'the ground ... too strongly occupied before I arrived there to give me any hope of success except by means that might (if I had succeeded) have also sent me to Newgate', and he was defeated with another Conservative at Ipswich the following month.[71] He successfully contested Berwick at the 1837 general election at an estimated cost of about £1,200, which was partly defrayed by a subscription got up by Lowther, to which Peel contributed £50. As Sir George Clerk*, the chief whip, and his assistants Charles Ross* and Bonham were not returned to the new Parliament, Holmes was ostensibly well placed to resume his former position; but senior Conservatives lost no time in advising Peel, who probably needed no telling, that his appointment as whip would be unacceptable to all the party except the Lowther set. He was passed over for Sir Thomas Fremantle*, who had Henry Bingham Baring* and George Cecil Weld Forester* as his assistants, though Holmes, who remained on personally friendly term with Peel, may have acted as an unofficial third, and he continued to do electoral work.[72] Defeat at Stafford at the 1841 general election ended his parliamentary career.

Holmes died at his London house in Grafton Street, January 1851. In his very brief will of 13 Aug. 1822 he had left the house and his property at Fulham to his wife, conferred £100 on Louisa Talbot, 'the child who has lived in my house', and made his son, then under age, his residuary legatee. A memorandum drawn up by his attorney on 1 July 1849, which was produced for purposes of probate, 12 June, and proved as his last will and testament, 9 Sept. 1851, recorded that he had confirmed the devise of the London house to his wife, whose jointure from her first husband would 'enable her to maintain a sufficient establishment', and who was to continue living there with a Miss Bennett as her companion. He had intended to provide the latter with a life annuity of £50, together with an additional like sum while she lived with Lady Stronge. Holmes's personal estate was sworn under £3,000.[73] Cyrus Redding, a political outsider and innocent, recalled him as 'a much-abused man by many', but paid tribute to his political consistency and commented:

I always found him, though differing in politics, a good-natured man, of talents peculiarly fitted for the office he undertook, and, I believe, that in every relation in life, without great abilities, he was strictly honourable.[74]

Yet on hearing of his death Cumberland, with whom he had fallen out, observed that 'at last that vagabond and ungrateful fellow, Billy Holmes, is gone: his conduct towards myself was incomprehensible and inexplicable, but, *De mortuis nil nisi bonum*'.[75]

[1] *Gent. Mag.* (1807), ii. 977. [2] *Colchester Diary*, iii. 76; Le Marchant, *Althorp*, 48; Buckingham, *Mems. Geo. IV*, ii. 133; Add. 40383, f. 304; 56540, ff. 31, 99. [3] Add. 38279, ff. 51, 53. [4] Add. 57371, f. 22; 57404, f. 48. [5] NLI, Vesey Fitzgerald mss 7858, p. 170. [6] TNA T64/261; *Salopian Jnl.* 1, 8, 15 Mar., 17 May, 7, 21 June 1820. [7] *The Times*, 22 May, 22 June 1824. [8] Buckingham, i. 142-3; *Hobhouse Diary*, 54. [9] TNA 30/29/6/3/93. [10] Bucks. RO, Fremantle mss D/FR/46/12/28. [11] Wellington mss WP1/754/26. [12] Inst. of Commonwealth Stud. M915/3/4; 4/1. [13] *Salopian Jnl.* 7, 14 June 1826. [14] Lonsdale mss; *Canning's Ministry*, 42. [15] *Croker Pprs.* i. 373; NLW, Powis mss, Holmes to Powis [c. 17 Nov. 1830]. [16] *Canning's Ministry*, 340; *Arbuthnot Corresp.* 83. [17] *Wellington Despatches*, iv. 77-79, 90-91, 93, 94-95, 96; *Arbuthnot Corresp.* 85. [18] Add. 40340, ff. 185, 191; *Arbuthnot Corresp.* 89; N. Gash, *Secretary Peel*, 663. [19] Lansdowne mss, Rice to Lansdowne, 25 Oct. 1827. [20] *Colchester Diary*, iii. 527; R. Stewart, *Foundation of Conservative Party*, 37-38. [21] *Arbuthnot Jnl.* ii. 148, 153-5; *Wellington and Friends*, 80; *Wellington Despatches*, iv. 171; *Arbuthnot Corresp.* 97; Aberdeen Univ. Lib. Arbuthnot mss, Holmes to Arbuthnot [8 Jan. 1828]. [22] Powis mss, Holmes to Powis, 17 Jan. 1828. [23] *Croker Pprs.* i. 409. [24] *Arbuthnot Jnl.* ii. 176. [25] Powis mss (History of Parliament Aspinall transcripts), Holmes to Powis [17], 27 May 1828. [26] *Croker Pprs.* ii. 7; Lonsdale mss, Lowther to Lonsdale, 19 Feb. [1829]. [27] W.G. Hoskins and H.P.R. Finsberg, *Devon Stud.* 414-16; Gash, *Secretary Peel*, 565; Add. 40399, f. 25. [28] The assertion in *Oxford DNB*, apparently based on the statement in *Gent. Mag.* (1851), i. 315, that Holmes was given permission by Wellington to vote against emancipation is erroneous. So is the suggestion by A. Aspinall, in 'English Party Organization', *EHR*, xli (1926), 397, that he was allowed to keep his place after doing so because of Wellington's fear of further enraging the king. [29] Add. 76369. [30] Wellington mss WP1/1030/24; 1031/17; 1032/14; 1034/22; 1035/5, 22. [31] Cornw. RO, Vyvyan mss, Vyvyan to Knatchbull, 31 Aug. 1829; Wellington mss WP1/1057/15. [32] *Wellington Despatches*, vi. 395. [33] *Greville Mems.* i. 369-70; *Ellenborough Diary*, ii. 193. [34] *Arbuthnot Jnl.* ii. 344-5. [35] Add. 40333, f. 88; 40400, f. 154; Wellington mss WP1/1111/9; *Arbuthnot Jnl.* ii. 349. [36] *Ellenborough Diary*, ii. 234. [37] Wellington mss WP1/1124/21; 1125/5; 1130/30, 33. [38] Lonsdale mss, Lowther to Lonsdale, 22 July [1830]. [39] St. Deiniol's Lib. Glynne-Gladstone mss 195, T. to J. Gladstone, 1 Oct. 1830. See QUEENBOROUGH. [40] *Creevey Pprs.* i. 213; Gash, *Secretary Peel*, 642-3. [41] *Arbuthnot Jnl.* ii. 389. [42] Hopetoun mss 167, f. 189; *Three Diaries*, 1, 20; *Greville Mems.* ii. 61, 63; Powis mss, Holmes to Powis [c. 17 Nov. 1830]. [43] *Croker Pprs.* ii. 80; Wellington mss WP1/1137/44; 1186/21; *Three Diaries*, 34; *PP* (1831), xiii. 403. [44] Stewart, 68-69; Gash, *Politics in Age of Peel*, 345-6; Aspinall, *Politics and the Press*, 329-31; *Three Diaries*, p. lxi; Add. 57404, f. 3; 57405, f. 39. [45] Lonsdale mss, Beckett to Lowther, 7 Jan. 1831; Gash, *Sir Robert Peel*, 7. [46] *Three Diaries*, 45, 46, 57; *Arbuthnot Corresp.* 143. [47] Glynne-Gladstone mss 197, T. to J. Gladstone, 21 Feb., 14 Mar. 1831; *Three Diaries*, 62; *Creevey Pprs.* ii. 221; *Macaulay Letters*, ii. 6. [48] *Three Diaries*, 76, 83, 90; *Croker Pprs.* ii. 114; Hatfield House mss 2M/Gen., Price to Salisbury, 23 Apr. 1831. [49] *Arbuthnot Corresp.* 146; *Three Diaries*, pp. xlviii-l, 93; Aspinall, *Politics and the Press*, 467-8. [50] Hatherton diary, 27 July [1831]; *Arbuthnot Corresp.* 146, 148. [51] Hatherton diary, 19 Sept. [1831]; *Arbuthnot Corresp.* 150. [52] *Arbuthnot Corresp.* 150; *Three Diaries*, 134, 135, 137; Wellington mss WP1/1199/13. [53] *Wellington Despatches*, viii. 56-57, 61, 75, 113; *Grey-Wellington Corresp.* i. 413-22. [54] Arbuthnot mss, Holmes to Mrs. Arbuthnot, 18 Nov. 1831; Add. 40402, ff. 118, 138, 159; Parker, *Peel*, ii. 191-2, 195; Gash, *Sir Robert Peel*, 25. [55] *Arbuthnot Corresp.* 154, 155; Add. 40402, ff. 138, 159; Powis mss, Holmes to Powis, 25 Nov.; Arbuthnot mss, Arbuthnot to wife, 15 Dec. 1831; Gash, *Sir Robert Peel*, 25 and *Politics in Age of Peel*, 395-6;; Aspinall, *Politics and the Press*, 335, 337; Stewart, 72; *Three Diaries*, pp. lii-liv. [56] Add. 40402, ff. 2, 50, 175, 181, 183; Gash, *Sir Robert Peel*, 27; *Arbuthnot Corresp.* 160. [57] *Three Diaries*, 180, 198; Holland House Diaries, 123. [58] *Raikes Jnl.* i. 11-12. [59] Glynne-Gladstone mss 199, T. to J. Gladstone, 16 Mar. 1832; *Three Diaries*, 222, 231, 232. [60] *Three Diaries*, 233, 269; Add. 57370, f. 87. [61] *Three Diaries*, 238, 257, 266; *Croker Pprs.* ii. 159; Holland House Diaries, 180. [62] *Shelley Diary*, ii. 219; Gash, *Sir Robert Peel*, 36; *Raikes Jnl.* i.

110; Add. 40403, f. 98; 57370, f. 94. [63] Gash, *Pillars of Government*, 120 and 'F.R. Bonham', *EHR*, lxiii (1948), 510; Add. 40617, f. 2. [64] Durham CRO, Londonderry mss D/Lo/C 83 (204) [65] *Three Diaries*, pp. lxii-lxiii; Add. 57404, ff. 48-76, 127, 156. [66] Add. 51587, Ellice to Holland [Sept. 1833]; 57370, f. 102; *Three Diaries*, 307. [67] A. Bird, *Damnable Duke of Cumberland*, 273; *Wellington Pol. Corresp.* i. 46, 63, 73-74, 100, 200-1, 394, 397; *Three Diaries*, 321-2, 340, 361, 365; *Arbuthnot Corresp.* 185; *Greville Mems.* ii. 400; iii. 158-9; Add. 40420, f. 141; 40421, ff. 23, 25, 37, 40, 46, 52. [68] Aspinall, *Politics and the Press*, 461; *Three Diaries*, pp. lxiii-lxv; Add. 57371, ff. 9, 19, 20, 26, 66, 68, 70; 57404, f. 46; 57405, ff. 25-26, 39-40; 57420, ff. 145, 149, 164, 167; 57421, f. 5. [69] *Greville Mems.* iii. 95-96, 163. [70] Add. 40341, f. 1. [71] Add. 40420, f. 141. [72] Gash, 'Influence of Crown', *EHR*, liv (1939), 660 and *Sir Robert Peel*, 196; Stewart, 120, 140; Add. 40333, f. 372; 40423, ff. 285, 310; 40424, ff. 1, 27, 47, 213; 40427, ff. 129, 131, 228. [73] PROB 11/2139/731; IR26/1903/673. [74] C. Redding, *Fifty Years' Recollections*, iii. 248-9. [75] *Hanover Letters* ed. C. Whibley, 219.

D.R.F.

HOLMES *see also* WORSLEY HOLMES

HOLMESDALE, Visct. *see* AMHERST, William Pitt

HOLME SUMNER (formerly SUMNER), George

(1760–1838), of Hatchlands Park, East Clandon, nr. Guildford, Surr.

ILCHESTER	24 Feb. 1787–1790
GUILDFORD	1790–1796
GUILDFORD	1806–16 Mar. 1807
SURREY	1807–1826
GUILDFORD	1830–1831

b. 10 Nov. 1760, at Calcutta, 1st s. of William Brightwell Sumner of Hatchlands, member of council, Bengal, and Catherine, da. of John Holme of Holme, Cumb. *educ.* Harrow 1770-1; by Dr. Samuel Parr, Stanmore; Emmanuel, Camb. 1778; L. Inn 1779. *m.* 17 Nov. 1787, Louisa, da. of Col. Charles Pemble, c.-in-c. Bombay, 3s. (1 *d.v.p.*) 3da. *d.v.p. suc.* uncle Thomas Holme 1794 and took additional name of Holme; fa. 1807. *d.* 26 June 1838.

Member, bd. of agriculture 1793.

Vol. London and Westminster light horse 1797-1807; lt.-col. commdt. 2 Surr. militia 1809, col. 1 regt. 1822.

Dir. British Fire Office 1811, Westminster Life Insurance 1816.

Holme Sumner, the heir of an Indian nabob, was returned for his county for the fourth time in 1820.[1] Lord Lowther's* personal assessment of him seven years later as 'an ill tempered morose fellow' appears to have been widely shared. Yet in 1822, after visiting a mutual friend at his 'most comfortable and superb home', Maria Edgeworth wrote: 'I hear from some who pretend to know him that Mr. Sumner is odd tempered and disagreeable, but from what

I heard ... I should think he must be one of the best natured of good friends'.[2] He continued to be a fairly regular attender who gave general support to Lord Liverpool's ministry and made frequent contributions to debate. He seconded the motion for Manners Sutton to continue as Speaker, 21 Apr. 1820. He spoke of the need to standardize weights and measures, 1 May. He attended meetings of Webb Hall's Central Agricultural Association that year.[3] He presented a Surrey petition complaining of agricultural distress, 9 May, and gave notice of his intention to propose an inquiry.[4] He maintained that the protection afforded by the 1815 corn law was inadequate, 25 May. In moving for inquiry, 30 May, he depicted an agricultural interest in a 'rapidly advancing state of decay', offered a robust argument against free trade and deprecated the calls for cheap bread emanating from manufacturing interests. He was as surprised as anyone when his motion was carried by 150-101. According to Edward Littleton*, many Members abstained from a fear, shared by ministers, of 'offending one of the suffering classes, either the agricultural or the manufacturing', and some who supported the motion did so 'without ... entertaining the slightest idea of raising the price of corn'.[5] Next day Holme Sumner was refreshingly candid in his reply to charges that he had packed the resulting select committee, insisting that 'he had only done what it would have been foolish in him not to have done in the situation in which he stood ... he had procured for himself a fair majority'; he assured the House that he approached the subject with an open mind. However, his triumph was short-lived as ministers carried an emasculatory amendment, which restricted the committee's remit to the investigation of fraud in the computation of the corn averages.[6] He emphasized that his support for the disfranchisement of corrupt boroughs did not signal his abandonment of the view that 'representation should rest on the principle of property, and not upon that of population, as the modern reformers so clamorously contended', 19 May 1820.

He unsuccessfully proposed a reduction of the grant to Queen Caroline to £30,000, 31 Jan. 1821, when he clashed with Matthew Wood over her alleged failure to pay bills. In what Thomas Creevey* described as a 'Billingsgate attack', he characterized her conduct since arriving in England as 'one continued effort to bring into contempt every institution in the country', and, though the adultery charge against her had been dropped, he stated his continued belief in her guilt.[7] Next day he repented of the warmth with which he had made the latter allegation, but he stood by the substance of his speech. However, as the radical Whig

Henry Grey Bennet* noted, when the gallery was cleared for the division on his amendment, Holme Sumner realized that 'no one would divide with him' and 'wisely abandoned his motion'. He told Grey Bennet that 'he had been hardly used, as many persons who had promised him their support now deserted him'.[8] He was hissed when he repeated his views at a county meeting, 2 Feb., and his defence of ministers and the wars against France likewise found little favour among the freeholders. William Cobbett†, who reciprocated the contempt which Holme Sumner often expressed for radicals, thought he had received a 'pretty decent lesson ... from the people of Surrey'.[9] He voted in defence of ministers' conduct towards the queen, 6 Feb., and denied that the Surrey meeting represented the generality of opinion in that county, 8 Feb. He approved of the transfer of Grampound's seats to Yorkshire, 12 Feb., but voted against Russell's general reform resolutions, 9 May. He divided against Catholic relief, 28 Feb. He expressed satisfaction with the government's proposed changes in the computation of corn averages, 26 Feb., and was reappointed to the committee on agricultural distress, 7 Mar. (and again, 18 Feb. 1822). He announced that while he had supported repeal of the tax on husbandry horses, he could not give his backing to remission of the additional malt tax, 21 Mar. He voted against Hume's economy and retrenchment motion, 27 June 1821. This was raised at two county meetings, 4, 18 Feb. 1822, when he faced strong criticism for his failure to vote for tax reductions, as he was supposed to have promised the previous year. Unrepentant, he replied that 'a passing word in a crowd could not be considered as a pledge or obligation', and maintained that tax remissions would do nothing to alleviate agricultural distress, which he ascribed to the post-war depression. He was similarly immovable on the subject of parliamentary reform.[10] He divided against more extensive tax reductions, 11, 21 Feb., having assured the House the previous day that he enjoyed neither office nor favour from ministers.[11] He voted against abolition of one of the joint-postmasterships, 13 Mar., explaining that he feared the growth not of crown influence, but of the popular clamour he had faced at county meetings. Returning to this theme, 2 May, he contended that even if 'a reduction proposed might be proper, it would not be made in a proper manner under the influence of such a spirit'. He thought reduction of the leather tax should have a higher priority than relief of that on salt, but preferred a partial remission of both, 1 May, 14, 28 June.[12] He divided against the leader of the Commons Lord Londonderry's resolution for a revised scale of corn duties, 9 May, presented a petition against Ricardo's

proposals for a fixed duty, 21 May,[13] and was a minority teller against the corn bill, 3 June. He voted against the removal of Catholic peers' disabilities, 30 Apr. He supported a bill to divide Yorkshire for electoral purposes, which would have limited the influence of the West Riding manufacturing interest, 7 June. He declared that no expense should be spared to relieve the Irish famine, 27 June.[14] Following Londonderry's suicide in August 1822 Holme Sumner confided to Lord Clive* that he could not support the government 'with the same confidence that I have done', if 'Canning is to be minister in the ... Commons'. Clive, alarmed that this comment might portend general discontent among the country gentlemen, reported it to the home secretary Lord Sidmouth. Henry Hobhouse, the home office under-secretary, subsequently tried to disabuse Holme Sumner of his conviction that Canning and Peel 'would never go on well together'.[15]

At a county meeting, 10 Feb. 1823, he was given another rough ride for his refusal to support its petition for parliamentary reform. Far less assured than hitherto, he lamely admitted that the agriculture select committee had sat 'for two years, without being able to devise a remedy for their distress', and, to the delight of Cobbett, he repented of his support for Peel's 1819 Currency Act.[16] In the House, 25 Feb., he conceded that the meeting had been 'numerous and regular', but claimed that nineteen-twentieths of the freeholders at large would not support its petition. In concurring with a call for returns on poor relief the next day, he asked that a distinction be drawn between regular and occasional recipients of relief.[17] He divided with ministers against repeal of the assessed taxes, 18 Mar., and inquiry into the currency, 12 June. He applauded their policy of neutrality in the Franco-Spanish war, 7 Mar., 28 Apr., and voted against the provision of information on the plot to murder the Irish lord lieutenant, 24 Mar., Scottish parliamentary reform, 2 June, and inquiry into delays in chancery, 5 June. On the other hand, he was in the minorities against the warehousing bill, 21 Mar., and for recommital of the silk manufacturing bill, 9 June. He opposed the reception of a petition against the game laws, 25 Apr., and unsuccessfully moved for postponement of the sale of game bill, 2 June 1823.[18] He was dismissive of a complaint against George Chetwynd's* conduct as a Staffordshire magistrate, 27 Feb., and opposed Hume's call for lists of the prison commitments made by individual magistrates in the metropolitan area, 2 Mar., 27 May 1824. He spoke against the clause in the Gaol Act amendment bill to restrict use of the treadmill, 5 Mar., for which he had been an apologist at an earlier Surrey magistrates' meeting.[19] He voted that day against abolition of flogging in the army and opposed any remission of the sugar duties, though he 'sincerely sympathized' with West Indian interests. He believed the coal trade had 'a paramount claim to relief', 1 Apr. He was a majority teller against repeal of the usury laws, 8 Apr. On 13 May he cited the complaint of hardship from retired clerks and civil servants as an example of how the cry for retrenchment had been 'listened to unjustly'. He supported a petition condemning the Catholic Association, 31 May, and wished it to be ascertained whether the existing law was 'sufficient to put an end to this evil', 10 June. Next day he divided against the motion condemning the prosecution of the Methodist missionary John Smith in Demerara. In December 1824 he consulted Peel, whom he addressed as 'our great Protestant defender', over whether to accept the vice-presidency of a national 'Protestant Union' contemplated by an existing organization of Southwark anti-Catholics. His sense of a 'formidable and appalling' threat to the Protestant ascendancy almost overcame his rooted distaste for mass organization, but in the end he accepted Peel's advice 'to wait at least and see whether the Protestant association of which you are already a Member (the House of Commons) will do its duty, before you attach yourself to any other'.[20] Holme Sumner duly voted for the Irish unlawful societies bill, 25 Feb. 1825. He divided against Catholic relief, 1 Mar., and paired against it, 10 May. He made a facetious suggestion for the wording of an oath not obnoxious to Catholics, 6 May, and demanded to know the government's attitude to the payment of priests, 8 May. He disapproved of Stuart Wortley's attempt to amend the game laws, 17 Feb., 29 Apr. He opposed a prohibition on Members voting on bills in which they had a pecuniary interest, 15 Mar. He wanted to see a clause added to the warehoused corn bill to limit Canadian imports and opposed a free trade amendment, 13 May. That day he objected to a further award of money to the road engineer Robert Macadam. Regarding his vote against the duke of Cumberland's annuity, 6 June, he explained that he was 'actuated by motives, the grounds of which he could not with propriety develop to those whom he now addressed'; he disclaimed any hostility to the duke in proposing that the grant be halved. He supported the investigation of allegations of misconduct made against the Welsh judge and Surrey resident William Kenrick[†], 28 June 1825. That autumn he thanked Peel for intelligence of the postponement of the dissolution, which was rumoured to have been taken 'against the opinions of Lord Liverpool, Lord Eldon, yourself and those in the cabinet who are my bonds of attachment to the present government', but observed that he could not

regard the delay as a material gain for the supporters of Catholic relief and therefore welcomed it.[21] He supported the London merchants' petition for relief, 23 Feb. 1826, with the admission that their distress had 'now assumed such a shape' as to render assistance necessary. However, this did not extend to conceding any relaxation of the corn laws, and he condemned the 'language of rebellion' in the Glasgow petition against them, 9 Mar. He remarked on 18 Apr. that free trade 'might do very well in commercial concerns', but 'it was a frightful and fearful doctrine to apply to the agricultural interest, the absolute ruin of which it might probably occasion'. He accused the government, which was now set on corn law revision, of seeking to stifle debate on the question, 4 May, and insinuated that Huskisson, the president of the board of trade, was beholden to mercantile interests by dint of his connection with Liverpool. Next day, denying that the threat of famine existed, he could find no justification for what he regarded as ministers' abandonment of the principle of protection, 'a *sine qua non* for the welfare of the landed interest'. Peel replied by asking what had happened to Holme Sumner's earlier intimations of flexibility on the issue. Ignoring the advice of his fellow agriculturists, he divided the House for an adjournment on the warehoused corn bill, 10 May, and was defeated by 174-2. He voted against the corn importation bill, 11 May, and regretted that he had been unable to get a county meeting called in time to strengthen his resistance, 17 May. He divided against reform of Edinburgh's representation, 13 Apr. He had harsh words for the design of the court of chancery building, 17 Apr. 1826, and clashed next day with Hume over an alleged miscarriage of justice in the court.

Holme Sumner spoke regularly in the 1820 Parliament on matters of local interest which, from his county's location, often encompassed London affairs. On 16 May 1820 he introduced a bill for a new church at Newington, Surrey, in the face of strong local opposition. He complained at the second reading stage, 26 May, of disorder at vestry meetings held to oppose it; it gained royal assent, 30 June 1820 (1 Geo. IV, c. 41).[22] His Newington select vestry bill of the following session was presumably a response to this problem. The second reading was carried by 128-80, 3 Mar., but it faced such concerted opposition thereafter that after several recommitals Holme Sumner was obliged to withdraw the bill, 24 May 1821. He was criticized for partiality in his chairmanship of the committee on the bill (on 6 Apr. there had been uproar over his refusal to allow the votes of latecomers), and Hume sarcastically informed the House that he had conducted himself upstairs with 'that suavity of temper, that mild forbearance and perfect command over himself, for which he was so remarkable'. (It was later reported that at some unspecified date before 1820 he had thrown an inkstand at a fellow Member in private committee.)[23] He pursued his earlier objections to proposed expenditure on a new post office which would have drawn on the Orphans' Fund, 11 May 1820. He privately complained to the prime minister of being ignored in favour of City interests and in the House, 22 July 1822, he alleged mismanagement of the fund.[24] He opposed a grant for public money for rebuilding Blackfriars Bridge, 3 Apr. 1821. He expressed disappointment with the plans to repair the old London Bridge, 5 Mar., and presented a Southwark petition for a new one, 26 Apr. 1822. He warmly supported the bill for rebuilding the bridge using public funds, 6, 16 June 1823.[25] He approved the Hammersmith Bridge bill, a private venture, 13 Apr. 1824. He was apparently noncommittal in introducing the South London Docks bill, 4 May 1824, but supported the St. Katharine's Docks bill on the principle of competition, 22 Feb., 9, 24 Mar. 1825.[26] In the autumn of 1824 he furnished Peel with lists of suitable candidates for the shrievalty of Surrey, with separate markings for 'Whigs' and 'incorrigible radicals'.[27] For all the hostility evinced towards him at county meetings, and the offence he realized he had given to commercial interests by his attitude to the corn laws, he was caught unawares by the challenge to him at the general election of 1826. On hearing of his likely defeat, Peel tried to persuade Liverpool of his entitlement to government support, but the premier replied that his opponent (a neighbour and connection of his own) had only been induced to come forward on account of Holme Sumner's personal unpopularity. According to Liverpool, he was 'hated by all parties in the county except his own immediate friends', because 'his temper and his manners are considered overbearing and offensive'.[28] Holme Sumner blamed his subsequent defeat on the 'tinkers and tailors', having 'always too sturdily set myself up against mobocracy to be a favourite with that class', and he told Peel that only his desire to help resist further inroads into the Protestant constitution, free trade and 'new theories of political economy', had induced him to abandon his plans for retirement.[29]

Out of the House, Holme Sumner made his presence felt at Surrey quarter sessions by opposing an attempt to exempt women from treadmill punishment in 1827, and by deprecating a motion against the game laws three years later. At a county meeting, 21 Mar. 1829, he accused the sheriff Felix Ladbroke of partiality in fixing the date and spoke strongly against the Wellington administration's plans to grant Catholic emancipation.[30] By late 1827 he was eyeing his former seat at Guildford, where he was returned at the general election of 1830 after a contest. At the county election he supported Hylton Jolliffe* against John Ivatt Briscoe, his chief liberal antagonist on the magistrates' bench. He failed to keep the poll open after Jolliffe retired, but queried the victor's property qualification and appeared to revel in the opprobrium of the crowd.[31] The ministry listed him as one of the 'moderate Ultras', with the hopeful endorsement 'friend'. He presented a petition from Jolliffe complaining of proceedings at the Surrey election, 12 Nov. 1830. On 15 Nov. he suggested that magistrates be granted additional powers to deal with the 'Swing' disturbances, but denied that a general state of disaffection prevailed in the agricultural counties; he appeared satisfied with Peel's response. Nevertheless, he voted against government in the crucial division on the civil list later that day, having explained that he was acting not to redeem any election pledge but purely out of personal dissatisfaction with the economies proposed by ministers. He said he expected better things from Lord Grey's ministry, 9 Dec. 1830, and trusted that they would show the way in effecting economies by volunteering 'fair and adequate' reductions in their own salaries. He joined in calls for the chancellor of the exchequer, Lord Althorp, to reconsider his budget proposal to tax the transfer of stock, 11 Feb. 1831, though he applauded the decision to reduce the duty on coal. He announced that he would support Hume's amendment for a greater reduction in the civil list than that proposed by ministers, 25 Mar. Early that year he evidently submitted to ministers a scheme for encouraging emigration.[32] He supported Weyland's bill to reform the law of settlement, 10 Feb., and noted the burden on the poor rates caused by immigrant Irish labourers, 17 Feb. In supporting an inquiry into secondary punishments in gaols, 17 Mar., he repelled Hunt's charges against visiting magistrates and extolled the benefits of solitary confinement. He did not explain his attitude to the government's reform bill, but he voted against its second reading, 22 Mar., and for Gascoyne's wrecking amendment, 19 Apr. 1831. At the ensuing general election, when he was described by Creevey as an 'arrant' anti-reformer, he was narrowly defeated by a supporter of the bill.[33]

Holme Sumner fought a spirited, though ultimately unsuccessful contest against two reformers in West Surrey in 1832.[34] He died in June 1838 and left his Surrey estate to his elder son William; his personalty was sworn under £45,000.[35]

¹ *County Chron.* 21 Mar. 1820. ² Lonsdale mss, Lowther to Lonsdale, 7 Jan. 1827; *Edgeworth Letters*, 358-9. ³ T.L. Crosby, *English Farmers and Politics of Protection*, 40, 54; B. Hilton, *Corn, Cash, Commerce*, 99-100. ⁴ *The Times*, 10 May 1820. ⁵ Hatherton diary, 10 May 1820. ⁶ Hilton, 102. ⁷ *Creevey's Life and Times*, 137. ⁸ HLRO, Hist. Coll. 379, Grey Bennet diary, 9. ⁹ Ibid. 10-11; *The Times*, 3 Feb.; *Pol. Reg.* 10 Feb. 1821; *Cobbett's Rural Rides* ed. G.D.H. and M. Cole, iii. 1036. ¹⁰ *The Times*, 5, 19 Feb. 1822; *Black Bk.* (1823), 195. ¹¹ *The Times*, 21 Feb. 1822. ¹² Ibid. 2 May, 15, 29 June 1822. ¹³ Ibid. 22 May 1822. ¹⁴ Ibid. 28 June 1822. ¹⁵ Devon RO, Sidmouth mss, Clive to Sidmouth, 22 Aug. 1822; Parker, *Peel*, i. 334. ¹⁶ *The Times*, 11 Feb.; *Pol. Reg.* 15 Feb. 1823. ¹⁷ *The Times*, 26 Feb. 1823. ¹⁸ Ibid. 3 June 1823. ¹⁹ Ibid. 15 Jan. 1824. ²⁰ Add. 40371, ff. 197-8, 234. ²¹ Add. 40381, f. 416. ²² *The Times*, 27 May 1820. ²³ Ibid. 17, 25 May 1821; *County Chron.* 20 June 1826. ²⁴ Add. 38282, ff. 221, 282; 38284, f. 261; *The Times*, 23 July 1822. ²⁵ *The Times*, 6 Mar., 27 Apr. 1822, 7 June 1823. ²⁶ Ibid. 5 May 1824, 10, 25 Mar. 1825. ²⁷ Add. 40368, ff. 103-8; 40370, ff. 36-38. ²⁸ Add. 40305, ff. 184-7; 40387, f. 159. ²⁹ *Baldwin's Weekly Jnl.* 17 June; *County Chron.* 20 June 1826; Add. 40387, f. 180. ³⁰ *Brighton Herald*, 17 Jan. 1827; *The Times*, 23 Mar. 1829; *County Chron.* 19 Jan. 1830. ³¹ *Brighton Herald*, 23 Oct. 1827; *Baldwin's Weekly Jnl.* 7, 14 Aug. 1830. ³² Grey mss, Graham to Howick, 3 Feb. 1831. ³³ Creevey mss, Creevey to Miss Ord, 30 Apr. 1831. ³⁴ Add. 51837, Denison to Holland [Dec. 1832]. ³⁵ PROB 11/1900/559; IR26/1499/532.

H.J.S.

HOME DRUMMOND, Henry (1783–1867), of Blair Drummond, Perth and 22 Fludyer Street, Mdx.

STIRLINGSHIRE   24 May 1821–1831

PERTHSHIRE   9 Mar. 1840–1852

b. 28 July 1783, 1st s. of George Home Drummond of Blair Drummond and Janet, da. of Rev. John Jardine, DD. *educ.* Edinburgh h.s.;¹ Corpus, Oxf. 1802; adv. 1808. *m.* 14 Apr. 1812, Christian, da. of Charles Moray of Abercairny, Perth, 2s. 1da. *d.v.p. suc.* fa. 1819. *d.* 12 Sept. 1867.

Adv. depute 1812.

Home Drummond, whose grandfather Henry Home had been a 'well known judge in the court of session' in the eighteenth century, sitting as Lord Kames, became an advocate depute in 1812 and 'gained ... rather an unenviable notoriety' for his part in the treason trials of Scottish radicals between 1817 and 1820.² In 1820 he agreed to contest the Haddington Burghs as a supporter of Lord Liverpool's ministry, after overcoming doubts that 'his going into Parliament would be considered as quitting the bar', but was defeated.³ He was returned for Stirlingshire at a by-election in May 1821, ahead of another ministerialist candidate backed by the 3rd duke of Montrose, thanks to support from a coalition of Tories dissatisfied with the duke's leadership and Whigs keen to strike a blow at his authority.⁴

He was a regular attender who gave general but independent support to ministers. He served on committees, usually dealing with Scottish matters, in most sessions. He divided against omitting the arrears from the duke of Clarence's grant, 18 June 1821. Later that year it was reported that he would 'probably be lord advocate' and have to seek re-election, in which case the Stirlingshire Whigs would 'not vote for him'; nothing came of this.⁵ He voted against abolition of one of the joint-postmasterships, 13 Mar., and repeal of the salt duty, 28 June 1822. He said it was a 'great honour' to present the Edinburgh dean and faculty of advocates' petition against the proposed permanent residence requirement for sheriffs, 29 Mar. He argued that the method envisaged was 'improper', as the financial inducements held out to sheriffs would destroy their independence, and 'inexpedient', as the residence requirement would conflict with their ability to continue in legal practice. The recent disturbances in Glasgow offered no justification, as it was impossible to 'legislate for such emergencies'. He secured the omission of a clause in the Scottish burghs accounts bill relating to exchequer proceedings against corrupt magistrates, so that this might be enacted separately, 17 June. He supported Kennedy's Scottish juries bill, 20 June, and declared that 'giving the right of challenge to persons placed upon trial ... would be a substantial benefit', 28 June. However, he 'did not like' the proposed alternative to the present unsatisfactory system of appointing juries and suggested that 'special juries, like those in England, might advantageously be introduced'.⁶ He divided against inquiry into the lord advocate's conduct towards the Scottish press, 25 June. He presented Perthshire petitions for relief from agricultural distress, 22, 29 Apr., and one from the Stirlingshire county meeting for removal of restrictions on the export of Scotch whisky, 21 May.⁷ He presented, without comment, petitions from the synod of Perth and Stirling and the inhabitants of Denny against the Catholic peers bill, 30 Apr.⁸ He voted against inquiry into Irish tithes, 19 June 1822. He was granted one month's leave on account of illness, 24 Feb. 1823. He divided against repeal of the Foreign Enlistment Act, 16 Apr. He denied that the Edinburgh petition for reform of its parliamentary representation 'expressed the sense of the population', 5 May, and voted against Hamilton's motion, 2 June. He was 'favourable to the principle' of Kennedy's Scottish transference of securities bill, to avoid heavy stamp duties, 4 June, but was 'afraid it could not be carried through in its present shape'.⁹ He had 'never heard a more singular attack' than Abercromby's against the lord advocate for his conduct in the Borthwick case, 8 June, and defended his chief from the 'grave accusation' of having 'not performed all the numerous duties of his office in person'. He maintained that

Borthwick had shown 'bad faith ... throughout' and that the 'whole transaction' had been a 'disgrace to all the parties concerned'. He divided against the Scottish juries bill, 20 June 1823. He hoped that petitions against the Scottish salmon fisheries bill, to prevent the rapid depletion of stocks in the Tay, would not impede its progress, 11 Mar. 1824.[10] He expressed his 'most determined hostility' to the Scottish poor law amendment bill, 7 May, and condemned its 'sweeping' provisions, 26 May.[11] He was a minority teller against recommitting the Scottish juries bill, 24 May, and explained that he agreed with its principle but had detailed objections, 28 May. The nomination of juries by judges was 'objectionable in theory', but he feared that the bill would 'lead to inextricable difficulties and great embarrassment in practice', aggravating the obstruction of court proceedings by 'technical niceties'. He 'joined in the entreaty for postponement' of the sale of beer bill and presented a hostile petition from Stirling, 17 May.[12] He pointed out 'one small defect' in Martin's horses slaughtering bill, which specified no penalty for ignoring the proposed regulations, 4 June 1824.[13] In letters at this time to the home secretary, Peel, he was anxious to ensure that Scottish church patronage was distributed in such a way as to be acceptable to all religious parties.[14]

He voted with the minority for the usury laws repeal bill, 17 Feb. 1825. He divided for the Irish unlawful societies bill, 25 Feb., and Catholic relief, 1 Mar., 21 Apr., 10 May. He introduced the Scottish debt recovery bill, to simplify proceedings in sheriffs' courts, 9 Mar.;[15] it gained royal assent, 20 May (6 Geo. IV, c. 24). He presented a petition from proprietors on the Rivers Dee and Don against the salmon fisheries bill and questioned whether its provisions could be 'equally applicable to all localities', 19 May.[16] He was a minority teller for the Edinburgh and Leith water bill at the report stage, 3 June. He gave 'cordial support' to the government's plan for a 'reasonable addition' to judges' salaries, 16 May. He voted for the financial provision for the duke of Cumberland, 30 May, 6 June 1825. He doubted whether the promissory notes bill would force one pound notes out of circulation, 27 Feb. 1826, and pointed to the experience in Scotland, where the 'facility with which debts could be recovered ... contributed to maintain the credit of bankers' notes'. He was convinced that Scottish public opinion had 'never been ... so unanimous' as it was against any alteration to the country's banking system, 14 Mar. When recommending an inquiry, 16 Mar., he disclaimed 'all feelings of jealousy of English influence or ... interference', recalling 'what Scotland was before the Union, distracted and impoverished by civil broils and dissen-

sions, and borne down by oppression of every form and degree', and he acknowledged the 'long catalogue of benefits and blessings' arising from the connection with England and expressed 'unmingled gratitude and respect for the wisdom and ... bounty of the British Parliament'. He thought it was 'uncandid' to criticize the Bank of England for the forgery of its notes, 21 Mar., observing that this resulted from the extent of their circulation, not from inferior production. He warned that under the Bank charter amendment bill it would be impossible for Scottish banks to draw bills on London and have them discounted as often as was necessary, 14 Apr. He introduced the Scottish assault and battery bill, to repeal statutes from the Scottish Parliament that had been 'found of great prejudice to the ends of justice', 8 Mar.;[17] it gained royal assent, 11 Apr. (7 Geo. IV, c. 19). He divided against reform of Edinburgh's representation, 13 Apr. He voted against the motion condemning the Jamaican slave trials, 2 Mar., and reduction of the salary of the president of the board of trade, 10 Apr. He divided with the minority to grant counsel to persons charged with felony, 25 Apr. According to Charles Tennyson's* list he voted against the spring guns bill, 27 Apr. 1826, despite having 'professed himself friendly' to it and secured the exemption of Scotland, where he maintained 'the law already stood right'.[18] At the general election that summer he was returned unopposed for Stirlingshire. He acknowledged the 'peculiar situation' in which he was placed, receiving support from 'both ... political parties', and promised to pursue an 'honest and independent course'. He predicted that the corn laws would 'not long remain on their present footing', as they 'broke down' whenever 'a great rise of prices took place ... though not without much angry and factious discussion'. In order to 'avoid ruinous fluctuations ... give people bread and the agriculturists their profit at a more ... certain rate', he favoured substituting a 'steady and efficient system of protection for the present wavering and impracticable attempt at prohibition', but would always 'err on ... the safe side' in fixing the level of duty. Alluding to the Catholic question, he considered it 'sound policy ... not ... to live in times that had gone by' and, while he 'spoke from no love of change', his awareness of 'the progress of the human mind' and desire to 'transmit unimpaired to posterity the blessings of the British constitution' made him 'anxious to prepare ... for the changes that time and circumstances imperiously require'.[19]

He presented a Stirling cotton spinners' petition for assistance to emigrate, 16 Feb. 1827.[20] He divided for Catholic relief, 6 Mar., and the Clarence annuity bill, 16 Mar. He argued that in fixing the corn averages data should be included from 'the maritime ports' and 'England generally', 19 Mar., and complained that 'the average price of corn in Scotland ... was also omitted'.[21] He warned that many interested parties would regard the Scottish salmon fisheries bill as a 'mere attempt' to transfer money from 'the pockets of one set of proprietors ... to ... another set', 22 Mar., and presented hostile petitions, 10 May.[22] He voted for the spring guns bill, 23 Mar., but secured an amendment stating that its provisions should be 'taken ... in addition and without prejudice to the common law of Scotland, which shall remain', 26 Mar.[23] He introduced the Scottish fraudulent bankrupts bill, to regulate their prosecution, 3 Apr.; it gained royal assent, 28 May (7 & 8 Geo. IV, c. 20). He also introduced the Scottish parochial settlements bill, to extend the period of residence required, 3 Apr.; it did not get through committee. He was a majority teller for an amendment to the Ayrshire roads bill, 21 May 1827. In January 1828 it was suggested to Huskisson, colonial secretary in Lord Goderich's coalition ministry, that Home Drummond's 'early and immediate attendance at the commencement of the session ... would have a good effect' among his countrymen, if he took a 'decided line', as he was 'possessed of ample estates and above the suspicion of having selfish views'.[24] Next month Herries, master of the mint in the duke of Wellington's government, recommended him for the finance committee 'as the representative of Scotland', adding that 'he is a discreet man and can I think be depended upon'; he was duly appointed, 15 Feb.[25] He divided against repeal of the Test Acts, 26 Feb.,[26] but for Catholic relief, 12 May. He endorsed Graham's Scottish vagrants bill, which would 'more equally distribute the burden ... attached to particular places', 19 Feb., and maintained that Scotland 'had a right to complain of her greater liabilities to the support ... of the paupers of all three kingdoms'. He reintroduced the Scottish parochial settlements bill, 28 Feb., which passed the Commons but did not reach the Lords. He 'approved entirely' of the Scottish justiciary court bill, to establish an additional circuit court at Glasgow, 11 Mar., as he 'feared immorality was increasing', partly because of the influx of Irish immigrants. He welcomed the removal of a clause giving sheriffs the power to transport convicts, which was best left to judges, but added that 'as some little doubt seemed still to lurk in the mind of the lord advocate' on this point, he must warn that he would 'decidedly ... oppose such a measure at any time it might be brought forward'. On 15 May he unsuccessfully suggested that the bill be postponed to allow time for consideration at county meetings, since it gave powers of taxation to justices.

He introduced the Scottish alehouses licensing bill, to regulate the granting of certificates by justices, 18 Mar., stating that it was 'similar' to the measure proposed for England. He explained that his object was to prevent abuses by 'giving publicity and regularity to the proceedings of the justices', 4 June; the bill gained royal assent, 15 July (9 Geo. IV, c. 58). He introduced the Scottish salmon fisheries bill, to preserve stocks by applying a uniform close season except in the Rivers Tweed and Solway, 28 Mar. He successfully resisted the exclusion of the River Thurso, 'an attempt to secure a private end at the expense of a public good', 23 June, but consideration of the Lords' amendments was postponed, 10 July. He thought that Dawson's revenue barristers bill would be 'of no advantage to Scotland', 2 Apr., as it gave English barristers 'a privilege in the Scotch courts which Scotch barristers will not possess in those of England'. He promised to give 'every assistance' to Littleton's turnpike trusts bill, 15 Apr., observing that 'no part of the country suffers more from the existing system than Scotland does'. He approved of the lord advocate's course on the Scottish gaols bill, 20 June. He voted against condemning delays in chancery, 24 Apr., and for the usury laws amendment bill, 19 June 1828. A recent historian has identified Home Drummond as one of those Members who apparently acted as an 'unofficial minister', in promoting legislation.[27]

In January 1829 Planta, the patronage secretary, mentioned Home Drummond as a possible mover or seconder of the address.[28] Next month he listed him as being 'with government' for Catholic emancipation, and he duly voted for the measure, 6, 30 Mar. He looked 'with pride and satisfaction as a Scotchman' at the favourable Edinburgh petition, 26 Mar., which represented the view of 'persons of education ... capable of forming a judgement', although he regretted that 'a vast number of the lower orders have been instigated by the clergy and by their landlords to sign anti-Catholic petitions'. He introduced the Scottish small debts recovery bill, to make legal proceedings cheaper, 3 Mar.; it gained royal assent, 19 June (10 Geo. IV, c. 55). He introduced the Scottish seisins bill, to amend the procedure for registering landed propriety, which was 'highly important to the mass of proprietors in burghs', 31 Mar.; it gained royal assent, 14 May (10 Geo. IV, c. 19). He 'despaired' of seeing the Scottish gaols bill come out of committee 'in a satisfactory shape', given the opposition to it, 5 May. He wanted the House to express an opinion on the Church of Scotland petition for the recovery of its records from Sion College, 20 May, as he believed 'public opinion will compel the fellows ... to perform the act of justice required of them'. He feared that an immediate increase in judges' salaries might 'throw a dangerous impediment in the way of the proposed improvements in the administration of justice in Scotland', 21 May, pointing out that it remained unclear what their future duties would be. He personally favoured abolishing the admiralty and commissary courts. He opposed an amendment to the anatomy regulation bill for a uniform penalty, 15 May 1829, maintaining that body-stealing was 'of all offences ... [the one] most liable to be varied by circumstances', depending on whether the accused was a scientist or a resurrectionist. He divided against the enfranchisement of Birmingham, Leeds and Manchester, 23 Feb., and the Galway franchise bill, 25 May 1830. He thought it was 'due to the dignity of ... our proceedings' that the evidence given before the committee on Lord Ellenborough's divorce bill should be printed, 1 Apr. That day he promised to 'give ... all the support in my power' to the Scottish judicature bill, although he disagreed with some of its details, wishing to separate the financial and judicial functions of the exchequer court and favouring the payment of fees rather than of salaries to court officials, to ensure 'prompt and proper discharge of duty'. He hoped 'the time is not far distant when an attempt will be made to remove those defects in the Scotch law which are not only an incumbrance to it, but also a serious source of unnecessary expense to ... suitors', 30 Apr. He said he would not press his own reform scheme, which raised 'complicated questions of compensation' and was best dealt with by government. He made several detailed suggestions for improving the court of session bill, 18 June. He expressed 'satisfaction', 8 Apr., that the sale of beer bill would not apply to Scotland, where the 'monopoly which forms the most objectionable feature in the manufacture ... in England' did not exist. He presented and 'entirely concurred' in the Stirlingshire and Clackmannanshire petitions against the proposed increase in the corn spirit duty, 11 May. He was a minority teller for the Perth navigation bill, 28 May. That day he defended the conduct of the committee on the Clyde navigation bill from complaints made by the provost of Dumbarton, who he suggested had personal financial motives, and said that it was the committee's unanimous wish that 'the responsibility of a decision in this case might rest anywhere but with them'. He moved that the bill be recommitted so that further evidence could be gathered, following the report of the committee of appeal, but was persuaded to withdraw, 10 June. He voted against abolition of the death penalty for forgery, 7 June 1830. He was again returned unopposed for Stirlingshire at the general election that

summer, after observing that his earlier advice to 'prepare for those innovations and improvements' which 'necessarily flow from the general diffusion of wealth, the rapid progress of knowledge, the increase of population and the consequent changes of manners and opinions', had been vindicated. He was convinced that 'the British constitution is [no] less firmly rooted in the hearts of the people' since the concession of Catholic emancipation. He urged those opposed to all reform to 'mark well the great moral and political lesson which the striking events ... now passing before our eyes' in France, a 'nation ... whose liberties have been trampled upon', taught 'all nations and their governments'. There was 'no fear of revolution' in Britain, thanks to Wellington's willingness to 'cautiously and gradually ... admit such changes as would any longer be more dangerous to reject than to adopt', and he expressed general confidence in the duke's government, although he had opposed some of its measures 'without scruple' if 'not without great reluctance'. He complained of being 'misrepresented' with regard to his Alehouses Licensing Act, which had been 'described as arming the justices with new and oppressive powers', when in fact the aim had been 'decidedly to impose restraints upon them and ... prevent the abuse of authority previously unlimited'; he blamed the increase of crime on cheap whisky.[29]

The ministry regarded him as one of their 'friends', and he voted with them in the crucial civil list division, 15 Nov. 1830; he was named to the resulting select committee. He said he had voted on an earlier occasion to postpone the election ballots, but could not agree to further delay, 23 Nov. He presented a Stirling anti-slavery petition, 6 Dec. 1830, and concurred with it that 'abolition should be cautious and gradual' and carried out with 'due regard' to the rights of the slave owners. He joined a deputation of Scottish Members to the chancellor of the exchequer, Lord Althorp, 5 Mar. 1831, to oppose the planned tax on steam vessels.[30] He divided against the second reading of the Grey ministry's reform bill, 22 Mar., and demanded that the House be given 'more accurate data' before reaching a final decision on the measure, 25 Mar. He asserted, 28 Mar., that a hostile petition from the Anstruther Burghs emanated not from 'close corporations' but from 'the inhabitants at large', who were being 'most unjustly treated' by the threat of disfranchisement. He argued that the electors were 'chosen out of a large population so that, in fact, the inhabitants themselves are electors'. Despite his opposition to reform, he told the chairman of a meeting at Grangemouth that he was willing to support an amendment to the Scottish bill to add Grangemouth and other towns to the Linlithgow Burghs.[31] He voted for Gascoyne's wrecking amendment, 19 Apr. 1831. At the ensuing dissolution he retired rather than face a contest against his former ally, Charles Elphinstone Fleeming, a reformer to whom he felt 'so much indebted for being placed during the last three Parliaments'. He maintained in his address that 'under any other circumstances' he would have stood again, to resist the government's 'dangerous and ill-digested innovations'.[32]

Home Drummond wrote from Perthshire to a friend, 6 Oct. 1831:

> It is not easy ... at a distance ... to speculate on the best form of resistance to revolution. But ever since I heard Lord John's [Russell's] expose, I have thought effectual resistance impossible, though I am very far from seeing in that any argument for concessions, such as the ministerial plan involves, which seem to me only calculated to hasten the catastrophe.[33]

He was returned for Perthshire in 1840 and sat as a 'Conservative of the Peel school', who supported repeal of the corn laws and was 'an ardent friend to agricultural improvement', until his retirement in 1852.[34] He died in September 1867 and was succeeded in turn by his elder son, George Stirling Home Drummond (1813-76), and his other son, Charles Stirling Home Drummond Moray (1816-91).

[1] *Gent. Mag.* (1867), ii. 548   [2] Ibid; P. Ellis and S. Mac a' Ghobhainn, *Scottish Insurrection of 1820*, pp. 111, 223, 233, 238, 246. [3] NLS mss 11, f. 24; NAS GD51/1/198/9/31. [4] *Glasgow Herald*, 25 May 1821. [5] Macleod of Macleod mss 1056/4, Macleod to wife, 28 Dec. 1821. [6] *The Times*, 21, 29 June 1822. [7] Ibid. 23, 30 Apr., 22 May 1822. [8] Ibid. 1 May 1822. [9] Ibid. 5 June 1823. [10] Ibid. 11 Mar. 1824. [11] Ibid. 8, 27 May 1824. [12] Ibid. 18 May 1824. [13] Ibid. 5 June 1824. [14] Add. 40364, f. 147; 40366, f. 17; Parker, *Graham*, i. 386. [15] *The Times*, 10 Mar. 1825. [16] Ibid. 20 May 1825. [17] Ibid. 9 Mar. 1826. [18] Norf. RO, Gunton mss 1/21, Tennyson's list. [19] *Greenock Advertiser*, 4 July 1826. [20] *The Times*, 17 Feb. 1827. [21] Ibid. 20 Mar. 1827. [22] Ibid. 11 May 1827. [23] Ibid. 27 Mar. 1827. [24] Add. 38754, f. 20. [25] Add. 40395, ff. 219-21. [26] *The Times*, 29 Feb. 1828. [27] P. Jupp, *British Politics on Eve of Reform*, 177. [28] Add. 40398, ff. 86-87. [29] *Stirling Jnl.* 20 Aug. 1830. [30] *Glasgow Herald*, 11 Mar. 1831. [31] *Stirling Jnl.* 15 Apr. 1831. [32] Ibid. 29 Apr., 13 May 1831. [33] Glasgow City Archives, Campbell of Succoth mss TD 219/11/62. [34] *Gent. Mag.* (1867), ii. 548.

T.A.J.

HONYWOOD, William Philip (1790–1831), of Sibton, Kent; Marks Hall, Essex, and 7 Charles Street, Berkeley Square, Mdx.

KENT   1818–1830

b. 15 Apr. 1790, 1st s. of William Honywood[†] of Sibton and Marks Hall and Mary Drake, da. of Rev. Ralph Drake Brockman of Beachborough, Kent. *educ.* Rugby 1800; Jesus, Camb. 1808. *m.* 11 Sept 1820, Priscilla, da. of Charles Hanbury, banker, of Sloe Farm, Halstead, Essex, at least 4s. (at least 1 *d.v.p.*). *suc.* fa. 1818. *d.* 22 Apr. 1831.

Capt. Ashford regt. Kent militia 1809.

Although a handful of his forebears had sat for Kent and Essex, as well as their former pocket borough of Steyning, Honywood's parliamentary career, which began in 1818, was restricted by his own personal and political failings. He inherited valuable properties in both counties in 1818 on the death of his father, whose personal wealth was sworn under £16,000, but he quickly ran into financial difficulties. His decision to reside at Marks Hall, near Coggeshall, rather than at Sibton, near Hythe, was constantly held against him, even by his supporters.[1] He differed in politics from his first cousin, Sir John Courtenay Honywood of Evington, Kent, and from their relation by marriage, Sir Edward Knatchbull, the other Kent Member, who were both highly influential. Instead he followed the Whig line of his father, but never appeared to be wholly committed to the cause. A valetudinarian, as his father had been, he divided regularly with opposition when present, notably during their campaign against the Liverpool administration over economies in the early 1820s; his absences became increasingly prolonged towards the end of the decade, and he was never very active in handling local petitions and legislation.[2] At the annual dinner of the Norfolk Fox Club in Norwich, 24 Jan. 1820, he admitted that he was 'little known in the political world', but boasted that he had been 'nursed in the lap of liberty'.[3] In an initial address, 23 Feb., he offered again for Kent at the general election and denounced the recent repressive legislation, 'passed in a moment of panic, artfully created'. On the discovery of the Cato Street conspiracy, he hurriedly issued a second address, 1 Mar., so that his words would not be misconstrued, but he was criticized for his apparent leniency, his pro-Catholic vote and his non-residence.[4] On the hustings, 18 Mar., he made clear that he had only opposed those laws, like the seditious meetings bill, which were attacks on the rights of the people. He explained that he had voted for the memorial of the Catholics of Ireland to be received in order 'to ascertain whether the alleged grievances were well-founded ... [and] whether the Catholics had claims which ought to be considered', but he promised to abide by the decision of any future county meeting on the subject. He also agreed with Knatchbull that agricultural distress should be relieved, but stated that any measures would fail unless taxes were lowered. The Tories attempted to challenge him, but nothing came of this and he was returned unopposed with Knatchbull.[5] According to his agent's accounts, he spent only £133 during the campaign, compared to £3,590 in 1818.[6] At a dinner in Canterbury to celebrate his election, 11 Apr. 1820, he praised 'liberty, freedom and independence' as the 'true principles of the British constitution', and he gave a toast to the cause of moderate reform.[7]

He voted with opposition against the civil list, 5, 8 May, and the appointment of an additional baron of exchequer in Scotland, 15 May, and for reducing the size of the army, 14 June, and economies in revenue collection, 4 July 1820. He presented and endorsed petitions complaining of distress from Kentish landowners, 11, 17 May.[8] He divided against Wilberforce's compromise motion on Queen Caroline, 22 June, and against the appointment of a secret committee on the affair, 26 June 1820. He signed the requisition for a county meeting, which the sheriff refused to hold, and attended the unofficial gathering at Maidstone, 18 Jan. 1821, when he declared his 'disapprobation of the shameful and scandalous bill of pains and penalties', and moved resolutions for petitions to both Houses for the restoration of Caroline's name to the liturgy.[9] He voted steadily in support of the opposition campaign on her behalf in early 1821. On 26 Jan. he warned that he 'feared much, that if these petitions should be treated with neglect, the people would be confirmed in an opinion which they had long entertained, namely that the House did not speak the sense, or represent the wishes of the country'. He brought up the Kent petition, 8 Feb., when he quarrelled with Knatchbull over the validity and respectability of the meeting which had approved it, and the following day he denied Wilbraham's allegation that the only man opposing it had been physically assaulted as he left the hall.[10] He voted for Catholic claims, 28 Feb. On the motion for the appointment of a committee on agricultural distress, 7 Mar., he complained of increases in the national debt and poor rates, the lack of effective protection for domestic producers and the corrupt influence of government, adding that he 'was one of those who lived among the people, who sympathized with their sufferings and who participated in their distresses. The only chance we had of maintaining the public faith, was by rigidly enforcing economies and retrenchment'. He voted to adjourn the House on Stuart Wortley's complaint against the *Morning Chronicle*, 9 Mar., and against going into the committee of supply until the question of distress had been considered, 6 Apr. He spoke in favour of reform at the *London Tavern* dinner, 4 Apr., arguing that it 'was not innovation, but renovation that was wanted'.[11] He had

divided for making Leeds a scot and lot borough if it was enfranchised in place of Grampound, 2 Mar., and, just before the adjournment of the debate on Lambton's motion for a committee to consider the representation, 17 Apr., he declared that 'although he was convinced of the necessity of a reform in Parliament, yet he was not prepared to go the length of his hon. friend's proposition'. He was not listed in the minority on it the next day, but divided for Russell's reform resolutions, 9 May. The radical *Black Book* noted that he had not voted for repeal of the Blasphemous and Seditious Libel Acts, 8 May, or inquiry into Peterloo, 16 May.[12] He had, however, been given a fortnight's leave, 14 May 1821, on account of the death of a near relation.

Honywood attended a meeting of local landowners in Canterbury on distress, 19 Dec. 1821, and the dinner in Norwich to venerate Fox's memory, 24 Jan. 1822.[13] He voted for Hume's amendment to the address, 5 Feb., and more extensive tax reductions to relieve distress, 11, 21 Feb. He sided with opposition on the Irish habeas corpus suspension and insurrection bills, 7, 8 Feb., Sir Robert Wilson's* removal from the army, 13 Feb., inquiry into Scottish royal burghs, 20 Feb., interference with Members' mail, 25 Feb., and the outrage against Alderman Waithman*, 28 Feb. He continued to divide steadily in favour of economies, but seems to have been absent for several weeks from early March and, for instance, did not vote for reform, 25 Apr.[14] He was, however, back in the House by mid-May, and voted for inquiry into the government of the Ionian Islands, 14 May, and law reform, 4 June, and against the aliens bill, 5, 14 June, 1 July. He was cheered at the Kent county meeting, 11 June, when he advocated lower taxation and reform, and told Knatchbull that ministers were not to be thanked for having been goaded into effecting what were only small reductions.[15] The following day he voted for Western's motion on the resumption of cash payments. He presented the ensuing Kent petition, 14 June, and repeatedly defended the conduct of the Whigs in failing to prevent William Cobbett[†] tacking on an addition to it for lowering the rate of interest on the national debt. He nevertheless endorsed its call for relief and reform, and opined that 'had government, two years ago, adopted that economy and retrenchment so loudly called for by the distresses of the country, they would never have heard such a sentiment from the freeholders of Kent'. This speech was his last major intervention in the House before 1830. He voted in condemnation of the influence of the crown, 24 June, and for inquiries into the conduct of the lord advocate and chancery administration, 25, 26 June 1822. He divided against the appointment of Lord Beresford as lieutenant-general of the ordnance in peacetime, 19 Feb., for reform, 20 Feb., 24 Apr., against Stuart Wortley's amendment approving British neutrality towards the French invasion of Spain, when most of the opposition voted with ministers, 30 Apr., and inquiry into the Middlesex county court, 19 June 1823. He briefly supported the Essex petition complaining of distress, 2 May, and continued to divide in favour of economies.[16] He voted for inquiries into the Irish church establishment, 4 Mar., the legal proceedings against the Dublin Orange rioters, 22 Apr., the disturbances in Ireland, 24 June, and Catholic complaints against the administration of justice there, 26 June 1823.

Honywood voted for papers on the government's conduct towards France and Spain, 17 Feb., reform of the representation of Edinburgh, 26 Feb., and Abercromby's complaint against the lord chancellor over an alleged breach of privilege, 1 Mar. 1824. He presented several Kentish anti-slavery petitions, 19 Mar., 6 Apr., and divided in condemnation of the trial of the Methodist missionary John Smith in Demerara, 11 June.[17] He voted for referring the reports of the commissioners of inquiry into the Scottish courts of justice to a committee of the whole House, 30 Mar., to permit defence by counsel in felony cases, 6 Apr., and for considering the evils of naval impressment, 10 June. He was also in opposition minorities on the advancement of capital to Ireland, 4 May, inquiry into the church establishment there, 6 May, the state of that country, 11 May, and the Irish insurrection bill, 14 June 1824. He divided against the Irish unlawful societies bill, 15, 21 Feb., and again for inquiry into the Irish church, 14 June 1825. He voted for Catholic relief, 1 Mar., 21 Apr., 10 May. He presented a local petition against the assessed taxes, 24 Feb., and another against alteration of the corn laws, 28 Apr., and he divided for repeal of the beer duties, 5 May, and the window tax, 17 May.[18] His only other known votes that session were to make puisne judges immoveable, 20 May, and for two amendments to the combination bill, 27 June 1825. He divided against going into committee on the Bank Charter Acts, 13 Feb., and was in the minority condemning the Jamaican slave trials, 2 Mar. 1826. He divided in favour of large reductions in the army, 3, 7 Mar., and to abolish flogging in it, 10 Mar., against receiving the report on the salary of the president of the board of trade, 10 Apr., and again for a bill to allow counsel to those facing felony charges, 25 Apr. He voted for alteration of the representation of Edinburgh, 13 Apr., parliamentary reform, 27 Apr., and resolutions to curb electoral bribery, 26 May. He voted against ministers on their resolution to admit foreign corn, 8 May, and the second reading of the importation bill, 11 May 1826.

Honywood offered again at the general election of 1826, on the basis of the 'same zeal in support of constitutional principles, and the same conviction of the necessity of diminishing the burden of excessive taxation, by every possible retrenchment in the public expenditure, which I have hitherto felt'. Although no contest was expected, a 'no Popery' cry was raised against him, as were doubts about his fitness. The Whig economist Sir Samuel Egerton Brydges[†] wrote that 'with every concession to the amiable private character and manly disposition' of Honywood, 'it would be contemptible flattery to assert that his habits fit him for a public man, and for the representative of a large and rich agricultural county, at this extraordinary and dangerous crisis!'[19] On 20 June Honywood declared that if demanding lower taxes 'was advocating cheap bread, then he was an advocate of it, but he was no advocate for opening the ports of this country to the admission of the wheat of the untithed, untaxed grower of foreign countries'. Although it meant differing with many of his supporters, he urged concessions to the Catholics, and he denied that 30 or 40 Catholic Members would endanger the constitution. He also expressed his strong opposition to slavery. He was again returned with Knatchbull, and his agent charged him only £12 12s. 11d. for his services between 3 and 22 June.[20] He was one of the diners at the party held by Abraham Wildey Robarts to celebrate his return at Maidstone, 23 Aug., but he refused to attend the meeting of the East Kent and Canterbury Agricultural Association, 15 Dec. 1826, because it was called at too short notice.[21] He voted in the minority for Catholic relief, 6 Mar. 1827. He divided for information on the mutiny at Barrackpoor, 22 Mar., and the Irish government's handling of the Lisburn Orange procession, 29 Mar., Tierney's amendment to postpone the committee of supply, 30 Mar., and against the second reading of the corn bill, 2 Apr. He was probably absent from the House for a lengthy period, as in mid-June there were alarming reports about his health.[22] It may have been at about this time that he wrote from Cheltenham to ask John Cam Hobhouse to present a petition against the Test Acts on his behalf, adding that 'I have been here some time, and am happy to say am better though still weak and not strong'.[23] This period also saw the culmination of his financial problems, which, possibly at the instigation of his wife, were taken out of the hands of his former agents. Sometime in the autumn of 1827 Samuel Forster of Lincoln's Inn visited Marks Hall to consult him about his 'pecuniary affairs, which he understood were in great disorder'.[24]

His only known vote in the following session was in favour of Catholic relief, 12 May 1828. Four days later a newspaper reported that he had returned to Marks Hall in order to convalesce.[25] Lord Clifton*, who observed that 'his stake in Kent is very inconsiderable', noted that Honywood was 'unfortunately *hors de combat*' and so unable to attend the stormy county meeting that narrowly decided in favour of an anti-Catholic petition, 24 Oct. 1828, when his opinion was represented to be strongly opposed to anything at variance with civil and religious liberties.[26] However, one freeholder argued in an address that, since he had pledged to follow his constituents' views, he should now oppose emancipation. He was named as a steward for the Kent anti-Brunswick dinner, though he was probably not able to attend.[27] He did not speak on the ensuing petition when it was debated in the House, 12 Feb. 1829, and that month he was listed by Planta, the Wellington ministry's patronage secretary, as one of those who would be absent on the emancipation bill. He made no known votes during that session and was less frequently named to committees on local legislation. He probably missed Knatchbull's amendment to the address on distress, 4 Feb. 1830, but he was present for much of the session, and having voted for lower army estimates, 22 Feb., he thereafter divided steadily in the opposition's renewed campaign for reduced expenditure and taxation.[28] He divided for enfranchising Birmingham, Leeds and Manchester, 23 Feb., transferring East Retford's seats to Birmingham, 1, 5, 15 Mar., and parliamentary reform, 28 May. He attended the Kent county meeting, 12 Mar., at which he acknowledged that the Commons was not representative of the nation, and declared that

> he thought that the contents of the petition might refer to no other subject than the distress of the country, the reduction of taxation and a reform of Parliament. And he would remind the meeting that he had never, in his whole parliamentary career, given a shy vote, or shied from giving his open and bold opinion on reform whenever it was found necessary.[29]

He backed the petition on its presentation, 29 Mar., stating that the 'distress is grievous', and avowing that, having been a reformer for 20 years, his mind derived 'from year to year additional strength of the value of my early impressions of that necessity'. He voted for abolition of the Irish lord lieutenancy, 11 May, Jewish emancipation, 17 May, the ending of capital punishment for forgery, 24 May, 7 June, inquiry into the civil government of Canada, 25 May, and reform of the divorce laws, 3 June 1830.

Writing on 9 July 1830, Thomas Law Hodges* noted that he had not heard of Honywood's intentions as to the general election, but gave his opinion that 'as he has within the last six weeks attended the House of Commons, he feels his health better, and that he will again offer himself as a candidate'.[30] Despite rumours of a groundswell of Whig opposition, he announced that he would stand, as the 'uncompromising advocate of reform, economy and retrenchment', 15 July. However, he withdrew by another address, 3 Aug., 'being informed that a general feeling prevails of the necessity of the Members of this county being resident amongst you, which condition is not in my power to comply with'.[31] Lord Darnley commented to Lord Holland, 4 Aug., that he had 'wisely retired', leaving the field open for Hodges who, as he explained at the election, 9 Aug. 1830, would 'on no consideration' have opposed him, had his health and place of residence allowed him to stand. After some wrangling, a vote of thanks to Honywood for his services was agreed.[32] He died, on the eve of another general election, in April 1831. By his will, dated 28 Nov. 1827, his estate was left in trust to his infant sons, of whom the eldest was his namesake, William Philip (1823-59). His personal wealth was initially sworn under £12,000, but notes in the death duty register indicate that his debts then amounted to at least £4,000 and the estate was declared insolvent in 1834.[33]

[1] F. Chancellor, *Ancient Sepulchral Mons. of Essex*, 116-22; *Gent. Mag.* (1818), i. 379; IR26/746/298; *Farington Diary*, xv. 5265. [2] *HP Commons, 1790-1820*, iv. 223-4. [3] *Kentish Chron.* 28 Jan.; *Norf. Chron.* 29 Jan. 1820. [4] *Kentish Gazette*, 25 Feb., 3, 10, 14 Mar. 1820. [5] *Kentish Chron.* 14, 21 Mar.; Add. 51571, Thanet to Lady Holland, 16 Apr. 1820. [6] Cent. Kent. Stud. Knocker coll. U55 E54. [7] *Kentish Chron.* 14 Apr. 1820. [8] *The Times*, 12, 18 May 1820. [9] *Kentish Chron.* 2, 12, 19 Jan. 1821. [10] *The Times*, 9, 10 Feb. 1821. [11] Ibid. 5 Apr. 1821. [12] *Black Bk.* (1823), 164. [13] *Kentish Chron.* 1 Jan.; *Norf. Chron.* 26 Jan. 1822. [14] *Black Bk.* (1823), 164. [15] *Kentish Chron.* 14 June 1822; A. de Staël-Holstein, *Letters on England* (1825), 191. [16] *The Times*, 3 May 1823. [17] Ibid. 3, 20 Mar., 7 Apr. 1824. [18] Ibid. 25 Feb., 29 Apr. 1825. [19] *Kentish Chron.* 6, 9, 20 June 1826. [20] Ibid. 23 June 1826; Knocker coll. E54. [21] *Kentish Chron.* 25 Aug., 19 Dec. 1826. [22] Knocker coll. E54, 15 June 1827. [23] Add. 36466, f. 251. [24] Knocker coll. E54, 9 July, 11 Oct. 1827. [25] *Kentish Gazette*, 16 May 1828. [26] Add. 51834, Clifton to Holland, 18 Oct.; *The Times*, 25 Oct.; *Kentish Chron.* 28 Oct. 1828. [27] *Kentish Chron.* 9 Dec.; *Kentish Gazette*, 12 Dec.; *The Times*, 23 Dec. 1828. [28] *Kentish Gazette*, 12 Feb. 1830. [29] *Kentish Chron.* 16 Mar. 1830. [30] Cent. Kent. Stud. Twisden mss U49 C13/151. [31] *Kentish Chron.* 6, 20 July; *Kentish Gazette*, 6 Aug. 1830. [32] Add. 51572; *Maidstone Jnl.* 10 Aug. 1830. [33] PROB 11/1786/333; IR26/1260/266.

S.M.F.

HOPE, **Hon. Sir Alexander** (1769–1837), of Farnham, Surr.

DUMFRIES BURGHS	1796–22 Apr. 1800
LINLITHGOWSHIRE	12 May 1800–1834

b. 9 Dec. 1769, 2nd s. of John, 2nd earl of Hopetoun [S] (*d.* 1781), and 3rd w. Lady Elizabeth Leslie, da. of Alexander, 5th earl of Leven and Melville [S]; bro. of Hon. Charles Hope[†] and half-bro. of Hon. John Hope[†]. *educ.* at home by Rev. John Gillies; grand tour. *m.* 23 Oct. 1805, Georgina Alicia, da. of George Brown, commr. of excise, of Elliestoun, Edinburgh, 5s. (3 *d.v.p.*) 1da. KB 29 June 1813, GCB 2 Jan. 1815. *d.* 19 May 1837.

Ensign 63 Ft. 1786; lt. 64 Ft. 1789; capt. army 1791; lt. and capt. 1 Ft. Gds. 1791; maj. 81 Ft. 1794; lt.-col. 90 Ft. Aug. 1794, 14 Ft. Dec. 1794; brigade maj.-gen. eastern district 1797-9, asst. adj.-gen., dep. adj.-gen. Dutch expedition 1799; brevet col. 1800; adj.-gen. [I] 1801; col. loyal Nottingham fencibles 1801, half-pay 1802; dep. q.m.g. 1802; brig.-gen. 1804; col. Cape regt., 5 W.I. regt. 1806; maj.-gen. 1808; col. 74 Ft. 1809; lt.-gen. 1813; col. 47 Ft. 1813; gen. 1830; col. 4 Ft. 1835-*d.*

Lt.-gov. Tynemouth 1797-8, Edinburgh Castle 1798-1812, 1819-24; gov. R.M.C. Sandhurst 1812-19, 1824-6; lt.-gov. Chelsea Hosp. 1826-*d.*

Hope, a veteran and well-connected Melvillite, who had lost an arm and been crippled in Flanders in 1795 (for which he received a disability pension of £450 a year), was on the continent when the death of George III in January 1820 necessitated a dissolution. He hurried back on hearing the news and at the general election in March was returned unopposed, and for the seventh consecutive time, for Linlithgowshire, on the now impregnable interest of his half-brother, the 4th earl of Hopetoun. Between Hopetoun's sudden death in August 1823 and the coming of age of the 5th earl, his nephew, in November 1824, Hope held the reins. He was secure in the seat for the rest of this period.[1]

He voted in defence of the Liverpool ministry's conduct towards Queen Caroline, 6 Feb. 1821. He was absent from the division on Catholic relief, 28 Feb., perhaps having already departed with his wife and five children on a two-year tour of Germany, Switzerland and Italy.[2] He was in the House to divide with government on the sinking fund, 3 Mar., against repeal of the assessed taxes, 10, 18 Mar., and of the Foreign Enlistment Act, 16 Apr., and for the grant for Irish glebe houses, 11 Apr. 1823. In debates on the army estimates he defended the votes of money for garrisons, 7 Mar., the Royal Military College (the governorship of which, an 'anxious and laborious' post, he had held from 1812 to 1819), 10 Mar., and the governorship of Edinburgh Castle, his current place,

24 Mar. 1823.[3] In March 1824 he resumed control at Sandhurst when Sir George Murray* was appointed to ministerial office. He voted, 5 Mar., and spoke, 11 Mar. 1824, against the abolition of flogging in the army, as he did again, 11 Mar. 1825. He presented petitions from Linlithgow for equalization of the duty on Scottish and Irish spirits, 6 May, and against alteration of the Scottish poor laws, 7 May 1824.[4] He voted for the Irish unlawful societies bill, 25 Feb. 1825. He defaulted on a call of the House, 28 Feb., appeared and was excused next day, but evidently did not then vote on the Catholic question. He presented a petition against relief, 18 Apr., and paired in that sense, 18 Apr.[5] He approved the army estimates, 4 Mar. He presented a constituency petition against interference with the corn laws, 9 May 1825. On 6 Mar. 1826 he assured Hume that while he had been absent from Sandhurst for two months on 'urgent private business' in 1825, 'his attention was not withdrawn from the establishment'. Claiming that after a total of ten years in the job he had 'not grown sixpence the richer', he explained that he was waiting to hand over to Sir Edward Paget[†] on his return from India. (This took place in September 1826, when Hope became lieutenant-governor of Chelsea Hospital.) He also defended governorships of garrisons as 'the only reward in the power of the crown to bestow upon officers who had become distinguished, wounded or worn out in the service of their country', and protested at Hume's description of Lord Charles Somerset[†], the controversial governor of the Cape, as 'a man whom everybody detested'. He presented a Linlithgowshire petition against restricting the circulation of small Scottish bank notes, 21 Apr. 1826.[6]

Hope again defended the public funding of Sandhurst, 19 Feb., garrison appointments, 20 Feb., and the selective use of corporal punishment to subdue 'the unruly passions' of miscreant soldiers, dismissing the views of 'visionary philanthropists', 12 Mar. 1827. He paired against Catholic relief, 6 Mar. 1827. In April he affirmed to John Hope, the Scottish solicitor-general, his unwavering attachment to the 2nd Lord Melville, who had declined to serve in the new ministry headed by Canning: 'as one of a cabinet he was most valuable when under the check of thinking men, but as *premier* without a cabinet which will control him I apprehend danger from his administration'.[7] He voted against repeal of the Test Acts, 26 Feb., and again paired against Catholic claims, 12 May 1828. He presented a constituency petition against the revised corn duties, 14 May. He expressed 'surprise' at Hume's objection to the appointment of Murray as colonial secretary in the duke of Wellington's administration, 30 May. On 13 June 1828, answering Hume's rant against the funding of Sandhurst, he complained that far from the finance committee's investigation having helped to expose the nonsense of 'garbled statements' about the military establishments, as he had hoped, 'insidious use' was being made of its findings by Hume and his cronies to spread 'poison'; he was drawn into further tart exchanges with Hume, Hobhouse and Waithman. He justified the grants for Kilmainham Hospital and the Royal Military Asylum, 20 June 1828. He was expected to side 'with government' for the concession of Catholic emancipation in 1829, but in the event he cast a token vote against the second reading of the relief bill, 18 Mar. He was appointed to the select committee on Scottish entails, 27 Mar., and called for urgent reform of the current laws, 2 June 1829. He voted against Lord Blandford's parliamentary reform scheme, 18 Feb. 1830. He presented but dissented from the prayer of a Cupar merchants' petition against the Dundee harbour bill, 19 Mar. 1830. Ministers listed him among their 'friends' after the 1830 general election (when he was joined in the House by his eldest son John Thomas as Member for Gatton), and he was in their minority in the crucial division on the civil list, 15 Nov. 1830. He presented a petition from Linlithgowshire distillers for revision of the regulations governing grain purchases, 28 Feb. 1831. He voted against the second reading of the Grey ministry's English reform bill, 22 Mar., and for Gascoyne's wrecking amendment, 19 Apr., but presented a constituency petition for reform, 14 Mar. He voiced fears that allowing Scottish clergymen to vote would infuse 'the poison of politics ... between the pastor and his flock', 25 Mar. His last recorded vote was against the second reading of the reintroduced reform bill, 6 July 1831. He paired against its passage, 21 Sept., and the second and third readings of the revised bill, 17 Dec. 1831, 22 Mar. 1832. He demanded to know if Lord Milton intended to move for repeal of the corn laws, 1 June 1832. He was given a month's leave on account of a family illness, 11 July 1832.

Hope narrowly retained his seat after a contest at the general election of 1832, when he gave 'as his definition of a Tory, which he avowed himself to be, that he was one anxious for every rational improvement, without dangerous and speculative experiments'.[8] He retired from Parliament at the dissolution of 1834, lost his eldest and youngest sons the following year and died at Chelsea Hospital in May 1837.[9] He was succeeded by his elder surviving son George William Hope (1808-63), Conservative Member for Windsor, 1859-63. His personalty was sworn under £30,000,

but with admitted debts in 1834 of £60,000 against assets of £54,000, his estate was deemed 'insolvent' for death duty purposes.[10]

[1] *Caledonian Mercury*, 19, 26 Feb., 27 Mar. 1820; Add. 40358, f. 359; 40370, f. 92. [2] *Black Bk.* (1823), 164. [3] *The Times*, 8, 11, 25 Mar. 1823. [4] Ibid. 7, 8 May 1824. [5] Ibid. 19 Apr. 1825. [6] Ibid. 22 Apr. 1826. [7] NAS GD364/289. [8] *Caledonian Mercury*, 20 Dec. 1832. [9] *Gent. Mag.* (1837), ii. 423-4. [10] PROB 11/1880/460; IR26/1453/389.

D.R.F.

HOPE, Henry Thomas (1807–1862), of The Deepdene, Dorking, Surr. and 1 Duchess Street, Mdx.

EAST LOOE	9 May 1829–1832
GLOUCESTER	9 Apr. 1833–1841
GLOUCESTER	1847–1852

b. 30 Apr. 1807,[1] 1st s. of Thomas Hope of The Deepdene and Louisa, da. of Hon. and Most Rev. William Beresford, abp. of Tuam. *educ.* privately by Rev. James Hitchings; Eton 1823; Trinity Coll. Camb. 1825. m. 6 Oct. 1851,[2] Anne Adele, da. of Joseph Bichat, 1 illegit. da. *suc.* fa. 1831. *d.* 4 Dec. 1862.

Groom of bedchamber Mar.-Nov. 1830; metropolitan improvement commr. 1842-51.

Dir. London and Westminster Bank.

Dep. recorder, East Looe 1830.

Hope came from a Scottish family, related to the Hopes of Hopetoun and Craighall, who had migrated to the Netherlands in the seventeenth century and became merchants in Rotterdam. The brothers Thomas and Adrian Hope laid the foundation of the family's great fortune by establishing a bank in Amsterdam in 1731, which was known as Hope and Company from 1762. Their cousin Henry (1736-1811) became the bank's active manager and his three sons, of whom the eldest, Thomas, was the father of this Member, were all sleeping partners until 1814, when they sold out to the Barings.[3] Thomas, who inherited a large personal fortune on his father's death, studied architecture and travelled extensively in southern Europe and the Middle East, adding to a large collection of paintings and *objets d'art* begun by his father. In 1794 the imminent French invasion of Holland drove the Hopes to take refuge in London, bringing the bulk of their moveable property with them. Five years later Thomas bought a town mansion in Duchess Street, which he enlarged, decorated in neoclassical style and filled with his collections; one visitor commented that it 'resembled a museum'.[4] A villainously ugly man, whom one contemporary described as 'disagreeable ... fastidious and conceited', and another as having 'a foolish manner and a very disagreeable voice', Thomas married the 'uncommonly pretty and very good natured' Irish aristocrat Louisa Beresford in 1806. Four years later Dubost's caricature painting of the couple as 'Beauty and the Beast' was mutilated in the Pall Mall exhibition room by Louisa's brother John.[5] Thomas's publications included an initially ridiculed but eventually influential treatise on *Household Furniture and Interior Decoration* (1807), which prompted the wags to dub him 'Furniture' Hope, *Design of Modern Costume* (1812), *Essay on the Origin and Prospects of Man* (1831), and *Historical Essay on Architecture* (1835).[6] Soon after his marriage he purchased The Deepdene, a large country house in Surrey with extensive grounds, which he improved and stuffed with pictures, statuary and marbles. It became a resort for intellectuals and men of letters, including Crabbe, Davy, Rogers, Scott and Sismondi, while Duchess Street, presided over by Louisa, was for many years one of the focal points of the fashionable London scene; the reviled princess of Wales was made welcome there.[7] During the French wars Thomas was said to be 'a little of an opposition man', though 'neither a Burdettite or a Jacobin'. Indeed, he coveted a peerage and there was an embarrassing episode in 1823 when a land agent named William Bromley, who turned out to be insane and was probably acting alone, tried to procure a title for him by offering £10,000 to the duke of York, the commander-in-chief, and to the duke of Wellington, a member of Lord Liverpool's cabinet.[8]

Henry Hope was groomed by his father for a parliamentary career. Soon after he went up to Cambridge (where he stayed only a year), Maria Edgeworth, who had earlier described him as an 'ugly' but 'simple good boy', unspoilt by Eton, wrote to his mother:

I am very glad that Henry is in a good set ... That is of much more consequence to a young man of his fortune and station in society than any temporary distinction he might gain. His father regrets, he says, that he is not more desirous of distinction; so do I. Yet he may be a very happy and a very useful and respectable man without ambition.[9]

Early in 1829 his father purchased the Trenant Park estate in Cornwall and the parliamentary patronage of East Looe which went with it, from James Buller Elphinstone*, and Henry was duly returned there in May. He divided with Wellington's ministry against Lord Blandford's reform scheme, 18 Feb., and the enfranchisement of Birmingham, Leeds and Manchester, 23 Feb. 1830. The following month he was appointed a groom of the bedchamber. Soon afterwards his mother, enlisting the support of her bastard cousin Lord Beresford, one of Wellington's Peninsular army comrades, unsuccessfully solicited a peerage for her husband, explaining to the duke:

Our family concerns both as Hopes and Beresfords are ... quite unobjectionable, and the fortune of our house ... is more than sufficient to maintain the dignity of any honour. We may fairly say that our eldest son will be one of the richest commoners in the kingdom. We have done everything, and we feel and believe not unsuccessfully, to give efficiency to his natural talents, and whatever they are we trust they may come to be useful to the support of your administration, and at a vast expense we have secured his being always in a situation to be so, as well as his younger brother [Adrian, *b.* 1811] as soon as his age will permit.[10]

Hope voted against Jewish emancipation, 17 May. He divided for the grant for South American missions and against abolition of the death penalty for forgery, 7 June 1830. He was retained in the household by William IV, a family friend, who made his mother, to the surprise of some, who thought it beneath her, a lady of the bedchamber.[11] He came in again for East Looe at the general election that summer.

The ministry of course regarded him as one of their 'friends', and he voted with them in the crucial civil list division, 15 Nov. 1830. He resigned from the household on the consequent change of government. On his father's death in February 1831 he inherited the Duchess Street house, all the pictures and works of art and an equal share with his three siblings in a residue which yielded over £361,000. His mother subsequently exercised the option of selling The Deepdene to him for £12,000.[12] Following the introduction of the Grey ministry's reform bill, which proposed to disfranchise East Looe, Hope's colleague, Thomas Kemmis, reported that he felt deterred from speaking on the issue because of his 'strong views' on it, and that 'he tells me ... he would be delighted to give up Looe and politics if he could make sure of keeping the remainder of his property'.[13] He presented an East Looe corporation petition with which he agreed in condemning the bill as 'a violation of the constitution', 18 Mar. He divided against the second reading, 22 Mar., and for Gascoyne's wrecking amendment, 19 Apr. 1831. He returned himself at the ensuing general election. He voted against the second reading of the reintroduced reform bill, 6 July, and in favour of using the 1831 census to determine the disfranchisement schedules, 19 July. He supported a futile attempt to have East and West Looe combined to return one

Member, 22 July, contending that the boroughs had 'never been under any other than ... just and natural influence'. He responded tartly to Daniel O'Connell's denunciation of them as 'nomination boroughs'. He divided against the partial disfranchisement of Chippenham, 27 July, may have supported a bid to have Rye combined with Winchelsea to return two Members, 30 July, and voted against the bill's passage, 21 Sept. He divided against the second reading of the revised bill, 17 Dec. 1831, the enfranchisement of Tower Hamlets, 28 Feb., and the third reading, 22 Mar. 1832. He voted against ministers on the Russian-Dutch loan, 12 July, and was credited with a vote in the minority against the crown colonies relief proposals, 3 Aug. 1832.

Hope was left without a seat at the general election of 1832. At a by-election in March 1833 he offered for Marylebone as an 'advocate [of] moderate Conservative principles', but was defeated. Shortly afterwards he was returned for Gloucester and sat until his defeat in 1841.[14] Later that year he asked Sir Robert Peel for a peerage as a reward for his services to the Conservative party, to no avail, but he eagerly accepted the premier's invitation to sit on the metropolitan improvement commission in 1842.[15] He came in again for Gloucester as a free trade Conservative in 1847, but was defeated there in 1852 and at a by-election the next year. He became very friendly with Benjamin Disraeli[†] and may have been a financial backer of the Young England group, though he was out of Parliament during its brief heyday. His youngest brother Alexander James Beresford Hope (1820-87), whom Disraeli privately dismissed as 'an imbecile' and 'a cretin', was a fellow-traveller.[16] Disraeli dedicated *Coningsby* (1844) to Hope, claiming that it had been conceived during conversations at The Deepdene, where his friend had created 'the most perfect Italian palace you can conceive', set in 'the most romantic grounds and surrounded by the most picturesque park I can well remember'.[17] In April 1843 a daughter, Adele Henrietta, was born to Hope and his lover Anne Adele Bichet, whom he married in 1851, soon after the death of his mother. He died in December 1862 and left the bulk of his property to his daughter, who had married the future 6th duke of Newcastle.

[1] *Gent. Mag.* (1807), i. 482. [2] IGI (Hants). [3] H.W. and I. Law, *Bk. of the Beresford Hopes*, 17, 267-74; D. Watkin, *Thomas Hope and the Neo-Classical Idea*, 1-3, 5. [4] Law, 18-19; Watkin, 6-8; *Farington Diary*, ii. 297; vi. 2314; xii. 4226, 4420. [5] Law, 27; Watkin, 16-17; *Farington Diary*, vii. 2754; x. 3674. [6] Watkin, *passim*; Law, 22; *Edgeworth Letters*, 55; *Smith Letters*, i. 352. [7] Watkin, 17; Law, 28-29; *VCH Surr.* iii. 143-4; *Edgeworth Letters*, 55-56, 188-9, 193-4, 196, 362-3; *Berry Jnls.* ii. 379-80, 382-3, 413. [8] Law,

38; Watkin, 24-25; *Lady Holland to Son*, 71; *Arbuthnot Jnl.* i. 222, 224; Wellington mss WP1/758/18, 24; 759/9. [9] Law, 46-49; *Edgeworth Letters*, 296, 299. [10] Law, 63-64; Watkin, 26; Wellington mss WP1/1107/2; 1111/49; 1129/14. [11] Law, 62; *Lady Holland to Son*, 110. [12] PROB 11/1783/153; IR26/1259/95. [13] Cornw. RO FS/3/1092/19. [14] *The Times*, 11, 14, 21 Mar., 8-10 Apr. 1833. [15] Add. 40497, ff. 223, 225. [16] *Disraeli Letters*, iv. 1213, 1264; Monypenny and Buckle, *Disraeli*, ii. 14, 92, 147-8, 183, 194, 197, 199, 200, 225-6, 239; C. Whibley, *Lord John Manners and his Friends*, i. 143, 146, 159; R. Faber, *Young England*, 111, 115-17. [17] *Disraeli Letters*, iii. 1104; iv. 126, 1343; Watkin, 181-5; Law, 106; Faber, 188.

D.R.F./H.J.S.

HOPE, John Thomas (1807–1835), of Luffness, Haddington.

GATTON	1830–1831
OKEHAMPTON	1831–1832

b. 10 Jan. 1807, 1st s. of Hon. Sir Alexander Hope* (*d.* 1837) and Georgina Alicia, da. of George Brown of Elliestoun, Edinburgh. *educ.* Christ Church, Oxf. 1823; L. Inn 1828. *m.* 2 Mar. 1835, Lady Frances Anne Lascelles, da. of Henry Lascelles[†], 2nd earl of Harewood, *s.p. d.v.p.* 17 Apr. 1835.
Lt.-col. Fife militia.

'Beauty' Hope, who was born while his father was governor of Edinburgh Castle, apparently went in 1821 with his father, pious mother and siblings on their two-year European tour, which took them to Dresden, Lausanne and Florence. While abroad he received tuition from the Rev. Joseph Langley Mills, chaplain to the forces. He took a first at Oxford, where he recited his Newdigate prize poem on 'The Arch of Titus' on the same day, 30 June 1824, that his father received an honorary doctorate. His brother James, who became a fellow of Merton and a leading figure in the Oxford Movement, later commented that John 'got nothing from Oxford but a good name', though 'from his situation' he had no 'need of much more'.[1] He revisited the continent under his own steam, 1827-8, before entering Lincoln's Inn.[2] At the general election of 1830 he was returned unopposed for Gatton on Lord Monson's interest.

The duke of Wellington's ministry listed him among their 'friends', and he probably voted with them in the crucial civil list division, 15 Nov. 1830. Two days before his father had asked the home secretary Peel to secure his appointment to the revived select committee on the East India Company, to which subject he had 'devoted some time ... and I hope not without profit'; but the ministry's fall intervened.[3] He may have been the 'young Hope' earlier referred to by Lord Ellenborough, a member of the outgoing cabinet, as one of the ministerialists who were supposedly 'very unwilling to vote against' parliamentary reform, 'thinking the public feeling too strong'.[4] However, in his maiden speech, 7 Mar. 1831, he opposed the Grey ministry's reform bill as an unnecessary concession to popular clamour, which would satisfy neither the 'middle classes', who wanted tax reductions, nor the 'crazy radicals and visionary anarchists', who wished to 'share amongst themselves the plunder of the country'. He also argued that it would drive a wedge between the landed and manufacturing interests, give too much power to the Commons and enfranchise men 'who have neither sufficient property nor sufficient education to guarantee a just and correct use of that privilege'. He divided against the second reading, 22 Mar., and for Gascoyne's wrecking amendment, 19 Apr. 1831. At the ensuing general election he offered for Haddingtonshire, where his kinsman Lord Hopetoun exercised considerable influence, but withdrew in order to avoid splitting the anti-reform vote. He had taken the precaution of 'securing a seat' for Okehampton on the Savile interest, and was returned unopposed.[5]

Hope joined in calls for gradual rather than immediate reduction of the barilla duties, 1 July 1831. He divided against the second reading of the reintroduced reform bill, 6 July, and for use of the 1831 census as a basis for the disfranchisement schedules, 19 July. Two days later he expressed regret at the extinction of Gatton as a parliamentary borough. He voted to postpone consideration of the partial disfranchisement of Chippenham, 27 July, and probably opposed the clause of the bill dealing with freeholders of city counties, 17 Aug. It is not clear whether it was he or Henry Thomas Hope who divided against the third reading, 19 Sept., but he certainly voted against the bill's passage, 21 Sept., and the second reading of the Scottish bill, 23 Sept. On 16 Dec. 1831 he claimed that many 'respectable' people were hostile to reform, and he divided against the second reading of the revised bill the next day. He dined at Peel's house, 5 Feb.,[6] and voted against going into committee on the bill, 20 Jan., the enfranchisement of Tower Hamlets, 28 Feb., and the third reading, 22 Mar. 1832. He asserted that 'a very large portion' of Scots, 'though ... not opposed to some change', considered the Scottish bill 'too sweeping and too extensive', 25 May. He voted against the second reading of the Irish bill that day. He divided against government on the Russian-Dutch loan, 26 Jan., 12 July, and criticized their foreign policy, 26 Mar., 20 July. He was a resolute opponent of Sadler's factories regulation bill.[7] He presented and endorsed a hostile petition from the flax spinners and linen manufacturers of Cupar, 8 Mar. He spoke at some length

against the bill's second reading, 16 Mar., contending that Parliament could not 'supply the place of parental affections on behalf of the child', that legislation was unnecessary and that the bill would be 'productive of great inconvenience' to both masters and workers. He asserted that 'ill health and wretchedness are by no means the necessary consequences of being employed in ... mills', 27 June, and presented hostile workers' petitions from Annan, Pendleton and Cupar, 3, 16 July. He called for the postponement of the Scottish cholera prevention bill to facilitate the introduction of a clause to cater for voluntary parish subscriptions, 27 Mar. 1832.

Okehampton was disfranchised by the Reform Act, and at the general election of 1832 Hope stood as a Conservative for Manchester, presumably on the strength of his opposition to the factories bill. He was shouted down on the hustings and finished a distant fourth in the poll.[8] On a tour of Norway in the summer of 1834 he fell 'alarmingly ill' with sunstroke,[9] and he had not fully recovered when the Haddingtonshire Conservatives put him up for the county at the general election of 1835; he was narrowly defeated by a Liberal and resolved never to stand again.[10] Two months later he married the eldest daughter of the 2nd earl of Harewood, but soon afterwards his 'brain fever' recurred and he died in April 1835, v.p. and aged 28. No will has been found. He was, according to Thomas Raikes, 'a very handsome man and much liked'.[11]

[1] R. Ornsby, *Mems. James Robert Hope Scott*, i. 1, 6-8, 21, 35, 53, 86. [2] His travel jnl. is in NAS GD364/263 (NRA 10172). [3] Add. 40340, ff. 246, 249. [4] *Ellenborough Diary*, ii. 426. [5] *Edinburgh Evening Courant*, 28 Apr.; *Western Times*, 7 May 1831; Northumb. RO, Hope Wallace mss ZHW/2/18. [6] NLW, Ormathwaite mss FG 1/6, p. 17. [7] NAS GD364/351. [8] *The Times*, 17 Oct., 7, 14, 17 Dec. 1832; NAS GD364/350, 352. [9] Keele Univ. Lib. Sneyd mss SC17/187; Ornsby, i. 65. [10] *Scottish Electoral Politics*, 221; *The Times*, 19, 21 Jan. 1835; Ornsby, i. 80-81; NAS GD364/156-62, 166, 741. [11] *Gent. Mag.* (1835), i. 428, 558; *Raikes Jnl.* ii. 90; Ornsby, i. 85-86.

D.R.F.

HOPE JOHNSTONE, John James (1796–1876), of Raehills, Dumfries.

DUMFRIESSHIRE	1830–1847
DUMFRIESSHIRE	12 Feb. 1857–1865

b. 29 Nov. 1796, 1st s. of Sir William Johnstone Hope* and 1st w. Lady Anne Hope Johnstone, da. of James, 3rd earl of Hopetoun [S]. *m.* 8 July 1816, Alicia Anne, da. of George Gordon of Hillhead, 7s. (4 *d.v.p.*) 3da. *suc.* mother to Dumfries estates of 2nd mq. of Annandale [S] 1818; fa. 1831. *d.* 11 July 1876.

Hered. kpr. Lochmaben Palace.

Hope Johnstone was only 19 when he married the ravishing Alicia Gordon in 1816; she bore him at least 11 children.[1] Two years later he succeeded his mother, a daughter of the 3rd earl of Hopetoun, to the extensive Dumfriesshire estates of the 2nd marquess of Annandale, who had died unmarried and insane in 1792. This property, with its mansion at Raehills, ten miles north-west of Lockerbie, made him the second largest landholder (after the dukes of Buccleuch) in a county for which his father, a naval hero, had sat as a Melvillite Tory since 1804. Like his maternal grandfather and mother before him, he pursued a claim to the Scottish earldom of Annandale and Hartfell, viscountcy of Annadale and barony of Johnstone as heir of line of Lord Hopetoun, Annadale's heir general and heir of entail. He also coveted a British peerage in the short term.[2] His petition claiming the titles was presented to the Lords by Lord Sidmouth, the home secretary, on 6 July 1820, but the first hearing before the committee of privileges did not take place until 1825. After further consideration in 1826 the proceedings were adjourned. They were resumed in 1830, when a number of other claimants came forward, but nothing was decided.[3] His kinsman James Hope Vere* reported that he was 'much out of humour at the delays of the House of Peers' and reflected that he had 'chosen a terrible sea of troubles to sail upon'.[4] Shortly before the dissolution in 1830 Hope Johnstone's father, now a commissioner of Greenwich Hospital, told him that he intended to retire from Parliament and that the new king, William IV, had 'most strongly solicited me to endeavour to persuade *you* to take my shoes, and added that it might be the means of forwarding your cause'.[5] He was initially reported to be 'very reluctant to come forward', but in the end he stood and was returned unopposed at the general election in August.[6]

The Wellington ministry of course reckoned him as one of their 'friends', and he divided in their minority on the civil list, 15 Nov. 1830. He was given three weeks' leave on account of illness in his family, 22 Nov. 1830. The new Grey ministry dismissed his father from his place but made him a privy councillor. Hope Johnstone presented a Moffat petition for Scottish parliamentary reform, 7 Mar., and voted for the second reading of the English reform bill, 22 Mar. 1831. This vote caused consternation among his county supporters, while William Douglas, Tory Member for Dumfries Burghs, told Buccleuch that Hope Johnstone was 'a man who is more open to flattery from inferiors than any person I am acquainted with. He is highly respectable in his domestic relations, but his judgement is weak and he has had no

experience of the world'.[7] On 27 Mar., having, as Hope Vere put it, 'suddenly become a great reformer', Hope Johnstone was elected to Brooks's, sponsored by the duke of Norfolk and Lord Essex.[8] He voted against Gascoyne's wrecking amendment to the reform bill, 19 Apr. 1831, and at the ensuing general election retained his seat unchallenged. He had renewed his petition for the committee of privileges to proceed with the peerage case on 28 Mar. 1831, but the business remained in abeyance.[9] He voted for the second reading of the reintroduced reform bill, 6 July, was given a month's leave on 'urgent private business', 11 July, but attended to give general support to its details, though he cast wayward votes on the cases of Appleby, 19 July, and Downton, 21 July, for the enfranchisement of £50 tenants-at-will, 18 Aug., and to withhold the borough franchise from weekly tenants and lodgers, 25 Aug. He voted to postpone the Dublin, 8 Aug., and Liverpool writs, 5 Sept. He divided for the third reading, 19 Sept., and passage of the reform bill, 21 Sept., the second reading of the Scottish bill, 23 Sept., and the motion of confidence in the ministry, 10 Oct. 1831.

Hope Johnstone voted for the second reading of the revised reform bill, 17 Dec. 1831, generally for its details (though he was probably in the minority against the enfranchisement of Gateshead, 5 Mar.) and for the third reading, 22 Mar. 1832. He divided against government on the Russian-Dutch loan, 26 Jan., but with them on relations with Portugal, 9 Feb., and against the production of information on military punishments, 16 Feb. He did not vote for the address calling on the king to appoint only ministers who would carry reform unimpaired, 10 May, but he voted against Conservative amendments to the Scottish reform bill, 1 June, when he criticized the removal of Selkirk from the Linlithgow district of burghs to Selkirkshire but accepted it as 'absolutely necessary', and 15 June. On 8 June 1832 he presented and largely endorsed a petition from ministers of the Church of Scotland praying that in the proposed scheme of Irish education all Protestant children should be allowed to attend daily Bible classes, though he considered the plan to be 'founded ... in reason and justice'; he also brought up hostile petitions from clergymen of Annan and Linlithgow.

At the general election of 1832 Hope Johnstone was returned unopposed for Dumfriesshire as a Conservative. He renewed his peerage claim in 1833 and seemed on the verge of 'a successful termination to so troublesome, vexatious and costly a job' the following year, but his hopes, raised by Lord Brougham, were again dashed.[10] Soon after Peel's accession to power in 1841 Hope Johnstone vainly asked him for a British peerage.[11] His Annandale claim was rejected by the committee of privileges on 25 June 1844.[12] A Peelite Conservative from 1846, he retired from Parliament in 1865.[13] He greatly extended the Raehills house, but struggled with estate debts.[14] He died of 'general decay' in July 1876. His eldest son William had died in 1850, and he was succeeded by his grandson and namesake (1842-1912), Conservative Member for Dumfriesshire, 1874-80, whose renewal of the Annandale claim was conclusively dismissed in 1881.

[1] Sir W. Fraser, *Annandale Fam. Bk.* ii. 411. [2] Ibid. vol. i, p. cccxxxix; ii. 356-82; NAS GD51/1/191. [3] Fraser, ii. 357-66; *LJ*, liii. 259-60; lvii. 62, 473, 1028, 1041, 1058; lviii. 49, 388; lxii. 139, 205, 262-3, 582-3, 650; lxiii. 171-2, 218; *The Times*, 23, 26 May 1826, 8, 22 May 1830. [4] Hopetoun mss 167, ff. 138, 140, 142. [5] Annandale mss (NRA [S] 217), 669, Johnstone Hope to Hope Johnstone, 12 July 1830. [6] NAS GD224/507/3/33. [7] NAS GD224/507/3/24, 25. [8] Hopetoun mss 167, f. 244. [9] *LJ*, lxiii. 387, 792, 982. [10] Fraser, ii. 366-79; *LJ*, lxv. 100; Annandale mss 932, Hope Johnstone to J. Hope, 16 May 1834; Heron, *Notes*, 238-9. [11] Add. 40493, f. 212. [12] *LJ*, lxx. 411-12; Fraser, ii. 379-81. [13] *Dod's Parl. Companion* (1859), 224-5. [14] Annandale mss 970, Hope Johnstone to J. Hope, 30 July 1845.

D.R.F.

HOPE VERE, James Joseph (1785–1843), of Craigie Hall, Linlithgow and Blackwood, Lanark.

ILCHESTER	1830–1831
NEWPORT I.o.W.	1831–1832

b. 3 June 1785, 1st surv. s. of William Hope Weir of Craigie Hall and Blackwood and Sophia, da. of Joseph Corrie of Dumfries. *educ.* privately; St. John's, Camb. 1801; L. Inn 1802, called 1820. *m.* 7 Sept. 1813, Lady Elizabeth Hay, da. of George, 7th mq. of Tweedale, 2s. 6da. *suc.* fa. 1811. *d.* 19 May 1843.

Hope Vere was the great-grandson of Charles Hope, 1st earl of Hopetoun (1681-1742), whose second son Charles (1710-91), Member for Linlithgowshire, 1743-68, succeeded to Craigie Hall on the death of his maternal uncle the 2nd marquess of Annandale in 1730. Through his marriage to Catherine, the only daughter of Sir William Weir, he obtained the Blackwood estate and an additional surname. It was he who held the office of commissary-general for musters in Scotland and not, as one source states, his eldest son William (1736-1811), this Member's father, who had a brief army career.[1] Hope Vere, who was educated in England, later described how he led a 'retired life at Cambridge', as 'my health had not been good ... and I

was advised to drink little wine, so I resolved to drink none at all'.[2] While at Lincoln's Inn he formed a life-long friendship with George Pryme, the Cambridge political economist, whose daughter recalled his 'elegant manners, refined yet vigorous mind, and delightful conversation'.[3] In his admission records he is entered as James Joseph Hope, but by the time of his marriage in 1813 he had adopted the additional family surname in its Anglo-Norman form of Vere. In 1811 he succeeded his father to valuable Scottish lowland estates, which later in the century were reckoned to exceed 8,000 acres.[4] He is not known to have practised after his belated call to the English bar.

Hope Vere emerges as a keen and occasionally ribald observer of politics in his surviving letters to John Philip Wood, an Edinburgh customs official and amateur historian with whom he corresponded regularly from 1823.[5] A moderate Whig, who joined the Edinburgh New Club in 1815 and Brooks's, sponsored by Lord Lansdowne, 18 July 1823, he was amused to acquire a radical connection in 1828, when his sister-in-law Lady Julia Hay married John Cam Hobhouse*.[6] At a Lanarkshire county meeting for a loyal address to the throne, 11 Jan. 1821, he moved and carried an amendment for economy, retrenchment and reconciliation, 11 Jan. 1821.[7] He claimed to have anticipated the recent financial crash by two years in December 1825, but was baffled by the Bank of England's decision to issue £1 notes.[8] At the Cambridge University election of 1826 he gave a plumper for Lord Palmerston, the war secretary, his near contemporary at St. John's, and recalled how he had cast a similar vote at an earlier contest, probably that of 1811, 'much to the annoyance of my Whig friends'.[9] Following the formation of Canning's ministry in 1827 he ruminated on the good fortune enjoyed by the new prime minister at crucial junctures in his career, but did not make his attitude towards him clear. He praised the duke of Wellington as a 'good economical premier' in 1830, though he disliked his interference with Lord Aberdeen's stewardship of the foreign office.[10] Claiming that he had attended a general assembly of the Church of Scotland purely out of curiosity, 30 May, he observed, 'I ... have long been satisfied that a gentleman should have no ambition to open his lips anywhere but in the House of Commons'.[11] At the 1830 dissolution, which he thought curiously timed, he decamped to London, mainly, he insisted, to avoid the Lanarkshire canvass, though with the evident aim of securing a seat for himself. He had apparently rejected Linlithgow Burghs as too expensive and denied a report that he would offer for St. Ives, 20 July.[12] He eventually settled on challenging the established patron at Ilchester, under the aegis of the 1st marquess of Cleveland. On the hustings he indicated his support for civil and religious liberty and the reduction of sinecures and pledged to 'oppose public oppression'. He was returned after a close contest which prompted a petition.[13] On 9 Nov. he described the prevailing view at Brooks's that the Wellington administration would not last a fortnight, though he was personally inclined to give them longer. Ministers had listed him among their 'friends', with a query, and though he 'made every enquiry' about the opposition to Wellington, he could 'discover no good grounds, except unjustifiable discontent and a determined spirit of faction, that is against him', 10 Nov. He expected ministers to win the anticipated showdown on reform, noting that the king was 'set against them going out', but was absent from the crucial division on the civil list which brought them down, 15 Nov., though present to witness the count. (Three days later he asserted that many of those listed as absent had actually voted with ministers, but it is unclear whether he did so himself.) Belatedly, he conceded that Wellington had made 'a sad mistake' by opposing parliamentary reform, 16 Nov.[14] Commenting on the petition against his return three days later, he observed, 'if I should be turned adrift it would not kill me', but admitted he would 'regret the loss' of his seat, 23 Nov. His return was upheld by the committee after a 'wearing and anxious' eight-day hearing, 17 Dec. 1830.[15] In the meantime, having been initially been unimpressed with the standard of oratory in the House, he found words of praise for Macaulay and Henry Brougham, while his remarks on the Liverpool by-election indicated his opposition to anything approaching universal suffrage.[16] He reported general dissatisfaction at the modest reductions proposed in the civil list, though personally he had 'never expected much, because I could not see how they could do it', 11 Feb., and described Lord Althorp's ill-fated budget as 'an unlucky affair', which ought to have been postponed, 28 Feb. 1831. He had expressed 'much doubt' about the success of any parliamentary reform plan, 17 Jan., and following the announcement of the Grey ministry's proposals, could not see 'either the necessity of the measure or the good expected to accrue from it', 4 Mar. 'You will see the Whig administration are about speedily to sweep away all us borough vermin as noxious animals that have not the good of our country at heart, and are blood suckers of the constitution', he informed Wood that day, adding that 'to be a successful speaker in the House one must have nerve enough to bawl out their opinions even though no one is attending, and all are talking. I have not yet made the attempt because that is a talent I

profess not'.[17] In spite of this, he voted for the reform bill's second reading, 22 Mar., telling Wood that for it 'to have been rejected at the outset might have led to unpleasant consequences'. He added that he did not expect this 'perilous experiment' to survive the committee stage, 4 Apr., but was surprised that it fell at the first hurdle, on Gascoyne's wrecking amendment, against which he voted, 19 Apr. 1831.[18]

At the 1831 dissolution he retired from Ilchester, where he had not expected to come in again, and disclaimed all knowledge of his prospects of finding another berth, 30 Apr. By then Cleveland had secured his return for Newport, Isle of Wight. He remained in Edinburgh for his wife's confinement and was notified of his unopposed return by 'a friend in London', 11 May.[19] One hazard of such an impersonal arrangement was demonstrated by the discovery that his Christian names had been recorded as John James on the return, probably due to confusion with his kinsman John James Hope Johnstone*. The published *Return* (Pt. II, vol. i, p. 333) inexplicably states that his name was substituted with that of George Augustus Frederick Villiers, but in fact the error was simply corrected by an order of the House, 28 June 1831, though only, as he complained, 'after much trouble ... and many walks about London in very bad weather'. The Speaker's absence the following day caused another delay in his taking the seat and he was finally sworn in, 30 June.[20] He voted for the second reading of the reintroduced reform bill, 6 July, and gave steady support to its details in committee, though he was sceptical about its chances and feared that its 'slow progress' would prejudice its success in the Lords.[21] He confided to Wood his lack of faith in the durability of the ministry and fears of an imminent rebellion in Ireland, 13 Aug., was in a minority of 11 against the Irish union of parishes bill, 19 Aug., but divided with ministers on the Dublin election controversy, 23 Aug.[22] He voted for the reform bill's passage, 21 Sept., but remained ambivalent about its consequences, recounting a Tory Member's forecast of ruin with the observation, 'he is a man of considerable sense', 6 Oct.[23] He was 'confounded' by the scale of its defeat in the Lords, 8 Oct., and despite the success of Lord Ebrington's confidence motion, for which he divided, reported that 'the faces at Brooks's are very long', 10 Oct. 1831.[24]

Hope Vere voted for the second reading of the revised bill, 17 Dec. 1831, following which he returned rapidly to Scotland, foregoing an overnight stop at Newcastle because of the cholera outbreak.[25] He was back in time to divide for going into committee on the bill, 20 Jan., and again voted steadily for its details, though he was in a minority of five to exempt Preston from the £10 householder franchise, 3 Feb. 1832. That day he predicted 'another tedious session' in both Houses.[26] He divided with ministers on the Russian-Dutch loan, 26 Jan., and relations with Portugal (as a pair), 9 Feb. That day he secured a return of cases referred to the Lords from the Scottish court of session. Given the attitude of Lord Grey and Smith Stanley, the Irish secretary, whom he considered the 'most useful of the whole cabinet', he privately expected no creation of peers and a thorough mauling of the reform bill in the Lords, naming the enfranchisement of metropolitan districts and the division of counties as the provisions most likely to go, 20 Mar. He voted for the bill's third reading, 22 Mar., and for the address calling on the king to appoint only ministers who would carry it unimpaired, 10 May. Reporting rumours of Wellington's return to office next day, he conjectured that Grey had been 'completely deceived' by the king.[27] He divided for the second reading of the Irish reform bill, 25 May, and against a Conservative amendment to increase Scottish county representation, 1 June. He was granted six weeks' leave on urgent business, 10 July 1832.

At the 1832 general election he stood unsuccessfully for Linlithgowshire against his distant kinsman Sir Alexander Hope, the incumbent Conservative, citing his 'independence of party'. (Eighteen months previously he had informed Wood that he would 'not be sorry' to be out of the reformed House, in which there would 'no longer be so many absent or silent Members'.)[28] He welcomed the opportunity to build a new Commons afforded by the fire of October 1834, observing that 'the avenues, the secret windings, and the curious pigeonhole offices of the *deceased* were something more intricate than it is possible to fancy'.[29] He viewed Wellington's actions as caretaker prime minister in December 1834 with some concern, but does not appear to have contemplated standing at the subsequent general election, or at any time thereafter.[30] He died in Park Lane, Mayfair, in May 1843. His will, dated 15 Dec. 1825, confirmed the entailment of the Craigie Hall and Blackwood estates on his elder son William Edward Hope Vere (1824-72), and by a codicil of 3 June 1836 he left £8,000 to his second son Charles (1828-1900).[31]

[1] See *Foster's Peerage* (1882), 353. [2] NRA [S] o888, Hopetoun mss 167, f. 173, Hope Vere to Wood, 10 Oct. 1830. [3] G. Pryme, *Autobiog. Recollections*, 69. [4] J. Bateman, *Great Landowners* (1872), 456. [5] Hopetoun mss 167, typescript intro. by M. Brock, *passim*. [6] *Members ... of the New Club* (1815), 27; Hopetoun mss 167, f. 40. [7] *Glasgow Herald*, 12, 15 Jan. 1821. [8] Hopetoun mss 167, f. 5. [9] Ibid. f. 10. [10] Ibid. ff. 17, 140. [11] Ibid. f. 138. [12] Ibid. ff. 151-6.

[13] Ibid. f. 157; *Western Flying Post*, 2 Aug.; *Sherborne Jnl.* 5 Aug. 1830. [14] Hopetoun mss 167, ff. 181-5, 187, 189. [15] Ibid. ff. 189, 193, 208; *CJ*, lxxxvi. 183. [16] Hopetoun mss 167, ff. 177, 193-7. [17] Ibid. ff. 214, 224. [18] Ibid. ff. 240, 248, 255, 257. [19] Ibid. ff. 261, 265-7; M. Brock, *Great Reform Act*, 197. [20] Hopetoun mss 167, ff. 273. [21] Ibid. ff. 272, 281. [22] Ibid. ff. 289-90. [23] Ibid. f. 311. [24] Ibid. ff. 313, 317. [25] Ibid. f. 323. [26] Ibid. f. 336. [27] Ibid. f. 368. [28] *The Times*, 20 Nov. 1832; Hopetoun mss 167, f. 244. [29] Hopetoun mss 167, f. 484. [30] Ibid. f. 495. [31] PROB 11/1985/603; IR26/1663/740.

H.J.S./P.J.S.

HORNBY, Edmund (1773–1857), of Dalton Hall, Westmld.

PRESTON   1812–1826

b. 16 June 1773, 1st s. of Rev. Geoffrey Hornby, rect. of Winwick, Lancs., and Lucy, da. of James Smith Stanley[†], Lord Strange, 1st s. of Edward Stanley[†], 11th earl of Derby. *educ.* Raikes's Sch., Neasden; Trinity Coll. Camb. 1790; I. Temple 1795, called 1798. *m.* 22 Aug. 1796, his cos. Lady Charlotte Smith Stanley, da. of Edward Smith Stanley[†], 12th earl of Derby, 2s. 2da. (1 *d.v.p.*).[1] *suc.* fa. to Scale Hall, Lancs. and Dalton 1812. *d.* 18 Nov. 1857. Sheriff, Lancs. 1828-9.

Hornby, whose estates straddled the Lancashire-Westmorland border, had devoted much of his life and skills as a barrister to promoting the Derby interest, and he continued to assist their candidates at elections between 1820 and 1832. The nephew and son-in-law of the Whig 12th earl and brother-in-law twice over of his son Lord Stanley*, he and his family were frequently at Knowsley and, since Lord Stanley's transfer to the county in 1812, he had represented Preston on the coalition (Derby-Horrocks) interest, as locum for his nephew Edward George Geoffrey Smith Stanley*. He did not intend to stand again, but agreed to do so when George III's death necessitated a general election shortly before Smith Stanley came of age in 1820.[2] After a riotous 13-day poll, with the radical Henry Hunt* and Whig barrister John Williams* as opponents, he and Samuel Horrocks prevailed at a cost of £11,560. On the hustings he defended the coalition by pointing to Williams's involvement in another Whig-Tory alliance at Chester in 1818. He declared for reform and a rate-based householder franchise and against annual parliaments, universal suffrage and the ballot, 'a cover for corruption', and stood by his votes for three of the Liverpool ministry's six repressive Acts (seditious meetings, military training and traverse) introduced after Peterloo. Defending the 'closed' Lancashire grand jury, of which he was a leading member, he spoke out against mass meetings and the deployment of 'physical force' by their agitators.[3] 'Detained by Hunt', he rallied late support in

Westmorland for the Whig lawyer Henry Brougham*, who lost to the Tory Lowthers.[4]

Generally acting with Lord Stanley, Hornby adhered to the main Whig opposition in the 1820 Parliament. He divided for Catholic relief, 28 Feb. 1821, 1 Mar., 21 Apr., 10 May 1825. He voted to make Leeds a scot and lot borough under the Grampound disfranchisement bill, 2 Mar., for Lord John Russell's reform proposal, 9 May (but not Lambton's, 18 Apr. 1821), and again for reform, 25 Apr. 1822, 24 Apr., 2 June 1823, 26 Feb. 1824, 27 Apr. 1826. In a rare speech, 7 Mar. 1821, he denied, as one of the visiting magistrates, the radical Nathan Broadhurst and his fellow petitioners' allegations of maltreatment in Lancaster gaol. He justified on grounds of economy and security the practices of putting prisoners to work, denying them newspapers and opening their mail. He was named to select committees on prisons, 30 Mar. 1821, 5 Mar. 1822, 14 May 1823, 1 Mar. 1824. Opposing the cotton factory bill, 16 May (after presenting unfavourable petitions on the 13th), he argued that as adult and child labour were interdependent, the proposed reduction in children's working hours would disrupt production at great cost, without benefiting the children it purported to assist. Despite their political differences, he supported the nomination of the anti-Catholic Tory barrister Thomas Greene* of Slyne, a fellow lobbyist for keeping the assizes at Lancaster, at the by-election there in 1824. Doing so, he explained that as 'much of the important business of the House was transacted without the walls of St. Stephen's, it was important to recruit men of Greene's calibre to serve on committees.[5] Together, they opposed the Liverpool-Manchester railway bill successfully on Derby's behalf in 1825, but failed to prevent its enactment in 1826.[6] He presented and endorsed Preston petitions against the beer bill, 7, 14 May 1824, and voted to permit adjourned sessions for alehouse licensing, 12 May 1826.[7] At the dissolution that month, he made way for Smith Stanley at Preston, where the coalition collapsed. He campaigned for Brougham in Westmorland, Greene at Lancaster and Lord Stanley in the county at the 1826 general election.[8]

Alluding to their adherence to Lord Goderich's ministry, he observed to Smith Stanley, through whom he sought patronage, 8 Dec. 1827, 'I always found it a great advantage of being in opposition, that it furnished me with a ready answer to all applications'.[9] He was sheriff of Lancashire during the 1828-9 Catholic agitation and a ready speaker for the ministerial reform bill at meetings and elections in Lancaster and the North-West, 1831-2.[10] He chaired the election committee of Smith Stanley (now Lord Stanley) in Lancashire North at the general election of 1832, when his eldest son Edmund George Hornby (1799-1865) came in for Preston as a Liberal. Hornby eventually went over to the Conservatives with his nephew.[11] He died at Dalton Hall in November 1857, recalled as a veteran electioneer and quarter sessions chairman, and was succeeded in his estates by Edmund.[12] His will, dated 30 June 1851 and proved at Lancaster, 6 Feb. 1858, also provided for his younger son Charles Hornby of Claret Rock, Dundalk, daughter Mary Margaret, the family of his late daughter Lucy Frances, wife of the Rev. Edward Pigot of Ashton, Lancashire, and other family members.

[1] Hornby's obituary in *Preston Chron.* 20 Nov. 1857 and his will show that he had four children, not one as stated in *HP Commons, 1790-1820*, iv. 233.   [2] *HP Commons, 1790-1820*, iv. 233-4; W. Dobson, *Parl. Rep. Preston*, 71. See LANCASTER and PRESTON.   [3] *Blackburn Mail*, 8 Mar.; *Preston Election Addresses* (1820), 4, 5, and *passim*.   [4] *Westmld. Advertiser*, 18, 25 Mar., 1 Apr. 1820.   [5] HLRO, Thomas Greene mss GRE/4/4; *Westmld. Advertiser*, 24 Apr.; *The Times*, 24 Apr. 1824.   [6] *The Times*, 22 Mar. 1825.   [7] Ibid. 8, 15 May 1824.   [8] *Preston Chron.* 22 Apr.; *The Times*, 3 May; *Lancaster Gazette*, 10, 17, 24 June; *Westmld. Advertiser*, 24 June 1826.   [9] Derby mss 920 Der (14) 61/1.   [10] *Lancaster Gazette*, 12 Mar.; *Lancaster Herald*, 12, 19 Mar., 30 Apr., 7 May 1831.   [11] *Lancaster Gazette*, 22 Dec. 1832; Greene mss 4/25.   [12] *Preston Chron.* 20 Nov.; *Westmld. Gazette*, 21, 28 Nov. 1857; *VCH Lancs.* vii. 333; viii. 185.

M.M.E.

HORNE, Sir William (1773–1860), of 19 Old Square, Lincoln's Inn; 49 Upper Harley Street, Mdx., and Epping House, Little Berkhampstead, Herts.

HELSTON	1812–1818
BLETCHINGLEY	18 Feb. 1831–1831
NEWTOWN I.o.W.	1831–1832
MARYLEBONE	1832–1834

b. 2 Dec. 1773, 2nd s. of Rev. Thomas Horne, DD (*d.* 1824), master of Manor House sch., Chiswick, Mdx. and his w. Frances Ann *née* Price of Weobley, Herefs.[1] *educ.* at his fa.'s sch.; L. Inn 1793, called 1798. *m.* (1) 12 Aug. 1799, Ann (*d.* 21 July 1823),[2] da. of James Hesse of Flitwick, Beds., 4s. (1 *d.v.p.*) 3da.; (2) c.1826, Ann Davison, wid., 1s. 1da.[3] kntd. 24 Nov. 1830. *d.* 13 July 1860.

Commr. of bankrupts 1807-18; KC 7 Aug. 1818; bencher, L. Inn 1818; att.-gen. to the queen July-Nov. 1830; solicitor-gen. Nov. 1830-Nov. 1832; att.-gen. Nov. 1832-Feb. 1834; master in chancery 1839-53.

Lt. Inns of Court vols. 1803.

Horne took silk soon after leaving the House in 1818 and continued his distinguished career as a leader in chancery, which was punctuated by the deaths of his first wife in 1823, his father in 1824 and his mother in 1826, and by a second marriage. He was appointed attorney-general to Queen Adelaide in July 1830 and four months later, when the Whigs came to power, was chosen by lord chancellor Brougham to be their solicitor-general. Horne, who was known to be 'a good Whig' (though he did not join Brooks's until 1835), was evidently quite willing to serve under the attorney-general Thomas Denman*, his professional junior.[4] The Grey ministry had some difficulty in finding him a seat, but eventually accommodated him at Bletchingley on the Russell interest. He apparently contributed £800 from his own pocket towards the £1,500 which was required for the first year's occupation of the seat.[5] At the general election of 1831 he came in for Newtown, where Lord Yarborough sold the seat to government.

Horne's first task in the House, 23 Feb. 1831, was to make an impromptu defence of Brougham in his squabble with the metropolitan lunacy commissioners. On 21 Mar. he spoke at length in support of the ministerial reform bill, which he believed to be

> perfectly safe and constitutional; and to furnish safe and adequate means of attaining the great object which we have in view, namely, the preservation of our constitution, the security of the throne, and the happiness and well-ordered liberty of the people.

He condemned the 'vexatious' series of adjournment divisions forced by the opponents of the revised bill, 12 July, when he was a government teller in the last of them. He was steady in his attendance during the bill's passage through committee, but his contributions to debate were confined to very occasional observations on technical points.[6] His attempt to explain the proposed leasehold franchise, 17 Aug., was frequently interrupted by a rowdy House, and a former Tory Member thought he had 'failed' in his attempts to defend the measure.[7] On 12 Oct. he and Denman, 'to their great fright at the time, and amusement afterwards', were mistaken for bishops and consequently 'hooted and pelted' by the crowd which converged on St. James's to support the metropolitan reform petition.[8] They were both 'quite decisive' in their professional view of the illegality of the plan for the organization of the Birmingham Political Union.[9] Horne was a member of the committee on general chancery practice formed by Brougham to assist him in his planned legal reforms; he 'would at first not hear of *viva voce* evidence, but rather than argue the point he soon conceded it'.[10] He

defended the appointment of lunacy commissioners by the chancellor, 26 Sept., and replied to criticism of the Scottish exchequer court regulation bill, 7 Oct. Taunted by Wetherell for his silence on Brougham's bankruptcy court bill, 12 Oct. 1831, Horne admitted his '*libido tacondi*', but thought it preferable to Wetherell's '*libido loquondi*', and he broke his 'habits of silence' to support the measure at length.

He spoke in defence of government on the Russian-Dutch loan, 26 Jan. 1832, but, in the opinion even of friends, he had never performed worse and failed to make out 'a tolerable case'.[11] He made a few technical contributions to the debates on the details of the revised reform bill. He opposed and defeated Knight's attempt to allow the Irish master of the rolls to try his right to appoint his own secretary, 22 Feb. He agreed with Alexander Baring that the House 'ought not to be made an asylum for insolvent debtors', but had strong reservations about his plan to exclude them, 6 June. He also had misgivings over John Campbell II's proposed alteration to the law of dower, 8 June; and later that month he was one of seven barrister Members who protested to Brougham against the unexpected passage through the Commons of four measures touching the laws of real property, which required 'much further consideration'.[12] He spoke and voted in favour of public inquests, 20 June, and later that day advised Lord Nugent to include marriages and deaths as well as births in his proposed registration bill. He welcomed Spence's chancery reform bill, 10 July, and again spoke in defence of government on the Russian-Dutch loan, 25 July. He landed himself in a scrape by failing, through a chapter of accidents, to apprize Brougham of Sugden's intention of raising in the House the appointment of the chancellor's brother James to two chancery sinecures. He was himself caught unawares, 25 July, and he had an awkward time in explaining his conduct the next day. In a letter of apology to Brougham he accepted the 'backhander or two' which the chancellor had given him in a speech in the Lords and pleaded for 'remission of any further punishment'.[13] He backed Denman's defence of the ecclesiastical courts contempts bill, 3 Aug., had something to say on the Deccan prize money dispute, 6 Aug., and regretted opposition hostility to government's proposal to allow extra time for the payment of rates and taxes as required for the registration of voters under the Reform Act, 7 Aug. 1832.

In November 1832 Horne, who planned to stand for the new constituency of Marylebone at the forthcoming general election, was promoted to the post of attorney-general on Denman's appointment as lord chief justice. Yet he was universally deemed to be 'obviously unfit for it', and it was only the failure of Brougham's attempts to create a vacancy for him on the bench which prevented his being passed over for Campbell.[14] His tenure of the office was brief and undistinguished. He was removed in humiliating circumstances in 1834, when the puisne judgeship which he was expected to take in compensation was unacceptable to him.[15] He reverted to private practice for a few years before becoming a master in chancery. Horne was described by Edward Littleton* as 'grave and somewhat pompous', but the Irish chancellor Lord Plunket thought him 'an honourable kind-hearted person'.[16] Both Brougham and Campbell, who between them were responsible for his 'abominable treatment' in 1834, condescended years later to acknowledge his good points. Brougham, writing of the Grey ministry's 'underlings', noted that Horne was 'inferior of course' to Denman, but that 'his admirable good nature was highly serviceable as a contrast to the coldness of John Russell and Althorp and Graham';[17] while Campbell claimed to have 'a sincere regard' for him on account of his 'many valuable qualities'.[18] Horne was widowed for a second time in 1849 and died in July 1860.

[1] IGI (Herefs.); PROB 11/1681/82; T. Faulkner, *Hist. Brentford*, 326. [2] *Gent. Mag.* (1823), ii. 190. [3] Horne's will, proved 20 Aug. 1860. She gave birth to a da. 2 Dec. 1827 and *d.* 12 Nov. 1849 (*Gent. Mag.* (1827), ii. 556; (1849), ii. 665). [4] *Life of Campbell*, i. 490-2; Wentworth Woodhouse mun. Althorp to Milton, 22 Nov. 1830. [5] Lonsdale mss, Lowther to Lonsdale, 12 Dec. 1830; PRO NI, Anglesey mss D619/28A-B/36. [6] See also Brougham mss, Horne to Brougham [9 Aug. 1831]. [7] Bucks. RO, Fremantle mss D/FR/139/20/32. [8] Hatherton diary, 12 Oct.. [9] *Holland House Diaries*, 82, 128; *Grey-William IV Corresp.* i. 399, 403, 424, 432, 434. [10] *Three Diaries*, 11. [11] Ibid. 197; Hatherton diary, 26 Jan. [1832]; *Greville Mems.* ii. 243-4. [12] Brougham mss, memo. [June 1832]. [13] Ibid. Horne to Brougham [27 July 1832]. [14] *Life of Campbell*, ii. 18-19, 40-41; *Three Diaries*, 282; *Greville Mems.* ii. 332-3. [15] *Greville Mems.* iii. 21; Le Marchant, *Althorp*, 61-62; Brougham, *Life and Times*, iii. 341-54, 426; Lord Campbell, *Lives of the Lord Chancellors*, viii. 424-6; *Holland House Diaries*, 265. [16] *Three Diaries*, 357-8. [17] Brougham, *Life and Times*, iii. 426; Brougham mss, autobiog. fragment. [18] *Life of Campbell*, ii. 41.

D.R.F.

HORROCKS, Samuel (1766–1842), of Lark Hill, Preston, Lancs.

PRESTON 17 Mar. 1804–1826

b. 27 Nov. 1766, 1st s. of John Horrocks of Bradshaw, nr. Bolton, Lancs. and Jane, da. of John Booth of Edgworth, nr. Bolton; bro. of John Horrocks†. *m.* 23 Aug. 1786, Alice, da. of Christopher Duckworth of Edgworth, 1s. 7da. (1 *d.v.p.*) *suc.* fa. 1816. *d.* 24 Mar. 1842.

Mayor, Preston 1802-3.

On the death in 1804 of his younger brother John, co-founder in 1796 of the Whig-Tory, Derby-Horrocks electoral coalition, Horrocks, an anti-Catholic Tory, had become the senior partner in the family cotton firm and Member for Preston, where he was the largest employer and an influential member of the corporation. His 'silence' in the House was ridiculed by his local opponents, but he had successfully defended his seat at great expense at each subsequent election.[1] He did so again in 1820, when, with the Whig 12th earl of Derby's nominee Edmund Hornby as his colleague, he prevailed over the radical Henry Hunt* and the Whig barrister John Williams* in a riotous 13-day poll, which cost him £11,560.[2]

Horrocks, who was granted a fortnight's leave on urgent private business, 4 July 1820, and a further six weeks, 9 Apr. 1821, when strikes and lay-offs closed his spinning factories, remained an important figure locally, but an insignificant one in Parliament, where his only reported speech was a brief defence of the Lancashire magistracy's treatment of Hunt and conditions in Lancaster gaol, 25 Feb. 1822.[3] He divided with the Liverpool government on the Queen Caroline case, 6 Feb., and against the additional malt duty repeal bill, 3 Apr. 1821, and Catholic relief, 30 Apr. 1822, 1 Mar., 21 Apr., having also brought up Preston's hostile petition, 18 Apr. 1825.[4] A radical publication of that session commented that he was a Member whose 'opinions and attendance are ... totally unknown to us'.[5] On 27 July 1823 Horrocks survived an attempt on his life by the disaffected cotton worker and trade unionist Andrew Ryding, who struck his head and arms with an iron cleaver. At Lancaster assizes, 18 Aug., he helped to secure a verdict of 'not guilty on account of insanity' against his assailant, who was detained for life.[6] Horrocks's retirement at the dissolution of 1826, when Hornby made way for Derby's grandson Edward George Geoffrey Smith Stanley, was unexpected and wrecked the coalition.[7] He supported Tory candidates and interests in Preston until his retirement from the corporation in 1833 and following his re-election to it in 1836, but he repeatedly declined to stand for Parliament or to sanction the candidature of his only son Samuel.[8] He died 'possessed of great wealth', at Lark Hill in March 1842, recalled as an 'unobtrusive and unostentatious character' and 'shrewd man of business', and was buried in St. George's churchyard, Preston. Samuel, who died without issue in 1846, succeeded him at Lark Hill and as head of Horrocks, Miller and Company.[9] His will, dated 28 Mar. 1840, provided for his six surviving daughters, and was proved at Chester, 27 Sept. 1842, and in London, 5 July 1843.[10]

[1] *Oxford DNB sub* Horrocks, John; *Fortunes Made in Business*, iii. (1887), 20-28; C. Brown, *Origins and Progress of Horrocks and Co.* (1925); W. Dobson, *Parl. Rep. Preston*, 68-71; D. Hunt, *Hist. Preston*, 156-7; *HP Commons, 1790-1820*, ii. 237; iv. 248. [2] Lancs. RO, Whittaker of Simonstone mss DDWh/4/99; *The Times*, 20 Mar. 1820; W. Bean, *Parl. Rep. Six Northern Counties*, 405; Dobson, 69. [3] *Preston Chron.* 20 Jan.; *The Times*, 10, 27 Apr. 1821. [4] *Preston Pilot*, 3 Feb., 9, 16, 23 Apr.; *The Times*, 19 Apr. 1825. [5] *Session of Parl. 1825*, p. 469. [6] *The Times*, 2, 4 Aug. 1823; *Account of the Trial of Andrew Ryding* ed. Wilkinson. [7] *Preston Pilot*, 22, 29 Apr.; *The Times*, 13, 20 June 1826. [8] *Preston Pilot*, 3 June, 5 Aug., 30 Sept. 1826; Lancs. RO, Preston corporation minutes, 1821-35 (unfol.) CNP3/1/5; Lancs. RO, Houghton mss DDH/76; *Manchester Guardian*, 13 Mar. 1830. [9] Hunt, 150-1, 154; *Preston Pilot.* 26 Mar., 2 Apr.; *Gent. Mag.* (1842), ii. 430; M. Burscough, *The Horrockses: cotton kings of Preston.* [10] PROB 8/236; 11/1982/483.

M.M.E.

HORT, Sir Josiah William, 2nd bt. (1791–1876), of Hortland, co. Kildare.

Co. Kildare   1831–1832

b. 6 July 1791, 1st. s. of Sir John Hort, 1st bt., of Hortland and Margaret, da. of Sir Fitzgerald Aylmer, 6th bt., of Donadea Castle. *educ.* Westminster; Trinity Coll. Camb. 1809. *m.* 31 Mar. 1823, Louisa Georgiana, da. and coh. of Sir John Caldwell, 5th bt., of Castle Caldwell, co. Fermanagh, 3s. 2da. *suc.* fa. as 2nd bt. 23 Oct. 1807. *d.* 24 Aug. 1876.

Sheriff, co. Kildare 1818-19.

Hort's father, second son of the archbishop of Tuam, 1741-51, had been appointed consul-general at Lisbon in 1767 and created a baronet the same year. On the death in 1786 of his elder brother Josiah George, Kildare's sheriff in 1758, he had acquired the 'fine estate' of Hortland, which Hort inherited on succeeding to the baronetcy in 1807, when he became the ward of Lord Henry Petty[†] (later 3rd marquess of Lansdowne). On meeting Hort and his brother for the first time in Paris in September 1818, Maria Edgeworth described him as

> a very pleasing young man ... [with] dark eyes, round good natured face, gentlemanlike figure, middle sized, good manners, no conceit, or *ennui* ... far above most of the young men of the present day. Literature enough for conversation, no pretension, a very good mechanic. At dinner one day Lord Grenville and all the gentlemen except himself were talking nonsense about the new magnetic perpetual motion. He modestly asked a question or two which showed he understood it was all nonsense and even the authority of Lord Grenville's eye and contradictory belief could not frighten him ... We became acquainted and to a certain degree intimate from that time forward. He always sits *where he ought to do at dinner*.

Later that month, however, she noted that he 'did not appear so agreeable when I saw more of him', adding that he 'was a good humoured young man and that was all. Nothing came out on further acquaintance'.[1] In December 1822 he sued Lord Newry for the price of a horse sold as 'quite in harness', which 'kicked' and threw a shoe during its trial in Oxford Street: he won the case and subsequent appeal.[2] At the 1830 general election he considered standing for an unexpected opening for county Kildare, but declined on finding that a 'friend' had already entered the field, promising to offer on the 'first suitable vacancy that may occur'.[3] At the 1831 general election he duly came forward as a 'reformer' opposed to 'monopoly and abuse in every shape', having secured the dominant interest of the 3rd duke of Leinster, whose 250 freeholders, together with his own, ensured him support from 350 of the 500 registered electors. A third candidate withdrew and he was returned unopposed.[4] Frederick Ponsonby[†] of Bishop's Court, brother of the 2nd Baron Ponsonby, told Lord Howick*, colonial undersecretary in the Grey ministry, that he had considered standing himself but had let Hort, who had 'pledged himself voluntarily to your bill, walk over'.[5] In the contest for Queen's County he controversially assisted the return of the former Tory Sir Charles Coote, who, as Leinster informed Lord Cloncurry, was an 'intimate friend and old acquaintance, and although they differ in politics, I should be sorry to see that carried too far'.[6]

Hort voted for the second reading of the reintroduced English reform bill, 6 July, at least twice against adjournment, 12 July, and gave generally steady support to its details, although he divided for the enfranchisement of £50 tenants-at-will, 18 Aug. 1831. He voted for the third reading, 19 Sept., and passage of the bill, 21 Sept., and Lord Ebrington's confidence motion, 10 Oct. On 30 July he joined Brooks's, sponsored by Lords Duncannon* and Killeen*, an earlier membership of 21 May 1817, when the sponsors were Sir Henry Parnell* and Lord Essex, apparently having lapsed. In his maiden speech, 5 Aug., he defended the practices of Maynooth College and called for a liberal system of Irish education with grants distributed so that all religions 'might derive an equal benefit'. On 11 Aug. he spoke and voted for printing the Waterford petition for disarming the Irish yeomanry, the 'last persons who ought to be employed on anything approaching military service in time of peace'. He divided with ministers on the Dublin election controversy, 23 Aug., and voted for legal provision for the Irish poor, 29 Aug. He divided for the second reading of the revised reform bill, 17 Dec. 1831, again supported its details, and voted for the third reading, 22 Mar., but was absent from the division on the motion for an address calling on the king to appoint only ministers who would carry it unimpaired, 10 May 1832. He voted to print the Woollen Grange petition for the abolition of Irish tithes, 16 Feb., and against the Irish tithes bill, 8 Mar. On the 23rd he presented and endorsed petitions for their total abolition, saying that the time had 'now come when the public must face the question' of the Irish church and that as 'a sincere Protestant' he was 'prepared to place all religious creeds on the same footing'. He divided for the second reading of the Irish reform bill, 25 May, but against the liability of Irish electors to pay municipal taxes before they could vote, 29 June. He was granted ten days' leave on account of family illness, 19 June, but was credited with a vote for Baring's bill to exclude insolvent debtors from Parliament, 27 June.[7] In his last known speech, 5 July, he explained that 'if on a former occasion' he had opposed the tithes bill because the Irish secretary Smith Stanley would not 'accompany' it with a measure of church appropriation, 'still more' did he now, after the 'emphatic manner' in which Smith Stanley had 'stated his intention to support the establishment in its present form'. He divided accordingly, 13 July. He voted with ministers on the Russian-Dutch loan, 12, 16, 20 July 1832.

At the 1832 general election Hort came third in a contest against two other Liberals. He died in Eaton Square, London, in August 1876 and was succeeded by his eldest son John Josiah (1824-82), an army officer.

[1] *Edgeworth Letters*, 95, 100-101. [2] *The Times*, 10 Dec. 1822, 24 Jan., 13 June 1823. [3] *Dublin Evening Post*, 20 July 1830. [4] Ibid. 26, 28 Apr., 3, 10 May 1831. [5] Grey mss, Ponsonby to Howick, 30 May 1831. [6] Add. 51568, Leinster to Cloncurry, 11 May 1831. [7] *The Times*, 28 June 1832.

P.J.S.

HORTON see WILMOT

HOSKINS, Kedgwin (1777–1852), of Strickstenning and Much Birch, Herefs. and 135 Regent Street, Mdx.

HEREFORDSHIRE 1831–1847

b. 26 May 1777, o. surv. s. of Rev. John Hoskins, rect. of Llandinabo, Herefs., and Sarah, da. of Kedgwin Hoskins of Newent, Glos. *m.* (1) 12 Apr. 1804, Harriet (*d.* 17 Sept. 1835), da. of William Elliott of Fawley Court, Herefs., *s.p.*; (2) 23 June 1836, Elizabeth, da. of Isaac Haynes of Ealing, Mdx., *s.p. d.* 24 Dec. 1852.

John Hoskins, who died in March 1827 at the age of 83 with next to nothing to leave to his son, was, like his wife, a member of the Newent branch of the family. Their relations, the Rogers family of Stanage, had appointed him to the Herefordshire living of Llandinabo, near Ross, where he was usually resident, and Cranford, Middlesex, which he held with the lectureship of Uxbridge.[1] Hoskins, his only surviving child, made his career in banking and may have been associated with the family bank in Crewkerne, Somerset, which was taken over in 1819, before becoming a partner with John and Richard Jones and the Quaker Nathaniel Morgan in establishments in Hereford and Ross-on-Wye.[2] A conscientious magistrate and regular attender at public meetings on popular Whig causes espoused by the 'Men of Ross', he chaired the hundred of Wormelow agriculturists' meeting at Harewood's End, 11 Feb. 1820, when they petitioned for government action to combat distress; and he was active in the establishment of local associations for the apprehension and prosecution of felons.[3] He encouraged the adoption of 'loyal addresses' incorporating declarations of support for Queen Caroline at Ross and Hereford, where he was also vice-chairman at the dinner and presentation to Joseph Hume*, 5 Dec. 1821.[4] Afterwards, he accompanied Hume, John Lucy Scudamore of Kentchurch Court, and the Whig Member for Herefordshire, Robert Price, to Monmouth, where the controlling anti-Beaufort party made them honorary freemen.[5] He was a requisitionist for and attended the contentious Herefordshire distress meeting attended by William Cobbett†, 17 Jan. 1823,[6] and joined in the protest against the corporation of Hereford's refusal to admit three of his political allies as freemen in 1824.[7] During the 1825-6 crisis, his bank, for whom Barclay, Tritton and Company were the London agents, 'stood the run nobly'. His auditing skills were now in high demand, and his presence with the Tory Kingsmill Evans at gentry dinners and meetings helped to restore confidence following the collapse of Garrett and Sons and Bodenhams' Hereford banks.[8] He chaired Price's dinner at the 1826 general election,[9] and subsequently helped to organize petitions on diverse subjects, including high rents, the shortage of specie, the Small Notes Act, the currency, capital punishment for forgery, and the 1830 Ross-on-Wye improvement bill.[10] He canvassed Hereford early on behalf of the sitting Whig Edward Bolton Clive at the 1830 general election, and the Ross bank became a place of signature for petitions against slavery and for parliamentary reform, 1830-1.[11] On 2 Apr. 1831 he attended the reform dinner for the self-proclaimed champion of the cause, Edmund Lechmere Charlton†, who announced his candidature for Herefordshire directly the Grey ministry's reform bill's defeat precipitated a dissolution.[12] However, a disagreement between Charlton and the eminent horticulturist and radical Thomas Andrew Knight of Downton made another choice imperative, and the Whig gentry selected Hoskins, whom the *Globe* described as a 'real reformer' with many friends and few enemies. According to his canvassing address, 26 Apr. 1831, he had agreed to stand free of expense for a single Parliament to accomplish 'the great work of reform'. Charlton desisted, the sitting Tory Sir John Cotterell retired, and he came in unopposed with Price.[13]

True to his promise, Hoskins, whose conduct was closely monitored by the *Hereford Journal* and *Monmouthshire Merlin*, divided for the reintroduced reform bill at its second reading, 6 July, against adjournment, 12 July, and steadily for its details; but he cast wayward votes for the total disfranchisement of Saltash, which ministers no longer pressed, 26 July, and for Lord Chandos's amendment to enfranchise £50 tenants-at-will, 18 Aug. 1831. He voted for the bill's third reading, 19 Sept., and passage, 21 Sept., the second reading of the Scottish measure, 23 Sept., and Lord Ebrington's confidence motion, 10 Oct. He was a requisitionist for the Herefordshire reform meeting which petitioned unanimously in protest at the reform bill's rejection by the Lords, and they thanked him for supporting it, 5 Nov. On the hustings, he said that he had not foreseen that his parliamentary duties would detain him so much in London, expressed disappointment at the bill's rejection, and, calling for patience and perseverance, urged the freeholders to place their confidence in the ministry and promised to vote conscientiously. Addressing the agriculturists' concerns, he insisted that the government's game bill had been a sound measure when it left the Commons for the Lords, and he therefore 'did not feel answerable' for its bad clauses.[14] He divided for the revised reform bill at its second reading, 17 Dec. 1831, and generally steadily for its details, but for the separate enfranchisement of Merthyr Tydfil, 5 Mar. 1832. He divided for the third reading, 22 Mar., and the address calling on the king to appoint only ministers who would carry it unimpaired, 10 May. He voted for the second reading of the Irish reform bill, 25 May, and against a Conservative amendment to the Scottish measure, 1 June, but in the minorities against the boundary bill's proposals for Stamford and Whitehaven, 22 June. He divided for the Liverpool disfranchisement bill at its second reading, 23 May, and annoyed the Liverpool Member William Ewart by presenting the corporation's petition against it, 24 May 1832, but he stood

his ground, insisting that he had no vested interest, but that he felt entitled to respond to the urgency of the Liverpool case. He divided with government against the Irish union of parishes bill, 19 Aug., in both divisions on the Dublin election controversy, 23 Aug. 1831, on the Russian-Dutch loan, 26 Jan., 12, 16, 20 July, and relations with Portugal, 9 Feb. 1832. Hoskins did not shy from voting against government when he felt his own judgement and constituency interests required it. He voted with the radicals for printing the Waterford petition for disarming the Irish yeomanry, 11 Aug. 1831, and to end military flogging, 16 Feb., and inquire into the Peterloo massacre, 15 Mar. 1832. He divided against the Vestry Act amendment bill, 23 Jan., and for inquiry into the distressed glove trade, which affected his constituents, 31 Jan. He presented a petition from bankers and others in Ross calling for an end to the death penalty for non-violent crimes, 24, and, supported by Clive and Price, he presented and endorsed several petitions from Herefordshire and elsewhere that day against West Indian slavery and voted against the government amendment to Buxton's motion for inquiry into abolition. He voted to make coroners' inquests public, 20 June, and to reduce the barrack grant, 28 June 1832.[15]

As Member for Herefordshire, Hoskins had patronized benefit societies, the Leominster races, and Herefordshire Association meetings at London's *Freemasons' Tavern*; and although he was a member of the established church, his stance on slavery and commutation of the death penalty guaranteed him Nonconformist support.[16] When it became apparent that the Conservatives were unlikely to field more than one candidate for the county's three seats at the first post-reform election in December 1832, and that if they did so Price would be their target, he issued a canvassing address, 1 Nov., and was duly returned.[17] He was admitted to Brooks's, 7 June 1834 (proposed by Clive and Price), topped the Herefordshire poll by over 1,000 votes in his only contest in 1835 and retained his seat for the Liberals until he retired through ill health in 1847.[18] He had remarried within a year of his first wife's death, but remained childless, and died at his home in Much Birch in December 1852. He bequeathed his interests as a trustee or mortgagee to Thomas Hardwick of Hereford and his heirs but otherwise left everything to his widow.[19]

[1] *Gent Mag.* (1827), i. 473; PROB 11/1730/542; IR26/1130. [2] *Gent. Mag.* (1853), i. 440. [3] *Hereford Jnl.* 9, 16 Feb. 1820, 24 Jan. 1821. [4] Ibid. 29 Nov., 20, 27 Dec. 1820, 10, 24 Jan., 12 Dec. 1821. [5] *Bristol Mercury*, 15 Dec. 1821. [6] *Hereford Jnl.* 18 Dec. 1822, 8, 15, 22 Jan. 1823; Herefs. RO, Pateshall mss A95/EB/40/4 *passim*. See HEREFORDSHIRE. [7] *Hereford Jnl.* 10, 17, 24 Nov., 15 Dec. 1824,

1 Jan.; *Hereford Independent*, 1 Jan. 1825. [8] *Hereford Independent*, 24 Dec. 1825, 7 Jan., 25 Feb., 18 Mar., 1, 15 Apr.; *Hereford Jnl.* 3 May 1826. [9] *Hereford Jnl.* 21 June 1826. [10] Ibid. 7, 21 Feb. 1827. [11] Ibid. 14 July 1830, 19 Jan., 2, 9, 23 Feb., 9, 16, 23 Mar. 1831. [12] Ibid. 6, 20, 27 Apr. 1831. [13] See LUDLOW and HEREFORDSHIRE; *Hereford Jnl.* 27 Apr., 4, 11 May; *Globe*, 30 Apr., 2 May; Herefs. RO, diaries of John Biddulph of Ledbury [Biddulph diary] G2/IV/J/59, 19 Mar.-1 May 1831. [14] *Hereford Jnl.* 2, 9 Nov. 1831. [15] Ibid. 8 Feb. 1832. [16] Ibid. 22 Feb., 2 May, 13 June 1832. [17] Biddulph diary G2/IV/J/61, 62, 11 Jan. 1832-10 Jan. 1833; *Hereford Jnl.* 23 June, 1, 15, 22 Dec. 1832. [18] *Hereford Jnl.* 26 June 1847. [19] Ibid. 29 Dec. 1852; *Hereford Times*, 1 Jan. 1853; *Gent. Mag.* (1853), i. 440; PROB 8/246; 11/2177/611.

M.M.E.

HOTHAM, Beaumont, 3rd Bar. Hotham [I] (1794–1870), of South Dalton, Yorks. and 36 Davies Street, Mdx.

LEOMINSTER   1820–1831

LEOMINSTER   22 Dec. 1831–1841

YORKSHIRE (EAST RIDING)   1841–1868

b. 9 Aug. 1794, 1st s. of Beaumont Hotham (*d.* 1799) of South Dalton and Philadelphia, da. of Sir John Dixon Dyke, 3rd bt., of Horeham, Suss. *educ.* Westminster 1806-8. *unm. suc.* grandfa. Beaumont Hotham[†] as 3rd Bar. Hotham [I] and 13th bt. 4 Mar. 1814. *d.* 12 Dec. 1870.

Ensign 2 Ft. Gds. 1810, capt. 1813, maj. Jan. 1819, half-pay Oct. 1819; lt.-col. 1825; col. 1838; maj.-gen. 1851; lt.-gen. 1858; gen. 1865.

Commr. on army recruitment 1859-60.

The Hothams, a family with a long and distinguished record of military and public service, were the descendants of Sir John de Trehouse, who came from Normandy with the Conqueror. Hotham, who, partly because of his old fashioned clothes, was considered somewhat eccentric in later life, was born at Lullington Castle in Kent and named after his soldier father and his paternal grandfather, an exchequer court judge and close friend of the prime minister, the 3rd duke of Portland. He was barely five when his father died at Weymouth in 1799, leaving a widow enceinte and two young children, and spent much of his childhood in a cottage close to his grandfather's home at East Molesey, Surrey, which led the admiralty secretary John Croker*, who later rented it, to suppose that he had been born there.[1] Like his relations, he attended Westminster School, leaving around the time of his mother's death in May 1808. In June 1810 he joined his father's old regiment, the Coldstream Guards, and served with them in the Peninsula from 1812-14. He fought at Nive, Nivelle, Salamanca (where he was wounded) and Vitoria, and was present at Waterloo, where, being occupied with the defence of Hougoumont, he saw

little of the action.[2] When he succeeded his grandfather in 1814, the family estates yielded only £7,075 a year from a nominal rental of £15,742, and he took half-pay in October 1819 to devote time to improving them and to enter Parliament, which his Yorkshire agent John Hall thought he would 'much like'.[3] He continued to live in London, and at the 1820 election he deliberately chose not to fall back on his family interests in Beverley and Hedon, where, as Hall pointed out, representation would require 'great expense and a great deal of personal application and trouble', especially during visits to South Dalton.[4] Hylton Joliffe*, a friend of his father, now returned him *in absentia* for Petersfield;[5] but he went to Leominster, which welcomed rich strangers. Drawing on his reputation as a soldier and sporting Waterloo blue, he topped the four-day poll.[6] He chose to sit for Leominster when Parliament met. That summer he sold part of his Scarborough estate for £14,448, and spent £29,590 on lands closer to South Dalton.[7]

Hotham was an anti-Catholic Tory who cherished his independence, attended the House regularly and served on many minor committees. He stated his opinions boldly and sought to remain aloof from Leominster politics. He divided with the Liverpool ministry on the revenue, 4 July 1820, Queen Caroline's case, 6 Feb., the malt duty repeal bill, 3 Apr., and the army estimates, 11 Apr., but in the minority for repeal of the agricultural horse tax, 5 Mar. 1821. He voted against Catholic relief, 28 Feb. 1821, 30 Apr. 1822, becoming one of its leading opponents. He divided against parliamentary reform, 9 May 1821, 26 Feb. 1824, and the proposed disqualification of civil officers of the ordnance from voting in parliamentary elections, 12 Apr. 1821. He voted against making forgery a non-capital offence, 23 May, and with government against omitting arrears from the grant to the duke of Clarence, 18 June, and on public expenditure, 27 June. He commended the unsuccessful Yorkshire polls bill in his maiden speech, 31 May 1821, which was 'quite inaudible in the gallery' and not reported.[8] He spoke and was a minority teller for a similar measure, 7 June 1822. That session he divided with government against more extensive tax reductions to relieve distress, 11, 21 Feb., but cast wayward votes for admiralty economies, 1 Mar., abolition of one of the joint-postmasterships, 2 May, and reductions in the Swiss embassy, 16 May. He voted against inquiries into Irish tithes, 19 June, and the lord advocate's treatment of the Scottish press, 25 June, and to renew the Aliens Act, 19 July. He also presented his constituents' petition for revision of the criminal code, 3 June 1822.[9]

The patronage secretary Arbuthnot suggested to Canning, as leader of the House*, that 'Lord Hotham would do famously if he could be prevailed upon' to move or second the 1823 address, but nothing came of it.[10] He voted with ministers on taxation, 3, 10, 13 Mar., and was one of their spokesmen on the mutiny bill, 14 Mar., but, not perceiving 'that any inconvenience would arise' thereby, he divided against them for information on, 24 Mar., and inquiry into the prosecution of the Dublin Orange rioters, 22 Apr., when they were defeated. He had warned that he would insist on the House being called over whenever the Catholic question was raised, 11, 12 Feb., and, challenging Plunket to explain its repeated postponement, he complained of the inconvenience this had caused him, 10 Apr. He protested again before presenting (as he had done, 10 May 1822) an anti-Catholic petition from Beverley, 16 Apr. 1823.[11] He divided with government for the grant for Irish churches and glebe houses, 11 Apr., on the Aliens Act, 16 Apr., and chancery delays, 5 June; but cast a critical vote on the lord advocate's handling of the Borthwick case, 3 June 1823. Hotham voted against altering the usury laws, 27 Feb. 1824 (and again, 17 Feb. 1825). He divided against abolishing flogging in the army, 5 Mar., and against condemning the indictment in Demerara of the Methodist missionary John Smith, 11 June. He had presented petitions from Leominster against the Insolvent Debtors Act, 20 Feb. 1823, and repeal of the assessed taxes, 10 May 1824, and an anti-slavery one from Maidstone, 15 Mar. 1824.[12] He was overlooked when Lord Morpeth† was appointed lord lieutenant of the East Riding in October 1824 and sent a letter of complaint to the home office under-secretary George Dawson*, whereupon the secretary Peel, confirming that he would have been well suited for the post, informed Lord Liverpool of this unintended slight to 'one of the best supporters of the government in the House of Commons'. Replying to Hotham, Peel deliberately praised his politics and 'high and independent character'; but Hotham remained highly critical of Morpeth, and annoyed that he had not pressed his own claim sooner, lest he 'give anyone even the shadow of a reason to suppose that in the line of conduct I have pursued during the time I have been in Parliament I had been looking only to my own private advantage'.[13] He naturally voted for the Irish unlawful societies bill, 25 Feb., and against Catholic relief, 1 Mar., 21 Apr., 10 May, and the Irish franchise bill, 26 Apr. 1825. His pertinent questions in committee had forced its supporters to concede that the intended changes in the franchise and financial provisions for the Irish clergy could not be enacted in the same bill, 23 Mar. A radical publication of 1825 noted that he 'attended frequently and voted in general with ministers'.[14] He was

expected to stand for Leominster and requisitioned for Yorkshire when a general election was anticipated that autumn, but refused to be harried into spending on a premature canvass and asked Peel to notify him promptly of a dissolution, lest he be defeated through neglect.[15] Before it was called in 1826, he presented an anti-slavery petition, 8 Feb., and another against the importation of foreign gloves, 16 Mar., and assisted with the Leominster canal bill, which was enacted, 26 May 1826.[16] He had turned down an offer of one of the duke of Newcastle's seats and topped the poll on both returns made for Leominster after a costly four-way contest. Hall, as usual, kept him abreast of developments in Yorkshire.[17]

Hotham drew attention to the peculiarity in his return when Parliament met, and the House decided that in his case it was not a double one, 21 Nov. 1826.[18] He defended the army estimates, 20 Feb. 1827.[19] Following Lord Liverpool's stroke, he divided against Catholic relief, 6 Mar., and with his partisans the 'three baronets' against the pro-Catholic Canning's corn bill, 2 Apr. He sent a supportive letter to Peel, who resigned rather than serve under Canning as premier, 12 Apr.[20] He nevertheless declared in the House, 7 May 1827, that he had 'never given a vote on the Catholic claims or on any other question, as a mere party question' and 'had fully made up his mind to give his support' to Canning's administration:

He felt unfeigned respect, at the same time, for those members of the late administration who had gone out, and regretted that in any allusions to them the word conspiracy, how casually soever, or with whatever qualifications, had been made use of. But, would anybody who observed the course which the business of tendering in their resignations had taken get up in his place and say that there had not been, at least, a tacit understanding?

He expressed 'great confidence' in Peel, but 'still more' in Canning, and, declaring party differences 'almost extinguished', he called on all able men to work together and for the divisive question of Catholic relief to be shelved. He assured Peel, as the Wellington ministry's home secretary in January 1828, that 'no one is more glad than myself to see you again in office'.[21] He voted against repealing the Test Acts, 26 Feb., and Catholic relief, 12 May, and ordnance reductions, 4 July. He presented an anti-slavery petition from Leominster, 20 May, and when his constituents complained that the glove trade had collapsed and advocated protection, he called on ministers to 'give their best attention to the subject' during the recess and address their grievances, 26 June 1828. Hotham was listed as a possible mover or seconder of the 1829 address which announced the concession of Catholic emancipation, but his hostility to it was undiminished and he refused to be swayed by ministers' change in policy. Informing Peel, 6 Feb., he wrote:

A sense of what is due to my own honour and conscience (for I am perfectly free from all electioneering engagements, and have no constituents to consult) will compel me to find myself opposed to you in every stage of such proceedings ... Upon other subjects I have no idea of acting otherwise than I have hitherto done, and further do express my sanguine hope that although until this unfortunate question be disposed of I may frequently be obliged to divide against you, yet, that the circumstance may not interfere with the friendship or interrupt the good feeling which has so long existed between us.[22]

Undeterred, though flattered, by the detailed explanation he received in reply, he apparently encouraged anti-Catholic petitioning in Yorkshire, where he was the patron of four church livings, and on presenting a similar one from Leominster, 3 Mar., he confirmed that although he regretted his differences with Peel, he would resolutely oppose concessions.[23] He observed:

Government, doubtless for their own reasons, have abstained from giving the details of the measure they intend to introduce, still ... [Wellington] has not hesitated to declare that its object is to remove all the disabilities which affect the Roman Catholics ... This in itself is sufficient for those who do not think that Papists can with safety be admitted into Parliament, and this it is which induces these petitioners to come forward. This is the opinion which the petitioners give, and in it I entirely concur, as I ever have done since I came into this House; and shall continue to do so, not, however, from any idea of the mere preservation of consistency, but because these are principles which I feel I can never either compromise or abandon.

He voted steadily against the measure and presented unfavourable petitions, 11, 17, 27 Mar. A 'serious accident [sustained] while out shooting' prevented him from stewarding the Leominster races in August 1829.[24] He voted to condemn the omission of distress from the address, 4 Feb. 1830, but does not seem to have attended again that Parliament. He was granted a fortnight's leave on account of ill health, 2 Mar., and concern about his physical well-being persisted until the dissolution. Poor health delayed his departure for Leominster, where the late arrival of Sir Stratford Canning* dashed his hopes of a cheap election. He was returned after a mere show of opposition, but afterwards engaged in a bitter correspondence with the deputy sheriff William Pateshall, whom he accused of trying to provoke a contest by delaying the writ.[25]

Contributing to a discussion on the business of the House, 3 Nov. 1830, Hotham suggested appointing a deputy Speaker and said that any plan to set a dining hour to prevent Members voting without hearing the discussion was bound to fail. Ministers had counted him among their 'friends', and he divided with them when they were brought down on the civil list, 15 Nov. He led the criticism of the Grey ministry's decision to create the office of inspector-general of marines for Sir James Cockburn and declared that he would vote against them 'strictly on public grounds ... to prevent ... a most unjust and unnecessary stigma being cast on the corps of marines', 25 Nov. Responding later in the debate to his fellow Tory Sir George Cockburn, who praised his brother's abilities, he insisted that he intended no personal slight to Sir James, but refused to moderate his views. Joining in the opposition offensive on the question, 28 Feb. 1831, he expressed dissatisfaction with the first lord of the admiralty Sir James Graham's explanation and dismay at the marines' lack of parliamentary influence. He voted against the government's reform bill, by which Leominster stood to lose a seat, at its second reading, 22 Mar. He apologized, 28 Mar., for his absence on the 25th when Peel criticized Tamworth's inclusion in schedule B, because Leominster was 'similarly unjustly treated', and although he deliberately refrained from accusing the government of partiality in its scheduling of boroughs, he denounced it:

It appears that sometimes the criterion adopted has been the population of the borough, and sometimes that of the parish. The consequence is, that in some cases a borough will retain its Members, because the population of the whole parish has been taken; and in others it will lose one or both representatives, because the population of the borough only has been selected. In the case of ... Leominster ... it appears that the population is only 3,650; but there is a note at the bottom of the page, by which it appears that the population of the parish now amounts to 4,640 persons. And I am sure it would be found to be so, if the census were again taken; and if the borough has such a population I think it ought not to be deprived of one of its representatives.

The leader of the House Lord Althorp promised to look into the matter, and Lord John Russell announced that Leominster would retain its second seat, 18 Apr. Undeterred, Hotham voted for Gascoyne's wrecking amendment, 19 Apr. 1831. He was defeated at Leominster by two reformers at the ensuing general election.[26] He did not, as initially expected, petition, but, calling for 'reaction' against the bill's excesses, he defeated the wealthy reformer William Fraser at a deliberately engineered by-election in Leominster in

December 1831.[27] Fraser's protests in *The Times* and elsewhere failed to yield a petition, which in any case Hotham was confident would fail.[28]

'Detained by business in the country', he was unable to vote on the revised reform bill at its committal, 20 Jan. 1832;[29] but he called for special provision for those freemen in the armed forces liable to be disfranchised through non-residence, 7 Feb., and voted against enfranchising Tower Hamlets, 28 Feb., and the bill's third reading, 22 Mar. He divided against the second reading of the Irish measure, 25 May, and against government on the Russian-Dutch loan, 12 July 1832. He voted for inquiry into the depressed glove trade, 3 Apr., and brought up the metropolitan cemetery bill, 17 May. He had opposed Nash's schemes for the London parks in 1828, and he ordered papers and accounts on the implementation of the Regent's Park and New Street Acts with a view to inquiry, 18 May 1832.[30]

Hotham retained his seat at Leominster as a Conservative until 1841, when he came in unopposed for the East Riding, which he represented until forced to retire through ill health in 1868. He died in December 1870, an army general, after being taken ill while on a visit to Sir James Walker at Sand Hutton, near York, and was buried in his new church in South Dalton. The *York Herald* noted that although a frequent visitor, well known in the county, Hotham had hardly resided there 'beyond a day or two'.[31] He never married, and his nephew Charles Hotham (1836-72), son of his late brother Admiral George Frederick Hotham (1799-1856), succeeded him in his titles and estates, which in 1873 comprised 20,352 acres, worth £20,126 a year.[32]

[1] *Oxford DNB sub* Hotham; Hotham, Beaumont, 2nd. Bar.; Hotham, Sir Henry; *Gent. Mag.* (1794), ii. 764; (1799), ii. 820; *Croker Pprs.* i. 432. [2] A.M.W. Stirling, *The Hothams*, 347, 351; *Gent. Mag.* (1794), ii. 764; (1799), ii. 820; *Oxford DNB*; Add. 34705, f. 196. [3] J.T. Ward, 'East Yorks. Landed Estates in 19th Cent.', *E. Yorks. Local Hist. Ser.* xxiii (1967), 26-27; Hull Univ. Lib. Hotham mss DDHO/8/2, Hall to Hotham, 7 Feb. 1820. [4] Hotham mss 8/2, Hall to Hotham, 7, 9, 13, 24 Feb., 5, 12 Mar. 1820; T. Lawson-Tancred, *Recs. of a Yorks. Manor*, 335. [5] Som. RO, Hylton mss DD/HY, box 17, Procs. at Petersfield Election (1820). [6] *Hereford Jnl.* 23 Feb., 8, 15 Mar. 1820. [7] Ward, 27. [8] *The Times*, 1 June 1821. [9] *Hereford Jnl.* 17 Apr.; *The Times*, 4 June 1822. [10] Add. 38744, f. 49. [11] *The Times*, 11 May 1822, 17 May 1823. [12] Ibid. 21 Feb. 1823, 16 Mar., 11 May 1824. [13] Add. 40304, ff. 269, 272, 276; 40396, ff. 115-17, 166. [14] *Session of Parl. 1825*, p. 469. [15] Add. 40380, f. 399; 40381, ff. 21, 379; *Hereford Independent*, 3 Dec.; Lincs. AO, Ancaster mss 3 Anc 9/10/10, Abercromby to Carlisle, 29 Dec. 1825. [16] *The Times*, 9 Feb., 17 Mar. 1826; *CJ*, lxxxi. 45, 99, 182, 222, 377. [17] Nottingham Univ. Lib. Ne2/F2/1, Newcastle diary, 22 May; *Hereford Jnl.* 7, 14, 21 June; *Cambrian*, 10 June; *Worcester Herald*, 17 June; Hotham mss 8/4, Hall to Hotham, 1, 6, 10, 11, 18, 20, 24 June 1826. [18] *CJ*, lxxxii. 10; *The Times*, 22 Nov. 1826. [19] *The Times*, 21 Feb. 1827. [20] Add. 40393, ff. 202, 235. [21] Add. 40395, f. 114. [22] Add. 40398, f. 167; N. Gash, *Secretary Peel*, 558. [23] Add. 40398, ff. 169, 202; Wentworth Woodhouse mun. F107/341. [24] *Hereford Jnl.* 24 June, 30 Sept. 1829. [25] Hotham mss 8/5, Hall to Hotham, 4, 11, 17, 22, 30, 31 July; St. Deiniol's Lib. Glynne-Gladstone mss 195, T. to J. Gladstone, 3-6 July; *Hereford Jnl.* 7, 14, 21, 28 July, 4, 11 Aug. 1830; Herefs. RO, Pateshall mss A95/V/W/C/382-94. [26] Hotham mss 8/5, Hall to Hotham, 30 Apr.; *Hereford Jnl.* 4 May 1831. [27] *Worcester Herald*, 7 May, 17, 24 Dec.; *Hereford Jnl.* 28 Dec. 1831. [28] *The Times*, 28 Dec.; *Worcester Jnl.* 29 Dec. 1831; *Hereford Jnl.* 4 Jan. 1832. [29] *The Times*, 25 Jan. 1832. [30] Northants. RO, Agar Ellis diary, 7 Mar. 1828. [31] *Hereford Times*, 15 Dec. 1832; *The Times*, 14, 21 Dec.; *York Herald*, 17, 24 Dec. 1870. [32] Ward, 27.

M.M.E.

HOULDSWORTH, Thomas (1771–1852), of Portland Place, Manchester, Lancs. and Sherwood Hall, nr. Epperstone, Notts.

PONTEFRACT	1818–1830
NEWTON	1830–1832
NOTTINGHAMSHIRE NORTH	1832–1852

b. 13 Sept. 1771, 2nd s. of Henry Houldsworth, yeoman, of Hagg Farm, Gonalstone and Anne, da. of Thomas Hooton of Newton. *unm. d.* 1 Sept. 1852.

Lt. S.W. Yorks. yeoman cav. 1820.

Houldsworth, a prosperous Manchester cotton manufacturer who had purchased a landed estate in Nottinghamshire, had a passion for horse racing; his stud and racing colours of gold and green were famous in the early nineteenth century and one of his horses won the Derby in 1816. According to the family historian, he was 'the possessor of a genial and popular personality'.[1] Reputedly he never made a bet, yet he took a chance in 1818 when he stood successfully for the open borough of Pontefract, where he also had a mill. He was returned at the head of the poll in 1820.

He was an irregular attender, but his politics became clearer than in the previous Parliament as he gave general though decidedly independent support to Lord Liverpool's ministry. He voted in defence of their conduct towards Queen Caroline, 6 Feb. 1821. He divided for Catholic relief, 28 Feb. He voted against repeal of the additional malt duty, 3 Apr., and was granted six weeks' leave for private business, 5 Apr. 1821. He divided against relieving Catholic peers of their disabilities, 30 Apr. 1822. He voted with ministers against inquiry into the conduct of the lord advocate towards the Scottish press, 25 June, but against them on the pensions bill the next day. He voted for Bennet's public house licensing bill, 27 June. He divided against repeal of the salt duties, 28 June, but for repeal of the window tax, 2 July 1822. He voted for the Irish churches grant, 11 Apr., but for inquiry into the prosecution of the Dublin Orange rioters, 22 Apr. 1823. He divided against repeal of the Foreign Enlistment Act, 16 Apr., and Scottish parliamentary reform, 2 June. He voted in the minorities on the silk bill, 9 June, and the beer duties bill, 13 June 1823. He gave no recorded votes during the 1824 session. He divided against repeal of the usury laws, 17 Feb., and for Catholic relief, 1 Mar., 21 Apr. 1825. It was said of him at this time that he 'attended frequently and voted sometimes with and sometimes against ministers'.[2] He presented a Pontefract anti-slavery petition, 28 Feb., yet voted against the motion condemning the Jamaican slave trials, 2 Mar. 1826.[3] He divided against reform of Edinburgh's representation, 13 Apr. 1826. At the general election that summer he was returned for Pontefract in second place, after an expensive contest in which the 'No Popery' cry was raised against him.[4]

A petition to the Commons accusing him of bribery was rejected, 14 Mar. 1827. Constituency considerations may account for his votes against Catholic relief, 6 Mar. 1827, 12 May 1828. He divided against the corn bill, 2 Apr. 1827. He presented a Pontefract petition for repeal of the Test Acts, 19 Feb., but voted against that measure, 26 Feb. 1828. He was in the small minority who believed a witness had not lied to the East Retford committee, 7 Mar. He voted against the appointment of a registrar for the archbishop of Canterbury, 16 June, but divided with the duke of Wellington's ministry against reduction of the salary of the lieutenant-general of the ordnance, 4 July 1828. In February 1829 Planta, the patronage secretary, predicted that he would side 'with government' for Catholic emancipation, but he voted against their measure, 6, 18 Mar., and paired against it, 23, 30 Mar. He maintained that 'much greater evil is attributed to the corn laws than has been produced by them', 19 May, and spoke 'on the authority of a vast number of the masters of Manchester' in denying that wage rates were low in Lancashire, 1 June. He voted in the minority for the issue of a new writ for East Retford, 2 June 1829. His name does not appear in the lists compiled that autumn by the Ultra leader Sir Richard Vyvyan*. He presented a Pontefract petition against renewal of the East India Company's charter, 15 Mar. 1830. Having presented a Market Harborough petition against the sale of beer bill, 4 May, he warned that the removal of the 'wholesome power' previously exercised by magistrates would 'let in every species of mischief' and that 'the difficulty of exercising any adequate control in popular places under the new system will be incalculable when the number of such houses come to be so greatly extended'; he believed that 'all

houses of licensed victuallers ought to be shut at seasonable hours'. Although he vowed to oppose the bill's second reading, his name does not appear in the list of those doing so. At the general election that summer he retired from Pontefract and came in for Newton on the interest of Thomas Legh*. It is not known whether there was any truth in the explanation for this switch provided by one Yorkshire newspaper, which claimed that

> a gentleman, the owner of a close borough, owes Mr. Houldsworth a large sum of money; that he is unable to pay it, unless Mr. H. will *take it out in boroughs*, the only article in which the aforesaid gent. *deals*; that therefore Mr. H. agrees to take the borough as a set off to the debt, and hence his resignation of the honour of representing us.[5]

The ministry regarded him as one of their 'friends', and he voted with them in the crucial division on the civil list, 15 Nov. 1830. He divided against the second reading of the Grey ministry's reform bill, 22 Mar., and paired for Gascoyne's wrecking amendment, 19 Apr. 1831. He was returned unopposed for Newton at the ensuing general election. He was in the small minority for the reduction of public salaries to 1797 levels, 30 June 1831. He divided against the second reading of the reintroduced reform bill, 6 July, and for an adjournment motion, 12 July. He paired against the partial disfranchisement of Chippenham, 27 July, and the enfranchisement of Merthyr Tydvil, 10 Aug.[6] On 19 Aug. he maintained that no person should be compelled to serve as a returning officer 'without some degree of remuneration', citing the need for the assistance of legal advisors and assessors. He expressed the opinion that the proposed two-day limit on voting was too stringent for the larger counties, 5 Sept. Next day he urged ministers to reconsider this matter and the number of places that could be used for polling. He was absent from the division on the reform bill's passage, 21 Sept. He voted against issuing a writ for Liverpool, 5 Sept., and to safeguard the West India interest when renewing the Sugar Refinery Act, 12 Sept. He was absent from the division on the second reading of the revised reform bill, 17 Dec. 1831, but voted against the enfranchisement of Tower Hamlets, 28 Feb., and the third reading, 22 Mar. 1832. He divided against ministers on the Russian-Dutch loan, 26 Jan. 1832.

With Newton disfranchised by the Reform Act, Houldsworth considered a return to Pontefract but instead offered for North Nottinghamshire, where he was elected in second place.[7] He sat as a Conservative until his retirement in 1852. Although he was a manufacturer, he voted against repeal of the corn laws in 1846.[8] He died in September 1852 and divided the bulk of his estate equally between his brothers; his personalty was sworn under £470,000.[9]

[1] W.H. Macleod, *Houldsworths of Coltness*, 114-17. [2] *Session of Parl. 1825*, p. 469. [3] *The Times*, 1 Mar. 1826. [4] *Leeds Intelligencer*, 15 June; *Leeds Mercury*, 17 June 1826. [5] *Leeds Mercury*, 10, 24 July 1830. [6] *The Times*, 1, 12 Aug. 1831. [7] Staffs. RO, Stafford Jerningham mss D641/B/P/3/14/69. [8] *Gent. Mag.* (1852), ii. 427. [9] PROB 11/2161/835; IR26/1936/909.

M.P.J.C.

HOWARD, Hon. Fulke Greville (1773–1846), of Levens Park, Milnthorp, Westmld.; Elford Hall, Staffs.; Ashtead Park, Surr.; Castle Rising, Norf., and 16 Grosvenor Square, Mdx.

CASTLE RISING   29 Jan. 1808–1832

b. 3 Apr. 1773, at Geneva, 2nd s. of Clotworthy Upton, 1st Bar. Templetown [I] (*d.* 1785), and Elizabeth, da. of Shuckburgh Broughton of Poston Court, Herefs.; bro. of Hon. Arthur Percy Upton* and John Henry Upton, 2nd Bar. Templetown [I]†. *educ.* Westminster 1786-91; Christ Church, Oxf. 1791; R. Mil. Acad. Berlin. *m.* 9 July 1807, Mary, da. and h. of Richard Howard (formerly Bagot) of Elford and Castle Rising, *s.p.*; took name of Howard 6 Aug. 1807. *d.* 4 Mar. 1846.
     Ensign 1 Ft. Gds. 1793, lt. and capt. 1794, capt. and lt.-col. 1804; lt.-col. 7 W.I. regt. May 1807; half-pay, Irish 9 garrison batt. July 1807; brevet col. 1813; ret. 1825.

A well-connected Anglo-Irish army officer and former aide-de-camp to the duke of York, Howard had lost the sight of one eye during the Helder expedition of 1799, and had represented the pocket borough of Castle Rising on his father-in-law's interest since 1808.[1] As stipulated in his marriage settlement, following his father-in-law's death in 1819 he held 'the castle, manor and chase of Rising, with its 60 burgages, 90 messuages, 20 tofts, 4 mills, 50 gardens, 2,000 acres of farmland, 1,500 acres of marsh and 1,000 acres of moorland' jointly with his wife, together with estates in Westmorland, Staffordshire and Surrey.[2] The poet Robert Southey*, his guest at Levens in January 1830, wrote to Charles Williams Wynn*:

> Of all our contemporaries at Westminster one should not have thought him the likeliest to obtain a large property by marriage; but I believe from what I saw and heard that good fortune of this kind has never been better bestowed.[3]

Like his brother Arthur Upton, Member for Bury St. Edmunds, 1818-1826, on the interest of their

brother-in-law, the 5th earl of Bristol, Howard was an indolent Member, who had given silent support to Lord Liverpool's administration and voted latterly for Catholic relief, which he did again, 28 Feb. 1821, 10 May 1825; but he voted against permitting Catholic peers to sit in the Lords, 30 Apr. 1822. In 1825, a radical publication noted that he 'appeared to attend very rarely and to vote with ministers'.[4] He divided with government against the additional malt duty repeal bill, 3 Apr. 1821, and tax reductions, 11 Feb. 1822, and in their minority against inquiry into the prosecution of the Dublin Orange rioters, 22 Apr. 1823. He voted for repeal of the usury laws, 27 June 1823. The death that September of his mother and of his sister-in-law Lady Templetown in August 1824 gave him much business to attend to, and his attempt to increase his influence in Castle Rising by purchasing additional burgages now failed.[5] He voted against condemning the indictment in Demerara of the Methodist missionary John Smith for inciting a slave riot, 11 June 1824. In the 1826 Parliament his only known votes were for Catholic relief, 6 Mar. 1827, 12 May 1828, and emancipation, 30 Mar. 1829. He presented a Waterford petition against the proposed alteration of the corn laws, 10 Mar. 1827,[6] and may have been the 'Mr. Howard' named to the select committee on the Catholic land tax, 1 May 1828. The Ultra leader Sir Richard Vyvyan* classified him as a Member whose attitude towards a putative coalition ministry in October 1829 was 'unknown'. He was listed among the Wellington ministry's 'friends' after the 1830 general election, but was absent from the division on the civil list by which they were brought down, 15 Nov. 1830. Castle Rising was to be disfranchised by the Grey ministry's reform bill, and Howard voted against its second reading, 22 Mar., and for Gascoyne's wrecking amendment, 19 Apr. 1831. He spoke against the principle of disfranchisement, but conceded that some reform of Scottish representation was necessary, 28 Mar. He voted against the reintroduced reform bill at its second reading, 6 July, to make the 1831 census the criterion for English borough disfranchisements, 19 July, and against taking a seat from Chippenham, 27 July, and the bill's passage, 21 Sept. He did not vote on the revised bill at its second reading, 17 Dec. 1831, but he divided against the enfranchisement of Tower Hamlets, 28 Feb., and the third reading, 22 Mar. 1832. He voted against the second reading of the Irish measure, 25 May 1832.

An astute man of business who employed effective agents, Howard did not stand for Parliament again, but he consolidated his Castle Rising holdings, renovated his mansions, travelled in Devon and kept a close watch over his estate and electoral interests.[7] He died without issue at Elford in March 1846.[8] His will, dated 2 June 1842, was proved under £120,000 in England and £4,000 in Ireland. His wife (d. 19 Oct. 1877) was the residuary legatee. The other main beneficiaries were the Bagot, Fortescue and Stuart Wortley families, who succeeded her to the English estates, and Howard's Upton nephews and nieces, for whom he had provided during his lifetime and upon whom his Irish property now devolved.[9]

[1] *HP Commons, 1790-1820*, iv. 250. [2] Norf. RO, Howard (Castle Rising) mss HOW 205-344x2; Norf. RO PR/DM. [3] *New Letters of Robert Southey* ed. K. Curry, ii. 349. [4] *Session of Parl. 1825*, p. 469. [5] Surr. Hist. Cent. Howard of Ashtead mss 203/33/14a-b, 20, 41-42, 45, 50, 53-54, 62, 79, 88, 89a, 94, 96, 98, 100, 102, 105. [6] *The Times*, 10 Mar. 1827. [7] Howard of Ashtead mss 203/28/1-12; 203/30/1-104; 203/31/1-71; 203/33/88, 102, 150, 161; Howard (Castle Rising) mss HOW 22-229x1; 23-339x2; 88-341x3; 650-349x1; 777-349x3; *Recs. Ashtead Estate* (1873), 109, 176. [8] *Gent. Mag.* (1846), i. 440. [9] PROB 8/239; 11/2037/428; IR26/1741/429; Howard of Ashtead mss 203/33/20, 41-42, 50.

M.M.E.

HOWARD, **George William Frederick**, Visct. Morpeth (1802–1864), of Howthorpe Manor, Yorks.[1]

MORPETH	1826–1830
YORKSHIRE	1830–1832
YORKSHIRE (WEST RIDING)	1832–1841
YORKSHIRE (WEST RIDING)	4 Feb. 1846–7 Oct. 1848

b. 18 Apr. 1802, 1st s. of George Howard[†], 6th earl of Carlisle, and Lady Georgiana Dorothy Cavendish, da. of William, 5th duke of Devonshire. *educ.* privately by Rev. Richard Roberts, Mitcham, Surr. 1811-13; Eton 1813; Christ Church, Oxf. 1819; continental tour 1823-4. *unm. styled* Visct. Morpeth 1825-48. *suc.* fa. as 7th earl of Carlisle 7 Oct. 1848; KG 7 Feb. 1855. *d.* 5 Dec. 1864.

Chief sec. to ld. lt. [I] Apr. 1835-Sept. 1841; PC 20 May 1835; chief commr. of woods, forests and land revenues July 1846-Mar. 1850; chan. of duchy of Lancaster Mar. 1850-Feb. 1852; ld. lt. [I] Feb. 1855-Mar. 1858, June 1859-Aug. 1864.

Ld. lt. Yorks. (E. Riding) 1847-*d.*; rect. Aberdeen Univ. 1853-*d.*

Howard (as he was known until 1825) was from a very early age expected to achieve great things. Variously described as reserved, studious, effeminate and dandified, he was always treated as a rare talent. In 1820 his aunt Lady Granville referred to him as a 'clever, pompous darling'.[2] He was always more interested in books than any physical activity, and when he visited Althorp in 1811, his cousin Sarah Spencer was so alarmed that she told her elder brother Robert, 'He talks of beauty, and dress, and poetry, and even novels, till I long to send him for a summer at sea'.[3] He was rather portly as a youth, but Lady Holland was able to report to her son, Henry Edward Fox*, his close friend and contemporary at Christ Church, 9 Feb. 1827, 'You would be agreeably surprised at the alteration for the better in George Howard. He is less full and swelled in his features, and though not slim yet his figure is less clumsy'.[4] His grandfather, the 5th earl of Carlisle, had been a close associate of Charles James Fox[†], to whom he remained loyal until 1792, when he became a supporter of Pitt's ministry. Carlisle's son, Lord Morpeth, this Member's father, who sat for Morpeth, 1795-1806, and Cumberland, 1806-20, was a personal friend and political associate of George Canning*, but from 1804 acted with the Grenvillite Whig opposition. Howard was greatly influenced by Canning, whom he regarded as some sort of political mentor, and during his years at Oxford he took every opportunity to travel to London to hear him speak. Always interested in politics, his ambition was to make his maiden speech in support of Catholic relief, and it was assumed that he would come into Parliament at the earliest opportunity. His mother assured him in February 1822, 'I know how much you have the ability and the knowledge to be a great statesman'.[5] Despite his affection for Canning, he was always more of a Whig than a liberal Tory, often dining with Henry Fox at Holland House. His connection with the Whig Cavendishes through his mother, and her own influence, doubtless helped to reinforce this inclination, but he was reluctant to upset his father and grandfather by airing his views. This natural reserve was noted by Granville Venables Vernon*, who told Howard's mother in 1825:

> George is so singularly cautious and reserved, it is difficult to know what his opinions are on any subject, not only on politics but about persons and things. He is fond of society, likes talking to ladies, his manner is open and agreeable, his friends dote on him, *but* they say the only drawback is that it is impossible to get at his opinions.[6]

The Rev. Sydney Smith, a close friend of the Howards, commented to Lady Holland, 25 Aug. 1825, that 'his nature is fine: he wants ease, but that will come, and indiscretion, which will never come'.[7] Howard nevertheless appears to have been the life and soul of all manner of social gatherings. A passionate dancer and keen cricketer, and an accomplished player of whist and croquet, he apparently delighted everyone. Lady Granville told his mother, 22 Sept. 1828: 'How anybody exists anyhow, anywhere, without [George] I do not know. From the moment he arrived all has been gaiety and animation'.[8]

At the 1820 general election his father reluctantly stood again for Cumberland, telling his wife, 6 Mar., that 'I undertake it for others and not myself' and 'I hope George may benefit by the attempt, but I think I could safely leave him to his own future exertions'.[9] Reporting the latest developments, 9 Mar., however, he wrote, 'All this you see is against George's future prospects, and to say the truth it would be embarking him on a sea of trouble'.[10] Morpeth relinquished the contest soon afterwards. Howard toured Scotland with Lord Ashley* in the summer of 1820, but kept in touch with the political developments involving Queen Caroline through correspondence with Henry Fox, to whom he confided, 1 Sept., that 'I cannot help, like you, feeling a little rebellious feeling in her favour, though this is the first time I have dared own it'. He informed Fox that 'no consideration shall prevent me attending the trial', 7 Oct. 1820, and he attended the Commons debates on the affair in January 1821, telling his mother, 28 Jan.:

> Your brother [the duke of Devonshire] and I agreed last night that having all our previous lives viewed the subject with abhorrence ... we both now see the expediency and necessity of reform. This *really* is my present impression, for when 310 Members vote that the exclusion from the liturgy was not inexpedient and ill advised, after the debate I heard, I think in spite of all risk a moderate reform becomes a desirable measure. You had better suppress this from my father if you think it may bring on another attack of his gout.[11]

In 1821 he was awarded University prizes for both his Latin and English verses. Reporting that the commemoration ceremony went extremely well, 25 July, his friend John Stuart Wortley*, son of the Member for Yorkshire, told Fox that 'his family ... were of course in ecstasies'. His fears that Howard would fall into 'idle habits' the following year by playing whist into the early hours were unfounded, however, as he secured a first in classics.[12] In October 1823 the Yorkshire Whigs turned their attention to deciding whom to put forward for the additional seats granted to the county. Lord Althorp* advised Lord Milton, the sitting Whig Member, that 'as to G. Howard he appears to me to be out of the question. Lord Carlisle is disliked and Morpeth not known'.[13] Stuart Wortley told Fox, 13 Oct., that he had received 'very melancholy epistles from poor George upon ... his prospects'.[14] Howard was on a continental tour from October 1823 and wintered in Rome, where he remained until the death of Lady Carlisle in March 1824, returning home at the

behest of James Loch*, Carlisle's estate manager, who needed his assistance to help sort out Carlisle's enormous debts. His agreement was needed for an arrangement with Coutts's bank for a loan of £220,000, which Loch hoped would not only put the estates back on a sound financial footing, but 'contribute materially to the future comfort and happiness of your life'.[15] On 2 Mar. Howard's brother-in-law George Agar Ellis* informed him that he had been unanimously elected a member of the Literary and Scientific Club, and he joined Brooks's, 11 May 1824, sponsored by Lords Holland and Duncannon*.[16]

By early 1825, when rumours of a dissolution surfaced, the Whig hierarchy of Yorkshire were apparently more inclined to support him, for Lady Holland told Fox, 18 Mar., that 'George will apparently come in without difficulty'.[17] He was in Paris, where his uncle Lord Granville was ambassador, for the coronation of Charles X, when his mother reported to him the latest news, 9 May, but she made no mention of his own involvement.[18] However, by the following month the notion was firmly established among the Yorkshire Whigs and on 24 June James Abercromby*, Devonshire's man of business, informed Howard's father that 'George's interest' would be taken into consideration over the potentially politically sensitive appointment of a new registrar for the West Riding.[19] Three days later Morpeth told Lady Holland that whether there was a dissolution or not, 'George will at all events attend the assizes at York the 16th of next month'.[20] The *Leeds Mercury* reported that it was 'pretty well understood' that Howard would be a candidate, and that 'in answer to certain enquiries on the subject, made at York', he had 'avowed himself a friend to parliamentary reform, and generally to the reform of all public abuses'.[21] On 24 Aug. Stuart Wortley told Fox that he was confident of Howard's election.[22] Following his father's succession to the peerage on the death of Lord Carlisle, 4 Sept., Howard took the courtesy title of Lord Morpeth. His candidacy appeared settled when Milton wrote to Carlisle, 18 Sept., to discuss who should nominate and second him and to decide on colours. Milton was concerned that he and Morpeth should between them appeal to the broad sweep of Yorkshire opinion and interests, and must therefore carefully co-ordinate their campaigns, but not officially make a joint appeal.[23] It had been anticipated that the pro-Catholic Richard Bethell* would come in alongside the like-minded sitting Member James Archibald Stuart Wortley on the Tory interest; but the incensed anti-Catholics were determined that the county would not have four pro-Catholic Members and therefore requisitioned Richard

Fountayne Wilson* and William Duncombe*. On 29 Nov. Townshend warned Fox, 'I am afraid Morpeth will have an opposition in Yorkshire, if so, I believe he cannot afford to stand a contest'.[24] Abercromby hinted that Devonshire would not be disposed to pay the cost of a poll, in which Morpeth's youth would make him the weakest candidate.[25] Carlisle voiced similar fears, 4 Dec., when he told Lady Holland that he was 'not sanguine' in view of the 'raging' anti-Catholicism of the West Riding.[26] However, John Ramsden, Whig Member for Malton, assured Milton, 6 Dec., that 'if Devonshire would only guarantee money to Morpeth and the Whigs hold their nerve they would see off the challenge without a contest.[27] Devonshire, however, was unwilling to give such a commitment and it was certain that Carlisle could not provide any money. Another of Morpeth's kinsmen, Lord George Cavendish*, was approached for funds, but declined.[28] On 29 Dec. 1825 Carlisle determined that Morpeth would have to refuse to stand, telling Milton that the requisitions that had been organized to his son should be answered 'openly and decidedly'.[29] This alarmed the leading Whigs, who sought to persuade Carlisle that the manner of retreat was of paramount importance to Morpeth's own future and the Whig cause.[30] Although the requisitions were ready, a delay was arranged to give Morpeth time to reconsider, but Carlisle insisted that the invitation had to be declined.[31] Morpeth consequently consulted the influential Whigs George Strickland*, Daniel Sykes* and Smith to advise on the wording of his reply, in which he emphasized his youth and inexperience and stated that circumstances beyond his control 'would not justify me in attempting to support the great and unavoidable expenses of a contested election'.[32] 'We had I think no alternative, without embarking in a sea of difficulty', Carlisle told Lady Holland, 13 Jan. 1826.[33] 'Morpeth is behaving admirably about it himself and bears the disappointment in a very manly and creditable manner', Althorp informed Milton, 22 Jan.[34] Loch commented to Lady Carlisle, 23 Jan.:

> I am sure ... it will be a source of infinite satisfaction to Lord Morpeth in after life to reflect that he has had the prudence and magnanimity to make so great a sacrifice ... I believe it is better for him to represent in the first place a smaller place; he may thus select as much of private business as he chooses and of the sort he chooses [giving him] time to make himself fully master on those great points of national policy by taking a share in the consideration of which, he is to give himself that place in the country which I am certain we shall soon see him fill.[35]

Holland suggested to Fox, 8 Feb., that Morpeth might come in for the current vacancy for Oxford University, but Carlisle explained to Lady Holland, 12 Feb., that he would have 'no chance', as 'the anti-Catholic prejudice is too strong' and that it was the same in Northumberland.[36] Devonshire was the official British representative at the coronation of Nicholas I in Russia and, as he was no longer required to fight an election, Morpeth accepted his invitation to be his attaché and was said to be 'much pleased with the prospect of his Russian trip'.[37] Townshend reported to Fox, 21 July, that 'Morpeth as usual is bursting with joy and happiness ... and puffing through many a dance, as if his legs had no connection with his body'.[38] After the coronation, 3 Sept. 1826, he came home via Berlin and Paris.

During his absence he was returned at the general election for his family's pocket borough of Morpeth, where his uncle William Howard made way and canvassed for him.[39] On 25 Nov. 1826 he told his mother, 'I have attended all the Houses this week, but have not yet had occasion to exercise my privilege of voting, having of course found myself unable to do so for Mr. Hume's amendment, and gone away before the division'.[40] Before the 1827 session, and after a reception in his honour at Newcastle, he visited his constituency, 12 Jan., when he presided at a dinner for 130 freemen.[41] By now his ambition of making his maiden speech on the Catholic question seemed a distinct possibility, as Sir Francis Burdett intended to bring on a motion early in the session. Burdett had paid a visit to Castle Howard the previous July, and Abercromby informed Carlisle in February 1827:

> Burdett told me last night that the duke of Norfolk had expressed to him a wish that Morpeth should second the motion on the Catholic question ... I have turned it in my mind, and feel doubts ... and on the whole I wonder whether it would not be as well for Morpeth to take his chance in debate. It is clear that ... Norfolk would wish a Howard to speak, and Burdett is perfectly happy to acquiesce if you wish it.[42]

Morpeth was eager to seize the chance, and in a magnificent début, his speech confirmed the expectations of many and established his reputation in the House. Seconding Burdett's motion, 5 Mar. 1827, he concentrated on questioning the propriety and consequences of not granting relief to the Catholics, a measure 'equally demanded by policy and by justice', which would probably pacify Ireland. The Orangeman George Dawson followed him and formally congratulated the House 'upon the acquisition of eloquence and talent which it had obtained'. Morpeth's political friends heaped praise on his speech, Mackintosh saying that he had never heard a maiden speech of more promise, whilst Henry Brougham declared it to be the best for 20 years. His parents, who were present, basked in his glory; Canning told Carlisle that it was 'all that ever a father could desire'.[43] Morpeth divided against the grant to the duke of Clarence, 16 Feb., and for a 50s. duty on corn, 9 Mar. He voted for inquiry into Leicester corporation, 15 Mar., the spring guns bill, 23 Mar., information on the Lisburn Orange procession, 29 Mar., to postpone the committee of supply, 30 Mar., and for inquiries into the Irish estimates and delays in chancery, 5 Apr. He was in the majority to disfranchise Penryn, 28 Apr. He presented a Morpeth petition for repeal of the Test Acts, 7 June. On 18 June 1827 he criticized the agriculturists in the Lords for amending the government's proposals on the corn bill, but he backed the government's revised scheme, which he considered as 'good as could be expected at that late period of the session'.[44]

After Lord Liverpool's incapacitation in February 1827, Carlisle had become one of the negotiators in Canning's attempts to form a ministry in association with the Whigs, and had reluctantly entered the cabinet as chief commissioner of woods and forests. On 10 Apr. Mackintosh informed Lady Holland of reports that Morpeth was destined 'for Canning's treasury', for which he was 'sorry' since 'it is an engagement for life'.[45] In the event no offer was forthcoming, and John Cam Hobhouse* advised him that having 'commenced his political career in such auspicious circumstances' with his speech on emancipation

> it is very well for less persons to begin with showing what is called a talent for business ... which some kind or kindred minister may call them to occupy ... [but] it would be inconsistent with your illustrious situation ever to have your name found amongst the sneaking sinecures and exceeding knaves of the treasury.[46]

Canning's death in August was deeply regretted by Morpeth, who felt 'a sense of individual affliction at his eternal loss', and despite his father's position in Lord Goderich's cabinet, he felt that there was not a 'less original, less guiding, less commanding minister' than the new premier.[47] Nevertheless, he was willing to move the address (as Huskisson wished him to do), although his mother had reservations as to the propriety of a cabinet minister's son doing so.[48] Following Goderich's resignation Morpeth went into opposition to the duke of Wellington's ministry for the opening of the 1828 session. He spent much of it defending Canning's reputation and fighting for a pension for his family. He took immediate offence at the apparent disavowal of Canning's foreign policy with the description of Navarino in the king's speech as 'an untoward affair' and, after brooding on it for two days,

condemned it, 31 Jan., as 'injudicious and unjust', and 'the most injurious and shabby epithet which could have been supplied', 31 Jan.[49] Lord Jersey, though acknowledging that Morpeth had talent, deprecated his style, telling Arthur Paget† that he 'spoke as a shouting schoolboy'.[50] During the postmortem debate on the Canning and Goderich ministries, 18 Feb., he was severely critical of Herries and Huskisson, whom he described as the '*arcades* of the present cabinet': he had looked to Huskisson to carry forward Canning's legacy, and accused him of desertion. After eulogizing Canning's foreign policy, he pronounced his cause to be now 'without a leader, an existence, or a name'. Soon afterwards he lamented to his mother: 'The only thing I should really mind in politics is coming to pass, the separation of the Whigs and liberal Tories. Never mind, we shall have our virtue and the memory of Mr. Canning to carry us through life'.[51] On 1 Apr. he gave notice that unless the government brought forward a measure to provide a pension for Canning's family, he would do so. Ministers apprised Morpeth of their intentions (£3,000 per annum and a peerage to his widow) in early May, and although Morpeth agreed with Lady Canning that it was insufficient, he feared that there was little more they could do. However, he assured her, 7 May, that whenever it was introduced, 'I shall be prepared to state what I think will meet your views'.[52] He described the proposal, 13 May, as 'not adequate to its avowed object ... to mark the merits of the dead ... the exigencies of the living, or to record, in a worthy manner, the sympathy and gratitude of a great nation'; but he accepted it, reasoning that it was desirable to secure 'all attainable unanimity', and quoting Canning's own words when a pension was granted to Pitt's family:

> We will not consent to receive the vote as an eleemosynary grant to posthumous necessities, not as the boon of pity or compassion, but as a public debt, due to a highly meritorious public servant.

Lord George Cavendish Bentinck* told Lady Canning, 14 May, that it was 'a beautiful speech', while John Backhouse informed her, 15 May, that it was 'beyond all praise'.[53] Irredeemably influenced by Canning's view of foreign policy, Morpeth welcomed with 'unequal satisfaction' Peel's announcement that the government would do all in its power to effect the pacification of Greece, 24 Mar. In April his verse tragedy *The Last of the Greeks; or the Fall of Constantinople*, inspired by the Greek war of independence, was published. On 30 June he urged Peel to pledge the government to a policy of 'fair neutrality' over Portugal. He voted for repeal of the Test Acts, 26

Feb., presented multiple petitions for Catholic relief, 29 Apr., 6 May, and divided thus, 12 May. Welcoming what he saw as 'hopeful signs of progress', he hoped 'that another session of Parliament will not be allowed to pass over without some measure [to] grant the claims of the Catholic to the fullest extent', 12 June. He voted against the extension of the East Retford franchise to the hundred, 21 Mar. He objected to the scale of corn duties proposed by government, 31 Mar., and voted for a pivot price of 60s. rather than 64s., 22 Apr. He divided for the production of information on civil list pensions, 20 May. He contended that 'the present system of game laws is an evil that ought no longer to be tolerated', 13 June. His motion to reduce the grant for the Royal Cork Institution by £500, 20 June, was rejected by 66-22. That month he was listed by Lords Palmerston* and Colchester among the Canningite rump. Before voting to reduce the salary of the lieutenant-general of the ordnance, 4 July, he warned that 'the country will certainly have much reason to be astonished if this House was, on the first opportunity, to nullify its own [finance] committee, in respect of a reduction which they have recommended'. He divided against the grant for North American fortifications, 7 July 1828.

On 24 Oct. 1828 Morpeth set out on his first visit to Ireland. His trip generated controversy when the Catholic Association invited him to a public dinner in his honour, through its 'Friends of Civil and Religious Liberty' offshoot.[54] Richard Sheil* and Daniel O'Connell* presented the invitation, 6 Nov., and although he was initially unsure whether to accept, Morpeth concluded in a letter to his mother that 'English liberals' had nothing to gain by being 'backward and lukewarm'. Abercromby advised him, 22 Nov., that, considering his family connections, a refusal could have been politically embarrassing, and told Carlisle, 24 Nov., that whatever their reservations, 'in this case there was no alternative but to act as he has done'.[55] In a widely reported speech at the dinner, 27 Nov., he alluded to his own family's association with Catholicism, praised Ireland and the Irish, urged the laying aside of jealousies to fight for a common cause, and, although he was in no doubt as to their ultimate success, urged 'those amongst you who suffer under the odious disabilities' to 'use every effort that human nature is capable of, but resistance' and 'to strive to conquer reluctant Protestantism, by a display of Catholic virtue [mixing] temperance with zeal'.[56] Before the 1829 session a rumour arose that he was to contest the vacant Cumberland seat, but there was no truth in it.[57] In the House, 10 Feb., he said that although he was willing to accept the supression of the Catholic

Association to secure emancipation, he believed that the only effective way of disbanding it was to grant that relief, for 'to talk of the other only seems a piece of tautology'. 'George spoke well the other night. He has gained in self-possession and manliness prodigiously by his journey last summer to Ireland', Lady Holland told Fox, 14 Feb.[58] He of course voted for the ministry's concession of emancipation, 6, 30 Mar., and he presented a number of favourable petitions that month. On 20 Mar. he stated that while he objected 'in principle' to the disfranchisement of the 40s. freeholders, he saw no option 'but to make virtue out of necessity, and with one hearty gulp, swallow [the securities] ... because we think we are contributing to help, to hasten, and to secure Catholic emancipation'. He reluctantly 'found himself unable to vote in support of the claim' of O'Connell to be allowed to take his seat without swearing the oath of supremacy, 18 May; but he welcomed the 'fair and legitimate' opportunity afforded by making an amendment to the bill, 21 May, which would allow O'Connell to take his seat. He voted to transfer East Retford's seats to Birmingham, 5 May, but when this was defeated declared that he must vote for the issue of a new writ rather than to 'transfer the franchise into the well known *dukery* of the already sufficiently represented county of Nottingham', 7 May. He was in the minority of 12 for a fixed duty on corn imports, 19 May, seconded Hobhouse's motion for a bill to regulate the working hours of children in factories, 21 May, and divided to reduce the hemp duties, 1 June 1829.

Morpeth voted for Knatchbull's amendment to the address drawing attention to the distressed state of the country, 4 Feb. 1830. On 12 Feb. he welcomed Sir James Graham's motion to reduce official salaries and paid tribute to the late George Tierney*. Lansdowne reported to Holland, 12 Feb., that his speech had been 'excellent' on the subject of finance, had shown 'taste and feeling' with respect to Tierney, and that 'all he said too on currency and retrenchment was exactly what it ought to be'.[59] He voted for tax cuts, 15 Feb., military reductions, 19, 22 Feb., 1 Mar., and argued that the Royal Military College ought to be self-financing, 26 Feb. He was absent from the meeting of Whigs held in early March to co-ordinate opposition to the administration, but, according to Graham, those who had attended 'considered you were assenting, though not present'.[60] He divided steadily with the revived opposition for economy and reduced taxation from that month onwards, but only started attending their meetings in July, reasoning that he had not done so previously because he had not considered them sufficiently hostile to ministers.[61] He voted to transfer East Retford's seats to Birmingham, 11 Feb., 5, 15 Mar. Before voting for the enfranchisement of Birmingham, Leeds and Manchester, 23 Feb., he outlined his view on the need for reform:

> The state of the country has undergone a great change within the last few years. The people are everyday acquiring intelligence, and with this intelligence they obtain moral power ... but they are at the same time becoming more distressed ... In my opinion a temperate and timely reform ... while it forms a safeguard against any virulent expression of popular feeling, is at the same time recommended by every consideration of justice, policy and prudence.

He voted for Russell's reform motion, 28 May. He divided for the production of papers on the Bombay judicature, 8 Mar. Speaking before voting in favour of Palmerston's critical motion on the interference of British troops in Portugal, 10 Mar., he condemned the government's actions and their explanation of it, declaring it an 'illiberal and retrograde policy'. He secured the appointment of a select committee to investigate the condition of the London to Edinburgh road, 10 Mar. Presenting its report and moving the first reading of the Northern roads bill, 20 May, he recommended the appointment of a commission to study the proposals and said that 30 miles could be saved from the existing route. On its second reading, 3 June, responding to criticism, he emphasized that the route alteration would occur on the northern stretches, would not affect the Midland and southern counties and would involve no expenditure. He was strenuously opposed by Lord Lowther, who claimed that it would only benefit the Scots at English expense, but the bill was committed. Morpeth presented petitions in its favour from the royal burghs of Scotland, 7 June, Ayr, 5 July, and Inverness and Nairn, 9 July, but petitioning by the various interested turnpike trusts and inn owners in the south led to its falling at the close of the session. He voted for Jewish emancipation, 5 Apr., when he asserted that 'every person who contributes to the exigencies of the state, who pays its taxes and defrays the wages of its public servants, has an equal right to all the privileges and distinctions of the constitution', and 17 May. He presented four petitions from Yorkshire against the East India Company's monopoly, 27 Apr., when he voted to alter the laws governing Irish vestries. He voted for abolition of the Irish lord lieutenancy, 11 May, and endorsed a Dublin petition against the assimilation of Irish and English stamp duties, 14 May. He divided for abolition of the death penalty for forgery, 24 May, 7 June, and for reform of the divorce laws, 3 June. On 22 Feb. he had given notice of a motion to repeal the banish-

ment clause of the Libels Act, which made those convicted of a second offence liable to transportation, but he postponed it, 3 May, and reluctantly again, 18 May, after Sir James Scarlett, the attorney-general, agreed to introduce an amendment to remove the clause, but also to raise by £100 the security that newspaper printers must provide, which Morpeth promised to oppose. Proposing his amendment, 6 July, he said that he did not seek to defend the excesses of the press, but that there were already adequate laws to deal with them. Although he triumphed by 26-21, Scarlett gave notice that he would seek to overturn the vote, and the penalty increase was reinserted on the third reading by 68-46, 9 July, when Morpeth again opposed it. He presented a petition from the printers of London and Westminster for reduction of the duty on newspapers and advertisements and promised to introduce his own measure to deal with the latter, 2 July. He seconded Brougham's motion for the abolition of slavery, 13 July, and brought up a relevant Leeds petition, 20 July 1830.

At the ensuing dissolution three of the four sitting Members for Yorkshire retired. Strickland had been sure as early as October 1829 that Morpeth would be one of the candidates, and his name was one of many mentioned by the Whig press.[62] Abercromby asked Lady Carlisle, 10 July:

> Would it really be an advantage to Morpeth to have it? I have always a scruple about his taking a seat which is inconsistent with his holding office ... To be sure it may be said that to represent Yorkshire is a distinction equal to that of a cabinet minister, if the election is obtained by the voice of the people, and the duties are well performed ... [but] I have always thought Morpeth was a very unlikely person to be thought of. He has all the requisites to please Whigs and people, except money. They may be shy of making an overture after what happened before, but they may make it, and it is right to be prepared.

Carlisle was apprehensive of damaging Morpeth, who was emerging as the favoured candidate amongst the Sheffield Whigs, by a second withdrawal if money were needed, and Abercromby again wondered whether Devonshire would help.[63] After meeting a number of North Riding Whigs at the quarter sessions in Northallerton, where they agreed that Morpeth ought to be invited, Strickland and Sir John Johnstone* of Hackness went to Leeds, 14 July, to sound the opinion of the West Riding liberals. Here Morpeth's name was received with 'some degree of coldness', but they persevered and secured backing for him, and an agreement to bring in their candidates free of expense.[64] Carlisle advised Morpeth to accept the requisition on these conditions, 17 July.[65] Following the adoption of Brougham as a second Whig candidate, Johnstone told Carlisle, 23 July, 'I consider Morpeth's position both as to success and expense unaltered and unalterable ... [and] as certain as ever'.[66] A requisition from Leeds, signed by 200 freeholders and pledging to bring them in free, was presented to both men, 26 July. Privately, however, Morpeth told his mother that 'coupling us (which is evidently their wish) is the difficult point, the management of which requires great delicacy', 25 July.[67] Lady Carlisle advised that there was no harm in being associated with Brougham 'as a public man', but warned Morpeth not to cross him privately, for 'I should dread his revenge'. Carlisle, equally worried, warned that 'if your friends show any jealousy of him you will go to the wall'.[68] Morpeth decided to have his own committee, but to go with Brougham, 27 July, to the Leeds Cloth Halls, where all the canvassing tours started. Introduced by John Marshall*, he quickly gained the crowds' confidence by invoking the name of William Wilberforce*. He acknowledged that he was a member of the aristocracy and had been proposed by the landed interest, but appealed for a chance to prove himself. He declared that he favoured a 'great amendment' in parliamentary representation and promised to back such a measure as he deemed 'practicable and most efficient'. He denounced all monopolies, especially that of the East India Company, objected to the corn and game laws, and advocated strict economy.[69] He was given an ecstatic reception, after which he returned to York, as he was 'labouring under a slight indisposition', which his sister Caroline Lascelles revealed to Lady Carlisle to be a boil on the leg.[70] After Brougham expressed concern that Morpeth was pandering too much to the landed interest, adding that he was having difficulty in preventing 'the good men' in the towns from starting Strickland with him as the second Whig, Morpeth spoke again with him at Bradford, 29 July, telling his mother that 'all is on a proper footing now; we are together when circumstances so arrange it, but we do not contrive it ourselves'.[71] He continued:

I have at one time a country gentleman representing to me that I had better not speak out of the same window [as Brougham], and at another a manufacturer begging I will get in the same carriage. However, as I receive so much of his support in the West Riding, I think for the sake of appearance he ought to have my father's.[72]

Strickland, a member of both committees, told Milton, 31 July, that 'after much discussion, it is decided to keep it separate from Brougham's, but the interests are so united in the West Riding, as to cause

some difficulties'.[73] Caroline Lascelles informed Lady Carlisle the same day that there were many local joint committees in the West Riding towns canvassing to return them both.[74] Even on the day before the nomination, 4 Aug., Brougham confided to Holland that some Whig squires were still pressing Morpeth to stand independently of him

and he has been weak enough to yield to their folly. But finding the West Riding to a man refused to support him if he persisted in such weakness he today has shown more spirit, and ... he knows to whom he owes his election.[75]

At the nomination Morpeth urged the necessity of domestic reform, applauded 'the triumphant and bloodless march of freedom ... [when] it sweeps away a Bourbon, a Dom Miguel, or a grand Turk', and called for the abolition of slavery.[76] Caroline Lascelles reported to her mother that 'George ... surpassed himself; his speech was the most beautiful, the most eloquent thing I ever heard, everybody is quite enthusiastic about it, and he was most rapturously received'.[77] He was returned at the head of the token poll. 'By dint of waiting when things went wrong till they got better, I flatter myself that everything has ended well and smoothly', he informed Lady Carlisle, 7 Aug., adding, 'I am not fonder of Brougham than I was before; but nothing in any way disagreeable has passed between us'.[78] Lascelles told Lady Carlisle, 7 Aug., that 'the enthusiastic feeling which was everywhere shown towards [Morpeth] was not of a party or political nature but was a general testimony of admiration and respect for his character from the whole county'.[79] Over the next month he attended a number of victory dinners and a Leeds Anti-Slavery Society meeting, 22 Sept. 1830.[80]

Morpeth joined Althorp at Brougham's, 29 Oct., and again at a larger meeting of leading Whigs in early November, when it was decided that Brougham would move for reform early in the session.[81] On 3 Nov. he spoke against the address, telling ministers that an improvement, not an overthrow, of national institutions was needed and warning them that unless there was a reform of Parliament he feared for the welfare and safety of the country. He presented the petition of Andrew Lawson, whose family were seeking to restore their interest at Boroughbridge, against the return there, 4 Nov., and Stapylton's petition demanding that all Members be required to swear an oath that they had acted on principles of purity at their elections, 9 Nov. He presented his first anti-slavery petition of the session, 4 Nov., when he said that its object was the most anxious desire of Yorkshire, another 254 from the county, 11 Nov, and many others that month, including one from Leeds with 15,000 signatures, 23 Nov. He had of course been listed by the ministry as one of their 'foes' and he voted against them in the crucial division on the civil list, 15 Nov. During the construction of Grey's ministry Lansdowne asked if Morpeth would take office, but he declined 'on account of Yorkshire'.[82] Carlisle entered the cabinet as minister without portfolio, while Agar Ellis became chief commissioner of woods and forests. Welcoming the new appointments, 23 Nov., Morpeth hoped that ministers would 'place slavery on its proper footing and be friends of retrenchment and reform ... pursuing a liberal and enlightened policy with respect to commercial affairs, and that the principle of their foreign policy may be summed up in the short, but comprehensive word – peace'. Brougham (whom Morpeth would have liked to have been lord privy seal) had accepted the great seal, thereby precipitating a by-election for his Yorkshire seat.[83] Johnstone emerged as the favourite, but at the nomination Strickland declared against him, forcing a brief contest that Johnstone won. Morpeth, a friend of both, felt obliged to support Johnstone after his efforts on his behalf at his own election, and accompanied him on his canvass.[84] Morpeth presented a Menlogh petition praying that Catholic freeholders be placed on an equal footing with Protestants, 2 Dec., and several other Irish petitions in similar terms during the Parliament. He gave his 'entire approbation' to the regency bill, 9 Dec., denied that there was any resemblance between the conditions of labourers in the south of England and those of slaves, 13 Dec., and said that despite his support for reform, he could not back the Tory call for inquiry into the Evesham election. He presented two Yorkshire petitions for repeal of the assessed taxes and abolition of 'all useless offices' and defended Plunket's appointment as Irish lord chancellor, 20 Dec. 1830.

He moved for an account of woollen exports, 3 Feb., and was appointed to the select committee on the East India Company, 4 Feb. 1831. He reminded ministers that they had promised to assist Lord Chandos's bill to reform the game laws, 8 Feb., and welcomed confirmation of this intention, 15 Feb. He spoke against a general amnesty for the 'Swing' rioters convicted by special commissions, 8 Feb. He presented Yorkshire petitions complaining of distress and in support of reform, 9, 14 Feb., 11 Mar. He welcomed the budget proposals for reductions and retrenchment, 11 Feb., and presented and endorsed petitions for the abolition of newspaper stamps, 14 Feb. Challenged that day by the radical Henry Hunt to state his opinion on the ballot, he said that he had not 'expressed either dissent or concurrence upon the proposition'. He welcomed

Hobhouse's proposals to regulate the hours of children in factories, 15 Feb., and was appointed to the committee on the ensuing bill, 14 Mar. On 17 Feb. Thomas Gladstone* told his father:

> I am much disappointed in Lord Morpeth, and believe the feeling is general. He deals too much in Latin quoting for the present day, and seems determined to make speeches whatever the subject matter may be.[85]

During discussion of the proposed increase in the army, 21 Feb., Morpeth denied accusations that he had abandoned his belief in the need for economy and said that he looked on 'this augmentation of our military force as a necessary, but temporary evil'. He presented several Yorkshire petitions for and against the numerous road and railway bills affecting the county, as well as steering through the Sheffield and Manchester railway bill. He presented 76 Yorkshire petitions against slavery, 28 Mar., and when Fowell Buxton's motion for abolition came before the House, 15 Apr., claimed to have presented in excess of 500, warning that 'if we forbear much longer to pronounce the sentence of emancipation, it will accomplish itself in the most appalling manner'. He presented a Leeds petition with 17,000 signatures for reform, 26 Feb., and several others, including one from Sheffield Political Union, that day. In a long speech welcoming the ministerial reform bill, 2 Mar., he insisted that there was 'nothing in it which need alarm the friends of order and existing establishments'. He presented multiple constituency petitions in its favour, 16 Mar., when he paid tribute to the non-resident freeholders of York for indicating their willingness to sacrifice their rights, and 21 Mar. He voted for the second reading of the bill next day. Bringing up another favourable petition, 28 Mar., he insisted that despite Yorkshire's size and diversity of interests, it had met with unanimous support, and defended the planned division of the county. When a hostile one from Doncaster was presented by Duncombe, 19 Apr., he protested that it did not represent majority opinion. He voted against Gascoyne's wrecking amendment, 19 Apr. Responding to Duncombe's assertion that ministers could not appeal with credit to the country, he declared that a dissolution would show 'spirit and wisdom' and admonished Duncombe for criticizing measures which he had shied from voting against, 21 Apr. 1831.

At the ensuing general election he offered again as a reformer. He was joined by Johnstone, Ramsden and Strickland, and, facing no opposition, they made a triumphant tour of the West Riding. At the nomination he declared that the bill would not only give the right of election to Leeds and Sheffield but would bring 'freedom of election to Newark and Knaresborough, and purity of election to Beverley and Pontefract', and that he 'fondly anticipated ... an increase of good understanding and a return of confidence between the different classes and various interests mixed up in our body politic'.[86] He celebrated his unopposed return by taking a three-week sojourn in Paris. He voted for the second reading of the reintroduced reform bill, 6 July 1831, and thereafter was a consistent and regular supporter of its details, casting no known wayward vote. On presenting a Bradford petition for annual parliaments, universal suffrage and the ballot, 11 July, he said he would always 'oppose those wishes of my constituents ... which appear to me to be impolitic and dangerous'. When Milton moved an amendment for two Members to be given to the boroughs in schedule D, 4 Aug., Morpeth said that although he agreed with the principle that two representatives were better than one, and that Bradford, Halifax and Huddersfield ought to have two, he must resist the proposal because 'the bill was intended as an adjustment between the two great interests, the agricultural and the commercial'. He supported the suggestion of Farrand that the town rather than the township of Bradford should form the borough, and denied Wrangham's assertion that Huddersfield would become a nomination borough, since the property there 'is all let out on building leases, which will, I think, effectually prevent nomination'. When Goulburn proposed that Sculcoates should have representation separate from Hull, 9 Aug., Morpeth said that although he would not oppose its having its own Member, he doubted whether it had a 'sufficient separateness and distinctness' from Hull, and pointed out that Goulburn had furnished the strongest argument against his own proposition when he had said that he had never heard of the place until the bill was brought in. He dismissed Wrangham's suggestion that Yorkshire should have ten, rather than six, county Members, 10 Aug., explaining that he supported the division of the county, with two Members for each Riding 'because I consider it a matter of necessity ... although I cannot adopt such a course without some feelings of regret'. He voted twice with government on the Dublin election controversy, 23 Aug. As a member of the committee investigating corruption at the Liverpool election, he described the motion to issue a new writ as merely a question of expediency, 5 Sept., and, holding out the reform bill as the cure for abuses, said that Liverpool ought to have both its Members in the House when 'a question of great and general importance is under consideration'. On Thomas Duncombe's attempt to disfranchise Aldborough, 14 Sept., he observed that while there were other places in Yorkshire which he would prefer to return Members, notably Doncaster, as Aldborough legitimately fell within the criteria laid down for the retention of one Member, he would 'not give a vote which will have the effect of placing it in a worse situation'; he was a teller for the hostile majority. In a long and wide-ranging speech, 19 Sept., he defended the principles and objectives of the reform bill, attacked those who predicted nothing but doom, and was particularly scathing of the criticisms of Scarlett. He was a majority teller for the third reading that day, voted for its passage, 21 Sept., and the second reading of the Scottish measure, 23 Sept. He divided for Lord Ebrington's confidence motion, 10 Oct. When Althorp presented a favourable Yorkshire petition of 40-50,000 signatures, 7 Dec. 1831, Morpeth said he had attended the meeting which produced it and declared it to be 'the strongest argument that can be adduced in favour of reform'.

Throughout this Parliament he acted as the principal medium for many Yorkshire petitions expressing local grievances and played a part in the passage of a number of regional road and railway bills. He led the opposition from Yorkshire to John Campbell II's general register bill, requesting that the county, which already had its own registration, be exempted from the bill's operation, 30 June 1831. Campbell appeared to agree, but when the bill came before the House, 4 Oct., no such exemption was included. Morpeth complained, and after Campbell had conceded that the change could be made in committee if it was still the wish of Yorkshire, he said he would consult his constituents. On 7 Dec. 1831, however, Campbell refused to leave out Yorkshire, and after a number of the county's Members had declared their hostility to the bill, Morpeth informed Campbell that he would bring in a motion of exemption. He presented dozens of Yorkshire petitions against it thereafter and was appointed to the select committee on it, 22 Feb., but Campbell abandoned it, 16 July 1832. He presented a West Riding petition from the magistracy and clergy complaining of the Beer Act, 3 Aug. 1831, but although he shared many of their concerns, he cautioned against 'taking any step which may infringe upon the comforts of the working classes'. On 10 Aug. he presented a Yorkshire petition for the introduction of a system of Irish poor relief, observing that while the English system could not 'with advantage' be introduced there, 'if the people are starving, the people must be fed'. He presented and endorsed three Yorkshire petitions in similar terms, 12 Aug., contending that 'the destitute [of Ireland] ought not to be supported by perpetual drains on English charity'. He welcomed Sadler's motions for the introduction of a system of Irish poor laws, 29 Aug., and his factory regulation bill restricting child labour, 15 Dec. 1831, and was ordered to bring it in with Sadler and Sir Richard Vyvyan that day. Over the ensuing months he brought up numerous Yorkshire petitions on the issue and on the bill's second reading, 16 Mar. 1832, approved its referral to a committee, to which he was appointed. Fearing that the committee would be unable to complete its work that session, he observed that 'sufficient evidence has been given there to convince me of the necessity of the legislature agreeing to some measure of regulation', 27 June. Sadler managed to present the report, 8 Aug. 1832, but there was insufficient time for further progress before the dissolution.

Morpeth voted for the second reading of the revised reform bill, 17 Dec. 1831, and was again an assiduous supporter of its details. He favoured York as the polling place for the North Riding, 24 Jan., and advised the House that his enquiries at Leeds had informed him that 'raising the qualification of voters' would 'be attended with the worst consequences', 3 Feb. 1832. On 5 Mar. he presented a Huddersfield petition complaining that the bill had restricted the area of the proposed constituency to the town, and by omitting the parish threatened to make it a nomination borough. He defended the decision to confine Wakefield to the town only, but criticized the limits imposed at Sheffield, 7 Mar. When Goulburn complained that Whitby was to receive a Member although it was in decline, 9 Mar., Morpeth retorted that it was a place of great local importance, connected with national shipping and commercial interests, suffering only a temporary downturn in prosperity. As the bill approached the end of its committee stages in the Commons, Althorp told Grey that if a number of new peers were not created to force it through the Lords, he would resign, and Brougham, Graham and Holland backed him. Morpeth warned Holland:

> An immediate creation of a certain number of peers, as a measure of demonstration, may be very proper and fitting; but if this is made the point of rupture, it being in your power to take office and carry the bill, I much question whether you would retain, and even whether you would deserve, the confidence of your party, or the support and sympathy of the sound portion of the community.[87]

He voted for the bill's third reading, 22 Mar. Before voting for Ebrington's motion for an address calling on the king to appoint only ministers who would carry it unimpaired, 10 May, he said that as a representative of the largest constituency in the kingdom, who

had refused office in order to remain so, he applauded Grey's ministry, believed that Peel would be unable to carry a satisfactory measure, and feared the 'victory of more extreme options' if Grey, the only man who could 'tread the path of safety', was not permitted to carry on. He presented multiple West Riding petitions for the withholding of supplies until the bill passed, 22 May, and voted for the second reading of the Irish reform bill, 25 May, and against a Conservative amendment to increase Scottish county representation, 1 June. He presented a Leeds petition for the relief of Ireland, 23 Jan., and a Dewsbury one supporting the new plan of Irish education, 28 Mar. He voted with ministers on the Russian-Dutch loan, 26 Jan., 12, 16 July, when he spoke of their 'debt of honour', and 20 July. He was reappointed to the select committee on the East India Company, 27 Jan., presented an 'enlightened' petition from the physicians and surgeons of Leeds in favour of the anatomy bill, 2 Feb., and spoke and acted as a majority teller against Courtenay's critical motion on relations with Portugal, 9 Feb. He presented and endorsed a petition of Leeds merchants claiming compensation for losses suffered in Brazil, 16 Apr. Acknowledging his 'personal prepossession in favour of Russia', 28 June, he nevertheless criticized its intervention in Poland. He welcomed the budget, 27 July 1832, but urged the chancellor to consider the reduction of duties on bills of exchange during the recess.

At the 1832 general election Morpeth was returned unopposed for the West Riding.[88] He played a prominent role in promoting factory reform and was elected unopposed in 1835. He moved the amendment to the address which preceded the downfall of Peel's first administration in 1835, and was appointed Irish secretary in Lord Melbourne's second ministry, defeating Stuart Wortley at the ensuing by-election. During his time in office he carried the Irish Tithe Act, Irish Municipal Reform Act and Irish Poor Law Act. Holland, reflecting on the younger generation of Whigs that he had helped to nurture, observed in 1836: 'It seems to me that Lord Morpeth, steady, firm, diligent, and conciliatory, has risen most rapidly and most surely in public estimation'.[89] In 1837 he won the first contested general election in the West Riding, securing the largest vote ever received by a candidate anywhere, and he came entered the cabinet in 1839.[90] His rise was interrupted when he unexpectedly lost his seat at the 1841 general election. He took the opportunity to indulge in travel, visiting the United States and Canada. During his absence his popularity in Ireland led to his unsolicited nomination for a vacant seat at Dublin in January 1842, but he was defeated. He regained his West Riding seat in 1846, and was drafted back into the cabinet. That year Campbell wrote:

> I am sorry that Lord Morpeth ... one of the most amiable and excellent of men, has rather gone down in the world lately. He had a brilliant reputation at the conclusion of Lord Melbourne's government, and I remember the duke of Sussex prophesizing to me that Morpeth would one day be prime minister ... He may rally again, but I would not give much for his chance of the premiership.[91]

In 1848 he succeeded to his father's earldom. From 1855 (with a brief interruption) until 1864, he was a remarkably popular Irish viceroy. Throughout his career his religious fervour coloured his actions. He believed in a common gospel of all Christians, and was closely associated with a group of Whig Liberal Anglicans who opposed the Evangelical movement. His belief was central to his social policy, and particularly influenced his views on education.[92] He had suffered bouts of dizziness since January 1864, and in March began periodically to lose the ability to speak or write. Diagnosed as suffering from a form of gout, he continued to work until his resignation. His left-hand side was paralyzed in September and he died peacefully at Castle Howard in December 1864. Obituaries concentrated on his amiable character, but noted that he 'left no enduring work behind him to make him known to future generations, or to illustrate his own time'.[93] Francis Thornhill Baring* noted:

> His virtues made his abilities underrated. As a public man his faults arose from his goodness; he was constantly getting into scrapes with the treasury from his kindness of heart. It was no small praise that in Ireland he had obtained the attachment, almost, and respect of all; and no small proof of ability.[94]

In 1870 a bronze statue was erected in Phoenix Park, Dublin, paid for by public subscription. He published a number of books, including a *Diary in Turkish and Greek Waters* (1854) and *The Second Vision of Daniel: a Paraphrase in Verse* (1859), and was a frequent contributor in prose and verse to various journals. By his will, dated 23 Aug. 1864, he left annuities of £2,000 to his surviving brothers and sisters and a number of smaller ones to his nephews and nieces. The rest of his personalty was placed in trust with the Castle Howard and Naworth estates. He never married, although he had briefly courted Lady Anne De Grey, daughter of the first Earl De Grey, in 1833, and was succeeded in the family estates and earldom by his younger brother, the Rev. William George Howard (1808-89).

[1] See D. D. Olien, *Morpeth, A Victorian Public Career* (1983). [2] *Countess Granville Letters*, i. 11. [3] *Lady Lyttelton Corresp.* 124. [4] *Lady Holland to Son*, 52. [5] Castle Howard mss J19/1/2/25. [6] Ibid. J19/1/3/17. [7] *Smith Letters*, i. 414. [8] *Countess Granville Letters*, i. 25. [9] Castle Howard mss. [10] Ibid. [11] Add. 52010; Castle Howard mss. [12] Add. 52011. [13] Fitzwilliam mss 114/2. [14] Add. 52011. [15] Castle Howard mss J19/1/2/27. [16] Ibid. J/19/1/2/53. [17] *Lady Holland to Son*, 40. [18] Castle Howard mss J19/1/3/4. [19] Ibid. [20] Add. 51580. [21] *Leeds Mercury*, 30 July 1825. [22] Add. 52011. [23] Castle Howard mss. [24] Add. 52017. [25] Castle Howard mss. [26] Add. 51580. [27] Fitzwilliam mss 123/7. [28] Castle Howard mss, Abercromby to Carlisle, 25 Dec. 1825. [29] Fitzwilliam mss 124/16. [30] Ibid. Althorp to Milton, 1 Jan. 1826. [31] Castle Howard mss J19/1/3/27. [32] Ibid. J19/1/3/28, 29, 30; *Leeds Mercury*, 21 Jan. 1826. [33] Add. 51580. [34] Fitzwilliam mss. [35] Castle Howard mss. [36] Add. 51749; 51580. [37] Add. 51580, Carlisle to Lady Holland, 2 May 1826. [38] Add. 52017. [39] *Newcastle Chron.* 10 June; *Tyne Mercury*, 20 June 1826. [40] Castle Howard mss. [41] Ibid. Morpeth to Lady Carlisle [Jan. 1827]. [42] Add. 51580, Carlisle to Lady Holland, 21 July 1826; Castle Howard mss. [43] Add. 52017, Townshend to Fox, 5 Mar.; Castle Howard mss, Canning to Carlisle, 6 Mar. 1827; Broughton, *Recollections*, iii. 173; *Lady Holland to Son*, 60. [44] *The Times*, 8 June 1827. [45] Add. 51655. [46] Add. 47226, f. 90. [47] Castle Howard mss, Morpeth to Percy, 28 Aug. 1827. [48] Ibid. Lady Carlisle to Huskisson [Dec.], same to Morpeth [12 Dec. 1827]. [49] *Howard Sisters*, 108. [50] Add. 48406, f. 147. [51] Castle Howard mss, Morpeth to Lady Carlisle [c. May 1828]. [52] Harewood mss. [53] Ibid. [54] *Morning Chron.* 22 Nov. 1828. [55] Castle Howard mss. [56] *Morning Chron.* 1 Dec. 1828. [57] Castle Howard mss, Abercromby to Carlisle, 14 Dec. 1828. [58] *Lady Holland to Son*, 98. [59] Add. 51687. [60] Castle Howard mss. [61] A. Mitchell, *Whigs in Opposition*, 228. [62] Wentworth Woodhouse mun. G83/95, Strickland to Milton, 14 Oct. 1829. [63] *Sheffield Mercury*, 10 July 1830; Castle Howard mss. [64] Wentworth Woodhouse mun. G2/23. [65] Castle Howard mss J19/1/5/3. [66] Ibid. [67] Ibid. [68] Ibid. J19/1/5/7. [69] *Leeds Mercury*, 31 July 1830. [70] Castle Howard mss. [71] Chatsworth mss 6DD/1961; Castle Howard mss. [72] Castle Howard mss. [73] Wentworth Woodhouse mun. G2/23. [74] Castle Howard mss. [75] Add. 51562. [76] *Leeds Mercury*, 7 Aug. 1830. [77] Castle Howard mss. [78] Ibid. [79] Ibid. [80] *Leeds Mercury*, 25 Sept. 1830. [81] *Howard Sisters*, 151; Mitchell, 244. [82] *Howard Sisters*, 165-6; Chatsworth mss, Brougham to Devonshire [18 Nov. 1830]. [83] *Howard Sisters*, 167. [84] Castle Howard mss, Morpeth to Lady Carlisle, 19 Jan. 1831. [85] St. Deiniol's Lib. Glynne-Gladstone mss 197, T. to J. Gladstone, 17 Feb. 1831. [86] *Leeds Mercury*, 7 May 1831. [87] Add. 51583, 10 Mar. 1832. [88] Le Marchant, *Althorp*, 447. [89] *Holland House Diaries*, 357. [90] *Leeds Mercury*, 15 Dec. 1837. [91] *Life of Campbell*, ii. 210. [92] See R. Brent, *Liberal Anglican Politics*, *passim*; B. Hilton, 'Whiggery, Religion and Social Reform: The Case of Lord Morpeth', *HJ*, xxxvii (1994), 829-59. [93] H. Martineau, *Biog. Sketches*, 369. [94] *Baring Jnls.* ii. 203.

M.P.J.C./P.J.S.

HOWARD, Henry (1802–1875), of Greystoke Castle, Cumb. and Thornbury Castle, Glos.

STEYNING	30 June 1824–1826
NEW SHOREHAM	1826–1832

b. 25 July 1802, o.s. of Lord Henry Thomas Howard Molyneux Howard* and Elizabeth, da. of Edward Long of Aldermaston, Berks., c.j. of vice-admiralty ct. of Jamaica. *educ.* privately by Rev. James Dalloway 1810-12, 1821; Dr. Thomas Redman Hooker's school, Rottingdean 1812; Harrow 1817-20; grand tour 1822-3. *m.* 6 Dec. 1849, his cos. Charlotte Caroline Georgiana, da. of Henry Lawes Long of Hampton Lodge, Surr., 4s.

2da. *suc.* kinsman Charles Howard, 11th duke of Norfolk, to Greystoke 1815; fa. to Thornbury 1824. *d.* 7 Jan. 1875. Sheriff, Cumb. 1832-3

Howard inherited an estate in Gloucestershire on his father's death in 1824,[1] when he also filled the resulting vacancy for Steyning, a pocket borough controlled by his uncle the 12th duke of Norfolk. Having joined Brooks's Club, 18 May 1824, he followed his family's accustomed line in the Commons by voting with the Whig opposition to Lord Liverpool's ministry, though he is not known to have spoken in his first Parliament. A keen field sportsman, he told his mother, 7 July 1824, that he hoped 'to be able to get out of town this week ... I merely lack a ride every day to keep myself in health'.[2] He divided against the Irish unlawful societies bill, 15 Feb. 1825, and declared himself to be 'delighted' with the associated debate.[3] He voted for Catholic relief, 1 Mar., 21 Apr., 10 May. He divided for repeal of the assessed taxes, 3 Mar., reduction of military expenditure, 7 Mar., and against the duke of Cumberland's grant, 9, 10 June. He voted to ban spring guns, 21 June, and to allow trial by jury to those accused of combination, 27 June 1825. He divided for reductions in military expenditure, 3, 6, 7 Mar., and to abolish flogging in the army, 25 Apr. 1826. He voted for the disfranchisement of non-resident voters in Irish boroughs, 9 Mar., and Russell's reform resolutions, 27 Apr. He voted to grant counsel to suspected felons, 25 Apr. He divided for Hume's motion on the state of the nation, 4 May 1826. At the general election that summer he offered for New Shoreham on his uncle's interest and was recommended as a 'young man of no avocations or employment'; he was returned after a sharp contest.[4]

He divided for Catholic relief, 6 Mar. 1827. He voted for inquiries into Leicester corporation, 15 Mar., the conduct of the Lisburn magistrates, 29 Mar., and delays in chancery, 5 Apr. He divided against Canning's ministry for the disfranchisement of Penryn, 28 May 1827. He voted for repeal of the Test Acts, 26 Feb., and Catholic relief, 12 May 1828. He divided against extending East Retford's franchise to Bassetlaw freeholders, 21 Mar. He presented a Steyning petition against the proposed sliding scale of corn duties, 1 May, and voted against restricting the circulation of small notes in Scotland and Ireland, 5 June. He voted against the duke of Wellington's ministry to deduct the salary of the governor of Dartmouth from the garrisons grant, 20 June, and to condemn the misapplication of public money for building work at Buckingham House, 23 June 1828. He presented a pro-Catholic petition from Worthing, 3 Mar. 1829, which

he took as an indication that opinion on the subject in Sussex had softened. He divided for the government's emancipation bill, 6, 30 Mar. Following its passage he wrote to his mother, 31 Mar.:

> Thank Heaven the Catholic question is over in the Commons forever. The bill passed this morning at a quarter before four o'clock with *tremendous cheers*. I never uplifted my small voice with greater delight, or to a greater purpose.[5]

He was in the minority against requiring O'Connell to swear the oath of supremacy before taking his seat, 18 May. He voted to transfer East Retford's seats to Birmingham, 5 May, and was against the additional grant for the sculpture of the marble arch, 25 May 1829. He divided for Knatchbull's amendment to the address on distress, 4 Feb. 1830, and acted with the revived Whig opposition on most major issues that session. He voted for the enfranchisement of Birmingham, Leeds and Manchester, 23 Feb., the transfer of East Retford's seats to Birmingham, 5 Mar., and Jewish emancipation, 5 Apr., 17 May. However, he paired against abolition of the death penalty for forgery, 7 June. On 9 Mar. he moved the second reading of the Shoreham bridge bill, a project of his uncle's, and chaired the resulting select committee; the bill gained royal assent, 29 May 1830.[6] Much was made of this success when he offered again for New Shoreham at the general election that summer. His nominator joked that 'it requires no little courage for a man to forsake the fox hounds, but I have known him many times forsake them to get you the new bridge and cheap beer', the last being a reference to his support for the government's beer bill, which he thought 'a good measure, if not the best'; he would have preferred a reduction in the malt duty. He rejoiced at the overthrow of Charles X in France and welcomed the accession of William IV, 'under whose benign government the principle of the "greatest good of the greatest number" will be in full operation'. He was returned unopposed.[7]

The ministry regarded Howard as one of their 'foes', and he duly voted against them in the crucial civil list division, 15 Nov. 1830. Afterwards, he wrote to his sister that there had 'never [been] a more complete victory', with 'almost all the county Members' voting in the majority. He thought that Lord Grey 'seems the only likely person' to become prime minister. He also lamented the recent incidents of machine breaking and rick burning in Sussex, observing that 'the farmers are now reaping the fruits of their hard hearted, short sighted policy'.[8] He presented anti-slavery petitions, 7 Feb., 28 Mar. 1831. On 11 Feb. he informed his mother that his hunting was to be curtailed by a 'call of the House' and that he had 'a private bill (for the Worthing and Littlehampton road) to get through the House, which will occupy me above a week'. He also wrote of his hopes for tax reductions in Lord Althorp's forthcoming budget, but five days later, after its introduction, he reported to his sister that 'everything appears ... to be going on as badly as possible'.[9] He presented Shoreham petitions for repeal of the coastwise coal duty and against revision of the timber duties, 7 Mar. He divided for the second reading of the Grey ministry's reform bill, 22 Mar., and against Gascoyne's wrecking amendment, 19 Apr. 1831. At the ensuing general election he was returned unopposed for New Shoreham, after recalling with 'great satisfaction' his vote on the civil list and expressing his 'fullest confidence' in the government.[10]

He divided for the second reading of the reintroduced reform bill, 6 July, and generally for its details, though he was against the partial disfranchisement of Guildford, 29 July, and for Lord Chandos's amendment to enfranchise £50 tenants-at-will, 18 Aug. 1831. He was absent from the division on the bill's passage, 21 Sept., owing to ill health, and informed a relative that if there were to be a call of the House the following week he would have to be excused, as 'I certainly shall not be in a fit state to make my appearance. I have not attempted to walk or get down stairs yet'.[11] He voted with ministers to punish only those guilty of bribery at the Dublin election, 23 Aug., but was in the minority for a legal provision for the Irish poor, 29 Aug. He divided for the second reading of the revised reform bill, 17 Dec. 1831, its details, and the third reading, 22 Mar. 1832. He was absent from the division on Lord Ebrington's motion for an address asking the king to appoint only ministers committed to carrying an unimpaired measure, 10 May, but attended to vote for the second reading of the Irish bill, 25 May. On 22 June he supported amendments to the division of counties bill aimed at reducing proprietorial influence in Whitehaven and Stamford, and he commended the choice of Thornbury as an additional polling place for Gloucestershire. He voted with ministers on the Russian-Dutch loan, 26 Jan., and relations with Portugal, 9 Feb. 1832.

He retired at the dissolution later that year and apparently never sought to enter the Commons again. He devoted much time to promoting the Lancashire and Cheshire Railway, of which he became a director. He died in January 1875 and left Greystoke Castle to his eldest son, Henry Charles Howard (1850-1914), and Thornbury Castle, which he had restored from

semi-dereliction, to his second son Edward Stafford Howard (1851-1916), Liberal Member for East Cumberland, 1876-85, and South Gloucestershire, 1885-86.[12]

[1] He received a one-fifth share of the residue of personal estate sworn under £90,000: PROB. 11/1689/469-70; IR26/1004/889. [2] R.M. Howard, *Longs of Jamaica*, ii. 533-9; Cumb. RO, Howard mss D/HW8/48/6. [3] Howard mss 48/7. [4] *Brighton Gazette*, 1, 15 June 1826. [5] Howard mss 48/14. [6] *Brighton Guardian*, 24 Mar. 1830. [7] *Brighton Gazette*, 5 Aug. 1830. [8] Hants RO, Carnarvon mss 75M91/L3, Howard to Lady Porchester, 16 Nov. 1830. [9] Howard mss 48/15; Carnarvon mss L3, Howard to Lady Porchester, 16 Feb. 1831. [10] *Brighton Gazette*, 5 May 1831. [11] Howard mss D/HC/1/21. [12] Brougham mss, Howard to J. Brougham, 2 Dec. 1832; Howard, ii. 533, 537.

H.J.S.

HOWARD, Henry Charles, earl of Surrey (1791–1856), of 21 St. James's Square, Mdx.

| HORSHAM | 4 May 1829–1832 |
| SUSSEX WEST | 1832–1841 |

b. 12 Aug. 1791, o.s. of Bernard Edward, 12th duke of Norfolk, and Lady Elizabeth Bellasyse, da. of Henry, 2nd earl of Fauconberg. *educ.* ?privately. *m.* 27 Dec. 1814, Lady Charlotte Sophia Leveson Gower, da. of George Granville Leveson Gower[†], 2nd mq. of Stafford, and Elizabeth, *s.j.* countess of Sutherland [S], 3s. (1 *d.v.p.*) 2da. *styled* earl of Surrey 1815-41; *summ.* to the Lords in his fa's barony as Lord Maltravers 16 Aug. 1841; *suc.* fa. as 13th duke of Norfolk 16 Mar. 1842. *d.* 18 Feb. 1856.

PC 1837; treas. of household July 1837-June 1841; capt. yeoman of the gd. July-Sept. 1841; earl marshal 1842-d.; master of the horse July 1846-Feb. 1852; KG 4 May 1848; ld. steward of household Jan. 1853-Jan. 1854.

Lt. Clumber yeoman cav. Mar. 1819, capt. June 1819; maj. Arundel and Bramber yeoman cav. May 1831.

Surrey, whose father succeeded to the dukedom of Norfolk in 1815 as a collateral heir, was the sole issue of his parents' ill-fated union which had ended in divorce in 1795. Details of his education are lacking, but he is known to have travelled in Sicily in 1811.[1] In 1814 he married the daughter of the fabulously wealthy marquess of Stafford and the formidable countess of Sutherland. A Catholic and a Whig, like his father, he joined Brooks's Club, 4 Apr. 1815. Thomas Grenville[†] described him about this time as 'plain, unaffected, reasonable and good natured'. However, Henry Brougham* feared that 'old mother Stafford' was determined to make him 'turn Protestant', and by 1819 Lord Grey was being warned about 'the state of Lord Surrey's politics', which were 'entirely under the influence of Lady Stafford'. The following year Sir James

Mackintosh* regretted to find him being 'seduced ... into Court politics', and on meeting him in 1823 concluded that he was 'almost a Tory and altogether a puppy, perfectly unworthy of his excellent father'.[2] Surrey's Catholicism prevented him from discharging his duties as deputy earl marshal at the coronation of George IV – 'a deprivation the more galling in proportion to the loyalty which fills my breast', as he assured the king – but he was allowed to act as a trainbearer.[3] His religion also barred his entry to the Commons until the passage of Catholic emancipation in 1829, directly upon which he was returned for his father's borough of Horsham, the sitting Member having retired in his favour. In a somewhat incoherent speech to his constituents, he insisted that his patriotism was undiminished by his upbringing in 'a religion in some trifling respects different to you', and he hoped that Catholics and Protestants would 'emulate each other ... in showing an attachment to the king and in maintaining the church as established by law'; the Catholic *Orthodox Journal* dismissed his remarks as 'cant'.[4]

He took the newly appointed oath for Catholic Members, 6 May 1829, and thus became the first man avowedly of his faith to take his seat in the Commons since the seventeenth century. It was reported that 'the circumstance occasioned some sensation, and the noble earl was warmly greeted by many of his friends'.[5] He presented a petition requesting measures to relieve depression in the wool trade, 13 May 1829, and another from local residents against the Horsham and Guildford road bill, 26 Feb. 1830. He divided against Lord Blandford's parliamentary reform motion, 18 Feb., but for the transfer of East Retford's seats to Birmingham, 5 Mar. He presented a Worksop petition in favour of Jewish emancipation, 13 May, and voted in this sense, 17 May 1830. It appears that his connection with the duke of Wellington's ministry went further than the division lists suggest, and that prior to the general election that summer he sought a seat outside his father's aegis. His brother-in-law Lord Francis Leveson Gower*, the Irish secretary, recommended to the home secretary Peel that support be given in the event of a vacancy at New Shoreham:

Lord Surrey has given proof of his dispositions towards government by very steadily voting with us at all hours, and has informed his father that he intends to continue the same course, with the only proviso that should a subject arise on which the duke's political feelings were much excited and engaged he ... would refrain from voting at all.

However, it was subsequently reported that Surrey had abandoned the intention of switching seats, and

he was again returned for Horsham, 'unfettered and without any promise on my part'.[6]

The ministry listed him as one of the 'good doubtfuls', with the additional note that he was 'a friend where not pledged', but he was absent from the crucial civil list division, 15 Nov. 1830. That winter he was closely involved in the measures taken to combat the 'Swing' riots in his Sussex locality. He instigated the revival of the Arundel and Bramber yeomanry and, as an Arundel clergyman noted, 'made himself very popular here by taking an active part in the proceedings for keeping the peace, and by patrolling the streets at night'. On the other hand, he was a founder member of the Sussex association for improving the condition of the labouring classes.[7] It is not clear whether these events influenced his subsequent political conduct, but he confounded Tory expectations by voting for the second reading of the Grey ministry's reform bill, 22 Mar., and against Gascoyne's wrecking amendment, 19 Apr. 1831. At the ensuing general election he offered for Sussex, with his father's blessing, but withdrew in the face of opposition from the duke of Richmond's brother Lord John George Lennox*. Richmond was willing to see Surrey as a county Member 'if the reform bill should pass', but in the meantime he was returned again for Horsham.[8] He divided for the second reading of the reintroduced reform bill, 6 July, and paired against giving urban freeholders the right to vote in boroughs, 17 Aug. 1831. However, he was noted as having been 'absent' from six divisions in committee, and his father was 'exceedingly mortified' to learn that this was being 'ascribed to so unfounded a motive' as lukewarmness on reform, when the real reason was that Lady Surrey had recently suffered a stillbirth.[9] He voted for the bill's passage, 21 Sept., and Lord Ebrington's confidence motion, 10 Oct. He was granted three weeks' leave 'on account of the disturbed state of his neighbourhood', 25 Nov. He returned to divide for the second reading of the revised reform bill, 17 Dec. 1831, the registration clause, 8 Feb., the enfranchisement of Tower Hamlets, 28 Feb., and Gateshead, 5 Mar., and the third reading, 22 Mar. 1832. He voted for the address asking the king to appoint only ministers committed to carrying an unimpaired measure, 10 May. In a letter to lord chancellor Brougham, 30 June, he made the not altogether disinterested suggestion that Arundel be made an additional polling place for the western division of Sussex.[10] He voted with ministers on relations with Portugal, 9 Feb. 1832.

He was returned as expected for West Sussex at the general election of 1832 and sat until he was raised to the peerage in 1841, shortly before his father's death. As duke of Norfolk he held various offices in the royal household and gained a reputation as an agricultural improver. However, his closure of the park at Arundel brought him much local opprobrium, and he was widely ridiculed for his speech at an agricultural dinner in 1845 when he recommended curry powder as a palliative for the starving poor: 'a pinch of this powder ... mixed with warm water ... warms the stomach incredibly ... and a man without food can go to bed comfortably on it'. He continued to be classed as a Whig, though he opposed repeal of the corn laws in 1846. He gained some political renown in 1851 for supporting the ecclesiastical titles bill, which sought to prevent the reintroduction of the Catholic hierarchy in England, and outwardly he conformed to the established church, although he never formally renounced Catholicism.[11] He died in February 1856 and was succeeded by his eldest son, Henry Granville Fitzalan Howard (1815-60), Liberal Member for Arundel, 1837-51. A deathbed reconciliation to the religion of his forebears did not prevent his son's biographer from asserting that he was 'a Catholic but in name'.[12]

[1] G. Brenan and E.P. Statham, *House of Howard*, ii. 643-4; Arundel Castle mss C 300. [2] *HMC Fortescue*, x. 392; *Creevey Pprs.* i. 245; Grey mss, Lambton to Grey, 4 Oct. 1819; Add. 52444, f. 92; 52445, f. 125. [3] *Geo. IV Letters*, iv. 442. [4] *Orthodox Jnl.* xi. (1829), 31-32; xii. (1830), 323. [5] *Parl. Deb.* (n.s.), xxi. 1105. [6] NAI, Leveson Gower letterbks. vol. 3; Add. 40338, f. 195; *Brighton Gazette*, 8 Aug. 1830. [7] W. Suss. RO, Burrell mss, Cartwright to Burrell, 10 Dec. 1830; *VCH Suss.* i. 355; ii. 209. [8] Arundel Castle mss, Richmond to Norfolk, 9 Apr. 1831. [9] Add. 51836, Norfolk to Holland [Aug. 1831]. [10] Brougham mss, Surrey to Brougham, 30 June 1832. [11] J.M. Robinson, *Dukes of Norfolk*, 195-7, 201-2; D. Roberts, *Paternalism in Early Victorian England*, 107. [12] Comte de Montalembert, *Biog. Sketch of duke of Norfolk*, 62.

H.J.S.

HOWARD, Philip Henry (1801–1883), of Corby Castle, Cumb.

CARLISLE   1830–1847

CARLISLE   14 Mar. 1848–1852

b. 22 Apr. 1801, 1st. s. of Henry Howard of Corby and Catherine Mary, da. of Sir Richard Neave, 1st. bt., of Dagnam Park, Essex. *educ.* Stonyhurst 1815-18.[1] *m.* 11 Nov. 1843, Elizabeth Minto, da. of Maj. John Canning Howard, E.I. Co., 1s. 3da. *suc.* fa. 1842. *d.* 1 Jan. 1883.
  Sheriff, Cumb. 1860-1.

Howard's father, a kinsman of the dukes of Norfolk, was the Catholic owner of the Corby Castle estate and founder in 1803 of the Cumberland Rangers volunteers. He remained a staunch supporter of the Cumberland and Westmorland Whigs in their long struggle against the Tory Lowthers, who made his right to vote without swearing allegiance to the established church a major issue at the Westmorland election of 1826.[2] Excluded from the universities on religious grounds, Howard was tutored privately and at Stonyhurst, and spent much of his early life on the continent.[3] He failed to impress when he toured the North of England with his father in 1823,[4] and had difficulty in persuading the Carlisle Whigs to back him at the first post-emancipation general election in 1830, when his father managed his campaign and a poll was narrowly averted.[5] On the hustings and at Whig dinners he promised to follow the political leadership of the county Member Sir James Robert George Graham: to promote retrenchment, 'a temperate but decisive reform in Parliament' and the gradual abolition of colonial slavery.[6] Graham thought Howard had 'obtained a seat, which by conduct and steady adherence to Whig principles he may keep for life'; his mother that he had realized 'the summit of his very earliest ambition'.[7]

Howard soon established himself as a regular contributor to debates and arranged for copies of the *Mirror of Parliament* to be dispatched to the Carlisle Commercial Newsroom to prove his diligence and counter any misreporting.[8] His maiden speech, 11 Nov. 1830, commonly misattributed to Viscount Boyle, was for Sadler's motion for a select committee on the state of the Irish poor, a sensitive issue in Carlisle on account of its proximity to the Solway ports. He stressed the unwelcome burden that the upkeep of the transient Irish placed on the English middle classes and the threat they posed to the status of English labourers, and called for a tax on absentee Irish landlords for their maintenance. He voted in Daniel O'Connell's minority for repeal of the Irish Subletting Act that day. The Wellington ministry had considered him as one of the 'bad doubtfuls' likely to vote with 'opposition', and he did so when they were brought down on the civil list, 15 Nov. 1830. He expressed qualified support for the Cumberland reform petition presented by Graham, 9 Feb. 1831, 'though the admission of inhabitant householders ... may seem to militate against the peculiar privileges of those ... I represent'; but he refused to endorse its plea for the ballot, and substantiated his case against it with illustrations from the classics and references to his personal experience of its operation in France. Countering, Warburton accused him of citing one side only of Cicero's *Dialogue*, but Sir Charles Wetherell praised his speech. He endorsed a Carlisle petition for repeal of the newspaper tax, 9 Feb., and called on ministers to amend the game bill so that the £5 fee for shooting licenses was dropped, 15 Mar. He divided for the Grey ministry's reform bill at its second reading, 22 Mar., and against Gascoyne's wrecking amendment, 19 Apr. He objected to the anti-reformers' time wasting speeches when he brought up a petition against taxing packet steamer passengers, 28 Mar. On his agents' advice, when the Carlisle guilds adopted hostile petitions, he warned ministers that they needed to reassess the impact of removing freemen's hereditary voting rights, 18 Apr. 1831.[9] He had to campaign jointly with the radical William James to safeguard his seat at the general election in May.[10] He informed his father afterwards that he 'was put out of his first speech by James, who had no sheet and somehow hit on all his ideas'.[11] He notified Graham, as one of the architects of the reform bill, that he had been made to promise to try to guarantee the voting rights of all freemen's children born of marriages solemnized before the measure was carried, and suggested minor alterations in phrasing to make the bill's wording on contingent parishes, wards, hundreds, rapes, wappentakes, and statutory miles less ambiguous.[12]

He divided for the reintroduced reform bill at its second reading, 6 July, against adjournment, 12 July 1831, and steadily for its details. He protested at attempts to delay its progress, 29 July, 27 Aug., and dismissed the proposed enfranchisement of £50 tenants-at-will as unconstitutional, 27 Aug. Endorsing a petition from Leath Ward that day against dividing the Cumberland constituency, he said that indisposition alone had prevented him from voting against the proposed county divisions (11 Aug.). He explained before dividing against Edmund Peel's amendment to preserve freemen's voting rights, 30 Aug., that he now considered the combination of a £10 householder vote and the enfranchisement of freemen resident within seven miles 'perfectly adequate'. He joined in the clamour against the anti-reformers' attempt to 'create collision' between the agricultural and commercial interests and cited extracts from the statutes of Henry VI and VIII as proof that non-resident freemen were not permitted to vote until 1774. He divided for the bill's passage, 21 Sept., and Lord Ebrington's confidence motion, 10 Oct. He objected to receiving a petition blaming the bishops for the bill's defeat in the Lords and urging their disfranchisement, 18 Oct. According to a hostile witness, Howard 'cut a sorry figure' at the Cumberland reform meeting at Wigton, 15 Nov.[13] He divided for the revised reform bill at its second reading, 17 Dec. 1831, and, apart from a minority vote against enfranchising £50 tenants-at-will, 1 Feb. 1832, he generally supported its

details. However, he was taken to task by the Carlisle Reform Association after the *Carlisle Journal* alleged that he had voted in the minority for the enfranchisement of £10 urban ratepayers, 3 Feb., which they interpreted as a sign that he aimed to promote the influence of 'aristocracy and wealth' in the constituency and 'exclude that of the mechanics and small tradesmen'.[14] He divided for the reform bill's third reading, 22 Mar., and the address requesting the king to appoint only ministers who would carry it unimpaired, 10 May. He voted against a Conservative amendment to the Scottish reform bill, 1 June. He had no qualms about supporting James and the Cumberland reformer William Blamire in their abortive attempt to alter the boundaries of Whitehaven to reduce the Lord Lonsdale's influence there, 22 June. Howard and his relations openly admitted that their pleasure at the passage of Catholic emancipation had been 'much dampened' by the restriction of the Irish freeholder franchise, and they regarded the removal of legal differences and restoration of the 40s. freeholder vote as welcome steps towards the greater assimilation of Ireland into the United Kingdom.[15] Howard therefore supported O'Connell's amendments for the enfranchisement of Irish 40s. and £5 freeholders, 13, 18 June, but he rebutted his charge that those who had benefited by emancipation now 'confederated with the opponents of reform in the attempt to crush the spirit in Ireland', 13 June 1832. He divided with government on the Dublin election controversy, 23 Aug. 1831, the Russian-Dutch loan, 26 Jan., 12, 16, 20 July, information on Portugal, 9 Feb., and the navy civil departments bill, 6 Apr. 1832. He voted against them for printing the radical Waterford petition for disbanding the Irish yeomanry, 11 Aug. 1831, but with them on military punishments, 16 Feb. 1832. He considered further inquiry into Peterloo 'inexpedient' 15 Mar. 1832.

Hoping to see district registries established according to the French plan, he initially declined to join Blamire in outright opposition to the locally unpopular general register bill, 27 Jan. 1832. He denounced central registration when presenting a hostile petition from Cumberland, 22 Feb., and criticized the appointment of a select committee on the English measure that day as a waste of time and money. He was in favour of committing the Irish registry of deeds bill, 9 Apr. He supported the principle of the factory regulation bill, but warned of its adverse effects in depressed textile towns like Carlisle, called for the exemption of 14-21-year-olds from its provisions and asked the select committee to consider its likely impact on poor rates, 14, 16 Mar. He disagreed with the Irish secretary Smith Stanley on the tithes question, 30 Mar., and claimed that he would never have voted for his resolutions had he realized that 'there was to be no difference in the appropriation of church property'. He explained that although he acquiesced in the continuance of the Church of Ireland, his priority was the establishment of a stable administrative and educational hierarchy within the Irish Catholic church. He suggested amending the Irish clandestine marriages bill by substituting the words 'Roman Catholic clergymen' for 'Popish priests', 29 June. He made several interventions in support of the anatomy bill, which he perceived as the only means of extending good surgical practice, but he objected to the appointment of political agents as coroners, 11 Apr., and voted to hold coroners' inquests publicly, 20 June. He endorsed Carlisle's petition against the bill to remove Scottish and Irish vagrants, 17 July 1832.

After a difficult canvass in which his Catholicism and refusal to support the ballot were major issues, he was returned for Carlisle as a Liberal with James at the general election of December 1832.[16] With a single interruption, brought about by his defeat at the voided election of 1847, when the appointment of Catholic bishops was the major issue, he represented Carlisle until he made way for Graham in 1852.[17] He succeeded his father to Corby Castle in 1842, but spent little time there, preferring the Warwickshire estate of Foxcote, which his wife (d. 1865), on whom £20,000 was settled when they married in 1843, inherited from her uncle Major Francis Canning.[18] Howard died at Ventnor on the Isle of Wight in January 1883 and was succeeded to his estates by his eldest son Philip John Canning Howard (1853-1924). His will was proved in London, 10 Apr. 1883, and resworn in November 1886.[19]

[1] Cumbria RO (Carlisle), Howard of Corby Castle mss D/HC/1/25. [2] H. Lonsdale, *Worthies of Cumb.* iii (1872); *Carlisle Patriot*, 24 Feb. 1827; J.R. McQuiston, 'Lonsdale Connection and its Defender', *Northern Hist.* xi (1975), 164-5. [3] Howard mss 1/25, *passim.* [4] Add. 51597, Morpeth to Lady Holland, 25 Dec. 1823. [5] Howard mss 1/21, corresp. 8-22 July; 1/27, *passim.*; Lonsdale mss, Lowther to Lonsdale, 19, 24 July; Brougham mss, Graham to Brougham, 16 Aug.; *Carlisle Jnl.* 17, 24, 31 Aug. 1830. [6] *Carlisle Patriot*, 31 July; Hants RO, Carnarvon mss 75M91/L3, H. Howard to Lady Porchester, 9 Aug. 1830. [7] Castle Howard mss J19/1/5/11; Howard mss 1/81, C.M. Howard, 'Reminiscences for my children'. [8] Howard mss 1/21, J. Steel to P.H. Howard, 5 Mar. 1831. [9] Ibid. Dobinson to P.H. Howard, 8, 9, 19, 21 Mar. 1831. [10] Ibid. Morley to P.H. Howard, 24 Apr.; Brougham mss, Blamire to J. Brougham [Apr.]; same to Lord Brougham, 30 Apr.; Northumb. RO, Hope-Wallace mss ZHW/2/16; Carnarvon mss L3, H. Howard to Lady Porchester, 4 May; *Westmld. Advertiser*, 7 May 1831. [11] Carnarvon mss L3, H. Howard to Lady Porchester May 1831. [12] Howard mss 1/21, P.H. Howard to Graham, 18 May 1831. [13] Lonsdale mss, Hodgson to Lonsdale, 17 Nov.; *Carlisle Patriot*, 19 Nov., 10 Dec. 1831. [14] *Carlisle Journal*, 11, 18, 25 Feb. 1832. [15] Brougham mss, H. Howard to Brougham, 10 Mar. 1829. [16] Ibid. H. Howard to J. Brougham, 6 Dec. 1832; Carlisle Pub. Lib. 3A/324.2; Wellington mss WP1/1240/4. [17] R. Torrens, *Sir James Graham*, 554-9. [18] Howard mss 1/29. [19] *The Times*, 3 Jan. 1883.

M.M.E.

HOWARD, Ralph (?1802–1873), of Bushy Park, co. Wicklow.

Co. WICKLOW	22 July 1829–1847
Co. WICKLOW	27 Apr. 1848–1852

b. ?1802, 1st s. of Hon. Hugh Howard, MP [I], and Catherine, da. of Rev. Robert Bligh, dean of Elphin. *educ.* Eton 1817; Brasenose, Oxf. 18 Dec. 1819, aged 17. *m.* July 1837, Charlotte Anne, da. and h. of Daniel Craufurd of Kilbirnie, Ayr, wid. of Sir James John Fraser, 3rd bt., of Ledeclune, Inverness, *s.p. cr.* bt. 26 July 1838; *suc.* fa. 1840. *d.* 15 Aug. 1873.

Col. co. Wicklow militia 1834-71.

Howard's father, Member for his family's borough of St. Johnstown, county Donegal, in the Irish Parliament, 1790-1800, was the fourth son of Ralph Howard, 1st Viscount Wicklow, Member for county Wicklow, 1761-76. A supporter of the Union, he was given an Irish commissionership of stamps worth £500 a year in 1796 and made postmaster-general in 1800.[1] At the 1826 general election Howard proposed his brother-in-law Granville Leveson Proby* for county Wicklow, where he had sat since 1816 on the combined interest of Lords Carysfort and Fitzwilliam.[2] Three years later Proby, an indifferent parliamentarian, made way for Howard with the approval of Fitzwilliam's son Lord Milton*, who had 'no objection whatever' and was 'perfectly willing to make a declaration in his favour'. He was returned unopposed.[3] He voted for the enfranchisement of Birmingham, Leeds and Manchester, 23 Feb., and divided with the revived Whig opposition to the Wellington ministry against the Bathurst and Dundas pensions, 26 Mar., and for abolition of the Irish viceroyalty, 11 May, and a reduction of the grant to South American missions, 7 June 1830.

At the 1830 general election Howard offered again, promising to support ministers only 'when their measures entitled them', and was returned unopposed.[4] The ministry listed him among the 'bad doubtfuls', though this was later queried, and he voted against them in the crucial division on the civil list, 15 Nov. 1830. He divided for repeal of the Irish Subletting Act, 11 Nov. 1830. On 16 Jan. 1831 Robert Chaloner*, Fitzwilliam's Wicklow agent, informed Milton that he had received a 'petition got up by Howard' against repeal of the Union, which 'was very short and tolerably mild', and which he would 'endeavour to get well signed'.[5] On 24 Mar. Howard endorsed a similar one from the governors of county Wicklow against repeal and argued for reintroduction of the Act to suppress seditious meetings, observing that even in countries admired for their 'liberal institutions', popular meetings could not 'be held without the permission of the local authorities'. He presented petitions for the abolition of slavery, 13 Apr. He voted for the second reading of the Grey ministry's reform bill, 22 Mar., and against Gascoyne's wrecking amendment, 19 Apr. 1831. At the ensuing general election he offered as a reformer with the support of Fitzwilliam. It was reported that his cousin, the Tory 4th earl of Wicklow, attempted to turn him out, but he was returned unopposed.[6]

On 31 July 1831 he joined Brooks's, sponsored by Lords Charlemont and Gosford. He voted for the second reading of the reintroduced reform bill, 6 July, against adjournment, 12 July, and gave steady support to its details, though he was in the minorities against the disfranchisement of Downton, 21 July, and for giving two Members to Stoke-on-Trent, 4 Aug. He divided with ministers on the Dublin election controversy, 23 Aug. He voted for the reform bill's passage, 21 Sept., and Lord Ebrington's confidence motion, 10 Oct. He may have been the 'young Howard' who, according to Denis Le Marchant[†], on 'merely making an observation in no loud tone to a friend as he entered the House was so generally and distinctly heard as to be loudly called to order' during Lord John Russell's speech introducing the revised reform bill, 13 Dec.[7] He divided for its second reading, 17 Dec. 1831, and again steadily supported its details, though he voted for an amendment to enfranchise all persons rated to the poor at £10, 3 Feb. 1832. He divided for the third reading, 22 Mar., and the address calling on the king to appoint only ministers who would carry it unimpaired, 10 May. He voted with government on the Russian-Dutch loan, 26 Jan., 12, 16, 20 July, relations with Portugal, 9 Feb., and the navy civil departments bill, 6 Apr. On 16 Apr. he criticized Smith Stanley, the Irish secretary, for suggesting that the oath taken by Catholic Members barred them from participating in debates on questions concerning the Protestant church, adding that there was a 'great distinction to be ... between maintaining the established church, with all proportionate and decent state, and keeping up the preposterous splendour which some of its dignitaries now affect'. He voted for the second reading of the Irish reform bill, 25 May, and was in the minority for a tax on Irish absentee landlords to provide permanent provision for the poor, 19 June 1832.

At the 1832 general election Howard stood for county Wicklow as a Liberal and topped the poll. He was given a baronetcy by the second Melbourne ministry and sat until 1847, when he unsuccessfully contested Evesham. He came in again for county Wicklow at a by-election the following year and retired in 1852. He died in August 1873.[8]

[1] Hist. Irish Parl. iv. 444. [2] Dublin Evening Post, 22 June 1826. [3] Fitzwilliam mss, Milton to Proby, 5 Apr.; Dublin Evening Post, 21, 25 July 1829. [4] Dublin Evening Post, 12 Aug. 1830. [5] Fitzwilliam mss. [6] Hants RO, Carnarvon mss 75M91/L3, H. Howard to Lady Porchester, 12 May 1831. [7] NLS mss 24762, f. 49. [8] The Times, 16 Aug. 1873.

P.J.S.

HOWARD, Hon. William (1781–1843).

MORPETH	1806–1826
MORPETH	1830–1832
SUTHERLAND	1837–20 Mar. 1840

b. 25 Dec. 1781, 2nd s. of Frederick, 5th earl of Carlisle (*d.* 1825), and Margaret Caroline, da. of Granville Leveson Gower[†], 1st mq. of Stafford; bro. of George Howard, Visct. Morpeth[†]. *educ.* Raikes's sch., Neasden 1789; Eton 1793; Christ Church, Oxf. 1799; L. Inn 1802. *m* bef. 7 Nov. 1842, Mary Ann.[1] *d.* 25 Jan. 1843.

2nd lt. 1 N. Yorks. riflemen vols. 1798, lt. 1803, capt. 1803; capt. E. Yorks. militia 1805.

Frustrated in his hopes of a diplomatic career, Howard, an associate of the diarist Charles Greville, Charles Henry Bouverie[†], Sidney Herbert[†], Thomas Raikes and Charles Baring Wall[*], had been brought in for the family borough of Morpeth in 1806.[2] An indolent and silent Member, he had usually voted with his elder brother Lord Morpeth, a pro-Catholic Whig and friend of Canning, opposed to sweeping parliamentary reform, differing from him only in his readiness to vote against the repressive measures introduced by Lord Liverpool's administration after Peterloo. He was returned for Morpeth at the general election of 1820 and not required to make way when his brother was unseated in Cumberland.[3]

From 5 May 1820-16 May 1822, Howard, who is not known to have voted on reform before 1831, divided consistently with the main Whig opposition on all other issues. His majority vote for inquiry into the prosecution of the Dublin Orange rioters, 22 Apr. 1823, was the only one recorded for him that session and his last until 1825, when (as on 28 Feb. 1821) he divided for Catholic relief, 1 Mar., 21 Apr., 10 May. A radical publication of that session noted that he 'attended occasionally and voted with the opposition'.[4] Concern at his long absence had caused his brother to consult Lord Holland, whom he informed on 10 Nov. 1824 that William had been 'heard of' in Paris and 'is probably in England at this time'.[5] He inherited £15,000 in addition to his 1801 settlement of £10,500, on his father's death, 4 Sept. 1825, but estate debts precluded full payment.[6] He voted for inquiry into the silk trade, 24 Feb., and for Hume's state of the nation motion, 4 May 1826. Having 'no wish to continue in Parliament', he retired at the dissolution that month to accommodate his nephew Lord Morpeth, who was then abroad, and deputized for him at the election. He also briefed his brother (now 6th earl of Carlisle) on the Northumberland contest and the festivities requisite at Morpeth before his nephew took his seat in 1827.[7]

Appointed clerk of the peace for the East Riding of Yorkshire, 5 Jan. 1828, a 'valuable office' he held for life, Howard assisted his nephew in the contest for that county at the general election of 1830 and came in again for Morpeth as what he termed his 'eager but inadequate substitute'.[8] The Wellington ministry listed him among their 'foes' and he divided against them when they were brought down on the civil list, 15 Nov. 1830. He received a fortnight's leave on account of ill health, 2 Dec. Obliged to support the new Grey administration of which Carlisle was a member, he divided for their reform bill, which threatened Morpeth's second seat, at its second reading, 22 Mar., and against Gascoyne's wrecking amendment, 19 Apr. 1831, after Morpeth had been reprieved. He presented a petition for the abolition of colonial slavery from Blyth, 13 Apr., and was returned for Morpeth as a reformer at the general election that month.[9] He divided for the reintroduced reform bill at its second reading, 6 July, and against the adjournment, 12 July 1831, but rarely for its details. He criticized the comparison made by its opponents between Appleby and Morpeth, 19 July, having defended his record that day as chairman of the select committee on the Arundel road bill, which was the subject of a critical petition presented by Lord Dudley Stuart from the Tory whip, Holmes. He voted for the reform bill's passage, 21 Sept., and Lord Ebrington's confidence motion, 10 Oct. He did not divide on the revised reform bill, which returned Morpeth to schedule B, at its second reading 17 Dec. 1831, or for the schedule B disfranchisements, 23 Jan.; but he voted for its proposals for Appleby, 21 Feb., Helston, 23 Feb., and Tower Hamlets, 28 Feb., and for its third reading, 22 Mar.

1832. He divided with government on the Russian-Dutch loan, 26 Jan., and presented a Morpeth petition against the general register bill, 28 Feb. 1832.

Howard stood down at the dissolution of 1832 and remained out of Parliament until 1837, when his kinswoman the dowager duchess of Sutherland returned him for Sutherland as a Conservative, which, as he had warned Peel the previous year would be the case, he was obliged by the 2nd duke to vacate in March 1840 on account of his politics.[10] He died in January 1843. On 10 Feb., correcting its obituary statement that Howard had been unmarried, the *Morning Herald* disclosed that though it was 'not mentioned in the *Peerages*', he had 'left an afflicted widow'. By his will, which was proved under £8,000, he left everything to his wife.[11]

[1] Howard was not, as stated in *HP Commons, 1790-1820*, iv. 256, unmarried. Details of his marriage are not known, but it is confirmed by his will, dated 7 Nov. 1842 and proved 13 Feb. 1843 (PROB 8/236; 11/1975/108; Castle Howard mss [NRA 24681] A5/159). [2] *Greville Mems.* i. 350; *Raikes Jnl.* i. 272; ii. 372. [3] *Newcastle Courant*, 18 Mar., 25 Mar.; *The Times*, 25 Mar. 1820. [4] *Session of Parl. 1825*, p. 469. [5] Add. 51578, Morpeth to Holland, 10 Nov. 1824. [6] Add. 51590, Agar Ellis to Lady Holland, 1 Aug. 1825; Castle Howard mss A5/129; J14/1/20; IR26/1039/1321. [7] Add. 51580, Carlisle to Lady Holland, 2 May; Castle Howard mss, Howard to Carlisle, 10 June 1826, 4 Jan. 1827; *The Times*, 12 June 1826. [8] Castle Howard mss [NRA 24681] W2; *Leeds Mercury*, 11 Feb. 1843; *Newcastle Chron.* 7 Aug. 1830. [9] *Tyne Mercury*, 26 Apr., 10 May 1831. [10] Add. 40246, f. 164; *The Times*, 18, 19, 21, 23, 27 Mar. 1840. [11] *Morning Herald*, 30 Jan., 10 Feb.; *Gent. Mag.* (1843), ii. 92; PROB 8/236; 11/1975/108.

M.M.E.

HOWARD MOLYNEUX HOWARD, Lord Henry Thomas (1766–1824), of Thornbury Castle, Glos.

ARUNDEL	1790–Feb. 1795
GLOUCESTER	11 Feb. 1795–1818
ARUNDEL	1818–1820
STEYNING	1820–17 June 1824

b. 7 Oct. 1766, 2nd s. of Henry Howard (*d.* 1787) of Glossop, Derbys. and Juliana, da. of Sir William Molyneux, 6th bt., of Teversall, Notts. *m.* 12 Sept. 1801, Elizabeth, da. of Edward Long of Aldermaston, Berks., c.j. vice-admiralty ct. of Jamaica, 1s. 4da. *suc.* cos. Edward Howard, 9th duke of Norfolk, to Thornbury 1777; mat. uncle Sir Francis Molyneux, 7th bt., to Teversall and Wellow, Notts. and took additional name of Molyneux by royal lic. July 1812. Having resumed surname of Howard, granted precedence as yr. s. of a duke (his bro. Bernard Edward Howard having *suc.* their cos. Charles Howard as 12th duke of Norfolk 16 Dec. 1815) and *styled* Lord Henry Thomas Howard Molyneux Howard 15 Oct. 1817–*d.* 17 June 1824.

Dep. earl marshal 1816-*d.*; high steward, Gloucester. Capt. N. Glos. militia 1790, maj. 1794, lt.-col. 1798.

Howard was returned unopposed for Steyning on the family interest in 1820, despite rumours that his brother, the 12th duke of Norfolk, would not bring him into Parliament again because of his refusal to vote against the Liverpool ministry's Six Acts.[1] His brother's Catholicism debarred him from exercising the ceremonial duties of his hereditary office of earl marshal and it fell to Howard as his deputy to supervise the arrangements for George IV's coronation. This work occupied much of his attention in 1820 and 1821, but illness prevented him from officiating at the ceremony itself, 19 July 1821.[2] Poor health also interfered with his parliamentary attendance. He is not known to have spoken in debate in this period and his name appears in none of the surviving division lists of the first three sessions of the 1820 Parliament. He was granted lengthy periods of leave for ill health, 12 Feb., 13 Apr. 1821. He resurfaced to vote with his Whig friends for repeal of the Foreign Enlistment Act, 16 Apr., parliamentary reform, 24 Apr., and the Scottish juries bill, 20 June 1823. He divided against the grant for building new churches, 9 Apr., and for repeal of the assessed taxes, 10 May 1824.

Described as a 'fat *bon vivant*, an accumulation of many years' turtle and venison', Howard died in June 1824. He left Thornbury Castle to his only son Henry Howard*, and other real estate and the residue of personal estate sworn under £90,000 was divided between all his children.[3]

[1] E. Suss. RO, Ashburnham mss 3242, Egremont to Ashburnham, 1 Mar. 1820. [2] *Geo. IV Letters*, ii. 927; Add. 38284, f. 263; 38286, f. 3; 38289, f. 210; *Gent. Mag.* (1824), ii. 81. [3] *Countess Granville Letters*, i. 138; PROB 11/1689/469-70; IR26/1004/889.

D.R.F.

HOWICK, Visct. *see* **GREY**, **Henry**

HOY, **James Barlow** (?1794–1843), of Midanbury and Thornhill, Hants and The Hermitage, I.o.W.

SOUTHAMPTON	13 Jan. 1830–1831
SOUTHAMPTON	1832–2 Apr. 1833
SOUTHAMPTON	1835–1837

b. ?1794,[1] *s.* of John Barlow of Dublin and w. Anne. *m.* 10 Sept. 1831, Marian D'Oyley, da. and h. of Shearman Bird of Harold's Park, Essex, 1 da. *suc.* kinsman Michael Hoy to Midanbury and Thornhill estates and The Hermitage 1828; took name of Hoy by royal lic. 26 Jan. 1829. *d.* 13 Aug. 1843.

2nd asst. surgeon, ordnance medical dept. 1813, half-pay 1819, returned to dept. 1825, 1st asst. surgeon 1827, ret. 1828.[2]

Hoy, originally Barlow, was said to have been 'a native of Ireland' by an obituarist.[3] His mother's name is given in his will, but the identification of his father rests on the assumption that his brother and executor, the Rev. Robert Joseph Barlow, was the individual admitted to Trinity College, Dublin, 6 Nov. 1820, aged 16, who had been born in that city to one John Barlow, possibly the printer of that name listed by the trade directories at 29 Bolton Street from the mid-1790s until about 1817.[4] No further details of Barlow's origins or education have been found. He was serving as a surgeon in the ordnance medical department when a fortunate inheritance dramatically altered his life. His benefactor was Michael Hoy, a former Russia merchant of Bishopsgate, London, and later of Walthamstow, Essex, who had purchased extensive landed property in Hampshire and the Isle of Wight. On his death, 26 June 1828, Barlow, a distant cousin described as a 'friend' in Hoy's will, succeeded to his estates and his personalty, which amounted to almost £90,000. Probate was granted, 9 July, and Barlow left the army, 21 July, indicating that his stroke of fortune may not have been unanticipated. In January 1829 he voluntarily adopted the name of Hoy out of 'grateful and affectionate regard' for his kinsman.[5]

In December 1819 he announced his candidacy for a vacancy at Southampton and, aided by the local prestige of his late relative, who had been an honorary burgess there since 1824, secured the support of the mercantile interest. In his first address, issued from Midanbury, he professed himself to be 'perfectly independent in principles and in politics'. A friendly newspaper added that he was 'a Protestant by education' and 'of independent fortune'. With the advantage of an early canvass and the alleged backing of the Tory sitting Member, he easily defeated his radically inclined opponent, and was chaired during a blizzard.[6] In his victory speeches, which contained no professions beyond a promise to judge each issue on its merits, he paid tribute to his benefactor, who, he claimed, had once been honoured with a handshake from the visiting Tsar Alexander I, and spoke of his 'family pride at being elevated to my present status by the mercantile and trading interests'. His return reputedly cost him £9,000.[7] He was belatedly elected a burgess of Southampton and sworn in as its Member, 5 Feb. 1830.[8] He voted for the transfer of East Retford's seats to Birmingham, 11 Feb., 5 Mar., and the enfranchisement of Birmingham, Leeds and

Manchester, 23 Feb. He divided for a reduction of the grant for army volunteers, 9 Mar., and for omission of the Bathurst and Dundas pensions from the civil list, 26 Mar., to the approval of local newspaper, which took these votes as evidence of his genuine independence.[9] He was in the minorities for abolition of the Irish lord lieutenancy, 11 May, returns of privy councillors' emoluments, 14 May, and against the provision of the beer bill allowing on-consumption, 21 June. Most sources list him in the majority for abolition of the death penalty for forgery, 7 June, but a local press report insisted that he had abstained.[10] At a meeting of the Southampton New Forest Archers in July 1830 he 'distinguished himself by the accuracy of his aim' and that September he took first prize in their competition.[11]

At the 1830 general election he offered again as 'a straightforward independent man ... not calling myself Whig or Tory, a servant of ministry or radical reformer', citing his efforts to lobby ministers for an upgrade in Southampton's port status and attachment to church and state, but insisting that he was 'no enemy to rational improvement'. He was returned unopposed.[12] That October he attended a meeting in support of the London and Southampton railway.[13] He was listed by the Wellington ministry as one of the 'bad doubtfuls', but divided with them in the crucial division on the civil list, 15 Nov. He presented petitions against slavery, 11, 16 Nov., 11 Dec. On 16 Dec. 1830 he clashed with Hume, who after presenting a radically inclined Southampton petition for parliamentary reform, commented that the Southampton Members had forfeited the confidence of their constituents. Hoy, who claimed to have attended the meeting at which it was drawn up, retorted that support for the petition had not been unanimous and attacked Hume's insufferable self-righteousness, for which he won press plaudits.[14] In January 1831 he made a donation of books to the Southampton Mechanics' Institution.[15] He presented an Isle of Wight petition against the proposed duty on steamboat passengers and secured returns of the relevant figures, 21 Feb. He denounced the tax as a 'check on the improvement of civilization', 28 Feb., and brought up a hostile Southampton petition, 14 Mar. That day he expressed concern that the Grey ministry's reform scheme would make future alterations of the corn laws impossible through its perpetuation of the dominant influence of landed proprietors, among whom, he curiously did not count himself. He asked Poulett Thomson, vice-president of the board of trade, whether any relaxation of restrictions on silk imports was contemplated, 18 Mar., and on receiving a negative response complained that

he had expected better from the ministry. He voted against the second reading of the reform bill, 22 Mar., and in a speech sprinkled with Latin tags, asserted that its disfranchisement provisions, in particular, were revolutionary, 30 Mar. He spoke against Hume's proposals for further reductions in the civil list, 18 Apr., and divided for Gascoyne's wrecking amendment to the reform bill, 19 Apr. His name was roundly hissed at a Southampton reform meeting, 25 Apr. 1831.[16]

At the 1831 general election Hoy defiantly offered again. On the hustings he claimed that 'he was always in his place; not an evening he had missed', and warned of the added influence that the reform bill would give to Ireland, and hence to Catholics. He welcomed the enfranchisement of new boroughs but was only willing to concede the disfranchisement of non-resident ancient right voters. Trailing badly, he retired after a four-day poll. In his parting address he defended his decision to make 'an example of resistance to the torrent, which in my opinion threatens our constitution'.[17] In September he married the young heiress to an estate near Waltham Abbey, Essex. He declined an invitation to serve as sheriff of Hampshire in February 1832, having been a deputy lieutenant since January 1831.[18] At the 1832 general election he narrowly regained his Southampton seat from his former rival, but was then unseated on petition, after offering no defence to charges of voter impersonation beyond a disclaimer of personal involvement or knowledge.[19] He topped the poll at the 1835 election, when he was reportedly returned free of expense and classed as a 'moderate reformer', but retired at the 1837 dissolution, his wife's declining health having forced him to go abroad.[20] In November 1841 Peel, the premier, sought his support for a new Conservative candidate at Southampton. Hoy, who addressed his reply from Thornhill, requested 'a few minutes conversation', but as Peel had surmised, had no intention of offering again.[21]

Hoy died in August 1843 at the Hospice de Vielle in the French Pyrenees. He had left England some month's earlier, once more, it was stated, for the sake of his wife's health, but met with a fatal accident in the pursuit of his hobby of collecting rare bird specimens. Whilst crossing a ravine just over the Spanish border with a shooting party his gun fell from his hand and fired, shattering his left arm. He was conveyed to hospital but died within twenty-four hours from tetanus.[22] By his will, dated 18 May 1843, his wife was given a choice of residence at The Hermitage or Thornhill, on which estate his mother was provided with a cottage for life. He made generous provision for one Eleanor

Maria Pera, an adopted daughter, but it is unclear to what extent his instructions were carried out, as his personal estate was dwarfed by mortgage debts of £58,500 and he was declared insolvent, suggesting another possible reason for his continental sojourns. Louisa Hoy, his only lawful child, probably derived little benefit as his residuary legatee, though at least a portion of The Hermitage estate seems to have eventually passed to her intact. In 1860 she married one Guadagno Guadagni, the son of a Tuscan aristocrat, while Hoy's widow took a second husband, the author John Richard Digby Beste of Botleigh, Hamphire.[23]

[1] Based on *Hants Advertiser*, 26 Dec. 1829, which gives his age as 35. [2] A. Peterkin and W. Johnson, *Medical Officers in British Army*, i. 3719. [3] *Gent. Mag.* (1843), ii. 547. [4] PROB 11/1990/851. [5] *Gent. Mag.* (1828), i. 647; PROB 11/1743/417; IR26/1166/556; Peterson and Johnson, i. 3719; *London Gazette*, 27 Jan. 1829. [6] *The Age*, 26 Dec.; *Hants Advertiser*, 11, 26 Dec. 1829, 16 Jan. 1830; *Southampton Corporation Jnls*. ed. A. Temple Patterson, 38. [7] *Hants Advertiser*, 23, 30 Jan. 1830. [8] Ibid. 6 Feb. 1830. [9] Ibid. 3 Apr. 1830. [10] Ibid. 19 June 1830. [11] *Salisbury Jnl.* 26 July, 23 Aug., 13 Sept. 1830. [12] *Southampton Mercury*, 7 Aug.; *Hants Advertiser*, 7 Aug. 1830. [13] Temple Patterson, *Hist. Southampton*, i. 166. [14] *Hants Advertiser*, 18 Dec. 1831. [15] Ibid. 15 Jan. 1831. [16] Ibid. 30 Apr. 1831. [17] Ibid. 7 May 1831. [18] *VCH Essex*, v. 159; Wellington mss WP4/3/1/2; 4/1/9. [19] *Hants Advertiser*, 15 Dec. 1831; Temple Patterson, i. 172-3. [20] *The Times*, 10 Jan. 1835, 12, 18 July 1837; *Dod's Parl. Companion* (1835), 130; Temple Patterson, ii. 33. [21] Add. 40496, ff. 26-28. [22] *Gent. Mag.* (1843), ii. 547; *Salisbury Jnl.* 26 Aug.; *Hants Independent*, 26 Aug.; *Hants Chron.* 28 Aug. 1843. [23] PROB 11/1990/851; IR26/1647/791.

H.J.S./P.J.S.

HUDSON, **Harrington** (1772–1826), of Bessingby Hall, nr. Bridlington, Yorks. and 16 New Norfolk Street, Mdx.

HELSTON   1818–1826

b. 11 Apr. 1772, o.s. of John Hudson of Bessingby and Susannah, da. of Sir George Trevelyan, 3rd bt., of Nettlecombe, Som. *educ.* Westminster 1783; St. John's, Camb. 1789. *m.* 26 Oct. 1795, Lady Anne Townshend, da. of George Townshend†, 1st Mq. Townshend, 5s. 3da. *suc.* fa. 1805.[1] *d.* 29 Nov. 1826.
    Ensign E. Yorks. militia 1791, lt. 1793, capt. 1794; capt. Bridlington vol. riflemen 1803.

Hudson, who inherited approximately 1,000 acres in the East Riding of Yorkshire from his father,[2] was returned for Helston for the second time in 1820 on his brother-in-law the 6th duke of Leeds's interest, after a contest forced by an 'independent' party among the freemen.[3] He was a silent Member and an infrequent attender, who continued to give general support to Lord Liverpool's ministry. He voted against repeal of the additional malt duty, 3 Apr. 1821, and more exten-

sive tax reductions, 11 Feb. 1822. However, he divided in the minorities for a 40s. fixed duty on corn, 8 May, and a permanent 18s. bounty on exports, 9 May, when he was against the proposed new scale of duties. He voted against the removal of Catholic peers' disabilities, 30 Apr. 1822. He divided against inquiry into the prosecution of the Dublin Orange rioters, 22 Apr. 1823. He paired against Catholic relief, 1 Mar., 21 Apr., 10 May 1825. He voted for the financial provision for the duke of Cumberland, 30 May, 6, 10 June 1825. It was said of him at this time that he 'appeared to attend seldom, and to vote with ministers'.[4] He retired at the dissolution in 1826 and died that November, leaving his estate to his eldest son Harrington Hudson (1798-1848); his personalty was sworn under £11,000.[5]

[1] There is a wall tablet in Bessingby church (N. Pevsner, *Buildings of England: York and East Riding* (1995), 276-7. [2] *VCH Yorks. E. Riding*, ii. 17-21. [3] *R. Cornw. Gazette*, 11 Mar. 1820. [4] *Session of Parl. 1825*, p. 469. [5] PROB 11/1723/164; IR26/1131/1031.

T.A.J.

HUDSON, **Thomas** (1772–1852), of Cheswardine Hill Hall, nr. Market Drayton, Salop and 6 Park Crescent, Portland Place, Mdx.

EVESHAM   1831–1834

b. 18 Oct. 1772, 3rd but o. surv. s. of Thomas Hudson (*d.* 1807) of Wigton, Cumb. and Ann, da. of William Dodgson of Wigton. *m.* Frances, da. of Robert Bamford Hesketh of Bamford, Lancs. and Gwyrch Castle, Denb., *s.p. d.* 14 Apr. 1852.

Hudson was a Cumbrian of humble origins. His father, a Wigton shopkeeper who is said to have died in 1807 aged 66, has been erroneously identified with the Thomas Hudson who was clerk to the cathedral chapter of Carlisle and still alive many years later. His eldest brother Robert, born in 1764, joined the navy but was killed in action on the *Magicienne*, 2 Jan. 1783. Another brother, Samuel, died an infant in 1771. His sister Elizabeth married Alexander Donaldson, a Wigton watchmaker, and bore several sons.[1] Thomas Hudson's early life is obscure, but by 1805 he was in business at 35 Mark Lane, London as a wine merchant, dealing mainly in the produce of Portugal. He seems to have retired from the firm in about 1827 and handed it over to one or more of his Donaldson nephews, with whom he had been in partnership since about 1813. (It traded as Donaldson and Dixon from 1828 to 1850.) He may have been involved in the wine business of Hudson and Williamson at 13 Berners Street, which was listed in the London directories between 1826 and 1828. In 1825 he invested some of his wealth in a Shropshire estate.

At the 1826 general election Hudson stood for Marlborough as part of an abortive bid by the independent association to overthrow the Ailesbury interest. His petition against the return was unsuccessful.[2] In 1831 he offered as a reformer for the open and venal borough of Evesham. Returned in second place after an expensive contest, he promised to 'steadily support' the reform bill, which would be 'beneficial to the king, the peers and the people'.[3] He duly voted for the second reading of the reintroduced bill, 6 July 1831, and gave steadfast support to its details, though he was in the minority against the enfranchisement of weekly tenants and lodgers, 25 Aug. He contended that Evesham was 'much superior to many boroughs that will continue to send two Members' and should keep both seats, but did not oppose its proposed loss of one, 28 July. (The borough subsequently retained both.) He divided with ministers on the Dublin election controversy, 29 July, 23 Aug., and for the issue of the Liverpool writ, 5 Sept. That day he secured returns of information concerning shipping, trade and the drawback on wine. He was in the minority of 20 against the quarantine duties, 6 Sept., and argued for printing the evidence given to the Pembrokeshire election committee. He voted for the third reading and passage of the reform bill, 19, 21 Sept., and for Lord Ebrington's confidence motion, 10 Oct. 1831.

Hudson divided for the second reading of the revised reform bill, 17 Dec. 1831, again steadily supported its details, and voted for the third reading, 22 Mar. 1832. He divided with ministers on the Russian-Dutch loan, 26 Jan., 12, 16, 20 July, and relations with Portugal, 9 Feb. He obtained more returns on trade, 9 Apr., and later that day voted against the recommittal of the Irish registry bill. He divided for the address calling on the king to appoint only ministers who would carry the reform bill unimpaired, 10 May, and paired for the second reading of the Irish bill, 25 May 1832. At that year's general election he successfully contested Evesham as a Liberal, but he retired at the dissolution of 1834. He died in London in April 1852. By his will, dated 29 June 1850 with a codicil made the day before his death, he provided his wife with a life annuity of £800, in addition to her benefits from their marriage settlement, and devised his real estate in Madeira to his nephew Robert Donaldson. Further annuities were given to the children of his nephew John Donaldson, Anne and Thomas Donaldson, to whom he also transferred a debt of £10,000 owed him by the firm of Henry and John Donaldson (as it

was now styled). His Shropshire property, subject to his widow's life interest, passed to John Donaldson's second son Charles (1840-93), Conservative Member for Newcastle-under-Lyme, 1880-85, who took the additional name of Hudson in 1862.[4]

[1] Wigton Reg. (Cumb. and Westmld. Antiq. and Arch. Soc.), ii. 294, 332, 305, 421, 473; Burke LG; C. R. Hudleston and R. S. Boumphrey, Cumb. Fams. 174; Brougham mss, T. Hudson to J. Brougham, 26 Oct. 1828. [2] The Times, 17 June 1826; VCH Wilts. v. 214. [3] Worcester Herald, 29 Apr., 6 May; Berrow's Worcester Jnl. 12 May 1831. [4] Gent. Mag. (1852), i. 634; PROB 8/245; 11/2156/566.

D.R.F./P.J.S.

HUGHES, James (1778–1845), of Llysdulas, Anglesey and Berkeley Square, Mdx.

GRANTHAM	1820–11 July 1820
GRANTHAM	1831–1832

b. 12 Nov. 1778, 3rd s. Rev. Edward Hughes (d. 1815) of Kinmel Park, Denb. and Mary, da. and coh. of Robert Lewis of Llysdulas; bro. of William Lewis Hughes*. m. 16 Mar. 1841, Frances Anne Jane, da. of Sir Francis Charles Stanhope, s.p. CB 4 June 1815. d. 28 Nov. 1845.
Cornet 16 Drag. 1800; lt. 18 Drag. 16 Sept. 1802, capt. 22 Sept. 1802, maj. 1812, lt.-col. 1817, half-pay 1821; col. 1837.

Hughes, unlike his elder brother William, Member for Wallingford, 1802-1831, played no active part in the family's copper mining business, whence came their immense wealth, but followed a military career. He saw active service in the Peninsula and was wounded in the cavalry assault at Mayorga. During the retreat from Corunna, he commanded the Hussars as they formed 'the last picket of the British cavalry, which remained until whole embarkation had taken place'. Later, while stationed in the south of France, he was 'severely wounded' in an action near Hellette.[1] He shared his brother's Whig politics and joined Brooks's, 7 May 1816. Whilst in France, he accepted an invitation from the Grantham freemen living in London to come forward at the 1818 general election in opposition to the candidates of the influential Brownlow and Manners famililes. Though first in the field, obtaining permission to leave delayed his departure and he arrived only just in time for the poll. His backers William Ostler, an attorney and the town clerk, and Sir John Thorold of nearby Syston Park urged to him continue, but he received only 14 votes. On his return to France he was court martialled on a charge of going absent without leave, but cleared after it was shown that his leave order had arrived before his departure.[2]

At the 1820 general election he offered again for Grantham, after an encouraging private canvass on his behalf and amid reports of support from the duke of Devonshire and Lord George Cavendish*. Branded by his opponents as a 'radical' and a 'coppermonger', who was 'totally unconnected' with the borough, on the hustings he clarified his alleged 'radicalism', saying that 'he did not exactly understand the meaning of that title, but if it means a Spencean, or a disciple of annual parliaments and universal suffrage, the accusation was unjust, as he was no advocate for such chimerical doctrines'. He assured them of his support for the 'glorious constitution' and added that nothing appeared more dangerous to him than attempts 'to control and influence elections'.[3] After a three-day poll he was returned in second place. Shortly after the declaration an address from 'H. Manners of Buckminster' appeared in the local press denouncing Hughes as 'an upstart coppermonger' and 'an ungentlemanlike exciter of tenants against landlords and workmen against masters', and claiming to have sufficient 'proofs of bribery against this adventurer' to unseat him on petition.[4] In a published response, Hughes named the writer as Sir William Manners†, as 'no one lives at Buckminster to whom the signature can apply but one of your sons, who is yet quite a boy', dismissed the comments about being 'a coppermonger, ironmonger, or any other monger that implied honest and honourable commerce', and explained that he demanded an explanation for the charge of ungentlemanlike conduct, to which he could not be 'permitted to ... be indifferent', but had received no reply. 'What can be expected from a man who, in the exercise of low scurrility, is unrestrained by the dignity of sex, rank or the general estimation in which the object of his impotent violence is held?', he asked, before conjecturing that Manners's motive was to close the borough.[5]

Hughes is not known to have spoken in debate. It is not clear whether it was he or his brother, a colonel in the militia, who was the 'Col. Hughes' listed in the minority on the civil list, 5 May, but he voted with opposition on the same issue, 8 May, and against the appointment of an additional Scottish baron of exchequer, 15 May, and the continuation of the Aliens Act, 1 June, and may have been the 'Col. Hughes' in the minority for reducing the standing army, 14 June 1820. He divided against the motion urging Queen Caroline to compromise her stance, 22 June. Following the presentation of Manners's petition an election committee was appointed, 10 July. Next day they unseated Hughes, citing his illegal payments to out-voters to 'indemnify them for loss of time', a practice which

they believed had been sufficiently general to necessitate a by-election, from which he was excluded.[6] In his parting address, 19 July 1820, Hughes claimed to have been unfairly targeted by Manners and promised that he would 'not abandon' the borough.[7] At the ensuing by-election he helped to bring up the London out-voters in the successful campaign against Manners's eldest son.[8]

At the 1831 general election he accepted an invitation from the London freemen to offer again for Grantham, following the unexpected retirement of the pro-reform Member because of ill health and the candidature of two of Manners's sons. In his campaign he claimed to have been 'content with his retirement, provided your independence was secure', but explained that he now felt compelled to act, adding that 'time had made no change to his principles', which 'remained what they had always been, most decidedly in favour of reform'. After a three-day poll he was returned in second place, ahead of Manners's sons.[9] He voted for the second reading of the reintroduced reform bill, 6 July, against the adjournment, 12 July, and gave generally steady support to the bill's details, though he was in the minority against the proposed division of counties, 11 Aug. Listed in error by *The Times* in the minority against Lord Chandos's amendment to enfranchise £50 tenants-at-will, 18 Aug., he wrote to explain that he had abstained:

> Entertaining the opinion that ... property, even to its minimum, should have a share in the election of representatives, I could not in the abstract object to the franchise being given to tenants paying £50 ... while I could not be insensible to the argument of Lord Milton about the derivative right of voting, which ... appears to me to have great weight ... particularly since ... the division of counties prevents the expansion of the voter's opinion out of that part of the country where he is irresistibly influenced by the immediate personal claims of his landlord ... Under the confliction of these considerations, I declined to vote ... I trust the division of counties will, at all events, become unnecessary.[10]

He voted for the third reading, 19 Sept., and passage of the bill, 21 Sept., and Lord Ebrington's confidence motion, 10 Oct. 1831. He divided for the second reading of the revised reform bill, 17 Dec. 1831, again silently supported its details, and voted for the third reading, 22 Mar. 1832. He was in the minority of 51 for printing the Woollen Grange petition for the abolition of Irish tithes, 16 Feb. He divided for the address calling on the king to appoint only ministers who would carry reform unimpaired, 10 May, the second reading of the Irish reform bill, 25 May, and against a Conservative amendment to increase Scottish county representation, 1 June, but was in the minority for O'Connell's motion to extend the Irish county franchise to £5 freeholders, 18 June. He voted with ministers on the Russian-Dutch loan, 26 Jan., 12, 16, 20 July, and relations with Portugal, 9 Feb. At the 1832 dissolution he retired from politics.

Hughes died intestate in Florence in November 1845. Administration of his estate passed to his widow.[11]

[1] *Gent. Mag.* (1846), i. 209. [2] UCNW, Hughes of Kinmel mss 1581. [3] *The Times,* 15 Feb. 1820; *Grantham Pollbook* (Ridge, 1820), 8, 19-20; (Storr, 1820), 8, 13. [4] *Drakard's Stamford News,* 24 Mar. 1820. [5] Ibid. 14 Apr. 1820. [6] *The Times,* 6, 12 July 1820. [7] *Lincoln, Rutland and Stamford Mercury,* 21 July 1820. [8] *The Times,* 20 Nov. 1820. [9] *Boston Gazette,* 3 May 1831; *Grantham Pollbook* (Ridge, 1831), *passim.* [10] *The Times,* 19, 20 Aug. 1831. [11] PROB 6/222/46; IR26/264/253.

M.P.J.C./P.J.S.

HUGHES, William Lewis (1767–1852), of Kinmel Park, nr. St. Asaph, Denb.

WALLINGFORD   1802–10 Sept. 1831

b. 10 Nov. 1767, 1st s. of Rev. Edward Hughes of Kinmel and Mary, da. and coh. of Robert Lewis of Llysdulas, Anglesey; bro. of James Hughes*. *educ.* Felsted; Christ Church, Oxf. 1786. *m.* (1) 8 Mar. 1804, Charlotte Margaret (*d.* 21 Jan. 1835), da. of Ralph William Grey of Backworth, Northumb., 2s. (1 *d.v.p.*) 8da. (6 *d.v.p.*); (2) 11 Feb. 1840, Gertrude, da. of Grice Blakeney Smyth of Ballynatray, co. Waterford, 2da. (1 *d.v.p.*). *suc.* fa. 1815; *cr.* Bar. Dinorben 10 Sept. 1831. *d.* 10 Feb. 1852.

Militia a.d.c. to Queen Victoria 1840-*d.*

Capt. (vols.) R. Anglesey militia 1794, maj. 1798, lt.-col. cmmdt. 1803, col. 1808.

Hughes derived his considerable wealth from the proceeds of the Parys Mountain copper mine in Anglesey, on which his father had founded the family's fortune. He had also inherited landed property in Anglesey, Caernarvonshire, Denbighshire and Flintshire, and was a partner in the Chester and North Wales Bank.[1] Although he was a Whig by conviction, a friend of Sir Francis Burdett* and John Cam Hobhouse* and their set and a contributor to party funds, he had never been the most dedicated of parliamentary attenders. He maintained the same relaxed attitude in this period, until the reform crisis belatedly stirred his interest. By dint of his wealth and acreage, he carried some weight in North Wales electoral politics, in particular by helping to prop up his brother-in-law Sir Robert Williams in Caernarvonshire; but he never forcefully asserted himself, and mostly avoided active involvement in political campaigns.[2] At the general election of 1820 he stood again for Wallingford, where venality and systematic bribery were entrenched, and where he had maintained a strong interest since 1802 on the basis of his money, though it was alleged that he was never seen in the borough from one election to the next. When the leaders of a new campaign to eradicate corruption, inspired by the Tory corporation, offered him their support, he apparently refused to subscribe to their resolutions in favour of electoral purity, which he said was a matter for electors rather than candidates. He topped the poll after a contest forced by the intrusion of another Whig, who ousted the Tory sitting Member. Just over two years later, it seems, the notorious 'Miller' of Wallingford, a local shoemaker, duly distributed packets of sovereigns to Hughes's supporters, who were mostly impoverished men.[3]

It is not clear whether it was Hughes or his brother James who voted with opposition on the civil list, 5 May 1820, but he was in their minorities on the same subject, 8 May, and the additional Scottish baron of exchequer, 15 May. He voted against the aliens bill, 1 June, 7 July. Either he or James voted to reduce the standing army, 14 June. He divided against Wilberforce's resolution calling for compromise in the Queen Caroline affair, 22 June, and the barrack agreement bill, 17 July. He was one of Hobhouse's minority of 12 in favour of a prorogation, 18 Sept. 1820. He joined in the opposition onslaught on government over their treatment of the queen in the first weeks of the 1821 session. He voted to condemn the Allies' repression of the liberal movement in Naples, 21 Feb., and for Catholic relief, 28 Feb. He was in small minorities for receiving the petition of Nathan Broadhurst complaining of his treatment in Lancaster gaol, 7 Mar., Creevey's motion for a reduction in the number of office-holders in the House, 9 Mar., and delaying the army estimates, 12 Mar.; but his only subsequent known votes that session were for repeal of the additional malt duty, 3 Apr., inquiry into Peterloo, 16 May, and economy and retrenchment, 27 June. Although he was listed as one of the stewards of the *London Tavern* reform dinner, 4 Apr. 1821, he did not attend.[4] Hughes voted for the amendment to the address, 5 Feb., against details of the Irish insurrection bill, 8 Feb., and in support of Sir Robert Wilson* over his dismissal from the army, 13 Feb. 1822. After voting for more extensive tax reductions to relieve distress, 21 Feb., he divided for the production of information on naval pay, 22 Feb., relaxation of the salt tax, 28 Feb., economies at the admiralty, 1 Mar., and in the army, 4 Mar., and inquiry into the duties of officers of the board of control, 14 Mar. He voted for Russell's parliamentary reform motion, 25 Apr., abolition of one of the joint-postmasterships, 2 May, the payment of naval and military pensions from the sinking fund, 3 May, and cuts in diplomatic expenditure, 15, 16 May. His only other known votes in 1822 were for inquiry into chancery administration and against the pensions bill, 26 June, and for repeal of the salt duties, 28 June. He was a conspicuously infrequent voter during the following four sessions. He divided against the national debt reduction bill, 13, 17 Mar., for a repeal of assessed taxes, 18 Mar., against the dead-weight pensions bill, 14 Apr., for repeal of the Foreign Enlistment Act, 16 Apr., and for inquiry into the prosecution of the Dublin Orange rioters, 22 Apr. 1823. He was in a minority of 13 against the trial of capital offenders in the army by court martial, 11 July 1823. His only recorded votes in 1824 were for inquiry into the state of Ireland, 11 May, and proper use of Irish first fruits revenues, 25 May. He was given a month's leave to deal with urgent private business, 15 Feb. 1825. He went up to vote for Catholic relief, 21 Apr., and against the Irish franchise bill, 26 Apr., and was present to divide against the duke of Cumberland's grant, 30 May, 2 June, and for a reduction in judges' salaries, 17 June 1825. In late October he wrote to Hobhouse from Kinmel Park that he had 'no thought of leaving the country before Christmas or indeed, unless compelled, before the meeting of Parliament'.[5] In the event, his first known votes in the 1826 session were against government on the salary of the president of the board of trade, 7, 10 Apr. He paired in favour of reform of Edinburgh's representation, 13 Apr., but voted in person for Russell's general reform proposals, 27 Apr. 1826.

From November 1825 Hughes had been vilified as a hypocrite and sham reformer in the Tory *Berkshire Chronicle*, which mounted a campaign to expose the 'Miller' system at Wallingford. In March 1826 he announced his intention of standing at the next election and, joining forces with his Whig colleague Robarts, canvassed in response to threats of opposition which then came to nothing.[6] At the election in June John Dodson*, an anti-Catholic Tory, started on the independent interest. On the hustings, Dodson's proposer, Alderman Charles Allnatt, repeatedly asked Hughes to renounce bribery, but he remained silent until, giving thanks after his return at the head of the poll, with Robarts in second place, he replied to his critics, assuming for himself the mantle of 'a genuine Whig', but disclaiming slavish adherence to a party line. He asserted that he had consistently voted for an extension of the franchise:

I have always felt convinced of the necessity for general parliamentary reform, but I never have been friendly to that species of reform which would have borne on the poor elector only while it left the borough proprietor in undisturbed possession of his property ... On this principle I refrained from voting for the disfranchising of Grampound, because I would not consent to disfranchise that borough, while so many equally corrupt were to be left untouched ... and which had for a series of years been held as property by individual patrons, which had been repeatedly been publicly brought to market.

He added that for this reason he had not felt able to vote for Russell's resolutions of 26 May 1826 aimed at curbing the practice of electoral bribery, 'which (however well intentioned) would have the effect of throwing a stronger fence around boroughs the property of individuals, and thus throw additional power and influence into the hands of the oligarchy'. When asked by a member of the corporation to confirm that he had voted for Russell's reform motion only seven weeks earlier, he was said to have replied, 'I suppose I did. I am not certain. *I have voted so often for reform*, that I really cannot recollect that motion in particular'.[7] It was alleged in some quarters that Hughes had deserted Williams, who was forced out of the Caernarvonshire seat by county hostility to his pro-Catholic views; but in fact he had done what he could for his brother-in-law before advising him to give up a hopeless cause.[8] When ill health forced Robarts to resign his seat for Wallingford in December 1826, Hughes publicly endorsed the candidature of the veteran Whig Robert Knight, who easily defeated the corporation man and so strengthened Hughes's hold on the borough.[9]

He voted for Catholic relief, 6 Mar. 1827. On 30 Mar. he was in the opposition minority for withholding supplies until the uncertainty over the new ministry had been resolved. His attitude to Canning's brief ministry is unknown. In the autumn of 1827 he was host at Kinmel to his friend the duke of Sussex (one of whose executors he was appointed in 1840) and his mistress Cecilia Buggin, 'a very agreeable person though perhaps not a very refined one'.[10] Hughes, who is not known to have spoken in debate in this period, presented a Wallingford inhabitants' petition in favour of Catholic relief, 8 May, and voted thus, 12 May 1828. He was reported to have paired in favour of the grant to Canning's family the following day.[11] He voted for reduction of the salary of the lieutenant-general of the ordnance, 4 July 1828. He was a virtual cypher for the rest of the Parliament. He presented petitions in favour of Catholic relief from Wallingford and a Suffolk parish, 19 Mar., and turned up to vote for the third reading of the relief bill, 30 Mar. 1829. He was granted a month's leave on account of ill health, 1 Mar. 1830; and his only known vote that session was against the administration of justice bill, 18 June.

At the general election of 1830 Hughes was returned again for Wallingford, with Knight, after a token contest.[12] Ministers of course numbered him among their 'foes', but he was not present to vote them out of office on the civil list, 15 Nov., and on 2 Dec. 1830 he was granted a month's sick leave. He attended to vote for the second reading of the Grey ministry's reform bill, by which Wallingford was to lose one seat, 22 Mar., presented a constituency petition in its favour, 18 Apr., and voted against Gascoyne's wrecking amendment the following day. He and Knight easily defeated a local Tory at the ensuing general election.[13] He voted for the second reading of the reintroduced reform bill, 6 July, and against the adjournment, 12 July. His steady support of its details in committee during the next five weeks contrasts strikingly with his previous idleness. His last known votes in the Commons were with ministers on the Dublin election controversy, 23 Aug. 1831. He was rewarded with a coronation peerage the following month. His nominee was returned for Wallingford in his place, after a contest, but his interest there was destroyed by the Reform and Boundary Acts.

As Lord Dinorben, he remained loyal to his Whig friends. His private life was studded with tragedy, for he lost six of the ten children produced by his first wife, and his only surviving son, William Lewis, born in 1821, was an imbecile. In a second marriage, made at the age of 72, he fathered two daughters, only one of whom survived him. He died in February 1852, having failed to recover consciousness after being seized with paralysis at dinner two days previously.[14] His will, dated 5 Jan. 1848, confirmed the provisions made by his father in 1805 for the benefit of his children.[15] His idiot son survived him by only eight months, and on his death the peerage became extinct. The entailed estates passed to Hughes's nephew, Hugh Robert Hughes (1827-1911), who unsuccessfully contested Flintshire as a Conservative in 1861.

[1] J.R. Harris, *Copper King*, pp. xvi, 26, 156-7, 182, 184; PROB 11/1570/374; IR26/645/486. [2] See CAERNARVONSHIRE and DENBIGHSHIRE. [3] E.A. Smith, 'Bribery and Disfranchisement', *EHR*, lxxv (1960), 621-2; *Trial and Conviction of Wallingford Whiggism* (1826), pp. vi-ix; *Reading Mercury*, 21 Feb., 6, 13 Mar. 1820. [4] *The Times*, 4, 5 Apr. 1821. [5] Add. 36461, f. 260. [6] *Berks. Chron.* 5, 19 Nov., 3, 10, 31 Dec. 1825, 14 Jan., 25 Feb., 4, 11, 18, 25 Mar., 22 Apr. 1826. [7] Ibid. 3, 10, 17 June, 1, 29 July, 5, 12 Aug.; *The Times*, 10, 15, 16 June 1826; *Trial*, 33, 42, 48-49; Smith, 621, 622-4. [8] *Berks. Chron.* 1 July 1826, citing *Courier*; see CAERNARVONSHIRE. [9] *Berks. Chron.* 9, 16, 23 Dec. 1826.

[10] Add. 36464, f. 85; 40528, f. 294. [11] *The Times*, 15 May 1828. [12] *Reading Mercury*, 2 Aug. 1830. [13] Ibid. 2 May 1831; Smith, 626. [14] *Gent. Mag.* (1852), i. 403; *Ann. Reg.* (1852), Chron. p. 317. [15] PROB 11/2150/298; IR26/1926/267.

D.R.F.

HUGHES HUGHES, William (1792–1874), of Clapham Common, Surr. and Belle Vue House, Ryde, I.o.W.

OXFORD	1830–1832
OXFORD	18 Mar. 1833–1837

b. 2 Sept. 1792,[1] 1st s. of John Hewitt (*d.* 1821) of St. Anne, Westminster and Sophia, da. of William Hughes of Clapham. *educ.* L. Inn 1822, called 1827. *m.* 23 Aug. 1814, Maria, da. of Richard Field of Brixton Rise, Surr.,[2] 1s. 6da. (1 *d.v.p.*). Took name of Hughes by royal lic. 25 May 1825 in compliance with will of grandfa. William Hughes and styled himself Hughes Hughes. *d.* 10 Oct. 1874.

Alderman, London Jan.-July 1832, 1843-8; sheriff, Hants 1843-4.

Little is known of Hughes's antecedents. His father, John Hewitt, who lived in Greek Street, Soho, married the daughter of William Hughes of Clapham, a wealthy property owner and urban landlord, on 20 Oct. 1791.[3] Just under a year later, their first child was baptized in the church of St. Anne as William Hughes Hewitt. They had at least three more sons and five daughters between 1793 and 1810.[4] On 10 Feb. 1809 William Hewitt was articled for five years to the attorney Emmanuel Allen of Carlisle Street, Soho, vestry clerk of St. Anne's. He was admitted as an attorney in common pleas on 16 Feb. 1814.[5] He appears to have practised initially at 5 Palgrave Place, Temple, but from 1817 his address was given in the *Law Lists* as Clapham Common. In August 1814 he married, and at about this time he became a liveryman of London as a member of the Cordwainers' Guild. His father died intestate in 1821. Administration of his estate, which was valued at under £800, was granted on 22 May to his widow, but she died soon afterwards, and administration was granted on 15 Nov. 1821 to their second son, Frederick Hewitt.[6] William was admitted to Lincoln's Inn the following year and withdrew his name from the register of attorneys in 1825, when he became a wealthy man, as the principal beneficiary of the will of his grandfather William Hughes, who died in May, worth about £90,000 in personalty alone. Hewitt's inheritance consisted of four leased freehold houses in Nicholson Lane, London, several dwellings and pieces of land at Battersea Rise and Clapham and a half-share in the residue of the estate, which was calculated for duty at almost £85,000.[7] In compliance with his grandfather's direction, he took the name of Hughes in lieu of Hewitt, and thereafter styled himself, ludicrously, as Hughes Hughes. He evidently used part of his windfall to acquire a property at Ryde, on the Isle of Wight, where he was an occasional resident, though his principal base remained at Clapham.

In February 1826 he offered for Oxford, where the ministerialist and anti-Catholic sitting Member, Sir Charles Wetherell, the solicitor-general, was expected to stand down to contest the current vacancy in the University representation. In the event, Wetherell decided to stay put, but Hughes and his main rival Robert Eden*, brother-in-law of Peel, the home secretary, announced their intention of standing for the city at the next general election, as did the other sitting Member, John Lockhart. In a series of addresses typical of an argumentative and verbose man, Hughes, who took 'independence' as his watchword, reported the progress of his continuing canvass of the non-resident voters, including those in London, and declared his utter hostility to Catholic relief, and his support for the 'mitigation, and gradual abolition' of slavery, 'a material alteration, if not total abandonment' of the corn laws, transfer of the duty on beer to malt, and such a repeal of taxes on necessities as was compatible with the public service.[8] Resuming his canvass of the out-voters in late April 1826, he made a virtue of the fact that, unlike Eden, a chancery lawyer, he was not 'engaged in any profession or business' which would distract him from his parliamentary duties. He expanded on this at the general election in June, when he said that the recent Commons resolutions regulating committees on bills made it imperative 'to return gentlemen of *complete leisure*, inasmuch as upon them additional duties will now devolve of the highest importance, and requiring a devotion of time incompatible with other engagements'. He suggested that the corn laws had received 'a death-blow' from the decision temporarily to open the ports, and welcomed the rejection of the Liverpool ministry's attempt to give the treasurer of the navy a separate ministerial salary. When Eden withdrew, Hughes seemed certain to come in unopposed with Lockhart, but many of the resident electors resented him as a stranger, and at the last minute they put up James Langston, a popular Oxfordshire Whig, who had just been defeated at Woodstock by the Blenheim interest. He topped the poll, and Hughes finished well adrift of Lockhart.[9]

Hughes, who continued to cultivate Oxford,[10] was called to the bar in 1827, but if he practised it

was only for a short time, on the home circuit and at Surrey sessions. Both Langston and Lockhart supported Catholic emancipation in 1829, when Hughes let it be known in Oxford that his attachment to the Protestant constitution remained 'firm and unalterable', and that in the gallery of the Commons he had 'heard with alarm and indignation the monstrous project' explained.[11] He did not, however, initially come forward for the city at the general election of 1830 when, after a rumour that he would offer for Maidstone had come to nothing, he accepted an invitation to stand for Rochester as an Ultra Protestant and canvassed the borough with some success. However, his leading supporters at Oxford, where Langston and Lockhart sought re-election, kept his name before the freemen and hinted that he might yet stand. He abandoned Rochester two days before the Oxford nomination, having apparently received private assurances of enough support to turn out Lockhart, who had become vulnerable. In both constituencies his conduct was the subject of complaint and recrimination, with the chairman of his Rochester committee alleging that he had been bought off by Lord Jersey, the father of his rival Lord Villiers*, with a promise to pay his Rochester expenses and give him such support as he commanded at Oxford by virtue of his property in the county. For his part, Hughes denied any such connivance, later claiming that Oxford had always been his 'first love'. He led the poll, in which he was heavily dependent on the support of non-resident, especially London, voters, for three of the five days and, although overtaken by Langston, finished comfortably ahead of Lockhart, who did not prosecute the petition which he lodged.[12]

The Wellington ministry listed Hughes among the 'good doubtfuls', while Henry Brougham* claimed him as a gain for opposition. (He never joined Brooks's.) From the outset of his parliamentary career, he was an unabashed contributor to debate. He presented and endorsed an Oxford Anglicans' petition for the abolition of slavery, 3 Nov. 1830, when, approving the address, after being reassured that there would be no unwarrantable interference in the internal affairs of Holland, he trusted that he would in future be able to support government, 'notwithstanding the confident predictions which had appeared to the contrary'. Disclaiming any attachment to 'a factious and irreconcilable opposition', he promised backing for ministers in their attempts to 'uphold whatever is excellent in those institutions under which this country has so long flourished, to introduce useful reforms, and, above all, to reduce the public burdens, and promote all practicable economy and retrenchment'. He applauded their 'judicious step' in advising the king not to go into the City for the lord mayor's jamboree, 8 Nov., but helped to vote them out of office on the civil list, 15 Nov. He presented an anti-slavery petition from Dissenting women of Oxford, 10 Nov. He opposed Alderman Thompson's bill to regulate charitable institutions, 7 Dec. His suggestions for amendments to the regency bill were ruled out as unnecessarily pedantic, 9, 10 Dec., but on the 13th Dec. he secured a change to the title of the Colonial Acts validity bill to provide for the longer duration of patents after a demise of the crown. On 17 Dec. he presented a bill to improve fire precautions in the erection of buildings and party walls within a 12-mile radius of London. It was printed for consideration, went through its second reading, 11 Feb. 1831, and was referred to a select committee, 14 Mar., but made no further progress in the 1830 Parliament. Hughes had the House counted out to adjourn the debate on Sugden's motion for returns concerning chancery administration, 20 Dec. 1830.

He presented petitions from the clergy of Bristol, 4 Feb., and Southampton, 18 Feb. 1831, for the introduction of a bill to encourage individuals to build and endow churches by allowing them to hold the perpetual presentation without the consent of the ecclesiastical authorities: he argued that it was the duty of government 'adequately to furnish the population with the means of sound religious instruction, according to the principles of the established church', but that in the current state of the finances public money should not be so applied. He presented similar petitions from Devon, Manchester, and Rutland, 2, 7, 10 and 18 Mar., when he expressed fears, discounted by the Grey ministry, that the additional churches bill which had just passed the Lords posed a threat to the Church of England. He presented a petition from the minister and congregation of Fitroy Episcopal Chapel, Fitzroy Square, London, for a day of 'public humiliation, fasting and prayer', 7 Feb. He brought up similar ones from Cheltenham, 8 Feb., when he rebuked the O'Gorman Mahon for casual 'invocation of the name of the Deity' but got no support from the Speaker, and from Ryde, 14 Feb., when he seconded Perceval's motion for a general fast. He expressed no personal opinion on the merits of a petition for inquiry by synod into the state of the church which he presented, 11 Feb. Frustrated in his attempt to have printed an anti-slavery petition from Fitzroy Chapel, 9 Feb., he threatened to read extracts from every subsequent one, and in many cases, particularly those concerned with additional churches, he proved as good as his word. He presented more anti-slavery petitions, 10, 15, 16 Feb., 9, 23 Mar., 14 Apr., and on

9 Mar. divided the House on his motion, defeated by 48-16, to have that from the women of Ryde printed. He complained that the proposed tax on steamboat passengers would be damaging to the Isle of Wight, 17 Feb., and supported the prayer of hostile petitions presented by others, 29 Mar. As requested by several London parishes, he urged objections to Hobhouse's Vestry Act amendment bill, 21 Feb., specifying as the main one in his own eyes the fact that it came near to 'the principle of universal suffrage, to which I am most decidedly opposed'. When Daniel O'Connell presented two Oxford parish petitions calling for parliamentary reform, 26 Feb., Hughes, professing ignorance of their existence, claimed that his 'enlightened constituency' wished him to come to the question unfettered. In a public letter to the mayor pleading a call of the House as his reason for not attending the city meeting to endorse the ministerial reform bill, 15 Mar., he stated that he, like 'the soundest and best part of the population', was 'altogether averse to ... *radical reform*', but wished to see 'such temperate, wise and practical amendments, as are consistent with the spirit of our constitution, and the advanced civilization of the age in which we live'. He therefore endorsed the bill, which he had at first considered to be 'too sweeping', as a 'timely concession', obstructive resistance to which would lead to disaster beneath 'the deluge of a ferocious democracy'. At the same time, he reserved his right to seek amendments to its details, notably its proposal to disfranchise non-resident freemen.[13] On the day of the Oxford meeting, he presented a petition from Tain for reform of the Scottish electoral system. When Langston presented the Oxford petition, 19 Mar., Hughes welcomed it and declared his support for the second reading of the bill, which he delivered silently, 22 Mar. During the following week he visited Oxford to canvass opinion on the measure.[14] In the House, 29 Mar., he supported the Hampshire reform petition, but was invited by the Speaker to explain his remark that its strong language was justified by the denials by the Members for Newport, in defiance of 'the sentiments of the people', of the need for reform; he felt that he had nothing for which to apologize. He was one of the Members bringing pressure to bear on ministers to allow the vote to the future children and apprentices of qualified freemen, as he explained at an Oxford dinner, 11 Apr., when he complained of 'a kind of guerilla warfare' against his 'honour and character' over the Rochester affair and denied a rumour that he did not intend to support the third reading of the bill.[15] He tried unsuccessfully to kill the Wolvercot enclosure bill, which was opposed by the Oxford authorities, 13 Apr. According to an Oxford

newspaper, he voted in Hume's minority of 17 for deducting royal pensions from the civil list, 14 Apr.[16] He voted against Gascoyne's wrecking amendment to the reform bill, 19 Apr. 1831. The next day he repudiated Hunt's assertions that it was 'a fraud or a delusion on the people of England' and that most of them did not understand it, and testified to the strength of support for it in Oxford. At the ensuing general election he and Langston were re-elected unopposed as its enthusiastic supporters. In reply to the allegation that it was inconsistent in him to support the entire bill after voicing reservations over its details, he argued that 'we must have the whole bill or no bill, its component parts being so nicely adjusted, that if you withdraw one point you destroy the equipoise and mar the whole'. He predicted that this regenerative measure of reform would strengthen the throne, aristocracy and church, and lead to the abolition of sinecure places and pensions and, ultimately, to a reduction in taxes on the poor. At the same election, he supported reformers in Oxfordshire, Surrey and Hampshire.[17]

Hughes secured a return of information on applications for the erection of new churches under the Acts of 1825 and 1827, 23 June, and drew attention to the filthy state of the interior of Westminster Hall, 8 July 1831. He had earlier written to Lord John Russell specifying various detailed changes which he wished to be made to the reform bill, and it was stated in the Oxford press that he would hesitate to support the second reading of the reintroduced measure unless ministers agreed to allow quarterly as well as half-yearly rent payers to vote.[18] In the event, he voted silently for it, 6 July. It was from the opposition benches that he deplored the 'gross act of injustice' of refusing Sir Abraham King compensation for the loss of his patent to supply official stationery, 11 July. He had given notices of motions to abandon the division of counties and to give the Isle of Wight two Members instead of the proposed one. On 13 July he supported the prayer of a petition to that effect, a few hours after voting steadily with ministers throughout the night against an adjournment.[19] For the next three weeks he was a steady supporter of the details of the bill in committee, though he was in the minority for the total disfranchisement of Saltash, 26 July. He spoke for the disfranchisement of Downton, 21 July, and Minehead, 22 July, and for the removal of one seat from Chippenham, 27 July, and Guildford, 29 July. He persuaded Lord Althorp to postpone consideration of the division of Lincolnshire, which he was prepared to exempt from his hostility to the general principle, 10 Aug., when he paired for the enfranchisement of Merthyr. The next day he pressed his amendment

against the division of counties, arguing that it would create 'districts' under the control of great landowners and lead inevitably to adoption of the ballot. He was defeated by 241-122, but announced on 16 Aug. that he would try again at the report stage. Later that day he unsuccessfully put the case for giving the Isle of Wight an additional Member, to look after its agricultural interest. He had earlier given notice of an amendment to clause 18 to get rid of the anomaly whereby freeholders of borough property, the tenants of which included an occupier paying £10 or more, would not be able to vote for the county by virtue of that property. He had been at the foreign office meeting of reform Members, 11 July, when Althorp had indicated that ministers planned to move this amendment themselves, and Hughes stated to the House, without contradiction, 13 Aug., that this was their intention. He was one of the Members accidentally locked out of the division on Davies's amendment to confine freeholders of cities and towns which were counties of themselves to the borough; he would have opposed it.[20] On 18 Aug. he voted for Chandos's successful amendment to enfranchise £50 tenants-at-will in the counties, after stating that he was unwilling to give landlords the power of withholding or conferring the vote by the arbitrary refusal or grant of a seven-year lease. He defended his action in a letter to *The Times*, where it had been criticized.[21] On 19 Aug. he gave notice that before the House next went into committee on the reform bill he would move a resolution that there should be no reduction in the current number of Members. When Althorp, responding to the reverse over the Chandos clause, 19 Aug., outlined proposed adjustments whereby borough copyholders and lease-holders were to be permitted to vote in counties, Hughes complained of a 'breach of faith' by ministers, and moved an amendment against the altered clause which was defeated by 187-1; Warburton was his only supporter. Attacked in *The Times* for trying to delay the bill, he wrote to defend his record of support for it, to justify dividing the House and to deny that in proposing that there should be no reduction in the number of Members he was resurrecting Gascoyne's wrecking amendment. He also wrote aggressively to the editor of the *Morning Herald*, whom he accused of trying to undermine his position at Oxford by portraying him as a covert enemy of the bill. He claimed that he had 'given a more undivided attention to the business of the House, and more votes personally, in favour of the bill, than any other Member', insisted on his right to exercise independent judgement on matters of detail, and said that if the division of counties went through he would vote for the ballot and triennial parliaments.[22]

In the House, 24 Aug., he announced that he had decided to postpone his motion regarding the number of Members until the report stage, when the fate of his renewed proposition concerning the division of counties would be known. Complaining that ministers had sanctioned and encouraged the slurs cast on him in the press, he sought to justify his conduct, and explained that he wished 32 hitherto unallocated seats to go to large towns, in order to counterbalance the effects of the division of counties and the Chandos clause. He opposed Campbell's amendment against enfranchising tenants who paid rent more frequently than by the quarter, because it would give too much power to landlords, 25 Aug. The following day, after adjusting the terms of an amendment of which he had given earlier notice, he proposed that, in order to prevent any 'system of jobbing in votes', notices to quit on weekly tenants should not have the effect of depriving them of the franchise at the next election. Althorp dismissed the notion as fanciful, and it was negatived. On 27 Aug. Hughes welcomed proposed changes to clauses 23 and 25, and suggested others which would make the division of counties relatively unobjectionable, namely that the boundary commissioners should be empowered to make a report of opinion, not determination, as to how to divide the schedule G counties, and that those not thus dealt with by Parliament should be left undivided with four Members. Later that day he voted in the minority of 17 to preserve existing voting rights, and he divided for attempts to preserve the rights of all freemen and of non-residents, 30 Aug. He defended these votes (on which Langston took the government side) in the Oxford press, asserting that he would rather resign his seat than be an 'automaton' in the House.[23] He protested against the appointment as boundary commissioners of the lord chief baron, two county Members and a clergyman, 1 Sept., but admitted that by making concessions government had now largely overcome his original objections to the unconstitutional powers of the commissioners. At the same time, he called on them to abandon the division of counties proposals, which would unduly delay the implementation of reform. Another self-exculpatory letter to *The Times* ensued.[24] He completed his retreat on this issue, 3 Sept., explaining that Althorp's statement of the previous day (when Hughes had voted with ministers on the franchise of the four sluiced freeholder boroughs), that either House would be able to send back the commissioners' reports for revision as often as they wished, had persuaded him to swallow the division of counties. He reproved Sugden for mischievously suggesting that the commissioners were already at work without official sanction, 5 Sept. The following day he got nowhere with his amendment to have the cost of erecting booths and hustings charged on the constituency authorities, which he peevishly withdrew, whining that trying to secure changes in the bill was a 'hopeless' task. The Speaker put an abrupt end to his attempted explanation of his reasons for dropping his motion relating to the number of Members, 7 Sept. He was in the minority for the disfranchisement of Aldborough, 14 Sept. He favoured a 15 rather than seven-mile limit for qualified non-resident freemen voters, 13 Sept. He voted for the third reading and passage of the reform bill, 19, 21 Sept., and for the second reading of the Scottish bill, 23 Sept. Four days later he hastened to the Isle of Wight to address the reform meeting at Newport, 28 Sept., when, according to one report, he was 'not received so cordially as he might have been'. He was back at his post in the Commons on the 30th, and on 10 Oct. 1831 divided for the motion of confidence in the ministry.[25]

Hughes called for permanent provision for the duchess of Kent as the mother of the heir presumptive, 3, 10 Aug. 1831. He wanted imposition of the penalty of hard labour for infractions of the game laws left to the discretion of magistrates, 8 Aug. That day he spoke for the issue of a new writ for Dublin, and he voted with ministers for the prosecution of only the bribers at the last election, 23 Aug. He promised support for Gordon's proposed motion for inquiry into pensions on the consolidated fund, 12 Aug. He was in the anti-Catholic minorities of 11 for the Irish union of parishes bill, 19 Aug., and of 47 for an end to the Maynooth grant, 26 Sept. He secured the second reading of his Churches Building Act amendment bill, 23 Aug., and on the 25th, when he handed it over to government, assured its critics that far from seeking to increase the powers of the official commissioners, it aimed to curb them and give more scope to individuals. He made suggestions on details of the measure, 26 Sept., 3 Oct. After the recent loss of the *Rothay Castle*, he recommended the appointment in every port of an official to monitor the seaworthiness of passenger vessels, 3 Sept.; he was named to the select committee on steam navigation, 6 Sept. He voted for inquiry into the effects of the Sugar Refinery Act on the West India interest, 12 Sept., and on 13 Oct. unsuccessfully moved the adjournment of the debate on the bill to renew it, which he said tended to encourage the foreign slave trade.[26] On 15 Sept. 1831 he voted in Hunt's minority of six for inquiry by committee of the whole House into the corn laws; but he subsequently wrote to *The Times* to explain that in doing so he had not committed himself to their repeal, which was unattainable, and that his preferred option was a 'moderate fixed duty'.[27]

In early December 1831 Hughes stood for election as an alderman of London for Portsoken ward against Michael Scales, who had been chosen there earlier in the year but been unseated by a judgment in king's bench. Scales won comfortably, but on 3 Jan. 1832 the court of aldermen, as expected, seated Hughes in his stead. He held the post until he was ousted by king's bench on a writ of quo warranto in July.[28] He voted on 17 Dec. 1831 for the second reading of the revised reform bill, which, as was pointed out in his favour in the local press, incorporated a number of the changes for which he had campaigned, including preservation of the voting rights of the future children and apprentices of qualified freemen.[29] He voted steadily for the bill in committee, though he was in the minority against the inclusion of Helston in schedule B, 23 Feb., and divided for its third reading, 22 Mar. 1832; but he is not reported to have uttered a syllable on it during its passage through the Commons. He voted against Hobhouse's vestry reform bill, 23 Jan. He secured a return of information on prisoners for debt in the Fleet, 27 Feb. The following day he stated that after consultations with surveyors and government officials he had decided to drop his previous bill to regulate the building of party walls and to introduce a new one, on the model of the present Act; but on 1 June he announced that he had given up the idea. On 20 Mar. he introduced, with government support, a bill to rectify the anomaly whereby the provisions of the Act of 1823 allowing courts to abstain from the formality of imposing the death penalty for certain offences had not been extended to London and Middlesex. To his frustration and annoyance, he encountered obstructive opposition from Colonel Sibthorp, the reactionary Tory Member for Lincoln, whom he took to task for saying that the cost of transporting criminals to New South Wales could be saved by executing them, 26 Mar. Hughes eventually got the measure through the Commons, 31 Mar., but it did not return from the Lords. He was forced to withdraw, with a bad grace, his notice of 30 Mar. for a motion to end proxy voting in the Lords, which the Speaker said might lead to 'a very unpleasant collision' between the two Houses. He decided not to press his contemplated changes to the friendly societies bill, 2 Apr. He advocated giving the current Irish registrar a salary of £1,500, rather than the lower sum proposed by some Irish Members, 3, 9 Apr., voted with ministers for the navy civil departments bill, 6 Apr., and endorsed the London corporation petition for the abolition of slavery, 4 Apr. 1832.

At the London common council meeting, 10 May 1832, Hughes, who was present with five other aldermen, objected to the resolution calling for the Commons to withhold supplies until the reform bill had been carried, arguing that it was absurd to deny support to a putative government of whose composition they were as yet ignorant. He moved an amendment expressing undiminished confidence in the Grey ministry and the hope that any new administration would carry a bill 'equally full and efficient' as the one before the Lords. Amid much confusion, he was forced to drop it, but he and his fellow aldermen signified their dissent from the resolution. In the House later that day, when the City Members endorsed and claimed unanimous council support for the petition, Hughes detailed these events and dissociated himself from the 'premature' and 'most dangerous step' of withholding the supplies. However, he voted for the motion for an address calling on the king to appoint only ministers who would carry the bill unimpaired. On 15 May he denied that he had 'committed a gross calumny' on his brother aldermen, as had been alleged by one of his detractors in common council the previous day.[30] He voted for the second reading of the Irish reform bill, 25 May, and against a Conservative amendment to the Scottish bill, 1 June. He was in the minority against the government's temporizing amendment to Fowell Buxton's motion for the abolition of slavery, 24 May, and voted to make coroners' inquests public, 20 June. He presented and endorsed an Oxford petition for relaxation of the criminal code, 30 May. He was one of the committee appointed to consider the agricultural labourers bill, 5 June, when he threw out the suggestion that it should not apply within ten miles of London. He presented hostile petitions from his area of Surrey, 8 June. He clashed again with Sibthorp, over the steam vessels bill, that day. On 19 June he obtained a return of information on the Act of 1831 giving additional powers to the commissioners for the erection of new churches, to substantiate his claim that it had proved to be ineffectual. He was named to the select committee on observance of the Sabbath, 3 July, and presented a number of petitions from retailers and tradesmen calling for steps to improve it, 8, 9, 11 Aug. He voted with government on the Russian-Dutch loan, 12, 16, 20 July 1832.

Hughes stood again for Oxford at the general election of 1832, was beaten into third place by a local Catholic Liberal, but was seated on petition.[31] He continued to support the Grey ministry, but was alienated by the Melbourne administration's programme of church reform, and it was as a Conservative that he topped the Oxford poll in 1835. His parliamentary career was ended by his defeat in 1837. In 1834 he published a new edition of De Lolme's *Constitution of England*. As master of the cordwainers he was elected alderman for Bread Street ward, after a scrutiny, in 1843, and served for almost five years.[32] The remainder of his life is obscure. He had left the Isle of Wight by 1857, and it was at Ilkley Wells, near Skipton, Yorkshire, that he died in October 1874. By his brief will, dated 15 Oct. 1872, he left small legacies to various relatives and to his 'highly valued friend Mary Ann Kemp'. He divided the residue of his estate equally between his only son, William Hughes Hughes, a barrister, his five surviving daughters, and the children of his late daughter Ann Hughes May. His effects were sworn under a derisory £300.

[1]*Ex inf.* Stephen Lees. [2] *The Times*, 24 Aug. 1814. [3] IGI (London). [4] Ibid. [5] TNA IND 1/4570, 4601. [6] PROB 6/197/82, 112. [7] *Gent. Mag.* (1825), i. 476; PROB 11/1699/264; IR26/1045/511. [8] *Oxford University and City Herald*, 18, 25 Feb., 4, 11, 18, 25 Mar. 1826. [9] Ibid. 29 Apr., 3, 10, 17 June; *The Times*, 26 May, 13, 16, 17 June; *Jackson's Oxford Jnl.* 17 June 1826. [10] *Jackson's Oxford Jnl.* 5 Aug., 14 Oct. 1826; *Oxford University and City Herald*, 19 June 1830. [11] *Oxford University and City Herald*, 14 Mar. 1829. [12] *Maidstone Gazette*, 25 May, 8 June, 6, 13, 20, 27 July; *Oxford University and City Herald*, 19 June, 10, 17, 24, 31 July, 7 Aug. 1830, 16 Apr. 1831; *Rochester Gazette*, 3 Aug.; *The Times*, 3 Aug. 1830. [13] *Oxford University, City and County Herald*, 19 Mar. 1831. [14] Ibid. 26 Mar. 1831. [15] Ibid. 16 Apr.; *The Times*, 18 Apr. 1831. [16] *Oxford University, City and County Herald*, 23 Apr. 1831. [17] Ibid. 30 Apr., 7, 21 May 1831. [18] Ibid. 2 July 1831. [19] Ibid. 16 July 1831. [20] M. Brock, *Great Reform Act*, 226-7, 370; *The Times*, 19 Aug. 1831. [21] *The Times*, 20 Aug. 1831. [22] Ibid. 23 Aug.; *Oxford University, City and County Herald*, 27 Aug., 3 Sept. 1831. [23] *The Times*, 29 Aug.; *Oxford University, City and County Herald*, 3 Sept. 1831. [24] *The Times*, 3 Sept.; *Oxford University, City and County Herald*, 10 Sept. 1831. [25] *Portsmouth Herald*, 2 Oct.; *Oxford University, City and County Herald*, 8 Oct. 1831. [26] *Oxford University, City and County Herald*, 17 Sept. 1831. [27] *The Times*, 17 Sept.; *Oxford University, City and County Herald*, 24 Sept. 1831. [28] *The Times*, 6, 7 Dec., 4 Jan. 1832; A.B. Beaven, *Aldermen of London*, i. 186, 188, 242. [29] *Oxford University, City and County Herald*, 17 Dec. 1831. [30] *The Times*, 11, 15 May 1832. [31] *Jackson's Oxford Jnl.* 14 July, 6 Oct., 17 Nov., 1, 8, 15 Dec. 1832. [32] *The Times*, 19-21 Sept., 19 Oct. 1843, 13 Apr. 1848; Beaven, i. 54

D.R.F.

HULSE, Sir Charles, 4th bt. (1771–1854), of Breamore, nr. Fordingbridge, Hants and 4 New Burlington Street, Mdx.

| WEST LOOE | 11 Mar. 1816–1826 |
| WEST LOOE | 6 Apr. 1827–1832 |

b. 12 Oct. 1771, 1st surv. s. of Sir Edward Hulse, 3rd bt., of Breamore and Mary, da. of Charles Lethieullier, LLD, fellow of All Souls, Oxf. *educ.* Eton 1782-9; Christ Church, Oxf. 1790; L. Inn 1793. *m.* 5 July 1808, Maria, da of John Buller[†] of Morval, Cornw., 5s. 1da. *suc.* fa. as 4th bt. 30 Sept. 1816. *d.* 19 Oct. 1854.

Capt. Fordingbridge yeomanry 1798, 1803; lt.-col. commdt. S.E. Hants militia 1812.

Sheriff, Hants 1836-7.

Hulse's great-grandfather Edward Hulse (c.1682-1759) became first physician to George II, was granted a baronetcy in 1739 and purchased Breamore in 1748. His father married the niece and heiress of the noted antiquary Smart Lethieullier, whose Huguenot family had made their fortune as London merchants. With the addition of property in Chigwell bequeathed by her aunt Elizabeth Goodere, she brought with her an Essex estate of over 1,500 acres centred on the mansion at Aldersbrook, as well as 'other interests in the city of London'. Hulse became heir to the baronetcy on the death of his elder brother Edward, 'of a putrid fever', in 1789.[1] Notwithstanding the sale of certain Essex properties, including Aldersbrook itself in 1786, his inheritance in 1816 consisted of land in Hampshire, Essex, Wiltshire, London and counties Cork and Tipperary. He derived no benefit as his father's residuary legatee (the personalty, sworn under £6,000, was exhausted by bequests), but he had made an advantageous marriage into a Cornish landowning family with multiple borough interests.[2] This family alliance was cemented when John Buller* married Hulse's youngest sister Harriet in 1814, and returned him for West Looe two years later.

In 1820, when Hulse was again returned unopposed for West Looe, he offered his interest in Hampshire to the Whig Sir Thomas Baring*, on the strength of his attention to county business and 'in preference to ... a second candidate whose political sentiments might perhaps be in general more in unison with my own'.[3] He continued to give general but silent support to Lord Liverpool's ministry, though he was prepared to oppose them on occasion. He voted in defence of their conduct towards Queen Caroline, 6 Feb. 1821. He divided against repeal of the additional malt duty, 3 Apr., reduction of the grant for the adjutant-general's office, 11 Apr., and Hume's economy and retrenchment motion, 27 June. He voted against parliamentary reform, 9 May. He was added to the select committee on poor returns, 31 May 1821, and reappointed to it in the next five sessions. He divided in the minority for the abolition of one the joint-postmasterships, 13 Mar. 1822, his only recorded vote that session. He voted against the production of papers on the alleged plot to murder the Irish lord lieutenant, 24 Mar., but for inquiry into the prosecution of the perpetrators, 22 Apr. 1823. He divided against Scottish parliamentary reform, 2 June, and inquiry into the currency, 12 June 1823. He voted against repeal of the usury laws, 27 Feb., and abolition of flogging in the navy, 5 Mar. 1824. He presented an anti-slavery petition from the corporation of West Looe, 6 Apr.[4] He was added to the select committee on county rates, 24 May, and reappointed in the next two sessions. He voted against inquiry into the prosecution of the Methodist missionary John Smith in Demerara, 11 June. He divided for the Irish insurrection bill, 14 June 1824, and the Irish unlawful societies bill, 25 Feb. 1825. Although he had voted in favour of Catholic relief in 1817, he divided against it, 1 Mar., 21 Apr., 10 May, and the Irish franchise bill, 26 Apr. He voted for the financial provision for the duke of Cumberland, 30 May, 2, 6, 10 June. In his only known parliamentary speech, 20 June 1825, he maintained that local opposition to the Berkshire and Hampshire Junction Canal bill was 'not so general as some ... gentlemen seemed to think'.[5] He voted to defend the salary of the president of the board of trade, 10 Apr., but was in the minority against empowering the government to admit foreign corn, 8 May 1826. He paired in favour of Russell's resolutions against electoral bribery, 26 May 1826.

At the general election of 1826 Buller returned himself for West Looe, but apparently this was no more than a stopgap measure, as he made way for Hulse at a by-election in April 1827. Hulse divided for repeal of the Test Acts, 26 Feb., and, having apparently undergone another change of heart, for Catholic relief, 12 May 1828. He presented a St. Ives petition against restrictions on the circulation of small notes, 22 May. He voted with the duke of Wellington's ministry against reduction of the salary of the lieutenant-general of the ordnance, 4 July 1828. In February 1829 Planta, the patronage secretary, predicted that he would side 'with government' for Catholic emancipation, and he voted accordingly, 6, 30 Mar. He divided in the minority against the grant for the sculpture of the marble arch, 25 May 1829. He voted against the enfranchisement of Manchester, Leeds and Birmingham, 23 Feb., but in favour of transferring East Retford's seats to Birmingham, 5 Mar. 1830. He presented a Wigan petition against renewal of the East India Company's charter, 17 Mar. He divided against Jewish emancipation, 5 Apr., 17 May 1830. He was in the minority for a reduction of the grant for public buildings, 3 May 1830. He was returned for West Looe as usual at the general election that summer.

The ministry regarded him as one of the 'good doubtfuls', with the optimistic endorsement 'a friend', but he was absent from the crucial civil list division, 15 Nov. 1830. He was granted a month's leave 'on account of the disturbed state of his neighbourhood', 30 Nov. 1830. As chairman of the committee on the Londonderry election, appointed on 8 Mar. 1831, Thomas Gladstone judged him to be 'a dull caller'.[6] He divided against the second reading

of the Grey ministry's reform bill, 22 Mar., and for Gascoyne's wrecking amendment, 19 Apr. 1831. He was returned unopposed at the ensuing general election. Thereafter his parliamentary attendance appears to have declined. He voted against the second reading of the reintroduced reform bill, 6 July, to use the 1831 census to determine the disfranchisement schedules, 19 July, and against the bill's passage, 21 Sept. 1831. He was absent from the divisions on the second and third readings of the revised bill, 17 Dec. 1831, 22 Mar., but divided against its entering committee, 20 Jan. 1832. He voted against ministers on the Russian-Dutch loan, 26 Jan., and the abolition of slavery, 24 May 1832.

West Looe was disfranchised by the Reform Act and Hulse apparently made no attempt to return to the Commons. Despite criticisms in 1830 that he was absent from Hampshire too often to be an effective magistrate, he served as sheriff in 1836.[7] A 'keen forester', he was responsible for the plantation of the Breamore estate, and he had Loxford Hall, near Ilford, Essex, rebuilt in 1830.[8] He died in October 1854 and was succeeded by his eldest son Edward Hulse (1809-99).[9]

[1] Oxford DNB sub Smart Lethieullier; A. Light and I. Dampney, Short Hist. Breamore, 8; C. Chown, Lethieullier Fam. 2-3, 19-22, 34-38; VCH Hants, iv. 574; Gent. Mag. (1789), ii. 866. [2] Chown, 37; VCH Essex, v. 203, 212; PROB 11/1588/16; IR26/709/5. [3] Baring mss deposit 189, Hulse to Baring, 20 Feb. 1820, cited in R. Foster, Politics of County Power, 134. [4] The Times, 7 Apr. 1824. [5] Ibid. 21 June 1825. [6] St. Deiniol's Lib. Glynne Gladstone mss 197, T. to J. Gladstone, 15 Mar. 1831. [7] Wellington mss WP4/2/1/3; 2/44. [8] Hist. Breamore and Hulse Fam. 19; Wellington mss WP4/4/2/3; VCH Essex, v. 207. [9] The Times, 21 Oct. 1854 confirms the date of death as the 19th; HP Commons, 1790-1820, iv. 261-2 incorrectly gives it as the 25th.

H.J.S.

HUME, Joseph (1777-1855), of 38 York Place, Portman Square and 6 Bryanston Square, Mdx. and Burnley Hall, Norf.[1]

WEYMOUTH & MELCOMBE REGIS	18 Jan. 1812-1812
ABERDEEN BURGHS	1818-1830
MIDDLESEX	1830-1837
KILKENNY	1837-1841
MONTROSE BURGHS	16 Apr. 1842-20 Feb. 1855

b. 22 Jan. 1777, yr. s. of James Hume, shipmaster, of Montrose, Forfar and w. Mary Allan.[2] educ. Montrose acad.; Edinburgh Univ. 1793-5;[3] Aberdeen Univ., MD 1799. m. 17 Aug. 1815, Maria, da. and h. of Hardin

Burnley, merchant, of Brunswick Square, Mdx., 3s. 4da.[4] *d.* 20 Feb. 1855.

Asst. surgeon, E.I. Co. naval service 1797, full asst. surgeon 1799; on Bengal medical establishment 1799-1808.

Rect. Aberdeen Univ. 1824-6, 1828-9.

By the start of this period Hume, a burly man with a massive head and virtually no neck, had established himself as an irritating and almost permanent fixture in the Commons, where he habitually occupied the same seat, against a post to the left of the Speaker's chair.[5] From there, between 1820 and 1832, he made over 4,000 speeches, interventions in debate, motions for papers and presentations of petitions. Most of his utterances were mercifully brief, consisting of comments, questions and interjections on a limited range of issues. His occasional long set-piece orations, during which he fortified himself with pears, could empty the chamber in minutes.[6] His capacity for inducing boredom in his listeners was enhanced during his first years in the House by an appalling, stuttering monotonous style of speaking; but with practice he improved considerably, and in 1837 one commentator wrote that 'without any pretensions to being a first-rate speaker', he had become an able performer.[7] He was no intellectual giant; indeed, he was rather dim in many respects, prone to making 'almost incredible blunders' in language (for example, using the word 'liable' as if it meant 'telling a lie'),[8] and often inept in judgement and wilfully perverse. He was industrious, earnest, stubborn and immensely thick-skinned, which made him largely impervious to the ridicule and abuse which he attracted from his political adversaries. A wealthy man, thanks to his early years as a surgeon in India and a lucrative marriage, he had repented of the independent Toryism which he had espoused during his first brief spell in the House in 1812, and reappeared in 1818 as a doctrinaire radical and political economist, with a political creed based on the theories of Bentham, David Ricardo* and his old Montrose school friend James Mill. He had been taken up by Francis Place, the Charing Cross radical tailor, who after initial doubts recognized his virtues and potential as a parliamentary spokesman for the causes in which they believed. His driving obsession was profusion and waste in public expenditure, against which he waged unremitting war. He regarded them as the cement of the corrupt spoils system and the cause of the unnecessarily high taxation which oppressed working people and hampered economic growth. He considered that the only effective antidote was radical parliamentary reform, which would make the Commons more responsive to popular opinion and

destroy the baneful influence of the crown and ministers; but he took no personal initiatives on this issue, concentrating instead on his anti-patronage economy crusade.[9]

At the general election of 1820 the Liverpool ministry tried to prevent Hume's re-election for Aberdeen Burghs, where he had been surprisingly returned in 1818, partly as a result of the privy council's inadvertent liberalization of the sett of Montrose the previous year. Their candidate John Mitchell*, a London merchant, seemed at first to be on the verge of success, with Aberdeen and Inverbervie definitely secured and Brechin reportedly all but committed to him. Hume, who refuted Mitchell's allegation that he was hostile to the linen bounties, a significant local issue, explaining that he was willing in the current state of the industry to waive temporarily his free trader's aversion to such imposts, was well received by the burgesses and populace of Aberdeen (where he never obtained the support of the council), to whom he made a promise that he 'would always be found at his post, watching with a jealous eye every encroachment upon the rights and privileges of his countrymen'. Brechin council, possibly in response to intimidation by a pro-Hume mob, gave him their backing, which, with that of the other Angus burghs of Arbroath and Montrose, was decisive. Mitchell's petition against the return was rejected.[10] Anticipating Hume's success ('the worst of our news today'), Charles Long*, a member of the government, predicted that 'he will be one of the most troublesome Members in the House'.[11] So he was.

Hume's name appears in almost every extant opposition division list in the 1820 Parliament. (He was absent from only a dozen of the 310 on which he might have been expected to vote against government.) He was frequently a teller. He condemned the civil list estimates as 'most extravagant', 2 May, and next day got 60 votes for his motion for inquiry into civil list expenditure since 1815. He was named to the select committee on the Scottish royal burghs, 4 May (and again, 16 Feb. 1821). He wanted an investigation of the involvement of the spy George Edwards in the Cato Street conspiracy, 9 May, arguing that there was a strong suspicion of ministerial incitement. As ever, he said that the increased protection for agriculture demanded in rural petitions would bring no relief and would worsen distress in the manufacturing districts, 12 May. He supported Lord Archibald Hamilton's motion for a return of the rolls of freeholders of the Scottish counties, 25 May. He disliked Littleton's proposed bill to abolish truck payments and maintained that repeal of the Combination Acts would be of more benefit to workers, 1, 23 June. He criticized the size and mystification of the ordnance, army, navy and miscellaneous estimates, 2, 6, 9, 16, 19 June. On the linen bounties, 30 June, he agreed with the ministerial view that while they should be continued for the time being, they should not become permanent. On 4 July 1820 he secured a very respectable vote of 99 (against 124) for his motion for the implementation of economies in revenue collection.

Hume took up the cause of Queen Caroline as a weapon against ministers, condemning their conduct towards 'this injured and oppressed' woman as 'one of the foulest and most disgraceful conspiracies which was ever formed', 18 Sept. 1820, but opposing Hobhouse's amendment for a prorogation. Hobhouse thought he made 'a bad speech', asserting that 'the attorney-general had charged the queen with adultery during six years and *proved it only for three*'. On 17 Oct. he moved for Sir Robert Baker, chief magistrate of Bow Street, to be called to the bar of the House to explain his role in the escape from custody of William Franklin, who had been charged with circulating a seditious handbill, in which he discerned more governmental 'conspiracy'; but Lord Castlereagh, the leader of the House, got the better of him, and he withdrew. Hobhouse, who seconded him, was again critical of his performance, thinking that he 'began too high' and 'did not prove the connection with government and ... made an assertion or two which ministers were able to contradict'.[12] Hume, who in late December 1820 confided to Place his view that the Whigs were 'in general despicable and quite unworthy of support from the people', presented and endorsed petitions in favour of restoration of Caroline's name to the liturgy, 24 Jan. 1821, but a few days later he apparently observed to Charles Arbuthnot*, the patronage secretary, that the queen's message refusing the offered £50,000 a year was 'great nonsense and all [Henry] Brougham's* doing, for ... people could not be expected to be upon stilts all their lives'.[13] On 31 Jan. he was called to order by the Speaker for accusing Castlereagh of lying on a matter affecting the queen; and on 14 Feb., opposing the additonal malt duties bill, he was forced to apologize for referring to the ministerial majority on the queen's affair as 'factious'. From early February Hume and his associates of the 'Mountain', notably Thomas Creevey, Thomas Davies, Henry Grey Bennet and John Maberly, began a concerted and deliberately obstructive parliamentary anti-patronage campaign against the estimates, which seized the initiative from the mainstream Whigs, who joined in it spasmodically. A Tory country gentleman complained later in the session that 'the choice knot of patriots ... with ...

Hume as their finance minister, contrive to obstruct and puzzle the examination of the annual estimates to an extent and with a degree of perseverance which is without example'.[14] As Hume explained on 9 Feb., 'the only way to procure some attention to the objects of economy was to deny ministers the means of lavish expenditure'. On 16 Feb. he moved for the printing of the ordnance estimates in full detail in what Grey Bennet thought 'a most excellent speech, with great details and sundry curious proofs of the waste and extravagance of the establishment'; a thin House divided 58-44 against him.[15] He divided silently for Catholic relief, 28 Feb. (and again, 1 Mar., 21 Apr., 10 May 1825). After voting in the minority of 38 for Creevey's motion to reduce the number of placemen and pensioners in the House, 9 Mar. 1821, he opposed going into committee on the army estimates by moving a series of resolutions encapsulating his argument that they could and should be reduced to the level of 1792, as recommended by the 1817 finance committee. The debate was adjourned to the 12th, when he resubmitted the resolutions, which were rejected by 98-74. He and his associates then divided an often disorderly House over a dozen times against details of the estimates, until four in the morning.[16] At about this time Castlereagh, reporting Tierney's resignation from the leadership of the Whig opposition in the Commons, told Lord Harrowby that 'we are to have a Pindari [marauding] warfare for the remainder of the session, conducted by a committee of which Hume, Creevey, Bennet and Davies are the chiefs!'; while Joseph Planta*, foreign office under-secretary, informed Stratford Canning*, envoy to the United States, that 'the guerillas' could create only 'useless trouble' which would 'recoil on their own heads'.[17] Hume's own motions for reduction of the army by 10,000 men (15 Mar.) and a revision of all official salaries to 1797 levels (30 Mar.) were defeated by 116-46 and 50-29 respectively. On 22 Mar. he proposed the abolition of the ten receiver-generalships and 95 distributorships of stamps, but settled for the select committee to investigate its feasibility which the government offered. His motion to disqualify civil officers of the ordnance from voting in parliamentary elections, which focused on abuses at Queenborough, was rejected by 118-60, 12 Apr., when the Tory independent Member Henry Bankes described him privately as 'the most indefatigable, meddling and vexatious universalist whom we have ever known in the House'.[18] When the Commons resumed after Easter, 30 Apr., Hume and Grey Bennet and their coadjutors, not a whit 'disheartened' by an evident 'diminution of zeal' for retrenchment in the House as whole, persevered with their sniping warfare, but they were more often than not in minorities of fewer than 30.[19] On 14 May they mustered 78 votes for Hume's motion to cut the ordnance estimates by £15,818, but Hume was lashed by the minister Robert Plumer Ward, who gleefully pointed out his errors of fact and arithmetic and mocked his 'dullness of intellect and gullibility'.[20] Three days later the cabinet minister William Wellesley Pole* wrote to Sir Charles Bagot:

> The system pursued by those wretched fellows ... is discountenanced by the high Whigs, and you will have perceived by the little dirty warfare on the estimates, and by the numbers in the numberless divisions upon them, that the great body of the opposition have taken little or no part in the proceedings. The whole House and the whole public are now tired out with Mr. Hume and company.[21]

The last observation was not accurate. Hume attacked the proposed grant for the duke of Clarence as too high by £2,500, 8 June, but withdrew his amendment to that effect to allow Harbord's against the inclusion of arrears since 1819 to be put to a vote. His own amendment to reduce the grant to £3,500 was defeated by 167-30, 18 June. He had a final defiant fling against the arrears on 29 June, when his amendment was defeated by 54-24. Grey Bennet noted that his 'vigorous reply' to Lord Londonderry (Castlereagh), in which he 'threw in his ... face all the acts of government relative to Her Majesty', notably her exclusion from the coronation, was 'much cheered, and I never knew him so pointed and forcible'. (Hume had been one of the Members who had dined with the queen at the Guildhall on 22 June.)[22] On 27 June he unsuccessfully moved, in what Grey Bennet deemed a 'clear good statement', a resolution condemning the 'Scotch job' of the building of the new Edinburgh stamp office, aiming particularly at Sir John Marjoribanks*. He then spoke for over three hours in support of resolutions calling for economy and retrenchment, specifying reduction of the army and deploying detailed statistics collected by Ricardo. Grey Bennet thought his speech was 'clear, forcible and well received', though 'perhaps the means of retrenchment were somewhat overcharged'. The Whig Lord Tavistock seconded the motion, but adopted a 'desponding' tone and criticized Hume for entering into such detail, which was the business of ministers. They, anticipating widespread backbench support for the resolutions, the contents of which Hume, 'in the openness of his heart and in his love of what he thinks to be *gentility*', as Grey Bennet put it, had communicated to them, set up the influential Bankes to move as an amendment an anodyne resolution affirming the government's commitment to retrenchment. Hume made a brief but spirited reply, denying Londonderry's jibe that he was 'a visionary in his plans of reduction', and his resolutions were rejected by 174-94.[23] On other issues, Hume supported the Grampound disfranchisement bill 'as a boon, small as it was', 5 Mar., having on the 2nd voted to give Leeds a ratepayer franchise if it received Grampound's seats. He was shut out of the snap division on Lambton's parliamentary reform motion, 18 Apr., but voted for Lord John Russell's proposal, 9 May, and Hamilton's for reform of the Scottish county representation, 10 May. He complained that the burghs select committee's report would be a nullity, for 'a majority ... had set themselves against every attempt at amelioration', 14 June. On 7 June he moved for a commission to be sent to the Ionian Islands to investigate the conduct of the governor, Sir Thomas Maitland†, whom he blamed 'for all the blood that had been shed, and all the property confiscated' after the disturbances provoked by 'his own ill government'. Grey Bennet reckoned that the three-hour speech 'made out a very good case, but more against the constitution and the government than against Sir Thomas'; the motion was defeated by 97-27.[24] Hume denounced Robert Owen's New Lanark socialist experiment, which would destroy human 'independence and spirit' and 'make us a race of beings very little removed from brutes, only ranging the four corners of a parallelogram, instead of the mazes of a forest', 26 June. On 10 July 1821 he presented and endorsed a petition alleging misconduct against Charles Hope†, lord president of the court of session. The junior minister Lord Binning rebuked him for bringing it up at the end of the session (it had been in his hands for three weeks); and Grey Bennet, who, with many Whigs, felt that Hume's timing was 'most unhappily selected', believed that if a more accomplished ministerial speaker had been present, he would have received 'the surest dressing (and well merited too) he has ever found in the House'. The following day he proposed an address to the king for the inclusion of Caroline in the coronation, but he was interrupted and silenced by the arrival of Black Rod to prorogue Parliament. Grey Bennet thought it 'but a foolish piece of business leading to no practical good'.[25]

The independent Whig Sir Robert Heron* reflected that the economical campaign of Hume and his associates was 'enthusiastically supported by the nation', and Hume was praised in the national press that summer. At the Holkham sheep-shearing in July, when he rubbed shoulders with Whig grandees, he responded to a toast to his health with the observation (after a long lecture on economy and reform) that he deserved no thanks for his efforts, because 'his taste naturally leaned towards the prosecution of this exposure, from which he derived as much pleasure' as his host Thomas Coke I* did from agricultural improvements.[26] Hume was voted thanks and given the freedom of the City of London by common council, 26 Oct.[27] Grey Bennet wrote in July that 'the perseverance of a few, with Mr. Hume at their head', had 'roused the spirit of the country' and 'frightened the boldest of the ministers' into giving ground on retrenchment. (They made a reduction of 12,000 in the army and, continuing their steady progress in economical reform, got rid of over 160 sinecures, as well as committing themselves to make further cuts.) Hume's popularity had risen 'every day', and 'the country has been taught to look into the details of its own affairs'.[28] John Whishaw commented to his fellow Whig Lord Holland, 16 July 1821, that the party remained 'much divided' and the 'Mountain' 'set no bounds to their triumph in Hume's success and the comparative inaction and obscurity of the leaders'.[29] Hume was involved with the radical Whigs Sir Robert Wilson* and Hobhouse in attempts to force the queen's funeral procession through the City, attended the inquest on the victims of the ensuing violence and urged Hobhouse to join him in encouraging the Whigs to take the outrage up 'with vigour'; and on Wilson's dismissal from the army commented that it was an example of 'what we are to expect and we must now live as slaves or meet the whole power of government'.[30] On 7 Dec. he was entertained at Hereford and presented with an engraved tankard and a hogshead of cider. In response, he spoke at inordinate length of the 'grievous malady' of 'excessive taxation' resulting from 'a long continuance of profuse and wasteful expenditure pervading every department of the state', and declared that the 'great polar star to lead us in our course was reform in Parliament', which would 'give an effectual control to the people over the expenditure'. A report of the proceedings, with a statistical appendix explaining and illustrating Hume's arguments, was published as a pamphlet in January 1822, when Hume was voted thanks at a public meeting of the householders of Reading.[31] On 21 Dec. 1821 he joined Russell, Brougham and three other Whigs at a *Freemasons' Tavern* meeting to organize a public gathering to express support for the Greeks in their struggle against Turkish oppression. To Hobhouse he mentioned rumours that 'the king and the Tories do not draw pleasantly at present', and speculated that if Lord Wellesley, the new Irish viceroy, had really been sent there 'to bring about Catholic emancipation, we shall have all the Tories up, and I hope, out of office 'ere six months are over'.[32]

On the eve of the 1822 session Planta reported a belief that 'Squire Hume will let alone the servants of the public and occupy himself entirely with an attack n the emoluments of the church', which turned out to be wide of the mark.[33] The duke of Bedford thought that the Whigs 'must enter with spirit into the guerrilla war, and support that efficient chief Joseph Hume in all his motions for retrenchment, diminution of taxes, etc.'.[34] Hume and the 'Mountain' began the session with some optimism. He gave notice of an amendment to the address, but was thought to have given it up on 4 Feb.[35] Next day, however, after Burdett's amendment for a postponement had been rejected, he did, in a speech larded indigestibly with figures, move an amendment to pledge the House to implement stringent economy and retrenchment. He also threw in an attack on the Grenvillites, who had recently joined the ministry and been handsomely rewarded for doing so. The Tory Member John Gladstone described him as 'very very noisy, very violent ... and on many points unintelligible, but quite satisfied with himself'.[36] He was called to order by the Speaker for saying that some Members entered the Commons 'to benefit themselves'. His amendment, which he modified at Newport's suggestion, was defeated by 171-89; Ricardo refused to vote for it and left the chamber. Lord Grey, the Whig leader, thought that Hume's speech, 'however dull it might be to the hearers', was 'calculated to produce great effect in the country' and strengthen the case for tax cuts.[37] After opposing the government's coercive measures for Ireland, 7, 8 Feb., supporting Wilson's demand for inquiry into his dismissal, 13 Feb., and voting for the Whig motions for further tax reductions, 11, 21 Feb., he resumed the tactics of the previous year, 22 Feb., by moving for a detailed account of the way in which the money required for seamen's wages was to be spent. After its rejection by 144-54, he became involved in a dispute with Croker, the secretary to the admiralty, who mockingly exposed what appeared to be egregious errors in his figures. Tierney was said to have left the House to avoid voting with him.[38] The wrangle with Croker was resumed on 27 Feb., when Hume secured 78 votes for his motion for the submission of detailed army estimates before money was granted. Creevey thought Hume had 'completely defeated' Croker and been 'raised again to the highest pinnacle of fame for his accuracy and arithmetic'; but the Whig Sir James Mackintosh* thought it boiled down to a mere difference 'in the mode of stating the account' and that 'even in that respect no serious impression was made on Joseph'. When he was detected in and owned up to another blunder, 22 Mar., Hobhouse noted privately that 'there is a general feeling of uneasiness on all sides respecting these details of Hume, and he daily produces less effect'. Mrs. Arbuthnot was gratified to write the following day that Hume's 'own party [the Whigs] are now beginning to turn against him as they are *jealous of his popularity*'.[39] Lord Palmerston*, the war secretary, told his brother:

I have not had half the trouble with estimates this year that I had last ... We had made such large reductions that little was left for Hume to object to, and the body of the opposition did not support him much in his objections even to that little. He is going downhill very fast: indeed, so dull and blunderheaded a fellow, notwithstanding all his perseverance and application, cannot long hold his ground in the ... Commons. It requires some degree of talent, and he does not come up to the mark.

He predicted that Hume would soon 'shrink into his proper dimensions'.[40] When Maberly had urged him in the House, 15 Mar., to 'abandon the useless task of disputing the estimates, item by item, since all his exertions were rendered unavailing by the overwhelming majorities of ministers', he expressed his 'determination to persevere'. He and his associates pressed on with their increasingly hopeless campaign, which secured sometimes embarrassingly small minorities, until Easter. On 20 Feb. he supported Hamilton's motion to refer the report of the burghs select committee to a committee of the whole House, protesting that while all the allegations of abuse and corruption had been substantiated, the lord advocate Sir William Rae and Binning had drawn up in Hamilton's absence a whitewash report which merely recommended cosmetic reforms; he duly denounced Rae's burghs accounts bill because it did not touch 'the root of all the evil ... the power of self-election', 17 June. His remark that army officers were 'the slaves of the crown', 12 Mar., provoked Frederick Trench to attack him in offensively personal terms, but the quarrel was brought to a peaceful conclusion by the Speaker. Hume presented and endorsed a petition from Monmouth for parliamentary reform, of which he predicted 'the ultimate triumph', 28 Mar. 1822. During the recess he was entertained by the Fishmongers' Company of London and introduced at Ricardo's to Maria Edgeworth, who did not 'like him much', as he 'attacks all things and all persons, never listens [and] has no judgement'.[41] He was appointed to the select committee on public accounts, 18 Apr. He voted for Russell's reform motion, 25 Apr., and reception of the Greenhoe reform petition, 3 June. He steadily attacked the 'delusion' of the naval and military deadweight pensions scheme, securing 56 votes for his proposal that the money should be taken from the sinking fund, 3 May. Renewed bids to effect this were defeated by 115-35 and 81-54, 24 May, 3 June. He divided with Ricardo for a 20s. duty on wheat imports, 9 May, but on the 13th approved the government's revision of the corn laws as a modest improvement. Next day he got 57 votes for another motion for inquiry into the Ionian Isles regime, but Wilberforce for one slept 'through great part' of his speech.[42] At the end of May he was caricatured as an ass in conversation with John Bull.[43] On 19 June he delivered a seemingly endless speech in support of his motion for the House next session to consider the state of the Irish established church and tithes collection, denying that he favoured 'spoliation and robbery', as his opponents alleged. He waived his own motion for Newport's amendment for a commutation of tithes. On the budget, 1 July, he declared that government had increased both the permanent and funded debt. He spoke and was a minority teller for Hobhouse's motion for repeal of the window tax next day, but Hobhouse thought he showed 'the frailty of man' by being lukewarm about his comments on the sinking fund, which Hume regarded as his special preserve.[44] He supported inquiry into the allegations in the Calcutta bankers' petition and was named to the select committee, 4 July. According to Mrs. Arbuthnot, her husband in the course of his work with Hume on the select committee on printing and stationery for the House (13 May) discovered that he had been 'exciting his clerks to tempt the treasury messengers to sell the paper to them at a cheap rate, which paper he has used for his own purposes'; Hume was 'in a fury' and had vowed vengeance against future estimates.[45] He dismissed the notion of introducing poor laws to Ireland, 24 July. A junior minister reported that the session was a long time dying, with 'everybody but Hume and Bennet ... sick of it, and literally very other opposition man gone out of town'.[46] As a finale, 25 July 1822, Hume proposed 38 resolutions on the national finances, the thrust of which was that the only true sinking fund consisted of the application of a genuine surplus of revenue to cancellation of the national debt and reduction of the interest on it. They were of course negatived. Heron thought that Hume had failed to build on his success of 1821:

His eternal interference on every question, and the many tedious hours he occupied in attempting trifling savings, only disgusted many from attending, and prevented more important questions from being brought forward. The climax of his vulgar assurance was the bringing forward of the Irish tithe question.[47]

Unchastened, but furious with the Whigs, Hume went in September 1822 to his constituency, where he was feted at Aberdeen and Montrose and spoke forcefully for parliamentary reform as the essential solution to the country's difficulties. He claimed to have succeeded in 'awakening the public to discern one great cause of their distress', namely the enormous national debt created by 'the Pitt system'. He urged the Whigs to 'disclose what they would do for the people if they were in power' and to 'pledge themselves to what extent they would go in promoting reform'. At a Perth dinner, he 'complained of the Whigs not having supported him as they ought to have done ... in burgh and parliamentary reform', but exempted Hamilton from his criticism. He was admitted as a freeman of Berwick on his way south.[48] Holland observed to Lord Duncannon*, 5 Oct., that Hume's 'censures on opposition do not disturb me', for 'if he is a violent reformer it is both natural and right that he should blame others for not being so. I only hope that his blame or his praise may not have the effect of making those who are to behave as if they were'.[49] Tierney wrote dismissively that Hume 'appears to set up for himself with the 40 gentlemen who have had the good fortune to meet with his approbation'.[50] Brougham, however was 'vexed', as he told Creevey

> at Hume's making such a stupid ass of himself ... by his stupid vanity ... His kind patronage of Archy [Hamilton] is only laughable, but to see him splitting on that rock (of egotism and vanity) is rather provoking. What right has *he* to talk of the Whigs never coming to his support on ... reform? I cannot reckon a man's conduct at all pure who shows up others at public meetings behind their backs, whom he never whispers a word against in their faces. There is extreme meanness in this sneaking way of ingratiating himself at their expense, and the utter falsehood of the charge is glaring. Parliamentary reform has never once been touched by him (luckily for the question). The motions on it last session were Lord John's and my own. His burgh reform professedly steered clear of the question. I trust he has been misrepresented, but I heard in Scotland that people were everywhere laughing at him for his arrogance and vanity.[51]

The Whig James Abercromby* wanted the party to make Ireland 'a leading topic' in the next session, and told Duncannon, 14 Oct. 1822, that it would 'never do to let it get into the hands of Hume. That of the Irish church is a question that requires to be very skilfully and delicately handled'.[52] The Edinburgh Whig lawyer Henry Cockburn observed in December 1822 that on Scottish questions, especially that of legal reform, Hume, whom he called 'Hum Drum', was 'ignorant'.[53]

With Hobhouse and Sir Francis Burdett*, Hume was invited to the Speaker's pre-session diner, 9 Feb. 1823, when, in 'uppish' mood, he 'amused' many 'by

talking his politics, particularly against the church, out loud'.[54] In the House, 12 Feb., he applauded the promises of economy and tax reductions in the king's speech, but urged Members to look beyond the 'sweet and honied words' of ministers to reality, specifying the recent appointment of Lord Beresford, whose family had plundered vast sums from the public coffers, as lieutenant-general of the ordnance, and moving a resolution that the appointment contradicted ministerial professions. Brougham and Burdett persuaded him to withdraw it, but on the 19th he brought it on again. Brougham, Tierney, Russell and other leading Whigs would not support him, Macdonald moved an unsuccessful amendment for inquiry and he was defeated by 200-73. Brougham, who had not forgiven Hume for his attack on the Whigs the previous autumn, told Duncannon that it was time for the party to dissociate itself from such 'absurd and untenable propositions' and that if Hume would not restrain himself after a private word they must oppose him 'openly, giving the reasons', when they judged that he had gone too far. He later reported that Lord Darlington 'expresses great annoyance at the way Hume, etc., are going on, and at our friends seeming resolved to do on every occasion ... whatever *anybody bawls out for*, without at all considering the character of the party'. Bedford, on the other hand, thought 'the *great guns* of the opposition behaved very ill' towards Hume, who seemed to have 'made good his case for the abolition of a useless office'; but he reflected that 'poor Joey is vulgar, and not so refined as some of our leaders, so he was abandoned, for the purpose of paying an unnecessary compliment to the duke of Wellington!'[55] Hume had on 10 Feb. denounced the 'perfect farce' of the sinking fund, 'a paying with one hand and borrowing with the other, without liquidating any portion of the amount of debt'. He moved an amendment that it was inexpedient to maintain a fund of £3,000,000 and that £2,000,000 could be remitted in taxation, 3 Mar., but was defeated by 110-39. His repeated attacks on the fund and the national debt reduction bill that month were all heavily crushed. In April he turned his fire against the related naval and military and naval pensions bill, which embodied a 'hole and corner' bargain with the Bank of England, but to no avail. Throughout the session he maintained his customary sniping against the estimates, though less intensively than in the previous two sessions. Peel, the home secretary, wrote facetiously to Croker of Babbage's 'scientific automaton', that 'if it can calculate what ... Babbage says it can, may be employed to the destruction of Hume'.[56] On the budget statement, 2 July, he declared himself 'somewhat satisfied' with the government's improved performance, admitting that the 'reduction which had taken place was certainly more than he had thought possible 18 months since', before the ministry had been reconstructed; he encouraged Robinson, the chancellor of the exchequer, to cut even more taxes. He supported and forced to a division, in which he was a teller for the minority of 25, Whitmore's motion for revision of the corn laws, 26 Feb. He favoured taxing malt rather than beer, 12, 28 May, 17 June; said that protectionist petitioners against the government's silk bill were deluded, 21 May; voted for equalization of the East and West Indian sugar duties, 22 May, and welcomed the government's trade reciprocity bill, 4 July. He did not divide the House on his proposition for savings in the collection and management of land tax revenues, 8 July. He voted for inquiry into the parliamentary franchise, 20 Feb., Russell's reform motion, 24 Apr., and reform of the Scottish representative system, 2 June. On 26 Mar. he supported Hamilton's motion for a copy of the royal warrant which had restored to power the old ruling oligarchy of Inverness and castigated the corrupt conduct of the magistrates of Aberdeen. He endorsed the prayer for reform of an Edinburgh householders' petition, 5 May. He presented and supported a petition from Mary Anne Carlile complaining of her fine and imprisonment for blasphemous libel, attacked the Society for the Suppression of Vice and the Constitutional Association and 'opened the whole question of religious persecution', which he raised regularly throughout this period, at the expense of being branded an atheist.[57] He was one of the supporters of Catholic relief who ostentatiously left the chamber before Plunket, the detested Irish attorney-general, proposed consideration of the question, 17 Apr.[58] He was among the 20 mainly ministerialist Members trapped in the chamber and counted as a minority (for which he acted as a teller) in the farcical division on the Franco-Spanish war, 30 Apr. 1823; he had, Brougham reported, stayed to 'take a note (which he loves to do) of a division'.[59]

Hume had outlined his scheme for Irish tithes and church reforms on the opening day of the session; and on 4 Mar. 1823 he proposed inquiry into the Irish church establishment, arguing that its property was public and as such liable to redistribution, that the income of its clergymen and their numbers, especially the non-residents, could be advantageously reduced and that Ireland would benefit from a commutation of tithes. The Whig Member George Agar Ellis thought he 'spoke forcibly in his rambling sort of way'.[60] The Speaker called him to order in his reply to the debate for accusing his opponents of 'grossly misrepresenting

him'. The motion was defeated by 167-62. Creevey evidently told the absent Brougham that 'there never was anything more triumphant than Joseph, that the church had got a body blow'; but Brougham, though he thought that the 'attack on the church was safer in his hands than in any others', expected Hume to 'throw away a great case' and told Duncannon that he, like most of the party, would support 'no general attack on the establishment'.[61] Bedford again sympathized with 'poor' Hume, who 'gets abused for everything he does because he is not *genteel* and his language and manner so *refined* as those of our opposition leaders', though he conceded that he was not the ideal person to take up 'the abuses of the Irish church', which would best be handled by 'an Englishman of some *calibre*'.[62] Proposing a reduction in the grant for Irish Protestant charter schools, for which he got 15 votes, 11 Apr., Hume declared that if the Irish people were to be made 'happy, we must give them education, revise the existing tithe system' and discourage absenteeism among landlords. On 23 Apr. he said that the government would soon be obliged to adopt his scheme for a general fund to pay Catholic as well as Protestant Irish clergy and caused a stir by asserting that the majority Catholic population should refuse to subsidize an alien church establishment through tithes and, if denied legal redress, should resort to 'physical force'. In the inquiry into the prosecution of the Dublin Orange rioters, 26 May, he insisted on his right to question a witness about Orange initiation ceremonies, as 'there could be no hope of peace in Ireland until Orangemen, as a body, should be destroyed'. On 16 June he spoke and voted in the minority of 36 against the government's Irish tithes composition bill, which he had decided contained 'nothing useful'. He proposed but did not divide the House on abolition of the Irish lord lieutenancy, 25 June. When the Methodist Joseph Butterworth damned Jesuits, 30 June, Hume replied that Methodists were 'the Jesuits from whom the Church of England had most to apprehend'; the ensuing angry exchanges obliged the chairman to intervene. His motions for inquiry into the excessive cost of the coronation (which the cabinet minister Charles Williams Wynn* privately admitted had been 'terrible')[63] were rejected by 119-65 (9 June) and 127-77 (19 June). In September 1823 he reported to Hobhouse that for all their efforts to raise money to support the Spanish liberals (he had just audited the accounts 'for about £17,000 expended by the Spanish committee'), he feared that 'things in Spain go on as badly as possible'. He was shocked and saddened by the premature death of his 'valuable' friend and tutor Ricardo.[64] On 20 Dec. 1823 Tierney observed to Lady

Holland that Hume's 'economical exertions have been crowned with signal success', for they had 'induced his father-in-law [who had died on 27 Nov.] to leave him all his own savings to the amount of £80,000'; certainly Hume profited from Burnley's will, but Tierney may have exaggerated the sum involved.[65]

On the address, 3 Feb. 1824, he voiced his dismay that 'the same ruinous policy which had so long distracted and divided Ireland was still to be persisted in' and that there had been no distinct statement of intended tax remissions. He said the navy estimates were 'extravagant', but was temporarily appeased by Canning's explanation, 16 Feb. On 20 Feb. he secured ten votes for his amendment against the proposed 4,000 increase in the army, observing that Lord Holland approved it because he was 'interested as a West Indian and he could not follow him now or at any time'.[66] On 23 Feb. he was left in a minority of eight on the same issue. Earlier that day, however, he had expressed his 'satisfaction at a great part' of Robinson's financial statement, especially that relating to the removal of restrictions on trade, but he felt that the chancellor had 'stopped at the half-way house' and could apply the £7,000,000 sinking fund to essential tax reductions. He spoke to the same effect, 7 May, specifying the taxes on timber and wool. He criticized the terms of the Austrian loan repayment, 24, 26 Feb. He was slightly disappointed with the ordnance estimates, 27 Feb., when he moved two amendments for economies, which were heavily defeated. He suggested that St. James's Palace should be demolished and rebuilt rather than have money wasted on it in 'tasteless repairs', 1 Mar. He spoke and voted for Hobhouse's motions for a repeal of assessed taxes, 2 Mar., 10 May, and endorsed the prayer of the Westminster petition for large tax remissions, 12 Mar., when he divided the House against details of the colonial estimates. He urged Robinson to reduce the wine duties, 19 Feb., and repeal those on seaborne coals, 29 Mar., and moved to postpone consideration of the grant for Windsor Castle repairs and refurbishment, 5 Apr., when he was defeated by 123-54. His wrecking amendment to the superannuation fund bill was negatived, 17 June. He again supported the government's silk trade proposals, 5, 9, 18 Mar., but wanted small shopkeepers to be given a bounty on surplus stocks of uncut material; his amendment for this was defeated by 76-30, 22 Mar. He spoke and voted for Grattan's motion for information on Irish Catholic office-holders, 19 Feb.; again opposed the grants for Protestant charter schools, 15 Mar.; called for a reform of Irish education, 29 Mar., 9 Apr.; denounced Irish magistrates who countenanced Orange processions,

30 Mar.; spoke and voted in the minority of ten for the reduction of the Irish militia, 5 May; got 79 votes for his renewed motion for inquiry into the Irish church establishment, 6 May, and supported Newport's motion to reform Irish first fruits revenues, 25 May. He voted for reform of Edinburgh's representation, 26 Feb. His attempts to end army flogging, 5, 15 Mar., were rejected by 50-24 and 127-47. His motion for inquiry next session into naval impressments was defeated by 108-38, 10 June. Hume's brother owned an estate in Trinidad, and he was conspicuously lukewarm on slavery abolition.[67] He called for reduction of the West Indian sugar duties, 8 Mar., but did not press it to a division. Presenting an abolitionist petition from Marylebone, 23 Mar., he promised on a future day to propose that emancipation of the slaves, who were 'undoubted property', must be accompanied by compensation to the owners. He was absent from the division on Brougham's motion condemning the prosecution of the Methodist missionary John Smith in Demerara, 11 June. He reacted strongly to the renewal of the Aliens Act, moving an unsuccessful wrecking amendment against its first reading, 23 Mar., when he alleged that the cabinet was split on the issue, and steadily opposing its progress thereafter. He was equally infuriated by the bill to promote the erection of new churches, which he denounced on 12 Apr. as a scheme to 'increase the church patronage and church influence, already too extensive'. He left the Westminster purity of election anniversary dinner, 24 May, before his health was given, telling Hobhouse, who was surprised at this 'unusual prudence', that if he had stayed he would have been obliged to 'controvert' the observations of Burdett and Lambton on 'the inutility of attending' Parliament.[68] On 27 May he moved for a return of commitments by magistrates, but Peel objected and he was defeated by 71-34. He then proposed a standing order to the effect that no Member with a vested interest in a private bill should be allowed to vote on it in committee upstairs, but was persuaded by Canning to withdraw this in return for the appointment of a select committee, to which he was named. In July and August 1824 he was centrally involved, as one of the three commissioners charged with managing and distributing the loan fund subscribed to support the Greek insurgents, in the internal squabble which threatened to scupper the plan to send Hobhouse to Greece to oversee distribution of the money. Hobhouse suspected that Hume wanted to send 'an agent of his own who would obey his orders and disperse his speeches in Greece', but in the end Hume backed down and assured Hobhouse that he had intended no personal slight.[69]

In 1822 Hume had told Place that he wished to propose and was confident of obtaining widespread support for repeal of the Combination Acts, which he believed impeded the labour market and were biased in favour of the masters. Place had him stay his hand for the moment and supplied him with detailed information on the subject. Early in the 1824 session Huskisson, president of the board of trade, persuaded Hume to drop his planned motion for a select committee on the laws in favour of one on artisans' emigration and the export of machinery. Place disliked this compromise and persuaded Hume to stick to his original plan; and after consultation with Huskisson he moved, in one of his most accomplished speeches, for the appointment of a select committee on all three issues, 29 Feb. Hume chaired the committee and drove it hard. Witnesses from the working class were coached beforehand by Place, who briefed Hume and gave evidence in favour of repeal, as did Malthus and McCulloch. Hume persuaded the committee to submit a series of short resolutions rather than a cumbersome report, and he revealed them to the House on 21 May: they recommended repeal of the Combination Acts, consolidation of the laws governing industrial disputes and removal of the restrictions on the emigration of skilled workers. He introduced two enabling bills, 25, 27 May, and saw them speedily through the Commons. He and Place lobbied successfully for support in the Lords, and the measures became law on 21 June 1824 (5 Geo. IV, cc. 95, 97).[70] Hume had naively expected repeal of the combination laws to obviate the need for unions, but of course they did not, and the later months of 1824 were marked by a series of violent disputes and strikes in manufacturing areas. Huskisson, afraid that repeal seemed to have put unions beyond the reach of common law, proposed the appointment of a select committee to reconsider the problem, 29 Mar. 1825, when Hume tried to attribute these difficulties to full employment rather than repeal, but admitted that both workers and employers 'carried their measures far beyond the point to which they should restrict themselves'. He was duly named to the committee, which decided that the unions were out of control, though it conceded that they had a legitimate role to play in wage negotiations. Hume's argument that a straight reversal of repeal would make matters worse had some effect, and the consequent bill confirmed that trade unionism and strikes were not illegal, while it outlawed intimidation and coercion. Hume felt obliged to oppose it, presenting hostile workers' petitions, 29 Apr., 3 May, defending the measure of 1824, 4 May, complaining that ministers had 'given the workman anything rather than fair play', 27 June, when his two amendments were beaten by 90-18 and 60-15, and securing only two votes for his amendment to deprive magistrates of the power of punishing men for 'molestation', 29 June. Hudson Gurney described his opposition on this occasion (when Place and a Glasgow delegate were spectators) as 'most violent and pertinacious': 'I never saw Hume lose temper so much before. He had been ill used at the beginning of the business, but there is nothing in the bill to justify ... [his] expressions about it'.[71] Hume registered his protest against the third reading, 1 July. The bill became law on 6 July 1825 (6 Geo. IV, c. 129).[72]

On the address, 4 Feb. 1825, Hume deplored the planned suppression of the Catholic Association and accused ministers of being 'anxious to bring on a crisis' in Ireland, where they planned 'to use the bayonet' in the hands of the unjustifiably augmented army. In committee on the bill to outlaw the Association, 22 Feb., he proposed a resolution to the effect that any man now holding or in future receiving an Irish office should be obliged to swear on oath that he did not and would not belong to an illegal organization; it was negatived. He spoke and voted, as previously, for repeal of the usury laws, 8, 17 Feb. He complained that the navy estimates still included 'useless expenditure', 21 Feb. On Robinson's financial statement, 28 Feb., he found fault with the 'immense military establishment', recommended reduction of the duties on tobacco and brandy and damned the sinking fund 'delusion', but gave the chancellor 'full credit' for his continued application of liberal commercial principles. His amendment questioning the need for so large an army, 7 Mar., when he attacked Lord Charles Somerset's[†] troubled regime in the Cape, was rejected by 102-8. He unsuccessfully proposed his ban on Members voting on private bills in which they had 'a direct pecuniary interest', 10 Mar; but on the Leith docks bill, 'one of the most shameful ... jobs that had ever been brought before the House', 20 May, he had Marjoribanks's vote for it discounted after pointing out his vested interest in the scheme. He welcomed Peel's juries regulation bill, but failed to persuade him to reform the chaos of the common law, 9 Mar., and he approved the government's Scottish juries bill, based on the efforts of the Whig Thomas Kennedy, 18 Apr. While he gave qualified support to the bill for the sale of waste lands in Canada, 15 Mar., he argued that the 'disgrace' of the colonial system (for which he would impeach the secretary Lord Bathurst in a reformed Parliament) needed urgent reform. He questioned Huskisson on some colonial matters, 21 Mar., when he said that diplomatic expenditure 'far exceeded what the country required'.

His motion for inquiry into the state of the Indian army, which was aimed at the governorship of Lord Amherst, was defeated by 58-15, 24 Mar.[73] He pressed for a reduction of the duties on Baltic timber and 'a careful and proper revision' of the corn laws, 25 Mar. He was in the minority of 47 for the latter, 28 Apr., and on 2 May protested, in the name of the manufacturing interest, against the assumption that the entire country was satisfied with the existing arrangements. He supported the West India Company bill, 29 Mar., 16 May. He asserted that the Glasgow merchants and bankers' petition for Catholic relief accurately reflected the views of 'the well-informed classes' of Scotland, 21 Apr. Next day and on 26 Apr. and 9 May he opposed the bill to disfranchise Irish 40s. freeholders, 'the most important measure' of his Commons experience, as an 'enormous invasion of the rights and privileges' of the electors.[74] His alternative proposal for inquiry into fraudulent Irish voting, 9 May, was negatived. He also opposed the other 'wing' of the Catholic relief bill, the payment of the Catholic priesthood because it was unjust to English and Irish Dissenters, 29 Apr., when his motion to inquire into paying all of them annual stipends was rejected by 205-162. He reckoned that the proposed increase in judges' salaries was 'ill-timed and uncalled-for', 16 May, spoke and voted for Brougham's motion to make puisne judges immoveable, 20 May, and contended that the lord chancellor should be paid by salary rather than fees, 27 May. That day he divided the House against the grant of £6,000 to the duke of Cumberland for the education of Prince George, and again, 30 May. His motion for leave to introduce a bill to end flogging in the navy was defeated by 45-23, 9 June, and that for early consideration next session of the Irish church and tithes by 126-37, 14 June. He urged ministers to regulate the paper currency by making it convertible into specie by 'a summary process', if necessary, 27 June 1825. Hume corresponded amicably with Huskisson in September about consular fees and the repeal of the duty on agricultural horses, which he thought had 'already done good'.[75] The following month he declined to accept pieces of plate and silver subscribed for him by Glasgow mechanics and artisans and colliers of the Glasgow area because, as he publicly explained to them, after the reversal of combination law repeal (for which he took his share of blame, though he complained that Huskisson and others had 'deserted him'), he did not think it appropriate to accept any token from operatives who thereby claimed him 'exclusively' as 'their advocate' while their employers regarded him as 'an enemy'. He enjoined the workmen to avoid intimidation or illegal action, for in that case he would be neither able nor willing to prevent reimposition of the old restrictions. He visited the Forfarshire burghs and 'found all right' in respect of the approaching general election. He had decided to avoid all public dinners for the moment, but was obliged by an earlier promise to attend one in Edinburgh in November 1825, when he boasted of his delight in 'hard labour' and spoke on his usual subjects.[76]

On the address, 2 Feb. 1826, Hume welcomed the government's proposal to facilitate the establishment of joint-stock banks, but complained that the army was still too large and taxation too heavy, and argued that the restriction of the circulation of small bank notes would do no good and that only the eradication of 'wasteful expenditure ... profligate sinecures and overgrown establishments' would serve. He attacked Amherst's Indian regime and denounced all monopolies, including the corn laws. Lord Fitzwilliam noted that 'Hume is at work again and taking everything under his consideration', but that 'it is supposed that his time is short', as a dissolution loomed.[77] Lord Althorp* heard that he liked the ministerial promissory notes bill, but he spoke and voted against it, 13 Feb.[78] Next day he praised ministers' free trade measures and made due allowance for their difficulties on the currency and bank questions, but denigrated the notion of an issue of exchequer bills. On 20 Feb. he attacked the promissory notes bill and proposed inquiry into the best means of placing the banking system on 'a better footing', but his motion was negatived. He secured the adjournment of the debate on the bill by threatening to divided continually against it, 24 Feb., and on the 27th moved an instruction to require banks to place in the exchequer deposits equal in amount to notes issued, which was defeated by 111-9. His amendment to empower magistrates to distrain on the property of any banker refusing to convert small notes into bullion was rejected by 163-19. He was in a minority of nine against the third reading, 7 Mar., when his attempt to oblige country bankers to make monthly returns of their notes in circulation was rejected by 143-24. Peel and Goulburn, the Irish secretary, thought he would 'give as much trouble as he can on the estimates', but Henry Hobhouse, the home office under-secretary, recalled that at the start of the session he 'evinced an intention of disputing every item in the estimates with the same pertinacity which he so successfully practised three or four years ago', only to be 'foiled by the want of support', as Members became preoccupied with the impending dissolution.[79] Hume attacked the navy estimates, 17, 21 Feb., when he got only 15 votes for his amendment for their reconsideration. His proposal to return to the army establishment of 1792 was defeated by 144-45, 3 Mar., and he was in minorities of 22 for cuts in the grants for the Royal Military College and garrisons, 6 Mar. He ranted against the army extraordinaries and colonial expenditure, 10 Mar., when his renewed attempt to end army flogging was thwarted by 99-42. On 17 and 21 Mar. he condemned the excesses of diplomatic expenditure, singling out the 'shameful' amount spent on repairs to the residence of the British ambassador to France; but Tierney, who would not have voted with him if he had divided the House, told Holland, 24 Mar., that 'I attended to all Joseph said and was convinced that he did not understand what he was talking about. He never means to act unfairly, but from haste or want of information he sometimes (and certainly he did so on this occasion) comes out with statements which I often wonder are not more exposed'.[80] He divided the Commons twice against grants for Irish charities, 23 Mar., but was in minorities of six and four. He declared against the precipitate abolition of slavery, 1 Mar., and did not vote for the motion condemning the slave trials in Jamaica next day. He called for repeal of the corn laws, 6, 9 Mar., and voted for their revision, 18 Apr. He supported ministerial motions for the appointment of select committees on emigration, 14 Mar., and Scottish gaols, 21 Mar., and was named to both. On 7 Apr. he secured 45 votes for his amendment that the £5,000 salary proposed for the president of the board of trade could be financed by abolition of the treasurership of the navy; and on 10 Apr. he welcomed the government's decision to settle for £2,000. He condemned the administration of chancery, 'by which justice was in effect denied to millions and the severest mental torture inflicted', 21 Apr. On 4 May he delivered a four-hour speech (during which Goulburn shirked the 'painful duty of listening to him' to write at length to his wife)[81] in support of his motion for an address requesting the king to order an inquiry into the causes of and remedies for distress, which he accompanied with 47 statistical resolutions embodying his views on taxation, the sinking fund and national accounting. He 'gave credit' to ministers for 'the liberal course of policy which had lately distinguished their administration', but urged them to go further and deplored continued high levels of expenditure; he was defeated by 152-51. He was appointed to the select committees on the allegations of James Silk Buckingham[†] concerning restrictions on freedom of the press in India and the Mauritius slave trade, 9 May. On 11 May he moved for leave for a bill to repeal the ban on the export of tools, but was persuaded by ministers to drop it. He attributed distress in the shipping industry to high taxation rather than ministerial legislation, 13 May. He spoke, 9 Mar., and

voted, 13 Apr., for reform of Edinburgh's representation. He divided silently for Russell's reform motion, 27 Apr., and spoke and voted for his resolution condemning electoral bribery, 26 May 1826, claiming to have received that day a letter asserting that an unnamed borough could be had for £2,500 in bribes and £500 legitimate expenses.

On his way to his constituency for the general election in late June 1826 Hume was summoned from Edinburgh to backtrack to Berwick in order to vote for the 'radical' Sir Francis Blake*. He came in unopposed for his burghs, where he claimed to have redeemed all his pledges of 1820 and expressed some hope of a relaxation of the corn laws.[82] That autumn it emerged that his inordinate love of money had led him to act a less than creditable part in the matter of the Greek loan: he had subscribed £10,000 in 1824, but when the bonds had depreciated the following year had persuaded the Greek agents to buy him out and so limit his loss to £1,300. When, however, the bonds subsequently rose in value, he insisted on being repaid that amount, plus interest. He made matters worse by sending unconvincing exculpatory letters to the national press, and the matter was unresolved when the new Parliament met in late November.[83] In consultation with Place and Mill he concocted a wide-ranging amendment to the address, which he proposed to 'a very unwilling audience', 21 Nov. 1826 Canning reported to the king that it was 'twice as long as the speech' from the throne, and Brougham, who, with Hobhouse and Burdett, had tried to persuade him not to oppose the address or at least to omit advocacy of reform and corn law repeal from his amendment, was infuriated by his 'absurd and wrongheaded' conduct and voted against him in the majority of 170 to 24. Several leading members of opposition had walked out of the chamber when he began to speak. Grey thought Brougham might have done more to restrain Hume, who 'more especially since this Greek business is no favourite of mine', but he chided his son Lord Howick, a new Member, for joining the minority.[84] The press revived the Greek loan scandal, but Hume, whom Place found at a low ebb and encouraged to persevere in his parliamentary efforts, refused to give way and repay the £1,300.[85] In the House, 27 Nov., when he pressed again for immediate revision of the corn laws, he referred to 'the malice and inveterate rancour pursued towards him' by some journalists. He secured returns concerning the sale of army commissions, 30 Nov. He presented and endorsed a petition for repeal of the 'absurd' ban on the export of machinery, 6 Dec., and urged ministers to legislate on emigration, 7 Dec., when he was persuaded to withdraw his motion for information on Somerset's rule at the Cape and the inquiry into it. According to Hobhouse, 'there was a general groan when Joe Hume got up' on 12 Dec. 1826 and 'proposed to have the House called over that day week', on the grounds that in the present distressed state of the country it was outrageous for the government to involve it in the Portuguese civil war; his proposal was negatived.[86]

Hume presented and endorsed the petition of 'starving weavers' of Blackburn for repeal of the corn laws and reform, including the ballot, 9 Feb. 1827. He badgered Robinson on the navy estimates but did not divide the House, 12 Feb. On 14 Feb. he clashed with Palmerston on the case of Colonel Bradley, who had been deprived of his Honduras command without a court martial, and was obliged to apologize for one of his intemperate remarks. He thought the government's plans for emigration would be 'a wasteful employment of the public capital', but that the proposed select committee might elicit some useful information, 15 Feb. Next day he denounced the granting of £9,000 to the duke of Clarence, the heir apparent, when Blackburn weavers were dying of starvation, and secured 65 votes against it. His subsequent amendment that it was inexpedient to vote supplies until ministers produced comprehensive accounts was negatived. He opposed the Clarence grant, 'a mean and scandalous waste of the public money', to the bitter end, 19, 26 Feb., 2, 16 Mar. His amendment to reduce the garrisons subsidy was defeated by 45-15, 20 Feb., and his usual motion against army flogging by 57-16, 26 Feb. He divided for Catholic relief, 6 Mar. He voted for a 50s. import price for corn, 9 May, and on the ministerial plan, 27 Mar., proposed a fixed duty of 15s., to be reduced by 1s. annually until it became a permanent 10s. tax; he got 16 votes. His motion for information on the Barrackpoor mutiny and its brutal suppression was rejected by 176-44, 22 Mar. He divided with opposition against voting supplies until the ministerial crisis which followed Lord Liverpool's incapacitation was resolved, 30 Mar. He moved for inquiry into the state of debtors' prisons and the operation of the laws of imprisonment for debt, but left the former issue in Peel's hands after a discussion. On 10 Apr. he got leave to introduce a bill to abolish arrest for debt on mesne process. He brought it in on 17 May, but it was thrown out on its second reading, 1 June. On the 21st he welcomed Peel's small debts recovery bill, which reached the statute book. He spoke and voted for referring the Irish miscellaneous estimates to a select committee and divided for information on chancery delays, 5 Apr. On the formation of Canning's ministry, when Peel and the seceding Tories crossed the floor, Hume stuck

to his customary seat.[87] He encouraged Canning to propose Catholic emancipation in due course, 2 May, seconded the vote of thanks to the Indian army, 8 May, and declared that from the new ministry the country 'expected ... a change of principle in financial matters', 11 May. He advised Canning to curb the recent increase in peerage creations, 14 May. He divided to separate bankruptcy from chancery administration, 22 May, and for the disfranchisement of Penryn and Althorp's election expenses bill, 28 May. His motion of 31 May for repeal of the Newspaper Stamp Duty Act of 1819, which was intended, as Canning saw it, 'to distress the new Whig allies of ... government', was crushed by 120-10; he had at first promised to drop it after a ministerial assurance that they planned to deal with it next session, but changed his mind and went ahead.[88] On Canning's budget statement, 1 June, he said that 'the finances presented the double spectacle of a diminished income and an increased expenditure', together with the 'delusive humbug' of the sinking fund. He consulted Place on a notion of moving an address to the king 'on the present state of the nation as to the state of trade', but Place talked him out of it.[89] He condemned continued British involvement in Portugal, 8 June, and gave Hobhouse to understand that he intended to oppose the vote of credit for that purpose, 11 June, but he did not speak.[90] He was a teller for the minority of 11 against the grant for Canadian water defences, 12 June. His motion for an address to the king for naval promotions to be restricted was negatived, 21 June 1827.

When presenting Irish petitions for Catholic relief, 4 Feb. 1828, Hume observed that it was 'a true Turkish domination which is exercised by this country over Ireland'. He duly voted for relief, 12 May, as he did for repeal of the Test Acts, 26 Feb., having declared on the 19th that 'no government can go on now that is not liberal', for 'the time of exclusion is at an end'. He secured a detailed account of the way in which the 1827 vote for seamen's wages had been spent, 11 Feb., and later that day attacked the navy estimates and said he was on the whole 'dissatisfied' with the start made by the new Wellington ministry, though he would judge them by their measures. He urged Members to

look with most scrupulous exactness at every possible reduction. The country is overspread with crime and pauperism; and the people are taxed to their utmost bearing to support useless places and pensions and to maintain a most extravagant appropriation of the public revenue.

In a wrangle with ministers over the victualling grant he was accused of a mathematical blunder, but he retorted that if they believed that they 'can put me down by calling me a fool ... they will find themselves very much mistaken'. His bid to reduce the grant for 30,000 seamen was defeated by 48-15. He went over the same ground the following day, and was in a minority of eight.[91] Ministers had decided to sanction the appointment of Hume and Maberly to the finance committee, believing that they would 'in some material points counteract each other'; but when the formal proposal was made, 15 Feb., Hume cast doubt on the efficacy of a single committee and recommended the appointment of a dozen with different remits. After his examination before the committee, 22 Feb., Croker privately denounced Hume and Maberly as 'two blockheads'.[92] In the House that day Hume complained that it was 'now understood that the finance committee cannot decide upon the amount of any naval and military establishments' and that nothing had changed in the treasury attitude, and urged Wellington to take 'the golden opportunity now before him' to cut £10,000,000 of taxes, though he applauded ministers for renouncing the sinking fund. His amendment to reduce the army by 10,000 men was defeated by 106-16. He supported Graham's motion for information on public salaries, arguing that the existence of the committee should not preclude the House from scrutinizing such matters, 27 Feb. When Peel moved for the appointment of a select committee on the increase in crime and the state of the metropolitan police, 28 Feb., Hume observed that he had omitted, in his 'great pomp of diction and much fluency of expression', to allude to the 'undeniable source' of the problem, namely 'excessive taxation' and low wages. He welcomed the government's Irish juries bill and called for equalization of the sugar duties, 5 Mar. He secured detailed returns concerning savings banks, which he wished to be brought under a uniform system of management, 12 Mar., when he also persuaded Palmerston to furnish information on army promotions. He objected to Peel's amendment limiting the duration of agreements under the tithes commutation bill, 17 Mar., and opposed the passenger regulation bill as a restriction on free emigration, 18, 24 Mar. He presented and endorsed a petition from Irish Catholics against the Vestry Acts, one of the many grievances which kept Ireland in turmoil, 20 Mar. In early February he had asked Place to draft a clause to authorize the voters of Birmingham to vote by secret ballot if that borough received East Retford's seats. Place sent him materials, but in the event he did not get the opportunity to raise the issue; he voted against throwing East Retford into the hundred of Bassetlaw, 21 Mar., 27 June.[93] He gave notice of a

motion on the ballot, but reluctantly agreed to postpone it for that session, 12 June. He criticized the plan to appropriate £2,164,000 from the trustees of the naval and military pensions fund to maintain the sinking fund, 24 Mar., accused the board of control of neglecting India and its 100,000,000 inhabitants, 25 Mar., and denied that the finance committee intended to recommend the abolition of annuities, 25 Mar. He presented a Montrose petition for repeal of the stamp duty on small receipts and approved the government's proposal to remove the tax on cards and dice as an acknowledgement of the truth that 'the revenue is injured by taxation', 2 Apr. 1828.

Hume opposed the ministerial bill to assist voluntary emigration through the poor rates as coercive, 17 Apr. 1828. On the 29th he argued for free trade in corn and reproduced his proposal for a 15s. fixed duty falling to 10s., which was defeated by 139-27. He supported Mackintosh's motion for information on the civil government of Canada, 2 May. He spoke and was a teller for the minority of 54 against the provision for Canning's family, 13 May; he moved an unsuccessful wrecking amendment, 22 May. On the 16th he objected to the navy estimates and defended the finance committee, claiming that it was overwhelmed with work. While he was expostulating, Croker observed to Peel, who was not best pleased with the remark, that 'we now see the folly, as we before saw the cowardice, of putting Hume and Maberly on this committee', for they were 'more troublesome than ever, because being placed on the committee has redeemed their characters and increased their information'. (Billy Holmes*, the government whip, privately commented the next day that he suspected that ministers had put Hume and the dithering chairman Parnell on the committee 'to retard all the proceedings'.)[94] Hume made a stubborn nuisance of himself in the Commons for the rest of the session. He moved for a return of civil list pensions, which he reckoned consumed almost a third of the revenue, 20 May, but was defeated by 131-52. His motion for inquiry into these payments, 10 June, went down by 85-13. He warned that extension of the restriction on the circulation of small notes to Scotland would do 'serious injury', 22 May, and voted for inquiry, 5 June. Moving in vain for a reduction in the allowances of distributors of stamps, 22 May, he remarked that there was 'no disposition on the part of ... ministers to commit the smallest crime of economy, unless they are forced to it'. On 30 May he deplored the appointment of the soldier Sir George Murray* as colonial secretary in the room of Huskisson, who had initiated 'a system of kindness and conciliation, calculated to produce union and peace in our colonies'. He criticized many details of the miscellaneous estimates, especially the lavish spending on Windsor Castle refurbishment, 6 June, and was a teller for the minority of 28 for his amendment against the grant for the Society for the Propagation of the Gospels in the colonies. He seconded Davies's motion for a reduction in all establishments, 13 June. Writing on 16 June 'amidst the discussion of the finance committee', Huskisson told John Gladstone, 'I am afraid what I have written must appear to you very like the blather with which J. Hume has been annoying us'.[95] That day he divided the House three times: twice against the archbishop of Canterbury's bill (83-49, 74-50), and against the small notes bill, 'the most stupid act of *felo de se* we can commit' (115-24). He was a teller for the minority of 13 against the third reading of the latter, 27 June. He presented and endorsed a petition from West India proprietors resident in Aberdeen for due consideration of their property rights in the event of emancipation, 20 June, when he spoke and voted against details of the army estimates, complaining that 'not a single man or a single farthing has been reduced'. He admitted that British ship owners were entitled to some relief, but deplored any significant abandonment of reciprocity, 23 June. He divided for inquiry into the Irish church next day. On 26 June he dismissed silk workers' demands for wage regulation, proposed but withdrew a motion for leave for a bill to compel banks to make quarterly returns of notes and spoke and was a teller for the minority of ten against the cider excise bill, which imposed a new tax. He moved a wrecking amendment to the second reading of the additional churches bill, objecting to 'the power it gives of taxing parishes without their consent', which was defeated by 66-28. His subsequent motions to adjourn the debate and to refer the measure to a select committee were also rejected. On 1 July he urged Tierney to attend the finance committee the following day when the important question of 'the appropriation of the surplus to redeem funded or discharge unfunded debt' was to be considered.[96] After voting for abolition of the post of lieutenant-general of the ordnance, 4 July, he moved to report progress, pointing out that as a member of the finance committee he had been in the House for 12 hours; he got only four votes. On 7 July he attacked the size of the ordnance estimates, but wondered if it was 'worth while opposing any of theses resolutions, being surrounded by empty benches'. He supported Maberly's bid to halve the grant for the Irish ordnance survey and spoke and voted against that for Canadian water defences. On 8 July he seconded the chancellor of the exchequer Goulburn's motion for leave for a bill to amend the statutes governing public pensions,

salaries and allowances, admitting that Goulburn had fairly stated the conclusions of the finance committee but urging him also to deal with army and navy promotions and diplomatic pensions. His condemnation of the expenditure on military works in Canada as 'a wanton and gratuitous waste of the capital of an impoverished country' was negatived. He welcomed the government's bill to repeal the Naval and Military Pensions Act, but noted that its author, Robinson, had since been rewarded with a peerage (Goderich) and a pension. On Goulburn's budget statement, 11 July, he declared that the chancellor had 'admitted that the established system of borrowing money to support the sinking fund is erroneous, and the finance committee has censured it as too bad to be continued any longer', though he would for a few years use the surplus of revenue to effect a reduction in customs duties rather than apply the whole to reduction of the debt, as the committee had recommended. He doubted the accuracy of revenue accounts. He objected to Goulburn's requesting 'the fullest confidence in ministers' on the national debt while he refused to disclose how the surplus was to be applied, 15 July, when he said that government seemed intimidated by the East India Company on trade matters. He spoke and voted for reduction of the duty on imported silk, 16 July. He applauded much of Huskisson's speech on the American tariff, but rebuked him for holding out the threat of retaliation and pointed out that the corn laws were a cause of aggravation to the United States. On 25 July he drew Peel's attention to the subject of imprisonment for debt and obtained detailed information. He had written to Peel on this subject three days earlier, hoping that further investigation would convince him of 'the incalculable evils that arise from such proceedings'. In late December 1828 he asked Peel to consider authorizing the early release from prison of Robert Taylor, having always considered 'the interpretation given to the laws of England on the subject of religious opinions to be as disgraceful as the sanction of the Inquisition would be'; but Peel would not be lenient on a man who had 'given public lectures recommending infidelity and turning into open ridicule the ceremonies and doctrines of the Christian religion'.[97]

Hume welcomed the government's concession of Catholic emancipation, 12 Feb. 1829, though he wished it had been done with 'a better grace' and without suppressing the Catholic Association. He presented and endorsed favourable petitions, 2, 10, 25 Mar., insisting that they reflected majority opinion in Scotland. He voted for emancipation, 6 Mar., but divided against the second reading of the bill to disfranchise Irish 40s. freeholders, 19 Mar. On the 26th he withdrew his opposition to this 'most objectionable and unjust' measure – claiming to be 'a decided radical reformer' – in order to secure emancipation. Next day he criticized the relief bill's outlawing of Jesuits as an 'extreme measure of harshness', but he duly voted for the third reading, 30 Mar. He voted to allow Daniel O'Connell to take his seat unhindered, 18 May. He was disappointed to learn from Goulburn, who evaded his question about ministerial intentions for the sinking fund, 13 Feb., that the finance committee was not to be reappointed, repeated his ludicrous notion of appointing many subcommittees and urged Goulburn to expedite the simplification of public accounts. On 20 Feb. he complained that last session ministers had 'tided over' some issues of economy by referring to the impending reports of the finance committee and accused them of now adopting the same stratagem to avoid grappling with high expenditure and oppressive taxation. He said that Sierra Leone should have been abandoned years ago and that half the present military force would suffice, and held out 'no hope' of a change for the better, 23 Feb. He ranted against the navy estimates and the dead weight pensions burden, 27 Feb., and the inflated ordnance estimates, 3 Mar. His motion to limit the number of lashes which could be prescribed by courts martial was negatived, 10 Mar. On the report of the committee of supply, 2 Apr., he called again for inquiry by select committee into feasible tax reductions, admitted that the change in the currency had damaged industry and commerce but damned the 'odious monopoly' of the agricultural interest, enjoyed by 'those landlords and gentlemen who formerly kept down the voice of the people at the point of the bayonet'. He objected to pensions for officials of the Irish linen board and the 'madness' of continuing to pour money into Canadian defences, 6 Apr. He supported the ministerial silk bill against the protectionists, 14 Apr., 1 May, and on 2 June deplored 'lawless combinations' among the Spitalfields workers and brought in a bill to extend the provisions of the 1823 Masters and apprentices Act to the silk trade, which became law on 19 June (10 Geo. IV, c. 52). He questioned the need for a militia force, 4 May, reckoning that £4,016,000 had been thus expended since 1815; but in committee on them he praised Sir Henry Hardinge, the new war secretary, for producing intelligible estimates and acquiesced in the grant. He also complimented Goulburn on his clear budget statement, 8 May, but could not share his optimism: he thought treasury officials were ignorant of 'the deplorable condition of some of the manufacturing districts' and demanded tax cuts. Goulburn accused him

of distorting the facts. Later that day he condemned the arrangement for an issue of exchequer bills as a 'ruinous and improvident bargain', defied attempts by rowdy Members to shout him down and declaimed that the House would 'stultify itself if it agreed to any such stupid proposal'. Supporting inquiry into the East Indian trade, 14 May, he said:

> I am accused of advocating strange opinions, and perhaps I sometimes do, but I like to see how many concur in these notions ... I have lived long enough to see measures which were rejected ... carried by the very ministers who previously had successfully opposed them. I like this well enough, but ... I like still better to carry things against ministers; because, when I do that, I am sure the people are with me. I do not say this in opposition to the government ... I am ready to make great allowances for the gentlemen belonging to it, whose difficulties are considerable. They do not know who are their friends or foes ... at present.

On 18 May he brought up a resolution signifying his protest against the exchequer bills scheme, but agreed to drop it. On the motion to pass the bill, 22 May, he moved a declaration to the effect that the conversion of £3,000,000 unfunded debt was unnecessary, which was negatived. Later that day, however, he applauded the sinking fund bill, which he hoped would mark the end of the delusion. He denounced the expenditure on Buckingham House as 'discreditable' and divided against the grant for the marble arch sculpture, 25 May, and on 28 May said that apart from carrying Catholic emancipation, ministers and Parliament had that session 'done nothing for the public interest'. He voted to reduce the hemp duties, 1 June. He presented petitions for repeal of the corn laws, 28 Apr., 1, 7, 8, 14, 18, 19 May, when he spoke at great length in favour of their relaxation. He divided the House, 'if ... only to ascertain how few there are of my opinion': the answer was 12 (to 154).[98] On 2 June he explained that he was not an advocate of a fixed duty *per se*, but as a means of transition to 'an entirely free trade'. He supported legislation to amend the debtors laws in Ireland, 17 Feb., 14 May, and Scotland, 3 Mar., 27 May. On Peel's bill to regulate justices of the peace he objected to its £300 qualification and wanted clergymen to be excluded, 25 Mar. He could not persuade Peel to drop the property qualification, 27 May, but did get him to agree to see if there would be a difficulty in finding suitably qualified men in some areas. He supported a Whig attempt to amend the power of Irish bishops and ecclesiastical corporations to make leases, 2 Apr., as it was 'monstrous that the clergy in Ireland should revel ... in unbounded luxury, in the enjoyment of princely incomes and laying by enormous fortunes for their families, while the mass of the people are living in poverty and degradation'. He secured from a dubious Goulburn agreement to furnish a return of the number of freemen, distinguishing non-residents, in Irish corporate boroughs, 7 Apr. He presented and endorsed petitions for repeal of the Vestries Act, which empowered Protestants to tax Catholics for their own purposes, 3 June. His opposition to the third reading of the archbishop of Canterbury's estate bill was unavailing, 10 Apr. He gave his approval to Peel's new metropolitan police force, 15 Apr. He supported Hobhouse's motion for a select committee on vestries, advocating the election by ratepayers of responsible financial managers; he was appointed to the committee. At the behest of his constituents, he presented petitions against the Scottish gaols bill, 5, 7, 8, 14 May. He supported Warburton's 'absolutely necessary' anatomy regulation bill, 15 May. On 21 May he opposed the increase in Scottish judicial salaries and the ecclesiastical courts bill, which perpetuated the proctors' monopoly; his wrecking amendment was defeated by 33-3. His proposal for a table of fees to be permanently displayed was rejected by 46-7, 5 June. On 2 June he spoke and voted for the Ultra Lord Blandford's reform resolutions, the truth of which he held to be 'self-evident', and divided for the issue of a new writ for East Retford. In September 1829 he tried without success to persuade James and John Stuart Mill to give active support to Dr. Bowring's *Westminster Review* as an antidote to the *Edinburgh*, the organ of the Whigs and 'the supporter of all kinds of bad principles and measures'.[99]

On the address, 4 Feb. 1830, when the Ultra Knatchbull moved an amendment which seemed to place the government in jeopardy, Hume 'and a large party of reformers' voted with them to give them a majority. Lord Castlereagh* asked Edward Littleton*, 8 Feb., 'who would have believed, ten years ago, that a government headed by the duke of Wellington would be *saved* by the support of *Joey Hume and Co*?'.[100] Hume was active and aggressive throughout the session, when he voted with opposition in almost every division for which lists have been found. He declared that the president of the board of control Lord Ellenborough's letter concerning the Bombay judicature (which he was suspected of having leaked to *The Times*) called into question his fitness for office.[101] He encouraged Peel to persevere in the tricky task of legislating to end imprisonment for debt, 9 Feb., when he was named to the select committee on renewal of the East India Company's charter. He welcomed the government's chancery reform bills, but jibbed at praise of Lord Eldon, 11 Feb.,

when he voted for the transfer of East Retford's seats to Birmingham. On 15 Feb. he spoke for three and a half hours in condemnation of excessive expenditure and taxation, said he had no confidence in ministers' promise to reduce them and moved an amendment, which was seconded by Howick, calling for action; it was rejected by 184-69. Althorp had decided the previous day to support the motion, and Lord Sefton* thought that Hume's speech was 'the best by far ... that he had ever made'. Howick's view was that if Hume 'could have arranged and compressed his speech into two hours and corrected his grammar it would have been very good'.[102] He stated his determination to support government in maintaining the gold standard, 17 Feb., and welcomed Peel's law reform bills, 18 Feb., when he seconded and was a minority teller for Blandford's renewed reform motion. He was dissatisfied with Goulburn's proposed economies and tax cuts, 19 Feb., but his motion to reduce the army by 10,000 men was defeated by 167-57. He provoked uproar on 22 Feb., when, claiming that many Tory backbenchers agreed with him that retrenchment was essential but feared to oppose ministers, so proving that 'gentlemen come here to serve themselves and not the country', he declared that as it was 'now almost hopeless to press for further reductions' in the existing House of Commons, the 'only remedy' for the people was a resort to 'force'. When Peel censured this 'appeal to physical force', Hume replied, 'Who are the real agitators? I, who wish to save the people, or the members of the government who press upon a distressed country with an iron hand?' His four amendments for reductions in items of the army estimates were all easily beaten. He voted for the enfranchisement of Birmingham, Leeds and Manchester, 23 Feb., reception of the Newark petition alleging electoral malpractice by the duke of Newcastle, 1 Mar., and the transfer of East Retford's seats to Birmingham, 5, 15 Mar., when he was a teller for the minority of 21 for O'Connell's amendment to incorporate the ballot in the disfranchisement bill. On 8 Mar. he became one of the council of 36 of the short-lived Metropolitan Union for radical reform.[103] Having concluded that it was 'hopeless' to try to secure reductions in the estimates he suggested that great savings were possible in revenue collection, 26 Feb., when he supported and was a teller for the minority of 26 for Harvey's bid to stop Members sitting on committees on bills in which they had a personal interest and got 17 votes for his own attempt to halve the grant for the Royal Military College. He made further vain bids to reduce estimates, 1, 9, 22 Mar., but on 5 and 8 Mar. merely registered his protest at the size of the army and the 'useless expense' of foreign garrisons. He said Newport's motion for inquiry into the Irish church was 'milk-and-water' and advocated wholesale reform and disestablishment, 4 Mar. He spoke and was a teller for the minority of 15 to condemn government interference with the Bombay judicature, 8 Mar. Next day he protested at the attorney-general Sir James Scarlett's 'sneer' at Bentham and urged him and Peel to apply Bentham's ideas to the promotion of a 'uniform code of law'. He denounced the appointment of a treasurer of the navy as further proof of ministers' 'vile disregard in the expenditure of the public money', 12 Mar. On Goulburn's budget statement, 15 Mar., he approved the proposed reduction of the beer and leather duties and removal of more trade restrictions, but wanted the surplus of £2,000,000 to be applied to remission of the oppressive taxes on coals and candles. He asserted that repeal of the corn laws would aid many of those who were 'in a worse state than common beggars', 16, 30 Mar. He stated his inflexible hostility to Littleton's new bill to abolish truck payments (on which Place had instructed him), 17 Mar., and he relentlessly opposed its progress thereafter.[104] He dissented from some Glasgow weavers' condemnation of the use of machinery, which had 'on the whole been greatly beneficial, though it may have produced much of personal inconvenience', 18 Mar. He spoke at length for Harvey's motion on crown lands revenues, advocating their sale and application of the proceeds to relief measures, 30 Mar. On 1 Apr. he tried to lower the voting qualification for ratepayers under the St. Giles's vestry bill, but was defeated by 57-27. He attacked the proposed increase in Scottish judicial salaries and said that the appointment of Abercromby as chief baron of the exchequer was 'a very considerable drawback to the professions of ministers with respect to retrenchment'. Next day, on the ordnance estimates, he said it was 'perfectly obvious that no reduction in this department is to be expected' and that he was 'now fighting in a cause altogether desperate'; but he detailed the excesses of the establishment and divided the House (80-40) against the grant for foreign stations. Hobhouse described his 'pertinacity' in questioning witnesses on the Ellenborough divorce bill, 31 Mar., 1 Apr., as 'inimitable': 'he wanted to know everything'.[105] Hume voted for Jewish emancipation, 5 Apr., 17 May. On 6 Apr. 1830 he spoke against the third reading of Ellenborough's divorce bill and was a teller for the minority of 16. Refuting allegations that he was conspiring against Ellenborough, he said, 'of sense ... I have little enough, but my conduct has always been decorous'. The minister Sir George Cockburn* commented that Hume's curious argu-

ments against the bill arose 'from the extraordinary formation of his mind'.

On 27 Apr. 1830 Hume advocated reform of the Irish church and the redistribution of all ecclesiastical property, before acting as a minority teller for O'Connell's bill to open Irish vestries. Complaining that the recommendation of the finance committee had been ignored, he divided the House (131-59) against the grant for the Royal Military College. He welcomed the ministerial bill to open the beer trade, 3 May, and supported it steadily, though he divided for Maberly's amendment to restrict on-sales, 1 July. On 3 May he sought leave to introduce a bill to end the obligation on army and navy officers to pay fees for the renewal of commissions on a demise of the crown, and persisted despite Goulburn's plea for him to drop it out of 'delicacy'. He carried a division by 11-9, but the House was counted out. He renewed the attempt, 10 May, when Goulburn persuaded him to make it simply a bill against the payment of fees, but, as Howick noted, he 'stupidly lost a stage by not moving at once for leave to bring it in'.[106] He introduced it next day, but it foundered when the Lords' amendments were rejected, 2 July. He produced a revised measure, which became law on 16 July (11 Geo. IV & 1 Gul. IV, c. 43). In late February Tavistock, hearing that Hume planned to proposes abolition of the Irish lord lieutenancy, had asked Hobhouse to let him know that his father Bedford, who had held that post, 1806-7, thought it 'useless ... for all purposes of good, and ... mischievous and powerful for objects of corruption', though he did not want Hume to cite this.[107] On 11 May Hume moved for abolition and got 115 votes. He then seconded Robinson's motion for inquiry into the state of the 'neglected and ... miserable colony' of Newfoundland and voted in the minority of 29. He seconded and was a teller for the minority of 12 for O'Connell's call for information on the Cork conspiracy trials, 12 May. Next day he advocated mitigation of the punishment for forgery to 'soften the sanguinary nature of laws which are a disgrace to the country'; he voted thus, 7 June. Before speaking and voting for Graham's motion for a return of privy councillors' emoluments (of which he had at one point been considered as the proposer by Littleton and Huskisson), 14 May, he moaned that it was 'utterly impossible that the country could go on with its present enormous establishments'. On 18 May he moved an amendment to the administration of justice bill to reduce Welsh judges' salaries to £4,000, but was prevailed on to withdraw it. When he tried again on 7 July, he was beaten by 37-11. His motion for information on the four-and-a-half per cent sugar duties was defeated by 78-42, 21 May, but he obtained it on the 24th. He spoke and voted for Stewart's motion for inquiry into the state of Ceylon, 27 May, describing ministerial resistance as typical of 'the way in which it is attempted to slur over ... every instance of abuse in our colonies'. He was a teller for the minority of 13 for O'Connell's radical reform scheme, 28 May, when he also divided for Russell's more moderate plan. He spoke and voted for reduction of the grants for South American missions, 7 June, O'Connell's renewed attempt to reform Irish vestries, 10 June, and Graham's motion against the consular services grant, 11 June, when he denied that his success in persuading ministers to change these arrangements had led to increased costs. When Goulburn spoke of the humanizing effects of religion, 8 June, Hume's smile prompted Goulburn to call him an atheist. Russell spoke up for him and Hume himself retorted that 'cant and hypocrisy are the vices of the day'. On 14 June he got 59 and 78 votes for his attempts to reduce the grants for Nova Scotia and Prince Edward Island; but Howick felt that the mess he had made of his own attack on the grant for the Society for Propagation of the Gospels was compounded by Hume's poor speech in his support.[108] Next day Hume secured the appointment of a select committee on Sierra Leone. He supported the amended bill to reform the court of session, but again condemned Abercromby's appointment, 18 June. He accused ministers of 'a complete violation' of a pledge on the sugar duties, 21 June. On 2 July Smith Stanley and other prominent Whigs attended the House intending to oppose going into committee of supply, but Hume, who had earlier privately sounded ministers as to whether they planned to oppose his candidature for Middlesex, would not back them. He acquiesced in the government's proposal to take a sum on account for the civil list, but reserved his right to oppose individual items.[109] He protested against the Irish arms bill, 3 July: 'it is time we should get rid of the principle of treating Ireland as a conquered country'. At a meeting at Brooks's to discuss the regency question, 4 July, Hume, 'who was there for the first time', according to Hobhouse (though he had joined the club on 22 Feb. 1822), 'said the only sensible thing ... namely that unless ... Grey and ... Holland and other party men would declare for cutting down places and for more decisive reform than they had ever yet done, the people would not sympathise with any parliamentary efforts of theirs'.[110] He spoke and voted against enhanced securities for newspaper publishers under the libel law amendment bill, 6 July, and said that Scarlett (who mistakenly alleged that Hume owned a paper) sought to 'impose additional shackles on the press'. Next day, on the consolidated fund bill,

he urged the electors of England to use the opportunity presented by the approaching general election to try to return 'a majority independent of ... the borough-holders and all the government patronage'. He blamed the self-interest of an aristocratic oligarchy for frustrating Wellington and Peel's good intentions on economy and urged voters to call defaulting Members to account. Hobhouse rebuked him for uttering 'this foolish and stale fallacy', and he later admitted that he had 'gone too far'.[111] He was in Brougham's minority of 27 for the speedy abolition of colonial slavery, 17 July 1830.

In October 1829 Hume had received an open challenge to his seat for Aberdeen Burghs from Sir James Carnegie*, a young baronet with a Forfarshire estate. He recognized the potential threat, but was not unduly perturbed and, after consulting Place, made it clear to the councils of the Forfarshire burghs that he intended to stand his ground.[112] By May 1830, as the king's life ebbed away, there was talk of his being invited to stand for Westminster, where Hobhouse, in Place's view, might be vulnerable to a 'sturdy parliamentary reformer'. According to Place, Hobhouse appreciated this, and suggested to Place that Hume should stand for Middlesex, where the ailing advanced Whig Samuel Charles Whitbread announced his intended retirement on 16 June. Place concurred in the idea, as did Burdett. The tight-fisted Hume initially shied at the expense of a contest, but at length agreed to be put up. Althorp privately endorsed his candidature and persuaded Grey to follow suit, though Bedford, the duke of Devonshire and other Whig grandees were hostile. Hume became 'undecided', but after much 'shabby' prevarication and vacillation, which annoyed Hobhouse and Place, agreed to stand.[113] Some of his supporters in the burghs, where Carnegie had been joined in the field by the Whig Horatio Ross*, were inclined to keep a door open for him until his fate in Middlesex was known, but it soon became clear that he and the sitting Member George Byng would walk over. Returning thanks, Hume portrayed himself as 'the representative of the people of England', applauded the revolution in France, boasted of his almost single-handed labours in the Commons and preached his usual sermon for economy, retrenchment and reform, including shorter parliaments and the ballot.[114] He subsequently intervened by letter in his former constituency on behalf of Ross, who was defeated by Carnegie through the defection of Brechin from the 'Angus union' created by Hume.[115]

He was fêted on a visit to Scotland in late August and September 1830. The celebrations included a jamboree appearance in Arbroath with Ross in tow, when Hume agreed to a request that he should take charge of petitions which his constituents did not wish to entrust to the Tory Carnegie.[116] He now had a more prestigious platform from which to air his views, and on his way south at Harrogate, 8 Oct. 1830, he asked Place to consider with Mill what subjects should be broached in the new Parliament 'in these times of sweeping reform', indicating that he intended to agitate for Scottish electoral and burgh reform in an attempt to 'break down the mockery of representation that exists there'. He was in touch also with Leslie Grove Jones, who planned a private dinner for him with O'Connell, Warburton and other parliamentary radicals. Hume, who was infuriated by Coke and Lord Braybrooke's continued profiteering from lighthouse dues, told Place at the end of October 1830 that report had it that 'concession of any kind is to be refused by the duke [of Wellington], as the Tories are not prepared for a moment to appear to meet the wishes and wants of the people'. He had also learned 'for the first time of the scandal of the patent of the king's printer', Andrew Spottiswoode*, which he planned to expose.[117] Howick thought that Hume (and others) 'spoke very ill' on the address, 2 Nov. 1830, when he said that the king's speech 'breathes nothing but war and expensive establishments and mentions not a syllable respecting the distress which pervades all parts of the empire'.[118] Next day he was disappointed to hear that Peel did not plan to legislate to end imprisonment for small debts. On 4 Nov. he urged ministers to give an early explanation of their foreign policy and moved for printed copies of treaties with Belgium, Holland and Portugal. Peel jibbed at the cost, but Hume insisted, prompting Peel to remark that he had 'become one of the most extravagant Members I have met with'. That day the lawyer John Campbell II* told his brother that Hume was 'inexpressibly disgusting, and nothing so strongly shows the fallen state of the House ... as his ascendancy. He is a low, vulgar, illiterate fellow, whom nothing can abash'.[119] On 5 Nov. he raised the issue of Spottiswoode's patent, moving for information and alleging that the holder was enabled to profit handsomely from the public purse while supporting ministers in the House; he obtained some of the material he wanted. He also denounced Wellington as 'incapable of government', confessed that he had been duped into believing Peel's promises of tax cuts at the end of the last session and seemed to suggest that Wellington might have authorized provocation of some of the 'Swing' outrages. When Alexander Baring accused him of using 'inflammatory language', Howick defended him.[120] He threatened to force an adjourn-

ment if he continued to be interrupted and baited by 'a set of men who are entirely unworthy of a place in the House'. According to Hobhouse, an alarmed Sir James Graham* asked him next day

> whether I thought Joe Hume meant mischief. I said, 'No'. 'What then did he mean by advising the people not to use premature force?' said Graham. 'He meant nothing', said I; 'he did not know the meaning of the word'.[121]

Hume objected to the government's proposal to regulate trade between the West Indies and America, which was 'robbing Peter to pay Paul', 8 Nov. He was a teller for the minority of 39 on this issue, 12 Nov. On 9 Nov. he criticized Peel's under-secretary George Dawson for describing O'Connell as 'the agitator of Ireland' and denouncing a petition for repeal of the Union (to which Hume was opposed) as the work 'of a mob'. He was a teller for the minority of 24 for repeal of the Irish Subletting Act, 12 Nov. He presented reform petitions from Marylebone, 10 Nov., Lanark, 11 Nov., and Perth, Arbroath and Brechin, 15 Nov., when he pointed out that in the last burgh, which had a population of over 7,000, only the 13 self-elected councillors had a say in parliamentary elections. Arguing that ministers' refusal to reform or retrench had driven men to violence, he said that the 'most effectual act of Parliament will be to remove the government'. He was in the majority for inquiry into the civil list, which achieved exactly that, 15 Nov., and was named to the select committee, as he was to that on the reduction of public salaries, 9 Dec. As he was declaiming on 16 Nov. 1830 that army and navy officers as well as placemen and pensioners should be excluded from the Commons, the Whig reformer General Sir Ronald Crauford Ferguson was walking through the chamber: 'He stopped and looked up at Hume and the whole House roared with laughter'.[122]

When the members of the Grey ministry and their supporters crossed the House to the right-hand benches, Hume, O'Connell and the other radicals remained in their old places. Princess Lieven urged her brother not to confuse 'the men now in power with the radicals of the Lower House', for Grey 'hates O'Connell and Mr. Hume more than the duke of Wellington does'; and Campbell, reflecting that it would be impossible for the new administration to 'satisfy the expectations they have raised', anticipated that 'in a short time Hume will be firing into them'.[123] Hume expressed his approval of the new metropolitan police force, 18 Nov. 1830, but, as he did repeatedly in the next two years, complained that it placed too heavy a financial burden on some parishes. Next day he pressed ministers to put the entire tithes system 'on a satisfactory footing'. Place wanted him to test the sincerity of the Whigs in office by asking them if they would include the ballot in their reform scheme, but he disregarded this.[124] On 22 Nov. he announced the postponement of his intended motion for a reduction of official salaries to 1796 levels, having been led to believe that it would have implied a want of confidence in the new government, whose accession to power had given him 'great satisfaction, because I think it offers the country hopes of a radical change in public measures'. Offering to give them a fair trial, he exhorted them to fulfil their pledges on reform, retrenchment, economy and free trade; otherwise he would be 'their steady opponent'. He was pleased to learn next day that no lieutenant-general of the ordnance was to be appointed and told Thomas Wyse that his notions of legislation for the employment of the Irish poor were nonsense. He presented petitions for the gradual abolition of slavery, 25 Nov. He took the government's decision not to fill the vacant office of Irish postmaster-general as 'an earnest of their disposition to economy' and welcomed their assurances that salary reductions were in the offing, 2 Dec., but he wanted more information about their intentions on tax cuts and the corn laws. He told Thomas Gladstone* that if no one else came forward he was willing to raise 'the present state of the Liverpool franchise', but Gladstone decided that it would be 'unwise' to place the relevant petitions in his hands 'from his want of popularity in the House'.[125] On 13 Dec. he lectured ministers on the need to abolish 'sinecures and highly paid useless offices', but he accepted the assurance of Althorp, leader of the House, that the matter was in hand. He pressed for a delay in naval and army promotions until it became clear how far the deadweight pensions could be reduced and called for the estimates to be presented in advance. Gladstone thought he 'really spoke well, but was ... very properly beaten' (by 167-27) when he opposed Littleton's reintroduced bill to abolish truck payments with an amendment for inquiry, 14 Dec.[126] His subsequent hostility to the measure was unwavering. He was 'well received' at the Middlesex reform meeting, 15 Dec., when he promised to vote for the ballot and dissented from Burdett's view that Members should withhold expression of their sentiments on reform, retrenchment and foreign policy until ministers had declared theirs: 'although many had changed sides with a change of ministry, he had never abandoned his favourite post, convinced that by maintaining this station he was the best friend to the ministry, as he kept them to their pledges'. Hobhouse thought he 'presses' ministers 'too much'.[127] On the 16th he urged ministers to open select vestries and

presented and endorsed a parliamentary reform petition from the mayor and inhabitants of Southampton, who had declined to entrust it to their own Members. When one of these, James Barlow Hoy, denounced him as the self-appointed 'receiver-general of petitions and redresser-general of wrongs', Hume replied that he was 'attentive to minute matters, because I want reform in everything', and bragged of his consistency. This prompted Goulburn to point out that he had deviated from his support of the sale of beer bill in July 1830 in order to vote for an amendment which appealed to his prospective Middlesex constituents. Later that day Hume welcomed Campbell's plan to establish a general register of deeds. He presented and supported several more petitions, including some from Aberdeen Burghs, for tax cuts and reform, 17, 18 Dec., when he declared that he was 'now convinced that no system of economy can be brought to bear without there previously existing a full, free and fair representation of the people in Parliament'. When he argued that the recorder of Dublin was not eligible to sit in the House, 20 Dec., he was attacked by Peel, to whom he retorted, 'I am not one of those men who pretend to be acquainted with everything, nor do I pretend to say that I am not ... liable to mistakes'. He accused Peel of holding out the French and Belgian revolutions as warnings to the advocates and supporters of reform and economy: Peel had 'read a lecture to the lower classes ... but why did he not read a similar lecture to the higher classes, who have brought the country to its present state?' Hobhouse thought he had answered Peel 'well'.[128] When Matthias Attwood on 21 Dec. accused Grey of having held out 'false and delusive hopes' on reform, Hume defended the premier, but his attempt to read from Grey's speech in the Lords landed him in trouble with the Speaker and forced him to adopt the expedient of quoting Grey as 'one of the chiefs' of 'a certain island called Brobdignag'. He said it was foolish to blame distress on the currency change and, endorsing an Essex petition concerning a local abuse of tithes, observed that 'when such cases of oppression and vexation occur ... it is no wonder that exasperation should be felt and violence take place'. On 23 Dec. 1830 he encouraged ministers to take their Irish retrenchments further, secured information bearing on the recorder of Dublin's case, colonial pensions and the pension given to Harriet Arbuthnot in 1823 and gave notice for 10 Feb. 1831 of a motion for inquiry into the king's printers scandal.

The ex-minister John Herries* told Mrs. Arbuthnot, 3 Jan. 1831, that Althorp was 'coaxing the ultra radicals' by feeding Hume 'and others of that stamp in small select parties'.[129] A week later Hume annoyed Place by telling a mutual acquaintance that he did not think ministers could reduce the stamp duty on newspapers at present.[130] Jones soon afterwards told O'Connell, who was facing arrest, that he and Hume were 'anxious to possess the means of contradicting false statements made against you'.[131] From 3 Feb. until the end of the month Hume presented and endorsed dozens of petitions (including several from his former constituency) calling for Scottish parliamentary and municipal reform, general reform, the ballot, the abolition of tithes, repeal of assessed taxes and vestry reform. He attended and addressed a Marylebone parish reform meeting, 16 Feb.[132] He was named to the reappointed East India select committee, 4 Feb. (and again, 28 June 1831, 27 Jan. 1832). He cast a critical eye over the government's civil list proposals and warned Althorp that he would oppose certain details, especially the pensions.[133] On 7 Feb. he called on the landed interest to 'act honestly and do justice' by surrendering the corn laws. Next day he seconded Hunt's motion for a pardon for convicted 'Swing' rioters, but subsequently urged him, unsuccessfully, to drop it; he was one of its two supporters in the division.[134] Later that day he objected to the demonization of O'Connell and told Althorp that he 'must not risk a civil war to maintain the Union, until he had recalled the lord lieutenant, abolished the tithe system ... and given to Ireland an establishment of her own'. Jones assured O'Connell that Hume's 'conduct was manly and straightforward. He only wants to have good assistants about him, someone who knows him well and can allow for his defects'.[135] On 10 Feb. Hume secured the appointment of a select committee on the king's printers, which he chaired. Place had again remonstrated with him for 'the folly of his conduct of confiding in ministers' on the newspaper stamp duties; but his note to Place, 15 Feb., satisfied the tailor that he had not 'given in to the delusion' that ministers had done all they could on taxation and the civil list.[136] In the House that day he declared that Lord Goderich (a member of the cabinet) deserved impeachment for misleading the Commons over the costs of the Buckingham Palace project. He generally approved of Althorp's budget, but on 16 Feb. pressed him not to tax imports of raw cotton and next day entreated him to drop the planned levy on steamboat passengers, which would hit hard in western Scotland. On the army estimates, 18 Feb., he said that 'I have had my expectations excited to the highest pitch, and have to regret being obliged to use the language of complaint with respect to the course ministers have pursued'. He deplored the increase in the army and said he 'knew of no purpose for which you can keep up these troops,

except to awe the people of England, of whom you are afraid', although he also suspected that they were to be deployed in European meddling. He was persuaded by Palmerston, the foreign secretary, to withdraw his motion for copies of protocols concerning Belgium. He sided with government on the sugar duties and pressed Lord Chandos to drop his proposal for immediate relief for West India planters, but again criticized the army estimates, 21 Feb. He was not inclined to divide the House, making due allowance for ministers' difficulties and hoping that they would redeem themselves on reform; but when Hunt did so, he voted in the minority of six. He supported Hobhouse's vestries reform bill. He registered his protest against the size of the navy estimates, 25 Feb., but on 28 Feb. 1831 he applauded as 'a decided improvement' Althorp's decision to transfer the tax on printed calicoes to raw cotton as a temporary measure.

Hume was 'delighted' with the ministerial reform scheme, revealed on 1 Mar. 1831, and a few days later assured Russell of 'his hearty support'.[137] In the House, 2 Mar., he confirmed that 'radical reformer as I am', the 'efficient' and 'manly' plan had 'far exceeded my expectations'. He endorsed the decision to exclude the ballot and shorter parliaments, which could wait for another day when the new system had been fairly tried. He thought the House could usefully be reduced to 500 Members, but urged all reformers to unite in support of the proposals. After welcoming them at a Marylebone meeting, 7 Mar., when he approved Althorp's assertion in the Commons that 'the time had gone by when the government could be carried on by patronage', he put off his planned motion for tithes reform. At a Tower Hamlets reform meeting, 14 Mar., he encouraged mass petitioning to strengthen ministers' position.[138] He initially agreed to become chairman of the Parliamentary Candidates Society, promoted by Erskine Perry and Place, but subsequently asked to be named merely as a committee member and at length (23 Mar.) had his name withdrawn entirely, having been attacked in the House for his involvement. The episode caused him and Place considerable public embarrassment.[139] In mid-March he predicted a majority of five for the second reading of the English reform bill, 'but leaving about 50 doubtful, most of whom he expected to get'.[140] He presented a backlog of over 60 petitions in support of the reform bills, 19 Mar., and voted silently for the second reading of the English measure, 22 Mar. On 11 Mar. he rebuked Poulett Thomson, vice-president of the board of trade, for seeming to talk of 'perpetual protection' and show 'a disposition to revert' to the discredited 'prohibition' system. He demanded a radical reform of Irish education, 14 Mar., when he again carped at the 'extravagant' army estimates, but sat down 'hoping for better things, when questions of pounds, shillings and pence may be attended to'. He advocated a purge of the diplomatic service, a refuge for well-connected mediocrities, 15 Mar. He remained unhappy with the proposed increase in the timber duties, and on 18 Mar. tried unsuccessfully to reduce them; but next day he complained that ministers had been defeated on this issue 'by the most factious vote I have ever known'. He asked Place at the end of March to tabulate the votes 'on all important subjects' during the last ten years of leading anti-reformers, so that the results could be circulated to the appropriate electors in time for the next general election, and promised to give him 1,000 copies of the division on the second reading of the reform bill marked 'in red and black, to be placed in the several places likely to be of most use'.[141] On 25 Mar. he said that 'from one end to the other' Scotland favoured reform and that its only opponents were 'a knot of gentlemen connected with the counties'. He gave details of the navy estimates a mixed reception, and on the civil list, as Hobhouse saw it, 'in the most laughable way seemed to assent and yet objected to the increase', moving an amendment to reduce the list to £423,470, but withdrawing it under pressure.[142] On the 28th he explained that he had decided to acquiesce in the grant, even though he hated its inclusion of pensions, in the hope that ministers would attend to this in due course; he acknowledged that it was only half the usual amount. When he objected to the grant of £3,600 to Babbage 'for making a machine', the treasury secretary Spring Rice replied that he should support it, as the device could perform many of his laborious calculations on the estimates. Hume defended the ministerial adjustments to the English reform bill, 12 Apr., when he also urged government to reform the jury system and extend it to Ireland. His attempts to lop sums off the civil list were negatived. He moaned that the reductions in the ordnance estimates did not add up to a row of beans, 13 Apr., and next day, while giving ministers credit for removing diplomatic expenses from the civil list and lowering their own salaries, proposed to strike out the £75,000 for pensions. Hunt seconded, but they were in a minority of 17. Hume presented a Glasgow merchants' petition for due consideration of all property rights if slavery was abolished, 15 Apr. On the 18th he disputed Hunt's assertion that a large portion of the Lancashire working classes were hostile to the reform bill because it did not go far enough. He voted in the ministerial minority against Gascoyne's wrecking amendment to the bill, 19 Apr. 1831, and on the 20th

said he would vote for all the supplies that might be needed to facilitate a quick dissolution – 'the first time I ever did so'. He had another row with Hunt later that day, arguing that 'the people of this country want ... good government' and that 'the system of rotten boroughs has led to anything but'. At his unopposed return for Middlesex at the 1831 general election he declared for the reform scheme without reservation and claimed to know that ministers would not make concessions. When asked by Jones if he would resign his seat in the event of a significant difference of opinion with his constituents, he refused to be dictated to, though he was ready to account for his conduct annually. Urging the electors to prepare themselves for the first reformed elections, which he expected in six months, he declared, 'The days of humbug were past, and reason now held sway'.[143] He subsequently sent a public letter to the promoters of the Dunfermline Political Union expressing his approval of such bodies, which he wanted to see established nationwide.[144]

On the address, 21 June 1831, Hume defended the decision to dissolve against Peel's attack, claimed that the government's appeal to the electorate had been emphatically answered, accused Peel of factiously opposing the timber duties and said he would swallow any changes to the details of the reform scheme which did not impair its principle. Next day he dissociated himself from the statement in the king's speech that ministers had maintained the stance on non-interference on Belgium, but conceded that the amended budget had been 'completely successful'. He advocated a low fixed duty on corn, 24 June, and protested at the 'immense' navy and army estimates, especially the 'monstrous charge' of £170,000 for the yeomanry, 27 June. Next day he pressed ministers to repeal the remaining coercive Acts of 1819, which most of them had opposed when in opposition. He secured the reappointment of his select committee on the king's printers, 28 June. On the 30th he said that Hunt was not justified in saying that ministers had not retrenched: 'I ... would not give a pin for reform, if I did not hope that the result of it would be the means of obtaining ... a good, cheap and efficient government'. He was a teller for the minority of 13 for Alderman Wood's motion to reduce public salaries to 1797 levels. His allegation that a contributor to the *Republican* had close links with the Tory opposition provoked angry exchanges, 29 June, 1 July. That day he called for repeal of the duty on tiles (and again, 21 July) and soap, but welcomed the remission of that on candles. He protested again at the 'confused and unintelligible' way in which the accounts were presented. On 4 July he appealed to the Speaker for a ruling on etiquette after finding his seat occupied at prayers by James Lindsay. He quizzed the Irish secretary Smith Stanley on the purpose of the advance of money for capital projects, 5 July 1831.

He voted for the second reading of the reintroduced reform bill next day. On 8 July 1831 Hunt stated that Hume had written to northern working class leaders to rally support for the measure, but Hume explained that he had merely seen three delegates who wanted hostile petitions to be presented and begged them not to harm the cause. On 12 July he voted at least twice against the adjournment, having told the Tory Wetherell that in changed times 'a popular ministry' was 'contending with an opposition consisting of a handful of factious men'. He voted steadily for the details of the bill, though he was in the minority on the case of Saltash, 26 July, and paired for divisions on 3, 5, 17 Aug. He had little to say on the measure as such. On 8 Aug. he objected to printing the petition, presented by Hunt, of the National Union of the Working Classes of the Metropolis in favour of the ballot and against compulsory emigration on account of its language, but said he would be 'very glad to see the sinecurists and public-paid drones of this country transported to the Canadas'. Like other radicals, he was suspicious of the proposed division of many English counties and he pressed ministers to reconsider it; but Littleton claimed that he 'frightened' Hume and company 'into support, by telling them that the county Members who wished a division ... would not compromise their principles about the *due amount* of the franchise, if they in return did not give way on this point'.[145] He brought up but refused to present, because of their 'unacceptable' reference to the 'improper motives' of antireformers, several Scottish petitions deploring the slow progress of the bill, 15 Aug., but he presented an inoffensive one from Edinburgh. His motion the following day to give the colonies 19 Members, including one for the Channel Islands, provoked much mirth and was negatived, despite receiving some Tory support. (The Ultra duke of Richmond unsuccessfully pressed colonial representation on his cabinet colleagues later in the year.) On 24 Aug. Hume gave notice of a motion for the 27th that to expedite reform orders should take precedence over notices on Tuesdays, Thursdays and Saturdays and the House convene for business at noon.[146] O'Connell seconded the motion, but Althorp, who said Hume had accused him of being 'slack', opposed it. The debate generated some bad temper, but Hume was persuaded by Lord Ebrington to drop the motion and make his peace with Althorp, whom he praised. He accused Hunt of practising 'delusion' on the people by speaking against but voting for details of the reform bill, 30 Aug. On 5 Sept. he endorsed the

appointment of boundary commissioners, but argued that the constituencies should pay for revising barristers; Althorp insisted that this was a case for the public purse. Replying to Sugden's denigration of reform Members who were anxious that their votes should be made known to their constituents, 7 Sept., Hume said that 'publicity is the only check on selfish views and improper proceedings; it is the dread of being hauled over the coals that keeps many men to their duty'. He voted for the third reading, 19 Sept., and passage of the bill, 21 Sept., when he attended a 'meeting of 90 Members ... all independent of ministers', who agreed that even if the bill was rejected by the Lords it would be 'a desertion of the king and country in the present ministers to resign'. Another report had it that Hume joined Ebrington in calling for a ministerial promise to press for a creation of peers to be made the condition of a vote of confidence, but that this was set aside as 'revolutionary'.[147] Hume voted silently for the second reading of the Scottish reform bill, 23 Sept. 1831.

On other issues, he pursued his usual dogged radical line. He spoke, 6, 18 July, 11 Aug. 1831, when he was a minority teller, for disarming the Irish yeomanry. He backed O'Connell's call for a fairer distribution of money for Irish education, 14, 15 July, 5 Sept. He urged Althorp to reduce the emoluments of the bishop of Londonderry before filling the vacancy, 18 July, but was satisfied with his promise of a general measure of redistribution, 6 Sept. On 19 July he expressed contempt for the Glasgow petition against the Maynooth grant, and on 31 Aug. described British universities as 'little better than hot-beds for everything that is illiberal'. He divided with O'Connell for swearing the Dublin election committee, 31 July, and against issuing a new writ, 8 Aug., but with government in both divisions on the issue, 23 Aug. On 10 Aug. he endorsed O'Connell's complaint that 'whatever may have been promised, nothing has been performed' by the ministry for Ireland, where the 'age of misrule' still prevailed. He questioned the need for a board of public works there, but was willing to acquiesce in the grant of £1,000,000 if placed 'on a proper footing'. His wrecking amendment to the Irish union of parishes bill was carried by 38-11, 19 Aug. He hoped for the early cessation of the grants for the Dublin Foundling Hospital, which promoted 'bad habits and immorality', 22 Aug., and the employment of the Irish poor, 29 Aug. He moved to reduce that for publishing Irish proclamations, 31 Aug., but withdrew when ministers promised an imminent cut. He said that Ireland would never be 'at peace' until ecclesiastical property was redistributed, 12 Sept. On the 16th, opposing the Irish public works bill, which would perpetuate the 'system of jobbing', he criticized ministers for appointing to or retaining in office men who were hostile to their measures: for example, the lords lieutenant of some counties. He welcomed their reduction in the grant for the Royal Dublin Society, 28 Sept. On 8 July he spoke and was a teller for the minority of 15 against the grant for professorial salaries at Oxford and Cambridge, where 'poor' people could not gain admittance and many fellows 'drive their carriage and four, and live in great state from the funds which are placed at their disposal'. He recommended sending the inmates of the 'useless' Millbank penitentiary to Botany Bay. He said that to repeal the Sale of Beer Act would be folly, 13 July, 24 Aug., but he wanted retailers to be treated the same as licensed publicans, 5 Sept. He accepted the grant for civil list salaries, reserving his right to object to the inclusion of pensions, 18 July, and opposed Robinson's amendment for a cut of £60,000. He condemned the 'enormous' provision for consular services and the grant for the Society for the Propagation of the Gospels, which 'cast a firebrand of jealousy and ill will' into the colonies, 26 July. He pressed for relaxation of the quarantine duties, 8 Aug., and spoke thus and divided in the minority of 20, 6 Sept. He asserted that by such 'extravagant application of the public money' as in the duchess of Kent's annuity bill, ministers were 'doing that which will tend to make royalty odious', 8 Aug. He objected to the proposed increase in the duties on Cape and Portuguese wines, 8 Aug., 7 Sept., but thanked Althorp for conceding on the former, 12 Sept. On 9 Aug. he damned the 'useless, unnecessary and extravagant manner in which the government are throwing away the public money by continuing to call out the militia'. He voted in Hunt's minority of six for reception of the Preston petition for repeal of the corn laws, 12 Aug., and supported, by request, the Coventry petition, 12 Sept.; but on 15 Sept. he opposed as untimely and disruptive to the reform bill Hunt's motion to consider repeal, preferring to look to a reformed Parliament 'not only for an alteration in our corn laws, but also for many other important and most desirable changes'. He spoke and was a teller for the minority of 12 against the compensation for Lesceyne and Escoffery, 22 Aug. On the 31st he said that the proposal to spend £50,000 on the coronation, which could be carried off for £5,000, was outrageous. On 1 Sept. he denounced the requirement for Members attending to wear court dress, but admitted defeat when the Speaker pointed out that this had been recommended by a committee of the House. Littleton recorded a pertinent ludicrous episode during the deliberations of the committee earlier that day:

While we were busy with our order of procession, in comes Mr. Economy Hume, to get some papers belonging to him out of the box. We paused. I began, 'Well ... I am assured by Rundell and Bridge that that the addition of these diamonds to the queen's crown will cost only £25,000. It would be miserable economy to boggle about such a trifle' ... Hume was staring at us in astonishment ... [He] left the room, went into the committee room of the civil government expenses, and out of mere ill humour cut off two aides-de-camp from the lord lieutenant of Ireland and when Wynn presented his report in the House ... attacked and ridiculed it.[148]

On coronation day, 8 Sept., Hume turned up at the House 'in a brand new suit, and was hailed with laughter and cheers'.[149] He spoke and voted for inquiry into the effects on the West India interest of continuing the Sugar Refinery Act, 12 Sept., because he felt they deserved the chance to make out their case, but stressed that he remained committed to freedom of trade. On 28 Sept., however, he sided with ministers, who had courted his support on this 'vital question', against further inquiry. But he supported the appointment of a select committee on the state of the West Indies, to which he was named, 6 Oct.[150] He moved unsuccessful wrecking amendments to the truck bill, 12 Sept., 5 Oct.; Littleton heard that news of its third reading had been celebrated in Gloucestershire by the firing of cannon and burning of Hume in effigy.[151] On 28 Sept. he moved to postpone consideration of the grant of £163,670 for Windsor Castle and Buckingham House repairs until a proper explanation was given; he got 12 votes to 110. He thanked ministers for reducing the salary of the president of the board of trade, 29 Sept. Next day he waived his objections to the £120,000 for civil list pensions, because ministers had shown 'every disposition' to facilitate inquiry (he was a member of the select committee of 12 Aug.); but he criticized the 'bad system' of navy victualling. On 3 Oct. he cavilled at the 'great amount' of national expenditure as detailed by Althorp. He was unwilling to depart from the principles laid down by the finance committee on army half-pay, 7 Oct. He supported investigation of the Deacles' allegations against the Hampshire magistrates, 21 July, 22 Aug., 14, 19, 27 Sept. He continued to speak on behalf of Taylor and others imprisoned for blasphemy, 15, 23 Aug., 5, 21 Sept., 5 Oct. He urged government to intervene on behalf of the Poles, who were 'struggling against tyranny and oppression for liberty', 16 Aug., but opposed interference in Belgium, 18 Aug. On the 17th he thanked ministers for ordering the emancipation of crown colonies slaves, but recommended a 'cautious' approach to abolition in general. He opposed the church building bill, 25 Aug. He wanted native Indians to be admitted to grand juries, 1 Sept. He spoke and voted in the minority for issuing the Liverpool writ, 5 Sept. Next day he seconded Hunt's motion for an Act of grace for all imprisoned crown debtors to mark the coronation and pressed ministers to end arrest and imprisonment for debt. On 15 Sept. he expressed his 'regret that a Whig administration should have been the first to imprison men' under the 1819 Newspaper Stamp Duty Act. He thought the Lords' amendments had ruined the lunatics bill, 26 Sept., when he revealed that he had been 'shocked' by what he had seen on a round of visits to asylums. His intervention that day in a spat between O'Connell and the Ultra Sir Richard Vyvyan, whom he seemed to accuse of ungentlemanly conduct, was ruled out of order by the Speaker and he had to apologize. On 30 Sept. he opposed a ministerial amendment to Hobhouse's vestries reform bill and spoke and was a teller for a minority of three against the Lords' amendments to the game bill. He dismissed the Scottish exchequer court bill as a 'half-and-half measure' and denounced the £2,000 pension granted to Abercromby as 'monstrous'. On Lord Brougham's bankruptcy court bill, 7 Oct., he remarked, 'I am a very unlearned man' and 'cannot understand ... why it is necessary that we should have a bankrupt court in addition to an insolvent court'. He condemned the bill's provision for the superannuation of officials, 14 Oct. 1831.

At the Middlesex meeting called to petition the Lords to pass the reform bill, 27 Sept. 1831, Hume said he looked on it as 'carried', for the peers would take a lesson from France on the wisdom of 'yielding gracefully'.[152] O'Connell reported that at a meeting of reform Members, 8 Oct., following the reform bill's defeat in the Lords

Hume ... [made] an energetic speech. He condemned the trivial policy of the Whigs, their unwise plan of supporting their enemies and promoting them and neglecting their friends. He insisted that they should now and at once start on a different line of policy. He was loudly cheered.[153]

At the mass Marylebone meeting called to address the king in support of ministers and reform, 10 Oct., he urged his listeners to avoid violence and tell 'the petty, spiteful majority of the ... Lords' that 'an oligarchy which had usurped their rights should be compelled to relinquish their tyrannical power':

Though ministers had not been so active in promoting the bill as they ought ... he hoped they would profit by experience and not coquet with the Tories, since it was in vain that the Tories could be induced to approve of measures favourable to the people ... There must be either reform or revolution ... It was because in case of

a revolution the working and useful classes would be the greatest sufferers that he wished to effect a reform by constitutional means.

He toned down a resolution urging the king to kick the bishops out of Parliament.[154] He spoke and voted for Lord Ebrington's confidence motion, 10 Oct., asserting that 'a miserable minority have withheld from the majority their just rights'. At the reform Members' meeting beforehand, according to John Hawkins*, he 'made a very judicious and sensible speech'.[155] On the 12th he and Byng, at the request of Lord Melbourne, the home secretary, persuaded the leaders of the trades' procession to St. James's to entrust their address to them as county Members.[156] In the House later that day he said that the subsequent disturbances by a mob had been 'trifling' and in any case provoked by the 'irritating language' of Tories who opposed reform in the hope of regaining their 'unhallowed power'. He came close to calling Trench a liar for saying that he had led and incited the rioters, but he retracted to the satisfaction of the Speaker. On 18 Oct. he endorsed the prayer of petitions for the exclusion of bishops from the Lords. In the absence of O'Connell, he presented on 19 Oct. a petition from the Birmingham Political Union for the Commons to address the king to create peers to carry reform. He defended the unions, which encouraged the people to 'seek by reason ... that which might otherwise be sought by riot' and blamed those in Derby and Nottingham on the absence of unions; but he saw no reason to force the king's hand on the use of his prerogative. On 20 Oct. he exhorted ministers to remove every lord lieutenant who had opposed the reform bill and argued that there 'must be no more attempts at conciliation'. In early November 1831 Hume enrolled as a member of the radical National Political Union. Later in the month he had published in *The Times* his letter to a churchwarden of Tunbridge Wells giving advice on the formation of a union and extolling their virtues as a means of preserving civil order and keeping the government up to the mark.[157] Soon afterwards Hobhouse

saw Joe Hume and his good little wife. He is a singular fellow indeed, and persuades many people he understands all the subjects he talks about. He is to be made lord rector of Glasgow University this year, for the second time ... and a paragraph in the *Herald* tells how great a linguist Joe is, and how much Greek and Latin, all Oriental, and most modern tongues he knows ... If he knows Greek and Latin, it is without learning them.[158]

Littleton was

not a little amused at a letter Duncannon ... showed me from the patriot and economist Joseph Hume, abusing him for not having given a servant of his one of the park gate keeper's lodges in Hyde Park. He had held out with Duncannon, and would not say whether he would accept the office or not during nine months, because he thought the salary should be raised, and now is in a fury and considers himself 'insulted' because it is given to another. I have often been assured by secretaries of the treasury during the last 15 years that no one has dabbled in little jobs of this sort more than this blustering declaimer against patronage.[159]

On 7 Dec. 1831 Hume clashed angrily in the House with Arthur Trevor over restrictions on press freedom, especially the stamp duties, and declared that those who hampered popular education were 'morally responsible for the consequences that may flow from a want of proper knowledge'. He concurred in that part of the king's speech which promised a speedy settlement of reform, but dissented from the notice of interference in Belgium and protested, as he did again on 9 Dec., at the continued excesses of expenditure and unwarranted increase in the army. He presented and endorsed a petition for the abolition of tithes, but passed no comment on the revised reform scheme. Holland, a member of the cabinet, noted that 'the only untoward appearance was the general complaint of the Irish at the small additional number (five) granted to their representation and the sympathy expressed by Hume and ... felt by many of our friends'.[160] He wanted some complex returns on Irish tithes, 14 Dec., but Spring Rice objected and he gave way with a bad grace. Place asked him to present a possibly objectionable petition from the council of the Northern Political Union concerning the reform bill's provision for the payment of rates, but the death of Hume's infant son Hardin on 15 Dec. kept him from the House that day and on 17 Dec. 1831, when the English reform bill was read a second time.[161] On 19 Jan. 1832 he answered Hunt's denunciation of the Scottish reform bill, and of the ministerial scheme in general said that while it had some defects, it was a major step forward. Next day he spoke and voted for going into committee on schedule A, and thereafter he gave generally steady support to the bill's details. He opposed Mackworth Praed's 'invidious and dangerous' proposal to exclude urban voters from the counties, 1 Feb. He defended the political unions, 6 Feb. On the registration clause, 10 Feb., he argued that claimants should be charged a fee to cover the costs, and next day reiterated his concern over the potentially 'tremendous' expense of this process. On 15 Feb. he supported and divided in the minority of four for Hunt's motion to limit the cost of booths and hustings. He acknowledged that ministers had had to play 'a difficult and weari-

some game' on reform, 2 Mar., when he supported the enfranchisement of Bradford. Hobhouse later recalled that that month a letter of Hume's was opened by the French authorities and copied to William IV, Grey and Melbourne:

> The imprudent man wrote of the reform bill as being a good measure as far as it went, and as certain of producing a better, by the destruction of our church establishment. This angered King William exceedingly, and did not add to his attachment to the Grey cabinet.[162]

Hume voted silently for the third reading of the bill, 22 Mar. 1832.

On other issues, he remained a thorn in ministers' flesh, though his pragmatic concern to see reform secured kept his recalcitrance largely within reasonable bounds. He demanded and received an assurance that the £75,000 earmarked for Buckingham House would complete the project, 17 Jan., but condemned the associated 'ridiculous and extravagant bargain' for the sale of crown lands, 19 Jan. 1832. He obtained returns to bolster his campaign for one general account of imports and exports, 24 Jan. He spoke and voted for inquiry into distress in the glove trade, 31 Jan., but only to demonstrate the folly of protectionist doctrine, and voted for inquiry into smuggling in the trade, 3 Apr., though he did not accept the premise of the motion. 'Anxious to dry up all the sources of corruption', he called for total abolition of the payment of officials by fees, 2 Feb., and secured a return of facts and figures, 7 Feb., when in passing he deplored 'the many improper appointments' that had been made in the colonies. He welcomed the ministerial promise to produce full estimates early in the session in future, 13 Feb., but criticized the half-pay element of the navy estimates. He conceded that the grant for civil contingencies was the 'least objectionable' for years, but still found fault with details. However, he welcomed the navy civil departments bill as a sign that 'ministers are determined that things shall not go on as they used to', 14 Feb., and he spoke and voted for it, 6 Apr. He wanted repeal of the duties on hemp and other shipbuilding materials, 17 Feb. Later that day he grilled Hobhouse, newly installed as war secretary, on the army estimates and complained that there were 20,000 more troops than in 1824. He did not oppose the estimates, recognizing that Hobhouse had inherited them, but registered his undiminished hostility to the grants for garrisons and the Royal Military College. Hobhouse recollected that Hume, 'when convicted of extravagant statements, said, as usual with him, "Well, I think so, and others think differently, that's all"'. Hobhouse 'soon found there was no arguing with this gentleman', for he was 'like the bookseller's customer, who lost one of a set of books, and could never be convinced that he ought to find the volume, or buy the whole set'.[163] He allowed the quarterly ordnance estimates through on an understanding that every item was to be detailed in the annual estimates, 22 Feb. He did not like the grant of £100,000 for hurricane damage relief in the West Indies, but acquiesced in it on humanitarian grounds, 29 Feb. He spoke and divided against government for the 'very moderate' reduction of the sugar duties proposed by Lord Chandos, 7 Mar., pressed ministers to come clean about their intentions on slavery, 15 Mar., and on the 23rd said that they must assure West Indian proprietors that they would receive due 'consideration and compensation' on emancipation. In mid-March Mrs. Arbuthnot heard from Herries that 'Hume says they Whigs have done more jobs and follies in one year than the Tories did in thirty'.[164] He again criticized the navy, 26 Mar., and army estimates, 28 Mar., but left it at that in the hope that ministers would economize when reform was safe. But he was a harsh critic of army pensions, 2, 4 Apr. On the miscellaneous estimates, 13 Apr. 1832, he recommended the demolition of all 'useless' royal residences, which were 'little better than barracks for destitute persons', and ranted against the cost of many other items.

Hume confirmed his support for the anatomy bill, 17, 24 Jan., 15 Feb., the general register bill, 19 Jan., and vestry reform, 23 Jan. 1832, when he voted in the minority for Hobhouse's bill to expedite his Vestry Act and angrily denounced ministers for opposing it.[165] On 26 Jan. he spoke and voted against government on the Russian-Dutch loan because, as he said, they had refused to reconsider their position on it;[166] but he divided with them on relations with Portugal, 9 Feb. His frank admission on 31 Jan. that he had made notes of Spencer Perceval's speech after the gallery had been cleared during the debate on his motion for a general fast, 26 Jan., and handed them to a journalist, whence they appeared as a report in *The Times*, astonished the Speaker, who said that every action of Hume's constituted a breach of privilege. He was unabashed. He had reservations about Sadler's bill to restrict the hours of child factory labour, 9, 10 Feb. That day he called for inquiry into the Peterloo massacre, and he seconded and was a minority teller for Hunt's motion to that effect, 15 Mar., when he said that 'time could never outrun crime'. On 13 Feb. he argued that the best way to combat cholera was not through quarantine but by giving decent food and clothing to the poor and promoting 'cleanliness amongst them'. On 16 Feb. he reacted to a proposal to include a reference to 'Almighty God' in the preamble of the Scottish cholera prevention bill with the comment, 'this is all humbug, cant and hypocrisy'; he divided the House against it, but was defeated by 55-10. He alleged that the City and the public had lost all confidence in the board of health, which had 'created unnecessary fears and alarm'. He supported and was a teller for the minority of 28 for Hunt's attempt to end army flogging, 16 Feb. He described the dismissal of Captain Sartorius as 'one of those many acts of weakness on the part of the government, which we meet with every day, in sacrificing their friends and principles to the sneers of this side of the House', 26 Mar. He voted with government for the malt drawback bill, 2 Apr. On the 10th he admitted to Dawson that the Scottish exchequer court bill was 'a job', but said that it had been brought in to 'undo a greater job', namely the appointment by the Wellington ministry of Abercromby to head a court with no business. Hobhouse was unimpressed with his allegations that British trade had been impeded by the protracted delay in settling claims against Brazil, 16 Apr. 1832:

> Hume ... said that, since the Whigs had been in office, the British flag had been disgraced in every part of the world. I often thought that this man was totally careless about his own assertions, as well as what had been said or done by others. This appeared to me strange enough in any politician; but, in a man of long experience, and much reputation, and very high popular position, I thought it totally inexplicable.[167]

When considering their plans to reform Irish tithes in December 1831, the cabinet had expected Hume to move an amendment for inquiry into the entire Irish church establishment.[168] He called for the abolition of tithes and a redistribution of Irish church property, 23, 24 Jan. 1832. On 14 Feb. he was pleased to hear Althorp's assurance that a report that Grey had threatened to 'deluge Ireland with blood for the purpose of collecting tithes' was 'altogether a mistake'. He voted in the minority of 51 for printing the Woollen Grange petition for tithes abolition, 16 Feb. At the meeting of government supporters called to explain and rally support for their plan for the gradual extinction of Irish tithes, 8 Mar., Hume, according to Littleton, 'expressed his individual dissent from the policy of arming the government with the power of placing itself in the situation of the clergy with respect to tithe rights and giving it summary powers for the collection of tithe rent, but approved of the general policy of the proposed arrangement, and promised support'. As Hawkins put it, Hume, 'after a few preliminary growls, gave his adhesion'.[169] He confirmed his qualified approval in the House, 13 Mar., but said that ultimately he desired a complete remodelling of the Irish church. In committee on the tithes resolutions, 30 Mar., he endorsed four but objected to that which gave the viceroy additional powers to enforce payment; he voted in the minority of 25 for an alternative means of funding relief of the clergy. On 6 Apr. he entreated ministers not to proceed with tithes collection until the composition bill had been brought in and voted in the minority of 21 against the arrears bill. He objected to any tithes money going to non-resident clergy, 9 Apr., when he spoke and was a minority teller against the Irish registrar of deeds bill. On 16 Apr. 1832 he said that Smith Stanley's attack on Sheil over tithes 'amounts very nearly to a declaration of war against Ireland' and accused him and his colleagues of breaking their promise to bring in a 'remedial' bill to complement the coercive one: 'Talk of agitation, if you please, but who is the agitator here? But it is in vain; the people, the millions will not be put down'. This provoked outraged protests.

Hume deplored 'the cry raised against these new beer shops' and denied that the Scottish clergy were unanimously hostile to the government's Irish education scheme, 7 May 1832. Next day he obtained returns of pluralities of benefices in England and Wales. When Althorp announced the government's resignation on the king's refusal to create peers, 9 May, Hume spoke 'violently', as the Conservative Member Sir John Beckett saw it, in approval of their action.[170] Supporting Ebrington's motion for an address asking the king to appoint only ministers who would carry an undiluted reform bill, 10 May, he contradicted Alexander Baring's assertion that 'the greater part of the wealth and intelligence of the country' was opposed to reform and deplored his description of the people as 'the brawlers out of doors'. He argued that only the Grey ministry could command national confidence, but he again rebuked them for allowing 'the avid enemies of reform' to stay in their offices. He dismissed the notion that Peel, a lifelong anti-reformer, could carry a bill; condemned the rotten borough system as the key to excessive expenditure; called for a reformed Parliament to appoint 'parliamentary commissioners to take charge of the public purse' (which provoked hilarity); denounced the 'mongrel set' of Conservative peers, and implied that William IV had betrayed his ministers. Littleton thought Hume, who was a teller for the ministerial majority, was 'excellent'.[171] On 11 May he accepted Baring's explanation of his 'brawlers' remark, but said that the king should not be allowed to ignore the reality that the people wanted and must have reform. He carried a motion to

hold a call of the House on the 14th, when he planned to submit one on the state of the nation. At a meeting at Brooks's, 13 May, he and Ebrington proposed the uncompromising course of opposing 'any [reform] bill' which the anticipated Conservative government might propose, but they were outvoted.[172] In the House, 14 May, he stated that Baring's speech that evening had dished any hope of a Conservative reform administration being formed, and secured an adjournment to forestall further debate.[173] Next day, when he spoke at the Kensington reform meeting of the 'silly ... cry of revolution' which had been raised to 'scare away the timid and trepan the well meaning', he deferred his call motion to the 18th, unless the Grey ministry had been reinstated by then.[174] He condemned the attack by a mob on the bishop of Lichfield at St. Bride's, Fleet Street, but suggested that it was the work of 'idle boys, or persons of no character'. On 17 May he arrived in the House fresh from a large and unanimous public meeting in favour of uncompromised reform, and warned whoever was now in power not to 'disappoint the well founded expectations of the people'. He had the House called over on 18 May, but elicited from Althorp confirmation that he and his colleagues were back in office with a 'sufficient' arrangement for getting reform through the Lords. He said that the conduct of the people during the crisis had been characterized by 'peace, order and unanimity' and their object gained 'not by physical force, but by moral power': in effect, they had rescued the king, whom he now praised, from the clutches of 'a monopolizing oligarchy'. That day Raikes recorded a story that Hume, 'the ... most vapouring radical in the House', had 'shown that courage is not amongst his peculiar virtues' by backing down when Ross, who had come in again for Aberdeen Burghs in 1831, libelled him as a liar for writing to his former constituents alleging that Ross was backsliding on reform.[175] Hume endorsed the Scottish reform bill at its second reading, 21 May. Next day he said that he would keep back 40 petitions for supplies to be withheld until reform was secured because he had faith in ministers' sincerity; he presented them on 10 July. He supported the prayer of the Birmingham Political Union's petition to that effect, 23 May. He divided for the second reading of the Irish reform bill, 25 May. Three days later Grey received from the king a querulous letter expressing alarm at 'the demoralizing designs and effects of a *third* party, which appears to be daily increasing in strength and audacity', having specifically in mind declarations by Hume, in and outside the House, to the effect that reform was only 'a stepping stone' to 'reformation of the church and of corporation property, etc.' The cabinet considered the letter and endorsed Grey's 'spirited and respectful reply'.[176] In early June Hume (like others) was duped by the charlatan Benjamin Disraeli[†] into commending him to the electors of Chipping Wycombe as a 'radical', but he recanted on discovering that Disraeli was standing against the interest of two local reformers.[177] On the Scottish reform bill, 1 June, he said that ideally he would have liked some minor changes, but he spoke and voted against a Conservative amendment to increase the number of county Members. His suggestion on 4 June that superiorities should be continued for the lives of their holders was dismissed by Althorp. He pressed Dixon to drop his proposal for a £5 voting qualification because there was no hope of its being adopted and he ought to 'take what he can get at present'. He welcomed the abandonment of the property qualification for Scottish Members, 27 June, and, while he agreed (as he had since the previous autumn) with Traill and others that Orkney and Shetland should logically have a Member each, argued that it was too late now to effect this.[178] On the Lords' amendments to the English reform bill, 5 June, he said that the 'dangers' of the political unions had 'no existence but in the disturbed imagination' of Conservatives, who had almost destroyed the monarchy. After attacking Peel personally, he declared his belief that 'the people should have complete control over the government'; and he supported the bill precisely because it would lead to further changes, having, like others, sacrificed personal preferences to secure a significant step towards the creation of a 'politically honest' Commons. He was in the minority of 23 on Whitehaven's boundaries, 22 June. In a discussion on the ballot, 24 July, he admitted that he had been 'anxious to guard against extending to the multitude the right of voting', but he wanted the issue to be 'speedily settled, for otherwise a great deal of unfair influence will be used'. On 18 June he rebuked O'Connell and Stanley for quarrelling over the Irish reform bill, but said that O'Connell was entitled to 'call in aid the physical force of the country', given that successive governments had 'oppressed' Ireland and ignored 'quiet remonstrance'. When challenged on this remark, he insisted that 'physical force' was a legitimate last resort for obtaining redress and argued that the measure short-changed Ireland by narrowing the franchise and not placing the country on the same footing as England and Scotland. He and Peel had angry words over his endorsement of violence, and the Speaker called him to order. He voted for amendments to enfranchise £5 freeholders and £30 rent payers, on which he was in a minority of nine. On 20 June Peel linked the attack on the king at Ascot races

with Hume's advocacy of 'physical force', but Hume accused Peel of 'uncandid and illiberal conduct'. He voted for Sheil's unsuccessful amendment to the Irish bill, 29 June, and on 2 July 1832 condemned it overall as 'disgraceful'.

Hume replied to a protectionist motion for a select committee on the state of trade and commerce, 22 May 1832, denying that he was 'one of those ultra political economists who profess doctrines to which the whole commercial community of England are opposed'. He failed to have the remit of the committee on renewal of the Bank of England's charter and small notes extended to Scotland, 4 June, when he attacked the Bank's monopoly. He pressed Lord Milton to save his motion for repeal of the corn laws for the first reformed Parliament, 30 May. He spoke and voted for the government's temporizing amendment to Fowell Buxton's motion for the abolition of slavery, 24 May, arguing that planters' rights must receive 'due regard' and that emancipation should be gradual. He supported the bill to abolish the death penalty for various offences, but wished it to be extended to all crimes except murder, 30 May. To salvage something of the measure, he recommended acceptance of the Lords' amendments, 6 July, but on 15 Aug. he decided that it had been rendered nugatory. He voted against Baring's bill to exclude insolvent debtors from the Commons, 6 June, because, as he explained on the 27th, it did not apply to the Lords. On 7 June, fending off Sadler's criticism, he said that he approved of his factories bill in so far as it restricted the labour of children under ten. He opposed Sadler's motion for a tax on Irish absentee landlords to provide for the poor, 19 June, when he seconded and was a teller for the minority of 15 for Hunt's motion to suspend army flogging. That day he raised the case of Alexander Somerville, a private in the Scots Greys, who had been flogged ostensibly for refusing to mount an unruly horse, but in reality, as his partisans believed, for radical political activities. Hume evidently discussed the business privately with Hobhouse, whom he told that he had raised it to prevent O'Connell from doing so and that 'the less said about it the better' if Hobhouse would secure Somerville an honourable discharge. This he did, but the process took several weeks; and Hobhouse was 'never more surprised than when Hume [on 3 July] got up and made a bitter speech against me' and moved for information. Hobhouse opposed this and Hume eventually dropped it; but Hobhouse, who was 'pledged against flogging', was embarrassed by the episode, exasperated by Hume's 'meddling' and considered resignation.[179] Hume moved an amendment for coroners to be qualified in medical law, which was defeated by 80-11, and voted for inquests to be made public, 20 June. He endorsed O'Connell's denunciation of the tsar as 'a monster in human form', 28 June, and, supporting De Lacy Evans's plea for intervention on behalf of the Poles, 7 Aug., described Russia's conduct since 1815 as 'one uninterrupted violation of all her pacific professions'. But he opposed as 'uncalled for' and was a teller for the minority of 16 against the government's Greek loan proposal, 6 Aug., which Hobhouse thought showed remarkable effrontery.[180] Hume said that the advance of £1,000,000 to the West Indies would be money down the drain, as the planters would be unable to repay it, 29 June; and he attacked the crown colonies relief bill, 3 Aug., when the colonial under-secretary Howick accused him of 'pursuing a course which is calculated to throw discredit upon those who wish to improve the state of slavery'. Hume was critical of the size of the ordnance estimates and voted to reduce the barracks grant, 2 July, but next day he postponed his motion to abolish unmerited pensions. He could not persuade Althorp not to fill the vacant governorship of Stirling Castle, 10 July. He gave Brougham the benefit of the doubt over the supposedly temporary appointment of his brother to a chancery sinecure, 25 July. He supported an unsuccessful motion of army reductions, 26 July, and opposed the 'vicious' tax on post horses, 27 July. He did not object to the award of a pension to Speaker Manners Sutton on his anticipated retirement, but did not think it should become automatic in future cases, 1 Aug. He approved in principle the proposal to pay the lord chancellor by salary rather than fees, but felt that it and the related pension were set too high, 2 Aug. His bid to reduce the salary from £14,000 to £12,000 was defeated by 56-6, 8 Aug.; and he supported and voted for Hunt's amendment to cut the pension by £1,000, 9 Aug. He argued for leaving the silk trade to market forces and could see no remedy for the 'evil' of dislocation caused by machinery, 7 Aug. On the consolidated fund bill next day, he said that he had acquiesced in numerous dubious grants that session in order not to obstruct reform. He praised ministers for reducing expenditure, especially in 'minor branches', but insisted that much remained to be done, particularly on pensions, and promised to demonstrate to the next Parliament how £5,000,000 could be lopped off the national expenditure. He criticized Hobhouse's proposal to allow army half-pay officers to hold civil posts as a departure from the advice of the finance committee; Hobhouse considered his opposition 'most unfair' in 'trying to make this act of justice appear as odious as possible'.[181] On 9 Aug. Hume moved but was persuaded to drop a resolution to restrict civil list pen-

sions to one year. He presented petitions for the abolition of tithes, 9, 24 July, and on the 10th pressed ministers to abandon their Irish tithes composition bill until the next session, as it begged the wider question of reform of the church establishment. He voted against the measure, 13 July. On 2 Aug. he divided the House for reception of an abolition petition, but was left in a minority of ten; and next day, when he spoke and voted in the minority of 12 for an amendment to the ecclesiastical courts contempt bill, he endorsed a petition from Preston against the use of troops to enforce tithes payment. On 6 Aug. he said that all tithes must be abolished, and on the 10th called for repeal of the provision which empowered the Irish viceroy and six privy councillors to suspend habeas corpus and ascertained from Stanley that an inquiry into Irish church revenues was in the offing. On 17 July he seconded and divided for Harvey's motion for inquiry into admissions to the Inns of Court. For all this, he voted with government on the Russian-Dutch loan, 12, 16, 20 July, frankly admitting that it was a 'wrong' measure but that he wished to keep the ministry in power: he would vote that black was white for that purpose if necessary.[182] He urged investigation of the parochial costs of the metropolitan police, 24 July, when he secured, by 36-16, leave to introduce a bill to exclude the recorder of Dublin from the Commons in future. On its second reading, 31 July, the House was counted out and the measure lapsed. He seconded Courtenay's motion for an address to ask the king to exercise his influence over the German Diet to protect the independence and freedom of German liberals, 2 Aug. He suggested an amendment to the electoral bribery bill to empower a committee of inquiry to disfranchise guilty electors, 6 Aug., but the matter was left undecided; and he supported an abortive attempt to construe payment of registration costs as bribery, 9 Aug. Next day and on 16 Aug. he questioned ministers closely on the fatal canvassing affray at Clitheroe. When he had raised the problem of the lack of time for £10 householders of Marylebone and other metropolitan constituencies to pay their rates in order to qualify for the vote, 10 July, Althorp had brushed him aside. He backed De Lacy Evans, who had been alerted to this threat of mass disfranchisement by Place, in his attempts to get ministers to take action, 7, 9 Aug.[183] On 15 Aug. he complained that the registration fee of 1s. would press most heavily on small tradesmen, who would make up the bulk of the metropolitan electorates, and declared that the Reform Act would 'never be thoroughly satisfactory to the country until it is so far modified as that the test of payment of rates should be removed altogether'. He brought up petitions on a wide range of issues, 16 Aug. 1832, when his last recorded act in the unreformed Parliament was the presentation of one from the political union of Bethnal Green praying that the name of the king should not be used to 'crush the liberty of Germany'.

At the general election of 1832 'the immaculate Joseph', as Bedford disparagingly called him, sent down the 'Benthamite baronet' Sir Francis Knowles to oppose Holland's son Charles Richard Fox* at Tavistock, notwithstanding the support which he received from Holland in Middlesex. Although he did not approve of personal canvassing, kept his purse strings tightly closed until the last minute and was embarrassed by public exposure of his 'shuffling' on slavery, he was returned at the head of the poll.[184] He was defeated there in 1837, but found other seats, which enabled him to bore and exasperate six reformed Parliaments until death stopped his mouth in February 1855. Tom Macaulay* was amused to receive a memorial poem from his son Joseph Burnley Hume:

'His body was a masterpiece; for force, endurance, speed
And every kind of action perfect; beautiful indeed'

Who but a son would have pronounced Joe the model of beauty? This son, I hear ... had but lately returned from his harlots and his hog trough to the fatted calf when the old gentleman died.[185]

Hobhouse called him in 1827 'the queerest mortal, if not malicious, I ever knew'; but he later wrote that Hume was 'essentially a part of the House of Commons for many years' and recollected 'a saying of Sir Robert Peel, that he could not conceive of a House of Commons without a Joseph Hume'.[186]

---

[1] See R.K. Huch and P.R. Zeigler, *Joseph Hume: the People's MP* (1985) and V. Chancellor, *The Political Life of Joseph Hume* (1986). Neither is up to much. For a fresh perspective on Hume see M. Taylor, *The Decline of British Radicalism* (1995) and 'Joseph Hume and the Reformation of India, 1819-33', in *Radicalism in English Political Thought, 1550-1850* ed. G. Burgess and M. Festenstein (2005). [2] According to *Willis's Current Notes* (1855), 48. [3] *The Times*, 26 Feb. 1855. [4] *Gent. Mag.* (1815), ii. 178; PROB 11/2210/326. She was *bap.* in July 1786 (IGI). [5] [J. Grant], *Random Recollections of Commons* (1837), 276, 278. [6] Huch and Zeigler, 20-21. [7] Grant, 79-80. [8] Broughton, *Recollections*, iii. 204. [9] B. Gordon, *Economic Doctrine and Tory Liberalism*, 8-9; G. Wallas, *Francis Place*, (1908), 183. [10] *HP Commons, 1790-1820*, ii. 592; *Inverness Courier*, 9, 16 Mar.; *Aberdeen Jnl.* 15, 22, 29 Mar., 5 Apr. 1820. [11] Lonsdale mss, Long to Lonsdale, 20 Mar. [1820]. [12] *Von Neumann Diary*, i. 41; Add. 56541, ff. 74, 84. [13] Huch and Zeigler, 23; *Arbuthnot Jnl.* i. 67. [14] *Colchester Diary*, iii. 217. [15] HLRO, Hist. Coll. 379, Grey Bennet diary, 21. [16] Ibid. 34-36. [17] Harrowby mss, Castlereagh to Harrowby, 8 Mar.; TNA FO352/8/4, Planta to Canning, 15 Mar.; Dorset RO, Bond mss D/BoH, Jekyll to Bond, 20 Mar. 1821. [18] Dorset RO D/BKL, Bankes jnl. 126. [19] Grey Bennet diary, 63. [20] Ibid. 81. [21] Bagot mss. [22] Grey Bennet diary, 100, 102, 104, 112-13. [23] Ibid. 79-81;

Bankes jnl. 129. [24] Grey Bennet diary, 98. [25] Ibid. 89; Buckingham, *Mems. Geo. IV*, i. 182. [26] Heron, *Notes*, 126; Huch and Zeigler, 25-26; *The Times*, 10, 14 July 1821. [27] *The Times*, 27 Oct. 1821. [28] Grey Bennet diary, 117, 121-3. [29] Add. 51659. [30] *Hobhouse Diary*, 73; Add. 36459, f. 115; 36460, f. 104. [31] *The Times*, 14 Dec. 1821, 8, 16 Jan. 1822. [32] Add. 36459, f. 183. [33] Bagot, *Canning and Friends*, ii. 123. [34] Add. 51663, Bedford to Holland, 22 Jan. [1822]. [35] Add. 52445, ff. 29, 30. [36] Gurney diary, 5 Feb.; Harewood mss, Gladstone to Canning, 6 Feb. [1822]. [37] Grey mss, Grey to Holland, 9 Feb. 1822. [38] NLW, Coedymaen mss 621. [39] *Creevey Pprs.* ii. 35; Add. 52445, f. 36; Huch and Zeigler, 28; *Arbuthnot Jnl.* i. 153. [40] Ashley, *Palmerston*, i. 88; Hants RO, Malmesbury mss 9M73/G2535/10. [41] *The Times*, 19 Apr. 1822; *Edgeworth Letters*, 398. [42] *Life of Wilberforce*, v. 127. [43] M.D. George, *Cat. of Pol. and Personal Satires*, x. 14369. [44] Broughton, ii. 190. [45] *Arbuthnot Jnl.* i. 166. [46] Buckingham, i. 354. [47] Heron, 133. [48] *The Times*, 12, 22, 25 Sept., 1 Oct. 1822. [49] Bessborough mss f 150. [50] Add. 51586, Tierney to Holland, 6 Oct. [1822]. [51] *Creevey Pprs.* ii. 50-51. [52] Bessborough mss f 1. [53] *Cockburn Letters*, 72, 164, 305. [54] Add. 52445, f. 112; Broughton, iii. 11. [55] *Creevey Pprs.* ii. 63; *Arbuthnot Jnl.* i. 216; Merthyr Mawr mss F/51/4, Sir J. Nicholl to son, 11 Mar.; Bessborough mss f 53, Brougham to Duncannon, 2 [4 Mar.]; Add. 51667, Bedford to Lady Holland [23 Feb. 1823]. [56] *Arbuthnot Jnl.* i. 224; *Croker Pprs.* i. 263. [57] Broughton, iii. 17. [58] *O'Connell Corresp.* ii. 1012. [59] Add. 40687, f. 1. [60] Northants. RO, Agar Ellis diary, 4 Mar. [1823]. [61] *Creevey Pprs.* ii. 66; Bessborough mss f 53, Brougham to Duncannon [10 Mar. 1823]. [62] Add. 51667, Bedford to Lady Holland, 7 Mar. [1823]. [63] Buckingham, i. 467. [64] Add. 36460, f. 123. [65] Add. 51586; *Gent. Mag.* (1823), ii. 571; PROB 11/1678/666; IR26/944/1880. [66] Add. 56548, f. 55. [67] *Life of Wilberforce*, v. 188. [68] Add. 56548. f. 93. [69] Broughton, iii. 73-75; Add. 36460, ff. 280-4. [70] Huch and Zeigler, 35-42; Wallas, 206-40; *Place Autobiog.* ed. M. Thale, p. xii; Gordon, 27-32. [71] Gurney diary, 29 June [1826]. [72] Gordon, 33-36; Huch and Zeigler, 42-44; *London Radicalism* ed. D.J. Rowe (London Rec. Soc. v), p. xi. [73] *Colchester Diary*, iii. 412. [74] Buckingham, ii. 242. [75] Add. 38747, ff. 73, 98. [76] *The Times*, 4, 12, 24 Oct., 1, 22 Nov. 1825; Add. 37949, f. 160; George, x. 14804; *Disraeli Letters*, i. 44. [77] Fitzwilliam mss 124/10, Fitzwilliam to Milton, 4 Feb. [1826]. [78] Ibid. 124/8, Althorp to Milton, 11 Feb. 1826. [79] Wellington mss WP1/850/9; Surr. Hist. Cent. Goulburn mss Acc 304/67A, Goulburn to wife, 12 Feb. 1826; *Hobhouse Diary*, 120. [80] Add. 51584. [81] Goulburn mss 67A. [82] Harewood mss, J. Gladstone to Canning, 22 June; *Aberdeen Jnl.* 14 June, 5 July; *Inverness Courier*, 28 June 1826. [83] *The Times*, 26-28 Nov. 1826; George, x. 15146; Huch and Zeigler, 47-50. [84] *Geo. IV Letters*, iii. 1271; Grey mss, Brougham to Grey, 20, 26 Nov., Grey to Howick, 24 Nov.; Castle Howard mss, Abercromby to Carlisle [22 Nov.] 1826; Huch and Zeigler, 50-52. [85] *Morning Chron.* 28 Nov.; *The Times*, 29 Nov. 1826; Huch and Zeigler, 53-54. [86] Broughton, iii. 159. [87] Nottingham Univ. Lib. Denison diary, 1 May [1827]. [88] *Geo. IV Letters*, iii. 1341; Huch and Zeigler, 56. [89] Add. 37949, f. 201; Huch and Zeigler, 57 [90] Broughton, iii. 201. [91] Add. 37949, f. 210. [92] Add. 40307, f. 50; 40395, ff. 219, 221; *Croker Pprs.* i. 407. [93] Add. 35148, ff. 24, 25. [94] *Croker Pprs.* i. 419; Powis mss 142. [95] St. Deiniol's Lib. Glynne-Gladstone mss 277. [96] Hants RO, Tierney mss 38. [97] Add. 40397, ff. 190, 407, 409. [98] Add. 37950, f. 5. [99] Add. 35145, f. 99. [100] *Greville Mems.* i. 370; Grey mss, Howick jnl. 4 Feb. [1830]; Hatherton mss. [101] *Ellenborough Diary*, ii. 179. [102] *Arbuthnot Jnl.* ii. 334; Le Marchant, *Althorp*, 235; Howick jnl. 14, 15 Feb.. [103] *London Radicalism*, 2. [104] Add. 35148, f. 40. [105] Add. 56554, f. 81. [106] Howick jnl. 10 May [1830]. [107] Add. 36466, ff. 23, 31. [108] Howick jnl. 14 June [1830]. [109] *Ellenborough Diary*, ii. 301; NAI, Leveson Gower letterbks. M. 738, p. 184; Howick jnl. 11 July [1830]. [110] Broughton, iv. 37. [111] Add. 56554, ff. 131, 133. [112] Add. 37950, ff. 45-52. [113] Add. 35146, ff. 114-16; 36466, ff. 161, 163, 256; 56554, ff. 119-20; Broughton, iv. 28-30; Glynne-Gladstone mss 195, T. to J. Gladstone, 29 June 1830; *Ellenborough Diary*, ii. 275; Huch and Zeigler, 64-69. [114] *The Times*, 16 June, 31 July, 6 Aug.; *Aberdeen Jnl.* 7, 14, 21, 28 July 1830; *Ellenborough Diary*, ii. 275, 313; Broughton,

iv. 43-44, 46-47. [115] *Aberdeen Jnl.* 11, 18 Aug. 1830. [116] *Scotsman*, 1 Sept. 1830. [117] Add. 35148, f. 66; 37950, ff. 91, 92, 94; *O'Connell Corresp.* iv. 1718. [118] Howick jnl. 2 Nov. [1830]. [119] *Life of Campbell*, i. 483. [120] Howick jnl. 5 Nov. [1830]. [121] Broughton, iv. 59. [122] Hopetoun mss 167, f. 189. [123] *Lieven Letters*, 275-6; *Life of Campbell*, i. 487. [124] Add. 35148, f. 73. [125] Glynne-Gladstone mss 196, T. to J. Gladstone, 13 Dec. 1830. [126] Ibid. T. to J. Gladstone, 15 Dec. 1830. [127] Add. 56555, ff. 74-75. [128] Broughton, iv. 78. [129] Aberdeen Univ. Lib. Arbuthnot mss. [130] Add. 35146, f. 130. [131] *O'Connell Corresp.* iv. 1751. [132] *The Times*, 17 Feb. 1831. [133] *Three Diaries*, 46. [134] Glynne-Gladstone mss 197, T. to J. Gladstone, 9 Feb. 1831. [135] *O'Connell Corresp.* iv. 1766. [136] Add. 35146, f. 131; 35149, ff. 26, 27. [137] Russell, *Recollections*, 72. [138] *The Times*, 8, 15 Mar. 1831. [139] Add. 35149, ff. 34, 40-49; *London Radicalism*, 16, 17, 20-23. [140] Glynne-Gladstone mss 197, T. to J. Gladstone, 14 Mar. 1831. [141] Add. 35149, f. 51. [142] Broughton, iv. 98. [143] *The Times*, 11 May 1831. [144] *Scotsman*, 8 June 1831. [145] Hatherton diary, 11 Aug. [1831]. [146] *Arbuthnot Corresp.* 148. [147] *Holland House Diaries*, 58; *Three Diaries*, 133. [148] Hatherton diary, 1 Sept. [1831]. [149] Ibid. 8 Sept. [1831]. [150] *Three Diaries*, 138. [151] Hatherton diary, 9 Oct. [1831]. [152] *The Times*, 28 Sept. 1831. [153] *O'Connell Corresp.* iv. 1839. [154] *London Radicalism*, 35-37; Hatherton diary, 11 Oct. [1831]. [155] Cornw. RO, Hawkins mss 10/2172. [156] *London Radicalism*, 43-44. [157] *The Times*, 5, 18 Nov. 1831. [158] Broughton, iv. 150. [159] Hatherton diary, 11 Nov. [1831]. [160] *Holland House Diaries*, 93. [161] Add. 35149, f. 132; *Gent. Mag.* (1831), ii. 570. [162] Broughton, iv. 201. [163] Ibid. iv. 182. [164] *Arbuthnot Corresp.* 163. [165] Add. 56556, f. 45. [166] *Three Diaries*, 188. [167] Broughton, iv. 215. [168] *Holland House Diaries*, 95. [169] *Three Diaries*, 206; Hawkins mss 10/2185. [170] Lonsdale mss, Beckett to Lord Lowther [9 May 1832]. [171] Hatherton diary, 10 May [1832]. [172] *Three Diaries*, 251-2; *Croker Pprs.* ii. 164. [173] *Croker Pprs.* ii. 166. [174] *The Times*, 16 May 1832. [175] *Raikes Jnl.* ii. 34-36. [176] *Grey-William IV Corresp.* ii. 449-50; *Holland House Diaries*, 186-7. [177] *Disraeli Letters*, i. 198-200. [178] Orkney Archives, Balfour mss D2/8/13, Traill to W. Balfour, 8 Oct. [1831]. [179] Broughton, iv. 246; Add. 56557, f. 15. [180] Add. 56557, f. 14. [181] Ibid. [182] *Holland House Diaries*, 199. [183] *London Radicalism*, 106. [184] Add. 37949, f. 269; 47223, f. 64; 51671, Bedford to Lady Holland [13 Dec.]; 51680, Russell to same, 2 Dec.; 51787, Holland to Fox, 12 Dec.; *Three Diaries*, 287; *The Times*, 20, 28 Dec. 1832. [185] *Macaulay Letters*, v. 449. [186] Broughton, iii. 202.

D.R.F.

HUNT, Henry (1773–1835), of Middleton Cottage, Andover, Hants and 36 Stamford Street, Mdx.[1]

PRESTON	17 Dec. 1830–1832

b. 6 Nov. 1773, 1st s. of Thomas Hunt of Widdington Farm, Upavon, Wilts. and Elizabeth *née* Powell of Week, nr. Devizes, Wilts. *educ.* Tilshead, Wilts. (Mr. Cooper); Hursley, Hants (Mr. Alner); Andover g.s. (Rev. Thomas Griffith); Salisbury, Wilts. (Rev. James Evans). *m.* 19 Jan. 1796[2] (*sep.* 6 Sept. 1802), Ann, da. of William Halcomb, innkeeper, of Devizes, 2s. 2da. (1 *d.v.p.*)[3]. *suc.* fa. 1797. *d.* 15 Feb. 1835.
Ensign Wilts. yeoman cav. Everleigh troop 1794-8; Marlborough troop 1798.

Arguably the 'best mob orator of the day', Hunt was a great-great-grandson of the royalist Colonel Thomas Hunt of Enford, whose escape from Ilchester gaol after the Somerset uprising, to join Charles II in exile, caused the family to forfeit Somerset and Wiltshire estates they had held since the Conquest.[4] Hunt's father Thomas, a successful farmer, restored the family to prosperity and added about 3,000 acres, including Littlecot, Glastonbury manor, property in Bath and the tenancies of Chisenbury and Widdington Farm on Salisbury Plain (Hunt's birthplace), to their holdings. When inherited in 1797 by Hunt, the eldest of his six children, they were worth £1,000-£1,500 a year.[5] A headstrong youth, he had resisted his socially ambitious parents' attempts to educate him for Oxford and the church, espoused the loyalist cause following the French revolution of 1789, enlisted in the yeomanry cavalry and become a gentleman farmer. Defying his father, who nevertheless assisted him at Widdington, he married the daughter of a well-to-do Devizes innkeeper with a dowry of £1,000. When they separated formally in September 1802, Ann was granted custody of their daughter and £250 a year and Hunt, who settled with his lifelong mistress Catherine Vince, took charge of their sons Thomas and Henry.[6] William Cobbett[†], during one of his many quarrels with Hunt, famously cautioned against associating with a man who 'rides about the country with a whore, the wife of another man, having deserted his own'.[7] Hunt's *Memoirs* date both his marital problems and his political awakening to 1799, when his defiance of his militia commander Lord Bruce prompted prosecutions for indiscipline and trespass for which he was fined and imprisoned in king's bench. There he came under the influence of the reformers Samuel Waddington and Henry Clifford.[8] Ostracized by the Wiltshire squirearchy and snubbed by Lord Pembroke, the lord lieutenant of Somerset, after he raised a volunteer militia troop at Enford in 1803, he rallied for Sir Francis 'Burdett* and independence' at the 1804 Middlesex by-election and campaigned in 1805 for the impeachment of the first lord of the admiralty Lord Melville. At the 1806 general election he promoted reform from the hustings in Somerset, Wiltshire and Bristol, where he had invested in the beleaguered Jacob's Well brewery.[9] As 'Bristol Hunt' he declared as an independent candidate after the 1807 election and established a Patriotic and Constitutional Association to promote local electoral reform. Politically motivated prosecutions ensued, including a successful one in 1809 for assaulting John Benett's* gamekeeper, for which he was consigned to king's bench prison, where he shared rooms with Cobbett. Lurching further into radicalism and distancing himself from the mainstream and Foxite Whigs, he joined Major John Cartwright's radical Union for Parliamentary Reform, whose demands for universal suffrage, short parliaments and the ballot, he promoted as a leader in 1830-2 of the National Metropolitan Union and the Great Northern Union of the Working Classes.[10] He polled last at both Bristol elections in 1812 and failed with a petition, but the evidence of charity abuse he acquired during its preparation enhanced his anti-corporation rhetoric and endeared him to the masses.[11] His Wiltshire tenancies had lapsed, and he took estates at Rowfant, near East Grinstead, Sussex, where he prospered, 1812-13, and Cold Henley, near Winchester, Hampshire, where the post-war collapse in prices and spurious legal actions, which dogged him for the rest of his life, terminated his farming career. He retained the lease of Middleton Cottage, Andover, with gaming rights over the 8,000-acre manor of Long Parish.[12]

Hunt entered London politics as a liveryman of the Loriners' Company in 1813. Verbal skirmishes with the 'City Cock' Robert Waithman* and the Whig moderates in Westminster, where he promoted Lord Cochrane's re-election in 1814 and opposed the property tax and the 1815 corn law, made him one of the leading radical demagogues, keen to denounce, in what Lord Holland termed his 'brawling eloquence (*loquentia potius quam eloquentia*)', the failure of the Whigs in office to prune the civil list and end jobbing.[13] In the winter of 1816-17 he addressed the radical meetings at Spa Fields, where, meeting him for the first time, the Middleton weaver-poet Samuel Bamford found him

> gentlemanly in his manner and attire, six feet and better in height, and extremely well formed. He was dressed in a blue lapelled coat, light waistcoat and kerseys, and topped boots; his leg and foot were about the firmest and neatest I ever saw. He wore his own hair; it was moderate in quantity and a little grey. His features were regular, and there was a kind of youthful blandness about them, which, in amiable discussion, gave his face a most agreeable expression. His lips were delicately thin and receding; but there was a dumb utterance about them, which in all portraits I have seen of him was never truly copied. His eyes were blue or light grey – not very clear nor quick, but rather heavy; except as I afterwards had opportunities for observing, when he was excited in speaking, at which times they seemed to distend and protrude; and if he worked himself furious, as he sometimes would, they became blood streaked, and almost started from their sockets. Then it was that the expression of his lip was to be observed – the kind smile was exchanged for the curl of scorn, or the curse of indignation. His voice was bellowing; his face swollen and flushed; his gripped hand beat as if it were to pulverise; and his whole manner gave token of a painful energy, struggling for utterance ... He was always beating against a tempest of his own or of others' creating.[14]

Backed by the northern delegates, 'Orator' Hunt (Robert Southey's* sobriquet) carried resolutions for reform including universal suffrage, the ballot and annual parliaments at the January 1817 Hampden Club convention and forced Cochrane to present a similar Bristol petition, 29 Jan. To distance himself from the Spencean revolutionaries, he sent 'loyalist' letters to the home secretary Lord Sidmouth, petitioned to ensure that these were recorded in the *Journals of the House of Commons*, 4 Feb. 1817, and offered to testify before the House.[15] Although his correspondence was intercepted, he evaded arrest under the Seditious Meetings Act, presided at the Palace Yard meetings, 23 Feb. 1817, 7 Sept. 1818, and campaigned against Waithman in the City and the Whigs in Westminster, where in 1818 he polled a poor fourth.[16] He petitioned the Commons personally against the Westminster hustings bill, 29 Jan., 2 Feb. 1819.[17]

Hunt first visited St. Peter's Fields, Manchester on 18 Jan. 1819, when, deputizing for the imprisoned Stockport radical John Bagguley, he carried the radical Palace Yard remonstrance. Its rejection by the regent spawned mass gatherings and the formation of unions in the major conurbations and culminated at Peterloo, 16 Aug. 1819.[18] Fresh from success at the Smithfield meeting, 21 July, and as author of the *Green Bag Plot*, criticizing Burdett and Lord Liverpool's Tory ministry, he had welcomed the opportunity to preside and publicize the campaign to secure radical reform by 'numerical force' and urge non-payment of taxes (from 1 Jan. 1820) until it was effected. His stance on the proposed elected national convention or anti-Parliament, which he described in his *Memoirs* as 'folly', was ambivalent, but he hoped to become a paid delegate to it with Cobbett, Cartwright and Thomas Wooler. He welcomed *The Times* reporter John Tyas and the editor of the *Manchester Observer*, John Thacker Saxton, to his entourage, and was apparently unaware that his Manchester host Joseph Johnson hoped for insurrection.[19] He ensured that the crowd of over 60,000 gathered peaceably, but at least 11 were killed and over 400 injured after the Manchester and Salford yeomanry, backed by the 15th Hussars, were sent in by the magistrates to arrest him for high treason under a warrant issued by their chairman, William Hulton of Hulton, a dandy he vilified as Polly Hulton.[20] He was charged with the lesser offence of seditious conspiracy and transferred to Lancaster gaol, 27 Aug. 1819. Bailed, he challenged the competence of the Lancashire grand jury and its foreman Lord Stanley*, and mustered popular support in the North-West and London, where, according to *The Times*, 300,000 watched his arrival, 9 Sept.[21] He vainly tendered affidavits in king's bench for the prosecution of the Manchester magistrates, petitioned Parliament alleging that his conduct had been misrepresented, 29 Nov. 1819, and encouraged petitioning for inquiry and redress.[22]

The Whigs hoped to use Peterloo to discredit the Liverpool ministry and the radicals, but Lord Grey's son-in-law John Lambton* warned Sir Robert Wilson* and the 'Mountain' to 'keep clear of ... [Hunt] as you would of infection'.[23] Hunt convened meetings against the Six Acts, chaired dinners to mark Cobbett's return from America and organized the production of 'Breakfast Powder' – a tax-free substitute for tea and coffee. It soon featured in caricatures of the period.[24] At the 1820 general election he used funds raised to cover his legal costs to contest Preston, where the franchise was almost universal and the representation vested in a Whig-Tory coalition to which Stanley's family was party.[25] Advocating inquiry into Peterloo, repeal of the Six Acts and the radical reform programme, he polled creditably, albeit in fourth place, prior to his departure for York.[26] At the trial, 16-27 Mar., his defence, which he conducted personally, was impressive and widely publicized but, to the relief of the royal household and the government, he was found guilty, 27 Mar. His appeal failed, and he was refused a retrial, 8 May. On 15 May he was sentenced to 30 months' imprisonment and bound over for £2,000 to keep the peace for a further five years.[27] Lord Grenville observed (29 Mar. 1820): 'It would have been a dreadful thing indeed if it had been established by the result of that trial that the Manchester meeting was under all its circumstances a legal assembly'.[28] In September 1828 the duke of Wellington as premier made Hunt's case his precedent for authorizing the detention of the editor of the *Irishman*, John Lawless, after the rioting at Ballibay.[29]

While imprisoned (on compassionate grounds at Ilchester), Hunt, who espoused Queen Caroline's cause, was commemorated by members of the Great Northern Union at dinners and celebrations throughout the North-West. He prepared radical addresses outlining plans for the popular democratic organization he hoped to lead, and drafted his *Memoirs* for serialization.[30] These convinced Bamford 'that my devoted *Patriot* was an overbearing *Tyrant*, one who would rather "Rule in Hell than serve in Heaven"', but they kept him in the eye of the public and the caricaturists.[31] Supported by the parliamentary radicals and the Liverpool Concentric Society (their leader, the Unitarian Dr. William Shepherd, later compared Cobbett to Robespierre and Hunt to Danton), Hunt

sought parliamentary inquiry into Peterloo, railed against Burdett's failure to secure it, 16 May 1821, and mounted a campaign on the Lancaster model against the Ilchester gaoler William Brindle and the visiting magistrates.[32] At least 40 petitions (including his own) were presented to the Commons in 1822 protesting at conditions in 'Ilchester Bastille' and urging remission of his sentence. Burdett's motion requesting this was defeated (by 223-84), 24 Apr., amid quips that all Hunt was deprived of was his mistress.[33] Despite reports of his waning popularity, his release on 30 Oct. 1822 was widely marked. He attended the processions and public celebrations in Somerset and London, where Johnson published a commemorative cartoon with the caption: 'They may *Hunt* me from Brixton to Ilchester again, before I will alter my conduct or *Vince*'.[34]

On 21 Jan. 1823, assisted by the radical Sir Charles Wolseley, he addressed a Somerset agricultural distress meeting he had instigated at Wells. The sheriff threw out his eight-point amendment for reform and retrenchment, but he carried it at another meeting the following week. John Hobhouse eventually presented the petition, 16 July 1823.[35] An excise board ruling that 'breakfast powder' was not tax exempt was rescinded, but in order to recoup financially Hunt turned to the manufacture and sale of the food dye amaretto and 'matchless' shoe and hearth blacking. He also invested unwisely on behalf of his son in a Peruvian mining company.[36] Caricatures depicting him as a 'blacking pot' boosted his sales, and he deployed his 'blacking vans' as election transport and wore his prison uniform when he contested Somerset, where he polled a poor third, at the general election of 1826. On the hustings he portrayed himself as the 'enemy to ... injustice ... corn laws ... game laws, and ... all laws that mark a degrading contrast between the lazy and the industrious'.[37] The *Bristol Mercury* commented:

> No one perhaps possesses greater tact in managing a mob; he mingles an indiscriminate abuse of the rich and the great with such an affectation of constitutional feeling and disinterested patriotism, that he never fails to carry the crowd along with him; they are led away by the enthusiasm of the moment ... they listen to the professions of the orator and they lose sight of his previous conduct.[38]

At Andover in September 1826, he took over proceedings at a protectionist meeting and carried a petition for corn law repeal.[39]

Hunt had re-entered City politics as a self-professed champion of reform and the rate-paying commonalty in 1824. As at Bristol, he campaigned for publication of the corporation accounts, and following his election as auditor in 1826 he exposed the system of

feasting ('guzzlings and gourmandizing') that prevailed and pressed for reform, retrenchment and
greater accountability. He failed to secure a seat on
the common council in 1827 and 1828, but exposed
the malpractices of the 'City Jobbers' in a petition to
the Lords concerning the London Bridge bill (June
1829). Before his term as auditor lapsed in December
1829 he carried resolutions compelling officials to keep
receipts and produce accounts promptly.[40] Bentham
grudgingly conceded his achievement, but doubted
his long-term utility to the reform movement. Squibs
and caricatures depicted him as a blacking man pol-
ishing the corporation accounts or hurling his wares.[41]
'Catechising', a satire marking the establishment
of King's College, London in 1828, gave as its tenth
commandment: 'Thou shalt not buy Hunt's matchless blacking, not his ink, nor his roasted grain, nor
anything that is his'.[42]

He had advocated Catholic relief since 1819 and,
nailing it firmly to reform, he opposed the restriction
of the Irish freehold franchise condoned by Burdett
in the 1825 bill and criticized Daniel O'Connell*, as
leader of the Catholic Association, for supporting it.[43]
He denounced the pro-Catholic Canning as an anti-
reformer at the 1827 and 1828 Westminster anniversary meetings and tried to extract a public pledge for
radical reform from O'Connell following his election
for Clare.[44] He accompanied Cobbett to the Kent
anti-Catholic meeting at Penenden Heath, 24 Oct.
1828, when they failed to carry an anti-tithe amendment. Hunt carried a similar one in Westminster in
1829 and criticized O'Connell and Burdett privately,
in the press and at the anniversary dinner for endorsing a bill that 'sacrificed' the 40s. Irish freeholder
vote, 25 May. He also deliberately stumbled when
the king was toasted and rose for reform.[45] Next day,
'to protect the poor from dissection', he and Cobbett
petitioned the Lords against relaxing restrictions on
anatomical dissection.[46] He campaigned to reform the
parish vestries at Christchurch and Lambeth, Surrey,
where he contended that the 'whole of the ... householders' were qualified to vote at Southwark elections, and defied Waithman by carrying a petition
for inquiry into distress at the City traders' meeting
at the Mansion House, 22 Feb. 1830.[47] His reform
manifesto (issued jointly with Cobbett, 4 July 1829)
was endorsed by the Radical Reform Association, but
denounced as extreme by the Westminster Whigs, the
Ultra Lord Blandford* and at Brooks's. He briefly
aspired to alignment with the Birmingham Political
Union established by Thomas Attwood[†], despite their
endorsement of Blandford's reform scheme.[48] On 8
Mar. 1830 he shared the platform with O'Connell at

the City's *Eagle House* tavern, to promote a petition for
reform, universal suffrage and the ballot. Advocating
'moral force', he called for 'no taxation without representation' and cajoled the Radical Reform Association
members present and their allies into forming the
Metropolitan Political Union.[49] The Charing Cross
tailor Francis Place later wrote that

> Hunt's acceptance of the office of treasurer ruined the
> Union. Several who had been named on the council [of
> 36] refused to act and nobody would subscribe money to
> be under the control or care of Mr. Hunt, and the Union
> was soon extinguished from want of money to pay its
> current expenses.[50]

He carried similar petitions in Surrey and in common
hall. According to Hobhouse, at the Westminster
dinner in May, Hunt met his match in the Newcastle
bookseller Eneas Mackenzie, who stifled his diatribes
against O'Connell.[51] Realizing his mistake in supporting Attwood and Blandford, he tried to seize supremacy for the Municipal Reform Union and the Radical
Reform Association before the general election in July.
Both subscribed towards his candidature for Preston
that month, when his quarry was Lord Stanley's son
and heir Edward George Geoffrey Smith Stanley*.
His supporters, a coalition of Tories, radicals and
the nascent political unions, mounted an ineffective campaign and he trailed throughout the five-day
poll.[52] His blacking business in Paris now failed, yet
he welcomed the recent revolution in France.[53] In
the Northern industrial towns and at the Rotunda in
Blackfriars Road that autumn he advocated reform
as a means of avoiding insurrection in England.[54] He
presented reform addresses at the levee, 3 Nov., and
similar petitions from the Rotunda and Glastonbury
were received in his name, 16 Nov., 6 Dec. 1830.[55]
Government informants, caricaturists and commentators erroneously associated Hunt with 'Captain Swing'
in Kent, plots for a Northern uprising and to disrupt
the king's visit to the City (which was cancelled), and
rioting at Blackfriars, 8 Nov.[56] According to Place:

> Information was given to the police commissioners that
> Henry Hunt was to lead 20,000 men from the Surrey side
> of the Thames over Blackfriars Bridge to Ludgate Hill to
> pay their respects to the king, and to let him hear the sen-
> timents of the people. That Hunt could collect and lead
> twice that number I have no doubt, but I do not believe
> that any such a procession would have taken place.[57]

Bruised by a public spat with Richard Carlile and the
deist Robert Taylor, he was on business in the West
country, where he helped to pacify the 'Swing' rioters
at Overton, Andover and Salisbury, when he learnt
on 7 Dec. 1830 of his nomination at the Preston by-

election caused by Smith Stanley's appointment as the Grey ministry's Irish secretary.[58] He arrived on the 13th with the poll 3,311-2,853 in his favour and made Smith Stanley's opposition to the ballot and the precipitate corn law repeal the main issues. He led by 3,730-3,392 when polling ceased, 15 Dec., and was declared the victor when the scrutiny was abandoned, 24 Dec. 1830.[59] The much caricatured success of the 'Preston Cock' in 'blacking' and 'hunting out' Smith Stanley embarrassed ministers, as did his rallying of 'the 3,730' and unionists throughout the North-West and Midlands, where he ranted about his tribulations after Peterloo, before making his 'grand entrance' to London with his Preston sponsor Mitchell, 10 Jan. 1831. He announced that 'like O'Connell, for Ireland', he would have his own parliamentary office 'for the people', requested funding for it and made the Irish Catholic reformer John Fitzgerald his clerk.[60] His celebrations exposed divisions and in-fighting in the London and northern unions.[61]

Thomas Creevey* quipped that Hunt was 'the best dressed country gentleman in the House' on 3 Feb. 1831, when he took his seat between Hume and Warburton on the opposition benches, 'side by side' with the Tories.[62] According to the *New Monthly Magazine*:

But once, and that for a moment, did his self-possession seem to fail him while going through the ceremonies ... After the Member has signed his name, and taken the oaths, he is formally introduced to the Speaker, who usually greets the new trespasser on his patience by a shake of the hand. The ceremony is generally performed by the present Speaker with a gloved hand towards those not particularly distinguished by wealth or pedigree. When the new Member for Preston was introduced to him, he was in the act of taking snuff with his glove off ... Hunt made a bow, not remarkable for its graceful repose, at a distance – apprehensive ... that the acknowledgement would be that of a *noli me tangere* (don't touch me) ... He was agreeably disappointed; the Speaker gave him his ungloved hand at once in a manner almost cordial.[63]

A self-professed independent, Hunt made over 1,000 parliamentary speeches between February 1831 and August 1832. He claimed to be the sole parliamentary spokesman for the unrepresented poor and the working classes and, from March 1832, 'the only self-avowed radical in the House'. He learnt to exploit his ignorance of procedure, became adept at raising procedural points and steadfastly refused to be tempted into bringing breach of privilege motions. A staunch critic of the Whigs and their reform bill, on which his stance was confusing, he alienated himself from its middle class supporters and the Midland unions and

was credited with fostering a schism between them and the Political Union of the Working Classes in Manchester.

Hunt gave qualified support to a petition he presented from Thorne Falcon, Somerset, for tithe commutation and declared firmly for radical reform, the ballot, and corn law repeal, for which he also brought up a petition from Manchester, 3 Feb. 1831. As again, 4, 7, 15 Feb., he promised to legislate for it as the only true means of relief. His criticism of the civil list as 'a bad earnest of ministers' intentions', 4 Feb., brought a patronizing response from the first lord of the admiralty Sir James Graham, and Thomas Gladstone* noted that his

natural enough ignorance of the forms of the House was very amusing. He constantly addressed Lord Althorp as 'You, Sir, have said and done' so and so, which according to the forms of the House, of course was applied to the Speaker.[64]

As announced in *The Times*, 22 Jan., he urged clemency towards the convicted 'Swing' rioters, 3, 4 Feb., and, with Hume seconding, requested it in an 'excessively prosy' two-hour speech and lost the division (by 269-2), 8 Feb. It prompted hostile exchanges with Benett, whose property the rioters had targeted, but when Admiral Sir Joseph Yorke claimed that Hunt would have responded differently had his blacking factory been attacked, he declined to 'treat the House with a battle between my blacking and his bilge-water'.[65] Greville deemed his 'manner and appearance very good, like a country gentleman of the old school, a sort of rural dignity about it, very civil, good humoured, and respectful to the House, but dull; listened to however, and very well received'.[66] The caricaturist Heath portrayed his 'matchless eloquence' as an exploding jar of blacking. Others depicted him as a 'handsome and promising pupil' on York's knee.[67] He demanded no taxation without representation, 8 Feb., and accused ministers that day and the next, when he brought up a petition from the Rotunda, of threatening to subdue Ireland by force: 'Repeal the tithe laws and you will hear no more of the repeal of the Union'. He presented the Dublin tin-workers' petition for the latter, 14 Feb. By the 28th, when he moved for and was named to the select committee of six on the reform petitions, he had presented and endorsed dozens forwarded to him daily by radicals and union branches. Most requested the ballot. Several called for short parliaments, universal suffrage, lower taxes, vestry reform, the abolition of tithes and corn law repeal. Making light of projected opposition to a wide-ranging ministerial measure, he said that 'government need not expect to satisfy the country without granting ... the ballot', 25 Feb., and made his support conditional on its concession, 26, 28 Feb. As the self-professed 'representative of the people', he applauded the removal of taxes in the budget but called for a reduction of the duty on soap instead of the 'disgusting weed' tobacco, for a property tax and 'significant reductions' in expenditure and official salaries, 11 Feb. (and again, 9 Dec. 1831, 27 Jan., 28 Feb. 1832). He reiterated his plea for a graduated property tax, criticized ministers for 'nibbling away at ... trivial taxes' and praised the Wellington ministry for carrying the repeal of the Test Acts, Catholic relief and the 1830 Sale of Beer Act, which, unlike most parliamentary radicals, he considered beneficial to the working classes, 14 Feb. 1831. (He opposed petitions for its repeal, 30 June, 3, 17, 24 Aug., 5 Sept. 1831, and Hill Trevor's 'premature' attempt to amend it by curtailing opening hours, 31 May 1832, but conceded that beer houses and public houses should keep the same hours. He echoed Hume's criticism of expenditure on Buckingham House, 'a wretched mix of mud and magnificence, built in such a place that no person could put his head out of a window without looking at the back door of some filthy public house', 15 Feb. 1831. He had testified before the 1828 Lords' select committee on the game laws,[68] and commenting that day on Lord Althorp's measure, he criticized game keepers, advised extending sales and commended Lord Radnor's policy of permitting tenants to shoot. He offered to back government on the sugar duties, 'principally because we are so near the 1st of March' and the introduction of the reform bill, 21 Feb. 1831. He nevertheless forced a division against the army estimates that day, which he lost by 250-6.

He speculated about the details of the reform bill with Henry Bulwer in the Commons tearoom before they were announced, and the magnitude of the proposed changes confused and confounded him.[69] He briefly declared for the bill, 2 Mar., but, later that day, drawing on his experience at Peterloo, Ilchester and Preston, he criticized the proposed £10 householder vote and the omission of the ballot, short parliaments and universal suffrage. According to Hobhouse, he 'talked like an ass about Ilchester gaol; indeed he is a very silly fellow'.[70] Hudson Gurney* thought that his 'speech would have been the best had he known where to stop'.[71] He presented and endorsed further radical reform petitions, 4, 9 Mar., and justified his support for the bill because it affected corporations like the City of London's, 4 Mar. Reporting from the select committee, 11 Mar., he explained that 280 of the 645 reform petitions received, 5 Nov. 1830-4 Mar. 1831, requested the ballot, 239 lower taxes, 182 short par-

liaments, and 70 the abolition of tithes; 179 sought reform of the Scottish electoral system. He confirmed that he intended dividing for the bill despite its shortcomings, but he refused to praise it and criticized the curtailment in the suffrage of Preston.[72] He brought up radical reform petitions, 14, 15, 17, 18, 19, 22 Mar., expressed support for the bill 'as a City liveryman', 16 Mar., but confirmed on the 19th that he sought 'more extensive reform'. Before dividing for the second reading, 22 Mar., he commended a concession giving resident freemen a 'life interest' in their constituencies, and claimed that his vote was 'justified in the eyes of the country'. To taunts and deliberate coughing by the anti-reformers (he offered them lozenges), he refuted Henry Bankes and John Calcraft's claims that he had been 'bought off' by Lord John Russell. Afterwards, his criticism of the bill intensified and he insisted that the potential increase in landlord and landowner influence made the ballot imperative, 24, 25 Mar. His objections to the civil list expenditure that day were shouted down from both sides of the House. Cobbett's *Political Register* accused him of colluding with the Tories to 'destroy the bill' by denying it unequivocal support and threatened to sponsor a pre-emptive campaign to unseat him at Preston (where his election expenses remained unpaid), unless he toed the line on reform like his colleague Wood. The 'Preston Cock' defended his parliamentary conduct in a scathing reply to the 'Kensington Dunghill'.[73] He rallied the extreme radicals, or 'Huntites' as they became known, during his Easter progress to Preston, where he maintained that the bill enfranchised the middle classes at the labourers' expense. Critics promptly exploited differences between Hunt's parliamentary and extra-parliamentary speeches.[74] Introducing a new tone to the latter, and with frequent references to distress in Lancashire's manufacturing districts, from 12 Apr. he declared daily to cheers from the anti-reformers (they issued free copies of his speeches) that the people were 'not quite so mad for the bill' as ministers surmised, now they realized it would 'not make bread and clothes cheaper'. He poured scorn on the promised £10 votes and predicted a hostile 'reaction' to reform.[75] The Tory Henry Goulburn* thought his pronouncement the 'severest blow' yet inflicted against the government and the bill. Greville observed: 'The man's drift is not very clear whether the bill is really unpalatable at Preston, or whether he wants to go further directly'.[76] Fearing his influence in the country and with the division on Gascoyne's wrecking amendment looming, O'Connell, Hume, and the ministerial reformers preempted and disputed his claims of 'reaction': Edward Littleton criticized his speech at Darleston, 14 Apr.,

Lord Stanley his inattention to Lancashire and constituency business, 18 Apr.[77] Replying, he maintained that only Archibald Prentice's *Manchester Times* and John Foster's *Leeds Patriot* accurately reported his 'country' speeches (he corresponded with both editors). He stood by his claim (of 24 Mar.) that the bill would only enfranchise ten per cent of the population and leave 7,000,000 unrepresented. Before dividing against Gascoyne, 19 Apr., he repeated that the bill would not 'bring ... cheaper food'. His vote failed to impress his critics. Hume denounced him in the Commons, 20 Apr., and he was caricatured 'Rat catching', 'Between two stools' (government and opposition) and 'Hunt-ing'.[78] In Manchester, 3 May 1831, he said that he preferred the 'open enmity of the Tories to [the] false friendship of the Whigs'.[79]

Ever disruptive, Hunt failed to dominate or unite the Lancashire unionists at the general election and only narrowly avoided a contest at Preston, where Hume and Place, acting on behalf of the Loyal and Patriotic Fund Committee, sent the reformer George De Lacy Evans* to oppose him.[80] He called on the hustings for corn law repeal and radical reform and vilified Wood for deferring to ministers and rejecting his political leadership. This alienated the *Manchester Times*, which cautioned that Hunt went 'too far'.[81] He was shouted down as a Tory turncoat when he proposed the Exeter radical Thomas Northmore at the Somerset election and strove afterwards to build up support for his brand of radicalism in the North, where he addressed over 65,000 in Manchester in June. He found the London-based National Union of the Working Classes less compliant. His *Address to the Radical Reformers of Lancashire and Yorkshire* (a damning critique of the bill) and meetings organized by the Manchester cotton-spinner John Doherty encouraged petitioning for universal suffrage on the Preston model (excluding paupers and convicts only), annual parliaments and the ballot.[82] The bill's advocates sought to undermine his influence through false reporting and a trumped up charge of short-payment of a hackney cab fare. The anti-reformers, with whom he engaged briefly in mutual flattery, planned to exploit his comments on the labourers' indifference to the bill and 'reaction'.[83] In late May 1831 the cartoon, *Thoughts on Reform, No. 2*, depicted him stating, 'This Reform will not do for me. I must cause a row somehow or other or my *matchless* oratory will be laid on the shelf'.[84] Assessing his prospects at the start of the session, he informed Foster, 17 June 1831:

We have chosen our old Speaker again (in spite of the lies of the London press) unanimously. It would have been a great loss if he had not been elected ... He is firm, courteous, and truly impartial, for this the Whigs and Tories hate him and would, if they had dared, put in a tool of their own, Littleton. Thank God they dare not attempt it ... I shall give notice of a motion the first day to rescind the ridiculous resolution wherein we resolve 'that it is a breach of our privileges for a peer ... to interfere in the election of Members' ... This all the world must see not only as a humbug, but a fraud upon the king ... I shall take leave in spite of *The Times* or the *Courier* and all the ministerial press, to do that which I think is best to serve the cause of my country and to say whatever I think will best serve the interest of my poor and suffering countrymen and, as long as I have health and strength, I will never cease to advocate the rights of the useful, the labouring classes of the community.[85]

(He vainly proposed his resolutions, 21, 22 June 1831.) On the address, 21 June, he called for assistance for the Poles against 'Russian tyranny' and information on the suppression of the riots in Merthyr Tydfil and Ireland. He predicted that the reintroduced reform bill would be carried by a large majority and explained that unless the Tories introduced a more extensive measure, he would vote for but speak against it, with a view to reducing the £10 qualification and amending its details. Bringing up petitions for the ballot from Preston and Somerset, 23 June, he denied O'Connell's charge that he was an 'enemy of reform' who had sold himself to the Tories and deceived the people, and condemned the Parliamentary Candidates Society for interfering at Preston. Waithman's caustic comment that he used the pronoun 'I' 75 times that day was caricatured in '*Cacoathes Loquendi*: the blacking bottle and the yard stick'.[86] He presented and endorsed the anti-reform petitions he had sought from the Northern radicals, 24, 30 June, 1, 4, 5 July, but divided for the reintroduced bill at its second reading, 6 July. He vented his spleen against *The Poor Man's Guardian*, the 'most abominable trash written', for misreporting, 29 June, and against Wood and Benjamin Heywood (who retaliated) for refusing to fully endorse the 19,409-signature radical reform petition of the Manchester working classes, 8 July; he introduced others 11, 12, 14 July.[87] Severely heckled for snubbing Wood, he taunted ministers about the production of celebratory reform medals and criticized the bill as 'undemocratic', 8, 12 July. He divided for adjournment that day and reaffirmed his intention of moving for a taxpayer franchise and new legislation to ensure that peers who influenced elections were punished. His call for a £10,000 fine and a years' imprisonment for the first offence was uproariously rejected. He voted to retain the 1821 census as the determinant of English borough disfranchisements, 19 July, and generally for the schedule A and B disfranchisements, but was a minority teller for that of Saltash, which ministers no longer pressed, 26 July. He held aloof when the anti-reformers' defended 'rotten' and nomination boroughs, but helped them almost daily to delay the bill by presenting petitions and preaching radical reform (18, 19, 21, 22, 25, 26, 28 July, 16 Aug.) and quibbling over the arrangements for Wiltshire's boroughs, 29, 30 July. On the schedule C and D enfranchisements, he contributed to the furore against the anti-reformers' proposals to unite Manchester and Salford, 2 Aug., welcomed the metropolitan borough representation for Greenwich, 3 Aug., and Finsbury, complained that Chelsea was not awarded it and voted to give an additional Member to Stoke, 4 Aug. (He did not share Burdett and Wood's preference for single Member constituencies.) He spoke against transferring Gateshead's seat to Merthyr, 5 Aug. On the 8th he presented and endorsed a temperate petition from the Manchester Political Union urging the prompt passage of the bill despite its faults, and declined to comment on that of the National Union of the Working Classes of the Metropolis for radical reform and against compulsory emigration. He objected to 'swamping Rochester' and Strood with the government borough of Chatham, 9 Aug. That day the *Poor Man's Guardian*, which on 16 July had reported that he was 'regularly insulted, and unsupported, even by that traitor O'Connell', criticized him for endorsing

> the enfranchising portions of the bill, though he knows how much opposed his constituents are to the principle, and how injurious it will be to the labouring classes, to have the middlemen added to the ranks of their already too powerful opponents. We must with candour say, we cannot reconcile his acts with the sentiments which he must entertain upon the subject.[88]

He repeated the parliamentary radicals' objections to the proposed county divisions, 11 Aug., especially the five Member Hampshire constituency, 16 Aug., without voting against them. However, his support for the enfranchisement of tenants-at-will, 18 Aug., with the ballot as imperative to it, 19 Aug., was wholehearted. Joining in the fray on renting and rating, he failed (by 123-1) with an amendment substituting a ratepayer franchise for a £10 householder vote, 24 Aug. (the anti-reformers opposed it as 'Utopian'), and (by 353-10) with one for the enfranchisement of 'tenpounders' paying rent quarterly, 25 Aug. His 'compromise proposal' to exempt the unfranchised from militia service and the payment of rates and taxes was not seconded, 26 Aug. It, however, satisfied the extreme radicals, whose support he courted in the wake of

Mitchell's declaration that month 'for Cobbett, the bill and gradual reform'. During his 'Northern tour' Hunt attacked Wood, Heywood and Manchester's wealthy mill-owning reformers and alluded to Lord Stanley by his Commons nickname, 'Tongs'.[89] Presenting the Westminster Union of the Working Classes' reform petition, 30 Aug. (and again, 13 Sept.), he pronounced *The Times*'s attempt to promote county reform meetings a failure and cited the lack of petitions endorsing the bill in its entirety as proof of its waning popularity. This provoked a furious response from Hume, O'Connell and his ally Richard Lalor Sheil, who denounced him as a 'false prophet'. He quibbled over the appointment of the boundary commission, to which he wanted Members seconded, 1, 5, 15 Sept. Drawing on his experience at Preston and Westminster, he criticized the bill's provisions for registration and polling, 5, 6, 13, 15 Sept., and objected to Lord Lansdowne's borough of Calne retaining two seats, 15 Sept. He protested at the House's refusal to consider the penalties he proposed for peers guilty of influencing elections, 7 Sept., and spoke similarly when a petition was introduced criticizing the marquess of Salisbury's influence at Hertford, 21 Sept. He divided for the bill's third reading, 19 Sept., and prefaced his vote for its passage, 21 Sept., with a hostile and frequently interrupted speech criticizing Althorp's failure to prevent the press inciting the lower classes to riot and testifying to the increasing apathy towards the bill's fate. He reserved the 'right of petitioning the … Lords to alter certain clauses'. He divided for the Scottish reform bill at its second reading, 23 Sept., presented and endorsed the unionists' petitions for the ballot, 26 Sept., 3 Oct., and when a motion for papers on the cancellation of the king's November 1830 visit to the City was refused, deemed himself the best qualified Member to comment, 4 Oct. Drawn into the debate on Lord Ebrington's confidence motion (which he voted against) by O'Connell's provocative claim that he had attended the Marylebone meeting that endorsed it, 10 Oct., he revealed that he had not been invited and had chaired the Rotunda meeting which rejected the motion by 2,000-7:

> I told the meeting that I had no confidence in … ministers … because they came in on pledges of economy, retrenchment and reform, which pledges they had violated. The kind of reform which they propose I have never advocated in my life; and I am sure it will give no satisfaction to the people at large.

He delivered a litany of complaints against the bill, the civil list, government expenditure on the Society for the Propagation of the Gospels and royal residences and their refusal to concede inquiry into the Deacles' case and treatment of the Newtownbarry rioters. He castigated the press for 'making the people believe ministers would achieve more than they have done':

> I have all my life contended that every man in the community should have a share in the representation; and I am sure that nothing less will satisfy the people of England than householders' suffrage and triennial parliaments. I am neither Whig nor Tory, but will join either party which will give something like a principle of reform, which will not draw an arbitrary line, saying that a man living in a £10 house shall have a vote, whilst he who lives in a £9 house shall have none. The principle of scot and lot voting would, if introduced, have had some reason to it, because it is founded on the constitution, and because a man, not then having a vote, would ... be able to see the reason why he should not have a vote.

He testified to the reform bill's unpopularity and the differences between the unionists of Birmingham who advocated non-payment of taxes to secure its passage (which, differing from Hume, he claimed was illegal) and those of Manchester who did not, and blamed the press for inciting trouble, 12, 13, 17 Oct., endorsed the unionists' petitions that Hume found too radical, 19 Oct. 1831, and had the Birmingham one printed. A cartoon, 'the led Bear', portrayed him and Attwood leading the king.[90] The Midland unions mistrusted his motives and remained suspicious of his conduct.[91] He received a particularly bad press in the wake of the reform bill's defeat in the Lords and the riots in Bristol, Derby and Nottingham.[92] Deeming libel actions pointless, he retaliated during the recess by issuing a series of self-congratulatory penny *Addresses* 'to the Radical Reformers of England, Ireland and Scotland, on the Whig Ministers, since they have been in place and power' and toured the North to rally the working classes with a view to reviving the Great Northern Union of the Working Classes.[93] Denouncing its architect Russell ('little Isaac'), he said the reform bill was a ploy to transfer power to the Whigs and Unitarians, adding: 'The *bill*, the eternal *Whig Bill*, as sent up to the House of Lords, is no more like the *bill* which was first submitted to Parliament, than a horse chestnut is like a chestnut horse'.[94] Pursuing a jealous vendetta against O'Connell, the darling of the Midland unions, he also publicized an allegation that his rival had fathered a child in 1818 by Ellen Courteney.[95] A vituperative article in *The Times*, 'Hunt turned author', claimed that his 'blacking' campaign was financed by the Tories. The Whig *Preston Chronicle* condemned him as a selfish and inflammatory speaker and inept legislator.[96] Through the *Poor Man's Guardian* and from January 1832 the

unstamped 'Letters from the 3,730' (which replaced his 'Addresses'), he made martyrs of his imprisoned followers William Ashmore, Nathan Broadhurst and Edward Curran, and launched inflammatory diversionary campaigns for inquiry into Peterloo and against the coroners' bill, which he termed the cannibal or dead body bill, so deploying arguments against anatomical dissection that he had used effectively in 1828-9 to curry favour with the City mob.[97]

He proposed an (unseconded) amendment to the address for a 24-hour adjournment which, like his speech prefacing it, attributed distress and the attendant unrest to the 1819 currency change 'without a correspondent reduction in taxation', provoked by the government's policy of 'prohibiting the importation of necessaries and encouraging that of luxuries', 6 Dec. 1831. He accused ministers of condoning the political unions when it suited them and turning against them when they asked for more, and confidently countered claims from both sides of the House when reform petitions were presented, 7 Dec.[98] He acknowledged improvements in the revised bill, such as the transfer of Calne to schedule B and the removal of restrictions on the mode of rent payment by £10 voters, but contended that it would leave nine-tenths of the population unfranchised (which ministers denied) and cited the case of Bolton, with its 680 £10 houses and 14,000 adult males, to prove his point, 12 Dec. He divided for its second reading, 17 Dec., but ministers failed to prevent him trumpeting its failings and criticizing their civil list immediately before the division. He featured in a cartoon of the debate, 'Rather Alarming, or the Reception of the New Bill', and subsequently as a thorn in John Bull's flesh.[99] On 11 Jan. 1832 he was tried on a trumped up assault charge, but discharged.[100] He endorsed the Manchester Political Union's petition criticizing the revised bill's failings (proprietorial control, long parliaments, no ballot and a £10 borough vote), and was trounced by Hume for denouncing the measure, 19 Jan. He opposed its committal and commenced his endless quibbling, 20 Jan. He objected to giving the sheriffs of Lancashire and Middlesex the right to appoint returning officers, 24 Jan., and spoke in favour of dividing counties but against 'unicorn' three and four Member constituencies, 27 Jan. He confirmed his support for the enfranchisement of tenants-at-will, 1 Feb. Pressing the case of Preston, where £6 houses predominated, he failed (by 290-11) to substitute scot and lot for the £10 borough franchise, 2 Feb., and opposed the anti-reformer Vernon's proposal for a £10 poor rate franchise on the grounds that it would reduce the size of the electorate, 3 Feb. He found little support that day for his proposal to exempt Preston from the bill's provisions (rejected by 206-5), or for a similar motion on Stamford, 19 Mar. He contributed to futile discussions on rating warehouses and farm buildings, 7 Feb. Three days later he announced that would vote to create peers to carry the bill, but complained that it placed too much power in the hands of lawyers. His amendment limiting the cost of the booths and hustings was a ploy to transfer the expense from the candidates to the constituencies and failed (by 154-4), 15 Feb. He spoke and voted to retain Appleby in schedule A, 21 Feb., Helston in schedule B, 23 Feb., and Tower Hamlets in schedule C, 28 Feb., and objected to the anti-reformers time-wasting attempt that day to procure separate representation for Toxteth Park. He was called to order several times for criticizing the yeomanry and making obstructive interventions on Helston and Dartmouth, 2 Mar. He thought Gateshead deserved separate enfranchisement, but voted in the minority to transfer its seat to Merthyr, 'a town penalized as a Methodist stronghold and on account of the 1831 riots', 5 Mar. Choosing between Doncaster and Wakefield on the 9th, he spoke sarcastically of the need to represent the Jockey Club at Doncaster and pressed Wakefield's claim. He welcomed the concession of a Monmouthshire seat to Merthyr, 14 Mar. Dixon ensured on the 22nd that Hunt's comments on the Glasgow Political Union's petition were not heard, but ministers failed to prevent him repeating his criticisms of the bill before dividing for its third reading that day. Aligning with the Tory opposition to the judges' compensation bill, 10 Apr., he explained:

> As long as Tories sit on this side of the House and take up the argument they now do, I myself am a Tory; but when they go to the other side of the House again, I shall remain here with the Whigs.

When the government's resignation over the king's refusal to create peers to carry the bill through the Lords was announced, 9 May, Hunt accused them of gross deceit, as the people had been led to believe that they had had that power for the past 12 months. He left without voting on Ebrington's confidence motion next day.[101] Before doing so, he expressed regret at the bill's defeat, projected it as an opportunity for political realignment and complained that the people had been duped into believing that William IV supported reform. He also ranted against the Whigs' failure to live up to their promises to reduce the civil list and the army and (as 18 Apr.) for financing Russian aggression in Poland. On 11 May he endorsed the 'temperate' Manchester petition for withholding supplies until reform was secured and concurred in Hume's bid to

adjourn the House to forestall premature debate. He approved Hume's statement that only a Whig administration could 'tranquilize' the country, 14 May.[102] He declared that he 'would vote to stop supply', when Lancashire cotton towns petitioned thus, 17 May, and objected to similar petitions being shelved, following the Grey ministry's reinstatement, 18 May. He praised the orderly conduct of his followers at mass meetings that month and on 13 June warned of disappointments in the aftermath of the bill's passage as expectations ran high.[103] He divided for the second reading of the Irish reform bill, 25 May, and called for the restoration of the 40s. Irish freeholder vote, 13, 14, 18 June. He divided in O'Connell's minority for a £5 freeholder franchise that day, for Sheil's unsuccessful amendment to the Irish borough franchise, 29 June, and complained that ministers had treated the Irish 'disgracefully', 13, 18, 29 June, 2 July. He was refused a hearing on the Scottish bill and voted silently for the proposed dismemberment of Perthshire, 15 June. He voted to alter Stamford's proposed boundaries, 22 June, and continued to press for the ballot, universal suffrage and annual parliaments, 14, 18, 24, June, 3 Aug. After much bantering that day he withdrew a petition for the enfranchisement of unmarried women. He criticized the Reform Act as a 'landlords' bill' to the last, 15 Aug. He opposed (as a minority teller) Alexander Baring's 'useless' bill to deny debtors parliamentary privilege, 'as it is self evident that persons who, by their improvidence have reduced themselves to poverty and rendered themselves liable to arrest, are not fit to be entrusted with the power of legislating for the property of others', and because it did not extend to the Lords, 30 May, 27 June 1832. When the Tory John Herries ordered papers on the Russian-Dutch loan, 17 Dec. 1831, Hunt said that he also supported investigation: the 'two extremes', the 'Radicals and Tories, will meet'. He opposed government on the issue, on grounds of economy and because they had attempted to interfere with the authority of the House, 26 Jan. 1832. However, perceiving it as a question between two great parties, 'one of whom desired to keep in office, and the other to get into it', he refrained from voting on the matter again, despite his objections to the payments to Russia, 20 July. He divided with government on Portugal, 9 Feb., and echoed Baring's claim that there was nothing to choose between Dom Pedro and Dom Miguel, 26 Mar. 1832.

Hunt's increasing radicalism and tendency to obfuscation through personal perspectives and repartee was better suited to public meetings than to the Commons, and was apparent on all issues. He voted in the minority for appointing 11 of its original members to the Dublin election committee, 29 July, was named to it, 31 July, and spoke and voted in favour of printing the evidence before issuing a new writ, 8 Aug. 1831. Impervious to Wood and O'Connell's arguments that it was a ploy to delay the reform bill, he promised to expose corruption at the highest level in Ireland. Refusing to be silenced by Smith Stanley, he defended the Grattans, exposed the viceroy's agent Baron Twyll's intrigues and voted to censure the Irish government for electoral interference, 23 Aug. Nor would he condone corruption in Liverpool, although he agreed that the town should be 'amply represented'. He voted against issuing a new writ, 5 Sept., and when it was authorized, 12 Oct., accused ministers of 'playing a little double in this affair'. He presented and endorsed the Westminster Political Union's petition condemning Russian aggression in Poland, 8 Aug., but refused to back the Ultra Sir Richard Vyvyan's 'time-wasting' motion for papers on the French annexation of Belgium, 18 Aug. On 23 Aug. the foreign secretary Lord Palmerston* told the cabinet that he had informed the French that no party in England, from Grey to Wellington to Hunt, would bear French interference in Dutch diplomatic negotiations.[104] Hunt considered corn law repeal more important to the labouring classes than parliamentary reform and ordered papers, 27 June, 1, 22 July, and presented and endorsed repeal petitions, 13, 19, 22, 25, 30 July, 9, 12 Aug. (including a Preston one rejected by 121-6), 13, 30 Aug. 1831 preparatory to moving for it. The motion's postponement to accommodate the reform bill infuriated its extra-parliamentary advocates, and the *Poor Man's Guardian* of 3 Sept. commented:

Why Master Hunt, we hardly understand this conduct of yours; do you, or do you not, approve of this reform bill, which you own will do more harm than good to the unrepresented millions, whose champion you profess to be? ... a measure which would lessen the price of bread is of paramount importance to such a canting hypocritical party measure as the middle man's reform.[105]

O'Connell, a fellow victim of Hetherington's pen, tactically raised the libellous comment when Hunt's 'untimely' call for corn law repeal was rejected (by 194-6), 15 Sept. Afterwards he placated the *Poor Man's Guardian* by having his speech printed, preparatory to renewing the attempt and by challenging Hume and Sadler to support a motion for repeal of the assessed taxes and the malt duties, 18 Oct., 19 Oct. 1831.[106] He was happy to let Lord Milton's corn law repeal motion take precedence over his own, 30 May, but clamoured successfully for its re-instatement directly Milton's was rescinded, 15 June, and promoted it as the only

effective means of reducing prices to assist the poor, 3 July 1832.

Hunt's criticism of the £170,000 grant for the yeomanry highlighted their use in recent civil disturbances and was attacked from both sides of the House, 27 June 1831. He presented and endorsed petitions against the East India Company's monopoly, 27 June, 15 July, and charged the government with profligacy and failure to retrench, 27, 30 June, 1, 8, 11, 18, 25 July. He voted to reduce official salaries to 1797 levels, 30 June, and against 'robbing the poor weavers' to finance professors' salaries, 8 July 1831, 13 Apr. 1832. He seconded a motion for civil list reductions (defeated by 142-41), 18 July 1831, and failed to curb spending on the Society for the Propagation of the Gospels (by 155-27), 25 July, the queen's coronation robes, 3 Aug., and the queen dowager, 19 Aug. He was unsupported on the last two occasions, and failed to goad Hume (who opposed it) into seeking reductions in the coronation expenditure, 31 Aug. However, Hume seconded his motion for deploying part of the award to discharge the debts of imprisoned crown debtors, 'as an act of grace' 6 Sept. When he attended the ceremony, 8 Sept., Littleton observed, 'strange to say [Hunt] seems always to dress himself with taste'.[107] He failed to make an issue of Princess Victoria's absence, 20 Sept. He objected to paying the balance of compensation payments due to the deported 'free coloureds' Louis Lecesne and John Escoffery, 22 Aug., and joined in the clamour against the Windsor Castle and Buckingham House expenditure, 28 Sept. Goaded by the anti-reformer Sir Charles Wetherell's references to charity management in Bristol, he opposed a ministerial amendment to Hobhouse's vestries reform bill, 30 Sept. He was a teller for a minority of three that day against the Lords' amendments to the game bill, which he complained was a 'landlord's bill' (18 Aug.) that left the powers of arrest and the treatment of poachers unchanged (19 Oct.). He opposed the general register bill as 'a job' which would 'bring grist to the lawyer's mill', 20 Sept., 4, 11 Oct. 1831, 20, 27 Jan., 2 Feb. 1832. He was against renewing the Sugar Refinery Act without prior inquiry, 7 Oct. He also objected to Wood's attempt to rush through lord chancellor Brougham's bankruptcy court bill, 'a great overpowering job', 12, 14, 17 Oct. 1831.

On Irish affairs, which he complained took up an inordinate amount of Parliament's time, 27 Sept., he drew parallels between Peterloo and the 'affrays' at Newtownbarry and Castle Pollard, 23, 30 June, 1, 11 July, 11 Aug. 1831, and voted that day to print the Waterford petition for disarming the yeomanry. To taunts from the government benches that he was the tool of the Tories and Irish radicals, which he denied, he introduced and supported petitions for repeal of the Union and tithe reform, 23, 27 June, 1, 4 July, 5 Aug. He refused to instigate breach of privilege proceedings when *The Times* repeated the allegations, 12 Aug. He agreed with Hume that land taken from Catholics at the reformation should be 'applied' to public purposes, 14 Sept., agitated for government assistance for the Irish poor and objected to delays in legislating for them, 25 July, 10, 12 Aug., 26 Sept. Taunted by O'Connell that day, he defended, as he had on 28 June, the principle, but not the administration, of the English Elizabethan poor law. He welcomed Sadler's relief scheme, 11 Oct. When he praised the Royal Dublin Society and criticized Smith Stanley's Irish grand jury bill as a cumbersome substitute for wholesale reform, Lord Sandon* informed Smith Stanley, 29 Sept., that 'Hunt opposes you out of spite and revenge at being treated by contempt by the Whigs, and because he can be more of a personage as a radical among the Tories, than as a mere follower with O'Connell and Hume.'[108] He supported investigation into the Deacles' allegations against the Hampshire magistracy (a popular issue in Preston), 21 July, 15, 16, 19, 22, 27 Sept. 1831, 23 Feb. 1832, and objected to their cause being taken up by O'Connell instead of De Lacy Evans, 19 Sept., 5 Oct. 1831. Although he had no time for their 'very Utopian doctrines', he presented petitions and raised complaints about the prison treatment of Taylor, 22 July, 15, 23 Aug., 13, 22 Sept., 7 Oct., 7 Dec., Carlile, 3 Aug., 22 Sept., the Rev. Samuel Seaton, 11 Aug., and the journalist William Carpenter, 22 Sept. 1831, and invariably drew parallels between their cases and his experience at Ilchester.

His recalcitrance and verbosity were unabated. He harried ministers for a select committee on the silk industry on behalf of the Bethnal Green weavers, 9 Dec. 1831, 21 Feb., and welcomed its concession, 1 Mar., but complained that by composition it was a 'free trade committee', 5 Mar. 1832. He supported inquiry into the distressed glove trade, 19, 31 Jan., protested at the proposed expenditure on the royal residences, 17 Jan., 23 Mar., and criticized the general lack of retrenchment, 6 Feb.[109] He prevaricated over the navy estimates, 13 Feb., and, condemning troop deployments to quell reform riots, he vainly called for a 10,000 (17 Feb.) or 8,000-man (28 Mar.) reduction in the army, 28 Mar. He protested at the cost of the Milford Haven establishment (under the navy civil departments bill), 27 Feb., and shipbuilding costs, 29 June. He opposed the payment to the lord privy seal, 13 Apr., and pressed pointless divisions

that day against the secret service grant. Ever critical, he voted to reduce the barrack grant, 2 July, raised several objections to the Irish, 18 July, and colonial estimates, 23 July, and welcomed the cut that day in the award for the Society for the Propagation of the Gospels. He supported inquiry into the Inns of Court, 17 July, and made his support for Hume's abortive bill to exclude the recorder of Dublin from the Commons conditional on an extension of its provisions to quarter sessions chairmen and others with pressing extra-parliamentary duties, 24 July. He acquiesced in the grant of £100,000 for hurricane damage in Barbados on humanitarian grounds, but called for similar assistance for Bristol and Bethnal Green, 29 Feb. Claiming that cleanliness (untaxed soap) and ventilation afforded the best means of combating cholera, he entertained Members with a reference to the 'hot air coming up in this House from a very impure source', 13 Feb., and stressed the inability of the metropolitan districts, especially poor and populous Bethnal Green, to implement the provisions of the cholera prevention bill, 14, 16 Feb. He voted in Hume's minority of ten that day against including a reference to 'Almighty God' in the preamble of the Scottish cholera bill. As requested by Foster and the Leeds Union, he supported Sadler's bill restricting the hours of child factory labour and endorsed favourable petitions, 1, 7, 10, 28 Feb., but cautioned against trapping the bill in a lengthy committee by legislating for workers up 23-years-old, 20, 29 Feb. He inveighed against those who would perpetuate child labour 'on grounds of political economy', 7, 14, 16 Mar. He supported the forgery mitigation bill as a committed opponent of capital punishment, 17, 29 May, and complained of the futility of sending popular measures to the Upper House when they returned to the Commons too late to be salvaged, 15 Aug. He supported the unions' campaign for the repeal of stamp duty on newsprint, but thought it best left to a reformed Parliament, so he 'refrained' from presenting 'no less than 40 petitions' he had received requesting it, 14 June. Goaded by references to the *Poor Man's Guardian* and the *Address of the Electors of Preston*, he defied government to put the Preston paper down, 24 July:

> That is not a periodical, but is called 'the 3,730' in honour of the number that sent me to Parliament. One of these 3,730 published an address every week; so that though there is no continuation within the law, we are likely to have 3,730 numbers of the address before the publication is at an end.

He presented petitions from the wives of printers imprisoned for selling unstamped papers, 1 Aug. 1832.

Hunt voted in the minority for vestry reform, 23 Jan., and a reduction in the sugar duties as a means of lower sugar and tea prices to assist the labouring classes, 7 Mar. 1832. He also acknowledged the 'real need' of the planters and accused the Whigs of changing their mind on equalization after attaining office. He opposed the crown colonies relief bill, 3 Aug. He had no objection to awarding a pension on his anticipated retirement to Manners Sutton, 'who has taken for his maxim that the House should be rode with a snaffle-bridle, and not with a curb' 1 Aug.,[110] or paying the lord chancellor by salary instead of fees, 8 Aug., but considering that suggested too high, he supported Hume's bid to reduce it, 8 Aug. He proposed a further £1,000 reduction (which was defeated by 60-2), 9 Aug. Althorp, whom he provoked on 18 June by threatening to move to exempt members of the Bank Charter committee from secrecy, was irritated by his repeated accusations that ministers were 'promising not performing' on retrenchment, 2, 9 Aug. 1832. Opposition to anatomical dissection and the coroners bill, which his colleague Wood praised, was (with radical reform, corn law repeal and inquiry into Peterloo), central to Hunt's campaign to win over the lower classes and secure re-election for Preston in 1832.[111] He objected to the introduction of the anatomy bill, 12, 15 Dec. 1831,[112] was a minority teller against its second reading, 17 Jan., and presented and endorsed hostile petitions, 24 Jan., 3, 15 Feb. 1832. He lost three obstructive divisions (by 87-4, 79-1 and 78-0), 24 Jan., condemned the sale of bodies, 6 Feb., and objected to the measure being timetabled at night when the House could be counted out, 9 Feb. The Preston '3,730' were informed that he stood 'alone against the principle of that bill' and 'only when he is occasionally absent in the early hours of the morning are its clauses carried'.[113] He tempered his harangue against its recommittal with citations from medical experts to little effect and the House divided against him (by 64-13 and 59-7), 27 Feb. The 'factious and popularity-hunting opposition ... set on foot by Hunt and Company' resumed with spurious amendments, time-wasting divisions and late night sittings, 11, 18 Apr., 8, 11 May, when he failed to prevent its passage.[114] He predicted that the coroners bill would fail to root out perjury and corruption and suggested that the post – reform franchise and constituency boundaries should apply at their elections, 7 May. On 20 June, in several interventions later caricatured by H.B., he seconded and was a teller for the minority of 11 for an amendment requiring coroners to be qualified in medical law, voted for inquests to be made public, opposed the appointment of attorneys as coroners and denied that the post-Peterloo inquests had

prompted rioting. He recommended paying coroners higher salaries to ensure proficiency, 6 July 1832.[115]

His call for inquiry into Peterloo was supported in petitions from the political unions, 3, 23 Feb., 15 Mar. 1832, but almost thwarted by 'this cursed humbug of a Whig bill for reform'. Seconded by Hume, he engaged Peel and intervened at least eight times before the motion was defeated (by 206-31) after a messy debate, 15 Mar. The *Manchester Guardian* criticized his 'absurd and violent speech' and the letter 'to the ... 3,730' commended it. Refusing to let the matter rest, between 27 Mar. and 2 Aug. he presented petitions and took up the cause of the martyred 'Huntites' imprisoned after the October and November 1831 St. Peter's Fields reform meetings (Ashmore, Broadhurst, Curran, Robert Gilchrist and John Pym) and other 'maltreated' detainees, including Cobbett, 21 May, 30 May, 21 June. He presented a 9,000-signature Manchester petition for inquiry into the 1819 'carnage', 17 July.[116] On 20 June he concurred in the adoption of an address congratulating William IV on surviving an assassination attempt at Ascot and blamed *The Times* for inciting recent insults to the king and queen at Hounslow, Hammersmith and Somerset House. On New South Wales (a ploy to revive the complaints against the former governor Charles Darling) he voted in the minorities for jury trial and a legislative assembly, 28 June, and ordered papers detailing complaints against Darling, 5 July, which he deemed proven, 5, 24 July 1832.

He renewed his pleas for the extension of the poor laws to Ireland, tithe abolition and a redistribution of Irish church property, 23 Jan., and criticized Smith Stanley's arguments for the government's Irish tithes bill as 'void' and 'threadbare', 24 Jan. 1832. He voted to print the radical Woollen Grange petition for the abolition of Irish tithes, 16 Feb., and to postpone the ministerial measure, which he vainly urged the Irish Members to reject, 8 Mar., and, clashing with Smith Stanley, 13, 27, 28, 30 Mar., 16 Apr., complained that it would do nothing to alleviate poverty, 27, 30 Mar., 16 Apr. He denounced the government's entire Irish policy that day, defended Sheil, and called for the 'separation of church and state as in America'. He referred to the widespread opposition to tithes in England and Wales, 20 June, urged ministers to abandon the Irish tithes composition bill that Parliament and divided against it, 1 Aug. (twice), 2 Aug. Addressing Sheil before leaving the House that day 'amid much laughter', he complained: 'I wish to get rid of this Irish bill, and to go home to bed. I am given the key of the door. I am locked in and I am no longer a free agent'. Sheil delayed presenting Preston's petition against deploying troops to enforce tithe payment in Ireland until 3 Aug., when Hunt, who claimed that it had been 'got up' by Smith Stanley's former supporters, endorsed it and read out its diatribe calling for his dismissal for attempting tithe enforcement, 'for the registration of arms, and for giving a reform bill to Ireland much more restricted and inequitable than that for England'. He expressed support for Benett's intended legislation for the labouring poor, 17 Feb., and Sadler's scheme to provide for the poor by taxing Irish absentee landlords, 19 June 1832, but would have preferred to see the English poor law introduced in Ireland and the Union abolished. He termed *The Times*'s report of his speech (20 June 1832) 'a pure invention', but added:

> The fault ... is attributable not to the editor of the paper, but to the reporter for the hour; because, in reference to what I said on the subject of flogging soldiers, I must say that my observations are fairly well reported.

Taking up the radical campaign against corporal punishment, he ordered returns on military punishments preparatory to moving to end army flogging, 16 Feb. 1832, when he had 28 in his minority. He tested opinion with similar motions, without proceeding to a division, 2, 5, 14, 28 Mar. He proposed an amendment to the mutiny bill to abolish flogging (in peacetime), 2 Apr., but much to the relief of the war secretary Hobhouse, who personally opposed the practice, he yielded to pressure and 'either from indifference or generosity, did not press his motion to a vote'.[117] He secured a minority of 15 for suspending military flogging, 19 June. His speech, which he repeated at the Kennington Common meeting, 27 June, was an obvious plagiarism of Burdett's correspondence with John Shipp. Targeting Hobhouse and Althorp, he seconded Hume's motion for papers on the case of Private Alexander Somerville, whose punishment was popularly attributed to his radicalism, 3 July, proposed a similar motion, 20 July,[118] and presented petitions from the political unions for inquiry into the case, 23, 24 July, 10, 15 Aug. The caricaturist Heath included him in 'Soldier Politicians "A la Somerville" on the Day of Battle'.[119] On 3 July, citing details from the *Blackburn Mail*, he drew attention to the fatal canvassing riot at Clitheroe, which John Irving's* committee had exploited to 'blacken' him as a radical. He questioned ministers and presented petitions from the Northern unions protesting at the suppression of public meetings following the 'affray', 10 Aug., and asked if the 'forthcoming elections are to be carried on under military escort', 15 Aug. 1832, before ending a time-wasting discussion on the 'impris-

oned blasphemites' Twort and Ward by forcing an adjournment.

Hunt was defeated at Preston, where aristocratic Liberal-Tory representation was restored, at the general election of 1832 and his subsequent petition failed.[120] Commentators tended to prefer Cobbett, who came in for Oldham in 1832, and most assessments of Hunt at this time resembled hostile obituaries. They influenced subsequent assessments of his career.[121] Sir Robert Heron* dismissed him as 'more odious and troublesome to the Members, than mischievous to the country: so small was the estimation in which he was held'.[122] James Grant observed:

> His parliamentary career was short ... It commenced at a time it might naturally have been least expected, and closed when it might rather have been expected to begin ... He was altogether a singular man ... He had something of the caprice of ... Cobbett, and a good deal of his irritable temper; but in intellect or information he could not be for a moment compared ... Hunt was not a man of much mind. He was unfitted for grappling with any great question. He never took an original view of any subject; and was altogether incapable of close and ingenious reasoning. He held certain principles of the most liberal kind, and had at his fingers' ends most of the principal arguments which other persons had urged in their favour. When these were exhausted, so were his means of vindicating his principles. His style was not good; it was rough and disjoined. What he excelled in was ready wit: he had few equals in this respect. All parties in the House, not even excepting the most ultra-radicals themselves, laboured hard to cough him down whenever he attempted to speak ... Nothing could disconcert him ... The fact was, he had been formed for scenes of confusion, and had all his life long been accustomed to them at meetings of his radical disciples ... His manner was as bad as his diction. It had no gracefulness in it. His gesture was awkward, and his voice was harsh and croaking. The bad effect produced by the latter was aggravated by a strongly marked provincial accent.[123]

Hunt's business suffered during his time in the House and he tried to supplement his income by lecturing on the history since 1807 of the Whig party.[124] He led the protest against the Cold Bath Fields 'massacre' in June 1833 and received an invitation to contest East Somerset in February 1834, but not Preston, which he coveted, and he realized that it was too late to recapture his popularity. He died in February 1835 at Arlesford, Hampshire, where he had suffered a stroke the previous month, and was buried in the Vince family mausoleum in Parnham Park, near Stormington, West Sussex. He was remembered as a successful farmer and enthusiastic radical and self-publicist who applied his great strength and energy to electoral endeavours and had the ability to link local and national issues.[125] The *Gentleman's Magazine* wrote: 'like other noisy demagogues, he soon found his level [in the Commons], and became harmless and insignificant, except in his votes'. *The Poor Man's Guardian* acknowledged his intense egotism and added: 'to sham reformers he was particularly obnoxious; while to turncoats and trading patriots he was a perfect raw head and bloody louse'.[126] Brougham's private secretary Denis Le Marchant† recalled him as a small landed proprietor in Somerset

> of broken fortune and profligate habits, ill informed, but clever and resolute, with a fine person, and (when he pleased), rather prepossessing manners; so that altogether he was able to gain an ascendancy in the disaffected districts greater than any man of the day.[127]

His holograph will, dated 23 Jan. 1835, by which he left his business and remaining property (the tithes of Edgerly, Somerset) to his sons, was proved under £800 by Mrs. Vince, the sole executrix.[128] His death left a void in English popular politics and was attributed as a reaction (broken heart) to the working people's failure to reject the reform bill *en masse*. A mock funeral was held in Manchester, where in 1842 the Chartist leader Fergus O'Connor laid the foundation stone to a monument in his memory. The Manchester Chartists conveniently forgot that Hunt had advocated moral not physical force and proclaimed him as their champion, which further 'blackened' his reputation as a Member.[129]

[1] The best modern biography is J. Belchem, *'Orator' Hunt: Henry Hunt and English Working Class Radicalism* (1985). Hunt's autobiography, *Mems. of Henry Hunt*, 3 vols. (1820-2), and R. Huish, *Hist. Private and Political Life of Henry Hunt*, 2 vols. (1836) are biased and unreliable. Hunt's parliamentary career is briefly reviewed in J.W. Osborne, 'Henry Hunt's Career in Parliament', *Historian*, xxxix (1976), 24-39. [2] IGI (Wilts.). Not 12 Jan. as Hunt specified in *Mems.* i. 295. [3] *Oxford DNB*. [4] Add. 27809, ff. 16, 22; Belchem, 'Henry Hunt and Evolution of Mass Platform', *EHR*, xciii (1978), 739-72; *VCH Wilts*. v. 149. [5] Belchem, *Hunt*, 16. [6] Ibid. 15-19, 22; *VCH Wilts*. x. 162, 261-2; Hunt, *Mems*. i. 271, 275, 284-99. [7] Melville, *Cobbett*, ii. 13. [8] H. Graham, *Annals of Yeomanry Cav. of Wilts*. 25-28; Hunt, *Mems*. i. 440-529; Belchem, *Hunt*, 21-22. [9] S. Maccoby, *English Radicalism, 1786-1832*, pp. 206, 314, 320-4; Belchem, *Hunt*, 23-25. [10] Melville, ii. 13, 141; N. LoPatin, *Political Unions, Popular Politics and the Great Reform Act*, 6, 98. [11] Hunt, *Mems*. iii. 115-37; *HP Commons, 1790-1820*, ii. 167-72; *CJ*, lxviii. 43, 303; R. Harrison, *Crowds and History*, 88, 125, 205, 208, 211-19. [12] Belchem, *Hunt*, 18-19. [13] Holland, *Further Mems*. 250; Melville, ii. 75, 84; Belchem, *Hunt*, 44-54; A. Mitchell, *Whigs in Opposition*, 94. [14] S. Bamford *Passages in Life of a Radical* ed. P. Dunkley, ii. 19. [15] R. Reid, *Peterloo Massacre*, 32-33; Belchem, *Hunt*, 54-69, 71-72; *CJ*, lxxii. 6, 26, 102-3; *LJ*, li. 22. [16] Reid, 70; A. Aspinall, *Lord Brougham and the Whig Party*, 67-72; Belchem, *Hunt*, 69-71, 73-84; *HP Commons, 1790-1820*, ii. 267-82; Maccoby, 347-8. [17] *CJ*, lxxiv. 45, 58. [18] Belchem, *EHR*, xciii. 751-3; D. Read, *Peterloo*, 106-121; Reid, 104-9. [19] Reid, 116-18, 158-61, 166-7; Read, 123-6; *The Times*, 19 Aug. 1819; W. Thomas, *Philosophic Radicals*, 86, 90-91. [20] Belchem, *Hunt*, 86-112 and *EHR*, xciii. 756-60; Reid, 124-9;

191. [21] Reid, 202-3. [22] Belchem, *Hunt*, 113-16; *CJ*, lxxv. 12, 13, 16, 38, 46, 65, 75, 79. [23] Mitchell, 126, 129, 137; Aspinall, *Brougham*, 97-98; E.A. Smith, *Lord Grey*, 217-20; Add. 30109, f. 78. [24] M.D. George, *Cat. of Pol. and Personal Satires*, x. 13503, 13534, 13561, 13563-4, 13714. [25] Belchem, *Hunt*, 115; *Blackburn Mail*, 23 Feb., 1, 8 Mar.; *Manchester Mercury*, 29 Feb., 7 Mar.; *The Times*, 1 Mar. 1820. [26] *Preston Election Addresses* (1820), 1-11, 15, 17-25, 31-32, 37-38, 48; *Lancaster Gazette*, 11 Mar. 1820. [27] Heron, *Notes*, 127; *Geo. IV Letters*, i. 800, 811. [28] Buckingham, *Mems. Geo. IV*, i. 15-16. [29] Wellington mss WP1/958/42. [30] Belchem, *Hunt*, 144-65 and *EHR*, xciii. 769-71; J. Epstein, 'Radical Dining, Toasting and Symbolic Expression in Early 19th Cent. Lancs.' *Albion*, xx (1988), 281-2, 287-8. [31] *Diaries of Samuel Bamford* ed. M. Hewitt and R. Poole, 74; George, x. 13879, 13895, 14122, 14139, 14187, 14194, 14206. [32] *The Times*, 22 May 1820, 24 Jan., 11 July 1821, 9 Feb. 1822; R. Walmsley, *Peterloo: the case reopened*, 400; *VCH Som*. iii. 186; Som. RO Q\AGi-15; W. Shepherd, *Three Letters ... on ... Ilchester Gaol Investigation* (1822); Brougham mss, Shepherd to Brougham, 29 Jan. 1823; Hunt, *Investigation at Ilchester Gaol*; *LJ*, lv. 100, 104; *CJ*, lxxvii. 47, 93, 201, 297. [33] *CJ*, lxxvii. 11, 41, 64, 72, 77, 81, 97, 104, 108, 118, 123, 127, 132, 149, 152, 167, 200; *Ann. Reg.* Hist. pp. 177-8; *The Times*, 4, 26 Apr. 1822; Melville, ii. 199; *Arbuthnot Jnl.* i. 158. [34] Belchem, *EHR*, xciii. 771; J. Johnson, *Letter to Henry Hunt* (1822); *Letters from Henry Hunt to the Radical Reformers* ed. J. Stevens Cox (Ilchester and District Occasional Pprs. no. 19, 1979); *The Times*, 19, 31 Oct., 1, 12 Nov. 1822; George, x. 14406. [35] *The Times*, 31 Oct.; *Taunton Courier*, 22, 29 Jan., 5 Feb.; *Keene's Bath Jnl.* 26 June, 3, 24 July 1823. [36] Belchem, *Hunt*, 167-72. [37] Ibid. 172-5; George, x. 15150, 15155; *The Times*, 27 May, 5, 21 June; *Taunton Courier*, 28 June 1826. [38] *Bristol Mercury*, 26 June 1826. [39] *Pol. Reg.* 7 Oct. 1826. [40] Belchem, *Hunt*, 177-9; *The Times*, 20 Dec. 1827, 25 June 1828, 25 June, 22 July 1829; *Coll. relative to Election of Common Councilmen for Farringdon Without 1827, 1828* (C. Wood, 1829 edn.). [41] J.E. Crimmins, 'Jeremy Bentham and Daniel O'Connell', *HJ*, xl (1997), 365; George, x. 15422, 15497; xi. 15783; Anon. *Wig v. Blackball* [BL 8132. ee. 15. (2).]. [42] George, x. 15542. [43] Belchem, *Hunt*, 185-7. [44] Ibid. 188, 191; *Pol. Reg.* 12, 19, 26 May; *The Times*, 24 May 1827; Add. 56550, f. 176; Crimmins, 371-3. [45] *The Times*, 18, 23, 24, 17, 28, 30 Oct. 1828, 17 Mar. 1829; Add. 51572, Darnley to Holland [24 Oct. 1828]; Belchem, *Hunt*, 191-4; G.I.T. Machin, *Catholic Question in English Politics*, 140-2; Hunt, *To the Member for Clare*; *Pol. Reg.* 14 Mar. 1829; Add. 56554, f. 17; Crimmins, 362, 364-5, 374. [46] *LJ*, lxi. 515. [47] Hunt, *Brief Hist. of Parish of Christ Church* (1830), p. 35 and *passim*; Belchem, *Hunt*, 181-4; *The Times*, 23 Feb. 1830. [48] Belchem, *Hunt*, 195-9; M. Brock, *Great Reform Act*, 79; Fitzwilliam mss, L. Jones to Milton, 8 Dec. 1829. [49] *London Radicalism* ed. D.J. Rowe (London Rec. Soc. v), 2-7; George, xi. 16070, 16075, 16079-80; Crimmins, 374. [50] Add. 27789, f. 145. [51] Add. 56554, ff. 97-98. [52] Belchem, *Hunt*, 202-4; *The Times*, 6 Apr.; *Preston Pilot*, 24 July, 7 Aug.; *Blackburn Gazette*, 28 July; *Preston Chron*. 7 Aug.; Lancs. RO DDPr 131/19/5-8; Hunt mss DDX113/25; Brougham mss, Shepherd to Brougham, 15 Aug. 1830; W. Proctor, 'Orator Hunt', *Trans. Hist. Soc. Lancs. and Cheshire*, cxiv (1962), 136-41. [53] Hunt mss 26. [54] *Manchester Guardian*, 14, 21 Aug.; Belchem, *Hunt*, 206-12. [55] George, xi. 16399; *CJ*, lxxxvi. 86, 149. [56] Wellington mss WP1/1154/9/2; 1160/11; George, xi. 16317, 16344, 16404; *Arbuthnot Jnl*. ii. 400; *Quarterly Rev*. xliv (1830), 299-300. [57] *London Radicalism*, 69-70. [58] *The Times*, 13 Nov., 11, 13 Dec.; Wellington mss WP4/2/2/34; Lansdowne mss, J. Benett to Lansdowne, 25, 27 Nov. 1830. [59] *Preston Chron*. 11, 18, 24 Dec.; St. Deiniol's Lib. Glynne-Gladstone mss 196, T. to J. Gladstone, 16 Dec.; *The Times*, 18 Dec. 1830; *Preston Pilot*, 1 Jan. 1831. [60] George, xi. 16539, 16551; PRO NI Anglesey mss D619/31D/6; Bucks. RO, Fremantle mss D/FR/139/20/36; Wilts. RO, Pembroke mss 2057/F4/50; *Morning Herald*, 27 Dec.; Derby mss 920 Der (14) 116/6, Winstanley to Smith Stanley, 29 Dec. 1830; Wellington mss WP1/1173/2; Hants RO, Carnarvon mss 75M91/F4/3; *Manchester Times*, 1 Jan.; *The Times*, 5, 11, 13 Jan.; *Bolton Chron*. 15 Jan. 1831. [61] Belchem, *Hunt*, 218-20. [62] Creevey

mss, Creevey to Miss Ord, 5 Feb., 23 June 1831. [63] *Crayons from Commons* (1831), 67; *New Monthly Mag.* Mar. 1831; Proctor, 146. [64] Glynne-Gladstone mss 197, T. to J. Gladstone, 5 Feb. 1831. [65] Ibid. 8, 9 Feb. 1831; Broughton, *Recollections*, iv. 83; *Three Diaries*, 48; Graham, 94-96. [66] *Greville Mems.* ii. 113. [67] George, xi. 16575, 16579. [68] *LJ*, lx. 77. [69] H.L. Bulwer, *Sir Robert Peel*, 87-88. [70] Broughton, iv. 89. [71] Brock, 165; Gurney diary, 2 Mar. 1831. [72] *PP* (1830-1), iii. 421-32. [73] *Pol. Reg.* 5, 12, 19 Mar. 1831; *The Preston Cock's Reply to the Kensington Dunghill* [BL Tracts 8138. f. 33.]; George, xi. 16634, 16636-8; Lancs. RO DDPr 130/23. [74] *Manchester Guardian*, 9, 16 Apr. 1831; *The Times*, 13 Apr. 1831; Proctor, 147; *Three Diaries*, 77, 79; *Croker Pprs.* ii. 114. [76] Surr. Hist. Cent. Goulburn mss Acc 304/67B; *Greville Mems.* ii. 136. [77] Hopetoun mss 167, f. 255; *Three Diaries*, 78; Glynne-Gladstone mss 198, T. to J. Gladstone, 18 Apr. 1831. [78] George, xi. 16643, 16653, 16656. [79] *Manchester Guardian*, 7 May 1831. [80] Hunt mss 27; Add. 36466, ff. 317, 333-5; Belchem, *Hunt*, 230-2; M.J. Turner, *Reform and Respectability*, 302, 307, 327. [81] Hatfield House mss bdle. 4, Leigh to Salisbury, 30 Apr.; *Manchester Times*, 30 Apr.; *Manchester Guardian*, 30 Apr.; *Preston Chron.* 30 Apr., 7 May; Brougham mss, Shepherd to Brougham [1831]; Proctor, 148-9. [82] *Taunton Courier*, 27 Apr., 4 May; *Manchester Guardian*, 18 June 1831; Belchem, *Hunt*, 232-6. [83] Wellington mss WP1/1187/1; Hunt mss 28; *The Times*, 18 May, 18 June 1831; *Arbuthnot Jnl.* ii. 426-7. [84] George, xi. 16695. [85] Hunt mss 28. [86] George, xi. 16722. [87] *Poor Man's Guardian*, 16 July 1831. [88] Ibid. 9 Aug. 1831. [89] Walmsley, 473; Belchem, *Hunt*, 237; *Preston Chron.* 3 Sept. 1831. [90] George, xi. 16756. [91] Coventry Archives 323/1; Norf. RO, Bulwer mss BUL1/5/57. [92] Walmsley, 481. [93] Hunt, *Addresses*, 20 Oct.-21 Nov.; Belchem, *Hunt*, 241-51; *The Times*, 3 Nov.; *Preston Chron.* 12 Nov. 1831. [94] Hunt, *Addresses*, 20, 27 Oct., 7 Nov. 1831. [95] O'Connell *Corresp.* iv. 1848, 1852; Crimmins, 374. [96] *The Times*, 1 Nov.; *Preston Chron.*, 5, 12, 19 Nov. 1831. [97] *Preston Chron.* 29 Oct.; *Poor Man's Guardian*, 19 Nov.; 17, 24, 31 Dec. 1831; Lancs. RO, 'Letters from the 3,730', Jan.-June 1832. [98] George, xi. 16831. [99] *Holland House Diaries*, 97; George, xi. 16919, 16923, 16935, 16940-1, 17131. [100] *The Times*, 12 Jan. 1831. [101] Ibid. 12 May 1831. [102] *Holland House Diaries*, 179; Add. 52058, C.R. to H.E. Fox, 15 May 1832. [103] Brock, 295. [104] *Holland House Diaries*, 38. [105] *Poor Man's Guardian*, 3 Sept. 1831. [106] Hunt, *Corn Laws*; *Poor Man's Guardian*, 19 Nov. 1831; Osborne, 27. [107] Hatherton diary, 8 Sept. 1831. [108] Derby mss (14) 127/3, Sandon to Smith Stanley, 16 Oct. 1831. [109] Add. 51573, Spring Rice to Lady Holland, 6 Feb. 1832. [110] George, xi. 17329. [111] 'Letters from the 3,730', Jan.-June 1832. [112] *Greville Mems.* ii. 230. [113] 'Letters from the 3,730', 11, 18, 25 Feb. 1832. [114] Cornw. RO, Hawkins mss 10/2192. [115] George, xi. 17057. [116] *Manchester Guardian*, 15, 22 Oct., 26 Nov, 3 Dec. 1831, 24 Mar. 1832; *Manchester Times*, 19, 26 Nov., 3 Dec.; *The Times*, 30 Nov. 1831; Hunt mss 30, 31; *CJ*, lxxxvii. 70, 90, 107, 139, 197, 226, 497; 'Letters from the 3,730', 25 Mar. 1832. [117] Broughton, iv. 208. [118] *Poor Man's Guardian*, 30 June 1832. [119] George, xi. 17343. [120] *The Times*, 3 July, 14, 15 Dec. 1832, 19 Mar. 1833; *Poor Man's Guardian*, 22 Dec. 1832; Proctor, 151-4; Belchem, *Hunt*, 264-9. [121] *Greville Mems.* ii. 351; Osborne, 38. [122] Heron, *Notes*, 200-1. [123] [J. Grant] *Random Recollections of Commons* (1837), 173-5. [124] Hunt, *Conduct of the Whigs to the Working Classes*. [125] Belchem, *Hunt*, 270-5; *The Times*, 3, 24 Feb.; *Ann. Reg.* (1835), App. pp. 215-16; Harrison, 219. [126] *Gent. Mag.* (1835), i. 545-7; *Poor Man's Guardian*, 21 Feb. 1835. [127] Le Marchant, *Althorp*, 196. [128] *Poor Man's Guardian*, 28 Feb. 1835; PROB 11/1884/172; IR26/1387/86. [129] *Preston Pilot*, 2 Apr. 1842; Belchem, *Hunt*, 276-7; M. Chase, *Chartism: a New Hist.* 13.

M.M.E.

HUNTER BLAIR, James (c.1780–1822), of Dunskey, Wigtown.

WIGTOWNSHIRE   2 Aug. 1816–24 June 1822

b. c.1780, 3rd s. of Sir James Hunter Blair[†], 1st bt., of Dunskey and Jane, da. and h. of John Blair of Dunskey. *unm. suc.* fa. to maternal estate of Dunskey and Robertland 1787. *d.* 24 June 1822.

Capt. Ayr militia 1802, maj. 1807, lt.-col. 1807; capt. Galloway rangers 1811.

Hunter Blair stood again for Wigtownshire in 1820 with the backing of the Liverpool ministry and came in without opposition.[1] He was named to the select committees on Scottish burgh reform, 4 May 1820, 16 Feb. 1821. He voted against economies in revenue collection, 4 July, and had something to say on the Desfourneaux compensation, 15 July 1820.[2] He voted in defence of ministers' conduct towards Queen Caroline, 6 Feb., and for Catholic relief, 28 Feb. 1821. On 27 Feb. he secured a return of information on the colonial corn trade since 1791.[3] He was appointed to the select committees on agricultural distress, 7 Mar. 1821, 18 Feb. 1822. He voted against government for repeal of the additional malt duty, 21 Mar., 3 Apr., and was named to the select committee on the subject, 13 Apr. 1821. He voted against parliamentary reform, 9, 10 May, but for criminal law reform, 4 June. He sided with ministers on the duke of Clarence's grant, 18 June, and economy, 27 June. He obtained information on Scottish distillation and coastal trade, 28 June 1821.[4] He voted against more extensive tax reductions to relieve distress, 11 Feb. 1822, and on 27 Feb., when presenting a constituency petition on the subject, gave his opinion that 'no immediate relief could be afforded to the agricultural interest, whose present distressed state he attributed to the superabundant produce of the two or three last years'.[5] Yet it is possible that it was he rather than James Blair who voted for admiralty reductions, 1 Mar., and abolition of one of the joint-postmasterships, 2 May. On 7 May he stated that agricultural distress in Scotland was widespread and unlikely to be ameliorated by the 'hopeful projects' proposed by government,[6] and he voted for repeal of the salt duties, 3 June. He moved for and was appointed to a select committee on Scottish turnpikes, 20 Mar., secured information on the consumption of spirits, 18 May, and presented Wigtown petitions for the removal of restrictions on their export from Scotland, 24 May.[7] It is not clear whether it was he or Blair who voted in the minority for the export of bonded corn as flour, 10 June 1822.

His friend John Vans Agnew reported to Lord Seaforth, 12 July 1822:

On ... Friday the 14th of June ... [Hunter Blair] was attacked with headache. On the Sunday he became delirious, and on Monday the 24th, having continued with little intermission in that state, he died [in London at Gordon's Hotel, Albemarle Street]. On inspecting the brain *ossification* was discovered, that being probably the physical tendency upon which the family complaint is dependent.[8]

He was not much older than 40. 'In private life', it was said, 'he was beloved by men of all parties'.[9] The Dunskey property passed to his younger brother Forbes, and eventually to the head of the family, Sir David Hunter Blair (1778-1857).[10]

[1] NAS GD51/1/198/14/19. [2] *The Times*, 17 July 1820. [3] Ibid. 28 Feb. 1821. [4] Ibid. 29 June 1821. [5] Ibid. 28 Feb. 1822. [6] Ibid. 8 May 1822. [7] Ibid. 21 Mar., 20, 25 May 1822. [8] NAS GD46/4/127. [9] *Gent. Mag.* (1822), ii. 89. [10] PROB 6/198/57.

D.R.F.

HURST, Robert (1750–1843), of Horsham Park, Suss.

SHAFTESBURY	1802–1806
STEYNING	1806–1812
HORSHAM	1812–13 Apr. 1829

bap. 19 Sept. 1750,[1] o.s. of Richard Hurst of Horsham and Mary (Barton?).[2] *educ.* M. Temple 1771, called 1776. *m.* 14 Oct. 1784,[3] Maria, da. of Adam Smith, 2s. 5da. *d.* 13 Apr. 1843.
  Bencher, M. Temple 1811, reader 1814, treas. 1821.
  Lt. Suss. yeomanry 1797.

Hurst, a 'Horsham gentleman and ... barrister of great reputation', was returned again for his native town in 1820 by the 12th duke of Norfolk, for whose family he had acted as an election agent.[4] He was a regular attender who continued to vote with the Whig opposition to Lord Liverpool's ministry on all major issues, including parliamentary reform, 9 May 1821, 25 Apr., 24 June 1822, 20 Feb., 24 Apr., 2 June 1823, 13 Apr. 1826. He divided for Catholic relief, 28 Feb. 1821, 1 Mar., 21 Apr., 10 May 1825. He was granted a week's leave to attend to urgent private business, 1 June, spoke and acted as a teller against the Sussex election bill, 23 June,[5] and was given another three weeks' leave, 28 June 1820. He approved of the enlargement of the marine force, 2 Feb. 1821. In supporting the enfranchisement of Leeds as a 'scot and lot' borough in place of Grampound, 2 Mar., he hoped that 'when the House was creating a new right, they would not overlook the claims of the poorer classes, who so largely

contributed to the burdens of the state and bore with such patience their unexampled privations'. He spoke in favour of a motion criticizing the use of excessive force in the preventive service, 22 Mar.[6] He thought the Lyme Regis petition complaining of a loss of elective rights should be attended to, but not by an election committee, 12 Apr. He was granted a week's leave for urgent private business, 14 May 1821. He described the vagrant laws as an 'ill-digested mass' which 'called loudly for revision', 29 Mar. 1822. He opposed a petition against the Insolvent Debtors Act, 10 Feb. 1823, on the grounds that 'in many cases the creditor was as much to blame for giving credit to improper persons as the debtor who requested and received it'.[7] He supported the bill to tackle abuses in the management of Limerick corporation, 6 May 1823.[8] Next day, during the inquiry into the conduct of the sheriff of Dublin, he offered his legal opinion that a grand juryman's oath did not prevent him from giving evidence. He suggested widening the brief of the committee on rate expenditure to include an examination of rate levels, which had remained static in some parishes 'notwithstanding great change of circumstance', 19 May 1824. The following day he endorsed the principle of a bill to repeal the settlement laws for mariners' apprentices. In supporting inquiry into delays in chancery, 7 June 1825, he recounted his personal experience of a lawsuit in which £8 17s. 6d. had been expended for every £10 recovered. He was again returned for Horsham at the general election of 1826.

He assured the House that the landed interest 'did not by any means feel the alarm on the subject of the corn laws which was attributed to them', 27 Nov. 1826, but he hoped to see swift action as 'landlords at present were embarrassed upon what terms to let their lands'. He divided for Catholic relief, 6 Mar. 1827. He was granted a month's leave for urgent business, 27 Mar., and returned to vote against Canning's ministry for the disfranchisement of Penryn, 28 May. He was in the minority of seven against the committal of Thomas Flanagan to Newgate for forging signatures on a petition, 19 June 1827. As a land tax commissioner of 30 years' standing he favoured remitting double payments by Catholics, 4, 21 Feb. 1828, predicting that the resultant loss of revenue would be minimal. He voted for repeal of the Test Acts, 26 Feb., and Catholic relief, 12 May. He warmly supported the division of counties bill as 'a boon ... to the poor suitor for justice', 27 Feb. He dismissed as 'libellous, false and scandalous' a petition alleging hardships in Horsham gaol, 2 May, but admitted that prisoners' allowances had been reduced owing to lack of funds. He supported Davies's bill for the better ordering of elections, 6 May, and lamented the 'confusion ... disturbance and tumult which took place by night as well as by day in all places where the polling booths were not so numerous as they ought to be'. He gave qualified backing to a proposal that trustees of turnpike roads should be personally liable for them, 3 June. In presenting an anti-slavery petition, 10 June, he recalled the royal declaration of 1823 and hoped the House would 'no longer suffer the matter to sleep in silence'. He voted against the duke of Wellington's ministry for the motion condemning the misapplication of public money for building work at Buckingham House, 23 June 1828. He divided for the government's Catholic emancipation bill, 6, 30 Mar., and presented a favourable petition from Horsham Baptists, 18 Mar. 1829. Following the bill's passage he resigned his seat in favour of his patron's son, the Catholic earl of Surrey. According to the historian of Horsham, 'it was certainly concluded by the ... people that Hurst had resigned his seat under pressure from the duke of Norfolk', but in his speech nominating the new Member, 4 May 1829, he cited 'advanced age' as the reason for his retirement and recalled with pride his 60 years spent 'upon the stage of public business'.[9]

In November 1830, during the 'Swing' riots, Hurst was involved in an incident when a group of discontented labourers demanded that local landowners hear their grievances about wages and tithe payments in Horsham church. A local lady recorded that

> they went in a large body for Mr. Hurst (who holds the great tithes) and as he endeavoured to excuse himself they seized a chariot from the *King's Head* yard and dragged it up to his house, but luckily he had just set off, supported by his two sons ... [The] gentlemen were stationed at the altar to receive the demands of the lawless multitude ... Mr. Hurst held out for so long it was feared that blood would be shed.

Another local diarist was convinced that 'had not some of Hurst's friends ... managed to take off the attention of the mob ... there would have been much risk of his being murdered'. Eventually the labourers' demands were met, much to the disgust of the home secretary Peel, who doubted Hurst's claim that 'it was expedient or necessary for the vestry to yield to the demands of the mob'.[10] Hurst died in April 1843. By dint of numerous land purchases he was able to dispose of more than 2,100 acres, most of which passed to his elder son Robert Henry Hurst, Radical Member for Horsham, 1832-41, 1844-7.[11]

[1] IGI (Suss.). [2] IGI (Bucks.). [3] IGI (London). [4] W. Albery, *Parl. Hist. Horsham*, 123, 127. [5] *The Times*, 24 June 1820. [6] Ibid. 23 Mar.

1821. [7] Ibid. 11 Feb. 1823. [8] Ibid. 7 May 1823. [9] Albery, 256. [10] E. Hobsbawm and G. Rudé, *Captain Swing* (1985), 85-86; J.L. and B. Hammond, *Village Labourer*, 258; Horsham museum mss 813, Browne diary. [11] *Gent. Mag.* (1843), ii. 93; *VCH Suss.* vi (2), 162-4; PROB 11/1978/252; IR26/1644/206.

H.J.S.

HUSKISSON, William (1770–1830), of Eartham, nr. Chichester, Suss. and Somerset Place, Mdx.[1]

MORPETH	1796–1802
LISKEARD	16 May 1804–1807
HARWICH	1807–1812
CHICHESTER	1812–8 Feb. 1823
LIVERPOOL	15 Feb. 1823–15 Sept. 1830

b. 11 Mar. 1770, 1st s. of William Huskisson of Oxley, nr. Wolverhampton, Staffs. and 1st w. Elizabeth, da. of John Rotton of Oxley. *educ.* Brewood; Albrighton, Staffs.; Appleby Magna g.s., Leics. 1782-3; Paris, privately from 1783. *m.* 6 Apr. 1799, Eliza Emily, da. of Adm. Mark Milbanke, *s.p. suc.* fa. 1790; gt.-uncle Dr. Richard Gem 1800. *d.* 15 Sept. 1830.

Supt. aliens office Jan. 1793-July 1794; chief clerk to sec. of state for war July 1794-Mar. 1795, under-sec. of state for war Mar. 1795-May 1801; agent, Cape of Good Hope 1799-1801, Ceylon 1801-4, 1807-23; sec. to treasury May 1804-Feb. 1806, Apr. 1807-Dec. 1809; PC 29 July 1814; commr. of woods, forests and land revenues Aug. 1814-Feb. 1823; member, bd. of trade Dec. 1814, pres. Feb. 1823-Sept. 1827; treas. of navy Feb. 1823-Sept. 1827; sec. of state for war and colonies Sept. 1827-May 1828.

Dir. Sun Fire Office 1814-*d.*

'Tall, slouching and ignoble-looking' but arguably the ablest practical financier of his generation, Canning's 'profound coadjutor' Huskisson was a plain, clumsy man with hair 'cropped as close as a ploughman'.[2] He compensated in the Commons for his appearance and feeble, uneducated voice with 'sheer political intellect', well-prepared speeches (of which his notes for some 300 survive), a facility with facts, occasional 'cutting and corrective looks' and by exuding composure and avoiding sarcasm.[3] Commending his contribution on trade, a radical publication of 1825 added that 'his manner is cold and formal, but his reasoning excellent'.[4] A follower of the younger Pitt, he was 'Mercury' in Canning's 'Pantheon', 'a man of the world of the best sort' to his friend John William Ward* (Lord Dudley), while Sir James Mackintosh*, a Whig who preferred him to Canning, thought him a 'good natured and kind hearted man'.[5] He was universally regarded as 'a very clever fellow', able administrator, and entertaining dinner guest, but suffered throughout his career from being disliked, at times intensely, at Court, and by leading City bankers, on account of his demeanour and background; for although he was 'not a new man of business', he had been half-raised in Paris among *philosophes*. In the 1820s he antagonized a growing number of Members on both sides of the House whose ambitions he thwarted. Tory agriculturists especially felt threatened by and mistrusted his 'liberal' policies on corn and trade.[6] As Canning's second fiddle, though vastly his superior on finance, in debate he too frequently became the scapegoat for him and Frederick Robinson. Furthermore, both as leader of the liberal Tories in the 1827-8 coalition ministries and subsequently, he rarely perceived the need to update Canning's policies or the weakness of executing them unamended.

By 1820 he had languished for more than five years as the Liverpool government's first commissioner of woods and forests, a brief he had long mastered and that bored him. Excluded from the cabinet he hankered for, he was an unpaid member of the board of trade yet a key member of the premier's policy committee. Adhering broadly to principles he had set out with Francis Horner[†] in the 1810 bullion committee's report and *The Question Concerning the Depreciation of Our Currency*, he advocated a gradual retreat from wartime depreciation and inflation, served on every major finance committee, rallied support for the 1815 corn law and 1819 Bank Act and condoned the repressive legislation after Peterloo. He also warned against reliance on government intervention to heal economic distress.[7] His re-election for Chichester, which since 1812 he had represented on the independent interest with Lord Egremont's acquiescence, was opposed at the 1820 general election, when he assisted the successful government candidate, Lord Ashburnham's nominee Edward Curteis, whom he mistrusted, in the bitter contest for Sussex. As the government whip William Holmes remarked, he 'escaped' a poll himself, but was sorely tested by the mob at the county one.[8] Drawing on this experience, on 24 Mar., five days before their pre-session meeting with Liverpool, he wrote to the patronage secretary Arbuthnot warning that the concessions opposition demanded on the civil list ('£30,000 more or less to the king's household') counted for little compared with the need for the cabinet to be seen to be appeasing the farmers:

> This dissolution has deprived us of nearly all our best and steadiest props ... and has substituted in their stead men of very different character ... We must not shut our eyes to the spirit which is spreading through the country even in the agricultural districts ... It is a soreness on

every subject connected with expense, a clamour for economy, a feeling growing out of the present straitened circumstances of the yeomanry contrasted with the ease which they enjoyed during the war ... The infection of radicalism, which is prevalent in the town is gradually making its way into the villages ... Government ... must not only forbear from provocation ... In my opinion the period may not be remote in which we may find it necessary to do something to secure the affection and more cordial goodwill of some great class in the state. To bid for the lower classes or the manufacturing population is out of the question. Duty and policy would equally forbid it, but the yeomanry are still within your reach and to them in my opinion we must look.[9]

Intervening regularly to support colleagues, he helped the chancellor of the exchequer Vansittart to counter attacks on the civil list, 27 Apr.-8 May. That day, he carried the division against further inquiry (by 256-157), praised the 1816 civil list report and dismissed opposition demands for reductions in diplomatic expenditure on the ground that ambassadors were accountable to the king, not Parliament.[10] On 12 May, anticipating the arrival of the Sussex agricultural distress petition (which Henry Brougham presented in his absence on the 16th), he urged that these petitions be presented silently. He countered James Stuart Wortley's arguments for repeal of the wool tax with the rejoinder, 'what else would give the treasury £250,000?', demonstrated statistically that the continental wool trade was depressed, and defeated the proposal (by 202-128), 26 May. Four days later he reinforced the president of the board of trade Robinson's arguments against referring the agricultural distress petitions to a select committee and insisted that as the Irish trade had resumed, the 1815 corn law and an 80s. pivot price afforded sufficient protection. When named to the select committee conceded next day, he immediately carried a motion confining its remit to the averages. Representing West Sussex interests, he had Curteis's bill authorizing the transfer of county polls from Chichester to Lewes postponed, 9 June, pending the arrival of hostile petitions, and defeated it (by 35-28) on the 23rd. He scotched a similar bill, 9 May 1827.[11] He disregarded quibbles on the estimates, 16, 21 June 1820, but he had to concede the shortcomings of the consolidated fund when the City banker William Heygate criticized it, 19 June, and admitted that without further savings the £5,000,000 sinking fund could not be retained.

His perspective on Queen Caroline's case was determined by his commitment to protecting and representing Canning, whose early liaison with her was common knowledge and an embarrassment to the cabinet, as George IV sought a divorce. When finance for the secret service was voted, 16 June, he was hard pressed to counter criticism of the undisclosed cost of proceeding against the queen by means of a bill of pains and penalties prosecuted by publicly funded government lawyers, using evidence acquired by the secret service, but he would not be drawn. He was a government teller for persisting with her prosecution, 26 June, and a key spokesman on 17 July against her counsel Lushington's motion for papers on the plate presented to her in 1808. (His decision, as treasury under-secretary that year, to remodel King William III's plate for her use, now enabled the foreign secretary and leader of the House Lord Castlereagh to designate it public not personal property.) He faced awkward questions on the prosecution's deployment of contingency and secret service funds to influence newspaper coverage of the queen's case, 18 Sept. He knew, through his early patron the 2nd marquess of Stafford's half-brother Lord Granville, that their friends opposed the bill in the Lords, and initially favoured forcing it through there and conceding defeat in the Commons, or carrying a resolution confined to its principle. However, Canning wrote from Paris scotching the proposal. As directed by him, on 22 Oct. he advised Liverpool to 'take the earliest opportunity of getting rid of the proceeding altogether', and retreated to Eartham to distance himself from further intrigue.[12] Lady Palmerston noted that the bill's abandonment and the forced prorogation, 23 Nov., which prompted Canning's resignation, left Huskisson feeling 'very low', despite talk of his promotion.[13] Canning had vainly suggested him for the board of trade. Reports that he would deputize for Canning at the India board, where Lord Bathurst was the substitute, were unfounded and he stayed on at woods and forests purely to allay suspicion of a 'job'.[14] With strong popular petitioning on the queen's behalf in Chichester and elsewhere, he feared that she might yet be the means of bringing down the government, and warned Canning in December 1820:

We may possibly struggle through the liturgy and the palace, but we shall be left weak and lingering to meet other questions and impressions and prepossessions, such ... as those growing out of the Milan Commission ... the final yielding to the king upon the divorce ... the £100,000 at least to be voted for the ... commission.[15]

Defending government's handling of the affair, 6 Feb. 1821, he attributed the recent industrial revival to the Six Acts, warned that the radicals' crusade for the queen threatened that recovery and rehashed and elaborated on the litany of misdemeanours she had been accused of in 1806 and 1813. It was his first major speech on a general question, and according to the radical Whig Henry Grey Bennet

the dullest and most stupid speech I ever heard. It was in fact, an entire failure, and he had better confine himself to finance and trade. He was repeatedly groaned at by his own friends and, when I, in my reply, sneeringly complimented him on the enlivening nature of his speech, the benches behind him cheered me.[16]

He justified the queen's £50,000 civil list pension, 12 Feb. He supported Londonderry (formerly Castlereagh) on the alleged libels against the judge William Draper Best[†], 23 Feb., 19 Apr., and by the *Morning Chronicle*, 26 Feb. Quoting from official papers, he refuted William Smith's claim that the duke of Clarence could live on his inheritance, 8 June, and defended the inclusion of arrears in his award, 8, 18, 29 June.[17] He was a government teller against inquiry into the preferential sale of the Llanllechyd slate quarries to Lord Penrhyn, in which his department was implicated, 21 June 1821, 8 July 1823. As agreed with Canning, he divided silently for Catholic relief, 28 Feb., and spoke against parliamentary reform, 18 Apr. 1821. His smile when Lambton, whose motion it was, returned to the chamber after missing the division, made him the target of the latter's wrath.[18] He was a majority teller against Lord John Russell's reform proposals, 9 May 1821.

Sparring frequently with John Maberly and the political economist Ricardo, whose works he had recently read, Huskisson defended the estimates in several speeches and interventions, 9 Feb.-18 May 1821.[19] He considered massive reductions in the sinking fund unsustainable and opposed all attempts to repeal or reduce the taxes on malt, 9 Feb., 21 Mar., husbandry horses, 5 Mar., windows, 6 Mar., and wool, 9 Apr. On 7 Mar., supported by Ricardo and Londonderry, he tried to confine the remit of the agriculture select committee deliberately conceded to Thomas Gooch to protection. 'Taking the leading oar', he colluded during it with Ricardo to carry (by 10-6) his own recommendation for a moderate fixed duty, removable in dearths, and included it in the report he drafted anonymously and presented on their behalf, 18 June.[20] To Lord Althorp, a Whig member of the committee, it was a 'masterly refutation of the views in which the inquiry had originated ... clearing the way for a more liberal system of legislation'.[21] Hence he was caricatured as the watering can used by 'the gardener' Londonderry to nourish the placemen 'thistles'.[22] He failed to prevent Curwen's resolution repealing the husbandry horse tax, which Londonderry had stifled, being revived and carried against government, 14 June.[23] Opposing Hume's economy and retrenchment motion, 27 June, he criticized the 'gloomy' account of the country given by Canning's nephew Lord Titchfield, scorned opposition's tactical use of statistics for 1792 and 1797 for comparison purposes and, arguing that the £4,000,000 savings Hume proposed would destroy the country's defence strategy, praised the modest ones already achieved. On the bank cash payments bill, 19 Mar. 1821, he objected to Lord Folkestone's defence of a paper currency and was glad to see Alexander Baring's amendment defeated.

When ministerial negotiations resumed in April 1821 preparatory to Canning's return, Huskisson was suggested for the navy treasurership, the mint and the Irish secretaryship but, rejecting all three, he informed Liverpool on the 25th that he would risk an election at Chichester 'only for the India board'.[24] He had set his terms too high. Although in contention, his threatened resignation and complaints of neglect, throughout the protracted discussions that preceded the January 1822 Grenvillite accession, when Charles Williams Wynn* became president of the India board 'with cabinet rank', dissipated the good will of Liverpool and Canning and their friends.[25] Liverpool had asked Arbuthnot, who found him 'unreasonable', and the duke of Wellington to soothe him, and he was talked of for Ireland, the war office and the exchequer. He and Palmerston quashed the first two suggestions, and Lord Buckingham reported to Lord Grenville that the last was never an option as the Bank 'would do no business or have any concern' with Huskisson.[26] Informing Granville on 3 Dec. 1821 of his decision to 'gulp Mr. Squeaker' [Williams Wynn] and stay on 'at least for the present', he attributed it to Charles Ellis's* influence and to Canning, who, to his relief, had yet to agree to go to Bengal as governor-general.[27] He wavered briefly when Grenvillites were substituted for his political allies Lord Binning* and William Sturges Bourne* on the India board, and complained formally to Liverpool of the hardship of his 'nearly eight years of lingering in expectation'.[28]

In February 1822 he vainly hoped that Londonderry could expedite repayment of the Austrian loan, so that borrowing through exchequer bills or a 'further inroad upon the feeble remnant of our sinking fund' could be avoided and 'our country gentlemen [put] in good humour before Parliament met'.[29] The session began badly for him. Opposing Hume's amendment to the address, 5 Feb., he became embroiled in hostile exchanges over his alleged 'jobbing' at woods and forests by investing incoming funds and pocketing the

interest before declaring them in the official returns. He gave a qualified endorsement only of the government's relief package, 15 Feb. He argued that distress could not be solved by emigration, reform or 'annihilation of the pretended national debt', and praised the vice-president of the board of trade Wallace's proposals for relaxing the navigation laws, but credited these to himself as a leading member of the 1820 and 1821 select committees on trade, which recommended the change. He attributed the low prices associated with distress to an excess of supply and the improved value of money and cautioned that the 1815 law had generated an artificial expectation that corn would fetch 80s. a quarter. He preferred bounties to sliding scales and gold coins to small banknotes, and endorsed the projected £4,000,000 exchequer loan as a means of boosting the money supply and the economy. Citing his 1821 report, he maintained that tax remissions afforded 'no immediate remedy to agricultural distress arising directly from low prices, but may benefit agriculture and other interests'. Speaking similarly on his reappointment to the agriculture select committee, 18 Feb., he also echoed criticism 'out of doors', and came under pressure from Curteis and others who accused him of having 'mystified' and 'misled' the committee, to acknowledge his authorship of the 1821 report.[30] He countered objections to the navy five per cents bill, 8, 11 Mar. He naturally divided against abolition of one of the joint-postmasterships, 13 Mar., 2 May, but conceded that there was a case for it, 2 May. He complained that the brewers' objections to the malt duty repeal bill were unjust, 18 Mar., presented petitions against Grey Benett's alehouses licensing bill, 6 May, and was instrumental in persuading Brougham to withdraw his, 18 July. He defended the concessions to colonial and American shipping under the colonial trade bills and disputed the abolitionists' spokesman Thomas Fowell Buxton's claim that they would boost the West Indian-North American slave trade, 1 Apr. He deliberately held aloof from the agriculture committee, whose report, based entirely on the 1821 evidence and recommending a 70s. pivot price and fixed countervailing duties was presented that day by its co-author Gooch. His relief proposal was one of seven it published and he submitted it to the House as an alternative to Londonderry's, 29 Apr.[31] Liverpool had freed him from making his differences with Londonderry on corn a resignation matter, and he now echoed Ricardo's preference for perpetual 'open' trade. He prefaced his resolutions (based on a 15s. duty on corn at 80s. a quarter with variable duties above and below this pivot price and provision for lesser grains and pulses) with a speech defending government's decision to extend the circulation period of small notes, and also reiterated his confidence in bounties and fixed term annuities. He sanctioned warehousing as a necessary evil.[32] Although he neither forced a division nor cast a wayward vote, his opposition to lending money on corn created a furore during a difficult period in the government's negotiations with the Bank, whose assistance was vital to the establishment of Londonderry's 'agricultural bank', 6 May. Londonderry rejected his proposals, 8, 13 May. He complained to Liverpool that he was being informed against, but that he did not consider this a resignation matter, 12 May.[33] Countering Ricardo's objections to the naval and military pensions bill, he denied that it infringed the sinking fund, 1, 24 May. Opposing Western's motion for inquiry into the resumption of cash payments, 11 June, he rendered his speech memorable by carrying as an amendment (by 194-30) the 1696 Commons resolution 'that this House will not alter the standard of gold and silver, in fineness, weight, or denomination'. The Whig George Agar Ellis* thought he spoke 'no better' than Western, 'except that he only spoke for two hours'.[34] He was a government teller for the aliens bill, 11 July, and against reducing the grant for publicizing Irish proclamations, 22 July 1822.

Directly Parliament was prorogued that month he renewed to Liverpool his threat to resign unless promoted, giving as reasons Canning's forthcoming departure for Bengal and his own long tenure of woods and forests 'less from a desire to hold it, than in the expectation of being removed to some other'. He emphasized also the loyalty he had shown by staying on after the Grenvillite accession. With Londonderry as intermediary, negotiations to find 'ways and means' of promoting him commenced on 30 July, but no agreement had been reached when Londonderry committed suicide, 12 Aug.[35] Any decision impacted on Chichester, where government expected a stiff contest, possibly defeat, should Huskisson retire; and Liverpool, where Canning had yet to vacate but he been requisitioned in June as his replacement. He had also accepted an invitation to Canning's farewell dinner.[36] On 9 Sept., ten days after the dinner, Canning was confirmed as foreign secretary and leader of the House. Huskisson had pressed his claims to both offices and deliberately stayed away from the Liverpool proceedings, only to see, as Palmerston put it, the premier 'clinch one point without embarrassing it with another'. Ruled out for the exchequer, and with only a chance of the India board, should Williams Wynn agree to move, it proved impossible to accommodate him and, after a month's speculation, his claim was relegated to the pre-session reshuffle.[37] John

Croker*, with whom he exchanged pleasantries and misinformation, commented:

> All that Huskisson can do for the government he can do best in his present rank ... He is *au fait* in all official and financial details, and has a great love of what the French call *administrative* experience. But the defects of his manner and voice prevent his being a useful speaker, for no one is useful whom the House merely tolerates.[38]

Hurt to be offered the presidency of the board of trade '*without cabinet*', 3 Oct., he vented his spleen on the Grenvillites and the '*via inertia* which has been so long Liverpool's principle of government'. He urged Canning as intermediary not to press his claim 'further than you feel to be conducive to some arrangement satisfactory to yourself, for improving gradually your position in the House' and took solace, as Canning knew he would, from Buckingham's exclusion from the cabinet.[39] Nothing came of a proposal to make him chancellor of the duchy of Lancaster, so giving him cabinet rank and influence in Liverpool, where the merchant elite were prepared to guarantee his election as Canning's replacement, but categorically refused to fund a by-election resulting from his subsequent promotion.[40] After sounding Wellington (who deplored his tactics) and half the ministry, partly through indecision, partly from what Arbuthnot indignantly called an attempt to 'carry the cabinet by storm', he heeded Ellis's warning that the political world would not sanction his refusal. On 5 Jan. 1823 he accepted the presidency of the board of trade with a written promise of cabinet later.[41] His exclusion was commonly credited to the king and communicated to him by Canning as such, 3 Jan. However, according to a letter of the previous day, cited by Liverpool's nineteenth-century biographer Yonge, the king had 'no objection'.[42] On the 7th Liverpool informed Wellington candidly of his decision, Canning's agreement and Huskisson's assent, 'though not with as good a grace as I should have desired for his credit', and requested that the 'secret' be kept from their colleagues. Wellington's letter to the home secretary Peel that day indicates that it was.[43] Canning touted Huskisson briefly for the India board, when Wallace refused to stay on as his deputy, claiming that he had no 'peculiar aptitude for the situation' and no 'marked accession of political weight to the government been obtained by his appointment'. Nevertheless, the arrangement endured and his promotion (financed by a second appointment as treasurer of the navy at £3,000 a year) was gazetted, 31 Jan.[44] He was directed with Arbuthnot to find a mover and seconder for the address and instrumental in securing Canning a £3,000 pension, should he leave office.[45] Reluctant to cast off his interest 'like an old shoe', he prevaricated over Chichester before coming in for Liverpool after a vexatious contest, during which he was placarded as an alien, a Jacobin and a placeman.[46] On the hustings and at the dinner afterwards he refuted these slurs, rejected claims that the economy could not sustain a war, eulogized Canning and endorsed his decision not to act to suppress the new liberal regime in Spain, as France intended. He saw no inconsistency in opposing domestic reform while condoning it abroad; defended, on economic grounds, the repressive measures taken after Peterloo and the use of government informers; and spoke of the advantages of having ministers in the Commons, where they were directly accountable to Members. He repeated much of the speech when thanking his Chichester friends for a gift of plate, 3 Apr. 1823.[47]

The commercial component of Canning's liberal Tory policies, executed by Huskisson and by Robinson as chancellor of the exchequer, was considered remarkable for the facility with which excise duties were reduced, antiquated trading restrictions abolished and protection perpetuated only where subsidized foreign competition threatened trade, or it was considered necessary to invoke colonial preference. Initially assisted by Wallace, whom Charles Grant replaced as vice-president in April 1823, Huskisson also relied heavily on his clerks (George Chalmers, Thomas Lack and the economist and codifier of the Customs Acts James Deacon Hume) and a staff of about 36, to whom he added his private secretary and biographer Edward Leeves (Leeves's brother William was his Chichester agent).[48] He drew too on the Liverpool Parliament Office in Fludyer Street and his merchant backers, especially reports supplied by the Liverpool merchant John Gladstone* (a potential rival for the Liverpool seat) and the Glasgow and Liverpool manufacturer Kirkman Finlay*. They expected him to add 'weight' to their petitions and suggestions for legislation. Between 1823 and 1830 he commented briefly on most of the diverse issues affecting Liverpool, doing so at length if they were matters of national concern.[49] In his first session as president of the board, he carried the Reciprocities Duties Act (4 Geo. IV, c. 77), an empowering measure permitting the king in council to grant foreign powers reciprocal concessions on duties, drawbacks and shipping, including carriage in foreign ships in breach of the Navigation Act. It was the basis for his 1824 and 1825 Acts and a raft of commercial treaties with Austria, Denmark, France, Hanover, the Hanse Towns, Mecklenburg, Prussia, South America and the United States. He negotiated them as a plenipotentiary with Canning and the latter's nephew Stratford Canning*.[50]

Drawn by Edmond Wodehouse's criticism of the 1821 report to comment on Whitmore's proposal for a corn bill based on a gradual reduction to 60s. in the pivot price, 26 Feb. 1823, Huskisson dismissed his case for separating the corn and currency questions as 'superficial', disputed Curwen's account of the benefits accruing from lowering taxes on household goods and cottages and, denying that the agriculturists had a right to protection because other taxes were high, hinted that he might support free trade 'at the right time'. Two days later, supporting Robinson in a prepared speech, he ridiculed Maberly's attempt to raid the entire £7,000,000 sinking fund to finance tax cuts and defended the policy of allowing it to accumulate at compound interest under the national debt reduction bill. Presenting a Liverpool petition for repeal of the window tax, 7 Mar., he conceded that he could not support its prayer[51] Floored by Baring's criticism of the naval and military pensions bill, whose committal ministers carried by only 11 votes, 11 Apr., he deemed his complaint 'irrelevant' and fudged a response based on the history of previous government dealings with the Bank. He fared no better at the bill's third reading, when Ricardo challenged him to explain the role of the Bank as its guarantor, 18 Apr. He made light work of opposing inquiry into the currency, despite being baited by Titchfield on behalf of the agriculturists, and it was rejected (by 96-27), 12 June. He justified the inflated salary awarded to the Grenvillite Henry Williams Wynn[†] as ambassador to the Swiss Cantons, 25 Mar. His merchant vessels apprentice bill (4 Geo. IV, c. 25), which involved the registration of shipping, impressments and wages, passed after several hostile exchanges with Ricardo, 13, 24 Mar., 18 Apr. 1823. Like the reform of the law of principal and factor (4 Geo. IV, c. 83) that he carried in the teeth of Scarlett's objections, 12 May, it was largely the product of mercantile pressure from Liverpool and London, and was hurriedly executed. Both required time-consuming remedial legislation in 1824, 1825 and 1826.[52] His legislation simplifying Commons procedures for dealing with trade bills (4 Geo. IV, c. 42) was not seriously opposed, and his measures for deregulating Scottish and Irish linen manufacture (4 Geo. IV, cc. 40, 90) were enacted, 18 July. That day, after two months of intense debate, petitioning and close divisions forced by City interests, he conceded that the Lords had wrecked the silk manufacture bill (repealing the Spitalfields Acts), which he had struggled to carry through the Commons with Whig support. Urged to accede to the demands of the Liverpool East and West India Associations, but anxious to stifle discussion of slavery, he decided that sugar prices should be determined by the world market, suggested restoring the 1814 import duties and refused to be directed towards equalization by Charles Grant, who voted in Whitmore's minority against him, 22 May.[53] His hostility to change and anxiety to stifle the issue persisted, and were apparent when he moved on behalf of the indisposed Robinson to prolong the 1823 duties for a year, 8 Mar. He refused to concede a committee to Whitmore, 13 May 1824. He described himself as 'sympathetic' to the ship owners' complaints, but refused to waver on the principles of the reciprocity bill, which he carried (by 75-15), 4 July 1823, having commended it to the House as a measure which would protect British shipping and assist commerce 'with a view not only to increase our wealth, but to securing the means of national defence against foreign states'. He accompanied Canning and the American envoy Richard Rush to the Liverpool dinner during their abortive negotiations in August. Amendments to the Reciprocity Acts in 1824 and 1825, in consequence of the Monroe doctrine, were endorsed in 1833 by the select committee on manufacturing, commerce and shipping.[54]

After three months of intrigue and in-fighting, on 6 Nov. 1823 the king authorized his admission to the cabinet when it met to discuss West Indian business on the 18th, but cautioned: 'Mr. Huskisson may be and no doubt is a very clever man, but he is not always a prudent one'.[55] He relinquished the Ceylon agency and £1,200 a year that month, lest it compromise his department, and resigned from the African Institution with Canning.[56] Briefed by Gladstone (a plantation owner) on the insurrection in Demerara, where Canning's 1823 order in council on slavery was not implemented, his *strictly private* reply on 2 Nov., endorsing the principle of emancipation but criticizing as unproductive the tactics of its parliamentary advocates and the role of Nonconformist missionaries, was misappropriated and printed in the *Jamaica Journal*, 21 Feb. 1824. As intended, it appeared in the London papers in late April, when the abolitionists agitated the case of Methodist missionary John Smith, indicted in Demerara, of whom Huskisson had written, 'it is difficult to presume that he was altogether innocent in the late conspiracy'.[57] He neither commented nor voted on Brougham's critical motion, 1, 11 June. He denied the Carlow petitioners' allegations that all slaves were cruelly treated, 15 June 1824. He had hinted at support for repeal of the combination laws when it was agitated by Moore, 3 Mar., but quashed his complicated proposals, 27 May 1823. Deliberately named to the 1824 committee, he delegated their inquiry, which included artisan emigration

and machinery exports, to Hume, directing him 'to filter out the good and bad from the current laws', 12 Feb.[58] He approved the repeal bill that Hume rushed through that session (5 Geo. IV, c. 95), but had to revive the committee himself, 21 Feb. 1825, in order to act to protect machinery, property and strike-breakers in the wake of the widespread industrial disruption it had legitimized. He promoted the revised act (6 Geo. IV, c. 129) in speeches on 29 Mar., 3 May, 27, 30 June, so attracting the opprobrium of the shipwrights and other disaffected artisans, who, as he predicted in debate, 29 Mar. 1825, encouraged opposition to him in Liverpool at the next election.[59] He advocated repeal of the 'oppressive' usury laws as government intended, 16, 27 Feb., but forfeited it on being outmanoeuvred by Littleton and the agriculturists, 8 Apr. 1824.[60] That session's silk bill was carried first by Lauderdale in the Lords, making Baring, with whom Huskisson had clashed over the hostile Spitalfields petition, 5 Mar., its only serious Commons opponent. Introducing it, 8 Mar., in a speech universally acknowledged as 'one the best, if not the very best ... ever heard on a trading question', he used evidence on the relatively unrestricted cotton trade to prove the case for replacing the current prohibitions and bounties with a 30 per cent tax on imported silks.[61] Supported by his colleagues, he intervened again in support of the bill 9, 10 18, 29 Mar., and it received royal assent, 12 Apr. (5 Geo. IV, c. 21). By May Huskisson was showing the strain of overwork after preparing reports on the Canada-United States border and transatlantic steam packets, while attending the House daily to defend policies which had increased his unpopularity at Court and on the Tory backbenches, where Canning rarely shielded him from attack.[62] He carried the government's warehoused wheat bill, 17, 27 May, to taunts that it had been introduced to benefit Liverpool; and was harassed over the marine insurance bill entrusted to him by Robinson, which was factiously delayed, 17 May, 3 June, before he carried its third reading (by 59-15), 14 June 1824. During the recess he travelled to Spa with Robert Wilmot Horton* and Ellis, ostensibly for his health, but also to negotiate a reciprocity treaty with the Netherlands, whose foreign minister Falk had rejected their terms. Writing to Granville, ambassador at The Hague, on his return in September, he expressed grave misgivings about Canning's 'private' visit to the Irish viceroy Lord Wellesley and its likely interpretation as a portent that Catholic relief would be carried, or of ministerial change.[63]

He mistrusted private bills and joint-stock companies and became increasingly critical of the protective measures sought by speculators and of their toll on Parliament's resources. This became evident in his interventions on the Irish Royal Mining Company, 6 May 1824, the Birmingham gas light bill, 6 May 1824, and the Manchester and Salford Loan Company, 10 May 1824, 28 Feb. 1825. Predicting 'many losses and disappointments', he agreed with lord chancellor Eldon that acquiring chartered status and appeals to law not Parliament should be used to check the 'wild and unreasonable speculation' in joint-stock companies 'which vanish into thin air and leave those who entertained them nothing but regret and disappointment', 18 Mar. 1825, and resisted Moore's assault on the 1720 Bubble Act, 29 Mar., but he had to concede it, 2 June 1825.[64] Initially wary of committing his support for schemes for a Liverpool-Birmingham or Liverpool-Manchester railway, he 'reluctantly' endorsed the latter as a public utility and boon to commerce, after ensuring that a clause was added to limit profiteering by shareholders, 2 Mar. 1825. He supported the revived bill, 6 Apr. 1826, and engineered a majority for it in the Lords.[65]

Huskisson played a part in the passage of most of the public bills enacted in 1825 and although his health held out, he found the session long and taxing.[66] On the budget, 28 Feb., he declared that the bounties on sugars would be abolished as part of a wholesale revision of the trade and tariff system, and he promised legislation to assist the West Indies before the close of the session, 11 Mar. He refused that day to concede a committee to investigate cutting duties on imported spirits, tobacco and tea, which he had hinted (28 Feb.) would be excluded from his list. He now classified most of the legislation his department had carried since 1822 as outmoded, and projected himself as 'an innovator only to the extent that colonial interests have changed', 21 Mar. He introduced his colonial trades and customs consolidation bills that day as revisionary measures (6 Geo. IV, cc. 104-13). Having established the principle of the colonial bill, he proceeded on the 25th with the attendant measures, intended to promote trade and manufacturing by relaxing prohibitions and lowering tariffs on raw materials and to encourage British shipping and navigation. Singling out Finlay, he paid tribute to the contribution of British manufacturers in formulating policy, discussed individual tariffs and reforms, including repeal of the quarantine duties and taxes on ship sales and debentures, and replacing the current unsatisfactory *ad hoc* system with a salaried consular service. Confident that 'public opinion and the … Commons' were on his side, 'although in detail everyone has an objection to my measures', he promoted them in further speeches, 13 May, 3, 14, 17, 24 June.[67] John Herries* deemed him

'one of the most dangerous men that ever was admitted into our councils', and warned the Arbuthnots in April and May 1825 that he was resented in the City on account of his 'indecent presumption', 'haste' and 'gross mistakes', for goods were 'not admitted in foreign ports on better terms than they were' and with trade 'turning against us', merchants were 'obliged to pay in gold'.[68] Huskisson's reforms did not weaken the principle of imperial preference, but his 'enumerated articles' were mostly imported from Europe in British ships, or the vessels of the country of production.[69]

He rightly interpreted Maberly's motion to repeal the assessed taxes, 3 Mar. 1825, as a tactical one, 'calculated to win over those who would not meddle with the sinking fund per se'. He did not rule out tax cuts but stipulated that the priority was to cut those affecting manufacturing, and amid fears of a shortfall in corn supplies, he strove to stifle discussion of the City petition, 28 Mar. Opposed in cabinet, 18 Apr., when he sought a pledge that government would consider revising the corn laws in 1826, he gave nothing away when baited by Gooch, 25 Apr. 1825, but bringing up a Liverpool petition next day, he hinted at concessions on warehousing.[70] Exceeding his brief, his speech opposing Whitmore's inquiry motion, 28 Apr., promised legislation leading to 'a free trade in corn, under proper and due protection' next session. He made the 'excessive speculation in shares, companies and foreign merchandise' his reason for delaying it, and warned that unless adequately restrained by the Bank and country banks, overspeculation would result in depression and financial exhaustion. His warehousing bill, introduced on 2 May (nominally effective from 15 Aug.) authorized the release of corn from bond at a 70s. pivot price with 10s. in duty, and proposed repealing the prohibit tariff on Canadian wheat. Amendments substituting 8s. for 10s., pressed by the Liverpool importers, 2 May, and for 7s., by the Newcastle merchants, 13 May, were easily defeated, but pressure from Baring, Gooch and Londonderry's brother-in-law Thomas Wood obliged him to concede a 5s. tariff on Canadian wheat, 2 May, 9 June.[71] Probably reflecting Canning's growing reluctance to make common cause with the Grenvillites on Catholic relief, his speech at the bill's third reading, 10 May 1825, included what William Fremantle* and Lord Grenville termed a 'strange declaration' that 'the spirit' of the suppressed Catholic Association would 'remain and start up in another shape'. This and the reservations he expressed over the franchise bill and provisions for the Irish clergy made them complain that he had cost them votes and set back the Catholic cause.[72] He told Granville on the 23rd that he did not despair at the measure's defeat in the Lords.[73]

During the recess he participated in negotiations in Paris and London with the French ministers Villèle and Polignac, which yielded another commercial treaty, and discussed the corn question at length with Liverpool.[74] Convinced that overspeculation by the Bank posed the risk of a 'stoppage or threat to public and private credit' that would be 'felt in their full extent' in late autumn, he suggested to Liverpool and Canning before the cabinet considered it, 22 Sept., that it would be better to hold a general election after the 1826 session, provided difficulties on corn, the Catholic question and slavery could be contained.[75] He stood firm when Pole, Thornton and Company crashed in December, bringing down 43 country banks and, with Liverpool, Canning and Wellington, he badgered the Bank, which only narrowly avoided suspending payments, 16 Dec., to co-operate in instigating inflationary measures.[76] Wellington, echoing the former chancellor Lord Bexley and the banker Rothschild, privately attributed the crisis to Huskisson's 'false policy' of encouraging foreign speculation and a rapid growth in country bank notes.[77] Critics denounced him as the 'French Jacobin in the English cabinet'. Defending his stance, he wrote on 21 Dec. to Gladstone, the rescuer of the Gloucester bank:

> For years I have been constantly labouring to prevail with the Bank of England to permit a modification of their charter. I have uniformly urged this concession on their part, in the double view of security to the country, and to themselves. To the country, by replacing the present system of individual bankers of little capital and often of less prudence or honesty, by joint – stock, or even locally chartered banks of ample capital, carrying on their business as bankers, and not making their credit the channel to feed, either in their own rash adventures, or those of their connections, every wild speculation. To the Bank, in preventing the periodical recourses of panics, with all their alarming consequences to their stability, such as that which is now, I hope, subsiding, but the traces of which will long remain. I have always urged too that the concession would, in fact, be no sacrifice, for that Parliament would secure to them the circulation of the metropolis and a certain district round it, which, together with the exclusive use of their paper in the receipt of the revenues and the payment of the dividends, would maintain it nearly, if not entirely at its accustomed level. Now I trust these considerations will have their weight; that the Bank, on the one hand, will no longer incur the odium of claiming the strict letter of its monopoly, and on the other, that the influence of the country bankers in Parliament will no longer be attended to, in opposition to so great and necessary an improvement.[78]

He rightly predicted a session 'less smooth and satisfactory than the last ... plagued with motions and inquiries' and that government would be 'called upon to devise means of relief where none can be afforded' in 1826.[79] Speaking after Peel and Canning on the address, 2 Feb., he justified the proposed joint-stock banks of six or more partners and the small notes bill and added that by being 'liberal and seasonable ... in saving others, the Bank had actually saved itself'.[80] His defence of the promissory notes bill, 10 Feb., a critical day for government, when the City, country bankers and squires combined against them, was according to John Denison*

> an admirable display of deep practical knowledge and of sound science proved by the test of experience. He took down Mr. Baring's 24,000,000 to about 14,000,000 ... He attributed the distress to the combined action of speculation and overissue of paper. He laid it down as an absolute rule that gold and paper cannot circulate together, the paper will drive out the gold ... Next, that no currency can be safe, where the bullion bears a very small relative proportion to the paper. That the substitution of gold for one pound notes will relieve the Bank from part of the enormous responsibility of standing as security for the 800 country banks of England, and for the banks of Ireland and Scotland, because with this portion of bullion in circulation, each country bank will have the same interest as the Bank of England in observing the exchanges and in regulating their issues accordingly.[81]

Agar Ellis thought his concluding speech on 13 Feb. 'the best ... I ever heard from him – clear, firm, and sound – and with a better manner and delivery than usual'.[82] Privately and to the dismay of Peel and Wellington, who saw it as evidence of his rashness, Huskisson now shared the bankers Hudson Gurney* and Baring's belief in the benefits of a bimetallic currency and he circulated a memorial to the cabinet accordingly.[83] Differing from Finlay and the parliamentary committee, he was also reluctant to concede 'a paper dram' instead of specie to the Scots.[84] Despite his reservations on policy he spoke for the Bank charter and promissory notes bills and exchequer loans, 20, 24, 27 Feb. 1826; but the City, where he was considered the 'real author of the finance measures of government', remained hostile.[85]

Though expected to yield, he successfully resisted the protectionists and the Coventry manufacturers' demands for higher protective tariffs on silk, 9, 14, 23 Feb. 1826.[86] Peel observed that his two-and-a-half-hour speech on the 23rd against conceding them an inquiry 'converted many who meant to vote against the government' and eclipsed that of his ablest opponent, John Williams.[87] He attributed stagnation in trade to the recent banking crisis and currency fluctuations and stated that the 'whole

principle of liberal commercial policy' was at stake
and that he was 'not for turning back'. Members
cheered, Lord Holland endorsed him, Lord Stafford
sent him a euphoric letter, and Canning commended
his performance to Lord Liverpool as 'far, far beyond
what anyone believed he could do'; but, as George
Tierney* reminded the Hollands, 'there is a strong
party against him and Canning and matters appear
to be fast coming to extremities'.[88] He intervened
briefly when challenged in a violent speech by Baring
on the 24th, and carried the division (by 222-40) only
after Canning's dazzling performance. Protectionists
and anti-Catholics begrudged him their support and
Canning avoided using him as a speaker on corn and
slavery before the question of his salary had been disposed of.[89] Implementing a treasury directive of 13
July 1825, and with a dissolution expected, Robinson
moved a resolution for a bill awarding the president of
the board of trade £5,000 a year and the navy treasurer £2,000, 6 Apr. 1826. Huskisson hoped to relinquish the treasurership without loss of income, and
maintained privately that he had 'no personal anxiety
upon the subject' beyond that of timing the change
to coincide with a general election, to avoid alienating his Liverpool sponsors.[90] In the House, 6 Apr., he
spoke of his overwhelming workload and the differences between the posts. The Whigs' personal tributes to him that day and the next were not reflected
in their votes. With the backbench Tories hostile or at
best apathetic, and Canning and Peel's speeches below
par, the resolution was delayed by spoiling motions
and divisions in committee, 7 Apr., and carried by
the embarrassingly narrow majority of 87-76, 10 Apr.
Sensing the mood of the House, Canning acceded to
opposition demands to unite the two offices at £5,000,
and the amended bill received royal assent, 5 May.[91]
Wellington's confidante Mrs. Arbuthnot blamed
Canning and Huskisson for the ministry's unpopularity and condemned the proceedings as 'a rank job'.
She also commented that 'it served them quite right'
as 'trade ... ought always to be subordinate to the
finances and always have [sic] been hitherto, but Mr.
Huskisson has quite emancipated himself from all
such control, and what a pretty mess he has made'.[92]

On 28 Apr. 1826, with full government backing, he
defeated Whitmore's motion to reduce agricultural
protection (by 250-81). Gloomy statistics procured
for the board of trade by William Jacob†, on which
the motion was based, were hinted at and the discussion highlighted Huskisson's failure to initiate the
inquiry promised in 1825. His citations from the 1821
agriculture report and allusions to his commercial
policies were stale. In consultations with Canning and

Liverpool afterwards, he explained that Jacob's figures
indicated a likely shortfall in supply, coinciding with a
depression in manufacturing. Legislation to open the
ports could not therefore be held back until the next
Parliament in November although he would be unable
to carry it himself in the Commons.[93] He therefore
schooled and supported Canning who led the debate,
2, 5, 8, 9 May, when they were opposed from both
sides of the House and the impact of the extra-parliamentary debate was evident. They forfeited the corn
admission bill, 9 May, but carried the warehoused corn
bill, permitting the privy council to authorize foreign
grain imports of only 500,000 quarters, on the 12th.
The Hollands delighted in the reports of Tory disu-
nity and rebellion at Boodle's, induced by Huskisson's
policies.[94] He redeemed himself with a definitive
speech on his reform of the navigation laws, 12 May
1826.[95] As requisitioned, and with Wilmot Horton in
reserve lest a serious contest ensued, he was returned
for Liverpool at the general election in June. He suspected his colleague Gascoigne, an anti-Catholic
Tory and recent opponent of his reforms on combinations, corn and shipping, of promoting the token poll
instigated by the shipwrights.[96] Afterwards, he was
dismayed to find his election speech and remarks to
the ship owners misreported by the radical Liverpool
Mercury. It added to his difficulties with Canning and
especially Wellington that summer.[97]

His main pre-session concerns were the deplorable
state of the revenue, the Catholic question and the
state of Ireland.[98] He had invoked the order in council
on corn during the recess, and as agreed beforehand
with Liverpool, Canning, Peel and Wellington, and in
cabinet subsequently, he moved the necessary indemnity bill, 24 Nov. 1826. It substituted 'an open trade
for prohibition' and regulated it with descending and
ascending scales, based on a 70s. remunerative price,
with corn flowing freely from 65s. but inhibited at
60s. It also set scales for pulses and inferior grains.[99]
According to Agar Ellis, 'he spoke ill, as did the country
gentlemen who followed him', and although the 'resolutions were agreed to nem. con.', Tierney observed
that unlike Canning, he had not gained ground recently
in the House and remained 'sadly abused as well as his
doctrines'.[100] Harried by Sir Henry Parnell to produce
import returns, 30 Nov., by Lord Folkestone on corn,
1 Dec., and by Hume on machinery exports, 6 Dec.,
he also had to comment on the dealings of the Arigna
Mining Company and other 'wild' and 'mischievous'
joint-stock schemes his colleagues had speculated in,
5 Dec. 1826. He did not escape the wave of intrigue
and sickness which swept through the cabinet after the
duke of York's funeral in January 1827, and was said

by Lady Palmerston to be in 'a very sickly state' from a 'constant inflammation of the trachea, and general derangement, and the moment he gets the least better and is able to move out of his bedroom, they come and talk to him about business and lay him up again'.[101] His recovery was slow, but, with Canning's illness worse, when a stroke disabled Liverpool he rescheduled the debates on corn and Catholics 'under the shadow of Liverpool's authority, though in abeyance' and, being housebound, hosted cabinet business meetings with Bathurst, Peel, Robinson and Wellington, and arranged for Thomas Frankland Lewis to represent Gladstone on the Berwick election committee (which unseated Gladstone).[102] He paired for Catholic relief, 6 Mar. 1827, and his 'accidental absence' was seen as an unavoidable factor in its defeat.[103] Binning, who saw him that day, found him 'very weak, and it is a poor little voice that comes from his chest, which is, and has long been sadly oppressed'.[104] He correctly predicted that the loss of Liverpool in the Lords would be 'a great blow to the corn question' which, as the main target of the agriculturists' hostility, he was ill placed to introduce in the Commons.[105] Barred by the City, the 'Protestants and corn aristocracy' from the exchequer his friends sought for him, the anti-Catholic exodus led by Wellington and Peel and the subsequent Lansdowne Whig adhesions to Canning's ministry afforded him little prospect of promotion. With Williams Wynn *in situ* and support for a Liverpool by-election as yet uncertain, he remained at the board of trade 'for the present' and 'because it is that against which an attack is threatened'.[106]

The assault on Canning's liberal economic policy and Huskisson's 'Reciprocity Acts' was enshrined in a motion for a select committee on the distressed shipping industry, announced on 21 Feb. 1827. Entrusted to Gascoyne, with Canning's office secretary Henry Thomas Liddell, representing the Tyne ship owners, as seconder, it was backed by favourable petitions from all the major ports and was moved on 7 May. Responding in a triumphant two-and-a-half-hour speech, after Charles Poulett Thomson had prepared the ground, Huskisson used statistics culled from different returns to Gascoyne's to contradict his account of recent trading losses and decline. Highlighting the achievements of his liberal policies, he reviewed and assessed the petitions submitted and made comparisons with silk, timber and other trades. He did not shy from dealing with their Irish and colonial dimensions, including slavery. The Great Yarmouth, Newcastle, Bristol and London Members, the agriculturists Wodehouse and Curwen, and Baring, Bernal and Peel were among those (about 40) whom

he won over during the debate and who openly withdrew their support from Gascoyne.[107] Encouraged by this endorsement of his policy and fêted,[108] he opposed Whitmore's motion for inquiry into the East India trade, a bid to secure equalization of the sugar duties, 15 May, and denied another on manufacturing distress to Edward Davies Davenport, 14 June. The attack had, however, switched to agriculture and to the Lords, where Wellington wrecked his corn bill by raising the pivot price from 60 to 66s., 1 June, supposedly in accordance with his written instructions of 24 May. Humiliated, he was castigated by Canning, the bill's pilot in the Commons, and engaged in open correspondence with the duke, which discredited both sides and proved Huskisson was correct. He quoted from their letters (as Wellington had done in the Lords) when supporting Canning's abortive corn resolutions, 18 June.[109] As his health was deteriorating rapidly, the king authorized his pension to be increased from £1,800 to £3,000, should he retire, and he went abroad on his doctor's orders for three months' complete rest.[110] Edward Ellice* informed his brother-in-law Lord Grey: 'From what the papers say, one would suppose Huskisson's mind was affected. His loss would be felt everywhere, however much people may differ as to the extent he carries his principles and his policy'.[111] Warning Granville, in Paris, to expect him, Huskisson wrote:

> Our session is now over, and our difficulties postponed. They were formidable enough without the necessity of trying our strength again upon a new corn bill at the commencement of the next session. However, I shall not despair of getting people into better humour if Canning keeps his health, and the king remains firm.[112]

News of Canning's death on 8 Aug. 1827 reached him in Switzerland on the 15th in letters from Granville and the treasury secretary Planta, who asked him to 'give us your best assistance'.[113] Travelling through Basle, he missed the couriers sent out to him. He arrived at the Paris embassy, to be briefed by Lambton and Granville, who had corresponded with their friends, 'shocked, fatigued and agitated', 20 Aug. It was too late for him to attend Canning's funeral.[114] He knew before he reached London on the 28th that Lord Goderich (Robinson) had kissed hands as premier on the 13th, that the Canningite-Whig coalition risked collapse unless the reluctant Sturges Bourne could be persuaded to take the exchequer instead of Herries, the king's choice, and that he was expected to resolve this impasse. The colonial office and leadership of the House were his, as 'the only person competent'.[115] Friends and foes feared lest what Croker termed his 'health ... disposition and habits would prevent his accepting'. Sturges Bourne, Dudley, the Grants, Lord Seaford (Ellis), Wilmot Horton, Frankland Lewis, Planta, Lord Howard de Walden and most of his ministerial colleagues were anxious that he should.[116] Holland and Baring for the Whigs suggested Althorp as an impractical alternative.[117] For the Tories, Peel's brother-in-law George Dawson* revived talk of Huskisson's stock-jobbing, and Arbuthnot intimated to Peel, 25 Aug.:

> We all know Huskisson well. Had he, upon coming home, found that the duke had refused the command, he would not I think have liked to embark with so feeble a government, but now I should not be at all surprised if he persuaded the Whigs to acquiesce in Herries's appointment'.[118]

The Whig James Abercromby*, for different reasons, agreed:

> He is a man of resource. But all my reflections lead to the conclusion that he is hostile. Canning being gone, he sees that he has no real protection against the growing influence and power of the Whigs, whom he hates and fears and is determined at all hazards to keep them out.[119]

He had decided by the 24th that retirement was no option. Accepting Goderich's offer two days later he wrote:

> I find myself upon the treasury bench almost the sole survivor not only of the generation under which I first entered it, but also of that which immediately succeeded Mr. Pitt's ministry and of which I was the contemporary. In the short space of six months the country has been deprived of Lord Liverpool and Mr. Canning, both born in the same year as myself, and both, I firmly believe, in a great degree prematurely destroyed by the anxiety and toil of public life. My labours, it is true, in point of importance, have been as dust in the balance compared to theirs; but however insignificant, they have not been the less wearing or incessant. The result has been that the greater part of these last six months has been passed by me in a very serious state of illness, and the unavoidable neglect of the public duties of my situation.[120]

He had met Tierney and the Whig peers Carlisle, Devonshire and Lansdowne by arrangement directly he returned, before going to Windsor.[121] Though 'harassed beyond measure', he impressed Lansdowne with his 'agreeableness, sagacity and firmness', but he proved as unwilling as Sturges Bourne, whose desertion he condemned, to take the exchequer as a way out: 'in that office I should lose the only chance of keeping well with the king and of acquiring his confidence'.[122] Although prepared to serve under Goderich without the Whigs, by telling Lansdowne otherwise

he persuaded them to swallow Herries and mediated between them.[123] The king's preference for a 'coalition with the old Tories' did not elude him.[124] Lord Grey condemned the arrangement, but Brougham was ambivalent, dangerous and unplaced.[125] Ellice thought he would 'lead the House well, if Brougham is got rid of, as 'Peel will do nothing against him', and informed James Brougham*:

> I sincerely wish success to Huskisson and *his* ministry and pray that prudence will create another miracle in inspiring the king with truth, constancy and firmness to support them through all the struggles and difficulties before them.[126]

Others noted the Canningites' lack of parliamentary influence, which Holland, who coveted the foreign secretaryship but was offered nothing, could have provided.[127] Consulted only over minor appointments, Huskisson agreed to take Edward Smith Stanley* as his under-secretary when Wilmot Horton (whom he had hoped to promote) vacated, and tried to find employment for Stafford's son Lord Francis Leveson Gower*.[128] Concern for his health persisted, and he feared that he had taken on a task beyond his strength.[129] But his was a popular appointment and the high point of his career.[130] The Whig John Fazakerley* wrote:

> My hope, and confidence and comfort of every sort is in Huskisson. I consider him not only to entertain all poor Canning's better opinions, but to be free from some of ... the ... prejudices of his friend and chief, and to want nothing but power to make him at least as efficient as a minister. But I tremble for his health'.[131]

As leader of the House, he was consulted on the Lanarkshire by-election and corresponded frequently with Binning on Scotland, where support for the ministry declined.[132] His departmental problems included refusals by the Jamaican and other assemblies to implement Canning's slavery resolutions and Wellington's fury after he failed to consult him as commander-in-chief before naming the duke of Gordon as governor of Lower Canada.[133] His early confidence in the foreign secretary Dudley's ability to handle the Navarino crisis, 'a nice kettle of fish', which would 'plague us to death until it gets settled', turned to despair when in late November he considered its implications for the coming session and realized that colleagues ignored his advice. The ministry's weakness troubled him: 'We have more heads (or rather noses) with less of the real work in the cabinet than I ever recollect'.[134] He was, according to Howard de Walden the only purposeful cabinet member ... the mainstay of the government and without him they could not go on a week ... In fact he is the person who directs everything, and I think the only one who understands anything about foreign politics.[135]

He took charge of the Canning pension and Kilbrahan peerage legislation, a potential problem as the revenue was in deficit and subject to finance committee scrutiny.[136] On 29 Nov. 1827 he warned the master of the mint Tierney that their choice of Althorp to chair the latter and discussion with Herries on its membership had been leaked. Herries delayed a month before making Althorp's appointment a resignation matter, and the wrangle, closely following another over overtures to Brougham, Holland and Wellesley, eventually destroyed the tottering ministry. Goderich resigned twice. Huskisson thrice drafted and threatened resignation, having between times dispatched summonses for the 1828 session and remained at the heart of negotiations between the king, Goderich, Harrowby and Lansdowne.[137] To Granville he described it as a 'worse scene, if possible, than that into which I was drawn on my arrival from the continent.[138] He explained in a draft resignation letter, 19 Dec.:

I can no longer conceal to myself that councils which ought to be, and which the king specially directs should be, held most strictly secret are not so kept. If on one occasion they are divulged to newspapers to secure any particular purpose, am I not justified in apprehending that in others they are betrayed to other quarters to serve some other purpose? Against such risks I cannot hope to be able to conduct the affairs of the government in the ... Commons. They open a door to intrigue against which no minister can contend, and no reputation can be safe. Neither can I venture to be one of the depositaries of confidence, which, however violated, must excite suspicion; and that suspicion may fall upon myself.[139]

With the ministry doomed, he wrote similarly, 29 Dec. 1827, 4 Jan. 1828, after seeing Palmerston and Wellington. Convinced that they could not go on, and of the king's secretary Knighton's intriguing, his official resignation letter (4 Jan.), which he knew would be fatal to the ministry, alluded directly to Herries, who had again agitated the finance committee, and made no mention of the Commons leadership.[140] Negotiations with Anglesey, Goderich and lord chancellor Lyndhurst ensued. Goderich vainly encouraged Herries, who denounced Huskisson, Lansdowne, Tierney and Holland, to yield and the ministry lingered until 8 Jan.[141] Having trusted Anglesey to expose 'all the petty intrigues and miserable weakness which have brought matters to their present helpless state', Huskisson was sorry when the latter's involvement

ceased.[142] Caricatured hanging on to Wellington's galloping charger scattering the Whigs, he was recruited by Lord Lyndhurst and the home secretary Peel (his replacement as leader of the House) the following week to serve 'with but not under' him as the Wellington ministry's colonial secretary. He had abandoned the Whigs, but the 'triumvirate', whom he consulted throughout, were in place: Dudley as foreign secretary, Palmerston at the war office and Charles Grant as president of the board of trade.[143] They demanded a free vote on Catholic emancipation, secured Herries's exclusion from the exchequer (he went to the mint) and Althorp's inclusion on the finance committee. Frankland Lewis, Smith Stanley and Scarlett (who resigned), were expected to remain in office and accept Huskisson's leadership. His wife's cousin William Lamb stayed on as Irish secretary and Planta remained at the treasury, but Leveson Gower initially refused office 'by the desire of his father' and Sturges Bourne again declined.[144] The Tory Lord Lowther* informed his father, 16 Jan. 1828:

There is a considerable difference of opinion amongst our best friends as to the admission of Huskisson. He will bring some votes, and *contra*. It is stated that his forming part of the government will indispose and make 90 country gentlemen as shy as hawks, and that the late cabinet intrigues only began when he was admitted into it. This is the theme of debate, but I don't think his wings would be so clipped ... Upon the whole I think it would be better to have him.[145]

The duke of Rutland and Sir Henry Hardinge* wrote similarly of the need to keep Huskisson in order: 'in short he is the dry rot of any cabinet into which he enters, but then he leads about 30 votes and is really an able fellow, and Peel is so short of aid in the Lower House'.[146] Non-Canningite Whigs condemned the Canningites in and out of office,[147] but Ellice, Hobhouse and Lord John Russell were among the few that 'at first' condoned Huskisson's conduct.[148] Tierney was disgusted:

The compromise between Herries and Huskisson is most curious. The objections urged against the former were pointed, it now seems, rather against the office than the man, for Mr. Herries appears to Huskisson a harmless cabinet minister when changed into the master of the mint.[149]

Carlisle's exclusion and Huskisson's failure to insist on leading the House caused a furore among their friends.[150] The unforgiving Lady Canning helped to accentuate the party split and gave Huskisson, whom she charged with 'delinquency and apostacy', a bad press.[151] He left London in late January suffering from stress and a bad chest.[152] He was anxious to reinforce Canning's London Treaty of July 1827, and in cabinet forced through euphemistic descriptions of Navarino and Portugal for inclusion in the king's speech. He also insisted on a government corn bill, with a view to enacting that forfeited in 1827.[153]

On 5 Feb. 1828 he went to Liverpool to be re-elected. The arrangements had been made when a resolution of support for Canning was carried the previous May, and he was asked to explain his changing political allegiance.[154] He sent Peel the following account:

> We had long speeches from some Whigs who had received their lessons from town; and in reply to which I was obliged to go into explanations much more at length than I could have wished. Lord Molyneux[†] was put in nomination, but no poll being demanded, everything was over by three o'clock, and without the least symptom of violence.[155]

However, his speech, as circulated in the press, greatly offended the Whigs, Tories and Lady Canning. In it he castigated Goderich, who reciprocated with a motion in the Lords, 11 Feb., inflated his status in Wellington's ministry and projected himself as the true heir to Canning. To make matters worse, he spoke as if he was in charge of the corn bill and commercial policy. Having no notes of the speech, he found the newspaper allegations difficult to deny.[156] He took Dudley's Downing Street house for the session.[157] He rallied to Peel's defence on the sinking find, 11 Feb., but his remarks, which echoed Maberly's, alarmed his colleagues.[158] He justified the anodyne selection of papers on Navarino and wanted 'Codrington's freedom from blame understood', 14 Feb., and pursued the matter in cabinet, 6, 10 Mar.[159] Contrary to his wishes, and certainly against Wellington's, on 15 Feb. he was added to the finance committee. He helped to carry the abolition of the sinking fund, and their fifth report, published on 10 July, exonerated his conduct in cutting the excise duties.[160] Briefed beforehand by Littleton and Lord Normanby*, he and Herries substantiated their explanations of the ministerial changes with correspondence, 18 Feb. His account, which highlighted Herries's silence, 2-26 Dec. 1827, accorded well with Carlisle's private memorandum and seemed the more reliable. In what was generally considered a satisfactory performance, he made no mention of Lyndhurst, Anglesey or any intermediary, and tried to correct assumptions based on his Liverpool election speech by citing relevant correspondence sent to him by the leading Liverpool reformer, the Rev. William Shepherd.[161] A caricature of the debate depicted Rothschild bribing Herries with Knighton's collusion, while 'a busy Husky fellow' ruled the king.[162]

He defended the corporation-sponsored Liverpool dock bill, 25 Feb., reluctantly acquiesced in the cabinet's decision to uphold the Test Acts as a government question and divided and apparently spoke against repeal, 26 Feb., but later complained that his 'views were misrepresented out of doors', 14 Mar. 1828. Agar Ellis and Lord George Cavendish Bentinck* thought his first speech 'wretched' and his argument that repeal would jeopardize Catholic relief 'contemptible'.[163] On corn, the issue that almost brought down the administration in March, he could not see beyond the 1827 bill wrecked by Wellington. He failed to steer the cabinet close enough to his scheme or to satisfy Grant or Wellington. He proposed stabilizing prices at 64-66s. a quarter, and threatened resignation should this be refused. Grant, in the event, avoided the debates.[164] He discussed the issue with George IV, 28 Mar., but according to Ellenborough the king only feigned a wish to keep him.[165] The duke of Bedford, writing on 31 Mar. to Holland, quipped: 'Corn will I think very likely upset the ministry. I always suspected that Huskisson would die by the sheaf'.[166] Deputizing for Grant, he quibbled over the statistics used by the agriculturists Waldo Sibthorp and Lethbridge to criticize his 1826 and 1827 bills, 31 Mar.; and when Grant moved the government bill in committee, 22 Apr. 1828, he fielded the agriculturists' questions himself and divided against Edward Portman II (202-58). He would not concede that the pivot price had changed, and tried to justify the fluctuation in the upward and downward scales which Canning had tried to carry for him. Smith Stanley condemned the tactic as 'disingenuous', while Peel and Herries could barely contain their laughter. Hobhouse, after discussing it with him next day, described him as 'a shabby unprincipled man, and cares not what he says'.[167] He and Grant sought Wellington's sanction to support John Benett's amendment for 'a higher duty at the low prices, and a lower duty at high prices' than the government's scale, but the tactic failed.[168] Citing from Jacob's 1826 report, and puffing his 1827 bill, he hinted at support, but failed to divide in Benett's minority.

He answered questions on the colonial assemblies and slavery, 27 Feb., 5, 6 Mar., and promised to support a bill 'to improve the civil and moral conditions of slaves', based on Canning's 1823 resolutions, 6 Mar. 1828. In cabinet, 4 Apr., he suggested keeping manumission compulsory and permitting the privy council to authorize slave transfers.[169] He defended the Canada Company, 27 Mar. His New South Wales bill was criticized for failing to provide trial by jury, 1, 18 Apr., an omission he justified in view of the colony's scattered population and high percentage of convicts. He gave qualified support to Wilmot Horton's emigration bills, 4 Mar., 17 Apr. Proposing a select committee on the Canadian government, 2 May, and backed by Wilmot Horton and Smith Stanley, he traced the background of the 1791 Act and, warning against making population density the determinant of representation, he described how it had left the French seigneuries overrepresented compared to the English ones. In June Lord Durham expressed astonishment at Huskisson's decision to make the matter one of open inquiry.[170] No longer trusted by Bathurst and Wellington, who found his meddling and obstinacy in cabinet irritating, especially on the Rideau Canal and foreign policy, Huskisson was, according to Ellenborough and Mrs. Arbuthnot, a target for ejection well before May.[171] The 3rd marquess of Londonderry, who blamed him for worrying his half-brother to his death, denounced him as 'this Machiavellian *parvenu*', the '*primum mobile* of all the Aeolian system', and 'Husky and his fag-end of the Canningites'.[172] He presented favourable petitions, 5 May, and spoke and voted for Catholic relief, 12 May. Lady Canning's fury remained unabated, despite his endeavours on her behalf and interviews with family members. He supported her brother-in-law the duke of Portland in cabinet (with Grant and Palmerston), 2, 5 May, when they failed to secure the £3,000 pension for two lives, but had it awarded to Canning's younger son.[173] In one of the best speeches for the pension bill he dwelt on Canning's political achievements, demonstrated the sacrifices he had made in turning down India and praised him 'above all Englishmen save Nelson', 13 May 1828.[174]

He found fault with Russell's proposal to transfer Penryn's franchise to Manchester, 24 Mar., but supported the principle behind the exchange. He vainly urged the postponement of the freeholders registration bill, 25 Mar., and opposed the Liverpool franchise bill, for which Smith Stanley presented a petition, 2 Apr., stating, 'it has never yet been held by this House desirable to give the franchise to a different class of voters, except for the purpose of punishing the former electors in cases of corruption'. He opposed it again, 9 June. On East Retford, 21 Mar., he maintained that the time had come to 'establish some general principle' for franchise transfer, and Lord Sandon duly claimed his vote for transferring the seats to Birmingham, 19 May. Backed by Dudley, Grant and Palmerston, he had stated in cabinet on the 17th that they 'must vote for a town', but on the morning of the 19th the cabinet agreed to follow Peel and support sluicing. In Grant's absence, Huskisson and Palmerston called for an adjournment until Penryn's fate was known.

Peel refused, and by not leaving the chamber with him they were counted in the minority. Huskisson's short speech argued that sluicing and a £20 ratepayer qualification would 'annihilate' the borough.[175] The votes caused a sensation. Huskisson's hasty draft to Wellington asking if he should resign was forwarded to the king as a formal resignation, and Wellington and the king denied him a second chance.[176] He later remarked: 'Where there is a will there is always a way. A most unimportant occurrence on a most trifling question afforded the way'.[177] Dudley, Grant and Palmerston resigned reluctantly and others, including Lamb, followed.[178] Among several caricatures, Huskisson was depicted in a fool's cap as 'a naughty boy turned out of school', being ordered back to Liverpool.[179] He spoke for government on the civil list while correspondence flew, 20 May, but informed Gladstone on the 21st that 'the time is now arrived when I shall probably have more leisure to look after my health, as well as other neglected concerns'.[180] Giving a personal perspective to Granville on the 23rd, he explained:

> I now incline to think it was a hasty step, taken under feelings of excitement, and that it would have been more discreet to have waited till daylight. At the same time I do not believe that the most cautious and guarded letter would have produced a different result, because ... the duke has his answer to the explanation which he treats as offensive. Be that as it may, this hasty letter (marked however *private and confidential*) was sent off in a breathless hurry to the king, and without any previous communication with me, as a positive absolute resignation. It is a breach of all the relations of confidence between a minister and the head of the government to have made such a use of a letter so marked.[181]

He received letters of sympathy, and the consensus was that he had been hard done by.[182] In Liverpool the *Albion* deprecated Wellington's 'cashiering of Mr. Huskisson and the retirement of his friends from office in consequence of that act of military severity'.[183] On 2 June, in a bitter and acrimonious speech, he gave the House a full account of events since 21 Mar., including all his correspondence with Wellington. He said that Peel had been well aware of the problem which the division on 19 May posed for him, and referred to his resignation in May 1822 and different treatment by Londonderry and Liverpool. He regretted his loss of office and influence on trade, commerce and industry, but acknowledged that he had lost the confidence of important colleagues. Peel, firm in reply, spoke of the painful failure of the coalition and maintained that Huskisson's precipitate action had given East Retford a singular importance.[184] Ellenborough noted that he 'spoke in a tone of exacerbation which will do him no good. The opposition did not take him up'. Ministers carried the division (by 258-152).[185] Lord Seaford and Wilmot Horton echoed Lord Morley's complaint to Granville that Huskisson was 'guilty of great omission in involving the interests of so many persons without consulting any of them'.[186] According to lists which Palmerston drafted, 3-7 June, the so-called Huskissonite party, or 'ejected liberals', could rely on at least 26 Members and 10 peers. Lord Colchester estimated their Commons strength at 21-35, but supplied only 17 names.[187]

Huskisson spoke against inquiry into small notes, warning that it might trigger a panic, 3, 5 June. He acquiesced in the continuance of the sugar duties for one year and, in view of his differences with Grant on their equalization, he deferred discussion of American involvement in the West Indian trade. He presented the Calcutta merchants' petition for equalizing the duties on all East and West Indian imports but deemed further discussion premature, 16 June. He replayed the shipping debate with Gascoyne to his own advantage next day and defended his policies as a minister when the Hull shipping petition was presented, 24 June. He intervened on the New South Wales bill, 20 June, Buckingham House expenditure, 23 June, and steam packets, 25 June. He supported his successor Sir George Murray's motion perpetuating the Slave Laws Consolidation Act, 1 July, and moved for a copy of his own letter of 22 Sept. 1827 to the governor of Jamaica. He divided with ministers on the ordnance estimates, 4 July, and defended his policies on Canada, 7, 14 July, and the silk trade, 14, 15 July, when opposition tried to exploit his humiliation. Citing from his correspondence with Gladstone, he ordered papers and accounts on American tariffs, 18 July 1828.[188] Before leaving for the continent that month, he arranged to bring in a new recruit (William Ewart) for Bletchingley.[189] To Denison he confided that he had thought it best 'to be quiet this session', as many recommendations 'opposed while they came from him', had subsequently been adopted.[190]

Huskisson returned from Switzerland in November 1828 in better health than at any time since 1826. He saw nothing extraordinary in Peel's Liverpool visit and was encouraged by growing talk of Catholic emancipation.[191] With Goderich, Melbourne (Lamb), Palmerston and Planta, he mustered his party at Eartham in late November. Their exact number is not reported.[192] Lady Cowper and others thought that his appetite for office had waned but that he remained as 'eager about politics' as ever. He considered an alliance

with the Holland House Whigs, and was preparing speeches on East Retford and Portugal. On Catholic emancipation, he anticipated that 'cabinet will neither originate nor attempt anything, except by every means of indiscreet influence and insinuation, to procure a majority'.[193] Following another 'Eartham conference' in January 1829, he was confident no Canningite would be 'backward or lukewarm' on emancipation, but 'the course of the Canning-hating Whigs ... [who] threw the country into the hands of the duke', troubled him.[194] On 6 Feb. he endorsed the Liverpool Dissenters' pro-emancipation petition, whose presenter John Wood criticized his opposition to Test Acts repeal. He also now praised Peel for conceding emancipation and endorsed his policy on Greece but not on Portugal.[195] Greville found him in 'good humour and spirits but rather bitter' at dinner at Grant's, 8 Feb., where they, Granville, Melbourne, Palmerston, Warrender 'and one or two more' agreed to support Duncombe's motion on Terceira.[196] Provoked by Henry Bankes, he spoke for the Irish unlawful societies bill, but added that he condoned it only to secure emancipation, 10 Feb. His interventions in favour of the measure were well received, 16, 24 Feb., 3, 6 Mar. Grey's son Lord Howick commended him for pressing the 'absolute necessity of carrying the question and the impossibility of any person in its favour consenting to form part of a neutral government', 3 Mar., which Lady Holland noted 'cuts off all hope of the king getting him'.[197] Clashing frequently with Gascoyne, he presented and endorsed petitions from Liverpool and elsewhere, 6, 9, 17, 19, 20 Mar., but he deplored the time-wasting involved, 19 Mar. To accusations of inconsistency, he criticized the disfranchisement of Irish 40s. freeholders 'as an enemy of parliamentary reform', and said that he regarded 'emancipation as uniting, consolidating and strengthening all the great interests of the empire' and reform as 'tending to destroy [not only] the church establishment, but every other important institution'. According to Howick, he added that he would not vote against the franchise bill.[198] He spoke, 23, 24, 27 Mar., and divided for the relief bill, 30 Mar. He was for permitting Daniel O'Connell to take his seat without swearing the oath of supremacy, 18 May, but wanted the issue deferred, 19 May. Attending to Liverpool business, he presented at least 40 minor petitions, 30 Mar.-12 June, including one against importing foreign boots, which he refused to endorse, and took charge of the St. Martin's church bill. In several speeches (9 Mar., 13 Apr., 8 May) he defended his policy on silk in 1824 and a gradual transition to free trade. Before voting for the transfer of East Retford's seats to Birmingham, 5 May, he joined in the clamour for its disfranchisement and argued that such towns as 'Birmingham must be represented when issues like the renewal of the East India Company and Bank charters are considered'. Supporting Peel, he said he would move to kill Villiers Stuart's resolutions for introducing the English poor law in Ireland, 7 May. Next day and on the 11th he clashed frequently on the budget with the banker Matthias Attwood, Baring, Poulett Thomson and Ward. He presented and endorsed Liverpool's petitions against renewing the East India charter and, opposing monopoly 'on political grounds', stated that if India was to be a permanent possession, the happiness of its people mattered, 12 May, 5 June. He also supported Whitmore's inquiry motion and welcomed its likely concession, 14 May. He defended his conduct as colonial secretary when Smith Stanley presented a petition for jury trial in Canada that day, and again when Labouchere ordered papers, 5 June. On corn, he doubted if the time for major reform had arrived, 19 May, and warned that a fixed permanent duty would be 'a perfect delusion' as protection for the agriculturist and impossible to levy. His definitive speech of 1 June on Portugal traced the origins of the dispute, defended Canning's foreign policy and gave a detailed account of his dealings with foreign ministers and consular officials. He portrayed Britain as deceived by Dom Miguel, argued that British intervention against Queen Maria at Terceira had been wrong and ordered papers to demonstrate that Canning had never given advice on the acceptance of the Portuguese constitution. He refuted Attwood's allegations that Members put party advantage before action on distress in 1825-6, 12 June 1829.

Speculation persisted that Wellington wanted to strengthen his ministry, and of a fresh approach to Melbourne or Palmerston, but reports of an overture to Huskisson were groundless.[199] Assessing his party and its potential, the secretary at war Hardinge wrote, 6 July:

> Huskissonian or liberal Tories ... unite the largest number of efficient public men. They embrace youth and talent in the House of Commons. They have a strong hold in the affection which the king displays for them; especially if they could join with them that portion of Whiggism connected with the House of Cavendish, which supported Canning's government. ... If they had such a partisan as the duke of Cumberland near the king's person and that ... [he] took as much pains for them as he is doing for his Tory adherents ... e're long he would establish them, making the Ultra Tories also join their standard. But the duke of Cumberland dislikes the Huskisson tribe, and rallying what he calls the king's friends, he makes his own party the sole consideration ... I believe the government the king would fancy, as most at his disposal, would be

formed out of the liberal Tory party, and His Majesty has even looked (as I am told) to Lord Melbourne as leader in the Lords, and Lord Palmerston in the Commons. It is, however, the policy of this junta not to commit themselves in any violent opposition, because they think it might widen them from the sovereign, who, they flatter themselves, will call on them in the first crisis. Their game is to remain '*en potence*'. They are satisfied of the duke's dislike. They see no hope of approximation, and they return the feelings the government displays towards them, with the most secret and cordial hate. Palmerston's able speeches at the close of the session were warmly eulogized, *in private*, by Huskisson and Co., and this is, I presume, the sort of battery that will be opened next session from that quarter.[200]

During the recess Huskisson visited Liverpool where he discussed politics with his merchant backers and free trade with Lord Harrowby.[201] He met Wellington at Sudbourne in October and Goulburn in November 1829, so encouraging rumours of a junction, which were duly lampooned, but he was 'indifferent to office', and believed that Wellington would meet Parliament unstrengthened and should be attacked on foreign policy.[202] After declining to join Wellington's ministry without him, on 3 Nov. Palmerston informed Lady Cowper that he had been told that

> there is so strong a prejudice among the country gentlemen that it would hardly be possible to bring them to join with him. ... I told them exactly the manner in which he and I had been thrown together; that we agreed generally in opinions and therefore were acting together, but that I looked upon him as entirely free to act for himself without reference to me, and held myself also equally free as to him.[203]

Convinced that the economic downturn was systemic, not cyclical, Huskisson complained before the 1830 session that Wellington 'does not allow that there is anything wrong in the state of the country' and wrongly assumed that he would fob off the distressed farmers with inquiry, as in 1820-22: 'This is always a convenient course for government. It gives them the chapter of accidents, and wears away the session without anything being done'.[204]

Confirming his opposition in a 'very bitter' speech drawing on his experience of distress in Sussex, he supported the amendment regretting its omission from the address, 4 Feb. 1830. He did not expect Wellington to propose a remedy.[205] Writing to Denison, he argued that the 'real evil of the country is not want of money ... but the want of profit in all the pursuits of industry' and that the remedy would 'only be found in a more general reduction of rents and a revision of ... taxation'.[206] He presented favourable petitions and demanded inquiry into the East India Company's monopoly, 9 Feb., was named to the select committee that day and presented further petitions, 11 Mar. He again advocated the transfer of East Retford's seats to Birmingham, 11 Feb. Equating the enfranchisement of large industrial towns to concessions on the Test Acts and Catholic emancipation, he explained: 'my principle is to deal with the evil before us in order to confine the remedy, if possible, to the immediate case, and to avoid a sweeping reform on principles too abstract and general'. Durham and Ellice thought his speech most 'hostile and mischievous' to the government, as it 'produced a great effect'.[207] On 12 Feb. the Huskissonites agreed to 'keep clear of all factious opposition, maintain strict independence, scrutinize measures on their own merit and avoid with all care petty causes of squabbling with government or anyone else'.[208] Probably the most active group in opposition, they eschewed all talk of coalition.[209] Still refusing to treat the enfranchisement of large towns as a party issue, Huskisson strongly advocated it for Birmingham, Leeds and Manchester, 23 Feb. He also realized that amid increasing calls for reform, waiting for transfers from corrupt boroughs had proved futile.[210] He demanded a comprehensive review of excise regulations on presenting petitions from the Liverpool tobacco trade, 2 Mar., and was named to the committee, 14 May. He presented petitions for Jewish emancipation, 11 Mar., 4 May, and supported Robert Grant's bill for it, 5 Apr., 17 May. He had annoyed Althorp on 9 Mar. by pre-empting the revived Whig opposition's intended criticism of government policy on pensions and superannuations, and his speech supporting Palmerston's unsuccessful motion for information on Portugal, 10 Mar., was considered 'very bad [and] dull'. Howick dismissed it as the 'most tiresome twaddle'.[211] He criticized Frankland Lewis's appointment as navy treasurer, but praised him personally, 12 Mar. Contributing to the debate on the state of the nation, 18 Mar., he cautioned against overemphasis on the currency and free trade as causes of distress and advocated inquiry into Irish poverty and banking.[212] Continuing his crusade against Wellington, he divided with the Whig opposition on taxation, but without endorsing a property tax, 25 Mar.[213] Responding to Peel's criticism of Canning's foreign policy, when intervention in Terceira was discussed, 28 Apr., he said it had been justified by a contravention of international law and that policy on Portugal was similarly defective. The speeches were regarded as a Whig-Canningite triumph, but the division (191-78) was a poor one.[214] He maintained close contact with the Whigs through Littleton and Sir

James Graham, whose motion for returns of privy councillors' emoluments he supported, 14 May.[215] He voted for Labouchere's resolutions on Canada, 25 May, but not for parliamentary reform, 28 May. He was not, as expected, entrusted with a select committee on banking, and bringing up petitions for currency reform, 3 June, he criticized paper currencies and promised to instigate a committee on banking in the next Parliament, 25 Mar., 6, 7 Apr., 8 June.[216] He voted to abolish the death penalty for forgery, 7 June. Petitions for action on vagrancy, 21 May, and for a reduction in the freight charges on bullion, 17 May, were among the many he presented from Liverpool that session. In a major speech supporting the Liverpool-Mexico Merchants' Association petition, 20 May, he traced the development of the trade since independence, regretted its recent interruptions and projected Mexico and its 7,000,000 inhabitants as a potential market and base from which to curb American aggrandisement. His request for information on Greece, 10 June, drew a hostile response from Peel, for he had cited extracts from particular letters which exposed ministers' botched attempt to effect reconciliation between Turkey and Russia.[217] He spoke briefly on the reciprocity agreement with Portugal, 15 June. He urged Chandos to withdraw his motion on the sugar duties until government's proposals were announced and, perceiving scope for reduction, he moved his own, 14 June. His speech of 21 June, proposing a tariff reduction from 27 to 20s. was considered 'almost fatal' to the ministry.[218] He stressed that his position as Liverpool Member had given him inside knowledge of the West India planters' plight and, criticizing the government's meddling, he urged that sugar production be boosted and used for spirits:

> We cannot deal with the vast commerce of this country with its immense and complicated many concerns, with the varied interests connected with its civil government and foreign policy, by a system of meeting every temporary difficulty by some expedient just suited to the occasion. We cannot put forward laws, as you would an advance guard, with instructions to fall back, or go to the right or left, as the occasion may require. There must be something like a well-adjusted, organized plan, undertaken deliberately, pursued firmly.

His amendment was defeated by 182-144. He quibbled over details of the government's and Chandos's tariff scales, 30 June, and although taken to task by Peel, he persevered in his attempt to secure a reduction in the sugar duties, 1, 2 July. He supported Littleton's bill to abolish truck payments, 23 June, 1, 5 July. He objected to deferring the regency question to the next Parliament and supported Robert Grant's motion for its immediate consideration, 5 July.[219] He also spoke on Irish distress and immigration, 13 July 1830. Speculation over his party's future and allegiance persisted. Both Grey and Wellington had recently made overtures to Melbourne and Palmerston, who feared they would 'lose character' by rejoining Wellington's administration.[220]

Huskisson was 'seized with a strangury' and other distressing symptoms at the king's funeral, was bled profusely and required surgery.[221] Recovering afterwards at his new house in Carlton Terrace, he remained 'wretchedly ill ... weak ... and very thin'. The Liverpool election was consequently delayed, but he remained unable to attend and was returned *in absentia* after a token poll.[222] He sympathized with Denison and Finlay in defeat and regretted that Ewart lacked a seat.[223] From Eartham and Cowes, where he was glad not to see the new king, he arranged to meet colleagues and rivals at the opening of the Liverpool-Manchester railway on 15 Sept.[224] He thought the Wellington ministry 'ought not to stand the shock of the next session', and wrote to Graham, whom he hoped to meet, 26 Aug.:

> The great captain [will] be there with all his tail. Of course one object is to throw me into the background at this ceremony; another is by extending his visit to Manchester ... [to] bid for a little popularity before Parliament meet.[225]

Wellington and members of all parties witnessed his fatal accident at Parkside, near Newton, struck down by the *Rocket* after panicking and 'trying to fling himself out of its way'. He spent his last hours at Eccles vicarage, his left leg reduced to pulp, and died that evening.[226] Arbuthnot, who was near him, wrote: 'If poor Huskisson had but stood still with his back towards our machine nothing could have happened'.[227] The inquest jury recorded a verdict of accidental death and 'acquitted the engineers and machinery of all blame'. He was buried with great pomp in the new St. James's cemetery in Liverpool, where, as in Chichester, a memorial was erected in his honour.[228] At Chichester, 13 Nov. 1830, their drafter, the Liverpool Parliament Office secretary Wainwright, testified to the authenticity of two holograph codicils had Huskisson made to his will, added after the accident. It was proved under £60,000 in the province of Canterbury and £40,000 in the province of York, 22 Nov. 1830. As he was childless, his Worcestershire and Staffordshire estates passed to his brothers and their heirs. He left his unentailed Sussex property and the bulk of his fortune to his widow, who died in 1856 worth £40,000.[229]

The manner of Huskisson's death made a great impression on his contemporaries. Tributes flowed, but within hours most acknowledged that his loss facilitated a political realignment.[230] His former partisan Thomas Spring Rice* wrote to Peel's brother-in-law George Dawson*, 20 Sept.:

> What an awful event has been the death of Huskisson. In point of knowledge and of that kind of knowledge just now most wanting, knowledge of commercial matters and political economy, he has not left his match behind. The Bank question, the East India question would all have brought him greatly prominent. The set-off was the want of confidence of all parties in his straightforwardness and sincerity. To *us* on the breaking up of Goderich's government he certainly did not act a chivalrous part. To Canning's personal friends he did not attach himself with the zeal that might have been expected. I leave you to decide your own cause of quarrel. But with all these defects, he was a mighty master in all the questions I have referred to and he is a prodigious loss to the country. Not so I think on party principles to his immediate clique. To them his unpopularity was a greater disadvantage than his abilities were a gain. This seems a paradox but the event will prove my prediction correct. One vessel may be over ballasted with gold as another with lead.[231]

Hardinge, then Irish secretary, fairly typically observed:

> He was a very agreeable, good natured man, and on all subjects very plausible and clever. If he had joined or not opposed the government, his views and measures would have been warped by the desire to please Liverpool at the expense of the state, but his death appears to me to be important as dissolving his party, and [as a means] of obtaining individuals [belonging to it] at less cost.[232]

By late September 1830, the Huskissonite party in the Commons was estimated by the Wellington administration at only 11.[233] Lamenting his loss and claiming 'a very sincere friendship for him', the duke of Gloucester added, 9 Oct.: 'I do no think it possible that the present administration can stand until Christmas and they have certainly not gained by the dissolution', or Huskisson's death.[234] He is generally recalled as portrayed by Greville, who knew him and had access to the kind and critical tributes paid to him:

> In society he was extremely agreeable, without much animation, generally cheerful, with a great deal of humour, information, and anecdote, gentlemanlike, unassuming, slow in speech, and with a downcast look, as if he avoided meeting anybody's gaze ... It is probably true that there is no man in Parliament, or perhaps out of it, so well versed in finance, commerce, trade and colonial matters, and that he is therefore a very great and irreparable loss. It is nevertheless remarkable that it is only within the last five

or six years that he acquired the great reputation which he latterly enjoyed. I do not think he was looked upon as more than a second-rate man till his speeches on the silk trade and the shipping interest; but when he became president of the board of trade he devoted himself with indefatigable application to the maturing and reducing to practice those commercial improvements with which his name is associated and to which he owes all his glory and most of his unpopularity.[235]

[1] There is no modern chronological biography of Huskisson. His life is treated kindly and thematically in A. Brady, *William Huskisson and Liberal Reform* (1928, 1967) and C.R. Fay, *Huskisson and his Age* (1951). Biographical articles of varying reliability are included in *Huskisson Speeches* ed. J. Wright, 3 vols. (1831) and *Huskisson Pprs.* ed. L. Melville (1931). B. Hilton, *Corn, Cash, Commerce* (1977) offers a detailed comprehensive survey of Huskisson's economic policy. S. Garfield, *The Last Journey of William Huskisson* (2002), combines biographical information with an account of the construction and opening of the Liverpool-Manchester railway. [2] *Greville Mems.* ii. 47-48. [3] [E. Leeves], 'Biog. Mem. of Huskisson', in *Huskisson Speeches*, i. 261-2. [4] *Session of Parl. 1825*, p. 470. [5] *HP Commons, 1790-1820*, iv. 270-6; J.E. Cookson, 'Canning's Pantheon', *History*, lxii (1977), 43-45; Ward, *Llandaff Letters*, 321; Add. 51655, Mackintosh to Lady Holland [27 Feb. 1827]. [6] P. Harling and P. Mandler, 'From fiscal military state to laissez-faire state', *JBS*, xxxii (1993), 61-62; *Countess Granville Letters*, i. 254; *Life of Campbell*, i. 402; *Lieven Letters*, 286. [7] *HP Commons, 1790-1820*, iv. 276-8. [8] *The Times*, 21 Feb., 21 Mar. 1820; J.R. McQuiston, 'Suss. Aristocrats and County Election of 1820', *EHR*, lxxxviii (1973), 534-58; Arundel Castle Archives, bdle. Fc 16, Holmes to Few, 10 Mar. 1820. [9] *Arbuthnot Corresp.* 14; Add. 38742, f. 6. [10] Dorset RO D/BKL, Bankes jnl. 116 (8 May 1820). [11] *The Times*, 10, 24 June 1820, 10 May 1827. [12] Add. 38742, ff. 29-46, 89-96, 109-14; *Huskisson Pprs.* 111-17; TNA 30/29/9/3/5-7. [13] Add. 38742, ff. 130, 146; Harewood mss WYL 250/8/26, Canning to wife, 24 Nov., 19 Dec. 1820; Buckingham, i. 93; *Lady Palmerston Letters*, 58. [14] TNA 30/58, Dacres Adams mss, T.P. Courtenay to Adams, 21 Dec.; NLW, Coedymaen mss, bdle. 29, Williams Wynn to Phillimore, 30 Dec. 1820. [15] *The Times*, 13, 20 Nov.; Harewood mss 26, Canning to wife, 24 Nov. 1820; Add. 38742, ff. 156, 171. [16] HLRO, Hist. Coll. 379, Grey Bennet diary, 14a. [17] *The Times*, 9, 19 June 1821. [18] Add. 38742, f. 125. [19] B. Semmell, *Rise of Free Trade Imperialism*, 137. [20] *PP* (1821), ix. 1-27; Add. 38743, ff. 148, 337-72; *The Times*, 15 June, 10 July; *Quarterly Rev.* xxv (1821), 466-70; Hilton, 104-9. [21] Le Marchant, *Althorp*, 220. [22] M.D. George, *Cat. of Pol. and Personal Satires*, x. 14195. [23] Grey Bennet diary, 85. [24] Add. 38742, ff. 201-10, 225. [25] *Croker Pprs.* i. 193; *Huskisson Pprs.* 120-31; Add. 38743, ff. 34, 56, 65; NAS GD249, Canning to Binning, 1 Dec., same to Morley, 12 Dec. 1821. [26] Hatherton diary, 20 Nov.; *Arbuthnot Jnl.* i. 127; Buckingham, i. 210; Add. 69044, memo. 30 Nov. 1821; Add. 38743, f. 76; 38829, f. 11. [27] TNA 30/29/9/3/9. [28] Add. 38743, ff. 72-132; Grey mss, Tierney to Grey, 23 Jan. 1822. [29] Wellington mss WP1/691/1, 2. [30] Buckingham, i. 288. [31] *PP* (1822), v. 1-92; Hilton, 151. [32] Ibid. 1-64, 75-84. [33] *Huskisson Pprs.* 137-9. [34] Northants. RO, Agar Ellis diary, 11 June 1822. [35] Add. 38743, ff. 176, 179, 192. [36] Harewood mss 83, Canning to J. Gladstone, 31 May, 1 June; Add. 38568, f. 115; 38743, ff. 156, 160; St. Deiniol's Lib. Glynne-Gladstone mss 275, Huskisson to J. Gladstone, 1 July 1822. [37] Add. 38743, ff. 192-218; Herts. Archives, Panshanger mss D/Elb F78, W. to F. Lamb, 16 Aug.; BL, Morley mss, Granville to Morley, 9 Sept.; Powis mss (History of Parliament Aspinall transcripts), Palmerston to Clive, 13 Sept.; Harewood mss 26, Canning to Liverpool, 14 Sept. 1822; Buckingham, i. 380-6; *Creevey Pprs.* ii. 70. [38] Add. 40319, f. 57; *Croker Pprs.* i. 227-32. [39] Add. 38743, ff. 217-243. [40] Harewood mss 83, J. Gladstone to

Canning, 8 Oct. 1822; Add. 38193, f. 171; 38291, f. 174; 38575, ff. 34-37; 38743, ff. 263, 266. [41] Add. 38743, ff. 263-9, 285-8, 294; 38744, ff. 2-6; 38291, f. 164; Wellington mss WP1/732/15; *Arbuthnot Jnl.* i. 200-1. [42] C.D. Yonge, *Lord Liverpool*, iii. 211. [43] Wellington mss WP1/754/13, 16; 772/18; Add. 40304, f. 106. [44] Add. 38744, ff. 14-38; 38291, ff. 335, 344, 398; Grey mss, Ellice to Grey, 21 Jan. 1823; Buckingham, i. 406-10. [45] Add. 38744, ff. 49, 53; Wellington mss WP1/754/26; Nottingham Univ. Lib. Portland mss PwH 132, Lord G. Cavendish Bentinck to Portland, 15 Feb. 1823. [46] Harewood mss 83, J. Gladstone to Canning, 21 Jan.; 84, Backhouse to same, 14, 15 Feb.; Glynne-Gladstone mss 275, J. Gladstone to Huskisson, 26 Jan., replies, 29 Jan., 3, 6 Feb.; *Huskisson Pprs.* 160-6; Add. 39948, f. 72; *Liverpool Mercury*, 14 Feb. 1823. [47] *The Times*, 19 Feb. 1823; *Huskisson Speeches*, iii. 647-62 and app. iv. [48] A.L. Lingelbach, 'Huskisson as president of board of trade', *AHR*, lxiii (1938), 759-74; L. Brown, *Board of Trade and Free Trade Movement*, 1-25 and *passim*.; Add. 38758, ff. 258, 317. [49] W.O. Henderson, 'Liverpool Office in London', *Economica*, xiii (1933), 473-9; G.S. Veitch, 'Huskisson and Liverpool', *Trans. Hist. Soc. Lancs. and Cheshire*, lxxx (1928), 1-50; Brougham mss, Shepherd to Brougham, 29 Jan. 1823. [50] Brown, 117-8; J.H. Clapham, 'Last Years of the Navigation Acts', *EHR*, xxv (1910) 480-501, 687-707. [51] *The Times*, 8 Mar. 1823. [52] Add. 38744, ff. 218-330; Glynne-Gladstone mss 275, Huskisson to J. Gladstone, 23 Mar.; T. Booth to Huskisson, 8 July 1823. [53] Add. 38744, ff. 153, 194-202. [54] Glynne-Gladstone mss 275, Huskisson to J. Gladstone, 3 Aug.; *Liverpool Courier*, 27 Aug.; *The Times*, 30 Aug. 1823; E. Halévy, *Liberal Awakening*, 200-2; *PP* (1833), vi. [55] Buckingham, i. 488-9, 494; ii. 6; *Arbuthnot Jnl.* i. 254, 259-60, 273; Wellington mss WP1/771/8, 12, 13, 15, 18; Add. 38568, f. 122; Harewood mss 87, Liverpool to Canning, 10 Nov. 1823; *Geo. IV Letters*, iii. 1109-10. [56] *Huskisson Pprs.* 166-73; Buckingham, i. 426; *Arbuthnot Jnl.* i. 278. See also P. Harling, 'Rethinking "Old Corruption"', *P and P*, cxlvii (1995), 146-7. [57] Glynne-Gladstone mss 353, *passim*.; 275, Huskisson to J. Gladstone, 2 Nov. 1823; 176, same to same, 8 Feb. 1824; *Courier*, 24, 27 Apr.; *Observer*, 25 Apr.; *Morning Herald*, 26 Apr.; *The Times*, 27, 30 Apr., 3, 5 May 1824. [58] Shakespeare Birthplace Trust (Stratford-on-Avon), Philips mss DR198/11. [59] Halévy, 203-10; N. Gash, *Secretary Peel*, 348-50. [60] *Ann. Reg.* (1824), p. 81. [61] TNA 30/29/6/3/92. [62] Wellington mss WP1/792/1, 2; 801/15; 805/2, 28; 806/21; 807/9; 808/4, 7; Buckingham, ii. 78. [63] TNA 30/29/9/3/10, 11; Glynne-Gladstone mss 276, Huskisson to J. Gladstone, 12, 29 July 1824; *Huskisson Pprs.* 176-8. [64] R. Harris, 'Political economy, interest groups and repeal of Bubble Act in 1825', *EcHR*, l (1997), 675-96. [65] Glynne-Gladstone mss 276, Huskisson to J. Gladstone, 12 July, 9 Nov. 1824; 350, *passim*.; Add. 38748, f. 17. [66] TNA 30/29/9/3/13, 14. [67] Ibid. 13. [68] *Arbuthnot Jnl.* i. 391. [69] Brown, 2-3. [70] *Arbuthnot Jnl.* i. 389. [71] *Huskisson Pprs.* 181-5. [72] Buckingham, ii. 249-50, 260-1. [73] TNA 30/29/9/3/14. [74] Ibid. 30/29/16/10; *Huskisson Pprs.* 194-9; Bagot, *Canning and Friends*, ii. 319. [75] Add. 38747, ff. 76, 100; Lansdowne mss, Baring to Lansdowne, 16 Sept. 1825; A.G. Stapleton, *Canning and his Times*, 225-7; *Croker Pprs.* i. 282. [76] Hilton, 210-12, 215-17; Glynne-Gladstone mss 276, Huskisson to J. Gladstone, 26 Jan. 1826. [77] *Arbuthnot Jnl.* i. 426-7. [78] Glynne-Gladstone mss 276. [79] TNA 30/29/9/3/15. [80] Grey mss, Ellice to Grey, 2 Feb. 1826. [81] Wellington mss WP1/849/13; Stapleton, 229; Nottingham Univ. Lib. Denison diary, 10 Feb. 1826. [82] Keele Univ. Lib. Sneyd mss SC8/79; TNA 30/29/9/38. [83] Gurney diary, 10 Feb. 1826; Wellington mss WP1/848/24, 30. [84] Glynne-Gladstone mss 276, Huskisson to J. Gladstone, 25 Mar., 11 Apr. 1826; Add. 38748, f. 35. [85] Add. 51574, Abercromby to Holland, 16 Feb. 1826; *Greville Mems.* i. 156-7. [86] Denison diary, 8 Feb. 1826. [87] Wellington mss WP1/851/3. [88] Denison diary, 23 Feb.; Add. 38833, f. 347; 51584, Tierney to Holland, 23 Feb.; 51784, Holland to C.R. Fox, 5 Mar.; 69366, Greville to G.M. Fortescue, 5 Mar.; Agar Ellis diary, 23 Feb. [1826]; Wellington mss WP1/851/3; Broughton, *Recollections*, iii. 127; *Huskisson Pprs.* 202; Stapleton, 236-7; *Greville Mems.* 159-60. [89] Add. 51574, Abercromby to Holland, 7 Mar.; 51584, Tierney to same, 12 Mar. 1826; TNA 30/29/9/3/16; 9/5/39. [90] *Arbuthnot Jnl.* ii.

17; *Huskisson Pprs.* 186-7. [91] Buckingham, ii. 297; *Creevey Pprs.* ii. 99; Add. 51584, Tierney to Holland, 10 Apr. 1826; Wellington mss WP1/854/10. [92] *Arbuthnot Jnl.* ii. 20, 26. [93] *Huskisson Pprs.* 202-4, Hilton, 273-5. [94] Add. 51569, Whishaw to Lady Holland, 14 May; 51574, Abercromby to Holland, 16 May; 51662, Bedford to same, 9 May 1826. [95] Gurney diary May; Denison diary, 12 May 1826. [96] *Liverpool Mercury*, 26 May, 2, 16 June; Glynne-Gladstone mss 276, Huskisson to J. Gladstone, 30 May, 24 June; Add. 38748, f. 40; Harewood mss 84, Huskisson to Canning, 12 June 1826. [97] *The Times*, 15, 21 June; *Liverpool Mercury*, 16, 23, 30 June; Wellington mss WP1/857/14; 858/11; Harewood mss 84, Huskisson to Canning, 22 Aug. 1826; *Huskisson Pprs.* 204-8; Stapleton, 239. [98] Add. 38748, f. 182. [99] *Huskisson Pprs.* 209-13; Hilton, 279-83. [100] Agar Ellis diary, 24 Nov.; Add. 51586, Tierney to Lady Holland, 25 Nov. [1826]. [101] *Canning's Ministry*, 30; TNA 30/29/9/3/17; *Lady Palmerston Letters*, 158; Glynne-Gladstone mss 277, Huskisson to J. Gladstone, 12 Feb. 1827. [102] Wellington mss WP1/883/11; *Huskisson Pprs.* 214-6; *Canning's Ministry*, 10, 12, 13, 19, 22-26, 32-34; *Lady Palmerston Letters*, 161; Glynne-Gladstone mss 277, Huskisson to J. Gladstone, 21, 24 Mar. 1827; *Croker Pprs.* i. 364-5. [103] *Canning's Ministry*, 48. [104] Ibid. 42. [105] Add. 38749, ff. 90, 112; *Croker Pprs.* i. 361. [106] Sneyd mss SC12/78; *Huskisson Pprs.* 220-3; *Geo. IV Letters*, iii. 1304; Glynne-Gladstone mss 277, J. Gladstone to Huskisson, 17 Apr., reply 21 Apr. 1827; *Canning's Ministry*, 192, 229-31, 269. [107] Glynne-Gladstone mss 123, Gascoyne to J. Gladstone, 9 May; 277, Huskisson to same, 8 May; Denison diary, 7 May 1827; Broughton, iii. 193. [108] *Lady Palmerston Letters*, 167. [109] Cent. Kent. Stud. Stanhope mss U1590 C190/2, J. Sinclair to Stanhope, 3 June 1827; Wellington mss WP1/889/23; 890/16; 891/1-5, 12; 892/3, 4; *Canning's Ministry*, 387-98; Bagot, ii. 406; *Creevey Pprs.* ii. 122; *Geo. IV Letters*, iii. 1357; Hilton, 283-7. W.D. Jones, *Prosperity Robinson*, 147-9 attributes the error to Huskisson. [110] Add. 52447, f. 88; Bagot, ii. 409-10; *Russell Letters*, ii. 92; *Geo. IV Letters*, iii. 1368; Broughton, iii. 216. [111] Grey mss, Ellice to Grey, 19 July 1827. [112] TNA 30/29/9/3/18. [113] Add. 38750, ff. 9, 19; TNA 30/29/9/3/19. [114] TNA 30/29/9/3/20; 14/4/8; *Geo. IV Letters*, iii. 1397; Add. 51584, Tierney to Holland, 25 Aug. [1827]. [115] *Huskisson Pprs.* 224-6; *Geo. IV Letters*, iii. 1399; Add. 38750, f. 81; 51578, Carlisle to Holland, 22 Aug.; 51586, Tierney to Lady Holland, 22 Aug.; 51687, Lansdowne to Holland, 24 Aug.; Castle Howard mss, Holland to Carlisle, 22 Aug. 1827. [116] Lonsdale mss, Croker to Lowther, 11 Aug., reply, 14 Aug. 1827; Add. 38750, ff. 28, 30, 39, 75; NLW, Harpton Court mss C/621; TNA 30/29/9/5/55; 14/4/8; *Croker Pprs.* i. 387; Buckingham, ii. 348. [117] Add. 76138, Holland to Spencer [19 Aug.]; Lansdowne mss, Baring to Lansdowne, 1 Sept. 1827. [118] Add. 40340, f. 195; 40394, f. 206. [119] Chatsworth mss, Abercromby to Devonshire [27 Aug. 1827]. [120] Add. 38750, f. 104; *Huskisson Pprs.* 231-3. [121] Add. 38750, ff. 81, 128, 132; Add. 51687, Lansdowne to Holland, 24 Aug. 1827. [122] TNA 30/29/9/3/21; 9/5/56; Add. 51584, Tierney to Holland, 31 Aug.; 51687, Lansdowne to Holland, 31 Aug.; Lansdowne mss, Huskisson to Lansdowne, 29 Aug.; Hants RO, Tierney mss 31M70/43d. [123] Add. 38750, ff. 132, 145-58, 166, 188; Denison diary, 1 Sept. 1827; *Huskisson Pprs.* 236-7. [124] TNA 30/29/9/3/21. [125] Fitzwilliam mss, Grey to Fitzwilliam, 30 Aug. 1827; NLS mss 24748, ff. 17, 27. [126] Brougham mss, same to J. Brougham, 9 Sept.; Grey mss, Ellice to Grey, 19 Sept. 1827. [127] *Baring Jnls.* i. 55; Lansdowne mss. [128] Add. 38750, ff. 180, 229, 264, 325; 38752, f. 38. [129] Add. 38750, f. 235; Glynne-Gladstone mss 277, Huskisson to J. Gladstone, 5 Sept. 1827. [130] A. Aspinall, 'Goderich Ministry', *EHR*, xlii (1927), 543-5. [131] Hatherton mss, Fazakerley to Littleton, 29 Sept. 1827. [132] Derby mss 920 Der (14) 62, Huskisson to Smith Stanley, 12 Sept., Stewart to J. Maxwell, 21 Sept. 1827; Add. 38750, ff. 280, 283; 38752, ff. 78, 84, 177, 280; 38753, f. 71; 38754, f. 20. [133] *Geo. IV Letters* iii. 1408, 1411; *Huskisson Pprs.* 238-43; Add. 38751, f. 42. [134] TNA 30/29/9/3/25, 26; Add. 38751, f. 124; 38752, f. 69. [135] TNA 30/29/14, Howard de Walden to Granville, 16 Nov. [1826]. [136] *Huskisson Pprs.* 240-1, 267, 272-4; *Geo. IV Letters*, 1431; Add. 38751, f. 88; 38753, ff. 3-6, 88, 92, 97, 98, 178. [137] Hilton, 243-6; Tierney mss 85b/1, 2; Add. 38752, ff. 104,

204, 221-40, 296; *Geo. IV Letters*, iii. 1443-5; Durham CRO, Londonderry mss D/LO/C83 (11); *Melbourne Pprs.* 115; TNA 30/29/9/30. [138] TNA 30/29/9/3/29. [139] Add. 38752, f. 306. [140] Add. 38753, ff. 122-6, 138-40, 167, 223, 232-3, 276; Grey mss, Ellice to Grey, 20 Dec. 1827; *Huskisson Pprs.* 268-70; TNA 30/29/9/3/17, 31; *Croker Pprs.* i. 400. [141] Add. 38753, ff. 185, 187, 199, 242, 282; 38754, f. 24; *Croker Pprs.* i. 401; Londonderry mss C83 (12). [142] *Huskisson Pprs.* 277-9. [143] George, xi. 15505; *Geo. IV Letters*, iii. 1461, 1469-70; TNA 30/29/9/3/34; Add. 38574, ff. 124, 126; 39948, f. 105. [144] Southampton Univ. Lib. Broadlands mss PP/GMC/26, 27, Palmerston to Lady Cowper, 17, 18 Jan. 1828; *Huskisson Pprs.* 282-3; Add. 38754, ff. 106, 154, 159, 162, 179, 188, 200, 215, 282, 300, 317, 325, 327; 40395, ff. 21, 26; TNA 30/29/9/3/37. [145] Lonsdale mss. [146] Aberdeen Univ. Lib. Arbuthnot mss, Rutland to Mrs. Arbuthnot, 18 Jan. 1828; Londonderry mss C83 (185). [147] Add. 36464, f. 166; 51785, Holland to C.R. Fox, 13 Jan. 1828. [148] Grey mss, Ellice to Grey, 12 Jan.; Lambton mss (History of Parliament Aspinall transcripts), Ellice to Lambton, 13 Jan. 1828; Add. 38754, f. 114; Broughton, iii. 237. [149] Tierney mss 85a. [150] *Huskisson Pprs.* 279-80; *Greville Mems.* i. 196-200; Harewood mss, Lord W. Cavendish Bentinck to Lady Canning, 21 Jan.; Bagot mss (History of Parliament Aspinall transcripts), Binning to Bagot, 25 Jan. 1828. [151] Add. 38754, f. 179; Agar Ellis diary, 17 Jan.; Devon RO, Sidmouth mss, J. Pearse to Sidmouth, 25 Jan. 1828; *Ellenborough Diary*, i. 6; Add. 38754, f. 234. [152] Castle Howard mss, Huskisson to Carlisle, 27 Jan. 1828. [153] *Ellenborough Diary*, i. 6, 9; Wellington mss WP1/913/7, 8; *Creevey Pprs.* ii. 144-5. [154] Glynne-Gladstone mss 277, Huskisson to J. Gladstone, 11, 17 May, 16 Sept. 1827, 7 Jan. 1828; Add. 38751, f. 20; *The Times*, 17, 21 Sept. 1827. [155] Add. 40395, f. 208. [156] *The Times*, 2, 5-7, 21, 26 Feb.; *Liverpool Chron.* 12, 19 Feb. 1828; *Greville Mems.* i. 204, 359; *Ellenborough Diary*, i. 20-21; *Huskisson Pprs.* 286-93; Add. 38755, f. 18; Wellington mss WP1/920/34. [157] Wellington mss WP1/916/9. [158] *Ellenborough Diary*, i. 29; *Creevey Pprs.* i. 152. [159] *Ellenborough Diary*, i. 48-53. [160] Add. 40395, f. 221; 40307, f. 50; *PP* (1828), v. 1-3, 553-9. [161] Hatherton diary, 10, 12, 16-18 Feb. 1828; *Ellenborough Diary*, i. 33-34; Sneyd mss SC12/86; 17/178; Manchester New Coll. Oxf. William Shepherd mss vii. ff. 89-91. [162] George, xi. 15522. [163] *Ellenborough Diary*, i. 36, 40; Portland mss PwH 146/1-3; Agar Ellis diary, 26 Feb. 1828. [164] *Ellenborough Diary*, i. 50-67; Add. 38755, ff. 155, 269; PRO NI, Anglesey mss D619/31A/49. [165] *Ellenborough Diary*, i. 72. [166] Add. 51663. [167] Broughton, iii. 257-8. [168] *Ellenborough Diary*, i. 90-91. [169] Ibid. i. 76. [170] Ibid. i. 141. [171] Wellington mss WP1/921/13; 922/11; 924/2; 925/29, 36; 930/7,8; *Ellenborough Diary*, i. 103-4; *Arbuthnot Jnl.* ii. 179. [172] *Arbuthnot Corresp.* 98. [173] *Huskisson Pprs.* 293-300; Agar Ellis diary, 20 Feb. 1828; *Ellenborough Diary*, i. 40, 78, 97, 100. [174] Harewood mss 87, Lord G. Cavendish Bentinck to Lady Canning, 14 May; Castle Howard mss, Abercromby to Carlisle, 17 May 1828. [175] *Ellenborough Diary*, i. 106. [176] *Croker Pprs.* i. 420; *Ellenborough Diary*, i. 111-15, 117; *Geo. IV Letters*, iii. 1517; *Arbuthnot Jnl.* ii. 187-9. [177] TNA 30/29/9/3/39. [178] Ward, *Letters to 'Ivy'*, 336-7; Aspinall, 'Last of the Canningites', *EHR*, l (1935), 639-69. [179] George, xi. 1531-2, 1535. [180] Glynne-Gladstone mss 277, Huskisson to J. Gladstone, 21 May 1828. [181] TNA 30/29/9/3/39. [182] *Croker Pprs.* i. 421; Add. 38756, f. 156. Add. 51567, Anglesey to Holland, 28 May, 1 June 1828. [183] *Albion*, 9 June 1828. [184] Broughton, iii. 275; *Ellenborough Diary* i. 136. [185] *Ellenborough Diary* i. 135. [186] TNA 30/29/6/69; 9/2/45,46; 9/5/72. [187] Aspinall, 'Canningite Party', *TRHS*, xvii (1934), 177-226. [188] Glynne-Gladstone mss 277, Huskisson to J. Gladstone, 5, 18 July 1828. [189] Ibid. Huskisson to J. Gladstone, 5, 18 July 1828. [190] Denison diary, 5 July 1828. [191] Glynne-Gladstone mss 277, Huskisson to J. Gladstone, 11 Nov., 7 Dec. 1828. [192] Add. 51580, Carlisle to Holland, 29 Nov. 1828; Cumbria RO (Carlisle), Howard (of Corby Castle) mss D/HC8/48/12, P.H. Howard to mother, 26 Nov. 1828. [193] Grey mss, Ellice to Grey, 11 Nov. 1828; Add. 51600, Lady Cowper to Lady Holland [15 Dec. 1828]; Nottingham Univ. Lib. Ossington mss OsC 62a, 67a; *Baring Jnls.* i. 60; Add. 38757, f. 147, 155, 184; Glynne-Gladstone mss 278, Huskisson to J. Gladstone, 2, 11 Jan.; Hatherton mss, Huskisson to

Littleton, 25 Jan. 1829. [194] Grey mss, Ellice to Grey, 20 Jan. 1829; TNA 30/29/9/38. [195] Grey mss, Howick jnl. 6 Feb. 1829; Suff. RO (Bury St. Edmunds), Hervey mss 941/56/60. [196] *Greville Mems.* i. 250. [197] Howick jnl. 3 Mar. 1829; *Russell Letters*, i. 120. [198] Howick jnl. 19 Mar. 1829. [199] NLW ms 10804 D, letterbk. iii, Williams Wynn to Cavendish Bentinck, 16 June 1829; *Greville Mems.* i. 298, 304. [200] Londonderry mss C83 (25). [201] Glynne-Gladstone mss 278, Huskisson to J. Gladstone, 11, 15 June; 355, reply 2 July, J. Bolton to same, 3 July, reply, 6 July 1829. [202] *Greville Mems.* i. 324-5; *Russell Letters*, i. 133; George, xi. 15702, 15899; PRO NI, Fitzgerald mss MIC639/13/7, 24; Hatherton mss, Huskisson to Littleton, 23 Sept., 12 Nov.; Glynne-Gladstone mss 278, Huskisson to J. Gladstone, 15 Nov., 19 Dec.; Add. 51574, Abercromby to Holland 20 Dec. 1829; Ossington mss OsC 72a. [203] Broadlands mss BR23AA/5/6. [204] Add. 38758, ff. 95-96; P. Harling, *Waning of Old Corruption*, 183. [205] Howick jnl. 4 Feb. 1830; *Geo. IV Letters*, iii. 1575. [206] Add. 38758, f. 95. [207] Grey mss, Durham to Grey, 12 Feb.; Ellice to same, 14 Feb. 1830. [208] Ossington mss OsC 74. [209] Howick jnl. 14 Feb., 7 Mar.; Add. 51785, Holland to C.R. Fox, 7, 20 Feb. 1830. [210] *Geo. IV Letters*, iii. 1579. [211] *Ellenborough Diary*, ii. 208; Add. 76369, Althorp to Brougham, 10 Mar.; Howick jnl. 10 Mar.; Agar Ellis diary, 10 Mar.; NAI, Leveson Gower letterbks. 7.B3.33, Leveson Gower to Singleton, 13 Mar. 1830. [212] Add. 38758, f. 155; Howick jnl. 14 Apr. 1830. [213] Grey mss, Ellice to Grey, 20 Mar. 1830. [214] Leveson Gower letterbks. 7.B3.33, Leveson Gower to Singleton, 29 Apr.; Christ Church, Oxf. Phillimore mss, J. to R. Phillimore, 29 Apr. 1830. [215] Hatherton mss, Huskisson to Littleton [May]; Howick jnl. 1, 5, 13 May 1830. [216] *Ellenborough Diary*, ii. 219; Add. 38758, f. 138. [217] Castle Howard mss, Abercromby to Carlisle, 4 June 1830. [218] Howick jnl. 21, 22 June 1830. [219] Glynne-Gladstone mss 195, T. to J. Gladstone, 28 June 1830. [220] *Croker Pprs.* ii. 58; Castle Howard mss, Abercromby to Lady Carlisle, 10 July; *Ellenborough Diary*, ii. 306, 312, 315-16; Devon RO, Earl Fortescue mss 1262M/FC86; Add. 38758, f. 193; 40340, f. 223, 226; Chatsworth mss, Brougham to Devonshire [12 July]; Broadlands mss, Palmerston's memo. [late June 1830]. [221] Ossington mss OsC 75. [222] Glynne-Gladstone mss 195, T. to J. Gladstone, 20, 22, 27 July, 8 Aug.; *The Times*, 4 Aug.; *Albion*, 5, 26 July; Sir James Graham mss (IHR microfilm XR 80), 1, bdle. 2, Palmerston to Graham, 25 or 28 July; Grey mss, Ellice to Grey [July]; Ossington mss OsC 76; *Liverpool Chron.* 7 Aug. 1830; Add. 38758, f. 220, 226. [223] Ossington mss OsC 76. [224] Add. 51534, T. Grenville to Holland, 9 Sept.; Glynne-Gladstone mss 195, T. to J. Gladstone, 13 Sept. 1830. [225] Parker, *Graham*, i. 86-87. [226] Add. 51604, Granville to Holland, 15 Sept. 1830. [227] Arbuthnot mss 3029/1/2/17. [228] *The Times*, 17, 18 Sept. 1830. For Huskisson's inquest, burial and printed obituaries, see also Garfield, 171-99. [229] PROB 11/1778/655; 2234/478; IR26/1229/551; 2067/522; *Albion*, 15 Nov. 1830. [230] Aspinall, *EHR*, l. 639-69; E.A. Wasson, *Whig Renaissance*, 173. [231] NLI, Monteagle mss 13370 (8). [232] *Arbuthnot Corresp.* 139. [233] Add. 40401, f. 195. [234] Dundee City Archives, Camperdown mss GD/Ca/(tin box EC/11), Gloucester to Duncan, 9 Oct. 1830. [235] *Greville Mems.* ii. 47-48.

M.M.E.

HUTCHINSON *see* HELY HUTCHINSON

HYDE, John (?1774–1832), of Castle Hyde, co. Cork.

YOUGHAL   1820–1826

b. ?1774, 1st s. of John Hyde, MP]I], of Castle Hyde and Sarah, da. of Benjamin Burton, MP [I], of Burton Hall, co. Carlow. *educ.* Eton 1788-92; Trinity, Dublin 25 Feb. 1794, aged 19. *m.* 13 Nov. 1802,[1] Hon. Elizabeth

O'Callaghan, da. of Cornelius O'Callaghan, MP [I], 1st Bar. Lismore [I], 4s. (2 *d.v.p.*) 4da. *suc.* fa. 1797. *d.* 13 Feb. 1832.

Sheriff, co. Cork 1808-9.

The Hydes of Castle Hyde were a branch of the Berkshire family that owned land at South Denchworth and Kingston Lisle and had supplied Members for the county, Abingdon, St. Germans and Tamworth between 1553 and 1601. Arthur Hyde (*d.* 1600) had settled in Ireland in the late sixteenth century and received a grant of 12,000 acres of confiscated lands at Carrigoneda, county Cork. His son and namesake (*d.* 1644) was knighted in 1624 and by 1670 the family were in possession of Castle Hyde. Hyde's father, a younger son, had in 1763 married a granddaughter of the 1st earl of Bessborough. The same year he replaced his father-in-law Benjamin Burton as Member for county Carlow in the Irish Parliament, where he sat until 1768 before representing county Cork, 1769-76. In 1772 he succeeded his unmarried brother Arthur to Castle Hyde, which at his death in 1797 passed to his elder son John, whom he had provided with a conventional education.[2] In 1798 Hyde's sister Sarah married their second cousin Henry Boyle (1771-1842), who became 3rd earl of Shannon in 1807, an alliance which was reinforced by Hyde's marriage to another second cousin, Boyle's first cousin Elizabeth, in 1802.

At the general election of 1820 Hyde was returned unopposed for Youghal, where Shannon, who had been in opposition to government since 1817, remained precariously in control of the representation but under threat from the reviving Devonshire interest.[3] A very lax attender, of whom a radical commentary of 1823 inaccurately stated there was 'no trace of attendance', Hyde is not known to have spoken in debate.[4] He was present to vote with the Whig opposition to the Liverpool ministry for the restoration of Queen Caroline's name to the liturgy, 13 Feb., and was granted three weeks' leave on urgent private business, 14 Mar. 1821. No evidence of parliamentary activity has been found for the next three sessions. Hyde clearly became something of a cypher, and in October 1822 James Abercromby*, after concluding negotiations which ensured the 6th duke of Devonshire's assumption of electoral control in Youghal, complained from Ireland:

> Mr. Hyde said nothing about resigning, which is very odd after he wrote to the people of Youghal to say he should do so, and he did not come to our dinner, which I regard as an act of total abdication.[5]

Hyde voted for Catholic relief, 1 Mar., 21 Apr., and was named to the select committee on the Irish prison laws bill, 2 May 1825. Writing from Sidmouth, Devon, he declined an invitation to attend the Catholic Association's dinner for the 'friends of civil and religious liberty', 24 Jan. 1826.[6] At that year's dissolution he made way for Devonshire's nominee at Youghal.[7] He did not seek re-election and died in February 1832. He was succeeded by his elder son and namesake, on whose death without issue in 1885 the Irish estates passed to his niece Mrs. Sarah Beck of Derwyn, Monmouthshire, who took the name of Hyde in 1888.

[1] *Reg. St. George Hanover Square*, ii. 269. [2] *Gent. Mag.* (1797), i. 172. [3] *Dublin Evening Post*, 18 Mar. 1820. [4] *Black Bk.* (1823), 166; *Session of Parl. 1825*, p. 470. [5] Bessborough mss F1, Abercromby to Duncannon, 14 Oct. 1822. [6] *O'Connell Corresp.* iii. 224. [7] *Southern Reporter*, 6 June 1826.

D.R.F./P.J.S.

INGESTRE, Visct. *see* **CHETWYND TALBOT, Henry John**

INGILBY *see* **AMCOTTS INGILBY**

INGLIS, Sir Robert Harry, 2nd bt. (1786–1855), of Milton Bryant, Woburn, Beds.

DUNDALK	5 May 1824–1826
RIPON	8 Feb. 1828–20 Feb. 1829
OXFORD UNIVERSITY	28 Feb. 1829–Jan. 1855

b. 12 Jan. 1786, o.s. of Sir Hugh Inglis[†], 1st bt., of Milton Bryant and 1st w. Catherine, da. and coh. of Harry Johnson of Milton Bryant. *educ.* Winchester 1799; Christ Church, Oxf. 1803; L. Inn 1806, called 1818. *m.* 10 Feb. 1807, Mary, da. of Joseph Seymour Biscoe of Pendhill Court, Bletchingley, Surr., *s.p. suc.* fa. as 2nd bt. 21 Aug. 1820. *d.* 5 May 1855.
Priv. sec. to sec. of state for home affairs Oct. 1812-Feb. 1814; Carnatic commr. 1814-30; commr. on ecclesiastical revenues and patronage 1832-5, improvement of metropolis 1842-51; PC 11 Aug. 1854.

Inglis's father, a native of Edinburgh, had a colourful career in the East India Company's naval and civil services before returning to England in 1775. Nine years later he married a Bedfordshire heiress and became a director of the Company, serving until 1813. A steady supporter of Henry Dundas[†] at East India House, he received a baronetcy from Addington, a personal friend, in 1801, and sat for Ashburton as a supporter of Addington and then Pitt in the 1802

Parliament.[1] Robert, his only son, whose mother died when he was six (his father married again in 1794) became a close friend at Christ Church of Robert Peel*, his junior by two years, who entered the House soon after going down and in little over a year was embarked on his ministerial career under Perceval, of whom Inglis was a warm admirer.[2] He shared Peel's Toryism and zeal for the interests of the established church, but not his talent. Another close friend from Oxford was Sir Thomas Dyke Acland*, who was returned as Member for Devon in 1812.[3]

That year Inglis's father secured his appointment as private secretary to Addington (now Lord Sidmouth) as home secretary in the Liverpool ministry.[4] In the summer of 1813 he toured Ireland, and on 23 Aug. he wrote from Killarney to Peel, who was in Dublin in his capacity as Irish secretary, to say that nothing he had seen had

weakened my conviction that it is necessary to stop short of any further concession of political power to the Roman Catholic body. If we could be morally certain that unconditional submission to their present demands would insure to us the permanent peace and union of all classes, we might, perhaps, admit the anomalies of the measure; but every concession has furnished only the disposition and the means to extort more ... Catholic emancipation will be followed by the abolition of the tithes, the erection of a Roman Catholic establishment, or the separation of the two countries, as successive objects of popular excitement.[5]

He left the home office in 1814 to become one of the three commissioners for investigating and settling the debts of the nabobs of the Carnatic, from whose premises at 11 Manchester Buildings, Westminster, he wrote many of his private letters; he remained on the commission until it was wound up in 1830. He was friendly with William Wilberforce*, his cousins the Thornton brothers (Robert Thornton[†] was a colleague of his father in the East India Company's direction) and other members of the Clapham Evangelical group. On the death of Henry Thornton[†] in 1815 Inglis and his wife became guardians of his nine children, and were associated in the trusts set up for them with Wilberforce, John Thornton, and Charles Grant* and Robert Grant*. They moved into Thornton's house at Battersea Rise, Clapham Common, and it was there that he introduced Wilberforce to the poet laureate and Tory polemicist Robert Southey* and the visiting Irish clergyman John Jebb, who became bishop of Limerick in 1822.[6] Inglis was belatedly called to the bar in 1818, but he never practised. On the death of his father in 1820 he came into his inheritance of Milton Bryant and, as residuary legatee, received about

£7,000 of personal estate sworn under £16,000.[7] After Peel replaced Sidmouth as home secretary in 1822 Inglis bombarded him with communications from Ireland by Jebb, his chaplain Charles Forster and others, which Peel evidently valued and found useful.[8]

In May 1824 Inglis was returned on a vacancy for Dundalk on the Roden interest, presumably under the aegis of the Liverpool ministry. He was in their majorities in defence of the prosecution of the Methodist missionary John Smith in Demerara, 11 June, and for the Irish insurrection bill, 14 June. On 9 June 1824 he was a teller for the majority against the orphans' fund debt bill, and for the minority against the coal exchange debt bill. He voted for the Irish unlawful societies bill, 15, 25 Feb., and against Catholic relief, 1 Mar., 21 Apr. and the Irish franchise bill, 26 Apr., 9 May. He voted for repeal of the usury laws, 17 Feb. Inglis, who was 'extremely entertaining, and most kind' to Wilberforce when he visited him in his retirement at Uxbridge, 24 Mar., and remained in touch with Jebb and Peel on Irish matters, was keen to speak on the Catholic question, but was initially 'guided in my silence' by Acland, who was 'not very eager for me to come forward'. He did not expect the relief bill to pass the Commons, let alone the Lords, though he admitted that his 'very strongest wish that it may never be carried' might be clouding his judgement.[9] He made his debut on the third reading, 10 May, when he delivered a lengthy set piece speech against concessions to the 'unchangeable' Catholic church, which Southey, a fellow spirit, thought contained 'good matter'.[10] On 18 May he objected to Henry Brougham's hostile remarks on lord chancellor Eldon after the measure's rejection by the Lords. It was later said of him that he habitually spoke 'in a drawling, whining sort of way. His enunciation is distinct, and he talks with ease and fluency; but there is a peculiar tone in his pronunciation, which were much better adopted to the pulpit than it is to the Senate'.[11] Accounting to Jebb for his silence on the Irish church rates bill, to counter which he had collected a good deal of information, he reckoned that he had been thwarted by technicalities of procedure and by some bad advice from friends. He intended to speak on Hume's motion for inquiry into the Irish church establishment, 14 June, but found the House 'unwilling to have much of a debate' on it.[12] He voted for the duke of Cumberland's grant, 30 May, 6, 10 June 1825.

That summer, so he later claimed, he received 'strong encouragement' from both Tories and Whigs to stand for Bedfordshire at the next general election. He 'waited to be asked to stand', but when a dissolution was expected in the autumn another Tory, Thomas Macqueen*, who had 'infinitely more wealth', took over the ground. Inglis was in any case very strongly disinclined to risk a contest and shy of canvassing openly while he was chairman of quarter sessions. One of the Whig sitting Members announced in December 1825 that he would retire at the dissolution rather than face a contest; but Macqueen was personally unpopular in the county and there remained a chance for Inglis, if he would commit himself. In the event, having made it known that he was unwilling to involve the county in a contest and would only stand 'in the case of its being the general wish of the country gentlemen' that he should do so, he 'very foolishly' withdrew his pretensions in January 1826, a decision which he came to regret at the time of the general election six months later. He predicted, wrongly, that 'sooner or later I shall represent it, if it shall please God to continue to me life and health and present inclinations'.[13] In February he was mentioned as a possible candidate for the current vacancy for Oxford University, for which his anti-Catholic credentials were ideal; but he knew that as a Christ Church man he had no chance, as the college already had one Member in the person of Peel. He dismissed Jebb's notion that he might put himself forward for Armagh.[14]

In November 1825 he had observed to Jebb:

I am thoroughly satisfied that the people of this country, though more blindly and madly violent against Papists in 1780, though louder in their war whoop in 1807, were never so firmly enlightened at any period in their opposition to the measures of emancipation as they are now. Their great instructors have been [Daniel] O'Connell*, [Richard] Sheil* and Doyle. Not all the Protestant speeches, sermons, tracts and petitions have done as much to rouse the people of England as the orations and letters of the Roman Catholic leaders themselves ... I am sure that the next Parliament will be a Protestant one. And I have a strong suspicion that partly by change of opinion or at least of vote, and partly by well contrived absences, the majority even in the present House of Commons would be very different next session from what it was in the last, if the Roman Catholics should be ill advised enough to bring the question forward.[15]

In the House, 16 Feb. 1826, when ministers countered Newport's resolutions against the levy of church rates in Ireland with a bill to deal with them, Inglis, while admitting that irregularities existed, defended the system and warned that he would oppose the measure if it took

from the existing authority, which was not only Protestant, but hierarchically Protestant, the control and expenditure of monies raised for the support of the ecclesiastical establishments of the country, and placed it in hands, which might be Roman Catholic, which might be latitudinarian.

To Jebb, who welcomed his speech, he wrote:

It is impossible to deny that legally speaking there has been a misapplication of the fund raised under the name of church rates. But the misapplication has been general and liberal and honest, instead of being selfish and bigoted and corrupt. And if the flow of the expenditure of that fund be in future narrowed by law and confined within the banks of a land, another stream must be turned to irrigate the lands which will otherwise be left dry and barren.[16]

He conferred with Goulburn, the Irish secretary, on the ministerial measure, detailing his own and Jebb's reservations and seeking amendments; but he was not satisfied, and on 21 Apr. he stated his objections in the House.[17] On the South American treaties bill, 22 Feb., he pressed ministers to secure fairer treatment for British residents in the matter of freedom of worship than was accorded to them in the arrangement with Colombia; his plan to institute an inquiry into the subject was later thwarted by Canning, the foreign secretary.[18] He was unable to attend for Newport's motion on Irish education grants, 7 Mar., being obliged to attend the Bedfordshire grand jury. In his view, Newport seemed determined to 'pursue the church establishment in every way and every place';[19] and he welcomed Goulburn's resistance to his attack on Irish first fruits revenues, 21 Mar. He voted with government in favour of a separate ministerial salary for the president of the board of trade, 10 Apr., and against reform of Edinburgh's representation, 13 Apr.; but he was in the protectionist minority against the corn bill, 11 May. He presented and as a Christian endorsed a petition in support of the Greeks in their struggle with Turkey, 19 May 1826.

The 4th duke of Newcastle, a leading champion of the Protestant interest, offered Inglis a seat for Aldborough at the general election the following month, but on interviewing him

soon found, which I was not before aware of, that he has a very lenient feeling towards, if not a very strong bias in favour of the Dissenters; besides this he is evidently friendly to the experimental system especially in what regards free trade. I therefore told him that we did not agree in our views and our parliamentary connection could not take place.[20]

Inglis failed to find a seat. He toured Switzerland and France for nine weeks that summer with his stepmother, sister and sickly wife. On his return in late September he found a letter of 6 Aug. from Jebb

referring to a possible, though unspecified opportunity to obtain a seat. He correctly assumed that it had now gone by, but remarked that it was 'exactly the kind of representation which under my circumstances I should like. An annual payment is in fact the only mode which would not be very inconvenient to me, though my ability to bear even that is not very great'. Before going abroad he had seen Southey who, having been returned for Downton by Lord Radnor as an opponent of Catholic claims without his knowledge and against his inclination, was about to write to Radnor to extricate himself from the situation. Inglis later reported that 'on paper he could not put, what he wished to have *said*, that he would think well of me to fill the vacant seat'. He heard no more of the matter, and in December 1826 joined in the abortive attempt to make Southey change his mind by purchasing a qualification for him, though he was under the impression that he was in any case disqualified by a pension.[21] He kept up his correspondence with Jebb and Peel on Irish church matters.[22] In November 1826 he reminded Peel of their conversation the previous year about his pretensions to the office of keeper of the state papers, asked him to bear them in mind in case of a future vacancy and expressed his keenness to serve on any new commission on the papers or the public records. (He was appointed to the latter in 1831 and performed his duties with great assiduity.)[23]

He took a close interest in political events following Lord Liverpool's stroke in February 1827, when, referring to the current speculation that Peel might go as prime minister to the Lords to avoid a clash with Canning in the Commons, he alerted Jebb to the possibility of his succeeding Peel in the Oxford University seat:

I cannot canvass for it, and should not indeed have now thought of it at all, if my name had not been most unexpectedly brought forward last year. I only mention it now since in case that your lordship or any other Irish prelate who may think me not unfit for the representation ... were unconnectedly and of your own mere motion to suggest my name in reference to it, you would probably serve my interest much.

His name continued to be mentioned in Oxford, 'as one of those who would be most anxious to do all for the maintenance of the religious and civil institutions of the country', while the rumours of Peel's elevation persisted.[24] Inglis rejoiced in the narrow defeat of Burdett's motion to consider Catholic claims, 6 Mar. 1827:

I believe in my conscience that the Protestant church would have sunk in Ireland and with it, to a minor object,

British connection, if the question had been otherwise decided. As it is, we are safe for this session, and one very high man said to me today, for the Parliament also, in his judgement.[25]

A member, like Acland, of Grillion's Club, in which 'we Protestants are in a woeful minority', he was in Peel's confidence at this time, but initially thought he was 'doubly wrong' in declining to 'form an administration on Protestant principles' or to head one including Canning, which led to the latter's accession to power and the resignation of Peel and the other Protestant ministers. However, he approved of the resignation, feeling that Peel was 'right in not swelling the ranks of a new government, at the head of which is a man who will certainly lead on his men as many a heathen to that assault' on the Protestant establishment; and was soon satisfied that Peel had acted correctly throughout.[26] In the early days of the Canning ministry he was invited by Lord Colchester to join in his discussion with Lord Kenyon of the chances of concocting a confidence motion in the Lords to overthrow it; and he told Colchester that Peel was 'not so zealous as he wished him to be' and that he himself 'thought "a divided cabinet" was desirable *per se*, on account of the state of Ireland'.[27] He made another continental tour in the summer of 1827, visiting the Pyrennees and the sites of Crecy and Agincourt.[28]

In February 1828, when Peel was back in power as home secretary in the duke of Wellington's administration, Inglis was returned on a vacancy for Ripon on the Lawrence interest. He presented petitions in favour of repeal of the Test Acts, 22 Feb., but on the 26th he spoke and voted against that measure: 'So long as the church remains in its present position, so long it will continue an object of dissatisfaction, and will need the protection of the Acts which it is the object of the motion to repeal'. He presented petitions against repeal, 24, 28 Mar. On the presentation by Hume of the Irish Catholics' petition against the Vestry Acts, 20 Mar., Inglis defended church rates and alleged that the opposition to them being stirred up by O'Connell and others was essentially 'an hostility, avowed, indeed, explicitly in the Roman Catholic Association, to the established church in Ireland'. He presented petitions against Catholic relief, 8 May, and the following day, replying to Burdett, opposed it at length:

The more you grant concessions to the Roman Catholics, the more they increase in their demands ... Let us not of our own accord break down the barriers which our ancestors erected for our preservation; and, if perish we must ... let us perish boldly in the face of the day, denying the assaults of our enemies, and not sinking under the treach-

ery of pretended friends, or the fatal consequences of our own credulity.

He voted in the hostile minority, 12 May. He was forced to withdraw an amendment to the pauper lunatics bill to stipulate the appointment of a resident surgeon in every asylum with 50 or more inmates, 1 Apr. He presented a petition from London apothecaries for measures to facilitate the study of anatomy, 1 May, and one from White Roothing, Essex, for the abolition of slavery, 4 June. He pressed for the settlement of outstanding claims on France over war damages, 5, 23 June. He defended the grant for the Society for the Propagation of the Gospels in the colonies, 6 June, and was in the ministerial majority on the ordnance estimates, 4 July 1828. That month he tried to persuade Peel to settle immediately the vexed question of the illegal return of O'Connell, as a Catholic, for Clare, in case the death of the ailing king during the recess precipitated a general election:

To an issue you must bring it: is it not better to choose your own time, with the summer before you, than to suffer the Roman Catholics to enjoy for six or seven months the fancy of a victory, and to try to undeceive them by a struggle at the last? Above all, when you consider that on the life of one man depends the recurrence of a contingency which will try the strongest nerves ... I do not understate (God forbid that anyone should reckon lightly) the evils of rebellion or civil war; but I feel that some such measures as I stated to you ... will, by a mere demonstration of our strength, and of our determination, suffice to prevent the necessity of a blood-shedding, which weak measures, or even the procrastination of strong men, may provoke, but cannot prevent.

Peel would have none of it.[29]

In January 1829, when rumours were rife that ministers intended to announce the concession of Catholic emancipation, Lord John Russell asked Lady Holland if there was any truth in the unlikely story that Inglis was to move the address: 'As a high flying Tory I should dread him, but in his quality of Saint he is slippery, and for good reasons would follow Antichrist. I don't know whether it is worth Peel's while to bag him, but perhaps he thinks so'.[30] In fact, Inglis was outraged at the government's decision, and on the address, 5 Feb., he angrily demanded a full explanation, in what the radical Whig Member John Hobhouse dismissed as 'a crazy and laughable harangue'.[31] He presented and endorsed petitions against emancipation from Ripon and elsewhere, 9, 10, 11 Feb., when he dissented from the suggestion that 'impregnable securities' would make emancipation acceptable: 'no securities ... would be sufficient. I see no safety but in exclusion alone'. He was the eventual choice of the leading Oxford University anti-Catholics to resist the attempt of the moderates to re-elect Peel after he had tendered his resignation on a point of conscience. A few days before he was formally adopted he wrote to Giffard, the editor of the *Standard*:

I never will compromise my opinions in religion or politics. Such as I am the University may reject or may elect me; but though the representation of Oxford be the highest external honour to which an English commoner can attain, there is still a higher honour, that of never betraying our principles to our supposed interests ... I should have thought that I had been too high church for the majority: I was certainly more high church than most of the bishops last year in the matter of the Test and Corporation Acts. Above all things, let not Oxford stultify itself, and precipitate the ruin of our cause by re-electing Mr. Peel. Upon that measure depends more than we can yet calculate, in reference to many other plans. Let the University choose the man who as against him will be likely to conciliate the largest support. Let us not be divided: and never think a second about me, unless in your sober judgement you should think that I am the individual.

Inglis, who was condemned by the liberal Tory Edward Littleton* as 'the prince of bigots' and by the Whig duke of Bedford as 'my sanctified and bigoted neighbour', was swept to victory over Peel largely by the 'conscience of the English clergy', as his ward Marianne Thornton put it. In his letter of thanks to the chairmen of his Oxford and London committees he exulted in this vindication of his stance on the Catholic question and asserted that 'we must ... remain a Protestant people with a Protestant legislature, the only security for a Protestant king'. This gave offence 'in some quarters', but in a letter to an Oxford correspondent he denied having meant to attribute corrupt motives to Peel's supporters and argued that it was perfectly plain that the Catholic question had been the 'real point ... in dispute'.[32] Sidney Herbert†, an undergraduate at Oriel, wished 'Inglis had not been elected', for he was 'not a man of calibre to represent such a body, and still less to be put forward as the champion of a party, since he only burlesques the cause he has to advocate by exaggerating it'.[33]

Presenting anti-Catholic petitions, 4 Mar. 1829, he asserted that his return showed that the 'rising talent' of the country was hostile to emancipation. He privately claimed that two pro-Catholics 'told me that I did not fail'.[34] The following day he criticized Peel's 'extraordinary change of policy' and attacked Wellington, 'whose skill in directing the energies of brute force is assuredly unrivalled [but who] has never learnt to calculate the powers and the resistance of opinion'. He described emancipation as the thin end of the wedge, leading inexorably to 'the destruction, or at least the irreparable injury of the Protestant church in Ireland', and called on the Lords to reject it. Hostile witnesses were contemptuous of his performance, contrasting it unfavourably with Peel's accomplished speech: Greville thought that the University 'should have been there in a body to hear the Member they have rejected and him whom they have chosen in his place'; while Mrs. Arbuthnot reckoned his effort was 'so bad a one as must have, I think, somewhat disconcerted his new constituents'.[35] He was one of the diehard opponents of emancipation in the division lobbies, 6, 18, 23, 27, 30 Mar. On the 9th, when he presented London and Glasgow petitions, he contended 'most fearlessly, that a large proportion of the good sense and intelligence of the people of England' was hostile to it and, in answer to a question as to why, if he did not think the Commons truly represented public opinion, he did not support parliamentary reform, said that he was 'satisfied with the constitution as it is'. He continued to present and defend hostile petitions, particularly from Scotland; and Lord Howick goaded him into 'a great rage' on this issue, 17 Mar.[36] On 23 Mar. he moved an amendment, which was defeated by 276-114, to stiffen the declaration of loyalty required of Catholics. In a final rant against the bill in the Commons, 30 Mar. 1829, which prompted the Whig James Abercromby* to condemn him privately as a 'conceited fool', he declared that 'this surrender to the Roman Catholics is a direct premium to intimidation' and 'destroys ... Protestantism, as the character of our institutions'.[37]

Inglis handled the third reading of the archbishop of Canterbury's estate bill, 10 Apr. 1829. On 15 May he moved an amendment to Warburton's anatomy regulation bill to repeal that part of it which directed that the bodies of criminals should be given for dissection. It was rejected by 40-8, but he subsequently carried one intended to ensure that dissected corpses were decently interred. He supported and was a teller for the minority for Osborne's attempt to kill the measure, 18 May. Although it galled him to subsidize erroneous Papist doctrines, he acknowledged that the faith of Parliament was pledged to vote the Maynooth grant for that year, 22 May; but he promised resistance to it in future. He defended church rates against Hume, 3 June; explained that the end of the Carnatic commissioners' labours were in sight and objected to the colonial secretary's observation that colonies should be left to their own devices in the matter of religious institutions, 5 June; and on 12 June presented a petition against compulsory attendance at Catholic worship for Protestant soldiers serving abroad. In October the Ultra leader Sir Richard Vyvyan*, making calculations for the possible formation of a coalition ministry, numbered Inglis among 'Tories strongly opposed to the present government'. On 12 Dec. 1829 Inglis wrote to Jebb:

> The proceedings in Ireland are a melancholy confirmation of the justice of the predictions of those who saw in concession nothing but a new fulcrum for a new power ... I wish for ... [Wellington's] own sake that I could think as well of his principles as to believe that he will ever admit a consciousness of any error. But I can see no comfort in the contemplation of his conduct public or private, and I shall look on his removal from power, at least from supreme power, as a relief to ourselves from a series of calamities ... No one knows whom to fight, or with whom to unite in the House of Commons in February next. Of two things only am I clear, that the duke cannot stand with the present ministry against the present opposition, a Cerberus of the old Tories, the old Whigs and the Huskissons, and that individually, I should have more confidence in any one of these three heads than in him.[38]

He duly voted against government on the address, 4 Feb., but he may have been in their majority against the enfranchisement of Birmingham, Leeds and Manchester, 23 Feb. 1830. On the presentation of a petition for Jewish emancipation, 22 Feb., he stated his objections to a measure which would 'sever the last link which connects the legislature with the religion of the country'. Despite illness, he led the opposition to Robert Grant's emancipation bill, 5 Apr., and he voted silently against it, 17 May.[39] He opposed interference in the affairs of Galway to remove the disabilities of local Catholics, 4 Mar., and voted in the minorities against the ensuing bill, 24, 25 May. On 4 Mar. he moved the previous question against Newport's motion for a commission of inquiry into the Irish church, but gave way when ministers proposed an alternative investigation. He called for action to deal with the problems created for certain English counties by the passage through them of Irish paupers, 9 Mar. He was talked out of insisting on the addition of James Grattan to the select committee on the Irish poor, 12 Mar. He voted against ministers on relations with Portugal, 10 Mar., and the Terceira incident, 28 Apr. He was in the minority of 16 against the third reading of Lord Ellenborough's divorce bill, 6 Apr. Next day he supported Agar Ellis's motion for the appointment of a select committee on the Commons library, to which he was named. He made a brief defence of the Irish church and the income of its bishops, 27 Apr., and on the presentation of a petition for tithe reform

by Hume, 18 May, 'protested against the doctrines and statements which he has now advanced with more than his usual hardihood'. He was, however, in Hume's majority for a bill to retain men in office on the death of the sovereign, 3 May, when the House was counted out. He voted against the second reading of the sale of beer bill the following day, and spoke and voted for a restrictive amendment to it, 1 July, when he squabbled with Brougham 'on the point whether drunkenness was a sin or only a vice'.[40] He recurred to the problem of compulsory attendance at alien religious ceremonies for Protestant soldiers, 30 Apr., 15, 17 June. He favoured referring petitions against the Clyde navigation bill to an appeals committee, 28 May, voted against the northern roads bill, 3 June, and advocated inquiry into the plan to construct a new road northwards from Waterloo Bridge, 4 June. He could see no point in a motion for a return of information on Irish absentees, 7 June, and opposed O'Connell's motion for a bill to reform Irish vestries, 10 June. He voted against the grants for South American missions, 7 June, and consular services, 11 June, and the abolition of the death penalty for forgery offences, 7 June. He again argued that government should promote and fund the established religion in the colonies, 14 June. Next day he opposed Hume's call for British withdrawal from Sierra Leone. He voted against going into committee on the bill to reform the Welsh judicature, 18 June, and on 2 July tried unsuccessfully to ensure that no business would be conducted under it on the four days following Good Friday. He presented petitions for the abolition of slavery, 1 July, and prevented the printing of a petition for reform of Irish corporations, 16 July 1830.

He was returned without opposition for the University at the general election of 1830, after which ministers listed him as one of the 'violent Ultras'.[41] He was in Paris in September.[42] He was an absentee from the division on the civil list which brought down the Wellington ministry, 15 Nov. A week later he told Jebb:

> To the late government I meant to have given support though I could not give confidence. To the present [Grey] government I can give neither support nor confidence. But, on the other hand, I don't desire at such a crisis to embarrass them by a vexatious every day opposition. I think that the appointment of Brougham [as lord chancellor], bad as it is in many respects, is almost redeemed by the fact that he must now support his 'order'. His weight is thrown into a scale which was kicking the beam, and he will bring it down to its fair level. I never was more convinced of the certainty of an event necessarily uncertain ... than [that] a reformed House of Commons will get

rid of an unreformed House of Lords. With the Lords will fall the king. As to yielding anything to satisfy the public will, it is more than idle, it is suicide. Little by little will with that view be conceded, till all be gone. Other nations, and indeed our own, might furnish sufficient example of this.[43]

In the House, 23 Nov. 1830, he agreed with Hume that the Grey ministry was as powerless as any other to create employment, but disputed his assertion that it could improve the condition of Ireland by interfering with church property. He opposed North's proposed bill to extend the provisions of the Act of 1819 allowing Protestant Dissenters to hold office without taking the sacrament, 2 Dec. Presenting a petition for the abolition of slavery, 13 Dec., he endorsed its prayer, but insisted that the proprietors would have to be fairly compensated. He objected to the printing of several anti-slavery petitions, 21 Dec. He declared his undiminished hostility to Jewish emancipation, 15 Dec. On 17 Dec. his attempt to have Ruthven called to order for calling for tax reductions to alleviate distress was not supported by the Speaker, who rebuked Inglis instead. He said that the abolition of tithes would benefit only landlords, 20 Dec., and when Hume raised a case of alleged abuse of tithes at Havering the following day, he denied church involvement and objected to attempts to make the Commons a court of appeal on such matters. Inglis, who was reported by Hobhouse early in the new year as believing that 'all our troubles, and amongst them the cry for reform, will subside quietly, and the old Tory principles and practice finally prevail',[44] denied in the House, 21 Dec., that there was widespread support for reform in the country:

The multitude – the uneducated and unthinking classes – may entertain opinions at the present crisis different from those which they held six months back, or from those which they will probably hold six months hence. I do not mean to deny that, from the late events in France and Belgium, the clamour for a reform of Parliament, excited by speeches in and out of this House, is now far louder and more general than it has been for a long time; but I do deny that the great mass of the intelligence of the country is in favour of reform; and I look forward with confidence to the return of a sound and healthy state of public opinion, generally, on that question.

On 23 Dec. 1830 he admitted that no previous government had contributed less to the burden of civil list pensions than Wellington's, even though 'no man ... had a greater want of confidence' in it. At the turn of the year, when he was busy with quarter sessions, he urged Giffard to do something to correct 'the system of misrepresentation which is now going on in the

London papers' on the subject of the recent trials at Winchester of 'Swing' rioters, who, far from being 'peasants starved into insurrection', were mostly 'well off'. He attributed the 'quiet' of Bedfordshire largely to 'the vigour and judgement of our lord lieutenant Lord Grantham in dividing the county into constabulary districts, and urging the justices to hold their petty sessions once a week instead of once a month, thus showing themselves on the spot at the time in the midst of the people'.[45]

Inglis, who was the subject of an 'absurd' rumour that he would second a motion by Hobhouse for repeal of the Catholic Emancipation Act,[46] led the opposition to Williams Wynn's 'sweeping' oaths in Parliament bill, which he feared would undermine the constitution by admitting to Parliament 'all persons of all sects and all modes of faith whatever', 4 Feb. 1831. He presented petitions for a general fast day, 8, 14 Feb. He acquiesced in Hume's motion for inquiry into the king's printers, 10 Feb., but advised against their hasty abolition. He defended tithes, 11, 16 Feb. He objected to the printing of an individual's petition complaining of corrupt electoral practices at Bridport, 17 Feb. On 1 Mar. he was the first to rise after Russell's motion for leave to introduce a reform bill had been seconded, and his doing so was 'a signal for a general rush of Members into the lobby, where they collected in groups to discuss the bill'. As another witness reported, his 'elaborate pamphlet against all reform', which occupied two hours, was 'not heard well' by 'those who remained', on account of 'his conversational style and the dryness of his matter', as well as 'the chattering that followed Lord John Russell's opening'. Inglis spoke of the 'destruction' of the constitution and predicted that in a reformed House 'the Members will be almost entirely confined to one interest, and no talent be admitted but the single one of mob oratory'.[47] He reported to Jebb two days later that it had been his own wish to divide the House against the introduction of the measure, declaring 'open war' on it; but that 'there are so many county Members who are pledged to their constituents on the subject, that at two meetings held at Sir Charles Wetherell's and at Sir Edward Knatchbull's (I was not present at either) it was resolved unanimously not to divide at present'.[48] He objected to Newport's proposed revaluation of Irish first fruits revenues, 14 Mar. He dismissed the petition of an individual complaining of ill-usage at the 1826 Leicester election and secured returns of the cost of select committees, disfranchisement bills and gaol building, 19 Mar. His allegation of breach of privilege by *The Times* for condemning the 'borough nominees' who opposed reform, 21 Mar., came to nothing. He voted against the second reading of the reform bill next day. He called on ministers to lay the 1831 census returns before the House to enable it to consider the details of the bill, 25 Mar., when he also argued that the crown had benefited the country by giving up substantial hereditary revenues in recent years. He objected to the printing of a petition for the promotion of new church building, 28 Mar., and presented one from West London against the reform bill, 28 Mar. He voted for Gascoyne's wrecking amendment, 19 Apr. 1831, and the following day reiterated his opposition to the oaths bill. He was returned unopposed at the ensuing general election.

On the report of the address, 22 June 1831, he complained at the omission from the king's speech of any reference to the beneficence of Providence. He upbraided Hunt for assuming to himself 'the sole manifestation of feeling for the poorer classes', 8 July. Inglis, who spoke at a meeting at Peel's to concert opposition tactics for dealing with the reintroduced reform bill,[49] voted against the second reading, 6 July. He presented a hostile Great Bedwyn petition against it, 11 July. The following night he voted at least twice for the adjournment, though he was reported eventually as objecting to the continuation of 'further useless opposition'. On 15 July, asserting that ministers were 'attempting to destroy that edifice of social greatness ... the constitution of England', he supported an attempt to save some of the condemned boroughs by grouping them, and observed that it was still not clear on what principles the disfranchisement proposals were based. He voted for use of the 1831 census, 19 July. He joined in protests against elections at Cricklade being held in the church, 20 July, and on the 22nd, seizing on a comment by O'Connell, said that it was now clear that ministers were 'not restoring and reforming the constitution, but reconstructing it ... through the means of the greatest revolution which this country has seen for centuries'. He voted for postponement of the consideration of the inclusion of Chippenham in schedule B, 27 July. He opposed the enfranchisement of Manchester, 2 Aug., because its representation had been filched from boroughs 'which have been convicted without examination, and condemned without hearing or trial'. On 9 Aug. he accused Tom Duncombe of 'a base and wicked calumny' in his allegation that Lord Durham, one of the framers of the original bill, had used his cabinet influence to secure an additional Member for the county of Durham. He saw no justification for giving the Isle of Wight separate representation, 16 Aug. He said that Grattan's admission that it had taken a year to register freeholders in four Irish counties indicated the practical difficulties

to be anticipated in implementing the registration provisions of the English reform bill, 30 Aug., when he was in the minority of 38 for the preservation of freemen's' rights. He demanded to know on what principle ministers would instruct the boundary commissioners to proceed, 1 Sept. He voted against the passage of the bill, 21 Sept., and the second reading of the Scottish reform bill, 23 Sept. 1831, and on the 27th argued that proprietors who had bought superiorities to create votes should be compensated for their abolition.

Inglis protested against the notion of not teaching the doctrines of the Church of England in schools, 14 July 1831, when he glanced at the Maynooth grant. He supported a Glasgow petition against it, 19 July; presented and endorsed a similar one from Irish Protestants, 31 Aug., when he exchanged words with O'Connell; disclaimed responsibility for alleged forgeries in it, 26 Sept., 13 Oct.; and spoke and was a teller for the minority of 47 for Perceval's motion to end the grant, 26 Sept. He defended the grant for the Society for the Propagation of the Gospels in the colonies, 25, 26 July. He raised objections to petitions brought up by Hunt against the grant for the education of Princess Victoria and for the dismissal of Lord Palmerston*, the foreign secretary, for his failure to support the Poles, 8 Aug. He took even more violent exception to the petition from Preston for repeal of the corn laws, which it said had been 'passed ... at the point of the bayonet', presented by Hunt, 12 Aug. He successfully opposed the intended retrospective operation of Grattan's bill to exclude the recorder of Dublin from Parliament, 12 Aug., and he spoke and voted for the motion of censure on the Irish government for interference in the Dublin election, 23 Aug. He objected to printing a Waterford petition for disarming the Irish yeomanry, 11 Aug., and one from Kilkenny for the abolition of tithes, which contained 'groundless' allegations of abuse, 16 Aug. He spoke and was a teller for the minority of 11 for the Irish union of parishes bill, 19 Aug., and voted for Sadler's motion for making legal provision for the Irish poor, 29 Aug. He presented and endorsed petitions for amendment of the Sale of Beer Act, 29 Aug., 7 Oct. On 27 Sept. he forced O'Connell to withdraw the word 'brutal' from his description of the assault on the Deacles. He said that it was too late to proceed that night with the vestries reform bill and deplored Protheroe's assertion that if thwarted, the people would 'legislate for themselves'. He was against reception of a petition, presented by Hunt, from an individual complaining of police brutality on Blackfriars Bridge, 11 Oct., but saw nothing offensive in one which called Roman Catholicism 'impious', 12 Oct. 1831.

On the address, 7 Dec. 1831, Inglis challenged Burdett's defence of Grey's communication with the Birmingham Political Union and said that the opponents of the revised reform bill could not give ground, if it retained its obnoxious features. In response to a conciliatory speech by Lord Clive, 12 Dec., he declared, on a personal note:

I am no party to any arrangement, if arrangement there is, that the new bill shall be met with a more limited hostility than the late bill encountered, if, on examination, the new bill should be found equally objectionable with the old one.

That day he secured the production of returns detailing tithes held by lay proprietors in Ireland. On 17 Dec. 1831 he spoke and voted against the second reading of the reform bill, which was 'not called for by the wants or wishes of the people', and was 'a poor return to God for his blessings'. He condemned the Irish secretary Smith Stanley's explanation that ministers had decided not to preserve the voting rights of Irish freemen because they did not wish to 'perpetuate a generation of Protestant freemen', 19 Jan. 1832. The reason for his inclusion in the list of the government majority for the first clause of the bill the following day was explained to Lady Holland by Thomas Spring Rice*: 'The best joke of the evening was a practical one. Sir R. Inglis fell asleep in the gallery, and in that state was *told* among the staunch reformers'.[50] Inglis, whom John Croker* deemed to be one of the few Ultras who were 'sincerely, actively and usefully' co-operative with Peel at this juncture,[51] had voted against going into committee on the bill, 20 Jan., and did so against the enfranchisement of Tower Hamlets, 28 Feb. On 19 Mar. he delivered a last tirade against the third reading of the measure, arguing that 'when once you begin this system of change on principle there is no stopping; you must go on carrying your principles to their fullest extent, and thus abandon everything to folly and wickedness'. He divided against the third reading, 22 Mar. 1832.

He was sorry that ministers had allowed Briscoe to promulgate the doctrine that crown property belonged to the public, 17 Jan. 1832. He voted in the majority against the vestry bill, 23 Jan. Disclaiming party objects, he moved and carried a motion for an address for information on the treaties of 1690 and 1704 concerning the protection of the Protestant Vaudois in Sardinia, 24 Jan. He divided against government on the Russian-Dutch loan, 26 Jan. He was named to the select committee on the East India Company, 27 Jan. He approved the principle of Warburton's anatomy bill, 6, 27 Feb., when he was twice a teller for majori-

ties for recommitting it. On 11 Apr. he secured, by 50-6, the adoption of an amendment requiring an application to the home secretary countersigned by two magistrates for the opening of a school of anatomy. He failed then and on 18 Apr. with other restrictive amendments, and on the third reading, 11 May, lamented their rejection, but did not divide the House against the bill. He was a persistent critic of the government's scheme for Irish education, 13 Feb., 6, 16 Mar. (when he presented hostile petitions), 9, 11, 16 Apr., 7 May, that day he took issue with O'Connell for denouncing the hostility to it as 'cant and hypocrisy'. He kept up his resistance to significant interference with Irish tithes. On 14 Feb. he said that by their statements ministers would 'establish a premium for discontent' and encourage a combination against rent and taxes as well; and on the 16th he successfully divided the House, by 130-51, against reception of a petition from Leinster for their total abolition. On the ministerial proposals to deal with the problem, 8 Mar., he defended tithes in his usual terms and asserted that the Irish Catholic Members, having contributed to 'the destruction of the constitution', were now claiming 'as their reward that they should be allowed to complete the destruction of the Protestant establishment of Ireland'. Privately, however, he thought Smith Stanley's 'speech in reply to the Forty was excellent'.[52] When Irish Members ironically cheered his question to Smith Stanley as to whether ministers intended to 'consider not merely the rights of the present incumbents, but also the rights of the church *in perpetuum*', 30 Mar., he retorted that those cheers would 'teach the Protestant people of England what they have to expect'. He thwarted the printing of a petition for the abolition of tithes and the disunion of church and state, 8 May. On 14 Feb. he called for permanent measures against cholera, and two days later he replied waspishly to Hume's observation that the reference in the preamble to the Scottish prevention bill to cholera as a visitation of the Almighty was 'humbug'. He did not oppose the introduction of Lord Nugent's bill for the establishment of a general register of births, 23 Feb., though he regarded it as an example of 'one of the great evils of the present day ... a pruriency of legislation which will allow no subject to remain in the state it now is'. He called for the correction of the injustice done to the Irish registrar of deeds over his salary, 9 Apr. He defended the hereditary revenues of the crown, the grant for the payment of Oxford and Cambridge professors and the salary of the chaplain of Millbank penitentiary, 13 Apr. He opposed a bill to abolish the death penalty for many coining offences, 16 Apr. He secured the appointment of a new select committee on the Commons library, 8 May 1832.

In the debate on the ministerial crisis, 14 May 1832, Inglis put the last nail in the coffin of Conservative attempts to form a ministry with what the Whig Denis Le Marchant† later termed his 'blundering officiousness', when he declared, as an inveterate opponent of Whig principles in general and the reform bill in particular, that if Wellington or any other Conservative agreed to take charge of the measure, it would be 'one of the most fatal violations of public confidence which could be inflicted'. At dinner later that day Croker, who had found Inglis's speech hard to follow because of his 'low' tone of voice, recorded Peel's verdict that it had been '*fatal*, and conclusive against any government to be formed of any class of anti-reformers'. Inglis called on Peel to discuss the situation the following day.[53] He trusted that the Catholic marriages bill would not be rushed through 'in a slovenly manner' and welcomed the bill to appoint a trustee of the British Museum, 21 May. That day he objected to the language of some Scottish petitions for supplies to be withheld until reform was safe, and he challenged the veracity of O'Connell's boast that the Dublin one had been carried at a meeting of 60,000 people, 1 June. He voted against the second reading of the Irish reform bill, 25 May. He presented more petitions against the Irish education scheme, 31 May, when he also supported a charge of breach of privilege against the *Dublin Evening Mail* for publishing the draft report of the tithes committee. On 5 June he claimed O'Connell's vote against it, on the ground that he had declared that unless certain improvements were made to the Irish reform bill he would oppose every Irish grant. He spoke and voted in the minority against the education grant, 23 July. He objected to the 'extraordinary' reference by Charles Grant, 5 June, to the 'calamities' perpetrated by previous administrations, and asserted that the reformed Commons would not be 'a deliberative assembly'. On the Scottish reform bill, 27 June, when he also voted for Alexander Baring's bill to exclude insolvent debtors from Parliament, he said that it was 'very essential' that Scottish Members should give 'some security' that they had 'interests in the property of England and Wales'. He was against the public disclosure of the proceedings of coroners' inquests, 20 June. He tried to kill the births registry bill, 20 June, but withdrew his amendment after the gallery had been cleared for a division. On 28 June he called on Palmerston to dissociate ministers from O'Connell's condemnation of the tsar as a 'miscreant conqueror' of the Poles. He found the labourers employment bill so radically altered that he did not press his planned

opposition, 9 July. He conceded that the description of Catholicism as 'idolatry' in a Glasgow petition against the Maynooth grant overstepped the bounds of propriety, 10 July, though he observed, without apparent irony, that one of the consequences of emancipation which he had always feared was that the presence of Catholics in the House would inhibit those who wished to hurl abuse at their religion. He voted against government on the Russian-Dutch loan, 12 July, but on the 20th, though he accused them of harrying Holland, 'the great support of Protestant freedom in Europe', he abstained on a technicality.[54] Recently named as one of the ecclesiastical commissioners, he defended the grants for the Canadian church establishment and the Society for the Propagation of the Gospels in the colonies, 23 July. The following day he opposed the production of information on the number of persons imprisoned for selling unstamped publications since the previous December and voted in the minority of 16 against disqualification from Parliament of the recorder of Dublin. He was persuaded to postpone proceedings on the report of the select committee on the Commons library, on the basis of which he intended to propose the erection of a new building, 25 July. When he brought this up, 4 Aug. he was forced to abandon it. He presented and endorsed a Bristol petition for the eradication of bull-baiting, 31 July, calling as well for 'the abolition of various practices which are pursued by ... more exalted classes of society'. He supported the £4,000 retirement pension for the Speaker, 1 Aug. He spoke and was a teller for the minority against the retrospective operation of the ecclesiastical courts contempts bill, 3 Aug. 1832.

Shortly before the general election of 1832, when he came in again unopposed for the University, Inglis wrote to Giffard:

If it be true that there is any hesitation on the part of the king to go all lengths with his present ministers (a hesitation which, I grieve to own, I do not believe to exist, since I think it too clear that they have under his own hand his concurrence in their introduction of the French into the city of Antwerp) that hesitation may be fixed in the right direction by addresses calling upon the king to permit this Parliament to assemble on the day named by himself in his last prorogation, viz. the 11 December, and to decide on the expediency of the Dutch war. The present ministers have no right to complain of the present House of Commons. The session might be limited to an address: if that address should be in their favour, they would have such weight as the House of Commons can give in their scale; if it should be against them, we shall be saved from a war, the probable failure of which is a much less[er] evil than its certain injustice.[55]

Inglis continued to sit for Oxford University, as the uncompromising champion and defender of the Protestant establishment, who opposed Peel on the Maynooth issue in 1845 and repeal of the corn laws in 1846, until he retired because of 'impaired health' in 1855. He died at his London house at 7 Bedford Square in May 1855. By his will, dated 6 Feb. 1854, he left Milton Bryant, his other Bedfordshire property and the town house to his wife.[56] His baronetcy became extinct, and on the death of his widow Milton Bryant passed to Marianne Thornton, who took possession of it in 1873.[57] Inglis's abilities were modest, but he enjoyed considerable 'consequence' among the more obscurantist Conservative backbenchers. It was said of him that 'there is this redeeming quality in his alleged bigotry – he cordially pities those whom his creed obliges him to condemn'.[58] Tom Macaulay* likened him to his hero Perceval, except in talent: 'the same opinions both religious and political, the same rectitude of principle, the same sweetness of temper, the same bigotry and narrowness'.[59] He became, as Hobhouse noted, 'essentially a part of the House of Commons for many years'; and an anonymous obituarist wrote that 'the younger Members ... will, for many years to come ... recall to mind the Member for Oxford University, moving quietly on towards his place ... with a fresh flower at his button-hole, and with a genial smile and courteous word for everyone'.[60]

[1] HP Commons, 1790-1820, iv. 283-4. [2] Macaulay Letters, ii. 44. [3] Add. 40182, f. 33. [4] Pellew, Sidmouth, iii. 108; Add. 41227, f. 5. [5] Add. 41229, ff. 189, 191; Pellew, 109-12. [6] E.M. Forster, Marianne Thornton, 75; TCD, Jebb mss 6396/40; Southey Letters ed. J.W. Warter, iii. 53; Macaulay Letters, i. 101, 109; Life of Wilberforce, iv. 320-1. [7] PROB 11/1634/525; IR26/827/904. [8] Add. 41345, f. 301; 41346, f. 194; 40352, ff. 285, 286; 41353, ff. 1, 200; 40356, f. 313; 41357, f. 33; 40360, f. 224; 40370, ff. 185, 248, 274; 40371, f. 28, 214; Jebb mss 6396/211. [9] Life of Wilberforce, v. 249; Jebb mss 6396/217, 218, 220. [10] Southey Letters, iii. 488. [11] [J. Grant], Random Recollections of Commons (1837), 132. [12] Jebb mss 6396/226. [13] Ibid. 6396/238, 245, 246; Add. 36461, ff. 347, 400; Beds. RO, Wynne ms WY 999/1; Bodl. MS. Eng. lett. c. 159; Lambeth Palace Lib. MS. 4243, f. 53. [14] Jebb mss 6396/245, 246. [15] Ibid. 6396/238. [16] Ibid. 6396/245. [17] Ibid. 6396/248, 249. [18] Southey Letters, iv. 39-40. [19] Jebb mss 6396/249. [20] Colchester Diary, iii. 435; Nottingham Univ. Lib. Newcastle mss Ne2 F2/1. [21] Jebb mss 6396/266; Add. 56368, f. 93; Life and Corresp. of Southey ed. C.C. Southey, v. 273-4. [22] Add. 40389, ff. 103, 105, 244; 40394, ff. 39, 286; 40397, f. 164; Jebb mss 6396/267, 269. [23] Add. 40390, ff. 21, 23; Oxford DNB. [24] Jebb mss 6396/274, 275, 277. [25] Ibid. 6396/275. [26] Ibid. 6396/276, 277, 279, 280. [27] Colchester Diary, iii. 496, 498. [28] Jebb mss 6396/289. [29] Add. 40397, ff. 164, 181, 183. [30] Add. 51680; Grey mss, Ellice to Grey [31 Jan. 1829]. [31] Colchester Diary, iii. 594, 596; Broughton, Recollections, iii. 302. [32] Oxford University and City Herald, 14, 21, 28 Feb., 7 Mar; The Times, 3 Mar.; Add. 34570, ff. 154, 172, 180, 184; 51669, Bedford to Lady Holland, 18 Feb.; Hatherton mss, Littleton to Leigh, 16 Feb. 1829; Forster, 88-90. [33] Wilts. RO, Pembroke mss 2057/F4/50, Herbert to sister, 8 Mar. 1829. [34] Add. 34570, f. 180. [35] Broughton, 309; Ellenborough Diary, i. 381; Greville Mems. i. 265; Arbuthnot Jnl. ii. 249. [36] Grey mss, Howick jnl. [37] Brougham mss, Abercromby to Brougham [31 Mar. 1829]. [38] Jebb mss 6397/376. [39] Add. 56368, f. 95. [40] Croker Pprs. ii. 68. [41] Add. 34570, f. 329. [42] Macaulay Letters, i. 293. [43] Jebb mss 6397/409. [44] Broughton, iv. 80. [45] Add. 56368, f. 96. [46] PRO NI, Anglesey mss, Stanley to Anglesey, 2 Feb. 1831. [47] Le Marchant, Althorp, 299; St. Deiniol's Lib. Glynne-Gladstone mss 197, T. to J. Gladstone, 2 Mar.; Gurney diary, 1 Mar. 1831. [48] Jebb mss 6397/427. [49] NLW, Ormathwaite mss FG1/5, p. 186. [50] Add. 51573. [51] Croker Pprs. ii. 151. [52] Add. 56368, f. 101. [53] Three Diaries, 252, 255-6; Le Marchant, 431-2; Croker Pprs. ii. 166; Greville Mems. ii. 299; Add. 52058, C.R. to H.E. Fox, 15 May; Surr. Hist. Cent. Goulburn mss Acc 304/67B, Goulburn to wife, 15 May 1831. [54] Three Diaries, 279. [55] Add. 56368, f. 103. [56] Gent. Mag. (1855), i. 640-1; PROB 11/2214/517; IR26/2033/557. [57] Forster, 75, 241. [58] Grant, 131, 133. [59] Macaulay Letters, ii. 44. [60] Broughton, iii. 75; Gent. Mag. (1855), i. 640.

D.R.F.

INNES, Sir Hugh, 1st bt. (?1764–1831), of Balmacara House, Lochalsh, Ross and Regent Street, Mdx.

ROSS-SHIRE	28 Nov. 1809–1812
TAIN BURGHS	1812–1830
SUTHERLAND	1831–16 Aug. 1831

b. ?1764, o. surv. s. of Rev. Hugh Innes of Calton, Glasgow and Jean, da. of Thomas Graham. educ. Glasgow Univ. 1777. unm. cr. bt. 7 Dec. 1818. d. 16 Aug. 1831.

Innes, a wealthy landowner whose fortune may have been derived from trade, was returned for Tain Burghs for the third time in 1820 on the combined interests of James Stewart Mackenzie* of Brahan Castle, a Whig, and the countess of Sutherland and her husband, the Grenvillite 2nd marquess of Stafford.[1] He continued to be an occasional attender who gave silent support to Lord Liverpool's ministry, despite the views of his patrons. He evidently gave close attention to local legislation relating to improvements in road and coastal communications.[2] The fact that he was 'severely hurt' when his carriage overturned during the election campaign may account for the absence of any recorded votes by him during the 1820 session.[3] It was reported that he had divided against the motion criticizing the omission of Queen Caroline's name from the liturgy, 26 Jan. 1821. Lady Stafford afterwards observed that her husband, who had opposed the bill of pains and penalties, believed 'it would not have done to urge Sir Hugh further, as he is so connected and in the habit of receiving and asking things from ministry, that doing more than telling him how his opinions might have distressed and embarrassed [us]' would have been undesirable 'in the circumstances'.[4] He voted in defence of ministers' conduct towards the queen, 6 Feb. He divided against Maberly's resolution on the state of the revenue, 6 Mar., repeal of the additional malt duty, 3 Apr., and the disfranchisement of civil officers of the ordnance, 12 Apr. He was granted six weeks' leave for urgent private business, 18 Apr. 1821. In March 1822 Lady Stafford said that she would write to him on the subject of Scottish burgh reform, 'to make him aware of the importance of the subject'; he gave no recorded votes that session.[5] Thereafter, Stafford's adherence to government must have made Innes's position much easier. He voted against inquiry into the prosecution of the Dublin Orange rioters, 22 Apr. 1823. There are no recorded votes by him for the 1824 session. He divided against repeal of the usury laws, 17 Feb. 1825. He voted for the Irish unlawful societies bill, 25 Feb., but for Catholic relief, 1 Mar., 21 Apr., 10 May. He divided for the financial provision for the duke of Cumberland, 30 May, 6, 10 June 1825. It was said of him at this time that he 'appeared to attend very seldom and to vote with government'.[6] He voted against the motion condemning the Jamaican slave trials, 2 Mar. 1826. He presented Dingwall and Kirkwall petitions against any alteration to the Scottish banking system, 10 Mar., 14 Apr.[7] He divided against reform of Edinburgh's representation, 13 Apr. 1826. At the general election that summer he was again returned unopposed for Tain Burghs.[8]

He divided for Catholic relief, 6 Mar. 1827. He voted against repeal of the Test Acts, 26 Feb., but paired for Catholic claims, 12 May 1828. He divided with the duke of Wellington's ministry against the motion condemning delays in chancery, 24 Apr. 1828. In February 1829 Planta, the patronage secretary, listed him as likely to be 'with government' for Catholic emancipation, and he voted accordingly, 6, 30 Mar. He presented Ross-shire petitions against any alteration to the law of entail in Scotland, 13, 16 Apr. 1829. Surprisingly, the Ultra Tory leader Sir Richard Vyvyan* listed him that autumn as one of those supporters of emancipation whose sentiments towards a putative coalition ministry were 'unknown'. He divided against the enfranchisement of Birmingham, Leeds and Manchester, 23 Feb., and Jewish emancipation, 17 May 1830. He was granted a month's leave for urgent private business, 7 Apr., but had returned by the 29th to present petitions from Wick council in favour of the Caithness statute labour bill and from Reay farmers and Caithness proprietors against it. He voted for the grant for South American missions and against abolition of the death penalty for forgery, 7 June 1830. At the dissolution that summer he retired to make way for James Loch, the auditor of Stafford's estates. However, Stafford, having switched his allegiance to Lord Grey's ministry, returned Innes for his wife's 'pocket' county of Sutherland at the general election of 1831 as a 'decided' supporter of the reform

bill and of economy, who hoped that on other issues 'his opinion ... would be found in unison with the voice of the nation'.[9] He divided for the second reading of the reintroduced reform bill, 6 July, and steadily for its details until 3 Aug. 1831. He died later that month 'in his sixty-eighth year' and his title 'expired with him'; no will or administration has been found.[10]

[1] NAS GD46/4/123, Innes to Loch, 29 Nov. 1819; *Inverness Courier*, 6 Apr. 1820. [2] NAS GD46/13/25 and 17/54 contain several letters from Innes on these matters. [3] *Glasgow Herald*, 31 Mar. 1820. [4] Macpherson Grant mss 361, Macpherson Grant to Lady Stafford, 27 Jan., reply, 1 Feb. 1821. [5] Ibid. 516, Lady Stafford to Macpherson Grant, 20 Mar. 1822. [6] *Session of Parl. 1825*, p. 470. [7] *The Times*, 11 Mar., 14 Apr. 1826. [8] *Inverness Courier*, 5 July 1826. [9] Ibid. 11 May, 1 June 1831. [10] *Gent. Mag.* (1831), ii. 373; *Inverness Jnl.* 26 Aug. 1831.

T.A.J.

INNES, John (1767–1838), of 9 Broad Street Buildings, London.

GRAMPOUND   1818–1826

bap. 28 Dec. 1767, s. of William Innes of Auldearn, Nairn and w. Anna née Smith.[1] *m.* Mary Anne, 2da.[2] *d.* 24 Nov. 1838.

Dir. Alliance Life and Fire Assurance Co. 1824–*d.*, London Dock Co. 1829–*d.*; commr. for issuing exch. bills 1829-30.

Capt. 6 Loyal London vols. 1803.

Innes, who was born in Nairnshire, was established in London by the beginning of the nineteenth century as a partner in the East India agency of Scott, Bonham, Hartwell, Innes and Company (later Fairlie, Bonham and Company) at 9 Broad Street Buildings.[3] He was connected in some way with the dissolute 4th duke of Gordon, who in 1816 offered him a superiority in Inverness-shire for £416 and later made him one of his trustees.[4] Indeed, Gordon was reputed to be the real father of Innes's younger daughter Matilda, who had the given name of Maxwell, the family name of the duke's first wife.[5] Innes lent money to and was on familiar terms with Gordon's eldest son Lord Huntly, who succeeded as 5th (and last) duke in 1827, and whose pious wife Elizabeth, the daughter of the Scottish nabob Alexander Brodie†, became a close family friend.[6]

At the general election of 1820 Innes was returned again for the venal borough of Grampound, which had been earmarked for disfranchisement as punishment for the corruption exposed by investigation of the 1818 election, but was temporarily reprieved by the intervention of the Lords.[7] He continued to give general support to Lord Liverpool's ministry, but was evidently a lax attender and is not known to have spoken in debate.[8] He was credited with presenting the Colchester election petition, 26 July 1820.[9] He voted in defence of ministers' conduct towards Queen Caroline, 6 Feb., and rallied to them against repeal of the additional malt duty, 3 Apr. 1821. He divided against Catholic relief, 28 Feb. He voted in the minority against the imprisonment of the author of an article in *John Bull* for breach of privilege, 11 May 1821. He divided against more extensive tax reductions, 11, 21 Feb. 1822. He voted against the removal of Catholic peers' disabilities, 30 Apr., and inquiry into Irish tithes, 19 June 1822. He voted against inquiry into the prosecution of the Dublin Orange rioters, 22 Apr., but was in the minority, with his colleague Alexander Robertson, against the reciprocity of duties bill, 4 July 1823. He may have been the 'J. Inglis' who divided against the motion condemning the prosecution of the Methodist missionary John Smith in Demerara, 11 June 1824. He voted for the Irish insurrection bill three days later. He divided for the Irish unlawful societies bill, 25 Feb., paired against Catholic relief, 1 Mar., and voted against it, 21 Apr., 10 May 1825. He was in the minorities against the government's emergency currency proposals, 13 Feb., and for revision of the corn laws, 18 Apr. 1826. The disfranchisement of Grampound, which became effective at the dissolution that summer, left him without a seat, and he is not known to have sought election elsewhere.

In March 1830 Innes observed stoically to Matilda (who in 1828 had married the impecunious Rev. William Scott Robinson, third son of Sir George Abercrombie Robinson†, an East India Company director) that he had 'met with so many disappointments for some time past and ... had to struggle against such a number of unexpected difficulties', that he was 'unable to gratify the anxious desire to add more amply to your [financial] comforts'.[10] The following year his other daughter Eliza married, rather against his wishes, Edward Grey, a younger brother of the prime minister, who was made bishop of Hereford soon afterwards. Grey was 20 years her senior, already had 13 children by two previous marriages and died in debt in 1837, leaving her with three infant children of her own.[11] On 4 July 1833 the Broad Street Buildings agency, 'one of the first standing in the East India trade', and now styled Fairlie, Clarke, Innes and Company, stopped payment. The duchess of Gordon wrote fatuously to Matilda four days later:

How very deeply I feel with you, and as another daughter, the affliction of your dear father. I have told him if all

who had felt his kindness joined in prayer for his comfort what a rich treasure he would have yet in store. I am sure there are many who will remember him at the Throne of Grace.

In the interim Innes, though doubtless consoled, had to sell 'sundry plate' for £70 in 1836.[12] He died in November 1838. By his brief will, he directed that two farms in Berkshire and Surrey and a total of 400 shares in the Alliance Fire and Life Assurance Company and the Alliance Marine Insurance Company, which he held as trustee for 'the late firm' of Fairlie, Clarke and Innes, should be sold for the benefit of its current representatives. He divided his personal estate, which was nominally sworn under £1,500 but realized only £165, between his two daughters. His Scottish friends drew up plans for the erection of a school at Auldearn 'to perpetuate the memory of a man of worth'.[13] One of the mysteries surrounding him is his relationship with Sarah Holder, 'otherwise Innes', who died at Bath in 1865, aged 85. On the burial certificate (14 Jan.) she was described as a widow, but the probate record of her will, which was executed by the Rev. William Scott Robinson, referred to her as a spinster. She divided the meagre residue of her estate between Matilda Robinson and Eliza Grey. Her unmarried daughter Sarah was probably Innes's child.[14]

[1] IGI (Nairn). [2] Ibid. (London). [3] *Scott Corresp.* ed. C.H. Philips (Cam. Soc. ser. 3, lxxvi.), 418, 443. [4] BL OIOC, Robinson Coll. MSS. Eur. F.142/38, Anderson to Innes, 6, 20 Apr. 1816; *LJ*, lxv. 49. [5] Intro. to NRA report (27534) on Robinson Coll. [6] MSS. Eur. F.142/38, Huntly to Innes, 19 Aug. 1826, 13 Nov. 1829; 44, Innes to Matilda Robinson [3 Aug. 1830]; 45 *passim*. [7] *West Briton*, 3, 10 Mar. 1820. [8] *Black Bk* (1823), 167; *Session of Parl. 1825*, p. 470. [9] *The Times*, 27 July 1820. [10] MSS. Eur. F.142/44, Innes to Matilda Robinson, 11 Mar. 1830. [11] Ibid. F.142/45, duchess of Gordon to Matilda Robinson, 24 Nov. 1831; *Gent. Mag.* (1837), ii. 311; Grey mss, Innes to Grey, 10, 15 Apr., reply, 11 Apr. 1838. [12] *The Times*, 5 July 1833; MSS. Eur. F.142/38, 45. [13] PROB 11/1904/763; IR26/1488/721; MSS. Eur. F.142/40. [14] MSS. Eur. F.142/51 *passim*.

D.R.F.

IRONMONGER, Richard (?1772–1826), of Effingham, Surr. and North Lodge, Brighton, Suss.

STAFFORD 1826–29 July 1826

b. ?1772, grands. of Richard Ironmonger of Derby. *m.* 30 June 1798, Ann Bradley, *s.p. d.* 29 July 1826.

Ironmonger's family came from Derby, where his sister Sarah married John Slack in 1793, but little is known about his parents.[1] His grandfather and namesake, a maltster who owned dwelling houses in Bold Lane, Sadler Gate and Wardwick, died there, 30 Apr. 1779, leaving his son William, who was presumably

Ironmonger's father, 'the sum of five shillings to be paid him weekly upon every Monday morning during his natural life', by his will of 9 Dec. 1777. His Derby properties, which were occupied by 15 tenants, were divided between his son-in-law Robert Grayson, his daughters Sarah Pollatt and Lydia Ironmonger and his grandson Richard. (His other grandchildren, Sarah, Dorothy and William Ironmonger, shared legacies totalling £200.)[2] In the 1790s Ironmonger moved to London, where he married at St. Martin-in-the-Fields, 30 June 1798.[3] By 1803 he was established at 35 Gerrard Street, Soho and working as a coachmaster from Charing Cross. In a civil action of that year, brought against the driver of a chaise-cart who had collided with one of his horses, he was described as 'a proprietor of several coaches, which ran between London and Brighton and places adjacent'.[4] These operated from the Swan Coach Office at Charing Cross, where he was registered in 1808, and from the *George and Blue Boar Inn* at Holborn, of which he owned the leasehold at his death. He did not trade under his own name, however, and was probably associated with Crossweller and Company, who operated coaches to and from the same locations. He was no longer recorded there in 1818, but was described as 'a coach proprietor in town' by Edward Littleton* two years later.[5] He moved to Effingham in Surrey and was 'an active Sussex magistrate' on the Brighton bench for a number of years.[6]

At the 1820 general election Ironmonger stood for Stafford, describing himself as 'an intimate friend of the late R.B. Sheridan', Member from 1780-1806, whom, it was later claimed, he had done much to 'comfort' during his final illness. In a published address, which he subsequently retracted as having been 'modified' by a friend without his knowledge and 'capable of misconstruction', he promised to help 'restore the depressed middle and lower classes of society to the independence and prosperity of other days ... to rescue their rights and privileges from the usurpations of the rich and powerful', and to 'oppose the unjust and scandalous system of taxation which fetters and depresses trade'. He also advocated 'shorter parliaments' and 'more frequent communications' between Members and their constituents. His 'official' address, published a week later, described him as 'an enemy of corruption' and a 'strenuous supporter of civil and religious liberty', 'the advocate of temperate reform' and 'a loyal subject to the king'. He was enrolled as a burgess by the corporation, 6 Mar. 1820.[7] Following his narrow defeat, he paid his election bills promptly and was considered to have 'terminated the contest in a manner most liberal and worthy

of his character'. Tributes from the town's inhabitants and corporation followed, and an address of thanks signed by 375 electors credited him with ensuring 'the unexampled tranquility which has prevailed during this contested election'.[8] Encouraged by this support, he offered again at the general election of 1826, when both the sitting Members retired. Considered 'more radical than most coachmasters', and later described as 'zealously devoted to all liberal institutions, and the amelioration of society', he pledged himself to support reform of the poor laws. With the support of the corporation he topped the poll.[9] His defeated opponent John Campbell I* observed that 'he sat all day at the right hand of the mayor, drinking porter and brandy', and had 'the appearance and manners of a coachman accustomed to drive the night heavy to Birmingham'.[10]

On 22 July 1826 it was reported that Ironmonger had been 'confined to his house through severe indisposition' and would be unable to keep an engagement in Stafford. A week later he died at North Lodge, his Brighton home, without taking his seat.[11] By his will, dated 28 Aug. 1825 and proved under £7,000, he provided annuities for his wife and sisters Sarah Slack and Dorothy Thompson, and left legacies to his nephew John Slack and his nieces Maria and Jane Slack. Costs were charged to six entrusted houses in Brighton, one at Worthing, three in Surrey, the *George and Blue Boar*, the Union Coffee House in Cockspur Street and property in Chancery Lane and at 24 Lincoln's Inn Fields, London.[12]

[1] *Gent. Mag.* (1793), ii. 766.   [2] Lichfield RO, consistory ct. 1779, Richard Ironmonger.   [3] IGI.   [4] *The Times,* 24 Mar. 1803.   [5] IR26/1089/697; Hatherton diary, 21 Mar. 1820.   [6] *Gent. Mag.* (1826) ii. 382; J.C. Wedgwood, *Staffs. Parl. Hist.* iii. 58.   [7] T. Moore, *Mem. Sheridan* (1825), 688; *Staffs. Advertiser,* 26 Feb., 4 Mar. 1820; Staffs. RO, town council order bk. D1323/A/1/4.   [8] *Staffs. Advertiser,* 11, 18, 25 Mar. 1820.   [9] Wedgwood, iii. 58; *Gent. Mag.* (1826) ii. 382; *Staffs. Advertiser,* 27 May, 10, 17 June 1826.   [10] *Life of Campbell,* i. 433; *Aris's Birmingham Gazette,* 12 June 1826.   [11] *Staffs. Advertiser,* 22 July, 5 Aug. 1826.   [12] PROB 11/1715/438; IR26/1089/697.

P.J.S.

IRVING, John (1766–1845), of Ashford, Mdx.

| BRAMBER | 1806–1832 |
| CO. ANTRIM | 1837–10 Nov. 1845 |

bap. 5 Oct. 1766,[1] 1st s. of John Irving of Cushathill and Burnfoot in Middlebie, Dumfries and his w. *née* Rae. *educ.* Middlebie parish sch. *unm. d.* 10 Nov. 1845.

Vol. London and Westminster light horse 1796-1814.

Dir. W.I. Dock Co. 1811-34; pres. Alliance Life and Fire Assurance Co. 1824-*d*.

Irving, a wealthy London merchant and financier of Scottish extraction, was a partner in Reid, Irving and Company, a concern of second-ranking importance whose dealings, originally concentrated in the West Indies, were increasingly extended worldwide; his partner Sir John Rae Reid* was a director of the Bank of England. He also collaborated with the better known merchant houses of Gurney, Montefiore, Baring and Rothschild, notably in the foundation of the Alliance Assurance company, and with the last two houses he was involved in negotiations over the Austrian loan at the Congress of Verona in 1823, 'a transaction requiring remarkable ability, and bringing him into contact with nearly all the great statesmen of that assembly'.[2]

He continued to sit undisturbed for Bramber throughout this period, on the interest of his friend the 5th duke of Rutland. A radical publication in 1820 classed him among 'the most determined adherents' of Lord Liverpool's ministry.[3] He was a regular attender who spoke more frequently than in previous Parliaments, mainly on subjects connected to his business interests. He was one of a handful of businessmen named to the select committees on agricultural distress in 1820, 1821 and 1822, and he was a fixture on those inquiring into foreign trade between 1820 and 1824. He delivered the select committee report on General Desfourneaux's compensation claim for losses incurred during the British occupation of Guadaloupe in 1794, 14 July 1820, and replied to objections to the proposed grant, 13, 15, 28 June 1821, although he could not prevent its substantial reduction.[4] He voted in defence of ministers' conduct towards Queen Caroline, 6 Feb. As a director of the West India Dock Company he replied to a petition against renewal of its charter, 27 Feb. Next day he voted against Catholic relief. He divided against Maberly's motion on the state of the revenue, 6 Mar., repeal of the additional malt duty, 3 Apr., reduction of the barracks grant, 28 May, omission of arrears from the duke of Clarence's grant, 18 June, and Hume's economy and retrenchment motion, 27 June. He expressed surprise at reports of the Bank of Ireland refusing gold currency as payment, 28 Mar. He approved the Bank of England's plan to augment the circulating metal currency, 9 Apr., explaining that while he had opposed the resumption of cash payments in 1819 he feared an inquiry would merely cause public alarm; inexplicably, his name appears in the minority list in favour of a select committee. He was a minority teller against the grant to pay exchequer bills, 26 June. He voted against the disfranchisement of ordnance officials, 12 Apr., and Russell's reform resolutions, 9 May 1821. He divided against more extensive

tax reductions, 11, 21 Feb., and abolition of one of the joint-postmasterships, 13 Mar. 1822. He voted against removing Catholic peers' disabilities, 30 Apr. He was the originator of the agriculture select committee's proposal for the government to subsidize farmers to warehouse surplus corn,[5] a plan that met with ridicule when it came before the Commons, 6 May. He diffidently confessed his authorship when pressed by the leader of the House, Lord Londonderry, who then withdrew the resolution 'seeing that [it] was not supported by those who brought it forward'. Two days later an offended Irving gave only grudging support to Londonderry's plan to revise the corn duties, comparing it unfavourably with his original scheme, which he complained had been tampered with by the committee. He voted in the minority for Canning's clause to permit the export of bonded corn, 10 June. He supported a compensation claim from a merchant whose ship had been destroyed by the Spanish, 26 July 1822.[6]

Irving divided against repeal of the Foreign Enlistment Act, 16 Apr., inquiries into delays in chancery, 5 June, and the currency, 12 June, and for repeal of the usury laws, 27 June 1823. He welcomed an attempt to reform the Irish banking system, 12 Mar. 1824. He voted against the motion condemning the trial of the Methodist missionary John Smith in Demerara, 11 June. He divided for the Irish insurrection bill, 14 June 1824, the Irish unlawful societies bill, 25 Feb., and against Catholic relief, 1 Mar., 21 Apr., 10 May 1825. He voted for the duke of Cumberland's annuity, 6, 10 June 1825. Like many other business Members he divided against the government's proposed alterations in the banking system following the recent crash, 13 Feb., but he was satisfied with their bill to restrict the circulation of small notes once a clause had been inserted to extend the life of those issued by the Bank, 20 Feb. 1826. He defended the Bank for its sale and purchase of exchequer bills, its lending policy and its close links with government, 15, 27 Feb. He also publicized its concern to produce a note less amenable to forgers, 21 Mar. He assured the House that 'a just reciprocity of advantages' had been secured in the South American treaties bill, 23 Feb., but was scathing about reciprocal trading arrangements in general when supporting a petition for a duty on foreign shipping, 17 Apr. He voted to receive the report on the salary of the president of the board of trade, 10 Apr. He divided against the motion condemning the Jamaican slave trials, 2 Mar., reform of Edinburgh's representation, 13 Apr., and Russell's resolutions against electoral bribery, 26 May. While defending the corn laws, 8 May 1826, he was prepared to admit some relaxation in their terms.

He divided against Catholic relief, 6 Mar. 1827, 12 May, and repeal of the Test Acts, 26 Feb. 1828. He voted for the duke of Clarence's annuity, 16 Mar. He supported a fixed duty on foreign flour, 19 Mar., and defended the existing corn laws against Hume's attack, 27 Mar., arguing that the latter's free trade principles were 'good in the abstract but ... unfortunately impractical' as they would 'subject the most important interest in the country to a course of slow but constant depression and decay'. He gave his 'hearty concurrence' to the Canning ministry's customs bill, 1 June, and voted with them against the Penryn disfranchisement bill, 28 May, 7 June 1827. That August he privately assured John Charles Herries*, the newly appointed chancellor of the exchequer in Lord Goderich's ministry, that he enjoyed broad support in the City.[7] In opposing a higher scale of corn duties, 29 Apr. 1828, his concern to protect the agricultural interest brought him into dispute with Lord Milton over manufacturing labour costs. Despite his general protectionist sympathies, he believed the free importation of wool was necessary to manufacturing industry, 3 June (a view which he repeated, 3 June 1829, 1 Mar. 1830). He favoured repeal of the usury laws, 19 June, but wished to retain restrictions on advances secured upon landed property, invoking the image of the feckless aristocrat 'ignorant of the principles of business' and needing protection. He paired with the duke of Wellington's ministry against the motion criticizing the expenditure on building work at Buckingham House, 23 June 1828. In February 1829 Planta, the patronage secretary, listed him as one who was 'doubtful' on the question of Catholic emancipation, but in the event he voted for it, 6 Mar. He spoke in favour of a grant to the West India docks, 14 Apr., and defended the dock company's purchase of the City canal, 16 Apr. He defended Sir Robert Townshend Farquhar*, the former governor of Mauritius, from allegations that he had been slow to suppress the slave trade there, 3 June 1829, and launched an attack on the *Anti-Slavery Reporter*, which responded that as a West India merchant Irving was 'in some measure entitled to be galled by our writings'.[8] He was named to the select committee on the East India Company, 9 Feb. 1830. He divided against transferring East Retford's seats to Birmingham, 11 Feb., Lord Blandford's reform plan, 18 Feb., and the enfranchisement of Birmingham, Leeds and Manchester, 23 Feb. On 16 Mar. he caused some annoyance by reading letters from manufacturing districts to contradict opposition claims about the extent of distress, and declared his support for the gold standard. He voted against a reduction in judges' salaries, 7 July 1830.

The ministry regarded Irving as one of their 'friends', and he voted with them in the crucial civil list division, 15 Nov. 1830. He was named to the renewed select committees on the East India Company, 4 Feb., 28 June, 28 Dec. 1831. He praised Alderman Waithman's exertions in the field of trade, 'however much I may differ from him', 15 Feb., but did not share his concern over the export of unfinished articles such as cotton twist. He spoke in favour of permitting the use of sugar and molasses in distilleries as a means of affording relief to the West India interest, 11 Mar. He raised the spectre of Buonaparte when supporting a grant to the recruiting service, 14 Mar., and denounced Hume's opposition as 'sordid economy'. He divided against the second reading of the Grey ministry's reform bill, 22 Mar., and for Gascoyne's wrecking amendment, 19 Apr. 1831. He never explained his anti-reform stance to the House, but according to the family historian his antipathy to constitutional innovation had been imbibed on an earlier visit to the United States.[9] He divided against the second reading of the reintroduced reform bill, 6 July, and its passage, 21 Sept. 1831. He reiterated his support for the corn laws, 24 June. That day he introduced a bill for the construction of the West India docks, which gained royal assent, 23 Aug. (1 & 2 Gul. IV, c. 52). He supported a reduction in the coffee duty, 25 July. He spoke against a bill to place restrictions on steam vessels, 29 Aug. He objected 'almost without exception' to the proposals made by the select committee on the reduction of official salaries (of which he was a member), 29 Sept., and ventured the opinion that many salaries were in fact too low. He opposed a government proposal to allow foreign sugar to be refined in Britain, 11 Oct. He divided against the second reading of the revised reform bill, 17 Dec. 1831, the enfranchisement of Tower Hamlets, 28 Feb., and the third reading, 22 Mar. 1832. He was named to the select committee on the renewal of the Bank of England's charter, 23 May, and spoke in the Bank's defence, 26, 27 July. He objected to the orders in council aimed at ending slavery in the West Indies, 4 June, 27 July, 8 Aug., mainly on the ground that they were unenforceable. In a letter the previous autumn to the colonial secretary Goderich he had gone further, refusing to condemn slavery and preferring to focus upon the continued trading in slaves in areas outside British jurisdiction, against which he advocated military action. He maintained that freed slaves 'almost invariably sink into a life of vagabondage', and he defended the use of whips in the colonies as necessary among 'a population so prone to indolence and idleness'. The *Anti-Slavery Reporter* congratulated

Goderich on his principled rejection of the 'miserable sophistry' of these arguments, but Irving continued to lobby him about the abolition of slavery in Mauritius, for whose proprietors he acted as an agent.[10] He voted against ministers on the Russian-Dutch loan, 12 July, and obtained no answer to a query about the ministerial response in the event of the Greek government defaulting on loan interest payments, 23 July. With Bramber disfranchised, he offered for Clitheroe, but his visit to that borough provoked a riot. He told the Commons, 10 Aug. 1832, that he regretted the consequent use of military force, and he ascribed his hostile reception to his support for the anatomy bill, 'the terms boroughmonger and Tory being much too general to excite the hatred displayed on that occasion'. At the general election later that year he was defeated by a Liberal.

Irving stood unsuccessfully for Poole in 1835 but was returned as a Conservative for County Antrim in 1837. Later business ventures, like his bank in Mauritius and the Royal Steam Packet Company, reflected the change in circumstances after the abolition of slavery, to which he seemed entirely reconciled. He was also involved in the project to build a railway across the isthmus of Panama. He died, 'aged 78', in November 1845 and left the bulk of his estates in London, Middlesex and Scotland to his nephew and namesake. His inability to bequeath his business acumen to his partners may perhaps account for the collapse of Reid, Irving and Company two years after his death.[11]

[1] IGI (Dumfries). [2] *Gent. Mag.* (1846), i. 93-95; R.W. Hidy, *House of Baring in American Trade*, 79; H. Cockerell and E. Green, *British Insurance Business*, 61. [3] *Black Bk.* (1820), 425, 434. [4] *The Times*, 15 July 1820, 14, 16, 29 June 1821. [5] B. Hilton, *Corn, Cash, Commerce*, 154-5. [6] *The Times*, 27 July 1822. [7] E. Herries, *Mems. Herries*, i. 227. [8] *Anti-Slavery Reporter* (June 1829), 11. [9] J.B. Irving, *The Irvings*, 216-19. [10] *PP* (1831-2), xlvi. 173; *Anti-Slavery Reporter* (Jan. 1832), 53; Add. 40879, ff. 206-14. [11] Irving, 216-19; PROB 11/2028/916.

H.J.S.

JAMES, William (1791–1861), of Barrock Lodge, Lower Heskett, Cumb.[1]

CARLISLE	31 May 1820–1826
CARLISLE	1831–1834
CUMBERLAND EAST	2 Sept. 1836–1847

b. 29 Mar. 1791, 1st. s. of William Evans James (*d.* 1795) of Clayton Square, Liverpool and Elizabeth, da. of Nicholas Ashton of Woolton Hall, Lancs. *educ.* Eton 1808; Jesus, Camb. 4 July, migrated to Trinity Coll. 17 Nov. 1808. *m.* 26 Feb. 1816, Frances, da. of William

Calton Rutson, cotton broker, of St. Anne's Street, Liverpool and Allerton Priory, Lancs., 10s. (6 *d.v.p.*) 3da. (1 *d.v.p.*). *suc.* grandfa. William James to Clifton Hill Plantation, Saint Thomas-in-the-East, Jamaica 1798. *d.* 4 May 1861.
Sheriff, Cumb. 1827-8.

James, a cradle radical, was baptized on 26 Apr. 1791 at Paradise Street Unitarian Chapel in Liverpool, where his paternal grandfather William James (1735-98) of Finch House, Knotty Ash (a younger son of John James of Culgarth, Cumberland and West Auckland, County Durham) had made his fortune as a West India merchant.[2] He was four when his father died leaving a widow enceinte and two young sons; and as residuary legatee under his grandfather's will proved on 16 Feb. 1798, he became heir to a Jamaican estate and a mercantile fortune entrusted to his maternal grandfather and uncles Richard Walker and John James until he reached the age of 26.[3] In 1801 his mother, heiress, through her maternal grandfather John Philpot of Chester, to the Warburton estate of Hefferton Grange, married the Liverpool radical and veteran of the American wars Lieutenant-Colonel George Williams†, from whom James derived his early political bias.[4] He boarded at Sumner's House at Eton with his mother's half-brothers Ellis and Henry Ashton, and after graduating from Cambridge in 1813 he purchased Barrock Lodge, the 3rd duke of Portland's former estate near Carlisle, from John Graham. He settled there on his marriage in 1816 to the only daughter of the cotton broker William Calton Rutson, sometime partner of William Ewart in Liverpool and Arthur Clegg in Manchester. He canvassed with his relations for the Whig lawyer Henry Brougham* in Liverpool in 1812, backed him and the anti-Lowther party in Cumberland and Westmorland in 1818, and made no secret of his own ambition to sit for Carlisle, where he could rely on radical support.[5] Shortly before the general election of 1820 he informed the Broughams, who thought their Westmorland campaign would benefit from an electoral diversion in Carlisle, that he was not prepared to sacrifice his

many comforts and enjoyments to party views or the empty pleasures of ambition, which would be the case were I to become Member for Carlisle. Besides, at present I am labouring under the same disadvantages and losses common to those whose incomes materially depend upon the prices of foreign produce, so much so indeed that this year I have scarcely sufficient to meet my current expenses, so that if I had even the inclination to stand for Carlisle it would under these circumstances be impossible.[6]

His late decision to contest the borough, where he came a poor third behind the sitting Members (the Whig John Christian Curwen and the Lowther nominee Sir James Graham) was accordingly seen as a ploy to further Curwen's return for Cumberland and secure Whig support as his replacement at Carlisle.[7] He topped the poll there in a tumultuous contest at the by-election in May at a personal cost of £17,000, £4,000 more than he would ever acknowledge.[8] He repeated his success at Lancaster races on 26 Sept. 1820, when his mount, owner up, defeated his opponent Sir Philip Musgrave's*, ridden by Sir Tatton Sykes.[9]

James, as a radical publication of 1825 observed, 'attended with great regularity and voted with the opposition'.[10] Making parliamentary reform his political priority, he divided almost daily with Hume and the Whig 'Mountain'. His frequent interventions in debate were bold, irreverent and occasionally humorous, but he had no pretensions as an orator and he made no major speeches before 1833.[11] He acknowledged his obligations as a West India planter and professed support for the abolition of slavery, but he presented no petitions requesting it, preferring instead to challenge the abolitionists to join him in campaigning on behalf of the 'white slaves' of England. He supported the 1820 and 1821 parliamentary and extra-parliamentary campaigns on behalf of Queen Caroline, and endorsed the strongly worded petition he presented from Carlisle condemning the bill of pains and penalties and its instigators, 26 Jan. 1821. He trounced the Lowthers and enabled opposition to capitalize on the deployment of troops at his election by tactically postponing consideration of Carlisle's petition for inquiry, 'on account of the queen's case', 28 June, 3 July 1820.[12] After obtaining information on barrack provision in the vicinity of Carlisle, 6 Mar., he revived the issue, in what his backbench colleague Henry Grey Bennet termed a 'a good, firm, popular, stout speech', 15 Mar. 1821, and the Lowthers and their partisans failed to prevent the matter being referred to the committee of privileges.[13] James was added to it, 30 Mar., and approved their report's finding that civil authority should have sufficed and their decision not to take further action against the summoning magistrates, 3 Apr. He had drawn an admission from the foreign secretary Lord Castlereagh, 24 Jan., that there was little prospect of early repayment of the Austrian loan, and, joining in the ensuing protests, he alluded to its damaging effect on the domestic tax burden and 'tyrannical' Austria's ability to wage war against 'independent' Naples, 1 Feb. He presented a Liverpool distress petition urging its repayment, 14 Mar., and spoke for Robert Smith's abortive motion for

further papers, 22 June.[14] On reform, he sent a letter of support to the Cumberland meeting, 5 Apr., and presented and endorsed their petition before dividing for Lord John Russell's resolutions, 9 May, having voted for Lambton's scheme, 18 Apr.[15] His connection with Williams and the reformers of the Liverpool Concentric Society made James a natural spokesman for the parliamentary campaign on behalf of radicals imprisoned after Peterloo. He confirmed on presenting a petition of complaint from Nathaniel Broadhurst, 7 Mar., that his Lancaster gaolers had opened letters addressed to him, but he failed (by 86-33) to have the matter declared a breach of privilege.[16] He presented further petitions from Broadhurst and his correspondents, including one from Williams, 15 May, 6 June 1821.[17]

To the acclaim of the Whig *Carlisle Journal*, whose editor Francis Jollie dedicated that year's edition of his *Political History of Carlisle* to him, James voted indefatigably with Hume for economy and retrenchment throughout the 1822 session.[18] Backed by petitions from Broadhurst and Edward Clayton in Lancaster gaol, he renewed his attempt to have interference with Members' mail declared a breach of privilege, 22 Feb. His case, based on legal opinions published by Sir Samuel Romilly[†] in 1812, had limited appeal outside radical circles and the motion was defeated (by 167-60), 25 Feb. Undeterred, he presented and endorsed similar petitions, 1, 7, 22 Mar.[19] He spoke in favour of receiving a petition of complaint against the Ilchester magistrates from the licensee William Priddle, 19 June.[20] Reflecting the influence of William Cobbett[†], whom he first met at Liverpool in November 1819, he called for parliamentary reform and universal suffrage on presenting a distress petition from Carlisle, 1 May, and attributed the petitioners' plight to 'excessive taxation', which could only be remedied by massive tax reductions. He disputed the political economist Ricardo's theories on the currency and the correlation between corn prices, supply and demand, and caused great mirth by referring him to the writings of Cobbett and citing his tenet that cash flow restriction would 'double the weight of taxation'. He was for receiving radical distress petitions from the Norfolk hundreds of Greenhoe, 3 June, and Grimshaw, 4 June.[21] He condemned the small notes bill as a measure for sanctioning 'a return to everlasting payments in paper', 2 July 1822, and, ignoring Curwen's admonitions to the contrary, he became a minority teller, with Lord Folkstone, against its passage. He voted for the amendment to the address censuring Lord Beresford's appointment as lieutenant-general of the ordnance (as an ally of the new foreign secretary Canning), 19 Feb.

1823, and continued to divide unstintingly with the radicals. He was responsible for mustering opposition to the corporation-sponsored Carlisle police bill that session, and rejoiced in its defeat, 21 Mar.[22] He was ridiculed for supporting Cobbett's Norfolk distress petition, which most Whigs, including its presenter Coke, denounced, 24 Apr., and made a great show of announcing, 18 June, and presenting a heavily signed radical reform petition from Newcastle-upon-Tyne, 19 June. He fully endorsed the petitioners' demands for the ballot and universal suffrage and blamed the repressive legislation carried by the Liverpool ministry after Peterloo in 1819 for making their plight worse than that of black slaves on his estates.[23] He urged the total repeal of the corn laws before voting to lower the pivot price to 60s., 26 Feb., and called again for their abolition together with that of the combination laws and restrictions on artisan emigration and machinery exports and other repressive measures when speaking against the silk bill, 11 June. He publicized Cobbett's opinions before voting for inquiry into the currency, 12 June, and presented the St. Pancras petition for reform of borough representation, 30 June 1823.[24]

Seizing on the recent acceptance without parliamentary sanction of a brokered deal on the Austrian loan, he harassed Canning and amused Members by questioning the legality of the arrangement, 6 Feb. 1824. He also suggested '*par ratione*', in a much-maligned quip he subsequently regretted, that the House was 'entitled to levy taxes in the like manner'.[25] He protested afresh when it emerged that £500,000 had been 'lost' through the transaction, 26 Feb. Backing Sir Francis Burdett, he disputed the home secretary Peel's statement that the employment of remand prisoners on treadmills had been considered by king's bench, 12 Feb., and was among those who opposed public expenditure on the royal residences until taxation had been reduced to pre-war levels, 1 Mar. He presented a petition against legacy duties from the Liverpool journalist Francis Bott, 9 Mar.[26] Equipped with a hostile petition from Cobbett, he joined in the clamour against the game bill, 23 Mar. Speaking in jest, he complained that as the measure 'made a species of property of a vast variety of wild fowl', 'wild geese' must have been excluded from it in deference to Shakespeare's words, 'the wild goose soars aloft, unclaimed by any man'. He presented further hostile petitions, 31 Mar., and failed (by 41-33) with an amendment legalizing game sales, 1 Apr.[27] He brought up the boot and shoemakers of Penrith's petition for repeal of the combination laws, 5 Apr., and called for an end to restrictions on the use of horse hides, 14 Apr.[28] Although James professed commitment to the established church, in which he had

been educated and now worshipped, he vehemently opposed the new churches bill, 6 Apr., 3 June, and presented unfavourable petitions from Carlisle, 12 Apr., and Manchester, 7, 12 May.[29] He criticized the severity of the prison sentence imposed for blasphemy on Joseph Swann, 11 May. Commenting on the superannuation fund, 13 May, he made it clear that he considered abolition of the assessed taxes a precondition of any increase in public salaries. His failure to vote in condemnation of the indictment in Demerara of the Methodist missionary John Smith, 11 June 1824, generated ill feeling in Carlisle, and the *Journal* rallied to him by printing several letters praising his diligence and advocacy of universal suffrage. It also welcomed him as a subscriber to the projected Newcastle-Carlisle railway.[30]

James moderated his opinions somewhat in the course of the 1825 session. He divided against the Irish unlawful societies bill, 21 Feb., for Catholic relief, 1 Mar., 21 Apr., 10 May, and against the attendant Irish franchise bill, 26 Apr. However, in a statement (9 May) he later regretted, he announced that he would vote for it, as a means of securing Catholic relief and 'because ... the freeholders were voters in name but not in reality'. He divided for the game bill, as the only means of making 'game the property of those who had been at the expense of rearing it', 7 Mar. Presenting Carlisle's petition for repeal of the corn laws, 25 Apr., he said he could no longer advocate an 'entirely free' trade in corn and made his support for the admission of foreign corn conditional on adequate remuneration of domestic growers, including allowances for labour and taxation costs. He suggested a pivot price of 80s. for free imports and a graduated scale from 55s.[31] He voted to consider relaxing the laws, 28 Apr., and consistently with his opposition colleagues until 9 June, when he endorsed their call for ending flogging in the navy, 9 June 1825. He spent the recess at Barrock, where he engaged in country pursuits.[32] Reports that he would stand down at the dissolution because of diminishing returns from his Jamaican estate circulated before the start of the 1826 session and were confirmed by his announcement on 24 Apr. that he 'did not wish under any circumstances to sit in the next Parliament'.[33] He had resumed his parliamentary attendance earlier that month, voted as hitherto to reform Parliament, 13, 27 Apr., and the corn laws, 18 Apr., and presented a petition from Hampshire for the latter, 18 Apr.[34] He supported a petition of complaint against the Lancashire justices for refusing to renew the Manchester publican Martha Johnson's license, 26 Apr., and was so infuriated to find his tales of woe from the distressed manufacturing districts ill received, that he vented his spleen against the 'Saints' for putting the needs of black slaves before those of the poor whites of Blackburn, 1 May.[35] He divided for Hume's state of the nation motion, 4 May, and for a reduction in salaries under the Irish prison laws bill, 5 May. He stayed away from Carlisle at the general election in June 1826, but he was nominated as previously and finished in third place.[36]

As sheriff of Cumberland, James was ineligible to stand for Carlisle at the 1827 by-election, and he declined nomination at the next vacancy in 1829.[37] He was one of the main speakers at the Cumberland distress meeting at Wigton, 26 Jan. 1830, when he pre-empted but failed to prevent the adoption of a cross-party petition, whose prayer for currency reform he opposed, by proposing another for 'an efficient reform' of Parliament.[38] He resisted attempts to make him spend at Carlisle at the general election of 1830 and backed William Ewart*, for whom his brother-in-law Rutson campaigned, at the Liverpool by-election in December.[39] He confirmed his support for reform and the ballot at the first lord of the admiralty Sir James Graham's re-election for Cumberland, 8 Dec. 1830, and declared wholeheartedly for the Grey ministry's reform bill at the county meeting, 15 Mar. 1831.[40] Certain that the Whig gentry would not dare to oppose him, he contested Carlisle successfully at the invitation of the Reform Association with the sitting Whig Philip Henry Howard at the 1831 general election, when his statement that '[Henry] Hunt* has deserted the cause of the people and become the oracle of the boroughmongers, their last hope', was loudly cheered.[41]

As the Reform Association kept a close watch on his parliamentary conduct, James took an early opportunity to distance himself from the radical opponents of reform, 23 June 1831, when, with frequent allusions to Carlisle, he contradicted Hunt's claim that Northern England demanded a 'sweeping reform'. Waiving his previous demands for universal suffrage and the ballot, he announced:

> As I think the reform now proposed will give the country good and cheap government, I shall be satisfied with it. If the measure should not prove as beneficial in its operation as I expected, I will then call for further improvement.

He divided for the reintroduced reform bill at its second reading, 6 July, and against adjournment, 12 July, stating that the frequent divisions that day afforded convincing proof of the 'factious nature' of the opposition to it. He divided fairly steadily for its details, but cast wayward votes for the total disfranchisement of Saltash, which ministers no longer

pressed, 26 July, against the proposed division of counties, 11 Aug., and for giving city freeholders borough votes, 17 Aug., and the enfranchisement of £50 tenants-at-will, 18 Aug. He observed that by partial disfranchisement Huntingdon would gain a Member, as Lord Sandwich would lose two, 29 July. When Hunt presented a massively signed petition for the ballot from the Westminster Union of the Working Classes, 30 Aug., James said the people of Carlisle had too much good sense to delay the bill in that way. He divided for its passage, 21 Sept., for the second reading of the Scottish reform bill, 23 Sept., whose provisions he also defended, 4 Oct., and for Lord Ebrington's confidence motion, 10 Oct. He was cheered at the Cumberland reform meeting when he proposed a petition endorsing the bill and the Grey ministry's conduct, 16 Nov.[42] He divided for the revised reform bill at its second reading, 17 Dec. 1831, and generally for its details. His return to Westminster after the Christmas recess was delayed by a fortnight and he cited a letter from the Carlisle Reform Association, complaining of his failure to vote against the amendment for a £10 poor rate franchise, 3 Feb. 1832, as proof that popular support for reform had not waned. He pressed for a large creation of peers to ensure the bill's passage, 10 Feb.[43] His vote for Hunt's amendment making the cost of booths and hustings chargeable to the rates or corporation funds, 15 Feb., was a wayward one. He divided for the bill's third reading, 22 Mar. When a ministry headed by the duke of Wellington was contemplated, he caused uproar by challenging Lord Althorp over ministerial resignations and stating that they should have advised the king to 'create any number of peers that might be necessary' to carry 'the only measure that can be adopted to prevent the collision of the two House of Parliament', 9 May. He voted for the address calling on the king to appoint only ministers who would carry the bill unamended, 10 May, and endorsed a Manchester petition against voting supplies until it was enacted, 11 May. Later that day, in what the Speaker, who chose to ignore it, interpreted as a breach of privilege provoked by 'the borough-mongering faction' around him, he ranted against military men who would resort to force to suppress the clamour for reform. He supported petitions for withholding supplies from Bolton, 17 May, and Carlisle, 1 June. He divided for the Irish reform bill at its second reading, 25 May, and against amending the Scottish measure, 1, 15 June. He referred to his intended vote on the 13th to restore the 40s. Irish freeholder franchise 'as the best reparation' he could make for voting to disfranchise them in 1825. Denouncing the 'farce' of abolishing one class of nomination boroughs in May and creating another through the boundary bill in June, he seconded and was a minority teller for altering the Whitehaven boundaries to neutralize Lonsdale's influence there, 22 June, and voted to amend the boundaries proposed for Stamford the same day. He divided with government on the Dublin election controversy, 23 Aug., and opposed John Bennet's 'time-wasting' Liverpool franchise bill, 5 Sept. 1831, 23 May 1832. He did not vote on the Russian-Dutch loan, 26 Jan., 12 July, but he spoke in support of ministers when it was considered in committee of supply, 6 Feb. 1832.

James's pragmatism rarely extended beyond reform, and he remained too bold, radical and self-opinionated to support the Grey ministry on most other issues. He called for repeal of the 1819 Select Vestry Act, which he complained deprived magistrates of the power of granting poor relief, 28 June, and praised the 1830 Beer Act, when petitions from his fellow county magistrates condemned it, 30 June, 27 Aug. 1831. He was unstinting in his support for Hunt's campaign for repeal of the corn laws, on which his opinions had again hardened, 24 June, 12, 13 Aug., 15 Sept. As a minority teller that day, he blamed the 1815 law for depriving the labouring classes of a market for the sale of their produce, making them worse fed than negro slaves. He voted in the minorities for printing the Waterford petition for disbanding the Irish yeomanry, 11 Aug., and against compensating two coloureds, Escoffery and Lescene, for their removal from Jamaica, 22 Aug. He spoke wildly of the coronation of William IV as unnecessary, 'except ... to make 50 or 100 new peers for the purpose of passing the reform bill', 13 Aug. After failing that day to limit spending to £10,000, he exhausted the patience of the House with questions on the allocation of the £50,000 voted and the seating arrangements for Members, of whom he was proud to be one, 31 Aug., 1 Sept. He spoke against the proposed expenditure on royal residences, 28 Sept. He opposed renewal of the Sugar Refinery Act with Burge and the West India Members, 12 Sept., and pressed for the immediate consideration of the report, 22 Sept., when (as again, 28 Sept.) he criticized the measure as nothing less than a bill for giving a premium to white sugar and promoting the Brazilian slave trade, 'a felony for any British subject in any way to connive at'. He presented and endorsed petitions from the Northern radicals for inquiry into the Deacles case and voted thus, 27 Sept. He did not apparently, as requested, endorse a Huddersfield Political Union petition for ending prosecutions for religious opinions (which named the Deist Robert Taylor) when it was presented, 22 Sept.[44] He called in vain on Graham to promote the use of chain cables manufactured by his Cumberland constituents by the navy, 13 Oct. 1831. He confirmed his radicalism in a series of votes and interventions on 16 Feb. 1832: for inquiry into Peterloo, printing the Woollen Grange petition for the abolition of Irish tithes, information on military punishments and omission of any reference to Providence in the preamble to the cholera bill, so providing ample fodder for Carlisle's Conservative squib writers.[45] His equivocal stance on the locally unpopular general register bill, 26 Feb., and the factories regulation bill, 1, 7 Mar., won him few friends, but this was partly remedied by his assertion that the factories bill would do less to assist poor children than tax reductions and his renewed plea for repeal of the corn laws, 16 Mar. Speaking 'freely' on the sugar duties, 'because I have the misfortune to be a West Indian planter', 7 Mar. 1832, he expressed a personal preference for an *ad valorem* duty, but professed himself ready to divide with government against reduction, so as to cause them embarrassment and 'because I believe that they will, as soon as they possibly can, do everything in their power to relieve the distress'.

Standing as a Liberal, James topped the poll at Carlisle in a three-man contest at the general election in December 1832, and he seconded the address in the ensuing Parliament. He made way for another Liberal in 1835, but came in for Cumberland East on a vacancy in September 1836 and defeated the 'turncoat' Graham in 1837 and a Conservative in 1841 to retain his seat until 1847, when he felt unable to sustain the cost of a contest.[46] He died at Barrock Lodge in May 1861, predeceased by his wife and seven of their 13 children, and remembered as an advocate of radical reform and free trade who in later life moderated his views. A Carlisle public house was named after him.[47] His will was proved in London, 28 May 1861, and honoured his obligations to his eldest son William James (1816-79), who as heir to his estates had assisted him financially at the 1841 election. His remaining money and effects were distributed equally among his children.

¹ Dates of death for William James (1735-98) and this Member are taken from H.E.M. and W.A. James, *Peds. James of Culgarth* (1913) and correct those given in *Burke LG* (1886). ² C.R. Hudleston and R.S. Boumphrey, *Cumb. Fams.*; IGI (Lancs.) ³ PROB 11/1302/108. ⁴ J. Picton, *Memorials of Liverpool* (1875), i. 351-8, 363-5, 368, 371-3, 376, 380, 390, 403, 414, 418, 429, 437, 443, 457, 461. ⁵ Ibid. 302, 307; James (Ashton and Rutson peds.). ⁶ Brougham mss, James to J. Brougham, 1 Feb. 1820. ⁷ Lonsdale mss, Hodgson to Lonsdale, 6 Feb., 1 Mar.; *Carlisle Jnl.* 12 Mar.; Brougham mss, James to J. Brougham, 18 Mar. 1820; Northumb. RO, Middleton mss ZMI/ S76/35/5-6. ⁸ *Carlisle Jnl.* 27 May, 3 June 1820; James, 7; J.T. Ward, *Sir James Graham*, 37-38. ⁹ James, 8. ¹⁰ *Session of Parl. 1825*, p. 470. ¹¹ J. Saunders, *Portraits and Mems. of Reformers*, 155. ¹² *The Times*, 29 June, 4 July 1820. ¹³ Ibid. 6, 20 Feb., 7, 16 Mar.; HLRO, Hist. Coll. 379,

Grey Bennet diary, 37. [14] *The Times*, 2 Feb., 15 Mar., 23 June. 1821. [15] *Carlisle Jnl.* 7 Apr.; *The Times*, 10 May 1821. [16] *The Times*, 8 Mar. 1821. [17] Ibid. 7 June 1821. [18] *Carlisle Jnl.* 16 Feb., 2 Mar., 11, 18 May 1822. [19] *The Times* 23, 26 Feb., 2, 8 Mar. 1822. [20] Ibid. 20 June 1822. [21] Ibid. 4, 5 June 1822. [22] *Carlisle Jnl.* 22, 29 Feb., 29 Mar. 1823. [23] *The Times*, 19, 20 June 1823. [24] Ibid. 1 July 1823. [25] *Carlisle Jnl.* 14 Feb. 1824. [26] *The Times*, 10 Mar. 1824. [27] Ibid. 1, 2 Apr. 1824. [28] Ibid. 6 Apr. 1824. [29] Ibid. 13 Apr., 8, 13 May 1824. [30] *Carlisle Jnl.* 15, 22 May, 10, 31 July, 9 Oct. 1824, 29 Apr. 1826. [31] *The Times*, 26 Apr. 1825. [32] *Recs. and Letters of Long Fam.* ed. R.M. Howard, ii. 505. [33] Brougham mss, Blamire to J. Brougham, 6 Feb.; Lonsdale mss, Porter to Lowther, 14, 26 Apr.; *Carlisle Jnl.* 29 Apr. 1826. [34] *The Times*, 19 Apr. 1826. [35] Ibid. 27 Apr. 1826. [36] *Carlisle Jnl.* 6 May, 10, 17 June; Lonsdale mss, Musgrave to Lowther, 9 June, R. Porter to Lonsdale, 11 June; *Manchester Guardian*, 17 June 1826. [37] Cumbria RO (Carlisle) D/DX/92/16; Lonsdale mss, Wood to Lonsdale, 17 Jan. 1829. [38] *Carlisle Jnl.* 23, 30 Jan.; *Cumb. Pacquet*, 2 Feb. 1830. [39] Reading Univ. Archives Printing coll. (Folio 324.4285 SQU), Carlisle election handbills, ff. 158-60; *Albion*, 6 Dec. 1830. [40] *Carlisle Jnl.* 11 Dec. 1830, 12, 19 Mar.; *Carlisle Patriot*, 19 Mar. 1831. [41] Sir James Graham mss (IHR microfilm XR 80),1, bdle. 5, Browne to Graham, 4 Apr.; ibid. 29, 'bdle. re Cumb. election 1831', Mounsey to same, 26 Apr.; Brougham mss, Blamire to Lord Brougham, 30 Apr.; *Carlisle Jnl.* 30 Apr., 7 May; *Carlisle Patriot*, 19 Mar., 7 May 1831. [42] *The Times*, 18 Nov.; *Carlisle Jnl.* 19 Nov. 1831. [43] *Carlisle Jnl.* 11, 18, 25 Feb. 1832. [44] *Poor Man's Guardian*, 17 Sept. 1831. [45] Carlisle Pub. Lib. 3A 324.2 (unbound squibs and handbills); *Carlisle Jnl.* 25 Feb. 1832. [46] Saunders, 153-5; Ward, 156, 160-1. [47] *Gent. Mag.* (1861), i. 708; James, 8-9.

M.M.E.

JEFFREY, Francis (1773–1850), of 24 Moray Place and Craigcrook, Costorphine, Edinburgh.[1]

PERTH BURGHS	13 Jan. 1831–28 Mar. 1831
MALTON	6 Apr. 1831–1831
PERTH BURGHS	1831–1832
EDINBURGH	1832–31 May 1834

b. 23 Oct. 1773, 1st s. of George Jeffrey (*d.* 1812) of Charles Street, Edinburgh, depute clerk of session, and Henrietta, da. of John Louden, farmer, of Lanark. *educ.* John Cockburn's sch., Edinburgh; Edinburgh h.s. 1781-7; Glasgow Univ. 1787-9; Edinburgh Univ. 1789-90, 1792-3; Queen's, Oxf. 1791-2; adv. 1794, dean of faculty 1829-30. *m.* (1) 1 Nov. 1801, Catherine (*d.* 8 Aug. 1805), da. of Prof. Charles Wilson of St. Andrews Univ., 1s. *d.v.p.*; (2) 1 Oct. 1813, in New York, Charlotte, da. of Charles Wilkes, banker, of New York, 1 da. *d.* 26 Jan. 1850.

Ld. advocate Dec. 1830-May 1834; ld. of session (Lord Jeffrey) 1834-*d.*

Ld. rect. Glasgow Univ. 1820-22.

In 1843 Tom Macaulay* described Jeffrey as 'more nearly an universal genius than any man of our time'; and his old friend Sydney Smith referred to him as 'the *maximus minimus*'.[2] Carlyle, who first met him when he was 50, at the pinnacle of his fame as a critic, advocate and orator, recalled him as 'a delicate, attractive, dainty little figure' ('perhaps hardly five feet four in height'), with 'uncommonly bright black eyes, instinct with vivacity, intelligence and kindly fire'.[3] When Lord Webb Seymour encountered him in 1814 he was entranced by the 'extraordinary little man', who 'in brilliancy of conversation ... is inferior to none'; but John William Ward*, who had known him since their Edinburgh University days, could not acquit him of 'affectation', the 'crying sin' of most Scottish 'men of talents', though he considered 'his coxcombry ... quite delightful' and 'would not for the world that he was natural'.[4] On first acquaintance in 1821 John Cam Hobhouse* dismissed him as 'a little, black eyed, smart, ill tempered, mannered man, not attentive to any'.[5] In 1828 Macaulay, who thought his 'talk has no very intellectual power', wrote of him:

> He has twenty faces ... As soon as he is interested ... there is a flash in his glance, a violent contortion in his frown, an exquisite humour in his sneer, and a sweetness and brilliancy in his smile beyond anything that ever I saw ... He possesses considerable powers of mimicry ... His familiar tone, his declamatory tone and his pathetic tone are quite different ... Sometimes his utterance is snappish and quick ... Sometimes it is remarkable for rotundity and mellowness ... His conversation is ... of immense variety ... He is a very shrewd observer ... Though not altogether free from affectation himself, he has a peculiar loathing for it in other people, and a great talent for discovering and exposing it.[6]

Jeffrey's mighty reputation raised great hopes of him when he belatedly entered Parliament, but his style of oratory did not take there and the routine drudgery of office ground him down.

The eldest son of a joyless Tory clerk in the court of session, he lost his mother when he was 12. His brother John became a partner in the mercantile business in Boston, Massachusetts, of their uncle, who had married a sister of John Wilkes† of *North Briton* notoriety. He was educated initially in his native city, studied at Glasgow University in the sessions of 1787-8 and 1788-9, and took law classes at Edinburgh University, 1789-90. He matriculated at Oxford in September 1791, but hated its domination by 'young men without any feeling, vivacity or passion', and left the following summer; he had shed his Scottish brogue and replaced it with what Carlyle described as 'a strange, swift, sharp-sounding, fitful modulation', which Henry Fox* thought 'absurd'.[7] He resumed his training for the Scottish bar, attended Dugald Stewart's lectures on moral philosophy and in December 1792 became a member of the Speculative Society, where he met Walter Scott, Francis Horner† and the brothers Charles* and Robert Grant*. He continued to write essays, verse and plays, as he had since his boyhood. Called to the bar in 1794, he faced an uncertain future, not least because, influenced by Stewart and his uncle William Morehead, he had espoused Whig politics, which in a Scotland then dominated by Henry Dundas† and his labyrinthine Tory connections, were a significant impediment to professional advancement. During the following six years he established himself as one of the coterie of Whig Edinburgh lawyers, doctors and literary men which included John Allen, Henry Brougham*, Henry Cockburn (his close and indulgent friend for life), Henry Erskine† and James Moncrieff, as well as Horner and Smith. A year after his call he wrote to his brother:

> I have been considering ... the probability of my success at the bar, and have but little comfort ... for all the employ-ment which I have has come entirely through my father, or those with whom I am otherwise connected. I have also been trying to consider some other occupation ... but find the prospect still more perplexing and obscure. I am determined, however, that I will not linger away the years of my youth and activity in an unprofitable and hopeless hanging about on our courts.[8]

In 1798 he made an abortive attempt to find an opening in London journalism. Back in Edinburgh he was encouraged by the advocate George Bell and his anatomist brother Charles, but the 'tinge of melan-choly' which was never far beneath the surface of his social vivacity sometimes got the better of him, as he told his cousin Robert Morehead, 6 July 1800:

> I have had fits of discontent and self-condemnation pretty severely ... My ambition, and my prudence, and indolence, will have a pitched battle, and I shall either devote myself to contention and toil, or lay quietly down in obscurity and mediocrity of attainment ... The unaspiring life, I believe, has the least positive wretch-edness. I have often thought of going to India, but I do not know for what station I should be qualified, or could qualify myself, and I have almost as little talent for solicitation as you have.[9]

In 1801 he married his distant kinswoman Catherine Wilson, who brought him no money. Their only child, a boy, was born in September 1802 but lived for only a few weeks.[10] Jeffrey transformed his life by joining Smith and Horner (who met for the purpose at his flat in Buccleuch Place) in deciding to start an independ-ent quarterly review of literature, economics, science and politics. Allen and Brougham gave support, and the first number of the *Edinburgh Review* appeared on 10 Oct. 1802. To Jeffrey's great surprise, it was an immediate success and went from strength to strength: by 1814 it was selling about 13,000 copies per issue.

After a few months of cumbersome management by committee, Jeffrey was made the responsible editor in January 1803. The following year, when Allen, Brougham, Horner and Smith had left Edinburgh, he became the sole controller of the magazine, which he fashioned into the leading organ of liberal opinion.[11] Between 1802 and 1829 he wrote some 220 articles for the *Edinburgh*, which under his editorship became the most feared arbiter of critical opinion. His prejudice against romanticism and mysticism in literature often betrayed him into unfairness: he was unduly harsh on Wordsworth and the Lakes poets, for example. In 1806 he and Tom Moore met at Chalk Farm, London, to fight a duel over the *Edinburgh*'s condemnation of his *Epistles*. They were arrested and bound over to keep the peace, and it was discovered that Jeffrey's pistol had been unloaded. (He and Moore soon afterwards became cordial friends.)[12] The *Edinburgh*'s political line was at first moderate, but by 1808, when Scott and other Tories, disgusted by the partisan line of Jeffrey and Brougham's 'Don Cevallos' article against British involvement in Spain (xiii. 215-34), decided to estab-lish the rival *Quarterly Review*, it was emphatically a Whig journal, with Brougham as its chief political contributor. While Jeffrey's Whiggism was genuine, he never joined Brooks's, was anything but an enthusi-ast, being pragmatic and desponding by temperament, and shied from extremes. He put out an article of his own in favour of parliamentary reform in July 1809 (xiv. 277-306), and at the end of the year told Allen, now an inmate of Holland House:

> Something must be yielded to the democratic party ... If the Whigs do not make some sort of coalition with the democrats, they are nobody, and the nation is ruined ... It is the duty of the Whigs to ... strengthen themselves by the alliance of those who will otherwise overwhelm both them and their antagonists.

His object was to convince the Whigs, whom he consid-ered to be too aristocratic in composition and outlook, to regain control of and moderate the popular reform movement.[13] In January 1810 he published his own piece on 'The State of Parties' (xv. 504-21), in which he advocated retrenchment and the abolition of sine-cures as well as concessions to the demand for parlia-mentary reform. Ward thought it typically 'ingenious and striking', but characteristically 'pert and hasty' and 'utterly mistaken ... in supposing that the whole population is divided into three parties'.[14] Jeffrey's connection with Allen gave him the entrée to Holland House, where he became a favourite: Lady Holland described him in 1814 as 'that dear little man, who has the best heart and temper, although the authors of the day consider him as their greatest scourge ... he is full of wit, anecdote and lively sallies'.[15]

He had persevered at the bar and begun to make his way, but the death of his wife 'in my arms', 8 Aug. 1805, following hard on that of his married sister Mary Napier in May 1804, made him 'inwardly sick of life'.[16] Yet he stuck to his profession, established a reputation as a very able advocate and secured a monopoly of one side before the general assembly for 20 years from 1807. In late 1810 he entertained the French refugee M. Simond and his wife, a sister of his kinsman Charles Wilkes, a New York banker. Wilkes's daughter Charlotte was with them, and Jeffrey fell in love with her before their return to America. In 1813 he resolved to pursue her, sailed from Liverpool on 29 Aug., arrived in New York on 7 Oct. and married Charlotte Wilkes soon afterwards. Armed with letters of introduction from Lord Holland, he saw President Madison and James Monroe, the secretary of state, with whom he had 'much conversation on the subject of our present differences'. He and his bride, who suffered from 'St. Vitus dance in her nose and chin' and was deemed by Henry Fox 'a poor creature ... not worth crossing the Atlantic for', though Macaulay liked her, landed back in Liverpool on 10 Feb. 1814.[17] Despite his former misgivings about the war, he welcomed the crushing of Buonaparte, who seemed 'the cause of my paying income tax, and having my friends killed by dysentery and gunshot wounds, and making my country unpopular, bragging and servile'. Shortly before Waterloo he took a lease of the old keep of Craigcrook, three miles north-west of Edinburgh, where he renovated and improved the house and garden and spent all his remaining summers, entertaining friends and guests with 'the finest pleasures of the head and of the heart'. The 'prevailing free-and-easy tone' and 'boisterous mirth' did not, however, suit Elizabeth Grant of Rothiemurchus.[18] In the autumn of 1815 he visited France and Holland for the first time. The introduction of jury trial in Scottish civil cases in 1816 gave him a new sphere in which to display his flashy skills to great effect. But according to John Whishaw, who thought his taste in literature was 'very much perverted' and that he was essentially a sophist, he 'did not add to his English reputation' on his sallies into London society in March 1817, when he was attending the Lords on a Scottish appeal case: 'though he showed great talents, neither his public nor private exhibitions were considered as successful'.[19] A year later Jeffrey told his father-in-law:

I am rather impatient to make a little money now ... My gains are in some degree precarious, and ... though I please myself with views of retirement and leisure, and travelling and reading, I am by no means perfectly convinced that I should be much happier in that state than my present one. Having long set my standard of human felicity at a very moderate pitch, and persuaded myself that men are *considerably* lower than the angels, I am not much given to discontent, and am sufficiently sensible that many things that appear and are irksome and vexatious, are necessary to help life along ... It is a foolish little thing this human life at the best; and it is half ridiculous and half pitiful to see what importance we ascribe to it, and to its little ornaments and distinctions.[20]

Although he had more or less given up political journalism by 1812, he became active as a rousing speaker at public meetings in Edinburgh. He delivered the main speech in favour of abolition of the property tax, 24 Feb. 1816. He made able but unsuccessful defences of prisoners charged with sedition in 1817 and 1820.[21] Immediately after Peterloo he told Wilkes that 'some reform' had become essential 'if it were only to convince and conciliate the people', for 'if they are met only with menaces and violence we shall be drenched in blood'. At an Edinburghshire county meeting to vote a loyal address to the regent, 15 Nov. 1819, he proposed 'an addition' to it intended to 'show that the higher classes were not indifferent to the distresses of the people'; this 'sophistry', as one Tory called it, was rejected by 87-18.[22] On 19 Dec. 1820, atoning, as he said, for 'his far too long supineness and want of sensibility to the public cause', he took the lead at the Edinburgh Pantheon meeting to address the king to dismiss ministers on account of their conduct towards Queen Caroline, arguing that 'the present system could not be continued without either the destruction of the public peace or of public liberty'.[23] At the Edinburgh Fox birthday dinner in January 1821 he toasted Brougham's work for the diffusion of knowledge with the observation that 'the general instruction of the people was at the bottom of all our glory and respectability'; and in January 1823 he saluted 'the cause of parliamentary reform', asserting that 'we require something better than a House of Commons only capable of putting down rebellion'.[24] In January 1822 he informed Wilkes that he had 'given a peremptory refusal, from taste as well as prudence', to 'two overtures to take a seat in Parliament': 'I am not in the least ambitious, and feel no desire to enter upon public life at such a moment as the present'.[25] He was involved with Cockburn and James Abercromby* in the promotion of a popular campaign for extension of the Edinburgh franchise to the resident householders in 1823 and 1824.[26] At the Edinburgh dinner in honour of Brougham, 5 Apr. 1825, he toasted Sir James Mackintosh* and spoke warmly of the United States. At that for Joseph Hume*, 18 Nov. 1825, he advocated support for the Spanish liberals and, in a speech subsequently published as a pamphlet, dealt with the combination laws, urging workmen to respect the rights of others while enjoying the right to strike. Scott sourly remarked in private that 'it takes only the hand of a Lilliputian to light a fire, but would require the diuretic powers of Gulliver to extinguish it'.[27] In August 1825, when a dissolution was expected, Brougham urged the duke of Norfolk to return Jeffrey for half the first session of the new Parliament so that he could 'give us a thundering speech on the Catholic question'. Jeffrey had apparently earlier declined to take part in this absurd scheme, and nothing came of it.[28] On the formation of Canning's ministry in April 1827 there was unfounded speculation that the Tory Sir William Rae* might be removed as lord advocate, and Cockburn told Thomas Francis Kennedy* that if this occurred he would 'decidedly force' Jeffrey to take the office, however unappealing it was to a working lawyer. Canning's early death prompted Jeffrey to observe that it marked 'an end ... for the present of this new and bold experiment of a liberal or rational government'.[29] That autumn, partly under the influence of some English friends, he developed 'a hankering' for a seat on the bench, having 'lately begun to feel that the more laborious parts of my professional duty may ... become burdensome'. He made his views known to Lord Landsdowne, home secretary in the Goderich ministry, but its collapse in January 1828 brought the duke of Wellington and Peel back to power.[30] Soon afterwards Jeffrey moved into a 'magnificent' new Edinburgh town house in Moray Place.[31] His speech at the Edinburgh meeting in support of Catholic emancipation, 14 Mar. 1829, was one of his most inspired efforts, full of 'fire and eloquence'.[32] On 2 July 1829 he was unanimously elected dean of the faculty of advocates when John Hope, the Scottish solicitor-general, withdrew in deference to his great popularity. He handed over the editorship of the *Edinburgh* to Macvey Napier, and thereafter contributed only five articles to it. Cockburn thought that 'the Scottish millennium' had arrived, and at the end of the year Smith quipped that when he was 'fairly on the bench, his robes ... will cost him little; one buck rabbit will clothe him to his heels'.[33] Jeffrey, who spoke at an Edinburgh meeting for the abolition of slavery in 1830, told Wilkes in March that 'I never have had so much hard work as this last session; and although I never made so much money, I should willingly have compounded for less of both'.[34]

On the formation of Lord Grey's administration in November 1830 Jeffrey and Cockburn were the obvious candidates for the office of lord advocate, which paid about £2,500 a year but 'nearly ruins the practice of any counsel' and entailed the considerable cost of obtaining a parliamentary seat. Cockburn was determined not to take it, and told Kennedy that while Jeffrey 'has a little of the same repugnance', it was 'not by a hundred degrees so much', and that 'he is rich, and if asked, will accept'. It was rumoured that ministers were inclined to appoint James Archibald Murray†, but they were warned by James Aytoun that if Jeffrey was slighted there would be 'universal disgust in Scotland' and the administration would 'at its commencement receive a shock in public opinion which it will perhaps ... find it impossible to recover'; and Murray himself urged Lansdowne to appoint Jeffrey, whose 'knowledge, eloquence and readiness in debate is so great that he may, though late in life to enter the House of Commons, make a distinguished figure there on questions of general interest'.[35] Jeffrey was offered the place (Cockburn was made solicitor-general) and took it with great misgivings, telling a niece that 'good reason I have for being sincerely sick and sorry at an elevation for which so many people are envying me'. Carlyle later recalled Jeffrey's 'considerable misgivings and gloomy forecasts', which proved all 'too true'.[36] Jeffrey resigned the deanship. Cockburn informed Kennedy, with whom he had drafted a plan of Scottish reform which they had given to ministers:

> I have no doubt of Jeffrey's doing well ... and I anticipate much good to Scotland from him and you, acting under a fair government and a strong public opinion. He requires in the conduct of business to be managed, but he is easily managed. He will probably not originate much, and he is very helpless in details. But expound to him what is wanted, and give him help in the manipulation, and you will find him an effective and able associate, and in the more difficult things a sagacious guide.

Jeffrey of course needed a seat, and in late December 1830 he began a canvass of the venal Perth district of burghs, where the last election had been declared void. He was opposed by the Tory William Ogilvy*, who secured Cupar and Forfar. Jeffrey had Perth, St. Andrews and Dundee, but the last was currently disfranchised. At a dinner there, 7 Jan. 1831, he portrayed himself as 'one of the signs of the times':

> A lord advocate ... not merely professing liberal and popular opinions, not merely avowing ... his love of economy and reform, but ... who has been promoted to that station for no other cause ... except that the whole of his past life has been spent in supporting those great objects.

He denounced the 'kind of hocus pocus' on which the Scottish electoral system rested and said that 'economy and reform' were 'the cardinal principles on which the government rests its claims'. At the election at Forfar, 13 Jan., when Jeffrey was jostled in the street by a hostile mob (Smith joked that he 'would have been killed had he been more visible'), the returning officer, on legal advice, received the disputed vote of the Dundee delegate and declared Jeffrey returned.[37] It was thought unlikely that he would survive his opponent's petition, and Cockburn, who incidentally warned Kennedy not to 'despair when you find him always wasting time at first, pouring out what may be said against you and not listening', as Jeffrey would 'always come right at last after his spare steam is let off', commented:

> He will probably have in his first two months of office spent a whole year's salary in attempting to get a seat, to say nothing of nearly the utter ruin of his professional practice. The condition of the lord advocate's office in relation to Parliament must be changed ... In the course of his canvass he has made many good speeches, but still I fear for him in Parliament. Nearly sixty years of age [in fact 57], a bad trachea, inexperience and a great reputation, are bad foundations for success in the House of Commons.

Jeffrey, 'not very well', set out for London on 28 Jan. 1831 with a 'shattered carcass and ... reluctant and half-desponding spirit', as he told a friend:

> There is not much fair weather before us ... politically ... and the only comfort is that we are honest and mean well ... Our other advantage, and our only one, is that the only party that can now turn us out must be mad ... to risk the experiment ... The real battle ... is ... between property and no property, Swing and the law. In that battle all our Tory opponents must be on the same side as us ... I am not very robustious, and have had a long and weakening cold.[38]

On 18 Feb. 1831 Jeffrey presented ten reform petitions from Scotland and one from Scots resident in Dublin, who, he remarked had 'not lost their nationality'. When Daniel O'Connell commented that they had 'acquired very little Irish nationality', Jeffrey retorted, 'I should be sorry if they had'. A ministerial backbencher reported next day that 'judging from ... [his] face and manner I would say that he finds himself much out of his element, and indeed a Scotch county Member told me ... that Jeffrey seemed at a loss about the House of Commons and not to know what to make of it'.[39] Cockburn was 'surprised' that Jeffrey was given sole responsibility for the Scottish reform bill, without the anticipated assistance of the

lawyer John Richardson and Kennedy, to whom he wrote:

> The failing which you mention ... has been his great failing always. He is too pure himself to suspect others. But he is very docile, and grateful to every teacher; so ... be quite plain ... [and] tell him to distrust words and villains.[40]

On 26 Feb. Jeffrey defended the Edinburgh reform petition, which he had signed before taking office, and said that there had been countless converts to the cause in Scotland. He made his eagerly anticipated full debut, which Macaulay, who hoped he 'must succeed', perceived that he was 'nervous' about, 4 Mar., when he defended the ministerial reform scheme in a speech of an hour and twenty minutes and declared his wish to 'unite all those who have property, and ... render the large body of the people interested in obeying the law and zealous in defending the institutions of the country'. The general reaction was one of disappointment.[41] The Tory Lord Ellenborough thought he spoke 'very indifferently', but this was too harsh.[42] Greville reckoned the speech was 'very able, but somewhat tedious'; Hobhouse admired 'his fluency and argumentative powers', but thought him 'too quick and too close for a popular assembly'; John Campbell II* decided that he 'got off very well ... but rather showed himself to be a very clever man than a very great orator'; and the Scot James Hope Vere* deemed it 'a *tolerably* successful hit, but by no means what I could have wished'.[43] Macaulay did not accept that it had been 'a complete failure', and told Napier that Jeffrey

> did wonders. His manner is not as yet suited to the House. But he fully sustained his character for talent; and that he should do so was extraordinary ... There were some beautiful passages in his speech.[44]

The patronage secretary Ellice assured Brougham next day that Jeffrey had 'distinguished himself, even more than I was prepared for. I had a little doubt as to his manner serving for the House, but his debut was eminently successful'.[45] On 9 Mar. he secured leave to introduce the Scottish reform bill and laid out its details. He presented petitions for the abolition of slavery, amendment of the Scottish grain purchase regulations, reform and repeal of the duties on solicitors' certificates, and against the East India Company's monopoly, 14 Mar. On the 19th he brought up about 40 Scottish reform petitions and one from Edinburgh for abolition of the death penalty for offences against property. At this time Maria Edgeworth reported him to be 'much broken' in bodily health.[46] He endorsed the Edinburgh householders' reform petition, 21 Mar., and next day voted silently for the second reading of the English reform bill. He defended the scheme as one of 'just and proper conciliation', 24 Mar. On the 28th he was unseated, as he had expected, by the decision of the Perth Burghs election committee, but nine days later he was brought in on a vacancy for Lord Fitzwilliam's borough of Malton. He 'called at 635 doors and shook 494 men by the hand' and spent about £500 on treating.[47] In the House, 14 Apr., he dismissed the Dunbartonshire anti-reform petition as unrepresentative of majority opinion. He voted against Gascoyne's wrecking amendment to the English bill, 19 Apr., and privately denounced the 'unspeakable baseness' of the Scottish Members who divided in the hostile majority. He wrote to a friend the following day:

> It was a beautiful, rosy, dead calm morning when we broke up a little before five ... and I took three pensive turns along the solitude of Westminster Bridge, admiring the sharp clearness of St. Paul's, and all the city spires soaring up in a cloudless sky, the orange and red light that was beginning to play on the trees of the Abbey, and the old windows of the Speaker's house, and the flat green mist of the river floating upon a few lazy hulks on the tide, and moving low under the arches. It was a curious contrast with the long previous imprisonment in the stifling roaring House, amidst dying candles, and every sort of exhalation.[48]

At the ensuing general election he stood for Edinburgh, but with so little hope of success that at the suggestion of ministers he asked Fitzwilliam's son Lord Milton* to return him again for Malton, which he readily agreed to do. He also stood again for the Perth district.[49] Since mid-March Cockburn had been worried by his apparent willingness to make changes to the Scottish reform bill in response to the plausible representations of interested parties and had urged Kennedy to keep him straight. He was 'very much disturbed' when Jeffrey's 'criminal candour and narrow minded liberality' led him at the time of the dissolution to hint that the Scottish county franchise qualification might be raised.[50] While in Edinburgh for the election, he told George Traill, Member for Orkney, that there was not 'the slightest hope' of his achieving his object of separate representation from Orkney.[51] At the election, 3 May, when he was defeated by an anti-reformer kinsman of Lord Melville (he was returned *in absentia* for Malton the same day), he declared that the measure was open to 'considerable modification' and that ministers were reviewing the possibility of changing the qualification from £10 to a higher figure. Cockburn and Kennedy were horrified and sought clarification from senior ministers: Lord Durham,

one of the framers of the English reform bill, assured Kennedy that '*no alteration of the qualification is under the consideration of the government*' and suggested that Jeffrey 'must have been misunderstood'. Cockburn had already 'sent an express to Perth' to 'warn him to correct' the impression his words had given, and Jeffrey did so in a speech at Perth, 7 May, claiming that he had been 'misrepresented'. Cockburn, who observed to Kennedy that 'our *risks* from that quarter are very distressing' but that Jeffrey 'must be upheld', was not quite satisfied. He talked with Abercromby, who thought Jeffrey's 'provoking' gaffe showed 'either that he does not understand the effect of what he says or does not attend to the wishes of others', about 'the best mode of repairing the mischiefs of the late *lapsus*' and persuaded Jeffrey to consult 'the chiefs'. A Scottish Tory noted that in Edinburgh Jeffrey had 'seemed ... very alarmed at his own plaything', but that his Perth speech 'was rather inclined to encourage it'. On 16 May the *Caledonian Mercury* published Jeffrey's letter of the 14th explaining what he had meant to say and stressing that the qualification would certainly be 'very low'.[52] At his unopposed return for the Burghs at Perth, 23 May 1831, Jeffrey asserted that the principal benefit of reform, which was supported by 'all the rank ... intelligence and ... opulence of the country', would be its 'tendency ... to knit together ... the higher and lower orders'.[53] He opted to sit for the Scottish seat.

In early June 1831 Abercromby suggested to Grey the appointment to junior office of a Scottish Member to advise on Scottish patronage requests and otherwise 'materially relieve the advocate from labour not necessarily connected with his office, such as taking charge of bills connected with Scotland'.[54] Nothing came of this, and Jeffrey's burden remained a heavy one. Two weeks later Cockburn wrote to Kennedy:

> I trust that there will be a good understanding established between Jeffrey and the new Whiggery which Scotland has lately sent to Parliament ... And still more earnestly do I trust that no past or even future mistakes will occasion any want of cordiality between him and you. I can easily understand how you should be annoyed and disappointed that ... [Jeffrey] has not ... turned out what all the wise would wish ... But we must all remember what, in other respects, the man is, and what he has done; and it is not only our public duty, but due to private friendship, that we should uphold him the more, the more he needs it ... Keep yourself in constant communication with him, upon all points of the bill especially, on which there ought not to be a misunderstood or unsettled word between you ... I don't hold out ... the hope that anything you may do will save you from the agony of his habits or defects. But I am clear that while we curse his failings, we

must patiently and good naturedly manage them to the best advantage.[55]

To Cockburn's 'hints as to my infirmities' Jeffrey replied, 23 June:

I am rather afraid to promise amendment, but I boldly promise never to be moved to anything but gratitude for having the course of amendment pointed out to me ... When the decision rests with myself, I ought probably to be more prompt and decided. But when I have in substance only to propose and report for others, I rather think that I ought to hear all, and discuss with all ... Many people have complained that I do not discuss enough, and that I am too peremptory and intractable ... It is very well for you ... to say that you adhere to the original arrangement of the bill, and that all the objections to it are nonsense. I must hear and discuss all these objections, and I cannot say to the minority that they are nonsense, for they are very much moved by them, and want me to obviate them by more decisive arguments than can always be produced.[56]

He went over the details of the bill with Lord Althorp, Lord John Russell, Sir James Graham, Brougham and Kennedy a few days later.[57] In the House, 27 June, he answered a question from his opponent at Edinburgh about prosecution of those involved in the riots which had marred a number of Scottish elections. He would not commit himself on the prayer of a Perth petition for the city to have separate representation, 30 June, when he presented a dozen Scottish reform petitions. Securing leave to reintroduce the Scottish reform bill, 1 July, he briefly stated the few changes which had been made to its details. He of course voted for the second reading of the English bill, 6 July, when he informed Cockburn that he had given up his plan to speak in the debate. Two days later he told Mrs. Laing that he pined for Craigcrook:

I have money enough to live there in independent idleness ... and the world would go on about as well, I dare say, although I passed my days in reading and gardening, and my nights in unbroken slumbers. Why, then, should I vex my worn and shattered frame with toils and efforts, and disturb the last sands in my hour-glass with the shaking of a foolish ambition?[58]

He was steady in his attendance in committee on the details of the reform bill, apart from a brief lapse in the second week of August, but it wore him down. On 15 July he opposed Agnew's amendment to group the doomed schedule A boroughs on the Scottish model; but next day, complaining to Cockburn that the home secretary Lord Melbourne had 'maliciously' fixed their 'conference' for four o'clock, so forcing him to 'give up the refreshment of a rural day at Greenwich', he said that

my voice was too weak for so full and stirring a House. I have always said that I was most afraid of that infirmity, and unless they are unusually quiet I am aware that I cannot make myself heard, which is very provoking.[59]

He gave sparse details of the fatal clash between Orangemen and police at Girvan and called for a ban on Irish processions in Scotland, 18 July. He was beginning to cut a forlorn figure, as Kennedy evidently reported to Cockburn, who replied:

What you say, and what from others I hear, of the advocate, sinks me to the ground. My love of the man, my admiration of his powers, my sorrow for his situation, have not even the consolation of thinking that his official failure is unjust. It is my conviction of the truth of what I hear that chiefly vexes me ... It is nothing to the disparagement of any man that at his age he has not succeeded in Parliament or in public official life. But it is very bad for the cause, and terrible to me to hear him slightingly thought of. But we must make the most of it.[60]

Carlyle recalled finding him 'much preoccupied and bothered' in London in August:

He lived in Jermyn Street, wife and daughter with him; in lodgings at £11 a week ... On the ground floor, in a room of fair size, was a kind of secretary, a blear-eyed, tacit Scotch figure ... On the first floor were the apartments of the family ... If I called in the morning ... I would find the family still at breakfast, ten a.m. or later; and have seen poor Jeffrey emerge in flowered dressing gown, with a most boiled and suffering expression of face: like one who had slept miserably, and now awoke mainly to paltry misery and bother, – poor official man! 'I am made a mere post office of!' I heard him once grumble, after tearing open several packets, not one of which was internally for himself.[61]

Jeffrey thought 'things look ominously for the Lords', who he expected to return the reform bill 'mutilated with amendments', and was 'in terror at the new war on the continent'.[62] He voted with his colleagues on the Dublin election controversy, 23 Aug., but was in a minority of 20 against the quarantine duties, 6 Sept., having presented a hostile Dundee ship owners' petition, 11 Aug. He denied that there had been any 'incaution' in the granting of a charter to the National Bank of Scotland, 6 Sept. He voted for the passage of the reform bill, 21 Sept. On the 23rd he moved the second reading of the Scottish bill, which he defended in detail and principle; it was carried by 209-94. Hobhouse observed that 'at last Jeffrey made a good speech'; and Campbell, who did 'not know why Scotland should be dissatisfied with Jeffrey', as 'he does all he can for his native country', thought it 'excellent'. At Jeffrey's request, he got Althorp to change the intended 'mode of conducting ... the bill'.[63] Soon afterwards Jeffrey fell ill and had to undergo a painful and debilitating operation on his trachea. He told Cockburn, 3 Oct., that he had 'lost quantities of blood and a good deal of flesh' and had 'come to the creed that continued pain is a far worse evil than a bad conscience, a bad character ... disappointment in love ... a bad government, a bad climate or an empty purse'.[64] After the English bill's defeat in the Lords, he advised Cockburn that it was essential that the country should express 'its adherence to the bill and the ministry in all firm and lawful ways'; and he personally wrote 'edifying letters to the sheriffs of the [Scottish] manufacturing counties', as well as arranging for 'additional troops' to be deployed.[65] He was unable to attend for the division on Lord Ebrington's confidence motion, 10 Oct. He was still 'suffering more pain than I could wish on an anti-reformer' and had 'a second cut', which relieved him but left him too weak to go to Scotland during the recess; he recuperated at Wimbledon. By 29 Nov. 1831, when he began to rally the attendance of Scottish reformers for the opening of the impending session and reckoned that he could thwart a scheme to restore the alternating system of election for Cromartyshire and Nairnshire, he claimed to be '*well*, being perfectly free from pain [and] able to walk three or four miles'.[66]

He had contemplated introducing 'a plan for a general police through Scotland', but 'suspended his operations in consequence of the announcement of a measure of the same kind in the king's speech'.[67] On 15 Dec. 1831 he got leave to bring in a bill to abolish the Scottish exchequer court and appoint an additional judge to do its business. He saw it through the House and it became law on 23 June 1832 (2 Gul. IV, c. 54). Still 'sound', he told Napier, 16 Dec. 1831, that 'we are just going into battle in good spirits but not very full ranks, on either side';[68] he was in the majority for the second reading of the revised English reform bill next day. He spoke against Mackworth Praed's amendment to exclude freeholders of parliamentary boroughs from county electorates, 1 Feb. 1832. He got leave to introduce the slightly altered Scottish reform bill, 19 Jan. On the 29th he informed Holland, for the benefit of his cabinet colleagues, that if 'reform were again to miscarry ... there would be a rebellion in Scotland, which it would require an army ten times as great as that the duke of Cumberland marched into that country in 1745 to subdue':

Though the great body of the people is at this moment unusually quiet ... the desire for reform is much more

deep and intense than ever ... The reports of *all* my informers concur in expressing their thorough conviction that a second rejection of the reform bills would be the signal, all over the populous and manufacturing districts, for a general defiance of authority and for scenes of violence and outrage ... The political *unions* (which I have endeavoured to discourage ... without exasperating them ...) have contributed greatly to preserve peace and good order ... but have also given a confidence and consciousness of strength to the reformers ... It is impossible ... to look to this new feature in the state of our society without much anxiety; but I feel the strongest assurance that, if the reform bills were once passed, the greater part of these associations would silently expire and the rest become quite insignificant.

He had given the same message to Grey and Melbourne during the recess to draw their attention to 'the inadequacy of the military force now stationed in Scotland in the event of disorder'.[69] He informed Napier, 7 Feb., that 'we are not yet on velvet in politics'; but a fortnight later he thought that on the problem of the Lords and the possible creation of peers, 'things are firmer and safer'.[70] He expressed willingness to apply the cholera prevention bill to Scotland if legally feasible, 15 Feb., but this proved not to be the case, and later that evening he brought in a separate measure to authorize assessments of rates according to local Police Acts. Next day he proposed and carried by 55-10 an amendment remedying his own oversight in omitting reference to Providence in the preamble. The measure received royal assent on 20 Feb. (2 Gul. IV, c. 11); but some defects in it (which made Cockburn lament 'the effect of unpractical habits on the highest intellect and the purest nature') forced Jeffrey on 10 Mar. to bring in an amendment bill, which became law on 9 Apr. (2 Gul. IV, c. 27).[71] After recovering from an illness which prevented him from attending the committee on the Dorset by-election petition, 3 Mar., he was said to have behaved 'more like a *hired counsel* than a member sworn to impartiality' in his unsuccessful attempts to secure the unseating of the Tory Lord Ashley.[72] On 21 Mar., the day before he voted for the third reading of the English reform bill, he told Cockburn's daughter of his 'life of late':

Getting up (with difficulty) at a little before ten, I usually found ten or fifteen letters to read; and before I had got half through them, was obliged to run down to a committee, where I was shut up till after four, when the House met, and seldom got finally home till after two o'clock in the morning.[73]

Even after the triumphant division, his 'anticipations' were 'anything but comfortable', and he thought that 'the odds seem to be heavily rising against us'.[74] He dismissed the notion of compensating the owners of Scottish voting superiorities for their abolition, 2 Apr., when he was one of the four Scottish Members present who abstained from the division on the malt drawback bill. He watched the 'excessively interesting' Lords debate on the English reform bill, 14 Apr., and at Easter took a week off to visit Sevenoaks, Tunbridge Wells and Hastings, though he felt 'more dyspeptical than when I was in the Dorset committee all day, and in the ... House all night'.[75] On 5 May Cockburn told Kennedy:

> Jeffrey once, about a month ago, wrote one word implying that he was making or had made great sacrifices, thanklessly. With this solitary exception ... he has never disclosed anything from which I could even guess that he felt any uneasiness. But if he thinks that endurance is his duty, I know him enough to know that he will endure long before he murmurs. I grieve for him more than I can describe. I perfectly agree with you about the *absolute necessity* of a Scottish secretary.[76]

When he called on Althorp to voice his 'dark apprehensions' about the political situation, 9 May, he was told, 'You need not be anxious about your Scottish bills tonight, as I have the pleasure to tell you, we are no longer His Majesty's ministers'. He was reported to be 'very tranquil' about this, but he wrote to Cockburn later that day:

> So ends the first act of our comedy. God grant that it may not fall too soon into the tragic vein ... Do what you can to *keep peace*, and ... conjure lovers of liberty to be lovers of order and tolerance. I tremble for Scotland, and think there is greater hazard there than in any other quarter.[77]

He voted for the address calling on the king to appoint only ministers who would carry reform unimpaired, 10 May. Back in office with his colleagues, he presented Cupar and Perth petitions endorsing the government's Irish education scheme, 17 May, and said that 'a large portion of the laity favoured it'. He voted for the second reading of the Irish reform bill, 25 May. He moved and carried without a division the second reading of the Scottish bill and presented five belated Scottish petitions for supplies to be withheld until reform was secured, 21 May. On the 23rd, as Cockburn had wished, he presented and endorsed the monster Edinburgh petition for 'unmutilated' reform.[78] On 1 June he defended the decision to throw the burghs of Peebles and Selkirk into their counties and opposed and defeated by 168-61 Murray's attempt to secure additional Scottish county Members. He gave a somewhat muddled explanation of the recent abandonment of the proposed property qualification for Scottish Members and denied that the £10 county

franchise would encourage the multiplication of fictitious votes (which it did), 4 June. On 15 June he got rid of an amendment against the annexation of a portion of Perthshire to Kinross-shire, justified the junction of Elginshire and Nairnshire and successfully resisted various changes to the make-up of some of the burgh districts. After the third reading of the bill, 27 June, he wrote to Cockburn:

> It is odd how strangely I felt as I walked home last night after all was over. Instead of being elated or relieved, I could not help feeling a deep depression and sadness ... A sense of the littleness and vanity even of those great contentions was uppermost in my mind. I have ever since had a most intense longing to get home, and ... it seems peculiarly hard on me to be chained for two or three weeks longer.[79]

He was in a minority with Hume and O'Connell against Baring's bill to exclude insolvent debtors from Parliament, 6 June. He defended the extension of the forgery punishment mitigation bill to Scotland, 31 July. On 8 Aug. 1832 he told Cockburn:

> For my comfort, there are still more flaws and awkwardnesses in the English [Reform] Act ... The torpor and apathy of voters to register, or to make the qualifying payments of votes and taxes is altogether astounding and disgusting ... In London I do not believe *one-fourth* of those substantially qualified will be found to have come forward, and in the counties, I believe, there will be nearly a half who have hung back out of mere laziness. This makes me a little anxious about Edinburgh after all.[80]

Before returning to Scotland he had an interview with Grey, who, heeding his complaints, promised to 'save the lord advocate from such ruinous attendance in future, by reducing his office in practice to its proper legal character, and devolving a great part of its political functions on another'.[81] Nothing material was done, however, though Kennedy was appointed to the treasury board with a Scottish brief towards the end of the year.

After initial doubts, Jeffrey stood for Edinburgh at the 1832 general election and was returned triumphantly with Abercromby.[82] He soldiered on as lord advocate, adding to his achievement by carrying a measure to reform the municipal government of the Scottish burghs, until May 1834, when he was released from his 'vexation' by being appointed to a vacant lordship of the court of session.[83] If he failed as a parliamentary speaker it was because, as Macaulay judged, his audience's 'expectations were extravagant'; and Brougham reckoned that 'he only failed by speaking too well for his audience – his shot went over their head'.[84] As a popular if sometimes voluble judge, he set aside his party allegiance. He died unexpectedly at Craigcrook in January 1850 after a brief bronchial illness. Cockburn wrote that Edinburgh would never seem the same without him, and that 'head and heart included, his was the finest nature I have ever known'.[85]

[1] See Lord Cockburn, *Life of Lord Jeffrey*, 2 vols. (1852). Vol. ii consists of a selection of Jeffrey's letters. On Jeffrey as critic and thinker, see J.A. Greig, *Francis Jeffrey of the Edinburgh Review* (1948) and P. Flynn, *Francis Jeffrey* (1978). [2] *Macaulay Letters*, iv. 167; *Smith Letters*, ii. 784. [3] T. Carlyle, *Reminiscences* (1887), ii. 230. [4] *Two Brothers*, 131; Ward, *Letters to 'Ivy'*, 243-4. [5] Broughton, *Recollections*, ii. 143. [6] *Macaulay Letters*, i. 237-9. [7] Cockburn, i. 1-47; Carlyle, ii. 262; *Fox Jnl.* 118. [8] Cockburn, ii. 51-54, 73, 77, 81, 97. [9] J. Taylor, *Lord Jeffrey and Craigcrook*, 30; Cockburn, i. 101-7. [10] Cockburn, i. 117-18, 144. [11] Ibid. i. 124-31; *Cockburn Mems.* 159; *Wellesley Index to Victorian Periodicals*, i. 416-19. [12] See *Jeffrey's Criticism* ed. P.F. Morgan; Cockburn, i. 171-4; *Oxford DNB*. [13] Cockburn, i. 195-7; ii. 126-7; Flynn, 95, 98, 121-6. [14] Ward, 92-93; Flynn, 126-9. [15] L.G. Mitchell, *Holland House*, 185-91; *Creevey Pprs.* i. 205. [16] Cockburn, i. 161, 163-8. [17] Ibid. i. 212, 215-31; Add. 51644, Jeffrey to Holland, 10 Feb. 1814; Broughton, ii. 143; *Fox Jnl.* 118; *Macaulay Letters*, i. 238. [18] Cockburn, i. 234-8; *Cockburn Jnl.* ii. 145; *Highland Lady*, 334-5; Taylor, 4. [19] Cockburn, i. 240; *The 'Pope' of Holland House* ed. Lady Seymour, 175. [20] Cockburn, ii. 177. [21] Ibid. i. 252-3, 259; Flynn, 131. [22] Cockburn, ii. 189; *The Times*, 16 Nov. 1819; NLS mss 1496, f. 148. [23] Cockburn, i. 261-2; Add. 51831, Gibson to Holland, 20 Dec.; *The Times*, 22 Dec. 1820. [24] Cockburn, i. 267-8; ii. 192-3; *The Times*, 17 Jan. 1821, 18 Jan. 1823. [25] Cockburn, ii. 196-7. [26] NLS mss 24749, f. 28; 24770, f. 4. [27] *The Times*, 9 Apr., 22 Nov. 1825; Cockburn, i. 269; *Cockburn Letters*, 132; *Scott Jnl.* 14. [28] *HMC Var. Coll.* ii. 346-7. [29] *Cockburn Letters*, 170; Cockburn, ii. 223-4. [30] NLS mss 24749, f. 37; Cockburn, i. 279; Lansdowne mss, Jeffrey to Lansdowne, 2 Nov. 1827. [31] *Macaulay Letters*, i. 240. [32] *The Times*, 18 Mar. 1829; Cockburn, i. 281; *Cockburn Letters*, 210; Taylor, 38. [33] *The Times*, i. 282-5; *Cockburn Letters*, 218; *Scott Jnl.* 646; *Smith Letters*, ii. 511. [34] *Buxton Mems.* 247-8; Cockburn, ii. 230. [35] *Cockburn Letters*, 255-7; Lansdowne mss, Aytoun to ?Lansdowne, 22 Nov., Murray to Lansdowne, 26 Nov. 1830. [36] Cockburn, i. 306-7; Carlyle, ii. 257. [37] Stair mss (History of Parliament Aspinall transcripts), Murray to Sir J. Dalrymple, 22 Dec. 1830; *Caledonian Mercury*, 13, 17, 20 Jan 1831; G.W.T. Omond, *Lord Advocates* (1883), ii. 308-9; *Smith Letters*, 527. [38] *Cockburn Jnl.* i. 2-3; *Cockburn Letters*, 287; Cockburn, ii. 232-3. [39] Hopetoun mss 167, f. 218. [40] *Cockburn Letters*, 294-5. [41] *Macaulay Letters*, i. 317, 319; [J. Grant], *Random Recollections of Commons* (1837), 184-6. [42] *Three Diaries*, 63. [43] *Greville Mems.* ii. 125; Broughton, iv. 90; *Life of Campbell*, i. 506; Hopetoun mss 167, f. 227. [44] *Macaulay Letters*, ii. 7. [45] Brougham mss. [46] *Edgeworth Letters*, 488. [47] Cockburn, i. 315-16; ii. 234-6; *The Times*, 4 Apr.; Fitzwilliam mss, Allen to Milton, 29 Mar., Cayley to same, 9 Apr. 1831. [48] Cockburn, i. 317. [49] *The Times*, 11 Apr.; Fitzwilliam mss, Jeffrey to Milton [22 Apr. 1831]; 732, p. 27; *Cockburn Jnl.* i. 6. [50] Cockburn, i. 300, 305, 309, 314, 315-16. [51] Orkney Archives, Balfour mss D2/3/14, Traill to J. Balfour, 13 May 1831. [52] *Caledonian Mercury*, 5, 14, 16 May; *The Times*, 7 May; *Cockburn Jnl.* i. 13-14; *Cockburn Letters*, 318-19, 321; Brougham mss, Abercromby to Brougham, 1 May 1831; NAS GD40/9/327/6. [53] *Caledonian Mercury*, 28 May 1831. [54] Grey mss, Abercromby to Grey, 6 June 1831. [55] *Cockburn Letters*, 324-5. [56] Cockburn, i. 319. [57] *Cockburn Letters*, 326. [58] Cockburn, ii. 237. [59] Ibid. i. 323. [60] *Cockburn Letters*, 334. [61] Carlyle, ii. 258-9. [62] Add. 34615, f. 116. [63] Wilts. RO, Hobhouse mss 145/2/6, Hobhouse to wife, 24 [Sept. 1831]; *Life of Campbell*, i. 521. [64] Ward, 375; Cockburn, i. 323-4. [65] Cockburn, i. 324; ii. 239. [66] Ibid. ii. 240;

Cockburn Letters, 354; NAS GD46/4/135/5. [67] *Cockburn Letters*, 360, 363, 364. [68] Add. 34615, f. 221. [69] Add. 51644. [70] Add. 34615, ff. 268, 278. [71] *Cockburn Letters*, 391. [72] *CJ*, lxxxvii. 162; Add. 51601, Lady Cowper to Lady Holland [9 Mar. 1832]. [73] Cockburn, ii. 245. [74] Add. 34615, f. 298. [75] Parker, *Graham*, i. 284; Cockburn, ii. 251-3. [76] *Cockburn Letters*, 403. [77] Le Marchant, *Althorp*, 421; *Life of Campbell*, ii. 9; Cockburn, i. 330-1. [78] *Cockburn Letters*, 407. [79] Cockburn, i. 334-5. [80] Ibid. ii. 254. [81] Ibid. i. 310; *Cockburn Jnl.* i. 35. [82] *Cockburn Letters*, 411; Cockburn, i. 337-9; ii. 255-8; *Cockburn Jnl.* i. 40-42; *Caledonian Mercury*, 8, 10, 13, 17, 20 Dec. 1832. [83] *Cockburn Jnl.* i. 59. [84] *Macaulay Letters*, iv. 167; Brougham mss, autobiog. fragment. [85] *Gent. Mag.* (1850), i. 313-15; *Cockburn Letters*, 535; *Cockburn Jnl.* ii. 253-4.

D.R.F.

JENKINS, Richard (1785–1853), of Bicton Hall, Salop and 7 Mansfield Street, Mdx.[1]

| SHREWSBURY | 1830–1832 |
| SHREWSBURY | 1837–1841 |

b. 18 Feb. 1785, 1st s. of Richard Jenkins of Bicton Hall and Constantia Harriet, da. of George Ravenscroft of Wrexham, Denb. *educ.* E.I. Coll. Fort William 1801-3. *m.* 31 Mar. 1824, at Hingnah, Elizabeth Helen, da. of Hugh Spottiswoode of E.I. Co. civil service, 4s. 4da. (2 *d.v.p.*). *suc.* fa. 1797; GCB 20 July 1838. *d.* 30 Dec. 1853.

Asst. writer E.I. Co. (Bombay) 1798; acting asst. in office of gov.-gen. 1803; asst. resident and acting sec. Hyderabad Feb. 1804, Burhanpur June 1804; acting resident, Nagpur 1807, resident 1810-27; ret. 1 May 1828.

Dir. E.I. Co. 1832-50, dep. chairman 1838-9, chairman 1839-40.

The Jenkins, a cadet branch of the Charlton (Salop) family of that name, had East India connections and a mansion in Shrewsbury's Abbey Foregate, built in 1698 by Thomas Jenkins. His descendants had intermarried with the county families of Wingfield of Preston Brockhurst, Charlton of Ludford, Leighton of Loton, Lloyd of Aston Hall and Muckleston of Bicton, through whom, by the death in childbirth in 1740 of Laetitia, the wife of Richard Jenkins (*d.* 1743), they had acquired that estate. Jenkins, the eldest of six children, was born at Cruckton and baptized at Portesbury, 2 June 1785.[2] References in his election addresses suggest that he attended Shrewsbury School,[3] but this cannot be confirmed. His father died intestate, 2 Nov. 1797, and shortly afterwards Jenkins was promised a writership and his brother Charles Edward Orlando (*d.* 16 July 1823) a military commission in the East India Company. Jenkins took up his post in 1800, arrived in Bombay, 8 Jan. 1801, and in May entered the college at Fort William, where he excelled as a translator and was awarded prizes in Arabic, Hindustani and Persian. Now intended for a diplomatic career, early in 1803 he was seconded to the office of the governor-general, Lord Wellesley, and came to be 'considered one of the family'. He was posted to the courts of Hyderabad and Dowlut Rao Scindia, where, following the death of the resident Joseph Webbe in November 1804, he remained 'virtually a prisoner' until Lord Lake demanded his release in October 1805, and Sir Barry Close arrived from Poona to negotiate a new treaty.[4] In 1807 he was sent to Nagpur to relieve the resident Lord Elphinstone, whose love of sport and literature he shared; his own appointment as resident was confirmed on Elphinstone's transfer to Poona in 1810. The annihilation of the Pindaris in 1812 was ordered on his advice, and he negotiated a treaty of perpetual defensive alliance between the Company and Nagpur, 27 May 1816, and effectively ruled that kingdom until the raja Rahuji came of age in December 1826. Reporting to the governor of Madras, Sir Thomas Munro, 4 May 1821, he observed that 'our general plan in all things has been to avoid innovation, and to regulate the old machinery and restore it where deficient'.[5] He was commended in dispatches and in a speech by Canning for his handling of the Appah Sahib rebellion, particularly the battle of Sitabaldi, 26 Nov. 1817; and following his marriage at Hingnah in 1824, he campaigned to have the increased allowance he had received since 1822 backdated to 1817 (an additional 75,000 rupees).[6] Forwarding a copy of his memorial, a 'last appeal ... to circulate privately amongst my friends at home', to the governor-general Lord Amherst in December 1825, he observed:

> I cannot help but feel mortified at the neglect which I have experienced from the authorities at home, now eight years since I was led to expect some special rank or favour ... Whatever may be the result I shall wish to be able to leave Nagpur early in 1827, and to embark from Calcutta towards the end of that year.[7]

The prospect of a vacancy for Shrewsbury may have induced him to apply to bring forward his departure on 'urgent family considerations ... pressed upon me in letters from home' in January 1826.[8] He stayed to negotiate a treaty with Nagpur in December 1826, but cut short his stay in Calcutta, where his *Report on the Territories of the Rajah of Nagpore*, an analytical document based on his dispatches and memorials to Amherst, Hastings and Munro, was published in 1827.[9] His homecoming was marked by a dinner for his friends at the *Raven*, Shrewsbury, 7 Aug. 1827, and 'a fine ox and three sheep decorated with colours and preceded by a band of music and flags were carried through the streets in procession to Bicton and Montford Bridge' for distribution to the poor.[10]

He supported his financial claim and his pretensions to a baronetcy for 'political services' by publishing *Extracts from Public Documents having Reference to the Services of Mr. Jenkins, 1804-1827* in 1828, and Sir John Malcolm*, the 1st earl of Powis and Lord Ashley* wrote to the duke of Wellington as premier on his behalf. He was turned down and his application to succeed Malcolm as governor of Bombay in 1829 was also rejected, making him, according to Malcolm, 'the only person unrewarded for his services in 1817 and 1818'.[11] Testifying before the Lords select committee on the Company, 23 Mar. 1830, he described revenue collection, the ryot system, criminal and civil jurisdiction and the customs and religion of Nagpur, but he could say little about its commerce or potential for sugar beet production. He insisted that the objectives of British 'superintendentship' had been 'to bring the country back to what it had been in its best times [rather] than to introduce any European principles into the general administration', so reinforcing the president of the India board Lord Ellenborough's view that a new treaty would be 'impolitic'.[12] Jenkins and his relations had been acclaimed at Shropshire Brunswick Club functions in 1829 and his return for Shrewsbury at the general election of 1830 was assured even before the Ultra Thomas Boycott stood down in his favour, for the interests of the 1st marquess of Cleveland and the 5th earl of Tankerville were his and he spent 'like a proper nabob'.[13] He refused to be bound by pledges, but was regarded as a government supporter. He stated on the hustings that he stood independently of and without the knowledge of the East India Company, as a defender of the constitution in church and state and promoter of the 'diffusion of education through all classes'. His declaration that he did not oppose necessary 'ameliorations and reforms' was loudly cheered and he described himself as

> an enemy to all regulations and restrictions which tend to shackle a man from doing the best for himself without injuring his neighbour. I am of opinion that legislation on such subjects is best left alone. I am an enemy to all monopolies, domestic and foreign, which tend to close any available markets for the produce of our manufactories. India and China are imagined to afford these fields; and should I be returned ... no vote of mine shall oppose the just claims of the public. But this question involves the destiny of many millions of people, and I cannot bring myself, therefore, to view it as a matter of commercial regulation.[14]

On the eve of the poll he refused 'for family reasons' to go to Persia as commander-in-chief, a posting approved by Wellington, and which Elphinstone had already rejected.[15]

Henry Brougham* thought that Jenkins might oppose the Wellington ministry, but they included him among their 'friends' and, perceiving that their existence 'depended on the result of that question', he divided with them on the civil list when they were brought down, 15 Nov. 1830, and corrected *The Times* for listing him as an absentee.[16] He remained a stockholder and East India Company affairs dictated his political career, but nothing came of his application to succeed Baring to a directorship in February 1831.[17] Declining attendance at the Shrewsbury reform meeting, 17 Mar., he wrote:

I am a friend to moderate reform, meaning thereby the admission of the great unrepresented towns to send Members to Parliament and the extension of the elective franchise to householders of a certain grade in towns and to leaseholders and copyholders in counties. I conceive, however, that these measures might be engrafted on the elective system as it stands, but I cannot see the necessity of subverting so many boroughs altogether, nor still less of taking away the right of voting from the lower classes, and of entirely reconstructing the elective system, which, however complicated, is interwoven with the habits and feelings, the patriotic feelings, of the lower classes. Any measure for checking bribery and corruption, and for lessening the expense and trouble of elections, both to the electors and the elected, I am also a good friend to; and in these views I dare say the subsidiary measures proposed may be useful and at least worth trying. With such opinions, I should not be disposed entirely to oppose the [Grey ministry's] plan, but I shall not be able finally to agree to it without considerable changes ... I am not inclined to be a violent anti-reformer, but I am convinced that we ought not to go too far in demolishing old institutions, with the view of correcting abuses, in conjunction with which the country has so long flourished, the envy and admiration of the world.[18]

When their petition in favour of the reform bill was presented, 21 Mar., he testified to the respectability of its 1,000 signatories, but dissented from their prayer and said that 'though not altogether an anti-reformer', he considered the government's measure 'too sweeping'. He divided against its second reading, 22 Mar., and for Gascoyne's wrecking amendment, 19 Apr. His supporters pressed their argument that most of Shrewsbury's freemen would be disfranchised by the bill, and he kept his seat at the general election that month, assisted by the retirement after the first day's poll of Boycott and the Manchester Unitarian mill owner Richard Potter[†]. He was denied a hearing on the hustings, and his opponents insisted that his votes did not match his professions of support for 'moderate reform'. In his intended speech, which he had printed, he said that he had voted against the Grey

administration on the timber duties, 18 Mar., because he thought lowering them would damage shipping 'for the theoretical advantage of free trade'. Directly after the chairing he returned to London, where his second son was born, 20 May 1831, and kept aloof from the Shropshire contest.[19]

Jenkins suggested holding anti-reform dinners and divided against the reintroduced reform bill at its second reading, 6 July, and to use the 1831 census to determine borough representation, 19 July 1831.[20] He voted against taking a Member from Chippenham, 27 July, paired against uniting Rochester with Chatham and Strood, 9 Aug. and divided against the bill's passage, 21 Sept., and the second reading of the Scottish measure, 23 Sept.[21] On 7 Oct. he was granted a month's leave because of ill health. He voted against the second reading, 17 Dec. 1831, committal, 20 Jan., and third reading of the revised reform bill, 22 Mar. 1832. He divided against administration on the Russian-Dutch loan, 26 Jan., 12 July, having also voted in the majority against the Vestry Act amendment bill, 23 Jan. 1832. Jenkins was excluded from the 1831 select committee on the East India Company, but appointed to its successor, 27 Jan., and elected a director of the Company in June 1832.[22] His mother, who had remained at Bicton, died in August 1832, and her estate proved awkward for Jenkins to administer.[23]

Jenkins had announced his candidature for Shrewsbury and canvassed early, but on 27 Oct. 1832 he stood down on health grounds, making way for another Conservative, Sir John Hanmer. He replaced Hanmer in 1837 after a severe contest and retired in 1841.[24] Though initially hostile, he voted (as a director) to accept the East India Company's 1833 charter vesting power in the crown, rather than paralyse business by opposition.[25] A baronetcy eluded him until 1838, when as deputy chairman he was made a knight commander of the Bath, on the recommendation of the president of the India board Sir John Hobhouse* and his predecessor Lord Glenelg. Wellesley considered the honour 'better suited to his services' than a baronetcy.[26] He became Company chairman for a single term in 1839, but his application to succeed Sir Henry Pottinger as envoy to China in 1843 was rejected.[27] He died 'somewhat impoverished' at his London home, Gothic Cottage, Blackheath, in December 1853 and was buried in Bicton Old Church. Recalling him, the *Shrewsbury Chronicle* praised him for securing East India posts for many from Shropshire.[28] He had entrusted his estates to his widow (described as 'of Paris'), Capel Sandys of Baddesley Clinton, Warwickshire and Major Thomas

Wilkinson of Hanover Square, and was succeeded at Bicton by his eldest son Richard (1828-80) and to the Abbey Foregate and Birmingham properties by his three younger sons.[29]

[1] Based unless otherwise stated on *Oxford DNB* and Salop Archives 1071/1 (F.A. Hagar, 'Richard Jenkins and the residency at Nagpore, 1807-1826', Univ. of California D. Phil. thesis, 1960). [2] BL OIOC J/1/18. [3] Salop Archives D45/1170/5b. [4] OIOC mss. Eur. F. 228/79-80. [5] Ibid. 151/76. [6] Ibid. 88/11; IOR/F/4/869/22981. [7] OIOC mss. Eur. F. 228/140/92. [8] Ibid. See SHREWSBURY. [9] OIOC mss. Eur. F. 151/101. [10] Salop Archives 6001/3057 ('Henry Pigeon's Salopian Annals', v. 30). [11] Wellington mss WP1/946/10; 973/38; 980/22, 38; 993/7; 1020/6; 1024/12; 1025/9; 1026/12; 1044/7; 1045/15; NLW, Aston Hall mss C.371. [12] OIOC L/PARL/2/64, pp. 140-8; Wellington mss WP1/1114/16; C.H. Philips, *E.I. Co.*, 271. [13] *Salopian Jnl.* 4 Feb. 1829; Aston Hall mss C.559; Salop Archives 840/442-3; D45/1170/1a-b, 3b, 4a-b, 5a-b, 8b, 11b; qD45/2-4; 6003/6 (Slaney jnl.), 4, 25 July, 2 Aug.; Add. 51835, Goodwin to Holland [Aug. 1830]; J.A. Phillips and C. Wetherell, 'Great Reform Bill of 1832 and Rise of Partisanship', *JMH*, lxiii (1991), 634. [14] E. Edwards, *Parl. Elections in Shrewsbury*, 25-26; *Shrewsbury Chron.* 6 Aug. 1830; Salop Archives D45/1170/6. [15] Wellington mss WP1/1129/2; 1134/12. [16] *The Times*, 22 Nov. 1830; *Shrewsbury Chron.* 29 Apr. 1831. [17] *Wolverhampton Chron.* 9 Feb., *The Times*, 24 Feb. 1831; Philips, 286. [18] *Shrewsbury Chron.* 18 Mar. 1831. [19] Ibid. 29 Apr., 6 May; *Wolverhampton Chron.* 4, 11 May 1831; Edwards, 29; Salop Archives D45/1170/14a-b, 15a-b; qD45/9; Phillips and Wetherell, 634-5. [20] Wellington mss WP1/1187/2. [21] *The Times*, 11 Aug. 1831. [22] *Shrewsbury Chron.* 29 June 1832. [23] PROB 6/208. [24] NLW, Coedymaen mss 230; *VCH Salop*, iii. 325-6; *Shrewsbury Chron.* 28 Sept., 2 Nov., 14 Dec.; *Spectator*, 27 Oct., 14 Dec. 1832; Phillips and Wetherell, 636-9; Edwards, 41-43. [25] Philips, 284, 286. [26] Add. 40419, f. 229; OIOC mss. Eur. F. 88/51; *Wellesley Pprs.* ii. 346-8. [27] Add. 40536, ff. 438-9. [28] Ibid.; *VCH* Salop, iii. 325; *Gent. Mag.* (1854), i. 197-9; *Shrewsbury Chron.* 6 Jan. 1854. [29] PROB 11/2184/39; IR26/1998/39; OIOC deRP, p.185.

M.M.E.

JENKINSON, Hon. Charles Cecil Cope (1784-1851), of Pitchford Hall, Salop and Buxted Park, Suss.

SANDWICH	1807-1812
BRIDGNORTH	1812-1818
EAST GRINSTEAD	1818-4 Dec. 1828

b. 29 May 1784, o.s. of Charles Jenkinson[†], 1st earl of Liverpool (*d.* 1808), and 2nd w. Catherine, da. of Sir Cecil Bisshopp[†], 6th bt., of Parham, Suss., wid. of Sir Charles Cope, 2nd bt., of Brewerne, Oxon.; half-bro. of Hon. Robert Banks Jenkinson[†]. *educ.* privately by Rev. Charles Richards; Christ Church, Oxf. 1801. *m.* 19 July 1810, Julia Evelyn Medley, da. and h. of Sir George Augustus William Shuckburgh Evelyn[†], 6th bt., of Shuckburgh Park, Warws., 3da. *suc.* cos. Adam Ottley to Pitchford estate 1807; half-bro. as 3rd earl of Liverpool 4 Dec. 1828; GCB 11 Dec. 1845. *d.* 3 Oct. 1851.

Page of honour 1793-4; précis writer, foreign office Apr. 1803-Apr. 1804; priv. sec. to sec. of state for home affairs May-July 1804; sec. of legation, Vienna 1804-7;

under-sec. of state for home affairs Nov. 1807-Nov. 1809, for war and colonies Nov. 1809-June 1810; prothonotary co. palatine of Lancaster 1838-*d.*; PC 3 Sept. 1841; ld. steward of household Sept. 1841-July 1846.

Cornet Surr. yeomanry 1803; lt.-col. cinque ports militia 1810.

In February 1820 Jenkinson's half-brother, the prime minister Lord Liverpool, encouraged him to consider standing for Sussex at the impending general election, but he preferred to come in again for East Grinstead on the interest of his cousin Lady Whitworth, widow of the 3rd duke of Dorset. His decision to decline the county was attributed by Lord Sheffield to his 'peculiar aversion to expenditure'.[1] He naturally continued to support Liverpool's ministry, though he was not the most assiduous of attenders. He voted in defence of their conduct towards Queen Caroline, 6 Feb. 1821. He divided against Catholic relief, 28 Feb. He voted against repeal of the additional malt duty, 3 Apr., and described as 'absurd and contemptible' a charge that members of the select committee on sewers were influenced by 'private considerations', 11 Apr.[2] He divided against parliamentary reform, 9 May, and paired against the forgery punishment mitigation bill, 23 May. Next day he spoke in support of Scarlett's poor relief bill, declaring that he 'deserved the thanks of the country for having brought before the House a measure on this most important subject'. He appeared in a list of placemen who supported payment of arrears to the duke of Clarence, 8 June 1821. He voted against more extensive tax reductions, 11, 21 Feb., and abolition of one of the joint-postmasterships, 13 Mar., and blamed agricultural distress on maladministration of the poor laws, which he also believed were intrinsically defective, 16 May 1822.[3] He divided against removing Catholic peers' disabilities, 30 Apr. 1822. Granted three weeks' leave to attend to urgent private business, 10 Apr., his next recorded vote was against inquiry into delays in chancery, 5 June 1823. He divided against the motion condemning the trial of the Methodist missionary John Smith in Demerara, 11 June 1824. He was granted two weeks' leave owing to illness in his family, 14 Apr., but returned to act as a minority teller for the immediate second reading of the Shrewsbury poor bill, 2 May 1825. He voted against Catholic relief, 10 May, and for the duke of Cumberland's annuity, 30 May 1825. At the general election of 1826 he was returned for East Grinstead by the new patrons, Lords Plymouth and De la Warr, having acted as an intermediary in their protracted negotiations over the borough with the 5th duke of Dorset.[4]

He divided against Catholic relief, 6 Mar. 1827. In January 1828 he briefly stepped out of his stricken half-brother's shadow when he offered to move the address on behalf of the duke of Wellington's newly formed ministry. This met with a mixed response from the colonial secretary Huskisson, who advised the leader of the House, Robert Peel:

> If he runs true the name is a great advantage. Should he bolt the mischief may be very embarrassing ... He must be very carefully tutored, but before you commit yourself, you will, I have no doubt, probe him very carefully in respect to the spirit in which he undertakes the task.

Accordingly, Peel provided Jenkinson with a 'general notion' of what should be said, which he duly followed in his speech on 29 Jan., notably in the avoidance of any reference to the previous coalition administrations, other than a personal tribute to Canning.[5] He used Liverpool's eminence to account for his own inconspicuousness, explaining that it had been 'needless for me to trouble the House with my own private opinions', which were 'on all public matters ... invariably in accordance' with his half-brother's. He commended Peel's inclusion in the government and, emphasizing that he spoke with Liverpool's approval but not at his behest, declared that 'I am not wrong, I think, in supposing in the general sense that [he] highly approves of the administration'. On specific issues, he sought to forestall discussion of the battle of Navarino by urging that it should be delayed until relevant papers were laid before the House. He announced the recall of British troops from Portugal and applauded the commercial treaties with Brazil and Mexico. He justified his 'most sanguine anticipations for the future' of the economy with historical examples of recovery from depression and hoped for a 'gradual and equal alleviation of distress'. He maintained that the government's 'great object' was 'the amelioration, as far as possible, of the condition of the poor'. His speech won praise from Peel, who called it 'excellent' and 'perfectly safe'. The Tory Henry Bankes* thought there was 'nothing ... remarkable' in it, apart from the intimation of Liverpool's opinions. Jenkinson privately observed that

> I had long intended to step forth the champion of my own opinion and the *representative* of those of my unfortunate brother. I chose myself the occasion and have not to regret or retract a syllable. Indeed, whatever my enemies may say, vanity or interest never have swayed me in politics. I have at least proved now that I was always capable of addressing Parliament and have assigned my reasons for *not* having done so, and I can say what no one I firmly believe could say before, that my brother was prime minister during 15 years during which time I never

asked or received a personal favour and always supported his government.[6]

His last recorded votes in the Commons were against repeal of the Test Acts, 28 Feb., and Catholic relief, 12 May 1828.

In December 1828 Jenkinson succeeded to his half-brother's title and Gloucestershire estates and received personalty worth £46,500.[7] He supported the government's Catholic emancipation bill in 1829. His interest in the poor laws resurfaced in 1836, when he published *An account of the operation of the poor law amendment in the Uckfield Union*, a defence of the workhouse system in his Sussex neighbourhood. He became closely attached to the duchess of Kent and her daughter Princess Victoria, to whom his own daughter Catherine was a lady-in-waiting, and he held a household appointment during Peel's second ministry. He died suddenly following an attack of pleurisy in October 1851, prompting Victoria to write of her 'great sorrow at the loss of a dear and faithful, excellent friend'.[8] The earldom became extinct on his death but was conferred on his grandson as a fresh creation in 1905.

[1] Add. 38191, f. 127; 38458, f. 282; Petworth House mss bdle. 69, Sheffield to Egremont, 20 Feb., 2 Mar. 1820. [2] *The Times*, 12 Apr. 1821. [3] Ibid. 17 May 1822. [4] See EAST GRINSTEAD. [5] Add. 38195, f. 201; 40395, ff. 26, 52, 103. [6] Add. 38195, f. 209; Dorset RO D/BKL, Bankes's jnl. 161; Salop RO, Weld-Forester mss 1224/37/219, Jenkinson to Lady Forester, 31 Jan. 1828. [7] PROB 11/1751/92; IR26/1200/33; N. Gash, *Lord Liverpool*, 215. [8] *Victoria Letters* (ser. 1), i. 207; ii. 390.

H.J.S.

JEPHSON, Charles Denham Orlando (1799–1888), of Mallow Castle, co. Cork.[1]

| MALLOW | 1826–1832 |
| MALLOW | 24 Apr. 1833–1859 |

b. 1 Dec. 1799, 3rd but 2nd surv. s. of William Jephson of Englefield Green, Surr. and 3rd w. Louisa, da. of Charles Kensington of Blackheath, Kent. *educ.* by Rev. Charles Delafosse at Richmond, Surr.; Brasenose, Oxf. 1817. *m.* 1821, Catherine Cecilia Jane, da. of William Franks of Carrig, co. Cork, 2s. *d.v.p.* 2da. *suc.* fa. 1813. Took additional name of Norreys by royal lic. 18 July 1838; *cr.* bt. 6 Aug. 1838. *d.* 11 July 1888.

Trustee, Incorporated General Steam Carriage Co.; chairman, Kerry Coach Co.

The Jephsons, who had acquired Mallow Castle in 1607 by marriage with the daughter of Sir Thomas Norreys, had represented Mallow intermittently since 1692. Jephson's grandfather William had sat in the Irish House, 1761-68, when he was replaced by Denham Jephson, Member, 1768-1800, and in the Imperial Parliament, 1802-12.[2] Denham succeeded to the family estates in 1781, by when his cousin William, Jephson's father, was his closest living relative. An army officer with a rakish reputation, William had married secretly while serving in New York in 1777, but shortly after the birth of a son, William Henry (1782-1867), had been divorced by his first wife for 'keeping women' in London and the West Indies. On his return to Ireland in 1783, he had married a daughter of the 10th Viscount Mountgarret, who died in childbirth two years later. His marriage to Jephson's mother, the daughter of a Kent wine merchant, took place in January 1798, after which they settled in Surrey. In 1803 William was sentenced by court martial to six months' suspension from pay and rank for a drunken brawl with another officer, and thereafter Denham came repeatedly to the family's aid. In 1812 he obtained the deputy barrackmastership of Nova Scotia for William, who informed his sister that he would go alone:

> Denham Jephson stayed with me from Saturday to Tuesday, and is very fond of the boy, who is, without partiality, a fine fellow and a good scholar, though not very quick ... He promised to take care of my family during my absence and I hope and believe that even should he marry he will not neglect my son.

William could not be found at his post on Denham's death in May 1813, and only learnt of his inheritance by chance. Taking the first available ship home, he arrived in Falmouth late that year, but was too ill to travel further and died a fortnight later. His will, written two days before sailing, named Charles Jephson as his chief beneficiary, making no mention of his eldest son in New York, who subsequently pursued the family for a settlement.[3]

At the 1820 general election Jephson, though still shy of his majority, came forward for Mallow in an attempt to regain it from the Catholic freeholders, who had assumed control during his minority. He stressed his support for Catholic claims and residence 'among them', and declared himself to be 'unshackled' by party. Daniel O'Connell*, his opponent's agent, described him as 'an unfledged boy of twenty, quite an English boy, confident and shallow, a man in his own opinion but not in that of others', who 'said simply that he was of no party and had no *political principles*'. After a four-day contest he was defeated.[4] He married a 'local beauty' the following year.[5] In June 1825 his agent recommended that O'Connell be retained for the

next election. He was invited by the local Catholics to a grand public dinner in Limerick as a Protestant supporter of emancipation, 22 Oct. 1825, and attended the Catholic Association dinner for the 'friends of civil and religious liberty', 2 Feb. 1826, having informed O'Connell, 23 Jan., that 'however short the notice', he would 'use every exertion to arrive in Dublin in time'.[6] On 3 May 1826 his brother-in-law William Hume Franks reported that Nicholas Philpot Leader* had told him that 'Lady Glengall has got from government a loan of £60,000 for the railroad between Waterford and Limerick' and 'says if we exerted ourselves in the county of Cork ... we might get a loan for the railroad from Cork to Mallow'.[7]

At the 1826 general election Jephson offered again for Mallow as a 'constant resident' and supporter of Catholic claims, paying tribute to the retiring Member, who now backed him. It was widely expected that as 'lord of the sod' he would be returned unopposed, but at the nomination another candidate was proposed *in absentia*. After a two-day contest in which his opponent's agents accused of him of failing to comply with the qualification procedures, he was returned with a large majority. Petitions against his return came to nothing.[8] He presented a petition for Catholic claims, 14 Feb., and voted thus, 6 Mar. 1827.[9] He divided for the duke of Clarence's annuity bill, 16 Mar., but he was in the minorities for information on the Barrackpoor mutiny, 22 Mar., and the Lisburn Orange procession, 29 Mar. He voted for the disfranchisement of Penryn, 28 May, and against the Coventry magistracy bill, 18 June 1827. He presented and endorsed petitions for Catholic claims, 14, 29 Feb., 7 Mar., when he denied that they were legally excluded from Parliament by the Treaty of Limerick, which had been 'violated', and voted accordingly, 12 May 1828. He divided for repeal of the Test Acts, 26 Feb. He voted against extending the franchise of East Retford to Bassetlaw, 21 Mar., and its disfranchisement, 27 June. On 26 Mar. he introduced a bill to amend the law of Irish distresses and replevins, which was read a first time, 9 May, but went no further. He divided for the Irish lessors bill, 12 June. He voted for the usury laws amendment bill, 19 June, when he warned that a bill for electoral registers, published and sold 'four times a year', would introduce the 'utmost confusion' and 'occasion a new species of taxation upon electors'. He obtained returns of Irish constabulary expenses, 27 June, and voted for the corporate funds bill, 10 July 1828. On 20 Jan. 1829 he spoke at a Dublin meeting of the Protestant supporters of Catholic emancipation.[10] He presented petitions against the Irish Subletting Act, 11 Feb., when he protested that its restriction on inheritance by more than one child left the others 'destitute' and was 'one of the most barbarous provisions ever enacted', 3 Apr. He sought assurances that Orange and Brunswick Clubs would be suppressed along with the Catholic Association, 13 Feb., brought up petitions for emancipation, 17 Feb., 12 Mar., 7 Apr., and one against, with which he differed, 9 Mar. He had, of course, been listed by Planta, the Wellington ministry's patronage secretary, as a supporter of emancipation, and he voted thus, 6, 30 Mar., though he regretted the continued exclusion of Catholics from Oxford University and the fact that O'Connell's return had been left 'undecided', 12 Mar. That day he reported to O'Connell:

> I spoke of the hardship of your being excluded from the benefit of a bill which purports to be a bill of relief to *all* Catholics. Robert Gordon* came to me subsequently and said he thought I was mistaken ... [and] that ... you ... were not required to take any oaths but those of abjuration, allegiance and supremacy ... He did not anticipate any difficulty.

O'Connell replied that Gordon was 'totally mistaken in his views'.[11] Jephson brought up a petition for repeal of the Irish Vestry Acts, 23 Feb. On 2 Mar. he complained that repeal of the drawback on Irish window glass had been 'very injurious to the lower orders' and 'completely put a stop' to the 'luxury of a single window'. He cautioned against interfering with Irish tobacco cultivation, which was 'highly advantageous to the agricultural interest', 13 Mar. He presented but dissented from a Mallow petition against the disfranchisement of the 40s. Irish freeholders, which was 'inseparably connected' with emancipation, 20 Mar., but objected to the restrictions on Catholic office-holders wearing insignia in their chapels, asking, 'Why should we stickle so about these robes, gowns, and habits of office?', 24 Mar. He acknowledged that the registration of freeholds in Irish boroughs gave 'every opportunity for fraud and perjury', but could not concur with a petition for the disfranchisement of Mallow's freeholders, as it would be better 'to regulate the ... franchise than to annihilate it', 26 Mar. On 6 May he attended the public meeting at the *London Tavern* to celebrate the passage of emancipation.[12] He called for a provision in the Irish fisheries bill against the washing of dye-cloths within a certain distance of fisheries, 15 May. He voted to allow O'Connell to take his seat unimpeded, 18 May 1829.

Jephson voted for the transfer of East Retford's seats to Birmingham, 11 Feb., 5, 15 Mar., and in the minority of 21 for O'Connell's motion for adoption of the secret ballot there, which would 'produce purity of election', 15 Mar. 1830. He complained that an 'immense

portion of the funds intended for the benefit' of the Irish poor was 'frittered away in the support of useless and unwieldy establishments', 17 Feb. He voted for parliamentary reform, 18 Feb., 28 May, and the enfranchisement of Birmingham, Leeds and Manchester, 23 Feb., and divided steadily with the revived Whig opposition for economy and retrenchment from March. He secured papers on the Cork summer assizes, where the trial of men 'who had been in gaol already for three months' had been 'unnecessarily' postponed, 3 Mar., and accused the magistrates of acting unlawfully and voted for information on the conduct of the Irish solicitor-general John Doherty* in the affair, 12 May. He complained that the British Museum reading room's closure at 4 p.m. prevented its use by a 'most numerous and respectable class of people', 8 Mar. He presented a petition for the abolition of slavery, 11 Mar. On 25 Mar. Jephson, who had read with horror newspaper accounts of the punishments received by convicts in New South Wales, agreed to withdraw a motion he had tabled for the introduction of trial by jury there after Sir George Murray, the colonial secretary, in a 'liberal concession', agreed to take it up.[13] He urged the necessity of its speedy implementation, 11 June, and called for inquiry into General Darling's sentencing, 17 June. He presented a petition against the Irish Subletting Act, 29 Mar. That month O'Connell urged him to attend the committee on the 'gross job' of the St. Giles vestry bill and to 'judge for yourself'.[14] He objected to the Irish constabulary bill, whereby government would receive information on the state of Ireland from police constables rather than magistrates, 30 Mar., and protested that the 'manner in which the police is armed is as improper as it is unnecessary', 20 May. He divided for Jewish emancipation, 5 Apr., 17 May. He was granted a month's leave on urgent private business, 6 Apr. He concurred with a petition against the increase in Irish stamp duties, 10 May, and presented one in similar terms, 17 May. He voted for repeal of the Irish coal duties, 13 May. On the 15th he and O'Connell obtained leave to bring in a bill to legalize Catholic marriages, which went no further.[15] He divided for the proper collection of Irish first fruits, 18 May. He presented a petition for repeal of the Irish Vestry Acts, 25 May, and voted thus, 10 June. He moved the report stage of the Irish county rates bill, 18 June. He spoke against the Irish witnesses bill, 6 July 1830. That month an address from the Cork chamber of commerce paid tribute to his support for 'retrenchment and reform' and hoped there would be no attempt 'to deprive the people of Mallow' of his services.[16]

At the 1830 general election Jephson offered again, saw off an expected opposition by securing endorsements from local Tories and was returned unopposed.[17] Probably as part of the terms of his endorsement, in October he attended a dinner for O'Connell in Cork and spoke 'strongly and decidedly against' repeal of the Union and made 'some converts'.[18] 'The regret I have felt at hearing the name of *Jephson* identified with that of the *Irish* Bolivar', remarked an anonymous 'sincere friend', 'is entirely removed and recompensed by your able and enlightened speech ... and your ... stand ... to stem the torrents of massacre and bloodshed ... I hope then, there is a repeal of the *apparent* union between the ancient name of Jephson, and O'Connell'.[19] He presented petitions against slavery, 3, 15 Nov. 1830. He voted for repeal of the Irish Subletting Act, 11 Nov., advocated its amendment next day and brought up a hostile petition, 19 Nov. He spoke and divided for reduction of West Indian wheat import duties, 12 Nov. He had been listed by the Irish agent Pierce Mahony† as 'contra' and by the Wellington ministry as one of their 'foes', and he voted against them on the civil list, 15 Nov. On 9 Dec. he condemned the Grey ministry's 'most unpopular' appointment of William Plunket* as Irish lord chancellor. He objected to the furnishing of information on the professions of Irish magistrates, which the clerks of the peace 'did not know', 15 Dec. 1830. That month he was asked by the Association for Abolishing Corporate Abuse in Londonderry to assist their campaign against the corporation.[20] He defended Irish tobacco growing as 'a source of enjoyment to the poor', 10 Mar. 1831. He voted for the second reading of the Grey ministry's English reform bill, 22 Mar., and welcomed the Irish measure, though he regretted that it did 'not go quite as far as might be wished' and called for an increase in the county representation, hoping 'some mistake has been made in this respect', 24 Mar. He divided against Gascoyne's wrecking amendment, 19 Apr., and brought up a petition for reform, 20 Apr. 1831, when he warned that the 'negligent and inaccurate' operation of the Irish registry office had become so 'frightful' as to prevent the transfer of landed property. At the ensuing general election he stood as a supporter of retrenchment and reform, but at the nomination protested that Ireland had 'not been put on that footing of equality with England and Scotland which I could desire' and demanded an additional representative for county Cork. On the hustings his proposer, John Dillon Croker, welcomed his earlier speech at Cork refuting 'an assertion industriously spread ... that he was a follower of O'Connell', who 'would not venture to think or vote differently from what that gentleman wished'. He was returned unopposed.[21]

He doubted that free trade would benefit manufacturers, as 'every ship coming to this country' would leave 'it in ballast, taking only our money', 24 June 1831. He voted for the second reading of the reintroduced reform bill, 6 July, at least twice against adjournment, 12 July, and gave generally steady support to its details, though he was in the minorities for the disfranchisement of Saltash, 26 July, separate representation for Merthyr, 10 Aug., and the disfranchisement of Aldborough, 14 Sept. He divided for the passage of the bill, 21 Sept., and the second reading of the Scottish bill, 23 Sept., but warned that he would vote in favour of giving additional Members to Scotland in view of its population, 4 Oct. He voted for Lord Ebrington's confidence motion, 10 Oct. He brought up petitions against the grant to the Kildare Place Society, 14, 19 July. He was in the minority of 41 for civil list reductions, 18 July, and was added to the select committee on the issue, 27 Aug.[22] He was appointed to and chaired that on steam carriages, 20 July, and brought up its report, 12 Oct. On 21 July he obtained leave for a bill to regulate the Irish registry of deeds office, which the president of the Irish Law Society Josias Dunn informed him was 'so well calculated to effect the intended purposes' that we 'feel it unnecessary to suggest any alterations, save in a few instances', 22 Sept.[23] The bill was read a first time, 1 Sept., deferred, 25 Sept. 1831, and reintroduced, 2 Feb. 1832. He successfully guided it through its various stages, acting as a majority teller, 9 Apr., 25 July, but his motion to increase the salary of the Irish registrar, whose duties had 'very considerably extended', was defeated by 23-21, 3 Apr., when he was a minority teller. It received royal assent, 4 Aug. 1832 (2 & 3 Gul. IV, c. 87). He divided against the issue of the Dublin writ, 8 Aug., but with ministers on the controversy, 23 Aug. 1831. He criticized the 'numerous accumulations of boards' in Ireland and demanded the appointment of a single officer of public works, 15 Aug., and complained that the public works bill was too 'cumbersome', 16 Sept. He asked for the introduction of lord lieutenants of Irish counties to be given a 'fair trial', 15 Aug., observing that they would provide better 'organs of communication between the government and the several counties' than chief constables, 20 Aug. He spoke and was a majority teller against the union of Irish parishes bill, 19 Aug., and endorsed petitions for the abolition of the Irish yeomanry, 26 Aug. He introduced a bill for the establishment of public hospitals in Ireland, 16 Sept., which was read a third time, 5 Oct., and received royal assent, 15 Oct. (1 & 2 Gul. IV, c. 48). He welcomed the general register bill for England and Wales, 20 Sept. He spoke and divided for inquiry into the conduct of the Winchester magistrates during the arrest of the Deacles, 27 Sept. He secured returns concerning Irish newspaper stamps, 10 Oct. 1831.

Jephson paired for the second reading of the revised reform bill, 17 Dec. 1831, voted for going into committee on it, 20 Feb., and again gave general support to its details, although he continued to advocate separate representation for Merthyr, describing its proposed connection with Cardiff as 'one of the most unfortunate that could have happened, as their interests are completely different', 5 Mar. 1832. He divided for the third reading, 22 Mar., but was absent from the division on the address calling on the king to appoint only ministers who would carry reform unimpaired, 10 May. He voted for the second reading of the Irish bill, 25 May, but was in the minorities for O'Connell's motion to extend the county franchise to £5 freeholders, 18 June, and against the liability of Irish electors to pay municipal taxes before they could vote, 29 June. On 25 June he proposed that the words 'or other building' should be inserted in the clause relating to the Irish £10 householder franchise, in keeping with the English bill, but after taking the sense of the House declined the 'trouble of dividing'. He presented a petition for retaining the ancient boundaries of the manor of Mallow and the separate enfranchisement of householders in the surrounding parish, 27 June. He argued that returning officers should have the power of summoning the constabulary, who had refused to attend on two occasions at Mallow, 6 July. He objected to the 'expense and trouble' of polling being carried out 'solely in county towns', citing the 'power of the city demagogues' who exist 'wherever there is a corporation', 6 July, and proposed an amendment for the division of Irish counties into polling districts, but desisted in the face of opposition, 18 July. He argued and moved successfully for the extension of the franchise of Dublin University to all Masters of Arts graduates, 9 July, and called for them to be given an opportunity to take up their degrees 'before the next election', 18 July. He regretted that the English bill had been 'spoiled' by preservation of the freeman franchise and warned that its continuation in Ireland would enable corporations to 'make as many fictitious votes as they please', 3 Aug. 1832.

Jephson left the House during the division on the Russian-Dutch loan, 26 Jan., but voted with ministers on the issue, 12, 16, 20 July, and on Portugal, 9 Feb. 1832.[24] He complained of recurrent delays in delivering mail to New South Wales, where a parcel sent in June had arrived before one sent in March, 2 Feb.

He divided for information on military punishments and for printing the Woollen Grange petition for the abolition of Irish tithes, 16 Feb. He welcomed a bill to remedy the Irish Subletting Act's 'unnatural and unjustifiable interference' with the right of property, 20 Feb. He presented a petition from mail coach contractors for a reduction of the fares charged by post office steam packets between Holyhead and Howth, 23 Feb., and was appointed to and chaired the committee on Irish postal communications, 16 Mar. On 6 Mar. he obtained leave to introduce a bill to regulate tolls on steam carriages, which passed its third reading, 9 Apr., but went no further. He urged the removal of 'every impediment thrown in the way of this new invention', 27 July. He apparently voted against the Irish secretary Smith Stanley's motion to consider Irish tithes, 8 Mar., for on the 20th Stephen Coppinger, chairman of the National Political Union of Ireland, wrote to express his thanks for 'the noble stand made by you and the other members of the minority of 31, who refused to agree to Stanley's motion'. (Jephson endorsed the letter, 'Opposed the consideration of the question until further evidence and until the whole question be considered together'.)[25] Denying that tithes were the 'real cause' of dissatisfaction in Ireland, he called for 'an entire and immediate revision' of the revenues of the established church, 13 Mar., recommended the granting of relief to the clergy, 6 Apr., and urged the necessity of proceeding 'at once to the question of appropriation', for as 'so long as this tax, however levied, is supplied to the support of one religion only, so long there will exist this opposition', 10 July. He voted against the Irish tithes resolutions, 27 Mar., and the composition bill, 13, 24 July, but was one of the Members 'usually opposing ministers' who divided for Crampton's amendment regarding the payment of arrears, 9 Apr., and in its support, 1 Aug., when he declared, 'I disapprove of tithes', but as 'this bill is to be carried, I should wish it to pass in as eligible a shape as possible'. He was in the minority of ten for the reception of a petition for the abolition of tithes next day. He voted with ministers on the navy civil departments bill, 6 Apr., but against their temporizing amendment on the abolition of slavery, 24 May. He divided for coroners' inquests to be made public, 20 June. He spoke and voted for Baring's bill to exclude insolvent debtors from Parliament, 27 June. He divided for a system of representation for New South Wales, 28 June. On 2 July he expressed concern at the spiralling costs of the survey of Ireland. He contended that the duties of the recorder of Dublin were 'quite inconsistent with an attendance in this House' and voted accordingly, 24 July 1832.

At the 1832 general election Jephson stood again for Mallow as a Liberal but was beaten by a Repealer, much to the delight of O'Connell and the officer with whom his father had brawled in 1803, who wrote:

Your father, although a drunken and profligate dog, was a loyal and good subject, drunk or sober. You, who by a fortunate accident have got into possession of luxury and comfort that he never enjoyed, have thought fit to apply your influence, and whatever talent you may possess, in aid of the enemies of your country and your religion ... You have already, I am happy to see, begun to feel the effects of your treason; you have been beaten out of your own borough by some nameless demagogue.[26]

Jephson was seated on petition the following year, re-elected unopposed in 1835 and 1837, and after a series of successful contests, was eventually defeated by a Liberal Conservative in 1859. He repeatedly sought but never achieved office with the Liberals, it being observed 'that he might have been chief secretary for Ireland, had not a certain infirmity of temper and want of tact interfered with a prospect of success in official life'.[27] Shortly before his defeat in 1832, Henry Lambert* had noted

one or two points of your character which unfit you in a considerable degree for the acquirement of popularity. You have the reality of a high and honourable mind, with what I may call a nervous susceptibility of conscience. Now, to be a popular man, to excite an extensive and powerful infatuation, you should know how to lie, to swagger, to boast of what you never did, to flatter men's passions with a view exclusively to your own interest, regardless of the mischief you might occasion ... Though you are so bare and destitute of these essential qualities of greatness, I still hope that the electors of Mallow will be pleased to recollect that you were the friend of the people.[28]

Jephson, who in 1838 assumed his ancestral name of Norreys and, after some hesitation, accepted the baronetcy which he had been offered on the accession of Queen Victoria, died a widower at Queenstown in July 1888. His last surviving son having predeceased him in May, the baronetcy became extinct and the Mallow estates, by now heavily indebted, passed to his eldest daughter Catherine Louisa (1827-1911).[29]

[1] See M.D. Jephson, *Anglo-Irish Misc.* 179-254. [2] *PP* (1831-2), xliii. 105; *Hist. Irish Parl.* iv. 480-1; *HP Commons, 1790-1820,* iv. 305. [3] Jephson, 149-69. [4] *Dublin Evening Post,* 4, 21, 25, 30 Mar. 1826; *O'Connell Corresp.* ii. 823. [5] Jephson, 183. [6] Ibid. 184, 188; *O'Connell Corresp.* iii. 1276, 1285. [7] Jephson, 204. [8] *Roscommon and Leitrim Gazette,* 3 June; *Southern Reporter,* 13, 15, 17 June; *Dublin Evening Post,* 17, 20 June 1826. [9] *The Times,* 15 Feb. 1827. [10] Ibid. 24 Jan. 1829. [11] *O'Connell Corresp.* iv. 1538-9. [12] Jephson, 186. [13] Ibid. 199. [14] *O'Connell Corresp.* iv. 1645. [15] Ibid. iv. 1643. [16] Jephson, 214.

[17] *Cork Constitution,* 3, 5 Aug. 1830. [18] Ibid. 5 May 1831. [19] Jephson, 190. [20] Ibid. 214. [21] *Cork Constitution,* 3, 5 May 1831. [22] *The Times,* 20 July 1831. [23] Jephson, 94. [24] *The Times,* 2 Feb. 1832. [25] Jephson, 217. [26] *O'Connell Corresp.* iv. 1944; Jephson, 196. [27] H.F. Twiss, *Mallow and Some Mallow Men,* cited in Jephson, 253. [28] Jephson, 254. [29] Ibid. 252; *The Times,* 4 July 1838, 12 July 1888.

P.J.S.

JERMYN, Earl *see* **HERVEY, Frederick William**

JERNINGHAM *see* **STAFFORD JERNINGHAM**

JERVOISE *see* **PUREFOY JERVOISE**

JOCELYN, Hon. John (1769–1828), of Tairhill, co. Louth.

Co. LOUTH	1807–9 Sept. 1809
Co. LOUTH	10 Aug. 1820–1826

b. 1769, 4th s. of Robert Jocelyn, 1st earl of Roden [I] (*d.* 1797), and Lady Anne Hamilton, da. and h. of James Hamilton†, 1st earl of Clanbrassill [I]. *m.* 1795, Margaret, da. of Richard Fitzgerald, MP [I], of Mount Ophaly, Queen's Co., 1da. *d.* 21 Jan. 1828.
MP [I] 1797-1800.
Port surveyor and storekeeper, Belfast 1796-1803; commr. of customs [I] 1803-7, 1809-20.
Sheriff, co. Louth 1801-2.

Jocelyn had acted as a seatwarmer for the family interest in Louth, headed since 1797 by his brother Robert, 2nd earl of Roden, until his nephew Viscount Jocelyn* came of age in 1809. His customs position gave him £650 per annum. Following the death of his brother in 1820 he came forward again as his nephew's nominee, with the additional backing of the Foster interest. Attempts to get up an opposition came to nothing.[1] A lax attender, who is not known to have spoken in debate, he was described by a radical publication of 1823 as having 'voted with ministers', but his only known votes were against the bill to relieve Catholic peers of their disabilities, 30 Apr., in the minority of 24 for a 40s. fixed duty on corn, 8 May 1822, and against the Liverpool ministry for inquiry into the prosecution of the Dublin Orange rioters, 22 Apr. 1823.[2] Next year he proposed his nephew's nominee Sir Robert Inglis* for the family seat at Dundalk.[3] Failing health accounts for his absenteeism during the remainder of this period, when it was repeatedly rumoured that he would retire. He was induced to hold on until the next general election by Lord Oriel, who persuaded a rival 'not to solicit, advertise or canvass, till a dissolution be announced, except in the case of Jocelyn's death', 12 Feb. 1825.[4] At the 1826 dissolution he duly stood down, explaining that 'the state of my health prevents me from offering'.[5] He died in January 1828, leaving a daughter, Anne Charlotte.

[1] *Belfast News Letter*, 1 Aug. 1820. [2] *Black Bk.* (1823), 167; *Session of Parl. 1825*, p. 470. [3] *Drogheda Jnl.* 8 May 1824. [4] PRO NI, Chilham (Foster) mss T.2519/4/2044, Oriel to Ferrard; A. Malcomson, *John Foster*, 140. [5] *Drogheda Jnl.* 7 June 1826.

P.J.S.

JOCELYN, Robert, Visct. Jocelyn (1788–1870).

Co. LOUTH	1806–1807
Co. LOUTH	10 Feb. 1810–29 June 1820

b. 27 Oct. 1788, 1st s. of Robert, 2nd earl of Roden [I], and 1st w. Frances Theodosia, da. of Very Rev. Robert Bligh, dean of Elphin. *educ.* Harrow 1801-5. *m.* (1) 9 Jan. 1813, Maria Frances Catherine Stapleton (*d.* 25 Feb. 1861), da. of Thomas, 12th Bar. Le Despenser, 4s. (2 *d.v.p.*) 3da.; (2) 16 Aug. 1862, Clementina Janet, da. of Thomas Andrews of Greenknowes, Dumfries, wid. of Capt. Robert Lushington Neilly of Scarva, co. Down, *s.p. suc.* fa. as 3rd earl of Roden [I] 29 June 1820; *cr.* Bar. Clanbrassill [UK] 17 July 1821; KP 20 Aug. 1821. *d.* 20 Mar. 1870.

Jt. auditor-gen. of exch. [I] 1800-20, auditor-gen. 1820-2; PC [GB] 26 Mar. 1812; treas. of household May-July 1812, v.-chamberlain Aug. 1812-Feb. 1821; ld. of bedchamber 1827-31; PC [I] 26 July 1858.

Sheriff, co. Louth 1812-13, custos rot. 1820-49.

Capt. Dundalk inf. 1809; lt.-col. Louth militia 1826-47.

Jocelyn, a steady supporter of the Liverpool ministry and implacable opponent of Catholic relief, was again returned unopposed for county Louth on the family interest in 1820.[1] He insisted that all Irish Members should be entitled to sit on the proposed committee on the expenses of returning officers, 3 May, carried an amendment to that effect, and was named to the inquiry.[2] On 5 June he was granted three weeks' leave on account of the death of his sister Frances, Lady Powerscourt. His father's death later that month removed him from the Commons. He relinquished his household post early in 1821 and received a United Kingdom peerage later that year. In 1822 he was compensated for the abolition of his Irish sinecure with a pension of £2,700 a year for life.

One of his last acts as a Member was to apply successfully to government in February 1820 for his uncle Percy Jocelyn, bishop of Ferns since 1809, to be promoted to the vacant see of Clogher.[3] His solicitude

was poorly rewarded, for on 19 July 1822 the bishop was caught in an act of gross indecency with one John Moverley, a private soldier, in a Westminster public house. He was arrested and charged, but released on bail of £1,000 the next day. He fled to France to avoid trial and in his absence was deprived of his see, 21 Oct. 1822.[4] The affair created 'a great noise', particularly as in 1811 the bishop had successfully prosecuted for libel a Dublin domestic servant who had accused him of making an immoral proposition. The man had been flogged almost to death as part of his punishment.[5] In 1823 Percy Jocelyn, evidently unrepentant, defiantly returned to Ireland. Ministers implored Roden, who 'owes it to the government as well as to his own family to prevent the scandal of a public trial', to impress on his uncle the certain consequences of his remaining in the United Kingdom. Roden, who, though mortified by the scandal, had provided Jocelyn with an annuity, needed no second bidding and prevailed on him to return to the continent. He later lived *incognito* in Glasgow and Edinburgh where he died and was buried as Thomas Wilson, an 'unhappy but apparently repentant transgressor', in 1843.[6]

The scandal must have been the more galling to Roden as a devout and proselytizing Protestant, whose home at Tollymore Park, county Down, was pervaded by an 'atmosphere of stern and uncompromising piety'.[7] A leading figure in the Evangelical movement within the Irish Church, he actively promoted the formation of Brunswick Clubs in Ireland in 1828 and later became Grand Master of the Orange Society. In 1831 he controversially returned the Scottish Evangelical proselytizer James Edward Gordon, founder of the Protestant Reformation Society (of which Roden was vice-president), for his pocket borough of Dundalk. 'But that Lord Roden is known to be an inveterate antagonist of reform', remarked Richard Sheil*, 'one would be tempted almost to believe that he intended to expose the monstrosities of the Irish borough system by the nomination of a man ... so obnoxious to the Irish people'. He was elected president of the Irish Protestant Conservative Society later that year and was one of the diehard minority of 22 who voted against the third reading of the reform bill in the Lords, 4 June 1832. On Peel's accession as premier in 1834 he was offered, but declined, the lord stewardship of the household, using the occasion to 'extract the maximum possible political gain from the endorsement thus given to his earlier activities'.[8] Lord Teignmouth wrote of him:

As a politician Lord Roden was steadfastly Conservative. In the support and public advocacy of the Protestant cause, and of institutions formed for the promotion of religion and religious education, he took a prominent part, and his personal example no less than his public and private efforts contributed materially to the growth and improvement of religious feeling amongst both the Irish clergy and laity.[9]

He expounded his anti-Catholicism and missionary zeal in his publications *Observations on Lord Alvanley's Pamphlet* (1841) and *Progress of the Reformation in Ireland* (1851), which advocated scriptural knowledge of the Bible as 'the great remedy for the ills of Ireland'. In 1849 he was removed from the commission of the peace of county Louth for alleged partiality in dealing with an Orange procession involved in a fatal affray between Catholics and Protestants at Dolly's Brae. Thereafter he played little part in public life. Like his wretched uncle, he died in Edinburgh in March 1870. Greville had condemned him as 'bigoted and obstinate, and virtuous moreover', but an obituarist wrote:

As a most fearless advocate of a somewhat narrow and antiquated creed ... it is not to be expected that in his public character he had no enemies. On the contrary, he had many. But none ever threw a doubt on the sincerity of his motives, though they often thought them mistaken and absurd, and hence he really secured, together with a character for religious eccentricity, a large amount of personal respect.[10]

[1] *Dublin Evening Post*, 18 Mar. 1820. [2] *The Times*, 4 May 1820. [3] Add. 38283, ff. 85, 87. [4] *Ann. Reg.* (1822), Chron., pp. 126, 432; *Von Neumann Diary*, i. 98. [5] *Greville Mems.* i. 125-6; H.M. Hyde, *The Other Love*, 83-86. [6] Add. 40304, ff. 184, 206; 40329, ff. 237, 249-53, 257, 261; 40359, ff. 266-9; *Gent. Mag.* (1844), i. 314. [7] Lady Airlie, *Lady Palmerston*, ii. 48. [8] J. Wolffe, *Protestant Crusade*, 37, 84; *Sketches, Legal and Political* ed. M. Savage, ii. 352; *Oxford DNB*. [9] Teignmouth, *Reminiscences*, ii. 177. [10] *Greville Mems.* iii. 184; *The Times*, 22 Mar. 1870.

D.R.F./P.J.S.

JOHNSON, **William Augustus** (1777–1863), of Witham-on-the Hill, Lincs.

BOSTON   16 Feb. 1821–1826

OLDHAM   1837–1847

b. 15 Oct. 1777, 2nd but 1st surv. s. of Rev. Robert Augustus Johnson, rect. of Wistanstow, Salop and Hamstall Ridware, Staffs., and Anna Rebecca, da. of Rev. John Craven, vic. of Stanton Lacy and rect. of West Felton, Salop. *educ.* Rugby 1785. *m*. 17 Feb. 1835, Lucy, da. of Rev. Kingsman Foster, rect. of Dowsby, Lincs., 3s. (1 *d.v.p.*) 6da. *suc.* uncle George William Johnson to Witham 1814. *d*. 26 Oct. 1863.

Ensign Independent Ft. 1793; lt. 32 Ft. 1794, capt. 1794, maj. 1803; lt.-col. 3 Ceylon Regt. (half-pay) 1810; col. 1819; maj.-gen. 1830; lt.-gen. 1841.

Sheriff, Lincs. 1830-1.

Johnson, who came from an old Lincolnshire family, well established as a clerical dynasty by the mid-eighteenth century, was a descendant of Archdeacon Robert Johnson, the Puritan divine and founder of the grammar schools at Oakham and Uppingham. His grandfather held a number of livings, including the vicarage of Witham-on-the-Hill, where he built the manor house and enclosed the park in 1752. His uncle George William Johnson inherited Witham and was sheriff of Lincolnshire, 1784-5, and his father held livings in Staffordshire and Shropshire.[1] Johnson entered the army in 1793 as an ensign in one of the independent companies of foot. He joined the duke of Cornwall's regiment as a lieutenant in January 1794 and served with them as a major in the Peninsular campaign of 1808-9. He was present at the battles of Roliça, Vimeiro, and Corunna, for which he received the war medal with three clasps. Six months after returning from Spain he took part in the ill-fated expedition to Walcheren. He was much engaged at the advanced posts during the siege of Flushing, where he caught the malignant fever which put his regiment out of action for almost a year. He did not see action in the Peninsular campaign of 1811-14, but appears to have served with the second battalion in Ireland. He was gazetted as lieutenant-colonel in the 3rd Ceylon regiment in 1810, and remained on the English half-pay list until 1830. He succeeded to Witham on his uncle's death in 1814 and became hereditary trustee of Oakham and Uppingham schools. Chairman of the Bourne bench since 1818, he was instrumental in directing the rebuilding of the house of correction at Folkingham from 1824-6.[2]

At the 1820 general election Johnson accepted an invitation to stand for Boston on the Blue or anti-corporation interest, following the unexpected retirement of William Alexander Madocks*. According to *Drakard's Stamford News*, a more 'upright, zealous and really independent' man could not have been selected. He declared his 'rigid regard' for economy and the freemen's independence, but was defeated after a two-day poll. He appeared on the hustings at the county election in company with his friend Sir Robert Heron* and, according to a correspondent of the *Stamford News*, his future success at Boston was certain.[3] He petitioned against the return of the corporation's absentee candidate Henry Ellis, 5 May, on the ground of his ineligibility as an office-holder under the crown, but after a number of postponements the petition was lost by the prorogation.[4] He addressed a meeting to promote the independence of Lincolnshire in company with Heron, 13 Oct. 1820, when he called for the establishment of associations and asked the Boston freemen to set an example by returning him free of expense.[5] His petition was renewed, 31 Jan. 1821, though neither he nor Heron was confident of success at a by-election in the event of Ellis's return being declared void. Johnson, who could ill afford another contest and had no wish to pay bribes, informed Richard Spooner*, a Birmingham banker, of his intention not to stand, but the election committee unexpectedly unseated Ellis in his favour, 16 Feb. 1821. William Garfit, the Boston banker, welcomed the prospect of seeing both Members voting on the liberal side, and assured Gilbert John Heathcote, the sitting Member, that he would find Johnson a 'useful and agreeable' colleague.[6]

Johnson took his seat, 28 Feb. 1821, and, according to the *Stamford News*, gave his first vote in favour of Catholic relief that day, though he does not appear in the known division lists. He divided in the same sense, 1 Mar., 21 Apr. 1825. A frequent attender, he voted with the Whig opposition to the Liverpool ministry on most major issues, including economy, retrenchment and reduced taxation.[7] He divided to make Leeds a scot and lot borough if it got Grampound's seats, 2 Mar., to exclude civil officers of the ordnance from voting in parliamentary elections, 12 Apr., for parliamentary reform, 9, 10 May 1821, 25 Apr. 1822, 20 Feb. 1823, 27 Apr. 1826, and inquiry into the Scottish burghs, 20 Feb. 1822, and reform of Edinburgh's representation, 26 Feb. 1824. In his maiden speech, 11 Apr. 1821, he drew on his experience in the Peninsula and declaimed against the adjutant-general's grant, saying that he had witnessed the embarkations at Corunna, Lisbon, and Mondego Bay, and on none of these occasions had the troops been assisted by staff officers. He presented and endorsed a Boston reform petition, 17 Apr. He paid his respects to the freemen and kept open house at the *Green Dragon*, 27 Apr. On 8 May 1821 he joined Brooks's, sponsored by Heron and the 2nd Earl Fitzwilliam.[8] Addressing a Lincolnshire county meeting to petition for agricultural relief, 29 Mar., he declared that parliamentary reform was the only means of redress and gave notice of a forthcoming county reform meeting, 19 Apr. 1822. He was one of the principal speakers on that occasion, when he reiterated his belief that without a 'thorough reform' nothing could be done, as the present House was incapable of making either the necessary retrenchments or stand against corruption and two sessions had provided little more

relief than one shilling off the malt tax.[9] He addressed a preliminary county reform meeting, 2 Jan. 1823, when he was appointed to the committee under the chairmanship of Heron, and succeeded in persuading the veteran reformer Major John Cartwright to attend the full meeting, 26 Mar., when he broke with Heron and seconded Cartwright's amendment for a radical reform, but failed to carry it. When Anderson Pelham, the county Member, presented the resulting petition, 21 Apr., he declared himself a 'radical, however unpalatable' the term might be to the House, and asserted that the 'great majority' of the people were in favour of reform.[10] He was a guest at the Nottingham election dinner to commemorate the triumph in 1820 of Birch and Denman, 24 Sept. 1823, when he argued that nothing less than reform could resolve the nation's difficulties and called on the Whigs to embrace it. That month he emerged as the leading opponent of Sir William Amcotts Ingilby in the county by-election caused by Anderson Pelham's succession as 2nd Baron Yarborough. He denounced Sir William, a renegade Tory, as an adventurer and Yarborough placeman, endorsed the proposal of Samuel Wells, the radical Huntingdon attorney, to put up the reluctant Sir John Hayford Thorold and nominated him at the election. In his analysis of Amcotts Ingilby's victory he attributed 1,400 votes to the influence of Whig lords and gentry. He continued to be associated with the cause of independence and chaired the committee established at Sleaford in February 1824 to promote it.[11]

Johnson presented a private petition against Catholic claims, 19 Apr. 1825, when he said that were he a Catholic, he could not take the oath as enjoined by the proposed relief bill. He spoke and voted against the accompanying Irish franchise bill, which he condemned as a 'wanton destruction of popular rights', 26 Apr., was a minority teller against it, 9 May, and next day told the House that he was familiar with Irish elections and did not think emancipation 'worth the price of this bill'. He spoke and was a minority teller against the 'unexplained augmentation' of the army, 7 Mar. On 11 Mar. he objected to the 'inequality' of military punishments, noting that there were regiments in which 100 lashes were the equivalent to 300 inflicted in others. He presented two petitions from Lincolnshire against revision of the corn laws, 28 Apr. 1825, when his proposed adjournment of the debate was lost and the House divided on Whitmore's proposal for inquiry.[12] Amid rumours of a dissolution that September he accepted a requisition to stand for the county, but refused to incur the cost of treating. According to Heron, his candidature on a radical platform opposed to 'aristocratical combination' risked dividing the cause of independence for 'many years to come'. At a county meeting to petition for more agricultural protection, 23 Dec. 1825, he argued that the petition ought to encompass tax reductions since the corn laws did not influence prices as much as the quantity of 'circulating medium'. He explained that he had supported Whitmore's proposal for inquiry into the laws not because he felt pledged to revision, but because ministers had fudged the issue, and he proposed the formation of district committees to protect the agricultural interest.[13] He seconded the motion to bring up William Cobbett's[†] petition against the promissory notes bill and was in the minority against the measure, 20 Feb. 1826. He spoke and voted for Hume's amendments to it, 27 Feb., 7 Mar., and contributed to the debate on the prohibition of small notes in Scotland, 14 Mar. He endorsed a Rochdale petition for reform and reduced taxation and complained that the 'baneful effects' of the circulation of small notes were already evident in the conviction of six men for forgery at Lancaster, 21 Mar. He 'denied the utility' of the yeomanry cavalry, 3 Mar., conceded that troops were better housed in barracks but objected to them in the heart of Westminster, 6 Mar., and was a minority teller for military reductions next day. He voted against the 'detestable punishment' of flogging in the army, 10 Mar. He spoke against the Irish chartered schools grant, 20 Mar. On 5 May he argued that reduced taxation was the best means of providing relief.[14] He voted against revision of the corn laws, 11 May, and to modify the alehouse licensing bill, 12 May 1826. That month he declared his intention of not seeking re-election at Boston in view of the freemen's rapaciousness.

At the 1826 general election he duly retired from Boston and offered for the county. Without the support of Thorold and Heron, who had unsuccessfully tried to rescind the resolution by which he had been adopted, his chances were bleak and he soon desisted, citing the divisions among the independents. According to Heron, who still valued him as a friend, he had become particularly unpopular by following the opinions of Cobbett. Johnson accepted Chaplin, the senior county Member, as the 'legitimate' Tory, but again denounced Amcotts Ingilby as a Yarborough nominee. He renewed his attack on the hustings, after a long and detailed speech on the economy, and declared the ballot to be the only way to stop coercion. He boasted of his own attempt to uphold the county's independence in 1823 and stigmatized the Whigs as 'old hacks' for carrying Amcotts Ingilby's election.[15] As sheriff of Lincolnshire in 1830-1, Johnson made 'numerous retrenchments' which the *Stamford*

Mercury thought would prove advantageous to his successors. With Johnson out of the running at the 1830 general election, the Sleaford independents tried to promote the candidature of two other local reformers, but neither was willing to come forward. Johnson officiated as returning officer at the county election and took a firm line with hecklers. He was a guest of honour at the dinner of Leicestershire independents in November 1830, when, after explaining the tactics of the Lincolnshire freeholders in 1823, he exhorted Thomas Paget*, the unsuccessful challenger at the last election, to persevere in his opposition to the duke of Rutland's interest. He acceded to the request for a county meeting to petition for reduced taxation and sweeping reforms in December 1830, presided at it, 28 Jan. 1831, and endorsed its petition.[16]

Shortly after the completion of his shrievalty Johnson announced his candidature for the Southern division of Lincolnshire in a reformed Parliament. He favoured the correction of 'all abuses', but was reluctant to engage in a personal canvass. He sought the support of Heathcote, already encouraged by Heron to stand, but met with a polite rebuff. He withdrew his candidature, pending the division of the county, after Yarborough's son signified his intention of standing.[17] He maintained a low profile during the 1831 election, but attended the festivities at Stamford following Tennyson's defeat of the Exeter interest there. At a county meeting in the aftermath of the defeat of the reform bill, 18 Nov. 1831, he attacked the peers and bishops who had rejected it, declared himself a champion of 'mechanics and farmers' (or a 'Huntite' as Heron now described him), opposed the resolution of confidence in ministers, called for the dismissal of all anti-reformers and the expulsion of bishops from the Lords, and vilified the 'hereditary principle' of the peerage. He added that the reform bill was too 'aristocratic' and envisaged the formation of associations to withhold taxes if steps were not taken to create new peers. Amcotts Ingilby lacked the courage to support him, but he carried his resolutions, including his violent attack on bishops, in the face of opposition from Heron and Tennyson. He did not, however, oppose a subsequent amendment expressing confidence in ministers.[18] In July 1832 he published an address to the electors of South Lincolnshire, in which he urged the freeholders to exercise their votes responsibly and denounced the 'profligacy' of the church as a 'gross abuse of religion', but did not commit himself to becoming a candidate.[19]

At the 1832 general election he was brought forward for North Leicestershire by Paget, in an abortive bid to resist Rutland's influence. In defeat he denounced the coercion of the gentry and clergy and spoke of the 'crying necessity' for the ballot. At the nomination of his friend Captain Joseph Wood, the unsuccessful radical candidate for Huddersfield, he argued the case for cheap government and further reform.[20] He was himself beaten at Huddersfield in 1835 but in 1837 he successfully contested Oldham, where he was returned unopposed in 1841. He retired in 1847 but, according to the *Stamford Mercury*, never lost his interest in 'liberal politics'.[21] He set up an institution to relieve distress and soften the 'asperities of the new poor law' in 1837 and established a lending library at Witham in 1856.[22] He died following a fall in his study in October 1863 and was buried in the family vault at Witham. By his will, dated 23 Mar. 1860, he devised the residue of his estate to his eldest surviving son Augustus Charles Johnson (*b.* 1837). His 'much beloved' relative Sir Robert Harry Inglis* (*d.* 1855) had devised the Bedfordshire property of his mother Catherine, daughter and coheiress of Harry Johnson of Milton Bryant (a junior branch of the family), to his wife for life, with reversion to Johnson as his nearest male heir. Lady Inglis died in 1872 and under the terms of Johnson's will the Milton Bryant and Teddington estates passed to his second surviving son George Woolsey Johnson (*b.* 1845).[23]

[1] E. Green, *Johnson of Wytham-on-the-Hill*, 5-8; R.J. Olney, *Rural Society in 19th Cent. Lincs.* 108-9. [2] Marquess of Anglesey, *One-Leg*, 106; H. Ross-Lewin, *The Thirty-Second*, 129-30; *Gent. Mag.* (1863), ii. 807. [3] *Drakard's Stamford News*, 10, 24 Mar., 20 Oct. 1820, 16 Feb. 1821; *Boston Gazette*, 7, 14 Mar.; *Lincoln, Rutland and Stamford Mercury*, 17, 24 Mar. 1820. [4] *CJ*, lxxv. 155, 213, 238, 245, 389. [5] *Drakard's Stamford News*, 20 Oct. 1820. [6] *CJ*, lxxvi. 18, 75-77, 84; Heron, *Notes*, 132-3; T. Lawson-Tancred, *Recs. of a Yorks. Manor*, 347; Lincs. AO, Ancaster mss XIII/B/10b, c, d, e, ff, gg. [7] *Black Bk.* (1823), 167; *Session of Parl. 1825*, p. 470. [8] *Drakard's Stamford News*, 2 Mar.; *Boston Gazette*, 27 Mar., 1 May; *The Times*, 12, 18 Apr. 1821. [9] *Boston Gazette*, 23 Apr. 1822. [10] *Lincoln, Rutland and Stamford Mercury*, 10 Jan., 21, 28 Mar. 1823; F.D. Cartwright, *Cartwright Corresp.* ii. 234-7; Heron, 148, 150. [11] *Boston Gazette*, 30 Sept., 2, 9, 16 Dec.; *Lincoln, Rutland and Stamford Mercury*, 14, 21 Nov.; *Drakard's Stamford News*, 21 Nov. 1823; Olney, 148; *The Times*, 7 Feb. 1824. [12] *The Times*, 29 Apr. 1825. [13] *Boston Gazette*, 27 Dec.; *Lincoln, Rutland and Stamford Mercury*, 30 Dec. 1825; Heron, 155-6. [14] *The Times*, 6 May 1826. [15] *Drakard's Stamford News*, 26 May, 2 June; *Lincoln, Rutland and Stamford Mercury*, 9 June 1826; Heron, 158-9. [16] Olney, 11-12; *Leicester Chron.* 27 Nov.; *Lincoln, Rutland and Stamford Mercury*, 12 Mar., 6, 13 Aug. 1830, 7 Jan., 4 Feb. 1831. [17] *Lincoln, Rutland and Stamford Mercury*, 15, 29 Apr. 1831; Ancaster mss XIII/B/6/g. [18] *Lincoln, Rutland and Stamford Mercury*, 27 May, 25 Nov. 1831; Heron, 193. [19] *Lincoln, Rutland and Stamford Mercury*, 6 July 1832. [20] *Leicester Jnl.* 21, 28 Dec.; *Leicester Chron.* 17, 24 Nov., 29 Dec. 1832; Leics. RO DG24/1058/12; 1060/31. [21] *Lincoln, Rutland and Stamford Mercury*, 30 Oct. 1863. [22] W. White, *Lincs.* (1882), 818; N.R. Wright, *Lincs. Towns and Industry, 1700-1914*, p. 114; [23] *Lincoln, Rutland and Stamford Mercury*, 30 Oct., 6 Nov. 1863; *Gent. Mag.* (1863), ii. 807.

S.R.H./P.J.S.

JOHNSTON, **Andrew** (1798–1862), of Rennyhill, Fife.

| ANSTRUTHER EASTER BURGHS | 1831–1832 |
| ST. ANDREWS BURGHS | 1832–1837 |

b. 1798, 1st s. of Andrew Johnston of Rennyhill. *educ.* adv. 1821. *m.* (1) 17 Apr. 1826, Barbara (*d.* 20 Jan. 1830), da. of Davis Pearson of Edinburgh; (2) 1 Aug. 1834, Priscilla, da. of Thomas Fowell Buxton*, 2s. 1da. *suc.* fa. 1844. *d.* 24 Aug. 1862.

Johnston's grandfather, Andrew Johnston of Rennyhill, was described in 1788 as a collector of customs (and thereby ineligible to vote in Fifeshire), with 'a very small estate' and 'a large family'. He died in about 1808 and was succeeded in the property by his son and namesake, this Member's father, who lived until 1844.[1] Nothing is known of Johnston's early life, beyond the fact that he was admitted an advocate on 10 July 1821. At the general election of 1826 (he told the House, 6 Aug. 1831), as one 'nearly connected with the landed interest' in Anstruther Easter Burghs, he used his 'small' influence there to support James Balfour in his successful contest against the Liverpool ministry's lord advocate. At the general election of 1831 he responded to an invitation from some 'independent men' in the burghs to stand against the Tory candidate of the Anstruther family. One observer, who would have preferred a more illustrious candidate, commented that 'although a radical reformer he has neither talents nor fortune to make it rational in him to go into Parliament'; but he persevered, secured the decisive backing of the returning burgh (one of the five was disfranchised at this time) and came in unopposed.[2]

In the House, 30 June 1831, he denied a story that the burghs had returned him as a reformer 'because they were given to understand that they would be disfranchised if they did not do so'. (They were scheduled for disfranchisement by the terms of the Grey ministry's first Scottish reform bill.) He voted for the second reading of the reintroduced English bill, 6 July, and steadily for its details. On 6 Aug. he had more to say on the subject of his burghs, defending ministers against a charge that they had deliberately ignored the problem of the disfranchised burgh of Kilrenny, and retorting to the Tory William Douglas that he would 'not be dictated to' by him 'as to the course which I may hold in dealing with the case of my constituents', preferring to hold back petitions against their disfranchisement until the Scottish bill was before the House. Later that day he argued that Perth deserved a Member of its own. He divided for the third reading, 19 Sept.,

and passage, 21 Sept., of the English bill. He presented petitions from the convention of royal burghs
in support of the Scottish reform bill and against the
disfranchisement of his constituency, and ones in the
same sense from each of the councils, 23 Sept., when
he divided for the second reading of the Scottish
measure. Three days later ministers announced that
they had decided to reprieve the Anstruther Burghs
by combining them with St. Andrews and Cupar and
giving Perth a separate Member. Johnston was in the
ministerial majority for Lord Ebrington's confidence
motion, 10 Oct. He voted in O'Connell's minority
for swearing the Dublin election committee, 29 July,
and also cast wayward votes for disarming the Irish
yeomanry, 11 Aug., and inquiry into the effects of
renewal of the Sugar Refinery Act on the West India
interest, 12 Sept. He was in the minority for issuing a
new writ for Liverpool rather than proceeding with a
bribery bill, 5 Sept. He had Evangelical inclinations,
and on 26 Sept. 1831, 'as an elder of the Church of
Scotland', which he said had 'done more good for a
people ... than almost any other church in existence',
he ranted against the grant to the Catholic seminary at
Maynooth, insisting that it was immoral to tax Scots
for the support of an institution 'for instruction in the
tenets of the Romish faith, which my church holds
to be idolatrous'. He attributed the 'evils' afflicting
Ireland 'mainly to the influence of the papistical faith'
and declared that the avowed hostility to the Protestant
establishment expressed by some Irish Members in a
House where they only sat on sufferance made him
question the wisdom of his approval of emancipation
in 1829.

Johnston voted for the second reading of the revised
English reform bill, 17 Dec. 1831, divided reliably for
its details and was in the majority for its third reading,
22 Mar. 1832. He voted with ministers on relations
with Portugal, 9 Feb., and against the production of
information on military punishments, 16 Feb., but was
in the minority against the malt drawback bill, 2 Apr.
On 2 Mar. he presented and supported the prayer of
a petition from ministers, elders and inhabitants of
Aberdeen against the government's scheme of Irish
education, which he condemned as 'unchristian in
principle' in its exclusion of scriptural instruction. He
returned to this theme on 6 Mar., when he said that
he was 'compelled to hold my views as a reformer in
subjection to my principles as a Christian', addressing
the issue 'on high grounds, as a Scottish Presbyterian'.
He condemned the scheme's 'false principle of expediency' and argued that the Protestant Kildare Place
Society had been 'productive of the greatest benefit',
28 Mar.; said that the ministerial proposals were 'cal-

culated to injure the interests of Protestant children
in Ireland, 21 May, and presented hostile petitions
from the presbyteries of Edinburgh and Hamilton,
23 May, and Haddington, 30 May. Yet when the Irish
secretary Smith Stanley explained on 5 June that in
practice Protestant children would have use of the
Bible at regulated times, Johnston welcomed 'so great
a modification', and on the 8th he agreed to give the
system a fair trial. He confirmed on 5 July (from the
opposition benches) that his initial objections had
'very much given way'; but on 23 July he regretted that
the plan had been proposed at a time of such excitement. He voted for the address calling on the king to
appoint only ministers who would carry reform unimpaired, 10 May. He supported the Scottish reform bill,
21 May, but remarked that the Church Patronage Act
of 1712 had alienated the affections of many Scottish
Presbyterians; that too many Scottish Members and
representative peers had hitherto attended to 'their
own individual interests ... [by] swelling ministerial majorities ... [and being] parties to gross jobs';
that the electoral regime in Scotland would significantly favour the agricultural interest, and that the
Scottish clergy should be kept out of politics. To the
last effect he moved an amendment to ban them from
voting in parliamentary elections, which was defeated
by 72-7, 6 June. He divided with government against
Conservative amendments to increase the Scottish
county representation, 1 June, and stop the dismemberment of Perthshire for electoral purposes, 15 June,
when he defended the annexation of Nairnshire to
Elginshire, but clashed with the lord advocate Jeffrey,
who accused him of seeking a political advantage,
over the proposed boundary of Crail in the new St.
Andrews district. He welcomed the government's
decision to abandon the planned property qualification for Scottish burgh Members and to modify their
original proposal for county Members, 27 June. On 6
July he looked forward to reform of Scottish municipal government in the next Parliament. He voted for
the second reading of the Irish reform bill, 25 May. On
4 June he divided the House on his motion to postpone
the third reading of the Edinburgh police bill, which
he said had been 'carried on ... by private arrangement
between private parties', and was a teller for the majority of 21 (to 18). He divided with government on the
Russian-Dutch loan, 12, 16, 20 July. He presented
and endorsed a petition from Aberdeen ministers and
elders against the Maynooth grant and condemned
the 'errors' of Catholicism, 11 Apr., and saw nothing
offensive in the language of a hostile Glasgow petition, 10 July. On 27 July he denounced the grant, the
failed Irish policy of conciliation and concession and

the 'system of terrorism' promoted by O'Connell and Richard Sheil* in their encouragement of 'passive resistance' to tithes collection. He divided the House against the grant and was a teller for the minority of eight. Johnston had long admired Thomas Fowell Buxton, the leading campaigner for the abolition of slavery, and as he later wrote, 'I introduced myself to him as one who aimed at being enlisted under his anti-slavery banner, and before long ... was honoured with ... [his] friendship'. He became one of the small 'select band of Members' who met daily when the House was sitting for prayers and scripture readings under Buxton's aegis. He spoke and voted for Buxton's motion for the appointment of a select committee on abolition, 24 May, when the government carried a restrictive amendment, and was one of Buxton's nominees for the committee, 30 May 1832.[3] He acted as Buxton's private secretary, 1834-7, and on 1 Aug. 1834, the official date of slave emancipation, married his daughter Priscilla.[4]

At the general election of 1832 Johnston, a man 'of a somewhat slender make', who spoke 'tolerably well' in a carefully prepared fashion, was returned for the St. Andrews district after a contest with a fellow Liberal. He came in unopposed in 1835. He made his parliamentary hobby horse repeal of the 1712 Patronage Act, but without success. His relations with his constituents broke down over his failure to fulfil a pledge to vote for the appropriation of surplus church revenues.[5] He sold the Fifeshire estate in 1853 and acquired one at Halesworth, Suffolk, where he lived at Holton Hall.[6] He died in August 1862 and was succeeded by his elder son Andrew Johnston, Liberal Member for Essex South, 1868-74, and a partner in the East London firm of Morewood and Company, iron manufacturers.[7]

[1] Pol. State of Scotland 1788, p. 130; (1790), 89; (1811), 60; Services of Heirs in Scotland. [2] Caledonian Mercury, 28 Apr., 5 May 1831; NAS GD46/132/23. [3] Buxton Mems. 384-6; Bodl. (Rhodes House), Buxton mss Brit. emp. S. 444, Hannah Buxton to the Cunninghams [25 May 1832]. [4] Ibid. 352-3, 383. [5] [J. Grant], Random Recollections of Commons (1837), 356-8; CJ, xc. 297. [6] J. Foster, MPs for Scotland, 196. [7] Dod's Parl. Companion (1869), 239-40.

D.R.F.

JOHNSTON, James (1801–1841), of Straiton, Edinburgh and Champfleurie, Linlithgow.

STIRLING BURGHS   1830–1832

bap. 15 Aug. 1801, o.s. of James Johnston of Straiton and Mary, da. of William Baillie of Linlithgow.[1] *educ.* Christ Church, Oxf. 1820. *unm. suc.* fa. 1814. *d.* 4 Sept. 1841.

Johnston's grandfather Alexander Johnston was served heir to his father, also Alexander, in the Straiton estate, just south of Edinburgh, on 27 Aug. 1766. He also had 'a very good estate' at Champfleurie, near Linlithgow.[2] Alexander Johnston was succeeded on 22 Jan. 1796 by his brother James, the father of this Member, who was served heir to him and his grandfather on 14 Nov. 1814, at the age of 13. He attended Oxford University. At the general election of 1826 he was chosen as delegate for Linlithgow in the interest of the Edinburgh banker Adam Hay, the successful candidate for Linlithgow Burghs.[3] In 1830 he stood for the venal district of Stirling Burghs against a supporter of the Wellington ministry and secured the votes of three of the five burghs. After his return, which was particularly popular with the operatives and weavers of Dunfermline, he declared that he would enter Parliament as 'a free and independent man, who would in all cases vote according to his conscience': he was 'under no pledge to government' and 'ministers had nothing to expect from him'. He observed that recent events in France had 'taught us the value of the constitution under which we live'.[4]

Ministerial head-counters evidently knew little of him, and they listed him among the 'good doubtfuls'; but he voted in Daniel O'Connell's minority of 34 for repeal of the Irish Subletting Act, 11 Nov., and the opposition majority on the civil list, 15 Nov. 1830, when the government fell. He did not hide his light under a bushel, and on 19 Nov. he delivered what John James Hope Vere* described as a 'curious' speech, 'more like a soliloquy than anything else', in support of Lord Nugent's bill to promote the employment of the labouring poor, citing evidence from letters to a friend to support his argument that Sussex, where labourers were combining to extort higher wages, was in 'a most alarming state'.[5] Later that day he gave notice of a motion proposing the appointment of a select committee of Members 'of long standing' to draw up instructions for the guidance of new Members balloted to serve on election committees, but he withdrew it, 22 Nov. He presented petitions for the abolition of slavery from United Associate Congregations in Dunfermline and Linlithgow, 23, 25 Nov., 2 Dec. He presented one from Edinburgh hammermen for reform of the municipal government of the royal burghs, 7 Dec., and next day brought up a like one from the incorporated trades of Stirling, but was ruled out of order by the Speaker when he referred to a comment by another Member on a previous day. On 9 Dec. he urged the Grey ministry, who had 'hitherto acted discreetly', to include wholesale reform of the 'corrupt' Scottish burghs in their impending scheme.

Observing that he had been returned by 70 men for a constituency which should have at least 3,000 electors, he claimed to 'have more constituents than any [other] Member ... for I consider myself the representative of the people of Scotland'. He presented several petitions for Scottish parliamentary and municipal reform, 11, 15, 18, 23 Dec. 1830, when he expressed his 'high opinion of ministers, and ... cordial approval' of their early measures. However, he disapproved of their proposed tax on steamboat passengers, 28 Feb. 1831. It was almost certainly he rather than the anti-reformer Sir James Carnegie, Member for Aberdeen Burghs (as attributed by the *Mirror of Parliament*), who, presenting reform petitions from two of his constituent burghs, 16 Feb., urged 'the necessity of reform in [Scottish] administration', and went on:

> I make no imputation against the present ministry ... The country is very much obliged to them for what they have done ... I hail ... the repeal of the duty on coals ... but ... a great deal more remains to be done ... The distress of the poor must be relieved; it is not known ... by the aristocratic portion of the community, who are wallowing in wealth. Look into the dwellings of the poor, not only in the country, but ... in London, and you will see the most abject state of poverty ... The state of the country is awful ... Look at the failings and backslidings of men ... We are doing evil; we forget our duty ... I would entreat government to remember the recent events which have taken place in France ... Scotland has hitherto been contented ... but it is impossible to say how long she will continue so ... If something be not immediately done to relieve the country from its present dreadful condition, the kingdom will be in a state of anarchy and confusion ... The people will not always ... implore the House to relieve them. An hour of retribution will arrive, when the voice of the people must be heard and attended to. The higher orders ... must make some sacrifice to relieve the distress of the poor.

On 9 Mar. he declared himself 'friendly' to the English and Scottish reform bills, though he admitted to reservations about the £10 householder franchise, and said that 'the people generally seem to be overjoyed at the prospect of reform'. He presented numerous petitions in favour of the scheme, 11, 14, 17, 18, 22, 25 Mar. He voted for the second reading of the English reform bill, 22 Mar., and against Gascoyne's wrecking amendment, 19 Apr. 1831. At the ensuing general election he was returned unopposed for the burghs.[6]

He voted for the second reading of the reintroduced English reform bill, 6 July, and at least twice against the adjournment, 12 July 1831. The following evening he deplored the opposition's behaviour and, taking up one Tory's reference to Cromwell, observed that 'we have now many Cromwells, who oppress us much

more than one could with his Round Parliament'. He was reminded by the chairman to speak to the question before the House, but he went on to remark that the Wellington ministry had 'acted very much like Catiline'. The chairman terminated these ramblings. He divided steadily for the details of the reform bill until early August; he paired for the proposal to unite Rochester with Chatham and Strood, 9 Aug., and for clause 15, 17 Aug. On 4 Aug. he endorsed the prayer of a petition from Linlithgow council urging ministers to expedite the progress of the measure, complaining that 'delays have been interposed ... which ought not to have been permitted, and with which the people ... have great reason to be dissatisfied'. He voted for the passage of the bill, 21 Sept., and the second reading of the Scottish measure, 23 Sept. He had on 8 July given notice that he would propose that burgh councillors elected for life before the bill was introduced should retain their parliamentary votes; nothing came of this. He said on 25 July that the country's present high taxation had its origins in 'the ruinous wars in which we so long engaged' and argued that repeal of the corn laws without compensatory relief of the agricultural interest from its peculiar burdens would condemn it to 'certain ruin'. He presented petitions against the use of molasses in brewing and distilling, 27 July, 5 Aug. He was in the ministerial majority for Lord Ebrington's confidence motion, 10 Oct. 1831, and on the 19th replied to Sir Richard Vyvyan's denunciation of political unions as 'lodges of carbonari' with the claim that in Birmingham and Manchester their effect had been 'to tranquillize the minds of the people' rather than to incite violence. Urging ministers to bring in the reform bills again as soon as possible, he argued that as a result of 'the spread of intelligence' during the last 100 years, the people had 'a moral strength which entitles them to the share of influence in the constitution which they ask for'.

Johnston voted for the second reading of the revised English reform bill, 17 Dec. 1831. He again divided for its details, and voted for its third reading, 22 Mar. 1832. He sided with government on the Russian-Dutch loan, 26 Jan., 12, 16, 20 July, relations with Portugal, 9 Feb., the malt drawback bill (unlike a number of Scottish reform Members), 2 Apr., and the navy civil departments bill, 6 Apr.; but he was in Hunt's minority of 31 for inquiry into Peterloo, 15 Mar., and the minority on the salary of the Irish registrar of deeds, 9 Apr. Protesting against the 'compulsory assessment' provisions of the Scottish cholera prevention bill, 15 Feb., he said that having been 'a great deal on the continent' he had witnessed 'many of the local and infectious diseases' there, but that he 'never saw, in any continental city, so much poverty and distress as in St. Giles's and Whitechapel'. He wanted it to be 'generally made known that cleanliness and sobriety are the best preventatives' against cholera and urged ministers to repeal the duty on soap. On 15 Mar. he moved for the appointment of a select committee to investigate cholera, with a view to its addressing the king for the repeal of all quarantine regulations, which 'cramp the trading and manufacturing interests', had created much distress and had made Britain 'a bugbear to the whole world'. He failed to find a seconder. He voted for the address calling on the king to appoint only ministers who would carry undiluted reform, 10 May. His comment on the assault on the duke of Wellington, 23 May, that while Scots respected his military achievements, they might not be sorry to see him dead in order to terminate 'his political course, which in Scotland is deemed to be mischievous', caused a minor stir. He divided for the second reading of the Irish reform bill, 25 May. On 1 June he reluctantly acquiesced in the proposal to throw the burghs of Peebles and Selkirk into their counties and voted against a Conservative attempt to increase the Scottish county representation. He divided against another opposition amendment to the Scottish reform bill, 15 June, but was in the minority for a tax on Irish absentee landlords to provide permanent relief for the poor, 19 June 1832. In August, 'as having been a supporter of the present government since they entered office', he successfully applied to the colonial secretary Lord Goderich for a place at Sierra Leone for a friend.[7]

Johnston, who never joined Brooks's Club, declared his candidature for Stirling Burghs for the 1832 general election, but he wrecked his chances of success by speaking at the Edinburgh public meeting, got up by the Conservatives, which carried resolutions condemning the government's bellicose attitude to Holland over the independence of Belgium, 22 Nov. Claiming that he would not have attended had he considered it a party meeting and that he had been worried by the government's stance and its likely effect on commerce for some time, he said that he still supported ministers on other issues but deemed them to have broken their pledge of non-interference in the affairs of foreign powers. He was savagely denounced by the Liberal press as 'a renegade and an apostate'. He retorted in a public letter and a statement to his constituents that 'it is *measures* and not *men* which I look to support', denied that he had ever been 'a radical of the most levelling order', as alleged, insisted that as he was also 'not a Whig' he could not fairly be accused of apostasy and argued that it was ministers who had 'become Ultra Tories' in their Belgian policy.[8]

At the general election in December 1832 he was opposed in the burghs by the 4th earl of Rosebery's son and heir Lord Dalmeny, a mainstream Liberal. On the hustings, Johnston stated that he was 'not a thick and thin supporter of the present ministry, and would never lend them his countenance in pursuing bad measures'. He was well supported by the newly enfranchised Dunfermline electors, but Dalmeny beat him by 127 votes in a poll of 863.[9] Johnston contested Linlithgowshire as a Liberal (or 'the mere cat's paw of the treasury', as *The* Times saw it) at a by-election in June 1838, but lost to a Conservative by 120 votes in a poll of 540.[10] He died, unmarried and intestate, at his London house in Bury Street, St. James's, in September 1841. Administration of his personal effects, which were sworn under £6,000 within the province of Canterbury, was granted the following month to Stair Hathorn Stewart of Physgill, Wigtownshire, the husband of his sister Margaret and father of Robert Hathorn Stewart (1824-99), who succeeded to the entailed Scottish estates and took the additional name of Stewart.[11]

[1] The *b.* date of 15 Sept. 1802 given in J. Foster, *MPs for Scotland*, 197, is that of James Johnston (*d.* 1886) of Kincardine, Perthshire, who was admitted an advocate, 14 Dec. 1824. [2] *Pol. State of Scotland 1788*, p. 229. [3] *Caledonian Mercury*, 8 July 1826. [4] *Edinburgh Evening Courant*, 31 July, 7, 26 Aug.; *Glasgow Herald*, 27 Aug. 1830. [5] Hopetoun mss 167, f. 191. [6] *Caledonian Mercury*, 23, 28, 30 Apr., 26 May 1831. [7] Add. 40879, ff. 174, 177. [8] *Caledonian Mercury*, 22, 26, 29 Nov., 1 Dec. 1832. [9] Ibid. 26, 29 Nov., 17, 22 Dec. 1832. [10] *The Times*, 9, 15 June 1838. [11] *Gent. Mag.* (1841), ii. 442; PROB 6/217/373.

D.R.F.

JOHNSTONE *see* **VANDEN BEMPDE JOHNSTONE**

JOHNSTONE HOPE, Sir William (1766-1831).

DUMFRIES BURGHS	22 May 1800-1802
DUMFRIESSHIRE	8 Nov. 1804-1830

b. 16 Aug. 1766, 3rd s. of John Hope† (*d.* 1785) of Cragiehall, Linlithgow and Mary, da. of Eliab Breton of Forty Hill, Enfield, Mdx.; bro. of Charles Hope†. *educ.* Edinburgh h.s. 1774-6. *m.* (1) 8 July 1792, Lady Anne Hope Johnstone (*d.* 28 Aug. 1818), da. of James, 3rd earl of Hopetoun [S], 4s. 2da.; (2) 30 Oct. 1821, Maria, da. of Sir John Eden†, 4th bt., of West Auckland, co. Dur., wid. of Frederik Willem, 6th earl of Athlone [I], *s.p.* Took name of Johnstone before Hope after 1st *m.* KCB 2 Jan. 1815; GCB 4 Oct. 1825. *d.* 2 May 1831.

Entered RN 1777, lt. 1782, cdr. 1790, acting capt. 1790, capt. 1794; col. marines 1811-12; r.-adm. 1812; c.-in-c. Leith 1813, 1816-18; v.-adm. 1819.

Ld. of admiralty Apr. 1807-Mar. 1809, Mar. 1820-May 1827; member of ld. high admiral's council May 1827-Mar. 1828; treas. Greenwich Hosp. 1828, commr. 1829-30; PC 24 Nov. 1830.

In March 1820 Johnstone Hope, a war hero and veteran Melvillite Scottish Member, was appointed to a place at the admiralty board, at £1,000 a year, in Lord Liverpool's ministry, under the 2nd Viscount Melville. At the general election he was returned unopposed for Dumfriesshire, where he had sat for 15 years on his own and the Buccleuch interest; he came in for the seventh time in 1826.[1] He could of course be relied on to vote with his colleagues when present, but he was evidently not an assiduous attender: for example, he paired against the opposition censure motion on the Queen Caroline affair, 6 Feb. 1821, and his only known vote in the 1824 session was a paired one in defence of the prosecution of the Methodist missionary John Smith in Demerara, 11 June 1824. He was absent from the division of 28 Feb. 1821 on Catholic relief, but paired against it, 30 Apr. 1822, 1 Mar., 10 May 1825, 6 Mar. 1827. On 8 May 1821 he denied that the Dumfriesshire petition against the Scottish juries bill had been factiously got up; and he presented the county's petition against interference with the Scottish banking system, 8 Mar. 1826.[2]

When the duke of Clarence was made lord high admiral after Melville's resignation with the Tory ministers who would not serve in Canning's ministry in April 1827, he asked Johnstone Hope to remain as one of his council, despite their 'violent quarrel' in the service in 1787, which had 'not [been] made up for ten years'.[3] He did so, but Canning subsequently vetoed as 'quite impossible' his 'pretension to be made a privy councillor', not least because he had recently 'waived his seniority ... by leaving the chief management in the hands' of Sir George Cockburn*.[4] He divided against repeal of the Test Acts, 26 Feb. 1828. A week later, on the recommendation of Clarence, which was endorsed by the new premier, the duke of Wellington, he was made treasurer of Greenwich Hospital at £800 a year.[5] Quietly re-elected for Dumfriesshire, he divided against Catholic relief, 12 May, and with government on the ordnance estimates, 4 July 1828. Wellington had by then turned down Clarence's request for Johnstone Hope to be made a privy councillor.[6] He voted against the concession of Catholic emancipation, 6, 18, and (as a pair) 30 Mar., and presented hostile petitions, 12 Mar. 1829. Two months later his office was abolished by statute and he was named as the first of the new commissioners responsible for managing the hospital's affairs and property, at a salary of £800 a year

and with the promise of a new house near Greenwich Park.[7] He presented petitions for the imposition of a duty on West Indian rum equivalent to that levied on Scottish spirits, 14 May 1830. On 12 July 1830 he told his eldest son John James Hope Johnstone, owner of the extensive Annandale estates in Dumfriesshire, that he intended to retire from Parliament at the impending dissolution and that Clarence (now William IV) was keen for him to come in in his room.[8] This duly occurred.

Johnstone Hope, who had married the widowed countess of Athlone in 1821, was removed from his commissionership by the incoming Grey ministry in November 1830, but was made a privy councillor in compensation. He died at Bath, where he had gone 'for the benefit of his health', in May 1831. He was remembered for his 'unvarying urbanity of manner and benevolence of heart'.[9] By his will, dated 26 May 1830 and sworn under £14,000 in the province of Canterbury and under £1,500 in that of Chester, he left his wife, his sole executrix, £6,000 of the £10,000 secured for her by their marriage settlement, and distributed the remaining £4,000 among his five younger children.[10]

[1] Annandale mss (NRA [S] 217) 452, Johnstone Hope to J. Hope, 7 Mar. 1820. [2] The Times, 9 May 1821, 9 Mar. 1826. [3] Colchester Diary, iii. 495. [4] Canning's Ministry, 264. [5] Wellington mss WP1/925/6; 1028/1. [6] Ibid. WP1/937/20; 939/19. [7] Ibid. WP1/1028/1; Annandale mss 687, Johnstone Hope to J. J. Hope Johnstone, 18 May 1829. [8] Annandale mss 669. [9] Glasgow Herald, 13 May 1831. [10] PROB 11/1786/335; IR26/1260/296.

D.R.F.

JOLLIFFE, Gilbert East (1802–1833), of Tilgate, nr. Crawley, Suss.

b. 13 Jan. 1802, 2nd s. of Rev. William John Jolliffe (d. 1835) of Merstham, rect. of Chelsworth, Suff., and Julia, da. and coh. of Sir Abraham Pytches of Streatham, Surr.; bro. of Sir William George Hylton Jolliffe, 1st bt.*. educ. privately by Mr. Knipe at Aldermaston, Berks. 1812-17.[1] m. 28 Aug. 1823, Margaret Ellen, da. of Sir Edward Banks of Mile Town, Sheerness, Kent, s.p. d.v.p. 18 Dec. 1833.
   Cornet 19 Drag. 1817, lt. 1820, half-pay 1821; lt. 15 Drag. 1822, half-pay 1823.

Jolliffe was named after Gilbert East (1764-1828) of Hall Place, Berkshire, the childless heir to a baronetcy and a fortune, who had married his paternal aunt Eleanor. When his grandfather William Jolliffe died in 1802 after 34 years as Member for Petersfield, he left

Jolliffe the modest sum of £200 'in the expectation that Mr. East, his uncle in law, or his aunt will provide for him', and the latter subsequently held out this incentive as a reward for good behaviour.[2] According to his mother's journal, from 1816-17 he toured France with his tutor and elder brother William, whom he followed into the army on his return. His brief military career was undistinguished. In February 1818 he was presented to the regent at a levée by his uncle Hylton Jolliffe*, whose enthusiasm for field sports he evidently shared.[3] Despite the misgivings of his father and aunt, in 1823 he married the daughter of Edward Banks, his father's partner in the firm of public works contractors, Jolliffe and Banks.[4] The couple returned from a sojourn abroad in November 1824 and settled at Hooley, Surrey, in a house belonging to Hylton Jolliffe. They travelled to Russia in 1827 and the following year moved to Tilgate, a gift from Banks.[5] Jolliffe was among the chief mourners at the funeral of his uncle Sir Gilbert East in December 1828, but was only left £500 out of his fortune of £300,000, which in the event he did not live to receive.[6]

At the 1830 general election Jolliffe came forward for Petersfield as the nominee of Hylton Jolliffe, though on the hustings he ritually declared himself to be 'perfectly unfettered'. His assertion that he had lived all his life in the borough, which was patently untrue, was greeted with derisive laughter, and he was goaded into a show of pique by a heckler. He and his brother William were returned after a two-day poll which was unsuccessfully challenged on petition.[7] Jolliffe, who is not known to have spoken in debate, was listed by the Wellington ministry as one of their 'friends', but he was absent from the crucial division on the civil list, 15 Nov. 1830. He voted against the second reading of the Grey ministry's reform bill, 22 Mar., and for Gascoyne's wrecking amendment, 19 Apr. 1831. At the ensuing dissolution his seat was reclaimed by his uncle, whose bid to transfer to Surrey in 1830 had proved unsuccessful. Jolliffe's father expressed himself

> sorry you are no longer in Parliament ... but the uneasiness it caused to your wife, which I hope will now cease, I trust will compensate ... enabling you both more agreeably to enjoy your tranquil home ... I wish the Penryn people would bring you in, in spite of all. You will say that is a mischievous wish, or at least Margaret will.[8]

Nothing came of this and Jolliffe made no bid to reenter Parliament. He died *v.p.* and *s.p.* in December 1833 'after a few days' illness'. By his will, executed four days before his death, he left a life interest in the Tilgate property and ample provision from funded investments of £20,000 to his wife, who survived him by less than three years, dying on 12 Oct. 1836. His real and personal estate, valued at £30,000, was left in trust to his brother's second son Hedworth Hylton Jolliffe (1829-99), later 2nd Baron Hylton.[9] A memorial plaque from his friends deplored his 'untimely loss', and according to the family historian his demise hastened that of his father, who died 31 Jan. 1835.[10]

[1] H.G.H. Jolliffe, *Jolliffes of Staffs.* 133-4. [2] Ibid. 159-60; PROB 11/1376/465. [3] Jolliffe, 152, 155, 157-9; *Sporting Mag.* (ser. 2), i. 418. [4] Jolliffe, 180, 183-4; *Oxford DNB sub* Banks. [5] Jolliffe, 188, 199, 203; C. and J. Greenwood, *Surr. Described*, 141. [6] *Gent. Mag.* (1829), i. 173-4; PROB 11/1751/76; IR26/1192/33. [7] Som. RO, Hylton mss DD/HY, box 17, Procs. at Petersfield Election (1830). [8] Jolliffe, 218-9. [9] PROB 11/1826/31; IR26/1355/28. [10] M.I. in Merstham church; Jolliffe, 224.

H.J.S./P.J.S.

JOLLIFFE, Hylton (1773–1843), of Merstham, Surr.

PETERSFIELD	1796–29 Dec. 1796
PETERSFIELD	29 Mar. 1802–1830
PETERSFIELD	1831–1832
PETERSFIELD	5 Mar. 1833–1834

b. 28 Feb. 1773, 1st. s. of William Jolliffe[†] of Merstham and Eleanor, da. and h. of Sir Richard Hylton, 5th bt., of Hayton Castle, Cumb. *educ.* Westminster 1783; L. Inn 1787. *m.* 6 Sept. 1804, Elizabeth Rose, illegit. da. of Robert Shirley, 7th Earl Ferrars, *s.p.*; 2s. illegit. *suc.* fa. 1802. *d.* 13 Jan. 1843.
Ensign 2 Ft. Gds. 1790, lt. and capt. 1793, capt. and lt.-col. 1799, ret. 1804.

'Hat Jolliffe' was renowned for his enthusiasm for field sports and outsize headgear, which proved a gift to cartoonists, but he achieved little in politics.[1] When the Merstham pack was disbanded in 1830, the *Sporting Magazine* paid tribute to the anachronistic figure that its master cut in town:

> The Colonel is one of the old school, and a very fine sample of it. Who has not seen him walk up St. James's Street with his venerable white head covered with a huge punt hat, a white neckcloth, neat blue coat with metal buttons, light vest and clean yellow leather shorts with long gaiters? He looks like what he is, a country gentleman and a fox-hunter ... When a younger man he must have been what we would call a 'devilish good-looking fellow', and though now rather corpulent, weighing above sixteen stone, he still retains most of his former good looks.[2]

A veteran of the campaigns in the Netherlands, Spain and Egypt, Jolliffe offered Lord Liverpool his services as a military commander in October 1819, but although he was aware of disaffection among the urban tradespeople of his Surrey neighbourhood, he was not an alarmist and had 'sanguine hopes from the rapid increase of the savings banks in this hundred that many of them will find it in their interest to change their sentiments'.[3]

At the 1820 general election he faced a challenge at Petersfield, where he had returned himself and paying guests since succeeding as its patron in 1802. On the hustings he criticized the recent modification of the corn laws, observing that of course 'no person will take me to be a radical', and strenuously denied allegations of financial impropriety in the management of Churcher's College, a local school of which he was the principal trustee. (He was exonerated by a chancery decree in February 1825.) He and his nominee were returned after a one-day poll and confirmed in their seats following a petition, 16 June 1820.[4] A lax and mostly silent attender, when present he continued to give general support to the Liverpool ministry, among whom he claimed his erstwhile political leader Canning as a 'very intimate friend'.[5] He presented a constituency petition calling for measures to alleviate agricultural distress, 25 May. On 21 June 1820 a motion for him to be given ten days' leave on urgent private business was negatived, after several Members had objected, causing general amusement.[6] He voted against censure of ministers' conduct towards Queen Caroline, 6 Feb. 1821. He divided for Catholic claims, 28 Feb. 1821, 10 May 1825. On 19 July 1821 he attended the coronation, telling his brother William Jolliffe that 'nothing could exceed the beauty of the scene and the enthusiasm of all present', and that as a result of the queen's attempt to disrupt proceedings, 'she has sunk as low as possible in the estimation of all, while the king has rose to the highest pinnacle'.[7] His nephew William George Hylton Jolliffe was created a baronet in the coronation honours, an honour apparently refused three years earlier by Jolliffe, for whom nothing less would suffice than the revival of the Hylton barony, which he claimed through the maternal line.[8] In 1824 he sought legal advice concerning his title to it and his elevation to the peerage was the subject of idle rumour in 1826.[9] In 1821 he moved into Merstham Hall, which had been let since 1813, and resided there 'a good deal', but the estate's extensive limeworks continued to be managed by his brother.[10] He voted against more extensive tax reductions, 11 Feb., and abolition of one of the joint-postmasterships, 13 Mar. 1822. He divided against inquiry into the parliamentary franchise, 20 Feb., repeal of the Foreign Enlistment Act, 16 Apr., reform of the

Scottish representative system, 2 June, and inquiries into chancery delays, 5 June 1823. No trace of activity has been found for 1824. He voted for the duke of Cumberland's annuity bill, 6 June, and the spring guns bill, 21 June 1825.

At the 1826 general election Jolliffe was returned unopposed for Petersfield.[11] He voted for Catholic relief, 6 Mar. 1827, 12 May 1828. He presented a constituency petition for repeal of the Test Acts, 21 Feb., and divided accordingly, 26 Feb. 1828. That June he was listed by Lord Colchester among 'the Huskisson party, or rather the rump of the Canning party'.[12] (He had not featured in other Canningite lists.) He was, of course, expected by Planta, the Wellington ministry's patronage secretary, to vote 'with government' for the concession of Catholic emancipation, and he divided accordingly, 6, 30 Mar. 1829. That July either Jolliffe, who was a director of a steamboat company, or his brother William vainly pestered Lord Ellenborough, the president of the board of control, for government backing for a scheme of steam navigation to India via the Red Sea.[13] No trace of activity has been found for 1830, although in support of his subsequent claims to be considered a free trader, Jolliffe cited his vote for the beer bill.[14]

At the 1830 general election Jolliffe came forward for Surrey, where he was so confident of success that he returned both his nephews for Petersfield. Sir William Jolliffe was informed of the arrangements by his aunt, Lady Eleanor East, who explained that it was 'understood that Hylton should vacate the county for you at the next election'.[15] Their plans were upset by the late appearance of a reform candidate. Pressed on the hustings, Jolliffe denied that he had ever sought or obtained ministerial favour, made a cautious promise to support 'step-by-step' retrenchment, but declined to say anything about parliamentary reform beyond an expression of opposition to the secret ballot. After admitting his discomfiture with public speaking he provoked 'hisses and laughter' by describing the French war as 'a war for our liberties (cries of "No, No!"). Well then, it was a war into which we had got, out of which we had got, and which must be paid for'. Opponents drew attention to his long silence in Parliament and proprietorship of a close borough, and he was catcalled with a play on his name, 'No jollop, no physic'.[16] His withdrawal from the contest after four days was seen as a blow to the Wellington ministry but did not surprise Lord Lowther*, who considered him to have been 'the most unpopular man who could be selected'.[17] His petition against the return, 12 Nov. 1830, was not pursued.[18] Through his nephews,

Jolliffe opposed the Grey ministry's reform bill and at the 1831 dissolution offered again for Petersfield as an opponent of that measure, which he predicted would be diluted on its reintroduction. On the hustings he expressed a willingness to support the enfranchisement of populous places and an enlargement of the electorate, but was hostile to any reduction in the number of English Members. He and his nominee were returned after a three-day contest.[19]

Jolliffe voted against the second reading of the reintroduced reform bill, 6 July, at least twice against its adjournment, 12 July, and for use of the 1831 census to determine the disfranchisement schedules, 19 July 1831. On the 22 July he broke nearly 30 years of silence to contend that Petersfield's parish population entitled it to return one Member and to assure the House that an enlargement of the borough along such lines would entirely deprive 'the present patron' of his influence. He divided against the bill's passage, 21 Sept., and despite reports of failing health, was present to vote against the second reading of the revised bill, by which Petersfield retained one Member, 17 Dec. 1831. A report in the local press claimed that he had promised to support the bill if this condition was met, an assertion swiftly denied by his agent, but he was in the ministerial majorities against an amendment to restrict polling to one day in smaller boroughs, 15 Feb., and against the transfer of Appleby to schedule B, which would have raised the possibility of complete disfranchisement for Petersfield, 21 Feb. 1832.[20] He was back in minorities against the enfranchisement of Tower Hamlets, 28 Feb., the third reading of the bill, 22 Mar., and the second reading of the Irish measure, 25 May. He voted against government on the Russian-Dutch loan, 26 Jan., 12 July 1832.

At the 1832 general election Jolliffe offered again for Petersfield, where he had established a bank, known by 1838 as Jolliffe, Butterfield and Company, to buttress his interest. Despite his earlier pessimism, he was only narrowly defeated by a reform candidate, following which Denis Le Marchant† reported that the 'rejoicing at Brooks's was almost as great as on the passing of schedule A, of which poor Jolliffe passed almost as the representative'.[21] He was seated on petition a few months later, but beaten by his former agent in 1835 and did not attempt a further return to the Commons, where he was one of the last Members to wear breeches and top boots.[22] He died in January 1843 at the house in Pall Mall where he had spent his declining years. By the terms of his will, dated 26 Sept. 1842, this residence and the residue of his estate passed to Sir William Jolliffe, who had also been given

the Mersham property on his marriage in 1825 and the Petersfield property in 1837. Jolliffe bequeathed stocks and shares to his two natural sons, Charles, aged 32, who inherited his Hylton estates in Cumberland and Durham, and George, aged 30, who received an annuity of £600.[23]

[1] Earl of Onslow, 'Hunting in Surr.', Surr. Arch. Colls. (1935), xliii. 7-8; M.D. George, Cat. of Pol. and Personal Satires, x. 14817, 14949; xi. 16211. [2] H.G.F. Jolliffe, Jolliffes of Staffs. 205-6; Sporting Mag. (ser. 2), i. 413. [3] Jolliffe, 111-17; Add. 38280, f. 222. [4] Som. RO, Hylton mss DD/HY, box 17, Procs. at Petersfield Election (1820); E.A. Minty, Hist. Petersfield, 39-40. [5] Black Bk. (1823), 169; Session of Parl. 1825, p. 470; Hylton mss box 17, Procs. at Petersfield Election (1820). [6] The Times, 26 May, 22 June 1820. [7] Jolliffe, 176. [8] Gent. Mag. (1843), i. 317-18. [9] Hylton mss box 22, J. Haworth to Jolliffe, 13 Dec. 1824; Jolliffe, 198. [10] Jolliffe, 176; A.B. de M. Hunter, Gentlemen of Merstham and Gatton, 108, 114. [11] Hants Telegraph, 12 June 1826. [12] Colchester Diary, iii. 567-8. [13] Jolliffe, 199; Ellenborough Diary, ii. 69, 139. [14] The Times, 7 Aug. 1830. [15] Jolliffe, 215. [16] County Chron., 3, 20 Aug.; Baldwin's Weekly Jnl. 7 Aug.; The Times, 9, 10 Aug. 1830. [17] Ellenborough Diary, ii. 338; Lonsdale mss, Lowther to Lonsdale, 20 Aug. 1830. [18] CJ, lxxxvi. 60, 136. [19] Hants Telegraph, 2, 16 May 1831. [20] Hylton mss box 22, W. Mitchell to J. Currie, 18 Nov., 27 Dec.; Hants Telegraph, 26 Dec. 1831. [21] Jolliffe, 222-3; Three Diaries, 287. [22] Jolliffe, 209, 225-6. [23] Gent. Mag. (1843), i. 317-8; Jolliffe, 193, 226-7; PROB 11/1973/37; IR26/1644/28.

H.J.S./P.J.S.

JOLLIFFE, Sir William George Hylton, 1st bt. (1800–1876), of Merstham, Surr.

PETERSFIELD	1830–1832
PETERSFIELD	1837–14 Feb. 1838
PETERSFIELD	1841–16 July 1866

b. 7 Dec. 1800, 1st s. of Rev. William John Jolliffe of Merstham, rect. of Chelsworth, Suff., and Julia, da. and coh. of Sir Abraham Pytches of Streatham, Surr.; bro. of Gilbert East Jolliffe*. educ. privately by Mr. Knipe at Aldermaston, Berks. 1812-17.[1] m. (1) 8 Oct. 1825, Eleanor (d. 23 July 1862), da. of Hon. Berkeley Paget*, 7s. (3 d.v.p.) 6da. (2 d.v.p.); (2) 19 Jan. 1867, Sophia Penelope, da. of Sir Robert Sheffield, 4th bt., of Normanby, Lincs., wid. of William Thomas Fox Strangways, 4th earl of Ilchester, s.p. cr. bt. 20 Aug. 1821; suc. fa. 1835; uncle Hylton Jolliffe* 1843; cr. Bar. Hylton 16 July 1866. d. 1 June 1876.

Cornet 15 Drag. 1817, lt. 1819, capt. 1824, half-pay 1824, out of service 1840.

Under-sec. of state for home affairs Mar.-Dec. 1852; sec. to treasury Mar. 1858-June 1859; PC 18 June 1859.

Lt.-col. Surr. yeoman cav. 1824-7, 1831;[2] sheriff, Surr. 1830-31.

Jolliffe's father William John Jolliffe (1774-1835) abandoned a legal career for the church, which he evidently found no more congenial. After the sudden death in 1802 of his father William Jolliffe, Member for Petersfield since 1768, he resigned his living in Suffolk and, armed with an inheritance of £13,000 and the support of his elder brother Hylton Jolliffe*, set about the exploiting the mineral wealth on the family's Merstham estates. To carry the stone from its rich lime workings the pioneering Surrey Iron Railway was built in 1805. With the overseer of this project, Edward Banks, William John Jolliffe entered into a business partnership in 1807. Jolliffe and Banks of Beauford Street, Strand, were listed in the London directories as lime burners, but as contractors for public works they were responsible for the construction of Waterloo Bridge, Sheerness dockyard, Dartmoor prison and the new London Bridge.[3]

Jolliffe was left £2,000 in his grandfather's will in 1802 and as his uncle Hylton Jolliffe produced no legitimate offspring was the family's heir presumptive.[4] He embarked on a tour of France with his tutor and younger brother Gilbert in April 1816 and returned to take up his army post at Birmingham in July 1817, following which his mother noted in her journal that he was 'much liked in his regiment'. The following February he was presented to the regent by his uncle at a levée.[5] A participant in the charge of the hussars at the Peterloo massacre in August 1819, 25 years later he provided Lord Sidmouth's biographer with a dispassionate and widely cited account of that day's events, in which he acknowledged that the actions of the yeomanry had 'greatly aggravated' the situation, and admitted, 'this was my first acquaintance with a large manufacturing population' and 'I had little knowledge of ... whether or no a great degree of distress then prevailed'.[6] At the time, however, he boasted to his father that it would 'be a long time before there is another meeting of this sort in the town', 19 Aug. Writing again from Bolton, 18 Dec. 1817, he had described his part in a raid

> to assist in the taking [of] radicals ... We should have succeeded in taking ten of them assembled at a house at Leigh ... had not the magistrate been an old fool ... I think I never was in such a rage as I was then and have been in ever since.[7]

Despite being nearly five months under age, in 1821 Jolliffe was gazetted a baronet in the coronation honours as a sop to his uncle's ambitions for a peerage. Following his marriage in 1825 the family's Merstham estate was made over to him, and in 1837 he was given additional property at Petersfield.[8] According to the family history, Jolliffe took half-pay in June 1824 so that he could devote himself to the command of the Surrey yeomanry. He evidently took these duties seriously and by the 1826 dissolution his profile in the county was sufficiently high

for him to be rumoured as a possible candidate, although in the event he did not offer.[9]

At the 1830 general election his uncle came forward for the Surrey seat, which he envisaged would soon pass to Jolliffe. In his capacity as sheriff, however, Jolliffe oversaw his uncle's unexpected defeat and won praise from the successful candidates for his strict impartiality.[10] At the same general election he and his younger brother were returned on their uncle's interest for Petersfield. On the hustings Jolliffe indicated his support for the disfranchisement of non-resident voters but refused to be drawn further on parliamentary reform. A petition against his return was unsuccessful.[11] On 10 Oct. 1830 he informed his cousin Thomas Robert Jolliffe:

> It is my intention during the sitting of Parliament to fix myself in London. I think that by so doing I shall be better able to make the business of the country my business, and during that period I shall therefore sacrifice the attention to the farm, the game and etc., but I do so with sincere regret, for I hate a London life and, above all things, I hate a London house. I trust in time my taste may become more civilised![12]

He was listed by the Wellington ministry among their 'friends', but was absent from the crucial division on the civil list, 15 Nov. 1830. He presented a Petersfield petition for the abolition of slavery, 25 Nov. 1830. He voted against the second reading of the Grey ministry's reform bill, 22 Mar., and for Gascoyne's wrecking amendment, 19 Apr.

At the ensuing general election he offered again for Petersfield, where he declared that the people had been 'gulled' by the bill, which would not diminish the influence of land and could not pass as it stood. He was returned with his uncle after a two-day poll.[13] A petition against the return was not pursued. He divided against the second reading of the reintroduced reform bill, 6 July, and at least five times for its adjournment, 12 July. He voted for use of the 1831 census to determine the disfranchisement schedules, 19 July. Endorsing his uncle's plea for Petersfield to be permitted to return one Member, 22 July, he insisted that ministers had misread its population returns and complained about the 'glaring cases of inconsistency' in the bill. To the same end he refuted John Bonham Carter's assertion that the mayor of Petersfield had no magisterial authority, 19 Aug. He voted against the inclusion of Chippenham in schedule B, 27 July, the third reading of the bill, 19 Sept., its passage, 21 Sept., and the second reading of the revised reform bill, 17 Dec. 1831. He was in the majority against the Vestry Act amendment bill, which would have opened vestries to a wider electorate, 23 Jan. 1832. With his uncle he was in the ministerial majority for keeping Appleby in schedule A, 21 Feb. (Its partial reprieve might have jeopardized Petersfield's retention of one seat in the final bill.) He divided against the enfranchisement of Tower Hamlets, 28 Feb., and the third reading of the reform bill, 22 Mar. He was in the minority for an amendment to preserve the rights of freemen in Irish boroughs, 2 July. He voted against ministers on the Russian-Dutch loan, 26 Jan., 12 July 1832.

At the 1832 dissolution Jolliffe was left without a seat. He remained out of Parliament until 1837, when he replaced his uncle on the family interest at Petersfield after a contest against their former agent.[14] He was unseated on petition the following year, but returned unopposed in 1841. Jolliffe, a Conservative Protectionist, held minor offices in the ministries of Lord Derby, who anticipated 'very useful results from his popularity and tact' on his appointment as Conservative chief whip in 1853.[15] He held this position until 1866, when he was elevated to the peerage in a fresh creation of the Hylton barony, the revival of which had been vainly sought by his grandfather and uncle.[16] Jolliffe, who had inherited the bulk of his uncle's remaining estates in 1843, died in June 1876 at Merstham.[17] His eldest son Hylton had been killed in the Crimea in 1854, and the title and Surrey estates passed to his second son Hedworth Hylton Jolliffe (1829-99), Conservative Member for Wells, 1855-68. By his will, dated 26 Feb. 1870, he directed that the estate at Ammerdown, Somerset, inherited from his cousin Thomas Robert Jolliffe in 1872 should also descend with the title, and left his son William Sydney Jolliffe (1841-1912) property at Liss, Hampshire, and his son Walter Hylton Jolliffe (1844-89) a freehold at Rogate, Sussex.[18] Further provision for them and his other surviving son Spencer Hylton Jolliffe (1853-1902) came out of his personal estate, while his second wife received a life interest in his Piccadilly house, with remainder to his eldest daughter Eleanor, the widowed Lady Blaquiere.

[1] H.G.H. Jolliffe, *Jolliffes of Staffs.* 133-4. [2] Ibid. 187, 200. [3] Ibid. 118, 121-5, 131; PROB 11/1376/465; K. Gravett and E. Wood, 'Merstham Limeworks', *Surr. Arch. Colls.* lxiv (1967), 129-30. [4] PROB 11/1376/465. [5] Jolliffe, 150, 155-6, 158-9. [6] Pellew, *Sidmouth*, 253-61. Republished in *Three Accounts of Peterloo* ed. F. Bruton (1921). [7] Jolliffe, 165, 171-2. [8] Ibid. 176, 193, 227. [9] Ibid. 186, 191; *Baldwin's Weekly Jnl.* 25 June, 1 July 1826. [10] Jolliffe, 215; *The Times*, 10 Aug. 1830. [11] Som. RO, Hylton mss DD/HY, box 17, Procs. at Petersfield Election (1830). [12] Hylton mss box 22. [13] *Hants Telegraph*, 16 May 1831. [14] Jolliffe, 225. [15] R. Stewart, *Foundation of Conservative Party*, 278-9. [16] Jolliffe, 57-8, 176, 227. [17] PROB 11/1973/37. [18] Jolliffe, 229.

H.J.S./P.J.S.

JONES, John (1777–1842), of Ystrad Lodge, Carm.

PEMBROKE BOROUGHS	3 July 1815–1818
CARMARTHEN	5 July 1821–1831
CARMARTHEN	25 Aug. 1831–1832
CARMARTHENSHIRE	1837–10 Nov. 1842

b. 15 Sept. 1777, 2nd. s. of Thomas Jones (*d.* 1790), attorney, of Job's Well and Capel Dewi, Carm. and Anna Maria, da. and h. of John Jones, attorney, of Crynfryn and Aberystwyth, Card. *educ.* Carmarthen; Eton 1791-3; Christ Church, Oxf. 1796; L. Inn 1798, called 1803. *unm. suc.* bro. Thomas Jones to Ystrad 1793. *d.* 10 Nov. 1842.

Mayor, Carmarthen 1809-10; recorder, Kidwelly 1814-*d.*

John Jones, a Welsh-speaking 'St. Peter's boy', whose politics were largely personal and frequently determined by local issues, was a leading advocate on the Carmarthen circuit and commanded political support in Cardiganshire, Carmarthenshire and Pembrokeshire. His father had been the agent for the Vaughan estate of Golden Grove, Carmarthenshire, bequeathed in 1804 to the Grenvillite 1st Baron Cawdor, and Jones had become mayor of Carmarthen on their Blue interest in 1809. Cawdor, however, refused to support his parliamentary ambitions and in 1812 and 1818 he had contested Carmarthen unsuccessfully on the rival Red interest of Lord Dynevor. Another West Wales Red, Sir John Owen*, had facilitated his election for Pembroke Boroughs on a vacancy in 1815, but in 1818 he had been obliged under a local arrangement to make way there for Cawdor's nominee John Hensleigh Allen*.[1] His personal following in Carmarthen ensured that 'there will be no peace in this borough until Mr. Jones will be our representative', and having increased Tory representation on the corporation, which had been under Whig control since the charter was renewed in 1764, he challenged Cawdor's heir John Frederick Campbell* there again in 1820, but desisted for fear of raising a Whig opposition to the election of Dynevor's son George Rice Rice (afterwards Trevor) for the county.[2] He contested Carmarthen successfully at no personal cost when Campbell succeeded to the peerage in 1821, and celebrated his return and the borough's liberation at Cardigan and towns throughout Carmarthenshire and Pembrokeshire.[3] Quo warranto proceedings against 21 known Cawdor supporters also succeeded, and by 1822 the Reds controlled Carmarthen corporation.[4]

Jones intervened readily in debate, but the Liverpool government could rarely be sure of his support, despite his professed allegiance to the new home secretary Peel. He presented Carmarthen's petition against the Insolvent Debtors Act, 20 Feb. 1822, and criticized the government's retrenchment measures as 'insufficient to afford effectual relief to the agricultural interest'. He acknowledged that lower malt duties would assist barley growing areas, but claimed that greater benefit, particularly for the poor, would be derived from reductions in the duties on salt and leather, and urged ministers to heed the 'sentiments of the country as they were expressed at county meetings ... except on the subject of parliamentary reform'.[5] He suggested a reduction in junior admiralty lords, an end to state lotteries, and a tax on gaming as possible remedies, before dividing against the government's relief proposals, 21 Feb., and voted for a gradual reduction in the salt duties, 28 Feb. He failed to persuade ministers that the agriculture committee should consider the relative benefits of lower taxes on malt and salt, 4 Mar., but renewed his efforts when the report on the malt tax was brought up, 6 Mar., on presenting petitions, 30 Apr., and again, 28 June, earning the sobriquet 'Jones yr Halen' (Jones the Salt) in Carmarthen.[6] He spoke in favour of the government's scheme to finance naval and military pensions from the sinking fund, 3 May, and against the vagrancy laws amendment bill, which affected Carmarthen as a popular stopover on the route to county Waterford, 21 May.[7] He voted to limit inquiry into Irish tithes, 19 June 1822.

Jones had sat on the 1817 select committee on the administration of justice in Wales and had sought since 1818 to legislate to reform the courts of great sessions, with a view to preventing their abolition, which the Blues now advocated. His remedial bill, which in 1820 he had entrusted to Charles Warren, had made no progress. A measure based on the 1817 and 1820-1 committee reports promoted by Cawdor (as Campbell had become) and Allen fared similarly, 23 May 1822. Jones agreed with them that the reports should be further considered and that Welsh judges should be appointed by the lord chancellor and barred from sitting in the Commons, and with Peel's acquiescence, on the 30th he introduced his bill 'to enlarge and extend the powers of the judges of the several courts of great sessions in Wales', which was printed and held over.[8] He reintroduced it, 18 Mar. 1823, but, as Hume revealed, it lacked provisions to prevent judges being Members. He brought up favourable petitions from the grand juries of Cardiganshire, 18 Apr., and Carmarthenshire, 2 May 1823, but the measure was repeatedly deferred and timed out.[9] He voted in Whitmore's minority of 25 for a gradual reduction to 60s. a bushel in the corn pivot price, 26 Feb., but against using the sinking fund to finance a £2,000,000

cut in taxation, 3 Mar. 1823. He was a speaker for the army estimates, 7 Mar., and tried to justify his vote for the national debt reduction bill at its third reading, 17 Mar., but could not be heard.[10] He voted against repealing the assessed taxes, 18 May, but against government for inquiry into the prosecution of the Dublin Orange rioters, 22 Apr. During it, he probed deeply into the background, political affiliation (especially Orange party connections) and whereabouts of the witnesses heard, 7, 8, 9, 23 May. He failed by 173-42 to 'consign the subject to oblivion' by adjournment, 27 May.[11] When the *Morning Chronicle* of 4 June published an account of the Commons proceedings on the Borthwick case (3 June) that ridiculed the majority in which he had voted, he raised it as breach of privilege, but had to withdrew his motion for want of government support.[12] He cast a wayward vote for recommittal of the silk manufacture bill, which was of local interest in Carmarthen, 9 June, but divided with ministers against inquiry into the currency, 12 June, and for the Scottish juries bill, 20 June. He abhorred and opposed flogging in prisons, 7 July 1823. Charles Williams Wynn* recommended him to Lord Liverpool for preferment that autumn and Jones himself sought Peel's intervention on behalf of constituents anxious to avoid appointments as sheriff.[13]

On 16 Feb. 1824 Jones obtained leave to introduce his bill to extend the power of judges in Wales.[14] Allen dismissed it as 'trifling in its remedy and likely to be most pernicious in its effects', but he failed (by 42-19) to kill it, 11 Mar., and it was 'passed with difficulty', 24 May, and enacted, heavily amended, 24 June 1824, after Dynevor and lord chancellor Eldon backed it in the Lords. The *Cambrian* saw 'great benefit' in 'Jones's Act' and commended 'his zeal and activity in framing and carrying the same into effect'.[15] He voted to consider the usury laws repeal bill, 27 Feb., but after a Carmarthenshire meeting declared against it, 30 Mar., he divided accordingly, 8 Apr. He brought up a private petition for revision of the insolvency laws, 2 Mar. 1824.[16] He divided with opposition on the aliens bill, 23 Mar., 2 Apr. After being turned down for employment as a commissioner on the Irish land valuation survey, he wrote to Peel, 26 Mar.:

I am far from thinking that *any* claim on government exists on my part. The support I have given to their measures has been dictated by principle; and whatever may be the result of this or any other application on my behalf, will continue disinterested ... Your public conduct has pointed you out to me as a proper political guide, and as the only individual of His Majesty's government who has had and who will most probably retain an influence over my vote. I have however written to Lord

Liverpool and Mr. [Stephen Rumbold] Lushington* on this occasion.[17]

He argued that to deny farmers and tenants access under the game laws to game on their land would be an 'unwarrantable invasion' of the rights of property, 1 Apr. He presented a petition against West Indian slavery from Milford Haven, 9 Apr., and others from Carmarthen for repeal of the window tax, 11 May, and in condemnation of the indictment in Demerara of the Methodist missionary John Smith, 26 May. *Seren Gomer* praised him for voting accordingly, 11 June.[18] He voted against ending military flogging, 5 Mar., and for the Irish insurrection bill, 14 June 1824. At the mayoral election in Carmarthen at Michaelmas he canvassed for the Red nominee Daniel Prytherch and was accused of insulting Cawdor's former agent, the Rev. Thomas Benyon. He was also a speaker at the corporation dinner and assisted with plans and the subscription for a memorial to the late Sir Thomas Picton†, whose brother Edward was one of his principal local supporters.[19]

Jones, according to a radical publication of 1825, 'attended frequently and voted in general with government'.[20] He received a month's leave on urgent private business, 14 Feb., and presented his constituents' petitions for repeal of the window tax, 21 Mar., and against the Western Ship Canal bill, 21 Apr.[21] A staunch churchman and freemason,[22] he divided against Catholic relief, 21 Apr., 10 May, having presented an unfavourable Carmarthen petition, 3 May. He voted against the attendant Irish franchise bill, 9 May.[23] He opposed the Welch Iron and Mining Company bill and criticized its backers for frequently absenting themselves from the select committee, 18 May. When the report on judges' salaries was considered, 20 May, he voted in a minority of 29 against making puisne judges immovable. He divided with administration for the duke of Cumberland's annuity bill, 30 May, 10 June. He called for extra time to consider the Hampshire and Berkshire canal bill and criticized those who had prevented it going forward, 20 June. He voted for the spring guns bill, 21 June. He pointed to inconsistencies in Hume's endorsement of the *Glasgow Free Press*'s petition criticizing unstamped papers, 29 June 1825.[24] During the recess he dealt with patronage requests and prepared for the next election by drawing up new electors' lists for Carmarthen.[25] Jones moved the first resolution at the Carmarthen anti-slavery meeting, 25 Jan., and presented their petition as requested, 13 Apr. 1826.[26] He was for legislating to give freeholders in counties corporate the right to vote in the counties from which they had been detached, 26 Apr., 2

May,[27] and in favour of bringing up the report on the corn bill, 8 May, because he thought that the admission of bonded corn might relieve distress. However, heeding the opposition of the Carmarthenshire clergy, who feared reduced tithe revenues, he reserved the right to vote against the measure and did so, 8 May, 11 June.[28] He voted to permit adjourned sessions to grant alehouse licences, 12 May 1826. At the general election in June he canvassed on behalf of Rice Trevor in Carmarthenshire and the Owens in Pembrokeshire and came in for Carmarthen unopposed. His expenses were defrayed by his constituents. Addressing a crowd of 5,000 afterwards, he said he would support retrenchment, religious liberty for all save Roman Catholics, and the abolition of colonial slavery. He also explained that although he supported the ministry's free trade proposals, he would oppose them on corn in order to protect agriculture.[29] The mayor and corporation of Kidwelly and the farmers celebrated his election, and the magistrates organized a subscription to mark his 'impartial conduct' as chairman of the quarter sessions with a gift of plate.[30]

Jones divided against Catholic relief, 6 Mar. 1827, and when Peel resigned rather than serve in the pro-Catholic Canning's ministry, he wrote to offer him his support, but made it clear that he would not vote against repeal of the Test Acts, 'as my own conviction as well as the wishes of the major part of my constituents incline me to support such repeal if the matter shall come before the House of Commons'.[31] During Canning's ministry, reporters found his speeches difficult to record 'as he sat under the gallery';[32] but he certainly deplored the way in which repeal 'had been suffered to sleep', 22 May, 6 June, and strenuously endorsed a favourable Carmarthen petition, 14 June.[33] He spoke and voted against the Canadian waterways grant, 12 June 1827.[34] He assisted with the Carmarthen corporation elections at Michaelmas and received a gift of plate worth £350 at the magistrates' dinner in October.[35] He led the dancing as usual at Llandovery ball and hosted a dinner for the magistrates, 17 Jan. 1828.[36] On 28 Jan. (and again, 19 Feb.) he attended meetings at Llanelli to organize resistance to Cawdor's attempt to levy local market tolls.[37] When Peel returned to office as home secretary and leader of the House in the duke of Wellington's ministry Jones, who had little private fortune, again requested 'one of the little subordinate stations in the treasury, admiralty or India board or in some other office where the change of administration may occasion a vacancy ... [or a] judgeship on the Brecon circuit'. Owen testified to his 'zeal, assiduity and abilities', and Dynevor to his exertion 'in all business relative to the Principality in the ... Commons and particularly the Welsh judicature bill'. Rice Trevor added:

> When ... Mr. Canning became premier he refused an offer made to him (I believe a judge in India) feeling that he could not consistently with his political principles accept of employment under that government.

However, it proved 'impossible to include the name of Mr. Jones in the recent arrangement'.[38] Presenting the Carmarthen Dissenters' petition for repeal of the Test Acts, 12 Feb. 1828, Jones demonstrated how a mayor or returning officer could have 'the unconstitutional power of electing a candidate of his choice' as Dissenters would not swear an oath, but Protestants occasionally conformed and could thereby take the Test. He brought up further repeal petitions from West Wales, 15, 20, 22 Feb., and divided for it, 26 Feb.[39] As a member of the committee on the Llanelli railroad and docks bill, he tried to convince a sceptical John Johnes of Dolaucothi that 'great public benefit will result from the adoption of the measure, inasmuch as there will be competition for coal'.[40] He divided against Catholic relief, 12 May, and strenuously opposed and was a minority teller against the borough polls bill 15 May, 6, 27 June, which he belittled as one of seven bills introduced by seven Members 'all suited to the meridians of their own boroughs and limiting the rights of electors'. He spoke against the alehouse licensing bill, whose object he claimed was 'to interfere like a side-wind with the rights and privileges of chartered towns and boroughs' to issue licences, 21 May. He presented and endorsed a hostile Carmarthen petition, 2 June, and voted against the small notes bill, 16, 27 June. He complained of the high stamp duty levied on the articles of attorneys' clerks, 16 June, supported the additional churches bill, 3 July, and divided with government against ordnance reductions, 4 July 1828. In August he was one of the principal speakers at the official opening of the Picton memorial in Carmarthen and a croupier at the celebration dinner.[41] After the borough elections, he encouraged Carmarthen to seek legislation to permit borough magistrates to try petty larcenies four times a year, but although they authorized him to introduce a bill, he delayed doing so.[42]

The patronage secretary Planta correctly observed in February 1829 that Jones remained opposed on principle to Catholic emancipation; but he also deprecated 'the attempts which I know are made to obtain signatures to anti-Catholic petitions', 4 Mar., and urged Members to

> suspend their judgement, until they know what is the nature of the measure intended to be brought forward by ... ministers. When I see what a sudden and unexpected

change has taken place in the highest quarters, I think we ought to give those persons credit for sincerity; and I must suppose that the change in their opinions has arisen from there being only a choice of evils.

He divided for emancipation, 6 Mar., giving what the anti-Catholic *Carmarthen Journal* of 17 Apr. described as a vote for Peel rather than the Catholics. Presenting Llanarthney's hostile petition, 12 Mar., he said he could not support its prayer, although it was prepared fairly, for he had 'made up my mind to vote in favour of the bill', thinking it 'more dangerous not to relieve Roman Catholics than to do so'.[43] He did not divide again on the measure, which Dynevor and his son opposed, but he voted against permitting Daniel O'Connell to take his seat without swearing the oath of supremacy, 18 May. He found fault with the county bridges bill, 12 May, and argued against making any distinction in the anatomy regulation bill between the unclaimed bodies of the rich and the poor, 15 May. John Nash, the architect of Carmarthen gaol, St. Peter's church and the Picton memorial, was his personal friend and he defended him against allegations of profiteering over the Buckingham House contract, 25, 27 May; he was appointed to the committee of inquiry that day. He presented a private petition calling for Sunday morning and evening services to be held in all churches and chapels, 1 June 1829. In Carmarthenshire during the recess he attended the races, sessions, borough elections and meetings on the Welsh judicature.[44]

The Whig lawyer Henry Brougham's speech on 7 Feb. 1828 had vilified the Welsh courts, and their future had been referred to a commission and discussed in Cawdor's pro-abolition *Letter ... to Lord Chancellor Lyndhurst*.[45] Responding to the commissioners' questionnaires, Jones praised and urged further reform of the courts, but denigrated the Welsh language and said that he regretted the way charity schools 'afforded the means of perpetuating the language which was before greatly in decline'. He saw no advantage in administering common law from Westminster because 'a few improvements easy of execution may be necessary' and 'a few wealthy individuals ... cry out for the measure', and disliked the proposed schemes to divide and amalgamate counties, but suggested separate circuits for North and South Wales, holding Brecon and Radnor assizes alternately in Brecon and Presteigne, and the assizes for Cardiganshire and Pembrokeshire in Cardigan.[46] Carmarthen magistrates countered pro-abolition memorials got up by Cawdor's agents in Cardiganshire, Carmarthenshire, Glamorgan and Merionethshire, and at the Carmarthenshire (23

Oct.) and Carmarthen (26 Oct.) meetings which petitioned against change, Jones, whom Allen accused of acting from self-interest as a lawyer, 'deprecated any party feeling being introduced', but poured scorn on Cawdor's supporters. He asserted that justice was both cheaper and more efficient in Wales than in England and predicted correctly that Carmarthen would not welcome the proposals just because its own assizes would continue. However, he conceded that there was 'little interest in the House of Commons in Welsh justice at present'.[47] His ability to oppose the 1830 administration of justice bill by which the change was enacted was hampered by Peel's reluctance to divulge its details, 1, 3 Mar., but he presented and endorsed petitions against change, 9 Mar., had the bill postponed to allow the magistrates time to comment, 17 Mar., and denounced it at its second reading, 27 Apr., as 'the veriest skeleton of a bill I have ever seen. It would take six months in a committee to put flesh on its bones'. Others agreed, and ministers admitted it was full of incongruities, but Jones, who raised further queries, 3, 18, 29 May, and presented hostile petitions, 14 May, 18 June, failed (by 129-30) to prevent its committal that day or to delay its enactment, 2, 5 July.[48] He ceased to practice when the new system came into operation, 12 Oct. 1830, but still coveted and was repeatedly denied 'the professional honour of a silk gown'.[49] Jones voted against Lord Blandford's parliamentary reform scheme, 18 Feb., and enfranchising Birmingham, Leeds and Manchester, 23 Feb. 1830. He presented petitions against the Kidwelly enclosure bill, 15 Mar., and the game laws, 17 Mar., and divided for Jewish emancipation, 17 May, and against the Galway franchise bill, 25 May 1830. In king's bench that month, he brought an action for debt (£240) against John Michael Goodere.[50] At the dissolution in July his constituents were reported to be ready to return him unopposed without cost, but he provided a pre-election *dejeuné* for the gentlemen and post-election beer for the populace at Ystrad. His stance on the Test Acts and the administration of justice bill was praised but he readily acknowledged that many disapproved of his pro-Catholic vote. He also mentioned his chance of office in India, which he now claimed to have refused in the interests of Carmarthen. He said that he remained a supporter of the ministry, but would vote against them as necessary. At the celebrations afterwards, the sheriff, Rees Goring Thomas, claimed that Jones had 'annihilated the Blue-Red divide' in Carmarthen.[51]

Ministers listed Jones among their 'friends' and he divided with them when they were brought down on the civil list, 15 Nov. 1830. At a Carmarthen meeting that month he challenged local abolitionists to prove the scriptural basis for opposition to West Indian slavery, but he nevertheless presented and endorsed many anti-slavery petitions from Carmarthenshire and Pembrokeshire between November 1830 and April 1831.[52] He brought up others against the coastwise coal duties, 11 Feb. 1831, campaigned against the drawback duties on printed calicoes, which were disliked in Carmarthen, and urged that the bridge across the River Blackwater be completed, 28 Mar.[53] A Carmarthen borough meeting, 22 Feb., amended the reform petition proposed by Cawdor's agent, the Unitarian attorney George Thomas, so that it included a resolution for the ballot.[54] Jones had stayed away, but he presented the petition, 28 Feb., and afterwards published an open letter declaring that he was 'friendly to reform'. He advocated transferring the franchise from decaying boroughs to populous towns, restricting the borough franchise to residents (and current voters), and enfranchising copyholders and long leaseholders in the counties, but he refused to support the ballot, short parliaments, universal suffrage, or the disfranchisement of existing voters.[55] He divided against the Grey ministry's reform bill at its second reading, 22 Mar. He said that it should be drafted by a national convention, not Parliament, 24 March, claimed that to disfranchise Criccieth but not Wiston was partisan, and asserted that as in Carmarthen, many resident lower class voters would be disfranchised by the measure, while many non-residents would retain their votes, 25 Mar. The bill lost much local support in Carmarthen once it was known that Llanelli would become its contributory, in what the *Carmarthen Journal* of 18 Mar. described as 'a piece of pure political meddling for which there exists not a shade of necessity'. Addressing a Carmarthen reform meeting disrupted by drunken intruders, 12 Apr., Jones, or 'Jack Slack' as he was subsequently called after the pugilist, showed that he could still use his fists. Justifying his anti-reform vote, he repeated his statement of 28 Feb., argued against disfranchising boroughs without proof of corruption, suggested petitioning for a separate Llanelli Boroughs constituency and projected himself as the defender of the rights of poor voters liable to disfranchisement.[56] He divided for Gascoyne's wrecking amendment, 19 Apr. 1831. His opponent at the ensuing general election was the naval captain and reformer John George Philipps of Cwmgwili, whose grandfather had represented the borough, 1796-1803. Assisted by Allen, Philipps criticized Jones's parliamentary record, but he stood by his statements of 28 Feb. and 12 Apr. and promised to vote for the principle of reform if not all its details.[57]

Carmarthen lived up to its reputation for violent contests and the poll was abandoned with three votes cast on each side. Philipps petitioned without success and on 10 Aug. a second election was called.[58] Jones spent at least £1,400 and received £300 from Tory Charles Street funds, for it was felt that his vote on the civil list had cost him support.[59] He outpolled Philipps, but the lampooning and physical violence continued and he was wounded in the head at his chairing, 25 Aug. 1831.[60]

He presented Kidwelly's petition to become a contributory of Carmarthen, 12 Sept., and divided for the passage of the reintroduced reform bill, 21 Sept., and the second reading of the Scottish reform bill, 23 Sept. 1831. He called for a new election writ for Pembrokeshire, 23, 26 Sept., and after it was issued received a fortnight's leave on urgent private business, 28 Sept., which he spent canvassing for the successful candidate Owen, another convert to reform. The aftermath of the by-election for Jones, who was never one to avoid the fray, was a duel with the reform candidate Robert Fulke Greville at *Tafarn Spite*, where, according to the *Cambrian*, he 'received Mr. Greville's shot, and refusing to apologise, fired his pistol in the air'.[61] He divided for the revised reform bill at its second reading, 17 Dec. 1831. On 1 Feb. 1832 he referred to the effect which Queen Anne's bounty and livings worth less than £10 a year could have on clergymen's voting rights, which the treasury admitted they had not allowed for, and pressed that they be retained. He argued against tinkering with the disfranchisement lists to replace Amersham with Midhurst and voted to retain Appleby in schedule A., 21 Feb. He divided for the bill's provisions for Helston, 23 Feb., and Tower Hamlets, 28 Feb., but against separate representation for Gateshead, 5 Mar., an issue of principle for those who hoped Merthyr Tydfil would receive its own Member.[62] He had to miss the division on the bill's third reading, 22 Mar., to attend the Carmarthenshire assizes, where George Thomas was fined £5 for insulting him in Pembrokeshire at the 1831 general election. A witness alleged that Jones had bought a pistol in order to shoot Thomas there 'like a dog'.[63] He voted for the address calling on the king to appoint only ministers who would carry the reform bill unimpaired, 10 May, and against a Conservative amendment to the Scottish reform bill, 1 June. He divided against government on the Russian-Dutch loan, 26 Jan., but on 12 July he was listed with the absent reformers. He voted with administration on relations with Portugal, 9 Feb., but in the minority against military punishments, 16 Feb. He spoke briefly on the use of the *Commons Journals* as evidence in courts of law, 25 June 1832.

Borough elections in Carmarthen remained unruly and it was rumoured that Jones would stand for the county's new second seat or that Hugh Owen Owen would make way for him in Pembroke Boroughs at the December 1832 general election. However, he contested the new Carmarthen and Llanelli constituency, where his surprise defeat by the Liberal William Henry Yelverton of Whitland Abbey was attributed to 'the tyrannical conduct of the magistracy to George Thomas [jailed after the borough election disturbances] ... which united the tradesmen of the town against him, even those who never interfered before'.[64] He did not contest Carmarthen again, but stood unsuccessfully for the county as a Conservative in 1835 and successfully in 1837. Though repeatedly denied party patronage, he retained the seat until his death in November 1842.[65] Although he had helped to endow Carmarthen's Welsh language church, St. David's, he was buried with masonic pomp at St. Peter's, and recalled as an 'able and active representative' who had endured a 'series of harassing electioneering struggles' to acquire 'probably the greatest influence of any private gentleman in the Principality'. His portrait by Thomas Brigstocke was presented to the county.[66] He bequeathed Ystrad, her home, to his unmarried sister Mary Ann, subject to yearly rent charges to provide for his 'natural son Richard Jones' and others. However, he was found to be insolvent and by August 1844 his assets, which included a library of 4,000 books, the 225-acre Ystrad and 159-acre Llanbadarn Fawr estates, tithes of St. Peter's commuted at £920 and rights to fees for the north chancel, had all been sold.[67]

[1] Add. 40363, f. 144; *Carmarthen Jnl.* 3 July 1818; Carm. RO, Cawdor mss 2/136; D. Williams, *Rebecca Riots* (1971), 24; M. Cragoe, *An Anglican Aristocracy: The Moral Economy of the Landed Estate in Carm. 1832-1895*, pp. 117-18; *HP Commons, 1790-1820*, iv. 322-3. [2] NLW, Dolaucothi mss V2/36; R.D. Rees, 'Parl. Rep. S. Wales 1790-1830' (Univ. of Reading Ph.D. thesis, 1962), 192-3, 389; *PP* (1835), xxiii. 341; *Cambrian*, 12, 26 Feb., 11 Mar.; *Carmarthen Jnl.* 25 Feb., 10 Mar. 1820; Cawdor mss 2/135; Dolaucothi mss V2/38. [3] *Carmarthen Jnl.* 15, 22, 29 June, 6, 13 July 1821; Cawdor mss 2/135-7; G.E. Evans, 'Morgan (Furnace) Pprs.', *Trans. Carm. Antiq. Soc.* xx (1926-7), 57-58. [4] Cawdor mss 2/137; *Carmarthen Jnl.* 11 Oct. 1822; *PP* (1835), xxiii. 347. [5] *The Times*, 21 Feb. 1822. [6] Ibid. 5, 7 Mar., 3 May 1822; Rees, 392. [7] *The Times*, 22 May 1822. [8] Ibid. 31 May 1822; *Seren Gomer*, v (1822), 221. [9] *The Times*, 19 Mar. 1823; *CJ*, lxxviii. 133, 135, 227, 276-8, 379. [10] *The Times*, 18 Mar. 1823. [11] Ibid. 8, 24 May 1823. [12] Ibid. 5 June 1823. [13] Add. 38296, f. 356; 40359, ff. 78-80; 40360, f. 66; 40370, ff. 133-5. [14] *The Times*, 17 Feb. 1824. [15] Ibid. 22 June; *Cambrian*, 26 June 1824, 7 Nov. 1829; *Seren Gomer*, vii (1824), 92, 224; *CJ*, lxxix.150, 249, 378, 407, 530, 536; M. Escott, 'How Wales lost its judicature: the making of the 1830 Act for the Abolition of the Courts of Great Sessions', *Trans. Hon. Soc. Cymmrodorion*, (2006), 135-59. [16] *The Times*, 3 Mar.; *Cambrian*, 26 Mar., 3 Apr. 1824. [17] Add 40364, f. 144. [18] *The Times*, 2, 10 Apr., 12, 27 May; *Seren Gomer*, vii (1824), 224-5.

[19] Cawdor mss 136, R.B. Williams to Cawdor, 19 Sept.; *Cambrian*, 8 Oct. 1824; Add. 40375, f. 70; 40377, ff. 215-18, 343. [20] *Session of Parl. 1825*, p. 471. [21] *The Times*, 22 Mar., 22 Apr. 1825. [22] *Oxford DNB*. [23] *Cambrian*, 30 Apr.; *The Times*, 4 May 1825. [24] *The Times*, 11, 21, 30 June 1825. [25] NLW mss 481 E; NLW, Glansevin mss 6. [26] *Cambrian*, 28 Jan.; *The Times*, 14 Apr. 1826. [27] *The Times*, 27 Apr. 1826. [28] *Cambrian*, 30 Apr. 1825. [29] *Carmarthen Jnl*. 26 May, 2, 9, 16, 23 June; *Cambrian*, 27 May, 17, 24 June 1826. [30] Evans, *Trans. Carm. Antiq. Soc.* xx. 61; *Cambrian*, 1 July 1826, 29 Apr. 1827. [31] Add. 40393, ff. 237, 264-6. [32] *The Times*, 23 May, 7 June 1827. [33] *Seren Gomer*, x (1827), 218; *The Times*, 12 May, 7, 15 June 1827. [34] *The Times*, 13 June 1827. [35] *Cambrian*, 6, 20 Oct. 1827. [36] Ibid. 1 Dec. 1827; Dolaucothi mss L3028. [37] *Cambrian*, 1 Mar.; *Carmarthen Jnl*. 7, 14 Mar. 1828. [38] Add. 40395, ff. 30-35, 57-59, 92. [39] *Cambrian*, 16 Feb., 1, 8 Mar.; *Carmarthen Jnl*. 29 Feb. 1828. [40] Dolaucothi mss L3029, 3030, 4095. [41] *Cambrian*, 9 Aug. 1828. [42] *Carmarthen Jnl*. 24 Oct.; *Cambrian*, 8 Nov. 1828. [43] *Cambrian*, 21 Mar. 1829. [44] Ibid. 26 Sept., 10, 24 Oct. 1829. [45] *Cambrian*, 16 Feb.; Cawdor, *Letter ... to Lyndhurst; Carmarthen Jnl*. 5, 19 Sept. 1828. [46] *PP* (1829), ix. 43-44, 62-63, 390-2, 427-30 and *passim.; Carmarthen Jnl*. 18 Apr. 1829. [47] *Cambrian*, 7 Mar., 2 May, 17, 31 Oct., 7 Nov.; *Carmarthen Jnl*. 16, 30 Oct. 1829. [48] *Cambrian*, 2, 9 July 1830. [49] Add. 40401, f. 199. [50] Glansevin mss 376. [51] *Carmarthen Jnl*. 2, 23, 30 July, 6, 13 Aug.; *Cambrian*, 7, 14 Aug. 1830. [52] *Carmarthen Jnl*. 19, 26 Nov. 1830, 4 Feb. 1831. [53] Ibid. 25 Feb. 1831. [54] Rees, 112; *Carmarthen Jnl*. 25 Feb. 1831. [55] *Carmarthen Jnl*. 22 Apr. 1831. [56] Ibid. 18 Mar., 15, 22 Apr.; *Cambrian*, 16 Apr. 1831. [57] *Carmarthen Jnl*. 29 Apr. 1831; Cawdor mss 2/136; Dolaucothi mss L3031, 4103. [58] D.J.V. Jones, 'Carmarthen Riots of 1831', *WHR*, iv (1968-9), 132-6; *Yr Erfangylydd*, i (1831), 193; E.V. Jones, 'Through Riot to Parl.' *Carm. Historian*, xiv (1977), 59-63; *Carmarthen Jnl*. 29 Apr., 6, 13, May, 3 June; *The Times*, 11 Aug. 1831; NLW, Highmead mss 3151, 3152. [59] Wellington mss, Holmes to Arbuthnot, 9 Aug., Arbuthnot to Wellington, 10 Aug. 1831. [60] Dolaucothi mss V21/40; G.E. Evans, 'Election Squibs', *Trans. Carm. Antiq. Soc.* vii (1911-12), 82-83; *Carmarthen Jnl*. 26 Aug. 1831; Jones, *WHR*, iv. 136-8. [61] *The Times*, 25 Oct.; *Cambrian*, 29 Oct. 1831; Jones, *Carm. Historian*, xiv. 64-65; D. Williams, 'Pemb. Elections of 1831', *WHR*, i (1960-3), 55-56. [62] *Carmarthen Jnl*. 16 Mar. 1832. [63] Ibid. 23 Mar.; *Cambrian*, 24, 31 Mar. 1832; *Seren Gomer*, xv (1832), 189; Williams, *WHR*, i. 51. [64] *Welshman*, 20 July 1832; Highmead mss 3156; *Welshman*, 21 Dec.; *Yr Efangylydd*, ii (1832), 355-6; Dynevor mss 159/4; 160/12; 161/5; *Carmarthen Jnl*. 3, 24 Aug., 28 Dec. 1832; M. Cragoe, *Culture, Politics and National Identity in Wales, 1832-1886*, pp. 51, 55, 243, and 'Carm. Co. Politics, 1804-37', *Carm. Antiquary*, xxx (1994), 75-79. [65] Add. 40414, f. 299; 40419, f. 348; 40473, ff. 6-8; 40510, f. 321; 40511, ff. 162-4; Dolaucothi mss L3032, 3163. [66] *Welshman*, 11, 18 Nov.; *Carmarthen Jnl*. 11, 18 Nov. 1842. [67] PROB 11/1979/331; IR26/1645/257; *Welshman*, 17 Feb., 17 July, 18 Aug. 1843; *Carmarthen Jnl*. 2 Aug. 1844.

M.M.E.

JONES, **Theobald** (1790–1868), of Bovagh House, co. Londonderry and 54 Curzon Street, Mdx.

Co. LONDONDERRY   1830–1857

b. 5 Apr. 1790,[1] 2nd s. of Rev. James Jones (*d.* 1835), rect. of Kilcronaghan, co. Londonderry, and 1st w. Lydia, da. of Theobald Wolfe of Blackhall, co. Kildare. *unm. d.* 7 Feb. 1868.

Vol. RN 1803, midshipman ?1804, lt. 1809, cdr. 1814, capt. 1828, ret. 1848; r.-adm. 1855, v.-adm. 1862, adm. 1865.

Jones's ancestor Bryan Jones (*d.* 1681), a Welshman, settled in Dublin in the early seventeenth century. Bryan's grandson Theophilus (1666-1742) of Headford, county Leitrim, sat for Sligo and county Leitrim in the Irish Parliament for a total of over 40 years. His grandson, another Theophilus (1729-1811), who married a Beresford, represented his native county as well as Coleraine and Monaghan at Dublin, 1761-1800, and county Leitrim at Westminster, 1801-2. His eldest son Walter (1754-1839), governor of Leitrim, was Member for Coleraine in both Parliaments in three spells between 1798 and 1809, while his second son Theophilus (1760-1835) served in the navy, becoming an admiral in 1819.[2] The third son, James Jones, whose address was often given as Merrion Square, Dublin, entered the church, becoming prebend of Killamery in 1783 and being resident in Kilcronaghan from 1786. It was there that his wife gave birth to this Member, 'Toby' Jones, who was perhaps so called in order to distinguish him from his similarly named elder brother, Theophilus.[3] Later that year James moved to Tamlaght O'Crilly and from 1814 until his death in 1835 he was the incumbent of Urney, in the diocese of Derry. In 1796, three years after the death of his first wife, he married the relict Anne Ryder, daughter of Sir John Blackwood of Ballyleidy House, county Down, Member for Killyleagh and Bangor, 1761-99.[4] The family were active in the Protestant suppression of the Irish volunteers in 1798, and from about that time James Jones held the grandmastership of the Orange order of the city and county of Londonderry.[5]

Jones entered the navy on 1 June 1803, serving as a first class volunteer in the *Melpomone* frigate, and the following year he was twice engaged as a midshipman in the bombardment of Le Havre. From November 1805 he served with his stepmother's brother Henry Blackwood in the *Euryalus*, and they were both on board the *Ajax* when it caught fire and exploded near the island of Tenedos on 14 Feb. 1807. He subsequently joined the *Endymion*, seeing action in the Dardanelles, and after a period in England, he was appointed to the *Warspite* under Blackwood in May 1808. Commissioned as a lieutenant in July 1809, he served in the skirmish with the Toulon fleet in July 1810, and in home waters until 1814. He went with the convoy to the Cape in the *Désirée*, returning to Britain the following year to find himself again promoted. Having commanded the *Cherokee* on the Leith station from February 1819 till at least 1822, he was in May 1827 made second captain of the *Prince Regent*, which for a while was Blackwood's flagship at the Nore. By the duke of Clarence, briefly lord high admiral, he was awarded the rank of captain, 25 Aug. 1828, but thereafter never again served at sea.[6]

A second cousin of the underage 3rd marquess of Waterford, Jones was in late 1829 considered by the family managers as a possible candidate to replace the now pro-Catholic George Dawson on their interest in county Londonderry. Henry Barré Beresford observed that 'I would think Theophilus Jones, as better known, would answer better than his brother', but considered that the 'Joneses are natives of Derry, well known and well liked and in certain parts of the county where they reside could gain many freeholders'.[7] In fact, perhaps because Theophilus held a legal appointment in the county, it was Theobald who offered at the general election in mid-1830, when he boasted that his Orange, anti-reform and retrenchment principles coincided perfectly with those of the electors.[8] Dawson's withdrawal meant that he was returned unopposed with the like-minded Sir Robert Bateson, 16 Aug. 1830, when Beresford reported that

> his speech was much approved. The uproar was great when he said he would have voted against the Roman Catholics [emancipation] bill, but it was from the lowest mob. His conduct is much approved by all and I have no doubt he will be a useful working man, diligent and persevering.[9]

Jones was expected to be 'pro-government', but Planta, the Wellington government's patronage secretary, listed him among the 'moderate Ultras' that autumn. He was noted as absent from the division on the civil list, 15 Nov. 1830, which led ministers to resign, though at the following election he asserted, apparently in vindication of his having divided with them on this occasion, that considerable economies had been made under the Tories.[10]

He attended the meeting of Apprentice Boys in Londonderry, 26 Jan. 1831, when resolutions were passed against repeal of the Union.[11] He voted silently against the second reading of the Grey ministry's reform bill, 22 Mar., but explained in a printed letter the following day that he had been unable conscientiously to support it, especially as the Irish measure would threaten the position of the church there.[12] He divided for Gascoyne's wrecking amendment, 19 Apr., which precipitated a dissolution. Calling for the preservation of the constitution inviolate, but conceding that some changes were required, he stood again for Londonderry and was returned in second place behind Bateson after a severe and violent contest against two reformers, who had government support.[13] He voted against the second reading of the reintroduced reform bill, 6 July, for using the 1831 census to determine the

boroughs in schedules A and B, 19 July, and to postpone consideration of the partial disfranchisement of Chippenham, 27 July. He defended the grant to the Kildare Place Society, 14 July, and presented a petition in its favour from Urney, 12 Aug. On Wyse introducing his Irish education bill, 8 Aug., he stated that his objection to it was 'so great and so decided' that, even if he were a junior Member, he would resist it to the full; the House was cleared for a division, but none took place. Having voted for Benett's amendment to the motion for issuing the Liverpool writ alleging that there had been gross bribery at the previous election, 5 Sept., he divided against the third reading, 19 Sept., and passage of the reform bill, 21 Sept. It was probably John Jones, Member for Carmarthen, who was granted a fortnight's leave on urgent private business, 28 Sept. 1831.

He voted against the second reading of the revised reform bill, 17 Dec. 1831, and its committal, 20 Jan. 1832. Although he was in the majority against limiting the polling in boroughs of fewer than 1,200 voters to one day, 15 Feb., he voted against the enfranchisement of Tower Hamlets, 28 Feb., and the third reading, 22 Mar. He divided against Hunt's motion for information on military punishments, 16 Feb. He brought up a petition for continuation of the grant to the Kildare Place Society, 23 Feb., and another against the government's plan for national education in Ireland, 8 Mar.; he denied that his opposition to the latter was political, 16 Mar. He supported the city petition for alteration of the grand jury laws, 5 Mar., and defended the conduct of the corporation of Londonderry, 1 June. He intervened in discussions on a case of tithes levied on a Catholic priest, 13, 30 Mar., 10 Apr., and got embroiled in a row concerning a Mayo magistrate, 3 Apr. He voted against the government amendment to the Irish arrears of tithes bill, 9 Apr., but for its general tithes bill, 13 July, and against an amendment to this measure, 1 Aug. He divided against the second reading of the Irish reform bill, 25 May, and to preserve the rights of freemen under it, 2 July, commenting on its details, 9, 25 July. He condemned the Irish party processions bill as unworkable and voted against it, 25 June. He sided with opposition against the Russian-Dutch loan, 26 Jan., 12 July. He voted against making the ecclesiastical courts bill retrospective, 3 Aug. Like his colleague he was thought likely to join the Protestant Conservative Society of Ireland that summer.[14] Beresford informed Lord Beresford, 2 June, that 'there is no doubt Jones has done his duty well, he is a zealous working man and stands high with all parties as an honest faithful representative, and he will be returned no doubt'.[15] He was duly re-elected unopposed at the general election of 1832 and sat for county Londonderry as a Conservative until his retirement in 1857.[16] He died in February 1868, presumably leaving his estate to his nephew Walter Henry Jones of 26 Upper Leeson Street, Dublin.[17] An accomplished lichenologist, who had contributed papers to the *Proceedings of the Natural History Society of Dublin*, Jones's library and valuable collection of lichens eventually passed to the National Museum.[18]

[1] IGI (co. Londonderry). [2] *Burke Commoners*, iii. 268-9; *Hist. Irish Parl.* iv. 503-7; *HP Commons, 1790-1820*, iv. 324, 327. [3] IGI (co. Londonderry) gives a speculative birth year for Theophilus of 1788. [4] Rev. J.B. Leslie, *Derry Clergy*, 303; *Hist. Irish Parl.* iii. 192. [5] *Belfast Guardian*, 22 June 1830. [6] W.R. O'Byrne, *Naval Biog.* ii. 594; Wellington mss WP1/952/4. [7] PRO NI, Primate Beresford mss D3279/A/4/39, 40. [8] PRO NI, Pack-Beresford mss D664/A/178; *Belfast News Letter*, 8 June, 13 July 1830; [W. Carpenter], *People's Bk.* (1831), 297-8. [9] *Belfast News Letter*, 20 July, 20 Aug. 1830; Pack-Beresford mss A/190. [10] *Belfast Guardian*, 20 May 1831. [11] *Belfast News Letter*, 1 Feb. 1831. [12] *Belfast Guardian*, 8 Apr. 1831. [13] Ibid. 17, 20, 24 May; *Belfast News Letter*, 17, 20, 24 May 1831. [14] NLI, Farnham mss 18611 (3), Lefroy to Farnham, 4 June 1832. [15] PRO NI, Carr Beresford mss T3396. [16] *Londonderry Sentinel*, 1, 29 Dec. 1832. [17] Ibid. 11 Feb.; *The Times*, 11 Feb. 1868; *Gent. Mag.* (1868), i. 404. [18] R.L. Praeger, *Some Irish Naturalists*, 110; R. Desmond, *Dict. British and Irish Botanists and Horticulturists*, 390.

S.M.F.

KAVANAGH, Thomas (1767–1837), of Borris House, co. Carlow.

| Co. CARLOW | 6 Apr. 1826–1831 |
| Co. CARLOW | 1835–20 Jan. 1837 |

b. 10 Mar. 1767, 4th s. of Thomas Kavanagh (*d.* 1790) of Borris and Lady Susanna Butler, da. of Walter Butler, *de jure* 16th earl of Ormonde [I]. *m.* (1) 24 Mar. 1799, his cos. Lady Elizabeth Butler (*d.* 14 Dec. 1823), da. of John Butler, MP [I], 17th earl of Ormonde [I], 1s. *d.v.p.* 9da.; (2) 28 Feb. 1825, Lady Harriet Margaret Le Poer Trench, da. of Richard Le Poer Trench†, 2nd earl of Clancarty [I], 3s. 1da. *suc.* bro. Walter Kavanagh 1813. *d.* 20 Jan. 1837.

MP [I] 1797-9.

Kavanagh, Member of the Irish House of Commons for Kilkenny, 1797-9, was a direct descendant of the ancient Catholic kings of Leinster, whose head was known as 'The MacMorrough' or 'monarch' in county Carlow. At an 'early period in his life' he entered the Austrian service, in which his uncle Field Marshal O'Kavanagh, governor of Prague, had been a 'highly distinguished' officer, and 'served throughout the war'. Following the death of his last surviving elder brother in 1813 Kavanagh, an 'unostentatious Christian' who had evidently conformed to the established church, succeeded to the family's

'extensive' estates in the counties of Carlow, Kilkenny and Wexford and so became 'one of the largest landed proprietors in Ireland'.[1] A resident landlord, he was considered 'charitable and benevolent' even by his political opponents.[2] In April 1826 he was returned unopposed on a vacancy for county Carlow, but owing to a 'severe illness' was not present to witness the rescue 'from death' of his 'personal representative' in the ensuing riot. He was too unwell to attend the general election two months later, when he came in unopposed with the sitting Member, his son-in-law Henry Bruen.[3]

Kavanagh, a lax attender, voted in the protectionist minority against the corn bill, 2 Apr. 1827. He presented a county Carlow petition for Catholic relief, 5 May, and divided thus, 12 May 1828. He denied that his constituents were 'hostile to the Catholic claims' and presented a Carlow petition in support of the Wellington ministry's concession of emancipation, 9 Mar. 1829, but was absent from the divisions on the issue that month, having been predicted to vote 'with government' by the patronage secretary Planta. He presented constituency petitions against the Subletting and Vestry Acts, 9 Mar. 1829, and the assimilation of Irish and English newspaper stamp duties, 29 May, 23 June 1830. He was granted a month's leave on account of ill health, 10 Mar., but was present to vote against reducing the grant for South African missions, 7 June. (His physician was highly recommended to the duke of Wellington by Lady Ormond that month.)[4] He presented petitions against increased taxation, 15 June, and the Irish spirit and stamp duties, 30 June 1830. At the 1830 general election he offered again for Carlow, where an opposition was started by the Catholic freeholders against the Members who 'do not represent them and who only now and then appear in Parliament to vote for ministers'. After a short contest he was returned in second place.[5] He was listed by the Wellington ministry as one of their 'friends', but was absent from the crucial division on the civil list, 15 Nov. 1830, and from those on the second reading of the Grey ministry's reform bill, 22 Mar., and Gascoyne's wrecking amendment, 19 Apr. 1831. At the ensuing dissolution Kavanagh, allegedly rather 'than risk the peace of the county', resigned, citing 'continued ill health'.[6]

At the 1832 general election he stood unsuccessfully as a Conservative for county Carlow. He was returned in 1835, but the result was challenged on petition and subject to a lengthy inquiry, during which he reminded the new premier, Sir Robert Peel, 'not to suffer to pass unnoticed and *unremedied* the outrageous practices of the Irish priests', as 'the result of future Irish elections will much materially depend on this being done'.[7] The original result being overturned he was defeated in the ensuing contest, but seated on petition later that year. Kavanagh died at Borris in January 1837. It was said of him that 'descended from a line of princes, he was princely in thought, word, and deed'. His funeral, 7 Feb. 1837, was reportedly attended by 10,000 mourners.[8] His estates and the 'MacMorrough' title passed through his two eldest sons (both of whom had died unmarried in their early twenties) to his third son Arthur (1831-89), Conservative Member for county Wexford, 1866-8, and county Carlow, 1868-80.

[1] Gent. Mag. (1837), i. 318; Burke's Irish Fam. Recs. (1976), 651-2. [2] Carlow Morning Post, 2 May 1831. [3] Westmeath Jnl. 13, 20 Apr., 8, 22 June; Wexford Evening Post, 23 June 1826. [4] Wellington mss WP1/1119/2. [5] Fitzwilliam mss, Rochfort to Milton, 7 June; Kilkenny Moderator, 11 Aug. 1830. [6] Carlow Morning Post, 28 Apr. 1831. [7] Add. 40417, f. 35. [8] Gent. Mag. (1837), i. 318

P.J.S.

KEARSLEY, John Hodson (1785–1842), of Standishgate, Wigan and Higher Hall, Westleigh, Lancs.

| WIGAN | 1 Mar. 1831–1832 |
| WIGAN | 1835–1837 |

b. 28 Feb. 1785, 3rd s. of Edward Kearsley (d. 1816), cotton manufacturer, of Aspull, nr. Wigan and Ann, da. of John Hodson of Standishgate.[1] m. (settlement) 23 Apr. 1811, Mary Anne, da. and coh. of George Bevan, attorney, of Tarbley Street and West Derby, Liverpool, s.p.[2] d. 2 Oct. 1842.

Mayor, Wigan 1813-14, 1819-20, 1825-6.

Capt. commdt. Wigan vol. light horse 1819-41.

Kearsley belonged to a family long established at Wigan and in the surrounding area of south Lancashire: they were part of the town's commercial and municipal elite by the end of the eighteenth century.[3] His father, Edward Kearsley, who was possibly the son of James Kearsley of Hulton, near Leigh, became a partner in the Wigan cotton and linen manufacturing business of his brother-in-law John Hodson of Ellerbeck, Member for Wigan, 1802-20. It is not clear whether he was also involved in the Manchester cotton manufacturing enterprise of James, Josiah (his brother), John and Edward Kearsley. John Hodson Kearsley, the third of his five sons, did not enter the trade, but took a partnership in the Wigan brewery of Henry Robinson and Company.[4] In 1811 he married the heiress Mary Anne Bevan, who owned prop-

erty in Wigan, Preston, Liverpool, Ireland and the West Indies, and soon afterwards came into her only sister's inheritance of property in Wigan, Hindley, Chorley, Adlington and Preston.[5] Kearsley's father, who was the leaseholder of New Brook House, Over Hulton, died in 1816, not long after his uncle Josiah of Manchester. By his father's will, Kearsley received an equal share with his seven siblings in a trust fund of almost £52,000, and by his great-uncle's a legacy of £1,000.[6] He was one of the prime movers in the formation of the Wigan volunteer light horse to combat unrest in the aftermath of Peterloo, and he commanded the regiment for over 20 years.[7]

As mayor of Wigan he presided at the general election of 1820, when his cousin James Alexander Hodson (John Hodson's nephew) and Lord Lindsay, son of the 6th earl of Balcarres, were returned after a contest; and that of 1826, when, Lindsay having succeeded to the peerage the previous year, his cousin James Lindsay came in unopposed with Hodson.[8] Shortly before the general election of 1830 the ailing Hodson indicated to his ally Balcarres that he wished to retire from Parliament, but could name none of his relatives as a replacement. He said that Kearsley, an obvious candidate, had 'become an active partner' in the brewery and would be too busy; and Kearsley himself was supposed to have assured Balcarres that he would not come forward. Hodson was persuaded to stand again with Lindsay, but on the day of the election, when the sitting Members faced a contest forced by dissidents who wished to extend the franchise to the ratepayers, Kearsley, to universal surprise, nominated himself with Hodson and attacked Lindsay as an aristocratic nominee and supporter of Catholic emancipation. In the ensuing poll Kearsley, who voted for himself and Hodson and received the votes of his brothers James and Thomas, came a distant third.[9] He had apparently already canvassed Wigan when Hodson told Balcarres in early November 1830 that he intended to retire. As Hodson's substitute, he defended the 1830 return against the petition of their radical opponents.[10] When Hodson vacated as soon as his election was confirmed in late February 1831 he stood and easily defeated one of the petitioners of 1830 in a poll held before a large hostile crowd. Kearsley, who was reported to have professed support for ending the East India Company's trade monopoly, was hit in the face by a stone when leaving the hustings.[11] He voted against the second reading of the Grey ministry's reform bill, 22 Mar., and for Gascoyne's wrecking amendment, 19 Apr. 1831, when he was added to the committee on the bill to revise the regulations governing the employment of apprentices in cotton and other factories. At the ensuing general election he stood again for Wigan, but such was the popular fury against him that he 'did not dare appear for fear of being murdered'. He was returned second in the poll behind a reformer. An angry mob smashed the windows of his town house in Standishgate, which was ransacked and wrecked in another attack three weeks later. He was forced to live thereafter at Higher Hall, six miles south-east of Wigan.[12] The story that the rioters 'got possession of his will, and read it aloud at the market cross', thereby fomenting 'dissension in the family', is almost certainly apocryphal.[13]

Kearsley proved to be 'the most singular' Member 'for many years past', as one commentator recalled in 1838:

> Mr. Kearsley's personal appearance is so much out of the beaten track, and is so expressive of his character, that it might be said, whenever he stood up in his full altitude, to constitute a speech in itself. I have seen him occasionally stand for a short time without uttering a word, and yet the eye of every honourable Member has been intently fixed on him as if he had been giving utterance to the most fascinating strains of eloquence that ever fell from mortal lips. And what may appear still more surprising, honourable gentlemen were delighted to see him rise, though they knew that when he did put himself into a perpendicular position, he never delivered half-a-dozen sentences. He had such a comfortable notion of his own senatorial qualifications, and this notion was so vividly imprinted on his little round pug-looking face, that it was impossible to look on him and not be pleased ... Never was man on better terms with himself ... A most expressive look of self-complacency always irradiated his globularly-formed, country-complexioned countenance; while his small bright eyes were ever peering triumphantly over his little cocked-up nose. Then there was his ample harvest of black, bushy hair, with a pair of excellent whiskers to match, not forgetting his well-developed cheeks. He is a little thick-set man, with an inclination to corpulency ... He never made a speech, and yet he often spoke ... A speech, according to the generally received acceptation of the term, has a beginning, a middle, and an end. This could not be predicated of anything which ever fell from the lips of Mr. Kearsley. His oratorical efforts had no middle; they were all beginning and end; the end being invariably the same as the beginning. In other words, Mr. Kearsley's addresses to the House always consisted of a single idea, and seldom of more sentences than one, though the reporters sometimes did such violence to prosody as to divide such sentence into two or three sentences. His ambition as a senator never soared any higher than to throw in, by way of episode to any discussion, some severe solitary observation on ministers, or on some of their supporters ... I never yet knew him open his mouth without setting the whole House in an uproar. Mr. Kearsley ... always contrived to speak at the same

hour. That hour was nine o'clock, that being the time he usually returned from dinner ... Nor do I recollect, except when there was to be a division on some important question, seeing him in the House after eleven.[14]

He divided against the second reading of the reintroduced reform bill, 6 July, and for at least four of the opposition adjournment motions, 12 July 1831. He voted for use of the census of 1831 to determine the borough disfranchisement schedules, 19 July, to postpone discussion of allocating Chippenham to schedule B, 27 July, and against the bill's passage, 21 Sept. He voted for inquiry into the effects of renewing the Sugar Refinery Act on the West India interest and to go into committee on the truck bill, 12 Sept. He was in the minority for ending the grant to Maynooth, 26 Sept. He presented a petition from Wigan for amendment of the Beer Act, 7 Oct. He voted against the second reading of the revised reform bill, 17 Dec. 1831, and the motion to go into committee on it, 20 Jan. 1832. He divided against government on the Russian-Dutch loan, 26 Jan. On 6 Feb. he seized on Thomas Duncombe's complaint that this issue had been raised 'as a means of tripping up' the ministry to observe that 'a government which can be so easily tripped up must be rotten indeed'. Edward Littleton* recorded that on 20 Feb. he travelled to London in the same coach as Kearsley's brother-in-law, the Rev. Thomas Pigot, vicar of St. Helens, whom he left at Islington but discovered later that day under the gallery of the Commons with Kearsley:

> The little brewer, who is a very violent vulgar little fellow, and an immoderate fool, thought he must show off to his relation in his grand character as legislator, and so went into his place, and made a short speech amidst roars of laughter at his language and manner, to the apparently deep mortification of his relation and guest.[15]

No intervention by Kearsley was reported that day, unless he was the unidentified Member who repudiated the extreme allegations of cruelty to children employed in cotton mills. Littleton may, however, have been referring to an episode on the 21st, when, having apparently responded to a speech by Sheil calling for the complete disfranchisement of Petersfield with certain 'musical exclamations' which were sarcastically noticed by Smith Stanley, the Irish secretary, he thanked the latter for his 'handsome compliment' and assured him that 'if it please God to spare my life' he would again hear 'that musical voice which so peculiarly struck him'. He voted against the enfranchisement of Tower Hamlets, 28 Feb. On 1 Mar. he condemned the government's handling of the silk industry as 'most improper' and asserted that 'there is not one merchant in the metropolis who places the least confidence in such "a Noodle and Doodle administration"'. In a debate on the reform bill the following day he said that ministers were

capable of saying anything whatever. One says, 'Wait until this reform bill is passed; be quiet, and we shall have what we want'. A second says, 'I will swallow anything, in order to support the reform bill'. A third says, 'I have voted black is white'; and a fourth adds, 'I have waded through the dirtiest job I ever had to encounter during the whole of my parliamentary career'.

After expressing mock concern that one of the participants in exchanges on Irish education had exhibited 'the incipient symptoms of cholera', 6 Mar., he observed, to 'loud laughter', that if the king 'called upon him to give his services, than which many things more unlikely had come to pass, the first thing he would do would be to order the "Rogue's March" to be beat for both parties'.[16] Supporting a Wigan mill owners' petition against Sadler's factories regulation bill, 8 Mar., he argued that 'any legislative interference on the subject will not only be detrimental to the real interests of the lower orders, but an act of injustice to the master spinners'. On the same theme, 16 Mar., he hoped that the measure would 'not be submitted to the investigation of a packed committee' and told Lord William Lennox, whom he had earlier interrupted, that he 'knows nothing whatever about cotton mills, nor indeed about anything else'. Lennox retorted that it would be 'far more parliamentary' for Kearsley to 'expose my mistakes in one of his speeches, so full of eloquence, and infinitely preferable to the unknown tongues of groans he so often indulges in'. Kearsley voted against the third reading of the reform bill, 22 Mar. Next day, ostensibly seconding Waldo Sibthorp's amendment to preserve the rights of Lincoln freeholders, he denounced 'this damnable bill'. According to Hawkins, Member for Tavistock, who described Kearsley as 'the impersonation of vulgarity, known in the House by his singular cheer, and a very un-senatorial addiction to inebriety', the Speaker 'stood for five minutes before his chair laughing, before he could summon a sufficient command of countenance to call the orator to order'.[17] Kearsley pressed on regardless:

Having carefully examined this bill, I have come to the conclusion that its complexion has very much varied since I had first the misfortune to look upon it. I can perceive in it the colours of black, brown, and grey, but nothing fair. It is an infernal pill, composed of two ingredients, in themselves most pernicious ... One of these venomous ingredients is called 'the Russell brown'; and the other is found on a certain tree, with a dingy-coloured stem, and a black top-knot, and it is called 'the Durham mustard'.

He was in the minority of 27. He divided against the second reading of the Irish reform bill, 25 May. He voted against government on the Russian-Dutch loan, 12 and 16 July, when he observed that his speeches were 'like angels' visits, few and far between', and not quite pertinently criticized ministers for their 'frequent desecrations of the Sabbath'. He voted in the minority against Hume's motion for leave to introduce a bill to disqualify the recorder of Dublin from sitting in the Commons, 24 July. When Burge insisted that he did not wish to 'take the sense of the House' on his proposal to reduce the duty on vinegar, 25 July 1832, Kearsley said that 'all the sense of the House is on this side' and complained that the reform bill had 'destroyed my property and done me all sorts of injury'.

He stood for Wigan at the general election of 1832, but finished bottom of the poll behind three Liberals.[18] He regained the seat in 1835, but lost it in 1837. He was defeated by two votes in a poll of 520 at a by-election in March 1839, and unsuccessfully petitioned. He decided against standing again in 1841.[19] Kearsley, who was widowed in 1837, died childless at Higher Hall in October 1842. By his will, dated 21 June 1842, he devised the Brickhouse estate at Westleigh to Alice, Ann and Jane Finch, who were then living with him, together with life annuities of £100, £100 and £150 respectively. He bequeathed a life annuity of £80 to Ellen Gregory, who also lived with him. He set up a trust fund of £5,000 for his brother Thomas, a recently bankrupt cotton spinner of Tyldesley, and made arrangements for a residuary fund to provide for his three other surviving siblings and the children of his late brother Josiah and sister Mary Anne Pigot.[20] An obituarist wrote that

his charity was unbounded, and the never-forgotten recipients of his bounteous liberality, the poor of Wigan and its neighbourhood, may mourn indeed in bitter grief for the loss of their best friend and benefactor. Seldom has an instance occurred in the neighbourhood, where the hand of death has spread a heavier gloom.[21]

[1] Lancs. RO, Hindley par. reg. [2] Lancs. RO, Mary Anne Kearsley's will; IGI (Lancs.). [3] G.T.O. Bridgeman, *Hist. Church and Manor of Wigan* (Chetham Soc. n. s. xvii), 595. [4] *Gent. Mag.* (1842), ii. 548; *Manchester Guardian*, 7 May 1831. [5] Mary Anne Kearsley's will. [6] *Gent. Mag.* (1816), i. 570; PROB 11/1580/263; 1584/530; IR26/683/876. [7] G. Derbyshire, *Wigan Military Chron.* i. 70. [8] NLS, Crawford mss 25/13/348. [9] Ibid. 25/13/353; *Manchester Guardian*, 31 July, 7 Aug.; *Wigan Pollbook* (1830). [10] Crawford mss 25/13/352, 354; *CJ*, lxxxvi. 65, 147-8. [11] *Bolton Chron.* 5 Mar. 1831. [12] Crawford mss 25/13/356; *VCH Lancs.* iii. 424; *Bolton Chron.* 30 Apr., 7, 14, 28 May; *Manchester Guardian*, 7 May; *Liverpool Mercury*, 13 May 1831. [13] *Moore Jnl.* iv. 1462-3. [14] [James Grant], *Random Recollections of Lords and Commons* (1838), ii. 29-34. [15] Hatherton

diary, 20 Feb. 1832. ¹⁶ *The Times*, 7 Mar. 1832. ¹⁷ Cornw. RO, Hawkins mss 10/2189. ¹⁸ *The Times*, 11-13 Dec. 1832. ¹⁹ Crawford mss 25/13/112-14. ²⁰ Lancs. RO, Kearsley's will; IR26/1648/114; *The Times*, 16 Apr. 1842. ²¹ *Gent. Mag.* (1842), ii. 548-9.

S.R.B./D.R.F.

KECK see LEGH KECK

KEKEWICH, Samuel Trehawke (1796–1873), of Peamore House, nr. Exeter, Devon.

EXETER	9 Feb. 1826–1830
DEVON SOUTH	6 Aug. 1858–1 June 1873

b. 31 Oct. 1796, o.s. of Samuel Kekewich of Bowden House, Totnes and Salome, da. of George Sweet of Tiverton. *educ.* Eton 1811-14; Christ Church, Oxf. 1814. *m.* (1) 3 Apr. 1820, Agatha Maria Sophia (*d.* 24 Sept. 1836), da. of John Langston of Sarsden, Oxon., 3s. (1 *d.v.p.*) 4da. (1 *d.v.p.*); (2) 9 June 1840, Louisa, da. of Lewis William Buck*, 1s. 3da. *suc.* fa. 1822. *d.* 1 June 1873.
   Sheriff, Devon 1834-5.

Kekewich's family, originally from Lancashire, had settled in Cornwall in the early sixteenth century, but by the eighteenth they resided in London, where his grandfather, William Kekewich, was a member of the Royal Exchange Assurance. His father, a barrister, acquired the Peamore estate, served as sheriff of Devon in 1805 and was remembered at Exeter for his charitable munificence.¹ Kekewich inherited Peamore in 1822 but had otherwise been 'sufficiently provided for by the settlements made on his marriage', according to his father's will.² In August 1825 he announced his candidature for Exeter at the next general election on the principle of 'strict independence ... unshackled by any party consideration whatever'. He was returned unopposed at a by-election in February 1826, caused by the sudden resignation of one of the Members, after admitting that he needed to master the currency question, hinting that he favoured a reduction in the corn duties and declaring his opposition to Catholic relief, while giving no pledges.³ His conduct in the House was markedly independent. He divided with Lord Liverpool's ministry against inquiry into the Jamaican slave trials, 2 Mar., and reform of Edinburgh's representation, 13 Apr., but was in the minorities for abolishing flogging in the army, 10 Mar., inquiring into the treasurership of the navy, 7 Apr., revising the corn laws, 18 Apr., and allowing defence by counsel in felony trials, 25 Apr. 1826. He was returned unopposed for Exeter at the general election that summer, when he confirmed his opposition to Catholic relief and support for relaxation of the corn laws, maintained

that he was 'not opposed in principle to the extinction of slavery', although the issue 'should not be precipitated', and admitted that he did not find the question of parliamentary reform 'a matter of great facility'.⁴

He divided against Catholic relief, 6 Mar. 1827, 12 May 1828. He presented petitions for repeal of the Test Acts, 31 May, 12 June 1827,⁵ and voted in this sense, 26 Feb., but presented a hostile petition from the Exeter chamber, 18 Mar. 1828. He voted against Canning's ministry for the disfranchisement of Penryn, 28 May, but with them for the grant to improve water communications in Canada, 12 June 1827. He opposed the duke of Wellington's ministry by voting against extending the East Retford franchise to Bassetlaw freeholders, 21 Mar., 27 June, and for a lower pivot price for the corn laws, 22 Apr. 1828. He attended the Exeter meeting to uphold the Protestant constitution, 15 Nov. 1828, when he announced that 'I fully concur in the petition you have adopted'.⁶ However, Planta, the patronage secretary, mentioned him as a possible mover or seconder of the address in January 1829, and the following month predicted that he would side 'with government' for Catholic emancipation. In presenting anti-Catholic petitions from the Exeter meeting and from the chamber, 2 Mar., Kekewich explained that 'my own opinions ... are not decidedly made up' and that he would judge the issue 'upon the grounds of the preservation and protection of ... [the] Protestant religion'. In the event, he divided for emancipation, 6, 30 Mar., and his effigy was burned at Exeter.⁷ He voted to reduce the grant for the sculpture of the marble arch, 25 May, and presented an Exeter petition for repeal of the coastwise coal duty, 28 May 1829. He divided against Lord Blandford's reform motion, 18 Feb., but for the enfranchisement of Birmingham, Leeds and Manchester, 23 Feb., and the transfer of East Retford's seats to Birmingham, 5, 15 Mar. 1830. He voted against Jewish emancipation, 17 May. He replied to an Exeter requisition in March by stating that he favoured repeal of the 'most partial and oppressive' coal duty and desired to lessen the burden of other taxes, but that he entertained 'great doubts whether (after the reduction which has already taken place) it would be ... conducive to the public interest to support any immediate remission of such taxes, unless ... by substituting a ... tax upon property ... to which I should most unwillingly consent'.⁸ Nevertheless, he voted with the Whig opposition to abolish the Bathurst and Dundas pensions, 26 Mar., reduce the grant for public buildings, 3 May, repeal the Irish coal duties, 13 May, inquire into privy councillors' emoluments, 14 May, and reduce the grant for consular services, 11 June. He presented an Exeter petition for abolition of the death penalty for forgery, 29 Mar., and voted in this sense, 24 May, 7 June 1830.

In late June 1830 Kekewich announced that he would not stand at the impending general election, having reluctantly decided that it was his 'duty to make a sacrifice of public ambition to considerations of a private character'. He trusted that 'those from whom I may have had the misfortune to differ will ... give me credit for the integrity of my motives'.[9] He stood unsuccessfully for Liskeard as a Conservative in 1835 and 1837, but was returned for South Devon in 1858. He died in June 1873 and the Peamore estate passed to his eldest son Trehawke Kekewich (1823-1909). His son from his second marriage was Sir George Kekewich (1841-1921), secretary to the education department and Conservative Member for Exeter, 1906-10.

[1] *Trewman's Exeter Flying Post*, 18 Aug. 1825. [2] The personalty was sworn under £16,000 (PROB 11/1663/596; IR26/918/987). [3] *Alfred*, 16, 30 Aug. 1825, 7, 14 Feb. 1826. [4] Ibid. 6, 13 June 1826. [5] *The Times*, 1, 13 June 1827. [6] *Woolmer's Exeter and Plymouth Gazette*, 22 Nov. 1828. [7] Bucks. RO, Fremantle mss D/FR/139/10/29. [8] *Western Times*, 27 Mar., 10 Apr. 1830. [9] *Woolmer's Exeter and Plymouth Gazette*, 3 July 1830.

T.A.J.

KEMEYS TYNTE, Charles Kemeys (1778–1860), of Halswell House, Goathurst, Som.; Cefn Mably, Glam.; Burhill, nr. Cobham, Surr., and 16 Hill Street, Hanover Square, Mdx.

BRIDGWATER   1820–1837

b. 29 May 1778, o.s. of John Johnson (afterwards Kemeys Tynte) of Burhill and Jane, da. of Ruisshe Hassell, maj. R. Horse Gds., niece and h. of Sir Charles Kemeys Tynte, 5th bt.†, of Halswell and Cefn Mably. *educ.* Eton 1791; St. John's, Camb. 1795. *m.* 25 Apr. 1798, Anne, da. of Rev. Thomas Leyson of Bassaleg, Mon., wid. of Thomas Lewis of St. Pierre, Mon., 1s. 4da. (1 *d.v.p.*). *suc.* fa. 1806. *d.* 23 Nov. 1860.
Sheriff, Som. 1808-9.
Lt.-col. W. Som. yeomanry cav. 1803, col. 1835.
Provincial grand master of freemasons 1820.[1]

Kemeys Tynte's father, a colonel in the Grenadier Guards who was appointed comptroller of the household of the prince of Wales in 1791, had changed his name by royal licence in 1785 on inheriting the estates of his wife's uncle, which comprised the extensive properties of two very old parliamentary families, the Kemeys of Glamorganshire and the Tyntes of Somerset. Charles was the residuary legatee of his father's estate, which was sworn under £10,000 in June

1806.[2] At the general election of 1820 he was invited to contest Bridgwater 'free of all expense' by the Foxite 'independent' party, after a deal had been struck with one of the sitting Members, William Astell, and the corporation interest. He was duly returned unopposed, pledged to support 'the cause of political integrity and independence', disclaiming 'a bigotted adherence to any party or any set of men' and declaring his warm attachment to 'the glorious constitution under which we live'.[3]

He was not the most assiduous of attenders, but he acted consistently with the Whig opposition to Lord Liverpool's ministry on all major issues, including parliamentary reform, 31 May 1821, 24 Apr. 1823. He was granted a month's leave for urgent private business, 15 Feb., and therefore missed the division on Catholic relief, 28 Feb. 1821, but he voted for it, 21 Apr., 10 May 1825. In presenting a Bridgwater petition in support of Queen Caroline, 24 Jan. 1821, he declared that the proceedings against her were 'in opposition to the established laws of the country' and represented 'a violent attack upon the constitution'. He supported inquiry into the Peterloo massacre, 16 May 1821, but was anxious to 'eulogise the yeomanry as a most valuable and peculiarly constitutional force' and said that they were 'the only party that could be entirely exculpated' from blame for the events at Manchester. In January 1822 he attended a public meeting at Taunton where he expressed support for a petition for relief from agricultural distress.[4] He argued that 'retrenchment ought to begin by the abolition of sinecures and the reduction of pensions', 15 Feb.[5] He defended the conduct of the Somerset magistrates in relation to the scandal at Ilchester gaol, 10 May 1822, contending that 'so general a charge ought not to be made' as 'many were not implicated in the transactions complained of'. He was granted a month's leave for urgent private business, 14 Feb. 1825. In February 1826 he was requisitioned to stand again for Bridgwater at the next general election and responded with a lengthy address announcing that despite his personal wish to retire from parliamentary life, with its attendant 'interruption to all domestic and social habits ... fatigue and injury to health' and other 'vexatious circumstances' which made it 'extremely irksome to me', he felt it his 'principal duty to submit to your wishes'.[6] At the dissolution in June handbills were circulated in the borough condemning his support for Catholic relief, and a 'Protestant' candidate was eventually found to stand against him, but his alliance with Astell remained firm and he was comfortably returned in second place.[7]

He voted to disfranchise Penryn, 28 May 1827. He divided for repeal of the Test Acts, 26 Feb., and Catholic relief, 12 May 1828. In February 1829 Planta, the Wellington ministry's patronage secretary, listed him as likely to be 'with government' for Catholic emancipation, and he duly voted for it, 6 Mar. He presented a Bridgwater petition for repeal of the house and window taxes, 12 Mar. 1829. He divided for Knatchbull's amendment to the address on distress, 4 Feb., and was granted a month's leave for urgent private business, 2 Mar. 1830. In presenting a Bridgwater licensed victuallers' petition against the sale of beer bill, 27 Apr., he stated that the petitioners also wished to have cider sellers put on the same footing as beer sellers, and observed that since the reduction in the cider tax there had been 'about a hundred little cider shops established in the town and immediate neighbourhood by the lowest description of persons, tending to demoralize the lower orders and increase pauperism'. He divided against the bill, 4 May, and paired for the amendment to prohibit on-consumption, 21 June. He voted to abolish the Irish lord lieutenancy, 11 May, for information on privy councillors' emoluments, 14 May, and reduction of the grant for South American missions, 7 June 1830, when he divided to abolish the death penalty for forgery. At the general election that summer he was again invited to stand for Bridgwater at no expense and was returned unopposed with Astell, boasting afterwards that it was 'without precedent in the annals of parliamentary history' for a Member to be elected 'for the same seat, a third time successively, at the call and by the unsolicited and free voice of the people'.[8]

The Wellington ministry listed Kemeys Tynte among the 'doubtful doubtfuls', with the optimistic parenthetical remark that he was 'a friend'. He was absent from the crucial civil list division, 15 Nov. 1830. He presented a Bridgwater anti-slavery petition, 18 Nov., and was granted a fortnight's leave on account of 'the disturbed state of his neighbourhood', 6 Dec. 1830. He presented a Bridgwater petition in favour of parliamentary reform, 1 Mar., and divided for the second reading of the Grey ministry's bill, 22 Mar., and against Gascoyne's wrecking amendment, 19 Apr. 1831. At the ensuing dissolution he received a requisition from Bridgwater signed by some 200 electors, which praised the 'steady, consistent and manly course you have pursued during this eventful period'. He campaigned independently of Astell, who was being challenged by another reformer, and said he looked forward to the bill's passage inaugurating an era of 'purity of election, confidence between representatives and electors, honest votes in Parliament, abolition of sinecure places and unmerited pensions, abolition of slavery and reduction of taxes'. He was returned at the head of the poll and promised to 'discharge my future duties in such a manner as may ... tend to the honour and dignity of the crown' and 'the support of the constitution'.[9] He divided for the second reading of the reintroduced reform bill, 6 July, supported its details in committee and voted for its passage, 21 Sept., and Lord Ebrington's confidence motion, 10 Oct. 1831. He voted to punish only those guilty of bribery at the Dublin election, 23 Aug. It was reported that his name was on the list for a coronation peerage, recommended by the duke of Sussex, but in the hasty arrangements that followed this was apparently 'refused'. His name continued to be mentioned in connection with the possible mass creation of peers by the government, and it was observed that 'his income amounts to more than twice the sum adequate to the support of the dignity of the peerage'.[10] He divided for the second reading of the revised reform bill, 17 Dec. 1831, supported it in committee and voted for the third reading, 22 Mar. 1832. He voted for Ebrington's motion for an address asking the king to appoint only ministers committed to carrying an unimpaired reform measure, 10 May. He paired against increasing Scotland's representation, 1 June. He divided with ministers on the Russian-Dutch loan, 26 Jan., and relations with Portugal, 9 Feb. 1832.

Kemeys Tynte was returned unopposed for Bridgwater at the general election of 1832 and sat, entertaining 'Whig opinions',[11] until his retirement in 1837. He belatedly joined Brooks's Club, 22 Feb. 1834. In 1845 the House of Lords committee of privileges declared him to be senior co-heir to the barony of Wharton, but no further proceedings were taken to revive this title in his lifetime and it was not until 1916 that his great-grandson was summoned to the Lords as the 8th baron. He died in November 1860 and was succeeded by his son, Charles Kemeys Tynte (1800-82), Liberal Member for West Somerset, 1832-37, and Bridgwater, 1847-65. It appears that he had several illegitimate children with Elizabeth Drewe, who went under the name 'Dowdney'.[12]

[1] *Bristol Mirror*, 30 Sept. 1820; *Gent. Mag.* (1861), i. 112. [2] PROB 11/1445/517; IR26/112/327. [3] Add. 51830, Symes to Holland, 26 Feb.; *Taunton Courier*, 23 Feb., 8 Mar. 1820. [4] *Taunton Courier*, 16 Jan. 1822. [5] *The Times*, 16 Feb. 1822. [6] Som. RO, Kemeys Tynte mss DD/S/WH 351; *Taunton Courier*, 15 Feb. 1826. [7] *Taunton Courier*, 14, 21 June 1826. [8] Ibid. 30 June, 7, 28 July, 4 Aug. 1830. [9] Kemeys Tynte mss DD/S/WH 352; *Bridgwater Herald*, 4 May; *Taunton Courier*, 18 May 1831. [10] *Bristol Mirror*, 13 Aug.; Heron, *Notes*, 199; Arundel Castle mss MD 2613, anon. to Burdett, 31 Oct. 1831. [11] *Dod's Parl. Companion* (1833), 169. [12] Kemeys Tynte mss, introduction to catalogue.

T.A.J.

KEMMIS, Thomas Arthur (1806–1858), of 98 Mount Street, Mdx.

EAST LOOE 1830–1832

b. 16 Mar. 1806, o.s. of Henry Kemmis, barrister, of Dublin and Maria, da. of Arthur Dawson, MP [I], of Castle Dawson, co. Londonderry. *educ.* Eton 1820-3; Christ Church, Oxf. 1825. *m.* 14 Sept. 1833, Henrietta Anne, da. of Charles Kemeys Kemeys Tynte*, 1s. *suc.* fa. 1857. *d.* 25 Dec. 1858.
Lt. 1 Ft. Gds. 1826, capt. 1830, half-pay 1834, ret. by 1844.

Kemmis belonged to a branch of the family (the name was otherwise spelt Kemeys) who came originally from Monmouthshire and settled in Ireland in the eighteenth century. His grandfather, also Thomas (1753-1823), held the office of Irish crown solicitor from 1801, and his father, who sat in the Irish Parliament for Tralee, 1798-1800, and supported the Union, subsequently practised at the Irish bar, took silk and chaired the Dublin quarter sessions.[1] Kemmis abandoned university for a military career and, while still a serving officer in the Guards, was returned unopposed for East Looe at the general election of 1830. His colleague Henry Thomas Hope, whose father had recently acquired a controlling interest in the borough, had been an Eton contemporary.[2]

The duke of Wellington's ministry regarded him as one of their 'friends' (his maternal uncle was Peel's brother-in-law George Dawson*, secretary to the treasury), and he voted with them in the crucial civil list division, 15 Nov. 1830. A week later he wrote to his mother:

> This country will owe much gratitude to any ministers who can ward off the impending storm, and I shall be glad of the change if those who succeed them show any capacity in managing affairs, for it is much more important to us all to see the country saved from revolution ... I am convinced that tranquillity will not be re-established until the higher classes make sacrifices which at present do not enter their thoughts. Although favourable to prerogative I hate practical oppression and most certainly the lower classes of this country suffer under it more than the labourers of despotic kingdoms.

He thought that if the Tories 'return within a year I shall not be sorry, as to have begun in opposition gives one a better chance of getting on in the House'. Following the introduction of the Grey ministry's reform bill he reported, 9 Mar. 1831, that

> the excitement here is extreme, nothing but the bill is talked about and no one gives a fair opinion. Those who are independent tell you their wishes when you ask their

opinions and the county Members who are in fear of dissolution will not speak out. I believe there are about 100 persons in that situation, wishing but afraid to vote against the bill, and their uncertainty makes each party claim the future victory. To my mind the argument is very simple, viz., whether society after 1831 will bear what has failed in all ages before 1831? I was thinking of speaking upon it ... thinking that it was unlucky for Henry Hope [who had recently succeeded his father] to have, at such a crisis, returned a Member who gave no assistance to his cause ... I sit more among the Tories than he does, the Tories who have not forgiven the apostates ... Yesterday when Mr. Praed attributed the present state of things to their yielding [Catholic] emancipation ... I thought him partly right, for though I do not attribute the feeling of the people to it, I think it the cause of the weakness of government.[3]

He divided against the bill's second reading, 22 Mar., and for Gascoyne's wrecking amendment, 19 Apr. 1831. At the ensuing general election he again came in unopposed for East Looe. He voted against the second reading of the reintroduced reform bill, 6 July, and in the minorities for Gordon's adjournment motion, 12 July, and use of the 1831 census to determine the disfranchisement schedules, 19 July. During the discussion on the proposed disfranchisement of East Looe, 22 July, he replied to Daniel O'Connell's jibe against its close borough status with a reference to the large number of Irish seats under his own 'nomination'. He voted to postpone consideration of the partial disfranchisement of Chippenham, 27 July, and against the bill's third reading, 19 Sept., and passage, 21 Sept. He paired against the second reading of the revised reform bill, 17 Dec. 1831, and divided against the enfranchisement of Tower Hamlets, 28 Feb., the third reading, 22 Mar., and the second reading of the Irish bill, 25 May 1832. He voted against ministers on the Russian-Dutch loan, 26 Jan. He defended the retention of flogging in the army as a punishment of last resort, 2 Apr., and recommended that courts martial be allowed greater powers to order custodial sentences, 19 June. He divided in the minority against a bill to ban Orange marches in Ireland, 25 June 1832.

Following the disfranchisement of East Looe Kemmis made no known attempt to continue his parliamentary career. Through his marriage to the daughter of Charles Kemeys Tynte* he forged a link with an English branch of his family, and by 1845 he was resident at Croham Hurst, near Croydon, Surrey, of which county he became a magistrate. On his father's death in 1857 he received a share of the family estates in King's County (Offaly), Queen's County (Leix), and counties Louth and Dublin.[4] He died in December

1858 and left a life interest in his Surrey property to his widow and his landed estates at Longford, Queen's County and Darrow, King's County, to his only child Arthur Henry Nicholas Kemmis (1834-1918).[5]

[1] W. Kemmis, *Fam. of Kemmis*, 1-5, 39-40; C.G. Bolton, 'Parl. Background to Irish Act of Union' (Oxford Univ. D. Phil. thesis, 1959), 47 and app.; *Gent. Mag.* (1857), i. 629. [2] *West Briton*, 13 Aug. 1830. [3] Cornw. RO FS/3/1092/9, 19. [4] *Gent. Mag.* (1859), i. 218; PROB 11/2255/555; IR26/2105/662. [5] Kemmis, 48.

H.J.S./T.A.J.

KEMP, **Thomas Read** (1782–1844), of Dale Park, Lewes Castle and Brighton, Suss.

LEWES	10 May 1811–28 Feb. 1816
ARUNDEL	21 Feb. 1823–1826
LEWES	1826–14 Apr. 1837

b. 23 Dec. 1782, o. surv. s. of Thomas Kemp† of Lewes and Ann, da. and h. of Henry Read of Brookland. *educ.* Westminster 1797; St. John's, Camb. 1801; M. Temple 1804. *m.* (1) 12 July 1806, Frances (*d.* 8 Mar. 1825), da. of Sir Francis Baring†, 1st bt., of Stratton Park, Hants, 4s. 6da.; (2) 26 Nov. 1832, Frances Margaretta, da. of Charles Watkin John Shakerley of Somerford, Cheshire, wid. of Vigors Harvey of Killaine Castle, co. Wexford, 1s. *suc.* fa. 1811. *d.* 20 Dec. 1844.
Lt. Ringmer yeoman cav. 1804-7.
Commr. Brighton 1825-7.

Kemp had resigned his Lewes seat in 1816 to join his brother-in-law the Rev. George Baring in founding a religious sect, which 'attracted notoriety, chiefly from the rank and fortune of some of ... its most prominent members'. Doctrinal details are sketchy, but it appears that Unitarian sentiment motivated their secession from the established church. As the 'leading citizen' in Brighton and Lewes, Kemp provided places of worship there and was a regular preacher, though he was no great orator. Disillusion with the vagaries of some of his co-religionists seems to have prompted his return to the Anglican fold in 1823, when he resumed a fashionable lifestyle and his political interests; the sect disintegrated two years later.[1] It was also in 1823 that work began on 'Kemptown', a development of over 100 large houses to the east of Brighton on land which Kemp held as joint lord of the manor. Financial necessity may have given rise to this speculation, as he had apparently run though much of his personal fortune as well as his wife's. The Nash-inspired estate was subsequently described as 'one of the most magnificent assemblages of private dwellings in the kingdom', but the houses were not taken up in large numbers until after 1830, by which time Kemp had been obliged to sell many of them incomplete, leaving others to realize the profits. Lack of funds prevented the completion of the project on the grand scale first envisaged, and scuppered plans for a similar venture on the other side of Brighton, giving credence to one historian's assessment that Kemp possessed 'no business capacity whatsover'. Similarly uncompleted was 'The Temple', the Brighton house where he resided after selling Hurstmonceaux Park in 1819. Replete with architectural eccentricities, this was built to the dimensions of Solomon's Temple, perhaps betraying the enthusiasm for freemasonry which led to his appointment as deputy grandmaster in Sussex. By 1827 he had ceased to live there, having adopted one of the Kemptown houses as his Brighton residence.[2] In 1822 he purchased Dale Park, possibly with a view to cultivating an interest at nearby Arundel. A vacancy for the borough occurred the following year and Kemp, professing 'the moderate principles of a Whig', was comfortably returned ahead of a radical.[3]

He was a fairly regular attender who voted with the Whig opposition to Lord Liverpool's ministry on most major issues. He would have divided for parliamentary reform, 24 Apr., had he not been shut out,[4] but did so, 2 June 1823, 27 Apr. 1826. However, he voted against Catholic relief, 21 Apr. 1825, as he had during his previous spell in the Commons. On 4 May 1824 he introduced a bill to establish a national registry of births, marriages and deaths, but it did not progress beyond its first reading.[5] Later that year he declined an invitation to contest New Shoreham and signalled his intention of returning to his former seat at Lewes, where his strong interest ensured that he topped the poll at the general election of 1826.[6] Having severed his connection with Arundel, he sold Dale Park to John Smith* the following year. He presented a Lewes anti-Catholic petition, 2 Mar.,[7] and divided against relief, 6 Mar. 1827. He presented a Sussex petition for relief of the landed interest, 27 Mar.,[8] and voted for information on the conduct of the Lisburn magistrates towards an Orange march, 29 Mar. 1827. He divided for repeal of the Test Acts, 26 Feb., but against Catholic relief, 12 May 1828. He opposed the duke of Wellington's ministry by voting against restricting the circulation of Scottish and Irish small notes, 5 June, and the additional churches bill, 30 June 1828. In February 1829 Planta, the patronage secretary, predicted that he would side 'with government' for Catholic emancipation, but in fact he continued to vote or pair against it, 6, 18, 30 Mar. 1829. He voted to transfer East Retford's seats to Birmingham, 5 May. He said he was 'not unwilling' to support a grant for the 'much criticized' improvements to Buckingham House, 12 May, but took the opportunity to condemn the window tax as a general cause of 'architectural deformities'. He presented a Sussex petition for inquiry into the state of the wool trade, 14 May 1829. He divided for Knatchbull's amendment to the address on distress, 4 Feb. 1830, and acted regularly with the revived Whig opposition later that session, particularly on economy and tax cutting motions. He voted for the enfranchisement of Birmingham, Leeds and Manchester, 23 Feb., inquiry into the Newark petition complaining of the duke of Newcastle's interference, 1 Mar., to transfer East Retford's seats to Birmingham, 5 Mar., and for Russell's reform motion, 28 May. He maintained that the agricultural interest would be 'exceedingly gratified' by the sale of beer bill, 23 Feb. He presented a Brighton petition in favour of Jewish emancipation, 13 May, and voted accordingly, 17 May: his earlier gift of land in Brighton for a Jewish cemetery is further indication that his 'rational' religious outlook found Judaism doctrinally more acceptable than Catholicism.[9] He voted for abolition of the death penalty for forgery, 24 May, 7 June 1830. Reports that his support for the sale of beer bill had placed his seat at Lewes in jeopardy proved groundless, and he topped the poll again at the general election that summer. At a celebratory dinner, he informed his audience that in Catholic countries 'they would see houses falling into decay and other effects of ignorance and superstition, whereas in a Protestant country all wore the appearance of cheerfulness and prosperity, resulting from the industry of the inhabitants'. At the election for Sussex he seconded Herbert Barrett Curteis, the successful Whig-inclined candidate.[10]

The ministry regarded Kemp as one of the 'bad doubtfuls', but he was absent from the crucial division on the civil list, 15 Nov. 1830, having 'retired to dinner, not anticipating so immediate a division'.[11] He presented anti-slavery petitions, 9 Dec. 1830, 15 Mar. 1831. At the Lewes meeting on parliamentary reform, 26 Jan., he declared his support for the ballot and remarked that, while 'he had never belonged to any party', he was proud that Lord Grey's ministry had solicited his support for their forthcoming measure;[12] he presented the resulting petition, 3 Feb. He proclaimed the 'general satisfaction of all classes' in Sussex with the bill and added his personal approval, 9 Mar. On presenting a friendly petition from Lewes, 15 Mar., he repeated his preference, shared with a 'great body' of his constituents, for the ballot, but accepted that the ministerial plan was sufficient. He also spoke in favour of extending that evening's session to allow more time for petitions to be received. He divided

for the bill's second reading, 22 Mar. Attending the Sussex meeting on reform, 9 Apr., he praised those borough owners who were willing to sacrifice their influence and support the bill.[13] He voted against Gascoyne's wrecking amendment, 19 Apr. 1831, when he dismissed Hardinge's claim that opinion in Lewes had turned against the bill and maintained that his own conduct had brought 'the most satisfactory assurances of success on all sides'. The ensuing dissolution apparently prevented him from presenting a Brighton petition for two Members to be given to the town. He was returned unopposed for Lewes, although he had been obliged to curtail his canvass owing to 'an affliction of the eyes'.[14]

He divided for the second reading of the reintroduced reform bill, 6 July 1831, and steadily for its details. He voted against the complete disfranchisement of Saltash, on which ministers declined to give a lead, 26 July. He believed the people of Brighton were 'too sensible of the benefit of the reform bill to the country at large to throw any obstacle in its way by making any unreasonable demands for themselves', 5 Aug. He defended the right of urban freeholders to vote in counties, 17 Aug., disputing the assertion that the Birmingham Political Union had wielded a disproportionate influence in recent Warwickshire elections. He voted for the bill's passage, 21 Sept., and Lord Ebrington's confidence motion, 10 Oct. He divided with the minorities for O'Connell's motion to swear in the Dublin election committee, 29 July, and for printing the Waterford petition urging that the Irish yeomanry be disarmed, 11 Aug. At a Sussex meeting on reform, 4 Nov., he expressed regret at the delay in settling the matter but was consoled that this had 'generated a more deep rooted and extensive conviction of its justice and expediency and had served to draw a palpable line between those who were friends of the people and those who were not'.[15] He divided for the second reading of the revised bill, 17 Dec. 1831, and steadily for its details, the third reading, 22 Mar., and Ebrington's motion for an address asking the king to appoint only ministers committed to carrying an unimpaired measure, 10 May 1832. He voted for the second reading of the Irish bill, 25 May. He divided with ministers on the Russian-Dutch loan, 26 Jan., 20 (paired), 26 July, and relations with Portugal, 9 Feb. However, he was in the minority for the immediate abolition of colonial slavery, 24 May 1832. At the general election later that year he was returned unopposed for Lewes.

Kemp's second marriage late in 1832, like his first, was to 'a lady of fortune', but this could not halt his slide into deep insolvency, which obliged him to resign his seat in 1837 and live abroad; most of his Brighton property was sold in 1842. He was declared an outlaw in January 1844 after failing to surrender to a suit brought against him. The family historian postulates that his sudden death in Paris in December 1844 may have been by his own hand, but this is contradicted by other sources. He made arrangements for clearing his debts and left his remaining Brighton estate to his son from his second marriage, Frederick Shakerley Kemp. While his 'mania for building' had ruined him, it left Kemptown as an enduring monument, and his 'many philanthropic acts' also helped shape the growth of Brighton.[16]

[1] R.H. Carne, *The Proper Deity* (1818); A. Dale, *Fashionable Brighton*, 51-52, 61; C. Musgrave, *Life in Brighton*, 194; *Gent. Mag.* (1845), i. 442. [2] Dale, 53-58, 61-62, 78; Musgrave, 178-81; E.W. Gilbert, *Brighton*, 18-19; *Gent. Mag.* (1845), i. 442. [3] *Brighton Gazette*, 13, 20, 27 Feb. 1823. [4] *The Times*, 26 Apr. 1823. [5] Ibid. 5, 6 May 1824. [6] Horsham Mus. mss 185, Kemp to Medwin, 13 Dec. 1824; *Brighton Gazette*, 6 Apr., 8, 15 June 1826. [7] *The Times*, 3 Mar. 1827. [8] Ibid. 28 Mar. 1827. [9] A. Dale, *Brighton: Town and People*, 179. [10] *Brighton Gazette*, 8 July, 12, 19 Aug. 1830. [11] *The Times*, 16 Nov. 1830. [12] Ibid. 28 Jan. 1831. [13] *Brighton Gazette*, 14 Apr. 1831. [14] Ibid. 21, 28 Apr.; *Brighton Guardian*, 11 May 1831. [15] *The Times*, 5 Nov. 1831. [16] Dale, *Fashionable Brighton*, 56, 65-69; F.H. Kemp, *Hist. Fams. Kemp and Kempe*, 27; PROB 11/2010/49.

H.J.S.

KENNEDY, Archibald, Lord Kennedy (1794-1832).

EVESHAM   1830-13 Dec. 1830

b. 4 June 1794, 1st s. of Archibald, 12th earl of Cassillis [S] (*d.* 1846), and Margaret, da. and h. of John Erskine of Dun, Forfar. *educ.* St. Andrews Univ. 1809-11. *m.* 1 May 1814, Eleanor, da. and h. of Alexander Allardyce† of Dunnottar, Kincardine, 9s. 3da. *styled* earl of Cassillis 10 Sept. 1831-*d. d.v.p.* 12 Aug. 1832.

David Kennedy, 1st earl of Cassillis (so created in 1509), was killed at Flodden in 1513. On the death without issue of the 8th earl in 1759 the peerage was disputed between William Douglas, earl of Ruglen, and Sir Thomas Kennedy of Culzean, whose claim was recognized by the Lords in 1762. He, who made Culzean Castle, spectacularly situated on the Ayrshire coast, the family's principal residence, died in 1775 and was succeeded by his brother David Kennedy, Member for the county, 1768-74, and a representative peer, 1776-90. He was responsible for the rebuilding and extension of Culzean by Robert Adam, and acted with the opposition to Pitt. On his death in 1792 he was succeeded by his cousin Archibald Kennedy, a retired naval officer, whose two wives, both American heiresses, had brought him considerable property

in New York, much of which he lost in the War of Independence. He died in 1794 and was succeeded by his eldest son and namesake, born in 1770, who raised and commanded the West Lowland Fencibles, supported Pitt and was elected a representative peer in 1796.[1] He broke with Pitt in 1803, when he joined Brooks's, and subsequently attached himself to Lord Grenville. He coveted an English peerage and a green ribbon, both of which he reckoned had been promised him by Pitt before their rupture. Grenville, as premier, obliged him with the barony of Ailsa in November 1806, but refused to entertain his bid for a vacant green ribbon less than a fortnight later.[2] Cassillis, who claimed to have declined the offer of a ribbon from the Portland ministry, urged his pretensions on the prince of Wales on another vacancy in 1810, but he was passed over. On the death of Lord Eglinton in December 1819, when he assured Grenville that he would 'support in future (generally speaking) ministers', he applied for the vacant green ribbon, but was again ignored. He was also annoyed, for all his professions of indifference, not to be offered the lord lieutenancy of Ayrshire. He considered the transfer of Lord Glasgow from Renfrewshire to be a 'flagrant' act of 'Scotch jobbing', motivated by the fears of 'the *Scotch ministry*' that 'such an appointment to me would throw the county into my hands altogether' at the next general election.[3] He overcame initial doubts to support the bill of pains and penalties in November 1820. The following summer he received a green ribbon as one of the extra knights of the Thistle created to mark the coronation of George IV, who conferred the honour on him without reference to Lord Liverpool.[4]

In December 1811 Cassillis had sought Grenville's advice on 'how to dispose of my son Lord Kennedy when he should ... leave St. Andrews':

Kennedy is one of the best scholars of his day in this country ... He has read a great deal upon most subjects and understands both modern and ancient history in an uncommon degree ... Even now ... he studies of his own accord seven hours every day ... I think preparatory to sending him to one of the English universities it would be advisable to put him for two years under the direction of some very eminent man (clergyman) in England, who would carry him on with attention and assiduity ... Kennedy is extremely ambitious to become a man of *some character in Parliament*. I mean to get him into the ... Commons as soon as the forms will permit and when there, *if he follows his father's advice*, he will look up for your guidance and direction ... I will not spare ... any expense which can contribute to turn him into the world a good and able man, and I really think he has all the seeds in him. Money is no object.[5]

Nothing much came of these plans and in 1814 Kennedy, still a minor, married a 17-year-old Mearns heiress, who was worth £30,000 in Bank stock and about £4,000 a year in landed property. Difficulties arose over the terms of the marriage settlement, which briefly became the subject of litigation.[6] In August 1817 the Edinburgh artist and antiquary Charles Kirkpatrick Sharpe wrote:

> Lord Kennedy called upon me today full of the same blushes and bashfulness he exhibited while a boy, which don't become the papa of two lusty children. What a pity it was that he did not first marry *Alma Mater* [Oxford], and then go abroad, in place of espousing Miss Allardyce and growing mouldy at Dunottar! However, neither his awkwardness, nor that of a country tailor, can spoil the look of blood and a very pleasing manner.[7]

Scholarship evidently forgotten, Kennedy made a reputation as an accomplished sportsman and first-rate shot. (A 'strange report' of his 'having shot at a boy in a tree and killed him' in 1822 turned out to be 'entire fiction'.) He also became an inveterate gambler, and ran through much of his own and his wife's fortunes.[8]

In 1824 Kennedy's sister Alicia married Jonathan Peel*, brother of the home secretary Robert, who had just become Cassillis's London neighbour in Whitehall (formerly Privy) Gardens. Cassillis was already on cordial personal terms with Peel, and on the collapse of the Liverpool ministry in April 1827 he pledged him his political adherence, reserving only his right to continue his support for Catholic relief. Cassillis was also friendly with the duke of Clarence (later William IV); and in July 1827 his second son John Kennedy, who had taken the additional name of Erskine on inheriting his mother's Forfarshire property, married Lady Augusta FitzClarence, one of the duke's illegitimate daughters with Mrs. Jordan. On Peel's return to office under the duke of Wellington in January 1828 Cassillis applied to him for the great seal of Scotland, in return for which he would 'endeavour to bring one, or both of my sons into Parliament at the first opening', in order to 'strengthen *permanently both of our families*'. He thought he might secure the election of Kennedy (still, in his view, 'a most excellent scholar') for Middlesex, on the strength of his stake in the county at St. Margaret's, near Twickenham. At all events, he would use the emoluments of the seal to 'purchase *two seats*, if I could find them on any reasonable terms', and open the Ayrshire seat, which was 'really going abegging' for 'any government man', but for which Kennedy was of course ineligible as the son of a Scottish peer. Though nettled by Peel's refusal to press his claims and unwilling to second the address

as requested, he promised to support the ministry on account of his personal attachment to Peel, and went on to back Catholic emancipation in 1829.[9]

At the general election of 1830 Kennedy, nursing broken ribs, offered for the open and venal borough of Evesham, having been introduced there by Benjamin Rotch, a barrister and friend of the family, who had himself declined an invitation to stand. Responding to concerns about his inexperience, he admitted that he was 'as yet untried' but promised that he would 'not disgrace' and would pursue a line of 'real independence'. After a controversial three-day poll he was returned in second place.[10] On 9 Nov. 1830 he gave notice that after Christmas he would move for leave to introduce a bill to permit Scottish peers to sit in the Commons. He presented petitions for the abolition of slavery from two Baptist congregations of Evesham, 15 Nov. He had been listed by ministers among their 'friends', but he was absent from the decisive division on the civil list later that day. He was granted a month's leave on account of family illness, 18 Nov. On 13 Dec. 1830 he was unseated on petition for bribery. Although the Evesham election was declared void, the order for a new writ was superseded pending parliamentary consideration of the borough's electoral corruption, and no new writ was issued before the dissolution in April 1831. Kennedy was again nominated for Evesham at that general election, but he remained in Scotland throughout and was reported to have 'withdrawn himself and declined the representation'. Even so, he finished a creditable third, only 21 votes behind the reform candidate.[11]

Kennedy died *v.p.*, aged 38, in August 1832. His widow, having borne him 12 children in 18 years, followed him to the grave three months later. In 1846 his eldest son Archibald Kennedy (1816-70), a soldier, succeeded to the peerage of his father, who had been promoted to the marquessate of Ailsa in the 1831 coronation honours and had given proxy votes for the reform bills.[12]

[1] S. Scott, *Culzean*, 3-10, 15, 20. [2] *Prince of Wales Corresp.* v. 2266; vi. 2302; Add. 58983, ff. 64, 66, 67, 71. [3] *Prince of Wales Corresp.* vii. 2794, 2815; Add. 58983, ff. 129, 133, 134, 136. [4] Add. 38288, ff. 60, 61; *Hobhouse Diary*, 69. [5] Add. 58933, f. 102. [6] *Ann. Reg.* (1818), Chron. pp. 293-4; *The Times*, 17 July 1818. [7] *CP*, i. 67-68. [8] Buckingham, *Mems. Geo. IV*, i. 342; Stirling, *Coke of Norf.* (1912), 393-4; *CP*, i. 68. [9] Add. 40355, f. 313; 40369, f. 158; 40393, f. 138; 40394, ff. 156, 189; 40395, ff. 64, 66, 107, 141. [10] G. May, *Hist. Evesham* (1845), 297-300; *Worcester Herald*, 17 July, 7 Aug. 1830. [11] *Worcester Herald*, 7 May 1831. [12] *Gent. Mag.* (1831), i. 382; *Von Neumann Diary*, i. 244.

D.R.F./P.J.S.

KENNEDY, Thomas Francis (1788–1879), of Dalquharran Castle and Dunure, Ayr.

AYR BURGHS 1818–4 Feb. 1834

b. 11 Nov. 1788, o.s. of Thomas Kennedy of Dunure and Dalquharran and Jean, da. of John Adam of Blair Adam, Kinross. *educ.* privately by James Pillans; Harrow 1801-5; Glasgow Univ. 1805; Edinburgh Univ. 1807; adv. 1811. *m.* 13 July 1820, Sophia, da. of Sir Samuel Romilly[†] of Tanhurst, Surr., 1s. *suc.* fa. 1819. *d.* 1 Apr. 1879.

Clerk of ordnance Feb.-Nov. 1832; ld. of treasury Nov. 1832-Apr. 1834; paymaster of civil service [I] 1837-50; PC [I] 1837; commr. of woods, forests, land revenues, works and buildings 1850-4.

In the spring of 1819 Kennedy, who had been admitted to Brooks's on 27 Jan., succeeded his estranged father to encumbered Ayrshire estates. The principal properties were Dalquharran Castle (described by John Campbell II* in 1822 as a 'very fine' house set in 'savage and desolate' rain-swept countryside), near Dailly, and the coastal estate of Dunure, midway between Dalquharran and Ayr.[1] At the general election of 1820 he was returned unopposed again for Ayr Burghs, where he had been elected in 1818 on the interest of the 6th duke of Argyll, having been recommended to him and other Whig aristocrats by his uncle William Adam[†], the former party manager and now head of the Scottish jury court.[2] Four months later he married the 'not handsome' but clever daughter of the late Whig legal reformer Romilly. This, as his close friend Henry Cockburn, the leading Edinburgh Whig lawyer, who admired his 'great judgement, high principle and ... love of work' for the benefit of Scotland, later wrote, 'introduced him to important English connections'.[3]

Kennedy was a respected figure in the Whig party and of course voted with them on most major issues, when present, but he was a spasmodic attender. His health periodically let him down, and his inherited financial problems discouraged him from maintaining a permanent London establishment: on at least two occasions in this period he seriously considered retiring from Parliament, but he was talked out of it by Cockburn (his regular correspondent and prompter) and others.[4] He was named to the revived select committees on reform of the Scottish royal burghs, 4 May 1820, 16 Feb. 1821. He backed Lord Archibald Hamilton's demand for action on the reports of the Scottish judicial commissioners, 4 July, and spoke and was a minority teller for his motion condemning the additional Scottish malt duty next day.[5] At the Ayrshire county meeting promoted by local Tories to

send a loyal address to the king in the context of the Queen Caroline affair, 30 Dec. 1820, he was one of the dissentients, arguing that the Liverpool ministry, for whose dismissal he called, had infringed the constitution, and advocating a policy of 'conciliation and correction, by which the thoughtless and misguided might be reclaimed, and the wicked satisfied that they were few in number'.[6] Responding to the Whig leader George Tierney's summons for an early attendance, and having been to the Edinburgh Fox birthday dinner, 12 Jan., he presented Scottish petitions for restoration of the queen's name to the liturgy, 26 Jan., 1 Feb., and on 31 Jan. 1821 disputed the lord advocate Rae's assertion that respectable Scottish opinion was hostile to her.[7] He was in the minority of 22 against the malt duties bill, 14 Feb., and voted silently for Catholic relief, 28 Feb. (as he did again, 1 Mar., 21 Apr., 10 May 1825). No other votes by him have been found for that session, and he evidently gave up attendance, having obtained an initial month's leave to deal with private business, 5 Mar. 1821. Before this he had got permission (14 Feb.) to introduce a bill to reform the 'most palpable and crying evil' of the manner in which juries were selected in Scottish criminal trials by the arbitrary choice of the presiding judge. His measure, chosen by himself and Cockburn as 'his first parliamentary effort', proposed a system of selection by ballot coupled with a right of peremptory challenge on behalf of the accused. He introduced it on 16 Feb. and had it formally read a second time and printed on the 22nd. Rae was opposed to it, and it made no further progress that session.[8] Cockburn composed an *Edinburgh Review* article (xxxvi. 176-219) explaining and justifying the bill, which Kennedy reintroduced in March 1822. Moving its second reading, 20 June, he challenged Rae to substantiate his earlier charge that it was 'uncalled for and unwise'. Rae remained hostile, but Peel, the home secretary, was willing to vote for the principle of the measure with a view to amending it in committee. There, 28 June, Kennedy explained that to 'obviate objections' he had acceded to Peel's proposition that he should limit it to providing the right of peremptory challenge. The measure, thus amended, passed the Commons on 2 July, was approved by the Lords, subject to an alteration requiring the judge to replace challenged jurors immediately, and became law on 26 July 1822 (3 Geo. IV, c. 85). While Cockburn told Kennedy that the impact of this limited success in Edinburgh was 'electrical' and had 'cheered the faithful', he stressed 'the necessity of carrying your whole scheme'.[9]

Kennedy spoke and was a minority teller for Hamilton's motion to refer the reports of the royal burghs select committee to a committee of the whole House, 20 Feb. 1822, when he highlighted the non-sense whereby the Member for Edinburgh, with a population of about 120,000, was effectively returned by 19 men. He criticized the government's palliative burghs accounts bill, 22 Mar.[10] Encouraged by Cockburn, he presented petitions against the contentious Edinburgh police bill, 8 Mar., and condemned it as 'an unwarrantable measure, introduced in defiance of the wishes of the inhabitants', 12 Mar.[11] He presented an Ayr trades' petition for burgh reform, 17 Apr.,[12] and divided for Lord John Russell's general reform scheme, 25 Apr., and reception of the Greenhoe reform petition, 3 June. He voted for reform of the criminal code, 4 June 1822. When Campbell visited him at Dalquharran in September he described Kennedy as 'a very clever and accomplished man'.[13] On 21 Dec. 1822 Cockburn, again urging him to persevere with the juries reform 'till the ballot be gained', pressed him to agree to the request of the committee organizing the impending Edinburgh Fox dinner to 'act as a steward'. Three days later Cockburn, who dismissed all his 'objections ... [as] singularly feeble', was horrified by Kennedy's 'intimation' of his 'intention of ceasing to be parliamentary':

> You seem to feel the step you are planning as a temporary one ... I trust it will prove so; but I have not the slightest expectation that it will. A man can neither dally with Parliament nor with his habits nor with time. You will become a mere Ayrshire gentleman before you know what you are about ... If you had been born and bred a clod of Dumbiedykes, it might have done very well. But any young man who has known higher things, and renounces them for the purpose of pacing over his own acres ... must either degenerate into a fool, or a tyrant, or both ... I daresay living with an establishment for half the year in London must be a severe addition to the calamities of the times ... But ... I am satisfied that by little occasional visits, not exceeding a month or six weeks in all, performed by yourself, you might do a deal of public good, without any private loss, and to your own ... satisfaction ... I don't believe any friend you have can approve of ... this cursed and nonsensical project.

In the event Kennedy, to Cockburn's delight, decided to give himself 'a year's probation' in Parliament, though not attending before Easter, and to adopt 'a system of severe retrenchment'.[14] His first recorded vote in the 1823 session was against the government's naval and military pensions bill, 14 Apr. He divided for Russell's reform motion, 24 Apr. He endorsed the Edinburgh inhabitants' petition for reform of the city's electoral system, 5 May, and supported Hamilton's motion for reform of the Scottish county

representation, which as it stood ensured that most such Members were 'always in adherence to the government of the day', 2 June; he was a teller for the respectable minority of 117 (to 152). He spoke and was a minority teller for Abercromby's motion condemning the lord advocate's role in the Borthwick affair, 3 June, and was a teller for the minority against the government's Scottish commissaries bill, 18 June. He introduced on 8 May a bill to make Scottish securities transferable from one creditor to another without penal duties. It passed the Commons on 12 June, but did not get to the Lords.[15] After consultation with Cockburn, he brought in another Scottish juries bill, which encompassed selection by ballot, 24 Apr. He carried its second reading by 47-42, 20 June, and its third by 60-56, 30 June, but it was thrown out by the Lords on 11 July 1823. After the second reading Cockburn wrote to him:

> I am sure you must be satisfied now of the good you have done by not deserting the public post ... Be assured that there is not a dissentient voice among liberal men here [Edinburgh], that if you can secure a permanent seat, and go on, a long vista of honourable usefulness is opened before you ... So persevere, and arrange your matters in such a way as to prevent all recurrence of the idea you once had.

After the failure in the Lords he consoled Kennedy with the reflection that 'carrying the thing in the Commons twice has advanced it a prodigious step, and I have no doubt whatever of ultimate success'.[16]

Kennedy backed a call for equalization of the Irish and Scottish spirit duties, 25 Feb., and advocated an extension of free trade in distillation, 12 Mar. 1824. Next day he supported Abercromby's motion for reform of Edinburgh's representation and taunted the Member William Dundas, who was 'not ... the representative of the people', with his silence; he was a teller for the minority of 75 (to 99). Egged on by Cockburn, he reintroduced his juries bill, 1 Mar. When he brought up the report, 14 Apr., Rae urged him to postpone it until after Easter, but Kennedy refused and divided the House, which was counted out. On 4 May he agreed to Peel's suggestion that the measure be recommitted. It was eventually passed on 28 May, but the Lords again threw it out, 16 June.[17] Kennedy was a teller for the minority for Hamilton's motion for further consideration of the Scottish judicial commissioners' reports, 30 Mar. That day he secured the appointment of a select committee, which he chaired, on the regulations governing salmon fisheries. He presented anti-slavery petitions, 16 Mar., 5 Apr.[18] He had revived his 1819 scheme for reform of the Scottish poor relief system, and concocted a measure in conjunction with Cockburn, Lord Minto and Dr. Thomas Chalmers. He got leave to introduce it on 6 Apr., after a spat with Rae, whom he accused of inciting 'the ignorant' to raise a misguided fuss about it, 7 May. Even Hamilton thought he ought to drop it, 24 May, and he did so, reluctantly, acknowledging the hostility which it had provoked but insisting that its object was not to introduce poor rates but to limit and subsequently abolish assessments. He vowed to try again. Cockburn, who urged him to promote 'some calm and full discussion of the whole subject', wrote an explanatory article for the *Edinburgh* (xli. 228-58).[19] On 17 June 1824 Kennedy expressed disappointment at ministers' withdrawal of their Scottish judicature bill in response to ill informed 'clamour'. He obtained ten days' leave on account of the illness of a near relation, 18 Feb. 1825. That session the government brought in a Scottish juries bill which conceded selection by ballot and became law as 6 Geo. IV, c. 22.[20] On its second reading, 18 Apr., Kennedy gave it his 'cordial support', but twitted Rae for his *volte face*. Later that day he introduced a salmon fisheries regulation bill (having secured reappointment of the select committee, 7 Mar.), which he saw to the report stage but allowed to lapse in the face of the strong opposition which it excited outside the House.[21] His only known votes that session, apart from those for Catholic claims, were against the Leith Docks bill and for Brougham's motion to make puisne judges immovable, 20 May, and against the grants to the duke of Cumberland, 30 May, and for repairs to Lyme Regis cobb, 3 June. He was absent from Parliament for the whole of the 1826 session. He chaired the Ayrshire meeting which petitioned against interference with the Scottish banking system, 4 Mar. 1826, and sent the petition to John Smith for presentation.[22]

Kennedy, whom the chancellor of the exchequer Frederick Robinson* described as a 'Whig M.P., but a gentleman', was returned unopposed for Ayr Burghs at the 1826 general election; a 'total change' in the composition of the council of Ayr had made him invulnerable.[23] On the eve of the meeting of the new Parliament Cockburn, exhorting him to co-operate with Abercromby 'in doing something ... about Scottish tailzies', gave him a list of ten topics which he could take on his 'own two personal shoulders'.[24] In the event he did not go up until February 1827, when he voted against the duke of Clarence's grant on the 16th. He presented Ayrshire petitions for subsidized emigration, 21 Feb., and against the duty on coal imports to Ireland, 26 Feb.[25] He voted for Catholic relief, 6 Mar., inquiry into alleged elec-

toral interference by Leicester corporation, 15 Mar., information on the Lisburn Orange march, 29 Mar., to withhold supplies until the ministerial crisis was resolved, 30 Mar., and against the Irish miscellaneous estimates and for inquiry into chancery delays, 5 Apr. He presented a Perth inhabitants' petition against the corn bill, 26 Mar.[26] He reintroduced his salmon fisheries bill, 23 Mar., and had it referred to a committee upstairs, 14 May, but it foundered at the report stage, 11 June.[27] After consultation with Cockburn, he brought in a measure to extend the period required to confer parochial settlements in Scotland, 5 Apr.; it lapsed on 11 June.[28] He was a minority teller for the Edinburgh oil gas bill, 1 June, and a majority one for the Edinburgh bridewell bill, 11 June. After the formation of Canning's ministry and the resignation of the Melvillite Tories, Cockburn advised him not to press the Lansdowne Whigs, who had joined Canning, to secure the removal of John Hope, the Scottish solicitor-general, but to let him 'distinctly understand that he must work pleasantly under the new system, or cease to get his corn'.[29] When it was reported that Canning's friend Lord Binning*, son of the earl of Haddington, was to become 'minister for Scotland', Kennedy, through Lords Lansdowne and Carlisle, let Canning know that the support of the Scottish Foxite Whigs 'depended on no such arrangement being made'. The plan was knocked on the head, but Cockburn, who told Kennedy that his and Abercromby's 'exertions in saving Scotland from Binning' were 'appreciated' in Edinburgh, urged him to remain in the alert for any more of 'that sort of mischief'.[30] On the question of whether the Whigs should press for Rae's replacement as lord advocate, Cockburn left it to Kennedy and other Scots on the spot in London, though he was keen that the office should be stripped in future of its political functions.[31] Rae remained in place. Kennedy voted against government for the disfranchisement of Penryn and Lord Althorp's election expenses bill, 28 May. On 12 June 1827 he gave notice that next session he would propose a remedial measure for Scottish entails.[32] Yet in the autumn he decided that leaving Parliament for financial reasons was 'indispensable'. Cockburn wrote to him:

> Your leaving ... is a very great loss to yourself, to those who wish to improve Scotland, and to the public ... [but] no man ... is justifiable in ruining his private fortune for patriotism, or can be called upon to make himself inwardly unhappy for the good of his party ... You ought clearly not to embarrass yourself in your private affairs ... My recollection of Thomson's views ... makes me suspect that he, and others, may be of opinion that you might manage in such a way as to give the House all the

attendance your duty requires without much expense ... If you be positively determined to retire, there is nothing more to be said ... Whatever you do, avoid the dangerous habit of letting the situation of your affairs prey upon your mind.

In the event Kennedy apparently reached a solution by placing his estates in trust.[33]

On 19 Feb. 1828 he joined in calls for the provision of 'slight relief' for western Scotland from the problems caused by casual Irish immigration. He reintroduced his parochial settlements bill, 28 Feb., had it read a second time, 10 Mar., and on the 24th denied that it aimed to exclude the Irish, but acquiesced in the home secretary Peel's suggestion that he postpone it until more information was to hand. It passed the Commons, 16 May, but foundered in the Lords on 17 June. Kennedy voted for repeal of the Test Acts, 26 Feb., and presented favourable petitions, 21, 25, 27 Mar., 29 Apr. He divided for Catholic relief, 12 May. On 6 Mar. he got leave to introduce his entails bill, which sought to lift the 'tyranny' of the existing law (under which he was himself a sufferer) while leaving existing arrangements untouched. He brought it in, 10 Mar., and after its second reading next day had it referred to a committee of 27. He produced their report on 9 June.[34] He welcomed the Wellington ministry's bill to establish an additional circuit judge in Glasgow, 11 Mar., but at the same time drew attention to the fearful state of Scottish gaols, where remand prisoners experienced 'such contamination that no punishment ... could be attended with any moral effect'. He spoke and voted for Whitmore's unsuccessful salmon fisheries bill, 20 Mar., explaining that he had given up the measure 'because I found my own time, as well as that of the committee, went for nothing'. He voted with opposition for information on civil list pensions, 20 May, and against the Irish and Scottish small bank notes bill, 5, 16 June, and the grant for Buckingham House, 23 June. He disputed a statement that the entire agricultural interest of Scotland wanted protection against foreign wool imports, 13 June 1828.

Kennedy divided for Catholic emancipation, 6, 30 Mar. 1829, and on the 24th said that majority intelligent opinion in his part of Scotland favoured it. On 27 Feb. he secured the renewal of his select committee on Scottish entails, in which he went 'into the whole case', with encouraging results. He presented the report on 23 Mar., and on the 27th got leave to introduce two bills in line with its recommendations: a tailzies regulation bill, which 'enacted the conditions on which lands now unentailed may be entailed

hereafter'; and a relief bill, which relieved heirs of tailzie from statutory burdens and debts incurred in the improvement of the property. Abercromby asked Lord Holland to request lord chancellor Lyndhurst to give Kennedy and his coadjutor James Loch* 'an hour' of his time to discuss the measures, which Lyndhurst 'caught at ... with eagerness'. Neither bill reached the Lords, and Kennedy postponed them to next session, 2 June. Cockburn nevertheless thought that merely by broaching the subject in detail he had 'given the old tailzie system an irrecoverable blow'.[35] Kennedy voted to transfer East Retford's seat to Birmingham, 5 May, to allow Daniel O'Connell to take his seat unhindered, 18 May, against the grant for the marble arch, 25 May, and to reduce the hemp duties, 1 June 1829. He was absent from Parliament for half the 1830 session, detained in Ayrshire by unspecified personal problems; he was given a nominal ten days' leave on urgent private business, 3 Mar.[36] He presented Ayr petitions against renewal of the East India Company's trade monopoly, 26 Apr., and next day divided with O'Connell for reform of Irish vestries. Thereafter he voted regularly with the revived Whig opposition, including for Russell's reform motion, 28 May. He voted for Jewish emancipation, 17 May. On the 14th he introduced a bill to facilitate the transfer of heritable securities in Scotland, which lapsed on 8 June. He approved the principle of the government's court of session bill, 27 May 1830, but wanted changes to details.

After his unopposed return at the 1830 general election ministers of course listed him among their 'foes'. In the autumn he began to draw up with Cockburn a plan for reform of the Scottish electoral system, and obtained the blessing of the leading Whig Sir James Robert George Graham*, who promised his 'most cordial co-operation'. Not the least of their motives for making an early start on this project was their wish (especially Cockburn's) to keep it out of the hands of Henry Brougham*, who they felt would do more harm than good. The rumour in Edinburgh was that Kennedy would 'move some kind of reform' when Parliament met, 'with the sanction of ministers': this would propose two Members for Edinburgh and Glasgow and one for Aberdeen.[37] When Kennedy went to London he duly got the permission of Althorp, the new Whig Commons leader, to take the initiative on the issue, and he gave notice accordingly, 3 Nov. 1830.[38] He was in the minority of 39 for reduction of the duty on wheat imported to the West Indies, 12 Nov. On the 15th he stated that there was 'anxious and deep feeling' for reform in Scotland, personally rejected adoption of the secret ballot, derided Dundas's claim that his elections for Edinburgh were 'popular' and secured a return of the number of £10-£20 householders in Scottish cities and royal burghs and of the number of their councillors. Later that day he helped to vote the government out of office on the civil list. On the change of ministry, which saw Francis Jeffrey* replace Rae as lord advocate and Cockburn become Scottish solicitor-general, Kennedy obtained an assurance from Graham, first lord of the admiralty, that he would impress on the premier Lord Grey the 'paramount importance of a good arrangement' in Scotland. He evidently sought for nothing for himself.[39] On 2 Dec. 1830 he welcomed Rae's bill to reform Scottish enfeoffments in heritable property. On the 8th he reintroduced his two 1829 tailzies bills, together with one to empower an unborn heir to make a settlement of estates; they did not receive a second reading, and lapsed on 15 Apr. 1831, Kennedy having decided that the subject was best set aside until reform was out of the way.[40] When ministers announced their intention of producing a comprehensive reform scheme, he waived his pretensions to propose a Scottish measure and at Russell's request sent him the details of the plan which he had concocted with Cockburn. This aimed to 'associate the middle with the higher orders of society in the love and support of the institutions and government of the country' by extending the franchise to men 'who possess property and knowledge'. It suggested a county qualification of £10 for residents in possession of land in perpetual fee and one of £20 for residents of non-parliamentary burghs. In the royal burghs, the franchise was to be conferred on £10 resident householders. Other notions were registration by parish, removal of the bar on the eldest sons of Scottish peers and some redistribution of seats, notably the disfranchisement of Anstruther Easter Burghs, joining the alternating counties of Buteshire and Caithness to Renfrewshire and Sutherland respectively, uniting Cromartyshire with Ross-shire, Nairnshire with Elginshire and Clackmannanshire with Kinross-shire, and giving the surplus seats to Glasgow, Edinburgh (which was to be united with Leith) and Dundee. Cockburn, who exhorted Kennedy to work with and guide the indecisive and often exasperating Jeffrey, continued to discuss difficulties and details of the plan with him, and in late December went to London to consult with Kennedy and Russell, Graham, and Lords Durham and Duncannon*, the committee of four charged with drawing up the ministerial scheme. Once they had settled on the £10 franchise, 'everything else resolved into mere detail and machinery'.[41] In the House, 13 Dec., Kennedy drew attention to the volume of Scottish petitions for burgh and par-

liamentary reform; he presented four himself, and several more, 20, 23 Dec. He had been named to the select committee on the reduction of public salaries, 8 Dec. (he was also appointed to the public accounts committee, 17 Feb. 1831), and on 13 Dec. he claimed that official returns underestimated Dundas's annual income from Scottish sinecures by £3,700. He conceded that few savings could be made in respect of efficient offices, but called for 'a sensible retrenchment' on 'inefficient and sinecure offices'. When Dundas complained that he had been traduced, 15 Dec. 1830, Kennedy retorted that his income for doing nothing was excessive. He sought privately to clarify the select committee's remit with his fellow member Alexander Baring.[42]

He presented petitions for repeal of the duty on candles and against truck payments, 3 Feb. 1831, having been summoned to attend that day by Althorp, leader of the House.[43] He brought up more Scottish reform petitions, 4, 10 Feb., and on the 26th, in the absence of Abercromby, presented and endorsed the 21,700-signature Edinburgh petition. Cockburn had assured him that he would 'instruct' Jeffrey 'to make you one of his chief councillors'; but in late February he was 'sorry and surprised' to learn that Jeffrey was to be 'deprived' of Kennedy's assistance with the Scottish reform bill. He urged Kennedy not to 'forget burgh reform', which was the 'next great Scottish subject', and to keep it on the political agenda.[44] Edward Ellice*, the patronage secretary, and Duncannon, the chief whip, picked his brains about his 'northern colleagues' as they scrutinized the list of Members before the reform scheme was introduced; and he was one of the delegation of Members for various ports who put their case against the proposed tax on steamboat passengers to Althorp.[45] On 9 Mar. he asserted that the government's reform plan had 'given unmixed and unbounded satisfaction in Scotland' and 'obtained the support of many hitherto opposed to all reform'. He presented favourable petitions, 11, 19, 21 Mar., and on the 19th denied an allegation that he was sure of his seat in perpetuity, as his influence at Ayr depended solely on 'goodwill' and the number of electors would increase from 85 to 1,026 after reform. He voted silently for the second reading of the English reform bill, 22 Mar. Meanwhile, Cockburn continued to bombard him with letters expressing his concern about some details of the Scottish measure, exhorting him to disregard Jeffrey and try, with Abercromby, to keep Russell and Duncannon straight and stop them making concessions to 'the local lies, which will be called knowledge, and the local intolerance, which will be held to be caution'. Kennedy, who defended the proposed disfranchisement of the Anstruther Burghs, 28 Mar., and said that support for reform was 'strong' even among the lower orders of Lanark and Paisley who would not be enfranchised, 14 Apr., was eventually able, on an assurance from Durham, to relieve Cockburn's anxieties about 'horrid plots' to raise the county franchise qualification to £15 or more, in which Jeffrey seemed at one point to be implicated. Cockburn agreed that Jeffrey was a liability, but urged Kennedy to uphold him in public whatever his private 'regrets'.[46] He divided against Gascoyne's wrecking amendment to the reform bill, 19 Apr. 1831. On the 21st he was a ministerial minority teller against adjourning the debate on electoral bribery at Liverpool. At the ensuing general election he proposed the reformer Richard Oswald[†] for Ayrshire and commended the reform scheme, but said that 'universal suffrage ... would prove the greatest curse imaginable'. He appealed in vain for calm when the mob rioted after Oswald's defeat. His own return for the Burghs was uneventful.[47]

Kennedy evidently carried around 'a list of disposable offices' in Scotland, and it was probably he whom Abercromby had in mind when on 6 June 1831 he suggested to Grey placing a Scottish Member 'of real character and honour' at the treasury 'or some other office' to advise objectively on the merits of patronage applications and relieve Jeffrey from 'labour not necessarily connected with his office, such as taking charge of bills connected with Scotland'.[48] Nothing immediately came of this, but Kennedy, who was implored by the neurotic Cockburn to bend over backwards to 'uphold' Jeffrey, in spite of everything, was summoned by Graham on 24 June to dine at the admiralty to 'discuss the Scottish reform bill' as 'an affair of life or death' with himself, Althorp, Russell, Durham and Jeffrey.[49] He admitted in the House, 27 June, that the Ayrshire rioters had behaved 'in an unjustifiable manner', but insisted that most 'respectable' Scots were well disposed to the government and the law. Prompted by Cockburn, he ascertained that there was no truth in the rumour that ministers intended to put off the Scottish reform bill until next session. His letter conveying this and other reassuring news was 'given to the flames' by Cockburn, who thought that 'so [long] as they carry us through this session, and leave us our £10 qualification, seven year leases, our proposed arrangement of towns and shires, and our 50 Members, all the details are comparatively immaterial'.[50] Kennedy voted for the second reading of the reintroduced English reform bill, 6 July, and on the 11th got Althorp formally to confirm ministers' intention of carrying the Scottish and Irish

measures that session.[51] Next day he denounced the Tory opposition's factious adjournment proceedings; he was a government teller in the seventh division of the night. He divided steadily for the details of the English reform bill (and at Ellice's request recorded the votes of Scottish Members on them) until 5 Aug., after which his attendance fell away for three weeks, though he paired at least twice. His health was apparently giving him trouble. He deplored the Glasgow Protestants' petition against the Maynooth grant, 19 July, observing that the ignorant were encouraged in their bigotry by 'individuals occupying a high station in society', a charge which he levelled against James Edward Gordon*, 9 Aug. He was in the minority for swearing the Dublin election committee, 29 July, but was absent from the divisions on government interference, 23 Aug. He voted to receive the Waterford petition for disarming the Irish yeomanry, 11 Aug., and to issue a new writ for Liverpool, 5 Sept. He was a teller for the government majorities for the third reading, 19 Sept., and passage of the reform bill, 21 Sept. During the summer he had been in constant contact with Cockburn on the details of the Scottish measure.[52] He dismissed the Edinburgh University petition for a seat to be given to the Scottish universities, 23 Sept., when he was a government teller for the second reading of the Scottish reform bill. He approved the changes made to the measure, 26 Sept., and next day argued that it did not 'deteriorate actual property' but removed 'the power of jobbing in political rights from the owners of superiorities'. Moving to go into committee on it, 3 Oct., he said that a Scottish gentleman had very little chance of representing a Scottish county, if 'he be not a supporter of the government of the day'. He defended the contentious decision to remove Peebles and Selkirk from their burgh districts and throw them into their respective counties, though he preferred the original plan to unite the latter for electoral purposes. In the absence of the unwell Jeffrey, he moved the second reading of the Scottish exchequer court bill, 6 Oct., admitting when he was interrupted by coughing that the subject was 'dry'; he was a majority teller in the division. He was named that day to the select committee on the West Indian colonies (and again, 15 Dec. 1831). He voted for the motion of confidence in the ministry, 10 Oct. 1831, and on the 19th claimed that on the whole the people had reacted with patience and determination to the Lords' rejection of the English reform bill.

In response to his transmission of addresses of support from Irvine and Maybole and information on the 'state of public feeling' in western Scotland, Grey assured Kennedy in early November 1831 that 'the public expectation will not be disappointed' by the revised reform scheme being prepared. A month later Cockburn urged him openly to condemn the contemplated reversion to the alternating system of county representation, which Althorp did not wish to be made generally known. In response to disorder in his locality, he evidently suggested to the home office the raising of 'a force of armed constables', but he was told that the only feasible option was 'a volunteer corps' with reliable officers.[53] He stayed in Ayrshire at the end of the year and paired for the second reading of the revised English reform bill, 17 Dec. 1831. He was present to refute Hunt's assertion that the people of Scotland were hostile to reform, 19 Jan. 1832, and next day voted to go into committee on the English bill. He was in the majorities for schedule A, 23 Jan., and the Russian-Dutch loan, 26 Jan. A few days later he was offered and accepted the office of clerk of the ordnance in the room of Charles Tennyson*, whose health had collapsed. The duke of Bedford thought he was 'worthy of his hire', and Cockburn wrote to him:

> You are not yet in the position I should have liked; because my scheme was that the lord advocate should be allowed to restrict himself to his proper professional or official duties, and that you should have been secretary for Scotland. But, thank God you are in office, and double thank God that the office is not a sinecure. Occupation will do infinite good to your body and soul; and office, especially with occupation, will add immensely to your weight in Scotland ... Go on, and work, and devise, and speak; and in all your proceedings and cogitations remember Scotland. And keep a horse, and keep up your heart, and be gay, and attend to the viscera, and become sagacious and potent. Devil take your anxieties, and your fears, and blue devils, and bad stomachs.[54]

In the event he fell ill almost immediately, and, while he was re-elected without difficulty, he was *hors de combat* for Parliament for over three months: he was forced to miss the division on the third reading of the English reform bill, 22 Mar.[55] In early April he informed Cockburn of some irritating points of detail of the Scottish bill on which ministers seemed inclined to make concessions. By early May he was optimistic about the prospects of its success; but Cockburn advised him not to make 'a newspaper topic' of 'the *absolute necessity* of a Scottish secretary', on which they were agreed.[56] He voted for the address calling on the king to appoint only ministers who would carry reform unimpaired, 10 May. He presented Scottish petitions for supplies to be withheld until reform was secured, 21 May. When Jeffrey presented the Edinburgh reform petition, 23 May, Kennedy denied Conservative allegations that the mass meeting which had produced it

had constituted a union-dominated threat to public order, and described it as a 'vent' for strong feelings, though he did admit that the wording of some of the placards on view had gone too far.[57] He voted for the second reading of the Irish reform bill, 25 May, and was a teller for the majority against a Conservative attempt to increase the Scottish county representation, 1 June. He denounced as 'monstrous' the notion of compensating holders of superiorities for their loss, and opposed an amendment to the Scottish registration machinery, 4 June. On 15 June he presented a number of petitions for the bill and opposed and was a majority teller against four amendments to its details, including one to remove Kilmarnock from Renfrew to Ayr Burghs and move Campbeltown and Inverary in the opposite direction. On the third reading, 27 June, he defended the government's decision to abandon the proposed property qualification for Scottish burgh Members and dismissed a suggestion that Dalkeith should replace Edinburgh as the polling place for Midlothian. He denied an allegation that mass treating was already going on in the burghs, 13 July. On 2 July he presented and explained the ordnance estimates and was a majority teller for the barracks grant. On the 17th he gave notice that in the next session he would again propose reform of Scottish entails law.[58] He was a ministerial teller against reception of a petition for the abolition of Irish tithes, 2 Aug., and for a clause of the Irish party processions bill, 9 Aug. 1832.

In mid-July 1832 Althorp asked Kennedy if he would transfer from the ordnance to a seat at the treasury board, 'with an understanding that he was to be consulted by government with regard to Scotch affairs, there being a want, in the present administration, of such an adviser'. Althorp did not tell him that behind this proposal lay the wish of his cabinet colleague Holland and his wife to obtain the clerkship of the ordnance for their son Charles Richard Fox*. According to John Whishaw, who spoke to Kennedy a few days later, his 'answer was that, having now settled and had some experience at the ordnance, he was unwilling to quit his present situation, but that he should be inclined to do so if the proposal respecting Scotland could be put on a practicable footing and form part of the arrangement'. After consulting Grey, Althorp told Kennedy that

> there seemed to be some difficulty with regard to that part of the proposal which related to Scotland; and, upon being asked by Kennedy what were the duties and attendance expected from a lord of the treasury ... [Althorp] gave such an account of the *attendance* as induced Kennedy to decline the appointment, intimating that a vacation of two or three months in the summer was

quite necessary to him, and that he would not accept or retain any office ... upon other terms.[59]

Lady Holland wanted Whishaw to press Kennedy to change his mind, but he refused:

> The situation of a lord of the treasury is certainly very inferior to the one he now holds, because he is now chief of a department in the House of Commons and his place also does not require a residence in London all year which will be required from our lords of the treasury. With respect to the salary there is not much difference ... I should be behaving ill to him if I pressed him upon the subject ... as he is a man who for many years has acted entirely with me and for whom I have the highest respect.

Lady Holland got Jeffrey to speak to Kennedy and tell him of her personal interest in the matter; but Jeffrey had to inform her that while Kennedy 'expressed himself most anxious to do anything to promote Colonel Fox's views, I rather fear that, unless the conditions can be modified ... he will still adhere to his resolution of remaining where he is'. Nor would Abercromby put further pressure on Kennedy, as Holland wished: even though he considered him to be the ideal man to take responsibility for Scottish patronage, he felt bound to respect Kennedy's 'private reasons which I know to be true and substantial'.[60] Althorp and Lansdowne (the latter at the behest of the Hollands) sought to relieve Kennedy from his uneasiness over thwarting the plan for Fox, and Althorp assured him that 'there may not be so much difficulty about your absence from town as I had apprehended' and that 'I should like to have you to work with here, instead of anyone else whom I do not know so well'.[61] In the event the arrangement was modified so that Kennedy replaced Lord Nugent*, who had been sent to govern the Ionian Islands, at the treasury, while William Leader Maberly* was promoted from surveyor-general to clerk of the ordnance and Fox took Maberly's place, which suited him better than Kennedy's. The reshuffle was implemented in November 1832 to coincide with the dissolution.[62]

Kennedy was returned for Ayr Burghs after a contest at the 1832 general election, but continued financial problems forced him to retire from Parliament and political office in 1834. In 1837 the second Melbourne ministry made him paymaster of the Irish civil service, charged with the task of introducing a new system of finance to Ireland. In August 1850 Russell appointed him a commissioner of woods and forests, but he was turned out without a pension in March 1854 after a dispute with a subordinate. He publicized his grievance in a *Letter to Lord John Russell* (1854). He devoted

the rest of his life to scientific farming, stock breeding and estate improvement. He died at Dalquharran in 1879 and was succeeded by his only child, Francis Thomas Romilly Kennedy (1842-92).[63]

[1] *Life of Campbell*, i. 413. [2] NLS mss 11, ff. 14, 24, 41. [3] *Edgeworth Letters*, 368; *Life of Campbell*, i. 413; *Cockburn Mems.* 361. [4] *Cockburn Letters*, 72-76, 181-2. [5] *The Times*, 5 July 1820. [6] *Glasgow Herald*, 5 Jan. 1821. [7] *Cockburn Letters*, 14-15; *The Times*, 17, 27 Jan., 2 Feb. 1821. [8] *Cockburn Mems.* 361-2; *Cockburn Letters*, 16-17; *The Times*, 23 Feb. 1821; *CJ*, lxxvi. 101, 318, 358. [9] *The Times*, 29 June 1822; *CJ*, lxxvii. 360, 385, 394, 442, 447, 467; *Cockburn Letters*, 26-34, 38, 41-45, 46, 58-59, 60-62. [10] *The Times*, 23 Mar. 1823. [11] *Cockburn Letters*, 41, 49; *The Times*, 9, 13 Mar. 1822. [12] *The Times*, 18 Apr. 1822. [13] *Life of Campbell*, i. 413. [14] *Cockburn Letters*, 70-77; NLS mss 24749, f. 28; *The Times*, 18 Jan. 1823. [15] *The Times*, 9 May, 7, 13 June 1823. [16] *Cockburn Letters*, 81, 88-90, 92; *The Times*, 25 Apr., 21 June, 1 July 1823; *CJ*, lxxviii. 251, 413, 440; *LJ*, lv. 869. [17] *Cockburn Letters*, 99-100, 106-7, 115; *The Times*, 2 Mar., 15 Apr., 5, 29 May 1824; *LJ*, lxi. 416. [18] *The Times*, 17 Mar., 6 Apr. 1824. [19] *Cockburn Letters*, 94-98, 100-6, 108-10, 116-19, 125-7; *The Times*, 7 Apr., 15, 27 May 1824. [20] *Cockburn Letters*, 128-30. [21] *The Times*, 19 Apr., 20 May 1825; *CJ*, lxxx. 318, 440. [22] *Glasgow Herald*, 6 Mar. 1826; *Cockburn Letters*, 138, 140-1. [23] Add. 57402, f. 16; NAS GD51/1/198/3/83. [24] *Cockburn Letters*, 145, 147. [25] *The Times*, 22, 27 Feb. 1827. [26] Ibid. 27 Mar. 1827. [27] Ibid. 24 Mar., 15 May, 12 June; *CJ*, lxxxii. 349, 457, 544. [28] *Cockburn Letters*, 149; *The Times*, 6 Apr. 1827; *CJ*, lxxxii. 391, 543. [29] *Cockburn Letters*, 156-7. [30] Ibid. 158-9, 161-4; *Canning's Ministry*, 278. [31] *Cockburn Letters*, 166-7. [32] *The Times*, 13 June 1827; *Cockburn Letters*, 173-4. [33] *Cockburn Letters*, 181-2, 186-7. [34] Ibid. 191-2. [35] Ibid. 206, 215-18; Add. 51574, Abercromby to Holland [Apr. 1829] [36] *Cockburn Letters*, 225-7. [37] NAS GD23/6/662. [38] *Cockburn Letters*, 239-41, 243-7, 248-51. [39] Ibid. 253-8, 267, 270. [40] Ibid. 294. [41] Ibid. 258-66, 270-9; *Cockburn Jnl.* i. 1; N. Gash, *Politics in Age of Peel*, 38-40. [42] *Cockburn Letters*, 280-4. [43] Ibid. 290-1. [44] Ibid. 287, 293-5. [45] Ibid. 299; *Glasgow Herald*, 11 Mar. 1831. [46] *Cockburn Letters*, 299-306, 309-14, 318-19. [47] *Glasgow Herald*, 20, 30 May 1831. [48] Grey mss. [49] *Cockburn Letters*, 324-6. [50] Ibid. 327-9. [51] Ibid. 331. [52] Ibid. 334-8, 346-8. [53] Ibid. 356-62. [54] Lincs. AO, Tennyson d'Eyncourt mss Td'E H111/3; Add. 51671, Bedford to Lady Holland [7 Feb.]; 75941, Althorp to Spencer, 31 Jan. 1832; *Cockburn Letters*, 384-6, 387. [55] *The Times*, 2, 26 Mar. 1832; *Cockburn Letters*, 392-4. [56] *Cockburn Letters*, 394-405. [57] Ibid. 406-8. [58] Ibid. 417. [59] Add. 51659, Whishaw to Lady Holland, 22 July [1832]. [60] Add. 51575, Abercromby to Holland, 21 July [1832]. [61] *Cockburn Letters*, 412-14. [62] Add. 51575, Abercromby to Holland, 27 [Nov.]; 51659, Whishaw to same, 31 Aug; 51786, Holland to Fox [?22 July] 1832; *Cockburn Letters*, 423. [63] *Oxford DNB*.

D.R.F.

KENYON, Hon. Lloyd (1805–1869), of 9 Portman Square, Mdx.

MITCHELL 1830–1832

b. 1 Apr. 1805, 1st s. of George, 2nd Bar. Kenyon, and his cos. Margaret Emma, da. of Sir Thomas Hanmer, 2nd bt., of Hanmer, Flints. *educ.* Harrow 1817-23; Christ Church, Oxf. 1823. *m.* 29 June 1833, Hon. Georgina De Grey, da. of Ven. Thomas, 4th Bar. Walsingham, 5s. (2 *d.v.p.*) 5da. *suc.* fa. as 3rd Bar. Kenyon 25 Feb. 1855. *d.* 14 July 1869.

Kenyon's grandfather Lloyd Kenyon† (1732-1802), whose mother brought the Flintshire estate of Gredington into the family, served as attorney-general under both Rockingham and Pitt, became master of the rolls in 1784 and chief justice of king's bench and a peer in 1788. A coarse-fibred man with a rough tongue, he was an able, industrious lawyer, who amassed a considerable fortune which he invested in landed property in Denbighshire and Flintshire.[1] Kenyon's father, a devout high churchman, was an implacable opponent of Catholic relief who emerged in the mid-1820s as one of the leading Ultra Tories, along with the duke of Newcastle and Lords Mansfield and Winchilsea. He was involved in their vain attempts to secure the formation of a solidly anti-Catholic ministry in 1827, and was made uneasy by the repeal of the Test Acts the following year. Later in 1828 he initiated the meetings which led to the formation of the Brunswick Constitutional Club, and in letters to the press he urged the Protestants of Britain to organize in order to stop the Wellington ministry's drift towards concession. Emancipation, when it came in 1829, infuriated him, and he was active in the Ultras' subsequent efforts to remove Wellington and form a Protestant ministry under the aegis of the duke of Cumberland.[2]

Kenyon, who was admitted a member of the Brunswick Club in August 1828, was returned for Mitchell at the general election of 1830 on the interest of the Ultra Lord Falmouth.[3] The ministry of course numbered him among the 'violent Ultras'. He took his seat on the opposition benches and in his maiden speech, 5 Nov. 1830, demanded to know what steps ministers intended to take to deal with the 'general and unexampled depression [which] exists in all interests'. (His father blamed 'the unexampled disorganized state of society now existing' largely on 'the loss of character which Parliament and public men have suffered from the course pursued by ... Wellington's government', and wanted to see order restored in the disturbed districts by reviving the yeomanry, imposing a curfew, suspending habeas corpus and introducing rewards for the exposure of miscreants.)[4] He voted against them in the crucial civil list division, 15 Nov. 1830. On 7 Feb. 1831 he moved for a return of the acreage of uncultivated waste in England and Wales, some of which he wished to make available to poor agricultural labourers, but he withdrew when it was explained that the materials for furnishing such information did not exist. He aligned himself with the group of Commons Ultras led by Sir Richard Vyvyan and Sir Edward Knatchbull, and on 19 Mar. complained to his father of Sir Robert Peel's obstinacy in refusing to endorse their plan to follow the anticipated defeat of the Grey

ministry's reform bill with a resolution in favour of moderate reform: he suspected that Peel 'wishes us to commit ourselves against *all* reform, so as to be totally dependent on him and his party'.[5] He divided against the bill's second reading, 22 Mar., and for Gascoyne's wrecking amendment, 19 Apr. 1831. He was again returned for Mitchell at the ensuing general election.

He was in the minority of 13 for a reduction of public salaries to their 1797 levels, 30 June 1831. He divided against the second reading of the reintroduced reform bill, 6 July, for an adjournment motion, 12 July, to use the 1831 census for the purpose of determining the disfranchisement schedules, 19 July, and against the partial disfranchisement of Chippenham, 27 July. He demanded 'as a claim of right' that all the Welsh counties should, like Glamorgan, be given an additional seat, 18 Aug., but dropped his motion for a mandatory instruction to the committee when the leader of the Commons, Lord Althorp, promised to consider the idea (Denbighshire was later given an additional Member). He divided against the bill's third reading, 19 Sept., and its passage, 21 Sept. Following its defeat in the Lords his father, who had recently made a fool of himself with a drunken outburst at a party meeting, was reportedly spoiling for a physical '*fight* with the people'.[6] He voted for the motion to censure the Irish administration for its conduct during the Dublin election, 23 Aug. He divided for the Liverpool bribery prevention bill, 5 Sept., and to investigate the complaints of West Indian sugar producers, 12 Sept. He voted against the second reading of the revised reform bill, 17 Dec. 1831, entering committee, 20 Jan., the enfranchisement of Tower Hamlets, 28 Feb., the third reading, 22 Mar., and the second reading of the Irish bill, 25 May 1832. In February John Croker* named him as one of the Ultras who, still unreconciled to Peel, afforded 'but a hollow support' to opposition and who, 'though they vote with us, are evidently a different party'.[7] He divided against ministers on the Russian-Dutch loan, 26 Jan., 12 July. On 9 Apr. he introduced a bill to encourage the employment of agricultural labourers through the enclosure of waste lands, his father having just abandoned an attempt to pilot the same measure through the Lords; it foundered at the report stage, 12 July. He was credited with an emphatic refusal to postpone the labourers' employment bill until the next session, 27 June, in terms which implied that it was his measure. This may have been a case of mistaken identity, for the bill, which gained royal assent, had been sponsored by Sir Charles Burrell. He voted to open coroners' inquests to the public, 20 June, and for Alexander Baring's bill to exclude insolvent debtors from the House, 27 June 1832.

At the general election of 1832 Kenyon made a bid for the extra Welsh county seat which he had helped to secure by standing for Denbighshire. He set much store by his support for agricultural protection and claimed to favour the abolition of slavery, but he was abused on account of the emoluments, totalling in excess of £9,400, which his father and uncle Thomas Kenyon derived from king's bench sinecures. He was beaten into third place and thereafter played little part in public life.[8] General Dyott, who met him in 1838, recorded that 'I never met a more agreeable man, with less pomp and pride of aristocratic superiority than usually falls to his grade'.[9] He succeeded to his father's title and estates in 1855. He died in July 1869 and, his eldest son having predeceased him, was succeeded by his grandson Lloyd Kenyon (1864-1927).

[1] *Oxford DNB sub* Lloyd, 1st Bar. Kenyon; R.L. Kenyon, *Kenyon Fam.* 43-44. [2] Add. 40396, f. 19; *Colchester Diary*, iii. 301-2, 496-7, 574-5; G.I.T. Machin, *Catholic Question in English Politics*, 3, 30, 96, 115, 131-4, 154, 167, 175-7, 181. [3] Kenyon mss, Chandos to Lord Kenyon, 27 Aug. [1828], Falmouth to same, 19 May, 15 Aug. 1830. [4] Add. 47591, f. 46. [5] Kenyon mss, Lloyd Kenyon to fa. 19 Mar. 1831; *Three Diaries*, 135, 220, 232; B.T. Bradfield, 'Vyvyan and Country Gentlemen', *EHR*, lxxxiii (1968), 732. [6] *Three Diaries*, 131; *Lady Holland to Son*, 120. [7] *Croker Pprs.* ii. 151. [8] *Carnarvon Herald*, 18 Aug., 29 Dec.; *Chester Chron.* 26 Oct. 1832. [9] *Dyott's Diary*, ii. 281.

D.R.F.

KEPPEL, **Augustus Frederick**, Visct. Bury (1794–1851), of 8 St. James's Place, Mdx.

ARUNDEL   1820–1826

b. 2 June 1794, 2nd but 1st surv. s. of William Charles Keppel, 4th earl of Albemarle, and 1st w. Elizabeth, da. of Edward Southwell, 20th Bar. de Clifford. *m.* 4 May 1816, Frances, da. of Charles Steer of Chichester, Suss., *s.p. styled* Visct. Bury 1804-49. *suc.* fa. as 5th earl of Albemarle 30 Oct. 1849. *d.* 15 Mar. 1851.
    Midshipman RN 1809; ensign 1 Ft. Gds. 1811; lt. and capt. 1814, ret. 1816.

Bury, whose family were of Dutch noble origin, had assumed the courtesy title on his elder brother's death in 1804, 'in consequence, as was believed in the family, of ill treatment at Harrow School'; this may explain why he was apparently educated privately. He followed in the military traditions of his family and was a midshipman aboard the *Superb* in 1809, before switching to the army in 1811 and serving in the Peninsula. According to his brother, 'in one action a bullet passed through his boot near the ankle. In another the rosette which concealed the socket of his feather was carried away – "a feather in his cap" as his comrades used to

say'. He was appointed aide-de-camp to the prince of Orange in 1815 and left the army the following year, having been awarded the Waterloo medal.[1] He joined Brooks's Club, 15 Apr. 1815. In October 1819 he stood at a by-election for Arundel on the duke of Norfolk's interest but withdrew the day before the poll. He successfully contested the seat at the 1820 general election.[2]

He was initially a fairly regular attender who, in keeping with his family's politics, voted with the Whig opposition to Lord Liverpool's ministry on all major issues, including parliamentary reform, 10 May 1821, 25 Apr. 1822, 26 Feb. 1824. In view of his background, his consistent support for military retrenchment is noteworthy. He divided for Catholic relief, 28 Feb. 1821, 1 Mar., 21 Apr., 10 May 1825. In February 1821 he read a letter from his father to the committee at Brooks's for the management of the subscription for Queen Caroline, which 'objected to the plan as doubting the chance of success, from the division of our friends' on the subject.[3] He praised the 'steadfast loyalty and patient obedience' of English Catholics in the face of the 'intolerable' exclusion laws, 28 Feb., and declared that Ireland 'called still more loudly for change', as 'no kingdom could be equitably ruled under laws which, of themselves, drew a line between the governors and the governed'. His only other reported speech, packed with rhetorical flourish, was in support of reform, 17 Apr. 1821, when he launched a wide-ranging attack on ministers, whom he derided as a 'faction'. He complained that Parliament as constituted, far from 'maintaining the political pre-eminence of England on the sound principles of civil and religious liberty', was called merely to 'ratify treaties with foreign powers leagued in one common principle of despotism', and he regretted that political abuses were so 'unblushingly practised' that 'those who seek reform [are] branded as being disaffected'. He predicted that 'reform must come and would come to teach Parliaments for what purpose they are delegated'.

Bury's decision not to seek re-election, announced in October 1824,[4] can safely be ascribed to his financial difficulties, which may also explain his lax attendance after 1823. As early as 1816 he had been obliged to resort to moneylenders and was in dispute with his father over the inadequacy of his £500 annual allowance, although Albemarle claimed to have paid him more than £1,500 in the previous year, partly to cover 'a gambling debt'. In April 1824 Thomas Creevey* reported seeing him gambling at Crockford's, where 'it appears inevitable that all the young ones must be ruined'.[5] After 1826 he resided in Paris, presumably to escape his creditors, but by January 1831 his insolvency was such that his furniture was seized in lieu of rent and his wife returned to her family. From Boulogne he informed his attorney:

> I owe in France long-standing debts to the amount of £700 which I am liable to be arrested upon any day and in England about £1,000 ... but of course it is my debts in this country that require the most immediate attention; then the next thing to be considered will be to save me from starvation. I am sorry to say since I wrote to you last ... I have been arrested for 1,000 Fr. and not having one shilling in the world they were taking me off to prison when my servant ... went to his box and paid over 1,000 Fr. ... and thus saved me from the everlasting disgrace that awaited me.

With Albemarle's own finances in a precarious state, it was left to another member of the family to send subsistence money. Bury had hoped that his wife's family might assist him, but his fecklessness and lack of tact had soured relations with them. His reputation also hampered his father's exertions to obtain an appointment for him from the Grey ministry, and the offer of a post in Ceylon was rejected as he could not pay his passage and feared for his health, recently impaired by serious illness.[6] In March Albemarle helpfully suggested that he should 'change his name and be concealed in Jersey ... or any country not subject to France or England'. In June he was in Calais, still destitute, and by October 1831 had been consigned to prison there 'by a usurer'. In a despairing letter to his attorney he complained that his family were bent on 'humiliating' him by threatening to withdraw all support unless he made a declaration that 'all that has occurred has been brought upon me by my own follies and extravagances' and promised to 'lead a new life for the future, repenting thoroughly my past conduct'; he claimed to have 'more than once meditated whether or not I would allow myself to survive my disgrace'. An advance from his attorney eventually secured his release, and he returned to England in February 1832, despite having earlier vowed never to do so. His rakish days were over, and he hoped to find 'some means to employ myself that I may not become a burden on my relations and friends' and to manage on £200 a year. However, his unsurprising omission from the recent batch of peerage creations prompted the bitter observation that 'I cannot see what I have gained by professing and acting upon Whig principles all my life', for 'now that the party is in power and ... I am in distress they will not give me the slightest assistance'.[7] He failed in his pretensions to his mother's family title of de Clifford in 1833, when doubts began to be aired

about his sanity.[8] In July 1849, three months before he succeeded to his father's title and encumbered estates,[9] he was confined to an asylum, his condition alternating between torpor and 'paroxysms of maniacal excitement'; on one occasion he nearly killed his keeper. He was certified by a commission of lunacy, 24 Nov. 1849, after several witnesses had described his deluded boasts of vast wealth and macabre stories of armed combat; one of them had 'always considered him eccentric'.[10] He died in March 1851 and was succeeded by his brother, George Thomas Keppel (1799-1891), Liberal Member for East Norfolk, 1832-4, and Lymington, 1847-9.

[1] G.T. Keppel, *Fifty Years of my Life* (1877), 2, 67-68. [2] W.D. Cooper, *Parl. Hist. Suss.* 8. [3] HLRO, Hist. Coll. 379, Grey Bennet diary, 24. [4] *The Times*, 14 Oct. 1824. [5] Suff. RO (Ipswich), Albemarle mss 461/365, Albemarle to Medcalfe, 23 June; 461/364, attorney's letter, 26 July 1816; *Creevey Pprs.* ii. 75. [6] Albemarle mss 461/396, Lady Bury to Bury, 11, 14 Jan., Bury to Medcalfe, 13 Jan., 3 Mar., replies, 16 Feb., 25 Mar., Albemarle to Medcalfe, 16 Feb., to Steer, 16 Aug. 1831. [7] Ibid. Albemarle to Medcalfe, 18 Mar., Bury to same, 21 Mar., 22 June, 23 Oct., 15 Nov. 1831, 7 Feb. 1832. [8] Ibid. 461/365, letter to Medcalfe, 17 Sept., Stephenson to Albemarle, 29 Sept. 1833. [9] His father left debts of over £10,000 and attached stringent conditions to his inheritance (PROB 11/2108/84). [10] TNA C/211/1(106); *The Times*, 13 Dec. 1849.

H.J.S.

KER, David Guardi (?1778–1844), of Portavo and Montalto, co. Down.

| ATHLONE | 2 June 1820–1826 |
| DOWNPATRICK | 1835–1841 |

b. ?1778, 1st s. of David Ker of Portavo and w. Maddalena Guardi of Venice. *educ.* Eton 1788-95; Christ Church, Oxf. 19 Apr. 1796, aged 17; I. Temple 1804. *m.* 22 Feb. 1814, Lady Selina Sarah Stewart, da. of Robert Stewart, 1st mq. of Londonderry [I], 2s. 2da. *suc.* fa. 1811. *d.* 30 Dec. 1844.

Ker's Scottish ancestors had originally settled in county Antrim before moving to Tottenham, Middlesex, from where his uncle Richard Gervas Ker, Member for Newport, Isle of Wight, 1802-6, and his father had returned to Ireland in the 1780s. The former went to Antrim and the latter to county Down, where he purchased lands at Clough and Magheraknock in 1785 and the Monalto estates of the earl of Moira in 1800. Ker, who promoted his uncle's abortive attempt to offer on the 'independent interest' for Antrim at the 1820 general election, was keen to 'get into Parliament', but owing to his connection with the Stewarts (he was the foreign secretary Lord Castlereagh's* brother-in-law), complained that he had 'been so much put down in jury lists, etc., etc., since I married into the family, that I feel it, and will endeavour to resist it whenever and where ever I can'.[1] He looked to his uncle 'to shove me into the House', writing to him, 4 Apr. 1820

> about a seat in Parliament for me, which I should be most anxious to obtain without delay and through you if possible, without interference with Castlereagh. There are many reasons why I should wish to avoid that interference, but nevertheless if you have no other avenue, and he can return me forthwith, I throw myself into his hands. I think in the main we agree in public politics and in county politics. I do not anticipate any disagreement, though I have determined views on that subject and am performing this act partly in reference to them.[2]

He was rumoured as a candidate for Downpatrick, where his family had considerable interest, but instead endorsed the return of his brother-in-law John Waring Maxwell, afterwards commenting that 'they are angry with me here for not getting the election in my own favour', but 'I should never have forgiven myself if I had, as I think it is the only thing for him'.[3] Three months later he came in unopposed on a vacancy for Athlone on the controlling interest of Lord Castlemaine.

Ker, a very poor attender who cast no recorded votes on the Catholic question and is not known to have spoken in debate in this period, voted in defence of the Liverpool ministry's conduct towards Queen Caroline, 6 Feb., and for their supplies, 6 Mar. 1821.[4] He was considered by Castlereagh for the vacancy in county Down which would be created on his succession to the Irish peerage as Lord Londonderry, but it was decided that although 'to pass by Ker might wound him, to put him forward would certainly offend the county'.[5] He voted against repeal of the additional malt duty, 3 Apr. 1821, more extensive tax reductions, 13 Mar., inquiry into the conduct of the lord advocate towards the Scottish press, 25 June, and repeal of the salt duties, 28 June 1822. No further votes have been found, though according to a commentary of 1825 he 'attended frequently and voted with ministers'.[6] His brother-in-law Charles, 3rd marquess of Londonderry, reviewing the prospects of forming 'a third party' at the end of 1822, considered Ker 'a very uncertain character', who 'I am afraid I have no hold over'.[7] He was granted a month's leave on account of ill health, 15 Apr. 1825.

At the 1826 general election Ker made way for Castlemaine's nephew. It had long been determined that he could 'never look to a seat' from Londonderry, who for county Down brought forward his son Lord

Castlereagh, to whom Ker wrote offering 'my presence or my votes ... in aid of yourself or your friends'.[8] The following year Ker 'kept himself quite neutral' in the controversy provoked by an anti-Catholic petition from Bangor, county Down, which 'all his tenants signed'.[9] At the 1830 general election he wrote from France to again place his 'interest in Down' at Castlereagh's disposal.[10] He was returned unopposed for Downpatrick in 1835, where he sat as a Conservative until his retirement in 1841. In 1844 he purchased the Downpatrick estates of the late Lord de Clifford. Ker died in December that year and was succeeded by his elder son David Stewart Ker (1816-78), Conservative Member for Downpatrick, 1841-47, 1859-67, and county Down, 1852-7.

[1] PRO NI, Ker mss D2651/3/28, 34. [2] Ibid. 3/35. [3] Ibid. 3/38. [4] *Black Bk.* (1823), 167. [5] PRO NI, Castlereagh mss D3030/Q2/2/256. [6] *Session of Parl. 1825*, p. 471. [7] Norf. RO, Blickling Hall mss, Londonderry to Emily, Lady Londonderry, 14, 29 Dec. 1822. [8] Castlereagh mss N/148, Turnley to Londonderry, 28 Oct. 1824; N/185, Ker to Castlereagh, 28 June 1826. [9] PRO NI, Perceval Maxwell mss, Cleland to Maxwell, 28 Feb. 1827. [10] Castlereagh mss N/275, Ker to Castlereagh, 15 July 1830.

P.J.S.

KERR, John William Robert, earl of Ancram (1794–1841).

HUNTINGDON   1820–27 Apr. 1824

b. 1 Feb. 1794, 1st s. of William, 6th mq. of Lothian [S], and 1st w. Lady Henrietta Hobart, da. and coh. of John Hobart[†], 2nd earl of Buckinghamshire, div. w. of Armar Lowry Corry, 1st Visct. Belmore [I]. *educ.* Harrow 1805; Christ Church, Oxf. 1813. *m.* 19 July 1831, Lady Cecil Chetwynd Talbot, da. of Charles, 2nd Earl Talbot, 5s. 2da. *styled* Lord Newbottle 1794-1815; earl of Ancram 1815-24. *suc.* fa. as 7th mq. of Lothian [S] 27 Apr. 1824. *d.* 14 Nov. 1841.
    Priv. sec. to sec. of state for foreign affairs July 1819-Jan. 1820; PC 14 Sept. 1841; capt. of yeomen of the guard Sept. 1841-*d.*
    Ld. lt. Roxburgh 1824-*d.*; recorder, Huntingdon.
    Col. Edinburgh militia 1824-*d.*

Ancram's grandfather William John, 5th marquess of Lothian (1737-1815), who was 'equally distinguished as a general and a *petit mâitre*', was deprived of his command of the Life Guards in 1789 for voting against the regency bill, but was reinstated as a colonel of dragoons in 1798.[1] With his wife Elizabeth Fortescue (1745-80) he had four sons and five daughters. After her death he evidently formed a liaison with one Elizabeth Parker, who died at Farnham, Surrey, in January 1793, leaving Lothian's infant daughters

Elizabeth and Mary. He took them in, raised them and provided for them in a codicil to his will, 1 Jan. 1814. Mary subsequently made an ill-advised marriage to a Mr. Hart, who declared that he required no money with her. Lothian consequently revoked the original bequest and instead left her £1,000, 2 Jan. 1815.[2] He died two days later. In about 1830 Mary Kerr Hart prefaced her book *Heath Blossoms: or Poems written in Obscurity and Seclusion* with the story of her life and the 'dark and melancholy fate' which had befallen her, her husband having been declared bankrupt and insane, leaving her at the mercy of his many creditors. What ultimately became of her is not clear. Ancram's father served in the army, and as colonel of the Midlothian cavalry was active against the Irish rebels in 1798. About eight years earlier he had begun to cohabit with Lady Belmore, who had been estranged from her husband since 1781. Lord Belmore obtained a ruling of crim. con. against Ancram (as he was styled until 1815), and in 1793 secured a divorce by an Act of the Irish Parliament (9 Apr.). Ancram and his mistress immediately married and their eldest child, the subject of this biography, was born ten months later. No confirmation has been found of an allegation that they had an illegitimate son in April 1792.[3] She died in 1805 and Ancram subsequently married a daughter of the 3rd duke of Buccleuch. He succeeded as marquess of Lothian in 1815, was elected a representative peer two years later and received a United Kingdom barony (Ker of Kersheugh) as part of the coronation honours in 1821.[4]

After a conventional education Ancram was appointed in July 1819 private secretary to his uncle by marriage Lord Castlereagh*, the foreign secretary, but he relinquished the position after only six months. At the 1820 general election he stood for Huntingdon on the interest of his half-sister Mary, dowager countess of Sandwich (his mother's only child with Belmore), and was returned after a token contest.[5] He took the family line and gave apparently silent support to the Liverpool government, when present. He was in their majority against economies in revenue collection, 4 July 1820. On 2 Feb. 1821 he informed Castlereagh's half-brother of their success in weathering the storm over Queen Caroline:

> We have been most triumphant, more so than the most sanguine could have anticipated considering the state of the country and the means that the Whigs took to commit the country gentlemen ... I think we may conclude that upon no one occasion has the sense of the respectable part of the country been more in favour of the acts of any ministry.[6]

Four days later he voted against the opposition censure motion. He probably voted against Catholic relief, 28 Feb., and he paired on that side from 2 Mar.[7] He divided against repeal of the additional malt duty, 3 Apr., and parliamentary reform, 9 May, paired against criminal law reform, 23 May, and voted against economy and retrenchment, 27 June 1821. He voted against reduction of the salt duties, 28 Feb., 28 June, and abolition of one of the joint-postmasterships, 13 Mar. 1822. He paired against Canning's Catholic peers relief bill, 30 Apr. 1822. Notwithstanding his politics, Ancram was a popular guest at Holland House. In early August 1822 he travelled to Scotland with Lord Holland's son Henry Edward Fox*, who found him 'agreeable, good-natured and well-informed'. He was thought at this time to be on the verge of marriage to Lord Grey's daughter Elizabeth, but nothing came of the romance. A bad fall from his horse did not prevent him from hastening back to London to comfort his aunt after Castlereagh's suicide. He evidently shared the anger of Castlereagh's family at Canning's appointment as his successor.[8] Ancram voted against repeal of the Foreign Enlistment Act, 16 Apr., inquiry into the prosecution of the Dublin Orange rioters, 22 Apr., and Scottish parliamentary reform, 2 June 1823. He paired against inquiry into chancery delays, 5 June 1823, and presented a Huntingdon innkeepers' petition against the licensing duties, 20 Feb. 1824.[9] Two months later his father's death removed him from the Commons.

He replaced his father as lord lieutenant of Roxburghshire, but turned down an invitation from Lord Melville, the government's Scottish manager, to do so in Midlothian until the 5th duke of Buccleuch came of age in 1828.[10] His estates were heavily encumbered, but he tried to reduce the debt and improve the property.[11] On the death of Castlereagh's widow in 1829 he got 'some thousands a year' which, as Lady Holland, with whom he was a 'bit of a favourite', reported, 'puts him quite at ease'. He was 'a convert to the Catholic question' that year.[12] In September 1841 he was given household office in Peel's second ministry, but he died two months later while staying at Blickling, Norfolk, which he would have inherited had he survived his aunt Caroline, dowager Lady Suffield.[13] As it was, the property passed to his eldest son and successor William Schomberg Robert Kerr (1832-70) on her death in 1850. That year his widow, who died in Rome in 1877, became a Catholic. His third son Ralph wrote of him:

> He was a most lovable character. It was, I believe, of him that Sir Walter Scott said that Lord Lothian was the most

perfect type of true gentleman that he knew. That he had the gift, when bestowing a favour, of making the recipient feel that it was he who was bestowing the favour rather than himself.[14]

[1] *Prince of Wales Corresp.* i. 251; ii. 247. [2] PROB 11/1565/91; *CP*, viii. 154, where, on the basis of a misleading reference in *N and Q* (ser. 3), viii. 48, the mother of Mary Kerr Hart is wrongly described as 'a supposed first wife' of the 6th marquess. [3] *CJ*, xv. 178-9, 182; *LJ*, vii. 103, 105, 125-6, 130, 131, 152; *Parl. Reg. [I]*, 398. [4] Add. 38276, f. 398; 38289, f. 239. [5] *Huntingdon, Bedford and Peterborough Gazette*, 26 Feb., 4, 11 Mar. 1820. [6] Add. 43212, f. 180. [7] Northants. RO, Agar Ellis diary, 1 Mar. [1821]. [8] *Fox Jnl.* 138-9, 140, 142, 148; Add. 40349, f. 191; Blakiston, *Lord William Russell*, 78; Agar Ellis diary, 7 Dec. [1822]; *Arbuthnot Corresp.* 30. [9] *The Times*, 21 Feb. 1824. [10] NAS GD51/5/134/1,2. [11] *Mem. Marchioness of Lothian* ed. C. Kerr, 10. [12] *Lady Holland to Son*, 97, 100. [13] *Gent. Mag.* (1842), i. 94. [14] *Mem. Marchioness of Lothian*, 32.

D.R.F.

KERRISON, **Sir Edward**, 1st bt. (1776–1853), of Oakley Park, Suff. and 21 Holles Street, Mdx.

SHAFTESBURY	19 Feb. 1813–1818
NORTHAMPTON	1818–1820
EYE	13 Feb. 1824–1852

b. 30 July 1776,[1] o.s. of Matthias Kerrison of Bungay and Mary, da. and h. of Edward Barnes of Barsham, Suff.[2] *m.* 20 Oct. 1810, Mary Martha, da. of Alexander Ellice of Pittencrief, Fife, 1s. 3da. kntd. 5 Jan. 1815; CB 22 June 1815; KCH 1821; *cr.* bt. 27 July 1821; *suc.* fa. 1827; GCH 1831; KCB 18 July 1840. *d.* 9 Mar. 1853.
Cornet 6 Drag. 1796, lt. 1798; capt. 47 Ft. 1798; capt. 7 Drag. 1798, maj. 1803, lt.-col. 1805-26; brevet col. 1813; maj.-gen. 1819; col. 14 Drag. 1830-*d.*; lt.-gen. 1837; gen. 1851.

Capt. Suff. Borderers yeoman cav. 1831-50.

Kerrison, an anti-Catholic Tory 'widely acclaimed for his long and distinguished military career, combined with his high regard for horses', did not stand for Parliament in 1820, although he canvassed at Norwich, where 'some pains had been taken to obtain a candidate in the ministerial interest'.[3] His father had made his fortune trading in coal, corn and timber from Bungay quay during the Napoleonic wars and invested the profits in mortgages and land, including the 2nd Viscount Maynard's estate of Hoxne, where Kerrison 'expended an immense sum' improving Oakley Park to the architect Sidney Smirke's designs: 'the furniture is costly in the extreme, vases, Buhl cabinets, porce-laine meet you at every turn', reported Sir John Benn Walsh*.[4] Kerrison was made a baronet at the coronation in 1821 and was already known to the premier Lord Liverpool as 'a very good man' and 'a very warm

and kind friend of the government', who should be accommodated.[5] His successful negotiations in 1823 to purchase the Brome Hall estate and a controlling interest in the borough of Eye from the 2nd Marquess Cornwallis gave him the opportunity to return to the House.[6] After some delay and disgruntlement on the part of the corporation, he was returned unopposed on a vacancy in February 1824.[7] He voted for the usury laws repeal bill, 8 Apr., against condemning the indict-ment in Demerara of the Methodist missionary John Smith, 11 June 1824, and against Catholic relief, 1 Mar., 21 Apr., 10 May and the Irish franchise bill, 26 Apr. 1825. He divided with government for the duke of Cumberland's grant, 2, 10 June 1825. Frederick Henniker, whose sudden death prevented a contest at Eye at the 1826 general election, had dismissed him in January 1825 as a Member of insufficient talent 'to command, nor even to excite attention' with 'little claim on patronage' and 'surely ... not capable of speaking'.[8]

Kerrison's attendance lapsed during his father's last illness and, notifying the home secretary Peel, 17 Mar. 1827, that he was 'unfortunately detained', he offered to go up 'for a day ... should any question of imme-diate urgency take place'.[9] He received three weeks' leave, 27 Mar., and another month, 4 May, to attend to urgent business following his father's death, 12 Apr. Allowing for fluctuating values in land and pos-sibly another £56,000 outstanding to the Cornwallis family, Matthias Kerrison had estimated his assets at between £721,320 and £826,878 in 1825. Kerrison, as his heir, calculated that he had been worth £852,389 in late 1826, and the will was proved under £250,000, 30 Apr. 1827 (adjusted to £126,389 in 1830).[10] He sold their mercantile interests in Bungay after serving there as reeve, 1827-8, and also toyed with purchas-ing Eye Park in 1828.[11] He wrote to congratulate Peel on his return to office, 17 Jan. 1828, and promised to be 'at my *post* with sincere satisfaction, when all your arrangements are made'.[12] He failed to vote on repeal of the Test Acts, 26 Feb., but did so against extend-ing the East Retford franchise to the freeholders of Bassetlaw, 21 Mar., and against Catholic relief, 12 May. He divided with the Wellington ministry against ordnance reductions, 4 July 1828. Their patronage secretary Planta anticipated that he would vote 'with government' for Catholic emancipation in 1829, but he had become involved with the Brunswick clubs, presented and endorsed hostile petitions, 13 Mar., and voted resolutely against the measure, 6, 18, 27, 30 Mar. 1829.[13] He acquired 13 Great Stanhope Street, Mayfair as his town house that summer and in October 1829 returned the duke of Clarence's son-in-law Philip Charles Sidney for a vacancy at Eye.[14] Cumberland, Lord Fitzroy Somerset*, the king's private secretary Sir Herbert Taylor* and the commander-in-chief Lord Hill suggested him for the command of the 17th Lancers in the reshuffle that followed Sir Thomas Garth's death, but by 29 Nov. 1829 the king had agreed to Sir John Elley's appointment and stipulated only that Kerrison should have 'the next occurring vacancy'. (In June 1830 he became colonel of the king's regiment of light dragoons.)[15] He presented and endorsed petitions from Eye and the hundred of Hoxne for relief from agricultural distress, 8, 15 Mar., which he said he was confident ministers could remedy; but he voted against them on the Bathurst and Dundas pensions, 26 Mar. 1830. He voted against Jewish emancipation, 17 May. He voted to restrict and delay licensing for on-consumption under the sale of beer bill, 21 June, 1 July, having presented and endorsed Eye's petition recommending this, 4 May 1830. He campaigned actively in Suffolk for the defeated sitting Tory Gooch at the general election that summer and returned Sidney and himself for Eye.[16]

Kerrison presented an anti-slavery petition, 9 Nov. 1830. Ministers now considered him to be one of the 'moderate Ultras', and he voted against them when they were brought down on the civil list, 15 Nov. 1830. The Grey ministry's reform bill, which caused Sidney, mindful of his obligations to William IV, to resign to avoid casting a hostile vote, proposed the disfranchisement of Eye and was bitterly opposed by Kerrison, who returned the anti-reformer and West India agent William Burge in Sidney's place and voted with him against the second reading, 22 Mar., and for Gascoyne's wrecking amendment, 19 Apr. 1831. They came in unopposed at the ensuing general election.[17] He voted against the reintroduced reform bill at its second reading, 6 July, spoke and voted to adjourn its committee stage, 12 July, and divided for making the 1831 census the criterion for English borough disfranchisements, 19 July 1831. Admitting that he felt 'put on trial', he spoke strongly in his borough's defence when the clause to disfranchise it was considered, 21 July. Supported by Burge and their fellow anti-reformers Sadler and Wetherell, he said that he opposed reform from a sense of duty to his constituents and country because of the threat it posed to the constitution, and based his case against Eye losing both seats on errors in the 1821 census, which, although the disfranchisement was carried without a division that day, were later confirmed. He voted against taking a seat from Chippenham, 27 July, and divided against the bill's third reading, 19 Sept., and passage, 21 Sept.

Following the bill's defeat in the Lords and Eye's reallocation to schedule B, he opposed it openly, and regularly dined Walsh and other anti-reformers, with whom he subsequently joined the Carlton Club.[18] In a letter to Earl Jermyn* approving the Suffolk anti-reform address to the king, 4 Dec. 1831, he explained that he had

> until now been unwilling to put myself forward in the cause, fearful *interested* motives might be assigned to me. God knows, this is the smallest *ill* we have to dread, and if they [reformers] could prove the country would be saved in prosperity, they should be welcome to the interest I have in my borough.[19]

He divided against the revised bill at its second reading, 17 Dec. 1831, and against its committal, 20 Jan., the enfranchisement of Tower Hamlets, 28 Feb., and the third reading, 22 Mar. 1832. He paired (with Bethel Walrond) for a Conservative amendment to the Scottish reform bill, 1 June.[20] He voted, 26 Jan., and paired, 12 July 1832, with opposition on the Russian-Dutch loan. He had presented petitions against the Sale of Beer Act from licensed victuallers in the Norfolk and Suffolk hundreds where he had estates, 11 July 1831; and on the 20th he confirmed the severity of the agricultural distress testified to by the Suffolk Members as presenters of Bungay's petition against permitting the use of molasses in brewing and distilling. He voted with Burge for inquiry into how far the Sugar Refinery Act could be renewed with due regard to the interests of the West Indies, 12 Sept. 1831.

Notwithstanding reports that he would be opposed at Eye by Lord Henniker's son John (a Liberal whom his daughter Anna married in 1836) at the general election of 1832, Kerrison retained the seat virtually unchallenged for the Conservatives until he made way for his only son Edward Clarence Kerrison (1821-88) in 1852, and strenuously supported the party in the county.[21] Even so, his request to Peel as premier in September 1841 for the peerage he coveted was rejected.[22] He died at his London home in March 1853 'after only an hour's illness', and was commemorated by a stained glass window in the church at Eye and his memorial to his 'favourite chargers' – the horses he claimed had saved his life in battle.[23] The baronetcy and estates passed to Edward and his will also made guardianship arrangements for his daughter Agnes and provided for his widow and daughters Emily, Lady Mahon, and Anna, Lady Henniker, to whose descendants his estates reverted following Edward's death without issue.[24]

[1] Bungay (Holy Trinity) par. reg. [Suff. RO (Lowestoft) FC148/01/3] has 31 July 1775; Kerrison's memorial tablet in Hoxne church and Suff. RO (Ipswich) CP Reds 30 (Kerrison Ped.) give 1774. [2] CP Reds 30 (Kerrison Ped.). [3] *HP Commons, 1790-1820,* iv. 33; J. Rushen, 'Squires of Oakley Park', *Suff. Fair,* iv (3) (1974), 28; *Bury and Norwich Post,* 15 Mar. 1820. [4] Suff. RO (Ipswich), Kerrison mss HA68/3116/447; HA85/662/384; 671/5; NLW, Ormathwaite mss FG/1/6, p. 158. [5] Kerrison mss HA85/671/22; Suff. RO (Bury St. Edmunds), Hervey mss 941/56/54. [6] Kerrison mss HA68/2593/1430; TNA 30/11/277, ff. 79-80; Lansdowne mss, Holland to Lansdowne, 15 Aug. 1823; Add. 38296, f. 68. [7] Add. 40357, f. 305; Kerrison mss HA68/3116/596; Suff. RO (Ipswich), Henniker mss S1/2/8/1.13; *Ipswich Jnl.* 14 Feb.; *Bury and Norwich Post,* 18 Feb. 1824. [8] Henniker mss S1/2/8/1.12, 13, 15; 8/2.3. [9] Add. 40392, f. 301. [10] Kerrison mss HA85/662/384; PROB 11/1724/244; IR26/1134/350. [11] Kerrison mss HA68/3116/662; E.D. King, *In Search of the Kerrison Millions,* 2; Henniker mss S1/2/8/1.13. [12] Add. 40395, f. 49. [13] Kerrison mss HA68/3116/565. [14] Henniker mss S1/2/8/1.1(15); *Suff. Chron.* 17, 24 Oct. 1829. [15] Wellington mss WP1/1057/14-23; *Arbuthnot Jnl.* ii. 318. [16] *Ipswich Jnl.* 31 July, 7, 14, 21 Aug. 1830. [17] *Bury and Norwich Post,* 9, 16, 30 Mar.; *Ipswich Jnl.* 19 Mar. 1831. [18] Ormathwaite mss FG/1/6, pp. 77, 81, 156, 158. [19] Hervey mss 941/56/24. [20] *The Times,* 4 June 1832. [21] Ibid. 19 June; *Suff. Chron.* 30 June, *Ipswich Jnl.* 15 Dec. 1832; *Bury and Norwich Post,* 16 Mar. 1853. [22] Add. 40490, ff. 218-20. [23] *Ann. Reg.* (1853), Chron. p. 219; Rushen, 29-30. [24] PROB 11/2170/288; IR26/1970/203-5.

M.M.E.

KERRY, knight of *see* **FITZGERALD, Maurice**

KILDERBEE (afterwards **DE HORSEY**), **Spencer Horsey** (1790–1860), of Great Glemham, Suff. and 8 Upper Grosvenor Street, Mdx.

ALDEBURGH	25 May 1829–1830
ORFORD	1830–1832
NEWCASTLE-UNDER-LYME	1837–1841

b./bap. 2 Sept. 1790,[1] o.s. of Rev. Dr. Samuel Kilderbee (*d.* 1847) of Great Glemham, rect. of Campsey Ash, and Caroline, da. of Samuel Horsey of Bury St. Edmunds, Suff., wid. of George Waddington, barrister, of Ely, Camb. and Cavenham Hall, Bury St. Edmunds. *educ.* Eton c.1802-5; Univ. Coll. Oxf. 1807, scholar 1812-16, (BA 1811, MA 1815). *m.* 23 Feb. 1824, Lady Louisa Maria Judith Rous, da. of John Rous†, 1st earl of Stradbroke, 2s. 1da.; *suc.* grandfa. 1813, fa. 1847. Took name of De Horsey by royal lic. 20 Apr. 1832. *d.* 20 May 1860.

A descendant of the seventeenth century Framlingham wool merchant and draper Francis Kilderbee, this Member was the only son of the wealthy Suffolk cleric and patron of the arts Samuel Kilderbee, and heir by birth and designation of his paternal grandfather, the Ipswich attorney and town clerk Samuel Kilderbee (*d.* 1813), who had prospered as the agent of the Tory Rous family of Henham Hall.[2] He was also a maternal half-brother of Harry Spencer

Waddington (1781-1864) of Cavenham Hall, Bury St. Edmunds, Conservative Member for West Suffolk, 1838-59, and the barrister John Horsey Waddington (1783-1864).[3] Following his grandfather's death Kilderbee relinquished his intended ecclesiastical career and returned to Great Glemham, where he managed the family estates and became a private secretary to his father's patron as rector of Easton, the 5th earl of Rochford, who signified his intention of making him his heir. Adhering to his family's 'church and state politics', he signed the 1821 Suffolk anti-reform declaration, became a founder member that year of the Suffolk Pitt Club and was appointed a burgess of Orford and Aldeburgh by his neighbour at Sudbourne, the 3rd marquess of Hertford, on account of his local influence.[4] It was enhanced by his marriage in 1824 with the 1st earl of Stradbroke's daughter and, predicting that 'our Kil will be a good man and true', Hertford decided to return him for a vacancy at Aldeburgh in 1829, tied down 'by a strong promise to *hold during pleasure* and to *follow my politics*'.[5] He duly voted against Jewish emancipation, 5 Apr., 17 May 1830. He was returned for Orford at the general election that summer, when Hertford reserved Aldeburgh for his former steward John Wilson Croker and the duke of Wellington's heir Lord Douro.[6] Rochford died, 3 Sept. 1830, after directing but failing to authorize changes in his will, 30 Aug., entailing his estates on Kilderbee, whose case in favour of the holograph will was rejected by the prerogative court of Canterbury, 28 Jan. 1831. According to Hertford, he had lost £7,000 a year, £12-14,000 in ready money, land and houses 'for want of a few visits'.[7]

Kilderbee was counted among the Wellington ministry's 'friends' and divided with them on the civil list when they were brought down, 15 Nov. 1830. He voted against the Grey ministry's reform bill, by which Aldeburgh and Orford were to be disfranchised, at its second reading, 22 Mar., and for Gascoyne's wrecking amendment, 19 Apr. 1831, and retained his seat at the general election that month.[8] He voted against the reintroduced reform bill at its second reading, 6 July 1831. When he seconded Croker's proposal for a combined Aldeburgh and Orford constituency, 22 July, it was variously reported that he testified from local knowledge to the close proximity and ties between the two of the two boroughs,[9] and that he argued for additional county rather than borough representation to serve the agricultural interest.[10] He voted against taking a seat from Chippenham, 27 July, and the bill's passage, 21 Sept. He voted against the revised reform bill at its second reading, 17 Dec. 1831, and against enfranchising Tower Hamlets, 28 Feb., and the third reading, 22 Mar. 1832. He voted against the second reading of the Irish reform bill, 25 May. He divided against government on the Russian-Dutch loan, 26 Jan., 12 July 1832.

A founder and lifelong member of the Carlton Club, Kilderbee, who assumed the name de Horsey in April 1832, as co-heir with his half-brother John to the estate of his maternal grandfather (d. 1771), was not a candidate at the 1832 and 1835 general elections, but came in for Newcastle-under-Lyme as the second Conservative in 1837. Nothing came of his endeavours at Barnstaple and Leicester in 1841 and he did not stand for Parliament again.[11] A widower since 1843, he died in May 1860 at Cowes, where he resided intermittently at Melcombe House with his father (d. 1847) and unmarried sister Carolina Kilderbee. The main beneficiaries of his will, which invoked indentures made prior to his marriage, were his sons General William Henry Beaumont de Horsey (1826-1915), his successor at Great Glemham, and Admiral Algernon Frederick Rous de Horsey (1827-1922), his only daughter Adeline Louisa Maria (1824-1915) having been 'amply provided for' on becoming the 7th earl of Cardigan's second wife in 1858.[12]

[1] IGI (Suff). [2] PROB 11/1544/257; IR26/584/320; Suff. RO (Ipswich), Charles Partridge peds. CP30; HA11/B1/1, 8; 61/436/874; B26/412/1358. [3] PROB 11/1130/283; Gent. Mag. (1863), i. 593. [4] Bury and Norwich Post, 4 Apr. 1821; Suff. Chron. 19 Aug. 1821, 20 Aug. 1822; PP (1835), xxvi. 14-16, 434-6. [5] Suff. RO HA11/C1/3; HB26/412/1358-9; Suff. Chron. 20 Aug. 1822; Add. 60288, ff. 122, 144, 295. [6] Ipswich Jnl. 7 Aug. 1830. [7] The Times, 25, 29 Jan. 1831; Add. 60288, f. 295. [8] Suff. Chron. 26 Mar., 23 Apr., 7 May 1831. [9] Parl. Deb. (ser. 3), v. 245-50; The Times, 23 July 1831. [10] Mirror of Parliament (1831), 783. [11] The Times, 10 Mar. 1832, 26 July 1837, 18, 30 June 1841; Add. 40485, ff. 325-6; 60288, ff. 295-6. [12] Gent. Mag. (1860), i. 101; Oxford DNB sub Lancastre Saldanha.

M.M.E.

KILLEEN, Lord see **PLUNKETT, Arthur James**

KING, Edward, Visct. Kingsborough (1795–1837).

Co. CORK   1818–1826

b. 10 Nov. 1795,[1] 1st s. of George, 3rd earl of Kingston [I] (d. 1839), and Lady Helena Moore, da. of Stephen, 1st Earl Mountcashell [I]; bro. of Hon. Robert Henry King*. educ. Eton;[2] Exeter, Oxf. 1814. unm. styled Visct. Kingsborough 1799-d. d.v.p. 27 Feb. 1837.

Kingsborough, a man 'of a retiring and studious disposition', had been returned unopposed for county Cork in 1818 on the combined interest of the 3rd Earl of Shannon, a recent convert to the Whigs, and his father 'Big George', 3rd Earl of Kingston, who subsequently rallied to the Liverpool ministry.[3] At the 1820 general election their electoral pact held firm and he was again returned unopposed.[4] A mostly silent Member, who was increasingly absorbed in the study of Mexican antiquities, when present he offered general support to government, by whom his father was listed as having obtained an inspectorate of fisheries and requested a revenue surveyorship.[5] He voted in defence of minister's conduct towards Queen Caroline, 6 Feb. 1821. He divided for Catholic claims, 28 Feb. 1821, 1 Mar., 21 Apr., 10 May 1825. He voted against revenue cuts, 6 Mar., repeal of the additional malt duty, 3 Apr., reductions to the duke of Clarence's grant, 18 June, an opposition call for economy and retrenchment, 27 June 1821, and more extensive tax reductions, 21 Feb. 1822. He was in the majority against providing information on the plot to murder the Irish viceroy Lord Wellesley, 24 Mar., but in the minorities for Newport's amendment to the Irish tithes bill, 19 June, and to limit the duration of the Irish insurrection bill, 8 July 1822. In his only known spoken intervention, he presented and endorsed a petition from Cove for repeal of the window tax, 1 May 1822.[6] He voted against repeal of the Foreign Enlistment Act, 16 Apr. 1823. He divided for the usury laws repeal bill, 27 Feb. 1824. He voted for the Irish insurrection bill, 14 June 1824, but against suppression of the Catholic Association, 15, 21, 25 Feb. 1825; Peel, the home secretary, remarked that Kingston, 'having written letters to me some time back accusing the government for not preventing the collection of rent and other evils of the Association, actually compelled his son ... to vote against the bill'.[7] Kingsborough was given a vote of thanks at an aggregate meeting of county Cork Catholics that June.[8] He voted for the duke of Cumberland's annuity bill, 6 June 1825. He declined to attend the Association dinner for the 'friends of civil and religious liberty', 2 Feb. 1826.[9] He divided against the emergency admission of foreign corn, 11 May 1826.

At the 1826 dissolution Kingsborough retired in favour of his younger brother Robert, citing 'ill health'; the local press surmised that he 'prefers the calm pursuits of literature to the troublesome career of a legislator'.[10] Thereafter he set about completing his Antiquities of Mexico (1831), for which he had been employing a Spanish artist to copy manuscripts, including those he had first seen in the Bodleian while up at Oxford, since 1824.[11] He signed a memorial to Wellesley for a new road between Cork and Limerick in 1827, and a county Cork Protestant declaration in support of Catholic emancipation in 1828.[12] By 1830 he was a recluse, 'too busy', as he informed his fellow bibliophile Sir Thomas Phillips, 'to make any engagements'.[13] Following his father's mental break-down that year he assumed responsibility for the running of the family estates, which were so encumbered that they were placed in chancery. His allowance from the Irish lord chancellor was reputedly £6,000 a year, which he unsuccessfully tried to increase, and in February 1837 he went to debtors' gaol, apparently 'in the hope that this extremity would induce the chancellor to relax the purse strings'. It has been said that he was 'imprisoned for a debt of his father, for which he had become security' and 'not from his own extravagance'; but the expenses of his book, which was published privately at an estimated total cost of £30,000, and his valuable collection of manuscripts, some of which he donated to the British Museum and Trinity College, Dublin, 'far exceeded his own resources'. A few days after being imprisoned he developed typhus fever and was released.[14] He died shortly thereafter. His vast library, comprising ancient manuscripts from all over the world, was sold at auction by an order of chancery in 1842.[15]

[1] IGI (Ireland); R.D. King-Harman, *The Kings, Earls of Kingston*, 84. *Oxford DNB* gives 16 Nov. [2] King-Harman, 84. [3] Ibid; Add. 38287, f. 287. [4] *Dublin Evening Post*, 9, 11, 16 Mar. 1820. [5] *Black Bk.* (1823), 168; *Session of Parl. 1825*, p. 471. [6] *The Times*, 2 May 1822. [7] Add. 37303, f. 196. [8] *Dublin Evening Post*, 18 June 1826. [9] *O'Connell Corresp.* iii. 1278. [10] *Southern Reporter*, 8, 17 June; *Cork Constitution*, 8 June 1826. [11] Add. 34569, ff. 61, 194, 210. [12] Add. 38103, f. 128; *Southern Reporter*, 13 Nov. 1828. [13] Bodl. mss Phillips Robinson b. 124, f. 245. [14] Ibid. b. 126, f. 152; King-Harman, 84-86; *Gent. Mag.* (1837), i. 537-8. [15] *Bibliotheca ... Edvardi vicecomitis de Kingsborough*; mss Phillips Robinson c. 478, f. 235; d. 143, ff. 1-8.

P.J.S.

KING, Edward Bolton (1801–1878), of Umberslade Hall, Tanworth-in-Arden, Warws.[1]

WARWICK	1831–1837
WARWICKSHIRE SOUTH	1857–1859

b. 15 July 1801, 1st s. of Edward King of Croston, Lancs. and 2nd w. Dorothea, da. of John Myers of Preston, Lancs. *educ.* Eton;[2] Corpus, Oxf. 1819; L. Inn 1821; continental tour 1823-4. *m.* (1) 7 Feb. 1828, Georgiana (*d.* 6 May 1858), da. of Robert Knight*, 1s. 6da.; (2) 19 July 1859, Louisa, da. of Rev. Charles Palmer of Lighthorne, Warws., 1s. 2da. *suc.* gt.-uncle Edward Bolton of Askham, Westmld. 1803; fa. 1824. *d.* 26 Mar. 1878.
  Sheriff, Warws. 1830-1.
  Capt. Warws. yeoman cav. 1827, 2nd troop 1831, maj. 1845, lt.-col. 1848, ret. 1876.

Bolton King (as he was known) was the scion of a northern family of distinguished Whig churchmen and lawyers. He was a paternal nephew of James King

(1750-84), the circumnavigator, Walker King (1755-1827), private secretary to Lord Rockingham as prime minister and the bishop of Rochester, and John King (1759-1830) who, as the Grenville ministry's patronage secretary in 1806, sat briefly for Enniskillen; but it was to his maternal great-uncle, the lawyer Edward Bolton of Askham (1734-1803), that he owed his name and the bulk of his fortune. His trustees, whom John King prosecuted in chancery on his behalf in 1818 for alleged mismanagement, had liquidated the Bolton estates for £125,699, which he invested in consols.[3] Raised in Lancashire, where his father, a bencher of Gray's Inn, was vice-chancellor of the duchy and the family lived successively at Croston, Askham Hall and Carr Hill House, Kirkham, Bolton King inherited the latter by his father's death in December 1824.[4] He did not, as intended, practice law but pursued the life of a country gentleman, initially at Kirkham, where he kept 'a fine pack [of harrier hounds] showing great breed and power', and subsequently at the former Archer estate of Umberslade Hall, ten miles north of Warwick, which, having disposed of his Kirkham property, he purchased for £76,000 in 1826.[5] His marriage in February 1828 to Georgiana Knight, daughter of the Member for Wallingford, term as sheriff, and captaincy in the county Member Francis Lawley's cavalry troop enhanced his standing in Warwickshire, where, at the county meeting of 4 Apr. 1831 he seconded the resolution thanking the Grey ministry for redeeming their promise to legislate for reform.[6] Two days later he publicized his candidature for Warwick, which his father-in-law had contested in 1792, and where a campaign to oust the anti-reformer and 'Warwick Castle Member' Sir Charles Greville was under way. After a fierce contest, he was returned at the general election in May with the sitting independent John Tomes, as a reformer and committed advocate of retrenchment.[7]

In his maiden speech, 1 July 1831, Bolton King, whose readiness to air his views earned him the nickname 'Bellows',[8] vainly opposed the chancellor Lord Althorp's decision to introduce a tariff on certain cottons, which he claimed (from Lancashire evidence) would assist foreign competitors already boosted by the export of British machinery. He also made a point of praising 'the repeal of the duty on printed cottons' in the previous Parliament. Possibly aligning with Knight and Lawley, he divided for the reintroduced reform bill at its second reading, 6 July, and generally for its details, but against the Saltash disfranchisement that ministers no longer pressed, 26 July. Reflecting local opinion, he voted against the proposed division of counties, 11 Aug., and for the enfranchisement of

£50 tenants-at-will, 18 Aug. On 30 Aug., having first raised the matter with ministers, who conceded that the 'defect' was genuine, he explained that constraints in the bill's registration clause left no time for current errors to be rectified prior to registration and that, unless amended, the bill would leave many Warwick voters unfranchised. He now refused to delay or jeopardize the bill by moving an amendment and defended the 'scot and lot' franchise:

> The rated inhabitants in the country towns, who are eventually to lose their franchise as such, are the very same class of persons who are so properly to be enfranchised in the large towns; and though many will continue to vote as £10 householders, yet as rents are in general much lower in these old boroughs than in the new ones the number of electors will be greatly diminished, and by that means you will tend to restore that nomination system we have been labouring so hard to destroy.

Travelling regularly between Warwick and London during the annual yeomanry training, he voted for the reform bill at its third reading, 19 Sept., and passage, 21 Sept., the second reading of the Scottish bill, 23 Sept., and Lord Ebrington's confidence motion, 10 Oct.[9] He was fêted at the Warwick mayor's feast, 1 Nov., and the county meeting which protested at the reform bill's Lords' defeat, 8 Nov., when he was one of the main speakers.[10] He divided for the revised reform bill at its second reading, 17 Dec. 1831, steadily for its details, and for the third reading, 22 Mar. 1832. He brought up the Leamington Political Union's petition for inclusion of their town in the Warwick constituency, 28 Feb., and several calling for the withdrawal of supplies pending its enactment, 21 May. He voted for Irish reform bill at its second reading, 25 May, and against amending the Scottish bill, 1 June, but to restore the 40s. Irish freeholder franchise, 18 June 1832. He divided with government in both divisions on the Dublin election controversy, 23 Aug. 1831, the Russian-Dutch loan, 26 Jan., 12 July, Portugal, 9 Feb., and the navy civil departments bill 6 Apr. 1832; but against them on civil service expenditure, 18 July 1831, the Irish registrar's salary, 9 Apr., and provision for the Irish poor, 19 June 1832. He also voted to make coroners' inquests public, 20 June 1832. He presented and endorsed a numerously signed petition from Warwick Political Society for the immediate abolition of colonial slavery, 11 Oct. 1831, and voted in Fowell Buxton's minority for a select committee to consider this, 24 May 1832.

Standing as a Liberal and staunch churchman, inclined to support the ballot, Bolton King contested Warwick successfully at the general election of 1832, when a petition against his return failed, and again in 1835.[11] Following his defeat in 1837, he joined Brooks's, 13 Mar. 1839, and tested the ground regularly in Warwick and the county before coming in for South Warwickshire for a single Parliament in 1857.[12] Preferring Chadshunt, the Knight estate he had consolidated and improved, he sold Umberslade that year to the Birmingham metal manufacturer George Frederick Muntz, whose father (of that name), the Liberal Member for Birmingham, 1840-57, had been his tenant there since 1850.[13] He died at Chadshunt in March 1878 and was succeeded in the entailed Knight estates by the son of his first marriage, Edward Raleigh King (1833-1900), and in his purchased estates by the son of his second marriage Bolton King (1860-1937). A specialist in Italian history, he was the defeated Liberal in Warwickshire South-West at the 'Khaki' by-election of 1901.[14]

[1] King's papers remain in private hands. The first paragraph of this biography draws on selected transcripts and a draft family history by Oliver Bolton King of High Wycombe (1953), made available to Warws. RO for filming [Bolton King mss TD 66/56], cited henceforth as King. [2] Not in school lists, but see *The Times*, 27 Mar. 1878. [3] IR26/425/72; King, 66-74. [4] PROB 8/218; 11/1694/27; *Gent. Mag.* (1824), ii. 645. [5] *VCH Lancs.* ii. 471; *VCH Warws.* v. 168; King, 79. [6] *Gent. Mag.* (1828), i. 175; H.A. Adderley, *Hist. Warws. Yeomanry Cav.* vii; *Warwick Advertiser*, 9 Apr. 1831. [7] Warws. RO, Moore and Tibbit mss CR 1097/330/60, 63, 98; *Warwick Advertiser*, 9, 30 Apr., 7 May; *The Times*, 12 Apr. 1831; Warws. RO, Greville of Warwick Castle mss CR 1886, box 613/11. [8] *Dyott's Diary*, ii. 303. [9] *Warwick Advertiser*, 17, 24 Sept., 1, 15 Oct. 1831. [10] Ibid. 29 Oct., 5, 12 Nov.; *The Times*, 10 Nov. 1831. [11] *Abstract of Commons Evidence respecting the Borough of Warwick and the Earl of Warwick* (1834), 6-7; *CJ*, lxxxviii. 97, 385; *VCH Warws.* viii. 503. [12] *Warwick Advertiser*, 29 July, 5, 12, 19 Aug. 1837; D. Paterson, 'Tory Political Influence in mid-19th Cent. Warwick', *Warws. Hist.* v (1975-8), 197-207. [13] Shakespeare Birthplace Trust RO, Verney (Lords Willoughby de Broke) mss DR 622/43, 45-47, 61-66, 88-99, 153, 163-4, 186; *VCH Warws.* v. 168; G. Tyack, *Country Houses of Warws.* 6. [14] *The Times*, 27 Mar., 17 May 1878; *VCH Warws.* iii. 180, 214; v. 32, 89; J.D. Browne, 'Stratford By-election of 1901', *Warws. Hist.* v (1981-4), 15-29, 157-63.

M.M.E.

KING, Hon. Henry (1776–1839).

Co. SLIGO   4 Dec. 1822–1831

b. 4 July 1776, 4th *s.* of Robert King, MP [I], 2nd earl of Kingston [I] (*d.* 1799), and Caroline, da. and h. of Richard Fitzgerald, MP [I], of Mount Ophaly, co. Kildare. *educ.* Eton 1785-9; Harrow 1789-93; Exeter, Oxf. 1794. *m.* (1) 9 Jan. 1802, Mary (*d.* 26 May 1821), da. of Hon. and Very Rev. John Hewitt, dean of Cloyne, 3s. 4da.; (2) 28 Feb. 1832, Catherine, da. of Rev. Edward Philipps, wid. of J. Richardson, *s.p.* KCB 28 Mar. 1835. *d.* 25 Nov. 1839.

Ensign 47 Ft. 1794, lt. 1795; capt. 56 Ft. 1796; capt. 1 Life Gds. 1799; capt. 43 Ft. 1802; maj. 5 Ft. 1804, lt.-col. 1809, col. 1814; maj.-gen. 1825; col. 1 W.I. Regt. 1834; lt.-gen. 1838.

Groom of bedchamber Jan. 1817-Feb. 1830.

King's father sat in the Irish Parliament for Boyle, 1776-83, and county Cork, 1783-90, 1791-97, before succeeding as 2nd earl of Kingston in 1797.[1] King was educated in England and entered the army on 7 Feb. 1794. After matriculating at Oxford that November he served 'with credit' in the Bahamas and at St. Domingo, where he obtained his captaincy. On the Helder expedition of September 1799 he was 'severely wounded' by musket balls in both legs, and although he managed to return to active service and 'remained a man of soldier-like gait and commanding presence', his injuries plagued him for life and were declared 'fully equal to the loss of a limb' by an army medical board, 21 May 1816. Ship-wrecked and taken prisoner by the Dutch on his way to Hanover in December 1805, he was subsequently exchanged, and in July 1807 commanded a wing in the attack on Buenos Aires, in which he was wounded in the left arm. He served with distinction in the Peninsula at Busaco and Salamanca, but by 1812 his legs had 'assumed so angry an appearance, that his medical attendants, apprehensive of a necessity for amputation, insisted on his quitting'. He resumed command of the 2nd battalion of the 5th Foot on its return to England in 1813 and, following the disbandment of his battalion in 1816, was appointed groom of the bedchamber to the prince regent the following year.[2]

In 1822 King started for a vacancy in county Sligo at the prompting of his elder brothers George, who had succeeded as 3rd earl of Kingston in 1799 and owned property there, and Robert, 1st Viscount Lorton. The local opposition complained that as Kingston's 'protegé brother' he would 'vote on political questions by the dictation of his lordship', and warned against electing a non-resident at the behest of 'two lordly brothers' and the 'aggrandizement of a proud family, whose head is without principle'.[3] Attempts by Charles King O'Hara, son of the late Member and an 'old friend' of Lorton, to avert a contest came to nothing.[4] At the nomination King dismissed the charges of non-residence by explaining that 'from a boy' it had been his profession to 'fight your enemies in distant lands' and 'bleed in the service of my country', which had prevented him from 'having a home'. After a seven-day contest he was returned amid complaints of intimidation and interference by Kingston, who allegedly 'induced' the Catholic priests to support him. (He

'let himself be put in by a junto of Popish priests', a Conservative publication later recalled.) Petitions against his return came to nothing.[5]

A regular but mostly silent attender, King gave steady support to the Liverpool ministry.[6] He voted against inquiry into the parliamentary franchise, 20 Feb., and reform of the Scottish representation, 2 June 1823, and of the representation of Edinburgh, 26 Feb. 1824, 13 Apr. 1826. He was in the majority for the grant for Irish churches and glebe houses, 11 Apr. 1823. He divided against repeal of the Foreign Enlistment Act, 16 Apr., and inquiry into the prosecution of the Dublin Orange rioters, 22 Apr. Commenting on 'why he, a mere tyro in the House', had risen to second Fowell Buxton's motion for inquiry into the capture in 1814 of the ship *Requin* by one Ogilvie, an army commissary, he explained that he had known the individual concerned for over 25 years and had 'served with him in the Peninsula', 2 July 1823. He presented a petition against the Irish tithes bill, 15 Apr. 1824.[7] He voted against condemnation of the trial in Demerara of the Methodist missionary John Smith, 11 June, and for the Irish insurrection bill, 14 June 1824. He voted for suppression of the Catholic Association, 15, 25 Feb. 1825. He was one of the Members who, having 'attended last session', ministers 'thought it impossible to omit' from the select committee on the state of Ireland, 17 Feb.[8] He divided against repeal of the usury laws that day. He voted against Catholic claims, 1 Mar., 21 Apr., 10 May. He was listed as having divided for the duke of Cumberland's annuity bill, 2, 10 June, but against it, 6 June 1825. He voted against Denman's motion condemning the Jamaican slave trials, 2 Mar. 1826.

At the 1826 general election King, having 'amply proved himself' to his former opponents, was returned unopposed.[9] He presented a petition against Catholic claims, 5 Mar. 1827, and voted thus next day.[10] He and his colleague Cooper introduced a bill to relieve persons from unlawful distresses for rent in Ireland, 8 Mar., which received royal assent, 2 July (7 & 8 Geo. IV. c. 69). He divided for the duke of Clarence's annuity, 17 Mar. He voted against the disfranchisement of Penryn, 28 May 1827. Affirming his 'firm and conscientious attachment to the principles of the constitution in church and state', on 28 Jan. 1828 he wrote to congratulate Peel, the home secretary, on the formation of the Wellington ministry, which he hoped would 'fully guarantee the blessings of civil and religious liberty in the *true* acceptance of the terms':

I am no *bigot*, nor can I assume to arrogate to myself the appellation of '*Saint*', though I believe I have already been *canonized* by *the Association*, at least *that assembly*

seem inclined to confer on me the distinctive consequences of *sanctity*, 'proscription and persecution'. I
trust ... government will shield me, and others similarly circumstanced, from eventual martyrdom. I wish
all ... cared as little for the malevolence of Papist agitators as myself, as I shall never shrink from giving my
humble support in or out of Parliament to the principles
I profess, under any circumstances of personal hazard
or threatened hostility ... Although *I* have long suffered
from severe and repeated attacks of illness, I shall be in
my place in the House.[11]

Admitting that he was 'no practised debator', 6 Feb.,
he complained that he had been 'denounced by an
illegal Association' as an 'enemy of my country', but
said he would 'never be intimidated by any menace
from any body ... to give my vote contrary to my conscience'. He brought up constituency petitions with
which he 'totally differed' in support of Catholic relief
that day, and 12, 14 Feb. He voted against repeal of
the Test Acts, 28 Feb. Next month Lorton sought to
dispel rumours 'industriously spreading' in Sligo
of King's 'intention to retire in consequence of an
intended appointment for him on a foreign station'.
'There is no foundation whatever for such a report,
nor any probability of his going abroad', he informed
O'Hara, 25 Mar.[12] King presented petitions against
Catholic relief, 25, 28 Apr., and voted thus, 12 May
1828. Later that month he told O'Hara of his 'regret'
at the Commons majority for the relief bill, which 'the
peers' would 'remedy'.[13] In February 1829 he was
listed by Planta, the patronage secretary, as 'opposed'
to Catholic emancipation but likely to support securities when the principle was carried. On 11 Feb. he
welcomed the bill to dissolve the Association and
'strangle a monster', but declared that 'after a residence of between three and four months in Ireland'
he was 'more determined than ever' to oppose 'any
concession'. He was a regular presenter of hostile
petitions, voted steadily against emancipation, 6, 18,
23, 27, 30 Mar., and was in the minority of 16 to raise
the new minimum Irish county freehold qualification
from £10 to £20, 27 Mar. (The 'Hon. King' listed in
the minority for Daniel O'Connell to be allowed to
take his seat unhindered, 18 May, was surely either
Robert Edward or Robert Henry King.) In October
1829 the Ultra Commons leader Sir Richard Vyvyan
numbered him among the 'Tories strongly opposed to
the present government'. He was in the minority for
Knatchbull's amendment to the address, 4 Feb., following which Wellington informed George IV that he
was 'concerned' that a member of the household had
'voted against the address', 7 Feb. 1830.[14] Next day
Lord Ellenborough recorded that he had been 'turned

out by the king himself; the duke having only mentioned the fact', but confirmation of his dismissal from
Sir Frederick Watson, master of the household, did
not reach Lord Winchester, groom of the stole, until
11 Feb.[15] That day King was in the majority against the
transfer of East Retford's seats to Birmingham. Next
day Peel complained to Wellington that King had not
been 'informed of his dismissal' but had 'read about
it in the newspapers', and regretted his removal as 'he
supported the government on the previous night and
would do so again'. Orders to confirm his dismissal
went out that day, when he voted with opposition to
condemn the filling of the vacant navy treasurership.[16]
'He became a sacrifice to political expediency and a
sense of duty superior to personal interests, being dismissed from his place ... for his conscientious votes',
it was later remarked.[17] On 19 Apr. King, 'having
reason to think that an opposition is in contemplation in consequence of my firm and devoted attachment to the constitution *as it was*', applied to O'Hara
for support in the event of a dissolution, but was told
that his 'non-residing alone' would preclude it.[18] He
was granted leave from the Rye election committee on
account of ill health, 6 May, and again, 10 May, when
he was excused further attendance after his physician
testified that he was 'now so ill as to be unable to attend
for three of four days'. He may have been the King
listed in the minority for repeal of the Irish coal duties,
13 May 1830.

At the 1830 general election King offered again,
claiming to be 'divested of all party bias'. Pressed at
the nomination about his beliefs, he explained that
he had opposed emancipation 'on principle alone'
but now 'bowed to that alteration', and promised to
oppose 'oppressive legislation' and 'uphold the liberty
of the press', even though he had 'been taunted as the
old general and the lame old pensioner' by the *Sligo
Observer*. 'Although I am no professed orator', he
added, 'I have made some speeches'. After a three-
day contest he was returned in second place.[19] He
was listed by the Wellington ministry as one of the
25 'violent Ultras' and he voted against them in the
crucial division on the civil list, 15 Nov. 1830. He presented petitions for the abolition of slavery, 18 Nov.
1830, 28 Feb. 1831. He challenged a petition from
county Roscommon for repeal of the Union and
argued that the Protestants of Ireland were 'almost
universally in favour of a continuance of the connection', 14 Feb. 1831. He brought up a petition from
Sligo borough for parliamentary reform, 28 Feb.,
and voted for the second reading of the Grey ministry's reform bill, 22 Mar. 'King, who is not bound up
with the rotten-borough system, has given his cordial

adhesion to the reform bill, and thus neutralizes ... his colleague', observed *The Times*.[20] He paired against Gascoyne's wrecking amendment, 19 Apr. 1831. At the ensuing general election he stood as a reformer, 'devoted' to the 'preservation of our established institutions'. (Pressed on the hustings, however, he admitted that he 'considered the qualification for voters too low'.) 'Refused assistance' by his brother Lorton, the local independents rallied to his support, but owing to 'the opening of an old wound' he was unable to attend and was proposed *in absentia*. After a two-day contest he was defeated by two anti-reformers, to the consternation of the *Dublin Evening Post*.[21] He did not stand again.

King was appointed colonel of the 1st West India Regiment in 1834, awarded the KCB the following year and promoted to lieutenant-general at the coronation brevet of 1838. He died at Grove Lodge, near Windsor, in November 1839, 'shattered by wounds that for 40 years preyed on his health without impairing his spirit', and attended by the same physician who had seen him 'struck to the earth on the sand-hills of Holland, crippled to all appearance for life, with grievous wounds, of which he bore the deeply entrenched scars to his grave'.[22] By his will, dated 29 Nov. 1838 and proved under £12,000, his first wife's 'fortune' of 3,000 Irish pounds and the £5,000 annuity 'charged upon the family estates' which had been left to him by his father was divided among the seven children of his first marriage. His second wife received an annuity of £500. The residue passed to his eldest son Henry Robert (1804-42).[23]

[1] *Hist. Irish Parl.* v. 31-32. [2] R.D. King-Harman, *The Kings, Earls of Kingston*, 116-21; *United Service Jnl.* (1840), ii. 519-29. [3] NLI, O'Hara mss 20331 (2), Lorton to O'Hara, 20 Sept.; 20316, Irwin to O'Hara, 30 Sept., Gethin to same, 1 Nov. 1822. [4] Ibid. 20331 (2), King to O'Hara, 13, 14 Nov. 1822. [5] *Roscommon and Leitrim Gazette*, 30 Nov. 1822; *The Times*, 12 Feb. 1823; PRO NI, Rossmore mss T2929/3/1, Westenra to Rossmore, 12 June 1824; *Portraits of Eminent Conservatives* ed. H. Ryall (ser. 2), 2. [6] *Session of Parl. 1825*, p. 471. [7] *The Times*, 16 Apr. 1824. [8] Add. 40373, f. 187. [9] *Roscommon and Leitrim Gazette*, 17, 24 June 1826. [10] *The Times*, 6 Mar. 1827. [11] Add. 40395, f. 152. [12] O'Hara mss 20331(2). [13] Ibid. King to O'Hara, 26 May 1828. [14] Wellington mss WP1/1098/12. [15] *Ellenborough Diary* ii. 188; Wellington mss WP1/1094/31. [16] Wellington mss WP1/1094/15; 1098/33. [17] *United Service Jnl.* (1840), ii. 528. [18] O'Hara mss 20308 (7), King to O'Hara with reply, 19 Apr. 1830. [19] *Sligo Jnl.* 29 July, 20 Aug. 1830. [20] *The Times*, 23 Apr. 1831. [21] *Sligo Jnl.* 6, 20 May; *Dublin Evening Post*, 21 May 1831. [22] *Gent. Mag.* (1840), i. 89-90; *United Service Jnl.* (1840), ii. 529. [23] PROB 11/1923/107; IR26/1553/35.

P.J.S.

KING, **Hon. Robert** (1804–1869), of Rockingham, co. Roscommon.

CO. ROSCOMMON   1826–1830

b. 17 July 1804, 1st s. of Robert Edward, 1st Visct. Lorton [I], and Lady Frances Harman, da. of Lawrence Harman Harman (formerly Parsons), 1st Visct. Oxmantown [I]. *educ.* ?Eton 1817; Trinity, Dublin 1823; continental tour 1825-6. *m.* 7 Dec. 1829, Anne, da. of Sir Robert Newcomen Gore Booth, 3rd bt., of Lissadill, co. Sligo, 2s. 1da. *suc.* fa. as 2nd Visct. Lorton [I] 20 Nov. 1854; cos. James as 6th earl of Kingston [I] 8 Sept. 1869. *d.* 16 Oct. 1869.

Sheriff, co. Roscommon 1835-6.

King's father, an army officer who once fought an inconsequential duel with his sister's disreputable lover, was the second son of the 2nd earl of Kingston, on whose death in 1799 he inherited the heavily indebted but subsequently much improved Rockingham estate in Roscommon.[1] Having been Member for Jamestown, 1796-7, and Boyle, 1798-1800, he was raised to the Irish peerage as Baron Erris at the Union, which he opposed, and became Viscount Lorton in 1806. His elder brother, the 3rd earl of Kingston, came into the family's principal estates in county Cork, which was represented during this period by his sons Viscount Kingsborough and Robert Henry King; his younger brothers were Edward, Member for Roscommon in the 1802 Parliament, and Henry, who was returned for county Sligo in 1822. Unlike his relatives, Lorton, who was elected a representative peer in 1822, was an anti-Catholic ministerialist: he wrote to Peel, the home secretary, to condemn the influence of the priests, 26 Feb., and voted against relief in the Lords, 17 May 1825.[2] King, who was brought up in a rigidly Evangelical household, celebrated his coming of age at a public dinner in Boyle that July, when it was reported that he would be put up by the unpopular Lorton against the pro-Catholic county Members. From August he travelled in Europe with his father, and on 26 Dec. 1825 he issued an address from Naples confirming that he would offer at the following general election.[3] Back in Ireland by early June 1826, he was returned unopposed for Roscommon after Stephen Mahon unexpectedly retired. He was considered by the Irish administration as 'a Protestant vote' gained, but, despite refusing to elucidate his principles on the hustings or in correspondence arising out of a Catholic meeting the following month, he made a conciliatory gesture to the Catholic freeholders at his election dinner which led to hopes that he might not, in fact, be hostile to their cause.[4]

However, he certainly voted against Catholic relief, 6 Mar. 1827, when his cousin and uncle were listed in the favourable minority. Opposition votes by the 'Hon. R. King' in that and later sessions were probably given by Robert Henry King; unless it was he who spoke for going into committee on the corn bill, 25 Apr. 1828, he was apparently silent in debate, as the presentation of numerous petitions in this Parliament can safely be attributed to the Member for county Cork. He missed the division on Catholic relief, 12 May, yet in reply to a letter from the O'Conor Don, the leading local Catholic, which was aired at a dinner in December 1828, he apparently revealed that he would now vote in its favour.[5] However, in February 1829 he was considered by Planta, the Wellington ministry's patronage secretary, to be one of the Protestants 'opposed to securities', and it is likely that he was absent from the divisions that session. If indeed it was he and not his namesake who voted for emancipation, 6, 30 Mar., his father, whom Lord Holland later described as a fanatical Orangeman, nevertheless divided against it in the Lords, 4, 10 Apr. 1829.[6] It was possibly this Member who voted against parliamentary reform and the enfranchisement of Birmingham, Leeds and Manchester, 18, 23 Feb., Jewish emancipation, 5 Apr., 17 May, and reducing the grant for South American missions, 7 June 1830. One county newspaper credited him with dividing for Davenport's motion for inquiry into agricultural distress, 23 Mar., and pairing against ministers on the Bathurst and Dundas pensions, 26 Mar., while he was correctly listed as being for abolition of the death penalty for forgery, 24 May (if not on 7 June).[7] He retired at the dissolution that summer, ostensibly because he no longer had time to devote to his parliamentary duties. But he may have abandoned his seat because of his inability to please both his father, who unsuccessfully brought forward another family member, and his influential Catholic constituents, who returned the O'Conor Don in his place.[8] Thereafter he played little part in Roscommon politics, although he signed the addresses congratulating Lorton on obtaining the lord lieutenancy of the county in December 1831 and urging the king to defend the Protestant interests of Ireland the following month.[9]

By the mid-1830s, when he suffered a stroke, King had started to feel the physical effects of his heavy drinking and by the 1840s he had debts of at least £40,000. He was almost entirely under the influence of his wife, the high living daughter of an Irish baronet, who was strongly disapproved of by her father-in-law. In 1840 Lorton managed to settle them into a more sober and regular lifestyle at Frankfurt, but from 1846 she contracted a relationship with a dubious and insolvent French nobleman, Vicomte Ernest Valentin de Satgé St. Jean. When she bore a son, Henry Ernest Newcomen, in 1848, King disowned the child, but continued to live with his wife and her lover despite pressure from his father; when he did sue for divorce in 1850 the legal proceedings failed because he was found to have committed adultery with his nursemaid and travelling companion, Julie Imhoff, who later lived openly with him as his mistress. In desperation, Lorton, who feared that his elder son and elder grandson's inheritance would be wrested from them, succeeded in gaining custody of his two grandchildren, Frances and Robert Edward, and, by various codicils to his will, left the unentailed parts of his estates to his second son Lawrence Harman King Harman of New Castle, county Longford. On succeeding to the viscountcy in 1854, King put Rockingham in trust for his acknowledged son and for many years lived quietly in London. However, his estranged wife was unceasing in her efforts to advance the interests of her second son, and he and his Kingston cousins were driven to extraordinary lengths to exclude 'the Frenchman', as they called him, from inheriting their patrimony. As a result, after the deaths of this Member, who had become the 6th earl of Kingston, in 1869 and Robert Edward, the 7th earl, in 1871, the peerage but not the hereditary lands, which were disastrously dispersed, passed to Henry Ernest Newcomen King Tenison, whose legitimacy was confirmed (as it could not be disproved) at the probate court in Dublin in 1870.[10]

[1] R.D. King-Harman, *The Kings, Earls of Kingston*, 73–78, 93–94, 101. [2] Add. 40373, f. 364. [3] King-Harman, 97, 103–7, 127; *Roscommon and Leitrim Gazette*, 16, 23 July, 22 Oct. 1825, 4 Feb. 1826. [4] *Roscommon and Leitrim Gazette*, 10, 24 June, 22 July, 5 Aug. 1826; Add. 40334, f. 171. [5] *O'Conor Pprs.* ed. G.W. and J.E. Dunleavy, 166; *Roscommon Jnl.* 3 Jan. 1829. [6] *Holland House Diaries*, 99, 140. [7] *Roscommon and Leitrim Gazette*, 10 Apr. 1830. [8] Ibid. 10 July, 14 Aug. 1830. [9] Ibid. 17 Dec. 1831, 4 Feb. 1832. [10] PRO NI, King-Harman mss D4168/C/11 (NRA 41002); King-Harman, 90–92, 108–13, 127–65, 173–96, 290–3; *The Times*, 23 Nov. 1854, 20 Oct. 1869.

S.M.F.

KING, Hon. Robert Henry (1796–1867), of Mitchelstown Castle, co. Cork.

CO. CORK   1826–1832

b. 4 Oct. 1796, 2nd but 1st surv. s. of George, 3rd earl of Kingston [I], and Lady Helena Moore, da. of Stephen, 1st Earl Mountcashell [I]; bro. of Edward King, Visct. Kingsborough*. *educ.* Eton;[1] Exeter, Oxf. 1818. *unm. styled* Visct. Kingsborough 1837–9; *suc.* fa. as 4th earl of

Kingston [I] and Bar. Kingston [UK] 18 Oct. 1839. *d.* 21 Jan. 1867.

Ensign 5 Ft. 1816, half-pay 1818; lt. 69 Ft. 1822, half-pay 1826.

Sheriff, co. Cork 1836.

King joined the army of occupation in France in 1816 and was remembered as 'good natured and popular in the service'. In 1825 he was granted leave of absence from his regiment pending a 'promotion to a company', which never occurred.[2] At the 1826 general election he came forward on the family interest for county Cork as a replacement for his elder brother. Pressed for his views on the hustings, he pledged support for Catholic emancipation and reform of the 'mischievous' tithe system, but on parliamentary reform he was 'neither able nor disposed to answer'. He was returned unopposed.[3] King, whose votes in this Parliament were subject to confusion with those of his Tory cousin Robert King, Member for county Roscommon, presented constituency petitions for Catholic claims, 12 Feb., 5 Mar., and voted accordingly, 6 Mar. 1827.[4] He divided against the duke of Clarence's grant, 16 Feb. He brought up a constituency petition against alteration of the corn laws, 21 Feb.[5] He voted for information on the Barrackpoor mutiny, 22 Mar., and the Lisburn Orange procession, 29 Mar. Next day he was in the opposition minority to postpone the supplies until the ministerial crisis was resolved. He divided against the corn bill, 2 Apr. In his maiden speech, 14 June 1827, he contended that the return to cash payments had created 'much of the distress' in Ireland and 'amounted to little else than a robbery upon the purse of every man'. That day he welcomed the accession of the Canning administration, whose formation represented 'not the triumph of party, but of principle and of public opinion'. He presented petitions for Catholic claims, 18, 27 Feb., 24 Apr., and voted thus, 12 May 1828. He divided for repeal of the Test Acts, 26 Feb. On 25 Apr. he recommended that 'before any experiment be tried' with the corn laws a 'measure for the alteration of the currency should be brought into full effect', as cash payments had brought 'greater ruin to the productive industry of the people than any other measure short of a revolution could have effected'. He was in the minority of 22 to reduce the grant to the Royal Cork Institution by £500, 20 June. In November 1828 he signed a county Cork Protestant declaration in support of Catholic emancipation.[6]

He was probably the 'Sir Robert King' who unsuccessfully attempted to present a petition defending the legitimacy of Daniel O'Connell's return for county Clare, 26 Feb., and he voted for allowing him to take his seat unhindered, 18 May 1829. He voted for the Wellington ministry's concession of Catholic emancipation, 6, 30 Mar., insisting that it was supported by the 'great majority' of his Protestant constituents, 9 Mar., when he dismissed a hostile county Cork petition brought up by Moore, Member for Dublin, as 'the machinations of a junto in the city of Cork, styled Brunswickers' who 'utter language ... almost treasonable'. He presented and endorsed a counter-petition, 12 Mar. It is not clear whether it was he or his namesake who had been listed by Planta, the Wellington ministry's patronage secretary, as being 'opposed to securities'; but on 12 Mar. he conceded the 'propriety of disfranchising the Irish 40s. freeholders' and urged the same to be applied in England, where there was no 'mode of doing this, except ... reform'. He brought up constituency petitions against militia reductions, 25 Mar. He presented and endorsed one against the 'disastrous' Irish Subletting Act, 7 May 1829, when he advocated the introduction of a 'modified system of poor laws', which would 'compel absentee proprietors, drawing large revenues ... to contribute ... to the relief and support of their suffering countrymen'. Speaking in similar terms, he called for a 'heavy tax upon the property of those who absent themselves', 5 Mar. 1830. It was probably his namesake who had been listed by the Ultra leader Sir Richard Vyvyan* as a supporter of the Wellington ministry in October 1829, and who voted against parliamentary reform, 18 Feb., the enfranchisement of Birmingham, Leeds and Manchester, 23 Feb., Jewish emancipation, 5 Apr., 17 May, and reducing the grant to South American missions, 7 June 1830. It was he, however, who divided in the minority with ministers on the Bathurst and Dundas pensions, 26 Mar., for on the hustings later that year he defended his vote, saying he had thought 'it was the custom to give superannuation pensions to persons filling these offices'.[7] He presented and endorsed a constituency petition against abuses in the Irish church by 'corrupt and profligate ministers', 27 Apr. He welcomed a bill to curb the 'baneful' effects of the truck system and demanded its extension to Ireland, 3 May. He presented and endorsed constituency petitions against increases in the duty on Irish stamps, tobacco and spirits, 25 May, 21 June, 2 July. He voted in favour of abolition of the death penalty for forgery, 7 June. He brought up a petition for repeal of the Irish Vestries Act, 10 June, and abolition of Irish tithes, 2 July 1830.

At the 1830 general election he was again returned unopposed.[8] He was listed by the Wellington ministry as one of the 'good doubtfuls', and he voted with them on the civil list, 15 Nov. 1830. He divided for the second reading of the Grey ministry's reform bill, 22 Mar., and against Gascoyne's wrecking amendment, 19 Apr. 1831. At the ensuing general election he offered as a 'determined supporter' of reform and the abolition of slavery, and was again returned unopposed.[9] He divided for the second reading of the reintroduced reform bill, 6 July, at least twice against adjournment, 12 July, and gave generally steady support to its detailed provisions, though he paired in the divisions on Greenwich, 3 Aug., Gateshead, 5 Aug., and Rochester, 9 Aug. He divided for the bill's third reading, 19 Sept., its passage, 21 Sept., and Lord Ebrington's confidence motion, 10 Oct. He presented two constituency petitions against the grant to the Kildare Place Society, 26 July. He divided with ministers on the Dublin election controversy, 23 Aug., but voted for legal provision for the Irish poor, 29 Aug. King voted for the second reading of the revised reform bill, 17 Dec. 1831, again gave general support to its details, and voted for the third reading, 22 Mar. 1832. He divided for Ebrington's motion for an address calling on the king to appoint only ministers who would carry reform unimpaired, 10 May, the second reading of the Irish bill, 25 May, and against a Conservative amendment to the Scottish bill, 1 June. He voted with government on the Russian-Dutch loan, 26 Jan., 12, 20 July, and relations with Portugal, 9 Feb. He was in the minority against the second reading of the Irish tithes bill, 6 Apr., but was one of the Members 'usually opposing ministers' on this issue who divided for Crampton's amendment regarding the payment of arrears, 9 Apr. He brought up a constituency petition for their abolition, 25 July. In June 1832 he applied to Lord Goderich, the colonial secretary, for a collectorship of customs in the Gambia for one Lloyd, who had 'distinguished himself in commanding the militia during the late disturbances', but was advised that it was in the gift of the treasury.[10]

At the 1832 general election he offered again for county Cork as a Liberal against two Repealers and two Conservatives and came bottom of the poll. He stood as a Conservative in 1837 but was again defeated. He succeeded his elder brother as Viscount Kingsborough that year, and his spendthrift father, who had started to go insane in 1830, as 4th earl of Kingston in 1839, by when the family estates were so indebted that creditors had begun to take action. In 1844 his Irish estates were seized by the encumbered estates court in Dublin, and by 1856 nearly 71,000 acres and 'a large quantity of silver and plate' had been sold.[11] In 1848 King came before the Marylebone magistrates charged with 'indecent assault' on a tradesman

in 'a gateway at the back of Marylebone station'. A trial was set in the criminal courts, at which he failed to appear, forfeiting bail of £10,000. (It later emerged that his alleged victim was a 'man of infamous character', who was subsequently transported.)[12] During the 1850s he appeared in the metropolitan police courts for drunkenness, assaulting the police, and refusing to pay cabmen, who complained of waiting for hours 'in expectation of their fare' outside the House of Lords, where his 'credit was so low ... that the contractor for the refreshment ... refused to bring up a dinner until paid in advance'. Following an incident at Chester in 1860, in which he attempted to walk through a railway tunnel, was ejected from the cathedral for refusing to remove his hat, and went 'out in the streets naked', he was committed to the local asylum. He was pronounced insane by a commission of lunacy next year, witnesses describing how 'his conversation repeatedly turned on unnatural crimes', with which he 'charged various distinguished persons', including 'a story of meeting a life guardsman in a urinal at St. James's, who made improper overtures to him'. King died in confinement in 1867 and was succeeded by his younger brother James, a barrister, on whose death two years later the United Kingdom barony became extinct.[13]

[1] R.D. King-Harman, *The Kings, Earls of Kingston*, 86. [2] Ibid; *Gent. Mag.* (1867), i. 381; Doncaster Archives, Kingston mss DD PC/P2/52. [3] *Southern Reporter*, 22 June 1826. [4] *The Times*, 13 Feb., 6 Mar. 1827. [5] Ibid. 22 Feb. 1827. [6] *Southern Reporter*, 13 Nov. 1828. [7] *Cork Constitution*, 14 Aug. 1830. [8] Ibid. 12, 14, 17 Aug. 1830. [9] *Southern Reporter*, 12 May 1831. [10] Add. 40879, f. 245. [11] King-Harman, 86-87. [12] *The Times*, 1, 3 Apr. 1848, 10 Apr. 1861. [13] Ibid. 22 Aug. 1855, 13 Apr., 12, 22 Sept. 1860, 10 Apr. 1861; *Gent. Mag.* (1867), i. 380-1.

P.J.S.

KING *see also* **DASHWOOD KING**

KINGSBOROUGH, Visct. *see* **KING**, **Edward**

KINNERSLEY, **William Shepherd** (1780–1823), of High Street, Newcastle-under-Lyme, Staffs. and Clough Hall, nr. Lawton, Cheshire.

NEWCASTLE-UNDER-LYME 1818–8 July 1823

b. 19 Nov. 1780, 1st s. of Thomas Kinnersley, banker, of Clough Hall and Mary, da. of Edward Shepherd of Sheffield, Yorks. *unm. suc.* fa. 1819. *d.* 8 July 1823.
Distributor of stamps, S. Staffs. 1807.
Mayor, Newcastle-under-Lyme 1810-11.
2nd lt. Newcastle vols. 1798, 1st lt. 1798, capt. 1803, (yeoman cav.) 1817-*d.*

Kinnersley's father, 'for many years an eminent banker' in Newcastle-under-Lyme, was a leading local corporator and businessman, closely connected with the Trentham interest of Lord Stafford. In 1790 he erected the Partridge Nest ironworks at nearby Chesterton and on his death, 3 Nov. 1819, devised land, buildings, and mining interests worth £35,041 19s. 4d. to Kinnersley, leaving him 'in most affluent circumstances'.[1] Like his father, Kinnersley, who assumed control of the family's banking concerns, was closely involved with the Fenton brothers, Thomas and Robert, who dominated Newcastle corporation. Their creation of 202 honorary freemen helped to ensure his return there in 1818, at a cost of 'more' than £6,000, when he was said to be 'the most popular man in and of the town'.[2]

At the 1820 general election Kinnersley, who had organized 'extensive' improvements to the local public roads, offered again with the backing of the corporation and was returned at the top of the poll with a much increased majority.[3] A poor attender, who is not known to have spoken in debate, when present he continued to give general support to the Liverpool ministry.[4] He was granted three weeks' leave on account of ill health, 26 June 1820. He divided against Catholic claims, 28 Feb. 1821, 30 Apr. 1822. He voted against parliamentary reform, 9 May 1821. On 21 Nov. 1821 Littleton, the county Member, noted in his diary how Kinnersley, 'the banker at Newcastle, and Member for that borough', was 'quite overwhelmed today at the duke's [Wellington] asking him to drink a glass of wine'.[5] In his last known vote, he divided against more extensive tax reductions, 11 Feb. 1822.

Kinnersley died at Clough Hall in July 1823, 'in the prime of life and the midst of usefulness', following a 'fall from his horse' and a 'violent haemorrhage'.[6] By his will, dated 15 Feb. 1820 and proved under £70,000, he left an annuity of £500 to his mother Mary (1757-1825), £1,000 to each of his sisters in a trust administered by Thomas Fenton and his brother-in-law George Attwood, and £15,000 to his youngest brother, Edward (1788-1868). On the death of his sister Mary Attwood her legacy, under a codicil of 22 Apr. 1823, was to be transferred to her daughter Georgina. The residue, including the Clough Hall estate, passed to his brother Thomas (1782-1855), later co-founder of the Staffordshire Conservative Club, who added Kinnersley's 'large property' to 'a larger property immediately inherited from his father', but despite many solicitations declined to come forward for the vacancy.[7]

[1] Gent. Mag. (1819), ii. 568; The Potteries ed. A. Phillips (1993), 90; Staffs. Advertiser, 12 July 1823; IR26/870/159. [2] S.M. Hardy and R.C. Baily, 'Downfall of Gower Interest in Staffs. Boroughs', Colls. Hist. Staffs. (1950-1), 276-78; Language, Print and Electoral Politics ed. H. Barker and D. Vincent, 160, 164; Derbys. RO, Catton ms D3155/WH/2932, Wilmot to Goderich, 18 Oct. 1827. [3] Staffs. Advertiser, 19 Feb., 11 Mar. 1820. [4] Black Bk. (1823), 168. [5] Hatherton diary. [6] Staffs. Advertiser, 12 July 1823. [7] PROB 11/1681/90; IR26/1007/190; Dyott's Diary, ii. 193; Add. 40369, f. 64; Staffs. Advertiser, 19 July 1823.

P.J.S.

KNATCHBULL, Sir Edward, 9th bt. (1781–1849), of Mersham Hatch, Kent and 30 Great George Street, Mdx.[1]

KENT	16 Nov. 1819–1831
KENT EAST	1832–19 Feb. 1845

b. 20 Dec. 1781, 1st s. of Sir Edward Knatchbull[†], 8th bt., of Mersham Hatch and 1st w. Mary, da. and coh. of William Western Hugessen of Provender, Kent. educ. Winchester 1794; Christ Church, Oxf. 1800; L. Inn 1803. m. (1) 25 Aug. 1806, Annabella Christiana (d. 4 Apr. 1814), da. of Sir John Honywood[†], 4th bt., of Sibton, Kent, 5s. (3 d.v.p.) 1da. d.v.p.; (2) 24 Oct. 1820, Fanny Catherine, da. of Edward Knight (formerly Austen), of Godmersham Park, Kent, 5s. 4da. (2 d.v.p.). suc. fa. as 9th bt. 21 Sept. 1819. d. 24 May 1849.

PC 16 Dec. 1834; paymaster-gen. Dec. 1834-May 1835, Sept. 1841-Feb. 1845.

Receiver-gen. E. Kent 1814-19; chairman, q. sess. Kent (Maidstone) 1819-35.

Capt. Provender cav. 1803; lt.-col. 2 E. Kent militia 1810; capt. Sandgate Castle 1817, E. Kent yeomanry 1819.

Imbued with the principles and prejudices of a Tory country gentleman, of which he was a typical specimen, Knatchbull was eventually forced by his stubborn commitment to the Protestant constitution and the agricultural interest into direct opposition to the government of Robert Peel* and the duke of Wellington. He had a strong and pious, but normally quiescent, sense of moral duty. This was revealed in a letter to his second wife, Jane Austen's favourite niece, 'Dearest Fanny', shortly after their engagement, when he was called away by the death of his aunt's husband, the naturalist Sir Joseph Banks (having obtained leave from the House, 21 June 1820). He wrote:

In all that I have undergone I have been supported by that Power from above without whose aid I must long ago have sunk; but, seriously as I have always regarded every occurrence of life, and attributing as I always do everything that happens to a superintending Power, I have never suffered these considerations to interfere with the duties or even the amusements of life. I have never felt that it could become one to find fault with the conduct of others, and dogmatically prescribe what course it is best to pursue. To act upon a uniform and steady principle, to adhere to what is right and to abstain from what is wrong, to afford the best example in my power, never to obtrude my opinions, but never upon proper occasions to be ashamed or afraid of avowing them – these have been the rules upon which I have acted, and I believe that they will bring peace at the last ... Your own principles as expressed to me are right: grounded on humility, admitting how unequal we are to perform our duties, but resolutely and constantly persevering to the utmost of our ability to discharge them properly – thinking seriously of everything that happens, constantly mixing with the world, but enjoying it more or less according as we meet with similar feelings and kindred spirits, and always hoping that our example and principles will effect some good and receive the respect to which they are entitled.[2]

As Banks's executor, he oversaw the distribution of his manuscripts to the British Museum and the Royal Society, though he was later criticized for holding back much of the material, some of which can now be found among his papers.[3]

After succeeding to his father's title, estates and parliamentary seat in 1819, he proved indefatigable in his application to county business, both inside and outside the House. He was a frequent attender at meetings all over Kent, as his wife's diaries attest, and was especially sensitive to the grievances of farmers.[4] He several times intervened with ministers to secure a postponement of the payment of the hop duties, and he led delegations opposed to the malt duties to the chancellor, 23 May 1829, 26 Feb. 1831.[5] He also took an active part in forwarding the interests of Kentish boroughs: for example, he was made an honorary freeman of Rochester, 24 July 1820, and was thanked by the corporation for his opposition to the alehouses licensing bill, 20 Oct. 1828.[6] He had a number of special concerns, notably as president of the Kent Auxiliary Church Missionary Society, which, despite the polemics of Wellington's crony, George Robert Gleig, perpetual curate of Ash, near Sandwich, he believed to be within the workings of the established church.[7] He was chairman of the east Kent quarter sessions and took his responsibilities as a magistrate, such as over the administration of Maidstone gaol, very seriously.[8] In the House, he defended the work of local justices, 20 Feb. 1821, 27 Mar. 1822, 27 May 1824, and he brought their resentment of increased expenses before Peel, 16 Nov. 1823, and before the House by petition, 10 Mar. 1826.[9] He was involved in the passage of a large number of local transport and improvement bills and presented a great many petitions, usually from specific economic interests in the county. Not even his

most inveterate Whig opponents could deny that he supervised Kent, and occasionally Sussex, affairs with marked endeavour and ability, particularly towards the end of the 1820s when his ailing colleague, William Philip Honywood, to whom he was distantly related by marriage, was increasingly absent.[10]

Despite the respect in which Knatchbull was usually held, he did have his detractors, like the headmaster of Winchester, William Stanley Goddard, who remarked on his 'general incivility of manners and sullenness of temper'.[11] His fussy and alarmist character, and dull and mediocre talents, were combined with a high-minded but entrenched conservatism.[12] According to Greville, he was 'anti-everything'.[13] While official opinion increasingly moved away from under-consumptionist theories, Knatchbull insisted that agricultural distress was caused not by overproduction but by lack of purchasing power. He therefore advocated reduced expenditure and taxation, repeal of Peel's Act of 1819 for the resumption of cash payments, which he said 'had mainly been the cause of all difficulties', and maintenance of the protectionist corn laws.[14] He frequently suffered at the hands of radical writers; for instance, over still owing £2,000 in 1820 in his former role as receiver-general, a sign of his sizeable financial problems.[15] William Cobbett[†], in one of his surveys of Kentish distress, 8 Dec. 1821, delivered just such an attack:

> Sir Edward Knatchbull, who is a child of the System, does appear to see no more of the cause of these sufferings than if he were a baby. How should he? Not very bright by nature; never listening to but one side of the question; being a man who wants high rents to be paid him; not gifted with much light, and that little having to strive against prejudice, false shame and self-interest, what wonder is it that he should not see things in their true light?[16]

His rejection of Catholic emancipation drew a similar response from Richard Lalor Sheil*:

> He seems a proud, obstinate, dogged sort of squire, with an infinite notion of his own importance as an English county Member and a corresponding contempt for seven millions of his fellow citizens. He has in his face and bearing many of the disagreeable qualities of John Bullism, without any of its frankness and plain-dealing. He is rude without being honest and offensive without being sincere.[17]

Knatchbull did eventually acknowledge some support for moderate parliamentary reform, but he remained deeply suspicious of such incursions into the established constitution. In the Commons he was initially a diffident, sometimes inaudible, speaker, but later became a competent performer. He reported to his wife that his speech on 4 Feb. 1830 was

> badly reported. The *Mirror of Parliament* people came to me. I rather complained. The reply was 'you speak so fluently, without stopping or hesitating, that it is most difficult to take down your words. We hear you well, but you never give us time to pause'.[18]

His local administrative experience was put to good use on a number of select committees, including those on poor returns in nearly every session from 1822 to 1828, and he served on very many others during this period. He made frequent minor interventions on a wide range of subjects and, during the period of disaffected Tory opposition around 1830, he often asked questions about the timetable of future business.

There was little expectation of a contest at the general election of 1820, when Knatchbull was returned with Honywood, after having defended his support for the recent repressive legislation as 'only temporary laws for temporary evils', condemned Catholic claims and endorsed some measures of economy to assist agriculture.[19] He moved the address to general commendation, 27 Apr. 1820, when he justified the use of force to put down acts of sedition, but clearly separated them from outbreaks of genuine agricultural distress, which needed to be treated in a non-partisan way, by measures of retrenchment.[20] He presented several Kentish petitions complaining of distress, 11, 15 May, and moved the second reading of, and acted as a teller for the majority for, the Kent coal meters bill, 9 June.[21] He urged ministers to accept Wilberforce's compromise motion on Queen Caroline, 6 June 1820, and voted in defence of their conduct towards her, 6 Feb. 1821. To save unnecessary expense, he opposed printing all the petitions in favour of restoring her name to the liturgy, 26 Jan., and when the Kentish one was brought up, 8 Feb., he defended the sheriff's refusal to call a county meeting, on the ground that the general feeling was against it. He voted against Catholic claims, 28 Feb. 1821, and the Catholic peers bill, 30 Apr. 1822. On 26 Feb. 1821 he commented that he hoped more was intended than changes in the method of calculating the corn averages, else agriculturists 'would sink down in utter despondency'.[22] He asked Maberly to delay his motion for economies so that the House could discuss agricultural distress and voted with ministers against him, 6 Mar. In seconding Gooch's motion the following day for a select committee, to which he was appointed, he spoke of the extensive distress, advocated various solutions, including the exclusion of foreign imports and the retention of lands in marginal cultivation, and concluded that it 'would be highly

serviceable also if a graduated scale of duties, varying according to the price of British corn, were fixed'. He divided against repeal of the malt tax, 3 Apr., but spoke and voted against the 'oppressive and objectionable' agricultural horse tax, 15 June.[23] He sided with ministers against parliamentary reform, 9 May 1821, and alteration of the Scottish representative system, 2 June 1823.

Knatchbull, who judged it inexpedient to attempt to get up a county meeting on this topic, was present at a meeting of agriculturists in Maidstone, 13 Dec. 1821, when he explained that he had not voted for the report in the committee on distress, because 'it did not do that which he conceived was necessary to afford relief'.[24] On 5 Feb. 1822 he admitted to being tempted by Hume's amendment, and 'had not ministers embodied in the address an admission of the existing agricultural distress, and similar principles of economy as disclosed in the amendment, he should have felt it his duty to vote against the proposition'. Two days later he repeated his point that opposition should wait to see what government proposed and only bring forward their plans if nothing satisfactory was forthcoming, and he was reappointed to the select committee on the subject, 18 Feb. He presented petitions for continued protection, 11, 13 Feb., 30 Apr., 6 May, but voted with ministers against further tax reductions to relieve distress, 11, 21 Feb.[25] Amid Whig charges of inconsistency, he asserted that voting for repeal of the salt tax, which he did, would not jeopardize the intended £5 million surplus, 28 Feb., and he divided for reducing the junior lords of the admiralty, 1 Mar. He commented that he could not vote for repeal of the leather, salt and tallow duties all at once, 1 May, but sided with opposition for abolition of one of the joint-postmasterships, 2 May. He acknowledged ministers' support for the agricultural committee's report, 6 May, and again backed relief measures, 10 May, but he divided in favour of Lord Althorp's amendment for permitting an 18*s*. bounty on wheat exports, 9 May.[26] On the 12th William Huskisson* complained to Liverpool, the prime minister, that 'it has come to my attention that the tone in which Sir E. Knatchbull and Mr. Wodehouse thought fit to animadvert upon the part which I have taken in the agricultural discussion is also the tone of the official connections of government'.[27] On the corn importation bill, 10 June, he objected to Canning's clause permitting foreign corn in bond to be ground into flour for export, and was teller for the majority against it.[28] He attended the county meeting which finally took place in Kent, 11 June, defending ministers' record on agricultural relief, but opposing a call for reform, which was embodied in the ensuing petition.[29] According to Baron de Staël-Holstein

> his speech was listened to without favour, but with impartiality; and the orator was respected for having acquitted himself of the task in a frank and *manly* manner, a term which, in the English language and spirit, is one of the greatest testimonies of esteem.[30]

When the petition was entered, 14 June, he condemned the rider calling for a reduction in the rate of interest on the national debt, which had been hitched to it by Cobbett in the face of Whig uneasiness, as a 'proposition for breaking faith with the public creditor', and he presented a Kent counter-petition, 4 July 1822.[31]

On bringing up three Kentish hop growers' petitions for repeal of the hop duties, he warned that if no relief was offered he would move for an inquiry, 21 Feb.; when the chancellor refused such a step, he admitted that there was an overproduction of hops, but again asked for assistance, 27 Feb. 1823. He voted in the minority for a bill to amend the corn laws by reducing the import price to 60s., 26 Feb., and presented a petition from the landowners of west Kent for relief, 24 Apr.[32] He voted for inquiry into the legal proceedings against the Dublin Orange rioters, 22 Apr., and was one of the Protestants who attended at Henry Bankes's* house to hear Peel, the home secretary, explain the government's policy on Lord Nugent's Catholic relief bill, 28 Apr.[33] He divided against ministers on the silk manufacture and Irish tithes composition bills, 9, 16 June 1823, but was in the majority against receiving papers on Catholic office – holders, 19 Feb. 1824, when he spoke in support of Peel's gaol and juries consolidation bills. He complained of the increase in the duty on exports of wool as amounting almost to a prohibition, 29 Mar., but successfully moved an amendment to equalize the duties on imported and exported wool by 102-83, 21 May.[34] He advocated lower duties on beer and voted against going into committee on this, 24 May, but on the warehoused wheat bill, 17 May, he stated that he was 'not disposed, when prices were rising, to withhold a liberal relief to the mercantile body, whose capital was employed in the warehoused wheat'. He moved the third reading of the Canterbury corn market bill, 3 June 1824, and spoke of its future contribution to the city's prosperity at a dinner to celebrate its opening, 5 Apr. 1825.[35] He objected to putting turnpike trusts into the hands of government, 'convinced that it would only lead to corruption and jobs, which he had always opposed', 17 Feb., when he voted against repeal of the usury laws. As he had been the previous year, he was named to select committee on the state

of Ireland, 17 Feb. He gave the Irish unlawful societies bill his hearty support, confirming that he had always opposed Catholic relief 'from conscientious motives', 21 Feb., and complained that anti-Catholic petitions had not been received by the House with proper respect, 21 Apr.[36] He voted against Catholic relief, 1 Mar., 21 Apr., 10 May, and the related Irish franchise bill, 26 Apr., 9 May. He opposed changes to the corn laws until they were proved necessary 'by the actual experience of some inconvenience', 25 Apr., and expressed his disapproval of either higher or lower rates of duty, 13 May.[37] He opposed ministers on the duke of Cumberland's grant, 'both by speaking and voting', 27 May, and divided against his annuity bill, 6 June. He chaired the annual dinner of the Pitt Club at the *London Tavern*, 28 May, after which Lord Eldon, the lord chancellor, wrote that 'I have hardly ever heard a display of good sense, excellent temper, appropriate language, etc., which pleased me more'.[38] He spoke at a meeting of the agriculturists of east Kent at Canterbury, 22 Oct. 1825, urging them not to support repeal of the corn laws, but also not to raise any agitation in their favour for the time being.[39]

He voted in the minority for a select committee on the silk trade petitions, 24 Feb. 1826. Sponsoring a bill for a new corn market in London, he was a teller for the majority against postponing consideration of its report, 17 Apr., and had a rider added, 25 Apr. He presented Kentish anti-slavery petitions, 14, 17 Mar., 13, 20 Apr.[40] He voted against reform of the representation of Edinburgh, 13 Apr. He defended Huskisson against the imputation of having communicated the government's plans to alter the corn laws to Liverpool merchants, 4 May, but regretted that such a delicate question was brought forward when there was no 'urgent necessity' for it. The following day he said that he had told his constituents 'that there would be no occasion for them to trouble the House with any petitions against an alteration in these laws. Under these circumstances, he could not think of acceding to the proposition'.[41] On 8 May he opposed empowering the government to admit foreign corn because it would only increase debate on the general question of protection and serve no purpose, 'except that of turning the odium of the distresses of the manufacturers upon the landed proprietors'. He added that he would have preferred ministers to act under discretionary powers and to seek parliamentary indemnity afterwards, and, as he feared that the measure was 'part of a system tending to do away with those laws, he considered it his duty to give it his opposition', which he did in the division. He offered no resistance to the second reading of the warehoused corn bill provided the importation bill was put off that night, 9 May, but felt 'compelled' to vote against the latter measure (as a teller), 11 May. He presented a petition from the landowners of east Kent against alteration of the corn laws, 12 May.[42] A rumour had circulated two years previously that he would be raised to the peerage as Lord Mersham, but nothing came of this, and no opposition was raised against him at the general election in 1826.[43] He spoke and voted in favour of Henry Dundas* at the Rochester election, 13 June.[44] On the hustings, 20 June, he restated his commitment to fulfil his parliamentary duties independently, urged the gradual abolition of slavery and defended the landed interest as 'the basis of our prosperity, and the foundation of all our greatness', especially as he was 'convinced that their interest combined the interest of every class'. He claimed to have constantly attended the committees on Ireland and Catholic relief, and had come to the conclusion that he could not support their claims.[45] At a dinner in Ashford to celebrate his election, 12 Sept., he confirmed his hostility to emancipation and reduced protection, and at the Canterbury mayoral dinner he repeated his commitment to the cause of agriculture, 30 Sept. 1826.[46]

He spoke in support of indemnifying ministers for opening the ports during the recess, 24 Nov. 1826, but again denied that there was a class basis to the corn laws and deplored attempts to stir up jealousy between landlords, manufacturers and the people. At a meeting of the East Kent Agricultural Association in Canterbury, 15 Dec., he justified government policy and advised toning down the proposed protectionist petitions in order not to alienate Members.[47] He repeated this point and pledged his continued support for the corn laws at the Maidstone Agricultural Association, 28 Dec. 1826.[48] He commended Lord Milton's moderation on presenting the Leeds petition, 21 Feb. 1827, and stated that the agriculturists' 'great object was to ensure a supply of corn equal to the demand of the country, at moderate and steady prices, as far as they could be regulated, save only where the vicissitudes of the season interposed'. He presented over 30 Kentish petitions against alteration of the corn laws, 23, 26, 27 Feb.[49] On 1 Mar. he 'thought himself bound to state (for he had given the subject the most mature consideration) that he was in favour of prohibition in preference to duty', and that his mind was filled with the 'greatest surprise and distrust' by the foreign secretary Canning's comment that he intended to 'cast the balance in favour of free trade'. Afterwards, Canning informed Knighton that

one only, a thorough malignant and furious *Ultra* in politics, as well as upon corn, attempted a feeble cry about

free trade. It fell flat and before he is six days older, he shall rue the attempt, if he gives me (as I trust he will) the opportunity.[50]

He brought up at least 45 anti-Catholic petitions, 2, 5, 19 Mar., and voted against relief, 6 Mar.[51] With what John Evelyn Denison* described as 'unfair and illiberal remarks', 8 Mar., he presented several more Kentish petitions for continued protection, expressed his regret at the change of policy by ministers whom he had once approved and (exempting Peel from his strictures) proceeded to quote a number of passages in which Canning, Huskisson and Liverpool had stressed the importance of self-sufficiency and restrictive duties.[52] He briefly offered an amendment to have the corn averages calculated over the previous six weeks, 19 Mar., and denied the existence of fictitious selling between agriculturists to raise the averages, 27 Mar.[53] He opposed relaxation of the corn laws unless accompanied by a reduction in taxes and prices, the scope for which he knew to be limited, 2 Apr., and he was a teller for the minority against the second reading of the corn bill. Given the mooted ministerial changes, he asked Lethbridge to withdraw his motion for an address to the king to that effect, 6 Apr., and proposed, only to withdraw, a minor amendment to the corn bill. He met Canning's appointment as prime minister with a prolonging baiting to the effect that only a man of Liverpool's 'high character, profound judgement and exalted rank' could hope to preside over so divided a cabinet, 3 May 1827. The new premier reported to the king that he 'indulged in a furious declamation against both the government *and* its supporters, which Mr. Canning felt it absolutely necessary to notice with part of the severity which it deserved and to declare that *the standard of opposition is now openly raised*'.[54] Mrs. Arbuthnot was indignant at his 'completely losing his temper in answering Sir Edward Knatchbull, one of our best country gentlemen'.[55] Peel spoke too, but apparently 'left the knight errant, his unfortunate *laudator*, wounded, overthrown and mud-bespattered'.[56] He drew up a series of questions to press Canning on how far he had offered places to members of the opposition, and sent them to Peel for his approval, but thereafter presumably abandoned the plan.[57] He stood forth in defence of protection, 18 June, when he was in the minority against the Coventry magistracy bill, but the following day Canning refused his request to delay the implementation of the corn bill.[58] He raised doubts over whether farmers would obtain a remunerating price and urged that the measure be made of only temporary duration, 21 June 1827. Lord Seaford commented on the 22nd that in Canning's first speech against him, 'which I heard, there was nothing to find fault with. And last night, as far as I can judge from the report, he was very temperate with Knatchbull'.[59]

While thinking that the 'list of the new ministry does not afford grounds for that unmixed satisfaction which I had anticipated', Knatchbull privately assured Peel of his support on his return to office under Wellington, 22 Jan. 1828. He was one of the ministerial 'supporters' appointed to the finance committee, 15 Feb.[60] He voted against repeal of the Test Acts, 26 Feb., and asked for a postponement in order to allow a compromise measure to be drawn up, 28 Feb., when he probably left the House with Peel before the division. He prepared and brought in a bill to allow appeals from minor jurisdictions to the county sessions, 27 Feb., and the following day supported the extension of the police force to populous areas of Kent near London. He asked whether the corn question would be brought on before the Easter recess, 24 Mar., and, facing insinuations of causing unnecessary delay, he declared he that he would 'make all the opposition the forms of the House will admit'. However, he wrote to Thomas Neame, chairman of the East Kent Agricultural Association, that he 'feared the legislature was so bent upon doing a something, that little in the way of prohibition could be accomplished'.[61] As well as presenting Kentish petitions for continued protection for corn and wool, he represented the agriculturists' hostility to any alteration, 22, 25 Apr. 1828, and on the latter day promised to vote for Portman's amendment to postpone consideration of it for six months if it was forced to a division, which it was. On 28 Apr. he made it clear that he had divided for Ferguson's amendment to raise the proposed level of duty on oats that day, and he endorsed (and probably divided in favour of) Western's motion to increase the duty on rye, peas and beans. He also raised concerns about growing unemployment, as he did on the hiring of servants, 29 Apr., and the exclusion of Irish paupers from parish relief, 6 May. He presented petitions against Catholic relief, 6 May, and voted in this sense, 12 May. He divided against provision for Canning's family, 13 May, and argued that a reduction of 2,000 men in the preventive service was not a true measure of economy, 16 May. Lord Ellenborough recorded that Sir Henry Hardinge* had said of Knatchbull that he was the 'best man to be got in the House of Commons', 17 May, and considered him one of the few who could be brought forward to strengthen the government.[62] He succeeded in delaying the third reading of the archbishop of Canterbury's bill for the appointment of a registrar, 5 June, and voted against it, 16 June. He supported the reintroduction of £1

notes, 6 June, and divided against going into committee on the Scottish and Irish small notes bill, 16 June. He advocated increased import duties on foreign wool in order to place it 'on a fair footing, which while it gives protection to the home grower, will in no respect be detrimental to the manufacturer', 12 June. Lord Bexley informed Lord Sidmouth, 16 Sept., that Knatchbull was one of those who had privately attempted to restrain Lord Winchilsea in his plan to establish a Brunswick Club at a meeting in Maidstone earlier that day.[63] However, Knatchbull spoke against those who opposed agitating the question, stating that when the Catholics 'will give full and undeniable security to the Protestant establishment in church and state, then he would agree to the concession of all they required, but till then he would never move his foot from his present position'.[64] He signed the requisition for the county meeting, held on 24 Oct., although he placed himself with Lord Camden on the sheriff's wagon, rather than amongst the Brunswickers. He was given a very stormy reception, but amid the catcalls of the radicals and Whigs, he stated that the opinions of those present confirmed his long held view that the county was decidedly anti-Catholic.[65] He thought the sheriff should have let Thomas Law Hodges's* pro-Catholic amendment be put to a vote rather than merely declaring that the majority was in favour of the Brunswick resolution, saying that 'it won't do; if we insist, they will deny it, and we are not in a condition to prove the contrary'.[66] He reiterated his staunch anti-Catholic views at various Brunswick dinners, including those at Maidstone, 31 Oct., and Ramsgate, 14 Nov. 1828.[67]

Knatchbull was, of course, listed by Planta, the patronage secretary, among those 'opposed to the principle' of Catholic emancipation in February 1829, and he was named as home secretary in one list of a putative Protestant ministry.[68] He gave his support to Peel's suppression of the Catholic Association as 'essential to the safety of the country and the dignity of the crown', 10 Feb., but spoke 'with a good deal of violence' against emancipation.[69] He also charged Peel with inconsistency and dishonesty, and, in making clear his separation from him, added that 'I state this with unspeakable distress and I lament the circumstance beyond anything that ever occurred in my life'. He presented and endorsed the Kent anti-Catholic petition, 12 Feb., declaring that 'Protestantism and the constitution of this country are about to be invaded and I will endeavour to the last moment, to defend them', but denying that he was entering a 'factious opposition'. According to John Wilson Croker*, he spoke 'moderately and, as I thought, fervently in general for

Peel, but he dropped a hint that it was a pity that the conversion had not taken place in Canning's time; this threw Peel into, or gave him occasion to assume, a fit of passion'.[70] He presented at least 30 more anti-Catholic petitions during the session, and voted against concessions, 6 Mar. He spoke against the incitement of popular clamour, 9 Mar., and in defence of the constitution of 1688, 11 Mar., and of his fellow anti-Catholic John Wells, Member for Maidstone, 16 Mar. Despite being ill, he went to the House to give a major speech against emancipation, 17 Mar., because 'my sense of public duty is paramount to every other feeling'. He found it 'utterly impossible', he said, to change his views for any of the reasons assigned by ministers: the state of Ireland was no worse than it had been, the Commons was as divided as ever on the issue and opinions in the cabinet were also still evenly matched. He insisted that it was only a religious question and made a deep impression by ending with the apt quotation, 'nusquam tuta fides', from Dido's upbraiding of Aeneas at his desertion, in order to emphasize that he could no longer place his trust in ministers.[71] John Cam Hobhouse* observed that he and Sadler 'had the best of the debate', while Hudson Gurney* noted that he 'did not make a bad speech, though mischievous and little to the purpose of the bill'.[72] Ellenborough, who thought his performance 'about as good as I expected', recorded that Thomas Wood had 'met Sir E. Knatchbull in the lobby. Sir E. said he was glad to see him there. Wood said he was there reluctantly, in obedience to his constituents. Sir E. said that was in reality his case; and yet he made a violent speech against the bill!'[73] He voted against the second reading, 18 Mar., for Bankes's amendment to prevent Catholics sitting in Parliament, 23 Mar., and against the report, 27 Mar., and third reading, 30 Mar. He made interventions on the oaths for Catholic Members, 23 Mar., for excluding them from the privy council, his amendment to this effect being defeated, 24 Mar., and to protect corporate funds, 27 Mar., but was reluctant to renew the debate on the 30th.[74] He defended Stephen Rumbold Lushington, who had refused to resign his seat at Canterbury on being appointed governor of Madras, 19 Mar. 1829, and busied himself for the rest of the session with legal and local legislation.

From the autumn of 1829 Knatchbull played a conspicuous part in the activities of the group of 20 to 30 disaffected Ultra Tories, who were led by Sir Richard Vyvyan*. In his later embittered memoirs, Vyvyan recalled that

> when I first ascertained the full extent of my influence, it was my impression that my age and isolation in the domi-

nant aristocracy of the country would interpose serious obstacles to my being the recognized head of the party. This induced me to put forward Sir Edward Knatchbull as its nominal chief. When I arranged all the combinations and acted oratorically as the mouthpiece of the section of the Tories, who opposed the duke of Wellington and Sir Robert Peel, I used my best endeavours to let it be understood, that Knatchbull was the ostensible leader. I issued summons for party meetings at *his house instead of my own* and committed the great mistake of making him the important personage, by which I inflamed his small ambition and perhaps generated his personal hostility to myself.[75]

Gatherings certainly took place at 30 Great George Street, where Knatchbull lived from 1827 to 1838, but they must have been equally convenient for Vyvyan, who had a house a few doors away at number 26. Knatchbull's disillusionment with Peel over the 'great betrayal' made him the prime target for his anger, and their relationship was further soured by his failure to advance his brother, Wyndham Knatchbull, to the regius chair of Hebrew at Oxford.[76] He refused even to forward patronage requests to Wellington,[77] but although hostility towards him was one of the defining features of the Ultras, it was not really the case with Knatchbull. After a visit to Mersham, Planta reported to Wellington, 8 Sept. 1829, that he had found him desponding over the scarcity of money and the prevailing distress:

> Sir Edward uses expressions like these: 'If old England should go on', 'If we shall last for five years', to which I answered, 'I suppose you do not, Sir Edward, really think it will *not*'. 'No I suppose it *will* go on after all,' he replied. He has a most established hatred for the Whigs; and, on that score, does not like the appointments of Rosslyn and Sir James Scarlett*. I explained to him, in general terms, the grounds on which they were made. He answered that 'that certainly palliated the matter very much, but then the world at large could not know these things and the impression was the other way'. Upon the whole I should say, quite unreservedly, that Sir Edward looks up wholly to your Grace, and that if anything can be done to propitiate the Ultras, he will hail it with great joy and cheerfully assist in the operation. On one occasion he said to me: 'I believe you must shake us all up in a bag together again, and see who will come out first'. I took up the expression of 'our being shaken up together again', and said *that* was what we wished; that we never willingly looked to the Whigs, but were always glad, standing on our own strength, to keep them between us and the radicals, reformers, etc. I made always more progress by insisting that there must be either the present government or a Whig government. The latter, the worthy baronet seemed to consider little short of *perdition*.[78]

Knatchbull was a subscriber to the defence of the Ultra *Morning Journal* in its libel action,[79] but as he wrote to Vyvyan, 2 Aug. 1829, he disliked its support for parliamentary reform and he was never one of those Ultras who were fully converted to its cause. In the same letter he revealed his desire to continue in personal opposition to ministers, his doubts about many of the 'high Tory party', and his inclination to side with Wellington as the only feasible alternative to merely standing aloof from politics. He added that 'our principles and policy should be what they always have been: to oppose the free traders and reformers, to assist in keeping together what yet remains of the constitution and to be a little more alive and active in all that relates to the public expenditure'. On 26 Aug. he wrote again, reluctantly agreeing to accept office (as home secretary and leader of the Commons) in any new Tory ministry, but 'full of distrust' at the idea of the duke of Cumberland, whom he had not even met, presiding over so unlikely a group of ministers as Vyvyan proposed. His preferred course was to strain for the removal of Peel, which would leave the Commons unmanageable and thus precipitate a change. He again hinted at some sort of arrangement with Wellington, 4, 11 Sept., but in Vyvyan's draft reply of 7 Sept., which flattered Knatchbull by revealing that he was 'the only person, to whom I have even given the *outlines* of [Cumberland's noncommittal] letter, or have mentioned the general tenor of what has passed already', he entirely ruled out any rapprochement with him or Peel.[80] Vyvyan received rebuffs not only from Cumberland, but also from Lord Palmerston*, who believed that the 'only government which could really answer the wants of the nation at the present moment would be one composed of men known and looked up to; fancy Knatchbull and Vyvyan secretaries of state!'[81] There was an untimely public dinner for Knatchbull at Maidstone, 13 Nov., and as he wrote to Vyvyan on the 15th

> I had enough to do, to talk without saying anything. It would not be difficult to create a stir in Kent, but there is no distinct and definite object that can justify me in taking such a course. It is more important to keep our body united, to prevent confusion and discord as long as possible, and also that when the proper moment does arise, we may all press together to gain the same object.[82]

Owing to a mixture of personal preference and adverse circumstances, Knatchbull thus spent the rest of the year in cautious but anxious inactivity, though he continued to inveigh against agricultural distress and signed the grand jury of Kent's letter of complaint about it to Wellington, 16 Dec. 1829.[83]

His decision to challenge the government, 4 Feb. 1830, was not the result of any prior preparations by the Ultras. He informed Lady Knatchbull a few days later that

> as I travelled to town, I thought it possible that an amendment might be wise, but I did not resolve upon moving my amendment till after two o'clock on Thursday, when I heard the king's speech. You know my opinion of the distress of the country and the assertion in the speech was by far too untrue and too insulting to pass without contradiction.[84]

Although agreeing with much of the speech, notably its pledge on economies, he argued that distress was not confined to 'some parts' of the country, but was general and required extensive relief. He also advocated restoration of a paper currency, and, while 'disposed to promote measures for a reform in Parliament', he was careful to distance himself from those whose object was to destroy, rather than to amend, the constitution. According to Sir James Willoughby Gordon*, he began 'with great apparent moderation, but as he proceeded and felt the House was with him, he became warm and hostile, and was cheered by a very large portion of the House'.[85] A variety of speakers rallied to him, but he was opposed by ministers and by Lord Grey's heir, Lord Howick, who thought Knatchbull had pounced 'very dexterously' on his amendment, as a slur on the Whigs' conduct. In the division (in which he was a teller), 28 opposition Members and many of the country gentlemen, who he had hoped would follow his lead, divided against the amendment, which was defeated by 158-105, despite Ultra, Whig and radical support. Knatchbull informed his wife, 8 Feb., that 'as to intrigues, if any there are, I am no party to them. I have very little communication with my party, but all seem very well satisfied with me, except the government, who are very angry, but they dare not show it or avow it'. His son Charles, who was present, confirmed that ministers 'never meant to leave such a nice little *lupe* hole in the speech on which an amendment could be moved. Peel was very angry with Papa'.[86] Although his manoeuvre had been unexpected, it nevertheless provided an impetus for Ultra attempts to beat down the administration's majority. Ellenborough reckoned that he led about 23 followers and, for instance, he had a 'good party' of leading Ultras at his house, 14 Feb.[87] During the succeeding months he presented a great many petitions for relief from distress and repeal of the malt duties, and against the sale of beer bill, and he often divided against ministers in favour of further economies. After voting with them against transferring East Retford's seats to Birmingham, 11 Feb., he told Hume that 'you saved the government the first night, and we have given them the majority tonight'.[88] He voted against parliamentary reform, 18 Feb., and Peel noted that on the motion to enfranchise Birmingham, Leeds and Manchester, 23 Feb. 1830, he and a 'great majority of those Members who usually act with him left the House without voting'.[89]

Knatchbull acknowledged the strategic necessity of maintaining the size of the army, but spoke and voted in favour of restricting its grant to six months, 19 Feb. 1830. In presenting and endorsing a Romney Marsh petition against the importation of foreign wool, 1 Mar., there was 'some incivility' between him and Sir Charles Burrell.[90] He agreed with the Suffolk petition against distress, 5 Mar., but warned ministers and its presenter, Gooch, that worse was yet to come, and that immediate relief could only be attained by an alteration of the currency. He attended the Kent county meeting which agreed to petition against distress, 12 Mar., but spoke against including a request for reform.[91] After bringing it up, 29 Mar., he made a major synoptic speech on the subject of distress, which drew together his hostility to excessive poor rates, free trade, the state of the currency and oppressive taxation, and he also reiterated his opposition to reform. He was given one month's leave of absence on urgent private business, 2 Apr. He spoke against soldiers being forced to participate in religious ceremonies with which they disagreed, 30 Apr. He later said that he had 'entirely concurred' with Graham's motion for a return of privy councillors' emoluments, 14 May, but had declined to vote for it in order to take advantage of the chancellor's offer of information.[92] He voted against Jewish emancipation, 17 May, and denied that there was a general feeling in Kent in favour of the abolition of tithes, 18 May. He objected to the Scottish and Irish poor removal bill, 26 May, on the ground that the burden would fall disproportionately on southern counties. While not questioning the *Morning Journal*'s libel of lord chancellor Lyndhurst, he raised constitutional doubts about his prosecution being financed out of the law charges, 4 June. He gave his opinion that a 'limited paper currency, founded on a secure basis and placed under proper regulations, will be the best means of affording relief to the country, which has been so long suffering from distress', 8 June. He voted against going into committee on the administration of justice bill, 18 June. Having divided against the second reading of the sale of beer bill, 5 Apr., he spoke against it, 21 May, and asked when it would come on, 14, 16 June. He complained about the House considering it at 1 a.m., 21 June, when he unsuccessfully moved two

amendments: to prevent the consumption of beer on the premises of beer houses, on which he was a teller for the minority of 108-138, and to limit the duration of the bill to an experimental period of three years. He again condemned it as ineffective in providing relief and as immoral and unjust, 1 July 1830, and he voted for postponing permission for the on-consumption of beer for two years that day.

Long before the general election of 1830 there were rumours that a Tory candidate might emerge to challenge Knatchbull, but he offered again and was not opposed.[93] He stressed his desire for an end to colonial slavery, further reductions to achieve agricultural relief and limited reform:

> If it is for the purpose of disfranchising those boroughs where ... corruption ... has been carried on to so great an extent and conferring it upon large towns, when the facts are properly proved, I shall support such a measure. But let us take care that in endeavouring to repair the fabric of our constitution we do not pull it down altogether.[94]

With the 'mild, gentlemanly and impressive manner with which he always speaks', he addressed the Hawkhurst dinner to celebrate his and Hodges's return, 8 Sept., stating, with typical modesty, that 'a Member of Parliament could ill perform his duty without the advice and assistance of his constituents; he had always received those, and from no one more than his present colleague'.[95] He ascribed the wave of 'Swing' unrest that swept Kent from mid-September to temporary agricultural distress, aggravated by outside *agents provocateurs*, rather than to any revolutionary disaffection.[96] He was very active in attending meetings of the local magistrates and in devising ways of containing the disturbances as peaceably as possible.[97] His curious leniency in sentencing guilty machine-breakers to only a few days' imprisonment, 24 Oct., met with widespread criticism, not least from Peel, but he continued to be involved with further efforts to end the outrages.[98] He was very reluctant to leave Mersham and had to delay a pre-session meeting with the Ultra duke of Richmond until 1 Nov.[99] He was present on the first day, 2 Nov., when he agreed with Hodges on the prevalence of distress in Kent, pointed out the basic loyalism of the peasantry and argued that had his former amendment been adopted it would have removed many of the present difficulties. He commended the actions of magistrates and of landowners who, at great expense, had taken on unemployed labourers, 9 Nov. He was granted one month's leave of absence on account of the disturbed state of his neighbourhood, 23 Nov., and supported the idea of a select committee on distress, 6 Dec. 1830.

Althorp wrote to Lord Milton*, 15 Nov. 1830, that Knatchbull and his friends might support Henry Brougham's intended reform motion the following day.[100] However, there was a meeting at his house in Great George Street on the morning of the 15th, at which it was decided that they would vote against government that day, perhaps in order to avoid having to show support for reform.[101] He duly voted in the majority which brought down the Wellington administration, on the establishment of a select committee on the civil list (to which he was appointed), an action which ministers attributed to personal pique.[102] He was sounded by Charles Wood*, at Grey's request, about whether he would accept the paymaster-generalship in his administration. Palmerston, who was similarly entrusted, reported to Edward John Littleton* on the 17th that he 'expresses himself favourably disposed ... but he declines office for himself, *bona fide* and handsomely'.[103] Brougham later commented that it was 'accidental circumstances' which prevented his joining the government at this point, but Ellenborough wrote, 19 Nov. 1830, that the Ultra leaders, the duke of Newcastle, Lord Falmouth, Knatchbull and Vyvyan

> will not support the new government. Having had their revenge they mean to put their knees in our backs and do all they can to get out the others. They are sorry for the work they have performed and regret their vote. They had intended to stay away on the question of reform – now they mean to vote against it.[104]

Knatchbull presented petitions against distress, 7 Feb. 1831, when he accepted ministers' explanation about the barilla duties, and stated that he would support them so long as they promoted the interests of the community at large. He informed his wife, 13 Feb., that he had held a party of Ultra friends the day before and had been summoned by Althorp, the chancellor, who 'gives up his plan of finance', 'to tell him what I thought of the matter: so I went and told him little enough of what I thought'.[105] He suggested that the House should regard with forbearance the difficulties in which the chancellor was placed and requested that the proposed duties on transfers of land, as well as those of stock, be dropped, 14 Feb. He asked Althorp when the coal duties would cease and if there would be a drawback on stock in hand, 23 Feb. A meeting of country gentlemen at his house, 2 Mar. 1831, apparently decided that they would henceforth take no part in such debates.[106]

In another letter to Lady Knatchbull, 27 Feb. 1831, he revealed the worries that were on his mind:

> I am sure you must have perceived from the papers, that I have been especially quiet and I do wish they would let me alone, for I wish I were out of all this turmoil and at home with you. On Tuesday [1 Mar.] we have reform and no one knows what I mean to do – but I am asked and asked and asked – all the world is anxiety and all sorts of changes are talked of – for me a peerage, disgraceful as it would be, might be the best thing; for then I could live at peace at home – but that will not do, it will be discreditable.[107]

Lord Lansdowne suggested his name to Grey, 5 Mar., adding that 'I do not know him personally, but hear him always represented as having considerable influence among the Tories, a good speaker and man of business and supposed to be not averse to office'.[108] However, he held a further 'crowded' meeting of Ultras, 5 Mar., perhaps to consolidate their opposition to ministers' reform proposals after Peel's refusal to denounce them. He told his wife that he was in better health, 6 Mar., though sickness continued to prevent his regular attendance, and he added some new reflections:

> I should not be at all surprised, and personally not sorry, if this reform question led to my quitting public life. If it is carried it may present a fair opportunity for me to retire. If it fails, it is likely to create an election in Kent, which might prevent my return, unless at much expense, which I will *never incur* – there now – of this I thought last night.[109]

He condemned threats of mass action to compel Parliament to accept reform and argued that public opinion should be expressed in a regular manner, 7 Mar.; but Sir James Mackintosh* wrote to Lady Holland, 8 Mar., that the 'temper of the Tories', as declared by Knatchbull, 'inclines them to yield passive obedience even to the present ministers'.[110] According to John Rickman, a Commons clerk, 'the coward of Kent (Sir E. K.) already shows the white feather in asking a fortnight's "leave of absence" [on the 9th], foreseeing ill health with careful eye'.[111] Although he presented a reform petition from Ashford, 19 Mar., he was expected to oppose the second reading of the bill like Vyvyan, and then to move a resolution for moderate changes in the following session. This tactic was adopted at a meeting at his house, 20 Mar., but he paired against the second reading on account of illness, 22 Mar.[112] Indisposition also prevented his attendance at a county meeting, 24 Mar., but he acknowledged his hostility to the bill in a letter, his declaration in favour of less extensive alterations being met with derision.[113] After communicating with him, Gleig wrote to Wellington, 8 Apr., that 'I don't know whether he thinks entirely with ... [you], but I believe he does. But he wants moral courage'. Writing again, 13 Apr., he confirmed that Knatchbull's 'sentiments accord perfectly with those of your grace, but he is timid; he believes that resistance is hopeless, and he is ready to concede everything that can be given up, short of the absolute acknowledgement that the bill is just and politic'.[114] He paired in favour of Gascoyne's wrecking amendment, 19 Apr. 1831.

Prior to the dissolution there were rumours that Knatchbull would bow to the growing criticism of his opposition to reform and decline to stand at the general election.[115] In the end no rival Tories offered, but he was opposed by two reformers, Hodges and Thomas Rider*. Several meetings in his favour took place and a large subscription was entered into. He made clear his hostility to reform by signing the Kentish declaration against it and, after repeated requests, he clarified his views in a second address, 27 Apr., in which he stated that

> the power of nominating representatives ought not to be exercised by any individual. This great object may be secured consistently with the rights of the electors. Large and populous towns ought to be directly represented; the amount of qualification is a matter of detail to be fixed on deliberate consideration. I think it would be injurious to divide counties and I am opposed to diminishing the number of English representatives.

In Canterbury, 30 Apr., he explained that he had initially supported the bill, but had opposed the second reading because ministers had declared against any modification in committee, and he argued that the real problem facing the country was the continued distress.[116] After an unsuccessful canvass, he announced his withdrawal in a bitter address, 4 May, but he was generally considered to have acted honourably.[117] Gleig wrote to Wellington, 9 May, that his retirement was 'scarcely to be deplored, for he had so committed himself on the subject of reform, that he could have done no good service'. However he confirmed, 29 June, that Knatchbull would use his influence in support of a Tory at Sandwich, and would have to be thought of at the next election because 'he had got such [a] hold of this county, that it would be foolish to think of shaking it'. Wellington replied, 30 June, that Kent 'would not be satisfied' unless Knatchbull was its Member. Gleig reported to Wellington, 14 July, that he had found Knatchbull 'as usual, doubting, hesitating, distrustful whether we should not do more harm than good', but had finally persuaded him 'to move heaven and earth in the good cause' of systematically organizing anti-reform petitions from Kent. He concluded by adding that 'though difficult to move, and wavering until his mind *is* made up, once he comes to a determi-

nation there is no man more obstinate'. Gleig continued to urge Wellington to co-operate with Knatchbull, 19 July, and Wellington expressed himself willing to do so, 21 July, though Gleig had to warn him to take Knatchbull's 'foreboding of evil ... *cum grano salis*', 27 July.[118] At a dinner in his honour at Sittingbourne, 3 Aug., Lord Mahon* praised him 'as the leader of what are called the country gentlemen. His opinion was always awaited with impatience, listened to with attention and generally followed by conviction'.[119] Gleig trusted that Mahon would 'talk Knatchbull into decision, if he be able', on opposing radical reform agitation in Kent, 21 Sept., but, fearful of making a poor impression, he absented himself from the county reform meeting, 30 Sept. 1831.[120]

Except for his temporary rise to prominence in early 1830, Knatchbull was never happy to act as a leader unless he was certain that he had the support of his colleagues in Parliament and of his constituents. From 1831 he began to move back into the mainstream of the Tory party and he was a founder member of the Carlton Club, 10 Mar. 1832. He gradually recovered the good opinion of the Kentish voters, for instance when he spoke at a meeting in Canterbury, 2 June, though Whigs such as Sir Samuel Egerton Brydges† continued to think that his inveterate and unbending Toryism disqualified him from returning to the House.[121] He was elected for Kent East behind a fellow Tory after a contest at the general election of 1832, and in late 1834, despite his notoriety as a leader of the mutiny which had overthrown the Wellington administration, he broke with Vyvyan and accepted the junior ministerial position offered to him by his erstwhile friend, Peel.[122] He was reappointed in 1841, but resigned in 1845 because of his growing unease at the liberal trend of ministerial policies, and also on account of personal distress over a number of family problems which had culminated with the death of his favourite daughter, Fanny Elizabeth. He died in May 1849, bequeathing the Mersham estate to his estranged heir, Norton Joseph (1808-68), who became the 10th baronet, and the Provender estate to his eldest son with his second wife, Edward Hugessen (1829-93), who was created Baron Brabourne in 1880.[123]

[1] Based on Sir H. Knatchbull-Hugessen, *Kentish Fam.* 164-260. [2] *Letters of Jane Austen* ed. Lord Brabourne, ii. 273-4. [3] *Gent. Mag.* (1820), ii. 381-2; *The Times*, 13 Jan. 1830; Cent. Kent. Stud. Knatchbull mss U951 Z32. [4] Knatchbull mss F24/17-29. [5] Add. 57418, f. 49; *Kentish Gazette*, 29 Apr., 10 June; *Kentish Chron.* 25 Mar., 6 June 1823, 26 May 1829, 1 Mar. 1831. [6] Medway Archives and Local Stud. Cent. Rochester city recs. RCA/A1/6, 209, 534. [7] G. R. Gleig, *Constitution and Tendency of Church Missionary Society* (1824). [8] *New Maidstone Gaol Order Bk.* ed. C.W. Chalklin, 126-43. [9] *The Times*, 21 Feb. 1821; Add. 40359, f. 30. [10] E.g. *Maidstone Jnl.*

17 May 1831. [11] Knatchbull mss C15/6, 7. [12] N. Gash, *Sir Robert Peel*, 72, 288. [13] *Greville Mems.* iii. 148. [14] *Kentish Chron.* 18 Dec. 1832. [15] *Extraordinary Red Bk.* (1821), 164; Knatchbull mss C53/16. [16] *Cobbett's Rural Rides* ed. G.D.H. and M. Cole, i. 42. [17] *New Monthly Mag.* (1828), ii. 479. [18] Knatchbull mss C127/43. [19] *Kentish Chron.* 29 Feb., 14, 21 Mar. 1820. [20] Dorset RO, Bankes mss D/BKL, Bankes jnl. 116; *Colchester Diary*, iii. 134. [21] *The Times*, 12, 16 May, 10 June 1820. [22] Ibid. 9, 27 Feb. 1821. [23] Ibid. 16 June 1821; HLRO, Hist. Coll. 379, Grey Bennet diary, 100. [24] Cent. Kent. Stud. Stanhope mss U1590 C190/1, Knatchbull to Stanhope, 14 Dec.; *Kentish Chron.* 21 Dec. 1821. [25] *The Times*, 12, 14 Feb., 1, 7 May 1822. [26] Ibid. 2, 11 May 1822. [27] *Huskisson Pprs.* 137. [28] *The Times*, 11 June 1822. [29] *Kentish Chron.* 14 June 1822. [30] A. de Staël-Holstein, *Letters on England* (1825), 191-2. [31] *The Times*, 5 July 1822. [32] Ibid. 22, 28 Feb., 25 Apr. 1823. [33] *Colchester Diary*, iii. 281. [34] *The Times*, 22 May 1824. [35] Ibid. 4 June 1824; *Kentish Chron.* 8 Apr. 1825. [36] *The Times*, 22 Apr. 1825. [37] Ibid. 14 May 1825. [38] Knatchbull mss C3/10; Twiss, *Eldon*, ii. 556. [39] *Kentish Gazette*, 25 Oct. 1825. [40] *The Times*, 15, 18 Mar., 14, 21, 26 Apr. 1826. [41] Ibid. 6 May 1826. [42] Ibid. 13 May 1826. [43] *Kent Herald*, 30 Dec. 1824; *Kentish Chron.* 6, 9 June 1826. [44] *Kentish Chron.* 16 June 1826. [45] Ibid. 23 June 1826. [46] *Kentish Gazette*, 15 Sept., 6 Oct. 1826. [47] Ibid. 19 Dec. 1826. [48] *Maidstone Jnl.* 2 Jan. 1827. [49] *The Times*, 24, 27, 28 Feb. 1827. [50] *Geo. IV Letters*, iii. 1292. [51] *The Times*, 3, 6, 20 Mar. 1827. [52] Ibid. 9 Mar.; Nottingham Univ. Lib. Ossulton mss acc. 636, Denison diary, 8 Mar. 1827. [53] *The Times*, 20 Mar. 1827. [54] *Geo. IV Letters*, iii. 1323. [55] *Arbuthnot Jnl.* ii. 116. [56] *Kent Herald*, 10 May 1827. [57] Add. 40394, ff. 124, 126. [58] Add. 52447, f. 82; *The Times*, 20 June 1827. [59] *Canning's Ministry*, 397. [60] Add. 40395, ff. 75, 221. [61] *Kentish Chron.* 15 Apr. 1828. [62] *Ellenborough Diary*, i. 107, 111, 112. [63] Devon RO, Sidmouth mss. [64] *Kentish Chron.* 23 Sept. 1828. [65] Ibid. 14, 28 Oct. 1828; *Report of Speeches at Kent County Meeting* (1828), 27-28. [66] *The Times*, 30 Oct. 1828. [67] *Kentish Chron.* 4, 18 Dec. 1828. [68] *Ellenborough Diary*, i. 365. [69] *Arbuthnot Jnl.* ii. 240. [70] *Croker Pprs.* ii. 9. [71] *Speech of Sir E. Knatchbull* (1829), 3-11; *Oxford DNB*. [72] Broughton, *Recollections*, iii. 310-11; Gurney diary. [73] *Ellenborough Diary*, i. 397, 399. [74] Bankes jnl. 166 [Mar. 1829]. [75] B. T. Bradfield, 'Sir Richard Vyvyan and Fall of Wellington's Government', *Univ. of Birmingham Hist. Jnl.* xi (1968), 142, 148, 154-6. [76] *Survey of London*, x. 50; Add. 40397, ff. 299, 301; 40398, ff. 73, 75; Knatchbull mss C14/13-20. [77] Wellington mss WP2/215/5. [78] Ibid. WP1/1044/4. [79] Hatfield House mss 2M/Gen., Crosbie to Salisbury, 8 Aug. 1829. [80] Cornw. RO, Vyvyan mss; Knatchbull-Hugessen, 182-6. [81] *Palmerston-Sulivan Letters*, 235. [82] *Maidstone Jnl.* 17 Nov. 1829; Vyvyan mss. [83] Knatchbull-Hugessen, 187-8; *Kentish Chron.* 22 Dec. 1829. [84] Knatchbull mss C127/43. [85] *Taylor Pprs.* 313. [86] Grey mss, Howick jnl.; Knatchbull mss C38/8; C127/43. [87] Knatchbull mss C127/42; *Ellenborough Diary*, ii. 186; *Arbuthnot Jnl.* ii. 332. [88] *Greville Mems.* i. 372. [89] *Geo. IV Letters*, iii. 1579. [90] *Ellenborough Diary*, ii. 204. [91] *Kentish Chron.* 16 Mar. 1830. [92] *Maidstone Jnl.* 10 Aug. 1830. [93] *Kent Herald*, 6 Nov. 1828; *Kentish Chron.* 6, 13 July 1830. [94] *Maidstone Jnl.* 10 Aug.; *Kentish Chron.* 10 Aug. 1830. [95] *Maidstone Jnl.* 14 Sept. 1830. [96] Knatchbull mss C177/28; J.L. and B. Hammond, *Village Labourer*, 245; E. Hobsbawm and G. Rudé, *Captain Swing* (1985 edn.), 187. [97] *Kent Herald*, 30 Sept. 1830; *Ellenborough Diary*, ii. 386-7; Knatchbull mss C14/12. [98] *The Times*, 25 Oct., 1 Nov. 1830; *Ellenborough Diary*, ii. 398, 403; Knatchbull mss C14/1-5; C.J. Griffin, '"Policy on the Hoof": Peel, Knatchbull and Trial of Elham Machine Breakers', *Rural Hist.* xv (2004), 127-48. [99] W. Suss. RO, Goodwood mss 1432, ff. 65-69. [100] Fitzwilliam mss. [101] Hopetoun mss 167, f. 189; *Greville Mems.* ii. 60. [102] *Three Diaries*, 109. [103] Ibid. p. xxviii; Le Marchant, *Althorp*, 261; Bankes mss HJ1/368; Hatherton mss; Knatchbull-Hugessen, 202-3. [104] Brougham, *Life and Times*, iii. 376; *Ellenborough Diary*, ii. 439. [105] Knatchbull mss C3/12. [106] TCD, Jebb mss, Inglis to Jebb, 3 Mar.; *Maidstone Gazette*, 8 Mar. 1831. [107] Knatchbull mss C3/14. [108] Grey mss. [109] *Three Diaries*, 14; Knatchbull mss C3/13. [110] Add. 51655. [111] O. Williams, *Life and Letters of Rickman*, 275-6. [112] *Three Diaries*, 67; M. Brock,

Great Reform Act, 172-3; B. T. Bradfield, 'Sir Richard Vyvyan and Country Gentlemen', *EHR*, lxxxiii (1968), 732; *Greville Mems.* ii. 133. [113] *Maidstone Jnl.* 29 Mar. 1831. [114] Wellington mss. [115] *Maidstone Jnl.*, 22 Mar., 5, 12 Apr. 1831. [116] Ibid. 26 Apr., 3 May; *Kentish Chron.* 19 Apr., 3 May; *Kentish Gazette*, 19, 26, 29 Apr., 3 May; *Maidstone Gazette*, 19 Apr. 1831; TNA 30/29/9/5/80. [117] *Three Diaries*, 90; *Maidstone Jnl.* 10, 17 May 1831; Knatchbull-Hugessen, 204-5. [118] Wellington mss; WP1/1188/6; 1190/17; 1191/4, 11, 12, 14, 18; *Wellington Despatches*, vii. 466-8, 473; G. R. Gleig, *Personal Reminiscences of Wellington*, 76-81, 85-87. [119] *Maidstone Jnl.* 9 Aug. 1831. [120] Wellington mss; Stanhope mss C381/1, Knatchbull to Mahon, 30 Sept. 1831. [121] *Kentish Gazette*, 5 June, 17 July 1832. [122] Torrens, *Melbourne*, ii. 65; *Greville Mems.* iii. 122; Add. 40405, ff. 56, 84-88. [123] *Gent. Mag.* (1849), ii. 89; *The Times*, 28 May 1849; Knatchbull mss F20; Knatchbull-Hugessen, 258-9; *Oxford DNB*.

S.M.F.

KNIGHT, James Lewis (1791–1866), of 1 New Square, Lincoln's Inn and Highwood Hill, Hendon, Mdx.

BISHOP'S CASTLE	1831–1832

b. 15 Feb. 1791, 3rd s. of John Knight (*d.* 1799) of Fairlinch, Devon and Margaret, da. and event. h. of William Bruce of Dyffryn and Llanblethian, Glam. *educ.* Bath g.s.; Sherborne 1799-1805; L. Inn 1812, called 1817. *m.* 20 Aug. 1812, Eliza, da. of Thomas Newte of Duvale, Devon, 3s. (2 *d.v.p.*) 2da. Took additional name of Bruce by royal lic. 4 Sept. 1837.[1] kntd. 15 Jan. 1842. *d.* 7 Nov. 1866.

KC 22 July 1829; bencher, L. Inn 1829, treas. 1842-3; vice-chanc. 1841-51; PC 15 Jan. 1842; member, jud. cttee. of PC 1842; ld. justice, ct. of appeal in chancery 1851-Oct. 1866.

Recorder, Brecon.

Knight's father, 'a gentleman of independent property in Devonshire', came from an old Shropshire family. His mother was descended from a branch of the Bruces of Kennet, Clackmannan. Her father William Bruce (1705-68), a navy agent and banker, bought property in Glamorgan, where he served as sheriff in 1756. Knight was educated initially at Bath, where his parents lived in the late 1790s and, after his father's death intestate in 1799, at Sherborne. He did not follow his brothers John (1784-1872), heir to the Welsh estates, and William (1785-1845), who entered the church, to university, but spent two years with a mathematical tutor and in 1807 was articled to the solicitor Bigoe Charles Williams of Lincoln's Inn Fields. His articles having expired, he entered Lincoln's Inn in 1812 and was called to the bar five years later. He practiced in the Welsh courts of great sessions before concentrating on the English equity courts, where his rise was rapid. On taking silk in 1829 he chose the vice-chancellor's court, where he vied unsuccessfully with Edward Sugden* for the lead. As a barrister he was noted for 'his marvellous rapidity in making himself master of the facts of a case' and 'his equally surprising memory in retaining what he had once mastered'.[2]

Nothing came of Knight's forays in Glamorgan as a Tory in 1830 and 1831,[3] but he was one of three king's counsel 'brought in to oppose' the reform bill in 1831. He reputedly sent '£500 to the boroughmongering committee' in Charles Street, and was returned for Bishop's Castle by its patrons the Clives, whom he had advised as counsel on the borough's franchise in 1821 and who now looked to him to prevent its disfranchisement.[4] He divided against the reintroduced reform bill at its second reading, 6 July, and for adjournment, 12 July 1831. In his maiden speech, 14 July, he challenged ministers to state unequivocally whether the guiding principle of the bill was 'nomination or population'. He insisted that Bishop's Castle was not a pocket borough and claimed to 'feel myself as independent as if I had been returned by the largest constituency in the country'. According to the Whig Denis Le Marchant[†], this 'absurd tirade' prompted Lord Clive* to remark that 'the choice which the burgesses had made of Knight was not theirs but Lord C.'s and it was not the independence but the absence of it which ought to have been defended'.[5] He voted to make the 1831 census the criterion for English borough disfranchisements, 19 July, and used the motion's defeat as his excuse for failing to divide the House against the inclusion of Bishop's Castle in Schedule A, 20 July, though he reserved his right to propose its retention of one Member at a future date. On 22 July he complained that the decision on the fate of Downton 'sets at nought all the supposed rules that were to bind us in regard to disfranchisement'. He voted with the Clives against taking a seat from Chippenham, 27 July, and the following day lost his temper in a snarling exchange with Smith Stanley over the 'absurd' case of Clitheroe. He opposed the plan to group Cardiff, where the 2nd marquess of Bute was the principal patron, with Merthyr Tydfil, whose stipendiary magistrate, his brother John Bruce Bruce, aspired to represent the latter as a separate constituency, arguing that each was sufficiently important to warrant a Member, 5 Aug.; and he suggested creating a joint Merthyr and Aberdare constituency to provide representation for the iron industry, 10 Aug. His remarks, as he informed Bute, 17 Aug, created

> a great outcry among some foolish people and a few who ought to have known better at Swansea in consequence of an erroneous report of something said by me in the … Commons on the Merthyr question. You will be at once

aware that I could not, being sane and sober, say anything so foolish as that Swansea or Neath desired to remain as at present in preference to the proposed change so plainly advantageous to them. What I said was that in my judgement Cardiff, Cowbridge and Llantrisant would prefer the existing state of things to the proposed alliance with Merthyr. Lord Althorp is the *Enemy*.[6]

He voiced misgivings at the proposal that the governor of the Isle of Wight, who might be a military man, should be the returning officer for that county, 16 Aug., 14 Sept., and thought the wording of clause 16 on the copyhold and leasehold franchise might open the way to the creation of fictitious votes, 19 Aug. He cavilled at the notion of £10 borough tenants being given the vote, 26 Aug., and asserted that the boundary commissioners would have 'a very dangerous power' to alter the whole constituency of the country, 1 Sept. He was in the small minority on clause 27, governing polling arrangements, 2 Sept., and unsuccessfully proposed that voters in Welsh contributory boroughs should be allowed to poll therein rather than at one central place, 6 Sept. He voted against the bill's passage, 21 Sept., and the second reading of the Scottish measure, 23 Sept. While Powis's other Members abstained, Knight voted against the second reading of the revised reform bill, 17 Dec. 1831. He joined in opposition protests at the provisions made for the boundary bill, arguing that it should not become operative until the reform bill was enacted, 23 Jan. 1832. Ministers accepted his amendment affecting the choice of returning officers for new constituencies, 24 Jan., and suggestions for changes to the clauses concerning votes derived from clerical livings, 1 Feb., and the appointment of revising barristers, 10 Feb. He thought the provisions for the punishment of misdemeanours under the bill were too severe, 16 Feb. He divided against enfranchising Tower Hamlets, 28 Feb., and the third reading, 22 Mar. 1832. Acting indirectly ('I cannot of course communicate very freely on such a subject with a friend of government') through Bute's brother Lord James Crichton Stewart*, he supported the campaign which resulted in the late concession of a Member to Merthyr Tydfil and Aberdare.[7] He voted against the Irish reform bill at its second reading, 25 May, made a heavy joke about Snugborough, a constituent part of one of the revamped Irish boroughs, 13 June, and argued that the measure would encourage fictitious votes and that the extension of voting rights to £10 freeholders had destroyed the principle of the borough franchise, 25 June. He divided against government on the Dublin election controversy, 23 Aug., the sugar refining bill, 12 Sept. 1831, and the Russian-Dutch loan, 26 Jan., 12 July 1832.

On his concerns as a lawyer, Knight, who was reported to have found attending the Commons disruptive to his professional practice and health,[8] took the side of the Irish master of the rolls McMahon in his dispute with the Irish chancellor Lord Plunket over his right to appoint his own secretary, 16 Sept. 1831. He introduced a bill to allow the master to try his case before a judge other than the chancellor, 5 Oct. He complained that the interpleader and arbitration bills, to which there were 'many serious objections', were rushed through the House, 7 Oct. On 11 Oct. 1831 he savaged lord chancellor Brougham's bankruptcy bill, which was 'considered by the profession to be wholly uncalled for and inadequate to the purposes for which it was framed'. Government opposed his Irish master of the rolls bill, introduced 19 Jan., and defeated it, by 88-84, 22 Feb. 1832. Knight was one of seven senior barrister Members who protested to Brougham against the unexpected passage through the Commons, 16 June, of four measures touching the laws of real property, which needed 'much further consideration'.[9] He clashed twice with Hume, 10 July: first on a dispute between certain creditors and the Bank; then on Hume's attack on duchy of Lancaster wine duties, which Knight considered an infringement of royal prerogative. He opposed and divided the House on Harvey's motion for inquiry into admissions to the inns of court, 17 July, and was a teller for the minority of two. In his last reported speech, 30 July 1832, he argued that 'a great error' had been perpetrated in the reorganization of the bankruptcy court, where one judge rather than four would have sufficed.

Bute and his agents considered sponsoring Knight as a Conservative candidate for the new two Member Glamorgan constituency at the 1832 general election, but rejected him for 'not having an estate in the county and most particularly from being a non-resident'.[10] He was beaten into third place by five votes at Cambridge in 1835 and defeated there again in 1837, when he denounced the Melbourne ministry as the tool of Daniel O'Connell*. At the same election his brother John Bruce Pryce (as he was now styled) lost to a Liberal at Merthyr, which returned his second son Henry Austin Bruce (1815-95), later Lord Aberdare, as a Conservative, 1852-68. Knight failed to secure church preferment from Peel for his brother William in 1842 but obtained a deanery for him the following year.[11] He was one of the counsel heard at the bar of the Lords against the municipal corporations bill in 1835 and was reputed to be earning £18,000 a year at the peak of his chancery practice in the late 1830s. One of two additional vice-chancellors

appointed in 1841, he was knighted on Peel's recommendation the following year and became one of the two lord justices of the court of appeal in chancery established in 1851. He was remarkable as a judge 'for his rapidity of apprehension, his accuracy of memory as regards both law and fact, and his determination to break down every barrier of form in order to arrive at the substance', although it was said that 'under the influence of a strong conviction, his judicial opinions sometimes went to the length of hardihood and temerity'.[12] He retired from the bench because of failing eyesight in October 1866 and died within a fortnight at Roehampton Priory, Surrey, his home since the early 1840s, predeceased by his wife (d. 4 Apr. 1866). He was buried in Cheriton churchyard, near Folkestone, Kent. His only surviving son, the barrister Lewis Bruce Knight Bruce (1820-1906), succeeded him at Roehampton. On hearing of his death his nephew wrote:

> How many memories ... it summoned up! Our walks to Highwood and Trent Park ... the ride by day, the evening of music and talk, while he sat at his brief-covered table, his glass to his eye, and his ear open to every word uttered ... He had little religiosity of temperament, but he had a strong sense of duty, and on that he acted.[13]

[1] *Oxford DNB* erroneously states 1838. [2] *The Times*, 8 Nov. 1866; PROB 6/175/298; A.C. Bruce, *Sir James Lewis Knight Bruce* (1867), 3-6; M.D. George, *Cat. of Pol. and Personal Satires*, xi. 16410. [3] *Cambrian*, 10, 17, 24 July 1830, 30 Apr. 1831. [4] *Life of Campbell*, i. 517; *The Times*, 27 Apr.; *Salopian Jnl.* 4 May 1831; Salop Archives, Clive-Powis mss 552/17/596, 597; 552/22/97 and uncat. Clark to Allen, 25 Apr.; Bishop's Castle corporation minutes, 1763-1861, pp. 289-93. [5] *Life of Campbell*, i. 517; *Three Diaries*, 168. [6] NLW, Bute mss L74/161. [7] Ibid. L74/28, 34. See GLAMORGAN. [8] Bruce, 7-10. [9] Brougham mss, memo. [June 1832]. [10] Cardiff Pub. Lib. Bute Estate Letterbks. ii. 347; iii. 21-23. [11] *The Times*, 6, 8, 10, 19 Jan. 1835, 18, 24-27 July 1837; Add. 40521, ff. 23, 25; 40543, f. 92. [12] Bruce, 7-10; H.A. Bruce, *Letters of Lord Aberdare*, i. 168. [13] Ibid. 11; *Gent. Mag.* (1866), i. 919; ii. 681, 833-5; *Aberdare Letters*, i. 243.

D.R.F./M.M.E.

KNIGHT, Robert (1768-1855), of Barrells Hall, Henley-in-Arden, Warws.

WOOTTON BASSETT	1806-1807
WOOTTON BASSETT	14 May 1811-1812
RYE	4 Mar. 1823-1826
WALLINGFORD	16 Dec. 1826-1832

b. 3 Mar. 1768, 1st illegit. s. of Robert Knight†, 1st earl of Catherlough [I], of Barrells and Jane Davies, da. of his tenant of Moat Farm, Ullenhall. *educ.* ?Queens', Camb. 1785. *m.* 12 June 1791, Hon. Frances Dormer, da. of Charles, 8th Bar. Dormer, 2s. (1 *d.v.p.*) 2da. *suc.* fa. to estates in Warws., Lincs., Mdx., Worcs., Salop, Chester, Mont. and Flints. 1772. *d*. 5 Jan. 1855.

Sheriff, Warws. 1797-8, Mont. 1803-4, 1808-9.

Knight, a former Friend of the People and an associate of Sir Francis Burdett*, joined the radical banker Douglas Kinnaird[†] in his attempt to wrest both seats at Bishop's Castle from the control of the Clive family in 1820. They were involved in a double return, but the inquiry proved favourable to their opponents after a redefinition of the right of election. When Knight did return to Westminster in March 1823 it was in the unlikely guise of Member for Rye, where the Lamb family had customarily returned ministerialists. The patron, the Rev. George Augustus Lamb, decided to 'introduce an opposition man' as an act of vengeance against the Liverpool government, whose refusal to give him church preferment he largely blamed for the 'poverty' which compelled him to make the maximum financial gain from his electoral interest. Thus he turned out the sitting Member John Dodson, his sister's brother-in-law, and sold the seat to Knight.[1]

Knight divided silently and somewhat spasmodically with the advanced wing of opposition. He was in small minorities for economy and retrenchment, 17, 18, 25 Mar., 9 June 1823. He voted against the naval and military pensions bill, 14 Apr., for repeal of the Foreign Enlistment Act, 16 Apr., and for parliamentary reform, 24 Apr. He paired in favour of Scottish reform, 2 June. He voted against the Irish insurrection bill, 12 May, 24 June, and in support of the Catholic petition on the administration of justice in Ireland, 26 June. He divided for abolition of the death penalty for larceny, 21 May, 25 June, and inquiry into the coronation expenses, 19 June 1823. He may have been in Rome in January 1824,[2] and his next recorded vote was not until 10 May of that year, when he supported repeal of the assessed taxes. He voted for inquiry into the state of Ireland, 11 May, and proper use of Irish first fruits revenues, 25 May. He presented a Rye petition for inquiry into the circumstances of the trial of the Methodist missionary John Smith in Demerara, 10 June,[3] and voted for Brougham's motion on the subject the following day. He was in the small minorities against the Irish insurrection bill and the new churches bill, 14 June 1824. He voted steadily against the Irish unlawful societies bill and for Catholic relief in 1825. He presented Rye petitions for repeal of the coal duties and the assessed taxes, 23 Feb.,[4] and voted for repeal of the window tax, 17 May. He divided against the duke of Cumberland's grant, 30 May, 6, 10 June, for inquiry into chancery delays, 7 June, and against the judicial salaries bill, 17 June 1825. He was one of the voters for

Hume's amendments to the promissory notes bill, 20, 27 Feb., 7 Mar. 1826. He voted for army reductions, 3, 6, 7 Mar., to exclude non-resident voters from Irish boroughs, 9 Mar., to abolish flogging in the army, 10 Mar., and against giving the president of the board of trade a ministerial salary, 7 Apr. He voted for Russell's motions on parliamentary reform, 27 Apr., and electoral bribery, 26 May, and for inquiries into the state of the nation, 4 May, and James Buckingham's grievances against the Indian government, 26 May 1826.

Knight did not find a seat at the 1826 general election, but in December that year he came forward on a vacancy for the venal borough of Wallingford, claiming the support of its long-serving Whig Member Hughes and emphasizing his opposition politics. Dodson, possibly seeking revenge for the Rye episode, threatened to oppose him but thought better of it. Knight defeated the corporation candidate.[5] His only known votes in the 1827 session were for Catholic relief, 6 Mar., relaxation of the corn laws, 9 Mar., and the opposition motion for supplies to be withheld until the ministerial crisis was resolved, 30 Mar. He presented a petition for repeal of the Test Acts, 21 Feb., and voted thus, 26 Feb. 1828. He was in minorities on the corn laws, 22 Apr., and chancery delays, 24 Apr., and voted for Catholic relief, 12 May. He divided against the provision for Canning's family, 13 May, and the additional churches bill, 30 June, and to reduce the salary of the lieutenant-general of the ordnance, 4 July 1828. Only his votes for Catholic emancipation, 6, 30 Mar., testify to his presence during the 1829 session. He was more active in 1830, after apparently missing the first few weeks, and voted for the transfer of East Retford's seats to Birmingham, 5, 15 Mar., and against British interference in the internal affairs of Portugal, 10 Mar., 28 Apr. He divided against government on the Bathurst and Dundas pensions, 26 Mar., and crown lands revenues, 30 Mar., and attended for most of the major divisions on economy forced by the reviving Whig opposition after Easter. He was for Jewish emancipation, 5 Apr., 17 May. He voted for Irish vestry reform, 27 Apr., abolition of the Irish lord lieutenancy, 11 May, and reform of the civil government of Canada, 25 May, but was not present to support parliamentary reform, 28 May. He voted for abolition of the death penalty for forgery, 7 June 1830.

At the general election that summer he was returned in second place for Wallingford after a contest.[6] The Wellington ministry naturally listed him among their 'foes', and he duly voted against them on the civil list, 15 Nov. 1830. He presented petitions for the abolition of slavery, 22 Nov., 8, 23 Dec. 1830. He supported his

Whig friends in power, voted for the second reading of their reform bill, 22 Mar., and against Gascoyne's wrecking amendment, 19 Apr., and addressed the Warwickshire county reform meeting, 4 Apr. 1831.[7] At the ensuing general election he came in again after a token contest.[8] He voted for the second reading of the reintroduced reform bill, 6 July 1831, and was a steady supporter of its details in committee, though he was one of the reformers who voted against the division of counties, 11 Aug. It is not clear whether it was he or James Lewis Knight who voted against government on the civil list grants, 18 July; but he was certainly in the minority of 27 in favour of halving the grant for the Society for the Propagation of the Gospels, 25 July. He voted for the passage of the reform bill, 21 Sept., the second reading of the Scottish bill, 23 Sept., and Lord Ebrington's motion of confidence in ministers, 10 Oct. He divided for the second reading of the revised reform bill, 17 Dec. 1831, again supported it in committee and divided for its third reading, 22 Mar. 1832. He voted with ministers on the Russian-Dutch loan, 26 Jan., 12, 16, 20 July, and relations with Portugal, 9 Feb., but was in the minority against recommitment of the Irish registry bill, 9 Apr. He voted for the address asking the king to appoint only ministers who would carry undiluted reform, 10 May, and the second reading of the Irish reform bill, 25 May, and against a Conservative amendment to the Scottish measure, 1 June 1832. He retired from Parliament at the dissolution that year.

Knight's first son Henry had died in Paris in 1800, aged five, and he evidently never acknowledged the paternity of his reputed second son Henry Charles (1813-87), who took holy orders in 1838. How far this repudiation was connected with his wife's adultery with his sister's brother-in-law, Colonel Joseph Fuller, for which he was awarded £7,000 damages in 1805, is not certain.[9] There clearly were grounds for doubting Henry Charles Knight's legitimacy, for his cousin Charles Raleigh Knight threatened to contest his right to take possession of the entailed Barrells estate on this score. Robert Knight apparently sought to depreciate its value through neglect. After his death in January 1855 a survey put the cost of necessary repairs to buildings and undrained lands at £25,000. Rather than risk litigation, Henry Charles Knight agreed with his cousin to sell the estate and share the proceeds, and it was sold in 1856 to William Newton of Whately Hall.[10] In his will, dated 28 July 1854, which made no mention of his son, Knight left the residue of his real and personal property to his then unmarried daughter Frances (she married Henry Edward Gooch in 1857), with remainder to his younger daughter Georgiana, wife of Edward Bolton King*. He allowed £1,000

for the expenses of his funeral and directed that his remains should be taken for interment in the family vault at Chadshunt from the nearest railway station, followed by one coach 'containing two of my men servants only and not to be followed by any other person'.[11]

[1] E. Suss. RO, Monk Bretton mss MOB 35. [2] *Jerningham Letters*, ii. 288. [3] *The Times*, 11 June 1824. [4] Ibid. 24 Feb. 1825. [5] *Berks. Chron.* 2, 9, 16, 23 Dec. 1826. [6] *Reading Mercury*, 2 Aug. 1830. [7] *The Times*, 11 Apr. 1831. [8] *Reading Mercury*, 2 May 1831. [9] *Gent. Mag.* (1800), ii. 1215; *The Times*, 12 Apr. 1805. [10] W. Cooper, *Henley-in-Arden*, 124-5, 130-1, 150-60; *VCH Warws*. iii. 141, 180, 212-14; v. 32. [11] PROB 11/2206/135; IR26/2037/70.

D.R.F.

KNIGHT *see also* **GALLY KNIGHT**

KNOX, **Hon. John Henry** (1788–1872).

NEWRY   1826–1832

> *b.* 26 July 1788, 3rd s. of Hon. Thomas Knox[†], 2nd Visct. Northland [I] (later 1st earl of Ranfurly [I]) (*d.* 1840), and Hon. Diana Jane Pery, da. and coh. of Edmund Sexton, 1st Visct. Pery [I]; bro. of Hon. John James Knox* and Hon. Thomas Knox*. *educ.* Harrow 1800; St. John's, Camb. 1806. *m.* 12 Feb. 1822, Lady Mabella Josephine Needham, da. of Francis Needham[†], 1st earl of Kilmorey [I], 4s. 6da. (2 *d.v.p.*). *d.* 27 Aug. 1872.
> Ensign 66 Ft. 1807; lt. 27 Ft. 1808; ensign 3 Ft. Gds. 1809, ret. 1813.
> Weighmaster of butter, Cork to 1830.

The Knoxes of Northland House (later known as Dungannon Park), originally descended from a Glasgow merchant family, took up residence at Dungannon in the seventeenth century and provided several of its representatives in the Irish Parliament. One of these, Thomas Knox (1729-1818), who was granted the Irish peerages of Baron Welles in 1781 and Viscount Northland in 1791, became a ministerialist representative peer in 1801. His Grenvillite Whig heir, another Thomas (1754-1840), who sat for county Tyrone before and after the Union, succeeded as 2nd Viscount Northland and eventually secured the United Kingdom barony and Irish earldom of Ranfurly. He, who had his father's Orange sympathies, was one of the instigators of the Dungannon yeomanry, which was claimed as the blueprint of the system established nationally in the 1790s. Of his brothers, three sat in Parliament, two became bishops and another shared his valuable Irish sinecure of prothonotary of common pleas. Of his four sons, Edmond Sexton Pery Knox became an admiral and the other three, including his eldest son and namesake, were Members in this period.[1]

Like Thomas and John James, John Henry Knox, whose army career apparently ended after he was wounded at the battle of Burgos, was a burgess of Dungannon, Northland's proprietary borough. However, he owed his return to Parliament not to his father, but to his father-in-law, Lord Kilmorey, who controlled Newry. At the general election of 1826, when his brother-in-law Lord Newry retired, he was elected after rowdy proceedings but, in the end, without a contest. Admittedly, he had had to promise to forward the town's expanding commercial interests, but in this his constituents were to be well rewarded.[2] It was perhaps his brother Thomas who was appointed to the select committee on the corporation of Northampton, 21 Feb., and he apparently missed the division on the Catholic question, 6 Mar. 1827. He brought up a Newry petition against the coal duties, 9 Mar., and, having been granted a week's absence owing to ill health, 14 May, may have voted in the minority against the Coventry magistracy bill, 18 June 1827.[3] He presented the Newry petition for Catholic relief, 18 Feb., but was absent from the division on this, 12 May 1828. Either he or Thomas objected to Waithman's slur that Members were dependent on their patrons, 27 June; both voted with the Wellington ministry against reducing the salary of the lieutenant-general of the ordnance, 4 July 1828. Although it was assumed in February 1829 by Planta, the patronage secretary, that Knox would side 'with government' for Catholic emancipation, he seems to have missed all the divisions the following month, even though it was probably he who brought up the favourable petition from Urney on 30 Mar. His inactivity may have derived from a perceived conflict between his father and brother's pro-Catholic votes and his patron and constituents' known hostility. His only reported vote that session was against allowing Daniel O'Connell to take his seat unimpeded, 18 May 1829. Knox voted against the enfranchisement of Birmingham, Leeds and Manchester, 23 Feb. 1830. He may have divided against Jewish emancipation, 5 Apr., when he brought up a Newry petition for the Broomielaw railway bill; he certainly did so on 17 May. 'However disposed I may be to give my support to the present ministers', as he declared on 10 May, he presented and endorsed the Newry petition against the proposed higher duties on Irish stamps and spirits, and three days later either he or Thomas voted for repeal of the Irish coal duties. He was a teller for the minority against amending the Galway franchise bill, 24 May, and voted against the third reading the following day. He divided against reducing the grant to South American missions and abolition of the death penalty for forgery, 7 June, but

for Maberly's attempt to postpone the sale of beer for on-consumption, 1 July. Claiming to be 'unfettered', he offered again at the general election of 1830, when he was praised for his quiet attention to the mercantile affairs of the town, notably its navigation, and was returned unopposed.[4] On the abolition of his sinecure office that year he was awarded a pension of £1,076.

Listed by ministers among their 'friends', Knox voted in their minority on the civil list, 15 Nov. 1830. He divided against the second reading of the Grey ministry's reform bill, 22 Mar. 1831, explaining in a letter to his disgruntled constituents that he favoured the redistribution of seats from rotten boroughs to large towns, but objected to the 'unicornation' of those in schedule B. Contrary to usual parliamentary practice, he claimed that in voting against the second reading he was not opposing the principle of the bill, and extricated himself by insisting that he would now defend the measure in committee. He duly voted with government against Gascoyne's wrecking amendment, which precipitated a dissolution, 19 Apr. With his position in Newry only just intact, he stood as a reformer and beat a local radical in a fierce contest, after repeatedly having to justify his conduct on the hustings. He missed his celebratory dinner through illness, 18 May, when he was again toasted as a 'hardworking' Member.[5] He paired for the second reading of the reintroduced reform bill, 6 July, and voted against using the 1831 census to determine the disfranchisement schedules, 19 July. At least until early August 1831 he divided for the bill's details in committee, as did his brother John James, who had replaced Thomas as Member for Dungannon. To the indignation of O'Connell, who noted that Northland had been given an earldom to secure his family's support, Knox voted against the passage of the bill, 21 Sept., and missed the division on the second reading of the revised bill, 17 Dec. 1831.[6] Although he was in the majority against enfranchising all £10 poor rate payers, 3 Feb., he voted against the enfranchisement of Tower Hamlets, 28 Feb., and the third reading, 22 Mar. 1832. His hostile votes incensed his liberal constituents, and he had to correct the report that he had divided against the second reading of the Irish bill, 25 May.[7] Either he or his brother voted against Alexander Baring's bill to exclude insolvent debtors from Parliament, 6 June, and the Irish party processions bill, 25 June, and for making permanent provision for the Irish poor, 19 June, and the Irish tithes bill, 13 July; but he was credited with dividing for preserving the voting rights of Irish freemen, 2 July. He spoke against the alteration of the boundaries of Newry, 9 July. His only other known votes were with opposition against the Russian-Dutch loan, 26 Jan., and again (although identified in the division list as John James Knox), 12 July 1832.

With other members of his family he resigned on 5 Sept. 1832 from the corporation of Dungannon, where the representation remained in the hands of his brother at the general election in December.[8] Much criticized for his recent conduct, he withdrew from Newry, where his brother-in-law (now Lord Kilmorey) refused to intervene; it was also reported that he did so for financial reasons.[9] Late in life he published several short collections of prose and verse.[10] He died at Chislehurst, Kent, in August 1872, presumably leaving his estate to his eldest son, the Rev. Dr. Thomas Francis Knox (1822-82), an army officer who became a priest at the Brompton Oratory.[11]

[1] *Hist. Irish Parl.* v. 39-49; *HP Commons, 1790-1820,* iv. 346-9; A. Blackstock, 'Knoxes of Dungannon and Irish Yeomanry', *Tyrone Hist. and Society* ed. C. Dillon and H.A. Jefferies, 489-509. [2] *Newry Commercial Telegraph,* 6, 9, 13, 16 June 1826. [3] *The Times,* 10 Mar. 1827. [4] *Newry Commercial Telegraph,* 15 June, 2, 9, 13, 16, 27, 30 July, 3 Aug. 1830. [5] Ibid. 5, 19, 26 Apr., 3, 6, 10, 13, 20 May 1831. [6] *O'Connell Corresp.* iv. 1854. [7] *Newry Commercial Telegraph,* 27 Mar., 5 June; *Newry Examiner,* 31 Mar., 30 May, 6 June 1832. [8] *PP* (1835), xxviii. 470. [9] *Newry Commercial Telegraph,* 11, 21 Dec.; *Newry Examiner,* 12, 22 Dec. 1832; Wellington mss WP1/1239/18. [10] J.H. Knox, *Norman Hamilton* (1860); *Ocean-Pilgrim's Jottings* (1870); *Critic-Vampyre* (1870). [11] *Illustrated London News,* 14 Sept. 1872.

S.M.F.

KNOX, Hon. John James (1790–1856).

DUNGANNON   28 Dec. 1830–1837

b. 3 Apr. 1790, 4th s. of Hon. Thomas Knox[†], 2nd Visct. Northland [I] (later 1st earl of Ranfurly [I]) (*d.* 1840), and Hon. Diana Jane Pery, da. and coh. of Edmund Sexton, 1st Visct. Pery [I]; bro. of Hon. John Henry Knox* and Hon. Thomas Knox*. *m.* 25 Sept. 1824, Mary Louisa, da. of Edward Taylor[†] of Bifrons, nr. Canterbury, Kent, 1da. *d.* 9 July 1856.
    Ensign 64 Ft. 1807; ensign 52 Ft. 1808; lt. 19 Ft. 1809; lt. 52 Ft. 1809; capt. 40 Ft. 1812; capt. 85 Ft. 1813, maj. 1817; lt.-col. 4 W.I. Regt. (half-pay) 1819, ret. 1832.
    Provost, Dungannon 1826-7, 1830.

James Knox was how this Member was usually known, in order to distinguish him from his brother John Henry, Member for Newry.[1] They both entered the army in 1807, but James, who several times purchased and exchanged commissions, had the longer career and remained in the service after the end of the Napoleonic wars. Having obtained his majority in May 1817, he joined the half-pay list as a lieutenant-colonel

in June 1819. On 14 September 1819 he was admitted a burgess of Dungannon, where his father, the 2nd Viscount Northland, controlled the corporation, and he served as interim provost from 7 Nov. 1826 until his resignation the following May and again, 29 Sept.-3 Oct. 1830.[2] He was returned for Dungannon on the retirement of his Tory brother Thomas in December 1830 and proved to be a silent reformer. He voted for the second reading of the Grey ministry's reform bill, 22 Mar., and, having obtained ten days' leave on urgent private business, 13 Apr., paired against Gascoyne's wrecking amendment, 19 Apr. 1831.

Again returned unopposed at the ensuing general election, he was absent from the division on the second reading of the reintroduced bill, 6 July, and sided with opposition for using the 1831 census to determine the disfranchisement schedules, 19 July 1831. But he voted for the disfranchisement of St. Germans, 26 July, and the partial disfranchisement of Guildford, 29 July, paired for the union of Rochester with Chatham and Strood, 9 Aug., and divided for the inclusion of Merthyr Tydfil in the Cardiff district, 10 Aug. He was listed in the ministerial majorities for prosecuting all those guilty of corrupt practices in the Dublin election, 23 Aug., and against preserving the rights of freemen, 30 Aug. His father having been granted an earldom in September as the apparent price of his family's continued support,[3] he missed the division on the passage of the reform bill, 21 Sept., but (unlike his brother John Henry) voted for the second reading of the Scottish bill, 23 Sept., and Lord Ebrington's confidence motion, 10 Oct. 1831. He was absent from the division on the second reading of the revised reform bill, 17 Dec. 1831, but divided for the enfranchisement of Tower Hamlets, 28 Feb., and Gateshead, 5 Mar., and paired for the third reading, 22 Mar. 1832. He voted with government against the production of information on Portugal, 9 Feb. He was absent from the division on Ebrington's motion for an address calling on the king to appoint only ministers who would carry the reform bill unimpaired, 10 May, but voted against increasing the county representation of Scotland, 1 June. It is not clear whether it was he or his brother who voted against Alexander Baring's bill to exclude insolvent debtors from Parliament, 6 June, for making permanent provision for the Irish poor, 19 June, against the Irish party processions bill, 25 June, and for the Irish tithes bill, 13 July. Narrowly retaining his reforming credentials, he saw off an ultimately abortive challenge from a Tory Brunswicker at the general election of 1832 and continued to sit as a Conservative for Dungannon until his retirement in 1837.[4]

Knox died at Brighton in July 1856, leaving his estate to his widow and their only child, Emily Louisa Diana, wife of Sir Robert Dundas of Arniston (1823-1909).[5]

[1] With whom he has sometimes been confused: e.g. *Harrow Reg. 1571-1800*, ii. 93, where his brother is credited with his army career. [2] PRO NI MIC547/1, Dungannon minute bk. [3] M. Brock, *Great Reform Act*, 233. [4] *Northern Whig*, 23 Aug., 3, 27 Sept., 13 Dec. 1832. [5] *Gent. Mag.* (1856), ii. 261.

S.M.F.

KNOX, **Hon. Thomas** (1786–1858), of Barham House, Elstree, Herts.

Co. TYRONE	1812–1818
DUNGANNON	1818–8 Dec. 1830
DUNGANNON	1837–1 June 1838

b. 19 Apr. 1786, 1st s. of Hon. Thomas Knox†, 2nd Visct. Northland [I] (later 1st earl of Ranfurly [I]), and Hon. Diana Jane Pery, da. and coh. of Edmund Sexton, 1st Visct. Pery [I]; bro. of Hon. John Henry Knox* and Hon. John James Knox*. *educ.* Harrow 1797; St. John's, Camb. 1803. *m.* 28 Feb. 1815, Mary Juliana, da. of Hon. and Most Rev. William Stuart, abp. of Armagh, 3s. (1 *d.v.p.*) 6da. *styled* Visct. Northland 1831-40; *suc.* fa. as 2nd earl of Ranfurly [I] and 2nd Bar. Ranfurly [UK] 26 Apr. 1840. *d.* 21 Mar. 1858.

1st capt. Dungannon inf. 1807.

Like his father, who joined Brooks's in July 1807, Knox entered Westminster politics as a supporter of Lord Grenville. In March 1809 he was presented at court and put up for Brooks's by the duke of Devonshire. The family were not thought to be especially loyal to the crown, despite their rich pickings from government. He soon returned to Ireland and, according to Mrs. Spencer Stanhope, was

> heartily glad to get from his mamma's introductions. When he was introduced to the duke of Gloucester, H.R.H. inquired what profession he was brought up to, and at the reply, exclaimed, 'What, *no* profession!' Mrs. Knox, who had presented him as an eldest son, coloured.[1]

In January 1810 he went with John Spencer Stanhope to the Peninsula, but after a few months in Portugal he abandoned his companion, who recorded that 'to quarrel with Knox was impossible, for there lives not a man of a more amiable or kind hearted disposition'.[2] He replaced his father as Member for Tyrone at the general election of 1812, and in 1818 was returned for Dungannon, where he was a burgess, by his father, who later that year succeeded as 2nd Viscount Northland. A member of the Grenvillite 'third party',

he continued to act sporadically with the opposition to Lord Liverpool's government, but he no longer voted in favour of the Catholics and at least once served on the committee of the Grand Orange Lodge.[3]

He was returned unopposed for Dungannon in 1820 and at the following two general elections. His only known vote that year was for inquiry into Anglo-Irish trade, 14 June. He divided in defence of ministers' conduct towards Queen Caroline, 6 Feb., against Catholic relief, 28 Feb., and for the forgery punishment mitigation bill, 4 June 1821. He followed the duke of Buckingham's lead in adhering to administration at the start of 1822 and was thereafter reckoned an inflexible ministerialist in the Commons, where he sat on several Irish select committees.[4] He divided against parliamentary reform, 20 Feb., and alteration of the Scottish representative system, 2 June 1823. He voted against inquiries into the legal proceedings against the Dublin Orange rioters, 22 Apr., and for the Irish insurrection, 14 June 1824, and unlawful societies bills, 15, 25 Feb. 1825. Perhaps now satisfied with the proposed securities, he for the first time since 1813 voted for Catholic relief, 1 Mar., 21 Apr., 10 May 1825. He presented anti-slavery petitions from Dungannon, 7 Apr., and elsewhere, 10, 20 Apr. 1826.[5] He voted against reforming the representation of Edinburgh, 13 Apr., and curbing electoral bribery, 26 May. That spring the premier again approached George IV about the promise of a United Kingdom peerage for Northland, which had been outstanding since the early 1820s. Liverpool claimed, of Grenville, that 'it was the only *personal* engagement at the close of his public life, about which he felt a deep interest and which really pressed upon his mind'. On 6 July 1826 Northland was given the barony of Ranfurly, the name of the family's original Renfrewshire property.[6]

Knox divided for Catholic relief, 6 Mar. 1827. It was probably he, not his brother John Henry, now Member for Newry, who was appointed to the select committee on the corporation of Northampton, 21 Feb., and who voted against the Coventry magistracy bill, 18 June 1827. Having brought up pro-Catholic petitions, including one from Drumglass parish, in which his constituency lay, 22 Feb., he voted for repeal of the Test Acts, 26 Feb., and Catholic relief, 12 May 1828. He complained about Waithman's comment that Members were slavish clients of their patrons, 27 June, unless this intervention was by his brother, whom he joined in voting with the Wellington ministry against the reduction of the salary of the lieutenant-general of the ordnance, 4 July 1828. Listed by Planta, the patronage secretary, as a possible mover or seconder of the address at the start of the 1829 session, he was considered likely to side 'with government' for Catholic emancipation.[7] He presented the favourable petition from the Catholics of Tyrone, 18 Mar., and voted for emancipation, 6, 30 Mar.; but he divided against allowing Daniel O'Connell to take his seat without swearing the oath of supremacy, 18 May 1829. He voted against transferring East Retford's seats to Birmingham, 11 Feb., Lord Blandford's reform scheme, 18 Feb., and the enfranchisement of Birmingham, Leeds and Manchester, 23 Feb. 1830. Either he or John Henry divided against Jewish emancipation, 5 Apr., and the Irish coal duties, 13 May. He voted against reducing the grant for South American missions, 7 June, when he apparently paired against abolition of the death penalty for forgery, but for Knatchbull's amendment to prohibit the sale of beer for on-consumption, 21 June. Listed by ministers among their 'friends', he divided in their minority on the civil list, 15 Nov. 1830. Three weeks later he resigned his seat in favour of his brother John James, who was perhaps thought more likely to support the Grey administration.

Knox's father, who voted by proxy for reform in the Lords, was rewarded with the Irish earldom of Ranfurly in September 1831. It was thus under the courtesy title of Viscount Northland that Knox, a Conservative, represented Dungannon as a stopgap, 1837-8. On Ranfurly's death in 1840 he succeeded to his titles and properties, including the bulk of personal wealth sworn under £30,000 in Ireland and £40,000 in England.[8] Described in 1841 by a Dungannon Presbyterian minister as having been 'always a rank Tory', he failed to gain an appointment on Peel's accession to power that year.[9] He died in March 1858 at his Irish seat, which since the 1840s had been known as Dungannon Park. He presumably left his estate to his eldest son, Thomas (b. 1816), Conservative Member for Dungannon, 1838-51.[10] Following his death in May 1858 the peerage passed in turn to his two sons, Thomas Granville Henry Stuart (1849-75), an army officer, and Uchter John Mark (1856-1933), a household and colonial official.

[1] *Spencer-Stanhope Letter-Bag*, i. 175-6, 178. [2] *Mems. of Anna Maria Wilhelmina Pickering* ed. S. Pickering, 51, 347, 376. [3] *HP Commons, 1790-1820*, iv. 348; PRO NI, Leslie mss MIC606/3/J/7/21/4. [4] J.J. Sack, *Grenvillites*, 196; *Black Bk.* (1823), 168; *Session of Parl. 1825*, p. 471. [5] *The Times*, 8, 11, 21 Apr. 1826. [6] Sack, 108, 191; *Geo. IV Letters*, iii. 1235; Add. 38301, f. 206. [7] Add. 40389, f. 87. [8] *Gent. Mag.* (1840), i. 90-91; PROB 11/1928/368; IR26/1558/339. [9] *O'Connell Corresp.* vii. 2813; Add. 40486, ff. 257-60. [10] *The Times*, 23 Mar. 1858; *Gent. Mag.* (1858), i. 439-40.

S.M.F.

KYNASTON POWELL, Sir John, 1st bt. (1753–1822), of Hardwick Hall, Salop.

SHROPSHIRE   1784–24 Oct. 1822

b. 5 Feb. 1753, 1st s. of Roger Kynaston of Shrewsbury and Mary, da. of Henry Powell of Worthen. *educ.* Pembroke, Oxf. 1770; All Souls, Oxf. by 1777. *m.* 19 Feb. 1778, Mary Elizabeth, da. of John Corbet of Sundorne, *s.p. suc.* fa. 1788; uncle John Powell to Worthen and took additional name of Powell 11 Feb. 1797; *cr.* bt. 3 Oct. 1818. *d.* 24 Oct. 1822.
    Mayor, Oswestry 1783, steward 1796-*d.*
    Lt.-col. Salop militia 1769, col. (West and North) 1797; brevet col. 1797; col. Salop vols. 1803.

Kynaston Powell, an anti-Catholic Tory whose parliamentary attendance was never more than sporadic, had represented his native Shropshire without interruption since 1784. He was a descendant of Bleddyn ap Cynfyn, king of Powys, and had developed the ambition of securing the revival in his favour of the barony of Grey de Powis, last applied for by John Kynaston[†] in 1731.[1] He had been consoled in December 1818 with a baronetcy with reversion, as he was childless, to his brother the Rev. Edward Kynaston, rector of Risby and Fornham, Suffolk, and his heirs, and was returned unopposed in 1820.[2] He had rarely spoken in debate and no speeches by him were reported during that Parliament. He was a signatory to Shopshire's loyal address to the king in January 1821,[3] and voted in defence of the Liverpool ministry's conduct towards Queen Caroline, 6 Feb., and against Catholic relief, 28 Feb. 1821. He died at Hardwick in October 1822, remembered for his integrity and urbanity.[4] His brother succeeded to the baronetcy and entailed estates as planned and, by his will, dated 10 Mar. 1798 and proved under £7,000, he left everything else to his wife. The baronetcy was extinguished on the death in 1866 of the 3rd baronet, his nephew the Rev. Sir John Roger Kynaston, whose sister and heir Amy Kynaston (*d.* 1868) devised the family estates to the descendants of her maternal grandfather, Robert Owen of Shrewsbury and Dublin, who assumed the name of Kynaston.[5]

[1] *HP Commons, 1715-54*, ii. 195; *HP Commons, 1790-1820*, iv. 350. [2] *Shrewsbury Chron.* 10, 17 Mar.; *Salopian Jnl.* 15 Mar. 1820; NLW, Aston Hall mss C.460, 461. [3] *Salopian Jnl.* 25 Jan. 1821. [4] *Gent. Mag.* (1822), ii. 471. [5] *The Times*, 2 Nov. 1822; PROB 11/1669/234; IR26/970/334.

R.M.H./M.M.E.